FOR REFERENCE

Do Not Take From This Room

DATE DUE

ROGET'S 21ST CENTURY THESAURUS

ROGET'S 21ST CENTURY THESAURUS

IN DICTIONARY FORM

The Essential Reference for Home, School, or Office

BARBARA ANN KIPFER, Ph.D.

Produced by The Philip Lief Group, Inc.

Delacorte Press

Published by
Delacorte Press
Bantam Doubleday Dell Publishing Group, Inc.
1540 Broadway
New York, New York 10036

Produced by The Philip Lief Group, Inc.
6 West 20th Street
New York, New York 10011

Design: Binns & Lubin / Martin Lubin

Library of Congress Cataloging in Publication Data

Kipfer, Barbara Ann
Roget's 21st century thesaurus in dictionary form: the essential reference
for home, school, or office / Barbara Ann Kipfer.
    p. cm.
Includes index.
ISBN 0-385-31606-2
1. English language—Synonyms and antonyms. I. Title.
II. Title: Roget's twenty-first century thesaurus in dictionary form.
PE1591.K54   1992
423'1.—dc20   91-37916
                                               CIP

Manufactured in the United States of America

Published simultaneously in Canada

August 1992

10 9 8 7 6 5 4 3 2

KPH

CONTENTS

PREFACE FROM THE EDITOR

Language and our ideas about language change as rapidly and inevitably as the world around us. The "Information Age" we now live in has been made possible by the sophisticated technology of computers and the potential of databases for information storage and retrieval; we receive and process more information than ever before. These innovations did not exist even a generation ago. Further, the research and development of artificial intelligence systems has led to a new examination of the complex cognitive relationships human beings form between their ideas and the words they choose—how this process works, and how it can be recreated. Current lexicographical research must go beyond traditional methods and techniques to consider these new discoveries and applications in developing viable contemporary reference materials for students, linguists, and writers.

The results of recent studies on students' ability to develop reference skills show that most people learn a new word by guessing, based on context, what that word means. Combining this proven trend with the advanced theories of language gained through electronic media, I have arrived at an "onomasiological" approach to understanding American English. That is, the capability of traveling successfully from a meaning to a word instead of the only other practical method to date—the straightforward dictionary approach of going from word to meaning.

Onomasiologically, readers move from the concepts of "yellow" and "flower" to a selection of words that describe the combination, or from the notion of a "positive state of mind" to its qualities, actions, and conditions.

For the general public, we cannot believe that the printed book will go out of style within our lifetime. Indeed, its popularity is increasing. I have searched for a method of presenting this lexical theory in a format that provides diversified access within one resource. In *Roget's 21st Century Thesaurus,* the text is designed to do just that: allowing users to search both from word to meaning and from meaning to word. The dictionary format lends familiarity of use, while the concept index illustrates the language's semantic structure and displays links between words. The A to Z listings further amplify the resonances between words by specifying syntactic function through part-of-speech and sense division.

The result is the most complete and comprehensive selection of synonyms published in print media: *Roget's* for the 21st-century reader.

BARBARA ANN KIPFER, PH.D.

INTRODUCTION

In 1805, P. M. Roget, a British surgeon and inventor, took up a peculiar hobby: the classification of words according to ideas. His intention: to present those words in a kind of verbal catalogue that would assist writers and linguists in their search for the right manner of expression. As he worked, he perhaps had in mind the ancient Sanskrit *Amarakosha,* arguably the first arrangement of words by subject, or the French *Pasigraphie,* published in 1797, which was an attempt to order words so they could be understood universally, without translation. Roget called his own work a "thesaurus"—a Latin word meaning "treasury" or "storehouse of knowledge."

Roget's pastime became a lifelong passion and in 1852, at the age of seventy-three, Roget published his *Thesaurus of English Words and Phrases, Classified and Arranged so as to Facilitate the Expression of Ideas and Assist in Literary Composition.* This new reference book became enormously popular and a second edition appeared only a year after the first. By the time of Roget's death in 1869, there had been over twenty-five editions and printings. Today, his name is synonymous with the thesaurus.

MAKING A BETTER THESAURUS

Because Roget's thesaurus assumes contemporary users share the compiler's ideas about language, Roget's 19th-century system is a difficult one for "21st-century" readers to use to advantage. Its abstruse classifications and indexes only present modern users with an agonizing labyrinth of possibility where each route deadends in a disappointing and many times inappropriate selection of synonyms. Synonyms are buried in the text in a way that is arcane and nearly impenetrable. All too often, the right word remains elusive and the thesaurus remains on the shelf.

While Roget's original idea was brilliant, his eccentrically organized hierarchy of the English language is demonstrably Victorian and outdated by today's standards. For over a century, thesaurus editors have strived to redefine the nature and function of the thesaurus, and to accomplish the primary objective of combining optimum accuracy with a highly usable format. Attempts to improve Roget's thesaurus began with Roget's own son, John Lewis, who expanded the selection of synonyms. Later, Thomas Y. Crowell acquired publishing rights to the thesaurus and his 1886 edition of Roget's provided a clearer page design and format that enhanced the book's readability. Subsequent generations of Crowells have added Americanisms, foreign expressions, slang and nonstandard speech, prefixes, suffixes, and quotations. However, Roget's structure of abbreviations, categories, cross-references, and indexes has only become further complicated by an elaborately conceived type design, boldface entries, numbered paragraphs, and a decimal system that requires an explanatory diagram.

Very few successful arrangements of lexical information have been devised to access words non-alphabetically. C. O. Sylvester Mawson was the first to attempt to simplify and reorganize Roget's thesaurus in dictionary form. In 1911, he issued his own alphabetical presentation of the famous Roget system. Twentieth-century editors quickly followed his lead, eager to arrive at an easier method for frustrated thesaurus users.

But because the dictionary style thesauri do not suggest any relationships between words beyond the simple aggregation of synonyms listed with a main entry, adoption of a strict dictionary format is but a limited improvement. Although these thesauri do offer a more straightforward presentation than the old Roget's, they neither help users organize thoughts nor do they infer broad conceptual links between ideas as expressed through language in words.

INNOVATION ON A CLASSIC THEME

Until *Roget's 21st Century Thesaurus,* no other thesaurus has been able to proficiently combine the utility of a dictionary format with the sophistication made possible by arranging words according to ideas. This revolutionary design supersedes the traditional Roget and all other thesauri as the new standard for thesaurus users. It is, simultaneously, a fast and efficient handbook for writers and a medium to facilitate the expression of ideas—both of Roget's objectives brought forward and reinterpreted for the 21st-century user.

Electronically compiled using state-of-the-art techniques, *Roget's 21st Century Theasurus* lists 17,000 main entries or headwords in alphabetical order that generate hundreds of thousands of synonyms—more than any other thesaurus in dictionary form.

Roget's 21st Century Thesaurus is the forerunner of the latest changes in the language. The editor's final selection of main entry words and synonyms reflects modern practices of speaking and writing, and appreciates contemporary linguistic sensitivities. Dialectic and obsolete terms have been replaced by timely words and phrases

recently evolved from new technologies and disciplines including computers, video equipment, biotechnology, and environmental chemistry. A nonsexist approach to language replaces outmoded epithets. Foreign words and phrases that reflect our global consciousness have been included, as well as hundreds of Americanisms. Drawing upon computer technology and recent innovations in typesetting and design, the pages are printed in a highly readable and contemporary format for ease in making skillful and effective decisions.

The synonym lists contain no superfluous cross-references, compendious usage labels, or cumbersome abbreviations to come between users and the words themselves. Like main entries, the synonym lists are arranged in alphabetical order. This is done so as not to proscribe or suggest any particular preference to the wealth of synonym choices available, and also for the user's convenience.

Synonyms that represent nonstandard usage are marked with an unobtrusive asterisk. These include both informal words and colloquial phrases and expressions common to the language.

THE CONCEPT INDEX

Thesaurus entries are enriched by directing users to related concepts in *Roget's 21st Century Thesaurus*'s Concept Index. This unique index offers users an up-to-the-minute language hierarchy that stimulates the path of thought into expression by mirroring the cognitive process of the human brain. By considering subject and concept as well as presenting an agglomeration of synonyms, *Roget's 21st Century Thesaurus*'s Concept Index actually helps writers organize their thoughts and generates possibilities for millions of word choices—far beyond the capabilities of traditional thesauri.

The Index lists over 800 individual numbered concepts to which each of the book's 17,000 headwords is referenced. The words "SEE CONCEPTS(S)" appear in small caps at the end of a main entry, followed by all relevant numerical assignments of concepts for that word. When an initial search does not yield adequate results, the Concept Index automatically provides users with alternative places to look when further exploration is desired.

For example, if none of the synonyms listed with the word "scintillating" seem appropriate, the Concept Index directs the writer to concepts #401, "attributes of behavior;" #529, "cognitive qualities;" and #617, "visual brightness." Each concept gathers together scores of headwords that share the same characteristics. Persistent writers or linguists can turn back in the A to Z listing to the synonym aggregates for any of these headwords again and again to accumulate a plethora of ideas for possible word choices.

In determining concept names and classifications, the most advanced theories of communication and learning avilable have been applied. The word hierarchies in *Roget's 21st Century Thesaurus* have been streamlined into categories that reflect contemporary ways of thinking. There are no misunderstandings or irksome inconsistencies about what concepts mean or confusion about how they are organized. Whether performing a speedy search through concepts referenced to a main entry in the A to Z listing, or entering the index with just a vague notion in mind, the Concept Index is a fast and reliable research tool.

HOW TO USE
ROGET'S 21ST CENTURY THESAURUS

Roget's 21st Century Thesaurus's sensible format ensures swift access to the right alternatives. For quick identification, each main entry in the A to Z listing is printed in boldface; its part of speech follows in bracketed italics. Some headwords have more than one listing; separate entries are included for each different part of speech and are ordered in the following manner: noun forms, adjectives, verbs, adverbs, conjunctions, and prepositions. "Pass," for example, has 13 entries in *Roget's 21st Century Thesaurus*—four noun forms and nine verb forms. Each sense of the word "pass" is treated exclusively to help writers pinpoint the precise sense of the word desired.

Although no thesaurus is intended to replace a dictionary, concise definitions accompany main entries in order to supply users with a basic reference point and help them to evaluate synonym choices. Semicolons sometimes appear within definitions to denote fine points of sense for a word's particular usage when the discernments are too subtle to warrant a separate entry.

Remember that no two words mean *exactly* the same thing; no two words are directly interchangeable. It is the subtle nuance and flavor of particular words that give the English language its rich and various texture. While we turn to a thesaurus to find different, more expressive ways of speaking and writing, we must turn to a dictionary, a sophisticated semantic tool, to determine meaning. Always consider synonyms in their desired context and consult a dictionary if there remains any doubt about a word or phrase's application.

The Concept Index follows the alphabetical listing of headwords and begins with a reference key to its 837 concepts. The concepts appear in the index in numerical order and are divided into ten overarching categories of interest: Actions, Causes, Fields of Human Activity, Life Forms, Objects, The Planet, Qualities, Senses, States, and Weights and Measures. All main entry words grouped under a specific concept are ordered alphabetically. Headwords that denote different parts of speech appear together in these lists, allowing users to enhance their prose from more than one perspective—and to think more about the relationships between the words they choose.

TOMORROW'S CLASSIC
FOR TODAY'S USER

In the minds of writers, Roget has always been the trademark of a dependable thesaurus. As we enter an era unimagined by P. M. Roget two hundred years ago, *Roget's 21st Century Thesaurus* secures that reputation. Adapting Roget's idea for his thesaurus to reflect today's concerns, this new text represents a living reference of American English.

ROGET'S 21ST CENTURY THESAURUS

A

abandon [n] *careless disregard for consequences*
disregard, freedom, impulse, licentiousness, recklessness, spontaneity, thoughtlessness, uninhibitedness, unrestraint, wantonness, wildness; SEE CONCEPTS *633,645*

abandon [v1] *leave behind, relinquish*
abdicate, back out, bail out*, bow out*, chicken out*, cop out*, cut loose*, desert, discard, discontinue, ditch, drop, drop out, duck, dump, dust*, flake out*, fly the coop*, give up the ship*, kiss goodbye*, leave, leg it*, let go, opt out, pull out, quit, run out on, screw*, ship out, stop, storm out*, surrender, take a powder*, take a walk*, throw over*, vacate, walk out on, wash hands of*, withdraw, yield; SEE CONCEPT *195*

abandon [v2] *leave in troubled state*
back out, desert, disown, forsake, jilt, leave, leave behind, quit, reject, renounce, throw over*, walk out on; SEE CONCEPTS *7,19,195*

abandoned [adj1] *left alone, deserted*
alone, cast aside, cast away, deserted, discarded, dissipated, dropped, dumped, eighty-sixed*, eliminated, empty, forgotten, forsaken, given up, godforsaken*, jilted, left, left in the cold*, left in the lurch*, neglected, on the rocks*, outcast, passed up*, pigeon-holed*, rejected, relinquished, shunned, sidelined*, side-tracked*, unoccupied, vacant, vacated; SEE CONCEPT *577*

abandoned [adj2] *free from moral restraint; uninhibited*
corrupt, depraved, dissolute, immoral, incontinent, incorrigible, licentious, profligate, shameless, sinful, uncontrolled, unprincipled, unrestrained, wanton, wicked, wild; SEE CONCEPT *545*

abase [v] *deprive of self-esteem, confidence*
belittle, debase, degrade, demean, diminish, disgrace, dishonor, humble, humiliate, lower, mortify, reduce, shame; SEE CONCEPTS *7,19*

abashed [adj] *exhibiting mental discomfort, ill at ease*
ashamed, bewildered, bugged, chagrined, confounded, confused, crushed, discombobulated*, disconcerted, embarrassed, fazed, fuddled, humbled, humiliated, in a tizzy*, mortified, rattled, shamed, taken aback; SEE CONCEPT *403*

abate [v] *lessen, grow or cause to grow less*
allay, chill out*, coast*, cool, cool it*, decline, decrease, diminish, dull, dwindle, ebb, go with the flow*, hang easy*, hang loose*, lay back*, let go, let it all hang out*, let up, mellow out*, moderate, quell, recede, reduce, slacken, slow, subdue, subside, take it easy*, taper, taper off; unlax, wane; SEE CONCEPTS *240,698*

abbey [n] *building that houses monks, nuns, or priests; church*
cloister, convent, friary, ministry, monastery, nunnery, priory, temple; SEE CONCEPTS *368,439*

abbreviate [v1] *shorten*
abridge, abstract, boil down*, clip, compress, condense, contract, cut, cut back, cut down, cut off, cut out, digest, get to the meat*, nutshell*, pare, prune, reduce, summarize, take out, trim; SEE CONCEPTS *236,247*

abbreviate [v2] *cut short an activity*
abort, curtail, restrict, stop short, truncate; SEE CONCEPT *234*

abbreviation [n] *something shortened*
abridgement, abstract, abstraction, clipping, compendium, compression, condensation, contraction, digest, outline, precis, reduction, sketch, summary, syllabus, synopsis; SEE CONCEPTS *283,652*

abdicate [v] *give up a right, position, or power*
abandon, abjure, abnegate, bag it*, bail out*, cede, demit, drop, forgo, give up, leave, leave high and dry*, leave holding the bag*, leave in the lurch*, opt out*, quit, quitclaim, relinquish, renounce, resign, retire, sell out*, surrender, vacate, waive, withdraw, yield; SEE CONCEPTS *133,298*

abdomen [n] *the stomach and area directly below in an animate being*
bay window*, belly, bowels, breadbasket*, corporation, gut*, guts, intestines, middle, midriff, midsection, paunch, pot*, potbelly*, spare tire*, tummy, venter, viscera; SEE CONCEPT *393*

abdominal [adj] *concerning the stomach and the area below it*
belly, duodenal, gastric, intestinal, stomachic, ventral, visceral; SEE CONCEPT *393*

abduct [v] *take by force and without permission*
carry off, dognap*, grab, kidnap, make off with, put the snatch on*, remove, seize, shanghai*, snatch, sneeze*, spirit away*; SEE CONCEPT *139*

aberrant [adj] *not normal; varying from the usual*
abnormal, atypical, deviant, different, flaky*, mental*, nonstandard, odd, off-base, off-color, out of line*, peculiar, psycho*, strange, unusual, weird; SEE CONCEPT *547*

aberration [n1] *state of abnormality*
delusion, eccentricity, oddity, peculiarity, quirk, strangeness, weirdness; SEE CONCEPT *647*

aberration [n2] *different from that expected*
departure, deviation, difference, distortion, divergence, diversion, irregularity, lapse, straying, wandering; SEE CONCEPT *665*

abet [v] *assist, help in wrongdoing*
advocate, back, condone, egg on, encourage, endorse, goad, incite, instigate, prod, promote, provoke, sanction, spur, support, urge; SEE CONCEPTS *14,110*

abeyance [n] *being inactive or suspended temporarily*
deferral, discontinuation, dormancy, inactivity, intermission, latency, pending, postponement, quiescence, recess, remission, suspension, waiting; SEE CONCEPTS *681,705*

abhor [v] *regard with contempt or disgust*
abominate, be allergic to*, be down on*, despise, detest, grossed out*, hate, have allergy to*, have no use for*, loathe, scorn; SEE CONCEPT **29**

abide [v1] *submit to, put up with*
accept, acknowledge, bear, bear with*, be big*, concede, consent, defer, endure, hang in*, hang in there*, hang tough*, live with*, put up with*, receive, sit tight*, stand, stand for, stomach, suffer, swallow, take, tolerate, withstand; SEE CONCEPTS **23,35**

abide [v2] *live in a certain place*
bide, bunk*, bunk out*, crash*, dwell, hang out*, inhabit, lodge, nest, perch, reside, room, roost, settle, squat, stay; SEE CONCEPT **226**

abide [v3] *remain or continue in a state*
continue, endure, keep on, last, persevere, persist, remain, survive; SEE CONCEPTS **23,239**

abide [v4] *stop temporarily and wait for*
anticipate, bide, expect, linger, pause, remain, rest, sojourn, stay, stick around, stop, tarry, wait; SEE CONCEPTS **119,681**

abiding [adj] *continuing or existing for an indefinite time*
constant, continuing, enduring, eternal, everlasting, fast, indissoluble, lasting, permanent, perpetual, persistent, persisting, steadfast, steady; SEE CONCEPT **551**

ability [n1] *power to act, perform*
aptitude, capability, capacity, competence, competency, comprehension, dexterity, endowment, facility, faculty, intelligence, might, potentiality, qualification, resourcefulness, skill, strength, talent, understanding; SEE CONCEPT **630**

ability [n2] *natural or acquired power in a particular activity*
adeptness, adroitness, bent, capability, cleverness, command, craft, cutting the mustard*, deftness, expertise, expertness, finesse, flair, genius, gift, handiness, ingenuity, knack, know-how, mastery, mind for, on the ball*, proficiency, savvy, skill, skillfulness, strength, talent, the goods*, the right stuff*, what it takes*; SEE CONCEPT **706**

abject [adj] *hopeless and downtrodden*
base, contemptible, degraded, dejected, deplorable, dishonorable, fawning, forlorn, groveling, hang dog, humiliating, low, miserable, outcast, pitiable, servile, submissive, worthless, wretched; SEE CONCEPT **571**

ablaze [adj1] *on fire*
afire, aflame, alight, blazing, burning, conflagrant, fiery, flaming, flaring, ignited, lighted; SEE CONCEPTS **485,605**

ablaze [adj2] *very excited*
afire, angry, aroused, enthusiastic, fervent, frenzied, fuming, furious, heated, impassioned, incensed, intense, on fire, passionate, raging, stimulated, vehement; SEE CONCEPT **550**

ablaze [adj3] *brightly illuminated*
aflame, aglow, brilliant, flashing, gleaming, glowing, luminous, radiant, refulgent, sparkling; SEE CONCEPT **617**

able [adj1] *capable of performing; having an innate capacity*
adept, adequate, adroit, agile, alert, apt, bright, capable, cleft, competent, cunning, dexterous, easy, effortless, endowed, equipped, facile, fitted, good, intelligent, knowing, powerful, ready, smart, strong, worthy; SEE CONCEPTS **402,527**

able [adj2] *able to perform well; having a proven capacity*
accomplished, adroit, agile, artful, au fait, brilliant, capable, clever, deft, dexterous, effective, effectual, efficient, equal to, experienced, expert, facile, gifted, ingenious, intelligent, keen, know backwards and forwards*, know one's onions*, know the ropes*, learned, masterful, masterly, paid dues*, powerful, practiced, prepared, proficient, qualified, responsible, savvy, sharp, skilled, skillful, smart, talented, there*, trained, up to it*, up to snuff*, up to speed*, with it*; SEE CONCEPTS **402,528**

able-bodied [adj] *physically strong and capable*
firm, fit, hale, hardy, healthy, hearty, lusty, powerful, robust, staunch, stout, strapping, sturdy, vigorous; SEE CONCEPTS **314,489**

abnegation [n] *denial, renouncement of something*
abandonment, abstinence, eschewal, fat chance*, forbearance, forget it*, giving up, nix, nothing doing*, no way*, refusal, rejection, relinquishment, renouncement, renunciation, sacrifice, self-denial, stonewall*, surrender; SEE CONCEPTS **18,25**

abnormal [adj] *different from standard or norm*
aberrant, anomalistic, anomalous, atypical, bizarre, curious, deviant, deviate, deviating, divergent, eccentric, exceptional, extraordinary, fantasmo*, funny, grody*, gross, heteroclite, heteromorphic, irregular, odd, off-base, off-color, out of line, peculiar, preternatural, queer, screwy*, spastic, strange, uncommon, unexpected, unnatural, unusual, weird; SEE CONCEPT **547**

abnormality [n] *being different from standard or norm*
aberrancy, aberrant, aberration, anomalism, anomaly, atypicalness, bizarreness, deformity, deviance, deviancy, deviation, eccentricity, exception, extraordinariness, flaw, irregularity, oddity, peculiarity, preternaturalness, singularity, strangeness, uncommonness, unnaturalness, unusualness, weirdness; SEE CONCEPT **647**

aboard [adj] *on or in a transportation object*
boarded, consigned, embarked, en route, in transit, loaded, on, on board, traveling; SEE CONCEPT **583**

abode [n] *building or place where one resides*
address, base, casa, condo, co-op, crash pad*, crib*, den, digs*, domicile, dwelling, flat, flop*, habitat, haunt, headquarters, hearth, hole*, home, home-

stead, house, joint*, lodging, pad, quarters, residence, roost*, sanctuary, seat; SEE CONCEPT *515*

abolish [*v*] *do away with or put an end to*
abate, abrogate, annihilate, annul, call off, cancel, destroy, disestablish, dissolve, end, eradicate, erase, expunge, extinguish, extirpate, finish, inhibit, invalidate, kibosh*, kill, negate, nix, nullify, obliterate, overthrow, overturn, prohibit, put an end to, put the kibosh on*, quash, repeal, repudiate, rescind, revoke, scrub*, set aside, squelch, stamp out, subvert, supersede, suppress, terminate, undo, vacate, vitiate, void, wipe out, zap*; SEE CONCEPTS *121,252,298*

abolition [*n*] *formal act of putting an end to, annulling*
abolishment, abrogation, annihilation, annulment, cancellation, destruction, dissolution, elimination, end, ending, eradication, extirpation, invalidation, negation, nullification, obliteration, overthrow, overturning, quashing, repeal, repudiation, rescinding, rescindment, rescission, revocation, subversion, suppression, termination, voiding, wiping out, withdrawal; SEE CONCEPTS *121,252,298*

abominable [*adj*] *awful, detestable*
abhorrent, atrocious, awful, base, beastly, contemptible, cursed, despicable, disgusting, foul, grim, grody*, gross*, hairy*, hateful, heinous, hellish, horrible, horrid, loathsome, lousy, nauseating, obnoxious, odious, offensive, repellent, reprehensible, repugnant, repulsive, revolting, rotten, sleazeball*, stinking, terrible, very bad, vile, wretched; SEE CONCEPTS *29,544,571*

abomination [*n1*] *object of extreme dislike, hate*
anathema, aversion, bother, curse, detestation, evil, hate, horror, nuisance, plague, shame, torment; SEE CONCEPTS *29,666*

abomination [*n2*] *wrongdoing*
crime, offense, wrong; SEE CONCEPT *691*

aboriginal [*adj*] *belonging to one, existing in a place since prehistory*
ancient, birth native, earliest, endemic, first, indigenous, original, primary, primeval, primitive, primordial; SEE CONCEPT *549*

abort [*v1*] *stop or cancel something*
arrest, break off, call it quits, call off, check, cut off, drop, end, fail, halt, interrupt, knock it off*, lay off*, nullify, scrap, scratch, scrub*, terminate; SEE CONCEPT *121*

abort [*v2*] *terminate or fail to complete pregnancy*
miscarry; SEE CONCEPTS *121,304,308*

abortion [*n*] *failure*
casting, disappointment, disaster, fiasco, misadventure, miscarriage, premature delivery; SEE CONCEPTS *304,308,674*

abortive [*adj*] *failing to achieve a goal*
failed, failing, fruitless, futile, ineffective, ineffectual, miscarried, unavailing, unproductive, unsuccessful, useless, vain, worthless; SEE CONCEPT *528*

abound [*v*] *overflowing; existing in abundance*
be alive with, be all over the place*, be knee deep in*, be no end to*, be plentiful, be thick with*, be up

to one's ears in*, crawl with*, crowd, flourish, flow, have a full plate*, infest, proliferate, swarm, swell, teem, thrive; SEE CONCEPT *141*

about [*adv1*] *in an opposite direction*
around, back, backward, in reverse, round; SEE CONCEPT *581*

about [*adv2*] *lying anywhere without order, arrangement*
anyhow, any which way*, around, here and there, in the ball park*, in the neighborhood*, practically, pretty near; SEE CONCEPT *583*

about [*prep1*] *near an amount, quantity*
almost, approximately, in general, nearly, roughly; SEE CONCEPT *771*

about [*prep2*] *concerning, relating to*
apropos, as concerns, as respects, dealing with, in connection with, in relation to, in respect to, referring to, regarding, relative to, touching, touching on; SEE CONCEPT *532*

about [*prep3*] *near or close to in position*
adjacent, beside, nearby; SEE CONCEPTS *586,778*

about [*prep4*] *on every side, in every direction*
around, encircling, round, surrounding, through, throughout; SEE CONCEPT *586*

about-face [*n*] *change in direction*
changeabout, double, doubleback, reversal, reverse, turn, turnabout, volte-face; SEE CONCEPT *697*

above [*prep1*] *higher in position*
aloft, atop, beyond, high, on high, on top of, over, overhead, raised, superior, upon; SEE CONCEPT *752*

above [*prep2*] *more, higher in amount, degree*
beyond, exceeding, greater than, larger than, over; SEE CONCEPT *793*

above [*prep3*] *superior to*
before, beyond, exceeding, prior to, superior to, surpassing; SEE CONCEPT *567*

aboveboard [*adj*] *candid*
forthright, frank, honest, open, overt, right on*, square, straight, straightforward, straight from shoulder*, true, trustworthy, truthful, up front*, veracious; SEE CONCEPT *404*

aboveboard [*adv*] *candidly*
frankly, honestly, on the up and up*, openly, overtly, truly, truthfully, veraciously; SEE CONCEPT *404*

abrasion [*n1*] *scraped area*
chafe, injury, scrape, scratch, scuff; SEE CONCEPT *309*

abrasion [*n2*] *scraping or wearing down by friction*
abrading, chafing, erosion, grating, rubbing, scratching, scuffing; SEE CONCEPT *186*

abrasive [*adj1*] *irritating in manner*
annoying, biting, caustic, cutting, galling, hard to take*, hateful, hurtful, nasty, rough, rubbing the wrong way*, sharp, spiky*, unpleasant; SEE CONCEPT *404*

abrasive [*adj2*] *scraping or wearing*
cutting, erosive, grinding, polishing, rough, scratching, scratchy, scuffing, sharpening, smoothing; SEE CONCEPT *606*

abreast [*adv1*] *next to, alongside*
beside, equal, in alignment, in line, level, opposite, shoulder to shoulder, side by side; SEE CONCEPT *586*

abreast [*adv2*] *up-to-date*
acquainted, au courant, au fait, contemporary, familiar, informed, in touch, knowledgeable, up, versed; SEE CONCEPT *402*

abridge [*v*] *shorten*
abbreviate, abstract, blue pencil*, chop, clip, compress, concentrate, condense, contract, curtail, cut, decrease, digest, diminish, lessen, limit, narrow, put in nutshell*, reduce, restrict, slash, snip*, summarize, trim, truncate; SEE CONCEPTS *236,247*

abridgement [*n*] *shortening, summary*
abbreviation, abstract, brief, compendium, condensation, conspectus, contraction, curtailment, cutting, decrease, digest, diminishment, diminution, lessening, outline, precis, reducing, reduction, synopsis; SEE CONCEPTS *283,652*

abroad [*adj*] *in a foreign country*
away, elsewhere, in foreign lands, in foreign parts, out of the country, overseas, touring, traveling; SEE CONCEPT *583*

abrogate [*v*] *formally put an end to*
abate, abolish, annul, cancel, dissolve, do in*, end, finish off*, invalidate, knock out*, negate, nix, nullify, quash, reject, renege, renig, repeal, retract, revoke, scrub*, torpedo*, undo, vacate, vitiate, void; SEE CONCEPT *121*

abrupt [*adj1*] *rude or brief in manner*
blunt, brusque, crude, crusty, curt, direct, discourteous, gruff, impetuous, impolite, matter-of-fact, rough, short, snappy, snippy, uncivil, ungracious; SEE CONCEPT *542*

abrupt [*adj2*] *happening suddenly and unexpectedly*
hasty, hurried, jerky, precipitate, precipitous, quick, rushing, sudden, surprising, unanticipated, unceremonious, unexpected, unforeseen; SEE CONCEPT *820*

abscond [*v*] *run away, leave confinement or threat*
beat it*, bolt*, break, clear out*, cut and run*, decamp, disappear, dog it*, duck out, escape, fade, flee, fly the coop*, get, go AWOL*, go south*, hightail*, jump*, leave, make a break*, make off, make scarce*, pull out, quit, run off, scram*, skedaddle*, skip out*, slip, sneak away, split*, steal away, take off*, vamoose*, vanish; SEE CONCEPTS *102,195*

absence [*n1*] *state of not being present*
absenteeism, AWOL*, cut*, French leave*, hooky*, nonappearance, nonattendance, no-show, truancy, vacancy; SEE CONCEPT *746*

absence [*n2*] *state of lacking something needed or usual*
dearth, deficiency, drought, inadequacy, insufficiency, lack, need, omission, privation, unavailability, void, want; SEE CONCEPT *646*

absent [*adj1*] *not present*
astray, away, AWOL*, elsewhere, ghost, gone, hooky*, missing, nobody home*, no-show, removed, vanished; SEE CONCEPT *583*

absent [*adj2*] *deficient in something needed or usual*
bare, blank, devoid, hollow, lacking, minus, missing, nonexistent, omitted, unavailable, vacant, vacuous, wanting; SEE CONCEPT *546*

absentee [*adj*] *not being present*
absent, distant, oblivious, remote; SEE CONCEPTS *403,583*

absenteeism [*n*] *state of not being present*
absence, defection, desertion, skipping, truancy; SEE CONCEPT *746*

absent-minded [*adj*] *unaware of events, surroundings*
absent, absorbed, abstracted, airheaded*, bemused, day dreaming, distracted, distrait, dreaming, dreamy, engrossed, faraway, forgetful, goofing off*, heedless, inattentive, inconscient, lost, mooning*, moony*, oblivious, out to lunch*, pipe dreaming*, popcorn-headed*, preoccupied, remote, removed, space cadet*, spacey*, unconscious, unheeding, unmindful, unobservant, unthinking, withdrawn, woolgathering*; SEE CONCEPT *403*

absolute [*adj1*] *without limit*
complete, consummate, downright, entire, flat out*, free, full, infinite, no catch*, no fine print*, no holds barred*, no ifs ands or buts*, no joke*, no strings attached*, outright, plenary, pure, sheer, simple, straight out, supreme, thorough, total, unabridged, unadulterated, unconditional, unlimited, unqualified, unrestricted, utter; SEE CONCEPT *554*

absolute [*adj2*] *in control or complete authority*
absolutist, arbitrary, authoritarian, autocratic, autonomous, despotic, dictatorial, full, monocratic, preemptory, sovereign, supreme, totalitarian, tyrannical, tyrannous; SEE CONCEPT *536*

absolute [*adj3*] *certain*
actual, categorical, conclusive, consummate, decided, decisive, definite, exact, factual, fixed, genuine, infallible, positive, precise, sure, unambiguous, undeniable, unequivocal, unmitigated, unquestionable; SEE CONCEPT *535*

absolute [*adj4*] *excellent, perfect*
categorical, complete, faultless, flawless, ideal, impeccable, thorough, ultimate, unblemished, unflawed, untarnished; SEE CONCEPT *574*

absolutely [*adv1*] *certainly, without question*
actually, categorically, certain, conclusively, decidedly, decisively, definitely, doubtless, easily, exactly, for sure*, no ifs ands or buts*, no strings attached*, on the button*, on the money*, on the nose*, positively, precisely, really, right on*, straight out*, sure as can be*, sure enough*, surely, sure thing*, the very thing*, truly, unambiguously, unconditionally, unquestionably; SEE CONCEPT *535*

absolutely [*adv2*] *in a complete manner, degree*
completely, consummately, entirely, fully, thoroughly, utterly, wholly; SEE CONCEPT *531*

absolve [*v*] *free from responsibility, duty*
acquit, bleach, blink at, clear, discharge, exculpate, excuse, exempt, exonerate, forgive, free, go easy on,

launder*, let off*, let off easy*, let off the hook*, let up on*, liberate, lifeboat*, loose, pardon, release, relieve, sanitize*, set free, spare, spring, vindicate, whitewash, wink at*, wipe it off*, wipe the slate clean*, write off*; SEE CONCEPTS *83,317*

absorb [*v1*] *physically take in a liquid*
blot, consume, devour, drink in, imbibe, ingest, ingurgitate, osmose, soak up, sop up*, sponge up*, suck in*, swallow, take in; SEE CONCEPT *256*

absorb [*v2*] *mentally take in information*
assimilate, comprehend, digest, follow, get, get into, grasp, incorporate, latch onto, learn, sense, soak up, take in, understand; SEE CONCEPT *31*

absorb [*v3*] *occupy complete attention*
captivate, concern, consume, employ, engage, engross, fascinate, fill, hold, immerse, involve, monopolize, obsess, preoccupy, rivet; SEE CONCEPT *17*

absorbed [*adj*] *being completely occupied mentally*
captivated, consumed, deep in thought, eat sleep and breathe*, engaged, engrossed, fascinated, fixed, gone*, head over heels*, held, immersed, intent, involved, lost, preoccupied, rapt, really into*, up to here*, wrapped up*; SEE CONCEPT *403*

absorbent [*adj*] *capable of physically taking in a liquid*
absorptive, bibulous, dry, imbibing, penetrable, permeable, porous, pregnable, retentive, spongy, thirsty; SEE CONCEPT *603*

absorbing [*adj*] *holding one's attention*
arresting, captivating, consuming, engrossing, enthralling, exciting, fascinating, gripping, interesting, intriguing, monopolizing, preoccupying, riveting, spellbinding; SEE CONCEPT *403*

absorption [*n1*] *assimilation, incorporation*
consumption, digestion, drinking in, exhaustion, fusion, imbibing, impregnation, ingestion, inhalation, intake, osmosis, penetration, reception, retention, saturation, soaking up, suction, taking in; SEE CONCEPTS *169,256*

absorption [*n2*] *total attention toward something*
captivation, concentration, engagement, engrossment, enthrallment, fascination, hang-up*, holding, immersion, intentness, involvement, occupation, preoccupation, raptness; SEE CONCEPT *410*

abstain [*v*] *hold back from doing*
abjure, abnegate, avoid, cease, constrain, curb, decline, deny oneself, do without, eschew, evade, fast, fence-sit*, forbear, forgo, give the go by*, give up, go on the wagon*, keep from, pass, pass up, quit, refrain, refuse, renounce, shun, sit on one's hands*, sit on the fence*, sit out, spurn, starve, stop, take the cure*, take the pledge*, withhold; SEE CONCEPTS *25,121*

abstemious [*adj*] *restraining behavior or appetite*
abstinent, ascetic, austere, continent, frugal, moderate, moderating, restraining, self-denying, self-restraining, sober, sparing, temperate; SEE CONCEPT *401*

abstinence [*n*] *restraint from desires, especially physical desires*
abnegation, abstaining, abstemiousness, asceticism, avoidance, chastity, continence, fasting, forbearance, frugality, moderation, refraining, renunciation, self-control, self-denial, self-restraint, soberness, sobriety, teetotalism, temperance; SEE CONCEPT *633*

abstract [*n*] *short document prepared from a longer one*
abridgment, brief, compendium, condensation, conspectus, digest, outline, precis, résumé, summary, synopsis; SEE CONCEPT *283*

abstract [*adj*] *conceptual, theoretical*
abstruse, complex, deep, hypothetical, ideal, indefinite, intellectual, nonconcrete, philosophical, recondite, transcendent, transcendental, unreal; SEE CONCEPT *582*

abstract [*v1*] *take away from*
detach, disconnect, disengage, dissociate, extract, isolate, part, remove, separate, steal, take out, uncouple, withdraw; SEE CONCEPTS *135,211*

abstract [*v2*] *prepare short document from longer one*
abbreviate, abridge, condense, digest, outline, review, shorten, summarize; SEE CONCEPTS *79,236,247*

abstraction [*n*] *state of being lost in thought*
absorption, aloofness, brooding, cogitation, consideration, contemplation, daydreaming, detachment, engrossment, entrancement, musing, pensiveness, pondering, preoccupation, reflecting, reflection, remoteness, reverie, ruminating, thinking, trance; SEE CONCEPT *410*

abstruse [*adj*] *difficult to understand*
abstract, clear as dishwater*, complex, complicated, deep, enigmatic, esoteric, Greek to me*, heavy, hidden, incomprehensible, intricate, involved, muddy, obscure, perplexing, profound, puzzling, recondite, subtle, unfathomable, vague; SEE CONCEPTS *402,562*

absurd [*adj*] *ridiculous, senseless*
batty, campy, crazy, daffy, dippy*, flaky*, fooling around, foolish, for grins*, freaky, gagged up*, goofy*, idiotic, illogical, inane, incongruous, irrational, jokey, joshing, laughable, loony, ludicrous, nonsensical, nutty, off the wall, preposterous, sappy*, screwy*, silly, stupid, tomfool, unreasonable, wacky; SEE CONCEPTS *544,552,558*

absurdity [*n*] *ridiculous situation or behavior*
applesauce*, bull*, craziness, farce, flapdoodle*, folly, foolishness, hot air*, idiocy, illogicality, illogicalness, improbability, inanity, incongruity, insanity, irrationality, jazz*, jive*, ludicrousness, ridiculousness, senselessness, silliness, sour grapes*, stupidity, unreasonableness, vanilla*; SEE CONCEPTS *650,656*

abundance [*n*] *great amount or supply*
affluence, ampleness, bounty, copiousness, fortune, opulence, plenitude, plenty, profusion, prosperity, prosperousness, riches, thriving, wealth; SEE CONCEPTS *710,767*

abundant [adj] plentiful, large in number
abounding, ample, bounteous, bountiful, copious, crawling with*, exuberant, filled, full, generous, heavy, lavish, liberal, lousy with*, luxuriant, mucho*, no end of*, overflowing, plate is full*, plenteous, plenty, profuse, rich, rolling in*, stinking with*, sufficient, teeming; SEE CONCEPT 781

abuse [n1] wrong use
corruption, crime, debasement, delinquency, desecration, exploitation, fault, injustice, misapplication, misconduct, misdeed, mishandling, mismanage, misuse, offense, perversion, prostitution, sin, wrong, wrongdoing; SEE CONCEPT 156

abuse [n2] physical hurting, injuring
crime, damage, defilement, harm, hurt, impairment, injury, malevolence, maltreatment, manhandling, misdeed, offense, pollution, violation, wrongdoing; SEE CONCEPT 246

abuse [n3] verbal attack
bad-mouthing*, blame, castigation, censure, curse, curses*, defamation, derision, hosing*, insults, invective, kicking around*, knifing*, libel, opprobrium, pushing around*, quinine*, reproach, revilement, scolding, signifying, slander, swearing, tirade, upbraiding, vilification, vituperation; SEE CONCEPT 54

abuse [v1] physically hurt or injure
bang up*, bung*, corrupt, cut up*, damage, defile, deprave, desecrate, harm, hose*, ill-treat, impair, maltreat, manhandle, mar, mess up*, mishandle, mistreat, misuse, molest, oppress, persecute, pollute*, roughhouse, rough up, ruin, shake up*, spoil, taint, total*, victimize, violate, wax*; SEE CONCEPT 246

abuse [v2] use wrongly
dissipate, exhaust, misemploy, mishandle, misuse, overburden, overtax, overwork, prostitute, spoil, squander, taint, waste; SEE CONCEPT 156

abuse [v3] attack with words
backbite, bad-mouth, bash, belittle, berate, blow off*, cap*, castigate, cuss out*, cut down*, cut to the quick*, decry, defame, derogate, discount, do a number on*, dump on*, give a black eye*, hurl brickbat*, insult, knock*, minimize, nag, offend, oppress, persecute, pick on, put down, rag on*, reproach, revile, ride*, rip up*, run down*, scold, signify, slam*, slap*, smear*, sound*, swear at*, tear apart*, trash*, upbraid, vituperate, zing*; SEE CONCEPTS 52,54

abuse [v4] take advantage of
do an injustice to, exploit, impose on, use, wrong; SEE CONCEPTS 156,384

abusive [adj] exhibiting unkind behavior or words
calumniating, castigating, censorious, contumelious, defamatory, derisive, disparaging, insolent, insulting, invective, libelous, maligning, obloquious, offensive, opprobrious, reproachful, reviling, rude, sarcastic, scathing, scolding, scurrilous, sharp-tongued, slanderous, traducing, upbraiding, vilifying, vituperative; SEE CONCEPT 267

abut [v] touch or be next to something
adjoin, be adjacent to, border on, butt against, join, neighbor; SEE CONCEPT 749

abysmal [adj1] great extent; immeasurable
bottomless, boundless, complete, deep, endless, extreme, illimitable, incalculable, infinite, profound, thorough, unending, unfathomable, vast; SEE CONCEPTS 772,793

abysmal [adj2] extending deeply
bottomless, fathomless, plumbless, plummetless; SEE CONCEPT 777

abyss [n] something very deep, usually a feature of land
abysm, chasm, crevasse, depth, fissure, gorge, gulf, hole, pit, void; SEE CONCEPTS 509,514

academic [n] scholar or university/college teacher
academician, don, fellow, lecturer, master, professor, pupil, scholar, scholastic, student, tutor; SEE CONCEPT 350

academic [adj1] relating to schooling, learning
bookish, book-learned, college, collegiate, erudite, intellectual, learned, pedantic, scholarly, scholastic, studious, university; SEE CONCEPT 536

academic [adj2] relating to theories, philosophy
abstract, closet, conjectural, formalistic, hypothetical, notional, speculative, theoretical; SEE CONCEPTS 402,529

academy [n1] school, especially for higher education
boarding school, brainery*, finishing school, halls of ivy*, institute, military school, preparatory school, prep school, secondary school, seminary; SEE CONCEPT 289

academy [n2] society or institution interested in learning
alliance, association, circle, council, federation, foundation, fraternity, institute, league; SEE CONCEPT 288

accede [v] agree or consent
accept, acquiesce, admit, allow, assent, be game*, cave in*, comply, concede, concur, cooperate, cry uncle*, endorse, enter into, fold, give the go-ahead*, give the green light*, go along with, grant, let, okay, permit, play ball*, roll over and play dead*, subscribe, throw in the towel*, yield; SEE CONCEPTS 8,50,82,88

accelerate [v] increase speed, timing
advance, drive, dust*, expedite, fire up*, forward, further, gun*, hammer on*, hasten, hurry, impel, lay a patch*, lay rubber*, make tracks*, nail it*, open up*, peel rubber*, precipitate, put on afterburners*, put pedal to metal*, quicken, railroad*, rev, rev up, roll*, speed up, spur, step on gas*, step up, stimulate, tool*; SEE CONCEPTS 234,242

acceleration [n] increasing speed, timing
dispatch, expedition, hastening, hurrying, quickening, speeding up, spurring, stepping up, stimulation; SEE CONCEPT 234

accent [*n1*] *importance, emphasis*
significance, stress, weight; SEE CONCEPT *668*

accent [*n2*] *stress or pitch in pronunciation*
accentuation, articulation, beat, cadence, emphasis, enunciation, force, inflection, intonation, meter, modulation, pronunciation, rhythm, stroke, timbre, tonality, tone; SEE CONCEPT *77*

accent [*v*] *place emphasis, importance*
accentuate, draw attention to, emphasize, highlight, intensify, stress, underline, underscore; SEE CONCEPTS *69,243*

accept [*v1*] *receive something given physically*
acquire, gain, get, obtain, secure, take, welcome; SEE CONCEPT *124*

accept [*v2*] *allow into group*
admit, receive, welcome; SEE CONCEPT *384*

accept [*v3*] *believe the goodness, realness of something*
acknowledge, affirm, approbate, approve, buy*, countenance, fancy, favor, go for*, hold, hold with, like, lump it*, recognize, relish, swallow*, take as gospel truth*, take stock in*, trust; SEE CONCEPT *12*

accept [*v4*] *put up with*
acknowledge, acquiesce, agree, assent, bear, bear with, bow, capitulate, defer to, don't make waves*, don't rock the boat*, endure, fit in, go along with, live with, play the game*, recognize, respect, sit still for*, stand, stand for, stomach, submit to, suffer, swallow, take, toe the mark*, tolerate, yield to; SEE CONCEPT *23*

accept [*v5*] *receive by agreeing, consenting*
accede, acknowledge, acquiesce, admit, adopt, affirm, agree to, approve, assent, assume, avow, bear, buy, check out*, comply, concur with, cooperate with, give stamp of approval*, give the go-ahead*, give the green light*, give the nod*, go for*, lap up*, okay, recognize, rubber-stamp*, set store by*, sign, sign off on*, take on*, take one up on*, thumbs up*, undertake; SEE CONCEPTS *8,82*

acceptable [*adj*] *satisfactory, agreeable*
adequate, admissible, all right, A-OK*, average, big*, common, cooking with gas*, cool*, decent, delightful, fair, hep*, hip*, hunky-dory*, in the swim*, kosher*, large, okay, on the ball*, on the beam*, passable, peachy keen*, pleasant, pleasing, respectable, right on*, standard, sufficient, swell*, tolerable, trendy, unexceptional, unobjectionable, up to code*, up to snuff*, welcome; SEE CONCEPTS *533,558*

acceptance [*n1*] *agreement, taking*
accepting, acknowledgment, acquiring, admission, agreement, approval, assent, compliance, consent, cooperation, gaining, getting, go-ahead*, green light*, nod*, obtaining, okay, permission, receipt, receiving, reception, recognition, securing, taking, taking on, undertaking, yes; SEE CONCEPTS *8,124*

acceptance [*n2*] *belief in goodness of something*
accedence, accession, acknowledgment, acquiescence, admission, adoption, affirmation, agreement,

approbation, approval, assent, concession, concurrence, favor, recognition, seal of approval; SEE CONCEPTS *12,32*

accepted [*adj*] *generally agreed upon*
accustomed, acknowledged, allowed, approved, arrived, authorized, card-carrying*, chosen, confirmed, conventional, credited, current, customary, endorsed, established, fashionable, in vogue, kosher*, legit*, made it*, normal, okayed, orthodox, passed, popular, preferred, received, recognized, regular, sanctioned, standard, straight*, time-honored, touted, universal, unopposed; SEE CONCEPTS *547,558*

access [*n*] *admission, means of entry, approach*
admittance, approach, avenue, connection, contact, course, door, entrance, entree, entry, in, ingress, introduction, key, open arms*, open door*, passage, path, road, route, way; SEE CONCEPTS *501,631*

accessible [*adj*] *approachable; ready for use*
attainable, available, door's always open*, employable, exposed, getatable, handy, near, obtainable, open, operative, possible, practicable, public, reachable, susceptible, unrestricted, usable; SEE CONCEPT *576*

accession [*n1*] *something that augments, adds to*
accretion, addition, augmentation, enlargement, extension, increase, increment, raise, rise; SEE CONCEPTS *700,775*

accession [*n2*] *coming to power*
assumption, attainment, inauguration, induction, investment, succession, taking on, taking over; SEE CONCEPTS *133,298*

accession [*n3*] *agreement*
accedence, acceptance, acquiescence, assent, concurrence, consent; SEE CONCEPTS *8,410*

accessory [*n1*] *ornament; accompanying item; supplementary part*
accent, addition, adjunct, adornment, appendage, appendix, appliance, appurtenance, attachment, component, decoration, extension, extra, frill, help, supplement, trim, trimming; SEE CONCEPT *834*

accessory [*n2*] *person peripherally involved in illegal activity*
abettor, accomplice, aid, aide, assistant, associate, co-conspirator, colleague, confederate, conspirator, helper, insider, partner, plant*, ringer*, shill*, stall*, subordinate; SEE CONCEPT *412*

accident [*n1*] *unexpected, undesirable event; often physically injurious*
blow, calamity, casualty, collision, crack-up*, disaster, fender-bender*, fluke*, hazard, misadventure, misfortune, mishap, pileup*, rear ender*, setback, smash*, smashup*, stack-up*, total*, wrack-up*; SEE CONCEPT *674*

accident [*n2*] *chance event*
adventure, circumstance, contingency, fate, fluke*, fortuity, fortune, happening, luck, occasion, occurrence; SEE CONCEPT *679*

accidental [adj] *happening unexpectedly*
adventitious, casual, chance, coincidental, contingent, fluky*, fortuitous, inadvertent, incidental, random, uncalculated, unexpected, unforeseen, unintended, unintentional, unplanned; SEE CONCEPTS *530,552*

acclaim [n] *expression of approval*
acclamation, acknowledgment, applause, approbation, celebration, cheering, clapping, commendation, commercial, eulogizing, exaltation, honor, kudos, pat on the back*, pat on the head*, plaudits, PR, praise, puff, pumping up*, rave, recognition, strokes*, stroking*; SEE CONCEPT *69*

acclaim [v] *give approval*
applaud, approve, blow horn*, boost, brag, celebrate, cheer, clap, commend, complement, eulogize, exalt, extol, give a bouquet*, give a posy*, hail, hand it to*, hear it for*, honor, kudize*, kudo*, laud, praise, puff up*, push*, rave, recommend, root, salute, stroke*; SEE CONCEPT *69*

acclamation [n] *enthusiastic expression of approval*
acclaim, adulation, applause, approbation, big hand*, cheer, cheering, cheers, hand, honor, jubilation, laudation, ovation, plaudits, salutation, standing O*, tribute; SEE CONCEPTS *69,377*

acclimate [v] *make or become adjusted, adapted*
acclimatize, accommodate, acculture, accustom, climatize, conform, get used to, habituate, harden, season, toughen; SEE CONCEPTS *202,701*

accolade [n] *strong praise, recognition of achievement*
approval, award, badge, decoration, distinction, honor, kudos*, laurels; SEE CONCEPT *69*

accommodate [v1] *make room, lodging available*
board, contain, domicile, entertain, furnish, harbor, hold, house, put up*, quarter, receive, rent, shelter, supply, take in, welcome; SEE CONCEPT *226*

accommodate [v2] *make, become suitable for something*
accord, accustom, adapt, adjust, agree, attune, bend over backwards*, comply, compose, conform, coordinate, correspond, don't make waves*, don't rock the boat*, fit, go by the book*, go with the flow*, harmonize, integrate, make consistent, modify, play the game*, proportion, reconcile, settle, shape up, suit, tailor, tailor-make, tune; SEE CONCEPTS *23,126*

accommodate [v3] *perform service*
afford, aid, arrange, assist, avail, benefit, bow, comfort, convenience, defer, favor, furnish, gratify, help, humor, indulge, oblige, pamper, please, provide, serve, settle, submit, suit, supply, support, sustain, yield; SEE CONCEPT *136*

accommodating [adj] *willing to help*
all around*, considerate, cooperative, friendly, handy, helpful, hospitable, kind, neighborly, obliging, on deck*, on tap*, polite, regular fellow*, unselfish, user friendly*; SEE CONCEPTS *542,555*

accommodation [n] *adjustment for different situation, circumstances*
adaptation, compliance, composition, compromise, conformity, deal fifty-fifty*, fitting, modification, reconciliation, settlement; SEE CONCEPT *697*

accommodations [n] *place of residence, usually temporary*
apartment, board, boardinghouse, crash pad*, crib*, digs*, hotel, house, housing, lodging, motel, pad*, quarters, roof, room and board, rooming house, rooms, shelter; SEE CONCEPT *516*

accompaniment [n1] *necessary part or embellishment*
accessory, adjunct, appendage, appurtenance, attachment, attendant, attribute, augmentation, complement, concomitant, enhancement, enrichment, supplement; SEE CONCEPTS *834,835*

accompaniment [n2] *music that supports a theme or performer in a composition*
back, background, backing, back-up, harmony, instrument, part; SEE CONCEPT *262*

accompany [v1] *go or be with something*
associate with, attend, chaperon, come along, conduct, consort, convoy, date, dog, draft, drag, escort, follow, go along, guard, guide, hang around with*, hang out*, keep company, lead, look after, shadow, schlepp along*, show about, show around, spook, squire, stick to*, string along*, tag along*, tailgate*, take out, usher; SEE CONCEPTS *113,224*

accompany [v2] *occur with something*
add, appear with, append, be connected, belong to, characterize, coexist, coincide with, come with, complete, co-occur, follow, go together, happen with, join with, occur with, supplement, take place with; SEE CONCEPT *643*

accomplice [n] *helper, especially in committing a crime*
abettor, accessory, aid, ally, assistant, associate, co-conspirator, collaborator, colleague, confederate, conspirator, henchman/woman, insider, partner, plant*, stall*; SEE CONCEPT *412*

accomplish [v] *succeed in doing*
achieve, arrive, attain, bring about, bring off, carry out, conclude, consummate, do, do a bang-up job*, do justice*, do one proud*, do the trick*, effect, finish, fulfill, gain, get someplace*, get there*, get to first base*, hit*, make hay*, make it, manage, nail it*, perform, produce, pull off*, put it over*, rack up*, reach, realize, score*, sew up*, take care of, win; SEE CONCEPTS *91,706*

accomplished [adj] *skilled in activity*
able, adept, brainy, consummate, cool*, cultivated, expert, gifted, hep*, hip*, masterly, polished, practiced, proficient, savvy, sharp, skillful, talented, wised up*, with it*; SEE CONCEPTS *326,528*

accomplishment [n] *something successfully done, completed*
ability, achievement, act, art, attainment, bringing about, capability, carrying out, completion, conclu-

sion, consummation, coup, deed, effecting, effort, execution, exploit, feat, finish, fulfillment, performance, production, proficiency, realization, skill, stroke, talent, triumph; SEE CONCEPT *706*

accord [*n*] *agreement, mutual understanding (often written)*
10-4, accordance, concert, concord, concurrence, conformity, congruence, correspondence, deal, good vibes*, good vibrations*, harmony, okay, pact, rapport, reconciliation, sympathy, treaty, unanimity, understanding; SEE CONCEPT *684*

accord [*v1*] *give approval, grant*
accede, acquiesce, admit, allow, award, bestow, concede, confer, endow, give, present, render, tender, vouchsafe; SEE CONCEPTS *50,83,88*

accord [*v2*] *come to agreement*
affirm, agree, assent, be in tune, concur, conform, correspond, fit, harmonize, jibe, match, square, suit, tally; SEE CONCEPTS *8,664*

accordingly [*adv*] *in an appropriate, suitable way*
appropriately, as a consequence, as a result, consequently, correspondingly, duly, equally, ergo, fitly, hence, in consequence, in respect to, in that event, properly, proportionately, respectively, resultantly, so, subsequently, suitably, then, therefore, thus, under the circumstances; SEE CONCEPT *558*

accost [*v*] *approach for conversation or solicitation*
address, annoy, bother, brace, buttonhole*, call, challenge, confront, cross, dare, entice, face, face off*, flag, greet, hail, proposition, run into, salute, welcome, whistle for*; SEE CONCEPTS *48,51*

account [*n1*] *written description of past events*
ABCs*, annual, blow by blow*, bulletin, chronicle, detail, explanation, history, lowdown*, make*, narration, narrative, play by play*, recital, report, rundown, score, story, tab, take, tale, the picture*, the whole picture*, version; SEE CONCEPT *282*

account [*n2*] *record of finances, fees, or charges*
bad news*, balance, bill, book, books, charge, check, computation, cuff*, grunt, inventory, invoice, IOU*, ledger, reckoning, record, register, report, score, statement, tab, tally; SEE CONCEPTS *331,332*

account [*n3*] *basis or consideration for action*
cause, ground, grounds, interest, justification, motive, rationale, rationalization, reason, regard, sake; SEE CONCEPT *240*

accountable [*adj*] *responsible for having done*
answerable, carry the load*, charged with, culpable, liable, obligated, obliged, on the hook*, straight*, surefire*; SEE CONCEPT *527*

accountant [*n*] *person who maintains financial accounts of a business*
actuary, analyst, auditor, bookkeeper, calculator, cashier, clerk, comptroller, CPA, examiner, public accountant, reckoner, teller; SEE CONCEPTS *348,353*

account for [*v*] *offer reason, explanation*
answer for, clarify, elucidate, explain, illuminate, justify, rationalize, resolve; SEE CONCEPT *57*

accredit [*v1*] *attribute responsibility or achievement*
ascribe, assign, charge, credit, input, lay, refer; SEE CONCEPTS *49,69*

accredit [*v2*] *give authorization or control*
appoint, approve, authorize, certify, commission, empower, enable, endorse, entrust, guarantee, license, okay, recognize, sanction, vouch for; SEE CONCEPTS *50,88*

accretion [*n*] *gradual growth, addition*
accession, accumulation, augmentation, build-up, increase, increment, raise, rise; SEE CONCEPT *780*

accrue [*v*] *increase by addition or growth, often financial*
accumulate, amass, build up, collect, enlarge, flow, gather, grow, increase; SEE CONCEPTS *763,780*

accumulate [*v*] *gather or amass something*
accrue, acquire, add to, agglomerate, aggregate, amalgamate, assemble, bring together, cache, clean up*, collect, collocate, compile, concentrate, cumulate, draw together, expand, gain, gather, grow, heap, heap together, hoard, incorporate, increase, load up, lump, make a bundle*, make a killing*, mass, pile, pile up, procure, profit, rack up*, roll up*, round up*, scare up*, stack up, stockpile, store, store up, swell, unite; SEE CONCEPTS *236,245*

accumulation [*n*] *gathering or amassing*
accession, accretion, addition, agglomeration, aggrandizement, aggregation, amassing, amassment, augmentation, build-up, chunk, collecting, collection, conglomeration, enlargement, gob, growth, heap, hoarding, hunk, increase, inflation, intensification, mass, multiplication, pile, quantity, stack, stock, store, trove, up, upping; SEE CONCEPTS *432,780*

accuracy [*n*] *being precise or correct*
accurateness, carefulness, certainty, closeness, correctness, definiteness, definitiveness, definitude, efficiency, exactitude, exactness, faultlessness, incisiveness, mastery, meticulousness, preciseness, precision, sharpness, skill, skillfulness, strictness, sureness, veracity, verity; SEE CONCEPTS *638,654*

accurate [*adj1*] *precise*
authentic, careful, close, concrete, correct, defined, definite, deft, detailed, discriminating, discriminative, distinct, exact, explicit, factual, faithful, genuine, judicious, just, literal, matter-of-fact, methodical, meticulous, on the button*, on the money*, on the nose*, particular, proper, punctilious, punctual, regular, right, rigid, rigorous, scientific, scrupulous, severe, sharp, skillful, solid, specific, strictness, systematic, true, ultraprecise, unerring, unmistakable, veracious; SEE CONCEPT *535*

accurate [*adj2*] *correct, without error*
absolute, actual, authentic, authoritative, certain, conclusive, correct, definite, definitive, errorless, exact, factual, faultless, final, flawless, genuine, infallible, irrefutable, official, perfect, right, straight, strict, true, truthful, undeniable, undisputed, unim-

peachable, unquestionable, unrefuted, valid, veracious; SEE CONCEPT *557*

accusation [*n*] *charge of wrongdoing, fault*
allegation, arraignment, attribution, beef*, blast*, bum rap*, censure, citation, complaint, denunciation, dido, exposé, gripe, impeachment, imputation, incrimination, indictment, insinuation, recrimination, roar*, rumble*, slur, squawk*, stink*; SEE CONCEPT *54*

accuse [*v*] *place blame for wrongdoing, fault*
allege, apprehend, arraign, arrest, attack, attribute, betray, blame, blow the whistle*, brand, bring charges, censure, charge, cite, complain, criminate, denounce, file claim, finger*, frame, hang something on*, hold accountable, impeach, implicate, impute, incriminate, inculpate, indict, lay at door*, let have it*, libel, litigate, lodge complaint, name, pin on*, point finger at*, prosecute, recriminate, serve summons, slander, slur, sue, summon, tax; SEE CONCEPT *44*

accustomed [*adj1*] *be or become prepared, used to*
acclimatized, acquainted, adapted, addicted, confirmed, disciplined, familiar, familiarized, given to, grooved*, habituated, habituated in, in the habit, inured, seasoned, settled in, trained; SEE CONCEPT *403*

accustomed [*adj2*] *normal, usual*
accepted, chronic, common, conventional, customary, established, everyday, expected, general, habitual, ordinary, regular, routine, set, traditional; SEE CONCEPT *547*

ace [*n*] *expert in some activity*
champion, genius, master, star, virtuoso, winner, wizard; SEE CONCEPT *416*

ace [*adj*] *exhibiting expertise in some activity*
brilliant, champion, distinguished, excellent, expert, first-rate, great, master, outstanding, superb, virtuoso; SEE CONCEPT *528*

acerbity [*n1*] *bitterness of taste*
acidity, acrimony, asperity, astringency, mordancy, sourness, tartness; SEE CONCEPTS *462,613*

acerbity [*n2*] *harsh speech, behavior*
causticity, ill temper, irritability, rancor, rudeness, sarcasm, sarcasticness, vitriolicism; SEE CONCEPTS *267,401*

ache [*n*] *sore feeling; dull pain*
anguish, hurt, misery, pang, pounding, smarting, soreness, spasm, suffering, throb, throbbing, throe, twinge; SEE CONCEPTS *316,410,728*

ache [*v*] *feeling soreness or dull pain, often physical*
be sore, hurt, pain, pound, smart, suffer, throb, twinge; SEE CONCEPTS *13,17,303,308,313*

achieve [*v*] *bring to successful conclusion; reach a goal*
accomplish, acquire, actualize, attain, bring about, bring off*, bring to pass, cap, carry out, carry through, close, complete, conclude, consummate, deliver, discharge, dispatch, do, earn, earn wings*, effect, effectuate, enact, end, execute, finish, follow

through, fulfill, gain, get, get done, manage, negotiate, obtain, perfect, perform, procure, produce, rack up*, reach, realize, resolve, score, seal, see through, settle, sign, solve, win, wind up, work out; SEE CONCEPT *706*

achievement [*n*] *something completed successfully; goal reached*
accomplishment, acquirement, acquisition, act, actualization, attainment, completion, conquest, consummation, contrivance, creation, deed, effectuation, effort, enactment, encompassment, execution, exploit, feat, fulfillment, hit, masterpiece, performance, production, realization, stroke, success, tour de force, triumph, victory; SEE CONCEPT *706*

acid [*adj1*] *bitter, sour in taste*
acerbic, acidulous, biting, piquant, pungent, sharp, tart, vinegarish, vinegary; SEE CONCEPT *613*

acid [*adj2*] *having acidic, corrosive properties*
acerbic, acidulous, acrid, anti-alkaline, biting, bleaching, corroding, disintegrative, dissolvent, eating away, eroding, erosive, oxidizing, rusting; SEE CONCEPT *485*

acid [*adj3*] *bitter in words or behavior*
acerbic, biting, caustic, cutting, dry, harsh, hateful, hurtful, mordant, nasty, offensive, sarcastic, sharp, stinging, trenchant, vitriolic; SEE CONCEPTS *267,401*

acidulous [*adj1*] *bitter, sour*
acerb, acerbic, acetose, dry, piquant, sharp, tart; SEE CONCEPT *613*

acidulous [*adj2*] *bitter in speech*
biting, cutting, ironical, mocking, sarcastic; SEE CONCEPT *267*

acknowledge [*v1*] *verbally recognize authority*
accede, accept, acquiesce, agree, allow, approve, attest to, certify, defend, defer to, endorse, grant, own, ratify, recognize, subscribe to, support, take an oath, uphold, yield; SEE CONCEPTS *8,50,88*

acknowledge [*v2*] *admit truth or reality of something*
accede, accept, acquiesce, allow, avow, come clean*, come out of closet*, concede, confess, cop a plea*, crack*, declare, fess up*, get off chest*, grant, let on*, open up*, own, profess, recognize, yield; SEE CONCEPTS *12,49*

acknowledge [*v3*] *verbally recognize receipt of something*
address, answer, get back to, greet, hail, notice, react, remark, reply, respond, return, salute, thank; SEE CONCEPTS *38,45,51,60*

acknowledgment [*n1*] *act of recognizing authority or truth of something*
acceptance, accession, acquiescence, admission, admitting, affirmation, allowance, allowing, assent, assertion, asseveration, avowal, compliance, conceding, concession, concurrence, confession, confirmation, corroboration, declaration, profession, ratification, realization, recognition, yielding; SEE CONCEPTS *8,50,88*

acknowledgment [*n2*] *physical symbol of recognition*
acclamation, addressing, answer, apology, applause, appreciation, bestowal, bow, card, confession, contract, credit, gift, gratitude, greeting, guarantee, hail, hailing, letter, nod, notice, reaction, receipt, reply, response, return, salutation, salute, signature, statement, support, thanks, token; SEE CONCEPTS *595,628*

acme [*n*] *pinnacle of achievement or physical object*
apogee, capstone, climax, culmination, height, highest point, high point, meridian, optimum, peak, summit, top, ultimate, vertex, zenith; SEE CONCEPTS *706,836*

acolyte [*n*] *attendant, usually in a church*
aid, assistant, follower, helper; SEE CONCEPT *361*

acquaint [*v*] *inform oneself or another about something new*
accustom, advise, apprise, bring out, clue, come out with*, disclose, divulge, do the honors*, enlighten, familiarize, fill in, fix up*, get together*, habituate, inform, intro, introduce, knock down*, let know, make familiar, notify, post, present, reveal, tell, warn; SEE CONCEPTS *31,60*

acquaintance [*n1*] *a person known informally*
associate, association, colleague, companion, contact, friend, neighbor; SEE CONCEPT *423*

acquaintance [*n2*] *knowledge of something through experience*
awareness, cognizance, conversance, familiarity, fellowship, grasp, intimacy, ken, relationship, understanding; SEE CONCEPT *409*

acquiesce [*v*] *agree with some reluctance*
accede, accept, accommodate, adapt, adjust, agree, allow, approve, bow to, buy, cave in*, come across, come around, comply, concur, conform, consent, cry uncle*, cut a deal*, ditto*, give in, give out, go along, jibe*, okay, pass, play ball*, reconcile, roll over and play dead*, say uncle*, set, shake on, submit, subscribe, yes, yield; SEE CONCEPTS *8,10,23,82*

acquiescence [*n*] *reluctant agreement*
acceptance, accession, approval, assent, compliance, concurrence, conformity, consent, giving in, obedience, permission, resignation, submission, submissiveness, yielding; SEE CONCEPTS *8,10*

acquire [*v*] *obtain or receive*
access, achieve, amass, annex, attain, bring in, buy, catch, collect, cop*, corral*, earn, gain, gather, get, get hands on, get hold of, grab, have, hustle, land, latch onto, lock up, pick up, procure, promote, rack up*, scare up*, secure, snag*, take, take possession, wangle*, win; SEE CONCEPTS *120,124,142*

acquisition [*n1*] *obtaining or receiving*
accretion, achievement, acquirement, acquiring, addition, attainment, buy, gain, gaining, learning, obtainment, possession, prize, procuration, procurement, procuring, property, purchase, pursuit, recovery, redemption, retrieval, salvage, winning; SEE CONCEPTS *120,124,142*

acquisition [*n2*] *something obtained, received*
accomplishment, achievement, allowance, annuity, award, benefit, bonus, commission, dividend, donation, earnings, fortune, gain, gift, grant, income, increment, inheritance, net, premium, prize, proceeds, profit, remuneration, return, reward, riches, salary, security, wages, wealth, winnings; SEE CONCEPTS *120,337,710*

acquisitive [*adj*] *eager to obtain knowledge or things*
avaricious, avid, covetous, demanding, desirous, grabbing, grabby, grasping, greedy, predatory, prehensile, rapacious; SEE CONCEPT *542*

acquit [*v1*] *announce removal of blame*
absolve, blink at*, clear, deliver, discharge, disculpate, exculpate, excuse, exonerate, free, let go, let off, let off the hook*, liberate, release, relieve, vindicate, whitewash*, wink at*, wipe off*; SEE CONCEPTS *50,83,88,317*

acquit [*v2*] *behave some way*
act, bear, carry, comport, conduct, deport, perform; SEE CONCEPT *633*

acquittal [*n*] *declaration removing blame*
absolution, acquitting, amnesty, clearance, deliverance, discharge, discharging, dismissal, dismissing, exculpation, exemption, exoneration, freeing, letting off, liberation, pardon, release, releasing, relief from, reprieve, vindication; SEE CONCEPTS *127,317,318*

acre [*n*] *piece of land, unit of area*
acreage, bit, estate, grounds, manor, plot, property; SEE CONCEPT *792*

acrid [*adj1*] *bitter, sour to taste*
acid, amaroidal, astringent, biting, burning, caustic, harsh, irritating, pungent, sharp, stinging; SEE CONCEPT *613*

acrid [*adj2*] *nasty in behavior or words*
acrimonious, austere, biting, bitter, caustic, cutting, harsh, mordant, sarcastic, sharp, trenchant, vitriolic; SEE CONCEPTS *267,401*

acrimonious [*adj*] *nastiness in behavior, speech*
acerbic, acid, angry, astringent, belligerent, biting, bitter, caustic, censorious, churlish, crabby, cranky, cross, cutting, indignant, irascible, irate, ireful, mad, mordant, peevish, petulant, rancorous, sarcastic, sharp, spiteful, splenetic, tart, testy, trenchant, wrathful; SEE CONCEPTS *267,401*

acrimony [*n*] *nasty behavior, speech*
acerbity, animosity, antipathy, asperity, astringency, belligerence, bitterness, churlishness, crankiness, harshness, ill will, irascibility, malevolence, malice, mordancy, peevishness, rancor, rudeness, sarcasm, spite, tartness, unkindness, virulence; SEE CONCEPTS *633,657*

acrobat [*n*] *performer who does tricks, physical feats*
aerialist, artist, athlete, balancer, clown, contortionist, dancer, funambulist, gymnast, performer, stunt man/woman, stunt person, trapezist, tumbler; SEE CONCEPT *352*

across [*prep*] *traversing a space, side to side*
athwart, beyond, cross, crossed, crosswise, opposite, over, side to side, transversely; SEE CONCEPT *581*

act [*n1*] *something done*
accomplishment, achievement, action, deed, doing, execution, exploit, feat, move, operation, performance, step, thing, undertaking; SEE CONCEPT *1*

act [*n2*] *legislative document*
amendment, announcement, bill, clause, code, commitment, decree, edict, enactment, judgment, law, measure, order, ordinance, resolution, statute, subpoena, summons, verdict, warrant, writ; SEE CONCEPTS *271,318*

act [*n3*] *part of a performance*
bit*, curtain, epilogue, gag*, introduction, number, piece, prologue, routine, scene, schtick*, show, sketch, spot, turn; SEE CONCEPT *264*

act [*n4*] *pretended behavior*
affectation, attitude, bit*, chaser*, dissimilation, fake, false front*, feigning, front, performance, phony, pose, posture, pretense, put-on, sham, show, shuck and jive*, soft soap*, stall, stance, stunt, sweet talk*; SEE CONCEPT *633*

act [*v1*] *do something*
accomplish, achieve, begin, carry on, carry out, consummate, cook, create, develop, do, do a number*, do one's thing*, enforce, execute, function, get in there*, go about, go for broke*, go for it*, go in for*, go that route*, go to town*, intrude, knock off*, labor, make progress, maneuver, move, officiate, operate, percolate*, perk*, perpetrate, persevere, persist, practice, preside, pursue, respond, serve, take effect, take part, take steps, take up, transport, undertake, work out; SEE CONCEPTS *1,4*

act [*v2*] *behave in a certain way*
appear, behave, carry, carry oneself, carry out, comport, conduct, do, enact, execute, exert, function, give the appearance, go about, impress as, operate, perform, play part, react, represent oneself, seem, serve, strike, take on; SEE CONCEPT *633*

act [*v3*] *entertain by playing a role*
be on*, bring down the house*, burlesque, characterize, do a turn*, dramatize, emote, enact, feign, go on, go over, ham*, ham it up*, impersonate, lay an egg*, make debut, mime, mimic, mug, parody, perform, personate, personify, play, play act, play gig, play part, play role, portray, pretend, put it over*, rehearse, represent, say one's piece*, simulate, star, stooge*, strut*, take part, tread the boards; SEE CONCEPT *292*

acting [*n*] *entertaining, performing*
assuming, characterization, depiction, dramatics, dramatizing, enacting, enactment, feigning, hamming*, histrionics, imitating, imitation, impersonation, improv, mime, mimicry, pantomime, performance, performing, play act, playing, portrayal, portraying, posing, posturing, pretending, pretense, putting, rendition, seeming, showing off, simulating, stagecraft, stooging*, theatre, theatricals; SEE CONCEPT *292*

acting [*adj*] *substituting in a role*
ad interim, adjutant, alternate, assistant, delegated, deputy, interim, pro tem, pro tempore, provisional, surrogate, temporary; SEE CONCEPT *560*

action [*n1*] *something done*
activity, agility, alacrity, alertness, animation, bag*, ballgame*, big idea*, bit*, business, bustle, commotion, dash, deal, energy, enterprise, flurry, force, functioning, game, going, happening, haste, hoopla*, hopper*, industry, in the works, life, liveliness, motion, movement, occupation, operation, pipeline*, plan, power, process, proposition, racket*, reaction, response, rush, scene, spirit, stir, stunt, trip, turmoil, vigor, vim, vitality, vivacity; SEE CONCEPT *1*

action [*n2*] *individual deed*
accomplishment, achievement, act, blow, commission, dealings, doing, effort, enterprise, execution, exercise, exertion, exploit, feat, handiwork, maneuver, manipulation, move, operation, performance, procedure, step, stroke, thrust, transaction, undertaking; SEE CONCEPTS *91,706*

action [*n3*] *a legal process*
case, cause, claim, lawsuit, litigation, proceeding, prosecution, suit; SEE CONCEPT *317*

action [*n4*] *an aggressive military deed*
battle, combat, conflict, contest, encounter, engagement, fight, fighting, fray, skirmish, warfare; SEE CONCEPT *320*

activate [*v*] *initiate something; start a function*
actify, actuate, arouse, call up, energize, impel, mobilize, motivate, move, prompt, propel, rouse, set in motion, start, stimulate, stir, switch on, take out of mothballs*, trigger, turn on; SEE CONCEPT *234*

active [*adj1*] *having movement*
alive, astir, at work, bustling, effective, efficacious, exertive, flowing, functioning, going, hasty, impelling, in force, in play, in process, mobile, movable, moving, operating, operative, progressive, pushing, rapid, restless, rolling, running, rushing, rustling, shifting, simmering, speeding, speedy, streaming, swarming, traveling, turning, walking, working; SEE CONCEPT *542*

active [*adj2*] *very involved in activity*
aggressive, agile, alert, alive, animated, assiduous, bold, brisk, bustling, busy, chipper, daring, dashing, determined, dexterous, diligent, dynamic, eager, energetic, engaged, enlivened, enterprising, enthusiastic, eventful, fireball*, forceful, forcible, fresh, frisky, hard-working, high-spirited, hyper, industrious, intense, inventive, jumping, keen, lively, nimble, on the move, perky, persevering, purposeful, pushing, quick, rapid, ready, resolute, sharp, sprightly, spry, whiz*, zealous; SEE CONCEPTS *401,542*

activity [*n1*] *state of being active*
action, activeness, animation, bustle, enterprise, exercise, exertion, hustle, labor, life, liveliness, motion, movement; SEE CONCEPTS *1,748*

activity [*n2*] *special interest or pursuit*
act, avocation, bag*, ballgame*, bit*, deed, endeavor, enterprise, entertainment, game, hobby, job, labor, occupation, pastime, project, racket, scene, scheme, stunt, task, trip, undertaking, venture, work, zoo*; SEE CONCEPT *32*

actor [*n*] *person who performs, entertains by role-playing*
amateur, artist, barnstormer, bit player, character, clown, comedian, entertainer, extra, foil, ham*, hambone*, headliner, idol, impersonator, ingénue, lead, leading man/woman, legiter, mime, mimic, pantomimist, performer, play-actor, player, soubrette, stand-in, star, stooge*, straight man/woman, television star, thesp*, thespian, trouper, understudy, ventriloquist, villain, walk-on; SEE CONCEPT *352*

actual [*adj1*] *truly existing, real*
absolute, authentic, categorical, certain, concrete, confirmed, definite, factual, for real*, genuine, hard, honest injun*, honest to God*, indisputable, indubitable, kosher*, no ifs ands or buts*, physical, positive, realistic, substantial, substantive, sure enough*, tangible, true, truthful, undeniable, unquestionable, verified; SEE CONCEPT *582*

actual [*adj2*] *existing at the present time*
current, exact, existent, extant, live, living, original, prevailing; SEE CONCEPT *799*

actuality [*n*] *something that truly exists, is real*
achievement, actualization, attainment, brass tacks*, fact, like it is*, live, materiality, materialization, reality, real world*, straight stuff*, substance, substantiality, truth, what it is*; SEE CONCEPT *725*

actually [*adj*] *truly real, existent*
absolutely, as a matter of fact, de facto, genuinely, indeed, in fact, in point of fact, in reality, in truth, literally, really, veritably, very; SEE CONCEPT *582*

actuate [*v*] *start a function or action, motivate*
activate, animate, arouse, cause, drive, egg on*, energize, excite, fire up*, impel, incite, induce, influence, inspire, instigate, key up*, mobilize, motivate, move, prompt, propel, put up to*, quicken, rouse, spur, stimulate, turn on*, work into lather*, work up*; SEE CONCEPTS *221,234*

acumen [*n*] *ability to understand and reason*
accuracy, acuity, acuteness, astuteness, awareness, brains, brilliance, cleverness, comprehension, cunning, discernment, discrimination, farsightedness, good taste, grasp, guile, ingenuity, insight, intellect, intelligence, intuition, judgment, keenness, perception, percipience, perspicacity, perspicuity, refinement, sagacity, sensitivity, sharpness, shrewdness, smartness, smarts, understanding, vision, wisdom, wit; SEE CONCEPT *409*

acute [*adj1*] *deeply perceptive*
astute, canny, clever, discerning, discriminating, incisive, ingenious, insightful, intense, intuitive, judicious, keen, observant, penetrating, perspicacious, piercing, quick-witted, sensitive, sharp, smart, subtle; SEE CONCEPT *402*

acute [*adj2*] *very important*
afflictive, critical, crucial, dangerous, decisive, desperate, dire, essential, grave, serious, severe, sudden, urgent, vital; SEE CONCEPT *568*

acute [*adj3*] *severe, intense*
cutting, distressing, excruciating, exquisite, fierce, keen, overpowering, overwhelming, piercing, poignant, powerful, racking, severe, sharp, shooting, stabbing, sudden, violent; SEE CONCEPT *569*

acute [*adj4*] *having a sharp end or point*
acicular, aciculate, acuminate, acuminous, cuspate, cuspidate, knifelike, needle-shaped, peaked, piked, pointed, sharpened, spiked; SEE CONCEPT *485*

adage [*n*] *saying or proverb*
aphorism, apothegm, axiom, byword, daffodil*, dictum, maxim, motto, precept, saw; SEE CONCEPT *276*

adamant [*adj1*] *unyielding*
determined, firm, fixed, hanging tough*, hard-nosed, immovable, inexorable, inflexible, insistent, intransigent, obdurate, pat*, relentless, resolute, rigid, set, set in stone*, standing pat*, stiff, stubborn, tough nut*, unbendable, unbending, uncompromising, unrelenting, unshakable, unswayable; SEE CONCEPT *401*

adamant [*adj2*] *hard like rock*
adamantine, flinty, impenetrable, indestructible, rock-hard, tough, unbreakable; SEE CONCEPT *604*

adapt [*v*] *adjust to a different situation or condition*
acclimate, accommodate, accustom, alter, change, come around, comply, conform, familiarize, fashion, fit, get act together*, get used to, grow used to, habituate, harmonize, make, match, modify, play the game*, prepare, qualify, readjust, reconcile, remodel, revise, roll with punches*, shape, shape up*, square, suit, tailor; SEE CONCEPTS *232,697*

adaptable [*adj*] *able and usually willing to change*
AC-DC*, adjustable, all around, alterable, can-do, changeable, compliant, conformable, convertible, ductile, easy-going, flexible, hanging loose*, malleable, modifiable, moldable, plastic, pliable, pliant, putty, resilient, rolling with punches*, supple, switch-hitting, tractable, variable, versatile; SEE CONCEPTS *550,576*

adaptation [*n1*] *ability and willingness to change*
adjustment, adoption, alteration, conversion, modification, refitting, remodeling, reworking, shift, transformation, variation; SEE CONCEPT *697*

adaptation [*n2*] *condition of something resulting from change*
acclimatization, accustomedness, agreement, compliance, correspondence, familiarization, habituation, naturalization; SEE CONCEPT *230*

add [*v1*] *simple arithmetical process of increase; accumulation*
calculate, cast, compute, count, count up, do addition, enumerate, figure, reckon, reckon up, sum, summate, tally, tot*, total, tote*, tot up*; SEE CONCEPT *764*

add [*v2*] *adjoin, increase; make further comment*
add fuel*, affix, annex, ante, append, augment, beef up, boost, build up, charge up, continue, cue in*, figure in, flesh out*, heat up*, hike, hike up*, hitch on*, hook on*, hook up with*, include, jack up*, jazz up*, join together, pad, parlay, piggyback*, plug into*, pour it on*, reply, run up*, say further, slap on*, snowball*, soup up*, speed up, spike, step up, supplement, sweeten*, tack on*, tag; SEE CONCEPTS *51,113,236,245*

addendum [*n*] *something conjoined, added*
addition, adjunct, appendage, appendix, attachment, augmentation, codicil, extension, extra, postscript, rider, supplement; SEE CONCEPTS *270,827*

addict [*n*] *person who has compulsion toward activity, often injurious*
aficionado, buff, devotee, enthusiast, fan, fanatic, fiend, follower, freak*, habitué, hound*, junkie*, nut, practitioner, zealot; SEE CONCEPTS *412,423*

addicted [*adj*] *dependent on something, compulsive*
absorbed, accustomed, attached, dependent, devoted, disposed, fanatic, fond, given over, given to, habituated, hooked, hyped*, imbued, inclined, obsessed, predisposed, prone, spaced out*, strung out*, under the influence, used to, wedded to; SEE CONCEPT *542*

addiction [*n*] *a habit of activity, often injurious*
bag*, bent, craving, dependence, enslavement, fixation, hang-up*, hook, inclination, jones*, kick*, monkey*, monkey on back*, obsession, shot*, sweet tooth*, thing*; SEE CONCEPTS *20,316,709*

addition [*n1*] *process of conjoining, adding*
accession, adding, adjoining, affixing, annexation, attachment, augmentation, enlargement, extension, inclusion, increasing; SEE CONCEPTS *236,245*

addition [*n2*] *something conjoined to or enlargement of something*
accession, accessory, accretion, accrual, addendum, additive, adjunct, aggrandizement, annex, appendage, appendix, attachment, augmentation, bonus, boost, commission, dividend, enhancement, enlargement, expansion, extension, extra, gain, hike, increase, increment, option, profit, raise, reinforcement, rise, supplement, wing; SEE CONCEPTS *640,835*

addition [*n3*] *arithmetical process of augmentation*
accretion, accruing, adding, computing, counting, enlarging, expanding, increasing, reckoning, summation, summing, tabulating, totaling, toting*; SEE CONCEPT *764*

additional [*adj*] *extra, supplementary*
added, affixed, appended, further, increased, lagniappe*, more, new, on the side, option, other, over-and-above, padding, perk, spare, supplementary; SEE CONCEPT *771*

addled [*adj*] *confused*
balled up*, befuddled, bewildered, fouled up*, gone*, mixed up, out of, punchy, rattled, shaken, shook, shook up, slap-happy, thrown, unglued*, woozy*; SEE CONCEPT *403*

address [*n1*] *place of residence or business where one can be contacted*
abode, box number, direction, domicile, dwelling, headquarters, home, house, living quarters, location, lodging, number, place of business, place of residence, street, whereabouts, zip code; SEE CONCEPT *516*

address [*n2*] *speech given to formal gathering*
chalk talk*, discourse, dissertation, lecture, oration, pep talk*, pitch, sermon, soapbox*, spiel*, talk; SEE CONCEPT *278*

address [*v1*] *write directions for delivery*
consign, dispatch, forward, inscribe, label, mark, postmark, remit, route, send, ship, superscribe, transmit; SEE CONCEPTS *60,79*

address [*v2*] *speak to a formal gathering*
approach, bespeak, call, deliver speech, deliver talk, discourse, discuss, get on a soapbox*, give speech, give talk, greet, hail, lecture, memorialize, orate, pitch, pontificate, root for, sermonize, spiel*, spout, stump*, take the floor, talk; SEE CONCEPTS *60,266,285*

address [*v3*] *devote effort to something*
apply, apply oneself to, attend to, concentrate on, devote oneself to, dig, direct, engage in, focus on, give, go at*, go for*, hammer away*, have a go at*, have at*, knuckle down to*, peg away*, pitch into*, plug*, take care of, take up, throw, try, turn, turn to, undertake; SEE CONCEPT *100*

adept [*adj*] *very able*
accomplished, adroit, brainy, capable, clean*, crack*, crackerjack*, deft, dexterous, expert, hot*, hotshot*, know stuff*, masterful, masterly, nobody's fool*, no dummy*, no slouch*, on the ball*, on the beam*, practiced, proficient, prosperous, quick, savvy, sharp, sharp as a tack*, skilled, skillful, slick, smooth, there*, up to speed*, versed, whiz*, wizard; SEE CONCEPTS *402,527*

adequacy [*n*] *ability, competency in some action*
capability, capacity, commensurateness, competence, enough, fairness, plenty, requisiteness, satisfactoriness, sufficiency, suitableness, tolerableness; SEE CONCEPTS *636,656*

adequate [*adj*] *enough, able*
acceptable, all right, capable, comfortable, commensurate, competent, decent, equal, fair, passable, requisite, satisfactory, sufficient, sufficing, suitable, tolerable, unexceptional, unobjectionable; SEE CONCEPTS *533,558*

adequately [*adv*] *sufficiently*
abundantly, acceptably, appropriately, capably, competently, copiously, decently, fairly well, fit-

tingly, modestly, pleasantly enough, presentably, satisfactorily, sufficiently, suitably, to an acceptable degree, tolerably, well enough; SEE CONCEPTS *558,560*

adhere [*v1*] *conform to or follow rules exactly*
abide by, be attached, be constant, be devoted, be devoted to, be faithful, be loyal, be true, cleave to, cling, comply, follow, fulfill, heed, keep, maintain, mind, obey, observe, practice, respect, stand by, support; SEE CONCEPTS *87,636*

adhere [*v2*] *stick or become stuck to, either physically or mentally*
attach, cement, cleave, cling, cling like ivy*, cohere, fasten, fix, freeze to*, glue, hold fast, hold on like bulldog*, paste, stay put, stick like a barnacle*, stick like glue*, unite; SEE CONCEPTS *85,113,160*

adhesive [*adj*] *sticking*
adherent, adhering, agglutinant, attaching, clinging, clingy, gelatinous, glutinous, gooey, gummed, gummy, holding, hugging, mucilaginous, pasty, resinous, sticky, tenacious, viscid, viscous, waxy; SEE CONCEPTS *488,606*

adieu [*n*] *parting remark or action*
adios, congé, farewell, goodbye, leave-taking, parting, so long, valediction; SEE CONCEPT *276*

ad infinitum [*adj*] *neverending*
ceaselessly, endlessly, forever, perpetually; SEE CONCEPT *798*

adjacent [*adj*] *next to, abutting*
adjoining, alongside, beside, bordering, close, close by, contiguous, near, neighboring, next door, touching; SEE CONCEPT *586*

adjective [*n*] *word that modifies a noun*
accessory, additional, adjunct, adnoun, attribute, attributive, dependent, descriptive, identifier, modifier, qualifier; SEE CONCEPT *275*

adjoin [*v1*] *be next to*
abut, approximate, be adjacent to, border, butt, communicate, connect, join, lie, lie beside, link, neighbor, touch, verge; SEE CONCEPT *747*

adjoin [*v2*] *attach*
add, affix, annex, append, combine, connect, couple, impinge, interconnect, join, link, unite; SEE CONCEPTS *85,113,160*

adjoining [*adj*] *being next to*
abutting, adjacent, approximal, bordering on, connecting, conterminous, contiguous, impinging, interconnecting, joined, joining, juxtaposed, near, neighboring, next door, touching, verging; SEE CONCEPT *586*

adjourn [*v*] *stop a proceeding*
curb, defer, delay, discontinue, hold off, hold over, hold up, postpone, prorogue, put off, recess, restrain, shelve, stay, suspend; SEE CONCEPTS *121,234*

adjournment [*n*] *discontinuation or delay of a proceeding*
break, deferment, deferral, intermission, interruption, pause, postponement, prorogation, putting off, recess, stay, suspension; SEE CONCEPTS *121,703*

adjudicate [*v*] *formally judge*
adjudge, arbitrate, decide, determine, mediate, referee, settle, umpire; SEE CONCEPTS *18,317*

adjunct [*n*] *addition; help*
accessory, addendum, appendage, appendix, appurtenance, associate, auxiliary, complement, detail, partner, subordinate, supplement; SEE CONCEPTS *484,835*

adjust [*v1*] *become or make prepared, adapted*
acclimatize, accommodate, accustom, adapt, alter, arrange, compose, conform, dispose, do as Romans do*, doctor*, fiddle with*, fine-tune, fit, fix, fix up, get act together*, get it together*, grin and bear it*, habituate, harmonize, make conform, modify, order, quadrate, reconcile, rectify, redress, regulate, remodel, settle, suit, swim with the tide*, tailor, tailor-make, tune; SEE CONCEPTS *35,232,697*

adjust [*v2*] *mechanically alter, especially to improve*
accommodate, align, balance, bring into line, calibrate, connect, correct, fine-tune, fit, fix, focus, grind, improve, mend, overhaul, polish, put in working order, readjust, rectify, regulate, renovate, repair, service, set, sharpen, square, tighten, troubleshoot, tune up; SEE CONCEPTS *202,212*

adjust [*v3*] *bring into agreement or to a standard*
accord, allocate, arrange, clarify, conclude, conform, coordinate, doctor*, fiddle with*, fine-tune, fix up, grade, methodize, modify, organize, reconcile, regulate, settle, sort, standardize, straighten, systematize, tally; SEE CONCEPTS *84,117*

adjustment [*n1*] *adaptation*
acclimation, acclimatization, alteration, arrangement, balancing, conformance, correcting, fitting, fixing, improvement, mending, modification, ordering, organization, organizing, orientation, readjustment, redress, regulating, regulation, repairing, setting, shaping, standardization, turning; SEE CONCEPT *697*

adjustment [*n2*] *financial retribution, payment of claim*
agreement, allotment, apportionment, benefit, compensation, compromise, pay, reconciliation, reimbursement, remuneration, settlement, share, stake, stipulation; SEE CONCEPT *332*

adjutant [*n*] *assistant*
aide, auxiliary, helper; SEE CONCEPT *348*

ad-lib [*adj*] *improvised*
extemporaneous, extempore, extemporized, impromptu, made-up, off-the-cuff, spontaneous, unprepared, unrehearsed; SEE CONCEPT *267*

ad-lib [*v*] *improvise speech*
extemporize, improvisate, invent, make up, speak extemporaneously, speak impromptu, speak off the cuff; SEE CONCEPT *266*

ad-lib [*adv*] *in an improvised manner*
extemporaneously, extempore, impromptu, off the cuff, off the top of one's head*, spontaneously, without preparation, without rehearsal; SEE CONCEPT *267*

administer [*v1*] *manage an organization or effort*
administrate, be in the driver's seat*, be in the saddle*, boss*, carry out, conduct, control, crack the whip*, direct, execute, govern, head, head up*, hold the reins*, oversee, pull the strings*, pull the wires*, render, ride herd on*, run, run the show*, sit on top of*, superintend, supervise; SEE CONCEPTS *117,298*

administer [*v2*] *dispense something needed*
apply, apportion, authorize, bring, contribute, deal, deliver, disburse, distribute, dole, execute, extend, furnish, give, impose, inflict, issue, measure out, mete out, offer, perform, portion, proffer, provide, regulate, serve, supply, tender; SEE CONCEPTS *108,136*

administration [*n1*] *management of an organization or effort*
administering, agency, application, authority, charge, command, conduct, conducting, control, directing, direction, dispensation, disposition, distribution, enforcement, execution, governing, government, guidance, handling, jurisdiction, legislation, order, organization, overseeing, oversight, performance, policy, power, provision, regulation, rule, running, strategy, superintendence, supervision, surveillance; SEE CONCEPTS *117,298*

administration [*n2*] *human or group who manages effort of an organization*
admiral, advisers, big brother*, board, bureau, cabinet, chairman/woman, chairperson, chargé d'affaires, command, commander, committee, consulate, department, directors, dome, embassy, executive, executives, feds*, front office*, general, governing body, headquarters, legislature, management, ministry, officers, officials, powers, presidency, president, presidium, stewards, superintendents, supervisors, top brass*, upstairs*; SEE CONCEPT *299*

administration [*n3*] *period during which a particular human group is in power*
dynasty, incumbency, presidency, regime, reign, stay, tenure, term; SEE CONCEPTS *298,816*

administrative [*adj*] *involved in managing or using power*
authoritative, bureaucratic, central, commanding, controlling, deciding, decisive, departmental, directing, directive, directorial, executive, governing, governmental, in charge, in control, jurisdictional, legislative, managerial, official, organizational, policy-making, presiding, regulative, regulatory, ruling, superintending, supervising, supervisory; SEE CONCEPTS *319,536*

administrator [*n*] *person who manages organization*
ambassador, authority, big brother*, boss, bureaucrat, captain, CEO, chairman/woman, chairperson, chief, commander, consul, controller, custodian, dean, director, exec, executive, front office, governor, head, head honcho*, head man/woman*, inspector, judge, leader, man/woman upstairs*, manager, master, mayor, minister, officer, official, organizer,

overseer, premier, president, prez*, producer, superintendent, supervisor; SEE CONCEPTS *347,354*

admirable [*adj*] *held in great respect*
A-1*, ace*, A-OK*, attractive, best ever, cat's pajamas*, choice, commendable, cool*, copacetic*, crackerjack*, deserving, dream*, estimable, excellent, exquisite, fine, good, great, greatest, hunky dory*, keen*, laudable, meritable, meritorious, neat*, out of sight*, out of this world*, peachy*, praiseworthy, rare, solid, super, super-duper*, superior, unreal*, valuable, wicked*, wonderful, worthy, zero cool*; SEE CONCEPTS *572,574*

admiration [*n*] *great respect*
account, adoration, affection, applause, appreciation, approbation, approval, deference, delight, esteem, estimation, favor, fondness, glorification, homage, honor, idolatry, idolization, liking, love, marveling, obeisance, pleasure, praise, prizing, recognition, regard, reverence, valuing, veneration, wonder, wonderment, worship; SEE CONCEPT *32*

admire [*v*] *hold in high regard*
adore, applaud, appreciate, approve, be crazy about*, be crazy for*, be crazy over*, be mad about*, be nuts about*, be stuck on*, be sweet on*, be wild about*, cherish, commend, credit, delight in, esteem, eulogize, extol, fall for*, get high on*, glorify, go for*, groove on*, hail, have the hots for*, hold in respect, honor, idolize, laud, look up to, marvel at, moon over*, pay homage to, praise, prize, rate highly, respect, revere, take pleasure in, think highly of, treasure, value, venerate, wonder at, worship; SEE CONCEPT *32*

admirer [*n*] *person who holds someone in high regard*
adherent, beau, believer, booster, boyfriend, buff, bug*, cat*, devotee, disciple, enthusiast, fan, fancier, fiend*, follower, freak*, girlfriend, groupie*, hound*, junkie*, lover, nut*, partisan, patron, rooter, suitor, supporter, swain, sweetheart, wooer, worshiper; SEE CONCEPT *423*

admissible [*adj*] *able or deserving of consideration; allowable*
acceptable, allowed, applicable, appropriate, concedable, fair, fitting, just, justifiable, lawful, legal, legitimate, licit, likely, logical, not impossible, not unlikely, okay, passable, permissible, permitted, pertinent, possible, probable, proper, rational, reasonable, relevant, right, suitable, tolerable, tolerated, warranted, worthy; SEE CONCEPT *533*

admission [*n1*] *entering or allowing entry*
acceptance, access, admittance, certification, confirmation, designation, door, entrance, entree, ingress, initiation, introduction, permission, reception, recognition, way, welcome; SEE CONCEPTS *83,159*

admission [*n2*] *confession or acknowledgment*
accession, admittance, affidavit, affirmation, allowance, assent, assertion, attestation, averment, avowal, concession, confirmation, declaration, deposition,

disclosure, divulgence, profession, revelation, statement, testimonial, testimony; SEE CONCEPT *57*

admit [*v1*] *allow entry*
accept, be big on*, bless, buy, concede, enter, entertain, give access, give the nod*, grant, harbor, house, initiate, introduce, let, let in, lodge, okay, permit, receive, shelter, sign*, sign off on*, suffer, take, take in, thumbs up*; SEE CONCEPT *83*

admit [*v2*] *confess, acknowledge*
accept, accord, acquiesce, adopt, affirm, agree, allow, approve, avow, bare, bring to light*, communicate, concede, concur, confide, confirm, consent, cop a plea*, credit, declare, disclose, divulge, enumerate, expose, go into details*, grant, indicate, let, let on, make known, narrate, number, open up, own, own up*, permit, proclaim, profess, recite, recognize, relate, reveal, spill*, subscribe to, talk, tell, tolerate, uncover, unveil, yield; SEE CONCEPTS *57,82*

admonish [*v*] *warn, strongly criticize*
advise, berate, call down, call on the carpet*, caveat, censure, check, chide, come down hard on*, counsel, ding*, draw the line*, enjoin, exhort, forewarn, give a going over*, give a piece of one's mind*, give comeuppance, glue*, growl*, hoist*, jack up*, notice, rap*, rap on knuckles*, rebuke, reprimand, reprove, scold, sit on, slap on wrist*, speak to, talk to, tell a thing or two*, tell off*, upbraid, warn; SEE CONCEPTS *52,78*

adolescence [*n*] *state of puberty, preadulthood*
boyhood, girlhood, greenness, juvenility, minority, pubescence, spring, teens, youth, youthfulness; SEE CONCEPT *817*

adolescent [*n*] *person in puberty, preadulthood*
juvenile, minor, stripling, sweet sixteen*, teen, teenager, teenybopper*, youngster, youth; SEE CONCEPT *424*

adolescent [*adj*] *preadult or immature*
boyish, girlish, growing, juvenile, pubescent, puerile, teen, teenage, young, youthful; SEE CONCEPTS *401,578,797*

adopt [*v1*] *choose or take something as one's own*
accept, adapt, affiliate, affirm, appropriate, approve, assent, assume, borrow, embrace, endorse, espouse, follow, go down the line*, go in for*, imitate, maintain, mimic, opt, ratify, seize, select, support, take on, take over, take up, tap, use, utilize; SEE CONCEPT *18*

adopt [*v2*] *legally care for another's child*
choose, foster, naturalize, pick, raise, select, take in; SEE CONCEPT *317*

adoption [*n1*] *choosing or taking something as one's own*
acceptance, approbation, appropriation, approval, assumption, choice, confirmation, embracement, embracing, enactment, endorsement, espousal, following, maintenance, ratification, selection, support, taking on, taking over, taking up; SEE CONCEPT *18*

adoption [*n2*] *legal taking of another's child*
adopting, fosterage, fostering, naturalizing, raising, taking in; SEE CONCEPT *317*

adorable [*adj*] *cute, lovable*
ambrosial, appealing, attractive, captivating, charming, cute, darling, dear, delectable, delicious, delightful, dishy*, dreamy*, fetching, heavenly, hot*, lulu*, luscious, pleasing, precious, sexy, suave; SEE CONCEPTS *579,589*

adoration [*n*] *intense love*
admiration, amore, ardor, attachment, crush, devotion, esteem, estimation, exaltation, glorification, hankering, honor, idolatry, idolization, infatuation, pash*, passion, puppy love*, reverence, shine*, veneration, weakness*, worship, worshipping, yen*; SEE CONCEPT *32*

adore [*v*] *love intensely*
admire, be crazy about*, be gone on*, be mad for*, be nuts about*, be serious about*, be smitten with*, be stuck on*, be sweet on*, be wild about*, cherish, delight in, dig*, dote on, esteem, exalt, fall for, flip over*, glorify, go for*, honor, idolize, prize, revere, reverence, treasure, venerate, worship; SEE CONCEPT *32*

adorn [*v*] *decorate*
array, beautify, bedeck, deck, doll up*, dress up, embellish, enhance, enrich, fix up, furbish, garnish, grace, gussy up, ornament, spruce up, trim; SEE CONCEPTS *162,177*

adornment [*n1*] *decorating, enhancing*
beautification, decoration, embellishment, gilding, ornamentation, trimming; SEE CONCEPTS *162,177*

adornment [*n2*] *a decoration*
accessory, dingbat, doodad, embellishment, fandangle*, floss*, frill, frippery, furbelow*, jazz*, ornament, thing, trimming; SEE CONCEPTS *446,484*

adrift [*adv1*] *floating out of control*
afloat, drifting, loose, unanchored, unmoored; SEE CONCEPT *488*

adrift [*adv2*] *without purpose*
aimless, directionless, goalless, purposeless; SEE CONCEPT *542*

adrift [*adv3*] *off course*
amiss, astray, erring, wrong; SEE CONCEPT *581*

adroit [*adj*] *very able or skilled*
adept, apt, artful, clean, clever, crack*, crackerjack*, cunning, cute, deft, dexterous, expert, foxy*, good, handy, have know-how*, heads up*, hot tamale*, ingenious, masterful, neat*, nifty*, nimble, on the ball*, on the beam*, proficient, quick on the trigger*, quick on the uptake*, quick-witted, savvy, sharp, skillful, slick, smart, up to speed*, whiz*, wizard; SEE CONCEPT *527*

adulation [*n*] *overenthusiastic praise*
applause, audation, blandishment, bootlicking*, commendation, fawning, flattery, sycophancy, worship; SEE CONCEPTS *32,69*

adult [*n*] *a mature, fully grown person*
gentleman/woman, grownup, lady, man, person, woman; SEE CONCEPTS *394,424*

adult [*adj*] *being mature, fully grown*
developed, grown, grown-up, of age, ripe, ripened; SEE CONCEPT *406*

adulterate [*v*] *alter or debase, often for profit*
alloy, amalgamate, attenuate, blend, cheapen, commingle, contaminate, cook, corrupt, cut*, defile, degrade, denature, depreciate, deteriorate, devalue, dilute, dissolve, doctor*, doctor up*, falsify, impair, infiltrate, intermix, irrigate, lace*, make impure, mingle, mix, phony up*, plant*, pollute, shave*, spike*, taint, thin, transfuse, vitiate, water down*, weaken; SEE CONCEPTS *240,254*

adulterated [*adj*] *debased or dirty*
attenuated, blended, contaminated, corrupt, defiled, degraded, depreciated, deteriorated, devalued, diluted, dissolved, impaired, mixed, polluted, tainted, thinned, vitiated, watered down, weakened; SEE CONCEPT *485*

adulterous [*adj*] *sexually promiscuous*
cheating, double-crossing*, extracurricular*, fast and loose*, illicit, immoral, moonlighting*, speedy*, two-faced*, two-timing*, unchaste, wicked; SEE CONCEPT *372*

adultery [*n*] *sexual promiscuousness*
affair, carrying on*, cheating, cuckoldry, extracurricular activity*, fling, fornication, hanky-panky*, immorality, infidelity, matinee*, playing around*, relationship, thing*, two-timing*, wickedness; SEE CONCEPT *633*

advance [*n1*] *forward movement*
advancement, headway, impetus, motion, progress, progression; SEE CONCEPTS *152,208*

advance [*n2*] *improvement, progress in development*
advancement, amelioration, betterment, boost, break*, breakthrough, buildup, development, enrichment, furtherance, gain, go-ahead*, growth, headway, increase, progress, promotion, rise, step, up, upgrade, upping; SEE CONCEPTS *700,704*

advance [*n3*] *money given beforehand*
accommodation, allowance, bite*, credit, deposit, down payment, floater*, front money*, hike, increase, loan, prepayment, retainer, rise*, score, stake, take*, touch*; SEE CONCEPTS *340,344*

advance(s) [*n4*] *desirous pursuit of someone*
approach, move, overture, proposal, proposition, suggestion; SEE CONCEPTS *20,384*

advance [*adj*] *ahead in position or time*
beforehand, earlier, early, first, foremost, forward, in front, in the forefront, in the lead, leading, previously, prior; SEE CONCEPTS *583,585,799*

advance [*v1*] *move something forward, often quickly*
accelerate, achieve, bring forward, come forward, conquer, continue ahead, continue on, dispatch, drive, elevate, forge ahead, gain ground, get ahead, get green light*, get there*, get with it*, go ahead, go forth, go forward, go great guns*, go places*, go to town*, hasten, launch, make headway, make the scene*, march, move on, move onward, move up, press on, proceed, progress, promote, propel, push ahead, push on, quicken, send forward, skyrocket*, speed, step forward, storm; SEE CONCEPTS *152,208,704*

advance [*v2*] *promote or propose an idea*
adduce, allege, ballyhoo, beat the drum for, benefit, boost, cite, encourage, foster, further, get ink for*, hype*, introduce, lay forward, make a pitch for*, offer, plug*, present, proffer, puff*, push, put forward, put on the map*, serve, set forth, splash, spot, submit, suggest, throw spotlight on*, urge; SEE CONCEPTS *49,60,68*

advance [*v3*] *give money beforehand*
furnish, lend, loan, pay, provide; SEE CONCEPT *341*

advance [*v4*] *increase in amount, number, or position*
boost, break the bank*, develop, elevate, enlarge, get fat*, get rich*, grade, grow, hit pay dirt*, hit the jackpot*, improve, magnify, make a killing*, make out*, multiply, pan out*, prefer, prosper, raise, strike gold*, strike it rich*, thrive, up, upgrade, uplift; SEE CONCEPTS *236,244,245*

advanced [*adj*] *ahead in position, time, manner*
avant-garde, breakthrough, cutting-edge, excellent, exceptional, extreme, first, foremost, forward, higher, late, leading, leading-edge, liberal, precocious, progressive, radical, state-of-the-art, unconventional; SEE CONCEPTS *574,578,585,797*

advancement [*n1*] *promotion, progress*
advance, amelioration, betterment, elevation, gain, growth, headway, improvement, preference, preferment, prelation, rise, upgrading; SEE CONCEPTS *700,704*

advancement [*n2*] *forward movement*
advance, anabasis, gain, headway, march, progress, progression; SEE CONCEPTS *152,208*

advantage [*n*] *benefit, favored position or circumstance*
aid, ascendancy, asset, assistance, authority, avail, blessing, boon, break, choice, comfort, convenience, dominance, edge, eminence, expediency, favor, gain, good, gratification, help, hold, improvement, influence, interest, lead, leeway, leg-up*, leverage, luck, mastery, odds, position, power, precedence, pre-eminence, preference, prestige, prevalence, profit, protection, recognition, resources, return, sanction, starting, superiority, support, supremacy, upper hand*, utility, wealth; SEE CONCEPT *574*

advent [*n*] *beginning or arrival of something anticipated*
appearance, approach, arrival, coming, entrance, occurrence, onset, rearing, visitation; SEE CONCEPTS *119,159*

adventure [*n*] *risky or unexpected undertaking*
chance, contingency, emprise, endangerment, enterprise, experience, exploit, feat, happening, hazard,

incident, jeopardy, occurrence, peril, scene, speculation, trip, undertaking, venture; SEE CONCEPTS *384,386*

adventurer [n] *person who takes risks*
charlatan, daredevil, entrepreneur, explorer, fortune-hunter, gambler, globetrotter, hero, heroine, knight, madcap, mercenary, opportunist, pioneer, pirate, rogue, romantic, soldier, soldier of fortune, speculator, stunt man/woman, swashbuckler, traveler, venturer, voyager, wanderer; SEE CONCEPT *423*

adventurous [adj] *daring, risk-taking*
adventuresome, audacious, bold, brave, courageous, dangerous, daredevil, enterprising, foolhardy, hazardous, headstrong, intrepid, rash, reckless, risky, temerarious, venturesome, venturous; SEE CONCEPTS *404,542*

adverb [n] *word modifying a verb*
limiter, modifier, qualifier; SEE CONCEPT *275*

adversary [n] *opponent*
antagonist, attacker, bad guy*, bandit, competitor, contestant, enemy, foe, match, opposer, opposite number*, oppugner, rival; SEE CONCEPT *412*

adverse [adj] *unfavorable, antagonistic*
allergic to*, conflicting, contrary, detrimental, disadvantageous, down on*, down side*, have no use for*, inimical, injurious, inopportune, negative, opposed, opposing, opposite, oppugning, ornery*, reluctant, repugnant, stuffy*, unfortunate, unfriendly, unlucky, unpropitious, unwilling; SEE CONCEPT *570*

adversity [n] *bad luck, situation*
affliction, bad break*, bummer*, calamity, can of worms*, catastrophe, clutch, contretemps, crunch*, difficulty, disaster, distress, downer*, drag*, evil eye*, hard knocks*, hardship, hard times, hurting, ill fortune, jam, jinx, kiss of death*, misery, misfortune, mishap, on the skids*, pain in the neck*, poison*, reverse, sorrow, suffering, the worst*, tough luck*, trial, trouble; SEE CONCEPT *674*

advertise [v] *publicize for the purpose of selling or causing one to want*
acquaint, advance, advise, announce, apprise, ballyhoo*, beat the drum for*, bill, blazon, boost*, build up, circularize, communicate, declare, disclose, display, divulge, drum*, endorse, exhibit, expose, flaunt, get on soapbox for*, hard sell, herald, hype, inform, make a pitch*, make known, notify, pitch, plug, press agent*, proclaim, promote, promulgate, puff*, push, put on the map*, reveal, show, soft sell, splash*, sponsor, spot, tout, uncover, unmask; SEE CONCEPTS *60,324*

advertisement [n] *public notice of sale*
ad, announcement, bill, blurb, broadcast, circular, classified ad, commercial, communication, declaration, display, endorsement, exhibit, exhibition, flyer, literature, notice, notification, placard, plug, poster, proclamation, promotion, promulgation, propaganda, publication, publicity, squib, throwaway, want ad; SEE CONCEPTS *270,277,278,280*

advertising [n] *public notice of sale; notices to increase consumer desire*
announcement, announcing, ballyhoo*, billing, blasting*, broadcasting, buildup, displaying, exhibiting, exhibition, exposition, hard sell, hoopla, hype, pitch, plug, posting, PR, proclamation, promo*, promoting, promotion, publicity, puff*, screamer*, spread, squib; SEE CONCEPTS *97,138,324*

advice [n] *recommendation*
admonition, advisement, advocacy, aid, bum steer*, caution, charge, consultation, counsel, directions, dissuasion, encouragement, exhortation, forewarning, guidance, help, information, injunction, input, instruction, judgment, kibitz*, lesson, news, opinion, persuasion, prescription, proposal, proposition, recommendation, steer, suggestion, teaching, telltale, tidings, tip, tip-off*, two cents' worth*, view, warning, word, word to the wise*; SEE CONCEPTS *75,274*

advisable [adj] *recommended, wise*
appropriate, apt, commendable, desirable, expedient, fit, fitting, judicious, politic, prudent, seemly, sensible, sound, suggested, suitable, tactical; SEE CONCEPT *574*

advise [v1] *offer recommendation*
admonish, advocate, caution, charge, commend, counsel, direct, dissuade, encourage, enjoin, exhort, forewarn, give a pointer*, give a tip*, guide, instruct, level with*, move, opine, point out, preach, prepare, prescribe, prompt, put bug in ear*, put in two cents*, recommend, steer, suggest, tout, update, urge, warn; SEE CONCEPT *75*

advise [v2] *offer information*
acquaint, apprise, clue*, clue in*, fill in, give the word*, inform, keep posted*, lay it out*, let in on*, make known, notify, post*, put next to*, put on the line*, put on to*, report, show, tell, tip off*, update, warn; SEE CONCEPT *60*

advisedly [adv] *with due consideration*
carefully, cautiously, consciously, deliberately, discreetly, intentionally, prudently, thoughtfully; SEE CONCEPT *544*

adviser/advisor [n] *person who recommends, teaches, or otherwise helps*
aide, attorney, authority, backseat driver*, buttinski*, clubhouse lawyer*, coach, confidant, consultant, counsel, counselor, director, doctor, Dutch uncle*, expert, friend, guide, helper, instructor, judge, kibitzer*, lawyer, mentor, monitor, partner, priest, quarterback*, referee, righthand man/woman, second-guesser, teacher, tutor; SEE CONCEPTS *348,350*

advisory [adj] *able, authorized to recommend*
advising, consultative, consultive, counseling, helping, recommending; SEE CONCEPT *537*

advocacy [n] *support for an idea or cause*
advancement, aid, assistance, backing, campaigning for, championing, defense, encouragement, justifica-

tion, pleading for, promotion, promulgation, propagation, proposal, recommendation, upholding, urging; SEE CONCEPT *689*

advocate [n] *person supporting an idea or cause publicly*
apostle, attorney, backer, campaigner, champion, counsel, defender, exponent, expounder, lawyer, pleader, promoter, proponent, proposer, speaker, spokesman/woman, spokesperson, supporter, upholder; SEE CONCEPTS *359,423*

advocate [v] *support idea or cause publicly*
advance, advise, argue for, back, be in corner*, bless, bolster, boost*, brace up*, build up, campaign for, champion, countenance, defend, encourage, favor, further, get on bandwagon*, give a leg up*, give a lift*, go for, go to bat for*, go with, hold with, justify, plead for, plug*, plump for*, press for, promote, propose, push, recommend, ride shotgun for*, root for*, run interference for*, say so*, side, speak for, spread around*, stump for*, support, tout, uphold, urge, vindicate; SEE CONCEPTS *10,49,75*

aerial [adj] *occurring in the air*
aeriform, aeronautical, airy, atmospheric, birdlike, ethereal, flying, lofty, pneumatic, up above, vaporous; SEE CONCEPT *583*

aesthetic/esthetic [adj] *beautiful or artful*
artistic, creative, gorgeous, inventive; SEE CONCEPTS *485,579*

afar [adv] *a great distance away*
distant, far away, far off, remote; SEE CONCEPT *778*

affable [adj] *friendly*
amiable, amicable, approachable, benevolent, benign, breezy, civil, clubby*, congenial, cordial, courteous, genial, gentle, good-humored, good-natured, gracious, kindly, mild, Mr./Ms. Nice Guy*, obliging, pleasant, polite, sociable, urbane, warm; SEE CONCEPT *401*

affair [n1] *matter or business to be taken care of; happening*
activity, assignment, avocation, calling, case, circumstance, concern, duty, employment, episode, event, hap, happening, incident, interest, job, mission, obligation, occupation, occurrence, office function, proceeding, profession, project, province, pursuit, question, realm, responsibility, subject, task, thing*, topic, transaction, undertaking; SEE CONCEPTS *2,349,362*

affair [n2] *illicit sexual relationship*
affaire, amour, carrying on*, extracurricular activity*, fling, goings-on*, hanky-panky*, intimacy, intrigue, liaison, love, playing around*, relationship, rendezvous, romance, thing together*, two-timing*; SEE CONCEPTS *32,375*

affair [n3] *party or celebration*
do, entertainment, function, gathering, reception, shindig, soiree; SEE CONCEPTS *377,383*

affect [v1] *influence, affect emotionally*
act on, alter, change, disturb, impinge, impress, induce, influence, inspire, interest, involve, modify,

move, overcome, perturb, prevail, regard, relate, stir, sway, touch, transform, upset; SEE CONCEPTS *7,19,22,228*

affect [v2] *pretend, imitate*
act, adopt, aspire to, assume, bluff, contrive, counterfeit, do a bit*, fake, feign, lay it on thick, make out like*, playact, put on, put up a front*, sham*, simulate, take on; SEE CONCEPT *59*

affectation [n] *pretended behavior to make an impression*
air, airs, appearance, artificiality, facade, false front*, front, going Hollywood*, imitation, insincerity, mannerism, pose, pretense, pretension, pretentiousness, put-on, putting on airs*, sham*, show, showing off, simulation; SEE CONCEPT *633*

affected [adj1] *deeply moved or hurt emotionally*
afflicted, altered, changed, compassionate, concerned, damaged, distressed, excited, grieved, impaired, impressed, influenced, injured, overwhelmed, overwrought, sorry, stimulated, stirred, sympathetic, tender, touched, troubled, upset; SEE CONCEPT *403*

affected [adj2] *changed in a bad or artificial way*
apish, artificial, assumed, awkward, campy*, chichi*, conceited, contrived, counterfeit, counterfeited, faked, false, feigned, fraud*, gone Hollywood*, ham*, hammy*, high falutin'*, hollow, imitated, insincere, melodramatic, ostentatious, overdone, pedantic, phony, playacting, pompous, precious, pretended, pretentious, put-on*, schmaltzy*, self-conscious, shallow, sham*, simulated, spurious, stiff, stilted, studied, superficial, theatrical, unnatural; SEE CONCEPTS *401,570*

affection [n] *strong fondness*
amore, ardor, attachment, care, case*, closeness, concern, crush, desire, devotion, emotion, endearment, feeling, friendliness, friendship, good will, hankering*, heart, inclination, itch*, kindness, liking, love, passion, predilection, propensity, puppy love*, regard, sentiment, shine*, soft spot*, solicitude, tenderness, warmth, weakness*, yen, zealousness; SEE CONCEPT *32*

affectionate [adj] *having or showing fondness*
all over*, attached, caring, crazy over*, dear, devoted, doting, fond, friendly, huggy*, kind, lovey-dovey*, loving, mushy*, nutty about*, partial, soft on*, sympathetic, tender, warm, warm-hearted; SEE CONCEPTS *401,403*

affidavit [n] *written legal declaration*
affirmation, oath, sworn statement, testimony; SEE CONCEPTS *271,318*

affiliate [n] *organization that is associated with another*
affil*, associate, branch, brother, offshoot, partner, sister; SEE CONCEPT *381*

affiliate [v] *associate or be associated with a larger organization*
ally, amalgamate, annex, associate, band together, combine, come aboard, confederate, connect, form

connection, go partners*, hook up*, incorporate, join, line up*, plug into*, relate*, team up, throw in with*, tie up, unite; SEE CONCEPTS *113,114*

affiliation [*n*] *association with an organization*
alliance, amalgamation, banding together, bunch, cahoots*, clan, coalition, combination, confederation, conjunction, connection, crew, crowd, gang, hookup*, incorporation, joining, league, merging, mob, outfit, partnership, relationship, ring, syndicate, tie-in, union; SEE CONCEPT *381*

affinity [*n1*] *liking or inclination toward something*
affection, attraction, closeness, compatibility, cotton*, cup of tea*, druthers, fondness, good vibrations*, leaning, partiality, rapport, same wavelength, simpatico, sympathy, thing*, weakness*; SEE CONCEPTS *20,32,709*

affinity [*n2*] *similarity*
alikeness, alliance, analogy, association, closeness, connection, correspondence, kinship, likeness, relation, relationship, resemblance, semblance, similitude; SEE CONCEPT *670*

affirm [*v*] *declare the truth of something*
assert, asseverate, attest, aver, avouch, avow, certify, cinch, clinch, confirm, cross heart, declare, guarantee, have a lock on*, ice*, insist, lock up*, maintain, nail down*, okay, predicate, profess, pronounce, put on ice*, ratify, repeat, rubber-stamp*, say so, set, state, swear, swear on bible*, swear up and down*, testify, vouch, witness; SEE CONCEPTS *49,50,88*

affirmation [*n*] *declaration of the truth of something*
affidavit, assertion, asseveration, attestation, averment, avouchment, avowal, certification, confirmation, declaration, green light*, oath, okay, pronouncement, ratification, stamp of approval*, statement, sworn statement, testimonial, testimony; SEE CONCEPT *49*

affirmative [*adj*] *being agreeable or assenting*
acknowledging, acquiescent, affirmatory, affirming, approving, complying, concurring, confirmative, confirmatory, confirming, consenting, corroborative, endorsing, favorable, positive, ratifying, supporting; SEE CONCEPTS *542,572*

affix [*v*] *attach or stick*
add, annex, append, bind, fasten, glue, hitch on*, join, paste, put on, rivet, slap on*, subjoin, tack, tack on*, tag, tag on*; SEE CONCEPTS *85,113,160*

afflict [*v*] *cause or become hurt*
agonize, annoy, beset, bother, burden, crucify, distress, grieve, harass, harrow, harry, irk, lacerate, martyr, oppress, pain, pester, plague, press, rack, smite, strike, torment, torture, trouble, try, vex, worry, wound; SEE CONCEPTS *7,19,246,313*

affliction [*n*] *hurt condition; something that causes hurt*
adversity, anguish, calamity, cross, crux, depression, difficulty, disease, disorder, distress, grief, hardship, illness, infirmity, misery, misfortune, ordeal, pain,

plague, plight, scourge, sickness, sorrow, suffering, torment, trial, tribulation, trouble, woe; SEE CONCEPTS *306,309,674,728*

affluent [*adj1*] *wealthy*
flush*, loaded*, moneyed*, opulent, prosperous, rich, stinking rich*, upper class, upscale, well-off, well-to-do; SEE CONCEPT *334*

affluent [*adj2*] *plentiful*
abundant, bountiful, copious, full, plenteous; SEE CONCEPT *771*

afford [*v1*] *able to have or do; within financial means*
allow, be able to, bear, be disposed to, have enough for, have the means for, incur, manage, spare, stand, support, sustain; SEE CONCEPTS *335,713*

afford [*v2*] *give, produce*
bestow, furnish, grant, impart, offer, provide, render, supply, yield; SEE CONCEPTS *108,143*

affront [*n*] *an insult*
abuse, backhanded compliment*, brickbat*, dirty deed*, indignity, injury, left-handed compliment*, offense, outrage, provocation, put-down*, slap*, slap in the face*, slight, slur, vexation, wrong; SEE CONCEPTS *7,19,44,54*

affront [*v*] *insult or involve in entanglement*
abuse, anger, annoy, confront, criticize, displease, dispraise, dump on*, encounter, face, give a zinger*, give the cold shoulder*, hit where one lives*, meet, offend, outrage, pique, provoke, put down*, slander, slight, taunt, vex; SEE CONCEPTS *7,19,44,54*

afraid [*adj1*] *fearful*
abashed, aghast, alarmed, anxious, apprehensive, aroused, blanched, cowardly, cowed, daunted, discouraged, disheartened, dismayed, distressed, disturbed, faint-hearted, frightened, frozen, have cold feet*, horrified, in awe, intimidated, nervous, panic-stricken, perplexed, perturbed, petrified, rattled, run scared*, scared, scared stiff*, scared to death*, shocked, spooked, startled, stunned, suspicious, terrified, terror-stricken, timid, timorous, trembling, upset, worried; SEE CONCEPTS *403,690*

afraid [*adj2*] *reluctant, regretful*
averse, backward, disinclined, hesitant, indisposed, loath, reluctant, sorry, uneager, unhappy, unwilling; SEE CONCEPT *529*

afresh [*adj*] *new or repeated*
again, anew, de novo, lately, newly, of late, once again, once more, over, over again, recently; SEE CONCEPTS *578,797*

after [*adj*] *following in position or time*
afterwards, back, back of, behind, below, ensuing, hind, hindmost, in the rear, later, next, posterior, postliminary, rear, subsequential, subsequently, succeeding, thereafter; SEE CONCEPTS *586,820*

aftermath [*n*] *situation following an event, occurrence*
after-effects, causatum, chain reaction*, consequences, end, eventuality, flak, impact, issue, outcome, payoff*, remainder, residual, residuum, results, upshot, waves*; SEE CONCEPT *230*

afternoon [*n*] *period after 12 noon and before sunset*
cocktail hour, P.M., post meridian, siesta, teatime;
SEE CONCEPTS *801,806,810*

afterthought [*n*] *idea that occurs after it is timely*
reconsideration, review, second thought; SEE CON-
CEPT *529*

afterward/afterwards [*adv*] *following a time, event*
after, another time, at a later time, a while later,
behind, by and by, ensuingly, eventually, in a while,
intra, late, later, latterly, next, on the next day, soon,
subsequently, then, thereafter, thereon, ultimately;
SEE CONCEPT *799*

again [*adv1*] *another time; repeated*
afresh, anew, anon, bis, come again, encore, freshly,
newly, once more, one more time, over, over and
over, recurrently, reiteratively, repeatedly; SEE CON-
CEPTS *553,799*

again [*adv2*] *in addition*
additionally, also, besides, further, furthermore,
moreover, on the contrary, on the other hand, then;
SEE CONCEPT *577*

age [*n1*] *period of animate existence*
adolescence, adulthood, boyhood, childhood, dotage, elderliness, girlhood, infancy, life, lifetime, majority, maturity, middle age, milestone, old age,
senility, seniority, wear and tear*, youth; SEE CON-
CEPTS *816,817*

age [*n2*] *a period of time*
aeon, blue moon*, century, date, day, duration, epoch, era, generation, interim, interval, life, lifetime,
millennium, span; SEE CONCEPT *807*

age [*v*] *become older*
decline, deteriorate, develop, get along, grow, grow
feeble, grow old, grow up, mature, mellow, push,
put mileage on*, ripen, wane; SEE CONCEPT *105*

aged [*adj*] *old*
age-old, ancient, antediluvian, antiquated, antique,
been around*, creaky*, elderly, getting on*, grand-
ma*, grandpa*, gray, moth-eaten*, oldie*, old lady*, old man*, over the hill*, passé*, rusty*,
senescent, senior citizen, shot*, timeworn, venerable, worn, worse for wear*; SEE CONCEPTS *578,797*

agency [*n1*] *organization, often business-related*
bureau, company, department, firm, office; SEE CON-
CEPTS *325,381,441*

agency [*n2*] *power, instrumentality*
action, activity, auspices, channel, efficiency, force,
influence, instrument, instrumentality, intercession,
intervention, means, mechanism, mediation, medium, operation, organ, vehicle, work; SEE CONCEPTS
376,658

agenda [*n*] *list of things to do*
calendar, card, diary, docket, lineup, plan, program,
schedule, timetable; SEE CONCEPT *283*

agent [*n1*] *person representing an organization or person in business*
abettor, actor, advocate, ambassador, assignee, assistant, attorney, broker, commissioner, delegate,
deputy, doer, emissary, envoy, executor, factor, factotum, functionary, go-between, handler, intermediary, lawyer, mediary, middleman/woman, middleperson, minister, mover, negotiator, officer, operative, operator, principal, proctor, promoter, proxy,
representative, salesman/woman, salesperson, servant, steward, substitute, surrogate, ten percenter*,
worker; SEE CONCEPT *348*

agent [*n2*] *power, instrument for achievement*
cause, channel, factor, force, means, medium, organ, power, vehicle; SEE CONCEPTS *376,658*

aggrandize [*v*] *cause something to seem or be greater,
bigger*
acclaim, applaud, augment, beef up*, boost, commend, dignify, distinguish, enlarge, ennoble, expand, extend, glorify, heighten, hike, hike up*,
honor, hype, increase, intensify, jack up*, jump,
magnify, multiply, parlay, praise; SEE CONCEPTS
50,69,88,236,245

aggravate [*v1*] *annoy*
be at*, be on the back of*, bother, bug, bum*, dog,
drive up the wall*, exasperate, gall, get, get on one's
nerves, get to, give a hard time, grate, hack, irk,
irritate, nag, needle, nettle, peeve, pester, pick on,
pique, provoke, tease, vex, wig*; SEE CONCEPTS *7,19*

aggravate [*v2*] *cause to become worse*
complicate, deepen, enhance, exacerbate, exaggerate, heighten, increase, inflame, intensify, magnify,
mount, rise, rouse, worsen; SEE CONCEPT *240*

aggravation [*n1*] *annoyance*
affliction, aggro*, bother, botheration*, difficulty,
distress, exasperation, hang-up*, headache*, irksomeness, irritation, pain, pain in the neck*, pet
peeve*, provocation, teasing, vexation, worry; SEE
CONCEPT *410*

aggravation [*n2*] *worsening of a situation, condition*
deepening, exacerbation, exaggeration, heightening,
increase, inflaming, inflammation, intensification,
magnification, sharpening, strengthening, worsening; SEE CONCEPT *240*

aggregate [*n*] *collection*
accumulation, agglomerate, agglomeration, all,
amount, assemblage, body, bulk, combination, conglomerate, conglomeration, gross, heap, lump, mass,
mixture, pile, quantity, sum, the works*, total, totality, whole, whole ball of wax*, whole enchilada*,
whole schmear*, whole shooting match; SEE CON-
CEPT *432*

aggregate [*adj*] *forming a collection from separate
parts*
accumulated, added, amassed, assembled, collected,
collective, combined, composite, corporate, cumulative, heaped, mixed, piled, total; SEE CONCEPT *781*

aggregate [*v*] *combine into a collection*
accumulate, add up, amass, amount, assemble, collect, combine, come, heap, mix, number, pile, sum,
total; SEE CONCEPT *109*

aggression [*n1*] *attack, often military*
assailment, assault, blitz, blitzkrieg, encroachment, injury, invasion, offense, offensive, onset, onslaught, push, raid; SEE CONCEPTS *86,320*

aggression [*n2*] *hostile or forceful behavior, attitude*
aggressiveness, antagonism, belligerence, blitz, combativeness, destructiveness, fight, hostility, pugnacity, push; SEE CONCEPTS *29,411*

aggressive [*adj1*] *belligerent, hostile*
advancing, antipathetic, assailing, attacking, barbaric, bellicose, combative, contentious, destructive, disruptive, disturbing, encroaching, hawkish, intruding, intrusive, invading, martial, offensive, pugnacious, quarrelsome, rapacious, threatening, warlike; SEE CONCEPT *550*

aggressive [*adj2*] *assertive*
assertory, ballsy*, bold, brassy*, cheeky*, cocky*, come on*, domineering, dynamic, energetic, enterprising, flip*, forceful, fresh*, get up and go*, go after, hard sell, imperious, masterful, militant, nervy*, pushing, pushy, sassy, shooting from the hip*, smart*, smart alecky*, strenuous, tough, vigorous, zealous; SEE CONCEPTS *404,542*

aggrieved [*adj*] *very distressed*
afflicted, depressed, disturbed, grieving, harmed, hurt, injured, oppressed, pained, peeved, persecuted, saddened, unhappy, woeful, wronged; SEE CONCEPT *403*

aghast [*adj*] *horrified; very surprised*
afraid, agape, agog, alarmed, amazed, anxious, appalled, astonished, astounded, awestruck, confounded, dismayed, dumbfounded, frightened, horror-struck, overwhelmed, shocked, startled, stunned, terrified, thunderstruck; SEE CONCEPTS *403,690*

agile [*adj*] *physically or mentally nimble, deft*
active, acute, alert, athletic, brisk, buoyant, bustling, clever, dexterous, easy-moving, energetic, fleet, frisky, limber, lithe, lively, mercurial, prompt, quick, quick on the draw*, quick on the trigger*, quick-witted, rapid, ready, sharp, spirited, sportive, spright, sprightly, spry, stirring, supple, swift, twinkle toes*, vigorous, vivacious, winged, zippy; SEE CONCEPTS *485,527,588*

agility [*n*] *physical or mental nimbleness, deftness*
activity, acuteness, adroitness, alacrity, alertness, briskness, celerity, cleverness, dexterity, dispatch, expedition, fleetness, friskiness, litheness, liveliness, promptitude, promptness, quickness, quick-wittedness, sharpness, sprightliness, spryness, suppleness, swiftness; SEE CONCEPTS *410,630,748*

aging [*n*] *becoming older*
crumbling, declining, developing, fading, fermenting, getting along*, getting on*, maturing, mellowing, senescent, slumping, stale, waning, wearing out*; SEE CONCEPT *701*

agitate [*v1*] *shake physically*
beat, churn, concuss, convulse, disturb, rock, rouse, stir, toss; SEE CONCEPT *152*

agitate [*v2*] *disturb, trouble someone*
alarm, argue, arouse, bug*, bug up*, burn up*, confuse, craze*, debate, discompose, disconcert, discuss, dispute, disquiet, distract, disturb, egg on*, examine, excite, ferment, flurry, fluster, get to*, incite, inflame, make flip*, move, perturb, psych*, push buttons*, rouse, ruffle, spook, stimulate, stir, trouble, turn on*, unhinge*, upset, ventilate*, work up*, worry; SEE CONCEPTS *7,19,46*

agitator [*n*] *person who disturbs, causes trouble*
adjy, advocate, agent, anarchist, champion, demagogue, disrupter, dissident, dogmatist, fighter, firebrand*, fomenter, hatchet man/woman*, heretic, incendiary, inciter, instigator, leftist, malcontent, mover, partisan, propagandist, provocateur, pusher, rabble-rouser, radical, reactionary, rebel, reformer, revisionist, revolutionary, ringleader, sparkplug*, troublemaker, wave maker*, zealot; SEE CONCEPT *412*

agnostic [*n*] *person unsure that God exists*
doubter, freethinker, materialist, skeptic, unbeliever; SEE CONCEPT *361*

ago [*adv*] *in the past*
ages ago, back, back when, before, from way back, from year one*, gone, since, since God knows when*, time was; SEE CONCEPT *820*

agonize [*v*] *suffer or cause another to suffer*
afflict, bleed, carry on, crucify, distress, disturb, eat heart out*, excruciate, harrow, hurt, labor, lament, martyr, pain, rack, sing the blues*, squirm, stew over, strain, strive, struggle, take it badly*, torment, torture, try, wince, worry, writhe; SEE CONCEPTS *7,19,410*

agonizing [*adj*] *difficult and painful, suffering*
disturbing, excruciating, extreme, fierce, harrowing, intense, racking, struggling, tearing, tormenting, tortuous, torturing, vehement, violent; SEE CONCEPTS *403,565*

agony [*n*] *suffering, pain*
affliction, anguish, distress, dolor, misery, pangs, passion, throes, torment, torture, woe; SEE CONCEPTS *410,728*

agrarian [*adj*] *concerning land, farming*
agricultural, natural, peasant, rural, rustic, uncultivated, undomesticated; SEE CONCEPT *536*

agree [*v1*] *be in unison, assent with another*
accede, acknowledge, acquiesce, admit, allow, be of the same mind*, bury the hatchet*, buy into*, check, clinch the deal*, come to terms, comply, concede, concur, consent, cut a deal*, engage, give blessing*, give carte blanche*, give green light*, give the go-ahead*, go along with, grant, make a deal*, okay, pass on, permit, play ball*, recognize, see eye to eye*, set, settle, shake on*, side with, sign*, subscribe, take one up on*, yes*; SEE CONCEPTS *8,10,45,235*

agree [*v2*] *be similar or consistent*
accord, answer, attune, be in harmony, blend, click, cohere, coincide, concert, concord, concur, conform,

consort, correspond, equal, fall in with*, fit, get along with, go hand in hand*, go together, go well with, harmonize, jibe, match, parallel, square, suit, synchronize, tally; SEE CONCEPTS *118,656,670*

agreeable [*adj1*] *pleasing*
acceptable, dandy, delicious, delightful, enjoyable, fair, fine, gratifying, hunky-dory*, mild, nice, peach*, peachy*, pleasant, pleasurable, pleasureful, pussycat*, ready, satisfying, spiffy*, swell*, to one's liking, to one's taste, welcome; SEE CONCEPT *572*

agreeable [*adj2*] *appropriate, in keeping*
befitting, compatible, congruous, consistent, consonant, fitting, proper; SEE CONCEPT *558*

agreeable [*adj3*] *willing to be in unison, assent*
acquiescent, amenable, approving, complying, concurring, congenial, consenting, favorable, grateful, in accord, responsive, sympathetic, well-disposed, willing; SEE CONCEPTS *401,542*

agreeably [*adv*] *willingly, assenting; pleasantly; in keeping*
affably, affirmatively, amiably, amicably, appropriately, benevolently, charmingly, cheerfully, convivially, favorably, genially, good-humoredly, good-naturedly, graciously, happily, kindly, mutually, obligingly, peacefully, pleasingly, politely, satisfactorily, sympathetically, well, wonderfully; SEE CONCEPTS *401,572*

agreement [*n1*] *concurrence*
acceding, accession, accomodation, accord, accordance, acknowledging, adjustment, affiliation, affinity, alliance, amity, approving, arbitration, arrangement, assenting, authorizing, bargaining, compatibility, compliance, complying, compromise, concert, concession, concord, concordance, concurring, conformity, congruity, consistency, correspondence, endorsing, granting, harmony, mediation, ratifying, reconciliation, similarity, suitableness, sympathy, understanding, union, unison, verification, verifying; SEE CONCEPT *684*

agreement [*n2*] *document of concurrence, contract*
acknowledgment, adjudication, affidavit, approval, arrangement, assent, avowal, bargain, bond, cartel, charter, codicil, compact, compromise, confirmation, covenant, deal, indenture, lease, negotiation, note, oath, okay, pact, piece of paper*, protocol, recognition, settlement, stipulation, the nod*, transaction, treaty, understanding, writ; SEE CONCEPTS *271,331*

agricultural [*adj*] *concerning farming, land*
aboricultural, aggie*, agronomical, floricultural, gardening, horticultural, ranch, rural, rustic; SEE CONCEPTS *536,583*

agriculture [*n*] *farming, crop production*
agronomics, agronomy, cultivation, culture, horticulture, husbandry, tillage; SEE CONCEPTS *205,257*

aground [*adv*] *on the bottom of*
ashore, beached, disabled, foundered, grounded, high and dry*, marooned, reefed, shipwrecked, stranded, stuck, swamped, wrecked; SEE CONCEPT *583*

ahead [*adv*] *in front or advance of*
advanced, advancing, ahead, along, ante, antecedently, at an advantage, at the head, before, beforehand, earlier, first, fore, foremost, forward, forwards, in the foreground, in the lead, leading, on, onward, onwards, precedent, precedently, preceding, previous, progressing, to the fore; SEE CONCEPTS *586,632,820*

aid [*n1*] *help, support*
advancement, advice, advocacy, alleviation, allowance, assist, assistance, attention, backing, backup, benefaction, benefit, benevolence, bounty, care, charity, comfort, compensation, cooperation, deliverance, encouragement, endowment, favor, furtherance, gift, giving, guidance, hand, handout, leg up*, lift, ministration, ministry, patronage, promotion, reinforcement, relief, rescue, reward, salvation, service, shot in the arm*, subsidy, sustenance, treatment; SEE CONCEPT *110*

aid/aide [*n2*] *person who helps*
abettor, adjutant, aide-de-camp, assistant, attendant, coadjutant, coadjutor, crew, deputy, girl Friday, helper, lieutenant, man Friday, second, supporter; SEE CONCEPT *348*

aid [*v*] *help, support*
abet, alleviate, assist, bail out, befriend, benefact, encourage, favor, go to bat for*, go with*, lend a hand*, lighten, mitigate, open doors for*, promote, relieve, serve, stick up for*, straighten out*, subsidize, sustain; SEE CONCEPT *110*

ailing [*adj*] *not feeling well*
below par, debilitated, diseased, down, down with, enfeebled, feeble, feeling awful, ill, indisposed, rocky*, run down*, sick, sick as a dog*, sickly, under the weather*, unwell, wasting, weak; SEE CONCEPT *314*

ailment [*n*] *mild sickness*
ache, bug, complaint, condition, disease, disorder, dose*, flu, illness, indisposition, infirmity, malady, syndrome; SEE CONCEPTS *306,316*

aim [*n*] *goal*
ambition, aspiration, course, desideratum, design, desire, direction, end, intent, intention, mark, object, objective, plan, purpose, scheme, target, where one is heading*, wish; SEE CONCEPT *659*

aim [*v*] *point or direct at a goal*
address, angle, aspire, attempt, cast, concentrate, contemplate, covet, design, direct, endeavor, essay, fix, focus, intend, level, mean, plan, propose, purpose, set one's sights on*, sight, slant, steer, strive, target, train, try, want, wish, zero in on, zoom in; SEE CONCEPTS *20,41,201*

aimless [*adj*] *having no goal*
accidental, any which way*, bits-and-pieces*, blind, capricious, careless, casual, chance, desultory, directionless, drifting, erratic, fanciful, fickle, fits and

starts*, flighty, fortuitous, frivolous, goalless, haphazard, heedless, hit-or-miss*, indecisive, indiscriminate, irresolute, objectless, pointless, purposeless, random, shiftless, stray, thoughtless, unavailing, undirected, unguided, unplanned, unpredictable, vagrant, wandering, wanton, wayward; SEE CONCEPTS *401,535,544*

air [*n1*] *gases forming the atmosphere*
blast, breath, breeze, draft, heavens, ozone, puff, sky, stratosphere, troposphere, ventilation, waft, whiff, wind, zephyr; SEE CONCEPT *437*

air [*n2*] *distinctive quality or character; style*
address, affectation, ambience, appearance, atmosphere, aura, bearing, comportment, demeanor, deportment, effect, feel, feeling, flavor, impression, look, manner, mannerism, mien, mood, pose, presence, property, quality, semblance, tone; SEE CONCEPTS *644,673*

air [*n3*] *musical tune*
aria, descant, lay, melody, song, strain, theme; SEE CONCEPTS *77,595*

air [*v1*] *put into the atmosphere; freshen*
aerate, aerify, air-condition, circulate, cool, eject, expel, expose, fan, open, oxygenate, purify, refresh, ventilate; SEE CONCEPT *255*

air [*v2*] *express opinion publicly*
broadcast, circulate, communicate, declare, disclose, display, disseminate, divulge, exhibit, expose, make known, make public, proclaim, publicize, publish, put, reveal, speak, state, tell, utter, ventilate, voice; SEE CONCEPTS *51,52*

airplane [*n*] *vehicle that transports cargo or passengers through the air*
aeroplane, airbus, aircraft, airliner, airship, cab*, crate*, jet, kite*, plane, ramjet*, ship*; SEE CONCEPT *504*

airport [*n*] *center for transportation by air*
aerodome, airdrome, airfield, airstrip, hangar, helipad, heliport, home plate*, installation, landing strip, runway, strip; SEE CONCEPTS *325,439*

airs [*n*] *affectation; pretended behavior*
affectedness, arrogance, false front, front, haughtiness, hauteur, mannerism, ostentation, pomposity, pose, pretense, pretension, pretentiousness, put-on*, show, superciliousness; SEE CONCEPT *633*

airtight [*adj1*] *sealed*
closed, impenetrable, impermeable, shut; SEE CONCEPTS *483,490*

airtight [*adj2*] *certain*
incontestable, indisputable, invulnerable, irrefutable, unassailable; SEE CONCEPT *535*

airy [*adj1*] *open to the atmosphere*
aerial, atmospheric, blowy, breezy, drafty, exposed, fluttering, fresh, gaseous, gusty, light, lofty, out-of-doors, uncluttered, vaporous, ventilated, well-ventilated, windy; SEE CONCEPT *583*

airy [*adj2*] *delicate or ethereal*
dainty, diaphanous, flimsy, fragile, frail, frivolous, illusory, imaginary, immaterial, intangible, light,

rare, rarefied, tenuous, thin, vaporous, visionary, volatile, weightless, wispy; SEE CONCEPTS *490,582*

airy [*adj3*] *buoyant, light, or lively in nature*
animated, blithe, bouncy, cheerful, cheery, effervescent, elastic, fanciful, flippant, frolicsome, gay, graceful, happy, high-spirited, jaunty, light, lighthearted, merry, nonchalant, resilient, sprightly, volatile, whimsical; SEE CONCEPTS *404,550*

aisle [*n*] *passageway dividing something*
alley, artery, avenue, clearing, corridor, course, egress, gangway, hallway, ingress, lane, opening, passage, path, walk, way; SEE CONCEPTS *440,513,830*

ajar [*adj/adv*] *slightly open*
open, unclosed, unlatched, unshut; SEE CONCEPT *586*

akin [*adj*] *related or connected*
affiliated, agnate, alike, allied, analogous, cognated, comparable, connate, consonant, corresponding, incident, kindred, like, parallel, similar; SEE CONCEPTS *487,563,573*

alacrity [*n*] *liveliness; promptness*
alertness, avidity, briskness, cheerfulness, dispatch, eagerness, enthusiasm, expedition, fervor, gaiety, hilarity, joyousness, promptitude, quickness, readiness, speed, sprightliness, willingness, zeal; SEE CONCEPTS *633,657*

alarm [*n1*] *feeling of sudden fear*
anxiety, apprehension, cold feet*, consternation, dismay, distress, dread, fright, horror, nervousness, panic, scare, strain, stress, tension, terror, trepidation, unease, uneasiness; SEE CONCEPTS *410,690*

alarm [*n2*] *warning, signaling device*
alert, bell, blast, buzzer, call, caution, clock, cry, drum, flap, flash*, forewarning, gong, high sign*, horn, Mayday*, nod*, scramble*, scream, shout, sign, signal, siren, SOS, squeal, tip, tip off, tocsin, trumpet, warning, whistle, wink*, yell; SEE CONCEPTS *269,463*

alarm [*v*] *upset*
amaze, astonish, chill, daunt, dismay, distress, frighten, give a turn*, make jump*, panic, scare, scare silly*, scare stiff*, scare to death*, spook*, startle, surprise, terrify, unnerve; SEE CONCEPTS *7,14,19,42*

album [*n*] *blank book for collecting; holder*
anthology, collection, depository, index, memento, memory book, miscellany, notebook, portfolio, register, registry, scrapbook; SEE CONCEPTS *271,446*

alcohol [*n*] *intoxicating, flammable liquid*
alky*, booze*, canned heat*, cocktail, drink, ethanol, firewater*, hard stuff*, hootch*, intoxicant, liquor, methanol, moonshine*, palliative*, red-eye*, rotgut*, sauce*, smoke*, spirits, tipple*, toddy*; SEE CONCEPTS *454,467*

alcoholic [*adj*] *intoxicating*
brewed, distilled, fermented, hard, inebriant, inebriating, sprituous, vinous; SEE CONCEPT *462*

alcove [n] *nook, secluded spot*
anteroom, bay, bower, compartment, corner, cubbyhole, cubicle, niche, recess, study; SEE CONCEPTS *440,448,513*

ale [n] *intoxicating, fermented beverage*
beer, brew, hops, malt, suds*; SEE CONCEPT *454*

alert [n] *warning*
admonition, alarm, flap*, high sign*, Mayday*, sign, signal, siren, SOS, tip off, wink*; SEE CONCEPTS *78,278,595,628*

alert [adj] *attentive, lively*
active, all ears*, bright, cagey*, careful, circumspect, clever, fast on the draw*, good hands*, heads up*, heedful, hip, intelligent, jazzed*, observant, on guard*, on one's toes*, on the ball*, on the job*, on the lookout*, on the qui vive*, perceptive, psyched up, quick, ready, sharp, spirited, switched on, vigilant, wary, watchful, wide-awake, wired, wise, with it*; SEE CONCEPTS *402,403*

alert [v] *warn*
alarm, flag, forewarn, give the high sign*, inform, notify, put on guard, signal, tip, tip off, wave flag*; SEE CONCEPT *78*

algae [n] *rootless, leafless plants living in water*
dulse, kelp, scum, seaweed; SEE CONCEPT *429*

alias [n] *false name*
AKA, anonym, assumed name, handle*, moniker, nickname, nom de guerre, nom de plume, pen name, pseudonym, stage name, summer name*; SEE CONCEPT *683*

alias [adv] *otherwise known as*
also called, also known as, otherwise; SEE CONCEPT *582*

alibi [n] *defense against charges of wrongdoing; evidence of absence*
account, affirmation, airtight case*, allegation, answer, assertion, assurance, avowal, case, cop-out*, cover, declaration, excuse, explanation, fish story*, justification, plea, pretext, profession, proof, reason, reply, retort, song and dance*, stall, statement, vindication; SEE CONCEPT *661*

alien [n] *foreign being*
blow in*, bum*, floater*, FOB*, foreigner, greenhorn*, guest, immigrant, incomer*, interloper, intruder, invader, migrant, newcomer, noncitizen, outsider, refugee, settler, squatter, stranger, visitor, weed*; SEE CONCEPT *423*

alien [adj] *foreign*
conflicting, contrary, estranged, exotic, extraneous, extrinsic, inappropriate, incompatible, incongruous, opposed, remote, separate, unusual; SEE CONCEPT *564*

alienate [v] *cause unfriendliness, hostility*
break off, come between, disaffect, disunite, divide, divorce, estrange, make indifferent, part, separate, set against, turn away, turn off, wean, withdraw the affections of; SEE CONCEPTS *7,19,231*

alienation [n] *unfriendliness*
breach, breaking off, coolness, disaffection, diverting, division, divorce, estrangement, indifference, remoteness, rupture, separation, setting against, turning away, variance, withdrawal; SEE CONCEPT *410*

align [v1] *line up, arrange next to*
adjust, allineate, coordinate, even, even up, fix, make parallel, order, range, regulate, straighten; SEE CONCEPT *158*

align [v2] *join; bring to agreement*
affiliate, agree, ally, associate, cooperate, enlist, follow, join sides, sympathize; SEE CONCEPTS *8,114*

alike [adj] *similar*
akin, allied, analogous, approximate, associated, carbon copy*, cognate, comparable, concurrent, correspondent, corresponding, dead ringer*, ditto*, double, duplicate, equal, equivalent, even, facsimile, identical, indistinguishable, kindred, like, look-alike, matched, matching, mated, parallel, proportionate, related, resembling, same, same difference, similar, spitting image*, undifferentiated, uniform, Xerox*; SEE CONCEPTS *487,566,573*

alike [adv] *similarly*
analogously, comparably, comparatively, consonantly, correspondingly, equally, equivalently, evenly, identically, in accordance with, in common, in the same degree, in the same manner, likewise, similarly, the same way, uniformly; SEE CONCEPTS *487,566,573*

alimentary [adj] *digestive*
comestible, dietary, digestible, nourishing, nutrient, nutritional, nutritious, nutritive, peptic, salutary, sustaining, sustentative; SEE CONCEPTS *406,485*

alimony [n] *money paid in support of a former spouse*
keep, livelihood, living, maintenance, provision, subsistence, sustenance, upkeep; SEE CONCEPT *344*

alive [adj1] *being animately existent*
animate, around, awake, breathing, cognizant, conscious, dynamic, existing, extant, functioning, growing, knowing, live, living, mortal, operative, running, subsisting, viable, vital, working, zoetic; SEE CONCEPT *539*

alive [adj2] *being active, full of life*
abounding, alert, animated, awake, brisk, bustling, cheerful, dynamic, eager, energetic, lively, overflowing, quick, ready, replete, rife, sharp, spirited, sprightly, spry, stirring, swarming, teeming, vigorous, vital, vivacious, zestful; SEE CONCEPTS *401,542*

alkali [n] *soluble base; opposite of an acid*
antacid, caustic soda, salt; SEE CONCEPT *472*

alkaline [adj] *being basic, not acid (chemically)*
acrid, alkalescent, alkali, antacid, bitter, caustic, neutralizing, salty, soluble; SEE CONCEPT *472*

all [n] *whole; totality*
accumulation, across the board, aggregate, aggregation, collection, ensemble, entirety, everyone, everything, gross, group, integer, jackpot*, lock stock and barrel*, mass, quantity, sum, sum total, total, unit,

utmost, wall to wall*, whole ball of wax*, whole enchilada*, whole nine yards*, whole schmear*, whole shooting match*, whole show*, works; SEE CONCEPTS *786,837*

all [*adj1*] *whole quantity*
complete, entire, full, greatest, gross, outright, perfect, total, utter; SEE CONCEPT *771*

all [*adj2*] *each; every one of a class*
any, bar none, barring no one, complete, each and every, entire, every, every bit of, every single, sum, total, totality, whole; SEE CONCEPT *772*

all [*adj3*] *exclusively*
alone, nothing but, only, solely; SEE CONCEPT *554*

all [*adv*] *completely, without exception*
all in all, altogether, entirely, exactly, fully, just, purely, quite, totally, utterly, wholly; SEE CONCEPTS *771,772*

allay [*v*] *reduce something, usually a pain or a problem*
abate, alleviate, assuage, calm, compose, cool out*, decrease, ease, lessen, lighten, make nice*, mitigate, moderate, mollify, pacify, play up to*, pour oil on*, quiet, square, take the bite out*, take the sting out*; SEE CONCEPTS *7,22,244*

allegation [*n*] *assertion placing blame*
accusation, affirmation, asseveration, avowal, charge, claim, declaration, deposition, overment, plea, profession, statement; SEE CONCEPT *49*

allege [*v*] *assert; claim*
adduce, advance, affirm, asseverate, aver, avouch, avow, charge, cite, declare, depose, lay, maintain, offer, plead, present, profess, put forward, recite, recount, state, testify; SEE CONCEPT *49*

alleged [*adj*] *asserted, often doubtful*
averred, declared, described, dubious, ostensible, pretended, professed, purported, questionable, so-called, stated, supposed, suspect, suspicious; SEE CONCEPT *552*

allegiance [*n*] *loyalty*
adherence, ardor, consecration, constancy, dedication, deference, devotion, duty, faithfulness, fealty, fidelity, homage, honor, obedience, obligation, piety; SEE CONCEPT *689*

allegorical [*adj*] *symbolic*
emblematic, figurative, illustrative, metaphorical, parabolic, symbolizing, typifying; SEE CONCEPT *582*

allegory [*n*] *indirect representation, storytelling*
apologue, emblem, fable, figuration, moral, myth, parable, story, symbol, symbolism, symbolization, tale, typification; SEE CONCEPT *282*

alleviate [*v*] *relieve; lessen*
allay, assuage, ease, lighten, mitigate, mollify, pacify, pour oil on*, soft-pedal*, take the bite out*, take the edge off*, take the sting out*; SEE CONCEPTS *7,22,110,236,247*

alley [*n*] *narrow passage*
alleyway, back street, lane, passageway, path, pathway, walk; SEE CONCEPT *501*

alliance [*n*] *friendly association, agreement*
accord, affiliation, affinity, betrothal, bond, coalition, coherence, collaboration, collusion, combination, communion, compact, concord, concurrence, confederacy, confederation, congruity, conjunction, connection, consanguinity, cooperation, engagement, entente, federation, fraternization, friendship, interrelation, kinship, league, marriage, matrimony, membership, mutuality, pact, participation, partnership, relation, support, tie, treaty, union; SEE CONCEPTS *301,423,684*

allied [*adj*] *friendly; united*
affiliated, agnate, akin, amalgamated, associated, bound, cognate, combined, confederate, connate, connected, incident, in league, joined, joint, kindred, linked, married, related, unified, wed; SEE CONCEPTS *555,563*

allocate [*v*] *assign; divide among*
admeasure, allot, apportion, appropriate, budget, cut, designate, dish out*, divvy, earmark, give, mete, set aside, share, slice; SEE CONCEPTS *41,98,108,129*

allot [*v*] *assign; give portion*
admeasure, allocate, appoint, apportion, appropriate, assign, budget, cut, cut the pie*, designate, distribute, divvy, dole, earmark, mete, set aside, share, shell out*, slice, split up; SEE CONCEPTS *41,108*

allotment [*n*] *portion assigned or given*
allocation, allowance, apportionment, appropriation, bite, chunk, cut, cut of pie*, end, grant, lot, measure, part, piece, piece of the action*, quota, rake off*, ration, share, slice, split, stint*; SEE CONCEPT *835*

all-out [*adj*] *complete*
absolute, determined, entire, exhaustive, full, full-blown, full-fledged, full-scale, maximum, optimum, resolute, supreme, thorough, total, undivided, unlimited, utmost; SEE CONCEPTS *531,772*

allow [*v1*] *admit; acknowledge*
acquiesce, avow, concede, confess, grant, let on, own; SEE CONCEPTS *60,82*

allow [*v2*] *permit an action*
accord, accredit, admit, approve, authorize, bear, be big*, be game for*, brook, certify, commission, consent, empower, endorse, endure, favor, free up, give a blank check*, give carte blanche, give leave, give permission, give the go-ahead, give the green light*, go along with, grant permission, hear of, hold with, indulge, let, license, live with*, oblige, okay, pass, pass on, put up with, recognize, release, sanction, sit still for*, stand, suffer, support, take kindly to, tolerate, warrant; SEE CONCEPTS *83,99*

allow [*v3*] *set aside*
admeasure, allocate, allot, apportion, assign, deduct, give, grant, lot, mete, provide, remit, spare; SEE CONCEPTS *41,108*

allowance [*n1*] *amount of money or other supply*
aid, alimony, allocation, allotment, annuity, apportionment, bequest, bite*, bounty, commission, con-

tribution, cut, endowment, fee, fellowship, gift, grant, honorarium, inheritance, interest, legacy, lot, measure, part, pay, pension, piece, portion, prize, quantity, quota, ration, recompense, remittance, salary, scholarship, share, slice, stint, stipend, subsidy, taste, wage; SEE CONCEPTS *337,340*

allowance [*n2*] *discount; concession*
accommodation, adaptation, adjustment, admission, advantage, cut, deduction, rebate, reduction, sanction, sufferance, toleration; SEE CONCEPT *775*

alloy [*n*] *mixture, usually of two metals*
admixture, adulterant, adulteration, amalgam, amalgamation, blend, combination, composite, compound, debasement, denaturant, fusion, hybrid, intermixture, reduction; SEE CONCEPTS *260,476*

alloy [*v1*] *mix metals*
admix, amalgamate, blend, combine, compound, fuse, intermix, mix; SEE CONCEPTS *109,113*

alloy [*v2*] *adulterate*
debase, denature, devalue, diminish, impair, reduce; SEE CONCEPT *240*

all right [*adj1*] *satisfactory*
acceptable, adequate, appropriate, average, decent, fair, fit, fitting, good, hunky-dory*, okay, okey-dokey*, passable, proper, satisfying, standard, sufficient, swell, tolerable, unexceptional, unobjectionable; SEE CONCEPTS *547,558*

all right [*adj2*] *in good condition or health*
hale, healthy, safe, sound, unharmed, unhurt, unimpaired, well, whole; SEE CONCEPT *572*

all right [*adj3*] *correct; excellent*
accurate, exact, good, great, precise, right; SEE CONCEPTS *557,574*

all right [*adv1*] *satisfactorily*
acceptably, adequately, okay, passably, tolerably, unobjectionably, well enough; SEE CONCEPTS *547,558*

all right [*adv2*] *yes*
agreed, certainly, definitely, of course, okay, positively, surely, very well, without a doubt; SEE CONCEPT *572*

all-time [*adj*] *unsurpassed and permanent*
best, champion, enduring, everlasting, perpetual; SEE CONCEPTS *574,798*

allude [*v*] *hint at*
advert, bring up, imply, insinuate, intimate, point, refer, suggest; SEE CONCEPTS *60,66*

allure [*n*] *appeal*
attraction, bedroom eyes*, charisma, charm, come-hither look*, come-on*, enchantment, enticement, glamor, inveiglement, lure, magnetism, seductiveness, temptation, the jazz*, witchery*; SEE CONCEPTS *673,720*

allure [*v*] *entice*
attract, bait, beguile, bewitch, cajole, captivate, charm, coax, come on*, decoy, draw, enchant, entrap, fascinate, hook*, inveigle, lead on, lure, magnetize, persuade, pull, seduce, suck in*, sweep off

feet*, tempt, turn on*, vamp, wile, win over; SEE CONCEPTS *7,22*

allusion [*n*] *indirect reference; hint*
casual remark, charge, citation, connotation, denotation, figure of speech, implication, imputation, incidental mention, indication, inference, innuendo, insinuation, intimation, mention, play on words, quotation, remark, statement, suggestion; SEE CONCEPTS *60,274*

ally [*n*] *something united with another, especially by treaty*
accessory, accomplice, associate, coadjutor, collaborator, colleague, confederate, co-worker, friend, helper, partner; SEE CONCEPTS *299,322,354,359*

alma mater [*n*] *school from which one has graduated*
academy, college, institution, old school, place of graduation, place of matriculation, university; SEE CONCEPTS *288,289*

almanac [*n*] *document containing information for a year*
annual, calendar, chronicle, ephemeris, journal, record, register, registry, yearbook; SEE CONCEPTS *280,801,809,823*

almighty [*adj1*] *having complete power, control*
absolute, all-powerful, invincible, mighty, omnipotent, puissant, supreme, unlimited; SEE CONCEPT *540*

almighty [*adj2*] *godlike*
all-knowing, all-seeing, boundless, celestial, deathless, deific, divine, enduring, eternal, everlasting, godly, heavenly, illimitable, immortal, infinite, omnipotent, omnipresent, omniscient, pervading; SEE CONCEPT *539*

almighty [*adj3*] *severe*
awful, desperate, enormous, excessive, extreme, great, intense, loud, terrible; SEE CONCEPT *569*

almost [*adv*] *nearly, very nearly*
about, about to, all but, approximately, around, as good as, bordering on, close to, close upon, essentially, for all practical purposes, for the greatest part, in effect, in the neighborhood of, in the vicinity of, just about, most, much, near to, nigh, not far from, not quite, on the brink of, on the edge of, on the point of, on the verge of, practically, pretty near, relatively, roughly, substantially, virtually, well-nigh, within sight of; SEE CONCEPTS *531,586,799*

alone [*adj1*] *separate; apart*
abandoned, batching it, by itself/oneself, companionless, deserted, desolate, detached, forlorn, forsaken, friendless, hermit, individual, in solitary, isolated, lone, lonely, lonesome, me and my shadow*, me myself and I*, onliest, only, on one's own, shag*, single, sole, solitary, solo, stag, traveling light*, unaccompanied, unaided, unassisted, unattached, unattended, unescorted, unmarried, widowed; SEE CONCEPTS *577,583*

alone [*adj2*] *to the exclusion of; unique*
incomparable, matchless, peerless, singly, singular, solely, unequalled, unique, unmatched, unparalleled, unrivaled, unsurpassed; SEE CONCEPTS *556,653*

along [*adv1*] *ahead*
forth, forward, on, onward; SEE CONCEPT *581*

along [*adv2*] *together with*
accompanying, additionally, also, as companion, as well, at same time, besides, coupled with, furthermore, in addition to, likewise, moreover, side by side, simultaneously, too, with; SEE CONCEPT *577*

along [*adv3*] *near*
adjacent, at, by; SEE CONCEPT *586*

alongside [*prep*] *close, near side of*
along the side of, apace with, at the side of, beside, by, by the side of, close at hand, close by, equal with, in company with, next to, parallel to, side by side; SEE CONCEPT *586*

aloof [*adj*] *remote*
above, apart, casual, chilly, cold, cold fish*, cool, detached, distant, forbidding, hard-boiled*, hard-hearted, haughty, incurious, indifferent, laid back*, loner*, lone wolf*, offish*, on ice*, putting on airs*, reserved, secluded, solitary, standoffish*, stuck up*, supercilious, thick-skinned*, unapproachable, unconcerned, unfriendly, uninterested, unresponsive, unsociable, unsympathetic, uppity*, withdrawn; SEE CONCEPTS *401,542*

aloud [*adv*] *in a spoken voice, usually not softly*
audibly, clearly, distinctly, intelligibly, loudly, lustily, noisily, out loud, plainly, vociferously; SEE CONCEPT *594*

alphabet [*n*] *letters of a writing system*
ABCs, characters, elements, fundamentals, graphic representation, hieroglyphs, ideograph, morphemes, phonemes, pictograph, rune, signs, syllabary, symbols; SEE CONCEPT *276*

alphabetical [*adj*] *in ascending order of a writing system*
A to Z, consecutive, graded, indexed, logical, ordered, progressive; SEE CONCEPT *585*

alphabetize [*v*] *place in order of a writing system*
index, order, systematize; SEE CONCEPT *84*

alpine [*adj*] *mountaintop; high altitude*
aerial, elevated, high, high-reaching, in the clouds, lofty, mountainous, rangy, snowcapped, soaring, towering; SEE CONCEPTS *779,836*

already [*adv*] *before expected time*
as of now, at present, before, before now, but now, by now, by that time, by then, by the time mentioned, by this time, earlier, even now, formerly, heretofore, in the past, just now, now, once, previously, then, up to now; SEE CONCEPT *799*

also [*adv*] *in addition to*
additionally, again, along, along with, and, as well, as well as, besides, conjointly, further, furthermore, including, in conjunction with, in like manner, likewise, more, moreover, more than that, on top of, over and above, plus, still, to boot*, together with, too, withal; SEE CONCEPT *577*

altar [*n*] *church table, pedestal*
chantry, font, reredos, retable, shrine, tabernacle; SEE CONCEPT *443*

alter [*v1*] *change*
adapt, adjust, amend, change, convert, cook, correct mid-course*, develop, dial back*, diversify, doctor, fine tune, make different, metamorphose, modify, mutate, phony up*, recalibrate, recast, reconstruct, refashion, reform, remodel, renovate, reshape, revamp, revise, shift, transform, transmute, turn, tweek, vary; SEE CONCEPT *232*

alter [*v2*] *sterilize animal*
caponize, castrate, change, desexualize, emasculate, fix, geld, mutilate, neuter, spay, unsex; SEE CONCEPTS *310,375*

alteration [*n*] *change*
about-face, accommodation, adaptation, adjustment, amendment, conversion, correction, difference, diversification, exchange, fixing, flip-flop*, metamorphosis, mid-course correction*, modification, mutation, reformation, remodeling, reshaping, revision, shift, switch, switch-over*, transformation, transmutation; SEE CONCEPT *701*

altercation [*n*] *fight, often verbal*
argument, beef*, bickering, blowup*, bone of contention*, brawl*, brush*, combat, contest, controversy, dispute, embroilment, flap*, fracas*, fuss, go*, hassle, quarrel, row, rumble*, run-in*, set-to*, squabbling, tiff*, words*, wrangle; SEE CONCEPTS *46,106*

altered [*adj*] *changed*
adapted, adjusted, amended, converted, cooked, corrected, diversified, doctored, fitted, fixed, modified, qualified, redone, refitted, reformed, remade, remodeled, renovated, reshaped, retailored, revised, spiked, transformed, turned, updated; SEE CONCEPT *564*

alter ego [*n*] *other side to personality*
doppelganger, evil twin*, second self; SEE CONCEPTS *410,423*

alternate [*n*] *substitute*
backup, double, equivalent, fill-in, proxy, replacement, stand-in, sub, surrogate; SEE CONCEPT *667*

alternate [*adj1*] *every other*
alternating, every second, intermittent, periodic, recurrent, recurring, rotating; SEE CONCEPT *553*

alternate [*adj2*] *substitute*
alternative, another, backup, different, interchanging, makeshift, second, surrogate, temporary; SEE CONCEPT *566*

alternate [*v*] *take turns, change back and forth*
act reciprocally, alter, blow hot and cold*, change, come and go, exchange, fill in for, fluctuate, follow, follow in turn, interchange, intersperse, oscillate, relieve, rotate, seesaw, shift, shilly-shally*, substitute, sway, vacillate, vary, waver, yo-yo*; SEE CONCEPTS *13,104,232,701*

alternative [*n*] *possible choice*
back-up, druthers, opportunity, option, other, other fish in sea*, other fish to fry*, pick, preference, re-

course, redundancy, selection, sub, substitute, take it or leave it*; SEE CONCEPT *529*

alternative [*adj*] *other, alternate*
another, back-up, different, flipside, other side, second, substitute, surrogate; SEE CONCEPT *564*

although [*conj*] *even though*
admitting, albeit, despite, despite the fact, even if, even supposing, granting, granting all this, in spite of, much as, notwithstanding, still, supposing, though, when, whereas, while; SEE CONCEPT *544*

altitude [*n*] *height in the sky*
apex, distance, elevation, eminence, loftiness, peak, summit; SEE CONCEPTS *739,752,791*

altogether [*adv1*] *as a whole*
all, all in all, all things considered, all told, bodily, by and large, collectively, conjointly, en masse, everything considered, everything included, for the most part, generally, in all, in sum, in toto, on the whole, taken together; SEE CONCEPT *771*

altogether [*adv2*] *completely*
absolutely, fully, perfectly, quite, thoroughly, totally, utterly, well, wholly; SEE CONCEPT *531*

altruistic [*adj*] *unselfish*
all heart, benevolent, big*, big-hearted*, bleeding heart*, charitable, considerate, generous, good, good scout, human, humanitarian, kind, magnanimous, openhanded, philanthropic, Robin Hood*, self-sacrificing; SEE CONCEPT *404*

alumnus/alumna [*n*] *graduate*
alum, old grad*, postgraduate; SEE CONCEPT *350*

always [*adv*] *forever; continually*
consistently, constantly, eternally, ever, everlastingly, evermore, forevermore, for keeps, in perpetuum, invariably, perpetually, regularly, repeatedly, till blue in the face*, till cows come home*, unceasingly, without exception; SEE CONCEPTS *551,798*

amalgam [*n*] *mixture*
admixture, alloy, amalgamation, blend, combo, composite, compound, fusion, mishmash*, soup; SEE CONCEPT *432*

amalgamate [*v*] *blend*
admix, alloy, ally, coalesce, combine, come together, compound, consolidate, fuse, hook up with*, incorporate, integrate, interface, intermix, join together, meld, merge, mingle, network, pool, team up*, tie in, tie up*, unite; SEE CONCEPT *113*

amass [*v*] *gather, accumulate*
aggregate, assemble, clean up*, collect, compile, corral*, garner, heap*, hoard, lay up*, make a killing*, make a pile*, pile, round up*, scare up*, stockpile, store; SEE CONCEPTS *109,120*

amateur [*n*] *casual participant*
abecedarian, apprentice, aspirant, beginner, bush, bush leaguer*, dabbler, dilettante, greenhorn, ham*, hopeful, layman, learner, neophyte, nonprofessional, novice, probationer, putterer, recruit, Sunday driver*, tenderfoot*; SEE CONCEPT *366*

amatory [*adj*] *affectionate, desirous*
admiring, amorous, aphrodisiac, ardent, attracted, devoted, doting, erotic, fervent, fond, languishing, lovesick, loving, passionate, rapturous, romantic, sentimental, tender, wooing, yearning; SEE CONCEPTS *372,403*

amaze [*v*] *surprise*
affect, alarm, astonish, astound, bewilder, blow away*, blow one's mind*, bowl over*, daze, dumbfound, electrify, flabbergast*, impress, move, perplex, put one away*, shock, stagger, startle, strike, stun, stupefy, touch*; SEE CONCEPT *42*

amazement [*n*] *state of surprise*
admiration, astonishment, awe, bewilderment, confoundment, confusion, marvel, one for the books*, perplexity, shock, something else*, stopper*, stunner*, stupefaction, wonder, wonderment; SEE CONCEPTS *230,410*

ambassador [*n*] *representative to a foreign country*
agent, consul, deputy, diplomat, emissary, envoy, minister, plenipotentiary; SEE CONCEPT *354*

amber [*n/adj*] *gold-colored*
brown, golden, tan, yellowish; SEE CONCEPT *618*

ambience [*n*] *environment*
ambient, atmosphere, climate, medium, surroundings; SEE CONCEPT *673*

ambiguity [*n*] *uncertainty of meaning*
double entendre, double meaning, doubt, doubtfulness, dubiety, dubiousness, enigma, equivocacy, equivocality, equivocation, incertitude, inconclusiveness, indefiniteness, indeterminateness, obscurity, puzzle, tergiversation, uncertainty, unclearness, vagueness; SEE CONCEPTS *638,682*

ambiguous [*adj*] *having more than one meaning*
clear as dishwater*, cryptic, doubtful, dubious, enigmatic, enigmatical, equivocal, inconclusive, indefinite, indeterminate, inexplicit, muddy, obscure, opaque, puzzling, questionable, tenebrous, uncertain, unclear, unintelligible, vague; SEE CONCEPTS *267,535*

ambition [*n1*] *strong desire for success*
appetite, ardor, aspiration, avidity, craving, desire, drive, eagerness, earnestness, emulation, energy, enterprise, enthusiasm, fire in belly*, get up and go*, hankering*, hope, hunger, initiative, itch*, keenness, longing, love, lust, moxie*, passion, pretension, push, right stuff*, spirit, striving, thirst, vigor, yearning; zeal; SEE CONCEPT *20*

ambition [*n2*] *something desired*
aim, aspiration, desire, dream, end, enterprise, goal, hope, intent, mark, objective, purpose, target, wish; SEE CONCEPT *659*

ambitious [*adj1*] *desiring success*
aggressive, anxious, ardent, aspiring, avid, ball of fire*, ballsy*, bent upon, climbing, come on, come on strong, designing, desirous, determined, driving, eager, eager beaver*, earnest, energetic, enterprising, enthusiastic, fireball*, get up and go*, goal-

oriented, go-getter*, hard ball*, high-reaching, hopeful, hungry, industrious, inspired, intent, longing, power-loving, purposeful, pushing, pushy*, resourceful, self-starting, sharp, soaring, striving, thirsty, vaulting, zealous; SEE CONCEPTS *326,542*

ambitious [*adj2*] *requiring great effort, ability*
arduous, bold, challenging, demanding, difficult, elaborate, energetic, exacting, formidable, grandiose, hard, impressive, industrious, lofty, pretentious, severe, strenuous, visionary; SEE CONCEPT *538*

ambivalent [*adj*] *conflicting*
clashing, contradictory, debatable, doubtful, equivocal, fluctuating, hesitant, inconclusive, irresolute, mixed, opposed, uncertain, undecided, unresolved, unsure, vacillating, warring, wavering; SEE CONCEPTS *534,564*

amble [*v*] *walk casually*
ankle*, boogie*, dawdle, drift, gander, gumshoe*, hoof it*, loiter, meander, mosey*, percolate*, ramble, sashay*, saunter, stroll, toddle*, wander; SEE CONCEPT *151*

ambulance [*n*] *emergency vehicle*
EMS, hospital wagon, rescue, transport; SEE CONCEPT *505*

ambulatory [*adj*] *changing position; able to move under own power*
ambulant, itinerant, nomadic, perambulant, perambulatory, peripatetic, roving, vagabond, vagrant; SEE CONCEPT *584*

ambush [*n*] *lying in wait; concealed position*
ambuscade, ambushment, camouflage, concealment, deception, hiding, hiding place*, lurking, pitfall, shelter, trap*, trick*, waiting, waylaying; SEE CONCEPTS *86,188*

ambush [*v*] *lie in wait; attack*
ambuscade, assail, assault, box in*, bushwhack*, decoy, dry gulch*, ensnare, entrap, hem in*, hide, hook*, jap*, jump, lay for, lurk, net, set trap, surprise, surround, trap, wait, waylay; SEE CONCEPTS *86,188*

ameliorate [*v*] *make, become better*
alleviate, amend, help, improve, lighten, meliorate, mitigate, relieve, step up, upgrade; SEE CONCEPT *244*

amenable [*adj1*] *willing, cooperative*
acquiescent, agreeable, biddable, docile, influenceable, manageable, obedient, open, persuadable, pliable, responsive, susceptible, tractable; SEE CONCEPT *404*

amenable [*adj2*] *able to be judged; responsible*
accountable, answerable, chargeable, liable, subject; SEE CONCEPT *402*

amend [*v*] *improve, correct*
alter, ameliorate, better, change, elevate, enhance, fix, help, lift, make up for, mend, modify, pay one's dues*, raise, rectify, reform, remedy, repair, revise, right, square*; SEE CONCEPTS *126,244*

amendment [*n1*] *correction, improvement*
alteration, amelioration, betterment, change, correction, enhancement, improvement, mending, modifi-

cation, rectification, reform, reformation, remedy, repair, revision; SEE CONCEPT *700*

amendment [*n2*] *addition to a document*
act, addendum, adjunct, alteration, attachment, bill, clarification, clause, codicil, measure, modification, motion, revision, rider, suggestion, supplement; SEE CONCEPT *270*

amends [*n*] *compensation*
apology, atonement, expiation, indemnification, indemnity, quittance, recompense, redress, reparation, reprisal, requital, restitution, restoration, satisfaction; SEE CONCEPTS *67,104,384*

amenity [*n1*] *pleasant thing*
advantage, betterment, comfort, convenience, enhancement, enrichment, excellence, extravagance, facility, frill, improvement, luxury, merit, quality, service, superfluity, virtue; SEE CONCEPT *712*

amenity [*n2*] *pleasing, agreeable behavior*
affability, agreeableness, amiability, attention, attractiveness, charity, charm, complaisance, cordiality, courtesy, delightfulness, enjoyableness, etiquette, gallantry, geniality, gentility, gratefulness, kindness, mildness, pleasantness, politeness, refinement, suavity, sweetness; SEE CONCEPT *633*

amiable [*adj*] *friendly, agreeable*
affable, amicable, attractive, benign, breezy, buddy-buddy*, charming, cheerful, clubby*, complaisant, cool*, copacetic*, cordial, cozy, delightful, downright neighborly*, easy, engaging, friendly, genial, good-humored, good-natured, gracious, home cooking*, kind, kindly, lenient, lovable, mellow, mild, Mr./Ms. Nice Guy*, obliging, palsy-walsy*, pleasant, pleasing, princely*, pussycat*, responsive, right, righteous, sociable, sweet-tempered, swell*, tight*, warm, warmhearted, winning; SEE CONCEPT *401*

amicable [*adj*] *friendly, especially regarding an agreement*
accordant, agreeing, amiable, brotherly, civil, clubby*, concordant, cordial, courteous, cozy, empathic, fraternal, good-humored, harmonious, kind, kindly, like-minded, mellow, neighborly, pacific, peaceable, peaceful, polite, regular, right nice*, sociable, square shooting*, sympathetic, understanding, white; SEE CONCEPTS *529,542*

amid/amidst [*prep*] *in middle of; among*
amongst, between, during, in the midst of, in the thick of, mid, over, surrounded by, throughout; SEE CONCEPTS *586,820*

amiss [*adj*] *wrong; defective*
awry, bad, confused, crooked, erring, erroneous, fallacious, false, faulty, flawed, foul, glitched up*, haywire, imperfect, improper, inaccurate, inappropriate, incorrect, mistaken, out of order, sick, unfair, unlawful, unsuitable, untoward; SEE CONCEPT *570*

amiss [*adv*] *wrongly; defectively*
afield, afoul, badly, erringly, erroneously, faultily, improperly, inappropriately, incorrectly, mistakenly,

out of turn, unfavorably, unsuitably; SEE CONCEPT *570*

amity [*n*] *friendship*
amicableness, benevolence, comity, concord, cordiality, friendliness, good vibrations*, goodwill, harmony, hitting it off*, in sync*, kindliness, neighborliness, same wavelength*, simpatico*, together*; SEE CONCEPT *388*

ammonia [*n*] *pungent gas, liquid*
alkali, salts, spirits, vapor; SEE CONCEPT *472*

ammunition [*n*] *projectiles for weaponry*
ammo*, armament, ball, bomb, buckshot*, bullet, cannonball, cartridge, charge, chemical, confetti*, explosive, fuse, grenade, gunpowder, iron rations*, materiel, missile, munition, napalm, powder, rocket, round, shell, shot, shrapnel, torpedo; SEE CONCEPTS *498,500*

amnesty [*n*] *pardon, often by government*
absolution, condonation, dispensation, forgiveness, immunity, reprieve; SEE CONCEPTS *298,300*

among [*prep1*] *in the middle of; between*
amid, amidst, betwixt, encompassed by, in dispersion through, in the midst of, in the thick of, mid, surrounded by, with; SEE CONCEPT *586*

among [*prep2*] *in a group*
by all of, by the whole of, in association with, in connection with, in the class of, in the company of, mutually, out of, together with, with, with one another; SEE CONCEPT *785*

amorous [*adj*] *loving, affectionate*
amative, amatory, aphrodisiac, ardent, attached, boy crazy*, doting, enamored, erotic, fond, girl crazy*, have a crush on*, horny*, hot, hot and heavy*, impassioned, infatuated, in love, lovesick, lovey dovey*, lustful, passionate, romantic, sexy, sweet for*, sweet on*, tender, turned on*; SEE CONCEPTS *372,403,555*

amorphous [*adj*] *without definite shape, character*
baggy, blobby, characterless, formless, inchoate, indeterminate, irregular, nebulous, nondescript, shapeless, unformed, unshaped, unstructured, vague; SEE CONCEPTS *404,490*

amount [*n1*] *quantity*
aplenty, bags*, bulk, bundle, chunk, expanse, extent, flock, gob, heap, hunk, jillion*, load, lot, magnitude, mass, measure, mess*, mint*, mucho*, number, oodles*, pack, passle, peck, pile, scads*, score, slat*, slew*, supply, ton*, volume, whopper*; SEE CONCEPTS *786,837*

amount [*n2*] *total*
addition, aggregate, all, bad news*, body, budget, cost, damage*, entirety, expense, extent, list, lot, net, outlay, output, price tag*, product, quantum, score, set-back*, sum, tab*, tidy sum*, whole; SEE CONCEPTS *329,784,786*

amount [*n3*] *whole effect*
body, burden, core, full value, import, matter, purport, result, sense, significance, substance, thrust, upshot, value; SEE CONCEPT *676*

amount [*v*] *equal, add up to*
aggregate, approach, approximate, become, be equivalent to, be tantamount to, check with, come to, correspond, develop into, effect, extend, grow, match, mean, number, purport, reach, rival, sum, tally, total, touch; SEE CONCEPT *667*

amour [*n*] *romance*
affair, entanglement, liaison, love, love affair, passion, relationship; SEE CONCEPT *32*

ample [*adj*] *more than necessary, sufficient*
abounding, abundant, big, bounteous, bountiful, broad, capacious, commodious, copious, enough, expansive, extensive, full, galore, generous, great, heavy, large, lavish, liberal, no end, plenteous, plentiful, plenty, profuse, rich, roomy, spacious, spare, substantial, unrestricted, voluminous, wide; SEE CONCEPTS *558,781*

amplification [*n*] *increase in size or effect*
addition, augmentation, boost, boosting, buildup, deepening, development, elaboration, enlargement, exaggeration, expansion, expatiation, extension, fleshing out, heightening, intensification, lengthening, magnification, padding, raising, strengthening, stretching, supplementing, upping, widening; SEE CONCEPTS *236,245,780*

amplify [*v*] *increase in size or effect*
add, augment, beef up*, boost, build up, deepen, develop, elaborate, enlarge, exaggerate, expand, expatiate, extend, flesh out*, heighten, hike up*, inflate, intensify, jack up*, lengthen, magnify, pad, pyramid, raise, soup up*, strengthen, stretch, supplement, swell, up, widen; SEE CONCEPTS *236,245*

amply [*adv*] *fully, sufficiently*
abundantly, acceptably, adequately, appropriately, bountifully, capaciously, completely, copiously, enough, extensively, fittingly, generously, greatly, lavishly, liberally, plenteously, plentifully, profusely, properly, richly, right, satisfactorily, substantially, suitably, thoroughly, well; SEE CONCEPTS *558,771*

amputate [*v*] *remove a limb*
cut away, cut off, dismember, eliminate, excise, lop, separate, sever, truncate; SEE CONCEPTS *176,211*

amuck [*adv*] *crazily*
berserk, destructively, ferociously, frenziedly, in a frenzy, insanely, madly, maniacally, murderously, savagely, uncontrollably, violently, wildly; SEE CONCEPT *401*

amulet [*n*] *charm*
fetish, lucky piece, ornament, talisman; SEE CONCEPTS *260,446*

amuse [*v*] *entertain; make laugh*
break one up*, charm, cheer, crack up*, delight, divert, fracture*, gladden, grab*, gratify, interest, kill*, knock dead*, lay in the aisles*, occupy, panic*, please, put away*, regale, slay*, tickle, wow*; SEE CONCEPTS *292,384*

amusement [n1] *entertaining, making someone laugh*
action, ball*, beguilement, cheer, delight, diversion, enjoyment, entertainment, field day*, fun, fun and games*, gladdening, gratification, grins*, high time*, hilarity, hoopla*, laughs*, laughter, merriment, merry go round*, mirth, picnic*, play, pleasing, pleasure, regalement, whoopee*; SEE CONCEPT 292

amusement [n2] *game, pastime*
distraction, diversion, entertainment, hobby, interest, joke, lark, play, prank, recreation, sport; SEE CONCEPT 364

amusing [adj] *entertaining, funny*
agreeable, ball*, boffo*, camp, campy, charming, cheerful, cheering, comical, cut up*, delightful, diverting, droll, enchanting, engaging, enjoyable, entertaining, for grins*, fun, gladdening, gratifying, gut-busting*, hoot*, humorous, interesting, jocular, jokey*, joshing*, laughable, lively, merry, pleasant, pleasing, priceless, riot*, scream*, screaming*, side-splitting*, too funny for words*, witty; SEE CONCEPTS 267,548

anachronism [n] *error in time placement*
antedate, chronological error, metachronism, misdate, misplacement, postdate, prolepsis, solecism; SEE CONCEPT 818

analgesic [n] *pain remover*
anesthetic, anodyne, painkiller, soother; SEE CONCEPT 307

analogous [adj] *agreeing, similar*
akin, alike, comparable, consonant, convertible, correspondent, corresponding, equivalent, homologous, interchangeable, kindred, like, parallel, related, resembling, undifferentiated, uniform; SEE CONCEPTS 487,573

analogy [n] *agreement, similarity*
affinity, alikeness, comparison, correlation, correspondence, equivalence, homology, likeness, metaphor, parallel, relation, relationship, resemblance, semblance, simile, similitude; SEE CONCEPTS 278,670

analysis [n1] *examination and determination*
assay, breakdown, dissection, dissolution, division, inquiry, investigation, partition, reasoning, resolution, scrutiny, search, separation, study, subdivision, test; SEE CONCEPTS 24,103

analysis [n2] *statement of results from examination*
estimation, evaluation, finding, interpretation, judgment, opinion, outline, reasoning, report, study, summary; SEE CONCEPTS 271,274

analyst [n] *person who examines and determines; psychoanalyst*
accountant, couch doctor*, examiner, guru*, head shrinker*, inquisitor, investigator, number cruncher*, psychiatrist, psychotherapist, questioner, shrink*; SEE CONCEPTS 348,357

analytic/analytical [adj] *examining and determining*
cogent, conclusive, detailed, diagnostic, discrete, dissecting, explanatory, expository, inquiring, inquisitive, interpretive, investigative, judicious, logical, organized, penetrating, perceptive, perspicuous, precise, problem-solving, questioning, ratiocinative, rational, reasonable, scientific, searching, solid, sound, studious, subtle, systematic, testing, thorough, valid, well-grounded; SEE CONCEPT 402

analyze [v1] *examine and determine*
assay, beat a dead horse*, chew over*, confab*, consider, estimate, evaluate, figure, figure out, get down to brass tacks*, hash*, inspect, interpret, investigate, judge, kick around*, rehash, resolve, scrutinize, sort out, spell out, study, talk game*, test, think through; SEE CONCEPTS 24,37,103

analyze [v2] *break down to components*
anatomize, break up, cut up, decompose, decompound, determine, disintegrate, dissect, dissolve, divide, electrolyze, hydrolyze, lay bare, parse, part, resolve, separate, x-ray; SEE CONCEPTS 135,310

anarchist [n] *person who opposes the idea of government and laws*
agitator, insurgent, insurrectionist, malcontent, mutineer, nihilist, rebel, revolter, revolutionary, terrorist; SEE CONCEPTS 359,412

anarchy [n] *lawlessness; absence of government*
chaos, confusion, disorder, disorganization, disregard, hostility, misrule, mob rule, nihilism, nongovernment, rebellion, reign of terror, revolution, riot, turmoil, unrest; SEE CONCEPTS 29,674

anathema [n1] *something hated*
abomination, bane, bugbear, detestation, enemy, hate, pariah; SEE CONCEPT 529

anathema [n2] *denouncement*
ban, censure, commination, condemnation, curse, damnation, denunciation, excommunication, execration, imprecation, malediction, proscription, reprehension, reprobation, reproof, taboo; SEE CONCEPT 278

anatomy [n1] *study of animal, plant structure*
analysis, biology, cytology, diagnosis, dissection, division, embryology, etiology, examination, genetics, histology, inquiry, investigation, medicine, morphology, physiology, zoology; SEE CONCEPT 349

anatomy [n2] *physical structure of animals, plants*
build, composition, figure, form, frame, framework, makeup, physique, shape; SEE CONCEPT 733

ancestor [n] *predecessor in family*
antecedent, antecessor, ascendant, forebear, forefather, foregoer, foremother, forerunner, founder, precursor, primogenitor, progenitor; SEE CONCEPT 414

ancestral [adj] *related to previous family or family trait*
affiliated, born with, congenital, consanguine, consanguineous, genealogical, inborn, inbred, inherited, innate, in the family, lineal, maternal, old, past, paternal, running in the family, totemic, tribal; SEE CONCEPT 549

ancestry [n] *family predecessors; family history*
ancestor, antecedent, antecessor, blood, breed, breeding, derivation, descent, extraction, forebear, forefather, foregoer, foremother, forerunner, genealogy, heritage, house, kindred, line, lineage, origin, parentage, pedigree, precursor, primogenitor, progenitor, race, source, stock; SEE CONCEPTS *414,648*

anchor [n] *something used to hold another thing securely*
ballast, bower, comfort, defense, fastener, foothold, grapnel, grappling iron, grip, hold, hook, kedge, mainstay, mooring, mud hook, pillar, protection, safeguard, security, staff, stay, support; SEE CONCEPTS *464,502,731*

anchor [v] *hold, be held securely*
attach, berth, catch, dock, drop, fasten, fix, imbed, make port, moor, plant, secure, stay, tie, tie up; SEE CONCEPTS *85,160,190*

ancient [adj] *old, often very old*
aged, age-old, antediluvian, antiquated, antique, archaic, back number*, been around*, bygone, creaky*, early, elderly, few miles on*, fossil*, hoary*, lot of mileage*, moth-eaten*, obsolete, older, old-fashioned, old goat*, oldie*, outmoded, out-of-date, primal, primeval, primordial, relic, remote, rusty, superannuated, timeworn, venerable, worse for wear*; SEE CONCEPTS *578,797*

ancillary [adj] *extra; supplementary*
accessory, accompanying, additional, adjuvant, appurtenant, attendant, attending, coincident, collateral, concomitant, contributory, incident, satellite, secondary, subordinate, subservient, subsidary; SEE CONCEPT *835*

and [conj] *in addition to; plus*
along with, also, as a consequence, as well as, furthermore, including, moreover, together with; SEE CONCEPT *577*

anecdote [n] *funny story*
chestnut*, episode, fairy tale*, fish story*, gag*, incident, long and short of it*, narration, narrative, old chestnut*, recital, relation, reminiscence, short story, sketch, tale, tall story*, tall tale*, yarn; SEE CONCEPT *282*

anemic [adj] *weak and pale*
bloodless, feeble, frail, infirm, pallid, sickly, wan, watery; SEE CONCEPTS *314,483,618*

anesthesia/anaesthesia [n] *induced sleep; induced absence of feeling*
analgesia, insentience, numbness, put under*, stupor, unconsciousness; SEE CONCEPTS *313,315,728*

anesthetic/anaesthetic [n] *sleep-inducing or numbing drug*
analgesic, anodyne, dope*, gas, hypnotic, inhalant, opiate, pain-killer, shot, soporific, spinal; SEE CONCEPT *307*

anew [adj/adv] *fresh; again*
afresh, another time, come again, de novo, from scratch, from the beginning, in a different way, in a new way, lately, new, newly, once again, once more, one more time, over, over again, recently; SEE CONCEPT *820*

angel [n1] *attendant of God*
archangel, celestial being, cherub, divine messenger, God's messenger, guardian, heavenly being, holy being, seraph, spirit, spiritual being, sprite, supernatural being; SEE CONCEPTS *361,370*

angel [n2] *sweet, kind person*
beauty, darling, dear, dream, gem, ideal, jewel, paragon, saint, treasure; SEE CONCEPT *416*

angelic [adj] *sweet, kind, and usually beautiful*
adorable, archangelic, beatific, beneficent, celestial, cherubic, devout, divine, entrancing, ethereal, godly, good, heavenly, holy, humble, innocent, lovely, otherworldly, pure, radiant, rapturous, righteous, saintly, self-sacrificing, seraphic, virtuous; SEE CONCEPT *572*

anger [n] *state of being mad, annoyed*
acrimony, animosity, annoyance, antagonism, blow up*, cat fit*, chagrin, choler, conniption, dander*, disapprobation, displeasure, distemper, enmity, exasperation, fury, gall, hatred, hissy fit*, huff, ill humor, ill temper, impatience, indignation, infuriation, irascibility, ire, irritability, irritation, mad, miff, outrage, passion, peevishness, pet peeve, petulance, pique, rage, rankling, resentment, slow burn*, soreness, stew, storm, tantrum, temper, tiff, umbrage, vexation, violence; SEE CONCEPTS *29,410*

anger [v] *make someone mad; become mad*
acerbate, affront, aggravate, agitate, annoy, antagonize, arouse, bait, blow up*, boil*, boil over*, bristle, burn, burn up, chafe, craze*, cross, displease, egg on*, embitter, enrage, exacerbate, exasperate, excite, fret, gall, get mad, get on one's nerves*, goad, incense, inflame, infuriate, irritate, lose one's temper, madden, make sore*, miff, nettle, offend, outrage, pique, provoke, rankle, rant, rave, rile, ruffle, seethe, steam up*, stew, stir up*, tempt, umbrage, vex; SEE CONCEPTS *7,19*

angle [n1] *shape formed by two lines meeting at a point*
bend, corner, crook, crotch, cusp, decline, divergence, dogleg, edge, elbow, flare, flection, flexure, fork, incline, intersection, knee, nook, notch, obliquity, point, slant, turn, turning, twist, V, Y; SEE CONCEPT *436*

angle [n2] *personal approach, purpose*
aim, approach, aspect, direction, hand, intention, outlook, perspective, plan, point of view, position, side, slant, standpoint, viewpoint; SEE CONCEPTS *660,661*

angle [v] *fish*
cast, dangle a line, drop a line; SEE CONCEPT *363*

angle for [v] *attempt to get*
aim for, be after, cast about for, connive, conspire, contrive, fish for, hint, hunt, invite, look for, ma-

neuver, plan, plot, scheme, seek, solicit, strive, try for; SEE CONCEPTS *20,87*

angry [*adj*] *being mad, often extremely mad*
affronted, annoyed, antagonized, bitter, chafed, choleric, convulsed, cross, displeased, enraged, exacerbated, exasperated, ferocious, fierce, fiery, fuming, furious, galled, hateful, heated, hot, huffy, ill-tempered, impassioned, incensed, indignant, inflamed, infuriated, irascible, irate, ireful, irritable, irritated, maddened, nettled, offended, outraged, piqued, provoked, raging, resentful, riled, sore, splenetic, storming, sulky, sullen, tumultous/tumultuous, turbulent, uptight, vexed, wrathful; SEE CONCEPT *403*

anguish [*n*] *severe upset or pain*
affliction, agony, distress, dole, dolor, grief, heartache, heartbreak, hurting, misery, pang, rue, sorrow, suffering, throe, torment, torture, woe, worried sick*, worried stiff*, wretchedness; SEE CONCEPT *410*

angular [*adj1*] *bent*
akimbo, bifurcate, cornered, crooked, crossing, crotched, divaricate, forked, intersecting, jagged, oblique, sharp-cornered, skewed, slanted, staggered, V-shaped, Y-shaped, zigzag; SEE CONCEPT *486*

angular [*adj2*] *thin, especially referring to people*
awkward, bony, gangling, gaunt, lank, lanky, lean, rangy, rawboned, scrawny, sharp, skinny, spare; SEE CONCEPT *773*

animal [*n*] *animate being; mammal*
beast, being, brute, bum*, creature, critter, invertebrate, living thing, mutt, pet, stray, varmint, vertebrate, wild thing; SEE CONCEPT *394*

animal [*adj*] *beastlike; carnal*
beastly, bestial, bodily, brute, brutish, corporeal, earthly, earthy, feral, fleshy, mammalian, muscular, natural, physical, sensual, untamed, wild, zoological; SEE CONCEPT *406*

animate [*adj1*] *alive*
breathing, live, living, mortal, moving, viable, vital, zoetic; SEE CONCEPT *539*

animate [*adj2*] *lively*
activated, active, alert, animated, dynamic, energized, gay, happy, spirited, vivacious; SEE CONCEPT *401*

animate [*v*] *bring to life*
activate, arouse, cheer, embolden, encourage, energize, enliven, exalt, excite, fire, gladden, hearten, impel, incite, inform, inspire, inspirit, instigate, invigorate, kindle, liven, make alive, move, quicken, revive, revivify, rouse, spark, spur, stimulate, stir, urge, vitalize, vivify; SEE CONCEPTS *231,241*

animated [*adj*] *lively*
activated, active, alert, animate, ardent, brisk, buoyant, dynamic, ebullient, elated, energetic, energized, enthusiastic, excited, fervent, gay, happy, passionate, peppy, quick, snappy, spirited, sprightly, vibrant, vigorous, vital, vitalized, vivacious, vivid, zealous, zestful, zingy, zippy; SEE CONCEPT *401*

animation [*n*] *liveliness; activity*
action, ardor, bounce, brio, briskness, buoyancy, dash, dynamism, ebullience, élan, elation, energy, enthusiasm, esprit, excitement, exhilaration, fervor, gaiety, high spirits, life, oomph, passion, pep, sparkle, spirit, sprightliness, verve, vibrancy, vigor, vim, vitality, vivacity, zap, zeal, zest, zing, zip; SEE CONCEPT *657*

animosity [*n*] *extreme dislike, hatred*
acrimony, animus, antagonism, antipathy, bad blood, bitterness, displeasure, enmity, hate, hostility, ill will, malevolence, malice, malignity, rancor, resentment, virulence; SEE CONCEPT *29*

ankle [*n*] *joint between leg and foot*
anklebone, astragalus, bone, talus, tarsus; SEE CONCEPTS *392,418*

annal(s) [*n*] *history, records*
account, archive, chronicle, journal, memorial, record, register; SEE CONCEPTS *271,281*

annex [*n*] *something added; extension*
addendum, addition, adjunct, affix, appendix, arm, attachment, ell, subsidiary, supplement, wing; SEE CONCEPTS *440,441,484*

annex [*v*] *join or add*
adjoin, affix, append, appropriate, associate, attach, connect, fasten, hitch on*, hitch up*, hook on*, hook up*, join, link, slap on*, subjoin, tack on*, tag, tag on*, take on, take over, unite; SEE CONCEPTS *85,113,160*

annexation [*n*] *adding, joining*
addition, annexing, appropriation, attachment, grab, incorporation, increase, increment, merger, takeover; SEE CONCEPTS *113,324*

annihilate [*v*] *destroy completely*
abate, abolish, abrogate, annul, blot out*, crush*, decimate, demolish, do in*, eradicate, erase, expunge, exterminate, extinguish, extirpate, finish off, invalidate, liquidate, massacre, murder, negate, nullify, obliterate, quash, quell, raze, root out*, rub out*, ruin, slaughter, take out*, undo, vitiate, wipe out*, wrack*, wreck; SEE CONCEPT *252*

anniversary [*n*] *yearly observance, celebration*
ceremony, commemoration, feast day, festival, holiday, jubilee, recurrence, red-letter day; SEE CONCEPTS *800,801,815,823*

annotate [*v*] *write explanatory notes*
comment, commentate, construe, define, elucidate, explain, expound, footnote, gloss, illustrate, interpret, note, remark; SEE CONCEPTS *51,57,79*

annotation [*n*] *explanatory note*
comment, commentary, definition, elucidation, exegesis, explanation, explication, footnote, gloss, glossary, illustration, interpretation, note, observation; SEE CONCEPTS *274,283*

announce [*v1*] *make a proclamation*
advertise, annunciate, blast, blazon, broadcast, call, communicate, declare, disclose, disseminate, divulge, drum*, give out, impart, intimate, issue, make

known, make public, pass the word*, proclaim, promulgate, propound, publicize, publish, release, report, reveal, run off at mouth*, sound off*, spread around*, state, tell, trumpet; SEE CONCEPT *49*

announce [*v2*] *declare arrival*
augur, forebode, forecast, forerun, foreshow, foretell, harbinger, herald, indicate, portend, predict, presage, signal, signify; SEE CONCEPTS *60,70*

announcement [*n*] *proclamation, declaration*
advertisement, advice, briefing, broadcast, broadcasting, bulletin, communication, communiqué, disclosure, dissemination, divulgence, edict, exposing, exposition, expression, intimation, message, narration, news, notice, notification, prediction, promulgation, publication, publishing, recitation, release, report, reporting, revelation, statement; SEE CONCEPTS *49,274*

announcer [*n*] *media commentator*
anchorperson, broadcaster, communicator, deejay, disc jockey, DJ, master of ceremonies, newscaster, reporter, rip and reader*, spieler*, talker, telecaster, veejay*; SEE CONCEPT *348*

annoy [*v*] *irritate, upset*
abrade, agitate, ask for it*, badger, be at*, bedevil, beleaguer, be on the back of*, bore, bother, break, bug, burn up, chafe, displease, distress, disturb, egg on*, exasperate, fire up*, gall, get, gnaw, harass, harry, heat up*, henpeck, hit where one lives*, irk, madden, make waves*, miff, nag, needle, nettle, nudge, peeve, perturb, pester, plague, provoke, push right button*, ride, rile, ruffle, tease, tick off*, T-off*, trouble, turn off*, vex, work on*, worry; SEE CONCEPTS *7,19*

annual [*n*] *book produced once a year*
annuary, report, summary, yearbook; SEE CONCEPT *271*

annual [*adj1*] *occurring, done yearly*
anniversary, each year, every year, once a year, year end; SEE CONCEPTS *541,823*

annual [*adj2*] *lasting for a year*
a year's worth, yearlong; SEE CONCEPT *798*

annually [*adv*] *occurring, done yearly*
by the year, each year, every year, once a year, per annum, per year, year after year; SEE CONCEPTS *541,823*

annul [*v*] *void an agreement*
abate, abolish, abrogate, annihilate, blot out*, call off, cancel, countermand, declare, delete, discharge, dissolve, efface, erase, expunge, get off the hook*, invalidate, kill, negate, neutralize, nix, nullify, obliterate, quash, recall, render null and void*, repeal, rescind, retract, reverse, revoke, scrub, undo, vacate, vitiate, wipe out*; SEE CONCEPTS *252,297,317*

annulment [*n*] *voiding an agreement*
abatement, abolition, abrogation, annihilation, breakup, cancellation, countermanding, dedomiciling, deletion, discharge, dissolution, erasing, going phffft*, invalidation, negation, neutralization, nullifi-

cation, obliteration, on the rocks*, recall, repeal, rescinding, rescindment, rescission, retraction, reversal, revocation, split*, split up*, undoing*, vitiation, voiding; SEE CONCEPTS *297,317,691*

anoint [*v*] *bless, usually with oil or water*
bless, consecrate, daub, embrocate, grease, hallow, rub, sanctify, smear; SEE CONCEPT *367*

anomalous [*adj*] *deviating from normal, usual*
aberrant, abnormal, atypical, bizarre, divergent, eccentric, exceptional, foreign, heteroclite, incongruous, inconsistent, irregular, odd, peculiar, preternatural, prodigous, rare, strange, unnatural, unrepresentative, untypical, unusual; SEE CONCEPT *547*

anomaly [*n*] *deviation from normal, usual*
aberration, abnormality, departure, deviation, eccentricity, exception, incongruity, inconsistency, irregularity, oddity, peculiarity, rarity, unconformity; SEE CONCEPT *647*

anonymous [*adj*] *unknown, usually by choice*
bearding*, incognito, innominate, Jane/John Doe*, nameless, pseudo, pseudonymous, secret, so and so*, such and such*, unacknowledged, unattested, unavowed, unclaimed, uncredited, undesignated, undisclosed, unidentified, unnamed, unsigned, unspecified, whatchamacallit*, what's his/her name*, whatsis*, X*, you know who*; SEE CONCEPT *683*

another [*n*] *other person*
addition, a different person, one more, someone else, something else; SEE CONCEPT *423*

another [*det/prep*] *additional, different*
added, a distinct, a further, a separate, else, farther, fresh, further, more, new, one more, other, some other, that; SEE CONCEPT *564*

answer [*n*] *reply; reaction*
acknowledgment, antiphon, backcap*, back talk, band-aid*, close, comeback, comment, cooler*, counterclaim, crack, defense, disclosure, echo, elucidation, explanation, feedback, guff*, interpretation, justification, key, lip*, observation, parting shot*, pay dirt*, plea, quick fix*, rebuttal, refutation, rejoinder, remark, repartee, report, resolution, response, result, retort, return, riposte, sign, solution, statement, thank-you note*, the ticket*, topper*, vindication, wisecrack; SEE CONCEPTS *274,278*

answer [*v1*] *reply, react*
acknowledge, answer back, argue, back at you*, back talk, be in touch*, claim, comeback, contest, counterclaim, defend, deny, disprove, dispute, echo, explain, feedback, field the question*, get back at*, get back to*, give a snappy comeback*, parry, plead, rebut, refute, rejoin, remark, resolve, respond, retaliate, retort, return, sass*, say, settle, shoot back*, solve, squelch, talk back, top*; SEE CONCEPTS *45,266*

answer [*v2*] *solve; fulfill*
clarify, conform, correlate, correspond, crack*, deal with*, do*, dope, dope out*, elucidate, fill, fit*, lick*, measure up, meet, pass, qualify, satisfy, serve,

suffice, suit, unzip*, work, work through; SEE CONCEPTS *87,664*

answerable [*adj*] *responsible*
accountable, amenable, bound, chargeable, compelled, constrained, liable, obligated, obliged, subject, to blame; SEE CONCEPT *545*

antagonism [*n*] *causing problem; opposition*
animosity, animus, antipathy, antithesis, clashing, competition, conflict, contention, contradistinction, contrariety, difference, disagreement, discord, dissension, enmity, friction, hatred, hostility, incongruity, oppugnancy, rancor, resistance, rivalry; SEE CONCEPT *29*

antagonist [*n*] *person causing problem*
adversary, angries*, bad guy*, bandit*, competitor, contender, crip*, enemy, foe, match, opponent, opposer, opposite number*, oppugnant, rival; SEE CONCEPT *412*

antagonize [*v*] *cause problem; oppose*
alienate, anger, annoy, counteract, estrange, insult, irritate, neutralize, offend, repel, struggle, work against; SEE CONCEPTS *7,19,231*

antecedent(s) [*n*] *predecessor(s) in family*
ancestor, ancestry, antecessor, blood, descent, extraction, forebears, forefather/mother, genealogy, line, primogenitor, progenitor, stock; SEE CONCEPT *414*

antecedent [*adj*] *prior*
anterior, earlier, foregoing, former, past, precedent, preceding, precursory, preliminary, previous; SEE CONCEPT *820*

antedate [*v*] *occur or cause to occur earlier*
accelerate, anachronize, antecede, backdate, date back, forerun, misdate, pace, precede, predate; SEE CONCEPT *84*

antediluvian [*adj*] *out-of-date; prehistoric*
age-old, ancient, antiquated, antique, archaic, hoary, obsolete, old, old-fashioned, passé, primeval, primitive, primordial, timeworn, venerable; SEE CONCEPTS *578,797,799*

antenna [*n*] *appendages for sensing, usually on insects or electronics*
aerial, bird snapper*, bullwhip*, ears*, feelers*, rabbit ears, receiver, sky wire*, whip*, wire; SEE CONCEPT *464*

anterior [*adj*] *beginning, prior*
antecedent, foregoing, former, past, precedent, preceding, previous; SEE CONCEPT *799*

anthem [*n*] *song*
canticle, chant, chorus, hymn, melody, paean; SEE CONCEPTS *263,595*

anthology [*n*] *literary collection*
album, analect, compendium, compilation, digest, garland, omnibus, selection, treasury; SEE CONCEPTS *280,432*

anthropology [*n*] *study of humans and their culture*
folklore, sociology; SEE CONCEPT *349*

antic [*n*] *funny act*
caper, dido, frolic, joke, lark, romp, shenanigan, tomfoolery, trick; SEE CONCEPT *292*

anticipate [*v1*] *expect; predict*
assume, await, bargain for*, be afraid*, conjecture, count chickens*, count on, cross the bridge*, divine, entertain*, figure, forecast, foresee, foretaste, foretell, have a hunch*, hope for, jump the gun*, look for, look forward to, plan on, prepare for, previse, prognosticate, promise oneself, prophesy, see, see coming*, see in the cards*, suppose, visualize, wait, wait for; SEE CONCEPTS *26,70*

anticipate [*v2*] *act in advance of*
apprehend, beat someone to it*, be early, be one step ahead of*, block, delay, forestall, hinder, hold back, intercept, precede, preclude, prepare for, prevent, provide against; SEE CONCEPTS *100,121*

anticipation [*n1*] *expectation*
apprehension, awaiting, contemplation, expectancy, foresight, foretaste, high hopes, hope, impatience, joy, looking forward, outlook, preconception, premonition, preoccupation, prescience, presentiment, promise, prospect, trust; SEE CONCEPTS *26,689*

anticipation [*n2*] *readiness; forethought*
apprehension, awareness, foreboding, forecast, foreseeing, foresight, foretaste, forethought, inkling, intuition, preconception, premonition, prescience, presentiment, prevision, prior knowledge, realization; SEE CONCEPTS *409,410*

anticlimax [*n*] *ineffective conclusion*
bathos, comedown, decline, descent, disappointment, drop, letdown, slump; SEE CONCEPTS *230,674*

antidote [*n*] *counteracting agent*
antitoxin, antivenin, corrective, counteractant, counteragent, countermeasure, counterstep, cure, medicine, negator, neutralizer, nullifier, preventive, remedy; SEE CONCEPT *307*

antipathy [*n*] *strong dislike, disgust*
abhorrence, allergy, animosity, animus, antagonism, aversion, avoidance, bad blood*, contrariety, distaste, dyspathy, enmity, escape, eschewal, evasion, hate, hatred, hostility, ill will, incompatibility, loathing, no use*, opposition, rancor, repellency, repugnance, repulsion; SEE CONCEPT *29*

antiquarian [*adj*] *old, ancient*
aged, antique, archaic, hoary, obsolete, primitive, timeworn, venerable; SEE CONCEPTS *578,797*

antiquated [*adj*] *obsolete*
aged, ancient, antediluvian, antique, archaic, dated, elderly, fusty*, hoary, moldy, obsolescent, old, old-fangled, old-fashioned, old hat*, outmoded, out-of-date, outworn, superannuated; SEE CONCEPTS *530,578,797*

antique [*n*] *old object, often of great value*
antiquity, artifact, bygone, heirloom, monument, objet d'art, rarity, relic, ruin, vestige; SEE CONCEPTS *259,443*

antique [*adj1*] *old*
aged, ancient, elderly, obsolescent, obsolete, out-dated, out-of-date, prehistoric, superannuated; SEE CONCEPTS *578,797*

antique [*adj2*] *old-fashioned*
antiquarian, archaic, classic, obsolete, olden, out-dated, vintage; SEE CONCEPTS *530,578,797*

antiquity [*n1*] *old object*
antique, relic, ruin; SEE CONCEPT *259*

antiquity [*n2*] *oldness*
age, ancientness, antiqueness, archaicism, archaism, elderliness, hoariness, old age, venerableness; SEE CONCEPT *715*

antiquity [*n3*] *distant past*
ancient time(s), classical times, days of old, days of yore, former age, old days, olden days, remote time, time immemorial; SEE CONCEPT *807*

antiseptic [*n*] *decontaminating agent*
bactericide, detergent, disinfectant, germicide, pre-servative, preventative, preventive, prophylactic, pu-rifier, sterilizer; SEE CONCEPTS *307,472,492*

antiseptic [*adj*] *completely clean, uncontaminated; decontaminating*
antibacterial, antibiotic, aseptic, bactericidal, clean, disinfectant, germ-destroying, germ-free, germi-cidal, hygienic, medicated, prophylactic, pure, puri-fying, sanitary, sterile, sterilized, sterilizing, unpolluted; SEE CONCEPT *485*

antisocial [*adj*] *nonparticipating; avoiding company*
alienated, ascetic, asocial, austere, cold, cynical, er-emetic, hermitlike, introverted, misanthropic, reclu-sive, remote, reserved, retiring, solitary, standoffish, uncommunicative, unfriendly, unsociable, with-drawn; SEE CONCEPT *555*

antithesis [*n1*] *exact opposite*
antipode, antipole, contra, contradictory, contrary, contrast, converse, counter, flip side*, inverse, other side, reverse; SEE CONCEPT *665*

antithesis [*n2*] *contrast, opposition*
antagonism, contradiction, contradistinction, contra-position, contrariety, inversion, opposure, reversal; SEE CONCEPTS *633,665*

antitoxin [*n*] *agent for negating the effect of an infec-tion or poison*
antibiotic, antibody, antipoison, antiseptic, antise-rum, counteractant, counteragent, medicine, neutral-izer, preventive, serum, vaccine; SEE CONCEPT *307*

antonym [*n*] *word with opposite meaning to another word*
opposite, reverse; SEE CONCEPT *275*

anxiety [*n*] *worry, tension*
all-overs*, angst, ants in pants*, apprehension, both-eration*, butterflies, care, cold sweat*, concern, creeps*, disquiet, disquietude, distress, doubt, down-er*, drag*, dread, fidgets*, flap*, foreboding, fret-fulness, fuss, goose bumps*, heebie-jeebies*, jitters, jumps*, misery, misgiving, mistrust, nail-biter*, needles*, nervousness, panic, pins and needles*,

restlessness, shakes*, shivers*, solicitude, suffering, suspense, sweat*, trouble, uncertainty, unease, un-easiness, watchfulness, willies*, worriment; SEE CONCEPTS *410,532,690*

anxious [*adj1*] *worried, tense*
afraid, aghast, antsy, apprehensive, basket case*, bugged*, butterflies, careful, choked*, clutched*, concerned, disquieted, distressed, disturbed, dread-ing, fearful, fidgety, fretful, hacked*, hyper, in a state*, in a tizzy*, in suspense*, jittery, jumpy, ner-vous, nervy, overwrought, restless, scared, shaking, shaky, shivery, shook up*, shot to pieces*, solici-tous, spooked*, strung out*, sweating bullets*, taut, troubled, uneasy, unglued*, unquiet, uptight*, watchful, wired*, worried sick*, wreck*; SEE CON-CEPTS *403,690*

anxious [*adj2*] *eager*
agog, ardent, avid, breathless, desirous, enthusiastic, expectant, fervent, impatient, intent, itching*, keen, thirsty, yearning, zealous; SEE CONCEPTS *401,542*

any [*det*] *one, some; unspecified, indiscriminate*
a bit, a little, all, each, each and every, either, in general, part of, several, whatever; SEE CONCEPT *762*

anybody [*n*] *one, some unspecified person or people*
all, any of, anyone, anyone at all, any person, a person, each and every one, everybody, everyone, masses, one, public, whole world; SEE CONCEPT *417*

anyhow [*adv*] *by any means*
about, anyway, any which way, around, at any rate, at random, haphazard, haphazardly, helter-skelter, however, in any case, in any respect, in any way, in either way, in one way or another, in whatever way, nevertheless, random, randomly, regardless, under any circumstances, whatever happens; SEE CONCEPT *544*

anyone [*n*] *one, some unspecified person*
all, anybody, anybody at all, any of, any person, a person, each and every one, everybody, everyone, masses, one, public, whole world; SEE CONCEPT *417*

anyplace [*n*] *unspecified area*
all over, anywhere, everywhere, in any place, in whatever place, wherever; SEE CONCEPT *198*

anything [*n*] *unspecified object or event*
all, any one thing, anything at all, everything, what-ever; SEE CONCEPTS *2,433*

anytime [*n*] *unspecified moment, period*
at all, at any moment, at one's convenience, every-time, no matter when, whenever, when one will; SEE CONCEPTS *807,819*

anyway [*adv*] *by any means*
anyhow, at all, at any rate, ever, however, in any case, in any event, in any manner, nevertheless, once; SEE CONCEPT *544*

anywhere [*n*] *unspecified area*
all over, anyplace, everywhere, in any place, in what-ever place, wherever; SEE CONCEPT *198*

apart [*adv*] *separate*
afar, alone, aloof, aside, away, by itself, cut off*, disassociated, disconnected, distant, distinct, di-

vorced, excluded, exclusively, freely, independent, independently, individually, isolated, lone wolf*, separated, separately, singly, special, to itself, to one side; SEE CONCEPTS *586,785*

apartment [*n*] *set of rooms for rent*
accommodation, cave*, chambers, cold-water*, condo, coop, cooperative, crash pad*, den*, digs*, dump*, flat, living quarters, lodging, pad, penthouse, rental, residence, suite, walk-up; SEE CONCEPTS *448,516*

apathetic [*adj*] *uncaring, disinterested*
blah, callous, cold, cool, couldn't care less*, draggy*, emotionless, flat, impassive, indifferent, insensible, laid-back, languid, moony*, passive, stoic, stolid, unconcerned, unemotional, unfeeling, uninterested, unmoved, unresponsive, untouched, wimpy*; SEE CONCEPTS *401,403*

apathy [*n*] *uncaring attitude, lack of interest*
aloofness, coldness, coolness, detachment, disinterest, dispassion, disregard, dullness, emotionlessness, halfheartedness, heedlessness, indifference, insensibility, insensitivity, insouciance, lassitude, lethargy, listlessness, passiveness, passivity, stoicism, unconcern, unresponsiveness; SEE CONCEPTS *410,633*

ape [*v*] *mimic*
affect, caricature, copy, counterfeit, ditto*, do*, do like*, echo, emulate, go like*, imitate, impersonate, make like*, mirror, mock, parody, parrot, take off*, travesty; SEE CONCEPTS *111,171*

aperture [*n*] *hole*
breach, break, chasm, chink, cleft, crack, cut, eye, fissure, gap, gash, interstice, opening, orifice, outlet, passage, perforation, pinhole, puncture, rift, rupture, slash, slit, slot, space, vent; SEE CONCEPT *757*

apex [*n*] *top, high point*
acme, apogee, climax, crest, crown, culmination, cusp, greatest, height, max*, maximum, meridian, most*, ne plus ultra, peak, pinnacle, point, roof, spire, sublimity, summit, tip, tops, up there*, vertex, zenith; SEE CONCEPTS *706,836*

aphorism [*n*] *saying expressing a belief, often true*
adage, apothegm, axiom, dictum, maxim, moral, precept, proverb, rule, saw, saying, truism; SEE CONCEPTS *275,278,689*

aphrodisiac [*n/adj*] *seductive; inducing sex*
amative, amatory, amorous, erotic, love drug, popper*, Spanish fly*, turn-on*, wampole*; SEE CONCEPTS *372,537*

apiece [*adv*] *each*
all, a pop*, aside, for each, from each, individually, one by one, per, respectively, separately, severally, singly, successively, to each; SEE CONCEPT *762*

apocryphal [*adj*] *questionable; fake*
counterfeit, doubtful, dubious, equivocal, false, fictitious, inaccurate, mythical, spurious, unauthenticated, ungenuine, unsubstantiated, untrue, unverified, wrong; SEE CONCEPTS *570,582*

apologetic [*adj*] *expressing remorse, regret*
atoning, attritional, compunctious, conciliatory, contrite, expiatory, explanatory, on one's knees*, penitent, penitential, propitiatory, regretful, remorseful, repentant, rueful, self-effacing, self-incriminating, sorry, supplicating; SEE CONCEPT *267*

apologize [*v*] *express remorse, regret*
admit guilt, ask forgiveness, ask pardon, atone, beg pardon, bow to*, clear oneself, confess, cop a plea*, cop out*, crawl*, excuse oneself, get down on knees*, give satisfaction*, make amends, make reparations, make up for, make up with, offer compensation, offer excuse, purge, retract, say one is sorry*, square*, withdraw; SEE CONCEPTS *48,67*

apology [*n*] *offering of remorse, regret*
acknowledgment, admission, amends, atonement, concession, confession, defense, excuse, explanation, extenuation, justification, mea culpa, mitigation, plea, redress, reparation, vindication; SEE CONCEPTS *48,67*

apoplexy [*n*] *loss of consciousness from blockage in vein or artery*
occlusion, seizure, stroke, thrombosis; SEE CONCEPTS *316,720*

apostate [*n*] *traitor*
backslider, defector, deserter, dissenter, heretic, nonconformist, rat*, recreant, renegade, turncoat*; SEE CONCEPTS *359,412*

apostle [*n*] *preacher; supporter*
advocate, champion, companion, converter, evangelist, follower, herald, messenger, missionary, pioneer, propagandist, proponent, proselytizer, witness; SEE CONCEPTS *359,361*

appall/appal [*v*] *horrify*
alarm, amaze, astound, awe, consternate, daunt, disconcert, dishearten, dismay, faze, frighten, get to, gross out, insult, intimidate, outrage, petrify, scare, shake, shock, terrify, throw, unnerve; SEE CONCEPTS *7,19,42*

appalling [*adj*] *horrifying*
alarming, astounding, awful, bad, bummer*, daunting, dire, disheartening, dismaying, downer*, dreadful, fearful, formidable, frightening, frightful, ghastly, grim, grody*, gross*, harrowing, heavy*, hideous, horrible, horrid, horrific, intimidating, mean, petrifying, scaring, shocking, terrible, terrifying, the end*, unnerving; SEE CONCEPT *529*

apparatus [*n1*] *equipment with a purpose*
accoutrement, appliance, black box*, contraption, dealie bob*, device, dingbat, doodad*, doohickey*, furnishings, gaff*, gear, gimcrack*, gimmick, gizmo*, grabber*, habiliments, idiot box*, implement, jigger*, job*, machine, machinery, means, mechanism, outfit, paraphernalia, provisions, setup, stuff, supplies, tackle, thingamajig*, tools, utensils, whatchamacallit*, whatsis*, whosis*, widget*; SEE CONCEPTS *260,463,499*

apparatus [n2] *organization or system*
bureaucracy, chain of command, hierarchy, network, setup, structure; SEE CONCEPTS *381,770*

apparel [n] *clothing; covering*
accoutrement, array, attire, clothes, costume, drapery*, dress, duds*, equipment, garb, garment, gear*, getup*, habiliment, habit, outfit, raiment, rig*, robe, suit, threads*, trapping*, vestment; SEE CONCEPTS *451,473*

apparent [adj1] *seeming, not proven real*
credible, illusive, illusory, likely, ostensible, outward, plausible, possible, probable, semblant, specious, superficial, supposed, supposititious; SEE CONCEPTS *552,582*

apparent [adj2] *obvious*
barefaced, big as life*, clear, clear cut, conspicuous, crystal clear, discernible, distinct, evident, glaring, indubitable, make no bones*, manifest, marked, noticeable, observable, open, open and shut*, out in the open*, overt, palpable, patent, perceivable, plain, self-evident, transparent, unambiguous, under one's nose*, understandable, unequivocal, unmistakable, visible; SEE CONCEPTS *535,582*

apparently [adv1] *seemingly*
allegedly, as if, as though, at a glance, at first sight, in all likelihood, intuitively, it appears that, it seems that, most likely, on the face of it, ostensibly, outwardly, plausibly, possibly, probably, professedly, reasonably, reputably, speciously, superficially, supposedly, tangibly, to all appearances; SEE CONCEPTS *552,582*

apparently [adv2] *obviously*
clearly, conspicuously, evident, evidently, expressly, indubitably, in plain sight, manifestly, officially, openly, overtly, palpably, patently, perceptibly, plainly, transparently, unmistakably; SEE CONCEPT *535*

apparition [n] *ghost*
bogeyman, bump in the night*, chimera, delusion, hallucination, haunt, illusion, phantasm, phantom, revenant, specter, spirit, spook, visitant; SEE CONCEPTS *370,689*

appeal [n1] *request for help*
address, adjuration, application, bid, call, claim, demand, entreaty, imploration, importunity, invocation, overture, petition, plea, prayer, proposal, proposition, question, recourse, requisition, solicitation, submission, suit, supplication; SEE CONCEPT *48*

appeal [n2] *power to attract, interest*
allure, attraction, attractiveness, beauty, charm, charmingness, engagingness, fascination, glamor, interestingness, pleasingness, seductiveness; SEE CONCEPTS *655,673*

appeal [v1] *request*
address, adjure, advance, apply, ask, beg, beseech, bid, call, call upon, claim, contest, crave, demand, entreat, hit on, implore, importune, petition, plead, pray, propose, proposition, question, refer, require,

resort to, solicit, strike, submit, sue, supplicate, urge; SEE CONCEPT *48*

appeal [v2] *attract, interest*
allure, beguile, captivate, catch the eye, charm, enchant, engage, entice, fascinate, intrigue, invite, please, tantalize, tempt; SEE CONCEPTS *7,19,22,384*

appear [v1] *come into sight*
arise, arrive, attend, be present, be within view, blow in*, bob up*, break through, breeze in*, check in*, clock in*, come, come forth, come into view, come out, come to light*, crop up*, develop, drop in*, emerge, expose, issue, loom, make the scene*, materialize, occur, pop in*, pop up*, present, punch in*, punch the clock*, recur, ring in*, rise, roll in*, show, show up, speak of the devil*, spring, surface, time in*, turn out, turn up; SEE CONCEPTS *159,261*

appear [v2] *seem*
have the appearance, look as if, look like, occur, resemble, sound, strike one as; SEE CONCEPTS *543,716*

appear [v3] *be obvious, clear*
be apparent, be evident, be manifest, be patent, be plain; SEE CONCEPT *725*

appear [v4] *be published; perform*
become available, be created, be developed, be invented, come into being, come into existence, come on, come on stage*, come out, enter, make an appearance, oblige, perform, play, play a part*, present oneself, take part; SEE CONCEPTS *292,324*

appearance [n1] *coming into sight*
actualization, advent, appearing, arrival, coming, debut, display, emergence, entrance, exhibition, introduction, manifestation, materialization, presence, presentation, representation, rise, showing up, turning up, unveiling; SEE CONCEPTS *159,261*

appearance [n2] *outward aspect, characteristic*
air, attitude, bearing, blind, carriage, cast, character, condition, countenance, demeanor, dress, expression, face, fashion, feature, figure, form, front, guise, image, look, looks, manner, mannerism, mien, mode, outline, pose, presence, presentation, screen, semblance, shape, stamp; SEE CONCEPTS *543,716*

appearance [n3] *outward show; pretense*
aura, beard, blind, countenance, dream, facade, front, guise, idea, illusion, image, impression, mirage, phenomenon, reflection, screen, seeming, semblance, sound, specter, vision; SEE CONCEPT *673*

appease [v] *satisfy, pacify*
allay, alleviate, assuage, be enough, blunt, calm, compose, conciliate, content, diminish, do*, ease, gratify, lessen, lull, make matters up, meet halfway, mitigate, mollify, patch things up, placate, propitiate, quell, quench, quiet, serve, soften, soothe, subdue, sweeten, tranquilize; SEE CONCEPTS *7,22,126*

appeasement [n] *satisfaction; pacification*
abatement, acceding, accommodation, adjustment, alleviation, amends, assuagement, blunting, compro-

mise, concession, conciliation, easing, grant, lessening, lulling, mitigation, moderation, mollification, peace offering, placation, propitiation, quelling, quenching, quieting, reconciliation, reparation, restoration, settlement, softening, solace, soothing, tranquilization; SEE CONCEPTS *7,22,126*

append [v] *add, join*
adjoin, affix, annex, attach, conjoin, fasten, fix, hang, subjoin, supplement, tack on*, tag on*; SEE CONCEPTS *85,113,160*

appendage [n] *limb; accessory*
addendum, addition, adjunct, ancillary, annex, appendix, appurtenance, attachment, auxiliary, extremity, member, projection, protuberance, supplement; SEE CONCEPT *835*

appendix [n] *added material at end of document*
addendum, addition, adjunct, appendage, appurtenance, attachment, codicil, excursus, index, notes, postscript, rider, sample, supplement, table, verification; SEE CONCEPT *270*

appertain [v] *belong, be connected*
apply, bear, be characteristic of, be part of, be pertinent, be proper, be relevant, have to do with, pertain, refer, relate, touch upon, vest; SEE CONCEPT *532*

appetite [n] *desire for food, worldly goods*
appetence, appetency, appetition, big eyes, craving, demand, fondness, gluttony, greed, hankering, hunger, inclination, itch*, liking, longing, lust, passion, penchant, proclivity, propensity, ravenousness, relish, soft spot*, stomach, sweet tooth*, taste, thirst, urge, voracity, weakness, willingness, yearning, yen, zeal, zest; SEE CONCEPTS *20,32*

appetizer [n] *snack before meal*
antipasto, aperitif, canapé, cocktail, dip, finger food, hors d'oeuvre, munchies, relish, sample, spread, taste; SEE CONCEPTS *457,828*

appetizing [adj] *tasting very good*
aperitive, appealing, delectable, delicious, delish*, divine*, flavorsome, heavenly, inviting, luscious, mouthwatering, palatable, saporous, savory, scrumptious, succulent, sugar-coated*, sweetened*, tantalizing, tasty, tempting, toothsome, yummy*; SEE CONCEPT *613*

applaud [v] *clap for; express approval*
acclaim, approve, boost, cheer, commend, compliment, encourage, eulogize, extol, give a hand*, give ovation, glorify, hail, hear it for*, kudo*, laud, magnify, plug, praise, rave, recommend, root*; SEE CONCEPTS *10,69,189*

applause [n] *clapping; expression of approval*
acclaim, acclamation, accolade, approbation, big hand, bring down the house*, cheering, cheers, commendation, eulogizing, hand, hand-clapping, hurrahs, laudation, ovation, plaudits, praise, rooting, round, standing ovation; SEE CONCEPTS *69,189*

appliance [n] *machine, usually with domestic purpose*
apparatus, device, gadget, implement, instrument, mechanism, tool; SEE CONCEPT *463*

applicable [adj] *appropriate*
applicative, applicatory, apposite, apropos, apt, associable, befitting, felicitous, fit, fitting, germane, kosher, legit*, material, on target*, on the button*, on the nose*, pertinent, relevant, right on*, suitable, suited, that's the idea*, that's the ticket*, to the point, to the purpose, useful; SEE CONCEPTS *558,563*

applicant [n] *person trying for position*
appellant, aspirant, candidate, claimant, hopeful, inquirer, petitioner, postulant, seeker, suitor, suppliant; SEE CONCEPTS *348,359*

application [n1] *use*
appliance, appositeness, employment, exercise, exercising, function, germaneness, operation, pertinence, play, practice, purpose, relevance, usance, utilization, value; SEE CONCEPTS *680,694*

application [n2] *request*
appeal, blank, claim, demand, draft, entreaty, form, inquiry, letter, paper, petition, requisition, solicitation, suit; SEE CONCEPT *48*

application [n3] *hard work*
assiduity, attention, attentiveness, busyness, commitment, concentration, consideration, dedication, deliberation, diligence, effort, industry, perseverance, study, zeal; SEE CONCEPTS *91,410*

application [n4] *putting substance on another*
administering, administration, applying, creaming, dosing, oiling, rubbing, treatment; SEE CONCEPT *200*

applied [adj] *used*
activated, adapted, adjusted, brought to bear, correlated, devoted, enforced, exercised, practiced, related, tested, utilized; SEE CONCEPTS *538,546*

apply [v1] *put into use*
administer, assign, bring into play, bring to bear, employ, engage, execute, exercise, exploit, handle, implement, practice, utilize; SEE CONCEPT *225*

apply [v2] *be appropriate, relevant*
affect, allude, appertain, be applicable, bear upon, be pertinent, concern, connect, fit, involve, pertain, refer, regard, relate, suit, touch; SEE CONCEPT *532*

apply [v3] *put substance on another*
administer, affix, anoint, bestow, cover, fasten, join, lay on, massage, paint, place, put on, rub, smear, spread, touch; SEE CONCEPT *200*

apply [v4] *ask, request*
appeal, claim, demand, inquire, petition, put in, put in for, requisition, solicit, sue; SEE CONCEPT *48*

apply [v5] *work hard*
address, bear down, be diligent, be industrious, bend, buckle down*, commit, concentrate, dedicate, devote, dig, direct, give, give all one's got*, give best shot*, give old college try*, grind, hammer away*, hit the ball*, hustle, knuckle down*, make effort, peg away*, persevere, plug*, pour it on*, pull out all stops*, scratch, study, sweat*, throw, try, turn; SEE CONCEPTS *87,100*

appoint [v1] *assign responsibility; decide*
accredit, allot, assign, choose, command, commission, decree, delegate, designate, determine, direct,

elect, enjoin, establish, finger, fix, install, name, nominate, ordain, select, set, settle, tap; SEE CONCEPTS *41,50,88*

appoint [*v2*] *furnish*
arm, equip, fit, fit out, gear, outfit, provide, rig, supply, turn out; SEE CONCEPT *140*

appointment [*n1*] *arrangement for meeting; prearranged meeting*
assignation, assignment, blind date*, consultation, date, engagement, errand, gig, interview, invitation, meet, rendezvous, session, something to do, tryst, zero hour*; SEE CONCEPTS *324,384*

appointment [*n2*] *assignment of responsibility*
allotment, approval, assigning, authorization, certification, choice, choosing, commissioning, delegation, deputation, designation, election, empowering, installation, naming, nomination, ordination, promotion, selection; SEE CONCEPTS *41,50,88*

appointment [*n3*] *job, position of responsibility*
appointee, assignment, berth, candidate, delegate, employment, nominee, office, officeholder, place, post, representative, situation, station, work; SEE CONCEPT *349*

appointment [*n4*] *furnishing(s)*
accoutrement, appurtenance, equipage, fitting, fixture, gear, outfit, paraphernalia, trappings; SEE CONCEPT *475*

apportion [*v*] *divide into shares*
accord, admeasure, administer, allocate, allot, assign, bestow, cut, cut up, deal, dispense, distribute, divvy, divvy up, dole out, give, lot, measure, mete, parcel, part, partition, piece up, prorate, quota, ration, slice, split, split up; SEE CONCEPTS *98,108*

appraisal [*n*] *judgment, estimation*
appraisement, assessment, estimate, evaluation, opinion, pricing, rating, reckoning, stock, survey, valuation; SEE CONCEPTS *18,328,766*

appraise [*v*] *judge, estimate*
adjudge, assay, assess, audit, calculate, check, check out*, cut in*, deem, evaluate, examine, eye*, figure, figure in, figure out, gauge, guesstimate, have one's number*, inspect, look over, peg, price, rate, read, review, set at, size, survey, take account of, valuate, value; SEE CONCEPTS *18,764*

appreciable [*adj*] *easily noticed; considerable*
apparent, ascertainable, clear-cut, definite, detectable, discernible, distinguishable, estimable, evident, goodly, good-sized, healthy, large, manifest, marked, material, measurable, noticeable, observable, obvious, perceivable, perceptible, plain, pronounced, recognizable, sensible, significant, sizable, substantial, tangible, visible; SEE CONCEPTS *619,781*

appreciate [*v1*] *be grateful, thankful*
acknowledge, be appreciative, be indebted, be obliged, enjoy, flip over*, freak out on*, get high on*, give thanks, groove on*, welcome; SEE CONCEPTS *12,32,76*

appreciate [*v2*] *increase in worth*
enhance, gain, grow, improve, inflate, raise the value of, rise; SEE CONCEPT *763*

appreciate [*v3*] *recognize worth*
acknowledge, apprehend, be aware of, be cognizant of, be conscious of, catch the drift, comprehend, dig, fathom, grasp, know, perceive, read, realize, recognize, savvy, see daylight*, sympathize with, take account of, understand, with it; SEE CONCEPT *15*

appreciate [*v4*] *value highly*
admire, adore, applaud, apprise, cherish, enjoy, esteem, extol, honor, like, look up to, love, praise, prize, rate highly, regard, relish, respect, savor, treasure; SEE CONCEPTS *10,32*

appreciation [*n1*] *thankfulness*
acknowledgment, gratefulness, gratitude, indebtedness, obligation, recognition, testimonial, thanks, tribute; SEE CONCEPTS *12,32*

appreciation [*n2*] *increase in worth*
enhancement, gain, growth, improvement, inflation, rise; SEE CONCEPTS *346,763*

appreciation [*n3*] *recognition of worth*
admiration, aesthetic sense, affection, appraisal, assessment, attraction, awareness, cognizance, commendation, comprehension, enjoyment, esteem, estimation, grasp, high regard, knowledge, liking, love, perception, realization, recognition, regard, relish, respect, responsivenesss, sensibility, sensitiveness, sensitivity, sympathy, understanding, valuation; SEE CONCEPTS *15,409*

appreciative [*adj1*] *thankful*
beholden, grateful, indebted, obliged, responsive; SEE CONCEPT *403*

appreciative [*adj2*] *understanding, recognizing worth*
admiring, affectionate, alive, aware, cognizant, conscious, considerate, cooperative, cordial, enlightened, enthusiastic, favorable, friendly, generous, keen, kindly, knowledgeable, magnanimous, mindful, perceptive, pleased, receptive, regardful, respectful, responsive, satisfied, sensitive, supportive, sympathetic, understanding; SEE CONCEPT *402*

apprehend [*v1*] *catch and arrest*
bag*, bust*, capture, collar, cop*, grab, nab, nail*, place under arrest, run in, seize, take in, take into custody, take prisoner*; SEE CONCEPTS *90,191,317*

apprehend [*v2*] *understand*
absorb, accept, appreciate, believe, catch, comprehend, conceive, digest, fathom, get, get the picture*, grasp, have, imagine, know, perceive, read, realize, recognize, sense, think, tumble; SEE CONCEPT *15*

apprehension [*n1*] *anxiety, fear*
alarm, apprehensiveness, concern, disquiet, doubt, dread, foreboding, misgiving, mistrust, premonition, presage, presentiment, suspicion, trepidation, uneasiness, worry; SEE CONCEPTS *27,690*

apprehension [*n2*] *catching and arresting*
booking, capture, collaring, detention, seizure, taking; SEE CONCEPTS *90,317*

apprehension [*n3*] *understanding*
awareness, comprehension, grasp, idea, intellect, intelligence, judgment, ken, knowledge, notion, perception, perspicacity, thought; SEE CONCEPT *409*

apprehensive [*adj*] *anxious, fearful*
afraid, alarmed, biting nails*, butterflies*, concerned, disquieted, doubtful, feel in bones*, foreboding, frozen*, get vibes*, have a hunch*, have cold feet*, have funny feeling*, have stage fright*, hung up*, in a cold sweat*, in a dither*, in a sweat*, jellyfish*, jittery, jumpy, lily-livered*, mistrustful, running scared*, scaredy-cat*, shaky*, stiff, suspicious, troubled, uncertain, uneasy, uptight, weak, worried, worried sick*; SEE CONCEPT *403*

apprentice [*n*] *novice/learner of a trade*
amateur, beginner, flunky*, freshman/woman, greenhorn*, heel*, neophyte, newcomer, new kid on block*, novitiate, probationer, pupil, rook*, rookie*, starter, student, tenderfoot*, tyro; SEE CONCEPTS *348,423*

approach [*n1*] *way, means of arriving*
access, accession, advance, advent, avenue, coming, drawing near, entrance, gate, landing, nearing, passage, path, reaching, road, way; SEE CONCEPTS *159,501*

approach [*n2*] *request, suggestion*
advance, appeal, application, offer, overture, proposal, proposition; SEE CONCEPT *278*

approach [*n3*] *plan of attack, resolution*
attitude, concept, course, crack, fling, go*, idea, lick, manner, means, method, mode, modus operandi, new wrinkle*, offer, procedure, program, shot, stab, style, technique, way, whack*, wrinkle; SEE CONCEPTS *655,660*

approach [*v1*] *come nearer*
advance, approximate, bear, be comparable to, be like, belly up to*, border, buzz, catch up, close in, come, come at, come close, compare with, contact, converge, correspond to, creep up, draw near, equal, gain on, go toward, impend, loom up, match, meet, move in on, move toward, near, progress, reach, resemble, surround, take after, threaten, verge upon; SEE CONCEPTS *159,198,701*

approach [*v2*] *make request, suggestion*
accost, address, advise, appeal to, apply to, beseech, confer, consult, entreat, feel, feel one out*, give a play*, give a tumble*, greet, implore, make advance, make overture, make up to, plead, propose, sound out, speak to, supplicate, take aside, talk to, thumb, tumble; SEE CONCEPTS *48,75*

approach [*v3*] *begin*
commence, embark, set about, start, undertake; SEE CONCEPT *234*

approachable [*adj1*] *accessible*
attainable, come-at-able*, convenient, door's always open*, getable*, obtainable, reachable; SEE CONCEPT *576*

approachable [*adj2*] *friendly*
affable, agreeable, congenial, cordial, open, receptive, sociable; SEE CONCEPT *404*

approbation [*n*] *praise*
admiration, approval, bells*, consent, endorsement, esteem, favor, go-ahead*, high regard, okay, permission, recognition, sanction, support, the nod; SEE CONCEPTS *10,69*

appropriate [*adj*] *suitable*
adapted, applicable, appurtenant, apropos, apt, becoming, befitting, belonging, congruous, convenient, correct, deserved, desired, due, felicitous, fit, fitting, germane, good, just, on the button*, on the nose*, opportune, pertinent, proper, relevant, right, rightful, seemly, tailor-made, true, useful, well-suited, well-timed; SEE CONCEPT *558*

appropriate [*v1*] *set aside; allocate*
allot, allow, appoint, apportion, assign, budget, devote, disburse, earmark, reserve, set apart; SEE CONCEPT *135*

appropriate [*v2*] *steal*
annex, borrow, clap, confiscate, cop, embezzle, filch, get fingers on*, get hands on*, glom on to*, grab, grab hold of*, hijack, liberate, lift, misappropriate, moonlight requisition*, pilfer, pocket, secure, snatch, swipe*, take over, usurp; SEE CONCEPT *139*

appropriation [*n1*] *allocation, setting aside*
allotment, allowance, apportionment, assignment, budgeting, concession, donation, earmarking, endowing, funding, giving, grant, provision, setting apart, sponsoring, stipend, stipulation, subsidy; SEE CONCEPTS *135,340*

appropriation [*n2*] *stealing*
confiscation, embezzlement, expropriation, grab, misappropriation, pilfering, seizure, takeover, taking, usurpation; SEE CONCEPT *139*

approval [*n1*] *authorization*
acquiescence, assent, bells, blessing, compliance, concurrence, confirmation, consent, countenance, endorsement, go-ahead*, green light*, leave, license, mandate, okay, permission, ratification, recommendation, sanction, support, the nod, validation; SEE CONCEPTS *10,685*

approval [*n2*] *good opinion*
acclaim, admiration, applause, appreciation, approbation, commendation, commercial, esteem, favor, liking, pat on the back*, pat on the head*, PR*, praise, puff, pumping up, regard, respect, strokes, stroking, wow; SEE CONCEPT *32*

approve [*v1*] *agree something is good*
accept, acclaim, admire, applaud, appreciate, approbate, be big on*, commend, countenance, esteem, face it, favor, go along with, grin and bear it*, handle, like, live with*, praise, put up with, regard highly, respect, roll with punches*, string along with*, take up on*, think highly of; SEE CONCEPT *10*

approve [v2] *allow, authorize*
accede, accept, accredit, acquiesce, advocate, affirm, agree, assent, authorize, back*, bless*, boost, buy, buy into, certify, charter, concur, confirm, consent, dig*, empower, encourage, endorse, establish, get behind, give go-ahead*, go along with, groove*, hats off to*, lap up*, license, maintain, make law, make valid, mandate, okay, permit, pronounce, push for, ratify, recommend, sanction, seal, second, sign, sign off on, stump for, subscribe to, support, thumbs up*, uphold, validate; SEE CONCEPTS *50,83,88*

approximate [adj1] *almost accurate, exact*
almost, close, comparative, near, proximate, relative, rough; SEE CONCEPT *557*

approximate [adj2] *inexact*
estimated, guessed, imperfect, imprecise, loose, rough, surmised, uncertain, unprecise, unscientific; SEE CONCEPT *557*

approximate [adj3] *similar*
alike, analogous, close, comparable, like, matching, near, relative, resembling, verging on; SEE CONCEPTS *487,573*

approximate [adj4] *near*
adjacent, bordering, close together, contiguous, nearby, neighboring; SEE CONCEPT *586*

approximate [v] *come close*
approach, border on, come near, estimate, near, reach, resemble, touch, verge on; SEE CONCEPT *664*

approximately [adv] *nearly*
about, almost, around, ballpark figure*, bordering on, circa, closely, close to, comparatively, generally, guesstimate, in the ballpark*, in the neighborhood of, in the region of, in the vicinity of, just about, loosely, more or less, most, much, not far from, not quite, proximately, relatively, roughly, upwards of*, very close; SEE CONCEPT *566*

apropos [adj] *relevant, suitable*
applicable, apposite, appropriate, apt, befitting, belonging, correct, fit, fitting, germane, kosher*, legit*, material, on the button*, on the nose*, opportune, pertinent, proper, related, right, right on, seemly; SEE CONCEPT *558*

apropos [adv] *relevantly, suitably*
appropriately, aptly, opportunely, pertinently, suitably, timely; SEE CONCEPT *558*

apropos [prep] *in respect of*
about, against, as for, as regards, as to, concerning, on the subject of, regarding, respecting, touching, toward, with reference to, with respect to; SEE CONCEPT *532*

apt [adj1] *suitable*
applicable, apposite, appropriate, apropos, befitting, correct, felicitous, fit, fitting, germane, happy, just, pertinent, proper, relevant, seemly, suitable, timely; SEE CONCEPT *558*

apt [adj2] *tending, inclined*
disposed, given, liable, likely, of a mind, prone, ready; SEE CONCEPT *542*

apt [adj3] *quick to learn*
able, adept, astute, bright, clever, expert, gifted, ingenious, intelligent, nobody's fool*, no dummy*, not born yesterday, prompt, quick on the trigger*, quick on the uptake*, ready, savvy, sharp, skilled, skillful, smart, talented, teachable; SEE CONCEPT *402*

aptitude [n1] *inclination*
bent, disposition, drift, leaning, predilection, proclivity, proneness, propensity, tendency; SEE CONCEPT *657*

aptitude [n2] *quickness at learning*
ability, capability, capacity, cleverness, competence, faculty, flair, gift, giftedness, intelligence, knack, proficiency, savvy, smarts, stuff*, talent, what it takes*; SEE CONCEPT *409*

aquarium [n] *fish tank*
aquatic museum, fishbowl, marine exhibit; SEE CONCEPTS *396,438,514*

aquatic [adj] *occurring in water*
amphibian, amphibious, floating, marine, maritime, natatory, oceanic, of the sea, sea, swimming, watery; SEE CONCEPTS *396,536*

aqueduct [n] *canal*
channel, conduit, course, duct, pipeline, water passage, waterworks; SEE CONCEPT *514*

arbiter [n] *person who settles dispute*
adjudicator, arbitrator, fixer, go-between, holdout, judge, maven, mediator, middleman/woman, middleperson, moderator, referee, umpire; SEE CONCEPT *354*

arbitrary [adj1] *whimsical, chance*
approximate, capricious, discretionary, erratic, fanciful, frivolous, inconsistent, injudicious, irrational, irresponsible, offhand, optional, random, subjective, supercilious, superficial, unaccountable, unreasonable, unscientific, wayward, willful; SEE CONCEPTS *534,542*

arbitrary [adj2] *dictatorial*
absolute, autocratic, bossy, despotic, dogmatic, domineering, downright, flat out, high-handed, imperious, magisterial, monocratic, no ifs ands or buts*, no joke*, overbearing, peremptory, straight out, summary, tyrannical, tyrannous; SEE CONCEPT *401*

arbitrate [v] *achieve settlement*
adjudge, adjudicate, adjust, bring to terms, come to school, come to terms, conciliate, decide, determine, hammer out a deal*, interpose, intervene, judge, make a deal, mediate, meet halfway, negotiate, parley, pass judgment, placate, play ball*, reconcile, referee, settle, smooth, soothe, step in, straighten out, strike happy medium*, trade off, umpire, work out a deal*; SEE CONCEPTS *126,300*

arbitration [n] *settlement of dispute*
adjudication, adjustment, agreement, compromise, decision, determination, judgment, mediation; SEE CONCEPTS *126,300*

arbitrator [*n*] *settler of a dispute*
adjudicator, arbiter, fixer, go-between, holdout, judge, maven, mediator, middleman/woman, middleperson, referee, umpire; SEE CONCEPTS *348,359*

arc [*n*] *curve*
arch, bend, bow, crescent, curvation, curvature, half-moon, round; SEE CONCEPT *436*

arcane [*adj*] *hidden, secret*
cabalistic, esoteric, impenetrable, mysterious, mystic, occult, recondite, unaccountable, unknowable; SEE CONCEPT *576*

arch [*n*] *curve, curved structure*
arc, archway, bend, bow, curvature, dome, semicircle, span, vault; SEE CONCEPT *436*

arch [*adj1*] *principal, superior*
accomplished, champion, chief, consummate, expert, finished, first, foremost, greatest, head, highest, leading, main, major, master, preeminent, premier, primary, top; SEE CONCEPT *574*

arch [*adj2*] *knowing, coy*
artful, frolicsome, mischievous, pert, playful, roguish, saucy, sly, waggish, wily; SEE CONCEPT *401*

arch [*v*] *curve*
arc, bend, bow, bridge, camber, extend, form, hook, hump, hunch, round, shape, span, stretch; SEE CONCEPT *184*

archaeologist [*n*] *student of the physical remains of ancient cultures or eras*
archaeologian, classicist, excavator, paleologist, paleontologist, prehistorian; SEE CONCEPT *348*

archaeology [*n*] *study of the physical remains of ancient cultures or eras*
antiquarianism, excavation, paleohistory, paleology, paleontology, prehistory; SEE CONCEPT *349*

archaic [*adj*] *very old*
ancient, antiquated, antique, bygone, obsolete, olden, old-fashioned, outmoded, out of date, passé, primitive, superannuated; SEE CONCEPTS *578,797*

archetype [*n*] *typical example*
classic exemplar, form, ideal, model, original, paradigm, pattern, perfect specimen, prime example, prototype, standard; SEE CONCEPTS *636,688*

architect [*n*] *person who designs buildings*
artist, builder, creator, designer, draftsman/woman, draftsperson, engineer, inventor, maker, master builder, originator, planner, prime mover; SEE CONCEPT *348*

architecture [*n1*] *design of buildings*
architectonics, building, construction, engineering, planning; SEE CONCEPTS *349,439*

architecture [*n2*] *design, structure of something*
composition, constitution, construction, formation, framework, make-up, style; SEE CONCEPTS *660,733*

archive [*n*] *collection, usually of records*
annals, chronicles, clippings, documents, excerpts, extracts, files, papers, registers, roll, scrolls, writings; SEE CONCEPTS *271,281,432*

archives [*n*] *place where records are stored*
athenaeum, library, museum, office, registry, repository, storage, treasury, vault; SEE CONCEPT *439*

archway [*n*] *curved opening*
entrance, passage; SEE CONCEPT *440*

arctic [*adj*] *very cold*
chill, chilly, cool, freezing, frigid, frosty, frozen, gelid, glacial, icy, nippy, polar; SEE CONCEPT *605*

ardent [*adj1*] *very enthusiastic*
agog, avid, blazing, burning, desirous, eager, fervent, fervid, fierce, fiery, horny*, hot*, hungry, impassioned, intense, keen, lovey-dovey*, lusty, passionate, spirited, thirsty, vehement, warm, zealous; SEE CONCEPTS *401,404*

ardent [*adj2*] *loyal*
allegiant, constant, devoted, faithful, resolute, steadfast, true; SEE CONCEPT *404*

ardor [*n*] *enthusiasm*
avidity, devotion, eagerness, earnestness, feeling, fervor, fierceness, fire, gusto, heat, intensity, jazz*, keenness, oomph*, passion, pep talk*, spirit, turn on*, vehemence, verve, warmth, weakness*, zeal, zest, zing; SEE CONCEPT *411*

arduous [*adj*] *difficult, hard to endure*
backbreaking, burdensome, exhausting, fatiguing, formidable, grueling, harsh, heavy, labored, laborious, murder, no picnic*, onerous, painful, punishing, rigorous, rough, severe, strenuous, taxing, tiring, toilsome, tough, troublesome, trying, uphill; SEE CONCEPT *565*

area [*n1*] *extent, scope of a surface*
breadth, compass, distance, expanse, field, operation, range, size, space, sphere, stretch, width; SEE CONCEPTS *651,792*

area [*n2*] *region, district*
belt, block, city, county, division, domain, dominion, enclosure, field, kingdom, locality, neck of the woods*, neighborhood, parcel, patch, plot, precinct, principality, quarter, section, sector, sphere, square, state, stretch, territory, township, tract, turf, vicinity, ward, zone; SEE CONCEPT *508*

arena [*n1*] *building or enclosure for entertainment or sports*
amphitheatre, boards*, bowl*, circus, coliseum, course, diamond, field, gridiron, ground, gym, gymnasium, hippodrome, ice, park, pit, platform, ring, rink, square, stadium, stage; SEE CONCEPT *438*

arena [*n2*] *area of activity*
battlefield, battleground, domain, field, province, realm, scene, sector, sphere, territory, theatre; SEE CONCEPT *198*

argue [*v1*] *verbally fight*
altercate, bandy, battle, bicker, break with, buck, bump heads, contend, cross, cross swords, disagree, dispute, face down, face off, feud, gang up on, go one on one, hammer, hammer away, hash, hash over, hassle, have at each other*, have at it*, in one's face*, jump, jump on, knock around, lock horns*,

mix it up*, pettifog, pick an argument, put up a fight, put up a struggle, quarrel, quibble, rehash, row, sass, set to, sock it to, squabble, stick it to, talk back, wrangle; SEE CONCEPT **46**

argue [v2] *try to convince; present support*
appeal, assert, attest, claim, contend, controvert, defend, demonstrate, denote, display, elucidate, establish, evince, exhibit, explain, hold, imply, indicate, justify, maintain, manifest, persuade, plead, present, prevail upon, reason, show, suggest, talk into, testify, vindicate, warrant, witness; SEE CONCEPT **68**

argue [v3] *discuss*
agitate, canvass, clarify, debate, dispute, expostulate, hold, maintain, question, reason, remonstrate, talk about; SEE CONCEPTS **46,56**

argument [n1] *verbal fight*
altercation, beef, bickering, blowup, bone, bone of contention, bone to pick*, brannigan, brawl, brush, clash, controversy, crusher*, debate, difference of opinion, disagreement, dispute, donnybrook, dust-up*, exchange, face-off, falling, feud, finisher*, flap, fuss, gin*, go*, hassle, knockdown*, knock down and drag out*, out, quarrel, rhubarb*, romp, row, ruckus, ruction, rumpus, run-in, scene, scrap, set-to, shindy*, spat, squabble, static*, stew*, talking heads*, tiff, words, wrangle; SEE CONCEPT **46**

argument [n2] *effort to convince; presentation of support*
argumentation, assertion, case, claim, contention, debate, defense, discussion, exchange, expostulation, grounds, line of reasoning, logic, plea, pleading, polemic, proof, questioning, reason, reasoning, remonstrance, remonstration; SEE CONCEPT **68**

argumentative [adj] *wanting to quarrel*
belligerent, combative, contentious, contrary, controversial, disputatious, factious, fire-eating, having a chip on one's shoulder*, litigious, opinionated, pugnacious, quarrelsome, salty, scrappy, spiky, touchy; SEE CONCEPT **401**

aria [n] *operatic solo*
descant, hymn, song; SEE CONCEPTS **263,595**

arid [adj1] *dry*
barren, bone-dry, desert, dry as a bone, dry as dust, dusty, moistureless, parched, thirsty, waterless; SEE CONCEPT **603**

arid [adj2] *uninterested, spiritless*
boring, colorless, drab, dreary, dry, dull, flat, insipid, lackluster, lifeless, tedious, unanimated, uninspired, vapid, wearisome; SEE CONCEPT **542**

arise [v1] *come into being; proceed*
appear, begin, come to light, commence, crop up, derive, emanate, emerge, ensue, flow, follow, happen, head, issue, occur, originate, result, rise, set in, spring, start, stem; SEE CONCEPT **105**

arise [v2] *get, stand, or go up*
ascend, climb, jump, mount, move upward, pile out*, rise, rise and shine*, roll out*, soar, stand, tower, turn out, wake up; SEE CONCEPTS **154,166**

aristocracy [n] *privileged class, government*
elite, gentility, gentry, haut monde, high society*, nobility, noblesse, patricians, patriciate, peerage, society, upper class, upper crust*; SEE CONCEPTS **296,423**

aristocrat [n] *privileged person*
blueblood, gentleman, gentleperson, lace curtain*, lady, nobleman/woman, patrician, peer, ritzy, silk stocking, swell*, upper cruster*; SEE CONCEPT **423**

aristocratic [adj] *privileged, elegant*
aloof, blue-blooded, courtly, dignified, elegant, elite, fine, haughty, noble, patrician, polished, refined, snobbish, stylish, upper-class, well-born, well-bred; SEE CONCEPT **555**

arithmetic [n] *mathematics*
addition, calculation, computation, division, estimation, figuring, multiplication, reckoning, subtraction; SEE CONCEPTS **349,764**

arm [n1] *limb, appendage*
bender, bough, bow, branch, fin, flapper, flipper, handle, hook, member, offshoot, projection, prong, rod, stump, wing; SEE CONCEPTS **392,471**

arm [n2] *subdivision, annex*
affiliate, authority, block, branch, command, department, detachment, division, ell, extension, force, offshoot, power, projection, section, sector, wing; SEE CONCEPTS **824,835**

arm [n3] *narrow body of water*
branch, brook, channel, creek, estuary, firth, inlet, rivulet, sound, strait, stream, subdivision, tributary; SEE CONCEPT **514**

arm [v] *equip with weapon or power*
accouter, appoint, array, deck, equalize, fortify, furnish, gear, gird, guard, heel, heel up, issue, load, load up, lug iron*, make ready, mobilize, outfit, pack, pack a rod*, prepare, prime, protect, provide, rig, rod up*, strengthen, supply, tote; SEE CONCEPTS **50,88,182**

armada [n] *group of ships or aircraft*
fleet, flotilla, force, navy, squadron; SEE CONCEPTS **432,504,506**

armament(s) [n] *weapon(s)*
ammunition, arms, defense, gun, hardware, heat, material, materiel, munitions, ordnance, protection, security, weaponry; SEE CONCEPT **500**

armistice [n] *peace-establishing agreement*
ceasefire, suspension, treaty, truce; SEE CONCEPTS **230,684**

armor [n] *protective covering, often made of metal*
bulletproof vest, defense, guard, mail, plate, protection, security, sheath, shield; SEE CONCEPTS **451,476**

armory [n] *military building, usually for storing weapons*
arsenal, center, depot, dump, factory, headquarters, magazine, plant, range; SEE CONCEPTS **321,439**

arms [n1] *weaponry*
accoutrements, armaments, artillery, equipment, firearms, guns, munitions, ordnance, panoply, weapons; SEE CONCEPT **500**

arms [n2] *family crest*
blazonry, coat, emblazonry, emblem, ensign, escutcheon, heraldry, insignia, shield, signet; SEE CONCEPTS *284,625*

army [n1] *military force, usually for land*
armed force, artillery, battalion, battery, brigade, cavalry, column, command, company, corps, detail, division, flight, formation, infantry, legion, men, outfit, patrol unit, platoon, regiment, soldiers, soldiery, squad, troops, wing; SEE CONCEPT *322*

army [n2] *group resembling military force*
array, cloud, company, crowd, division, flock, horde, host, legion, mob, multitude, outfit, pack, regiment, scores, swarm, throng, unit; SEE CONCEPT *417*

aroma [n] *distinctive smell*
balm, bouquet, fragrance, incense, odor, perfume, redolence, scent, spice; SEE CONCEPT *599*

aromatic [adj] *distinctive smelling*
ambrosial, balmy, fragrant, odoriferous, perfumed, pungent, redolent, savory, scented, spicy, sweet, sweet-smelling; SEE CONCEPT *598*

around [adv1] *situated on sides, circumference, or in general area*
about, all over, any which way, encompassing, everywhere, in the vicinity, in this area, neighboring, over, throughout; SEE CONCEPT *581*

around [adv2] *close to a place*
about, almost, approximately, close at hand, near, nearby; SEE CONCEPT *586*

arouse [v] *excite, entice*
agitate, alert, animate, awaken, call, challenge, electrify, enliven, fire up, foment, foster, goad, heat up, incite, inflame, instigate, kindle, move, provoke, rally, rouse, send, spark, spur, stimulate, stir, thrill, turn on, waken, wake up, warm, whet, whip up, work up; SEE CONCEPTS *7,19,22*

arraign [v] *accuse*
blame, charge, criminate, hang on, incriminate, inculpate, indict, lay at one's door*, pin it on*, pin on*, point the finger at*, summon; SEE CONCEPTS *44,317*

arrange [v1] *put in an order*
align, array, class, classify, clear the decks, dispose, file, fix up, form, group, line up, methodize, organize, police, police up, position, put in good shape*, put in order*, put in shape*, put to rights*, range, rank, regulate, sort, spruce, spruce up, systematize, tidy, whip into shape*; SEE CONCEPTS *84,158*

arrange [v2] *make plans, often involving agreement*
adapt, adjust, agree to, blueprint, chart, come to terms, compromise, concert, construct, contrive, decide, design, determine, devise, direct, draft, establish, frame*, get act together*, get ready, hammer out a deal*, harmonize, iron out*, lay out, line up, make a connection, make ready, manage, map out, negotiate, organize, prepare, project, promote, pro-vide, pull a wire, pull things together, quarterback*, resolve, schedule, scheme, set stage, settle, shape up, tailor, work out, work out a deal; SEE CONCEPTS *36,84*

arrange [v3] *prepare musical composition differently*
adapt, instrument, orchestrate, score; SEE CONCEPT *292*

arrangement [n1] *an understanding*
adjustment, agreement, compact, compromise, deal, frame-up*, game plan*, layout*, organization, package*, package deal*, pecking order*, plan, preparation, provision, schedule, settlement, setup, terms; SEE CONCEPT *684*

arrangement [n2] *something that has been ordered*
alignment, array, classification, combination, composition, design, display, disposition, distribution, form, grouping, lineup, method, ordering, organization, pattern, ranging, rank, sequence, setup, structure, system; SEE CONCEPTS *84,727*

arrangement [n3] *musical adaptation*
chart, composition, instrumentation, interpretation, lead sheet, orchestration, score, version; SEE CONCEPTS *262,595*

array [n1] *collection, considerable group*
arrangement, batch, body, bunch, bundle, clump, cluster, design, display, disposition, exhibition, formation, host, lineup, lot, multitude, order, parade, pattern, set, show, supply, throng; SEE CONCEPTS *432,769,786*

array [n2] *fine clothes*
apparel, attire, drapes*, dress, duds*, finery, full dress, garb, garments, getup*, rig*, threads*; SEE CONCEPT *451*

array [v1] *arrange in collection or order*
align, display, exhibit, form, group, line up, methodize, organize, parade, range, set, show, systematize; SEE CONCEPT *84*

array [v2] *dress in fine clothes*
attire, bedeck, clothe, deck, deck out, decorate, dog out, doll up*, drape, dud, dude up*, fit, fit out, garb, outfit, suit up, tog, try on, turn out, wrap; SEE CONCEPT *167*

arrears [n] *debt*
back payment, balance due, claim, debit, deficiency, deficit, liability, obligation, unpaid bill; SEE CONCEPTS *332,335*

arrest [n1] *taking into custody*
accommodation, apprehension, appropriation, bag*, booby trap*, bust, captivity, capture, collar, commitment, confinement, constraint, crimp*, detention, drop*, fall*, gaff*, glom*, grab*, heat*, hook*, imprisonment, incarceration, jailing, mitt*, nab*, nail*, nick*, nip*, pickle*, pick up*, pinch*, preventive custody, protective custody, pull*, pull in*, restraining, run in*, sequestering, snare, sweep*; SEE CONCEPTS *90,317*

arrest [n2] *slowing or stopping*
blockage, cessation, check, checking, delay, end, halt, hindrance, inhibition, interruption, obstruction,

prevention, restraining, restraint, stalling, stay, staying, stoppage, suppression, suspension; SEE CONCEPTS *121,234*

arrest [*v1*] *take into authorized custody*
apprehend, bag*, book, brace*, bust, capture, catch, collar, detain, drop*, gaff*, get*, glom*, grab*, hook*, imprison, incarcerate, jail, kick*, nab*, nail*, net*, nick*, pick up*, pinch*, pull*, pull in*, put the arm on*, put the cuffs on*, round up*, roust*, run in*, secure*, seize*, sidetrack*, snag*, tab*, tag*, take in, take prisoner, toss in jail; SEE CONCEPTS *90,317*

arrest [*v2*] *stop or slow*
block, can, check, delay, drop, end, freeze, halt, hinder, hold, inhibit, interrupt, knock off, obstruct, prevent, restrain, restrict, retard, scrub, shut down, stall, stay, suppress; SEE CONCEPTS *121,234*

arrest [*v3*] *get someone's attention*
absorb, catch, engage, engross, fascinate, grip; SEE CONCEPTS *7,19,22*

arrival [*n1*] *coming to a destination*
accession, advent, alighting, appearance, approach, arriving, debarkation, disembarkation, dismounting, entrance, happening, homecoming, influx, ingress, landing, meeting, occurrence, return; SEE CONCEPT *159*

arrival [*n2*] *something that makes it to a destination*
addition, arriver, caller, cargo, comer, conferee, delegate, delivery, entrant, envoy, freight, guest, mail, newcomer, package, parcel, passenger, representative, shipment, tourist, traveler, visitant, visitor; SEE CONCEPTS *337,423,712*

arrive [*v1*] *come to a destination*
access, alight, appear, attain, barge in, blow in, bob up*, breeze in*, bust in, buzz, check in, clock in, disembark, dismount, drop anchor, drop in, enter, fall by, fall in, get to, hit*, hit town*, land*, make it*, make the scene*, pop in*, pop up*, pull in*, punch the clock*, reach, report, roll in*, show, show up, sign in, sky in, take place, turn up, visit, wind up at; SEE CONCEPT *159*

arrive [*v2*] *achieve recognition*
accomplish, become famous, flourish, make good, make it, make the grade, prosper, reach the top, score, succeed, thrive; SEE CONCEPT *706*

arrogance [*n*] *exaggerated self-opinion*
airs, aloofness, audacity, bluster, braggadocio, brass*, cheek*, chutzpah*, conceit, conceitedness, contemptuousness, crust*, disdain, disdainfulness, ego, egotism, gall, haughtiness, hauteur, high-handedness, hubris, imperiousness, insolence, loftiness, nerve, ostentation, overbearance, pomposity, pompousness, presumption, pretension, pretentiousness, pride, priggishness, scornfulness, self-importance, self-love, smugness, superciliousness, swagger, vanity; SEE CONCEPTS *411,633*

arrogant [*adj*] *having exaggerated self-opinion*
aloof, assuming, audacious, autocratic, biggety*, bossy, bragging, cavalier, cheeky, cocky*, cold

shoulder*, conceited, contemptuous, cool*, disdainful, domineering, egotistic, haughty, high and mighty*, high-handed, imperious, insolent, know-it-all*, lordly, on an ego trip*, overbearing, peremptory, pompous, presumptuous, pretentious, proud, puffed up*, scornful, self-important, smarty, smug, sniffy*, snippy*, snooty*, snotty*, stuck up*, supercilious, superior, swaggering, uppity*, vain, wise guy*; SEE CONCEPTS *401,404*

arrogate [*v*] *claim without justification*
accroach, appropriate, assume, commandeer, confiscate, demand, expropriate, preempt, presume, seize, take, usurp; SEE CONCEPTS *142,266*

arsenal [*n*] *storage of weapons*
armory, depository, depot, dump, factory, magazine, ordnance, plant, repository, stock, stockpile, store, storehouse, supply, warehouse; SEE CONCEPTS *432,439*

arson [*n*] *intentional burning*
firing, incendiarism, pyromania, setting fire, torching, touch off; SEE CONCEPT *249*

art [*n1*] *skill, creativity*
adroitness, aptitude, artistry, craft, craftsmanship, dexterity, expertise, facility, imagination, ingenuity, inventiveness, knack, know-how, knowledge, mastery, method, profession, trade, virtuosity; SEE CONCEPT *706*

art [*n2*] *cunning*
artfulness, artifice, astuteness, canniness, craftiness, deceit, duplicity, guile, slyness, trickery, wiliness; SEE CONCEPT *411*

art [*n3*] *creation meant to communicate or appeal to senses or mind*
abstraction, carving, description, design, illustration, imitation, modeling, molding, painting, pictorialization, portrayal, representation, sculpting, shaping, simulation, sketching, symbolization; SEE CONCEPT *349*

artery [*n*] *channel*
avenue, boulevard, canal, conduit, corridor, course, duct, highway, line, passage, pathway, road, route, sewer, thoroughfare, track, tube, way; SEE CONCEPT *501*

artful [*adj*] *skillful; cunning*
adept, adroit, clever, crafty, designing, dexterous, foxy*, ingenious, masterly, politic, proficient, resourceful, scheming, sharp, shrewd, slick*, sly, smart, smooth*, tricky, wily; SEE CONCEPTS *404,528*

article [*n1*] *item, object*
commodity, dojigger*, gizmo*, piece, substance, thing, thingamabob*, thingamajig*, unit; SEE CONCEPT *433*

article [*n2*] *piece of writing*
beat, blurb*, column, commentary, composition, discourse, editorial, essay, exposition, feature, item, paper, piece, scoop*, spread, story, theme, think piece*, treatise; SEE CONCEPTS *270,271,280*

article [n3] *section of document*
branch, chapter, clause, detail, division, element, head, heading, item, matter, paragraph, part, passage, piece, point, portion, provision; SEE CONCEPTS *270,318*

articulate [adj] *clearly, coherently spoken*
clear, coherent, comprehensible, definite, distinct, eloquent, expressive, fluent, intelligible, lucid, meaningful, understandable, well-spoken; SEE CONCEPT *267*

articulate [v1] *say clearly, coherently*
enunciate, express, mouth, pronounce, say, sound off, speak, state, talk, utter, verbalize, vocalize, voice; SEE CONCEPTS *47,55*

articulate [v2] *connect*
concatenate, couple, fit together, hinge, integrate, join, link; SEE CONCEPT *113*

articulation [n1] *clear, coherent speech*
delivery, diction, enunciation, expression, pronunciation, saying, speaking, statement, talking, utterance, verbalization, vocalization, voicing; SEE CONCEPT *55*

articulation [n2] *connection*
coupling, hinge, joining, joint, junction, juncture, unification, union; SEE CONCEPT *113*

artifice [n1] *hoax; clever act*
con, contrivance, device, dodge, expedient, gambit, gimmick*, know-how*, machination, maneuver, play, ploy, racket*, ruse, savvy, stratagem, subterfuge, tactic, wile; SEE CONCEPT *59*

artifice [n2] *cunning; deception*
artfulness, chicanery, craftiness, dishonesty, duplicity, guile, scheming, slyness, trickery, wiliness; SEE CONCEPT *411*

artifice [n3] *skill, cleverness*
ability, adroitness, deftness, facility, finesse, ingenuity, invention, inventiveness, know-how*, skill; SEE CONCEPT *630*

artificial [adj1] *fake; imitation*
bogus, counterfeit, ersatz, fabricated, factitious, faked, false, falsie*, hyped up*, man-made, manufactured, mock, phony*, plastic, sham, simulated, specious, spurious, substitute, synthetic, unnatural, unreal; SEE CONCEPT *582*

artificial [adj2] *pretended; affected*
assumed, contrived, false, feigned, forced, hollow, insincere, labored, mannered, meretricious, phony*, put-on, spurious, theatrical, unnatural; SEE CONCEPT *401*

artillery [n] *weaponry or military unit*
arms, battery, bazooka, big guns*, cannon, cannonry, force, gunnery, heavy stuff*, munitions, ordnance, rainmakers*, stovepipe, weapons; SEE CONCEPTS *322,500*

artist [n] *person skilled in creative activity*
artisan, artiste, authority, composer, craftsman/woman, craftsperson, creator, expert, handicrafter, inventor, painter, virtuoso, whiz*; SEE CONCEPT *352*

artistic [adj1] *beautiful, satisfying to senses*
aesthetic, creative, cultivated, cultured, decorative, dramatic, elegant, exquisite, fine, graceful, grand, harmonious, ideal, imaginative, musical, ornamental, pictorial, picturesque, pleasing, poetic, refined, rhythmical, sensitive, stimulating, stylish, sublime, tasteful; SEE CONCEPT *579*

artistic [adj2] *being skilled in creative activity*
accomplished, artful, artsy-craftsy, arty, crafty, discriminating, gifted, imaginative, inventive, skillful, talented; SEE CONCEPT *527*

artistry [n] *great skill in creative endeavors*
ability, accomplishment, artfulness, brilliance, craftsmanship, creativity, finesse, flair, genius, mastery, proficiency, style, talent, taste, touch, virtuosity; SEE CONCEPTS *630,655*

artless [adj] *simple*
direct, genuine, guileless, honest, ingenious, innocent, naive, natural, open, plain, pure, sincere, straight, straightforward, talking turkey*, true, unadorned, unaffected, uncontrived, unpretentious, unsophisticated, up front*; SEE CONCEPTS *267,562*

arty [adj] *pretended expertise in art; affected interest*
affected, deceptive, ephemeral, false, flaunting, illusory, imitative, overblown, popular, popularized, pretentious, pseudo, tasteless; SEE CONCEPT *582*

as [conj1] *while, when*
at the time that, during the time that, in the act of, in the process of, just as, on the point of; SEE CONCEPT *544*

as [conj2] *in the way that; to a degree*
acting as, being, by its nature, comparatively, equally, essentially, for instance, functioning as, in the manner that, in the same manner with, just as, just for, like, serving as, similarly, such as; SEE CONCEPT *544*

as [conj3] *because*
as long as, being, cause, considering, for, for the reason that, inasmuch as, now, seeing that, since, whereas; SEE CONCEPT *544*

as [prep] *in the role of*
being, in the character of, under the name of; SEE CONCEPT *544*

ascend [v] *go up*
arise, climb, escalate, float, fly, lift off, mount, move up, rise, scale, soar, sprout, take off, tower; SEE CONCEPTS *149,166*

ascendancy/ascendency [n] *domination*
advantage, authority, command, control, dominance, dominion, edge, influence, jump*, leg up*, mastery, on top, power, predominance, preeminence, prepotence, prevalence, reign, rule, sovereignty, superiority, supremacy, sway, upper hand*, whip hand*; SEE CONCEPTS *376,671*

ascension [n] *going up*
ascent, climbing, escalating, flying, mounting, rise, rising, scaling, soaring, towering; SEE CONCEPTS *149,166*

ascent [n1] *upward movement*
ascendance, ascending, ascension, clambering, climb, climbing, lift, mounting, rise, rising, scaling, spring, take off; SEE CONCEPT *166*

ascent [n2] *upward slope*
acclivity, grade, gradient, incline, ramp, rise; SEE CONCEPTS *738,757*

ascertain [v] *make sure*
catch on, check*, check out*, check up on*, confirm, determine, dig*, discover, divine, double-check, establish, eye*, eyeball*, find out, fix, get down cold*, get down pat*, get hold of*, get it down*, get the hang of*, identify, learn, learn the ropes*, look-see*, make certain, make sure, peg*, pick up*, pick up on*, read, see, settle, size, size up*, tell, verify; SEE CONCEPTS *31,34,38*

ascribe [v] *assign to source*
accredit, attribute, charge, credit, hang on, impute, lay, pin on*, put down, refer, reference, set down; SEE CONCEPTS *39,49*

ash(es) [n] *remains of burning*
charcoal, cinders, dust, embers, powder, relics, remains, ruins, slag, soot; SEE CONCEPT *260*

ashamed [adj] *regretting, remorseful*
abashed, apologetic, bashful, blushing, chagrined, compunctious, conscience-stricken, contrite, crestfallen, debased, demeaned, discomfited, disconcerted, distraught, distressed, embarrassed, flustered, guilty, hesitant, humble, humbled, humiliated, meek, mortified, muddled, penitent, regretful, reluctant, repentant, shamed, shamefaced, sheepish, shy, sorry, stammering, stuttering, submissive; SEE CONCEPT *550*

ashore [adv] *toward, onto land from water*
aground, beached, on dry land, on land, on shore, shorewards; SEE CONCEPT *583*

aside [n] *confidential statement*
departure, digression, discursion, interpolation, interposition, parenthesis, tangent, throwaway*; SEE CONCEPT *51*

aside [adv] *away from; to the side*
abreast, afar, alone, alongside, apart, away, beside, by oneself, down, in isolation, in reserve, near, nearby, neck and neck, out, out of the way, privately, separately, sidewise; SEE CONCEPT *586*

ask [v1] *question*
buzz*, canvass, catechize, challenge, cross-examine, demand, direct, enjoin, examine, give the third degree*, go over, grill*, hit*, hunt for*, inquire, institute, interrogate, investigate, needle*, pick one's brains*, pop the question*, pry into, pump, put the screws to*, put through the wringer*, query, quiz, request, roast*, strike, sweat*; SEE CONCEPT *48*

ask [v2] *request*
angle, appeal, apply, beg, beseech, bite*, bum*, call for, charge, claim, command, contend for, crave, demand, entreat, file for, hit*, hustle*, implore, impose, knock*, levy, mooch*, order, petition, plead,

pray, promote*, request, requisition, seek, solicit, sue, supplicate, touch*, urge; SEE CONCEPT *53*

ask [v3] *invite*
bid, call upon, propose, suggest, summon, urge; SEE CONCEPT *75*

askew [adj] *crooked*
askance, askant, aslant, awry, bent, buckled, catawampus*, cockeyed*, crookedly, curved, knotted, lopsided, oblique, obliquely, off-center, slanted, slanting, to one side, topsy-turvey*, turned, twisted, yaw ways*, zigzag*; SEE CONCEPT *586*

asleep [adj] *unconscious*
catching some zzz's*, comatose*, conked*, crashed*, dormant, dozing, dreaming, flaked out*, getting shut-eye*, hibernating, inactive, in dreamland*, inert, in repose, napping, on the kip*, out*, out cold*, out like a light*, out of it*, reposing, resting, sacked out*, sleeping, slumbering, snoozing, snoring, somnolent, taking forty winks*; SEE CONCEPTS *210,315,681*

aspect [n1] *visible feature*
air, appearance, attitude, bearing, condition, countenance, demeanor, expression, face, facet, form, look, manner, mien; SEE CONCEPTS *434,628,673*

aspect [n2] *element to consider*
angle, bearing, direction, facet, feature, gimmick, hand, outlook, perspective, phase, point of view, position, prospect, regard, scene, side, situation, slant, switch, twist, view, vista; SEE CONCEPT *668*

asperity [n] *harshness; bad temper*
acerbity, acrimony, bitterness, churlishness, crabbiness, crossness, difficulty, disagreeableness, irascibility, irritability, meanness, moroseness, peevishness, roughness, sharpness, sourness, sullenness, tartness; SEE CONCEPT *633*

aspersion [n] *verbal exhibition of bad temper*
abuse, animadversion, backbiting, backhanded compliment, black eye*, calumny, defamation, detraction, dirty dig*, dump*, hit*, invective, knock*, libel, obloquy, put-down*, rap*, slam*, slander, smear*, vituperation; SEE CONCEPTS *52,54,58*

asphyxiate [v] *cut off air*
choke, drown, smother, stifle, strangle, strangulate, suffocate; SEE CONCEPTS *121,246*

aspiration [n] *goal, hope*
aim, ambition, ambitiousness, craving, desire, direction, dream, eagerness, endeavor, fire in the belly*, hankering, inclination, longing, object, objective, passion, pursuit, push, right stuff, urge, vocation, wish, work, yearning; SEE CONCEPTS *20,659*

aspire [v] *aim, hope*
be ambitious, be eager, crave, desire, dream, hanker, long, pursue, seek, strive, struggle, try, want, wish, yearn; SEE CONCEPT *20*

aspiring [adj] *hopeful*
ambitious, aspirant, eager, eager beaver*, endeavoring, enthusiastic, impassioned, longing, on the

make*, striving, wishful, would-be, zealous; SEE CONCEPT *403*

ass [n] *stupid person*
blockhead*, dolt, donkey*, dope, dunce, fool, half-wit*, idiot, imbecile, jackass*, jerk*, nitwit*, numb-skull*, simpleton*, twit*; SEE CONCEPT *412*

assail [v] *attack, usually with words*
abuse, assault, bash, berate, beset, blast, blister, bust, charge, come at, criticize, encounter, have at*, impugn, invade, lambaste, lay into*, malign, mal-treat, molest, revile, set upon*, trash*, vilify, work over; SEE CONCEPTS *52,86*

assailant [n] *attacker*
aggressor, antagonist, assaulter, bushwhacker*, en-emy, foe, goon*, hit man, invader, mugger, opposite number*, trigger man/woman, trigger person; SEE CONCEPT *412*

assassin [n] *murderer of prominent or important per-son*
butcher*, clipper*, dropper*, eliminator, enforcer, executioner, guerrilla*, gun*, gunman/woman, hatchet man/woman, hit man/woman, killer, liquida-tor, piece man/woman*, plugger*, slayer, soldier, torpedo*, triggerman/woman; SEE CONCEPT *412*

assassinate [v] *murder prominent or important person*
bump off*, do in*, eliminate, execute, gun down, hit, kill, knock off*, liquidate, slaughter, slay; SEE CONCEPT *252*

assault [n] *attack*
advance, aggression, charge, incursion, invasion, of-fensive, onset, onslaught, rape, storm, storming, strike, violation; SEE CONCEPT *86*

assault [v] *attack*
abuse, advance, assail, bash, beset, blast, blitz, bush-whack, charge, come down on*, go for, haul off on*, invade, jump, jump down one's throat*, jump on one's case*, lay into, let have it*, light into*, rape, ruin, set upon, shoot down, slam, slap around, storm, strike, trash, violate, work over, zap*; SEE CONCEPTS *52,86*

assay [n] *analysis*
appraisal, assessment, estimation, evaluation, exam-ination, inspection, investigation, measurement, rat-ing, survey, test, trial, valuation; SEE CONCEPTS *24,103,290*

assay [v] *analyze*
appraise, apprise, assess, check, check out, estimate, evaluate, examine, eyeball*, inspect, investigate, measure, peg*, prove, rate, read, see, size, size up*, survey, test, try, valuate, value, weigh; SEE CON-CEPTS *24,103*

assemblage [v] *gathering of people*
aggregation, assembly, association, collection, com-pany, congregation, convergence, crowd, group, throng; SEE CONCEPT *417*

assemble [v1] *congregate*
accumulate, agglomerate, amass, bring together, bunch, bunch up, call, call together, capture*, col-lect, come together, convene, convoke, corral*, flock, gang up*, gather, group, hang around*, hang out*, huddle, lump, make the scene*, meet, meet up, mobilize, muster, rally, reunite, round up, scare up*, summon, unite; SEE CONCEPT *114*

assemble [v2] *put together*
compile, connect, construct, contrive, erect, fabri-cate, fashion, fit, form, join, make, manufacture, model, mold, piece together, produce, set up, shape, unite, weld; SEE CONCEPT *113*

assembly [n1] *congregation*
accumulation, aggregation, assemblage, association, band, body, bunch, clambake*, cluster, coffee klatch*, collection, company, conclave, confab*, conference, convocation, council, crew, crowd, fac-tion, flock, gathering, get-together*, group, huddle, mass, meet*, meeting, multitude, rally, sit-in*, throng, turnout*; SEE CONCEPTS *381,432*

assembly [n2] *putting together*
adjustment, attachment, building, collection, con-necting, construction, erection, fabrication, fitting to-gether, joining, manufacture, manufacturing, modeling, molding, piecing together, setting up, shaping, welding; SEE CONCEPT *113*

assent [n] *agreement*
acceptance, accession, accord, acknowledgment, ac-quiescence, admission, affirmation, approval, autho-rization, compliance, concurrence, consent, nod, permission, sanction; SEE CONCEPTS *8,684*

assent [v] *agree*
accede, accept, accord, acquiesce, adopt, allow, ap-prove, buy, cave in*, comply, concur, conform, con-sent, cut a deal*, defer, ditto*, embrace, espouse, give five*, give in, go along with, grant, knuckle under*, okay*, pass on*, permit, recognize, sanc-tion, say uncle*, shake on*; SEE CONCEPT *8*

assert [v] *insist, declare, maintain*
advance, affirm, allege, argue, asservate, attest, aver, avouch, avow, butt in*, cite, claim, contend, defend, horn in, justify, mouth off*, pop off*, predicate, press, proclaim, profess, pronounce, protest, put for-ward, say, shoot off one's mouth*, shoot one's wad*, stand up for, state, stress, swear, uphold, vindicate, warrant; SEE CONCEPT *49*

assertion [n] *declaration, positive statement*
affirmation, allegation, asseveration, attestation, avowal, contention, defense, insistence, mainte-nance, mouthful, okay, predication, profession, pro-nouncement, report, say so*, stamp of approval, stressing, two cents' worth*, vindication; SEE CON-CEPTS *49,278*

assertive [adj] *aggressive*
absolute, assured, certain, confident, decided, deci-sive, demanding, dogmatic, domineering, emphatic, firm, forceful, forward, insistent, militant, overbear-ing, positive, pushy, self-assured, self-confident, strong-willed, sure; SEE CONCEPT *404*

assess [*v1*] *evaluate, determine*
appraise, apprise, assay, check*, check out*, compute, determine, dig it*, estimate, figure*, fix, gauge, guess, judge, nick*, peg*, rate, reckon, set, size*, size up, survey, take measure*, valuate, value, weigh; SEE CONCEPT *24*

assess [*v2*] *assign fee, amount*
charge, demand, evaluate, exact, fix, impose, levy, rate, tax, value; SEE CONCEPT *330*

assessment [*n1*] *evaluation*
appraisal, computation, determination, estimate, estimation, judgment, rating, reckoning, valuation, value judgment; SEE CONCEPT *24*

assessment [*n2*] *assignment of fee, amount*
appraisal, charge, demand, duty, estimate, fee, levy, rate, rating, tariff, tax, taxation, toll, valuation; SEE CONCEPT *332*

asset [*n1*] *advantage*
aid, benefit, blessing, boon, credit, distinction, help, resource, service, treasure; SEE CONCEPT *661*

asset(s) [*n2*] *property or money possessed*
ace in the hole*, ace up sleeve*, backing, bankroll, budget, capital, credit, equity, estate, funds, goods, holdings, kitty*, mattress*, means, nest egg*, nut*, possessions, rainy day, reserve(s), resources, riches, sock*, something put aside, something put away, stake, stash*, stuff, valuables, wealth; SEE CONCEPTS *332,340,710*

assiduous [*adj*] *hard-working*
active, attentive, busy, constant, diligent, eager beaver*, exacting, grinding, indefatigable, industrious, laborious, persevering, plugging, scrupulous, sedulous, steady, studious, unflagging, untiring, whiz, zealous; SEE CONCEPTS *538,542*

assign [*v1*] *select and give a responsibility*
accredit, allow, appoint, ascribe, attach, attribute, authorize, cast, charge, choice, commission, commit, credit, delegate, deputize, designate, draft, elect, empower, enroll, entrust, hang on, hire, hold responsible, impute, name, nominate, ordain, pin on*, refer, reference, select, slot, tab, tag; SEE CONCEPTS *41,50,88*

assign [*v2*] *set apart for a reason*
allocate, allot, appoint, apportion, appropriate, consign, designate, detail, determine, dish out*, distribute, divide, earmark, fix, fork out*, give, grant, hand out*, hand over, indicate, mete, prescribe, relegate, shell out*, specify, stipulate; SEE CONCEPTS *129,135*

assignation [*n*] *clandestine meeting*
affair, appointment, date, engagement, heavy date*, illicit meeting, love nest*, one-night stand*, quickie*, rendezvous, secret meeting, tryst; SEE CONCEPTS *375,386*

assignment [*n1*] *responsibility, task*
appointment, beat, charge, chore, commission, drill, duty, homework, job, mission, position, post, practice, stint; SEE CONCEPT *362*

assignment [*n2*] *selecting or setting apart*
allocation, allotment, appointment, apportionment, appropriation, ascription, assignation, attribution, authorization, choice, consignment, delegation, designation, determination, distribution, giving, grant, nomination, selection, specification, stipulation; SEE CONCEPTS *41,129*

assimilate [*v1*] *absorb mentally*
comprehend, digest, grasp, incorporate, ingest, learn, osmose, sense, soak up, take in, take up, understand; SEE CONCEPT *15*

assimilate [*v2*] *become adjusted; adjust*
acclimatize, accommodate, acculturate, accustom, adapt, become like, become similar, blend in, conform, fit, go native*, homogenize, homologize, intermix, match, mingle, parallel, standardize; SEE CONCEPTS *232,701*

assist [*n*] *help*
abetment, aid, assistance, backing, benefit, boost, collaboration, comfort, compensation, cooperation, facilitation, furtherance, hand, helping hand, lift, reinforcement, relief, service, support; SEE CONCEPT *110*

assist [*v*] *help*
abet, aid, back, bail out, benefit, boost, collaborate, cooperate, do for*, expedite, facilitate, further, give a boost*, give a leg up*, give a lift*, go down the line for*, go for, go to bat for*, go with, grease the wheels*, hype*, lend a hand*, make a pitch for*, open doors*, plug*, puff*, push*, put on the map*, reinforce, relieve, ride shotgun*, root for*, run interference*, serve, stand up for, stump*, support, sustain, take care of, thump*, work for, work with; SEE CONCEPT *110*

assistance [*n*] *help*
abetment, aid, assist, backing, benefit, boost, collaboration, comfort, compensation, cooperation, facilitation, furtherance, hand, help, helping hand, lift, reinforcement, relief, service, support, sustenance; SEE CONCEPT *110*

assistant [*n*] *helper*
abettor, accessory, accomplice, adherent, adjunct, aide, ally, appointee, apprentice, associate, attendant, auxiliary, backer, backup*, coadjutant, coadjutor, collaborator, colleague, companion, confederate, cooperator, deputy, fellow worker, flunky*, follower, friend, gal Friday*, girl Friday*, gofer*, help, helpmate, man Friday*, mate, partner, patron, peon*, representative, right-hand man/woman, right-hand person, secretary, serf*, slave*, subordinate, supporter, temp*, temporary worker; SEE CONCEPTS *348,423*

associate [*n*] *colleague*
accessory, accomplice, affiliate, aid, ally, assistant, auxiliary, branch, buddy, chum, clubber*, cohort, collaborator, companion, compatriot, comrade, confederate, consort, cooperator, co-worker, crony, dweeb*, fellow, friend, helper, joiner, kissing

cousin, mate, offshoot, one of the boys/girls*, pal, pard*, partner, peer, playmate, sidekick; SEE CONCEPTS 348,423

associate [v1] *connect in the mind*
affiliate, blend, bracket, combine, concord, conjoin, correlate, couple, group, identify, join, league, link, lump together, mix, pair, relate, think of together, unite, yoke; SEE CONCEPT 39

associate [v2] *befriend*
accompany, amalgamate, be friends, be in cahoots*, buddy up, bunch up, come together, confederate, consort, fraternize, gang up, get in on, get into, get in with, get together, go along with, go partners*, hang around, hang out, hang out with*, hobnob, join, join up with, line up with, mingle, mix, pal up, play footsie with*, pool, run around with, run with, string along with, swing with, take up with, team up, throw in together, tie in, tie up, truck with, work with; SEE CONCEPTS 114,384

association [n1] *group with common interest or pursuit*
affiliation, alliance, band, brotherhood, bunch, circle, clan, clique, club, coalition, combination, combo, company, confederacy, confederation, congress, cooperative, corporation, crew, crowd, family, federation, fellowship, fraternity, gang, guild, hookup*, league, mob, order, organization, outfit, partnership, pool, rat pack*, ring, sisterhood, society, sorority, syndicate, tie-in, tie-up, tribe, troops, troupe, union, zoo*; SEE CONCEPTS 325,387

association [n2] *friendship*
acquaintance, acquaintanceship, affiliation, agreement, assistance, camaraderie, companionship, comradeship, conjunction, cooperation, familiarity, fellowship, fraternization, frequenting, friendliness, hookup*, intimacy, membership, participation, partnership, relation, relationship; SEE CONCEPTS 387,388

association [n3] *mental connection*
bond, combination, concomitance, concordance, connotation, correlation, identification, impression, joining, juxtaposition, linkage, linking, lumping together, mixing, mixture, pairing, recollection, relation, remembrance, tie, train of thought, union; SEE CONCEPT 39

assorted [adj] *various*
different, diverse, diversified, heterogeneous, hybrid, indiscriminate, miscellaneous, mixed, motley, sundry, varied, variegated; SEE CONCEPT 564

assortment [n] *variety*
array, choice, collection, combination, combo, diversity, garbage, group, hodgepodge, jumble, kind, medley, mélange, miscellany, mishmash, mixed bag, mixture, potpourri, selection, sort; SEE CONCEPTS 432,665

assuage [v] *soothe, relieve*
allay, alleviate, appease, calm, compose, conciliate, cool*, ease, fill, lessen, lighten, lull, make nice*, mitigate, moderate, mollify, pacify, palliate, placate, pour oil on*, propitiate, quench, quiet, sate, satisfy, soften, still, surfeit, sweeten, take the edge off*, take the sting out*, temper, tranquilize; SEE CONCEPTS 7,22,244

assume [v1] *believe, take for granted*
accept, ascertain, be afraid, be inclined to think, conclude, conjecture, consider, count upon, deduce, deem, divine, estimate, expect, fall for, fancy, find, gather, get the idea*, guess, have a hunch*, have sneaking suspicion, hypothesize, imagine, infer, judge, posit, postulate, predicate, presume, presuppose, speculate, suppose, surmise, suspect, theorize, think, understand; SEE CONCEPTS 12,26

assume [v2] *take, undertake*
accept, acquire, appropriate, arrogate, attend to, begin, confiscate, don, embark upon, embrace, enter upon, seize, set about, take on, take over, take up; SEE CONCEPTS 87,142

assume [v3] *pretend*
act, adopt, affect, bluff, counterfeit, fake, feign, imitate, impersonate, mimic, pretend, put on, simulate; SEE CONCEPT 59

assume [v4] *adopt, acquire*
annex, appropriate, arrogate, borrow, clap hands on*, commandeer, confiscate, expropriate, get fingers on*, get hands on*, glom onto*, grab, grab hold of*, hijack, kipe*, liberate, moonlight requisition*, preempt, seize, snatch, swipe, take over, usurp; SEE CONCEPTS 139,142

assumed [adj1] *pretended*
affected, artificial, bogus, counterfeit, fake, false, feigned, fictitious, imitation, made-up, make-believe, phony, pretended, put-on, sham, simulated, spurious; SEE CONCEPT 582

assumed [adj2] *expected*
accepted, conjectured, connoted, counted on, given, granted, hypothesized, hypothetical, inferred, postulated, presumed, presupposed, supposed, suppositional, surmised, tacit, taken as known, taken for granted, understood; SEE CONCEPTS 403,689

assuming [adj] *presumptuous, arrogant*
bold, conceited, disdainful, domineering, egotistic, forward, haughty, imperious, overbearing, pushy, rude; SEE CONCEPT 404

assumption [n1] *taking something for granted; something expected*
acceptance, accepting, assuming, belief, conjecture, expectation, fancy, guess, hunch, hypothesis, inference, posit, postulate, postulation, premise, presumption, presupposition, shot*, shot in the dark*, sneaking suspicion, stab, supposal, supposition, surmise, suspicion, theorization, theory; SEE CONCEPT 689

assumption [n2] *assuming possession, power*
acceptance, accepting, acquisition, adoption, appropriation, arrogation, assuming, embracing, grab, seizure, shouldering, takeover, taking, taking on, taking

up, undertaking, usurpation; SEE CONCEPTS *129,142*

assumption [*n3*] *arrogance*
brass, chutzpah, cockiness, conceit, imperiousness, insolence, nerve, presumption, pride, sass*, self-importance; SEE CONCEPT *411*

assurance [*n1*] *statement to relieve doubt*
affirmation, assertion, declaration, guarantee, insurance, lock*, lock on*, oath, pledge, profession, promise, rain or shine*, security, sewed up*, shoo-in*, support, sure thing*, vow, warrant, warranty, word, word of; SEE CONCEPTS *71,278*

assurance [*n2*] *confidence*
aggressiveness, aplomb, arrogance, assuredness, audacity, boldness, bravery, certainty, certitude, conviction, coolness, courage, effrontery, faith, firmness, impudence, nerve, poise, positiveness, presumption, security, self-confidence, self-reliance, sureness, surety, temerity, trust; SEE CONCEPT *410*

assure [*v1*] *convince, relieve doubt*
bag*, bet on*, comfort, encourage, hearten, inspire, persuade, reassure, satisfy, sell*, sell on*, soothe; SEE CONCEPT *68*

assure [*v2*] *promise*
affirm, attest, aver, brace up, buck up, certify, confirm, give one's word, guarantee, pledge, swear, vouch for, vow; SEE CONCEPT *71*

assure [*v3*] *make certain*
cinch, clinch, complete, confirm, ensure, guarantee, have a lock on*, ice*, insure, lock, lock on, lock up, make sure, nail down*, put on ice*, seal, secure, set; SEE CONCEPTS *36,91*

assured [*adj1*] *absolutely certain*
beyond doubt, cinched, clear-cut, clinched, confirmed, decided, definite, dependable, ensured, fixed, guaranteed, indubitable, insured, in the bag*, irrefutable, made certain, nailed down*, on ice*, pronounced, racked*, sealed, secure, set, settled, sure, surefire, undoubted; SEE CONCEPT *535*

assured [*adj2*] *confident*
assertive, audacious, bold, brazen, certain, cocksure*, collected, complacent, composed, confident, cool, gung ho*, gutsy*, high*, imperturbable, overconfident, poised, positive, puffed up*, pumped up*, pushy, rosy*, sanguine, secure, self-assured, self-confident, self-possessed, sure, unflappable, unhesitating, upbeat*; SEE CONCEPTS *401,404*

astern [*adv*] *backward*
abaft, aft, rear, rearward; SEE CONCEPT *581*

astonish [*v*] *surprise*
amaze, astound, bewilder, blow away*, blow one's mind*, boggle, bowl over*, confound, daze, dumbfound, flabbergast, floor*, knock over*, overwhelm, put one away*, shock, spring on, stagger, startle, stun, stupefy, take aback, throw a curve*; SEE CONCEPT *42*

astonishing [*adj*] *surprising*
amazing, astounding, bewildering, breathtaking, extraordinary, impressive, marvelous, miraculous, spectacular, staggering, startling, striking, stunning, stupefying, stupendous, wonderful, wondrous; SEE CONCEPTS *547,572*

astonishment [*n*] *state of surprise*
amazement, astoundment, awe, bewilderment, confusion, consternation, dumbfoundment, one for the books*, shock, something else, stunner, stupefaction, wonder, wonderment; SEE CONCEPTS *230,410*

astound [*v*] *amaze*
astonish, bewilder, blow away, bowl over*, confound, confuse, daze, dumbfound, flabbergast, knock over with feather*, overwhelm, shock, stagger, startle, stun, stupefy, surprise, take aback; SEE CONCEPT *42*

astray [*adj*] *off the path or right direction*
adrift, afield, amiss, awry, gone, lost, off, off course, off the mark, roaming, straying, vanished, wandering, wrong; SEE CONCEPTS *545,581*

astride [*adj*] *with a leg on either side*
astraddle, athwart, on the back of, piggyback, sitting on, straddling; SEE CONCEPT *583*

astringent [*adj*] *harsh*
acetic, acrid, biting, bitter, cutting, sharp, tonic; SEE CONCEPTS *598,613*

astrology [*n*] *prophesy of the future by observation of stars and planets*
astrometry, horoscope; SEE CONCEPT *70*

astronaut [*n*] *space explorer*
cosmonaut, moonman/woman, moonwalker, pilot, rocketeer, rocket scientist, spaceman/woman, starman/woman; SEE CONCEPT *348*

astronomy [*n*] *study of the stars and planets other than Earth*
astrochemistry, astrography, astrolithology, astrometry, astrophysics, selenology, sky-watching, stargazing, uranology; SEE CONCEPT *349*

astute [*adj*] *perceptive*
adroit, brainy, bright, calculating, canny, clever, crafty, discerning, foxy, insightful, intelligent, keen, knowing, not born yesterday*, on the ball*, perspicacious, quick on the uptake*, sagacious, savvy, sharp, sharp as a tack*, shrewd, sly; SEE CONCEPT *402*

asunder [*adv*] *apart; into pieces*
disconnected, disjoined, divided, in half, loose, separated, split, torn, to shreds; SEE CONCEPT *785*

asylum [*n1*] *refuge*
cover, den, harbor, haven, hideaway, hideout, hole, ivory tower*, port, preserve, refuge, retreat, safe house, safety, sanctuary, security, shelter; SEE CONCEPTS *435,515*

asylum [*n2*] *psychiatric hospital*
institution, loony bin*, madhouse*, mental hospital, mental institution, sanatorium; SEE CONCEPTS *312,439,516*

at [*prep*] *about; in the direction of*
appearing in, by, found in, in the vicinity of, near to, on, placed at, situated at, through, toward; SEE CONCEPTS *581,583,799*

atheism [n] *belief that no God exists*
disbelief, doubt, freethinking, Godlessness, heresy, iconoclasm, impiety, infidelity, irreligion, irreverence, nihilism, nonbelief, paganism, skepticism, unbelief; SEE CONCEPT *689*

athlete [n] *person involved in sports*
amateur, animal, challenger, competitor, contender, contestant, games player, gorilla*, iron man/woman*, jock, jockey, muscle man/woman*, player, professional, shoulders, sport, sportsman/woman, sportsperson, superjock*; SEE CONCEPT *366*

athletic [adj1] *agile; prepared to participate in sports*
able-bodied, active, brawny, energetic, fit, lusty, muscular, powerful, robust, strapping, strong, sturdy, vigorous; SEE CONCEPTS *406,489*

athletic [adj2] *relating to sports*
competitive, contesting, exercise-related, recreational, sporting, team; SEE CONCEPT *536*

athletics [n] *sports*
contest, drill, events, exercises, games, practice, races, recreation, workout; SEE CONCEPT *363*

atmosphere [n1] *gases around the earth*
air, envelope, heavens, pressure, sky, substratosphere, troposphere; SEE CONCEPT *437*

atmosphere [n2] *general feeling or mood*
air, ambience, aura, background, character, climate, color, environment, feel, feeling, flavor, impression, local color, medium, mood, place, property, quality, scene, semblance, sense, space, spirit, surroundings, taste, tone; SEE CONCEPT *673*

atom [n] *smallest part of something*
bit, crumb, dot, fragment, grain, iota, jot, minimum, mite, modicum, molecule, morsel, mote, ounce, particle, scintilla, scrap, shred, smidgen, speck, spot, tittle, trace, whit; SEE CONCEPT *831*

atom bomb [n] *nuclear weapon*
A-bomb, backpack nuke*, doomsday machine*, fission bomb, H-bomb, hydrogen bomb, neutron bomb, nuclear bomb, nuke*, thermonuclear weapon; SEE CONCEPT *500*

atomic [adj1] *tiny*
diminutive, fragmentary, granular, microscopic, minute; SEE CONCEPT *773*

atomic [adj2] *nuclear*
atom-powered, fissionable, thermonuclear; SEE CONCEPT *485*

atone [v] *compensate; make amends for former misdoing*
absolve, answer, apologize, appease, balance, correct, counterbalance, do penance, expiate, make amends, make redress, make reparation, make up for, offset, outweigh, pay, pay one's dues*, propitiate, recompense, reconcile, redeem, redress, repair, set off, square, take one's medicine*; SEE CONCEPTS *108,126*

atonement [n] *compensation*
amends, expiation, indemnification, payment, penance, propitiation, recompense, redemption, redress,
reparation, restitution, satisfaction; SEE CONCEPTS *126,337*

atrocious [adj1] *outrageous; widely condemned*
awful, bad, barbaric, beastly, desperate, diabolical, fiendish, flagrant, godawful*, grody*, gross*, hairy, heinous, lousy, monstrous, nefarious, rotten, scandalous, shocking, villainous, wicked; SEE CONCEPTS *545,571*

atrocious [adj2] *offensive*
appalling, awful, bad, beastly, detestable, disgusting, dreadful, execrable, foul, godawful*, grody*, gross*, horrible, horrid, horrifying, icky*, loathsome, noisome, obscene, repulsive, rotten, sickening, terrible; SEE CONCEPTS *548,571*

atrocity [n1] *outrageous behavior*
atrociousness, barbarity, barbarousness, enormity, fiendishness, heinousness, horror, infamy, monstrousness, nefariousness, shockingness, villianousness, wickedness; SEE CONCEPTS *411,657*

atrocity [n2] *cruelness, offensiveness; widely condemned action*
abomination, barbarity, brutality, crime, enormity, evil, horror, inhumanity, iniquity, monstrosity, offense, outrage, ruthlessness, savagery, viciousness, wrong; SEE CONCEPTS *29,645*

atrophy [n] *wasting away, disintegration*
decline, degeneracy, degeneration, deterioration, diminution, downfall, downgrade; SEE CONCEPTS *674,698*

attach [v1] *join, fasten*
add, adhere, affix, annex, append, bind, connect, couple, fix, hitch on, hitch up, hook on, hook up, latch onto, link, make fast, prefix, rivet, secure, slap on, stick, tag on*, tie, unite; SEE CONCEPTS *85,113,160*

attach [v2] *socially join*
accompany, affiliate, associate, become associated with, combine, enlist, join forces with, latch onto, sign on with, sign up with, unite with; SEE CONCEPT *114*

attach [v3] *attribute, ascribe*
allocate, allot, appoint, assign, associate, connect, consign, designate, detail, earmark, impute, invest with, lay, name, place, put, second, send; SEE CONCEPTS *62,73*

attachment [n1] *fastening*
adapter, bond, clamp, connection, connector, coupling, fastener, joint, junction, link, tie; SEE CONCEPT *471*

attachment [n2] *something joined, fastened to another*
accessory, accoutrement, adapter, addition, adjunct, annex, appendage, appurtenance, auxiliary, extension, extra, fitting, fixture, part, supplement; SEE CONCEPT *824*

attachment [n3] *affection, high regard*
affinity, amore, attraction, bond, case, crush, devotion, fidelity, fondness, friendship, hankering*, liking, love, loyalty, partiality, possessiveness, regard,

shine*, tenderness, weakness, yen; SEE CONCEPT *32*

attack [*n1*] *physical assault*
advance, aggression, assailing, assailment, barrage, blitz, blitzkrieg, charge, defilement, dirty deed, drive, encounter, encroachment, foray, incursion, initiative, inroad, intervention, intrusion, invasion, irruption, mugging, offense, offensive, onrush, onset, onslaught, outbreak, push, raid, rape, rush, skirmish, storming, strike, thrust, violation, volley; SEE CONCEPT *86*

attack [*n2*] *verbal assault*
abuse, aggression, belligerence, blame, calumny, censure, combativeness, criticism, denigration, denunciation, impugnment, libel, pugnacity, slander, vilification; SEE CONCEPTS *52,54*

attack [*n3*] *sudden dysfunction or disorder*
access, ailment, bout, breakdown, convulsion, disease, failure, fit, illness, paroxysm, relapse, seizure, spasm, spell, stroke, throe; SEE CONCEPT *308*

attack [*v1*] *assault physically*
advance, aggress, ambush, assail, assault, bash, bat, bean*, beat, beset, besiege, biff, blast, blister, boff*, bombard, boot*, bop*, brain*, bust, charge, chop down, clip, clock, club, combat, cook*, harm, hit, hurt, infiltrate, invade, jump, kick, knock block off*, knock cold*, knock for a loop*, larrup, lay siege to, light into*, molest, mug, overwhelm, pounce upon, punch, raid, rush, set upon, slog, soak, stab, storm, strike, take the offensive, turn on, wallop*, whop*; SEE CONCEPT *86*

attack [*v2*] *assault verbally*
abuse, berate, blame, blitz, censure, criticize, impugn, jump down one's throat*, jump on one's case*, lay into, malign, refute, reprove, revile, shoot down*, stretch, vilify; SEE CONCEPTS *52,54*

attack [*v3*] *set to work*
buckle down*, deal with, dive into, plunge into, set to, start in on, tackle, take up, tear into*; SEE CONCEPT *112*

attain [*v*] *achieve, accomplish*
accede to, acquire, arrive, arrive at, bring off, come through, complete, cop*, earn, effect, fulfill, gain, get*, get fat*, get hands on, get there, glom onto*, grasp, hit, latch onto, make it, obtain, procure, promote, pull off*, rack up, reach, realize, reap, score, secure, snag, succeed, unzip*, win; SEE CONCEPTS *120,706*

attainable [*adj*] *within reach; achievable*
accessible, accomplishable, at hand, available, cherry pie*, duck soup*, easy, feasible, gettable, likely, no problem*, no sweat*, obtainable, piece of cake*, possible, potential, practicable, probable, procurable, reachable, realizable, securable; SEE CONCEPTS *528,552*

attainment [*n*] *achievement, accomplishment*
acquirement, acquisition, arrival, completion, feat, finish, fulfillment, gaining, getting, obtaining, procurement, reaching, realization, reaping, securing, succeeding, winning; SEE CONCEPT *706*

attempt [*n*] *try, effort*
all one's got*, attack, bid*, crack*, dry run*, endeavor, exertion, experiment, fling, go, header*, lick*, one's all, one's darnedest*, one's level best*, pursuit, shakedown, shot, stab, striving, struggle, trial, try, tryout, undertaking, venture, whack, workout; SEE CONCEPT *87*

attempt [*v*] *try, make effort*
aim, attack, do level best*, endeavor, essay, exert oneself, experiment, give a fling*, give a whirl*, give best shot*, give it a go*, give it a try*, give old college try*, go the limit*, have a crack*, have a go at*, make a run at*, pursue, push, seek, shoot the works*, solicit, strive, tackle, take a stab at*, take best shot*, take on, try one's hand at*, undertake, venture; SEE CONCEPT *87*

attend [*v1*] *be present at*
appear, be a guest, be at, be present, be there, bob up*, catch, check in, clock in*, come to light*, drop in, frequent, go to, haunt, make an appearance, make it*, make the scene*, pop up*, punch in*, punch the clock*, ring in*, show, show up, sit in on, speak of the devil*, time in, turn up; SEE CONCEPT *114*

attend [*v2*] *care for*
be in the service of, doctor, do for, look after, mind, minister to, nurse, serve, take care of, tend, wait upon, watch, work for; SEE CONCEPT *110*

attend [*v3*] *pay attention; apply oneself*
catch, concentrate on, devote oneself, follow, get a load of*, hear, hearken, heed, keep one's eye on*, lend an ear*, listen, listen up*, look after, look on, mark, mind, note, notice, observe, occupy oneself with, pay heed, pick up, regard, see to, watch; SEE CONCEPTS *34,596,623*

attend [*v4*] *accompany*
bear, be associated with, be connected with, catch, follow, issue from, make the scene, occur with, result from; SEE CONCEPT *714*

attend [*v5*] *escort*
accompany, chaperon, companion, consort, convoy, escort, guard, squire, usher; SEE CONCEPTS *114,714*

attendance [*n1*] *being present*
appearance, attending, being in evidence, being there, participation, presence; SEE CONCEPT *388*

attendance [*v2*] *people present at event*
assemblage, assembly, audience, box office, company, congregation, crowd, draw, gate, gathering, gross, house, observers, onlookers, patrons, public, spectators, turnout, witnesses; SEE CONCEPT *417*

attendant [*n*] *person who serves others*
aide, alarm clock*, assistant, auxiliary, baby sitter, bird dog, chaperon, companion, custodian, domestic, escort, follower, guide, helper, lackey, maid, nurse, orderly, secretary, servant, steward, stewardess, understudy, usher, valet, waitperson; SEE CONCEPT *348*

attendant [adj] being present or related
accessory, accompanying, ancillary, associated, attending, coincident, concomitant, consequent, incident; SEE CONCEPT 577

attention [n1] concentration
absorption, application, assiduity, consideration, contemplation, debate, deliberation, diligence, engrossment, heed, heedfulness, immersion, industry, intentness, mind, scrutiny, study, thinking, thought, thoughtfulness; SEE CONCEPT 409

attention [n2] consideration, care
awareness, big rush*, brace, concern, consciousness, looking after, ministration, notice, observation, recognition, regard, spotlight, tender loving care, TLC*, treatment; SEE CONCEPTS 32,410

attention(s) [n3] courtesy
amenity, assiduities, care, civility, compliment, consideration, deference, gallantry, mindfulness, politeness, regard, respect, service; SEE CONCEPT 644

attentive [adj1] concentrating
alert, all ears*, awake, aware, conscientious, enrapt, enthralled, fascinated, glued, hanging on every word*, heedful, hooked, immersed, intent, interested, listening, mindful, observant, on one's toes*, on the ball*, on the job*, on the lookout*, on the qui vive*, preoccupied, regardful, studious, vigilant, watchful; SEE CONCEPT 403

attentive [adj2] considerate
accommodating, civil, courteous, devoted, gallant, gracious, kind, obliging, polite, respectful, solicitous, thoughtful; SEE CONCEPT 401

attenuate [v] weaken
abate, constrict, contract, cripple, debilitate, deflate, disable, dissipate, enfeeble, extenuate, lessen, mitigate, sap, shrink, thin, undermine, vitiate; SEE CONCEPT 240

attest [v] affirm, vouch for
adjure, announce, argue, assert, asserverate, authenticate, aver, bear out, bear witness, certify, confirm, corroborate, countersign, declare, demonstrate, display, exhibit, give evidence, indicate, prove, ratify, seal, show, substantiate, support, sustain, swear, testify, uphold, verify, warrant, witness; SEE CONCEPT 49

attic [n] space under the roof of a house
garret, loft, sky parlor*, top floor; SEE CONCEPTS 440,448

attire [n] clothing
accoutrements, apparel, array, bib and tucker*, clothes, costume, drapes, dress, duds*, garb, garments, gear, getup, habiliments, habit, outfit, raiment, things, threads*, togs, uniform, vestment, wear; SEE CONCEPT 451

attire [v] clothe
accoutre, array, clad, costume, deck, deck out*, doll up*, drape, dress, dud*, dude up*, equip, fit out, outfit, suit up, tog, turn out; SEE CONCEPT 167

attitude [n1] mental outlook
air, angle, approach, belief, bent, bias, character, demeanor, disposition, frame of mind, headset*, inclination, leaning, like it is*, mental state, mindset*, mindtrip*, mood, notion, opinion, perspective, philosophy, point of view, position, posture, predilection, prejudice, proclivity, reaction, routine, say so*, sensibility, sentiment, set, slant, stance, stand, standing, standpoint, temper, temperament, twist, view, where one is at*; SEE CONCEPTS 410,689

attitude [n2] stance
aspect, bearing, carriage, manner, mien, pose, position, posture, stand; SEE CONCEPT 757

attorney [n] lawyer
advocate, ambulance chaser*, barrister, counsel, counselor, DA, fixer, front, legal beagle*, legal eagle*, lip*, mouthpiece*, pleader*, proxy, spieler*; SEE CONCEPT 355

attract [v] draw attention
allure, appeal to, bait, beckon, beguile, bewitch, bring, captivate, charm, come on*, court, drag, draw, enchant, endear, engage, enthrall, entice, entrance, exert influence, fascinate, freak out*, give the come-on*, go over big, grab, hook, induce, interest, intrigue, inveigle, invite, kill, knock dead*, knock out*, lure, magnetize, make a hit with*, mousetrap, pull, rope in*, score, seduce, send*, slay*, solicit, spellbind, steer, suck in*, sweep off one's feet*, tempt, turn on, vamp, wile, wow; SEE CONCEPTS 7,11,22

attraction [n] ability to draw attention; something that draws attention
allure, allurement, appeal, attractiveness, bait, captivation, charm, chemistry, come-on*, courting, draw, drawing power, enchantment, endearment, enthrallment, enticement, fascination, gravitation, inclination, inducement, interest, invitation, it*, lure, magnetism, pull, seduction, solicitation, temptation, tendency; SEE CONCEPTS 14,676

attractive [adj] appealing, drawing attention
adorable, agreeable, alluring, beaut*, beautiful, beckoning, bewitching, captivating, charming, comely, enchanting, engaging, enthralling, enticing, fair, fascinating, fetching, glamorous, good-looking, gorgeous, handsome, hunky*, interesting, inviting, looker*, lovely, luring, magnetic, mesmeric, pleasant, pleasing, prepossessing, pretty, provocative, seductive, stunning, taking, tantalizing, teasing, tempting, winning, winsome; SEE CONCEPTS 529,579

attribute [n] feature
aspect, character, characteristic, facet, idiosyncrasy, indication, mark, note, particularity, peculiarity, point, property, quality, quirk, sign, speciality, symbol, trait, virtue; SEE CONCEPTS 411,673,834

attribute [v] ascribe, assign to source
account for, accredit, apply, associate, blame, charge, connect, credit, fix upon, hang on, hold re-

sponsible, impute, lay, pin on, refer, reference, trace; SEE CONCEPT *73*

attrition [*n1*] *wearing down or away*
abrasion, attenuation, debilitation, depreciation, disintegration, erosion, grinding, rubbing, thinning, weakening, wear; SEE CONCEPTS *469,776*

attrition [*n2*] *regret*
contriteness, penance, penitence, remorse, remorsefulness, repentance; SEE CONCEPTS *410,689*

attune [*v*] *adjust*
acclimatize, accommodate, accord, accustom, adapt, balance, compensate, conform, coordinate, counterbalance, familiarize, harmonize, integrate, make agree, proportion, reconcile, regulate, tune; SEE CONCEPT *232*

atypical [*adj*] *nonconforming*
aberrant, abnormal, anomalous, deviant, different, divergent, exceptional, heteroclite, irregular, odd, peculiar, preternatural, strange, unnatural, unrepresentative; SEE CONCEPTS *547,564*

auburn [*n*] *reddish-brown color*
chestnut, copper, hazel, henna, nut, russet, rust, tawny, titian; SEE CONCEPT *622*

auction [*n*] *competitive sale; sale by bid*
bargain, jam, sell-off; SEE CONCEPTS *324,345*

audacious [*adj1*] *reckless, daring*
adventurous, aweless, ballsy*, bold, brassy, brave, cheeky*, courageous, daredevil, dauntless, enterprising, fearless, foolhardy, gutty*, intrepid, nervy, rash, resolute, risky, unafraid, uncurbed, undaunted, ungoverned, valiant, venturesome; SEE CONCEPT *401*

audacious [*adj2*] *arrogant, presumptuous*
assuming, ballsy*, bantam, bold, brash, brassy, brazen, cheeky*, defiant, disrespectful, forward, impertinent, impudent, insolent, nervy, rude, saucy, shameless; SEE CONCEPTS *401,404*

audacity [*n1*] *recklessness, daring*
adventurousness, audaciousness, boldness, bravery, courage, dauntlessness, enterprise, fearlessness, guts, intrepidity, nerve, rashness, valor, venturesomeness; SEE CONCEPT *633*

audacity [*n2*] *arrogance, presumptuousness*
assurance, audaciousness, balls*, brass, cheek*, chutzpah*, cockiness*, crust, defiance, disrespectfulness, effrontery, forwardness, gall, guts*, gutsiness, hardiness, impertinence, impudence, insolence, moxie, nerve, rudeness, shamelessness, spunk, stuff*, temerity; SEE CONCEPTS *411,633*

audible [*adj*] *able to be heard*
aural, auricular, clear, deafening, detectable, discernible, distinct, hearable, loud, loud enough, perceptible, plain, resounding, roaring, sounding, within earshot; SEE CONCEPTS *591,594*

audience [*n1*] *group observing an entertainment or sporting event*
admirers, assemblage, assembly, congregation, crowd, devotees, fans, following, gallery, gathering, hearers, house, listeners, market, moviegoers, onlookers, patrons, playgoers, public, showgoers, spectators, theatergoers, turnout, viewers, witnesses; SEE CONCEPT *417*

audience [*n2*] *hearing*
audition, conference, consideration, consultation, conversation, discussion, interview, meeting, reception; SEE CONCEPT *266*

audit [*n*] *inspection of financial records*
analysis, balancing, check, checking, examination, investigation, report, review, scrutiny, survey, verification, view; SEE CONCEPT *330*

audit [*v*] *inspect financial records*
analyze, balance, check, examine, go over, go through, investigate, report, review, scrutinize, sit in, survey, verify; SEE CONCEPTS *103,330*

audition [*n*] *test of ability*
audience, demo, hearing, reading, trial, try on, tryout; SEE CONCEPT *290*

auditor [*n*] *person who inspects financial records*
accountant, actuary, bookkeeper, cashier; SEE CONCEPT *348*

auditorium [*n*] *room, building for entertainment events*
amphitheater, assembly hall, barn*, concert hall, hall, movie house, music hall, opera house, playhouse, reception hall, theater; SEE CONCEPTS *293,439,448*

augment [*v*] *make greater; improve*
add to, aggrandize, amplify, beef up*, boost, build, build up, compound, develop, enhance, enlarge, expand, extend, grow, heighten, increase, inflate, intensify, magnify, mount, multiply, pad, piggyback*, progress, raise, reinforce, strengthen, sweeten, swell, tag on; SEE CONCEPTS *236,244,245*

augmentation [*n*] *making greater; improving*
accession, accretion, addition, amplification, beefing up*, boost, buildup, development, enhancement, enlargement, enrichment, expansion, extension, fleshing out, growth, heightening, hike, increase, increment, inflation, intensification, magnification, multiplication, raise, reinforcement, rise, strengthening, swelling, up, upping; SEE CONCEPTS *244,245*

augur [*n*] *predictor*
diviner, forecaster, harbinger, herald, oracle, prognosticator, prophet, seer, soothsayer; SEE CONCEPT *423*

augur [*v*] *predict; be an omen of*
adumbrate, bespeak, bode, call it*, call the shots*, crystal-ball, figure out, forecast, foreshadow, foretell, harbinger, have a hunch, herald, portend, presage, prognosticate, promise, prophesy, psych out*, read, signify, soothsay; SEE CONCEPT *70*

augury [*n1*] *omen*
auspice, boding, forerunner, foretoken, forewarning, harbinger, herald, portent, precursor, presage, prognostication, promise, prophecy, sign, token, warning; SEE CONCEPT *284*

augury [n2] *prediction*
divination, prediction, prophecy, soothsaying; SEE CONCEPT *70*

august [adj] *dignified, noble*
baronial, brilliant, eminent, exalted, glorious, grand, grandiose, highfalutin', high-minded, high-ranking, honorable, imposing, impressive, kingly, lofty, lordly, magnificent, majestic, monumental, pompous, princely, regal, resplendent, stately, superb, venerable; SEE CONCEPTS *404,567*

aura [n] *air, character*
ambience, appearance, aspect, atmosphere, background, emanation, feel, feeling, mood, quality, scent, semblance, suggestion, tone; SEE CONCEPT *673*

auspices [n] *protection; support*
advocacy, aegis, authority, backing, care, charge, control, countenance, guidance, influence, patronage, sponsorship, supervision; SEE CONCEPTS *94,376*

auspicious [adj] *encouraging; favorable*
advantageous, bright, favorable, felicitous, fortunate, golden, halcyon, happy, hopeful, lucky, opportune, promising, propitious, prosperous, rosy, timely, well-timed; SEE CONCEPT *572*

austere [adj1] *severe in manner*
ascetic, astringent, cold, earnest, exacting, forbidding, formal, grave, grim, hard, harsh, inexorable, inflexible, obdurate, rigid, rigorous, serious, sober, solemn, somber, stern, stiff, strict, stringent, unfeeling, unrelenting; SEE CONCEPT *550*

austere [adj2] *refraining; abstinent*
abstemious, ascetic, chaste, continent, economical, puritanical, self-denying, self-disciplined, sober, straitlaced, strict, subdued, unrelenting; SEE CONCEPT *401*

austere [adj3] *grim, barren*
bald, bare, bare-bones, bleak, clean, dour, plain, primitive, rustic, severe, simple, spare, spartan, stark, subdued, unadorned, unembellished, vanilla*; SEE CONCEPT *485*

austerity [n1] *severity*
acerbity, asperity, astringence, coldness, exactingness, exactness, formality, formalness, gravity, grimness, hardness, harshness, inclemency, inflexibility, obduracy, rigidity, rigor, seriousness, solemnity, sternness, stiffness, strictness, stringency; SEE CONCEPT *644*

austerity [n2] *refraining; abstinence*
abstemiousness, asceticism, chasteness, chastity, continence, determination, economy, prudence, puritanism, self-denial, self-discipline, sobriety, stoicism, strictness, temperance; SEE CONCEPT *633*

austerity [n3] *grimness, barrenness*
baldness, bareness, dourness, economy, plainness, primitiveness, rusticism, severity, simplicity, spareness, spartanism, starkness, unadornment; SEE CONCEPT *723*

authentic [adj] *real, genuine*
accurate, actual, authoritative, bona fide, certain, convincing, credible, creditable, dependable, factual, faithful, for real*, legit*, legitimate, official, original, pure, reliable, sure, true, trustworthy, trusty, twenty-four carat*, valid, veritable; SEE CONCEPT *582*

authenticate [v] *establish as real, genuine*
accredit, attest, authorize, bear out, certify, confirm, corroborate, endorse, guarantee, justify, prove, substantiate, validate, verify, vouch, warrant; SEE CONCEPTS *12,103*

author [n] *composer of written work*
biographer, columnist, composer, creator, essayist, ghost, ghostwriter, ink slinger*, journalist, originator, playwrite, poet, producer, prose writer, reporter, scribbler*, scribe, scripter, word slinger*, wordsmith, work-for-hire*, writer; SEE CONCEPT *348*

authoritarian [n] *domineering person*
absolutist, autocrat, despot, dictator, disciplinarian, tyrant; SEE CONCEPTS *354,412*

authoritarian [adj] *domineering*
absolute, authoritative, autocratic, despotic, dictatorial, disciplinarian, doctrinaire, dogmatic, harsh, imperious, magisterial, rigid, severe, strict, totalitarian, tyrannical, unyielding; SEE CONCEPTS *319,401*

authoritative [adj1] *recognized as true, valid*
accurate, attested, authentic, authenticated, circumstantiated, confirmed, definitive, dependable, documented, factual, faithful, learned, legit*, proven, reliable, righteous, scholarly, sound, straight from horse's mouth*, supported, trustworthy, truthful, validated, verified, veritable; SEE CONCEPT *582*

authoritative [adj2] *being domineering*
assertive, authoritarian, autocratic, commanding, confident, decisive, dictatorial, doctrinaire, dogmatic, dominating, imperative, imperious, imposing, masterly, officious, peremptory, powerhouse, self-assured; SEE CONCEPT *550*

authoritative [adj3] *official, authorized*
administrative, approved, bureaucratic, canonical, departmental, ex cathedra, executive, ex officio, imperial, lawful, legal, legitimate, magisterial, mandatory, ruling, sanctioned, sovereign, supreme; SEE CONCEPTS *319,536*

authority [n1] *power, control*
ascendancy, authorization, beef*, charge, clout*, command, credit, domination, dominion, edge, esteem, force, goods*, government, guts*, influence, juice*, jump, jurisdiction, leg up*, license, mastery, might, might and main*, permission, permit, pizzazz*, pow*, powerhouse, prerogative, prestige, punch, right, ropes*, rule, say, say-so*, steam, strength, strong arm*, stuff*, supremacy, sway, upper hand*, warrant, weight, what it takes*, whip hand*, word, zap*; SEE CONCEPTS *376,685,687*

authority [n2] *expert, animate or inanimate*
arbiter, aristocrat, bible, big cheese*, big shot*, big wig*, boss, brains*, brass*, buff*, CEO, city hall*, connoisseur, czar, egghead*, establishment*, exec, expert, feds*, front office*, governor, guru, ivory

dome*, judge, kingfish*, kingpin*, law*, master, Mr./Ms. Big*, power elite, pro, professional, professor, pundit, scholar, specialist, textbook*, top brass*, top dog*, top hand*, upstairs*, veteran, virtuoso, whiz, wizard; SEE CONCEPTS *280,348,354*

authorize [*v1*] *give power or control*
accredit, bless, commission, empower, enable, entitle, give authority, give the go-ahead*, give the green light*, give the word, invest, license, okay, rubberstamp*, say the word*, vest; SEE CONCEPTS *50,88*

authorize [*v2*] *permit, allow*
affirm, approve, confirm, countenance, endorse, give leave, let, license, qualify, ratify, sanction, suffer, tolerate, warrant; SEE CONCEPTS *10,83*

autobiography [*n*] *written account of one's own life*
adventures, bio, biography, confession, diary, experience, journal, letter, letters, life, life story, memoir, personal history, reminiscences, self-portrayal; SEE CONCEPT *280*

autocracy [*n*] *government by one*
absolutism, czarism, despotism, dictatorship, monarchy, monocracy, oppression, totalitarian government, tyranny; SEE CONCEPTS *354,691*

autocratic [*adj*] *holding power exclusively*
absolute, all-powerful, arbitrary, bossy, czarlike, despotic, dictatorial, domineering, driving, imperious, monocratic, pushing, tyrannical, tyrannous; SEE CONCEPTS *319,536*

autograph [*n*] *handwritten signature*
endorsement, handwriting, inscription, John Hancock*, seal, token, undersignature, writing; SEE CONCEPT *284*

autograph [*v*] *write signature*
endorse, engross, handwrite, ink, inscribe, pen, sign, signature, subscribe, write by hand; SEE CONCEPT *79*

automated [*adj*] *made or done by a machine*
automatic, computerized, electrical, electronic, mechanical, mechanized, motorized, programmed, robotic; SEE CONCEPTS *538,549*

automatic [*adj1*] *done or made by machine*
automated, electric, electronic, mechanical, mechanized, motorized, robotic, self-moving, self-regulating, self-starting; SEE CONCEPTS *538,549*

automatic [*adj2*] *done by habit*
autogenetic, habitual, impulsive, instinctive, instinctual, intuitive, involuntary, knee-jerk, mechanical, natural, perfunctory, reflex, routine, spontaneous, unconscious, unforced, unintentional, unmeditated, unthinking, unwilled; SEE CONCEPTS *403,538*

automatic [*adj3*] *occurring as natural consequence*
assured, certain, inescapable, inevitable, necessary, routine, unavoidable; SEE CONCEPTS *530,535*

automation [*n*] *machine control*
computerization, industrialization, mechanization; SEE CONCEPT *770*

automobile [*n*] *land vehicle; car*
auto, bucket of bolts*, bug*, buggy*, bus, clunker*, compact, convertible, crate*, four-wheeler*, gas

guzzler*, go-cart*, hardtop, hatchback, heap*, jalopy*, junker*, lemon*, limousine, motor car, oil burner*, passenger car, pickup truck, ride*, sedan, sports car, station wagon, subcompact, taxi, transportation, truck, tub*, van, wheels*, wreck*; SEE CONCEPT *505*

autonomous [*adj*] *independent*
free, self-determining, self-governing, self-ruling, sovereign, uncontrolled; SEE CONCEPT *554*

autonomy [*n*] *independence*
freedom, liberty, self-determination, self-government, self-rule, sovereignty; SEE CONCEPT *652*

autopsy [*n*] *examination of dead body*
dissection, necropsy, pathological examination, postmortem; SEE CONCEPTS *103,310*

autumn [*n*] *season between summer and winter*
autumnal equinox, fall, harvest, Indian summer; SEE CONCEPT *814*

auxiliary [*n*] *helper*
accessory, accomplice, adjutant, ally, assistant, associate, companion, confederate, crutch*, partner, reserve, subordinate, supporter; SEE CONCEPT *423*

auxiliary [*adj*] *supplementary*
abetting, accessory, adjuvant, ancillary, appurtenant, backup, complementary, contributory, extra, reserve, secondary, spare, subordinate, subservient, subsidiary, supporting; SEE CONCEPTS *546,824*

avail [*n*] *use*
account, advantage, applicability, appropriateness, fitness, service, usefulness; SEE CONCEPT *680*

avail [*v*] *be of use; use*
account, advantage, answer, be adequate, benefit, fill, fulfill, meet, profit, satisfy, serve, suffice, work; SEE CONCEPTS *91,225*

available [*adj*] *ready for use*
accessible, achievable, applicable, at hand, at one's disposal*, attainable, come-at-able*, convenient, derivable from, feasible, free, getatable, handy, obtainable, on deck*, on hand*, on tap*, open to, possible, prepared, procurable, purchasable, reachable, ready willing and able*, realizable, securable, serviceable, up for grabs*, usable; SEE CONCEPT *576*

avalanche [*n*] *falling large mass; sudden rush of large quantity*
barrage, deluge, flood, inundation, landslide, landslip, snowslide, torrent; SEE CONCEPTS *509,524,786*

avant-garde [*adj*] *unconventional, forward-looking*
beat*, experimental, head*, hip*, innovative, lead, leading-edge*, liberal, new, new wave, pioneering, progressive, radical, state-of-the-art, vanguard; SEE CONCEPTS *564,585*

avarice [*n*] *extreme greed*
avidity, close-fistedness*, covetousness, cupidity, frugality, grabbiness, greediness, miserliness, niggardliness, parsimony, penny-pinching*, penuriousness, rapacity, stinginess, thrift; SEE CONCEPTS *335,410*

avenge [v] *retaliate*
chasten, chastise, come back at, even the score, get back at, get even, payback, punish, redress, repay, requite, retribute, revenge, stick it to, take satisfaction, take vengeance, venge, vindicate; SEE CONCEPTS *122,126*

avenue [n] *street; path*
access, alley, approach, boulevard, channel, course, drive, entrance, entry, exit, outlet, parkway, passage, pathway, promenade, road, route, thoroughfare, way; SEE CONCEPT *501*

average [n] *normal, typical amount*
mean, median, medium, middle, midpoint, norm, par, rule, standard, usual; SEE CONCEPTS *647,786*

average [adj1] *normal, typical*
boilerplate*, common, commonplace, customary, dime a dozen, everyday, fair, fair to middling*, familiar, garden*, garden-variety*, general, humdrum*, intermediate, mainstream, mediocre, medium, middle of the road*, middling, moderate, nowhere, ordinary, passable, plastic*, regular, run of the mill*, so-so*, standard, tolerable, undistinguished, unexceptional, usual; SEE CONCEPT *547*

average [adj2] *numerical mean*
intermediate, median, medium, middle; SEE CONCEPT *762*

average [v] *obtain numerical mean*
balance, equate, even out; SEE CONCEPT *764*

averse [adj] *opposing*
afraid, allergic, antagonistic, antipathetic, contrary, disinclined, disliking, have no use for*, hesitant, hostile, ill-disposed, indisposed, inimical, loath, nasty, perverse, reluctant, uneager, unfavorable, unfriendly, unwilling; SEE CONCEPTS *403,564*

aversion [n] *dislike; opposition*
abhorrence, abomination, allergy, animosity, antagonism, antipathy, detestation, disfavor, disgust, disinclination, disliking, displeasure, dissatisfaction, distaste, dread, hate, hatred, having no use for*, horror, hostility, indisposition, loathing, odium, reluctance, repugnance, repulsion, revulsion, unwillingness; SEE CONCEPT *29*

avert [v] *thwart; ward off*
avoid, deflect, deter, fend off, foil, forestall, frustrate, halt, look away, preclude, prevent, rule out, shove aside, shunt, stave off, turn, turn aside, turn away; SEE CONCEPTS *121,623*

aviation [n] *flying an aircraft; study of flying aircraft*
aerodynamics, aeronautics, flight, navigation, piloting; SEE CONCEPTS *148,187,324*

aviator [n] *person who flies aircraft*
ace, aeronaut, airman/woman, barnstormer, bird legs*, birdman*, eagle*, flier, flyboy*, hotshot*, jockey*, navigator, pilot; SEE CONCEPTS *348,366*

avid [adj] *enthusiastic*
ardent, athirst, avaricious, breathless, covetous, desirous, devoted, dying to*, eager, fanatical, fervent, gotta have*, grasping, greedy, hungry, impatient, insatiable, intense, keen, passionate, rapacious, ravenous, thirsty, voracious, zealous; SEE CONCEPTS *20,401,403*

avocation [n] *hobby*
amusement, diversion, kick*, occupation, pastime, recreation, schtick*, shot*, side interest, sideline, thing; SEE CONCEPT *364*

avoid [v] *refrain or stay away from; prevent*
abstain, avert, bypass, circumlocute, circumvent, deflect, desist, ditch, divert, dodge, duck, elude, escape, eschew, evade, fake out*, fend off, flee, give the slip*, hide, hold off, jump, keep clear, lay low, obviate, recoil, run for cover*, shake, shake and bake*, shake off, shirk, shrink from, shuffle off, shun, shy, sidestep, skip*, skip out on*, skip town*, skirt*, stay away, stay out, steer clear of*, step aside, turn aside, ward off, weave, withdraw; SEE CONCEPTS *102,121*

avoidance [n] *eluding; preventing*
absention, circumvention, delay, departure, dodge, dodging, elusion, escape, escapism, eschewal, evasion, flight, forbearance, nonparticipation, parry, passive resistance, prevention, recession, recoil, restraint, retreat, run-around, self-restraint, shirking, shunning, steering clear of*; SEE CONCEPTS *102,121*

avow [v] *state; profess*
acknowledge, admit, affirm, allow, assert, aver, avouch, concede, confess, cross one's heart*, declare, grant, maintain, own up, proclaim, swear, swear on bible*, swear up and down*; SEE CONCEPTS *49,60,71*

await [v] *wait with expectation*
anticipate, attend, be prepared for, be ready for, cool one's heels*, count on, hang around*, hang in*, hang out*, hope, look for, look forward to, stay, sweat, sweat it out*; SEE CONCEPT *26*

awake [adj] *conscious; alert*
alive, aroused, attentive, awakened, aware, cognizant, excited, heedful, knowing, observant, on guard, roused, vigilant, wakeful, waking, watchful; SEE CONCEPTS *402,406*

awake [v1] *become alert or cause to rise from sleep*
arise, awaken, call, gain consciousness, get up, roll out, rouse, stir, wake, wake up; SEE CONCEPTS *250,315*

awake [v2] *become or make aware*
activate, alert, animate, arouse, awaken, call forth, enliven, excite, incite, kindle, provoke, revive, stimulate, stir up, vivify; SEE CONCEPT *231*

awaken [v] *make conscious or alert*
activate, animate, arouse, awake, call, enliven, excite, fan, incite, kindle, pile out*, provoke, rally, revive, rise and shine*, roll out, rouse, show a leg*, stimulate, stir up, turn out*, vivify, wake; SEE CONCEPTS *7,19,22,105,231*

awakening [n] *making conscious or alert*
activation, animating, arousal, awaking, birth, enlivening, incitement, kindling, provocation, rebirth, re-

newal, revival, rousing, stimulation, stirring up, vivication, waking, waking up; SEE CONCEPTS *13,105,231*

award [*n*] *prize or reward*
accolade, adjudication, allotment, bestowal, citation, conferment, conferral, decision, decoration, decree, distinction, donation, endowment, feather in cap*, gift, gold, gold star*, grant, honor, order, presentation, scholarship, trophy, verdict; SEE CONCEPT *337*

award [*v*] *give prize or reward*
accord, adjudge, allocate, allot, apportion, assign, bestow, concede, confer, decree, dish out*, distribute, donate, endow, fork out*, gift, grant, hand out, present, render, reward, shell out, sweeten the kitty*; SEE CONCEPT *132*

aware [*adj*] *knowledgeable*
acquainted, alert, alive, appraised, appreciative, apprehensive, apprised, attentive, au courant, awake, cognizant, conscious, cool*, enlightened, familiar, go-go*, groovy, grounded*, heedful, hip*, informed, in the know, in the picture*, into, knowhow, knowing, know the score*, know what's what*, latched on*, mindful, on the beam*, on to*, perceptive, plugged in*, really into*, receptive, savvy, sensible, sentient, sharp, tuned in, up on, wise, wised up*, wise to, with it*; SEE CONCEPT *402*

awareness [*n*] *knowledge*
acquaintance, acquaintanceship, alertness, aliveness, appreciation, apprehension, attention, attentiveness, cognizance, comprehension, consciousness, discernment, enlightenment, experience, familiarity, information, keenness, mindfulness, perception, realization, recognition, sensibility, sentience, understanding; SEE CONCEPT *409*

away [*adv1*] *in another direction; at a distance*
abroad, absent, afar, apart, aside, beyond, distant, elsewhere, far afield, far away, far off, far remote, forth, from here, hence, not present, off, out of, out of the way, over, to one side; SEE CONCEPTS *581, 778*

away [*adv2*] *continuously*
endlessly, forever, incessantly, interminably, on and on, relentlessly, repeatedly, tirelessly, unremittingly, without break, without end, without rest, without stopping; SEE CONCEPT *553*

awe [*n*] *amazement*
admiration, apprehension, astonishment, consternation, dread, esteem, fear, fright, horror, regard, respect, reverence, shock, stupefaction, terror, veneration, wonder, wonderment, worship; SEE CONCEPTS *230,410*

awe [*v*] *amaze*
alarm, appall, astonish, blow away*, cow*, daunt, dazzle, flabbergast, frighten, grandstand, horrify, hotdog*, impress, intimidate, knock socks off*, overawe, scare, showboat*, startle, strike, stun, stupefy, terrify; SEE CONCEPTS *7,19,22,42*

awesome [*adj*] *amazing*
alarming, astonishing, awe-inspiring, awful, beautiful, breathtaking, daunting, dreadful, exalted, fearful, fearsome, formidable, frantic, frightening, gone*, grand, hairy*, horrible, horrifying, imposing, impressive, intimidating, magnificent, majestic, mean, mind-blowing*, moving, nervous, overwhelming, real gone*, shocking, something else*, striking, stunning, stupefying, terrible, terrifying, wonderful, wondrous, zero cool*; SEE CONCEPTS *537,572*

awful [*adj*] *very bad; terrible*
abominable, alarming, appalling, atrocious, deplorable, depressing, dire, disgusting, distressing, dreadful, fearful, frightful, ghastly, grody*, gross*, gruesome, grungy*, harrowing, hideous, horrendous, horrible, horrific, horrifying, nasty, offensive, raunchy, repulsive, shocking, stinking, synthetic, tough, ugly, unpleasant, unsightly; SEE CONCEPTS *570,571*

awfully [*adv1*] *badly*
clumsily, disgracefully, disreputably, dreadfully, inadequately, incompletely, poorly, reprehensibly, shoddily, unforgivably, unpleasantly, wickedly, wretchedly; SEE CONCEPTS *570,571*

awfully [*adv2*] *very*
badly, dreadfully, excessively, extremely, greatly, hugely, immensely, indeed, much, quite, terribly, truly, very much; SEE CONCEPT *569*

awhile [*adv*] *for a short period*
briefly, for a bit, for a little while, for a moment, for a spell, for a while, for the moment, momentarily, not for long, temporarily, transiently; SEE CONCEPT *798*

awkward [*adj1*] *clumsy, inelegant*
all thumbs*, amateurish, artless, blundering, bulky, bumbling, bungling, butterfingers*, coarse, floundering, gawky, graceless, green*, having two left feet*, having two left hands*, incompetent, inept, inexpert, klutzy*, lumbering, maladroit, oafish, rude, stiff, stumbling, uncoordinated, uncouth, unfit, ungainly, ungraceful, unhandy, unpolished, unrefined, unskilled, unskillful; SEE CONCEPTS *406,480,527*

awkward [*adj2*] *difficult to handle*
annoying, bulky, chancy, cramped, cumbersome, dangerous, disagreeable, discommodious, hard to use, hazardous, incommodious, inconvenient, perilous, risky, troublesome, uncomfortable, unhandy, unmanageable, unwieldy; SEE CONCEPTS *558,565*

awkward [*adj3*] *embarrassing*
compromising, delicate, difficult, embarrassed, ill at ease, inconvenient, inopportune, painful, perplexing, sticky*, thorny*, ticklish*, troublesome, trying, uncomfortable, unpleasant, untimely; SEE CONCEPT *555*

awkwardness [*n1*] *clumsiness; inelegance*
amateurishness, artlessness, boorishness, coarseness, crudeness, gawkiness, gracelessness, greenness*, ignorance, inability, incompetence, ineptitude, inept-

ness, inexpertness, maladroitness, oafishness, rudeness, tactlessness, uncoordination, uncouthness, ungainliness, unskillfulness; SEE CONCEPTS *405,630, 717*

awkwardness [*n2*] *difficulty*
bulkiness, chanciness, cumbersomeness, danger, hazardousness, inconvenience, peril, perilousness, risk, troublesomeness, uncomfortableness, unhandiness, unmanageability, unwieldiness; SEE CONCEPTS *656,666*

awkwardness [*n3*] *embarrassment*
delicacy, difficulty, discomfort, inconvenience, inopportuneness, painfulness, stickiness*, thorniness*, ticklishness*, trouble, uncomfortableness, unpleasantness, untimeliness; SEE CONCEPT *388*

awning [*n*] *canopy*
covering, door cover, marquee, protection, shade, shelter, sunshade, tent; SEE CONCEPTS *440,473*

awry [*adj*] *off course; amiss*
afield, askance, askew, aslant, astray, badly, bent, cockeyed, crooked, curved, slanting, turned, wrong, zigzag; SEE CONCEPTS *537,581*

ax/axe [*n*] *large cutting tool*
adz, chopper, hatchet, tomahawk; SEE CONCEPT *499*

ax/axe [*v1*] *cut with large blade*
chop, cut, cut down, fell, hew; SEE CONCEPT *176*

ax/axe [*v2*] *dismiss from service*
boot*, bounce*, can*, cancel, cut back, discharge, dispense with, eliminate, fire, get rid of, give a pink slip*, give the boot*, kick out, lay off, remove, sack*, terminate, throw out; SEE CONCEPT *351*

axiom [*n*] *principle*
adage, aphorism, apothegm, device, dictum, fundamental, law, maxim, moral, postulate, precept, proposition, proverb, saying, theorem, truism, truth; SEE CONCEPTS *278,687,689*

axiomatic [*adj*] *understood; aphoristic*
absolute, accepted, aphoristic, apophthegmatic, assumed, certain, fundamental, given, indubitable, manifest, obvious, presupposed, proverbial, self-evident, unquestioned; SEE CONCEPT *529*

axis [*n*] *point around which something revolves*
arbor, axle, hinge, pivot, pole, shaft, spindle, stalk, stem, support, turning point; SEE CONCEPT *830*

axle [*n*] *shaft around which wheels rotate*
arbor, axis, gudgeon, mandrel, pin, pivot, pole, rod, shaft, spindle, stalk, stem, support; SEE CONCEPTS *464,830*

B

babble [*n*] *trivial talk, often incessant*
blubbering, burble, chatter, clamor, drivel, gab, gabble, gibberish, gossip, gushing, idle talk, jabber, jabbering, jargon, murmur, muttering, prattle, ranting, tattling; SEE CONCEPTS *266,278*

babble [*v*] *talk trivially, often incessantly*
blab, blubber, blurt, burble, cackle, chat, chatter,

gibber, go on, gossip, gush, jabber, mumble, murmur, mutter, patter, prate, prattle, rant, rave, run off at the mouth*, run on, spill the beans*, squeal*, talk foolishly, talk incoherently, talk nonsensically, tattle, trivialize, yackety yak*, yak*; SEE CONCEPTS *51,266*

babe [*n*] *baby*
bairn, child, infant, little one, newborn, suckling; SEE CONCEPTS *414,424*

baby [*n*] *infant*
angelface*, babe, bairn, bambino, bundle, buttercup*, button, cherub, chick, child, crawler, deduction*, dividend*, dumpling*, kid, little angel*, little darling*, little doll*, little one*, newborn, nipper*, nursling, papoose, preemie*, suckling, tad*, toddler, tot, write-off*, youngster; SEE CONCEPTS *414,424*

baby [*adj*] *miniature*
babyish, diminutive, dwarf, little, midget, mini, minute, petite, small, tiny, wee, youthful; SEE CONCEPT *773*

baby [*v*] *treat like a child*
cater to, cherish, coddle, cosset, cuddle, dandle, dote on, foster, humor, indulge, nurse, overindulge, pamper, pet, please, satisfy, serve, spoil; SEE CONCEPTS *110,295*

babyhood [*n*] *period of infancy*
childhood, diaper days*, infanthood; SEE CONCEPT *817*

babyish [*adj*] *acting like an infant*
baby, childish, foolish, immature, infantile, juvenile, kid stuff, puerile, silly, sissy, spoiled; SEE CONCEPTS *401,550*

baby-sit [*v*] *care for a child*
guard, sit, take care, tend, watch; SEE CONCEPT *295*

bachelor [*n*] *unmarried man or woman*
available*, celibate, eligible, misogamist, misogynist, single, single man, single woman, stag*, unattached; SEE CONCEPTS *419,423*

back [*n*] *end part*
aft, back end, backside, extremity, far end, hindpart, hindquarters, posterior, rear, reverse, stern, tail, tail end, tailpiece; SEE CONCEPTS *392,471,827,833*

back [*adj1*] *end*
aback, abaft, aft, after, astern, back of, backward, behind, final, following, hind, hindmost, in the wake of, posterior, rear, rearmost, rearward, tail; SEE CONCEPTS *827,833*

back [*adj2*] *from earlier time*
delayed, elapsed, former, overdue, past, previous; SEE CONCEPT *820*

back [*v1*] *support*
abet, abide by, advocate, ally, angel*, assist, bankroll, boost, champion, countenance, encourage, endorse, favor, finance, give a boost, give a leg up*, give a lift*, go to bat for*, grubstake, sanction, second, side with, sponsor, stake, stand behind, stick

by, stick up for, subsidize, sustain, underwrite, uphold; SEE CONCEPTS *8,50,88*

back [*v2*] *put in reverse direction*
backtrack, drive back, fall back, recede, regress, repel, repulse, retire, retract, retreat, reverse, turn tail, withdraw; SEE CONCEPTS *195,208*

backbiting [*n*] *hateful talk*
abuse, aspersion, backstabbing*, belittlement, calumniation, calumny, cattiness, defamation, denigration, depreciation, detraction, disparagement, gossip, invective, lie, malice, obloquy, scandal, slander, spite, spitefulness, tale, traducement, vilification, vituperation; SEE CONCEPTS *54,58,63*

backbone [*n1*] *strength of character*
courage, determination, firmness, fortitude, grit, guts, hardihood, heart, intestinal fortitude, mettle, moral fiber, nerve, pluck, resolution, resolve, spunk, stamina, steadfastness, tenacity, toughness, will, willpower; SEE CONCEPT *411*

backbone [*n2*] *spinal column of vertebrate*
base, basis, foundation, spine, support, vertebrae, vertebral column; SEE CONCEPTS *420,442*

back down [*v*] *withdraw from agreement or statement*
abandon, accede, admit, back off, back out, back pedal*, backtrack, balk, beg off*, cancel, chicken out*, concede, cop out*, defeat, demur, give in, give up, go back on, hold back, recant, recoil, renege, resign, retreat, surrender, take back, withdraw, yield; SEE CONCEPTS *266,697*

backer [*n*] *supporter*
advocate, ally, angel*, benefactor, champion, endorser, fairy godmother*, follower, grubstaker, meal ticket*, money, patron, promoter, protagonist, sponsor, staker, underwriter, well-wisher; SEE CONCEPT *359*

backfire [*v*] *have an opposite effect*
backlash, boomerang, bounce back, disappoint, fail, flop, miscarry, rebound, recoil, ricochet, spring back; SEE CONCEPTS *42,701*

background [*n*] *experience or circumstances*
accomplishments, acquirement, actions, atmosphere, attainment, aura, backdrop, breeding, capacity, credentials, cultivation, culture, deeds, education, environment, framework, grounding, history, practice, preparation, qualification, rearing, seasoning, tradition, training, upbringing; SEE CONCEPTS *673,678, 706*

backing [*n*] *support*
abetment, accompaniment, adherence, advocacy, aegis, aid, assistance, auspices, championing, championship, encouragement, endorsement, funds, grant, help, patronage, reinforcement, sanction, secondment, sponsorship, subsidy; SEE CONCEPTS *110,332*

backlash [*n*] *adverse reaction*
backfire, boomerang, counteraction, kickback, reaction, recoil, repercussion, resentment, resistance, response, retaliation, retroaction, tangle; SEE CONCEPT *230*

backlog [*n*] *uncompleted work; accumulation*
excess, hoard, inventory, quantity, reserve(s), reservoir, resources, stock, stockpile, store, supply; SEE CONCEPTS *432,786*

backpack [*n*] *sack carried on the back*
haversack, knapsack, pack, rucksack; SEE CONCEPT *446*

backside [*n*] *rear end*
behind, bottom, butt*, buttocks, derrière, fanny*, posterior, rear, rump*, seat*, tail*, tush*; SEE CONCEPT *392*

back talk [*n*] *nasty reply*
cheek, guff, lip, mouth, sass; SEE CONCEPTS *46,278*

backward [*adj1*] *toward the rear*
astern, behind, inverted, rearward, regressive, retrograde; SEE CONCEPT *581*

backward [*adj2*] *bashful*
afraid, averse, demure, diffident, disinclined, hesitant, hesitating, humble, indisposed, late, loath, modest, reluctant, reserved, retiring, shy, sluggish, tardy, timid, uneager, unwilling, wavering; SEE CONCEPT *401*

backward [*adj3*] *slow in growth*
arrested, behind, checked, delayed, dense, dull, feeble-minded, imbecile, late, moronic, retarded, stupid, subnormal, underdeveloped, underprivileged, undeveloped; SEE CONCEPTS *402,562*

backward [*adv*] *toward the rear*
aback, abaft, about, astern, back, behind, in reverse, inverted, rearward, turned around; SEE CONCEPT *581*

backwash [*n*] *repercussion*
aftermath, result, wake; SEE CONCEPTS *230,674*

backwoods [*n/adj*] *forests; land distant from settled area*
backcountry, boondocks, frontier, hinterland, interior, isolation, outback, rural area, sticks*, timberland; SEE CONCEPT *509*

backyard [*n*] *expanse behind house*
courtyard, garden, grass, lawn, patio, play area, terrace, yard; SEE CONCEPT *513*

bacteria [*n*] *microorganisms*
bacilli, germs, microbes, organisms, pathogens; SEE CONCEPTS *306,393*

bad [*adj1*] *poor quality*
abominable, amiss, atrocious, awful, bad news*, beastly, blah*, bottom out, bummer*, careless, cheap, cheesy*, crappy*, cruddy*, crummy*, defective, deficient, diddly*, dissatisfactory, downer*, dreadful, erroneous, fallacious, faulty, garbage, godawful*, grody*, gross*, grungy*, icky*, imperfect, inadequate, incorrect, inferior, junky*, lousy*, not good, off, poor, raunchy*, rough, sad, sleazy*, slipshod, stinking, substandard, synthetic, the pits*, unacceptable, unsatisfactory; SEE CONCEPT *571*

bad [*adj2*] *harmful*
damaging, dangerous, deleterious, detrimental, hurtful, injurious, ruinous, unhealthy; SEE CONCEPTS *537,570*

bad [*adj3*] *immoral*
base, corrupt, criminal, delinquent, evil, iniquitous, mean, reprobate, sinful, vicious, vile, villainous, wicked, wrong; SEE CONCEPT *545*

bad [*adj4*] *mischievous*
disobedient, ill-behaved, misbehaving, naughty, unruly, wrong; SEE CONCEPT *401*

bad [*adj5*] *decayed*
moldy, off, putrid, rancid, rotten, sour, spoiled; SEE CONCEPTS *485,613*

bad [*adj6*] *severe*
disastrous, distressing, grave, harsh, intense, painful, serious, terrible; SEE CONCEPT *569*

bad [*adj7*] *sick*
ailing, diseased, ill, in pain, unwell; SEE CONCEPT *314*

bad [*adj8*] *sorry*
apologetic, conscience-stricken, contrite, crestfallen, dejected, depressed, disconsolate, down, downcast, downhearted, guilty, low, regretful, remorseful, sad, upset, woebegone; SEE CONCEPT *403*

bad [*adj9*] *distressing*
adverse, disagreeable, discouraged, discouraging, displeasing, distressed, gloomy, grim, melancholy, troubled, troubling, unfavorable, unfortunate, unhappy, unpleasant; SEE CONCEPTS *403,529*

badge [*n*] *emblem worn*
brand, cordon, device, identification, insignia, mark, marker, medallion, motto, pin, ribbon, scepter, shield, sign, stamp, symbol, token; SEE CONCEPTS *260,284,476*

badger [*v*] *nag, bother*
annoy, bait, bug, bully, eat*, give the business*, goad, harass, harry, hassle, heckle, hound, importune, insist on, needle, nudge, pester, plague, ride, tease, torment, work on; SEE CONCEPTS *14,51*

badly [*adv1*] *inadequately*
abominably, awkwardly, blunderingly, carelessly, clumsily, crudely, defectively, erroneously, faultily, feebly, haphazardly, imperfectly, incompetently, ineffectively, ineptly, maladroitly, negligently, poorly, shoddily, stupidly, unfavorably, unfortunately, unsatisfactorily, unskillfully, unsuccessfully, weakly, wrong, wrongly; SEE CONCEPT *571*

badly [*adv2*] *immorally*
criminally, evilly, improperly, naughtily, shamefully, unethically, wickedly; SEE CONCEPT *545*

badly [*adv3*] *very much; desperately*
acutely, deeply, exceedingly, extremely, gravely, greatly, hard, intensely, painfully, roughly, seriously, severely; SEE CONCEPT *569*

baffle [*v1*] *perplex*
addle, amaze, astound, befuddle, bewilder, buffalo*, confound, confuse, daze, disconcert, dumbfound, elude, embarrass, faze, floor*, get, mix up, muddle, mystify, nonplus, puzzle, rattle, stick*, stump, stun, throw; SEE CONCEPTS *7,19,42*

baffle [*v2*] *hinder*
beat, block, check, circumvent, dash, defeat, disappoint, foil, frustrate, impede, obstruct, prevent, ruin, thwart, upset; SEE CONCEPT *121*

bag [*n1*] *container for one's possesions*
attaché, backpack, briefcase, carryall, carry-on, case, duffel, gear, handbag, haversack, holdall, kit, knapsack, pack, packet, pocket, pocketbook, poke, pouch, purse, rucksack, sac, sack, saddlebag, satchel, suitcase, tote; SEE CONCEPTS *339,450,494*

bag [*n2*] *special interest*
expertise, favorite activity, hobby, preference, speciality, thing; SEE CONCEPTS *32,529*

bag [*v1*] *catch*
acquire, apprehend, capture, collar, gain, get, hook, kill, land, nab, nail, net, seize, shoot, take, trap; SEE CONCEPT *90*

bag [*v2*] *droop*
balloon, billow, bulge, flap, flop, hang, lop, sag, swell; SEE CONCEPTS *754,757*

baggage [*n*] *gear*
accoutrements, bags, belongings, carry-on, effects, equipment, fortnighter*, gear, impedimenta, luggage, paraphernalia, parcels, slough, suitcases, things, tote, tote bag, trappings, two-suiter*; SEE CONCEPT *494*

baggy [*adj*] *drooping*
billowing, bulging, droopy, flabby, floppy, ill-fitting, loose, oversize, roomy, sagging, slack, unshapely; SEE CONCEPTS *486,490*

bail [*n*] *money for assurance*
bond, collateral, guarantee, pawn, pledge, recognizance, security, surety, warrant, warranty; SEE CONCEPTS *318,332*

bail out [*v1*] *help*
aid, deliver, release, relieve, rescue, spring; SEE CONCEPT *110*

bail out [*v2*] *escape*
flee, quit, retreat, withdraw; SEE CONCEPT *102*

bait [*n*] *something for luring*
allurement, attraction, bribe, come-on*, drag, enticement, inducement, lure, seducement, shill, snare, temptation, trap; SEE CONCEPT *709*

bait [*v1*] *lure*
allure, attract, bedevil, beguile, draw, entice, fascinate, lead on, seduce, tempt; SEE CONCEPTS *9,14*

bait [*v2*] *needle*
anger, annoy, badger, bother, gall, harass, heckle, hound, irk, irritate, nag, persecute, provoke, tease, torment; SEE CONCEPTS *7,19*

bake [*v*] *cook in oven*
heat, melt, scorch, simmer, stew, warm; SEE CONCEPT *170*

baked [*adj*] *cooked in oven*
dried, heated, melted, scorched, simmered, stewed, warmed; SEE CONCEPT *462*

baker [*n*] *person who cooks baked goods*
chef, cook, dough puncher*, pastry maker; SEE CONCEPT *348*

bakery [n] *cooking business where baked goods are produced*
bake shop, confectionery, pastry shop, pâtisserie; SEE CONCEPTS *325,439,449*

balance [n1] *equilibrium*
antithesis, correspondence, counterbalance, equity, equivalence, evenness, even-steven*, hang, harmony, parity, proportion, stasis, symmetry, tension; SEE CONCEPTS *664,667*

balance [n2] *composure*
equanimity, poise, self-control, self-possession, stability, steadfastness; SEE CONCEPT *633*

balance [n3] *money remaining in account*
difference, dividend, excess, profit, remainder, residue, rest, surplus; SEE CONCEPT *332*

balance [v1] *make equal; cause to have equilibrium*
accord, adjust, attune, cancel, collate, come out, come out even, compensate, correspond, counteract, counterbalance, equalize, equate, even, harmonize, level, make up for, match, neutralize, nullify, offset, oppose, pair off, parallel, poise, readjust, redeem, set, square, stabilize, steady, tie, weigh; SEE CONCEPTS *197,697*

balance [v2] *compare*
assess, consider, deliberate, estimate, evaluate, weigh; SEE CONCEPT *17*

balance [v3] *make equal numerically*
adjust, audit, calculate, compute, count, enumerate, equate, estimate, figure, settle, square, sum up, tally, total; SEE CONCEPT *764*

balanced [adj1] *equalized*
counterbalanced, equitable, equivalent, evened, fair, just, offset, proportional, stabilized, symmetrical, uniform; SEE CONCEPT *566*

balanced [adj2] *settled financially*
certified, confirmed, validated; SEE CONCEPT *334*

balance sheet [n] *financial statement including gains and losses for a period*
account, annual report, assets and liabilities, budget, ledger, report; SEE CONCEPTS *271,332*

balcony [n] *porch or structure above the ground*
balustrade, box*, catwalk, gallery, mezzanine, piazza, platform, porch, portico, stoop, terrace, veranda; SEE CONCEPT *440*

bald [adj1] *having no covering*
baldheaded, bare, barren, depilated, exposed, glabrous, hairless, head*, naked, shaven, skin head, smooth, stark, uncovered; SEE CONCEPT *485*

bald [adj2] *simple, unadorned*
austere, bare, blunt, direct, downright, forthright, outright, plain, severe, straight, straightforward, unembellished; SEE CONCEPTS *485,589*

bale [n] *bunch*
bundle, package, parcel; SEE CONCEPT *432*

baleful [adj] *menacing*
calamitous, deadly, dire, evil, foreboding, harmful, hurtful, injurious, malevolent, malignant, noxious, ominous, pernicious, ruinous, sinister, threatening,

venomous, vindictive, woeful; SEE CONCEPTS *537,570*

balk [v1] *stop short*
cramp, crimp, demur, desist, dodge, evade, flinch, hesitate, recoil, refuse, resist, shirk, shrink from, shy, turn down, upset apple cart*; SEE CONCEPTS *119,121,188*

balk [v2] *thwart*
baffle, bar, beat, check, circumvent, counteract, cramp, cramp one's style*, dash, defeat, disappoint, disconcert, foil, forestall, frustrate, hinder, obstruct, prevent, ruin, stall, stop, throw a curve*, throw monkey wrench in*, upset apple cart*; SEE CONCEPT *121*

balky [adj] *uncooperative*
averse, contrary, hesitant, immovable, indisposed, inflexible, intractable, loath, negative, negativistic, obstinate, ornery, perverse, reluctant, stubborn, unbending, unmanageable, unpredictable, unruly; SEE CONCEPT *401*

ball [n] *dance party*
hoedown, hoodang, hop, jump, mingle, prom, promenade, reception, shindig; SEE CONCEPT *386*

ball [v1] *globe, sphere*
apple, balloon, drop, globule, orb, pellet, pill, round, spheroid; SEE CONCEPT *436*

ballad [n] *narrative song*
carol, chant, ditty, serenade; SEE CONCEPT *595*

ballast [n] *something giving balance*
balance, brace, bracket, counterbalance, counterweight, equilibrium, sandbag, stability, stabilizer, support, weight; SEE CONCEPT *712*

ballet [n] *graceful, expressive dancing*
choreography, dance, toe dancing; SEE CONCEPT *263*

ballet dancer [n] *person who performs graceful dance*
company, coryphee, dancer, danseur, danseuse, figurant, figurante, hoofer*, prima ballerina; SEE CONCEPT *352*

balloon [n] *inflated material or vehicle*
airship, bladder, blimp, dirigible, zeppelin; SEE CONCEPTS *293,504*

balloon [v] *billow out; bloat*
belly, blow up, bulge, dilate, distend, enlarge, expand, inflate, puff out, swell; SEE CONCEPTS *208,756*

ballot [n1] *voting; recording of vote*
election, franchise, plebiscite, poll, polling, referendum, slate, tally, ticket; SEE CONCEPTS *300,301*

ballot [n2] *candidates from political party*
choice, lineup, slate, ticket; SEE CONCEPT *301*

balm [n1] *oily substance*
analgesic, application, balsam, cerate, compound, cream, demulcent, dressing, embrocation, emollient, formula, lotion, medicine, ointment, potion, poultice, preparation, prescription, salve, soother, soothing agent, unction, unguent; SEE CONCEPTS *307,466*

balm [n2] *something soothing*
alleviation, anodyne, assuagement, comfort, consolation, curative, cure, easement, mitigation, pallia-

tive, refreshment, relief, remedy, restorative, solace, soother; SEE CONCEPTS *337,529*

balmy [*adj1*] *comfortable with respect to weather*
mild, moderate, moist, pleasant, refreshing, summerlike, summery, temperate, tropical; SEE CONCEPTS *603,605*

balmy [*adj2*] *insane*
absurd, bugged out*, cracked*, crazed, crazy, daft, deranged, dotty*, foolish, harebrained*, idiotic, loony, mentally incompetent, moronic, nuts*, nutty*, odd, potty*, preposterous, silly, stupid, wacky; SEE CONCEPT *403*

bamboozle [*v*] *fool; cheat*
baffle, befuddle, bilk, con, confound, confuse, deceive, defraud, delude, dupe, flimflam*, hoax, hoodwink*, hornswoggle*, mystify, perplex, puzzle, stump, swindle; SEE CONCEPT *59*

ban [*n*] *official forbiddance*
a don't*, a thou-shalt-not*, boycott, censorship, embargo, injunction, interdiction, limitation, no-no*, off limits*, out of bounds*, prohibition, proscription, refusal, restriction, stoppage, suppression, taboo; SEE CONCEPTS *50,88,121,687*

ban [*v*] *officially forbid*
banish, bar, blackball*, close down, close up, curse, declare illegal, disallow, enjoin, exclude, halt, ice out*, illegalize, inhibit, interdict, outlaw, pass by, pass up, prevent, prohibit, proscribe, restrict, shut out, suppress; SEE CONCEPTS *50,88,121*

banal [*adj*] *commonplace*
blah*, bland, bromidic, clichéd, common, conventional, cornball*, cornfed*, corny, dull as dishwater*, dumb, everyday, flat, hackneyed, ho hum*, hokey*, humdrum*, insipid, mundane, noplace, nothing, nowhere, old hat*, ordinary, pablum*, pedestrian, platitudinous, square, stale, stereotyped, stock, stupid, tired, tripe, trite, unimaginative, unoriginal, vapid, watery, wishy-washy*, zero*; SEE CONCEPT *530*

banality [*n*] *common saying*
adage, boiler*, buzzword, chestnut*, cliché, corn*, dullsville*, familiar tune*, high camp*, hokum*, old chestnut*, old saw*, plate*, platitude, prosaicism, prosaism, saw*, trite phrase, trivia, triviality, truism; SEE CONCEPT *275*

band [*n1*] *something which encircles*
bandage, bandeau, belt, binding, bond, braid, cable, chain, circle, circuit, copula, cord, fillet, harness, hoop, ligature, line, link, manacle, ribbon, ring, rope, sash, scarf, shackle, snood, stay, strap, string, strip, tape, tie, truss; SEE CONCEPTS *470,751*

band [*n2*] *group of people with same interest*
assembly, association, bevy, body, bunch, clique, club, cluster, collection, company, corps, coterie, covey, crew, gang, gathering, horde, menagerie, outfit, party, society, troop, troupe; SEE CONCEPTS *387,391,417*

band [*n3*] *musical group*
combo, ensemble, orchestra, philharmonic, symphony, troupe; SEE CONCEPT *294*

band [*v*] *group or join group*
affiliate, ally, amalgamate, belt, coadjute, combine, conjoin, consolidate, federate, gather, league, merge, team, unite; SEE CONCEPTS *113,114*

bandage [*n*] *covering for wound*
cast, compress, dressing, gauze, plaster; SEE CONCEPT *311*

bandage [*v*] *cover a wound*
bind, dress, swathe, truss, wrap; SEE CONCEPT *310*

bandanna [*n*] *colorful scarf*
handkerchief, kerchief, neckerchief, silk; SEE CONCEPT *450*

bandit [*n*] *thief*
badman, brigand, criminal, crook, desperado, forager, gangster, gunman, highwayman, hijacker, holdup man, hooligan, marauder, mobster, outlaw, pillager, pirate, plunderer, racketeer, raider, ravager, robber, villain; SEE CONCEPT *412*

bane [*n*] *cause of misery*
affliction, bête noir, blight, burden, calamity, curse, despair, destruction, disaster, downfall, fatal attraction, misery, nuisance, pest, plague, poison, ruin, ruination, scourge, torment, trial, trouble, undoing, venom, woe; SEE CONCEPTS *529,674*

baneful [*adj*] *ruinous, injurious*
baleful, calamitous, deadly, deleterious, destructive, disastrous, evil, fatal, harmful, hurtful, malefic, noxious, pernicious, pestilent, pestilential, poisonous, venomous, wicked; SEE CONCEPTS *537,570*

bang [*n1*] *explosive noise*
blast, boom, burst, clang, clap, clash, crack, detonation, discharge, howl, peal, pop, report, roar, roll, rumble, salvo, shot, slam, smash, sound, thud, thump, thunder, wham; SEE CONCEPT *595*

bang [*n2*] *loud hit or knock*
bash, bat, belt, blow, box, bump, collide, crack, cuff, punch, slam, smack, smash, sock, stroke, wallop, whack, whop; SEE CONCEPT *189*

bang [*n3*] *thrilling situation*
enjoyment, excitement, kick, pleasant feeling, smash, wallop, wow; SEE CONCEPT *230*

bang [*v1*] *hit or knock loudly*
boom, burst, clang, clatter, crash, detonate, drum, echo, explode, make noise, peal, rattle, resound, sound, thump, thunder; SEE CONCEPTS *65,189*

bang [*v2*] *moving by hitting hard*
bash, beat, bump, clatter, collide, crash, hammer, hit, knock, pound, pummel, rap, slam, smash, strike, thump, whack; SEE CONCEPT *189*

bang [*adv*] *suddenly, with force*
abruptly, hard, headlong, head on, noisily, precisely, smack, straight, suddenly; SEE CONCEPT *540*

banish [*v*] *expel from place or situation*
ban, cast out, deport, discard, discharge, dislodge, dismiss, dispel, drive away, eject, eliminate, eradi-

69

cate, evict, exclude, excommunicate, exile, expatriate, expulse, extradict, get rid of, isolate, ostracize, oust, outlaw, proscribe, relegate, remove, rusticate, sequester, shake off, shut out, transport; SEE CONCEPTS *121,217*

banister [*n*] *railing of stairs*
baluster, balustrade, handrail, rail, support; SEE CONCEPT *443*

bank [*n1*] *financial institution*
coffer, countinghouse, credit union, depository, exchequer, fund, hoard, investment firm, repository, reserve, reservoir, safe, savings, stock, stockpile, store, storehouse, thrift, treasury, trust company, vault; SEE CONCEPTS *333,339,439*

bank [*n2*] *ground bounding waters*
beach, cay, cliff, coast, edge, embankment, lakefront, lakeshore, lakeside, ledge, levee, oceanfront, reef, riverfront, riverside, seabank, seaboard, seafront, shore, strand, streamside, waterfront; SEE CONCEPT *509*

bank [*n3*] *row or tier of objects*
array, dashboard, group, line, rank, row, sequence, series, succession; SEE CONCEPT *464*

bank [*v1*] *collect money or advantage*
amass, deposit, heap, hill, hoard, invest, lay aside, lay away, mass, mound, pile, put by, salt away, save, sock away, speculate, squirrel, stash; SEE CONCEPTS *109,330*

bank [*v2*] *lean or tilt*
bend, camber, cant, incline, pitch, slant, slope; SEE CONCEPTS *148,213*

banker [*n*] *professional in financial institution*
broker, capitalist, croupier, dealer, financier, house, investor, manager, money-lender, officer, teller, treasurer, usurer; SEE CONCEPTS *347,348,353*

bank on [*v*] *depend upon*
assume, believe in, be sure about, bet on, build on, count on, gamble on, lean on, look to, reckon on, rely on, stake, trust, venture, wager; SEE CONCEPT *12*

bankrupt [*adj*] *unable to pay debts*
broke, depleted, destitute, exhausted, failed, impoverished, in Chapter 11*, insolvent, lacking, lost, out of business, ruined, spent, tapped out; SEE CONCEPT *334*

bankruptcy [*n*] *inability to pay debts*
Chapter 11*, defalcation, default, destituteness, destitution, disaster, exhaustion, failure, indebtedness, indigence, insolvency, lack, liquidation, loss, nonpayment, overdraft, pauperism, privation, repudiation, ruin, ruination; SEE CONCEPT *335*

banner [*n*] *flag, usually with message*
banderole, burgee, colors, emblem, ensign, gonfalon, heading, headline, pennant, pennon, standard, streamer; SEE CONCEPTS *270,277,278*

banquet [*n*] *formal dinner, usually ceremonial*
feast, festivity, fete, meal, reception, regale, repast, spread, treat; SEE CONCEPTS *377,459*

bantam [*adj*] *small*
diminutive, little, petite, tiny; SEE CONCEPTS *491,773*

banter [*n*] *teasing*
badinage, chaff, chaffing, chitchat, derision, dissing*, exchange, fun, gossip, jeering, jesting, joking, joshing, kidding, mockery, persiflage, play, raillery, repartee, ribbing, ridicule, small talk; SEE CONCEPTS *59,278*

banter [*v*] *tease*
chaff, deride, fool, fun, jeer, jest, jive*, joke, josh, kid, make fun of, mock, rag*, razz*, rib, ridicule, satirize, taunt; SEE CONCEPTS *59,273*

baptism [*n*] *church rite; initiation*
ablution, baptismal, christening, debut, dedication, dunking, immersion, introduction, launching, lustration, purgation, purge, purification, rite of passage, ritual, sanctification, sprinkling; SEE CONCEPTS *367,377*

baptize [*v*] *initiate in church rite*
admit, asperse, besprinkle, call, christen, cleanse, denominate, dip, dub, entitle, immerse, name, purify, regenerate, sprinkle, term, title; SEE CONCEPT *367*

bar [*n1*] *rod; straight length of material*
batten, billet, boom, crossbar, crosspiece, ingot, lever, paling, pig, pole, rail, rib, rule, shaft, slab, spar, spoke, stake, stick, streak, strip, stripe, stroke; SEE CONCEPTS *470,471*

bar [*n2*] *barrier; blockage*
barricade, blank wall, block, clog, deterrent, encumbrance, fence, hindrance, hurdle, impediment, obstacle, obstruction, pale, rail, railing, restraint, road block, snag, stop, stumbling block, traverse, wall; SEE CONCEPTS *470,652,680*

bar [*n3*] *establishment serving alcohol*
alehouse, barroom, beer garden, bistro, canteen, cocktail lounge, drinkery, inn, lounge, pub, public house, rathskeller, saloon, tap, taproom, tavern, watering hole*; SEE CONCEPTS *325,439*

bar [*n4*] *legal system*
attorneys, barristers, bench, counsel, counselors, court, courtroom, dock, judgment, judiciary, jurists, law, law court, law practice, lawyers, legal fraternity, solicitors, tribunal; SEE CONCEPTS *318,381*

bar [*v1*] *secure, usually with a length of material*
barricade, block, blockade, bolt, caulk, clog, close, dam, deadbolt, dike, fasten, fence, jam, latch, lock, plug, seal, secure, trammel, wall; SEE CONCEPTS *121,130*

bar [*v2*] *prohibit*
ban, boycott, circumvent, condemn, debar, deny, disallow, discountenance, discourage, eliminate, enjoin, except, exclude, exile, forbid, freeze out, frustrate, hinder, interdict, interfere, keep out, limit, obstruct, ostracize, outlaw, override, preclude, prevent, refuse, reject, restrain, rule out, segregate, shut out, stop, suspend; SEE CONCEPTS *50,61,88*

barb [*n1*] *point*
arrow, bristle, dart, prickle, prong, quill, shaft, spike, spur, thistle, thorn; SEE CONCEPTS *434,836*

barb [*n2*] *pointed comment*
affront, criticism, cut, dig, gibe, insult, rebuff, sarcasm, scoff, sneer; SEE CONCEPTS *52,54*

barbarian [*n*] *crude, savage person*
beast, bigot, boor, brute, cannibal, clod, hooligan, hun, ignoramus, lout, monster, philistine, rascal, ruffian, troglodyte, vandal; SEE CONCEPT *412*

barbarian [*adj*] *crude, savage*
barbaric, barbarous, boorish, brutal, coarse, cruel, inhuman, lowbrow, merciless, philistine, primitive, rough, rude, uncivil, uncivilized, uncouth, uncultivated, uncultured, unsophisticated, untamed, vicious, vulgar, wild; SEE CONCEPT *401*

barbaric [*adj*] *crude, savage*
barbarian, barbarous, boorish, brutal, coarse, cruel, fierce, graceless, inhuman, lowbrow, primitive, rough, rude, tasteless, uncivilized, uncouth, vulgar, wild; SEE CONCEPT *401*

barbarism [*n*] *crudity, savagery, especially in speech*
atrocity, barbarity, brutality, catachresis, coarseness, corruption, cruelty, impropriety, inhumanity, localism, malapropism, misusage, misuse, primitive culture, provincialism, solecism, uncivilizedness, vernacularism, vernacularity, vulgarism; SEE CONCEPTS *275,633*

barbarity [*n*] *crudity, savagery*
boorishness, brutality, crudeness, cruelty, inhumanity, ruthlessness, savageness, viciousness, vulgarity; SEE CONCEPT *633*

barbarous [*adj*] *crude, savage*
atrocious, barbarian, barbaric, brutal, brutish, coarse, cruel, ferocious, heartless, ignorant, inhuman, inhumane, monstrous, primitive, rough, rude, ruthless, sadistic, truculent, uncivil, uncivilized, uncouth, uncultured, vicious, vulgar, wicked, wild, wolfish; SEE CONCEPT *401*

barbecue [*n1*] *meal cooked on grill*
bake, clam bake, cookout, party, picnic, weinie roast; SEE CONCEPT *459*

barbecue [*n2*] *grill for cookout*
broiler, charcoal grill, fireplace, gas grill, griddle, pit of coals, roaster, spit; SEE CONCEPT *493*

barbecue [*v*] *cook outside, usually on a grill*
broil, charcoal, fry, grill, rotisserie, sear; SEE CONCEPT *170*

barber [*n*] *hair cutter*
beautician, coiffeur, coiffeuse, cosmetologist, hairdresser, hair stylist, shaver, tonsorial artist; SEE CONCEPT *348*

bare [*adj1*] *without clothing*
bald, bareskinned, denuded, disrobed, divested, exposed, in one's birthday suit*, naked, nude, peeled, shorn, stripped, unclad, unclothed, uncovered, undressed, unrobed; SEE CONCEPT *485*

bare [*adj2*] *without covering or content*
arid, barren, blank, bleak, clear, desert, desolate, empty, lacking, mean, open, poor, scanty, scarce, stark, unfurnished, vacant, vacuous, void, wanting; SEE CONCEPT *490*

bare [*adj3*] *simple, unadorned*
austere, bald, basic, blunt, chaste, cold, essential, hard, literal, meager, mere, modest, scant, severe, sheer, simple, spare, stark, unembellished, unornamented; SEE CONCEPT *562*

bare [*v*] *reveal*
disclose, divulge, exhibit, expose, publish, show, uncover, unroll, unveil; SEE CONCEPTS *60,138*

barefaced [*adj*] *shameless; open*
apparent, arrant, audacious, blatant, blunt, bold, brash, brassy, brazen, candid, clear, flagrant, frank, glaring, immodest, impudent, insolent, manifest, naked, obvious, palpable, temerarious, transparent, unabashed, unconcealed; SEE CONCEPT *401*

barefoot [*adj*] *wearing no shoes*
barefooted, discalceate, discalced, shoeless, unshod; SEE CONCEPT *406*

barely [*adj*] *not quite*
almost, hardly, just, only just, scantily, scarcely; SEE CONCEPT *772*

bareness [*n*] *state of being unclothed*
dishabille, nakedness, nudity, starkness, unadornment, undress; SEE CONCEPT *453*

bargain [*n1*] *agreement*
arrangement, bond, business, compact, contract, convention, covenant, deal, engagement, negotiation, pact, pledge, promise, stipulation, transaction, treaty, understanding; SEE CONCEPT *684*

bargain [*n2*] *something bought at cheap price*
budget price, buy, closeout, deal, discount, giveaway, good buy, good deal, good value, low price, markdown, nominal price, reduction, steal, value; SEE CONCEPTS *332,338*

bargain [*v*] *negotiate terms of sale or agreement*
agree, arrange, barter, buy, compromise, confer, contract, covenant, deal, dicker, do business, haggle, make terms, palter, promise, sell, stipulate, trade, traffic, transact; SEE CONCEPTS *56,330*

bargain for [*v*] *expect*
aim for, anticipate, contemplate, count on, foresee, imagine, look for, plan on, reckon on; SEE CONCEPT *26*

barge [*n*] *large work boat*
ark, canal boat, dory, flatboat, freight ship, lighter, raft, scow; SEE CONCEPT *506*

barge in/barge into [*v*] *charge*
break in, burst in, collide, infringe, interrupt, intrude, muscle in, push, shove, stumble; SEE CONCEPTS *150,208*

bark [*n1*] *plant covering*
case, casing, coat, cortex, crust, husk, peeling, rind, shell, skin; SEE CONCEPT *428*

bark [*n2*] *animal yelp*
bay, growl, grunt, howl, roar, snarl, woof, yap, yip;
SEE CONCEPT *64*

bark [*v1*] *yelp*
arf, bay, cry, gnarl, growl, howl, snap, snarl, woof,
yap, yip; SEE CONCEPT *64*

bark [*v2*] *shout*
bawl, bellow, berate, clamor, cry, growl, grumble,
mutter, roar, snap, snarl, yell; SEE CONCEPT *77*

barn [*n*] *animal shelter*
farm building, outbuilding, shed; SEE CONCEPTS
439,517

baroque [*adj*] *decorative, especially architecture*
bizarre, convoluted, elaborate, embellished, extravagant, flamboyant, florid, gilt, grotesque, ornamented, ornate, overdecorated, rich, rococo; SEE
CONCEPTS *562,589*

barracks [*n*] *shelter for military*
billet, bivouac, camp, cantonment, dormitory, encampment, enclosure, garrison, headquarters, hut,
prefab, quarters, Quonset hut, tent; SEE CONCEPTS
321,516

barrage [*n1*] *weapon fire*
battery, blast, bombardment, broadside, cannonade,
crossfire, curtain of fire, discharge, enfilade, fire, fusillade, gunfire, hail, salvo, shelling, shower, storm,
volley; SEE CONCEPT *320*

barrage [*n2*] *profusion of something*
assault, attack, blast, bombardment, burst, deluge,
hail, mass, onslaught, plethora, rain, shower, storm,
stream, surge, torrent; SEE CONCEPT *786*

barrel [*n*] *cylindrical container*
butt, cask, cylinder, drum, firkin, hogshead, keg,
pipe, receptacle, tub, tun, vat, vessel; SEE CONCEPT
494

barren [*adj1*] *unable to support growth*
arid, depleted, desert, desolate, dry, effete, empty,
fallow, fruitless, impotent, impoverished, infecund,
infertile, parched, sterile, unbearing, uncultivable,
unfertile, unfruitful, unproductive, waste; SEE CON-
CEPTS *485,527*

barren [*adj2*] *unprofitable*
dull, flat, fruitless, futile, lackluster, profitless, stale,
uninspiring, unproductive, unrewarding, useless,
vain, vapid; SEE CONCEPT *560*

barricade [*n*] *blocking object*
bar, barrier, blank wall, block, blockade, bulwark,
fence, obstruction, palisade, rampart, roadblock,
stockade, stop, wall; SEE CONCEPT *470*

barricade [*v*] *block, usually to protect*
bar, blockade, defend, fortify, obstruct, shut in; SEE
CONCEPTS *130,201*

barrier [*n1*] *obstruction*
bar, barricade, blank wall, blockade, bound, boundary, confines, curtain, ditch, enclosure, fence, fortification, gully, hurdle, impediment, limit, moat,
obstacle, pale, palisade, railing, rampart, roadblock,
stop, trench, wall; SEE CONCEPTS *435,470,513*

barrier [*n2*] *obstruction to goal*
bar, check, difficulty, drawback, encumbrance,
handicap, hindrance, hurdle, impediment, limitation,
obstacle, pale, preventive, restraint, restriction,
stumbling block; SEE CONCEPT *532*

barter [*v*] *trade goods or services*
bargain, exchange, haggle, swap, trade, traffic,
truck; SEE CONCEPT *104*

base [*n1*] *foundation*
basement, basis, bed, bedrock, bottom, foot, footing, ground, groundwork, infrastructure, pedestal,
rest, root, seat, seating, stand, substratum, substructure, support, underpinning; SEE CONCEPT *442*

base [*n2*] *fundamental part*
authority, backbone, basis, chief constituent, core,
essence, essential, evidence, foundation, fundamental, groundwork, heart, important part, infrastructure, key, origin, primary element, principal,
principle, root, source, underpinning; SEE CONCEPT
826

base [*n3*] *headquarters*
camp, center, depot, dock, field, garrison, hangar,
harbor, home, port, post, settlement, site, starting
point, station, strip, terminal; SEE CONCEPTS *435,449*

base [*adj*] *vulgar, low*
abject, abominable, cheap, coarse, common, contemptible, corrupt, depraved, despicable, disgraceful, dishonorable, disreputable, foul, grovelling,
humble, ignoble, immoral, indelicate, loathsome,
lowly, mean, menial, offensive, paltry, pitiful, plebeian, poor, scandalous, servile, shameful, shoddy,
sleazy, sordid, sorry, squalid, trashy, ugly, unworthy, vile, worthless, wretched; SEE CONCEPTS
542,570

base [*v*] *build plan or opinion on*
construct, depend, derive, establish, found, ground,
hinge, locate, plant, predicate, prop, rest, set up,
station, stay; SEE CONCEPT *36*

baseless [*adj*] *without substantiation*
bottomless, flimsy, foundationless, gratuitous,
groundless, reasonless, unconfirmed, uncorrobo-
rated, unfounded, ungrounded, unjustifiable, unjustified, unsubstantiated, unsupported, untenable, unwarranted; SEE CONCEPT *582*

basement [*n*] *room on lower floor of building*
bottom, cellar, crypt, excavation, furnace room, storage, substructure, subterranean room, underbuilding,
understructure, vault; SEE CONCEPT *440*

bashful [*adj*] *shy*
abashed, backward, blushful, blushing, chary, confused, constrained, coy, demure, diffident, embarrassed, humble, modest, nervous, overmodest,
recoiling, reserved, reticent, retiring, self-conscious,
self-effacing, shamefaced, sheepish, shrinking, silent, timid, timorous, unassertive; SEE CONCEPT *404*

basic [*adj*] *elementary, fundamental*
basal, capital, central, chief, elemental, essential, indispensable, inherent, intrinsic, key, main, neces-

sary, primary, primitive, principal, radical, substratal, underlying, vital; SEE CONCEPT *568*

basically [*adv*] *fundamentally*
at heart, at the bottom, essentially, firstly, in essence, inherently, in substance, intrinsically, mostly, primarily, radically; SEE CONCEPT *568*

basin [*n*] *container or area where water is held*
bay, bowl, concavity, depression, dip, ewer, gulf, hole, hollow, lagoon, pan, pool, pot, sag, sink, sinkage, sinkhole, tub, valley, vessel, watershed; SEE CONCEPTS *494,509,514*

basis [*n1*] *physical foundation*
base, bed, bottom, foot, footing, ground, groundwork, rest, resting place, seat, substructure, support; SEE CONCEPT *442*

basis [*n2*] *foundation for belief, action*
antecedent, assumption, authority, axiom, backbone, background, backing, base, bedrock, cause, center, chief ingredient, core, crux, data, essence, essential, evidence, explanation, footing, fundamental, hard fact, heart, infrastructure, justification, keynote, keystone, law, nexus, nucleus, postulate, premise, presumption, presupposition, principal element, principle, proof, reason, root, rudiment, sanction, security, source, substratum, support, theorem, theory, underpinning, warrant; SEE CONCEPTS *661,687, 689*

bask [*v1*] *lie in sunlight*
laze, loll, lounge, relax, sun, sunbathe, swim in, toast oneself*, warm oneself; SEE CONCEPTS *162,210*

bask [*v2*] *lie in glory*
delight in, derive pleasure, enjoy, indulge, luxuriate, relish, revel, rollick, savor, take comfort, take pleasure, wallow, welter; SEE CONCEPT *32*

basket [*n*] *woven container*
bassinet, bin, box, bushel, cradle, crate, creel, hamper, nacelle, pannier; SEE CONCEPT *494*

bastard [*n*] *illegitimate male*
bantling, by-blow, colt, come-by-chance*, illegitimate, love child*, mongrel, natural child, scoundrel, spurious issue*, whoreson, woods colt*; SEE CONCEPTS *414,419*

bastard [*adj*] *illegitimate*
adulterated, baseborn, counterfeit, fake, false, fatherless, imperfect, impure, inferior, irregular, misbegotten, misborn, mixed, mongrel, natural, phony, sham, spurious, suppositious, unfathered, ungenuine; SEE CONCEPT *549*

bastardize [*v*] *debase*
adulterate, bestialize, brutalize, corrupt, debauch, declare illegitimate, degrade, demoralize, deprave, pervert, vitiate, warp; SEE CONCEPT *44*

baste [*v1*] *moisten during cooking*
brush with liquid, drip, grease, lard, season; SEE CONCEPT *170*

baste [*v2*] *sew temporarily*
catch, fasten, stitch, tack; SEE CONCEPT *218*

baste [*v3*] *pummel, thrash*
batter, beat, berate, blister, clobber, club, drub, lambaste, lash, maul, pelt, revile, scold, trounce, wallop, whip, whomp; SEE CONCEPTS *52,189*

bastion [*n*] *support; fortified place*
breastwork, bulwark, citadel, defense, fortification, fortress, mainstay, parapet, prop, protection, rock, stronghold, support, tower of strength; SEE CONCEPT *712*

bat [*n*] *a hit with a solid object*
bang, belt, blow, bop, crack, knock, rap, slam, smack, sock, strike, swat, thump, thwack, wallop, whack, whop; SEE CONCEPT *189*

bat [*v*] *hit with solid object*
bang, belt, bop, crack, hit, lob, loft, rap, slam, smack, sock, strike, swat, thump, thwack, wallop, whack, whop; SEE CONCEPT *189*

batch [*n*] *group of same objects*
accumulation, aggregation, amount, array, assemblage, assortment, bunch, bundle, clump, cluster, clutch, collection, crowd, group, lot, pack, parcel, quantity, set, shipment, volume; SEE CONCEPTS *432,786*

bath [*n1*] *washing with water and, usually, soap*
ablution, cleansing, dip, douche, dousing, gargle, laving, scrubbing, shower, soak, soaking, soaping, sponging, tub, wash; SEE CONCEPTS *161,165*

bath [*n2*] *room for bathing*
bathroom, lavatory, powder room, restroom, sauna, shower, shower room, spa, steam room, toilet, washroom; SEE CONCEPT *448*

bathe [*v*] *wash with water and, usually, soap*
bath, clean, cleanse, dip, douse, dunk, flood, hose, imbathe, imbue, immerse, moisten, rinse, scour, scrub, shower, soak, soap, sponge, steep, submerge, suffuse, tub, water, wet; SEE CONCEPTS *161,165*

bathing suit [*n*] *clothing for swimming, sunning*
bathing costume, beach costume, bikini, maillot, one-piece, swimsuit, trunks, two-piece; SEE CONCEPT *451*

bathroom [*n*] *room for bathing, toilet use*
bath, lavatory, powder room, restroom, sauna, shower, shower room, spa, steam room, toilet, washroom, water closet; SEE CONCEPT *448*

baton [*n*] *stick used for conducting or for protection*
billy, billy club, club, cudgel, mace, nightstick, rod, staff, truncheon, wand; SEE CONCEPTS *262,470,500*

battalion [*n*] *military division*
army, brigade, company, contingent, corps, force, horde, host, legion, multitude, regiment, squadron, throng, unit; SEE CONCEPT *322*

batten [*v1*] *fasten securely*
board up, clamp down, cover up, fix, nail down, secure, tie, tighten; SEE CONCEPTS *85,160*

batten [*v2*] *grow fat*
burgeon, feed on, grow, prosper, thrive, wax; SEE CONCEPT *704*

batter [n] *mixture before baking*
concoction, dough, mix, mush*, paste, preparation, recipe; SEE CONCEPTS *457,466*

batter [v] *strike and damage*
assault, bash, beat, break, bruise, buffet, clobber, contuse, cripple, crush, dash, deface, demolish, destroy, disable, disfigure, drub, hurt, injure, lacerate, lambaste, lame, lash, mangle, mar, maul, mutilate, pelt, pommel, pound, pummel, punish, ruin, shatter, smash, thrash, wallop, wreck; SEE CONCEPTS *189, 246,252*

battery [n1] *series of similar things*
array, batch, body, bunch, bundle, chain, clot, clump, cluster, group, lot, ring, sequence, set, suite; SEE CONCEPT *432*

battery [n2] *physical abuse*
assault, attack, beating, mayhem, mugging, onslaught, thumping, violence; SEE CONCEPTS *189,246*

battery [n3] *group of weapons*
artillery, cannon, cannonry, gunnery unit, guns; SEE CONCEPTS *321,500*

battle [n1] *military fight*
action, assault, attack, barrage, blitzkreig, bloodshed, bombing, brush, campaign, carnage, clash, combat, conflict, contention, crusade, encounter, engagement, fighting, fray, havoc, hostility, onset, onslaught, press, ravage, scrimmage, significant contact, skirmish, sortie, strife, struggle, war, warfare; SEE CONCEPT *106*

battle [n2] *struggle*
agitation, campaign, clash, conflict, contest, controversy, crusade, debate, disagreement, dispute, strife; SEE CONCEPTS *46,106*

battle [v] *fight, struggle*
agitate, argue, clamor, combat, contend, contest, dispute, feud, oppugn, skirmish, strive, tug, war, wrestle; SEE CONCEPTS *46,106*

battlefield [n] *location of military fights*
arena, Armageddon, battleground, combat zone, field, front, front line, salient, theater of operations, theater of war; SEE CONCEPTS *198,321*

bawdy [adj] *vulgar, dirty*
blue, cheap, coarse, dirty, erotic, gross, indecent, indecorous, indelicate, lascivious, lecherous, lewd, libidinous, licentious, lustful, obscene, prurient, ribald, risqué, rude, salacious, suggestive; SEE CONCEPT *545*

bawl [v1] *yell*
bark, bellow, bluster, call, cheer, clamor, holler, howl, roar, rout, scream, screech, shout, shriek, vociferate; SEE CONCEPT *77*

bawl [v2] *cry*
blubber*, boohoo*, howl, shed tears, sob, squall, wail, weep, yowl; SEE CONCEPTS *77,185*

bay [n1] *shoreline indentation*
anchorage, arm, basin, bayou, bight, cove, estuary, fiord, firth, gulf, harbor, inlet, lagoon, loch, mouth, narrows, sound, strait; SEE CONCEPTS *509,514*

bay [n2] *alcove in wall*
bow window, compartment, niche, nook, opening, oriel, picture window, recess; SEE CONCEPT *440*

bay [n3] *howl*
bark, bellow, clamor, cry, growl, howl, ululation, wail, yelp; SEE CONCEPT *64*

bazaar [n] *fair; sale place*
exchange, exposition, fete, market, marketplace, mart; SEE CONCEPTS *345,438,449*

be [v1] *exist*
abide, act, be alive, breathe, continue, do, endure, go on, have being, have place, hold, inhabit, last, live, move, obtain, persist, prevail, remain, rest, stand, stay, subsist, survive; SEE CONCEPT *407*

be [v2] *happen*
befall, come about, come to pass, occur, take place, transpire; SEE CONCEPT *2*

beach [n] *sandy area by body of water*
bank, coast, lakeshore, lakeside, littoral, margin, oceanfront, seaboard, seafront, seashore, seaside, shingle, shore, strand, waterfront; SEE CONCEPTS *509,514*

beached [adj] *grounded*
abandoned, aground, ashore, deserted, high and dry, marooned, stranded, wrecked; SEE CONCEPT *583*

beacon [n] *light used as signal, guide*
alarm, alert, balefire, beam, bonfire, flare, guidepost, heliograph, lamp, lantern, lighthouse, lodestar, pharos, radar, rocket, sign, signal fire, smoke signal, warning signal, watchtower; SEE CONCEPT *628*

bead [n] *droplet, blob*
bean, bubble, dab, dot, driblet, drop, globule, grain, particle, pea, pellet, pill, shot, speck, spherule, stone; SEE CONCEPT *436*

beads [n] *string of small, often round, objects*
chaplet, choker, necklace, necklet, pearls, pendant, rosary, wampum; SEE CONCEPTS *368,446*

beak [n] *nose of animal*
bill, mandible, neb, nib, nozzle, pecker, proboscis, projection, prow, snout; SEE CONCEPT *392*

beam [n1] *length of material used as support*
axle, bail, balk, bolster, boom, brace, cantilever, column, crossbar, crosspiece, girder, jamb, joist, lath, lintel, pile, piling, pillar, plank, pole, post, prop, rafter, reach, scaffolding, scantling, shaft, sill, spar, stanchion, stay, stringer, strip, strut, stud, timber, transverse, trestle, two-by-four; SEE CONCEPTS *471,479*

beam [n2] *ray of light*
bar, beacon, chink, column, dartle, emission, finger, flicker, glare, gleam, glimmer, glint, glitter, glow, laser, radiation, ray, shaft, shimmer, shoot, sparkle, streak, stream, twinkle; SEE CONCEPTS *624,628*

beam [v1] *broadcast on air waves*
emit, give off, give out, glare, glimmer, glow, radiate, send, shed, shine, throw off, transmit; SEE CONCEPTS *519,624*

beam [v2] *smile broadly*
gleam, glow, grin, laugh, radiate, shine, smirk; SEE CONCEPT *185*

beam [v3] *shine, as a light*
burn, emit, glare, gleam, glitter, glow, radiate, yield; SEE CONCEPT *624*

beaming [adj1] *radiant; beautiful*
bright, brilliant, effulgent, flashing, fulgent, gleaming, glistening, glittering, glowing, incandescent, lambent, lucent, luminous, refulgent, scintillating, sparkling; SEE CONCEPT *617*

beaming [adj2] *very happy*
animated, cheerful, genial, grinning, joyful, radiant, shining, smiling, sparkling, sunny; SEE CONCEPT *401*

bear [v1] *bring*
buck, carry, convey, deliver, ferry, fetch, lug, move, pack, take, tote, transfer, transport; SEE CONCEPTS *108,143*

bear [v2] *support mentally*
cherish, entertain, exhibit, harbor, have, hold, hold up, maintain, possess, shoulder, sustain, uphold, weigh upon; SEE CONCEPTS *8,12*

bear [v3] *endure*
abide, admit, allow, brook, encounter, experience, permit, put up with, stomach, suffer, tolerate, undergo; SEE CONCEPTS *23,239*

bear [v4] *give birth*
be delivered of, beget, breed, bring forth, create, develop, engender, form, fructify, generate, invent, make, parturitate, produce, propagate, provide, reproduce, yield; SEE CONCEPTS *173,251,302,373*

bearable [adj] *endurable*
acceptable, admissible, allowable, livable, manageable, passable, satisfactory, sufferable, supportable, sustainable, tolerable; SEE CONCEPT *529*

beard [n1] *facial hair on human*
bristles, brush, five-o-clock shadow*, fuzz, goatee, imperial*, muttonchops*, Santa Claus*, stubble, Van Dyke*; SEE CONCEPT *418*

beard [n2] *decoy*
false face, front, mask; SEE CONCEPT *716*

beard [v] *confront*
brave, face, oppose, stand up to; SEE CONCEPTS *46,96*

bearded [adj] *having facial hair*
barbate, beardy, bewhiskered, bristly, bushy, goateed, hairy, hirsute, shaggy, stubbled, stubbly, unshaven, whiskered; SEE CONCEPTS *406,485*

bearer [n1] *person who carries messages or delivery*
agent, beast of burden*, carrier, conveyor, courier, drogher, emissary, envoy, internuncio, messenger, porter, runner, servant, shipper, transporter; SEE CONCEPT *348*

bearer [n2] *person who requests payment of bill*
beneficiary, casher, collector, consignee, payee; SEE CONCEPT *353*

bearing [n1] *person's conduct, posture*
address, air, aspect, attitude, behavior, carriage, comportment, demeanor, deportment, display, front, look, manner, mien, poise, port, pose, presence, set, stand; SEE CONCEPTS *411,633*

bearing [n2] *significance*
application, connection, import, meaning, pertinence, reference, relation, relevance, weight; SEE CONCEPT *668*

bearing/bearings [n3] *position, usually of water vehicle*
aim, course, direction, location, orientation, point of compass, position, situation, track, way, whereabouts; SEE CONCEPTS *739,746*

bear on/bear upon [v] *concern*
affect, appertain to, apply, belong to, involve, pertain to, refer to, relate to, touch upon; SEE CONCEPT *532*

bear out [v] *substantiate*
authenticate, confirm, corroborate, endorse, justify, prove, substantiate, support, uphold, validate, verify, vindicate; SEE CONCEPTS *50,88,97*

bear with [v] *tolerate*
be patient, endure, forbear, make allowance, put up with, suffer, wait; SEE CONCEPT *23*

beast [n] *large wild animal; brute*
barbarian, beastie, creature, critter, fiend, gargoyle, glutton, hun, lower animal, monster, monstrosity, pig, quadruped, swine, varmint; SEE CONCEPT *394*

beastly [adv1] *savage; vulgar*
abominable, animal, barbarous, base, bestial, boorish, brutal, brute, brutish, carnal, coarse, cruel, degraded, depraved, disgusting, feral, ferine, foul, gluttonous, gross, inhuman, irrational, loathsome, low, monstrous, obscene, piggish, prurient, repulsive, sadistic, swinish, unclean, vile; SEE CONCEPT *401*

beastly [adv2] *offensive*
awful, disagreeable, disgusting, foul, gross, mean, nasty, revolting, rotten, terrible, unpleasant, vile; SEE CONCEPTS *537,542*

beat [n1] *throbbing*
cadence, cadency, flow, flutter, measure, meter, oscillation, palpitation, pound, pressure, pulsation, pulse, quake, quiver, rhyme, rhythm, ripple, shake, surge, swell, swing, throb, thump, tick, undulation, vibration; SEE CONCEPTS *150,185*

beat [n2] *blow, stroke*
hit, lash, punch, shake, slap, strike, swing, thump; SEE CONCEPT *189*

beat [n3] *area of responsibility*
circuit, course, march, path, patrol, precinct, rounds, route, walk, way; SEE CONCEPTS *513,532*

beat [adj] *very tired*
dog tired*, exhausted, fatigued, kaput*, wearied, weary, worn out; SEE CONCEPTS *316,720*

beat [v1] *injure by striking*
bang, bash, bat, batter, belt, box, break, bruise, buffet, cane, castigate, clout, club, collide, crush, cudgel, drub, flagellate, flail, flog, hammer, hit, knock, lambaste, lash, lick, maltreat, mash, maul, pelt,

pommel, pound, punch, punish, ram, rap, slap, slug, smack, spank, strike, swat, thrash, thresh, thump, thwack, trounce, wallop, whale, whip; SEE CONCEPTS *189,246*

beat [*v2*] *defeat, surpass*
best, better, be victorious, conquer, exceed, excel, outdo, outplay, outrival, outrun, outshine, outstrip, overcome, overtake, overwhelm, shoot ahead of, subdue, top, transcend, triumph, vanquish, whip; SEE CONCEPTS *95,141*

beat [*v3*] *forge*
fashion, form, hammer, malleate, model, pound, shape, work; SEE CONCEPTS *137,175*

beat [*v4*] *throb*
agitate, alternate, bob, bounce, buffet, flap, flicker, fluctuate, flutter, heave, jerk, jounce, oscillate, palpitate, pitch, pound, pulsate, pulse, quake, quaver, quiver, ripple, shake, shiver, swing, thrill, throb, thump, tremble, twitch, undulate, vibrate, writhe; SEE CONCEPTS *150,185*

beat [*v5*] *mix*
stir, whip; SEE CONCEPT *170*

beaten [*adj1*] *defeated*
baffled, bested, circumvented, conquered, cowed, crushed, disappointed, discomfited, disheartened, frustrated, humbled, licked, mastered, overcome, overpowered, overthrown, overwhelmed, routed, ruined, subjugated, surmounted, thwarted, trounced, undone, vanquished, worsted; SEE CONCEPTS *403,674*

beaten [*adj2*] *forged*
formed, hammered, milled, pounded, rolled, shaped, stamped, tamped, tramped, tramped down, trodden, worked; SEE CONCEPTS *486,490*

beaten [*adj3*] *mixed*
aerated, blended, bubbly, churned, creamy, foamy, frothy, meringued, stirred, whipped, whisked; SEE CONCEPTS *491,606*

beatnik [*n*] *unc013onventional, free-sprited person*
beat, Bohemian, demonstrator, dropout, flower child, hippie, iconoclast, maverick, nonconformist, peacenik, protester, radical; SEE CONCEPT *423*

beau [*n*] *boyfriend*
admirer, beloved, cavalier, escort, fiancé, flame, gentleman caller, gentleman friend, honey, inamorato, love, lover, paramour, squire, steady, suitor, swain, sweetheart, true love; SEE CONCEPT *423*

beautiful [*adj*] *physically attractive*
admirable, alluring, angelic, appealing, beauteous, bewitching, charming, classy, comely, cute, dazzling, delicate, delightful, divine, elegant, enticing, excellent, exquisite, fair, fascinating, fine, foxy, good-looking, gorgeous, graceful, grand, handsome, ideal, lovely, magnificent, marvelous, nice, pleasing, pretty, pulchritudinous, radiant, ravishing, refined, resplendent, shapely, sightly, splendid, statuesque, stunning, sublime, superb, symmetrical, taking,

well-formed, wonderful; SEE CONCEPTS *485,579, 589*

beautifully [*adv*] *in an attractive or pleasing manner*
alluringly, appealingly, attractively, bewitchingly, celestially, charmingly, cutely, delightfully, divinely, elegantly, entrancingly, excellently, exquisitely, gorgeously, gracefully, handsomely, ideally, magnificently, prettily, seductively, splendidly, sublimely, superbly, tastefully, wonderfully; SEE CONCEPT *544*

beautify [*v*] *make more physically attractive*
adorn, array, bedeck, deck, decorate, dress up, embellish, enhance, garnish, gild, glamorize, grace, improve, make up, ornament, prettify, set off, trim; SEE CONCEPT *162*

beauty [*n1*] *physical attractiveness*
adorableness, allure, allurement, artistry, attraction, bloom, charm, class, comeliness, delicacy, elegance, exquisiteness, fairness, fascination, glamor, good looks, grace, handsomeness, loveliness, polish, pulchritude, refinement, shapeliness, style, symmetry, winsomeness; SEE CONCEPT *718*

beauty [*n2*] *good-looking person*
Adonis*, Apollo*, beaut*, belle, charmer, dream, dreamboat*, enchanter, enchantress, eyeful*, femme fatale, goddess, good-looker*, head turner*, hunk*, knockout*, looker*, lovely, ornament*, seducer, seductress, siren, stunner*, Venus*, vision*; SEE CONCEPTS *415,424*

beauty [*n3*] *advantage*
asset, attraction, benefit, blessing, boon, excellent, feature, good thing, importance, merit, value, worth; SEE CONCEPT *668*

because [*conj/prep*] *on account of*
as, as a result of, as long as, as things go, being, by cause of, by reason of, by virtue of, considering, due to, for, for the reason that, for the sake of, in as much as, in behalf of, in that, in the interest of, in view of, now that, on the grounds that, over, owing to, seeing, since, thanks to, through, whereas; SEE CONCEPT *676*

beckon [*v*] *call, signal, or lure*
allure, ask, attract, bid, coax, command, demand, draw, entice, gesticulate, gesture, invite, motion, nod, pull, sign, summon, tempt, wave; SEE CONCEPTS *7,22,53,74*

become [*v1*] *evolve into*
alter to, assume form of, be converted to, be reduced to, be reformed, be remodeled, be transformed into, change into, come, come to be, convert, develop into, emerge as, eventually be, grow into, incline, mature, metamorphose, pass into, ripen into, shift, turn into, turn out, wax; SEE CONCEPT *701*

become [*v2*] *enhance*
accord, adorn, agree, augment, be appropriate, belong to, display, embellish, enrich, fit, flatter, garnish, go together, go with, grace, harmonize,

heighten, make handsome, match, ornament, set off, suit; SEE CONCEPT *244*

becoming [*adj1*] *flattering*
acceptable, agreeable, attractive, beautiful, comely, cute, effective, enhancing, excellent, fair, graceful, handsome, neat, nice, presentable, pretty, seemly, tasteful, welcome, well-chosen; SEE CONCEPTS *579,589*

becoming [*adj2*] *suitable; appropriate*
befitting, comme il faut, compatible, conforming, congruous, correct, decent, decorous, fit, fitting, in keeping, nice, proper, right, seemly, worthy; SEE CONCEPT *558*

bed [*n1*] *furniture for sleeping*
bassinet, bedstead, berth, bunk, chaise, cot, couch, cradle, crib, davenport, divan, mattress, pallet, platform, sack, trundle; SEE CONCEPT *443*

bed [*n2*] *patch of ground for planting*
area, border, frame, garden, piece, plot, row, strip; SEE CONCEPTS *509,513*

bed [*n3*] *base, foundation*
basis, bedrock, bottom, ground, groundwork, rest, seat, substratum, understructure; SEE CONCEPT *442*

bed [*v*] *plant*
base, embed, establish, fix, found, implant, insert, settle, set up; SEE CONCEPTS *234,257*

bedazzle [*v*] *captivate*
astound, bewilder, blind, confuse, daze, dazzle, dumbfound, enchant, overwhelm, stagger, stun; SEE CONCEPTS *7,22,42*

bedding [*n*] *covering for sleeping furniture*
bedclothes, bed linen, bedspread, blanket, comforter, cover, coverlet, eiderdown, electric blanket, linen, pillow, pillowcase, quilt, sheet, spread, thermal blanket; SEE CONCEPTS *444,473*

bedlam [*n*] *chaotic situation*
chaos, clamor, commotion, confusion, din, disquiet, disquietude, furor, hubbub, madhouse, maelstrom, noise, pandemonium, racket, shambles, tumult, turmoil, uproar; SEE CONCEPTS *230,674*

bedraggled [*adj*] *unkempt*
decrepit, dilapidated, dirty, disheveled, disordered, dowdy, drenched, dripping, faded, messy, muddied, muddy, run-down, seedy, shabby, sloppy, slovenly, sodden, soiled, stained, sullied, tacky, tattered, threadbare, untidy, wet; SEE CONCEPT *589*

bedroom [*n*] *place for sleeping*
bedchamber, bunk room, chamber, cubicle, guest room; SEE CONCEPT *448*

bedspread [*n*] *thick, often quilted, covering for bed*
bedcover, blanket, counterpane, cover, coverlet, spread; SEE CONCEPT *444*

bee [*n1*] *honey-making, stinging insect*
bumblebee, drone, honey bee, killer bee, queen bee; SEE CONCEPT *398*

bee [*n2*] *collective task*
communal gathering, harvest, party, social, work party; SEE CONCEPTS *362,386*

beef [*n1*] *strong physical makeup*
arm, brawn, flesh, force, heftiness, meat, might, muscle, physique, power, robustness, sinew, steam, strength, thew, vigor; SEE CONCEPT *757*

beef [*n2*] *complaint*
bickering, criticism, dispute, grievance, gripe, grouse, grumble, objection, protestation, quarrel, rhubarb*; SEE CONCEPT *52*

beer [*n*] *alcoholic beverage made from malted grain*
a chill*, ale, amber brew*, barley pop*, brew, brewski*, brown bottle*, cold coffee*, cold one*, hops, lager, malt, malt liquor, oil*, stout*, suds*; SEE CONCEPT *455*

befall [*v*] *happen to; take place*
action, bechance, betide, break, chance, come down, come off, come to pass, cook*, cook up a storm*, cook with gas*, develop, ensue, fall, fall out, follow, gel, go, go down, hap*, happen, jell*, materialize, occur, shake*, smoke*, supervene, transpire; SEE CONCEPT *4*

befitting [*adj*] *appropriate*
according to Hoyle*, apt, becoming, behooving, beseeming, comme il faut, conforming, correct, decent, decorous, felicitous, fit, fitting, happy, just, kosher*, nice, on the button*, on the nose*, proper, right, right on*, seemly, suitable, what the doctor ordered*; SEE CONCEPTS *533,558*

before [*adv*] *earlier*
afore, aforetime, ahead, ante, antecedently, anteriorly, back, before present, ere, fore, former, formerly, forward, gone, gone by, heretofore, in advance, in days of yore, in front, in old days, in the past, past, precedently, previous, previously, since, sooner, up to now, vanward; SEE CONCEPT *820*

before [*prep*] *earlier than*
ahead of, ante, antecedent to, anterior to, ere, in advance of, in front of, preceding, previous to, prior to, since; SEE CONCEPT *820*

beforehand [*adj/adv*] *early*
advanced, ahead, ahead of time, already, ante, antecedently, before, before now, earlier, fore, in advance, in anticipation, precedently, precocious, previous, previously, sooner; SEE CONCEPT *820*

befriend [*v*] *make social acquaintance; support*
advise, aid, assist, back, benefit, buddy up*, case out*, come on to*, cotton to*, encourage, favor, get chummy with, get in with*, help, hit it off*, patronize, side with, stand by, sustain, take up with, take under one's wing*, uphold, welcome; SEE CONCEPTS *110,384*

befuddle [*v*] *confuse*
addle, baffle, ball up*, bewilder, bother, daze, disorient, distract, dumbfound, fluster, inebriate, intoxicate, make punchy*, mix up, muddle, puzzle, shake, stupefy, throw off*; SEE CONCEPTS *7,19,42*

beg [*v1*] *request*
abjure, advocate, apply to, ask, beseech, besiege, call to, canvass, conjure, crave, desire, entreat, im-

petrate, implore, importune, invoke, nag, obsecrate, obtest, petition, plead, pray, press, requisition, solicit, sue, supplicate, urge, woo, worry; SEE CONCEPT *48*

beg [*v2*] *seek charity*
ask alms, benefit, bite*, brace, bum*, burn*, buzz*, cadge*, call on, call upon, chisel*, clamor for, dime up*, ding*, freeload*, hit up*, hustle, knock, live hand to mouth*, mendicate, mooch*, nick*, nickel up*, panhandle, pass the hat*, put the bite on*, put the touch on*, score*, scrounge, solicit charity, sponge*, sponge on*, tap*, touch*, want; SEE CONCEPT *53*

beget [*v*] *create, bear*
afford, breed, bring, bring about, cause, effect, engender, father, generate, get, give rise to, multiply, occasion, procreate, produce, progenerate, propagate, reproduce, result in, sire; SEE CONCEPTS *173,251,374*

beggar [*n1*] *person asking for charity*
asker, borrower, bum, deadbeat, hobo, mendicant, panhandler, rustler, scrounger, supplicant, supplicator, tramp, vagabond; SEE CONCEPTS *412,423*

beggar [*n2*] *person in financial trouble*
almsman/woman, bankrupt, dependent, destitute, down-and-out*, guttersnipe*, indigent, mendicant, pauper, poor person, poverty-stricken person, street person*, suppliant, vagrant, ward of state; SEE CONCEPT *423*

begin [*v1*] *start*
activate, actualize, break ground, break the ice*, bring about, bring to pass, cause, commence, create, do, drive, effect, embark on, enter on, enter upon, establish, eventuate, found, generate, get going, give birth to, give impulse, go ahead, go into, impel, inaugurate, induce, initiate, instigate, institute, introduce, launch, lay foundation for, lead, make, make active, motivate, mount, occasion, open, originate, plunge into, prepare, produce, set about, set in motion, set up, trigger, undertake; SEE CONCEPTS *234,241*

begin [*v2*] *come into being; become functional*
appear, arise, be born, bud, come forth, come into existence, come out, commence, crop up, dawn, derive from, emanate, emerge, enter, germinate, get going, get show on road*, get under way, grow out of, happen, issue forth, kick off, make tick*, occur, originate, proceed from, result from, rise, sail, send off, set, spring, sprout, start, stem from, take off; SEE CONCEPTS *105,680*

beginner [*n*] *person unskilled in something*
abecedarian, amateur, apprentice, buckwheater*, catechumen, colt, fish*, fledgling, freshman, greenhorn, greenie*, initiate, learner, neophyte, new boy/girl, newcomer, new kid on the block*, novice, novitiate, probationer, recruit, starter, student, tenderfoot*, trainee, tyro*; SEE CONCEPTS *423,424*

beginning [*n1*] *start of an event or action*
alpha, basis, birth, blastoff*, commencement, creation, dawn, dawning, day one*, genesis, inaugura-tion, inception, induction, infancy, initiation, installation, introduction, kickoff, onset, opener, opening, origin, origination, outset, point of departure, preface, prelude, presentation, rise, root, rudiment, source, spring, square one*, starting point, takeoff, threshold, top; SEE CONCEPTS *815,833*

beginning [*n2*] *origin, cause*
antecedent, birth, conception, egg, embryo, font, fount, fountain, fountainhead, generation, genesis, germ, heart, principle, resource, root, seed, stem, well; SEE CONCEPT *240*

begrudge [*v*] *wish that someone did not have*
be jealous, be reluctant, be stingy, covet, eat one's heart out, envy, grudge, pinch, resent, stint; SEE CONCEPTS *17,21*

beguile [*v1*] *fool*
betray, bluff, burn*, cheat, chisel, con, deceive, delude, double-cross, dupe, entice, exploit, finesse, flimflam*, gyp*, have, hoodwink*, impose on, jockey, juggle, lure, manipulate, mislead, play, play for a sucker*, rook*, rope in*, scam, seduce, shave*, snow*, stick*, string along, suck in*, take, take in, trick; SEE CONCEPT *59*

beguile [*v2*] *charm*
amuse, attract, cheer, delight, distract, divert, engross, entertain, entice, knock dead, knock out, lure, occupy, seduce, send, slay, solace, sweep off one's feet, tickle, tickle pink*, tickle to death*, turn on, vamp, wow; SEE CONCEPTS *7,19,22*

behalf [*n*] *personal interest*
account, advantage, aid, assistance, benefit, cause, concern, countenance, defense, encouragement, favor, furtherance, good, help, part, place, profit, recommendation, representation, sake, service, side, stead, support, welfare; SEE CONCEPTS *410,532*

behave [*v1*] *function*
act, operate, perform, react, run, take, work; SEE CONCEPTS *1,4*

behave [*v2*] *act reasonably, properly*
act correctly, act one's age, act with decorum, be civil, be good, be nice, be on best behavior*, be orderly, comport oneself, conduct oneself properly, control, demean oneself, deport oneself, direct, discipline oneself, keep one's nose clean*, keep the peace, live up to, manage, manage oneself, mind one's manners*, mind p's and q's*, observe golden rule*, observe the law*, play fair, shape up, toe the mark*, watch one's step*; SEE CONCEPT *633*

behavior [*n*] *manner of conducting oneself*
act, action, address, air, attitude, bag, bearing, carriage, code, comportment, conduct, convention, course, dealings, decency, decorum, deed, delivery, demeanor, deportment, ethics, etiquette, expression, form, front, guise, habits, management, mien, mode, morals, nature, observance, performance, practice, presence, propriety, ritual, role, routine, savoir-faire, seemliness, social graces, speech, style, tact, talk,

taste, tenue, tone, way, way of life, ways, what's done; SEE CONCEPTS *633,655*

behead [*v*] *decapitate*
bring to the block, decollate, execute, guillotine, head, kill, neck; SEE CONCEPT *176*

behest [*n*] *order; personal decree*
bidding, charge, command, commandment, demand, dictate, direction, expressed desire, injunction, instruction, mandate, order, precept, prompting, request, solicitation, wish, word; SEE CONCEPTS *20,53*

behind [*n*] *buttocks*
backside, bottom, breech, can*, derrière, fanny*, fundament, posterior, rear, rump, seat, tail, tush*; SEE CONCEPT *392*

behind [*adv1/prep1*] *position farther back; following*
abaft, after, afterwards, at the heels of*, at the rear of, back of, bringing up the rear*, eating the dust*, in the background, in the wake, later than, next, off the pace, subsequently, trailing; SEE CONCEPTS *586,820*

behind [*adv2*] *in debt; late*
backward, behindhand, behind schedule, behind time, belated, delayed, dilatory, have to play catch up*, in arrears, laggard, overdue, slow, sluggish, tardy; SEE CONCEPTS *334,799*

behind [*prep2*] *being the reason for*
at the bottom of, causing, concerning the circumstances, initiating, instigating, responsible for; SEE CONCEPT *532*

behind [*prep3*] *in support*
backing, for, in agreement, on the side of, supporting; SEE CONCEPT *388*

behold [*v*] *regard; look at*
catch, consider, contemplate, descry, discern, distinguish, earmark, eye, eyeball*, feast one's eyes*, flash*, lay eyes on*, note, notice, observe, perceive, regard, scan, see, spot, spy, survey, view, watch, witness; SEE CONCEPTS *34,626*

beholden [*adj*] *indebted*
bound, grateful, in hock, into, obligated, obliged, on a string*, on the arm*, on the cuff*, on the tab*, owe one, owing, responsible, under obligation; SEE CONCEPT *403*

behoove [*v*] *be necessary, proper*
be expected, befit, be fitting, be incumbent upon, be needful, be one's obligation, be required, be requisite, be right, beseem, owe it to, suit; SEE CONCEPT *646*

beige [*n/adj*] *light brown color*
biscuit, buff, café au lait, camel, cream, ecru, fawn, khaki, mushroom, neutral, oatmeal, off-white, sand, tan, taupe; SEE CONCEPTS *618,622*

being [*n1*] *existence*
actuality, animation, journey, life, living, presence, reality, subsistence, vitality, world; SEE CONCEPT *407*

being [*n2*] *essential nature*
character, entity, essence, essentia, essentiality, individuality, marrow, personality, quintessence, self-

dom, soul, spirit, substance, texture; SEE CONCEPTS *411,673*

being [*n3*] *animate object*
animal, beast, body, conscious thing, creature, entity, human, human being, individual, living thing, mortal, organism, person, personage, soul, thing; SEE CONCEPT *389*

belated [*adj*] *late, slow*
behindhand, behind time, delayed, long-delayed, overdue, remiss, tardy, unpunctual; SEE CONCEPT *820*

belch [*v*] *burp; spew*
discharge, disgorge, emit, eruct, eructate, erupt, give off, gush, hiccup, irrupt, repeat, ventilate, vomit; SEE CONCEPT *185*

beleaguer [*v*] *harass, besiege*
annoy, badger, bedevil, beset, blockade, bother, gnaw, harry, nag, persecute, pester, plague, put upon, set upon, siege, storm, tease, vex, worry; SEE CONCEPTS *7,19*

belfry [*n*] *tower; part of tower*
bell tower, campanile, carillon, clocher, cupola, dome, head, minaret, spire, steeple, turret; SEE CONCEPT *440*

belie [*v1*] *disprove*
confute, contradict, contravene, controvert, deny, disaffirm, disagree, explode, gainsay, negate, negative, oppose, repudiate; SEE CONCEPTS *54,58*

belie [*v2*] *deceive*
color, conceal, disguise, distort, falsify, garble, give the lie to, gloss over, hide, miscolor, mislead, misrepresent, misstate, pervert, trump up, twist, warp; SEE CONCEPT *63*

belief [*n1*] *putting regard in as true*
acceptance, admission, assent, assumption, assurance, avowal, axiom, certainty, conclusion, confidence, conjecture, conviction, credence, credit, deduction, divination, expectation, faith, fancy, feeling, guess, hope, hypothesis, idea, impression, intuition, judgment, knowledge, mind, mindset, notion, opinion, persuasion, position, postulation, presumption, presupposition, profession, reliance, supposition, surmise, suspicion, theorem, theory, thesis, thinking, trust, understanding, view; SEE CONCEPTS *410,529*

belief [*n2*] *something regarded as true, trustworthy*
assumption, concept, credence, credo, creed, doctrine, dogma, faith, fundamental, gospel, gospel truth*, hypothesis, idea, ideology, law, opinion, postulate, precept, principle, say-so*, tenet, theorem, theory; SEE CONCEPT *689*

believable [*adj*] *trustworthy*
aboveboard, acceptable, authentic, colorable, conceivable, convincing, credential, credible, creditable, fiduciary, honest to God*, imaginable, impressive, likely, persuasive, plausible, possible, presumable, presumptive, probable, rational, reasonable, reliable, satisfying, straight, supposable, tena-

ble, tried, trusty, unquestionable, up front*; SEE CONCEPTS *403,582*

believe [*v1*] *trust, rely on*
accept, accredit, admit, affirm, attach weight to, be certain of, be convinced of, be credulous, be of the opinion, buy, conceive, conclude, consider, count on, credit, deem, fall for*, give credence to, have, have faith in, have no doubt, hold, keep the faith, lap up*, opine, place confidence in, posit, postulate, presume true, presuppose, reckon on, regard, rest assured, suppose, swallow*, swear by, take as gospel*, take at one's word, take for granted, take it, think, trust, understand; SEE CONCEPT *12*

believe [*v2*] *assume or suppose*
conjecture, consider, credit, deem, expect, feel, gather, guess, hold, imagine, judge, maintain, postulate, presume, reckon, sense, speculate, suppose, suspect, take, think, understand; SEE CONCEPT *28*

believer [*n*] *person who has trust, faith in something*
acceptor, adherent, apostle, canonist, convert, devotee, disciple, doctrinaire, dogmatist, follower, freak, orthodox, prophet, proselyte, religionist, religious person, supporter, upholder, zealot; SEE CONCEPTS *361,423*

belittle [*v*] *detract*
bad-mouth, blister, criticize, cut down to size*, cut to the quick*, decry, deprecate, depreciate, deride, derogate, diminish, discount, discredit, disparage, dispraise, downgrade, downplay, dump on*, knock*, lower, minimize, pan, pooh pooh*, poor mouth*, put down, rip*, roast*, run down, scoff at, scorch*, scorn, shoot down*, shoot full of holes*, slam*, smear, sneer at, sour grapes*, squash*, squelch, take a swipe at*, take down, take down a peg*, tear down*, underestimate, underrate, undervalue, write off; SEE CONCEPTS *52,54*

bell [*n*] *signaling object or sound*
alarm, buzz, buzzer, carillon, chime, clapper, curfew, ding-dong, dinger, gong, peal, ringer, siren, tintinnabulum, tocsin, toll, vesper; SEE CONCEPT *595*

belligerent [*adj*] *nasty, argumentative*
aggressive, antagonistic, ardent, at loggerheads*, battling, bellicose, cantankerous, combative, contentious, fierce, fighting, flip, have a bone to pick*, have chip on shoulder*, have it in for*, hostile, hot, hot-tempered, mean, militant, on the outs*, ornery, pugnacious, quarrelsome, scrappy, truculent, warlike; SEE CONCEPTS *401,404*

bellow [*v*] *holler*
bark, bawl, bay, beller, blare, bluster, bray, call, clamor, cry, howl, low, roar, rout, scream, shout, shriek, wail, whoop, yawp, yell, yelp; SEE CONCEPT *77*

belly [*n*] *stomach*
abdomen, bay window*, beer belly*, breadbasket*, corporation*, front porch*, gut, insides, intestines, paunch, pelvis, pot*, pot belly*, solar plexus, spare tire*, tank, tummy, venter; SEE CONCEPT *393*

belong [*v1*] *be part of, be in proper place*
accord, agree, appertain, apply, associate, attach to, be a component, be a constituent, be a part, be akin, be an adjunct of, bear, bear upon, become, be connected with, befit, be fitting, be linked with, be related, be relevant, chime, concern, correlate, correspond, exist, fit, go, go with, harmonize, have relationship to, have respect to, have to do with, inhere, match, permeate, pertain, refer, regard, reside, set, suit, touch, vest; SEE CONCEPTS *532,543*

belong [*v2*] *be affiliated with*
be allied to, be a member, be a member of, be associated with, be classified among, be contained in, be included in, be one of, be one of the family, be part of, fit in, have a place, in, in with, owe allegiance, owe support, run with*, swing*, swing with*, take one's place with; SEE CONCEPTS *114,388*

belonging [*n*] *sense of security in friendship*
acceptance, affinity, association, attachment, fellowship, inclusion, kinship, loyalty, rapport, relationship; SEE CONCEPTS *388,410*

belongings [*n*] *personal possessions*
accouterments, appurtenances, assets, chattels, effects, gear, goods, paraphernalia, personal property, property, stuff, things; SEE CONCEPTS *446,710*

beloved [*n*] *someone adored*
baby*, beau, boyfriend, darling, dear, dearest, doll*, fiancé, flame, girlfriend, heartbeat*, heartthrob, honey, idol, inamorato, love, love of my life*, lover, number one*, numero uno*, object of affection, old lady*, old man*, one and only, pet*, prize, rave*, significant other, steady, sugar*, sweetheart, tootsie*, treasure, true love; SEE CONCEPT *423*

beloved [*adj*] *adored*
admired, cared for, cherished, darling, dear, dearest, doted on, endeared, esteemed, fair-haired, favorite, hallowed, highly regarded, highly valued, idolized, loved, near to one's heart*, pet*, pleasing, popular, precious, prized, respected, revered, sweet, treasured, venerated, well-liked, worshiped; SEE CONCEPTS *568,572*

below [*adv/prep*] *lower*
beneath, down, down from, under, underneath; SEE CONCEPTS *581,586,735*

below [*prep2*] *less than; beneath*
inferior, lesser, lower, subject, subordinate, unworthy; SEE CONCEPTS *567,771*

belt [*n1*] *supporting band*
cincture, cummerbund, girdle, ribbon, ring, sash, strap, string, waistband; SEE CONCEPT *450*

belt [*n2*] *strip of land with characteristic feature*
area, district, layer, region, stretch, territory, tract, zone; SEE CONCEPTS *513,517*

belt [*v*] *hit hard*
bash, bat, biff, blast, blow, bop, clobber, slam, slug, smack, smash, sock, strap, switch, wallop, whip, whop; SEE CONCEPT *189*

bemoan [v] *express sorrow*
beat one's breast*, bewail, complain, cry over spilled milk*, deplore, grieve for, lament, moan over, mourn, regret, rue, sing the blues*, weep for; SEE CONCEPTS *49,51*

bemuse [v] *confuse*
addle, amaze, bewilder, daydream, daze, gather wool*, moon, muddle, overwhelm, paralyze, perplex, pipe dream*, puzzle, stun, stupefy; SEE CONCEPTS *7,19,22*

bench [n1] *furniture for sitting*
bank, chair, form, lawn seat, pew, seat, settee, settle, stall; SEE CONCEPT *443*

bench [n2] *large table*
board, counter, desk, easel, ledge, shelf, trestle, workbench, work table; SEE CONCEPT *443*

bench [n3] *group of judges*
court, courtroom, his/her honor, judiciary, magistrate, the bar, tribunal; SEE CONCEPTS *318,355*

benchmark [n] *reference point*
criterion, gauge, measure, standard, touchstone, yardstick; SEE CONCEPT *687*

bend [n] *curve*
angle, arc, bending, bow, corner, crook, curvation, curvature, deflection, deviation, flection, flexure, hook, lean, loop, round, sag, shift, tack, tilt, turn, twist, yaw, zigzag; SEE CONCEPT *436*

bend [v1] *form or cause a curve*
angle away, angle off, arch, bow, buckle, camber, careen, circle, contort, crimp, crinkle, crook, crouch, curl, deflect, deform, detour, double, droop, flex, genuflect, hook, incline, incurvate, lean, loop, pervert, round, spiral, stoop, swerve, tilt, turn, twist, veer, verge, warp, waver, wilt, wind, yaw, zigzag; SEE CONCEPTS *149,184*

bend [v2] *persuade; influence*
change mind, compel, direct, mold, shape, subdue, submit, sway, yield; SEE CONCEPT *68*

beneath [adv] *in a lower place*
below, underneath; SEE CONCEPT *586*

beneath [prep] *inferior*
below, lesser, less than, lower than, subject, subordinate, unbefitting, under, underneath, unworthy of; SEE CONCEPT *567*

benediction [n] *closing prayer*
amen, approbation, approval, beatitude, benedictus, benison, blessing, consecration, favor, grace, gratitude, invocation, laying on of hands, okay, orison, praise, sanctification, thanks, thanksgiving; SEE CONCEPT *69*

benefactor [n] *donor*
aid, altruist, angel, assistant, backer, contributor, fairy godmother*, fan, good Samaritan, grubstaker, helper, humanitarian, mark, patron, philanthropist, promoter, protector, Santa Claus*, sponsor, subscriber, subsidizer, supporter, well-wisher; SEE CONCEPTS *416,423*

beneficial [adj] *advantageous*
benign, constructive, favorable, favoring, gainful, good, good for what ails you*, healthful, helpful, profitable, propitious, salubrious, salutary, serviceable, toward, useful, valuable, what the doctor ordered*, wholesome, worthy; SEE CONCEPTS *567,572*

beneficiary [n] *person who gains, benefits*
almsman, assignee, charity case, devisee, donee, grantee, heir, heiress, inheritor, legatee, payee, pensioner, possessor, receiver, recipient, stipendiary, successor; SEE CONCEPTS *355,423*

benefit [n1] *advantage, profit*
account, aid, asset, assistance, avail, benediction, betterment, blessing, boon, cream*, egg in one's beer*, extras, favor, gain, godsend*, good, gravy*, help, interest, perk*, profit, prosperity, use, welfare, worth; SEE CONCEPTS *337,346,661*

benefit [n2] *event to raise money*
ball, bazaar, charitable affair, charity performance, concert, dance, dinner, exhibit, exhibition, fair, pancake breakfast, raffle; SEE CONCEPT *386*

benefit [v] *help, enhance*
advance, advantage, aid, ameliorate, assist, avail, be good for, better, build, contribute to, do for one, do the trick, favor, fill the bill*, further, improve, make a killing*, make it*, pay, pay off*, profit, promote, relieve, serve, succor, work for; SEE CONCEPTS *110,244*

benevolence [n] *charity*
altruism, amity, comity, compassion, feeling, friendliness, friendship, generosity, gift, goodness, good will, humanity, kindheartedness, kindness, sympathy; SEE CONCEPT *633*

benevolent [adj] *charitable, kind*
all heart, altruistic, beneficent, benign, big, bighearted, bounteous, bountiful, caring, chivalrous, compassionate, considerate, generous, helpful, humane, humanitarian, kindhearted, liberal, magnanimous, philanthropic, tenderhearted, warmhearted, well-disposed; SEE CONCEPT *401*

benign [adj1] *kindly*
amiable, beneficent, benevolent, benignant, complaisant, congenial, favorable, friendly, generous, genial, gentle, good, goodhearted, gracious, kind, liberal, merciful, mild, obliging, sympathetic; SEE CONCEPT *542*

benign [adj2] *mild, especially describing weather*
auspicious, balmy, bright, favorable, fortunate, gentle, healthful, propitious, refreshing, temperate, warm; SEE CONCEPT *605*

benign [adj3] *advantageous*
auspicious, beneficent, benevolent, bright, charitable, dexter, encouraging, favorable, fortunate, good, lucky, merciful, propitious, salutary, smiling; SEE CONCEPTS *537,572*

benign [adj4] *not cancerous*
curable, early stage, harmless, limited, remediable, slight, superficial; SEE CONCEPT *314*

bent [n] *inclination; talent*
ability, aim, aptitude, bag*, disposition, druthers*, facility, faculty, flair, forte, genius, gift, head-set*, inclining, knack, leaning, mind-set*, nose, penchant, predilection, predisposition, preference, proclivity, propensity, set, tack, tendency, thing for*, tilt, turn, weakness for; SEE CONCEPTS *409,630*

bent [adj1] *curved*
angled, arced, arched, arciform, bowed, contorted, crooked, curvilinear, doubled over, drooping, droopy, hooked, humped, hunched, inclined, limp, looped, round, rounded, sinuous, slouchy, slumped, stooped, twined, twisted, warped, wilted; SEE CONCEPT *486*

bent [adj2] *determined*
bound, decided, decisive, dedicated, disposed, firm, fixed, inclined, insistent, intent, leaning, predisposed, resolute, resolved, set, settled, tending; SEE CONCEPT *403*

bequeath [v] *give in a will*
bestow, commit, devise, endow, entrust, grant, hand down, hand on, impart, leave, leave to, legate, pass on, transmit, will; SEE CONCEPTS *108,317*

bequest [n] *something given in will*
bequeathal, bequeathment, bestowal, devisal, devise, dower, endowment, estate, gift, heritage, inheritance, legacy, settlement, trust; SEE CONCEPTS *318,337*

berate [v] *criticize hatefully*
bawl out, blister, call down, castigate, censure, chew*, chew out*, chide, cuss out*, eat out*, give one hell*, give what for*, jaw*, jump all over*, rail at*, rake over the coals*, rate, rebuke, reprimand, reproach, reprove, revile, scold, scorch, tell off, tongue-lash, upbraid, vituperate; SEE CONCEPT *52*

bereavement [n] *death; loss*
affliction, deprivation, distress, misfortune, sorrow, tribulation; SEE CONCEPTS *230,674*

bereft [adj] *lacking; missing*
beggared, bereaved, cut off, deprived, destitute, devoid, dispossessed, divested, fleeced, impoverished, left without, minus, naked, parted from, robbed, shorn, stripped, wanting, without; SEE CONCEPTS *546,576*

berry [n] *small fruit*
bean, drupe, drupelet, grain, haw, hip, kernel, pome, seed; SEE CONCEPT *426*

berth [n1] *harbor; bunk*
anchorage, bed, bedroom, billet, compartment, cot, dock, hammock, haven, jetty, levee, pier, port, quay, slip, wharf; SEE CONCEPTS *513,516*

berth [n2] *position of responsibility*
appointment, billet, capacity, connection, employment, job, living, office, place, post, profession, situation, spot; SEE CONCEPTS *362,668*

beseech [v] *beg*
adjure, appeal, ask, call upon, crave, entreat, implore, importune, invoke, petition, plead, pray, solicit, sue, supplicate; SEE CONCEPT *48*

beset [v] *plague; hem in*
aggress, assail, attack, badger, bedevil, beleaguer, besiege, bug*, circle*, compass, dog*, drive up the wall*, embarrass, encircle, enclose, encompass, entangle, environ, fall on, fall upon, girdle, give a bad time*, give a hard time*, give one the business*, give the needle*, harass, harry, hassle, infest, invade, jump on one's case*, nag, nudge, overrun, perplex, pester, pick on, put the squeeze on*, ride, ring, start in on, storm, strike, surround; SEE CONCEPTS *7,19*

beside [adv/prep] *next to*
abreast of, adjacent to, adjoining, alongside, aside, a step from, at one's elbow, at the edge of, at the side of, bordering on, by, cheek by jowl*, close at hand, close to, close upon, connected with, contiguous to, fornent, in juxtaposition, near, nearby, neck and neck*, neighboring, next door to, nigh, opposite, overlooking, round, side by side, verging on, with; SEE CONCEPT *586*

besides [adv] *in addition; as well*
added to, additionally, along with, also, and all, apart from, aside from, as well as, beyond, conjointly, else, exceeding, exclusive of, extra, further, furthermore, in conjunction with, in distinction to, in excess of, in other respects, likewise, more, moreover, more than, not counting, on the side, on top of everything, other than, otherwise, over and above, plus, secondly, supplementary to, to boot*, together with, too, what's more*, with the exception of, yet; SEE CONCEPT *772*

besides [prep1] *apart from*
aside from, bar, barring, beside, but, except, excepting, excluding, exclusive of, in addition to, other than, outside of, over and above, save, without; SEE CONCEPT *772*

besides [prep2] *in addition to*
added to, along with, as well as, beside, beyond, in excess of, more than, on top of, other than, over and above, plus, supplementary, together with; SEE CONCEPTS *542,772*

besiege [v1] *surround; assault*
assail, attack, beleaguer, beset, blockade, come at from all sides, confine, congregate, encircle, encompass, environ, hem in, invest, lay siege to, shut in, trap, work on, work over; SEE CONCEPTS *86,90*

besiege [v2] *bother*
badger, beleaguer, bug*, buttonhole*, harass, harry, hound*, importune, nag, pester, plague, trouble; SEE CONCEPTS *7,19*

best [n1] *most outstanding thing in class*
choice, cream, cream of the crop*, elite, fat, favorite, finest, first, flower, gem, model, nonpareil, paragon, pick, prime, prize, select, top; SEE CONCEPT *668*

best [n2] *highest personal effort*
all one's got, best shot, hardest, highest endeavor, one's level best*, Sunday best*, utmost; SEE CONCEPT *411*

best [*adj1*] *most excellent*
10*, A-1*, ace, bad*, beyond compare, boss*, capital, champion, chief, choicest, cool*, culminating, finest, first, first-class, first-rate, foremost, greatest, highest, incomparable, inimitable, leading, matchless, nonpareil, number 1*, optimum, out-of-sight*, outstanding, paramount, peerless, perfect, preeminent, premium, prime, primo*, principal, sans pareil, second to none, super, superlative, supreme, terrific, tops, tough, transcendent, unequaled, unparalleled, unrivaled, unsurpassed; SEE CONCEPTS *568,572*

best [*adj2*] *correct, right*
advantageous, apt, desirable, golden, most desirable, most fitting, preferred, presentable; SEE CONCEPT *558*

best [*adj3*] *most*
biggest, bulkiest, greatest, largest; SEE CONCEPT *771*

best [*v*] *defeat; gain advantage*
beat, beat up*, better, blank*, blast*, bulldoze*, clobber*, conquer, cream*, deck*, drub*, exceed, excel, flax*, floor*, get the better of, KO, knock off*, lambaste, let have it*, lick*, master, outclass, outdo, outshine, outstrip, overcome, prevail, put away, shoot down*, shut down*, surpass, take care of, take down*, tan*, thrash*, top, total, transcend, trash*, triumph, triumph over, trounce, wallop, waste*, wax*, whip*, whomp*, whop*, wipe, wipe out, wipe the floor with*, zap; SEE CONCEPT *95*

best [*adv*] *most excellently*
advantageously, attractively, creditably, extremely, gloriously, greatly, honorably, illustriously, magnanimously, most deeply, most fortunately, most fully, most highly, sincerely; SEE CONCEPTS *568,572*

bestow [*v*] *give, allot*
accord, apportion, award, bequeath, come through, commit, confer, devote, donate, entrust, favor, gift, give away, grant, hand out, honor with, impart, kick in, lavish, offer, present, put out, render to; SEE CONCEPTS *98,108*

bet [*n*] *game of chance; money gambled*
action, ante, betting, chance, down on, hazard, long shot, lot, lottery, odds, odds on, parlay, play, pledge, plunge, pot, raffle, random shot, risk, shot, shot in the dark*, speculation, stake, sweepstakes, uncertainty, venture, wager; SEE CONCEPTS *28,293,329*

bet [*v*] *gamble*
ante, buy in on, chance, dice, game, hazard, lay down, lay odds, play against, play for, play the ponies*, pledge, pony up*, put, put money on, risk, set, speculate, tempt fortune*, toss up, trust, venture, wager; SEE CONCEPTS *292,330*

betray [*v1*] *be disloyal*
abandon, be unfaithful, bite the hand that feeds you*, blow the whistle*, bluff, break faith, break promise, break trust, break with, commit treason, cross, deceive, deliver up*, delude, desert, double-cross, finger*, forsake, go back on, inform against, inform on, jilt, knife*, let down, mislead, play false*, play Ju-

das*, seduce, sell down the river*, sell out, stab in the back*, take in*, trick, turn in, turn informer, turn state's evidence, walk out on; SEE CONCEPT *384*

betray [*v2*] *divulge, expose information*
blurt out, disclose, evince, fink on*, give away, inform, lay bare, let slip, make known, manifest, rat on*, reveal, show, sing*, snitch*, spill, squeal*, stool*, tattle, tell, tell on, turn in, uncover, unmask; SEE CONCEPTS *44,60*

betrayal [*n1*] *exhibition of disloyalty*
deception, dishonesty, double-crossing, double-dealing, duplicity, falseness, giveaway, Judas kiss*, let-down, perfidy, sellout, treachery, treason, trickery, unfaithfulness; SEE CONCEPT *633*

betrayal [*n2*] *divulgence of information*
blurting out, disclosure, giving away, ratting*, revelation, snitching*, spilling*, squealing*, tattling, telling; SEE CONCEPTS *44,60*

betroth [*v*] *marry*
affiance, become engaged, bind, commit, contract, engage, espouse, give one's hand, make compact, plight faith, plight troth, promise, tie oneself to, vow; SEE CONCEPT *297*

betrothal [*n*] *marriage*
affiancing, betrothing, engagement, espousal, plight, promise, troth, vow; SEE CONCEPT *297*

better [*adj1*] *excelling, more excellent*
bigger, choice, exceeding, exceptional, finer, fitter, greater, higher quality, improved, larger, more appropriate, more desirable, more fitting, more select, more suitable, more useful, more valuable, preferable, preferred, prominent, sharpened, sophisticated, souped up*, superior, surpassing, worthier; SEE CONCEPTS *568,572*

better [*adj2*] *improved in health*
convalescent, cured, fitter, fully recovered, healthier, improving, less ill, mending, more healthy, on the comeback trail*, on the mend, on the road to recovery*, out of the woods*, over the hump*, progressing, recovering, stronger, well; SEE CONCEPT *314*

better [*adj3*] *larger*
bigger, greater, longer, more, preponderant, weightier; SEE CONCEPTS *771,773*

better [*v*] *improve performance; outdo*
advance, ameliorate, amend, beat, best, cap, correct, enhance, exceed, excel, forward, further, help, meliorate, mend, outshine, outstrip, promote, raise, rectify, refine, reform, revamp, surpass, top, transcend; SEE CONCEPTS *141,244*

better [*adv*] *in a more excellent manner*
finer, greater, in a superior way, more, more advantageously, more attractively, more competently, more completely, more effectively, more thoroughly, preferably, to a greater degree; SEE CONCEPTS *568,572*

betterment [*n*] *improvement*
advancement, amelioration, mastery, melioration, progress, prosperity, upgrading; SEE CONCEPT *244*

between [*adv/prep*] *middle from two points*
amid, amidst, among, at intervals, betwixt, bounded by, centrally located, enclosed by, halfway, in, in the middle, in the midst of, in the seam, in the thick of, inserted, interpolated, intervening, medially, mid, midway, separating, surrounded by, 'tween, within; SEE CONCEPTS *586,820*

beverage [*n*] *liquid refreshment*
cooler, draft, drink, drinkable, libation, liquor, potable, potation; SEE CONCEPT *454*

bevy [*n*] *swarm*
assembly, band, bunch, cluster, collection, company, covey, crew, crowd, flight, flock, gathering, group, pack, party, troupe; SEE CONCEPT *432*

bewail [*v*] *cry over, lament*
bemoan, deplore, eat heart out*, express sorrow, grieve for, moan, mourn, regret, repent, rue, sing the blues*, take on, wail, weep over; SEE CONCEPT *266*

beware [*v*] *be careful*
attend, avoid, be cautious, be wary, guard against, heed, keep eyes open*, keep on one's toes*, keep one's distance, look out, mind, mind p's and q's*, notice, refrain from, shun, steer clear of*, take care, take heed, walk on eggs*, watch one's step, watch out; SEE CONCEPT *34*

bewilder [*v*] *confuse*
addle, baffle, ball up*, befuddle, bemuse, confound, daze, disconcert, distract, floor*, fluster, mess with one's head*, mix up, muddle, mystify, perplex, puzzle, rattle, snow*, stump, stupefy, throw, upset; SEE CONCEPTS *14,42*

bewildered [*adj*] *confused*
addled, agape, aghast, agog, appalled, astonished, astounded, awed, awe-struck, baffled, befuddled, bowled over*, dazed, dazzled, disconcerted, dizzy, dumbfounded, dumbstruck, flabbergasted, flipped out*, floored*, flustered, giddy, in a dither*, lost, misled, muddled, mystified, perplexed, punchy*, puzzled, rattled, reeling, shocked, shook up, speechless, staggered, startled, stumped, stunned, stupefied, surprised, taken aback, thrown, thunderstruck*, uncertain, unglued*; SEE CONCEPTS *402,403*

bewitch [*v*] *charm*
allure, attract, bedevil, beguile, captivate, capture, control, dazzle, draw, enchant, enrapture, enthrall, entrance, fascinate, hex, hypnotize, knock dead*, knock out, put horns on*, put the whammy on*, put under magic spell*, send*, slay*, spell*, spellbind, sweep off one's feet*, take, tickle*, tickle pink*, tickle to death*, trick, turn on*, vamp, voodoo, wile, wow*; SEE CONCEPTS *7,22*

bewitched [*adj*] *charmed*
captivated, enamored, enchanted, enraptured, ensorcelled, entranced, fallen for, fascinated, gaga about*, have a bug in one's ear*, have a thing about*, head over heels*, hooked*, hung up*, mad about, mesmerized, possessed, spellbound, transformed, turned on*, under a spell; SEE CONCEPTS *32,403*

beyond [*adv/prep*] *further; outside limits*
above, after, ahead, apart from, as well as, at a distance, away from, before, behind, besides, beyond the bounds, clear of, farther, free of, good way off, hyper, in addition to, in advance of, long way off, moreover, more remote, on the far side, on the other side, out of range, out of reach, outside, over, over and above, over there, past, remote, superior to, without, yonder; SEE CONCEPTS *554,772,778*

bias [*n1*] *belief in one way; partiality*
bent, bigotry, disposition, favoritism, flash, headset*, illiberality, inclination, intolerance, leaning, mind trip*, mind-set*, narrowmindedness, onesidedness, penchant, preconception, predilection, predisposition, preference, prejudice, prepossession, proclivity, proneness, propensity, spin, standpoint, tendency, tilt, turn, unfairness, viewpoint; SEE CONCEPT *689*

bias [*n2*] *diagonal weave of fabric*
angle, cant, cross, incline, oblique, slant; SEE CONCEPT *606*

bias [*v*] *cause to favor*
distort, incline, influence, make partial, prejudice, prepossess, slant, sway, twist, warp, weight; SEE CONCEPTS *7,19*

bible [*n*] *holy book*
authority, Book, Book of Books, creed, doctrine, God's word, guide, guidebook, handbook, Holy Scriptures, Holy Writ, manual, sacred writ, sacred writings, scripture, testament, text, the Good Book, the good news, the Word; SEE CONCEPTS *280,368*

bicker [*v*] *nastily argue*
altercate, brawl, caterwaul, cause a scene*, cavil, dig, disagree, dispute, fall out, fight, hassle, pick at, quarrel, quibble, row, scrap, scrape, spar, spat, squabble, tiff, trade zingers*, wrangle; SEE CONCEPT *46*

bicycle [*n*] *pedal-driven recreational vehicle*
bike, cycle, tandem, two-wheeler, velocipede, wheels; SEE CONCEPTS *364,505*

bid [*n1*] *offering of money or services*
advance, amount, declaration, feeler, hit, invitation, offer, pass, price, proffer, proposal, proposition, request, submission, suggestion, sum, summons, tender; SEE CONCEPTS *67,330*

bid [*n2*] *endeavor*
attempt, crack, effort, essay, try, venture; SEE CONCEPT *87*

bid [*v1*] *offer money or services*
present, proffer, propose, render, submit, tender, venture; SEE CONCEPTS *67,330*

bid [*v2*] *say*
call, greet, tell, wish; SEE CONCEPT *266*

bid [*v3*] *ask for; command*
call, charge, demand, desire, direct, enjoin, instruct, invite, make a pass at*, make a pitch*, make a play for*, order, proposition, request, require, solicit, summon, tell, warn; SEE CONCEPT *53*

bidding [n1] *command*
behest, call, charge, demand, dictate, direction, injunction, instruction, invitation, mandate, order, request, summons, word; SEE CONCEPT *53*

bidding [n2] *offering of money, services*
advance, auction, invitation, offer, proffering, proposal, proposition, request, submission, suggestion, tender; SEE CONCEPTS *67,330*

bide [v] *wait*
abide, attend, await, continue, dwell, hang around, hang in*, hang out*, hold the phone*, lie in wait*, linger, live, remain, reside, sit tight*, stay, stick around, sweat it*, tarry, watch for; SEE CONCEPT *681*

big [adj1] *large, great*
ample, awash, a whale of a*, brimming, bulky, bull*, burly, capacious, chock-full, colossal, commodious, considerable, copious, crowded, enormous, extensive, fat, full, gigantic, heavy-duty*, heavyweight, hefty, huge, hulking, humungous*, husky, immense, jumbo, king-sized, mammoth, massive, mondo*, monster*, oversize, packed, ponderous, prodigious, roomy, sizable, spacious, strapping, stuffed, substantial, super colossal*, thundering, tremendous, vast, voluminous, walloping, whopper, whopping; SEE CONCEPTS *771,773*

big [adj2] *important*
big league*, big-time*, consequential, considerable, eminent, heavy-duty*, heavyweight, influential, leading, main, major league*, material, meaningful, momentous, paramount, popular, powerful, prime, principal, prominent, serious, significant, substantial, super, super colossal*, valuable, weighty; SEE CONCEPT *568*

big [adj3] *grown*
adult, elder, full-grown, grown-up, mature, tall; SEE CONCEPTS *578,797*

big [adj4] *generous*
altruistic, benevolent, bighearted, chivalrous, considerate, free, gracious, greathearted, heroic, liberal, lofty, magnanimous, noble, princely, unselfish; SEE CONCEPT *404*

big [adj5] *arrogant*
arty, boastful, bragging, conceited, flamboyant, haughty, high-sounding, imperious, imposing, inflated, overblown, pompous, presumptuous, pretentious, proud; SEE CONCEPT *401*

bigot [n] *intolerant, prejudiced person*
diehard, doctrinaire, dogmatist, enthusiast, extremist, fanatic, fiend, male chauvinist pig*, maniac, monomaniac, opinionated person, partisan, persecutor, puritan, racist, sectarian, segregationist, sexist person, stickler, superpatriot, zealot; SEE CONCEPTS *359,423*

bigoted [adj] *intolerant, prejudiced*
biased, conservative, dogmatic, illiberal, narrow, narrow-minded, obstinate, opinionated, partial, partisan, sectarian, slanted, small-minded, twisted, unfair, warped; SEE CONCEPTS *403,555*

bigotry [n] *intolerance, prejudice*
bias, conservatism/conservativism, discrimination, dogmatism, fanaticism, ignorance, injustice, Jim Crowism*, mindlessness, narrow-mindedness, partiality, provincialism, racialism, racism, sectarianism, sexism, unfairness; SEE CONCEPTS *388,410*

bilateral [adj] *having two sides*
mutual, reciprocal, respective, two-sided; SEE CONCEPT *562*

bilk [v] *cheat*
bamboozle*, beat, circumvent, con, deceive, defraud, disappoint, do*, fleece*, flimflam*, foil, frustrate, gyp*, overreach, rook*, ruin, snow*, swindle, thwart, trick; SEE CONCEPTS *59,139*

bill [n1] *account of charges; money owed*
bad news*, check, chit, damage*, debt, invoice, IOU, itemized account, knock*, note, reckoning, request for payment, score*, statement, statement of indebtedness, tab; SEE CONCEPTS *329,332*

bill [n2] *list; circular*
advertisement, affiche, agenda, bulletin, card, catalogue, flyer, handbill, handout, inventory, leaflet, listing, notice, placard, playbill, poster, program, roster, schedule, syllabus; SEE CONCEPTS *280,283*

bill [n3] *piece of legislation*
act, draft, measure, projected law, proposal, proposed act; SEE CONCEPTS *271,318*

bill [n4] *piece of paper money*
bank note, buck, certificate, currency, dollar, greenback*, long green*, skin*; SEE CONCEPT *340*

bill [n5] *beak of animal*
mandible, neb, nib, pecker, projection; SEE CONCEPT *399*

bill [v1] *charge money for goods, services*
bone, chase, debit, draw upon, dun, figure, invoice, put the arm on*, put the bite on*, put the squeeze on*, reckon, record, render, solicit; SEE CONCEPTS *330,342*

bill [v2] *advertise*
announce, book, give advance notice, post; SEE CONCEPTS *60,292*

billow [n] *surging mass*
beachcomber, breaker, crest, roller, surge, swell, tide, wave; SEE CONCEPTS *437,514*

billow [v] *surge*
balloon, belly, bloat, bounce, bulge, ebb and flow, heave, pitch, puff up, ripple, rise and fall, rise up, rock, roll, swell, toss, undulate, wave; SEE CONCEPTS *159,208*

billowy [adj] *surging*
bouncing, bouncy, bulgy, distended, ebbing and flowing, heaving, puffy, rippled, rippling, rising, rising and falling, rolling, swelling, swirling, swollen, undulating, waving, wavy; SEE CONCEPTS *486,584*

bind [n] *predicament*
between a rock and a hard place*, crunch*, difficulty, dilemma, hot water*, no-win situation*, nuisance, pickle*, predicament, quandary, sticky

situation*, tight situation, tight spot*; SEE CONCEPTS *230,674*

bind [*v1*] *fasten, secure*
adhere, attach, bandage, border, chain, cinch, clamp, connect, constrict, cover, dress, edge, encase, enchain, enfetter, fetter, finish, fix, fold, furl, glue, hamper, handcuff, hem, hitch, hitch on, hobble, hook on, hook up, lace, lap, lash, leash, manacle, moor, muzzle, paste, peg down, pin, pin down, pinion, put together, restrain, restrict, rope, shackle, stick, strap, swathe, tack on, tether, tie, tie up, trammel, trim, truss, unite, wrap, yoke; SEE CONCEPTS *85,160*

bind [*v2*] *obligate; restrict*
compel, confine, constrain, detain, engage, enslave, force, hamper, hinder, hogtie*, indenture, lock up, necessitate, oblige, prescribe, put half nelson on*, put lock on*, require, restrain, restrict, yoke; SEE CONCEPTS *14,130*

binding [*n*] *cover; something which fastens*
adhesive, belt, fastener, jacket, tie, wrapper; SEE CONCEPT *475*

binding [*adj1*] *necessary*
bounden, compulsory, conclusive, counted upon, essential, imperative, incumbent on, indissoluble, irrevocable, mandatory, obligatory, required, requisite, unalterable; SEE CONCEPT *546*

binding [*adj2*] *confining*
attached, enslaved, fastened, indentured, limiting, restraining, tied, tying; SEE CONCEPT *554*

binge [*n*] *spree*
affair, bender, blind*, bout*, carousal, compotation, drunk*, fling, jag*, orgy*, toot*; SEE CONCEPT *386*

biography [*n*] *account of person's life*
adventures, autobiography, bio, biog, close-up, confessions, diary, experiences, journal, letters, life, life history, life story, memoir, personal account, personal anecdote, personal narrative, personal record, picture, profile, résumé, saga, sketch, vita; SEE CONCEPTS *280,282*

bird [*n*] *flying animal*
feathered creature, fowl, game; SEE CONCEPT *395*

birth [*n1*] *becoming alive*
act of God, bearing, beginning, birthing, blessed event*, childbearing, childbirth, creation, delivery, labor, nascency, natality, nativity, parturition, producing, travail, visit from stork*; SEE CONCEPTS *302,373*

birth [*n2*] *beginning*
commencement, dawn, dawning, emergence, fountainhead, genesis, onset, opening, origin, outset, rise, source, start; SEE CONCEPT *119*

birth [*n3*] *heritage*
ancestry, background, blood, breeding, derivation, descent, extraction, forebears, genealogy, heritance, legacy, line, lineage, nobility, noble extraction, parentage, pedigree, position, race, rank, station, status, stock, strain; SEE CONCEPTS *296,648*

birth control [*n*] *method of preventing pregnancy*
abstinence, condom, contraception, contraceptive, diaphragm, IUD, pill, planned parenthood, rhythm method, rubber, safety, tied tubes, vasectomy, virginity; SEE CONCEPTS *121,375*

bisect [*v*] *divide in two*
bifurcate, branch off, cleave, cross, cut across, cut in half, cut in two, dichotomize, dimidiate, divaricate, divide in two, fork, furcate, halve, hemisect, intersect, separate, split, split down the middle; SEE CONCEPTS *98,137,176*

bisexual [*adj*] *having relations with either gender*
AC-DC*, ambidextrous, androgynous, bi*, double-gaited*, epicene, gynandrous, hermaphroditic, hits both ways*, intersexual, monoclinous, swings both ways*, switch-hitting*; SEE CONCEPT *372*

bit [*n1*] *tiny piece*
atom, butt, chicken feed*, chip, chunk, crumb, dab, dash, division, dollop, dose, dot, driblet, droplet, end, excerpt, flake, fraction, fragment, grain, iota, item, jot, lick*, lump, mite, modicum, moiety, molecule, morsel, niggle, parcel, part, particle, peanuts*, pinch, portion, sample, scale, scintilla, scrap, section, segment, shard, share, shaving, shred, slice, sliver, smidgen, snatch, snip, snippet, specimen, speck, splinter, sprinkling, stub, stump, taste, tittle, trace, trickle; SEE CONCEPTS *831,835*

bit [*n2*] *short period of time*
instant, jiffy, little while, minute, moment, second, space, spell, stretch, tick, while; SEE CONCEPT *807*

bite [*n1*] *injury from gripping, tearing*
chaw*, chomp*, gob*, itch*, laceration, nip, pain, pinch, prick, smarting, sting, tooth marks*, wound; SEE CONCEPT *309*

bite [*n2*] *mouthful of food*
brunch, drop, light meal, morsel, nibble, nosh*, piece, refreshment, sample, snack, sop*, taste; SEE CONCEPTS *457,459*

bite [*n3*] *pungency; stinging sensation*
burn, edge, guts, kick, piquancy, punch, spice, sting, zap*, zip*; SEE CONCEPT *614*

bite [*n4*] *allotment*
allowance, cut, lot, part, piece, portion, quota, share, slice; SEE CONCEPT *835*

bite [*v1*] *grip or tear with teeth*
champ, chaw, chaw on, chew, chomp, clamp, crunch, crush, cut, eat, gnaw, hold, lacerate, masticate, munch, nibble, nip, pierce, pinch, rend, ruminate, seize, sever, snap, take a chunk out of*, taste, tooth, wound; SEE CONCEPTS *185,616*

bite [*v2*] *corrode, eat away*
burn, consume, decay, decompose, deteriorate, dissolve, eat into, engrave, erode, etch, oxidize, rot, rust, scour, sear, slash, smart, sting, tingle, wear away; SEE CONCEPTS *215,250*

bite [*v3*] *take a chance*
be victim, get hooked, nibble, risk, volunteer; SEE CONCEPT *384*

biting [*adj1*] *piercing, sharp*
bitter, bleak, blighting, cold, crisp, cutting, freezing, harsh, nipping, penetrating, raw; SEE CONCEPTS *569,605*

biting [*adj2*] *sarcastic*
acerbic, acrimonious, bitter, caustic, cutting, incisive, mordant, scathing, severe, sharp, stinging, trenchant, withering; SEE CONCEPT *267*

bitter [*adj1*] *pungent, sharp*
absinthal, absinthian, acerbic, acid, acrid, amaroidal, astringent, harsh, sour, tart, unsweetened, vinegary; SEE CONCEPT *613*

bitter [*adj2*] *hostile, nasty*
acrimonious, alienated, antagonistic, begrudging, biting, caustic, crabby, divided, embittered, estranged, fierce, freezing, hateful, intense, irreconcilable, morose, rancorous, resentful, sardonic, severe, sore, sour, stinging, sullen, virulent, vitriolic, with chip on shoulder*; SEE CONCEPTS *267,404*

bitter [*adj3*] *painful, distressing*
afflictive, annoying, bad, brutal, calamitous, cruel, dire, disagreeable, displeasing, distasteful, disturbing, galling, grievous, hard, harsh, heartbreaking, hurtful, inclement, intemperate, intense, merciless, offensive, poignant, provoking, rigorous, rugged, ruthless, savage, severe, sharp, stinging, unpalatable, unpleasant, vexatious, woeful; SEE CONCEPT *537*

bitterness [*n1*] *sourness*
acerbity, acidity, acridity, astringency, brackishness, brininess, piquancy, pungency, sharpness, tartness, vinegariness; SEE CONCEPT *614*

bitterness [*n2*] *agony*
acrimoniousness, anguish, asperity, distress, grievousness, harshness, hostility, mordancy, pain, painfulness, sarcasm, venom, virulence; SEE CONCEPTS *410,633*

bizarre [*adj*] *strange, wild*
bugged out*, camp*, comical, curious, eccentric, extraordinary, fantastic, far-out, freakish, grody*, grotesque, kooky, ludicrous, odd, oddball, offbeat, off the wall*, outlandish, outré, peculiar, queer, ridiculous, singular, unusual, way-out*, weird; SEE CONCEPTS *547,564*

blab [*v*] *gossip*
babble, betray, blather, blurt out, chatter, disclose, divulge, gab, gabble, give away, go on, jabber, let out, let slip, mouth, peach*, prattle, reveal, run off at the mouth*, run on, shoot the breeze*, spill*, spill the beans*, squeal*, talk through one's hat*, tattle, tell, tell on, yackety-yak*, yak*; SEE CONCEPTS *55,60*

black [*n*] *African-American*
African, Afro-American, Negro; SEE CONCEPT *413*

black [*adj1*] *dark, inky*
atramentous, brunet, charcoal, clouded, coal, dingy, dusky, ebon, ebony, inklike, jet, livid, melanoid, murky, nigrescent, nigrous, obsidian, onyx, piceous, pitch, pitch-dark, raven, sable, shadowy, slate, sloe, somber, sombre, sooty, starless, stygian, swart, swarthy; SEE CONCEPT *618*

black [*adj2*] *hopeless*
atrocious, bleak, depressing, depressive, dismal, dispiriting, distressing, doleful, dreary, foreboding, funereal, gloomy, horrible, lugubrious, mournful, ominous, oppressive, sad, sinister, sombre, threatening; SEE CONCEPTS *529,570*

black [*adj3*] *dirty*
dingy, filthy, foul, grimy, grubby, impure, nasty, soiled, sooty, spotted, squalid, stained, unclean, uncleanly; SEE CONCEPT *589*

black [*adj4*] *angry*
enraged, fierce, furious, hostile, menacing, resentful, sour, sullen, threatening; SEE CONCEPT *403*

black [*adj5*] *evil*
bad, diabolical, iniquitous, mean, nefarious, villainous, wicked; SEE CONCEPT *545*

blacken [*v1*] *darken*
befoul, begrime, blot, cloud, deepen, ebonize, grow dark, grow dim, ink, make dark, nigrify, shade, smudge, soil; SEE CONCEPT *250*

blacken [*v2*] *malign; smear*
asperse, attack, bad-mouth*, blot, blotch, calumniate, decry, defame, defile, denigrate, dishonor, do a number on*, give a black eye*, knock*, libel, malign, rip*, rip up and down*, slander, slur, smudge, stain, sully, taint, tarnish, traduce, vilify; SEE CONCEPT *54*

blacklist [*v*] *ban*
banish, bar, blackball, boycott, debar, exclude, expel, hit list*, ostracize, preclude, proscribe, put on hit list*, reject, repudiate, snub, thumbs down*, vote against; SEE CONCEPT *25*

black magic [*n*] *sorcery*
diabolism, magic, necromancy, voodoo, witchcraft, wizardry; SEE CONCEPTS *370,689*

blackmail [*n*] *intimidation for money; money to quiet informer*
bribe, bribery, exaction, extortion, hush money*, milking*, payoff, protection, ransom, slush fund*, tribute; SEE CONCEPTS *123,192*

blackmail [*v*] *intimidating for money*
badger, bleed, coerce, compel, demand, exact, extort, force, hold to ransom, milk*, put the shake on*, ransom, shake, shake down, squeeze*, threaten; SEE CONCEPTS *192,342*

black out [*v1*] *delete; cover*
batten, conceal, cover up, cross out, cut off, darken, eclipse, eradicate, erase, hold back, make dark, obfuscate, rub out, shade, squash, squelch; SEE CONCEPT *250*

black out [*v2*] *faint*
collapse, crap out*, draw a blank*, go out like a light*, lose consciousness, pass out*, slip into coma, swoon*, zone out*; SEE CONCEPT *303*

blade [n] *cutting tool*
brand, cutlass, edge, épée, knife, shank, sword; SEE CONCEPTS *495,499*

blah [adj] *dull, lifeless*
banausic, bland, boring, dim, dreary, humdrum*, monotone, monotonous, pedestrian, plodding, yawn producing; SEE CONCEPT *544*

blame [n1] *condemnation*
accusation, animadversion, arraignment, attack, attribution, castigation, censure, charge, chiding, complaint, criticism, denunciation, depreciation, diatribe, disapprobation, disapproval, disfavor, disparagement, expostulation, exprobation, impeachment, implication, imputation, incrimination, inculpation, indictment, invective, objurgation, obloquy, opposition, rebuke, recrimination, remonstrance, reprehension, reprimand, reproach, reprobation, reproof, repudiation, slur, tirade; SEE CONCEPT *54*

blame [n2] *responsibility*
accountability, answerability, burden, culpability, fault, guilt, incrimination, liability, onus, rap*; SEE CONCEPTS *639,661*

blame [v] *accuse; place responsibility*
admonish, ascribe, attribute, blast, blow the whistle on*, censure, charge, chide, climb all over*, condemn, criticize, denounce, denunciate, disapprove, express disapprobation, find fault with, finger*, frame, give hell*, hold responsible, impute, indict, jump all over*, jump down one's throat*, knock*, lay a bad trip on*, lay at one's door*, lay to*, let one have it*, lower the boom*, pass the buck*, point the finger*, rap, rebuke, reprehend, reproach, reprove, roast, saddle, skin, stick it to*, tax, upbraid; SEE CONCEPT *44*

blameless [adj] *not responsible*
above suspicion, clean, clean-handed, clear, crimeless, exemplary, faultless, good, guilt-free, guiltless, immaculate, impeccable, inculpable, innocent, irreprehensible, irreproachable, in the clear, lily-white, not guilty, perfect, pure, righteous, stainless, unblemished, unimpeachable, unoffending, unspotted, unsullied, untarnished, upright, virtuous; SEE CONCEPT *555*

blanch [v] *become afraid*
flinch, pale, recoil, shrink, start, wince; SEE CONCEPT *27*

bland [adj1] *tasteless; undistinctive*
banal, blah*, boring, dull, dull as dishwater*, flat, flavorless, ho hum*, humdrum*, insipid, milk-and-water*, monotonous, nerdy*, nothing, pablum*, sapless*, tame, tedious, unexciting, uninspiring, uninteresting, unstimulating, vanilla*, vapid, waterish, watery, weak, wimpy, wishy-washy*, zero*; SEE CONCEPTS *589,613*

bland [adj2] *friendly, gracious*
affable, amiable, civilized, congenial, courteous, gentle, good-natured, ingratiating, oily*, pleasant,

smooth, suave, unctuous, unemotional, urbane; SEE CONCEPT *401*

bland [adj3] *mild, temperate*
balmy, calm, calmative, clear, lenient, mollifying, nonirritant, nonirritating, smooth, soft, soothing; SEE CONCEPTS *485,605*

blank [n] *empty space*
abyss, cavity, chasm, emptiness, gap, gulf, hiatus, hole, hollow, hollowness, interstice, interval, nihility, nothingness, nullity, omission, opening, preterition, pretermission, skip, tabula rasa, vacancy, vacuity, vacuum, void, womb; SEE CONCEPT *513*

blank [adj1] *clear*
bare, barren, clean, empty, fresh, new, pale, plain, spotless, uncompleted, unfilled, unmarked, untouched, unused, vacant, vacuous, virgin, virginal, void, white; SEE CONCEPTS *485,562*

blank [adj2] *expressionless*
deadpan, dull, empty, fruitless, hollow, immobile, impassive, inane, inexpressive, inscrutable, lifeless, masklike, meaningless, noncommittal, poker-faced, stiff, stupid, uncommunicative, unexpressive, vacant, vacuous, vague; SEE CONCEPT *406*

blank [adj3] *dumbfounded*
at a loss, awestruck, bewildered, confounded, confused, dazed, disconcerted, muddled, nonplussed, stupefied, uncomprehending, wonderstruck; SEE CONCEPT *402*

blank [adj4] *absolute, utter*
black, complete, downright, out-and-out, outright, perfect, regular, sheer, straight-out, thorough, total, unconditional, unqualified; SEE CONCEPT *531*

blanket [n] *cover, covering*
afghan, carpet, cloak, coat, coating, comforter, covering, coverlet, envelope, film, fleece, layer, mat, puff, quilt, rug, sheath, sheet, strip, throw, wrapper; SEE CONCEPTS *473,475*

blanket [adj] *comprehensive*
absolute, across-the-board, all-inclusive, overall, powerful, sweeping, unconditional, wide-ranging; SEE CONCEPT *772*

blanket [v] *cover*
bury, cloak, cloud, coat, conceal, crown, eclipse, envelop, hide, mask, obscure, overcast, overlay, overspread, suppress, surround; SEE CONCEPT *172*

blare [v] *make loud noise*
bark, bellow, blast, boom, bray, clamor, clang, honk, hoot, peal, resound, roar, scream, shout, shriek, sound out, toot, trumpet; SEE CONCEPTS *65,77*

blarney [n] *flattery*
a line*, adulation, baloney*, blandishment, cajolery, coaxing, compliments, exaggeration, eyewash*, fawning*, honey*, incense, ingratiation, inveiglement, oil*, overpraise, soft soap*, soft words, sweet talk, wheedling; SEE CONCEPT *69*

blasé [adj] *nonchalant*
apathetic, been around twice*, bored, cloyed, cool*, disenchanted, disentranced, done it all*, fed up*,

glutted, indifferent, jaded, knowing, laid-back*, lukewarm*, mellow, mondaine, offhand, satiated, sick of, sophisticate, sophisticated, surfeited, unconcerned, unexcited, uninterested, unmoved, weary, worldly, world-weary; SEE CONCEPT *404*

blasphemous [*adj*] *irreverent*
cursing, disrespectful, godless, impious, insulting, irreligious, profanatory, profane, sacrilegious, swearing, ungodly; SEE CONCEPT *545*

blasphemy [*n*] *irreverence*
abuse, cursing, cussing, desecration, execration, heresy, impiety, impiousness, imprecation, indignity, lewdness, profanation, profaneness, profanity, reviling, sacrilege, scoffing, scurrility, swearing, vituperation; SEE CONCEPT *645*

blast [*n1/v1*] *loud sound; make loud sound*
bang, blare, blow, burst, clang, clap, crack, din, honk, peal, roar, scream, slam, smash, toot, trumpet, wail, wham; SEE CONCEPTS *65,521,595*

blast [*n2*] *explosion*
bang, blow-up, burst, crash, detonation, discharge, dynamite, eruption, outbreak, outburst, salvo, volley; SEE CONCEPTS *179,521*

blast [*n3*] *gust of wind*
blow, draft, gale, squall, storm, strong breeze, tempest; SEE CONCEPTS *437,524*

blast [*n4*] *fun time*
amusement, bash*, blow out*, excitement, good time, great time, party, riot; SEE CONCEPT *386*

blast [*v2*] *explode*
annihilate, blight, blow up, bomb, break up, burst, damage, dash, demolish, destroy, detonate, dynamite, injure, kill, ruin, shatter, shrivel, spoil, stunt, torpedo, wither, wreck; SEE CONCEPTS *86,179*

blast [*v3*] *lambaste; defeat mentally*
attack, beat, castigate, clobber*, criticize, drub*, flay, lash out at, lick*, rail at, shellac*, whip*; SEE CONCEPT *52*

blatant [*adj1*] *obvious; brazen*
arrant, bald, barefaced, brassy, brazenfaced, clear, conspicuous, crying, flagrant, flashy, flaunting, garish, gaudy, glaring, glitzy, impudent, loud, meretricious, naked, obtrusive, ostentatious, outright, overbold, overt, pizzazz, plain, prominent, pronounced, protrusive, screaming, shameless, sheer, showy, snazzy, unabashed, unblushing, unmitigated; SEE CONCEPTS *540,569*

blatant [*adj2*] *deafening*
boisterous, clamorous, crying, ear-splitting, harsh, loud, loudmouthed, noisy, obstreperous, obtrusive, piercing, screaming, scurrilous, strident, vociferant, vociferous, vulgar; SEE CONCEPTS *592,594*

blaze [*n1*] *fire*
bonfire, burning, combustion, conflagration, flame, flames, holocaust, wildfire; SEE CONCEPTS *478,521*

blaze [*n2*] *flash of light*
beam, brilliance, burst, flare, glare, gleam, glitter, glow, radiance; SEE CONCEPT *628*

blaze [*n3*] *torrent*
blast, burst, eruption, flare-up, flash, fury, outbreak, outburst, rush, storm; SEE CONCEPT *673*

blaze [*v*] *burn brightly*
beam, burst out, coruscate, explode, fire, flame, flare, flash, flicker, fulgurate, glare, gleam, glow, illuminate, illumine, incandesce, jet, light, radiate, scintillate, shimmer, shine, sparkle; SEE CONCEPT *249*

bleach [*v*] *whiten*
achromatize, blanch, blench, decolor, decolorize, etiolate, fade, grow pale, lighten, make pale, peroxide, wash out; SEE CONCEPT *250*

bleachers [*n*] *seating for watching event*
benches, boxes, grandstand, Ruthville*, seats, stands; SEE CONCEPTS *440,443*

bleak [*adj1*] *barren*
austere, bare, blank, blighted, bombed, bulldozed, burned, chilly, cleared, cold, deforested, desert, deserted, desolate, dreary, exposed, flat, gaunt, grim, open, raw, scorched, stripped, unpopulated, unsheltered, weather-beaten, wild, windswept; SEE CONCEPT *490*

bleak [*adj2*] *depressing*
black, cheerless, comfortless, dark, discouraging, disheartening, dismal, drear, dreary, funereal, gloomy, grim, hard, harsh, hopeless, joyless, lonely, melancholy, mournful, oppressive, sad, somber, unpromising; SEE CONCEPTS *403,537*

bleed [*v1*] *cause blood to flow*
drain, exude, gush, hemorrhage, leech, ooze, open vein, phlebotomize, run, seep, shed, spurt, trickle, weep; SEE CONCEPT *185*

bleed [*v2*] *extort*
blackmail, confiscate, deplete, drain, exhaust, extract, fleece, impoverish, leech*, milk, mulct, overcharge, pauperize, put the screws to*, rook*, sap*, skin*, squeeze*, steal, stick*, strong-arm; SEE CONCEPTS *192,342*

bleed [*v3*] *grieve*
ache, agonize, be in pain, feel for, pity, suffer, sympathize; SEE CONCEPTS *12,17*

blemish [*n*] *flaw*
beauty spot, birthmark, blackhead, blister, bloom*, blot, blotch, blot on the landscape*, blur, brand, bruise, bug*, catch, chip, cicatrix, defacement, defect, deformity, dent, discoloration, disfigurement, disgrace, dishonor, eyesore, fault, freckle, hickey*, imperfection, impurity, lentigo, lump, macula, maculation, mark, mole, nevus, nodule, patch, pimple, pock, pockmark, scar, second, sight, smudge, snag, speck, speckle, spot, stain, stigma, taint, tarnish, vice, wart, whitehead, zit*; SEE CONCEPT *580*

blemish [*v*] *flaw, disfigure*
blot, blotch, blur, damage, deface, distort, harm, hurt, impair, injure, maim, mangle, mar, mark, mutilate, pervert, prejudice, scar, smudge, spoil, spot,

stain, sully, taint, tarnish, twist, vitiate, wrench; SEE CONCEPTS *54,246*

blend [*n*] *composite, mix*
alloy, amalgam, amalgamation, brew, combination, commixture, composite, compound, concoction, fusion, interfusion, intermixture, mixture, synthesis, union; SEE CONCEPT *432*

blend [*v1*] *mix*
amalgamate, cement, coalesce, combine, commingle, commix, compound, fuse, integrate, interblend, intermix, meld, merge, mingle, synthesize, unite, weld; SEE CONCEPT *109*

blend [*v2*] *harmonize*
arrange, complement, fit, go well, go with, integrate, orchestrate, suit, symphonize, synthesize, unify; SEE CONCEPT *656*

bless [*v1*] *sanctify*
absolve, anoint, baptize, beatify, canonize, commend, confirm, consecrate, cross, dedicate, enshrine, eulogize, exalt, extol, give thanks to, glorify, hallow, honor, invoke benefits, invoke happiness, laud, magnify, make holy, offer, offer benediction, ordain, panegyrize, praise, pray for, pronounce holy, sacrifice, sign, sprinkle, thank; SEE CONCEPTS *69,367*

bless [*v2*] *grant, bestow*
celebrate, endow, favor, give, glorify, grace, laud, magnify, praise, provide; SEE CONCEPTS *50,88*

blessed [*adj1*] *sanctified*
adored, among the angels, beatified, consecrated, divine, enthroned, exalted, glorified, hallowed, holy, inviolable, redeemed, resurrected, revered, rewarded, sacred, sacrosanct, saved, spiritual, unprofane; SEE CONCEPTS *536,568*

blessed [*adj2*] *happy*
blissful, content, contented, endowed, favored, fortunate, glad, granted, joyful, joyous, lucky; SEE CONCEPT *404*

blessing [*n1*] *sanctification*
absolution, benedicite, benediction, benison, commendation, consecration, dedication, divine sanction, grace, invocation, laying on of hands, thanks, thanksgiving; SEE CONCEPT *367*

blessing [*n2*] *good wishes, approval*
approbation, backing, concurrence, consent, favor, Godspeed, leave, okay, permission, regard, sanction, support, valediction; SEE CONCEPTS *10,50,88*

blessing [*n3*] *advantage*
asset, benediction, benefit, boon, bounty, break, favor, gain, gift, godsend, good, good fortune, good luck, help, kindness, lucky break, manna from heaven*, miracle, profit, service, stroke of luck*, windfall; SEE CONCEPTS *230,679*

blight [*n*] *disease; plague*
affliction, bane, blot on the landscape*, canker, contamination, corruption, curse, decay, dump, evil, eyesore, fungus, infestation, mildew, pest, pestilence, pollution, rot, scourge, sight, withering, woe; SEE CONCEPTS *306,674*

blight [*v*] *ruin, destroy*
annihilate, blast, crush, damage, dash, decay, disappoint, foul up*, frustrate, glitch up*, injure, mar, mess up, nip in the bud*, nullify, shrivel, spoil, taint, trash*, wither, wreck; SEE CONCEPT *252*

blind [*n*] *screen, covering*
blinder, blindfold, blinker, camouflage, cloak, cover, curtain, facade, front, mask, trap, veil; SEE CONCEPT *716*

blind [*adj1*] *sightless*
amaurotic, blind as a bat*, dark, destitute of vision, eyeless, groping, in darkness, purblind, typhlotic, undiscerning, unseeing, unsighted, visionless; SEE CONCEPT *619*

blind [*adj2*] *indifferent*
careless, heedless, ignorant, imperceptive, inattentive, inconsiderate, indiscriminate, injudicious, insensitive, myopic, nearsighted, neglectful, oblivious, thoughtless, unaware, unconscious, undiscerning, unmindful, unobservant, unperceiving, unreasoning, unseeing; SEE CONCEPT *402*

blind [*adj3*] *uncontrolled*
hasty, heedless, impetuous, inconsiderate, irrational, mindless, rash, reckless, senseless, shortsighted, thoughtless, unseeing, unthinking, violent, wild; SEE CONCEPT *544*

blind [*adj4*] *hidden or covered*
blocked, closed, closed at one end, concealed, dark, dead-end, dim, disguised, impassable, leading nowhere, obscured, obstructed, secluded, unmarked, without egress, without exit; SEE CONCEPTS *490,576*

blindly [*adv1*] *without direction, purpose*
aimlessly, at random, confusedly, frantically, in all directions, indiscriminately, instinctively, madly, pell-mell, purposelessly, wildly; SEE CONCEPT *542*

blindly [*adv2*] *carelessly*
foolishly, heedlessly, impulsively, inconsiderately, obtusely, passionately, purblindly, recklessly, regardlessly, senselessly, thoughtlessly, tumultuously, unreasonably, unreasoningly, willfully, without rhyme or reason; SEE CONCEPT *401*

blindness [*n*] *sightlessness*
amaurosis, anopsia, astigmatism, cataracts, darkness, defect, myopia, presbyopia, purblindness, typhlosis; SEE CONCEPT *629*

blink [*v1*] *wink of eye; twinkle*
bat, flash, flicker, flutter, glimmer, glimpse, glitter, nictate, nictitate, peek, peep, peer, scintillate, shimmer, sparkle, squint; SEE CONCEPTS *185,624*

blink [*v2*] *ignore*
bypass, condone, connive, cushion, discount, disregard, fail, forget, neglect, omit, overlook, overpass, pass by, slight, turn a blind eye; SEE CONCEPT *30*

bliss [*n*] *ecstasy*
beatitude, blessedness, cool*, euphoria, felicity, gladness, gone*, happiness, heaven*, joy, paradise, rapture; SEE CONCEPTS *32,230*

blissful [adj] happy
beatific, cool*, crazy, delighted, delightful, dreamy, ecstatic, elated, enchanted, enraptured, euphoric, floating*, flying*, gone*, heavenly, in ecstasy, in seventh heaven*, in the twilight zone*, joyful, joyous, mad, on cloud nine*, rapturous, sent*, spaced-out*, turned-on*; SEE CONCEPT 403

blister [n] swelling
abscess, blain, bleb, boil, bubble, bulla, burn, canker, carbuncle, cyst, furuncle, pimple, pustule, sac, sore, ulcer, vesication, vesicle, wale, weal, welt, wheal; SEE CONCEPT 309

blithe [adj] happy
animated, buoyant, carefree, cheerful, cheery, chirpy, gay, gladsome, gleeful, jaunty, jocund, jolly, jovial, joyful, lighthearted, merry, mirthful, sprightly, sunny, vivacious; SEE CONCEPT 404

blitz [n] heavy attack
assault, blitzkrieg, bombardment, bombing, lightning attack, offensive, onslaught, raid, shelling, strike; SEE CONCEPTS 86,320

blizzard [n] snow storm
blast, gale, precipitation, snowfall, squall, tempest, whiteout; SEE CONCEPT 526

bloat [v] blow up like a balloon
balloon, belly, bilge, billow, dilate, distend, enlarge, expand, inflate, puff up, swell; SEE CONCEPTS 184,208

block [n1] mass of material
bar, brick, cake, chunk, cube, hunk, ingot, loaf, lump, oblong, piece, section, segment, slab, slice, solid, square; SEE CONCEPTS 470,471

block [n2] obstruction
bar, barrier, blank wall, blockage, chunk, clog, hindrance, impediment, jam, mass, obstacle, obstruction, roadblock, snag, stop, stoppage, wall; SEE CONCEPTS 470,652

block [v] obstruct
arrest, bar, barricade, blockade, block out, brake, catch, charge, check, choke, clog, close, close off*, close out, congest, cut off, dam, deter, fill, halt, hang up*, hinder, hold up, impede, intercept, interfere with, occlude, plug, prevent, shut off*, shut out, stall, stonewall, stop, stop up*, stopper, stymie, tackle, take out of play*, thwart; SEE CONCEPTS 121,130

blockade [n] barrier
bar, barricade, blank wall, clog, closure, embolus, encirclement, hindrance, impediment, infarct, infarction, obstacle, obstruction, restriction, roadblock, siege, snag, stop, stoppage, wall; SEE CONCEPTS 470,652

block out [v1] plan course
arrange, chart, map out, outline, prepare, sketch; SEE CONCEPT 36

block out [v2] try to forget
close, conceal, cover, hide, obscure, obstruct, screen, shroud, shut off, shut out; SEE CONCEPT 40

blond/blonde [adj] having light-colored hair
albino, auricomous, bleached, champagne, fair, fair-haired, flaxen, golden-haired, light, pale, pearly, platinum, sallow, sandy-haired, snowy, straw, strawberry, towheaded*, washed-out, yellow-haired; SEE CONCEPT 618

blood [n1] red body fluid
claret, clot, cruor, gore, hemoglobin, juice, plasma, sanguine fluid, vital fluid; SEE CONCEPTS 393,420

blood [n2] ancestry
birth, consanguinity, descendants, descent, extraction, family, kindred, kinship, line, lineage, noble extraction, origin, pedigree, relations, stock; SEE CONCEPT 296

bloodless [adj1] unfeeling
anesthetic, cold, coldhearted, dull, impassible, indolent, insensible, insensitive, languid, lazy, lifeless, listless, passionless, slow, sluggish, spiritless, torpid, unemotional, unkind; SEE CONCEPT 404

bloodless [adj2] pale
anemic, ashen, cadaverous, chalky, colorless, ghostly, lifeless, pallid, pasty, sallow, sickly, wan, watery; SEE CONCEPT 618

bloody [adj1] bleeding
blood-soaked, blood-spattered, bloodstained, crimson, ensanguined, gaping, gory, grisly, hematic, hemic, imbrued, open, raw, sanguinary, sanguine, unstaunched, unstopped, wounded; SEE CONCEPT 485

bloody [adj2] hard-fought
bloodthirsty, cruel, cutthroat, decimating, ferocious, fierce, gory, grim, heavy, homicidal, murderous, sanguinary, sanguine, savage, slaughterous; SEE CONCEPTS 540,569

bloom [n] flowering
blossom, blossoming, bud, efflorescence, floret, flourishing, flower, floweret, opening; SEE CONCEPT 425

bloom [v] flower; flourish
bear fruit, be in flower, blossom, blow, bud, burgeon, burst, develop, effloresce, fare well, fructify, germinate, grow, open, prosper, sprout, succeed, tassel out, thrive, wax; SEE CONCEPTS 427,706

blooper [n] blunder
boner*, boo-boo*, bungle, error, faux pas, fluff*, gaffe, impropriety, indecorum, lapse, mistake, slip, solecism, trip*; SEE CONCEPTS 384,674

blossom [n] flower
bloom, bud, efflorescence, floret, floweret, inflorescence, posy, spike; SEE CONCEPT 425

blossom [v1] flower
bloom, blow, burgeon, burst, effloresce, leaf, open, outbloom, shoot, unfold; SEE CONCEPT 427

blossom [v2] flourish
batten, bloom, develop, grow, mature, progress, prosper, succeed, thrive; SEE CONCEPT 706

blot [n] mark; flaw
black eye*, blemish, blotch, blur, brand, defect, discoloration, disgrace, fault, odium, onus, patch, slur,

smear, smudge, speck, spot, stain, stigma, taint; SEE CONCEPTS *230,580*

blot [*v1*] *disgrace, disfigure*
bespatter, blemish, dirty, discolor, mark, smudge, smut, soil, spoil, spot, stain, sully, tarnish; SEE CONCEPT *240*

blot [*v2*] *soak up*
absorb, dry, take up; SEE CONCEPT *211*

blotch [*n*] *smudge*
acne, blemish, blot, breakout, eruption, mark, mottling, patch, splash, spot, stain, stigma; SEE CONCEPT *580*

blouse [*n*] *shirt for woman*
bodice, bodysuit, middy, pullover, shell, slipover, T-shirt, turtleneck, V-neck; SEE CONCEPT *451*

blow [*n1*] *blast, rush of air, wind*
draft, flurry, gale, gust, hurricane, puff, squall, strong breeze, tempest, typhoon; SEE CONCEPT *526*

blow [*n2*] *hard hit*
bang, bash, bat, belt, biff, blindside, bop, buffet, bump, clip, clout, clump, collision, concussion, crack, cut, ding*, impact, jab, jar, jolt, kick, knock, knockout, knuckle sandwich*, KO*, lick, percussion, poke, pound, punch, rap, shock, slam, slap, slug, smack, smash, sock, strike, stroke, swat, swing, swipe, thrust, thump, thwack, uppercut, wallop, whack, whomp, zap*; SEE CONCEPT *189*

blow [*n3*] *catastrophe*
affliction, balk, bolt from the blue*, bombshell*, calamity, casualty, chagrin, comedown, debacle, disappointment, disaster, disgruntlement, frustration, jolt, letdown, misadventure, misfortune, mishap, reverse, setback, shock, tragedy, upset; SEE CONCEPT *674*

blow [*v1*] *blast, rush of air, wind*
breathe, buffet, drive, exhale, fan, flap, flow, flutter, gasp, heave, huff, inflate, pant, puff, pump, ruffle, rush, stream, swell, swirl, waft, wave, whiff, whirl, whisk, whisper, whistle; SEE CONCEPTS *185,526*

blow [*v2*] *make sound, usually with instrument*
blare, blast, honk, mouth, pipe, play, sound, toot, trumpet, vibrate; SEE CONCEPT *65*

blow [*v3*] *leave suddenly*
depart, go, hit the road*, split, take a hike*, take a powder*; SEE CONCEPT *195*

blow [*v4*] *ruin chance*
fail, flounder, goof*, miscarry, miss; SEE CONCEPT *699*

blow [*v5*] *use up money*
dissipate, lay out, pay out, spend, squander, waste; SEE CONCEPT *341*

blowout [*n1*] *explosion; something exploded*
blast, break, burst, detonation, eruption, escape, flat tire, leak, puncture, rupture, tear; SEE CONCEPT *179*

blowout [*n2*] *wild party*
bash, binge, feast, riot, shindig, spree; SEE CONCEPT *383*

blow up [*v1*] *inflate*
billow, bloat, distend, enlarge, expand, fill, inflate, puff up, pump up, swell; SEE CONCEPTS *208,236,245*

blow up [*v2*] *explode*
blast, bomb, burst, detonate, dynamite, erupt, go off, mushroom, rupture, shatter; SEE CONCEPTS *179,320*

blow up [*v3*] *magnify importance*
enlarge, exaggerate, heighten, overstate; SEE CONCEPTS *49,59*

blow up [*v4*] *burst with anger*
become angry, become enraged, erupt, go off the deep end*, hit the roof*, lose control, lose temper, rage, rave; SEE CONCEPTS *29,44*

blue [*adj1*] *sky, sea color*
azure, beryl, cerulean, cobalt, indigo, navy, royal, sapphire, teal, turquoise, ultramarine; SEE CONCEPT *618*

blue [*adj2*] *sad*
dejected, depressed, despondent, disconsolate, dismal, dispirited, down in the dumps*, downcast, downhearted, fed up, gloomy, glum, low, melancholy, moody, unhappy, woebegone; SEE CONCEPT *403*

blue [*adj3*] *vulgar*
bawdy, dirty, indecent, lewd, naughty, obscene, off-color, racy, risqué, salty, shady, smutty, spicy, suggestive, wicked; SEE CONCEPT *545*

blues [*n*] *depression*
dejection, despondency, doldrums, dumps*, gloom, gloominess, glumness, heavy heart*, low spirits, melancholy, moodiness, mournfulness, sadness, the dismals*, the mopes*, unhappiness; SEE CONCEPT *410*

bluff [*n1*] *boast; deceit*
bluster, braggadocio, bragging, bravado, deception, delusion, facade, fake, false colors, false front, feint, fraud, front, humbug*, jiving*, lie, pretense, pretext, ruse, sham, show, snow*, stall, subterfuge, trick; SEE CONCEPTS *58,59*

bluff [*n2*] *precipice*
bank, cliff, crag, escarpment, headland, hill, mountain, peak, promontory, ridge, rock; SEE CONCEPT *509*

bluff [*adj*] *abrupt*
barefaced, bearish, blunt, blustering, breviloquent, brief, brusque, candid, crusty, curt, direct, downright, forthright, frank, gruff, hearty, honest, laconic, no-nonsense, open, outspoken, plain-spoken, rough, rude, short, short-spoken, sincere, snippety, snippy, straightforward, tactless, tart, terse, unceremonious; SEE CONCEPT *267*

bluff [*v*] *deceive*
affect, beguile, betray, bunco*, con, counterfeit, defraud, delude, double-cross, fake*, fake out*, feign, fool, humbug*, illude, jive*, juggle, lie, mislead, pretend, psych out*, put on*, sham*, shuck*, simulate, take in*, trick; SEE CONCEPTS *58,59*

blunder [n] *mistake*
blooper, boner*, boo-boo*, bungle, dumb move*, dumb thing to do*, error, fault, faux pas, flub*, flub-up*, fluff*, gaffe, goof*, howler*, impropriety, inaccuracy, indiscretion, lapse, muff*, oversight, slip*, slip-up*, solecism, trip*; SEE CONCEPTS *101,230*

blunder [v] *make mistake*
ball up*, blow, bobble, botch, bumble, bungle, confuse, drop the ball*, err, flounder, flub, foul up, fumble, gum up*, louse up, mess up, misjudge, screw up*, slip up*, stumble; SEE CONCEPT *101*

blunt [adj1] *not sharp*
dull, dulled, edgeless, insensitive, obtuse, pointless, round, rounded, unsharpened; SEE CONCEPTS *485,486*

blunt [adj2] *straightforward*
abrupt, bluff, brief, brusque, candid, crusty, curt, discourteous, explicit, forthright, frank, gruff, impolite, matter-of-fact, outspoken, plain-spoken, rude, short, snappy, snippy, tactless, trenchant, unceremonious, uncivil, unpolished; SEE CONCEPT *267*

blunt [v] *make dull*
attenuate, benumb, cripple, dampen, deaden, debilitate, desensitize, disable, enfeeble, numb, obtund, sap, soften, take the edge off*, undermine, water down, weaken; SEE CONCEPT *240*

blur [v1] *cloud, fog*
becloud, bedim, befog, blear, blind, darken, daze, dazzle, dim, glare, make hazy, make indistinct, make vague, mask, muddy, obscure, shade, soften; SEE CONCEPT *627*

blur [v2] *make dirty*
besmear, blemish, blot, discolor, smear, smudge, spot, stain, taint, tarnish; SEE CONCEPT *254*

blush [n] *pink coloring*
bloom, blossom, burning, color, flush, flushing, glow, glowing, mantling, pink tinge, reddening, redness, rosiness, rosy tint, ruddiness, scarlet; SEE CONCEPT *622*

blush [v] *become colored, pink*
color, crimson, flush, glow, have rosy cheeks, mantle, pink, redden, rouge, turn red, turn scarlet; SEE CONCEPT *250*

bluster [n] *bullying, intimidation*
bluff, boasting, boisterousness, bombast, braggadocio, bragging, bravado, crowing, rabidity, rampancy, swagger, swaggering; SEE CONCEPT *633*

bluster [v] *bully, intimidate*
badger, boast, brag, brazen, browbeat, bulldoze*, cow*, crow*, domineer, gloat, hector, rant, rave, ride the high horse*, roar, roister, shoot off one's mouth*, show off, storm, strut, swagger, swell, talk big*, vapor*, vaunt, yap*; SEE CONCEPTS *49,78*

board [n1] *piece of wood*
lath, panel, plank, slat, strip, timber; SEE CONCEPT *479*

board [n2] *meal*
daily bread*, eats*, fare, food, keep*, mess, provisions, victuals; SEE CONCEPT *459*

board [n3] *group of advisers*
advisers, advisory group, brass, cabinet, committee, conclave, council, directorate, directors, execs, executives, executive suite, front office*, jury, panel, trustees, upstairs*; SEE CONCEPTS *323,333,417*

board [v1] *embark on vehicle*
catch, climb on, embus, emplane, enter, entrain, get on, hop on, mount; SEE CONCEPTS *159,195*

board [v2] *provide food and sleeping quarters*
accommodate, bed, canton, care for, feed, harbor, house, let crash*, lodge, put up, quarter, room; SEE CONCEPT *136*

boast [n] *brag; source of pride*
avowal, bluster, bombast, braggadocio, bravado, exaggeration, gasconade, grandiloquence, heroics, joy, pretension, pride, pride and joy, self-satisfaction, swank, treasure, vaunt; SEE CONCEPTS *410,710*

boast [v1] *brag*
advertise, aggrandize, attract attention, blow, blow one's own horn*, blow smoke*, bluster, bully, cock-a-doodle-doo*, con, congratulate oneself, crow, exaggerate, exult, fake, flatter oneself, flaunt, flourish, gasconade, give a good account of oneself, gloat, glory, grandstand*, hug oneself*, jive*, lay on thick*, prate, preen, psych, puff*, shoot*, shovel*, show off, showboat*, shuck, sling, sound off, strut, swagger, talk big*, triumph, vapor*; SEE CONCEPT *49*

boast [v2] *to have advantage*
be proud of, claim, exhibit, have in keeping, own, possess, pride oneself on, show off; SEE CONCEPT *261*

boastful [adj] *bragging*
arrogant, big, big-headed, bombastic, cocky, conceited, crowing, egotistic, egotistical, exultant, full of hot air*, hifalutin*, hot stuff*, know-it-all, loudmouth, on ego trip*, pompous, pretentious, puffed-up, self-aggrandizing, self-applauding, smart-alecky*, snooty, strutting, stuck-up, swaggering, swanky, swollen-headed, too big for one's britches*, vainglorious, vaunting, windbag*; SEE CONCEPTS *267,404*

boat [n] *vehicle for water travel*
ark, barge, bark, bateau, bottom, bucket, canoe, catamaran, craft, dinghy, dory, hulk, ketch, launch, lifeboat, pinnace, raft, sailboat, schooner, scow, ship, skiff, sloop, steamboat, tub, yacht; SEE CONCEPT *506*

boating [n] *travel, recreation in water*
canoeing, cruising, drifting, paddling, rowing, sailing, sculling, trawling, yachting; SEE CONCEPT *363*

bob [v] *bounce up and down*
bow, duck, genuflect, hop, jerk, jounce, leap, nod, oscillate, quaver, quiver, ricochet, seesaw, skip, waggle, weave, wobble; SEE CONCEPT *147*

bodily [adj] *concerning animate structure*
actual, animal, carnal, corporal, corporeal, fleshly, gross, human, material, natural, normal, organic,

physical, sensual, somatic, substantial, tangible, un-spiritual; SEE CONCEPT *406*

bodily [*adv*] *totally*
absolutely, altogether, as a body, as a group, collectively, completely, en masse, entirely, fully, totally, wholly; SEE CONCEPTS *531,772*

body [*n1*] *physique*
anatomy, bag of bones*, beefcake*, bod*, booty*, build, carcass, chassis, constitution, embodiment, figure, form, frame, makeup, mortal part, protoplasm, shaft, shape, tenement, torso, trunk; SEE CONCEPT *405*

body [*n2*] *corpse*
ashes, bones, cadaver, carcass, carrion, clay, corpus delicti, dead body, deceased, dust, relic, remains, stiff*; SEE CONCEPT *390*

body [*n3*] *human being*
being, creature, human, individual, mortal, party, person, personage, soul; SEE CONCEPTS *389,417*

body [*n4*] *bulk; central portion*
assembly, basis, bed, box, chassis, core, corpus, crux, essence, frame, fuselage, gist, gravamen, groundwork, hull, main part, majority, mass, material, matter, pith, skeleton, staple, substance, substructure, sum, tenor, total, trunk, whole; SEE CONCEPT *829*

body [*n5*] *crowd*
array, batch, bunch, bundle, clump, cluster, group, horde, lot, majority, mass, mob, multitude, parcel, party, set, society, throng; SEE CONCEPT *432*

body [*n6*] *main part of written work*
argument, burden, core, discourse, dissertation, evidence, exposition, gist, heart, material, meat, pith, sense, substance, text, thesis, treatise, upshot; SEE CONCEPT *270*

bog [*n*] *swamp*
fen, lowland, marsh, marshland, mire, morass, moss, peat, quag, quagmire, slough, sump, wetlands; SEE CONCEPT *509*

bog down [*v*] *stick; become stuck*
decelerate, delay, detain, halt, hang up, impede, retard, set back, sink, slacken, slow down, slow up, stall; SEE CONCEPT *121*

bogus [*adj*] *counterfeit*
artificial, dummy, ersatz, fake, false, fictitious, forged, fraudulent, imitation, not what it is cracked up to be*, phony, pretended, pseudo, sham*, simulated, spurious; SEE CONCEPT *582*

boil [*n*] *blister*
abscess, blain, blister, carbuncle, excrescence, furuncle, pimple, pustule, sore, tumor, ulcer; SEE CONCEPT *309*

boil [*v1*] *heat to bubbling*
agitate, bubble, churn, coddle, cook, decoct, effervesce, evaporate, fizz, foam, froth, parboil, poach, seethe, simmer, smolder, steam, steep, stew; SEE CONCEPTS *170,255*

boil [*v2*] *be angry*
be indignant, blow up, bristle, burn, flare, foam at the mouth*, fulminate, fume, rage, rave, sputter, storm; SEE CONCEPT *29*

boiling [*adj1*] *very hot*
baking, blistering, broiling, burning, fiery, hot, red-hot, roasting, scalding, scorching, sizzling, torrid, tropical, warm; SEE CONCEPT *605*

boiling [*adj2*] *angered*
angry, enraged, fuming, furious, incensed, indignant, infuriated, mad, raging; SEE CONCEPT *403*

boisterous [*adj*] *noisy and mischievous*
bouncy, brawling, clamorous, disorderly, effervescent, impetuous, loud, obstreperous, rambunctious, raucous, riotous, rollicking, rowdy, strident, tumultous/tumultuous, unrestrained, unruly, uproarious, vociferant, vociferous, wild; SEE CONCEPT *401*

bold [*adj1*] *brave*
adventurous, assuming, audacious, aweless, bantam, courageous, daring, dauntless, enterprising, fearless, forward, gallant, heroic, intrepid, resolute, unafraid, undaunted, valiant, valorous; SEE CONCEPT *401*

bold [*adj2*] *brazen, insolent*
assuming, audacious, barefaced, brash, brassy, cheeky, coming on strong*, confident, forward, fresh, gritty, gutsy, immodest, impudent, insolent, nervy, pert, presumptuous, rude, sassy, saucy, shameless, smart, smart-alecky*, spunky; SEE CONCEPTS *401,404*

bold [*adj3*] *bright, striking*
clear, colorful, conspicuous, definite, evident, eye-catching, flashy, forceful, lively, loud, manifest, plain, prominent, pronounced, showy, spirited, strong, vivid; SEE CONCEPTS *589,617,618*

bolster [*v*] *help*
aid, assist, bear up, boost, brace, buck up, bulwark, buoy, buttress, carry, cushion, help, hold up, maintain, pick up, pillow, prop, reinforce, shore up, stay, strengthen, support, sustain, uphold; SEE CONCEPT *110*

bolt [*n1*] *lock; part of lock*
bar, brad, catch, coupling, dowel, fastener, lag, latch, lock, nut, padlock, peg, pin, pipe, rivet, rod, screw, skewer, sliding bar, spike, stake, staple, stud; SEE CONCEPTS *470,471,680*

bolt [*n2*] *flash; projectile*
arrow, dart, fulmination, missile, shaft, thunderbolt, thunderstroke; SEE CONCEPTS *624,686*

bolt [*n3*] *large roll of material*
coil, curl, cylinder, package, spindle, spiral, twist; SEE CONCEPT *432*

bolt [*v1*] *run quickly away*
abscond, bail out*, bound, cop out*, cut loose*, cut out*, dart, dash, ditch*, drop out*, dump*, escape, flee, flight, fly, hightail*, hotfoot*, hurtle, jump, kiss goodbye*, leap, leave flat*, leave high and dry*, leave holding the bag*, leave in the lurch*, make a break for it*, make off*, make tracks*, opt out*, run

like scared rabbit*, run out on, rush, scamper, scoot, skedaddle*, skip, spring, sprint, start, startle, step on it*, take flight, take off*, walk out on; SEE CONCEPTS *150,195*

bolt [*v2*] *fasten securely*
bar, deadbolt, latch, lock, secure; SEE CONCEPT *225*

bolt [*v3*] *eat very fast*
consume, cram, devour, englut, gobble, gorge, gulp, guzzle, ingurgitate, inhale, scarf*, slop, slosh, stuff, swallow whole, wolf*; SEE CONCEPT *169*

bomb [*n*] *exploding weapon*
atom bomb, bombshell, charge, device, explosive, grenade, hydrogen bomb, mine, missile, Molotov cocktail, nuclear bomb, projectile, rocket, shell, ticker, torpedo; SEE CONCEPT *500*

bomb [*v1*] *detonate weapon*
attack, blast, blitz, blow up, bombard, cannonade, destroy, napalm, prang, raid, rain destruction*, rake, shell, strafe, torpedo, wipe out*, zero in*; SEE CONCEPTS *86,252*

bomb [*v2*] *fail miserably*
blow it*, flop, flummox, go out of business, lose, wash out*, wipe out*; SEE CONCEPT *699*

bombard [*v*] *assault, attack*
assail, barrage, batter, beset, besiege, blast, blitz, bomb, cannonade, catapult, fire upon, harass, hound, launch, open fire, pester, pound, shell, strafe, strike; SEE CONCEPTS *7,19,86*

bombastic [*adj*] *pompous, grandiloquent*
aureate, balderdash, big-talking*, declamatory, euphuistic, flowery, full of hot air*, fustian, grandiose, highfalutin, high-flown, histrionic, inflated, loud-mouthed, magniloquent, orotund, ostentatious, overblown, ranting, rhapsodic, rhetorical, sonorous, stuffed shirt*, swollen, tumid, turgid, verbose, windbag*, windy, wordy; SEE CONCEPT *267*

bond [*n1*] *binder or fastener*
band, binding, chain, connection, cord, fastening, fetter, gunk, handcuff, hookup, irons, ligature, link, linkage, manacle, network, nexus, rope, shackle, stickum*, tie, tie-in, wire; SEE CONCEPT *497*

bond [*n2*] *association, relation*
affiliation, affinity, attachment, connection, connective, friendship, hookup, interrelationship, liaison, link, marriage, network, obligation, relationship, restraint, tie, tie-in, union; SEE CONCEPT *388*

bond [*n3*] *guarantee; contract*
agreement, bargain, certificate, collateral, compact, convention, covenant, debenture, guaranty, obligation, pact, pledge, promise, security, transaction, warrant, warranty, word; SEE CONCEPTS *318,684*

bond [*v*] *fasten; stick*
bind, connect, fix, fuse, glue, gum, paste, stickum*; SEE CONCEPTS *85,160*

bondage [*n*] *slavery*
chains, enslavement, helotry, peonage, serfage, serfdom, servility, servitude, subjection, subjugation, thrall, thralldom, villenage, yoke; SEE CONCEPTS *136,652*

bone [*n*] *piece of animate skeleton*
bony process, cartilage, ossein, osseous matter; SEE CONCEPTS *393,420*

bonus [*n*] *unexpected extra*
additional compensation, benefit, bounty, commission, dividend, fringe benefit, frosting*, gift, golden parachute*, goody, gratuity, gravy*, hand-out*, honorarium, ice*, perk*, plus*, premium, prize, reward, special compensation, tip; SEE CONCEPT *337*

book [*n1*] *published document*
album, atlas, bestseller, bible, booklet, brochure, codex, compendium, copy, dictionary, dissertation, edition, encyclopedia, essay, fiction, folio, handbook, hardcover, leaflet, lexicon, magazine, manual, monograph, nonfiction, novel, octavo, offprint, omnibus, opus, opuscule, pamphlet, paperback, periodical, portfolio, preprint, primer, publication, quarto, reader, reprint, roll, scroll, softcover, speller, text, textbook, thesaurus, tome, tract, treatise, vade mecum, volume, work, writing; SEE CONCEPT *280*

book [*n2*] *account; diary*
agenda, album, list, notebook, pad, record, register, roster; SEE CONCEPTS *271,331*

book [*v1*] *register, arrange for*
bespeak, bill, charter, engage, enroll, enter, hire, line up*, make reservation, order, organize, pencil in*, preengage, procure, program, reserve, schedule, set up, sew up*; SEE CONCEPT *36*

book [*v2*] *arrest*
accuse, charge, prefer charges, take into custody; SEE CONCEPT *317*

boom [*n1*] *loud sound; crash*
bang, barrage, blare, blast, burst, cannonade, clap, crack, drumfire, explosion, reverberation, roar, rumble, slam, smash, thunder, wham; SEE CONCEPTS *521,595*

boom [*n2*] *prosperity*
advance, boost, development, expansion, gain, growth, improvement, increase, inflation, jump, prosperousness, push, rush, spurt, upsurge, upswing, upturn; SEE CONCEPTS *230,335,700*

boom [*v1*] *crash; make loud sound*
bang, blast, burst, clap, crack, drum, explode, resound, reverberate, roar, roll, rumble, slam, smash, sound, thunder, wham; SEE CONCEPT *65*

boom [*v2*] *prosper*
appreciate, bloom, develop, enhance, expand, flourish, flower, gain, grow, increase, intensify, rise in value, spurt, strengthen, succeed, swell, thrive; SEE CONCEPTS *700,704*

boomerang [*v*] *backfire*
backlash, bounce back, come back, come home to roost*, kick back, react, rebound, recoil, return, reverse, ricochet; SEE CONCEPTS *242,695*

boon [*n*] *advantage*
benefaction, benefit, benevolence, blessing, break, compliment, donation, favor, gift, godsend, good,

good fortune, grant, gratuity, help, largess, present, windfall; SEE CONCEPTS *337,661*

boor [*n*] *clod*
barbarian, bear, boob*, brute, buffoon, cad, churl, dork*, goon*, lout, oaf, peasant, philistine, rube, vulgarian; SEE CONCEPT *423*

boorish [*adj*] *crude, awkward*
bad-mannered, barbaric, bearish, cantankerous, churlish, cloddish, clodhopping*, clownish, clumsy, coarse, countrified, gross*, gruff, ill-bred, ill-mannered, impolite, inurbane, loud, loutish, low-bred, oafish, ornery, out-of-line, out-of-order, provincial, rough, rude, rustic, swinish, tasteless, ugly, uncivilized, uncouth, uncultured, uneducated, ungracious, unpoised, unpolished, unrefined, vulgar; SEE CONCEPT *404*

boost [*n1*] *increase*
addition, advance, breakthrough, expansion, hike, improvement, increment, jump, lift, raise, rise, step-up, up, upgrade, wax; SEE CONCEPTS *700,780*

boost [*n2*] *encouragement*
aid, assistance, backup, buildup, goose*, hand*, handout, help, helping hand, improvement, leg*, leg up*, lift, praise, promotion, shot in the arm*, support; SEE CONCEPT *110*

boost [*n3*] *push, usually up*
advance, goose*, heave, hoist, lift, raise, shove, thrust; SEE CONCEPTS *196,208*

boost [*v1*] *further, improve*
advance, advertise, assist, encourage, foster, inspire, plug, praise, promote, push, support, sustain; SEE CONCEPT *244*

boost [*v2*] *push, usually up*
advance, elevate, heave, heighten, hoist, lift, raise, shove, thrust, upraise, uprear; SEE CONCEPTS *196,208*

boost [*v3*] *increase*
add to, aggrandize, amplify, augment, beef up*, develop, enlarge, expand, extend, heighten, hike, jack up*, jump, magnify, multiply, put up, raise, up; SEE CONCEPTS *236,245*

boot [*n*] *heavy, often tall, shoe*
brogan, footwear, galoshes, mukluk, oxford, snow shoes, waders*, waters*; SEE CONCEPT *450*

boot [*v*] *kick; oust*
ax, bounce, can*, chase, chuck*, cut, discharge, dismiss, drive, dropkick*, eighty-six*, eject, evict, expel, extrude, fire, heave, kick out, knock, punt*, sack*, shove, terminate, throw out; SEE CONCEPTS *180,189*

booth [*n*] *small enclosure or building*
berth, box, carrel, compartment, coop, corner, cote, counter, cubbyhole, cubicle, dispensary, hut, hutch, nook, pen, pew, repository, shed, stall, stand; SEE CONCEPTS *439,440,443*

border [*n1*] *outermost edge, margin*
bound, boundary, bounds, brim, brink, circumference, confine, end, extremity, fringe, hem, limit, line, lip, outskirt, perimeter, periphery, rim, selvage, skirt, trim, trimming, verge; SEE CONCEPTS *484,827*

border [*n2*] *boundary; frontier*
beginning, borderline, door, edge, entrance, line, march, marchland, outpost, pale, perimeter, sideline, threshold; SEE CONCEPTS *484,513*

border [*v*] *bound on; be on the edge*
abut, adjoin, be adjacent to, bind, circumscribe, communicate, contour, decorate, define, delineate, edge, encircle, enclose, flank, frame, fringe, hem, join, line, march, margin, mark off, neighbor, outline, rim, set off, side, skirt, surround, touch, trim, verge; SEE CONCEPT *747*

borderline [*adj*] *inexact*
ambiguous, ambivalent, doubtful, dubitable, equivocal, indecisive, indefinite, indeterminate, marginal, open, problematic, uncertain, unclassifiable, unclear, undecided, unsettled; SEE CONCEPT *534*

border on [*v*] *come close to; approximate*
abut, adjoin, approach, be like, be similar to, come near, compare, connect, contact, echo, impinge, join, lie near, lie next to, march, match, near, neighbor, parallel, resemble, touch, verge on; SEE CONCEPTS *667,749*

bore [*n*] *nuisance*
bother, bromide, bummer*, creep*, deadhead*, downer*, drag*, drip*, dull person, flat tire*, headache, nag, nudge, pain*, pain in the neck*, pest, pill*, soporific, stuffed shirt*, tedious person, tiresome person, wet blanket*, wimp, yawn*; SEE CONCEPT *423*

bore [*v1*] *drill hole*
burrow, gouge out, mine, penetrate, perforate, pierce, pit, prick, punch, puncture, ream, riddle, sink, tunnel; SEE CONCEPT *178*

bore [*v2*] *cause weariness, disinterest*
afflict, annoy, be tedious, bend one's ear*, bother, burn out, cloy, discomfort, drag, exhaust, fatigue, irk, irritate, jade, pall, pester, put to sleep*, send to sleep*, talk one's ear off*, tire, trouble, turn one off*, vex, wear, wear out, weary, worry; SEE CONCEPTS *7,19*

boredom [*n*] *disinterest; weariness*
apathy, detachment, disgust, distaste, doldrums, dullness, ennui, fatigue, flatness, incuriosity, indifference, irksomeness, jadedness, lack of interest, lassitude, lethargy, listlessness, monotony, pococurantism, sameness, taedium vitae, tediousness, tedium, tiresomeness, unconcern, weariness, world-weariness, yawn; SEE CONCEPT *410*

boring [*adj*] *uninteresting*
arid, bomb*, bromidic, bummer*, characterless, cloying, colorless, commonplace, dead*, drab, drag*, drudging, dull, flat*, ho hum*, humdrum*, insipid, interminable, irksome, lifeless, monotonous, moth-eaten*, mundane, nothing, nowhere, platitudinous, plebeian, prosaic, repetitious, routine, spiritless, stale, stereotyped, stodgy, stuffy, stupid, tame, tedious, threadbare, tiresome, tiring, trite, unexcit-

ing, uninteresting, unvaried, vapid, wearisome, well-worn, zero*; SEE CONCEPT *529*

born [*adj*] *innate*
built-in, congenital, constitutional, deep-seated, essential, inborn, inbred, ingenerate, inherent, intrinsic, natural; SEE CONCEPTS *549,550*

borrow [*v1*] *take for temporary use*
accept loan of, acquire, beg, bite, bum, cadge*, chisel*, give a note for*, hire, hit up*, lift, mooch*, negotiate, obtain, pawn, pledge, raise money, rent, run into debt, scrounge, see one's uncle*, soak, sponge*, take on loan, tap, touch, use temporarily; SEE CONCEPT *89*

borrow [*v2*] *adopt from another source; appropriate*
acquire, adopt, assume, copy, filch, imitate, make one's own, obtain, pilfer, pirate, plagiarize, simulate, steal, take, use, usurp; SEE CONCEPT *225*

bosom [*n1*] *breast*
bust, chest, melons, rack, rib cage, teats; SEE CONCEPT *418*

bosom [*n2*] *heart; core*
affections, center, circle, conscience, emotions, feelings, inside, interior, sentiments, soul, spirit, sympathies; SEE CONCEPTS *410,826*

boss [*n*] *manager over other employees*
administrator, big cheese*, big gun*, big man/woman*, chief, chieftain, controller, director, dominator, employer, exec, executive, foreman/woman, head, head honcho*, honcho*, leader, master, overseer, owner, person in charge, superintendent, supervisor, taskmaster, top dog*, wheel*; SEE CONCEPT *347*

boss [*adj*] *great*
awesome*, bang-up*, capital, champion, excellent, fine, first-rate, fly*, top, whiz-bang*, wonderful; SEE CONCEPT *572*

boss [*v*] *control; command*
administrate, chaperon, direct, employ, manage, overlook, oversee, quarterback, run, superintend, supervise, survey, take charge; SEE CONCEPT *117*

botany [*n*] *study of plants*
anatomy, cytology, dendrology, ecology, floristics, genetics, horticulture, morphology, natural history, paleobotany, pathology, physiology, phytogeography, phytology, pomology, study of flora, study of vegetation, taxonomy; SEE CONCEPT *349*

botch [*v*] *blunder*
blow*, bobble*, boggle*, bollix*, boot, bumble, bungle, butcher*, distort, err, fall down*, flounder, flub*, fumble, goof up*, gum up*, louse up*, mar, mend, mess, mess up*, misapply, miscalculate, miscompute, misconjecture, misconstrue, mishandle, misjudge, mismanage, muck up*, muddle, muff, mutilate, patch, pull a boner*, ruin, screw up*, spoil, stumble, wreck; SEE CONCEPT *101*

both [*det*] *two together*
one and the other, the couple, the pair, the two, twain; SEE CONCEPT *714*

bother [*n*] *trouble, inconvenience*
ado, aggravation, annoyance, anxiety, bellyache*, botheration, bustle, care, concern, difficulty, distress, drag, exasperation, flurry, fuss, headache*, irritant, irritation, molestation, nudge, nuisance, pain*, pain in the neck*, perplexity, pest, plague, pother*, pressure, problem, strain, to-do*, trial, trouble, vexation, worriment, worry; SEE CONCEPT *532*

bother [*v1*] *harass, annoy; give trouble*
afflict, aggravate, agitate, alarm, badger, bedevil, bore, browbeat, carp at, concern, cross, discommode, disconcert, disgust, dismay, displease, disquiet, distress, disturb, eat, embarrass, exacerbate, exasperate, goad, grate on, grieve, harry, hinder, hurt, impede, inconvenience, insult, intrude upon, irk, irritate, molest, nag, needle, nudge, pain, perplex, perturb, pester, pick on, plague, provoke, pursue, put out, ride, scare, spite, tantalize, taunt, tease, torment, trouble, upset, vex, worry; SEE CONCEPTS *7,19*

bother [*v2*] *take the trouble*
be concerned about, concern oneself, exert oneself, fuss over, go out of one's way*, make a fuss about*, make an effort, put oneself out*, take pains, try, worry about; SEE CONCEPT *87*

bothersome [*adj*] *troubling*
aggravating, annoying, distressing, disturbing, exasperating, incommodious, inconvenient, irritating, remote, tiresome, troublesome, vexatious, vexing; SEE CONCEPT *529*

bottle [*n*] *container, usually for liquids*
canteen, carafe, cruet, dead soldier, decanter, ewer, flagon, flask, glass, jar, jug, phial, soldier, urn, vacuum bottle, vial; SEE CONCEPT *494*

bottle up [*v*] *keep feeling inside oneself*
box up, check, collar, contain, coop up, corner, cramp, curb, keep back, restrain, restrict, shut in, suppress, trap; SEE CONCEPT *35*

bottom [*n1*] *foundation*
base, basement, basis, bed, bedrock, belly, deepest part, depths, floor, foot, footing, ground, groundwork, lowest part, nadir, nether portion, pedestal, pediment, rest, seat, sole, substratum, substructure, support, terra firma, underbelly, underneath, underside; SEE CONCEPT *442*

bottom [*n2*] *base, core*
basis, bottom line, cause, essence, essentiality, ground, heart, mainspring, marrow, origin, pith, principle, quintessence, root, soul, source, stuff, substance, virtuality; SEE CONCEPTS *648,826*

bottom [*n3*] *rear end*
backside, behind, breech, bum*, butt*, buttocks, derriere, fanny*, fundament, posterior, rear, rump, seat, tail, tush*; SEE CONCEPT *418*

bottom [*adj*] *lowest; fundamental*
basal, base, basement, basic, foundational, ground, last, lowermost, lowest, meat-and-potatoes*, nether-

most, primary, radical, rock-bottom, underlying, undermost; SEE CONCEPTS *585,586,735,799*

bottom line [*n*] *conclusion*
determination, final decision, income, last word, loss, main point, net, profit; SEE CONCEPT *230*

bough [*n*] *branch*
arm, fork, limb, offshoot, shoot, sprig, sucker; SEE CONCEPT *428*

boulevard [*n*] *street, often lined with trees*
artery, avenue, drag, highway, passage, path, road, thoroughfare, track, way; SEE CONCEPT *501*

bounce [*n*] *spring*
animation, bound, dynamism, elasticity, energy, give, go, life, liveliness, pep, rebound, recoil, resilience, springiness, vigor, vitality, vivacity, zip; SEE CONCEPTS *150,411*

bounce [*v1*] *spring up; rebound*
backlash, bob, boomerang, bound, buck, bump, carom, fly back, glance off, hop, hurdle, jerk up and down*, jounce, jump, kick back, leap, rebound, recoil, resile, ricochet, saltate, snap back, spring back, thump, vault; SEE CONCEPTS *150,194*

bounce [*v2*] *evict*
ax*, boot out*, can*, discharge, dismiss, eighty-six*, eject, fire, give one notice, give the heave ho*, heave*, kick out*, oust, sack*, terminate, throw; SEE CONCEPTS *211,351,384*

bound/bounds [*n*] *farthest limit*
boundary, compass, confine, edge, end, environs, extremity, fringe, limit, limitation, line, march, margin, pale, periphery, precinct, purlieus, rim, term, termination, verge; SEE CONCEPTS *484,787*

bound [*adj*] *obligated; destined*
apprenticed, articled, bent, bounden, certain, coerced, compelled, constrained, contracted, doomed, driven, duty-bound, enslaved, fated, firm, forced, having no alternative, impelled, indentured, intent, made, necessitated, obligated, obliged, pledged, pressed, required, restrained, sure, under compulsion, under necessity, urged; SEE CONCEPT *554*

bound [*v1*] *jump, bounce*
bob, caper, frisk, gambol, hop, hurdle, leap, pounce, prance, recoil, ricochet, saltate, skip, spring, vault; SEE CONCEPT *194*

bound [*v2*] *restrict*
circumscribe, confine, define, delimit, delimitate, demarcate, determine, encircle, enclose, hem in, limit, mark, mark out, measure, restrain, restrict, surround, terminate; SEE CONCEPT *130*

boundary [*n*] *outer limit*
abuttals, ambit, barrier, beginning, border, borderland, borderline, bounds, brink, circumference, circumscription, compass, confines, edge, end, environs, extent, extremity, frame, fringe, frontier, hem, horizon, limits, line, line of demarcation, march, margin, mark, mere, mete, outline, outpost, pale, perimeter, periphery, precinct, purlieus, radius,

rim, side, skirt, terminal, termination, terminus, verge; SEE CONCEPTS *5,484,745*

bounded [*adj*] *limited, confined*
belted, bordered, boundaried, circumscribed, compassed, contiguous, defined, definite, delimited, determinate, edged, encircled, enclosed, encompassed, enveloped, fenced, finite, flanked, fringed, girdled, hedged, hog-tied*, limitary, restricted, rimmed, ringed, surrounded, walled; SEE CONCEPTS *554,772*

boundless [*adj*] *endless, without limit*
great, illimitable, immeasurable, immense, incalculable, indefinite, inexhaustible, infinite, limitless, measureless, no catch*, no end of, no end to, no holds barred*, no strings*, no strings attached*, tremendous, unbounded, unconfined, unending, unlimited, untold, vast, wide open; SEE CONCEPTS *554,772*

bountiful [*adj*] *abundant*
ample, aplenty, bounteous, copious, crawling with*, dime a dozen*, exuberant, free, galore, generous, handsome, lavish, liberal, luxuriant, magnanimous, munificent, no end*, plenteous, plentiful, plenty, prolific, stink with*, unsparing; SEE CONCEPT *771*

bounty [*n*] *bonus; compensation*
donation, gift, grant, gratuity, largess, pay, premium, present, prize, recompense, reward; SEE CONCEPTS *337,344*

bouquet [*n1*] *flower arrangement*
boutonniere, buttonhole, corsage, festoon, garland, lei, nosegay, posy, pot, spray, vase, wreath; SEE CONCEPTS *425,429*

bouquet [*n2*] *aroma*
aura, balm, fragrance, incense, odor, perfume, redolence, savor, scent, smell, spice; SEE CONCEPT *599*

bourgeois [*adj*] *commonplace*
common, conservative, conventional, hidebound, illiberal, materialistic, middle-class, old-line, Philistine, traditional, Victorian; SEE CONCEPTS *530,589*

bout [*n1*] *period of time in which something occurs*
bender, binge, bust, course, fit*, go*, round, run, session, shift, spell, spree, stint, stretch, tear, term, toot*, tour, trick*, turn, winging*; SEE CONCEPT *807*

bout [*n2*] *competitive fight*
bat, battle, boxing match, competition, contest, encounter, engagement, go, match, round, set-to, struggle; SEE CONCEPTS *92,106*

bow [*n1*] *bend from waist*
angle, arc, arch, bend, bending, bob, curtsy, curvation, curvature, curve, flection, flexure, genuflection, inclination, kowtow*, nod, obeisance, round, salaam, turn, turning; SEE CONCEPTS *154,201*

bow [*n2*] *front of boat*
beak, bowsprit, fore, forepart, head, nose, prow, stem; SEE CONCEPT *502*

bow [*v1*] *bend over*
arch, bob, cower, crook, curtsy, curve, debase, dip, do obeisance, droop, duck*, genuflect, hunch, incline, nod, round, stoop; SEE CONCEPT *213*

bow [v2] *submit, concede*
accept, acquiesce, bend, be servile, capitulate, cave, comply, defer, give in, knuckle*, knuckle under*, kowtow*, relent, succumb, surrender, yield; SEE CONCEPT *23*

bowels [n] *insides*
belly, core, deep, depths, entrails, guts, hold, innards, interior, intestines, penetralia, recesses, viscera, vitals; SEE CONCEPTS *393,830*

bowl [n] *scooped out container*
basin, boat, casserole, crock, deep dish, dish, porringer, pot, saucer, tureen, urn, vessel; SEE CONCEPTS *493,494*

bowl [v] *roll a ball down a lane*
fling, hurl, pitch, play duckpins, play tenpins, revolve, rotate, spin, throw, trundle, whirl; SEE CONCEPT *363*

box [n] *container, often square or rectangular*
bin, carton, case, casket, chest, coffer, crate, pack, package, portmanteau, receptacle, trunk; SEE CONCEPT *494*

box [v1] *place in square or rectangular container*
case, confine, crate, encase, pack, package, wrap; SEE CONCEPT *209*

box [v2] *punch competitively*
buffet, clout, cuff, duke, exchange blows, hit, mix, scrap, slap, slug, sock, spar, strike, wallop, whack; SEE CONCEPTS *106,189*

boxing [n] *punching competition*
battle, glove game*, mill*, prelim*, prizefighting, pugilism, slugfest*, sparring, the ring*; SEE CONCEPTS *92,363*

boy [n] *young man*
buck, cadet, chap, child, dude*, fellow, gamin, guy, half-pint*, junior, lad, little gentleman, little guy*, little shaver*, master, punk*, puppy*, runt*, schoolboy, shaver*, small fry*, sonny*, sprout*, squirt*, stripling, tadpole*, whippersnapper*, youngster, youth; SEE CONCEPTS *419,424*

boycott [v] *ban; refrain from using*
avoid, bar, blackball*, blacklist, brush off, cut off, embargo, exclude, hold aloof from, ice out*, ostracize, outlaw, pass by*, pass up*, prohibit, proscribe, refuse, reject, shut out*, snub, spurn, strike, withhold patronage; SEE CONCEPTS *25,130*

boyfriend [n] *amorous male acquaintance*
admirer, baby*, beau, companion, crush, daddy*, date, escort, fiancé, flame*, follower, gentleman caller, gentleman friend, heartthrob, honey*, inamorato, lover, main squeeze*, paramour, steady, suitor, swain, sweetheart, truelove, wooer, young man; SEE CONCEPTS *419,423*

boyhood [n] *period before adulthood for male*
adolescence, childhood, formative period, juniority, schoolboy days, teens, young manhood, youth; SEE CONCEPT *816*

boyish [adj] *youthful*
adolescent, boylike, childish, immature, innocent, juvenile, puerile, young; SEE CONCEPTS *578,797*

brace [n] *support*
arm, band, bar, bearing, block, bolster, boom, bracer, bracket, buttress, cantilever, clamp, girder, grip, guy, lever, mainstay, peg, prop, rafter, reinforcement, rib, shore, skid, splice, splint, staff, stanchion, stave, stay, stirrup, strengthener, strut, sustainer, truss, underpinning, vice; SEE CONCEPTS *470,475,499*

brace [v] *support*
bandage, bind, bolster, buttress, fasten, fortify, gird, hold up, prepare, prop, ready, reinforce, shove, steady, steel, strap, strengthen, support, tie, tighten, uphold; SEE CONCEPT *191*

bracelet [n] *wrist jewelry*
arm band, armlet, bangle, circlet, manacle, ornament, trinket, wristlet; SEE CONCEPT *446*

bracing [adj] *brisk; exhilarating*
animating, chilly, cool, crisp, energizing, exhilarative, fortifying, fresh, invigorating, lively, quickening, refreshing, restorative, reviving, rousing, stimulating, stimulative, tonic, vigorous; SEE CONCEPTS *537,605*

brag [v] *talk boastingly*
blow one's own horn*, bluster*, boast, crow*, exult, gasconade, gloat, grandstand, hotdog*, jive*, mouth*, pat oneself on the back*, prate, puff*, rodomontade, showboat*, shuck*, swagger, vaunt; SEE CONCEPTS *49,51*

braggart [n] *person who talks boastingly*
bag of wind*, bigmouth, big talker*, big-timer*, blowhard*, blusterer, boaster, brag, braggadocio, bragger, egotist, exhibitionist, gasbag*, gascon*, grandstander, hotshot*, know-it-all, peacock*, ranter, raver, show-off, strutter, swaggerer, swashbuckler*, swelled head*, trumpeter*, windbag*; SEE CONCEPTS *412,423*

braid [n] *interwoven hair style*
pigtail, plait, ponytail, queue; SEE CONCEPTS *418,716*

braid [v] *interweave*
complect, cue, entwine, interknit, interlace, intertwine, lace, mesh, pigtail, plait, ravel, twine, twist, weave; SEE CONCEPTS *184,202*

brain [n1] *very smart person*
academician, doctor, egghead*, Einstein*, genius, highbrow, intellect, intellectual, mastermind, prodigy, pundit, sage, scholar; SEE CONCEPT *350*

brain [n2] *mind, intelligence*
cerebellum, cerebrum, encephalon, gray matter*, head, intellect, medulla oblongata, mentality, upper story*, wit; SEE CONCEPTS *393,409,420*

brainwash [v] *force to believe or do things*
alter, catechize, condition, convert, convince, educate, indoctrinate, influence, instill, persuade, proselytize, teach; SEE CONCEPT *14*

brake [n] *stopping device; check*
anchor, binders, cinchers, constraint, control, curb, damper, deterrent, discouragement, hamper, hin-

drance, hurdle, obstacle, rein, restraint, retarding device; SEE CONCEPTS *130,463*

brake [*v*] *check; stop*
bar, block, dam, decelerate, halt, hinder, impede, moderate, obstruct, reduce speed, slacken, slow, slow down, stop; SEE CONCEPT *121*

bramble [*n*] *thorny bush*
brier, burr, catch weed, cleaver, furze, goose grass, gorse, hedge, nettle, prick, prickly shrub, shrub, spray, thistle, thistle sage, thorn; SEE CONCEPT *429*

branch [*n1*] *department*
annex, arm, bureau, category, chapter, classification, connection, dependency, derivative, division, extension, local, member, office, outpost, part, portion, section, subdivision, subsection, subsidiary, tributary, wing; SEE CONCEPTS *325,378*

branch [*n2*] *arm, limb*
bough, branchlet, bug, detour, divergence, extension, fork, growth, offshoot, prong, scion, shoot, spray, sprig, wing; SEE CONCEPTS *392,428,471,835*

branch off/branch out [*v*] *extend beyond main part*
add to, develop, diverge, diversify, divide, enlarge, expand, extend, fork, grow, increase, multiply, part, proliferate, ramify, separate, spread out; SEE CONCEPT *756*

brand [*n1*] *type, kind*
cast, character, class, description, grade, make, quality, sort, species, variety; SEE CONCEPT *378*

brand [*n2*] *distinctive label, mark*
brand name, emblem, hallmark, heraldry, imprint, logo, logotype, marker, sign, stamp, symbol, trademark, welt; SEE CONCEPT *284*

brand [*n3*] *stigma*
bar sinister, black eye, blot, blur, disgrace, infamy, mark, mark of Cain, odium, onus, reproach, slur, smirch, spot, stain, stigma, taint; SEE CONCEPT *388*

brandish [*v*] *flaunt, swing around*
come on strong*, display, disport, exhibit, expose, flash, gesture, parade, raise, shake, show, show off, sport, swing, threaten, throw weight around*, trot out*, warn, wield; SEE CONCEPT *261*

brash [*adj*] *impulsive, brazen*
audacious, bold, brazenfaced, cheeky*, cocksure*, cocky*, effervescent, flip, foolhardy, forward, hasty, headlong, heedless, hotheaded, ill-advised, impertinent, impetuous, impolitic, impudent, incautious, inconsiderate, indiscreet, insolent, madcap, maladroit, nervy, precipitate, presuming, presumptuous, pushing, rash, reckless, rude, self-asserting, self-assertive, tactless, thoughtless, undiplomatic, untactful, uppity, vivacious; SEE CONCEPTS *401,404*

brass [*n*] *impulsiveness; nerve*
assumption, audacity, brashness, cheek*, chutzpah*, confidence, effrontery, gall, impertinence, impudence, insolence, presumption, rudeness; SEE CONCEPT *633*

brassy [*adj*] *vulgar, loud to the senses*
arrant, barefaced, blaring, blatant, bold, brash, brazen, flashy, flirtatious, forward, garish, gaudy, grat-

ing, hard, harsh, impudent, insolent, jarring, jazzy, loudmouthed, noisy, obtrusive, overbold, pert, piercing, rude, saucy, shameless, showy, shrill, strident, unabashed, unblushing; SEE CONCEPTS *401,589, 592,594*

brat [*n*] *spoiled child*
devil*, enfant terrible*, holy terror*, impudent child, kid, punk*, rascal, unruly child, urchin, whippersnapper*, wild one*, youngster; SEE CONCEPT *424*

bravado [*n*] *boastfulness*
blowing, bluff, bluster, boasting, bombast, braggadocio, bragging, bullying, crowing*, fancy talk*, fuming*, gasconade, grandiosity, guts, hot air*, macho*, pomposity, pretension, raging, railing, rant, self-glorification, storming, swaggering, swelling, talk, tall talk*; SEE CONCEPTS *49,51*

brave [*adj*] *bold*
adventurous, audacious, chin-up*, chivalrous, confident, courageous, daring, dashing, dauntless, defiant, doughty, fearless, firm, foolhardy, forward, gallant, game, gritty, gutsy, hardy, heroic, herolike, imprudent, indomitable, intrepid, lionhearted, manly, militant, nervy, plucky, reckless, resolute, spirited, spunky, stalwart, stout, stouthearted, strong, unabashed, unafraid, unblenching, undauntable, undaunted, undismayed, unfearful, valiant, valorous, venturesome; SEE CONCEPT *401*

brave [*v*] *endure bad situation*
bear, beard, challenge, confront, court, dare, defy, face, face off, fly in the face of*, go through, outdare, risk, stand up to, suffer, support, take on, venture, withstand; SEE CONCEPT *23*

bravery [*n*] *boldness*
courage, daring, dauntlessness, fearlessness, fortitude, gallantry, grit, guts, hardiness, heroism, indomitability, intrepidity, mettle, pluck, pluckiness, spirit, spunk, valor; SEE CONCEPTS *411,633*

brawl [*n*] *nasty fight*
affray, altercation, argument, battle, battle royal*, bickering, broil, clash, disorder, dispute, donnybrook, duke out*, feud, fight, fracas, fray, free-for-all*, fuss, hassle, hell broke loose*, melee, quarrel, rhubarb*, riot, row, ruckus, rumble, rumpus, scrap, scuffle, squabble, tumult, uproar, wrangle; SEE CONCEPTS *46,106*

brawl [*v*] *fight nastily*
altercate, argue, battle, bicker, buck*, caterwaul, dispute, kick up a row*, quarrel, raise Cain*, roughhouse*, row, rumble, scrap, scuffle, spat, squabble, tiff, tussle, wrangle, wrestle; SEE CONCEPTS *46,106*

brawn [*n*] *muscular strength and breadth*
beef, beefiness, clout, energy, flesh, kick, meat, might, moxie, muscle, muscularity, power, punch, robustness, sinews, sock, steam, thew, vigor; SEE CONCEPTS *723,732*

brawny [*adj*] *muscular, strong*
able-bodied, athletic, beefy, bulky, burly, fleshy, hardy, hefty, herculean, husky, powerful, robust,

sinewy, stalwart, strapping, sturdy, thewy, tough, vigorous, vital; SEE CONCEPTS *485,489*

brazen [*adj*] *brash, unashamed*
audacious, barefaced, blatant, bold, brassy, cheeky, cocky, contumelious, defiant, flashy, flip, forward, gritty, gutsy, hotshot*, immodest, impertinent, impudent, indecent, insolent, loud, meretricious, nervy, overbold, pert, saucy, shameless, smart-alecky*, spunky, tawdry, unabashed, unblushing; SEE CONCEPTS *267,401*

breach [*n1*] *gap*
aperture, break, chasm, chip, cleft, crack, discontinuity, fissure, hole, opening, rent, rift, rupture, slit, split; SEE CONCEPT *513*

breach [*n2*] *violation of a law*
contravention, delinquency, dereliction, disobedience, disregard, infraction, infringement, neglect, noncompliance, nonobservance, offense, transgression, trespass, violation; SEE CONCEPT *192*

breach [*n3*] *change from friendly to unfriendly relationship*
alienation, break, difference, disaffection, disagreement, discord, disharmony, dissension, disunity, division, estrangement, falling-out, fissure, fracture, parting of the ways, quarrel, rent, rift, rupture, schism, secession, separation, severance, split, strife, variance, withdrawal; SEE CONCEPT *388*

bread [*n1*] *daily food*
aliment, bed and board, comestibles, diet, fare, feed, grub*, necessities, nourishment, nurture, nutriment, provender, provisions, shingle*, staff of life*, subsistence, sustenance, viands, victuals; SEE CONCEPT *457*

bread [*n2*] *money*
cabbage*, cash, coin, dollars, dough*, finance, funds, greenbacks*, mazuma*, scratch*; SEE CONCEPT *340*

breadth [*n1*] *width*
broadness, diameter, distance across, latitude, span, spread, wideness; SEE CONCEPT *760*

breadth [*n2*] *extent*
amplitude, area, compass, comprehensiveness, dimension, expanse, extensiveness, fullness, gamut, greatness, inclusiveness, largeness, magnitude, measure, orbit, range, reach, scale, scope, size, space, spread, stretch, sweep, vastness; SEE CONCEPTS *651,756,787*

break [*n1*] *fissure, opening*
breach, cleft, crack, discontinuity, disjunction, division, fracture, gap, gash, hole, rent, rift, rupture, schism, split, tear; SEE CONCEPTS *230,757*

break [*n2*] *interruption of activity*
blow, breather, breathing space, caesura, coffee break, cutoff, downtime, halt, hiatus, interlude, intermission, interval, lacuna, layoff*, letup*, lull, pause, recess, respite, rest, suspension, ten*, time off, time out; SEE CONCEPT *807*

break [*n3*] *change from friendly to unfriendly relationship*
alienation, altercation, breach, clash, difference of opinion, disaffection, dispute, divergence, estrangement, fight, misunderstanding, rift, rupture, schism, separation, split, trouble; SEE CONCEPT *388*

break [*n4*] *lucky happening*
accident, advantage, chance, favorable circumstances, fortune, good luck, luck, occasion, opening, opportunity, shot, show, stroke of luck, time; SEE CONCEPT *679*

break [*v1*] *destroy; make whole into pieces*
annihilate, batter, burst, bust, bust up, crack, crash, crush, damage, demolish, disintegrate, divide, eradicate, finish off, fracture, fragment, make hash of*, make mincemeat of*, part, pull to pieces, rend, separate, sever, shatter, shiver, smash, snap, splinter, split, tear, torpedo, total, trash; SEE CONCEPT *252*

break [*v2*] *violate law*
breach, contravene, disobey, disregard, infract, infringe, offend, renege on, transgress, violate; SEE CONCEPT *192*

break [*v3*] *weaken, cause instability*
bankrupt, bust, confound, confute, controvert, cow, cripple, declass, degrade, demerit, demoralize, demote, disconfirm, dispirit, disprove, downgrade, enervate, enfeeble, humiliate, impair, impoverish, incapacitate, pauperize, rebut, reduce, refute, ruin, subdue, tame, undermine; SEE CONCEPT *240*

break [*v4*] *stop an action*
abandon, cut, discontinue, give up, interrupt, pause, rest, suspend; SEE CONCEPT *121*

break [*v5*] *tell news*
announce, come out, communicate, convey, disclose, divulge, impart, inform, let out, make public, pass on, proclaim, reveal, tell, transmit; SEE CONCEPT *60*

break [*v6*] *better a performance*
beat, cap, exceed, excel, go beyond, outdo, outstrip, surpass, top; SEE CONCEPT *141*

break [*v7*] *emerge, happen*
appear, befall, betide, burst out, chance, come forth, come off, come to pass, develop, erupt, go, occur, transpire; SEE CONCEPT *4*

break [*v8*] *run away*
abscond, bust out, clear out*, cut and run*, dash, decamp, escape, flee, fly, get away, get out, run away; SEE CONCEPTS *102,195*

break [*v9*] *cushion something's effect*
diminish, lessen, lighten, moderate, reduce, soften, weaken; SEE CONCEPT *110*

breakable [*adj*] *easily hurt or destroyed*
brittle, crisp, crispy, crumbly, delicate, flimsy, fracturable, fragile, frail, frangible, friable, shatterable, shattery, splintery, vitreous, weak; SEE CONCEPTS *489,606*

breakdown [*n1*] *nervous collapse*
basket case*, crackup*, disintegration, disruption, failure, mishap, nervous prostration, neurosis, psychasthenia, stoppage; SEE CONCEPT *410*

breakdown [*n2*] *account of finances or other business*
analysis, categorization, classification, detailed list, diagnosis, dissection, itemization, resolution; SEE CONCEPT *283*

break in [*v1*] *intrude*
barge in, breach, break and enter, burglarize, burgle, burst in*, butt in*, interfere, interject, interrupt, intervene, invade, meddle, raid, rob, steal, trespass; SEE CONCEPTS *139,192*

break in [*v2*] *train in new skill*
accustom, condition, educate, gentle, get used to, habituate, initiate, instruct, prepare, tame; SEE CONCEPT *285*

break off [*v1*] *snap off something*
detach, disassemble, divide, part, pull off, separate, sever, splinter, take apart; SEE CONCEPT *211*

break off [*v2*] *end activity*
cease, desist, discontinue, end, finish, halt, pause, stop, suspend, terminate; SEE CONCEPT *234*

break out [*v1*] *happen, emerge*
appear, arise, begin, burst forth, commence, erupt, explode, occur, set in, spring up, start; SEE CONCEPT *701*

break out [*v2*] *escape*
abscond, bolt, break loose, burst out, bust out, depart, flee, get free, leave; SEE CONCEPTS *102,195*

breakthrough [*n*] *advance, progress*
boost, development, discovery, find, finding, gain, hike, improvement, increase, invention, leap, progress, quantum leap, rise, step forward; SEE CONCEPT *704*

breakup [*n*] *end of relationship*
breakdown, breaking, crackup*, disintegration, dispersal, dissolution, divorce, ending, parting, rift, separation, split, splitsville*, splitting, termination, wind-up; SEE CONCEPT *385*

break up [*v*] *end relationship, activity*
adjourn, disassemble, disband, dismantle, disperse, disrupt, dissolve, divide, divorce, end, halt, part, put an end to, scatter, separate, sever, split, stop, sunder, suspend, take apart, terminate; SEE CONCEPT *234*

breast [*n1*] *front of upper body*
bosom, bust, chest, front, mammary glands, mammilla, nipple, rack, set, teat, udder; SEE CONCEPT *418*

breast [*n2*] *feelings, conscience*
being, bosom, character, core, emotions, essential nature, heart, mind, psyche, seat of affections, sentiments, soul, spirit, thoughts; SEE CONCEPTS *410,529*

breath [*n1*] *respiration*
animation, breathing, eupnea, exhalation, expiration, gasp, gulp, inhalation, inspiration, insufflation, pant, wheeze; SEE CONCEPT *163*

breath [*n2*] *wind or something in the air*
aroma, faint breeze, flatus, flutter, gust, odor, puff, sigh, smell, vapor, waft, whiff, zephyr; SEE CONCEPTS *437,599*

breath [*n3*] *respite, break*
blow*, breather, breathing space*, instant, moment, pause, rest, second, ten*; SEE CONCEPT *807*

breath [*n4*] *hint, suggestion*
dash, murmur, shade, soupçon, streak, suspicion, touch, trace, undertone, whiff, whisper; SEE CONCEPTS *278,831*

breathe [*v1*] *take air in and let out*
draw in, exhale, expire, fan, gasp, gulp, inhale, insufflate, open the floodgates*, pant, puff, respire, scent, sigh, sniff, snore, snort, use lungs, wheeze; SEE CONCEPTS *163,601*

breathe [*v2*] *inspire action*
imbue, impart, infuse, inject, instill, transfuse; SEE CONCEPT *242*

breathe [*v3*] *tell information*
articulate, confide, express, murmur, say, sigh, utter, voice, whisper; SEE CONCEPT *60*

breathless [*adj1*] *unable to respire normally*
asthmatic, blown, choking, emphysematous, exhausted, gasping, gulping, out of breath, panting, short of breath, short-winded, spent, stertorous, wheezing, winded; SEE CONCEPT *406*

breathless [*adj2*] *astounded*
agog, anxious, avid, eager, excited, flabbergasted, open-mouthed, thunderstruck, with bated breath; SEE CONCEPT *403*

breathtaking [*adj*] *beautiful, awesome*
amazing, astonishing, awe-inspiring, exciting, hairraising, heart-stirring, heart-stopping, impressive, magnificent, moving, overwhelming, spine-tingling, stunning, thrilling; SEE CONCEPT *529*

breed [*n*] *kind, class*
brand, character, extraction, family, feather, genus, ilk, likes, line, lineage, lot, nature, number, pedigree, progeny, race, sort, species, stamp, stock, strain, stripe, type, variety; SEE CONCEPT *378*

breed [*v1*] *generate, bring into being*
bear, beget, bring about, bring forth, cause, create, deliver, engender, father, give birth to, give rise to, hatch, impregnate, induce, make, mother, multiply, originate, procreate, produce, progenerate, propagate, reproduce, sire; SEE CONCEPTS *173,251,302,373*

breed [*v2*] *raise, nurture*
bring up, cultivate, develop, discipline, educate, foster, instruct, nourish, nurture, raise, rear; SEE CONCEPTS *285,295*

breeding [*n*] *cultivation of person*
ancestry, civility, conduct, courtesy, culture, development, gentility, grace, lineage, manners, nurture, polish, raising, rearing, refinement, schooling, training, upbringing, urbanity; SEE CONCEPT *388*

breeze [*n*] *light wind*
air, airflow, breath, current, draft, flurry, gust, puff, waft, whiff, zephyr; SEE CONCEPTS *437,524*

breeze [*v*] *work quickly through task*
cruise, flit, glide, hurry, move, pass, sail, sally, skim, slide, slip, sweep, trip, waltz, zip; SEE CONCEPT *704*

breezy [*adj1*] *windy*
airy, blowing, blowy, blusterous, blustery, drafty, fresh, gusty, squally, stormy; SEE CONCEPT *525*

breezy [*adj2*] *easy, lighthearted*
airy, animated, blithe, buoyant, carefree, casual, cheerful, debonair, easy-going, effervescent, free

and easy*, gay, informal, jaunty, light, lively, low-pressure, peppy, racy, relaxed, sparkling, spicy, spirited, sprightly, sunny, unconstrained, vivacious; SEE CONCEPT *544*

brevity [*n*] *shortness, briefness*
conciseness, concision, condensation, crispness, curtness, economy, ephemerality, impermanence, pithiness, pointedness, succinctness, terseness, transience, transitoriness; SEE CONCEPTS *730,804*

brew [*n*] *concoction*
beverage, blend, broth, compound, distillation, drink, fermentation, hash, hodgepodge*, infusion, instillation, liquor, melange, miscellany, mishmash*, mixture, potpourri, preparation; SEE CONCEPTS *260,454,457*

brew [*v1*] *prepare by boiling*
boil, concoct, cook, ferment, infuse, mull, seethe, soak, steep, stew; SEE CONCEPT *170*

brew [*v2*] *plan, devise*
breed, compound, concoct, contrive, develop, excite, foment, form, gather, hatch, impend, loom, mull, plot, project, scheme, start, stir up, weave; SEE CONCEPT *36*

bribe [*n*] *payoff for silence*
allurement, bait, blackmail, buyoff, compensation, contract, corrupting gift, corrupt money, enticement, envelope*, feedbag*, fringe benefit, gift, goody*, graft, gratuity, gravy*, grease*, hush money*, ice*, incentive, inducement, influence peddling, kickback, lagniappe, lure, payola*, perk*, perquisite, present, price, protection*, remuneration, reward, sop*, sweetener*, sweetening*, take; SEE CONCEPTS *192,329*

bribe [*v*] *request silence, action, or inaction for money*
approach, black market, buy, buy back, buy off, coax, corrupt, do business*, entice, fix*, get at, get to, grease palm*, influence, instigate, lubricate, lure, make a deal, oil palm*, pay off, pervert, reward, seduce, soap, square, suborn, sugar, sweeten the pot*, take care of, tamper, tempt, tip; SEE CONCEPTS *53,192*

bridal [*adj*] *concerning marriage*
conjugal, connubial, epithalamic, espousal, hymeneal, marital, matrimonial, nubile, nuptial, prewedding, prothalamic, spousal; SEE CONCEPT *536*

bride [*n*] *female marriage partner*
helpmate, mate, newly married woman, newlywed, old lady*, spouse, wife; SEE CONCEPTS *296,415*

bridegroom [*n*] *male marriage partner*
benedict, groom, helpmate, husband, mate, newlywed, old man*, spouse; SEE CONCEPTS *296,419*

bridge [*n*] *structure or something that makes connection*
arch, bond, branch, catwalk, connection, extension, gangplank, link, overpass, platform, pontoon, scaffold, span, tie, transit, trestle, viaduct, wing; SEE CONCEPTS *501,721*

bridge [*v*] *connect, extend*
arch over, attach, bind, branch, couple, cross, cross over, go over, join, link, reach, span, subtend, traverse, unite; SEE CONCEPTS *113,756*

bridle [*n*] *restraining device*
check, control, curb, deterrent, hackamore, halter, headstall, leash, rein, restraint, trammels; SEE CONCEPT *497*

bridle [*v*] *check, hold back*
constrain, control, curb, govern, inhibit, keep in check, master, moderate, repress, restrain, rule, subdue, suppress, withhold; SEE CONCEPT *121*

brief [*n*] *abridgment*
abstract, argument, boildown*, case, condensation, conspectus, contention, data, defense, digest, epitome, outline, précis, sketch, summary, synopsis; SEE CONCEPTS *283,318*

brief [*adj1*] *short, compressed*
abrupt, bluff, blunt, boiled down*, breviloquent, brusque, compendiary, compendious, concise, crisp, curt, hasty, laconic, limited, little, pithy, sharp, short and sweet*, skimpy, small, snippy, succinct, surly, terse, to the point; SEE CONCEPTS *267,773*

brief [*adj2*] *short in time*
concise, curtailed, ephemeral, fast, fleeting, hasty, instantaneous, little, meteoric, momentary, passing, quick, short-lived, short-term, swift, temporary, transient, transitory; SEE CONCEPT *798*

brief [*v*] *inform of facts*
abridge, advise, apprise, edify, enlighten, epitomize, explain, fill in, give rundown*, give the lowdown*, inform, initiate, instruct, let in on*, orient, prepare, prime, recapitulate, show the lay of the land*, show the ropes*, summarize, tip off*, update; SEE CONCEPT *60*

briefcase [*n*] *carrier for work papers*
attaché, bag, baggage, case, dispatch, folder, portfolio; SEE CONCEPTS *446,494*

briefing [*n*] *preparation by informing of facts*
background meeting, conference, directions, discussion, guidance, information, initiation, instruction, meeting, preamble, priming, rundown, update; SEE CONCEPT *60*

brigade [*n*] *fleet of trained people*
army, band, body, company, contingent, corps, crew, detachment, force, group, organization, outfit, party, posse, squad, team, troop, unit; SEE CONCEPTS *322,381*

bright [*adj1*] *shining, glowing in appearance*
ablaze, aglow, alight, argent, auroral, beaming, blazing, brilliant, burning, burnished, coruscating, dazzling, effulgent, flashing, fulgent, fulgid, glaring, gleaming, glistening, glittering, glossy, golden, illuminated, illumined, incandescent, intense, irradiated, lambent, light, lighted, limpid, luminous, lustrous, mirrorlike, moonlit, phosphorescent, polished, radiant, relucent, resplendent, scintillating,

shimmering, shiny, silvery, sparkling, sunlit, sunny, twinkling, vivid; SEE CONCEPT *617*

bright [*adj2*] *sunny, clear (weather)*
clement, cloudless, fair, favorable, limpid, lucid, mild, pellucid, pleasant, translucent, transparent, unclouded; SEE CONCEPT *525*

bright [*adj3*] *intelligent*
acute, advanced, alert, astute, aware, brain, brainy, brilliant, clear-headed, clever, discerning, eggheaded*, Einstein*, having smarts*, ingenious, inventive, keen, knowing, precocious, quick, quick-witted, sharp, smart, whiz kid*, wide-awake; SEE CONCEPT *402*

bright [*adj4*] *hopeful, promising*
airy, auspicious, benign, breezy, cheering, encouraging, excellent, favorable, golden, good, optimistic, palmy, propitious, prosperous, rosy, white; SEE CONCEPT *537*

bright [*adj5*] *cheerful*
alert, animated, gay, genial, glad, happy, jolly, joyful, joyous, keen, lighthearted, lively, merry, optimistic, sanguine, spirited, sprightly, vivacious; SEE CONCEPT *404*

bright [*adj6*] *famous, outstanding*
distinguished, eminent, glorious, illustrious, magnificent, prominent, remarkable, splendid; SEE CONCEPT *568*

bright [*adj7*] *vivid in color*
brave, brilliant, clear, colored, colorful, deep, flashy, fresh, gay, glitzy, hued, intense, psychedelic, razzle-dazzle, rich, ruddy, sharp, showy, tinged, tinted; SEE CONCEPT *618*

brighten [*v1*] *make shine or glow*
buff up, burnish, clear up, enliven, gleam, grow sunny, illuminate, illumine, intensify, kindle, lighten, light up, polish, punch up*, spiff up*; SEE CONCEPTS *244,250*

brighten [*v2*] *make happy, feel better*
become cheerful, buck up, buoy up, cheer, cheer up, clear up, encourage, enliven, gladden, hearten, improve, look up, perk up; SEE CONCEPTS *7,22*

brilliant [*adj1*] *shining, glowing in appearance*
ablaze, bright, coruscating, dazzling, effulgent, flashy, fulgent, gleaming, glittering, glossy, incandescent, intense, lambent, lucent, luminous, lustrous, radiant, refulgent, resplendent, scintillating, showy, sparkling, vivid; SEE CONCEPT *617*

brilliant [*adj2*] *famous, outstanding*
celebrated, distinguished, eminent, excellent, exceptional, glorious, illustrious, magnificent, prominent, splendid, superb; SEE CONCEPT *568*

brilliant [*adj3*] *very intelligent*
accomplished, acute, astute, brainy*, bright, clever, discerning, eggheaded*, Einstein*, expert, genius, gifted, ingenious, intellectual, inventive, knowing, knowledgeable, masterly, penetrating, profound, quick, quick-witted, sharp, smart, smart as a*, talented, whip, whiz kid*; SEE CONCEPT *402*

brim [*n*] *edge of object, usually the top*
border, brink, circumference, fringe, hem, lip, margin, perimeter, periphery, rim, skirt, verge; SEE CONCEPT *836*

brim [*v*] *flow over the top*
fill, fill up, hold no more, overflow, run over, spill, swell, teem, well over; SEE CONCEPT *740*

brimming/brimful [*adj*] *overflowing; up to the top*
awash, chock-full, crammed, crowded, filled, flush, full, full to the top, jammed, level with, loaded, overfull, packed, running over, stuffed, topfull; SEE CONCEPTS *481,771,774*

brine [*n*] *salt solution*
alkali, blue, brackish water, deep, drink, marinade, ocean, pickling solution, preservative, saline, salt water, sea water, sodium chloride solution, vinegar; SEE CONCEPT *514*

bring [*v1*] *transport or accompany*
attend, back, bear, buck*, carry, chaperon, companion, conduct, consort, convey, deliver, escort, fetch, gather, guide, gun*, heel*, import, lead, lug, pack, pick up, piggyback*, ride, schlepp*, shoulder, take, take along, tote, transfer, transport, truck, usher; SEE CONCEPT *143*

bring [*v2*] *cause; influence*
begin, compel, contribute to, convert, convince, create, dispose, effect, engender, force, induce, inflict, lead, make, move, occasion, persuade, prevail on, prevail upon, produce, prompt, result in, sway, wreak; SEE CONCEPT *242*

bring [*v3*] *command a price*
afford, bring in, draw, earn, fetch, gross, net, produce, return, sell for, take, yield; SEE CONCEPTS *330,335*

bring [*v4*] *file charges in court*
appeal, arraign, cite, declare, indict, initiate legal action, institute, prefer, serve, sue, summon, take to court; SEE CONCEPT *317*

bring about [*v*] *cause success*
accomplish, achieve, beget, bring to pass, compass, create, do, draw on, effect, effectuate, engender, generate, give rise to, make happen, manage, occasion, produce, realize, secure, succeed; SEE CONCEPTS *244,706*

bring around [*v*] *convince, induce*
argue, convert, draw, get, indoctrinate, persuade, prevail upon, prompt, prove, talk into, win over; SEE CONCEPT *68*

bring down [*v*] *reduce or hurt*
abase, cut down, damage, drop, fell, floor, injure, knock down, KO*, lay low, level, lower, mow down, murder*, overthrow, overturn, prostrate, pull down, shoot down, slay*, throw down, tumble, undermine, upset, wound; SEE CONCEPTS *7,19,252*

bring in [*v*] *make a profit*
accrue, acquire, bear, be worth, bring, cost, earn, fetch, gain, get, gross, make, pay, produce, realize, return, sell, yield; SEE CONCEPTS *124,330*

bring off [v] *accomplish*
achieve, bring home the bacon*, bring to pass, carry off, carry out, discharge, effect, effectuate, execute, perform, pull off, realize, succeed; SEE CONCEPTS *704,706*

bring up [v1] *raise youngster*
breed, cultivate, develop, discipline, educate, feed, form, foster, nourish, nurture, provide for, rear, school, support, teach, train; SEE CONCEPT *295*

bring up [v2] *initiate, mention in conversation*
advance, advert, allude to, broach, discuss, introduce, moot, move, offer, point out, propose, put forward, raise, raise a subject, refer, submit, tender, touch on, ventilate; SEE CONCEPT *51*

brink [n] *edge of an object or area*
border, boundary, brim, fringe, frontier, limit, lip, margin, perimeter, periphery, point, rim, skirt, threshold, verge; SEE CONCEPTS *484,513*

brisk [adj1] *fast-moving; active*
adroit, agile, alert, animated, bustling, busy, energetic, lively, nimble, quick, speedy, sprightly, spry, vigorous, vivacious, zippy; SEE CONCEPTS *542,584*

brisk [adj2] *chilly, refreshing (weather)*
biting, bracing, crisp, exhilarating, fresh, invigorating, keen, nippy, sharp, snappy, stimulating; SEE CONCEPT *605*

bristle [n] *short, prickly hair*
barb, feeler, fiber, point, prickle, quill, spine, stubble, thorn, vibrissa, whisker; SEE CONCEPT *418*

bristle [v] *become upset, excited*
be angry, be infuriated, be maddened, blow up*, boil, boil over, bridle, flare, flare up, fume, get one's dander up*, rage, rise, ruffle, see red*, seethe, spit*, stand on end*, swell; SEE CONCEPT *410*

brittle [adj1] *fragile*
breakable, crisp, crumbling, crumbly, delicate, fragile, frail, frangible, friable, inelastic, shatterable, shivery, vitreous, weak; SEE CONCEPTS *488,606*

brittle [adj2] *tense*
curt, edgy, irritable, nervous, prim, short, stiff, stilted; SEE CONCEPT *401*

broach [v1] *bring up a topic*
advance, approach, bring up, hint at, interject, interpose, introduce, mention, moot, move, offer, open up, propose, raise subject, speak of, submit, suggest, talk of, touch on, ventilate; SEE CONCEPT *51*

broach [v2] *open, pierce*
begin, crack, decant, draw off, puncture, start, tap, uncork; SEE CONCEPTS *142,225*

broad [adj1] *wide physically*
ample, capacious, deep, expansive, extended, extensive, full, generous, immense, large, latitudinous, outspread, outstretched, roomy, spacious, splay, squat, thick, vast, voluminous, widespread; SEE CONCEPTS *773,796*

broad [adj2] *extensive*
all-embracing, all-inclusive, comprehensive, copious, encyclopedic, expansive, extended, far-flung, far-reaching, general, inclusive, nonspecific, scopic, sweeping, ubiquitous, undetailed, universal, unlimited, wide, wide-ranging, widespread; SEE CONCEPT *772*

broad [adj3] *full, obvious*
apparent, clear, explicit, open, plain, straightforward, undisguised, unequivocal; SEE CONCEPT *576*

broad [adj4] *liberal-minded*
advanced, cultivated, experienced, open, open-minded, permissive, progressive, radical, tolerant, unbiased, wide; SEE CONCEPT *403*

broad [adj5] *vulgar*
blue, coarse, dirty, gross, improper, indecent, indelicate, low-minded, off-color, purple, racy, risqué, salty, saucy, smutty, spicy, suggestive, unrefined, unrestrained, wicked; SEE CONCEPT *545*

broadcast [n] *information on electronic media*
advertisement, air time, announcement, newscast, performance, program, publication, radiocast, show, simulcast, telecast, transmission; SEE CONCEPTS *274,293*

broadcast [v1] *put forth on electronic media*
air, announce, beam, be on the air, cable, circulate, colorcast, communicate, get out, go on the air, go on the airwaves, put on the air, radio, radiograph, relay, send, show, simulcast, telecast, telegraph, telephone, televise, transmit; SEE CONCEPTS *60,292*

broadcast [v2] *make public*
advertise, announce, annunciate, blare, blazon, circulate, communicate, declare, disseminate, distribute, proclaim, promulgate, publish, report, sow, spread, strew, troll; SEE CONCEPT *60*

broadcasting [n] *informing via electronic media*
airing, air time, announcing, auditioning, newscasting, performing, posting online, putting on program, radio, reporting, telecasting, television, transmission, transmitting; SEE CONCEPTS *263,293*

broaden [v] *extend, supplement*
augment, breadthen, develop, enlarge, expand, fatten, grow, increase, open up, ream, spread, stretch, swell, widen; SEE CONCEPT *239*

broad-minded [adj] *liberal*
advanced, catholic, cosmopolitan, dispassionate, flexible, free-thinking, indulgent, liberal, open, open-minded, permissive, progressive, radical, receptive, responsive, tolerant, unbiased, unbigoted, undogmatic, unprejudiced, wide; SEE CONCEPT *403*

brochure [n] *short, printed document*
advertisement, booklet, circular, flyer, folder, handbill, handout, leaflet, pamphlet; SEE CONCEPT *280*

broil [v] *cook under direct heat*
burn, melt, roast, scorch, sear, swelter; SEE CONCEPT *170*

broiling [adj] *very hot*
baking, burning, fiery, on fire, red-hot, roasting, scalding, scorching, sizzling, sweltering, torrid; SEE CONCEPT *605*

broke [adj] *without money*
bankrupt, beggared, bust*, cleaned out*, destitute, dirt poor*, flat broke*, impoverished, in Chapter 11*, in debt, indebted, indigent, insolvent, needy, penniless, penurious, poor, ruined, stone broke*, strapped, tapped out; SEE CONCEPT *334*

broken [adj1] *destroyed; made into pieces from a whole*
burst, busted, collapsed, cracked, crippled, crumbled, crushed, damaged, defective, demolished, disintegrated, dismembered, fractured, fragmentary, fragmented, hurt, injured, in pieces, mangled, mutilated, pulverized, rent, riven, ruptured, separated, severed, shattered, shivered, shredded, slivered, smashed, split; SEE CONCEPT *485*

broken [adj2] *discontinuous*
disconnected, disturbed, erratic, fragmentary, incomplete, intermittent, interrupted, irregular, spasmodic, spastic; SEE CONCEPT *482*

broken [adj3] *mentally defeated*
beaten, browbeaten, crippled, crushed, defeated, demoralized, depressed, discouraged, disheartened, heartsick, humbled, oppressed, overpowered, subdued, tamed, vanquished; SEE CONCEPT *403*

broken [adj4] *not working*
busted, coming unglued, coming unstuck, defective, disabled, down, downtime, exhausted, fallen apart, faulty, feeble, gone, gone to pieces*, gone to pot*, haywire, imperfect, in disrepair, in need of repair, in the shop*, inoperable, kaput*, not functioning, on the blink*, on the fritz*, on the shelf*, out, out of commission*, out of kilter*, out of order, out of whack*, ruined, run-down, screwed up*, shot, spent, unsatisfactory, weak, wracked*, wrecked; SEE CONCEPTS *485,560*

broken [adj5] *forgotten, ignored (promise)*
abandoned, dishonored, disobeyed, disregarded, ignored, infringed, isolated, retracted, traduced, transgressed, violated; SEE CONCEPT *544*

broken [adj6] *stuttering in speech*
disjointed, halting, hesitant, hesitating, imperfect, incoherent, mumbled, muttered, stammering, unintelligible, weak; SEE CONCEPT *267*

brokenhearted [adj] *devastated*
crestfallen, crushed, desolate, despairing, despondent, disappointed, disconsolate, grief-stricken, grieved, heartbroken, heartsick, heartsore, inconsolable, miserable, mournful, prostrated, sorrowful, wretched; SEE CONCEPT *403*

broker [n] *financial expert*
agent, businessman/woman, dealer, entrepreneur, factor, financier, go-between, interagent, interceder, intercessor, intermediary, intermediate, mediator, merchant, middleman, negotiator, stockbroker; SEE CONCEPTS *348,353*

bronze [adj] *coppery-brown color*
brownish, burnished, chestnut, copper, copper-colored, metallic brown, reddish-brown, reddish-tan, russet, rust, tan; SEE CONCEPT *618*

brooch [n] *ornamental pin*
bar pin, breastpin, clip, cluster, jewelry; SEE CONCEPT *446*

brood [n] *cluster of children*
begats, breed, chicks, clutch, descendants, family, flock, hatch, infants, issue, litter, offspring, posterity, progeniture, progeny, scions, seed, young; SEE CONCEPT *296*

brood [v] *agonize over*
be in brown study*, bleed, chafe inwardly*, consider, daydream, deliberate, despond, dream, dwell upon, eat one's heart out*, fret, gloom, grieve, lament, languish, meditate, mope, mull over, muse, ponder, reflect, repine, ruminate, sigh, speculate, stew over*, sulk, sweat out*, sweat over*, think about, think upon, worry; SEE CONCEPT *17*

brook [n] *stream of water*
beck, branch, burn, creek, rill, rindle, river, rivulet, run, runnel, streamlet, watercourse; SEE CONCEPT *514*

brook [v] *endure, accept*
abide, allow, bear, be big*, countenance, go, hang in, hang in there*, hear of, live with, put up with, sit tight*, stand, stomach, suffer, support, swallow, take, tolerate; SEE CONCEPT *23*

broom [n] *device for cleaning floors*
besom, carpet sweeper, feather duster, floor brush, mop, swab, sweeper, whisk; SEE CONCEPT *499*

broth [n] *soup, usually clear*
borscht, bouillon, bowl, brew, chowder, concoction, consommé, decoction, dishwater*, distillation, elixir, fluid, gumbo, hodge-podge*, liquor, olio, porridge, potage, potpourri, pottage, puree, splash, stock, vichyssoise, water; SEE CONCEPTS *457,467*

brothel [n] *house of prostitution*
bagnio, bawdy house*, bordello, call house*, cathouse*, den of iniquity*, house of assignation, house of ill repute, house with red doors*, massage parlor, red-light district, whorehouse; SEE CONCEPT *449*

brother [n1] *male sibling*
blood brother, kin, kinsman, relation, relative, twin; SEE CONCEPTS *414,419*

brother [n2] *peer*
associate, bro*, buddy, chum, colleague, companion, compeer, comrade, confrere, fellow, mate, pal, partner; SEE CONCEPT *423*

brotherhood [n1] *group or organization acting as brothers*
alliance, association, clan, clique, club, community, comradeship, coterie, fellowship, fraternity, guild, league, order, secret society, society, sodality, union; SEE CONCEPTS *381,387*

brotherhood [n2] *friendship*
affiliation, amity, association, brotherliness, camaraderie, companionship, comradeship, consanguinity, equality, family, family connection, fellowship, filiation, friendliness, intimacy, kinship, race, relationship, society; SEE CONCEPT *388*

brotherly [adj] kind, friendly
affectionate, altruistic, amicable, benevolent, chari-table, compassionate, comprehending, comradely, cordial, disinterested, forgiving, fraternal, generous, humane, intimate, kindly, neighborly, personal, phil-anthropic, selfless, solicitous, sympathetic, tender, understanding; SEE CONCEPT 555

brow [n] forehead
countenance, eyebrow, face, frons, front, mien, tem-ple, top; SEE CONCEPT 418

browbeat [v] castigate, nag
badger, bludgeon, bluster, bulldoze*, bully, coerce, cow, despotize, domineer, dragoon, frighten, harass, hector, intimidate, lean on*, lord it over*, oppress, overawe, overbear, put heat on*, put the chill on*, put through the wringer*, threaten, tyrannize; SEE CONCEPTS 14,52

brown [adj] dark, burnished color
amber, auburn, bay, beige, bister, brick, bronze, buff, burnt sienna, chestnut, chocolate, cinnamon, cocoa, coffee, copper, drab, dust, ecru, fawn, gin-ger, hazel, henna, khaki, mahogany, nut, ochre, puce, russet, rust, sepia, snuff-colored, sorrel, tan, tawny, terra-cotta, toast, umber; SEE CONCEPT 618

browse [v] look around; look through
check over, dip into*, examine cursorily, feed, flip through, get the cream*, give the once over*, glance at, graze, hit the high spots*, inspect loosely, leaf through, nibble*, once over lightly*, pass an eye over*, peruse, read, read here and there, riffle through, riff through, run through, scan, skim, skip through, survey, thumb through; SEE CONCEPT 623

bruise [n] black and blue mark under skin
abrasion, black eye, black mark, blemish, boo-boo*, contusion, discoloration, injury, mark, mouse*, swelling, wale, wound; SEE CONCEPT 309

bruise [v] break blood vessel; discolor
bang up, batter, beat, black, blacken, blemish, bung up*, contuse, crush, damage, deface, do a number on*, injure, mar, mark, pound, pulverize, wound, zing*; SEE CONCEPTS 137,246,250

brunette/brunet [adj] dark hair and/or skin
bistered, brown, dusky, pigmented, swart, swarthy, tanned, tawny; SEE CONCEPTS 406,579,618

brunt [n] bad end of a situation
burden, force, full force, impact, pressure, shock, strain, stress, tension, thrust, violence; SEE CONCEPT 674

brush [n1] tool with bristles for cleaning
besom, broom, hairbrush, mop, polisher, sweeper, toothbrush, waxer, whisk; SEE CONCEPT 499

brush [n2] fight
clash, conflict, confrontation, encounter, engage-ment, fracas, rub, run-in, scrap, set-to, skirmish, tap, touch, tussle; SEE CONCEPT 106

brush [n3] scrappy bushes
boscage, bracken, brushwood, chaparral, coppice, copse, cover, dingle, fern, gorse, grove, hedge, scrub, sedge, shrubbery, spinney, thicket, under-growth, underwood; SEE CONCEPT 429

brush [v1] touch lightly
caress, contact, flick, glance, graze, kiss, scrape, shave, skim, smooth, stroke, sweep, tickle; SEE CON-CEPT 612

brush [v2] clean, prepare by whisking
buff, clean, paint, polish, sweep, wash, whisk, wipe; SEE CONCEPTS 165,202

brush aside/brush off [v] ignore; refuse
boycott, cold-shoulder*, contradict, cut, deny, dis-claim, dismiss, disown, disregard, get rid of, have no time for*, ostracize, override, rebuff, reject, repudi-ate, scorn, send away, slight, snub, spurn, sweep aside; SEE CONCEPT 30

brush up [v] improve condition
clean up, cram, go over, look over, polish up, read up, refresh one's memory, refurbish, relearn, reno-vate, reread, retouch, review, revise, study, touch up; SEE CONCEPTS 202,244

brusque [adj] curt, surly
abrupt, bluff, blunt, brief, crusty, discourteous, gruff, hasty, impolite, sharp, short, snappy, snippy, tart, terse, unmannerly; SEE CONCEPTS 267,401

brutal [adj1] cruel, remorseless
barbarous, bloodthirsty, callous, ferocious, gruff, hard, harsh, heartless, impolite, inhuman, insensi-tive, merciless, pitiless, remorseless, rough, rude, ruthless, savage, severe, uncivil, uncivilized, unfeel-ing, unmannerly, unmerciful, vicious; SEE CONCEPT 401

brutal [adj2] crude, rough
animal, bearish, beastly, bestial, brute, brutish, car-nal, coarse, feral, ferine, inhuman, inhumane, rude, savage, swinish, unfeeling; SEE CONCEPT 544

brutality [n] cruel treatment
atrocity, barbarism, barbarity, bloodthirstiness, brut-ishness, choke hold, cruelty, ferocity, fierceness, grossness, inhumanity, ruthlessness, sadism, savage-ness, savagery, third degree*, unfeelingness, vi-ciousness; SEE CONCEPTS 14,86

brutally [adv] cruelly, without remorse
atrociously, barbarically, barbarously, brutishly, cal-lously, demoniacally, diabolically, ferally, fero-ciously, fiercely, hardheartedly, heartlessly, in cold blood, inexorably, inhumanely, inhumanly, meanly, mercilessly, murderously, pitilessly, relentlessly, re-morselessly, ruthlessly, savagely, something fierce, something terrible, unkindly, unrelentingly, vi-ciously; SEE CONCEPT 544

brute [n] barbarian
animal, beast, cannibal, creature, critter, degenerate, devil, fiend, lout, monster, ogre, ruffian, sadist, sav-age, scamp, swine, wild animal; SEE CONCEPTS 394,423

brute [adj] very strong; animallike
animal, beastly, bestial, bodily, carnal, feral, ferine, fleshly, instinctive, mindless, physical, senseless, swinish, unthinking; SEE CONCEPTS 489,540

bubble [n] *globule of air*
air ball*, balloon, barm, bead, blister, blob, drop, droplet, effervescence, foam, froth, lather, sac, spume; SEE CONCEPT *437*

bubble [v] *foam, froth up, especially with sound*
boil, burble, churn, eddy, effervesce, erupt, fester, fizz, gurgle, gush, issue, moil, murmur, percolate, ripple, seep, seethe, simmer, smolder, sparkle, spume, stir, swash, trickle, well; SEE CONCEPTS *179,469*

buck [n] *male animal*
blade, bull, man, sir, stag; SEE CONCEPTS *394,419*

buck [v] *resist, kick off*
bound, combat, contest, dislodge, dispute, duel, fight, jerk, jump, leap, oppose, prance, repel, start, throw, traverse, trip, unseat, vault, withstand; SEE CONCEPTS *180,222*

bucket [n] *container, often for liquids, with handle*
brazier, can, canister, cask, hod, kettle, pail, pot, scuttle, vat; SEE CONCEPT *494*

buckle [n] *fastener with long pin*
catch, clamp, clasp, clip, fastening, harness, hasp; SEE CONCEPT *450*

buckle [v] *contort, warp*
bend, bulge, cave in, collapse, crumple, distort, fold, twist, yield; SEE CONCEPT *702*

buckle down [v] *concentrate on*
address, apply oneself, attend to, bend, dedicate oneself, devote oneself to, exert oneself, give, give oneself over to, keep close to, keep one's mind on, launch into, occupy oneself with, pitch in, set to, throw, turn; SEE CONCEPTS *17,87*

bud [n] *new sprout on plant*
bloom, blossom, embryo, floret, germ, incipient flower, nucleus, shoot, spark; SEE CONCEPT *428*

bud [v] *sprout*
burgeon, burst forth, develop, grow, pullulate, shoot; SEE CONCEPT *427*

budding [adj] *developing, flowering*
beginning, blossoming, burgeoning, bursting forth, embryonic, fledgling, fresh, germinal, germinating, growing, incipient, maturing, nascent, opening, potential, promising, pubescent, pullulating, shooting up, sprouting, vegetating, young; SEE CONCEPT *490*

buddy [n] *friend*
associate, chum, co-mate, co-worker, companion, comrade, confidant, crony, fellow, intimate, mate, pal, peer, sidekick; SEE CONCEPT *423*

budge [v] *dislodge from staid position*
bend, change, change position, convince, give way, inch, influence, locomote, move, persuade, propel, push, remove, roll, shift, slide, stir, sway, yield; SEE CONCEPTS *68,147*

budget [n] *financial plan*
account, aggregate, allocation, allowance, bulk, cost, estimated expenses, finances, fiscal estimate, funds, means, planned disbursement, quantity, quantum, resources, spending plan, statement, total; SEE CONCEPT *332*

budget [v] *plan money or action*
allocate, apportion, calculate, compute, cost, estimate, predict, ration; SEE CONCEPTS *36,330*

buff [n] *enthusiast*
addict, admirer, aficionado, connoisseur, devotee, expert, fan, fiend, freak, habitué, hound, lover, votary; SEE CONCEPTS *352,423*

buff [adj] *sandy color*
bare, blonde, canary, ecru, lemon, light brown, nude, ochre, straw, tan, tawny, yellow-brown, yellowish; SEE CONCEPT *618*

buff [v] *polish to a shine*
brush, burnish, furbish, glaze, gloss, pumice, rub, sandpaper, scour, shine, smooth; SEE CONCEPTS *202,215*

buffer [n] *safeguard*
bulwark, bumper, cushion, defense, fender, intermediary, screen, shield, shock absorber; SEE CONCEPTS *484,729*

buffet [n] *meal set out on table for choosing*
café, cafeteria, cold table, counter, cupboard, lunch wagon, salad bar, shelf, sideboard, snack bar; SEE CONCEPTS *443,459*

buffet [v] *hit repeatedly*
bang, batter, beat, blow, box, bump, clobber, cuff, flail, jolt, knock, pound, pummel, push, rap, shove, slap, smack, spank, strike, thrash, thump, wallop; SEE CONCEPT *189*

buffoon [n] *clownlike person*
antic, bozo, clown, comedian, comic, droll, fool, harlequin, jester, joker, merry-andrew, wag, zany; SEE CONCEPT *423*

bug [n1] *bacterium, microorganism*
bacillus, disease, germ, infection, microbe, virus; SEE CONCEPT *306*

bug [n2] *insect*
ant, beetle, cootie, flea, gnat, louse, pest, vermin; SEE CONCEPT *398*

bug [n3] *obsession*
craze, enthusiasm, fad, mania, rage, zeal; SEE CONCEPT *532*

bug [v1] *bother, disturb*
abrade, annoy, badger, chafe, gall, get on someone*, harass, irk, irritate, needle, nettle, pester, plague, provoke, vex; SEE CONCEPTS *7,19*

bug [v2] *listen to without permission*
eavesdrop, listen in, overhear, spy, tap, wiretap; SEE CONCEPTS *192,596*

bugle [n] *musical horn*
clarion, cornet, misery pipe, trumpet; SEE CONCEPT *262*

build [n] *physical structure, form*
body, conformation, constitution, figure, frame, habit, habitus, physique, shape; SEE CONCEPT *757*

build [v1] *construct structure*
assemble, bring about, carpenter, cast, compile, compose, contrive, engineer, erect, evolve, fabri-

cate, fashion, fit together, forge, form, frame, jerry-build, knock together*, make, manufacture, model, prefab, produce, put together, put up, raise, rear, reconstruct, sculpture, set up, superstruct, synthesize, throw together*, throw up*; SEE CONCEPT *168*

build [*v2*] *initiate, found*
base, begin, constitute, establish, formulate, inaugurate, institute, originate, set up, start; SEE CONCEPT *234*

build [*v3*] *increase, accelerate*
aggrandize, amplify, augment, boost, compound, develop, enlarge, escalate, expand, extend, heighten, improve, intensify, magnify, mount, multiply, strengthen, swell, wax; SEE CONCEPTS *236,245*

builder [*n*] *construction worker*
architect, artisan, constructor, contractor, craftsman, erector, fabricator, framer, inventor, maker, manufacturer, mason, originator, producer; SEE CONCEPT *348*

building [*n*] *constructed dwelling*
architecture, construction, domicile, edifice, erection, fabric, framework, home, house, hut, pile, superstructure; SEE CONCEPTS *439,441*

buildup [*n*] *development; accumulation*
accretion, advertising, enlargement, escalation, expansion, gain, growth, heap, hype, increase, load, mass, plug, promotion, publicity, puff, stack, stockpile, store; SEE CONCEPTS *230,704,786*

build up [*v*] *amplify, advertise*
add to, boost, develop, enhance, expand, extend, fortify, heighten, hype, improve, increase, intensify, plug*, promote, publicize, puff*, reinforce, spotlight, strengthen; SEE CONCEPTS *236,245,266*

built-in [*adj*] *included*
congenital, constitutional, deep-seated, essential, implicit, inborn, inbred, in-built, incorporated, indwelling, ingrained, inherent, innate, inseparable, integral, part and parcel*; SEE CONCEPT *549*

bulb [*n*] *globular object*
ball, bunch, corm, corn, globe, head, knob, nodule, nub, protuberance, swelling, tube, tumor; SEE CONCEPT *436*

bulge [*n*] *swollen object*
appendage, bagginess, blob, bump, bunch, bunching, convexity, dilation, distention, excess, excrescence, gibbosity, growth, hump, intumescence, jut, lump, nodulation, nodule, outgrowth, outthrust, projection, prominence, promontory, protrusion, protuberance, sac, sagging, salience, salient, superfluity, swelling, tuberosity, tumefaction, tumor, wart; SEE CONCEPTS *436,470*

bulge [*v*] *project outward*
bag, balloon, beetle, belly, bilge, billow, bloat, blob, bug out, dilate, distend, enlarge, expand, extrude, jut, overhang, poke, pop out, pouch, protrude, protuberate, puff out, sag, stand out, stick out, swell; SEE CONCEPTS *208,780*

bulk [*n1*] *size, largeness*
aggregate, amount, amplitude, bigness, dimensions, extent, immensity, magnitude, mass, massiveness, quantity, quantum, substance, total, totality, volume, weight; SEE CONCEPT *730*

bulk [*n2*] *main part, most*
best part, better part, biggest share, body, generality, greater number, greater part, gross, lion's share*, major part, majority, mass, nearly all, plurality, predominant part, preponderance, principal part; SEE CONCEPTS *635,829*

bulky [*adj*] *huge*
awkward, beefy, big, colossal, cumbersome, cumbrous, enormous, gross, heavy, hefty, high, hulking, immense, large, long, mammoth, massive, ponderous, substantial, unhandy, unmanageable, unwieldy, voluminous, weighty; SEE CONCEPT *781*

bulldoze [*v1*] *demolish*
drive, elbow, flatten, force, jostle, level, press, propel, push, raze, shove, thrust; SEE CONCEPTS *208,252*

bulldoze [*v2*] *bully, intimidate*
bludgeon, bluster, browbeat, coerce, cow, dragoon, harass, hector; SEE CONCEPT *14*

bullet [*n*] *small missile*
ammo*, ammunition, ball, bolt, cap, cartridge, dose*, lead, love letter*, pellet, projectile, rocket, shot, slug, trajectile; SEE CONCEPT *500*

bulletin [*n*] *message, notification*
account, announcement, break, calendar, communication, communiqué, dispatch, flash*, handout, hot wire*, item, list, news, news flash, notice, program, publication, release, report, scoop*, skinny*, statement, the dope*, what's going down*, what's happening*; SEE CONCEPTS *271,274*

bully [*n*] *domineering person*
annoyer, antagonizer, browbeater*, bulldozer*, coercer, harrier, hector, insolent, intimidator, oppressor, persecutor, pest, rascal, rowdy, ruffian, tease, tormenter, tough; SEE CONCEPT *423*

bully [*v*] *intimidate, push around*
bludgeon, bluster, browbeat, buffalo, bulldoze, coerce, cow, despotize, domineer, dragoon, enforce, harass, hector, lean on, lord over*, menace, oppress, overbear, persecute, ride roughshod*, showboat*, swagger, terrorize, threaten, torment, torture, turn on the heat*, tyrannize, walk heavy*; SEE CONCEPT *14*

bulwark [*n*] *fortification, support*
barrier, bastion, buffet, buttress, citadel, defense, embankment, fort, fortress, guard, mainstay, outwork, parapet, partition, protection, rampart, redoubt, safeguard, security, stronghold, vallation; SEE CONCEPTS *96,729*

bum [*n*] *beggar*
bindle*, black sheep*, derelict, drifter, floater, gutterpup*, guttersnipe*, hobo, homeless person, stiff*, tramp, transient, vagabond, vagrant; SEE CONCEPTS *412,423*

bump [v1] *collide, hit, usually with sound*
bang, bounce, box, buck, bunt, butt, carom, clap, clatter, crack, crash, impinge, jar, jerk, jolt, jostle, jounce, knock, pat, plop, plunk, pound, punch, rap, rattle, shake, slam, slap, smack, smash into, strike, thud, thump, thunder, thwack, whack; SEE CONCEPT *189*

bump [v2] *move over, dislodge*
budge, displace, remove, shift; SEE CONCEPT *213*

bump into [v] *happen upon*
chance upon, come across, encounter, hit, light, light upon, luck, meet, meet up with, run across, run into, stumble, tumble; SEE CONCEPT *114*

bun [n] *baked roll*
bread, cruller, Danish, doughnut, eclair, muffin, pastry, scone, sweet roll; SEE CONCEPT *457*

bunch [n] *collection of something*
agglomeration, assemblage, assortment, band, batch, bevy, blob, bouquet, bundle, caboodle*, chunk, clump, cluster, covey, crew, crowd, fascicle, flock, galaxy, gang, gathering, group, heap, host, hunk, knot, lot, mass, mess, mob, multitude, number, oodles*, pack, parcel, party, passel, pile, quantity, sheaf, shebang*, shock, shooting match*, spray, stack, swarm, team, thicket, troop, tuft; SEE CONCEPT *432*

bunch [v] *gather in group*
assemble, bundle, cluster, collect, congregate, cram, crowd, flock, group, herd, huddle, mass, pack; SEE CONCEPT *109*

bundle [n] *accumulation, package of something*
array, assortment, bag, bale, batch, box, bunch, carton, clump, cluster, collection, crate, group, heap, lot, mass, pack, package, packet, pallet, parcel, pile, quantity, roll, set, stack, wad; SEE CONCEPTS *432,786*

bundle [v] *accumulate, package*
bale, bind, clothe, fasten, pack, palletize, tie, truss, wrap; SEE CONCEPTS *158,202*

bungle [v] *blunder, mess up*
ball up*, boggle, botch, butcher*, drop the ball*, err, flub, foul up, fudge*, fumble, goof up*, gum up*, louse up*, make a mess of, mar, mess up, miscalculate, mishandle, mismanage, muff*, ruin, screw up*, spoil; SEE CONCEPT *101*

bungler [n] *person who blunders*
addlebrain*, blockhead*, blunderer, bonehead*, botcher*, butcher*, butterfingers*, clod, clumsy oaf*, dolt, donkey*, duffer*, dunce, featherbrain*, fool, foul-up*, fumbler*, goofball*, goof off*, harebrain*, idiot, ignoramus, incompetent, klutz, mismanager, muddler, muffer*, numskull*, screw up*, spoiler; SEE CONCEPTS *412,423*

bunk [n1] *nonsense*
applesauce*, balderdash*, baloney*, bilge*, claptrap*, eyewash*, flimflam*, garbage*, hogwash*, hooey*, horsefeathers*, jazz*, piffle*, poppycock*, rot*, rubbish*, tomfoolery*, tommyrot*, trash*, twaddle*; SEE CONCEPTS *63,278*

bunk [n2] *twin bed, usually stacked; place to sleep*
berth, cot, doss, hay, kip, pallet, sack; SEE CONCEPT *443*

bunt [v] *hit half-heartedly*
butt, lay it down, meet, sacrifice, throw, toss; SEE CONCEPTS *189,363*

buoy [n] *floating device*
beacon, drift, float, guide, marker, signal; SEE CONCEPT *628*

buoy (up) [v] *make light, encourage*
bolster, boost, buck up, cheer, cheer up, encourage, hearten, keep afloat, lift, prop, raise, support, sustain, uphold; SEE CONCEPTS *7,22*

buoyancy/buoyance [n1] *lightness in weight*
airiness, ethereality, floatability, levity, weightlessness; SEE CONCEPT *734*

buoyancy/buoyance [n2] *lightness in spirit*
animation, bounce, cheerfulness, cheeriness, ebullience, effervescence, exuberance, gaiety, good feeling, good humor, happiness, high spirits, jollity, liveliness, pep, spiritedness, sunniness, vim and vigor, zing, zip; SEE CONCEPTS *410,411*

buoyant [adj1] *light in weight*
afloat, airy, bouncy, floatable, floating, resilient, supernatant, unsinkable, weightless; SEE CONCEPT *491*

buoyant [adj2] *light in spirit*
animated, blithe, bouncy, breezy, bright, carefree, cheerful, debonair, effervescent, elastic, expansive, full of zip, gay, happy, invigorated, jaunty, jovial, joyful, laid back*, lighthearted, lively, peppy, resilient, sunny, supple, vivacious; SEE CONCEPTS *403,404*

burden [n] *mental weight; stress*
accountability, affliction, albatross*, anxiety, ball and chain*, blame, care, charge, clog, concern, deadweight, difficulty, duty, encumbrance, excess baggage*, grievance, hardship, Herculean task, hindrance, load, millstone, misfortune, mishap, obstruction, onus, punishment, responsibility, sorrow, strain, task, tax, thorn in one's side*, trial, trouble, weary load, work, worry; SEE CONCEPTS *532,690*

burden [v] *encumber, strain*
afflict, bear down on, bother, crush, cumber, depress, dish it out*, dish out*, dump on*, encumber, give it to, hamper, handicap, hinder, impede, lade, load, make heavy, obligate, oppress, overcharge, overload, overwhelm, pile, press, saddle with, snow*, snow under*, stick it to, strain, tax, trouble, try, vex, weigh down, worry; SEE CONCEPTS *7,14,19*

burdensome [adj] *troublesome*
carking, crushing, demanding, difficult, disturbing, exacting, exigent, headache*, heavy*, irksome, onerous, oppressive, superincumbent, taxing, tough, trying, wearing, wearying, weighty; SEE CONCEPT *529*

bureau [n1] *branch of an organization*
agency, authority, board, commission, committee, department, division, front office*, office, salt

mines*, service, setup, shop, store; SEE CONCEPTS *325,441,449*

bureau [*n2*] *chest of drawers*
chiffonier, commode, desk, dresser, highboy, sideboard, writing desk; SEE CONCEPT *443*

bureaucracy [*n*] *system which controls organization*
administration, authority, beadledom, city hall*, civil service, directorate, government, management, ministry, officialdom, officials, powers that be*, red tape*, regulatory commission, the Establishment*, the system*; SEE CONCEPTS *325,770*

burglar [*n*] *person who steals*
cat burglar, crook, filcher*, housebreaker, midnighter*, owl*, picklock*, pilferer*, porch-climber*, prowler, robber, safecracker, second-story man*, sneakthief*, thief; SEE CONCEPT *412*

burglary [*n*] *stealing from residence, business*
break-in, breaking and entering, caper, crime, filching, heist, housebreaking, larceny, owl job*, pilferage, prowl, robbery, safecracking, second-story work*, sting, theft, thieving; SEE CONCEPT *139*

burial [*n*] *laying in of dead body*
burying, deep six*, deposition, entombment, exequies, funeral, inhumation, interment, last rites, obsequies, sepulture; SEE CONCEPT *367*

burlesque [*n*] *bawdy show; vaudeville*
burly*, caricature, farce, lampoon, lampoonery, mock, mockery, parody, pastiche, peep show, revue, satire, send-up, spoof, strip, takeoff, travesty; SEE CONCEPT *263*

burlesque [*adj*] *farcical*
caricatural, comic, ironical, ludicrous, mock, mocking, parodic, satirical, travestying; SEE CONCEPT *555*

burly [*adj*] *husky*
able-bodied, athletic, beefcake*, beefy*, big, brawny, bruising, bulky, gorillalike, hefty, hulking, hulky, hunk, muscle man*, muscular, portly, powerful, stocky, stout, strapping, strong, sturdy, thickset, well-built; SEE CONCEPT *773*

burn [*v1*] *be on fire; set on fire*
bake, be ablaze, blaze, brand, broil, calcine, cauterize, char, combust, conflagrate, cook, cremate, enkindle, flame, flare, flash, flicker, glow, heat, ignite, incinerate, kindle, light, melt, parch, reduce to ashes, rekindle, roast, scald, scorch, sear, set a match to, singe, smoke, smolder, toast, torch, wither; SEE CONCEPT *249*

burn [*v2*] *feel stinging pain*
bite, hurt, pain, smart, sting, tingle; SEE CONCEPT *590*

burn [*v3*] *be excited about; yearn for*
be angry, be aroused, be inflamed, be passionate, be stirred up, blaze, boil, breathe fire*, bristle, desire, eat up*, fume, lust, rage, seethe, simmer, smoulder, tingle, yearn; SEE CONCEPTS *20,29,34*

burn [*v4*] *cheat*
beat, bilk, chisel, cozen, deceive, defraud, gyp, overreach, ream, swindle, take, trick, use; SEE CONCEPTS *59,142*

burning [*adj1*] *blazing, flashing*
afire, aflame, alight, blistering, broiling, conflagrant, enkindled, fiery, flaming, flaring, gleaming, glowing, heated, hot, ignited, illuminated, in flames, incandescent, kindled, on fire, oxidizing, red-hot*, scorching, searing, sizzling, smoking, smouldering, torrid, white-hot*; SEE CONCEPTS *485,605*

burning [*adj2*] *fervent, excited*
all-consuming, ardent, blazing, eager, earnest, fervid, feverish, frantic, frenzied, heated, hectic, impassioned, intense, passionate, red-hot*, vehement, white-hot*, zealous; SEE CONCEPT *403*

burning [*adj3*] *stinging, painful*
acrid, biting, caustic, irritating, painful, piercing, prickling, pungent, reeking, sharp, smarting, tingling; SEE CONCEPTS *314,537*

burning [*adj4*] *important*
acute, clamant, clamorous, compelling, critical, crucial, crying, dire, essential, exigent, imperative, importunate, instant, pressing, significant, urgent, vital; SEE CONCEPT *568*

burnish [*v*] *polish, brighten*
buff, furbish, glance, glaze, gloss, luster, patina, put on a finish, rub, sheen, shine, smooth, wax; SEE CONCEPTS *202,215*

burrow [*n*] *hole dug by animal*
couch, den, hovel, lair, retreat, shelter, tunnel; SEE CONCEPT *517*

burrow [*v*] *dig a hole*
delve, excavate, hollow out, scoop out, tunnel, undermine; SEE CONCEPT *178*

burst [*n*] *blow-up, blast*
access, bang, barrage, blowout, bombardment, breach, break, cannonade, crack, discharge, eruption, explosion, fit, flare, fusillade, gush, gust, outbreak, outpouring, round, rupture, rush, sally, salvo, shower, spate, split, spurt, storm, surge, torrent, volley; SEE CONCEPTS *86,179,208*

burst [*v*] *blow up, break out*
barge, blow, break, crack, detonate, discharge, disintegrate, erupt, explode, fly open, fracture, fragment, gush forth, perforate, pierce, pop, prick, puncture, rend asunder, run, rupture, rush, shatter, shiver, splinter, split, spout, tear apart; SEE CONCEPTS *179,252*

bury [*v1*] *lay to rest after death*
coffin, consign to grave, cover up, deposit, embalm, ensepulcher, enshrine, entomb, hold last rites for*, hold services for, inearth, inhume, inter, inurn, lay out, mummify, plant*, put away*, put six feet under*, sepulcher, sepulture, tomb; SEE CONCEPT *367*

bury [*v2*] *conceal, cover*
cache, cover up, ensconce, enshroud, hide, occult, plant, screen, secrete, shroud, stash, stow away; SEE CONCEPTS *172,188*

bury [*v3*] *plant in ground*
drive in, embed, engulf, implant, sink, submerge; SEE CONCEPTS *172,257*

bury [v4] *engross oneself*
absorb, concentrate, engage, immerse, interest, occupy, rivet, throw oneself into; SEE CONCEPT 24

bush [n] *shrubs; woodland*
backcountry, backwoods, boscage, bramble, briar, brush, chaparral, creeper, forest, hedge, hinterland, jungle, outback, plant, scrub, scrubland, shrubbery, the wild, thicket, vine; SEE CONCEPT 429

bushy [adj] *shaggy, unkempt*
bristling, bristly, disordered, feathery, fluffy, fringed, full, furry, fuzzy, hairy, heavy, hirsute, leafy, luxuriant, nappy, prickly, rough, rumpled, spreading, stiff, thick, tufted, unruly, wiry, woolly; SEE CONCEPTS 406,606

busily [adv] *actively; intently*
agilely, animatedly, ardently, arduously, assiduously, briskly, carefully, diligently, eagerly, earnestly, energetically, enthusiastically, expeditiously, fervently, hastily, hurriedly, indefatigably, industriously, laboriously, like all get out*, like the devil*, like the dickens*, nimbly, painstakingly, perseveringly, persistently, purposefully, restlessly, seriously, speedily, spiritedly, strenuously, studiously, unremittingly, unweariedly, vigilantly, vigorously, vivaciously, zealously; SEE CONCEPT 544

business [n1] *job, profession*
bag*, biz*, calling, career, craft, dodge*, employment, field, function, game, line, livelihood, métier, occupation, pursuit, racket*, specialty, trade, vocation, what one is into*, work; SEE CONCEPT 360

business [n2] *company, enterprise*
cartel, concern, corporation, establishment, factory, firm, fly-by-night operation*, house, institution, market, megacorp*, mill, Mom and Pop*, monopoly, organization, outfit, partnership, setup, shoestring operation*, shop, store, syndicate, trust, venture; SEE CONCEPTS 325,449

business [n3] *commerce, trade*
affairs, bargaining, barter, buying and selling, capital and labor, commercialism, contracts, deal, dealings, exchange, free enterprise, game, industrialism, industry, manufacturing, market, merchandising, production and distribution, racket*, sales, selling, trading, traffic, transaction, undertaking; SEE CONCEPTS 325,770

business [n4] *personal concern*
affair, assignment, beeswax*, carrying on, duty, function, goings-on*, hanky-panky*, happening, interest, issue, lookout, matter, palaver, point, problem, question, responsibility, subject, task, topic; SEE CONCEPT 532

businesslike [adj] *efficient, professional*
accomplished, careful, concentrated, correct, diligent, direct, disciplined, earnest, effective, enterprising, expeditious, hardworking, industrious, intent, matter-of-fact, methodical, orderly, organized, painstaking, practical, practiced, purposeful, regular, routine, sedulous, serious, skillful, systematic, thorough, well-ordered, workaday; SEE CONCEPTS 326,544

businessman/businesswoman [n] *professional working person*
baron, big-time operator*, big wheel*, capitalist, dealer, employer, entrepreneur, executive, financier, franchiser, gray flannel suit*, industrialist, manager, merchandiser, merchant, operator, organization man/woman, robber baron*, small potatoes*, storekeeper, suit*, the bacon*, tradesperson, trafficker, tycoon, wheeler-dealer*; SEE CONCEPTS 347,348

bust [n1] *chest of human*
bosom, breast, chest, front, rack; SEE CONCEPT 392

bust [n2] *arrest for illegal action*
apprehension, arrest, capture, cop, detention, nab, pickup, pinch, raid, search, seizure; SEE CONCEPTS 298,317

bust [v1] *ruin, impoverish*
become insolvent, break, crash, fail, fold up, go bankrupt, go into Chapter 11*, pauperize; SEE CONCEPT 330

bust [v2] *arrest for illegal action*
apprehend, catch, collar, cop, detain, nab, pick up, pinch, pull in, raid, run in, search; SEE CONCEPTS 298,317

bust [v3] *physically break*
burst, fold, fracture, rupture; SEE CONCEPT 252

bustle [n] *quick and busy activity*
ado, agitation, clamor, commotion, do*, excitement, flurry, furor, fuss, haste, hubbub, hurly-burly*, hurry, pother, rumpus, stir*, to-do*, tumult, turmoil, uproar, whirl, whirlpool, whirlwind; SEE CONCEPT 386

bustle [v] *move around quickly, busily*
bestir, dash, dust, flit, flutter, fuss, hasten, hum, hurry, hustle, run, rush, scamper, scramble, scurry, scuttle, stir, tear, whirl, whisk; SEE CONCEPT 150

busy [adj1] *engaged, at work*
active, already taken*, assiduous, at it*, buried, diligent, employed, engaged, engrossed, having a full plate*, having enough on one's plate*, having fish to fry*, having many irons in the fire*, hustling, in a meeting, in conference, industrious, in someone else's possession*, in the field, in the laboratory, occupied, on assignment, on duty, on the go, overloaded, persevering, slaving, snowed*, swamped*, tied up, unavailable, up to one's ears*, with a customer, working; SEE CONCEPTS 326,544,555

busy [adj2] *active, on the go*
bustling, busy as a beaver*, energetic, full, fussy, hectic, humming*, hustling, lively, popping*, restless, strenuous, tireless, tiring; SEE CONCEPT 542

busy [adj3] *nosy, impertinent*
butting in, curious, forward, inquisitive, interfering, intrusive, meddlesome, meddling, nebby, obtrusive, officious, prying, pushy, snoopy, stirring, troublesome; SEE CONCEPT 404

busybody [n] *nosy, impertinent person*
backseat driver*, butt-in*, buttinsky*, eavesdropper, fink*, fussbudget, gossip, intermeddler, intruder, meddler, newsmonger*, nosey Parker*, pragmatist, rubberneck*, scandalmonger*, sidewalk superintendent*, snoop, snooper*, tattletale, troublemaker, yenta*; SEE CONCEPT *423*

butcher [n] *meat killer, seller*
boner*, meat man/woman, meatmarket man/woman, processor, skinner*, slaughterer, slayer*; SEE CONCEPT *348*

butcher [v1] *slay and prepare animal for meat*
beef up, carve, clean, cure, cut, cut down, dress, joint, liquidate, salt, slaughter, smoke, stick; SEE CONCEPTS *170,252*

butcher [v2] *ruin*
bollix up*, botch, destroy, goof up*, louse up*, make a mess of*, mutilate, screw up*, spoil, wreck; SEE CONCEPT *101*

butler [n] *male servant*
head servant, house boy, man, manservant, steward, valet; SEE CONCEPT *348*

butt [n1] *end, shaft*
base, bottom, edge, extremity, fag end, foot, fundament, haft, handle, hilt, shank, stock, stub, stump, tail, tip; SEE CONCEPT *827*

butt/buttocks [n2] *animate rear end*
back end, backside, behind, bottom, bum*, buttocks, derrière, fanny*, fundament, gluteus maximus, haunches, hindquarters, posterior, rear, rump, seat, tush*; SEE CONCEPT *392*

butt [n3] *object of joking*
chump*, clay pigeon*, derision, dupe*, easy mark*, fall guy, fool, goat, jestee*, joke, laughing stock, mark, patsy, pigeon*, sap, setup*, sitting duck*, softie*, subject, sucker, target, turkey, victim; SEE CONCEPT *423*

butt [v1] *bang up against with head*
batter, buck, buffet, bump, bunt, collide, gore, hook, horn, jab, knock, poke, prod, punch, push, ram, run into, shove, smack, strike, thrust, toss; SEE CONCEPT *189*

butt [v2] *touch, adjoin*
abut, border, bound, communicate, join, jut, meet, neighbor, project, protrude, verge; SEE CONCEPTS *113,747*

buttress [n] *brace, support*
abutment, column, mainstay, pier, prop, reinforcement, shore, stanchion, stay, strut, underpinning; SEE CONCEPT *440*

buttress [v] *support, bolster*
back up, beef up*, brace, build up, bulwark, carry, jack up*, jazz up*, prop, reinforce, shore, step up, strengthen, sustain, uphold; SEE CONCEPT *250*

buxom [adj] *bosomy*
ample, built, busty, chubby, comely, curvaceous, curvy, full-bosomed, full-figured, healthy, hearty, lusty, plump, robust, shapely, stacked*, voluptuous, well-made, well-proportioned, well-rounded, zaftig*; SEE CONCEPTS *371,406*

buy [n] *something purchased*
acquisition, bargain, closeout, deal, good deal, investment, purchase, steal, value; SEE CONCEPT *710*

buy [v1] *purchase*
acquire, bargain for, barter for, contract for, get, get in exchange, go shopping, invest in, market, obtain, pay for, procure, purchase, redeem, score, secure, shop for, sign for, take; SEE CONCEPT *327*

buy [v2] *bribe*
corrupt, fix, grease palm*, have, land, lubricate, oil palm*, ransom, reach, redeem, sop*, square, suborn, tamper; SEE CONCEPTS *192,341*

buyer [n] *someone who purchases*
client, consumer, customer, easy make*, emptor, end user, patron, prospect, purchaser, representative, shopper, sucker*, user, vendee; SEE CONCEPT *348*

buzz [n1] *droning sound*
drone, fizz, fizzle, hiss, hum, murmur, purr, ring, ringing, sibilation, whir, whisper; SEE CONCEPT *595*

buzz [n2] *gossip*
comment, cry, grapevine*, hearsay, news, on dit, report, rumble*, rumor, scandal, scuttlebutt*, talk, whisper; SEE CONCEPT *274*

buzz [v1] *make droning sound*
bombinate, bumble, drone, fizz, fizzle, hum, murmur, reverberate, ring, sibilate, whir, whisper, whiz; SEE CONCEPT *65*

buzz [v2] *gossip*
call, chatter, inform, natter, rumor, tattle; SEE CONCEPT *60*

by [adv] *near*
aside, at hand, away, beyond, close, handy, in reach, over, past, through, to one side; SEE CONCEPT *586*

by [prep1] *next to*
along, alongside, beside, by way of, close to, near, nearby, nigh, over, past, round, via; SEE CONCEPT *586*

by [prep2] *by means of*
at the hand of, in the name of, on, over, supported by, through, through the agency of, through the medium of, under the aegis of, with, with the assistance of; SEE CONCEPT *544*

bygone [adj] *in the past*
ancient, antiquated, archaic, belated, dated, dead, defunct, departed, down memory lane*, erstwhile, extinct, forgotten, former, gone, gone by, in oblivion, late, lost, of old, of yore, olden, oldfangled, old-fashioned, old-time, one-time, out-of-date, previous, quondam, sometime, vanished, water over the dam*, water under the bridge*; SEE CONCEPT *820*

bypass [v] *avoid*
blink at, burke, circumnavigate, circumvent, depart from, detour, deviate from, finesse, get around, go around, go around the barn*, ignore, let go, neglect, omit, outflank, pass around, sidestep, skirt, take back road*, wink at*; SEE CONCEPTS *30,102*

bystander [n] *person who watches*
eyewitness, gaper*, kibitzer*, looker-on, observer, onlooker, passerby, spectator, viewer, watcher, witness; SEE CONCEPT *423*

byword [n] *saying*
adage, aphorism, apophthegm, axiom, catchphrase, catchword, dictum, epithet, gnome, gnomic saying, handle, maxim, motto, nickname, precept, proverb, saw, shibboleth, slogan, standing joke; SEE CONCEPT *275*

C

cab [n] *car for hire*
carriage, hack, hackney, jitney, taxi, taxicab, tourist car; *see concept 505*

cabaret [n] *nightclub with musical performances*
after-hours joint*, bar, café, disco, discothèque, dive, hideaway, hot spot*, nightery, night spot, speakeasy, supper club, tavern, watering hole*; SEE CONCEPTS *447,449*

cabin [n] *tiny house; lodging*
berth, box, caboose, camp, chalet, compartment, cot, cottage, crib, deckhouse, home, hovel, hut, lodge, log house, quarters, room, shack, shanty, shed, shelter; SEE CONCEPT *516*

cabinet [n1] *cupboard for storage*
case, chiffonier, closet, commode, container, depository, dresser, escritoire, locker, repository, wardrobe; SEE CONCEPTS *443,494*

cabinet [n2] *executives serving a leader*
administration, administrators, advisers, assembly, assistants, authority, brain trust*, bureau, bureaucracy, committee, council, counselors, department heads, governing body, government, kitchen cabinet*, ministry, official family; SEE CONCEPT *299*

cache [n] *hidden supply*
accumulation, assets, drop, drop joint, drop-off, fund, hideout, hiding place, hoard, kitty*, nest egg*, plant, repository, reserve, shade, stake, stash, stockpile, store, storehouse, supplies, treasure, treasury, wealth; SEE CONCEPTS *446,710*

cache [v] *hide a supply of something*
accumulate, bury, conceal, cover, ditch, duck, ensconce, lay away, maintain, park, plant, put away, put in the hole*, save, screen, secrete, squirrel*, squirrel away*, stash, stash away, store; SEE CONCEPT *188*

cackle [n] *a loud laugh*
chortle, chuckle, cluck, crow, gibber, giggle, gobble, guffaw, quack, snicker, snigger, titter; SEE CONCEPT *77*

cackle [v] *laugh irritatingly*
babble, blather, burble, chat, chatter, chortle, chuckle, cluck, crow, gab, gabble, gas, gibber, giggle, gobble, jabber, jaw, prattle, quack, run on, snicker, snigger, titter; SEE CONCEPT *77*

cacophonous [adj] *harsh sounding*
clinking, discordant, disharmonic, dissonant, grating, ill-sounding, immusical, inharmonious, jangly, jarring, noisy, raucous, sour, strident, unmusical; SEE CONCEPTS *592,594*

cad [n] *sly, dastardly person*
boor, bounder*, clown, creep, cur*, dog*, heel, knave, louse, lout, rake, rascal, rat*, rogue, rotter*, rounder*, scoundrel, stinker, worm; SEE CONCEPT *412*

cadaver [n] *dead body*
body, cage, carcass, corpse, deceased, mort*, remains, skeleton, stiff*; SEE CONCEPT *390*

cadaverous [adj] *pale, corpselike*
ashen, bag of bones, blanched, bloodless, consumptive, dead, deathlike, deathly, emaciated, exsanguinous, gaunt, ghastly, ghostly, haggard, pallid, peaked, peaky, sallow, shadowy, sick, skeletal, skeletonlike, skin and bones*, spectral, stack of bones, thin, wan, wasted; SEE CONCEPTS *406,491,618*

cadence [n] *rhythm*
accent, beat, count, inflection, intonation, lilt, measure, meter, modulation, pulse, rhythmus, swing, tempo, throb; SEE CONCEPT *65*

cadre [n] *nucleus of effort*
core, force, framework, infrastructure, key group, officers, organization, personnel, staff; SEE CONCEPTS *417,432*

café [n] *small, informal restaurant*
bistro, burger joint, cafeteria, cake shop, chophouse, coffee bar, coffee shop, diner, eating house, grease joint, greasy spoon*, hash house, luncheonette, lunchroom, noshery, pit stop, quick-lunch, snack bar, soup house, tearoom; SEE CONCEPT *449*

cage [n] *enclosure with bars*
coop, corral, crate, enclosure, fold, jail, mew, pen, pinfold, pound; SEE CONCEPT *494*

cage [v] *hold in enclosure*
close in, confine, coop up, enclose, envelop, fence in, hem, immure, impound, imprison, incarcerate, jail, lock up, mew, pen, restrain, shut in, shut up; SEE CONCEPT *191*

cajole [v] *attempt to coax; flatter*
apple polish*, argue into, banter, beguile, blandish, bootlick*, brownnose*, build up, butter up*, con, crowd, deceive, decoy, delude, dupe, entice, entrap, get around, get next to*, hand a line*, induce, influence, inveigle, jolly, lay it on thick*, lure, make up to, maneuver, massage, mislead, oil*, play up to, push, rub the right way*, seduce, snow*, soap*, soften, soft-soap*, spread it on*, stroke, suck up to*, sweeten up, sweet-talk*, tantalize, tempt, urge, wheedle, work on, work over*; SEE CONCEPTS *59,68,75*

cake [n] *bar of something*
block, brick, loaf, lump, mass, slab; SEE CONCEPT *470*

calamitous [*adj*] *disastrous; tragic*
adverse, afflictive, blighting, cataclysmic, catastrophic, deadly, deplorable, devastating, dire, fatal, grievous, harmful, heartbreaking, lamentable, messy, pernicious, regrettable, ruinous, unfavorable, unfortunate, woeful; SEE CONCEPT 537

calamity [*n*] *disaster; tragedy*
adversity, affliction, blue ruin*, cataclysm, catastrophe, collapse, cross, curtains, distress, downfall, hardship, holy mess*, misadventure, mischance, misfortune, mishap, reverse, ruin, scourge, the worst*, trial, tribulation, unholy mess*, visitation, Waterloo*, woe, wreck, wretchedness; SEE CONCEPTS 674,675

calculable [*adj*] *able to be computed or estimated*
accountable, ascertainable, computable, countable, discoverable, estimable, foreseeable, measurable, predictable, reckonable; SEE CONCEPTS 402,762

calculate [*v1*] *compute or estimate amount*
account, add, adjust, appraise, assay, cast, cipher, consider, count, determine, divide, dope out*, enumerate, figure, forecast, foretell, gauge, guess, judge, keep tabs*, measure, multiply, number, rate, reckon, size up, subtract, sum, take account of, tally, tot, tote up*, value, weigh, work out; SEE CONCEPT 764

calculate [*v2*] *plan on*
aim, anticipate, assume, bank on, build, count on, depend on, design, intend, judge, plan, reckon, rely on, suppose, think likely, trust; SEE CONCEPTS 26,36

calculating [*adj*] *scheming to manipulate*
artful, canny, careful, cautious, chary, circumspect, considerate, contriving, crafty, cunning, designing, devious, discreet, gingerly, guarded, guileful, intelligent, Machiavellian, manipulative, politic, premeditating, safe, scheming, sharp, shrewd, sly, wary, wily; SEE CONCEPTS 401,403

calculation [*n1*] *computing, estimating amount*
adding, arithmetic, ciphering, computation, counting, dividing, estimate, estimation, figuring, forecast, judgment, multiplying, prediction, reckoning, subtracting, summation, totaling; SEE CONCEPTS 28,764

calculation [*n2*] *computed or estimated amount*
answer, computation, divination, estimate, estimation, figuring, forecast, judgment, prediction, prognosis, prognostication, reckoning, reply; SEE CONCEPT 786

calculation [*n3*] *forethought*
canniness, caution, circumspection, contrivance, deliberation, discretion, foresight, forethought, planning, precaution, prudence, thought; SEE CONCEPT 660

calendar [*n*] *schedule of events*
agenda, almanac, annal, bulletin, card, chronology, daybook, diary, docket, journal, lineup, list, log, logbook, menology, pipeline, program, record, register, sked, system of reckoning, tab, table, time, timetable; SEE CONCEPTS 274,281,809

calf [*n1*] *leg between knee and ankle*
foreleg, shin; SEE CONCEPT 392

calf [*n2*] *baby cow*
dogie, freemartin, heifer, maverick, veal, yearling, young bull, young cow; SEE CONCEPT 394

caliber [*n1*] *capacity; character*
ability, appetency, capability, competence, constitution, dignity, distinction, endowment, essence, faculty, force, gifts, habilitation, merit, nature, parts, power, quality, scope, stature, strength, talent, value, virtue, worth, worthiness; SEE CONCEPT 411

caliber [*n2*] *size of ammunition*
bore, class, diameter, gauge, grade, length, measure, measurement, quality, striking power, weight; SEE CONCEPT 730

call [*n1*] *yelled statement*
alarm, calling, command, cry, hail, holler, invitation, scream, shout, signal, whoop, yawp, yell; SEE CONCEPT 278

call [*n2*] *demand, announcement*
appeal, bidding, command, invitation, notice, order, plea, proposal, request, solicitation, subpoena, summons, supplication, visit; SEE CONCEPT 53

call [*n3*] *need, cause for action*
claim, excuse, grounds, justification, necessity, obligation, occasion, reason, right, urge; SEE CONCEPT 709

call [*n4*] *normal sound of animal*
cheep, chirp, cry, note, peep, roar, shriek, song, tweet, twitter, warble; SEE CONCEPT 64

call [*v1*] *yell declaration*
announce, arouse, awaken, bawl, bellow, cry, cry out, exclaim, hail, holler, hoot, howl, proclaim, roar, rouse, scream, screech, shout, shriek, vociferate, waken, whoop, yawp, yoo hoo*, yowl; SEE CONCEPTS 47,266

call [*v2*] *arrange meeting*
ask, assemble, bid, collect, contact, convene, convoke, gather, invite, muster, phone*, rally, request, ring up, subpoena, summon, telephone; SEE CONCEPT 114

call [*v3*] *entitle*
address, baptize, christen, denominate, describe as, designate, dub, label, name, style, term, title; SEE CONCEPT 62

call [*v4*] *demand or announce action*
appeal to, appoint, ask, challenge, charge, claim, command, declare, decree, elect, entreat, exact, ordain, order, postulate, pray to, proclaim, require, requisition, set apart, solicit, summon; SEE CONCEPT 53

call [*v5*] *estimate, consider*
adumbrate, approximate, augur, forecast, foretell, guess, judge, make rough guess, place, portend, predict, presage, prognosticate, prophesy, put, reckon, regard, think, vaticinate; SEE CONCEPTS 28,70

call [*v6*] *attempt to communicate by telephone*
beep, blast, bleep, buzz, contact, get back to, phone, ring, telephone; SEE CONCEPTS 74,266

call [*v7*] *visit at residence or business*
come by, come over, crash, drop by, drop in, fall by, fall down, hit, look in on, look up, play, pop in*, run in, see, stop by, stop in, swing by; SEE CONCEPT *227*

call for [*v*] *demand; entail*
ask for, inquire, involve, lack, necessitate, need, occasion, request, require, suggest, want; SEE CONCEPT *646*

calling [*n*] *chosen profession*
art, business, career, craft, day gig*, do*, dodge*, employment, gig*, go*, handicraft, hang*, life's work, lifework, line, métier, mission, nine-to-five*, occupation, play, province, pursuit, racket*, rat race*, slot*, swindle*, trade, vocation, walk of life, work; SEE CONCEPT *360*

callous [*adj*] *cruel, insensitive*
apathetic, blind to, careless, case-hardened, cold, cold-blooded, deaf to, hard, hard-bitten, hard-boiled, hardened, hardhearted, heartless, impassive, impenitent, indifferent, indurated, inflexible, insensate, insensible, insensitive, insentient, inured, obdurate, soulless, spiritless, stiff, stony, stubborn, thick-skinned, torpid, tough, toughened, unaffected, unbending, uncaring, uncompassionate, unconcerned, unfeeling, unimpressionable, unresponsive, unsusceptible, unsympathetic; SEE CONCEPT *404*

callow [*adj*] *immature*
crude, green, guileless, inexperienced, infant, jejune, jellybean*, juvenile, kid, low tech*, naive, not dry behind ears*, puerile, raw, sophomore, tenderfoot, unbaked, unfledged, unripe, unsophisticated, untrained, untried, young; SEE CONCEPTS *578,678,797*

calm [*n*] *quietness, composure*
calmness, dispassion, doldrums, hush, impassivity, imperturbation, lull, patience, peace, peacefulness, peace of mind, placidity, quiet, repose, rest, restraint, serenity, silence, stillness, stoicism, tranquility; SEE CONCEPTS *388,411,720*

calm [*adj1*] *peaceful, quiet (inanimate)*
at a standstill, at peace, bland, bucolic, cool, halcyon, harmonious, hushed, inactive, in order, low-key, mild, motionless, pacific, pastoral, placid, quiescent, reposeful, reposing, restful, rural, serene, slow, smooth, soothing, still, stormless, tranquil, undisturbed, unruffled, waveless, windless; SEE CONCEPTS *544,705*

calm [*adj2*] *composed, cool (animate)*
aloof, amiable, amicable, civil, collected, cool as cucumber*, cool-headed*, detached, disinterested, dispassionate, equable, gentle, impassive, imperturbable, inscrutable, kind, laid back, levelheaded, listless, moderate, neutral, patient, placid, pleased, poised, relaxed, restful, satisfied, sedate, self-possessed, serene, still, temperate, unconcerned, undisturbed, unemotional, unexcitable, unexcited, unflappable, unimpressed, unmoved, unruffled, untroubled; SEE CONCEPTS *401,404*

calm [*v*] *make composed, quiet*
allay, alleviate, appease, assuage, balm, becalm, compose, cool, cool it*, cool out*, hush, lay back, lull, mitigate, mollify, pacify, placate, quiet, quieten, relax, relieve, sedate, settle, simmer down, soft-pedal*, soothe, steady, still, stroke, take it easy*, take the edge off*, tranquilize; SEE CONCEPT *231*

camaraderie [*n*] *friendship*
brotherhood, brotherliness, cheer, companionability, companionship, comradeship, conviviality, esprit de corps, fellowship, fraternization, good-fellowship, gregariousness, intimacy, jollity, sociability, togetherness; SEE CONCEPT *388*

camouflage [*n*] *disguise*
beard*, blind, cloak, concealment, cover, coverup, deceit, deceptive marking, dissimulation, faking, false appearance, front, guise, mask, masking, masquerade, mimicry, paint, plain brown wrapper*, protective coloring, red herring*, screen, shade, shroud, smokescreen, veil; SEE CONCEPT *260*

camouflage [*v*] *disguise, cover*
beard, becloud, befog, cloak, conceal, cover up, deceive, dim, dissemble, dissimulate, dress up, hide, mask, obfuscate, obscure, screen, throw on makeup, veil; SEE CONCEPTS *172,188*

camp [*n*] *site for outdoor living*
bivouac, campfire, campground, camping ground, caravansary, chalet, cottage, encampment, hut, lean-to, lodge, log cabin, shack, shanty, shed, summer home, tent, tent city, tepee, tilt, wigwam; SEE CONCEPTS *198,516*

camp [*adj*] *consciously affecting the unfashionable, weird, or bizarre*
affected, arch, artificial, avant-garde, Daliesque*, far out*, in, mannered, mod, ostentatious, pop, posturing, wild; SEE CONCEPT *544*

campaign [*n*] *attempt to win; attack*
crusade, drive, expedition, fight, movement, offensive, operation, push, warfare; SEE CONCEPTS *87,320*

campaign [*v*] *attempt to win political election*
agitate, barnstorm, canvass, contend for, contest, crusade, electioneer, go to grass roots*, hit the trail*, lobby, mend fences*, muckrake, mudsling*, politick, press the flesh*, ring doorbells*, run, run for, shake hands and kiss babies*, solicit votes, stand for, stump*, tour, whistle-stop*; SEE CONCEPT *300*

can [*n1*] *container, usually metallic*
aluminum, bottle, bucket, canister, cannikin, gunboat*, gutbucket*, jar, package, pop top*, receptacle, tin, vessel; SEE CONCEPTS *476,494*

can [*n2*] *toilet*
head*, john*, johnny*, latrine, lavatory, litter box*, outhouse, pot*, potty, privy, restroom, sandbox*, throne*, washroom, water closet; SEE CONCEPT *443*

can [*n3*] *buttocks*
backside, behind, butt*, derrière, fanny*, fundament, gluteus maximus, hind end, posterior, rump, seat, tush*; SEE CONCEPT *418*

can [*v1*] *preserve fruit, vegetable*
bottle, keep, put up; SEE CONCEPT *170*

can [*v2*] *be able*
be capable of, be equal to, be up to, be within one's area, be within one's control, can do*, commit, could, cut the mustard*, have it made*, lie in one's power, make it*, make out, make the grade*, manage, may, take care of; SEE CONCEPT *630*

can [*v3*] *fire from job*
ax*, boot*, bounce*, cashier, discharge, dismiss, expel, give the heave ho*, kick out*, let go, sack*, terminate; SEE CONCEPT *351*

canal [*n*] *waterway*
aqueduct, bottleneck, channel, choke point, conduit, course, cove, ditch, duct, estuary, firth, trench, water, watercourse; SEE CONCEPT *514*

cancel [*v1*] *call off; erase*
abolish, abort, abrogate, annul, ax, black out, blot out, break, break off, call off, countermand, cross out, cut, deface, delete, destroy, do away with, do in, efface, eliminate, eradicate, erase, expunge, finish off*, go back on one's word*, kill, obliterate, off, omit, quash, remove, render invalid, repeal, repudiate, rescind, revoke, rub out, scratch out, scrub*, sink*, smash, squash, stamp across, strike out, torpedo*, total*, trash*, trim*, undo, wash out*, wipe out*, wipe slate clean*, X-out*, zap*; SEE CONCEPTS *18,211,234*

cancel [*v2*] *equal out*
abort, abrogate, annul, balance out, call off, compensate for, counteract, counterbalance, countercheck, countermand, counterpoise, declare invalid, discard, discharge, frustrate, ignore, invalidate, make up for, negate, neutralize, nullify, offset, overthrow, put an end to, recall, recant, redeem, redress, refute, render inert, render null and void, repeal, repudiate, rescind, retract, revoke, rule out, set aside, suppress, vacate, void; SEE CONCEPTS *232,667*

cancellation [*n*] *calling off; erasure*
abandoning, abandonment, abolishing, abolition, abrogation, annulment, canceling, deletion, dissolution, dissolving, elimination, invalidating, invalidation, nullification, overruling, quashing, recall, recalling, repeal, repudiation, retirement, retracting, retraction, reversal, reversing, revocation, revoking, undoing, withdrawing; SEE CONCEPT *119*

cancer [*n*] *malignant growth*
big C*, C*, canker, carcinoma, corruption, disease, long illness, malignancy, sickness, tumor; SEE CONCEPT *306*

candid [*adj*] *honest*
aboveboard, bluff, blunt, equal, equitable, fair, forthright, frank, free, frontal, genuine, guileless, impartial, ingenuous, just, objective, open, outspoken, plain, right up front*, scrupulous, sincere, straightforward, talking turkey*, telling it like it is*, truthful, unbiased, uncolored, unequivocal, unprejudiced, unpretended, up front*, upright; SEE CONCEPT *267*

candidate [*n*] *person desiring political office, job*
applicant, aspirant, bidder, claimant, competitor, contender, contestant, dark horse*, entrant, favorite son*, handshaker*, hopeful*, job-hunter, nominee, office-seeker, petitioner, possibility, possible choice, pothunter, runner, seeker, solicitant, stumper, successor, suitor, whistle-stopper*, write-in*; SEE CONCEPT *359*

candlestick [*n*] *holder for candles*
candelabra, candelabrum, menorah, pricket, sconce, taper holder; SEE CONCEPT *444*

candor [*n*] *complete honesty*
artlessness, directness, fairness, forthrightness, frankness, guilelessness, honesty, impartiality, ingenuousness, naïveté, openness, outspokenness, probity, simplicity, sincerity, straightforwardness, truthfulness, unequivocalness, uprightness, veracity; SEE CONCEPT *411*

candy [*n*] *confection*
bonbon, confectionery, confit, hokum*, jawbreaker*, sugarcoated, sweet, sweetmeat; SEE CONCEPT *457*

cane [*n*] *stick to aid walking of disabled*
pikestaff, pole, rod, staff, vademecum, walking stick; SEE CONCEPT *479*

canker [*n*] *blistered infection*
bane, blight, blister, boil, cancer, corrosion, corruption, lesion, rot, scourge, smutch, sore, ulcer; SEE CONCEPT *306*

canker [*v*] *blight, corrupt*
animalize, bestialize, consume, corrode, debase, debauch, demoralize, deprave, embitter, envenom, inflict, pervert, poison, pollute, rot, ruin, scourge, sore, stain, ulcer, vitiate; SEE CONCEPT *240*

cannibal [*n*] *beast, beastlike human*
aborigine, anthrophagite, anthropophaginian, anthropophagus, brute, bushman, bushwoman, cruel person, head-hunter, man-eater, ogre, ogress, primitive, ruffian, savage; SEE CONCEPT *412*

canny [*adj*] *clever, artful*
able, acute, adroit, astute, cagey, careful, cautious, circumspect, cunning, dexterous, discreet, foxy*, frugal, having fancy footwork*, hep*, ingenious, intelligent, judicious, knowing, nimble-witted, perspicacious, prudent, quick, quick-witted, sagacious, shrewd, skillful, slick, slippery*, sly, smart, smooth*, street smart*, streetwise*, subtle, wary, watchful, wise, with it*, worldly-wise; SEE CONCEPT *402*

canoe [*n*] *light, paddled boat*
coracle, dugout, kayak, outrigger, piragua, pirogue; SEE CONCEPT *506*

canon [*n*] *rule, edict*
assize, catalogue, command, commandment, criterion, declaration, decree, decretum, dictate, doctrine, dogma, formula, law, list, maxim, order, ordinance, precept, principle, regulation, roll, screed, standard, statute, table, tenet, touchstone, yardstick; SEE CONCEPTS *318,687*

canonical [*adj*] *accepted, recognized*
approved, authoritative, authorized, lawful, legal, official, orthodox, received, sanctioned, sound, statutory; SEE CONCEPTS *319,535*

canonize [*v*] *sanctify; idolize*
apotheosize, beatify, besaint, bless, consecrate, dedicate, deify, glorify, idolatrize, love, put on a pedestal*, saint, worship; SEE CONCEPTS *32,367*

canopy [*n*] *overhanging covering*
awning, baldachin, cover, marquee, shade, sunshade, umbrella; SEE CONCEPTS *440,444*

cant [*n1*] *hypocritical statement*
affected piety, deceit, dishonesty, humbug, hypocrisy, hypocriticalness, insincerity, lip service*, pecksniffery, pharisaicalness, pious platitudes, pomposity, pretense, pretentiousness, sanctimoniousness, sanctimony, sham holiness, show; SEE CONCEPT *63*

cant [*n2*] *jargon*
argot, dialect, diction, idiom, language, lingo, patois, patter, phraseology, slang, vernacular, vocabulary; SEE CONCEPTS *275,278*

cant [*v*] *lean, slant*
angle, bevel, careen, grade, heel, incline, list, recline, rise, slope, tilt, tip; SEE CONCEPTS *154,201*

cantankerous [*adj*] *difficult, crabby*
bad-tempered, bearish, captious, choleric, contrary, cranky, critical, cross, crotchety*, crusty*, disagreeable, dour, grouchy*, grumpy*, huffy*, ill-humored, ill-natured, irascible, irritable, morose, obstinate, ornery*, peevish, perverse, petulant, prickly, quarrelsome, snappish*, sour, stuffy*, testy, vinegarish, vinegary; SEE CONCEPT *401*

canteen [*n1*] *portable kitchen*
chuck wagon, mobile kitchen, snack bar, snack shop; SEE CONCEPT *449*

canteen [*n2*] *container for liquids, used in travels*
bota, bottle, flacon, flask, flasket, jug, thermos, water bottle; SEE CONCEPT *494*

canvas [*n1*] *coarse material*
10-ounce, 12-ounce, awning cloth, duck, fly, sailcloth, shade, tarp, tarpaulin, tenting; SEE CONCEPT *473*

canvas [*n2*] *painting on coarse material*
art, artwork, oil, picture, piece, portrait, still life, watercolor; SEE CONCEPT *259*

canvass [*v*] *poll; discuss issues*
agitate, analyze, apply, argue, campaign, check, check over, consult, debate, dispute, electioneer, examine, inspect, investigate, review, run, scan, scrutinize, sift, solicit, study, survey, ventilate; SEE CONCEPTS *24,48,56,300*

canyon [*n*] *gulf in mountain area*
coulee, glen, gorge, gulch, gully, ravine, valley; SEE CONCEPTS *509,513*

cap [*n*] *small hat*
beanie*, beret, bonnet, dink*, fez, pillbox, skullcap, tam, tam o'shanter; SEE CONCEPT *450*

cap [*v*] *outdo a performance*
beat, best, better, button down*, button up*, can*, clinch*, cob, complete, cover, crest, crown, do to a T*, eclipse, exceed, excel, finish, outshine, outstrip, pass, put the lid on*, surmount, surpass, top, top it off*, transcend, trump, wrap up*; SEE CONCEPT *141*

capability [*n*] *ability to perform*
adequacy, aptitude, art, capacity, competence, craft, cunning, effectiveness, efficacy, efficiency, facility, faculty, means, might, potency, potential, potentiality, power, proficiency, qualification, qualifiedness, skill, wherewithal; SEE CONCEPT *630*

capable [*adj*] *able to perform*
able, accomplished, adapted, adept, adequate, apt, au fait, clever, competent, dynamite, efficient, experienced, fireball*, fitted, gifted, good, green thumb*, has what it takes*, having the goods*, having the right stuff*, intelligent, know-how*, knowing the ropes*, knowing the score*, like a one-man band*, like a pistol*, masterly, old hand*, old-timer*, on the ball*, proficient, proper, qualified, skillful, suited, talented, there*, up*, up to it*, up to snuff*, up to speed*, veteran; SEE CONCEPT *527*

capacious [*adj*] *ample, extensive*
abundant, broad, comfortable, commodious, comprehensive, dilatable, distensible, expandable, expansive, extended, generous, liberal, plentiful, roomy, sizable, spacious, substantial, vast, voluminous, wide; SEE CONCEPTS *481,772,773,774*

capacity [*n1*] *volume; limit of volume held*
accommodation, amplitude, bulk, burden, chock full, compass, contents, dimensions, expanse, extent, full, holding ability, holding power, latitude, magnitude, mass, measure, proportions, quantity, range, reach, retention, room, scope, size, space, spread, standing room only*, sufficiency, sweep; SEE CONCEPTS *481,736,774,794*

capacity [*n2*] *ability; competency*
adequacy, aptitude, aptness, bent, brains, caliber, capability, cleverness, compass, competence, efficiency, facility, faculty, forte, genius, gift, inclination, intelligence, knack, might, power, qualification, readiness, skill, stature, strength, talent, the goods*, up to it*, what it takes*; SEE CONCEPTS *409,630*

cape [*n1*] *promontory into water*
arm, beak, bill, cheronese, finger, foreland, head, headland, jetty, jutty, mole, naze, neck, ness, peninsula, point, tongue; SEE CONCEPTS *509,514*

cape [*n2*] *sleeveless coat*
bertha, capote, cardinal, cloak, cope, dolman, fichu, gabardine, manteau, mantelletta, mantilla, mantle, overdress, paletot, pelerine, pelisse, poncho, shawl, tabard, talma, tippet, Vandyke, victorine, wrap, wrapper; SEE CONCEPT *451*

caper [*n*] *antic, lark*
escapade, gag*, gambol, high jinks*, hop, hot foot*, jest, joke, jump, leap, mischief, monkeyshines*, practical joke, prank, put on*, revel, rib*, rollick,

shenanigan*, sport, stunt, tomfoolery*, trick; SEE CONCEPT 386

caper [v] *frolic, cavort*
blow the lid off*, bounce, bound, cut capers*, cut loose*, dance, frisk, gambol, go on a tear*, hop, horse around*, jump, kick up one's heels*, leap, let loose*, play, raise hell*, rollick, romp, skip, spring, whoop it up*; SEE CONCEPT 384

capital [n1] *financial assets*
business, cash, CD, estate, finances, financing, fortune, funds, gold, interests, investment, IRA, kitty, means, money, nest egg, principal, property, resources, savings, stake, stock, substance, treasure, ways and means, wealth, wherewithal; SEE CONCEPTS 332,710

capital [n2] *city of governmental seat*
control, county seat, metropolis, municipality, political front, principal city, the Hill*; SEE CONCEPTS 507,512

capital [n3] *upper case written symbol*
cap, initial, majuscule, small cap, uncial; SEE CONCEPT 284

capital [adj1] *main, essential*
basic, cardinal, central, chief, controlling, dominant, first, foremost, fundamental, important, leading, major, number one*, outstanding, overruling, paramount, predominant, preeminent, primary, prime, principal, prominent, underlying, vital; SEE CONCEPTS 546,568,829

capital [adj2] *superior*
best, champion, choice, crack, dandy, delightful, deluxe, excellent, famous, fine, first, first-class*, first-rate*, five-star*, fly, great, prime, splendid, superb, top, top-notch*; SEE CONCEPT 574

capitalism [n] *economic system of private ownership*
commercialism, competition, democracy, free enterprise, free market, industrialism, laissez faire economics, mercantilism, private enterprise; SEE CONCEPTS 299,689,770

capitalist [n] *person engaged in private ownership of business*
backer, banker, bourgeois, businessperson, entrepreneur, financier, investor, landowner, moneybags*, one who signs the checks*, plutocrat, the boss*, the money*; SEE CONCEPT 347

capitalize [v] *benefit from situation*
avail oneself of, exploit, gain, make capital of, obtain, profit, realize, subsidize, take advantage of; SEE CONCEPT 120

capitol [n] *building or buildings housing chief governmental offices*
Capitol Hill, center, dome, legislative hall, political scene*, seat of government, statehouse, the political front; SEE CONCEPTS 299,449

capitulate [v] *give in*
bow, buckle under, cave in, cede, come across, come to terms, concede, defer, fold, give away the store*, give out, give up, knuckle under, put out, relent,

submit, succumb, surrender, yield; SEE CONCEPTS 35,83

capitulation [n] *giving in*
accedence, bowing, buckling, conceding, giving up, knuckling under, relenting, resignation, submission, succumbing, surrender, yielding; SEE CONCEPTS 83,410

caprice [n] *sudden change of behavior*
bee, caper*, changeableness, contrariety, crotchet, fad, fancy, fickleness, fitfulness, fool notion*, freak, gag*, humor, impulse, inconsistency, inconstancy, jerk, kink, mood, notion, peculiarity, perversity, put on*, quirk, rib*, temper, thought, vagary, vein, whim, whimsy; SEE CONCEPTS 13,410

capricious [adj] *given to sudden behavior change*
any way the wind blows*, arbitrary, blowing hot and cold*, careless, changeful, contrary, crotchety, effervescent, erratic, every which way*, fanciful, fickle, fitful, flaky*, flighty, freakish, gaga*, helter-skelter*, humorsome, impulsive, inconstant, kinky*, lubricious, mercurial, moody, mutable, notional, odd, picky*, punchy*, queer, quirky, temperamental, ticklish, unpredictable, unreasonable, unstable, up and down*, vagarious, variable, volatile, wayward, whimsical, yo-yo*; SEE CONCEPT 401

capsize [v] *overturn*
invert, keel over, roll, tip over, turn over, turn turtle*, upset; SEE CONCEPTS 150,152

capsule [n] *tablet, usually medicine*
bolus, cap, dose, lozenge, pellet, pill, troche; SEE CONCEPTS 260,307

capsule [adj] *shortened form*
abridged, canned, condensed, epitomized, pocket, potted, tabloid; SEE CONCEPTS 531,773

captain [n] *chief of vehicle, effort*
authority, boss, cap, CEO, CFO, chieftain, commander, director, exec*, executive, four-striper*, guide, head, head honcho*, higher up*, leader, master, mistress, number one*, officer, operator, owner, pilot, royalty, skip*, skipper*, top*, top dog*; SEE CONCEPT 347

caption [n] *heading; short description*
explanation, head, inscription, legend, rubric, subtitle, title, underline; SEE CONCEPT 283

captious [adj] *very critical*
acrimonious, cantankerous, carping, caviling, cavillous, censorious, contrary, crabby, cross, demanding, deprecating, disparaging, exacting, exceptive, fault-finding, finicky, hypercritical, irritable, nagging, nit-picking, overcritical, peevish, perverse, petulant, sarcastic, severe, testy, touchy; SEE CONCEPTS 267,404

captivate [v] *attract, enchant*
allure, beguile, bewitch, charm, dazzle, delight, draw, enamour, enrapture, enslave, ensnare, entertain, enthrall, entrance, fascinate, gratify, grip, hold, hook, hypnotize, infatuate, intrigue, lure, magnetize, make a hit with*, mesmerize, please, rope in*, se-

duce, spellbind, sweep off one's feet*, take, turn one on, vamp, wile, win; SEE CONCEPTS *7,22*

captive [*n*] *person held physically*
bondman, bondservant, bondwoman, con, convict, detainee, hostage, internee, prisoner, prisoner of war, slave; SEE CONCEPTS *412,423*

captive [*adj1*] *physically held by force*
bound, caged, confined, enslaved, ensnared, imprisoned, incarcerated, incommunicado, in custody, jailed, locked up, penned, restricted, subjugated, under lock and key*; SEE CONCEPTS *536,554*

captive [*adj2*] *mentally enchanted, held*
beguiled, bewitched, charmed, delighted, enraptured, enthralled, fascinated, hypnotized, infatuated; SEE CONCEPT *403*

captivity [*n*] *physical detention by force*
bondage, committal, confinement, constraint, custody, durance, duress, enslavement, enthrallment, entombment, impoundment, imprisonment, incarceration, internment, jail, limbo, restraint, serfdom, servitude, slavery, subjection, thralldom, vassalage; SEE CONCEPTS *191,652*

capture [*n*] *catching, forceful holding*
abduction, acquirement, acquisition, apprehension, appropriating, appropriation, arrest, bag*, bust*, catch, collar*, commandeering, confiscation, drop*, ensnaring, fall, gaining, grab*, grasping, hit the jackpot*, hook*, imprisonment, knock off*, laying hold of*, nab*, nail*, obtaining, occupation, pick up*, pinch*, pull*, run in*, securing, seizing, seizure, snatching*, sweep*, taking, taking captive, taking into custody, trapping, trip, winning; SEE CONCEPT *90*

capture [*v*] *catch and forcefully hold*
apprehend, arrest, bag*, bust*, catch, collar*, conquer, cop, gain control, get, grab*, hook*, land, nab*, nail*, net, occupy, overwhelm, pick up*, pinch*, prehend, pull in, put the cuffs on*, round up*, run in*, secure, seize, snare, snatch, take, take captive, take into custody, take prisoner, trap, tumble; SEE CONCEPT *90*

car [*n*] *vehicle driven on streets*
auto, automobile, bucket*, buggy*, bus, clunker*, compact, convertible, conveyance, coupe, gas guzzler*, hardtop, hatchback, heap*, jalopy*, jeep, junker*, limousine, machine, motor, motorcar, pickup, ride*, roadster, sedan, station wagon, subcompact, touring car, truck, van, wagon, wheels*, wreck*; SEE CONCEPT *505*

caravan [*n*] *group traveling together*
band, camel train*, campers, cavalcade, expedition, procession, safari, train, troop; SEE CONCEPTS *432,503*

carbohydrate [*n*] *organic compound composed of carbon, hydrogen, and oxygen*
cellulose, dextrin, dextrose, disaccharide, fructose, galactose, glucose, glycogen, lactose, maltose, monosaccharide, polysaccharide, starch, sucrose, sugar; SEE CONCEPT *478*

carcass/carcase [*n*] *dead body; framework, base structure*
body, cadaver, corpse, framework, hulk, mort*, remains, shell, skeleton, stiff*; SEE CONCEPTS *390,434*

card [*n*] *piece of paper, often with purposeful writing*
agenda, badge, billet, calendar, cardboard, check, docket, fiberboard, identification, label, pass, poster, program, schedule, sheet, square, tally, ticket, timetable, voucher; SEE CONCEPTS *260,271*

cardinal [*adj*] *important, key*
basal, basic, central, chief, constitutive, essential, first, foremost, fundamental, greatest, highest, indispensable, leading, main, overriding, overruling, paramount, pivotal, preeminent, primary, prime, principal, ruling, vital; SEE CONCEPTS *568,574*

care [*n1*] *personal interest, concern*
affliction, aggravation, alarm, anguish, annoyance, anxiety, apprehension, bother, burden, chagrin, charge, consternation, discomposure, dismay, disquiet, distress, disturbance, encumbrance, exasperation, fear, foreboding, fretfulness, handicap, hardship, hindrance, impediment, incubus, load, misgiving, nuisance, onus, oppression, perplexity, pressure, responsibility, solicitude, sorrow, stew, strain, stress, sweat, tribulation, trouble, uneasiness, unhappiness, vexation, woe, worry; SEE CONCEPTS *410,532*

care [*n2*] *carefulness, attention to detail*
alertness, caution, circumspection, concentration, concern, conscientiousness, consideration, diligence, direction, discrimination, effort, enthusiasm, exactness, exertion, fastidiousness, forethought, heed, interest, management, meticulousness, nicety, pains, particularity, precaution, prudence, regard, scrupulousness, solicitude, thought, trouble, vigilance, wariness, watchfulness; SEE CONCEPT *657*

care [*n3*] *custody of person, usually child*
administration, aegis, auspices, charge, control, direction, guardianship, keeping, management, ministration, protection, safekeeping, superintendence, supervision, trust, tutelage, ward, wardship; SEE CONCEPTS *285,295,388*

care [*v1*] *tend to*
attend, baby-sit, consider, foster, keep an eye on*, keep tabs on*, look after, mind, mind the store*, minister, mother, nurse, nurture, pay attention to, protect, provide for, ride herd on*, sit, take pains, tend, treasure, wait on, watch, watch over; SEE CONCEPTS *110,295*

care [*v2*] *regard highly*
be crazy about*, be fond of*, cherish, desire, enjoy, find congenial, hold dear, like, love, prize, respect, take to, want; SEE CONCEPTS *20,32*

careen [*v*] *tilt; move wildly down path*
bend, lean, lurch, pitch, sway, tilt; SEE CONCEPT *147*

career [*n1*] *occupation*
bag*, calling, course, dodge*, employment, field, game*, job, lifework, livelihood, number*, pilgrim-

age, profession, pursuit, racket*, specialty, thing*, vocation, work; SEE CONCEPTS *349,360*

career [*n2*] *course, path*
course, orbit, passage, pilgrimage, procedure, progress, race, walk; SEE CONCEPTS *501,678,692*

carefree [*adj*] *lighthearted, untroubled*
airy, at ease, blithe, breezy, buoyant, calm, careless, cheerful, cheery, cool, easy, easy-going, feelgood*, happy, happy-go-lucky, insouciant, jaunty, jovial, laid back*, radiant, secure, sunny, unanxious, unbothered; SEE CONCEPT *404*

careful [*adj*] *cautious; painstaking*
accurate, alert, apprehensive, assiduous, attentive, chary, choosy, circumspect, concerned, conscientious, conservative, cool, deliberate, discreet, exacting, fastidious, finicky, fussy, going to great lengths*, guarded, heedful, judicious, leery, meticulous, mindful, observant, particular, playing safe*, precise, prim, protective, provident, prudent, punctilious, regardful, religious, rigorous, scrupulous, self-disciplined, shy, sober, solicitous, solid, thorough, thoughtful, vigilant, wary; SEE CONCEPTS *326,542*

carefully [*adv*] *cautiously; painstakingly*
anxiously, attentively, circumspectly, concernedly, conscientiously, correctly, deliberately, delicately, dependably, discreetly, exactly, faithfully, fastidiously, fully, gingerly, guardedly, heedfully, honorably, in detail, laboriously, meticulously, particularly, precisely, providently, prudently, punctiliously, regardfully, reliably, rigorously, scrupulously, solicitously, thoroughly, thoughtfully, trustily, uprightly, vigilantly, warily, watchfully, with forethought, with reservations; SEE CONCEPT *542*

careless [*adj1*] *without sufficient attention*
absent-minded, abstracted, casual, cursory, disregardful, forgetful, hasty, heedless, improvident, imprudent, inaccurate, inadvertent, incautious, inconsiderate, indifferent, indiscreet, indolent, injudicious, irresponsible, lackadaisical, lax, loose, mindless, napping, negligent, nonchalant, oblivious, offhand, perfunctory, pococurante, reckless, regardless, remiss, slipshod, sloppy, thoughtless, uncircumspect, unconcerned, unguarded, unheeding, unmindful, unobservant, unreflective, unthinking, wasteful; SEE CONCEPT *542*

careless [*adj2*] *artless*
casual, modest, naive, natural, nonchalant, simple, unstudied; SEE CONCEPT *557*

caress [*n*] *loving touch*
cuddle, embrace, endearment, feel, fondling, hug, kiss, pat, pet, petting, snuggle, squeeze, stroke; SEE CONCEPTS *375,590*

caress [*v*] *touch lovingly*
bear hug*, brush, buss, clinch, clutch, coddle, cosset, cuddle, dandle, embrace, feel, fondle, graze, handle, hug, kiss, make love, massage, mug, neck, nestle, nuzzle, pat, pet, play around*, rub, squeeze, stroke, toy; SEE CONCEPTS *375,612*

caretaker [*n*] *person who maintains something*
baby sitter*, concierge, curator, custodian, housesitter*, janitor, keeper, porter, sitter, super*, superintendent, supervisor, warden, watchman; SEE CONCEPT *348*

cargo [*n*] *baggage; something to be delivered*
burden, consignment, contents, freight, goods, haul, lading, load, merchandise, payload, shipload, shipment, tonnage, ware; SEE CONCEPTS *338,446*

caricature [*n*] *exaggerated description in writing, drawing*
burlesque, cartoon, distortion, farce, imitation, lampoon, libel, mimicry, mockery, parody, pasquinade, pastiche, put-on*, ridicule, satire, send-up*, sham, takeoff*, travesty; SEE CONCEPTS *271,386,625*

carillon [*n*] *set of bells*
angelus, chimes, glockenspiel, gong, lyra, peal, tintinnabulation, tocsin; SEE CONCEPT *595*

carnage [*n*] *massacre*
annihilation, blitz, blood, blood and guts*, blood bath*, bloodshed, butchering, butchery, crime, extermination, gore, havoc, hecatomb, holocaust, homicide, killing, liquidation, manslaughter, mass murder, murder, offing*, rapine, search and destroy*, shambles, slaughter, slaying, taking out*, warfare, wasting; SEE CONCEPT *252*

carnal [*adj*] *erotic, sensual*
animal, bodily, corporal, corporeal, earthly, fleshly, genital, impure, lascivious, lecherous, lewd, libidinous, licentious, lustful, physical, prurient, salacious, sensuous, temporal, unchaste, venereal, voluptuous, vulgar, wanton, worldly; SEE CONCEPTS *372,403*

carnival [*n*] *outdoor celebration*
amusement park, bacchanal, carny*, carousal, circus, conviviality, exposition, fair, feasting, festival, fete, fiesta, frolic, gala, grind show*, heyday, jamboree, jollification, jubilee, Mardi Gras, masquerade, merrymaking, orgy, ragbag*, revelry, rout, Saturnalia, side show, spree, street fair; SEE CONCEPTS *377,386*

carnivorous [*adj*] *eating animal flesh*
cannibal, flesh-eating, hungry, omnivorous, predatory, rapacious; SEE CONCEPT *401*

carol [*n*] *joyful hymn*
ballad, canticle, canzonet, chorus, Christmas song, ditty*, lay, madrigal, noel, song, strain; SEE CONCEPTS *263,595*

carouse [*v*] *make merry, often with liquor*
booze, drink, frolic, go on a spree*, have fun, imbibe, paint the town*, paint the town red*, play, quaff, raise Cain*, revel, riot, roister, wassail, whoop it up*; SEE CONCEPT *384*

carp [*v*] *nag*
bother, cavil, censure, complain, criticize, find fault, fuss, grumble, henpeck*, hypercriticize, knock, nit-

pick*, objurgate, pan, peck*, pick at, quibble, reproach; SEE CONCEPT *52*

carpenter [*n*] *person who works with wood*
artisan, builder, cabinetmaker, carps*, chips*, craftsperson, joiner, laborer, mason, woodworker, worker; SEE CONCEPT *348*

carpet [*n*] *nappy floor covering*
carpeting, matting, rug, runner, tapestry, throw rug, wall-to-wall*; SEE CONCEPT *473*

carriage [*n1*] *delivery of freight*
carrying, conveyance, conveying, delivering, freight, transit, transport, transportation; SEE CONCEPTS *148,217*

carriage [*n2*] *posture, physical and mental*
air, aspect, attitude, bearing, behavior, cast, comportment, conduct, demeanor, deportment, gait, look, manner, mien, pace, positure, presence, stance, step; SEE CONCEPTS *633,720*

carry [*v1*] *transport physical object*
backpack*, bear, bring, cart, channel, conduct, convey, convoy, displace, ferry, fetch, freight, funnel, give, haul, heft*, hoist*, import, lift, lug*, move, pack, pipe, portage, relay, relocate, remove, schlepp*, shift, shoulder*, sustain, take, tote*, traject, transfer, transmit, transplant, truck*, waft; SEE CONCEPTS *148,217*

carry [*v2*] *win; accomplish*
affect, be victorious, capture, drive, effect, gain, get, impel, impress, influence, inspire, move, prevail, secure, spur, strike, sway, touch, urge; SEE CONCEPTS *68,706*

carry [*v3*] *broadcast electronically*
air, bear, communicate, conduct, convey, display, disseminate, give, offer, pass on, publish, relay, release, send, transfer, transport; SEE CONCEPTS *217,266*

carry on [*v1*] *continue activity*
achieve, endure, hang on, keep going, last, maintain, perpetuate, persevere, persist, proceed; SEE CONCEPT *239*

carry on [*v2*] *manage operations*
administer, conduct, direct, engage in, keep, operate, ordain, run; SEE CONCEPT *117*

carry on [*v3*] *lose control emotionally*
act up, be indecorous, blunder, cut up, lose it, make a fuss*, misbehave, rage, raise Cain*; SEE CONCEPT *633*

carry out [*v*] *complete activity*
accomplish, achieve, carry through, consummate, discharge, effect, effectuate, execute, finalize, fulfill, implement, meet, perform, realize; SEE CONCEPT *706*

cart [*n*] *small attachment for transporting*
barrow, buggy, curricle, dolly, dray, gig, gurney, handcart, palanquin, pushcart, rickshaw, tilbury, truck, tumbrel, two-wheeler, wagon, wheelbarrow; SEE CONCEPTS *499,505*

cart [*v*] *carry*
bear, bring, convey, ferry, haul, move, schlepp*, take, tote; SEE CONCEPTS *148,217*

carte blanche [*n*] *full power, authority*
blank check, freedom, free hand, free rein, license, permission, power of attorney, prerogative, sanction, say, say-so, unconditional right; SEE CONCEPT *376*

cartel [*n*] *group which shares business interest*
bunch*, chain, combine, conglomerate, consortium, corporation, crew*, crowd*, gang*, holding company, megacorp*, mob*, monopoly, multinational*, outfit*, plunderbund*, pool, ring*, syndicate, trust; SEE CONCEPTS *323,325*

carton [*n*] *box for holding items*
bin, case, casket, chest, coffer, container, corrugated box, crate, pack, package, packet; SEE CONCEPT *494*

cartoon [*n*] *funny drawing, often with dialogue or caption*
animation, caricature, comic strip, drawing, lampoon, parody, representation, satire, sketch, takeoff; SEE CONCEPTS *280,625*

cartoonist [*n*] *person who draws cartoons*
artist, caricaturist, comic artist, gag man*, gagster*, gag woman*, illustrator, social critic; SEE CONCEPT *348*

carve [*v*] *cut carefully with sharp instrument*
block out, chip, chisel, cleave, dissect, dissever, divide, engrave, etch, fashion, form, grave, hack, hew, incise, indent, insculpt, model, mold, mould, pattern, rough-hew, sculpt, shape, slash, slice, stipple, sunder, tool, trim, whittle; SEE CONCEPTS *137, 176,184*

cascade [*n*] *something falling, especially water*
avalanche, cataract, chute, deluge, downrush, falls, flood, force, fountain, outpouring, precipitation, rapids, shower, spout, torrent, watercourse, waterfall; SEE CONCEPTS *514,786*

cascade [*v*] *fall in a rush*
descend, disgorge, flood, gush, heave, overflow, pitch, plunge, pour, spew, spill, spit up, surge, throw up, tumble, vomit; SEE CONCEPT *179*

case [*n1*] *container; items in container*
bag, baggage, basket, bin, box, cabinet, caddy, caisson, canister, capsule, carton, cartridge, casing, casket, chamber, chassis, chest, coffer, compact, cover, covering, crate, crating, crib, drawer, envelope, folder, grip, holder, integument, jacket, receptacle, safe, scabbard, sheath, shell, suitcase, tray, trunk, wallet, wrapper, wrapping; SEE CONCEPT *494*

case [*n2*] *circumstance, conditions*
context, contingency, crisis, dilemma, event, eventuality, fact, incident, occurrence, plight, position, predicament, problem, quandary, situation, state, status; SEE CONCEPT *696*

case [*n3*] *example*
case history, exemplification, illustration, instance, occasion, occurrence, representative, sample, sampling, specimen; SEE CONCEPT *688*

case [*n4*] *matter brought before a court*
action, argument, cause, claim, dispute, evidence, lawsuit, litigation, petition, proceedings, process, proof, suit, trial; SEE CONCEPT *318*

case [v] *check something in detail*
canvass, check out, check over, check up, examine, inspect, scrutinize, study, view; SEE CONCEPT *103*

cash [n] *money; assets*
banknote, bread*, buck*, bullion, cabbage*, chicken feed*, coin, coinage, currency, dinero*, dough*, funds, green stuff*, investment, legal tender, lot, mazumah*, note, payment, pledge, principal, ready assets, refund, remuneration, reserve, resources, riches, savings, scratch*, security, skins*, stock, supply, treasure, wampum*, wherewithal; SEE CONCEPTS *340,710*

cash [v] *exchange for real money*
acknowledge, break a bill*, change, discharge, draw, honor, liquidate, make change, pay, realize, redeem; SEE CONCEPT *330*

cashier [n] *bank worker*
accountant, banker, bursar, clerk, collector, paymaster, purser, receiver, teller, treasurer; SEE CONCEPT *348*

cashier [v] *discard, expel*
ax, boot, bounce, break, can*, cast off, discharge, dismiss, displace, drum out*, fire, give a pink slip*, give the heave ho*, heave*, remove, sack*, terminate; SEE CONCEPTS *211,324*

casino [n] *gambling establishment*
bank, betting house, big store*, club, clubhouse, dance hall, dice joint*, dive, gambling den, hall, honky-tonk, house, joint, Monte Carlo, pool hall, roadhouse, rotunda, saloon, track; SEE CONCEPT *447*

cask [n] *rounded container for liquids*
barrel, barrelet, butt, firkin, hogshead, keg, pipe, tun, vat; SEE CONCEPT *494*

casket [n] *burial box*
bin, carton, case, chest, coffer, crate, funerary box, pine box, pinto, sarcophagus, wood overcoat*; SEE CONCEPTS *368,494*

casserole [n] *dish consisting of a combination of cooked food*
covered dish, goulash, hash, meat pie, pot pie, pottage, stew, stroganoff; SEE CONCEPT *457*

cast [n1] *a throw to the side*
casting, ejection, expulsion, fling, flinging, heave, heaving, hurl, hurling, launching, lob, lobbing, pitch, pitching, projection, propulsion, shooting, sling, slinging, thrust, thrusting, toss, tossing; SEE CONCEPT *222*

cast [n2] *appearance; shade of color*
air, complexion, countenance, demeanor, embodiment, expression, face, hue, look, manner, mien, semblance, stamp, style, tinge, tint, tone, turn, visage; SEE CONCEPTS *622,716*

cast [n3] *actors in performance*
actors, actresses, artists, characters, company, dramatis, list, parts, personae, players, roles, troupe; SEE CONCEPT *294*

cast [n4] *molded structure*
conformation, copy, duplicate, embodiment, facsimile, figure, form, mold, plaster, replica, sculpture, shape; SEE CONCEPTS *470,475*

cast [v1] *throw aside*
boot, bung*, chuck*, drive, drop, fire*, fling, heave, hurl, impel, launch, lob, peg, pitch, project, shed, shy, sling, thrust, toss; SEE CONCEPT *222*

cast [v2] *emit, give*
aim, bestow, deposit, diffuse, direct, distribute, point, radiate, scatter, shed, spatter, spray, spread, sprinkle, strew, train; SEE CONCEPTS *108,624*

cast [v3] *calculate*
add, compute, count, figure, foot, forecast, number, reckon, sum, summate, tot, total; SEE CONCEPT *764*

cast [v4] *select for activity*
allot, appoint, arrange, assign, blueprint, chart, choose, decide upon, delegate, design, designate, detail, determine, devise, give parts, name, pick, plan, project; SEE CONCEPT *41*

caste [n] *social class*
cultural level, degree, estate, grade, lineage, order, position, race, rank, social order, species, sphere, standing, station, status, stratum; SEE CONCEPTS *378,388*

castigate [v] *criticize severely*
baste, bawl out*, beat, berate, blister, cane, censure, chasten, chastise, chew out*, come down on*, correct, criticize, discipline, drag over the coals*, dress down*, drub, excoriate, flay, flog, jump down one's throat*, lambaste, lash, lay out*, lean on*, penalize, pummel, punish, rail, rate, read the riot act*, ream, rebuke, reprimand, scarify, scathe, scold, scorch, scourge, thrash, tongue-lash*, upbraid, whip; SEE CONCEPT *52*

castle [n] *magnificent home, often for royalty*
acropolis, alcazar, château, citadel, donjon, estate house, fasthold, fastness, fort, fortification, fortress, hold, keep, manor, mansion, palace, peel, safehold, seat, stronghold, tower, villa; SEE CONCEPT *516*

castrate [v] *remove sexual organs*
alter, asexualize, caponize, change, cut, deprive of virility, desexualize, effeminize, emasculate, eunuchize, fix, geld, mutilate, neuter, spay, sterilize, unman, unsex; SEE CONCEPT *310*

casual [adj1] *chance, random*
accidental, adventitious, by chance, contingent, erratic, extemporaneous, extempore, fluky, fortuitous, impromptu, improvised, impulsive, incidental, infrequent, irregular, occasional, odd, offhand, serendipitous, spontaneous, uncertain, unexpected, unforeseen, unintentional, unplanned, unpremeditated; SEE CONCEPTS *541,544*

casual [adj2] *nonchalant, relaxed in manner*
aloof, apathetic, blasé, breezy, cool*, cursory, detached, down home*, easygoing, folksy*, homey*, incurious, indifferent, informal, insouciant, lackadaisical, laid back*, loose*, low-pressure, mellow, offhand, perfunctory, pococurante, purposeless, remote, unconcerned, unfussy, uninterested, withdrawn; SEE CONCEPTS *401,542,589*

casualty [n1] *accident*
blow, calamity, catastrophe, chance, contingency,

debacle, disaster, misadventure, misfortune, mishap; SEE CONCEPT *674*

casualty [*n2*] *victim*
dead, death toll, fatality, injured, killed, loss, missing, prey, sufferer, wounded; SEE CONCEPTS *407,423*

casuistry [*n*] *overgeneral reasoning*
chicanery, deception, deceptiveness, delusion, equivocation, evasion, fallacy, lie, oversubtleness, sophism, sophistry, speciousness, spuriousness, trick; SEE CONCEPTS *54,63*

cat [*n*] *feline animal, sometimes a pet*
bobcat, cheetah, cougar, grimalkin, jaguar, kitten, kitty, leopard, lion, lynx, malkin, mouser, ocelot, panther, puma, puss, pussy, tabby, tiger, tom, tomcat; SEE CONCEPTS *394,400*

cataclysm [*n*] *disaster*
calamity, cataract, catastrophe, collapse, convulsion, crunch*, curtains*, debacle, deluge, disaster, disturbance, double trouble*, flood, flooding, holy mess*, inundation, misadventure, ruin, torrent, tragedy, unholy mess*, upheaval, Waterloo*, woe; SEE CONCEPTS *674,675*

catalog/catalogue [*n*] *written or printed matter featuring a selection of objects*
archive, brief, bulletin, calendar, cartulary, charts, classification, compendium, directory, docket, draft, enumeration, gazette, gazetteer, hit list, index, inventory, list, prospectus, record, register, roll, roster, schedule, slate, specification, syllabus, synopsis, table; SEE CONCEPTS *271,280*

catalyst [*n*] *something which incites activity*
adjuvant, agitator, enzyme, goad, impetus, impulse, incendiary, incentive, incitation, incitement, motivation, radical stimulus, reactant, reactionary, spark plug*, spur, stimulant, synergist, wave maker*; SEE CONCEPT *712*

catapult [*n*] *implement for shooting weapon*
arbalest, ballista, heaver, hurler, pitcher, propeller, shooter, sling, slingshot, tosser, trebuchet; SEE CONCEPTS *463,500*

catastrophe [*n*] *calamity; unhappy conclusion*
accident, adversity, affliction, alluvion, bad luck, bad news*, blow, calamity, casualty, cataclysm, contretemps, crash, culmination, curtain*, debacle, denouement, desolation, devastation, disaster, emergency, end, failure, fatality, fiasco, finale, grief, hardship, havoc, ill, infliction, meltdown*, misadventure, mischance, misery, misfortune, mishap, reverse, scourge, stroke, termination, the worst*, tragedy, trial, trouble, upshot, Waterloo*, wreck; SEE CONCEPT *674*

catch [*n1*] *fastener*
bolt, buckle, clamp, clasp, clip, hasp, hook, hook and eye, latch, snap; SEE CONCEPT *497*

catch [*n2*] *trick, hidden disadvantage*
Catch-22, conundrum, deception, decoy, drawback, fly in the ointment*, hitch, joke, puzzle, puzzler, snag, stumbling block, trap; SEE CONCEPTS *674,679*

catch [*v1*] *ensnare, apprehend*
arrest, bag*, bust*, capture, clasp, claw, clench, clutch, collar*, cop, corral*, entangle, entrap, get one's fingers on*, glom, glove, grab, grasp, grip, hook, lasso, lay hold of, nab, nail*, net, pick, pluck, pounce on, prehend, secure, seize, snag, snare, snatch, take, take hold of, trap; SEE CONCEPT *90*

catch [*v2*] *find out, discover*
descry, detect, encounter, expose, hit upon, meet with, spot, surprise, take unawares, turn up, unmask; SEE CONCEPT *31*

catch [*v3*] *contract an illness*
become infected with, break out with, come down with, develop, fall ill with, fall victim to, get, incur, receive, sicken, succumb to, suffer from, take; SEE CONCEPTS *93,308*

catch [*v4*] *come from behind and grab*
board, climb on, come upon, cotch, get, go after, grab, hop on, jump, make, overhaul, overtake, pass, ram, reach, run down, take; SEE CONCEPT *164*

catch [*v5*] *hear and understand*
accept, apprehend, comprehend, discern, feel, follow, get, grasp, perceive, recognize, see, sense, take in, understand; SEE CONCEPT *15*

catching [*adj*] *contagious (disease)*
communicable, dangerous, endemic, epidemic, epizootic, infectious, infective, miasmatic, pandemic, pestiferous, pestilential, taking, transferable, transmittable; SEE CONCEPT *314*

catchword [*n*] *motto*
byword, catchphrase, household word, maxim, password, refrain, shibboleth, slogan, watchword; SEE CONCEPTS *275,278*

catchy [*adj*] *captivating, addictive*
fetching, haunting, having a good hook*, memorable, popular; SEE CONCEPT *544*

catechize [*v*] *instruct and question*
ask, cross-examine, drill, educate, examine, grill, inquire, interrogate, query, quiz, teach, train; SEE CONCEPTS *48,285*

categorical [*adj*] *explicit, unconditional*
absolute, all out*, certain, clear-cut, definite, definitive, direct, downright, emphatic, express, flat out*, forthright, no holds barred*, no strings attached*, positive, specific, straight out, sure, ultimate, unambiguous, unequivocal, unmitigated, unqualified, unreserved; SEE CONCEPT *535*

categorize [*v*] *sort by type, classification*
assort, button down*, class, classify, group, identify, peg*, pigeonhole*, put down as, rank, tab, typecast; SEE CONCEPT *39*

category [*n*] *classification, type*
class, department, division, grade, group, grouping, head, heading, kind, league, level, list, order, pigeonhole*, rank, section, sort, tier; SEE CONCEPT *378*

cater [*v*] *provide, help*
baby, coddle, cotton, furnish, gratify, humor, indulge, minister to, outfit, pamper, pander to, pro-

cure, provision, purvey, spoil, supply, victual; SEE
CONCEPT *136*

caterwaul [*v*] *make screeching, crying noise*
bawl, bicker, howl, quarrel, scream, screech, shriek,
squall, wail, yell, yowl; SEE CONCEPT *77*

catharsis [*n*] *purging, purification*
ablution, abreaction, cleansing, expurgation, lustration, purgation, purification, release; SEE CONCEPTS
13,165,230

cathedral [*n*] *large church*
basilica, bishop's seat, chancel, holy place, house of
God, house of prayer, house of worship, minster,
place of worship, sanctuary, temple; SEE CONCEPTS
368,439

catholic [*adj*] *all-embracing, general*
all-inclusive, broad-minded, charitable, comprehensive, cosmic, cosmopolitan, diffuse, eclectic, ecumenical, extensive, generic, global, inclusive,
indeterminate, large-scale, liberal, open-minded,
planetary, receptive, tolerant, unbigoted, universal,
unprejudiced, unsectarian, whole, wide, world-wide;
SEE CONCEPTS *557,772*

cattle [*n*] *bovine animals*
beasts, bovid mammals, bulls, calves, cows,
dogies*, herd, livestock, longhorn*, moo cows*,
shorthorns, stock, strays; SEE CONCEPT *394*

catty [*adj*] *nasty, malicious*
backbiting, evil, hateful, ill-natured, malevolent,
mean, rancorous, spiteful, venomous, vicious,
wicked; SEE CONCEPT *404*

caucus [*n*] *group gathered to make decision*
assembly, conclave, convention, council, gathering,
get-together, meeting, parley, session; SEE CONCEPTS
301,417

cause [*n1*] *agent, originator*
account, agency, aim, antecedent, author, basis, beginning, causation, consideration, creator, determinant, doer, element, end, explanation, foundation,
genesis, ground, grounds, incitement, inducement,
instigation, leaven, mainspring, maker, matter, motivation, motive, object, occasion, origin, prime
mover*, principle, producer, purpose, root, source,
spring, stimulation; SEE CONCEPTS *229,661*

cause [*n2*] *belief; undertaking for belief*
attempt, conviction, creed, enterprise, faith, goal,
ideal, intention, movement, object, objective, plan,
principles, purpose; SEE CONCEPT *689*

cause [*v*] *bring into being; bring about*
be at the bottom of*, begin, brainstorm*, break in*,
break the ice*, breed, bring to pass, come out with*,
compel, cook up*, create, dream up*, effect, elicit,
engender, evoke, fire up*, generate, get things rolling*, give rise to, hatch, incite, induce, introduce,
kickoff*, kindle, lead to, let, make, make up, motivate, muster, occasion, open, originate, precipitate,
produce, provoke, result in, revert, secure, sow the
seeds, start the ball rolling*, think up, work up; SEE
CONCEPTS *228,231,241*

caustic [*adj1*] *burning, corrosive*
abrasive, acerbic, acid, acrid, alkaline, astringent,
biting, corroding, erosive, keen, mordant, pungent,
tart; SEE CONCEPT *485*

caustic [*adj2*] *sarcastic*
acerb, acrimonious, bitter, cutting, harsh, incisive,
pithy, pungent, rough, salty, satiric, scathing, severe, sharp, stinging, trenchant, virulent; SEE CON-
CEPT *267*

caution [*n1*] *alertness, carefulness*
attention, canniness, care, circumspection, deliberation, discreetness, discretion, Fabian policy, foresight, forethought, heed, heedfulness, providence,
prudence, vigilance, watchfulness; SEE CONCEPT *410*

caution [*n2*] *warning*
admonition, advice, bug in one's ear*, caveat, commonition, counsel, forewarning, hint, injunction,
monition, notice, omen, premonition, sign, tip*, tip-
off*; SEE CONCEPTS *78,274*

caution [*v*] *warn, advise*
admonish, alert, exhort, flag, forewarn, give the high
sign*, give the lowdown on*, pull one's coat*, put
one wise*, tip*, tip off*, urge, wave a red flag*, wise
one up*; SEE CONCEPT *78*

cautious [*adj*] *careful, guarded*
alert, all ears*, cagey, calculating, chary, circumspect, considerate, discreet, forethoughtful, gingerly,
hedging one's bets*, heedful, judicious, keeping on
one's toes*, leery, on the lookout*, playing it cool*,
playing safe*, politic, provident, prudent, pussyfoot*, safe, shrewd, taking it easy, taking it slow*,
tentative, thinking twice*, vigilant, walking on
eggs*, wary, watchful, watching one's step*, watching out, with one's eyes peeled*; SEE CONCEPTS
401,403

cavalcade [*n*] *parade*
array, drill, march-past, procession, promenade, review, spectacle, train; SEE CONCEPT *432*

cavalier [*adj*] *arrogant*
condescending, curt, disdainful, haughty, high-and-
mighty*, insolent, lofty, lordly, offhand, overbearing, proud, scornful, snooty, snotty, supercilious,
superior; SEE CONCEPT *401*

cavalry [*n*] *troops riding horses*
army, bowlegs*, chasseurs, cuirassiers, dragoons,
horse, horsemen, horse soldiers, hussars, lancers,
mounted men, mounted troops, Mounties, rangers,
squadron, uhlans; SEE CONCEPT *322*

cave [*n*] *hole in land formation*
cavern, cavity, den, grotto, hollow, pothole, rock
shelter, subterrane, subterranean area; SEE CONCEPT
509

caveat [*n*] *warning*
admonition, alarm, caution, commonition, forewarning, monition, sign; SEE CONCEPTS *78,274*

cavern [*n*] *hollow in land formation*
cave, grotto, hole, pothole, subterrane, subterranean
area; SEE CONCEPT *509*

cavernous [adj] *hollow and large*
alveolate, broad, chambered, chasmal, commodious, concave, curved inward, deep, deep-set, echoing, gaping, huge, resonant, reverberant, roomy, sepulchral, socketed, spacious, sunken, vast, wide, yawning; SEE CONCEPTS *490,773,796*

cavity [n] *sunken or decayed area*
atrium, basin, bursa, caries, chamber, crater, decay, dent, depression, gap, hole, hollow, pit, pocket, sinus, socket, vacuity, void; SEE CONCEPT *513*

cavort [v] *frolic, prance*
caper, caracole, carry on*, cut loose*, cut up*, dance, fool around, frisk, gambol, go places and do things*, horse around*, horseplay, monkey around*, play, revel, rollick, romp, roughhouse*, sport; SEE CONCEPTS *114,384*

cease [v] *stop, conclude*
back off, break off, bring to an end, call it a day*, call it quits*, close, close out, come to an end, culminate, cut it out*, desist, deval, die, discontinue, drop, end, fail, finish, give over, halt, intermit, knock off*, leave off, pack in*, quit, quit cold turkey*, refrain, shut down, stay, surcease, terminate, wind up*; SEE CONCEPT *234*

ceaseless [adj] *never-ending*
amaranthine, constant, continual, continuous, day and night*, endless, eternal, everlasting, incessant, indefatigable, interminable, nonstop, on a treadmill*, perennial, perpetual, round the clock*, unceasing, unending, uninterrupted, unremitting, untiring, world-without-end*; SEE CONCEPT *798*

cede [v] *abandon, surrender*
abalienate, abdicate, accord, alien, alienate, allow, capitulate, come across with*, communicate, concede, convey, deed, drop, fold*, fork over*, give in*, give up, grant, hand over*, leave, make over, part with, relinquish, remise, renounce, resign, sign over, throw in the sponge*, throw in the towel*, transfer, vouchsafe, waive, yield; SEE CONCEPTS *108,127*

ceiling [n1] *top of a room*
baldachin, beam, canopy, covert, dome, fan vaulting, groin, highest point, housetop, plafond, planchement, plaster, roof, roofing, timber, topside covering; SEE CONCEPT *440*

ceiling [n2] *maximum*
legal price, record, superiority, top; SEE CONCEPT *836*

celebrate [v] *commemorate occasion, achievement*
beat the drum*, bless, blow off steam*, carouse, ceremonialize, commend, consecrate, dedicate, drink to, eulogize, exalt, extol, feast, fete, glorify, hallow, have a ball*, honor, jubilate, keep, kick up one's heels*, laud, let loose*, lionize, live it up*, make merry, make whoopee*, mark with a red letter*, memorialize, observe, paint the town red*, party*, perform, praise, proclaim, publicize, raise hell*, rejoice, revel, revere, ritualize, signalize, solemnize; SEE CONCEPT *377*

celebrated [adj] *distinguished, famous*
acclaimed, big*, eminent, famed, glorious, great, high powered, illustrious, immortal, important, large, laureate, lionized, notable, number one*, numero uno*, outstanding, popular, preeminent, prominent, renowned, revered, storied, up there*, w.k.*, well-known; SEE CONCEPT *568*

celebration [n] *commemoration of occasion, achievement*
anniversary, bash*, birthday, blast*, blowout*, carousal, ceremony, conviviality, festival, festivity, fete, frolic, gaiety, gala, glorification, hilarity, honoring, hoopla, hullabaloo*, jollification, joviality, jubilation, jubilee, keeping, magnification, memorialization, merriment, merrymaking, observance, party, performance, recognition, remembrance, revelry, Saturnalia, solemnization, spree, triumph, wingding*; SEE CONCEPT *377*

celebrity [n1] *dignitary*
ace, big cheese*, big deal*, big gun*, big name*, big shot*, big stuff*, bigwig*, celeb*, cynosure, famous person, figure, heavyweight, hero, hotshot*, immortal, lion*, luminary, magnate, mahatma, major leaguer*, man/woman of note, Mr./Ms. Big*, name, notable, personage, personality, somebody, someone, star, superstar, the cheese*, VIP, worthy; SEE CONCEPT *423*

celebrity [n2] *fame, notoriety*
distinction, eclat, eminence, glory, honor, notability, popularity, preeminence, prestige, prominence, renown, reputation, repute, stardom; SEE CONCEPTS *388,668*

celerity [n] *swiftness*
alacrity, briskness, dispatch, expedition, expeditiousness, fleetness, gait, haste, hurry, hustle, legerity, promptness, quickness, rapidity, speed, speediness, swiftness, velocity, vivacity; SEE CONCEPT *755*

celestial [adj] *heavenly*
angelic, astral, beatific, blessed, divine, elysian, empyral, empyrean, eternal, ethereal, godlike, hallowed, holy, immortal, Olympian, otherworldly, seraphic, spiritual, sublime, supernal, supernatural, transcendental, transmundane; SEE CONCEPTS *536,673*

celibacy [n] *abstinence from sexual activity*
abstention, chastity, continence, frigidity, impotence, maidenhood, purity, singleness, virginity, virtue; SEE CONCEPT *388*

celibate [adj] *abstaining from sexual activity*
chaste, continent, impotent, maiden, pure, virgin, virginal, virtuous; SEE CONCEPT *372*

cell [n1] *smallest living organism*
bacterium, cellule, corpuscle, egg, embryo, follicle, germ, haematid, microorganism, spore, unit, utricle, vacuole; SEE CONCEPTS *389,478*

cell [n2] *small room, container*
alcove, antechamber, apartment, bastille, booth, burrow, cage, cavity, chamber, cloister, closet, compartment, coop, crib, crypt, cubicle, den, dungeon, hold, hole, keep, lockup, nook, pen, receptacle, recess, retreat, stall, tower, vault; SEE CONCEPTS *448,494,513*

cellar [n] *underground story of building*
apartment, basement, subbasement, subterrane, underground room, vault; SEE CONCEPTS *440,448*

cement [n] *gluing, binding material*
adhesive, binder, birdlime, bond, concrete, epoxy, glue, grout, gum, gunk*, lime, lute, mortar, mucilage, mud*, paste, plaster, putty, rubber cement, sand, sealant, size, solder, stickum*, tar; SEE CONCEPT *475*

cement [v] *attach securely, often with sticky material*
bind, blend, bond, cohere, combine, connect, fasten, fuse, glue, gum, join, merge, mortar, paste, plaster, seal, solder, stick together, unite, weld; SEE CONCEPTS *85,160*

cemetery [n] *burial ground*
boot hill*, catacomb, charnel, charnel house, churchyard, city of the dead*, crypt, eternal home*, funerary grounds, garden, God's acre*, Golgotha, grave, graveyard, marble town*, memorial park, mortuary, necropolis, ossuary, polyandrium, potter's field, resting place, sepulcher, tomb, vault; SEE CONCEPTS *305,368*

censor [v] *forbid; ban; selectively remove*
abridge, blacklist, black out*, bleach, bleep*, blue-pencil*, bowdlerize, clean up, conceal, control, cork*, criticize, cut, decontaminate, delete, drop the iron curtain*, edit, examine, excise, expurgate, exscind, inspect, launder*, narrow, oversee, prevent publication, purge, purify, put the lid on*, refuse transmission, repress, restrain, restrict, review, revile, sanitize, scissor out*, squelch, sterilize, strike out, supervise communications, suppress, withhold; SEE CONCEPTS *121,266*

censorious [adj] *very critical*
accusatory, captious, carping, caviling, cavillous, chiding, complaining, condemnatory, condemning, critical, culpatory, denouncing, disapproving, disparaging, fault-finding, hypercritical, overcritical, reprehending, reproaching, severe; SEE CONCEPT *267*

censorship [n] *forbiddance; ban*
blackout*, blue pencil*, bowdlerization, control, forbidding, hush up*, infringing on rights, iron curtain*, restriction, suppression, thought control*; SEE CONCEPTS *376,388*

censure [n] *severe criticism*
admonishment, admonition, blame, castigation, condemnation, disapproval, dressing down, objection, obloquy, rebuke, remonstrance, reprehension, reprimand, reproach, reproof, stricture; SEE CONCEPTS *52,410*

censure [v] *condemn; criticize severely*
abuse, admonish, animadvert, asperse, attack, backbite, berate, blame, carp at, castigate, cavil, chastise, chide, contemn, cut up, denigrate, denounce, deprecate, disapprove, discipline, disparage, exprobate, find fault with, get after, impugn, incriminate, judge, knock, lecture, look askance, ostracize, pick apart, pull apart, read out*, rebuff, rebuke, remonstrate, reprehend, reprimand, reproach, reprove, scold, take to task*, tear apart*, tell off, upbraid; SEE CONCEPT *52*

center [n1] *middle point*
axis, bull's-eye, centrality, centriole, centrum, core, cynosure, equidistance, essence, focal point, focus, gist, heart, hotbed, hub, inside, interior, intermediacy, kernel, mainstream*, marrow, middle of the road*, midpoint, midst, nave, navel, nucleus, omphalos, pith, pivot, place, polestar, quick, radial point, root, seat, straddle the fence*; SEE CONCEPT *830*

center [n2] *point of attraction for visitors, shoppers, travelers*
capital, city, club, concourse, crossroads, focal point, focus, heart, hub, mall, market, marketplace, mart, meeting place, metropolis, nerve center, plaza, polestar, shopping center, social center, station, town, trading center; SEE CONCEPTS *435,438,507*

center [adj] *middle*
at halfway point, centermost, deepest, equidistant, inmost, inner, innermost, inside, interior, intermediary, intermediate, internal, mean, medial, mid, middlemost, midway; SEE CONCEPTS *583,585,830*

center [v] *concentrate, draw together*
attract, bring to a focus, bring together, centralize, close on, collect, concenter, consolidate, converge upon, focalize, focus, gather, intensify, join, medialize, meet, unify; SEE CONCEPTS *35,84*

central [adj] *main, principal; in the middle*
axial, basic, cardinal, center, centric, centroidal, chief, dominant, equidistant, essential, focal, foremost, fundamental, important, inmost, inner, interior, intermediate, key, leading, master, mean, median, mid, middle, middlemost, midmost, midway, nuclear, outstanding, overriding, paramount, pivotal, predominant, primary, prime, radical, ruling, salient, significant, umbilical; SEE CONCEPTS *567,583,830*

centralize [v] *concentrate, draw toward a point*
accumulate, amalgamate, assemble, compact, concenter, condense, consolidate, converge, focus, gather, incorporate, integrate, organize, rationalize, streamline, systematize, unify; SEE CONCEPTS *35,84*

centrifugal [adj] *radiating from a central point*
deviating, diffusive, divergent, diverging, eccentric, efferent, outward, radial, spiral, spreading; SEE CONCEPTS *581,584*

ceremonial [adj] *ritual, formal*
august, conventional, imposing, liturgical, lofty, mannered, ritualistic, solemn, stately, studied, stylized; SEE CONCEPT *548*

ceremonious [adj] *ritual, formal*
civil, courteous, courtly, decorous, deferential, dignified, exact, grandiose, impressive, majestic, moving, precise, proper, punctilious, seemly, solemn, starchy, stately, stiff, striking; SEE CONCEPT *548*

ceremony [n1] *ritual; celebratory observation*
ceremonial, commemoration, custom, formality, function, liturgy, observance, ordinance, parade, rite, sacrament, service, show, solemnity, tradition; SEE CONCEPT *386*

ceremony [n2] *etiquette*
ceremonial, conformity, decorum, form, formal courtesy, formalism, formality, nicety, politeness, pomp, preciseness, prescription, propriety, protocol, strictness, usage; SEE CONCEPT *388*

certain [adj1] *confident*
assertive, assured, believing, calm, cocksure*, convinced, positive, questionless, sanguine, satisfied, secure, self-confident, sure, unconcerned, undisturbed, undoubtful, undoubting, unperturbed, untroubled; SEE CONCEPT *403*

certain [adj2] *undoubtable, valid*
absolute, ascertained, authoritative, clear, conclusive, confirmable, definite, demonstrable, destined, determined, establishable, evident, firm, fixed, genuine, guaranteed, having down pat*, incontrovertible, indubitable, infallible, in the bag*, irrefutable, known, on ice*, plain, positive, predestined, provable, real, reliable, safe, salted away*, set, sound, supreme, sure, sure thing*, true, trustworthy, unambiguous, undeniable, undoubted, unequivocal, unerring, unmistakable, verifiable; SEE CONCEPTS *535,582*

certain [adj3] *fixed*
assured, bound, certified, concluded, decided, definite, determined, ensured, established, guaranteed, insured, set, settled, stated, stipulated, sure, warranted; SEE CONCEPT *535*

certain [adj4] *referring to a specifically known amount*
a couple, a few, defined, divers, express, individual, many, marked, numerous, one, particular, precise, regular, several, singular, some, special, specific, specified, sundry, upwards of, various; SEE CONCEPT *557*

certainly [adv] *without doubt*
absolutely, assuredly, cert*, exactly, for a fact, of course, positively, posolutely*, right on*, surely, unquestionably, without fail; SEE CONCEPT *535*

certainty [n1] *positive assurance*
all sewn up*, authoritativeness, belief, certitude, cinch, confidence, conviction, credence, definiteness, dogmatism, faith, firmness, indubitableness, inevitability, lock*, lockup*, open and shut case*, positiveness, positivism, rain or shine*, setup, shoo-in*, staunchness, steadiness, stock, store, sure bet*, surefire*, sureness, sure thing*, surety, trust, validity, wrap-up; SEE CONCEPTS *638,725*

certainty [n2] *fact, resulting truth*
consequence, foregone conclusion, inevitable result, reality, sure thing*, surety; SEE CONCEPT *230*

certificate [n] *authorizing document*
affidavit, affirmation, attestation, authentication, authorization, certification, coupon, credential, deed, diploma, docket, documentation, endorsement, guarantee, license, paper, pass, permit, receipt, record, sheepskin*, shingle, testament, testification, testimonial, testimony, ticket, voucher, warrant, warranty; SEE CONCEPTS *271,685*

certify [v] *declare as true*
accredit, approve, ascertain, assure, attest, authenticate, authorize, aver, avow, commission, confirm, corroborate, endorse, guarantee, license, notify, okay, profess, reassure, rubber-stamp*, sanction, show, state, swear, testify, validate, verify, vouch, witness; SEE CONCEPTS *50,88*

cessation [n] *ending*
abeyance, arrest, break, break-off*, breather*, cease, ceasing, close, conclusion, cutoff*, desistance, discontinuance, downtime*, end, finish, freeze*, grinding halt, halt, halting, hiatus, intermission, interruption, interval, layoff*, let-up*, pause, recess, remission, respite, rest, screaming halt*, standstill, stay, stop, stoppage, suspension, termination, time off, time-out*; SEE CONCEPT *119*

chafe [v1] *rub, grind against*
abrade, bark, corrode, damage, erode, excoriate, gall, grate, graze, hurt, impair, inflame, irritate, peel, ruffle, scrape, scratch, skin, wear; SEE CONCEPT *215*

chafe [v2] *annoy*
abrade, anger, annoy, bother, exasperate, exercise, fret, fume, gall, grate, harass, incense, inflame, irk, irritate, itch, offend, provoke, rage, rasp, rub, ruffle, scrape, scratch, vex, worry; SEE CONCEPTS *7,19*

chaff [n] *waste*
crust, debris, dregs, husks, pod, refuse, remains, rubbish, shard, shell, trash; SEE CONCEPT *679*

chaff [v] *joke, ridicule*
banter, deride, fun, jeer, jolly, josh, kid, mock, rag*, rally, razz*, rib*, scoff, taunt, tease; SEE CONCEPT *273*

chagrin [n] *displeasure*
annoyance, balk, blow, crushing, discomfiture, discomposure, disgruntlement, dismay, disquiet, dissatisfaction, embarrassment, fretfulness, frustration, humiliation, ill-humor, irritation, letdown, mortification, peevishness, shame, spleen, upset, vexation; SEE CONCEPTS *410,674*

chagrin [v] *cause displeasure*
abash, annoy, confuse, crush, discomfit, discompose, disconcert, disgrace, dismay, displease, disquiet, dissatisfy, embarrass, humiliate, irk, irritate, mortify, peeve, perturb, shame, upset, vex; SEE CONCEPTS *7,19*

chain [n1] *succession, series*
alternation, catena, concatenation, conglomerate, consecution, continuity, group, order, progression, row, sequence, set, string, syndicate, train, trust; SEE CONCEPTS *432,727,769*

chain [n2] *connected metal links; jewelry made of such links*
bond, bracelet, cable, clinker*, connection, coupling, fetter, iron, lavaliere, link, locket, manacle, pendant, shackle, trammel; SEE CONCEPTS *446, 476,499*

chain [v] *manacle in metal*
attach, bind, confine, connect, enslave, fetter, handcuff, hold, moor, restrain, shackle, tether, tie up, trammel; SEE CONCEPTS *85,160*

chair [n1] *single-seat furniture*
armchair, bench, cathedra, recliner, rocker, sling*; SEE CONCEPT *443*

chair [n2] *person in authority*
captain, chairman/woman, chairperson, director, fellowship, helm, instructorship, leader, master, monitor, position of control, principal, professorate, professorship, saddle, throne, tutor, tutorship; SEE CONCEPTS *348,376*

chairperson [n] *person in charge of proceedings*
administrator, captain, chair, chairman, chairwoman, director, introducer, leader, master of ceremonies, moderator, monitor, president, presider, principal, prolocutor, speaker, spokesman/woman, spokesperson, symposiarch, toastmaster; SEE CONCEPTS *348,376*

challenge [n] *dispute, question*
claiming, confrontation, dare, defiance, demanding, demur, interrogation, objection, protest, provocation, remonstrance, summons to contest, test, threat, trial, ultimatum; SEE CONCEPTS *53,532*

challenge [v] *dispute, question*
accost, arouse, ask for, assert, beard, brave, call for, call out, claim, confront, cross, dare, defy, demand, denounce, dispute, exact, face down, face off, face the music*, fly in the face of*, hang in*, impeach, impose, impugn, inquire, insist upon, investigate, invite competition, make a point of, make a stand, object to, provoke, query, reclaim, require, search out, stand up to, stick it out, stimulate, summon, tax, test, throw down the gauntlet*, try, vindicate; SEE CONCEPT *53*

chamber [n1] *small compartment, room*
alcove, antechamber, apartment, bedchamber, bedroom, box, case, cavity, cell, chest, container, cubicle, enclosure, flat, hall, hollow, lodging, pocket, room, socket; SEE CONCEPTS *448,494*

chamber [n2] *legislative body*
assembly, council, legislature, organization, representatives; SEE CONCEPT *299*

champion [n] *defeater in competition; preeminent supporter*
advocate, ally, backer, challenger, champ, conqueror, defender, endorser, exponent, expounder, guardian, hero, heroine, master, medalist, nonpareil, number one*, numero uno*, paladin, partisan, patron, proponent, protector, supporter, sympathizer, the greatest*, titleholder, top dog*, upholder, van-

quisher, victor, vindicator, warrior, white knight*, winner; SEE CONCEPT *366*

champion [adj] *best, excellent*
blue-ribbon, boss, capital, chief, choice, cool, dandy, distinguished, first, greatest, head, illustrious, out of sight*, out of this world*, outstanding, premier, prime, principal, prize-winning, splendid, super, superior, tip top*, top drawer*, topflight*, top-notch*, tops*, unbeaten, undefeated, world class*; SEE CONCEPT *574*

champion [v] *advocate, support*
back, battle, contend, defend, espouse, fight for, go to bat for*, patronize, plead for, promote, put in a good word for*, ride shotgun for*, side with, stand behind, stand up for, support, thump for, uphold; SEE CONCEPTS *10,69*

chance [n1] *possibility, probability*
break, contingency, fair shake*, fighting chance*, indications, liability, likelihood, long shot*, look-in, occasion, odds, opening, opportunity, outlook, prospect, scope, shot*, show, squeak, time, wager; SEE CONCEPT *650*

chance [n2] *fate, luck*
accident, advantage, adventure, bad luck, break, cast, casualty, coincidence, contingency, destination, destiny, doom, even chance, fluke, fortuity, fortune, future, gamble, good luck, hap*, haphazard, happening, hazard, heads or tails*, hit*, in the cards*, kismet, Lady Luck*, lot, lottery, luck out*, lucky break, misfortune, occurrence, odds, outcome, peradventure, peril, providence, risk, stroke of luck*, throw of the dice*, toss-up*, turn of the cards*, way the cookie crumbles*, wheel of fortune*; SEE CONCEPT *679*

chance [n3] *gamble, risk*
bet, craps game*, fall of the cards*, hazard, jeopardy, lottery, raffle, speculation, stake, throw of the dice*, try, venture, wager; SEE CONCEPT *363*

chance [adj] *accidental, unforeseeable*
adventitious, at random, casual, contingent, fluky, fortuitous, fortunate, happy, inadvert, incidental, lucky, odd, offhand, unforeseen, unintentional, unlooked for, unplanned; SEE CONCEPT *552*

chance [v1] *risk, endanger*
attempt, cast lots, draw lots, gamble, go out on a limb, have a fling at, hazard, jeopardize, play with fire*, plunge, put eggs in one basket*, put it on the line*, roll the dice*, run the risk, skate on thin ice*, speculate, stake, stick one's neck out*, take shot in the dark*, tempt fate*, tempt fortune*, toss up*, try, venture, wager, wildcat; SEE CONCEPT *87*

chance [v2] *happen*
arrive, befall, be one's fate, betide, blunder on, break, bump, come, come about, come off, come to pass, fall out, fall to one's lot, go, hap*, hit upon, light, light upon, luck, meet, occur, stumble, stumble on, transpire, tumble, turn up; SEE CONCEPT *4*

chancy [*adj*] *dangerous, risky*
capricious, contingent, dicey, erratic, fluctuant, flukey, hazardous, iffy, incalculable, precarious, problematic, problematical, rocky, speculative, ticklish, touchy, tricky, uncertain, unpredictable, unsound, whimsical; SEE CONCEPTS *552,587*

chandelier [*n*] *light hanging from ceiling*
candelabrum, candleholder, corona, crown, electrolier, gasolier, light fixture, luster; SEE CONCEPT *444*

change [*n1*] *something made different; alteration*
about-face*, addition, adjustment, advance, break, compression, contraction, conversion, correction, development, difference, distortion, diversification, diversity, innovation, metamorphosis, modification, modulation, mutation, novelty, permutation, reconstruction, refinement, remodeling, reversal, revision, revolution, shift, surrogate, switch, tempering, transformation, transition, transmutation, turn, turnover, variance, variation, variety, vicissitude; SEE CONCEPTS *230,260,701*

change [*n2*] *substitution; replacement*
conversion, exchange, flip-flop*, interchange, swap, switch, trade, turnaround; SEE CONCEPT *128*

change [*n3*] *smaller currency in exchange for larger*
chicken feed*, coins, copper, dimes, nickels, pennies, pin money*, pocket money, quarters, silver, spending money; SEE CONCEPT *340*

change [*v1*] *make or become different*
accommodate, adapt, adjust, alter, alternate, commute, convert, diminish, diverge, diversify, evolve, fluctuate, make innovations, make over, merge, metamorphose, moderate, modify, modulate, mutate, naturalize, recondition, redo, reduce, reform, regenerate, remake, remodel, renovate, reorganize, replace, resolve, restyle, revolutionize, shape, shift, substitute, tamper with, temper, transfigure, transform, translate, transmute, transpose, turn, vacillate, vary, veer, warp; SEE CONCEPTS *228,232,701*

change [*v2*] *substitute, replace*
alternate, barter, convert, displace, exchange, interchange, invert, remove, reverse, shift, supplant, swap, switch around, trade, transmit, transpose; SEE CONCEPT *128*

changeable [*adj*] *erratic*
agitated, capricious, changeful, commutative, convertible, fickle, fitful, flighty, fluctuating, fluid, impulsive, inconstant, indecisive, irregular, irresolute, irresponsible, kaleidoscopic, mercurial, mobile, movable, mutable, permutable, protean, restless, reversible, revocable, shifting, skittish, spasmodic, transformable, transitional, uncertain, unpredictable, unreliable, unsettled, unstable, unsteady, vacillating, vagrant, variable, variant, varying, versatile, volatile, wavering, whimsical; SEE CONCEPT *534*

channel [*n1*] *pathway, usually containing water*
approach, aqueduct, arroyo, artery, avenue, canal, canyon, carrier, chamber, chase, conduit, course, dig, ditch, duct, fluting, furrow, gouge, groove, gully, gutter, main, means, medium, pass, passage, pipe, raceway, route, runway, sewer, slit, sound, strait, tideway, trough, tube, tunnel, vein, watercourse, way; SEE CONCEPTS *501,514*

channel [*n2*] *means*
agency, agent, approach, avenue, course, instrument, instrumentality, instrumentation, medium, ministry, organ, route, vehicle, way; SEE CONCEPTS *6,660,770*

channel [*v*] *direct, guide*
carry, conduct, convey, funnel, pipe, route, send, siphon, traject, transmit, transport; SEE CONCEPTS *187,217*

chant [*n*] *chorus of song*
carol, croon, hymn, incantation, intonation, lilt, melody, psalm, shout, singing, song, trill, tune, warble; SEE CONCEPTS *263,595*

chant [*v*] *sing simple song or song part*
cantillate, carol, chorus, croon, descant, doxologize, drone, intone, recite, shout, tune, vocalize, warble; SEE CONCEPTS *65,77*

chaos [*n*] *utter confusion*
anarchy, ataxia, bedlam, clutter, disarray, discord, disorder, disorganization, entropy, free-for-all*, holy mess*, lawlessness, misrule, mix-up, mobocracy, muddle, pandemonium, rat's nest*, snarl, topsy-turviness*, tumult, turmoil, unruliness; SEE CONCEPTS *230,674*

chaotic [*adj*] *utterly confused*
anarchic, deranged, disordered, disorganized, every which way*, harum-scarum*, helter-skelter*, lawless, purposeless, rampageous, riotous, topsy-turvy*, tumultuous, turbid, turbulent, uncontrolled; SEE CONCEPT *548*

chaperon [*n*] *person who accompanies for supervision*
alarm clock*, baby-sitter*, bird dog*, chaperone, companion, duenna, escort, governess; SEE CONCEPT *423*

chaperon [*v*] *accompany for supervision*
attend, carry, conduct, consort with, convoy, escort, guide, oversee, protect, safeguard, shepherd, supervise, watch over; SEE CONCEPTS *114,714*

chaplain [*n*] *minister in church*
clergyman/woman, cleric, Holy Joe*, pastor, preacher, preacher man/woman*, priest, rabbi, turnaround collar*; SEE CONCEPT *361*

chapter [*n*] *section of book or group of items*
affiliate, branch, clause, division, episode, member, offshoot, part, period, phase, stage, topic, unit, wing; SEE CONCEPTS *270,382,832*

char [*v*] *scorch, sear*
burn, carbonize, cauterize, singe; SEE CONCEPT *249*

character [*n1*] *individuality*
appearance, aspect, attribute, badge, bent, caliber, cast, complex, complexion, constitution, crasis, disposition, emotions, estimation, ethos, frame, frame of mind, genius, grain, habit, humor, kind, makeup, mettle, mood, morale, mystique, nature, personality,

quality, record, reputation, repute, sense, set, shape, singularity, sort, specialty, spirit, standing, streak, style, temper, temperament, tone, trait, turn, type, vein; SEE CONCEPT *411*

character [*n2*] *integrity*
courage, fame, honor, intelligence, mind, name, place, position, rank, rectitude, rep, report, reputation, repute, standing, station, status, uprightness; SEE CONCEPT *668*

character [*n3*] *odd person*
card*, case*, clown, crank*, customer*, duck*, eccentric, figure, freak, nut, oddball, oddity, original*, personage, personality, psycho*, queer, spook*, wack*, weirdo, zombie*; SEE CONCEPTS *412,423*

character [*n4*] *written symbol*
cipher, device, emblem, figure, hieroglyph, letter, logo, mark, monogram, number, numeral, rune, sign, type; SEE CONCEPT *284*

character [*n5*] *portrayal of another*
impersonation, part, personification, role; SEE CONCEPTS *263,352*

characteristic [*n*] *typical feature, trait*
affection, aspect, attribute, badge, bag, bearing, bent, caliber, cast, complexion, component, differentia, disposition, distinction, earmark, endowment, essence, essential, faculty, flavor, frame, idiosyncrasy, inclination, individuality, lineament, mannerism, mark, mood, nature, originality, particularity, peculiarity, personality, point, property, quality, singularity, specialty, streak, stripe, style, symptom, temperament, tendency, thing, thumbprint, tinge, tone, trademark, turn, virtue; SEE CONCEPT *411*

characteristic [*adj*] *typical; distinguishing*
appropriate, diagnostic, differentiating, discriminating, discriminative, distinctive, distinguishing, emblematic, especial, essential, exclusive, fixed, idiosyncratic, inborn, inbred, indicative, individual, individualistic, individualizing, ingrained, inherent, innate, local, marked, native, normal, original, particular, peculiar, personal, private, proper, regular, representative, singular, special, specific, symbolic, symptomatic, unique; SEE CONCEPTS *542,547,550*

characterize [*v*] *typify, distinguish*
belong to, brand, button down*, constitute, define, delineate, describe, designate, differentiate, discriminate, feature, identify, indicate, individualize, individuate, inform, make up, mark, outline, peculiarize, peg, personalize, pigeonhole*, portray, represent, signalize, singularize, stamp, style, symbolize, tab, typecast; SEE CONCEPT *644*

charade [*n*] *pretense*
deception, disguise, fake, farce, make-believe, mimicry, pageant, pantomime, parody, pretension, pretentiousness, put-on, travesty, trick; SEE CONCEPT *59*

charge [*n1*] *accusation*
allegation, beef, complaint, gripe, imputation, indictment, plaint, stink; SEE CONCEPTS *44,317*

charge [*n2*] *attack*
assault, blitz, blitzkrieg, dirty deed*, invasion, mugging, onset, onslaught, outbreak, push, rush, sortie; SEE CONCEPT *86*

charge [*n3*] *burden*
care, commitment, committal, concern, custody, deadweight, duty, millstone, must, need, obligation, office, onus, ought, responsibility, right, safekeeping, task, tax, trust, ward, weight; SEE CONCEPTS *532,709*

charge [*n4*] *price asked for something*
amount, bad news*, bite, cost, damage, expenditure, expense, nick, outlay, payment, price, price tag, rate, squeeze, tab, tariff, tick; SEE CONCEPT *329*

charge [*n5*] *command*
behest, bidding, dictate, direction, exhortation, injunction, instruction, mandate, order, precept, word; SEE CONCEPTS *53,274*

charge [*n6*] *supervisory responsibility*
care, conduct, custody, handling, intendance, management, oversight, running, superintendence, superintendency, supervision, ward; SEE CONCEPT *117*

charge [*v1*] *accuse*
arraign, blame, blow the whistle on*, censure, criminate, drag into court*, finger, hang something on*, impeach, impugn, impute, incriminate, inculpate, indict, involve, peg, point the finger at*, reprehend, reproach, tax, turn on, whistle-blow*; SEE CONCEPTS *44,317*

charge [*v2*] *attack*
assail, assault, blindside, bolt, buck, bushwhack*, chase, dash, invade, jump on, lunge, mug, rush, smash, stampede, storm, tear; SEE CONCEPT *86*

charge [*v3*] *load, tax*
afflict, burden, choke, clog, commit, cram, crowd, cumber, encumber, entrust, fill, heap, impregnate, instill, lade, pack, penetrate, permeate, pervade, pile, ram, saddle, saturate, suffuse, transfuse, weigh; SEE CONCEPTS *107,156,740*

charge [*v4*] *order something done*
adjure, ask, bid, command, direct, enjoin, entrust, exhort, instruct, request, require, solicit, tell, warn; SEE CONCEPTS *53,78*

charge [*v5*] *ask a price*
demand, fix price at, impose, levy, price, require, sell for; SEE CONCEPTS *330,345*

charge [*v6*] *pay with credit card*
book, buy on credit, chalk up, cuff, debit, encumber, go into hock*, incur debt, nick, paste, put on account, put on one's card, put on the cuff, put on the tab, receive credit, run up; SEE CONCEPTS *327,330*

charisma [*n*] *great personal charm*
allure, animal magnetism*, appeal, dazzle, drawing power, fascination, flash, glamour, it*, magnetism, pizzazz*, something*, star quality, witchcraft, witchery; SEE CONCEPT *411*

charitable [*adj1*] *giving, generous*
accommodating, all heart, altruistic, beneficent, benevolent, benign, big*, bighearted*, bountiful, elee-

mosynary, good, helpful, humane, humanitarian, kind, kindly, lavish, liberal, obliging, philanthropic, sympathetic; SEE CONCEPTS *334,542*

charitable [*adj2*] *kind, lenient*
all heart*, benevolent, big*, bighearted*, broad-minded, clement, considerate, easy, favorable, forbearing, forgiving, gracious, humane, indulgent, kindly, lenient, magnanimous, merciful, sympathetic, thoughtful, tolerant, understanding; SEE CONCEPT *404*

charity [*n1*] *generosity, gift*
a hand*, alms, alms-giving, assistance, benefaction, beneficence, contribution, dole, donation, endowment, fund, gifting, hand-out, helping hand*, largesse, oblation, offering, philanthropy, relief, write-off; SEE CONCEPTS *337,657*

charity [*n2*] *kindness, compassion*
affection, agape, altruism, amity, attachment, benevolence, benignity, bountifulness, bounty, caritas, clemency, fellow feeling, generosity, goodness, goodwill, grace, humaneness, humanity, indulgence, kindliness, lenity, love, magnanimity, mercy, tenderheartedness; SEE CONCEPTS *32,411*

charm [*n1*] *enchantment, allure*
agreeableness, allurement, appeal, attraction, attractiveness, beauty, bewitchery, charisma, chemistry, conjuration, delightfulness, desirability, fascination, glamour, grace, it*, lure, magic, magnetism, pizzazz*, something*, sorcery, spell, star quality, witchery; SEE CONCEPTS *411,673*

charm [*n2*] *talisman*
amulet, fetish, good-luck piece, juju, lucky piece, madstone, mascot, phylactery, rabbit's foot, trinket, zemi; SEE CONCEPTS *284,446*

charm [*v*] *enchant*
allure, attract, beguile, bewitch, cajole, captivate, delight, draw, enamor, enrapture, ensorcell, enthrall, entrance, fascinate, grab, hex, hypnotize, inveigle, kill*, knock dead*, knock out*, magnetize, mesmerize, please, possess, put under a spell*, send*, slay*, spell*, sweep off feet*, take*, tickle, tickle pink*, transport, turn on*, vamp, voodoo, wile, win, win over, wow*; SEE CONCEPTS *7,22*

charming [*adj*] *captivating*
absorbing, alluring, amiable, appealing, attractive, bewitching, charismatic, choice, cute, dainty, delectable, delicate, delightful, desirable, electrifying, elegant, enamoring, engaging, engrossing, enthralling, entrancing, eye-catching, fascinating, fetching, glamorous, graceful, infatuating, inviting, irresistible, likable, lovable, lovely, magnetizing, nice, pleasant, pleasing, provocative, rapturous, ravishing, seducing, seductive, sweet, tantalizing, tempting, titillating, winning, winsome; SEE CONCEPT *404*

chart [*n*] *map, plan*
blueprint, diagram, graph, outline, plat, plot, rough draft, scheme, sketch, table, tabulation; SEE CONCEPTS *625,660*

chart [*v*] *plan, map out*
arrange, block out, blueprint, cast, delineate, design, devise, draft, graph, lay out, outline, plot, project, shape, sketch; SEE CONCEPTS *36,174*

charter [*n*] *treaty, agreement*
allotment, bond, code, concession, constitution, contract, conveyance, deed, document, endowment, franchise, grant, indenture, license, pact, patent, permit, prerogative, privilege, right, settlement; SEE CONCEPTS *684,685*

charter [*v*] *reserve, commission*
allow, authorize, borrow, contract, employ, engage, hire, lease, let, license, permit, rent, sanction; SEE CONCEPTS *48,50,88,89*

chary [*adj*] *careful, cautious*
cagey, calculating, canny, circumspect, considerate, constrained, discreet, economical, fastidious, frugal, gingerly, guarded, heedful, hesitant, inhibited, leery, loath, miserly, particular, prudent, reluctant, restrained, safe, scrupulous, sparing, stingy, suspicious, thrifty, uneasy, wary, watchful; SEE CONCEPTS *401,587*

chase [*n*] *pursuit*
hunt, hunting, quest, race, venery; SEE CONCEPT *207*

chase [*v*] *run after, pursue*
bird-dog*, charge, chivy, course, drive, drive away, expel, follow, go after, hound, hunt, run down, rush, seek, shag, speed, take off after*, tear, track, track down, trail; SEE CONCEPT *207*

chasm [*n*] *gap, abyss*
abysm, alienation, arroyo, blank, breach, cavity, cleavage, cleft, clough, clove, crater, crevasse, fissure, flume, gorge, gulch, gulf, hiatus, hole, hollow, omission, opening, oversight, preterition, ravine, rent, rift, schism, skip, split, void, yawn; SEE CONCEPT *513*

chaste [*adj*] *pure, incorrupt*
austere, celibate, clean, continent, controlled, decent, decorous, elegant, frigid, immaculate, impotent, inexperienced, innocent, intemerate, maidenly, modest, monogamous, moral, neat, platonic, proper, prudish, quiet, refined, restrained, simple, spotless, stainless, subdued, unaffected, unblemished, uncontaminated, undefiled, unstained, unsullied, unwed, vestal, virginal, virtuous, wholesome; SEE CONCEPTS *372,404*

chasten [*v*] *correct, humiliate*
abase, admonish, afflict, berate, call down, castigate, chastise, chide, cow, curb, discipline, exprobate, fulminate against, have on the carpet*, humble, objurgate, penalize, punish, rake over the coals*, rebuke, reprehend, repress, reprimand, reproach, reprove, restrain, scold, scourge, soften, subdue, take to task, tame, tongue-lash*, try, upbraid; SEE CONCEPTS *52,122*

chastise [*v*] *scold, discipline*
baste, beat, berate, castigate, censure, chasten, chew out*, climb all over*, correct, ferule*, flog*, lash*,

lay into*, lean on*, pummel, punish, ream, scourge, skelp, slap down*, spank, thrash, upbraid, whip; SEE CONCEPTS *52,122*

chastity [*n*] *celibacy, purity*
abstemiousness, abstinence, chasteness, cleanness, continence, decency, demureness, devotion, honor, immaculacy, innocence, integrity, modesty, monogamy, morality, naïveté, restraint, singleness, sinlessness, spotlessness, temperance, uprightness, virginity, virtue; SEE CONCEPT *633*

chat [*n*] *talk, often short*
babble, bull session, chatter, conversation, converse, gab*, gas*, gossip, heart-to-heart, hot air*, jabber*, palaver, prattle*, rap*, rap session*, tête-à-tête, visit, yak*; SEE CONCEPT *278*

chat [*v*] *talk, gossip*
babble, blab*, burble, cackle, chatter, chew the fat*, chew the rag*, converse, gab*, go on*, jaw, prate, prattle*, run on*, shoot the breeze*, yap*; SEE CONCEPT *266*

chatter [*n*] *constant or rapid talk*
babble, blather, chat, chitchat, gas*, gossip, jabber*, palaver, prattle*, twaddle, yakking*; SEE CONCEPTS *266,278*

chatter [*v*] *speak fast and non-stop*
babble, blab*, blather, cackle, chat, chitchat, clack, gab*, gabble, gas*, gibber, go on and on, gossip, jabber*, jaw, natter, palaver, prate, prattle*, tattle, twaddle, twiddle, yak*; SEE CONCEPT *266*

chatty [*adj*] *talkative*
colloquial, communicative, conversational, familiar, friendly, gabby, garrulous, gossipy, informal, intimate, loose-lipped, loquacious, multieloquent, spontaneous, talky; SEE CONCEPT *267*

chauvinism [*n*] *devotion to a belief or nation*
bellicism, fanatical patriotism, fanaticism, jingoism, nationalism; SEE CONCEPT *689*

cheap [*adj1*] *inexpensive*
at a bargain, bargain, bargain-basement*, bargain-counter, bought for a song*, budget, buy, cheapo*, competitive, cost next to nothing*, cut-price, cut-rate, depreciated, dime a dozen*, easy on the pocketbook*, economical, half-priced, irregular, low-cost, lowered, low-priced, low tariff, marked down, moderate, nominal, on sale, popularly priced, real buy*, reasonable, reduced, sale, slashed, standard, steal, uncostly, undear, utility, worth the money*; SEE CONCEPT *334*

cheap [*adj2*] *inferior, low in quality*
bad, base, bogus, catchpenny, cheesy, common, commonplace, crap, crappy*, cruddy, dud, flashy, garbage, garish, glitzy, junky*, lousy, mangy, mean, mediocre, meretricious, no bargain*, no good, ordinary, paltry, poor, ratty, raunchy, rinky-dink*, rotten, rubbishy, scroungy, second-rate, shoddy, sleazy, small-time*, tatty, tawdry, terrible, trashy, trumpery, two-bit, valueless, white elephant*, worthless; SEE CONCEPT *589*

cheap [*adj3*] *low, vulgar*
abject, base, beggarly, contemptible, despicable, dirty, dishonest, mean, pitiable, scurvy, shabby, sordid, sorry, tawdry, vile; SEE CONCEPT *542*

cheap [*adj4*] *concerned with saving money*
mean, mingy, miserly, penny-pinching*, stingy, thrifty, tight*, tight-wad*; SEE CONCEPT *332*

cheapen [*v*] *diminish worth*
abase, beat down, belittle, corrupt, damage, debase, decline, decry, degrade, demean, denigrate, depreciate, derogate, devalue, discredit, disparage, downgrade, drop, fall, lose value, lower, mar, mark down, minimize, reduce, render worthless, ruin, spoil, undervalue, write off; SEE CONCEPT *240*

cheat [*n1*] *person who fools others*
bluff, charlatan, chiseler, confidence man, con man, conniver, cozener, crook, deceiver, decoy, defrauder, dodger, double-crosser*, double-dealer*, enticer, fake, hypocrite, impostor, inveigler, jockey, knave, masquerader, pretender, quack, rascal, rogue, scammer*, shark, sharper, shyster, swindler, trickster; SEE CONCEPT *412*

cheat [*n2*] *trick*
artifice, baloney, bamboozlement*, bill of goods*, bunco, chicanery, con, con game, cover up, cozening, deceit, deception, dirty pool*, dirty trick*, dodge, double-dealing*, fake, fast one, fast shuffle*, fix, flimflam, frame, fraud, gyp*, hanky-panky*, hoax, hoaxing, humbug, hustle, imposture, jazz, jive, plant, put-on, racket, rip-off, run around, sell, shady deal, sham, shell game, snow job*, spoof, sting, stunt, swindle, trickery, whitewash, wrong; SEE CONCEPT *59*

cheat [*v1*] *defraud, fool*
bamboozle*, beat, beguile, bilk, bleed, bunco, burn, caboodle, chisel, con, cozen, crib, cross, deceive, defraud, delude, diddle*, do*, do a number on*, double-cross, double-deal, dupe, fast talk, finagle, fleece, flimflam, fudge*, give bum steer*, gouge, gyp*, hoodwink, hose, jerk around, milk, mislead, pull one's leg*, ream*, rip off*, rook*, rope in*, sandbag, scam, screw, shaft, short, shuck, skin, snow, stiff, sucker, swindle, take, take for a ride*, take in, take out, trick, trim, two-time, victimize; SEE CONCEPTS *59,139,192*

cheat [*v2*] *frustrate, thwart*
baffle, check, defeat, deprive, foil, prevent; SEE CONCEPT *121*

check [*n1*] *inspection, examination*
analysis, audit, checkup, control, inquiry, investigation, poll, rein, research, review, scrutiny, test; SEE CONCEPT *103*

check [*n2*] *restraint, hindrance*
blow, constraint, control, curb, damper, disappointment, frustration, grunt, harness, holdup, impediment, inhibition, limitation, obstruction, rebuff, rejection, restrainer, reversal, reverse, setback, stoppage, trouble; SEE CONCEPTS *121,130,230*

check [n3] *symbol for ticking off*
cross, dot, line, mark, score, sign, stroke, tick, X*;
SEE CONCEPT *284*

check [n4] *pattern of squares*
checkerboard, patchwork, plaid, quilt, tartan; SEE
CONCEPT *436*

check [v1] *inspect, examine*
analyze, ascertain, audit, balance account, candle,
case, compare, confirm, correct, count, enquire
about, eyeball*, find out, frisk, go through, investigate, keep account, look at, look over, look see,
make sure, monitor, note, overlook, probe, prove,
quiz, review, scout out, scrutinize, study, take stock,
tell, test, try, verify; SEE CONCEPTS *24,103*

check [v2] *hinder, restrain*
arrest, baffle, bar, bit, bottleneck*, bridle, checkmate, choke, circumvent, constrain, control, counteract, curb, cut short, delay, discourage, foil,
frustrate, halt, harness, hold, hold back, hold down,
hold in, impede, inhibit, interrupt, keep back, limit,
moderate, neutralize, nip in the bud*, obstruct, obviate, pause, play for time, preclude, prevent, rebuff,
reduce, rein in, repress, repulse, retard, slacken pace,
slow down, snub, squelch, stay, stop, suppress,
tame, terminate, thwart, withhold; SEE CONCEPTS
121,130

checkered [adj] *patterned*
checky, diversified, motley, mutable, patchwork,
plaid, quilted, spotted, variegated; SEE CONCEPT *486*

cheek [n1] *side of human face*
chop*, choppers*, gill, jowl; SEE CONCEPT *418*

cheek [n2] *audacity, boldness*
brashness, brass*, brazenness, chutzpah*, confidence, disrespect, effrontery, gall, impertinence, impudence, insolence, lip*, nerve*, presumption,
rudeness, sauce*, temerity; SEE CONCEPT *633*

cheep [v] *vocalize as a bird*
chip, chipper, chirp, chirrup, peek, tweedle, tweet,
twitter; SEE CONCEPT *64*

cheer [n1] *happiness*
animation, buoyancy, cheerfulness, cheeriness, comfort, delight, encouragement, exuberance, gaiety, geniality, gladness, glee, good cheer, hilarity,
hopefulness, jauntiness, jocundity, joy, joyousness,
lightheartedness, liveliness, merriment, merrymaking, mirth, optimism, solace; SEE CONCEPT *410*

cheer [n2] *applause, supportive yell*
acclamation, approbation, approval, cry, encouragement, hurrah, hurray, huzzah, ovation, plaudits,
roar, shout; SEE CONCEPTS *69,77*

cheer [v1] *make someone feel happier*
animate, brace up, brighten, buck up*, buoy, comfort, console, elate, elevate, embolden, encourage,
enliven, exhilarate, give a lift*, gladden, hearten,
help, incite, inspirit, let the sun shine in*, perk up,
pick up, put on cloud nine*, put on top of the world*,
snap out of it*, solace, steel, strengthen, uplift, upraise, warm; SEE CONCEPTS *7,22*

cheer [v2] *encourage in activity*
acclaim, applaud, clap, hail, hurrah, plug*, rise to,
root, salute, sound off for, support, yell; SEE CON-
CEPT *69*

cheerful [adj] *happy*
airy, animated, blithe, bouncy, bright, bucked, buoyant, cheery, chipper, chirpy, contented, effervescent,
enlivening, enthusiastic, full of pep, gay, glad, gladsome, good-humored, good-natured, hearty, high,
hilarious, hopeful, in good spirits, in high spirits,
jaunty, jocund, jolly, joyful, lighthearted, lively,
merry, optimistic, peppy, perky, pleasant, roseate,
rosy, sanguine, snappy, sparkling, sprightly, sunny,
sunny side up*, up, upbeat, vivacious, winsome,
zappy, zingy, zippy; SEE CONCEPTS *403,404*

cheering [adj] *encouraging*
auspicious, bright, comforting, heartening, hopeful,
promising, propitious; SEE CONCEPT *529*

cheerless [adj] *depressing, unhappy*
austere, black, bleak, blue, comfortless, dark, dejected, dejecting, depressed, desolate, despondent,
disconsolate, dismal, dispiriting, dolorous, drab,
draggy, drearisome, dreary, dull, forlorn, funereal,
gloomy, grim, in the dumps*, jarring, joyless, melancholy, miserable, mopey, mournful, oppressive,
sad, somber, sorrowful, sullen, tenebrific, uncomfortable, wintry, woebegone, woeful; SEE CONCEPT *403*

chemical [adj] *concerned with atom and molecule
change*
actinic, alchemical, enzymatic, synthesized, synthetic, synthetical; SEE CONCEPT *536*

cherish [v] *care about deeply*
admire, adore, appreciate, apprise, care for, clasp,
cleave to, cling to, coddle, comfort, cosset, cultivate, defend, dote on, embrace, encourage, enshrine,
entertain, fancy, fondle, foster, guard, harbor, hold
dear, hold in high esteem, honor, hug, idolize, like,
love, nourish, nurse, nurture, pet, preserve, prize,
revere, reverence, safeguard, shelter, shield, support,
sustain, treasure, value, venerate, worship; SEE CON-
CEPT *32*

cherry [adj] *bright red color*
blooming, blushing, bright red, cerise, claret, crimson, dark red, erubescent, Harvard crimson, incarnadine, reddish, rosy, rubescent, rubicund, ruddy;
SEE CONCEPT *618*

chest [n1] *box for storage*
bin, bureau, cabinet, carton, case, casket, chiffonier,
coffer, commode, crate, exchequer, pyxis, receptacle, reliquary, strongbox, treasury, trunk; SEE CON-
CEPT *494*

chest [n2] *upper front of body*
bosom, breast, bust, heart, mammary glands, peri-
toneum, pulmonary cavity, rib cage, ribs, thorax,
upper trunk; SEE CONCEPT *392*

chew [v1] *grind with teeth*
bite, champ, chaw, chomp, crunch, dispatch, feast
upon, gnaw, gulp, gum, manducate, masticate,

munch, nibble, rend, ruminate, scrunch; SEE CON-CEPTS *169,185*

chew [*v2*] *think about deeply*
consider, deliberate, meditate, mull, mull over, muse on, ponder, reflect upon, ruminate, weigh; SEE CON-CEPT *24*

chew out [*v*] *scold*
bawl out, carpet*, criticize, dress down, jaw, revile, tell off, tongue-lash*, vituperate, wig, yell at; SEE CONCEPT *52*

chic [*adj*] *fashionable*
chichi, clean, current, dap, dapper, dashing, elegant, exclusive, faddish, last word*, latest thing*, mod*, modern, modish, natty, sharp, smart, stylish, swank, trendy, voguish, with-it*; SEE CONCEPT *589*

chicanery [*n*] *deception, trickery*
artifice, cheating, chicane, deviousness, dishonesty, dodge, double-crossing, double-dealing*, duplicity, feint, fourberie, fraud, furtiveness, gambit, hanky-panky, intrigue, machination, maneuver, plot, ploy, ruse, sharp practice, skullduggery, sophistry, strata-gem, subterfuge, surreptitiousness, underhanded-ness, wiles; SEE CONCEPTS *59,660*

chicken [*n1*] *person afraid to try something*
coward, craven, dastard, funk, poltroon, quitter, rec-reant, scaredy cat*, yellow belly*; SEE CONCEPT *423*

chicken [*n2*] *farm fowl*
banty, barnyard fowl, biddy, capon, chick, cock, cock-a-doodle-do*, cockalorum, cockerel, gump*, heeler, hen, poultry, pullet, rooster; SEE CONCEPTS *394,395*

chide [*v*] *criticize, lecture*
admonish, berate, blame, call down*, call on the carpet*, castigate, censure, check, condemn, expro-bate, find fault, flay, give a hard time*, lesson, mon-ish, rate, rebuke, reprehend, reprimand, reproach, reprove, scold, slap on the wrist*, speak to, take down*, take down a peg*, talk to, tell off, tick off*, upbraid; SEE CONCEPT *52*

chief [*n*] *person in charge*
big cheese*, big gun*, big wheel*, bigwig*, boss, captain, chieftain, commander, dictator, director, duke, foreman, general, governor, head, head hon-cho*, head man/woman*, honcho*, key player*, king, leader, lord, manager, master, monarch, over-lord, overseer, president, prince/princess, principal, proprietor, queen, ringleader, ruler, sovereign, su-perintendent, supervisor, suzerain, top brass*, top cat*; SEE CONCEPTS *347,376*

chief [*adj*] *most important, essential*
arch, capital, cardinal, central, champion, conse-quential, controlling, crucial, effective, especial, first, foremost, grand, head, highest, key, leading, main, major, master, momentous, number one*, out-standing, paramount, potent, predominant, preemi-nent, premier, primal, primary, prime, principal, ruling, significant, star, stellar, superior, supreme,

telling, uppermost, vital, weighty; SEE CONCEPTS *568,574,829*

chiefly [*adv*] *most importantly*
above all, especially, essentially, in general, in the first place, in the main, largely, mainly, mostly, on the whole, overall, predominantly, primarily, princi-pally, usually; SEE CONCEPTS *567,772*

child [*n*] *very young person*
adolescent, anklebiter*, babe, baby, bairn, bambino, brat, cherub, chick, cub, descendant, dickens*, imp, infant, innocent, issue, juvenile, kid, kiddie*, lamb*, little angel*, little darling*, little doll*, little one, minor, mite, moppet, neonate, nestling, newborn, nipper, nursling, offspring, preteen, progeny, pubes-cent, shaver, small fry*, sprout, squirt, stripling, suckling, tadpole, teen, teenager, teenybopper, tod-dler, tot, tyke, urchin*, whippersnapper*, young one, youngster, youth; SEE CONCEPTS *414,424*

childbirth [*n*] *giving birth*
accouchement, bearing children, blessed event*, childbed, confinement, delivering, delivery, labor, lying-in, nativity, parturience, parturition, procre-ation, producing, propagation, reproduction, travail, visit from the stork*; SEE CONCEPTS *302,373*

childhood [*n*] *period of being young*
adolescence, babyhood, boyhood, cradle, girlhood, immaturity, infancy, juniority, juvenility, minority, nonage, nursery, puberty, pupilage, schooldays*, teens, tender age, youth; SEE CONCEPT *816*

childish [*adj*] *immature, silly*
baby, babyish, boyish, childlike, foolish, frivolous, girlish, green, imbecile, infantile, infantine, juvenile, kid stuff*, naive, pedomorphic, petty, prekindergar-ten, primitive, puerile, simple, slow, soft, stupid, trifling, unsophisticated, weak, young, youthful; SEE CONCEPTS *401,402*

childlike [*adj*] *innocent, naive*
artless, childish, credulous, guileless, immature, in-genuous, natural, simple, spontaneous, trustful, trusting, unaffected, unfeigned; SEE CONCEPT *404*

chill [*n*] *cold conditions*
bite, coldness, coolness, crispness, frigidity, gelid-ity, iciness, nip, rawness, rigor, sharpness; SEE CON-CEPT *524*

chill [*adj1*] *cold, raw*
arctic, biting, bleak, brisk, chilly, cool, freezing, frigid, frosty, gelid, glacial, icy, nippy, sharp, win-try; SEE CONCEPT *605*

chill [*adj2*] *unfriendly, aloof*
cool, depressing, discouraging, dismal, dispiriting, distant, emotionless, formal, frigid, glacial, hateful, hostile, icy, indifferent, reserved, solitary, standoff-ish, stony, uncompanionable, unemotional, unge-nial, unhappy, unresponsive, unwelcoming, wintry, withdrawn; SEE CONCEPTS *401,404*

chill [*v1*] *make cold*
air-condition, congeal, cool, freeze, frost, ice, refrig-erate; SEE CONCEPTS *255,521*

chill [v2] *discourage*
cloud, dampen, dash, deject, demoralize, depress, dishearten, dismay, disparage, dispirit; SEE CONCEPTS *7,19*

chilly [adj1] *cold*
arctic, biting, blowy, breezy, brisk, cool, crisp, drafty, freezing, fresh, frosty, glacial, hawkish, icebox, icy, nippy, penetrating, sharp, snappy, two-dog night*, wintry; SEE CONCEPT *605*

chilly [adj2] *unfriendly, aloof*
cold, frigid, hostile, unfriendly, unresponsive, unsympathetic, unwelcoming; SEE CONCEPT *404*

chime [v] *ring, peal*
bell, bong, boom, clang, dong, jingle, knell, sound, strike, tinkle, tintinnabulate, toll; SEE CONCEPT *65*

chimera [n] *dream, fantasy*
bogy, bubble, delusion, fabrication, fancy, figment, fool's paradise*, hallucination, ignis fatuus, illusion, monster, monstrosity, pipe dream*, rainbow*, snare, specter; SEE CONCEPT *529*

chimney [n] *smokestack for building*
chase, chimney pot, chimney stack, fireplace, flue, funnel, furnace, hearth, pipe, smokeshaft, stack, vent, ventilator; SEE CONCEPT *440*

chin [n] *area under mouth*
button, jaw, jawbone, mandible, mentum, point; SEE CONCEPT *399*

china [n] *dishes, often valuable*
ceramics, crockery, porcelain, pottery, service, stoneware, tableware, ware; SEE CONCEPT *493*

chip [n] *shard, flaw*
dent, flake, fragment, gobbet, nick, notch, paring, part, scrap, scratch, shaving, slice, sliver, wafer, wedge; SEE CONCEPTS *580,831*

chip [v] *knock a piece out of*
break, chisel, chop, clip, crack, crack off, crumble, cut away, cut off, damage, flake, fragment, gash, hack, hackle, hew, incise, nick, notch, shape, shear, slash, slice, sliver, snick, snip, splinter, split, whack, whittle; SEE CONCEPTS *137,189,246,250*

chip in [v] *contribute*
ante up*, break in*, chime in*, come through*, conate, go Dutch*, interpose, interrupt, pay, pitch in, subscribe; SEE CONCEPT *110*

chipper [adj] *happy*
alert, animate, animated, bright, brisk, gay, in good spirits, keen, lively, spirited, sprightly, vivacious; SEE CONCEPT *403*

chips [n] *substitute for money; money*
coin, currency, markers, play money, scratch; SEE CONCEPT *340*

chirp [v] *peep, cheep*
call, chip, chipper, chirrup, lilt, pipe, purl, quaver, roll, sing, sound, trill, tweedle, tweet, twitter, warble; SEE CONCEPT *64*

chisel [n] *shaping tool*
adze, blade, edge, gouge, knife; SEE CONCEPTS *495,499*

chisel [v] *cut, wear away*
carve, hew, incise, roughcast, rough-hew, sculpt, sculpture, shape; SEE CONCEPTS *137,176,184*

chivalrous [adj] *valiant*
benevolent, big, bold, brave, considerate, courageous, courteous, courtly, gallant, gentlemanly, great-hearted, heroic, high-minded, honorable, intrepid, knightly, lofty, magnanimous, noble-minded, polite, quixotic, spirited, sublime, true, valorous; SEE CONCEPT *401*

chivalry [n] *valor, gallantry*
courage, courtesy, courtliness, fairness, gentlemanliness, knight-errantry, knighthood, politeness, valiance; SEE CONCEPT *633*

choice [n] *power to select; selection*
alternative, appraisal, choosing, cull, cup of tea*, decision, determination, discretion, discrimination, distinction, druthers, election, evaluation, extract, favorite, finding, free will, judgment, opportunity, option, pick, preference, rating, say, substitute, variety, verdict, volition, vote, weakness; SEE CONCEPTS *41,376*

choice [adj] *best, superior*
10*, 24-karat*, A-1*, elect, elite, excellent, exceptional, exclusive, exquisite, fine, hand-picked, nice, popular, precious, preferential, preferred, prime, prize, rare, select, solid gold*, special, top-drawer*, uncommon, unusual, valuable, winner; SEE CONCEPT *574*

choke [v] *smother, block*
asphyxiate, bar, check, clog, close, congest, constrict, dam, die, drown, fill, gag, garrote, gasp, gibbet, kill, noose, obstruct, occlude, overpower, retard, squeeze, stifle, stop, stopper, strangle, strangulate, stuff, stunt, suffocate, suppress, throttle, wring; SEE CONCEPTS *121,219*

choose [v] *pick, select*
accept, adopt, appoint, call for, cast, commit oneself, co-opt, crave, cull, decide on, designate, desire, determine, discriminate between, draw lots, elect, embrace, espouse, excerpt, extract, fancy, favor, feel disposed to, finger, fix on, glean, judge, love, make choice, make decision, make up one's mind, name, opt for, predestine, prefer, see fit, separate, set aside, settle upon, sift out, single out, slot, sort, tab, tag, take, take up, tap, want, weigh, will, winnow, wish, wish for; SEE CONCEPT *41*

choosy [adj] *fussy, discriminating*
dainty, eclectic, exacting, fastidious, finical, finicky, nice, overparticular, particular, persnickety*, picky*, prissy, select, selective; SEE CONCEPT *404*

chop [v] *cut up with tool*
axe, cleave, clip, cube, dice, divide, fell, fragment, hack, hackle, hash, hew, lop, mangle, mince, sever, shear, slash, truncate, whack; SEE CONCEPT *176*

choppy [adj] *wavy*
inclement, ripply, rough, uneven, violent, wild; SEE CONCEPT *488*

chore [n] *task*
assignment, burden, devoir, duty, effort, errand, grind, housework, job, KP*, routine, scutwork, stint, trial, tribulation, workout; SEE CONCEPT *362*

chortle [v] *laugh gleefully*
cackle, chuckle, crow, giggle, guffaw, hee-haw*, snicker, sniggle, snort, teehee*, titter; SEE CONCEPT *77*

chorus [n1] *group of singers*
carolers, choir, chorale, choristers, ensemble, glee club, singing group, vocalists, voices; SEE CONCEPT *294*

chorus [n2] *refrain*
bob, burden, chorale, main section, melody, motif, music, recurrent verse, response, ritornelle, song, strain, theme, tune, undersong; SEE CONCEPT *264*

chorus [n3] *agreement*
accord, concert, concord, consonance, harmony, tune, unison; SEE CONCEPTS *673,684*

chosen [adj] *preferred*
called, conscript, elect, exclusive, got the nod*, named, pegged, pick, picked, popular, preferential, select, selected, tabbed; SEE CONCEPTS *546,567,574*

christen [v] *named in religious rite*
asperse, baptize, bless, call, dedicate, denominate, designate, dub, entitle, godfather/mother, immerse, sprinkle, style, term, title; SEE CONCEPTS *62,367*

chronic [adj] *incessant, never-ending*
abiding, ceaseless, confirmed, constant, continual, continuing, continuous, deep-rooted, deep-seated, enduring, ever-present, fixed, habitual, inborn, inbred, incurable, ineradicable, ingrained, intermittent, inveterate, lasting, lifelong, lingering, long-lived, long-standing, obstinate, perennial, persistent, persisting, prolonged, protracted, recurrent, recurring, rooted, routine, settled, stubborn, sustained, tenacious, unabating, unmitigated, unyielding, usual; SEE CONCEPTS *534,551,798*

chronicle [n] *account, narrative*
annals, archives, diary, history, journal, narration, prehistory, recital, record, recountal, register, report, story, version; SEE CONCEPTS *271,282*

chronicle [v] *report, recount*
enter, narrate, record, register, relate, set down, tell; SEE CONCEPTS *60,79*

chronological [adj] *in consecutive time order*
archival, chronographic, chronologic, chronometric, chronometrical, chronoscopic, classified, dated, historical, horological, horometrical, in due course, in due time, in order, in sequence, junctural, ordered, progressive, sequent, sequential, tabulated, temporal; SEE CONCEPTS *548,585*

chubby [adj] *slightly fat*
ample, bearish, big, butterball*, buxom, chunky, fatty, flabby, fleshy, full-figured, hefty, husky, pleasingly plump*, plump, plumpish, podgy, portly, pudgy, roly-poly*, rotund, round, stout, tubby, zaftig*; SEE CONCEPTS *491,773*

chuck [v] *throw aside, throw away, throw out*
abandon, can, cast, desert, discard, ditch, eighty-six*, eject, fire, fling, flip, forsake, give the heave ho*, heave, hurl, jettison, junk, launch, pitch, quit, reject, relinquish, renounce, scrap, shed, shy, sling, slough, toss; SEE CONCEPTS *180,222*

chuckle [v] *giggle*
cackle, chortle, crow, exult, guffaw, hee-haw*, laugh, smile, snicker, snigger, sniggle, teehee*, titter; SEE CONCEPT *77*

chum [n] *friend*
associate, bro*, buddy, comate, companion, comrade, crony, mate, pal, playmate, sis*; SEE CONCEPT *423*

chummy [adj] *friendly*
affectionate, buddy-buddy*, close, confidential, constant, cozy, familiar, intimate, pally*, palsy-walsy*, thick*; SEE CONCEPTS *401,555*

chunk [n] *mass, slab of something*
block, clod, dollop, glob, gob, hunk, lump, nugget, part, piece, portion, wad; SEE CONCEPT *471*

chunky [adj] *fat, plump*
beefy*, chubby, dumpy, heavyset, husky, rotund, scrub, squat, stocky, stout, stubby, thick-bodied, thickset; SEE CONCEPTS *491,773*

church [n1] *religious institution, building*
abbey, basilica, bethel, cathedral, chancel, chantry, chapel, fold, house of God, house of prayer, house of worship, Lord's house, minster, mission, mosque, oratory, parish, sacellum, sanctuary, shrine, synagogue, tabernacle, temple; SEE CONCEPTS *368,449*

church [n2] *religious belief, group*
affiliation, body, chapter, communion, congregation, connection, creed, cult, denomination, doctrine, faction, faith, gathering, ism, order, persuasion, religion, schism, sect, society; SEE CONCEPTS *369,689*

churl [n] *rude and ill-bred, a boor; person overly concerned with saving money*
beast, chuff, clodhopper*, miser, mucker*, niggard*, oaf, peasant, provincial, rustic, tightwad*, yokel*; SEE CONCEPT *423*

churlish [adj] *crude, boorish*
base, blunt, brusque, cantankerous*, cloddish*, clodhopping*, crabbed, crude, crusty, curt, cussed*, discourteous, dour, grouchy, gruff, grumpy, harsh, ill-tempered, impolite, loutish, lowbred, mean, miserly, morose, oafish, ornery*, rude, rustic, snippy*, sullen, surly, touchy*, ugly, uncivil, uncivilized, uncultured, unmannerly, unneighborly, unpolished, unsociable, vulgar; SEE CONCEPT *404*

churn [v] *mix up, beat*
agitate, boil, bubble, convulse, ferment, foam, froth, jolt, moil, seethe, simmer, stir up, swirl, toss; SEE CONCEPTS *147,170*

chute [n] *ramp, slope*
channel, course, fall, gutter, incline, rapid, runway, slide, trough; SEE CONCEPTS *440,471*

cinder [n] *hot ash*
clinker, ember, hot coal, soot; SEE CONCEPT *260*

cinema [n] *movie industry; movie arena*
big screen*, bijou, cine, drive-in, film, flicks*, motion pictures, movie house, movie theater, moving pictures, nabes*, photoplay, pictures, picture show, playhouse, show, silver screen*; SEE CONCEPTS *293,349*

cipher [n] *zero; nothingness*
blank, diddly squat*, goose egg*, insignificancy, nada, naught, nil, nobody, nonentity, nothing, nought, nullity, squat, zilch, zip, zippo*, zot*; SEE CONCEPTS *668,786*

cipher [v] *figure out code*
break, calculate, clear up, compute, count, decipher, estimate, figure, reckon, resolve, solve, unravel; SEE CONCEPT *37*

circa [prep] *approximately*
about, around, close on, in the region of, near, nearby, nigh, roughly; SEE CONCEPT *820*

circle [n1] *orb, loop, round figure*
amphitheater, aureole, band, belt, bowl, bracelet, circlet, circuit, circumference, circus, cirque, coil, colure, compass, cordon, corona, crown, cycle, disc, disk, ecliptic, enclosure, equator, full turn, globe, halo, hoop, horizon, lap, meridian, orbit, parallel of latitude, perimeter, periphery, record, revolution, ring, ringlet, round, sphere, stadium, tire, turn, vortex, wheel, wreath, zodiac; SEE CONCEPT *436*

circle [n2] *group of close friends, associates*
assembly, bunch, cabal, camarilla, camp, clan, class, clique, club, companions, company, comrades, coterie, crew, cronies, crowd, crush, fellowship, fraternity, gang, in-group, insiders, intimates, lot, Mafia*, mob, outfit, party, posse, ring, school, set, society, sorority; SEE CONCEPTS *387,417*

circle [v] *go around, circumnavigate*
begird, belt, cincture, circuit, circulate, circumduct, circumscribe, coil, compass, curve, embrace, encircle, enclose, encompass, ensphere, envelop, gird, girdle, gyrate, gyre, hem in, loop, mill around, pivot, revolve, ring, roll, rotate, round, spiral, surround, tour, wheel, whirl, wind about; SEE CONCEPT *758*

circuit [n] *revolution, track, boundary*
ambit, area, bounds, circle, circling, circulation, circumference, circumnavigation, circumscription, circumvolution, compass, course, cycle, district, gyration, gyre, journey, lap, limit, line, orbit, perambulation, perimeter, periphery, range, region, round, route, tour, tract, turn, turning, twirl, way, wheel, whirl, wind, winding, zone; SEE CONCEPTS *484,501,770*

circuitous [adj] *going around, indirect*
back road*, by way of, circular, collateral, complicated, devious, labyrinthine, long way*, long way around*, meandering, oblique, rambling, roundabout, tortuous, winding around; SEE CONCEPTS *544,581*

circular [n] *handbill*
advertisement, booklet, broadside, brochure, flyer, handout, insert, leaflet, literature, notice, pamphlet, poster, publication, throwaway*; SEE CONCEPT *271*

circular [adj] *going around*
annular, circling, disklike, indirect, oblique, orbicular, round, rounded, spheroid; SEE CONCEPT *486*

circulate [v1] *make known*
bring out, broadcast, diffuse, disperse, disseminate, distribute, exchange, interview, issue, promulgate, propagate, publicize, publish, radiate, report, spread, strew, troll; SEE CONCEPTS *60,138*

circulate [v2] *flow*
actuate, circle, fly about, get about, get around, go about, gyrate, mill around, mobilize, move around, radiate, revolve, rotate, set off, travel, wander; SEE CONCEPT *147*

circulation [n1] *distribution*
apportionment, currency, dissemination, spread, transmission; SEE CONCEPTS *631,651*

circulation [n2] *moving circularly*
circling, circuit, circumvolution, current, flow, flowing, gyration, gyre, motion, revolution, rotation, round, turn, twirl, wheel, whirl; SEE CONCEPTS *147,738*

circumference [n] *edge, perimeter*
ambit, border, boundary, bounds, circuit, compass, confines, extremity, fringe, girth, limits, lip, margin, outline, periphery, rim, verge; SEE CONCEPT *484*

circumlocution [n] *indirect speech*
beating around the bush*, circumambages, diffuseness, discursiveness, euphemism, gassiness, indirectness, periphrase, periphrasis, pleonasm, prolixity, roundabout, tautology, verbal evasion, verbality, verbiage, wordiness; SEE CONCEPTS *51,266*

circumscribe [v] *mark off, delimit*
bar, bound, call a spade a spade*, confine, define, delineate, demarcate, encircle, enclose, encompass, environ, girdle, hamper, hem in*, limit, nail down*, outline, prelimit, restrain, restrict, surround, trammel; SEE CONCEPTS *18,130*

circumspect [adj] *cautious, discreet*
attentive, cagey, calculating, canny, careful, chary, considerate, deliberate, discriminating, gingerly, guarded, handle with kid gloves*, heedful, judicious, meticulous, observant, play safe*, politic, prudent, punctilious, safe, sagacious, sage, scrupulous, vigilant, wary, watchful, watch step*; SEE CONCEPTS *403,544*

circumstance [n] *situation, condition*
accident, action, adjunct, affair, article, case, cause, coincidence, concern, contingency, crisis, destiny, detail, doom, element, episode, event, exigency, fact, factor, fate, feature, fortuity, go, happening, happenstance, incident, intervention, item, juncture, kismet, lot, matter, Moira, occasion, occurrence, particular, phase, place, point, portion, proviso, re-

spect, scene, status, stipulation, supervention, thing, time, where it's at*; SEE CONCEPT *696*

circumstances [*n*] *state of affairs in one's life*
assets, capital, chances, class, command, degree, dowry, financial status, footing, income, lifestyle, lot, means, net worth, outlook, position, precedence, prestige, property, prospects, prosperity, rank, rating, resources, situation, sphere, standing, state, station, status, substance, times, way of life, worldly goods; SEE CONCEPTS *335,388*

circumstantial [*adj*] *incidental*
amplified, coincidental, concomitant, concurrent, conjectural, contingent, detailed, environmental, fortuitous, inconclusive, indirect, inferential, itemized, minute, particular, precise, presumptive, provisional, specific, uncertain; SEE CONCEPTS *556,582,653*

circumvent [*v*] *fool, mislead*
avoid, beat, beguile, bilk, bypass, circumnavigate, cramp, crimp, deceive, detour, disappoint, dodge, dupe, elude, ensnare, entrap, escape, evade, foil, frustrate, get around, hoodwink, outflank, outwit, overreach, prevent, queer, ruin, shun, sidestep, skirt, stave off, steer clear of*, stump, stymie, thwart, trick, ward off; SEE CONCEPTS *59,102,121*

circus [*n*] *fair with entertainment*
bazaar, big top, festival, gilly*, hippodrome, kermis, show, spectacle, three-ring*; SEE CONCEPT *293*

citadel [*n*] *top, tower*
bastion, blockhouse, castle, fastness, fort, fortification, fortress, keep, manor, redoubt, stronghold; SEE CONCEPTS *321,836*

citation [*n1*] *excerpt*
example, illustration, mention, passage, quotation, quote, quoting, reference, saying, source; SEE CONCEPT *283*

citation [*n2*] *award*
bidding, charge, commendation, encomium, mention, panegyric, reward, salutation, summons, tribute; SEE CONCEPTS *69,337*

cite [*v1*] *note, quote*
adduce, advance, allege, allude to, appeal to, enumerate, evidence, excerpt, exemplify, extract, get down to brass tacks*, give as example, illustrate with, indicate, instance, lay, mention, name, number, offer, point out, present, recite, recount, reference, refer to, rehearse, remember, reminisce, repeat, specify, spell out, tell; SEE CONCEPT *57*

cite [*v2*] *subpoena*
arraign, call, command, name, order, summon; SEE CONCEPT *317*

citizen [*n*] *person native of country*
aborigine, burgess, burgher, civilian, commoner, cosmopolite, denizen, dweller, freeman/woman, householder, inhabitant, John Q. Public*, member of body politic, member of community, national, native, naturalized person, occupant, resident, settler, subject, taxpayer, townsman/woman, urbanite, villager, voter; SEE CONCEPT *413*

city [*n*] *large town*
apple*, boom town, borough, burg, capital, center, conurbation, downtown, hamlet, megalopolis, metropolis, metropolitan area, municipality, place, polis, port, urban place, urbs*; SEE CONCEPT *507*

city [*adj*] *metropolitan*
burghal, citified, civic, civil, interurban, intraurban, megalopolitan, municipal, oppidian, urban; SEE CONCEPT *536*

civic [*adj*] *community*
borough, civil, communal, local, metropolitan, municipal, national, oppidian, public, urban; SEE CONCEPTS *536,583*

civil [*adj1*] *civic, community*
civilian, domestic, governmental, home, interior, local, municipal, national, political, public; SEE CONCEPTS *536,583*

civil [*adj2*] *obliging, kind*
accommodating, affable, civilized, complaisant, cordial, courteous, courtly, cultivated, diplomatic, formal, genteel, gracious, mannerly, polished, polite, politic, refined, suave, urbane, well-bred, well-mannered; SEE CONCEPT *401*

civilian [*n*] *nonmilitary person*
citizen, civ*, civvie*, commoner, noncombatant, private citizen, subject; SEE CONCEPT *423*

civilian [*adj*] *nonmilitary*
noncombatant, noncombative, nonmilitant, not in armed forces, pacificist, private, unhostile; SEE CONCEPT *555*

civilization [*n1*] *culture, sophistication*
acculturation, advancement, breeding, civility, cultivation, development, edification, education, elevation, enlightenment, illumination, polish, progress, refinement, social well-being; SEE CONCEPT *388*

civilization [*n2*] *society*
civilized life, community, customs, literate society, modern humanity, mores, nation, people, polity, way of life; SEE CONCEPTS *388,417*

civilize [*v*] *make cultured; develop*
acculturate, acquaint, advance, better, cultivate, edify, educate, elevate, enlighten, ennoble, enrich, ethicize, foster, help forward, humanize, idealize, improve, indoctrinate, inform, instruct, polish, promote, reclaim, refine, sophisticate, spiritualize, tame, uplift; SEE CONCEPTS *244,385*

claim [*n*] *property, right demanded or reserved*
affirmation, allegation, application, assertion, birthright, call, case, counterclaim, declaration, demand, dibs, due, entreaty, interest, lien, part, petition, plea, postulation, prerogative, pretense, pretension, privilege, profession, protestation, reclamation, request, requirement, requisition, suit, title, ultimatum; SEE CONCEPTS *278,318,376,709*

claim [*v*] *demand, maintain property or right*
adduce, advance, allege, ask, assert, believe, call for, challenge, collect, declare, defend, exact, have dibs on something*, hit, hit up*, hold, hold out for*,

insist, justify, knock, lay claim to, need, pick up, pop the question*, postulate, pretend, profess, pronounce, require, requisition, solicit, stake out, take, uphold, vindicate; SEE CONCEPTS 53,129

clairvoyance [n] *intuition*
acumen, discernment, ESP, feeling, foreknowledge, insight, omen, penetration, perception, precognition, premonition, psyche, sixth sense*, telepathy; SEE CONCEPTS 409,410

clairvoyant [n] *person who is psychic*
augur, channeller, diviner, fortune-teller, haruspex, horoscopist, medium, oracle, palm reader, prophet, prophetess, seer, sibyl, soothsayer, telepath, telepathist, visionary, voodoo man/woman*; SEE CONCEPT 423

clairvoyant [adj] *intuitive, psychic*
clear-sighted, discerning, extrasensory, farseeing, far-sighted, fey, judicious, long-sighted, new age*, oracular, penetrating, perceptive, prescient, prophetic, second-sighted, sibylline, spiritualistic, telepathic, vatic, visionary; SEE CONCEPTS 402,403

clam [n] *bivalve living in ocean*
cherrystone, littleneck, mollusk, quahog; SEE CONCEPT 394

clammy [adj] *damp*
close, dank, drizzly, moist, mucid, mucous, muculent, pasty, slimy, soggy, sticky, sweating, sweaty, wet; SEE CONCEPT 603

clamor [n] *loud cry; commotion*
agitation, babel, blare, brouhaha*, bustle, buzz, clinker, complaint, convulsion, din, discord, exclamation, ferment, hassle, hoo-ha*, hubba-hubba*, hubbub, hullabaloo*, hurly-burly*, lament, noise, outcry, pandemonium, protesting, racket, remonstrance, row, ruckus, shout, shouting, to-do, tumult, turmoil, upheaval, uproar, vociferation; SEE CONCEPTS 386, 595,674

clamor [v] *cry out, make commotion*
agitate, bark, bawl, bellow, bluster, claim, debate, demand, dispute, holler, put up a howl*, raise Cain*, raise the roof*, roar, rout, shout; SEE CONCEPTS 77,106

clamp [n] *fastener*
bracket, catch, clasp, grip, hold, lock, nipper, press, snap, vice; SEE CONCEPT 499

clamp [v] *fasten*
brace, clench, clinch, fix, impose, make fast, secure; SEE CONCEPTS 85,160

clan [n] *family, clique*
association, band, brotherhood, bunch, coterie, crew, crowd, crush, faction, folks, fraternity, gang, group, house, insiders, kinfolks, mob, moiety, organization, outfit, race, ring, sect, set, society, sodality, stock, tribe; SEE CONCEPTS 296,387

clandestine [adj] *secret, sly*
artful, cloak-and-dagger, closet, concealed, covert, foxy, fraudulent, furtive, hidden, hush-hush*, illegitimate, illicit, in holes and corners*, on the Q.T.*,

on the quiet, private, sneaky, stealthy, surreptitious, undercover, underground, underhand, under-the-counter*, under wraps*; SEE CONCEPTS 555,576

clank [n] *metallic noise*
bang, bong, clash, clink, jangle, ring; SEE CONCEPT 595

clank [v] *clang, clatter*
bong, clash, clink, jangle, make noise, resound, reverberate, ring, toll; SEE CONCEPT 65

clannish [adj] *exclusive, select*
akin, alike, associative, cliquish, close, insular, like, narrow, related, reserved, restricting, restrictive, sectarian, unfriendly, unreceptive; SEE CONCEPT 555

clap [n] *loud hitting noise*
applause, bang, blast, boom, burst, crack, crash, handclap, pat, slam, slap, smash, strike, thrust, thunder, thunderclap, thwack, wallop, whack, wham; SEE CONCEPTS 189,595

clap [v] *applaud; slap with approbation*
acclaim, approve, bang, cheer, give a big hand*, give a hand*, hear it for*, pat, praise, slap, strike gently, thwack, whack; SEE CONCEPTS 185,189

clarification [n] *explanation*
description, elucidation, exposition, illumination, interpretation, resolution, simplification, solution, unravelment, vivification; SEE CONCEPTS 57,274

clarify [v1] *explain, make clear*
analyze, break down, clear up, define, delineate, draw a picture, elucidate, formulate, illuminate, illustrate, interpret, make perfectly clear, make plain, resolve, settle, shed light on*, simplify, spell out*, straighten out, throw light on; SEE CONCEPT 57

clarify [v2] *purify*
clean, cleanse, depurate, distill, filter, rarefy, refine; SEE CONCEPT 165

clarion [adj] *clear, stirring sound*
blaring, definite, inspiring, loud, ringing, sharp, shrill, strident; SEE CONCEPTS 562,592,594

clarity [n] *clearness*
accuracy, articulateness, brightness, certainty, cognizability, comprehensibility, conspicuousness, decipherability, definition, directness, distinctness, evidence, exactitude, exactness, explicability, explicitness, intelligibility, legibility, limpidity, limpidness, lucidity, manifestness, obviousness, openness, overtness, palpability, penetrability, perceptibility, perspicuity, plainness, precision, prominence, purity, salience, simplicity, tangibility, transparency, unambiguity, unmistakability; SEE CONCEPTS 409,638

clash [n1] *disagreement or fight, often brief*
affray, argument, battle, brawl, break, broil, brush, bump, collision, concussion, conflict, confrontation, crash, difference of opinion, discord, discordance, disharmony, dispute, donnybrook*, embroilment, encounter, engagement, fracas, fray, have a go at each other*, impact, jam, jar, jolt, jump, melee, misunderstanding, mix up, opposition, rift, riot, row, rumpus, run-in, rupture, scrap, scrimmage, set-to,

shock, showdown, skirmish, smash, wallop; SEE
CONCEPTS *46,106*

clash [*v1*] *hit with a loud noise*
bang, bump, clang, clank, clatter, collide, crash,
grate, grind, jangle, jar, jolt, prang, rattle, scrap,
scrimmage, shock, smash, wallop; SEE CONCEPTS
65,189

clash [*v2*] *fight about, often verbally*
argue, bang heads*, battle, brawl, buck, combat,
conflict, contend, cross swords, differ, disagree, encounter, feud, fret, gall, grapple, grate, mix it up*,
quarrel, raise Cain*, row, try, war, wrangle; SEE
CONCEPTS *46,106*

clash [*v3*] *do not match*
be dissimilar, conflict, contrast, differ, disaccord,
discord, disharmonize, mismatch, not go with; SEE
CONCEPTS *655,664*

clasp [*n*] *fastener; hold on something*
brooch, buckle, catch, clamp, clench, clinch, clip,
clutch, embrace, fastening, grapple, grasp, grip,
hasp, hold, hook, hug, pin, safety pin, snap; SEE
CONCEPTS *497,641*

clasp [*v*] *grab tightly*
attack, bear hug*, buckle, clamp, clinch, clip,
clutch, coll, concatenate, connect, embrace, enfold,
fasten, glom onto*, grapple, grasp, grip, hold, hug,
pin, press, seize, snatch, squeeze, take; SEE CON-
CEPTS *85,160,191,219*

class [*n1*] *kind, sort, category*
branch, brand, breed, cast, caste, character, classification, collection, color, degree, denomination, department, description, designation, distinction, division,
domain, estate, family, feather, frame, genre, genus,
grade, grain, grouping, hierarchy, humor, ilk, kidney,
league, make, mold, name, nature, order, origin, property, province, quality, range, rank, rate, school, sect,
section, selection, set, source, species, sphere, standing, status, stripe, style, suit, temperament, value, variety; SEE CONCEPT *378*

class [*n2*] *societal group, background*
ancestry, birth, bourgeoisie, breed, caliber, caste,
circle, clan, clique, club, company, condition, connection, coterie, cultural level, degree, derivation,
descent, estate, extraction, family, genealogy, grade,
hierarchy, influence, intelligentsia, league, lineage,
moiety, nobility, origin, pecking order*, pedigree,
pigeonhole*, place, position, prestige, quality, sect,
social rank, source, sphere, standing, state, station,
status, stock, strain, stratum, the right stuff*, tier,
title; SEE CONCEPTS *296,387,388,417*

class [*n3*] *group in school*
academy, colloquium, course, course of study, division, form, grade, homeroom, lecture group, line,
quiz group, recitation, room, round table, section,
seminar, seminary, session, study, study group, subdivision, subject; SEE CONCEPTS *286,287,288,289*

class [*adj*] *stylish; with panache*
chic, classy, dashing, fashionable, fine, fly, foxy,
sharp; SEE CONCEPT *589*

class [*v*] *categorize*
account, allot, appraise, assess, assign, assort, brand,
classify, codify, consider, designate, divide, evaluate, gauge, grade, group, hold, identify, judge,
mark, part, pigeonhole*, rank, rate, reckon, regard,
score, separate; SEE CONCEPTS *39,135*

classic [*n*] *model*
chef d'oeuvre, exemplar, magnum opus, masterpiece, masterwork, paradigm, prototype, standard,
tour de force; SEE CONCEPTS *259,655,688*

classic/classical [*adj1*] *best, model*
archetypal, capital, champion, consummate, definitive, distinguished, esthetic, excellent, exemplary,
famous, fine, finest, first-rate, flawless, ideal, master, masterly, paradigmatic, paramount, perfect,
prime, quintessential, ranking, standard, superior,
top, top-notch, vintage, well-known; SEE CONCEPT
574

classic [*adj2*] *characteristic, regular*
prototypal, prototypical, representative, simple, standard, time-honored, typical, usual, vintage; SEE CON-
CEPTS *533,547*

classical [*adj1*] *concerning ancient culture*
academic, Attic, Augustan, belletristic, bookish,
canonic, canonical, classic, classicistic, Doric, Gre-
cian, Greek, Hellenic, Homeric, humanistic, Ionic,
Latin, Roman, scholastic, Virgilian; SEE CONCEPTS
536,549

classical [*adj2*] *simple, chaste*
classic, elegant, harmonious, pure, refined, restrained, symmetrical, understated, well-proportioned; SEE CONCEPT *589*

classicism [*n*] *simple style; regularity, restraint*
aesthetic principle, Atticism, balance, Ciceronian-
ism, clarity, class, classicalism, conventional formality, dignity, elegance, excellence, finish, formality,
formal style, grandeur, grand style, Hellenism, high
art, lucidity, majesty, neoclassicism, nobility, objectivity, polish, proportion, propriety, pure taste, purity, rationalism, refinement, rhythm, severity,
simplicity, sobriety, sublimity, symmetry; SEE CON-
CEPT *655*

classification [*n*] *categorization*
allocation, alloting, allotment, analysis, apportionment, arrangement, assignment, assortment, cata-
loguing, categorizing, codification, collocation,
consignment, coordination, denomination, department, designation, disposal, disposition, distribut-
ing, distribution, division, echelon, gradation, grade,
grading, graduation, group, grouping, kind, order,
ordering, ordination, organization, pigeonholing*,
regulation, sizing, sorting, systematization, tabulating, taxonomy, typecasting; SEE CONCEPTS
18,39,135,378

classify [*v*] *categorize*
allocate, allot, alphabetize, analyze, arrange, assort,
brand, break down, button down*, catalogue, class,
codify, collocate, coordinate, correlate, dispose, dis-

tinguish, distribute, divide, docket, embody, file, grade, group, incorporate, index, label, match, name, number, order, organize, peg*, pigeonhole*, put away, put down as, put down for, range, rank, rank out, rate, regiment, segregate, size, size up, sort, systematize, tab, tabulate, tag, take one's measure, ticket, type, typecast; SEE CONCEPTS *18,39,135*

classy [*adj*] *stylish, having panache*
chic, dashing, elegant, exclusive, fashionable, high-class, in vogue, mod, modish, posh, select, sharp, superior, swank, swanky, tony, uptown; SEE CONCEPT *589*

clatter [*n*] *loud noise*
ballyhoo*, bluster, clack, clangor, hullabaloo*, pandemonium, racket, rattle, rumpus, shattering, smashing; SEE CONCEPTS *181,189,595*

clatter [*v*] *crash; make racket*
bang, bluster, bump, clang, clank, clash, hurtle, noise, rattle, roar, shatter, smash; SEE CONCEPTS *65,181,189*

clause [*n*] *provision in document*
article, catch*, chapter, codicil, condition, fine print*, heading, item, joker*, kicker*, limitation, paragraph, part, passage, point, provision, proviso, requirement, section, small print*, specification, stipulation, string attached to something*, ultimatum; SEE CONCEPTS *270,275*

claw [*n*] *nail of animal; tool shaped like nail of an animal*
barb, cant hook, clapperclaw, crook, fang, fingernail, grapnel, grappler, hook, manus, nail claw, nipper, paw, pincer, retractile, spur, talon, tentacle, unguis, ungula; SEE CONCEPT *392*

claw [*v*] *using sharp nail*
break, dig, graze, hurt, itch, lacerate, mangle, maul, open, rip, scrabble, scrap, scrape, scratch, tear; SEE CONCEPTS *178,214,220*

clay [*n*] *workable earth material*
adobe, argil, argillaceous earth, bole, brick, china material, clunch, earth, kaolin, loam, loess, marl, mud, porcelain material, pottery, slip, terra cotta, till, wacke; SEE CONCEPT *509*

clean [*adj1*] *not dirty; uncluttered*
apple-pie order*, blank, bright, cleansed, clear, delicate, dirtless, elegant, faultless, flawless, fresh, graceful, hygienic, immaculate, laundered, neat, neat as a button*, neat as a pin*, orderly, pure, sanitary, shining, simple, snowy, sparkling, speckless, spic and span*, spotless, squeaky, stainless, taintless, tidy, trim, unblemished, unpolluted, unsmudged, unsoiled, unspotted, unstained, unsullied, untarnished, vanilla*, washed, well-kept, white; SEE CONCEPT *485*

clean [*adj2*] *sterile*
antiseptic, aseptic, clarified, decontaminated, disinfected, hygienic, pure, purified, sanitary, sterilized, unadulterated, uncontaminated, uninfected, unpolluted, unsullied, wholesome; SEE CONCEPTS *314,485*

clean [*adj3*] *chaste, virtuous*
blameless, crimeless, decent, exemplary, faultless, good, guiltless, honorable, inculpable, innocent, modest, moral, respectable, sinless, undefiled, unguilty, unsullied, upright, wholesome; SEE CONCEPT *404*

clean [*adj4*] *precise, sharp*
clear, clear-cut, correct, definite, distinct, legible, neat, plain, readable, simple, trim, uncluttered; SEE CONCEPT *535*

clean [*adj5*] *complete, thorough*
absolute, conclusive, decisive, entire, final, perfect, total, unimpaired, whole; SEE CONCEPT *531*

clean [*v*] *make undirty, uncluttered*
absterge, bath, bathe, blot, brush, cauterize, clarify, cleanse, clear the decks*, clear up, deodorize, depurate, deterge, disinfect, do up*, dredge, dust, edulcorate, elutriate, erase, expunge, expurgate, flush, hackle, launder, lave, mop, neaten, pick, pick up, polish, purge, purify, rake, rasp, refine, rinse, rout out, sanitize, scald, scour, scrape, scrub, shake out, shampoo, soak, soap, sponge, spruce up, sterilize, straighten up, swab, sweep, tidy up, vacuum, wash, whisk, winnow, wipe; SEE CONCEPTS *161,165*

clean-cut [*adj*] *neat, clearly outlined*
categorical, chiseled, clear, definite, definitive, etched, explicit, express, sharp, specific, unambiguous, well-defined; SEE CONCEPTS *490,535*

cleanse [*v*] *make undirty; wash*
absolve, clarify, clean, clear, depurate, disinfect, expurgate, launder, lustrate, purge, purify, refine, restore, rinse, sanitize, scour, scrub, sterilize; SEE CONCEPT *165*

cleanser [*n*] *strong disinfectant, solvent*
abrasive, abstergent, antiseptic, cathartic, deodorant, detergent, fumigant, lather, polish, purgative, purifier, scourer, soap, soap powder, suds; SEE CONCEPT *492*

clear [*adj1*] *cloudless, bright*
clarion, crystal, fair, fine, halcyon, light, luminous, pleasant, rainless, shining, shiny, sunny, sunshiny, unclouded, undarkened, undimmed; SEE CONCEPTS *525,617,627*

clear [*adj2*] *understandable, apparent*
apprehensible, audible, clear-cut, coherent, comprehensible, conspicuous, crystal, definite, distinct, evident, explicit, express, graspable, incontrovertible, intelligible, knowable, legible, loud enough, lucent, lucid, manifest, obvious, open and shut*, palpable, patent, perceptible, perspicuous, plain, precise, pronounced, readable, recognizable, sharp, simple, spelled out*, straightforward, transparent, transpicuous, unambiguous, unblurred, uncomplicated, unequivocal, unmistakable, unquestionable; SEE CONCEPTS *402,562*

clear [*adj3*] *open, unhindered*
bare, empty, free, smooth, stark, unhampered, unimpeded, unlimited, unobstructed, vacant, vacuous, void; SEE CONCEPT *490*

clear [adj4] *transparent*
apparent, cloudless, crystal, crystal clear, crystalline, glassy, limpid, pellucid, pure, see-through, thin, tralucent, translucent, translucid; SEE CONCEPTS *618,619*

clear [adj5] *not guilty*
absolved, blameless, clean, cleared, discharged, dismissed, exculpated, exonerated, guiltless, immaculate, innocent, pure, sinless, stainless, unblemished, uncensurable, undefiled, untarnished, untroubled; SEE CONCEPTS *319,404*

clear [adj6] *certain in one's mind*
absolute, confirmed, convinced, decided, definite, positive, resolved, satisfied, sure; SEE CONCEPT *403*

clear [v1] *clean, clear away*
ameliorate, break up, brighten, burn off, clarify, cleanse, disencumber, disengage, disentangle, eliminate, empty, erase, extricate, free, lighten, loosen, lose, meliorate, open, purify, refine, rid, rule out, shake off, sweep, throw off, tidy, unblock, unburden, unclog, unload, unloose, unpack, untie, vacate, void, wipe; SEE CONCEPTS *165,211*

clear [v2] *liberate; free from uncertainty*
absolve, acquit, clarify, defog*, discharge, disculpate, emancipate, exculpate, exonerate, explain, find innocent, let go, let off, let off the hook*, release, relieve, set free, vindicate; SEE CONCEPTS *7,22,127*

clear [v3] *pass over, often by jumping*
hurdle, leap, miss, negotiate, overleap, surmount, vault; SEE CONCEPT *194*

clear [v4] *profit*
accumulate, acquire, clean up*, earn, gain, gather, get, glean, make, net, obtain, pick up, realize, reap, receive, secure, win; SEE CONCEPTS *129,342*

clearance [n1] *permission for activity*
approval, authorization, consent, endorsement, go-ahead*, green light*, leave, okay, sanction, say-so; SEE CONCEPT *376*

clearance [n2] *gap above something*
allowance, assart, defoliated area, empty space, expanse, gap, headroom, margin, opening, open space; SEE CONCEPT *513*

clear-cut [adj] *definite*
assured, categorical, crystalline, decided, definitive, distinct, evident, explicit, express, indubitable, lucent, lucid, obvious, plain, precise, pronounced, sharp-cut, specific, straightforward, unambiguous, undisputed, undoubted, unequivocal, unquestioned, well-defined; SEE CONCEPT *535*

clearing [n] *gap in area*
allowance, assart, clearance, defoliated area, dell, empty space, expanse, gap, glade, headroom, margin, opening, open space; SEE CONCEPT *513*

clearly [adv] *without any doubt*
acutely, apparently, audibly, beyond doubt, certainly, conspicuously, decidedly, definitely, discernibly, distinctly, evidently, incontestably, incontrovertibly, indubitably, lucidly, manifestly, markedly, noticeably, obviously, openly, overtly, patently, penetratingly, perceptibly, plainly, positively, precisely, prominently, purely, recognizably, seemingly, sharply, sonorously, surely, translucently, transparently, undeniably, undoubtedly, unmistakably; SEE CONCEPTS *535,552*

clear out [v1] *empty something*
clean out, dispose of, eliminate, exhaust, get rid of, remove, sort, tidy up; SEE CONCEPT *211*

clear out [v2] *leave, often quickly*
beat it*, begone, decamp, depart, go, hightail*, kite*, make oneself scarce*, remove oneself, retire, scram, skedaddle*, split, take a hike*, take off, vamoose*, withdraw; SEE CONCEPT *195*

clear up [v1] *explain; resolve*
answer, cipher, clarify, decipher, dissolve, elucidate, figure out, illuminate, illustrate, make plausible, make reasonable, puzzle out, resolve, solve, straighten out, tidy, unfold, unravel; SEE CONCEPTS *37,57*

clear up [v2] *become improved*
become fair, become sunny, blow over, brighten, die away, die down, improve, lapse, lift, pick up, run its course*; SEE CONCEPT *700*

cleavage [n] *gap*
break, chasm, cleft, discontinuity, divide, division, fracture, hole, rift, schism, separation, severance, split, valley; SEE CONCEPT *513*

cleave [v1] *divide, split*
carve, chop, crack, cut, dissect, dissever, disunite, divorce, hack, hew, open, part, pierce, rend, rip, rive, separate, sever, slice, stab, sunder, tear asunder, whack; SEE CONCEPTS *98,137,176*

cleave [v2] *stand by, stick together*
abide by, adhere, agree, associate, attach, be devoted to, be tight with*, be true*, cling, cohere, combine, freeze to*, hold, join, link, remain, stay put, unite; SEE CONCEPTS *8,113*

cleft [n] *break, gap*
aperture, arroyo, breach, canyon, chasm, chink, cleavage, clough, clove, crack, cranny, crevice, fissure, fracture, gorge, gulch, opening, ravine, rent, rift, rima, rimation, rime, schism, slit; SEE CONCEPT *513*

cleft [adj] *separated, split*
broken, cloven, cracked, crannied, crenelated, parted, perforate, pierced, rent, riven, ruptured, separated, sundered, torn; SEE CONCEPT *490*

clemency [n] *forgiveness*
caritas, charity, compassion, endurance, equitableness, fairness, forbearance, gentleness, grace, humanity, indulgence, justness, kindness, lenience, leniency, lenity, lifesaver, mercifulness, mercy, mildness, moderation, soft-heartedness, sufferance, tenderness, tolerance, toleration; SEE CONCEPTS *410,644*

clement [adj1] *calm, mild (weather)*
balmy, clear, fair, fine, moderate, peaceful, temperate, warm; SEE CONCEPT *525*

clement [*adj2*] *forgiving*
benevolent, benign, benignant, charitable, compassionate, easy, forbearing, gentle, humane, humanitarian, indulgent, kind, kind-hearted, kindly, lenient, merciful, mild, soft-hearted, sympathetic, tender, tolerant; SEE CONCEPTS *404,550*

clench [*v*] *grasp*
clamp, clasp, clinch, clutch, constrict, contract, double up, draw together, grapple, grip, hold; SEE CONCEPT *191*

clergy [*n*] *ministry of church*
canonicate, canonry, cardinalate, churchmen/women, clerics, conclave, deaconry, diaconate, ecclesiastics, first estate, holy order, pastorate, prelacy, priesthood, rabbinate, the cloth, the desk, the pulpit; SEE CONCEPT *369*

clergyman/woman [*n*] *minister of church*
abbey, archbishop, bishop, cardinal, cassock, chaplain, churchman/woman, cleric, clerk, curate, dean, divine, ecclesiast, ecclesiastic, evangelist, father, man/woman of God, man/woman of the cloth, missionary, monsignor, padre, parson, pastor, pontiff, preacher, predicant, priest, primate, pulpitarian, pulpiteer, rabbi, rector, reverend, sermonizer, shepherd, vicar; SEE CONCEPT *361*

clerical [*adj1*] *secretarial*
accounting, bookkeeping, clerkish, clerkly, office, pink collar*, scribal, stenographic, subordinate, typing, white collar*, written; SEE CONCEPT *536*

clerical [*adj2*] *concerning clergy*
apostolic, canonical, churchly, cleric, ecclesiastic, ecclesiastical, episcopal, holy, ministerial, monastic, monkish, papal, parsonical, parsonish, pastoral, pontifical, prelatic, priestly, rabbinical, sacerdotal, sacred, theocratical; SEE CONCEPT *536*

clerk [*n*] *assistant*
agent, amanuensis, auditor, bookkeeper, cashier, copyist, counter jumper*, counterperson, employee, notary, office helper, operator, paper pusher*, paper shuffler*, pencil pusher*, pen pusher*, pink collar*, receptionist, recorder, registrar, salesperson, secretary, seller, shopman, stenographer, teller, transcriber, white collar*, worker; SEE CONCEPT *348*

clever [*adj*] *bright, ingenious*
able, adept, adroit, alert, apt, astute, brainy, brilliant, cagey, canny, capable, competent, crackerjack*, cunning, deep, dexterous/dextrous, discerning, egghead*, expert, foxy*, gifted, good, handy, intelligent, inventive, keen, knowing, knowledgeable, many-sided, masterly, nimble, nobody's fool*, pretty, pro, qualified, quick, quick on trigger*, quick-witted, rational, resourceful, sagacious, savvy, sensible, sharp, shrewd, skilled, skillful, slick, sly, smart, sprightly, talented, versatile, wise, witty; SEE CONCEPT *402*

cleverness [*n*] *brightness, ingenuity*
ability, adroitness, astuteness, brains, calculation, canniness, dexterity, discernment, flair, gift, gump-

tion, intelligence, quickness, quick wit, resourcefulness, sagacity, sense, sharpness, shrewdness, skill, smartness, talent, wisdom, wit; SEE CONCEPT *409*

cliché [*n*] *overused, hackneyed phrase*
adage, banality, boiler plate*, bromide, buzzword, chestnut*, commonplace, corn*, counterword, familiar tune, high camp*, motto, old story*, platitude, potboiler, prosaism, proverb, rubber stamp*, saying, shibboleth, slogan, stale saying, stereotype, threadbare phrase, triteness, trite remark, triviality, truism, vapid expression; SEE CONCEPTS *275,278*

click [*n/v1*] *metallic sound*
bang, beat, clack, snap, tick; SEE CONCEPTS *65,595*

click [*v2*] *fall into place*
become clear, be compatible, be on same wavelength*, come off*, feel a rapport*, get on*, go, go off well*, go over, hit it off*, make a hit*, make sense, match, meet with approval, pan out*, prove out, succeed, take to each other*; SEE CONCEPT *704*

client [*n*] *customer*
applicant, believer, buyer, chump, consumer, dependent, disciple, follower, front, habitué, head, mark, patient, patron, protégé, protégée, purchaser, shopper, walk-in, ward; SEE CONCEPT *348*

clientele [*n*] *customers of business*
audience, business, clientage, clientry, clients, constituency, cortege, dependents, following, market, patronage, patrons, public, regulars, trade; SEE CONCEPTS *325,417*

cliff [*n*] *overhang on hill or mountain*
bluff, crag, escarpment, face, precipice, rock face, rocky height, scar, scarp, steep rock, wall; SEE CONCEPT *509*

climactic/climacteric [*adj*] *decisive*
acute, climactical, critical, crucial, desperate, dire, paramount, peak; SEE CONCEPT *567*

climate [*n1*] *weather of region*
altitude, aridity, atmospheric conditions, characteristic weather, clime, conditions, humidity, latitude, meteorological character, meteorologic conditions, temperature; SEE CONCEPT *524*

climate [*n2*] *mood of situation*
ambience, ambient, atmosphere, disposition, environment, feeling, medium, milieu, mise-en-scène, mood, surroundings, temper, tendency, trend; SEE CONCEPT *673*

climax [*n*] *peak, culmination*
acme, apex, apogee, ascendancy, capsheaf, capstone, climacteric, crest, crowning point, extremity, head, height, highlight, high spot*, intensification, limit, maximum, meridian, ne plus ultra, orgasm, payoff*, pinnacle, pitch, summit, tiptop, top, turning point, utmost, zenith; SEE CONCEPTS *706,836*

climax [*v*] *come to top; culminate*
accomplish, achieve, break the record*, cap, come, come to a head*, conclude, content, crown, end, finish, fulfill, hit high spot*, orgasm, peak, please, reach a peak, reach the zenith, rise to crescendo*,

satisfy, succeed, terminate, top, tower; SEE CONCEPTS *375,704,706*

climb [*v*] *crawl, move up*
ape up*, ascend, clamber, escalade, escalate, go up, mount, rise, scale, soar, top; SEE CONCEPT *166*

clinch [*v1*] *secure a goal*
assure, cap, conclude, confirm, decide, determine, seal, seize, set, settle, sew up, verify; SEE CONCEPT *706*

clinch [*v2*] *hold securely; grab*
bolt, clamp, clasp, clench, clutch, cuddle, embrace, enfold, fasten, fix, grab hold of, grapple, grasp, grip, hug, lay hands on, make fast, nail, press, rivet, secure, seize, snatch, squeeze; SEE CONCEPTS *191,219*

cling [*v*] *attach to*
adhere, be true to, cherish, clasp, cleave to, clutch, cohere, continue, embrace, endure, fasten, freeze to, grasp, grip, hang in, hang onto, hold fast, hug, last, linger, squeeze, stay put, stick, stick like glue*; SEE CONCEPTS *85,160,190*

clinic [*n*] *medical center*
dispensary, hospital, infirmary, sick bay, surgery center; SEE CONCEPTS *312,439,449*

clinical [*adj*] *dispassionate*
analytic, antiseptic, cold, detached, disinterested, emotionless, impersonal, objective, scientific, unemotional; SEE CONCEPT *404*

clink [*n/v*] *bang against, ring*
chink, clang, jangle, jingle, sound, tingle, tinkle; SEE CONCEPTS *65,595*

clip [*v1*] *cut short*
bob, crop, curtail, cut, cut back, decrease, dock, lower, mow, pare, prune, reduce, shave, shear, shorten, skive, slash, snip, trim, truncate; SEE CONCEPTS *137,176*

clip [*v2/n*] *punch*
blow, box, clout, cuff, knock, punch, smack, sock, thump, wallop, whack; SEE CONCEPT *189*

clique [*n*] *group of friends*
bunch, cabal, camarilla, camp, circle, clan, club, coterie, crew, crowd, crush, faction, gang, in-group, insiders, lobby, Mafia, mob, organization, outfit, pack, posse, ring, set, society; SEE CONCEPTS *387,417*

cloak [*n*] *cover; coat*
beard, blind, camouflage, cape, capote, disguise, facade, face, front, guise, manteau, mantle, mask, pretext, semblance, shawl, shield, show, veneer, wrap; SEE CONCEPTS *451,475,680*

cloak [*v*] *disguise*
blanket, camouflage, coat, conceal, cover, curtain, dissemble, dissimulate, dress up, hide, mask, obscure, pretext, screen, shroud, veil; SEE CONCEPT *188*

clobber [*v*] *hit, beat*
belt, blast, drub, lambaste, lick, shellac, slam, slug, smash, smear, smother, thrash, trim, wallop, whip; SEE CONCEPTS *189,252*

clock [*n*] *timekeeping device*
alarm, Big Ben*, chroniker, chronograph, chronometer, digital watch, hourglass, pendulum, stopwatch, sundial, tattler, ticker*, tick-tock*, timekeeper, timemarker, timepiece, timer, turnip, watch; SEE CONCEPTS *463,819*

clockwork [*n*] *being on time; precision*
accuracy, consistency, perfect timing, regularity, smoothness; SEE CONCEPT *818*

clod [*n*] *stupid person*
blockhead*, boor, chump, clown, dimwit*, dolt, dope*, dumbbell, dummy, dunce, fool, imbecile, lame-brain*, lout, oaf, simpleton; SEE CONCEPTS *412,423*

clog [*n*] *blockage*
bar, block, blockade, burden, cumbrance, dead weight, drag, encumbrance, hindrance, impedance, impediment, obstruction, snag; SEE CONCEPTS *121,674*

clog [*v*] *block, hinder*
burden, choke, close, congest, curb, dam up, encumber, entrammel, fetter, fill, glut, hamper, impede, jam, leash, obstruct, occlude, plug, seal, shackle, stopper, stop up, stuff, tie, trammel; SEE CONCEPTS *121,130,190*

cloister [*n*] *secluded religious place*
abbey, cell, chapter house, convent, friary, hermitage, house, lamasery, monastery, nunnery, order, priorate, priory, religious community, retreat, sanctuary; SEE CONCEPTS *368,516*

cloistered [*adj*] *secluded*
cloistral, confined, hermitic, hidden, insulated, recluse, reclusive, restricted, secluse, seclusive, sequestered, sheltered, shielded, shut off, withdrawn; SEE CONCEPTS *554,583*

close [*n*] *ending*
adjournment, cease, cessation, completion, conclusion, culmination, denouement, desistance, end, finale, finish, period, stop, termination, windup; SEE CONCEPTS *119,832*

close [*adj1*] *near, nearby*
abutting, across the street, adjacent, adjoining, approaching, around the corner, at hand, contiguous, convenient, give or take a little*, handy, hard by, immediate, imminent, impending, in spitting distance*, in the ball park*, near-at-hand, nearest, nearly, neighboring, next, nigh, proximate, under one's nose*, warm; SEE CONCEPT *586*

close [*adj2*] *dense, cramped*
circumscribed, close-grained, compact, confined, confining, congested, consolidated, cropped, crowded, firm, impenetrable, impermeable, jam-packed, narrow, packed, restricted, short, solid, substantial, thick, tight; SEE CONCEPTS *481,483,774*

close [*adj3*] *accurate, precise*
conscientious, exact, faithful, lifelike, literal, resembling, similar, strict; SEE CONCEPTS *535,563*

close [*adj4*] *intimate*
attached, buddy-buddy*, chummy, confidential, cozy with, dear, devoted, familiar, inseparable, kissing cousins*, loving, making it with*, on top of each other*, palsy-walsy*, private, related, thick*, thick as thieves*, thick with*; SEE CONCEPTS *372,555*

close [*adj5*] *oppressive, humid*
airless, breathless, choky, confined, fusty, heavy, moldy, motionless, muggy, musty, stagnant, stale, stale-smelling, sticky, stifling, stuffy, suffocating, sultry, sweltering, sweltry, thick, tight, uncomfortable, unventilated; SEE CONCEPTS *525,605*

close [*adj6*] *secret, reserved*
buttoning one's lip*, buttoning up*, clamming up*, close-lipped, closemouthed, hidden, hush-hush*, mum's the word*, on the Q.T.*, private, reticent, retired, secluded, secretive, silent, taciturn, tight chops*, tight-lipped*, uncommunicative, unforthcoming, zipping one's lips*; SEE CONCEPTS *267,576*

close [*adj7*] *stingy*
chintzy*, closefisted, illiberal, mean, mingy, miserly, narrow, niggardly, parsimonious, penny-pinching, penurious, Scotch*, skimpy, skinflint*, tight, tight-fisted, ungenerous; SEE CONCEPTS *334,404*

close [*v1*] *obstruct, seal*
bang, bar, block, bolt, button, caulk, choke, clap, clench, clog, confine, congest, cork, dam, exclude, fasten, fill, lock, occlude, plug, prevent passage, put to, retard flow, screen, secure, shut, shut off, shutter, slam, stopper, stop up, stuff, turn off; SEE CONCEPTS *113,121,201*

close [*v2*] *complete, finish, stop*
button down*, button up*, call it a day*, call off, cap, cease, clear, clinch, conclude, consummate, culminate, cut loose, determine, discontinue, do, drop the curtain*, end, fold, fold up, halt, pack it in*, put a lid on*, put to bed*, sew up*, shut down, shutter, terminate, ultimate, wind down*, wind up*, wrap up*; SEE CONCEPT *234*

close [*v3*] *join, unite*
agree, bind, chain, coalesce, come together, connect, couple, encounter, fuse, grapple, inclose, meet, put together, tie, tie up; SEE CONCEPT *113*

closed [*adj1*] *shut, out of service*
bankrupt, dark, fastened, folded, gone fishing*, locked, not open, out of business*, out of order*, padlocked, sealed, shut down; SEE CONCEPT *576*

closed [*adj2*] *finished, terminated*
concluded, decided, ended, final, over, resolved, settled; SEE CONCEPT *548*

closed [*adj3*] *exclusive, independent*
restricted, self-centered, self-contained, self-sufficient, self-sufficing, self-supported, self-supporting, self-sustained, self-sustaining; SEE CONCEPT *550*

closely [*adv*] *approximately, carefully*
by the skin of one's teeth*, exactly, firmly, hard, heedfully, in conjunction with, intently, intimately,

jointly, meticulously, mindfully, minutely, nearly, punctiliously, scrupulously, searchingly, sharply, similarly, strictly, thoughtfully; SEE CONCEPTS *487,557,573*

closemouthed [*adj*] *silent, reserved*
buttoned up*, clammed up*, close, close-lipped, dummied up*, Garbolike*, have tight chops*, hush-hush, on the Q.T.*, quiet, reticent, sedate, taciturn, tight-lipped, uncommunicative, zipped one's lips*; SEE CONCEPT *267*

closet [*n*] *storage cupboard, usually tall*
ambry, bin, buffet, cabinet, chest of drawers, clothes room, cold storage, container, depository, locker, receptacle, recess, repository, room, safe, sideboard, vault, walk-in, wardrobe; SEE CONCEPT *440*

closure [*n1*] *conclusion*
cease, cessation, close, closing, desistance, end, ending, finish, stop, stoppage, termination; SEE CONCEPT *119*

closure [*n2*] *plug, seal*
blockade, bolt, bung, cap, cork, fastener, latch, lid, obstruction, occludent, occlusion, padlock, stop, stopper, stopple, tampon, tap; SEE CONCEPTS *471,680*

clot [*n*] *blockage, mass of coagulation*
array, batch, battery, body, bulk, bunch, bundle, clotting, clump, cluster, coagulum, coalescence, conglutination, consolidation, curd, curdling, embolism, embolus, glob, gob, group, grume, lump, occlusion, precipitate, set, thickness, thrombus; SEE CONCEPTS *432,466,470*

clot [*v*] *coagulate*
clabber*, coalesce, congeal, curdle, gel, gelate, gelatinize, glop up*, jell, jellify, jelly, lopper*, lump, set, solidify, thicken; SEE CONCEPT *469*

cloth [*n*] *fabric*
bolt, calico, cotton, dry goods, goods, material, stuff, synthetics, textiles, tissue, twill, weave, yard goods; SEE CONCEPT *473*

clothe [*v*] *cover with apparel*
accouter, apparel, array, attire, bedizen, bedrape, breech, bundle up, caparison, cloak, coat, costume, dandify, deck, disguise, dizen, do up*, drape, dress, dress up, dud*, endow, endue, enwrap, equip, fit, fit out, garb, gown, guise, habilitate, habit, invest, jacket, livery, mantle, outfit, panoply, primp, raiment, rig, robe, spruce, suit up, swaddle, swathe, tog, turn out, vest; SEE CONCEPT *167*

clothes/clothing [*n*] *personal attire*
accouterment, apparel, array, caparison, civvies*, costume, covering, drag*, drapery*, dress, duds*, ensemble, equipment, finery, frippery, frock, full feather*, garb, garments, gear, get-up*, habiliment, habit, hand-me-downs, livery, mufti, outfit, overclothes, panoply, rags*, raiment, regalia, rigging*, sack*, sportswear, Sunday best*, tailleur, tatters*, things*, threads*, tog*, toggery*, tout ensemble, trappings, trousseau, underclothes, vestment, ves-

ture, vines*, wardrobe, wear, weeds*, zoot suit*;
SEE CONCEPT *451*

cloud [*n1*] *mass of water particles in air*
billow, brume, darkness, dimness, film, fog, fogginess, frost, gloom, haze, haziness, mare's tail*, mist, murk, nebula, nebulosity, obscurity, ol' buttermilk sky*, overcast, pea soup*, pother, puff, rack, scud, sheep, smog, smoke, smother, steam, thunderhead, vapor, veil, woolpack; SEE CONCEPTS *437,524*

cloud [*n2*] *crowd*
army, dense mass, flock, horde, host, legion, multitude, rout, scores, shower, swarm, throng; SEE CONCEPTS *417,432*

cloud [*v1*] *become foggy or obscured*
adumbrate, becloud, befog, blur, darken, dim, eclipse, envelop, fog, gloom, mist, obfuscate, overcast, overshadow, shade, shadow, veil; SEE CONCEPTS *469,526*

cloud [*v2*] *confuse*
addle, becloud, befuddle, disorient, distort, distract, impair, muddle, muddy, obscure, perplex, puzzle; SEE CONCEPTS *7,19*

cloudy [*adj*] *hazy; darkened*
blurred, confused, dark, dense, dim, dismal, dull, dusky, emulsified, foggy, gloomy, heavy, indefinite, indistinct, leaden, lowering, misty, mucky, muddy, murky, mushy, nebulous, nontranslucent, nontransparent, not clear, nubilous, obscure, opaque, overcast, somber, sullen, sunless, vaporous; SEE CONCEPT *525*

clown [*n1*] *joking person*
antic, buffoon, comedian, comic, cut-up*, dolt, droll, farceur, fool, funnyman/woman, funster, gagman*, gagster*, harlequin, humorist, jester, joker, jokesmith, jokester, life of the party*, madcap, merry-andrew, merrymaker, mime, mountebank, mummer, picador, pierrot, prankster, punch, punchinello*, quipster, ribald, wag, wisecracker, wit*, zany*; SEE CONCEPT *423*

clown [*n2*] *stupid, ignorant person*
blockhead*, boor, bucolic, buffoon, bumpkin*, chuff, churl, clodhopper*, gawk, hayseed*, hick*, hind, jake, lout, mucker*, oaf, peasant, rube, rustic, swain, yahoo*, yokel; SEE CONCEPTS *412,423*

clown [*v*] *joke*
act crazy, act the fool*, bug out*, cut up*, fool around, have fun, jest, kid around; SEE CONCEPT *386*

cloy [*v*] *overfill*
disgust, fill, glut, gorge, jade, nauseate, pall, sate, satiate, satisfy, sicken, stall, stodge, suffice, surfeit, weary; SEE CONCEPT *740*

club [*n1*] *bat, stick*
baton, billy*, blackjack, bludgeon, business*, conk buster*, convincer*, cosh, cudgel, hammer, hickory, mace, mallet, nightstick, persuader*, quarterstaff, rosewood, sap, shill, shillelagh, staff, swatter, truncheon, works*; SEE CONCEPTS *470,499*

club [*n2*] *social organization*
alliance, association, brotherhood, bunch, circle, clique, company, crew, faction, fellowship, fraternity, gang, guild, hangout*, league, lodge, meeting, mob, order, outfit, ring, set, sisterhood, society, sodality, sorority, stamping ground*, union; SEE CONCEPTS *387,439*

club [*n3*] *golfing tool*
brassie, cleek, driver, iron, mashie, midiron, niblick, putter, spoon, stick, wedge, wood; SEE CONCEPT *364*

club [*v*] *hit hard with object*
bash, baste, batter, beat, blackjack, bludgeon, clobber, clout, cosh, cudgel, fustigate, hammer, pommel, pound, pummel, strike, whack; SEE CONCEPT *189*

clue [*n*] *hint, evidence*
cue, dead giveaway*, hot lead*, indication, inkling, intimation, key, lead, mark, notion, pointer, print*, proof, sign, solution, suggestion, suspicion, telltale, tip, tip-off*, trace, track, wind; SEE CONCEPT *274*

clue [*v*] *give information*
acquaint, advise, apprise, fill in, give the lowdown*, give the skinny on*, hint, indicate, inform, intimate, lead to, leave evidence, leave trace, leave tracks*, notify, point to, post, suggest, tell, warn, wise up; SEE CONCEPT *60*

clump [*n1*] *mass of something*
array, batch, blob, body, bunch, bundle, chunk, cluster, clutter, gob, group, hodgepodge, hunk, jumble, knot, lot, lump, nugget, parcel, set, shock, wad; SEE CONCEPTS *432,470*

clump [*n2*] *thumping noise*
clatter, clomp, galumph, scuff, stomp, stumble, thud; SEE CONCEPT *595*

clump [*v*] *make thumping noise*
barge, bumble, clatter, clomp, galumph, hobble, limp, lumber, plod, scuff, stamp, stomp, stumble, stump, thud, thump, tramp; SEE CONCEPTS *65,595*

clumsy [*adj*] *not agile; awkward*
all thumbs*, blundering, blunderous, bulky, bumbling, bungling, butterfingered*, clownish, crude, elephantine, gauche, gawkish, gawky, graceless, hamhanded*, heavy, heavy-handed, helpless, hulking, ill-shaped, incompetent, inelegant, inept, inexperienced, inexpert, lubberly, lumbering, lumpish, maladroit, oafish, ponderous, splay, stumbling, unable, unadept, uncoordinated, uncouth, undexterous, uneasy, ungainly, unhandy, unskillful, untactful, untalented, untoward, unwieldy, weedy; SEE CONCEPTS *401,402,584*

cluster [*n*] *group of something*
array, assemblage, band, batch, bevy, blob, body, bunch, bundle, chunk, clump, clutch, collection, covey, crew, gathering, hunk, knot, lot, pack, party, set; SEE CONCEPT *432*

cluster [*v*] *assemble, group*
accumulate, aggregate, associate, bunch, bunch up, bundle, collect, crowd around, cumulate, flock, gang

around, gather, package, parcel, round up; SEE CON-
CEPT *109*

clutch [n] *strong hold*
clamp, clasp, clench, clinch, connection, coupling,
grapple, grasp, grip, gripe, link; SEE CONCEPT *190*

clutch [v] *grab, snatch*
catch, cherish, clasp, clench, clinch, cling to, collar,
embrace, fasten, glom*, grapple, grasp, grip, harbor, hold, hook, keep, nab, nail*, put the snare on*,
seize, snag, snatch, take; SEE CONCEPTS *190,191*

clutches [n] *personal power*
claws, control, custody, grasp, grip, hands, keeping,
possession, sway; SEE CONCEPTS *388,641,710*

clutter [n] *disarray, mess*
ataxia, chaos, confusion, derangement, disorder,
hodgepodge, huddle, jumble, litter, medley, melange, muddle, rummage, scramble, shuffle, tumble,
untidiness; SEE CONCEPTS *432,674*

clutter [v] *cause mess, disarray*
dirty, jumble, litter, muddle, scatter, snarl, strew;
SEE CONCEPT *254*

coach [n1] *instructor, usually in recreation*
drillmaster, educator, mentor, physical education instructor, skipper, taskmaster, teacher, trainer, tutor;
SEE CONCEPTS *350,366*

coach [n2] *carriage*
bus, car, chaise, charabanc, fourwheeler, gocart, per-
ambulator, stage, tallyho, train, vehicle, victoria; SEE
CONCEPT *505*

coach [v] *instruct, usually in recreation*
break in*, cram, drill, educate, hone, lay it out for*,
lick into shape*, prepare, pull one's coat*, put
through the grind*, put through the mill*, ready,
school, teach, train, tutor; SEE CONCEPTS *285,363*

coagulate [v] *clot*
clabber*, coalesce, compact, concentrate, concrete,
condense, congeal, consolidate, curdle, dry, gel, gelate, gelatinize, glop up*, harden, inspissate, jell,
jellify, jelly, lopper*, set, solidify, thicken; SEE CON-
CEPT *469*

coagulation [n] *clotting*
agglomeration, caseation, concentration, concretion,
condensation, congelation, consolidation, curdling,
embolism, gelatination, incrassation, inspissation,
jellification, thickening; SEE CONCEPT *469*

coalesce [v] *blend, come together*
adhere, amalgamate, associate, bracket, cleave,
cling, cohere, combine, commingle, commix, conjoin, connect, consolidate, fraternize, fuse, hook up
with*, incorporate, integrate, join, join up with, link,
merge, mingle, mix, relate, stick, tie in with*, unite,
wed; SEE CONCEPTS *112,113*

coalition [n] *allied group, association*
affiliation, alliance, amalgam, amalgamation, anschluss, bloc, coadunation, combination, combine,
compact, confederacy, confederation, conjunction,
consolidation, conspiracy, faction, federation, fusion, integration, league, melding, mergence,

merger, merging, party, ring, unification, union; SEE
CONCEPT *381*

coarse [adj1] *not fine, rude*
base, bawdy, blue*, boorish, brutish, cheap, common,
crass, crude, dirty, earthy, filthy, foul, foul-mouthed,
gross, gruff, immodest, impolite, improper, impure,
incult, indelicate, inelegant, loutish, low, lowbred,
lowdown and dirty*, mean, nasty, obscene, off-color,
offensive, raffish, raunchy, raw, ribald, rough, roughneck*, rude, scatological, smutty*, tacky, uncivil, uncouth, uncultivated, uncultured, unrefined, vulgar,
vulgarian; SEE CONCEPTS *401,545*

coarse [adj2] *rough, unrefined*
chapped, coarse-grained, crude, grainy, granular,
harsh, homespun, impure, inferior, loose, lumpy,
mediocre, particulate, poor quality, rough-hewn,
rugged, unfinished, unpolished, unprocessed, unpu-
rified; SEE CONCEPTS *574,606*

coarseness [n] *rudeness, vulgarity*
bawdiness, boorishness, callousness, crassness, crudity, earthiness, harshness, indelicacy, offensiveness, poor taste, rawness, ribaldry, roughness,
smut*, smuttiness*, uncouthness, unevenness, unre-
finement; SEE CONCEPTS *633,645*

coast [n] *border by water*
bank, beach, coastline, littoral, margin, seaboard,
seacoast, seashore, seaside, shore, shoreline, strand;
SEE CONCEPTS *509,514*

coast [v] *glide along without much effort*
cruise, drift, float, freewheel, get by, ride on current,
sail, skate, slide, smooth along, taxi; SEE CONCEPTS
150,704

coastal [adj] *bordering the water*
along a coast, littoral, marginal, marshy, riverine,
seaside, skirting; SEE CONCEPT *583*

coat [n1] *animal hair*
crust, ectoderm, epidermis, fell, fleece, fur, hide,
husk, integument, leather, membrane, pelage, pellicle, pelt, peltry, protective covering, rind, scale,
scarfskin, shell, skin, wool; SEE CONCEPT *399*

coat [n2] *covering*
bark, coating, crust, finish, glaze, gloss, lacquer,
lamination, layer, overlay, painting, plaster, priming, roughcast, set, tinge, varnish, wash, whitewashing; SEE CONCEPTS *259,475*

coat [n3] *personal outerwear*
cape, cloak, cutaway, flogger, frock, greatcoat,
jacket, mackinaw, mink, overcoat, pea, raincoat,
slicker, suit, tails, threads, topcoat, trench, tux, tuxedo, ulster, windbreaker, wrap; SEE CONCEPT *451*

coat [v] *cover with layer of material*
apply, cover, crust, enamel, foil, glaze, incrust, laminate, paint, plaster, plate, smear, spread, stain, surface, varnish; SEE CONCEPTS *172,202*

coating [n] *covering*
blanket, bloom, coat, crust, dusting, encrustation,
film, finish, glaze, lamination, layer, membrane, patina, sheet, skin, varnish, veneer; SEE CONCEPT *475*

coax [v] *persuade*
allure, argue into, arm-twist*, barter, beguile, blandish, blarney, butter up*, cajole, come on, con, decoy, entice, flatter, get, hook, importune, induce, influence, inveigle, jawbone*, lure, pester, plague, press, prevail upon, rope in*, soft-soap*, soothe, sweet-talk, talk into, tease, tempt, urge, wangle, wheedle, work on, worm; SEE CONCEPT *68*

cobweb [n] *entanglement; filament*
fiber, gossamer, labyrinth, mesh, net, network, snare, tissue, toil, web, webbing; SEE CONCEPTS *517,674*

cock [n] *rooster*
capon, chanticleer, chicken, cock-a-doodle-doo*, cockalorum, cockerel; SEE CONCEPT *394*

cock [v] *aim up toward*
erect, hump, perk up, pile, prick, raise, stack, stand erect, stand up, stick up; SEE CONCEPT *201*

cockeyed [adj] *crooked, askew*
absurd, askance, askant, asymmetrical, awry, cam, canted, crazy, crooked, cross-eyed, esophoric, lopsided, ludicrous, nonsensical, preposterous, squint, strabismic; SEE CONCEPT *586*

cocky/cocksure [adj] *self-assured, full of oneself*
arrogant, brash, bumptious, certain, conceited, confident, egotistical, hotdogging*, hotshot*, hubristic, know-it-all*, lordly, nervy, overconfident, overweening, positive, presumptuous, self-confident, smart aleck*, smart guy*, smarty*, smarty pants*, sure, swaggering, swollen-headed, vain, wise guy*; SEE CONCEPTS *401,404*

cocoon [v] *protect with covering*
cushion, encase, envelop, insulate, pad, swaddle, swathe, truss, wrap; SEE CONCEPTS *130,134*

coddle [v1] *indulge, pamper*
baby, caress, cater to, cosset, cotton, favor, humor, make much of, make over, mollycoddle, nurse, pet, play up to, spoil; SEE CONCEPTS *110,295*

coddle [v2] *boil lightly, usually eggs*
brew, cook, poach, simmer, steam; SEE CONCEPT *170*

code [n1] *secret language system*
cipher, cryptograph; SEE CONCEPTS *276,284*

code [n2] *law, rule*
canon, charter, codex, constitution, convention, custom, digest, discipline, ethics, etiquette, manners, maxim, method, regulation, system; SEE CONCEPTS *318,687*

codicil [n] *added part to document*
addendum, addition, appendix, postscript, rider, supplement; SEE CONCEPT *270*

codify [v] *systematize*
arrange, catalogue, classify, code, collect, condense, digest, order, organize, summarize, tabulate; SEE CONCEPTS *39,84*

coerce [v] *compel, press*
beset, browbeat, bulldoze*, bully, concuss, constrain, cow, dragoon, drive, force, high pressure*, hinder, impel, intimidate, lean on, make, make an offer they can't refuse*, menace, oblige, pressurize, push, put the squeeze on*, repress, restrict, shotgun, strong-arm, suppress, terrorize, threaten, twist one's arm*, urge; SEE CONCEPTS *14,68*

coercion [n] *compulsion, pressure*
browbeating, bullying, constraint, duress, force, intimidation, menace, menacing, persuasion, restraint, strong-arm tactic*, threat, threatening, violence; SEE CONCEPTS *14,68*

coexistence [n] *happening or being at same time, place*
accord, coetaneousness, coevality, coincidence, concurrence, conformity, conjunction, contemporaneousness, harmony, order, peace, simultaneousness, synchronicity; SEE CONCEPT *407*

coffee [n] *hot beverage made from beans of a tree*
battery acid*, brew, café, café au lait, café noir, cappuccino, decaf, decoction, demitasse, espresso, forty weight*, hot stuff*, ink*, jamocha*, java*, joe*, mocha*, mud*, perk*, varnish remover*; SEE CONCEPT *454*

coffer [n] *large box*
case, casket, chest, exchequer, repository, strongbox, treasure chest, treasury, war chest; SEE CONCEPT *494*

coffin [n] *box for dead person*
casket, catafalque, crate, funerary box, pall, pine box, pine drape*, sarcophagus; SEE CONCEPTS *368,479,494*

cog [n] *main part of device*
cogwheel, differential, fang, gear, pinion, prong, rack, ratchet, tine, tooth, transmission, tusk, wheel; SEE CONCEPT *464*

cogency [n] *effectiveness*
bearing, concern, connection, conviction, convincingness, force, forcefulness, pertinence, point, potency, power, punch, relevance, strength, validity, validness; SEE CONCEPTS *376,676*

cogent [adj] *effective*
apposite, apt, compelling, conclusive, consequential, convictive, convincing, fitting, forceful, forcible, inducing, influential, irresistible, justified, meaningful, momentous, persuasive, pertinent, potent, powerful, puissant, relevant, satisfactory, satisfying, significant, solid, sound, strong, suasive, telling, urgent, valid, weighty, well-grounded; SEE CONCEPT *537*

cogitate [v] *think deeply about*
brainstorm, cerebrate, chew the cud*, conceive, consider, contemplate, deliberate, envisage, envision, figure, flash on*, imagine, kick around*, meditate, mull over, muse, noodle around*, ponder, reason, reflect, ruminate, speculate, stew over*; SEE CONCEPTS *17,24*

cogitation [n] *deep thought*
brainwork, cerebration, consideration, contemplation, deliberation, meditation, reflection, rumination, speculation; SEE CONCEPT *410*

cognate [*adj*] *alike, associated*
affiliated, agnate, akin, allied, analogous, comparable, connate, connatural, connected, consanguine, general, generic, incident, kindred, like, related, same, similar, universal; SEE CONCEPTS *487,573*

cognizance/cognition [*n*] *understanding*
acknowledgment, apprehension, attention, awareness, comprehension, discernment, insight, intelligence, knowledge, mind, need, note, notice, observance, observation, perception, percipience, reasoning, recognition, regard; SEE CONCEPT *409*

cognizant [*adj*] *aware*
acquainted, alive, apprehensive, au courant, awake, conscious, conversant, down with, familiar, grounded, hep to*, hip to*, informed, in on, in the know, in the picture*, judicious, knowing, knowledgeable, observant, on the beam*, on to*, perceptive, plugged in, savvy, sensible, sentient, tuned in*, up on*, versed, wise to*, with it*, witting; SEE CONCEPT *402*

cohabit [*v*] *live together*
be roommates with, conjugate, couple, have relations, live illegally, live with, mingle, play house*, room together, shack up*, share address, take up housekeeping*; SEE CONCEPTS *226,375,384*

cohere [*v1*] *stick to, cling*
adhere, associate, bind, blend, cleave, coalesce, combine, connect, consolidate, fuse, glue, hold, join, merge, unite; SEE CONCEPTS *85,113,160*

cohere [*v2*] *agree, conform*
accord, be connected, be consistent, check, check out, comport, conform, correspond, dovetail, fit in, go, hang together, harmonize, hold, hold water, make sense, relate, square; SEE CONCEPTS *8,636,667*

coherence [*n*] *agreement*
adherence, attachment, bond, cementation, cling, clinging, comprehensibility, concordance, conformity, congruity, connection, consistency, consonance, construction, continuity, correspondence, inseparability, inseparableness, integrity, intelligibility, rationality, relations, solidarity, stickage, tenacity, union, unity; SEE CONCEPTS *388,684*

coherent [*adj*] *understandable*
articulate, comprehensible, consistent, identified, intelligible, logical, lucid, meaningful, orderly, organized, rational, reasoned, sound, systematic; SEE CONCEPT *402*

cohort [*n*] *partner in activity*
accomplice, adherent, aide, ally, assistant, associate, companion, company, comrade, confrere, consociate, contingent, disciple, fellow, follower, friend, hand, henchman, legion, mate, myrmidon, pal, partisan, regiment, satellite, sidekick, stall, supporter; SEE CONCEPT *423*

coiffure [*n*] *hairstyle*
afro, beehive, blow dry*, braids, corn rows, crew cut, DA*, dreadlocks, dreads, flip, fuzz cut*, hair, hair-comb, haircut, hairdo, permanent, pigtails, plait, ponytail, razor cut*, tail, tease, trim, wave; SEE CONCEPTS *418,718*

coil [*n*] *thread that curls*
bight, braid, circle, convolution, corkscrew, curlicue, gyration, helix, involution, lap, loop, ring, roll, scroll, spiral, tendril, turn, twine, twirl, twist, whorl, wind; SEE CONCEPT *436*

coil [*v*] *curl around, entwine*
convolute, convolve, corkscrew, fold, intertwine, intervolve, lap, loop, make serpentine, rotate, scroll, sinuate, snake, spiral, spire, turn, twine, twist, wind, wrap around, wreathe, writhe; SEE CONCEPTS *201,758*

coin [*n*] *metallic money*
bread*, cash, change, chicken feed*, chips*, coinage, copper, currency, dough, gold, jack*, legal tender, meter money*, mintage, money, piece, scratch*, silver, small change*, specie; SEE CONCEPT *340*

coin [*v*] *create, invent*
brainstorm, compose, conceive, contrive, counterfeit, dream up, fabricate, forge, formulate, frame, head trip*, make up, make up off the top of one's head*, manufacture, mint, mold, originate, spark, spitball*, stamp, strike, think up, trump up*; SEE CONCEPTS *36,173*

coincide [*v*] *go along with; coexist*
accompany, accord, acquiesce, agree, be concurrent, befall, be the same, come about, concert, concur, correspond, equal, eventuate, harmonize, identify, jibe, match, occur simultaneously, quadrate, square, sync, synchronize, tally; SEE CONCEPTS *667,714*

coincidence [*n1*] *agreement; coexistence*
accompaniment, accord, accordance, collaboration, concomitance, concurrence, conformity, conjunction, consonance, correlation, correspondence, parallelism, synchronism, union; SEE CONCEPTS *667, 684,714*

coincidence [*n2*] *accidental happening*
accident, chance, eventuality, fate, fluke, fortuity, happening, happy accident, incident, luck, stroke of luck; SEE CONCEPTS *4,230*

coincident [*adj*] *concurring, happening together*
ancillary, attendant, attending, coinciding, collateral, concomitant, consonant, contemporaneous, contemporary, coordinate, correspondent, incident, satellite, simultaneous, synchronous; SEE CONCEPTS *548,820*

coincidental [*adj*] *accidental*
casual, chance, circumstantial, fluky, fortuitous, incidental, unintentional, unplanned; SEE CONCEPT *548*

cold [*n*] *frigid conditions*
ague, algidity, algor, chill, chilliness, coldness, congelation, draft, freeze, frigidity, frost, frostbite, frostiness, frozenness, gelidity, gelidness, glaciation, goose flesh, iciness, inclemency, rawness, refrigeration, shivering, shivers, snow, wintertime, wintriness; SEE CONCEPTS *524,610*

cold [*adj1*] *chilly, freezing*
algid, arctic, below freezing, below zero, benumbed, biting, bitter, blasting, bleak, boreal, brisk, brumal, chill, chilled, cool, crisp, cutting, frigid, frore, frosty, frozen, gelid, glacial, have goose bumps*, hawkish, hiemal, hyperborean, icebox, iced, icy, inclement, intense, keen, nipping, nippy, numbed, numbing, one-dog night*, penetrating, piercing, polar, raw, rimy, severe, sharp, shivery, Siberian, sleety, snappy, snowy, stinging, two-dog night*, wintry; SEE CONCEPT **605**

cold [*adj2*] *aloof, unresponsive*
apathetic, cold-blooded, cool, dead, distant, emotionless, frigid, frosty, glacial, icy, impersonal, imperturbable, indifferent, inhibited, inhospitable, joyless, lukewarm, matter-of-fact, passionless, phlegmatic, reserved, reticent, spiritless, standoffish, stony, unconcerned, undemonstrative, unenthusiastic, unfeeling, unimpassioned, unmoved, unresponsive, unsympathetic; SEE CONCEPT **404**

cold-blooded [*adj*] *cruel, heartless*
barbarous, brutal, callous, cold, dispassionate, hard-boiled, hardened, hard-hearted, imperturbable, inhuman, matter-of-fact, merciless, obdurate, pitiless, relentless, ruthless, savage, steely, stony-hearted, uncompassionate, unemotional, unfeeling, unmoved; SEE CONCEPT **542**

coliseum [*n*] *arena for events*
amphitheater, bowl, hippodrome, open-air theater, stade, stadium, theater; SEE CONCEPT **438**

collaborate [*v*] *work together*
be in cahoots*, coact, cofunction, collude, come together, concert, concur, conspire, cooperate, coproduce, do business with, fraternize, get together, glue oneself to*, go partners*, hook on, hook up*, interface, join forces, join together, join up with, participate, team up, throw in together*, throw in with*, tie in, work with; SEE CONCEPTS **100,351,384**

collaborator [*n*] *person who works with another*
assistant, associate, colleague, confederate, co-worker, fellow traveller, fraternizer, helper, partner, quisling, running dog, teammate, team player*; SEE CONCEPTS **348,423**

collage [*n*] *mixture of pictures*
abstract composition, found art, photomontage; SEE CONCEPT **259**

collapse [*n*] *downfall, breakdown*
bankruptcy, basket case*, cataclysm, catastrophe, cave-in, conk out*, crackup*, crash, debacle, destruction, disintegration, disorganization, disruption, exhaustion, failure, faint, flop, prostration, ruination, ruining, smash, smashup, subsidence, undoing, wreck; SEE CONCEPTS **230,316,410,674**

collapse [*v*] *fall apart, break down*
belly up*, bend, break, cave in, conk out*, crack up*, crumple, deflate, disintegrate, droop, drop, exhaust, fail, faint, fall down, flag, flake out, fold, founder, give, give in, give out, give way, go*, go to

pieces*, keel over, languish, shatter, subside, succumb, tire, topple, weaken, weary, wilt, yield; SEE CONCEPTS **252,469,702**

collar [*n*] *neck attire*
bertha, choker, dicky, Eton, fichu, fraise, frill, jabot, neckband, ruff, torque, Vandyke; SEE CONCEPTS **450,452**

collar [*v*] *apprehend*
abduct, appropriate, arrest, bag, capture, catch, cop, corner, get, grab, hook, lay hands on, nab, nail, prehend, secure, seize, take, tree; SEE CONCEPTS **90,317**

collate [*v*] *sort collection*
adduce, analogize, assemble, bracket, collect, compare, compose, contrast, examine, gather, group, match, order, relate, verify; SEE CONCEPTS **84,158**

collateral [*n*] *monetary deposit*
assurance, bond, endorsement, guarantee, pledge, promise, security, surety, warrant, wealth; SEE CONCEPT **344**

collateral [*adj*] *indirect, secondary*
accessory, accompanying, added, adjunctive, adjuvant, ancillary, appurtenant, attendant, auxiliary, circuitous, coincident, complementary, concomitant, concurrent, confirmatory, coordinate, corresponding, corroborative, dependent, incident, lateral, not lineal, parallel, related, roundabout, satellite, side, sub-, subordinate, subservient, subsidiary, supporting, tributary, under; SEE CONCEPTS **546,567,831**

colleague [*n*] *associate, fellow worker*
aide, ally, assistant, auxiliary, buddy, chum, coadjutor, cohort, collaborator, companion, compatriot, compeer, comrade, confederate, confrere, co-worker, crony, fellow, friend, helper, pal, partner, teammate, workmate; SEE CONCEPTS **348,423**

collect [*v1*] *accumulate, come together*
aggregate, amass, array, assemble, cluster, compile, congregate, congress, convene, converge, convoke, corral, flock, flock together, gather, get hold of, group, heap, hoard, muster, rally, rendezvous, round up, save, scare up, stockpile; SEE CONCEPTS **109,114**

collect [*v2*] *obtain (money)*
acquire, dig up, muster, pass the hat*, raise, requisition, secure, solicit; SEE CONCEPT **342**

collected [*adj*] *composed, calm*
composed, confident, cool, easy, easygoing, level-headed, nonchalant, peaceful, placid, poised, possessed, quiet, sanguine, self-possessed, serene, still, sure, temperate, together, tranquil, unflappable, unperturbable, unperturbed, unruffled; SEE CONCEPT **401**

collection [*n*] *group, accumulation*
accumulating, acquiring, acquisition, agglomeration, amassing, amassment, anthology, assemblage, assembling, assembly, assortment, batch, bringing together, caboodle, clump, cluster, collation, combination, company, compilation, congeries, congregation, convocation, crowd, cumulation, digest,

gathering, heap, hoard, kit, levy, lot, mass, medley, mess, miscellany, mobilization, muster, number, obtaining, omnibus, pile, quantity, securing, selection, set, stack, stock, stockpile, store; SEE CONCEPTS *109,432*

collective [*adj*] *composite*
aggregate, assembled, collated, combined, common, compiled, concentrated, concerted, conjoint, consolidated, cooperative, corporate, cumulative, gathered, grouped, heaped, hoarded, joint, massed, mutual, piled, shared, unified, united; SEE CONCEPT *585*

college [*n*] *institution of higher education*
alma mater, association, brainery*, halls of ivy*, halls of knowledge*, institute, lyceum, organization, seminary, university; SEE CONCEPTS *287,288,289*

collide [*v*] *slam into*
bang, beat, break up, bump, clash, conflict, crash, crunch*, disagree, fender-bend*, fragment, hit, jolt, meet head-on*, pile up*, plow into*, pulverize*, scrap*, shatter, sideswipe, smash, splinter, strike, wrack up*; SEE CONCEPTS *189,248*

collision [*n*] *accident*
blow, bump, butt, concussion, contact, crash, demolishment, destruction, dilapidation, encounter, fender bender*, head-on*, hit, impact, jar, jolt, knock, percussion, pileup*, rap, ruin, shock, sideswipe, slam, smash, strike, thud, thump, wreck; SEE CONCEPTS *189,230,674*

collocate [*v*] *compile*
accumulate, assemble, collect, collimate, gather, parallel; SEE CONCEPT *84*

colloquial [*adj*] *particular, familiar to an area, informal*
chatty, common, conversational, demotic, dialectal, everyday, idiomatic, jive*, popular, street*, vernacular; SEE CONCEPT *267*

colloquy [*n*] *conversation, debate*
buzz session, chat, chinfest*, chitchat, clambake*, colloquium, confab*, confabulation, conference, converse, dialogue, discourse, discussion, flap*, gab fest*, gam*, groupthink*, huddle*, palaver, parley, powwow*, rap*, rap session*, seminar, talk, talkfest*; SEE CONCEPT *266*

collusion [*n*] *secret understanding, often with intent to defraud*
bait and switch*, bill of goods*, bunco*, cahoots*, complicity, con game*, connivance, conspiracy, craft, deceit, diddling*, dodge, double-cross, fast shuffle, flam*, flimflam*, fradulent artifice, graft, guilt, guiltiness, gyp, intrigue, plot, racket, scam, scheme, shell game*, skunk*, sting*, trick, whitewash; SEE CONCEPTS *114,660*

colonial [*adj*] *pioneering, relating to a nonindependent or new territory*
crude, dependent, dominion, early American, emigrant, frontier, immigrant, new, outland, pilgrim, pioneer, prerevolutionary, primitive, provincial, puritan, territorial, transplanted, uncultured, unset-

tled, unsophisticated, wild; SEE CONCEPTS *549,799*

colonization [*n*] *settlement of area*
clearing, establishment, expanding, expansion, founding, immigration, migration, opening up, peopling, pioneering, populating, settlement, settling, squatting, transplanting; SEE CONCEPTS *198,298*

colony [*n*] *community*
antecedents, clearing, dependency, dominion, mandate, new land, offshoot, outpost, possession, protectorate, province, satellite, settlement, subject state, swarm, territory; SEE CONCEPTS *379,512*

color [*n1*] *pigment, shade*
blush, cast, chroma, chromaticity, chromatism, chromism, colorant, coloration, coloring, complexion, dye, glow, hue, intensity, iridescence, luminosity, paint, pigmentation, polychromasia, saturation, stain, tinct, tincture, tinge, tint, undertone, value, wash; SEE CONCEPT *622*

color [*n2*] *deceptive appearance*
deception, disguise, excuse, facade, face, false show, front, guise, mask, plea, pretense, pretext, put-on, semblance, show; SEE CONCEPTS *59,716*

color [*v1*] *make pigmented; shade*
adorn, bloom, blush, burn, chalk, crayon, crimson, darken, daub, dye, embellish, emblazon, enamel, enliven, flush, fresco, gild, glaze, gloss, illuminate, imbue, infuse, lacquer, paint, pigment, pinken, redden, rouge, stain, stipple, suffuse, tinge, tint, tone, turn red, variegate, wash; SEE CONCEPTS *250,469*

color [*v2*] *distort, exaggerate*
angle*, belie, cook up*, disguise, doctor*, embroider*, fake, falsify, fudge*, garble, gloss over, magnify, misrepresent, misstate, overstate, pad*, pervert, prejudice, slant*, taint, twist*, warp*; SEE CONCEPTS *49,63*

colored [*adj1*] *not white*
dyed, flushed, glowing, hued, shaded, stained, tinged, tinted, washed; SEE CONCEPT *618*

colored [*adj2*] *distorted*
angled, biased, false, falsified, jaundiced, misrepresented, one-sided, partial, partisan, perverted, prejudiced, prepossessed, tampered with, tendentious, warped; SEE CONCEPT *582*

colorful [*adj1*] *brilliant, intensely hued*
bright, chromatic, flashy, florid, gaudy, gay, hued, intense, jazzy, kaleidoscopic, loud, motley, multicolored, picturesque, prismatic, psychedelic, rich, showy, splashy, variegated, vibrant, vivid; SEE CONCEPTS *617,618*

colorful [*adj2*] *full of life, interesting*
brave, characterful, distinctive, flaky, gay, glamorous, graphic, jazzy, lively, picturesque, rich, stimulating, unusual, vivid; SEE CONCEPT *404*

colorless [*adj1*] *without hue*
achromatic, achromic, anemic, ashen, ashy, blanched, bleached, cadaverous, doughy, drab, dull, faded, flat, ghastly, livid, lurid, neutral, pale, sickly, uncolored, wan, washed out, waxen, white; SEE CONCEPT *618*

colorless [*adj2*] *unlively, uninteresting*
characterless, dreary, dull, insipid, lackluster, lifeless, prosaic, run-of-the-mill*, tame, unmemorable, unpassioned, vacuous, vapid; SEE CONCEPT *404*

colossal [*adj*] *very large*
barn door*, behemothic, blimp*, cyclopean, elephantine, enormous, gargantuan, giant, gigantic, huge, humongous*, immense, jumbo, mammoth, mondo*, monstrous, mountainous, super, titanic, vast; SEE CONCEPT *781*

colt [*n*] *young horse*
filly, fledgling, foal, rookie, sapling, yearling, youngling, youngster; SEE CONCEPT *394*

column [*n1*] *line, procession*
cavalcade, company, file, list, platoon, queue, rank, row, string, train; SEE CONCEPTS *432,727*

column [*n2*] *pillar*
brace, buttress, caryatid, colonnade, cylinder, mast, minaret, monolith, monument, obelisk, pedestal, peristyle, pier, pilaster, post, prop, pylon, shaft, standard, stay, stele, support, totem, tower, underpinning, upright; SEE CONCEPT *440*

coma [*n*] *deep unconsciousness*
blackout, dullness, faint, hebetude, insensibility, lethargy, oblivion, sleep, slumber, somnolence, stupor, swoon, syncope, torpidity, torpor, trance; SEE CONCEPT *315*

comatose [*adj*] *unconscious*
cold, dead, dead to the world*, dopey, drowsy, drugged, hebetudinous, inconscious, insensible, lethargic, out, out cold*, out to lunch*, PVS, senseless, sleepy, sluggish, slumberous, somnolent, soporose, stupefied, stupid, stuporous, torpid, vegged out*; SEE CONCEPT *539*

comb [*v1*] *arrange hair*
adjust, card, cleanse, curry, disentangle, dress, groom, hackle, hatchel, lay smooth, rasp, scrape, separate, smooth, sort, straighten, tease, untangle; SEE CONCEPT *162*

comb [*v2*] *search by ransacking*
beat, beat the bushes*, examine, finecomb, forage, go through with fine-tooth comb*, grub, hunt, inspect, investigate, leave no stone unturned*, look high and low*, probe, rake, ransack, rummage, scour, screen, scrutinize, search high heaven*, sift, sweep, turn inside out*, turn upside down*; SEE CONCEPT *216*

combat [*n*] *battle*
action, affray, battle royal*, brush, brush-off, conflict, contest, encounter, engagement, fight, flap, fray, jackpot*, mix-up*, run-in*, service, shoot-out*, skirmish, struggle, war, warfare; SEE CONCEPTS *86,106*

combat [*v*] *fight*
battle, buck, clash, contend, contest, cope, cross swords with*, defy, dispute, do battle with, duel, engage, fight, go up against, oppose, put up a fight*, repel, resist, shoot it out*, strive, struggle, traverse, war, withstand; SEE CONCEPTS *86,106*

combative [*adj*] *aggressive*
antagonistic, bellicose, belligerent, cantankerous, contentious, cussed, energetic, fire-eating*, gladiatorial, hawkish, manly, militant, ornery*, pugnacious, quarrelsome, ructious, scrappy, strenuous, trigger-happy*, truculent, warlike, warring; SEE CONCEPTS *401,404*

combination [*n1*] *mixture, blend*
aggregate, amalgam, amalgamation, blending, brew, coalescence, combo, composite, compound, connection, consolidation, everything but the kitchen sink*, fusion, junction, medley, merger, miscellany, mishmash*, mix, olio, order, sequence, solution, soup, stew, succession, synthesis, unification, union; SEE CONCEPT *432*

combination [*n2*] *alliance, association*
affiliation, bloc, cabal, cahoots, camarilla, cartel, circle, clique, club, coadunation, coalition, combine, compound, confederacy, confederation, conjunction, connection, consolidation, consortium, conspiracy, coterie, faction, federation, gang, guild, hookup, Mafia, melding, mergence, merger, merging, partnership, party, pool, ring, set, syndicate, tie-up, trust, unification, union; SEE CONCEPT *381*

combine [*v*] *connect, integrate*
amalgamate, associate, band, bind, blend, bond, bracket, bunch up, coadjute, coalesce, commingle, compound, conjoin, cooperate, couple, dub, fuse, get together, glue oneself to, hitch on*, hook on*, incorporate, interface, join, league, link, marry, merge, mingle, mix, network, plug into, pool, put together, relate, slap on*, stand in with, synthesize, tack on*, tag on*, team up with*, throw in together*, tie up with*, unify, unite, wed; SEE CONCEPT *113*

combustible [*adj*] *able to be exploded*
burnable, comburent, combustive, explosive, fiery, firing, flammable, ignitable, incendiary, inflammable, kindling, volatile; SEE CONCEPTS *485,537*

combustion [*n*] *explosion; on fire*
agitation, candescence, disturbance, flaming, ignition, kindling, oxidization, thermogenesis, tumult, turmoil; SEE CONCEPTS *521,676,724*

come [*v1*] *advance, approach*
appear, arrive, attain, be accessible, be at disposal, become, be convenient, be handy, be obtainable, be ready, blow in*, bob up, breeze in*, burst, buzz*, check in*, clock in*, close in, draw near, drop in, enter, fall by, fall in, flare*, get, get in, happen, hit, hit town*, make it, make the scene*, materialize, move, move toward, near, occur, originate, pop in*, pop up*, punch in*, punch the clock*, reach, ring in*, roll in*, show, show up, sign in, sky in*, spring in, turn out, turn up, wind up at; SEE CONCEPT *159*

come [*v2*] *happen*
befall, betide, break, chance, come to pass, develop, fall, hap*, occur, take place, transpire, turn out; SEE CONCEPT *4*

come [v3] *extend, reach*
add up, aggregate, amount, become, come over, develop, expand, get, go, grow, join, mature, number, run, run into, spread, stretch, sum to, total, turn, wax; SEE CONCEPTS *239,701*

come about [v] *happen*
arise, befall, come to pass, occur, result, take place, transpire; SEE CONCEPT *701*

come across [v] *encounter, find*
bump into, chance upon, discover, happen upon, hit upon, light upon, meet, notice, stumble upon, uncover, unearth; SEE CONCEPTS *38,183*

come along [v] *progress, develop*
do well, get on, improve, mend, perk up, pick up, rally, recover, recuperate, show improvement; SEE CONCEPT *700*

come at [v1] *reach, attain*
accomplish, achieve, discover, feel for, find, grasp, succeed, touch, win; SEE CONCEPTS *34,706*

come at [v2] *attack*
assail, assault, charge, fall upon, fly at, go for, invade, light into, rush; SEE CONCEPT *86*

comeback [n1] *recovery, triumph*
improvement, rally, rebound, resurgence, return, revival, victory, winning; SEE CONCEPT *706*

comeback [n2] *snappy retort*
answer back, quip, rejoinder, repartee, reply, response, retaliation, riposte; SEE CONCEPT *278*

come back [v] *return*
come again, do better, reappear, recover, recur, reenter, remigrate, resume, triumph; SEE CONCEPT *239*

come between [v] *alienate*
divide, estrange, interfere, interpose, interrupt, intervene, meddle, part, put at odds, separate; SEE CONCEPTS *14,386*

come by [v1] *acquire*
get, lay hold of, obtain, procure, secure, take possession of, win; SEE CONCEPTS *124,129*

come by [v2] *visit someone*
call, come over, drop by, drop in, look in, look up, meet, pay a call, pop in, run in, see, step in, stop by, visit; SEE CONCEPT *227*

come clean [v] *acknowledge information*
admit, confess, explain, make clean breast*, own up, reveal; SEE CONCEPTS *49,57*

comedian [n] *funny person, often professional*
actor, banana*, card*, clown, comic, cutup, droll, entertainer, farceur, funnyman/woman, humorist, jester, joker, jokester, laugh, merry-andrew, million laughs*, quipster, stand-up comic, stooge*, top banana*, wag, wisecracker, wit*, zany*; SEE CONCEPTS *352,423*

comedown [n] *letdown, blow*
anticlimax, blow, collapse, comeuppance, crash, cropper*, decline, defeat, deflation, demotion, descent, disappointment, discomfiture, dive, down, downfall, failure, fall, flop*, humiliation, pratfall*,

reverse, ruin, setback, undoing, wreck; SEE CONCEPTS *674,699*

come down [v] *worsen*
decline, decrease, degenerate, descend, deteriorate, fail, fall, go downhill, reduce, suffer; SEE CONCEPT *698*

come down on [v] *criticize strongly*
attack, dress down, jump on, land on, rebuke, reprimand, scold; SEE CONCEPT *52*

come down with [v] *contract illness*
be stricken with, catch, contract, fall ill, fall victim to, sicken, take, take sick; SEE CONCEPTS *93,303*

comedy [n] *funny entertainment*
ball*, burlesque, camp, chaffing, comicality, comicalness, comic drama, drollery, drollness, facetiousness, farce, field day*, fun, fun and games*, funnies, funniness, gag show, grins, high camp*, high time, hilarity, hoopla, humor, humorousness, interlude, jesting, joking, laughs, light entertainment, merry-go-round*, picnic, play on, satire, schtick*, send-up, sitcom, slapstick, takeoff, travesty, wisecracking, witticism, wittiness; SEE CONCEPTS *263,293*

come forward [v] *volunteer services*
appear, make proposal, offer services, present oneself, proffer oneself; SEE CONCEPT *67*

come from [v] *arise, emanate*
accrue, derive from, ejaculate, emerge, end up, flow, hail from, issue, originate, proceed, result, rise, spring, stem, turn out; SEE CONCEPTS *105,179*

come in [v] *enter place*
alight, appear, arrive, cross threshold, disembark, finish, immigrate, intrude, land, pass in, reach, set foot in, show up; SEE CONCEPT *159*

come in for [v] *be eligible for something*
acquire, bear brunt, endure, get, receive, suffer; SEE CONCEPTS *23,124*

comely [adj] *beautiful*
attractive, beauteous, becoming, being a ten*, blooming, buxom, fair, fine, good-looking, gorgeous, graceful, handsome, nice, pleasing, pretty, pulchritudinous, stunning, wholesome, winsome; SEE CONCEPT *579*

come off [v] *transpire*
befall, betide, break, chance, click, come about, develop, go, go off, go over, hap*, happen, occur, pan out, prove out, succeed, take place; SEE CONCEPT *4*

come on [v1] *advance, progress*
develop, gain, improve, increase, make headway, proceed; SEE CONCEPT *704*

come on [v2] *appear, enter*
begin, come across, come into, come upon, encounter, meet, pass in, set foot in*, take place; SEE CONCEPT *119*

come out [v1] *make public*
appear, be announced, be brought out, be disclosed, be divulged, be exposed, be issued, be made known, be promulgated, be published, be released, be re-

ported, be revealed, break*, debut, get out, leak*, out, transpire; SEE CONCEPT *60*

come out [*v2*] *conclude*
end, result, terminate, transpire; SEE CONCEPT *119*

come out with [*v*] *disclose information*
acknowledge, bring out, chime in*, come clean, declare, deliver, divulge, lay open, own, own up, say, state, tell, throw out, utter; SEE CONCEPT *60*

come through [*v1*] *accomplish goal*
achieve, be successful, be victorious, carry out, chip in, contribute, kick in, pitch in, prevail, score, succeed, triumph, win; SEE CONCEPT *706*

come through [*v2*] *survive bad situation*
endure, live through, persist, pull through, ride, ride out, survive, weather storm*, withstand; SEE CONCEPT *23*

come up [*v*] *happen suddenly*
arise, crop up, occur, rise, spring up, turn up; SEE CONCEPT *119*

come up to [*v*] *meet expectations*
admit of comparison with, approach, arrive, bear comparison with, come near, compare with, equal, extend, get near, match, measure up to, rank with, reach, resemble, rival, stand comparison with; SEE CONCEPT *667*

come up with [*v*] *suggest, create*
advance, bring forth, compose, detect, discover, find, furnish, invent, offer, originate, present, produce, propose, provide, recommend, stumble upon, submit, uncover; SEE CONCEPTS *75,173*

comfort [*n1*] *good feeling; ease*
abundance, alleviation, amenity, assuagement, bed of roses*, cheer, cheerfulness, complacency, contentment, convenience, coziness, creature comforts, enjoyment, exhilaration, facility, gratification, happiness, luxury, opulence, peacefulness, pleasure, plenty, poise, quiet, relaxation, relief, repose, rest, restfulness, satisfaction, snugness, succor, sufficiency, warmth, well-being; SEE CONCEPTS *230, 410,720*

comfort [*n2*] *aid, help*
alleviation, assist, compassion, compensation, consolation, encouragement, hand, lift, pity, relief, secours, solace, succor, support, sympathy; SEE CONCEPTS *337,712*

comfort [*v*] *make to feel better*
abate, aid, allay, alleviate, ameliorate, assist, assuage, bolster, buck up*, calm, cheer, commiserate with, compose, condole, confirm, console, delight, divert, ease, encourage, enliven, free, gladden, grant respite, hearten, help, inspirit, invigorate, lighten burden, make well, mitigate, nourish, put at ease, quiet fears, reanimate, reassure, refresh, relieve, remedy, revitalize, revive, salve, soften, solace, soothe, strengthen, stroke, succor, support, sustain, sympathize, uphold, upraise; SEE CONCEPTS *7,22,572*

comfortable [*adj1*] *good feeling*
adequate, agreeable, appropriate, at rest, cared for, cheerful, complacent, contented, convenient, cozy,

delightful, easy, enjoyable, enjoying, gratified, hale, happy, healthy, hearty, loose, loose-fitting, made well, pleasant, pleased, protected, relaxed, relaxing, relieved, rested, restful, restored, satisfactory, satisfying, serene, sheltered, snug, snug as a bug in a rug*, soft, soothed, strengthened, untroubled, useful, warm, well-off; SEE CONCEPT *572*

comfortable [*adj2*] *affluent, wealthy*
ample, easy, enough, prosperous, substantial, sufficient, suitable, well-heeled, well-off, well-to-do; SEE CONCEPT *334*

comfortable [*adj3*] *more than adequate*
ample, commodious, cushy, luxurious, palatial, rich, roomy, spacious; SEE CONCEPT *485*

comforting [*adj*] *cheering*
abating, allaying, alleviating, analeptic, assuaging, consolatory, consoling, curing, encouraging, freeing, health-giving, heart-warming, inspiriting, invigorating, lightening, mitigating, reassuring, refreshing, relieving, remedying, restoring, revitalizing, revivifying, softening, solacing, soothing, succoring, sustaining, tranquilizing, upholding, warming; SEE CONCEPT *529*

comic [*n*] *funny person, often professional*
banana*, buffoon*, card*, clown, comedian, droll, funnyman/woman, gag man/woman, humorist, jester, joker, jokester, life of the party*, million laughs*, quipster, stand-up comic, stooge*, top banana*, wag*, wit*; SEE CONCEPTS *352,423*

comic/comical [*adj*] *amusing*
absurd, batty, boffo*, camp*, comical, crazy, dippy, diverting, dizzy, droll, entertaining, facetious, farcical, flaky*, fool, foolheaded, for grins*, freaky, funny, gelastic, goofus*, goofy, gump*, horse's tail*, humorous, ironic, jerky, jocular, joking, joshing, laughable, light, loony, ludicrous, Mickey Mouse*, nutty, off the wall*, priceless, ridiculous, risible, screwy, schtick*, side-splitting, silly, wacky, waggish, whimsical, witty; SEE CONCEPTS *401,529*

coming [*n*] *arrival*
accession, advent, approach, landing, reception; SEE CONCEPTS *119,159*

coming [*adj*] *approaching, promising*
about to happen, advancing, almost on one, anticipated, aspiring, at hand, certain, close, converging, deserving, docking, drawing near, due, en route, eventual, expected, fated, foreseen, forthcoming, future, gaining upon, getting near, immediate, imminent, impending, in prospect, instant, in store, in the offing, in the wind*, in view, marked, near, nearing, next, nigh, oncoming, ordained, predestined, preparing, progressing, prospective, pursuing, running after, subsequent, to be, up-and-coming; SEE CONCEPTS *537,799*

command [*n1*] *directive, instruction*
act, adjuration, ban, behest, bidding, call, canon, caveat, charge, citation, commandment, decree, demand, devoir, dictate, dictation, dictum, direction,

duty, edict, enactment, exaction, fiat, imperative, imposition, injunction, interdiction, law, mandate, notification, obligation, order, ordinance, precept, prescript, proclamation, prohibition, proscription, regulation, request, requirement, requisition, responsibility, rule, subpoena, summons, ultimatum, warrant, will, word, writ; SEE CONCEPTS *274,662*

command [*n2*] *rule, power*
ability, absolutism, aplomb, authority, authorization, charge, coercion, compulsion, constraint, control, despotism, domination, dominion, expertise, expertism, expertness, government, grasp, grip, hold, jurisdiction, know-how*, leadership, management, mastership, mastery, might, prerogative, primacy, restraint, right, royalty, skill, sovereignty, strings*, supervision, supremacy, sway, tyranny, upper hand*; SEE CONCEPT *376*

command [*v1*] *demand*
adjure, appoint, authorize, ban, bar, beckon, bid, call, call for, call on, call the signals*, call upon, charge, check, cite, compel, debar, dictate, direct, enact, enjoin, exact, forbid, force upon, give directions, give orders, grant, impose, inflict, inhibit, instruct, interdict, lay down the law, mark out, oblige, ordain, order, ordinate, proclaim, prohibit, put foot down*, require, requisition, restrain, rule out, send for, set, subpoena, summon, take charge, take lead, task, tell, warn; SEE CONCEPT *53*

command [*v2*] *rule, have power*
administer, boss, charge, check, coach, coerce, compel, conduct, conquer, constrain, control, curb, determine, dictate, direct, dominate, domineer, exact, exercise power, force, govern, guide, have authority, head, hinder, hold office, influence, lead, lord, manage, master, officiate, oppress, overbear, override, predominate, prescribe, preside over, prevail, push, regulate, reign, reign over, repress, restrain, run, stop, subdue, superintend, supervise, sway, take over, tyrannize, wield; SEE CONCEPTS *133,298*

commandeer [*v*] *seize, take over*
accroach, activate, annex, appropriate, arrogate, assume, confiscate, conscript, draft, enslave, expropriate, grab, hijack, liberate, moonlight requisition*, preempt, requisition, sequester, sequestrate, snatch, take, usurp; SEE CONCEPTS *90,142*

commander [*n*] *leader of military or other organization*
administrator, big cheese*, boss, captain, chief, CO*, commandant, czar, director, don, exec, guru, head, head honcho*, head man/woman*, higher up, high priest*, king, kingfish*, kingpin*, lead-off man/woman*, lord, mastermind, Mr./Ms. Big*, officer, point man/woman*, ruler, skipper, top banana*, top brass*, top dog*; SEE CONCEPTS *347,358*

commanding [*adj*] *superior, authoritative*
advantageous, arresting, assertive, autocratic, bossy, compelling, controlling, decisive, dictatorial, dominant, dominating, forceful, imperious, imposing, impressive, in charge, lofty, peremptory, striking; SEE CONCEPTS *536,574*

commemorate [*v*] *honor, observe occasion*
admire, celebrate, immortalize, keep, memorialize, monument, monumentalize, observe, pay tribute to, perpetuate, remember, salute, solemnize; SEE CONCEPTS *69,377,384*

commemoration [*n*] *honoring, observance*
celebration, ceremony, custom, memorial service, monumentalization, recognition, remembrance, tribute; SEE CONCEPT *377*

commemorative [*adj*] *in honor of something*
celebratory, commemoratory, dedicatory, in memory, in remembrance, memorial, observing; SEE CONCEPT *555*

commence [*v*] *start action*
arise, begin, come into being, come into existence, embark on, enter upon, get cracking*, get going, get one's feet wet*, get show on road*, hit the ground running*, inaugurate, initiate, jump into, kick off, launch, lead off, open, originate, start the ball rolling*, take up, tear into; SEE CONCEPTS *119,234*

commencement [*n*] *ceremony marking the beginning of stage*
admission, alpha, birth, bow, celebration, convocation, countdown, curtain-raiser*, dawn, dawning, genesis, graduation, initiation, kickoff, onset, opener, opening, outset, proem, services, start, starting point, tee off; SEE CONCEPT *377*

commend [*v1*] *recommend, praise*
acclaim, accredit, advocate, applaud, approve, boost, build, build up, compliment, countenance, endorse, eulogize, extol, give a posy*, gold star*, hail, hand it to*, hats off to*, hear it for*, kudize, laud, pat on the back*, puff up, sanction, speak highly of, stroke, support; SEE CONCEPTS *69,75*

commend [*v2*] *hand over with confidence*
assign, commit, confer, confide, consign, deliver, entrust, proffer, relegate, resign, tender, trust, turn over, yield; SEE CONCEPTS *108,132*

commendable [*adj*] *praiseworthy*
admirable, creditable, deserving, estimable, excellent, exemplary, laudable, meritable, meritorious, praisable, thankworthy, worthy; SEE CONCEPTS *527,572*

commendation [*n*] *giving of praise; acclaim*
acclamation, approbation, approval, award, bouquet, Brownie points*, credit, encomium, encouragement, good opinion, honor, panegyric, pat on the back*, pat on the head*, pay, plum, points, posy, PR*, puff, pumping up*, rave, recommendation, shot in the arm*, stroke, stroking, tribute; SEE CONCEPTS *69,337*

commensurate [*adj*] *adequate, corresponding*
appropriate, coextensive, comparable, compatible, consistent, due, equal, equivalent, fit, fitting, in accord, proportionate, sufficient, symmetrical; SEE CONCEPTS *563,566*

comment [n] *statement of opinion; explanation*
animadversion, annotation, backtalk*, buzz*, comeback*, commentary, crack*, criticism, dictum, discussion, editorial, elucidation, exposition, footnote, gloss, hearsay, illustration, input, judgment, mention, mouthful, note, obiter, observation, opinion, remark, report, review, two cents' worth*, wisecrack*; SEE CONCEPTS *51,278*

comment [v] *make statement of opinion, explanation*
affirm, animadvert, annotate, assert, bring out, clarify, commentate, conclude, construe, criticize, disclose, elucidate, explain, explicate, expound, express, gloss, illustrate, interject, interpose, interpret, mention, note, notice, observe, opine, pass on, point out, pronounce, reflect, remark, say, state, touch upon; SEE CONCEPTS *51,57*

commentary [n] *analysis*
annotation, appreciation, comment, consideration, criticism, critique, description, discourse, exegesis, explanation, exposition, gloss, narration, notes, obiter dictum, observation, remark, review, treatise, voice-over; SEE CONCEPTS *51,278*

commentator [n] *reporter*
analyst, annotator, announcer, correspondent, critic, expositor, interpreter, observer, pundit, reviewer, sportscaster, writer; SEE CONCEPT *356*

commerce [n] *buying and selling*
business, dealing, dealings, economics, exchange, industry, marketing, merchandising, merchantry, retailing, trade, traffic, truck, wholesaling; SEE CONCEPTS *325,770*

commercial [adj1] *concerning business, marketing*
across the counter*, bartering, commissary, economic, exchange, financial, fiscal, for sale, in demand, in the market, market, marketable, mercantile, merchandising, monetary, pecuniary, popular, profitable, profit-making, retail, retailing, saleable, sales, supplying, trade, trading, wholesale, wholesaling; SEE CONCEPT *536*

commercial [adj2] *intended for financial gain*
exploited, for profit, investment, materialistic, mercenary, monetary, money-making, pecuniary, profitmaking, venal, Wall Street*; SEE CONCEPT *334*

commercialize [v] *prepare for saleability*
advertise, cheapen, degrade, depreciate, develop as business, lessen, lower, make bring returns, make marketable, make pay, make profitable, make saleable, market, sell; SEE CONCEPT *324*

commingle [v] *blend*
amalgamate, combine, commix, compound, inmix, integrate, intermingle, intermix, join, merge, mingle, unite; SEE CONCEPT *109*

commiserate [v] *listen to woes of another*
ache, compassionate, condole, console, feel, feel for, have mercy, pity, share sorrow, sympathize; SEE CONCEPTS *110,596*

commission [n1] *task, duty*
agency, appointment, authority, brevet, certificate, charge, consignment, delegation, deputation, diploma, embassy, employment, errand, function, instruction, legation, mandate, mission, obligation, office, permit, power of attorney, proxy, trust, warrant, work; SEE CONCEPT *362*

commission [n2] *share of a profit*
allowance, ante, bite*, bonus, brokerage, chunk, compensation, cut, cut-in*, discount, end*, factorage, fee, indemnity, juice, pay, payment, percentage, piece, piece of the action*, rake-off, remuneration, royalty, salary, slice*, stipend, taste, vigorish; SEE CONCEPTS *329,344*

commission [n3] *group working together toward goal*
board, commissioners, committee, delegation, deputation, representative; SEE CONCEPT *381*

commission [v] *authorize or delegate task*
accredit, appoint, assign, bespeak, bid, charge, command, commit, confide to, consign, constitute, contract, crown, depute, deputize, dispatch, employ, empower, enable, engage, enlist, enroll, entrust, hire, inaugurate, induct, instruct, invest, license, name, nominate, ordain, order, select, send; SEE CONCEPTS *50,88,324,351*

commit [v1] *perform an action*
accomplish, achieve, act, carry out, complete, contravene, do, effectuate, enact, execute, go for broke*, go in for*, go out for*, offend, perpetrate, pull, pull off*, scandalize, sin, transgress, trespass, violate, wreak; SEE CONCEPTS *6,87*

commit [v2] *deliver, entrust*
allocate, allot, apportion, authorize, charge, commend, commission, confer trust, confide, consign, convey, delegate, deliver, depend upon, deposit, depute, deputize, destine, dispatch, employ, empower, engage, give, give to do, grant authority, hand over, hold, ice, imprison, institutionalize, intrust, invest, leave to, make responsible for, move, offer, ordain, promise, put away, put in the hands of, relegate, rely upon, remove, send, shift, submit, transfer, turn over to, vest; SEE CONCEPTS *108,143,217*

commitment [n] *assurance; obligation*
charge, committal, devoir, duty, engagement, guarantee, liability, must, need, ought, pledge, promise, responsibility, undertaking, vow, word; SEE CONCEPTS *71,271,274*

committee [n] *group working on project*
board, bureau, cabinet, chamber, commission, consultants, convocation, council, investigators, jury, panel, representatives, task force, trustees; SEE CONCEPT *381*

commodious [adj] *ample, spacious*
big, capacious, comfortable, convenient, expansive, extensive, large, loose, roomy, wide; SEE CONCEPTS *773,781*

commodity [n] *merchandise, possession*
article, asset, belonging, chattel, goods, line, material, object, produce, product, property, specialty, stock, thing, vendible, ware; SEE CONCEPTS *338,710*

common [*adj1*] *average, ordinary*
accepted, banal, bourgeois, casual, characteristic, colloquial, comformable, commonplace, conventional, current, customary, daily, everyday*, familiar, frequent, general, habitual, hackneyed, homely, humdrum, informal, mediocre, monotonous, natural, obscure, passable, plain, prevailing, prevalent, probable, prosaic, regular, routine, run-of-the-mill*, simple, stale, standard, stereotyped, stock, trite, trivial, typical, undistinguished, universal, unvaried, usual, wearisome, workaday, worn-out; SEE CONCEPT *547*

common [*adj2*] *generally known; held in common*
accepted, coincident, collective, communal, communistic, community, commutual, congruous, conjoint, conjunct, constant, corporate, correspondent, customary, general, generic, in common, intermutual, joint, like, mutual, popular, prevailing, prevalent, public, reciprocal, shared, social, socialistic, united, universal, usual, well-known, widespread; SEE CONCEPT *530*

common [*adj3*] *low, coarse behavior*
baseborn, characterless, cheap, colorless, crass, declassé, hack, hackneyed, impure, inferior, low-grade, mean, middling, nondescript, passable, pedestrian, Philistine, plebeian, poor, prosy, raffish, second-class, second-rate, shoddy, sleazy, stale, trite, undistinguished, vulgar; SEE CONCEPTS *401,545*

commonly [*adv*] *usually*
as a rule, by ordinary, frequently, generally, more often than not, ordinarily, regularly; SEE CONCEPTS *530,541*

commonplace [*n*] *clichéd saying or idea*
banality, bromide*, chestnut*, cliché, corn*, inanity, motto, platitude, prosaicism, prosaism, prose, rubber stamp*, shallowness, shibboleth, stereotype, tag, triteness, truism, triviality; SEE CONCEPTS *278,689*

commonplace [*adj*] *usual, everyday*
boiler plate*, characterless, clichéd, colorless, conventional, corny, customary, dime-a-dozen*, familiar, familiar tune, garden variety*, hackneyed, humdrum, lowly, mainstream, matter-of-course, mediocre, middle-of-the-road*, middling, mundane, natural, normal, obvious, ordinary, pedestrian, plebeian, prevalent, prosaic, run-of-the-mill*, stale, starch, stereotyped, threadbare, trite, typical, uneventful, unexceptional, uninteresting, unnoteworthy, vanilla*, widespread, workaday, worn-out; SEE CONCEPT *530*

common sense [*n*] *good reasoning*
acumen, cool, good sense, gumption, horse sense*, intelligence, levelheadedness, practicality, prudence, reasonableness, sense, sound judgment, soundness, wisdom, wit; SEE CONCEPT *409*

common-sense [*adj*] *reasonable*
astute, commonsensical, cool, down-to-earth, hard-headed, judicious, levelheaded, matter-of-fact, practical, rational, realistic, sane, sensible, shrewd, sound; SEE CONCEPT *402*

commonwealth [*n*] *political or geographic area*
body politic, citizenry, citizens, commonality, democracy, federation, nation, people, polity, republic, society; SEE CONCEPTS *301,512*

commotion [*n*] *clamor, uproar*
ado, agitation, annoyance, backwash, ballyhoo*, bedlam, big scene*, big stink*, brouhaha, bustle, clatter, combustion, confusion, convulsion, discomposure, disquiet, dither, excitement, ferment, fermentation, flap, flurry, furor, fuss, hell broke loose*, hubbub, hurly-burly, insurgence, insurrection, lather*, mutiny, outcry, pandemonium, perturbation, pother, racket, rebellion, revolt, riot, rumpus, stew, stir, to-do, tumult, turbulence, upheaval, uprising, upset, upturn, vexation, welter, whirl; SEE CONCEPTS *388,674*

communal [*adj*] *collective; shared*
common, communistic, community, conjoint, conjunct, cooperative, general, intermutual, joint, mutual, neighborhood, public; SEE CONCEPTS *536,708*

commune [*n*] *group living together*
collective, commonage, commonality, community, cooperative, family, kibbutz, municipality, neighborhood, rank and file, village; SEE CONCEPT *379*

commune [*v*] *communicate, experience with another*
confer, confide in, contemplate, converse, discourse, discuss, mediate, muse, parley, ponder, reflect; SEE CONCEPTS *17,266*

communicable [*adj*] *able to be contracted*
catching, communicative, contagious, expansive, infectious, pandemic, taking, transferable, transmittable; SEE CONCEPT *314*

communicate [*v1*] *give or exchange information, ideas*
acquaint, advertise, advise, announce, be in touch, betray, break, broadcast, carry, connect, contact, convey, correspond, declare, disclose, discover, disseminate, divulge, enlighten, get across, get through, hint, impart, imply, inform, interact, interface, keep in touch, let on, let out, make known, network, pass on, phone, proclaim, publicize, publish, raise, reach out, relate, report, reveal, ring up, signify, spread, state, suggest, tell, touch base, transfer, transmit, unfold, write; SEE CONCEPT *266*

communicate [*v2*] *mutually exchange information*
answer, associate with, be close to, be in touch, be near, buzz, cable, chat, commune with, confabulate, confer, converse, correspond, discourse, drop a line*, drop a note*, establish contact, get on the horn*, give a call, give a ring*, have confidence of, hear from, reach, reply, talk, telephone, wire, write; SEE CONCEPTS *56,266*

communication [*n1*] *giving, exchanging information, ideas*
advice, advisement, announcing, articulation, assertion, communion, connection, contact, conversation,

converse, correspondence, corresponding, declaration, delivery, disclosing, dissemination, elucidation, expression, intelligence, interchange, intercommunication, intercourse, link, making known, mention, notifying, publication, reading, reception, revelation, talk, talking, telling, transfer, translating, transmission, utterance, writing; SEE CONCEPT *266*

communication [*n2*] *information transmitted*
account, advice, announcement, briefing, bulletin, communiqué, conversation, converse, declaration, directive, disclosure, dispatch, excerpt, goods*, hot story*, ideas, info*, information, inside story*, intelligence, language, lowdown, message, missive, news, note, pipeline, poop*, precis, prophecy, publicity, report, revelation, scoop*, skinny*, speech, statement, summary, tidings, translation, utterance, warning, word, work; SEE CONCEPT *274*

communications [*n*] *systems of information exchange*
information technology, means, media, publicity, public relations, route, telecommunications, transport, travel; SEE CONCEPTS *349,770*

communicative [*adj*] *informative*
candid, chatty, communicable, conversable, conversational, demonstrative, effusive, enlightening, expansive, forthcoming, frank, garrulous, gushing, loquacious, open, outgoing, talkative, unreserved, voluble; SEE CONCEPT *267*

communion [*n1*] *affinity, agreement*
accord, association, closeness, close relationship, communing, concord, contact, converse, fellowship, harmony, intercommunication, intercourse, intimacy, participation, rapport, sympathy, togetherness, unity; SEE CONCEPT *684*

communion [*n2*] *sacrament in church; body of believers sharing a sacrament*
breaking of bread, church, creed, denomination, Eucharist, faith, Lord's Supper, Mass, persuasion, religion, sacrament; SEE CONCEPT *367*

communism [*n*] *socialist government*
Bolshevism, collectivism, Leninism, Marxism, rule of the proletariat, socialism, state ownership, totalitarianism; SEE CONCEPT *301*

community [*n1*] *society, area of people*
association, body politic, brotherhood, center, colony, commonality, commonwealth, company, district, general public, hamlet, locality, nation, neck of the woods*, neighborhood, people, populace, public, residents, society, state, stomping ground*, territory, turf; SEE CONCEPTS *379,512*

community [*n2*] *agreement, similarity*
affinity, identity, kinship, likeness, sameness, semblance; SEE CONCEPTS *664,670*

commute [*v1*] *travel to work*
drive, go back and forth, take the bus, take the subway, take the train; SEE CONCEPT *224*

commute [*v2*] *reduce punishment*
alleviate, curtail, decrease, mitigate, modify, remit, shorten, soften; SEE CONCEPTS *236,247,317*

commute [*v3*] *exchange, trade*
barter, change, convert, interchange, metamorphose, substitute, switch, transfer, transfigure, transform, translate, transmogrify, transmute, transpose; SEE CONCEPTS *104,232*

commuter [*n*] *daily traveler, usually for work*
city worker, driver, straphanger*, suburbanite, traveler; SEE CONCEPT *348*

compact [*n*] *agreement*
alliance, arrangement, bargain, bond, concordat, contract, convention, covenant, deal, engagement, entente, gentlemen's agreement, indenture, pact, settlement, stipulation, transaction, treaty, understanding; SEE CONCEPTS *271,684*

compact [*adj1*] *condensed*
appressed, bunched, close, compressed, crowded, dense, firm, hard, impenetrable, impermeable, packed, pressed, solid, thick, tight; SEE CONCEPTS *481,483,774*

compact [*adj2*] *short, brief*
boiled down, compendious, concise, epigrammatic, in a nutshell*, laconic, make a long story short*, marrowy, meaty, pithy, pointed, short and sweet*, succinct, terse, to the point; SEE CONCEPTS *773,798*

compact [*v*] *make condensed*
combine, compress, concentrate, condense, consolidate, contract, cram, integrate, pack, set, solidify, stuff, unify, unite; SEE CONCEPTS *137,208,250*

compact disc [*n*] *recording of music or speech*
album, CD, cut, cylinder, demo, digital recording, disk, laser disk, record, release, track; SEE CONCEPT *262*

companion [*n*] *helper, friend*
accompaniment, accomplice, aide, ally, amigo, assistant, associate, attendant, bro*, brother, buddy, chaperon, chum, colleague, comate, complement, comrade, concomitant, confederate, consort, convoy, counterpart, cousin, coworker, crony, cuz*, double, duenna, escort, fellow, governess, guide, match, mate, matron, nurse, pal, pard*, partner, playmate, protector, roomie*, safeguard, sidekick, sis*, sister, squire; SEE CONCEPT *423*

companionable [*adj*] *friendly*
affable, amicable, buddy buddy*, clubby*, complacent, congenial, conversable, convivial, cordial, cozy, cozy with, familiar, genial, good-natured, gregarious, intimate, mellow, neighborly, outgoing, pally, palsy*, sociable, social, tight, tight with*; SEE CONCEPT *555*

companionship [*n*] *friendship, accompaniment*
amity, brotherhood, camaraderie, company, comradeship, conviviality, esprit de corps, fellowship, fraternity, rapport, society, togetherness; SEE CONCEPT *388*

company [*n1*] *crowd of people*
aggregation, assemblage, assembly, association, band, body, circle, clan, clique, club, collection, community, concourse, congregation, convention,

corps, cortege, coterie, crew, ensemble, gang*, gathering, group, horde, jungle*, league, mob*, muster, order, outfit, pack, party, retinue, ring, ruck, set, team, throng, troop, troupe, turnout, zoo*; SEE CONCEPT 417

company [n2] *business concern*
association, business, concern, corporation, enterprise, establishment, firm, house, megacorp, multinational, outfit, partnership, syndicate; SEE CONCEPT 325

company [n3] *social friend, guest*
boarder, caller, companionship, cortege, fellowship, fraternity, party, presence, retinue, society, visitor; SEE CONCEPTS 417,423

comparable [adj1] *worthy of comparison*
a match for, as good as, commensurable, commensurate, equal, equipollent, equipotential, equivalent, in a class with, on a par, proportionate, tantamount; SEE CONCEPT 566

comparable [adj2] *corresponding, similar*
agnate, akin, alike, analogous, cognate, consonant, corresponding, like, parallel, related, relative, similar, undifferenced, uniform; SEE CONCEPTS 487,573

comparative [adj] *approximate, close to*
allusive, analogous, approaching, by comparison, comparable, conditional, connected, contingent, contrastive, correlative, corresponding, equivalent, in proportion, like, matching, metaphorical, near, not absolute, not positive, parallel, provisional, qualified, related, relative, restricted, rivaling, similar, vying, with reservation; SEE CONCEPTS 487,566,573

compare [v1] *examine in contrast*
analyze, approach, balance, bracket, collate, confront, consider, contemplate, contrast, correlate, divide, equal, examine, hang, hold a candle to*, inspect, juxtapose, match, match up, measure, observe, oppose, parallel, place in juxtaposition, ponder, rival, scan, scrutinize, segregate, separate, set against, set side by side, size up, stack up against, study, touch, weigh, weigh against another; SEE CONCEPTS 24,103

compare [v2] *liken, equate*
allegorize, approach, approximate to, assimilate, balance, bear comparison, be in the same class as*, be on a par with*, bring near, come up to, compete with, connect, correlate, distinguish between, draw parallel, equal, equate, hold a candle to*, identify with, link, make like, match, notice similarities, parallel, put alongside, relate, resemble, show correspondence, stack up with*, standardize, tie up, vie; SEE CONCEPT 39

comparison [n] *contrasting; corresponding*
allegory, analogizing, analogy, analyzing, association, balancing, bringing together, collating, collation, comparability, connection, contrast, contrasting, correlation, corresponding, discrimination, distinguishing, dividing, estimation, example, exemplification, identification, illustration, juxtaposition, like-

ness, likening, measuring, metaphor, observation, opposition, paralleling, ratio, relating, relation, resemblance, segregation, separation, similarity, testing, weighing; SEE CONCEPTS 24,39,529

compartment [n] *section, subdivision*
alcove, area, bay, berth, booth, carrel, carriage, category, cell, chamber, corner, cubbyhole, cubicle, department, division, hole, locker, niche, nook, part, piece, pigeonhole, place, portion, slot, stall; SEE CONCEPT 434

compass [n] *boundary, periphery*
ambit, area, bound, circle, circuit, circumference, circumscription, confines, domain, enclosure, environs, expanse, extent, field, limit, limitation, orbit, perimeter, precinct, purlieus, purview, radius, range, reach, realm, restriction, round, scope, sphere, stretch, sweep, zone; SEE CONCEPTS 484,651,787

compass [v1] *enclose*
beset, besiege, blockade, circle, circumscribe, encircle, encompass, environ, gird, girdle, hem in, ring, round, surround; SEE CONCEPT 758

compass [v2] *achieve, get*
accomplish, annex, attain, bring about, effect, execute, fulfill, gain, have, land, obtain, perform, procure, realize, secure, win; SEE CONCEPTS 142,706

compassion [n] *tender feeling*
benevolence, charity, clemency, commiseration, compunction, condolence, consideration, empathy, fellow feeling, grace, heart, humaneness, humanity, kindness, lenity, mercy, softheartedness, softness, sorrow, sympathy, tenderheartedness, tenderness, yearning; SEE CONCEPTS 410,633

compassionate [adj] *having tender feelings*
all heart, being big, benevolent, bleeding heart, charitable, commiserative, forbearing, going easy on*, humane, humanitarian, indulgent, kindhearted, kindly, lenient, living with, merciful, old softie*, piteous, pitying, responsive, softhearted, soft shell*, sparing, sympathetic, tender, tenderhearted, understanding, warm, warmhearted; SEE CONCEPTS 401, 403

compatibility [n] *harmony in relationship*
affinity, agreeableness, agreement, amity, congeniality, congruity, consonance, empathy, fit, likemindedness, rapport, single-mindedness, sympathy, unity; SEE CONCEPT 388

compatible [adj] *agreeable, in harmony*
accordant, adaptable, appropriate, congenial, congruent, congruous, consistent, consonant, cooperative, cotton to*, fit, fitting, getting along with, harmonious, having good vibes*, hitting it off*, in keeping, in sync with, in the groove*, like-minded, meet, on the same wavelength*, proper, reconcilable, simpatico, suitable, sympathetic, together; SEE CONCEPT 555

compel [v] *force to act*
bulldoze*, coerce, concuss, constrain, crack down, dragoon, drive, enforce, exact, hustle, impel, make,

make necessary, necessitate, oblige, put the arm on*, put the chill on*, restrain, shotgun*, squeeze, throw weight around*, turn on the heat*, urge; SEE CONCEPTS *14,384*

compendious [*adj*] *abridged*
abbreviated, breviloquent, brief, close, compact, compendiary, comprehensive, concise, condensed, contracted, curt, inclusive, laconic, short, short and sweet*, succinct, summarized, summary, synoptic; SEE CONCEPTS *773,789*

compendium [*n*] *abridgment*
abstract, aperçu, brief, conspectus, digest, epitome, essence, guide, handbook, manual, overview, pandect, precis, sketch, summary, survey, syllabus, sylloge; SEE CONCEPT *283*

compensate [*v1*] *make restitution*
atone, come down with*, commit, guerdon, indemnify, make good*, pay, pay up, plank out*, pony up*, recompense, recoup, refund, reimburse, remunerate, repay, requite, reward, satisfy, shell out*, take care of, tickle the palm*; SEE CONCEPTS *108,126,341*

compensate [*v2*] *offset, make up for*
abrogate, annul, atone for, balance, better, cancel out, counteract, counterbalance, counterpoise, countervail, fix, improve, invalidate, make amends, negate, negative, neutralize, nullify, outweigh, redress, repair, set off; SEE CONCEPTS *126,212*

compensation [*n*] *repayment; rectification*
advantage, allowance, amends, atonement, benefit, bonus, bread*, consideration, counterclaim, coverage, damages, defrayal, deserts*, earnings, fee*, gain, honorarium, indemnification, indemnity, meet, pay, payment, payoff, premium, profit, quittance, reciprocity, reckoning, recompense, recoupment, redress, reimbursement, remittal, remittance, remuneration, reparation, reprisal, requital, restitution, reward, salary, salt, satisfaction, scale, settlement, shake, stipend, take*, take-home*, wage; SEE CONCEPTS *337,344*

compete [*v*] *go up against in contest*
attempt, bandy, battle, be in the running*, bid, challenge, clash, collide, contend, contest, cope with, emulate, encounter, essay, face, fence, fight, go after, go for*, go for broke*, go for the gold*, grapple, in the hunt*, jockey for position*, joust, lock horns*, match strength, match wits*, oppose, participate in, pit oneself against*, play, rival, run for, scramble for*, seek prize, spar, strive, struggle, take on, take part, tilt, try, tussle, vie, wrestle; SEE CONCEPT *92*

competence [*n*] *ability*
adequacy, appropriateness, capability, capacity, competency, cutting it*, cutting the mustard*, expertise, fitness, hacking it*, know-how*, makings, making the grade*, might, moxie, proficiency, qualification, qualifiedness, savvy, skill, suitability, the goods*, the right stuff*, what it takes*; SEE CONCEPT *630*

competent [*adj*] *able*
adapted, adequate, all around, appropriate, au fait, being a pistol*, capable, clever, complete, crisp, decent, dynamite, efficient, endowed, enough, equal, fireball*, fit, fool, good, have savvy, know ins and outs*, know one's business*, know one's stuff*, know the answers*, know the ropes*, know the score*, masterly, no slouch*, one-man band*, on the ball*, paid one's dues*, pertinent, polished, proficient, qualified, satisfactory, skilled, sufficient, suitable, there, up to it, up to snuff*, up to speed*, wicked*; SEE CONCEPT *527*

competition [*n*] *contest*
antagonism, athletic event, bout, candidacy, championship, clash, concours, contention, controversy, counteraction, dog eat dog*, do or die*, emulation, encounter, engagement, event, fight, game, go for it, go for the gold*, horse race*, jungle*, match, matchup, meeting, one on one*, one-upmanship, opposition, pairing off, puzzle, quiz, race, racing, rat race*, rivalry, run, sport, strife, striving, struggle, tilt, tournament, trial, tug-of-war, warfare; SEE CONCEPTS *92,363*

competitive [*adj*] *willing to oppose*
aggressive, ambitious, antagonistic, at odds, combative, competing, cutthroat, dog-eat-dog*, emulous, killer*, killer instinct*, opposing, rival, streetwise, vying; SEE CONCEPT *542*

competitor [*n*] *person willing to enter contest*
adversary, antagonist, challenger, competition, contestant, corrival, dark horse*, emulator, favorite, me and you*, opponent, opposition, rival; SEE CONCEPTS *366,423*

compilation [*n*] *assemblage*
accumulating, accumulation, aggregating, anthology, assembling, assortment, collecting, collection, collocating, combining, compiling, consolidating, garner, garnering, gathering, incorporating, joining, treasury, unifying; SEE CONCEPTS *109,432*

compile [*v*] *assemble, accumulate*
abridge, amass, anthologize, arrange, assemble, bring together, collate, collect, colligate, collocate, compose, concentrate, congregate, consolidate, cull, draw together, edit, garner, gather, get together, glean, group, heap up, marshal, muster, organize, put together, recapitulate, unite; SEE CONCEPTS *79,84,109*

complacent [*adj*] *contented*
conceited, confident, easy-going, egoistic, egotistic, gratified, happy, obsequious, pleased, satisfied, self-assured, self-contented, self-pleased, self-possessed, self-righteous, self-satisfied, serene, smug, unconcerned; SEE CONCEPTS *401,403*

complain [*v*] *grumble about*
accuse, ascribe, attack, beef*, bellyache*, bemoan, bewail, bitch, carp, cavil, charge, contravene, criticize, defy, demur, denounce, deplore, deprecate, differ, disagree, disapprove, dissent, expostulate, find

fault, fret, fuss, gainsay, grieve, gripe, groan, grouse, growl, grumble, impute, indict, kick up a fuss*, lament, lay, look askance, make a fuss, moan, nag, object, oppose, protest, refute, remonstrate, repine, reproach, snivel, sound off, take exception to, wail, whimper, whine, yammer; SEE CONCEPT 52

complaint [n1] *statement of disagreement, discontent*
accusation, annoyance, beef*, cavil, CC*, charge, clamor, criticism, dissatisfaction, expostulation, fault-finding, grievance, gripe, grouse, grumble, guff*, jeremiad, kick, lament, moan, objection, plaint, protest, protestation, rap, remonstrance, remonstration, representation, reproach, rumble*, squawk, stink, trouble, wail, where's the beef*, whine; SEE CONCEPTS 52,689

complaint [n2] *illness, affliction*
affection, ailment, condition, disease, disorder, ill, indisposition, infirmity, malady, sickness, syndrome, upset; SEE CONCEPTS 306,316

complaisance [n] *agreeableness*
accommodativeness, acquiescence, compliance, courtesy, deference, friendliness, kindness, obligingness, politeness, respect; SEE CONCEPT 633

complaisant [adj] *agreeable*
accommodating, amiable, compliant, conciliatory, deferential, easy, easy-going, friendly, generous, good-humored, good-natured, good-tempered, indulgent, lenient, mild, obliging, polite, solicitous, submissive; SEE CONCEPT 401

complement [n] *companion, counterpart*
accompaniment, addition, aggregate, augmentation, balance, capacity, completion, consummation, correlate, correlative, counterpart, enhancement, enrichment, entirety, filler, finishing touch, makeweight, pendant, quota, remainder, rest, rounding-off*, supplement, total, totality; SEE CONCEPTS 635,824

complement [v] *complete*
accomplish, achieve, cap, clinch, conclude, consummate, crown, finish, fulfill, integrate, perfect, round off, top off; SEE CONCEPTS 91,119,234

complementary [adj] *filling, completing*
commutual, complemental, completing, completory, conclusive, correlative, correspondent, corresponding, crowning, equivalent, fellow, integral, integrative, interconnected, interdependent, interrelated, interrelating, matched, mated, paired, parallel, reciprocal; SEE CONCEPTS 577,824

complete [adj1] *total, not lacking*
all, entire, exhaustive, faultless, full, full-dress, gross, hook line and sinker*, imperforate, intact, integral, integrated, lock stock and barrel*, organic, outright, plenary, replete, the works*, thorough, thoroughgoing, unabbreviated, unabridged, unbroken, uncondensed, uncut, undiminished, undivided, undocked, unexpurgated, unimpaired, unitary, unreduced, whole, whole enchilada*, whole-hog*, whole-length, whole nine yards*; SEE CONCEPT 531

complete [adj2] *finished*
accomplished, achieved, all-embracing, all-inclusive, all over, all over but the shouting*, attained, compassed, concluded, consummate, done, done with, down, effected, ended, entire, executed, fini*, finished off, full, full-fledged, home free*, perfect, plenary, realized, sweeping, terminated, that's it*, through; SEE CONCEPT 528

complete [adj3] *utter, absolute*
blank, blanket, categorical, consummate, downright, dyed-in-the-wool*, flawless, impeccable, out-and-out, outright, perfect, positive, sheer, thorough, thoroughgoing, total, unblemished, unconditional, unmitigated, unqualified, whole; SEE CONCEPTS 531,535

complete [v] *carry out action*
accomplish, achieve, actualize, bring to fruition, bring to maturity, call it a day*, cap, carry off, close, conclude, consummate, crown, determine, develop, discharge, do, do thoroughly, effect, effectuate, elaborate, end, equip, execute, fill, finalize, finish, fulfill, furnish, get through, go the limit*, go through with, go whole hog*, halt, make good*, make up, perfect, perform, put to bed*, realize, refine, round off, round out, settle, sew up*, supplement, terminate, ultimate, wind up*, wrap up*; SEE CONCEPT 91

completely [adv] *entirely*
absolutely, all the way*, altogether, competently, comprehensively, conclusively, effectively, en masse, exclusively, exhaustively, extensively, finally, from A to Z*, from beginning to end*, fully, heart and soul*, hook line and sinker*, in all, in entirety, in full, in toto*, on all counts*, painstakingly, perfectly, quite, solidly, thoroughly, totally, to the end, to the limit, to the max*, to the nth degree*, ultimately, unabridged, unanimously, unconditionally, undividedly, utterly, wholly, without omission; SEE CONCEPT 531

completion [n] *accomplishment, finishing*
achievement, ain't no more*, attainment, close, conclusion, consummation, culmination, curtains*, dispatch, end, expiration, finalization, finish, fruition, fulfillment, hips*, integration, perfection, realization, swan song*, that's all folks*, that's all there is*, windup*, wrap-up; SEE CONCEPTS 119,706

complex [n1] *composite, aggregate*
association, compound, conglomerate, ecosystem, entanglement, group, network, organization, scheme, structure, syndrome, synthesis, system, totality; SEE CONCEPTS 432,770

complex [n2] *psychological problem*
anxiety, a thing about something*, exaggerated reaction, fear, fixation, fixed idea, hang-up*, idée fixe, insanity, mania, neurosis, obsession, phobia, preoccupation, repression; SEE CONCEPT 410

complex [adj1] *involved, intricate*
circuitous, complicated, composite, compound, compounded, confused, conglomerate, convoluted,

elaborate, entangled, heterogeneous, knotty, labyrinthine, manifold, mingled, miscellaneous, mixed, mixed-up, mosaic, motley, multifarious, multiform, multiple, multiplex, tangled, tortuous, variegated; SEE CONCEPT *562*

complex [*adj2*] *difficult to understand*
abstruse, bewildering, Byzantine, circuitous, complicated, confused, convoluted, crabbed, cryptic, Daedalean, discursive, disordered, disturbing, enigmatic, entangled, excursive, Gordian, hidden, impenetrable, inscrutable, interwoven, intricate, involved, jumbled, knotted, knotty, labyrinthine, mazy, meandering, mingled, mixed, muddled, obscure, paradoxical, perplexing, puzzling, rambling, recondite, round-about, sinuous, snarled, sophisticated, tangled, tortuous, undecipherable, unfathomable, winding; SEE CONCEPTS *402,529*

complexion [*n1*] *skin coloring, appearance*
cast, color, coloration, coloring, flush, front, glow, hue, looks, mug*, phiz*, pigmentation, skin, skin tone, texture, tinge, tint, tone; SEE CONCEPTS *405,622*

complexion [*n2*] *someone's character*
appearance, aspect, cast, countenance, disposition, guise, humor, ilk, individualism, individuality, kind, light, look, make-up, nature, personality, seeming, semblance, sort, stamp, style, temper, temperament, type; SEE CONCEPT *411*

complexity [*n*] *complicatedness*
complication, convolution, elaboration, entanglement, intricacy, involvement, multiplicity, ramification; SEE CONCEPT *663*

compliance [*n*] *agreement*
acquiescence, amenability, assent, complaisance, concession, concurrence, conformity, consent, deference, docility, obedience, observance, passivity, resignation, submission, submissiveness, tractibility, yielding; SEE CONCEPTS *411,684*

complicate [*v*] *confuse, make difficult*
add fuel to fire*, bedevil, clog, combine, confound, convolute, derange, disarrange, disorder, elaborate, embroil, entangle, fold, foul up*, handicap, impede, infold, interfuse, interrelate, interweave, involve, jumble, make intricate, make waves*, mix up, muck up*, muddle, multiply, obscure, open can of worms*, perplex, ravel, render unintelligible, screw up*, snafu*, snag, snarl up*, tangle, twist, upset; SEE CONCEPTS *7,19*

complicated [*adj*] *difficult, complex*
abstruse, arduous, Byzantine, can of worms*, convoluted, Daedalean, difficult, elaborate, entangled, fancy, gasser*, Gordian, hard, hi tech*, interlaced, intricate, involved, knotty, labyrinthine, mega factor*, mind blower*, mixed, perplexing, problematic, puzzling, rat's nest*, recondite, snake pit*, sophisticated, troublesome, various, wheels within wheels*; SEE CONCEPTS *562,565*

complication [*n*] *difficult situation*
aggravation, complexity, confusion, development, difficulty, dilemma, drawback, embarrassment, entanglement, factor, intricacy, obstacle, problem, snag, web; SEE CONCEPTS *230,674*

complicity [*n*] *conspiracy*
abetment, agreement, collaboration, collusion, complot, concurrence, confederacy, connivance, engineering, guilt, guiltiness, implication, intrigue, involvement, machination, manipulation, partnership; SEE CONCEPTS *388,660*

compliment [*n*] *praise, flattery*
acclaim, acclamation, admiration, adulation, applause, appreciation, approval, blessing, bouquet*, buttering up*, cajolery, commendation, comp, confirmation, congratulations, courtesy, encomium, endorsement, eulogy, favor, felicitation, good word, homage, honor, kudo*, laud, laudation, notice, orchid*, ovation, panegyric, pat on the back*, posy*, regard, respects, sanction, sentiment, trade-last, tribute, veneration; SEE CONCEPTS *69,278*

compliment [*v*] *praise, flatter*
acclaim, adulate, applaud, butter up*, cajole, celebrate, charm, cheer, commemorate, commend, congratulate, endorse, eulogize, exalt, extol, fawn upon, felicitate, give bouquet*, glorify, hail, hand it to*, honor, ingratiate oneself with, kudize*, laud, magnify, make much of, panegyrize, pat on the back*, pay respects, pay tribute to, please, puff up*, recommend, roose, salute, sanction, satisfy, sing praises of, soothe, speak highly of, take off hat to*, toast, trade last, warm fuzzy*, wish joy to, worship; SEE CONCEPT *69*

complimentary [*adj1*] *flattering*
adulatory, appreciative, approbative, approbatory, approving, celebrating, commendatory, congratulatory, courtly, encomiastic, encomiastical, eulogistic, fair-spoken, fawning, highly favorable, honeyed, honoring, laudatory, panegyrical, plauditory, polite, praiseful, respectful, sycophantic, unctuous, well-wishing, with highest recommendation, with high praise; SEE CONCEPT *267*

complimentary [*adj2*] *free*
as a perk*, chargeless, comp, costless, courtesy, donated, free lunch*, free of charge, gratis, gratuitous, honorary, on the house*; SEE CONCEPT *334*

comply [*v*] *abide by, follow agreement or instructions*
accede, accord, acquiesce, adhere to, agree to, cave in, come around, conform to, consent to, cry uncle*, defer, discharge, ditto, don't make waves*, don't rock the boat*, fit in, fold, fulfill, give in, give out, give up, go along with, go with the flow*, keep, knuckle to*, knuckle under*, mind, obey, observe, perform, play ball*, play the game*, put out, quit, respect, roll over and play dead*, satisfy, shape up, stay in line*, straighten up, submit, throw in towel*, toss it in*, yes one*, yield; SEE CONCEPTS *8,35,91*

component [*n*] *part, element*
constituent, factor, fixings, ingredient, item, making, makings, peripheral, piece, plug-in, segment, unit; SEE CONCEPTS *831,834*

component [*adj*] *constituent*
basic, composing, elemental, fundamental, inherent, integral, intrinsic, part and parcel of*, part of; SEE CONCEPTS *546,567*

compose [*v1*] *be part of construction*
be an adjunct, be an element of, belong to, be made of, build, compound, comprise, consist of, constitute, construct, enter in, fashion, form, go into, make, make up, merge in; SEE CONCEPTS *168,642*

compose [*v2*] *create writing, artwork, or music*
author, bang out*, cast, clef*, coin a phrase, comp, conceive, contrive, cook up*, design, devise, discover, draw up, dream up, fabricate, forge, form, formulate, frame*, fudge together*, ghost*, ghostwrite, imagine, indite, invent, knock off*, knock out*, make up, note down, orchestrate, originate, pen, poetize, produce, push pencil*, put down, put pen to paper*, score, scribble, script, set type, set up, time, turn out, whip up*, write; SEE CONCEPTS *79,173,174*

compose [*v3*] *calm, bring under control*
adjust, allay, appease, arrange, assuage, balm, becalm, check, collect, comfort, console, contain, control, cool, ease, ease up, hold in, lessen, let up, lull, mitigate, moderate, modulate, pacify, placate, quell, quiet, re-collect, reconcile, regulate, rein, relax, repress, resolve, restrain, settle, simmer down, slacken, smother, soften, solace, soothe, still, suppress, temper, tranquilize, tune down; SEE CONCEPTS *7,22,117*

composed [*adj*] *calm, collected*
at ease, calmed, clearheaded, commonsensical, confident, cool, cool as cucumber*, disimpassioned, easy, easygoing, have one's act together*, imperturbable, keeping a stiff upper lip*, keeping one's shirt on*, levelheaded, nonchalant, not turn a hair*, placid, poised, possessed, quieted, relaxed, repressed, sedate, self-assured, self-possessed, sensible, serene, serious, soothed, staid, suppressed, sure of oneself, temperate, together, tranquil, unflappable, unruffled, untroubled; SEE CONCEPT *401*

composite [*n*] *combination, mixture*
amalgam, amalgamation, blend, combo, commixture, complex, compost, compound, conglomerate, fusion, immixture, intermixture, medley, mix, olio, pasteup*, stew*, synthesis, union; SEE CONCEPTS *260,432*

composite [*adj*] *combined, mixed*
blended, complex, compound, conglomerate, melded, synthesized; SEE CONCEPT *490*

composition [*n1*] *structure, arrangement*
agreement, architecture, balance, beauty, combination, concord, configuration, consonance, constitution, content, design, distribution, form, formation, harmony, layout, make-up, placing, proportion, relation, rhythm, spacing, style, symmetry, weave; SEE CONCEPTS *733,757*

composition [*n2*] *written or musical creation*
arrangement, article, chart, concerto, dissertation, drama, essay, exercise, exposition, fiction, getup*, literary work, manuscript, melody, music, novel, number, opus, paper, piece, play, poetry, rhapsody, romance, score, setup*, short story, song, stanza, study, symphony, theme, thesis, tune, verse, work, writing; SEE CONCEPTS *259,260,263,271*

compost [*n*] *organic material*
admixture, blend, commixture, composition, compound, fertilizer, fusion, humus, manure, mix, mixture, mulch, ordure, pile; SEE CONCEPT *509*

composure [*n*] *calmness, collectedness*
accord, aplomb, assurance, balance, calm, contentment, control, cool*, cool head*, coolheadedness, coolness, dignity, dispassion, ease, equanimity, equilibrium, evenness, even temper, fortitude, harmony, imperturbability, inexcitability, levelheadedness, moderation, nonchalance, peace of mind, placidity, poise, polish, presence of mind, quietude, repose, sang-froid, sedateness, self-assurance, self-control, self-possession, serenity, sobriety, stability, tranquility; SEE CONCEPT *410*

compound [*n*] *combination, mixture*
admixture, aggregate, alloy, amalgam, amalgamation, blend, combo, commixture, composite, composition, compost, conglomerate, fusion, goulash, lorelei, medley, mishmash*, soup, stew, synthesis, union; SEE CONCEPTS *260,432*

compound [*v1*] *mix, combine*
admix, amalgamate, associate, blend, bracket, coadunate, coagment, coalesce, comingle, commingle, commix, concoct, connect, couple, fuse, immix, intermingle, join, link, make up, meld, mingle, synthesize, unite; SEE CONCEPTS *109,113*

compound [*v2*] *make difficult; complicate*
add to, aggravate, augment, confound, confuse, exacerbate, extend, heighten, intensify, magnify, make complex, make intricate, multiply, worsen; SEE CONCEPTS *231,240*

comprehend [*v1*] *understand*
appreciate, apprehend, assimilate, capeesh*, catch, click, cognize, conceive, dig*, discern, envisage, envision, fathom, get*, get the picture*, gotcha*, grasp, have, know, make out*, perceive, read, savvy*, see, take in, tumble*; SEE CONCEPT *15*

comprehend [*v2*] *include*
comprise, contain, embody, embrace, enclose, encompass, have, involve, subsume, take in; SEE CONCEPT *118*

comprehensible [*adj*] *understandable*
apprehensible, clear, coherent, comprehendible, conceivable, explicit, fathomable, graspable, intelligible, knowable, lucid, luminous, plain; SEE CONCEPTS *402,529*

comprehension [*n*] *understanding*
aha*, apperception, apprehension, awareness, capacity, cognizance, conception, discernment, double

comprehension take*, grasp, intelligence, judgment, ken, knowledge, perception, prehension, realization, sense, slow take*, take*; SEE CONCEPT *409*

comprehensive [*adj*] *inclusive*
absolute, across the board*, all-embracing, all-inclusive, blanket, broad, catholic, compendious, complete, comprising, containing, discursive, encircling, encyclopedic, exhaustive, expansive, extensive, far-reaching, full, general, global, in depth, infinite, lock stock and barrel*, of great scope, overall, sweeping, syoptic, the big picture*, the whole shebang*, the works*, thorough, umbrella, wall-to-wall*, whole, wide, widespread; SEE CONCEPTS *531,772*

compress [*v*] *compact, condense*
abbreviate, abridge, abstract, bind, boil down*, coagulate, concentrate, consolidate, constrict, contract, cram, cramp, crowd, crush, decrease, dehydrate, densen, densify, epitomize, force into space, make brief, narrow, pack, press, press together, ram, reduce, restrict, shorten, shrink, shrivel, squash, squeeze, stuff, summarize, syncopate, telescope*, tighten, wedge, wrap; SEE CONCEPTS *208,236,247*

comprise [*v*] *make up, consist of*
add up to, amount to, be composed of, be contained in, compass, compose, comprehend, constitute, contain, cover, embody, embrace, encircle, enclose, encompass, engross, form, hold, include, incorporate, involve, span, subsume, sum up, take in; SEE CONCEPT *643*

compromise [*n*] *agreement, give-and-take*
accommodation, accord, adjustment, arrangement, bargain, compact, composition, concession, contract, copout*, covenant, deal, fifty-fifty*, half and half, half measure, happy medium*, mean, middle course, middle ground, pact, sellout, settlement, trade-off, understanding, win-win situation*; SEE CONCEPTS *230,684*

compromise [*v1*] *give and take*
adjust, agree, arbitrate, compose, compound, concede, conciliate, find happy medium*, find middle ground*, go fifty-fifty*, make a deal, make concession, meet halfway, negotiate, play ball with*, settle, split the difference*, strike balance, trade off; SEE CONCEPT *8*

compromise [*v2*] *put in jeopardy*
blight, cop out*, discredit, dishonor, embarrass, endanger, explode, expose, give in, hazard, imperil, implicate, jeopardize, mar, menace, peril, prejudice, put under suspicion, risk, ruin, sell out, spoil, weaken, whore; SEE CONCEPTS *101,240*

compulsion [*n*] *drive, obligation*
coercion, constraint, demand, drive, driving, duress, duty, engrossment, exigency, force, hang-up, have on the brain*, monkey*, necessity, need, obsession, preoccupation, prepossession, pressure, tiger by the tail*, urge, urgency; SEE CONCEPTS *410,532*

compulsive [*adj*] *driving, obsessive*
besetting, compelling, enthusiastic, irresistible, overwhelming, passionate, uncontrollable, urgent; SEE CONCEPT *401*

compulsory [*adj*] *binding*
compulsatory, de rigueur, forced, imperative, imperious, mandatory, necessary, obligatory, required, requisite; SEE CONCEPT *546*

compunction [*n*] *regret, sorrow*
attrition, conscience, contrition, misgiving, penitence, penitency, pity, punctiliousness, qualm, reluctance, remorse, repentance, rue, ruth, second thoughts, shame, stab of conscience, sympathy; SEE CONCEPT *410*

computation [*n*] *performing arithmetic*
calculation, ciphering, computing, counting, data processing, estimating, estimation, figuring, gauge, guess, reckoning, summing, totalling; SEE CONCEPT *764*

compute [*v*] *calculate, estimate*
add up, cast up, cipher, count, count heads, count noses, cut ice*, dope out*, enumerate, figure, figure out, gauge, keep tabs*, measure, rate, reckon, run down, size up, sum, take account of, take one's measure, tally, tot*, total, tote*, tote up*; SEE CONCEPT *764*

computer [*n*] *calculating, data processing machine*
abacus, adding machine, analog, artificial intelligence, brain*, calculator, clone, CPU, data processor, digital, electronic brain*, laptop*, MAC, mainframe, micro, microcomputer, mini, minicomputer, number cruncher*, PC, personal computer, thinking machine*; SEE CONCEPTS *269,463*

comrade [*n*] *ally*
associate, bosom buddy, buddy, chum, colleague, comate, companion, compatriot, compeer, confederate, confidant, confidante, coworker, crony, fellow, friend, intimate, mate, pal, partner, sidekick; SEE CONCEPT *423*

con [*n*] *trick*
bluff, cheat, crime, deception, double-cross, dupe, fraud, gold brick*, graft, gyp*, mockery, swindle, take in; SEE CONCEPT *59*

con [*v*] *deceive, defraud*
bamboozle*, bilk, cajole, cheat, chicane, coax, double-cross, dupe, flimflam*, fool, hoax, hoodwink, hornswoggle*, humbug, inveigle, mislead, rip off*, rook, sweet-talk*, swindle, trick, wheedle; SEE CONCEPT *59*

concatenation [*n*] *connection, sequence*
chain, connecting, continuity, integration, interlocking, link, linking, nexus, series, succession, uniting; SEE CONCEPTS *721,727*

concave [*adj*] *curved, depressed*
biconcave, cupped, dented, dimpled, dipped, excavated, hollow, hollowed, incurvate, incurvated, incurved, indented, round, rounded, sagging, scooped, sinking, sunken; SEE CONCEPT *486*

conceal [v] *hide, disguise*
beard, burrow, bury, cache, camouflage, cloak, couch, cover, cover up, dissemble, ditch, duck, ensconce, enshroud, harbor, hole up*, keep dark, keep secret, lie low*, lurk, mask, masquerade, obscure, plant*, put in a hole*, screen, secrete, shelter, skulk, slink, sneak, stash, stay out of sight, stow, tuck away, veil, wrap; SEE CONCEPT *188*

concealed [adj] *hidden, secret*
buried, cached, camouflaged, covered, covered up, covert, enshrouded, guarded, holed up, hushed up, hush-hush*, incog*, incognito, inconspicuous, masked, obscure, obscured, on the Q.T.*, perdu, planted, privy, put in the hole*, recondite, screened, secreted, shrouded, stashed, tucked away, ulterior, under wraps*, unseen, veiled; SEE CONCEPTS *576,619*

concealment [n] *hiding, secrecy*
beard, blind, camouflage, cover, covering, cover-up, curtain, disguise, dissimulation, fig leaf*, front, hideaway, hide-out, laundromat, mask, obliteration, obscuration, occultation, privacy, red herring*, secretion, smoke screen*, veil, wraps*; SEE CONCEPTS *188,631*

concede [v] *acknowledge, give in*
accept, accord, admit, allow, avow, award, bury the hatchet*, capitulate, cave in, cede, confess, cry uncle*, ditto, fess up*, fold, give up, go along with, go with the flow*, grant, hand over, knuckle under, let on, own, own up, play ball with*, quit, relinquish, say uncle*, surrender, throw in the towel*, waive, yes one*, yield; SEE CONCEPTS *35,57,82,235*

conceit [n] *egotism*
amour-propre, arrogance, complacence, complacency, consequence, immodesty, narcissism, outrecuidance, pomposity, pride, self-admiration, self-exaltation, self-importance, self-love, self-regard, smugness, snottiness, stuffiness, swagger, swelled head*, vainglory, vainness, vanity; SEE CONCEPT *411*

conceited [adj] *egotistical*
arrogant, bigheaded*, big talking, cocky, conceity, full of hot air*, gall, ham*, hot stuff*, immodest, know-it-all, loudmouth, narcissistic, overweening, phony, puffed up*, self-important, smart-alecky*, snotty*, stuck up*, swollen-headed*, vain, vainglorious, windbag*; SEE CONCEPT *404*

conceivable [adj] *reasonable, easy to understand*
believable, convincing, credible, earthly, imaginable, likely, mortal, possible, probable, supposable, thinkable; SEE CONCEPTS *529,552*

conceive [v1] *understand*
accept, appreciate, apprehend, assume, believe, catch, compass, comprehend, deem, dig, envisage, expect, fancy, feel, follow, gather, get, grasp, imagine, judge, perceive, realize, reckon, suppose, suspect, take, twig; SEE CONCEPT *15*

conceive [v2] *create*
become pregnant, brainstorm, cogitate, consider, contrive, cook up*, depicture, design, develop, devise, dream up, envisage, envision, fancy, feature, form, formulate, head trip*, image, imagine, make up, meditate, originate, ponder, produce, project, purpose, realize, ruminate, spark, speculate, spitball, think up, trump up*, visualize; SEE CONCEPTS *35,173,251*

concentrate [v1] *think about closely*
apply, attend, be engrossed in, bring to bear, brood over, center, consider closely, contemplate, crack one's brains*, direct attention, establish, examine, fixate, fix attention, focus, focus attention, get on the beam*, give attention, hammer*, hammer away at*, head trip*, intensify, knuckle down, meditate, muse, need, occupy thoughts, peruse, ponder, pour it on, put, put mind to, rack one's brains*, rivet, ruminate, scrutinize, set, settle, study, sweat, think hard, weigh; SEE CONCEPT *17*

concentrate [v2] *gather, collect*
accumulate, agglomerate, aggregate, amass, assemble, bunch, center, centralize, cluster, coalesce, collect, combine, compact, compress, congest, conglomerate, congregate, consolidate, constrict, contract, converge, cramp, crowd, draw together, eliminate, embody, focalize, focus, forgather, garner, get to the meat*, heap, heap up, hoard, huddle, integrate, intensify, localize, mass, muster, narrow, nutshell*, pile, reduce, salt away, store, strengthen, swarm, unify, zero in*; SEE CONCEPTS *84,109*

concentrated [adj1] *condensed, reduced*
boiled down, complete, crashed*, entire, evaporated, fixed, full-bodied, lusty, potent, rich, robust, straight, strong, stuffed*, telescoped*, thick, thickened, total, unadulterated, undiffused, undiluted, undivided, unmingled, unmixed, whole; SEE CONCEPTS *483,554*

concentrated [adj2] *intense*
all-out, deep, desperate, exquisite, fierce, furious, hard, intensive, terrible, vehement, vicious; SEE CONCEPTS *326,569*

concentration [n1] *consolidation of effort*
absorption, amassing, application, assembly, bringing to bear, centering, centralization, close attention, clustering, coalescing, combination, compacting, compression, concern, congregation, consolidation, convergence, converging, debate, deliberation, fixing, flocking, focusing, heed, huddling, intensification, massing, narrowing, need, single-mindedness, study, unity; SEE CONCEPT *677*

concentration [n2] *aggregation*
accumulation, army, array, audience, band, cluster, collection, company, concourse, convergence, flock, group, herd, horde, mass, miscellany, mob, party; SEE CONCEPT *432*

concept [n] *idea*
abstraction, apprehension, approach, big idea*, brainchild*, brain wave*, conceit, conception, conceptualization, consideration, fool notion*, hypothesis, image, impression, intellection, notion,

perception, slant, supposition, theory, thought, twist, view, wrinkle; SEE CONCEPTS *532,689*

conception [*n1*] *understanding; idea*
apperception, appreciation, apprehension, clue, cogitating, cognition, communing, comprehension, conceit, concentrating, concept, consideration, considering, deliberating, design, dreaming, envisaging, explanation, exposition, fancy, fancying, image, imagining, impression, inkling, intellection, interpretation, meditating, meditation, mental grasp, musing, notion, perception, philosophizing, picture, plan, realization, representation, speculating, speculation, thought, version; SEE CONCEPTS *409,410,689*

conception [*n2*] *beginning, birth*
fertilization, formation, germination, impregnation, inception, initiation, insemination, invention, launching, origin, outset, start; SEE CONCEPTS *119,302, 373,375*

concern [*n1*] *business, responsibility*
affair, burden, care, charge, company, corporation, deportment, entanglement, enterprise, establishment, field, firm, house, interest, involvement, job, jungle*, matter, megacorp, mission, multinational, occupation, organization, outfit, shooting match*, task, thing, transaction, worry, zoo*; SEE CONCEPTS *325,362,532*

concern [*n2*] *interest; anxiety*
apprehension, attention, bearing, care, carefulness, concernment, consideration, disquiet, disquietude, distress, heed, heedfulness, important matter, matter, reference, regard, relation, relevance, solicitude, tender loving care, unease, worry; SEE CONCEPTS *410,690*

concern [*v1*] *affect personally*
apply to, bear on, become involved, be relevant to, bother, disquiet, distress, disturb, interest, involve, make anxious, make uneasy, pertain to, perturb, regard, take pains, touch, trouble, worry; SEE CONCEPTS *7,19,22*

concern [*v2*] *relate to, have reference to*
answer to, appertain to, apply to, be about, be applicable to, bear on, bear upon, be connected with, be dependent upon, be interdependent with, belong to, be pertinent to, be well taken, deal with, depend upon, have a bearing on, have connections with, have implications for, have relation to, have significance for, have to do with, involve, pertain to, refer to, regard; SEE CONCEPT *532*

concerned [*adj1*] *worried*
anxious, biting one's nails*, bothered, butterflies in stomach*, distressed, disturbed, exercised, in a stew*, on pins and needles*, perturbed, tied up in knots*, troubled, uneasy, upset, uptight, worried sick*; SEE CONCEPT *403*

concerned [*adj2*] *involved with*
active, affected, attentive, caring, down with, implicated, in on, interested, mixed up, privy to, solicitous; SEE CONCEPTS *401,403*

concert [*n1*] *musical performance*
gig, jam session, musical, musicale, recital, rockfest, selections, show; SEE CONCEPT *263*

concert [*n2*] *agreement, harmony*
accord, chorus, collaboration, concord, concordance, consonance, joint, league, togetherness, tune, unanimity, union, unison; SEE CONCEPTS *388,684*

concerted [*adj*] *coordinated*
agreed upon, collaborative, combined, joint, mutual, planned, prearranged, united; SEE CONCEPT *538*

concession [*n*] *yielding, adjustment*
acknowledgment, admission, allowance, assent, authorization, boon, buyback, compromise, confession, copout*, deal, giveback, giving in, grant, indulgence, permission, permit, privilege, rollback, sellout, surrender, trade-off, warrant; SEE CONCEPTS *13,50,67,88*

conciliatory [*adj*] *placid, yielding*
appeasing, assuaging, calm, civil, disarming, irenic, mollifying, pacific, peaceable, placating, placatory, propitiative, quiet, willing; SEE CONCEPT *401*

concise [*adj*] *short, to the point*
abridged, boiled down*, breviloquent, brief, compact, compendiary, compendious, compressed, condensed, curt, epigrammatic, in a nutshell*, laconic, lean, marrowy, meaty, pithy, short and sweet*, succinct, summary, synoptic, terse; SEE CONCEPTS *773,798*

conclave [*n*] *secret meeting*
assembly, buzz session*, cabinet*, confab*, conference, council, encounter, gathering, get-together, huddle, meet, parley, powwow*, private meeting, session; SEE CONCEPTS *324,384*

conclude [*v1*] *finish, come to an end*
achieve, bring down curtain*, call it a day*, cease, cinch, clinch, close, close out, complete, consummate, crown, desist, draw to close, end, halt, knock off, put the lid on*, put to bed*, round off, stop, terminate, top off, ultimate, wind up, wrap up; SEE CONCEPTS *119,234*

conclude [*v2*] *decide, deduce*
add up to, adjudge, analyze, assume, be afraid, boil down to*, collect, derive, draw, figure, gather, have a hunch*, infer, intuit, judge, make, make out, presume, ratiocinate, reason, reckon, sum up, suppose, surmise, the way one sees it*; SEE CONCEPTS *18,37*

conclude [*v3*] *settle, resolve*
accomplish, achieve, bring about, carry out, clinch, confirm, decide, determine, effect, establish, fix, pull off, rule, work out; SEE CONCEPTS *18,91,126*

conclusion [*n1*] *end*
cease, cessation, close, closure, completion, consequence, culmination, denouement, desistance, development, ending, end of the line, eventuality, finale, finish, issue, outcome, payoff, period, result, stop, termination, that's all folks*, upshot, when the fat lady sings*, windup, wrap; SEE CONCEPTS *119,832*

conclusion [n2] *judgment, decision*
agreement, conviction, corollary, deduction, determination, illation, inference, opinion, ratiocination, resolution, resolve, sequitur, settlement, verdict; SEE CONCEPT *689*

conclusive [adj] *definite, final*
absolute, all out*, clear, clinching, cogent, compelling, convincing, deciding, decisive, demonstrative, determinant, determinative, flat out*, incontrovertible, indisputable, irrefragable, irrefrangible, irrefutable, irrevocable, litmus test*, precise, resolving, revealing, settling, straight out, telling, ultimate, unambiguous, unanswerable, unarguable, unconditional, undeniable, unmistakable, unquestionable, what you see is what you get*; SEE CONCEPT *535*

concoct [v] *formulate, think up*
ad lib, batch*, brew*, compound, contrive, cook up, create, design, devise, discover, dream up, envisage, envision, fabricate, frame*, hatch, invent, make up, mature, originate, plan, plot, prefab*, prepare, project, scheme, slap together*, throw together*, vamp; SEE CONCEPTS *36,173,251*

concoction [n] *creation, blend*
brew, combination, compound, contrivance, intention, medley, mixture, plan, preparation, project, solution; SEE CONCEPTS *260,432,660*

concomitant [adj] *contributing, accompanying*
accessory, adjuvant, agreeing, ancillary, associated with, associative, attendant, attending, belonging, coefficient, coetaneous, coeval, coexistent, coincident, coincidental, collateral, complementary, concordant, concurrent, conjoined, conjoined with, connected, contemporaneous, contemporary, coordinate, corollary, coterminous, coupled with, fellow, incident, in tempo, in time, isochronal, isochronous, joint, satellite, synchronal, synchronous, synergetic, synergistic; SEE CONCEPT *577*

concord [n1] *unity, harmony*
accord, agreement, amity, calmness, chime, comity, concert, concordance, consensus, consonance, friendship, goodwill, peace, placidity, rapport, serenity, tranquility, tune, unanimity, understanding, unison; SEE CONCEPT *388*

concord [n2] *agreement, treaty*
compact, concordat, contract, convention, entente, pact, protocol; SEE CONCEPTS *271,684*

concourse [n1] *passageway*
avenue, boulevard, entrance, foyer, hall, highway, lobby, lounge, meeting place, path, rallying point*, road, street; SEE CONCEPTS *440,501*

concourse [n2] *crowd, group*
assemblage, assembly, collection, concursion, confluence, convergence, crush, gang, gathering, joining, junction, linkage, meeting, mob, multitude, rout, throng; SEE CONCEPT *432*

concrete [adj1] *actual, factual*
accurate, corporeal, definite, detailed, explicit, material, objective, particular, precise, real, sensible, solid, specific, substantial, tangible; SEE CONCEPTS *535,582*

concrete [adj2] *hardened*
caked, calcified, cemented, compact, compressed, congealed, conglomerated, consolidated, dried, firm, indurate, monolithic, petrified, poured, precast, set, set in stone*, solid, solidified, steeled, strong, unyielding; SEE CONCEPT *604*

concur [v] *agree, approve*
accede, accord, acquiesce, assent, band, be consonant with, be in harmony, coadjute, coincide, collaborate, combine, come together, consent, cooperate, cut a deal*, equal, harmonize, jibe*, join, league*, meet, okay, pass on, shake on, unite; SEE CONCEPTS *8,10,82*

concurrent [adj1] *simultaneous*
circumstantial, coeval, coexisting, coincident, concerted, concomitant, contemporaneous, incidental, in sync, parallel, synchronal, synchronous; SEE CONCEPT *799*

concurrent [adj2] *agreeing, converging*
allied, at one, centrolineal, coinciding, compatible, concerted, confluent, consentient, consistent, convergent, cooperating, coterminous, harmonious, in agreement, in rapport, joined, like-minded, meeting, mutual, of the same mind, unified, uniting; SEE CONCEPT *563*

concussion [n] *collision, shaking*
blast, blow, buffeting, bump, clash, clout, crack, crash, hit, impact, injury, jar, jarring, jolt, jolting, jounce, pounding, punch, shock, trauma; SEE CONCEPTS *189,309,521*

condemn [v] *blame, convict*
adjudge, belittle, blow whistle on*, call down*, castigate, censure, chide, come down on*, criticize, damn, decry, denounce, denunciate, deprecate, depreciate, disapprove, disparage, doom, find fault with, find guilty, frame, hang something on*, judge, knock, lay at one's door*, let have it*, name, pass sentence on*, pin it on*, point finger at*, pronounce, proscribe, punish, put away, put down, reprehend, reproach, reprobate, reprove, send up, send up the river*, sentence, skin, thumbs down on*, upbraid; SEE CONCEPTS *44,52,317*

condemnation [n] *blaming, conviction*
accusation, blame, censure, damnation, denouncement, denunciation, disapproval, doom, judgment, proscription, reproach, reprobation, reproof, sentence, stricture; SEE CONCEPTS *44,52,317*

condensation [n1] *abridgment*
abstract, boildown*, breviary, brief, compendium, compression, concentration, consolidation, conspectus, contraction, curtailment, digest, epitome, essence, precis, reduction, summary, synopsis; SEE CONCEPTS *283,730*

condensation [n2] *water buildup*
condensate, crystallization, deliquescence, dew, distillation, liquefaction, precipitate, precipitation, rainfall; SEE CONCEPT *514*

condense [v] *abridge*
abbreviate, blue pencil*, boil down, chop, coagulate, compact, compress, concentrate, constrict, contract, curtail, cut, cut down, decoct, densen, digest, edit, encapsulate, epitomize, inventory, nutshell*, precipitate, precis, press together, reduce, shorten, shrink, snip, solidify, sum, summarize, summate, synopsize, telescope, thicken, trim; SEE CONCEPTS *236,247*

condescend [v] *stoop, humble oneself*
accommodate, accord, acquiesce, agree, be courteous, bend, come down off high horse*, comply, concede, degrade oneself, deign, demean oneself, descend, favor, grant, high hat*, lower oneself, oblige, see fit, submit, talk down to, toss a few crumbs*, unbend, vouchsafe, yield; SEE CONCEPT *633*

condescending [adj] *snobby, lordly*
arrogant, complaisant, disdainful, egotistic, la-dee-da*, lofty, patronizing, snobbish, snooty*, snotty*, supercilious, superior, uppish, uppity; SEE CONCEPT *401*

condescension [n] *disdain, superiority*
airs, civility, deference, haughtiness, loftiness, lordliness, patronage, patronizing attitude, superciliousness, toleration; SEE CONCEPT *633*

condition [n1] *circumstances*
action, ballgame, case, estate, happening, how it goes*, how things are*, how things stack up*, lay of the land*, like it is, mode, order, plight, position, posture, predicament, quality, rank, repair, reputation, riff, scene, shape, situation, size of it, sphere, spot, standing, state, state of affairs, status, status quo, trim, way things are*, way things shape up*, where it's at*; SEE CONCEPT *639,696*

condition [n2] *requirement, limitation*
arrangement, article, catch, codicil, contingency, demand, essential, exception, exemption, fine print*, kicker*, modification, must, necessity, postulate, precondition, prerequisite, provision, proviso, qualification, requisite, reservation, rule, sine qua non, small print*, stipulation, strings*, terms; SEE CONCEPTS *270,687*

condition [n3] *physical shape, fitness*
appearance, aspect, build, constitution, fettle, form, health, kilter, mint, order, phase, repair, state, status, tone, trim; SEE CONCEPTS *316,757*

condition [n4] *illness*
affection, ailment, complaint, disease, ill, infirmity, malady, predicament, problem, syndrome, temper, weakness; SEE CONCEPT *306*

condition [v] *adapt, prepare*
accustom, brainwash, build up, educate, equip, habituate, inure, loosen up, make ready, modify, practice, program, ready, shape up, sharpen, tone up, toughen up, train, warm up, whip into shape*, work out, work over; SEE CONCEPTS *35,202*

conditional [adj] *dependent*
codicillary, contingent, depending on, fortuitous, granted on certain terms, guarded, iffy*, incidental, inconclusive, limited, modified, not absolute, obscure, provisional, provisory, qualified, relative, reliant, relying on, restricted, restrictive, subject to, tentative, uncertain, with grain of salt*, with reservations, with strings attached*; SEE CONCEPT *554*

condolence [n] *sympathy*
comfort, commiseration, compassion, condolement, consolation, fellow feeling, solace; SEE CONCEPT *633*

condone [v] *make allowance for*
buy*, disregard, excuse, forget, forgive, give green light*, go along with, ignore, lap up*, let it by*, let it come*, let pass*, look the other way*, nod at*, okay, overlook, pardon, pass over, remit, wink at*; SEE CONCEPTS *10,23*

conducive [adj] *favorable for*
accessory, calculated to produce, contributive, contributory, helpful, leading, productive of, promotive, tending, useful; SEE CONCEPT *542*

conduct [n1] *administration*
care, carrying on*, channels, charge, control, direction, execution, guidance, handling, intendance, leadership, management, manipulation, organization, oversight, plan, policy, posture, red tape*, regimen, regulation, rule, running, strategy, superintendence, supervision, tactics, transaction, treatment, wielding; SEE CONCEPT *117*

conduct [n2] *behavior*
address, attitude, bearing, carriage, comportment, demeanor, deportment, manner, manners, mien, posture, stance, tenue, ways; SEE CONCEPT *633*

conduct [v1] *administer*
accompany, attend, call the tune*, carry on*, chair, chaperon, control, convey, direct, engineer, escort, govern, guide, handle, head, keep, lead, manage, operate, ordain, order, organize, oversee, pilot, preside over, regulate, ride herd on*, rule, run, run things, shepherd, steer, supervise, trailblaze*, usher, wield baton*; SEE CONCEPT *117*

conduct [v2] *comport oneself*
acquit, act, bear, behave, carry, demean, deport, go on, quit; SEE CONCEPT *384*

conduct [v3] *transport*
accompany, attend, bring, carry, chaperon, companion, convoy, escort, guide, lead, move, pass on, pilot, route, send, shepherd, show, steer, transfer; SEE CONCEPT *187*

conduit [n] *passage*
aqueduct, cable, canal, channel, conductor, course, culvert, duct, flow, flume, gully, gutter, lead-in, lead-out, main, pipe, pipeline, race, sewer, spout, trough, tube, watercourse; SEE CONCEPTS *499,501*

cone [n] *circular-shaped object with pointed end*
conoid, pyramid, raceme, strobile, strobiloid; SEE CONCEPT *436*

confection [n] *sweet food*
cake, candy, dainty, jam, pastry, sweet; SEE CONCEPT *457*

confederacy [n] *coalition*
alliance, anschluss, bond, compact, confederation, conspiracy, covenant, federation, government, league, organization, union; SEE CONCEPTS *299, 301*

confederate [n] *abettor*
accessory, accomplice, ally, associate, coconspirator, collaborator, colleague, conspirator, fellow, fellow traveler, partner, rebel; SEE CONCEPT *412*

confederate [adj] *allied*
amalgamated, associated, combined, corporate, federal, federated, in alliance, incorporated, leagued, organized, syndicated, unionized; SEE CONCEPT *536*

confer [v1] *discuss, deliberate*
advise, argue, bargain, blitz*, brainstorm, breeze*, collogue, confab*, confabulate, consult, converse, deal, debate, discourse, flap*, gab*, get heads together*, give meeting*, groupthink*, huddle, jaw, kick ideas around*, negotiate, parley, pick one's brain*, powwow*, speak, talk, toss ideas around*, treat; SEE CONCEPT *56*

confer [v2] *giving honor, award*
accord, allot, award, bestow, donate, gift with, give, grant, lay on, present, provide, sweeten the kitty*, vouchsafe; SEE CONCEPT *132*

conference [n1] *convention, colloquium*
appointment, argument, chat, colloquy, confabulation, conferring, congress, consultation, conversation, convocation, deliberation, discussion, forum, gabfest*, groupthink*, huddle, interchange, interview, meeting, palaver, parley, powwow*, round robin, round table, seminar, symposium, talk, think-in*, ventilation; SEE CONCEPTS *56,324,386*

conference [n2] *league of athletic teams*
association, athletic union, circuit, league, loop, organization, ring; SEE CONCEPT *365*

confess [v] *admit, confirm*
acknowledge, affirm, allow, assert, attest, aver, avow, blow, blurt out, chirp, clue in, come clean*, come out, concede, confide, declare, disclose, divulge, dump on*, evince, finger*, fink*, grant, humble oneself, leak*, let on*, level with, make clean breast of*, manifest, narrate, open one's heart*, own, own up, post, profess, prove, rat on, recognize, relate, reveal, sing*, snitch*, sound off*, spill the beans*, spit out*, squeal*, tip hand*, unload*, vent, weasel*; SEE CONCEPT *60*

confession [n] *admittance of information*
acknowledgment, admission, affirmation, allowance, assenting, assertion, avowal, concession, declaration, disclosing, disclosure, divulgence, enumeration, exposé, exposure, making public, narration, owning up, proclamation, profession, publication, recitation, relation, revealing, revelation, song*,

squawk*, squeal*, statement, story, telling, unbosoming, utterance; SEE CONCEPTS *60,274*

confidant [n] *close friend*
acquaintance, adherent, adviser, alter ego, bosom buddy, companion, crony, familiar, intimate, mate, pal; SEE CONCEPT *423*

confide [v1] *divulge information*
admit, bend an ear*, breathe, buzz*, confess, crack to, disclose, hint, impart, insinuate, intimate, lay it on*, lay the gaff*, let in on*, reveal, spill to, suggest, tell, unload on*, whisper; SEE CONCEPT *57*

confide [v2] *entrust*
bestow, charge, commend, commit, consign, delegate, hand over, present, relegate, trust; SEE CONCEPT *108*

confidence [n1] *belief in oneself*
aplomb, assurance, backbone, boldness, brashness, certainty, cool, courage, daring, dash, determination, elan, faith in oneself, fearlessness, firmness, fortitude, grit, hardihood, heart, impudence, intrepidity, mettle, morale, nerve, pluck, poise, presumption, reliance, resoluteness, resolution, self-possession, self-reliance, spirit, spunk, sureness, tenacity; SEE CONCEPT *411*

confidence [n2] *belief in something*
assurance, credence, dependence, faith, hope, reliance, stock, store, sure bet, trust; SEE CONCEPT *689*

confident [adj1] *certain, assured*
bet on*, bold, brave, cocksure*, convinced, counting on, courageous, dauntless, depending on, expectant, expecting, fearless, having faith in, high*, hopeful, intrepid, positive, presuming, presumptuous, puffed up*, pushy, racked, sanguine, satisfied, secure, self-assured, self-reliant, self-sufficient, sure, trusting, unafraid, undaunted, upbeat, uppity, valiant; SEE CONCEPTS *403,404*

confidential [adj] *secret*
arcane, backdoor, classified, closet, hushed, hush-hush*, inside, intimate, off the record*, private, privy; SEE CONCEPTS *267,576*

confidentially [adv] *in secret*
behind closed doors*, between ourselves, between us, between you and me*, covertly, don't breathe a word*, hushedly, in confidence, in on the ground floor*, off the cuff*, off the record*, personally, privately, sub rosa; SEE CONCEPTS *267,576*

confine [v] *enclose, limit*
bar, bastille, bind, bound, cage*, circumscribe, constrain, cool, cool down, cramp, delimit, detain, enslave, fix, hem in, hinder, hog-tie*, hold back, ice*, immure, imprison, incarcerate, intern, jail, keep, put a lid on*, put away, put on ice*, repress, restrain, restrict, send up, shorten, shut up; SEE CONCEPTS *121,130*

confined [adj] *limited, enclosed*
bedfast, bedridden, bottled up, bound, chilled, circumscribed, compassed, cooped up, cramp, cramped, detained, flattened out, grounded, ham-

pered, held, hog-tied*, iced*, immured, imprisoned, incarcerated, in chains, incommodious, indisposed, in jail, invalided, jailed, laid up, locked up, on ice*, pent, restrained, restricted, sealed up, shut in, sick; SEE CONCEPT *554*

confinement [*n1*] *imprisonment; restriction*
bonds, bounding, bounds, check, circumscription, coercion, constrainment, constraint, control, cramp, curb, custody, delimitation, detention, immuration, incarceration, internment, jail, keeping, limitation, repression, safekeeping, trammels; SEE CONCEPTS *90,191*

confinement [*n2*] *pregnancy and childbirth*
accouchement, childbed, delivery, labor, lying-in, one's time, parturition, travail; SEE CONCEPTS *302,316,373*

confines [*n*] *boundaries*
borders, bounds, circumference, compass, country, dimension, edge, end, environs, extent, limits, orbit, periphery, precinct, proportions, purlieus, purview, radius, range, reach, region, scope, sweep, term, terrain, territory; SEE CONCEPTS *484,745,787*

confirm [*v1*] *ratify, validate, prove*
affirm, approve, attest, authenticate, back, bear out, bless, buy, certify, check, check out, circumstantiate, corroborate, debunk, double-check, endorse, establish, explain, give green light*, give high sign*, give stamp of approval*, give the go-ahead*, give the nod*, justify, lap up, make good*, make sure, okay, rubber-stamp*, sanction, settle, sign, sign off on*, size up, subscribe, substantiate, support, thumbs up*, underpin, uphold, verify, vouch, warrant, witness; SEE CONCEPTS *57,103*

confirm [*v2*] *reinforce*
assure, buttress, clinch, establish, fix, fortify, invigorate, make firm, settle, strengthen; SEE CONCEPTS *244,250*

confirmation [*n*] *ratification, validation, proof*
acceptance, accepting, accord, admission, affirmation, affirming, agreement, approval, assent, attestation, authenticating, authentication, authorization, authorizing, avowal, consent, corroborating, corroboration, endorsement, evidence, go ahead*, green light*, nod, okay, passage, passing, proving, recognition, sanction, sanctioning, stamp of approval*, substantiation, support, supporting, testament, testimonial, testimony, validating, verification, verifying, visa, witness; SEE CONCEPTS *661,685*

confirmed [*adj*] *habitual; rooted*
accepted, accustomed, chronic, deep-rooted, deepseated, dyed-in-the-wool*, entrenched, firmly established, fixed, habituated, hardened, hard-shell*, ingrained, inured, inveterate, long-established, proved, rooted, seasoned, settled, staid, valid, worn; SEE CONCEPTS *542,798*

confiscate [*v*] *steal; seize*
accroach, annex, appropriate, arrogate, assume, commandeer, confisticate, expropriate, glom on

to*, grab, hijack, impound, liberate, moonlight requisition*, possess oneself of, preempt, sequester, sequestrate, swipe, take, take over, usurp; SEE CONCEPTS *139,142*

conflagration [*n*] *large fire*
blaze, bonfire, burning, flaming, holocaust, inferno, rapid oxidation, up in smoke*, wildfire; SEE CONCEPTS *249,478*

conflict [*n1*] *fight, warfare*
battle, clash, collision, combat, competition, contention, contest, emulation, encounter, engagement, fracas, fray, rivalry, set-to, strife, striving, struggle, tug-of-war, war; SEE CONCEPTS *106,320*

conflict [*n2*] *disagreement, discord*
affray, animosity, antagonism, bad blood*, brush, competition, concours, contention, contest, dance, difference, disaccord, dispute, dissension, dissent, dissidence, disunity, divided loyalties, faction, factionalism, flap, fray, friction, fuss, hassle, hostility, interference, meeting, opposition, row, ruckus, run-in, set-to, strife, variance; SEE CONCEPTS *106,388, 674*

conflict [*v*] *be at odds*
brawl, bump heads with*, clash, collide, combat, contend, contest, contrast, cross swords with*, differ, disaccord, disagree, discord, disharmonize, disturb, fight, interfere, jar, lock horns with*, mismatch, oppose, romp, run against tide*, scrap, slug, square off with, strive, struggle, tangle, vary; SEE CONCEPTS *46,106*

conflicting [*adj*] *contradictory*
adverse, antagonistic, antipathetic, at odds with, clashing, contrariant, contrary, disconsonant, discordant, discrepant, dissonant, incompatible, incongruent, incongruous, inconsistent, inconsonant, opposed, opposing, paradoxical, unfavorable, unmixable; SEE CONCEPTS *542,570*

confluence [*n*] *coming together*
assemblage, assembly, concourse, concurrence, concursion, conflux, convergence, crowd, gathering, host, junction, meeting, mob, multitude, union; SEE CONCEPTS *109,114*

conform [*v1*] *adjust, adapt*
accommodate, attune, be guided by, clean up act*, comply, coordinate, don't make waves*, don't rock the boat*, fall in with, fit, follow, follow beaten path*, follow the crowd, go by the book*, go with the flow*, harmonize, integrate, keep, make room, meet halfway, mind, move over, obey, observe, play the game, proportion, quadrate, reconcile, reconciliate, roll with punches*, run with the pack*, shape up, square, straighten up, suit, tailor, tailor-make*, toe the line*, tune, yield; SEE CONCEPT *13*

conform [*v2*] *correspond, match*
accord, agree, assimilate, be regular, dovetail, fit in, fit the pattern, go, harmonize, jibe, square, suit, tally; SEE CONCEPT *664*

conformable [*adj*] *appropriate; matching*
adapted, agreeable, alike, amenable, applicable, assorted, comparable, compliant, consistent, docile, fitted, fitting, harmonious, in agreement, like, matched, obedient, orderly, proper, regular, resembling, similar, submissive, suitable, suited, tractable, unified, useable, well-regulated; SEE CONCEPTS *487,558,563,573*

conformation [*n*] *shape*
anatomy, arrangement, build, cast, configuration, figure, form, formation, frame, framework, outline, structure, symmetry, type; SEE CONCEPTS *754,757*

conformity [*n1*] *compliance*
acquiescence, allegiance, assent, consent, conventionality, docility, obedience, observance, orthodoxy, resignation, submission, willingness; SEE CONCEPTS *13,689*

conformity [*n2*] *correspondence, harmony*
accord, affinity, agreement, coherence, conformance, congruity, consistency, consonance, likeness, resemblance, similarity; SEE CONCEPT *664*

confound [*v*] *confuse*
abash, amaze, astonish, astound, baffle, befog, bewilder, blend, bug*, commingle, confute, discombobulate*, discomfit, discountenance, dumbfound, embarrass, faze, fiddle, flabbergast, jumble, metagrobolize, misidentify, mix, mix up*, mystify, nonplus, perplex, pose, puzzle, rattle, screw up*, startle, surprise, throw*; SEE CONCEPTS *16,42*

confront [*v*] *challenge*
accost, affront, beard, brave, call one's bluff*, come up against*, dare, defy, encounter, face down*, face up to*, face with*, flout, front, go one-on-one*, go up against*, make my day*, meet, meet eyeball-to-eyeball*, oppose, repel, resist, scorn, stand up to, tell off, withstand; SEE CONCEPTS *46,52,54*

confrontation [*n*] *conflict*
affray, battle, contest, crisis, dispute, encounter, fight, meeting, set-to, showdown, strife; SEE CONCEPTS *46,106*

confuse [*v1*] *bewilder someone*
abash, addle, amaze, astonish, baffle, becloud, bedevil, befuddle, bemuse, cloud, clutter, complicate, confound, darken, daze, demoralize, discomfit, discompose, disconcert, discountenance, disorient, distract, embarrass, faze, fluster, fog, frustrate, fuddle, involve, lead astray, mess up*, misinform, mislead, mortify, muddle, mystify, nonplus, obscure, perplex, perturb, puzzle, rattle, render uncertain, shame, stir up, stump, throw off, throw off balance*, trouble, unhinge, unsettle, upset, worry; SEE CONCEPT *16*

confuse [*v2*] *mix up; involve*
bedlamize, blend, clutter, confound, disarrange, disarray, discombobulate*, discreate, disorder, disorganize, embroil, encumber, entangle, intermingle, involve, jumble, litter, mess up*, mingle, mistake, muddle, muss up, rumple, snarl up, tangle, tousle, tumble; SEE CONCEPT *112*

confused [*adj1*] *disoriented mentally*
abashed, addled, at a loss*, at sea*, at sixes and sevens*, baffled, befuddled, bewildered, come apart*, dazed, discombobulated*, disconcerted, disorganized, distracted, flummoxed, flustered, fouled up*, glassy-eyed*, gone*, misled, mixed up, muddled, nonplussed, not with it*, out to lunch*, perplexed, perturbed, punch-drunk*, punchy*, puzzled, screwy*, shook up*, shot to pieces*, slaphappy, spaced out*, stumped, taken aback, thrown, thrown off balance*, unglued*, unscrewed*, unzipped*; SEE CONCEPT *403*

confused [*adj2*] *mixed up, disordered*
anarchic, blurred, chaotic, disarranged, disorderly, disorganized, haywire, in a muddle, in disarray, involved, jumbled, messy, miscalculated, miscellaneous, mistaken, misunderstood, obscured, out of order, snafu*, snarled, topsy-turvy, unsettled, untidy; SEE CONCEPT *585*

confusion [*n1*] *disorientation*
abashing, abashment, addling, agitation, befuddlement, befuddling, bemusement, bewilderment, blurring, chagrin, cluttering, commotion, confounding, demoralization, disarranging, discomfiting, discomfiture, disorientation, distraction, disturbing, dither, dumbfounding, embarrassing, embarrassment, embroiling, flap, fluster, lather, mixup, mystification, obscuring, perplexing, perplexity, perturbation, pother, puzzlement, stew, stirring up, tangling, tumult, turbulence, turmoil, unsettling, upsetting; SEE CONCEPT *14*

confusion [*n2*] *disoriented state*
abashment, ado, anarchy, astonishment, bustle, chaos, clutter, commotion, complexity, complication, consternation, daze, difficulty, disarray, discomposure, dislocation, disorganization, distraction, emotional upset, ferment, fog, fracas, haze, hodgepodge, imbroglio, intricacy, jumble, labyrinth, mess, mistake, muddle, mystification, pandemonium, perturbation, racket, riot, row, shambles, stir, stupefaction, surprise, tangle, trouble, tumult, turmoil, untidiness, upheaval, uproar, wilderness; SEE CONCEPTS *410,727*

confute [*v*] *disprove, refute*
blow sky high*, break, bring to naught, confound, contradict, controvert, defeat, demolish, dismay, disprove, expose, invalidate, knocks props out from under*, negate, oppugn, overcome, overthrow, overturn, overwhelm, parry, prove false, prove wrong, put down, rebut, set aside, shut up, silence, subvert, tap, upset, vanquish; SEE CONCEPTS *46,95*

congeal [*v*] *coagulate*
cake, clabber, clot, concrete, condense, curdle, dry, freeze, gel, gelate, gelatinate, gelatinize, glob up*, harden, indurate, jell, jellify, jelly, refrigerate, set, solidify, stiffen, thicken; SEE CONCEPTS *250,469*

congenial [*adj*] *friendly, compatible*
adapted, affable, agreeable, amical, clubby, companionable, compatible, complaisant, congruous, consis-

tent, consonant, conversable, convivial, cooperative, cordial, delightful, favorable, fit, genial, good-humored, gracious, happy, harmonious, jovial, kindly, kindred, like-minded, mellow, pleasant, pleasing, regular fellow, right neighborly, sociable, social, suitable, sympathetic, well-suited; SEE CONCEPT *555*

congenital [*adj*] *inborn*
complete, connate, connatural, constitutional, inbred, indigenous, indwelling, ingrained, inherent, inherited, innate, intrinsic, inveterate, latent, native, natural, thorough, unacquired, utter; SEE CONCEPTS *314,549*

congested [*adj*] *blocked, clogged*
chock-full, choked, closed, crammed, crowded, filled, glutted, gorged, gridlocked, jam-full, jammed, jam-packed, massed, mobbed, obstructed, occluded, overcrowded, overfilled, overflowing, packed, packed like sardines*, plugged, stopped, stoppered, stuffed, stuffed-up, teeming, up to the rafters*; SEE CONCEPTS *481,483,774*

congestion [*n*] *blockage*
bottleneck*, clogging, crowdedness, crowding, excess, jam, mass, overcrowding, overdevelopment, overpopulation, press, profusion, rubber-necking*, snarl-up*, surfeit, surplus, traffic jam; SEE CONCEPTS *230,432*

conglomerate [*n*] *composite organization*
agglomerate, agglomeration, aggregate, aggregation, cartel, chain, combine, conglomeration, group, multinational, pool, syndicate, trust; SEE CONCEPTS *323,325*

conglomerate [*adj*] *composite*
amassed, assorted, blended, clustered, heterogeneous, indiscriminate, massed, melded, miscellaneous, mixed, motley, multifarious, promiscuous, varied, variegated; SEE CONCEPTS *490,589*

conglomeration [*n*] *accumulation, potpourri*
agglomeration, aggregate, aggregation, amassment, assortment, collection, combination, combo, composite, cumulation, everything but the kitchen sink*, hoard, hodge-podge, mass, medley, miscellany, mishmash*, mixed bag, trove; SEE CONCEPT *432*

congratulate [*v*] *compliment on achievement, luck*
applaud, bless, boost, felicitate, give a big cigar*, give bouquet*, give regards, gold star*, have to hand it to*, hear it for*, laud, pat on back, praise, rejoice with, salute, stroke, toast, wish happy returns*, wish joy to, wish one well; SEE CONCEPTS *51,69*

congratulations [*n*] *complimentation on achievement, luck*
best wishes, compliments, felicitations, give a "hear-hear"*, good going*, good wishes, good work, greetings, hail; SEE CONCEPTS *69,278*

congregate [*v*] *assemble, come together*
besiege, bunch up*, collect, concentrate, congress, convene, converge, convoke, corral, flock*, forgather, gang around, gang up, gather, hang out*, make the scene*, mass, meet, meet up, muster, pack,

raise, rally, rendezvous, round up, swarm, teem, throng; SEE CONCEPTS *109,114*

congregation [*n*] *assembled group, especially concerned with church-going*
aggregation, assemblage, assembly, audience, brethren, churchgoers, collection, company, confab*, crowd, disciples, fellowship, flock, following, gathering, get-together, group, host, laity, meet, meeting, multitude, muster, parish, parishioners, public, sit-in, throng, turnout; SEE CONCEPTS *369,387,417*

congress [*n*] *delegation of representatives*
assembly, association, brotherhood, caucus, chamber, club, committee, conclave, conference, convention, convocation, council, delegates, diet, fellowship, fraternity, government, guild, league, legislative body, legislature, meeting, order, parliament, senate, sisterhood, society, sorority, the Hill, the house, union; SEE CONCEPTS *299,387*

congruent [*adj*] *agreeable, harmonious*
coinciding, compatible, concurring, conforming, consistent, corresponding, identical, in agreement; SEE CONCEPT *563*

congruous [*adj*] *corresponding, suitable*
accordant, appropriate, apt, becoming, coincidental, compatible, concordant, congruent, consistent, consonant, correspondent, fit, fitting, harmonious, meet, proper, seemly, sympathetic; SEE CONCEPTS *558,563*

conical/conic [*adj*] *shaped cylindrically and with a point*
coned, cone-shaped, conoid, conoidal, funnel-shaped, pointed, pyramidal, sharp, strobilate, strobiloid, tapered, tapering; SEE CONCEPT *486*

conjectural [*adj*] *speculative*
academic, assumed, doubtful, figured, guessing, guesstimated, hypothetical, on a hunch*, on a long shot*, putative, reputed, supposed, suppositional, suppositious, suppositive, surmised, surmising, suspect, tentative, theoretical, uncertain, unresolved; SEE CONCEPT *582*

conjecture [*n*] *speculation, assumption*
conclusion, fancy, guess, guesstimate, guesswork, hunch, hypothesis, inference, notion, opinion, perhaps, presumption, shot in the dark*, sneaking suspicion, stab in the dark*, supposition, surmise, theorizing, theory; SEE CONCEPTS *28,274,689*

conjecture [*v*] *speculate*
assume, believe, conceive, conclude, deem, estimate, expect, fancy, feel*, figure, gather, glean, guess, guesstimate*, hazard a guess*, hypothesize, imagine, infer, judge, presume, pretend, suppose, surmise, suspect, take a shot*, take a stab*, take for granted, theorize, think; SEE CONCEPTS *28,51*

conjugal [*adj*] *marital*
bridal, connubial, hymeneal, married, matrimonial, nuptial, spousal, wedded; SEE CONCEPT *555*

conjunction [*n*] *combination*
affiliation, agreement, alliance, association, cahoots, coincidence, concomitance, concurrence, congru-

ency, conjointment, hookup, juxtaposition, parallelism, partnership, tie-up, union; SEE CONCEPTS *388,714*

conjure [*v1*] *appeal to, implore*
adjure, ask, beg, beseech, brace, crave, entreat, importune, pray, supplicate, urge; SEE CONCEPT *48*

conjure [*v2*] *cast spell*
bewitch, call upon, charm, enchant, ensorcel, entrance, exorcise, fascinate, invoke, levitate, play tricks, raise, rouse, summon, voodoo; SEE CONCEPT *14*

conjure up [*v*] *bring to mind*
call, contrive, create, evoke, materialize, produce as by magic, recall, recollect, remember, review, summon, urge; SEE CONCEPT *38*

connect [*v*] *combine, link*
affix, ally, associate, attach, bridge, cohere, come aboard, conjoin, consociate, correlate, couple, equate, fasten, get into, hitch on, hook on, hook up, interface, join, join up with, marry, meld with, network with, plug into, relate, slap on, span, tack on, tag, tag on, tie in, tie in with, unite, wed, yoke; SEE CONCEPTS *85,113,160*

connected [*adj*] *related, affiliated*
akin, allied, applicable, associated, banded together, bracketed, coherent, combined, consecutive, coupled, in on with*, joined, linked, pertinent, undivided, united; SEE CONCEPTS *482,577*

connection [*n1*] *person who aids another in achieving goal*
acquaintance, agent, ally, associate, association, contact, friend, go-between, intermediary, kin, kindred, kinship, mentor, messenger, network, reciprocity, relation, relative, sponsor; SEE CONCEPTS *348,423*

connection [*n2*] *something that connects, links*
affiliation, alliance, association, attachment, bond, combination, conjointment, conjunction, coupling, fastening, hookup, joining, joint, junction, juncture, link, linkage, network, partnerhip, seam, tie, tie-in, tie-up, union; SEE CONCEPTS *499,720*

connection [*n3*] *something that communicates, relates*
affinity, application, association, bearing, bond, commerce, communication, correlation, correspondence, intercourse, interrelation, kinship, link, marriage, nexus, partnership, reciprocity, relation, relationship, relevance, tie-in, togetherness; SEE CONCEPTS *388,664*

connive [*v*] *plot, scheme*
angle, be in cahoots with*, cabal, cogitate, collude, conspire, contrive, cook up, devise, diddle*, finagle, frame, frame up, intrigue, machinate, operate, promote, wangle, wire, work hand in glove*; SEE CONCEPT *36*

connoisseur [*n*] *authority*
adept, aesthete, aficionado, appreciator, arbiter, bon vivant, buff, cognoscente, critic, devotee, dilettante, epicure, expert, fan, freak*, gourmet, judge, maven,

nut*, one into*, savant, specialist; SEE CONCEPTS *352,376*

connotation [*n*] *implication*
association, coloring, essence, hint, meaning, nuance, overtone, significance, suggestion, undertone; SEE CONCEPTS *682,689*

connote [*v*] *imply*
add up to, betoken, denote, designate, evidence, express, hint at, import, indicate, insinuate, intend, intimate, involve, mean, signify, spell, suggest; SEE CONCEPTS *75,118*

connubial [*adj*] *marital*
conjugal, hymeneal, married, matrimonial, nuptial, spousal, wedded; SEE CONCEPT *555*

conquer [*v1*] *defeat, overcome*
beat, bring to knees*, checkmate, circumvent, clobber, control, cream, crush, discomfit, drub, foil, frustrate, get the better of*, humble, lick, master, outwit, overmaster, overpower, override, overthrow, prevail, quell, reduce, rout, shut down, subdue, subjugate, succeed, surmount, throw, thwart, total, trample underfoot, trash, triumph, vanquish, whip, wipe off map*, worst, zap*; SEE CONCEPT *95*

conquer [*v2*] *win; obtain*
achieve, acquire, annex, best, master, occupy, overcome, overrun, prevail, seize, succeed, triumph; SEE CONCEPTS *90,141,706*

conqueror [*n*] *champion*
conquistador, defeater, hero, lord, master, subduer, subjugator, vanquisher, victor, winner; SEE CONCEPTS *354,358*

conquest [*n1*] *defeat, victory*
acquisition, annexation, appropriation, big win, clean sweep*, conquering, coup, defeating, discomfiture, grand slam*, invasion, killing*, mastery, occupation, overthrow, rout, routing, score, splash*, subdual, subjection, subjugation, success, takeover, triumph, vanquishment, win; SEE CONCEPTS *95,706*

conquest [*n2*] *enchantment; person enchanted*
acquisition, adherent, admirer, captivation, catch, enthralment, enticement, fan, feather in cap*, follower, prize, seduction, supporter, worshiper; SEE CONCEPTS *410,423*

consanguinity [*n*] *family relationship*
affiliation, affinity, agnate, blood-relationship, brotherhood, cognate, connection, family tie, filiation, kin, kindred, kindredship, kinship, lineage, race, sisterhood, strain; SEE CONCEPTS *296,388*

conscience [*n*] *moral sense*
censor, compunction, demur, duty, inner voice, morals, principles, qualms, right and wrong, scruples, shame, small voice*, squeam, still small voice*, superego; SEE CONCEPTS *645,689*

conscientious [*adj1*] *thorough, careful*
complete, diligent, exact, exacting, faithful, fastidious, fussy, hanging in*, hanging tough*, heart and soul into*, heedful, meticulous, minding p's and q's*, painstaking, particular, playing safe, punctili-

ous, punctual, reliable, tough, walking on eggs*; SEE CONCEPTS *531,538*

conscientious [*adj2*] *moral, upright*
conscionable, high-minded, high-principled, honest, honorable, incorruptible, just, pious, principled, responsible, right, scrupulous, straightforward, strict, true; SEE CONCEPT *545*

conscious [*adj1*] *alert, awake*
able to recognize, acquainted, aesthetic, alive to, apperceptive, apprised, assured, attentive, au courant, aware, certain, cognizant, conversant, discerning, felt, hep to*, informed, in on*, in right mind, keen, knowing, known, mindful, noticing, noting, observing, on to*, perceiving, percipient, recognizing, remarking, responsive, seeing, sensible, sensitive to, sentient, supraliminal, sure, understanding, vigilant, watchful, wise to*, with it*, witting; SEE CONCEPTS *402,539*

conscious [*adj2*] *intentional*
affected, calculated, deliberate, knowing, mannered, premeditated, rational, reasoning, reflective, responsible, self-conscious, studied, willful; SEE CONCEPTS *403,535*

consciousness [*n*] *knowledge*
alertness, apprehension, awareness, care, carefulness, cognizance, concern, heed, heedfulness, mindfulness, realization, recognition, regard, sensibility; SEE CONCEPT *409*

consecrate [*v*] *hold in high religious regard*
anoint, beatify, bless, dedicate, devote, exalt, hallow, honor, ordain, sanctify, set apart, venerate; SEE CONCEPTS *69,367*

consecutive [*adj*] *in sequence*
after, chronological, connected, constant, continuing, continuous, ensuing, following, going on, increasing, in order, in turn, later, logical, numerical, one after another, progressive, running, sequent, sequential, serial, serialized, seriate, seriatim, succedent, succeeding, successional, successive, understandable, uninterrupted; SEE CONCEPTS *585,799*

consensus [*n*] *general agreement*
accord, concord, concurrence, consent, harmony, unanimity, union, unity; SEE CONCEPTS *684,689*

consent [*n*] *agreement; concession*
accord, acquiescence, allowance, approval, assent, authorization, blank check, blessing, carte blanche, compliance, concurrence, go-ahead*, green light*, leave, okay, permission, permit, right on*, sanction, say so*, stamp of approval*, sufferance, understanding, yes; SEE CONCEPTS *684,685*

consent [*v*] *agree*
accede, accept, acquiesce, allow, approve, assent, bless, comply, concede, concur, fold, give in, give the nod*, give up, knuckle under, let, make a deal, okay, permit, roll over, sanction, say uncle*, say yes, sign off on*, subscribe, throw in the towel*, yes, yield; SEE CONCEPTS *8,50,88*

consequence [*n1*] *result, outcome of action*
aftereffect, aftermath, bottom line*, can of worms*, chain reaction*, effect, end, event, fallout, follow through, follow-up, issue, outgrowth, payback, reaction, repercussion, sequel, sequence, spin-off, upshot, waves*; SEE CONCEPT *230*

consequence [*n2*] *importance, significance*
account, concern, exigency, fame, honor, import, interest, magnitude, moment, momentousness, need, note, pith, portent, renown, reputation, repute, signification, value, weight, weightiness; SEE CONCEPT *668*

consequence [*n3*] *person's status*
cachet, dignity, distinction, eminence, notability, position, prestige, rank, repute, standing, state, stature, status; SEE CONCEPT *388*

consequent [*adj*] *resultant*
consistent, ensuing, following, indirect, inferable, intelligent, logical, rational, reasonable, resulting, sensible, sequential, sound, subsequent, successive, understandable; SEE CONCEPTS *537,548*

consequential [*adj*] *significant*
big, considerable, eventful, far-reaching, grave, important, material, meaningful, momentous, serious, substantial, weighty; SEE CONCEPT *568*

conservation [*n*] *preservation*
attention, care, cherishing, conservancy, conserving, control, custody, directing, economy, governing, guardianship, guarding, husbanding, husbandry, keeping, maintenance, management, managing, preserval, preserving, protecting, protection, safeguarding, safekeeping, salvation, saving, storage, supervising, supervision, sustentation, upkeep; SEE CONCEPTS *134,257*

conservative [*n*] *person who is cautious, moderate; an opponent of change*
bitter-ender*, classicist, conserver, conventionalist, diehard, hard hat*, middle-of-the-roader*, moderate, moderatist, obstructionist, old guard*, old liner*, preserver, reactionary, redneck*, right, rightist, right-winger, silk-stocking*, standpat, stick-in-the-mud*, Tory*, traditionalist, unprogressive; SEE CONCEPT *359*

conservative [*adj*] *cautious, moderate, tending to preserve the status quo*
bourgeois, constant, controlled, conventional, die-hard, fearful, firm, fogyish*, fuddy-duddy*, guarded, hard hat*, hidebound, holding to, illiberal, in a rut*, inflexible, middle-of-the-road*, not extreme, obstinate, old guard*, old line*, orthodox, quiet, reactionary, redneck*, right, right of center*, right-wing, sober, stable, steady, timid, Tory*, traditional, traditionalistic, unchangeable, unchanging, uncreative, undaring, unimaginative, unprogressive, white bread*; SEE CONCEPT *542*

conservatory [*n*] *greenhouse*
cold frame, glasshouse, hot house, nursery; SEE CONCEPTS *439,449,517*

conserve [v] *save, protect*
cut back, cut down on, go easy on, hoard, husband, keep, maintain, nurse, preserve, safeguard, scrimp, skimp, sock away*, squirrel*, squirrel away*, stash, store up, support, sustain, take care of, use sparingly; SEE CONCEPT *134*

consider [v1] *turn over in one's mind*
acknowledge, allow for, assent to, chew over*, cogitate, concede, consult, contemplate, deal with, deliberate, dream of, envisage, examine, excogitate, favor, flirt with*, grant, inspect, keep in mind, look at, meditate, mull over, muse, perpend, ponder, provide for, reason, reckon with, recognize, reflect, regard, revolve, ruminate, scan, scrutinize, see, see about, speculate, study, subscribe to, take into account, take under advisement, take up, think out, think over, toss around; SEE CONCEPT *24*

consider [v2] *regard a certain way*
analyze, appraise, bear in mind, believe, care for, count, credit, deem, estimate, feel, hold, hold an opinion, judge, keep in view, look upon, make allowance for, reckon with, reflect, remember, respect, sense, set down, suppose, take for, take into account, think, think of, view; SEE CONCEPT *12*

considerable [adj1] *abundant, large*
ample, appreciable, astronomical, big, bountiful, comfortable, commodious, extensive, goodly, great, hefty, huge, large-scale, lavish, major, marked, much, noticeable, plentiful, pretty, reasonable, respectable, sizable, substantial, tidy, tolerable; SEE CONCEPT *781*

considerable [adj2] *important*
big, consequential, distinguished, doozie*, dynamite, essential, fab*, fat, influential, material, meaningful, momentous, mondo*, noteworthy, renowned, significant, solid gold*, something, something else*, substantial, super, super-duper*, to the max*, unreal*, venerable, weighty; SEE CONCEPT *568*

considerably [adv] *significantly*
appreciably, far, greatly, markedly, noticeably, quite, rather, remarkably, somewhat, substantially, very much, well; SEE CONCEPT *569*

considerate [adj] *respectful of others*
accommodating, amiable, attentive, benevolent, big, charitable, chivalrous, circumspect, compassionate, complaisant, concerned, cool, discreet, forbearing, generous, kind, kindly, like a sport*, magnanimous, mellow, mindful, obliging, patient, polite, regular fellow*, solicitous, sympathetic, tactful, tender, thoughtful, unselfish, warmhearted; SEE CONCEPT *401*

consideration [n1] *mental analysis*
application, attention, cogitation, concentration, contemplation, debate, deliberation, discussion, examination, forethought, heed, reflection, regard, review, scrutiny, study, thinking, thought; SEE CONCEPT *24*

consideration [n2] *concern; something mentally examined*
development, difficulty, emergency, estate, evidence, exigency, extent, factor, fancy, idea, incident, issue, items, judgment, magnitude, minutiae, notion, occasion, occurrence, particulars, perplexity, plan, point, problem, proposal, puzzle, scope, situation, state, thought, trouble; SEE CONCEPT *532*

consideration [n3] *high regard*
attentiveness, awareness, concern, considerateness, esteem, estimation, favor, forbearance, friendliness, heed, heedfulness, kindliness, kindness, mercy, mindfulness, respect, solicitude, tact, thoughtfulness, tolerance; SEE CONCEPTS *32,410*

consideration [n4] *payment*
commish*, commission, fee*, payback, percentage, perk, perquisite, recompense, remuneration, reward, salary, something to sweeten pot*, tip, wage; SEE CONCEPT *344*

considered [adj] *deliberate, thought-out*
advised, aforethought, contemplated, designed, designful, examined, express, given due consideration, gone into, intentional, investigated, mediated, premeditated, prepense, studied, studious, thought-about, thought-through, treated, voluntary, weighed, well advised, well chosen, willful; SEE CONCEPTS *402,529*

considering [adj] *taking everything in mind*
all in all, all things considered*, as, as long as, because, everything being equal*, for, forasmuch as, inasmuch as, in consideration of, in light of, insomuch as, in view of, now, pending, seeing, since, taking into account; SEE CONCEPT *529*

consign [v] *entrust, hand over for care*
address, appoint, assign, authorize, commend to, commission, commit, confide, convey, delegate, deliver, deposit with, dispatch, forward, give, issue, put in charge of, relegate, remit, route, send, ship, transfer, transmit, turn over; SEE CONCEPTS *108, 143,217*

consignment [n1] *entrusting, handing over*
assignment, committal, dispatch, distribution, relegation, sending shipment, transmittal; SEE CONCEPTS *108,143,217*

consignment [n2] *something entrusted to another's care*
batch, delivery, goods, shipment; SEE CONCEPT *338*

consist [v] *exist, reside*
abide, be, be contained in, be expressed by, be found in, dwell, inhere, lie, repose, rest, subsist; SEE CONCEPT *539*

consistency [n1] *thickness*
bendability, bendableness, compactness, density, elasticity, fabric, firmness, flexibility, frangibility, hardness, limberness, moldability, organization, plasticity, pliability, softness, solidity, suppleness, texture, viscidity, viscosity, viscousness; SEE CONCEPTS *611,722*

consistency [n2] *constancy, regularity*
accord, agreement, apposition, appropriateness, aptness, coherence, cohesion, compatibility, concord, concurrence, conformability, congruity, consonance, correspondence, evenness, fitness, harmony, homo-

geneity, invariability, likeness, proportion, similarity, stability, steadfastness, steadiness, suitability, symmetry, uniformity, union, unity; SEE CONCEPTS *637,656,670*

consistent [*adj1*] *constant, regular*
dependable, even, expected, homogeneous, invariable, logical, of a piece, persistent, rational, same, steady, true, true to type, unchanging, undeviating, unfailing, uniform, unvarying; SEE CONCEPT *534*

consistent [*adj2*] *agreeing, compatible*
accordant, according to, agreeable, all of a piece, coherent, compatible, conforming with, congenial, congruous, consonant, equable, harmonious, like, logical, matching, sympathetic; SEE CONCEPT *563*

consist of [*v*] *made up of*
amount to, be composed of, comprise, contain, embody, include, incorporate, involve; SEE CONCEPT *643*

consolation [*n*] *relief, comfort*
alleviation, assuagement, cheer, comfort, compassion, ease, easement, encouragement, fellow feeling, help, lenity, pity, solace, succour, support, sympathy; SEE CONCEPTS *32,410*

console [*v*] *relieve, comfort*
animate, assuage, buck up*, calm, cheer, condole with, encourage, express sympathy, gladden, inspirit, lift, solace, soothe, tranquilize, untrouble, upraise; SEE CONCEPTS *7,22*

consolidate [*v*] *combine; make firm*
add to, amalgamate, amass, band, bind, blend, build up, bunch up, cement, centralize, combine, compact, compound, concatenate, concentrate, condense, conjoin, connect, densen, develop, federate, fortify, fuse, harden, hitch, hitch on, hook up with, incorporate, join, league, mass, meld, mix, plug into, pool, reinforce, render solid, secure, set, slap on, solidify, stabilize, strengthen, tack on, tag on, team up with*, thicken, throw in together*, tie in, tie up with, unify; SEE CONCEPTS *109,250*

consolidation [*n*] *combination, fortification*
alliance, amalgamation, association, coadunation, coalition, compression, concentration, condensation, federation, fusion, incorporation, melding, mergence, merger, merging, reinforcement, solidification, strengthening, unification; SEE CONCEPTS *109,469*

consonance [*n*] *agreement, consistency*
accord, chime, chorus, concert, concord, conformity, congruence, congruity, correspondence, harmony, suitableness, tune; SEE CONCEPT *664*

consonant [*adj*] *agreeing, consistent*
accordant, according, agnate, akin, alike, analogous, blending, coincident, comformable, comparable, compatible, concordant, congenial, congruous, correspondent, corresponding, harmonious, in agreement, in rapport, like, parallel, similar, suitable, sympathetic, uniform; SEE CONCEPT *563*

consort [*n*] *associate, partner*
accompaniment, companion, concomitant, fellow,

friend, husband, mate, spouse, wife; SEE CONCEPT *423*

consort [*v1*] *be friendly with; fraternize*
accompany, associate, attend, bear, befriend, bring, carry, chaperon, chum together*, chum with*, clique with, company, conduct, convoy, gang up with*, go around with*, hang around with*, hang out with*, hang with*, join, keep company, mingle, mix, pal, pal around with, pal with, run around with*, run with, take up with, tie up with; SEE CONCEPTS *114,384*

consort [*v2*] *agree*
accord, coincide, comport, concur, conform, correspond, dovetail, harmonize, march, square, tally; SEE CONCEPT *664*

conspicuous [*adj1*] *obvious, easily seen*
apparent, clear, discernible, distinct, evident, manifest, noticeable, open-and-shut*, patent, perceptible, plain, visible; SEE CONCEPT *619*

conspicuous [*adj2*] *important, prominent*
arresting, arrestive, blatant, celebrated, commanding, distinguished, eminent, famed, famous, flagrant, flashy, garish, glaring, glitzy, illustrious, influential, jazzy, loud, marked, notable, noted, notorious, outstanding, pointed, rank, remarkable, renowned, salient, screaming, showy, signal, splashy, stick out like sore thumb*, striking, tony, well-known; SEE CONCEPTS *542,567*

conspiracy [*n*] *collusion in plan*
cabal, complot, confederacy, connivance, countermine, counterplot, covin, disloyalty, fix, frame*, game, hookup*, intrigue, league, little game*, machination, perfidy, plot, practice, put-up job*, scheme, sedition, treacherousness, treachery, treason, trick, trickery; SEE CONCEPT *660*

conspire [*v1*] *plot, scheme with someone*
be in cahoots*, cabal, cogitate, collogue, collude, confederate, connive, contrive, cook up*, cooperate, devise, get in bed with*, hatch, intrigue, machinate, maneuver, operate, promote, put out a contract*, wangle, wire, work something out*; SEE CONCEPTS *36,192*

conspire [*v2*] *agree, concur*
cabal, colleague, combine, complot, conduce, consort, contribute, cooperate, join, tend, unite, work together; SEE CONCEPT *8*

constancy [*n*] *fixedness*
abidingness, adherence, allegiance, ardor, attachment, certainty, decision, dependability, determination, devotedness, devotion, doggedness, eagerness, earnestness, endurance, faith, fealty, fidelity, firmness, honesty, honor, integrity, love, loyalty, passion, permanence, perseverance, principle, regularity, resolution, stability, staunchness, steadfastness, steadiness, surety, tenacity, trustiness, trustworthiness, truthfulness, unchangeableness, unfailingness, uniformity, zeal; SEE CONCEPTS *32,410,637*

constant [*adj1*] *fixed*
connected, consistent, continual, equable, even,

firm, habitual, homogeneous, immutable, invariable, like the Rock of Gibralter*, monochrome, monophonic, monotonous, nonstop, of a piece, permanent, perpetual, regular, regularized, solid as rock*, stabile, stable, standardized, steadfast, steady, together, unalterable, unbroken, unchanging, unflappable, unfluctuating, uniform, uninterrupted, unvarying; SEE CONCEPT *534*

constant [*adj2*] *neverending*
abiding, ceaseless, chronic, continual, continuous, endless, enduring, eternal, everlasting, incessant, interminable, lasting, nonstop, perpetual, persistent, persisting, relentless, sustained, unending, uninterrupted, unrelenting, unremitting; SEE CONCEPTS *649,798*

constant [*adj3*] *loyal, determined*
allegiant, attached, dependable, devoted, dogged, faithful, fast, persevering, resolute, staunch, tried-and-true, true, trustworthy, trusty, unfailing, unflagging, unshaken, unwavering; SEE CONCEPT *542*

consternation [*n*] *dismay, distress*
alarm, amazement, anxiety, awe, bewilderment, confusion, distraction, dread, fear, fright, horror, muddle, muddlement, panic, perplexity, shock, stupefaction, terror, trepidation, trepidity, wonder; SEE CONCEPT *230*

constituency [*n*] *voting public*
balloters, body of voters, body politic, citizenry, city, county, district, electorate, electors, faction, nation, people, precinct, state, system, voters, voting area, ward; SEE CONCEPT *379*

constituent [*n*] *element*
board, component, division, essential, factor, fixins*, fraction, ingredient, makings, part, part and parcel, plug-in, portion, principle, unit; SEE CONCEPTS *826,834*

constituent [*adj1*] *component, part*
basic, combining, composing, constituting, division, elemental, essential, factor, forming, fraction, fundamental, ingredient, integral, portion; SEE CONCEPTS *826,834,835*

constituent [*adj2*] *voting*
balloter, citizen, electing, electoral, official, overruling; SEE CONCEPT *536*

constitute [*v1*] *comprise, form*
aggregate, complement, complete, compose, compound, construct, cook up*, create, develop, dream up*, embody, enact, establish, fill out, fix, flesh out*, found, frame, fudge together*, incorporate, integrate, make, make up, set up; SEE CONCEPTS *173,184,251*

constitute [*v2*] *authorize*
appoint, commission, decree, delegate, depute, deputize, designate, draft, empower, enact, establish, legislate, make, name, nominate, ordain, order; SEE CONCEPTS *50,88*

constitution [*n1*] *physical make-up and health*
architecture, build, character, composition, construction, content, contents, design, disposition, essence, form, formation, frame, habit, habitus, nature, physique, structure, temper, temperament, type, vitality; SEE CONCEPT *757*

constitution [*n2*] *establishment*
charter, code, composition, custom, formation, lawmaking, legislation, organization, written law; SEE CONCEPTS *271,318*

constitutional [*n*] *walk*
airing, ambulation, footwork, legwork, perambulation, ramble, saunter, stroll, turn, walk; SEE CONCEPT *149*

constitutional [*adj1*] *inherent*
built-in, congenital, deep-seated, essential, inborn, inbred, ingrained, innate, intrinsic, natural, organic, vital; SEE CONCEPT *549*

constitutional [*adj2*] *provided for by law*
approved, chartered, democratic, ensured, lawful, legal, representative, statutory, vested; SEE CONCEPT *319*

constrain [*v*] *force; restrain*
ban, bar, bind, bottle up, bridle, chain, check, coerce, compel, concuss, confine, constrict, cool off*, cork, curb, deny, deprive, disallow, drive, hem in*, hog-tie*, hold back, hold down, hold in, immure, impel, imprison, incarcerate, inhibit, intern, jail, keep lid on*, make, necessitate, oblige, pressure, pressurize, put half nelson on*, shotgun*, stifle, urge, withhold; SEE CONCEPTS *14,121,130*

constraint [*n1*] *force*
a must*, coercion, compulsion, driving, duress, goad, hang-up*, impelling, impulsion, monkey*, motive, necessity, no-no*, pressure, repression, restraint, spring, spur, suppression, violence; SEE CONCEPTS *14,121*

constraint [*n2*] *shyness*
bashfulness, diffidence, embarrassment, hang-up, humility, inhibition, modesty, repression, reservation, reserve, restraint, timidity; SEE CONCEPT *411*

constraint [*n3*] *restriction*
arrest, captivity, check, circumscription, confinement, constrainment, cramp, curb, damper, detention, deterrent, hindrance, limitation, restraint; SEE CONCEPTS *130,652*

constrict [*v*] *inhibit*
astringe, choke, circumscribe, clench, compress, concentrate, condense, confine, constringe, contract, cramp, curb, draw together, limit, narrow, pinch, restrain, restrict, shrink, squeeze, strangle, strangulate, tauten, tense, tighten, tuck; SEE CONCEPTS *130,191,219*

constriction [*n*] *blockage*
binding, choking, compression, constraint, contraction, cramp, impediment, limitation, narrowing, pressure, reduction, restriction, squeezing, stenosis, stricture, tightness; SEE CONCEPTS *130,191,219*

construct [*v*] *assemble, build*
build up, cobble up*, compose, compound, constitute, cook up*, create, design, dream up*, elevate,

engineer, envision, erect, establish, fabricate, fashion, forge, form, formulate, found, frame, fudge together*, hammer out*, hoke up*, imagine, invent, make, manufacture, organize, prefab*, produce, put out, put together, put up, raise, rear, set up, shape, throw together, throw up*, trump up*, uprear, whip up*; SEE CONCEPTS *168,173,251*

construction [n1] *creation, building*
architecture, arrangement, assembly, build, cast, composition, conception, constitution, contour, cut, development, disposition, edifice, elevation, erecting, erection, fabric, fabricating, fabrication, figuration, figure, form, format, formation, foundation, improvisation, invention, makeup, making, manufacture, mold, origination, outline, plan, planning, prefab, prefabrication, putting up, raising, rearing, roadwork, shape, structure, system, systematization, turn, type; SEE CONCEPTS *168,439,757*

construction [n2] *explanation*
apprehension, construal, definition, exegesis, explication, exposé, exposition, inference, interpretation, reading, rendering, rendition, translation, version; SEE CONCEPT *274*

constructive [adj] *helpful*
effective, positive, practical, productive, useful, valuable; SEE CONCEPT *401*

construe [v] *deduce; explain*
analyze, decipher, define, explicate, expound, figure it to be*, infer, interpret, one's best guess*, parse, read, render, spell out, take, translate, understand; SEE CONCEPTS *37,57*

consul [n] *representative*
delegate, emissary, envoy, lawyer, legate; SEE CONCEPTS *354,355*

consulate [n] *embassy*
consular office, government office, ministry; SEE CONCEPTS *439,449*

consult [v] *ask, confer*
argue, ask advice of, be closed with, brainstorm, call in, cogitate, collogue, commune, compare notes, confab, confabulate, consider, debate, deliberate, discuss, examine, flap*, groupthink*, huddle, interrogate, interview, kick ideas around*, negotiate, parlay, pick one's brains*, powwow*, put heads together*, question, refer to, regard, respect, review, seek advice, seek opinion of, take account of, take a meeting*, take counsel, talk over, toss ideas around*, treat, turn to; SEE CONCEPTS *17,48,56*

consultation [n] *asking, conference*
appointment, argument, buzz session*, clambake*, confab*, conference, council, deliberation, dialogue, discussion, examination, groupthink*, hearing, huddle, interview, meeting, powwow*, second opinion*, session; SEE CONCEPTS *48,114,324*

consume [v1] *use up*
absorb, apply, avail oneself of, deplete, devour, dissipate, dominate, drain, drivel, eat up, employ, engross, exhaust, expend, finish, finish up, fritter away,

frivol away, go, go through, have recourse to, lavish, lessen, monopolize, obsess, preoccupy, profit by, put away, put to use, run out of, run through, spend, squander, throw away, trifle, utilize, vanish, wash up, waste, wear out; SEE CONCEPT *225*

consume [v2] *eat, drink*
absorb, bolt, chow down*, devour, down, eat up, feed, gobble*, gorge, gulp, guzzle, hoover*, ingest, ingurgitate, inhale, meal, mow*, nibble, partake, polish off*, punish, put away*, put down*, scarf*, snack, stuff one's face*, swallow, swill, take, toss down*, wolf*; SEE CONCEPT *169*

consume [v3] *destroy*
annihilate, crush, decay, demolish, devastate, eat up, exhaust, expend, extinguish, lay waste, overwhelm, ravage, raze, ruin, suppress, waste, wreck; SEE CONCEPT *252*

consumer [n] *person who buys merchandise, services*
buyer, customer, end user, enjoyer, purchaser, shopper, user; SEE CONCEPT *348*

consummate [adj] *ultimate, best*
able, absolute, accomplished, complete, conspicuous, downright, faultless, finished, flawless, gifted, ideal, impeccable, inimitable, matchless, out-and-out, peerless, perfect, perfected, polished, positive, practiced, ripe, skilled, superb, superlative, supreme, talented, thoroughgoing, total, trained, transcendent, unmitigated, unqualified, unsurpassable, utter, virtuosic, whole; SEE CONCEPTS *528,572*

consummate [v] *achieve, finish*
accomplish, button down*, call a day*, can*, carry out, clean up, clinch, close, come, come through, compass, complete, conclude, crown, drop curtain*, effectuate, end, fold up, get it together*, go the route*, halt, knock off, mop up, perfect, perform, polish off*, put away*, put finishing touch on*, put lid on*, put to bed*, sew up, sign, take care of, terminate, top it off, ultimate, wind up, wrap, wrap up; SEE CONCEPTS *234,704,706*

consummation [n] *achievement, fulfillment*
cleanup, completion, culmination, doing it to a T*, end, mop-up, payoff, perfection, realization, to a finish, wind-up*, wrap, wrap-up*; SEE CONCEPT *706*

consumption [n] *devouring; use*
burning, consuming, damage, decay, decrease, depletion, desolation, destruction, devastation, diminution, dispersion, dissipation, drinking, eating, exhaustion, expenditure, loss, misuse, ruin, swallowing, using up, utilization, waste, wear and tear; SEE CONCEPTS *156,169,225,252*

contact [n1] *form of communication*
acquaintance, association, channel, commerce, communion, companionship, connection, fellowship, influence, intercourse, junction, meeting, network, touch, union, unity; SEE CONCEPTS *278,388,686*

contact [n2] *touching*
approximation, closeness, collision, connection, contiguity, contingence, hit, impingement, junction,

juxtaposition, nearness, propinquity, proximity, relation, strike, taction, touch, union; SEE CONCEPT *747*

contact [*v*] *communicate with*
approach, be in touch with, buzz*, call, check with, connect, get, get ahold of, get in touch with, interact, interface, network, phone, reach, reach out, relate, speak to, talk, telephone, touch base*, visit, write to; SEE CONCEPT *266*

contagion [*n*] *infection*
bane, contamination, corruption, illness, miasma, pestilence, plague, poison, pollution, taint, transmission, venom, virus; SEE CONCEPT *306*

contagious [*adj*] *communicable*
catching, deadly, endemic, epidemic, epizootic, impartible, infectious, inoculable, pestiferous, pestilential, poisonous, spreading, taking, transmissible, transmittable; SEE CONCEPT *314*

contain [*v1*] *include, hold*
accommodate, be composed of, comprehend, comprise, consist of, embody, embrace, enclose, encompass, have, have capacity for, hold, incorporate, involve, seat, subsume, take in; SEE CONCEPTS *112,736,742*

contain [*v2*] *hold back, control*
bottle up*, check, collect, compose, control, cool*, cork*, curb, harness, hog-tie*, hold in, keep back, keep lid on*, put half nelson on*, rein, repress, restrain, restrict, simmer down, smother, stifle, stop; SEE CONCEPTS *94,191*

container [*n*] *holder for physical object*
alembic, bag, beaker, bin, bottle, bowl, box, bucket, bunker, caisson, can, canister, canteen, capsule, carafe, carton, cask, casket, cauldron, chamber, chest, churn, cistern, cradle, crate, crock, dish, ewer, firkin, flask, hamper, hod, hopper, humidor, hutch, jar, jeroboam, jug, kettle, magnum, package, packet, pail, pit, pod, poke, pot, pottery, pouch, purse, receptacle, reliquary, repository, sac, sack, scuttle, stein, storage, tank, tub, utensil, vase, vat, vessel, vial; SEE CONCEPT *494*

contaminate [*v*] *adulterate*
alloy, befoul, corrupt, debase, debauch, defile, deprave, desecrate, dirty, harm, infect, injure, muck up, pervert, poison, pollute, profane, radioactivate, soil, spoil, stain, sully, taint, tarnish, vitiate; SEE CONCEPTS *252,254*

contamination [*n*] *adulteration*
contagion, corruption, decay, defilement, dirtying, disease, epidemic, filth, foulness, impurity, infection, pestilence, plague, poisoning, pollution, radioactivation, rottenness, spoliation, taint; SEE CONCEPTS *230,306,674*

contemplate [*v1*] *think about seriously; plan*
aim, aspire to, brood over, chew over, consider, cool out*, deliberate, design, envisage, excogitate, expect, foresee, intend, kick around*, mean, meditate on, mind, mull over, muse over, observe, percolate, perpend, ponder, propose, purpose, reflect upon, ru-

minate, size up, speculate, study, take in, think of, weigh; SEE CONCEPTS *17,36*

contemplate [*v2*] *gaze at*
audit, behold, consider, examine, eye, inspect, notice, observe, peer, penetrate, peruse, pierce, pore over, probe, pry, regard, scan, scrutinize, see, stare at, study, survey, view, witness; SEE CONCEPT *623*

contemplation [*n1*] *deep thought; planning*
ambition, cogitation, consideration, deliberation, design, intention, meditation, musing, plan, pondering, purpose, reflection, reverie, rumination, study; SEE CONCEPT *410*

contemplation [*n2*] *gazing at*
examination, inspection, looking at, observation, scrutiny, survey, viewing; SEE CONCEPT *623*

contemplative [*adj*] *deep in thought*
attentive, cogitative, in brown study*, intent, introspective, lost, meditative, musing, pensive, pondering, rapt, reflecting, reflective, ruminative, speculative, thinking, thoughtful; SEE CONCEPTS *402, 403*

contemporary [*adj1*] *modern*
abreast, à la mode*, au courant, contempo, current, existent, extant, hot off press*, in fashion, instant, in vogue, just out*, latest, leading-edge*, mod*, new, newfangled, now, present, present-day, recent, redhot*, state-of-the-art, today*, topical, ultramodern, up*, up-to-date, up-to-the-minute, voguish, with it*; SEE CONCEPTS *578,589,797*

contemporary [*adj2*] *existing, occurring at same time*
accompanying, associated, attendant, coetaneous, coeval, coexistent, coexisting, coincident, concomitant, concurrent, connected, contemporaneous, current, linked, present, related, simultaneous, synchronal, synchronic, synchronous; SEE CONCEPT *820*

contempt [*n1*] *disdain, disrespect*
antipathy, audacity, aversion, condescension, contumely, defiance, derision, despisal, despisement, despite, disesteem, disregard, distaste, hatred, indignity, malice, mockery, neglect, recalcitrance, repugnance, ridicule, scorn, slight, snobbery, stubbornness; SEE CONCEPT *29*

contempt [*n2*] *state of disgrace*
discredit, disesteem, disfavor, dishonor, disrepute, humiliation, ignominy, infamy, insignificancy, opprobrium, shame, stigma; SEE CONCEPTS *388,674*

contemptible [*adj*] *despicable, shameful*
abhorrent, abject, abominable, bad, base, beggarly, cheap, crass, currish, degenerate, despisable, detestable, dirty, disgusting, fink*, hateful, heel, ignoble, ignominious, inferior, low, low-down*, lowest, mean, odious, outcast, paltry, pitiable, pitiful, poor, rat*, sad, scummy*, scurvy*, shabby, shameful, sordid, sorry*, swinish, unworthy, vile, worthless, wretched; SEE CONCEPT *550*

contemptuous [*adj*] *arrogant, insolent*
audacious, bold, cavalier, cheeky, cold-shoulder, condescending, contumelious, cool, derisive, derisory, disdainful, disrespectful, dog it*, hard, hard-

nosed, haughty, high and mighty*, high hat*, insulting, on high horse*, opprobrious, sardonic, scornful, sneering, snippy, snobbish, snooty*, snotty*, supercilious, temperamental, uppity, upstage; SEE CONCEPT *401*

contend [v1] *compete, fight*
argue, battle, clash, confront, contest, controvert, cope, dispute, emulate, encounter, face, give all one's got*, give one's all*, go after, go for, go for broke*, go for it*, go for jugular*, grapple, have at*, jockey for position*, jostle, knock oneself out, litigate, lock horns*, make play for*, meet, mix it up with*, oppose, oppugn, push, push for, resist, rival, scramble for, shoot at, shoot for, skirmish, stand, strive, struggle, tangle with, tug, vie, withstand; SEE CONCEPTS *92,106*

contend [v2] *argue*
affirm, allege, assert, aver, avow, blast, charge, claim, come at, cross, debate, defend, dictate, dispute, enjoin, fly in face of*, gang up on, go at, have at*, have bone to pick*, hold, insist, jump on, justify, lace into*, lay into*, let have it*, light into*, lock horns with*, maintain, mix, mix it up*, prescribe, put up argument, report, rip*, say, set to, sock it to one*, stick it to*, take on, tell, urge, vindicate, warrant, zap*; SEE CONCEPT *46*

content [n1] *comfort, happiness*
contentment, ease, gratification, peace, peace of mind, pleasure, satisfaction; SEE CONCEPT *410*

content [n2] *essence, meaning*
burden, composition, constitution, gist, idea, matter, significance, subject, subject matter, substance, text, thought; SEE CONCEPT *682*

content [n3] *capacity, volume*
filling, load, measure, packing, size; SEE CONCEPTS *719,740*

content [adj] *happy, agreeable*
appeased, at ease, can't complain*, comfortable, complacent, contented, fat dumb and happy*, fulfilled, gratified, pleased as punch*, satisfied, smug, tickled pink*, willing; SEE CONCEPT *403*

content [v] *please*
appease, bewitch, captivate, charm, delight, enrapture, gladden, gratify, humor, indulge, make happy, mollify, placate, reconcile, satisfy, suffice, thrill, tickle; SEE CONCEPTS *7,22*

contented [adj] *at ease; happy*
at peace, cheerful, comfortable, complacent, content, glad, gratified, pleased, satisfied, serene, thankful; SEE CONCEPT *403*

contention [n1] *competition*
altercation, argument, battle, beef*, belligerency, bone of contention*, bone to pick*, combat, conflict, contest, controversy, difference, disaccord, discord, dispute, dissension, dissent, dissidence, disunity, enmity, feuding, fight, flak, hassle, hostility, quarrel, rivalry, run-in, scene, scrap, set-to*, squabble, static, strife, struggle, variance, war, wrangle, wrangling; SEE CONCEPTS *92,106*

contention [n2] *argument for idea*
advancement, affirmation, allegation, assertion, asseveration, avowal, belief, charge, claim, contestation, declaration, demurrer, deposition, discussion, explanation, ground, hurrah, hypothesis, idea, maintaining, opinion, plea, position, predication, profession, rumpus, stand, thesis, view; SEE CONCEPTS *46,278,689*

contentment [n] *comfort, happiness*
complacency, content, contentedness, ease, equanimity, fulfillment, gladness, gratification, peace, pleasure, repletion, satisfaction, serenity; SEE CONCEPT *410*

contents [n] *elements of larger object*
capacity, cargo, chapters, connotation, constituents, details, divisions, essence, filling, freight, furnishing, gist, guts, implication, ingredients, innards, inside, lading, load, meaning, nub, packing, shipment, significance, size, space, stuffing, subject matter, subjects, substance, sum, text, themes, topics, volume; SEE CONCEPT *835*

contest [n1] *competition*
challenge, concours, discussion, game, match, meet, meeting, proving, rencounter, sport, testing, tournament, trial, trying; SEE CONCEPTS *92,363*

contest [n2] *fight, struggle*
action, affray, altercation, battle, battle royal*, beef*, brawl, brush, combat, conflict, controversy, debate, discord, dispute, duke out*, emulation, encounter, engagement, fray, go*, hassle, rivalry, row, rumble*, run-in, scrap, set-to*, shock, skirmish, static, strife, striving, tug-of-war, warfare, wrangle; SEE CONCEPTS *106,320*

contest [v1] *argue, challenge*
blast, call in question, debate, dispute, doubt, give it one's all*, go for it*, go for jugular*, jockey for position*, jump on, litigate, mix it up with*, object to, oppose, push, question, scramble for, shoot for, stand up for, tangle; SEE CONCEPT *46*

contest [v2] *fight*
altercate, attack, battle, brawl, break with, buck, compete, conflict, contend, cross, defend, duel, feud, fight over, gang up on, hassle, knuckle with, lay a finger on*, lay out, put on gloves*, put up dukes*, quarrel, repel, rival, row, rumpus, scrap, scuffle, set to*, sock*, square off, strike, struggle, take on, tilt, traverse, vie, withstand, wrangle; SEE CONCEPT *106*

contestant [n] *competitor*
adversary, antagonist, aspirant, battler, candidate, challenger, combatant, contender, contester, dark horse*, disputant, entrant, favorite son*, hopeful, member, participant, player, rival, scrapper*, team member, warrior, white hope*; SEE CONCEPT *366*

context [n] *framework, circumstances*
ambience, background, conditions, connection, frame of reference, lexicon, relation, situation, substance, text, vocabulary; SEE CONCEPTS *682,696*

contiguous [*adj*] *adjacent, in contact*
abutting, adjoining, approximal, beside, bordering, close, contactual, conterminous, juxtaposed, juxtapositional, meeting, near, near-at-hand, nearby, neighboring, next, next door to, next to, touching; SEE CONCEPTS *586,778*

continent [*adj*] *chaste, pure*
abstemious, abstentious, abstinent, ascetic, austere, bridled, celibate, curbed, inhibited, modest, restrained, self-restrained, sober, temperate; SEE CONCEPT *550*

contingency [*n*] *chance happening; possibility*
accident, break, chance, crisis, crossroads, emergency, event, eventuality, exigency, fortuity, happening, if it's cool*, incident, juncture, likelihood, occasion, odds, opportunity, pass, pinch, predicament, probability, strait, turning point, uncertainty, zero hour*; SEE CONCEPTS *650,679,693*

contingent [*n*] *group of followers*
batch, body, bunch, deputation, detachment, disciples, mission, quota, sect, section, set; SEE CONCEPT *417*

contingent [*adj*] *conditional; possible*
accidental, casual, chance, controlled by, dependent, fluky, fortuitous, haphazard, incidental, likely, odd, probable, probably, random, subject to, unanticipated, uncertain, unexpected, unforeseeable, unforeseen, unpredictable; SEE CONCEPT *552*

continual [*adj*] *constant, incessant*
aeonian, around-the-clock, ceaseless, connected, consecutive, continuous, dateless, endless, enduring, eternal, everlasting, frequent, interminable, oft-repeated, permanent, perpetual, persistent, persisting, recurrent, regular, relentless, repeated, repetitive, running, staying, steady, timeless, unbroken, unceasing, unchanging, unending, unfailing, unflagging, uninterrupted, unremitting, unvarying, unwaning; SEE CONCEPTS *534,798*

continuance [*n*] *duration*
constancy, continuation, endurance, extension, guts*, longevity, period, permanence, perpetuation, protraction, run, survival, term, vitality; SEE CONCEPTS *637,804,807*

continuation [*n*] *addition; maintenance*
assiduity, augmenting, continuance, continuing, continuity, duration, endurance, enduring, extension, furtherance, going on, increase, increasing, line, maintaining, perpetuating, perpetuation, persisting, postscript, preservation, preserving, producing, production, prolongation, prolonging, propagation, protracting, protraction, sequel, succession, supplement, sustaining, sustenance, tenacity; SEE CONCEPTS *640,651,804*

continue [*v1*] *persist, carry on*
abide, advance, carry forward, draw out, endure, extend, forge ahead, get on with it*, go on, hang in*, keep at, keep on, keep on truckin'*, keep the ball rolling*, keep up, last, lengthen, linger, live on, loi-

ter, maintain, make headway, move ahead, never cease, outlast, outlive, perdure, persevere, persist in, press on, progress, project, prolong, promote, pursue, push on, reach, remain, rest, ride, run on, stand, stay, stay on, stick at, stick to, survive, sustain, uphold; SEE CONCEPT *239*

continue [*v2*] *begin again; resume*
begin over, begin where one left off, carry on, carry over, go on with, pick up, proceed, recapitulate, recommence, reestablish, reinstate, reinstitute, renew, reopen, restart, restore, return to, take up; SEE CONCEPT *234*

continuity [*n*] *progression*
chain, cohesion, connection, constancy, continuance, continuousness, continuum, dovetailing, durability, duration, endurance, extension, flow, interrelationship, linking, perpetuity, persistence, prolongation, protraction, sequence, stability, stamina, succession, survival, train, uniting, unity, vitality, whole; SEE CONCEPT *721*

continuous [*adj*] *constant, unending*
connected, consecutive, continued, day and night*, endless, everlasting, extended, for ever and ever, interminable, looped, no end of*, no end to, on a treadmill*, perpetual, prolonged, regular, repeated, stable, steady, timeless, unbroken, unceasing, undivided, unfaltering, uninterrupted; SEE CONCEPTS *482,798*

contort [*v*] *disfigure, distort*
bend, convolute, curve, deform, gnarl, knot, misshape, torture, twist, warp, wind, wrench, writhe; SEE CONCEPTS *147,184*

contortion [*n*] *distortion, mutilation*
anamorphosis, crookedness, deformation, deformity, dislocation, grimace, malformation, misproportion, misshapement, pout, twist, ugliness, unsightliness, wryness; SEE CONCEPTS *436,580*

contour [*n*] *outline, profile*
curve, delineation, figuration, figure, form, lineament, lines, relief, shape, silhouette; SEE CONCEPT *436*

contraband [*n*] *black-market production*
bootlegging, counterfeiting, crime, dealing, goods*, moonshine*, piracy, plunder, poaching, rum-running*, smuggling, stuff, swag, theft, trafficking, violation, wetbacking*; SEE CONCEPTS *192,338*

contraband [*adj*] *black-market; unlawful*
banned, bootleg, bootlegged, disapproved, excluded, forbidden, hot*, illegal, illicit, interdicted, prohibited, proscribed, shut out, smuggled, taboo, unauthorized, verboten*; SEE CONCEPTS *319,545*

contraceptive [*n*] *birth control method*
armor, coil, condom, diaphragm, douche, foam, hormone, intrauterine device, IUD, jelly, loop, pill, planned parenthood, preventative, preventive medicine, prophylactic, rhythm method, ring, rubber, safety, shield, spermicidal cream, sponge, vaginal douche, vaginal suppository; SEE CONCEPTS *307,446*

contract [n] *agreement, deal*
arrangement, bargain, bond, commission, commitment, compact, concordat, convention, covenant, deposition, dicker*, engagement, evidence, gentleman's agreement, guarantee, handshake*, indenture, liability, mise, obligation, pact, paper, pledge, promise, proof, record, settlement, stipulation, treaty, understanding; SEE CONCEPTS *271,684*

contract [v1] *condense*
abate, abbreviate, abridge, become smaller, clench, compress, confine, constrict, consume, curtail, decline, decrease, deflate, draw in, dwindle, ebb, edit, epitomize, evaporate, fall away, fall off, grow less, lessen, lose, narrow, omit, purse, recede, reduce, shrink, shrivel, subside, syncopate, take in, tighten, wane, waste, weaken, wither, wrinkle; SEE CONCEPTS *169,236,247*

contract [v2] *come to terms*
accept offer, adjust, agree, arrange, assent, bargain, become indebted, bound, buy, circumscribe, clinch, close, come around, commit, consent, covenant, dicker*, engage, enter into, firm a deal*, give one's word, go along with*, hammer out deal*, initial*, ink*, it's a deal*, limit, make terms, negotiate, obligate, owe, pact, pledge, promise, put in writing, set, settle, shake hands on it*, sign for, sign papers, sign up, stipulate, swear to, undertake, work out details, you got it*, you sold me*; SEE CONCEPTS *8,50,88*

contract [v3] *catch disease*
acquire, afflict, be afflicted with, become infected with, be ill with, bring on, cause, come down with, decline, derange, develop, disorder, fall, fall victim to, get, go down with, incur, indispose, induce, obtain, sicken, sink, succumb to, take, take one's death, upset, weaken; SEE CONCEPTS *93,308*

contraction [n] *drawing in; shortening*
abbreviating, abbreviation, abridging, abridgment, compression, condensation, condensing, confinement, confining, constriction, curtailing, curtailment, cutting down, decrease, decreasing, deflating, deflation, diminishing, diminution, drawing together, dwindling, elision, evaporating, evaporation, lessening, lopping, narrowing, omission, omitting, receding, recession, reducing, reduction, shrinkage, shrinking, shrivelling, tensing, tightening, withdrawal, withdrawing; SEE CONCEPTS *469,776*

contradict [v] *be at variance with*
belie, buck, call in question*, challenge, confront, contravene, controvert, counter, counteract, cross, dare, deny, differ, disaffirm, disclaim, disprove, dispute, fly in the face of*, gainsay, have bone to pick*, impugn, negate, negative, oppose, refuse to accept, repudiate, take on, thumbs down*, traverse; SEE CONCEPTS *46,54,665*

contradiction [n] *variance to something*
bucking, conflict, confutation, contravention, defiance, denial, difference, disagreement, discrepancy, dispute, dissension, gainsaying, incongruity, inconsistency, negation, opposite, opposition; SEE CONCEPTS *46,278,665*

contradictory [adj] *antagonistic*
adverse, against, agin, anti, antipodal, antipodean, antithetic, antithetical, con, conflicting, contrary, converse, counter, counteractive, diametric, discrepant, incompatible, incongruous, inconsistent, irreconcilable, negating, no go*, nullifying, opposing, opposite, ornery*, paradoxical, polar, repugnant, reverse; SEE CONCEPT *542*

contrary [adj] *antagonistic; opposite*
adverse, anti, antipathetic, antipodal, antipodean, antithetical, balky, clashing, conflicting, contradictory, contrariant, contumacious, converse, counter, diametric, discordant, dissentient, dissident, froward, headstrong, hostile, inconsistent, inimical, insubordinate, intractable, negative, nonconforming, nonconformist, obstinate, opposed, ornery*, paradoxical, perverse, rebellious, recalcitrant, recusant, refractory, restive, reverse, stubborn, unruly, wayward, wrongheaded; SEE CONCEPT *401*

contrast [n] *difference*
adverse, antithesis, comparison, contradiction, contradistinction, contraposition, contrariety, converse, differentiation, disagreement, disparity, dissimilarity, dissimilitude, distinction, divergence, diversity, foil, heterogeneity, incompatibility, incongruousness, inconsistency, inequality, inverse, oppositeness, opposition, reverse, unlikeness, variance, variation; SEE CONCEPTS *561,665*

contrast [v] *compare, differ*
balance, be a foil to*, be contrary to, be dissimilar, be diverse, be unlike, be variable, bracket, collate, conflict, contradict, depart, deviate, differentiate, disagree, distinguish, diverge, hang, hold a candle to*, match up, mismatch, oppose, separate, set in opposition, set off, stack up against*, stand out, vary, weigh; SEE CONCEPTS *39,561,665*

contravene [v] *go against, contradict*
abjure, breach, break, combat, conflict with, counteract, cross, defy, disaffirm, disobey, encroach, exclude, fight, gainsay, hinder, impugn, infract, infringe, interfere, interpose, intrude, negate, offend, oppose, overstep, refute, reject, repudiate, resist, spurn, thwart, transgress, traverse, trespass, violate; SEE CONCEPTS *46,106,121,192*

contribute [v1] *donate, provide*
accord, add, afford, ante up, assign, bequeath, bequest, bestow, chip in, come through, commit, confer, devote, dispense, dole out*, dower, endow, enrich, furnish, give, give away, go Dutch*, grant, hand out, kick in*, pitch in*, pony up*, present, proffer, sacrifice, share, subscribe, subsidize, supply, sweeten the kitty*, tender, will; SEE CONCEPTS *108,140*

contribute [v2] *be partly responsible for*
add to, advance, aid, assist, augment, be conducive, be instrumental, conduce, do one's bit, finger in the

pie*, fortify, get in the act*, have a hand in*, help, lead, put in two cents*, redound, reinforce, sit in on, strengthen, supplement, support, tend, uphold; SEE CONCEPTS *83,110,244*

contribution [n] *gift, offering*
addition, a hand, alms, augmentation, benefaction, beneficence, bestowal, charity, donation, do one's part*, gifting, grant, handout, helping hand, improvement, increase, input, offering, present, significant addition, subscription, supplement, write-off; SEE CONCEPTS *337,340*

contrite [adj] *regretful*
apologetic, attritional, chastened, compunctious, conscience-stricken, humble, penitent, penitential, remorseful, repentant, sorrowful, sorry; SEE CONCEPT *403*

contrition [n] *regret*
attrition, compunction, contriteness, humiliation, penance, penitence, penitency, remorse, repentance, rue, ruth, self-reproach, sorrow; SEE CONCEPT *410*

contrivance [n1] *plan, fabrication*
angle, artifice, brainchild, coinage, design, dodge, expedient, formation, gimmick, intrigue, invention, inventiveness, machination, measure, plot, project, ruse, scheme, slant, stratagem, switch, trick, twist; SEE CONCEPT *660*

contrivance [n2] *gadget*
apparatus, appliance, brainchild, coinage, contraption, convenience, creation, device, discovery, engine, equipment, gear, gimcrack*, harness, implement, instrument, invention, machine, material, mechanism, tackle, thingamabob*, thingamajig*, tool, utensil, whatsis*, widget*; SEE CONCEPTS *260,463,499*

contrive [v1] *invent, design*
come up with, concoct, construct, cook up, create, devise, dream up*, engineer, fabricate, fashion, forge, form, formulate, frame*, handle, hatch, improvise, make, make up*, manipulate, manufacture, move, plan, plot, project, rig*, scheme, throw together*, trump up*, vamp, wangle, whip up*; SEE CONCEPTS *36,173*

contrive [v2] *bring about, succeed with difficulty*
achieve, angle, arrange, carry out, cogitate, collude, compass, concoct, connive, develop, devise, effect, elaborate, engineer, execute, finagle*, hatch, hit upon, intrigue, jockey*, machinate, manage, maneuver, manipulate, mastermind, negotiate, pass, plan, play games*, plot, project, scheme, shift, swing, work out, wrangle; SEE CONCEPTS *36,91,94*

control [n] *command, mastery*
ascendancy, authority, bridle, charge, check, clout, containment, curb, determination, direction, discipline, domination, dominion, driver's seat*, force, government, guidance, inside track, juice, jurisdiction, limitation, management, manipulation, might, oversight, power, predomination, qualification, regimentation, regulation, restraint, restriction, ropes,

rule, strings*, subjection, subordination, superintendence, supervision, supremacy, sway, upper hand*, weight, wire pulling*; SEE CONCEPT *376*

control [v1] *have charge of*
administer, administrate, advise, be in saddle*, boss, bully, call, call the signals*, command, conduct, deal with, direct, discipline, dominate, domineer, govern, guide, handle, head, head up*, hold purse strings*, hold sway over*, hold the reins*, instruct, lead, manage, manipulate, mastermind, overlook, oversee, pilot, predominate, push buttons*, quarterback*, regiment, regulate, reign over, rule, run, run the show*, run things*, steer, subject, subjugate, superintend, supervise, wear the pants*; SEE CONCEPT *117*

control [v2] *curb, hold back*
adjust, awe, bridle, check, collect, compose, constrain, contain, cool, corner, cow, limit, master, monopolize, quell, regulate, rein in, repress, restrain, simmer down*, smother, subdue; SEE CONCEPT *130*

controversial [adj] *at issue*
arguable, argumentative, contended, contentious, contestable, controvertible, debateable, disputable, disputatious, disputed, doubtable, doubtful, dubious, dubitable, in dispute, litigious, moot, open to discussion*, open to question*, polemical, questionable, suspect, uncertain, under discussion; SEE CONCEPTS *535,546*

controversy [n] *debate, dispute*
altercation, argument, beef*, bickering, brush, contention, difference, discussion, disputation, dissention, embroilment, falling-out*, flak, fuss, hurrah, miff, polemic, quarrel, row, rumpus, scene, scrap, squabble, strife, tiff*, words, wrangle, wrangling; SEE CONCEPTS *46,278,665*

controvert [v] *oppose, argue*
break, challenge, confound, confute, contest, contradict, counter, debate, deny, disconfirm, discuss, disprove, dispute, oppugn, question, rebut, refute, wrangle; SEE CONCEPTS *21,46*

contumacious [adj] *headstrong, obstinate*
alienated, contrary, disaffected, estranged, factious, froward, haughty, inflexible, insubordinate, insurgent, intractable, intransigent, irreconcilable, mutinous, obdurate, perverse, pig-headed, rebellious, recalcitrant, refractory, seditious, stubborn, unyielding; SEE CONCEPT *401*

contusion [n] *bruise, injury*
bang, bump, cut, discoloration, knock, mouse, swelling, wale, wound; SEE CONCEPT *309*

conundrum [n] *puzzle*
brain-teaser, closed book*, enigma, mystery, mystification, poser*, problem, puzzlement, riddle, why*; SEE CONCEPTS *532,666,690*

convalescent [adj] *improving, recuperating*
ambulatory, discharged, dismissed, gaining strength, getting better, getting over something*, getting well, healing, mending, on the mend*, past crisis, perked up, rallying, recovering, rejuvenated, rejuvenating,

released, restored, strengthening; SEE CONCEPT *314*

convene [v] *bring together; meet*
assemble, call, call in, collect, come together, congregate, convoke, corral, gather, get together, hold meeting, muster, open, rally, round up, scare up, sit, summon, unite; SEE CONCEPTS *60,114,324*

convenience [n1] *availability, usefulness; useful thing*
accessibility, accessory, accommodation, advancement, advantage, agreeableness, aid, amenity, appliance, appropriateness, assistance, avail, benefit, comfort, comforts, contribution, cooperation, decency, ease, enjoyment, facility, fitness, furtherance, handiness, help, life, luxury, means, ministration, ministry, openness, opportuneness, promotion, receptiveness, relief, satisfaction, service, serviceability, succor, suitability, suitableness, support, time saver, use, utility; SEE CONCEPTS *658,712*

convenience [n2] *spare time*
chance, freedom, hour, leisure, liberty, occasion, one's own sweet time*, opportunity, place, preference, spare moment*, suitable time, whenever; SEE CONCEPT *807*

convenient [adj1] *appropriate, useful*
acceptable, accommodating, adaptable, adapted, advantageous, agreeable, aiding, assisting, available, beneficial, comfortable, commodious, conducive, contributive, decent, favorable, fit, fitted, good, handy, helpful, in public interest, opportune, proper, ready, roomy, seasonable, serviceable, suitable, suited, timely, time-saving, user-friendly*, well-planned; SEE CONCEPT *560*

convenient [adj2] *nearby*
accessible, adjacent, adjoining, all around, at elbows*, at fingertips*, at hand, available, central, close, close at hand, close-by, contiguous, easy to reach, handy, immediate, in neighborhood, next, next door, nigh, on deck*, on tap*, under one's nose*, within reach; SEE CONCEPT *586*

convent [n] *nunnery*
abbey, cloister, monastery, religious community, retreat, school; SEE CONCEPTS *368,516*

convention [n1] *conference*
assemblage, assembly, clambake, confab*, congress, convocation, council, delegates, delegation, get together, meet*, meeting, members, powwow*, rally, representatives, show; SEE CONCEPTS *114, 324,417*

convention [n2] *practice, tradition*
canon, code, covenance, custom, etiquette, fashion, form, formality, habit, law, percept, precept, propriety, rule, understanding, usage; SEE CONCEPT *687*

convention [n3] *agreement*
bargain, bond, compact, concord, concordat, contract, covenant, pact, protocol, stipulation, transaction, treaty; SEE CONCEPTS *271,684*

conventional [adj1] *common, normal*
accepted, accustomed, button-down, commonplace, correct, current, customary, decorous, everyday, expected, fashionable, formal, general, habitual, in established usage, ordinary, orthodox, plain, popular, predominant, prevailing, prevalent, proper, regular, ritual, routine, square, standard, stereotyped, straight, traditional, tralatitious, typical, usual, well-known, wonted; SEE CONCEPTS *530,547*

conventional [adj2] *unoriginal*
bigoted, bourgeois, commonplace, conforming, conservative, demure, doctrinal, dogmatic, drippy, hackneyed, hidebound, humdrum, illiberal, inflexible, in rut, insular, isolationist, lame, literal, moderate, moral, narrow, narrow-minded, not heretical, obstinate, parochial, pedestrian, prosaic, puritanical, rigid, routine, rube, run-of-the-mill, sober, solemn, square, stereotyped, straight, straight-laced, strict, stuffy, uptight; SEE CONCEPT *550*

converge [v] *gather*
assemble, coincide, combine, come together, concenter, concentrate, concur, encounter, enter in, focalize, focus, join, meet, merge, mingle, rally, unite; SEE CONCEPTS *113,114*

conversant [adj] *experienced, familiar with*
abreast, acquainted, alive, apprehensive, au courant, au fait, aware, cognizant, comprehending, conscious, cool*, down with*, hep*, hip*, informed, into, kept posted, knowing, knowledgeable, learned, on the beam*, perceptive, percipient, plugged in, practiced, proficient, sensible, sentient, skilled, up*, up-to-date, versant, versed, well-informed, witting; SEE CONCEPT *402*

conversation [n] *dialogue, discourse*
chat, colloquy, comment, communication, communion, confab*, confabulation, conference, consultation, converse, debate, discussion, exchange, expression, gab*, gossip, hearing, intercourse, jive*, observation, palaver, parley, pillow talk*, powwow*, questioning, remark, repartee, speech, talk, talkfest*, tête-à-tête*, ventilation*, visit, yak*; SEE CONCEPT *266*

converse [n] *opposite*
antipode, antipole, antithesis, contra, contrary, counter, counterpole, inverse, obverse, other side, reverse; SEE CONCEPT *665*

converse [adj] *opposite*
antipodal, antipodean, antithetical, contradictory, contrary, counter, counterpole, different, reverse, reversed, transposed; SEE CONCEPT *564*

converse [v] *talk*
chat, chew the fat*, chitchat*, commune, confer, discourse, exchange, gab*, parley, rap*, schmooze*, speak, use, yak*; SEE CONCEPT *266*

conversion [n] *change, adaptation*
about-face*, alteration, born again*, change of heart*, changeover, exchange, flip-flop*, flux, growth, innovation, metamorphosis, metanoia, metasis, modification, novelty, passage, passing, permutation, progress, proselytization, qualification, reclamation, reconstruction, reformation, regeneration, remodelling, reorganization, resolution, resolving, reversal,

see the light*, switch, transfiguration, transformation, translation, transmogrification, transmutation, turning, turning around; SEE CONCEPTS *232,701*

convert [*n*] *new believer*
catechumen, disciple, follower, neophyte, novice, novitiate, proselyte; SEE CONCEPT *361*

convert [*v1*] *change; adapt*
alter, apply, appropriate, commute, interchange, make, metamorphose, modify, remodel, reorganize, restyle, revise, switch, switch over, transfigure, transform, translate, transmogrify, transmute, transpose, turn; SEE CONCEPTS *232,701*

convert [*v2*] *change belief, especially regarding religion*
actuate, alter conviction, assimilate to, baptize, be born again*, bend, bias, brainwash, bring, bring around, budge, cause to adopt, change into, change of heart*, convince, create anew, impel, incline, lead, lead to believe, make over, move, persuade, proselyte, proselytize, redeem, reform, regenerate, save, see the light*, sway, turn; SEE CONCEPTS *12,14,35*

convex [*adj*] *rounded, curving outward*
arched, bent, biconvex, bulged, bulging, bulgy, gibbous, outcurved, protuberant, raised; SEE CONCEPT *486*

convey [*v1*] *transport*
back, bear, bring, carry, channel, conduct, dispatch, ferry, fetch, forward, funnel, grant, guide, hump, lead, lug, move, pack, pipe, ride, schlepp*, send, shoulder, siphon, support, tote, traject, transfer, transmit, truck; SEE CONCEPTS *187,217*

convey [*v2*] *express message*
break, carry, communicate, conduct, disclose, impart, make known, pass on, project, put across, relate, reveal, send, tell, transmit; SEE CONCEPT *60*

conveyance [*n*] *transport*
car, carriage, carrying, communication, machine, movement, transfer, transference, transmission, transportation, vehicle; SEE CONCEPTS *143,501,503*

convict [*n*] *criminal*
captive, con, culprit, felon, jailbird*, long-termer*, loser*, malefactor, prisoner, repeater*; SEE CONCEPT *412*

convict [*v*] *find guilty*
adjudge, attaint, bring to justice, condemn, declare guilty, doom, frame, imprison, pass sentence on, pronounce guilty, put away, put the screws to*, rap*, send up*, send up the river*, sentence, throw the book at*; SEE CONCEPTS *18,317*

conviction [*n1*] *belief, opinion*
confidence, creed, doctrine, dogma, eye, faith, feeling, judgment call, mind, persuasion, principle, reliance, say so, sentiment, slant, tenet, view; SEE CONCEPT *689*

conviction [*n2*] *guilty sentence; assurance*
assuredness, certainty, certitude, condemnation, condemning, confidence, determining guilt, earnestness,

fall, fervor, firmness, rap, reliance, sureness, surety, unfavorable verdict; SEE CONCEPTS *317,410*

convince [*v*] *gain the confidence of*
argue into, assure, brainwash, bring around, bring home to*, bring to reason*, change, demonstrate, draw, effect, establish, get, hook*, induce, make a believer*, overcome, persuade, prevail upon, prompt, prove, put across, refute, satisfy, sell*, sell one on*, sway, talk into, turn, twist one's arm*, win over; SEE CONCEPT *68*

convincing [*adj*] *persuasive*
acceptable, authentic, believeable, cogent, conclusive, credible, dependable, faithful, hopeful, impressive, incontrovertible, likely, moving, plausible, possible, powerful, presumable, probable, rational, reasonable, reliable, satisfactory, satisfying, solid, sound, swaying, telling, trustworthy, trusty, valid; SEE CONCEPTS *267,537,552*

convivial [*adj*] *fun-loving*
back-slapping*, cheerful, clubby*, companionable, conversible, entertaining, festal, festive, friendly, gay, genial, glad-handing*, happy, hearty, hilarious, holiday, jocund, jolly, jovial, lively, merry, mirthful, pleasant, sociable, vivacious; SEE CONCEPTS *401,404*

convocation [*n*] *assembly*
assemblage, conclave, concourse, confab*, conference, congregation, congress, convention, council, diet, get-together, meet, meeting, powwow*, synod, turnout; SEE CONCEPT *114*

convolution [*n*] *loop, spiral*
coil, coiling, complexity, contortion, curlicue, flexing, gyration, helix, intricacy, involution, serpentine, sinuosity, sinuousness, snaking, swirl, tortuousness, twist, undulation, winding; SEE CONCEPT *436*

convoy [*n*] *guard, escort*
attendance, attendant, companion, protection; SEE CONCEPT *423*

convoy [*v*] *protect, escort*
accompany, attend, bear, bring, chaperon, companion, company, conduct, consort, defend, guard, pilot, safeguard, shepherd, shield, usher, watch; SEE CONCEPTS *96,110*

convulsion [*n1*] *muscle spasm*
algospasm, attack, contortion, contraction, cramp, epilepsy, fit, paroxysm, seizure, throe, tremor; SEE CONCEPT *308*

convulsion [*n2*] *disturbance*
agitation, cataclysm, clamor, commotion, disaster, ferment, furor, outcry, quaking, rocking, seism, shaking, shock, tottering, trembling, tumult, turbulence, upheaval, upturn; SEE CONCEPTS *152,748*

cook [*n*] *person who prepares food*
baker, chef, hash slinger*, mess sergeant, servant, sous chef; SEE CONCEPT *348*

cook [*v*] *prepare food, usually using heat*
bake, barbecue, blanch, boil, braise, brew, broil, brown, burn, coddle, cremate, curry, decoct, deep

fry, devil, doctor*, escallop, fix, French fry, fricassee, fry, griddle, grill, heat, imbue, melt, microwave, mull, nuke*, panfry, parboil, parch, percolate, poach, pressure-cook, reduce, roast, ruin, sauté, scald, scorch, sear, seethe, simmer, sizzle, spoil, steam, steep, stew, toast, warm up; SEE CONCEPT *170*

cook up [*v*] *devise*
arrange, concoct, contrive, dream up, fabricate, falsify, formulate, frame, hatch, improvise, invent, make up, plan, plot, prepare, scheme, vamp; SEE CONCEPTS *17,36*

cool [*adj1*] *cold, nippy*
air-conditioned, algid, arctic, biting, chill, chilled, chilling, chilly, coldish, frigid, frore, frosty, gelid, hawkish, nipping, refreshing, refrigerated, shivery, snappy, wintry; SEE CONCEPT *605*

cool [*adj2*] *calm, collected*
assured, composed, coolheaded, deliberate, detached, dispassionate, impassive, imperturbable, levelheaded, nonchalant, philosophical, phlegmatic, placid, quiet, relaxed, self-controlled, self-possessed, serene, stolid, together, tranquil, unagitated, unemotional, unexcited, unflappable, unruffled; SEE CONCEPT *401*

cool [*adj3*] *aloof, disapproving*
annoyed, apathetic, distant, frigid, impertinent, impudent, incurious, indifferent, insolent, lukewarm, offended, offhand, offish, procacious, reserved, solitary, standoffish, unapproachable, uncommunicative, unenthusiastic, unfriendly, uninterested, unresponsive, unsociable, unwelcoming, withdrawn; SEE CONCEPT *404*

cool [*adj4*] *excellent*
boss*, dandy, divine, glorious, hunky-dory*, keen, marvelous, neat, nifty, sensational, swell; SEE CONCEPT *572*

cool [*v1*] *chill*
abate, air-condition, air-cool, ally, calm, freeze, frost, infrigidate, lessen, lose heat, mitigate, moderate, reduce, refrigerate, temper; SEE CONCEPT *255*

cool [*v2*] *take a break; abate*
allay, assuage, calm, calm down, chill, compose, control, dampen, lessen, mitigate, moderate, quiet, reduce, rein, repress, restrain, simmer down, suppress, temper; SEE CONCEPTS *240,384*

cooperate [*v*] *aid, assist*
abet, advance, agree, back up, band, befriend, be in cahoots, chip in, coadjute, coincide, collaborate, combine, comply with, concert, concur, conduce, conspire, contribute, coordinate, espouse, forward, fraternize, further, go along with, help, join forces, join in, league, lend a hand*, participate, partner, pitch in*, play ball*, pool resources, pull together, second, share in, show willingness, side with, stick together, succor, take part, unite, uphold, work side by side, work together; SEE CONCEPTS *110,112*

cooperation [*n*] *mutual effort*
aid, alliance, assistance, cahoots*, coaction, coadjuvancy, coalition, collaboration, combination, combined effort, communion, company, concert, concurrence, confederacy, confederation, confunction, conspiracy, doing business with, esprit de corps, federation, fusion, give-and-take, harmony, help, helpfulness, logrolling*, participation, partisanship, partnership, playing ball*, reciprocity, responsiveness, service, society, symbiosis, synergism, synergy, teaming, teamwork, unanimity, union, unity; SEE CONCEPTS *110,112,388,677*

cooperative [*adj1*] *joint, unified*
agreeing, coacting, coactive, coadjuvant, coefficient, collaborating, collaborative, collective, collegial, collusive, combined, combining, common, concerted, concurring, coordinated, hand in glove*, harmonious, in league, interdependent, joining, participating, reciprocal, shared, symbiotic, synergetic, synergic, team, united, uniting; SEE CONCEPT *538*

cooperative [*adj2*] *helpful*
accommodating, companionable, obliging, responsive, sociable, supportive, useful; SEE CONCEPTS *538,555*

coordinate [*adj*] *equivalent*
alike, coequal, correlative, correspondent, counterpart, equal, equalized, like, parallel, same, tantamount; SEE CONCEPT *566*

coordinate [*v*] *match, relate*
accommodate, adjust, agree, atune, combine, conduce, conform, correlate, get it together*, get one's act together*, harmonize, integrate, mesh, organize, pool, proportion, pull together, quarterback*, reconcile, reconciliate, regulate, shape up, synchronize, systematize, team up; SEE CONCEPTS *36,84,158*

cope [*v*] *manage, contend*
battle with, buffet, carry on, confront, deal, dispatch, encounter, endure, face, get a handle on*, get by, grapple, hack*, hack it*, handle, hold one's own*, live with, make go of it*, make it*, make out*, make the grade*, manage, pit oneself against*, rise to occasion, struggle, struggle through, suffer, survive, tangle, tussle, weather, wrestle; SEE CONCEPTS *23,35*

copious [*adj*] *abundant*
alive with, a mess of*, ample, aplenty, bounteous, bountiful, coming out of ears*, crawling with*, extensive, exuberant, full, galore, generous, heavy, lavish, liberal, lush, luxuriant, no end*, overflowing, plenteous, plentiful, plenty, profuse, prolix, replete, rich, superabundant, thick with, verbose, wordy; SEE CONCEPT *771*

copiousness [*n*] *abundance*
affluence, amplitude, bountifulness, bounty, cornucopia, exuberance, fullness, horn of plenty*, lavishness, luxuriance, plentifulness, plenty, richness, superabundance; SEE CONCEPT *767*

cop out [*v*] *abandon, quit*
back down, back off, back out, backpedal, desert, dodge, excuse, give the slip*, have alibi, rationalize, renege, renounce, revoke, skip, use pretext, welsh, withdraw; SEE CONCEPTS *121,156*

copulate [v] *have sexual relations*
be carnal, bed, breed, cohabit, conjugate, couple, do it*, fool around*, fornicate, go all the way*, go to bed*, have coition, have relations, have sex, lay, lie with, make love, make out*, mate, sleep together, sleep with, unite; SEE CONCEPT *375*

copy [n] *duplicate, imitation*
archetype, carbon, carbon copy*, cast, clone, counterfeit, counterpart, ditto, ectype, effigy, ersatz, facsimile, forgery, hard copy, image, impersonation, impression, imprint, likeness, microfiche, mimeograph, miniature, mirror, model, offprint, parallel, pattern, photocopy, photograph, photostat, portrait, print, reflection, replica, replication, representation, reprint, reproduction, rubbings, similarity, simulacrum, simulation, study, tracing, transcript, transcription, type, Xerox*; SEE CONCEPTS *269,667,716*

copy [v1] *duplicate*
carbon, cartoon, clone, counterfeit, delineate, depict, ditto, draw, dupe, engrave, engross, fake, forge, imitate, knock off*, limn, manifold, mimeo, mirror, mold, paint, paraphrase, photocopy, photostat, picture, plagiarize, portray, reduplicate, reflect, repeat, replicate, represent, reproduce, rewrite, sculpture, simulate, sketch, stat, trace, transcribe, Xerox*; SEE CONCEPT *171*

copy [v2] *imitate*
act like, ape, burlesque, do, do a take-off*, do like*, echo, embody, emulate, epitomize, fake, follow, follow example, follow suit, go like*, illustrate, incarnate, knock off*, make like*, mimic, mirror, mock, model, parody, parrot, personify, phony, pirate, play a role, prefigure, repeat, sham, simulate, steal, take leaf out of book*, take off*, travesty, typify; SEE CONCEPTS *59,139,242*

coquet [v] *tease*
dally, flirt, fool, gold-dig*, lead on, make eyes at*, operate, philander, string along, titillate, toy, trifle, vamp, wanton, wink at*; SEE CONCEPTS *375,384*

cord [n] *rope*
bond, connection, cordage, fiber, line, link, string, tendon, tie, twine; SEE CONCEPTS *470,680*

cordial [adj] *friendly, sociable*
affable, affectionate, agreeable, amicable, buddy-buddy*, cheerful, clubby*, companionable, congenial, convivial, cozy, earnest, genial, glowing, gracious, happy, heartfelt, heart-to-heart, hearty, invigorating, jovial, mellow, neighborly, palsy-walsy*, polite, red-carpet*, responsive, sincere, social, sympathetic, tender, warm, warmhearted, welcoming, wholehearted; SEE CONCEPT *401*

cordiality [n] *friendliness, sociability*
affability, agreeability, agreeableness, amenity, amiability, approbation, approval, earnestness, enjoyableness, favor, geniality, gratefulness, heartiness, mutuality, pleasantness, reciprocity, responsiveness, sincerity, sweetness and light*, sympathy, understanding, warmth, wholeheartedness; SEE CONCEPT *633*

core [n] *center, gist*
amount, base, basis, body, bottom line, bulk, burden, consequence, corpus, crux, essence, focus, foundation, heart, import, importance, kernel, main idea, mass, meat*, meat and potatoes*, middle, midpoint, midst, nitty gritty*, nub, nucleus, origin, pith, pivot, purport, quick, root, significance, staple, substance, thrust, upshot; SEE CONCEPTS *442,668,826*

corner [n1] *angle*
bend, branch, cloverleaf, crook, crossing, edge, fork, intersection, joint, junction, projection, ridge, rim, shift, V*, veer, Y*; SEE CONCEPTS *436,484,513*

corner [n2] *niche*
angle, cavity, compartment, cranny, hideaway, hideout, hole, indentation, nook, recess, retreat; SEE CONCEPTS *440,471,513*

corner [n3] *predicament*
box, difficulty, dilemma, distress, fix, hole, impasse, impediment, jam, knot, pickle, plight, scrape, tight spot; SEE CONCEPTS *674,675*

corner [v] *trap*
bottle, bring to bay, capture, catch, collar*, fool, get on ropes*, have up a tree*, mousetrap*, nab, put out, seize, tree, trick, trouble; SEE CONCEPTS *59,90*

corny [adj] *trite, clichéd*
banal, commonplace, dull*, feeble, hackneyed, mawkish, melodramatic, old-fashioned, old hat*, sentimental, shopworn, stale, stereotyped, stupid, tired, warmed-over*; SEE CONCEPT *550*

corollary [n] *conclusion, deduction*
aftereffect, analogy, consequence, culmination, effect, end, end product, induction, inference, issue, precipitate, result, sequel, sequence, upshot; SEE CONCEPTS *230,410,529*

corporal [adj] *bodily, physical*
anatomical, carnal, corporeal, fleshly, fleshy, gross, human, material, objective, phenomenal, sensible, somatic, substantial, tangible; SEE CONCEPT *542*

corporation [n] *business organization, usually large*
association, bunch, business, clan, company, corporate body, crew, crowd, enterprise, gang, hookup*, jungle*, legal entity, megacorp*, mob, multinational, octupus*, outfit, partnership, ring, shell, society, syndicate, zoo*; SEE CONCEPT *325*

corporeal [adj] *bodily, physical*
anatomical, carnal, corporal, fleshly, fleshy, human, material, mortal, objective, phenomenal, sensible, somatic, substantial, tangible; SEE CONCEPT *542*

corps [n] *group trained for action*
band, body, brigade, company, contingent, crew, detachment, division, outfit, party, posse, regiment, squad, squadron, team, troop, troupe, unit; SEE CONCEPTS *294,322,417*

corpse [n] *dead body*
body, bones*, cadaver, carcass, carrion, mort*, remains, stiff*, the deceased, the departed; SEE CONCEPTS *390,417*

corpulent [adj] fat, chubby
baby elephant*, beefy*, blimp*, bulky, burly, embonpoint, fat, fleshy, gross, having a bay window*, having a spare tire*, heavy, hefty, husky, large, lusty, obese, overblown, overweight, plump, portly, roly-poly*, rotund, stout, tubby, weighty, well-padded*; SEE CONCEPTS 406,491,773

corpus [n] body of text
bulk, collection, compilation, complete works, core, entirety, extant works, mass, oeuvre, opera omnia, staple, substance, whole; SEE CONCEPT 271

correct [adj1] accurate, exact
according to Hoyle*, actual, amen*, appropriate, cooking with gas*, dead on*, equitable, factual, faithful, faultless, flawless, for sure, free of error, impeccable, just, legitimate, nice, okay, on target*, on the ball*, on the beam*, on the button*, on the money*, on the nose*, on track*, perfect, precise, proper, regular, right, right as rain*, righteous, right on*, right stuff*, rigorous, stone, strict, true, undistorted, unmistaken, veracious, veridical; SEE CONCEPTS 542,557,574

correct [adj2] proper, appropriate
acceptable, becoming, careful, comme il faut, conforming, conventional, decent, decorous, diplomatic, done, fitting, meticulous, nice, okay, punctilious, right, right stuff*, scrupulous, seemly, standard, suitable; SEE CONCEPTS 401,558

correct [v1] fix, adjust
alter, ameliorate, amend, better, change, clean up, clean up act*, cure, debug*, doctor*, do over, edit, emend, fiddle with, fix up, get with it*, go over, help, improve, launder, make over, make right, make up for, mend, pay dues*, pick up, polish, put in order, reclaim, reconstruct, rectify, redress, reform, regulate, remedy, remodel, reorganize, repair, retouch, review, revise, right, scrub*, set right, set straight, shape up, straighten out, touch up, turn around, upgrade; SEE CONCEPT 126

correct [v2] discipline, chastise
administer, admonish, castigate, chasten, chide, penalize, punish, reprimand, reprove; SEE CONCEPTS 52,122

correction [n1] adjustment; fixing
alteration, amelioration, amending, amendment, changing, editing, emendation, improvement, indemnification, mending, modification, rectification, redress, reexamination, remodeling, repair, reparation, rereading, revisal, revising, righting; SEE CONCEPTS 126,700

correction [n2] discipline
admonition, castigation, chastisement, punishment, punition, reformation, reproof, rod; SEE CONCEPT 122

corrective [adj] healing, curing
antidotal, counteracting, curative, disciplinary, palliative, penal, punitive, reformatory, rehabilitative, remedial, restorative, therapeutic; SEE CONCEPT 537

correctly [adv] right
accurately, befittingly, decently, decorously, fitly, fittingly, justly, nicely, perfectly, precisely, properly, rightly, to a T*, well; SEE CONCEPT 558

correctness [n1] accuracy
definiteness, definitiveness, definitude, exactitude, exactness, faultlessness, fidelity, preciseness, precision, regularity, truth; SEE CONCEPTS 638,654

correctness [n2] propriety
bon ton, civility, correctitude, decency, decorousness, decorum, fitness, good breeding, order, orderliness, properness, rightness, seemliness; SEE CONCEPTS 633,656

correlate [v] equate, compare
associate, be on same wavelength*, connect, coordinate, correspond, have good vibes*, interact, parallel, relate mutually, tie in*, tune in on*; SEE CONCEPT 39

correlation [n] equating, equivalence
alternation, analogue, complement, correspondence, correspondent, counterpart, interaction, interchange, interconnection, interdependence, interrelation, interrelationship, match, parallel, pendant, reciprocity, relationship; SEE CONCEPTS 388,667

correspond [v1] agree, complement
accord, amount, approach, assimilate, be consistent, be identical to, be similar to, coincide, compare, conform, correlate, dovetail, equal, fit, harmonize, lip sync, match, partake of, reciprocate, resemble, rival, square, tally, touch; SEE CONCEPT 664

correspond [v2] communicate in writing
answer, drop a kite*, drop a line*, drop a note*, epistolize, exchange letters, have pen pal, hear from, keep in touch, pen, put pen to paper*, reply, scribble, send letter, send word, write; SEE CONCEPTS 79,266

correspondence [n1] agreement
accord, analogy, coherence, coincidence, comparability, comparison, concurrence, conformity, congruity, consistency, correlation, equivalence, fitness, harmony, likeness, match, regularity, relation, resemblance, similarity, symmetry; SEE CONCEPT 664

correspondence [n2] communication by writing
exchange of letters, letters, mail, messages, post, reports, writing; SEE CONCEPTS 79,277,278

correspondent [n] person communicating in writing
contributor, epistler, epistolarian, freelancer, gazetteer, journalist, letter writer, pen pal, reporter, stringer*, writer; SEE CONCEPTS 348,423

corresponding [adj] equivalent, matching
agnate, akin, alike, analogous, answering, comparable, complementary, consonant, correlative, correspondent, coterminus, identical, interrelated, kin, kindred, like, parallel, reciprocal, similar, synonymous, undifferentiated; SEE CONCEPT 566

corridor [n] hallway
aisle, couloir, entrance hall, entranceway, foyer, hall, ingress, lobby, passage, passageway; SEE CONCEPT 440

corroborate [v] *back up information, story*
approve, authenticate, bear out, certify, check on, check out, check up, confirm, declare true, document, double check, endorse, establish, give nod*, justify, okay, prove, ratify, rubber-stamp*, strengthen, substantiate, support, sustain, validate, verify; SEE CONCEPTS *49,57*

corrode [v] *wear away; eat away*
bite, canker, consume, corrupt, destroy, deteriorate, erode, gnaw, impair, oxidize, rot, rust, scour, waste; SEE CONCEPTS *156,169,186,250*

corrosive [adj] *consuming, wearing; bitter*
acerb, acerbic, acrid, archilochian, biting, caustic, corroding, cutting, destructive, erosive, incisive, sarcastic, strongly acid, trenchant, venomous, virulent, wasting; SEE CONCEPT *537*

corrugated [adj] *ridged, grooved*
channelled, creased, crinkled, crumpled, flexed, fluted, folded, furrowed, puckered, roughened, rumpled, wrinkled; SEE CONCEPTS *485,606*

corrupt [adj1] *dishonest*
base, bent, bribable, crooked, debauched, double-dealing, exploiting, extortionate, faithless, fast and loose*, fixed, foul, fraudulent, gone to the dogs*, inconstant, iniquitous, knavish, mercenary, nefarious, on the take*, open, padded*, perfidious, praetorian, profiteering, racket up*, reprobate, rotten, shady, snide, suborned, tainted, treacherous, two-faced, underhanded, unethical, unfaithful, unprincipled, unscrupulous, untrustworthy, venal, wide open*; SEE CONCEPT *545*

corrupt [adj2] *debased, vicious*
abandoned, abased, baneful, boorish, degenerate, degraded, deleterious, depraved, dishonored, dissolute, evil, flagitious, infamous, loose, low, miscreant, monstrous, nefarious, perverse, profligate, rotten, villainous; SEE CONCEPTS *401,545*

corrupt [adj3] *adulterated, rotten*
altered, contaminated, decayed, defiled, distorted, doctored, falsified, foul, infected, noxious, polluted, putrescent, putrid, tainted; SEE CONCEPTS *485,613*

corrupt [v] *pervert; pollute*
abase, abuse, adulterate, animalize, bastardize, blemish, blight, bribe, contaminate, damage, debase, debauch, decay, decompose, deface, defile, deform, degrade, demean, demoralize, deprave, depreciate, despoil, disfigure, disgrace, dishonor, fix, grease palm*, harm, hurt, ill-treat, impair, infect, injure, lower, lure, maltreat, mar, mistreat, misuse, outrage, pull down, putrefy, ravage, reduce, rot, ruin, spoil, square, stain, suborn, subvert, taint, undermine, violate, vitiate, warp, waste; SEE CONCEPTS *14,240*

corruption [n1] *dishonesty*
breach of trust, bribery, bribing, crime, crookedness, demoralization, dishonesty, exploitation, extortion, fiddling, fraud, fraudulency, graft, jobbery, malfeasance, misrepresentation, nepotism, on the take*, payoff, payola*, profiteering, racket*, shadiness*, shady deal*, shuffle, skimming, squeeze*, unscrupulousness, venality; SEE CONCEPT *645*

corruption [n2] *baseness*
atrocity, decadence, degeneration, degradation, depravity, evil, immorality, impurity, infamy, iniquity, looseness, lubricity, perversion, profligacy, sinfulness, turpitude, vice, viciousness, vulgarity, wickedness; SEE CONCEPTS *633,645*

corruption [n3] *adulteration*
debasement, decay, defilement, distortion, doctoring, falsification, foulness, infection, noxiousness, pollution, putrefaction, putrescence, rot, rottenness; SEE CONCEPT *723*

cosmetic [adj] *beautifying; relating to appearance*
corrective, gooky*, improving, makeup, nonessential, painted, remedial, restorative, superficial, surface, touching-up; SEE CONCEPT *579*

cosmic [adj] *limitless; universal*
catholic, cosmogonal, cosmogonic, cosmopolitan, ecumenical, empyrean, global, grandiose, huge, immense, infinite, measureless, planetary, vast, worldwide; SEE CONCEPT *772*

cosmopolitan [adj] *worldly-wise*
catholic, cultivated, cultured, ecumenical, global, gregarious, metropolitan, planetary, polished, public, smooth, sophisticated, universal, urbane, well-travelled, worldly, worldwide; SEE CONCEPT *589*

cosmos [n1] *universe*
creation, galaxy, macrocosm, macrocosmos, megacosm, nature, solar system, star system, world; SEE CONCEPTS *511,770*

cosmos [n2] *ordered system*
harmony, order, organization, scheme, structure; SEE CONCEPTS *727,770*

cost [n1] *expense; price paid*
amount, arm and a leg*, bad news*, bite*, bottom dollar*, bottom line*, charge, damage*, disbursement, dues, expenditure, figure, line, nick*, nut*, outlay, payment, price, price tag, rate, score*, setback*, squeeze*, tab, tariff, ticket, toll, top dollar*, value, worth; SEE CONCEPTS *328,336*

cost [n2] *penalty, sacrifice*
damage, deprivation, detriment, expense, forfeit, forfeiture, harm, hurt, injury, loss, suffering; SEE CONCEPTS *676,679*

cost [v1] *command a price of*
amount to, be asked, be demanded, be given, be marked at, be needed, be paid, be priced at, be received, be valued at, be worth, bring in, come to, mount up, move back, nick*, rap*, require, sell at, sell for, set back, take, to the tune of*, yield; SEE CONCEPTS *328,336*

cost [v2] *harm; exact a penalty*
do disservice to, expect, hurt, infuriate, lose, necessitate, obligate, require; SEE CONCEPT *246*

costly [adj1] *expensive*
an arm and leg*, cher*, dear*, excessive, executive, exorbitant, extortionate, extravagant, fancy, high,

highly priced, high-priced, inordinate, precious, premium, pricey, steep, stiff*, top, valuable; SEE CONCEPT 334

costly [adj2] *priceless*
gorgeous, inestimable, invaluable, lavish, luxurious, opulent, precious, rich, splendid, sumptuous, valuable; SEE CONCEPT 567

costly [adj3] *harmful, damaging*
catastrophic, deleterious, disastrous, loss-making, ruinous, sacrificial; SEE CONCEPT 537

costume [n] *set of clothes*
apparel, attire, clothing, dress, ensemble, fashion, garb, getup*, guise, livery, mode, outfit, rig*, robes*, style, suit, uniform, wardrobe; SEE CONCEPT 451

cot [n] *temporary bed*
army bed, berth, bunk, camp bed, folding bed, gurney, small bed, trundle; SEE CONCEPT 443

cottage [n] *tiny house; lodging*
box, bungalow, cabana, cabin, caboose, camp, carriage house, chalet, cot, home, hut, lean-to, lodge, ranch, shack, shanty, small house; SEE CONCEPT 516

couch [n] *sofa; long, upholstered furniture*
bed, chair, chaise longue, chesterfield, davenport, daybed, divan, lounge, love seat, ottoman, resting place, settee; SEE CONCEPT 443

couch [v] *express in particular way*
formulate, frame, phrase, put, set forth, utter, word; SEE CONCEPT 51

cough [n] *expelled air with sound*
ahem, bark, cold, croup, frog in throat*, hack, hem, tickle in throat*, whoop; SEE CONCEPTS 65,316

cough [v] *expelling air with sound*
bark, choke, clear throat, convulse, expectorate, hack, hawk, hem, spit up, vomit, whoop; SEE CONCEPTS 65,308

council [n] *people assembled for purpose*
assembly, board, body, brain trust*, cabinet, chamber, clan, committee, conclave, confab*, conference, congregation, congress, convention, convocation, diet, directorate, gang, gathering, governing body, groupthink*, huddle*, kitchen cabinet*, meet, ministry, mob, official family, outfit, panel, parliament, powwow*, ring, senate, synod; SEE CONCEPTS 299,325,381

counsel [n1] *guidance*
admonition, advice, advisement, caution, consideration, consultation, deliberation, direction, forethought, information, instruction, kibitz*, recommendation, steer, suggestion, tip, tip-off*, two cents' worth*, warning, word to the wise*; SEE CONCEPTS 75,274

counsel [n2] *legal representative*
adviser, advocate, attorney, barrister, bomber*, counselor, legal adviser, legal beagle*, legal eagle*, lip*, mouthpiece*, patch*, shyster*, solicitor; SEE CONCEPT 355

counsel [v] *give advice*
admonish, advise, advocate, caution, charge, confab*, direct, enjoin, exhort, give pointer, give two cents*, guide, huddle*, inform, instruct, keep posted, order, prescribe, prompt, put bug in ear*, put heads together*, put on to, recommend, reprehend, show the ropes*, steer, suggest, teach, tip, tip off*, tout, urge, warn, wise one up*; SEE CONCEPTS 75,317

counselor [n] *legal representative; adviser*
advocate, ambulance chaser*, attorney, counsel, front*, guide, instructor, legal beagle*, legal eagle*, lip*, mentor, mouthpiece*, pleader, solicitor, squeal*, teacher*; SEE CONCEPT 355

count [n] *tally; number*
calculation, computation, enumeration, numbering, outcome, poll, reckoning, result, sum, toll, total, whole; SEE CONCEPT 766

count [v1] *add, check in order*
add up, calculate, cast, cast up, cipher, compute, enumerate, estimate, figure, foot, keep tab, number, numerate, reckon, run down, score, sum, take account of, tally, tell, tick off, total, tot up; SEE CONCEPT 764

count [v2] *consider, deem*
await, esteem, expect, hope, impute, judge, look, look upon, rate, regard, think; SEE CONCEPTS 18,43

count [v3] *have importance*
carry weight, cut ice*, enter into consideration, import, matter, mean, militate, rate, signify, tell, weigh; SEE CONCEPT 668

count [v4] *include*
await, expect, hope, look, number among, take into account, take into consideration; SEE CONCEPTS 26,112

count on/count upon [v] *depend on; rely*
aim for, bank on, bargain for, believe, believe in, bet bottom dollar*, bet on, expect from, heed, lean on, pin faith on, place confidence in, plan on, reckon on, rest on, score, stake on, swear by, tab, take as gospel truth*, take for granted, take on trust, trust; SEE CONCEPTS 12,26

countenance [n1] *appearance, usually of the face*
aspect, biscuit*, cast, expression, face, features, gills*, kisser*, look, looks, map*, mask, mien, mug, phizog*, physiognomy, poker face*, potato*, puss*, visage; SEE CONCEPTS 716,718

countenance [n2] *self-control*
calmness, composure, presence of mind, self-composure; SEE CONCEPT 633

countenance [v] *approve, support*
abet, accept, advocate, aid, applaud, approbate, back, bear with, champion, commend, condone, confirm, cope, encourage, endorse, favor, get behind, give green light*, give stamp of approval*, give the nod*, go along with, go for, grin and bear it*, handle, help, hold with, invite, live with*, nod at, okay, put John Hancock on*, put up with, sanction, sign off on*, sit still for*, smile on*, stand for, stomach

something*, swallow*, thumbs up*, uphold; SEE CONCEPTS *10,50,88*

counter [adj] *opposite, opposing*
adverse, against, antagonistic, anti, antipodal, antipodean, antithetical, conflicting, contradictory, contrary, contrasting, converse, diametric, hindering, impeding, obstructive, obverse, opposed, polar, reverse; SEE CONCEPTS *544,581*

counter [v] *answer, respond in retaliation*
backtalk, beat, bilk, buck, circumvent, contravene, counteract, counterwork, cross, dash, disappoint, fly in the face of*, foil, frustrate, have bone to pick*, hinder, hit back, match, meet, offset, oppose, parry, pit, play off, resist, respond, retaliate, return, ruin, take on, thumbs down*, vie, ward off; SEE CONCEPTS *45,121*

counter [adv] *contrary, reverse*
against, at variance with, contrarily, contrariwise, conversely, in defiance of, opposite, versus; SEE CONCEPTS *544,581*

counteract [v] *do opposing action*
annul, buck, cancel, cancel out, check, contravene, correct, counterbalance, countercheck, countervail, counterwork, cross, defeat, fix, foil, frustrate, go against, halt, hinder, invalidate, negate, negative, neutralize, offset, oppose, prevent, rectify, redress, resist, right, thwart; SEE CONCEPTS *87,96,126*

counterbalance [v] *offset an action*
amend, atone for, balance, cancel, compensate, correct, counteract, counterpoise, countervail, equalize, make up for, outweigh, rectify, redeem, set off; SEE CONCEPTS *87,96,126*

counterfeit [n] *fake, forgery*
actor, bogus*, bum, copy, deceit, deception, dummy, facsimile, fake, fraud, gyp*, hoax, humbug, imitation, imposture, junque*, phony, pseudo, put-on*, reproduction, sell*, sham, simulacrum; SEE CONCEPTS *648,725*

counterfeit [adj] *fake, simulated*
affected, assumed, bent, bogus*, brummagem, copied, crock, deceptive, delusive, delusory, ersatz, faked, false, feigned, fictitious, fishy*, forged, framed, fraudulent, Hollywood*, imitation, misleading, mock, not genuine, not kosher*, phony*, pirate, plant*, pretended, pretentious, pseudo, put-on*, queer, sham, snide, soft shell*, spurious, supposititious, two-faced*, won't fly*, wrong; SEE CONCEPTS *549,582*

counterfeit [v] *make deceitful imitation*
act like, affect, ape, assume, bluff, carbon, cheat, circulate bad money, clone, coin, copy, defraud, delude, ditto, do, do like*, dupe, fabricate, fake, feign, forge, go like*, imitate, impersonate, knock off, make like*, make money, mimeo, mimic, mint, phony*, phony up*, pretend, put on*, sham, simulate, stat, Xerox*; SEE CONCEPTS *59,171*

countermand [v] *annul, cancel a command*
override, recall, repeal, rescind, retract, retreat, reverse, revoke; SEE CONCEPTS *50,53,88*

counterpart [n] *match; identical part or thing*
analogue, carbon copy*, complement, copy, correlate, correlative, correspondent, dead ringer*, ditto, doppelganger, duplicate, equal, equivalent, fellow, like, look alike, mate, obverse, opposite, opposite number, peas in a pod*, pendant, ringer*, spit and image*, spitting image*, supplement, tally, twin, two of a kind; SEE CONCEPTS *667,834*

countless [adj] *innumerable*
bags of*, endless, gobs*, heap*, immeasurable, incalculable, infinite, innumerous, jillion*, legion, limitless, loads*, lots of, many, measureless, mess*, mint*, mucho*, multitudinous, myriad, numberless, oodles*, passel of*, peck, pile, raft*, scads*, slew*, stack*, tidy sum, umpteen*, uncountable, uncounted, untold, wad*, whole slew*, zillion*; SEE CONCEPTS *762,781*

count out [v] *disregard, exclude*
bar, bate, debar, eliminate, except, get rid of, leave out, leave out of account, mark off, pass over, rule out, suspend; SEE CONCEPT *25*

country [n1] *political territory; nation*
citizenry, citizens, commonwealth, community, constituents, electors, fatherland, grass roots, homeland, inhabitants, kingdom, land, motherland, native land, patria, people, polity, populace, public, realm, region, society, soil, sovereign state, state, terrain, voters; SEE CONCEPTS *379,508,510*

country [n2] *rural area; area away from city*
back country, backwoods, boondocks*, boonies*, bush, countryside, cow country*, farmland, farms, forests, green belt*, hinterland, middle of nowhere*, outback, outdoors, province, sticks*, up country*, wide open space*, wilds, woodlands, woods; SEE CONCEPTS *508,513*

country [adj] *rural, pastoral*
agrarian, agrestic, Arcadian, bucolic, campestral, countrified, georgic, homey, out-country, outland, provincial, rustic, uncultured, unpolished, unrefined, unsophisticated; SEE CONCEPTS *401,536,589*

county [n] *province or district of area*
canton, constituency, division, shire; SEE CONCEPTS *508,513*

coup [n] *achievement, often by maneuver*
accomplishment, action, coup de mâitre, coup d'état, deed, exploit, feat, mastery, overthrow, plot, revolution, stratagem, stroke, stroke of genius*, stunt, successful stroke, tour de force, upset; SEE CONCEPT *706*

coup d'état [n] *violent seizure*
coup, overthrow, palace revolution, power play*, Putsch*, rebellion, revolt, revolution, takeover; SEE CONCEPTS *86,90,320*

coup de grâce [n] *finishing blow*
blow, clincher*, comeuppance, deathblow, defeat, final blow, final stroke, kill, knockout, mercy stroke, mortal blow, quietus; SEE CONCEPTS *95,252*

couple [*n*] *pair of things*
brace, couplet, deuce it*, doublet, duo, dyad, item, man and wife, newlyweds, pair off, set, span, team, twain, twosome, yoke; SEE CONCEPTS *432,766*

couple [*v*] *join two things*
bracket, bring together, buckle, clasp, coalesce, co-habit, come together, conjoin, conjugate, connect, copulate, harness, hitch, hook up, link, marry, match, pair, unite, wed, yoke; SEE CONCEPTS *113,114,297,375*

coupon [*n*] *discount ticket*
advertisement, box top*, card, certificate, credit slip, detachable portion, order blank, premium certificate, ration slip, redeemable part, redemption slip, slip, token, voucher; SEE CONCEPT *331*

courage [*n*] *boldness, braveness*
adventuresomeness, adventurousness, audacity, backbone, bravery, bravura, daring, dash, dauntless-ness, determination, élan, endurance, enterprise, fearlessness, firmness, fortitude, gallantry, game-ness, grit, guts, hardihood, heroism, intrepidity, lion-heartedness, manliness, mettle, nerve, pluck, power, prowess, pugnacity, rashness, recklessness, resolu-tion, spirit, spunk, stoutheartedness, temerity, tenac-ity, valor, venturesomeness; SEE CONCEPTS *411,633*

courageous [*adj*] *brave, bold*
adventuresome, adventurous, assured, audacious, cool, daredevil, daring, dauntless, doughty, fearless, fiery, fire-eating*, gallant, game, gritty*, gutsy*, hardy, heroic, high-spirited, impavid, indomitable, intrepid, lionhearted, manly, martial, nervy, plucky*, red-blooded*, resolute, Spartan, stalwart, stand tall*, stouthearted, strong, tenacious, tough, Trojan*, unafraid, undaunted, valiant, valorous, ven-turesome, venturous; SEE CONCEPTS *401,404*

courier [*n*] *messenger*
bearer, carrier, dispatcher, emissary, envoy, express, go-between, gofer*, gopher*, herald, intelligencer, internuncio, runner; SEE CONCEPT *348*

course [*n1*] *progress, advance*
advancement, chain, channels, consecution, continu-ity, development, flow, furtherance, line, manner, march, movement, order, plan, policy, polity, pro-cedure, program, progression, red tape*, row, scheme, sequel, sequence, series, string, succession, system, unfolding, way; SEE CONCEPTS *704,727*

course [*n2*] *path, channel*
aisle, aqueduct, boards, byway, canal, circuit, con-duit, direction, duct, flow, groove, itinerary, lap, line, movement, orbit, passage, range, road, route, run, rut, scope, stream, tack, track, trail, trajectory, watercourse, way; SEE CONCEPTS *501,514*

course [*n3*] *length of action*
duration, elapsing, lapse, passage, passing, progress, sweep, term, time; SEE CONCEPT *804*

course [*n4*] *plan of study*
class, conference, curriculum, discussion group, in-terest, laboratory, lecture, matriculation, meeting, method, period, preparation, procedure, program, regimen, schedule, seminar, session, speciality, sub-ject; SEE CONCEPT *287*

course [*v*] *flow; run*
career, chase, dart, dash, follow, gallop, gush, has-ten, hunt, hurry, hustle, pursue, race, rush, scamper, scoot, scurry, speed, spring, stream, surge, tumble; SEE CONCEPTS *150,152*

court [*n1*] *yard, garden of building*
cloister, close, compass, courtyard, curtilage, enclo-sure, forum, patio, piazza, plaza, quad, quadrangle, square, street; SEE CONCEPTS *509,513*

court [*n2*] *ruler's attendants*
castle, cortege, entourage, hall, lords and ladies, pal-ace, retinue, royal household, staff, suite, train; SEE CONCEPTS *296,348*

court [*n3*] *judicial system*
bar, bench, court of justice, forum, judge, justice, kangaroo court*, law court, magistrate, seat of judg-ment, session, tribunal; SEE CONCEPTS *299,318*

court [*n4*] *building for legal proceedings*
bar, bench, city hall, county courthouse, courthouse, courtroom, federal building, hall of justice, justice building, law court, municipal building, tribunal; SEE CONCEPTS *318,439*

court [*n5*] *wooing*
address, attention, homage, love, respects, suit; SEE CONCEPT *32*

court [*v*] *fawn over, pay attention to*
allure, ask in marriage, attract, beseech, bid, boot-lick, captivate, charm, chase, cultivate, curry favor, date, entice, entreat, flatter, follow, gallant, go out with, go steady, go together, go with, grovel*, im-portune, invite, keep company with, make love to, make overture, make time with*, pander to, pay ad-dresses to, pay court to, please, pop the question*, praise, propose, pursue, run after*, seek, seek the hand of, serenade, set one's cap*, solicit, spark, spoon*, sue, sweetheart, take out, WOO; SEE CON-CEPTS *32,384*

courteous [*adj*] *gentle, mannerly*
affable, attentive, ceremonious, civil, civilized, com-plaisant, considerate, courtly, cultivated, debonair, elegant, gallant, genteel, gentlemanly, gracious, la-dylike, polished, polite, refined, respectful, soft-spoken, suave, thoughtful, urbane, well-behaved, well-bred, well-mannered, well-spoken; SEE CON-CEPTS *267,401*

courtesy [*n1*] *good manners*
address, affability, amenities, amiability, attentive-ness, ceremony, chivalry, civility, comity, complai-sance, consideration, cordiality, courteousness, courtliness, cultivation, culture, deference, elegance, familiarity, favor, friendliness, gallantness, gal-lantry, generosity, geniality, gentleness, good behav-ior, good breeding, graciousness, indulgence, kindness, polish, politeness, refinement, respect, rev-

erence, solicitude, suavity, sympathy, tact, thoughtfulness, urbanity; SEE CONCEPTS. *633,644*

courtesy [*n2*] *favor, indulgence*
accommodation, benevolence, bounty, charity, chivalry, compassion, consent, consideration, dispensation, generosity, kindness, liberality, service, unselfishness; SEE CONCEPTS *337,388,633*

courtly [*adj*] *refined manner*
adulatory, affable, aristocratic, august, ceremonious, chivalrous, civil, civilized, complimentary, conventional, cultured, decorous, dignified, elegant, flattering, formal, gallant, gracious, high-bred, imposing, lofty, lordly, obliging, polished, polite, preux, prim, refined, stately, studied, urbane; SEE CONCEPT *401*

courtship [*n*] *dating, romance*
courting, engagement, keeping company*, love, lovemaking, pursuit, suit, wooing; SEE CONCEPT *388*

cove [*n*] *inlet, small niche*
anchorage, arm, bay, bayou, bight, cave, cavern, creek, estuary, firth, frith, gulf, harbor, hole, lagoon, nook, retreat, slough, sound, wash; SEE CONCEPT *509*

covenant [*n*] *pact, promise*
agreement, arrangement, bargain, bond, commitment, compact, concordat, contract, convention, deal, deed, dicker*, handshake*, papers, stipulation, transaction, treaty, trust; SEE CONCEPT *684*

covenant [*v*] *agree*
bargain, concur, contract, engage, pledge, plight, promise, stipulate, swear, undertake, vow; SEE CONCEPTS *8,71,317*

cover [*n1*] *wrapping, cover-up*
awning, bark, binding, camouflage, canopy, canvas, cap, caparison, case, ceiling, cloak, clothing, coating, covering, coverlet, disguise, dome, dress, drop, envelope, facade, false front*, fig leaf, front, guise, hood, integument, jacket, lid, marquee, mask, masquerade, overlay, paint, parasol, polish, pretense, put-on*, roof, screen, seal, semblance, sheath, sheet, shroud, smoke screen*, spread, stopper, tarp, tarpaulin, tegument, tent, top, umbrella, varnish, veil, veneer, window-dressing, wrapper, wraps; SEE CONCEPTS *484,750*

cover [*n2*] *hiding place*
asylum, camouflage, concealment, covert, defense, drop, front, guard, harbor, harborage, haven, port, protection, refuge, retreat, safety, sanctuary, screen, security, shelter; SEE CONCEPT *198*

cover [*v1*] *wrap, hide*
blanket, board up, bury, bush up, cache, camouflage, canopy, cap, carpet, cloak, clothe, coat, conceal, cover up, crown, curtain, daub, disguise, do on the sly*, dress, eclipse, encase, enclose, enfold, ensconce, enshroud, envelop, hood, house, invest, layer, mantle, mask, obscure, overcast, overlay, overspread, protect, put on, screen, secrete, set on, shade, shield, shroud, stash, superimpose, superpose, surface, veil; SEE CONCEPTS *172,188*

cover [*v2*] *protect, guard*
bulwark, defend, fend, house, reinforce, safeguard, screen, secure, shelter, shield, watch over; SEE CONCEPT *96*

cover [*v3*] *include, contain*
be enough, comprehend, comprise, consider, deal with, embody, embrace, encompass, examine, incorporate, involve, meet, provide for, reach, refer to, suffice, survey, take account of; SEE CONCEPT *643*

cover [*v4*] *describe in published writing*
broadcast, detail, investigate, narrate, recount, relate, report, tell of, write up; SEE CONCEPTS *60,79*

cover [*v5*] *fill in for, compensate*
balance, counterbalance, double for, insure, make good, make up for, offset, relieve, stand in for*, substitute, take over, take the rap for*; SEE CONCEPTS *110,126*

cover [*v6*] *travel across area*
cross, do, journey over, pass over, pass through, range, track, traverse, trek; SEE CONCEPT *224*

covert [*adj*] *clandestine, underhanded*
buried, camouflaged, cloaked, concealed, disguised, dissembled, furtive, hidden, hush-hush*, incog*, incognito, masked, obscured, private, privy, QT*, secret, shrouded, stealthy, sub rosa, surreptitious, ulterior, undercover, underhand, under-the-table*, under wraps*, unsuspected, veiled; SEE CONCEPTS *544,548*

covertly [*adv*] *clandestine, underhandedly*
by stealth, clandestinely, furtively, hush-hush*, in camera, in holes and corners*, on the QT*, on the quiet, on the sly, privately, secretly, slyly, stealthily, sub rosa, surreptitiously, undercover, under wraps*, wildcat*; SEE CONCEPTS *544,548*

covet [*v*] *desire strongly*
aspire to, begrudge, choose, crave, desiderate, envy, fancy, hanker for*, have eye on*, have hots for*, itch for*, long for, lust after, spoil for, thirst for, want, wish for, yearn for, yen for*; SEE CONCEPT *20*

covetous [*adj*] *greedy; very desirous*
acquisitive, avaricious, avid, close-fisted, eager, ensurient, envious, gluttonous, grabby, grasping, green-eyed*, grudging, hogging, itchy*, jealous, keen, mercenary, piggish*, prehensile, rapacious, ravenous, selfish, swinish*, voracious, yearning; SEE CONCEPT *401*

cow [*v*] *browbeat, intimidate*
abash, appall, awe, bludgeon, bluster, buffalo, bulldoze, bully, daunt, discomfit, disconcert, dishearten, dismay, dragoon, embarrass, enforce, faze, frighten, hector, lean on*, overawe, push around*, rattle, scare, showboat*, strong-arm*, subdue, terrorize, turn on the heat*, unnerve, walk heavy*; SEE CONCEPTS *7,19,52*

coward [*n*] *person who is scared, easily intimidated*
alarmist, baby*, caitiff, chicken*, chicken heart*, chicken liver*, craven, cur, dastard, deserter, faintheart, faint-of-heart, fraidy-cat*, funk, gutless*, in-

vertebrate*, jellyfish*, lily liver, malingerer, mouse*, pessimist, poltroon, quitter, rabbit*, recreant, scaredy cat*, shirk, shirker, sissy*, skulker, sneak, weakling, weak sister*, white liver*, wimp*, yellow*, yellow belly*; SEE CONCEPT *423*

cowardly [*adj*] *fearful*
afraid, anxious, apprehensive, backward, base, caitiff, chicken-hearted, cowering, cowhearted, craven, dastardly, diffident, dismayed, fainthearted, frightened, gutless, having the willies*, jittery, lacking courage, lily-livered*, nervous, no guts, panicky, paper tiger*, pigeonhearted*, pusillanimous, recreant, retiring, running scared, scared, shrinking, shy, soft*, spineless*, timid, timorous, unmanly, weak, weak-kneed*, worthless, yellow*, yellow-bellied*; SEE CONCEPT *401*

cower [*v*] *hide, hover in fear*
apple-polish*, blench, bootlick*, brownnose*, cringe, crouch, draw back, fawn, flinch, grovel, honey*, kowtow*, quail*, recoil, shrink, skulk, sneak, toady*, tremble, truckle, wince; SEE CONCEPTS *188,384*

coy [*adj*] *very modest*
backward, bashful, blushing, coquettish, demure, diffident, evasive, flirtatious, humble, kittenish, overmodest, prudish, rabbity, reserved, retiring, self-effacing, shrinking, shy, skittish, timid, unassertive; SEE CONCEPTS *401,404*

cozy [*adj*] *comforting, soft, warm*
comfortable, comfy, cuddled up, cushy, easeful, in clover, intimate, in velvet*, on bed of roses*, restful, safe, secure, sheltered, snug, snug as bug in rug*, snuggled down, tucked up; SEE CONCEPTS *485,605,606*

crabby/crabbed [*adj*] *in a bad mood*
acid, acrid, acrimonious, awkward, bad-tempered, blunt, brusque, captious, choleric, churlish, cranky*, cross, crotchety, crusty*, cynical, difficult, dour, fretful, gloomy, glum, grouchy*, harsh, huffy, ill-humored, ill-tempered, irascible, irritable, misanthropic, morose, nasty-tempered, peevish, perverse, petulant, prickly, saturnine, snappish, snappy, sour, splenetic, sulky, sullen, surly, tart, testy, tough, trying, unsociable; SEE CONCEPTS *401,403*

crack [*n1*] *break, crevice*
breach, chink, chip, cleft, cranny, crevasse, crevice, cut, discontinuity, division, fissure, fracture, gap, hole, interstice, interval, rent, rift, rima, rimation, rime, split; SEE CONCEPTS *469,513*

crack [*n2*] *loud sound, usually from hitting*
bang, bash, belt, blast, blow, boom, buffet, burst, clap, clip, clout, crash, cuff, explosion, go, noise, pop, report, shot, slam, slap, smack, smash, snap, splintering, splitting, stab, stroke, thump, thwack, wallop, whack, wham; SEE CONCEPTS *189,595*

crack [*n3*] *attempt to do something*
fling, go, opportunity, pop, shot, stab, try, whack, whirl; SEE CONCEPT *87*

crack [*n4*] *joke*
dig, funny remark, gag, insult, jest, jibe, quip, remark, return, smart remark, wisecrack, witticism; SEE CONCEPT *273*

crack [*adj*] *super, first-rate*
able, ace, adept, best, capital, choice, crackerjack*, deluxe, elite, excellent, expert, first-class, handpicked, master, masterful, masterly, pro, proficient, skilled, skillful, superior, talented; SEE CONCEPTS *528,542,574*

crack [*v1*] *break, usually into parts*
burst, chip, chop, cleave, crackle, crash, damage, detonate, explode, fracture, hurt, impair, injure, pop, ring, rive, sever, shiver, snap, splinter, split; SEE CONCEPT *248*

crack [*v2*] *lose self-control*
become deranged, become insane, blow one's mind*, blow up, break, break down, bug out*, collapse, flip*, give way*, go bonkers*, go crazy, go to pieces*, lose it*, succumb, yield; SEE CONCEPT *13*

crack [*v3*] *hit very hard*
bash, buffet, clip, clout, cuff, slap, thump, thunder, wallop, whack; SEE CONCEPT *189*

crack [*v4*] *discover meaning, answer*
break, cryptanalyze, decipher, decode, decrypt, fathom, figure out, get answer, solve, work out; SEE CONCEPTS *37,38*

cracker [*n*] *hard, often salted, baked wafer*
biscuit, bun, cookie, hardtack, pretzel, rusk, saltine; SEE CONCEPT *457*

crack up [*v*] *break down mentally*
become demented, become psychotic, blow a fuse*, collapse, come apart at seams*, decline, derange, deteriorate, fail, flip out*, freak out*, go bonkers*, go crazy, go nuts, go off deep end*, go off rocker*, go out of mind*, go to pieces*, have breakdown, schizz out*, sicken; SEE CONCEPT *13*

cradle [*n1*] *small bed for baby*
baby bed, bassinet, cot, crib, hamper, Moses basket, pannier, trundle bed; SEE CONCEPT *443*

cradle [*n2*] *early childhood; origins*
babyhood, beginning, birthplace, fount, fountain, fountainhead, infancy, nativity, nursery, origin, source, spring, ultimate cause, wellspring; SEE CONCEPTS *648,817*

cradle [*v*] *hold in arms; nurture*
lull, nestle, nourish, nurse, rock, support, tend, watch over; SEE CONCEPTS *190,295*

craft [*n1*] *expertise, skill*
ability, adeptness, adroitness, aptitude, art, artistry, cleverness, competence, cunning, dexterity, expertness, ingenuity, knack, know-how*, proficiency, technique, workmanship; SEE CONCEPTS *409,706*

craft [*n2*] *deceit, scheme*
art, artfulness, artifice, cageyness, canniness, contrivance, craftiness, cunning, disingenuity, duplicity, foxiness, guile, ruse, shrewdness, slyness, strata-

gem, strategy, subterfuge, subtlety, trickery, wiles, wiliness; SEE CONCEPTS *645,660*

craft [*n3*] *business, discipline*
art, calling, career, employment, handicraft, line, metier, occupation, profession, pursuit, trade, vocation, work; SEE CONCEPT *360*

craft [*n4*] *water or air vehicle*
aircraft, airplane, air ship, barge, blimp, boat, bottom, plane, ship, shipping, spacecraft, vessel, watercraft, zeppelin; SEE CONCEPTS *504,506*

craftsperson [*n*] *person skilled in art*
artificer, artisan, journeyman, machinist, maker, manufacturer, master, mechanic, skilled worker, smith, specialist, technician, wright; SEE CONCEPT *348*

crafty [*adj*] *clever, scheming*
adroit, artful, astute, cagey, calculating, canny, crazy like fox*, cunning, deceitful, deep, designing, devious, disingenuous, duplicitous, foxy*, fraudulent, guileful, insidious, intelligent, keen, knowing, sharp, shrewd, slick, slippery*, sly, smart, smooth, street smart*, streetwise*, subtle, tricky, vulpine, wily; SEE CONCEPT *401*

craggy [*adj*] *jagged*
asperous, broken, cragged, harsh, precipitous, rockbound, rocky, rough, rugged, scabrous, scraggy, stony, uneven, unlevel, unsmooth; SEE CONCEPTS *490,606*

cram [*v1*] *fill to overflowing; compress*
charge, chock, choke, compact, crowd, crush, devour, drive, force, gobble, gorge, guzzle, heap, ingurgitate, jam, jam-pack*, load, overcrowd, overeat, overfill, pack, pack 'em in*, pack in, pack it in*, pack like sardines*, press, ram, sardine*, satiate, shove, slop, slosh, squash, squeeze, stive, stuff, tamp*, thrust, wedge, wolf*; SEE CONCEPTS *208,740*

cram [*v2*] *study intensely*
burn midnight oil*, heavy booking*, hit the books*, megabook*, mug up*, read, review, revise; SEE CONCEPT *17*

cramp [*n*] *muscle spasm*
ache, charley horse*, circumscription, confinement, constipation, contraction, convulsion, crick, hindrance, impediment, kink, obstruction, pain, pang, restriction, shooting pain, stiffness, stitch, stricture, twinge; SEE CONCEPTS *308,728*

cramp [*v*] *hinder, restrain*
bottle up*, box up*, check, circumscribe, clamp, clasp, clog, confine, constrain, coop up*, encumber, fasten, grip, hamper, hamstring, handicap, impede, inhibit, limit, object, obstruct, restrict, shackle, stymie, thwart; SEE CONCEPTS *130,191*

cramped [*adj*] *congested, overcrowded*
awkward, circumscribed, close, closed in, confined, crabbed, crowded, hemmed in*, illegible, incommodious, indecipherable, irregular, jammed in, little, minute, narrow, packed, pent, restricted, small,

squeezed, tight, tiny, tucked up, two-by-four*, uncomfortable; SEE CONCEPTS *483,773*

cranky [*adj*] *in bad mood*
bad-humored, bearish, cantankerous, choleric, crabby, cross, crotchety, cussed, disagreeable, got up on wrong side of bed*, grouchy, grumpy, hot-tempered, ill-humored, irascible, irritable, like a bear*, mean, ornery*, out of sorts, perverse, quick-tempered, ratty, snappish, tetchy, ugly, vinegary; SEE CONCEPTS *401,403*

cranny [*n*] *nook, opening*
breach, byplace, chink, cleft, crack, crevice, fissure, gap, hole, interstice, niche; SEE CONCEPTS *440,513*

crash [*n1/v1*] *bang; banging sound*
blast, boom, burst, clang, clap, clash, clatter, clattering, crack, din, peal, racket, slam, smash, smashing, sound, thunder, thunderclap, wham; SEE CONCEPTS *65,521,595*

crash [*n2*] *collision, accidental hitting*
accident, bump, collapse, concussion, crack-up*, crunch, debacle, ditch, fender bender*, fender tag*, impact, jar, jolt, percussion, pileup, ram, rear-ender*, shock, sideswipe, smash, smashup*, splashdown*, stack-up*, thud*, thump*, total*, washout*, wreck; SEE CONCEPT *189*

crash [*v2*] *break into pieces*
bang into, crack up, crunch, dash, disintegrate, fracture, fragment, pile up, shatter, shiver, sideswipe, smash, smash up, splinter, total, wrack up; SEE CONCEPT *248*

crash [*v3*] *fall*
bite the dust*, bump, collapse, collide, crash-land, ditch, dive, drive into, drop, fall flat*, fall headlong, fall prostrate, give way, go in*, hurtle, lurch, meet, overbalance, overturn, pancake*, pitch, plough into*, plunge, prang, slip, smash, splash down, sprawl, topple, tumble, upset, washout*; SEE CONCEPT *181*

crass [*adj*] *coarse, insensitive*
asinine, blundering, boorish, bovine, churlish, dense, doltish, gross, indelicate, inelegant, loutish, lowbrow, lumpish, oafish, obtuse, Philistine, raw, rough, rude, stupid, uncouth, unrefined, vulgar, witless; SEE CONCEPT *401*

crate [*n*] *wooden container*
box, cage, carton, case, chest, package; SEE CONCEPT *494*

crave [*v1*] *desire intensely*
ache for, covet, cry out for, die for*, dream, eat one's heart out*, fancy, give eyeteeth for*, hunger for*, itch for*, long for, lust after, need, pine for*, require, sigh for, spoil for, suspire, thirst for*, want, yearn for, yen for*; SEE CONCEPT *20*

crave [*v2*] *beg*
ask, beseech, call for, demand, entreat, implore, necessitate, petition, plead for, pray for, require, seek, solicit, supplicate, take; SEE CONCEPTS *48,53*

craven [n] *timid person*
caitiff, chicken*, coward, dastard, fraidy cat*, nebbish, poltroon, quitter, recreant, scaredy cat*, weakling, wheyface, wimp*, wuss*, yellow belly*; SEE CONCEPT *423*

craven [adj] *weak, timid*
chicken*, cowardly, dastardly, fearful, gutless, lily-livered*, mean-spirited, poltroonish, pusillanimous, scared, timorous, unmanly, weak-kneed*, wimpish*, wimpy*, wussy*, yellow*, yellow-bellied*; SEE CONCEPTS *401,550*

craving [n] *strong desire*
appetite, appetition, hankering, hunger, hurting, itch*, longing, lust, munchies*, need, passion, thirst, urge, yearning, yen*; SEE CONCEPTS *20,709*

crawl [v1] *move very slowly*
clamber, creep, drag, drag oneself along, go on all fours, go on belly, grovel, hang back, inch, lag, loiter along, lollygag*, move at snail's pace*, move on hands and knees, plod, poke, pull oneself along, scrabble, slide, slither, squirm, worm, wriggle, writhe; SEE CONCEPT *151*

crawl [v2] *humble oneself*
abase oneself, apple-polish*, brownnose*, cringe, fawn, grovel, toady, truckle; SEE CONCEPTS *35,48*

craze [n] *fad, strong interest*
chic, cry, enthusiasm, fashion, fever, furor, infatuation, in thing*, kick, mania, mode, monomania, newest wrinkle*, novelty, passion, preoccupation, rage, the last word*, the latest thing*, trend, vogue, wrinkle; SEE CONCEPTS *532,690*

craze [v] *make insane*
bewilder, confuse, dement, derange, distemper, distract, drive mad, enrage, frenzy, infatuate, inflame, madden, unbalance, unhinge; SEE CONCEPTS *7,19*

crazy [adj1] *mentally strange*
ape, barmy, batty, berserk, bonkers*, cracked, crazed, cuckoo, daft, delirious, demented, deranged, dingy*, dippy*, erratic, flaky, flipped*, flipped out*, freaked out*, fruity*, idiotic, insane, kooky, lunatic, mad, maniacal, mental*, moonstruck*, nuts, nutty, nutty as fruitcake*, of unsound mind, out of one's mind, out of one's tree*, out to lunch*, potty*, psycho*, round the bend*, schizo*, screwball*, screw loose*, screwy*, silly, touched*, unbalanced, unglued*, unhinged*, unzipped*, wacky; SEE CONCEPT *403*

crazy [adj2] *unrealistic, fantastic*
absurd, balmy, beyond all reason, bizarre, cockeyed, derisory, eccentric, fatuous, foolhardy, foolish, goofy*, half-baked*, harebrained*, idiotic, ill-conceived, impracticable, imprudent, inane, inappropriate, insane, irresponsible, loony, ludicrous, nonsensical, odd, out of all reason, outrageous, peculiar, preposterous, puerile, quixotic, ridiculous, senseless, short-sighted, silly, strange, unworkable, weird, wild; SEE CONCEPT *529*

crazy [adj3] *infatuated, in love*
ardent, beside oneself*, devoted, eager, enamoured, fanatical, hysterical, keen, mad, passionate, smitten, wild, zealous; SEE CONCEPT *403*

creak [v] *grind, grate with high noise*
chirr, crepitate, groan, rasp, scrape, scratch, screech, sound, squeak, squeal; SEE CONCEPTS *65,186,215*

cream [n1] *lotion, oil*
cerate, chrism, cosmetic, demulcent, emulsion, essence, jelly, liniment, moisturizer, ointment, paste, salve, unction, unguent; SEE CONCEPTS *466,467,468*

cream [n2] *the best*
choice, crème de la crème*, elite, fat, favorite, finest, flower*, pick, pride, prime*, prize, skim*, top; SEE CONCEPT *668*

creamy [adj] *smooth, buttery*
creamed, feathery, fluffy, gloppy*, gooey, gooky*, goopy*, greasy, gunky, luscious, lush, milky, oily, rich, soft, velvety; SEE CONCEPT *606*

crease [n] *fold, wrinkle*
bend, bulge, cockle, corrugation, furrow, groove, line, overlap, pleat, plica, pucker, ridge, rimple, rivel, ruck, rugosity, tuck; SEE CONCEPTS *452,757*

crease [v] *fold, rumple*
bend, cockle, corrugate, crimp, crinkle, crumple, dog-ear*, double up, plait, pleat, pucker, purse, ridge, ruck up, screw up*, wrinkle; SEE CONCEPTS *158,219*

create [v] *develop in mind or physically*
actualize, author, beget, bring into being, bring into existence, bring to pass, build, cause to be, coin, compose, conceive, concoct, constitute, construct, contrive, design, devise, discover, dream up, effect, erect, establish, fabricate, fashion, father, forge, form, formulate, found, generate, give birth to, give life to, hatch, imagine, initiate, institute, invent, invest, make, occasion, organize, originate, parent, perform, plan, procreate, produce, rear, set up, shape, sire, spawn, start; SEE CONCEPTS *173,239,251*

creation [n1] *development of entity*
conception, constitution, establishment, formation, formulation, foundation, generation, genesis, imagination, inception, institution, laying down, making, nascency, nativity, origination, procreation, production, setting up, siring; SEE CONCEPT *173*

creation [n2] *all living things*
cosmos, life, living world, macrocosm, macrocosmos, megacosm, nature, totality, universe, world; SEE CONCEPTS *389,429*

creation [n3] *invention, concoction*
achievement, brainchild, chef-d'oeuvre, concept, handiwork, magnum opus, opus, piece, pièce de résistance, production, work, work of genius; SEE CONCEPTS *259,260*

creative [adj] *artistic, imaginative*
clever, cool*, demiurgic, deviceful, fertile, formative, gifted, hip*, ingenious, innovational, innovative, innovatory, inspired, inventive, leading-edge*,

original, originative, productive, prolific, stimulating, visionary, way out*; SEE CONCEPT *402*

creator [*n*] *inventor; God*
architect, author, begetter, brain, deity, designer, father, founder, framer, generator, initiator, maker, mastermind, originator, patriarch, prime mover, producer, sire; SEE CONCEPTS *348,352,361*

creature [*n*] *being, beast*
animal, body, brute, creation, critter*, fellow, individual, living being, living thing, lower animal, man, mortal, party, person, personage, quadruped, soul, varmint*, woman; SEE CONCEPT *389*

credence [*n*] *trust, acceptance*
accepting, admission, admitting, assurance, belief, certainty, confidence, credit, dependence, faith, reliance, stock, store; SEE CONCEPT *689*

credentials [*n*] *references, attestation*
accreditation, authorization, card, certificate, character, deed, diploma, docket, document, documentation, endorsement, letter of credence, letter of introduction, license, missive, papers, passport, proof, recommendation, sanction, testament, testimonial, title, token, voucher, warrant; SEE CONCEPTS *271,685*

credibility [*n*] *believeableness*
believability, chance, integrity, likelihood, plausibility, possibility, probability, prospect, reliability, satisfactoriness, solidity, solidness, soundness, tenability, trustworthiness, validity; SEE CONCEPTS *650,725*

credible [*adj*] *believable*
aboveboard, colorable, conceivable, conclusive, creditable, dependable, determinative, honest, honest to God*, imaginable, likely, plausible, possible, probable, probably, rational, reasonable, reliable, satisfactory, satisfying, seeming, sincere, solid, sound, straight, supposable, tenable, thinkable, trustworthy, trusty, up front*, valid; SEE CONCEPTS *552,582*

credit [*n1*] *recognition; trust*
acclaim, acknowledgment, approval, attention, belief, Brownie points*, commendation, confidence, credence, distinction, faith, fame, glory, honor, kudos*, merit, notice, pat on the back*, points*, praise, reliance, strokes*, thanks, tribute; SEE CONCEPTS *69,410*

credit [*n2*] *reputation, status*
authority, character, clout, esteem, estimation, fame, good name, influence, position, prestige, regard, renown, repute, standing, weight; SEE CONCEPT *388*

credit [*n3*] *deferred payment arrangement; assets*
balance, bond, capital outlay, continuance, debenture, extension, installment buying, installment plan, lien, loan, mortgage, on account, on the arm*, on the cuff*, plastic*, respite, securities, stock, surplus cash, tab, trust, wealth; SEE CONCEPT *335*

credit [*v1*] *believe, depend on*
accept, bank on, buy, consider, deem, fall for*, feel, hand it to one, have faith in, hold, pat on back, rely on, sense, swallow*, take as gospel truth*, take stock in*, think, trust; SEE CONCEPT *12*

credit [*v2*] *accredit, assign to*
ascribe to, attribute to, chalk up to, charge to, defer, impute, lay, refer; SEE CONCEPT *18*

creditable [*adj*] *praiseworthy*
admirable, batting a thousand*, believeable, commendable, decent, deserving, estimable, excellent, exemplary, honest, honorable, laudable, meritorious, nasty*, not too shabby*, organic, palmary, reputable, reputed, respectable, salt of the earth*, satisfactory, suitable, well-thought-of, worthy; SEE CONCEPT *542*

credulous [*adj*] *gullible, naive*
accepting, believing, born yesterday*, dupable, easy mark*, falling for*, green, overtrusting, simple, swallow whole, taken in, take the bait*, trustful, trusting, uncritical, unquestioning, unsophisticated, unsuspecting, unsuspicious, unwary; SEE CONCEPT *404*

creed [*n*] *belief, principles*
articles of faith, canon, catechism, church, confession, conviction, cult, doctrine, dogma, faith, ideology, persuasion, profession, religion, tenet, Weltanschauung; SEE CONCEPTS *687,689*

creek [*n*] *stream of water*
brook, brooklet, burn, crick, ditch, race, rill, rindle, river, rivulet, run, runnel, spring, streamlet, tributary, watercourse; SEE CONCEPT *514*

creep [*v*] *crawl along, usually on ground*
approach unnoticed, crawl on all fours, edge, glide, grovel, gumshoe*, inch, insinuate, lurk, pussyfoot, scrabble, scramble, skulk, slink, slither, snake*, sneak, squirm, steal, tiptoe, worm, wriggle, writhe; SEE CONCEPT *151*

creepy [*adj*] *nasty, scary*
awful, direful, disgusting, disturbing, dreadful, eerie, frightening, ghoulish, gruesome, hair-raising, horrible, itching, itchy, macabre, menacing, nightmarish, ominous, shuddersome, sinister, terrifying, threatening, unpleasant, weird; SEE CONCEPT *570*

crescent [*n*] *sickle-shaped object*
bow, concave figure, convex figure, cresentoid, curve, demilune, half-moon, horned moon, lune, meniscus, new moon, old moon, sickle; SEE CONCEPT *436*

crescent [*adj*] *sickle-shaped*
bowed, bow-shaped, concave, convex, crescentic, crescentiform, curved, falcate, semicircular; SEE CONCEPT *486*

crest [*n1*] *highest point*
acme, apex, apogee, climax, crescendo, crown, culmination, fastigium, head, height, noon, peak, pinnacle, ridge, roof, summit, top, vertex; SEE CONCEPT *836*

crest [*n2*] *emblem, symbol*
badge, bearings, charge, device, insignia; SEE CONCEPT *284*

crest [n3] *topknot on head of animal*
aigrette, caruncle, chine, cockscomb, comb, crown, feather, hogback, mane, panache, plume, ridge, tassel, tuft; SEE CONCEPT *399*

crestfallen [adj] *disappointed*
ass in a sling*, blue, cast down, chapfallen, dejected, depressed, despondent, disconsolate, discouraged, disheartened, dispirited, down, downcast, downhearted, down in the dumps*, in a funk*, inconsolable, low, sad, singing the blues*, taken down*; SEE CONCEPT *403*

crevice/crevasse [n] *crack, gap*
abyss, chasm, chink, cleft, crack, cranny, cut, division, fissure, fracture, hole, interstice, opening, precipice, rent, rift, slit, split; SEE CONCEPTS *509,513*

crew [n] *group working together*
aggregation, assemblage, band, bevy, bunch, cluster, collection, company, complement, congregation, corps, covey, crowd, faction, gang, hands, herd, horde, lot, mob, organization, pack, party, posse, retinue, sailors, seamen, sect, set, squad, swarm, team, troop, troupe, workers, working party; SEE CONCEPTS *381,417*

crib [n] *baby bed*
bassinet, bin*, box*, bunk, cot, cradle, manger, Moses basket*, rack*, stall*, trundle bed; SEE CONCEPT *443*

crick [n] *muscle spasm*
ache, charley horse*, convulsion, cramp, jarring, kink, pain, stitch, twinge, wrench; SEE CONCEPTS *308,728*

crime [n] *offense against the law*
abomination, antisocial behavior, atrocity, breach, break, caper, case, corruption, criminality, delict, delictum, delinquency, depravity, dereliction, enormity, evil, evil behavior, fast one*, fault, felony, hit, illegality, immorality, infraction, infringement, iniquity, job, lawlessness, malefaction, malfeasance, misconduct, misdeed, misdemeanor, mortal sin, outrage, quickie*, racket, scandal, sneak, tort, transgression, trespass, unlawful act, vice, villainy, violation, wickedness, wrong, wrongdoing; SEE CONCEPT *192*

criminal [n] *person who breaks the law*
bad actor*, blackmailer, black marketeer, con, convict, crook, culprit, delinquent, desperado, deuce, evildoer, ex-con, felon, fugitive, gangster, guerilla, hatchet man*, heavy*, hood*, hoodlum, hooligan*, hustler, inside man/woman*, jailbird, lawbreaker, malefactor, mobster, moll, mug, muscle*, offender, outlaw, racketeer, repeater, scofflaw, sinner, slippery eel*, thug*, transgressor, trespasser, wrongdoer, yardbird*; SEE CONCEPT *412*

criminal [adj] *lawless, felonious*
bent, caught, corrupt, crooked, culpable, deplorable, dirty, heavy, hung up*, illegal, illegitimate, illicit, immoral, indictable, iniquitous, nefarious, off base*, out of line*, peccant, racket, scandalous, senseless, shady*, smoking gun*, unlawful, unrighteous, vicious, villainous, wicked, wildcat*, wrong; SEE CONCEPT *545*

crimp [v] *fold or curl*
coil, crease, crimple, crinkle, crisp, crumple, flow, frizz, pleat, rimple, ruck, screw, scrunch, set, swirl, undulate, wave, wrinkle; SEE CONCEPTS *137,213,250*

cringe [v] *flinch, recoil from danger*
blench, cower, crawl, crouch, dodge, draw back, duck, eat dirt, grovel, kneel, quail, quiver, shrink, shy, start, stoop, tremble, wince; SEE CONCEPTS *188,195*

crinkle [v] *crumple, ruffle*
cockle, coil, crackle, crease, crimp, crimple, curl, fold, hiss, pucker, ruck, rumple, rustle, scallop, screw, scrunch, seam, swish, twist, whisper, wind, wreathe, wrinkle; SEE CONCEPTS *65,137,213,250*

cripple [v1] *disable; make lame*
attenuate, blunt, debilitate, disarm, dislimb, dismember, enfeeble, hamstring*, hurt, immobilize, incapacitate, injure, lame, maim, mangle, mutilate, palsy, paralyze, prostrate, sap, sideline*, stifle, undermine, unstrengthen, weaken; SEE CONCEPT *246*

cripple [v2] *hinder action, progress*
bring to standstill, cramp, damage, destroy, halt, hamstring*, impair, put out of action*, ruin, spoil, stifle, vitiate; SEE CONCEPT *121*

crippled [adj] *disabled*
bedridden, broken, damaged, defective, deformed, enfeebled, game, gimp*, halt, hamstrung*, handicapped, harmed, hog-tied*, housebound, impaired, incapacitated, laid up*, lame, maimed, mangled, marred, mutilated, out of commission*, paralyzed, sidelined*; SEE CONCEPTS *314,485*

crisis [n] *critical situation*
big trouble*, catastrophe, change, climacteric, climax, confrontation, contingency, corner, crossroad, crunch*, crux, culmination, deadlock, dilemma, dire straits*, disaster, embarrassment, emergency, entanglement, exigency, extremity, height, hot potato*, hour of decision*, imbroglio, impasse, juncture, mess, moment of truth*, necessity, pass, perplexity, pickle*, pinch*, plight, point of no return*, predicament, pressure, puzzle, quandary, situation, stew, strait, trauma, trial, trouble, turning point, urgency; SEE CONCEPT *674*

crisp [adj1] *brittle, dry*
crispy, crumbly, crunchy, crusty, firm, fresh, friable, green, plump, ripe, short, unwilted; SEE CONCEPT *606*

crisp [adj2] *fresh, chilly*
bracing, brisk, clear, cloudless, invigorating, refreshing, stimulating; SEE CONCEPTS *525,605*

crisp [adj3] *short, curt in presentation*
abrupt, biting, brief, brusque, clear, clear-cut, cutting, incisive, penetrating, piquing, pithy, provoking, stimulating, succinct, tart, terse; SEE CONCEPT *267*

crisp [*adj4*] *smart, snappy in appearance*
clean-cut, neat, orderly, spruce, tidy, well-groomed, well-pressed; SEE CONCEPT *579*

criterion [*n*] *test, gauge for judgment*
archetype, basis, benchmark, canon, example, exemplar, fact, foundation, law, measure, model, norm, opinion, original, paradigm, pattern, point of comparison, precedent, principle, proof, prototype, rule, scale, standard, touchstone, yardstick; SEE CONCEPTS *290,687*

critic [*n1*] *analyst, interpreter*
analyzer, annotator, arbiter, authority, caricaturist, cartoonist, commentator, connoisseur, diagnostic, evaluator, expert, expositor, judge, master, pundit, reviewer, sharpshooter; SEE CONCEPT *348*

critic [*n2*] *faultfinder, detractor*
aristarch, attacker, backseat driver*, belittler, blamer, carper, caviler, censor, censurer, complainant, complainer, defamer, disapprover, disparager, disputer, doubter, fretter, hypercritic, maligner, muckraker, mud-slinger*, nagger*, nit-picker*, panner*, quibbler, reviler, scolder, sidewalk superintendent*, slanderer, vilifier, worrier, zapper*; SEE CONCEPT *412*

critical [*adj1*] *fault-finding, detracting*
analytical, belittling, biting, calumniatory, captious, carping, caviling, cavillous, censorious, censuring, choleric, condemning, critic, cutting, cynical, demanding, demeaning, derogatory, diagnostic, disapproving, discerning, discriminating, disparaging, exacting, exceptive, finicky, fussy, hairsplitting, humbling, hypercritical, lowering, nagging, niggling, nit-picking*, overcritical, particular, penetrating, reproachful, sarcastic, satirical, scolding, severe, sharp, trenchant, withering; SEE CONCEPT *267*

critical [*adj2*] *urgently important*
acute, all-important, climacteric, conclusive, consequential, crucial, dangerous, deciding, decisive, desperate, determinative, dire, exceptive, grave, hairy, hazardous, high-priority, integral, momentous, perilous, pivotal, precarious, pressing, psychological, risky, serious, significant, strategic, urgent, vital, weighty; SEE CONCEPT *568*

criticism [*n1*] *interpretation, analysis*
appraisal, appreciation, assessment, comment, commentary, critique, elucidation, essay, estimate, evaluation, examination, exposition, judgment, lemon, notice, observation, opinion, pan*, rating, rave*, review, reviewal, scorcher, sideswipe*, sleighride*, study, write-up; SEE CONCEPTS *271,277,278*

criticism [*n2*] *verbal disapproval*
animadversion, aspersion, bad press*, blast, brickbats, Bronx cheer*, call down*, carping, cavil, caviling, censure, critical remarks, cut*, denunciation, disparagement, faultfinding, flak*, hit*, knock*, nitpicking, objection, opprobrium, pan, panning, put down, quibble, rap on knuckles*, roast*, slam*,

slap*, slap on wrist*, static, stricture, swipe*, vitriol, zapper*; SEE CONCEPT *52*

criticize [*v1*] *disapprove, judge as bad*
animadvert on, bash, blame, blast, blister, carp, castigate, censure, chastise, chide, clobber, come down on, condemn, cut down*, cut to bits*, cut up*, denounce, denunciate, disparage, do a number on*, dress down*, excoriate, find fault, fluff*, fulminate against, fustigate, give bad press*, hit, jump on*, knock*, lambaste, nag at, nit-pick, pan, pick at, rap*, reprehend, reprimand, reprobate, reprove, rip*, roast*, scathe, scorch*, skin*, skin alive*, slam*, slog*, slug*, take down*, trash*, trim*, zap*; SEE CONCEPT *52*

criticize [*v2*] *analyze, interpret*
appraise, assess, comment upon, evaluate, examine, give opinion, judge, pass judgment on, probe, review, scrutinize, study; SEE CONCEPTS *37,103*

critique [*n*] *analysis, essay*
appraisal, assessment, comment, commentary, criticism, editorial, examination, exposition, flak*, judgment, notice, pan*, putdown*, rap*, rave*, review, reviewal, slam*, slap*, study, takedown*, write-up, zapper*; SEE CONCEPTS *51,52,271*

croak [*v*] *make husky, squawking noise*
caw, crow, gasp, grunt, quack, squawk, utter huskily, utter throatily, wheeze; SEE CONCEPT *77*

crony [*n*] *ally, companion*
accomplice, acquaintance, associate, bosom buddy*, buddy, chum, colleague, comate, comrade, confidant, friend, good buddy*, intimate, mate, pal, partner, sidekick*; SEE CONCEPT *423*

crook [*n*] *criminal, thief*
cheat, filcher, knave, pilferer, purloiner, racketeer, robber, rogue, scoundrel, shark*, shyster*, swindler, villain; SEE CONCEPT *412*

crook [*v*] *bend, angle*
bow, curve, flex, fork, hook, meander, notch, round, slither, snake, wind, zigzag; SEE CONCEPTS *213,738*

crooked [*adj1*] *bent, angled*
agee, anfractuous, angular, asymmetric, awry, bowed, catawampus*, circuitous, cockeyed*, contorted, crippled, curved, curving, deformed, deviating, devious, disfigured, distorted, errant, gnarled, hooked, incurving, indirect, irregular, kinky, knurly, lopsided, meandering, misshapen, not straight, oblique, out of shape, rambling, roundabout, screwy*, serpentine, sinuous, skewed, slanted, snaky, spiral, tilted, topsy-turvy*, tortile, tortuous, twisted, twisting, uneven, warped, winding, zigzag; SEE CONCEPTS *486,490,581*

crooked [*adj2*] *evil, corrupt*
crafty, criminal, deceitful, devious, dishonest, dishonorable, double-dealing, dubious, fraudulent, illegal, indirect, iniquitous, knavish, lying, nefarious, questionable, ruthless, shady, shifty, suborned, treacherous, underhand, unlawful, unprincipled, unscrupulous, untruthful; SEE CONCEPT *545*

crop [*n*] *harvest of fruit, vegetable*
annual production, byproduct, crops, fruitage, fruits, gathering, gleaning, output, produce, product, reaping, season's growth, vintage, yield; SEE CONCEPT *429*

crop [*v*] *cut, trim off*
chop, clip, curtail, detach, detruncate, disengage, hew, lop, mow, pare, pollard, prune, reduce, shave, shear, shorten, skive, slash, snip, top, truncate; SEE CONCEPT *176*

cross [*adj*] *very angry; in a bad mood*
annoyed, cantankerous, captious, caviling, choleric, churlish, crabby*, cranky, crotchety*, crusty, disagreeable, faultfinding, fractious, fretful, grouchy, grumpy, ill-humored, ill-tempered, impatient, irascible, irritable, jumpy, out of humor, peeved, peevish, pettish, petulant, put out*, querulous, quick-tempered, ratty, short, snappy, splenetic, sullen, surly, testy, tetchy, touchy, vexed, waspish; SEE CONCEPTS *401,403*

cross [*v1*] *traverse an area*
bridge, cruise, cut across, extend over, ford, go across, meet, move across, navigate, overpass, pass over, ply, sail, span, transverse, voyage, zigzag; SEE CONCEPTS *159,224*

cross [*v2*] *intersect, lie across*
bisect, crisscross, crosscut, decussate, divide, intercross, intertwine, lace, lie athwart of, rest across; SEE CONCEPTS *738,747*

cross [*v3*] *hybridize, mix*
blend, crossbreed, cross-fertilize, cross-mate, cross-pollinate, interbreed, intercross, mingle, mongrelize; SEE CONCEPTS *250,257*

cross [*v4*] *betray, hinder*
backtalk, block, bollix, buck, crab, cramp, crimp, deny, double-cross, flummox, foil, foul up*, frustrate, have bone to pick*, impede, interfere, knock props out*, louse up*, obstruct, oppose, resist, sell*, sell out*, snafu*, stab in the back*, stonewall*, stump, stymie, take on, take wind out of sails*, thwart; SEE CONCEPTS *7,19,59,121*

cross-examine [*v*] *ask pointed questions*
catechize, check, cross-question, debrief, examine, grill, interrogate, investigate, pump, put the screws to*, question, quiz, sweat, third-degree*; SEE CONCEPTS *48,53,317*

crossing [*n*] *pathway to traverse larger path*
bridge, cloverleaf, crossroad, crosswalk, crossway, decussation, exchange, grade crossing, grating, gridiron, interchange, intersection, junction, loop, network, overpass, passage, screen, traversal, traverse, underpass; SEE CONCEPTS *501,513*

crosswise/crossways [*adj*] *across, at an angle*
angular, aslant, athwart, at right angles, awry, contrariwise, crisscross, cross, crossing, diagonally, from side to side, horizontally, longways, on the bias, over, perpendicular, sideways, thwart, trans-versal, transverse, transversely, traverse, vertically; SEE CONCEPT *581*

crotchety [*adj*] *irritable, often due to old age*
awkward, bad-tempered, bearish, cantankerous, contrary, crabby*, cranky, cross, cross-grained, crusty, curmudgeonly, difficult, disagreeable, eccentric, fractious, grouchy, grumpy, irritable, obstinate, obstreperous, odd, ornery*, peevish, queer, surly, testy, unusual, vinegary*, waspish, waspy; SEE CONCEPTS *401,403,578,797*

crouch [*v*] *stoop low; cringe*
bend, bend down, bow, cower, dip, duck, grovel, huddle, hunch, hunker down, kneel, quail, quat, scrooch down, squat, stoop, wince; SEE CONCEPT *213*

crow [*v*] *brag, exult*
babble, blow, bluster, boast, cackle, caw, cock-a-doodle-doo*, cry, flourish, gas, gloat, glory in, gurgle, jubilate, mouth, prate, puff, rodomontade, squawk, strut, swagger, triumph, vaunt, whoop; SEE CONCEPT *49*

crowd [*n1*] *large assembly*
army, array, blowout, bunch, cattle, circle, clique, cloud, cluster, company, concourse, confluence, conflux, congeries, congregation, coterie, crew, crush, deluge, drove, everybody and his brother*, faction, flock, flood, gaggle, great unwashed*, group, herd, horde, host, jam, legion, lot, mass, masses, meet, mob, multitude, muster, organization, pack, party, people, posse, press, rabble, rank and file*, scores, sellout, set, stream, surge, swarm, throng, troupe, tumult; SEE CONCEPTS *381,417*

crowd [*n2*] *special group of friends*
bunch, circle, clique, coterie, faction, group, in-crowd, lot, posse, push, set; SEE CONCEPTS *387,417*

crowd [*v*] *cram, press into area*
bear, bunch, bundle, chock, cluster, congest, congregate, crush, deluge, elbow, flock, gather, huddle, jam, jam-pack*, justle, mass, muster, overcrowd, pack, pack 'em in*, pack like sardines*, pile, push, ram, sardine*, shove, squash, squeeze, squish*, stream, surge, swamp, swarm, throng, top off, troop; SEE CONCEPTS *208,740*

crowded [*adj*] *busy, congested*
awash, brimful, brimming, chock-full, clean, close, compact, crammed, cramped, crushed, dense, elbow-to-elbow*, filled to the rafters*, fit to bust*, full, full house*, full up*, huddled, jammed, jam-packed*, loaded, lousy with*, massed, mobbed, mob scene*, overflowing, packed, populous, sardined*, sold out, SRO*, standing room only*, stiff with*, stuffed, swarming, teeming, thick, thickset, thronged, tight, topped off, up to here*, up to the hilt*, wall-to-wall*; SEE CONCEPTS *481,483,774*

crown [*n1*] *top; best*
acme, apex, climax, crest, culmination, fastigium, head, meridian, peak, perfection, pinnacle, roof, summit, tip, top, ultimate, vertex, zenith; SEE CONCEPTS *706,836*

crown [n2] *tiara for royalty*
chaplet, circlet, coronal, coronet, diadem, garland, headband, headdress, wreath; SEE CONCEPT *452*

crown [n3] *royalty*
crowned head, emperor, empress, king, monarch, monarchy, potentate, queen, ruler, sovereign, sovereignty, supreme ruler, the throne; SEE CONCEPT *422*

crown [v1] *reward, dignify*
adorn, arm, authorize, commission, coronate, delegate, determine, dignify, dower, enable, endow, endue, ennoble, enthrone, erect, establish, exalt, festoon, fix, heighten, honor, inaugurate, induct, install, invest, raise, sanction, settle, set up, stabilize, strengthen; SEE CONCEPTS *50,69,88*

crown [v2] *be the culmination of*
cap, climax, complete, consummate, crest, finish, fulfill, perfect, put finishing touch on, round off, surmount, terminate, top, top off; SEE CONCEPTS *234,706*

crown [v3] *hit, usually on head*
biff, box, cuff, knock, punch, smite, strike; SEE CONCEPT *189*

crowning [adj] *climactic*
consummate, culminating, excellent, final, paramount, principal, sovereign, supreme, ultimate; SEE CONCEPTS *531,548*

crucial [adj] *critical, important*
acute, central, clamorous, climacteric, climatic, compelling, deciding, decisive, desperate, dire, essential, hanging by thread*, high-priority, imperative, insistent, momentous, necessary, on thin ice*, pivotal, pressing, searching, showdown*, touch and go*, touchy, urgent, vital; SEE CONCEPT *568*

crucify [v1] *execute; torture near to death*
excruciate, hang, harrow, kill, martyr, martyrize, nail to cross, persecute, rack, torment, torture; SEE CONCEPT *252*

crucify [v2] *browbeat, destroy with words*
afflict, agonize, bedevil, bother, harrow, ill-treat, lampoon, pan, ridicule, smite, tear to pieces*, torment, torture, try, wipe the floor with*; SEE CONCEPTS *7,19,52*

crude [adj1] *vulgar, unpolished in manner*
awkward, backward, barnyard*, boorish, cheap, cloddish, clumsy, coarse, crass, dirty, earthy, filthy, foul, grody*, gross*, ignorant, ill-bred, indecent, indelicate, inelegant, insensible, lewd, loud, loud-mouthed, loutish, lowbred, oafish, obscene, raunchy*, raw, rough, rude, savage, smutty*, tacky*, tactless, uncouth, unenlightened, ungainly, unskillful; SEE CONCEPTS *267,401*

crude [adj2] *unrefined, natural*
amateurish, callow, coarse, green, harsh, homemade, homespun, immature, impure, inexpert, in the rough*, makeshift, outline, prentice, primitive, raw, rough, rough-hewn, rude, rudimentary, rustic, simple, sketchy, thick, undeveloped, unfinished, unformed, ungraded, unmatured, unmilled, unpolished,

unprepared, unprocessed, unproficient, unsorted, untaught, untrained, unworked, unwrought; SEE CONCEPTS *562,578,589,797*

cruel [adj] *vicious, pitiless; causing pain*
atrocious, barbarous, bestial, bitter, bloodthirsty, brutal, brutish, callous, cold-blooded, degenerate, demoniac, depraved, evil, excruciating, ferocious, fierce, flinty, hard, hard-hearted, harsh, hateful, heartless, hellish, implacable, inexorable, inhuman, inhumane, malevolent, merciless, monstrous, painful, pernicious, poignant, rancorous, relentless, revengeful, ruthless, sadistic, sinful, spiteful, tyrannical, unfeeling, unkind, unnatural, unrelenting, vengeful, vicious, virulent, wicked; SEE CONCEPTS *401,570*

cruelty [n] *brutality, harshness*
animality, barbarism, barbarity, bestiality, bloodthirstiness, brutishness, callousness, coarseness, coldness, depravity, despotism, ferocity, fiendishness, fierceness, hard-heartedness, heartlessness, inhumanity, insensibility, insensitiveness, malice, malignity, masochism, mercilessness, murderousness, persecution, rancor, ruthlessness, sadism, savageness, savagery, severity, spite, spitefulness, torture, truculence, unfeelingness, unkindness, venom, viciousness, wickedness; SEE CONCEPT *633*

cruise [n] *sailing expedition*
boat trip, crossing, jaunt, journey, sail, sailing, sea trip, voyage; SEE CONCEPTS *224,292,363*

cruise [v] *sail*
boat, coast, drift, fare, gad, gallivant, go, hie, jaunt, journey, keep steady pace, meander, navigate, pass, proceed, push on, repair, travel, voyage, wander about, wend; SEE CONCEPTS *147,151,159,224*

crumb [n] *tiny bit, morsel*
atom, dab, dash, dram, drop, grain, iota, jot, mite, ounce, particle, pinch, scrap, seed, shred, sliver, smidgen, snippet, soupçon, speck; SEE CONCEPT *831*

crumble [v] *break or fall into pieces*
break up, collapse, crumb, crush, decay, decompose, degenerate, deteriorate, disintegrate, dissolve, fragment, go to pieces, granulate, grind, molder, perish, powder, pulverize, putrefy, triturate, tumble; SEE CONCEPTS *181,248,469*

crumbly [adj] *brittle*
breakable, corroded, crisp, crunchy, decayed, degenerated, deteriorated, deteriorating, disintegrated, eroded, fragile, frail, frangible, friable, oxidized, perishing, powdery, pulverizable, rotted, rotten, rusted, shivery, short, soft, worn; SEE CONCEPTS *485,606*

crumple [v] *make or become wrinkled*
break down, buckle, cave in, collapse, crease, crimp, crimple, crinkle, crush, fall, fold, give way, go to pieces, pucker, rimple, ruck, rumple, screw, scrunch, shrivel, wad, wrinkle; SEE CONCEPTS *184,208,252*

crunch [n] *crucial point*
crisis, critical point, crux, difficulty, emergency, hour of decision*, moment of truth*, problem, test, trouble, trying time*; SEE CONCEPTS *388,674,675*

crunch [v] *grind, chew*
beat, bite, champ, chaw, chomp, crush, gnaw, masticate, munch, ruminate, scrunch; SEE CONCEPTS *169,186*

crusade [n] *campaign for cause*
cause, demonstration, drive, evangelism, expedition, holy war, jihad, march, movement, push; SEE CONCEPT *300*

crush [n1] *crowd of animate beings*
drove, gathering, horde, huddle, jam, multitude, party, press, push, throng, tumult; SEE CONCEPTS *417,432*

crush [n2] *infatuation*
beguin, desire, flame, love affair, passion, puppy love, torch; SEE CONCEPT *20*

crush [v1] *compress, smash*
beat, bray, break, bruise, buck, comminute, contriturate, contuse, crease, crowd, crumble, crunch, embrace, enfold, express, hug, jam, kablooey*, mash, pound, powder, press, pulverize, push, romp, rumple, smash, squash, squeeze, squish, total*, trample, tread, triturate, wrinkle; SEE CONCEPTS *208,219, 246,252*

crush [v2] *defeating soundly*
annihilate, bear down, beat, blot out*, blow away*, conquer, defeat, demolish, extinguish, force down, ice*, kill, obliterate, overcome, overpower, overwhelm, quelch, quell, reduce, ruin, squelch, stamp out*, strangle, subdue, subjugate, suppress, vanquish, wreck; SEE CONCEPTS *95,252*

crush [v3] *humiliate*
abash, browbeat, chagrin, dispose of, dump, hurt, mortify, overwhelm, put away*, put down*, quash, quell, shame, suppress; SEE CONCEPTS *7,19*

crust [n] *stiff outer layer; coating*
band, bloom, border, caking, coat, concretion, covering, edge, encrustation, film, hull, incrustation, integument, layer, outside, rind, scab, shell, skin, surface, verge; SEE CONCEPT *484*

crusty [adj1] *irritable, often due to old age*
abrupt, bluff, blunt, brief, brusque, cantankerous, captious, choleric, crabbed, crabby*, cranky, cross, curt, dour, gruff, harsh, ill-humored, irascible, peevish, prickly, sarcastic, saturnine, scornful, short, short-tempered, snappish, snarling, snippety, snippy, splenetic, surly, testy, touchy, vinegary; SEE CONCEPT *401*

crusty [adj2] *brittle on outside*
crisp, crispy, crunchy, friable, hard, short, well-baked, well-done; SEE CONCEPTS *462,606*

crux [n] *most important part*
body, bottom line*, core, decisive point, essence, gist, heart, kernel, matter, meat, meat and potatoes*, nitty-gritty, nub, pith, purport, substance, thrust; SEE CONCEPTS *668,826*

cry [n1] *weeping and making sad sounds*
bawl, bawling, bewailing, blubber, blubbering, howl, howling, keening, lament, lamentation, mourning, shedding tears, snivel, snivelling, sob, sobbing, sorrowing, tears, the blues*, wailing, weep, whimpering, yowl; SEE CONCEPTS *77,469*

cry [n2] *calling out; yelling*
acclamation, bark, bawl, bay, bellow, cackle, call, caw, chatter, cheer, clack, clamor, cluck, coo, crow, ejaculation, exclamation, expletive, fuss, gobble, groan, grunt, hiss, holler, hoot, howl, hullabaloo, hurrah, meow, mewling, moo, motto, nicker, note, outcry, pipe, quack, report, roar, ruckus, scream, screech, shout, shriek, song, squall, squawk, squeak, trill, uproar, vociferation, wail, whine, whinney, whistle, whoop, yammer, yawp, yell, yelp, yoo-hoo; SEE CONCEPTS *47,77,278*

cry [v1] *weep and make sad sounds*
bawl, bemoan, bewail, blub, blubber, boohoo*, break down, burst into tears*, caterwaul, choke up, complain, crack up*, deplore, dissolve in tears*, fret, grieve, groan, howl, keen, lament, let go, let it all out*, mewl, moan, mourn, put on the weeps*, regret, ring the blues*, shed bitter tears*, shed tears, sigh, sniff, snivel, sob, sorrow, squall, turn on waterworks*, wail, weep, whimper, whine, yammer, yowl; SEE CONCEPTS *77,469*

cry [v2] *call out, yell*
bark, bawl, bay, bellow, bleat, cackle, call, caw, chatter, cheer, clack, clamor, cluck, coo, croak, crow, ejaculate, exclaim, gabble, growl, grunt, hail, hiss, holler, holler out, hoot, howl, low, meow, moo, nicker, pipe, quack, roar, scream, screech, shout, shriek, sing out, snarl, squawk, trill, tweet, twitter, vociferate, whinney, whistle, whoop, yawp, yell, yelp; SEE CONCEPTS *47,77*

cry [v3] *advertise*
announce, bark*, broadcast, build up, hawk, hype*, press-agent*, proclaim, promulgate, publicize, publish, puff*, trumpet*; SEE CONCEPT *324*

crypt [n] *burial place*
catacomb, cave, cavern, cell, chamber, compartment, grave, grotto, mausoleum, room, sepulcher, tomb, undercroft, vault; SEE CONCEPT *305*

cryptic [adj] *secret; obscure in meaning*
abstruse, ambiguous, apocryphal, arcane, cabbalistic, dark, Delphian, Delphic, enigmatic, equivocal, esoteric, evasive, hidden, incomprehensible, inexplicable, murky, mysterious, mystic, mystical, mystifying, occult, opaque, oracular, perplexing, puzzling, recondite, secretive, strange, tenebrous, unclear, unfathomable, uninformative, vague, veiled; SEE CONCEPTS *267,576,682*

crystal [adj] *clear, transparent*
clear-cut, limpid, lucent, lucid, luminous, pellucid, translucent, transpicuous, unblurred; SEE CONCEPTS *617,618*

cuddle [v] *hold fondly, closely*
bundle, burrow, caress, clasp, cosset, curl up, dandle, embrace, enfold, fondle, huddle, hug, kiss, love, nestle, nuzzle, pet, snug, snuggle, touch; SEE CONCEPTS *190,375*

cuddly [adj] *huggable, embraceable*
caressible, cuddlesome, kissable, lovable, plump, snuggly, soft, warm; SEE CONCEPT *485*

cudgel [n] *baton for hitting*
bastinado, bat, billy, billyclub, birch, blackjack, bludgeon, cane, club, cosh, ferule, mace, nightstick, paddle, rod, sap, shill, shillelagh, spontoon, stick, switch, truncheon; SEE CONCEPT *500*

cue [n] *signal to act*
catchword, clue, hint, hot lead*, idea, indication, inkling, innuendo, in the wind*, intimation, job, key, lead, mnemonic, nod, notion, prod, prompt, prompting, reminder, sign, suggestion, telltale*, tip-off, warning; SEE CONCEPTS *278,284,628*

cuff [n] *beating with hands*
belt, biff, box, buffet, chop, clip, clout, hit, knock, poke, punch, rap, slap, smack, sock, thump, wallop, whack; SEE CONCEPT *189*

cuff [v] *beat with hands*
bat, belt, biff, box, buffet, clap, clobber, clout, hit, knock, pummel, punch, slap, smack, spank, thump, whack; SEE CONCEPT *189*

cull [v1] *pick out for reason*
choose, discriminate, elect, extract, glean, mark, optate, opt for, pluck, prefer, select, sift, single out, take, thin, thin out, winnow; SEE CONCEPTS *41, 142*

cull [v2] *gather*
accumulate, amass, collect, extract, garner, glean, pick up, round up; SEE CONCEPT *109*

culminate [v] *come to a climax*
cap, climax, close, come to a head*, conclude, crown, end, end up, finish, go over the mountain*, go the route*, rise to crescendo, round off, shoot one's wad*, terminate, top off*, wind up*; SEE CONCEPT *119*

culmination [n] *conclusion; climactic stage*
acme, all the way*, apex, apogee, blow off*, capper*, climax, completion, consummation, critical mass, crown, crowning touch, finale, finish, height, limit, maximum, meridian, ne plus ultra, noon, payoff, peak, perfection, pinnacle, punch line*, summit, top, zenith; SEE CONCEPTS *230,635,676*

culpable [adj] *responsible for action*
amiss, answerable, at fault, blamable, blameful, blameworthy, caught, caught in the act*, caught red-handed*, censurable, demeritorious, dirty, found wanting, guilty, hung up, impeachable, indictable, in the wrong, liable, off base, out of line, punishable, reprehensible, responsible, sinful, smoking gun*, to blame, unholy, wrong; SEE CONCEPTS *404,545*

culprit [n] *person responsible for wrongdoing*
con, convict, criminal, delinquent, evildoer, ex-con*, felon, fugitive, guilty party, jailbird*, male-

factor, miscreant, offender, rascal, sinner, transgressor, wrongdoer, yardbird*; SEE CONCEPT *412*

cult [n1] *group sharing belief*
band, body, church, clan, clique, creed, denomination, faction, faith, following, party, persuasion, religion, school, sect; SEE CONCEPTS *369,387*

cult [n2] *worship; form of ceremony*
admiration, ceremony, craze, creed, cultus, devotion, faddism, faith, idolization, liturgy, persuasion, religion, reverence, rite, ritual, veneration; SEE CONCEPTS *410,689*

cultivate [v1] *develop land for growing*
breed, crop, dress, farm, fertilize, garden, harvest, labor, manage, mature, plant, plow, prepare, propagate, raise, ripen, seed, tend, till, work; SEE CONCEPTS *253,257*

cultivate [v2] *enrich situation; give special attention*
advance, ameliorate, better, bolster, bring on, brownnose*, butter up*, cherish, civilize, court, develop, discipline, elevate, encourage, enrich, foster, further, get in with*, get next to*, get on good side of*, improve, nourish, nurse, nurture, play up to*, polish, promote, refine, run after, seek friendship, shine up to*, suck up to*, take pains with, train; SEE CONCEPTS *244,384*

cultivate [v3] *nurture, take care of*
aid, ameliorate, better, cherish, devote oneself to, educate, encourage, forward, foster, further, help, improve, instruct, nurse, patronize, promote, pursue, raise, rear, refine, support, teach, train; SEE CONCEPTS *110,295*

cultivation [n1] *development of land for growing*
agrology, agronomics, agronomy, farming, gardening, horticulture, husbandry, planting, plowing, tillage, tilling, working; SEE CONCEPT *257*

cultivation [n2] *culture, sophistication, education*
advancement, aestheticism, breeding, civility, civilization, delicacy, discernment, discrimination, enlightenment, gentility, good taste, grounding, improvement, learning, letters, manners, polish, progress, refined taste, refinement, schooling, taste; SEE CONCEPTS *411,655,673*

cultivation [n3] *nurture, help*
advancement, advocacy, development, encouragement, enhancement, fostering, furtherance, patronage, promotion, support; SEE CONCEPTS *110,657*

cultural [adj] *educational, enlightening*
adorning, advancing, artistic, beautifying, beneficial, broadening, civilizing, constructive, corrective, developmental, dignifying, disciplining, edifying, educative, elevating, ennobling, enriching, expanding, glorifying, helpful, humane, humanizing, influential, inspirational, instructive, learned, liberal, liberalizing, nurturing, ornamenting, polishing, promoting, raising, refined, refining, regenerative, socializing, stimulating, uplifting, widening; SEE CONCEPTS *537,555,589*

culture [n1] *breeding, education, sophistication*
ability, accomplishment, address, aestheticism, art, capacity, civilization, class, courtesy, cultivation, delicacy, dignity, discrimination, dress, elegance, elevation, enlightenment, erudition, experience, fashion, finish, gentility, good taste, grace, improvement, kindness, learning, manners, nobility, perception, polish, politeness, practice, proficiency, refinement, savoir-faire, science, skill, tact, training, urbanity; SEE CONCEPTS *388,633,678*

culture [n2] *ideas, values of a people*
arts and sciences, civilization, convention, customs, development, ethnology, folklore, folkways, grounding, habit, humanism, knowledge, lifestyle, mores, society, the arts, way of life; SEE CONCEPTS *388,689*

culture [n3] *development of land*
agriculture, agrology, agronomics, agronomy, cultivation, farming, gardening, husbandry, raising, tending; SEE CONCEPT *257*

cultured [adj] *well-bred, experienced*
able, accomplished, advanced, aesthetic, appreciative, au courant, blue-stocking*, chivalrous, civilized, courteous, cultivated, distingue, educated, elegant, enlightened, erudite, gallant, genteel, highbrow*, high-class, informed, intellectual, intelligent, knowledgeable, lettered, liberal, literary, literate, mannerly, polished, polite, refined, savant, scholarly, sensitive, sophisticated, tasteful, tolerant, traveled, understanding, up-to-date, urbane, versed, well-informed; SEE CONCEPT *550*

culvert [n] *ditch for flow of water*
canal, channel, conduit, drain, duct, gutter, pipe, watercourse; SEE CONCEPT *509*

cumbersome [adj] *clumsy, awkward*
bulky, burdensome, clunker, clunking, clunky, cumbrous, embarrassing, galumphing, heavy, hefty, incommodious, inconvenient, leaden, massive, oppressive, ponderous, tiresome, unhandy, unmanageable, unwieldy, wearisome, weighty; SEE CONCEPTS *544,773*

cumulative [adj] *accruing; growing in size or effect*
accumulative, additive, additory, advancing, aggregate, amassed, augmenting, chain, collective, heaped, heightening, increasing, increscent, intensifying, magnifying, multiplying, snowballing*, summative; SEE CONCEPTS *540,548,788*

cunning [adj1] *devious*
acute, artful, astute, cagey, canny, crafty, crazy like fox*, deep, fancy footwork*, foxy, guileful, insidious, keen, knowing, Machiavellian, sharp, shifty, shrewd, slick, slippery, sly, sly boots*, smart, smarts, smooth, street-smart*, streetwise*, subtle, tricky, wary, wily; SEE CONCEPTS *401,545*

cunning [adj2] *imaginative*
able, adroit, canny, clever, crackerjack*, deft, dexterous, ingenious, intelligent, masterful, skillful, slighty, sly, smart, smooth, subtle, well-laid, well-planned; SEE CONCEPT *402*

cup [n] *container for drinking*
beaker, bowl, cannikin, chalice, cupful, demitasse, draught, drink, goblet, grail, mug, potion, stein, taster, teacup, tumbler, vessel; SEE CONCEPT *494*

cupboard [n] *storage cabinet*
buffet, closet, depository, facility, locker, press, repository, sideboard, storeroom, wardrobe; SEE CONCEPT *443*

cupidity [n] *greed, strong desire*
acquisitiveness, avarice, avariciousness, avidity, covetousness, craving, eagerness, graspingness, greediness, hunger, infatuation, itching, longing, lust, passion, possessiveness, rapaciousness, rapacity, voracity, yearning; SEE CONCEPTS *20,709*

cur [n1] *rotten, lowly animate being*
blackguard, black sheep*, bum, cad, coward, dog*, good-for-nothing*, heel*, hound*, ne'er-do-well*, rat*, riffraff*, scoundrel, scum*, skunk*, snake*, stinker*, toad*, villain, worm*, wretch, yellow dog*; SEE CONCEPTS *389,412*

cur [n2] *animal of mixed breed*
Heinz 57*, mongrel, mutt; SEE CONCEPT *394*

curable [adj] *able to be improved, fixed*
amenable, capable, correctable, corrigible, healable, improvable, mendable, not hopeless, not too bad, reparative, restorable, subject to cure; SEE CONCEPTS *314,485*

curative [adj] *healing, health-giving*
alleviative, beneficial, corrective, curing, healthful, helpful, invigorating, medicable, medicative, medicinal, pick-me-up*, remedial, remedying, restorative, salutary, sanative, shot in the arm*, therapeutic, tonic, vulnerary, what the doctor ordered*, wholesome; SEE CONCEPTS *314,537*

curb [n] *restraining device; check*
barrier, border, brake, bridle, chain, control, deterrent, edge, harness, hindrance, ledge, limitation, lip, rein, restrainer, restraint, restriction, rim; SEE CONCEPTS *376,497,652,745*

curb [v] *repress, restrict*
abstain, bit, bottle up*, box in, bridle, bring to screeching halt*, check, clog, constrain, contain, control, cook*, cool down, cool off, deny, entrammel, fetter, hamper, hinder, hobble, hog-tie*, hold back, hold down, hold in, ice*, impede, inhibit, keep lid on*, keep tight rein on*, leash, manacle, moderate, muzzle, refrain, rein in, restrain, retard, scrub, send up, shackle, subdue, suppress, tame, tie, tie up, withhold; SEE CONCEPTS *121,130*

curdle [n] *sour; change into coagulated substance*
acerbate, acidify, acidulate, clabber*, clot, coagulate, condense, congeal, curd, ferment, go off, spoil, thicken, turn, turn sour; SEE CONCEPT *456*

cure [n] *solution to problem, often health*
aid, alleviation, antidote, assistance, catholicon, corrective, counteractant, counteragent, countermeasure, drug, elixir, elixir vitae, fix, healing, healing agent, help, medicament, medicant, medication,

medicine, nostrum, panacea, pharmacon, physic, placebo, proprietary, quick fix*, recovery, redress, remedy, reparation, restorative, therapeutic, treatment; SEE CONCEPTS *110,307,311*

cure [*v1*] *heal, ease bad situation*
alleviate, ameliorate, attend, better, cold turkey*, correct, doctor, dose, dress, dry out*, help, improve, kick, kick the habit*, make better, make healthy, make whole, medicate, mend, minister to, nurse, palliate, quit cold*, rectify, redress, rehabilitate, relieve, remedy, repair, restore, restore to health, right, shake, sweat it out*, treat; SEE CONCEPTS *126,244,310*

cure [*v2*] *cook, age food*
dry, fire, harden, keep, kipper, pickle, preserve, salt, smoke, steel, temper; SEE CONCEPT *170*

curio [*n*] *knickknack*
antique, bauble, bibelot, bygone, collectible, collector's item, objet d'art, toy, trifle, trinket, whatnot; SEE CONCEPT *446*

curiosity [*n1*] *intense desire to know, understand*
concern, eagerness, inquiring mind, inquiringness, inquisitiveness, interest, interestingness, intrusiveness, investigation, meddlesomeness, meddling, mental acquisitiveness, nosiness, officiousness, prying, questioning, regard, searching, snoopiness, snooping, thirst for knowledge; SEE CONCEPTS *20,410*

curiosity [*n2*] *odd item*
anomaly, bibelot, bygone, conversation piece, curio, exoticism, freak, knickknack, marvel, monstrosity, nonesuch, objet d'art, oddity, peculiar object, prodigy, rarity, singular object, trinket, unusual object, wonder; SEE CONCEPT *260*

curious [*adj1*] *desiring knowledge, understanding*
analytical, disquisitive, examining, impertinent, inquiring, inquisitive, inspecting, interested, interfering, intrusive, investigative, meddlesome, meddling, nosy, peeping, peering, prurient, prying, puzzled, questioning, scrutinizing, searching, snoopy, tampering; SEE CONCEPTS *403,542*

curious [*adj2*] *very odd*
bizarre, exotic, extraordinary, marvelous, mysterious, novel, oddball, peculiar, puzzling, quaint, queer, rare, remarkable, singular, strange, unconventional, unexpected, unique, unorthodox, unusual, weird, wonderful; SEE CONCEPTS *547,564*

curl [*n*] *loop, ringlet, curve*
coil, crimp, crispation, curlicue, flourish, frizz, kink, quirk, spiral, swirl, twist, wave, whorl; SEE CONCEPTS *418,436*

curl [*v*] *bend, loop*
buckle, coil, contort, convolute, corkscrew, crimp, crinkle, crisp, crook, curve, entwine, fold, form into ringlets, frizz, indent, kink, lap, meander, ringlet, ripple, roll, scallop, snake, spiral, swirl, turn, twine, twirl, twist, undulate, wave, wind, wreathe, writhe, zigzag; SEE CONCEPTS *147,184,213*

curly [*adj*] *looping, forming ringlets*
coiled, convoluted, corkscrew, crimped, crimpy, crinkling, crinkly, crisp, curled, curling, frizzed, frizzy, fuzzy, kinky, looped, permed, spiralled, waved, waving, wavy, winding, wound; SEE CONCEPTS *406,486*

currency [*n*] *paper and coin money of a country*
almighty dollar*, bills, bread*, cabbage*, cash, chicken feed*, coinage, coins, cold cash*, dinero*, dough*, folding money, green stuff*, legal tender, medium of exchange, moolah*, notes, piece of change*, roll*, specie*, wad*; SEE CONCEPT *340*

current [*n*] *flow of something, usually water*
course, draught, drift, ebb and flow, flood, flux, jet, juice, progression, river, run, rush, spate, stream, tidal motion, tide; SEE CONCEPTS *514,519,738*

current [*adj*] *contemporary; common*
accepted, accustomed, afoot, circulating, common knowledge, customary, cutting-edge*, doing, existent, extant, fad, fashionable, general, going around, hot*, in, in circulation, in progress, instant, in the mainstream, in the news, in use, in vogue, leading-edge*, mod*, modern, now*, on front burner*, ongoing, popular, present, present-day, prevailing, prevalent, rampant, regnant, rife, ruling, state-of-the-art, swinging, topical, trendy, up-to-date, widespread; SEE CONCEPTS *530,820*

curse [*n1*] *hateful, swearing remark*
anathema, ban, bane, blaspheming, blasphemy, commination, cursing, cussing, cuss word, damning, denunciation, dirty name*, dirty word*, double whammy*, execration, expletive, four-letter word*, fulmination, imprecation, malediction, malison, naughty words*, no-no*, oath, objuration, obloquy, obscenity, profanation, profanity, sacrilege, swearing, swear word, vilification, whammy*; SEE CONCEPTS *54,278*

curse [*n2*] *misfortune wished upon someone*
affliction, bane, burden, calamity, cancer, cross, disaster, evil, evil eye*, hydra, jinx, ordeal, pestilence, plague, scourge, torment, tribulation, trouble, vexation, voodoo; SEE CONCEPTS *674,675*

cursed [*adj1*] *damned, doomed for bad ending*
accursed, bedeviled, blankety-blank*, blasted, blessed, blighted, cast out, confounded, doggone*, excommunicate, execrable, fey, foredoomed, hell fire*, ill-fated, infernal, snakebit*, star-crossed, unholy, unsanctified, villainous, voodooed*; SEE CONCEPTS *548,571*

cursed [*adj2*] *detestable, hateful*
abominable, accursed, atrocious, damnable, detestable, devillish, disgusting, execrable, fiendish, flatitous, heinous, infamous, infernal, loathsome, odious, pernicious, pestilential, vile; SEE CONCEPTS *404,571*

cursory [*adj*] *casual, hasty*
brief, careless, depthless, desultory, fast, half-assed*, half-baked*, haphazard, hit or miss*, hurried, offhand, passing, perfunctory, quick, random, rapid, shallow, short, sketchy, slapdash, slight, sloppy, speedy, summary, superficial, swift, uncritical; SEE CONCEPTS *562,588,589*

curt [*adj*] *abrupt, rude*
blunt, breviloquent, brief, brusque, churlish, compendiary, compendious, concise, crusty, gruff, imperious, laconic, offhand, peremptory, pithy, sharp, short, short and sweet, snappish, snippety, snippy, succinct, summary, tart, terse, unceremonious, uncivil, ungracious; SEE CONCEPT *267*

curtail [*v*] *cut short; abridge*
abbreviate, boil down, chop, clip, contract, cramp, cut, cut back, decrease, diminish, dock, downsize, get to meat*, halt, lessen, lop, minify, nutshell*, pare down, reduce, retrench, roll back, shorten, slash, trim, truncate; SEE CONCEPTS *130,236,247*

curtain [*n*] *window covering*
blind, decoration, drape, drapery, film, hanging, jalousie, oleo, portiere, rag, roller, screen, shade, shield, shroud, shutter, valance, veil, Venetian blind; SEE CONCEPT *444*

curvaceous [*adj*] *voluptuous, full-figured*
attractive, beautiful, bosomy, built*, buxom, comely, curves, curvesome, curvilinear, curvy, Junoesque, pleasing, rounded, shapely, stacked*, statuesque, well-developed, well-proportioned, well-rounded, zaftig; SEE CONCEPTS *406,490*

curvature [*n*] *rounded part of thing, usually body part*
arc, arch, arching, bend, bow, curve, curving, curvity, deflection, flexure, incurvation, round, shape; SEE CONCEPTS *754,757*

curve [*n*] *arched, rounded line or object*
ambit, arc, arch, bend, bight, bow, camber, catenary, chord, circle, circuit, circumference, compass, concavity, contour, crook, curlicue, curvation, curvature, ellipse, festoon, flexure, hairpin, half-moon, helix, horseshoe, hyperbola, incurvation, incurvature, loop, meniscus, ogee, parabola, quirk, rondure, round, sinuosity, sweep, swerve, trajectory, turn, vault, whorl; SEE CONCEPT *436*

curve [*v*] *bending in a shape or course*
arc, arch, bend, bow, buckle, bulge, coil, concave, convex, crook, crumple, curl, deviate, divert, gyrate, hook, incurve, inflect, loop, round, skew, snake, spiral, stoop, swerve, turn, twist, veer, wind, wreathe; SEE CONCEPTS *147,184,213,738*

curved [*adj*] *bowed, bent*
arced, arched, arciform, arrondi, biflected, circular, compass, crooked, curly, curvaceous, curvilinear, declinate, elliptical, enbowed, humped, incurvate, incurved, looped, loopy, round, rounded, serpentine, sigmoid, sinuous, skewed, snaky, S-shaped, sweeping, swirly, turned, twisted, twisting, twisty, wreathed; SEE CONCEPTS *486,490*

cushion [*n*] *pillow, pad*
beanbag, bolster, buffer, bumper, fender, hassock, headrest, mat, rest, seat, sham, squab, woolsack; SEE CONCEPTS *444,464,484*

cushion [*v*] *pad, protect from blow*
bolster, buttress, cradle, dampen, deaden, insulate, muffle, pillow, seclude, soften, stifle, support, suppress; SEE CONCEPT *680*

custodian [*n*] *caretaker, maintenance person*
baby sitter, bodyguard, cerebus, claviger, cleaner, cleaning person, concierge, curator, escort, governess, governor, guardian, housesitter, keeper, maintenance, manager, overseer, protector, sitter, steward, super*, superintendent, supervisor, swamper*, warden, watchdog, watchman; SEE CONCEPT *348*

custody [*n1*] *supervision, charge of something*
aegis, auspices, care, conservation, custodianship, guardianship, keeping, management, observation, preservation, protection, safekeeping, salvation, superintendence, supervision, trusteeship, tutelage, ward, wardship, watch; SEE CONCEPTS *117,376,710*

custody [*n2*] *confinement, jailing*
arrest, detention, duress, imprisonment, incarceration, jail, keeping; SEE CONCEPTS *90,691*

custom [*n1*] *habitual action*
addiction, beaten path*, characteristic, consuetude, daily grind*, fashion, form, grind*, groove, habit, habitude, hang-up*, into*, manner, matter of course, mode, observance, practice, praxis, precedent, procedure, proprieties, routine, rule, second nature*, shot, swim, thing, trick, usage, use, way, wont; SEE CONCEPT *633*

custom [*n2*] *ritual, traditional action*
attitude, canon, ceremony, character, convention, conventionalism, design, dictates, established way, etiquette, fashion, folkways, form, formality, inheritence, manner, matter of course, method, mode, mold, mores, observance, observation, pattern, performance, policy, practice, praxis, precedent, precept, rite, ritual, routine, rule, second nature*, style, system, taste, type, unwritten law, unwritten rule, usage, use, vogue, way; SEE CONCEPTS *644,687*

customarily [*adv*] *ordinarily; as a rule*
as a matter of course, as usual, commonly, consistently, conventionally, frequently, generally, habitually, naturally, normally, regularly, routinely, traditionally, usually, wontedly; SEE CONCEPTS *530,547*

customary [*adj*] *usual, established*
accepted, according to Hoyle*, accustomed, acknowledged, by the numbers*, chronic, common, confirmed, conventional, established, everyday, familiar, fashionable, frequent, general, habitual, household, in a rut*, in the groove*, normal, ordinary, orthodox, playing it safe*, popular, prescriptive, recognized, regular, regulation, routine, same old*, SOP*, standard, standard operating procedure*, stipulated, traditional, understood, universal, wonted; SEE CONCEPTS *530,547*

customer [*n*] *buyer of goods, services*
client, clientele, consumer, habitué, patron, prospect, purchaser, regular shopper; SEE CONCEPT *348*

cut [*n1*] *incision*
carving, chip, chop, cleavage, cleft, dissection, fissure, furrow, gash, graze, groove, intersection, kerf, laceration, mark, nick, nip, notch, opening, passage,

penetration, pierce, prick, rabbet, rent, rip, scarification, sculpture, section, shave, slash, slit, slot, snip, stab, stroke, trench, trim, wound; SEE CONCEPT *309*

cut [*n2*] *reduction, diminution*
cutback, decrease, decrement, economy, fall, lessening, lowering, reduction, saving; SEE CONCEPTS *698,776*

cut [*n3*] *portion of profit*
allotment, allowance, bite, chop, division, kickback, lot, member, moiety, part, partage, percentage, piece, quota, section, segment, share, slice; SEE CONCEPT *344*

cut [*n4*] *style, shape of clothing*
configuration, construction, fashion, figure, form, look, mode; SEE CONCEPTS *655,754*

cut [*n5*] *insult*
abuse, hateful remark, indignity, offense; SEE CONCEPT *52*

cut [*n6*] *type, kind*
cast, description, feather, ilk, lot, mold, sort, stamp; SEE CONCEPT *378*

cut [*v1*] *sever, chop with sharp instrument; incise*
amputate, behead, bisect, bite, carve, chine, chip, chisel, cleave, clip, crop, curtail, decussate, dice, dissect, dissever, divide, facet, fell, flitch, gash, guillotine, hack, hash, hew, intersect, lacerate, lay open, lop, mince, mow, nick, notch, part, penetrate, perforate, pierce, prune, puncture, quarter, rabbet, reap, rend, rip, rive, saber, saw, scarify, scissor, score, scythe, separate, shave, shear, sickle, skive, slash, slice, slit, sliver, snip, split, sunder, transect, truncate, whack; SEE CONCEPTS *137,176*

cut [*v2*] *shorten, reduce*
abbreviate, abridge, bob, clip, condense, contract, crop, curtail, cut back, cut down, decrease, delete, dock, ease up, edit out, excise, lessen, lower, mark down, mow, pare, precis, ration, reduce, shave, slash, slim, trim, truncate; SEE CONCEPTS *236, 247*

cut [*v3*] *ignore, avoid*
cold-shoulder*, disregard, ditch*, duck, dump*, evade, freeze someone out*, grieve, hurt, insult, look straight through*, neglect, ostracize, pain, play hooky*, play truant, shirk, skip, slam door on*, slight, snob, snub, spurn, stay away, sting, turn aside, turn one's back on, wound; SEE CONCEPTS *38,188,633*

cut [*v4*] *dilute*
impair, thin, undermine, weaken; SEE CONCEPT *240*

cutback [*n*] *reduction*
curtailment, cut, decrease, decrement, economy, lessening, retrenchment, shortening; SEE CONCEPTS *335,776*

cut back [*v*] *economize*
abbreviate, abridge, check, clip, curb, curtail, cut, cut down, decrease, lessen, lower, mark down, mark off, pare, prune, reduce, retrench, shave, shorten, slash, trim; SEE CONCEPTS *236,247*

cut down [*v*] *kill; fell*
dispatch, hew, level, lop, massacre, mow, mow down, raze, slaughter, slay; SEE CONCEPT *252*

cute [*adj*] *perky, attractive*
adorable, beautiful, charming, dainty, delightful, pleasant, pretty; SEE CONCEPTS *404,579*

cut in [*v*] *interrupt*
break in, butt in*, chisel in*, horn in*, interfere, interpose, intervene, intrude, move in, obtrude; SEE CONCEPT *234*

cut off [*v1*] *prevent; interrupt*
block, break in, bring to end, catch, close off, disconnect, discontinue, halt, insulate, intercept, intersect, intervene, intrude, isolate, obstruct, renounce, segregate, separate, sequester, suspend; SEE CONCEPT *234*

cut off [*v2*] *disinherit in will*
cut out of will, disown, renounce; SEE CONCEPT *317*

cut out [*v*] *excise, remove*
carve, cease, delete, displace, eliminate, exclude, exsect, extirpate, extract, give up, oust, pull out, refrain from, sever, stop, supersede, supplant, usurp; SEE CONCEPT *211*

cut out for [*adj*] *adapted*
adequate, competent, designed, equipped, fit, fitted, good for, qualified, suitable, suited; SEE CONCEPT *558*

cut short [*v*] *bring to an end; leave unfinished*
abbreviate, abort, abridge, break off, check, diminish, end, finish, halt, hinder, intercept, interrupt, postpone, quit, shorten, stop, terminate; SEE CONCEPTS *121,234*

cutting [*adj*] *nasty, hateful*
acerbic, acid, acrimonious, barbed, biting, bitter, caustic, clear-cut, crisp, hurtful, incisive, ingoing, malicious, penetrating, piercing, pointed, probing, raw, sarcastic, sardonic, scathing, severe, sharp, stinging, trenchant, wounding; SEE CONCEPT *267*

cut up [*v1*] *make fun of; criticize*
censure, condemn, crucify, denounce, give a rough time, knock, pan, rap, reprehend, reprobate, ridicule, skin, vilify; SEE CONCEPT *52*

cut up [*v2*] *be rowdy*
act up, caper, carry on*, cavort, clown, fool around, horse, horseplay, joke, misbehave, play, play jokes, romp, roughhouse, show off, whoop it up*; SEE CONCEPT *384*

cut up [*v3*] *chop, mince*
carve, dice, divide, slice; SEE CONCEPT *176*

cycle [*n*] *era, phase*
aeon, age, alternation, chain, circle, circuit, course, eon, isochronism, loop, orbit, period, periodicity, revolution, rhythm, ring, rotation, round, run, sequel, sequence, series, succession, wheel; SEE CONCEPTS *816,817*

cynic [n] *nonbeliever*
carper, caviler, detractor, disbeliever, doubter, doubting Thomas*, egoist, egotist, flouter, misanthrope, misanthropist, misogamist, misogynist, mocker, pessimist, questioner, satirist, scoffer, skeptic, sneerer, unbeliever; SEE CONCEPTS *361,423*

cynical [adj] *nonbelieving; doubtful*
contemptuous, derisive, ironic, misanthropic, misanthropical, mocking, pessimistic, sarcastic, sardonic, scoffing, scornful, skeptical, sneering, suspicious, unbelieving, wry; SEE CONCEPTS *267,403*

cyst [n] *unusual growth*
bag, bleb, blister, injury, pouch, sac, sore, vesicle, wen; SEE CONCEPT *306*

D

dab [n] *small quantity*
bit, blob, dollop, drop, fleck, flick, pat, peck, smidgen, smudge, speck, spot, stroke, tap, touch; SEE CONCEPT *835*

dab [v] *blot up; touch lightly*
bedaub, besmear, daub, pat, peck, plaster, smear, smudge, stipple, swab, tap, wipe; SEE CONCEPT *612*

dabble [v] *play at; tinker*
amuse oneself with, be amateur, dally, dilly-dally*, fiddle with*, flirt with*, horse around*, idle, kid around*, mess around*, monkey*, monkey around*, muck around*, not be serious*, play, play around*, play games with, toy with, trifle, trifle with, work superficially; SEE CONCEPT *87*

dabbler [n] *amateur*
abecedarian, beginner, dilettante, loafer, nonprofessional, novice, potterer, pretender, smatterer, tinkerer, trifler, tyro, uninitiate; SEE CONCEPTS *348,366*

daft [adj] *stupid; crazy*
absurd, asinine, baked*, bedlamite, bonkers, cracked*, crackers*, daffy*, demented, deranged, dopey*, flaky, foolish, fried*, giddy, idiotic, inane, insane, in the ozone*, lunatic, mad, mental*, nuts, nutty*, off the wall*, out of one's gourd*, ridiculous, screwy*, silly, simple, touched*, unbalanced, unhinged*, unsound, wacky, whacko*, witless; SEE CONCEPT *403*

daily [adj] *occurring every day; during the day*
circadian, common, commonplace, constantly, cyclic, day after day, day by day, day-to-day, diurnal, everyday, from day to day, often, once a day, once daily, ordinary, per diem, periodic, quotidian, regular, regularly, routine; SEE CONCEPTS *541,801*

dainty [adj1] *delicate, fragile, fine*
airy, attractive, beautiful, bonny, charming, choice, comely, cute, darling, delectable, delicious, delightful, diaphanous, elegant, ethereal, exquisite, fair, feeble, fragile, frail, graceful, lacy, ladylike, light, lovely, neat, nice, palatable, petite, pleasing, precious, pretty, rare, recherché, refined, savory, select, soft, subtle, superior, sweet, tasteful, tasty, tender, thin, toothsome, trim, well-made; SEE CONCEPTS *490,491,606*

dainty [adj2] *finicky, particular*
acute, choosy, delicate, fastidious, finical, finicking, fussy, ladylike, mincing, nice, perceptive, persnickety*, refined, scrupulous, tasteful; SEE CONCEPT *404*

dairy [n] *producer of milk products*
buttery, cow barn, creamery, dairy farm, factory, farm, pasteurizing plant; SEE CONCEPTS *449,517*

dalliance [n1] *dawdling*
dabbling, delay, delaying, dilly-dallying*, frittering, frivoling, idling, loafing, loitering, playing, poking*, procrastinating, procrastination, puttering, toying, trifling; SEE CONCEPTS *151,210,681*

dalliance [n2] *love affair*
affair, a little on the side*, amorous play, billing and cooing*, caressing, carrying on*, coquetry, cuddling, fling, flirtation, flirting, fondling, fooling around*, frolicking, hanky-panky*, making out*, messing around*, necking, petting, relationship, seduction, spooning, stringing along*, toying*, working late at office*; SEE CONCEPTS *114,375,388*

dally [v1] *dawdle, delay*
boondoggle, drag, fool around, fool with, fritter away, hang about*, horse around*, idle, jerk off*, lag, linger, loiter, lollygag*, play around*, play games with*, procrastinate, put off, putter, tarry, trail, trifle with, waste time, while away; SEE CONCEPTS *151,210,681*

dally/dally with [v2] *have love affair*
be insincere with, caress, carry on, coquet, cosset, cuddle, flirt, fondle, fool around, frivol, frolic, gambol, have a fling, lead on, play around*, rollick, romp, tamper, tease, toy, trifle, wanton; SEE CONCEPTS *114,375*

dam [n] *embankment, wall*
bank, barrage, barrier, dike, ditch, gate, grade, hindrance, levee, milldam, millpond, obstruction, weir; SEE CONCEPT *470*

dam [v] *hold back; block*
bar, barricade, brake, check, choke, clog, close, confine, hinder, hold in, impede, obstruct, repress, restrain, restrict, retard, slow, stop up, suppress; SEE CONCEPTS *130,191*

damage [n1] *injury, loss*
accident, adulteration, adversity, affliction, bane, blemish, blow, breakage, bruise, casualty, catastrophe, cave-in, contamination, corruption, debasement, depreciation, deprivation, destruction, deterioration, detriment, devastation, disservice, disturbance, evil, hardship, harm, hurt, illness, impairment, infliction, knockout, marring, mischief, mishap, mutilation, outrage, pollution, ravage, reverse, ruin, ruining, spoilage, stroke, suffering, waste, wound, wreckage, wrecking, wrong; SEE CONCEPTS *309,674*

damage(s) [n2] *cost for problem*
amends, bill, charge, compensation, expense, fine, forfeit, indemnity, reimbursement, reparation, satisfaction, total; SEE CONCEPTS *123,329*

damage [v] *cause injury, loss*
abuse, bang up*, batter, bleach, blight, break, burn, contaminate, corrode, corrupt, crack, cripple, deface, defile, dirty, discolor, disfigure, disintegrate, dismantle, fade, gnaw, harm, hurt, impair, incapacitate, infect, injure, lacerate, maim, maltreat, mangle, mar, mutilate, pollute, ravage, rot, ruin, rust, scathe, scorch, scratch, smash, split, spoil, stab, stain, tamper with, tarnish, tear, undermine, vitiate, weaken, wear away, wound, wreak havoc on*, wreck, wrong; SEE CONCEPTS *246,252*

damaged [adj] *broken, not working*
beat-up, bent, blemished, busted, dinged, down, flawed, flubbed, fouled up, glitched, gone, hurt, impaired, imperfect, injured, in need of repair, in poor condition, in smithereens*, kaput*, loused up*, marred, messed up*, mucked up*, no go*, on the blink*, on the fritz*, out of action*, out of kilter*, out of whack*, run-down, screwed up*, shot, snafued, spoiled, sunk*, totaled*, unsound; SEE CONCEPTS *485,560*

damaging [adj] *hurtful to reputation*
bad, deleterious, detrimental, disadvantageous, evil, harmful, injurious, mischievous, nocent, nocuous, prejudicial, ruinous; SEE CONCEPT *537*

damn [v] *condemn, denounce*
abuse, anathematize, attack, ban, banish, blaspheme, blast, castigate, cast out, censure, complain of, confound, convict, criticize, cry down, curse, cuss, darn, denunciate, doom, drat, excommunicate, excoriate, execrate, expel, flame, fulminate against, imprecate, inveigle against, jinx, object to, objurgate, pan, penalize, proscribe, punish, revile, sentence, slam, swear, thunder against*; SEE CONCEPTS *52,54*

damnable [adj] *atrocious, horrible*
abhorrent, abominable, accursed, blamed, blessed, culpable, cursed, dang, darn, depraved, despicable, detestable, dratted, execrable, hateful, odious, offensive, outrageous, wicked; SEE CONCEPTS *545,570*

damned [adj] *hateful, unwelcome*
accursed, all-fired, anathematized, bad, blankety-blank*, blasted*, blessed*, bloody*, blooming*, condemned, confounded, cursed, cussed, damnable, dang*, darn*, darned*, despicable, detestable, dog-gone*, done for*, doomed, dratted*, execrable, gone to blazes*, infamous, infernal*, loathsome, lost, lousy, reprobate, revolting, unhappy, voodooed*; SEE CONCEPTS *545,570*

damp [adj] *wet, humid*
clammy, cloudy, dank, dewy, drenched, dripping, drippy, drizzly, irriguous, misty, moist, muggy, oozy, saturated, soaked, soaking, sodden, soggy, sopping, steam bath*, steamy, sticky, vaporous, waterlogged, wettish; SEE CONCEPT *603*

dampen [v1] *make wet*
bedew, besprinkle, dabble, humidify, moisten, rinse, spray, sprinkle, water, wet; SEE CONCEPT *256*

dampen [v2] *spoil spirits*
allay, check, chill, cloud, cool, curb, dash, deaden, deject, depress, diminish, discourage, dismay, dispirit, dull, humble, inhibit, moderate, muffle, mute, restrain, stifle; SEE CONCEPTS *7,19*

dance [n1/v] *moving feet and body to music*
bob*, boogie, boogie down*, bunny hop, caper, careen, cavort, Charleston, conga, cut a rug*, disco, flit*, foot it*, foxtrot, frolic*, gambol*, get down*, hoof it*, hop, hustle, jig, jitter*, jitterbug, jive*, jump, leap, one-step, prance, promenade, rhumba, rock, rock 'n' roll, samba, shimmy, skip, spin, step, strut, sway, swing, tango, tap, tread, trip, trip the light fantastic*, twist, two-step, waltz, whirl; SEE CONCEPTS *292,363*

dance [n2] *party for moving to music*
ball, brawl, disco, formal, hoedown, hop, jump, masquerade, mingle, prom, promenade, shindig, social, sock hop; SEE CONCEPT *383*

dandle [v] *caress, cuddle*
amuse, cosset, cradle, dance, fondle, love, nuzzle, pet, play, ride on knee, rock, sport, toss, toy*, toy with*; SEE CONCEPTS *147,190*

dandy [adj] *fine, excellent*
capital, cool*, exemplary, famous, first-class, first-rate, five-star*, fly*, glorious, grand, great, groovy*, hunky-dory*, keen, marvelous, model, neat, nifty, paragon, peachy*, prime, splendid, superior, swell, terrific; SEE CONCEPT *574*

danger [n] *hazard, troublesome situation*
clouds, crisis, double trouble*, dynamite, emergency, endangerment, exigency, exposure, hot potato*, insecurity, instability, jeopardy, menace, peril, pitfall, possibility, precariousness, precipice, probability, risk, risky business*, slipperiness, storm, thin ice*, threat, uncertainty, venture, vulnerability; SEE CONCEPT *675*

dangerous [adj] *hazardous, troubling*
alarming, bad, breakneck*, chancy, critical, dangersome, deadly, delicate, dynamite, exposed, fatal, formidable, hairy*, heavy*, hot*, impending, impregnable, insecure, jeopardous, loaded, malignant, menacing, mortal, nasty, on collision course*, parlous, perilous, portentous, precarious, pressing, queasy, risky, serious, serpentine, shaky, speculative, terrible, thorny*, threatening, ticklish*, touch-and-go*, touchy, treacherous, ugly*, unhealthy, unsafe, unstable, urgent, viperous, vulnerable, wicked; SEE CONCEPT *548*

dangerously [adv] *precariously*
alarmingly, carelessly, critically, daringly, desperately, gravely, harmfully, hazardously, perilously, precariously, recklessly, riskily, seriously, severely, unsafely, unsecurely; SEE CONCEPT *548*

dangle [v] *suspend*
brandish, depend, droop, entice, flap, flaunt, flourish, hang, hang down, lure, sling, sway, swing, tantalize, tempt, trail, wave; SEE CONCEPTS *153,190*

dank [adj] clammy
chilly, close, damp, dewy, dripping, humid, moist, muggy, slimy, soggy, steamy, sticky, wet, wettish; SEE CONCEPT 603

dapper [adj] well-groomed, neat
bandbox, brisk, chic, chichi, classy, clean, dainty, dashing, doggy, dressed to kill*, dressed to nines*, jaunty, natty, nice, nifty, nimble, nobby, posh, prim, rakish, ritzy, sassy, sharp, showy, smart, snazzy*, snug, spiff*, spiffy*, spruce, spry, stylish, swank, swanky, swell, trim, turned out*, well turned out*; SEE CONCEPT 579

dappled [adj] mottled, freckled
brindle, brindled, checkered, discolored, flecked, motley, multicolor, multicolored, multihued, particolored, piebald, pied, speckled, spotted, stippled, varicolored, variegated, versicolor, versicolored; SEE CONCEPT 618

dare [n] challenge, defiance
cartel, defy, provocation, stump, taunt; SEE CONCEPTS 53,87

dare [v1] challenge, defy someone
beard, brave, bully, call one's bluff, confront, cope, denounce, disregard, face, face off, front, goad, insult, knock chip off shoulder*, laugh at, make my day, meet, mock, muster courage, oppose, outdare, provoke, resist, run the gauntlet, scorn, spurn, square off, step over the line, take one on, taunt, threaten, throw down gauntlet; SEE CONCEPTS 14,53

dare [v2] take a risk; be courageous
adventure, attempt, be bold, brave, endanger, endeavor, gamble, go ahead, hazard, make bold, pluck up, presume, risk, run the risk, speculate, stake, take a chance, take heart, try, try one's hand*, undertake, venture; SEE CONCEPTS 35,87

daring [adj] adventurous
adventuresome, audacious, bold, brassy*, brave, cheeky, cocky*, courageous, crusty, fearless, fire eating*, foolhardy, forward, game, go for broke*, gritty, gutsy*, gutty*, hot shot*, impudent, impulsive, intrepid, nervy, obtrusive, out on a limb*, pizzazz*, play with fire*, plucky, rash, reckless, salty*, smart, smart-alecky*, spunky*, temerarious, valiant, venturesome; SEE CONCEPT 401

dark [n1] place, time without light
caliginosity, darkness, dead of night, dimness, dusk, duskiness, evening, gloom, midnight, murk, murkiness, night, nightfall, nighttime, nigritude, obscurity, opacity, semi-darkness, shade, shadows, twilight, witching hour; SEE CONCEPTS 620,810

dark [n2] ignorance; mystery
concealment, denseness, inscrutability, seclusion, secrecy, thickness; SEE CONCEPTS 409,410

dark [adj1] lack of light
aphotic, atramentous, black, blackish, caliginous, Cimmerian, clouded, cloudy, crepuscular, darkened, dim, dingy, drab, dull, dun, dusk, dusky, faint, foggy, gloomy, grimy, ill-lighted, indistinct, inky, lightless, lurid, misty, murky, nebulous, obfuscous, obscure, opaque, overcast, pitch-black, pitch-dark, pitchy, rayless, shaded, shadowy, shady, somber, sooty, stygian, sunless, tenebrous, unlighted, unlit, vague; SEE CONCEPT 617

dark [adj2] shaded complexion, hair
adumbral, bistered, black, brunet, brunette, colored, dark-complexioned, dark-skinned, dusky, ebon, ebony, sable, swart, swarthy, tan; SEE CONCEPTS 406,618

dark [adj3] hidden, secret
abstruse, anagogic, arcane, cabalistic, complicated, concealed, cryptic, deep, Delphian, enigmatic, esoteric, intricate, knotty, mysterious, mystic, mystical, mystifying, not known, obscure, occult, puzzling, recondite; SEE CONCEPTS 402,576,582

dark [adj4] grim, hopeless
bleak, cheerless, dismal, doleful, drab, foreboding, gloomy, joyless, morbid, morose, mournful, ominous, sinister, sombre, unpropitious; SEE CONCEPT 548

dark [adj5] evil, satanic
atrocious, bad, corrupt, damnable, foul, hellish, horrible, immoral, infamous, infernal, nefarious, sinful, sinister, vile, wicked; SEE CONCEPT 545

dark [adj6] ignorant
benighted, uncultivated, unenlightened, unlettered, unread; SEE CONCEPT 402

dark [adj7] angry, upset
dour, forbidding, frowning, glowering, glum, ominous, scowling, sulky, sullen, threatening; SEE CONCEPT 401

darken [v] become shaded, unlit
becloud, bedim, blacken, cloud over, cloud up, deepen, dim, eclipse, fog, gray, haze, make dim, murk, obfuscate, obscure, overcast, overshadow, shade, shadow, tone down; SEE CONCEPTS 250,469

darkness [n1] place, time that is unlit
black, blackness, blackout, brownout, calignosity, Cimmerian shade, cloudiness, crepuscule, dark, dimness, dusk, duskiness, eclipse, gloom, lightlessness, murk, murkiness, nightfall, nigritude, obscurity, pitch darkness, shade, shadiness, shadows, smokiness, tenebrosity, twilight; SEE CONCEPT 620

darkness [n2] ignorance; mystery
blindness, concealment, denseness, inscrutability, isolation, privacy, seclusion, secrecy, unawareness; SEE CONCEPTS 409,410

darling [n] sweetheart, favorite person
angel*, apple of one's eye*, baby*, beloved, boyfriend, dear, dearest, dearie*, dear one, fair-haired boy*, flame, friend, girlfriend, heart's desire*, honeybunch, lamb*, light of my life*, love, lover, one and only*, pet*, precious, sugar*, sweetie, treasure*, truelove; SEE CONCEPTS 296,423

dart [v] race away; propel
bound, career, cast, course, dash, flash, fling, flit, float, fly, gallop, hasten, heave, hurry, hurtle,

launch, move quickly, pitch, plunge, run, rush, sail, scamper, scoot, scud, scurry, shoot, skim, speed, spring, sprint, spurt, start, tear, throw, thrust, whiz; SEE CONCEPTS *150,195,222*

dash [*n1*] *fast race for short distance*
birr, bolt, dart, haste, onset, run, rush, sortie, sprint, spurt, zip; SEE CONCEPT *150*

dash [*n2*] *flair, style*
animation, birr, brio, éclat, élan, energy, esprit, flourish, force, impressiveness, intensity, life, might, oomph*, panache, power, spirit, strength, vehemence, verve, vigor, vim, vivacity, zing, zip; SEE CONCEPTS *411,655,673*

dash [*n3*] *small amount; suggestion*
bit, drop, few drops, flavor, grain, hint, lick, little, part, pinch, scattering, seasoning, smack, smidgen, soupçon, sprinkle, sprinkling, squirt, streak, suspicion, taste, tincture, tinge, touch, trace, trifle, zest; SEE CONCEPT *831*

dash [*v1*] *run very fast for short distance*
boil, bolt, bound, career, charge, chase, course, dart, fly, gallop, get on it, haste, hasten, hurry, lash, make a run for it*, make it snappy*, race, rush, rush at, scamper, scoot, scurry, shoot, speed, spring, sprint, tear; SEE CONCEPT *150*

dash [*v2*] *break by hitting or throwing violently*
beat, bludgeon, cast, charge, crash, cudgel, destroy, fling, hit, hurl, hurtle, lunge, plunge, shatter, shiver, slam, sling, smash, splash, splatter, splinter, throw; SEE CONCEPTS *189,222,248*

dash [*v3*] *discourage, frustrate*
abash, baffle, balk, beat, bilk, blast, blight, chagrin, chill, circumvent, cloud, confound, dampen, disappoint, discomfort, dismay, dispirit, foil, nip, ruin, spoil, thwart; SEE CONCEPTS *7,19,121*

dashing [*adj*] *bold, flamboyant*
adventurous, alert, animated, chic, dapper, daring, dazzling, debonair, elegant, exclusive, exuberant, fashionable, fearless, gallant, gay, jaunty, keen, lively, modish, plucky, rousing, showy, smart, spirited, sporty, stylish, swank, swashbuckling, swish, vivacious; SEE CONCEPTS *404,589*

data [*n*] *information in visible form*
abstracts, brass tacks*, chapter and verse*, circumstances, compilations, conclusions, details, documents, dope, dossier, evidence, experiments, facts, figures, goods, info, input, knowledge, materials, measurements, memorandums, notes, picture, proof, reports, results, scoop, score, statistics, testimony, whole story*; SEE CONCEPT *274*

date [*n1*] *point in time; particular day or time*
age, century, course, day, duration, epoch, era, generation, hour, juncture, moment, period, quarter, reign, span, spell, stage, term, time, while, year; SEE CONCEPTS *800,801,802,815*

date [*n2*] *social engagement*
appointment, assignation, call, interview, meeting, rendezvous, tryst, visit; SEE CONCEPTS *114,386*

date [*n3*] *person accompanying another socially*
blind date, boyfriend, companion, escort, friend, girlfriend, lover, partner, steady, sweetheart; SEE CONCEPT *423*

date [*v1*] *assign a time*
affix a date to, belong to, carbon-date, chronicle, come from, determine, exist from, fix, fix the date of, isolate, mark, measure, originate in, put in its place, record, register; SEE CONCEPTS *18,37*

date [*v2*] *see person socially*
associate with, attend, consort with, court, deuce it*, escort, fix up, go around together*, go around with*, go out with, go steady, go together, keep company, make a date, see*, step around, take out, woo; SEE CONCEPT *114*

date [*v3*] *become obsolete*
antiquate, archaize, obsolesce, obsolete, outdate, show one's age; SEE CONCEPT *105*

daub [*v*] *coat; make dirty*
begrime, besmear, bespray, blur, cover, dab, deface, dirty, fleck, grime, paint, plaster, slap on, smear, smirch, smudge, spatter, speckle, splatter, spot, spread, stain, sully, variegate, varnish; SEE CONCEPTS *172,250*

daunt [*v*] *frighten, alarm*
appall, baffle, browbeat, bully, consternate, cow, deter, discourage, dishearten, dismay, dispirit, foil, horrify, intimidate, overawe, put off*, scare, shake, subdue, terrify, thwart; SEE CONCEPTS *7,19*

dauntless [*adj*] *bold, courageous*
aweless, brave, daring, doughty, fearless, gallant, game, heroic, indomitable, intrepid, invincible, lionhearted, resolute, stouthearted, unafraid, unconquerable, undaunted, unfearing, unflinching, valiant, valorous; SEE CONCEPT *401*

dawdle [*v*] *delay; waste time*
amble, bum around*, dally, diddle-daddle*, dillydally*, drag, fool around*, fritter away, get no place fast*, goof off*, hang around*, hang out*, idle, lag, laze, lazy, loaf, loiter, loll, lounge, mosey*, poke*, procrastinate, put off, saunter, scrounge around, schlepp along*, sit around*, sit on one's butt*, stay, stroll, tarry, toddle, trifle, wait, warm a chair*, waste; SEE CONCEPTS *210,681*

dawn [*n1*] *beginning of day*
aurora, break of day, bright, cockcrow, crack of dawn, dawning, daybreak, daylight, day peep, early bright, first blush, first light, light, morn, morning, sunrise, sunup, wee hours; SEE CONCEPTS *810,815*

dawn [*n2*] *a beginning*
advent, alpha, birth, commencement, dawning, emergence, foundation, genesis, head, inception, onset, opening, origin, outset, outstart, rise, source, start, unfolding; SEE CONCEPT *832*

dawn [*v*] *start*
appear, begin, develop, emerge, glimmer, initiate, lighten, loom, open, originate, rise, show itself, unfold; SEE CONCEPT *119*

day [n1] *light part of every 24 hours*
astronomical day, bright, dawn-to-dark, daylight, daytime, diurnal course, early bright, light, light of day, mean solar day, nautical day, sidereal day, sunlight, sunrise-to-sunset, sunshine, working day; SEE CONCEPTS *801,803,810,821*

day [n2] *era*
age, ascendancy, cycle, epoch, generation, height, heyday, period, prime, term, time, years, zenith; SEE CONCEPTS *802,816*

daybreak [n] *beginning of light hours*
aurora, break of day, bright, cockcrow, crack of dawn, dawn, dawning, daylight, day peep, dayspring, early bright, first light, morn, morning, sunrise, sunup; SEE CONCEPTS *810,815*

daydream [n] *fantasy thought of when awake*
castle in the air*, conceiving, dream, fancy, fancying, figment of imagination, fond hope, fool's paradise*, head trip*, imagination, imagining, in a zone*, mind trip*, musing, phantasm, phantasy, pie in the sky*, pipe dream*, reverie, stargazing*, trip*, vision, wish, woolgathering*; SEE CONCEPT *529*

daydream [v] *make up fantasy*
build castles in air*, conceive, dream, envision, fancy, fantasize, hallucinate, imagine, moon, muse, pipe dream*, stargaze*, trip out*, woolgather*; SEE CONCEPTS *17,36*

daylight [n] *light part of 24 hours*
aurora, dawn, day, daybreak, daytime, during the day, light, light of day, sunlight, sunrise, sunshine; SEE CONCEPT *810*

daze [n] *confusion*
befuddlement, bewilderment, distraction, gauze, glaze, haze, lala-land*, maze, muddledness, Nadaville*, narcosis, shock, stupefaction, stupor, trance; SEE CONCEPT *410*

daze [v] *confuse, shock*
addle, amaze, astonish, astound, befog, befuddle, benumb, bewilder, blind, blur, confound, dazzle, disorder, distract, dizzy, dumbfound, flabbergast, fuddle, mix up, muddle, mystify, numb, overpower, overwhelm, paralyze, perplex, petrify, puzzle, rock, stagger, startle, stun, stupefy, surprise; SEE CONCEPTS *16,42*

dazzle [v] *confuse, amaze*
astonish, awe, bedazzle, blind, blur, bowl over*, daze, excite, fascinate, glitz, hypnotize, impress, overawe, overpower, overwhelm, razzle-dazzle, strike dumb*, stupefy, surprise; SEE CONCEPTS *16,42*

dead [adj1] *no longer alive*
asleep, bereft of life, bloodless, bought the farm*, breathless, buried, cadaverous, checked out*, cold, cut off, deceased, defunct, departed, done for*, erased, expired, extinct, gone, gone to meet Maker*, gone to reward*, inanimate, inert, late, lifeless, liquidated, mortified, no more, not existing, offed*, out of one's misery*, passed away, perished, pushing up

daisies*, reposing, resting in peace, spiritless, stiff, unanimated, wasted; SEE CONCEPT *539*

dead [adj2] *indifferent, cold*
anesthetized, apathetic, asleep, boring, callous, deadened, dull, flat, frigid, glazed, inert, insensitive, insipid, lukewarm, numb, numbed, paralyzed, senseless, spiritless, stagnant, stale, still, tasteless, torpid, unfeeling, uninteresting, unresponsive, vapid, wooden; SEE CONCEPT *550*

dead [adj3] *not working*
barren, bygone, defunct, departed, exhausted, extinct, gone, inactive, inoperable, inoperative, lost, obsolete, spent, stagnant, sterile, still, tired, unemployed, unprofitable, useless, vanished, wearied, worn, worn out; SEE CONCEPT *560*

dead [adj4] *complete, total*
absolute, bloody, downright, entire, final, out-and-out*, outright, perfect, sure, thorough, unconditional, unmitigated, unqualified, utter, whole; SEE CONCEPT *531*

dead [adv] *completely, totally*
absolutely, direct, directly, due, entirely, ·exactly, right, straight, straightly, undeviatingly, wholly; SEE CONCEPTS *531,772*

deaden [v] *diminish, muffle, quiet*
abate, alleviate, anesthetize, benumb, blunt, check, chloroform*, consume, cushion, damp, dampen, depress, deprive, desensitize, destroy, devitalize, dim, dope, drown, dull, etherize, exhaust, freeze, frustrate, gas, hush, impair, incapacitate, injure, knock out, KO*, lay out, lessen, mute, numb, paralyze, put out of order*, put to sleep*, quieten, reduce, repress, retard, slow, smother, soften, stifle, stun, stupefy, suppress, tire, tone down, unnerve, weaken; SEE CONCEPTS *130,240*

deadlock [n] *stalemate, impasse*
box*, Catch-22*, cessation, checkmate, corner, dead end, dead heat, dilemma, draw, full stop*, gridlock, halt, hole*, pause, pickle*, plight, posture, predicament, quandary, standoff, standstill, tie, wall*; SEE CONCEPT *674*

deadly [adj1] *causing end of life*
baleful, baneful, bloodthirsty, bloody, cannibalistic, carcinogenic, cruel, dangerous, death-dealing, deathly, deleterious, destroying, destructive, fatal, grim, harmful, homicidal, injurious, internecine, killing, lethal, malignant, mortal, mortiferous, murderous, noxious, pernicious, pestiferous, pestilent, pestilential, poisonous, ruthless, savage, slaying, suicidal, toxic, unrelenting, venomous, violent, virulent; SEE CONCEPT *537*

deadly [adj2] *ghostly*
ashen, corpselike, dead, deadened, deathful, deathlike, deathly, ghastly, pallid, wan, white; SEE CONCEPT *539*

deaf [adj1] *without hearing*
deafened, earless, hard of hearing, stone deaf, unable to hear; SEE CONCEPT *591*

deaf [*adj2*] *unwilling to listen*
blind, bullheaded*, headstrong, indifferent, intractable, mulish*, oblivious, obstinate, pertinacious, perverse, pigheaded*, self-willed, strong-willed, stubborn, unaware, unconcerned, unhearing, unmoved; SEE CONCEPT *401*

deal [*n1*] *agreement, bargain*
accord, arrangement, buy, compromise, conception, contract, pact, pledge, prearrangement, transaction, understanding; SEE CONCEPT *684*

deal [*n2*] *amount, share*
abundance, degree, distribution, extent, plenty, plethora, portion, quantity, shake, superabundance, transaction; SEE CONCEPTS *344,786,835*

deal [*n3*] *distribution of playing cards*
appointment, chance, cut and shuffle*, fresh start, game, hand, opportunity, round; SEE CONCEPT *363*

deal/deal with [*v1*] *handle, manage*
act, approach, attend to, behave, behave toward, clear, concern, conduct oneself, consider, control, cope with, direct, discuss, get a handle on something*, hack it*, handle, have to do with, live with*, make a go of it*, make it*, oversee, play, review, rid, see to, serve, take, take care of, treat, unburden, use; SEE CONCEPTS *94,117*

deal [*v2*] *do business*
bargain, barter, bicker, buy and sell, dicker*, hammer out deal*, handle, horse trade*, knock down price*, negotiate, sell, stock, swap, trade, traffic, treat, work out deal; SEE CONCEPT *324*

deal [*v3*] *distribute*
administer, allot, apportion, assign, bestow, come across with*, deliver, disburse, dish out*, dispense, disperse, disseminate, distribute, divide, divvy*, dole out*, drop, fork out*, fork over*, give, hand out, impart, inflict, measure, mete out, partake, participate, partition, render, reward, share, strike; SEE CONCEPTS *108,140*

dealer [*n*] *business owner*
banker, bursar, businessman/woman, chandler, changer, dispenser, marketer, merchandiser, merchant, retailer, trader, tradesman/woman, trafficker, vendor, wholesaler; SEE CONCEPT *347*

dealings [*n*] *business relations*
affairs, balls in air*, business, commerce, concerns, doings, intercourse, irons in fire*, matters, proceedings, ropes*, sale, strings*, trade, traffic, transactions, truck, wire pulling*, wires*; SEE CONCEPT *324*

dean [*n*] *leader of institution*
administrator, authority, college leader, dignitary, doyen, ecclesiastic, guide, headmaster, lead, legislator, pilot, preceptor, president, principal, professor, senior, tack; SEE CONCEPT *350*

dear [*n*] *beloved person*
darling, favorite, heartthrob, honey, love, loved one, lover, pet, precious, sweetheart, treasure; SEE CONCEPT *423*

dear [*adj1*] *beloved, favorite*
blue-eyed*, cherished, close, darling, endeared, esteemed, fair-haired*, familiar, intimate, loved, pet, precious, prized, respected, treasured; SEE CONCEPTS *555,567*

dear [*adj2*] *very expensive*
an arm and a leg*, at a premium*, cher*, costly, fancy, high, high-priced, out of sight*, overpriced, pretty penny*, pricey*, prized, steep, stiff*, valuable; SEE CONCEPT *334*

dearly [*adv1*] *extremely*
greatly, profoundly, to a great extent, very, very much; SEE CONCEPT *772*

dearly [*adv2*] *lovingly*
affectionately, devotedly, fondly, tenderly, yearningly; SEE CONCEPT *403*

dearth [*n*] *insufficiency, scarcity*
absence, default, defect, deficiency, exiguousness, famine, inadequacy, infrequency, lack, meagerness, miss, need, paucity, poverty, privation, rareness, scantiness, scantness, shortage, slim pickings*, sparsity, uncommonness, want; SEE CONCEPTS *646,674,709*

death [*n*] *end of life*
afterlife, annihilation, bereavement, casualty, cessation, curtains*, darkness, decease, demise, departure, destruction, dissolution, downfall, dying, end, ending, eradication, eternal rest, euthanasia, exit, expiration, extermination, extinction, fatality, finis*, finish, grave, grim reaper*, heaven, loss, mortality, necrosis, obliteration, oblivion, paradise, parting, passing, passing over, quietus, release, repose, ruin, ruination, silence, sleep, termination, tomb; SEE CONCEPT *304*

deathly [*adj1*] *suggesting end of life*
appalling, cadaverous, corpselike, deathlike, defunctive, dreadful, gaunt, ghastly, grim, gruesome, haggard, horrible, macabre, pale, pallid, wan, wasted; SEE CONCEPTS *579,618*

deathly [*adj2*] *fatal*
deadly, extreme, intense, lethal, mortal, mortiferous, noxious, pestilent, pestilential, terrible; SEE CONCEPT *537*

debacle [*n*] *catastrophe*
beating, blue ruin*, breakdown, collapse, crack-up*, crash, defeasance, defeat, devastation, disaster, dissolution, downfall, drubbing, failure, fiasco, havoc, licking, overthrow, reversal, rout, ruin, ruination, shellacking*, smash, smashup, trouncing, vanquishment, washout, wreck; SEE CONCEPT *674*

debase [*v1*] *degrade, shame*
abase, bemean, cast down, cheapen, corrupt, cripple, debauch, debilitate, demean, demoralize, deprave, devaluate, devalue, disable, disgrace, dishonor, drag down*, dump on*, enfeeble, fluff off*, humble, humiliate, lower, put away, put down, reduce, sap, shoot down, sink, take down*, take down a peg*, undermine, weaken; SEE CONCEPTS *7,19,52,54*

debase [*v2*] *adulterate*
abase, animalize, bastardize, bestialize, contaminate, corrupt, damage, defile, depreciate, doctor, dope up*, impair, load, pervert, pollute, sophisticate, spoil, taint, vitiate, weight, worsen; SEE CONCEPTS *240,250*

debatable [*adj*] *controversial*
arguable, between rock and hard place*, between sixes and sevens*, betwixt and between*, borderline, chancy*, contestable, disputable, doubtful, dubious, iffy*, in dispute, moot, mootable*, open to question, problematic, problematical, questionable, the jury's out*, touch and go*, uncertain, undecided, unsettled, up for discussion; SEE CONCEPTS *267,535*

debate [*n*] *discussion of issues; consideration*
agitation, altercation, argument, argumentation, blah-blah*, bone of contention*, cogitation, contention, contest, controversy, controverting, deliberation, dialectic, disputation, dispute, forensic, hassle, match, meditation, mooting, polemic, rebutting, reflection, refuting, tiff, words, wrangle; SEE CONCEPTS *56,532*

debate [*v*] *argue, discuss*
agitate, altercate, answer, bandy, bicker, bump heads*, canvass, chew the fat*, cogitate, confab*, confute, consider, contend, contest, controvert, cross swords*, deliberate, demonstrate, differ, discept, disprove, dispute, hammer away at*, hash over*, hassle, have at it*, kick around*, knock around*, lock horns*, moot, oppose, pettifog, pick a bone*, prove, put up argument, question, reason, rebut, refute, rehash, set to, talk back*, talk game*, thrash out*, toss around*, wrangle; SEE CONCEPTS *24,56*

debauch [*v*] *deprave, corrupt*
abuse, bastardize, bestialize, betray, brutalize, debase, defile, deflower, demoralize, fornicate, fraternize, go bad*, go to hell*, intrigue, inveigle, lead astray*, live in the gutter*, lure, pervert, pollute, ravish, ruin, seduce, subvert, tempt, violate, vitiate, warp; SEE CONCEPTS *14,240,375*

debauched [*adj*] *violated, corrupted*
abandoned, corrupt, debased, defiled, degenerate, degraded, depraved, deteriorated, dissipated, dissolute, fast, gone bad*, gone to the dogs*, immoral, in the gutter*, licentious, perverted, profligate, reprobate, vitiate, vitiated, wanton, wicked; SEE CONCEPT *545*

debauchery [*n*] *immoral self-indulgence*
bender*, binge, blowout*, burning candle at both ends*, bust, carousal, depravity, dissipation, dissoluteness, drunk*, excess, fast living*, fornication, fraternization, gluttony, incontinence, indulgence, intemperance, intimacy, jag*, la dolce vita*, lasciviousness, lechery, lewdness, license, licentiousness, life in fast lane*, lust, orgy, overindulgence, revel, revelry, seduction, sensuality, sybaritism, tear*; SEE CONCEPTS *633,645*

debilitate [*v*] *incapacitate*
attenuate, blunt, cripple, devitalize, disable, emasculate, enervate, enfeeble, eviscerate, exhaust, extenuate, harm, hurt, injure, mar, prostrate, relax, sap, spoil, unbrace, undermine, unstrengthen, weaken, wear out*; SEE CONCEPTS *240,246*

debility [*n*] *incapacity, weakness*
decrepitude, disease, enervation, enfeeblement, exhaustion, faintness, feebleness, frailty, infirmity, languor, malaise, sickliness, unhealthiness; SEE CONCEPT *316*

debonair [*adj*] *charming, elegant*
affable, buoyant, casual, cheerful, courteous, dashing, detached, happy, jaunty, lighthearted, nonchalant, pleasant, refined, smooth, sprightly, suave, urbane, well-bred; SEE CONCEPT *401*

debris [*n*] *litter, waste*
bits, crap, detritus, dregs, dross, fragments, garbage, junk, offal, pieces, refuse, remains, riffraff, rubbish, rubble, ruins, trash, wreck, wreckage; SEE CONCEPT *260*

debt [*n*] *money owed to others*
albatross*, arrearage, arrears, bad news*, baggage*, below the line*, bill, bite*, capital, check, chit*, claim, commitment, credit, cuff*, damage*, dead horse*, debenture, debit, deficit, due, dues, duty, encumbrance, indebtedness, in hock*, in the hole*, in the red*, invoice, IOU*, liability, manifest, mortgage, note, obligation, outstandings*, price tag*, promissory note, receipt, reckoning, red ink*, responsibility, score, tab, tally, voucher; SEE CONCEPTS *329,344*

debunk [*v*] *disprove, ridicule*
cut down to size*, deflate, demystify, discover, disparage, expose, lampoon, mock, puncture, show up*, uncloak, unmask, unshroud; SEE CONCEPTS *49,60*

debut [*n*] *first public appearance*
admission, appearance, beginning, bow, coming out*, coming out party*, entrance, entree, first step*, graduating, graduation, inauguration, incoming, initiation, introduction, launching, opener, presentation; SEE CONCEPT *386*

decadence [*n*] *perversion; deterioration of morality*
corruption, debasement, decay, declension, decline, degeneracy, degeneration, degradation, devolution, dissipation, dissolution, downfall, downgrade, evil, excess, fall, gluttony, incontinence, intemperance, lasciviousness, lechery, lewdness, licentiousness, regression, sensuality, sybaritism; SEE CONCEPT *645*

decadent [*adj*] *corrupt, self-indulgent*
debased, debauched, decaying, declining, degenerate, degraded, depraved, dissolute, effete, evil, gone bad*, gone to hell*, gone to the dogs*, immoral, lost, moribund, overripe, perverted, wanton, wicked; SEE CONCEPT *545*

decay [*n*] *breaking down, collapse*
adulteration, atrophy, blight, caries, cariosity, consumption, corrosion, crumbling, decadence, decline,

decomposition, decrease, decrepitude, degeneracy, degeneration, depreciation, deterioration, dilapidation, disintegration, disrepair, dissolution, downfall, dying, extinction, fading, failing, gangrene, impairment, mortification, perishing, putrefaction, putrescence, putridity, putridness, rot, rotting, ruin, ruination, rust, senescence, spoilage, spoilation, wasting, wasting away, withering; SEE CONCEPTS *230,674,716*

decay [v] *deteriorate, crumble*
atrophy, become contaminated, be impaired, blight, break up, collapse, corrode, crumble, curdle, decline, decompose, defile, degenerate, depreciate, discolor, disintegrate, dissolve, dry-rot, dwindle, fade, fail, get worse, go bad, go to seed*, go to the dogs*, hit rock bottom*, hit the skids*, lessen, mildew, mold, molder, mortify, pejorate, perish, pollute, putrefy, putresce, reach depths, rot, sap, shrivel, sicken, sink, slump, spoil, suppurate, turn, wane, waste away, weaken, wear away, wither; SEE CONCEPTS *240,246,469*

decayed [adj] *rotten, falling apart*
addled, bad, carious, carrion, corroded, decomposed, effete, gangrenous, moldered, overripe, perished, putrefied, putrescent, putrid, rank, riddled, rotted, ruined, spoiled, wasted, withered; SEE CONCEPT *485*

decease [n] *death*
buying the farm*, curtains*, defunction, demise, departure, dissolution, dying, grim reaper*, passing, passing away, passing over, quietus, release, silence, sleep, taps*, the end; SEE CONCEPT *304*

decease [v] *pass away; expire*
buy a one-way ticket*, call off all bets*, cease, check out*, cool off*, croak*, deep six*, depart, die, drop, go, pass, pass away, pass on, pass over, perish, succumb; SEE CONCEPT *304*

deceased [adj] *dead*
asleep, bit the dust*, cold*, defunct, departed, exanimate, expired, extinct, finished, former, gave up the ghost*, gone, inanimate, kicked the bucket*, late, lifeless, lost, passed on, pushing up daisies*; SEE CONCEPT *539*

deceit [n1] *practice of misleading*
ambidexterity, ambidextrousness, artifice, cheating, chicane, chicanery, cozening, craft, craftiness, cunning, deceitfulness, deception, defrauding, dirty dealing*, dirty pool*, dishonesty, dissemblance, dissimulation, double-dealing, duplicity, entrapping, fraud, fraudulence, guile, hypocrisy, imposition, overreaching, pretense, slyness, smoke and mirrors*, trapping, treachery, trickery, two-facedness*, two-timing*, underhandedness; SEE CONCEPTS *59,633*

deceit [n2] *particular type of trick, misleading*
artifice, blind, cheat, chicanery, crocodile tears*, deception, dirty trick*, dirty work*, duplicity, fake, feint, flimflam*, fraud, fraudulence, gyp, hoax, humbug*, imposture, misrepresentation, pretense, ruse,

sell, sellout, sham, shift, smoke and mirrors*, snow job*, soft soap*, spoof, stratagem, subterfuge, sweet talk*, swindle, trick, whitewash*, wile; SEE CONCEPTS *59,660*

deceitful [adj] *dishonest, insincere*
artful, astucious, astute, beguiling, clandestine, counterfeit, crafty, cunning, deceiving, deceptive, delusive, delusory, designing, disingenuous, double-dealing, duplicitous, fallacious, false, feline, foxy, fraudulent, furtive, guileful, hypocritical, illusory, impostrous, indirect, insidious, insincere, knavish, lying, mendacious, misleading, rascal, roguish, shifty, slick, sly, sneaky, stealthy, subtle, treacherous, tricky, two-faced*, underhand, underhanded, untrustworthy, untruthful, wily; SEE CONCEPT *401*

deceive [v] *mislead; be dishonest*
bamboozle*, beat, beat out of, beguile, betray, bilk, buffalo*, burn, cheat, circumvent, clip, con, cozen, cross up, defraud, delude, disappoint, double-cross, dupe, ensnare, entrap, fake, falsify, fleece, fool, gouge, gull, gyp*, hoax, hoodwink, hook*, humbug*, impose upon, lead on, outwit, play joke on, pull fast one*, put on, rob, scam, screw, sell, skin, suck in*, swindle, take advantage of, take for, take for ride*, take in, take to cleaners*, trick, victimize; SEE CONCEPTS *7,19,59*

decency [n] *respectable behavior*
appropriateness, ceremoniousness, civility, conventionality, correctness, courtesy, decorum, dignity, etiquette, fitness, fittingness, formality, good form, good manners, honesty, modesty, propriety, respectability, righteousness, seemliness, virtue; SEE CONCEPT *633*

decent [adj1] *respectable, appropriate*
approved, becoming, befitting, chaste, clean, comely, comme il faut, conforming, continent, correct, decorous, delicate, ethical, fit, fitting, good, honest, honorable, immaculate, mannerly, modest, moral, nice, noble, on the up and up*, polite, presentable, proper, prudent, pure, reserved, right, seemly, spotless, stainless, standard, straight, straight arrow*, straight shooting*, suitable, trustworthy, unblemished, undefiled, untarnished, upright, virtuous, worthy; SEE CONCEPTS *401,558*

decent [adj2] *kind, generous*
accommodating, courteous, friendly, gracious, helpful, obliging, thoughtful, virtuous; SEE CONCEPTS *404,542*

decent [adj3] *sufficient, tolerable*
acceptable, adequate, all right, ample, average, comfortable, common, competent, enough, fair, fair to middling*, good, mediocre, middling, moderately good, passable, presentable, reasonable, respectable, right, satisfactory, sufficing, tolerable, unexceptional, unimpeachable, unobjectionable; SEE CONCEPTS *533,558,572*

deception [n1] *misleading; being dishonest*
beguilement, betrayal, blarney*, boondoggle*, cheat, circumvention, cozenage, craftiness, cunning,

deceit, deceitfulness, deceptiveness, defraudation, dirt, disinformation, dissimulation, double-dealing, dupery, duplicity, equivocation, falsehood, fast one*, flimflam*, fraud, fraudulence, guile, gyp*, hokum*, hypocrisy, imposition, insincerity, juggling, legerdemain, lying, mendacity, pretense, prevarication, snow job*, sophism, treachery, treason, trickery, trickiness, trumpery, untruth; SEE CONCEPTS **7,19,59**

deception [*n2*] *trick*
artifice, bilk, bluff, catch, cheat, chicane, con, confidence game, con game*, cover-up, crock, decoy, device, dodge, fallacy, fast one*, fast shuffle*, feint, fib, fraud, gimmick, hoax, hogwash*, hustle, illusion, imposture, jive*, lie, malarkey*, mare's-nest*, pretext, ride*, ruse, scam, sham, shift, shuck, snare, snow job*, stall, sting, story, stratagem, subterfuge, swindle, trap, trick, whitewash*, wile, wrinkle*; SEE CONCEPTS **59,230**

deceptive [*adj*] *dishonest*
ambiguous, astucious, beguiling, bum*, catchy, crafty, cunning, deceitful, deceiving, deluding, delusive, delusory, designing, disingenuous, fake, fallacious, false, fishy*, foxy, fraudulent, illusory, imposturous, indirect, insidious, knavish, lying, misleading, mock, oblique, off*, phony, plausible, rascal, roguish, scheming, seeming, serpentine, shifty, slick, slippery, sly, sneaky, snide, specious, spurious, subtle, treacherous, tricky, two-faced*, underhand, underhanded, unreliable, wily; SEE CONCEPTS **401,582**

decide [*v*] *make a determination; settle an issue*
adjudge, adjudicate, agree, arrive at conclusion, award, call shots*, cast the die*, choose, cinch, clinch, come to agreement, come to conclusion, come to decision, commit oneself, conclude, conjecture, decree, determine, draw a conclusion, elect, end, establish, figure, fix upon, form opinion, gather, go down line*, guess, have final word*, judge, make a decision, make up mind, mediate, opt, pick, poll, purpose, reach decision, resolve, rule, select, set, surmise, take a stand, tap, vote, will; SEE CONCEPT **18**

decided [*adj1*] *certain, definite*
absolute, all locked up*, assured, categorical, cinched, clear, clear-cut, clinched, destined, determined, distinct, emphatic, explicit, express, fated, for sure*, indisputable, in the bag*, nailed*, on ice*, positive, prearranged, predetermined, pronounced, resolved, runaway*, settled, sure, unalterable, unambiguous, undeniable, undisputed, unequivocal, unmistakable, unquestionable; SEE CONCEPT **535**

decided [*adj2*] *determined, strong-willed*
assertive, bent, certain, cocksure*, decisive, deliberate, earnest, emphatic, established, firm, fixed, inflexible, intent, iron-jawed*, mulish*, positive, purposeful, resolute, resolved, serious, set, settled, strong-minded, sure, unbending, unfaltering, unhes-

itating, unwavering, unyielding; SEE CONCEPTS **401,403**

decidedly [*adv*] *certainly*
absolutely, bloody*, by all means, clearly, decisively, determinedly, distinctly, downright, emphatically, flat out*, for a fact*, in spades*, no catch*, no holds barred*, no ifs ands or buts*, no mistake*, no strings attached*, of course, positively, powerful, real, really, right, straight out, strongly, sure, surely, terribly, terrifically, unequivocally, unmistakably, you said it*; SEE CONCEPT **535**

deciding [*adj*] *determining*
chief, conclusive, critical, crucial, decisive, important, influential, key, necessary, prime, principal, significant; SEE CONCEPTS **546,568**

decipher [*v*] *figure out, understand*
analyze, break, break down, bring out, cipher, construe, crack, decode, deduce, disentangle, dope out, elucidate, encipher, explain, expound, find the key, interpret, make clear, make out, puzzle out, read, render, reveal, solve, spell, translate, understand, unfold, unravel, unriddle; SEE CONCEPTS **15,31,37**

decision [*n1*] *conclusion; resolution reached*
accommodation, accord, adjudication, adjudicature, adjustment, agreement, arbitration, arrangement, choice, compromise, declaration, determination, end, finding, judgment, opinion, outcome, prearrangement, preference, reconciliation, resolution, result, ruling, selection, sentence, settlement, showdown, the call, the nod, understanding, verdict; SEE CONCEPTS **278,689**

decision [*n2*] *strength of mind or will*
backbone*, decidedness, decisiveness, determination, doggedness, earnestness, firmness, fortitude, grit, iron will*, obstinacy, obstinance, perseverance, persistence, pluck*, purpose, purposefulness, purposiveness, resoluteness, resolution, resolve, seriousness, spine*, stubbornness, volition, will, will power; SEE CONCEPTS **410,411**

decisive [*adj*] *definite*
absolute, all out*, assured, bent, certain, conclusive, crisp, critical, crucial, decided, definitive, determined, fateful, final, firm, flat out*, forceful, imperative, imperious, incisive, influential, intent, litmus test*, momentous, peremptory, positive, resolute, resolved, set, settled, significant, straight out*, strongminded, trenchant; SEE CONCEPT **535**

deck [*v*] *put on clothing, usually nice*
accouter, adorn, appoint, array, attire, beautify, bedeck, clothe, decorate, dress, dress up, embellish, festoon, garland, garnish, grace, gussy up*, ornament, prettify, primp, slick, trim; SEE CONCEPT **167**

declaim [*v*] *proclaim; get on a soapbox*
attack, bloviate, blow hot air*, declare, decry, denounce, harangue, hold forth, inveigh, lecture, mouth, orate, perorate, pile it on*, proclaim, rail, rant, recite, soapbox*, speak, spiel*, spout*, talk big*; SEE CONCEPTS **49,51**

declaration [n1] *assertion of belief or knowledge*
acknowledgment, admission, advertisement, affirmation, allegation, announcement, answer, attestation, averment, avowal, bomb*, broadcast, communication, deposition, disclosure, enunciation, explanation, exposition, expression, hot air*, information, notice, notification, oath, pitch, presentation, profession, promulgation, protestation, publication, remark, report, revelation, saying, say so, spiel*, statement, story, testimony, two cents' worth*, utterance; SEE CONCEPTS *49,274,278*

declaration [n2] *official proclamation*
acclamation, affidavit, allegation, announcement, article, attestation, bulletin, canon, charge, confirmation, constitution, credo, creed, denunciation, deposition, document, edict, gospel, indictment, manifesto, notice, notification, plea, proclamation, profession, promulgation, pronouncement, pronunciamento, resolution, testament, testimony, ultimatum; SEE CONCEPTS *271,274,278*

declare [v1] *make known clearly or officially*
acknowledge, advance, advocate, affirm, allegate, allege, announce, argue, assert, asservate, attest, aver, avow, be positive, blaze, bring forward, certify, cite, claim, confess, confirm, contend, convey, demonstrate, disclose, enunciate, give out, inform, insist, maintain, manifest, notify, pass, proclaim, profess, promulgate, pronounce, propound, publish, put forward, reaffirm, reassert, render, repeat, reveal, set forth, show, sound, state, stress, swear, tell, testify, validate, vouch; SEE CONCEPTS *49,60*

declare [v2] *claim as possession*
acknowledge, admit, avouch, avow, confess, convey, disclose, divulge, impart, indicate, manifest, notify, own, profess, represent, reveal, state, swear; SEE CONCEPTS *57,60*

decline [n1] *lessening*
abatement, backsliding, comedown, cropper*, decay, decrepitude, degeneracy, degeneration, descent, deterioration, devolution, diminution, dissolution, dive, downfall, downgrade, downturn, drop, dwindling, ebb, ebbing, enfeeblement, failing, failure, fall, falling off, flop, lapse, on the skids*, pratfall, recession, relapse, senility, skids*, slump, wane, waning, weakening, worsening; SEE CONCEPTS *674,698,699*

decline [n2] *downward change in value, position*
declivity, decrease, depression, descent, dip, downslide, downswing, downtrend, downturn, drop, drop-off, fall-off, hill, incline, lapse, loss, lowering, pitch, sag, slide, slip, slope, slump; SEE CONCEPTS *336,346,738*

decline [v1] *say no*
abjure, abstain, avoid, balk, beg to be excused, bypass, demur, deny, desist, disapprove, dismiss, don't buy*, forbear, forgo, gainsay, nix*, not accept, not hear of, not think of, pass on, refrain, refuse, reject, renounce, reprobate, repudiate, send regrets, shy, spurn, turn down, turn thumbs down*; SEE CONCEPTS *45,51*

decline [v2] *lessen, become less*
abate, backslide, cheapen, decay, decrease, degenerate, depreciate, deteriorate, diminish, disimprove, disintegrate, droop, drop, dwindle, ebb, fade, fail, fall, fall off, flag, go downhill*, go to pot*, go to the dogs*, hit the skids*, languish, lapse, lose value, lower, pine, recede, relapse, retrograde, return, revert, rot, sag, settle, shrink, sink, slide, subside, wane, weaken, worsen; SEE CONCEPTS *240,698*

decline [v3] *descend*
dip, droop, drop, fall, go down, lower, sag, set, settle, sink, slant, slope; SEE CONCEPTS *151,181*

decompose [v1] *rot, break up*
break down, crumble, decay, disintegrate, dissolve, fall apart, fester, molder, putrefy, putresce, spoil, taint, turn; SEE CONCEPT *469*

decompose [v2] *analyze by taking apart*
anatomize, atomize, break down, break up, decompound, disintegrate, dissect, dissolve, distill, resolve, separate; SEE CONCEPTS *24,103*

decomposition [n] *rot, breakdown*
atomization, corruption, decay, disintegration, dissipation, dissolution, division, putrefaction, putrescence, putridity; SEE CONCEPTS *230,674*

decor [n] *colors, furnishings of a place*
adornment, color scheme, decoration, interior design, ornamentation; SEE CONCEPTS *622,723*

decorate [v1] *beautify, embellish*
add finishing touches, adorn, bedeck, bedizen, brighten, burnish, color, deck, do up*, dress out*, dress up*, enhance, enrich, festoon, finish, fix up, frill, furbish, garnish, gild, grace, gussy up*, idealize, illuminate, jazz up*, ornament, paint, perfect, prank, renovate, spruce up*, trim; SEE CONCEPTS *162,177*

decorate [v2] *honor and give medal*
cite, laureate, pin medal on, plume; SEE CONCEPT *132*

decoration [n1] *beautification, embellishment*
adornment, beautifying, bedecking, bedizenment, designing, elaboration, enhancement, enrichment, festooning, flounce, flourish, frill, furbelow, garnish, garnishing, illumination, improvement, ornament, ornamentation, redecorating, spangle, trimming; SEE CONCEPTS *162,177*

decoration [n2] *particular type of embellishment*
appliqué, arabesque, bauble, braid, color, curlicue, design, dingbat*, doodad*, extravagance, fandangle*, festoon, filigree, finery, flounce, flourish, fretwork, frill, frippery, furbelow, fuss, garbage*, garnish, garniture, gewgaws*, gilt, gimcracks*, gingerbread*, inlay, jazz*, lace, ornament, parquetry, plaque, ribbon, scroll, sequin, spangle, thing*, tinsel, tooling, trimming, trinket, wreath; SEE CONCEPTS *259,260*

decoration [n3] *medal of honor*
accolade, award, badge, bays, citation, colors, cross, distinction, emblem, garter, kudos, laurels, medal, mention, order, purple heart, ribbon, star; SEE CONCEPT *337*

decorative [adj] *beautifying*
adorning, cosmetic, embellishing, enhancing, fancy, florid, nonfunctional, ornamental, prettifying, pretty; SEE CONCEPT *579*

decorous [adj] *appropriate, suitable*
au fait*, becoming, befitting, ceremonial, ceremonious, civilized, comely, comme il faut*, conforming, conventional, correct, decent, demure, de rigueur*, dignified, done, elegant, fit, fitting, formal, good, mannerly, meet, moral, nice, polite, prim, proper, punctilious, refined, respectable, right, seasonable, sedate, seemly, staid, well-behaved; SEE CONCEPTS *401,558*

decorum [n] *appropriate behavior, good manners*
breeding, civility, conduct, convenance, convention, correctitude, correctness, courtliness, decency, demeanor, deportment, dignity, etiquette, form, formality, gentility, good grace, gravity, habits, order, orderliness, politeness, politesse, properness, propriety, protocol, punctilio, respectability, seemliness, tact, usage; SEE CONCEPT *633*

decoy [n] *bait, trap*
allurement, attraction, beard*, blind, blow off*, booster, camouflage, catch, chicane, chicanery, come-on, come-on man*, deception, drawing card, ensnarement, enticement, facade, fake, front, imitation, inducement, inveiglement, lure, nark, plant, pretense, seducement, shill, sitting duck*, snare, stick, stoolie*, stool pigeon*, temptation, trick, trickery; SEE CONCEPTS *59,230,680*

decoy [v] *bait, entrap*
allure, come on, con, deceive, delude, egg one on*, ensnare, ensorcell, entice, fascinate, inveigle, lead on*, lead up garden path*, lure, mislead, mousetrap*, rope in*, seduce, shill, steer, suck in*, tempt, toll, tout, trap, wile; SEE CONCEPTS *16,59*

decrease [n] *diminishing, lessening*
abatement, compression, condensation, constriction, contraction, cutback, decline, declining, decrescence, depression, diminution, discount, downturn, dwindling, ebb, falling off, loss, reduction, shrinkage, striction, subsidence, waning; SEE CONCEPT *698*

decrease [v] *grow less or make less*
abate, calm down, check, contract, crumble, curb, curtail, cut down, decay, decline, degenerate, depreciate, deteriorate, devaluate, die down, diminish, droop, drop, drop off, dry up, dwindle, ease, ebb, evaporate, fade, fall off, lessen, let up, lighten, lose edge, lower, modify, narrow down, peter out, quell, quiet, reduce, restrain, run low, settle, shrink, shrivel, sink, slacken, slack off, slash, slow down, slump, soften, subside, tail off, wane, waste,

weaken, wear away, wear down, wither; SEE CONCEPTS *240,698*

decree [n] *mandate, legal order*
act, announcement, behest, bidding, charge, charging, command, commandment, declaration, decretum, dictum, direction, directive, edict, enactment, injunction, instruction, judgment, law, order, ordinance, precept, prescript, proclamation, promulgation, pronouncement, rap, regulation, rule, ruling, say, statute, the riot act, the word, ukase; SEE CONCEPTS *318,685*

decree [v] *order rule or action*
announce, command, compel, constrain, decide, declare, demand, determine, dictate, enact, force, impose, lay down the law*, oblige, ordain, prescribe, proclaim, pronounce, put one's foot down*, read the riot act*, require, rule, set; SEE CONCEPTS *50,53,81, 88,317*

decrepit [adj] *deteriorated, debilitated, especially as a result of age*
aged, anile, antiquated, battered, bedraggled, broken-down, creaky, crippled, dilapidated, doddering, effete, feeble, flimsy, fragile, frail, haggard, incapacitated, infirm, insubstantial, old, quavering, ramshackle, rickety, run-down, seedy, senile, shabby, shaking, superannuated, tacky, threadbare, tired, tottering, tumble-down, unsound, used, wasted, weak, weakly, weather-beaten, worn, worn-out; SEE CONCEPTS *406,485*

decry [v] *criticize, blame*
abuse, asperse, bad-mouth*, belittle, calumniate, censure, condemn, cry down, defame, denounce, depreciate, derogate, detract, devalue, diminish, discount, discredit, disgrace, disparage, do a number on*, downgrade, dump on*, hit*, knock*, lower, malign, mark down, minimize, opprobriate, pan*, poor-mouth*, put down*, rail against, rap, reprehend, reprobate, run down, slam*, take away, take swipe at*, throw stones at*, traduce, underestimate, underrate, undervalue, vilify, write off; SEE CONCEPTS *44,52*

dedicate [v1] *donate, set aside for special use*
address, allot, apply, apportion, appropriate, assign, commit, consign, devote, give, give over to, inscribe, offer, pledge, restrict, surrender; SEE CONCEPTS *18,50,88,135*

dedicate [v2] *sanctify*
anoint, bless, consecrate, hallow, set apart; SEE CONCEPTS *69,367*

dedicated [adj] *loyal, hard-working*
committed, devoted, enthusiastic, given over to, old faithful*, purposeful, single-hearted, single-minded, sworn, true blue*, true to the end*, wholehearted, zealous; SEE CONCEPTS *404,542*

dedication [n1] *faithfulness, loyalty*
adherence, allegiance, commitment, devotedness, devotion, single-mindedness, wholeheartedness; SEE CONCEPTS *411,657*

dedication [n2] *speech of praise; sanctification*
address, celebration, consecration, devotion, envoy, glorification, hallowing, inscription, message; SEE CONCEPTS *69,367*

deduce [v] *figure out, understand*
add up, analyze, assume, be afraid, boil down, cogitate, collect, conceive, conclude, consider, deduct, deem, derive, draw, fancy, figure, figure out, gather, glean, have a hunch*, imagine, infer, judge, make, make out, presume, presuppose, ratiocinate, read into, reason, regard, surmise, take to mean; SEE CONCEPTS *15,24*

deducible [adj] *understandable*
a priori, consequent, deductive, derivable, dogmatic, following, inferable, inferential, provable, reasoned, traceable; SEE CONCEPTS *402,529*

deduct [v] *take away or out; reduce*
abstract, allow, bate, cut back, decrease by, diminish, discount, dock, draw back, knock off, lessen, rebate, reduce, remove, roll back, subtract, take, take from, take off, withdraw, write off; SEE CONCEPTS *236,247,330*

deduction [n1] *conclusion, understanding*
answer, assumption, cogitation, concluding, consequence, consideration, contemplation, corollary, deliberation, derivation, finding, illation, inference, inferring, judgment, meditation, mulling, musing, opinion, pondering, ratiocination, reasoning, reflection, result, rumination, sequitur, speculation, thinking, thought; SEE CONCEPTS *15,24,689*

deduction [n2] *something subtracted*
abatement, abstraction, allowance, credit, cut, decrease, decrement, depreciation, diminution, discount, dockage, excision, rebate, reduction, removal, subtraction, withdrawal, write-off; SEE CONCEPTS *763,776*

deed [n1] *achievement*
accomplishment, act, action, adventure, ballgame, big idea*, bit, byplay, cause, commission, crusade, do*, enterprise, exploit, fact, feat, follow through, game, happenin'*, mitzvah*, performance, plan, quest, reality, securing, stunt, thing*, tour de force, truth, winning; SEE CONCEPTS *4,706*

deed [n2] *legal paper assigning property; contract*
agreement, bargain, certificate, charter, compact, conveyance, covenant, document, indenture, instrument, lease, papers, proof, record, release, security, title, transaction, voucher, warranty; SEE CONCEPTS *271,318*

deem [v] *regard, consider*
account, allow, appraise, assume, be afraid, believe, calculate, conceive, conjecture, credit, daresay, divine, esteem, estimate, expect, feel, guess, hold, imagine, judge, know, presume, reckon, sense, set store by, suppose, surmise, suspect, think, understand, view; SEE CONCEPTS *12,28*

deep [n] *the sea*
blue*, brine, briny*, Davy Jones's locker*, drink*, main, middle, ocean, Poseidon's realm*, the high seas; SEE CONCEPT *514*

deep [adj1] *extending very far, usually down*
abysmal, abyssal, below, beneath, bottomless, broad, buried, deep-seated, distant, downreaching, far, fathomless, immersed, inmost, low, profound, rooted, subaqueous, submarine, submerged, subterranean, sunk, underground, unfathomable, wide, yawning; SEE CONCEPTS *737,777*

deep [adj2] *abstract, complicated in meaning*
abstruse, acute, arcane, complex, concealed, Delphic, difficult, discerning, esoteric, hard to understand, heavy*, hermetic, hidden, incisive, intricate, learned, mysterious, obscure, occult, Orphic, penetrating, profound, recondite, sagacious, secret, serious, Sibylline, wise; SEE CONCEPTS *402,529*

deep [adj3] *scheming, devious*
acute, artful, astute, canny, contriving, crafty, cunning, designing, foxy, guileful, insidious, intriguing, keen, knowing, plotting, sharp, shrewd, sly, tricky, wily; SEE CONCEPT *404*

deep [adj4] *absorbed, engrossed in activity*
abstracted, centered, concentrated, enfolded, engaged, fixed, focused, immersed, intent, into, lost, musing, preoccupied, rapt, set, wrapped, wrapped up; SEE CONCEPT *542*

deep [adj5] *intense in effect on senses*
bass, booming, dark, extreme, full-toned, grave, great, hard, low, low-pitched, low-toned, profound, resonant, rich, sonorous, strong, vivid; SEE CONCEPTS *537,594,618*

deepen [v1] *make depth greater*
dig, dig out, dredge, excavate, expand, extend, hollow, scoop out, scrape out; SEE CONCEPT *250*

deepen [v2] *make more intense*
aggravate, develop, enhance, expand, extend, grow, heighten, increase, intensate, intensify, magnify, mount, redouble, reinforce, rise, rouse, strengthen; SEE CONCEPTS *236,245,697*

deeply [adv] *completely, intensely*
acutely, affectingly, distressingly, feelingly, genuinely, gravely, intensely, mournfully, movingly, passionately, profoundly, sadly, seriously, severely, surely, thoroughly, to the quick; SEE CONCEPTS *531,772*

deface [v] *mar, mutilate*
blemish, contort, damage, deform, demolish, destroy, dilapidate, disfigure, distort, harm, impair, injure, mangle, misshape, obliterate, ruin, scratch, spoil, sully, tarnish, trash, vandalize, wreck; SEE CONCEPTS *246,252*

de facto [adv] *in reality*
actual, actually, existing, genuinely, in effect, in fact, real, really, tangible, truly, veritably; SEE CONCEPT *582*

defamation [n] *libel, slander*
aspersion, backbiting, backstabbing, belittlement, black eye*, calumny, character assassination, cheap shot*, denigration, depreciation, detraction, dirt*, dirty laundry*, disparagement, dump, dynamite, hit, knock, lie, low-down dirty*, mud, obloquy, oppro-

brium, scorcher, slam*, slap in face*, slime, slur, smear, tale, traducement, vilification; SEE CONCEPT *54*

defamatory [adj] *libelous, slanderous*
abusive, calumnious, contumelious, denigrating, derogatory, detracting, detractive, disparaging, injurious, insulting, maligning, opprobrious, traducing, vilifying, vituperative; SEE CONCEPTS *267,537*

defame [v] *inflict libel or slander*
asperse, bad-mouth*, belie, besmirch, blacken, blister, calumniate, cast aspersions on, cast slur on, denigrate, detract, discredit, disgrace, dishonor, disparage, do a number on*, knock, malign, pan, put zingers on*, roast, scandalize, scorch, slam, smear, speak evil of*, stigmatize, throw mud at*, traduce, vilify, villainize, vituperate; SEE CONCEPTS *7,19,54*

default [n] *failure; want*
absence, blemish, blunder, dearth, defect, deficiency, delinquency, dereliction, disregard, error, fault, imperfection, inadequacy, insufficiency, lack, lapse, miss, neglect, nonpayment, offense, omission, overlooking, oversight, privation, shortcoming, slight, transgression, vice, weakness, wrongdoing; SEE CONCEPTS *335,699,709*

default [v] *dodge payment*
bilk, defraud, dishonor, evade, fail, leave town*, meet under arch*, neglect, put on the cuff*, rat*, repudiate, run out on*, shirk, skate*, skip, skip out on*, stiff*, swindle, welch, welsh; SEE CONCEPTS *59,63,330*

defeat [n1] *overthrow, beating*
ambush, annihilation, beating, blow, break, breakdown, check, collapse, conquest, count, debacle, defeasance, destruction, discomfiture, downthrow, drubbing*, embarrassment, extermination, failure, fall, insuccess, killing*, KO*, lacing, licking, loss, massacre, mastery, nonsuccess, paddling, rebuff, repulse, reverse, rout, ruin, scalping, setback, shellacking*, slaughter, subjugation, thrashing, trap, trashing, trimming, triumph, trouncing, vanquishment, waxing, whaling, whipping*, whitewashing*; SEE CONCEPT *95*

defeat [n2] *frustration*
disappointment, discomfiture, downfall, failure, foil, loss, rebuff, repulse, reversal, reverse, setback, thwarting; SEE CONCEPT *410*

defeat [v1] *conquer in military manner*
ambush, annihilate, bar, bear down, beat, best, block, butcher, crush, decimate, demolish, discomfit, drown, entrap, finish off, halt, hinder, impede, lick, mow down*, obliterate, obstruct, outflank, outmaneuver, overpower, overrun, overthrow, overwhelm, parry, prevail over, quell, reduce, repel, repress, repulse, roll back, rout, route, sack, scatter, shipwreck, sink, slaughter, smash, subdue, subjugate, suppress, surmount, swamp, torpedo*, trample, trash, upset, vanquish, whip, wipe out*; SEE CONCEPTS *95,320*

defeat [v2] *conquer in athletic contest*
beat, bust*, clobber*, cream*, deck*, drop*, drub*, edge, flax*, flog*, floor*, knock out*, KO*, lambaste, lick, outhit, outjump, outplay, outrun, overpower, plow under*, pommel*, pound*, powder*, pulverize*, run roughshod over*, skin*, steamroll*, take, take it all*, take to cleaners*, tan*, thrash, total, trounce, wallop*, whack*, whomp*, win, work over*, zap*; SEE CONCEPTS *95,363*

defeat [v3] *frustrate*
baffle, balk, beat down*, beat the system*, blank, block, bury, cast down, cause setback, checkmate, circumvent, confound, contravene, cook*, counterplot, cross, disappoint, discomfit, disconcert, disprove, edge out*, foil, invalidate, neutralize, nonplus, nose out*, nullify, outwit, overturn, put end to*, puzzle, quell, reduce, refute, ruin, scuttle, shave*, shellac*, skunk*, spoil, squash, stump, subdue, subjugate, surmount, take wind out of sails*, throw for loop*, thwart, undo, victimize; SEE CONCEPTS *14,121*

defect [n] *blemish, imperfection*
birthmark, blot, blotch, break, bug, catch, check, crack, deficiency, deformity, discoloration, drawback, error, failing, fault, flaw, foible, frailty, gap, glitch, gremlin, hole, infirmity, injury, irregularity, kink, knot, lack, mark, marring, mistake, patch, rift, rough spot, scar, scarcity, scratch, seam, second, shortage, shortcoming, sin, speck, spot, stain, taint, unsoundness, vice, want, weakness, weak point; SEE CONCEPTS *309,580,646*

defect [v] *break from belief, faith*
abandon, abscond, apostatize, back out, break faith*, change sides, depart, desert, fall away from, forsake, go, go back on, go over, go over the fence*, lapse, leave, pull out, quit, rat*, rebel, reject, renege, renounce, revolt, run out, schism, sell out*, spurn, take a walk*, tergiversate, tergiverse, turn, turn coat*, walk out on, withdraw; SEE CONCEPTS *198,367*

defection [n] *abandonment*
alienation, apostasy, backsliding, deficiency, dereliction, desertion, disaffection, disloyalty, disownment, divorce, estrangement, failing, failure, faithlessness, forsaking, lack, parting, rebellion, recreancy, rejection, repudiation, retreat, revolt, separation, severance, sundering, tergiversation, withdrawal; SEE CONCEPTS *195,198,367*

defective [adj] *broken, not working*
abnormal, amiss, blemished, damaged, deficient, faulty, flawed, impaired, imperfect, inadequate, incomplete, injured, insufficient, lacking, on the bum*, out of order, poor, retarded, seconds, sick, subnormal, unfinished, unhealthy, unsound, wanting; SEE CONCEPTS *560,565*

defend [v1] *protect*
avert, battle, beat off, bulwark, care for, cherish, conserve, contend, cover, entrench, espouse, fend off, fight, fight for, fortify, foster, garrison, guard, guard against, hedge, hold, hold at bay, house, in-

sure, keep safe, look after, maintain, mine, nourish, oppose, panoply, preserve, prevent, protect, provide sanctuary, repel danger, resist, retain, safeguard, save, screen, secure, shelter, shield, stave off, sustain, take in, uphold, war, ward off, watch, watch over, withstand; SEE CONCEPTS *96,110*

defend [v2] *show support for*
advocate, aid, air, apologize for, argue, assert, back, back up, bear one out*, befriend, champion, come to defense of, cover for, endorse, espouse, exculpate, exonerate, explain, express, go to bat for, guarantee, justify, maintain, plead, prove a case, put in a good word*, rationalize, recommend, ride shotgun for*, say in defense, second, speak up for, stand by*, stand up for, stick up for, stonewall*, support, sustain, thump for, uphold, vent, vindicate, voice, warrant; SEE CONCEPTS *10,49*

defense [n1] *armament; protection system*
aegis, armor, arms, barricade, bastille, bastion, bulwark, buttress, citadel, cover, deterrence, dike, embankment, fastness, fence, fort, fortification, fortress, garrison, guard, immunity, munitions, palisade, parapet, position, protection, rampart, redoubt, resistance, safeguard, security, shelter, shield, stockade, stronghold, trench, wall, ward, warfare, weaponry, weapons; SEE CONCEPTS *321,322,500*

defense [n2] *explanation, justification*
answer, apologetics, apologia, apologizing, apology, argument, cleanup, copout*, exculpation, excuse, excusing, exoneration, explaining, extenuation, fish story, jive*, justifying, off-time*, plea, rationalization, rejoinder, reply, response, retort, return, song and dance*, story, vindication, whitewash*; SEE CONCEPTS *57,278*

defenseless [adj] *powerless, vulnerable*
caught, endangered, exposed, hands tied*, helpless, indefensible, in line of fire*, like a clay pigeon*, like a sitting duck*, naked*, on the line*, on the spot*, open, out on limb*, pigeon*, poor, unarmed, unguarded, unprotected, up the creek*, weak, wide open*; SEE CONCEPTS *555,576*

defensible [adj] *justifiable*
condonable, defendable, excusable, fit, logical, pardonable, permissible, plausible, proper, tenable, valid, vindicable, warrantable; SEE CONCEPT *528*

defensive [adj] *protective, watchful*
arresting, averting, balking, checking, conservative, coping with, defending, foiling, forestalling, frustrating, guarding, in opposition, interrupting, opposing, preservative, preventive, protecting, resistive, safeguarding, thwarting, uptight, warding off, withstanding; SEE CONCEPTS *401,550*

defer [v1] *hold off, put off*
adjourn, block, delay, detain, extend, give rain check*, hang fire*, hinder, hold up, impede, intermit, lay over, lengthen, obstruct, postpone, procrastinate, prolong, prorogue, protract, put on back burner*, put on hold, put on ice*, remit, retard, set

aside, shelve, slow, stall, stay, suspend, table, waive; SEE CONCEPTS *121,130*

defer [v2] *yield*
accede, accommodate, acquiesce, adapt, adjust, admit, agree, assent, bow, buckle, capitulate, cave, comply, concede, cringe, fawn*, give in to*, knuckle*, knuckle under*, kowtow to*, obey, submit, succumb, truckle; SEE CONCEPT *83*

deference [n1] *obedience, compliance*
acquiescence, capitulation, complaisance, condescension, docility, obeisance, submission, yielding; SEE CONCEPT *633*

deference [n2] *attention, homage*
acclaim, civility, consideration, courtesy, esteem, honor, obeisance, politeness, regard, respect, reverence, thoughtfulness, veneration; SEE CONCEPTS *10,410*

deferential [adj] *respectful, considerate*
civil, complaisant, courteous, disarming, duteous, dutiful, ingratiating, ingratiatory, insinuating, insinuative, obedient, obeisant, obsequious, polite, regardful, reverential, saccharine, silken, silky, submissive; SEE CONCEPT *401*

deferment/deferral [n] *postponement*
adjournment, delay, moratorium, pause, putting off*, stay, suspension; SEE CONCEPTS *121,130*

deferred [adj] *put off till a later time*
adjourned, assessed, charged, delayed, funded, held up, indebted, in waiting, negotiated, on hold*, on the shelf*, pigeonholed*, postponed, prolonged, protracted, remanded, renegotiated, retarded, scrubbed, stalled, staved off, temporized; SEE CONCEPT *820*

defiance [n] *disobedience, disregard*
affront, audacity, back talk*, big talk*, boldness, bravado, brazenness, call, cartel, challenge, command, confrontation, contempt, contrariness, contumacy, dare, defy, effrontery, enjoinder, factiousness, gas, guts*, hot air*, impudence, impugnment, insolence, insubordination, insurgence, insurgency, intractableness, lip*, macho*, muster*, opposition, order, perversity, provocation, rebellion, rebelliousness, recalcitrance, revolt, sass*, spite, stump, summons, temerity, the gauntlet*, unruliness; SEE CONCEPTS *633,657*

defiant [adj] *disobedient, disregardful*
aggressive, audacious, bold, challenging, contumacious, daring, gutsy*, insolent, insubmissive, insubordinate, macho*, mutinous, obstinate, provocative, rebellious, recalcitrant, reckless, refractory, resistant, resistive, sassy*, truculent; SEE CONCEPT *401*

deficiency [n] *imperfection, inadequacy*
absence, bug*, dearth, defalcation, default, defect, deficit, demerit, dereliction, failing, failure, fault, flaw, frailty, glitch*, inability to hack it, inadequacy, insufficience, insufficiency, lack, loss, need, neglect, paucity, privation, scantiness, scarcity, shortage, shortcoming, sin, want, weakness; SEE CONCEPTS *635,666,674*

deficient [adj] imperfect, inadequate

amiss, bad, damaged, defective, exiguous, faulty, flawed, found wanting, impaired, incomplete, inferior, infrequent, injured, insufficient, lacking, marred, meager, not cut out for*, not enough, not make it*, not up to scratch*, outta gas*, rare, scant, scanty*, scarce, second fiddle*, second string, short, shy, sketchy, skimpy, third string*, unassembled, unequal, unfinished, unsatisfactory, wanting, weak; SEE CONCEPTS 531,565

deficit [n] shortage of something needed, required

arrears, dead horse*, defalcation, default, deficiency, due bill, dues, inadequacy, in hock*, insufficience, insufficiency, in the hole*, in the red*, lack, loss, paucity, red ink*, scantiness, shortcoming, shortfall, underage; SEE CONCEPTS 335,646

defile [v] corrupt, violate

abuse, adulterate, befoul, besmirch, contaminate, debase, deflower, degrade, desecrate, dirty, discolor, disgrace, dishonor, hurt, maculate, make foul, mess up*, molest, muck up*, pollute, profane, rape, ravish, scuzz up*, seduce, shame, smear, soil, stain, sully, taint, tar, tarnish, trash, vitiate; SEE CONCEPTS 54,156,246

defiled [adj] corrupted, violated

besmirched, common, cooked, desecrated, dirty, dishonored, exposed, impure, mucked up*, polluted, profaned, ravished, spoilt, tainted, trashed*, unclean, vitiated; SEE CONCEPT 570

define [v1] give description

ascertain, assign, call spade a spade*, characterize, construe, decide, delineate, denominate, denote, describe, designate, detail, determine, dub, elucidate, entitle, etch, exemplify, explain, expound, formalize, illustrate, interpret, label, lay it out*, nail it down*, name, prescribe, represent, specify, spell out, tag, translate; SEE CONCEPTS 55,57,62

define [v2] delimit, outline

belt, border, bound, circumscribe, compass, confine, curb, delineate, demarcate, distinguish, edge, encircle, enclose, encompass, envelop, establish, fence in, fix, flank, gird, girdle, limit, mark, mark out, rim, set, set bounds to, settle, stake out, surround, verge, wall in; SEE CONCEPTS 18,60,758

definite [adj1] exact, clear

audible, bold, categorical, clean-cut, clear-cut, clearly defined, complete, crisp, definitive, determined, distinct, distinguishable, downright, explicit, express, fixed, forthright, full, graphic, incisive, marked, minute, not vague, obvious, palpable, particular, plain, positive, precise, pronounced, ringing, severe, sharp, silhouetted, specific, straightforward, tangible, unambiguous, undubitable, unequivocal, unmistakable, visible, vivid, well-defined, well-grounded, well-marked; SEE CONCEPT 557

definite [adj2] fixed, certain, positive

assigned, assured, beyond doubt, circumscribed, convinced, decided, defined, determinate, deter-

mined, established, guaranteed, limited, narrow, precise, prescribed, restricted, set, settled, sure; SEE CONCEPT 535

definitely [adv] certainly

absolutely, beyond any doubt, categorically, clearly, decidedly, doubtless, doubtlessly, easily, explicitly, expressly, far and away*, finally, indubitably, no ifs ands or buts about it*, obviously, plainly, positively, specifically, surely, undeniably, unequivocally, unmistakably, unquestionably, without doubt, without fail, without question; SEE CONCEPTS 535,552

definition [n] description

analogue, annotation, answer, characterization, clarification, clue, comment, commentary, cue, delimitation, delineation, demarcation, denotation, determination, diagnosis, drift, elucidation, exemplification, explanation, explication, exposition, expounding, fixing, formalization, gloss, individuation, interpretation, key, outlining, rationale, rendering, rendition, representation, settling, signification, solution, statement of meaning, terminology, translation; SEE CONCEPTS 274,278,689

definitive [adj] authoritative

absolute, actual, categorical, clear-cut, closing, complete, completing, concluding, conclusive, decisive, definite, determining, downright*, ending, exhaustive, express, final, finishing, flat out*, last, limiting, nailed down, perfect, plain, precise, real, reliable, settling, specific, straight out, terminal, terminating, ultimate, unambiguous; SEE CONCEPTS 531,535,574

deflate [v1] reduce or cause to contract

collapse, contract, decrease, depreciate, depress, devalue, diminish, empty, exhaust, flatten, puncture, shrink, squash, void; SEE CONCEPTS 236,247,776

deflate [v2] humiliate

chasten, cut down to size*, dash, debunk, disconcert, dispirit, humble, kick in the teeth*, knock down*, let down easy*, let wind out of sails*, mortify, puncture balloon*, put down*, shoot down*, take down*; SEE CONCEPTS 7,19

deflect [v] bounce off; turn aside

avert, bend, bounce, cover up, curve, deviate, disperse, diverge, divert, fend, glance off, hold off, hook, keep off, parry, pivot, ricochet, sheer, shy, sidetrack, slew, slip, swerve, turn, twist, veer, volteface, wheel, whip, whirl, wind; SEE CONCEPTS 147,189,194

deflower [v] take virginity; ravish

assault, defile, deflorate, depredate, desecrate, despoil, devour, force, harm, have, mar, molest, outrage, possess, ruin, seduce, spoil, violate; SEE CONCEPT 375

deform [v] distort, disfigure

batter, blemish, buckle, contort, cripple, damage, deface, flaw, gnarl, grimace, impair, injure, knot, maim, malform, mangle, mar, misshape, mutilate, ruin, skew, spoil, twist, warp, wince; SEE CONCEPTS 246,250

deformed [adj] disfigured, distorted
askew, awry, bent, blemished, bowed, buckled, contorted, cramped, crippled, crooked, curved, damaged, disjointed, dwarfed, gnarled, grotesque, humpbacked, hunchbacked, ill-made, irregular, knotted, lame, maimed, malformed, mangled, marred, misbegotten, misconceived, misproportioned, misshapen, out of shape, scarred, twisted, ugly, unnatural, unseemly, warped; SEE CONCEPTS 485,486

deformity [n] disfigurement, distortion
aberration, abnormality, asymmetry, buckle, contortion, corruption, crookedness, damage, defacement, defect, depravity, evil, grossness, hideousness, impairment, injury, irregularity, knot, malconformation, malformation, misproportion, misshape, misshapenness, repulsiveness, ugliness, unattractiveness, unnaturalness, unsightliness, warp; SEE CONCEPT 580

defraud [v] cheat, bilk
bamboozle*, beguile, burn, chouse, circumvent, clip*, con, cozen, deceive, delude, do, do number on*, do out of*, dupe*, embezzle, fleece, flimflam, foil, gyp*, hoax, jive*, milk*, outwit, pilfer, pull fast one*, rip off*, rob, shaft*, shuck*, stick*, sucker into*, swindle, take*, take in*, take to cleaner's*, trick, victimize; SEE CONCEPT 59

deft [adj] agile, clever
able, adept, adroit, apt, crack, crackerjack*, cute, dexterous, expert, fleet, handy, having good hands, having know-how*, ingenious, neat, nimble, proficient, prompt, quick, ready, skilled, skillful; SEE CONCEPT 527

defunct [adj] extinct, not functioning
asleep, bygone, cold, dead, deceased, departed, done for*, down the drain*, exanimate, expired, gone, had it*, inanimate, inoperative, invalid, kaput*, late, lifeless, lost, nonexistent, obsolete, out of commission*, vanished; SEE CONCEPTS 539,560

defy [v] challenge, frustrate
baffle, beard, brave, confront, contemn, dare, defeat, deride, despise, disregard, elude, face, flout, fly in face of*, foil, front, gibe*, hang tough*, hurl defiance at, ignore, insult, make my day*, mock, oppose, outdare, provoke, repel, repulse, resist, ridicule, scorn, slight, spurn, stick*, stick fast*, take one on*, thwart, venture, violate, withstand; SEE CONCEPTS 78,87

degeneracy [n1] corruption
abasement, decadence, degradation, depravity, dissoluteness, downfall, immorality, inferiority, meanness, poorness; SEE CONCEPT 645

degeneracy [n2] decay, deterioration
atrophy, debasement, declination, decline, decrease, depravation, devolution, downfall, downgrade; SEE CONCEPTS 230,469

degenerate [adj] corrupt, deteriorated
base, debased, debauched, decadent, decayed, degenerated, degraded, demeaned, depraved, dissolute, effete, failing, fallen, flatitious, immoral, infamous, low, mean, miscreant, nefarious, overripe, perverted, retrograde, retrogressive, rotten, sinking, unhealthy, vicious, villainous, vitiated, wicked, worsen; SEE CONCEPTS 545,570

degenerate [v] decay, deteriorate
backslide, come apart at seams*, corrode, corrupt, decline, decrease, deprave, descend, die on vine*, disimprove, disintegrate, fall off, go downhill*, go to pieces*, go to the dogs*, lapse, lessen, regress, retrogress, return, revert, rot, sink, slip, vitiate, worsen; SEE CONCEPTS 469,698,702

degradation [n] depravity, shame
abasement, debasement, decadence, decline, degeneracy, degeneration, demotion, derogation, deterioration, discredit, disgrace, dishonor, downgrading, evil, humiliation, ignominy, mortification, perversion, reduction, shame; SEE CONCEPTS 230,410

degrade [v] shame, humiliate
abase, belittle, bemean, bench, break, bump, bust, canker, cast down, cheapen, corrupt, cut down to size*, debase, debauch, declass, decry, degenerate, demean, demote, depose, deprave, derogate, deteriorate, detract, diminish, disbar, discredit, disgrace, dishonor, disparage, downgrade, humble, impair, injure, lessen, lower, mudsling*, pan*, pervert, put down, reduce, rule out, run down*, shoot down*, sink, slam, take down*, take down a peg*, tear down*, vitiate, weaken; SEE CONCEPTS 7,19,240

degree [n1] unit of measurement
amount, caliber, dimension, division, extent, gauge, gradation, grade, height, intensity, interval, limit, line, link, mark, measure, notch, period, plane, point, proportion, quality, quantity, range, rate, ratio, reach, rung, scale, scope, severity, shade, size, space, stage, stair, standard, step, stint, strength, tenor, term, tier; SEE CONCEPTS 651,783,792

degree [n2] recognition of achievement
amplitude, approbation, approval, baccalaureate, caliber, class, compass, credentials, credit, development, dignification, dignity, distinction, eminence, expanse, extent, grade, height, honor, intensity, length, level, magnitude, order, pitch, point, position, potency, proportion, qualification, quality, quantity, range, rank, reach, scope, sheepskin, shingle, sort, stage, standard, standing, station, status, strength, testimonial, testimony; SEE CONCEPTS 388,706

dehydrate [v] take moisture out of
cotton-mouth, desiccate, drain, dry, dry out, dry up, evaporate, exsiccate, parch, sear; SEE CONCEPTS 250,469

deify [v] elevate, glorify
adore, apotheosize, consecrate, ennoble, enthrone, exalt, extol, idealize, idolize, immortalize, venerate, worship; SEE CONCEPTS 69,367

deign [v] lower oneself
condescend, consent, deem worthy, patronize, see fit, stoop, think fit, vouchsafe; SEE CONCEPT 35

deity [n] *god, worshiped being*
celestial, celestial being, creator, divine being, divinity, goddess, godhead, idol, immortal, supreme being; SEE CONCEPTS *368,370*

dejected [adj] *depressed, blue*
abject, all torn up*, atrabilious, black, bleak, broody, bummed out*, cast down, cheerless, clouded, crestfallen, dampened, dashed, despondent, disconsolate, discouraged, disheartened, dismal, dispirited, doleful, down*, downcast, downhearted, down in dumps*, down in the mouth*, dragged, drooping, droopy, gloomy, glum, heavyhearted, hurting*, in the pits*, low, low-spirited, melancholy, miserable, moody, mopey*, mopish*, morose, sad, sagging, shot down*, spiritless, woebegone, wretched; SEE CONCEPT *403*

delay [n] *deferment, interruption*
adjournment, bind, check, cooling-off period*, cunctation, dawdling, demurral, detention, discontinuation, downtime*, filibuster, hangup*, hindrance, holding, holding pattern*, hold-up*, impediment, interval, jam, lag, lingering, logjam*, loitering, moratorium, obstruction, postponement, problem, procrastination, prorogation, putting off*, remission, reprieve, retardation, retardment, setback, showstopper*, stall, stay, stop, stoppage, surcease, suspension, tarrying, tie-up, wait; SEE CONCEPTS *121,130, 666*

delay [v] *cause stop in action*
adjourn, arrest, bar, bide time, block, check, choke, clog, confine, curb, dawdle, defer, detain, deter, dilly-dally*, discourage, drag, encumber, filibuster, gain time, hamper, hold, hold over, impede, inhibit, interfere, intermit, keep, keep back, lag, lay over, linger, loiter, obstruct, postpone, prevent, procrastinate, prolong, prorogue, protract, put off, remand, repress, restrict, retard, shelve, slacken, stall, stave off, stay, stop, suspend, table, tarry, temporize, withhold; SEE CONCEPTS *121,130,237*

delectable [adj] *delicious, enjoyable*
adorable, agreeable, ambrosial, appetizing, charming, choice, dainty, darling, delicate, delightful, delish, divine, enticing, exquisite, gratifying, heavenly, inviting, luscious, lush, palatable, pleasant, pleasurable, rare, sapid, satisfying, savory, scrumptious, tasty, toothsome, yummy; SEE CONCEPTS *574,579, 613*

delegate [n] *representative, often governmental*
agent, alternate, ambassador, appointee, catchpole*, commissioner, congressman, consul, deputy, emissary, envoy, factor, front*, legate, member, minister, mouthpiece, nominee, people's choice, pinch hitter*, plenipotentiary, proxy, regent, rep*, replacement, senator, spokesman, stand-in, substitute, surrogate, vicar, viceroy; SEE CONCEPT *354*

delegate [v1] *give authority; empower*
accredit, appoint, assign, authorize, cast, charge, choose, commission, constitute, depute, deputize,

designate, elect, give nod, invest, license, mandate, name, nominate, ordain, place trust in, select, swear in, warrant; SEE CONCEPTS *50,88*

delegate [v2] *assign responsibility*
authorize, consign, devolve, entrust, give, hand over, hold responsible for, parcel out*, pass on*, relegate, send on errand, send on mission, shunt, transfer; SEE CONCEPTS *50,88,143*

delegation [n1] *assignment of responsibility*
appointment, apportioning, authorization, charge, commissioning, committal, consigning, consignment, conveyance, conveying, deputation, deputization, deputizing, devolution, entrustment, giving over, installation, investiture, mandate, nomination, ordination, reference, referring, relegation, sending away, submittal, submitting, transferal, transference, transferring, trust; SEE CONCEPTS *50,88,143,685*

delegation [n2] *group of representatives*
commission, contingent, deputation, embassy, envoys, gathering, legation, mission, organization; SEE CONCEPTS *299,301*

delete [v] *erase, remove*
annul, black out, bleep, blot out, blue-pencil*, cancel, clean, clean up, cross out, cut, cut out, decontaminate, destroy, drop, edit, efface, eliminate, exclude, expunge, obliterate, omit, pass up, rub, rub out, rule out, sanitize, snip, squash, squelch, sterilize, strike out, trim, wipe out, X-out*; SEE CONCEPT *211*

deleterious [adj] *harmful, damaging*
bad, destroying, destructive, detrimental, hurtful, injurious, mischievous, nocent, nocuous, pernicious, prejudicial, prejudicious, ruining, ruinous; SEE CONCEPTS *537,570*

deliberate [adj] *intentional*
advised, aforethought, calculated, careful, cautious, cold-blooded, conscious, considered, cut-and-dried*, designed, designful, done on purpose, express, fixed, intended, judged, meticulous, planned, pondered, prearranged, predesigned, predeterminate, predetermined, premeditated, prepense, projected, provident, prudent, purposed, purposeful, purposive, reasoned, resolved, schemed, scrupulous, studied, studious, thoughtful, thought out, voluntary, wary, weighed, willful, with forethought, witting; SEE CONCEPTS *401,542*

deliberate [v] *think about seriously; discuss*
argue, bat it around*, cerebrate, chew over*, cogitate, consider, consult, contemplate, debate, discuss, excogitate, hammer away at*, judge, kick around, knock around, meditate, mull over, muse, ponder, pour it on*, put on thinking cap*, rack brains*, reason, reflect, revolve, roll, ruminate, run up a flagpole*, speculate, stew over*, study, sweat over*, talk over, think, turn over, weigh; SEE CONCEPTS *17,24,56*

deliberately [adv] *intentionally*
advisedly, after consideration, apurpose, by design, calculatingly, consciously, designed, determinedly,

emphatically, freely, in cold blood, independently, knowingly, meaningfully, on purpose, pointedly, premeditatively, prepensely, purposely, purposively, resolutely, studiously, to that end, voluntarily, willfully, with a view to, with eyes wide open*, with malice aforethought*, without qualms, wittingly; SEE CONCEPTS *401,542*

deliberation [n] *serious thought, discussion*
application, attention, brainwork, calculation, care, carefulness, caution, cerebration, circumspection, cogitation, confabulation, conference, consideration, consultation, debate, forethought, heed, meditation, prudence, purpose, rap, ratiocination, reflection, speculation, study, ventilation, wariness; SEE CONCEPTS *17,24,56*

delicacy [n1] *daintiness, fineness of structure*
airiness, debility, diaphaneity, elegance, etherealness, exquisiteness, fragility, frailness, frailty, gossameriness, infirmity, lightness, slenderness, smoothness, softness, subtlety, tenderness, tenuity, translucency, transparency, weakness; SEE CONCEPTS *611,733*

delicacy [n2] *delicious, gourmet food*
ambrosia, banquet, bonne bouche, dainty, delight, dessert, feast, goody, indulgence, luxury, morsel, nectar, pleasure, rarity, regale, relish, savory, special, sweet, tidbit, treat; SEE CONCEPT *457*

delicate [adj1] *dainty, weak*
aerial, balmy, breakable, choice, delectable, delicious, delightful, elegant, ethereal, exquisite, faint, filmy, fine, fine-grained, finespun, flimsy, fracturable, fragile, frail, frangible, gauzy, gentle, gossamery, graceful, hairline, mild, muted, nice, pale, pastel, rare, recherché, select, shatterable, shattery, slight, soft, subdued, subtle, superior, tender; SEE CONCEPTS *490,574,606*

delicate [adj2] *sickly*
ailing, debilitated, decrepit, feeble, flimsy, fragile, frail, infirm, shatterable, shattery, sick, slender, slight, susceptible, tender, unhealthy, weak; SEE CONCEPT *314*

delicate [adj3] *fussy, discriminating*
alert, careful, critical, dainty, fastidious, finical, finicking, finicky, gentle, nice, particular, persnickety, prudish, pure, refined, scrupulous, sensitive, squeamish, thin-skinned; SEE CONCEPT *404*

delicate [adj4] *difficult, sticky (situation)*
critical, hair-trigger*, precarious, sensitive, ticklish, touchy, tricky, uncertain, unpredictable, volatile; SEE CONCEPT *565*

delicate [adj5] *careful, tactful*
accurate, adept, cautious, considerate, deft, detailed, diplomatic, discreet, expert, foresighted, heedful, masterly, minute, politic, precise, proficient, prudent, sensitive, skilled, tactical, wary; SEE CONCEPTS *401,542*

delicately [adv] *carefully*
beautifully, cautiously, daintily, deftly, elegantly, exquisitely, fastidiously, finely, gracefully, lightly,

precisely, sensitively, skillfully, softly, subtly, tactfully; SEE CONCEPTS *542,544*

delicious [adj] *pleasing, especially to the taste*
adorable, ambrosial, appetizing, choice, dainty, darling, delectable, delightful, delish*, distinctive, divine, enjoyable, enticing, exquisite, fit for king*, good, gratifying, heavenly, luscious, lush, mellow, mouthwatering, nectarous, nice, palatable, piquant, rare, rich, sapid, savory, scrumptious, spicy, sweet, tasteful, tasty, tempting, titillating, toothsome, very pleasant, well-prepared, well-seasoned, yummy*; SEE CONCEPTS *572,613*

delight [n] *enjoyment, happiness*
contentment, delectation, ecstasy, enchantment, felicity, fruition, gladness, glee, gratification, hilarity, jollity, joy, joyance, mirth, pleasure, rapture, relish, satisfaction, transport; SEE CONCEPT *410*

delight [v] *make happy; experience happiness*
allure, amuse, arride, attract, be the ticket*, charm, cheer, content, delectate, divert, enchant, enrapture, entertain, exult, fascinate, freak out, gladden, glory, go over big*, gratify, groove, happify, hit the spot*, jubilate, knock dead*, knock out*, please, pleasure, ravish, rejoice, satisfy, score, send, slay, thrill, tickle pink*, tickle to death*, turn on, wow; SEE CONCEPTS *7,22*

delighted [adj] *very happy*
captivated, charmed, ecstatic, elated, enchanted, entranced, excited, fulfilled, gladdened, gratified, joyous, jubilant, overjoyed, pleasantly surprised, pleased, thrilled; SEE CONCEPT *403*

delightful [adj] *pleasant, charming*
adorable, agreeable, alluring, ambrosial, amusing, attractive, beautiful, captivating, cheery, clever, congenial, darling, delectable, delicious, enchanting, engaging, enjoyable, entertaining, fair, fascinating, gratifying, heavenly, ineffable, lovely, luscious, lush, pleasing, pleasurable, rapturous, ravishing, refreshing, satisfying, scrumptious, thrilling, yummy*; SEE CONCEPTS *401,404*

delight in [v] *take pleasure from*
admire, adore, amuse oneself, appreciate, be content, be pleased, cherish, dig*, eat up*, enjoy, feast on, get a kick out of*, get high on*, get off on*, glory in, groove on*, indulge in, like, live a little*, live it up*, love, luxuriate in, relish, revel in, savor; SEE CONCEPTS *32,410*

delinquency [n] *misconduct*
crime, default, dereliction, failure, fault, lapse, misbehavior, misdeed, misdemeanor, neglect, nonobservance, offense, oversight, weakness, wrongdoing; SEE CONCEPTS *192,645*

delinquent [n] *criminal, often young*
behind, blackguard, black sheep*, culprit, dawdler, deadbeat*, deadhead*, debtor, defaulter, derelict, desperado, evader, fallen angel*, felon, hoodlum*, jailbird*, JD*, juvenile delinquent, juvie*, lawbreaker, loafer, lounger, malefactor, miscreant, ne-

glecter, no show*, offender, outlaw, punk*, recreant, reprobate, sinner, wrongdoer, young offender; SEE CONCEPT 412

delinquent [adj] irresponsible, defaulting
behind, blamable, blameworthy, careless, censurable, criminal, culpable, defaultant, derelict, disregardful, faulty, guilty, lax, neglectful, negligent, offending, overdue, procrastinating, red-handed*, remiss, reprehensible, shabby, slack, tardy, unpaid; SEE CONCEPTS 401,570

delirious [adj1] mentally imbalanced
aberrant, bewildered, confused, crazed, crazy, demented, deranged, deviant, deviate, disarranged, disordered, distracted, disturbed, flipped*, flipped out*, hallucinatory, incoherent, insane, irrational, lightheaded, lunatic, mad, maniac, maniacal, manic, off one's head*, out of head*, out of skull*, rambling, raving, unhinged, unreasonable, unsettled, wandering; SEE CONCEPTS 402,403

delirious [adj2] excited; very happy
beside oneself*, carried away*, corybantic, crazy, delighted, drunk*, ecstatic, enthused, frantic, frenetic, frenzied, furious, hysterical, intoxicated, mad, overexcited, overwrought, rapturous, thrilled, transported, wild; SEE CONCEPTS 401,403

delirium [n] madness
aberration, ardor, dementia, derangement, ecstasy, enthusiasm, fervor, fever, frenzy, furor, fury, hallucination, hysteria, insanity, lunacy, mania, passion, rage, raving, transport, zeal; SEE CONCEPT 410

deliver [v1] transfer, carry
bear, bring, cart, come across with*, convey, dish out*, distribute, drop, fork over*, gimme*, give, hand, hand-carry, hand over, pass, put on, put out, remit, transport, truck; SEE CONCEPTS 108,217

deliver [v2] relinquish possession
abandon, cede, commit, give up, grant, hand over, let go, resign, surrender, transfer, turn over, yield; SEE CONCEPTS 116,131

deliver [v3] free, liberate
acquit, discharge, emancipate, loose, ransom, redeem, release, rescue, save, set free, unshackle; SEE CONCEPT 127

deliver [v4] announce, proclaim
address, bring out, broach, chime in, come out with, communicate, declare, express, give, give forth, impart, present, pronounce, publish, read, say, state, tell, throw out, utter, vent, voice; SEE CONCEPTS 51,60

deliver [v5] administer; throw
aim, deal, direct, dispatch, fling, give, hurl, inflict, launch, pitch, send, strike, transmit; SEE CONCEPTS 217,222

deliver [v6] discharge, give forth
accouch, bear, birth, born, dispense, feed, find, give, hand, hand over, produce, provide, release, supply, turn over; SEE CONCEPTS 179,374

delivery [n1] transfer, transmittal
carting, commitment, consignment, conveyance, dispatch, distribution, drop, freighting, giving over, handing over, impartment, intrusting, mailing, parcel post, portage, post, rendition, shipment, surrender, transferal, transmission; SEE CONCEPTS 108,217

delivery [n2] articulation of message
accent, diction, elocution, emphasis, enunciation, inflection, intonation, modulation, pronunciation, speech, utterance; SEE CONCEPTS 47,595

delivery [n3] childbirth
accouchement, bearing, birth, birthing, bringing forth, Caesarian section, childbearing, confinement, geniture, labor, lying-in, parturition, travail; SEE CONCEPTS 302,373,374

delivery [n4] giving of freedom
deliverance, emanication, escape, freeing, liberation, pardon, release, rescue, salvage, salvation; SEE CONCEPT 127

delude [v] deceive, fool
beguile, betray, bluff, caboodle*, cheat, con, cozen, disinform, do a number on*, double-cross, dupe*, gull*, hoax*, hoodwink*, illude, impose on, jive*, juggle*, lead up garden path*, misguide, mislead, mousetrap*, outfox, play trick on, snow*, string along, sucker*, take in, trick; SEE CONCEPT 59

deluge [n] downpour, flood of something
avalanche, barrage, cataclysm, cataract, drencher, flux, inundation, niagara, overflowing, overrunning, pour, rush, spate, torrent; SEE CONCEPTS 432,524,786

deluge [v1] inundate with water
douse, drench, drown, engulf, flood, flush, gush, overflow, overrun, overwhelm, pour, sluice, soak, sop, souse, stream, submerge, swamp, wet, whelm; SEE CONCEPT 256

deluge [v2] overwhelm
abound, crowd, engulf, flood, glut, inundate, overcome, overcrowd, overload, overrun, oversupply, snow*, snow under*, swamp, teem, whelm; SEE CONCEPTS 42,140

delusion [n] misconception, misbelief
apparition, blunder, casuistry, chicanery, daydream, deception, deceptiveness, dream, eidolon, error, fallacy, false impression, fancy, fantasy, figment*, fool's paradise*, ghost, hallucination, head trip*, ignis fatuus, illusion, lapse, mirage, misapprehension, mistake, optical illusion, oversight, phantasm, phantom, pipedream*, self-deception, shade, speciousness, spuriousness, trickery, trip, vision; SEE CONCEPTS 409, 410,689

delusive [adj] deceptive
apparent, beguiling, chimerical, deceiving, deluding, fallacious, false, fanciful, fantastic, illusive, illusory, imaginary, misleading, ostensible, quixotic, seeming, specious, spurious, visionary; SEE CONCEPT 582

deluxe [adj] superior, plush
choice, costly, dainty, delicate, elegant, exclusive, expensive, exquisite, first-class, grand, luscious,

lush, luxuriant, luxurious, opulent, palatial, posh, rare, recherché, rich, ritzy, select, special, splendid, sumptuous, super, swank, swanky; SEE CONCEPT *574*

delve [*v*] *dig into task, action*
burrow, dig, dredge, examine, excavate, explore, ferret out*, go into, gouge out, inquire, investigate, jump into, leave no stone unturned*, look into, probe, prospect, ransack, really get into*, research, rummage, scoop out, search, seek, shovel, sift, spade, trowel, turn inside out*, unearth; SEE CONCEPTS *87,103,216*

demagogue [*n*] *agitating person*
agitator, fanatic, firebrand*, fomenter, haranger, hothead*, incendiary, inciter, inflamer, instigator, politician, rabble-rouser*, radical, rebel, revolutionary, soapbox orator*, troublemaker; SEE CONCEPTS *359, 412*

demand [*n*] *question, request*
appeal, application, arrogation, bid, bidding, call, call for, charge, claim, clamor, command, counterclaim, entreatment, entreaty, exaction, impetration, imploration, importunity, imposition, inquiry, insistence, interest, interrogation, lien, necessity, need, occasion, order, petition, plea, prayer, pursuit, requirement, requisition, rush, sale, search, solicitation, stipulation, suit, supplication, trade, ultimatum, use, vogue, want; SEE CONCEPT *662*

demand [*v1*] *ask strongly for something*
abuse, appeal, apply, arrogate, badger, beg, beseech, besiege, bid, challenge, charge, cite, claim, clamor for, coerce, command, compel, constrain, counterclaim, direct, dun, enjoin, entreat, exact, expect, force, hit, hit up, impetrate, implore, importune, inquire, insist on, interrogate, knock, nag, necessitate, oblige, order, pester, petition, postulate, pray, press, question, request, require, requisition, solicit, stipulate, sue for, summon, summons, supplicate, tax, urge, whistle for; SEE CONCEPT *53*

demand [*v2*] *require*
ask, call for, command, crave, cry out for, fail, involve, lack, necessitate, need, oblige, take, want; SEE CONCEPTS *26,646*

demanding [*adj*] *challenging, urgent*
ambitious, backbreaker*, bothersome, clamorous, critical, dictatorial, difficult, exacting, exhausting, exigent, fussy, grievous, hard, imperious, importunate, insistent, nagging, onerous, oppressive, pressing, querulous, strict, stringent, taxing, tough, troublesome, trying, wearing, weighty; SEE CONCEPTS *542,565*

demarcation [*n*] *boundary, division*
bound, confine, delimitation, differentiation, distinction, enclosure, limit, margin, separation, split, terminus; SEE CONCEPT *745*

demean [*v*] *humble, humiliate*
abase, bad-mouth*, belittle, bemean, cast down, contemn, cut down to size*, cut rate, debase, decry,

degrade, derogate, descend, despise, detract, dis*, disparage, dump on*, knock down*, lower, pan*, poor-mouth*, scorn, sink, stoop*; SEE CONCEPTS *7,19,54*

demeanor [*n*] *behavior, manner*
address, air, attitude, bearing, carriage, comportment, conduct, deportment, disposition, mien, poise, port, presence, set; SEE CONCEPTS *411,633*

demented [*adj*] *crazy, insane*
bananas*, bemused, crackbrained*, crazed, daft, delirious, deranged, distracted, distraught, flipped out*, foolish, frenzied, fruity*, hysterical, idiotic, in the ozone*, lunatic, mad, maniac, maniacal, manic, non compos mentis, nutty as fruitcake*, out of gourd*, out of tree*, psycho, psychopathic, psychotic, schitzy*, schizoid*, unbalanced, unglued*, unhinged*, unsound, whacko*; SEE CONCEPT *403*

demise [*n*] *fate, usually death*
annihilation, collapse, curtains, decease, departure, dissolution, downfall, dying, end, ending, expiration, extinction, failure, fall, final thrill*, last out*, last roundup*, lights out*, number's up*, passing, quietus, ruin, silence, sleep, termination; SEE CONCEPTS *105,304,679*

democracy [*n*] *government in which people participate*
commonwealth, egalitarianism, emancipation, equalitarianism, equality, freedom, justice, liberal government, representative government, republic, suffrage; SEE CONCEPTS *299,687,689*

democratic [*adj*] *representative, self-governing*
autonomous, common, communal, constitutional, egalitarian, equal, free, friendly, individualistic, informal, just, libertarian, orderly, popular, populist, self-ruling, socialist; SEE CONCEPTS *319,536*

demolish [*v*] *destroy; consume*
annihilate, break, bulldoze, burst, crack, crush, decimate, defeat, devastate, devour, dilapidate, dismantle, eat, flatten, gobble up, knock down, level, obliterate, overthrow, overturn, pulverize, put away, put in toilet*, raze, ruin, sink, smash, take apart, take out, tear down, torpedo*, total*, trash*, unbuild, undo, wax*, wipe off map*, wrack, wreck; SEE CONCEPTS *169,252*

demolition [*n*] *destruction*
annihilation, bulldozing, explosion, extermination, knocking down, leveling, razing, wrecking; SEE CONCEPT *252*

demon [*n*] *evil, devilish being or influence*
archfiend, beast, brute, devil, evil spirit, fiend, goblin, hellion, imp, incubus, little devil*, malignant spirit, monster, rascal, rogue, Satan, vampire, villain; SEE CONCEPTS *370,412*

demonic/demoniac/demoniacal [*adj*] *evil*
aroused, crazed, devilish, diabolic, diabolical, fiendish, fired, frantic, frenetic, frenzied, hellish, impious, infernal, insane, inspired, mad, maniacal,

manic, possessed, satanic, serpentine, unhallowed, violent, wicked; SEE CONCEPTS *404,545*

demonstrable [*adj*] *provable, evident*
ascertainable, attestable, axiomatic, certain, conclusive, deducible, evident, evincible, incontrovertible, indubitable, inferable, irrefutable, obvious, palpable, positive, self-evident, undeniable, unmistakable, verifiable; SEE CONCEPTS *529,535*

demonstrate [*v1*] *display, show*
authenticate, determine, establish, evidence, evince, exhibit, expose, flaunt, indicate, make evident, make out, manifest, prove, roll out*, show and tell*, test, testify to, trot out*, try, validate; SEE CONCEPT *97*

demonstrate [*v2*] *explain, illustrate*
confirm, debunk, describe, express, give for instance, make clear, ostend, proclaim, set forth, show how, teach, testify to, walk one through*; SEE CONCEPT *57*

demonstrate [*v3*] *display or take public action for a cause*
exhibit, fast, lie in, manifest, march, march on, parade, picket, protest, rally, sit in, stage walkout, strike, walkout; SEE CONCEPTS *261,300*

demonstration [*n1*] *display of proof*
affirmation, confirmation, description, evidence, exhibition, explanation, exposition, expression, illustration, induction, manifestation, presentation, proof, show, spectacle, substantiation, test, testimony, trial, validation; SEE CONCEPT *261*

demonstration [*n2*] *display of belief in cause by taking public action*
fast, lie-in*, love-in*, march, mass lobby, parade, peace march, picket, picket line, protest, rally, sit-in*, strike, teach-in*, walkout; SEE CONCEPTS *261,300*

demonstrative [*adj1*] *expressive, communicative*
affectionate, candid, effusive, emotional, evincive, expansive, explanatory, expository, frank, gushing, histrionic, illustrative, indicative, loving, open, outgoing, outpouring, outspoken, plain, profuse, symptomatic, tender, unconstrained, unreserved, unrestrained, warmhearted; SEE CONCEPTS *267,401*

demonstrative [*adj2*] *conclusive*
authenticating, certain, convincing, decisive, definite, final, proving, showing, specific, validating; SEE CONCEPTS *531,537*

demoralize [*v1*] *depress, unnerve*
abash, blow out, blow up, chill, cripple, damp, dampen, daunt, debilitate, deject, disarrange, disconcert, discountenance, discourage, dishearten, disorder, disorganize, disparage, dispirit, disturb, embarrass, enfeeble, get to*, jumble, muddle, nonplus, psych out*, rattle, sap, send up*, shake, snarl, take apart*, take steam out*, undermine, unglue*, unman, unsettle, unzip*, upset, weaken; SEE CONCEPTS *7,19*

demoralize [*v2*] *corrupt, pervert*
bastardize, bestialize, brutalize, debase, debauch, deprave, lower, vitiate, warp; SEE CONCEPT *14*

demote [*v*] *downgrade, lower in rank*
bench*, break, bump, bust, declass, degrade, demean, demerit, dismiss, disrate, hold back, kick downstairs*, lower, reduce, relegate, set back; SEE CONCEPTS *233,351*

demur [*v*] *disagree*
balk, cavil, challenge, combat, complain, deprecate, disapprove, dispute, doubt, fight, hem and haw*, hesitate, object, oppose, pause, protest, pussyfoot*, refuse, remonstrate, resist, scruple, shy, stick, stickle, strain, take exception*, vacillate, wait and see*, waver; SEE CONCEPTS *46,54*

demure [*adj*] *reserved, affected*
backward, bashful, blushing, close, coy, decorous, diffident, earnest, humble, modest, nice, prim, prissy, proper, prudish, reticent, retiring, sedate, serious, shy, silent, skittish, sober, solemn, staid, strait-laced, timid, unassertive, unassuming, unassured; SEE CONCEPTS *401,404*

den [*n1*] *cavern, hideaway*
atelier, burrow, cave, cloister, couch, cubbyhole, haunt, hideout, hole, hotbed, lair, lodge, nest, retreat, sanctuary, sanctum, shelter, snuggery, study; SEE CONCEPTS *448,513*

den [*n2*] *room for relaxation or informal entertaining*
family room, library, media room, playroom, recreation room, rec room*, rumpus room, studio, TV room; SEE CONCEPTS *440,448*

denial [*n*] *dismissal, refusal of belief in statement*
abnegation, abstaining, adjuration, brush-off, cold shoulder*, contradiction, controversion, declination, disallowance, disapproval, disavowal, disclaimer, dismissing, disproof, dissent, forswearing, gainsaying, nay, negation, negative, nix*, nonacceptance, noncommittal, no way*, prohibition, protestation, rebuff, rebuttal, refraining, refusing, refutal, refutation, rejecting, rejection, renegement, renouncement, renunciation, repudiating, repudiation, repulse, retraction, turndown, veto; SEE CONCEPTS *45,54*

denigrate [*v*] *belittle, malign*
asperse, bad mouth*, besmirch, blacken, blister, calumniate, decry, defame, dis*, disparage, give black eye*, impugn, knock*, libel, mudsling*, put down*, revile, rip up*, roast*, run down*, scandalize, slander, tear down*, traduce, vilify; SEE CONCEPTS *52,54*

denizen [*n*] *resident*
citizen, dweller, habitant, indweller, inhabitant, inhabiter, liver, national, native, occupant, resider, subject; SEE CONCEPT *413*

denomination [*n1*] *religious belief*
church, communion, connection, creed, cult, faith, group, persuasion, religion, school, sect; SEE CONCEPTS *368,689*

denomination [*n2*] *classification*
body, category, class, grade, group, size, type, unit, value; SEE CONCEPT *378*

denomination [*n3*] *name*
appellation, appellative, brand, cognomen, compellation, designation, flag, handle, identification, la-

bel, moniker, nomen, slot, style, surname, tab, tag, term, title; SEE CONCEPT *683*

denotation [*n*] *meaning, description*
designation, explanation, implication, indication, signification, specification; SEE CONCEPTS *268,682*

denote [*v*] *designate, mean*
add up, announce, argue, bespeak, betoken, connote, evidence, express, finger, flash, hang sign on, imply, import, indicate, insinuate, intend, make, mark, peg, prove, put down for, put finger on*, show, signify, spell, stand for, symbol, symbolize, tab, tag, typify; SEE CONCEPTS *55,682*

denounce [*v*] *condemn, attack*
accuse, adjudicate, arraign, blacklist, blame, boycott, brand, castigate, censure, charge, charge with, criticize, damn, declaim, decry, denunciate, derogate, dress down, excoriate, expose, finger*, hang something on*, impeach, implicate, impugn, incriminate, indict, inveigh against, knock, ostracize, proscribe, prosecute, rap, rat*, rebuke, reprehend, reprimand, reproach, reprobate, reprove, revile, scold, show up, skin*, smear, stigmatize, take to task, threaten, upbraid, vilify, vituperate; SEE CONCEPTS *44,52*

dense [*adj1*] *compressed, thick*
close, close-knit, compact, condensed, crammed, crowded, heaped, heavy, impenetrable, jammed, jam-packed*, massed, opaque, packed, packed like sardines*, piled, solid, substantial, thickset; SEE CONCEPT *483*

dense [*adj2*] *slow, stupid*
blockheaded*, boorish, doltish, dull, dumb, fatheaded*, half-witted, ignorant, imbecilic, impassive, lethargic, numskulled*, oafish, obtuse, phlegmatic, simple, slow-witted, sluggish, stolid, thick, torpid; SEE CONCEPT *402*

density [*n*] *bulk, mass*
body, closeness, compactness, concretion, consistency, crowdedness, denseness, frequency, heaviness, impenetrability, massiveness, quantity, solidity, substantiality, thickness, tightness; SEE CONCEPT *722*

dent [*n*] *depression, scrape, chip*
cavity, concavity, crater, crenel, cut, dimple, dint, dip, embrasure, furrow, hollow, impression, incision, indentation, nick, notch, pit, scallop, score, scratch, sink, trough; SEE CONCEPT *580*

dent [*v*] *chip, scrape, depress*
dig, dimple, dint, furrow, gouge, hollow, imprint, indent, make concave, mark, nick, notch, perforate, pit, press in, push in, ridge, scratch; SEE CONCEPTS *176,189,208,246*

denunciation [*n*] *condemnation, criticism*
accusation, arraignment, blame, castigation, censure, charge, cursing, damning, denouncement, derogation, dressing down*, fulmination, incrimination, indictment, invective, knock*, obloquy, rap*, reprehension, reprimand, reprobation, smearing, stigmatization, upbraidment, vilification; SEE CONCEPT *52*

deny [*v*] *disagree, renounce, decline*
abjure, abnegate, ban, begrudge, call on, contradict, contravene, controvert, curb, decline, disacknowledge, disallow, disavow, disbelieve, discard, disclaim, discredit, disown, disprove, doubt, enjoin from, eschew, exclude, forbid, forgo, forsake, gainsay, hold back, keep back, negate, negative, not buy, nullify, oppose, rebuff, rebut, recant, refuse, refute, reject, repudiate, restrain, revoke, sacrifice, say no to, spurn, taboo, take exception to, turn down, turn thumbs down, veto, withhold; SEE CONCEPTS *46,49,52*

deodorant [*n*] *something that freshens*
air freshener, antiperspirant, cleanser, cosmetic, deodorizer, disinfectant, fumigant, fumigator, smoke screen*; SEE CONCEPT *492*

depart [*v1*] *leave, retreat*
abandon, abdicate, absent, beat it*, blast off*, cut and run*, cut out*, decamp, desert, disappear, emigrate, escape, evacuate, exit, get away, git*, go, go away, go forth, hit the bricks*, hit the road*, hit the trail*, make a break*, march out, migrate, move on, move out, part, perish, pull out, quit, remove, retire, sally forth*, say goodbye*, scram*, secede, set forth, shove off*, slip away*, split*, start, start out, take leave, tergiversate, troop*, vacate, vanish, withdraw; SEE CONCEPT *195*

depart [*v2*] *diverge from normal, expected*
abandon, cast, desert, deviate, differ, digress, disagree, discard, dissent, excurse, forsake, ramble, reject, repudiate, stray, swerve, turn aside, vary, veer, wander; SEE CONCEPTS *665,697*

department [*n1*] *section of organization, area*
administration, agency, area, arena, beat, board, branch, bureau, canton, circuit, commission, commune, constituency, division, force, office, parish, precinct, quarter, range, staff, station, subdivision, territory, tract, unit, ward; SEE CONCEPTS *381,440,508*

department [*n2*] *area of interest, expertise*
activity, administration, assignment, avocation, bailiwick, berth, bureau, business, capacity, class, classification, domain, dominion, duty, field, function, incumbency, jurisdiction, line, niche, occupation, office, province, realm, responsibility, slot, specialty, sphere, spot, station, vocation, walk of life, wing; SEE CONCEPT *349*

departure [*n1*] *leaving*
abandonment, adieu, bow out*, congé, decampment, departing, desertion, egress, egression, embarkation, emigration, escape, evacuation, exit, exodus, expatriation, farewell, flight, getaway*, going, going away, goodbye*, hegira, leave-taking, migration, parting, passage, powder*, quitting, recession, removal, retirement, retreat, sailing, separation, setting forth, setting out, stampede, start, takeoff, taking leave, taking off, vacation, vanishing act*, walkout, withdrawal, withdrawing; SEE CONCEPT *195*

departure [n2] *deviation from normal, expected*
aberration, branching off, branching out, change, declination, deflection, difference, digression, divergence, diversion, innovation, in thing*, last word*, latest thing*, new wrinkle*, novelty, rambling, shift, straying, turning, variance, variation, veering, wandering; SEE CONCEPTS *665,697*

depend [v1] *count on, rely upon*
bank on*, bet bottom dollar on*, bet on*, build upon, calculate on, confide in, gamble on*, lay money on*, lean on*, reckon on, trust in, turn to; SEE CONCEPT *26*

depend [v2] *be contingent on*
be at mercy of, be based on, be conditioned, be connected with, be determined by, be in control of, be in the power of, be subject to, be subordinate to, bottom, found, ground, hang, hang in suspense, hang on, hinge on, pend, rest, rest on, rest with, revolve around, revolve on, stand on, stay, trust to, turn on; SEE CONCEPT *711*

dependable [adj] *reliable, responsible*
always there, carrying the load*, certain, constant, faithful, good as one's word*, loyal, rocklike*, secure, stable, staunch, steadfast, steady, sturdy, sure, to be counted on, tried, tried-and-true, true, trustworthy, trusty, unfailing; SEE CONCEPTS *542,560*

dependence/dependency [n1] *confidence, reliance*
assurance, belief, credence, expectation, faith, hope, interdependence, responsibility, responsibleness, stability, steadiness, stock, trust, trustiness, trustworthiness; SEE CONCEPTS *410,689*

dependence/dependency [n2] *addiction, need*
attachment, contingency, habit, helplessness, hook, inability, security blanket, servility, subjection, subordination, subservience, vulnerability, weakness, yoke; SEE CONCEPTS *20,709*

dependent [adj1] *weak, helpless*
abased, clinging, counting on, debased, defenseless, humbled, immature, indigent, inferior, lesser, minor, poor, reliant, relying on, secondary, subordinate, tied to apron strings*, under, under thumb*, unsustaining, vulnerable; SEE CONCEPTS *404,574*

dependent [adj2] *contingent, determined by*
accessory to, ancillary, appurtenant, conditional, controlled by, counting, depending, incidental to, liable to, provisory, reckoning, regulated by, relative, reliant, relying, subject to, subordinate, subservient, susceptible, sustained by, trusting, under control of; SEE CONCEPT *546*

depict [v] *describe, render in drawing or writing*
characterize, delineate, design, detail, draw, illustrate, image, interpret, limn, narrate, outline, paint, picture, portray, relate, report, represent, reproduce, sculpt, sketch, state; SEE CONCEPTS *79,174*

depiction [n] *description, rendering*
delineation, drawing, illustration, image, likeness, outline, picture, portraiture, portrayal, presentment, representation, sketch; SEE CONCEPTS *259,268*

deplete [v] *consume, exhaust supply*
bankrupt, bleed*, decrease, dig into, diminish, drain, draw, dry up, empty, evacuate, expend, finish, impoverish, lessen, milk*, reduce, sap, spend, squander, suck dry*, undermine, use up, wash up, waste, weaken; SEE CONCEPTS *142,169,225*

depleted [adj] *consumed, exhausted*
all in*, bare, bleary*, collapsed, decreased, depreciated, destitute, devoid of, drained, effete, emptied, far-gone*, in want, kaput*, lessened, out of, pooped out*, reduced, sapped, short of, sold, sold out, spent, sucked out*, used, used up, vacant, washed out, wasted, weakened, without resources, worn, worn out; SEE CONCEPTS *576,771*

deplorable [adj] *unfortunate, shameful*
afflictive, awful, blameworthy, bummer*, calamitous, dire, dirty, disastrous, disgraceful, dishonorable, disreputable, distressing, dolorous, downer*, dreadful, execrable, faulty, godawful*, grievous, grim, heartbreaking, heartrending, horrifying, intolerable, lamentable, lousy, melancholy, miserable, mournful, opprobrious, overwhelming, pitiable, poor, regrettable, reprehensible, rotten, sad, scandalous, sickening, stinking, terrible, tragic, unbearable, unsatisfactory, woeful, wretched; SEE CONCEPTS *529,570,574*

deplore [v] *regret; condemn*
abhor, be against, bemoan, bewail, carry on, censure, complain, cry, denounce, deprecate, disapprove of, eat one's heart out*, grieve for, hate, hurt, lament, moan, mourn, object to, regret, repent, rue, sing the blues*, sorrow over, take on, weep; SEE CONCEPTS *21,29*

deploy [v] *redistribute, station troops or weapons*
arrange, display, dispose, expand, extend, fan out, form front, open, position, put out patrol, set out, set up, spread out, take battle stations, unfold, use, utilize; SEE CONCEPTS *158,213,320*

deport [v] *banish*
cast out, dismiss, displace, exile, expatriate, expel, expulse, extradite, oust, relegate, ship out, transport; SEE CONCEPTS *198,211,217*

deportation [n] *banishment*
displacement, eviction, exile, expatriation, expulsion, extradition, ostracism, relegation, removal, transportation; SEE CONCEPTS *198,211,217*

deportment [n] *carriage, manner of person*
actions, address, air, appearance, aspect, bearing, behavior, cast, comportment, conduct, demeanor, manners, mien, port, posture, set, stance; SEE CONCEPT *633*

depose [v] *oust from position*
boot out, bounce, break, can*, cashier, chuck, degrade, demote, dethrone, discrown, dismiss, displace, downgrade, drum out, eject, freeze out*, give heave-ho*, impeach, kick out*, overthrow, remove from office, ride out on rail*, run out of town*, send packing*, subvert, throw out, throw out on ear*,

uncrown, unfrock, unmake, unseat, upset; SEE CONCEPTS *133,298,320*

deposit [*n1*] *down payment; money saved*
drop, installment, money in the bank, partial payment, pledge, retainer, security, stake, warranty; SEE CONCEPTS *340,344*

deposit [*n2*] *accumulation of solid*
alluvium, delta, deposition, dregs, drift, grounds, lees, precipitate, precipitation, sediment, settlings, silt; SEE CONCEPTS *432,470,471*

deposit [*v*] *locate, put in place for safekeeping*
accumulate, amass, bank, collect, commit, deliver, ditch, drop, entrust, garner, give in trust, hoard, install, invest, keep, lay, lay away, park, place, plant*, plop*, plunk*, plunk down*, precipitate, put aside, put by, repose, rest, salt away*, save, settle, sit down, sock away*, squirrel*, squirrel away*, stash, stock up, store, stow, transfer, treasure; SEE CONCEPTS *134,201,330*

deposition [*n1*] *dethroning, ousting*
degradation, discharge, dismissal, displacement, ejection, impeachment, overthrow, removal, unfrocking; SEE CONCEPTS *133,298,320*

deposition [*n2*] *attestation of truth, especially in legal matters*
affidavit, affirmation, allegation, announcement, declaration, evidence, sworn statement, testimony; SEE CONCEPTS *271,318*

depository [*n*] *storage place*
archive, arsenal, bank, bunker, cache, collection, depot, gallery, magazine, museum, repertory, repository, safe, safe-deposit box, store, storehouse, tomb, vault, warehouse; SEE CONCEPT *435*

depot [*n*] *storage place; station*
annex, armory, base, depository, destination, garage, halting-place, haven, junction, loft, lot, magazine, office, repository, stopping-place, store, storehouse, storeroom, terminal, terminus, waiting room, warehouse, yard; SEE CONCEPTS *435,449*

deprave [*v*] *corrupt, lead astray*
bastardize, bestialize, brutalize, debase, debauch, degrade, demoralize, pervert, seduce, subvert, vitiate, warp; SEE CONCEPT *14*

depraved [*adj*] *corrupt, immoral*
abandoned, bad, base, corrupted, debased, debauched, degenerate, degraded, dirty*, dirty-minded, dissolute, evil, fast*, filthy*, flagitous, gone to hell*, gone to the dogs*, kinky*, lascivious, lewd, licentious, low, mean, miscreant, nefarious, perverted, profligate, putrid, rotten, shameless, sinful, twisted, unhealthy, unnatural, vicious, vile, villainous, vitiate, vitiated, wanton, warped, wicked; SEE CONCEPT *545*

depravity [*n*] *corruption, immorality*
abandonment, baseness, contamination, criminality, debasement, debauchery, degeneracy, degradation, depravation, evil, iniquity, lewdness, licentiousness, perversion, profligacy, sensuality, sinfulness, vice, viciousness, vitiation, wickedness; SEE CONCEPT *645*

deprecate [*v*] *belittle, condemn*
cut down to size*, depreciate, derogate, detract, disapprove of, discommend, discountenance, disesteem, disfavor, disparage, expostulate, frown, mudsling*, not go for*, object, pooh pooh*, poor mouth*, protest against, put down*, rip*, run down*, take dim view of, take down, take exception to; SEE CONCEPTS *7,19,52*

depreciate [*v1*] *devalue, lose value*
abate, cheapen, decay, decrease, decry, deflate, depress, deteriorate, devalorize, devaluate, diminish, downgrade, drop, dwindle, erode, fall, lessen, lower, mark down, reduce, soften, underrate, undervalue, worsen, write down, write off; SEE CONCEPTS *698,776*

depreciate [*v2*] *belittle, ridicule*
abuse, asperse, attack, calumniate, censure, clamor against, condemn, contemn, decry, defame, denigrate, denounce, deprecate, deride, derogate, detract, discount, discountenance, discredit, disgrace, disparage, dispraise, fault, find fault with, humble, knock, look down on*, lower, malign, minimize, put down, rap, revile, roast*, run down*, scoff at, scorn, slam, slander, slight, slur, smear, sneer at, spurn, take down a peg*, traduce, underestimate, underrate, undervalue, vilify; SEE CONCEPTS *7,19,52*

depredation [*n*] *devastation, destruction*
burglary, crime, desecration, desolation, despoiling, laying waste, marauding, pillage, plunder, ransacking, rapine, ravaging, robbery, sacking, spoliation, stealing, theft, wasting; SEE CONCEPTS *192,252*

depress [*v1*] *deject, make despondent; exhaust*
abase, afflict, ail, bear down, beat, beat down*, bother, bug*, bum out*, cast down, chill*, cow*, damp, dampen, darken, daunt, debase, debilitate, degrade, desolate, devitalize, discourage, dishearten, dismay, dispirit, distress, disturb, drag*, drain, dull, enervate, faze, keep under, lower, mock, mortify, oppress, perturb, press, put down*, reduce, reduce to tears*, run down*, sadden, sap*, scorn, slow, throw cold water on*, torment, trouble, try, turn one off*, upset, weaken, weary, weigh down*; SEE CONCEPTS *7,19,240*

depress [*v2*] *devalue*
cheapen, debase, depreciate, devaluate, diminish, downgrade, impair, lessen, lower, reduce; SEE CONCEPTS *240,330*

depress [*v3*] *push down*
couch, demit, dip, droop, flatten, let down, level, lower, press down, settle, sink, smoosh, squash; SEE CONCEPT *208*

depressed [*adj1*] *discouraged*
bad, bleeding*, blue*, bummed out*, cast-down, crestfallen, crummy*, dejected, despondent, destroyed, disconsolate, dispirited, down, down and out*, downcast, downhearted, down in dumps*, down in the mouth*, dragged*, fed up*, glum, grim, hurting, in a blue funk*, in pain*, in the dumps*, in

the pits*, in the toilet*, let down, low, low-down, low-spirited, lugubrious, melancholy, moody, morose, on a downer*, pessimistic, ripped, sad, sob story*, spiritless, taken down*, torn up*, unhappy, weeping, woebegone; SEE CONCEPT *403*

depressed [*adj2*] *concave, pushed down*
hollow, indented, recessed, set back, sunken; SEE CONCEPT *490*

depressed [*adj3*] *disadvantaged*
cheapened, depreciated, deprived, destitute, devalued, distressed, ghetto, ghost, impaired, needy, poor, poverty-stricken, run-down, shanty, skid row*, underprivileged, weakened; SEE CONCEPTS *334,555*

depressing [*adj*] *discouraging, upsetting*
black, bleak, daunting, dejecting, depressive, discouraging, disheartening, dismal, dispiriting, distressing, dreary, funereal, gloomy, heartbreaking, hopeless, joyless, melancholic, melancholy, mournful, oppressive, sad, saddening, somber; SEE CONCEPT *529*

depression [*n1*] *low spirits; despair*
abasement, abjection, abjectness, blahs*, bleakness, blue funk*, bummer, cheerlessness, dejection, desolation, desperation, despondency, disconsolation, discouragement, dispiritedness, distress, dole, dolefulness, dolor, downheartedness, dreariness, dullness, dumps, ennui, gloom, gloominess, heaviness of heart, heavyheartedness, hopelessness, lowness, lugubriosity, melancholia, melancholy, misery, mortification, qualm, sadness, sorrow, the blues*, trouble, unhappiness, vapors*, woefulness, worry; SEE CONCEPT *410*

depression [*n2*] *economic decline*
bad times*, bankruptcy, bear market*, big trouble*, bottom out*, bust, crash, crisis, deflation, dislocation, downturn, drop, failure, hard times*, inactivity, inflation, overproduction, panic, paralysis, rainy days*, recession, retrenchment, sag, slide, slowness, slump, stagflation, stagnation, unemployment; SEE CONCEPTS *324,330,335*

depression [*n3*] *concavity, cavity*
basin, bowl, crater, dent, dimple, dip, excavation, hole, hollow, impression, indentation, pit, pocket, sag, scoop, sink, sinkage, sinkhole, vacuity, vacuum, valley, void; SEE CONCEPT *513*

deprivation [*n*] *taking, keeping away; need*
denial, deprival, destitution, detriment, disadvantage, dispossession, distress, divestiture, divestment, expropriation, hardship, loss, privation, removal, seizure, want, withdrawal, withholding; SEE CONCEPTS *121,142,709*

deprive [*v*] *keep or take away something wanted, needed*
bankrupt, bare, bereave, cold turkey*, denudate, denude, despoil, disinherit, dismantle, dispossess, disrobe, divest, dock, expropriate, hold back, lose, oust, rob, seize, skim, stiff, strip, wrest; SEE CONCEPTS *121,142*

depth [*n1*] *distance down or across*
base, bottom, declination, deepness, draft, drop, expanse, extent, fathomage, intensity, lower register, lowness, measure, measurement, pit, pitch, profoundness, profundity, remoteness, sounding; SEE CONCEPTS *737,790*

depth [*n2*] *insight, wisdom*
acuity, acumen, astuteness, brain, discernment, intellect, intelligence, keenness, penetration, profoundness, profundity, sagacity, sense, sharpness, weightiness; SEE CONCEPT *409*

deputy [*n*] *assistant, agent*
aide, ambassador, appointee, assemblyman/woman, backup, commissioner, councilor, delegate, dogcatcher*, factor, legate, lieutenant, minister, proxy, regent, replacement, representant, representative, second-in-command, sub, subordinate, substitute, surrogate; SEE CONCEPTS *348,354*

derange [*v*] *make crazy; confuse*
confound, craze*, dement, disarrange, disarray, discommode, discompose, disconcert, disorder, disorganize, displace, distract, disturb, drive crazy*, drive mad, frenzy, madden, make insane, mess up*, misplace, muss*, perplex, ruffle, rummage, unbalance, unhinge*, unsettle, upset; SEE CONCEPTS *16,84*

deranged [*adj*] *crazy, insane*
ape*, baked*, bananas*, berserk, cracked*, crazed, delirious, demented, disarranged, disconcerted, disordered, displaced, distracted, dotty*, flipped*, flipped out*, frantic, frenzied, fried*, irrational, loco*, lunatic, mad, maddened, maniac, maniacal, nuts*, perplexed, schizzo*, unbalanced, unglued*, unhinged*, unscrewed*, unsettled, unsound, unzipped*, whacko*; SEE CONCEPT *403*

derelict [*n*] *worthless or down-and-out person*
beggar, bum, bummer, castaway, dawdler, delinquent, drifter, floater, good-for-nothing*, grifter, hobo, leper*, loafer, lounger, ne'er-do-well*, outcast, pariah, renegade, skidrow bum, stiff, stumblebum*, tramp, untouchable, vagabond, vagrant, wastrel; SEE CONCEPTS *412,423*

derelict [*adj1*] *careless, negligent*
behindhand, delinquent, disregardful, irresponsible, lax, regardless, remiss, slack, undependable, unreliable, untrustworthy; SEE CONCEPT *542*

derelict [*adj2*] *deserted, forsaken*
abandoned, castoff, desolate, dilapidated, dingy, discarded, faded, lorn, neglected, ownerless, relinquished, ruined, run-down, seedy, shabby, solitary, threadbare, uncouth; SEE CONCEPT *560*

deride [*v*] *make fun of; insult*
banter, chaff, contemn, detract, dis*, disdain, disparage, do number on*, dump on*, flout, gibe, jeer, jolly, kid, knock, laugh at, lout, mock, pan, poohpooh*, put down*, quiz, rag*, rally, razz*, rib*, ridicule, roast*, scoff, scorn, slam, sneer, taunt, twit; SEE CONCEPTS *52,54*

de rigeur [adj] proper, right
au fait, becoming, comme il faut, conventional, correct, decent, decorous, done, fitting, necessary, nice, required; SEE CONCEPT *558*

derision [n] insult, disrespect
backhanded compliment*, brickbat*, Bronx cheer*, butt*, comeback, contempt, contumely, crack, dig*, disdain, disparagement, dump*, jab, jest, joke, laughingstock, laughter, mockery, object of ridicule, parting shot, pilgarlic, put-down, raillery, ridicule, satire, scoffing, scorn, slam*, slap, sneering; SEE CONCEPTS *52,278,689*

derisive [adj] ridiculing
cheeky*, cocky, contemptuous, crusty, derisory, disdainful, flip*, fresh, gally, insulting, jeering, mocking, nervy, out-of-line, rude, sarcastic, sassy, scoffing, scornful, smart*, smart-alecky*, taunting; SEE CONCEPT *267*

derivable [adj] deducible
a priori, attributable, available, determinable, dogmatic, extractable, inferable, likely, obtainable, reasoned, resultant, traceable; SEE CONCEPT *529*

derivation [n] root, source
ancestry, basis, beginning, descent, etymology, foundation, genealogy, inception, origin, provenance, provenience, spinoff, well, wellspring, whence it came; SEE CONCEPT *648*

derivative [n] product, descendant
by-product, derivation, offshoot, outgrowth, spinoff, wave; SEE CONCEPT *260*

derivative [adj] borrowed, transmitted from source
acquired, ancestral, caused, cognate, coming from, connate, copied, derivate, derivational, derived, evolved, hereditary, imitative, inferential, inferred, not original, obtained, plagiaristic, plagiarized, procured, rehashed, secondary, secondhand, subordinate, uninventive, unoriginal; SEE CONCEPT *549*

derive [v] deduce a conclusion
acquire, arrive, assume, collect, conclude, deduct, determine, develop, draw, educe, elaborate, elicit, evolve, excogitate, extract, follow, formulate, gain, gather, get, glean, infer, judge, make, make out, obtain, procure, put together, reach, receive, trace, work out; SEE CONCEPTS *15,18*

derive from [v] come from; arise
descend, emanate, flow, head, issue, originate, proceed, rise, spring from, stem from; SEE CONCEPT *648*

derogatory [adj] offensive, uncomplimentary
aspersing, belittling, calumnious, censorious, contumelious, critical, damaging, decrying, defamatory, degrading, demeaning, deprecatory, depreciative, despiteful, detracting, discreditable, disdainful, dishonoring, disparaging, fault-finding, humiliating, injurious, malevolent, malicious, maligning, minimizing, opprobrious, reproachful, sarcastic, scornful, slanderous, slighting, spiteful, unfavorable, unflattering, vilifying; SEE CONCEPTS *267,570*

descend [v1] move down, lower
alight, cascade, cataract, cave in, coast, collapse, crash, crouch, decline, deplane, detrain, dip, disembark, dismount, dive, dribble, drop, fall, fall prostrate, get down, get off, go down, gravitate, ground, incline, light, lose balance, lower, penetrate, pitch, plop, plummet, plunge, prolapse, set, settle, sink, slant, slide, slip, slope, slough off, slump, stoop, stumble, submerge, subside, swoop, toboggan, topple, trickle, trip, tumble, weep; SEE CONCEPTS *147,181,213*

descend [v2] condescend
abase oneself, concede, degenerate, deteriorate, humble oneself, lower oneself, patronize, stoop; SEE CONCEPTS *23,35*

descend [v3] trace ancestry from; be passed or handed down
arise, derive, issue, originate, proceed, spring; SEE CONCEPT *108*

descendant [n] person in line of ancestry
brood, child, children, chip off old block*, get*, heir, issue, kin, offshoot, offspring, posterity, product, progeniture, progeny, scion, seed, spin-off*; SEE CONCEPTS *296,414*

descent [n1] moving down; lowering
cave-in, coast, coming down, crash, declension, declination, decline, declivity, dip, downgrade, droop, drop, drop-off, fall, falling, grade, gradient, header, hill, inclination, incline, landslide, plummeting, plunge, plunging, precipitation, prolapse, sag, settlement, sinkage, sinking, slant, slide, slip, slope, swoop, tailspin, topple, tumble; SEE CONCEPTS *147,181,213,738*

descent [n2] line of ancestry
blood, extraction, family, family tree, genealogy, heredity, lineage, origin, parentage, pedigree, relationship; SEE CONCEPT *296*

descent [n3] deterioration
abasement, anticlimax, cadence, comedown, debasement, decadence, decline, degradation, discomfiture, down, downcome, downfall, lapse, pathos, slump; SEE CONCEPTS *230,674*

descent [n4] assault, attack
advance, foray, incursion, invasion, pounce, raid, swoop; SEE CONCEPTS *86,320*

describe [v] explain in speech, writing
call, characterize, chronicle, communicate, construe, convey image, define, delineate, depict, detail, distinguish, draw, elucidate, epitomize, exemplify, explicate, expound, express, illuminate, illustrate, image, impart, interpret, label, limn, make apparent, make clear, make sense of, make vivid, mark out, name, narrate, outline, paint, particularize, picture, portray, recite, recount, rehearse, relate, report, represent, sketch, specify, state, tell, term, trace, transmit, write up; SEE CONCEPT *55*

description [n1] account in speech, writing
ABCs*, blow by blow, brief, characterization, chronicle, confession, declaration, definition, delin-

eation, depiction, detail, explanation, explication, fingerprint, information, make, monograph, narration, narrative, picture, portraiture, portrayal, presentment, recital, recitation, record, recountal, rehearsal, report, representation, rundown, sketch, specification, statement, story, summarization, summary, tale, version, vignette, writeup, yarn; SEE CONCEPT **268**

description [n2] *class, kind*
brand, breed, category, character, classification, feather, genre, genus, ilk, kidney, nature, order, sort, species, stripe, type, variety; SEE CONCEPT **378**

descriptive [adj] *explanatory*
anedotic, characteristic, characterizing, circumstantial, classificatory, clear, definitive, delineative, depictive, describing, designating, detailed, eloquent, explicative, expository, expressive, extended, graphic, identifying, illuminating, illuminative, illustrative, indicative, interpretive, lifelike, narrative, particularized, pictorial, picturesque, revealing, specific, true to life, vivid; SEE CONCEPTS **267,557**

desecrate [v] *abuse, violate*
befoul, blaspheme, commit sacrilege, contaminate, defile, depredate, desolate, despoil, devastate, devour, dishonor, make lose face*, mess up*, pervert, pillage, pollute, profane, prostitute, ravage, sack*, spoil, spoliate, waste; SEE CONCEPTS **246,252**

desecration [n] *violation, abuse*
blasphemy, debasement, defilement, impiety, irreverence, profanation, sacrilege; SEE CONCEPTS **246,252**

desert [n] *wasteland; dry area*
arid region, badland, barren, barren land, flats, lava bed, Sahara, sand dunes, solitude, waste, wild, wilderness, wilds; SEE CONCEPTS **508,517**

desert [adj] *barren, uncultivated*
arid, bare, desolate, infertile, lonely, solitary, sterile, uninhabited, unproductive, untilled, waste, wild; SEE CONCEPT **560**

desert [v] *abandon, defect*
abscond, apostatize, bail out*, beach, betray, bolt, chuck, cop out*, crawl out, decamp, depart, duck*, escape, flee, fly, forsake, give up, go, go AWOL*, go back on, go over the hill*, go west*, jilt, leave, leave high and dry*, leave in the lurch*, leave stranded, light, maroon, opt out, play truant, pull out, quit, relinquish, renounce, resign, run out on*, sneak off*, split*, strand, take a hike*, take off, tergiversate, throw over, vacate, violate oath, walk; SEE CONCEPTS **195,297**

deserted [adj] *abandoned, unoccupied*
bare, barren, bereft, cast off, derelict, desolate, empty, forlorn, forsaken, godforsaken*, isolated, left, left in lurch*, left stranded, lonely, lorn, neglected, relinquished, solitary, uncouth, uninhabited, vacant; SEE CONCEPTS **485,577**

deserter [n] *fugitive from responsibility*
absconder, apostate, AWOL*, backslider, betrayer, criminal, defector, delinquent, derelict, escapee, es-

caper, fugitive, hookey player*, lawbreaker, maroon, no-show*, recreant, refugee, renegade, runaway, shirker, slacker, traitor, truant; SEE CONCEPTS **358,412,423**

desertion [n] *abandonment*
abrogation, absconding, apostasy, avoidance, backsliding, betrayal, castoff, defecting, departing, departure, derelict, dereliction, disaffection, disavowal, disavowing, divorce, elusion, escape, evasion, falling away, falseness, flight, forsaking, going back on*, leaving, marooning, perfidy, recreancy, rejection, relinquishment, renunciation, repudiation, resignation, retirement, retreat, running out on*, secession, tergiversation, treachery, truancy, withdrawal; SEE CONCEPTS **195,297**

deserts [n] *what is due one*
chastening, chastisement, comeuppance, compensation, deserving, discipline, disciplining, due, get hers*, get his*, guerdon, just deserts*, lumps*, meed, merit, payment, penalty, punishment, recompense, requital, retribution, return, revenge, reward, right, talion, what is coming to one*, what one is asking for*; SEE CONCEPTS **129,710**

deserve [v] *be entitled to*
be given one's due*, be in line for*, be worthy of, demand, earn, gain, get, get comeuppance*, get what is coming to one*, have it coming*, have the right to, justify, lay claim to, merit, procure, rate, warrant, win; SEE CONCEPT **129**

deserving [adj] *worthy, meritorious*
admirable, commendable, due, estimable, fitting, laudable, meritable, needy, praisable, praiseworthy, righteous, rightful, thankworthy; SEE CONCEPT **404**

desiccate [v] *take moisture out of*
anhydrate, dehydrate, deplete, devitalize, divest, drain, dry, dry up, evaporate, exsiccate, parch, sear, shrivel, wither, wizen; SEE CONCEPTS **137,250**

design [n1] *sketch, draft*
architecture, arrangement, blueprint, chart, comp, composition, conception, constitution, construction, delineation, depiction, diagram, doodle, drawing, dummy, form, formation, idea, layout, makeup, map, method, model, outline, paste-up, pattern, perspective, picture, plan, rough draft, scheme, study, tracery, tracing, treatment; SEE CONCEPTS **268, 625,660**

design [n2] *artful conception*
arrangement, configuration, construction, depiction, device, doodle, drawing, figure, form, illustration, motif, motive, organization, painting, pattern, picture, portrait, shape, sketch, style; SEE CONCEPT **259**

design [n3] *intention*
action, aim, angle, animus, big picture*, brainchild*, child*, conation, conspiracy, deliberation, end, enterprise, game plan*, gimmick, goal, intendment, intent, intrigue, lay of the land*, machination, meaning, notion, object, objective, picture, pitch, plan, play, plot, point, project, proposition, purport, purpose,

recipe, reflection, scenario, scene, schema, scheme, setup, story, target, thinking, thought, trick, undertaking, view, volition, what's cooking*, will; SEE CONCEPTS *410,660*

design [*v1*] *plan, outline*
accomplish, achieve, arrange, block out, blueprint, cast, chart, construct, contrive, create, delineate, describe, devise, diagram, dope out, draft, draw, effect, execute, fashion, form, frame, fulfill, invent, lay out, perform, plan, produce, project, set out, sketch, sketch out, trace, work out; SEE CONCEPT *36*

design [*v2*] *create, conceive*
compose, contrive, cook up*, devise, dream up*, fabricate, fashion, form, frame, invent, make up, originate, produce, think up; SEE CONCEPTS *43,173*

design [*v3*] *intend, mean to do*
aim, contemplate, contrive, destine, devise, make, mind, plan, prepare, project, propose, purpose, scheme, set apart, tailor; SEE CONCEPTS *35,36*

designate [*v1*] *name, entitle*
baptize, call, christen, cognominate, denominate, dub, entitle, label, nickname, nominate, style, term, title; SEE CONCEPT *62*

designate [*v2*] *specify as selection*
allocate, allot, appoint, apportion, appropriate, assign, authorize, button down*, characterize, charge, choose, commission, connote, constitute, define, delegate, denote, depute, deputize, describe, dictate, earmark*, elect, evidence, favor, finger*, indicate, individualize, make, mark, mete, name, nominate, opt, peg*, pick, pin down, pinpoint, prefer, put down for*, reserve, select, set apart, set aside, show, single, slot, stipulate, tab*, tag*, tap*; SEE CONCEPTS *41,129*

designation [*n1*] *name, label, mark*
appellation, appellative, class, classification, cognomen, compellation, denomination, description, epithet, identification, key word, moniker, naming, nickname, nomen, style, title; SEE CONCEPT *683*

designation [*n2*] *delegation, selection*
appointment, classification, identification, indication, pigeonhole*, recognition, specification; SEE CONCEPT *41*

designedly [*adv*] *intentionally*
apurpose, by design, calculatedly, deliberately, knowingly, on purpose, prepensely, purposedly, purposely, purposively, studiously, willfully, wittingly; SEE CONCEPTS *402,535*

designing [*adj*] *plotting, crafty*
artful, astute, conniving, conspiring, crooked, cunning, deceitful, devious, heedful, intriguing, Machiavellian, observant, scheming, sharp, shrewd, sly, treacherous, tricky, unscrupulous, wily; SEE CONCEPT *542*

desirable [*adj1*] *attractive, seductive*
adorable, alluring, charming, covetable, drop-dead beautiful*, enticing, fascinating, fetching, sexy; SEE CONCEPTS *372,579*

desirable [*adj2*] *advantageous, good*
acceptable, advisable, agreeable, beneficial, covetable, eligible, enviable, expedient, grateful, gratifying, helpful, pleasing, preferable, profitable, useful, welcome, worthwhile; SEE CONCEPTS *560,572*

desire [*n1*] *want, longing*
admiration, ambition, appetite, ardor, aspiration, attraction, avidity, concupiscence, covetousness, craving, craze, cupidity, devotion, doting, eagerness, fancy, fascination, fervor, fondness, frenzy, greed, hankering*, hunger, inclination, infatuation, itch*, lasciviousness, lechery, libido, liking, love, lust, mania, motive, need, passion, predilection, proclivity, propensity, rapaciousness, rapture, ravenousness, relish, salacity, solicitude, thirst, urge, voracity, will, wish, yearning; SEE CONCEPTS *20,709*

desire [*n2*] *request*
appeal, entreaty, hope, importunity, petition, solicitation, supplication, want, wish; SEE CONCEPT *662*

desire [*v1*] *want, long for*
aim, aspire to, be smitten, be turned on by*, choose, cotton to, covet, crave, desiderate, die over*, enjoy, fall for*, fancy, give eyeteeth for*, go for*, hanker after*, have eyes for*, have the hots for*, hunger for, like, lust after, make advances to, partial to, pine, set heart on*, spoil for, sweet on*, take a liking to*, take a shine to*, take to*, thirst, wish for, yearn for; SEE CONCEPT *20*

desire [*v2*] *ask, request*
beg, bespeak, entreat, importune, petition, seek, solicit; SEE CONCEPT *48*

desirous [*adj*] *aspiring, hopeful*
acquisitive, ambitious, amorous, anxious, avid, covetous, craving, desiring, eager, enthusiastic, grasping, greedy, hoping, hot*, itchy*, keen, longing, lustful, passionate, prehensile, ready, stimulated, turned on*, willing, wishful, wishing, yearning; SEE CONCEPT *529*

desist [*v*] *stop, refrain from*
abandon, abstain, avoid, break off, cease, discontinue, end, forbear, give over, give up, halt, have done with*, knock off*, leave off, not do, pause, quit, relinquish, resign, surcease, suspend, yield; SEE CONCEPTS *119,234*

desolate [*adj1*] *unused, barren*
abandoned, bare, bleak, derelict, desert, destroyed, dreary, empty, forsaken, godforsaken*, isolated, lonely, lonesome, lorn, ruined, solitary, uncouth, unfrequented, uninhabited, unoccupied, vacant, waste, wild; SEE CONCEPTS *485,560*

desolate [*adj2*] *depressed, despondent*
abandoned, acheronian, bereft, black, bleak, blue, cheerless, comfortless, companionless, dejected, depressing, disconsolate, dismal, dolorous, down, downcast, forlorn, forsaken, funereal, gloomy, hurting, in a blue funk*, inconsolable, joyless, lonely, lonesome, lorn, melancholy, miserable, somber, tragic, wretched; SEE CONCEPT *403*

desolate [v] *ravage, destroy*
depopulate, depredate, desecrate, despoil, devastate, devour, lay low, lay waste, pillage, plunder, ruin, sack, spoliate, waste; SEE CONCEPT 252

desolation [n1] *uninhabited area; barrenness*
bareness, bleakness, desert, desolateness, devastation, dissolution, extinction, forlornness, isolation, loneliness, ruin, solitariness, solitude, waste, wildness, wreck; SEE CONCEPTS 517,710

desolation [n2] *distress, unhappiness*
anguish, dejection, despair, gloom, gloominess, loneliness, melancholy, misery, mourning, sadness, sorrow, woe, wretchedness; SEE CONCEPT 410

despair [n] *depression, hopelessness*
anguish, dashed hopes, dejection, desperation, despondency, discouragement, disheartenment, forlornness, gloom, melancholy, misery, ordeal, pain, sorrow, trial, tribulation, wretchedness; SEE CONCEPT 410

despair [v] *give up hope*
abandon, abandon hope, be hopeless, despond, destroy, drop, flatten, give way, have heavy heart*, have no hope, let air out*, lose faith, lose heart, lose hope, relinquish, renounce, resign, surrender, take down, yield; SEE CONCEPT 21

despairing [adj] *upset, despondent*
anxious, at end of rope*, blue, broken-hearted, can't win*, cynical, dejected, depressed, desperate, disconsolate, downcast, forlorn, frantic, grief-stricken, hopeless, inconsolable, in dumps*, in pain*, in the pits*, in the soup*, melancholic, melancholy, misanthropic, miserable, not a prayer*, no-win*, oppressed, pessimistic, sad, shot down*, strabilious, suicidal, sunk*, weighed down*, wretched; SEE CONCEPT 403

desperado [n] *criminal*
badman, bandido, bandit, bravo, convict, cutthroat, gangster, gunman, hoodlum, lawbreaker, mugger, outlaw, ruffian, thug; SEE CONCEPT 412

desperate [adj1] *reckless, outrageous*
atrocious, audacious, bold, careless, crying, dangerous, daring, death-defying, determined, devil-may-care, foolhardy, frantic, frenzied, furious, hasty, hazardous, headlong, headstrong, heinous, impetuous, incautious, madcap, monstrous, precipitate, rash, risky, scandalous, shocking, venturesome, violent, wild; SEE CONCEPT 401

desperate [adj2] *extreme, intense*
acute, climacteric, concentrated, critical, crucial, dire, drastic, exquisite, extreme, fierce, furious, great, terrible, urgent, vehement, very grave, vicious, violent; SEE CONCEPTS 537,540,569

desperate [adj3] *hopeless*
at end of rope*, back to the wall*, can't win*, dead duck*, despairing, despondent, desponding, downcast, forlorn, futile, gone*, goner*, hard up*, inconsolable, in the soup*, in the toilet*, irrecoverable, irremediable, irretrievable, no-chance*, no-way*,

no-win*, running out of time*, sad, sunk*, up against it*, up the creek*, useless, vain, wretched; SEE CONCEPT 548

desperately [adv1] *severely*
badly, carelessly, dangerously, dramatically, fiercely, gravely, greatly, harmfully, hysterically, like crazy*, like mad*, perilously, seriously; SEE CONCEPT 569

desperately [adv2] *frightfully*
appallingly, fearfully, hopelessly, shockingly; SEE CONCEPT 403

desperation [n1] *hopelessness*
agony, anguish, anxiety, concern, dejection, depression, desolation, despair, despondency, discomfort, disconsolateness, distraction, distress, fear, gloom, grief, heartache, hopelessness, melancholy, misery, pain, pang, sorrow, torture, trouble, unhappiness, worry; SEE CONCEPT 410

desperation [n2] *rashness*
carelessness, defiance, foolhardiness, frenzy, heedlessness, impetuosity, madness, recklessness; SEE CONCEPT 633

despicable [adj] *hateful; beyond contempt*
abject, awful, base, bastard, beastly, cheap, contemptible, degrading, detestable, dirty, disgraceful, disreputable, down, ignominious, infamous, insignificant, loathsome, low, low-life*, mean, no-good*, pitiful, reprehensible, shameful, slimy*, sordid, vile, worthless, wretched; SEE CONCEPTS 404,570

despise [v] *look down on*
abhor, abominate, allergic to*, contemn, deride, detest, disdain, disregard, eschew, execrate, feel contempt for, flout, hate, have no use for*, loathe, look down nose at*, misprize, neglect, put down*, reject, renounce, repudiate, revile, scorn, shun, slight, snub, spurn, undervalue, wipe out*; SEE CONCEPT 29

despite [prep] *in spite of, regardless of*
against, although, even though, even with, in contempt of, in defiance of, in the face of, notwithstanding, undeterred by; SEE CONCEPT 544

despoil [v] *ravage, destroy*
denude, depopulate, depredate, deprive, desecrate, desolate, devastate, devour, dispossess, divest, loot, maraud, pillage, plunder, raid, rifle, rob, sack, spoil, spoliate, strip, vandalize, waste, wreak havoc, wreck; SEE CONCEPT 252

despondent [adj] *depressed*
all torn up*, blue*, bummed-out*, cast-down, dejected, despairing, disconsolate, discouraged, disheartened, dispirited, doleful, down, downcast, downhearted, forlorn, gloomy, glum, griefstricken, grieving, hopeless, in a blue funk*, in despair, in the pits*, low, low-spirited, melancholy, miserable, morose, mourning, sad, shot down*, sorrowful, woebegone, wretched; SEE CONCEPT 403

despot [n] *dictator*
autocrat, czar, duce, Hitler*, monocrat, oppressor, slave driver, strong man, tyrant; SEE CONCEPTS 354,412

destination [n] *goal; place one wants to go*
aim, ambition, design, end, harbor, haven, intention, journey's end, landing-place, object, objective, purpose, resting-place, station, stop, target, terminal, terminus; SEE CONCEPTS *198,659*

destine [v] *predetermine, ordain*
allot, appoint, assign, consecrate, decide, decree, dedicate, design, determine, devote, doom, doom to, earmark*, fate, foreordain, intend, mark out, predestine, preform, preordain, purpose, reserve; SEE CONCEPT *18*

destined [adj1] *bound for, fated in near future*
at hand, brewing*, certain, closed, coming, compelled, compulsory, condemned, designed, directed, doomed, foreordained, forthcoming, hanging over*, impending, ineluctable, inescapable, inevitable, inexorable, in prospect, instant, in store, intended, in the cards*, in the wind*, looming, meant, menacing, near, ordained, overhanging, predesigned, predestined, predetermined, que sera sera*, sealed, settled, stated, that is to be, that will be, threatening, to come, unavoidable, way the ball bounces*; SEE CONCEPTS *537,820*

destined [adj2] *en route, on the road to*
appointed, appropriated, assigned, bent upon, booked, bound for, chosen, consigned, delegated, designated, determined, directed, entrained, heading, ordered to, prepared, routed, scheduled, specified; SEE CONCEPT *584*

destiny [n] *fate*
afterlife, break*, breaks*, certainty, circumstance, conclusion, condition, constellation, course of events, cup, design, divine decree, doom, expectation, finality, foreordination, fortune, future, happenstance, hereafter, horoscope, inevitability, intent, intention, karma, kismet*, lot, luck, Moira, objective, ordinance, portion, predestination, predetermination, prospect, serendipity, the stars*, way the ball bounces*, way the cookie crumbles*, what is written*, wheel of fortune*, world to come*; SEE CONCEPT *679*

destitute [adj] *down and out; wanting*
bankrupt, beggared, bereft, busted, dead broke*, deficient, depleted, deprived of, devoid of, dirt poor*, divested, drained, empty, exhausted, flat*, flat broke*, impecunious, impoverished, indigent, in need of, insolvent, lacking, moneyless, necessitous, needy, on breadline*, on the rocks*, penniless, penurious, pinched, played out*, poor, poverty-stricken, stony, strapped, stripped, totaled, wiped out*, without; SEE CONCEPT *334*

destroy [v] *demolish, devastate*
abort, annihilate, annul, axe*, blot out, break down, butcher*, consume, cream*, crush, damage, deface, desolate, despoil, dismantle, dispatch, end, eradicate, erase, exterminate, extinguish, extirpate, gut*, impair, kill, lay waste, level, liquidate, maim, mar, maraud, mutilate, nuke*, nullify, overturn, quash,

quell, ravage, ravish, raze, ruin, sabotage, shatter, slay, smash, snuff out*, spoliate, stamp out, suppress, swallow up*, tear down, torpedo*, total, trash*, vaporize, waste, wax*, wipe out, wreck, zap*; SEE CONCEPT *252*

destruction [n] *demolition, devastation*
abolishing, abolition, annihilation, assassinating, bane, carnage, crashing, crushing, demolishing, disintegrating, disrupting, dissolving, downfall, elimination, end, eradication, extermination, extinction, extinguishing, extirpation, havoc, invalidating, invalidation, liquidation, loss, massacre, murder, overthrow, ravaging, ruin, ruination, sacking, shattering, slaughter, slaying, subjugation, subversion, subverting, undoing, wreckage, wrecking; SEE CONCEPTS *230,252*

destructive [adj1] *injurious, devastating*
annihilative, baleful, baneful, calamitous, cancerous, cataclysmic, catastrophic, consumptive, cutthroat, damaging, deadly, deleterious, detrimental, dire, disastrous, eradicative, evil, extirpative, fatal, fell, harmful, hurtful, internecine, lethal, lethiferous, mortal, noisome, noxious, pernicious, pestiferous, pestilential, ruinous, slaughterous, suicidal, toxic, venomous, wrackful, wreckful; SEE CONCEPT *537*

destructive [adj2] *hurtful, disparaging*
abrasive, adverse, antagonistic, cankerous, caustic, contrary, corrosive, deleterious, derogatory, detrimental, discouraging, discrediting, erosive, hostile, injurious, invalidating, negative, offensive, opposed, troublesome, undermining, vicious; SEE CONCEPTS *267,537*

detach [v] *disconnect, cut off*
abstract, disaffiliate, disassemble, disassociate, disengage, disentangle, disjoin, dismount, dissociate, disunite, divide, divorce, free, isolate, loose, loosen, part, remove, segregate, separate, sever, sunder, take apart, tear off, uncouple, unfasten, unfix, unhitch, withdraw; SEE CONCEPT *135*

detached [adj1] *disconnected*
alone, apart, discrete, disjoined, divided, emancipated, free, isolate, isolated, loose, loosened, removed, separate, severed, unaccompanied, unconnected; SEE CONCEPT *490*

detached [adj2] *aloof, disinterested; neutral*
abstract, apathetic, casual, cool*, dispassionate, distant, impartial, impersonal, incurious, indifferent, laid-back*, objective, out of it*, poker-faced*, remote, removed, reserved, spaced-out, spacey*, staid, stolid, unbiased, uncommitted, unconcerned, uncurious, uninvolved, unpassioned, unprejudiced, withdrawn; SEE CONCEPTS *401,404*

detachment [n1] *disconnection*
disengagement, disjoining, dissolution, disunion, division, divorce, divorcement, partition, rupture, separation, severing, split-up; SEE CONCEPTS *388,747*

detachment [n2] *aloofness*
brown study*, coldness, coolness, disinterestedness, dreaminess, impartiality, incuriosity, indifference,

neutrality, nonpartisanship, objectivity, preoccupation, remoteness, reverie, unconcern, woolgathering*; SEE CONCEPT *633*

detachment [n3] *military troop*
army, body, detail, division, force, organization, party, patrol, special force, squad, task force, troupe, unit; SEE CONCEPT *322*

detail [n1] *feature, specific aspect*
ABCs*, accessory, article, brass tacks*, chapter and verse*, circumstantiality, component, count, cue, design, dope*, element, fact, factor, fine point, fraction, item, meat and potatoes*, minor point, minutia, nicety, nitty-gritty*, nuts and bolts*, part, particular, peculiarity, plan, point, portion, respect, schedule, singularity, specialty, specific, specification, structure, technicality, thing, trait, trivia, triviality; SEE CONCEPT *831*

detail [n2] *military troop*
army, assignment, body, detachment, duty, fatigue, force, kitchen police, KP*, organization, party, special force, squad, unit; SEE CONCEPT *322*

detail [v1] *specify, make clear*
analyze, catalog, circumstantiate, communicate, delineate, depict, describe, designate, elaborate, embellish, enumerate, epitomize, exhibit, fly speck*, get down to brass tacks*, individualize, itemize, lay out, narrate, particularize, portray, produce, quote chapter and verse*, recapitulate, recite, recount, rehearse, relate, report, reveal, set forth, show, specialize, specificate, spell out, spread, stipulate, summarize, sweat details*, tell, uncover; SEE CONCEPTS *55,57,60*

detail [v2] *assign specific task*
allocate, appoint, assign, charge, commission, delegate, detach, send; SEE CONCEPTS *50,88*

detailed [adj] *itemized, particularized*
abundant, accurate, all-inclusive, amplified, at length, blow-by-blow*, circumstantial, circumstantiated, clocklike, complete, complicated, comprehensive, copious, definite, described, developed, disclosed, elaborate, elaborated, enumerated, exact, exhausting, exhaustive, finicky*, full, fussy*, individual, individualized, intricate, meticulous, minute, narrow, nice, particular, point-by-point, precise, seriatim, specific, specified, thorough, unfolded; SEE CONCEPT *557*

detain [v] *hold, keep back; arrest*
apprehend, bog down*, bust*, buttonhole*, check, confine, constrain, decelerate, delay, hang up*, hinder, hold, hold up*, ice*, impede, inhibit, intern, jail, keep, mire, nab*, pick up, pinch*, pull in*, put away*, reserve, restrain, retard, run in, send up, set back, slow down, slow up, withhold; SEE CONCEPTS *191,317*

detect [v] *discover*
ascertain, catch, descry, dig up*, disclose, distinguish, encounter, espy, expose, find, hit on*, hit upon*, identify, meet, meet with, nose out*, note,

notice, observe, recognize, reveal, scent, see, smell out*, smoke out*, spot, stumble on, track down, tumble into, turn up, uncover, unmask, wise up to*; SEE CONCEPTS *38,183*

detection [n] *discovery*
apprehension, disclosure, espial, exposé, exposure, ferreting out, find, revelation, strike, tracking down, uncovering, unearthing, unmasking; SEE CONCEPTS *38,183*

detective [n] *investigator of crime*
agent, analyst, bird dog*, bloodhound*, bull*, constable, cop, dick*, eavesdropper, eye*, fed*, fink*, flatfoot*, G-man*, gumshoe*, informer, nark*, P.I.*, peeper*, plainclothesman/woman, policeman/woman, private eye, private investigator, prosecutor, reporter, roper, scout, sergeant, shadow*, shamus*, Sherlock Holmes*, shoofly*, sleuth, slewfoot*, snoop*, spy, tail*; SEE CONCEPT *348*

detention [n] *confinement, imprisonment*
apprehension, arrest, arrestation, bust*, custody, delay, detainment, hindrance, holding back, holding pen*, immurement, impediment, incarceration, internment, keeping in, nab, pen*, pickup, pinch*, quarantine, restraint, retention, time up the river*, withholding; SEE CONCEPTS *191,317*

deter [v] *check, inhibit from action*
act like wet blanket*, avert, block, caution, chill, cool, damp, dampen, daunt, debar, disadvise, discourage, dissuade, divert, forestall, forfend, frighten, hinder, impede, intimidate, obstruct, obviate, preclude, prevent, prohibit, put damper on, put off, restrain, rule out, scare, shut out, stave off, stop, talk out of, throw cold water on*, turn off, warn; SEE CONCEPT *121*

deteriorate [v] *decay, degenerate*
adulterate, alloy, become worse, be worse for wear*, break, corrode, corrupt, crumble, debase, debilitate, decline, decompose, degrade, deprave, depreciate, descend, disimprove, disintegrate, ebb, fade, fail, fall apart, flag, go downhill*, go to pieces*, go to pot*, go to the dogs*, hit the skids*, impair, injure, languish, lapse, lessen, lose it, lose quality, lower, mar, pervert, regress, retrograde, retrogress, rot, sink, skid, slide, spoil, undermine, vitiate, weaken, wear away, worsen; SEE CONCEPT *698*

deterioration [n] *decay, degeneration*
abasement, adulteration, atrophy, corrosion, crumbling, debasement, decadence, decaying, declension, declination, decline, decomposition, degenerateness, degradation, degringolade, depreciation, descent, devaluation, dilapidation, disintegration, dislocation, disrepair, downfall, downgrade, downturn, drop, fall, lapse, lessening, perversion, retrogression, rotting, ruin, slump, spoiling, vitiation, worsening; SEE CONCEPTS *230,698*

determination [n1] *perseverance*
assurance, backbone*, boldness, bravery, certainty, certitude, constancy, conviction, courage, dauntless-

ness, decision, dedication, doggedness, dogmatism, drive, energy, fearlessness, firmness, fortitude, grit, guts*, hardihood, heart*, independence, indomitability, intrepidity, nerve*, obstinacy, persistence, pluck*, purpose, purposefulness, resoluteness, resolution, resolve, self-confidence, single-mindedness, spine*, spunk*, steadfastness, stiff upper lip*, stubbornness, tenacity, valor, willpower; SEE CONCEPTS *411,657*

determination [*n2*] *conclusion*
decision, judgment, measurement, opinion, perception, purpose, resolution, resolve, result, settlement, solution, verdict, visualization; SEE CONCEPTS *685,689*

determine [*v1*] *conclude, decide*
actuate, arbitrate, call the shots, cinch, clinch, complete, dispose, drive, end, figure, finish, fix upon, halt, impel, incline, induce, move, nail down*, opt, ordain, persuade, pin down*, predispose, regulate, resolve, rule, settle, take a decision, tap, terminate, ultimate, wind up*, wrap up*; SEE CONCEPTS *18,35,234*

determine [*v2*] *discover, find out*
add up to, ascertain, boil down to*, catch on, certify, check, demonstrate, detect, divine, establish, figure, figure out, have a hunch*, hear, learn, make out, see, size up, tell, tumble, unearth, verify, work out; SEE CONCEPTS *15,31*

determine [*v3*] *choose, decide*
destine, doom, elect, establish, fate, finger*, fix, foreordain, make up mind, predestine, predetermine, preform, preordain, purpose, resolve, settle; SEE CONCEPT *18*

determine [*v4*] *dictate, govern, regulate*
affect, bound, circumscribe, command, condition, control, decide, delimit, devise, direct, impel, impose, incline, induce, influence, invent, lead, limit, manage, mark off, measure, modify, plot, rule, shape; SEE CONCEPT *94*

determined [*adj*] *driven, persistent*
bent, bent on, buckled down, constant, decided, decisive, dogged, earnest, firm, fixed, hard-as-nails*, hardboiled*, intent, mean business*, obstinate, on ice*, pat, persevering, purposeful, resolute, resolved, serious, set, set on, settled, single-minded, solid, steadfast, strong-minded, strong-willed, stubborn, tenacious, unfaltering, unflinching, unhesitating, unwavering; SEE CONCEPTS *404,542*

deterrent [*n*] *impediment, restraint*
bridle, check, curb, defense, determent, discouragement, disincentive, hindrance, leash, obstacle, preventative, preventive, rein, shackle; SEE CONCEPT *680*

detest [*v*] *hate; feel disgust toward*
abhor, abominate, be allergic to, despise, dislike intensely, down on, execrate, feel aversion toward, feel hostility toward, feel repugnance toward, have

no use for*, loathe, recoil from, reject, repudiate; SEE CONCEPT *29*

detestable [*adj*] *loathsome, abominable*
abhorred, abhorrent, accursed, atrocious, awful, despicable, disgusting, execrable, godawful*, grody*, gross*, hateable, hateful, heinous, horrid, lousy, low-down, maggot, monstrous, obnoxious, odious, offensive, outrageous, repugnant, repulsive, revolting, rotten, shocking, sorry, vile; SEE CONCEPTS *529,542*

dethrone [*v*] *oust*
degrade, depose, discrown, dismiss, displace, oust, uncrown, unmake; SEE CONCEPTS *298,320*

detonate [*v*] *set off bomb*
bang, blast, blow up, burst, discharge, explode, fulminate, kablooey*, let go, mushroom*, push the button, shoot off, touch off, va-voom*; SEE CONCEPT *179*

detour [*n*] *indirect course*
alternate route, back road, branch, bypass, bypath, byway, circuit, circuitous route, circumbendibus*, circumnavigation, circumvention, crotch, deviation, divergence, diversion, fork, roundabout way, runaround, secondary highway, service road, substitute, temporary route; SEE CONCEPT *501*

detract [*v*] *take away a part; lessen*
backbite*, belittle, blister, cheapen, cut rate, decrease, decry, depreciate, derogate, devaluate, diminish, discount, discredit, disesteem, draw away, knock*, laugh at, lower, minimize, misprize, reduce, subtract from, underrate, undervalue, vilipend, withdraw, write off; SEE CONCEPTS *52,54,236,247*

detraction [*n*] *misrepresentation; slander*
abuse, aspersion, backbiting*, backstabbing*, belittlement, calumny, damage, defamation, denigration, deprecation, derogation, disesteem, disparagement, harm, hit, hurt, injury, injustice, innuendo, insinuation, knock*, libel, libeling, lie, maligning, minimization, muckraking*, obloquy, pejorative, revilement, ridicule, running down*, scandal, scandalmongering, scurrility, slam, slandering, smear campaign*, tale, traducement, traducing, vilification, vituperation, wrong; SEE CONCEPTS *52,54,63*

detriment [*n*] *disadvantage*
damage, disability, disservice, drawback, handicap, harm, hurt, impairment, injury, liability, loss, marring, mischief, prejudice, spoiling; SEE CONCEPTS *309,674*

detrimental [*adj*] *damaging, disadvantageous*
adverse, bad, baleful, deleterious, destructive, disturbing, evil, harmful, hurtful, ill, inimical, injurious, mischievous, negative, nocuous, pernicious, prejudicial, unfavorable; SEE CONCEPTS *537,570*

devalue [*v*] *depreciate*
cheapen, cut rate, debase, decrease, decry, devalorize, devaluate, knock off, lower, mark down, nose dive, revalue, take down, underrate, undervalue, write down, write off; SEE CONCEPTS *330,335*

devastate [v] *demolish, destroy*
depredate, desecrate, desolate, despoil, devour, do one in*, lay waste, level, pillage, plunder, raid, ravage, raze, ruin, sack, smash, spoil, spoliate, stamp out*, take apart, total*, trash*, waste, wipe off map*, wreck; SEE CONCEPTS *246,252*

devastation [n] *destruction*
confusion, defoliation, demolition, depredation, desolation, havoc, loss, pillage, plunder, ravages, ruin, ruination, spoliation, waste; SEE CONCEPT *674*

develop [v1] *cultivate, prosper*
advance, age, enroot, establish, evolve, expand, flourish, foster, grow, grow up, maturate, mature, mellow, progress, promote, ripen, thrive; SEE CONCEPTS *253,427,704*

develop [v2] *expand, work out*
actualize, advance, amplify, augment, beautify, broaden, build up, cultivate, deepen, dilate, elaborate, enlarge, enrich, evolve, exploit, extend, finish, heighten, improve, intensify, lengthen, magnify, materialize, perfect, polish, promote, realize, refine, spread, strengthen, stretch, unfold, widen; SEE CONCEPTS *700,775*

develop [v3] *begin; occur*
acquire, arise, befall, betide, break, break out, breed, chance, come about, come off, commence, contract, ensue, establish, follow, form, generate, go, happen, invest, originate, pick up, result, start, transpire; SEE CONCEPT *119*

develop [v4] *unfold; be made known*
account for, acquire, actualize, disclose, disentangle, elaborate, evolve, exhibit, explain, explicate, foretell, form, materialize, produce, reach, realize, recount, state, uncoil, uncover, unfurl, unravel, unroll, untwist, unwind; SEE CONCEPTS *60,261*

development [n1] *growth*
adding to, addition, adulthood, advance, advancement, advancing, augmentation, augmenting, boost, buildup, developing, elaborating, enlargement, evolution, evolvement, evolving, expansion, flowering, growing, hike, improvement, increase, increasing, making progress, maturation, maturing, maturity, ongoing, perfecting, progress, progression, reinforcement, reinforcing, ripening, spread, spreading, unfolding, unraveling, upgrowth, upping; SEE CONCEPTS *700,704,775*

development [n2] *happening, incident*
change, circumstance, conclusion, denouement, event, eventuality, eventuation, issue, materialization, occurrence, outcome, phenomenon, result, situation, transpiration, turn of events, upshot; SEE CONCEPT *3*

deviant [adj] *abnormal, different*
aberrant, anomalous, atypical, bent, deviate, deviative, devious, divergent, freaky, heretical, heteroclite, irregular, kinky, off-key, perverse, perverted, preternatural, queer, twisted, unorthodox, unrepre-

sentative, untypical, variant, varying, wandering, wayward, weird; SEE CONCEPT *564*

deviate [v] *stray from normal path*
aberrate, angle off, avert, bear off, bend, bend the rules*, break pattern, circumlocate, contrast, deflect, depart, depart from, differ, digress, divagate, diverge, drift, edge off*, err, get around, go amiss, go haywire*, go off on tangent*, go out of control*, go out of way, leave beaten path*, not conform, part, shy, swerve, swim against stream*, take a turn, turn, turn aside, vary, veer, wander; SEE CONCEPTS *195,665,697*

deviation [n] *change, departure*
aberration, alteration, anomaly, breach, crotch, deflection, detour, difference, digression, discrepancy, disparity, divergence, diversion, fluctuation, fork, hereticism, inconsistency, irregularity, modification, shift, transgression, turning, variance, variation; SEE CONCEPTS *665,697,738*

device [n1] *instrument, tool*
accessory, agent, apparatus, appliance, arrangement, article, construction, contraption, contrivance, creation, doohickey*, equipment, expedient, gadget, gear, gimmick, implement, invention, machine, makeshift, material, means, mechanism, medium, outfit, resort, resource, rigging*, Rube Goldberg invention*, shift, tackle, thingamabob*, thingamajig*, utensil, whatchamacallit*, whatnot*, whatsit*; SEE CONCEPTS *463,499*

device [n2] *ploy, scheme, maneuver*
artifice, cabal, chicanery, clever move, craft, craftiness, cunningness, design, dodge, evasion, expedient, fake, feint, finesse, gambit, game, gimmick, improvisation, loophole*, machination, method, pattern, plan, plot, project, proposition, purpose, racket, ruse, shift, stratagem, strategy, stunt, subterfuge, trap, trick, wile; SEE CONCEPT *660*

device [n3] *symbol, emblem*
badge, colophon, crest, design, ensign, figure, insignia, logo, motif, motto, pattern, scroll, sign, slogan, token; SEE CONCEPT *284*

devil [n] *demon*
adversary, archfiend, beast, Beelzebub, bête noire, brute, common enemy, dastard, diablo, dybuk, enfant terrible*, evil one, fiend, hellion, imp, knave, Lucifer, Mephistopheles, monster, ogre, Prince of Darkness, rogue, Satan, scamp, scoundrel, the dickens*, villain; SEE CONCEPTS *370,412*

devilish [adj] *wicked*
accursed, atrocious, bad, brutish, cloven-footed, cursed, damnable, demoniac, demonic, detestable, diabolic, diabolical, evil, execrable, fiendish, hellborn, hellish, infernal, inhuman, iniquitous, Mephistophelian, nefarious, satanic, serpentine, unhallowed, villainous; SEE CONCEPT *545*

devious [adj1] *dishonest, crafty*
artful, calculating, crooked, deceitful, dishonorable, double-dealing, duplicitous, errant, erring, evasive,

faking one out*, fishy*, foxy*, fraudulent, guileful, indirect, insidious, insincere, not straightforward, oblique, obliquitous, playing games, playing politics*, put on, roundabout, scheming, shady, shifty, shrewd, sly, sneaking, sneaky, surreptitious, treacherous, tricky, underhanded, wily; SEE CONCEPTS *401,404*

devious [adj2] *crooked; indirect*
ambiguous, bending, circuitous, confounding, confusing, curving, detouring, deviating, digressing, digressory, diverting, errant, erratic, excursive, flexuous, misleading, obscure, out-of-the-way, rambling, remote, removed, roundabout, serpentine, straying, tortuous, twisting, wandering; SEE CONCEPT *581*

devise [v] *conceive, dream up*
ad-lib, arrange, blueprint*, brainstorm*, cast, chart, cogitate, come up with, concoct, construct, contrive, cook up*, craft, create, design, discover, dope out*, fake it, forge, form, formulate, frame*, get off*, hatch, head trip*, imagine, improvise, intrigue, invent, machinate, make up, mastermind*, plan, play it by ear*, plot, prepare, project, scheme, shape, spark, think up, throw together, trump up*, vamp, whip up*, work out; SEE CONCEPTS *36,43*

devoid [adj] *empty, wanting*
bare, barren, bereft, deficient, denuded, destitute, free from, innocent, lacking, needed, sans, unprovided with, vacant, void, without; SEE CONCEPTS *483,485*

devote [v] *commit one's energies, thoughts*
allot, apply, apportion, appropriate, assign, bestow, bless, concern oneself, confide, consecrate, consign, dedicate, donate, enshrine, entrust, give, give away, hallow, hand out, occupy oneself, pledge, present, reserve, sanctify, set apart, vow; SEE CONCEPTS *17,108,112*

devoted [adj] *committed, loyal*
adherent, affectionate, ardent, behind one, caring, concerned, consecrated, constant, crazy about*, dear, dedicated, devout, doting, dutiful, faithful, fervid, fond, gone on*, lovesome, loving, staunch, steadfast, stuck on*, thoughtful, true, true-blue*, wild about*, zealous; SEE CONCEPT *542*

devotee [n] *ardent supporter; fan*
addict, adherent, admirer, aficionado, amateur, believer, booster, buff, disciple, enthusiast, fanatic, fancier, fiend, follower, groupie, habitué, junkie, lover, rooter, supporter, votarient, votary; SEE CONCEPT *423*

devotion [n] *commitment; loyalty*
adherence, adoration, affection, allegiance, ardor, attachment, consecration, constancy, dedication, deference, devotedness, devotement, devoutness, earnestness, enthusiasm, faithfulness, fealty, fervor, fidelity, fondness, intensity, love, observance, passion, piety, reverence, sanctity, service, sincerity, spirituality, worship, zeal; SEE CONCEPTS *32,657*

devour [v] *swallow, consume*
absorb, annihilate, appreciate, be engrossed by, be preoccupied, bolt, bolt down*, chow down*, cram*, delight in, destroy, dispatch, do compulsively, do voraciously, drink in, eat, enjoy, exhaust, feast on, feed on, gloat over, gobble, gorge*, go through, gulp, guzzle, hoover*, imbibe, ingest, inhale, partake of, pig out*, polish off*, ravage, rejoice in, relish, revel in, scarf down*, spend, stuff, take, take in, use up, waste, wipe out, wolf*, wolf down*; SEE CONCEPTS *169,225*

devout [adj] *sincerely believing; devoted*
adherent, adoring, ardent, deep, earnest, faithful, fervent, fervid, genuine, godly, goody-goody*, goody two-shoes*, heart-and-soul, heartfelt, holy, intense, orthodox, passionate, pietistic, pious, prayerful, profound, religious, reverent, revering, serious, sincere, venerating, worshiping, zealous; SEE CONCEPT *542*

dexterity [n] *aptitude, ability*
address, adroitness, aptness, art, artistry, cleverness, craft, cunning, deftness, effortlessness, expertise, expertness, facility, finesse, handiness, ingenuity, knack, know-how, mastery, neatness, nimbleness, proficiency, readiness, skill, skillfulness, smoothness, tact, touch; SEE CONCEPTS *409,630*

dexterous [adj] *ingenious, proficient*
able, active, acute, adept, adroit, agile, apt, artful, canny, clever, crack*, crackerjack*, deft, effortless, expert, facile, handy, having the know-how*, masterly, neat, nimble, nimble-fingered, prompt, quick, savvy, skilled, skillful, slick, sly, smooth; SEE CONCEPTS *402,527*

diabolic [adj] *evil, fiendish*
atrocious, cruel, damnable, demoniac, demonic, devilish, hellish, impious, infernal, Mephistophelian, monstrous, nasty, nefarious, satanic, serpentine, shocking, unhallowed, unpleasant, vicious, vile, villainous, wicked; SEE CONCEPT *545*

diagnose [v] *identify problem, disease*
analyze, determinate, determine, diagnosticate, distinguish, interpret, investigate, pinpoint, place, pronounce, recognize, spot; SEE CONCEPTS *38,310*

diagnosis [n] *identification of problem, disease*
analysis, conclusion, examination, interpretation, investigation, opinion, pronouncement, scrutiny, summary; SEE CONCEPTS *283,689*

diagonal [adj] *angled*
askew, bevel, beveled, bias, biased, cater-cornered, catty-cornered, cornerways, cross, crossways, crosswise, inclining, kitty-cornered*, oblique, skewing, slanted, slanting, transversal, transverse; SEE CONCEPT *581*

diagonally [adv] *at an angle*
askew, aslant, cater-corner, catty-corner, cornerwise, crosswise, kitty-corner*, obliquely, on a slant, on the bias, slantingways, slantways, slantwise, slaunchways; SEE CONCEPT *581*

diagram [n] *drawing, sketch of form or plan*
big picture*, blueprint, chart, description, design, draft, figure, floor plan, game, game plan, ground plan, layout, outline, perspective, representation, rough draft; SEE CONCEPTS *625,660*

dial [v] *tune to desired position*
punch, ring, rotate, turn, twist, wheel, zero in on*; SEE CONCEPT *201*

dialect [n] *local speech*
accent, argot, can, idiom, jargon, language, lingo, localism, patois, patter, pronunciation, provincialism, regionalism, slang, terminology, tongue, vernacular, vocabulary; SEE CONCEPT *276*

dialectic [n] *logic, reasoning*
argumentation, contention, debate, deduction, discussion, disputation, forensic, logical argument, mooting, persuasion, polemics, question-and-answer method, ratiocination; SEE CONCEPT *37*

dialectic [adj] *logical, rational*
analytic, argumentative, controversial, dialectical, persuasive, polemical, rationalistic; SEE CONCEPT *529*

dialogue/dialog [n] *talk, exchange of ideas*
chat, colloquy, communication, confab*, confabulation, conference, conversation, converse, discourse, discussion, duologue, interlocution, lines*, parlance, parley, powwow, remarks, repartee, script, sides, small talk*; SEE CONCEPTS *56,278*

diameter [n] *measurement across object*
bore, breadth, broadness, caliber, module, width; SEE CONCEPT *760*

diametric/diametrical [adj] *opposed, conflicting*
adverse, antipodal, antipodean, antithetical, contradictory, contrary, contrasting, converse, counter, facing, opposite, polar, reverse; SEE CONCEPT *564*

diaphanous [adj] *fine, see-through*
chiffon, clear, cobweblike, delicate, filmy, flimsy, gauzy, gossamer, light, pellucid, pure, sheer, thin, translucent, transparent; SEE CONCEPTS *490,606*

diary [n] *recounting of activities in writing*
account, agenda, appointment book, chronicle, daily record, daybook, engagement book, journal, log, minutes, notebook, record; SEE CONCEPT *283*

diatribe [n] *harangue, criticism*
abuse, castigation, denunciation, disputation, invective, jeremiad, objection, onslaught, philippic, reviling, screed, stricture, tirade, vituperation; SEE CONCEPT *52*

dicey [adj] *risky*
capricious, chancy, dangerous, difficult, erratic, fluctuant, iffy*, incalculable, ticklish, tricky, uncertain, unpredictable, whimsical; SEE CONCEPTS *535,552*

dicker [v] *bargain; argue about*
barter, buy and sell, chaffer, cut a deal*, haggle*, hammer out a deal*, huckster*, negotiate, palter, trade, work out a deal*; SEE CONCEPTS *46,330*

dictate [n] *command; rule*
behest, bidding, code, decree, dictum, direction, edict, fiat, injunction, law, mandate, order, ordi-

nance, precept, principle, requirement, statute, ultimatum, word; SEE CONCEPTS *274,318,687*

dictate [v1] *command; give instructions*
bid, bulldoze*, call the play*, call the shots*, call the tune*, charge, control, decree, direct, enjoin, govern, guide, impose, instruct, lay down, lay down the law, lead, manage, ordain, order, prescribe, pronounce, put foot down*, read the riot act*, regiment, rule, set, take the reins*, walk heavy*; SEE CONCEPTS *53,60*

dictate [v2] *read out for the record*
compose, deliver, draft correspondence, emit, formulate, give account, give forth, interview, orate, prepare draft, record, say, speak, talk, transmit, utter, verbalize; SEE CONCEPTS *60,324*

dictator [n] *absolute ruler*
absolutist, adviser, authoritarian, autocrat, baron, boss, Caesar, caliph, chief, commander, czar, despot, disciplinarian, duce, emir, fascist, Hitler*, kaiser, lama, leader, lord, magnate, martinet, master, mogul, oligarch, oppressor, overlord, rajah, ringleader, sachem, shah, sheik, slavedriver, strongman, sultan, taskmaster, totalitarian, tycoon, tyrant, usurper; SEE CONCEPT *354*

dictatorial [adj] *tyrannical, authoritarian*
absolute, arbitrary, arrogant, authoritative, autocratic, bossy, clamorous, crack-the-whip*, despotic, dictative, doctrinaire, dogmatic, domineering, egotistic, firm, haughty, imperative, imperious, ironhanded, lordly, magisterial, masterful, oppressive, overbearing, peremptory, pompous, proud, stern, throwing weight around, totalitarian, unlimited, unrestricted; SEE CONCEPT *542*

dictatorship [n] *absolute rule*
absolutism, authoritarianism, autocracy, coercion, despotism, fascism, garrison state, Nazism, reign of terror*, totalitarianism, tyranny, unlimited rule; SEE CONCEPTS *133,299,641*

diction [n] *style of speech; articulation*
command of language, delivery, elocution, eloquence, enunciation, expression, fluency, gift of gab*, inflection, intonation, language, line, lingo, locution, oratory, parlance, phrase, phraseology, phrasing, pronunciation, rhetoric, usage, verbalism, verbiage, vocabulary, wordage, wording; SEE CONCEPTS *47,276*

dictionary [n] *book of word meanings*
concordance, cyclopedia, encyclopedia, glossary, language, lexicon, palaver, promptory, reference, terminology, vocabulary, wordbook; SEE CONCEPT *280*

dictum [n1] *saying; proverb*
adage, aphorism, apothegm, axiom, brocard, gnome, maxim, moral, motto, precept, rule, saw, truism; SEE CONCEPTS *278,689*

dictum [n2] *decree, pronouncement*
affirmation, assertion, command, declaration, dictate, edict, fiat, order; SEE CONCEPT *278*

didactic [adj] *educational*
academic, advisory, donnish, edifying, enlightening, exhortative, expository, homiletic, hortative, instructive, moral, moralizing, pedagogic, pedantic, preachy, preceptive, schoolmasterist, sermonic, sermonizing, teacherish, teacherly, teachy; SEE CONCEPT 548

die [v1] *pass away; stop living*
be no more*, be taken, breathe one's last*, cease to exist, conk*, croak*, decease, demise, depart, drop, drop dead, drown, expire, finish, give up ghost*, go way of all flesh*, kick the bucket*, perish, relinquish life, rest in peace, succumb, suffocate; SEE CONCEPT 304

die [v2] *wither, dwindle*
abate, bate, break down, crumble, decay, decline, degenerate, deteriorate, dilapidate, diminish, disappear, droop, ease off, ebb, end, expire, fade, fade away, fade out, fail, fall, fizzle out*, go bad*, go downhill*, halt, lapse, let up, lose power, melt away, moderate, molder, pass, peter out*, rankle, recede, retrograde, rot, run down, run low, run out, sink, slacken, stop, subside, vanish, wane, weaken, wear away, wilt; SEE CONCEPTS 469,698

diehard [n] *overenthusiastic person*
bitter ender*, Bourbon*, dyed-in-the-wool*, extremist, fanatic, fogy, fundamentalist, intransigent, mossback*, old liner*, praetorian, pullback*, reactionary, right, rightist, right-winger, standpat, standpatter, stick-in-the-mud*, Tory*, true blue*, ultraconservative, zealot; SEE CONCEPTS 359,423

die-hard [adj] *uncompromising*
conservative, convinced, dyed-in-the-wool*, extremist, firm, fogyish, immovable, inflexible, intransigent, old-line*, orthodox, Philistine, reactionary, right, standpat, Tory*, traditionalistic, ultraconservative, unreconstructed; SEE CONCEPTS 404,542

diet [n1] *abstinence from food*
dietary, fast, nutritional therapy, regime, regimen, restriction, starvation, weight-reduction plan; SEE CONCEPT 660

diet [n2] *daily intake of food*
aliment, bite, comestibles, commons, daily bread, edibles, fare, goodies, grubbery, menu, nourishment, nutriment, nutrition, provisions, rations, snack, subsistence, sustenance, viands, victuals; SEE CONCEPTS 457,459

diet [v] *abstain from food*
count calories*, eat sparingly, fall off, fast, go without, lose weight, reduce, skinny down*, slim, slim down, starve, tighten belt*, watch weight*; SEE CONCEPT 169

differ [v1] *be dissimilar, distinct*
alter, bear no resemblance, be distinguished from, be off beaten path*, be unlike, clash with, conflict with, contradict, contrast, depart from, deviate from, digress, disagree, divaricate from, diverge, diversify, jar with, lack resemblance, modify, not conform, not

look like, qualify, reverse, run counter to, show contrast, sing different tune*, stand apart, take exception, turn, vary; SEE CONCEPT 665

differ [v2] *clash; hold opposing views*
bicker*, bump heads*, clash, contend, debate, demur, disaccord, disagree, discept, discord, dispute, dissent, divide, fight, go after each other, go at it*, hit a clinker*, hit a sour note*, jar*, lock horns*, object, oppose, protest against, quarrel, squabble, take issue, vary, war; SEE CONCEPT 46

difference [n1] *dissimilarity, distinctness*
aberration, alteration, anomaly, antithesis, asymmetry, change, characteristic, contrariety, contrariness, contrast, departure, deviation, differentiation, digression, discongruity, discrepancy, disparity, dissemblance, distinction, divergence, diversity, exception, heterogeneity, idiosyncrasy, inequality, irregularity, nonconformity, opposition, particularity, peculiarity, separateness, separation, singularity, unconformity, unlikeness, unorthodoxness, variance, variation, variety; SEE CONCEPT 665

difference [n2] *opposing views*
argument, beef*, blowup*, bone to pick*, brannigan, brawl, brush*, brush-off*, catamaran, clash, conflict, contention, contrariety, contretemps, controversy, debate, disaccord, disagreement, discord, discordance, dispute, dissension, dissent, dissidence, disunity, dustup*, estrangement, hassle, quarrel, row*, run-in*, scrap*, set-to*, spat*, strife, tiff*, variance, words*, wrangle; SEE CONCEPTS 46,388

different [adj1] *dissimilar, unlike*
a far cry from*, altered, antithetic, at odds, at variance, changed, clashing, colorful, contradistinct, contradistinctive, contrary, contrasting, contrastive, deviating, differential, discrepant, disparate, distant, distinct, distinctive, divergent, divers, diverse, incommensurable, incomparable, inconsistent, individual, like night and day*, mismatched, mismated, offbeat, opposed, other, otherwise, particular, peculiar, poles apart, single, unalike, unequal, unrelated, unsimilar, variant, various; SEE CONCEPTS 487,564,573

different [adj2] *separate, distinct*
another, another story, atypical, bizarre, discrete, distinctive, diverse, especial, express, extraordinary, individual, novel, original, other, out of the ordinary, particular, peculiar, rare, several, singular, something else, special, specialized, specific, startling, strange, uncommon, unconventional, unique, unusual, various; SEE CONCEPT 564

different [adj3] *miscellaneous, various*
anthologized, assorted, asymmetrical, collected, disparate, dissonant, divergent, divers, diverse, diversified, diversiform, heterogeneous, incongruous, inconsistent, indiscriminate, jarring, manifold, many, multifarious, multiform, numerous, omnifarious, omniform, several, some, sundry, varicolored,

varied, variegated, varietal, variform; SEE CONCEPT *772*

differentiate [*v1*] *make a distinction*
antithesize, characterize, comprehend, contrast, demarcate, difference, discern, discrepate, discriminate, distinguish, extricate, individualize, individuate, know, know what's what*, mark, mark off, redline*, separate, set apart, set off, sever, severalize, split hairs*, tell apart, understand; SEE CONCEPTS *15,38*

differentiate [*v2*] *change; make different*
adapt, alter, assort, convert, diversify, mismatch, mismate, modify, transform, variegate, vary; SEE CONCEPT *232*

differently [*adv*] *in another way; otherwise*
abnormally, adversely, antagonistically, antithetically, asymmetrically, conflictingly, contradictorily, contrarily, contrastingly, contrastively, discordantly, disparately, dissimilarly, distinctively, divergently, diversely, hostilely, in a different manner, incompatibly, incongruously, individually, negatively, nonconformably, on the contrary, on the other hand, oppositely, poles apart, separately, uniquely, unorthodoxly, unusually, variously, vice versa; SEE CONCEPT *564*

difficult [*adj1*] *hard on someone; hard to do*
ambitious, arduous, backbreaker*, bothersome, burdensome, challenging, crucial, demanding, difficile, easier said than done*, effortful, exacting, formidable, galling, Gargantuan*, hard, hard-won, heavy, Herculean*, immense, intricate, irritating, labored, laborious, man-sized*, no picnic*, not easy, onerous, operose, painful, problem, problematic, prohibitive, rigid, severe, stiff, strenuous, titanic, toilsome, tough, troublesome, trying, unyielding, uphill, upstream, wearisome; SEE CONCEPT *538*

difficult [*adj2*] *complicated; hard to comprehend*
abstract, abstruse, baffling, bewildering, complex, confounding, confusing, dark, deep, delicate, enigmatic, enigmatical, entangled, esoteric, formidable, hard, hard to explain, hard to solve, hidden, inexplicable, intricate, involved, knotty, labyrinthine, loose, meandering, mysterious, mystical, mystifying, nice, obscure, obstinate, paradoxical, perplexing, problematical, profound, puzzling, rambling, subtle, tangled, thorny, ticklish, troublesome, unclear, unfathomable, unintelligible, vexing; SEE CONCEPT *529*

difficult [*adj3*] *unmanageable socially*
argumentative, bearish, boorish, dark, demanding, fastidious, finicky, fractious, fussy, grim, hard to please, impolite, intractable, irritable, oafish, obstreperous, perverse, picky, refractory, rigid, rude, tiresome, tough, troublesome, trying, unaccommodating, unamenable; SEE CONCEPTS *404,542,555*

difficulty [*n1*] *problem; situation requiring great effort*
adversity, arduousness, awkwardness, barricade, check, complication, crisis, crux, dead end, dead-

lock, deep water*, dilemma, distress, emergency, exigency, fix*, frustration, hardship, hazard, hindrance, hitch*, hot water*, impasse, knot*, labor, laboriousness, mess, misfortune, muddle, obstacle, obstruction, pain, painfulness, paradox, perplexity, pickle*, predicament, quagmire, quandary, scrape*, snag*, stew*, strain, strait, strenuousness, struggle, stumbling block*, tribulation, trouble; SEE CONCEPTS *674,677*

difficulty [*n2*] *mental burden*
ado, aggravation, annoyance, anxiety, bafflement, bother, care, charge, complication, crisis, depression, discouragement, distress, embarrassment, emergency, exigency, frustration, grievance, hangup, harassment, imbroglio, inconvenience, irritation, jam, maze, mess, millstone*, misery, oppression, perplexity, pickle*, pinch, predicament, pressure, puzzle, quandary, ramification, responsibility, scrape*, setback, strain, strait, stress, strife, struggle, to-do*, trouble, vicissitude, weight, worry; SEE CONCEPTS *410,532,690*

difficulty [*n3*] *argument*
altercation, beef*, bickering, controversy, dispute, falling-out*, fight, hassle, misunderstanding, quarrel, squabble, strife, trouble; SEE CONCEPT *46*

diffidence [*n*] *hesitancy; lack of confidence*
backwardness, bashfulness, constraint, doubt, fear, hesitation, humility, insecurity, meekness, modesty, mousiness, reluctance, reserve, self-consciousness, sheepishness, shyness, timidity, timidness, timorousness, unassertiveness; SEE CONCEPT *633*

diffident [*adj*] *hesitant; unconfident*
backward, bashful, blenching, chary, constrained, coy, demure, distrustful, doubtful, dubious, flinching, humble, insecure, meek, modest, mousy, rabbity, reluctant, reserved, retiring, self-conscious, self-effacing, sheepish, shrinking, shy, suspicious, timid, timorous, unassertive, unassuming, unassured, unobtrusive, unpoised, unsure, withdrawn; SEE CONCEPT *401*

diffuse [*adj1*] *spread out*
broadcast, catholic, circulated, diluted, dispersed, disseminated, distributed, expanded, extended, general, prevalent, propagated, radiated, scattered, separated, strewn, thin, unconcentrated, universal, widespread; SEE CONCEPTS *530,583,772*

diffuse [*adj2*] *wordy*
circumlocutory, copious, diffusive, digressive, discursive, dull, exuberant, lavish, lengthy, long, long-winded, loose, meandering, palaverous, profuse, prolix, rambling, random, redundant, vague, verbose, waffling, windy; SEE CONCEPT *267*

diffusion [*n*] *spread; wide distribution*
circulation, dispersal, dispersion, dissemination, dissipation, expansion, propaganda, propagation, scattering; SEE CONCEPTS *634,651*

dig [*n*] *insult*
crack, cut, cutting remark, gibe, innuendo, jeer, quip, slur, sneer, taunt, wisecrack; SEE CONCEPT *54*

dig [v1] *delve into; hollow out*
bore, break up, bulldoze, burrow, cat, channel, clean, concave, deepen, depress, dig down, discover, dredge, drill, drive, enter, excavate, exhume, fork out, go into, gouge, grub, harvest, hoe, investigate, mine, penetrate, pierce, pit, probe, produce, quarry, root, root out, rout, sap, scoop, scoop out, search, shovel, sift, spade, till, tunnel, turn over, uncover, undermine, unearth; SEE CONCEPT *178*

dig [v2] *thrust object into*
drive, gouge, jab, jog, nudge, plunge, poke, prod, punch, ram, sink, stab, stick; SEE CONCEPT *208*

dig [v3] *investigate; discover*
bring to light*, come across, come up with, delve, dig down, expose, extricate, find, go into, inquire, look into, probe, prospect, research, retrieve, root, search, search high and low*, shake down*, sift*, turn inside out*, turn upside down*, uncover, unearth; SEE CONCEPTS *31,103,216*

dig [v4] *enjoy, like*
appreciate, follow, go for*, groove*, love, mind, relish, understand; SEE CONCEPT *32*

dig [v5] *understand*
accept, apprehend, catch, comprehend, follow, grasp, recognize, see, take, take in; SEE CONCEPT *15*

digest [n] *abridgement of something written*
abstract, aperçu, brief, compendium, condensation, epitome, pandect, précis, résumé, short form, sketch, summary, survey, syllabus, sylloge, synopsis; SEE CONCEPT *271*

digest [v1] *assimilate food*
absorb, chymify, consume, dissolve, eat, incorporate, macerate, swallow, take; SEE CONCEPT *169*

digest [v2] *make shorter; abridge*
abbreviate, abstract, boil down, classify, codify, compress, condense, cut, cut down, cut to bone*, decrease, epitomize, get to meat*, inventory, methodize, nutshell*, put in nutshell*, reduce, shorten, sum, summarize, summate, sum up, survey, synopsize, systematize, tabulate, trim; SEE CONCEPTS *236,247*

digest [v3] *come to understand*
absorb, analyze, assimilate, consider, contemplate, deliberate, grasp, master, meditate, ponder, study, take in, think about, think over, understand; SEE CONCEPT *15*

digest [v4] *tolerate, endure*
abide, bear, brook, go, stand, stomach, swallow, take; SEE CONCEPT *23*

dig in [v] *begin with enthusiasm*
bite, burrow, chew, commence, consume, delve, eat, rise, set about, spring, start eating; SEE CONCEPTS *100,169*

digit [n1] *number*
arabic, chiffer, cipher, figure, integer, notation, numeral, symbol, whole number; SEE CONCEPTS *765,784*

digit [n2] *small appendage of animate being*
claw, extremity, fang, feeler, finger, fork, hook, index finger, phalange, pinkie, pointer, ring finger, thumb, toe; SEE CONCEPT *392*

dignified [adj] *honorable*
aristocratic, august, chic, classic, classical, classy, courtly, cultured, decorous, distingué, distinguished, elegant, eminent, exalted, exquisite, formal, gentlemanly, glorious, grand, grave, great, haughty, highbrow*, highfalutin'*, imperial, imperious, imposing, kingly, ladylike, lofty, lordly, magisterial, magnificent, nifty*, noble, of consequence, ornate, princely, proud, queenly, refined, regal, reserved, respected, solemn, somber, stately, sublime, superior, upright; SEE CONCEPTS *404,555,574*

dignify [v] *make honorable; glorify*
adorn, advance, aggrandize, distinguish, elevate, ennoble, erect, exalt, grace, honor, magnify, prefer, promote, raise, sublime, uprear; SEE CONCEPTS *244,700*

dignity [n] *excellence, nobility*
address, cachet, character, consequence, courtliness, culture, decency, decorum, distinction, elevation, eminence, ethics, etiquette, glory, grace, grandeur, gravity, greatness, hauteur, honor, importance, loftiness, majesty, merit, morality, nobleness, perfection, poise, prestige, propriety, quality, rank, regard, renown, respectability, seemliness, self-respect, significance, solemnity, splendor, standing, state, stateliness, station, stature, status, sublimity, virtue, worth, worthiness; SEE CONCEPTS *388,411,668*

digress [v] *stray, deviate*
aberrate, beat about bush*, be diffuse, circumlocute, depart, divagate, drift, excurse, get off the point, get off the subject, get sidetracked, go by way of*, go off on tangent*, long way*, meander, ramble, roam, stray, swerve, turn aside, veer, wander, wander away; SEE CONCEPTS *195,266,697*

digression [n] *deviation; straying*
apostrophe, aside, deflection, departure, detour, difference, discursion, divagation, divergence, diversion, drifting, episode, excursion, excursus, footnote, incident, note, obiter dictum, parenthesis, rambling, variation, wandering; SEE CONCEPTS *278,665,697*

dilapidated [adj] *falling apart; in ruins*
battered, beat-up, broken-down, crumbling, crumbly, crummy*, damaged, decayed, decaying, decrepit, derelict, dingy, dog-eared*, faded, fallen-in, impaired, in a bad way*, injured, marred, neglected, old, ramshackle, ratty*, raunchy, rickety, rinky-dink*, ruined, ruinous, run-down, seedy, shabby, shaky, slummy, tacky, threadbare, tumble-down, uncared for, unimproved, unkempt, used-up, worn-out; SEE CONCEPTS *485,560*

dilate [v] *stretch, widen*
amplify, augment, be profuse, be prolix, broaden, develop, distend, enlarge, expand, expatiate, ex-

pound, extend, increase, inflate, lengthen, prolong, protract, puff out, spin off, swell; SEE CONCEPTS *57,236,245*

dilatory [*adj*] *procrastinating*
backward, behindhand, dallying, delaying, deliberate, laggard, late, lax, lazy, leisurely, lingering, loitering, moratory, neglectful, negligent, putting off, remiss, slack, slow, sluggish, snail-like*, tardy, tarrying, time-wasting, unhasty, unhurried; SEE CONCEPTS *542,799*

dilemma [*n*] *crisis*
bind*, box*, Catch-22*, corner, difficulty, double bind*, embarrassment, fix, hole, hooker*, impasse, jam, mess, mire, perplexity, pickle*, plight, predicament, problem, puzzle, quandary, scrape, spot, strait, tight corner*; SEE CONCEPTS *674,675*

dilettante [*n*] *amateur*
abecedarian, aesthete, connoisseur, dabbler, dallier, greenhorn*, nonprofessional, rookie, smatterer, tenderfoot*, trifler, tyro, uninitiate; SEE CONCEPT *423*

dilettante [*adj*] *amateurish*
artsy fartsy*, dabbling, dilettantish, green*, half-baked*, half-cocked*, rookie, tenderfoot*, unaccomplished, ungifted, unskilled; SEE CONCEPT *527*

diligence [*n*] *perseverance in carrying out action*
activity, alertness, application, assiduity, assiduousness, attention, attentiveness, briskness, care, carefulness, constancy, earnestness, exertion, heed, heedfulness, industry, intensity, intent, intentness, keenness, laboriousness, pertinacity, quickness, sedulousness, vigor; SEE CONCEPTS *657,677*

diligent [*adj*] *persevering, hard-working*
active, assiduous, attentive, busy, careful, conscientious, constant, eager, eager beaver*, earnest, grind*, indefatigable, industrious, laborious, occupied, operose, painstaking, persistent, persisting, pertinacious, plugging*, sedulous, steadfast, studious, tireless, unflagging, unrelenting, untiring; SEE CONCEPTS *326,538,542*

dilute [*v*] *make thinner; weaken*
adulterate, alter, attenuate, cook, cut, decrease, deliquesce, diffuse, diminish, doctor*, doctor up*, irrigate, lace, lessen, liquefy, mitigate, mix, moderate, modify, needle*, phony up*, plant, qualify, reduce, shave*, spike, temper, thin, thin out, water, water down; SEE CONCEPT *250*

diluted/dilute [*adj*] *thinned, weakened*
adulterated, attenuated, cut, impaired, impoverished, laced, light, moderated, reduced, shaved*, spiked, tempered, washy, watered down, waterish, watery, weak, wishy-washy*; SEE CONCEPTS *485,606*

dim [*adj1*] *darkish*
blah, bleary, blurred, caliginous, cloudy, dark, dingy, dreary, dull, dusk, dusky, faded, faint, flat, fuzzy, gloomy, gray, grey, ill-defined, indistinct, lackluster, lightless, mat, monotone, monotonous, murky, muted, obscured, opaque, overcast, pale, poorly lit, shadowy, sullied, tarnished, tenebrous,

unclear, unilluminated, vague, weak; SEE CONCEPT *617*

dim [*adj2*] *unfavorable with regard to opinion*
depressing, disapproving, discouraging, gloomy, skeptical, somber, suspicious, unpromising; SEE CONCEPT *542*

dim [*adj3*] *not very intelligent*
boorish, dense, dim-witted, doltish, dull, dumb, oafish, obtuse, slow, slow on uptake*, stupid, thick*, weak-minded; SEE CONCEPT *402*

dim [*v*] *darken; obscure*
becloud, bedim, befog, blear, blur, cloud, dull, eclipse, fade, fog, haze, lower, muddy, obfuscate, pale, tarnish, turn down; SEE CONCEPTS *250,627*

dimensions/dimension [*n*] *proportions; range*
admeasurement, ambit, amplitude, bigness, bulk, capacity, compass, depth, dimensionality, extension, extensity, extent, greatness, height, importance, largeness, length, magnitude, measure, measurement, reach, scale, scope, size, volume, width; SEE CONCEPTS *730,792*

diminish [*v1*] *become or cause to be less*
abate, abbreviate, attenuate, become smaller, close, contract, curtail, cut, decline, decrease, depreciate, die out, drain, dwindle, ebb, extenuate, fade away, lessen, lower, minify, moderate, peter out, recede, reduce, retrench, shrink, shrivel, slacken, subside, taper, temper, wane, weaken; SEE CONCEPTS *698,776*

diminish [*v2*] *belittle*
abuse, bad-mouth*, cheapen, cut down to size*, decry, demean, depreciate, derogate, detract from, devalue, dispraise, dump on*, give comeuppance*, knock off high horse*, minimize, pan*, poormouth*, put away*, put down*, run down*, tear down*; SEE CONCEPT *54*

diminution [*n*] *lessening, reduction*
abatement, alleviation, contraction, curtailment, cut, cutback, decay, decline, decrease, deduction, retrenchment, weakening; SEE CONCEPTS *698,776*

diminutive [*adj*] *tiny, petite*
bantam, bitsy*, bitty*, button*, Lilliputian, little, midget, mini, miniature, minute, peewee*, pint-sized, pocket, pocket-sized, pygmy, small, teensy*, teensy-weensy*, teeny*, teeny-weeny*, undersize, wee*, weeny*; SEE CONCEPT *789*

din [*n*] *loud, continuous noise*
babel, bedlam, boisterousness, brouhaha*, buzz, clamor, clangor, clash, clatter, commotion, confusion, crash, disquiet, hoo-ha*, hubbub*, hullabaloo*, hurly-burly*, jangle, music, outcry, pandemonium, percussion, racket, row, shout, sound, stridency, tintamarre*, tintinnabulation, tumult, uproar; SEE CONCEPT *595*

dine [*v*] *eat, often formally*
banquet, breakfast, consume, do lunch*, eat out*, fall to*, feast, feed on, lunch, sup, supper; SEE CONCEPT *169*

diner [n] *casual restaurant with varied menu*
Automat*, bistro, booth, café, canteen, chuck wagon*, coffee shop, concession, dump*, eatery*, eating house, facility, fast-food outlet, greasy spoon*, grill, hash house*, ice-cream parlor, lunch counter, lunchroom, lunch wagon, mess hall, quick-lunch, saloon, sandwich shop, snack bar, tearoom; SEE CONCEPT *449*

dingy [adj] *soiled, tacky*
bedimmed, broken-down, colorless, dark, darkish, dilapidated, dim, dirty, discolored, drab, dreary, dull, dusky, faded, gloomy, grimy, muddy, murky, obscure, run-down, seedy, shabby, smirched, somber, sullied, tarnished, threadbare, tired; SEE CONCEPTS *485,617*

dinky [adj] *tiny, small*
bush-league*, dainty, insignificant, lesser, Lilliputian, mini, miniature, minor, minor-league*, neat, petite, secondary, second rate*, small-fry*, small-time*, trim; SEE CONCEPT *789*

dinner [n] *evening meal*
banquet, blowout*, chow*, collation, din-din*, eats*, feast, feedbag*, fete, main meal, major munch*, potluck, principal meal, refection, regale, repast, ribs*, spread*, supper, table d'hôte; SEE CONCEPT *459*

dip [n1] *submersion in liquid*
bath, dive, douche, drenching, ducking, immersion, plunge, soak, soaking, swim; SEE CONCEPT *256*

dip [n2] *something for dunking*
concoction, dilution, infusion, mixture, preparation, solution, suffusion, suspension; SEE CONCEPTS *260,466*

dip [n3] *depression; decline*
basin, concavity, declivity, descent, downslide, downswing, downtrend, drop, fall, fall-off, hole, hollow, inclination, incline, lowering, pitch, sag, sink, sinkage, sinkhole, slip, slope, slump; SEE CONCEPTS *513,697,738*

dip [v1] *put into liquid*
baptize, bathe, douse, drench, duck, dunk, immerse, irrigate, lave, lower, moisten, pitch, plunge, rinse, slop, slosh, soak, souse, splash, steep, submerge, submerse, wash, water, wet; SEE CONCEPTS *201,256*

dip [v2] *lower, descend*
bend, decline, disappear, droop, drop down, fade, fall, go down, incline, nose-dive, plummet, plunge, reach, recede, sag, set, settle, sheer, sink, skew, skid, slant, slip, slope, slue, slump, spiral, subside, swoop, tilt, tumble, veer, verge; SEE CONCEPT *181*

dip [v3] *scoop, ladle*
bail, bale, bucket, decant, dish, draft off, draw, draw out, dredge, handle, lade, lift, offer, reach into, shovel, spoon, strain; SEE CONCEPTS *196,225*

dip into [v] *try, sample*
appropriate, browse, dabble, flip through, get, glance at, glance over, leaf through, peruse, play at, rifle through*, run over, run through, scan, seize, skim,
take, taste, thumb through*; SEE CONCEPTS *87,623*

diploma [n] *certificate for achievement*
authority, award, charter, commission, confirmation, credentials, degree, honor, recognition, sheepskin, shingle, voucher, warrant; SEE CONCEPTS *271,337*

diplomacy [n] *tact, statesmanship*
address, artfulness, craft, delicacy, delicatesse, discretion, expedience, finesse, negotiation, poise, politics, savoir-faire, skill, statecraft, subtlety; SEE CONCEPTS *388,633*

diplomat [n] *politician, statesman*
agent, ambassador, attaché, cabinet member, chargé d'affaires, conciliator, consul, emissary, envoy, expert, go-between, legate, mediator, minister, moderator, negotiator, nuncio, plenipotentiary, public relations person, representative, tactician; SEE CONCEPTS *354,359*

diplomatic [adj] *politic, tactful*
adept, arch, artful, astute, bland, brainy, cagey, calculating, capable, clever, conciliatory, conniving, contriving, courteous, crafty, cunning, deft, delicate, dexterous, discreet, gracious, guileful, intriguing, opportunistic, polite, prudent, savvy, scheming, sensitive, sharp, shrewd, sly, smooth, strategic, suave, subtle, wily; SEE CONCEPTS *401,542*

dire [adj1] *urgent; crucial*
acute, burning, clamant, clamorous, climacteric, critical, crying, desperate, drastic, exigent, extreme, immoderate, imperative, importunate, instant, pressing; SEE CONCEPTS *546,568,799*

dire [adj2] *terrible, ominous*
afflictive, alarming, appalling, awful, black, calamitous, cataclysmic, catastrophic, cruel, deplorable, depressing, direful, disastrous, dismal, distressing, dreadful, fearful, fierce, frightful, gloomy, grievous, grim, heartbreaking, horrible, horrid, lamentable, oppressing, portentous, redoubtable, regrettable, ruinous, scowling, shocking, terrific, ugly, unfortunate, woeful; SEE CONCEPTS *537,548,570*

direct [adj1] *honest*
absolute, bald, blunt, candid, categorical, downright, explicit, express, forthright, frank, matter-of-fact, open, outspoken, person-to-person, plain, plainspoken, point-blank, sincere, straight, straightforward, straight from shoulder*, talk turkey*, unambiguous, unconcealed, undisguised, unequivocal, unreserved; SEE CONCEPT *267*

direct [adj2] *undeviating; uninterrupted*
beeline*, continuous, even, horizontal, in beeline*, in straight line, linear, nonstop, not crooked, point-blank, right, shortest, straight, straight ahead, straightaway, through, true, unbroken, unswerving; SEE CONCEPTS *482,581*

direct [adj3] *face-to-face; next to*
contiguous, firsthand, head-on, immediate, lineal, next, personal, primary, prompt, proximate, resultant, succeeding; SEE CONCEPTS *585,586*

direct [*v1*] *manage, oversee*
administer, advise, be in driver's seat*, boss, call the shots*, carry on, conduct, control, control the affairs of, dispose, dominate, govern, guide, handle, have the say, head up*, influence, keep, lead, mastermind*, operate, ordain, preside over, quarterback*, regulate, rule, run, run the show*, run things*, shepherd, superintend, supervise, take the reins*; SEE CONCEPTS *94,117*

direct [*v2*] *give instructions; teach*
address, advise, bid, charge, command, deliver, dictate, enjoin, give directions, give orders, inform, instruct, lecture, order, read, tell, warn; SEE CONCEPTS *53,61*

direct [*v3*] *point in a direction; guide*
address, aim, beam, cast, conduct, escort, fix, focus, head, incline, indicate, intend, lay, lead, level, mean, move in, pilot, point, point the way, present, route, see, set, shepherd, show, sight, sight on, slant, steer, target, train, turn, zero in; SEE CONCEPTS *187,201*

direct [*v4*] *send, usually by mail system*
address, designate, inscribe, label, mail, mark, route, superscribe; SEE CONCEPT *217*

direct [*v5*] *put all of efforts toward*
address, aim, apply, bend, buckle down, devote, endeavor, fix, give, set, settle, strive, throw, try, turn; SEE CONCEPTS *87,677*

direction [*n1*] *management*
administration, charge, command, control, government, guidance, leadership, order, oversight, superintendence, supervision; SEE CONCEPTS *299,325*

direction [*n2*] *course, route*
aim, angle, area, aspect, bearing, beeline*, bent, bias, current, drift, end, inclination, line, objective, orientation, outlook, path, point of compass, proclivity, range, region, road, set, side, slant, spot, standpoint, stream, tack, tendency, that-a-way, tide, track, trajectory, trend, viewpoint, way; SEE CONCEPTS *657,738*

direction(s) [*n3*] *instructions, guidance*
advice, advisement, assignment, briefing, directive, guidelines, indication, lowdown*, notification, plan, prescription, recommendation, regulation, sealed order, specification, specs*, steer*, summons, tip, word*; SEE CONCEPTS *271,274*

directive [*n*] *command, instruction*
charge, communication, decree, dictate, edict, injunction, mandate, memo, memorandum, message, notice, order, ordinance, regulation, ruling, ukase, word; SEE CONCEPTS *271,274,662*

directly [*adv1*] *the shortest route*
as crow flies*, beeline*, dead, direct, due, exactly, plump, precisely, right, slam bang*, slap, smack, smack dab*, straight, straightly, undeviatingly, unswervingly, without deviation; SEE CONCEPTS *581,778*

directly [*adv2*] *as soon as possible*
anon, at once, contiguously, dead*, due, first off, forthwith, immediately, in a second, instantaneously, instanter, instantly, presently, promptly, pronto*, quickly, right away, shortly, soon, speedily, straightaway, straight off; SEE CONCEPT *820*

directly [*adv3*] *straightforwardly*
candidly, face-to-face, honestly, in person, literally, openly, personally, plainly, point-blank, truthfully, unequivocally, verbatim, without prevarication, word for word; SEE CONCEPT *267*

director [*n*] *manager*
administrator, big man/woman*, boss, chairman/woman*, chief, controller, exec, executive, executive officer, governor, head, head honcho*, key player*, kingpin*, leader, man/woman upstairs*, organizer, overseer, player, principal, producer, skipper*, supervisor, top dog*, top man/woman*; SEE CONCEPTS *347,352*

directory [*n*] *reference book; guide*
agenda, almanac, atlas, blue book, book, catalogue, charts, gazeteer, hit list*, index, laundry list*, lineup, list, little black book*, record, register, roster, scorecard, short list*, social register, syllabus, white pages*, who's who*, yellow pages*; SEE CONCEPTS *280,283*

direful [*adj*] *fearful; horrible*
apocalyptic, appalling, awful, baleful, baneful, calamitous, dire, dreadful, fateful, ghastly, gloomy, horrid, ill-boding, inauspicious, ominous, shocking, terrible, terrific, unlucky, unpropitious; SEE CONCEPTS *537,570*

dirge [*n*] *sad song*
chant, coronach, cry, death march, death song, elegy, funeral song, hymn, jeremiad, keen, lament, march, monody, requiem, threnody; SEE CONCEPT *595*

dirt [*n1*] *grime, impurity*
crud*, dreck, dregs, excrement, feculence, filth, filthiness, gook*, ground, gunk*, mire, muck*, mud, rottenness, scuz*, sleaze*, slime*, smudge, smut*, soil, stain, tarnish; SEE CONCEPT *509*

dirt [*n2*] *obscenity; immorality*
chicanery, deception, dishonesty, double-dealing, filth, fourberie, fraud, hanky-panky*, indecency, lubricity, pornography, smut; SEE CONCEPT *645*

dirt [*n3*] *soil*
clay, dust, earth, loam, real estate, terra firma; SEE CONCEPT *509*

dirty [*adj1*] *soiled, unclean*
bedraggled, begrimed, black, contaminated, cruddy*, crummy, defiled, disarrayed, dishabille, disheveled, dreggy, dungy, dusty, filthy, foul, fouled, greasy, grimy, grubby, grungy*, icky*, lousy, messy, mucky*, muddy, mung*, murky, nasty, pigpen*, polluted, raunchy, scummy*, scuzzy*, skank, slatternly, slimy, sloppy, slovenly, smudged, smutty, sooty, spattered, spotted, squalid, stained, straggly, sullied,

undusted, unhygienic, unkempt, unlaundered, unsanitary, unsightly, unswept, untidy, unwashed, yucky*; SEE CONCEPT *485*

dirty [*adj2*] *obscene, pornographic*
base, blue, coarse, contemptible, despicable, filthy, immoral, impure, indecent, lewd, low, mean, nasty, off-color, ribald, risqué, salacious, scatological, scurvy, smutty, sordid, squalid, unchaste, unclean, uncleanly, vile, vulgar; SEE CONCEPTS *542,545*

dirty [*adj3*] *violent, stormy with regard to weather*
blustering, blustery, coarse, dark, furious, gusty, lowering, raging, rainy, rough, squally, storming, tempestuous, wild; SEE CONCEPT *525*

dirty [*v*] *cause to be soiled*
begrime, besoil, blacken, blotch, blur, botch, coat, contaminate, corrupt, debase, decay, defile, discolor, draggle, encrust, foul, grime, make dusty, make impure, mess up, mold, muddy, pollute, rot, smear, smirch, smoke, smudge, smutch, soil, spatter, spoil, spot, stain, sully, sweat, taint, tar, tarnish; SEE CONCEPT *254*

disability [*n*] *handicap*
affliction, ailment, complaint, defect, demoralization, detriment, disablement, disadvantage, disorder, disqualification, drawback, enervation, enfeeblement, exhaustion, feebleness, impairment, impotency, inability, incapacity, incompetency, inexperience, infirmity, injury, invalidity, lack, malady, palsy, paralysis, unfitness, weakness; SEE CONCEPTS *309,316,410,720*

disable [*v*] *render inoperative; cripple*
attenuate, batter, blunt, damage, debilitate, disarm, disenable, disqualify, enervate, enfeeble, exhaust, hamstring*, handicap, harm, hock*, hogtie*, hurt, immobilize, impair, incapacitate, invalidate, kibosh*, knock out*, maim, mangle, mar, mutilate, muzzle, paralyze, pinion, prostrate, put out of action*, render incapable, ruin, sabotage, sap, shatter, shoot down*, spoil, take out*, throw monkey wrench in*, total*, unbrace, undermine, unfit, unstrengthen, weaken, wreck; SEE CONCEPTS *130,246*

disabled [*adj*] *crippled*
bedridden, broken-down, castrated, confined, decrepit, disarmed, game, halting, hamstrung*, handicapped, helpless, hurt, imbecile, impotent, incapable, incapacitated, infirm, laid-up, lame, maimed, mangled, mutilated, out-of-action*, out-of-commission*, palsied, paralyzed, paraplegic, powerless, run-down, senile, sidelined, silenced, stalled, superannuated, taken out, unable, useless, weak, weakened, worn-out, wounded, wrecked; SEE CONCEPTS *314,527*

disadvantage(s) [*n1*] *difficulty, trouble*
adverse circumstance, bar, blocking, burden, defect, deficiency, deprivation, detriment, disability, discommodity, drawback, failing, fault, flaw, fly in ointment*, hamper, handicap, hardship, hindrance, impediment, imperfection, imposition, inadequacy, inconvenience, inutility, lack, liability, limitation, minus, nuisance, objection, obstacle, privation, problem, restraint, snag, stumbling block*, weakness, weak point; SEE CONCEPTS *666,674*

disadvantage [*n2*] *hurt, loss*
damage, deprivation, detriment, disservice, harm, injury, prejudice; SEE CONCEPTS *230,309,679*

disadvantaged [*adj*] *deprived, handicapped*
boxed-in*, cornered, depressed, destitute, discriminated against, down-and-out*, had by the tail*, hard-up*, have-not*, impoverished, in a corner*, locked-out, poor, struggling, truly needy*, underdog*, underprivileged, vulnerable; SEE CONCEPTS *334,555*

disadvantageous [*adj*] *detrimental, inconvenient*
adverse, contrary, damaging, debit-side, deleterious, depreciative, depreciatory, derogatory, detracting, disparaging, downside, dyslogistic, harmful, hurtful, ill-timed, inexpedient, injurious, inopportune, objectionable, on the debit side, pejorative, prejudicial, slighting, uncomplimentary, unfavorable, unprofitable; SEE CONCEPTS *334,537,555*

disaffect [*v*] *lose affection for, estrange*
agitate, alien, alienate, antagonize, discompose, disquiet, disturb, disunify, disunite, divide, repel, upset, wean; SEE CONCEPTS *7,19,135,384*

disaffected [*adj*] *alienated, estranged*
antagonistic, discontented, disloyal, dissatisfied, hostile, indifferent, mutinous, rebellious, seditious, uncompliant, unfriendly, unsubmissive; SEE CONCEPTS *403,555*

disaffection [*n*] *alienation, estrangement*
animosity, antagonism, antipathy, aversion, breach, disagreement, discontent, dislike, disloyalty, dissatisfaction, hatred, hostility, ill will, repugnance, resentment, unfriendliness; SEE CONCEPTS *388,410*

disagree [*v1*] *be different*
be discordant, be dissimilar, clash, conflict, contradict, counter, depart, deviate, differ, discord, disharmonize, dissent, diverge, run counter to, vary, war; SEE CONCEPT *665*

disagree [*v2*] *argue; hold differing opinion*
altercate, battle, bicker, brawl, break with, bring action, clash, contend, contest, controversialize, controvert, debate, differ, disaccord, discept, discord, dispute, dissent, divide, fall out*, feud, fight, go for jugular*, haggle, have words*, jump on*, lay into*, let have it, logomachize, object, oppose, palter, quarrel, quibble, rip, row, scrap, set to, skirmish, spar, spat, sue, take issue, take on, war, wrangle, zap*; SEE CONCEPTS *12,46*

disagree [*v3*] *be injurious*
be distasteful, be disturbing, be sickening, be unsuitable, bother, discomfort, distress, go against grain*, hurt, injure, make ill, nauseate, sicken, trouble, upset; SEE CONCEPT *246*

disagreeable [*adj1*] *bad-tempered, irritable*
bellicose, brusque, cantankerous, churlish, contentious, contrary, cross, difficult, disobliging, disputatious, eristic, grouchy, ill-natured, nasty, obnoxious,

offensive, out of sorts, peevish, pettish, petulant, querulous, rude, snappy, surly, ugly, unfriendly, ungracious, unlikable, unpleasant, uptight, waspish, whiny; SEE CONCEPT *401*

disagreeable [*adj2*] *disgusting, offensive*
annoying, awful, bad, bothersome, displeasing, distasteful, distressing, drag, nasty, objectionable, obnoxious, pain, repellent, repugnant, repulsive, rotten, sour, unhappy, uninviting, unpalatable, unpleasant, unsavory, upsetting, woeful; SEE CONCEPTS *537,548*

disagreement [*n1*] *dispute, quarrel*
altercation, animosity, antagonism, argument, atmospherics, bickering, breach, break, clash, clashing, conflict, contention, contest, controversy, cross-purposes, debate, difference, discord, dissent, dissidence, disunion, disunity, division, divisiveness, falling out, feud, fight, friction, hassle, hostility, ill feeling, ill will, jarring, misunderstanding, opposition, quarrel, quarreling, rupture, spat, split, squabble, strife, tension, variance, vendetta, words, wrangle; SEE CONCEPTS *46,388*

disagreement [*n2*] *difference, unlikeness*
clash, disaccord, discordance, discrepancy, disharmonism, disharmony, disparity, dissimilarity, dissimilitude, divergence, divergency, diversity, incompatibility, incongruity, incongruousness, inconsistency, variance; SEE CONCEPT *665*

disallow [*v*] *reject, prohibit*
abjure, cancel, censor, debar, deny, disacknowledge, disavow, disclaim, dismiss, disown, embargo, exclude, forbid, keep back, kill, nix*, pass on, proscribe, put down, rebuff, refuse, repudiate, shut out, taboo*, veto, withhold, zing*; SEE CONCEPTS *21,25,30*

disappear [*v*] *vanish; cease*
abandon, abscond, be done for, be gone, be lost, be no more*, be swallowed up, cease to exist, clear, come to naught, decamp, dematerialize, depart, die, die out, disperse, dissipate, dissolve, drop out of sight*, ebb, end, end gradually, escape, evanesce, evanish, evaporate, exit, expire, fade, fade away, flee, fly, go, go south*, leave, leave no trace, melt, melt away, pass, pass away, perish, recede, retire, retreat, sink, take flight, vacate, vamoose*, wane, withdraw; SEE CONCEPTS *102,105,195*

disappearance [*n*] *vanishing*
ceasing to exist, decline and fall, dematerialization, departure, desertion, disappearing, disappearing act, disintegration, dispersal, dissipation, dissolution, ebbing, eclipse, escape, evanescence, evaporation, exit, exodus, fading, flight, going, loss, melting, passing, receding, recession, removal, retirement, vanishing point, vanishment, wane, wearing away, withdrawal; SEE CONCEPTS *102,105,195*

disappoint [*v*] *sadden, dismay; frustrate*
abort, baffle, balk, break a date*, bring to naught, bungle, cast down, chagrin, circumvent, come to

nothing, dash, dash hopes*, deceive, delude, disconcert, disenchant, disgruntle, dishearten, disillusion, dissatisfy, dumbfound, embitter, fail, fall down on, fall flat, fall short of, foil, founder, hamper, hinder, leave in lurch*, let down, miscarry, mislead, not show, put out, ruin prospects, stand up, tease, thwart, torment, vex; SEE CONCEPTS *7,19,699*

disappointed [*adj*] *let down, saddened*
aghast, balked, beaten, chapfallen, complaining, crestfallen, defeated, depressed, despondent, disconcerted, discontented, discouraged, disenchanted, disgruntled, disillusioned, dissatisfied, distressed, down, downcast, downhearted, down in dumps*, foiled, frustrated, hopeless, objecting, shot down, taken down, thwarted, unhappy, unsatisfied, upset, vanquished, worsted; SEE CONCEPT *403*

disappointment [*n1*] *saddening situation; letdown*
bitter pill*, blind alley*, blow, blunder, bringdown, bummer, bust*, calamity, defeat, disaster, discouragement, downer*, downfall, drag, dud, error, failure, false alarm*, faux pas*, fiasco, fizzle, flash in pan*, impasse, inefficacy, lemon*, miscalculation, miscarriage, mischance, misfortune, mishap, mistake, obstacle, old one-two*, setback, slip, washout; SEE CONCEPTS *230,674*

disappointment [*n2*] *mental upset; displeasure*
adverse fate, adversity, bafflement, blow, chagrin, defeat, despondency, discontent, discouragement, disenchantment, disgruntlement, disillusion, disillusionment, dissatisfaction, distress, failure, frustration, lack of success, letdown, mortification, nonsuccess, regret, setback, the knocks*, unfulfillment; SEE CONCEPT *410*

disapproval [*n*] *condemnation*
blackball*, black list*, blame, boo*, boycott, brickbat, call down, castigation, catcall*, censure, criticism, denunciation, deprecation, disapprobation, discontent, disfavor, dislike, disparagement, displeasure, dissatisfaction, hiss*, nix*, objection, opprobrium, ostracism, reproach, reproof, slap on wrist*, stricture, thumbs down*, vitriol, zing*; SEE CONCEPTS *278,689*

disapprove [*v*] *condemn*
blame, censure, chastise, criticize, damn, decry, denounce, deplore, deprecate, detract, disallow, discommend, discountenance, disesteem, disfavor, dislike, dismiss, dispraise, expostulate, find fault with, find unacceptable, frown on, look askance at, look down on, nix*, object to, oppose, pan*, pass on, refuse, reject, remonstrate, reprehend, reprobate, reprove, set aside, slam, spurn, take dim view of, take exception to, turn down, veto, zing*; SEE CONCEPTS *18,21,52*

disarm [*v1*] *render defenseless*
conciliate, cripple, deactivate, debilitate, deescalate, demilitarize, demobilize, disable, disband, disqualify, incapacitate, invalidate, neutralize, occupy, pacify, paralyze, prostrate, skin, strip, subdue, sub-

jugate, unarm, weaken; SEE CONCEPTS *142,211,320*

disarm [*v2*] *persuade*
allure, attract, bewitch, captivate, charm, coax, convince, enchant, fascinate, seduce, set at ease, unarm, urge, win over; SEE CONCEPTS *7,19,22,68*

disarmament [*n*] *reduction of weapons*
arms limitation, arms reduction, conquest, crippling, deescalation, demilitarization, demobilization, disablement, disqualification, freeze, neutralizing, occupation, pacification, paralyzing, rendering powerless, subjugation; SEE CONCEPTS *142,211,320*

disarming [*adj*] *charming*
bewitching, convincing, deferential, ingratiating, ingratiatory, insinuating, insinuative, inveigling, irresistible, likable, persuasive, saccharine, seductive, silken, silky, winning; SEE CONCEPT *401*

disarray [*n*] *disorder, confusion, mess*
anarchy, ataxia, chaos, clutter, disarrangement, discomposure, disharmony, dishevelment, disorganization, holy mess*, indiscipline, jumble, muddle, shambles*, snarl, tangle, topsy-turviness*, unholy mess*, unruliness, untidiness, upset; SEE CONCEPTS *230,727*

disaster [*n*] *accident, trouble*
act of God*, adversity, affliction, bad luck, bad news*, bale, bane, blight, blow, bust, calamity, casualty, cataclysm, catastrophe, collapse, collision, crash, debacle, defeat, depression, emergency, exigency, failure, fall, fell stroke*, fiasco, flood, flop, grief, hard luck, harm, hazard, holocaust, hot water*, ill luck, misadventure, mischance, misfortune, mishap, reverse, rock, rough, ruin, ruination, setback, slip, stroke, the worst*, tragedy, undoing, upset, washout*, woe; SEE CONCEPTS *674,675*

disastrous [*adj*] *detrimental, devastating*
adverse, calamitous, cataclysmal, cataclysmic, catastrophic, destructive, dire, dreadful, fatal, fateful, hapless, harmful, ill-fated, ill-starred, luckless, ruinous, terrible, tragic, unfavorable, unfortunate, unlucky, unpropitious, untoward; SEE CONCEPTS *537,548*

disavow [*v*] *reject*
abjure, contradict, deny, disacknowledge, disallow, disclaim, disown, drop out, forswear, gainsay, go back on word*, impugn, negate, negative, refuse, renege, renig, repudiate, wash hands of*, weasel out of*, welsh, worm out of*; SEE CONCEPTS *18,25*

disbelief [*n*] *doubt, skepticism*
atheism, distrust, dubiety, incredulity, mistrust, nihilism, rejection, repudiation, spurning, unbelief, unbelievingness, unfaith; SEE CONCEPTS *21,689*

disbelieve [*v*] *doubt*
discount, discredit, distrust, eschew, give no credence to, mistrust, not accept, not buy, not credit, not swallow*, question, reject, repudiate, scoff at, scorn, scout, suspect, unbelieve; SEE CONCEPT *21*

disbelieving [*adj*] *suspicious, doubting*
aporetic, cagey, cynical, incredulous, leery, mistrustful, questioning, quizzical, show-me, skeptical, unbelieving; SEE CONCEPT *403*

disburse [*v*] *spend money*
acquit, ante up*, come across, come through, come up with, contribute, cough up*, deal, defray, dispense, disperse, distribute, divide, divvy*, dole out*, expend, foot the bill*, give, lay out*, measure out, outlay, partition, pay out, pony up*, put out, shell out*, use; SEE CONCEPTS *108,341*

disbursement [*n*] *payment*
cost, disposal, expenditure, expense, outgoing, outlay, spending; SEE CONCEPT *344*

discard [*v*] *get rid of*
abandon, abdicate, abjure, adios*, banish, can*, cancel, cashier, cast aside, chuck, deep-six*, desert, dispatch, dispense with, dispose of, dispossess, ditch, divorce, do away with, drop, dump, eject, eliminate, expel, forsake, free of, give up, have done with, jettison, junk*, oust, part with, protest, put by, reject, relinquish, remove, renounce, repeal, repudiate, scrap, shake off, shed, sweep away, throw away, throw out, throw overboard*, toss, toss aside, write off; SEE CONCEPT *180*

discern [*v*] *catch sight of; recognize and understand*
anticipate, apprehend, ascertain, behold, decern, descry, detect, determine, difference, differentiate, discover, discrepate, discriminate, distinguish, divine, espy, extricate, figure out, find out, focus, foresee, get a load of*, get the picture*, get wise to, judge, know, make distinction, make out, note, notice, observe, perceive, pick out, read, remark, rubberneck*, secern, see, see the light*, see through, separate, severalize, spot, take in, view; SEE CONCEPTS *15,38*

discernible [*adj*] *recognizable; distinct*
apparent, appreciable, audible, clear, detectable, discoverable, distinguishable, noticeable, observable, obvious, palpable, perceivable, perceptible, plain, sensible, tangible, visible; SEE CONCEPTS *535, 576, 619*

discerning [*adj*] *discriminating*
acute, astute, bright, brilliant, clear-sighted, clever, critical, gnostic, ingenious, insighted, insightful, intelligent, judicious, knowing, knowledgeable, penetrating, perceptive, percipient, perspicacious, piercing, sagacious, sage, sensitive, sharp, shrewd, subtle, wise; SEE CONCEPT *402*

discharge [*n1*] *setting free*
acquittal, clearance, disimprisonment, exoneration, liberation, pardon, parole, probation, release, remittance; SEE CONCEPT *127*

discharge [*n2*] *dismissal from responsibility*
ax, bounce, bum's rush*, congé, demobilization, door, ejection, gate, old heave ho*, pink slip*, the boot*, walking papers*; SEE CONCEPTS *324,351*

discharge [*n3*] *detonation*
barrage, blast, burst, discharging, explosion, firing, fusillade, report, salvo, shot, shower, volley; SEE CONCEPT *521*

discharge [*n4*] *pouring forth*
elimination, emission, emptying, excretion, exudation, flow, ooze, pus, secretion, seepage, shower,

suppuration, vent, voiding; SEE CONCEPTS *179,748*

discharge [n5] *unloading*
disburdening, emptying, unburdening, unlading; SEE CONCEPT *211*

discharge [n6] *carrying out of responsibility*
accomplishment, achievement, execution, fulfillment, observance, performance; SEE CONCEPT *706*

discharge [n7] *payment of debt*
acquittal, disbursement, liquidation, satisfaction, settlement; SEE CONCEPTS *341,344*

discharge [v1] *set free*
absolve, acquit, allow to go, clear, disimprison, dismiss, emancipate, exonerate, expel, free, liberate, loose, loosen, manumit, oust, pardon, release, unbind, unchain, unimprison, unshackle; SEE CONCEPT *127*

discharge [v2] *dismiss from responsibility*
absolve, ax, boot*, boot out, bounce, bump, bust, can*, cashier, disburden, discard, disencumber, dispense, displace, eject, excuse, exempt, expel, fire, freeze out*, give one notice, kick out, lay off, let go, let off, let one go, let out, lock out*, nix*, oust, privilege from, relieve, remove, replace, ride out on rail*, run out of town*, show the door*, spare, supersede, supplant, terminate, unload; SEE CONCEPTS *324,351*

discharge [v3] *detonate weapon*
blast, explode, fire, let off, set off, shoot, shoot off; SEE CONCEPT *179*

discharge [v4] *pour forth*
break out, disembogue, dispense, ejaculate, emit, empty, erupt, excrete, exude, give off, gush, leak, ooze, pour, release, send forth, spew, void, vomit; SEE CONCEPTS *152,179*

discharge [v5] *unload*
carry away, disburden, empty, off-load, remove, remove cargo, send, take away, take off, unburden, unlade, unpack, unship, unstow; SEE CONCEPT *211*

discharge [v6] *carry out responsibility*
accomplish, achieve, do, execute, fulfill, meet, observe, perform; SEE CONCEPT *91*

discharge [v7] *pay, settle debt*
clear, honor, liquidate, meet, pay up, quit, relieve, satisfy, square, square up; SEE CONCEPT *341*

discharge [v8] *invalidate agreement*
abrogate, annul, cancel, dissolve, quash, render void, vacate, void; SEE CONCEPT *121*

disciple [n] *believer, follower*
adherent, apostle, attendant, booster, buff, bug*, catechumen, cohort, convert, devotee, enthusiast, fan, fanatic, fiend, freak, groupie, henchman, hound*, junkie*, learner, nut*, partisan, proselyte, pupil, rooter*, satellite, sectary, sectator, student, supporter, votary, witness, zealot; SEE CONCEPTS *361,423*

disciplinarian [n] *person who makes others work hard*
authoritarian, bully, despot, drill sergeant, enforcer, formalist, hard master, martinet, master, sergeant, stickler, strict teacher, sundowner, taskmaster,

teacher, trainer, tyrant; SEE CONCEPTS *350,354,423*

discipline [n1] *regimen, training*
conduct, control, cultivation, curb, development, domestication, drill, drilling, education, exercise, inculcation, indoctrination, limitation, method, orderliness, practice, preparation, regulation, restraint, self-command, self-control, self-government, self-mastery, self-restraint, strictness, subordination, will, willpower; SEE CONCEPTS *94,326,410*

discipline [n2] *punishment*
castigation, chastisement, comeuppance, correction, getting yours*, hell to pay*, punition, rod; SEE CONCEPTS *122,123*

discipline [n3] *field of study; subject of interest*
area, branch of knowledge, course, curriculum, specialty, subject; SEE CONCEPT *349*

disclaim [v] *deny*
abandon, abjure, abnegate, belittle, contradict, contravene, criticize, decline, deprecate, disacknowledge, disaffirm, disallow, disavow, discard, disown, disparage, divorce oneself from, forswear, gainsay, minimize, negate, recant, refuse, reject, renounce, repudiate, retract, revoke, spurn, traverse, turn back on, wash hands of*; SEE CONCEPT *54*

disclose [v] *reveal, make public*
acknowledge, admit, avow, bare, betray, blab, bring to light*, broadcast, come out of closet*, communicate, confess, discover, display, divulge, exhibit, expose, give away, impart, lay bare, leak, let slip, make known, mouth*, open, own, publish, relate, reveal, show, snitch*, spill, spill the beans*, squeal*, tell, unclose, uncover, unfurl, unveil, utter; SEE CONCEPT *60*

disclosure [n] *announcement, revelation*
acknowledgment, admission, advertisement, betrayal, blow by blow*, broadcast, confession, declaration, discovery, divulgation, divulgence, enlightenment, exposal, exposé, exposure, handout, impartance, impartation, leak, make, picture, publication, revealing, revealment, rundown, snitch*, squeal*, tip*, tip-off*, uncovering, unveilment, ventilation; SEE CONCEPT *274*

discolor [v] *fading, dirtying of hue*
besmear, besmirch, blot, defile, fade, mar, mark, rust, smear, soil, stain, streak, sully, tar, tarnish, tinge; SEE CONCEPTS *250,469*

discomfit [v] *defeat, frustrate; confuse*
abash, annoy, baffle, balk, beat, bother, checkmate, confound, demoralize, discompose, disconcert, discountenance, disturb, embarrass, faze, fluster, foil, irk, outwit, overcome, perplex, perturb, prevent, rattle, ruffle, take aback, thwart, trump, unsettle, upset, vex, worry, worst; SEE CONCEPTS *7,19,95*

discomfiture [n] *embarrassment, frustration*
abashment, agitation, beating, chagrin, comedown, confusion, conquest, defeasance, defeat, demoralization, descent, disappointment, discomposure, disconcertion, disconcertment, disquiet, failure, humiliation, overthrow, perturbation, rout, ruin,

shame, undoing, unease, uneasiness, upset, vanquishment, vexation; SEE CONCEPTS *410,674*

discomfort [n] *irritation, pain*
ache, annoyance, discomfiture, discomposure, displeasure, disquiet, distress, embarrassment, hardship, hurt, inquietude, malaise, nuisance, soreness, trouble, uneasiness, unpleasantness, upset, vexation; SEE CONCEPTS *410,728*

discomfort [v] *irritate; cause pain*
discomfit, discompose, disquiet, distress, disturb, embarrass, make uncomfortable, nettle, perturb, upset, vex; SEE CONCEPTS *7,19,246,313*

discommode [v] *annoy*
bother, burden, disoblige, disquiet, disturb, fluster, harass, incommode, inconvenience, irk, molest, perturb, put out, trouble, upset, vex; SEE CONCEPTS *7,19*

discompose [v] *provoke, agitate*
annoy, bewilder, bother, confuse, discombobulate*, discomfit, disconcert, dismay, disorganize, displease, disquiet, disturb, embarrass, faze, flurry, fluster, harass, harry, irk, irritate, nettle, perplex, perturb, pester, plague, rattle, ruffle, unhinge, unsettle, upset, vex, worry; SEE CONCEPTS *7,19*

disconcert [v] *shake up; confuse*
abash, agitate, baffle, balk, bewilder, bug*, confound, demoralize, disarrange, discombobulate*, discomfit, discompose, discountenance, disturb, embarrass, faze, fluster, foul up*, frustrate, get to*, hinder, nonplus, perplex, perturb, psych out*, put off, puzzle, rattle, ruffle, take aback, throw off balance, trouble, unbalance, undo, unsettle, upset, upset apple cart*, worry; SEE CONCEPTS *7,16,19*

disconcerted [adj] *confused; shaken*
annoyed, bewildered, caught off balance, come apart, distracted, disturbed, embarrassed, fazed, flustered, in botheration, messed-up, mixed-up, nonplussed, out of countenance, perturbed, psyched-out*, rattled, ruffled, shook-up*, spaced-out*, taken aback, thrown, troubled, unglued, unzipped*, upset; SEE CONCEPT *403*

disconnect [v] *take apart; uncouple*
abstract, break it off, break it up, cut, cut off, detach, disassociate, disengage, disjoin, dissever, dissociate, disunite, divide, drop, drop it, part, separate, sever, sideline, unfix; SEE CONCEPTS *98,135*

disconnected [adj] *confused; discontinuous*
broken, detached, disjointed, disordered, garbled, illogical, inchoate, incoherent, incohesive, interrupted, irrational, irregular, jumbled, loose, mixed-up, muddled, rambling, separated, uncontinuous, uncoordinated, unintelligible, wandering; SEE CONCEPTS *267,482*

disconsolate [adj] *depressed, unhappy*
bad, black, blue, cheerless, cold, comfortless, crestfallen, crushed, dark, dejected, desolate, despairing, destroyed, dispirited, distressed, doleful, down, downcast, downhearted, dreary, forlorn, gloomy, grief-stricken, heartbroken, hopeless, hurting, inconsolable, in pain*, in the pits*, low, melancholy, miserable, ripped*, sad, somber, sorrowful, torn-up*, woebegone, woeful, wretched; SEE CONCEPT *403*

discontent [n] *dissatisfaction*
depression, discontentment, displeasure, envy, fretfulness, regret, restlessness, uneasiness, unhappiness, vexation; SEE CONCEPT *410*

discontented/discontent [adj] *unhappy, dissatisfied*
blue, complaining, crabby*, disaffected, disgruntled, displeased, disquieted, disturbed, exasperated, fed up, fretful, griping, kvetching*, malcontent, malcontented, miserable, perturbed, picky, restless, ungratified, upset, vexed; SEE CONCEPT *403*

discontinuance [n] *stop, suspension of activity*
adjournment, alternation, cease, cessation, close, closing, desistance, desuetude, discontinuation, disjunction, disruption, end, ending, finish, intermission, interruption, separation, stoppage, stopping, termination; SEE CONCEPT *119*

discontinue [v] *prevent activity from going on*
abandon, bag it*, blow off*, break off*, call it quits, cease, close, desist, disconnect, disjoin, dissever, disunite, drop, end, finish, give over, give up, halt, interpose, interrupt, intervene, kill, knock off*, leave off, part, pause, put end to, quit, refrain from, scrub, separate, stop, surcease, suspend, terminate; SEE CONCEPTS *121,234*

discontinuous [adj] *broken; intermittent*
alternate, broken off, desultory, disconnected, disjointed, disordered, fitful, gaping, inchoate, incoherent, incohesive, interrupted, irregular, muddled, spasmodic, unconnected, unorganized; SEE CONCEPT *482*

discord [n1] *conflict, disagreement*
animosity, antagonism, antipathy, clash, clashing, collision, contention, difference, disaccord, discordance, discrepancy, disharmony, dispute, dissension, dissent, dissidence, dissonance, disunion, disunity, division, enmity, friction, fuss, hassle, hostility, incompatibility, incongruity, inharmony, lack of concord, mischief, opposition, polarization, rancor, row, ruckus, rupture, scene, spat, split, static, strife, variance, wrangling; SEE CONCEPT *388*

discord [n2] *noise*
cacophony, clamor, clinker, din, disharmony, dissonance, harshness, jangle, jarring, racket, sour note, tumult; SEE CONCEPT *595*

discordant [adj] *not in harmony; conflicting*
antagonistic, antipathetic, at odds, cacophonous, clashing, contradictory, contrarient, contrary, different, disagreeing, discrepant, dissonant, divergent, grating, harsh, incompatible, incongruous, inconsistent, inconsonant, inharmonious, jangling, jarring, on a sour note*, opposite, quarreling, strident, uncongenial, unharmonious, unmelodious, unmixable; SEE CONCEPTS *558,564,592,594*

discount [n] *reduction in cost*
abatement, allowance, commission, concession, cut, cut rate, decrease, deduct, deduction, depreciation,

diminution, drawback, exemption, knock-off*, mark-down, modification, percentage, premium, qualification, rebate, remission, rollback, salvage, something off, subtraction, tare; SEE CONCEPTS *335,763*

discount [*v1*] *lower, reduce cost*
abate, allow, deduct, depreciate, diminish, hold a sale, knock off*, make allowance for, mark down, modify, rebate, redeem, remove, sell at discount, strike off, subtract, take away, take off, undersell; SEE CONCEPTS *236,247,330*

discount [*v2*] *ignore; treat as insignificant*
belittle, blink at*, brush off*, depreciate, derogate, detract from, disbelieve, discredit, dispraise, disregard, doubt, fail, forget, minimize, mistrust, neglect, omit, overlook, overpass, pass over, question, reject, scoff at, scout, slight; SEE CONCEPTS *21,30*

discountenance [*v1*] *reject, oppose*
condemn, count me out*, deprecate, disapprove, discommend, discourage, disesteem, disfavor, dispute, frown on*, hold no brief for*, not go for*, not stand for*, object to, put down, resist, take a dim view of, take exception to; SEE CONCEPT *21*

discountenance [*v2*] *embarrass, disconcert*
abash, chagrin, confuse, discomfit, discompose, faze, humiliate, rattle, shame; SEE CONCEPTS *7,19,54*

discourage [*v1*] *dishearten, dispirit*
abash, afflict, alarm, appall, awe, beat down, bother, break one's heart*, bully, cast down, chill, confuse, cow, damp, dampen, dash, daunt, deject, demoralize, deprecate, depress, dismay, disparage, distress, droop, frighten, intimidate, irk, overawe, prostrate, repress, scare, throw cold water on*, trouble, try, unnerve, vex, weigh; SEE CONCEPT *14*

discourage [*v2*] *deter, dissuade; restrain*
check, chill, control, curb, deprecate, disadvise, discountenance, disfavor, disincline, divert, frighten, hinder, hold back, hold off, impede, indispose, inhibit, interfere, keep back, obstruct, prevent, put off, quiet, repress, scare, shake, talk out of, throw cold water on*, turn aside, turn off, warn, withhold; SEE CONCEPTS *68,121*

discouraged [*adj*] *disheartened*
beat, beat-down, blue, caved-in, come-apart, crestfallen, dashed, daunted, depressed, deterred, dismayed, dispirited, down, downbeat, downcast, down-in-mouth*, glum*, gone to pieces*, in a funk*, in blue funk*, in the dumps*, lost momentum, pessimistic, sad; SEE CONCEPT *403*

discouragement [*n1*] *despondency*
cold feet*, dejection, depression, despair, disappointment, discomfiture, dismay, downheartedness, hopelessness, loss of confidence, low spirits, melancholy, pessimism, sadness, the blues*; SEE CONCEPT *410*

discouragement [*n2*] *restraint*
bar, constraint, curb, damper, deterrent, disincentive, hindrance, impediment, obstacle, opposition, rebuff, setback; SEE CONCEPT *674*

discouraging [*adj*] *upsetting*
black, bleak, dampening, daunting, depressing, depressive, deterring, disadvantageous, disappointing, disheartening, dismal, dismaying, dispiriting, dissuading, dreary, gloomy, hindering, inopportune, off-putting, oppressive, repressing, unfavorable, unpropitious; SEE CONCEPTS *403,529*

discourse [*n*] *dialogue; dissertation*
address, article, chat, communication, conversation, converse, descant, discussion, disquisition, essay, gabfest*, homily, huddle, lecture, memoir, monograph, monologue, oration, paper, rhetoric, sermon, speaking, speech, talk, thesis, tractate, treatise, utterance, verbalization; SEE CONCEPT *266*

discourse [*v*] *discuss, speak about*
argue, chew*, comment, commentate, confab*, confer, converse, debate, declaim, descant, develop, dilate upon, dispute, dissert, dissertate, elaborate, enlarge, expand, expatiate, explain, expound, give a meeting, harangue, hold forth, lecture, modulate, orate, perorate, remark, sermonize, talk, treat, voice; SEE CONCEPTS *51,56*

discourteous [*adj*] *rude, impolite*
abrupt, bad-mannered, boorish, brusque, cavalier, cheeky*, churlish, contumelious, crude, crusty*, curt, disrespectful, flip, fresh, ill-bred, ill-mannered, impertinent, impolite, inaffable, indelicate, insolent, inurbane, oafish, offhand, rude, rustic, sassy, smart-alecky*, uncivil, uncouth, ungenteel, ungentlemanly, ungracious, unladylike, unmannerly, unrefined; SEE CONCEPT *401*

discover [*v*] *find, uncover*
ascertain, bring to light, catch, come across, come upon, conceive, contrive, debunk, design, detect, determine, devise, dig up, discern, disclose, distinguish, elicit, espy, explore, ferret out*, find out, get wind of*, get wise to*, glimpse, hear, identify, invent, learn, light upon, locate, look up, nose out*, notice, observe, originate, perceive, pick up on*, pioneer, realize, recognize, reveal, see, sense, smoke out*, spot, think of, turn up, uncover, unearth; SEE CONCEPTS *31,183*

discovery [*n1*] *finding, uncovering*
analysis, ascertainment, authentication, calculation, certification, detection, determination, diagnosis, discernment, disclosure, distinguishing, empiricism, encounter, espial, experimentation, exploration, exposition, exposure, feeling, find, hearing, identification, introduction, invention, learning, locating, location, origination, perception, revelation, sensing, sighting, strike, uncovering, unearthing, verification; SEE CONCEPTS *31,183*

discovery [*n2*] *treasure; invention*
algorithm, bonanza*, breakthrough, conclusion, contrivance, coup, data, design, device, find, finding, formula, godsend*, innovation, law, luck, luck out*, machine, method, principle, process, result, secret, theorem, way; SEE CONCEPTS *260,532*

discredit [*v1*] *blame, detract from*
blow up*, bring into disrepute, bring to naught, censure, defame, degrade, destroy, disconsider, disesteem, disfavor, disgrace, dishonor, disparage, disprove, explode, expose, frown upon*, knock bottom out of*, mudsling*, poke full of holes*, poohpooh*, puncture, put down, reflect on, reproach, ruin, run down, shoot, show up, slander, slur, smear, take rug out from under*, tear down*, vilify; SEE CONCEPTS *44,54*

discredit [*v2*] *doubt, question*
challenge, deny, disbelieve, discount, dispute, distrust, mistrust, put under suspicion, reject, scoff at, unbelieve; SEE CONCEPT *21*

discreet [*adj*] *cautious, sensible*
alert, attentive, awake, cagey, calculating, careful, chary, circumspect, civil, conservative, considerate, controlled, diplomatic, discerning, discriminating, gingerly, guarded, having foresight, heedful, intelligent, judicious, like a clam*, moderate, noncommittal, not rash, observant, on lookout*, politic, precautious, prudent, reasonable, reserved, restrained, safe, sagacious, strategic, tactful, temperate, thoughtful, unexcessive, unextreme, vigilant, wary, watchful, wise, worldly-wise; SEE CONCEPT *401*

discrepancy [*n*] *conflict, disagreement*
alterity, contrariety, difference, discordance, disparity, dissemblance, dissimilarity, dissimilitude, dissonance, distinction, divergence, divergency, error, far cry*, incongruity, inconsistency, miscalculation, otherness, split, unlikeness, variance, variation; SEE CONCEPT *665*

discrepant [*adj*] *disagreeing*
at variance, conflicting, contradictory, contrary, different, differing, disagreeing, disconsonant, discordant, disparate, dissonant, divergent, diverse, incompatible, incongruent, incongruous, inconsistent, inconsonant, unmixable, varying; SEE CONCEPT *564*

discrete [*adj*] *individual*
detached, different, disconnected, discontinuous, distinct, diverse, separate, several, unattached, various; SEE CONCEPT *564*

discretion [*n*] *caution, judgment*
acumen, attention, calculation, canniness, care, carefulness, chariness, circumspection, concern, considerateness, consideration, deliberation, diplomacy, discernment, discrimination, foresight, forethought, good sense, gumption, heed, heedfulness, judiciousness, maturity, observation, perspicacity, precaution, presence of mind, providence, prudence, responsibility, sagacity, sense, shrewdness, solicitude, tact, thoughtfulness, vigilance, wariness, warning, watchfulness, wisdom; SEE CONCEPT *657*

discretionary [*adj*] *open to choice*
at the call, elective, facultative, judge and jury, leftover, nonmandatory, nonobligatory, open, optional, unrestricted; SEE CONCEPT *546*

discriminate [*v1*] *show prejudice*
be bigot, be partial, contradistinguish, disfavor, favor, hate, incline, judge, segregate, separate, set apart, show bias, single out, treat as inferior, treat differently, victimize; SEE CONCEPTS *32,384*

discriminate [*v2*] *differentiate, distinguish*
assess, collate, compare, contradistinguish, contrast, difference, differentiate, discern, discrepate, draw distinction, evaluate, extricate, judge, know, know what's what*, make out*, note, perceive, remark, segregate, separate, sever, severalize, sift, specify, split hairs*, tell apart, tell the difference; SEE CONCEPTS *15,38*

discriminating [*adj*] *critical*
acute, astute, careful, choicy, choosy, cultivated, discerning, distinctive, eclectic, fastidious, finical, finicky, fussy, individualizing, judicious, keen, particular, persnickety*, picky, prudent, refined, select, selective, sensitive, tasteful, wise; SEE CONCEPTS *404,542*

discrimination [*n1*] *bias*
bigotry, favoritism, hatred, inequity, injustice, intolerance, partiality, prejudice, unfairness, wrong; SEE CONCEPTS *29,689*

discrimination [*n2*] *particularity in taste*
acumen, acuteness, astucity, astuteness, clearness, decision, difference, differentiation, discernment, distinction, judgment, keenness, penetration, perception, percipience, perspicacity, preference, refinement, sagacity, sense, separation, shrewdness, subtlety, taste, understanding; SEE CONCEPTS *32,410,655*

discuss [*v*] *talk over with another*
altercate, argue, bounce off*, canvass, compare notes, confabulate, confer, consider, consult with, contend, contest, converse, debate, deliberate, descant, discept, discourse about, dispute, dissert, dissertate, examine, exchange views on*, explain, figure, get together, go into, groupthink*, hash over*, hold forth, jaw*, kick about*, knock around*, moot, put heads together*, reason about, review, sift, take up, talk about, thrash out*, toss around*, ventilate, weigh; SEE CONCEPT *56*

discussion [*n*] *talk with another*
altercation, analysis, argument, argumentation, canvass, colloquy, confabulation, conference, consideration, consultation, contention, controversy, conversation, debate, deliberation, dialogue, discourse, disputation, dispute, dissertation, examination, exchange, excursus, groupthink*, huddle, interview, meet, meeting, powwow*, quarrel, review, scrutiny, symposium, ventilation, wrangling; SEE CONCEPT *56*

disdain [*n*] *hate; indifference*
antipathy, arrogance, aversion, contempt, contumely, derision, despisal, despisement, despite, dislike, disparagement, hatred, haughtiness, hauteur, insolence, loftiness, morgue, pride, ridicule, scorn,

sneering, snobbishness, superbity, superciliousness; SEE CONCEPT *29*

disdain [*v*] *scorn*
abhor, be allergic to*, belittle, chill, contemn, deride, despise, disregard, hate, ignore, look down nose at*, look down on, misprize, pooh-pooh*, put down*, refuse, reject, scout, slight, sneer at, spurn, undervalue; SEE CONCEPTS *29,30*

disdainful [*adj*] *scornful*
aloof, antipathetic, arrogant, averse, cavalier, contemning, contemptuous, cool, derisive, despising, egotistic, haughty, high-and-mighty*, hoity-toity*, indifferent, insolent, lordly, overbearing, proud, rejecting, repudiating, scouting, sneering, snooty*, supercilious, superior, toplofty, unsympathetic, uppity*; SEE CONCEPT *401*

disease [*n*] *ailment, affliction*
ache, affection, attack, blight, breakdown, bug*, cancer, canker, collapse, complaint, condition, contagion, contamination, convulsions, debility, decrepitude, defect, disorder, distemper, endemic, epidemic, feebleness, fever, fit, flu, hemorrhage, ill health, illness, indisposition, infection, infirmity, inflammation, malady, misery, pathosis, plague, seizure, sickliness, sickness, spell, stroke, syndrome, temperature, unhealthiness, unsoundness, upset, virus, visitation; SEE CONCEPT *306*

diseased [*adj*] *unhealthy*
afflicted, ailing, indisposed, infected, infectious, infirm, rotten, sick, sickly, tainted, unsound, unwell, unwholesome; SEE CONCEPT *314*

disembark [*v*] *get off transportation*
alight, anchor, arrive, come ashore, debark, deplane, detrain, dismount, go ashore, land, put in, step out of; SEE CONCEPT *159*

disenchanted [*adj*] *let down*
blasé, cynical, disappointed, disenthralled, disentranced, disillusioned, embittered, indifferent, jaundiced, knowing, mondaine, out of love, sick of, sophisticate, sophisticated, soured, undeceived, worldly, worldly-wise; SEE CONCEPT *403*

disengage [*v*] *free from connection*
abstract, back off, back out, cut loose, cut out, detach, disassociate, disconnect, disentangle, disjoin, dissociate, disunite, divide, drop out, ease, extricate, liberate, loose, loosen, opt out, pull the plug, release, separate, set free, unbind, uncouple, undo, unfasten, unfix, unloose, untie, weasel out*, withdraw; SEE CONCEPT *135*

disentangle [*v*] *unwind, disconnect; solve*
bail one out*, clear up, detach, discumber, disembroil, disencumber, disengage, disinvolve, emancipate, expand, extricate, free, let go, let off, loose, open, part, resolve, separate, sever, simplify, sort out, sunder, unbraid, undo, unfold, unravel, unscramble, unsnarl, untangle, untie, untwine, untwist, work out; SEE CONCEPTS *127,135*

disfavor [*n*] *dislike; disgrace*
aversion, disapprobation, disapproval, discredit, disesteem, dishonor, disinclination, disliking, displeasure, disregard, disrepute, disrespect, dissatisfaction, distaste, distrust, doghouse*, indisposition, mistrust, shame, thumbs down*, unpopularity; SEE CONCEPTS *29,388*

disfigure [*v*] *make ugly*
blemish, damage, deface, defile, deform, disfashion, disfeature, distort, hurt, injure, maim, mangle, mar, mutilate, scar; SEE CONCEPTS *137,246,250*

disgrace [*n*] *state of shame; bad reputation*
abasement, abuse, baseness, black eye*, blemish, blur, brand, comedown, contempt, contumely, corruption, culpability, debasement, debasing, defamation, degradation, derision, disbarment, discredit, disesteem, disfavor, dishonor, disrepute, disrespect, humbling, humiliation, ignominy, ill repute, infamy, ingloriousness, meanness, obloquy, odium, opprobrium, pollution, prostitution, put-down, reproach, scandal, scorn, slander, slight, slur, spot, stain, stigma, taint, tarnish, turpitude, venality; SEE CONCEPT *388*

disgrace [*v*] *bring shame upon*
abase, attaint, besmirch, blot, debase, defame, defile, degrade, depress, deride, derogate, desecrate, discredit, disfavor, dishonor, disparage, disregard, disrespect, expel, give black eye*, humble, humiliate, libel, lose face*, lower, mock, put down, reduce, reproach, ridicule, shame, slander, slur, snub, stain, stigmatize, sully, taint, take down a peg*, tar and feather*, tarnish; SEE CONCEPTS *14,54,384*

disgraceful [*adj*] *shameful, low*
blameworthy, contemptible, degrading, detestable, discreditable, dishonorable, disreputable, ignoble, ignominious, infamous, inglorious, mean, offensive, opprobrious, scandalous, shabby, shady, shocking, shoddy, unrespectable, unworthy; SEE CONCEPT *555*

disgruntled [*adj*] *unhappy; critical*
annoyed, bad tempered, bellyaching*, crabbing*, crabby, cranky, disappointed, discontent, discontented, displeased, dissatisfied, griping, grouchy, grousing, grumpy, irritable, irritated, kicking, kvetching*, malcontent, malcontented, peeved, peevish, petulant, put out, sulky, sullen, testy, uncontent, ungratified, vexed; SEE CONCEPTS *401,403*

disguise [*n*] *covering, makeup for deception*
beard, blind, camouflage, charade, cloak, color, coloring, concealment, costume, counterfeit, cover, cover-up, dissimulation, dress, facade, face, faking, false front*, fig leaf*, front*, get-up, guise, illusion, make-believe, mask, masquerade, pageant, pen name, pretense, pretension, pretentiousness, pseudonym, put-on, red herring*, screen, semblance, smoke screen*, trickery, veil, veneer; SEE CONCEPTS *446,451,680*

disguise [*v*] *mask; misrepresent*
affect, age, alter, antique, assume, beard, belie, camouflage, change, cloak, color, conceal, counterfeit,

cover, cover up, deceive, dissemble, dissimulate, doctor up*, dress up, fake, falsify, feign, front, fudge*, garble, gloss over, hide, make like, make up, masquerade, muffle, obfuscate, obscure, pretend, put on a front*, put on an act*, put on false front*, put up a front*, redo*, screen, secrete, sham, shroud, simulate, touch up, varnish, veil, wear cheaters*, whitewash*; SEE CONCEPTS *59,137,172,188,202*

disguised [*adj*] *unrecognizable*
bearded, camouflaged, changed, cloaked, covered, covert, fake, false, feigned, hidden, incognito, in disguise, masked, pretend, undercover; SEE CONCEPTS *547,619*

disgust [*n*] *aversion; repulsion*
abhorrence, abomination, antipathy, detestation, dislike, distaste, hatefulness, hatred, loathing, nausea, nauseation, nauseousness, objection, repugnance, revolt, revulsion, satiation, satiety, sickness, surfeit; SEE CONCEPTS *410,720*

disgust [*v*] *cause aversion; repel*
abominate, be repulsive, bother, cloy on, disenchant, displease, disturb, fill with loathing, gross out*, insult, irk, make one sick*, nauseate, offend, offend morals of, outrage, pall, pique, put off, reluct, repulse, revolt, scandalize, shock, sicken, surfeit, turn off, turn one's stomach*, upset; SEE CONCEPTS *7,19*

disgusted [*adj*] *sickened; offended*
abhorred, appalled, displeased, fastidious, fed up*, full up*, grossed out*, had bellyful*, had enough*, had it*, nauseated, nauseous, outraged, overwrought, queasy, repelled, repulsed, revolted, satiated, scandalized, sick, sick and tired of*, sick of*, squeamish, t'd off*, tired, turned off*, unhappy, up to here*, weary; SEE CONCEPT *403*

disgusting [*adj*] *sickening; repulsive*
abominable, awful, beastly, cloying, creepy, detestable, distasteful, foul, frightful, ghastly, grody*, gross*, gruesome, hateful, hideous, horrid, horrific, icky*, loathsome, lousy, macabre, monstrous, nasty, nauseating, nerdy*, noisome, objectionable, obnoxious, odious, offensive, outrageous, repellent, repugnant, revolting, rotten, satiating, scandalous, scuzzy*, shameless, shocking, skank, sleazeball*, sleazy*, stinking, surfeiting, vile, vulgar, yecchy*, yucky*; SEE CONCEPTS *485,548*

dish [*n1*] *eating receptacle*
bowl, casserole, ceramic, china, container, cup, mug, pitcher, plate, platter, porringer, pot, pottery, salver, saucer, tray, vessel; SEE CONCEPT *494*

dish [*n2*] *main part of meal*
course, eats*, entreé, fare, food, helping, recipe, serving; SEE CONCEPTS *457,460,461*

disharmony [*n*] *conflict, discord*
clash, contention, difference, disaccord, discordance, dissension, dissonance, dissonancy, friction, inharmoniousness, strife, unpeace, variance; SEE CONCEPTS *388,665*

dishearten [*v*] *depress, ruin one's hopes*
cast down, chill*, crush, damp, dampen, dash, daunt, deject, demoralize, depress, deter, discourage, disincline, dismay, disparage, dispirit, get down*, humble, humiliate, indispose, put a damper on*, put down, shake, throw a pall over*; SEE CONCEPTS *7,19*

disheveled [*adj*] *wrinkled, unkempt in appearance*
bagged out*, beat up*, bedraggled, blowzy*, dirty, disarranged, disarrayed, disordered, frowzy*, grubby*, ill-kempt, messed up, messy, mussed up*, mussy, ruffled, rumpled, scuzzy, slipshod, sloppy, slovenly, tousled, unbuttoned, uncombed, unfastidious, untidy, unzipped*; SEE CONCEPTS *485,579*

dishonest [*adj*] *lying, untruthful*
backbiting*, bent, bluffing, cheating, corrupt, crafty, crooked, cunning, deceitful, deceiving, deceptive, designing, disreputable, double-crossing, double-dealing, elusive, false, fraudulent, guileful, hoodwinking*, knavish, mendacious, misleading, perfidious, recreant, roguish, shady, shifty, sinister, slippery*, sneaking, sneaky, swindling, traitorous, treacherous, tricky, two-faced*, two-timing*, unctuous, underhanded, unfair, unprincipled, unscrupulous, untrustworthy, villainous, wily; SEE CONCEPT *267*

dishonesty [*n*] *lying; unwillingness to tell the truth*
artifice, bunk, cheating, chicane, chicanery, corruption, craft, criminality, crookedness, cunning, deceit, double-dealing, duplicity, faithlessness, falsehood, falsity, flimflam*, fourberie, fraud, fraudulence, graft, guile, hanky-panky*, hocus-pocus*, improbity, infamy, infidelity, insidiousness, knavery, knavishness, mendacity, perfidiousness, perfidy, racket, rascality, sharp practice*, slyness, stealing, swindle, treachery, trickery, trickiness, unscrupulousness, wiliness; SEE CONCEPTS *59,633,657*

dishonor [*n*] *state of shame*
abasement, abuse, affront, blame, degradation, discourtesy, discredit, disesteem, disfavor, disgrace, disrepute, ignominy, indignity, infamy, insult, obloquy, odium, offense, opprobrium, outrage, reproach, scandal, shame, slight; SEE CONCEPT *388*

dishonor [*v*] *shame, degrade*
abase, attaint, blacken, blot, corrupt, debase, debauch, defame, defile, disconsider, discredit, disgrace, disoblige, give black eye*, libel, make lose face*, reflect on, slander, sully; SEE CONCEPT *54*

dishonorable [*adj*] *shameful, corrupt*
base, blackguardly, contemptible, crooked, deceitful, despicable, devious, discreditable, disgraceful, disreputable, fraudulent, ignoble, ignominious, infamous, inglorious, low, miscreant, offensive, opprobious, putrid, scandalous, shabby, shady, shameless, treacherous, unprincipled, unrespectable, unscrupulous, untrustworthy; SEE CONCEPT *555*

dish out [*v*] *distribute*
allocate, deliver, dispense, dole out*, fork over*, furnish, give out, hand, hand out, hand over, inflict,

ladle, mete out, present, produce, scoop, serve, serve up, spoon, supply, transfer, turn over; SEE CONCEPT *140*

disillusioned [*adj*] *disappointed*
blasé, broken, brought down to earth*, debunked, disabused, disenchanted, disenthralled, disentranced, embittered, enlightened, freed, indifferent, knowing, let-down, mondaine, out of love*, punctured, sadder and wiser*, shattered, sophisticated, undeceived, worldly, worldly-wise*; SEE CONCEPT *403*

disinclination [*n*] *unwillingness to do, believe something*
alienation, antipathy, aversion, demur, disfavor, dislike, disliking, displeasure, disrelish, dissatisfaction, distaste, hatred, hesitance, indisposition, lack of desire, lack of enthusiasm, loathness, objection, opposition, reluctance, repugnance, resistance; SEE CONCEPTS *29,410,657*

disinclined [*adj*] *unwilling*
afraid, antipathetic, averse, backward, balking, doubtful, dubious, hesitating, indisposed, loath, not in the mood*, objecting, opposed, protesting, reluctant, resistant, shy, shying, slow, sticking, uneager, unsympathetic; SEE CONCEPTS *403,542*

disinfect [*v*] *make clean, pure*
antisepticize, clean, cleanse, decontaminate, deodorize, fumigate, purify, sanitize, sterilize; SEE CONCEPT *165*

disingenuous [*adj*] *insincere*
artful, crooked, cunning, deceitful, designing, dishonest, duplicitous, false, feigned, foxy, guileful, indirect, insidious, left-handed*, mendacious, oblique, shifty*, sly, tricky, two-faced*, uncandid, underhanded, unfair, unfrank, wily; SEE CONCEPTS *401,542*

disinherit [*v*] *cut off in will of bequeathal*
bereave, cut off without cent*, deprive, disaffiliate, disherit, disown, dispossess, divest, evict, exclude, exheridate, neglect, oust, repudiate, rob; SEE CONCEPTS *25,317*

disintegrate [*v*] *fall apart; reduce to pieces*
atomize, break apart, break down, break up, come apart, crumble, decay, decline, decompose, degenerate, deliquesce, descend, detach, dilapidate, disband, disconnect, disimprove, dismantle, disorganize, disperse, disunite, divide, fade away, fall to pieces*, molder, pulverize, putrefy, reduce, rot, separate, sever, shatter, sink, splinter, spoil, taint, take apart, turn, turn to dust*, unmake, wash away, wash out, wither, worsen; SEE CONCEPTS *252,469*

disinterested [*adj*] *detached, uninvolved*
aloof, candid, casual, dispassionate, equitable, even-handed, impartial, impersonal, incurious, indifferent, just watching the clock*, lackadaisical, negative, neutral, nonpartisan, not giving a damn*, outside, perfunctory, remote, unbiased, unconcerned, uncurious, unprejudiced, unselfish, withdrawn; SEE CONCEPTS *401,403*

disjointed [*adj*] *loose, disconnected*
aimless, confused, cool, discontinuous, disordered, displaced, disunited, divided, far-out, fitful, fuzzy, inchoate, incoherent, incohesive, irrational, jumbled, muddled, out-of-it*, out-to-lunch*, rambling, separated, spaced-out*, spacey*, spasmodic, split, unattached, unconnected, unorganized; SEE CONCEPTS *267,482,585*

disk [*n*] *round object*
circle, disc, discoid, discoidal, discus, dish, flan, plate, platter, quoit, sabot, saucer, shell; SEE CONCEPT *436*

dislike [*n*] *antagonism, hatred toward something*
animosity, animus, antipathy, aversion, deprecation, detestation, disapprobation, disapproval, disesteem, disfavor, disgust, disinclination, displeasure, dissatisfaction, distaste, enmity, hate, hostility, indisposition, loathing, mislike, objection, offense, opposition, prejudice, repugnance; SEE CONCEPT *29*

dislike [*v*] *be antagonistic toward something; hate*
abhor, abominate, antipathize, avoid, be allergic to*, bear malice toward, be averse to, be turned off to*, condemn, contemn, deplore, despise, detest, disapprove, disesteem, disfavor, disrelish, eschew, execrate, gross out on*, have hard feelings*, have no stomach for*, have no taste for, loathe, look down on, lose interest in, make faces at*, mind, not appreciate, not care for, not endure, not feel like, not take kindly to, object to, regret, resent, scorn, shudder at, shun; SEE CONCEPT *29*

dislocate [*v*] *displace*
break, disarticulate, disconnect, disengage, disjoint, disorder, disrupt, disturb, disunite, divide, jumble, misplace, mix up, move, put out of joint, remove, rummage, separate, shift, transfer, unhinge, upset; SEE CONCEPTS *135,147,213*

dislocation [*n*] *displacement*
break, confusion, disarray, disarticulation, disconnection, discontinuity, disengagement, disorder, disorganization, disruption, disturbance, division, luxation, misplacement, unhinging; SEE CONCEPTS *316,720,727*

dislodge [*v*] *knock loose*
bump loose, dig out, disentangle, dislocate, displace, disturb, eject, evict, extricate, force out, oust, remove, uproot; SEE CONCEPTS *147,213*

disloyal [*adj*] *unfaithful*
alienated, apostate, cheating, disaffected, double-crossing, estranged, faithless, false, perfidious, recreant, seditious, snaky*, subversive, traitorous, treacherous, treasonable, two-faced*, two-timing*, unfaithful, unloyal, unpatriotic, untrue, untrustworthy, wormlike*; SEE CONCEPT *401*

disloyalty [*n*] *unfaithfulness*
apostasy, bad faith, betrayal of trust, betrayment, breach of trust, breaking of faith, deceitfulness, disaffection, double-dealing, faithlessness, falseness, falsity, inconstancy, infidelity, perfidiousness, per-

fidy, recreancy, sedition, seditiousness, subversive activity, treachery, treason, unfaithfulness, untrueness, violation; SEE CONCEPT *633*

dismal [adj] *bleak, dreary, gloomy*
afflictive, black, boring, cheerless, cloudy, dark, depressed, depressing, desolate, despondent, dim, dingy, disagreeable, discouraging, disheartening, dispiriting, doleful, dolorous, dull, forlorn, frowning, funereal, ghastly, gruesome, hopeless, horrible, horrid, inauspicious, in the pits*, joyless, lonesome, lowering, lugubrious, melancholy, miserable, monotonous, morbid, murky, oppressive, overcast, sad, shadowy, somber, sorrowful, tedious, tenebrous, troublesome, unfortunate, unhappy; SEE CONCEPTS *525,536,548*

dismantle [v] *take apart*
annihilate, bankrupt, bare, break down, break up, decimate, demolish, denudate, denude, deprive, destroy, disassemble, dismember, dismount, disrobe, divest, fell, knock down, level, part out, pull down, raze, ruin, strike, strip, subvert, take down, take to pieces, tear down, unbuild, undo, unrig, wrack, wreck; SEE CONCEPTS *135,168,252*

dismay [n] *disappointed feeling; distress*
agitation, alarm, anxiety, apprehension, blue funk*, blues*, bummer*, chagrin, cold feet*, consternation, disappointment, discouragement, disheartenment, disillusionment, downer*, dread, dumps*, fear, fright, funk*, hassle, horror, letdown, panic, terror, the blahs*, trepidation, upset; SEE CONCEPTS *27,410,690*

dismay [v] *disappoint, fill with consternation*
abash, affright, agitate, alarm, appall, bewilder, bother, chill, confound, consternate, daunt, discomfit, discompose, disconcert, discourage, dishearten, disillusion, dispirit, disquiet, distress, disturb, dumbfound, embarrass, faze, flummox*, fluster, foul up*, frighten, get to, horrify, louse up*, mess up*, muck up*, mystify, nonplus, paralyze, perplex, put off, puzzle, rattle, scare, screw up*, shake, snafu*, take aback, terrify, terrorize, throw, throw into tizzy*, unhinge*, unnerve, upset; SEE CONCEPTS *7,19*

dismember [v] *cut into pieces*
amputate, anatomize, cripple, disassemble, disjoint, dislimb, dislocate, dismantle, dismount, dissect, divide, maim, mutilate, part, rend, sever, sunder, take down; SEE CONCEPTS *98,135,176*

dismiss [v1] *send away, remove; free*
abolish, banish, boot*, brush off*, bundle, cast off*, cast out*, chase, chuck, clear, decline, deport, detach, disband, discard, dispatch, dispense with, disperse, dispose of, dissolve, divorce, do without, drive out, eject, expel, force out, have done with*, kick out*, let go, let out, lock out*, outlaw, push aside, push back, reject, release, relegate, relinquish, repel, repudiate, rid, send off, send packing*, shed, show out*, slough off, supersede, sweep away*, turn out; SEE CONCEPTS *127,217*

dismiss [v2] *remove from job, responsibility*
ax*, boot*, boot out*, bounce*, bump*, can*, cashier*, defrock, depone, depose, deselect, discharge, disemploy, disfrock, displace, disqualify, drop, fire, furlough, give notice to, give the ax*, give the gate*, give the heave-ho*, give walking papers*, give warning, impeach, kick out*, lay off, let go*, let out*, oust, pension, pink-slip*, put away*, recall, retire, sack*, send packing*, shelve*, shut out*, suspend, terminate, turn away, unfrock, unseat, wash out*; SEE CONCEPTS *324,351*

dismiss [v3] *put out of one's mind*
banish, contemn, deride, despise, discard, disdain, dispel, disregard, drop, flout, gibe, gird, jeer, kiss off*, laugh away*, lay aside, mock, pooh-pooh*, rally, reject, relegate, repudiate, repulse, ridicule, scoff, scorn, scout, set aside, shelve*, spurn, taunt, twit; SEE CONCEPT *35*

dismissal [n] *release*
adjournment, banishment, bounce, brush-off, cold shoulder*, congé, deportation, deposal, deposition, discharge, dislodgment, displacement, dispossession, dissolution, door*, end, eviction, exile, exorcism, expatriation, expulsion, freedom, freeing, housecleaning*, kiss-off*, layoff, liberation, marching orders*, notice, old heave-ho*, ostracism, ouster, permission, pink slip*, relegation, removal, suspension; SEE CONCEPTS *127,217,351*

dismount [v] *get off something higher*
alight, debark, deplane, descend, detrain, disembark, get down, light; SEE CONCEPT *195*

disobedience [n] *misbehavior; noncompliance with rules*
defiance, dereliction, disregard, indiscipline, infraction, infringement, insubmission, insubordination, insurgence, intractableness, mutiny, neglect, nonobservance, perversity, rebellion, recalcitrance, refractoriness, revolt, revolution, riot, sabotage, sedition, strike, stubbornness, transgression, unruliness, violation, waywardness; SEE CONCEPT *633*

disobedient [adj] *defiant, mischievous*
contrary, contumacious, disorderly, fractious, froward, headstrong, insubordinate, intractable, naughty, noncompliant, nonobservant, obstreperous, perverse, recalcitrant, refractory, resistive, uncompliant, undisciplined, unruly, wayward, willful; SEE CONCEPT *401*

disobey [v] *disregard rules; refuse to conform*
balk, be remiss, break rules, contravene, counteract, dare, decline, defy, desert, differ, disagree, evade, flout, fly in face of*, go counter to, ignore, infringe, insurrect, misbehave, mutiny, neglect, not conform, not heed, not listen, not mind, object, overstep, pay no attention to, rebel, recalcitrate, resist, revolt, revolution, revolutionize, riot, rise in arms*, run riot*, set aside, shirk, strike, take law into own hands*, transgress, violate, withstand; SEE CONCEPTS *30,192,384*

disoblige [v] *displease, annoy*
affront, bother, discommode, disturb, incommode, inconvenience, insult, offend, put about, put out, slight, trouble, upset, vex; SEE CONCEPTS *7,19*

disobliging [adj] *rude, annoying*
awkward, disagreeable, discourteous, ill-disposed, ill-natured, rude, unaccommodating, unamiable, uncivil, uncongenial, uncooperative, unhelpful, unobliging, unpleasant; SEE CONCEPT *401*

disorder [n1] *chaos, clutter*
anarchy, ataxia, confusion, derangement, disarrangement, disarray, discombobulation, disorderliness, disorganization, huddle, irregularity, jumble, mess, muddle, rat's nest*, shambles, snarl, topsy-turviness*, untidiness; SEE CONCEPT *230*

disorder [n2] *social commotion; mental confusion*
agitation, anarchism, anarchy, brawl, bustle, chaos, clamor, commotion, complication, convulsion, discombobulation*, discord, disorganization, distemper, disturbance, dither*, entanglement, fight, flap*, fracas, fuss, hubbub*, hullabaloo*, imbroglio, insurrection, lawlessness, mayhem, misrule, mob rule*, quarrel, rebellion, reign of terror*, revolution, riot, rioting, ruckus, rumpus, static, strike, terrorism, tizzy*, trouble, tumult, turbulence, turmoil, unrest, unruliness, uproar; SEE CONCEPTS *388,410*

disorder [n3] *illness*
affliction, ailment, cachexia, complaint, disease, diseasedness, indisposition, infirmity, malady, sickness, unhealth, upset; SEE CONCEPT *306*

disorder [v] *mix up, disarrange*
clutter, confound, confuse, derange, discompose, discreate, dishevel, disjoint, dislocate, disorganize, disrupt, distemper, disturb, embroil, jumble, mess up, muddle, muss up*, rummage, rumple, scatter, shuffle, tumble, unsettle, upset; SEE CONCEPTS *240,250*

disordered [adj] *in a mess*
all over the place*, confused, deranged, disarranged, discombobulated*, disconnected, discontinuous, disjointed, dislocated, disorganized, displaced, incoherent, in confusion, jumbled, mislaid, misplaced, molested, moved, muddled, out-of-place, removed, roiled, ruffled, rumpled, shifted, shuffled, stirred-up, tampered with, tangled, tossed, tousled, tumbled, unsettled, untidy; SEE CONCEPTS *485,535*

disorderly [adj1] *messy, untidy*
all over the place*, chaotic, cluttered, confused, dislocated, disorganized, heterogeneous, indiscriminate, irregular, jumbled, messed-up, mixed-up, out-of-control*, out-of-line*, out-of-step*, out-of-whack*, scattered, scrambled, slovenly, topsy-turvy*, tumult, uncombed, undisciplined, unkempt, unmethodical, unrestrained, unsystematic, untrained; SEE CONCEPTS *485,535*

disorderly [adj2] *causing trouble; unlawful*
boisterous, disobedient, disruptive, drunk, fractious, indisciplined, intemperate, lawless, noisy, obstreperous, off-base*, on-a-tear*, out-of-line*, out-of-order*, raucous, rebellious, refractory, riotous, rowdy, stormy, termagant, tumultous/tumultuous, turbulent, uncompliant, uncontrollable, ungovernable, unmanageable, unruly, wayward; SEE CONCEPTS *401,545*

disorganization [n] *unordered situation or thing*
anarchy, chaos, confusion, derangement, disarray, disjointedness, disorder, disruption, dissolution, disunion, foul-up*, incoherence, mix-up, rat's nest*, screw-up*, unconnectedness, unholy mess*; SEE CONCEPTS *674,727*

disorganize [v] *disrupt arrangement; make shambles of*
break down, break up, clutter, complicate, confound, confuse, demobilize, derange, destroy, disarrange, disarray, disband, discompose, discreate, dishevel, dislocate, disorder, disperse, disturb, embroil, jumble, litter, mess up, mislay, misplace, muddle, perturb, put out of order, scatter, scramble, shuffle, toss, turn topsy-turvy, unsettle, upset; SEE CONCEPTS *250,252,384*

disorganized [adj] *unmethodical; messed up*
chaotic, confused, disordered, disorderly, haphazard, jumbled, like a Chinese fire drill*, mixed up, muddled, screwed up*, shuffled, unsystematic; SEE CONCEPTS *485,585*

disoriented [adj] *confused, unstable*
adrift, all at sea*, astray, bewildered, discombobulated*, lost, mixed-up, not adjusted, off-beam*, off-course*, out-of-joint*, perplexed, unbalanced, unhinged*, unsettled; SEE CONCEPT *403*

disown [v] *refuse to acknowledge*
abandon, abjure, abnegate, cast off, deny, disacknowledge, disallow, disavow, discard, disclaim, divorce oneself from, refuse to recognize, reject, renounce, repudiate, retract; SEE CONCEPTS *50,54,88*

disparage [v] *criticize; detract from*
abuse, belittle, chill*, cry down, decry, defame, degrade, deject, demoralize, denigrate, deprecate, depreciate, deride, derogate, dis*, discourage, discredit, disdain, dishearten, dismiss, dispirit, dispraise, downcry, dump on*, lower, malign, minimize, pan*, put down, put hooks in*, rap*, ridicule, roast*, run down*, scorch, scorn, slam*, slander, smear*, sour grapes*, tear down, traduce, underestimate, underrate, undervalue, vilify, write off; SEE CONCEPTS *7,19,52,54*

disparagement [n] *strong criticism; detraction*
aspersion, backbiting*, backstabbing*, belittlement, blame, calumny, censure, condemnation, contempt, contumely, debasement, degradation, denunciation, depreciation, derision, derogation, discredit, disdain, impairment, lessening, lie, prejudice, reproach, ridicule, scandal, scorn, slander, tale, underestimation; SEE CONCEPTS *52,54*

disparate [adj] *at odds, different*
at variance, contrary, contrasting, discordant, discrepant, dissimilar, distant, distinct, divergent,

diverse, far cry, incommensurate, incompatible, inconsistent, inconsonant, like night and day*, poles apart, separate, unalike, unequal, unequivalent, uneven, unlike, unsimilar, various; SEE CONCEPT 564

disparity [n] *difference*
alterity, discrepancy, disproportion, dissemblance, dissimilarity, dissimilitude, distinction, divergence, divergency, diverseness, gap, imbalance, imparity, incongruity, inequality, otherness, unevenness, unlikeness, variation; SEE CONCEPT 665

dispassionate [adj] *unfeeling, impartial*
abstract, aloof, calm, candid, cold-blooded, cold-fish*, collected, composed, cool, cool cat*, couldn't care less*, detached, disinterested, fair, iceberg*, impersonal, imperturbable, indifferent, judicial, just, laid back, moderate, neutral, nondiscriminatory, nonpartisan, objective, poker-faced*, quiet, serene, sober, temperate, tough, unbiased, unemotional, unexcitable, unexcited, unflappable, uninvolved, unmoved, unprejudiced, unruffled; SEE CONCEPTS *401,404*

dispatch [n1] *speed in carrying out action*
alacrity, celerity, expedition, expeditiousness, haste, hurry, hustle, precipitateness, promptitude, promptness, quickness, rapidity, rustle, speediness, swiftness; SEE CONCEPTS *755,818*

dispatch [n2] *communication*
account, bulletin, communiqué, document, instruction, item, letter, message, missive, news, piece, report, story; SEE CONCEPTS *271,277,278*

dispatch [v1] *hurry, send fast*
accelerate, address, consign, dismiss, express, forward, hand-carry, hasten, issue, quicken, railroad*, remit, route, run with, run with ball*, ship, speed, transmit, walk through; SEE CONCEPTS *152,217*

dispatch [v2] *finish; consume*
conclude, devour, discharge, dispose of, eat up, expedite, lay low, perform, polish off*, scarf down*, settle; SEE CONCEPTS *169,234*

dispatch [v3] *kill*
assassinate, bump off*, butcher*, destroy, eliminate, execute, finish, finish off*, murder, put away*, put end to, slaughter, slay, take out*; SEE CONCEPTS *238,252*

dispel [v] *drive away thought, belief*
allay, banish, beat off*, break it up*, break up*, bust up*, cancel, chase away, crumble, deploy, disband, disintegrate, dismiss, disperse, dissipate, distribute, eject, eliminate, expel, oust, repel, resolve, rout, scatter, scramble, split up*; SEE CONCEPTS *14,35*

dispensable [adj] *not necessary; able to be thrown away*
disposable, excessive, expendable, inessential, minor, needless, nonessential, removable, superfluous, trivial, unimportant, unnecessary, unrequired, useless; SEE CONCEPT 546

dispensation [n1] *allocation of supply*
allotment, appointment, apportionment, award, bestowal, conferment, consignment, courtesy, dealing out, disbursement, distribution, dole, endowment, favor, indulgence, kindness, part, portion, quota, service, share, supplying; SEE CONCEPTS *140,337*

dispensation [n2] *management*
administration, direction, economy, plan, regulation, scheme, stewardship, system; SEE CONCEPTS *325,660,770*

dispensation [n3] *permission*
exception, exemption, immunity, indulgence, license, privilege, relaxation, relief, remission, reprieve; SEE CONCEPT 685

dispense [v1] *dole out supply*
allocate, allot, apportion, assign, come across with, deal, deal out, disburse, dish out*, distribute, divide, divvy*, fork out*, furnish, give, give away, give with, hand out, hand over, lot, measure, mete out, partition, portion, prepare, prorate, share, shell out*, supply; SEE CONCEPT 140

dispense [v2] *operate, administer*
apply, carry out, command, direct, discharge, enforce, execute, handle, implement, manage, maneuver, manipulate, swing, undertake, wield; SEE CONCEPT 117

dispense [v3] *exempt from responsibility*
absolve, discharge, except, excuse, exonerate, let off, privilege from, release, relieve, reprieve, spare; SEE CONCEPT 110

dispense with [v] *omit; do away with*
abolish, abstain from, brush aside, cancel, dispose of, disregard, do without, forgo, get rid of, give up, ignore, pass over, relinquish, render needless, shake off, waive; SEE CONCEPT 30

disperse [v] *distribute; scatter*
banish, besprinkle, break up, broadcast, cast forth, circulate, deal, diffuse, disappear, disband, disburse, discharge, dislodge, dismiss, dispel, disseminate, dissipate, dissolve, divvy*, dole out, eject, intersperse, measure out, partition, propagate, radiate, rout, scatter, scramble, send off, separate, shed, sow, split up, spray, spread, strew, take off in all directions*, vanish; SEE CONCEPTS *135,217*

dispirited [adj] *dejected, sad*
blue*, bummed-out*, crestfallen, dejected, depressed, despondent, disconsolate, discouraged, disheartened, down*, downbeat, downcast, downhearted, dragged*, funky*, gloomy, glum, in the doldrums, low, melancholy, morose, shot-down*, spiritless, woebegone; SEE CONCEPT 403

displace [v1] *move, remove from normal place*
change, crowd out, derange, disarrange, disestablish, dislocate, dislodge, displant, dispossess, disturb, eject, evict, expel, expulse, force out, lose, mislay, misplace, relegate, shift, transpose, unsettle, uproot; SEE CONCEPTS *147,213*

displace [v2] *remove from position of responsibility*
banish, can*, cashier*, cut out*, deport, depose, dethrone, discard, discharge, discrown, disenthrone, dismiss, disthrone, exile, expatriate, fire, oust, rele-

gate, remove, replace, sack*, step into shoes of*, succeed, supersede, supplant, take over, take the place of, transport, uncrown, unmake, usurp; SEE CONCEPTS *133,298,300*

display [*n*] *public showing; spectacle*
affectation, an act, arrangement, array, arrayal, blaze, bravura, dash, demonstration, example, exhibit, exhibition, expo*, exposition, exposure, fanfare, flourish, for show, frame-up*, frippery, front, grandstand play*, layout, manifestation, ostentation, ostentatiousness, pageant, panorama, parade, pedantry, pomp, presentation, pretension, pretentiousness, revelation, sample, scheme, shine, show, showboat*, splash, splendor, splurge, spread, unfolding, vanity; SEE CONCEPTS *261,386*

display [*v*] *show for public viewing, effect*
advertise, arrange, bare, betray, boast, brandish, bring to view, demonstrate, disclose, emblazon, evidence, evince, exhibit, expand, expose, extend, feature, flash, flaunt, flourish, glaze, grandstand*, illustrate, impart, lay bare*, lay out, make clear, make known, manifest, model, open, open out, parade, perform, present, promote, promulgate, publish, represent, reveal, set out, showcase, show off, sport, spread out, stretch out, trot out*, uncover, unfold, unfurl, unmask, unroll, unveil, vamp; SEE CONCEPT *261*

displease [*v*] *make unhappy*
aggravate, anger, annoy, antagonize, bother, cap, chagrin, cool, curdle*, cut to the quick*, disappoint, discontent, disgruntle, disgust, disoblige, dissatisfy, enrage, exasperate, fret, frustrate, gall, hurt, incense, irk, irritate, nettle, offend, perplex, pique, play dirty, provoke, put out, repel, revolt, rile, roil, sound, turn off*, upset, vex, wing*, worry, zing*; SEE CONCEPTS *7,19*

displeasure [*n*] *unhappiness, anger*
annoyance, aversion, disapprobation, disapproval, discontentment, disfavor, disgruntlement, disinclination, dislike, disliking, disrelish, dissatisfaction, distaste, incensement, indignation, indisposition, irritation, offense, pique, resentment, umbrage, vexation, wrath; SEE CONCEPT *410*

disposal [*n1*] *parting with or throwing something away*
auctioning, bartering, chucking, clearance, conveyance, demolishing, demolition, destroying, destruction, discarding, dispatching, dispensation, disposition, dumping, ejection, jettison, jettisoning, junking, relegation, relinquishment, removal, riddance, sacrifice, sale, scrapping, selling, throwing away, trading, transfer, transference, vending; SEE CONCEPT *180*

disposal [*n2*] *conclusion, settlement of situation*
action, allocation, arrangement, array, assignment, assortment, bequest, bestowal, consignment, control, conveyance, determination, dispensation, disposition, distribution, division, effectuation, end,

gift, grouping, order, ordering, placing, position, provision, sequence, transfer, winding up; SEE CONCEPTS *119,230*

dispose [*v*] *place, order; deal with*
actuate, adapt, adjust, arrange, array, bend, bias, call the tune*, condition, determine, distribute, fix, govern, group, incline, induce, influence, lay down the law*, lead, locate, make willing, marshal, methodize, motivate, move, organize, predispose, prepare, promote, prompt, put, put one's foot down*, put to rights, range, rank, read the riot act*, regulate, ride herd on*, set, set in order, settle, shepherd, stand, sway, systematize, tailor, tempt; SEE CONCEPTS *84,117,158*

disposed [*adj*] *inclined to a type of behavior*
apt, at drop of hat*, biased, fain, game*, game for, given, liable, likely, minded, of a mind to*, partial, predisposed, prone, ready, subject, tending toward, willing; SEE CONCEPTS *542,552*

dispose of [*v1*] *throw away*
adios*, bestow, chuck*, deep six*, destroy, discard, dump, eighty-six*, eliminate, file in circular file*, get rid of, give, jettison, junk*, kiss*, kiss off*, make over, part with, relinquish, scrap, sell, throw out, throw over, throw overboard*, transfer, unload; SEE CONCEPT *180*

dispose of [*v2*] *settle a matter*
chop, cut, cut off, deal with, decide, determine, do the trick*, end, finish, knock off*, polish off*, put away, take care of; SEE CONCEPTS *18,234*

disposition [*n1*] *personal temperament*
bag*, being, bent, bias, cast, character, complexion, constitution, cup of tea*, druthers*, emotions, flash, frame of mind, groove*, habit, humor, identity, inclination, individualism, individuality, leaning, make-up, mind-set*, mood, nature, penchant, personality, predilection, predisposition, proclivity, proneness, propensity, readiness, spirit, stamp, temper, tendency, tenor, thing*, tone, type, vein; SEE CONCEPT *411*

disposition [*n2*] *arrangement, management of situation*
adjustment, classification, control, decision, direction, disposal, distribution, grouping, method, order, ordering, organization, placement, plan, regulation, sequence; SEE CONCEPTS *6,660*

disproportion [*n*] *imbalance*
asymmetry, difference, discrepancy, disparity, imparity, inadequacy, inequality, insufficiency, irregularity, lopsidedness, unevenness, unsuitableness; SEE CONCEPTS *665,667*

disproportionate [*adj*] *out of balance*
asymmetric, excessive, incommensurate, inordinate, irregular, lopsided, nonsymmetrical, off-balance, out of proportion, overbalanced, superfluous, too much, unbalanced, unequal, uneven, unreasonable, unsymmetrical; SEE CONCEPTS *564,566,771*

disprove [v] *prove false*
belie, blow sky high*, blow up*, break, confound, confute, contradict, contravene, controvert, deny, disconfirm, discredit, explode, expose, find unfounded, impugn, invalidate, knock bottom out of*, knock props out*, negate, negative, overthrow, overturn, poke holes in*, puncture, rebut, refute, set aside, shoot, shoot holes in*, tear down*, throw out, traverse, weaken; SEE CONCEPT *58*

disputable [adj] *debatable; open to discussion*
arguable, controversial, doubtful, dubious, moot, mootable, problematic, questionable, uncertain; SEE CONCEPTS *529,535*

disputation [n] *controversy*
argumentation, debate, dialectic, dispute, dissension, forensic, mooting, polemics; SEE CONCEPTS *278,532*

disputatious [adj] *argumentative*
cantankerous, captious, caviling, contentious, controversial, dissentious, litigious, polemical, pugnacious, quarrelsome; SEE CONCEPTS *401,542*

dispute [n] *argument*
altercation, beef*, bickering, bone*, bone of contention*, brawl, broil, brouhaha*, commotion, conflict, contention, controversy, debate, difference of opinion, disagreement, discord, discussion, dissension, disturbance, embroilment, falling-out*, feud, fireworks*, flare-up*, fracas, friction, fuss*, hubbub*, miff*, misunderstanding, polemic, quarrel, row*, rumpus*, squabble, squall, strife, tiff*, uproar, variance, words*, wrangle; SEE CONCEPTS *46,106,278*

dispute [v] *argue*
agitate, altercate, bicker, brawl, bump heads*, canvass, challenge, clash, confute, contend, contest, contradict, controvert, debate, deny, disaffirm, discept, discuss, disprove, doubt, gainsay, hassle, have at*, impugn, jump on one's case*, kick around*, lock horns*, moot, negate, pick a bone*, quarrel, question, quibble, rebut, refute, squabble, take on, thrash out, toss around*, wrangle; SEE CONCEPT *46*

disqualification [n] *disability; rejection for participation*
awkwardness, clumsiness, debarment, disablement, disenablement, disentitlement, elimination, exclusion, incapacitation, incapacity, incompetence, incompetency, ineligibility, ineptitude, lack, unfitness, unproficiency; SEE CONCEPT *630*

disqualify [v] *be unfit for; be ineligible*
bar, bate, debar, declare ineligible, disable, disenable, disentitle, disfranchise, eighty-six*, except, exclude, impair, incapacitate, invalidate, nix*, not make the cut*, paralyze, preclude, prohibit, rule out, suspend, unfit, weaken; SEE CONCEPTS *121,699*

disquiet [n] *worry; mental upset*
ailment, alarm, angst, anxiety, care, concern, concernment, disquietude, distress, disturbance, fear, ferment, foreboding, fretfulness, inquietude, nervousness, restiveness, restlessness, solicitude, storm, trouble, turmoil, unease, uneasiness, unrest; SEE CONCEPTS *410,532,690*

disquiet [v] *worry; make uneasy*
agitate, annoy, bother, concern, discompose, distress, disturb, fluster, fret, harass, incommode, perplex, perturb, pester, plague, trouble, unhinge, unsettle, upset, vex; SEE CONCEPTS *7,19*

disquieting [adj] *upsetting*
annoying, bothersome, disconcerting, distressing, disturbing, irritating, perplexing, perturbing, troublesome, troubling, unnerving, unsettling, vexing, worrying; SEE CONCEPT *529*

disregard [n] *ignoring*
apathy, brush-off*, contempt, disdain, disesteem, disfavor, disinterest, disrespect, forgetting, heedlessness, inadvertence, inattention, indifference, insouciance, lassitude, lethargy, listlessness, neglect, neglecting, negligence, oblivion, omission, omitting, overlooking, oversight, scorn, slight, slighting, the cold shoulder*, unconcern, unmindfulness; SEE CONCEPTS *30,633*

disregard [v] *ignore; make light of*
blink at*, brush aside, brush away, brush off, cold-shoulder*, contemn, despise, discount, disdain, disobey, disparage, fail, forget, have no use for*, laugh off*, leave out of account, let go, let off easy*, let pass*, live with*, look the other way*, miss, neglect, omit, overlook, overpass, pass over, pay no attention to, pay no heed to, pay no mind*, pooh pooh*, scorn, shut eyes to*, slight, snub, take no notice of, tune out*, turn blind eye*, turn deaf ear*, vilipend, wink at*; SEE CONCEPT *30*

disrepair [n] *state of deterioration*
collapse, decay, decrepitude, dilapidation, ruination; SEE CONCEPTS *230,674*

disrepair [adj] *broken; deteriorated*
busted*, damaged, dead, decayed, decrepit, down, kaput*, not functioning, on the blink*, on the fritz*, out of commission*, out of order, worn out, wracked*; SEE CONCEPT *485*

disreputable [adj] *dishonorable, lowly*
abject, bad, base, beggarly, cheap, contemptible, derogatory, despicable, discreditable, disgraceful, disorderly, dissolute, ignominious, in bad, infamous, inglorious, in low esteem, lewd, libidinous, licentious, mean, no good*, notorious, opprobrious, pitiable, scandalous, scurvy, shabby, shady, shameful, shocking, shoddy, sordid, sorry, unprincipled, unrespectable, vicious, vile; SEE CONCEPT *404*

disrepute [n] *dishonor, shame*
blemish, blot, brand, cloud, discredit, disesteem, disfavor, disgrace, ignominy, ill fame, ill favor, ill repute, infamy, ingloriousness, notoriety, obloquy, odium, opprobrium, reproach, scandal, scar, slur, smear, spot, stain, stigma, taint, unpopularity; SEE CONCEPT *411*

disrespect [n] *disregard, rudeness toward someone*
boldness, coarseness, contempt, discourtesy, dishonor, flippancy, hardihood, impertinence, impiety,

impoliteness, impudence, incivility, insolence, insolency, insolentness, irreverence, lack of respect, sacrilege, unmannerliness; SEE CONCEPTS *29,633*

disrespectful [*adj*] *insulting, rude*
aweless, bad-mannered, blasphemous, bold, cheeky*, contemptuous, discourteous, disgracious, flip*, flippant, fresh, ill-bred, ill-mannered, impertinent, impious, impolite, impudent, insolent, irreverent, misbehaved, nervy*, out-of-line*, profanatory, profane, sacrilegious, sassy*, saucy*, smart-alecky*, snippy*, uncivil, unfilial, ungracious; SEE CONCEPTS *267,401*

disrobe [*v*] *take off one's clothes*
bare, denudate, denude, deprive, dismantle, divest, doff, husk*, peel*, remove, shed, shuck*, slip out of, strip, take it off, unbutton*, unclothe, uncover, undress; SEE CONCEPT *167*

disrupt [*v1*] *upset, disorganize*
agitate, bollix, confuse, disarray, discombobulate*, discompose, disorder, disturb, mess up, mix up, muck up*, muddle, muddy the waters*, psych out*, put off, rattle, rattle one's cage*, rummage, screw up*, shake, spoil, throw, unsettle, upset apple cart*; SEE CONCEPTS *16,84,234*

disrupt [*v2*] *break, interrupt*
breach, break into, break up, fracture, hole, interfere with, intrude, obstruct, open, rupture, unsettle, upset; SEE CONCEPTS *98,135*

disruptive [*adj*] *causing trouble, confusion*
confusing, disorderly, distracting, disturbing, obstreperous, off-base*, out-of-line*, out-of-order*, rowdy, troublemaking, troublesome, unruly, unsettling, upsetting; SEE CONCEPTS *401,537*

dissatisfaction [*n*] *discontent, unhappiness*
annoyance, anxiety, aversion, boredom, chagrin, complaint, desolation, disapproval, discomfort, discontentment, discouragement, disfavor, disgruntlement, disinclination, dislike, disliking, dismay, displeasure, disquiet, disrelish, distaste, distress, ennui, envy, exasperation, fretfulness, frustration, heartburn, hopelessness, indisposition, irritation, jealousy, lamentation, malcontent, malcontentment, oppression, querulousness, regret, resentment, trouble, uneasiness, weariness, worry; SEE CONCEPTS *29,410*

dissatisfied [*adj*] *discontented, unhappy*
annoyed, begrudging, bothered, complaining, crabby*, critical, disaffected, disappointed, discontent, disgruntled, displeased, ennuied, envious, faultfinding, fed-up*, fretful, fretting, frustrated, griping, grudging, grumbling, grumpy*, insatiable, irked, jaundiced, jealous, kvetching*, malcontent, malcontented, not satisfied, offended, picky, plaintive, put-out*, querulous, sniveling, sulky, sullen, unappeased, unassuaged, unfulfilled, ungratified, unsated, unsatisfied, vexed; SEE CONCEPT *403*

dissect [*v1*] *cut up; take apart*
anatomize, break up, cut, cut apart, dichotomize, disjoin, disjoint, dislimb, dismember, dissever, di-

vide, exscind, exsect, lay open, operate, part, prosect, quarter, section, sever, slice, sunder; SEE CONCEPTS *98,176*

dissect [*v2*] *analyze*
anatomize, break down, decompose, decompound, examine, explore, inquire about, inspect, investigate, resolve, scrutinize, study; SEE CONCEPT *24*

dissection [*n1*] *cutting up, particularly of a dead body*
anatomization, anatomy, autopsy, dismemberment, examination, necropsy, operation, postmortem, vivisection; SEE CONCEPTS *176,310*

dissection [*n2*] *thorough analysis*
breakdown, breakup, criticism, critique, examination, inquest, inspection, investigation, resolution, review, scrutiny, study; SEE CONCEPTS *24,290*

dissemble [*v*] *disguise, pretend*
affect, camouflage, cloak, conceal, counterfeit, cover, cover up, dissimulate, doublespeak*, double talk*, dress up, fake, falsify, feign, four-flush*, hide, let on*, make like*, mask, pass, play possum*, pussyfoot*, put on a front*, put on an act*, put on false front*, put up a front*, put up smoke screen*, sham*, shroud, shuck and jive*, signify, simulate, stonewall*, whitewash*; SEE CONCEPTS *59,188,716*

disseminate [*v*] *distribute, scatter*
advertise, announce, annunciate, blaze, blazon, broadcast, circulate, declare, diffuse, disject, disperse, dissipate, proclaim, promulgate, propagate, publicize, publish, radiate, sow, spread, strew; SEE CONCEPTS *108,140,201,222*

dissemination [*n*] *distribution*
airing, broadcasting, circulation, diffusion, dissipation, promulgation, propagation, publication, publishing, spread; SEE CONCEPTS *651,746*

dissension [*n*] *conflict of opinion*
altercation, argument, bad vibes*, bickering, clinker*, contention, controversy, difference, disaccord, disagreement, discord, discordance, dispute, dissent, dissidence, disunity, faction, factionalism, flak*, friction, fuss, quarrel, scene, sour note*, static, strife, trouble, variance, wrangle; SEE CONCEPTS *46,278,665*

dissent [*n*] *disagreement, disapproval*
bone*, bone of contention*, bone to pick*, clinker*, conflict, contention, denial, difference, disaccord, discord, dissension, dissidence, disunity, far cry*, flak*, forget it, hassle, heresy, heterodoxy, misbelief, nonagreement, nonconcurrence, nonconformism, nonconformity, nope*, objection, opposition, poles apart*, protest, refusal, resistance, schism, sour note*, spat, split, strife, unorthodoxy, variance; SEE CONCEPTS *29,665,689*

dissent [*v*] *disagree*
argue, balk, break with, buck, contradict, decline, demur, differ, disaccord, discord, divide, fly in the face of*, object, oppose, pettifog, protest, put up a fight*, put up an argument, refuse, say not a chance*,

say nothing doing*, say no way*, shy, stickle, vary, wrangle; SEE CONCEPTS *21,46*

dissertation [*n*] *scholarly thesis*
argumentation, commentary, critique, discourse, disputation, disquisition, essay, exposition, memoir, monograph, tractate, treatise; SEE CONCEPTS *271,287*

disservice [*n*] *unkindness*
bad turn, detriment, disfavor, harm, hurt, injury, injustice, insult, outrage, prejudice, wrong; SEE CONCEPTS *309,645,674*

dissidence [*n*] *difference of opinion*
bad vibes*, contention, disaccord, disagreement, discordance, disharmony, dispeace, dispute, dissension, dissent, feud, heresy, heterodoxy, misbelief, nonconformism, nonconformity, rupture, schism, sour note*, strife, unorthodoxy; SEE CONCEPTS *278,633,689*

dissident [*n*] *person who holds different belief*
agitator, dissenter, heretic, misbeliever, nonconformist, protester, rebel, recusant, schismatic, schismatist, sectary, separatist; SEE CONCEPTS *359,423*

dissident [*adj*] *disagreeing, differing*
discordant, dissentient, dissenting, heretical, heterodox, nonconformist, schismatic, sectarian, unorthodox; SEE CONCEPT *403*

dissimilar [*adj*] *not alike; not capable of comparison*
antithetical, antonymous, contradictory, contrary, different, disparate, distant, divergent, diverse, far cry*, heterogeneous, individual, like night and day*, march to different drummer*, mismatched, mismated, not similar, offbeat, opposite, poles apart*, unequal, unique, unlike, unrelated, unsimilar, various, weird*; SEE CONCEPT *564*

dissimilarity [*n*] *unlikeness*
alterity, contrast, difference, discord, discordance, discrepancy, disparity, dissemblance, dissimilitude, distance, distinction, divarication, divergence, divergency, diversity, heterogeneity, incomparability, incongruity, inconsistency, inconsonance, nonuniformity, offset, otherness, separation, severance, unrelatedness, variance, variation; SEE CONCEPT *665*

dissimulate [*v*] *conceal, disguise*
beard*, camouflage, cloak, deceive, dissemble, dress up, fake, feign, hide, make-believe, mask, present a false face*, present a false front*, pretend; SEE CONCEPTS *59,172,188*

dissipate [*v1*] *expend, spend*
be wasteful with, blow*, burn up*, consume, deplete, dump*, fritter away, indulge oneself, kiss goodbye*, lavish, misspend, misuse, run through, squander, throw away, trifle away, use up, waste; SEE CONCEPTS *156,169*

dissipate [*v2*] *disappear*
dispel, disperse, dissolve, drive away, evanesce, evaporate, melt away, run dry, scatter, spread, vanish; SEE CONCEPTS *105,469*

dissipated [*adj1*] *used up*
blown, burnt out*, consumed, destroyed, exhausted, kaput*, played out*, scattered, spent, squandered, wasted; SEE CONCEPTS *560,576*

dissipated [*adj2*] *self-indulgent*
abandoned, corrupt, debauched, dissolute, gone bad*, gone to seed*, gone to the dogs*, hellbent*, intemperate, profligate, rakish, wicked; SEE CONCEPTS *401,545*

dissipation [*n1*] *amusement, entertainment, occasionally to excess*
bender*, binge, blow-out, bust*, celebration, circus, distraction, diversion, divertissement, gratification, party, recreation, self-indulgence, tear*, toot*, winging*; SEE CONCEPTS *363,386*

dissipation [*n2*] *wantonness*
abandonment, debauchery, dissoluteness, dissolution, drunkenness, evil, excess, extravagance, freeliving, high-living*, indulgence, intemperance, lavishness, life in the fast lane*, prodigality, profligacy, self-gratification, squandering, to waste; SEE CONCEPT *633*

dissipation [*n3*] *disappearance*
diffusion, disintegration, dispersal, dispersion, dissemination, dissolution, distribution, emission, extravagance, improvidence, radiation, scattering, spread, vanishing, wastage, waste; SEE CONCEPTS *230,651,720*

dissociate [*v*] *part company with; separate*
abstract, alienate, break off, detach, disassociate, disband, disconnect, disengage, disjoin, disperse, disrupt, distance, disunite, divide, divorce, estrange, isolate, quit, scatter, segregate, set apart, uncouple, unfix; SEE CONCEPTS *135,384*

dissociation [*n*] *detachment, separation*
break, disconnection, disengagement, disjunction, distancing, disunion, division, divorce, isolation, segregation, severance; SEE CONCEPT *388*

dissolute [*adj*] *immoral*
abandoned, corrupt, debauched, degenerate, depraved, dissipated, evil, fast*, fast and loose*, gone bad*, high living*, in fast lane*, intemperate, lascivious, lax, lecherous, lewd, libertine, licentious, light, loose*, nighthawk*, night owl*, on the take*, open, playboy*, player*, profligate, raffish, rakish, reprobate, slack, swift, sybaritic, unconstrained, unprincipled, unrestrained, vicious, wanton, wayward, wicked, wild; SEE CONCEPTS *401,545*

dissolution [*n1*] *separation, rupture*
breaking up, detachment, disintegration, disunion, division, divorce, divorcement, parting, partition, resolution, split-up; SEE CONCEPTS *230,388*

dissolution [*n2*] *death; destruction*
adjournment, conclusion, curtains, decay, decease, decomposition, defunction, demise, disappearance, disbandment, discontinuation, dismissal, dispersal, end, ending, evaporation, extinction, finish, liquefaction, melting, overthrow, passing, quietus, release, resolution, ruin, silence, sleep, solution, suspension, termination; SEE CONCEPTS *105,304, 469,703*

dissolve [*v1*] *melt from solid to liquid; mix in*
defront, deliquesce, diffuse, fluidify, flux, fuse, liquefy, liquesce, render, run, soften, thaw, waste away; SEE CONCEPTS *469,702*

dissolve [*v2*] *disappear, disintegrate*
break down, break into pieces, break up, crumble, decline, decompose, diffuse, dilapidate, disband, disperse, dissipate, dwindle, evanesce, evaporate, fade, melt away, perish, separate, unmake, vanish, waste away; SEE CONCEPTS *105,469*

dissolve [*v3*] *annul, discontinue*
abrogate, adjourn, annihilate, break up, cancel, collapse, decimate, demolish, destroy, destruct, discharge, dismiss, disorganize, disunite, divorce, do away with, end, eradicate, invalidate, loose, overthrow, postpone, put an end to, quash, render void, repeal, resolve into, ruin, separate, sever, shatter, shoot, suspend, terminate, unmake, vacate, void, wind up, wrack, wreck; SEE CONCEPTS *121,234,252*

dissonance [*n1*] *disagreement*
antagonism, conflict, contention, controversy, difference, disaccord, discord, discrepancy, disharmony, disparity, dissension, dissidence, incongruity, inconsistency, strife, variance; SEE CONCEPTS *278,665,689*

dissonance [*n2*] *noise, discord*
cacophony, discordance, harshness, jangle, jarring, unmelodiousness; SEE CONCEPT *595*

dissonant [*adj1*] *different, conflicting*
anomalous, at variance, differing, disagreeing, disconsonant, discordant, discrepant, dissentient, incompatible, incongruent, incongruous, inconsistent, inconsonant, irreconcilable, irregular, sour note*, unmixable; SEE CONCEPT *564*

dissonant [*adj2*] *unharmonious*
cacophonic, cacophonous, discordant, disharmonic, disharmonious, grating, harsh, immusical, inharmonic, inharmonious, jangling, jarring, out of tune, raucous, strident, tuneless, unmelodious, unmusical; SEE CONCEPTS *592,594*

dissuade [*v*] *talk out of*
advise against, caution against, chicken out*, counsel, cry out against, deprecate, derail, deter, disadvise, discourage, disincline, divert, exhort, expostulate, faze, hinder, lean on*, persuade not to, prevent, prick, put off, remonstrate, throw cold water on*, throw off, throw wet blanket on*, thwart, turn off*, urge not to, warn; SEE CONCEPTS *68,78*

distance [*n1*] *interval, range*
absence, ambit, amplitude, area, bit, breadth, compass, country mile*, expanse, extension, extent, farness, far piece*, gap, good ways*, heavens, hinterland, horizon, lapse, length, objective, orbit, outpost, outskirts, provinces, purlieu, purview, radius, reach, remoteness, remove, scope, separation, size, sky, space, span, spread, stretch, sweep, way, width; SEE CONCEPTS *651,739,790*

distance [*n2*] *aloofness*
coldness, coolness, frigidity, reserve, restraint, stiffness; SEE CONCEPT *633*

distance [*v*] *dissociate oneself; leave behind*
break away from the pack, outdistance, outdo, outpace, outrun, outstrip, pass, put in proportion, separate oneself; SEE CONCEPT *195*

distant [*adj1*] *faraway*
abroad, abstracted, apart, a piece, arm's length*, asunder, away, backwoods, beyond range, far, far back, far-flung, far-off, farther, further, inaccessible, in background, indirect, in distance, in the boonies*, in the sticks*, isolated, middle of nowhere*, not home*, obscure, outlying, out-of-the-way, out of earshot*, out of range, out of reach, remote, removed, retired, secluded, secret, separate, sequestered, telescopic, unapproachable, ways*, wide of*, yonder*; SEE CONCEPTS *576,778*

distant [*adj2*] *aloof*
arrogant, ceremonious, cold, cool, formal, haughty, insociable, laid back, modest, offish, on ice*, proud, put on airs*, remote, reserved, restrained, reticent, retiring, shy, solitary, standoff, standoffish, stiff, stuck-up*, unapproachable, uncompanionable, unconcerned, unfriendly, unsociable, uppity*, withdrawn; SEE CONCEPTS *401,404*

distaste [*n*] *dislike, hate*
abhorrence, antipathy, aversion, detestation, disfavor, disgust, disinclination, disliking, displeasure, disrelish, dissatisfaction, hatred, horror, hostility, indisposition, loathing, repugnance, repulsion, revolt, revulsion; SEE CONCEPT *29*

distasteful [*adj*] *repulsive, unpleasant*
abhorrent, abominable, afflictive, bitter, detestable, disagreeable, dislikable, displeasing, flat, flavorless, galling, grievous, grody*, gross*, hateful, icky*, insipid, loathsome, nauseous, objectionable, obnoxious, odious, offensive, painful, repellent, repugnant, savorless, tasteless, unappetizing, undesirable, uninviting, unlikable, unpalatable, unsavory, yicky*, yucky*; SEE CONCEPTS *529,589,613*

distend [*v*] *bulge, swell*
amplify, augment, balloon, bloat, bulge, dilate, distort, enlarge, expand, increase, inflate, lengthen, puff, stretch, widen; SEE CONCEPTS *157,469,780*

distill [*v*] *make pure; draw out something*
boil down, brew, clarify, concentrate, condense, cook, cut, cut down, cut to bone*, dribble, drip, drop, evaporate, express, extract, ferment, get to the meat*, infuse, precipitate, press, press out, purify, rarefy, rectify, refine, squeeze out, steam, sublimate, trickle, trim, vaporize, volatilize; SEE CONCEPTS *165,170,211,219*

distinct [*adj1*] *apparent, obvious*
audible, categorical, clean-cut, clear, clear-cut, decided, definite, enunciated, evident, explicit, express, incisive, lucid, manifest, marked, noticeable, palatable, patent, perspicuous, plain, prescribed, recognizable, sharp, sharp-cut, specific, transparent, trenchant, unambiguous, unequivocal, unmistakable, well-defined; SEE CONCEPTS *535,591,619*

distinct [*adj2*] *different; unconnected*
detached, discrete, disparate, dissimilar, distinctive, disunited, divergent, diverse, especial, individual, offbeat, particular, peculiar, poles apart*, separate, separated, several, single, sole, special, specific, unassociated, unattached, unique, various; SEE CONCEPT *564*

distinction [*n1*] *differentiation; feature*
acumen, acuteness, alterity, analysis, characteristic, clearness, contrast, diagnosis, difference, differential, discernment, discrepancy, discreteness, discretion, discrimination, dissemblance, dissimilarity, dissimilitude, distinctiveness, divergence, divergency, division, earmark, estimation, individuality, judgment, mark, marking, nicety, otherness, particularity, peculiarity, penetration, perception, qualification, quality, refinement, sensitivity, separation, sharpness, tact, unlikeness; SEE CONCEPTS *411,665*

distinction [*n2*] *prominence; achievement*
accolade, account, award, badge, bays, celebrity, consequence, credit, decoration, eminence, excellence, fame, flair, greatness, illustriousness, importance, kudos, laurels, manner, merit, name, note, perfection, preeminence, prestige, prominency, quality, rank, renown, reputation, repute, style, superiority, worth; SEE CONCEPTS *388,671,706*

distinctive [*adj*] *different, unique*
characteristic, cool, diacritic, diagnostic, discrete, distinct, distinguishing, excellent, extraordinary, far cry, gnarly*, idiosyncratic, individual, like night and day*, offbeat, original, outstanding, peculiar, perfect, poles apart*, proper, separate, single, singular, special, superior, typical, uncommon, unreal, weird, wicked; SEE CONCEPTS *564,574*

distinguish [*v1*] *tell the difference*
analyze, ascertain, categorize, characterize, classify, collate, decide, demarcate, determinate, determine, diagnose, diagnosticate, difference, differentiate, discriminate, divide, estimate, extricate, figure out, finger*, identify, individualize, individuate, judge, know, label, make out, mark, mark off, name, part, pinpoint, place, qualify, recognize, select, separate, set apart, set off, sift, signalize, single out, singularize, sort out, specify, spot, tag, tell apart, tell between, tell from; SEE CONCEPTS *15,18,38*

distinguish [*v2*] *discern, identify*
beam*, catch, decern, descry, detect, dig, discover, discriminate, eye, eyeball*, flash*, focus, get a load of*, get an eyeful*, know, make out, mark, note, notice, observe, perceive, pick out, pick up on*, read, recognize, remark, see, spot, spy, take in, tell, view; SEE CONCEPTS *38,626*

distinguish [*v3*] *make famous*
acknowledge, admire, celebrate, dignify, honor, immortalize, pay tribute to, praise, signalize; SEE CONCEPT *69*

distinguished [*adj*] *famous, outstanding*
acclaimed, aristocratic, arresting, big name*, brilliant, celebrated, conspicuous, dignified, distingué, eminent, especial, esteemed, extraordinary, famed, foremost, glorious, great, highly regarded, honored, illustrious, imposing, marked, memorable, name, noble, nonpareil, notable, noted, noteworthy, peerless, prominent, remarkable, renowned, reputable, royal, salient, shining, signal, singular, special, stately, striking, superior, talked of, unforgettable, venerable, well-known; SEE CONCEPT *574*

distort [*v*] *deform; falsify*
alter, angle, belie, bend, bias, buckle, change, collapse, color, con, contort, crush, curve, deceive, decline, deteriorate, deviate, disfigure, doctor*, fake, fudge*, garble, gnarl, knot, lie, make out like, mangle, melt, misconstrue, misinterpret, misrepresent, misshape, pervert, phony up*, put one on, sag, scam*, slant, slump, snow*, torture, trump up*, twist, warp, whitewash*, wind, wrench, writhe; SEE CONCEPTS *63,137,232,250*

distortion [*n*] *deformity; falsification*
baloney*, bend, bias, buckle, coloring, contortion, crock, crookedness, exaggeration, intorsion, jazz*, jive*, lie, line, malconformation, malformation, misinterpretation, misrepresentation, misshape, misstatement, misuse, mutilation, perversion, slant, smoke*, story*, tall story*, torture, twist, twistedness, warp; SEE CONCEPTS *63,580*

distract [*v*] *divert attention; confuse*
abstract, addle, agitate, amuse, befuddle, beguile, bewilder, call away, catch flies*, confound, derange, detract, discompose, disconcert, disturb, divert, draw away, engross, entertain, fluster, frenzy, harass, lead astray*, lead away, madden, mislead, mix up, occupy, perplex, puzzle, sidetrack, stall, throw off*, torment, trouble, turn aside, unbalance, unhinge*; SEE CONCEPTS *14,16*

distraction [*n*] *having one's attention drawn away*
aberration, abstraction, agitation, amusement, beguilement, bewilderment, commotion, complication, confusion, disorder, dissipation, disturbance, diversion, divertissement, engrossment, entertainment, frenzy, game, interference, interruption, pastime, perplexity, preoccupation, recreation; SEE CONCEPTS *293,410,532,690*

distraught [*adj*] *very upset, worked-up*
addled, agitated, anxious, beside oneself, bothered, concerned, confused, crazed*, crazy, discomposed, distracted, distrait, distressed, flustered, frantic, harassed, hysterical, in a panic, like chicken with head cut off*, mad, muddled, nonplussed, nuts*, out of one's mind*, overwrought, perturbed, rattled, raving, shook up, thrown*, tormented, troubled, unglued*, unscrewed*, unzipped*, wild, worried; SEE CONCEPTS *401,403,690*

distress [*n1*] *pain, agony*
ache, affliction, anguish, anxiety, bad news*, blues*, care, concern, cross, dejection, desolation, disappointment, discomfort, disquietude, dolor, embarrassment, grief, headache, heartache, heartbreak,

irritation, malaise, misery, mortification, ordeal, pain, pang, perplexity, sadness, shame, sorrow, stew, suffering, throe, torment, torture, trial, tribulation, trouble, twinge, unconsolability, unhappiness, vexation, visitation, woe, worriment, worry, wretchedness; SEE CONCEPTS *410,532,690,720,728*

distress [*n2*] *hardship, adversity*
bad luck, bummer*, calamity, can of worms*, catastrophe, crunch*, destitution, difficulty, disaster, downer*, drag*, exigency, hard knocks*, hard time*, holy mess*, hot water*, indigence, jam*, misfortune, need, pickle*, pinch*, poverty, privation, rigor, rotten luck*, scrape*, straits, throe, ticklish spot*, tough break*, tough luck*, trial, trouble, unholy mess*, vicissitude, want; SEE CONCEPT *674*

distress [*v*] *worry, upset*
afflict, aggrieve, agonize, ail, be on one's case*, bother, break, bug, burn up, depress, desolate, discombobulate*, disquiet, disturb, dog*, do number on*, eat*, get*, get to*, give a hard time*, grieve, harass, harry, hound, hurt, injure, irk, irritate, make it tough for*, miff, nag, needle, nit-pick, oppress, pain, peeve, perplex, pester, pick on, plague, push, push buttons*, rack, sadden, strain, strap, stress, tick off*, torment, torture, trouble, try, vex, weigh, wound; SEE CONCEPTS *7,19,313*

distressed [*adj*] *upset*
afflicted, agitated, all torn up*, antsy, anxious, basket case*, bothered, bugged, bummed out*, bundle of nerves*, concerned, cut up*, discombobulated*, disconsolate, distracted, distrait, distraught, dragged, exercised, fidgety, harassed, hyper*, inconsolable, in a stew*, in a tizzy*, jittery, jumpy, miffed, peeved, perturbed, ripped*, saddened, shaky, shook*, shook up*, shot down*, spooked*, strung out*, tormented, troubled, unconsolable, unglued*, up the wall*, uptight*, wired, worried, wrecked*, wretched; SEE CONCEPT *403*

distribute [*v1*] *allocate, deliver, spread*
administer, allot, apportion, appropriate, assign, bestow, circulate, consign, convey, cut up, deal, deal out, deliver, diffuse, disburse, dish out*, dispense, disperse, dispose, disseminate, divide, divvy up*, dole out*, donate, endow, fork out*, give, give away, hand out, issue, lot out, measure out, mete, parcel, partition, pass out, pay out, present, prorate, radiate, ration, scatter, share, shell out*, slice up, sow, strew; SEE CONCEPTS *98,140,217*

distribute [*v2*] *classify*
arrange, assort, categorize, class, file, group, order; SEE CONCEPT *84*

distribution [*n1*] *allocation, dispersion*
administration, alloting, allotment, apportioning, apportionment, assessment, assigning, circulating, circulation, dealing, delivery, diffusion, dispensation, dispersal, disposal, disposing, dissemination, dissipating, division, dole, handing out, handling, mailing, marketing, partition, partitioning, propagation, prorating, rationing, scattering, sharing, spreading, trading, transport, transportation; SEE CONCEPTS *98,140,217*

distribution [*n2*] *classification*
arrangement, assortment, disposal, disposition, grouping, location, order, ordering, organization, placement, sequence; SEE CONCEPTS *109,727*

district [*n*] *geographical area*
commune, community, department, locale, locality, neck of woods*, neighborhood, parcel, parish, precinct, quarter, region, section, sector, stomping ground*, territory, turf*, vicinage, vicinity, ward; SEE CONCEPT *508*

distrust [*n*] *lack of faith in something*
disbelief, doubt, misdoubt, misgiving, mistrust, qualm, question, skepticism, suspicion, wariness; SEE CONCEPTS *21,689*

distrust [*v*] *be suspicious, skeptical of*
be wary of, disbelieve, discredit, doubt, misbelieve, mistrust, question, smell a rat*, suspect, wonder about; SEE CONCEPT *21*

distrustful [*adj*] *disbelieving*
been hit before*, cagey, cautious, chary, cynical, distrusting, doubtful, doubting, dubious, fearful, jealous, leery, mistrustful, skeptical, suspicious, uneasy, uptight, wary; SEE CONCEPTS *403,542*

disturb [*v1*] *bother, upset*
afflict, agitate, ail, alarm, amaze, annoy, arouse, astound, badger, burn up*, complicate, confound, confuse, depress, discompose, dishearten, disrupt, distract, distress, excite, fluster, frighten, gall, grieve, harass, interfere, interrupt, intrude, irk, irritate, make uneasy, molest, muddle, outrage, pain, perplex, perturb, pester, pique, plague, provoke, puzzle, rattle, rouse, ruffle, shake, shake up*, startle, tire, trouble, unhinge*, unnerve, unsettle, vex, worry; SEE CONCEPTS *7,19*

disturb [*v2*] *disorder; dislocate*
confuse, derange, disarrange, disarray, discompose, disorganize, displace, distort, foul up*, interfere, jumble, louse up*, mess up, mix up, move, muddle, remove, replace, shift, tamper, unsettle, upset; SEE CONCEPTS *84,137,250*

disturbance [*n*] *commotion; upset*
agitation, annoyance, big scene*, big stink*, bother, brawl, brouhaha*, clamor, confusion, convulsion, derangement, disarrangement, disorder, disruption, distraction, eruption, explosion, ferment, fisticuffs, flap, fracas, fray, fuss, hindrance, hubbub*, hullabaloo*, insurrection, interruption, intrusion, molestation, perturbation, quake, quarrel, racket, rampage, restlessness, riot, ruckus, rumble, shock, spasm, stink*, stir*, storm, to-do*, tremor, tumult, turmoil, upheaval, uprising, uproar, violence; SEE CONCEPTS *388,410,674,720*

ditch [*n*] *gulley*
canal, channel, chase, cut, dike, drain, excavation, furrow, gutter, mine, moat, trench, watercourse; SEE CONCEPTS *509,513*

ditch [v] *get rid of*
abandon, desert, discard, dispose of, drop, dump*, eighty-six*, forsake, jettison, junk*, leave, reject, scrap*, throw away, throw out, throw overboard*; SEE CONCEPT *180*

dive [n1] *descent, usually underwater*
belly flop*, dash, dip, duck, ducking, fall, header* headlong* jump, leap, lunge, nosedive, pitch, plunge, spring, submergence, submersion, swoop; SEE CONCEPTS *147,181,194*

dive [n2] *dirty, sleazy establishment*
bar, barroom, beer garden* cabaret, dump, flea trap*, flophouse*, hangout, hole, honky-tonk*, joint, lounge, night club, pool hall, pub, saloon, taproom, tavern; SEE CONCEPT *449*

dive [v] *descend, usually going underwater*
belly flop*, dip, disappear, drop, duck, fall, go head-first, gutter, header*, jump, leap, lunge, nose-dive, pitch, plumb, plummet, plunge, spring, submerge, swoop, vanish, vault; SEE CONCEPTS *147,181,194*

diverge [v1] *go in different directions*
bend, bifurcate, branch, branch off, depart, deviate, digress, divagate, divaricate, divide, excurse, fork, part, radiate, ramble, separate, split, spread, stray, swerve, veer, wander; SEE CONCEPTS *195,738*

diverge [v2] *be different from; be at odds*
argue, conflict, contrast, depart, deviate, differ, digress, disagree, disapprove, dissent, oppose, stray, swerve, turn aside, vary, wander; SEE CONCEPTS *46,665*

divergence [n] *branching out; difference*
aberration, alteration, alterity, branch, crotch, deflection, departure, detour, deviation, differing, digression, disagreeing, discrepancy, disparity, dissemblance, dissimilarity, dissimilitude, distinction, divagation, divergency, diversity, division, fork, mutation, otherness, parting, radiation, ramification, separation, turning, unlikeness, variety, varying; SEE CONCEPTS *665,738*

divergent [adj] *differing*
aberrant, abnormal, anomalous, antithetical, atypical, conflicting, contradictory, contrary, deviating, different, disagreeing, disparate, dissimilar, dissonant, distant, diverging, diverse, factional, factious, irregular, off-key, opposite, poles apart*, separate, unalike, unequal, unlike, unnatural, unsimilar, untypical, variant, various; SEE CONCEPT *564*

diverse [adj] *different; various*
assorted, contradictory, contrary, contrasted, contrasting, contrastive, differing, discrete, disparate, dissimilar, distant, distinct, divergent, diversified, diversiform, incommensurable, like night and day*, manifold, miscellaneous, mixed bag*, multifarious, opposite, separate, several, sundry, unalike, unequal, unlike, varied, varying; SEE CONCEPTS *564,772*

diversify [v] *spread out; branch out*
alter, assort, change, expand, mix, modify, transform, variegate, vary; SEE CONCEPTS *232,697*

diversion [n1] *change in a course, path*
aberration, alteration, deflection, departure, detour, deviation, digression, divergence, fake out*, red herring*, turning, variation; SEE CONCEPTS *501,738*

diversion [n2] *entertainment, recreation*
amusement, ball, beguilement, delectation, delight, disport, dissipation, distraction, divertissement, enjoyment, field day*, frivolity, fun, fun and games*, game, gratification, grins*, high time*, hoopla*, laughs*, levity, merry-go-round*, pastime, picnic*, play, pleasure, relaxation, relish, sport, whoopee*; SEE CONCEPTS *292,363,386*

diversity [n] *variety, difference*
assortment, dissimilarity, distinction, distinctiveness, divergence, diverseness, diversification, heterogeneity, medley, mixed bag*, multeity, multifariousness, multiformity, multiplicity, range, unlikeness, variance, variegation, variousness; SEE CONCEPTS *651,665*

divert [v1] *turn a different direction*
alter, avert, change, deflect, modify, pivot, redirect, sheer, swerve, switch, turn aside, veer, volte-face, wheel, whip, whirl; SEE CONCEPTS *187,213*

divert [v2] *amuse, entertain*
beguile, break one up*, delight, fracture one*, get one's jollies*, gladden, gratify, knock 'em dead*, make happy, panic, please, put 'em away*, recreate, regale, relax, slay, tickle, wow; SEE CONCEPT *9*

divert [v3] *take attention away*
abstract, attract attention, bend the rules*, catch flies*, circumlocute, detach, deter, detract, disadvise, discourage, disengage, dissuade, distract, disturb, draw away, get around, lead astray, lead away, send on wild-goose chase*, sidetrack, stall; SEE CONCEPTS *7,19,22*

divest [v] *dispossess; take off*
bankrupt, bare, bereave, bleed, denudate, denude, deprive, despoil, disinherit, dismantle, disrobe, ditch*, doff, dump, eighty-six*, lose, milk*, oust, plunder, remove, rob, seize, spoil, strip, take from, unclothe, uncover, undress, unload; SEE CONCEPTS *139,142,211*

divide [v1] *separate, disconnect*
abscind, bisect, branch, break, break down, carve, chop, cleave, cross, cut, cut up, demarcate, detach, dichotomize, disengage, disentangle, disjoin, dislocate, dismember, dissect, dissever, dissociate, dissolve, disunite, divorce, fork, halve, intersect, isolate, loose, part, partition, pull away, quarter, rend, rupture, section, segment, segregate, sever, shear, split, subdivide, sunder, tear, unbind, undo; SEE CONCEPTS *98,135,137*

divide [v2] *distribute*
allocate, allot, apportion, articulate, cut, cut in*, cut one in*, cut up, deal, deal out, disburse, dish out*, dispense, disperse, divvy up*, dole out*, factor, fork out*, go fifty-fifty*, hand out, hand over, lot out, measure out, parcel, partition, piece up, portion, pro-

rate, quota, ration, share, shell out*, shift, slice, slice up, split up; SEE CONCEPTS *98,140*

divide [v3] *put in order; classify*
arrange, categorize, grade, group, separate, sort; SEE CONCEPT *84*

divide [v4] *disagree, alienate*
break up, cause to disagree, come between, differ, disaccord, dissent, disunite, estrange, part, pit against, separate, set against, set at odds*, sow dissension*, split, vary; SEE CONCEPTS *46,266*

dividend [n] *one's share, profit*
allotment, allowance, appropriation, bonus, carrot*, check, coupon, cut*, dispensation, divvy*, extra, gain, gravy*, guerdon, interest, lagniappe*, meed, pay, portion, premium, prize, proceeds, remittance, returns, reward, surplus, taste*; SEE CONCEPTS *337,344*

divine [adj] *godlike, perfect*
all-powerful, almighty, ambrosial, angelic, anointed, beatific, beautiful, blissful, celestial, consecrated, deific, deistic, eternal, exalted, excellent, glorious, godly, hallowed, heavenly, holy, immaculate, magnificent, marvelous, mystical, omnipotent, omnipresent, omniscient, perfect, rapturous, religious, sacramental, sacred, sacrosanct, sanctified, spiritual, splendid, superhuman, superlative, supernatural, supreme, theistic, transcendent, transcendental, transmundane, unearthly, wonderful; SEE CONCEPTS *568,574*

divine [v] *prophesy*
anticipate, apprehend, conjecture, deduce, discern, forebode, forefeel, foreknow, foresee, foretell, go out on a limb*, guess, infer, intuit, perceive, predict, previse, prognosticate, see, see in the cards*, suppose, surmise, suspect, take a shot*, take a stab*, understand, visualize; SEE CONCEPT *28*

divinity [n] *godliness; god*
celestial, deity, divine nature, genius, goddess, godhead, godhood, godship, guardian spirit, higher power, holiness, lord, prime mover, sanctity, spirit; SEE CONCEPTS *368,370,689*

division [n1] *separation, disconnection*
analysis, apportionment, autopsy, bisection, breaking, breaking down, breaking up, carving, contrasting, cutting up, demarcation, departmentalizing, detaching, detachment, diagnosis, disjuncture, dismemberment, disparting, disseverance, dissolution, distinguishing, distribution, disunion, disuniting, dividing, divorce, parceling, parting, partition, reduction, rending, rupture, segmentation, selection, separating, severance, splitting up, subdivision, vivisection; SEE CONCEPTS *98,135*

division [n2] *something produced from separating*
affiliate, associate, border, boundary, branch, category, chunk, class, compartment, cut, degree, demarcation, department, divide, dividend, divider, dividing line, divvy*, end, fraction, fragment, grouping, head, kind, lobe, lump, member, moiety, offshoot, parcel, partition, piece, piece of action*,

portion, rake-off*, ramification, section, sector, segment, share, slice, sort, split, subdivision, wedge; SEE CONCEPTS *378,382,710,835*

division [n3] *breach, estrangement*
conflict, difference of opinion, difficulty, disaccord, disagreement, discord, disharmony, dispute, dissension, dissent, dissidence, dissonance, disunion, feud, rupture, split, trouble, variance, words; SEE CONCEPT *388*

divorce [n] *split-up of marriage*
annulment, breach, break, breakup, decree nisi, dedomiciling, detachment, disparateness, dissociation, dissolution, disunion, division, divorcement, on the rocks*, parting of the ways*, partition, rupture, separate maintenance, separation, severance, split, splitsville*; SEE CONCEPT *297*

divorce [v] *split up a marriage*
annul, break up, cancel, disconnect, disjoin, dissever, dissociate, dissolve, disunite, divide, nullify, part, put away, separate, sever, split, split up, sunder, unmarry; SEE CONCEPT *297*

divulge [v] *make known; confess*
admit, betray, blab, blow the whistle*, broadcast, communicate, cough up*, declare, disclose, discover, exhibit, expose, fess up*, give away, go public*, gossip, impart, leak, let hair down*, let slip*, mouth, open up*, own up*, proclaim, promulgate, publish, reveal, spill, spill the beans*, spring, tattle, tell, tip off*, uncover; SEE CONCEPT *60*

dizzy [adj1] *lightheaded, confused*
addled, befuddled, bemused, bewildered, blind, blinded, dazed, dazzled, distracted, disturbed, dumb, dumbfounded, faint, gaga*, giddy, groggy*, hazy, light, muddled, off balance*, out of control*, punchdrunk*, punchy*, puzzled, reeling, shaky, slaphappy*, staggered, staggering, swimming*, tipsy, unsteady, upset, vertiginous, weak in knees*, weakkneed*, whirling, wobbly, woozy; SEE CONCEPTS *314,480*

dizzy [adj2] *flighty, scatterbrained*
capricious, changeable, crazy, empty-headed, fatuous, featherbrained, fickle, foolish, frivolous, giddy, harebrained, heady, inane, light-headed, silly, skittish, unstable; SEE CONCEPT *402*

do [v1] *carry out*
accomplish, achieve, act, arrange, be responsible for, bring about, cause, close, complete, conclude, cook*, create, determine, discharge, do one's thing*, effect, end, engage in, execute, finish, fix, fulfill, get ready, get with it*, go for it*, look after, make, make ready, move, operate, organize, perform, perodate*, prepare, produce, pull off*, see to, succeed, take care of business*, take on, transact, undertake, wind up*, work, wrap up*; SEE CONCEPT *91*

do [v2] *be sufficient*
answer, avail, be adequate, be enough, be good enough for, be of use, be useful, give satisfaction*,

pass muster*, satisfy, serve, suffice, suit; SEE CON-CEPTS *646,656*

do [*v3*] *figure out, solve*
adapt, decipher, decode, interpret, puzzle out, render, resolve, translate, transliterate, transpose, work out; SEE CONCEPTS *15,37*

do [*v4*] *act, behave*
acquit oneself, appear, bear, carry, come on like*, comport, conduct, demean, deport, discourse, enact, fare, get along, get by, give, go on, impersonate, make out*, manage, muddle through*, operate, perform, personate, play, playact, portray, present, produce, put on*, quit, render the role, seem, stagger along*; SEE CONCEPT *633*

do [*v5*] *travel, visit*
cover, explore, journey, look at, pass through, stop in, tour, track, traverse; SEE CONCEPT *224*

do [*v6*] *cheat*
beat, bilk, chouse, con, cozen, deceive, defraud, dupe, fleece*, flimflam*, gyp*, hoax, overreach, swindle, take for a ride*, trick; SEE CONCEPT *59*

do away with [*v*] *get rid of; destroy*
abolish, bump off*, cancel, discard, discontinue, do in*, eliminate, exterminate, finish, kill, liquidate, murder, put an end to, put to death, remove, slaughter, slay, take away, wipe out*; SEE CONCEPTS *180,252*

docile [*adj*] *compliant, submissive*
accommodating, acquiescent, adaptable, agreeable, amenable, biddable, childlike, complacent, compliant, cool, docious, ductile, easily influenced, easy, easygoing, gentle, governable, humble, laid-back, manageable, meek, mellow, mild, obedient, obliging, orderly, pliable, pliant, quiet, resigned, soft, tame, teachable, tractable, usable, weak-kneed*, well-behaved, willing, yielding; SEE CONCEPTS *401,404*

dock [*n*] *waterfront*
berth, embarkment, harbor, jetty, landing, landing pier, levee, lock, marina, pier, quay, slip, wharf; SEE CONCEPT *439*

dock [*v*] *land on the waterfront*
anchor, berth, drop anchor, hook up, join, link up, moor, put in, rendezvous, tie up, unite; SEE CONCEPT *159*

docket [*n*] *program, agenda*
calendar, card, schedule, sked, tab, tally, ticket, timetable; SEE CONCEPT *271*

doctor [*n*] *medical practitioner*
bones*, doc*, expert, general practitioner, healer, intern, MD, medic, medical man/woman, medicine man/woman, medico, physician, professor*, quack*, scientist, specialist, surgeon; SEE CONCEPT *357*

doctor [*v1*] *fix up, treat*
administer, apply medication, attend, do up, fix, give treatment, medicament, medicate, mend, overhaul, patch up*, rebuild, recondition, reconstruct, repair, revamp, supply, treat; SEE CONCEPTS *110,310*

doctor [*v2*] *adulterate, pervert*
add to, alter, change, cut, deacon, debase, dilute, disguise, dope up*, falsify, fudge*, gloss, load, misrepresent, mix with, sophisticate, spike*, tamper with, water down, weight; SEE CONCEPT *240*

doctrinaire [*adj*] *dogmatic, opinionated*
authoritarian, authoritative, biased, bigoted, bull-headed*, dictative, dictatorial, dogged, fanatical, impractical, inflexible, insistent, magisterial, mulish, obstinate, one-sided, pertinacious, pigheaded*, rigid, speculative, stiff-necked*, stubborn, unrealistic; SEE CONCEPTS *267,401*

doctrine [*n*] *opinion; principle*
article, article of faith, attitude, axiom, basic, belief, canon, concept, convention, conviction, credenda, creed, declaration, dogma, fundamental, gospel, implantation, inculcation, indoctrination, instruction, position, precept, principle, pronouncement, propaganda, proposition, regulation, rule, statement, teaching, tenet, tradition, universal law, unwritten rule; SEE CONCEPTS *687,689*

document [*n*] *written communication*
archive, certificate, credentials, deed, diary, evidence, form, instrument, language, pages, paper, record, report, script, testimony, token; SEE CONCEPT *271*

doddering [*adj*] *aged, feeble*
anile, decrepit, doddery, dotard, faltering, floundering, infirm, senile, shaky, tottering, trembling, unsteady, weak; SEE CONCEPTS *314,488,578,797*

dodge [*n*] *trick, feint*
contrivance, device, machination, method, plan, plot, ploy, ruse, scheme, stratagem, strategy, subterfuge, wile; SEE CONCEPT *660*

dodge [*v*] *avoid*
circumlocute, dark, deceive, ditch, duck, elude, equivocate, escape, evade, fence, fend off, fudge*, get around, get out of, give the slip*, hedge, juke, lurch, malinger, move to the side*, parry, pussyfoot*, put the move on*, shake, shake off*, shift, shirk, short-circuit, shuffle, sidestep, skip out on*, skirt, slide, slip, swerve, tergiversate, tergiverse, trick, turn aside, weasel*; SEE CONCEPTS *59,102*

do for [*v1*] *destroy*
defeat, deprive, finish, kill, ruin, shatter, slaughter, slay; SEE CONCEPTS *238,252*

do for [*v2*] *help*
abet, aid, assist, benefact, care for, help out, lend a hand*, look after, provide for, steady, support; SEE CONCEPT *110*

dog [*n*] *canine mammal*
bitch, bowwow*, cur, doggy, fido*, flea bag*, hound, man's best friend*, mongrel, mutt, pooch*, pup, puppy, stray, tail-wagger*, tyke; SEE CONCEPT *400*

dog [*v*] *chase after; bother*
bedog, haunt, hound, plague, pursue, shadow, tag, tail, track, trail, trouble; SEE CONCEPT *207*

dogged [adj] determined, persistent
adamant, bullheaded*, firm, hanging tough*, hardheaded*, hard-nosed*, indefatigable, inexorable, inflexible, insistent, mulish, obdurate, obstinate, perseverant, perseverative, persevering, persisting, persistive, pertinacious, pigheaded*, relentless, resolute, rigid, single-minded, staunch, steadfast, steady, stubborn, tenacious, tough nut*, unbending, unflagging, unshakable, unyielding; SEE CONCEPTS 401,542

dogma [n] belief, principle
article, article of faith, canon, conviction, credenda, credo, creed, doctrine, gospel, opinion, persuasion, precept, rule, teachings, tenet, view; SEE CONCEPTS 687,689

dogmatic [adj1] dictatorial, opinionated
arbitrary, arrogant, assertive, bigoted, bullheaded*, categorical, cocksure*, confident, definite, despotic, determined, dictative, doctrinaire, domineering, downright, egotistical, emphatic, fanatical, fascistic, formal, high and mighty*, imperious, intolerant, magisterial, narrow-minded, obdurate, obstinate, one-sided, overbearing, peremptory, pigheaded*, prejudiced, rednecked*, stiff-necked, stubborn, stupid, tenacious, tyrannical, unequivocal, wrongheaded; SEE CONCEPTS 267,542

dogmatic [adj2] based on absolute truth
a priori, as a matter of course, assertive, authoritarian, authoritative, axiomatic, by fiat, by natural law, by nature, canonical, categorical, deducible, deductive, derivable, doctrinaire, doctrinal, eternal, excathedra, formal, imperative, inevitable, on faith, oracular, orthodox, peremptory, positive, pragmatic, prophetic, reasoned, systematic, theoretical, unchangeable, unerring, unqualified; SEE CONCEPTS 530,567,582

do in [v] destroy; exhaust
assassinate, bankrupt, bump off*, butcher*, cool*, dilapidate, dispatch, do away with*, eliminate, execute, fatigue, finish, frazzle*, kill, knock out*, liquidate, murder, put away*, ruin, shatter, slaughter, slay, tire, wear out, weary, wreck; SEE CONCEPTS 137,250,252

doing [n] achievement
accomplishing, accomplishment, achieving, act, action, carrying out, deed, execution, exploit, handiwork, implementation, performance, performing, thing; SEE CONCEPT 706

doldrums [n] depression
apathy, black mood*, blahs*, blue funk*, blues*, boredom, bummer*, dejection, disinterest, dismals, downer, dullness, dumps*, ennui, funk*, gloom, inactivity, indifference, inertia, lassitude, letdown, listlessness, malaise, mopes*, slump, stagnation, stupor, tedium, torpor, yawn*; SEE CONCEPT 410

dole [n] allowance, allocation
allotment, alms, apportionment, benefit, charity, dispensation, distribution, division, donation, gift, grant, gratuity, handout, living wage, mite, modicum, parcel, pittance, portion, quota, relief, share, subsistence, trifle; SEE CONCEPTS 337,344

doleful [adj] depressing
afflicted, cast down, cheerless, crestfallen, dejected, depressed, dirgeful, dismal, dispirited, distressing, dolent, dolorous, down, downcast, downhearted, down in the mouth*, dreary, forlorn, funereal, gloomy, grieving, lamentable, lugubrious, melancholy, mournful, painful, piteous, pitiful, plaintive, rueful, sad, somber, sorrowful, woebegone, woeful, wretched; SEE CONCEPTS 403,529

dole out [v] allocate, distribute
administer, allot, apportion, assign, deal, deal out, dispense, disperse, divide, divvy*, give, hand out, lot, measure, mete, mete out, parcel, partition, share, share out; SEE CONCEPTS 108,140

doll [n] toy person
baby, dolly, effigy, figure, figurine, manikin, marionette, model, moppet*, puppet; SEE CONCEPT 446

dollar [n] paper money
ace*, bank note, bill, buck*, certificate, cucumber, currency, folding money, greenback*, legal tender, note, one-spot*, single; SEE CONCEPT 340

doll up [v] beautify oneself; dress up
deck out*, fix up, gussy up*, preen, primp, put on best clothes, smarten up*, spiff*, spruce up*; SEE CONCEPTS 162,167,202

dolor [n] misery, anguish
agony, distress, grief, heartache, heartbreak, passion, ruth, sadness, sorrow, suffering; SEE CONCEPT 410

dolorous [adj] miserable, anguished
afflicted, afflictive, calamitous, deplorable, dire, distressing, doleful, dolent, dolesome, grievous, harrowing, heart-rending, lamentable, lugubrious, melancholy, mournful, painful, plaintive, regrettable, rueful, ruthful, sad, sorrowful, woebegone, woeful, wretched; SEE CONCEPTS 401,403

dolt [n] stupid person
airhead*, blockhead*, boob*, chump*, dimwit*, dodo*, dope, dork*, dumbbell*, dumdum*, dunce, fool, goon*, idiot, ignoramus, lamebrain*, lunkhead*, meathead*, nitwit*, sap*, simpleton, stupid, yo-yo*; SEE CONCEPTS 412,423

domain [n] area of expertise, rule
area, authority, bailiwick, concern, demesne, department, discipline, district, dominion, empire, estate, field, home park*, jurisdiction, kingdom, land, neck of the woods*, occupation, orbit*, power, province, quarter, realm, region, scope, slot, specialty, sphere, stomping grounds*, terrain, territory, turf, walk, wing; SEE CONCEPTS 349,518,710

dome [n] arched part of ceiling
arcade, arch, bubble, bulge, covering, cupola, mosque, roof, span, top, vault; SEE CONCEPT 440

domestic [n] housecleaning servant
butter, chamberperson, cleaning lady/man, help, houseboy, live-in, maid, servant, slave*; SEE CONCEPT 348

domestic [*adj1*] *household*
calm, devoted, domesticated, domiciliary, family, home, homelike, home-loving, homely, indoor, pet, private, sedentary, settled, stay-at-home, subdued, submissive, tame, trained, tranquil; SEE CONCEPT *542*

domestic [*adj2*] *not foreign*
handcrafted, home-grown, homemade, indigenous, inland, internal, intestine, intramural, municipal, national, native; SEE CONCEPTS *536,549*

domesticate [*v*] *tame; habituate*
acclimatize, accustom, break, break in, breed, bring up, bust, corral, domesticize, domiciliate, familiarize, gentle, herd, hitch, housetrain, master, naturalize, raise, reclaim, round up, subdue, teach, train, yoke; SEE CONCEPTS *202,285*

domicile [*n*] *human habitat*
abode, accommodation, apartment, castle, commorancy, condo*, condominium, co-op, crash pad*, dump, dwelling, habitation, home, house, joint, legal residence, mansion, pad*, rack*, residence, residency, roof over head*, roost*, settlement; SEE CONCEPTS *439,516*

dominance [*n*] *supremacy*
ascendancy, authority, command, control, domination, dominion, government, influence, masterdom, mastery, paramountcy, power, preeminence, preponderance, prepotence, prepotency, rule, sovereignty, sway, upper hand, whip hand; SEE CONCEPTS *376,668*

dominant [*adj1*] *superior, controlling*
ascendant, assertive, authoritative, bossy, chief, commanding, demonstrative, despotic, domineering, effective, first, foremost, governing, imperative, imperious, leading, lordly, main, master, obtaining, outweighing, overbalancing, overbearing, overweighing, paramount, powerful, predominant, predominate, preeminent, preponderant, presiding, prevailing, prevalent, principal, regnant, reigning, ruling, sovereign, supreme, surpassing, transcendent; SEE CONCEPT *574*

dominant [*adj2*] *main, primary*
capital, chief, influential, major, number one*, outstanding, paramount, predominant, preeminent, prevailing, prevalent, principal, prominent, stellar; SEE CONCEPT *568*

dominate [*v1*] *govern, rule*
boss, call the shots*, command, control, detract from, dictate, direct, domineer, eclipse, handle, have one's way*, have upper hand*, head, hold sway over*, influence, keep under thumb*, lay down the law*, lead, lead by nose*, manage, master, monopolize, outshine, overbear, overrule, overshadow, play first fiddle*, predominate, preponderate, prevail, prevail over, reign, rule the roost*, run, run the show*, sit on top of*, subject, subjugate, superabound, sway, tyrannize, wear the pants*; SEE CONCEPTS *94,117,298*

dominate [*v2*] *tower above*
bestride, look down upon, loom over, overlie, overlook, overtop, stand over, survey; SEE CONCEPTS *741,752*

domination [*n*] *control; subjection*
ascendancy, authority, command, despotism, dictatorship, dominance, dominion, influence, jurisdiction, masterdom, mastery, might, oppression, power, preponderancy, prepotence, prepotency, repression, rule, sovereignty, strings*, subordination, superiority, suppression, supremacy, sway, tyranny; SEE CONCEPT *376*

domineer [*v*] *oppress; assume authority*
be in the saddle*, bend, bluster, boss around*, browbeat, bulldoze*, bully*, call the shots*, dominate, hector, henpeck*, in the driver's seat*, intimidate, keep under thumb*, kick around*, lead by nose*, menace, overbear, predominate, preponderate, prevail, push the buttons*, reign, rule, rule the roost*, run the show*, run things*, swagger, threaten, throw weight around*, tyrannize, wear the pants*; SEE CONCEPTS *14,94*

domineering [*adj*] *oppressive, authoritarian*
arrogant, autocratic, bossy, coercive, crack the whip*, despotic, dictatorial, egotistic, high-handed, imperative, imperial, imperious, in driver's seat*, insolent, iron-handed*, lordly, magisterial, masterful, on high horse*, overbearing, peremptory, tyrannical; SEE CONCEPT *401*

dominion [*n*] *area of rule; authority*
ascendancy, authorization, bailiwick, command, commission, control, country, demesne, district, domain, dominance, domination, empire, enclave, field, government, jurisdiction, kingdom, lordship, management, masterdom, mastership, mastery, power, preeminence, prepotence, prepotency, prerogative, privilege, property, province, realm, regency, regiment, regimentation, region, reign, rule, seniority, sovereignty, sphere, state, stomping grounds*, supremacy, sway, terrain, territory, turf, walk; SEE CONCEPTS *198,376,710*

donate [*v*] *make a gift of*
accord, ante up*, award, bequeath, bestow, chip in*, confer, contribute, devote, dole out*, do one's part*, feed the kitty*, get in the act*, get it up*, gift, give, give away, grant, hand out, lay on, pass the hat*, present, provide, subscribe, sweeten the pot*; SEE CONCEPT *108*

donation [*n*] *gift*
a hand*, aid, allowance, alms, appropriation, assistance, benefaction, beneficence, bequest, boon, charity, contribution, dole, do one's part*, endowment, gifting, grant, gratuity, handout, help, helping hand* largess, lump, offering, philanthropy, pittance, present, presentation, ration, relief, subscription, subsidy, subvention, write-off*; SEE CONCEPTS *337,340*

done [*adj1*] *accomplished, finished*
all in*, all over*, a wrap*, brought about, brought to pass, buttoned up*, compassed, complete, completed, concluded, consummated, depleted, down, drained, effected, effete, ended, executed, exhausted, fixed, fulfilled, over, perfected, performed,

realized, rendered, set, spent, succeeded, terminated, through, used up, wired, wrought; SEE CONCEPTS *528,531*

done [*adj2*] *thoroughly cooked*
baked, boiled, brewed, broiled, browned, cooked enough, cooked sufficiently, cooked to a turn*, crisped, fried, ready, stewed; SEE CONCEPTS *462,613*

done [*adj3*] *approved, agreed upon*
compacted, determined, okay, settled, you're on*; SEE CONCEPT *558*

done for [*adj*] *beaten, defeated*
broken, conquered, dashed, destroyed, doomed, finished, foiled, lost, ruined, through, undone, vanquished, washed-up*, wrecked; SEE CONCEPTS *537, 570*

done in [*adj*] *exhausted*
all in*, bushed*, dead, depleted, done, effete, fagged, far-gone*, on last leg*, ready to drop*, spent, tired, used up, washed-out*, weary, worn-out; SEE CONCEPTS *314,485*

donkey [*n*] *small domestic horselike mammal*
ass, burro, hee-haw*, horse, jackass, jennet, jenny, maud, moke, mule, neddy, pony, Rocky Mountain canary*; SEE CONCEPT *400*

donor [*n*] *giver of gift*
almsgiver, altruist, angel*, backer, benefactor, benefactress, bestower, conferrer, contributor, donator, fairy godmother*, Good Samaritan*, grantor, heavy hitter*, patron, patroness, philanthropist, presenter, Santa Claus*, savior, subscriber; SEE CONCEPTS *359,423*

doom [*n*] *fate or decision, usually unpleasant*
annihilation, calamity, cataclysm, catastrophe, circumstance, conclusion, condemnation, death, decree, destination, destiny, destruction, disaster, downfall, end, fixed future, foreordination, fortune, handwriting on wall*, judgment, Judgment Day, karma, kismet, lap of the gods*, lot, Moira, opinion, portion, predestination, predetermination, ruin, sentence, tragedy, verdict, way ball bounces*, way cookie crumbles*, weird; SEE CONCEPT *679*

doomed [*adj*] *condemned, hopeless*
bedeviled, bewitched, convicted, cursed, cut down, damned, dead duck*, destroyed, done, done for*, fated, foreordained, ill-fated, ill-omened, in the cards*, kiss of death*, lost, luckless, menaced, overthrown, overwhelmed, predestined, que sera sera*, reprobate, ruined, sentenced, star-crossed, sunk, suppressed, threatened, thrown down, undone, unfortunate, unredeemed, wrecked; SEE CONCEPT *537*

door [*n*] *entrance to room, building*
aperture, doorway, egress, entranceway, entry, entryway, exit, gate, gateway, hatch, hatchway, ingress, opening, portal, postern, slammer; SEE CONCEPT *440*

do out of [*v*] *cheat*
balk, beat out of*, bilk, con, deceive, deprive, steal, swindle, trick; SEE CONCEPTS *59,139*

dope [*n1*] *stupid person*
ass, blockhead*, dimwit*, dolt, donkey*, dunce, fool, idiot, lame-brain*, simpleton; SEE CONCEPTS *412,423*

dope [*n2*] *drug*
narcotic, opiate, stimulant; SEE CONCEPT *307*

dope [*n3*] *inside news*
account, details, developments, facts, info*, information, inside information, knowledge, lowdown*, tip*; SEE CONCEPT *274*

dope [*v*] *drug someone*
adulterate, anesthetize, deaden, debase, inject, knock out*, load, narcotize, put to sleep, sedate, soak, sophisticate, stupefy; SEE CONCEPTS *156,310*

dopey [*adj*] *stupid*
comatose, dense, dumb, foolish, heavy, hebetudinous, idiotic, lethargic, senseless, silly, simple, slow, sluggish, slumberish, thick, torpid; SEE CONCEPT *402*

dormant [*adj*] *inactive; sleeping*
abeyant, asleep, closed down, comatose, down, fallow, hibernating, inert, inoperative, latent, lethargic, lurking, on the shelf*, out of action*, passive, potential, prepatent, quiescent, sidelined, slack, sluggish, slumbering, smoldering, suspended, torpid; SEE CONCEPT *539*

dose [*n*] *portion of drug or other consumable*
application, dosage, dram, draught, fill, fix*, hit*, lot, measure, measurement, nip*, potion, prescription, quantity, share, shot*, slug*, spoonful; SEE CONCEPTS *307,835*

dot [*n*] *tiny mark, drop*
atom, circle, dab, droplet, fleck, flyspeck, grain, iota, jot, mite, mote, particle, period, pinpoint, point, speck, spot, tittle; SEE CONCEPTS *284,831*

dot [*v*] *make spot(s)*
bespeckle, dab, dabble, fleck, freckle, pepper, pimple, sprinkle, stipple, stud; SEE CONCEPTS *79,174*

dotage [*n*] *feebleness, old age*
advanced age, age, decrepitude, elderliness, fatuity, imbecility, infirmity, second childhood*, senectitude, senility, weakness; SEE CONCEPTS *405,715*

dote on/dote upon [*v*] *lavish affection on*
admire, adore, be fond of, be infatuated with, be sweet on*, cherish, enjoy, fancy, hold dear, idolize, like, love, pet, prize, treasure, worship; SEE CONCEPT *32*

doting [*adj*] *indulgent; serving*
adoring, affectionate, devoted, fascinated, fatuous, fond, foolish, lovesick, lovesome, loving, silly, simple, struck; SEE CONCEPT *401*

double [*n*] *something which exactly resembles another*
angel, clone, companion, coordinate, copy, counterpart, dead ringer*, duplicate, fellow, image, impersonator, lookalike*, match, mate, picture, portrait, reciprocal, replica, ringer*, simulacrum, spitting image*, stand-in*, twin; SEE CONCEPTS *664,716*

double [*adj*] *in a pair*
as much again, bifold, binary, binate, coupled, double-barreled, doubled, dual, dualistic, duple, du-

plex, duplicate, duplicated, geminate, paired, repeated, second, twice, twin, twofold, two times; SEE CONCEPT *771*

double [*v*] *make two of; make twice as large*
amplify, augment, dualize, dupe, duplicate, duplify, enlarge, fold, grow, increase, infold, loop, magnify, multiply, plait, pleat, plicate, redouble, repeat, replicate, supplement; SEE CONCEPTS *236,245*

double back [*v*] *reverse path*
backtrack, circle, dodge, loop, retrace one's steps, return, turn; SEE CONCEPTS *224,232*

double-cross [*v*] *betray*
beguile, bluff, cheat, con, cross, deceive, defraud, four-flush*, hoodwink*, humbug*, illude, juggle, mislead, sell, sell out*, split, swindle, take in, trick, two-time*; SEE CONCEPTS *7,19,59*

double-dealing [*n*] *betrayal, cheating*
bad faith, chicane, chicanery, deceit, deception, dishonesty, duplicity, foul play*, fourberie, fraud, hanky-panky*, hypocrisy, mendacity, perfidy, sharp practice*, treachery, trickery, two-timing*; SEE CONCEPT *59*

double-dealing [*adj*] *cheating, deceitful*
ambidextrous, crooked, dishonest, double, duplicitous, fraudulent, hypocritical, insincere, left-handed*, lying, perfidious, sneaky, swindling, treacherous, tricky, two-faced*, two-timing*, underhanded, untrustworthy, wily; SEE CONCEPT *401*

double entendre [*n*] *play on words*
ambiguity, amphibiology, double meaning, equivocality, equivocation, equivoque, innuendo, joke, pun, tergiversation; SEE CONCEPTS *278,682*

double-talk [*n*] *nonsense communicated*
amphibiology, balderdash, baloney*, bull*, drivel, equivocation, flimflam*, gibberish, jazz*, mumbo jumbo*, rigmarole; SEE CONCEPT *278*

doubt [*n*] *lack of faith, conviction; questioning*
agnosticism, ambiguity, apprehension, confusion, demurral, difficulty, diffidence, dilemma, disbelief, discredit, disquiet, distrust, dubiety, dubiousness, faithlessness, faltering, fear, hesitancy, hesitation, incertitude, incredulity, indecision, irresolution, lack of confidence, misgiving, mistrust, perplexity, problem, qualm, quandary, rejection, reluctance, scruple, skepticism, suspense, suspicion, uncertainty, vacillation, wavering; SEE CONCEPTS *21,410,689,690*

doubt [*v*] *lack confidence in; question*
be apprehensive of, be curious, be dubious, be in quandary, be puzzled, be uncertain, be undetermined, call in question, challenge, demur, disbelieve, discredit, dispute, distrust, fear, fluctuate, give no credence, harbor suspicion, have qualms, hesitate, imagine, impugn, insinuate, misdoubt, misgive, mistrust, not buy*, query, question, read differently, scruple, shilly-shally*, skepticize, smell a rat*, surmise, suspect, take dim view of, vacillate, waver, wonder at; SEE CONCEPT *21*

doubter [*n*] *person who does not believe*
agnostic, cynic, disbeliever, doubting Thomas*, headshaker*, questioner, skeptic, unbeliever, zetetic; SEE CONCEPTS *361,423*

doubtful [*adj1*] *questionable, unclear*
ambiguous, borderline, chancy, clouded, contingent, debatable, dicey, disreputable, doubtable, dubious, dubitable, equivocal, far-fetched, fat chance, fishy*, hazardous, hazy, iffy*, impugnable, inconclusive, indecisive, indefinite, indeterminate, indistinct, insecure, long shot*, obscure, on thin ice*, open, pending, precarious, problematic, shady, sneaky*, speculative, suspect, suspicious, touch-and-go*, touchy, uncertain, unconfirmed, undecided, uneasy, unsettled, unstable, unsure, up for grabs*; SEE CONCEPTS *529,535*

doubtful [*adj2*] *not believing*
agnostic, baffled, confused, discomposed, disconcerted, distracted, distrustful, disturbed, doubting, dubious, equivocal, faithless, faltering, flustered, hesitant, hesitating, in a quandary, in clouds*, indecisive, in dilemma, irresolute, like doubting Thomas*, lost, not following, of two minds*, perplexed, puzzled, questioning, skeptical, suspicious, tentative, theoretical, troubled, uncertain, unconvinced, undecided, unresolved, unsettled, unsure, vacillating, wavering, without belief; SEE CONCEPTS *403,542*

doubtless [*adj*] *certainly; most likely*
absolutely, apparently, assuredly, clearly, doubtlessly, easily, for sure, indisputably, no ifs ands or buts*, of course, ostensibly, positively, precisely, presumably, probably, seemingly, supposedly, sure as hell*, surely, truly, undoubtedly, unequivocally, unquestionably, without doubt; SEE CONCEPTS *535,552*

doughnut [*n*] *sweet baked ring*
bun, cruller, danish, dunker*, fried cake, pastry, sinker*, sweet roll; SEE CONCEPTS *457,461*

do up [*v*] *physically prepare; fix*
clean, doctor, enclose, finish, fix, gift-wrap, launder, mend, overhaul, package, patch, rebuild, recondition, reconstruct, repair, revamp, wash, wrap; SEE CONCEPTS *126,165,182,202*

dour [*adj*] *gloomy, grim*
bleak, crabbed, dismal, dreary, forbidding, glum, hard, harsh, morose, saturnine, severe, sour, stringent, sulky, sullen, surly, ugly, unfriendly; SEE CONCEPTS *401,542*

douse [*v*] *drench, extinguish with liquid*
blow out, deluge, drown, duck, dunk, immerse, plunge, put out, quench, saturate, slop, slosh, smother, snuff, snuff out, soak, sop, souse, spatter, splash, splatter, squench, steep, submerge, submerse, wet; SEE CONCEPTS *250,256*

dovetail [*v*] *link, fit together*
accord, agree, check out, coincide, conform, correspond, fit, go, harmonize, interlock, jibe, join,

match, mortise, square, sync*, sync up*, tally, tenon, unite; SEE CONCEPTS *113,664*

dowdy [*adj*] *poorly dressed; old-fashioned*
antiquated, archaic, baggy, bedraggled, blowsy*, bygone, dated, dingy, drab, dull, frowzy*, frumpy*, homely, mince, moldy, old hat*, outdated, outmoded, out-of-date, passé, plain, run-down, scrubby*, shabby, slatternly, sloppy, slovenly, stodgy, tacky, tasteless, unfashionable, unkempt, unseemly, unstylish, untidy, vintage, wrinkled; SEE CONCEPT *589*

do without [*v*] *get along without*
abstain from, dispense, endure, forgo, give up; SEE CONCEPTS *23,646*

down [*adj1/adv*] *below; physically lower*
bottomward, cascading, declining, depressed, descending, downgrade, downhill, downward, dropping, earthward, falling, gravitating, groundward, inferior, nether, precipitating, sagging, sinking, sliding, slipping, slumping, subjacent, to the bottom, under, underneath; SEE CONCEPTS *583,586,735*

down [*adj2*] *unhappy*
bad, blue*, cast down, chapfallen, crestfallen, dejected, depressed, disheartened, dispirited, downcast, downhearted, low, miserable, off, sad, slack, sluggish, unhappy; SEE CONCEPT *403*

down-and-out [*adj*] *poverty-stricken*
beaten, beggared, defeated, derelict, destitute, finished, impoverished, needy, outcast, penniless, ruined, vagabond, vagrant; SEE CONCEPT *334*

downcast [*adj*] *depressed, unhappy*
bad, blue*, brooding, bummed out*, cast down, chapfallen, cheerless, crestfallen, daunted, dejected, depressed, despondent, disappointed, disconsolate, discouraged, disheartened, dismayed, dispirited, distressed, doleful, down, downhearted, down-in-the-mouth*, down in dumps*, dragged*, droopy, dull, forlorn, gloomy, glum, heartsick, in pain, listless, low, low-spirited, miserable, moody, mopey*, morose, oppressed, sad, shot down*, singing the blues*, sunk*, troubled, weighed down*, woebegone; SEE CONCEPT *403*

downfall [*n*] *disgrace, ruin*
atrophy, bane, breakdown, ceclination, cloudburst, collapse, comedown, comeuppance, debacle, decadence, declension, degeneracy, degeneration, deluge, descent, destruction, deterioration, devolution, discomfiture, down, drop, failure, fall, flood, on the rocks*, overthrow, rack and ruin*, road to ruin*, ruination, storm, the skids*, undoing; SEE CONCEPTS *674,679,699*

downgrade [*n*] *slope*
decline, declivity, descent, dip, hill, inclination, pitch; SEE CONCEPTS *509,738*

downgrade [*v*] *lower in opinion or rank*
abase, bench*, break*, bump*, bust*, declass, decrease, decry, degrade, demerit, demote, denigrate, depreciate, detract from, devalorize, devalue, disparage, disrate, humble, mark down, minimize, reduce,

run down, set back, take down a peg*, undervalue, write off*; SEE CONCEPTS *7,19,54,240*

downhearted [*adj*] *depressed, unhappy*
blue*, chapfallen, crestfallen, dejected, despondent, disconsolate, discouraged, disheartened, dismayed, dispirited, down, downcast, low, low-spirited, sad, sorrowful, spiritless, woebegone; SEE CONCEPT *403*

downpour [*n*] *tremendous pouring of rain*
cloudburst, deluge, drencher, flood, inundation, monsoon, rainstorm, storm, torrential rain; SEE CONCEPT *526*

downright [*adj*] *thorough, absolute*
blatant, blunt, categorical, certain, clear, complete, damned, explicit, flat, gross, honest, indubitable, open, out-and-out, outright, plain, positive, simple, sincere, straight, straightforward, sure, thoroughgoing, total, undisguised, unequivocal, unmitigated, unqualified, unquestionable, utter, whole; SEE CONCEPT *531*

down-to-earth [*adj*] *reasonable, practical*
common, commonsense, easy, hard, hard-boiled, hardheaded, matter-of-fact, mundane, no-nonsense, plainspoken, pragmatic, rational, realistic, sane, sensible, sober, unfantastic, unidealistic, unsentimental; SEE CONCEPTS *402,558*

downtrodden [*adj*] *afflicted, abused*
abject, a slave to*, at one's beck and call*, at one's feet*, at one's mercy*, destitute, distressed, exploited, have-not, helpless, in one's clutches*, in one's pocket*, in one's power*, led by the nose*, maltreated, mistreated, needy, oppressed, overcome, persecuted, subjugated, subservient, suppressed, tyrannized, underdog*, underfoot*, under one's thumb*; SEE CONCEPT *542*

downy [*adj*] *fluffy*
featherlike, feathery, fleecy, fuzzy, light, plumate, plumose, pubescent, silky, soft, velutinous, velvety, woolly; SEE CONCEPTS *604,606*

doze [*n*] *light sleep*
catnap, drowse, forty winks*, nap, shut-eye*, siesta, slumber, snooze*; SEE CONCEPTS *315,681*

doze [*v*] *take a nap*
catch a wink*, catnap, cop some z's*, drift off*, drop off*, drowse, nod off*, sleep, sleep lightly, slumber, snooze; SEE CONCEPTS *315,681*

drab [*adj*] *dull, colorless*
arid, blah*, bleak, boring, brown, characterless, cheerless, desolate, dingy, dismal, dreary, dry, dull as dishwater*, faded, flat, gloomy, gray, grungy, lackluster, lusterless, muddy, murky, run-down, same, shabby, somber, subfuse, unchanging, uninspired, vapid, zero*; SEE CONCEPTS *536,617,618*

draft [*n1*] *something formulated; plan*
abstract, blueprint, delineation, outline, preliminary form, rough, sketch, version; SEE CONCEPTS *271,660*

draft [*n2*] *check for paying money*
bank draft, bill, bond, cheque, coupon, debenture, IOU, letter of credit, money order, order, promissory note, receipt, warrant; SEE CONCEPTS *332,344*

draft [*n3*] *gust of air*
breeze, current, eddy, puff, wind; SEE CONCEPT *437*

draft [*n4*] *military conscription*
allotment, assignment, call of duty, call-up*, greetings*, impressment, induction, letter from Uncle Sam*, levy, lottery, recruiting, registration, roll call*, selection, selective service; SEE CONCEPT *321*

draft [*n5*] *drink of beverage*
drag*, drain, drench, glass, peg*, quaff, swallow, swig*, swill*; SEE CONCEPTS *169,454*

draft [*v1*] *formulate*
adumbrate, block out, characterize, compose, concoct, contrive, delineate, design, devise, draw, draw up, fabricate, fashion, forge, form, frame, invent, make, manufacture, outline, plan, prepare, project, rough, shape, skeleton, sketch; SEE CONCEPTS *36,79,173*

draft [*v2*] *select for military force*
call up, choose, conscribe, conscript, dragoon, enlist, enroll, impress, indite, induct, muster, press, recruit, sign on, sign up; SEE CONCEPTS *8,320*

drag [*n1*] *bad situation*
annoyance, bore, bother, burden, encumbrance, hang-up, hindrance, impediment, nuisance, pain, pest, pill, sway, trouble; SEE CONCEPT *674*

drag [*n2*] *a puff while smoking*
breathing, draw, inhalation, pull, smoke; SEE CONCEPT *185*

drag [*v1*] *haul something to new place*
draw, hale, lug, magnetize, move, pull, schlepp*, tow, trail, transport, truck, tug, yank; SEE CONCEPTS *206,213*

drag [*v2*] *move very slowly*
be delayed, be quiescent, crawl, creep, dally*, dawdle*, delay, encounter difficulty*, hang*, inch*, lag, lag behind, limp along, linger, loiter, mark time*, poke*, procrastinate, put off*, sag, shamble, shuffle, slow down, stagnate, straggle, tarry, trail behind*, traipse; SEE CONCEPTS *151,681*

dragging [*adj*] *tiresome, monotonous*
boring, drawn-out, dull, going slowly, humdrum, lengthy, long, overlong, prolonged, protracted, tedious, wearisome; SEE CONCEPTS *482,798*

drag on/drag out [*v*] *extend time of action*
continue, draw out, endure, extend, go on slowly, keep going, lengthen, persist, prolong, protract, spin out, stretch out; SEE CONCEPT *239*

drain [*n*] *channel through which liquid runs off*
cesspool, cloaca, conduit, culvert, ditch, duct, outlet, pipe, sewer, sink, trench, watercourse; SEE CONCEPT *501*

drain [*v1*] *remove liquid; remove supply*
abate, bankrupt, bleed, bleed white*, catheterize, consume, debilitate, decrease, deplete, devitalize, diminish, dissipate, divert, draft, draw off, drink up, dry, empty, evacuate, exhaust, expend, fatigue, filter off, finish, free from, get last drop*, get rid of, gulp down, impoverish, lessen, milk*, pump, pump out,

quaff, reduce, sap, siphon, spend, strain, suck, suck dry*, swallow, tap, tax, tire out, use up, waste, wear, wear down, weary, withdraw; SEE CONCEPTS *142,211,225*

drain [*v2*] *seep, discharge liquid*
abate, decline, decrease, diminish, dwindle, effuse, exude, filter off, flow, flow out, leak, leave dry, ooze, osmose, percolate, reduce, run off, taper off, trickle, well; SEE CONCEPTS *179,698*

drained [*adj*] *used up; exhausted*
all in*, beat*, bleary, burned out*, dead, dead tired*, depleted, dragging, effete, far-gone, hacked*, pooped*, spent, washed-out, weary, wiped-out*, worn-out; SEE CONCEPTS *485,560*

drama [*n1*] *theatrical piece; acting*
boards*, Broadway*, climax, comedy, dramatic art, dramatization, dramaturgy, farce, footlights, histrionic art, melodrama, play, production, scene, show, show business, showmanship, stagecraft, stage show, tear-jerker*, theater, theatricals, thespian art, tragedy, vehicle*; SEE CONCEPTS *263,271,293*

drama [*n2*] *turmoil in real life*
climax, comedy, crisis, dramatics, emotion, excitement, farce, histrionics, melodrama, scene, spectacle, tension, theatrics, tragedy; SEE CONCEPT *674*

dramatic [*adj*] *exciting, moving*
affecting, breathtaking, climactic, comic, effective, electrifying, emotional, expressive, farcical, histrionic, impressive, melodramatic, powerful, sensational, startling, striking, sudden, suspenseful, tense, theatrical, thespian, thrilling, tragic, vivid; SEE CONCEPTS *537,548*

dramatize [*v*] *make a performance of*
act, amplify, burlesque, enact, exaggerate, execute, farcialize, give color to, ham it up*, lay it on*, make a production of, melodramatize, overdo, overstate, perform, playact, play on heartstrings*, play to gallery, play up, present, produce, show, splash, stage, tragedize; SEE CONCEPTS *49,59,292*

drape [*v*] *hang over, adorn*
array, cloak, clothe, cover, dangle, display, don, dress, droop, drop, enclose, enswathe, envelop, enwrap, fold, hang, lean over, let fall, line, model, roll, sprawl, spread, spread-eagle, suspend, swathe, wrap; SEE CONCEPT *172*

drastic [*adj*] *severe, extreme*
desperate, dire, exorbitant, extravagant, forceful, harsh, immoderate, radical, strong; SEE CONCEPTS *537,569*

draw [*n*] *tie in competition*
dead end*, dead heat*, deadlock, even steven*, Mexican standoff*, photo finish*, stalemate, standoff, tie; SEE CONCEPT *706*

draw [*v1*] *move something by pulling*
attract, bring, carry, convey, cull, draft, drag, drain, educe, elicit, evoke, extract, fetch, gather, haul, hook, jerk, lug, magnetize, pick, pluck, pull, pump,

rake, siphon, tap, tow, trail, trawl, tug, wind in, wrench, yank; SEE CONCEPT 206

draw [v2] *create a likeness in a picture*
caricature, chart, compose, crayon, delineate, depict, describe, design, draft, engrave, etch, express, form, formulate, frame, graph, limn, map out, mark, model, outline, paint, pencil, portray, prepare, profile, sketch, trace, write; SEE CONCEPTS 79,174

draw [v3] *deduce*
collect, conclude, derive, gather, get, infer, judge, make, make out, take; SEE CONCEPT 15

draw [v4] *allure, influence*
argue into, attract, bewitch, bring around, bring forth, call forth, captivate, charm, convince, elicit, enchant, engage, entice, evoke, fascinate, get, induce, invite, lure, magnetize, persuade, prompt, take, wile, win over; SEE CONCEPTS 7,19,22,68

draw [v5] *take out, extend*
attenuate, choose, drain, elongate, extort, extract, lengthen, pick, pull out, respire, select, single out, stretch, suck, take; SEE CONCEPTS 142,163,239

drawback [n] *disadvantage*
check, defect, deficiency, detriment, difficulty, disability, evil, failing, fault, flaw, fly in ointment*, handicap, hindrance, hitch, ill, impediment, imperfection, inconvenience, lack, nuisance, obstacle, shortcoming, snag, stumbling block*, trouble, weakness; SEE CONCEPTS 666,674

draw back [v] *retract from position*
deduct, discount, pull back, recede, recoil, reel in, retreat, sheathe, shrink, start back, subtract, take away, withdraw; SEE CONCEPTS 195,213

drawing [n] *illustration*
cartoon, commercial art, comp, delineation, depiction, design, doodle, etching, graphics, layout, likeness, outline, painting, picture, portrayal, representation, sketch, storyboard, study, tracing, work of art; SEE CONCEPT 625

drawl [v] *lengthen, draw out*
chant, drag out, drone, extend, intone, nasalize, prolong, pronounce slowly, protract, utter; SEE CONCEPTS 77,239

drawn [adj] *tense, fatigued*
fraught, haggard, harassed, harrowed, peaked, pinched, sapped, starved, strained, stressed, taut, thin, tired, worn; SEE CONCEPT 485

draw on [v] *use to advantage*
effect, employ, exploit, extract, fall back on, have recourse to, make use of, rely on, require, take from; SEE CONCEPT 225

draw out [v] *prolong*
attract, continue, drag, drag out, draw, elongate, extend, lead on, lengthen, make longer, prolongate, protract, pull, spin, spin out*, stretch, string out*, tug; SEE CONCEPTS 236,239,245

draw up [v] *draft document*
compose, formulate, frame, indite, make, prepare, write, write out; SEE CONCEPT 79

dread [n] *fear*
affright, alarm, apprehension, aversion, awe, cold feet*, consternation, creeps*, dismay, fright, funk*, goose bumps*, horror, jitters, panic, phobia, stage fright, terror, trepidation, trepidity, worriment; SEE CONCEPT 27

dread [adj] *horrible, terrifying*
alarming, awe-inspiring, awful, creepy*, dire, dreaded, dreadful, frightening, frightful, shuddersome, terrible; SEE CONCEPT 537

dread [v] *anticipate with horror*
apprehend, be afraid, cringe, fear, have cold feet*, misdoubt, quake, shrink from, shudder, tremble; SEE CONCEPT 27

dreadful [adj] *horrible, frightening*
abominable, alarming, appalling, atrocious, awful, bad, beastly, creepy*, dire, distressing, dread, fearful, formidable, frightful, frozen, ghastly, godawful*, grievous, grim, grody*, gross*, hideous, horrendous, horrific, icky*, lousy, mean, monstrous, rotten, shameful, shocking, shuddersome, spooky, terrible, terrific, tragic, tremendous, wicked, yucky*; SEE CONCEPTS 537,550

dream [n1] *illusion, vision*
bubble*, castle in the air*, chimera, daydream, delusion, fancy, fantasy, hallucination, head trip*, idea, image, imagination, impression, incubus, mental picture, nightmare, pie in the sky*, pipe dream*, rainbow, reverie, specter, speculation, thought, trance, vagary, wraith; SEE CONCEPT 529

dream [n2] *goal*
ambition, aspiration, design, desire, flight of fancy*, hope, notion, pipe dream*, wish; SEE CONCEPT 659

dream [v] *conjure up scenario*
be delirious, be moonstruck, be up in clouds*, brainstorm, build castles in air*, conceive, concoct, cook up*, crave, create, daydream, devise, envisage, fancy, fantasize, formulate, hallucinate, hanker*, hatch, have a vision, have flash*, have nightmare*, have notion*, hunger, idealize, imagine, invent, long, lust, make up, picture, pine, search for pot of gold*, sigh, stargaze*, sublimate, think, think up, thirst, visualize; SEE CONCEPTS 17,529

dream up [v] *concoct plan*
contrive, cook up*, create, devise, frame, hatch*, imagine, invent, make up, spin*, think up; SEE CONCEPTS 17,36

dreamy [adj] *illusory, romantic*
abstracted, astral, calming, chimerical, daydreaming, dreamlike, excellent, fanciful, fantastic, gentle, idealistic, imaginary, immaterial, impractical, intangible, introspective, introvertive, lulling, marvelous, misty, musing, mythical, nightmarish, otherworldly, out of this world*, pensive, phantasmagoric, phantasmagorical, preoccupied, quixotic, relaxing, shadowy, soothing, speculative, unreal, unsubstantial, utopian, vague, visionary, whimsical; SEE CONCEPT 582

dreary [adj] *gloomy, lifeless*
black, blah, bleak, boring, cheerless, colorless, comfortless, damp, depressing, depressive, dingy, dismal, dispiriting, doleful, downcast, drab, dull, forlorn, funereal, glum, humdrum, joyless, lonely, lonesome, melancholy, monotonous, mournful, oppressive, pedestrian, raw, routine, sad, somber, sorrowful, tedious, uneventful, uninteresting, wearisome, windy, wintry, wretched; SEE CONCEPTS *525,544*

drench [v] *wet thoroughly*
deluge, dip, douse, drown, duck, dunk, flood, imbrue, immerse, impregnate, inundate, pour, saturate, seethe, soak, sodden, sop, souse, steep, submerge, teem; SEE CONCEPT *256*

dress [n] *clothing; woman's garment*
accouterment, apparel, attire, attirement, civvies*, clothes, costume, covering, drape, dry goods, duds*, ensemble, evening clothes, frock, garb, gear, gown, guise, habiliment, habit, muumuu, outfit, raiment, robe, shift, skirt, smock, suit, Sunday best*, things*, threads*, tog, toga, toggery, trappings, uniform, vestment, wardrobe; SEE CONCEPT *451*

dress [v1] *put on clothing*
adorn, apparel, array, attire, bedeck, bundle up, change, clad, clothe, costume, cover, deck, decorate, don, drape, embellish, fit out, furbish, garb, ornament, outfit, primp, put on, raiment, rig, robe, slip into, slip on, spruce up, suit up, trim, turn out, wear; SEE CONCEPT *167*

dress [v2] *physically prepare; groom*
adjust, align, arrange, comb, decorate, dispose, do up, fit, make ready, ornament, set, straighten, trim; SEE CONCEPT *202*

dress [v3] *cover a wound*
attend, bandage, bind, cauterize, cleanse, give first aid, heal, plaster, sew up, sterilize, treat; SEE CONCEPTS *172,310*

dress down [v] *scold*
bawl out, berate, carpet, castigate, censure, chew out*, lash, rail, rake over coals*, ream, rebuke, reprimand, reprove, tear into*, tell off*, tongue-lash*, upbraid; SEE CONCEPT *52*

dress up [v] *put on one's best clothes*
array, attire, beautify, clothe, deck out*, embellish, fit out*, fix up, gussy up*, improve, overdress, preen, prettify, primp, prink, slick, smarten, spiff up*, spruce up*, titivate; SEE CONCEPT *167*

dressy [adj] *formal, fashionable*
chic, classy, dressed to kill*, dressed to nines*, dressed up*, elaborate, elegant, fancy, in high feather*, looking sharp, ornate, ritzy, smart, stylish; SEE CONCEPTS *579,589*

dribble [v] *trickle*
distill, drip, drivel, drizzle, drool, drop, fall in drops, leak, ooze, run, salivate, seep, slaver, slobber, spout, squirt, trill, weep; SEE CONCEPTS *179,185*

drift [n1] *accumulation*
alluvion, bank, batch, bunch, bundle, clump, cluster, deposit, heap, hill, lot, mass, mound, mountain, parcel, pile, set, shock, stack; SEE CONCEPTS *432,524*

drift [n2] *meaning, significance of communication*
aim, design, direction, end, gist, implication, import, intention, object, progress, progression, purport, scope, significance, tendency, tenor; SEE CONCEPT *682*

drift [v] *move aimlessly*
accumulate, aim, amass, amble, be carried along, coast, dance, draw near, flicker, flit, flitter, float, flow, flutter, gad*, gallivant*, gather, go-that-a-way*, go with tide*, gravitate, hover, kick around*, linger, malinger, meander, mosey*, move without effort, muck*, ride, sail, saunter, scud, skim, slide, stray, stroll, tend, waft, wander, wash*; SEE CONCEPT *147*

drill [n1] *practice, exercise*
assignment, call, conditioning, constitutional, daily dozen*, discipline, dress, drilling, dry run*, gym, homework, instruction, learning by doing, maneuvers, marching, preparation, repetition, runthrough*, shakedown*, training, tryout, warm-up, workout; SEE CONCEPTS *87,290*

drill [n2] *tool for boring*
auger, awl, bit, borer, corkscrew, countersink, dibble, gimlet, implement, jackhammer, punch, riveter, rotary tool, trepan, trephine, wimble; SEE CONCEPT *499*

drill [v1] *train, discipline*
accustom, break, break in, exercise, get into shape, habituate, hone, instruct, lick into shape, practice, rehearse, teach, tune up, walk through, work out; SEE CONCEPTS *117,285*

drill [v2] *bore hole*
dig, penetrate, perforate, pierce, prick, punch, puncture, sink in; SEE CONCEPT *220*

drink [n] *beverage; alcoholic beverage*
alcohol, booze*, brew, cup, draft, glass, gulp, libation, liquid, liquor, potable, potation, potion, refreshment, shot, sip, slug*, spirits, spot*, swallow, swig, taste, thirst quencher*, toast; SEE CONCEPT *454*

drink [v] *take in liquid*
absorb, belt*, booze*, consume, dissipate, down, drain, gargle, gulp, guzzle*, hit the bottle*, imbibe, indulge, inhale, irrigate, lap*, liquor up*, nip*, partake of, put away, quaff, sip, slosh, slurp, soak up, sop, sponge, suck, sup, swallow, swig, swill, tank up*, thirst, tipple*, toast, toss off*, wash down*, wet whistle*; SEE CONCEPT *169*

drip [v] *drop, trickle*
dribble, drizzle, exude, filter, plop, rain, splash, sprinkle, trill, weep; SEE CONCEPT *181*

drive [n1] *journey by vehicle*
airing, commute, excursion, expedition, hitch, jaunt, joyride, lift, outing, pickup, ramble, ride, run, spin,

Sunday drive*, tour, trip, turn, whirl; SEE CONCEPT *224*

drive [*n2*] *campaign for cause*
action, advance, appeal, crusade, effort, enterprise, get-up-and-go*, initiative, push, surge; SEE CONCEPTS *87,300*

drive [*n3*] *person's will to achieve*
ambition, clout, effort, energy, enterprise, fire in belly*, get-up-and-go, goods*, gumption*, guts*, impellent, impetus, impulse*, initiative, momentum, motivation, motive, moxie*, pep, pressure, punch*, push*, right stuff*, spunk*, steam*, stuff*, vigor, vitality, what it takes*, zip*; SEE CONCEPTS *411,706*

drive [*v1*] *move or urge on*
actuate, act upon, animate, arouse, bulldoze*, chase, coerce, compel, constrain, dog*, egg on*, encourage, force, goad, goose*, harass, hasten, herd, hound*, hurl, hurry, hustle, impel, induce, inspire, instigate, kick, lean on*, make, motivate, nag, oblige, overburden, overwork, pound, press, pressure, prod, prompt, propel, provoke, push, put up to*, railroad*, ride herd on*, rouse, rush, send, shepherd, shove, spirit up, spur, steamroll*, stimulate, work on, worry; SEE CONCEPTS *68,147,208*

drive [*v2*] *moving, controlling a vehicle*
actuate, advance, bear down, bicycle, bike, burn rubber*, burn up the road*, coast, cruise, cycle, dash, direct, drag, fire up*, floor it*, fly, guide, handle, impel, lean on it*, make sparks fly*, manage, mobilize, motor, move, operate, pour it on*, propel, push, ride, roll, run, send, speed, spin, start, steer, step on it*, step on the gas*, tailgate, tool*, transport, travel, turn, vehiculate*, wheel; SEE CONCEPTS *148,187*

drive [*v3*] *hit with heavy blow*
batter, beat, butt, dash, dig, hammer, jackhammer, knock, maul, plunge, pop, punch, ram, run, shoot, sink, smite, sock, stab, stick, strike, throw, thrust, thump, twack*, whack*, wham*; SEE CONCEPT *189*

drive at [*v*] *mean, suggest as meaning*
aim, allude to, contemplate, design, get at, have in mind, hint at, imply, indicate, intend, intimate, propose, refer to, signify; SEE CONCEPTS *73,682*

drivel [*n*] *foolish talk*
babble, balderdash*, blather, bunk*, double-talk, gibberish, gobbledygook*, Greek*, hogwash*, hooey*, jabber*, nonsense, poppycock*, prating, rot*, rubbish*, tripe*, twaddle*; SEE CONCEPT *278*

drivel [*v1*] *talk foolishly*
babble, blabber, blather*, blethe, gab, gabble, prate, prattle, ramble, twaddle*, waffle*; SEE CONCEPT *266*

drivel [*v2*] *drool*
dribble, salivate, slaver, slobber; SEE CONCEPTS *185,256*

driver [*n*] *person who engineers vehicle*
autoist, automobilist, cabbie, chauffeur, coachman, cowboy, hack*, handler, jockey, leadfoot*, motor-

ist, operator, road hog*, trainer, wheelman, whip*; SEE CONCEPT *423*

driving [*adj*] *forceful*
active, compelling, dynamic, energetic, enterprising, galvanic, impellent, lively, propulsive, sweeping, urging, vigorous, violent; SEE CONCEPT *540*

drizzle [*v*] *fine rain*
dribble, drip, drop, mist, mizzle, shower, spit, spray, sprinkle; SEE CONCEPT *526*

droll [*adj*] *amusing, farcical*
absurd, camp, campy, clownish, comic, comical, crack-up*, diverting, eccentric, entertaining, for grins*, funny, gagged up*, gelastic, humorous, jocular, joshing, laffer, laughable, ludicrous, odd, preposterous, quaint, queer, quizzical, ridiculous, riot, risible, waggish, whimsical; SEE CONCEPTS *267,548*

drone [*n1*] *person who is lazy*
idler, leech, loafer, lounger, parasite, slug, sluggard, sponger*; SEE CONCEPT *412*

drone [*n2*] *continuous noise*
buzz, hum, murmuring, purr, sound, vibration, whirr, whirring; SEE CONCEPT *595*

drone [*v*] *making noise continuously*
bombinate, buzz, chant, drawl, hum, intone, nasalize, purr, sound, strum, thrum, vibrate, whirr; SEE CONCEPTS *65,77*

drool [*v1*] *salivate*
dribble, drivel, froth, ooze, run, slabber, slaver, slobber, spit, water, water at the mouth; SEE CONCEPTS *185,256*

drool [*v2*] *desire, lust after*
dote on, enthuse, fondle, gush, lick chops*, make much of, pet, rave, rhapsodize, rhapsody, slobber over*, spoil, want; SEE CONCEPT *20*

droop [*v*] *hang down; languish*
bend, dangle, decline, depress, diminish, drop, fade, fail, faint, fall down, flag, lean, let down, loll, lop, sag, settle, sink, sling, slouch, slump, subside, suspend, weaken, wilt, wither; SEE CONCEPTS *181,699*

droopy [*adj*] *limp*
bent, drooping, flabby, floppy, languid, languorous, lassitudinous, pendulous, sagging, saggy, slouchy, stooped, wilting; SEE CONCEPT *485*

drop [*n1*] *globule*
bead, bit, bubble, crumb, dab, dash, dewdrop, driblet, drip, droplet, iota, molecule, morsel, nip, ounce, particle, pearl, pinch, sip, smidgen, speck, splash, spot, taste, tear, teardrop, trace, trickle; SEE CONCEPTS *467,468,831,835*

drop [*n2*] *steep decline; hole*
abyss, chasm, declivity, deepness, depth, descent, dip, fall, plunge, precipice, slope, tumble; SEE CONCEPTS *181,509*

drop [*n3*] *decrease*
cut, decline, descent, deterioration, dip, downfall, downslide, downswing, downtrend, downturn, fall, fall-off, landslide, lapse, lowering, precipitation, re-

duction, sag, slide, slip, slump, tumble, upset; SEE CONCEPTS *698,776*

drop [*v1*] *fall in globules*
bead, bleed, descend, distill, drain, dribble, drip, emanate, hail, leak, ooze, percolate, precipitate, seep, snow, splash, trickle, trill; SEE CONCEPT *179*

drop [*v2*] *let go of; fall*
abandon, bring down, cave in, collapse, decline, depress, descend, dive, duck, dump, fell, floor, flop, give up, go down, ground, keel over*, knock, loosen, lower, nose-dive*, pitch, plummet, plump, plunge, release, relinquish, shed, shoot, sink, slide, slip, slump, topple, tumble, unload; SEE CONCEPTS *181,200*

drop [*v3*] *abandon; ignore*
abort, adios*, be alienated from, break with, call off, cancel, cast off, cease, desert, discontinue, dismiss, disown, ditch*, divorce, dust off*, eighty-six*, end, forfeit, forget about, forsake, give up, have done with*, interrupt, jilt, kick*, leave, lose, part from, part with, quit, reject, relinquish, remit, renounce, repudiate, resign, sacrifice, scratch*, scrub*, separate, shake, stop, terminate, throw over, wash out*, waste one*, wipe out*, write off*; SEE CONCEPTS *30,121,195*

drop in [*v*] *visit*
blow in*, call, call upon, come by, come over, go and see*, look in on, look up, pop in*, run in*, stop, stop by, stop in, turn up; SEE CONCEPT *227*

drop off [*v1*] *decrease*
decline, diminish, dwindle, fall away, fall off, lessen, sag, slacken, slide, slip, slump; SEE CONCEPTS *698,776*

drop off [*v2*] *deliver*
deposit, give, hand over, leave, let off, present, set down, unload; SEE CONCEPT *108*

drop off [*v3*] *fall asleep*
catnap, doze, doze off*, drowse, have forty winks*, nod, nod off*, snooze; SEE CONCEPTS *210,315*

drop out [*v*] *stop doing an activity*
abandon, back out, cease, forsake, give notice, give up, leave, quit, renege, retreat, withdraw; SEE CONCEPT *121*

drought [*n*] *dryness; shortage of supply*
aridity, dearth, deficiency, dehydration, desiccation, dry spell, insufficiency, lack, need, parchedness, rainlessness, scarcity, want; SEE CONCEPTS *607,646*

drove [*n*] *large gathering*
collection, company, crowd, crush, drive, flock, herd, horde, mob, multitude, pack, press, rout, run, swarm, throng; SEE CONCEPTS *397,432*

drown [*v*] *submerge in liquid; submerge and die*
asphyxiate, deluge, dip, douse, drench, engulf, flood, go down, go under, immerse, inundate, knock over, obliterate, overcome, overflow, overpower, overwhelm, plunge, prostrate, sink, soak, sop, souse, stifle, submerge, suffocate, swamp, whelm, wipe out; SEE CONCEPTS *252,256*

drowsy [*adj*] *sleepy*
comatose, dazed, dopy, dozing, dozy, dreamy, drugged, half asleep, heavy, indolent, lackadaisical, languid, lazy, lethargic, lulling, napping, nodding, out of it*, restful, sleepy, sleepy head*, sluggish, slumberous, snoozy, somnolent, soothing, soporific, tired, torpid; SEE CONCEPTS *406,539*

drudge [*n*] *slave, very hard worker*
factotum, grind*, laborer, maid, menial, nose to grindstone*, peon*, plodder*, servant, toiler, workaholic, worker, workhorse; SEE CONCEPT *348*

drudge [*v*] *work very hard*
back to salt mines*, dig, grind*, hammer*, keep nose to grindstone*, labor, muck*, perform, plod, plow, plug away*, pound*, schlepp*, slave, slog, sweat, toil, travail; SEE CONCEPTS *87,100,324*

drudgery [*n*] *hard, tedious work*
backbreaker*, chore, daily grind*, elbow grease*, grind*, gruntwork*, labor, menial labor, rat race, slavery, struggle, sweat, toil, travail, workout; SEE CONCEPT *362*

drug [*n*] *medication*
biologic, cure, depressant, dope, essence, medicament, medicinal, medicine, narcotic, opiate, pharmaceutic, pharmaceutical, physic, pill, poison, potion, prescription, remedy, sedative, stimulant, tonic; SEE CONCEPT *307*

drug [*v*] *put under influence of medication*
analgize, anesthetize, benumb, blunt, deaden, desensitize, dope, dope up*, dose, dose up*, fix, hit, knock out*, medicate, narcotize, numb, poison, relax, sedate, stupefy, treat; SEE CONCEPT *310*

drugged [*adj*] *under the influence of medication*
benumbed, blown away*, coked*, comatose, dazed, doped, dopey*, floating*, flying*, high*, junked-up*, loaded*, narcotized, on a trip*, out of it*, ripped*, smashed*, spaced-out*, stoned*, strung out*, stupefied, unconscious; SEE CONCEPT *314*

drum [*v*] *beat, tap a beat*
boom*, pulsate, rap, reverberate, roar, strum, tattoo, throb, thrum, thunder*; SEE CONCEPTS *65,189*

drum into [*v*] *make a point strongly*
din into, drive home*, hammer away*, harp on*, instill, reiterate; SEE CONCEPTS *49,75*

drum up [*v*] *gather support for something*
attract, bid for, canvass, discover, obtain, petition, round up, solicit, succeed in finding; SEE CONCEPTS *68,300*

drunk/drunkard [*n*] *person who is inebriated*
alcoholic, boozer*, carouser*, dipsomanic, drinker, guzzler*, inebriate, lush*, sot*, sponge*, wino*; SEE CONCEPT *423*

drunk [*adj*] *intoxicated by alcohol*
bashed, befuddled, boozed up*, buzzed*, crocked*, drinking, drunken, feeling no pain*, flushed*, flying*, fuddled, glazed*, groggy, high*, inebriated, juiced*, laced*, liquored up*, lit*, lush, muddled, plastered*, potted*, seeing double*, sloshed*,

stewed*, stoned*, tanked*, three sheets to wind*, tight*, tipsy, totaled*, under the influence, under the table*, wasted*; SEE CONCEPTS *314,545*

dry [*adj1*] *moistureless*
anhydrous, arid, athirst, baked, bald, bare, barren, dehydrated, depleted, desert, desiccant, desiccated, drained, dried-up, droughty, dusty, evaporated, exhausted, hard, impoverished, juiceless, not irrigated, parched, rainless, sapless, sapped, sear, shriveled, stale, thirsty, torrid, unmoistened, waterless; SEE CONCEPT *603*

dry [*adj2*] *dull, uninteresting*
apathetic, blah, boring, bromidic, draggy, dreary, dull as dishwater*, dusty, ho hum*, impassive, inelaborate, insipid, matter-of-fact, modest, monotonous, naked, phlegmatic, plain, simple, tedious, tiresome, trite, weariful, wearisome; SEE CONCEPT *529*

dry [*adj3*] *sarcastic, sharp-tongued*
acerbic, arcane, biting, caustic, cutting, cynical, deadpan, droll, harsh, humorous, ironical, keen, low-key, restrained, salty, sardonic, satirical, sharp, sly, sour, subtle, tart; SEE CONCEPT *267*

dry [*v*] *take moisture out of*
anhydrate, bake, blot, concentrate, condense, dehumidify, dehydrate, deplete, desiccate, drain, empty, evaporate, exhaust, exsiccate, freeze-dry, harden, kiln, make dry, mummify, parch, scorch, sear, shrivel, soak up, sponge, stale, swab, torrefy, towel, wilt, wipe, wither, wizen; SEE CONCEPTS *250,469*

dual [*adj*] *two-fold*
bifold, binal, binary, coupled, double, doubleheader, duple, duplex, duplicate, matched, paired, twin; SEE CONCEPTS *762,771*

dub [*v*] *name, label something*
baptize, bestow, call, christen, confer, denominate, designate, entitle, knight, nickname, style, tag, term, title; SEE CONCEPT *62*

dubious [*adj1*] *doubtful*
arguable, chancy, debatable, diffident, disputable, dubitable, equivocal, far-fetched, fishy*, fly-by-night*, hesitant, iffy*, improbable, indecisive, moot, mootable, open, perplexed, problematic, questionable, reluctant, shady, skeptical, suspect, suspicious, touch and go*, trustless, unassured, uncertain, unclear, unconvinced, undecided, undependable, unlikely, unreliable, unsure, untrustworthy, untrusty, wavering; SEE CONCEPT *552*

dubious [*adj2*] *vague, unclear*
ambiguous, debatable, disinclined, doubtful, equivocal, indefinite, indeterminate, mistrustful, obscure, open, problematic, problematical, skeptical, undecided, unsettled; SEE CONCEPTS *535,576*

duck [*v*] *drop down; avoid*
bend, bob, bow, crouch, dip, dive, dodge, double, elude, escape, evade, fence, lower, lurch, move to side, parry, plunge, shirk, shun, shy, sidestep, stoop, submerge; SEE CONCEPTS *102,154,181*

duct [*n*] *channel, pipe*
aqueduct, canal, conduit, course, funnel, passage, tube, vessel, watercourse; SEE CONCEPT *501*

ductile [*adj*] *pliant, flexible*
adaptable, amenable, biddable, docile, extensile, malleable, manageable, moldable, plastic, pliable, responsive, submitting, supple, tractable, yielding; SEE CONCEPTS *488,490*

dud [*n*] *failure*
bomb, bummer, bust, debacle, flop, lemon, loser, washout; SEE CONCEPT *674*

dude [*n*] *man who feigns worldliness*
beau, buck, city slicker*, clotheshorse, coxcomb, dandy, exquisite, flash, fop, hotshot*, snappy dresser*, sport, swell; SEE CONCEPTS *419,423*

due [*n*] *expected reward*
be in line for*, claim, comeuppance, compensation, deserts*, entitlement, guerdon, interest, merits, need, payment, perquisite, prerogative, privilege, rate, recompense, repayment, reprisal, retaliation, retribution, revenge, right, rights, satisfaction, title, vengeance, what is coming to one*; SEE CONCEPTS *337,710*

due [*adj1*] *unpaid; owing money*
chargeable, collectible, expected, in arrears, IOU, mature, not met, outstanding, overdue, owed, payable, receivable, scheduled, to be paid, unliquidated, unsatisfied, unsettled; SEE CONCEPT *334*

due [*adj2*] *appropriate, proper*
becoming, coming, condign, deserved, earned, equitable, fair, fit, fitting, good, just, justified, merited, obligatory, requisite, rhadamanthine, right, rightful, suitable; SEE CONCEPT *558*

due [*adv*] *directly*
dead, direct, exactly, right, straight, straightly, undeviatingly; SEE CONCEPTS *581,799*

dues [*n*] *payment for membership*
ante, arrearage, assessment, charge, charges, collection, contribution, custom, debit, debt, duty, fee, kickback, levy, liability, obligation, pay, protection, rates, tax, toll; SEE CONCEPTS *344,679*

dull [*adj1*] *unintelligent*
addled, backward, besotted, boring, brainless, daffy, daft, dense, dim, dim-witted, doltish, dumb, feebleminded, half-baked, half-witted, ignorant, imbecilic, indolent, insensate, low, moronic, not bright, numskulled, obtuse, retarded, scatterbrained, shallow, simple, simple-minded, slow, sluggish, stolid, stupid, tedious, thick, unintellectual, vacuous, wearisome, witless; SEE CONCEPT *402*

dull [*adj2*] *insensitive*
accustomed, apathetic, blank, boring, callous, colorless, dead, depressed, empty, even, flat, heavy, impassible, inactive, indifferent, inert, insensible, jejune, languid, lifeless, listless, lumpy, monotonous, passionless, placid, prosaic, quiet, regular, routine, slack, slow, sluggish, spiritless, stagnant,

still, stolid, torpid, unexciting, unresponsive, unsympathetic, usual, vacuous; SEE CONCEPT 542

dull [adj3] boring, uninteresting
abused, archaic, arid, big yawn*, blah, colorless, common, commonplace, dead, dismal, dreary, driveling, dry, familiar, flat, hackneyed, heavy, hoary, ho hum*, humdrum*, insipid, jejune, longwinded, monotonous, oft-repeated*, ordinary, out-of-date, plain, pointless, prolix, prosaic, prosy, repetitious, repetitive, routine, run-of-the-mill*, senile, soporific, stale, stock, stupid, tame, tedious, tired, tiresome, trite, unimaginative, uninspiring, usual, usual thing, vapid, worn-out; SEE CONCEPTS 529,530

dull [adj4] not sharp
blunt, blunted, edentate, edgeless, flat, not keen, obtuse, pointless, round, square, toothless, turned, unpointed, unsharpened; SEE CONCEPT 486

dull [adj5] uneventful
accustomed, apathetic, blah, boring, dead, depressed, draggy*, even, falling off*, flat, inactive, inert, languid, lifeless, listless, monotonous, placid, quiet, regular, routine, sitting tight*, slack, slothful, slow, sluggish, stagnant, still, stolid, tight, torpid, unexciting, unresponsive, usual, without incident, yawn; SEE CONCEPT 548

dull [adj6] drab, lackluster in effect on senses
ashen, black, blind, cloudy, cold, colorless, dark, dead, dim, dingy, dismal, dun, dusky, faded, feeble, flat, grimy, hazy, indistinct, leaden, lifeless, low, matte, mousy, muddy, muffled, murky, muted, obscure, opaque, overcast, plain, shadowy, sober, soft, softened, somber, sooty, subdued, subfusc, toned-down, unlit; SEE CONCEPTS 594,617

duly [adv] accordingly, properly
appropriately, at the proper time, befittingly, correctly, decorously, deservedly, on time, punctually, rightfully, suitably; SEE CONCEPTS 558,799

dumb [adj1] unable to speak
at loss for words*, impaired, inarticulate, incoherent, mousy*, mum, mute, quiet, silent, soundless, speechless, tongue-tied, uncommunicative, voiceless, wordless; SEE CONCEPT 593

dumb [adj2] stupid, unintelligent
dense, dim-witted, doltish, dull, feebleminded, foolish, moronic, simple-minded, thick*; SEE CONCEPT 402

dumbbell [n] stupid person
dodo*, dolt, dullard, dumb bunny*, dumb cluck*, dumb head*, dumbo*, dumb ox*, dumdum*, dummy, dunce, idiot, ignoramus, moron, simpleton; SEE CONCEPTS 412,423

dumbfound [v] astound, confuse
amaze, astonish, bewilder, blow away*, blow one's mind*, boggle, bowl over*, confound, flabbergast, knock over with feather*, nonplus, overwhelm, puzzle, stagger, startle, stun, surprise, take aback, throw, throw into tizzy*; SEE CONCEPTS 16,42

dumbfounded [adj] astounded, confused
agape, aghast, amazed, astonished, bamboozled*, beat, bewildered, blown away*, bowled over*, breathless, buffaloed*, confounded, dismayed, dumb, flabbergasted, floored, knocked, licked, nonplused, overcome, overwhelmed, puzzled, shocked, speechless, staggered, startled, stuck, stumped, stunned, surprised, taken aback, thrown, thunderstruck*; SEE CONCEPT 403

dummy [n1] mannequin
copy, counterfeit, duplicate, figure, form, imitation, manikin, model, ringer*, sham*, stand-in, sub, substitute; SEE CONCEPTS 436,716

dummy [n2] stupid person
blockhead*, dimwit*, dolt*, dullard*, dunce, fool, idiot, ignoramus, moron, numskull, oaf, simpleton; SEE CONCEPTS 412,423

dump [n1] junkyard
ash heap*, cesspool, depot, discard, dumping ground, garbage lot, junk pile*, magazine, refuse heap, rubbish pile, swamp; SEE CONCEPTS 438,449, 680

dump [n2] slummy establishment
hole, hovel, joint*, mess*, pigpen*, pigsty*, shack, shanty, slum, sty; SEE CONCEPTS 449,673

dump [v] drop, throw away
cast, chuck, clear out, deep-six*, deposit, discard, discharge, dispose of, ditch, drain, eject, empty, evacuate, expel, exude, fling, fling down, get rid of, jettison, junk, leave, let fall, scrap, throw down, throw out, throw overboard*, tip, unload, unpack; SEE CONCEPTS 180,181

dunce [n] stupid person
ass, birdbrain*, blockhead*, bonehead*, buffoon, dimwit*, dolt, donkey*, dope, dork*, drip*, dullard*, dunderhead*, fool, goof, goof ball*, half-wit, idiot, ignoramus, imbecile, jerk, knucklehead*, lamebrain*, lightweight*, moron, nerd*, nincompoop*, ninny*, nitwit, numskull, oaf, pinhead*, scatterbrain*, schnook*, simpleton, twit*; SEE CONCEPTS 412,423

dunk [v] dip in liquid
douse, duck, immerse, saturate, soak, sop, souse, submerge, submerse; SEE CONCEPT 256

duo [n] twosome
brace, couple, doublet, dyad, pair; SEE CONCEPT 786

dupe [n] person who is fooled
butt*, chump*, easy mark*, fish*, fool, mark*, patsy*, pigeon*, pushover*, sap*, sitting duck*, sucker, victim; SEE CONCEPT 423

dupe [v] fool someone
baffle, bamboozle*, beguile, betray, catch, cheat, chicane, circumvent, con, cozen, deceive, defraud, delude, double-cross, dust*, flimflam*, gull, hoax, hoodwink*, hornswoggle, jerk around*, kid, mislead, outwit, overreach, pull one's leg*, pull something*, rip off*, rook*, rope in*, shaft, spoof, swindle, trick, victimize; SEE CONCEPT 59

duplicate [n] *copy, reproduction*
analogue, carbon, carbon copy*, chip off old block*, clone, companion, coordinate, copycat*, correlate, counterfeit, counterpart, counterscript, dead ringer*, ditto*, double, dupe*, duplication, facsimile, fake, fellow, germination, imitation, knockoff*, likeness, lookalike, match, mate, obverse, parallel, phony, photocopy, photostat, pirate*, reciprocal, recurrence, repetition, replica, replication, repro*, ringer*, second, similarity, spitting image*, stat, twin, Xerox*; SEE CONCEPTS *664,667,716*

duplicate [adj] *matching*
alike, corresponding, dualistic, duple, duplex, equal, equivalent, identic, identical, indistinguishable, matched, same, self-same, tantamount, twin, twofold, very same; SEE CONCEPTS *563,566*

duplicate [v] *make a copy; repeat*
act like, clone, copy, counterfeit, ditto*, do again, do a takeoff*, do like*, double, dualize, dupe, echo, fake, go like*, imitate, knock off*, make like*, make replica, make twofold, manifold, mirror, multiply, phony, photocopy, photostat, pirate*, redo, redouble, reduplicate, remake, replicate, repro, reproduce, rework, stat, take off as*, trace, Xerox*; SEE CONCEPTS *91,171*

duplicity [n] *deception*
artifice, chicanery, cunning, deceit, dirty dealing*, dirty pool*, dirty trick*, dirty work*, dishonesty, dissemblance, dissimulation, double-dealing, dualism, duality, faithlessness, falsehood, fraud, gamesmanship, guile, hypocrisy, Judas kiss*, one-upmanship, perfidiousness, perfidy, skullduggery, stab in back*, treacherousness, treachery, two-facedness*, twoness; SEE CONCEPTS *59,63*

durability [n] *sturdiness over time*
backbone, constancy, durableness, endurance, grit, guts*, gutsiness, hard as nails*, heart*, imperishability, intestinal fortitude, lastingness, moxie*, permanence, persistence, stamina, starch*, staying power*, stick-to-itiveness*; SEE CONCEPTS *721,731,732*

durable [adj] *sturdy, long-lasting*
abiding, constant, dependable, diuturnal, enduring, fast, firm, fixed, impervious, lasting, long-continued, perdurable, perduring, permanent, persistent, reliable, resistant, sound, stable, stout, strong, substantial, tenacious, tough; SEE CONCEPTS *482,488, 489*

duration [n] *length of action, event*
continuance, continuation, continuity, endurance, extent, period, perpetuation, persistence, prolongation, run, span, spell, stretch, term, tide, time; SEE CONCEPT *804*

duress [n] *threat, hardship*
bondage, captivity, coercion, compulsion, confinement, constraint, control, detention, discipline, force, imprisonment, incarceration, pressure, restraint, violence; SEE CONCEPTS *14,674*

during [prep] *concurrently with an activity, event*
all along, all the while, amid, as, at the same time as, at the time, for the time being, in the course of, in the interim, in the meanwhile, in the middle of, in the time of, meanwhile, mid, midst, over, pending, the time between, the whole time, throughout, until, when, while; SEE CONCEPT *820*

dusk [n] *early evening*
dark, dimday, dimmet, evening, eventide, gloaming, gloom, night, nightfall, sundown, sunset, twilight; SEE CONCEPT *810*

dusky [adj] *dark-hued; murky*
adusk, bistered, bleak, brunette, caliginous, cheerless, cloudy, crepuscular, dark, dark-complexioned, darkish, desolate, dim, dismal, dull, funereal, gloomy, joyless, lightless, obscure, overcast, sable, shadowy, shady, swart, swarthy, tenebrous, twilight, twilit, unilluminated, veiled; SEE CONCEPTS *617, 618*

dust [n] *tiny particles in the air*
ashes, cinders, dirt, dust bunnies*, earth, filth, flakes, fragments, gilings, granules, grime, grit, ground, lint, loess, powder, refuse, sand, smut, soil, soot; SEE CONCEPT *437*

dust [v] *sprinkle tiny particles*
besprinkle, cover, dredge, powder, scatter, sift, spray, spread; SEE CONCEPTS *172,222*

dusty [adj] *filled with or covered with powdery particles*
arenaceous, arenose, chalky, crumbly, dirty, friable, granular, grubby, sandy, sooty, unclean, undusted, unswept, untouched; SEE CONCEPT *485*

dutiful [adj] *obedient*
binding, compliant, conscientious, deferential, devoted, docile, duteous, faithful, filial, incumbent on, obligatory, punctilious, regardful, respectful, reverential, submissive; SEE CONCEPT *542*

duty [n1] *responsibility, assignment*
burden, business, calling, charge, chore, commission, commitment, committal, contract, devoir, dues, engagement, function, hook*, job, load, millstone*, minding the store*, mission, must, need, obligation, occupation, office, onus, ought*, pains, part, province, role, service, station, string*, taking care of business*, task, trouble, trust, undertaking, weight, work; SEE CONCEPTS *362,376,679*

duty [n2] *tax on foreign goods*
assessment, cess, custom, customs, due, excise, impost, levy, rate, revenue, tariff, toll; SEE CONCEPT *329*

duty [n3] *moral obligation*
accountability, accountableness, allegiance, amenability, answerability, burden, call of duty, charge, conscience, deference, devoir, faithfulness, good faith, honesty, integrity, liability, loyalty, obedience, pledge, respect, reverence, sense of duty; SEE CONCEPT *388*

dwarf [n] *very small person*
bantam, dwarfling, gnome, half-pint*, homunculus, knee high*, Lilliputian*, little person, manikin,

midget, peanut*, peewee*, pygmy, runt, shorty*, shrimp*, squirt*, Tom Thumb*, tot; SEE CONCEPT *424*

dwarf [*adj*] *miniature, tiny*
baby, diminutive, dwarfed, low, petite, pocket, small, undersized; SEE CONCEPT *773*

dwarf [*v*] *minimize*
belittle, check, detract from, dim, diminish, dominate, hinder, look down upon, lower, make small, micrify, minify, overshadow, predominate, retard, rise above, stunt, suppress, tower above, tower over; SEE CONCEPTS *7,19,698,741*

dwell [*v*] *live in*
abide, bide, bunk*, continue, crash*, establish oneself, exist, flop*, hang one's hat*, hang out*, hole up*, inhabit, keep house, live at, locate, lodge, make one's home, nest, occupy, park*, perch*, pitch tent*, quarter, remain, rent, reside, rest, room, roost*, settle, sojourn, squat*, stay, stop, tarry, tenant, tent; SEE CONCEPT *226*

dwelling [*n*] *home*
abode, castle, commorancy, den, digs*, domicile, dump*, establishment, habitat, habitation, haunt, hole in the wall*, house, lodging, pad, quarters, residence, residency; SEE CONCEPT *516*

dwell on/dwell upon [*v*] *linger over; be engrossed in*
consider, continue, elaborate, emphasize, expatiate, harp on*, involve oneself, tarry over; SEE CONCEPTS *17,239*

dwindle [*v*] *waste away; taper off*
abate, bate, become smaller, close, contract, decay, decline, decrease, die away, die down, die out, diminish, drain, drop, ebb, fade, fall, grow less, lessen, peter out*, pine, shrink, shrivel, sink, slack off*, subside, taper, wane, weaken, wither; SEE CONCEPTS *698,776*

dye [*n*] *coloring agent*
color, colorant, coloring, dyestuff, pigment, stain, tincture, tinge, tint; SEE CONCEPT *259*

dye [*v*] *change color with mixture*
color, impregnate, pigment, stain, tincture, tinge, tint; SEE CONCEPT *250*

dying [*adj*] *failing, expiring*
at death's door*, at end of rope*, decaying, declining, disintegrating, done for*, doomed, ebbing, fading, fated, final, giving up the ghost*, going, in extremis, moribund, mortal, one foot in grave*, on last leg*, passing, perishing, sinking, vanishing, withering; SEE CONCEPT *539*

dynamic [*adj*] *active, vital*
activating, aggressive, changing, charismatic, coming on strong*, compelling, driving, effective, electric, energetic, energizing, enterprising, forceful, forcible, go-ahead*, go-getter*, go-getting*, high-powered, hyped-up, influential, intense, lively, lusty, magnetic, peppy*, play for keeps*, play hard ball*, potent, powerful, productive, progressive, red-

blooded*, strenuous, vehement, vigorous, vitalizing, zippy*; SEE CONCEPTS *404,540,542*

dynasty [*n*] *area of rule*
absolutism, ascendancy, dominion, empire, government, house, regime, rule, sovereignty, sway; SEE CONCEPTS *435,508,710*

E

each [*adj*] *every*
all, any, exclusive, individual, one by one*, particular, personal, piece by piece*, respective, separate, several, single, specific, various, without exception; SEE CONCEPT *577*

each [*adv*] *apiece; for each one*
all, a pop*, a shot*, aside, a throw*, by the, every, for each, for one, from each, individually, per, per capita, per head, per person, per unit, proportionately, respectively, separately, singly, to each, without exception; SEE CONCEPT *577*

each [*prep*] *each one*
each and every one*, each for himself*, each in his own way*, each other, every last one, every one, one, one and all*, one another; SEE CONCEPT *577*

eager [*adj*] *anxious, enthusiastic*
acquisitive, agog, ambitious, antsy, appetent, ardent, athirst, avid, breathless, champing at the bit*, covetous, craving, desiring, desirous, dying to, earnest, fervent, fervid, greedy, gung ho*, hankering, heated, hot*, hot to trot*, hungry*, impatient, intent, keen, longing, pining, rarin' to go*, ready and willing*, restive, restless, self-starting, solicitous, thirsty, vehement, voracious, warmblooded*, wild, wishful, yearning, zealous; SEE CONCEPTS *326,401,542*

eagerness [*n*] *enthusiasm, anxiousness*
alacrity, ambition, anticipation, ardor, avidity, earnestness, excitement, fervor, greediness, gusto, heartiness, hunger, impatience, impetuosity, intentness, keenness, longing, promptness, quickness, solicitude, thirst, vehemence, voracity, yearning, zeal, zest, zing*; SEE CONCEPTS *20,633,657*

ear [*n*] *attention*
appreciation, consideration, discrimination, hearing, heed, mark, mind, note, notice, observance, observation, perception, regard, remark, sensitivity, taste; SEE CONCEPT *532*

early [*adj1*] *in the beginning*
a bit previous, aboriginal, ancient, antecedent, antediluvian, antiquated, brand-new, budding, early bird*, fresh, initial, maiden, new, original, preceding, premier, prevenient, previous, primal, prime, primeval, primitive, primordial, prior, pristine, proleptical, raw, recent, undeveloped, virgin, young; SEE CONCEPTS *799,828*

early [*adj2*] *sooner than expected*
advanced, ahead of time, anticipative, anticipatory, before appointed time, beforehand, direct, immature, immediate, matinal, on short notice*, on the dot*, overearly, oversoon, preceding, precipitant, precocious, preexistent, premature, previous, prompt,

pronto, punctual, quick, seasonable, soon, speedy, unanticipated, unexpected, untimely; SEE CONCEPT *820*

early [*adv1*] *sooner than expected*
a bit previous, ahead of time, anon, beforehand, before long, betimes, briefly, bright and early*, directly, early bird*, ere long, far ahead, immediately, in advance, in good time*, in the bud*, in time, on short notice*, on the dot*, oversoon, prematurely, presently, previous, promptly, pronto, proximately, quick, shortly, soon, too soon, unexpectedly, with time to spare*; SEE CONCEPT *820*

early [*adv2*] *immediately*
at once, betimes, directly, first, freshly, in a jiffy*, in an instant*, in no time*, instantaneously, instantly, newly, presto, primitively, promptly, recently, right away, seasonably, soon, straightaway, summarily, thereon, thereupon, timely, without delay; SEE CONCEPTS *799,828*

earmark [*n*] *signature characteristic*
attribute, differential, distinction, feature, hallmark, label, marking, pecularity, quality, signature, stamp, tag, token, trademark, trait; SEE CONCEPT *644*

earmark [*v*] *reserve*
allocate, designate, keep back, label, maintain, mark out, name, set aside, slot, tab, tag; SEE CONCEPT *129*

earn [*v1*] *make money*
acquire, attain, be gainfully employed, be in line for*, bring home*, bring home the bacon*, bring home the groceries*, bring in, clean up*, clear*, collect, consummate, cop*, derive, draw, effect, gain, gather, get, gross, hustle, make, make fast buck*, make it big*, net, obtain, pay one's dues*, perform, pick up, procure, profit, pull*, pull down*, rate, realize, reap, receive, scare up*, score*, scrape together*, secure, snag*, sock*, turn, wangle, win; SEE CONCEPTS *330,351*

earn [*v2*] *deserve a reward*
acquire, attain, bag, be entitled to, be worthy of, come by, gain, harvest, merit, net, rate, reap, score, warrant, win; SEE CONCEPTS *120,129*

earnest [*adj1*] *very enthusiastic*
ardent, busy, devoted, diligent, eager, fervent, fervid, heartfelt, impassioned, industrious, keen, passionate, perseverant, purposeful, sedulous, sincere, urgent, vehement, warm, wholehearted, zealous; SEE CONCEPTS *326,401,542*

earnest [*adj2*] *serious; very important*
close, constant, determined, firm, fixed, for real, grave, intent, mean business, meaningful, no-fooling, no-nonsense, playing hard ball*, resolute, resolved, sedate, sincere, sober, solemn, somber, stable, staid, steady, thoughtful, weighty; SEE CONCEPT *568*

earnestness [*n*] *determination; seriousness*
absorption, ardor, attentiveness, concentration, decision, deliberation, devotion, doggedness, eagerness, earnest, engrossment, enthusiasm, fervor, firmness,

gravity, intensity, intentness, keenness, passion, perseverance, persistence, purposefulness, resolution, resolve, serious-mindedness, sincerity, sobriety, solemnity, stress, tenacity, urgency, vehemence, warmth, zeal; SEE CONCEPTS *633,657*

earnings [*n*] *money for work performed*
balance, bottom line*, emolument, gain, gate, groceries*, income, in the black*, lucre, net, pay, payoff, piece of the pie*, proceeds, profit, receipts, remuneration, return, revenue, reward, salary, salt*, stipend, take-home*, takings, wages; SEE CONCEPT *344*

earth [*n1*] *the world*
apple*, big blue marble*, cosmos, creation, dust*, globe, macrocosm, orb, planet, spaceship Earth*, sphere, star, sublunary world, terra, terra firma, terrene, terrestrial sphere, universe, vale; SEE CONCEPT *511*

earth [*n2*] *ground, soil*
alluvium, clay, clod, coast, compost, deposit, dirt, dry land, dust, fill, glebe, gravel, humus, land, loam, marl, mold, muck, mud, peat moss, sand, shore, sod, subsoil, surface, terra firma, terrain, terrane, topsoil, turf; SEE CONCEPT *509*

earthly [*adj1*] *physically concerning land or its inhabitants*
alluvial, carnal, corporeal, earthy, geotic, global, human, in all creation, material, mortal, mundane, nonspiritual, physical, profane, secular, subastral, sublunary, tellurian, telluric, temporal, terraqueous, terrene, terrestrial, uncelestial, under the sun*, unspiritual, worldly; SEE CONCEPT *536*

earthly [*adj2*] *conceivable*
feasible, imaginable, likely, mortal, possible, potential, practical, probable; SEE CONCEPT *552*

earthquake [*n*] *tremor from inside the earth*
convulsion, fault, macroseism, microseism, movement, quake, quaker*, seimicity, seism, seismism, shake, shock, slip, temblor, trembler*, undulation, upheaval; SEE CONCEPTS *144,526*

earthy [*adj*] *unsophisticated*
bawdy, coarse, crude, down, down home*, down-to-earth*, dull, easygoing, folksy, funky*, hard-boiled*, home folk*, homely, homey, indelicate, lowbred, lusty, mundane, natural, pragmatic, ribald, robust, rough, simple, unidealistic, uninhibited, unrefined; SEE CONCEPT *542*

ease [*n1*] *peace, quiet; lack of difficulty*
affluence, ataraxia, bed of roses*, calm, calmness, comfort, content, contentment, easiness, enjoyment, gratification, happiness, idleness, inactivity, inertia, inertness, leisure, luxury, passivity, peace of mind*, prosperity, quietness, quietude, relaxation, repose, requiescence, rest, restfulness, satisfaction, security, serenity, supinity, tranquility; SEE CONCEPTS *388,410,673*

ease [*n2*] *facility, freedom*
adroitness, affability, aplomb, breeze, child's play*, cinch, cleverness, composure, dexterity, dispatch,

duck soup*, easiness, easygoingness, efficiency, effortlessness, expertise, expertness, familiarity, flexibility, fluency, freedom, informality, insouciance, knack, liberty, naturalness, nonchalance, poise, pushover, quickness, readiness, relaxedness, setup, simplicity, skillfulness, smoothness, smooth sailing*, snap, unaffectedness, unconstraint, unreservedness; SEE CONCEPTS *376,388,630*

ease [*v1*] *alleviate, help*
abate, aid, allay, ameliorate, anesthetize, appease, assist, assuage, attend to, calm, cheer, clear the way*, comfort, cure, disburden, disengage, doctor, expedite, facilitate, forward, free, further, improve, lessen, let up on, lift, lighten, make easier, meliorate, mitigate, moderate, mollify, nurse, open the door*, pacify, palliate, promote, quiet, relax, release, relent, relieve, run interference for*, simplify, slacken, smooth, soften, soothe, speed, speed up, still, tranquilize, untighten; SEE CONCEPTS *110,310*

ease [*v2*] *guide, move carefully*
disentangle, ease off, edge, extricate, facilitate, handle, inch, induce, insert, join, loose, loosen, maneuver, relax, remove, right, set right, slack, slacken, slide, slip, squeeze, steer, untighten; SEE CONCEPT *187*

easily [*adv1*] *without difficulty*
calmly, comfortably, competently, conveniently, coolly, dexterously, efficiently, effortlessly, evenly, facilely, fluently, freely, handily, hand over fist*, hands down*, just like that*, lightly, like nothing*, no sweat*, nothing to it*, piece of cake*, plainly, quickly, readily, regularly, simply, smoothly, steadily, surely, swimmingly, uncomplicatedly, well, with ease, with no effort, without a hitch*, without trouble; SEE CONCEPT *565*

easily [*adv2*] *without a doubt*
absolutely, actually, almost certainly, assuredly, beyond question, by far, certainly, clearly, decidedly, definitely, doubtless, doubtlessly, far and away, indeed, indisputably, indubitably, no doubt, plainly, positively, probably, really, surely, truly, undeniably, undoubtedly, unequivocally, unquestionably; SEE CONCEPTS *535,552*

easy [*adj1*] *not difficult*
accessible, apparent, basic, child's play*, cinch, clear, easily done, easy as pie*, effortless, elementary, evident, facile, inconsiderable, light, little, manageable, manifest, mere, no bother*, no problem*, no sweat*, not burdensome, nothing to it*, no trouble*, obvious, painless, paltry, picnic*, piece of cake*, plain, plain sailing*, pushover*, royal, simple, simple as ABC*, slight, smooth, snap, straightforward, uncomplicated, undemanding, uninvolved, untroublesome, wieldy, yielding; SEE CONCEPT *565*

easy [*adj2*] *leisurely, relaxed*
at ease, calm, carefree, comfortable, comfy, commodious, composed, content, contented, cozy, cursive, cushy, easeful, easygoing, effortless, flowing, fluent, forthright, gentle, in clover*, languid, light, mild, moderate, peaceful, pleasant, prosperous, quiet, running, satisfied, secure, serene, slow, smooth, snug, soft, spontaneous, substantial, successful, temperate, thriving, tranquil, undemanding, undisturbed, unexacting, unhurried, untroubled, unworried, well-to-do; SEE CONCEPTS *542,544*

easy [*adj3*] *tolerant, permissive*
accommodating, amenable, benign, biddable, charitable, clement, compassionate, compliant, condoning, deceivable, deludable, dupable, easygoing, excusing, exploitable, fleeceable, flexible, forbearing, forgiving, gentle, gullible, humoring, indulgent, kindly, lax, lenient, liberal, light, merciful, mild, moderate, mollycoddling*, naive, pampering, pardoning, soft, spoiling, submissive, susceptible, sympathetic, temperate, tractable, trusting, unburdensome, unoppressive, unsuspicious; SEE CONCEPT *401*

easy [*adj4*] *good-humored*
affable, amiable, at ease, carefree, casual, complaisant, diplomatic, easygoing, familiar, friendly, gentle, good-natured, good-tempered, graceful, gracious, gregarious, informal, mild, natural, obliging, open, pleasant, polite, relaxed, secure, smooth, sociable, suave, tolerant, unaffected, unanxious, undemanding, unforced, unpretentious, urbane; SEE CONCEPT *404*

easygoing [*adj*] *complacent, permissive*
amenable, breezy, calm, carefree, casual, collected, complaisant, composed, devil-may-care*, easy, even-tempered*, flexible, free and easy*, hang-loose*, happy-go-lucky*, indolent, indulgent, informal, insouciant, laid-back*, lazy, lenient, liberal, low-pressure, mild, moderate, nonchalant, offhand, outgiving, patient, placid, poised, relaxed, self-possessed, serene, tolerant, tranquil, unconcerned, uncritical, undemanding, unhurried, uninhibited; SEE CONCEPT *404*

eat [*v1*] *consume food*
absorb, attack, banquet, bite, bolt*, break bread*, breakfast, chew, chow down*, cram*, devour, digest, dine, dispatch, dispose of, fall to, feast upon, feed, gobble up*, gorge, gormandize, graze*, have a bite*, have a meal, have for, ingest, inhale*, lunch, make pig of oneself*, masticate, munch, nibble, nosh*, partake of, peck at*, pick, pig out*, polish off*, pork out*, put away*, ruminate, scarf*, scoff, snack, sup, swallow, take food, take in, take nourishment, wolf; SEE CONCEPT *169*

eat [*v2*] *erode, wear away; use up*
bite, condense, corrode, crumble, decay, decompose, disappear, disintegrate, dissipate, dissolve, drain, exhaust, gnaw, liquefy, melt, nibble, rot, run through, rust, spill, squander, vanish, waste away; SEE CONCEPTS *225,469*

eatable [*adj*] *able to be consumed*
appetizing, comestible, culinary, delicious, delish*, dietary, digestible, edible, esculent, fit, good, harm-

less, kosher*, nutritious, nutritive, palatable, piquant, safe, satisfying, savory, scrumptious, succulent, tasty, tempting, wholesome, yummy*; SEE CONCEPTS *462,613*

eavesdrop [v] *listen without permission*
be all ears*, bend an ear*, bug, ears into*, listen in, monitor, overhear, pry, snoop, spy, tap, tune in on*, wire, wiretap; SEE CONCEPTS *188,596*

ebb [n] *regression; decline*
abatement, backflow, decay, decrease, degeneration, depreciation, deterioration, diminution, drop, dwindling, fading away, flagging, going out, lessening, low tide, low water, outward flow, petering out*, recession, refluence, reflux, retreat, retrocession, retroflux, shrinkage, sinking, slackening, subsidence, sweep, wane, waning, weakening, withdrawal; SEE CONCEPTS *195,698*

ebb [v] *subside; decline*
abate, decay, decrease, degenerate, deteriorate, die down, die out, diminish, drop, dwindle, ease off, fade away, fall, fall away, fall back, flag, flow back, go out, languish, lessen, let up, melt, moderate, peter out, recede, relent, retire, retreat, retrocede, shrink, sink, slacken, wane, weaken, withdraw; SEE CONCEPTS *195,698*

ebullience [n] *enthusiasm*
agitation, animation, buoyancy, effervescence, effusiveness, elation, excitement, exhilaration, exuberance, exuberancy, ferment, gaiety, high-spiritedness, high spirits, liveliness, vitality, vivaciousness, vivacity, zest; SEE CONCEPT *633*

ebullient [adj] *enthusiastic*
agitated, bouncy, brash, buoyant, chipper*, chirpy*, effervescent, effusive, elated, excited, exhilarated, exuberant, frothy*, gushing, high-spirited, in high spirits*, irrepressible, vivacious, zestful, zippy*; SEE CONCEPT *401*

eccentric [n] *person who is bizarre, unusual*
beatnik, character, freak, heretic, hippie, kook, loner, maverick, nonconformist, nut*, oddball, oddity, odd person, original, queer duck*, rare bird*, three-dollar bill*, weirdo; SEE CONCEPT *423*

eccentric [adj] *bizarre, unusual*
aberrant, abnormal, anomalous, beat*, bent*, bizarre, capricious, characteristic, cockeyed, crazy, curious, droll, erratic, far out*, flaky, freak, freakish, funky*, funny, idiosyncratic, irregular, kooky, nutty, odd, oddball, offbeat, off-center, off the wall*, out in left field*, outlandish, peculiar, quaint, queer, quirky, quizzical, singular, strange, uncommon, unconventional, unnatural, way out*, weird, whimsical, wild; SEE CONCEPTS *547,564*

eccentricity [n] *bizarreness, unusualness*
aberration, abnormality, anomaly, caprice, capriciousness, foible, freakishness, hereticism, idiocrasy, idiosyncrasy, irregularity, kink, nonconformity, oddity, oddness, outlandishness, peculiarity, queerness, quirk, singularity, strangeness, unconventionality,

unorthodoxness, waywardness, weirdness, whimsicality, whimsicalness; SEE CONCEPTS *647,665*

echelon [n] *class, level*
degree, file, grade, line, office, place, position, queue, rank, row, string, tier; SEE CONCEPTS *378,388*

echo [n] *repeat, copy*
answer, imitation, mirror, mirror image, onomatopoeia, parallel, parroting, rebound, reflection, reiteration, repercussion, repetition, reply, reproduction, reverberation, ringing, rubber stamp*; SEE CONCEPTS *595,695,716*

echo [v] *repeat, copy*
ape, ditto*, do like*, go like*, imitate, impersonate, make like*, mimic, mirror, parallel, parrot, react, recall, redouble, reflect, reiterate, reproduce, resemble, resound, respond, reverberate, ring, rubberstamp*, second, vibrate; SEE CONCEPTS *91,171*

eclectic [adj] *comprehensive, general*
all-embracing, assorted, broad, catholic, dilettantish, diverse, diversified, heterogeneous, inclusive, liberal, many-sided, mingled, mixed, multifarious, multiform, selective, universal, varied, wide-ranging; SEE CONCEPTS *537,772*

eclipse [n] *shadowing of the sun*
concealment, darkening, decline, diminution, dimming, extinction, extinguishment, obliteration, obscuration, occultation, penumbra, shading, shadow, shroud, veil; SEE CONCEPTS *522,624*

eclipse [v1] *obscure, veil*
adumbrate, becloud, bedim, blot out, cloud, darken, dim, extinguish, murk, overshadow, shadow, shroud; SEE CONCEPT *250*

eclipse [v2] *surpass achievement*
exceed, excel, outdo, outshine, overrun, surmount, tower above, transcend; SEE CONCEPT *141*

economic [adj] *business-related; financial*
bread-and-butter*, budgetary, commercial, fiscal, industrial, material, mercantile, monetary, money-making, pecuniary, productive, profitable, profit-making, remunerative, solvent, viable; SEE CONCEPTS *334,536*

economical [adj1] *conservative with resources; careful*
avaricious, canny, careful, chary, circumspect, close, closefisted, cost-effective, curmudgeonly, economizing, efficient, frugal, meager, mean, methodical, miserly, money-saving, on the rims*, parsimonious, penny-pinching*, penny-wise*, penurious, practical, provident, prudent, prudential, saving, Scotch*, scrimping, skimping, spare, sparing, stingy, thrifty, tight, time-saving, unwasteful, watchful, work-saving; SEE CONCEPT *542*

economical [adj2] *inexpensive*
bought for a song*, cheap, cost next to nothing*, cost nothing, cut rate, dime a dozen*, dirt cheap*, dog cheap*, el cheapo*, fair, low, low-priced, low tariff, marked down, moderate, modest, on sale, quite a buy*, reasonable, reduced, sound, steal*; SEE CONCEPT *334*

economize [v] *save money*
be economical, be frugal, be prudent, be sparing, conserve, cut back, cut corners*, cut down, husband, keep within means, make ends meet*, manage, meet a budget, pay one's way*, pinch pennies*, retrench, run tight ship*, save, scrimp, shepherd, skimp, stint, stretch a dollar*, tighten one's belt*; SEE CONCEPT *330*

economy [n] *saving, frugality*
abridgement, austerity, care, carefulness, caution, curtailment, cutback, decrease, deduction, direction, discretion, husbandry, layoff, meanness, miserliness, moratorium, niggardliness, parcity, parsimony, providence, prudence, recession, reduction, regulation, restraint, retrenchment, rollback, scrimping, shrinkage, skimping, sparingness, stinginess, supervision, thrift, thriftiness; SEE CONCEPTS *117,330,335*

ecstasy [n] *bliss*
beatitude, blessedness, cool*, delectation, delight, delirium, ebullience, elation, enchantment, enthusiasm, euphoria, exaltation, felicity, fervor, frenzy, gladness, happiness, heaven, inspiration, intoxication, joy, joyfulness, paradise, rapture, ravishment, rhapsody, seventh heaven*, trance, transport, twilight zone*; SEE CONCEPT *403*

ecstatic [adj] *very happy, blissful*
athrill, beatific, crazy, delirious, dreamy, elated, enraptured, enthusiastic, entranced, euphoric, fervent, floating, flying high*, frenzied, gone*, high*, in exaltation, in seventh heaven*, joyful, joyous, mad, on cloud nine*, out, overjoyed, pleased as punch*, rapturous, ravished, rhapsodic, sent*, sunny, thrilled, tickled pink*, tickled to death*, transported*, turned on*, upbeat, wild; SEE CONCEPT *403*

ecumenical [adj] *general*
all-comprehensive, all-inclusive, all-pervading, catholic, comprehensive, cosmic, cosmopolitan, global, inclusive, planetary, unifying, universal, worldwide; SEE CONCEPTS *537,772*

edge [n1] *border, outline*
bend, berm, bound, boundary, brim, brink, butt, circumference, contour, corner, crook, crust, curb, end, extremity, frame, fringe, frontier, hem, hook, ledge, limb, limit, line, lip, margin, molding, mouth, outskirt, peak, perimeter, periphery, point, portal, rim, ring, shore, side, skirt, split, strand, term, threshold, tip, trimming, turn, verge; SEE CONCEPTS *484,513*

edge [n2] *advantage*
allowance, ascendancy, bulge, dominance, draw, handicap, head start, lead, odds, start, superiority, upper hand*, vantage; SEE CONCEPT *712*

edge [v1] *border, trim*
bind, bound, decorate, fringe, hem, margin, outline, rim, shape, skirt, surround, verge; SEE CONCEPTS *751,758*

edge [v2] *defeat narrowly*
creep, ease, inch, infiltrate, nose out*, sidle, slip by, slip past, squeeze by*, squeeze past*, steal, worm*; SEE CONCEPT *95*

edge [v3] *sharpen*
file, grind, hone, polish, sharpen, strop, whet; SEE CONCEPTS *137,250*

edgy [adj] *nervous*
anxious, critical, excitable, excited, high-strung, ill at ease, impatient, irascible, irritable, keyed up*, on edge, overstrung, restive, restless, skittish, tense, touchy, uneasy, uptight; SEE CONCEPT *401*

edible [adj] *able to be eaten*
comestible, digestible, eatable, esculent, fit, good, harmless, nourishing, nutritious, nutritive, palatable, savory, succulent, tasty, toothsome, wholesome; SEE CONCEPTS *462,613*

edict [n] *pronouncement, order*
act, canon, command, commandment, decree, decretum, dictate, dictum, directive, enactment, fiat, injunction, instrument, judgment, law, mandate, manifesto, order, ordinance, precept, prescript, proclamation, pronunciamento, regulation, rule, ruling, statute, ukase, writ; SEE CONCEPTS *278,662,687*

edification [n] *improvement, education*
betterment, elevation, elucidation, enhancement, enlightenment, guidance, illumination, information, instruction, irradiation, knowledge, learning, nurture, schooling, teaching, tuition, uplifting; SEE CONCEPTS *31,287,700*

edifice [n] *structure*
building, construction, erection, habitation, house, monument, pile, rockpile*, skyscraper, towers; SEE CONCEPT *439*

edit [v] *rewrite, refine*
adapt, alter, amplify, analyze, annotate, arrange, assemble, assign, blue-pencil*, boil down*, butcher, censor, check, choose, compile, compose, condense, correct, cut, delete, discard, doctor, draft, emend, excise, feature, fine-tune, finish, fly speck*, go over, make up, massage*, polish, prepare, prescribe, proofread, publish, put together, rearrange, recalibrate, rectify, redact, regulate, rehash, rephrase, report, revise, scrub*, select, set up, strike out, style, tighten, trim, write over; SEE CONCEPTS *79,126,203*

edition [n] *issue of publication*
copy, impression, imprint, number, printing, program, publication, reissue, release, reprint, reprinting, version, volume; SEE CONCEPT *280*

educate [v] *teach information, experience*
brainwash*, brief, civilize, coach, cultivate, develop, discipline, drill, drum into, edify, enlighten, exercise, explain, foster, improve, indoctrinate, inform, instruct, let in on, mature, nurture, put hip*, put through the grind*, rear, school, show the ropes*, train, tutor; SEE CONCEPTS *61,285*

educated [adj] *learned, experienced*
accomplished, acquainted with, brainy, civilized, coached, corrected, cultivated, cultured, developed, enlightened, enriched, erudite, expert, finished, fitted, formed, informed, initiated, instructed, intelligent, knowledgeable, lettered, literary, literate,

nurtured, polished, prepared, professional, refined, scholarly, schooled, scientific, shaped, skilled, tasteful, taught, trained, tutored, versed in, well-informed, well-read, well-taught, well-versed; SEE CONCEPT *402*

education [*n*] *instruction, development of knowledge*
apprenticeship, background, book learning*, brainwashing*, breeding, catechism, civilization, coaching, cultivation, culture, direction, discipline, drilling, edification, enlightenment, erudition, finish, guidance, improvement, inculcation, indoctrination, information, knowledge, learnedness, learning, literacy, nurture, pedagogy, preparation, propagandism, proselytism, reading, rearing, refinement, scholarship, schooling, science, study, teaching, training, tuition, tutelage, tutoring; SEE CONCEPTS *285,287,409*

educe [*v*] *bring out, elicit*
bring forth, come out, conclude, deduce, derive, develop, distill, drag, draw, draw out, evince, evoke, evolve, excogitate, extort, extract, gain, get, infer, milk*, obtain, procure, pull, reason, secure, think out, wrest, wring; SEE CONCEPTS *37,142*

eerie [*adj*] *spooky*
awesome, bizarre, crawly, creepy, fantastic, fearful, frightening, ghostly, mysterious, scary, spectral, spookish, strange, supernatural, superstitious, uncanny, unearthly, weird; SEE CONCEPT *537*

effect [*n1*] *result*
aftereffect, aftermath, backlash, backwash, can of worms*, causatum, chain reaction*, conclusion, consequence, corollary, denouement, development, end, end product, event, eventuality, fallout, flak*, follow through, follow-up, fruit, issue, outcome, outgrowth, precipitate, pursuance, ramification, reaction, reflex, repercussion, response, sequel, sequence, side effect, spin-off, upshot*, waves*; SEE CONCEPT *230*

effect [*n2*] *impact, impression*
action, clout, drift, effectiveness, efficacy, efficiency, enforcement, essence, execution, fact, force, implementation, import, imprint, influence, mark, meaning, power, purport, purpose, reality, sense, significance, strength, tenor, use, validity, vigor, weight; SEE CONCEPT *686*

effect [*v*] *carry out, accomplish*
achieve, actualize, actuate, begin, bring about, bring off, bring on, buy, carry through, cause, complete, conceive, conclude, consummate, create, do a number*, do one's thing*, do the job*, do the trick*, do to a T*, draw on, effectuate, enact, enforce, execute, fulfill, generate, get across, get to, give rise to, implement, induce, initiate, invoke, make, make it*, make waves*, perform, procure, produce, pull it off*, put across, realize, render, secure, sell, turn out, turn the trick*, unzip*, yield; SEE CONCEPTS *91,706*

effective [*adj1*] *productive, persuasive*
able, active, adequate, capable, cogent, compelling, competent, convincing, direct, effectual, efficacious,

efficient, emphatic, energetic, forceful, forcible, having lead in pencil*, impressive, live, moving, on the ball*, operative, playing hardball*, potent, powerful, powerhouse*, practical, producing, resultant, serviceable, serving, sound, striking, sufficient, telling, trenchant, useful, valid, virtuous, wicked*, yielding; SEE CONCEPTS *537,540*

effective [*adj2*] *in use at the time*
active, actual, current, direct, dynamic, in effect, in execution, in force, in operation, operative, real; SEE CONCEPTS *560,582,799*

effectiveness [*n*] *influence*
capability, clout, cogency, effect, efficacy, efficiency, force, forcefulness, performance, point, potency, power, punch, strength, success, use, validity, validness, verve, vigor, weight; SEE CONCEPTS *676,686*

effectual [*adj*] *influential; authoritative*
accomplishing, achieving, adequate, binding, capable, conclusive, decisive, determinative, effecting, effective, efficacious, efficient, forcible, fulfilling, in force, lawful, legal, licit, potent, powerful, practicable, productive, qualified, serviceable, sound, strong, successful, telling, useful, valid, virtuous, workable; SEE CONCEPTS *319,528,537*

effeminate [*adj*] *not manly*
delicate, epicene, feminine, overnice, soft, tender, unmanly, unvirile, womanish, womanlike, womanly; SEE CONCEPTS *401,404*

effervescence [*n1*] *fizz, foam*
bubbles, bubbling, ebullition, ferment, fermentation, fizzing, foaming, froth, frothing, sparkle; SEE CONCEPTS *437,522*

effervescence [*n2*] *enthusiasm, vivacity*
animation, buoyancy, ebullience, excitedness, excitement, exhilaration, exuberance, exuberancy, gaiety, happiness, high spirits, joy, liveliness, vim, vitality, volatility, zing*; SEE CONCEPTS *633,657*

effervescent [*adj1*] *fizzing, foaming*
airy, boiling, bouncy, bubbling, bubbly, carbonated, elastic, expansive, fermenting, fizzy, foamy, frothing, frothy, resilient, sparkling, volatile; SEE CONCEPTS *462,485*

effervescent [*adj2*] *enthusiastic, vivacious*
animated, bouncy, brash, bubbly, buoyant, ebullient, excited, exhilarated, exuberant, gleeful, happy, high-spirited, hilarious, in high spirits*, irrepressible, jolly, joyous, lively, merry, mirthful, sprightly, vital, zingy; SEE CONCEPTS *401,542*

effete [*adj1*] *spoiled, exhausted*
burnt out*, corrupt, debased, decadent, decayed, declining, decrepit, degenerate, dissipated, dissolute, drained, enervated, enfeebled, far-gone*, feeble, immoral, ineffectual, obsolete, overrefined, overripe, played out*, soft, spent, used up, vitiated, washed-out*, wasted, weak, worn out; SEE CONCEPT *560*

effete [*adj2*] *unproductive*
barren, fruitless, impotent, infecund, infertile, sterile, unfruitful, unprolific; SEE CONCEPT *527*

efficacious [adj] efficient, productive
active, adequate, capable, competent, effective, effectual, energetic, influential, operative, potent, powerful, puissant, serviceable, strong, successful, useful, virtuous; SEE CONCEPTS 528,537

efficacy [n] efficiency; productiveness
ability, adequacy, capability, capableness, capacity, competence, effect, effectiveness, efficaciousness, energy, force, influence, performance, potency, power, strength, success, sufficiency, use, vigor, virtue, weight; SEE CONCEPTS 641,676,706

efficiency [n] adeptness, effectiveness
ability, abundance, adaptability, address, adequacy, capability, capableness, competence, competency, completeness, economy, effectualness, efficacy, energy, expertise, facility, faculty, know-how, performance, potency, power, powerfulness, productiveness, productivity, proficiency, prowess, quantity, readiness, resourcefulness, response, skill, skillfulness, suitability, suitableness, talent, thoroughness; SEE CONCEPTS 409,630,658

efficient [adj] adept, effective
able, accomplished, active, adapted, adequate, apt, businesslike, capable, clever, competent, conducive, decisive, deft, dynamic, economic, economical, effectual, efficacious, energetic, equal to, experienced, expert, familiar with, fitted, good at, good for, handy, masterly, organized, potent, powerful, practiced, productive, proficient, profitable, qualified, ready, saving, shrewd, skilled, skillful, systematic, talented, tough, useful, valuable, virtuous, well-organized, workmanlike; SEE CONCEPTS 402,527,560

effigy [n] dummy
figure, icon, idol, image, likeness, model, picture, portrait, puppet, representation, statue; SEE CONCEPT 436

effort [n] work, exertion
accomplishment, achievement, act, aim, application, aspiration, attempt, battle, crack*, creation, deed, discipline, drill, elbow grease*, endeavor, energy, enterprise, essay, exercise, feat, fling*, force, go*, industry, intention, job, labor, old college try*, pains, power, product, production, pull, purpose, push, resolution, shot*, spurt, stab*, strain, stress, stretch, strife, striving, struggle, sweat, tension, toil, training, travail, trial, trouble, try, tug*, undertaking, venture, whack*; SEE CONCEPTS 87,362,677,724

effortless [adj] easy
child's play*, cursive, duck soup*, easy as pie*, facile, flowing, fluent, light, no problem*, no sweat*, offhand, painless, picnic*, piece of cake*, royal, running, simple, smooth, snap*, uncomplicated, undemanding, untroublesome; SEE CONCEPT 565

effrontery [n] nerve, boldness
arrogance, assurance, audacity, backtalk, brashness, brass*, brazenness, cheek*, cheekiness, chutzpah*, crust*, disrespect, face, gall, guff, hardihood, impertinence, impudence, incivility, insolence, lip*, nerve, presumption, rudeness, sass, sauce*, self-assurance, self-confidence, shamelessness, smart talk, temerity; SEE CONCEPTS 411,633

effulgent [adj] glowing, luminous
beaming, blazing, bright, brilliant, dazzling, flaming, fluorescent, incandescent, lambent, lucent, lustrous, radiant, refulgent, resplendent, shining, splendid, vivid; SEE CONCEPT 617

effusion [n] outpouring
address, diffusion, discharge, effluence, effluvium, efflux, emanation, emission, exudate, gush, gushing, ooze, outflow, pouring, shedding, stream, verbosity, wordiness; SEE CONCEPTS 179,266

effusive [adj] gushing, profuse
all jaw*, big mouthed*, demonstrative, ebullient, enthusiastic, expansive, extravagant, exuberant, free-flowing, fulsome, gabby*, gushy*, lavish, outpouring, overflowing, prolix, talkative, unconstrained, unreserved, unrestrained, verbose, windbag*, windy*, wordy; SEE CONCEPTS 267,542

egg [n] seed, cell; embryo of animal
bud, cackle*, cackleberry*, germ, nucleus, oospore, ovum, roe, rudiment, spawn, yellow eye*; SEE CONCEPTS 389,392

egg on [v] push to do something
agitate, arouse, drive, encourage, excite, exhort, goad, incite, instigate, pique, prick, prod, prompt, propel, rally, sic, spur, stimulate, stir up, urge, whip up; SEE CONCEPT 68

ego [n] personality
character, individuality, power, psyche, self, self-admiration, selfdom, self-pride; SEE CONCEPT 411

egocentric [adj] thinking very highly of oneself
conceited, egoistic, egoistical, egomaniacal, egotistic, egotistical, individualist, individualistic, megalomaniac, narcissistic, pompous, self-absorbed, self-centered, self-concerned, self-indulgent, self-interested, selfish, self-loving, self-serving, stuck-up, vainglorious, wrapped up in oneself; SEE CONCEPT 404

egoism/egotism [n] self-centeredness
arrogance, assurance, boastfulness, boasting, bragging, conceit, conceitedness, egocentricity, egomania, gasconade, haughtiness, insolence, megalomania, narcissism, ostentation, overconfidence, preoccupation with self, presumption, pride, self-absorption, self-admiration, self-confidence, self-importance, self-interest, selfishness, self-love, self-possession, self-regard, self-worship, superiority, swellheadedness, vainglory, vanity, vaunting; SEE CONCEPT 411

egotistic/egoistic [adj] thinking very highly of oneself
affected, aloof, autocratic, boastful, boasting, bragging, conceited, egocentric, egoistical, egomaniacal, egotistical, haughty, individualistic, inflated, inner-directed, intimate, intrinsic, introverted, isolated, narcissistic, obsessive, opinionated, personal, pompous, prideful, proud, puffed up*, self-absorbed, self-

admiring, self-centered, self-important, snobbish, stuck on oneself*, stuck-up*, subjective, superior, swollen, vain, vainglorious; SEE CONCEPT *404*

egregious [*adj*] *outstandingly bad; outrageous*
arrant, atrocious, capital, deplorable, extreme, flagrant, glaring, grievous, gross*, heinous, infamous, insufferable, intolerable, monstrous, nefarious, notorious, outright, preposterous, rank, scandalous, shocking, stark; SEE CONCEPTS *545,548,570*

egress [*n*] *passage out*
departure, doorway, egression, emanation, emergence, escape, exit, exiting, exodus, issue, opening, outlet, setting-out, vent, way out, withdrawal; SEE CONCEPTS *195,440*

eject [*v*] *throw or be thrown out*
banish, bounce*, bump, cast out, debar, disbar, discharge, disgorge, dislodge, dismiss, displace, dispossess, ditch, do away with*, drive off, dump*, eighty-six*, ejaculate, eliminate, emit, eradicate, eruct, erupt, evict, exclude, expel, expulse, extrude, fire, force out, get rid of, give the boot*, heave out*, irrupt, kick out*, kiss goodbye*, oust, reject, rout, sack, send packing*, show the gate to*, spew, spit out, spout, squeeze out, throw out, throw overboard*, turn out, unloose, vomit; SEE CONCEPTS *179,222*

eke out [*v*] *make something last*
barely exist, be economical with, be frugal with, be sparing with, economize on, get by*, husband, stretch out; SEE CONCEPT *239*

elaborate [*adj*] *intricate; involved*
busy, careful, complex, complicated, decorated, detailed, elegant, embellished, exact, extensive, extravagant, fancy, fussy, garnished, highly wrought, high tech*, imposing, knotty, labored, labyrinthine, luxurious, many-faceted, minute, ornamented, ornate, ostentatious, overdone, overworked, painstaking, perfected, plush, posh, precise, prodigious, refined, showy, skillful, sophisticated, studied, thorough, with all the extras*, with all the options*, with bells and whistles*; SEE CONCEPT *562*

elaborate [*v*] *make detailed; expand*
add detail, amplify, bedeck, clarify, comment, complicate, deck, decorate, develop, devise, discuss, embellish, enhance, enlarge, evolve, expatiate, explain, expound, flesh out, garnish, improve, interpret, ornament, particularize, polish, produce, refine, specify, unfold, work out; SEE CONCEPT *57*

élan [*n*] *vivacity*
animation, ardor, brio, dash, esprit, flair, impetuosity, impetus, life, oomph*, panache, spirit, style, verve, vigor, vim, zest, zing*; SEE CONCEPT *411*

elapse [*v*] *go by; slip away*
expire, flow, glide by, go, lapse, pass, pass away, pass by, roll by, roll on, run out, slip by, transpire, vanish; SEE CONCEPTS *6,144,818*

elastic [*adj1*] *pliant, rubbery*
adaptable, bouncy, buoyant, ductile, extendible, extensible, flexible, irrepressible, limber, lithe, mallea-ble, moldable, plastic, pliable, resilient, rubberlike, springy, stretchable, stretchy, supple, tempered, yielding; SEE CONCEPTS *490,606*

elastic [*adj2*] *adaptable, tolerant*
accommodating, adjustable, airy, animated, bouncy, buoyant, complaisant, compliant, ebullient, effervescent, expansive, flexible, gay, high-spirited, lively, recuperative, resilient, soaring, spirited, sprightly, supple, variable, vivacious, volatile, yielding; SEE CONCEPT *404*

elated [*adj*] *very happy*
animated, aroused, blissful, cheered, delighted, ecstatic, elevated, enchanted, enraptured, euphoric, exalted, excited, exhilarated, exultant, fired up*, flying*, flying high*, gleeful, high, hopped up*, in heaven*, in high spirits*, in seventh heaven*, intoxicated, joyful, joyous, jubilant, looking good*, on cloud nine*, overjoyed, proud, puffed up*, roused, set up, transported, turned-on*; SEE CONCEPT *403*

elation [*n*] *extreme happiness*
bliss, buoyancy, buzz, charge, cloud nine*, delight, ecstasy, enthusiasm, euphoria, exaltation, excitement, exhilaration, exultation, glee, high, high spirits, intoxication, jollies*, joy, joyfulness, joyousness, jubilation, kick*, kicks*, rapture, stars in one's eyes*, transport, triumph, up*, upper*; SEE CONCEPT *410*

elbow [*n*] *angular part of arm; angularly-shaped item*
ancon, angle, bend, bow, corner, crazy bone*, crook, crutch, curve, fork, funny bone*, half turn, hinge, joint, turn; SEE CONCEPTS *418,436*

elbow [*v*] *push aside*
bend, bulldoze, bump, crowd, hook, hustle, jostle, knock, nudge, press, push, push around, rough and tumble*, shoulder, shove; SEE CONCEPT *208*

elder [*n*] *older person*
ancestor, ancient, first-born, forefather, golden ager*, matriarch, older adult, oldest, old fogey*, old man, oldster*, old-timer, old woman, patriarch, senior, senior citizen, superior, veteran; SEE CONCEPT *424*

elder [*adj*] *born earlier*
ancient, earlier, first-born, more mature, older, senior; SEE CONCEPTS *578,797*

elderly [*adj*] *in old age*
aged, aging, ancient, been around*, declining, gray*, hoary, long in tooth*, lot of mileage*, no spring chicken*, old, olden, one foot in grave, one foot in grave*, on last leg*, over the hill*, retired, tired, venerable; SEE CONCEPTS *578,797*

elect [*v*] *select as representative; choose*
accept, admit, appoint, ballot, conclude, cull, decide upon, designate, determine, go down the line, judge, mark, name, nominate, optate, opt for, pick, pick out, prefer, receive, resolve, select, settle, settle on, single out, take, tap, vote, vote for; SEE CONCEPTS *41,300*

election [n] *choosing; voting*
alternative, appointment, ballot, balloting, choice, decision, determination, franchise, judgment, option, poll, polls, preference, primary, referendum, selection, ticket, vote, vote-casting; SEE CONCEPTS *41,300*

elective [adj] *able to be chosen*
constituent, discretionary, electoral, facultative, nonobligatory, not compulsory, optional, selective, voluntary, voting; SEE CONCEPT *535*

electric/electrical [adj] *charged; energetic*
AC, DC, dynamic, electrifying, exciting, juiced*, magnetic, motor-driven, power-driven, rousing, stimulating, stirring, tense, thrilling, voltaic; SEE CONCEPT *540*

electricity [n] *energized matter, power*
AC, current, DC, electromagneticism, electron, galvanism, heat, hot stuff*, ignition, juice*, light, magneticism, service, spark, tension, utilities, voltage; SEE CONCEPT *520*

electrify [v] *thrill, stimulate*
amaze, animate, astonish, astound, charge, commove, disturb, dynamize, energize, enthuse, excite, fire, frenzy, galvanize, invigorate, jar, jolt, magnetize, power, provoke, rouse, send, shock, stagger, startle, stir, strike, stun, take one's breath away*, wire*; SEE CONCEPTS *7,22,42*

elegance [n] *cultivated beauty, taste*
breeding, charm, class, courtliness, cultivation, culture, delicacy, dignity, discernment, distinction, exquisiteness, felicity, gentility, good taste, grace, gracefulness, grandeur, hauteur, lushness, luxury, magnificence, nicety, nobility, noblesse, ornateness, polish, politeness, poshness, propriety, purity, refinement, restraint, rhythm, sophistication, splendor, style, sumptuousness, symmetry, tastefulness; SEE CONCEPTS *655,671,718*

elegant [adj] *beautiful, tasteful*
affected, appropriate, apt, aristocratic, artistic, august, chic, choice, classic, clever, comely, courtly, cultivated, cultured, dainty, delicate, dignified, effective, exquisite, fancy, fashionable, fine, genteel, graceful, grand, handsome, ingenious, luxurious, majestic, modish, neat, nice, noble, opulent, ornamented, ornate, ostentatious, overdone, polished, rare, recherché, refined, rich, select, simple, stately, stuffy, stylish, stylized, sumptuous, superior, turgid, well-bred; SEE CONCEPTS *574,579,589*

element [n1] *essential feature*
aspect, basic, basis, bit, component, constituent, detail, drop, essential, facet, factor, feature, fundamental, hint, ingredient, item, material, matter, member, part, particle, particular, piece, portion, principle, root, section, stem, subdivision, trace, unit, view; SEE CONCEPTS *668,826,829*

element [n2] *place where one feel comfortable*
domain, environment, field, habitation, medium, milieu, sphere; SEE CONCEPTS *198,516*

elementary [adj] *simple, basic*
ABCs, abecedarian, basal, basic, beginning, child's play*, clear, duck soup*, easy, elemental, essential, facile, foundational, fundamental, initial, introductory, meat and potatoes*, original, plain, prefatory, preliminary, primary, primitive, primo*, rudimentary, simplest, simplex, simplified, straightforward, substratal, uncomplex, uncomplicated, underlying; SEE CONCEPTS *546,562*

elevate [v1] *lift up*
erect, fetch up*, heighten, hike up*, hoist, jack up*, levitate, lift, poise, pump, put up, pyramid*, raise, ramp, rear, shoot up*, stilt, take up, tilt, uphold, uplift, upraise; SEE CONCEPT *196*

elevate [v2] *promote; augment*
advance, aggrandize, appoint, boost, build up, dignify, enhance, ennoble, exalt, further, glorify, heighten, honor, increase, intensify, magnify, prefer, put up, skip, swell, upgrade; SEE CONCEPTS *69,351,700*

elevate [v3] *raise spirits*
animate, boost, brighten, bring up, buoy up*, cheer, elate, excite, exhilarate, glorify, hearten, inspire, lift up*, perk up*, raise, refine, rouse, sublimate, uplift; SEE CONCEPTS *7,22*

elevated [adj1] *highly moral or dignified*
animated, big-time*, bright, elated, eloquent, eminent, ethical, exalted, exhilarated, formal, grand, grandiloquent, heavy, high, high-flown*, high-minded, honorable, inflated, lofty, noble, righteous, stately, sublime, superb, upright, upstanding, virtuous; SEE CONCEPTS *402,545,567*

elevated [adj2] *raised up*
aerial, high, high-rise, lifted, raised, stately, tall, towering, upheaved, uplifted, upraised, uprisen; SEE CONCEPT *779*

elevation [n1] *height; high ground*
acclivity, altitude, ascent, boost, eminence, heave, hill, hillock, hoist, levitation, mountain, platform, ridge, rise, roof, top, uplift, upthrow; SEE CONCEPTS *509,741*

elevation [n2] *advancement, promotion*
advance, aggrandizement, apotheosis, boost, deification, eminence, ennoblement, exaltation, exaltedness, glorification, grandeur, immortalization, lionization, loftiness, magnification, nobility, nobleness, preference, preferment, prelation, raise, sublimity, upgrading; SEE CONCEPTS *69,351,668*

elf [n] *small, fairytale character*
brownie, elfin, fairy, fay, leprechaun, nisse, pixie; SEE CONCEPT *370*

elicit [v] *draw out*
arm-twist*, badger, bite*, bring, bring forth, bring out, bring to light*, call forth, cause, derive, educe, evince, evoke, evolve, exact, extort, extract, fetch, give rise to, milk*, obtain, put muscle on*, put the arm on*, rattle, shake, shake down*, squeeze, wrest, wring; SEE CONCEPTS *68,142*

eligible [adj] *fit, worthy*
acceptable, appropriate, becoming, capable of, desirable, discretionary, elective, employable, equal to, fitted, in line for*, in the running*, licensed, likely, marriageable, nubile, preferable, privileged, proper, qualified, satisfactory, seemly, suitable, suited, trained, up to*, usable; SEE CONCEPTS *527,558*

eliminate [v] *remove, throw out*
annihilate, blot out*, bump off*, cancel, cast out, count out, cut out, defeat, discard, discharge, dismiss, dispense with, dispose of, disqualify, disregard, do away with, drive out, drop, eject, eradicate, erase, evict, exclude, expel, exterminate, get rid of, ignore, invalidate, kill, knock out*, leave out, liquidate, murder, omit, oust, phase out, put out, reject, rub out*, rule out, set aside, shut the door on*, slay, stamp out*, take out, terminate, waive, waste, wipe out*; SEE CONCEPTS *30,211*

elite [n] *high-class persons*
aristocracy, beautiful people*, best, blue blood*, carriage trade*, celebrity, choice, cognoscenti, country club set*, cream, crème de la crème*, crowd, elect, establishment, fast lane*, fat*, flower, gentility, gentry, glitterati, high society*, in-crowd*, jet-set*, main line*, nobility, old money*, optimacy, pride, prime, prize, quality, select, society, top, upper class, upper crust*; SEE CONCEPTS *387,388,417*

elite [adj] *best, first-class*
aristocratic, best, choice, cool*, crack*, elect, exclusive, gilt-edged, greatest, noble, out of sight*, out of this world*, pick, selected, super, tip-top*, top, top drawer*, topflight, top-notch, upper-class, world-class; SEE CONCEPTS *555,574*

elliptical [adj] *oval-shaped*
egg-shaped, ellipsoidal, oblong, ovoid; SEE CONCEPT *486*

elocution [n] *articulation*
declamation, delivery, diction, dramatic, eloquence, enunciation, expression, locution, oratory, pronunciation, public speaking, reading, rhetoric, speech, speechcraft, speechmaking, utterance, voice culture, voice production; SEE CONCEPT *47*

elongate [v] *make longer*
drag one's feet*, drag out, draw, draw out, extend, fill, lengthen, let out, pad*, prolong, prolongate, protract, put rubber in*, spin out, stretch; SEE CONCEPTS *137,239,250*

elope [v] *run away to be married*
abscond, bolt, decamp, disappear, escape, flee, fly, go secretly, go to Gretna Green*, leave, run away, run away with, run off, skip*, slip away, slip out, steal away; SEE CONCEPT *297*

eloquence [n] *skillful way with words*
ability, appeal, articulation, command of language, delivery, diction, dramatic, expression, expressiveness, expressivity, facility, facundity, fervor, flow, fluency, force, forcefulness, gift of gab*, grandiloquence, loquacity, meaningfulness, mellifluousness, oration, oratory, passion, persuasiveness, poise, power, rhetoric, spirit, style, vigor, vivacity, volubility, wit, wittiness; SEE CONCEPTS *68,278,630*

eloquent [adj] *having a skillful way with words*
affecting, ardent, articulate, expressive, facund, fervent, fervid, fluent, forceful, glib, grandiloquent, graphic, impassioned, impressive, indicative, magniloquent, meaningful, moving, outspoken, passionate, persuasive, poignant, potent, powerful, revealing, rhetorical, sententious, significant, silver-tongued*, smooth-spoken*, stirring, suggestive, telling, touching, vivid, vocal, voluble, well-expressed; SEE CONCEPT *267*

elsewhere [adv] *in another place*
abroad, absent, away, formerly, gone, hence, not here, not present, not under consideration, otherwhere, outside, remote, removed, somewhere, somewhere else, subsequently, to another place; SEE CONCEPT *586*

elucidate [v] *explain in detail*
annotate, clarify, clear, clear up, decode, demonstrate, draw a picture*, enlighten, enucleate, exemplify, explain, explicate, expound, get across*, gloss, illuminate, illustrate, interpret, make perfectly clear, make plain, make see daylight*, prove, shed light on*, spell out*, throw light on*, unfold; SEE CONCEPT *57*

elude [v] *avoid; escape*
baffle, beat around the bush*, be beyond someone*, bilk, circumvent, confound, cop out*, ditch, dodge, double, duck, eschew, evade, flee, fly, foil, frustrate, get around, get away from, give the runaround*, give the slip*, give wide berth to*, hem and haw*, not touch, outrun, outwit, pass the buck*, pass up, puzzle, run around, shirk, shuck, shun, shy, stall, stay shy of*, steer clear of*, stonewall*, stump, thwart; SEE CONCEPTS *30,38,59,102*

elusive [adj] *evasive, mysterious*
ambiguous, baffling, cagey, deceitful, deceptive, difficult to catch, elusory, equivocal, evanescent, fallacious, fleeting, fraudulent, fugacious, fugitive, greasy, illusory, imponderable, incomprehensible, indefinable, insubstantial, intangible, misleading, occult, phantom, puzzling, shifty, shy, slippery, stonewalling*, subtle, transient, transitory, tricky, unspecific, volatile; SEE CONCEPTS *529,542*

emaciated [adj] *undernourished; thin*
anorexic, atrophied, attenuate, attenuated, bony, cadaverous, consumptive, famished, gaunt, haggard, lank, lean, like a bag of bones*, meager, peaked, pinched, scrawny, skeletal, skeletonlike, skin-and-bones*, skinny, starved, thin as rail*, underfed, wasted, wizened; SEE CONCEPTS *490,491*

emanate [v] *come forth; give off*
arise, birth, come out, derive, discharge, egress, emerge, emit, exhale, exit, exude, flow, give out, initiate, issue, originate, proceed, radiate, rise, send forth, spring, stem; SEE CONCEPTS *179,221,648*

emanation [n] *emergence, discharge*
arising, beginning, derivation, drainage, effluence, effluent, efflux, effusion, ejaculation, emerging, emission, escape, exhalation, exudation, flow, flowing, gush, issuance, issuing, leakage, oozing, origin, origination, outflow, outpour, proceeding, radiation, springing, welling; SEE CONCEPTS *179,221,648*

emancipate [v] *set free*
affranchise, deliver, discharge, disencumber, disenthral, enfranchise, free, liberate, loose, loosen, manumit, release, unbind, unchain, unfetter, unshackle; SEE CONCEPT *127*

emasculate [v] *weaken, deprive of force*
alter, castrate, cripple, debilitate, devitalize, enervate, fix*, geld, impoverish, mutilate, soften, unman, unnerve, unstring, vitiate; SEE CONCEPTS *240,250*

embalm [v] *preserve, immortalize*
anoint, cherish, consecrate, conserve, enshrine, freeze, lay out, mummify, prepare, process, store, treasure, wrap; SEE CONCEPT *202*

embargo [n] *prohibition, restriction*
ban, bar, barrier, blockage, check, hindrance, impediment, interdict, interdiction, proscription, restraint, stoppage; SEE CONCEPTS *119,130*

embark [v] *get on transportation object*
board, commence, emplane, enter, entrain, go aboard ship, launch, leave port, plunge into, put on board, set about, set out, set sail, take on board, take ship; SEE CONCEPTS *159,195,224*

embark on [v] *begin undertaking, journey*
broach, commence, engage, enter, get off, initiate, jump off, launch, open, plunge into, set about, set out, set to, start, take up, tee off*, undertake; SEE CONCEPTS *100,221*

embarrass [v] *cause mental discomfort*
abash, agitate, annoy, bewilder, bother, bug, catch one short*, chagrin, confuse, discombobulate*, discomfit, discomfort, discompose, disconcert, discountenance, distract, distress, disturb, dumbfound, faze, fluster, give a bad time*, give a hard time*, hang up*, irk, let down*, make a monkey of*, mortify, nonplus, perplex, perturb, plague, put in a hole*, put in a spot*, put on the spot*, put out of countenance*, puzzle, rattle, shame, show up*, stun, tease, throw, throw into a tizzy*, upset; SEE CONCEPTS *7,19,54*

embarrassing [adj] *humiliating, shaming*
awkward, bewildering, compromising, confusing, delicate, difficult, disagreeable, discomfiting, discommoding, discommodious, disconcerting, distracting, distressing, disturbing, equivocal, exasperating, impossible, incommodious, inconvenient, inopportune, mortifying, perplexing, puzzling, rattling, sensitive, shameful, sticky, ticklish, touchy, tricky, troublesome, troubling, uncomfortable, uneasy, unpropitious, unseemly, upsetting, worrisome; SEE CONCEPTS *537,548*

embarrassment [n] *humiliation, shame*
awkwardness, awkward situation, bashfulness, bind, boo boo*, chagrin, clumsiness, complexity, confusion, destitution, difficulty, dilemma, discomfiture, discomposure, disconcertion, distress, egg on face*, faux pas, fix, hitch, hot seat*, hot water*, impecuniosity, indebtedness, indiscretion, inhibition, mess, mistake, mortification, pickle*, pinch, plight, poverty, predicament, puzzle, quandary, scrape, self-consciousness, shyness, snag, stew, strait, tangle, timidity, unease, uneasiness; SEE CONCEPTS *410,674*

embassy [n] *residence, offices of overseas representatives*
commission, committee, consular office, consulate, delegation, diplomatic office, legation, ministry, mission; SEE CONCEPTS *439,449,516*

embed [v] *sink, implant*
bury, deposit, dig in, drive in, enclose, fasten, fix, hammer in, impact, infix, ingrain, inlay, insert, install, lodge, pierce, plant, plunge, press, put into, ram in, root, set, stick in, stuff in, thrust in, tuck in; SEE CONCEPTS *178,188*

embellish [v] *make beautiful; decorate*
add bells and whistles*, adorn, amplify, array, beautify, bedeck, color, deck, dress up*, elaborate, emblaze, embroider, enhance, enrich, exaggerate, festoon, fix up*, fudge*, garnish, gild, give details, grace, gussy up*, magnify, ornament, overstate, spiff up*, spruce up*, trim; SEE CONCEPTS *49,162,177,700*

embellishment [n] *beautification; decorating*
adornment, coloring, decoration, doodad*, elaboration, embroidering, embroidery, enhancement, enrichment, exaggeration, fandangle*, floridity, flowery speech, frill, froufrou*, fuss*, garnish, gilding, gingerbread*, hyperbole, icing on the cake*, jazz*, ornament, ornamentation, ostentation, overstatement; SEE CONCEPTS *177,278,700,718*

embers [n] *hot ashes from fire*
ash, brand, cinders, clinkers, coals, firebrand, live coals, slag, smoking remnants, smoldering remains; SEE CONCEPTS *260,478*

embezzle [v] *steal money, often from employer*
abstract, appropriate, defalcate, filch, forge, loot, misapply, misappropriate, misuse, peculate, pilfer, purloin, put hand in cookie jar*, put hand in till*, skim, thieve; SEE CONCEPT *139*

embezzlement [n] *stealing money, often from employer*
abstraction, appropriation, defalcation, filching, fraud, larceny, misapplication, misappropriation, misuse, peculation, pilferage, pilfering, purloining, skimming, theft, thieving; SEE CONCEPT *139*

embitter [v] *upset, alienate*
acerbate, acidulate, aggravate, anger, annoy, bitter, bother, disaffect, disillusion, envenom, exacerbate, exasperate, irritate, make bitter, make resentful, poison, sour, venom, worsen; SEE CONCEPTS *7,14,19*

emblem [n] *crest*
adumbration, arms, attribute, badge, banner, brand, character, coat of arms, colophon, colors, design, device, figure, flag, hallmark, identification, image, impress, insignia, logo, mark, marker, medal, memento, miniature, monogram, motto, pennant, regalia, reminder, representation, scepter, seal, sign, standard, symbol, token, trademark, type; SEE CONCEPTS *259,284,625*

embodiment [n] *representation, manifestation*
apotheosis, archetype, cast, collection, comprehension, conformation, embracement, encompassment, epitome, example, exemplar, exemplification, expression, form, formation, incarnation, inclusion, incorporation, integration, manifestation, matter, organization, personification, prosopopoeia, quintessence, realization, reification, structure, symbol, systematization, type; SEE CONCEPTS *118,688*

embody [v1] *represent; materialize*
actualize, complete, concretize, demonstrate, emblematize, epitomize, evince, exemplify, exhibit, express, exteriorize, externalize, hypostatize, illustrate, incarnate, incorporate, manifest, mirror, objectify, personalize, personify, realize, reify, show, stand for, substantiate, symbolize, typify; SEE CONCEPT *118*

embody [v2] *include, integrate*
absorb, amalgamate, assimilate, blend, bring together, codify, collect, combine, comprehend, comprise, concentrate, consolidate, contain, embrace, encompass, establish, fuse, have, incorporate, involve, merge, organize, subsume, systematize, take in, unify; SEE CONCEPTS *112,113*

embrace [v1] *hold tightly in one's arms*
bear hug*, clasp, clinch, cling, clutch, coll-, cradle, cuddle, encircle, enfold, entwine, envelop, fold, fondle, grab, grasp, grip, hug, lock, nuzzle, press, seize, snuggle, squeeze, take in arms*, wrap; SEE CONCEPTS *190,191*

embrace [v2] *include in one's beliefs; take into account*
accept, accommodate, admit, adopt, avail oneself of, comprehend, comprise, contain, cover, deal with*, embody, enclose, encompass, espouse, get into*, go in for*, grab, have, incorporate, involve, make use of, provide for, receive, seize, subsume, take advantage of, take in, take on, take up, welcome; SEE CONCEPTS *12,15,112*

embroider [v1] *add fancy stitching, adornment*
beautify, bedeck, braid, color, cross-stitch, deck, decorate, embellish, fix up, garnish, gild, gussy up*, knit, ornament, pattern, quilt, spruce up*, stitch, weave pattern, work; SEE CONCEPTS *177,218*

embroider [v2] *exaggerate information*
aggrandize, amplify, blow-up*, build up, color, distend, dramatize, elaborate, embellish, enhance, enlarge, expand, falsify, fudge*, heighten, hyperbolize, lie, magnify, make federal case*, make

mountain out of molehill*, overdo, overelaborate, overembellish, overemphasize, overestimate, overstate, pad*, play up*, puff*, romanticize, spread on thick*, stretch, stretch the truth*, yeast*; SEE CONCEPTS *58,63*

embroidery [n] *fancy stitching*
adornment, appliqué, arabesque, bargello, brocade, crewel, crochet, cross-stitch, decoration, lace, lacery, needlepoint, needlework, quilting, sampler, tapestry, tatting, tracery; SEE CONCEPTS *218,259*

embroil [v] *involve in dispute; complicate*
cause trouble, compromise, confound, confuse, derange, disorder, disturb, disunite, encumber, enmesh, ensnare, entangle, implicate, incriminate, involve, mire, mix up, muddle, perplex, snarl, tangle, trouble; SEE CONCEPTS *7,19,86*

emend [v] *correct*
alter, amend, better, edit, emendate, improve, polish, rectify, redact, retouch, revise, right, touch up; SEE CONCEPT *126*

emerge [v] *come out, arise*
appear, arrive, become apparent, become known, become visible, come forth, come into view, come on the scene, come to light, come up, crop up, dawn, derive, develop, egress, emanate, flow, gush, issue, loom, make appearance, materialize, originate, proceed, rise, show, spring, spring up, spurt, steam, stem, surface, transpire, turn up; SEE CONCEPTS *105,118*

emergency [n] *crisis, danger*
accident, climax, clutch*, compulsion, crossroad, crunch*, depression, difficulty, distress, exigency, extremity, fix, hole, impasse, juncture, meltdown*, misadventure, necessity, pass, pinch*, plight, predicament, pressure, push, quandary, scrape, squeeze, strait, tension, turning point, urgency, vicissitude, zero hour*; SEE CONCEPTS *674,675*

emergent [adj] *resulting*
appearing, budding, coming, developing, efflorescent, emanant, emanating, emerging, issuing forth, outgoing, rising; SEE CONCEPT *537*

emigrant [n] *person who leaves his or her native country*
alien, colonist, departer, displaced person, émigré, evacuee, exile, expatriate, fugitive, migrant, migrator, outcast, pilgrim, refugee, traveler, wanderer, wayfarer; SEE CONCEPTS *413,423*

emigrate [v] *move to new country*
depart, migrate, move abroad, quit, remove, transmigrate; SEE CONCEPT *198*

eminence [n1] *importance, fame*
authority, celebrity, credit, dignity, distinction, esteem, famousness, glory, greatness, honor, illustriousness, influence, kudos, loftiness, notability, note, power, preeminence, prepotency, prestige, prominence, prominency, rank, renown, reputation, repute, significance, standing, superiority, weight; SEE CONCEPTS *388,668,671*

eminence [n2] *high ground*
altitude, elevation, height, highland, highness, hill, hillock, knoll, loftiness, peak, project, prominence, promontory, raise, ridge, rise, summit, upland; SEE CONCEPTS *509,741*

eminent [adj] *very important; famous*
august, big-gun*, big-league*, big-name*, big-time*, celeb*, celebrated, celebrious, conspicuous, distinguished, dominant, elevated, esteemed, exalted, famed, grand, great, high, high-ranking, illustrious, lionlike, lofty, name, noble, notable, noted, noteworthy, of note, outstanding, page-oner*, paramount, preeminent, prestigious, prominent, redoubted, renowned, star, superior, superstar, VIP*, well-known; SEE CONCEPTS *555,568*

eminently [adv] *exceptionally; well*
conspicuously, exceedingly, extremely, greatly, highly, notably, outstandingly, prominently, remarkably, strikingly, suitably, surpassingly, very; SEE CONCEPT *574*

emissary [n] *deputy*
agent, ambassador, bearer, carrier, consul, courier, delegate, envoy, front, go-between, herald, hired gun*, intermediary, internuncio, legate, messenger, rep*, representative, scout, spy; SEE CONCEPTS *348,423*

emission [n] *issuance, diffusion*
discharge, ejaculation, ejection, emanation, exhalation, exudation, issue, radiation, shedding, transmission, utterance, venting; SEE CONCEPT *179*

emit [v] *diffuse, discharge*
afford, beam, belch, breathe, cast out, disembogue, drip, eject, emanate, erupt, evacuate, excrete, exhale, expectorate, expel, expend, expire, extrude, exude, give off, give out, give vent to, gush, issue, jet, let off, loose, ooze, pass, perspire, pour, pronounce, purge, radiate, reek, secrete, send forth, send out, shed, shoot, speak, spew, spill, spit, squirt, throw out, transmit, utter, vent, voice, void, vomit, yield; SEE CONCEPTS *108,179,266*

emotion [n] *mental state*
affect, affection, affectivity, agitation, anger, ardor, commotion, concern, desire, despair, despondency, disturbance, drive, ecstasy, elation, empathy, excitability, excitement, feeling, fervor, grief, gut reaction, happiness, inspiration, joy, love, melancholy, passion, perturbation, pride, rage, remorse, responsiveness, sadness, satisfaction, sensation, sensibility, sensitiveness, sentiment, shame, sorrow, sympathy, thrill, tremor, vehemence, vibes, warmth, zeal; SEE CONCEPT *410*

emotional [adj] *demonstrative about feelings*
affecting, ardent, disturbed, ecstatic, emotive, enthusiastic, excitable, exciting, falling apart*, fanatical, feeling, fervent, fervid, fickle, fiery, heartwarming, heated, histrionic, hot-blooded*, hysterical, impassioned, impetuous, impulsive, irrational, moving, nervous, overwrought, passionate, pathetic, poi-

gnant, responsive, roused, sensitive, sentient, sentimental, spontaneous, stirred, stirring, susceptible, tear-jerking*, temperamental, tender, thrilling, touching, warm, zealous; SEE CONCEPTS *403,542*

emotionless [adj] *unfeeling, undemonstrative*
blank, chill, cold, cold-blooded*, cold fish*, cool, cool cat*, deadpan, detached, dispassionate, distant, flat, frigid, glacial*, heartless, ice maiden*/ice man*, icy, immovable, impassive, impersonal, in cold blood*, indifferent, laid back*, matter-of-fact, nonemotional, nowhere*, poker face*, remote, reserved, stony-eyed*, thick-skinned*, toneless, undemonstrative, unemotional, unfeeling, unimpassioned, with straight face; SEE CONCEPTS *401,403,542*

empathy [n] *understanding*
affinity, appreciation, being on same wavelength*, being there for someone*, communion, community of interests, compassion, comprehension, concord, cottoning to*, fellow feeling, good vibrations*, hitting it off*, insight, picking up on*, pity, rapport, recognition, responsiveness, soul, sympathy, warmth; SEE CONCEPTS *32,409,411*

emphasis [n] *importance, prominence*
accent, accentuation, attention, decidedness, force, headline, highlight, impressiveness, insistence, intensity, moment, positiveness, power, preeminence, priority, significance, strength, stress, underlining, underscoring, weight; SEE CONCEPTS *668,682*

emphasize [v] *stress, give priority to*
accent, accentuate, affirm, articulate, assert, bear down, charge, dramatize, dwell on, enlarge, enunciate, headline, highlight, hit*, impress, indicate, insist on, italicize, labor the point*, limelight*, maintain, make a point, make clear, make emphatic, make much of*, mark, pinpoint, play up*, point out*, point up*, press, pronounce, punctuate, put accent on*, reiterate, repeat, rub in*, spotlight*, underline, underscore, weight; SEE CONCEPTS *49,57*

emphatic [adj] *insistent, unequivocal*
absolute, accented, assertive, assured, categorical, certain, cogent, confident, decided, definite, definitive, determined, direct, distinct, dogmatic, dynamic, earnest, energetic, explicit, express, flat, for a face*, forceful, forcible, important, impressive, insistent, insistive, marked, momentous, no mistake*, pointed, positive, potent, powerful, pronounced, resounding, significant, sober, solemn, stressed, striking, strong, sure, telling, trenchant, unmistakable, vigorous; SEE CONCEPTS *267,535*

empire [n] *place ruled by sovereign; rule*
authority, command, commonwealth, control, domain, dominion, federation, government, kingdom, people, power, realm, sovereignty, supremacy, sway, union; SEE CONCEPTS *198,299,376*

empirical/empiric [adj] *practical; based on experience*
experient, experiential, experimental, factual, observational, observed, pragmatic, provisional, speculative; SEE CONCEPTS *548,582*

employ [*v1*] *make use of*
apply, bestow, bring to bear*, engage, exercise, exert, exploit, fill, handle, keep busy*, manipulate, occupy, operate, put to use*, spend, take up*, use, use up*, utilize; SEE CONCEPT *225*

employ [*v2*] *give money in exchange for work performed*
bring on board*, come on board*, commission, contract, contract for, engage, enlist, hire, ink*, obtain, place, procure, put on*, retain, secure, sign on*, sign up*, take on, truck with*; SEE CONCEPT *351*

employed [*adj*] *working*
active, at it*, at work, busy, engaged, hired, in a job, in collar*, in harness*, inked*, in place, laboring, occupied, on board*, on duty*, on the job*, on the payroll*, operating, plugging away*, selected, signed*; SEE CONCEPTS *538,560*

employee [*n*] *person being paid for working for another or a corporation*
agent, apprentice, assistant, attendant, blue collar*, breadwinner*, clerk, cog*, company man/woman, craftsman/woman, craftsperson, desk jockey*, domestic, flunky*, hand, help, hired gun*, hired hand*, hireling, jobholder, laborer, lackey*, member, operator, peon*, pink collar*, plug*, punk*, representative, sales help, salesman/woman, salesperson, servant, slave, staff member, wage-earner, white collar*, worker, working stiff*, workman/woman; SEE CONCEPT *348*

employer [*n*] *person, business who hires workers*
big cheese*, big shot*, boss, boss lady, boss man, businessman, capitalist, CEO*, chief, CO*, company, corporation, director, entrepreneur, establishment, executive, firm, front office, hammer man/woman*, head, head honcho*, juice*, kingpin*, lord, management, manager, manufacturer, master, meal ticket*, organization, outfit, overseer, owner, patron, president, proprietor, slave driver*, superintendent, supervisor, taskmaster; SEE CONCEPT *347*

employment [*n1*] *working for a living; engagement in activity*
application, assignment, avocation, awarding, business, calling, carrying, commissioning, contracting, craft, employ, engaging, enlistment, enrollment, exercise, exercising, exertion, field, function, game*, hire, hiring, job, line, métier, mission, number, occupation, occupying, office, position, post, profession, pursuit, racket*, recruitment, retaining, service, servicing, setup, signing on*, situation, taking on, thing*, trade, using, vocation, what one is into*, work; SEE CONCEPTS *349,351,360*

employment [*n2*] *using something*
adoption, appliance, application, disposition, exercise, exercising, exertion, exploitation, handling, operation, play, purpose, usage, usance, use, utilization; SEE CONCEPTS *225,658,694*

emporium [*n*] *market*
bazaar, boutique, chain, co-op, cut-rate store*, discount store, five-and-dime*, flea market, galleria, mall, mart, outlet, outlet store, shop, shopping center, shopping plaza, stand, store, supermarket, thrift shop; SEE CONCEPT *449*

empower [*v*] *authorize*
accredit, allow, capacitate, charge, commission, delegate, enable, entitle, entrust, grant, invest, license, okay, permit, privilege, qualify, sanction, vest, warrant; SEE CONCEPTS *50,88*

emptiness [*n*] *void, bareness*
blank, blankness, chasm, depletedness, desertedness, desolation, destitution, exhaustion, gap, hollowness, inanition, vacancy, vacuity, vacuum, waste; SEE CONCEPTS *720,733*

empty [*adj1*] *containing nothing*
abandoned, bare, barren, blank, clear, dead, deflated, depleted, desert, deserted, desolate, despoiled, destitute, devoid, dry, evacuated, exhausted, forsaken, godforsaken*, hollow, lacking, stark, unfilled, unfurnished, uninhabited, unoccupied, vacant, vacated, vacuous, void, wanting, waste; SEE CONCEPTS *481,774,788*

empty [*adj2*] *fruitless, ineffective*
aimless, banal, barren, cheap, dead, deadpan, devoid, dishonest, dumb, expressionless, fatuous, flat, frivolous, futile, hollow, idle, ignorant, inane, ineffective, ineffectual, inexpressive, insincere, insipid, jejune, meaningless, nugatory, otiose, paltry, petty, purposeless, senseless, silly, trivial, unintelligent, unreal, unsatisfactory, unsubstantial, vacuous, vain, valueless, vapid, worthless; SEE CONCEPTS *402,570,575*

empty [*adj3*] *hungry*
famished, ravenous, starving, unfed, unfilled; SEE CONCEPT *406*

empty [*v*] *remove contents*
clear, consume, decant, deplete, discharge, disgorge, drain, drink, dump, ebb, eject, escape, evacuate, exhaust, expel, flow out, gut, leak, leave, make void, pour out, purge, release, run out, rush out, tap, unburden, unload, use up, vacate, void; SEE CONCEPT *211*

empty-headed [*adj*] *flighty, scatterbrained*
brainless, dizzy, featherbrained, frivolous, giddy, harebrained, ignorant, illiterate, inane, know-nothing, silly, skittish, stupid, uneducated, unschooled, untaught, vacant, vacuous; SEE CONCEPT *402*

emulate [*v*] *copy the actions of*
challenge, compete, compete with, contend, contend with, copy, ditto*, do*, do like*, follow, follow in footsteps*, follow suit*, follow the example of*, go like*, imitate, make like*, mimic, mirror, outvie, pattern after*, rival, rivalize, take after*, vie with; SEE CONCEPTS *87,171*

enable [*v*] *allow, authorize*
accredit, approve, capacitate, commission, condition, empower, endow, facilitate, fit, give power, implement, invest, let, license, make possible, per-

mit, prepare, provide the means*, qualify, ready, sanction, set up, warrant; SEE CONCEPTS 50,83,88,99

enact [v1] *act out; accomplish*
achieve, act, appear as, depict, discourse, do, execute, go on*, perform, personate, play, playact, play the part of, portray, represent; SEE CONCEPTS 91,292

enact [v2] *authorize, legislate*
accomplish, appoint, bring about, carry through, command, constitute, decree, determine, dictate, effect, effectuate, establish, execute, fix, formulate, get the floor*, institute, jam through*, make, make into law, make laws, ordain, order, pass, proclaim, put in force, put through, railroad*, railroad through*, ratify, sanction, set, steamroll*, transact, vote favorably*, vote in*; SEE CONCEPTS 50,88,298,317

enactment [n1] *playacting*
achievement, acting, depiction, execution, impersonation, performance, personation, personification, playing, portrayal, representation; SEE CONCEPTS 263,292

enactment [n2] *law; authorization*
command, commandment, decree, dictate, edict, execution, legislation, order, ordinance, proclamation, ratification, regulation, statute; SEE CONCEPTS 318,685

enamel [n] *paint, often shiny*
cloisonné, coating, finish, glaze, gloss, japan, lacquer, polish, stain, topcoat, varnish, veneer; SEE CONCEPTS 259,260,467

enamor [v] *fascinate, captivate*
attract, bewitch, charm, enchant, endear, enrapture, enthrall, entice, entrance, fall in love with*, grab, infatuate, make hit with*, please, slay*, sweep off feet*, turn on*, vamp; SEE CONCEPTS 7,22,375

enamored [adj] *in love*
amorous, attracted, besotted, bewitched, captivated, charmed, crazy about*, devoted, dotty, enchanted, enraptured, entranced, fascinated, fond, gone*, has a thing about*, hooked*, infatuated, loving, nuts about*, silly about*, smitten, stuck on*, swept off one's feet*, taken*, wild about*; SEE CONCEPTS 32,403

enchant [v] *delight, mesmerize*
allure; beguile, bewitch, captivate, carry away*, cast a spell on*, charm, delectate, draw, enamor, enrapture, ensorcell, enthrall, entice, entrance, fascinate, grab, gratify, hex, hypnotize, kill*, knock dead*, magnetize, make happy*, make hit with*, please, send*, slay*, spell, spellbind, sweep off feet*, take, thrill, turn on*, voodoo*, wile, witch, wow*; SEE CONCEPTS 7,22

enchanting [adj] *fascinating, delightful*
alluring, appealing, attractive, beguiling, bewitching, captivating, charming, delectable, endearing, enthralling, entrancing, exciting, glamorous, intriguing, lovely, pleasant, pleasing, ravishing, seductive, siren, sirenic, winsome, witching; SEE CONCEPTS 404,529

encircle [v] *circumscribe*
band, begird, cincture, circle, circuit, compass, cover, enclose, encompass, enfold, enring, envelop, environ, gird in, girdle, halo, hem in*, inclose, invest, ring, surround, wreathe; SEE CONCEPT 758

enclose [v] *put inside, surround*
blockade, block off, bound, box up, cage, circle, circumscribe, close in, confine, coop, corral, cover, encase, encircle, encompass, enfold, enshroud, environ, fence, fence off*, hedge, hem in*, imbue, immure, implant, impound, imprison, include, induct, insert, intern, jail, limit, lock in*, lock up*, mew, mure, pen, restrict, set apart, shut in, veil, wall in, wrap; SEE CONCEPTS 112,209,758

enclosure [n1] *area bounded by something*
asylum, aviary, bowl, building, cage, camp, cell, close, coliseum, coop, corral, court, courtyard, den, dungeon, garden, ghetto, hutch, jail, pale, park, patch, pen, place, plot, pound, precinct, prison, quad, quadrangle, region, room, stadium, stockade, sty, vault, walk, yard, zone; SEE CONCEPTS 439,448,513

enclosure [n2] *something included with letter*
check, circular, copy, document, form, information, money, printed matter, questionnaire; SEE CONCEPT 271

encompass [v1] *surround, circumscribe*
beset, circle, compass, encircle, enclose, envelop, environ, gird, girdle, hem in, ring; SEE CONCEPT 758

encompass [v2] *include, contain*
admit, comprehend, comprise, cover, embody, embrace, have, hold, incorporate, involve, subsume, take in; SEE CONCEPT 112

encore [n] *another round of applause; repeat*
acclamation, cheers, number, plaudits, praise, reappearance, repeat performance, repetition, response, return; SEE CONCEPT 264

encounter [n1] *chance meeting*
appointment, brush, concurrence, confrontation, interview, rendezvous; SEE CONCEPT 384

encounter [n2] *fight, argument*
action, battle, bout, brush, clash, collision, combat, conflict, contention, contest, dispute, engagement, flap*, fray, hassle, quarrel, rumpus*, run-in*, scrap, set-to*, skirmish, velitation, violence; SEE CONCEPTS 46,86,106

encounter [v1] *happen upon*
alight upon, bear, bump into, chance upon, close, come across, come upon, confront, cross the path*, descry, detect, espy, experience, face, fall in with*, find, front, happen on, hit upon, meet, meet up with, rub eyeballs*, run across, run into, run smack into*, suffer, sustain, turn up, undergo; SEE CONCEPTS 38,384

encounter [v2] *fight, attack*
affront, battle, clash with, collide, combat, conflict, confront, contend, cross swords*, do battle*, en-

gage, face, grapple, meet, strive, struggle; SEE CON-
CEPTS *86,106*

encourage [*v1*] *stimulate spiritually*
animate, applaud, boost, brighten, buck up*, buoy,
cheer, cheer up, comfort, console, embolden, energize, enhearten, enliven, excite, exhilarate, fortify,
galvanize, give shot in arm*, gladden, goad, hearten,
incite, inspire, inspirit, instigate, praise, prick, prop
up*, psych up*, push, rally, reassure, refresh, restore, revitalize, revivify, rouse, spur, steel, stimulate, stir, strengthen, sway; SEE CONCEPTS *7,22*

encourage [*v2*] *give support; help*
abet, advance, advocate, aid, approve, assist, back,
back up, befriend, bolster, boost, brace, comfort,
console, countenance, develop, ease, egg on*, endorse, favor, fortify, forward, foster, further, get behind, give a leg up*, go for*, improve, instigate,
invite, pat on the back, prevail, promote, pull for*,
push, reassure, reinforce, relieve, root for*, sanction, second, serve, side with*, smile upon*, solace,
spur, strengthen, subscribe to, subsidize, succor,
support, sustain, uphold; SEE CONCEPTS *8,110*

encouragement [*n*] *help, support*
advance, advocacy, aid, animation, assistance, backing, boost, cheer, comfort, confidence, consolation,
consoling, easement, enlivening, faith, favor, firmness, fortitude, helpfulness, hope, incentive, incitement, inspiration, inspiritment, invigoration,
optimism, promotion, reassurance, reassuring, refreshment, relief, relieving, reward, shot in the arm*,
softening, solacing, stimulation, stimulus, succor,
supporting, trust, urging; SEE CONCEPTS *7,22,110,410*

encroach [*v*] *invade another's property, business*
appropriate, arrogate, barge in*, butt in*, crash, elbow in*, entrench, horn in*, impinge, infringe, interfere, interpose, intervene, intrude, invade, make
inroads*, meddle, muscle in*, overstep, put two
cents in*, squeeze in*, stick nose into*, trench, trespass, usurp, work in, worm in*; SEE CONCEPTS
7,19,86,159

encumber [*v*] *bother, burden*
block, charge, clog, cramp, discommode, embarrass,
hamper, handicap, hang up, hinder, hog-tie*, hold
up, impede, incommode, inconvenience, lade, load,
make difficult, obstruct, oppress, overburden, overload, retard, saddle, saddle with*, slow down, tax,
trammel, weigh down, weight; SEE CONCEPTS
121,130

encyclopedic [*adj*] *comprehensive*
all-embracing, all-encompassing, all-inclusive,
broad, catholic, complete, discursive, exhaustive, extensive, general, thorough, thorough-going, universal, vast, wide-ranging, widespread; SEE CONCEPTS
267,772

end [*n1*] *extreme, limit*
borderline, bound, boundary, butt end, confine,
cusp, deadline, edge, extent, extremity, foot, head,
heel, limitation, neb, nib, point, prong, spire, stub,
stump, tail, tail end, term, terminal, termination, terminus, tip, top, ultimate; SEE CONCEPTS *745,827,833*

end [*n2*] *completion; stop*
accomplishment, achievement, adjournment, attainment, bottom line*, cease, cessation, close, closing,
closure, conclusion, consequence, consummation,
culmination, curtain, denouement, desistance, desuetude, determination, discontinuance, ending, execution, expiration, expiry, finale, finis, finish,
fulfillment, issue, last word*, omega, outcome, payoff, perfection, realization, resolution, result, retirement, sign-off*, stop, target, termination, terminus,
upshot*, windup, wrap-up*; SEE CONCEPTS
119,230,832

end [*n3*] *intention, aim*
aspiration, design, drift, goal, intent, mark, object,
objective, point, purpose, reason, where one's heading*; SEE CONCEPT *659*

end [*n4*] *leftover part*
bit, butt end, dregs, fragment, leaving, lees, leftover,
part, particle, piece, portion, remainder, remnant,
residue, scrap, share, side, stub, tag end; SEE CON-
CEPT *835*

end [*n5*] *death, destruction*
annihilation, demise, dissolution, doom, expiration,
extermination, extinction, finish, passing, ruin, ruination; SEE CONCEPT *304*

end [*v1*] *bring to an end*
abolish, abort, accomplish, achieve, break off, break
up, call it a day*, call off*, cease, close, close out,
complete, conclude, consummate, crown, culminate,
cut short, delay, determine, discontinue, dispose of,
dissolve, drop, expire, finish, get done, give up, halt,
interrupt, pack it in*, perorate, postpone, pull the
plug*, put the lid on*, quit, relinquish, resolve, settle, sew up*, shut down*, stop, switch off*, terminate, top off*, ultimate, wind up*, wrap, wrap up*;
SEE CONCEPT *234*

end [*v2*] *die or kill*
abolish, annihilate, cease, depart, desist, destroy,
die, expire, exterminate, extinguish, lapse, put to
death, ruin, run out, wane; SEE CONCEPTS *252,304*

endanger [*v*] *put in jeopardy*
be careless, chance, chance it*, expose, hazard, imperil, jeopard, lay on the line*, lay open*, leave
defenseless, leave in the middle*, make liable, menace, peril, play into one's hands*, put at risk, put in
danger, put on the spot*, risk, stick one's neck out*,
subject to loss, threaten, venture; SEE CONCEPTS
246,252,384

endear [*v*] *attract attention*
attach, bind, captivate, charm, cherish, engage,
prize, treasure, value, win; SEE CONCEPTS *7,22,32*

endeavor [*n*] *attempt to achieve something*
aim, all*, best shot*, crash project*, dry run*, effort,
enterprise, essay, exertion, fling, full blast*, full
court press*, full steam*, go, header*, labor, lick*,
old college try*, one's all*, one's level best*, push,

shot*, stab*, striving, struggle, toil, travail, trial, try, try-on*, undertaking, venture, whack*, whirl*, work; SEE CONCEPT *87*

endeavor [*v*] *attempt to achieve something*
address, aim, apply, aspire, assay, bid for, buck, determine, dig, do one's best*, drive at, essay, go for*, go for broke*, grind, hammer away*, hassle, have a crack at*, have a shot at*, have a swing at*, hump*, hustle, intend, labor, make an effort, make a run at*, offer, peg away*, plug, pour it on*, purpose, push, risk, scratch, seek, strain, strive, struggle, sweat, take on, take pains*, try, undertake, venture; SEE CONCEPT *87*

ending [*n*] *conclusion*
catastrophe, cessation, close, closing, closure, completion, consummation, coup de grace, culmination, denouement, desistance, dissolution, end, epilogue, expiration, finale, finish, lapse, omega, outcome, period, resolution, stop, summation, swan song*, termination, terminus, upshot, wane, windup; SEE CONCEPTS *119,230,832*

endless [*adj*] *not stopping, not finishing*
amaranthine, boundless, ceaseless, constant, continual, continuous, countless, deathless, enduring, eternal, everlasting, illimitable, immeasurable, immortal, incalculable, incessant, indeterminate, infinite, interminable, limitless, measureless, monotonous, multitudinous, never-ending, no end of, no end to, numberless, overlong, perpetual, self-perpetuating, unbounded, unbroken, undivided, undying, unending, unfathomable, uninterrupted, unlimited, unsurpassable, untold, without end; SEE CONCEPTS *482,551,798*

endorse [*v1*] *support, authorize*
accredit, advocate, affirm, approve, attest, authenticate, back, back up*, bless, boost, certify, champion, commend, confirm, countenance, defend, favor, give a boost to, give green light*, give one's word*, give the go-ahead*, give the nod*, go along with*, go to bat for*, go with, guarantee, lend one's name to, okay, praise, push, ratify, recommend, rubber-stamp*, sanction, second, stand behind, stand up for*, stump for*, subscribe to, sustain, underwrite, uphold, vouch for, warrant, witness; SEE CONCEPTS *10,50,69,88,300*

endorse [*v2*] *countersign a check*
add one's name to, authenticate, autograph, cosign, notarize, put John Hancock on*, put signature on, rubber-stamp*, say amen to*, sign, sign off on, sign on dotted line*, subscribe, superscribe, undersign, underwrite; SEE CONCEPTS *50,79,88,330*

endorsement [*n*] *support, authorization*
advocacy, affirmation, approbation, approval, backing, championing, commercial, confirmation, countersignature, favor, fiat, go-ahead*, green light*, hubba-hubba*, okay, pat on back*, permission, qualification, ratification, recommendation, sanction, seal of approval, signature, stroke, subscription to, superscription, the nod*, warrant; SEE CONCEPT *685*

endow [*v*] *give large gift*
accord, award, back, bequeath, bestow, come through with, confer, contribute, donate, empower, enable, endue, enhance, enrich, establish, favor, finance, found, fund, furnish, gift with, grant, heighten, invest, lay on*, leave, make over*, organize, promote, provide, settle on, sponsor, subscribe, subsidize, supply, support, vest in, will; SEE CONCEPTS *108,341*

endowment [*n1*] *large gift*
award, benefaction, benefit, bequest, bestowal, boon, bounty, dispensation, donation, fund, funding, gifting, grant, gratuity, income, inheritance, largess, legacy, nest egg, pension, presentation, property, provision, revenue, stake, stipend, subsidy, trust; SEE CONCEPTS *337,340*

endowment [*n2*] *personal talent, ability*
aptitude, attribute, capability, capacity, faculty, flair, genius, gift, habilitation, power, qualification, quality, turn; SEE CONCEPTS *411,630*

end up [*v*] *become eventually; come to a close*
arrive finally, cease, come to a halt, finish, finish as, finish up, stop, turn out to be, wind up; SEE CONCEPT *119*

endurable [*adj*] *tolerable*
bearable, livable, sufferable, supportable, sustainable; SEE CONCEPT *548*

endurance [*n1*] *bearing hardship; staying power*
ability, allowance, backbone, bearing, capacity, continuing, cool, coolness, courage, enduring, forebearance, fortitude, grit, guts, gutsiness, heart*, holding up*, intestinal fortitude, mettle, moxie*, patience, perseverance, persistence, pertinacity, pluck, resignation, resistance, resolution, restraint, spunk, stamina, standing, starch*, strength, submission, sufferance, suffering, suffering, tenacity, tolerance, toleration, undergoing, vitality, will, withstanding; SEE CONCEPTS *411,633*

endurance [*n2*] *continuity, lastingness*
continuance, continuation, durability, duration, immutability, longevity, permanence, persistence, stability; SEE CONCEPT *804*

endure [*v1*] *bear hardship*
abide, accustom, allow, bear, bear the brunt*, be patient with, brave, brook, cope with, countenance, eat, encounter, experience, face, feel, go through, grin and bear it*, hang in*, keep up, know, live out, live through, meet with, never say die*, permit, put up with, repress feelings, resign oneself, ride out*, sit through, stand, stick, stick it out*, stomach*, subject to, submit to, suffer, support, sustain, swallow*, take, take it*, take patiently, tolerate, undergo, weather, withstand; SEE CONCEPT *23*

endure [*v2*] *continue; be durable*
abide, be, be left, be long lived, be timeless, bide, carry on, carry through, cling, exist, go on, hang on*, have no end, hold, hold on, hold out, keep on,

last, linger, live, live on, never say die*, outlast, outlive, perdure, persist, prevail, remain, ride out*, run on, stand, stay, stay on, stick to*, superannuate, survive, sustain, wear, wear on, wear well*; SEE CONCEPTS *239,407,804*

enemy [n] *someone hated or competed against*
adversary, agent, antagonist, archenemy, asperser, assailant, assassin, attacker, backbiter, bad guy*, bandit, betrayer, calumniator, competitor, contender, criminal, defamer, defiler, detractor, disputant, emulator, falsifier, fifth column*, foe, guerrilla, informer, inquisitor, invader, murderer, opponent, opposition, other side*, prosecutor, rebel, revolutionary, rival, saboteur, seditionist, slanderer, spy, terrorist, traducer, traitor, vilifier, villain; SEE CONCEPTS *322,412*

energetic [adj] *full of life; forceful*
active, aggressive, animated, ball of fire*, breezy, brisk, demoniac, driving, dynamic, enterprising, forcible, fresh, hardy, high-powered, indefatigable, industrious, kinetic, lively, lusty, peppy, potent, powerful, red-blooded*, rugged, snappy, spirited, sprightly, spry, stalwart, strenuous, strong, sturdy, tireless, tough, unflagging, untiring, vigorous, vital, vivacious, zippy*; SEE CONCEPTS *404,542*

energize [v] *activate; give more life*
actify, activize, animate, arm, build up, electrify, empower, enable, enliven, excite, fortify, goose*, innervate, inspirit, invigorate, jazz up*, juice up*, liven up, motivate, pep up, prime, pump up*, put zip into*, quicken, reinforce, start up, stimulate, strengthen, sustain, switch on, trigger, turn on, vitalize, work up, zap*; SEE CONCEPTS *7,22,231,700*

energy [n1] *person's spirit and vigor*
activity, animation, application, ardor, birr, dash, drive, effectiveness, efficacy, efficiency, élan, endurance, enterprise, exertion, fire, force, forcefulness, fortitude, get-up-and-go*, go, hardihood, initiative, intensity, juice, life, liveliness, might, moxie*, muscle, operativeness, pep, pizzazz, pluck, potency, power, puissance, punch, spirit, spontaneity, stamina, steam, strength, toughness, tuck, vehemence, verve, vim, virility, vitality, vivacity, zeal, zest, zing, zip*; SEE CONCEPT *411*

energy [n2] *generated power*
application, burn, conductivity, current, dynamism, electricity, force, friction, gravity, heat, horsepower, juice, kilowatts, magnetism, potential, pressure, radioactivity, rays, reaction, response, service, steam, strength, voltage, wattage; SEE CONCEPT *520*

enervate [v] *tire, wear out*
bush, castrate, debilitate, devitalize, disable, emasculate, enfeeble, exhaust, fatigue, incapacitate, jade, paralyze, prostrate, sap, unman, unnerve, unstring, vitiate, wash out, weaken, wear, weary; SEE CONCEPTS *156,225,250*

enervated [adj] *exhausted, worn out*
debilitated, deteriorated, devitalized, done in, enfeebled, exhausted, fatigued, feeble, gone to seed*, in-

capacitated, lackadaisical, languid, languishing, languorous, limp, listless, on the ropes*, out of condition*, out of gas*, out of shape*, paralyzed, prostrate, prostrated, run-down, rusty, sapped, soft, spent, spiritless, tired, undermined, unnerved, vitiated, washed out, weak, weakened; SEE CONCEPTS *485,560*

enfeeble [v] *make very weak*
attenuate, blunt, castrate, cripple, debilitate, deplete, devitalize, diminish, disable, exhaust, fatigue, incapacitate, sap, unbrace, undermine, unhinge, unnerve, weaken, wear out; SEE CONCEPTS *240,252*

enfold [v] *embrace, hug*
bear hug, cinch, clasp, clinch, clutch, cover, drape, encase, enclose, encompass, enshroud, envelop, envelope, enwrap, fold, girdle, grab, hold, invest, press, shroud, squeeze, surround, swathe, veil, wrap, wrap up; SEE CONCEPTS *191,219*

enforce [v] *put a rule, plan in force*
accomplish, administer, administrate, apply, carry out, coerce, commandeer, compel, constrain, crack down, demand, dictate, discharge, dragoon, drive, effect, egg on*, emphasize, exact, execute, exert, expect, extort, force upon, fortify, fulfill, goad, hound, impel, implement, impose, incite, insist on, invoke, lash, lean on, make, necessitate, oblige, perform, press, prosecute, put into effect, put screws to*, reinforce, require, sanction, spur, strain, stress, strong-arm, support, urge, whip, wrest; SEE CONCEPTS *50,88,133,298,317*

enforcement [n] *requirement to obey; implementation of rule(s)*
administration, application, carrying out, coercion, compulsion, compulsory law, constraint, duress, enforcing, exaction, execution, fulfilling, imposition, impulsion, insistence, lash, martial law, necessitation, obligation, prescription, pressure, prosecution, reinforcement, spur, whip; SEE CONCEPTS *133,298, 317,685*

engage [v1] *hire for job, use*
appoint, bespeak, book, bring on board*, charter, come on board*, commission, contract, employ, enlist, enroll, ink*, lease, place, prearrange, put on, rent, reserve, retain, secure, sign on, sign up, take on, truck with*; SEE CONCEPTS *129,351*

engage [v2] *occupy oneself; engross*
absorb, allure, arrest, bewitch, busy, captivate, catch, charm, draw, embark on, employ, enamor, enchant, enter into, enthrall, fascinate, give a try*, give a whirl*, go for broke*, go in for*, go out for*, grip*, have a fling at*, have a go at*, have a shot at*, imbue, immerse, interest, involve, join, keep busy, monopolize, partake, participate, pitch in, practice, preengage, preoccupy, set about, soak, tackle*, take part, tie up, try on for size*, undertake; SEE CONCEPTS *87,363*

engage [v3] *promise to marry*
affiance, agree, betroth, bind, catch, commit, contract, covenant, give one's word*, guarantee, hook,

obligate, oblige, pass, pledge, tie, troth, turn on*, undertake, vouch, vow; SEE CONCEPT *297*

engage [*v4*] *start a fight; attack*
assail, assault, combat, do battle with, encounter, face, fall on, fight, give battle to, join battle with, launch, meet, strike, take on; SEE CONCEPTS *86,106,320*

engage [*v5*] *interconnect; bring into operation*
activate, apply, attach, dovetail, energize, fasten, get going, interact, interlace, interlock, intermesh, interplay, join, lock, mesh, switch on; SEE CONCEPTS *85,113,160,221*

engaged [*adj1*] *promised to be married*
affianced, asked for, betrothed, bound, committed, contracted, future, given one's word*, going steady*, hooked*, intended, matched, pinned, pledged, plighted, ringed, spoken for, steady; SEE CONCEPT *555*

engaged [*adj2*] *operating; busy*
absorbed, at work, committed, connected with, dealing in, deep, doing, employed, engrossed, immersed, in place, intent, interested, in use, involved, occupied, performing, practicing, preoccupied, pursuing, rapt, signed, tied up, unavailable, working, wrapped up*; SEE CONCEPTS *542,555,576*

engagement [*n1*] *pledge to marry*
assurance, betrothal, betrothing, betrothment, bond, commitment, compact, contract, espousal, match, oath, obligation, pact, plight, promise, troth, undertaking, vow, word; SEE CONCEPT *297*

engagement [*n2*] *meeting; date*
appointment, arrangement, assignation, blind date*, commission, commitment, date, errand, get-together, gig, going out*, interview, invitation, meet, seeing one*, stint, tryst, visit; SEE CONCEPT *384*

engagement [*n3*] *battle*
action, combat, conflict, confrontation, contest, encounter, fight, fray, skirmish; SEE CONCEPTS *106,320*

engaging [*adj*] *charming*
agreeable, alluring, appealing, attractive, bewitching, captivating, enchanting, enticing, entrancing, fascinating, fetching, glamorous, interesting, intriguing, inviting, likable, lovable, magnetic, mesmeric, pleasant, pleasing, prepossessing, siren, sweet, winning, winsome; SEE CONCEPT *404*

engender [*v*] *cause to happen; cause an action*
arouse, beget, breed, bring about, bring forth, cause, create, develop, excite, father, foment, generate, give birth to, give rise to, hatch, incite, induce, instigate, lead to, make, muster, occasion, precipitate, procreate, produce, propagate, provoke, quicken, rouse, sire, spawn, stimulate, stir, work up; SEE CONCEPTS *221,242*

engine [*n*] *device that drives a machine*
agent, apparatus, appliance, barrel, contrivance, cylinder, diesel, dynamo, fan, generator, horses*, implement, instrument, means, mechanism, motor, piston, pot*, powerhouse, power plant, power train, putt-putt*, rubber band*, tool, transformer, turbine,

weapon, what's under the hood*; SEE CONCEPTS *463,464*

engineer [*n*] *person who puts together things*
architect, builder, contriver, designer, deviser, director, inventor, manager, manipulator, motorman, originator, planner, schemer, sights*, surveyor, techie*, technie*; SEE CONCEPT *348*

engineer [*v*] *devise; bring about*
angle, arrange, cause, come up with, con, concoct, contrive, control, cook*, create, direct, doctor, effect, encompass, finagle*, jockey*, machinate, manage, maneuver, manipulate, mastermind, negotiate, operate, originate, plan, plant, play games*, plot, pull strings*, pull wires*, put one on*, put one over*, put over*, put through, rig*, scam, scheme, set up, superintend, swing, upstage, wangle, work; SEE CONCEPTS *36,173,251*

engrave [*v*] *carve letters or designs into*
bite, burn, chase, chisel, crosshatch, cut, diaper, embed, enchase, etch, fix, grave, hatch, impress, imprint, infix, ingrain, initial, inscribe, instill, intaglio, lithograph, lodge, mezzotint, ornament, print, scratch, stipple; SEE CONCEPTS *79,174,176*

engraving [*n*] *carving of letters or design into something*
blocking, chasing, chiselling, cutting, dry point, enchasing, etching, illustration, impression, inscribing, inscription, intaglio, lithograph, mezzotint, photoengraving, photogravure, print, rotogravure, scratch, woodcut; SEE CONCEPTS *79,174,176,625*

engross [*v*] *hold one's attention*
absorb, apply, arrest, assimilate, attract, become lost, be hung*, bewitch, busy, captivate, consume, corner, engage, engulf, enrapture, enthrall, fascinate, fill, grip, hog*, hold, immerse, involve, monopolize, occupy, preoccupy, sew up*, soak, take up, up on*; SEE CONCEPTS *14,17*

engrossed [*adj*] *preoccupied; attentive to*
absorbed, all wound up*, assiduous, bugged*, busy, captivated, caught up, caught up in, consumed, deep, diligent, engaged, enthralled, fascinated, fiend for*, gone*, gripped, head over heels*, heavily into*, hooked, hung up, immersed, industrious, intent, into*, intrigued, lost, monopolized, occupied, rapt, really into*, riveted, sedulous, submerged, taken up with, tied up, turned on*, up to here in*, wrapped up*; SEE CONCEPTS *403,542*

engrossing [*adj*] *very interesting*
absorbing, all-consuming, captivating, compelling, consuming, controlling, enthralling, exciting, fascinating, gripping, intriguing, monopolizing, obsessing, preoccupying, provoking, riveting, stimulating; SEE CONCEPT *529*

engulf [*v*] *absorb, overwhelm*
bury, consume, deluge, drown, encompass, engross, envelop, flood, imbibe, immerse, inundate, overflow, overrun, overwhelm, plunge, submerge, swallow up, swamp, whelm; SEE CONCEPTS *169,172,256*

enhance [v] *improve, embellish*
add to, adorn, aggrandize, amplify, appreciate, augment, beautify, boom, boost, build up, complement, elevate, embroider, enlarge, exaggerate, exalt, flesh out*, heighten, increase, intensify, lift, magnify, pad*, pyramid*, raise, reinforce, strengthen, swell, upgrade; SEE CONCEPTS *162,177,244*

enigma [n] *mystery*
bewilderment, cliffhanger, conundrum, crux, cryptogram, Gordian knot*, grabber*, knot*, mind-boggler*, mind-twister*, mystification, parable, perplexity, problem, puzzle, puzzlement, puzzler, question, question mark, riddle, secret, sixty-four dollar question*, sphinx*, sticker, stickler, stumper, teaser, tough nut to crack*, twister, why*; SEE CONCEPT *532*

enigmatic/enigmatical [adj] *mysterious*
ambiguous, cryptic, dark, Delphian*, doubtful, equivocal, imcomprehensible, indecipherable, inexplicable, inscrutable, obscure, occult, oracular, perplexing, puzzling, recondite, secret, Sibylline*, sphinxlike, stickling, stumping, teasing, uncertain, unfathomable, unintelligible; SEE CONCEPTS *529,576, 582*

enjoin [v1] *order, command*
adjure, admonish, advise, appoint, bid, call upon, caution, charge, counsel, decree, demand, dictate, direct, forewarn, impose, instruct, ordain, prescribe, require, rule, tell, urge, warn; SEE CONCEPTS *53,78*

enjoin [v2] *forbid*
ban, bar, deny, disallow, inhibit, interdict, outlaw, place injunction on, preclude, prohibit, proscribe, restrain, taboo; SEE CONCEPTS *50,53,88,130*

enjoy [v1] *take pleasure in, from something*
adore, appreciate, be entertained, be fond of, be pleased, cotton to*, delight in, dig*, dote on*, drink in*, eat up*, fancy, flip over*, freak out on*, get a charge out of*, get a kick out of*, get high on*, go, have a ball*, have a good time, have fun, like, live a little*, live it up*, love, luxuriate in, mind, paint the town*, pleasure in, rejoice in, relish, revel in, savor, take joy in, thrill to; SEE CONCEPTS *32,384*

enjoy [v2] *have the benefit or use of*
be blessed, be favored, boast, command, experience, have, hold, maintain, occupy, own, possess, process, reap the benefits*, retain, use; SEE CONCEPT *710*

enjoyable [adj] *pleasing; to one's liking*
agreeable, amusing, clear sailing*, delectable, delicious, delightful, entertaining, fun, genial, gratifying, groovy*, just for grins*, just for kicks*, just for laughs*, just for the heck of it*, likable, lots of laughs*, pleasant, pleasurable, preferable, relishable, satisfying, welcome; SEE CONCEPTS *529,548*

enjoyment [n1] *delight in something*
amusement, delectation, diversion, enjoying, entertainment, fruition, fun, gladness, gratification, gusto, happiness, hedonism, indulgence, joy, loving, luxury, pleasure, recreation, rejoicing, relaxation, relish, satisfaction, savor, self-indulgence, sensuality, thrill, triumph, zest; SEE CONCEPTS *32,410*

enjoyment [n2] *possession; use of*
advantage, benefit, exercise, having, indulgence, ownership, spending, using; SEE CONCEPT *710*

enlarge [v] *make or grow bigger; increase*
add to, aggrandize, amplify, augment, beef up*, blow up*, boost, broaden, build, bulk, develop, diffuse, dilate, distend, elaborate, elongate, embroider, exaggerate, expand, expatiate, extend, give details, grow, grow larger, heighten, inflate, jack up*, jazz up*, lengthen, magnify, make larger, mount, multiply, pad*, pyramid*, rise, slap on*, snowball*, spread, stretch, swell, upsurge, wax, widen; SEE CONCEPTS *137,236,245,780*

enlargement [n] *increase, expansion*
aggrandizement, amplification, augmentation, blow up, elongation, extension, growth, spread; SEE CONCEPT *780*

enlighten [v] *explain thoroughly; make aware*
acquaint, advise, apprise, brief, catechize, cause to understand, civilize, convert, counsel, direct, disclose, divulge, edify, educate, elucidate, give faith*, give the lowdown*, give the word*, guide, illume, illuminate, illumine, imitate, improve, inculcate, indoctrinate, inform, inspirit, instruct, let in on, open up, persuade, preach, put on to*, reveal, save, school, teach, tell, train, update, uplift; SEE CONCEPTS *57,60,75*

enlightened [adj] *informed, educated*
aware, broad-minded, civilized, cultivated, hip to*, instructed, in the picture*, knowing what's what*, knowledgeable, learned, liberal, literate, open-minded, plugged in*, reasonable, refined, savvy, sharp, sophisticated, tuned in*, wised up*; SEE CONCEPT *402*

enlightenment [n] *awareness, understanding*
broad-mindedness, civilization, comprehension, cultivation, culture, edification, education, information, insight, instruction, knowledge, learning, literacy, open-mindedness, refinement, sophistication, teaching, wisdom; SEE CONCEPT *409*

enlist [v] *sign up for responsibility*
admit, appoint, assign, attract, call to arms, call up, conscribe, conscript, draft, embody, employ, engage, enroll, enter, enter into, gather, get, hire, hitch, incorporate, induct, initiate, inscribe, interest, join, join up, levy, list, mobilize, muster, oblige, obtain, place, press into service, procure, record, recruit, register, reserve, secure, serve, sign on, take on, volunteer; SEE CONCEPTS *8,320*

enliven [v] *inspire, vitalize*
animate, brace up, brighten, buck up, buoy, cheer, cheer up, divert, entertain, excite, exhilarate, fire, fire up, galvanize, give a lift, give life to, gladden, hearten, inspirit, invigorate, jazz up*, juice up*, let sunshine in*, pep up*, perk up*, pick up, put pep

into, quicken, recreate, refresh, rejuvenate, renew, restore, rouse, snap out of it*, spark, spice, spice up*, stimulate, vivificate, vivify, wake up, work up*, zap*; SEE CONCEPTS 7,22

en masse [adj] *all at once*
all in all, all together, altogether, as a body, as a group, as a whole, as one, bodily, by and large*, ensemble, generally, in a body, in a group, in a mass, jointly, on the whole, together; SEE CONCEPT 577

enmesh [v] *involve in situation*
box in, catch, drag into*, draw in, embroil, ensnare, entangle, entrap, hook, implicate, incriminate, lay a trap for*, lay for*, make party to*, net, snare, snarl, tangle, trammel, trap; SEE CONCEPTS 59,112

enmity [n] *hatred, animosity*
acrimony, alienation, animus, antagonism, antipathy, aversion, bad blood*, bitterness, daggers*, detestation, dislike, hate, hostility, ill will, loathing, malevolence, malice, malignancy, malignity, rancor, spite, spleen, uncordiality, unfriendliness, venom; SEE CONCEPT 29

ennui [n] *boredom*
apathy, blahs, blues, dejection, depression, dissatisfaction, doldrums, dumps*, fatigue, ho hums*, lack of interest, languidness, languor, lassitude, listlessness, melancholy, sadness, satiety, spiritlessness, surfeit, tedium, weariness, yawn*; SEE CONCEPT 410

enormity [n1] *horribleness*
abomination, atrociousness, atrocity, crime, depravity, disgrace, evil, evilness, flagrancy, grossness, heinousness, horror, monstrosity, monstrousness, nefariousness, outrage, outrageousness, rankness, turpitude, vice, viciousness, vileness, villainy, wickedness; SEE CONCEPTS 645,666

enormity [n2] *extreme largeness*
bigness, bulk, enormousness, greatness, hugeness, immensity, magnitude, massiveness, size, tremendousness, vastness; SEE CONCEPT 730

enormous [adj] *very large*
astronomic, barn door*, blimp*, colossal, excessive, gargantuan, gigantic, gross, huge, humongous, immense, jumbo*, king-sized*, mammoth, massive, monstrous, mountainous, prodigious, stupendous, super-colossal*, titanic*, tremendous, vast, whopping; SEE CONCEPT 773

enough [n] *plenty*
abundance, adequacy, ampleness, ample supply, competence, plenitude, right amount, sufficiency, sufficient; SEE CONCEPTS 646,767

enough [adj] *plenty*
abundant, acceptable, adequate, all right already*, ample, bellyful*, bounteous, bountiful, comfortable, competent, complete, copious, decent, enough already*, fed up*, full, had it*, last straw*, lavish, plenteous, plentiful, replete, satisfactory, satisfying, sick and tired of*, sufficient, sufficing, suitable, unlimited, up to here*; SEE CONCEPTS 546,771

enough [adv] *adequately*
abundantly, acceptably, admissibly, amply, averagely, barely, commensurately, decently, fairly, moderately, passably, proportionately, rather, reasonably, satisfactorily, so-so*, sufficiently, tolerably; SEE CONCEPTS 546,558,771

enrage [v] *make very upset*
aggravate, anger, ask for it*, exasperate, get under skin*, hack*, incense, incite, inflame, infuriate, ire, irritate, madden, make blood boil*, make see red*, needle, provoke, rile, steam up*, T-off*, umbrage, whip up*; SEE CONCEPTS 7,14,19

enrapture [v] *captivate*
allure, attract, beguile, bewitch, charm, delight, elate, enamor, enchant, enthrall, entrance, fascinate, gladden, gratify, please, ravish, rejoice, score, send, spellbind, transport; SEE CONCEPTS 7,22

enrich [v] *improve, embellish*
adorn, aggrandize, ameliorate, augment, beef up*, better, build, build up, cultivate, decorate, develop, endow, enhance, figure in, flesh out*, grace, hike up*, hop up*, jack up*, jazz up*, make rich, ornament, pad, parlay, pour it on*, pyramid*, refine, run up*, soup up*, spike*, step up, supplement, sweeten*, up*, upgrade; SEE CONCEPTS 177,244

enroll [v1] *sign up for membership*
accept, admit, become student, call up, employ, engage, enlist, enter, join, join up, matriculate, muster, obtain, recruit, register, serve, sign on, subscribe, take course, take on; SEE CONCEPTS 114,129

enroll [v2] *list, record*
affix, bill, book, catalog, chronicle, engross, enlist, enter, file, fill out, index, inscribe, insert, inventorize, mark, matriculate, note, poll, register, schedule, slate; SEE CONCEPTS 79,125

enrollment [n] *registration for membership*
acceptance, accession, admission, conscription, engagement, enlistment, entrance, entry, induction, influx, listing, matriculation, rally, reception, record, recruitment, response, student body, students, subscription; SEE CONCEPTS 288,388,417

en route [adj] *on the way to destination*
advancing, along the way, bound, driving, entrained, en voyage*, flying, heading toward, in passage, in transit, making headway*, midway, on the road*, pressing on, progressing, travelling; SEE CONCEPTS 577,586

ensconce [v] *hide; tuck away*
bury, cache, conceal, cover, curl up, ditch, establish, fix, install, locate, nestle, place, plant, protect, screen, seat, secrete, set, settle, shelter, shield, situate, snuggle up, stash, station; SEE CONCEPTS 188,201

ensemble [n1] *collection*
aggregate, assemblage, band, cast, choir, chorus, company, composite, entirety, gathering, glee club, group, octet, orchestra, organization, outfit, quartet,

quintet, set, sextet, sum, total, totality, trio, troupe, whole, whole thing; SEE CONCEPTS *294,432*

ensemble [*n2*] *clothing outfit*
coordinates, costume, garb*, get-up*, suit, togs*; SEE CONCEPT *451*

ensemble [*adv*] *at the same time*
all at once, all together, altogether, as a body, as a group, as a whole, as one, at once, en masse, in concert; SEE CONCEPT *577*

enshrine [*v*] *hold as sacred*
apotheosize, bless, cherish, consecrate, dedicate, embalm, exalt, hallow, idolize, preserve, revere, sanctify, treasure; SEE CONCEPTS *69,367*

enslave [*v*] *make someone a servant*
bind, capture, chain, check, circumscribe, coerce, compel, confine, deprive, disenfranchise, disfranchise, dominate, enchain, enclose, enthrall, fetter, get hooks into*, hobble, hold, immure, imprison, incarcerate, indenture, jail, keep under thumb*, oppress, put in irons*, reduce, restrain, restrict, secure, shackle, shut in, subdue, subject, subjugate, suppress, tether, tie, yoke; SEE CONCEPTS *14,90,130,191*

ensnare [*v*] *trap*
bag*, bat eyes at*, benet, capture, catch, cheat, come on, deceive, decoy, embroil, enmesh, entangle, entice, entrap, hook, inveigle, lure, mislead, net, rope in, snag, snare, snarl, suck in*, tangle, trick; SEE CONCEPTS *59,90*

ensue [*v*] *start to happen; come to pass*
appear, arise, attend, be consequent on, befall, be subsequent to, come after, come next, come up, derive, develop, emanate, eventualize, eventuate, flow, follow, issue, occur, proceed, result, stem, succeed, supervene, turn out, turn up; SEE CONCEPTS *119,242*

ensuing [*adj*] *resultant*
after, coming, coming up, consequent, consequential, following, later, next, next off, posliminary, posterior, subsequent, subsequential; SEE CONCEPTS *548,820*

ensure [*v*] *guarantee; make secure*
arrange, assure, certify, cinch, clinch, confirm, effect, establish, guard, insure, lock on*, lock up*, make certain, make safe, make sure, nail down*, okay, protect, provide, put on ice*, safeguard, secure, set out, warrant; SEE CONCEPTS *71,96*

entail [*v*] *require; result in*
bring about, call for, cause, demand, encompass, entangle, evoke, give rise to, impose, involve, lead to, necessitate, occasion, require, tangle; SEE CONCEPTS *242,646*

entangle [*v*] *involve, mix up*
benet, bewilder, burden, catch, clog, come on, complicate, compromise, confuse, corner, dishevel, duke in, embarrass, embrangle, embroil, enchain, enmesh, ensnare, entrap, fetter, hamper, hook, impede, implicate, intertangle, intertwine, interweave, jumble, knot, lead on, mat, muddle, perplex, puzzle, ravel, rope in, set up, snag, snare, snarl, swindle, tangle,

trammel, trap, twist, unsettle; SEE CONCEPTS *59,90,112*

entanglement [*n*] *complication, predicament*
affair, association, cobweb, complexity, confusion, difficulty, embarrassment, embroilment, enmeshment, ensnarement, entrapment, imbroglio, intricacy, intrigue, involvement, jumble, knot, liaison, mesh, mess, mix-up, muddle, snare, tangle, tie-up, toil, trap, web; SEE CONCEPTS *666,674*

enter [*v1*] *come, put into a place*
access, arrive, barge in*, blow in*, break in, breeze in*, burst in, bust in*, butt in*, come, come in, crack, crawl, creep, crowd in*, drive in, drop in, fall into, gain entree, get in, go in, horn in*, immigrate, infiltrate, ingress, insert, insinuate, introduce, intrude, invade, jump in, make an entrance, make way, move in, pass into, penetrate, pierce, pile in, pop in*, probe, rush in, set foot in, slip, sneak, work in, worm in*, wriggle; SEE CONCEPT *159*

enter [*v2*] *embark on; take part in*
become member, begin, commence, commit oneself, enlist, enroll, get oneself into*, inaugurate, join, join up, lead off, muster*, open, participate in, set about, set out on, set to, sign on, sign up, start, subscribe, take up, tee off*; SEE CONCEPTS *114,234*

enter [*v3*] *record, list*
admit, docket, inject, inscribe, insert, intercalate, interpolate, introduce, log, note, post, put in, register, set down, take down; SEE CONCEPT *125*

enterprise [*n1*] *adventure, undertaking*
action, activity, affair, attempt, baby*, bag*, ballgame*, biggie*, big idea*, bit*, business, campaign, cause, company, concern, crusade, deal, deed, do*, effort, endeavor, engagement, essay, establishment, firm, flier*, follow through*, game*, happening, hazard, house, move, operation, outfit, performance, pet project*, plan, plunge*, program, project, proposition, purpose, pursuit, risk, scheme, speculation, stake, striving, stunt, task, thing*, trade, try, venture, work; SEE CONCEPTS *87,324,325,362*

enterprise [*n2*] *resourcefulness, energy*
activity, adventurousness, alertness, ambition, audacity, boldness, courage, daring, dash, drive, eagerness, enthusiasm, force, foresight, get-up-and-go*, gumption, hustle, industry, initiative, inventiveness, pluck, push, readiness, resource, self-reliance, spirit, venturesomeness, vigor, zeal; SEE CONCEPTS *411,657*

enterprising [*adj*] *resourceful, energetic*
active, advancing, adventurous, aggressive, alert, ambitious, aspiring, audacious, bold, busy, coming on strong*, craving, daring, dashing, diligent, driving, eager, enthusiastic, go-ahead*, go-go*, gumptious, hard ball*, hardworking, hungry, hustling, industrious, intrepid, itching, keen, lively, lusting, peppy, progressive, pushing, ready, self-starting, snappy, spanking, spark plug*, spirited, stirring, take-over, up-and-coming*, venturesome, vigorous,

yearning, zealous, zippy*; SEE CONCEPTS *326,404, 542*

entertain [*v1*] *amuse*
absorb, beguile, captivate, charm, cheer, comfort, crack up*, delight, distract, divert, ecstasize, elate, engross, enliven, enthrall, gladden, grab, gratify, humor, indulge, inspire, inspirit, interest, knock dead*, make merry, occupy, pique, please, recreate, regale, relax, satisfy, slay, solace, stimulate, tickle; SEE CONCEPTS *9,292*

entertain [*v2*] *accommodate visitors*
admit, be host, board, chaperone, dine, do the honors*, feed, foster, give a party, harbor, have a do*, have a get-together*, have company, have guests, have visitors, house, invite, lodge, nourish, pick up the check*, pop for*, put up*, quarter, receive, recreate, regale, room, show hospitality, spring for*, throw a party*, treat, welcome, wine*, wine and dine*; SEE CONCEPTS *377,384*

entertain [*v3*] *think about seriously*
cherish, cogitate on, conceive, consider, contemplate, deliberate, foster, harbor, heed, hold, imagine, keep in mind, maintain, muse over, ponder, recognize, support, think over; SEE CONCEPT *17*

entertaining [*adj*] *amusing, pleasing*
absorbing, affecting, be a ball*, captivating, charming, cheerful, cheering, clever, compelling, delightful, diverting, droll, enchanting, engaging, engrossing, enjoyable, enthralling, enticing, entrancing, exciting, fascinating, fun, funny, gas*, gay, humorous, impressive, inspiring, interesting, lively, moving, piquant, pleasant, pleasurable, poignant, priceless, provocative, recreative, relaxing, restorative, riot, rousing, scream, side-splitting, stimulating, stirring, striking, thrilling, witty; SEE CONCEPTS *529,537*

entertainment [*n*] *amusement, pleasure*
ball*, bash*, big time*, blast*, blow out*, celebration, cheer, clambake*, delight, dissipation, distraction, diversion, divertissement, enjoyment, feast, frolic, fun, fun and games*, gaiety, game, good time*, grins*, high time*, laughs*, leisure activity, lots of laughs*, merriment, merrymaking, party, pastime, picnic, play, recreation, regalement, relaxation, relief, revelry, satisfaction, shindig*, sport, spree, surprise, treat, wingding*; SEE CONCEPTS *383,384,386,388*

enthrall [*v*] *captivate*
absorb, beguile, bewitch, charm, enchant, engage, enrapture, enslave, entrance, fascinate, grab, grip, hold spellbound, hook, hypnotize, intrigue, master, mesmerize, preoccupy, rivet, spellbind, subdue, subject, subjugate; SEE CONCEPTS *7,19,22*

enthusiasm [*n*] *keen interest, excitement*
activity, ardency, ardor, avidity, conviction, craze, dash, devotion, eagerness, earnestness, ecstasy, elan, emotion, energy, exhilaration, fad, fanaticism, feeling, fervor, fever, fieriness, fire, flame, flare, frenzy, fury, gaiety, glow, go*, heat, hilarity, hobby, impetuosity, intensity, interest, joy, joyfulness, keenness, life, mania, mirth, nerve, oomph*, orgasm, passion, pep, rapture, red heat*, relish, snap, spirit, transport, vehemence, verve, vim, vivacity, warmth, zeal, zealousness, zest; SEE CONCEPTS *633,657*

enthusiast [*n*] *person active in interest*
addict, admirer, aficionado, believer, buff, bug*, bum*, devotee, eccentric, fan, fanatic, follower, freak, gate, habitué, lover, maniac, monomaniac, nut*, optimist, participant, partisan, rooter, supporter, votary, worshiper, zealot; SEE CONCEPT *423*

enthusiastic [*adj*] *interested, excited*
agog, animated, anxious, ardent, athirst, attracted, avid, bugged*, concerned, crazy about*, devoted, dying to*, eager, earnest, ebullient, exhilarated, exuberant, fanatical, fascinated, fervent, fervid, forceful, gaga*, gone on*, gung ho*, hearty, intent, keen, keyed up*, lively, nutty*, obsessed, passionate, pleased, rabid, red-hot*, rhapsodic, spirited, tantalized, thrilled, titillated, unqualified, vehement, vigorous, wacky*, warm, wholehearted, willing, zealous; SEE CONCEPTS *401,542*

entice [*v*] *allure; persuade*
attract, bait, bat eyes at*, beguile, cajole, coax, decoy, draw, entrap, inveigle, lead on, lure, prevail on, seduce, tempt, toll, turn on*, wheedle; SEE CONCEPTS *7,19,22,68*

enticement [*n*] *allurement; persuasion*
attraction, bait, blandishment, cajolery, coaxing, come hither*, come-on*, decoy, fascination, inducement, inveiglement, lure, mousetrap*, promise, seduction, snare, sweetener*, sweetening, temptation, trap; SEE CONCEPTS *7,19,22,68*

entire [*adj*] *complete, whole*
absolute, all, choate, consolidated, continuous, full, gross, intact, integral, integrated, outright, perfect, plenary, sound, thorough, total, unbroken, undamaged, undiminished, undivided, unified, unimpaired, uninjured, unmarked, unmarred, unmitigated, unreserved, unrestricted, untouched; SEE CONCEPTS *482,531*

entirely [*adv*] *completely*
absolutely, alone, altogether, exclusively, fully, in every respect, only, perfectly, plumb, quite, reservedly, solely, thoroughly, totally, undividedly, uniquely, utterly, well, wholly, without exception, without reservation; SEE CONCEPTS *531,535*

entirety [*n*] *wholeness, whole*
absoluteness, aggregate, all, allness, collectiveness, collectivity, completeness, complex, comprehensiveness, ensemble, entireness, everything, fullness, gross, intactness, integrality, integrity, omneity, omnitude, oneness, perfection, plenitude, sum, sum total, the works*, total, totality, undividedness, unity, universality, whole ball of wax*, whole bit*, whole enchilada*, whole nine yards*; SEE CONCEPTS *635,837*

entitle [v1] *name, label*
baptize, call, characterize, christen, denominate, designate, dub, nickname, style, subtitle, term, title; SEE CONCEPT *62*

entitle [v2] *hold right to*
accredit, allow, authorize, be in line for*, confer a right, empower, enable, enfranchise, fit for, have coming*, let, license, make eligible, permit, qualify for, rate, warrant; SEE CONCEPTS *50,83,88,129*

entity [n1] *object that exists*
article, being, body, creature, existence, individual, item, material, matter, organism, presence, quantity, single, singleton, something, stuff, subsistence, substance, thing; SEE CONCEPT *433*

entity [n2] *nature of a being*
actuality, essence, existence, integral, integrate, quiddity, quintessence, reality, subsistence, substance, sum, system, totality; SEE CONCEPTS *411,644*

entourage [n] *followers*
associates, attendants, companions, company, cortege, court, courtiers, escort, following, groupies*, hangers-on*, retainers, retinue, staff, suite, sycophants, toadies*, train; SEE CONCEPTS *387,417*

entrance [n1] *a way into a place*
access, approach, archway, avenue, corridor, door, doorway, entry, entryway, gate, gateway, hall, hallway, ingress, inlet, lobby, opening, passage, passageway, path, porch, port, portal, portico, staircase, threshold, vestibule, way; SEE CONCEPT *440*

entrance [n2] *coming into a place; introduction*
access, accession, adit, admission, admittance, appearance, approach, arrival, baptism, beginning, commencement, debut, enlistment, enrollment, entree, entry, immigration, import, importation, inception, incoming, ingoing, ingress, ingression, initiation, invasion, outset, passage, penetration, progress, start, trespass; SEE CONCEPTS *119,159*

entrance [v] *captivate, hypnotize*
anesthetize, attract, bewitch, charm, delight, enchant, enrapture, enthrall, fascinate, gladden, mesmerize, please, put in a trance, ravish, rejoice, spellbind, transport; SEE CONCEPTS *7,14,22*

entrant [n] *person entering competition, starting new activity*
aspirant, beginner, candidate, competitor, contestant, convert, entry, incomer, initiate, neophyte, newcomer, new member, novice, participant, petitioner, player, probationer, rival, solicitor, suitor, tenderfoot*; SEE CONCEPTS *366,423*

entrap [v] *capture, involve*
allure, bag*, beguile, benet, box in*, catch, decoy, embroil, enmesh, ensnare, entangle, entice, hook, implicate, inveigle, lay for*, lead on, lure, net, reel in*, rope in*, seduce, set up, snare, suck in*, tempt, trap, trick; SEE CONCEPTS *59,90,112*

entreat [v] *plead with*
appeal to, ask, beg, beseech, blandish, coax, conjure, crave, enjoin, exhort, implore, importune, in-

voke, pester, petition, plague, pray, press, request, supplicate, urge, wheedle; SEE CONCEPTS *48,53*

entreaty [n] *plea*
appeal, application, imploration, imprecation, petition, prayer, request, suit, supplication; SEE CONCEPTS *318,662*

entree [n] *admittance*
access, adit, admission, connection, contact, debut, door, entrance, entry, importation, in, incoming, induction, ingress, introduction, open arms*, open door*, way; SEE CONCEPTS *388,685*

entrench [v1] *establish, make inroads*
anchor, confirm, define, dig in, embed, ensconce, fence, fix, fortify, found, ground, hole up, implant, infix, ingrain, install, lodge, plant, protect, root, seat, set, settle, strengthen; SEE CONCEPTS *518,710*

entrench [v2] *trespass*
break in on, encroach, impinge, infringe, interfere, interlope, intervene, intrude, invade, make inroads*, stick nose into*; SEE CONCEPT *192*

entrepreneur [n] *person who starts a business alone*
administrator, backer, businessman, contractor, executive, founder, impressario, industrialist, manager, organizer, producer, promoter, undertaker; SEE CONCEPT *347*

entrust [v] *give custody, authority to*
allocate, allot, assign, authorize, bank, bend an ear*, charge, commend, commit, confer, confide, consign, count, delegate, deliver, depend, deposit with, hand over, impose, invest, leave with, reckon, relegate, rely, trust, turn over; SEE CONCEPTS *50,88,108*

entry [n1] *way in to a place*
access, adit, approach, avenue, door, doorway, entrance, foyer, gate, hall, ingress, ingression, inlet, lobby, opening, passage, passageway, portal, threshold, vestibule; SEE CONCEPT *440*

entry [n2] *introduction; permission to enter*
access, adit, admission, admittance, appearance, coming in, entering, entrance, entree, free passage*, ingress, initiation, introgression, way; SEE CONCEPTS *388,685*

entry [n3] *person participating in competition; effort*
attempt, candidate, competitor, contestant, entrant, participant, player, submission; SEE CONCEPT *366*

entry [n4] *listing in a record*
account, item, jotting, memo, memorandum, minute, note, registration; SEE CONCEPT *270*

entwine [v] *twist around*
braid, coil, corkscrew, curl, embrace, encircle, enmesh, entangle, interlace, interplait, intertwine, interweave, knit, lace, plait, spiral, surround, twine, weave, wind, wreathe; SEE CONCEPTS *147,201,754*

enumerate [v] *list, count*
add up, calculate, cite, compute, count noses*, detail, figure, identify, inventory, itemize, keep tabs*, mention, name, number, particularize, quote, recapitulate, recite, reckon, recount, rehearse, relate, run down, run off*, specialize, specify, spell out, sum,

take account of, tally, tell, tick off*, total; SEE CON-
CEPTS *57,125,764*

enunciate [v] *speak clearly*
affirm, announce, articulate, declare, deliver, develop, enounce, express, intone, lay down, modulate,
outline, phonate, postulate, proclaim, promulgate,
pronounce, propound, publish, say, show, sound,
state, submit, utter, vocalize, voice; SEE CONCEPTS
47,51

envelop [v] *encase, hide*
blanket, cage, cloak, conceal, contain, coop, corral,
cover, drape, embrace, encircle, enclose, encompass, enfold, engulf, enshroud, enwrap, fence, gird,
girdle, guard, hem, hide, immure, invest, obscure,
overlay, overspread, pen, protect, roll, sheathe,
shield, shroud, shut in, superimpose, surround,
swaddle, swathe, veil, wrap, wrap up; SEE CONCEPTS
172,188

envelope [n] *wrapper*
bag, box, case, casing, cloak, coat, coating, container, cover, covering, enclosure, hide, jacket,
pocket, pouch, receptacle, sheath, shell, skin, vesicle, wrapping; SEE CONCEPT *494*

enviable [adj] *desired, blessed*
advantageous, covetable, desirable, excellent, favored, fortunate, good, lucky, privileged, superior,
welcome; SEE CONCEPT *574*

envious [adj] *jealous, resentful*
appetent, aspiring, begrudging, coveting, covetous,
craving, desiring, desirous, distrustful, fain, grasping, greedy, green-eyed*, green with envy*, grudging, hankering, invidious, jaundiced, longing for,
malicious, spiteful, suspicious, umbrageous, watchful, wishful, yearning; SEE CONCEPTS *401,403*

environment [n] *surroundings, atmosphere*
ambiance, aura, backdrop, background, circumstances, climate, conditions, context, domain, element, encompassment, entourage, habitat, hood*,
jungle*, locale, medium, milieu, neck of the
woods*, neighborhood, purlieus, scene, scenery, setting, situation, status, stomping ground*, surroundings, terrain, territory, turf, zoo*; SEE CONCEPTS
515,673,696

environs [n] *neighborhood*
bound, boundary, compass, confine, district, fring-
es*, limits, locality, outskirts, precinct, purlieus, suburb, surroundings, territory, turf, vicinity; SEE
CONCEPT *516*

envisage/envision [v] *picture in one's mind*
anticipate, behold, conceive, conceptualize, contemplate, externalize, fancy, feature, foresee, form mental picture of*, grasp, have a picture of*, image,
imagine, look upon, materialize, objectify, predict,
realize, regard, see, survey, think up, view, view in
mind's eye*, vision, visualize; SEE CONCEPTS *17,43*

envoy [n] *deputy*
agent, ambassador, attaché, bearer, carrier, chargé
d'affaires, consul, courier, delegate, diplomat, em-

issary, intermediary, internuncio, legate, medium,
messenger, minister, nuncio, plenipotentiary, representative, vicar; SEE CONCEPTS *348,354*

envy [n] *jealousy*
backbiting, bad sportsmanship*, coveting, covetousness, enviousness, evil eye*, green-eyed monster*,
grudge, grudging, grudgingness, hatred, heartburn,
ill will, invidiousness, jaundiced eye*, lusting, malevolence, malice, maliciousness, malignity, opposition, prejudice, resentfulness, resentment, rivalry,
spite; SEE CONCEPT *410*

envy [v] *be jealous of another*
be envious, begrudge, covet, crave, desire, die
over*, eat one's heart out*, grudge, hanker, have
hard feelings*, hunger, long, lust, object to, resent,
thirst, turn green*, want, yearn; SEE CONCEPTS *10,20*

ephemeral [adj] *momentary, passing*
brief, episodic, evanescent, fleeting, flitting, fugacious, fugitive, impermanent, short, short-lived, temporary, transient, transitory, unenduring, volatile;
SEE CONCEPTS *798,801*

epic [n] *long story*
heroic poem, legend, narrative, saga, tale; SEE CON-
CEPT *282*

epicurean [n] *gourmet*
bon vivant, connoisseur, critic, epicure, gastronome,
gastronomer, glutton, gourmand, hedonist, pleasure
seeker, sensualist, specialist, sybarite; SEE CONCEPT
423

epicurean [adj] *loving food and finer things*
gluttonous, gourmandizing, gourmet, hedonistic, libertine, lush, luxurious, pleasure-seeking, self-
indulgent, sensual, sensuous, sybaritic, voluptuous;
SEE CONCEPT *401*

epidemic [n] *widespread disease*
contagion, endemic, growth, outbreak, pest, pestilence, plague, rash, scourge, spread, upsurge, wave,
what's going around*; SEE CONCEPTS *306,316*

epidemic [adj] *widespread*
catching, communicable, contagious, endemic, general, infectious, pandemic, prevailing, prevalent,
rampant, rife, sweeping, wide-ranging; SEE CON-
CEPTS *314,537*

epigram [n] *witticism*
aphorism, bon mot, joke, motto, pithy saying, quip,
quirk; SEE CONCEPT *278*

epilogue [n] *afterword*
coda, concluding speech, conclusion, ending, finale,
follow-up, peroration, postlude, postscript, sequel,
summation, swan song*; SEE CONCEPTS *264,270,278*

episode [n] *adventure; scene*
affair, business, chapter, circumstance, doings,
event, experience, goings-on*, happening, incident,
installment, interlude, matter, occasion, occurrence,
part, passage, section, thing*, what's going down*;
SEE CONCEPTS *3,4*

episodic [adj] *intermittent; composed of several tales*
anecdotal, digressive, disconnected, discursive, disjointed, incidental, irregular, occasional, picaresque,

rambling, roundabout, segmented, soap opera*, sporadic, wandering; SEE CONCEPT *482*

epistle [*n*] *letter*

billet doux*, cannonball*, card, communication, Dear John*, dispatch, FYI*, get-well, invite, kite*, line*, love letter, memo, message, missive, note, poison pen*, postcard, scratch*, tab*, thank-you; SEE CONCEPT *271*

epitaph [*n*] *inscription on a gravestone*

commemoration, elegy, epigraph, eulogy, hic jacet, legend, memorial, monument, remembrance, requiscat in pacem, sentiment; SEE CONCEPT *278*

epithet [*n*] *nickname*

appellation, description, designation, name, sobriquet, tag, title; SEE CONCEPT *683*

epitome [*n1*] *perfect example*

apotheosis, archetype, embodiment, essence, exemplar, exemplification, illustration, last word*, personification, quintessence, representation, type, typification, ultimate; SEE CONCEPT *688*

epitome [*n2*] *abbreviation*

abridgment, abstract, brief, compendium, condensation, conspectus, contraction, digest, precis, recapitulation, résumé, summary, summation, syllabus, synopsis; SEE CONCEPT *283*

equable [*adj*] *steady, calm*

agreeable, composed, consistent, constant, easygoing, even, even-tempered, imperturbable, levelheaded, methodical, orderly, placid, regular, serene, smooth, stabile, stable, systematic, temperate, tranquil, unchanging, unexcitable, unflappable, unfluctuating, uniform, unruffled, unvarying; SEE CONCEPTS *401,542,544*

equal [*n*] *peer*

alter ego, brother, coequal, companion, compeer, competitor, complement, copy, counterpart, double, duplicate, equivalent, fellow, like, likeness, match, mate, parallel, rival, sister, twin; SEE CONCEPT *423*

equal [*adj1*] *alike*

according, balanced, break even, commensurate, comparable, coordinate, correspondent, corresponding, double, duplicate, egalitarian, equivalent, evenly matched, fifty-fifty*, homologous, identic, identical, indistinguishable, invariable, level, look-alike, matched, matching, one and the same, parallel, proportionate, same, same difference*, spit and image*, stack up with*, tantamount, to the same degree, two peas in pod*, uniform, unvarying; SEE CONCEPTS *487,566,573*

equal [*adj2*] *fair, unbiased*

dispassionate, egalitarian, equable, even-handed, impartial, just, nondiscriminatory, nonpartisan, objective, uncolored, unprejudiced, without distinction; SEE CONCEPTS *401,542*

equal [*v*] *make even, be even with*

agree, amount to, approach, balance, be commensurate, be identical, be level, be tantamount, break even, come up to, compare, comprise, consist of, coordinate, correspond, emulate, equalize, equate, equipoise, equiponderate, keep pace with*, level, live up to*, match, measure up, meet, parallel, partake of, rank with, reach, rise to, rival, run abreast, square with, tally, tie, touch; SEE CONCEPT *667*

equality [*n*] *similarity, balance; egalitarianism*

adequation, brotherhood, civil rights, commensurateness, coordination, correspondence, equal opportunity, equatability, equilibrium, equipoise, equivalence, evenness, fairness, fair play*, fair practice, fair shake*, fellowship, homology, identity, impartiality, isonomy, likeness, par, parallelism, parity, sameness, sisterhood, tolerance, uniformity; SEE CONCEPTS *388,645,667*

equalize [*v*] *make the same; balance*

adjust, commeasure, communize, compare, coordinate, democratize, emulate, equal, equate, establish, even, even up, handicap, level, match, parallel, regularize, rival, smooth, socialize, square, standardize, trim; SEE CONCEPTS *126,232*

equanimity [*n*] *levelheadedness*

aplomb, assurance, ataraxia, ataraxy, calm, calmness, composure, confidence, cool, coolness, detachment, equability, imperturbability, patience, peace, phlegm, placidity, poise, presence of mind*, sangfroid, self-possession, serenity, steadiness, tranquillity; SEE CONCEPTS *410,633*

equate [*v*] *balance; think of together*

agree, assimilate, associate, average, be commensurate, compare, consider, correspond to, correspond with, equalize, even, hold, level, liken, make equal, match, offset, pair, paragon, parallel, regard, relate, represent, similize, square, tally, treat; SEE CONCEPTS *37,39,667*

equilibrium [*n*] *balance; evenness*

calm, calmness, composure, cool, coolness, counterbalance, counterpoise, equanimity, equipoise, poise, polish, rest, serenity, stability, stasis, steadiness, steadying, symmetry; SEE CONCEPTS *633,731*

equip [*v*] *make ready with supplies*

accouter, adorn, appoint, arm, array, attire, deck, deck out*, decorate, dress, endow, feather nest*, fit out, fix up, furnish, gear, gear up*, heel*, implement, line nest*, man, outfit, prep*, prepare, provide, qualify, ready, rig, set up, stake, stock, supply, turn out; SEE CONCEPTS *140,182*

equipment [*n*] *supplies, gear for activity*

accessories, accompaniments, accouterments, apparatus, appliances, appurtenances, articles, attachments, baggage, belongings, contraptions, contrivances, devices, equipage, facilities, fittings, fixtures, furnishings, furniture, gadgets, habiliments, impedimenta, kit and kaboodle*, machinery, material, materiel, miscellaneous, outfit, paraphernalia, provisioning, provisions, rig*, setup, shebang*, stock, store, stuff, supply, tackle, things, tools, trappings, traps, utensils; SEE CONCEPTS *364,446,496*

equitable [*adj*] *impartial*
candid, cricket, decent, disinterested, dispassionate, due, ethical, even-handed, even-steven*, fair, fair and square*, fair shake*, fair-to-middling*, honest, impersonal, just, level, moral, nondiscriminatory, nonpartisan, objective, proper, proportionate, reasonable, right, rightful, square, square deal*, stable, unbiased, uncolored, unprejudiced; SEE CONCEPTS *542,545*

equity [*n1*] *impartiality*
disinterestedness, equitableness, even-handedness, fair-mindedness, fairness, fair play, honesty, integrity, justice, justness, nonpartisanship, piece, reasonableness, rectitude, righteousness, square deal*, uprightness; SEE CONCEPTS *645,657*

equity [*n2*] *money invested in possession*
capital, investment, outlay; SEE CONCEPTS *332,344*

equivalence [*n*] *sameness, similarity*
adequation, agreement, alikeness, compatibility, conformity, correlation, correspondence, equality, evenness, exchangeability, identity, interchangeability, interchangeableness, likeness, match, par, parallel, parity, synonym, synonymy; SEE CONCEPTS *667,670*

equivalent [*n*] *equal, counterpart*
carbon copy*, correspondent, dead ringer*, ditto, like, match, obverse, opposite, parallel, peer, reciprocal, same difference*, spitting image*, substitute, twin; SEE CONCEPTS *667,670*

equivalent [*adj*] *same, similar*
agnate, akin, alike, analogous, carbon*, commensurate, comparable, convertible, copy, correlative, correspondent, corresponding, ditto*, duplicate, equal, even, homologous, identical, indistinguishable, interchangeable, like, of a kind, parallel, proportionate, reciprocal, same difference*, substitute, synonymous, tantamount; SEE CONCEPTS *487,566, 573*

equivocal [*adj*] *doubtful, uncertain*
ambiguous, ambivalent, amphibological, borderline, clear as mud*, clouded*, disreputable, dubious, evasive, fishy*, fuzzy*, hazy*, indefinite, indeterminate, indistinct, misleading, muddled, muzzy*, oblique, obscure, open, problematic, puzzling, questionable, suspect, suspicious, tenebrous, unclear, undecided, unexplicit, unintelligible, vague, with mixed feelings*; SEE CONCEPTS *529,535*

equivocate [*v*] *avoid an issue*
beat around the bush*, beg the question*, blow hot and cold*, cavil, cloud the issue*, con, cop a plea*, cop out*, cover up*, dodge, double-talk, elude, escape, eschew, evade, falsify, fence, fib, flip-flop*, fudge*, give run around*, hedge, hem and haw*, jive*, lie, mince words, palter, parry, pass the buck*, prevaricate, pussyfoot, quibble, run around, shuck, shuffle, sidestep, sit on the fence*, stonewall*, tell white lie*, tergiversate, tergiverse, waffle*, weasel*; SEE CONCEPTS *63,102*

equivocation [*n*] *avoidance of an issue*
ambiguity, amphibology, casuistry, coloring, con, cop out, cover, cover-up, deceit, deception, deceptiveness, delusion, dissimulation, distortion, double entendre, double meaning, double talk, doubtfulness, duplicity, equivocality, evasion, fallacy, fib, fibbing, hedging, lie, line*, lying, misrepresentation, prevarication, quibbling, routine, run-around, shuffling, song*, song and dance*, sophistry, speciousness, spuriousness, stall, stonewall*, tergiversation, waffle*; SEE CONCEPTS *63,278*

era [*n*] *time period in history*
aeon, age, cycle, date, day, days, eon, epoch, generation, stage, term, time; SEE CONCEPTS *807,816*

eradicate [*v*] *destroy; remove*
abate, abolish, annihilate, blot out*, demolish, deracinate, do away with, efface, eliminate, erase, expunge, exterminate, extinguish, extirpate, liquidate, mow down*, obliterate, off*, purge, raze, root out*, rub out*, scratch*, scrub, shoot down, squash, stamp out*, take out*, torpedo*, total, trash, unroot, uproot, wash out, waste, weed out*, wipe out*; SEE CONCEPTS *211,252*

erase [*v*] *remove; rub out*
abolish, annul, black out, blank, blot, blue pencil*, cancel, cross out, cut, cut out, delete, disannul, dispatch, efface, eliminate, excise, expunge, extirpate, gut, kill, launder*, negate, nullify, obliterate, remove, rub out*, scratch out*, stamp out*, strike, strike out, take out, trim, wipe out*, withdraw, X-out*; SEE CONCEPTS *211,215*

erect [*adj*] *straight up*
arrect, cocked, elevated, erectile, firm, perpendicular, raised, rigid, standing, stiff, straight, upright, upstanding, vertical; SEE CONCEPTS *485,581,604*

erect [*v*] *build; establish*
assemble, bring about, cobble up*, cock, compose, construct, create, effect, elevate, fabricate, fashion, fit together, forge, form, found, frame, fudge together*, heighten, hoist, initiate, institute, join, knock together*, lift, make, make up, manufacture, mount, organize, pitch, plant, prefab*, produce, put together, put up, raise, rear, run up, set up, shape, stand, stand up, throw together*, throw up, upraise, uprear; SEE CONCEPTS *168,221*

ergo [*adv*] *for that reason*
accordingly, consequently, hence, in consequence, so, then, therefore, thereupon, thus, thusly; SEE CONCEPT *544*

erode [*v*] *deteriorate; wear away*
abrade, bite, consume, corrode, crumble, destroy, disintegrate, eat, gnaw, grind down, scour, spoil, waste, wear down; SEE CONCEPTS *252,469*

erosion [*n*] *deterioration; wearing away*
abrasion, attrition, consumption, corrasion, corrosion, decrease, desedimentation, despoliation, destruction, disintegration, eating away, grinding

down, spoiling, washing away, wear, wearing down; SEE CONCEPTS 252,257,698

erotic [adj] *sexy*
amative, amatory, amorous, aphrodisiac, bawdy, blue*, carnal, concupiscent, earthy, erogenous, fervid, filthy, fleshly, hot*, impassioned, kinky*, lascivious, lecherous, lewd, obscene, off-color*, prurient, purple*, raunchy, raw, romantic, rousing, salacious, seductive, sensual, sexual, spicy, steamy, stimulating, suggestive, titillating, venereal, voluptuous; SEE CONCEPTS 372,545

err [v] *make a mistake; do wrong*
be inaccurate, be incorrect, be in error, be mistaken, blow*, blunder, bollix*, boo-boo*, deviate, drop the ball*, fall, flub*, foul up*, go astray, goof*, go wrong, lapse, louse up*, make a mess of*, mess up*, misapprehend, misbehave, miscalculate, misjudge, mistake, muff*, offend, screw up*, sin, slip up*, snafu*, snarl up, stray, stumble, transgress, trespass, wander; SEE CONCEPT 101

errand [n] *task*
assignment, charge, commission, duty, job, message, mission; SEE CONCEPT 362

errant [adj] *wrong; deviant*
aberrant, deviating, devious, drifting, errable, erratic, erring, fallible, heretic, meandering, misbehaving, mischievous, miscreant, naughty, offending, off straight and narrow*, rambling, ranging, roaming, roving, shifting, sinning, stray, straying, unorthodox, unreliable, wandering, wayward; SEE CONCEPTS 542,545,581

erratic [adj] *unpredictable; wandering*
aberrant, abnormal, anomalous, arbitrary, bizarre, capricious, changeable, desultory, devious, dicey, directionless, dubious, eccentric, fitful, flaky*, fluctuant, idiosyncratic, iffy*, incalculable, inconsistent, inconstant, irregular, meandering, mercurial, nomadic, oddball*, peculiar, planetary, rambling, roving, shifting, spasmodic, strange, stray, uncertain, undirected, unnatural, unreliable, unstable, unusual, vagarious, variable, volatile, wayward, weird, whimsical; SEE CONCEPTS 535,542,581

erroneous [adj] *wrong, incorrect*
all off*, all wet*, all wrong, amiss, askew, awry, defective, fallacious, false, faulty, flawed, inaccurate, inexact, invalid, misguided, mistaken, off, specious, spurious, unfounded, unsound, untrue, way off, wrong number*; SEE CONCEPTS 267,570,582

error [n] *mistake; wrong*
absurdity, bad job*, blunder, boner*, boo-boo*, delinquency, delusion, deviation, erratum, failure, fall, fallacy, falsehood, falsity, fault, faux pas, flaw, glitch, goof*, howler*, inaccuracy, lapse, misapprehension, misbelief, miscalculation, misconception, miscue, misdeed, misjudgment, mismanagement, miss, misstep, misunderstanding, offense, omission, oversight, screamer*, screw-up*, sin, slight, slip, slipup, solecism, stumble, transgression, trespass,

untruth, wrongdoing, X*; SEE CONCEPTS 101, 230,674,699

ersatz [adj] *artificial*
bogus, copied, counterfeit, fake, false, imitation, manufactured, phony, pretended, sham, simulated, spurious, substitute, synthetic; SEE CONCEPT 582

erstwhile [adj] *former*
bygone, ex, late, old, once, one-time, past, preceding, previous, quondam, recent, sometime; SEE CONCEPT 820

erudite [adj] *well-educated, cultured*
brainy, cultivated, educated, highbrow, in the know, into*, knowledgeable, learned, lettered, literate, savvy, scholarly, scholastic, studious, well-read, wised to, wise up; SEE CONCEPT 402

erudition [n] *higher education*
bookishness, brains, cultivation, culture, enlightenment, intellectuality, knowledge, learnedness, learning, letters, literacy, lore, pedantry, refinement, savvy, scholarliness, scholarship, science, studiousness; SEE CONCEPTS 287,409

erupt [v] *give forth, eject with force*
appear, belch, blow up, boil, break out, burst, cast out, detonate, discharge, emit, eruct, explode, extravasate, flare up*, go off*, gush, hurl, jet, pour forth, rupture, spew, spit, spout, spurt, throw off*, touch off*, vent, vomit; SEE CONCEPTS 179,222

eruption [n] *ejection*
access, blast, blow-up, breakout, burst, discharge, explosion, flare-up, flow, gust, outbreak, outburst, sally, venting, vomiting; SEE CONCEPTS 179,467

escalate [v] *increase, be increased*
amplify, ascend, broaden, climb, enlarge, expand, extend, grow, heighten, intensify, magnify, make worse, mount, raise, rise, scale, step up, widen; SEE CONCEPTS 236,245

escapade [n] *adventure, usually lighthearted*
antic, caper, fling, folly, frolic, gag, high jinks, lark, mischief, monkeyshines*, prank, rib*, roguery, rollick, romp, scrape, shenanigans*, spree, stunt, trick, vagary; SEE CONCEPTS 384,386

escape [n] *breaking away; getaway*
abdication, avoidance, AWOL*, beat, bolt, break, breakout, bypassing, circumvention, decampment, deliverance, departure, desertion, disappearance, dodging, ducking, elopement, elusion, elusivensss, eschewal, evasion, evasiveness, extrication, fadeout, flight, freedom, hegira, lam, leave, liberation, out, outbreak, powder, release, rescue, retreat, runaround, shunning, sidestepping, slip, spring, withdrawal; SEE CONCEPT 102

escape [v] *break away from*
abscond, avoid, bail out*, bolt, break, break free, break loose, break out, burst out, circumvent, cut and run*, cut loose*, decamp, depart, desert, disappear, dodge, double, duck, duck out*, elope, elude, emerge, evade, flee, fly, fly the coop*, gafiate, get away with*, get off*, go scot-free*, leave, make

getaway*, make off*, make oneself scarce*, pass, play hooky*, run, run away, run off*, run out on*, shun, skip, slip, slip away, steal away, take a powder*, take flight, take on the lam*, vanish, work out of, wriggle out*; SEE CONCEPT *102*

eschew [v] *have nothing to do with*
abandon, abjure, abstain, avoid, double, duck, elude, evade, forgo, forswear, give up, have no truck with*, let well enough alone*, not touch, refrain, renounce, sacrifice, shun, shy, shy away from, steer clear of*, swear off*; SEE CONCEPTS *30,102*

escort [n] *protection; accompaniment*
alarm clock*, attendant, beau, bird dog*, bodyguard, boyfriend, cavalier, chaperon, companion, company, consort, convoy, convoyer, cortege, date, entourage, fellow, gallant, gigolo*, guard, guide, henchman/woman*, partner, protector, retinue, safeguard, squire, train, warden*; SEE CONCEPTS *419,423*

escort [v] *act as a companion, guard*
accompany, attend, bear, bring, carry, chaperon, company, conduct, consort with, convoy, date, direct, drag, go with, guide, lead, partner, pilot, protect, route, see, shepherd, show, squire, steer, take out, usher; SEE CONCEPTS *114,384,714*

esoteric [adj] *mysterious, obscure*
abstruse, acroamatic, arcane, cabbalistic, cryptic, deep, Delphic, heavy, hermetic, hidden, inner, inscrutable, mystic, mystical, occult, Orphic, private, profound, recondite, secret, Sibylline; SEE CONCEPTS *529,576,582*

especial [adj] *exceptional, particular*
chief, distinguished, dominant, exclusive, express, extraordinary, individual, marked, notable, noteworthy, outstanding, paramount, peculiar, personal, predominant, preeminent, preponderant, principal, private, set, signal, singular, special, specific, supreme, surpassing, uncommon, unique, unusual; SEE CONCEPTS *535,564,574*

especially [adv] *exceptionally, particularly*
abnormally, above all, before all else, chiefly, conspicuously, curiously, eminently, exclusively, expressly, extraordinarily, in particular, in specie, mainly, markedly, notably, oddly, outstandingly, peculiarly, preeminently, primarily, principally, remarkably, signally, singularly, specially, specifically, strangely, strikingly, supremely, unaccountably, uncommonly, uncustomarily, uniquely, unusually, wonderfully; SEE CONCEPTS *535,564,574*

espouse [v1] *stand up for; support*
accept, adopt, advocate, approve, back, champion, defend, embrace, get into*, go in for*, maintain, stand behind*, take on, take up, uphold; SEE CONCEPT *10*

espouse [v2] *marry*
betroth, catch, take as spouse, unite, wed; SEE CONCEPT *297*

essay [n1] *written discourse*
article, composition, discourse, discussion, disquisition, dissertation, explication, exposition, manu-

script, paper, piece, study, theme, thesis, tract, treatise; SEE CONCEPT *271*

essay [n2] *try, attempt*
aim, bid, dry run*, effort, endeavor, exertion, experiment, hassle, labor, one's all*, one's level best*, shot*, striving, struggle, test, toil, travail, trial, try, try on*, tryout, undertaking, venture, whack*, work; SEE CONCEPT *87*

essay [v] *try, attempt*
aim, assay, endeavor, have a crack*, have a go*, have a shot*, have at it*, labor, make a run at*, offer, put to the test*, seek, strive, struggle, take a stab at*, take a whack at*, take on, test, toil, travail, try out, undertake, venture, work; SEE CONCEPT *87*

essence [n1] *heart, significance*
aspect, attribute, backbone, base, basis, be-all and end-all*, being, bottom, bottom line*, burden, caliber, character, chief constituent, constitution, core, crux, element, entity, essentia, essentiality, fiber, form, fundamentals, germ, grain, kernel, life, lifeblood, main idea, marrow, meaning, meat*, name of game*, nature, nitty-gritty*, nub, nucleus, pith, point, principle, property, quality, quiddity, quintessence, reality, root, soul, spirit, structure, stuff, substance, timber, vein, virtuality; SEE CONCEPTS *411,661,668,687*

essence [n2] *distillate, concentrate*
balm, cologne, distillation, drug, effusion, elixir, extract, fragrance, juice, liquor, perfume, potion, scent, spirits, tincture; SEE CONCEPTS *260,467*

essential [n] *necessity, basic*
ABCs*, bottom line*, brass tacks*, condition, element, essence, fire and ice*, fundamental, groceries*, guts*, heart, meat and potatoes*, must, name of the game*, nitty-gritty*, nuts and bolts*, part and parcel*, precondition, prerequisite, principle, quintessence, requirement, requisite, rudiment, sine qua non, stuff, substance, vital part, where one's at*; SEE CONCEPTS *646,661,826*

essential [adj1] *important, vital*
capital, cardinal, chief, constitutive, crucial, foremost, fundamental, imperative, indispensable, leading, main, necessary, necessitous, needed, needful, prerequisite, principal, required, requisite, righthand, wanted; SEE CONCEPT *567*

essential [adj2] *basic, fundamental*
absolute, basal, cardinal, cold, complete, congenital, connate, constitutional, deep-seated, elemental, elementary, ideal, inborn, inbred, inherent, innate, intrinsic, key, main, material, meat and potatoes*, name of the game*, nitty-gritty*, nub, perfect, primary, prime, primitive, principal, quintessential, substratal, underlying; SEE CONCEPTS *546,549*

establish [v1] *set up, organize*
authorize, base, build, constitute, create, decree, domiciliate, enact, endow, ensconce, entrench, erect, father, fix, form, found, ground, implant, inaugurate, inculcate, install, institute, land, lay founda-

tion, live, lodge, moor, mother, originate, place, plant, practice, provide, put, ring in, rivet, root, secure, set down, settle, stabilize, start, start ball rolling*, station, stick; SEE CONCEPTS *168,173,221,251*

establish [v2] *authenticate; demonstrate*
ascertain, authorize, base, certify, circumstantiate, confirm, constitute, corroborate, decree, determine, discover, enact, find out, formulate, learn, legislate, make, make out, predicate, prescribe, prove, ratify, rest, show, stay, substantiate, validate, verify; SEE CONCEPTS *49,50,88,97*

establishment [n1] *organization; creation*
enactment, endowment, formation, formulation, foundation, founding, inauguration, installation, institution, setting up; SEE CONCEPTS *173,221*

establishment [n2] *business, institution*
abode, building, company, concern, corporation, enterprise, factory, firm, foundation, house, institute, office, organization, outfit, plant, quarters, residence, setup, structure, system, workplace; SEE CONCEPTS *323,325,449*

establishment [n3] *ruling class; bureaucracy*
authority, city hall*, conservatives, diehards*, established order, Old Guard*, powers that be*, them, the system*, they*; SEE CONCEPTS *347,354*

estate [n1] *extensive manor and its property*
acreage, area, country home, country place, demesne, domain, dominion, farm, finca, freehold, grounds, holdings, lands, parcel, plantation, quinta, ranch, residence, rural seat, territory, villa; SEE CONCEPT *516*

estate [n2] *person's possessions, property, wealth*
assets, belongings, bequest, capital, chattels, devise, earthly possessions, effects, endowment, fortune, goods, heritage, inheritance, legacy, patrimony, substance; SEE CONCEPTS *340,710*

estate [n3] *class, rank*
bracket, caste, category, classification, condition, echelon, footing, form, grade, level, lot, order, period, place, position, quality, repair, shape, situation, sphere, standing, state, station, status, stratum; SEE CONCEPTS *378,388*

esteem [v1] *think highly of*
admire, appreciate, apprise, be fond of, cherish, consider, hold dear, honor, idolize, like, look up to*, love, prize, regard, regard highly, respect, revere, reverence, think the world of*, treasure, value, venerate, worship; SEE CONCEPT *32*

esteem [v2] *consider, believe*
account, calculate, deem, estimate, hold, judge, rate, reckon, regard, think, view; SEE CONCEPT *12*

estimable [adj] *honorable, worthy*
admirable, admired, appreciable, august, big name*, big time*, commendable, decent, deserving, esteemed, excellent, good, high-powered, honored, in limelight*, laudable, major league*, meretorious, meritable, name, noble, palmary, praisable, praiseworthy, reputable, reputed, respectable, respected,

sterling, valuable, valued, venerable, well-thought-of*; SEE CONCEPTS *567,572*

estimate [n] *approximate calculation; educated guess*
appraisal, appraisement, assay, assessment, ballpark figure*, belief, conclusion, conjecture, estimation, evaluation, gauging, guess, guesstimate*, impression, judgment, measure, measurement, mensuration, opinion, point of view, projection, rating, reckoning, sizing up*, stock, surmise, survey, thought, valuation; SEE CONCEPTS *28,37,689,784*

estimate [v] *guess, try to value*
account, appraise, assay, assess, believe, budget, calculate roughly, cast, cipher, class, classify, compute, conjecture, consider, count, decide, deduce, determine, enumerate, evaluate, examine, expect, figure, form opinion, gauge, guess, guesstimate*, judge, look into, look upon, number, outline, plan, predict, prophesy, rank, rate, reason, reckon, regard, run over*, scheme, set a figure*, size up*, sum, suppose, surmise, suspect, tax, think, think through*, value; SEE CONCEPTS *28,37,764*

estimation [n] *belief, guess*
admiration, appraisal, appreciation, arithmetic, assessment, calculating, ciphering, computation, consideration, considered opinion, credit, esteem, estimate, estimating, evaluation, favor, figuring, impression, judgment, opinion, predicting, reckoning, regard, respect, stock, valuation, veneration, view; SEE CONCEPTS *28,689*

estrange [v] *destroy the affections of*
alien, alienate, antagonize, break up, disaffect, disunify, disunite, divert, divide, divorce, drive apart, leave, make hostile, part, put on the outs*, separate, set at odds*, sever, split, sunder, turn off*, wean, withdraw, withhold; SEE CONCEPTS *7,19,297,384*

estrangement [n] *destruction of affections*
alienation, antagonization, breach, break-up, disaffection, disassociation, disunity, division, divorce, hostility, leave, leaving, parting, removal, schism, separation, split, withdrawal, withholding; SEE CONCEPTS *297,388*

et cetera [adj] *and so forth*
along with others, and, and all, and on and on, and others, and so on, and the like, and the rest, blah blah blah*, et al., whatever, whatnot; SEE CONCEPTS *267,577*

etch [v] *carve*
compose, corrode, cut, define, delineate, depict, describe, eat into, engrave, erode, execute, furrow, grave, impress, imprint, incise, ingrain, inscribe, outline, picture, portray, reduce, represent, set forth, stamp; SEE CONCEPTS *174,176*

etching [n] *art created by carving*
carving, engraving, impression, imprint, inscription, mezzotint, old master*, photoengraving, photogravure, print, reproduction, rotogravure, transferring; SEE CONCEPT *259*

eternal [adj] *without pause; endless*
abiding, ageless, always, amaranthine, boundless, ceaseless, constant, continual, continued, continuous, dateless, deathless, enduring, everlasting, forever, illimitable, immemorial, immortal, immutable, imperishable, incessant, indefinite, indestructible, infinite, interminable, lasting, never-ending, perdurable, perennial, permanent, perpetual, persistent, relentless, termless, timeless, unbroken, unceasing, undying, unending, unfading, uninterrupted, unremitting, without end; SEE CONCEPTS *482,798*

eternally [adv] *endlessly*
always, continually, ever, evermore, forever, forevermore, for ever so long*, for keeps, in perpetuum, perpetually, regularly, till the cows come home*; SEE CONCEPT *798*

eternity [n] *forever*
aeon, afterlife, age, ages, blue moon*, dog's age*, endlessness, endless time, everlastingness, forever and a day*, forever and ever, future, immortality, imperishability, infiniteness, infinitude, infinity, kingdom come*, other world*, perpetuity, timelessness, time without end, wild blue yonder*, world without end*; SEE CONCEPTS *370,804,818*

ethereal [adj] *delicate, heavenly*
aerial, airy, celestial, dainty, divine, empyreal, empyrean, exquisite, fairy, filmy, fine, gaseous, ghostly, gossamer, impalpable, insubstantial, intangible, light, rarefied, refined, spiritual, sublime, subtle, supernal, tenuous, unearthly, unsubstantial, unworldly, vaporous, vapory; SEE CONCEPTS *491,549,582,606*

ethical [adj] *moral, righteous*
Christian, clean, conscientious, correct, decent, elevated, equitable, fair, fitting, good, high-principled, honest, honorable, humane, just, kosher*, moralistic, noble, principled, proper, respectable, right, right-minded, square, straight, true blue*, upright, upstanding, virtuous; SEE CONCEPT *545*

ethics/ethic [n] *moral philosophy, values*
belief, conduct, conscience, convention, conventionalities, criteria, descency, ethos, goodness, honesty, honor, ideal, imperative, integrity, moral code, morality, mores, natural law, nature, practice, principles, right and wrong, rules of conduct, standard, standards, the Golden Rule*, value; SEE CONCEPTS *645,687,689*

ethnic [adj] *racial, cultural*
indigenous, national, native, traditional, tribal; SEE CONCEPT *549*

etiquette [n] *manners, politeness*
amenities, civility, code, convention, courtesy, customs, decency, decorum, deportment, dignity, form, formalities, good behavior*, mores, p's and q's*, politesse, proper behavior, propriety, protocol, rules, seemliness, social graces, suavities, usage; SEE CONCEPT *633*

eulogize [v] *praise, glorify*
acclaim, applaud, bless, celebrate, commend, compliment, cry up, exalt, extol, flatter, give a bouquet*, give a posy*, hymn, idolize, laud, magnify, panegyrize, pay tribute to, sing praises; SEE CONCEPT *69*

eulogy [n] *praise, acclamation*
acclaim, accolade, adulation, applause, citation, commendation, compliment, encomium, exaltation, glorification, laudation, paean, panegyric, plaudit, salutation, tribute; SEE CONCEPTS *69,278*

euphemism [n] *nice way of saying something*
circumlocution, delicacy, floridness, grandiloquence, inflation, pomposity, pretense, purism; SEE CONCEPTS *275,278*

euphoria [n] *extreme happiness*
bliss, dreamland, ecstasy, elation, exaltation, exhilaration, exultation, frenzy, glee, health, high spirits, intoxication, joy, joyousness, jubilation, madness, rapture, relaxation, transport, twilight zone*; SEE CONCEPT *410*

evacuate [v] *clear an area; empty*
abandon, bail out*, cut out, decamp, depart, desert, discharge, displace, eject, expel, forsake, hightail, leave, move out, pack up, pull out, quit, relinquish, remove, run for hills*, skidaddle*, vacate, withdraw; SEE CONCEPTS *179,195*

evade [v] *get away from*
avoid, baffle, balk, beat around bush*, beg the question*, bypass, cavil, circumvent, conceal, confuse, cop out, deceive, decline, dodge, double, duck, elude, equivocate, escape, eschew, fence, fend off*, flee, fly, fudge*, get around, give the runaround*, hedge, hide, keep distance*, lay low*, lead on a merry chase*, lie, parry, pass up, pretend, prevaricate, pussyfoot, put off, shift, shirk, shuck, shuffle, shun, shy, sidestep, slip out, sneak away*, steer clear of*, tergiversate, trick, waffle*, weasel*; SEE CONCEPTS *30,102*

evaluate [v] *judge*
appraise, assay, assess, calculate, check, check out, class, classify, criticize, decide, estimate, figure out, fiture, gauge, grade, guesstimate*, look over, peg*, price out, rank, rate, read, reckon, set at, size, size up*, survey, take account of, take measure, valuate, value, weigh; SEE CONCEPTS *18,24,103*

evaluation [n] *judgment*
appraisal, appraisement, assessment, calculation, decision, estimate, estimation, guesstimation*, interpretation, opinion, rating, stock, take, valuation; SEE CONCEPTS *24,103,689*

evaporate [v] *dry up, dissolve*
clear, concentrate, dehumidify, dehydrate, dematerialize, desiccate, disappear, dispel, disperse, dissipate, dry, evanesce, evanish, fade, fade away, melt, parch, pass, vanish, vaporize, weaken; SEE CONCEPTS *469,698*

evaporation [n] *drying up; dissolution*
dehydration, dematerialization, desiccation, disappearance, dispelling, dispersal, dissipation, drying, escape, evanescence, fading, melting, vanishing, va-

porescence, vaporization; SEE CONCEPTS *469,607, 698*

evasion [n] *escape, avoidance*
artifice, circumvention, cop-out*, cunning, ditch*, dodge*, dodging, elusion, equivocating, equivocation, escaping, eschewal, evading, evasiveness, excuse, fancy footwork*, fudging*, jive, lie, obliqueness, pretext, prevarication, quibble, routine, runaround, ruse, shift, shirking, shuffling, shunning, slip*, sophism, sophistry, stall, stonewall*, subterfuge, trick, trickery; SEE CONCEPTS *59,63,102*

evasive [adj] *deceitful, tricky*
ambiguous, cagey, casuistic, casuistical, cunning, deceptive, devious, dissembling, elusive, elusory, equivocating, false, fugitive, greasy, indirect, intangible, lying, misleading, oblique, prevaricating, shifty, shuffling, slippery, sly, sophistical, stonewalling*, unclear, vague; SEE CONCEPTS *267,401,542*

even [adj1] *flat, uniform*
alike, balanced, consistent, constant, continual, continuous, direct, equal, flush, homogenous, horizontal, level, like, matching, metrical, parallel, planate, plane, plumb, proportional, regular, right, same, smooth, square, stabile, stable, steady, straight, surfaced, true, unbroken, unchanging, undeviating, unfluctuating, uninterrupted, unvaried, unvarying, unwavering, unwrinkled; SEE CONCEPTS *480,490*

even [adj2] *calm, undisturbed*
composed, cool, equable, equanimous, even-tempered, imperturbable, peaceful, placid, serene, stable, steady, tranquil, unexcitable, unruffled, well-balanced; SEE CONCEPT *401*

even [adj3] *commensurate; having no advantage*
balanced, coequal, comparable, coterminous, drawn, equal, equalized, equivalent, even-steven*, exact, fifty-fifty*, horse to horse*, identical, level, like, matching, neck and neck*, on a par*, parallel, proportional, proportionate, same, similar, smack in the middle*, square, tied, uniform; SEE CONCEPT *566*

even [adj4] *fair, impartial*
balanced, disinterested, dispassionate, equal, equitable, fair and square*, honest, just, matching, nonpartisan, square, straightforward, unbiased, unprejudiced; SEE CONCEPTS *267,542*

even [v] *balance, make smooth*
align, equal, equalize, flatten, flush, grade, lay, level, match, pancake*, plane, regularize, roll, smooth, square, stabilize, steady, symmetrize, uniform; SEE CONCEPTS *231,757*

even [adv] *still, yet*
all the more, despite, disregarding, even so much as, indeed, in spite of, much, notwithstanding, so much as; SEE CONCEPT *544*

evening [n] *latter part of a day*
black, close, dark, decline, dim, dusk, duskiness, early black*, eve, even, eventide, late afternoon, nightfall, sundown, sunset, twilight; SEE CONCEPTS *801,806,810*

event [n1] *occurrence, happening*
accident, act, action, advent, adventure, affair, appearance, business, calamity, case, catastrophe, celebration, ceremony, chance, circumstance, coincidence, conjuncture, crisis, deed, development, emergency, episode, experience, exploit, fact, function, holiday, incident, juncture, marvel, matter, milestone, miracle, misfortune, mishap, mistake, occasion, occurrence, pass, phase, phenomenon, predicament, proceeding, shift, situation, story, thing*, tide, transaction, triumph, turn, wonder; SEE CONCEPT *2*

event [n2] *effect, result*
aftereffect, aftermath, case, causatum, chance, conclusion, consequence, end, end result, eventuality, fortuity, hap, happenstance, issue, offshoot, outcome, outgrowth, product, resultant, sequel, sequent, termination, upshot; SEE CONCEPT *230*

event [n3] *performance, competition*
bout, contest, game, match, meet, tournament; SEE CONCEPTS *263,363*

eventful [adj] *significant, busy*
active, consequential, critical, crucial, decisive, exciting, fateful, full, historic, important, lively, memorable, momentous, notable, noteworthy, outstanding, remarkable, signal, significant; SEE CONCEPT *548*

eventual [adj] *future, concluding*
closing, conditional, consequent, contingent, dependent, down the pike*, down the road*, ending, endmost, ensuing, final, hindmost, indirect, inevitable, in the cards*, last, later, latter, overall, possible, prospective, resulting, secondary, succeeding, terminal, ulterior, ultimate, vicarious; SEE CONCEPTS *552,820*

eventuality [n] *something that probably will happen*
aftereffect, aftermath, any case, case, chance, consequence, contingency, effect, event, go-down*, goings-on*, hap*, happening, issue, likelihood, outcome, possibility, probability, result, sequel, toss-up, upshot*; SEE CONCEPTS *230,650*

eventually [adv] *in the course of time*
after all, at last, at the end of the day*, finally, hereafter, in future, in the end, in the long run*, one day, someday, sometime, sooner or later*, ultimately, when all is said and done*, yet; SEE CONCEPTS *552,820*

eventuate [v] *be a consequence*
be consequent, befall, come about, come to pass, end, ensue, eventualize, follow, happen, issue, occur, result, stop, take place, terminate; SEE CONCEPTS *2,242*

ever [adv] *always, at any time*
anytime, at all, at all times, at any point, by any chance*, consistently, constantly, continually, endlessly, eternally, everlastingly, evermore, forever, for keeps, in any case*, incessantly, in perpetuum, invariably, on any occasion*, perpetually, regularly, relentlessly, till the cows come home*, to the end of

time*, unceasingly, unendingly, usually; SEE CONCEPTS *798,799*

everlasting [adj] *infinite, never-ending*
abiding, amaranthine, boundless, ceaseless, constant, continual, continuous, deathless, endless, eternal, immortal, imperishable, incessant, indestructible, interminable, lasting, limitless, perdurable, permanent, perpetual, termless, timeless, unceasing, undying, unending, uninterrupted, unremitting; SEE CONCEPT *798*

every [adj] *each, all*
each one, whole, without exception; SEE CONCEPT *531*

everybody/everyone [n] *all involved, all human beings; the whole world*
all, all and sundry*, anybody, each one, each person, everyman/woman, every person, generality, masses, people, populace, the public, the whole, young and old*; SEE CONCEPT *417*

everyday [adj] *common*
accustomed, average, commonplace, conventional, customary, daily, dime a dozen*, dull, familiar, frequent, garden variety*, habitual, informal, lowly, mainstream, middle-of-the-road*, mundane, normal, ordinary, per diem, plain, prosaic, quotidian, routine, run-of-the-mill*, stock, unexceptional, unimaginative, unremarkable, usual, vanilla*, whitebread*, wonted, workaday; SEE CONCEPTS *530,547*

everything [n] *entirety*
aggregate, all, all in all, all that, all things, business, complex, each thing, every little thing*, fixins'*, lock stock and barrel*, lot, many things, sum, the works*, total, universe, whole, whole ball of wax*, whole caboodle*, whole enchilada*, whole lot*, whole shebang*; SEE CONCEPTS *432,837*

everywhere [adv] *in all places*
all around, all over, all over creation*, all over the map*, far and wide*, here and there*, here till Sunday*, high and low*, in all quarters, in each place, in every direction, in every place, inside and out, near and far*, omnipresent, overall, pole to pole*, the world over*, throughout, ubiquitous, ubiquitously, universally, wherever; SEE CONCEPT *583*

evict [v] *throw out from residence*
boot out*, bounce*, chase, dislodge, dismiss, dispossess, eject, expel, extrude, force out, heave-ho*, kick out*, oust, out, put out, remove, send packing*, show out, show the door*, shut out, toss out on ear*, turn out; SEE CONCEPTS *122,198,211*

eviction [n] *throwing out of a residence*
boot*, bounce*, bum's rush*, clearance, dislodgement, dispossession, ejection, expulsion, kicking out*, ouster, removal, rush, the gate*, walking papers*; SEE CONCEPTS *123,198,211*

evidence [n] *proof*
affirmation, attestation, averment, cincher*, clincher*, clue, confirmation, corroboration, cue, data, declaration, demonstration, deposition, documentation, dope*, goods*, gospel, grabber*, grounds, index, indication, indicia, info*, information, manifestation, mark, sign, significant, smoking gun*, substantiation, symptom, testament, testimonial, testimony, token, witness; SEE CONCEPTS *274,318*

evidence [v] *prove*
attest, bespeak, betoken, confirm, connote, demonstrate, denote, designate, display, evince, exhibit, expose, illustrate, indicate, manifest, mark, ostend, proclaim, reveal, show, signify, testify to, witness; SEE CONCEPTS *57,97,317*

evident [adj] *apparent, clear*
axiomatic, barefaced*, clear-cut, conspicuous, crystal clear*, distinct, fact, incontestable, incontrovertible, indisputable, logical, manifest, noticeable, obvious, open-and-shut*, palpable, patent, perceptible, plain, plain as day*, reasonable, straightforward, tangible, unambiguous, unmistakable, visible; SEE CONCEPTS *529,535*

evidently [adv] *apparently, clearly*
doubtless, doubtlessly, incontestably, incontrovertibly, indisputably, it seems, it would seem, manifestly, obviously, officially, ostensibly, outwardly, patently, plainly, professedly, seemingly, to all appearances*, undoubtedly, unmistakably, without question; SEE CONCEPT *535*

evil [n] *badness, immorality; disaster*
affliction, baseness, blow, calamity, catastrophe, corruption, crime, criminality, curse, debauchery, depravity, devilry, diabolism, disaster, harm, hatred, heinousness, hurt, ill, impiety, indecency, infamy, iniquity, injury, knavery, lewdness, licentiousness, looseness, malevolence, malignity, meanness, mischief, misery, misfortune, obscenity, outrage, pain, perversity, ruin, sin, sinfulness, sorrow, suffering, turpitude, vice, viciousness, vileness, villainy, wickedness, woe, wrong, wrongdoing; SEE CONCEPT *645*

evil [adj] *sinful, immoral*
angry, atrocious, bad, baneful, base, beastly, calamitous, corrupt, damnable, depraved, destructive, disastrous, execrable, flagitious, foul, harmful, hateful, heinous, hideous, iniquitous, injurious, loathsome, low, maleficent, malevolent, malicious, malignant, nefarious, no good, obscene, offensive, pernicious, poison, rancorous, reprobate, repugnant, repulsive, revolting, spiteful, stinking, ugly, unpleasant, unpropitious, vicious, vile, villainous, wicked, wrathful, wrong; SEE CONCEPTS *545,570*

evoke [v] *induce, stimulate*
arouse, awaken, call, call forth, conjure, educe, elicit, evince, evolve, excite, extort, extract, give rise to, invoke, milk*, provoke, raise, rally, recall, rouse, stir up, summon, waken; SEE CONCEPTS *228,242*

evolution [n] *development, progress*
change, enlargement, evolvement, expansion, flowering, growth, increase, maturation, natural process,

progression, transformation, unfolding, working out;
SEE CONCEPT *704*

evolve [*v*] *develop, progress*
advance, derive, disclose, educe, elaborate, emerge, enlarge, excogitate, expand, get, grow, increase, mature, obtain, open, result, ripen, unfold, work out;
SEE CONCEPTS *236,245,704*

exacerbate [*v*] *infuriate; make worse*
add insult to injury*, aggravate, annoy, egg on*, embitter, enrage, envenom, exasperate, excite, fan the flames*, feed the fire*, go from bad to worse*, heat up*, heighten, hit on*, increase, inflame, intensify, irritate, madden, provoke, push one's button*, rattle one's cage*, rub salt in wound*, vex, worsen;
SEE CONCEPTS *7,19*

exact [*adj1*] *accurate, precise*
bull's-eye*, careful, clear, clear-cut, correct, dead on*, definite, distinct, downright, explicit, express, faithful, faultless, identical, literal, methodical, nailed down*, nice, on target*, on the button*, on the money*, on the numbers*, orderly, particular, perfect, right, right on*, rigorous, sharp, specific, true, unequivocal, unerring, veracious, verbal, verbatim; SEE CONCEPTS *535,557*

exact [*adj2*] *careful, painstaking*
conscientious, conscionable, demanding, exacting, finicky, fussy, heedful, meticulous, punctilious, punctual, rigorous, scrupulous, severe, strict; SEE CONCEPT *542*

exact [*v*] *demand, call for*
assess, bleed, call, challenge, claim, coerce, command, compel, constrain, extort, extract, force, gouge, impose, insist upon, lean on, levy, oblige, pinch, postulate, put on, require, requisition, shake down*, solicit, squeeze, wrench, wrest, wring; SEE CONCEPTS *53,142*

exacting [*adj*] *demanding*
burdensome, by the book*, careful, critical, difficult, exigent, finicky, fussy, grievous, hard, harsh, hypercritical, imperious, nit-picking, onerous, oppressive, painstaking, particular, persnickety, picky, precise, rigid, rigorous, severe, stern, strict, stringent, taxing, tough, trying, unsparing, weighty; SEE CONCEPTS *401,404*

exactly [*adv*] *accurately, particularly*
absolutely, altogether, bang*, carefully, completely, correctly, definitely, explicitly, expressly, faithfully, faultlessly, for a fact, for certain, for sure*, indeed, in every respect, just, literally, methodically, no mistake, on the dot*, on the money*, on the nail*, on the nose*, positively, precisely, quite, right, rigorously, scrupulously, severely, sharp, specifically, square, strictly, the ticket*, totally, truly, truthfully, unequivocally, unerringly, utterly, veraciously, wholly; SEE CONCEPTS *535,557*

exactness [*n*] *accuracy, precision*
carefulness, correctness, definiteness, definitiveness, definitude, exactitude, faithfulness, faultlessness,

nicety, orderliness, painstakingness, preciseness, promptitude, regularity, rigor, rigorousness, scrupulousness, strictness, truth, unequivocalness, veracity;
SEE CONCEPTS *638,654*

exaggerate [*v*] *overstate, embellish*
amplify, blow out of proportion*, boast, boost, brag, build up, caricature, color, cook up*, corrupt, distort, embroider, emphasize, enlarge, exalt, expand, fabricate, falsify, fudge*, go to extremes*, heighten, hike, hyperbolize, inflate, intensify, lay it on thick*, lie, loud talk*, magnify, make too much of*, misquote, misreport, misrepresent, overdo, overdraw, overemphasize, overestimate, pad*, pretty up*, puff, put on, pyramid*, romance, romanticize, scam, stretch, up*; SEE CONCEPT *63*

exaggerated [*adj*] *overstated, embellished*
a bit thick*, abstract, amplified, artificial, bouncing, caricatural, distorted, embroidered, exalted, excessive, extravagant, fabricated, fabulous, false, fantastic, farfetched, hammy, highly colored, histrionic, hyperbolic, impossible, inflated, magnified, melodramatic, out of proportion, overblown, overdone, overestimated, overkill, overstated, overwrought, preposterous, pretentious, schmaltzy, sensational, spectacular, steep, strained, stylized, tall, too much*, too-too*, unrealistic; SEE CONCEPTS *267,542,562*

exaggeration [*n*] *overstatement, embellishment*
aggrandizement, amplification, baloney*, boasting, caricature, coloring, crock*, elaboration, embroidery, emphasis, enlargement, exaltation, excess, extravagance, fabrication, falsehood, fancy, fantasy, figure of speech, fish story*, flight of fancy*, hogwash*, hyperbole, inflation, jazz*, line*, magnification, misjudgment, misrepresentation, overemphasis, overestimation, pretension, pretentiousness, rant, romance, stretch, tall story*, untruth, whopper*, yarn*; SEE CONCEPTS *63,278,663*

exalt [*v*] *promote, praise*
acclaim, advance, aggrandize, apotheosize, applaud, bless, boost, build up*, commend, dignify, distinguish, ennoble, erect, eulogize, extol, glorify, halo, honor, idolize, intensify, laud, magnify, pay homage to, pay tribute to, raise, revere, set on pedestal*, sublime, transfigure, upgrade, uprear, worship; SEE CONCEPTS *10,69*

exaltation [*n1*] *promotion, praise*
acclaim, acclamation, advancement, aggrandizement, apotheosis, applause, blessing, dignity, elevation, eminence, ennoblement, extolment, glorification, glory, grandeur, high rank, homage, honor, idolzation, laudation, lionization, loftiness, magnification, panegyric, plaudits, prestige, reverence, rise, tribute, upgrading, uplifting, worship; SEE CONCEPTS *69,278*

exaltation [*n2*] *great joy*
animation, bliss, delectation, delight, ecstasy, elation, elevation, euphoria, excitement, exhilaration, exultation, inspiration, intoxication, joy, joyousness,

jubilation, rapture, stimulation, transport, uplift; SEE CONCEPTS *32,410*

exalted [*adj*] *praised; held in high esteem*
astral, august, dignified, elevated, eminent, exaggerated, excessive, first, grand, high, highest, highest-ranking, high-minded, high-ranking, honorable, honored, ideal, illustrious, immodest, imposing, inflated, intellectual, leading, lofty, magnificent, noble, number one, outstanding, overblown, pompous, prestigious, pretentious, proud, self-important, sublime, superb, superior, top-drawer*, top-ranking, uplifting; SEE CONCEPTS *404,529*

examination [*n1*] *test, analysis*
assay, audit, battery, blue book*, breakdown, canvass, catechism, checking, checkup, cross-examination, diagnosis, dissection, exam, experiment, exploration, final, grilling, inquest, inquiry, inquisition, inspection, interrogation, investigation, legwork*, make-up, observation, once-over*, oral, perlustration, perusal, probe, quest, questioning, questionnaire, quiz, raid, reconnaissance, research, review, scan, scrutiny, search, study, survey, the eye*, third degree*, trial, tryout, view, written; SEE CONCEPT *290*

examination [*n2*] *medical checkup*
autopsy, biopsy, exam, inquiry, medical, observation, physical, postoperative, probe, test; SEE CONCEPTS *103,310*

examine [*v1*] *analyze, test*
appraise, assay, audit, canvass, case, check, check out, chew over*, consider, criticize, delve into, dig into, explore, eye*, finger*, frisk, go into, go over, go through, gun*, inquire, inspect, investigate, look over, look see*, parse, pat down, peruse, pick at, ponder, pore over, probe, prospect, prove, read, reconnoiter, research, review, scan, scope, screen, scrutate, scrutinize, search into, sift, size up*, study, survey, sweep, take stock of*, test, try, turn over*, vet, view, weigh, winnow*; SEE CONCEPTS *24,103*

examine [*v2*] *ask questions pointedly*
catechize, check, cross-examine, experiment, give the third*, give the third degree*, grill, inquire, interrogate, judge, measure, pump, put through the wringer*, query, question, quiz, try, try out, weigh; SEE CONCEPT *48*

example [*n*] *instance, model*
archetype, case, case history, case in point, citation, copy, excuse, exemplar, exemplification, for instance, ideal, illustration, kind of thing, lesson, object, original, paradigm, paragon, part, pattern, precedent, prototype, quotation, representation, sample, sampling, specimen, standard, stereotype, symbol; SEE CONCEPT *688*

exasperate [*v*] *upset, provoke*
aggravate, agitate, anger, annoy, bug*, disturb, drive up the wall*, embitter, enrage, exacerbate, excite, gall, get*, get under one's skin*, incense, inflame,

infuriate, irk, irritate, madden, make waves*, needle*, nettle, peeve, pique, rankle, rile, roil, rouse, T-off*, try the patience of, vex, work up; SEE CONCEPTS *7,19*

exasperation [*n*] *upset, provocation*
aggravation, anger, annoyance, besetment, bother, botheration, displeasure, exacerbation, fury, ire, irritant, irritation, nuisance, passion, pest, pique, plague, rage, resentment, vexation, wrath; SEE CONCEPTS *29,410*

excavate [*v*] *dig up*
burrow, cut, delve, dig, empty, gouge, grub, hollow, mine, quarry, scoop, scrape, shovel, spade, trench, tunnel, uncover, unearth; SEE CONCEPT *178*

excavation [*n*] *site of digging; digging*
blasting, burrow, cavity, cut, cutting, dig, diggings, disinterring, ditch, dugout, exhuming, hole, hollow, mine, mining, pit, quarry, removal, scooping, shaft, shoveling, trench, trough, unearthing; SEE CONCEPTS *178,509,513*

exceed [*v*] *be superior to; surpass*
beat, best, better, break record*, cap, distance, eclipse, excel, get upper hand*, go beyond, go by, have advantage, have a jump on*, have it all over*, out-distance, outdo, outpace, outreach, outrun, outshine, outstrip, overstep, overtake, overtax, pass, rise above*, run circles around*, surmount, top, transcend; SEE CONCEPT *141*

exceedingly [*adv*] *very; exceptionally*
awfully, enormously, especially, excessively, extraordinarily, extremely, greatly, highly, hugely, immoderately, in a marked degree, inordinately, powerful, really, remarkably, strikingly, superlatively, surpassingly, terribly, too much, unusually, vastly, vitally; SEE CONCEPT *569*

excel [*v*] *be superior; surpass*
beat, be good, be master of, be proficient, be skillful, best, be talented, better, cap, come through, eclipse, exceed, go beyond, go to town*, improve upon, make it, outdo, outrival, outshine, outstrip, pass, predominate, shine, show talent, surmount, take precedence, top, transcend, wax*; SEE CONCEPTS *141,671,706*

excellence [*n*] *superiority*
arete, class, distinction, éclat, eminence, excellency, fineness, goodness, greatness, high quality, merit, perfection, preeminence, purity, quality, superbness, supremacy, transcendence, virtue, worth; SEE CONCEPT *671*

excellent [*adj*] *superior, wonderful*
A-1*, accomplished, admirable, attractive, capital, certified, champion, choice, choicest, desirable, distinctive, distinguished, estimable, exceptional, exemplary, exquisite, fine, finest, first, first-class, first-rate, good, great, high, incomparable, invaluable, magnificent, meritorious, notable, noted, outstanding, peerless, piked*, premium, priceless, prime, select, skillful, sterling, striking, superb, superlative,

supreme, tiptop*, top-notch, transcendent, world-class; SEE CONCEPT *574*

except [*v*] *leave out*
ban, bar, bate, count out, debar, disallow, eliminate, exclude, exempt, expostulate, inveigh, object, omit, pass over, protest, reject, remonstrate, rule out, suspend, taboo; SEE CONCEPTS *25,30,211*

except [*prep*] *other than*
apart from, aside from, bar, barring, besides, but, excepting, excluding, exclusive of, exempting, if not, lacking, leaving out, minus, not for, omitting, outside of, rejecting, save, saving, short of, without, with the exception of; SEE CONCEPT *577*

exception [*n1*] *leaving out*
barring, debarment, disallowment, excepting, exclusion, excusing, expulsion, noninclusion, omission, passing over, rejection, repudiation, reservation; SEE CONCEPTS *25,30,211*

exception [*n2*] *special case; irregularity*
allowance, anomalism, anomaly, departure, deviation, difference, dispensation, eccentricity, exemption, freak, inconsistency, nonconformity, oddity, peculiarity, perquisitor, privilege, privileged person, quirk; SEE CONCEPTS *423,665*

exceptional [*adj1*] *irregular*
aberrant, abnormal, anomalous, atypical, deviant, distinct, extraordinary, inconsistent, infrequent, notable, noteworthy, odd, peculiar, phenomenal, rare, remarkable, scarce, singular, special, strange, uncommon, uncustomary, unheard-of, unimaginable, unique, unordinary, unprecedented, unthinkable, unusual; SEE CONCEPT *564*

exceptional [*adj2*] *excellent, wonderful*
brainy, extraordinary, fine, first-class, first-rate, good, high, marvelous, outstanding, phenomenal, premium, prodigious, remarkable, singular, special, superior, wizard*, world-class; SEE CONCEPTS *572,574*

excerpt [*n*] *citation; something taken from a whole*
extract, fragment, notation, note, part, passage, pericope, piece, portion, quotation, quote, saying, section, selection; SEE CONCEPTS *270,274,835*

excerpt [*v*] *take a part from a whole*
choose, cite, cull, extract, glean, note, pick, pick out, quote, select, single out; SEE CONCEPTS *41,142,211*

excess [*n1*] *overabundance of something*
balance, by-product, enough, exorbitance, exuberance, fat, fulsomeness, glut, inundation, lavishness, leavings, leftover, luxuriance, nimiety, overdose, overflow, overkill, overload, overmuch, overrun, oversupply, overweight, plenty, plethora, profusion, recrement, redundance, redundancy, refuse, remainder, residue, rest, spare, superabundance, supererogation, superfluity, surfeit, surplus, the limit, too much*, too much of good thing*, waste, wastefulness; SEE CONCEPTS *786,824,835*

excess [*n2*] *overindulgence in personal desires*
debauchery, dissipation, dissoluteness, exorbitance, extravagance, extreme, extremes, extremity, immoderacy, immoderation, indulgence, inordinateness, intemperance, overdoing, prodigality, saturnalia, self-indulgence, unrestraint; SEE CONCEPTS *633,645*

excessive [*adj*] *too much; overdone*
boundless, disproportionate, dissipated, dizzying, enormous, exaggerated, exorbitant, extra, extravagant, extreme, immoderate, indulgent, inordinate, intemperate, limitless, more, needless, over, overboard, overkill, overmuch, plethoric, prodigal, profligate, recrementitious, redundant, self-indulgent, sky-high*, steep, stiff, stratospheric*, super, superabundant, superfluous, supernatural, too many, towering, unbounded, unconscionable, undue, unmeasurable, unreasonable, way out*; SEE CONCEPTS *560,771,781*

exchange [*n1*] *trade; deal*
barter, buying and selling, castling, change, commerce, commutation, conversion, correspondence, dealing, interchange, interdependence, interrelation, network, quid pro quo, rearrangement, reciprocation, reciprocity, replacement, revision, shift, shuffle, shuffling, substitution, supplanting, supplantment, swap, switch, tit for tat*, traffic, transaction, transfer, transposing, transposition, truck*; SEE CONCEPTS *104,324*

exchange [*n2*] *place where stocks are bought, sold*
curb, market, net, network, over the counter, stock exchange, store, the Big Board*, the Street*, Wall Street*; SEE CONCEPTS *325,449*

exchange [*v*] *trade*
alternate, bandy, bargain, barter, buy and sell, cash in, castle, change, change hands*, commute, contact with, convert into, correspond, deal in, displace, flip-flop*, give and take*, go over to*, hook up, horse trade, interchange, invert, link up, market, network, pass to, pay back, rearrange, reciprocate, replace, return the compliment*, reverse, revise, seesaw, shift, shuffle, shuttle, substitute, swap, swap horses*, switch, traffic, transact, transfer, transpose, truck*, turn the tables*; SEE CONCEPT *104*

excise [*n*] *tax on goods*
customs, duty, import tax, levy, surcharge, tariff, toll; SEE CONCEPT *329*

excise [*v*] *remove, delete*
amputate, black out, blot out*, blue pencil*, cross out, cut, cut off, cut out, cut up, destroy, edit, elide, eradicate, erase, expunge, exscind, exsect, exterminate, extirpate, extract, gut, knock off*, launder*, lop off*, resect, scissor out, scratch out, slash, stamp out*, strike, trim, wipe out, X out*; SEE CONCEPT *211*

excitable [*adj*] *easily upset or inspired*
agitable, alarmable, demonstrative, edgy, emotional, enthusiastic, fidgety, fierce, fiery, galvanic, hasty, high-strung, hot-headed, hot-tempered, hysterical, impatient, impetuous, impulsive, inflammable, intol-

erant, irascible, mercurial, moody, nervous, neurotic, overzealous, passionate, peevish, quick, quick-tempered, rash, reckless, restless, sensitive, short fused, skittish, susceptible, temperamental, testy, touchy, uncontrolled, uneasy, vehement, violent, volatile, volcanic; SEE CONCEPTS *401,404*

excite [v] *inspire; upset*
accelerate, agitate, amaze, anger, animate, annoy, arouse, astound, awaken, bother, chafe, delight, discompose, disturb, electrify, elicit, energize, evoke, feed the fire*, fire, fluster, foment, galvanize, goad, incite, induce, inflame, infuriate, instigate, intensify, irritate, jar, jolt, kindle, madden, mock, move, offend, precipitate, provoke, quicken, rouse, start, stimulate, stir up, taunt, tease, thrill, titillate, touch off, vex, waken, wake up, warm, whet, work up, worry; SEE CONCEPTS *7,14,19,22*

excited [adj] *inspired; upset*
aflame, agitated, animated, annoyed, aroused, awakened, beside oneself*, charged, delighted, discomposed, disconcerted, disturbed, eager, enthusiastic, feverish, fired up*, frantic, high*, hot*, hot and bothered*, hyperactive, hysterical, in a tizzy*, inflamed, juiced up*, jumpy*, keyed up*, moved, nervous, on edge*, on fire*, overwrought, passionate, piqued, provoked, roused, ruffled, steamed up*, stimulated, stirred, thrilled, tumultous/tumultuous, wild, wired*, worked up, zipped up*; SEE CONCEPTS *401,403*

excitement [n] *enthusiasm; incitement*
action, activity, ado, adventure, agitation, animation, bother, buzz*, commotion, confusion, discomposure, disturbance, dither*, drama, elation, emotion, excitation, feeling, ferment, fever, flurry, frenzy, furor, fuss, heat*, hubbub*, hullabaloo*, hurry, hysteria, impulse, instigation, intoxication, kicks*, melodrama, motivation, motive, movement, passion, perturbation, provocation, rage, stimulation, stimulus, stir, thrill, titillation, to-do*, trepidation, tumult, turmoil, urge, warmth, wildness; SEE CONCEPTS *388,410,633*

exciting [adj] *inspiring, exhilarating*
agitative, animating, appealing, arousing, arresting, astonishing, bracing, breathtaking, commoving, dangerous, dramatic, electrifying, exhilarant, eye-popping*, far-out*, fine, flashy, groovy*, hair-raising*, heady*, hectic, impelling, impressive, interesting, intoxicating, intriguing, lively, melodramatic, mind-blowing, moving, neat, overpowering, overwhelming, provocative, racy, rip-roaring*, rousing, sensational, showy, spine-tingling*, stimulating, stirring, thrilling, titillating, wild, zestful; SEE CONCEPTS *529,542,548*

exclaim [v] *shout out*
assert, bellow, blurt, burst out, call, call aloud, call out, cry, cry out, declare, ejaculate, emit, figure, holler, proclaim, rend the air*, roar, say loudly, shout, state, utter, vociferate, yawp*, yell; SEE CONCEPTS *47,49*

exclamation [n] *shout; assertion*
bellow, call, clamor, cry, ejaculation, expletive, holler, interjection, outcry, pfaugh*, roar, shout, utterance, vociferation, yawp*, yell; SEE CONCEPTS *49,77*

exclude [v] *expel, forbid*
ban, bar, bate, blackball*, blacklist, block, bounce, boycott, close out, count out, debar, disallow, drive out, eject, eliminate, embargo, estop, evict, except, expel, force out, get rid of, ignore, interdict, keep out, leave out, lock out, obviate, occlude, omit, ostracize, oust, pass over, preclude, prevent, prohibit, proscribe, put out, refuse, refuse admittance, reject, remove, repudiate, rule out, set aside, shut out, shut the door on*, sideline, suspend, throw out, veto, ward off; SEE CONCEPTS *25,30,121*

exclusion [n] *expulsion; forbiddance*
ban, bar, blackball*, blockade, boycott, coventry, cut, debarment, debarring, discharge, dismissal, ejection, elimination, embargo, eviction, exception, excommunication, interdict, interdicting, interdiction, keeping out, lockout, nonadmission, occlusion, omission, ostracism, ousting, preclusion, prevention, prohibition, proscription, refusal, rejection, relegation, removal, repudiation, segregation, separation, suspension, veto; SEE CONCEPTS *25,30,121*

exclusive [adj] *unshared, restricted*
absolute, aloof, aristocratic, chic, choice, chosen, circumscribed, clannish, classy, cliquish, closed, complete, confined, country club, discriminative, elegant, entire, exclusionary, exclusory, fashionable, full, independent, licensed, limited, narrow, only, particular, peculiar, posh, preferential, private, privileged, prohibitive, restrictive, ritzy, segregated, select, selfish, single, snobbish, socially correct, sole, swank, total, undivided, unique, upper crust*, whole; SEE CONCEPTS *554,567*

exclusively [adv] *particularly*
alone, but, completely, entirely, one and only, onliest, only, singularly, solely, wholly; SEE CONCEPT *554*

exclusive of [prep] *except for*
aside from, bar, barring, bating, besides, but, debarring, except, excepting, excluding, leaving aside, not counting, omitting, outside of, restricting, ruling out, save; SEE CONCEPT *554*

excogitate [v] *think about seriously*
conceive, consider, contemplate, contrive, deliberate, derive, develop, devise, educe, evolve, frame, invent, mind, mull over, perpend, ponder, ruminate, study, think out, think up, weigh, work out; SEE CONCEPTS *17,24*

excommunicate [v] *banish*
anathematize, ban, cast out, curse, denounce, dismiss, eject, exclude, expel, oust, proscribe, remove, repudiate, unchurch; SEE CONCEPTS *317,367*

excoriate [v1] *scrape layers off*
abrade, chafe, flay, fret, gall, peel, rub, scarify, scratch, skin, strip; SEE CONCEPTS *211,215*

excoriate [v2] *denounce, criticize*
attack, berate, blister, castigate, censure, chastise, condemn, flay, lambaste, lash, rebuke, reproach, reprove, revile, scathe, scold, scorch, slash, tear into, upbraid, vilify; SEE CONCEPT 52

excrete [v] *discharge, usually liquified substance*
defecate, egest, ejaculate, eject, eliminate, emanate, evacuate, exhale, expel, exudate, exude, give off, leak, pass, perspire, produce, remove, secrete, sweat, throw off, urinate, void; SEE CONCEPTS 179,185

excruciating [adj] *torturous, painful*
acute, agonizing, burning, chastening, consuming, exquisite, extreme, grueling, harrowing, insufferable, intense, piercing, punishing, racking, rending, searing, severe, sharp, shooting, stabbing, tearing, tormenting, torturesome, torturing, unbearable, unendurable, violent; SEE CONCEPTS 314,548,609

exculpate [v] *forgive*
absolve, acquit, amnesty, clear, condone, discharge, disculpate, dismiss, excuse, exonerate, explain, free, justify, let off*, pardon, rationalize, release, remit, vindicate, wipe slate clean*; SEE CONCEPTS 10,127, 317

excursion [n] *journey*
circuit, cruise, day trip, digression, expedition, jaunt, junket, outing, picnic, pleasure trip, ramble, round trip, safari, tour, trek, trip, walk, wandering; SEE CONCEPTS 224,384

excusable [adj] *allowable*
all right, condonable, defensible, exculpatory, explainable, fair, forgivable, justifiable, minor, moderate, not too bad*, okay, pardonable, passable, permissible, plausible, reasonable, remittable, reprievable, slight, specious, temperate, tenable, trivial, understandable, venial, vindicable, vindicatory, warrantable, within limits; SEE CONCEPT 558

excuse [n] *reason, explanation*
alibi, apology, cleanup*, cop-out*, cover*, cover story*, coverup, defense, disguise, evasion, expedient, extenuation, fish story*, grounds, jive*, justification, makeshift, mitigation, plea, pretext, rationalization, regrets, routine, semblance, shift, song*, song and dance*, stall, stopgap*, story, substitute, subterfuge, trick*, vindication, whitewash*, why and wherefore*; SEE CONCEPTS 59,661

excuse [v] *forgive, absolve; justify*
absolve, acquit, alibi, apologize for, appease, bear with, clear, condone, cover, defend, discharge, dispense from, exculpate, exempt, exempt from, exonerate, explain, extenuate, forgive, free, give absolution, grant amnesty, indulge, justify, let go*, let off*, liberate, make allowances for, mitigate, overlook, pardon, pass over*, plead ignorance, pretext, purge, rationalize, release, relieve, remit, reprieve, shrive, shrug off*, spare, take rap for*, tolerate, vindicate, whitewash*, wink at*; SEE CONCEPTS 10,57,83

execrable [adj] *horrible, sickening*
abhorrent, abominable, accursed, atrocious, confounded, cursed, damnable, defective, deplorable, despicable, detestable, disgusting, foul, hateful, heinous, horrific, loathsome, low, monstrous, nauseous, obnoxious, odious, offensive, repulsive, revolting, vile, wretched; SEE CONCEPT 542

execrate [v] *hate*
abhor, abominate, accurse, anathematize, censure, condemn, curse, damn, denounce, deplore, despise, detest, excoriate, imprecate, loathe, objurgate, reprehend, reprobate, reprove, revile, vilify; SEE CONCEPT 29

execration [n] *hating*
abhorrence, abomination, anathema, blasphemy, condemnation, contempt, curse, cursing, cussing, damnation, denunciation, detestation, detesting, excoriation, hate, hatred, imprecation, loathing, malediction, odium, profanity, swearing, vilification; SEE CONCEPT 29

execute [v1] *kill*
assassinate, behead, bump off*, do in*, electrocute, eliminate, finish, gas, guillotine, hang, knock off*, liquidate, murder, purge, put away*, put to death, shoot; SEE CONCEPT 252

execute [v2] *carry out a task*
accomplish, achieve, act, administer, administrate, bring off, bring to fruition, cause, come through, complete, consummate, deal with, discharge, do, do the job*, do the trick*, do to a T*, earn wings*, effect, enact, enforce, finish, fulfill, get there*, govern, hack it*, hit*, implement, make it*, meet, percolate*, perform, play, polish off*, prosecute, pull off*, put into effect, put over*, put through, realize, render, sail through*, score*, take care of, take care of business*, transact; SEE CONCEPTS 91,706

execution [n1] *killing*
beheading, capital punishment, contract killing*, crucifixion, decapitation, electrocution, gassing, guillotining, hanging, hit, impalement, lethal injection, necktie party*, punishment, rub out*, shooting, strangling, strangulation; SEE CONCEPT 252

execution [n2] *carrying out of a task*
accomplishment, achievement, administration, completion, consummation, delivery, discharge, doing, effect, enactment, enforcement, fulfilling, implementation, nuts and bolts*, operation, performance, prosecution, realization, rendering, style; SEE CONCEPTS 91,706

executive [n] *person who manages organization*
administration, administrator, baron, big man/woman*, big wheel*, boss, brass, businessman/woman, CEO*, chief, CO*, commander, director, directorate, don, entrepreneur, exec*, godfather*, government, governor, head, head honcho*, head man/woman*, heavyweight*, hierarchy, higher-up*, high priest*, industrialist, key player*, kingfish*, kingpin*, leader, leadership, management, manager,

officer, official, skipper*, supervisor, top brass*, tycoon, VIP*; SEE CONCEPTS *347,354*

executive [*adj*] *administrative*
controlling, decision-making, directing, governing, managerial, managing, ruling; SEE CONCEPT *527*

exemplar [*n*] *ideal*
archetype, copy, criterion, epitome, example, exemplification, illustration, instance, mirror, model, paradigm, paragon, pattern, prototype, specimen, standard, type; SEE CONCEPT *688*

exemplary [*adj*] *ideal*
admirable, batting a thousand*, blameless, bueno*, characteristic, classic, classical, commendable, correct, estimable, excellent, good, guiltless, honorable, illustrative, inculpable, innocent, irreprehensible, laudable, meritorious, model, neato*, not bad*, not too shabby*, paradigmatic, praiseworthy, prototypical, punctilious, pure, quintessential, representative, righteous, sterling, typical, virtuous, worthy; SEE CONCEPTS *404,572,574*

exemplify [*v*] *serve as an example*
body, cite, clarify, clear up, demonstrate, depict, display, elucidate, emblematize, embody, enlighten, epitomize, evidence, exhibit, illuminate, illustrate, instance, manifest, mirror, personify, quote, represent, show, spell out, symbolize, typify; SEE CONCEPTS *97,118*

exempt [*adj*] *freed from responsibility*
absolved, beat the rap*, clear, cleared, discharged, excepted, excluded, excused, favored, free, immune, let go*, let off*, liberated, not liable, not responsible, not subject, off the hook*, outside, privileged, released, set apart, spared, special, unbound, unchecked, unrestrained, unrestricted, unshackled, void of, walked*; SEE CONCEPTS *319,554*

exempt [*v*] *relieve, absolve*
clear, discharge, dispense, except, excuse, exonerate, free, go easy on*, grant immunity, let off*, let off the hook*, liberate, pass by, privilege from, release, spare, wipe the slate*, write off; SEE CONCEPTS *50,83,88,127*

exemption [*n*] *freedom from a responsibility*
absolution, discharge, dispensation, exception, exoneration, immunity, impunity, privilege, release; SEE CONCEPTS *652,685,691*

exercise [*n1*] *work, effort*
act, action, activity, calisthenics, constitutional*, daily dozen*, discharge, discipline, drill, drilling, examination, exercising, exertion, gym, labor, lesson, movement, occupation, operation, performance, problem, pursuit, recitation, schoolwork, study, task, test, theme, toil, training, warm-up, workout; SEE CONCEPTS *87,290,362,363*

exercise [*n2*] *accomplishment, use*
application, discharge, employment, enjoyment, exercising, exertion, fulfillment, implementation, operation, performance, practice, pursuit, utilization; SEE CONCEPTS *225,706*

exercise [*v1*] *put to use*
apply, bestow, bring to bear, devote, drill, employ, enjoy, execute, exert, exploit, handle, operate, practice, put into practice, rehearse, sharpen, use, utilize, wield; SEE CONCEPT *225*

exercise [*v2*] *do repeatedly, especially to improve*
break, break in, condition, cultivate, develop, discipline, drill, dry run*, exert, fix, foster, groom, habituate, hone, improve, inure, labor, lick into shape*, limber up, loosen up, maneuver, ply, practice, prepare, pump iron*, put out, put through grind*, put through mill*, rehearse, run through, set, strain, teach, train, tune up, walk through, warm up, work, work out; SEE CONCEPTS *87,363*

exercise [*v3*] *upset, worry*
abrade, afflict, agitate, annoy, bother, burden, chafe, distress, disturb, gall, irk, occupy, pain, perturb, preoccupy, provoke, trouble, try, vex; SEE CONCEPTS *7,19*

exert [*v*] *make use of*
apply, apply oneself, bring into play*, bring to bear*, dig*, employ, endeavor, exercise, expend, give all one's got*, give best shot*, labor, make effort, peg away*, plug*, ply, pour it on*, push, put forth, put out, strain, strive, struggle, sweat it*, throw, toil, try hard, use, utilize, wield, work; SEE CONCEPTS *87,225*

exertion [*n*] *hard work*
action, activity, application, attempt, effort, elbow grease*, employment, endeavor, exercise, hard pull*, industry, labor, long pull*, operation, pains, strain, stretch, striving, struggle, toil, travail, trial, trouble, use, utilization; SEE CONCEPTS *87,362,677*

exhale [*v*] *breathe out*
breathe, discharge, eject, emanate, emit, evaporate, expel, give off, issue, let out, outbreathe, respire, steam, vaporize; SEE CONCEPT *163*

exhaust [*v1*] *tire or wear out*
bankrupt, burn out*, conk out*, cripple, debilitate, disable, do in*, drain, draw, enervate, enfeeble, fag, fatigue, frazzle, impoverish, overdo, overexert, overextend, overfatigue, overtire, overwork, peter out*, poop*, poop out*, prostrate, run ragged*, sap*, suck dry*, tire, tucker*, use up, weaken, wear down, weary; SEE CONCEPTS *250,469*

exhaust [*v2*] *consume, use up*
bankrupt, bleed white*, deplete, devour, dispel, disperse, dissipate, drain, draw, dry, eat, eat up*, empty, expend, finish, impoverish, run out, run through, spend, squander, strain, suck dry*, take last of, void, wash up, waste; SEE CONCEPTS *169,225*

exhausted [*adj1*] *extremely tired*
all in*, beat*, bleary, bone-weary, bushed, crippled, dead*, dead tired*, debilitated, disabled, dog-tired*, done for*, done in*, drained, effete, enervated, frazzled, had it*, kaput*, limp, out on one's feet*, outta gas*, prostrated, ready to drop*, run-down, sapped*, shot*, spent, tired out, wasted*, weak, weakened, wearied, worn, worn out; SEE CONCEPTS *406,485*

exhausted [*adj2*] *used up*
all gone, at an end, bare, consumed, depleted, dissipated, done, drained, dry, empty, expended, finished, gone, spent, squandered, used, void, washed-out, wasted; SEE CONCEPTS *560,771*

exhaustion [*n*] *tiredness*
burnout*, collapse, consumption, debilitation, debility, enervation, expenditure, fatigue, feebleness, lassitude, prostration, weariness; SEE CONCEPTS *410,720*

exhaustive [*adj*] *all-inclusive, complete*
all-embracing, all-encompassing, all-out, catholic, comprehensive, embracive, encyclopedic, extensive, far-reaching, from A to Z*, full, full-blown, full-dress*, full-scale, in-depth, intensive, no stone unturned*, out-and-out*, profound, radical, sweeping, the word, thorough, thoroughgoing, total, whole-hog*; SEE CONCEPTS *531,772*

exhibit [*n*] *viewing; presentation*
display, exhibition, exposition, fair, illustration, model, performance, show; SEE CONCEPTS *259,261*

exhibit [*v*] *put on view; present*
advertise, air, brandish, demonstrate, disclose, display, disport, evidence, evince, expose, express, feature, flash, flaunt, illustrate, indicate, let it all hang out*, make clear, make plain, manifest, mark, offer, ostend, parade, parade wares*, proclaim, reveal, roll out, show, show and tell*, showcase, show off, strut stuff*, trot out*, wave around*; SEE CONCEPT *261*

exhibition [*n*] *showing, demonstration*
advertisement, airing, an act*, a scene*, carnival, display, exhibit, expo, exposition, fair, fireworks, flash*, front*, manifestation, offering, pageant, performance, presentation, representation, show, sight, spectacle; SEE CONCEPTS *261,386*

exhilarate [*v*] *make very happy*
animate, boost, buoy, cheer, commove, delight, elate, enliven, exalt, excite, gladden, inspire, inspirit, invigorate, juice*, lift, pep up*, perk up*, pick up, put zip into*, quicken, rejoice, send, snap up*, stimulate, thrill, turn on*, uplift, vitalize; SEE CONCEPTS *7,22*

exhilarating [*adj*] *stimulating, cheering*
animating, animative, bracing, breathtaking, electric, elevating, enlivening, exalting, exciting, exhilarant, exhilarative, exhilaratory, eye-popping*, gladdening, inspiring, inspiriting, intoxicating, invigorating, quickening, rousing, stimulating, stimulative, stirring, thrilling, tonic, uplifting, vitalizing; SEE CONCEPTS *529,548*

exhilaration [*n*] *great happiness, excitement*
animation, a rush*, cheerfulness, delight, elation, electrification, elevation, enlivenment, euphoria, exaltation, excitation, firing, gaiety, galvanization, gladness, gleefulness, head rush*, high spirits*, hilarity, inspiration, invigoration, joy, joyfulness, liveliness, mirth, quickening, sprightliness, stimulation, uplift, vitalization, vivacity, vivification; SEE CONCEPT *410*

exhort [*v*] *urge, warn*
admonish, advise, beseech, bid, call upon, caution, counsel, egg on*, encourage, enjoin, entreat, goad, incite, insist, persuade, plead, preach, press, pressure, prick, prod, prompt, propel, spur, stimulate; SEE CONCEPTS *75,78*

exhortation [*n*] *warning, urging*
admonition, advice, beseeching, bidding, caution, counsel, encouragement, enjoinder, entreaty, goading, incitement, instigation, lecture, persuasion, preaching, sermon; SEE CONCEPTS *75,78,274*

exhume [*v*] *dig up, especially the dead*
disclose, disembalm, disentomb, disinhume, disinter, exhumate, resurrect, reveal, unbury, uncharnel, unearth; SEE CONCEPT *178*

exigency/exigence [*n*] *difficulty; demand*
acuteness, constraint, contingency, crisis, criticalness, crossroad, demandingness, dilemma, distress, duress, emergency, extremity, fix, hardship, imperativeness, jam, juncture, necessity, need, needfulness, pass, pickle*, pinch, plight, predicament, pressingness, pressure, quandary, requirement, scrape*, stress, turning point*, urgency, vicissitude, want, wont, zero hour*; SEE CONCEPTS *646,674,709*

exigent [*adj1*] *urgent, pressing*
acute, burning, clamant, clamorous, constraining, critical, crucial, crying, imperative, importunate, insistent, instant, menacing, necessary, needful, threatening; SEE CONCEPTS *548,568*

exigent [*adj2*] *difficult, taxing*
arduous, burdensome, demanding, exacting, grievous, hard, harsh, onerous, oppressive, rigorous, severe, stiff, strict, stringent, superincumbent, tough, weighty; SEE CONCEPTS *537,542*

exiguous [*adj*] *scanty*
bare, confined, diminutive, inadequate, limited, little, meager, narrow, negligible, paltry, petty, poor, restricted, scant, skimpy, slender, slight, small, spare, sparse, tenuous, thin, tiny; SEE CONCEPTS *771,789*

exile [*n1*] *deportation from place*
banishment, diaspora, dispersion, displacement, exclusion, expatriation, expulsion, extradition, migration, ostracism, proscription, relegation, scattering, separation; SEE CONCEPT *298*

exile [*n2*] *person deported from place*
deportee, displaced person, DP*, émigré, expatriate, expellee, fugitive, man without country*, nonperson*, outcast, outlaw, refugee; SEE CONCEPTS *354,412,423*

exile [*v*] *deport from place*
banish, cast out, displace, dispossess, drive out, eject, evacuate, expatriate, expel, expulse, extradite, ostracize, oust, outlaw, proscribe, relegate, transport, turn out; SEE CONCEPTS *122,198,298*

exist [*v1*] *be living*
abide, be, be extant, be latent, be present, breathe, continue, endure, happen, last, lie, live, move, ob-

tain, occur, prevail, remain, stand, stay, subsist, survive; SEE CONCEPT *407*

exist [v2] *get along in life*
consist, dwell, eke out a living*, endure, get by*, go on, inhere, kick*, lie, live, make it*, reside, stay alive*, subsist, survive; SEE CONCEPTS *100,226*

existence [n] *life*
actuality, animation, being, breath, continuance, continuation, duration, endurance, entity, essence, hand one is dealt*, individuality, journey, lifing, permanence, perseverance, presence, rat race*, reality, real world*, something, subsistence, survival, the big game*, world; SEE CONCEPTS *407,639*

exit [n1] *way out of a place*
avenue, door, egress, fire escape, gate, hole, opening, outlet, passage out, vent; SEE CONCEPT *440*

exit [n2] *leaving*
adieu, death, demise, departure, egress, egression, evacuation, exodus, expiration, expiry, farewell, going, goodbye, leave-taking, offgoing, retirement, retreat, stampede, withdrawal; SEE CONCEPT *195*

exit [v] *leave a place*
bid farewell, blow*, depart, do vanishing act*, flake off*, get*, get away, get off, git*, go, go away, go out, issue, move, move out, quit, retire, retreat, say goodbye, split*, take a hike*, take one's leave*, withdraw; SEE CONCEPT *195*

exodus [n] *leaving*
departure, egress, egression, emigration, evacuation, exit, exiting, flight, going out, journey, migration, offgoing, retirement, retreat, withdrawal; SEE CONCEPT *195*

exonerate [v] *excuse, clear of responsibility or blame*
absolve, acquit, disburden, discharge, dismiss, except, exculpate, excuse, exempt, free, justify, let off*, let off hook*, liberate, pardon, release, relieve, sanitize, vindicate, whitewash*, wipe slate clean*; SEE CONCEPTS *10,127,317*

exorbitant [adj] *extravagant, excessive*
absonant, dear, enormous, exacting, expensive, extortionate, extreme, high, highway robbery*, immoderate, inordinate, out of sight*, outrageous, overboard, overmuch, over one's head*, preposterous, pricey, steep*, stiff*, towering, unconscionable, undue, unreasonable, unwarranted, up to here*, wasteful; SEE CONCEPTS *334,547,558*

exotic [adj] *not native or usual; mysterious*
alien, alluring, avant garde, bizarre, colorful, curious, different, enticing, external, extraneous, extraordinary, extrinsic, far out*, fascinating, foreign, glamorous, imported, introduced, kinky*, outlandish, outside, peculiar, peregrine, romantic, strange, striking, unfamiliar, unusual, way out*, weird*; SEE CONCEPTS *542,549*

expand [v1] *extend, augment*
aggrandize, amplify, beef up*, bloat, blow up*, bolster, broaden, bulk up*, burgeon, detail, develop, diffuse, dilate, distend, elaborate, embellish, en-large, explicate, fan out*, fatten, fill out, grow, heighten, hike, increase, inflate, lengthen, magnify, mount, multiply, mushroom, open, open out, outspread, pad, piggyback*, prolong, protract, puff up*, pyramid*, slap on*, soup up*, spread, spread out, stretch, stretch out, swell, tack on*, thicken, unfold, unfurl, unravel, unroll, upsurge, wax*, widen; SEE CONCEPTS *236,245*

expand [v2] *go into detail*
amplify, beef up*, build up, develop, dilate, discourse, drag out*, elaborate, embellish, enlarge, expatiate, expound, extend, flesh out*, spell out, sweeten; SEE CONCEPT *57*

expanse [n] *large space, usually open*
amplitude, area, belt, breadth, compass, distance, domain, extension, extent, field, immensity, latitude, length, margin, orbit, plain, radius, range, reach, region, remoteness, room, scope, span, sphere, spread, stretch, sweep, territory, tract, uninterrupted space, width, wilderness; SEE CONCEPTS *509,513, 651,787*

expansion [n] *growth*
amplification, augmentation, breadth, development, diffusion, dilation, distance, distension, enlargement, evolution, expanse, extension, increase, inflation, magnification, maturation, multiplication, opening out, space, spread, stretch, swelling, unfolding, unfurling; SEE CONCEPTS *700,704,780*

expansive [adj1] *broad, comprehensive*
all-embracing, ample, big, dilatant, elastic, expanding, expansile, extensive, far-reaching, great, inclusive, large, scopic, scopious, stretching, thorough, unrepressed, unsuppressed, voluminous, wide, wide-ranging, widespread; SEE CONCEPT *772*

expansive [adj2] *talkative*
affable, communicative, demonstrative, easy, effervescent, effusive, extroverted, free, friendly, garrulous, generous, genial, gregarious, gushy, lavish, liberal, loquacious, open, outgoing, sociable, unconstrained, uninhibited, unreserved, unrestrained, warm; SEE CONCEPT *267*

expatriate [n] *person thrown out of country*
departer, deportee, displaced person, emigrant, émigré, evacuee, exile, expellee, migrant, outcast, refugee; SEE CONCEPTS *354,412,423*

expatriate [v] *throw out of country*
banish, deport, displace, exile, expel, expulse, ostracize, oust, proscribe, relegate, transport; SEE CONCEPTS *130,198,211*

expect [v1] *believe strongly; anticipate*
apprehend, assume, await, bargain for, bargain on, be afraid, calculate, conjecture, contemplate, count on, divine, envisage, feel, figure, forecast, foreknow, foresee, gather, hope, hope for, imagine, in the cards*, look, look ahead to, look for, look forward to*, predict, presume, presuppose, reckon, see coming*, sense, suppose, surmise, suspect, take,

think, trust, understand, wait for, watch for; SEE CONCEPTS *12,26*

expect [*v2*] *want, wish*
call for, count on, demand, exact, insist on, look for, rely upon, require; SEE CONCEPT *20*

expectancy [*n*] *anticipation*
assumption, assurance, belief, calculation, confidence, conjecture, expectation, hope, likelihood, looking forward, outlook, prediction, presentation, presentiment, presumption, probability, prospect, reliance, supposition, surmise, suspense, trust, view, waiting; SEE CONCEPTS *410,689*

expectant [*adj1*] *anticipating*
alert, anticipative, anxious, apprehensive, awaiting, breathless, eager, expecting, hopeful, hoping, in suspense, looking for, on edge*, on tenterhooks*, prepared, raring*, ready, vigilant, waiting, waiting on, watchful, with bated breath*; SEE CONCEPTS *403,406*

expectant [*adj2*] *preparing to give birth*
enceinte, expecting, gravid, parturient, pregnant, with child*; SEE CONCEPT *485*

expectation [*n*] *belief, anticipation*
apprehension, assumption, assurance, calculation, chance, confidence, conjecture, design, expectancy, fear, forecast, hope, intention, likelihood, looking forward, motive, notion, outlook, possibility, prediction, presumption, probability, promise, prospect, reliance, supposition, surmise, suspense, trust, view; SEE CONCEPTS *410,689*

expediency/expedience [*n1*] *appropriateness; worth*
advantage, advantageousness, advisability, appositeness, aptness, benefit, convenience, desirability, effectiveness, efficiency, fitness, helpfulness, judiciousness, meetness, opportunism, opportunity, order, policy, practicality, pragmatism, profitability, profitableness, properness, propitiousness, propriety, prudence, rightness, suitability, usefulness, utilitarianism, utility; SEE CONCEPTS *656,658*

expediency/expedience [*n2*] *resource*
band-aid*, contrivance, design, device, dodge, easy way out*, expedient, gimmick*, makeshift*, maneuver, means, measure, method, recourse, resort, scheme, shift, step, stopgap*, stratagem, strategy, substitute, surrogate, tactic, trick; SEE CONCEPTS *660,712*

expedient [*n*] *resource*
agency, contrivance, device, expediency, instrument, instrumentality, makeshift, maneuver, means, measure, medium, method, recourse, refuge, resort, scheme, shift, stopgap, stratagem, substitute; SEE CONCEPTS *660,712*

expedient [*adj*] *worthwhile, appropriate*
ad hoc, advantageous, advisable, appropriate, beneficial, convenient, desirable, discreet, effective, feasible, fit, fitting, helpful, judicious, meet, opportune, politic, possible, practicable, practical, pragmatic, profitable, proper, prudent, seasonable, suitable, tac-

tical, timely, useful, utilitarian, wise; SEE CONCEPTS *558,560*

expedite [*v*] *make happen faster*
accelerate, advance, assist, cut red tape*, dispatch, facilitate, fast track*, forward, grease wheels*, hand-carry, handle personally, hand-walk*, hasten, hurry, precipitate, press, promote, quicken, railroad*, run interference*, run with ball*, rush, shoot through*, speed, speed up, urge, walk it through*; SEE CONCEPT *242*

expedition [*n1*] *journey; people on a journey*
campaign, caravan, cavalcade, company, crew, crowd, cruise, crusade, enterprise, entrada, excursion, exploration, explorers, fleet, jaunt, junket, mission, outing, party, patrol, peregrination, picnic, posse, quest, safari, squadron, swing, team, tour, travel, travellers, trek, trip, undertaking, voyage, voyagers, wayfarers; SEE CONCEPTS *224,417*

expedition [*n2*] *speed; speeding up*
alacrity, celerity, dispatch, expeditiousness, goodwill, haste, hurry, hustle, promptitude, promptness, punctuality, quickness, rapidity, readiness, speediness, swiftness; SEE CONCEPTS *242,755*

expeditious [*adj*] *immediate, speedy*
active, alert, breakneck, brisk, diligent, effective, effectual, efficient, fast, fleet, hasty, instant, nimble, prompt, punctual, quick, rapid, ready, swift; SEE CONCEPTS *542,588*

expel [*v1*] *discharge*
belch, blow out, cast out, discharge, disgorge, dislodge, drive out, ejaculate, eruct, erupt, evacuate, exhaust, exudate, exude, get rid of, irrupt, pass, remove, spew, throw out, vomit; SEE CONCEPT *179*

expel [*v2*] *throw out, banish*
ban, bar, blackball*, bust, cast out, chase, deport, discharge, dismiss, displace, dispossess, drum out, eject, eliminate, evict, exclude, exile, expatriate, expulse, fire, give the boot*, give the hook*, give walking papers*, kick, kick out, oust, proscribe, send packing*, show the door*, suspend, throw out on ear*, turn out; SEE CONCEPTS *122,130,198*

expend [*v*] *exhaust; spend*
ante up*, blow*, consume, disburse, dish out*, dispense, dissipate, distribute, employ, finish, foot the bill*, fork out*, give, go through*, lay out, outlay, pay, pay out, put out*, shell out*, splurge*, spring for*, throw money at*, use up, wash up*; SEE CONCEPTS *225,341*

expendable [*adj*] *not important*
dispensable, disposable, excess, inessential, nonessential, replaceable, superfluous, unimportant; SEE CONCEPTS *546,575*

expenditure [*n*] *payment*
amount, application, bottom line*, cash on barrelhead*, charge, come to*, consumption, cost, disbursement, dissipation, expense, figure, investment, kickback*, outgo, outlay, output, payoff, price, rate, setback*, spending, splurge, squander, throw*,

tune*, use, valuation, value, waste; SEE CONCEPT *344*

expense [*n*] *cost, payment*
amount, assessment, bite*, bottom line*, budget, charge, consumption, debit, debt, decrement, deprivation, disbursement, duty, expenditure, forfeit, forfeiture, insurance, investment, liability, loan, loss, mortgage, obligation, outdo*, outlay, out of pocket*, output, overhead, payroll, price, price tag, rate, responsibility, risk, sacrifice, spending, sum, surcharge, tariff, toll, upkeep, use, value, worth; SEE CONCEPTS *328,329,336,344*

expensive [*adj*] *high-priced*
an arm and a leg*, at a premium, big-ticket*, cher*, costly, dear, excessive, exorbitant, extravagant, fancy, high, highway robbery*, holdup*, immoderate, inordinate, invaluable, lavish, out of sight*, overpriced, plush, posh, pretty penny*, pricey*, rich, ritzy*, sky-high*, steep*, stiff*, swank*, too high, uneconomical, unreasonable, upscale*, valuable; SEE CONCEPT *334*

experience [*n1*] *knowledge*
acquaintance, action, actuality, background, caution, combat, contact, doing, empiricism, evidence, existence, exposure, familiarity, forebearance, intimacy, involvement, inwardness, judgment, know-how*, maturity, observation, participation, patience, perspicacity, practicality, practice, proof, reality, savoir-faire, seasoning, sense, skill, sophistication, strife, struggle, training, trial, understanding, wisdom, worldliness; SEE CONCEPT *409*

experience [*n2*] *happening, occurrence*
adventure, affair, encounter, episode, event, incident, ordeal, test, trial, trip; SEE CONCEPTS *2,696*

experienced [*adj*] *knowledgeable, knowing*
accomplished, accustomed, adept, been around*, been there*, broken in*, capable, competent, cultivated, dynamite, expert, familiar, having something on the ball*, instructed, in the know*, knowing one's stuff*, knowing the score*, master, mature, matured, old, old hand*, practical, practiced, pro, professional, qualified, rounded, seasoned, skillful, sophisticated, sport, tested, the right stuff*, trained, tried, versed, vet, veteran, well-versed, wise, worldly, worldly-wise*; SEE CONCEPTS *402,527*

experiment [*n*] *investigation, test*
agreement, analysis, assay, attempt, check, dissection, dry run*, enterprise, essay, examination, exercise, experimentation, fling*, measure, observation, operation, practice, probe, procedure, proof, quiz, R and D*, rehearsal, research, research and development, scrutiny, search, speculation, study, trial, trial and error*, trial run*, try, try-on, tryout, undertaking, venture, verification; SEE CONCEPTS *103,290*

experiment [*v*] *investigate, test*
analyze, assay, diagnose, examine, explore, fool with*, futz around*, mess around*, play around with*, practice with, probe, prove, put to the test*, research, sample, scrutinize, search, shake down*, speculate, study, try, try on, try on for size*, try out, venture, verify, weigh; SEE CONCEPTS *24,87,103*

experimental [*adj*] *exploratory*
beginning, developmental, empirical, experiential, first stage, laboratory, momentary, on approval, pilot, preliminary, preparatory, primary, probationary, provisional, rodential, speculative, temporary, tentative, test, trial, trial-and-error, unconcluded, under probation, unproved; SEE CONCEPT *535*

expert [*n*] *master, specialist*
ace*, adept, artist, artiste, authority, buff, connoisseur, doyen, graduate, guru*, hot shot*, maven, old hand*, old pro*, phenomenon, pro, professional, proficient, shark*, virtuoso, whiz*, wizard; SEE CONCEPTS *348,350,416*

expert [*adj*] *knowledgeable, proficient*
able, adept, adroit, apt, big league*, clever, crack, crackerjack*, deft, dexterous, experienced, facile, handy, master, masterful, masterly, practiced, professional, qualified, savvy, schooled, sharp, skilled, skillful, slick, trained, virtuoso; SEE CONCEPTS *402,527*

expertise/expertness [*n*] *knowledge, proficiency*
ability, ableness, adroitness, aptness, art, cleverness, command, competence, craft, cunning, deftness, dexterity, dodge*, expertness, facility, finesse, goods*, ingeniousness, judgment, knack*, knowhow*, line*, makings*, masterliness, mastery, oil*, one's thing*, prowess, readiness, savvy, sharpness, skill, skillfulness, stuff*; SEE CONCEPTS *409,630*

expiate [*v*] *make amends for*
absolve, amend, appease, atone, atone for, compensate, correct, do penance, excuse, forgive, pay one's dues*, rectify, redeem, redress, remedy, square things*; SEE CONCEPTS *67,126*

expiration [*n*] *finish, demise*
cessation, close, closing, conclusion, death, decease, departure, dying, elapsing, end, expiry, finish, going, passing, termination, terminus; SEE CONCEPTS *119,304*

expire [*v1*] *come to an end*
bite the dust*, buy it*, cash in chips*, cease, close, conclude, croak*, decease, depart, die, elapse, end, finish, go, kick the bucket*, lapse, pass, pass away, pass on, pass over, perish, quit, run out, stop, strike out*, terminate, up and die*; SEE CONCEPTS *119,304*

expire [*v2*] *breathe out*
emit, exhale, expel, outbreathe; SEE CONCEPTS *163,185*

explain [*v*] *make clear; give a reason for*
account for, analyze, annotate, break down, bring out, clarify, clear up, construe, decipher, define, demonstrate, describe, diagram, disclose, elucidate, excuse, explicate, expound, get across*, go into detail, illustrate, interpret, justify, make plain*, manifest, paraphrase, point out, put across, put in plain English*, rationalize, read, refine, render, resolve,

reveal, set right, solve, spell out*, teach, tell, throw light upon*, translate, unfold, unravel, untangle; SEE CONCEPT 57

explanation [n] *clarification; reason*
account, annotation, answer, breakdown, brief, cause, comment, commentary, confession, definition, demonstration, description, details, display, elucidation, evidence, example, excuse, explication, exposition, expression, gloss, history, illustration, information, interpretation, justification, meaning, mitigation, motive, narration, note, recital, rendition, report, resolution, sense, showing, significance, specification, statement, story, summary, tale, talking, telling, vindication, writing; SEE CONCEPTS *271,274,661*

explanatory [adj] *descriptive*
allegorical, analytical, annotative, critical, declarative, demonstrative, diagrammatic, discursive, elucidatory, enlightening, exegetic, exegetical, explicative, expositional, expository, graphic, guiding, hermeneutic, illuminative, illustrative, informative, informing, instructive, interpretive, justifying, summary, supplementary; SEE CONCEPT *267*

expletive [n] *swear word; exclamation*
curse, cuss, cuss word, interjection, oath, swear; SEE CONCEPT *275*

explicate [v] *clarify, expand*
amplify, clear up, construe, demonstrate, develop, dilate, elucidate, enlarge upon, enucleate, expatiate, explain, expound, give the big picture*, illustrate, interpret, make clear, make explicit, make plain*, run down, spell out*, tell why, unfold, untangle, work out; SEE CONCEPT *57*

explicit [adj] *specific, unambiguous*
absolute, accurate, categorical, certain, clean-cut, clear, clear-cut, correct, definite, definitive, direct, distinct, exact, express, frank, lucid, obvious, on the nose*, open, outspoken, patent, perspicuous, plain, positive, precise, stated, straightforward, sure, understandable, unequivocal, unqualified, unreserved; SEE CONCEPTS *267,529,535*

explode [v1] *blow up*
backfire, blast, blaze, blow out, blow to kingdom come*, break out, burst, collapse, convulse, detonate, discharge, erupt, flame up, flare up, fracture, jet, kablooey*, let go*, mushroom*, rupture, set off, shatter, shiver, split, thunder; SEE CONCEPTS *179,320*

explode [v2] *discredit*
belie, confute, debunk, deflate, discard, disprove, invalidate, puncture, refute, repudiate, shoot down*, shoot full of holes*; SEE CONCEPT *54*

exploit [n] *achievement*
accomplishment, adventure, attainment, coup, deed, do, effort, enterprise, escapade, feat, job, maneuver, performance, stroke, stunt, tour de force, venture; SEE CONCEPT *706*

exploit [v] *take advantage of; misuse*
abuse, apply, avail oneself of, bleed*, capitalize on, cash in on*, employ, exercise, finesse, fleece*, get

mileage out of*, handle, impose upon, jockey*, make capital of, make use of, maneuver, manipulate, milk*, mine*, play*, play on, profit by, profit from, put to use, skin*, soak*, stick*, use, utilize, work; SEE CONCEPTS *156,225*

exploration [n] *investigation; survey*
analysis, examination, expedition, inquiry, inspection, probe, reconnaissance, research, scrutiny, search, study, tour, travel, trip; SEE CONCEPTS *216,224*

explore [v] *investigate; survey*
analyze, burrow, delve into, dig into, examine, go into*, have a look*, hunt, inquire into, inspect, leave no stone unturned*, look into, probe, prospect, question, reconnoitre, research, scout, scrutinize, search, seek, sift, test, tour, travel, traverse, try, turn inside out*; SEE CONCEPTS *103,216,224*

explosion [n] *eruption, discharge*
access, backfire, bang, blast, blowout, blowup, burst, clap, combustion, concussion, crack, detonation, firing, fit, flare-up, fulmination, gust, ignition, outbreak, outburst, paroxysm, percussion, pop, report, roar, salvo; SEE CONCEPTS *179,320,521*

explosive [n] *something that blows up*
ammunition, bomb, booby trap*, charge, detonator, dynamite, fireworks, grease*, grenade, gunpowder, mine, missile, mulligan, munition, nitroglycerin, pineapple*, powder, propellant, shell, shot, soup*, TNT*; SEE CONCEPT *500*

explosive [adj] *volatile, dangerous*
at the boiling point*, bursting, charged, consequential, convulsive, detonating, detonative, ebullient, eruptive, fiery, forceful, frenzied, fulminant, fulminating, hazardous, impetuous, meteoric, overwrought, perilous, raging, rampant, stormy, tense, touchy, ugly, uncontrollable, unstable, vehement, violent, wild; SEE CONCEPT *542*

exponent [n1] *person who supports, advocates*
advocate, backer, booster, champion, defender, demonstrator, expositor, expounder, interpreter, partisan, promoter, propagandist, proponent, protagonist, second, seconder, spokesman/woman, spokesperson, supporter, upholder; SEE CONCEPT *423*

exponent [n2] *example*
denotation, exemplar, illustration, index, indication, model, representative, sample, sign, specimen, token, type; SEE CONCEPTS *284,688*

export [v] *sell or trade abroad*
consign, convey, dump, find market, find outlet, freight, send out, ship, smuggle, transport, transship; SEE CONCEPTS *217,324*

exposé [n] *disclosure*
betrayal, confession, construction, divulgence, exegesis, explanation, explication, exposal, exposition, exposure, interpretation, revelation, truth, uncovering; SEE CONCEPT *274*

expose [v1] *reveal*
advertise, air, bare, betray, brandish, bring to light*, broadcast, crack, debunk, denude, dig up*, disclose,

display, disport, divulge, exhibit, feature, flash, flaunt, give away, lay bare*, lay open*, leak, let cat out of bag*, let out*, make known, manifest, open, open to view, parade, present, prove, publish, put on view, report, reveal, show, show off, smoke out*, spill, streak, tip off*, trot out*, unclothe, uncover, unearth, unfold, unmask, unshroud, unveil; SEE CONCEPTS *60,261*

expose [*v2*] *subject to danger*
endanger, hazard, imperil, jeopardize, lay open*, leave open*, make liable, make vulnerable, peril, put in harm's way*, risk; SEE CONCEPT *246*

exposed [*adj1*] *made public*
apparent, bare, bared, brought to light*, caught, clear, debunked, defined, denuded, disclosed, discovered, divulged, dug up*, evident, exhibited, for show, found out, laid bare*, made manifest, manifest, naked, on display, on the spot*, on view, open, peeled, resolved, revealed, shown, solved, stripped, unconcealed, uncovered, unhidden, unmasked, unprotected, unsealed, unsheltered, unveiled, visible; SEE CONCEPT *576*

exposed [*adj2*] *in danger*
accessible, in peril, laid bare*, laid open*, left open*, liable, menaced, open, prone, sensitive, subject, susceptible, threatened, unguarded, unprotected, vulnerable; SEE CONCEPTS *485,548*

exposition [*n1*] *written description*
account, analysis, annotation, article, comment, commentary, composition, construal, construction, critique, delineation, details, discourse, discussion, disquisition, dissertation, editorial, elucidation, enucleation, enunciation, essay, exegesis, explanation, explication, exposé, expounding, history, illustration, interpretation, monograph, paper, piece, position paper, presentation, report, review, statement, story, study, tale, text, theme, thesis, tract, tractate, treatise; SEE CONCEPTS *268,271*

exposition [*n2*] *fair*
bazaar, circus, county fair, demonstration, display, exhibition, expo, marketplace, mart, pageant, presentation, production, show, showing; SEE CONCEPT *386*

expository [*adj*] *descriptive*
critical, disquisitional, elucidative, exegetic, explanatory, explicative, explicatory, hermeneutic, illustrative, informative, interpretive; SEE CONCEPT *267*

expostulate [*v*] *reason with*
argue, dissuade, oppose, protest, remonstrate; SEE CONCEPT *46*

exposure [*n*] *uncovering; putting in view or danger*
acknowledgment, airing, baring, betrayal, confession, danger, defenselessness, denudation, denunciation, disclosure, display, divulgence, divulging, exhibition, exposé, giveaway, hazard, introduction, jeopardy, laying open, liability, manifestation, nakedness, openness, peril, presentation, publicity, revelation, risk, showing, susceptibility, susceptive-

ness, susceptivity, uncovering, unfolding, unmasking, unveiling, vulnerability, vulnerableness; SEE CONCEPTS *60,261*

expound [*v*] *talk about in great detail*
clarify, comment, construe, delineate, describe, discourse, elucidate, enucleate, exemplify, explain, explicate, express, illustrate, interpret, present, set forth, spell out, state, unfold; SEE CONCEPT *57*

express [*adj1*] *certain, precise*
accurate, categorical, clean-cut*, clear, clear-cut, considered, definite, definitive, deliberate, designful, direct, distinct, especial, exact, explicit, expressed, individual, intended, intentional, out-and-out*, outright, particular, plain, pointed, premeditated, set, singular, special, specific, unambiguous, unconditional, unmistakable, unqualified, uttered, voiced, voluntary, willing, witting; SEE CONCEPTS *535,556, 653*

express [*adj2*] *direct, speedy*
accelerated, fast, high-speed, nonstop, quick, rapid, swift, velocious; SEE CONCEPTS *548,588*

express [*v1*] *articulate; signify, mean*
add up to*, air, assert, asseverate, bespeak, broach, circulate, communicate, connote, convey, couch, declare, denote, depict, designate, disclose, divulge, embody, enunciate, evince, exhibit, formulate, frame*, give, hint, import, indicate, insinuate, intend, intimate, make known, manifest, phrase, pop off*, proclaim, pronounce, put, put across, put into words*, represent, reveal, say, show, speak, spell, stand for, state, suggest, symbolize, tell, testify, utter, vent, ventilate, verbalize, voice, word; SEE CONCEPTS *51,682*

express [*v2*] *discharge by squeezing or force*
crush, dispatch, distill, expel, extract, force out, forward, press out, ship, squeeze out; SEE CONCEPT *179*

expression [*n1*] *verbalization*
announcement, argument, articulation, assertion, asseveration, choice of words, commentary, communication, declaration, definition, delivery, diction, elucidation, emphasis, enunciation, execution, explanation, exposition, formulation, idiom, interpretation, intonation, issue, language, locution, mention, narration, phrase, phraseology, phrasing, pronouncement, remark, rendition, set phrase, speaking, speech, statement, style, term, turn of phrase, utterance, vent, voice, voicing, word, writ; SEE CONCEPTS *47,268,276*

expression [*n2*] *facial appearance*
air, aspect, cast, character, contortion, countenance, face, grimace, grin, look, mien, mug*, pout*, simper, smile, smirk, sneer, visage; SEE CONCEPT *716*

expressionless [*adj*] *having a blank look on face*
dead*, deadpan, dull, empty, fish-eyed*, impassive, inexpressive, inscrutable, lackluster, lusterless, nobody home*, poker-faced*, stolid, straight-faced, stupid, unexpressive, vacant, vacuous, wooden; SEE CONCEPT *406*

expressive [*adj*] *telling, revealing*
alive, allusive, articulate, artistic, brilliant, colorful, demonstrative, dramatic, eloquent, emphatic, energetic, forcible, graphic, indicative, ingenious, lively, masterly, meaningful, mobile, moving, passionate, pathetic, pictorial, picturesque, poignant, pointed, pregnant, representative, responsive, revelatory, showy, significant, silver-tongued*, spirited, stimulating, stirring, striking, strong, suggestive, sympathetic, tender, thoughtful, touching, understanding, vivid, warm; SEE CONCEPTS *267,537*

expressly [*adv1*] *purposely*
especially, exactly, in specie, intentionally, on purpose, particularly, precisely, specially, specifically; SEE CONCEPT *556*

expressly [*adv2*] *definitely, unambiguously*
absolutely, categorically, clearly, decidedly, directly, distinctly, explicitly, in no uncertain terms*, manifestly, outright, plainly, pointedly, positively, specifically, unequivocally, unmistakably; SEE CONCEPT *535*

expressway [*n*] *large, well-travelled road*
freeway, interstate, parkway, superhighway, thruway, turnpike; SEE CONCEPT *501*

expropriate [*v*] *seize*
accroach, annex, appropriate, arrogate, assume, commandeer, confiscate, deprive of property, dispossess, impound, preempt, requisition, sequester, take, take over; SEE CONCEPTS *90,142*

expulsion [*n*] *banishing*
banishment, boot*, bounce, debarment, deportment, discharge, dislodgment, dismissal, displacement, dispossession, driving out, ejection, eviction, exclusion, exile, expatriation, extrusion, forcing out, ostracism, ouster, ousting, proscription, purge, relegation, removal, rush, suspension; SEE CONCEPTS *130,211,298*

expunge [*v*] *destroy, obliterate*
abolish, annihilate, annul, black, black out*, blot out, blue pencil*, call all bets off*, call off, cancel, cut, delete, discard, drop, efface, eradicate, erase, exclude, exterminate, extinguish, extirpate, gut, kayo*, kill, knock off*, KO*, launder*, omit, raze, remove, scrub*, strike out, take out, trim, wipe out, X out*, zap*; SEE CONCEPTS *211,252*

expurgate [*v*] *censor, cut*
bleep*, bleep out*, blip*, blue pencil*, bowdlerize, cleanse, clean up, decontaminate, lustrate, purge, purify, sanitize, screen, scrub*, squash, sterilize; SEE CONCEPTS *165,232*

exquisite [*adj1*] *beautiful, excellent, finely detailed*
admirable, attractive, charming, choice, comely, consummate, cultivated, dainty, delicate, delicious, discerning, discriminating, elegant, errorless, ethereal, fastidious, fine, flawless, impeccable, incomparable, irreproachable, lovely, matchless, meticulous, outstanding, peerless, perfect, pleasing, polished, precious, precise, rare, recherché, refined, select, selective, splendid, striking, subtle, superb, superior, superlative; SEE CONCEPTS *574,579,589*

exquisite [*adj2*] *intense*
acute, concentrated, consummate, desperate, excruciating, extreme, fierce, furious, keen, piercing, poignant, sharp, terrible, transcending, vehement, vicious, violent; SEE CONCEPT *569*

extant [*adj*] *in existence*
actual, alive, around, being, contemporary, current, existent, existing, immediate, in current use, instant, living, not lost, present, present-day, real, remaining, subsisting, surviving, undestroyed; SEE CONCEPTS *539,582*

extemporaneous/extemporary [*adj*] *unrehearsed, improvised*
ad hoc, ad lib, at first glance, automatic, autoschediastic, by ear*, casual, expedient, extempore, free, immediate, impromptu, improv*, improvisatory, improviso, informal, jamming*, made-up, makeshift, offhand, off the cuff*, off the top of head*, on impulse, on-the-spot*, snap, spontaneous, spur-of-the-moment*, taking for ride*, thought out loud*, tossed off*, tossed out*, unplanned, unpremeditated, unprepared, unstudied, winging it*; SEE CONCEPTS *267,799*

extemporize [*v*] *improvise*
ad-lib, dash out, devise, do offhand*, improvisate, invent, knock off*, make up, play by ear*, toss off*; SEE CONCEPT *51*

extend [*v1*] *make larger, longer*
add to, aggrandize, amplify, augment, beef up*, boost, broaden, carry on, continue, crane, develop, dilate, drag one's feet*, drag out, draw, draw out, elongate, enhance, enlarge, expand, fan out, go on, heighten, increase, last, lengthen, let out, magnify, mantle, multiply, open, pad, prolong, prolongate, protract, run on, spin out, spread, spread out, stall, stretch, string out, supplement, take, unfold, unfurl, unroll, widen; SEE CONCEPTS *236,239,245*

extend [*v2*] *offer*
accord, advance, allocate, allot, award, bestow, bring forward, confer, donate, give, grant, hold out, impart, place at disposal, pose, present, proffer, put forth, put forward, reach out, stretch out, submit, tender, yield; SEE CONCEPTS *66,67*

extended [*adj1*] *lengthened*
continued, drawn-out, elongate, elongated, enlarged, lengthy, long, prolonged, protracted, spread, spread out, stretched out, unfolded, unfurled, very long; SEE CONCEPTS *782,798*

extended [*adj2*] *widespread, comprehensive*
broad, enlarged, expanded, expansive, extensive, far-flung, far-reaching, large-scale, outspread, scopic, scopious, spread, sweeping, thorough, wide; SEE CONCEPT *772*

extension [*n*] *enlargement, continuation*
addendum, addition, adjunct, amplification, annex, appendage, appendix, arm, augmentation, branch,

broadening, compass, continuing, delay, development, dilatation, distension, drawing out, elongation, expansion, extent, increase, lengthening, orbit, postponement, production, prolongation, protraction, purview, radius, reach, scope, span, spread, spreading out, stretch, stretching, supplement, sweep, widening, wing; SEE CONCEPTS *236,245,824*

extensive [*adj*] *far-reaching, thorough*
across the board*, all-encompassing, all-inclusive, big, blanket*, boundless, broad, capacious, commodious, comprehensive, comprising, considerable, expanded, extended, far-flung*, general, great, hefty, huge, inclusive, indiscriminate, large, large-scale, lengthy, long, major, pervasive, prevalent, protracted, roomy, scopic, scopious, sizable, spacious, sweeping, unexclusive, universal, unrestricted, vast, voluminous, wall to wall*, wholesale, wide, wide-ranging, widespread; SEE CONCEPTS *772,773*

extent [*n*] *range, magnitude*
admeasurement, ambit, amount, amplitude, area, bounds, breadth, bulk, capaciousness, compass, degree, dimensions, duration, elbowroom*, expanse, expansion, extension, intensity, leeway, length, limit, mass, matter, measure, neighborhood, orbit, order, period of time, play, proliferation, proportions, purview, quantity, radius, reach, scope, size, space, spaciousness, span, sphere, stretch, sweep, term, territory, time, tract, tune, vicinity, volume, wideness, width; SEE CONCEPTS *651,730,743,745, 783,787,804*

extenuating [*adj*] *serving as an excuse*
condoning, diminishing, excusing, justifying, lessening, mitigating, moderating, palliating, qualifying, reducing, sanitizing, softening, varnishing, whitewashing*; SEE CONCEPT *537*

exterior [*n*] *visible part*
appearance, aspect, coating, cover, covering, exteriority, external, facade, face, finish, outside, polish, rind, shell, skin, superficies, superstratum, surface; SEE CONCEPT *484*

exterior [*adj*] *outside*
alient, exoteric, external, extraneous, extraterrestrial, extraterritorial, extrinsic, foreign, marginal, outdoor, outer, outermost, outlying, outmost, outward, over, peripheral, superficial, surface; SEE CONCEPT *583*

exterminate [*v*] *kill*
abolish, annihilate, blot out*, decimate, destroy, do away with*, eliminate, eradicate, erase, execute, extinguish, extirpate, finish off, massacre, obliterate, put an end to*, rub out*, send to kingdom come*, slaughter, stamp out*, wipe out*; SEE CONCEPT *252*

external [*adj*] *outside, extrinsic*
alien, apparent, exterior, extraneous, foreign, independent, out, outer, outermost, outmost, outward, over, peripheral, superficial, surface, visible; SEE CONCEPT *583*

extinct [*adj*] *dead, obsolete*
abolished, archaic, asleep, bygone, cold*, dead and gone*, deceased, defunct, departed, disappeared,

done for*, doused, ended, exanimate, exterminated, extinguished, fallen, gone, inactive, late, lifeless, lost, no longer known, out, outmoded, passé, passed on, snuffed out*, superseded, terminated, unknown, vanished, vanquished, void; SEE CONCEPT *539*

extinguish [*v1*] *put out a fire*
blot out, blow out, choke, douse, drown, out, quench, smother, snuff out, stamp out, stifle, suffocate, trample; SEE CONCEPT *256*

extinguish [*v2*] *kill; quash*
abate, abolish, annihilate, blot out*, check, crush, destroy, eliminate, end, eradicate, erase, expunge, exterminate, extirpate, obliterate, obscure, put down, put the lid on*, quell, remove, squash, stamp out, suppress, wipe out*; SEE CONCEPTS *95,252*

extirpate [*v*] *destroy; uproot*
abate, abolish, annihilate, blot out*, cut out, demolish, deracinate, efface, eliminate, eradicate, erase, excise, expunge, exsect, exterminate, extinguish, kill, raze, remove, root out, wipe out*; SEE CONCEPTS *211,252*

extol [*v*] *sing the praises of*
acclaim, applaud, bless, boost, brag about, celebrate, commend, cry up*, eulogize, exalt, give a boost to, give a bouquet*, glorify, hand it to*, hats off to*, hear it for*, hymn, laud, magnify, make much of, panegyrize, pay tribute to, praise, puff up*, push, rave, root, stroke*; SEE CONCEPT *69*

extort [*v*] *cheat; blackmail*
bleed*, bully, clip, coerce, demand, educe, elicit, evince, exact, extract, fleece, force, get, gouge, hold up*, ice*, make pay through nose*, milk*, obtain, pinch, pull one's leg*, put screws to*, put the arm on*, secure, shake down*, skin*, soak, squeeze, stick, sting, wrench, wrest, wring; SEE CONCEPTS *53,59,139,342*

extortion [*n*] *blackmail; cheating*
arm, badger, bite, coercion, compulsion, demand, exaction, force, fraud, oppression, payoff, payola*, pressure, protection, racket, rapacity, shake, shakedown*, squeeze, stealing, swindle, theft; SEE CONCEPTS *53,139,192,342*

extra [*n*] *accessory*
addendum, addition, adjunct, affix, appendage, appurtenance, attachment, bonus, complement, extension, supernumerary, supplement; SEE CONCEPT *824*

extra [*adj*] *accessory; excess*
added, additional, ancillary, another, auxiliary, beyond, button*, extraneous, extraordinary, fresh, further, fuss*, gingerbread*, gravy*, ice*, in addition, inessential, in reserve, in store, lagniappe*, leftover, more, needless, new, one more, optional, other, over and above*, perk*, plus, redundant, reserve, spare, special, superfluous, supernumerary, supplemental, supplementary, surplus, tip, unnecessary, unneeded, unused; SEE CONCEPTS *546,771*

extra [adv] *particularly*
considerably, especially, exceptionally, extraordinarily, extremely, markedly, noticeably, rarely, remarkably, uncommon, uncommonly, unusually; SEE CONCEPTS *557,569*

extract [n] *something condensed from whole*
abstract, citation, clipping, concentrate, cutting, decoction, distillate, distillation, elicitation, essence, excerpt, infusion, juice*, passage, quotation, selection; SEE CONCEPTS *270,835*

extract [v1] *physically remove, draw out*
avulse, bring out, catheterize, cull, derive, distill, draw, eke out, elicit, eradicate, evoke, evulse, exact, express, extirpate, extort, extricate, garner, gather, get, glean, obtain, pick up, pluck, press out, pry, pull, reap, secure, select, separate, siphon, squeeze, take, tear, uproot, weed out*, withdraw, wrest, wring, yank; SEE CONCEPTS *206,211*

extract [v2] *select a quotation*
abridge, abstract, bring forth, choose, cite, condense, copy, cull, cut out, deduce, derive, educe, elicit, evolve, excerpt, glean, quote, shorten; SEE CONCEPTS *79,142,211*

extraction [n1] *removal from whole; distillation*
abstraction, derivation, drawing, elicitation, eradication, evocation, evulsion, expression, extirpation, extrication, pulling, separation, taking out, uprooting, withdrawal, wrenching, wresting; SEE CONCEPT *211*

extraction [n2] *ancestry, origin*
birth, blood, derivation, descent, family, lineage, parentage, pedigree, race, stock; SEE CONCEPTS *296,648*

extradite [v] *send to another place by force*
abandon, apprehend, arrest, bring to justice, bring to trial, deliver, give up, release, surrender; SEE CONCEPTS *217,317*

extraneous [adj1] *unneeded; irrevelant*
accidental, additional, adventitious, beside the point, extra, foreign, immaterial, impertinent, inadmissible, inapplicable, inapposite, inappropriate, incidental, inessential, needless, nonessential, off the subject, peripheral, pointless, redundant, superfluous, supplementary, unconnected, unessential, unnecessary, unrelated; SEE CONCEPT *546*

extraneous [adj2] *foreign*
adventitious, alien, exotic, external, extrinsic, out of place, strange; SEE CONCEPT *549*

extraordinary [adj] *strange and wonderful*
amazing, bizarre, boss*, curious, exceptional, fab*, fantastic, flash*, gnarly*, heavy*, inconceivable, incredible, marvelous, odd, off beaten path*, out of the ordinary, outstanding, particular, peculiar, phenomenal, rare, remarkable, singular, special, strange, stupendous, surprising, terrific, uncommon, unfamiliar, unheard-of, unimaginable, unique, unprecedented, unthinkable, unusual, unwonted, weird, wicked*; SEE CONCEPTS *564,572*

extravagance [n] *indulgence; waste*
absurdity, amenity, dissipation, exaggeration, excess, exorbitance, expenditure, folly, frill, icing on the cake*, immoderation, improvidence, lavishness, luxury, outrageousness, overdoing, overindulgence, overspending, preposterousness, prodigality, profligacy, profusion, recklessness, squander, squandering, superfluity, unreasonableness, unrestraint, unthrift, wastefulness, wildness; SEE CONCEPTS *335, 337,786*

extravagant [adj] *indulgent, wasteful*
absurd, bizarre, costly, crazy, exaggerated, excessive, exorbitant, expensive, extortionate, extreme, fanciful, fancy, fantastic, flamboyant, flashy, foolish, garish, gaudy, grandiose, immoderate, implausible, improvident, imprudent, inordinate, lavish, ludicrous, nonsensical, ornate, ostentatious, outrageous, overpriced, preposterous, pretentious, prodigal, profligate, reckless, ridiculous, showy, silly, spendthrift, steep, unbalanced, unconscionable, unreasonable, unrestrained; SEE CONCEPTS *334,560,771*

extravaganza [n] *spectacle*
caricature, display, divertissement, flight of fancy*, pageant, parody, show, spectacular; SEE CONCEPTS *263,293*

extreme [n] *ultimate; limit*
acme, apex, apogee, bitter end, boundary, ceiling, climax, consummation, crest, crown, culmination, depth, edge, end, excess, extremity, height, inordinancy, maximum, nadir, nth degree*, peak, pinnacle, pole, termination, top, utmost, uttermost, zenith; SEE CONCEPTS *484,706,745,836*

extreme [adj1] *very great*
acute, consummate, great, greatest, high, highest, intense, maximal, maximum, severe, sovereign, supreme, top, ultimate, utmost, uttermost; SEE CONCEPTS *569,771,781*

extreme [adj2] *beyond reason and convention*
absolute, desperate, dire, downright, drastic, egregious, exaggerated, exceptional, excessive, extraordinary, extravagant, fabulous, fanatical, flagrant, gross, harsh, immoderate, improper, imprudent, inordinate, intemperate, irrational, nonsensical, out-and-out*, out of proportion, outrageous, overkill, preposterous, rabid, radical, remarkable, rigid, severe, sheer, stern, strict, thorough, unbending, uncommon, uncompromising, unconventional, unreasonable, unseemly, unusual, utter, zealous; SEE CONCEPTS *547,558,569*

extreme [adj3] *faraway*
far-off, farthest, final, furthermost, last, most distant, outermost, outmost, remotest, terminal, ultimate, utmost, uttermost; SEE CONCEPT *778*

extremely [adv] *greatly, intensely*
acutely, almighty, awfully, drastically, exceedingly, exceptionally, excessively, exorbitantly, extraordinarily, highly, hugely, immensely, immoderately, inordinately, intensely, markedly, mortally, notably,

over, overly, overmuch, parlous, plenty, powerful, prohibitively, quite, radically, rarely, remarkably, severely, strikingly, surpassingly, terribly, terrifically, to nth degree*, too, too much*, totally, ultra*, uncommonly, unduly, unusually, utterly, very*, violently, vitally; SEE CONCEPTS *569,771,781*

extremist [n] *person zealous about belief*
agitator, die-hard, fanatic, radical, revolutionary, revolutionist, ultra, ultraist, zealot; SEE CONCEPTS *359,423*

extremity [n1] *ultimate; limit*
acme, acuteness, adversity, apex, apogee, border, bound, boundary, brim, brink, butt, climax, consummation, crisis, depth, dire straits, disaster, edge, end, excess, extreme, extremes, frontier, height, last, margin, maximum, nadir, outside, pinnacle, plight, pole, remote, rim, setback, terminal, termination, terminus, tip, top, trouble, verge, vertex, zenith; SEE CONCEPTS *484,706,745,836*

extremity [n2] *animate being's appendage*
backside, finger, flipper, foot, hand, leg, limb, paw, posterior, toe; SEE CONCEPT *392*

extricate [v] *get out of situation; relieve of responsibility*
bail out*, clear, deliver, detach, difference, differentiate, disburden, discumber, disembarrass, disencumber, disengage, disentangle, disinvolve, extract, free, get off the hook*, get out from under*, let go, let off*, liberate, loose, loosen, pull out, release, remove, rescue, resolve, save one's neck*, separate, sever, untie, withdraw, wriggle out of*; SEE CONCEPTS *102,127*

extrinsic [adj] *foreign*
acquired, alien, exotic, exterior, external, extraneous, gained, imported, outer, outside, outward, superficial; SEE CONCEPT *549*

extrovert [n] *sociable person*
character*, exhibitionist, gregarious person, life of the party*, showboat*, show-off*; SEE CONCEPT *423*

extrude [v] *force out*
boot*, chase, dismiss, eject, evict, expel, kick out, press, project, squeeze*, throw out, thrust; SEE CONCEPTS *208,222*

exuberance [n1] *energy, enthusiasm*
abandon, animation, ardor, bounce, buoyancy, cheerfulness, eagerness, ebullience, effervescence, excitement, exhilaration, fervor, friskiness, gayness, get up and go*, high spirits, juice*, life, liveliness, pep, pepper*, spirit, sprightliness, vigor, vitality, zap*, zest*, zip*; SEE CONCEPT *633*

exuberance [n2] *profusion*
abundance, affluence, copiousness, effusiveness, exaggeration, excessiveness, fulsomeness, lavishness, lushness, luxuriance, plenitude, plenty, prodigality, richness, superabundance, superfluity, teemingness; SEE CONCEPTS *710,767*

exuberant [adj1] *energetic, enthusiastic*
animated, ardent, bouncy, brash, buoyant, cheerful, chipper, eager, ebullient, effervescent, elated, ex-

cited, exhilarated, feeling one's oats*, frolicsome, gay, high-spirited, lively, passionate, sparkling, spirited, sprightly, vigorous, vivacious, zappy*, zestful, zingy*, zippy*; SEE CONCEPT *401*

exuberant [adj2] *profuse*
abundant, affluent, copious, diffuse, effusive, exaggerated, excessive, fecund, fertile, fruitful, fulsome, lavish, lush, luxuriant, opulent, overdone, overflowing, plenteous, plentiful, prodigal, profusive, prolific, rampant, rich, riotous, superabundant, superfluous, teeming; SEE CONCEPT *781*

exude [v] *display, emit*
bleed, discharge, emanate, emit, evacuate, excrete, exhibit, expel, flow out, give forth, give off, issue, leak, manifest, ooze, pass, percolate, radiate, secrete, seep, show, sweat, throw off, trickle, weep; SEE CONCEPTS *118,179*

exult [v1] *be joyful*
be delighted, be elated, be happy, be in high spirits*, be jubilant, be overjoyed, celebrate, cheer, jubilate, jump for joy*, make merry*, rejoice; SEE CONCEPTS *32,266*

exult [v2] *boast*
bluster, brag, bully, crow, gloat, glory, revel, show off, take delight in*, triumph, vaunt; SEE CONCEPT *49*

exultant [adj] *very happy*
blown away*, delighted, ecstatic, elated, exulting, flipping, flushed, flying, gleeful, high, joyful, joyous, jubilant, overjoyed, rejoicing, revelling, transported, triumphant, turned on*, wowed*; SEE CONCEPT *403*

exultation [n] *celebration, revelling*
crowing, delight, elation, glee, gloating, glory, happiness, high spirits, joy, joyousness, jubilance, jubilation, merriment, rejoicing, satisfaction, transport, triumph; SEE CONCEPTS *32,410*

eye [n1] *judgment, opinion*
appreciation, belief, conviction, discernment, discrimination, eagle eye*, feeling, mind, perception, persuasion, point of view, recognition, scrutiny, sentiment, surveillance, tab, taste, view, viewpoint, watch; SEE CONCEPTS *411,689*

eye [n2] *optical organ of animate being*
baby blue*, blinder*, eyeball, headlight*, lamp*, ocular, oculus, optic, peeper*, pie*; SEE CONCEPT *392*

eye [v] *gaze at, scrutinize*
check out, consider, contemplate, eyeball*, gape, give the eye*, glance at, have a look, inspect, keep eagle eye on*, leer, look at, ogle, peruse, regard, rubberneck*, scan, size up*, stare at, study, survey, take a look, take in, view, watch; SEE CONCEPTS *17,623,626*

eyeful [n] *spectacular-looking person*
beauty, dazzler*, knockout*, looker, lovely, show, spectacle, stunner*, vision; SEE CONCEPT *424*

eyesore [n] *mess, ugliness*
atrocity, blemish, blight, blot, blot on landscape*, deformity, disfigurement, disgrace, distortion,

dump, horror, monstrosity, sight, ugly thing; SEE CONCEPTS *674,716*

eyewitness [*n*] *person who sees an event occur*
beholder, bystander, looker-on, observer, onlooker, passer-by, spectator, viewer, watcher, witness; SEE CONCEPT *423*

F

fable [*n*] *fantasy, story*
allegory, apologue, bestiary, bunk*, crock*, fabrication, fairy story, fairy tale, falsehood, fantasy, fib, fiction, figment, fish story*, hogwash*, invention, legend, lie, myth, old chestnut*, old saw*, one for the birds*, parable, romance, tale, tall story, untruth, white lie*, whopper*, yarn; SEE CONCEPT *282*

fabled [*adj*] *legendary*
fabulous, famed, famous, fanciful, fictional, mythical, mythological, storied, unreal; SEE CONCEPT *568*

fabric [*n1*] *cloth, material*
bolt, fiber, goods, stuff, textile, texture, web; SEE CONCEPT *473*

fabric [*n2*] *structure*
building, consistency, constitution, construction, foundation, frame, framework, infrastructure, make-up, mold, organization, stamp, substance, texture; SEE CONCEPTS *733,757*

fabricate [*v1*] *manufacture*
assemble, brainstorm, build, cobble up*, compose, concoct, construct, contrive, cook up*, create, devise, dream up, erect, fashion, fit together, form, formulate, frame, head trip*, invent, join, knock together*, make, make up, mix, organize, piece together, prefab*, produce, put together, shape, structure, think up, throw together*, throw up*, turn out, whip up*, whomp up*; SEE CONCEPTS *36,173, 205,251*

fabricate [*v2*] *falsify, make up story*
coin, concoct, contrive, counterfeit, devise, fake, feign, fib, forge, form, fudge*, invent, jive*, lie, make like*, misrepresent, pretend, prevaricate, trump up*; SEE CONCEPT *63*

fabrication [*n1*] *lie*
artifact, concoction, deceit, fable, fairy story*, fake*, falsehood, fib, fiction, figment, forgery, hogwash*, invention, jazz*, jive*, lie, line*, myth, opus, smoke*, song and dance*, untruth, work, yarn; SEE CONCEPTS *63,278*

fabrication [*n2*] *something manufactured*
assemblage, assembly, building, construction, creation, erection, manufacture, product, production; SEE CONCEPTS *205,260,338*

fabulous [*adj*] *amazing, wonderful*
10*, A-1*, aces*, A-OK*, astonishing, astounding, awesome, best, breathtaking, cool*, doozie*, extravagant, fab*, fantastic, fictitious, first-class, greatest, groovy*, immense, inconceivable, incredible, legendary, marvelous, mind-blowing*, okay, out-of-

sight*, out-of-this-world*, outrageous, peachy*, phenomenal, primo*, prodigious, rad*, remarkable, spectacular, striking, stupendous, super, superb, terrific, top drawer*, tops*, turn-on*, unbelievable, unreal, wicked*, wonderful; SEE CONCEPTS *529,572*

facade [*n*] *appearance, often deceptive*
beard*, bluff, color, disguise, exterior, face, fake, false colors*, false front*, front, frontage, guise, look, mask, phony, pretense, put-on*, semblance, show, veneer, window dressing*; SEE CONCEPT *716*

face [*n1*] *front of something; expression, exterior*
air, appearance, aspect, cast, clock, countenance, dial*, disguise, display, facet, features, finish, front, frontage*, frontal, frontispiece, frown, glower, grimace, guise, kisser*, light*, lineaments, look, makeup, map*, mask, mug*, obverse, paint*, physiognomy, potato*, pout, presentation, profile, puss*, scowl, seeming, semblance, show, showing, silhouette, simulacrum, smirk, surface, top, visage; SEE CONCEPTS *484,716,836*

face [*n2*] *pretense, nerve*
air, audacity, boldness, brass*, cheek*, chutzpah*, cloak, confidence, cover, disguise, effrontery, facade, false front*, front, gall, impertinence, impudence, mask, presumption, semblance, show, veil; SEE CONCEPTS *633,657*

face [*n3*] *authority, status*
dignity, honor, image, prestige, reputation, self-respect, social position, standing; SEE CONCEPT *388*

face [*v1*] *come up against situation*
abide, accost, affront, allow, bear, beard, be confronted by, bit the bullet*, brace, brave, brook, challenge, confront, contend, cope with, countenance, court, cross, dare, deal with, defy, encounter, endure, experience, eyeball*, fight, fly in face of*, go up against*, grapple with, make a stand*, meet, oppose, resist, risk, run into, square off*, stand, stomach*, submit, suffer, sustain, swallow*, take, take bull by horns*, take it, take on, tell off*, tolerate, venture, withstand; SEE CONCEPTS *23,35,117*

face [*v2*] *be opposite; look at*
be turned toward, border, confront, front, front onto, gaze, glare, look, meet, overlook, stare, watch; SEE CONCEPTS *623,747*

face [*v3*] *put paint or finish on*
clad, coat, cover, decorate, dress, finish, front, level, line, overlay, plaster, polish, redecorate, refinish, remodel, sheathe, shingle, side, skin, smooth, surface, veneer; SEE CONCEPTS *172,202*

facet [*n*] *surface; aspect*
angle, appearance, character, face, feature, front, hand, level, obverse, part, phase, plane, side, slant, switch, twist; SEE CONCEPT *835*

facetious [*adj*] *tongue-in-cheek, kidding*
amusing, blithe, capering, clever, comic, comical, droll, dry, fanciful, farcical, flip*, flippant, frivolous, funny, gay, humorous, indecorous, ironic, irreverent, jesting, jocose, jocular, joking, joshing,

laughable, ludicrous, merry, not serious, playful, pleasant, pulling one's leg*, punning, putting one on*, ridiculous, salty, sarcastic, satirical, smart, sportive, sprightly, waggish, whimsical, wisecracking, witty, wry; SEE CONCEPT 267

facile [*adj*] *easy; easily mastered*
accomplished, adept, adroit, apparent, articulate, breeze, child's play*, cursory, deft, dexterous, easy as pie*, effortless, fast talk*, flip*, fluent, glib, hasty, light, obvious, picnic*, practiced, proficient, pushover*, quick, ready, royal, shallow, simple, skillful, slick*, smooth, superficial, uncomplicated, untroublesome, voluble; SEE CONCEPTS *527,565*

facilitate [*v*] *assist the progress of*
aid, ease, expedite, forward, further, grease the wheels*, hand-carry*, help, make easy, open doors*, promote, run interference for*, simplify, smooth, speed, speed up, walk through*; SEE CONCEPTS *110,242*

facility [*n1*] *ease; ability*
address, adroitness, aptitude, bent, child's play*, competence, dexterity, efficiency, effortlessness, expertness, fluency, knack, leaning, lightness, poise, proficiency, propensity, quickness, readiness, skill, skillfulness, smoothness, smooth sailing*, spontaneity, tact, turn, wit; SEE CONCEPTS *630,666*

facility [*n2*] *convenience*
accommodation, advantage, aid, amenity, appliance, comfort, equipment, fitting, material, means, opportunity, resource, tool; SEE CONCEPTS *693,712*

facsimile [*n*] *reproduction*
carbon, carbon copy*, chip off old block*, clone, copy, copycat*, dead ringer*, ditto*, double, dupe*, duplicate, knock-off*, likeness, look-alike, mimeo, miniature, mirror, photocopy, photostat, print, reduplication, replica, replication, repro*, ringer*, spitting image*, stat, transcript, twin, Xerox*; SEE CONCEPTS *271,625,716*

fact [*n1*] *verifiable truth; reality*
actuality, appearance, authenticity, basis, bottom line*, brass tacks*, case, certainty, certitude, concrete happening, dope*, evidence, experience, genuineness, gospel, gospel truth*, how it is*, intelligence, law, like it is*, matter*, naked truth*, palpability, permanence, scene, scripture, solidity, stability, substantiality, verity, what's what*; SEE CONCEPTS *687,725*

fact [*n2*] *event; detail of action*
accomplishment, act, action, actuality, adventure, affair, being, case, circumstance, conception, consideration, construction, creation, data, datum, deed, entity, episode, evidence, experience, factor, fait accompli, feature, happening, incident, information, item, manifestation, occurrence, organism, particular, performance, phenomenon, point, proceeding, specific, statistic, transaction, truism; SEE CONCEPTS *2,274,433*

faction [*n1*] *group sharing a belief or cause*
band, bloc, bunch, cabal, camp, caucus, cell, circle, clan, clique, club, coalition, combination, combine, combo, concern, conclave, confederacy, conspiracy, contingent, coterie, crew, crowd, design, division, entente, gang, guild, insiders, intrigue, junta, knot, lobby, machine, minority, mob, network, offshoot, outfit, partnership, party, pressure group, ring, schism, sect, section, sector, set, side, splinter group, team, unit, wing; SEE CONCEPTS *301,387*

faction [*n2*] *conflict, strife*
disagreement, discord, disharmony, dissension, disunity, division, divisiveness, friction, infighting, quarrelsomeness, rebellion, sedition, tumult, turbulence; SEE CONCEPTS *106,684*

factious [*adj*] *conflicting, warring*
alienated, belligerent, contending, contentious, contumacious, disaffected, disputatious, dissident, divisive, estranged, fighting, hostile, insubordinate, insurgent, insurrectionary, litigious, malcontent, mutinous, partisan, quarrelsome, rebellious, refractory, rival, sectarian, seditious, troublemaking, tumultous/tumultuous, turbulent; SEE CONCEPT *542*

factor [*n*] *determinant*
agency, agent, aid, antecedent, aspect, board, cause, circumstance, component, consideration, constituent, element, fixin's*, influence, ingredient, instrument, instrumentality, item, makin's*, means, part, part and parcel*, point, portion, thing; SEE CONCEPTS *831,835*

factory [*n*] *manufacturing plant*
branch, cooperative, firm, forge, foundry, industry, laboratory, machine shop, manufactory, mill, mint, salt mines*, shop, sweatshop*, warehouse, workroom, works, workshop; SEE CONCEPTS *439,441,449*

facts [*n*] *inside information*
bottom line*, brass tacks*, certainty, clue, cue, data, details, dope*, gospel, info*, inside dope*, like it is*, lowdown*, numbers, poop*, reality, scoop*, score*, story, whole story*; SEE CONCEPT *274*

factual [*adj*] *real, correct*
absolute, accurate, actual, authentic, card-carrying*, certain, circumstantial, close, credible, descriptive, exact, faithful, genuine, hard, kosher*, legit*, legitimate, literal, objective, on the level*, positive, precise, righteous, specific, straight from horse's mouth*, sure, sure-enough*, true, true-to-life*, unadorned, unbiased, undoubted, unquestionable, valid, veritable; SEE CONCEPTS *535,582*

faculty [*n1*] *ability, skill*
adroitness, aptitude, aptness, bent, capability, capacity, cleverness, dexterity, facility, flair, forte, genius, gift, instinct, intelligence, knack, knowing way around*, leaning, nose*, peculiarity, penchant, pistol*, power, predilection, proclivity, propensity, property, quality, readiness, reason, right stuff*, sense, strength, talent, turn, up to snuff*, what it takes*, wits; SEE CONCEPT *630*

faculty [n2] *teachers in educational institution*
academics, advisers, body, clinic, college, corps, department, dons, employees, fellows, institute, instructors, lecturers, literati, mentors, organization, pedagogues, personnel, professorate, professors, profs*, researchers, scholars, society, staff, tutors, university, workers; SEE CONCEPTS *288,350*

fad [n] *craze*
affectation, amusement, caprice, chic, conceit, cry, custom, dernier cri, eccentricity, fancy, fantasy, fashion, fool notion*, frivolity, furor, hobby, humor, in, innovation, in thing*, kick, kink, latest word*, mania, mode, newest wrinkle*, new look*, passing fancy*, passion, quirk, rage, sport, style, thing, trend, vagary, vogue, whim, whimsy, wrinkle; SEE CONCEPT *655*

fade [v1] *lose color*
achromatize, become colorless, blanch, bleach, blench, clear, decolorize, dim, disappear, discolor, dissolve, dull, etiolate, evanish, evaporate, grow dim, lose brightness, lose luster, muddy, neutralize, pale, tarnish, tone down, vanish, wash out; SEE CONCEPTS *250,469,622*

fade [v2] *dwindle, die out*
abate, attenuate, clear, decline, deliquesce, deteriorate, die away, die on vine*, dim, diminish, disappear, disperse, dissolve, droop, ebb, etiolate, evanesce, evanish, evaporate, fag out*, fail, fall, flag, fold, hush, languish, lessen, melt, melt away, moderate, perish, peter out*, poop out*, quiet, rarefy, shrivel, sink, slack off*, taper, thin, tire, tucker out*, vanish, wane, waste away, weaken, wilt, wither; SEE CONCEPTS *105,698*

faded [adj] *bleached; used*
achromatic, ashen, bedraggled, dim, dingy, discolored, dull, etiolated, indistinct, lackluster, lusterless, murky, not shiny, pale, pallid, run-down, seedy, shabby, shopworn, tacky, tattered, threadbare, tired, wan, washed out, wasted, worn; SEE CONCEPTS *560,617,618*

fail [v1] *be unsuccessful*
abort, backslide, back wrong horse*, be defeated, be demoted, be found lacking*, be in vain*, be ruined, blunder, break down, come to naught, come to nothing, decline, deteriorate, fall, fall flat*, fall short*, fall through*, fizzle, flop, flounder, fold, founder, go astray, go down*, go downhill*, go down swinging*, go up in smoke*, go wrong, hit bottom*, hit the skids*, lose control, lose out, lose status, meet with disaster, miscarry, miss, miss the boat*, play into, run aground*, slip, turn out badly; SEE CONCEPT *699*

fail [v2] *abandon, forsake*
abort, back out, blink, break one's word, desert, disappoint, discount, disregard, fault, forget, funk, go astray, ignore, let down, miscarry, neglect, omit, overlook, overpass, slight, slip; SEE CONCEPTS *7,19*

fail [v3] *lose money*
be cleaned out*, become insolvent, be in arrears, be ruined, be taken to cleaners*, break, close, close down*, close one's doors*, crash, defalcate, default, dishonor, drop, drop a bundle*, end, finish, fold, go bankrupt, go belly up*, go broke*, go bust*, go into chapter 11*, go out of business*, go to the wall*, go under*, go up*, lose big*, lose one's shirt*, overdraw, repudiate, terminate; SEE CONCEPTS *330,335*

failing [n] *lapse, shortcoming*
blind spot*, defect, deficiency, drawback, error, failure, fault, flaw, foible, frailty, imperfection, infirmity, miscarriage, misfortune, vice, weakness, weak point*; SEE CONCEPTS *411,674*

failing [adj] *not well, weak*
declining, defeated, deficient, faint, feeble, inadequate, insufficient, scant, scanty, scarce, short, shy, unavailing, unprosperous, unsuccessful, unsufficient, unthriving, vain, wanting; SEE CONCEPTS *485,489*

failure [n1] *lack of success*
abortion, bankruptcy, bomb, botch*, breakdown, bungle*, bust, checkmate, collapse, decay, decline, defeat, deficiency, deficit, deterioration, downfall, failing, false step*, faux pas, fiasco, flash in the pan*, flop*, frustration, implosion, inadequacy, lead balloon*, lemon*, loser, loss, mess, misadventure, miscarriage, misstep, nonperformance, nonsuccess, overthrow, rout, rupture, sinking ship*, stalemate, stoppage, total loss, turkey*, washout*, wreck; SEE CONCEPTS *699,706*

failure [n2] *person who does not succeed*
also-ran*, bankrupt, beat*, born loser*, bum, castaway, deadbeat, defaulter, derelict, disappointment, dud*, flop, good-for-nothing*, has-been, incompetent, insolvent, loafer, loser, lumpy*, might-have-been*, moocher*, nobody, no-good, nonperformer, prodigal, turkey*, underachiever, washout*; SEE CONCEPTS *412,423*

faint [n] *unconsciousness*
blackout, collapse, dizziness, grayout, insensibility, knockout, stupor, swoon, syncope, vertigo; SEE CONCEPTS *308,316*

faint [adj1] *have little effect on senses*
aside, bated, bland, bleached, blurred, breathless, deadened, deep, delicate, dim, distant, dull, dusty, faded, faltering, far-off, feeble, gentle, hazy, hoarse, hushed, ill-defined, imperceptible, inaudible, indistinct, lenient, light, low, low-pitched, mild, moderate, muffled, murmuring, muted, muttering, obscure, out of earshot*, padded, pale, piano, quiet, remote, shadowy, slight, smooth, soft, softened, soothing, stifled, subdued, tenuous, thin, unclear, vague, wan, weak, whispered; SEE CONCEPTS *537,594,617*

faint [adj2] *weak*
delicate, dizzy, drooping, enervated, exhausted, faltering, fatigued, feeble, fragile, languid, lethargic,

lightheaded, slight, tender, unenthusiastic, woozy; SEE CONCEPTS *314,485*

faint [v] *lose consciousness*
become unconscious, be overcome, black out, collapse, drop, fade, fail, fall, flicker, go out like light*, keel over, languish, pass out, succumb, swoon, weaken; SEE CONCEPTS *303,308*

fair [n] *exposition, carnival*
bazaar, celebration, centennial, display, exhibit, exhibition, expo*, festival, fete, gala, market, observance, occasion, pageant, show, spectacle; SEE CONCEPTS *377,386*

fair [adj1] *impartial, unprejudiced*
aboveboard, benevolent, blameless, candid, civil, clean, courteous, decent, disinterested, dispassionate, equal, equitable, even-handed, frank, generous, good, honest, honorable, impartial, just, lawful, legitimate, moderate, nonpartisan, objective, on the level*, on up-and-up*, open, pious, praiseworthy, principled, proper, reasonable, respectable, righteous, scrupulous, sincere, square, straight, straightforward, temperate, trustworthy, unbiased, uncolored, uncorrupted, upright, virtuous; SEE CONCEPT *542*

fair [adj2] *light-complexioned, light-haired*
argent, blanched, bleached, blond, blonde, chalky, colorless, creamy, faded, fair-haired, fair-skinned, flaxen-haired, light, milky, neutral, pale, pale-faced, pallid, pearly, sallow, silvery, snowy, tow-haired, tow-headed, white, whitish; SEE CONCEPTS *406,618*

fair [adj3] *mediocre, satisfactory*
adequate, all right, average, common, commonplace, decent, fairish, indifferent, intermediate, mean, medium, middling, moderate, not bad*, okay, ordinary, passable, pretty good*, reasonable, respectable, satisfactory, so-so*, tolerable, up to standard*, usual; SEE CONCEPT *530*

fair [adj4] *beautiful*
attractive, beauteous, bonny, charming, chaste, comely, dainty, delicate, enchanting, exquisite, good-looking, handsome, lovely, pretty, pulchritudinous, pure; SEE CONCEPT *579*

fair [adj5] *bright, cloudless (weather)*
balmy, calm, clarion, clear, clement, dry, favorable, fine, mild, placid, pleasant, pretty, rainless, smiling, sunny, sunshiny, tranquil, unclouded, undarkened, unthreatening; SEE CONCEPT *525*

fairly [adv1] *somewhat*
adequately, averagely, enough, kind of, moderately, more or less, passably, pretty well, quite, rather, ratherish, reasonably, some, something, sort of, so-so*, tolerably; SEE CONCEPT *788*

fairly [adv2] *justly*
deservedly, equitably, honestly, honorably, impartially, objectively, properly, reasonably, without favor, without fear; SEE CONCEPT *542*

fairness [n] *justice*
candor, charitableness, charity, civility, consideration, courtesy, decency, decorum, disinterested-

ness, due, duty, equitableness, equity, exactitude, fair-mindedness, fair shake*, give and take*, good faith, goodness, honesty, honor, humanity, impartiality, integrity, justness, legitimacy, moderation, open-mindedness, propriety, rationality, reasonableness, right, righteousness, rightfulness, rightness, seemliness, square deal*, suitability, tolerance, truth, uprightness, veracity; SEE CONCEPTS *645,657*

fairy [n] *supernatural being*
bogie, brownie, dwarf, elf, enchantress, fay, genie, gnome, goblin, gremlin, hob, imp, leprechaun, mermaid, nisse, nymph, pixie, puck, siren, spirit, sprite, sylph; SEE CONCEPT *370*

faith [n1] *trust in something*
acceptance, allegiance, assent, assurance, belief, certainty, certitude, confidence, constancy, conviction, credence, credit, credulity, dependence, faithfulness, fealty, fidelity, hope, loyalty, reliance, stock, store, sureness, surety, troth, truth, truthfulness; SEE CONCEPT *689*

faith [n2] *belief in a higher being; community of believers*
canon, church, communion, confession, connection, conviction, credo, creed, cult, denomination, doctrine, dogma, doxy, gospel, orthodoxy, persuasion, piety, piousness, principle, profession, religion, revelation, sect, teaching, tenet, theism, theology, worship; SEE CONCEPTS *368,689*

faithful [adj1] *loyal, reliable*
affectionate, allegiant, ardent, attached, behind one, circumspect, confiding, conscientious, constant, dependable, devoted, dutiful, dyed-in-the-wool*, enduring, fast, firm, genuine, hard-core*, honest, honorable, incorruptible, loving, obedient, on the level*, patriotic, resolute, scrupulous, sincere, staunch, steadfast, steady, straight, string along with*, sure, tried, tried and true*, true, true-blue*, trustworthy, trusty, truthful, unchanging, unswerving, unwavering, upright, veracious; SEE CONCEPTS *401,545*

faithful [adj2] *authentic, accurate*
close, credible, exact, just, lifelike, precise, right, similar, strict, true, trusty, undistorted, veracious, veridical; SEE CONCEPTS *487,573*

faithfulness [n] *devotion*
adherence, adhesion, allegiance, ardor, attachment, care, constancy, dependability, duty, fealty, fidelity, loyalty, piety, trustworthiness, truth; SEE CONCEPTS *633,645,689*

faithless [adj] *disloyal*
capricious, changeable, changeful, cheating, deceitful, dishonest, double-crossing*, double-dealing*, doubting, dubious, false, fickle, fluctuating, inconstant, perfidious, recreant, skeptical, traitorous, treacherous, two-faced*, two-timing*, unbelieving, unconverted, unfaithful, unloyal, unreliable, unstable, untrue, untrustworthy, untruthful, wavering; SEE CONCEPTS *401,545*

faithlessness [n] *disloyalty*
betrayal, disbelief, dishonesty, doubt, falseness, fickleness, fraud, inconstancy, infidelity, perfidiousness, perfidy, skepticism, treacherousness, treachery, treason, unfaithfulness; SEE CONCEPTS *633,645*

fake [n] *imposter, copy*
actor, bluffer, charlatan, cheat, counterfeit, deception, fabrication, faker, flimflam*, forgery, four-flusher*, fraud, gold brick*, gyp*, hoax, imitation, imposition, imposture, junque, make-believe, mountebank, phony, plant*, pretender, pretense, pseudo*, put-on, reproduction, scam, sham*, sleight, spoof, swindle, trick; SEE CONCEPTS *260,412*

fake [adj] *false, imitation*
affected, artificial, assumed, bogus, concocted, counterfeit, fabricated, fictitious, forged, fraudulent, invented, make-believe, mock, phony, pretended, pseudo*, reproduction, sham, simulated, spurious; SEE CONCEPTS *401,582*

fake [v] *pretend*
act, affect, assume, bluff, copy, counterfeit, disguise, dissimulate, fabricate, feign, forge, put on, put on an act*, sham, simulate, spoof; SEE CONCEPT *59*

fall [n1] *descent; lowering*
abatement, belly flop*, cut, decline, declivity, decrease, diminution, dip, dive, downgrade, downward slope, drop, dwindling, ebb, falling off, header*, incline, lapse, lessening, nose dive*, plummet, plunge, pratfall*, recession, reduction, slant, slip, slope, slump, spill, tumble; SEE CONCEPTS *152,181,776*

fall [n2] *defeat, overthrow*
abasement, breakdown, capitulation, collapse, death, degradation, destruction, diminution, disaster, dive, downfall, drop, failure, humiliation, loss, resignation, ruin, surrender, tumble; SEE CONCEPTS *116,230,674,699*

fall [v1] *descend; become lower*
abate, backslide, be precipitated, break down, buckle, cascade, cave in, collapse, crash, decline, decrease, depreciate, diminish, dip, dive, drag, droop, drop, drop down, dwindle, ease, ebb, fall off, flag, flop, fold up, go down, gravitate, hit the dirt*, keel over, land, lapse, lessen, lower, nose-dive, pitch, plummet, plunge, recede, regress, relapse, settle, sink, slip, slope, slump, spin, stumble, subside, take a header*, tip over, topple, totter, trail, trip, tumble, wane; SEE CONCEPTS *152,181,776*

fall [v2] *be overthrown by enemy; surrender*
back down, be casualty, be destroyed, be killed, be lost, bend, be taken, capitulate, defer to, die, drop, eat dirt*, fall to pieces*, give in, give up, give way, go down, go under, lie down, obey, pass into enemy hands*, perish, resign, slump, submit, succumb, yield; SEE CONCEPTS *116,699*

fall [v3] *happen*
arrive, become, befall, chance, come about, come to pass, fall out, occur, take place; SEE CONCEPT *119*

fallacious [adj] *false, wrong*
beguiling, deceiving, deceptive, deluding, delusive, delusory, erroneous, fictitious, fishy*, fraudulent, illogical, illusory, incorrect, invalid, irrational, mad, misleading, mistaken, off*, phony, reasonless, sophistic, sophistical, spurious, unfounded, ungrounded, unreal, unreasonable, unreasoned, unsound, untrue, way off*; SEE CONCEPTS *267,570,582*

fallacy [n] *illusion, misconception*
aberration, ambiguity, artifice, bias, casuistry, cavil, deceit, deception, deceptiveness, delusion, deviation, elusion, equivocation, erratum, erroneousness, error, evasion, falsehood, faultiness, flaw, heresy, illogicality, inconsistency, inexactness, invalidity, misapprehension, miscalculation, misconstrual, misinterpretation, mistake, non sequitur, notion, paradox, perversion, preconception, prejudice, quibbling, quirk, solecism, sophism, sophistry, speciousness, subterfuge, untruth; SEE CONCEPTS *410,689,725*

fall back [v] *retreat*
back, draw back, give back, recede, recoil, retire, retrocede, retrograde, surrender, withdraw, yield; SEE CONCEPT *195*

fallen [adj1] *disgraced, ruined*
collapsed, decayed, dishonored, immoral, loose, ruinous, shaken, shamed, sinful, unchaste; SEE CONCEPTS *539,555*

fallen [adj2] *dead*
casualty, killed, lost, perished, slain, slaughtered; SEE CONCEPT *539*

fall for [v] *become infatuated with*
desire, fall in love with, flip over, go head over heels*, lose one's head over*, succumb; SEE CONCEPT *32*

fallible [adj] *able, prone to err*
careless, deceptive, errable, errant, erring, faulty, frail, heedless, human, ignorant, imperfect, in question, liable, mortal, questionable, uncertain, unreliable, untrustworthy, weak; SEE CONCEPT *542*

fall out [v1] *argue*
altercate, bicker, clash, differ, disagree, fight, quarrel, spar, squabble; SEE CONCEPT *46*

fall out [v2] *come to pass*
befall, chance, happen, occur, result, take place, turn out; SEE CONCEPT *4*

fallow [adj] *inactive*
dormant, idle, inert, neglected, quiescent, resting, slack, uncultivated, undeveloped, unplanted, unplowed, unproductive, unseeded, untilled, unused, vacant, virgin; SEE CONCEPTS *485,560*

fall to [v] *set about doing*
apply oneself to, begin, be up to, buckle down*, commence, jump in, pitch in*, start, undertake, wade into*; SEE CONCEPTS *100,221*

false [adj1] *wrong, made up*
apocryphal, beguiling, bogus, casuistic, concocted, contrary to fact, cooked-up*, counterfactual, deceitful, deceiving, delusive, dishonest, distorted, erroneous, ersatz*, fake, fallacious, fanciful, faulty,

fictitious, fishy, fraudulent, illusive, imaginary, improper, inaccurate, incorrect, inexact, invalid, lying, mendacious, misleading, misrepresentative, mistaken, off the mark*, phony, sham, sophistical, specious, spurious, trumped up*, unfounded, unreal, unsound, untrue, untruthful; SEE CONCEPTS 267, 570,582

false [adj2] *dishonest, hypocritical*
apostate, base, beguiling, canting, corrupt, crooked, deceitful, deceiving, deceptive, deluding, delusive, devious, dishonorable, disloyal, double-dealing*, duplicitous, faithless, falsehearted, forsworn, foul, knavish, lying, malevolent, malicious, mean, misleading, mythomaniac, perfidious, perjured, rascally, recreant, renegade, roguish, scoundrelly, traitorous, treacherous, treasonable, two-faced*, underhanded, unfaithful, unscrupulous, untrustworthy, venal, villainous, wicked; SEE CONCEPTS 267,401

false [adj3] *fake, counterfeit*
adulterated, alloyed, artificial, assumed, bent, bogus*, brummagem, bum*, colored, contrived, copied, crock*, deceptive, disguised, ersatz*, fabricated, factitious, feigned, fishy*, forged, framed*, gyp*, hollow, imitation, made-up, make-believe, manufactured, meretricious, mock, ostensible, phony, pretended, pseudo*, queer, seeming, shady, sham*, simulated, snide, so-called*, spurious, substitute, synthetic, unreal, wrong; SEE CONCEPT 582

falsehood [n] *lie*
canard, cover-up, deceit, deception, dishonesty, dissimulation, distortion, equivocation, erroneousness, error, fable, fabrication, fakery, fallaciousness, fallacy, falseness, falsity, feigning, fib, fibbery, fiction, figment, fraud, half truth, hogwash*, line, mendacity, misstatement, perjury, pretense, prevarication, sham*, story, tale, tall tale*, untruism, untruth, untruthfulness, whopper*, yarn; SEE CONCEPTS 63,278

falsely [adv] *deceitfully*
basely, behind one's back*, crookedly, dishonestly, dishonorably, disloyally, faithlessly, falseheartedly, knavishly, malevolently, maliciously, perfidiously, roguishly, traitorously, treacherously, underhandedly, unfaithfully, unscrupulously; SEE CONCEPTS 267,401

falsify [v] *alter, misrepresent*
adulterate, belie, change, color, con, contort, contradict, contravene, cook, counterfeit, deacon, deceive, deny, distort, doctor, dress up*, embroider, equivocate, exaggerate, fake, fake it, fib, forge, four-flush*, frame up*, garble, gloss, lie, misquote, misstate, palter, pervert, phony up*, prevaricate, promote, put on an act*, salt*, tamper with, traverse, trump up*, twist, warp; SEE CONCEPT 63

falsity [n] *dishonesty, deception*
canard, cheating, deceit, deceptiveness, disingenuousness, double-dealing, duplicity, erroneousness, error, faithlessness, fake, fallacy, falsehood, fib,

fraud, fraudulence, hypocrisy, inaccuracy, infidelity, insincerity, lie, mendacity, misrepresentation, perfidiousness, perfidy, prevarication, sham, story, tale, treachery, uncandidness, unfaithfulness, unreality, untruth; SEE CONCEPTS 278,645,725

falter [v] *stumble, stutter*
be undecided, bobble, break, drop the ball*, flounder, fluctuate, fluff, halt, hem and haw*, hesitate, lurch, quaver, reel, rock, roll, scruple, shake, speak haltingly, stagger, stammer, stub toe*, teeter, topple, totter, tremble, trip up, vacillate, waver, whiffle, wobble; SEE CONCEPTS 18,147,266

fame [n] *celebrity*
acclaim, acclamation, account, acknowledgment, character, credit, dignity, distinction, éclat, elevation, eminence, esteem, estimation, exaltation, favor, glory, greatness, heyday, honor, illustriousness, immortality, kudos, laurels, luster, majesty, name, nobility, note, notoriety, place, popularity, position, preeminence, prominence, public esteem, rank, recognition, regard, renown, rep*, report, reputation, repute, splendor, standing, stardom, station, superiority; SEE CONCEPT 388

familiar [adj1] *common, well-known*
accustomed, commonplace, conventional, customary, domestic, everyday, frequent, garden variety*, habitual, homespun, household, humble, informal, intimate, known, matter-of-fact, mundane, native, natural, old hat*, ordinary, plain, prosaic, proverbial, recognizable, repeated, routine, simple, stock, unceremonious, unsophisticated, usual, well-known, wonted, workaday; SEE CONCEPTS 530,547

familiar [adj2] *knowledgeable*
abreast, acquainted, apprised, at home with*, au courant, au fait, aware, cognizant, conscious, conversant, grounded*, informed, in on*, in the know*, introduced, kept posted*, mindful, no stranger to*, plugged in*, savvy, tuned in*, up*, up on*, versant, versed in, well up in*, with it*; SEE CONCEPT 402

familiar [adj3] *friendly, bold*
affable, amicable, buddy-buddy*, chummy*, close, comfortable, confidential, cordial, cozy, dear, easy, forward, free, free-and-easy*, fresh, genial, gracious, impudent, informal, intimate, intrusive, near, neighborly, nervy, obtrusive, officious, open, palsy, palsy-walsy*, presuming, presumptuous, relaxed, sassy*, smart, snug, sociable, thick, tight, unceremonious, unconstrained, unreserved, wise; SEE CONCEPT 555

familiarity [n1] *friendliness*
acquaintance, acquaintanceship, boldness, closeness, ease, fellowship, forwardness, freedom, freshness, friendship, informality, intimacy, liberty, naturalness, openness, presumption, sociability, unceremoniousness; SEE CONCEPT 388

familiarity [n2] *knowledgeableness*
acquaintance, awareness, cognition, comprehension, experience, feel, grasp, knowledge, sense, understanding; SEE CONCEPT 409

familiarize [v] *make or become acquainted with, knowledgeable about*
accustom, acquaint, adapt, adjust, awaken to, become adept in, become aware of, break the ice*, bring into use, case*, check out, coach, come to know, condition, enlighten, gain friendship, get in, get lay of land*, get lowdown on*, get together, get to know, get with it*, habituate, inform, instruct, inure, let down hair*, let know, let next to, make conversant, make used to, mix, naturalize, popularize, post, prime, put on to*, school, season, tip off*, train, use, wont; SEE CONCEPTS *15,38*

family [n] *kin, offspring; classification*
ancestors, ancestry, birth, blood, brethren, brood, children, clan, class, descendants, descent, dynasty, extraction, folk, forebears, forefathers, genealogy, generations, genre, group, heirs and assigns, house, household, inheritance, in-laws, issue, kind, kindred, kith and kin, line, lineage, ménage, network, offspring, parentage, paternity, patrimony, pedigree, people, progenitors, progeny, race, relations, relationship, relatives, siblings, strain, subdivision, system, tribe; SEE CONCEPTS *296,378,397*

famine [n] *hunger*
dearth, destitution, drought, misery, paucity, poverty, scarcity, starvation, want; SEE CONCEPTS *674,709*

famished [adj] *starving*
could eat a horse*, dog-hungry*, empty, flying light*, having the munchies*, hollow, hungering, hungry, ravening, ravenous, starved, starved to death*, voracious; SEE CONCEPTS *20,406,546*

famous [adj] *legendary, notable to many*
acclaimed, applauded, august, brilliant, celebrated, conspicuous, distinguished, elevated, eminent, exalted, excellent, extraordinary, foremost, glorious, grand, great, honored, illustrious, important, imposing, influential, in limelight*, in spotlight*, leading, lionized, memorable, mighty, much-publicized, noble, noted, noteworthy, notorious, of note, outstanding, peerless, powerful, preeminent, prominent, recognized, remarkable, renowned, reputable, signal, splendid, talked about*, well-known; SEE CONCEPT *568*

fan [n1] *blower of air*
air conditioner, blade, draft, flabellum, leaf, palm leaf, propeller, thermantidote, vane, ventilator, windmill; SEE CONCEPT *463*

fan [n2] *person enthusiastic about interest*
addict, adherent, admirer, aficionado, amateur, buff, devotee, enthusiast, follower, freak*, groupie*, habitué, hound, lover, rooter, supporter, votary, zealot; SEE CONCEPTS *352,366,423*

fan [v1] *blow on*
aerate, air-condition, air-cool, cool, refresh, ruffle, spread, ventilate, wind, winnow; SEE CONCEPTS *199,208*

fan [v2] *provoke*
add fuel, agitate, arouse, enkindle, excite, expand, extend, impassion, increase, rouse, stimulate, stir up, whip up, work up; SEE CONCEPT *14*

fanatic [n] *person overenthusiastic about interest*
activist, addict, bigot, bug*, crank*, crazy, demon, devotee, enthusiast, extremist, fiend*, fool, freak, maniac, militant, monomaniac, nut*, radical, ultraist, visionary, zealot; SEE CONCEPTS *352,359,366*

fanatical [adj] *overenthusiastic*
biased, bigoted, bugged*, burning*, contumacious, credulous, devoted, dogmatic, domineering, enthusiastic, erratic, extreme, fervent, feverish, fiery, frenzied, headstrong, high on*, immoderate, impassioned, impulsive, incorrigible, infatuated, mad, monomaniacal, narrow-minded, nuts for*, obsessed, obsessive, obstinate, opinionated, partial, partisan, passionate, possessed, prejudiced, rabid, radical, raving, single-minded, stubborn, turned on*, unruly, violent, visionary, wild, willful, zealous; SEE CONCEPT *401*

fanaticism [n] *overenthusiasm*
abandonment, arbitrariness, bias, bigotry, contumacy, dedication, devotion, dogma, enthusiasm, extremism, faction, frenzy, hatred, illiberality, immoderation, incorrigibility, infatuation, injustice, intolerance, madness, monomania, obsessiveness, obstinacy, partiality, partisanship, passion, prejudice, rage, single-mindedness, stubbornness, superstition, tenacity, transport, unfairness, unreasonableness, unruliness, violence, willfulness, zeal, zealotry; SEE CONCEPTS *633,689*

fanciful [adj] *imaginary, romantic*
absurd, aerial, bizarre, blue sky*, capricious, castles in the air*, chimerical, curious, dreamlike, extravagant, fabulous, fairy-tale, fancied, fantastic, fantastical, fictional, fictitious, fictive, flaky*, floating, ideal, illusory, imaginative, imagined, incredible, kinky*, legendary, mythical, notional, offbeat, on cloud nine*, pie in the sky*, pipe dream*, poetic, preposterous, shadowy, suppositious, unreal, visionary, whimsical, wild; SEE CONCEPTS *529,572*

fancy [n1] *impulse, urge*
caprice, conceit, conception, contrariness, creation, cup of tea*, desire, druthers*, flash, fool's paradise*, groove*, humor, idea, image, imagination, impression, inclination, irrationality, liking, mind, notion, perverseness, pleasure, thing*, thought, vagary, velleity, visualization, weakness for, whim, will; SEE CONCEPTS *20,532*

fancy [n2] *liking, dream*
big eyes*, chimera, conception, daydream, delusion, envisagement, envisioning, eyes for*, fabrication, fantasy, figment, fondness, hallucination, hankering, idea, illusion, imagination, imaginativeness, inclination, invention, itch*, mirage, nightmare, notion, partiality, penchant, phantasm, picture, pie in the sky*, pipe dream*, predilection, preference, relish,

reverie, romancing, sweet tooth*, vision, yearning, yen; SEE CONCEPTS 20,32,409

fancy [adj] extravagant, ornamental
adorned, baroque, beautifying, chichi*, complicated, cushy, custom, decorated, decorative, deluxe, elaborate, elegant, embellished, fanciful, florid, frilly, frou frou*, garnished, gaudy, gingerbread*, intricate, lavish, ornamented, ornate, ostentatious, resplendent, rich, rococo, showy, special, spiffy*, sumptuous, unusual; SEE CONCEPTS 562,579

fancy [v1] imagine, create
be inclined to think, believe, conceive, conjecture, dream up, envisage, envision, fantasize, feature*, guess, head trip*, image, infer, make up, make up off top of one's head*, phantom, picture, realize, reckon, spark, spitball*, suppose, surmise, think, think likely, think up, trump up*, vision, visualize; SEE CONCEPT 43

fancy [v2] love, desire
approve, be attracted to, be captivated by, be enamored of, be in love with, care for, crave, crazy about*, desire, dream of, endorse, fall for, favor, like, long for, lust after, mad for*, prefer, relish, sanction, set one's heart on*, take a liking to*, take to, wild for*, wish for, yearn for; SEE CONCEPTS 17,20,32

fanfare [n] cheering
alarum, array, ballyhoo*, demonstration, display, flourish, hullabaloo*, panoply, parade, pomp, shine, show, trump, trumpet call*; SEE CONCEPT 377

fantasize [v] dream about desires
build castles in air*, daydream, envision, hallucinate, head trip*, imagine, invent, live in dream world*, moon, romance, trip out*, woolgather*; SEE CONCEPT 17

fantastic [adj1] strange, different; imaginary
absurd, artificial, capricious, chimerical, comical, crazy, eccentric, erratic, exotic, extravagant, extreme, fanciful, far-fetched, fictional, foolish, foreign, freakish, grotesque, hallucinatory, illusive, imaginative, implausible, incredible, insane, irrational, ludicrous, mad, misleading, nonsensical, odd, outlandish, out of sight*, peculiar, phantasmagorical, preposterous, quaint, queer, ridiculous, singular, suppositious, unbelievable, unlikely, unreal, wacky*, weird, whimsical; SEE CONCEPTS 564,582

fantastic [adj2] enormous
cracking, extreme, great, huge, humongous, massive, monstrous, monumental, overwhelming, prodigious, severe, stupendous, towering, tremendous; SEE CONCEPT 781

fantastic [adj3] wonderful, excellent
A-1*, awesome, best, best ever, cat's meow*, delicious, far out*, first-class, first-rate, great, like wow*, marvelous, out of sight*, out of this world*, primo*, sensational, superb, unreal*; SEE CONCEPTS 572,574

fantasy [n] imagination, dream
air castle, apparition, appearance, Atlantis*, bubble*, chimera, conceiving, creativity, daydream, delusion, envisioning, externalizing, fabrication, fairyland*, fancy, fancying, fantasia, figment*, flight, flight of imagination, fool's paradise*, hallucination, head trip*, illusion, imaginativeness, imagining, invention, mind trip*, mirage, nightmare, objectifying, originality, rainbow*, reverie, trip, Utopia, vagary, vision; SEE CONCEPTS 20,529,689

far [adj/adv1] at a great distance
afar, a good way, a long way, bit, deep, distant, end of rainbow*, faraway, far-flung*, far-off, far piece*, far-removed, good ways*, miles, outlying, out-of-the-way*, piece, remote, removed, stone's throw*, ways*; SEE CONCEPTS 586,778

far [adv2] considerably
decidedly, extremely, greatly, incomparably, much, notably, quite, significantly, somewhat, very, very much, well; SEE CONCEPTS 772,781

faraway [adj] remote, distant
absent, abstracted, beyond the horizon, distant, dreamy, far, far-flung*, far-off, far-removed, lost, outlying, preoccupied, quite a ways*, removed, well away; SEE CONCEPTS 586,778

farce [n] nonsense, satire
absurdity, broad comedy, buffoonery, burlesque, camp, caricature, comedy, high camp*, horseplay*, interlude, joke, low camp*, mock, mockery, parody, play, pratfall comedy, ridiculousness, sham*, skit, slapstick, travesty; SEE CONCEPTS 263,293

farcical [adj] absurd
amusing, camp, campy*, comic, comical, derisory, diverting, droll, for grins*, funny, gelastic, joshing, laughable, ludicrous, nonsensical, outrageous, preposterous, ridiculous, risible, slapstick, stupid; SEE CONCEPTS 267,542

fare [n1] amount charged for transportation
book, charge, check, expense, passage, price, slug, tariff, ticket, token, toll, transportation; SEE CONCEPT 329

fare [n2] food served at meals
commons, diet, eatables, eats*, edibles, meals, menu, provision, rations, slop*, sustenance, swill*, table, victuals; SEE CONCEPTS 457,459

fare [v] get along; turn out
advance, do, get by, get on, go, handle, happen, hie, journey, make headway, make out, manage, muddle through, pass, proceed, progress, prosper, prove, shift, stagger; SEE CONCEPTS 100,117,704

farewell [n] departing saying; departure
adieu, adieus, adieux, adios, bye-bye, cheerio, ciao, goodbye, hasta la vista, have a nice day, leave-taking, parting, salutation, sendoff, so long, ta-ta, valediction; SEE CONCEPTS 195,278

far-fetched [adj] hard to believe
bizarre, doubtful, dubious, eccentric, fantastic, fishy*, forced, hard to swallow*, illogical, implau-

sible, improbable, incoherent, inconsequential, incredible, labored, preposterous, queer, recondite, strained, strange, suspicious, unbelievable, unconvincing, unlikely, unnatural, unrealistic; SEE CONCEPTS *529,552,582*

farm [*n*] *land for agriculture or animal breeding*
acreage, acres, arboretum, claim, demense, enclosure, estate, farmstead, field, freehold, garden, grange, grassland, holding, homestead, land, lawn, meadow, nursery, orchard, pasture, patch, plantation, ranch, soil, vineyard; SEE CONCEPTS *258, 449,509,517*

farm [*v*] *produce crops, raise animals*
bring under cultivation, crop, cultivate, direct, dress, garden, graze, grow, harrow, harvest, homestead, husband, landscape, look after, operate, pasture, plant, plow, practice husbandry, produce crops, raise, ranch, reap, run, seed, sow, subdue, superintend, tend, till, till the soil, work; SEE CONCEPTS *117,253,324*

farmer [*n*] *person who produces crops, raises animals*
agriculturalist, agriculturist, agronomist, breeder, clodhopper*, cob*, country boy/girl, cropper, cultivator, feeder, gardener, gleaner, grazer, grower, harvester, hired hand, homesteader, horticulturist, husbandman, laborer, peasant, planter, plowman/woman, producer, rancher, ranchman/woman, reaper, sharecropper, sower, tender, tiller, villein, yeoman; SEE CONCEPTS *347,348*

farming [*n*] *producing crops, raising animals*
agriculture, agronomics, agronomy, breeding, crop-raising, cultivation, culture, feeding, fertilizing, gardening, geoponics, gleaning, grazing, growing, harvesting, homesteading, husbandry, hydroponics, landscaping, operating, production, ranching, reaping, seeding, share-cropping, soil culture, threshing, tillage; SEE CONCEPTS *117,253,324*

far-reaching [*adj*] *broad, widespread*
extensive, far-ranging, important, momentous, pervasive, significant, sweeping, wide; SEE CONCEPT *772*

far-sighted [*adj*] *looking ahead wisely*
acute, canny, cautious, clairvoyant, commonsensical, cool-headed*, discerning, judicious, level-headed, perceptive, politic, prescient, provident, prudent, sagacious, sage, shrewd, well-balanced, wise; SEE CONCEPT *402*

farther [*adv*] *at a greater distance*
beyond, further, longer, more distant, more remote, remoter, yon, yonder; SEE CONCEPTS *586,778*

farthest [*adv*] *most distant*
extreme, farthermost, furthermost, furthest, last, lattermost, outermost, outmost, remotest, ultimate, utmost, uttermost; SEE CONCEPTS *586,778*

fascinate [*v*] *captivate, hold spellbound*
absorb, allure, animate, arouse, attach, attract, beguile, bewitch, charm, compel, delight, draw, enamor, enchant, engage, engross, enrapture, enslave, ensnare, enthrall, entice, entrance, excite, fire, gladden, hypnotize, infatuate, interest, intoxicate, intrigue, invite, kindle, lure, mesmerize, overpower, overwhelm, pique, please, provoke, ravish, rivet, seduce, spellbind, stimulate, stir, subdue, tantalize, tempt, thrill, titillate, transfix, transport, win; SEE CONCEPTS *7,11,22*

fascinated [*adj*] *captivated, spellbound*
absorbed, aroused, attracted, beguiled, bewitched, captivated, charmed, dazzled, delighted, enamored, enchanted, engrossed, enraptured, enthralled, enticed, entranced, excited, fond of, hypnotized, infatuated, in love with, intoxicated, mesmerized, overpowered, seduced, sent, smitten, sold on*, stuck on*, tantalized, thrilled, titillated, transfixed, transported, under a spell*; SEE CONCEPTS *32,403*

fascinating [*adj*] *interesting, spellbinding*
alluring, appealing, attractive, bewitching, captivating, charming, compelling, delectable, delightful, enchanting, engaging, engrossing, enticing, glamorous, gripping, intriguing, irresistible, ravishing, riveting, seducing, seductive, siren; SEE CONCEPT *529*

fascination [*n*] *strong interest*
allure, appeal, attraction, bug*, charisma, charm, enchantment, enthrallment, glamour, grabber*, hang-up*, lure, magic, magnetism, obsession, piquancy, power, pull*, sorcery, spell, thing*, thing for*, trance, witchcraft, witchery; SEE CONCEPTS *20,32,532,690*

fascism [*n*] *political system of dictatorship*
absolutism, authoritarianism, autocracy, bureaucracy, despotism, Nazism, one-party system, party government, racism, regimentation, totalitarianism; SEE CONCEPTS *299,301,689*

fashion [*n1*] *latest style, prevailing taste*
appearance, bandwagon*, chic, configuration, convention, craze, cry, cultism, cultus, custom, cut, dernier cri, fad, faddism, figure, form, furor, in thing*, last word*, latest*, latest thing*, line*, look, make, mode, model, mold, newest wrinkle*, pattern, rage, shape, thing*, tone, trend, usage, vogue; SEE CONCEPT *655*

fashion [*n2*] *attitude, manner*
convention, custom, demeanor, device, etiquette, form, formality, formula, guise, method, mode, modus operandi, mores, observance, order, practice, precedent, prescription, prevalence, procedure, sort, style, system, technique, tendency, tone, trend, usage, vein, vogue, way; SEE CONCEPTS *644,657*

fashion [*v*] *adjust, design, create*
accommodate, adapt, build, carve, construct, contrive, cook up*, cut, devise, dream up*, erect, fabricate, fit, forge, form, frame*, knock together*, make, manufacture, model, mold, plan, plot, produce, sculpture, shape, suit, tailor, throw together*, turn out*, work; SEE CONCEPTS *168,173,232*

fashionable [*adj*] *stylish, up-to-date*
a go-go*, à la mode*, all the rage*, chic, chichi*, contemporary, current, customary, dashing, faddy*,

favored, fly*, genteel, hot*, in style, in-thing*, in vogue, last word*, latest*, latest thing*, mod*, modern, modish*, natty*, new, newfangled, now, popular, prevailing, rakish, smart, swank, trendsetting, trendy, upscale*, up-to-the-minute*, usual, well-liked, with it*; SEE CONCEPTS *579,589*

fast [*n*] *abstention from eating*
abstinence, diet, fasting, xerophagy; SEE CONCEPT *169*

fast [*adj1*] *speedy*
accelerated, active, agile, blue streak*, breakneck*, brisk, chop-chop*, dashing, double-time*, electric, expeditious, expeditive, flashing, fleet, fleeting, flying, hairtrigger*, hasty, hot*, hurried, hypersonic, in a jiffy*, in nothing flat*, lickety split*, like a bat out of hell*, like all get out*, like crazy*, like mad*, nimble, on the double*, PDQ*, posthaste, presto, pronto, quick, racing, rapid, ready, screamin'*, snap*, snappy*, speedball*, supersonic, swift, velocious, winged; SEE CONCEPTS *588,799*

fast [*adj2*] *fixed, immovable*
adherent, ardent, attached, close, constant, constrained, durable, faithful, fastened, firm, fortified, glued, held, impregnable, indelible, inextricable, lasting, loyal, permanent, resistant, resolute, secure, set, sound, stable, staunch, steadfast, stuck, sure, tenacious, tight, true, true blue*, unwavering, wedged; SEE CONCEPTS *488,542*

fast [*adj3*] *immoral, promiscuous*
bawdy, careless, debauched, depraved, devil-may-care*, dissipated, dissolute, easy, extravagant, flirtatious, frivolous, gadabout*, giddy, incontinent, indecent, intemperate, lascivious, lecherous, lewd, libertine, libidinous, licentious, light, loose, lustful, profligate, rakish, reckless, salacious, self-gratifying, self-indulgent, sportive, sporty, unchaste, wanton, wild; SEE CONCEPT *545*

fast [*v*] *go without food*
abstain, deny oneself, diet, famish, forbear, go hungry, not eat, refrain, starve; SEE CONCEPT *169*

fast [*adv1*] *speedily*
apace, chop-chop*, expeditiously, flat-out*, fleetly, full tilt*, hastily, hurriedly, in a flash*, in haste, in nothing flat*, in short order*, like a flash*, like a shot*, like greased lightning*, like wildfire*, posthaste, presto, promptly, pronto, quick, quickly, rapidly, soon, swift, swiftly; SEE CONCEPTS *588,799*

fast [*adv2*] *fixedly*
deeply, firm, firmly, hard, securely, solidly, soundly, steadfastly, tight, tightly; SEE CONCEPT *488*

fasten [*v*] *make secure; join together*
adhere, affix, anchor, attach, band, bar, batten, belt, bind, bolt, bond, brace, button, catch, cement, chain, cleave, close, cohere, connect, couple, embed, establish, fix, freeze to*, girth, glue, grip, hitch, hitch on, hold, hook, hook up, implant, infix, jam, knot, lace, leash, link, lock, lodge, make firm, moor, mortise, nail, rivet, rope, screw, seal, secure, set, settle,

solder, stay put, stick, strengthen, string, tack on, tag, tie, tighten, truss, unite, wedge, weld; SEE CONCEPTS *85,113,160*

fastidious [*adj*] *very careful, meticulous*
captious, choosy, critical, dainty, demanding, difficult, discriminating, easily disgusted, exacting, finical, finicky, fussbudgety*, fussy, hard to please*, hypercritical, nice, nit-picky, overdelicate, overnice, particular, persnickety*, picky, punctilious, queasy, squeamish, stickling; SEE CONCEPTS *542,550*

fat [*n*] *overweight, adipose tissue*
blubber, bulk, cellulite, corpulence, excess, fatness, flab, flesh, grease, lard, obesity, overabundance, overflow, paunch, plethora, suet, superfluity, surfeit, surplus, tallow; SEE CONCEPTS *723,734*

fat [*adj1*] *overweight*
beefy*, big, blimp, bovine, brawny, broad, bulging, bulky, bull, burly, butterball*, chunky*, corpulent, distended, dumpy, elephantine, fleshy, gargantuan, gross, heavy, heavyset*, hefty, husky, inflated, jelly-belly*, lard, large, meaty*, obese, oversize, paunchy, plump, plumpish, ponderous, porcine, portly, potbellied, pudgy*, roly-poly*, rotund, solid, stout, swollen, thickset*, weighty, whalelike*; SEE CONCEPT *491*

fat [*adj2*] *containing oily substance*
adipose, fatlike, fatty, greasy, oily, oleaginous, suety, unctuous; SEE CONCEPT *485*

fat [*adj3*] *productive, rich*
affluent, cushy, fertile, flourishing, fruitful, good, lucrative, lush, profitable, prosperous, remunerative, thriving; SEE CONCEPT *334*

fatal [*adj1*] *deadly, lethal*
baleful, baneful, calamitous, cataclysmic, catastrophic, deathly, destructive, disastrous, fateful, final, ill-fated, ill-starred, incurable, inevitable, killing, lethal, malefic, malignant, mortal, mortiferous, noxious, pernicious, pestilent, pestilential, poisonous, ruinous, terminal, virulent; SEE CONCEPTS *537,539*

fatal [*adj2*] *critical, very important*
crucial, decisive, destined, determining, doomed, fateful, final, foreordained, inevitable, predestined, unlucky; SEE CONCEPTS *531,568*

fatalism [*n*] *resignation to a fate*
acceptance, destinism, determinism, necessitarianism, passivity, predestinarianism, predestination, stoicism; SEE CONCEPT *689*

fatality [*n*] *death, loss; ability to cause such*
accident, casualty, deadliness, destructiveness, disaster, dying, inevitability, lethality, lethalness, mortality, necrosis, noxiousness, poisonousness, virulence; SEE CONCEPTS *304,675*

fate [*n*] *predetermined course*
break, chance, circumstance, consequence, cup*, destination, destiny, divine will*, doom, effect, end, ending, fortune, future, handwriting on wall*, horoscope, inescapableness, issue, karma, kismet, Lady Luck*, lot, luck, Moira, nemesis, outcome, portion,

predestination, providence, stars*, termination, up-shot, wheel of fortune*; SEE CONCEPT *679*

fateful [*adj1*] *significant*
acute, apocalyptic, conclusive, critical, crucial, decisive, determinative, direful, doomful, eventful, important, inauspicious, momentous, ominous, portentous, resultful; SEE CONCEPT *568*

fateful [*adj2*] *deadly*
calamitous, cataclysmic, catastrophic, destructive, disastrous, fatal, lethal, mortal, ominous, ruinous; SEE CONCEPT *537*

father [*n1*] *male person who begets children; forefather*
ancestor, begetter, dad, daddy*, forebear, head, pa, padre, papa, parent, pop*, predecessor, procreator, progenitor, sire; SEE CONCEPTS *414,419*

father/mother [*n2*] *founder, inventor*
administrator, architect, author, builder, creator, dean, elder, encourager, generator, initiator, introducer, leader, maker, mother of invention, motor*, mover, organizer, originator, patriarch, patron, prime mover*, promoter, promulgator, publisher, sire, sponsor, supporter; SEE CONCEPTS *347,423*

father [*n3*] *priest*
abbé, clergyman, confessor, curé, ecclesiastic, minister, padre, parson, pastor, preacher, reverend; SEE CONCEPT *361*

father [*v*] *create; generate*
beget, breed, engender, establish, found, get, hatch, institute, invent, make, originate, parent, procreate, produce, progenerate, sire, spawn; SEE CONCEPTS *173,205,221,251,374*

fatherly [*adj*] *acting as a male parent*
affectionate, benevolent, benign, forbearing, indulgent, kind, kindly, paternal, patriarchal, protective, supportive, tender; SEE CONCEPT *401*

fathom [*v*] *discern, understand*
appreciate, apprehend, catch, cognize, comprehend, dig, divine, estimate, figure out, follow, gauge, get, get to the bottom*, grasp, have, interpret, know, measure, penetrate, perceive, pierce, pinpoint, plumb, probe, recognize, savvy, sound, unravel; SEE CONCEPTS *15,38*

fatigue [*n*] *tiredness*
brain fag*, burnout*, debility, dullness, enervation, ennui, exhaustion, faintness, fatigation, feebleness, heaviness, languor, lassitude, lethargy, listlessness, overtiredness, weakness, weariness; SEE CONCEPTS *316,405*

fatigue [*v*] *tire, wear out*
bedraggle, burn out*, bush*, conk out*, debilitate, deplete, disable, drain, droop, drop, enervate, exhaust, fag, fizzle, flag, jade*, knock out*, languish, overtire, peter out*, poop*, poop out*, prostrate, sag, sink, succumb, take, tucker, weaken, wear, wear down, weary; SEE CONCEPTS *137,225,240,250*

fatigued [*adj*] *tired*
all in*, beat*, bedraggled, blasé, burned out*, bushed*, dead*, dead-beat*, dead-tired*, dog-tired*,

dog-weary*, done in*, droopy, dropping, enervated, exhausted, fagged out*, jaded*, languid, languorous, lassitudinous, listless, out of gas*, overtired, played out*, pooped*, prostrate, ready to drop*, spent*, tuckered*, washed out*, wasted*, weary, worn, worn-out, zonked*; SEE CONCEPT *485*

fatness [*n*] *overweight*
adiposity, breadth, bulkiness, corpulence, distension, flab*, flesh, fleshiness, girth, grossness, heaviness, heftiness, inflation, largeness, obesity, plumpness, portliness, protuberance, pudginess, rotundity, size, stoutness, tumidity, weight; SEE CONCEPT *734*

fatten [*v*] *grow or make bigger; nourish*
augment, bloat, broaden, build up, coarsen, cram, distend, expand, feed, fill, gain weight, increase, overfeed, plump, put flesh on*, put on weight, round out, spread, stuff, swell, thicken, thrive, wax; SEE CONCEPTS *236,245,250*

fatty [*adj*] *full of adipose tissue*
blubbery, fatlike, greasy, lardaceous, lardy, oily, oleaginous, rich, suety, unctuous; SEE CONCEPT *485*

fatuous [*adj*] *stupid*
absurd, asinine, birdbrained*, boneheaded*, brainless*, dense, dull, foolish, idiotic, imbecile, inane, insensate, jerky*, lamebrained*, ludicrous, lunatic, mad, mindless, moronic, puerile, sappy, silly, simple, vacuous, witless; SEE CONCEPT *402*

fault [*n1*] *blame, sin; mistake*
accountability, answerability, blunder, crime, culpability, defect, delinquency, dereliction, error, evil doing, failing, flaw, foible, frailty, guilt, impropriety, inaccuracy, indiscretion, infirmity, lapse, liability, loss of innocence, malfeasance, malpractice, misconduct, miscue, misdeed, misdemeanor, negligence, offense, omission, onus, oversight, peccancy, responsibility, slip, slip-up*, solecism, transgression, trespass, vice, weakness, wrong, wrongdoing; SEE CONCEPTS *101,192,699*

fault [*n2*] *physical defect*
blemish, debility, deficiency, demerit, imperfection, infirmity, lack, pimple, shortcoming, weakness, weak point, zit*; SEE CONCEPT *580*

faultless [*adj*] *having nothing wrong with it*
above reproach, accurate, blameless, classic, clean, correct, crimeless, errorless, exemplary, exquisite, faithful, flawless, foolproof, guiltless, ideal, immaculate, impeccable, inculpable, innocent, intact, irreproachable, model, on target*, perfect, pure, right on*, sinless, spotless, stainless, supreme, textbook*, unblemished, unguilty, unspotted, unsullied, whole; SEE CONCEPTS *545,572*

faulty [*adj*] *not working; incorrect*
adulterated, amiss, awry, bad, below par, blamable, blemished, botched, broken, cracked, damaged, debased, defective, deficient, distorted, erroneous, fallacious, fallible, false, flawed, frail, impaired, imperfect, imprecise, inaccurate, inadequate, incom-

plete, incorrect, inexact, injured, insufficient, invalid, lame, leaky, lemon, maimed, malformed, malfunctioning, marred, out of order, rank, sick, tainted, unfit, unreliable, unretentive, unsound, warped, weak, wrong; SEE CONCEPTS *560,570*

faux pas [*n*] *blunder in etiquette*
blooper*, boo-boo*, breach, break, bungle, error, flop, flub*, gaffe*, goof*, impropriety, indecorum, indiscretion, mess-up, misconduct, misjudgment, misstep, mistake, oversight, solecism; SEE CONCEPTS *101,384*

favor [*n*] *approval, good opinion; help*
accommodation, account, admiration, aid, approbation, assistance, backing, benediction, benefit, benevolence, benignity, bias, blessing, boon, championship, compliment, consideration, cooperation, courtesy, dispensation, encouragement, esteem, estimation, friendliness, gift, good turn*, good will*, grace, indulgence, kindness, largess, obligement, okay, partiality, patronage, present, regard, respect, service, support, token; SEE CONCEPTS *10,110,689*

favor [*v1*] *pamper, reward; help*
abet, accommodate, advance, aid, assist, befriend, be partial to, do a kindness, do right by*, esteem, facilitate, further, gratify, humor, indulge, make exception, oblige, play favorites*, promote, pull strings*, show consideration, side with, smile upon*, spare, spoil, treat well, value; SEE CONCEPT *110*

favor [*v2*] *prefer, like*
accept, advocate, appreciate, approbate, approve, back, be in favor of, be on one's side*, buck for*, champion, choose, commend, cotton to*, countenance, encourage, endorse, esteem, eulogize, fancy, flash on*, for, go for*, hold with, honor, incline, lean toward, look up to, opt for, patronize, pick, praise, prefer, prize, regard highly, root for, sanction, single out*, support, take a liking to*, take a shine to*, take to*, think well of, tilt toward*, value; SEE CONCEPT *32*

favor [*v3*] *look like*
be the image of*, be the picture of*, feature, resemble, simulate, take after*; SEE CONCEPT *716*

favorable [*adj1*] *approving, friendly*
acclamatory, affirmative, agreeable, amicable, approbative, approbatory, assenting, benevolent, benign, benignant, commending, complimentary, encouraging, enthusiastic, inclined, in favor of, kind, kindly, laudatory, okay, positive, praiseful, predisposed, reassuring, recommendatory, supportive, sympathetic, understanding, welcoming, well-disposed, well-intentioned; SEE CONCEPT *401*

favorable [*adj2*] *good, timely, advantageous*
appropriate, auspicious, benefic, beneficial, benign, bright, cheering, convenient, encouraging, fair, fit, fortunate, full of promise, gratifying, happy, healthful, helpful, hopeful, kindly, lucky, nice, opportune, pleasant, pleasing, pleasurable, pleasureful, promising, propitious, prosperous, providential, reassuring,

seasonable, suitable, toward, useful, welcome, well-timed, wholesome, worthy; SEE CONCEPTS *537,558,572*

favorably [*adv1*] *genially, in a kindly manner*
agreeably, amiably, approvingly, cordially, courteously, enthusiastically, fairly, generously, graciously, heartily, helpfully, kindly, positively, receptively, usefully, willingly, with approbation, with approval, without prejudice; SEE CONCEPT *401*

favorably [*adv2*] *opportunely, advantageously*
auspiciously, conveniently, fortunately, happily, profitably, prosperously, satisfyingly, successfully, swimmingly, to one's advantage, well; SEE CONCEPTS *537,558,572*

favored [*adj*] *popular*
advantaged, best-liked, blessed, chosen, elite, fair-haired*, favorite, golden-haired*, lucky, pet*, preferred, privileged, recommended, selected, singled out, sweetheart, well-liked; SEE CONCEPTS *529,568*

favorite [*n*] *something or someone cherished, prized*
apple of eye*, beloved, blue-eyed*, chalk*, choice, darling, dear, evergreen*, fair-haired*, fave*, front-runner*, ideal, idol, love, main, minion, number one*, paramour, pet*, pick, preference, shoo-in*, teacher's pet*; SEE CONCEPTS *423,446*

favorite [*adj*] *preferred*
admired, adored, beloved, best-loved, blue-eyed*, cherished, choice, darling, dear, dearest, desired, especial, esteemed, fair-haired*, favored, intimate, liked, main, number one*, personal, pet*, pleasant, popular, precious, prized, revered, sweetheart*, treasured, wished-for; SEE CONCEPTS *529,568*

favoritism [*n*] *bias, partiality*
discrimination, inclination, inequity, nepotism, one-sidedness, partisanship, preference, preferential treatment, unfairness; SEE CONCEPTS *41,388,645*

fawn [*n*] *baby deer*
baby buck, baby doe, yearling; SEE CONCEPTS *394,400*

fawn [*v*] *ingratiate oneself to; serve*
abase, apple-polish*, be at beck and call*, be obsequious, be servile, blandish, bow, brownnose*, buddy up*, butter up*, cajole, cater to, cave in to*, cotton*, court, cower, crawl, creep, cringe, crouch, curry favor*, debase, defer, fall all over, fall on one's knees*, flatter, grovel, honey up*, invite, jolly, kneel, kowtow*, lay it on*, lick boots*, make up to, massage*, oil*, pander, pay court*, play up to*, scrape, slaver, snow*, stoop, stroke*, submit, toady*, truckle*, woo*, yield; SEE CONCEPTS *110,384*

fawning [*adj*] *deferential, grovelling*
abject, adulatory, bootlicking*, bowing, brownnosing*, compliant, cowering, crawling, cringing, flattering, humble, ingratiating, kowtowing*, mealy-mouthed*, obsequious, parasitic, prostrate, scraping, servile, slavish, sniveling, spineless, submissive,

subservient, sycophant, sycophantic; SEE CONCEPT *401*

faze [*v*] *embarrass*
abash, annoy, appall, bother, confound, confuse, daunt, discomfit, disconcert, discountenance, dismay, dumbfound, horrify, irritate, muddle, mystify, nonplus, perplex, puzzle, rattle, vex; SEE CONCEPTS *7,19*

fear [*n*] *alarm, apprehension*
abhorrence, agitation, angst, anxiety, apprehensiveness, aversion, awe, bête noire, chickenheartedness*, cold feet*, cold sweat*, concern, consternation, cowardice, creeps, despair, discomposure, dismay, disquietude, distress, doubt, dread, faintheartedness, foreboding, fright, funk*, horror, jitters, misgiving, nightmare, panic, phobia, presentiment, qualm, recreancy, reverence, revulsion, scare, suspicion, terror, timidity, trembling, tremor, trepidation, unease, uneasiness, worry; SEE CONCEPT *27*

fear [*v*] *feel alarm; be scared of*
anticipate, apprehend, avoid, be afraid, be anxious, be apprehensive, be disquieted, be frightened, be in awe, blanch, break out in sweat*, cower, crouch, dare not, dread, expect, falter, feel concern, flinch, foresee, fret, have butterflies*, have qualms, lose courage*, quail, quaver, shrink, shudder, shun, shy, start, suspect, tremble, wilt, worry; SEE CONCEPT *27*

fearful [*adj1*] *alarmed, apprehensive*
aflutter, afraid, aghast, agitated, anxious, chicken, chickenhearted*, diffident, discomposed, disquieted, disturbed, fainthearted, frightened, goose-bumpy*, have cold feet*, hesitant, in a dither*, intimidated, jittery, jumpy, lily-livered*, mousy, nerveless, nervous, nervy, panicky, perturbed, phobic, pusillanimous, quivery, rabbity*, running scared*, scared, shaky, sheepish*, shrinking, shy, skittish, solicitous, spineless, tense, timid, timorous, tremulous, uneasy, unmanly, weak-kneed*, worried, yellow*; SEE CONCEPT *401*

fearful [*adj2*] *horrifying*
appalling, astounding, atrocious, awful, baleful, bloodcurdling, creepy, dire, distressing, dreadful, eerie, formidable, frightful, ghastly, ghoulish, grievous, grim, grisly, gruesome, hair-raising*, hideous, horrendous, horrible, horrific, lurid, macabre, monstrous, morbid, overwhelming, redoubtable, shocking, shuddersome, sinister, strange, sublime, terrible, tremendous, unearthly, unspeakable; SEE CONCEPTS *529,537,570*

fearless [*adj*] *brave, unafraid*
assured, aweless, bodacious, bold, brassy, cheeky, chesty*, cocky, confident, cool hand*, courageous, crack*, daring, dashing, dauntless, doughty, flip*, fresh*, gallant, game, gritty, gutsy, heroic, icy*, indomitable, intrepid, lionhearted, nervy, plucky, salty*, sanguine, sassy*, smart, spunky, sure, temerarious, unabashed, undaunted, unflinching, valiant, valorous, wise; SEE CONCEPT *401*

feasible [*adj*] *possible, doable*
achievable, advantageous, appropriate, attainable, beneficial, breeze, cinch, duck soup*, easy as pie*, expedient, fit, fitting, likely, no sweat*, performable, pie*, piece of cake*, practicable, practical, probable, profitable, pushover, realizable, reasonable, simple as ABC*, snap, suitable, viable, workable, worthwhile; SEE CONCEPTS *528,552,558*

feast [*n*] *banquet and celebration*
barbecue, big feed*, blow*, blowout*, carnival, carousal, clambake, dinner, entertainment, fest, festival, festivity, fete, fiesta, gala, jollification, merrymaking, picnic, refreshment, regale, repast, spread, treat, wassail; SEE CONCEPTS *377,459*

feast [*v*] *eat a great amount or very well*
banquet, dine, eat sumptuously, entertain, gorge, gormandize, indulge, overindulge, regale, stuff, stuff one's face*, treat, wine and dine*; SEE CONCEPT *169*

feat [*n*] *achievement*
accomplishment, act, action, adventure, attainment, conquest, consummation, coup, deed, effort, enterprise, execution, exploit, performance, stunt, tour de force, triumph, venture, victory; SEE CONCEPTS *1,706*

feather [*n*] *tuft of bird; plumage*
calamus, crest, down, fin, fluff, fringe, penna, pinion, pinna, plume, plumule, pompon, quill, shaft, spike, wing; SEE CONCEPT *399*

feature [*n1*] *characteristic*
affection, angle, article, aspect, attribute, character, component, constituent, detail, differential, earmark*, element, facet, factor, gag*, gimmick, hallmark, idiosyncrasy, individuality, ingredient, integrant, item, mark, notability, particularity, peculiarity, point, property, quality, savor, slant*, speciality, specialty, trait, twist*, unit, virtue; SEE CONCEPTS *831,834,835*

feature [*n2*] *highlight, special attraction*
big show*, crowd puller*, draw, drawing card*, headliner*, innovation, main item, peculiarity, prominent part, special, speciality, specialty; SEE CONCEPTS *386,829*

feature [*n3*] *special article in publication*
column, comment, item, piece, report, story; SEE CONCEPT *270*

feature [*v*] *give prominence to*
accentuate, advertise, blaze*, call attention to, emphasize, headline*, italicize, make conspicuous, mark, play up*, point up*, present, promote, set off*, spotlight*, star, stress, underline, underscore; SEE CONCEPT *60*

features [*n*] *facial characteristics*
appearance, countenance, face, lineaments, looks, mien, mug*, physiognomy, puss*, visage; SEE CONCEPT *418*

featuring [*adj*] *giving prominence to*
calling attention to, displaying, drawing attention to, giving center stage to*, headlining*, highlighting, making much of*, pointing up*, presenting, promot-

ing, pushing, recommending, showing, showing off*, starring, turning, turning the spotlight on*; SEE CONCEPT *292*

febrile [*adj*] *feverish*
delirious, fevered, fiery, flushed, hallucinatory, hot, inflamed, pyretic; SEE CONCEPTS *314,605*

feckless [*adj*] *without purpose*
aimless, carefree, careless, feeble, fustian, futile, good-for-nothing*, hopeless, incautious, incompetent, ineffective, ineffectual, irresponsible, meaningless, purposeless, reckless, shiftless, uncareful, unpurposed, useless, weak, wild, worthless; SEE CONCEPTS *404,542*

fecund [*adj*] *productive*
breeding, fertile, fructiferous, fruitful, generating, pregnant, proliferant, prolific, propagating, reproducing, rich, spawning, teeming; SEE CONCEPT *537*

federation [*n*] *partnership, organization*
alliance, amalgamation, association, bunch, coalition, combination, confederacy, crew, crowd, entente, family, federacy, gang, league, mob, outfit, pool, ring, syndicate, syndication, tribe, union; SEE CONCEPTS *323,381,417*

fed up [*adj*] *disgusted with*
annoyed, blasé, blue*, bored, depressed, discontented, dismal, dissatisfied, down, gloomy, glum, jaded, sated, satiated, sick and tired*, surfeited, tired, up to here*, weary; SEE CONCEPT *403*

fee [*n*] *charge for service, privilege*
account, ante*, bill, bite*, chunk*, commission, compensation, consideration, cost, cut*, emolument, end*, expense, gravy*, handle, hire, honorarium, house*, juice*, pay, payment, percentage, piece*, piece of the action*, price, rake-off*, recompense, remuneration, reward, salary, share, slice*, stipend, take*, take-in*, toll, wage; SEE CONCEPTS *329,344*

feeble [*adj*] *not strong; ineffective*
aged, ailing, chicken*, debilitated, decrepit, delicate, doddering, dopey*, effete, emasculated, enervated, enfeebled, etiolated, exhausted, failing, faint, flabby*, flat, fragile, frail, gentle, helpless, impotent, inadequate, incompetent, indecisive, ineffectual, inefficient, infirm, insubstantial, insufficient, lame, languid, low, out of gas*, paltry, poor, powerless, puny, sapless, sickly, slight, strengthless, tame, thin, unconvincing, vitiated, weak, weakened, weakly, wimpy*, woozy*, zero*; SEE CONCEPTS *267, 489,527*

feebleness [*n*] *lack of strength; ineffectiveness*
debility, decrepitude, delicacy, disease, effeteness, enervation, etiolation, exhaustion, flimsiness, frailness, frailty, inability, inadequacy, incapacity, incompetence, ineffectualness, infirmity, infirmness, insignificance, insufficiency, lameness, languor, lassitude, malaise, senility, sickliness, unhealthiness, weakness; SEE CONCEPTS *630,676,732*

feed [*v*] *give nourishment; augment*
banquet, bolster, cater, cram, deliver, dine, dish out*, dispense, encourage, fatten, feast, fill, find,

foster, fuel, furnish, give, gorge, hand, hand over, maintain, minister, nourish, nurse, nurture, provide, provision, regale, satisfy, stock, strengthen, stuff, supply, support, sustain, victual, wine and dine*; SEE CONCEPTS *107,140*

feed on [*v*] *consume*
devour, eat, exist on, fare, feast, graze, have a bite*, ingest, live on*, meal, munch, nibble, nurture, partake, pasture*, peck*, pig out*, prey on, scarf*, snack, sponge, subsist, take, take nourishment; SEE CONCEPT *169*

feel [*n*] *texture; air*
ambience, atmosphere, aura, feeling, finish, impression, mood, palpation, quality, semblance, sensation, sense, surface, tactility, taction, touch, vibes; SEE CONCEPTS *611,673*

feel [*v1*] *touch, stroke*
apperceive, caress, clasp, clutch, explore, finger, fondle, frisk, fumble, grapple, grasp, grip, grope, handle, manipulate, maul, palm, palpate, paw, perceive, pinch, ply, poke, press, run hands over*, sense, squeeze, test, thumb, tickle, touch, try, twiddle, wield; SEE CONCEPT *612*

feel [*v2*] *experience*
accept, acknowledge, appear, appreciate, be affected, be aware of, be excited, be impressed, be sensible of, be sensitive, be turned on to*, comprehend, discern, encounter, endure, enjoy, exhibit, get*, get in touch*, get vibes*, go through*, have, have a hunch*, have funny feeling*, have vibes*, know, meet, note, notice, observe, perceive, receive, remark, resemble, savor, see, seem, sense, suffer, suggest, take to heart*, taste, undergo, understand, welcome; SEE CONCEPTS *15,34,38*

feel [*v3*] *believe*
assume, be convinced, be of the opinion, conclude, conjecture, consider, credit, deduce, deem, esteem, gather, guess, have a hunch*, have the impression*, hold, infer, intuit, judge, know, presume, repute, sense, suppose, surmise, suspect, think; SEE CONCEPT *12*

feeling [*n1*] *sensation, especially of touch*
activity, awareness, consciousness, enjoyment, excitability, excitation, excitement, feel, innervation, motility, motor response, pain, perceiving, perception, pleasure, reaction, receptivity, reflex, responsiveness, sense, sensibility, sensitivity, sensuality, tactility, tangibility, titillation, touch; SEE CONCEPT *608*

feeling [*n2*] *idea, impression*
apprehension, belief, consciousness, conviction, eye*, hunch*, inclination, inkling, instinct, mind, notion, opinion, outlook, persuasion, point of view, presentiment, reaction, sense, sentiment, suspicion, thought, view; SEE CONCEPTS *532,689,690*

feeling [*n3*] *a state of mind, often strong*
action, affection, appreciation, ardor, behavior, capacity, compassion, concern, cultivation, culture,

delicacy, discernment, discrimination, emotion, empathy, faculty, fervor, fondness, heat, imagination, impression, intelligence, intensity, intuition, judgment, keenness, palpability, passion, pathos, pity, reaction, refinement, sensibility, sensitivity, sentiment, sentimentality, sharpness, spirit, sympathy, tangibility, taste, tenderness, understanding, warmth; SEE CONCEPTS *409,410*

feeling [*n4*] *ambience*
air, atmosphere, aura, feel, impression, imprint, mood, quality, semblance; SEE CONCEPT *673*

feign [*v*] *pretend*
act, affect, assume, bluff*, counterfeit, devise, dissemble, dissimulate, do a bit*, fabricate, fake, forge, four-flush*, give appearance of, imagine, imitate, invent, make show of*, phony up*, play, play possum*, put on, put on act*, put up a front*, sham*, simulate, stonewall*; SEE CONCEPTS *59, 63,292*

feigned [*adj*] *pretended*
affected, artificial, assumed, counterfeit, fabricated, fake, faked, false, fictitious, imaginary, imagined, imitation, insincere, phony, pretended, pseudo*, put-on*, sham*, simulated, spurious; SEE CONCEPTS *401,582*

feint [*n*] *pretense*
artifice, bait, blind, bluff, cheat, deceit, distraction, dodge, duck, expedient, fake, gambit, hoax, hoodwinking*, imposture, make-believe, maneuver, mock attack, play, ploy, pretension, pretext, ruse, sham*, shift, snare, stall, stratagem, subterfuge, trick, wile; SEE CONCEPTS *633,660,725*

felicitate [*v*] *congratulate*
commend, compliment, praise, recommend, rejoice with, salute, wish joy to; SEE CONCEPT *69*

felicitous [*adj*] *appropriate, suitable*
applicable, apposite, apropos, apt, convincing, fit, fitting, germane, happy, inspired, just, meet, neat, opportune, pat, pertinent, proper, propitious, relevant, seasonable, telling, timely, well-chosen, well-timed; SEE CONCEPTS *558,799*

fell [*v*] *chop down*
blow down, bowl over*, bring down, cause to fall, cleave, cut, cut down, dash, demolish, down, drop, flatten, floor*, gash, ground, hack, hew, knock down, knock over, lay low*, level, mangle, mow down*, prostrate, pull down, raze, rive, sever, shoot, shoot down*, slash, split, strike down, sunder, throw down, tumble; SEE CONCEPTS *176,181*

fellow [*n1*] *male person*
adolescent, apprentice, beau, bloke*, boy, brother, buck*, cadet, chap*, character, customer, daddy*, dude*, gentleman, guy, hunk*, individual, juvenile, kid, lad, man, master, novice, pubescent, punk*, scion, squirt, stallion, stripling, stud*, teenager, whippersnapper*, youngster, youth; SEE CONCEPT *419*

fellow [*n2*] *colleague, friend*
assistant, associate, cohort, companion, compeer, comrade, concomitant, confrere, consort, coordinate, counterpart*, coworker, double, duplicate, equal, instructor, lecturer, match, mate, member, partner, peer, professor, reciprocal, twin; SEE CONCEPTS *348,423*

fellowship [*n*] *sociability, brotherhood*
acquaintance, affability, alliance, amity, association, camaraderie, club, communion, companionability, companionship, company, comradeship, conviviality, familiarity, fraternity, fraternization, friendliness, guild, intimacy, kindliness, league, order, sisterhood, society, sodality, togetherness; SEE CONCEPTS *387,388*

felon [*n*] *criminal*
con, convict, delinquent, ex-con*, jailbird*, lawbreaker, lifer*, loser*, malefactor, offender, outlaw, yardbird*; SEE CONCEPT *412*

female [*n*] *woman*
beauty, daughter, dowager, feminist, femme, gal, gentlewoman, girl, grandmother, lady, lesbian, madam, madonna, mama, matron, Miss/Mrs./Ms., mom, mother, she, sister; SEE CONCEPTS *408,415*

femininity/feminine [*n/adj*] *womanly*
effeminate, effete, fertile, ladylike, womanhood, womanish, womanliness; SEE CONCEPTS *371,372, 408,648*

fence [*n*] *barrier used to enclose a piece of land*
backstop, balustrade, bar, barbed wire, barricade, block, boards, chains, Cyclone, defense, dike, guard, hedge, net, paling, palisade, pickets, posts, rail, railing, rampart, roadblock, shield, stakes, stockade, stop, wall; SEE CONCEPTS *260,476,479*

fence [*v1*] *enclose, separate an area*
bound, cage, circumscribe, confine, coop, corral, defend, encircle, fortify, girdle, guard, hedge, hem, immure, mew, mure, pen, protect, rail, restrict, secure, surround, wall; SEE CONCEPT *758*

fence [*v2*] *dodge; beat around the bush*
avoid, baffle, cavil, duck, equivocate, evade, feint, foil, hedge, maneuver, outwit, parry, prevaricate, quibble, shift, shirk, sidestep, stonewall*, tergiversate; SEE CONCEPTS *30,59*

fend [*v*] *defend*
bulwark, cover, dodge, guard, oppose, parry, protect, repel, resist, safeguard, screen, secure, shield; SEE CONCEPT *96*

fender [*n*] *piece protecting part of a vehicle*
apron, buffer, bumper, cover, curb, cushion, frame, guard, mask, mudguard*, protector, screen, shield, splashboard, ward; SEE CONCEPT *502*

fend for [*v*] *take care of*
eke out existence*, look after, make do, make provision for, provide for, stay alive*, subsist, support, survive, sustain; SEE CONCEPTS *100,117*

fend off [*v*] *keep at bay*
avert, avoid, beat off*, deflect, drive back*, hold at bay*, keep at a distance, keep at arm's length*, keep

off, parry, rebuff, rebuke, rebut, refuse, reject, repel, repulse, resist, snub, spurn, stave off, turn aside, ward off; SEE CONCEPT **96**

ferment [*n1*] *substance causing chemicals to split into simpler substances*
bacteria, bacterium, barm, ebullition, enzyme, fermentation agent, leaven, leavening, mold, seethe, simmer, yeast; SEE CONCEPT **478**

ferment [*n2*] *agitation, uprising*
ailment, brouhaha*, clamor, commotion, convulsion, disquiet, disquietude, disruption, disturbance, excitement, fever, flap, frenzy, furor, fuss, heat, hell broke loose*, hubbub*, imbroglio, outcry, restiveness, restlessness, row*, rumble*, scene*, state of unrest, stew*, stink*, stir, storm, to-do*, tumult, turbulence, turmoil, unrest, upheaval, uproar, upturn; SEE CONCEPTS **106,674**

ferment [*v*] *split into simpler substances; be agitated*
acidify, agitate, be violent, boil, brew, bubble, churn, concoct, dissolve, effervesce, evaporate, excite, fester, fizz, foam, foment, froth, heat, incite, inflame, leaven, moil, overflow, provoke, ripen, rise, rouse, seethe, simmer, sour, sparkle, stir up, work; SEE CONCEPTS **7,19,22,250**

ferocious [*adj*] *violent, barbaric*
barbarous, bloodthirsty, brutal, brutish, cruel, fell, feral, fierce, frightful, grim, implacable, inhuman, inhumane, lupine, merciless, murderous, pitiless, predatory, rapacious, ravening, ravenous, relentless, ruthless, sanguinary, savage, tigerish, truculent, unmerciful, unrestrained, untamed, vehement, vicious, voracious, wild, wolfish; SEE CONCEPTS **401,542**

ferret out [*v*] *trace, search out*
ascertain, be on to, bring to light*, chase, determine, dig up*, disclose, discover, drive out, elicit, extract, follow, get at*, hunt, learn, nose out*, penetrate, pick up on, pierce, probe, pry, pursue, quest, root out*, seek, smell out*, smoke out*, track down, trail, unearth; SEE CONCEPTS **183,216**

ferry [*n*] *transportation boat*
barge, ferryboat, packet, packet boat, passage boat; SEE CONCEPT **506**

ferry [*v*] *carry across*
bear, buck, carry, chauffeur, convey, lug*, move across, pack, run, schlepp*, send, ship, shuttle, tote*, transport; SEE CONCEPTS **187,217**

fertile [*adj*] *ready to bear, produce*
abundant, arable, bearing, black, bountiful, breeding, breedy, bringing forth, childing, fecund, feracious, flowering, flowing with milk and honey*, fruitful, generative, gravid, hebetic, loamy, lush, luxuriant, plenteous, plentiful, pregnant, procreant, producing, productive, proliferant, prolific, puberal, pubescent, rank, rich, spawning, teeming, uberous, vegetative, virile, with child*, yielding; SEE CONCEPTS **372,485**

fertility [*n*] *readiness to bear, produce*
abundance, copiousness, fecundity, feracity, fruitfulness, generative capacity, gravidity, luxuriance,

plentifulness, potency, pregnancy, productiveness, productivity, prolifacacy, prolificity, puberty, pubescence, richness, uberty, virility; SEE CONCEPTS **372, 723**

fertilize [*v*] *make ready to bear, produce*
beget, breed, compost, cover, dress, enrich, fecundate, feed, fructify, generate, germinate, impregnate, inseminate, lime, make fruitful, make pregnant, manure, mulch, pollinate, procreate, propagate, topdress, treat; SEE CONCEPTS **257,374,375**

fertilizer [*n*] *dressing to aid production of crops*
buffalo chips*, compost, cow chips*, dung, guano, humus, manure, maul*, mulch, peat moss, plant food, potash, top dressing*; SEE CONCEPTS **260, 399,429**

fervent/fervid [*adj*] *enthusiastic, excited*
animated, ardent, blazing, burning, devout, dying to*, eager, earnest, ecstatic, emotional, enthused, falling all over oneself*, fiery, glowing, go great guns*, heartfelt, hearty, hot*, hot-blooded*, impassioned, intense, passionate, perfervid, pious, religious, responsive, serious, sincere, tender, unfeigned, vehement, warm, warmhearted, wholehearted, zealous; SEE CONCEPTS **401,542**

fervor [*n*] *excitement, enthusiasm*
animation, ardency, ardor, devoutness, eagerness, earnestness, fervency, fire*, heartiness, heat*, hurrah, intensity, jazz*, love, oomph*, passion, pep talk*, piety, piousness, religiousness, seriousness, sincerity, solemnity, vehemence, warmth, weakness, wholeheartedness, zeal, zealousness; SEE CONCEPTS **633,657**

fester [*v*] *intensify; become inflamed*
aggravate, blister, canker, chafe, decay, gall, gather, irk, maturate, putrefy, rankle, rot, smolder, suppurate, ulcer, ulcerate; SEE CONCEPTS **469,698**

festival [*n*] *celebration*
anniversary, carnival, commemoration, competition, entertainment, fair, feast, festivities, fete, field day, fiesta, gala, holiday, jubilee, merrymaking, treat; SEE CONCEPT **377**

festive [*adj*] *decorated, celebratory*
blithe, bouncy, carnival, cheery, chipper*, chirpy, convivial, festal, gala, gay, gleeful, go-go*, grooving, happy, hearty, holiday, jocund, jolly, jovial, joyful, joyous, jubilant, juiced up*, jumping, lighthearted, merry, mirthful, peppy*, perky, rocking*, snappy*, swinging, upbeat, zippy*; SEE CONCEPTS **403,548**

festivity [*n*] *celebration, revelry*
amusement, bash*, blowout*, carousal*, clambake*, conviviality, do*, entertainment, festival, fun, fun and games*, gaiety, happiness, hilarity, hoopla, jamboree, jollity, joviality, joyfulness, levity, merriment, merrymaking, mirth, party, pleasure, revel, reveling, revelment, revelry, shindig*, sport, whoopee*, wingding*; SEE CONCEPTS **377,383**

fetch [*v*] *go get, bring in*
back, bear, be sold for, bring, bring back, bring to, buck, call for, carry, conduct, convey, deliver, draw

forth, earn, elicit, escort, get, give rise to, go for, gun, heel, lead, lug*, make, obtain, pack, piggyback*, produce, realize, retrieve, ride, sell, sell for, shoulder*, tote, transport, truck*, yield; SEE CONCEPTS *90,124,131*

fetching [*adj*] *alluring, attractive*
beautiful, captivating, charming, cute, enchanting, enticing, fascinating, intriguing, luring, pleasing, sweet, taking, tempting, winsome; SEE CONCEPTS *537,579*

fete [*n*] *celebration, party*
ball, banquet, bazaar, do*, fair, festival, fiesta, gala; SEE CONCEPT *377*

fete [*v*] *throw a party for someone*
celebrate, entertain, feast, festival, hold reception for, holiday, honor, lionize, make much of*, roll out red carpet*, treat, wine and dine*; SEE CONCEPT *384*

fetid [*adj*] *foul, rancid*
corrupt, fusty, grody*, gross*, icky*, loathsome, lousy, malodorous, mephitic, noisome, noxious, offensive, putrid, rank, reeking, repugnant, repulsive, revolting, rotten, smelly, stenchy, stinking, stinky, strong, yecchy*, yucky*; SEE CONCEPT *598*

fetish [*n1*] *obsession*
bias, craze*, desire, fixation, golden calf*, idée fixe, leaning, luck, mania, partiality, penchant, periapt, predilection, prejudice, preoccupation, prepossession, proclivity, propensity, stimulant, thing*; SEE CONCEPTS *529,689*

fetish [*n2*] *object believed to have supernatural powers*
amulet, charm, cult object, idol, image, juju*, mascot, phylactery, superstition object, talisman, voodoo doll*, zemi; SEE CONCEPTS *446,686*

fetter [*v*] *tie up, hold*
bind, chain, check, clog, confine, cuff, curb, drag feet, encumber, hamper, hamstring*, handcuff, hang up, hinder, hobble, hog-tie*, hold captive, leash, manacle, put straitjacket on*, repress, restrain, restrict, shackle, throw monkey wrench in*, tie, trammel; SEE CONCEPTS *130,191*

fetters [*n*] *bindings; bondage*
bilboes, bonds, captivity, chains, check, cuffs, curb, handcuffs, hindrance, irons, manacles, obstruction, restraint, shackles, trammels; SEE CONCEPTS *130, 191,500*

feud [*n*] *major argument; estrangement*
altercation, argument, bad blood*, bickering, broil*, combat, conflict, contention, contest, controversy, disagreement, discord, dispute, dissension, enmity, estrangement, faction, falling out*, fight, fracas, grudge, hostility, quarrel, rivalry, row, run-in*, squabble, strife, vendetta; SEE CONCEPTS *46,106,388*

feud [*v*] *fight bitterly; fall out*
be at daggers with*, be at odds*, bicker, brawl, clash, contend, dispute, duel, quarrel, row, squabble, war; SEE CONCEPTS *46,106*

fever [*n*] *state of high temperature or agitation*
burning up*, delirium, ecstasy, excitement, febrile disease, ferment, fervor, fire, flush, frenzy, heat, intensity, passion, pyrexia, restlessness, running a temperature*, the shakes*, turmoil, unrest; SEE CONCEPTS *410,610*

feverish [*adj1*] *having high temperature*
above normal*, aguey, burning, burning up*, febrile, fevered, fiery, flushed, having the shakes*, hectic, hot, inflamed, on fire, pyretic, running a temperature*; SEE CONCEPT *605*

feverish [*adj2*] *excited, agitated*
burning, distracted, fervid, fevered, frantic, frenetic, frenzied, furious, heated, hectic, high-strung*, impatient, keyed up*, nervous, obsessive, overwrought, passionate, restless; SEE CONCEPT *401*

few [*adj*] *hardly any*
a few, any, exiguous, few and far between*, imperceptible, inconsequential, inconsiderable, infrequent, insufficient, lean, less, meager, middling, minor, minority, minute, negligible, not many, not too many*, occasional, paltry, petty, piddling, rare, scant, scanty, scarce, scarcely any, scattered, scattering, seldom, semioccasional, short, skimpy, slender, slight, slim, some, sparse, sporadic, stingy, straggling, thin, trifling, uncommon, unfrequent, widely spaced; SEE CONCEPTS *771,789*

few [*prep*] *scarcely any*
not many, not too many*, scattering, several, slim pickings*, small number, smatter, smattering, some, spattering, sprinkling; SEE CONCEPT *786*

fiancé/fiancée [*n*] *person engaged to marry*
affianced person, betrothed, bride-to-be, engaged person, future*, going steady*, husband-to-be, intended, prospective spouse, steady*, wife-to-be; SEE CONCEPTS *414,423*

fiasco [*n*] *catastrophe*
abortion, blunder, botched situation, breakdown, debacle, disaster, dumb thing to do*, dumb trick*, embarrassment, error, failure, farce, flap, flop, mess, miscarriage, route, ruin, screwup*, stunt, washout*; SEE CONCEPT *674*

fiat [*n*] *order, proclamation*
authorization, command, decree, dictate, dictum, edict, endorsement, mandate, ordinance, permission, precept, sanction, ukase, warrant; SEE CONCEPT *685*

fib [*n*] *undetailed lie*
canard, crock*, equivocation, evasiveness, fabrication, fairy tale*, falsehood, falsity, fiction, invention, jazz*, line*, mendacity, misrepresentation, prevarication, spinach*, story, tale, untruth, untruthfulness, white lie*, whopper*, yarn*; SEE CONCEPTS *278,282*

fib [*v*] *tell undetailed lie*
concoct, create fiction, equivocate, fabricate, falsify, invent, jive*, lie, make up, palter, plant, prevaricate, promote, shovel*, speak with forked tongue*, stretch the truth*, tell little white lie*, trump up*; SEE CONCEPT *63*

fiber [*n1*] *strand of material*
cilia, cord, fibril, filament, footlet, grain, grit, hair, shred, staple, string, strip, tendril, thread, tissue,

tooth, vein, warp, web, woof; SEE CONCEPTS *392,428,611,831*

fiber [*n2*] *texture*
essence, fabric, feel, hand, nap, nature, pile, spirit, substance; SEE CONCEPTS *411,682*

fibrous [*adj*] *stringy*
coarse, fibroid, hairy, muscular, pulpy, ropy, sinewy, stalky, threadlike, tissued, veined, wiry, woody; SEE CONCEPT *606*

fickle [*adj*] *vacillating, blowing hot and cold*
arbitrary, capricious, changeable, cheating, coquettish, double-crossing, faithless, fitful, flighty, frivolous, inconstant, irresolute, lubricious, mercurial, mutable, quicksilver, sneaking, temperamental, ticklish, two-timing, unfaithful, unpredictable, unstable, unsteady, untrue, variable, volatile, whimsical, yo-yo*; SEE CONCEPTS *401,534,545*

fiction [*n*] *made-up story*
anecdote, best seller, book, cliff-hanger*, clothesline*, concoction, crock*, drama, fable, fabrication, falsehood, fancy, fantasy, fib, figment of imagination*, fish story*, hooey*, imagination, improvisation, invention, legend, lie, misrepresentation, myth, narrative, novel, old wives' tale*, potboiler*, prevarication, romance, smoke*, story, storytelling, tale, tall story*, terminological inexactitude, untruth, whopper*, work of imagination, yarn*; SEE CONCEPTS *63,271,280,282*

fictitious [*adj*] *untrue, made-up*
apocryphal, artificial, assumed, bogus*, chimerical, concocted, cooked-up*, counterfeit, created, deceptive, delusive, delusory, dishonest, ersatz*, fabricated, factitious, fake, faked, false, fanciful, fantastic, fashioned, feigned, fictional, fictive, figmental, hyped up*, illusory, imaginary, imagined, improvised, invented, made, make-believe, misleading, mock, mythical, phony, queer, romantic, sham*, simulated, spurious, suppositious, supposititious, synthetic, trumped-up*, unreal; SEE CONCEPTS *267,582*

fiddle [*v*] *mess with, tinker*
dabble, doodle, feel, fidget, finger, fool, handle, interfere, mess, mess around*, monkey*, play, potter, puddle, putter, tamper, touch, toy, trifle, twiddle; SEE CONCEPTS *87,291*

fidelity [*n1*] *faithfulness in a relationship*
allegiance, ardor, attachment, constancy, dependability, devotedness, devotion, faith, fealty, integrity, loyalty, piety, reliability, staunchness, steadfastness, true-heartedness, trustworthiness; SEE CONCEPTS *32,388*

fidelity [*n2*] *conformity to standard*
accuracy, adherence, adhesion, attachment, closeness, constancy, correspondence, exactitude, exactness, faithfulness, loyalty, naturalism, preciseness, precision, realism, scrupulousness, verism; SEE CONCEPT *636*

fidget [*v*] *move restlessly*
be antsy*, be hyper*, be nervous, be on pins and needles*, be spooked*, be wired*, bustle, chafe, fiddle, fret, fuss, hitch, jiggle, jitter, joggle, jump, play, squirm, stir, toss, trifle, twiddle, twitch, wiggle, worry; SEE CONCEPT *147*

fidgety [*adj*] *restlessly moving*
antsy*, apprehensive, high-strung*, hyper*, impatient, jerky, jittery, jumpy, nervous, nervous wreck*, nervy, on edge*, on pins and needles*, restive, restless, spooked*, spooky*, twitchy, uneasy, unrestful, up the wall*, wired*; SEE CONCEPT *401*

field [*n1*] *open land that can be cultivated*
acreage, cropland, enclosure, farmland, garden, glebe, grassland, green, ground, lea, mead, meadow, moorland, pasture, patch, plot, ranchland, range, terrain, territory, tillage, tract, vineyard; SEE CONCEPTS *509,517*

field [*n2*] *persons taking part in competition*
applicants, candidates, competition, competitors, contestants, entrants, entries, nominees, participants, possibilities, runners; SEE CONCEPTS *325,365,417*

field [*n3*] *sphere of influence, activity, interest, study*
area, avocation, bailiwick, bounds, calling, champaign, circle, compass, confines, cup of tea*, demesne, department, discipline, domain, dominion, environment, job, jurisdiction, limits, line, long suit*, margin, métier, occupation, orbit, precinct, province, purview, racket, range, reach, region, scope, speciality, specialty, sweep, terrain, territory, thing, vocation, walk, weakness, work; SEE CONCEPT *349*

field [*n4*] *arena with special use, as athletics*
amphitheater, battlefield, circuit, course, court, diamond, fairground, golf course, green, gridiron, grounds, landing strip, lot, park, playground, playing area, racecourse, race track, range, rink, stadium, terrain, theater, track, turf; SEE CONCEPTS *364,438,449*

field [*v*] *catch a hit or thrown object*
cover, deal with, deflect, handle, hold, occupy, patrol, pick up, play, retrieve, return, stop, turn aside; SEE CONCEPT *164*

fiend [*n1*] *dastardly person*
barbarian, beast, brute, degenerate, demon, devil, diablo*, evil spirit, hellcat, hellion, imp, little devil*, Mephistopheles, monster, ogre, Satan, savage, serpent, troll; SEE CONCEPT *412*

fiend [*n2*] *person overenthusiastic about interest*
addict, aficionado, bigot, devotee, enthusiast, fan, fanatic, freak, maniac, monomaniac, nut*, votarist, votary, zealot; SEE CONCEPT *423*

fierce [*adj*] *violent, menacing*
angry, animal, ape, awful, barbarous, bloodthirsty, blustery, boisterous, bold, brutal, brutish, cruel, cutthroat*, dangerous, enraged, fell, feral, ferocious, fiery, flipped*, frightening, furious, horrible, howling, impetuous, infuriated, intense, malevolent, ma-

lign, murderous, passionate, powerful, primitive, raging, raving, relentless, savage, stormy, strong, tempestuous, terrible, threatening, tigerish, truculent, tumultous/tumultuous, uncontrollable, untamed, vehement, venomous, vicious, wild; SEE CONCEPTS *525,537,540*

fiercely [*adv*] *violently, menacingly*
angrily, awfully, boldly, brutally, ferociously, forcefully, forcibly, frantically, frenziedly, frighteningly, furiously, hard, horribly, impetuously, in a frenzy, irresistibly, like cats and dogs*, madly, maleficiently, malevolently, malignly, mightily, monstrous, no holds barred*, passionately, riotously, roughly, savagely, severely, stormily, tempestuously, terribly, threateningly, tigerishly, tooth and nail*, turbulently, uncontrollably, vehemently, venomously, viciously, wildly, with bared teeth*; SEE CONCEPTS *525,537,540*

fiery [*adj*] *passionate; on fire*
ablaze, afire, aflame, agitable, alight, blazing, burning, choleric, combustible, conflagrant, enthusiastic, excitable, febrile, fervid, fevered, feverish, fierce, flaming, flaring, flickering, flushed, glowing, heated, hot, hot-blooded, hot-headed*, hot-tempered*, igneous, ignited, impassioned, impetuous, impulsive, inflamed, in flames, intense, irascible, irritable, madcap, peppery, perfervid, precipitate, red-hot*, spirited, unrestrained, vehement, violent; SEE CONCEPTS *401,542,605*

fiesta [*n*] *day of rest; religious celebration*
carnival, feast, festival, holiday, holy day, saint's day, vacation; SEE CONCEPTS *377,386*

fight [*n1*] *physical encounter*
action, affray, altercation, argument, battle, battle royal*, bout, brawl, broil, brush, clash, combat, conflict, confrontation, contention, contest, controversy, difficulty, disagreement, dispute, dissension, dogfight, duel, engagement, exchange, feud, fisticuffs*, fracas, fray, free-for-all*, fuss, hostility, joust, match, melee, quarrel, riot, rivalry, round, row, ruckus, rumble, scrap*, scrimmage, scuffle, set-to*, skirmish, sparring match, strife, struggle, tiff, to-do*, tussle, war, wrangling; SEE CONCEPT *106*

fight [*n2*] *courage, will to resist*
aggression, aggressiveness, attack, backbone, belligerence, boldness, combativeness, gameness, hardihood, mettle, militancy, pluck, pugnacity, resistance, spirit; SEE CONCEPT *411*

fight [*v1*] *engage in physical encounter*
altercate, assault, attack, bandy with*, battle, bear arms, bicker, box, brawl, brush with*, buck, carry on war, challenge, clash, contend, cross swords, dispute, do battle, duel, exchange blows, feud, flare up, go to war, grapple, joust, meet, mix it up*, oppugn, ply weapons, protect, quarrel, repel, resist, rowdy, scrap, scuffle, skirmish, spar, strive, struggle, take all comers*, take the field*, take up the gauntlet*,

tiff*, tilt*, traverse, tug, tussle, wage war, war, withstand, wrangle, wrestle; SEE CONCEPT *106*

fight [*v2*] *oppose action, belief*
argue, bicker, buck*, buckle down*, carry on, combat, conduct, contest, continue, defy, dispute, effect, endure, engage in, exert oneself, fall out, force, further, hammer away*, hassle, lay into*, light into*, maintain, make a stand against*, oppose, persevere, persist, prosecute, push forward, put up an argument*, repel, resist, row, spare no effort*, squabble, stand up to*, strive, struggle, support, take on, take pains*, tangle with, toil on, travail, traverse, uphold, wage, withstand, wrangle; SEE CONCEPTS *46,100,384*

fight back/fight off [*v*] *defend oneself*
beat off*, bottle up*, check, contain, control, curb, fend off, hold at bay*, hold back, keep at bay*, oppose, put up fight, repel, reply, repress, repulse, resist, restrain, retaliate, stave off, ward off; SEE CONCEPTS *96,106*

fighter [*n*] *person engaged in hostile encounter*
aggressor, antagonist, assailant, battler, belligerent, boxer, brawler, bruiser*, bully, champion, combatant, competitor, contender, contestant, disputant, duelist, GI, gladiator, heavy*, jouster, man-at-arms, mercenary, militant, opponent, pugilist, punching bag*, rival, scrapper, serviceman/woman, serviceperson, slugger, soldier, tanker*, warrior, wildcat*; SEE CONCEPTS *358,366,412*

fighting [*n*] *battle, encounter*
argument, battle royal*, beef*, bloodshed, blowup, bout, brannigan, brawling, brush, combat, conflict, contention, dispute, donnybrook*, exchange, flap*, fracas, free-for-all*, go, hassle, hell broke loose*, hostility, joust, match, melee, mix, punch out*, riot, roughhouse*, row, rowdy, rumble, rumpus, run-in*, scramble, scrap*, scrimmage, scuffle, set-to*, spat, strife, struggle, tiff, war, warfare, words, wrangle; SEE CONCEPT *106*

fighting [*adj*] *aggressive, warlike*
angry, argumentative, battling, bellicose, belligerent, boxing, brawling, combative, contending, contentious, determined, disputatious, disputative, fencing, ferocious, hawkish, hostile, jingoistic, jousting, martial, militant, militaristic, pugnacious, quarrelsome, ready to fight, resolute, scrappy, skirmishing, sparring, tilting, truculent, unbeatable, under arms*, up in arms*, warmongering, wrestling; SEE CONCEPT *401*

figment [*n*] *creation in one's mind*
bubble*, castle in the air*, chimera, daydream, dream, fable, fabrication, falsehood, fancy, fantasy, fiction, illusion, improvisation, invention, lie, nightmare, production; SEE CONCEPT *529*

figurative [*adj*] *not literal, but symbolic*
allegorical, denotative, descriptive, emblematic, emblematical, fanciful, florid, flowery, illustrative, metaphoric, metaphorical, ornate, pictorial, poetical,

representative, signifying, typical; SEE CONCEPTS *267,582*

figure [*n1*] *numeral; numeric value*
amount, character, chiffer, cipher, cost, digit, integer, number, price, quotation, rate, sum, symbol, terms, total, worth; SEE CONCEPTS *784,786*

figure [*n2*] *form, shape; physical structure*
anatomy, appearance, attitude, bod*, body, build, carriage, cast, chassis*, configuration, conformation, constitution, delineation, development, frame, mass, measurements, outline, physique, pose, posture, proportions, shadow, silhouette, substance, torso; SEE CONCEPTS *733,754,757*

figure [*n3*] *object with design; depiction*
cast, composition, decoration, design, device, diagram, drawing, effigy, embellishment, emblem, illustration, image, model, mold, motif, motive, ornamentation, pattern, piece, portrait, representation, sketch, statue; SEE CONCEPTS *259,625*

figure [*n4*] *famous person*
celebrity, character, dignitary, force, leader, notability, notable, personage, personality, presence, somebody, worthy; SEE CONCEPTS *354,423*

figure [*v1*] *calculate, compute*
add, cast, cipher, count, count heads*, count noses*, cut ice*, dope out*, enumerate, estimate, fix a price, foot*, guess, keep tabs*, number, reckon, run down, sum, summate, take account of, tally, tot*, total, totalize, tote*, tot up*, work out; SEE CONCEPTS *197,764*

figure [*v2*] *understand; decide, infer*
catch on to, cipher, clear up, comprehend, conclude, crack, decipher, decode, determine, discover, disentangle, dope out*, fathom, follow, get*, make heads or tails of*, make out*, master, opine, puzzle out, reason, resolve, rule, see, settle, solve, suppose, think, think out, unfold, unravel, unriddle, unscramble, untangle; SEE CONCEPTS *15,18,37*

figurehead [*n*] *person who is leader in name only*
cipher, front*, man/woman of straw*, mouthpiece*, nominal head, nonentity, nothing, puppet*, straw boss*, titular head, token; SEE CONCEPTS *354,423*

figure in [*v*] *contribute to*
act, appear, be conspicuous, be featured, be included, be mentioned, have a place in, play a part*; SEE CONCEPT *112*

figure of speech [*n*] *communication that is not meant literally; stylistic device*
adumbration, allegory, alliteration, allusion, analogue, anaphora, anticlimax, antistrophe, antithesis, aposiopesis, apostrophe, asyndeton, bathos, comparison, conceit, echoism, ellipsis, euphemism, euphuism, exaggeration, hyperbole, image, imagery, irony, litotes, metaphor, metonymy, onomatopoeia, oxymoron, parable, paradox, parallel, personification, proteron, rhetoric, satire, simile, synecdoche, trope, tropology, turn of phrase, understatement; SEE CONCEPTS *275,278*

filch [*v*] *steal*
cop*, crib*, embezzle, hustle*, lift*, misappropriate, pilfer*, pinch*, purloin, rip off*, rob, scrounge, sneak, snipe, snitch*, swipe, take, thieve, walk off with*; SEE CONCEPTS *139,142*

file [*n1*] *system of order, placement for ease of use*
book, cabinet, case, census, charts, circular file*, data, directory, docket, documents, dossier, folder, index, information, list, notebook, pigeonhole*, portfolio, record, register, repository; SEE CONCEPTS *271,770*

file [*n2*] *line, queue*
column, echelon, list, parade, rank, row, string, tier, troop; SEE CONCEPT *727*

file [*v1*] *put in place, order*
alphabetize, arrange, catalog, catalogue, categorize, classify, deposit, docket, document, enter, index, list, pigeonhole*, record, register, slot, tabulate; SEE CONCEPTS *84,158*

file [*v2*] *rub down, grind*
abrade, burnish, erode, finish, furbish, grate, level, polish, rasp, raze, refine, rub, scrape, shape, sharpen, smooth; SEE CONCEPTS *137,186,215,250*

filibuster [*n*] *obstruction of progress, especially in verbal argument*
delay, hindrance, holding the floor*, interference, opposition, postponement, procrastination, stonewalling*, talkathon*; SEE CONCEPT *298*

fill [*n*] *capacity*
all one wants, ample, enough, filler, padding, plenty, satiety, stuffing, sufficiency, sufficient; SEE CONCEPTS *719,736,794*

fill [*v1*] *to put in and occupy the whole of*
block, blow up, brim over, bulge out, charge, choke, clog, close, congest, cram, crowd, distend, fulfill, furnish, glut, gorge, heap, impregnate, inflate, jampack, lade, load, meet, overflow, overspread, pack, pack like sardines*, permeate, pervade, plug, puff up*, pump up, ram, ram in*, replenish, sate, satiate, satisfy, saturate, shoal, stock, stopper*, store, stretch, stuff, supply, swell, take up, top, top off*; SEE CONCEPTS *107,209*

fill [*v2*] *execute, fulfill*
answer, assign, carry out, discharge, dispatch, distribute, elect, engage, fix, hold, meet, name, occupy, officiate, perform, satisfy, take up; SEE CONCEPT *91*

fill in [*v1*] *answer in writing*
advise, apprise, clue, complete, fill out, inform, insert, notify, post, sign, tell, warn, write in; SEE CONCEPTS *45,79*

fill in [*v2*] *act as substitute*
act for, deputize, insinuate, interject, interpose, replace, represent, stand in, substitute, substract, take the place of, understudy; SEE CONCEPT *128*

filling/filler [*n*] *something that takes up capacity*
batting, bushing, cartridge, center, content, contents, cylinder, dressing, fill, guts*, impletion, inlay, in-

nards, inside, layer, liner, mixture, pack, packing, pad, padding, refill, replenishment, shim, stuffing, wad, wadding; SEE CONCEPTS *826,830*

film [*n1*] *coating, tissue; mist*
blur, brume, cloud, coat, covering, dusting, fabric, foil, fold, gauze, haze, haziness, integument, layer, leaf, membrane, mistiness, nebula, obscuration, opacity, partition, pellicle, scum*, sheet, skin, transparency, veil, web; SEE CONCEPTS *478,524*

film [*n2*] *movie*
cinema, dailies*, flick*, footage, motion picture, moving picture, photoplay, picture, picture show, rushes, show, silent*, talkie*; SEE CONCEPT *293*

film [*v*] *take photographs*
lens, photograph, put in the can*, record, roll, shoot, take, turn; SEE CONCEPTS *173,205*

filmy [*adj1*] *finespun, fragile*
chiffon, cobwebby*, dainty, delicate, diaphanous, fine, fine-grained, flimsy, floaty, gauzy, gossamer, insubstantial, see-through*, sheer, tiffany, transparent, wispy; SEE CONCEPT *606*

filmy [*adj2*] *covered with mist; blurry*
bleary, blurred, cloudy, dim, hazy, membranous, milky, misty, opalescent, opaque, pearly; SEE CONCEPTS *525,603*

filter [*v*] *separate to refine; seep through*
clarify, clean, distill, drain, dribble, escape, exude, filtrate, leak, metastasize, ooze, osmose, penetrate, percolate, permeate, purify, refine, screen, sieve, sift, soak through, strain, trickle, winnow; SEE CONCEPTS *135,165*

filth [*n*] *dirt, pollution*
carrion, contamination, corruption, crud*, defilement, dregs, dung, excrement, feces, feculence, filthiness, foul matter, foulness, garbage, grime, impurity, manure, mire, muck, mud, nastiness, ordure, putrefaction, putrescence, putridity, refuse, rottenness, sediment, sewage, silt, sleaze, slime, slop, sludge, slush, smut, trash, uncleanness; SEE CONCEPTS *260,674*

filthy [*adj1*] *dirty, polluted*
begrimed, black, blackened, cruddy*, crummy*, disheveled, fecal, feculent, foul, grimy*, gross*, grubby*, grungy*, impure, loathsome, miry, mucky*, muddy, nasty, obscene, offensive, putrid, repulsive, revolting, scummy, sleazy, slimy, slipshod, sloppy, slovenly, smoky, soiled, soily, sooty, squalid, unclean, uncleanly, unkempt, unwashed, verminous, vile, yecchy*; SEE CONCEPTS *485,570*

filthy [*adj2*] *vulgar, obscene*
base, bawdy, blue*, coarse, contemptible, corrupt, depraved, despicable, dirty-minded*, foul, foulmouthed, impure, indecent, lewd, licentious, low, mean, nasty, offensive, pornographic, raunchy, scatological, scurvy, smutty, suggestive, vicious, vile; SEE CONCEPTS *267,545*

final [*adj1*] *ending, last*
bitter-end*, bottom-line*, closing, concluding, crowning, curtains*, end, eventual, finishing, hind-

most, lag, last hurrah*, last-minute, latest, latter, supreme, swan song*, terminal, terminating, ultimate; SEE CONCEPTS *531,820*

final [*adj2*] *conclusive, definitive*
absolute, decided, decisive, definite, determinate, determinative, finished, incontrovertible, irrefutable, irrevocable, settled, unanswerable, unappealable; SEE CONCEPT *535*

finale [*n*] *ending of an event*
afterpiece, blow-off*, button*, cessation, chaser*, climax, close, closer*, conclusion, consummation, crowning glory*, culmination, denouement, end, end piece, epilogue, finis, finish, last act, payoff*, peroration, summation, swan song*, termination, wind-up*; SEE CONCEPT *832*

finality [*n*] *definiteness, conclusiveness*
certitude, completeness, decidedness, decisiveness, entirety, finish, inevitableness, intactness, integrity, irrevocability, perfection, resolution, terminality, totality, unavoidability, wholeness; SEE CONCEPTS *635,638,832*

finalize [*v*] *finish, complete action*
agree, clinch*, conclude, consummate, decide, ice*, put on ice*, settle, sew up*, tie up*, work out, wrap up; SEE CONCEPT *91*

finally [*adv1*] *beyond any doubt*
assuredly, beyond recall*, beyond shadow of doubt*, certainly, completely, conclusively, convincingly, decisively, definitely, determinately, done with, enduringly, for all time*, for ever, for good*, in conclusion, inescapably, inexorably, irrevocably, lastly, once and for all*, past regret*, permanently, settled, with conviction; SEE CONCEPT *535*

finally [*adv2*] *in the end; after period of time*
after all, after a while, already, as a sequel, as it may be, at last, at length, at long last*, at the end, at the last moment, belatedly, despite delay*, eventually, in conclusion, in spite of all*, in the eleventh hour*, in the long run*, it's about time*, lastly, long time coming*, someday, sometime, sooner or later*, subsequently, tardily, ultimately, when all is said and done*, yet; SEE CONCEPT *799*

finance [*n*] *economic affairs*
accounts, banking, business, commerce, economics, financial affairs, investment, money, money management; SEE CONCEPTS *360,770*

finance [*v*] *offer loan money; set up in business*
back, bank, bankroll, capitalize, endow, float*, fund, go for*, grubstake*, guarantee, juice*, lay on one*, loan shark*, patronize, pay for, pick up the check*, pick up the tab*, prime the pump*, promote, provide funds, provide security, put up money, raise dough*, sponsor, stake, subsidize, support, underwrite; SEE CONCEPTS *108,115,341*

finances [*n*] *person or corporation's money, property*
affairs, assets, balance sheet, budget, capital, cash, condition, funds, net, net worth, resources, revenue, wealth, wherewithal, worth; SEE CONCEPTS *340,710*

financial [adj] having to do with money
banking, budgeting, business, commercial, economic, fiscal, monetary, numbers*, numeric, pecuniary, pocket; SEE CONCEPT 334

financier [n] person who lends money, advises
backer, banker, bankroller, baron, broker, businessman/woman, businessperson, capitalist, entrepreneur, fairy godmother*, fat cat*, grubstaker*, lady bountiful*, man/woman who writes the checks*, manipulator*, merchant, money, moneybags*, money lender, operator*, rich man/woman, robber baron*, Santa Claus*, speculator, sponsor, staker, stockbroker, sugar daddy*, tycoon, usurer; SEE CONCEPTS 347,348,353

financing [n] money for operating expenses
costs, expenditure, expense, expenses, funding, loan, matching funds, outgo, outlay, payment; SEE CONCEPTS 340,344

find [n] discovery
acquisition, asset, bargain, boast, bonanza, catch, gem, good buy, jewel, one in a million*, pride, treasure, treasure trove; SEE CONCEPTS 337,712

find [v1] catch sight of, lay hands on
arrive at, bring to light*, bump into*, catch, chance upon, collar*, come across, come upon, come up with*, corral, descry, detect, dig up*, discern, discover, distinguish, encounter, espy, expose, fall in with*, ferret out, happen upon*, hit upon*, identify, lay fingers on, light upon*, locate, make out, meet, notice, observe, perceive, pinpoint, recognize, recover, run across, run into, scare up*, sight, smoke out*, spot, strike, stumble upon, track down, trip on*, turn up*, uncover, unearth; SEE CONCEPT 183

find [v2] achieve, win
acquire, attain, be one's lot*, earn, fall to the lot*, gain, get, meet, meet with, obtain, procure; SEE CONCEPTS 124,706

finding [n] judgment, verdict
award, conclusion, data, decision, decree, discovery, pronouncement, recommendation, sentence; SEE CONCEPT 685

find out [v] discover, learn
ascertain, catch, catch on, detect, determine, disclose, divine, expose, hear, identify, note, observe, perceive, realize, reveal, see, uncover, unearth, unmask; SEE CONCEPTS 31,183

fine [n] penalty in money
amends, amercement, assessment, damages, forfeit, mulct, punishment, reparation, rip; SEE CONCEPT 123

fine [adj1] excellent, masterly
accomplished, aces*, admirable, attractive, beautiful, capital, choice, cool*, crack*, dandy*, elegant, enjoyable, exceptional, expensive, exquisite, fashionable, first-class, first-rate, first-string, five-star*, gilt-edged*, gnarly*, good-looking, great, handsome, lovely, magnificent, mean, neat*, not too shabby*, ornate, outstanding, pleasant, rare, refined, select, showy, skillful, smart, solid, splendid, strik-

ing, subtle, superior, supreme, top, top-notch, unreal*, well-made, wicked*; SEE CONCEPTS 528, 574,579

fine [adj2] cloudless, sunshiny (weather)
balmy, bright, clarion, clear, clement, dry, fair, pleasant, rainless, sunny, undarkened; SEE CONCEPT 525

fine [adj3] dainty, delicate; sheer
diaphanous, ethereal, exquisite, filmy, fine-drawn, fine-grained, fine-spun, flimsy, fragile, gauzy, gossamer, gossamery, granular, impalpable, light, lightweight, little, loose, minute, porous, powdered, powdery, pulverized, quality, slender, small, thin, threadlike, transparent; SEE CONCEPTS 491,606

fine [adj4] discriminating, exact
abstruse, acute, clear, critical, cryptic, delicate, distinct, enigmatic, esoteric, fastidious, finespun, hairline, hairsplitting, intelligent, keen, minute, nice, obscure, petty, precise, pure, quick, recondite, refined, sensitive, sharp, sterling, strict, subtle, tasteful, tenuous, trifling, unadulterated, unpolluted; SEE CONCEPT 557

fine [v] penalize in monetary way
alienate, amerce, confiscate, dock*, exact, extort, hit with*, levy, make pay, mulct, pay through the nose*, punish, sconce, seize, sequestrate, slap with*, tax, throw book at*; SEE CONCEPTS 122,342

finery [n] best clothing
apparel, bib and tucker*, black tie, caparison, decoration, fancy dress, formals, frippery*, full dress, gear, regalia, splendor, suit, Sunday best* trappings, trimmings, trinkets, white tie*; SEE CONCEPT 451

finesse [n] know-how, maneuver
acumen, adeptness, adroitness, artfulness, artifice, big stick*, bluff, cleverness, competence, con, craft, craftiness, cunning, delicacy, diplomacy, discernment, discretion, feint, gamesmanship, gimmick, grift, guile, one-upmanship*, polish, quickness, racket*, run-around*, ruse, savoir-faire, savvy, skill, sophistication, stratagem, subtlety, tact, trick, wile; SEE CONCEPTS 409,657

finesse [v] maneuver, manipulate
angle, beguile, bluff, exploit, finagle*, jockey*, operate, play, play games*, pull strings*, pull wires*, rig*, wangle; SEE CONCEPTS 36,59

finger [n] appendage of hand
antenna*, claw, digit, extremity, feeler*, hook*, pinky*, pointer*, ring finger, tactile member, tentacle*, thumb; SEE CONCEPT 392

finger [v1] touch lightly
feel, fiddle, grope, handle, manipulate, maul, meddle, palpate, paw, play with, thumb, toy with; SEE CONCEPT 612

finger [v2] choose, designate
appoint, determine, identify, indicate, locate, make, name, nominate, pin down*, point out, specify, tap; SEE CONCEPT 41

finicky [*adj*] *overparticular*
choosy, critical, dainty, difficult, fastidious, finical, finicking, fussbudget*, fussy, granny*, hard to please, nice, nit-picking, overnice, particular, persnickety*, picky, picky-picky*, scrupulous, squeamish, stickling; SEE CONCEPTS *401,404,556*

finish [*n1*] *conclusion; completion*
accomplishment, achievement, acquirement, acquisition, all he/she wrote*, annihilation, attainment, cease, cessation, close, closing, culmination, curtain*, curtains*, death, defeat, denouement, desistance, end, ending, end of road*, end of the line*, finale, finis, last, last stage, ruin, stop, termination, terminus, winding-up*, wind-up, wrap, wrap-up*; SEE CONCEPTS *119,832*

finish [*n2*] *coating; perfecting*
appearance, beauty, burnish, cultivation, culture, elaboration, glaze, grace, grain, lacquer, luster, patina, perfection, polish, refinement, shine, smoothness, surface, texture, veneer; SEE CONCEPTS *611,655*

finish [*v1*] *bring to a conclusion; get done*
accomplish, achieve, bag it*, break up, bring to a close, carry through, cease, clinch, close, complete, conclude, crown*, culminate, deal with, determine, discharge, do, effect, end, execute, finalize, fold, fulfill, get out of the way*, halt, hang it up*, have done with*, make, make short work of*, mop up*, perfect, put finishing touches on*, round off*, round up*, scratch, scrub, settle, sew up*, shut down, shutter*, stop, terminate, top off*, ultimate, wind up*, wrap, wrap up*; SEE CONCEPTS *91,234,706*

finish [*v2*] *consume, use up*
deplete, devour, dispatch, dispose of, drain, drink, eat, empty, exhaust, expend, go, run through*, spend, use, wash up*; SEE CONCEPTS *169,225*

finish [*v3*] *defeat; kill*
annihilate, assassinate, best*, bring down*, carry off*, destroy, dispatch, dispose of, do in*, down, execute, exterminate, get rid of*, liquidate, overcome, overpower, put an end to, put away*, rout, rub out*, ruin, slaughter, slay, take off*, take out*, vaporize, worst*; SEE CONCEPTS *95,252*

finish [*v4*] *put a coating on; perfect*
coat, develop, elaborate, face, gild, lacquer, polish, refine, smooth, stain, texture, veneer, wax; SEE CONCEPTS *172,202*

finished [*adj1*] *cultivated, refined*
accomplished, all-around, classic, consummate, cultured, elegant, expert, exquisite, flawless, impeccable, many-sided, masterly, perfected, polished, professional, proficient, skilled, smooth, suave, urbane, versatile; SEE CONCEPTS *404,528*

finished [*adj2*] *complete, done*
accomplished, achieved, brought about, ceased, closed, come to an end, compassed, completed, concluded, consummated, decided, discharged, dispatched, disposed of, done for, done with, effected, effectuated, elaborated, ended, entire, executed, fi-

nal, finalized, fulfilled, full, in the past, lapsed, made, over, over and done*, perfected, performed, put into effect*, realized, resolved, satisfied, settled, sewn up*, shut, stopped, terminated, through, tied up*, worked out*, wound up*, wrapped up*; SEE CONCEPTS *528,531*

finished [*adj3*] *consumed, used up*
bankrupt, devastated, done, done for*, done in*, drained, empty, exhausted, gone, liquidated, lost, played out*, ruined, spent, through, undone, washed up*, wiped out*, wrecked*; SEE CONCEPTS *334,560*

finite [*adj*] *subject to limitations*
bound, bounded, circumscribed, conditioned, confined, definable, definite, delimited, demarcated, determinate, exact, fixed, limited, precise, restricted, specific, terminable; SEE CONCEPTS *535,554*

fire [*n1*] *burning*
blaze, bonfire, campfire, charring, coals, combustion, conflagration, devouring, element, embers, flame and smoke, flames, flare, glow, hearth, heat, holocaust, hot spot*, incandescence, inferno, luminosity, oxidation, phlogiston, pyre, rapid oxidation, scintillation, scorching, sea of flames*, searing, sparks, tinder, up in smoke*, warmth; SEE CONCEPTS *478,521*

fire [*n2*] *barrage of projectiles*
attack, bombarding, bombardment, bombing, cannonade, cannonading, crossfire, explosion, fusillade, hail, round, salvo, shelling, sniping, volley; SEE CONCEPTS *86,320*

fire [*n3*] *animation, vigor*
ardor, brio, calenture, dash, drive, eagerness, élan, energy, enthusiasm, excitement, exhilaration, fervency, fervor, force, ginger*, gusto, heartiness, heat, impetuosity, intensity, life, light, liveliness, luster, passion, pep*, punch*, radiance, red heat*, scintillation, snap*, sparkle, spirit, splendor, starch, verve, vigor, vim, virtuosity, vivacity, white heat*, zeal, zing, zip; SEE CONCEPT *411*

fire [*v1*] *cause to burn*
burn, enkindle, ignite, kindle, light, put a match to*, set ablaze, set aflame, set alight, set fire to, set on fire, start a fire, touch off*; SEE CONCEPT *249*

fire [*v2*] *detonate or throw weapon*
cast, discharge, eject, explode, fling, heave, hurl, launch, let off*, loose, pitch, pull trigger, set off*, shell, shoot, throw, toss, touch off*; SEE CONCEPTS *179,222*

fire [*v3*] *excite, arouse*
animate, electrify, enliven, enthuse, exalt, galvanize, heighten, impassion, incite, inflame, inform, inspire, inspirit, intensify, intoxicate, irritate, provoke, quicken, rouse, stir, thrill; SEE CONCEPT *14*

fire [*v4*] *dismiss from responsibility*
ax*, boot*, can*, discharge, drop, eject, expel, give bum's rush*, give marching orders*, give one notice*, give pink slip*, give the sack*, hand walking

papers*, kick out*, lay off, let one go*, oust, pink slip*, sack*, terminate; SEE CONCEPTS *50,88,351*

fireplace [*n*] *hearth for burning wood*
bed of coals, blaze, chimney, fireside, furnace, grate, hearthside, hob, ingle, inglenook, ingleside, settle, stove; SEE CONCEPTS *440,443*

fireproof [*adj*] *resistant to burning*
asbestos, concrete, fire-resistant, incombustible, non-candescent, noncombustible, nonflammable, noninflammable; SEE CONCEPT *485*

fireworks [*n*] *pyrotechnic display at celebrations*
bottle rockets, bursts, firecrackers, fire flowers, illuminations, pyrotechnics, pyrotechny, rockets, Roman candles, sparklers; SEE CONCEPT *293*

firm [*n*] *business*
association, bunch, company, concern, conglomerate, corporation, crew, crowd, enterprise, gang, house, megacorp, mob, multinational, organization, outfit, partnership, ring; SEE CONCEPTS *323,325*

firm [*adj1*] *inflexible*
close, close-grained, compact, compressed, concentrated, concrete, condensed, congealed, dense, fine-grained, hard, hardened, heavy, impenetrable, impermeable, impervious, inelastic, jelled, nonporous, refractory, rigid, set, solid, solidified, stiff, sturdy, substantial, thick, tough, unyielding; SEE CONCEPTS *604,606*

firm [*adj2*] *stable, unmoving*
anchored, bolted, braced, cemented, closed, durable, embedded, fast, fastened, fixed, immobile, immovable, motionless, mounted, nailed, petrified, riveted, robust, rooted, screwed, secure, secured, set, settled, soldered, solid, sound, spiked, stationary, steady, strong, sturdy, substantial, taut, tenacious, tight, tightened, unfluctuating, unshakable, welded; SEE CONCEPT *488*

firm [*adj3*] *unalterable, definite*
abiding, adamant, bent, bound, consistent, constant, dead set on*, determined, enduring, established, exact, explicit, fixed, flat, going, hang tough*, inflexible, intent, never-failing, obdurate, persevering, persistent, prevailing, resolute, resolved, set, settled, specific, stable, stand pat*, stated, staunch, steadfast, steady, stipulated, strict, strong, sure, tenacious, true, unbending, unchangeable, undeviating, unflinching, unqualified, unshakable, unshaken, unwavering, unyielding; SEE CONCEPTS *267,403,542*

firmament [*n*] *heaven*
empyrean, heavens, lid*, sky, the blue*, the skies, vault, welkin, wild blue yonder*; SEE CONCEPT *437*

firmly [*adv1*] *immovably*
durably, enduringly, fast, firm, fixedly, hard, inflexibly, like a rock*, motionlessly, rigidly, securely, solid, solidly, soundly, stably, steadily, stiffly, strongly, substantially, thoroughly, tight, tightly, unflinchingly, unshakeably; SEE CONCEPTS *488,489,604*

firmly [*adv2*] *with determination*
adamantly, constantly, decisively, determinedly, doggedly, indefatigably, intently, obdurately, obsti-

nately, perseveringly, persistently, pertinaciously, purposefully, resolutely, staunchly, steadfastly, stolidly, strictly, stubbornly, tenaciously, through thick and thin*, unchangeably, unwaveringly, with heavy hand*; SEE CONCEPTS *534,542*

firmness [*n1*] *stiffness*
compactness, density, durability, fixedness, hardness, impenetrability, impermeability, imperviousness, impliability, inelasticity, inflexibility, resistance, rigidity, solidity, temper, tensile strength, toughness; SEE CONCEPTS *722,726*

firmness [*n2*] *immovability*
durability, solidity, soundness, stability, steadiness, strength, substantiality, tautness, tension, tightness; SEE CONCEPTS *731,732*

firmness [*n3*] *resolution, resolve*
constancy, decidedness, decision, determination, fixedness, fixity, inflexibility, obduracy, obstinacy, purposefulness, purposiveness, resoluteness, staunchness, steadfastness, strength, strictness; SEE CONCEPTS *410,633*

first [*adj1*] *earliest in order*
aboriginal, ahead, antecedent, anterior, basic, beginning, cardinal, early, elementary, first off*, front, fundamental, head, headmost, inaugural, inceptive, incipient, initial, in the beginning, introductory, key, leading, lead off*, least, maiden, number one*, numero uno*, opening, original, pioneer, premier, primary, prime, primeval, primitive, primogenial, primordial, pristine, right up front*, rudimentary, slightest, smallest; SEE CONCEPTS *585,632,820*

first [*adj2*] *highest in importance*
advanced, A-number-1*, arch, champion, chief, dominant, eminent, first-class, first-string*, foremost, greatest, head, head of the line*, leading, main, number one*, outstanding, paramount, predominant, preeminent, premier, primary, prime, primo*, principal, ranking, ruling, sovereign, supreme, topflight*, top of the list; SEE CONCEPT *568*

first [*adv*] *at the beginning*
at the outset, before all else, beforehand, firstly, initially, in the first place, originally, to begin with, to start with; SEE CONCEPTS *585,820*

first-class/first-rate [*adj*] *superior, excellent*
capital, choice, dandy, fine, first-string*, five-star*, in class by itself*, prime*, shipshape, sound, supreme, tiptop*, top, top-notch*, very good; SEE CONCEPT *574*

firsthand [*adj*] *direct*
eyewitness, immediate, primary, straight, straight from horse's mouth*; SEE CONCEPT *267*

fiscal [*adj*] *monetary*
budgetary, commercial, economic, financial, money, pecuniary, pocket; SEE CONCEPT *334*

fish [*v*] *throwing bait to catch seafood*
angle, bait, bait the hook*, bob, cast, cast one's hook*, cast one's net*, chum, extract, extricate,

find, go fishing, haul out*, net, produce, pull out, seine, trawl, troll; SEE CONCEPT *363*

fish for [*v*] *look for; hint*
angle, angle for, elicit, hope for, hunt for, invite, search for, seek, solicit, try to evoke; SEE CONCEPTS *20,75*

fishy [*adj*] *doubtful, suspicious*
ambiguous, doubtable, dubious, dubitable, equivocal, far-fetched, funny, implausible, improbable, odd, problematic, queer, questionable, shady, suspect, uncertain, unlikely; SEE CONCEPT *552*

fit [*n*] *seizure; sudden emotion*
access, attack, blow, bout, burst, caprice, conniption*, convulsion, epileptic attack, frenzy, humor, jumps*, mood, outbreak, outburst, paroxysm, rage, rush, spasm, spate, spell, stroke, tantrum, throe, torrent, turn, twitch, whim, whimsy; SEE CONCEPTS *13,303*

fit [*adj1*] *suitable, appropriate*
able, adapted, adequate, advantageous, apposite, apt, becoming, befitting, beneficial, capable, comely, comme il faut, competent, conformable, convenient, correct, correspondent, deserving, desirable, due, equipped, equitable, expedient, favorable, feasible, felicitous, fitted, fitting, good enough, happy, just, likely, meet, opportune, practicable, preferable, prepared, proper, qualified, ready, right, rightful, seasonable, seemly, tasteful, timely, trained, well-suited, wise, worthy; SEE CONCEPT *558*

fit [*adj2*] *healthy, in good physical shape*
able-bodied, competent, fit as fiddle*, hale, in good condition, muscled, robust, slim, sound, strapping*, toned, trim, up to snuff*, well, wholesome, wrapped tight*; SEE CONCEPTS *314,485*

fit [*v1*] *belong, correspond*
accord, agree, answer, apply, be apposite, be apt, become, be comfortable, be consonant, befit, be in keeping, click*, concur, conform, consist, correspond, dovetail*, go, go together, go with, harmonize, have its place, interlock, join, match, meet, parallel, relate, respond, set, suit, tally; SEE CONCEPT *664*

fit [*v2*] *equip*
accommodate, accoutre, arm, fix, furnish, get, implement, kit out*, make, make up, outfit, prepare, provide, ready, rig*; SEE CONCEPT *182*

fit [*v3*] *adapt, change*
adjust, alter, arrange, conform, dispose, fashion, modify, place, position, quadrate, reconcile, shape, square, suit, tailor, tailor-make*; SEE CONCEPT *232*

fitful [*adj*] *irregular, sporadic*
bits and pieces*, broken, capricious, catchy*, changeable, desultory, disturbed, erratic, flickering, fluctuating, haphazard, herky-jerky*, hit-or-miss*, impulsive, inconstant, intermittent, interrupted, on-again-off-again, periodic, random, recurrent, restive, restless, shifting, spasmodic, spastic*, spotty, unstable, variable; SEE CONCEPTS *482,534*

fitness [*n1*] *good condition*
fettle*, good health, health, kilter*, repair, robustness, shape, strength, trim, vigor; SEE CONCEPTS *316,723*

fitness [*n2*] *appropriateness*
accommodation, accordance, adaptation, adequacy, admissibility, agreeableness, applicability, appositeness, aptitude, aptness, assimilation, auspiciousness, compatibility, competence, concurrency, congeniality, congruousness, consistency, consonance, convenience, correspondence, decency, decorum, eligibility, expediency, harmony, keeping, order, patness, pertinence, preparedness, propriety, qualification, readiness, relevancy, rightness, seasonableness, seemliness, suitability, timeliness; SEE CONCEPT *656*

fitted [*adj1*] *appropriate, right*
adapted, conformable, cut out for, equipped, fit, matched, proper, qualified, suitable, suited, tailor-made; SEE CONCEPT *558*

fitted [*adj2*] *equipped*
accoutered, appointed, armed, furnished, implemented, outfitted, provided, rigged out*, set up, supplied; SEE CONCEPTS *560,589*

fitting [*n*] *accessory*
accouterment, appointment, attachment, component, connection, convenience, equipment, extra, furnishing, furniture, instrument, paraphernalia, part, piece, trimming, unit; SEE CONCEPT *824*

fitting [*adj*] *appropriate, suitable*
applicable, apt, becoming, comme il faut, correct, decent, decorous, desirable, due, felicitous, happy, just, just what was ordered*, meet, on the button*, on the nose*, proper, right, right on*, seemly, that's the ticket*; SEE CONCEPT *558*

fix [*n*] *difficult or ticklish situation*
box*, corner*, difficulty, dilemma, embarrassment, hole*, hot water*, jam*, mess*, pickle*, plight, predicament, quandary, scrape, spot*; SEE CONCEPT *674*

fix [*v1*] *establish, make firm*
affix, anchor, attach, bind, catch, cement, congeal, connect, consolidate, couple, embed, entrench, fasten, freeze to*, glue, graft, harden, implant, inculcate, infix, ingrain, install, instill, link, locate, lodge, moor, nail down*, pin, place, plant, position, rigidify, rivet, root, secure, set, settle, solidify, stabilize, stay put, steady, stick, stiffen, thicken, tie; SEE CONCEPTS *85,113,160,201*

fix [*v2*] *determine, decide*
agree on, appoint, arrange, arrive at, conclude, define, establish, limit, name, resolve, set, settle, solve, specify, work, work out; SEE CONCEPT *18*

fix [*v3*] *mend, repair*
adjust, amend, correct, debug, doctor, do up*, emend, face-lift*, fiddle with, overhaul, patch, put to rights*, rebuild, recondition, reconstruct, regulate, restore, retread, revamp, revise, see to*, sort, tune up; SEE CONCEPTS *126,212*

fix [*v4*] *prepare, plan ahead*
arrange, dispose, frame, prearrange, precontrive, predesign, preorder, preplan, put up, rig*, set up, stack the deck*; SEE CONCEPT 36

fix [*v5*] *focus on*
concenter, concentrate, direct, fasten, fixate, level at, put, rivet; SEE CONCEPT 623

fix [*v6*] *cook a meal*
fit, get, get ready, heat, make, make up, microwave, prepare, ready, warm, whip up*; SEE CONCEPT 170

fix [*v7*] *manipulate, influence an event*
bribe, buy, buy off, corrupt, fiddle*, have, lubricate, maneuver, pull strings*, reach, square, suborn, tamper with; SEE CONCEPTS 192,232

fix [*v8*] *wreak vengeance on*
cook someone's goose*, get*, get even, get revenge, hurt, pay back, punish, take retribution; SEE CONCEPT 86

fixation [*n*] *obsession*
addiction, case, complex, craze, crush, fascination, fetish, hang-up*, idée fixe, infatuation, mania, preoccupation, thing; SEE CONCEPTS 532,690

fixed [*adj1*] *permanent, steady*
anchored, attached, established, fast, firm, hitched, hooked, immobile, immotile, immovable, located, locked, made fast, nailed*, quiet, rigid, rooted, secure, set, settled, situated, solid, stable, steadfast, stiff, still, tenacious, tight; SEE CONCEPTS 488,551,583,649

fixed [*adj2*] *intent, resolute; established*
abiding, agreed, arranged, certain, changeless, circumscribed, confirmed, decided, defined, definite, definitive, determinate, enduring, firm, inalterable, inflexible, in the bag*, inveterate, level, limited, narrow, never-failing, planned, prearranged, precise, resolved, restricted, rigged, rooted, set, settled, set-up, stated, steadfast, steady, still, stipulated, sure, unbending, unblinking, unchangeable, undeviating, unfaltering, unflinching, unmodifiable, unmovable, unqualified, unwavering; SEE CONCEPTS 535,554

fixed [*adj3*] *repaired*
back together, going, in order, in working order, mended, put right, rebuilt, refitted, repaired, sorted, whole; SEE CONCEPT 560

fix up [*v*] *prepare, beautify*
deck*, dress up, furnish, gussy up*, primp, provide, rehabilitate, repair, smarten, spiff*, spruce up*; SEE CONCEPTS 162,202

fizz [*v*] *bubble*
buzz, effervesce, fizzle, froth, hiss, seethe, sibilate, simmer, sparkle, sputter, whisper, whoosh; SEE CONCEPT 469

fizzle [*v*] *collapse, fall through*
abort, be fiasco*, come to nothing*, die, end, end in defeat*, end in disappointment*, fail, fold, miscarry, misfire, miss the mark*, peter out*, wane; SEE CONCEPT 699

flabbergast [*v*] *surprise*
abash, amaze, astonish, astound, blow away*, bowl over*, confound, daze, disconcert, dumbfound, make speechless, nonplus, overcome, overwhelm, put away*, shock, stagger, stun, throw, throw for a loop*; SEE CONCEPT 42

flabby [*adj*] *baggy, fat*
drooping, enervated, flaccid, flexuous, floppy*, gone to seed*, hanging, irresilient, lax, limp, loose, out of condition*, out of shape*, pendulous, rusty, sagging, shapeless, slack, sloppy, soft, tender, toneless, unfit, yielding; SEE CONCEPTS 486,490

flaccid [*adj*] *drooping*
debilitated, emasculated, enervated, enfeebled, flabby, flimsy, inelastic, irresilient, lax, limp, loose, nerveless, quaggy, sapped, slack, soft, weak, weakened; SEE CONCEPTS 485,604

flag [*n*] *pennant, symbol*
banderole, banner, bannerol, burgee, colors, emblem, ensign, gonfalon, jack, pennon, standard, streamer; SEE CONCEPTS 284,473

flag [*v1*] *decline, fall off*
abate, deteriorate, die, droop, ebb, fade, fail, faint, fall, languish, peter out*, pine, sag, sink, slump, succumb, taper off*, wane, weaken, weary, wilt; SEE CONCEPTS 698,699

flag [*v2*] *signal*
gesture, give a sign to, hail, indicate, motion, salute, signalize, warn, wave; SEE CONCEPT 74

flagrant [*adj*] *flaunting, blatant; without shame*
arrant, atrocious, awful, bare-faced*, bold, brazen, capital, conspicuous, crying, disgraceful, dreadful, egregious, enormous, flagitous, flaming, flashy*, glaring, grody*, gross*, hanging out*, heinous, immodest, infamous, noticeable, notorious, obvious, open, ostentatious, out-and-out*, outrageous, rank, scandalous, shameful, shameless, shocking, stick out like sore thumb*, striking, undisguised, wicked; SEE CONCEPTS 401,545,576

flair [*n*] *talent, style*
ability, accomplishment, aptitude, aptness, bent, chic, dash, elegance, faculty, feel, genius, gift, glamour, head, knack, mastery, panache, pizzazz*, presence, shine*, splash*, taste, turn, zip*; SEE CONCEPTS 630,706

flak [*n*] *complaint, criticism*
abuse, bad press*, brickbat*, censure, condemnation, disapprobation, disapproval, disparagement, fault-finding, hostility, knock*, opposition, pan*, rap*, swipe*; SEE CONCEPTS 52,278

flake [*n*] *scale, peel*
cell, disk, drop, foil, lamella, lamina, layer, leaf, membrane, pellicle, plate, scab, section, shaving, sheet, skin, slice, sliver, wafer; SEE CONCEPT 831

flake [*v*] *peel off*
blister, chip, delaminate, desquamate, drop, exfoliate, pare, scab, scale, shed, slice, sliver, trim, wear away; SEE CONCEPTS 157,469

flamboyant [*adj*] *extravagant, theatrical*
baroque, bombastic, brilliant, camp, chichi*, colorful, dashing, dazzling, elaborate, exciting, flaky*, flaming, flashy, florid, gassy*, gaudy, glamorous, jazzy*, luscious, luxuriant, ornate, ostentatious, peacockish, pretentious, resplendent, rich, rococo, showy, splashy, sporty, swank*, swashbuckling*; SEE CONCEPTS *401,589*

flame [*n1*] *fire*
blaze, brightness, conflagration, flare, flash, holocaust, light, rapid oxidation, wildfire; SEE CONCEPTS *478,521*

flame [*n2*] *lover; passion*
affection, ardor, baby, beau, beloved, boyfriend, darling, dear, desire, enthusiasm, fervor, fire, girlfriend, heartthrob, honey, inamorata, inamorato, keenness, ladylove, love, paramour, spark, steady, swain, sweetheart, sweetie, truelove; SEE CONCEPTS *32,423*

flame [*v*] *burn*
blaze, coruscate, fire, flare, flare up, flash, glare, glint, glow, ignite, kindle, light, oxidize, shine; SEE CONCEPT *249*

flaming [*adj1*] *burning*
ablaze, afire, aflame, alight, blazing, brilliant, conflagrant, fiery, flaring, glowing, ignited, in flames, raging, red, red-hot*; SEE CONCEPT *485*

flaming [*adj2*] *very angry, vehement*
ardent, aroused, blazing, bright, burning, fervent, frenzied, hot, hot-blooded*, impassioned, intense, passionate, raging, red-hot*, scintillating, vivid, white-hot*; SEE CONCEPTS *267,403*

flammable [*adj*] *easily started afire*
burnable, combustible, ignitable, incendiary, inflammable; SEE CONCEPT *485*

flank [*n*] *haunch of animate being*
ham, hand, hip, loin, pleuron, quarter, side, thigh, wing; SEE CONCEPT *392*

flap [*n1*] *winged or extended part of object*
accessory, adjunct, appendage, apron, cover, drop, fly, fold, hanging, lapel, lobe, lug, overlap, pendant, pendulosity, ply, queue, skirt, strip, tab, tag, tail, tippet, wing; SEE CONCEPTS *471,824*

flap [*n2*] *commotion*
agitation, banging, brouhaha*, confusion, dither*, fluster, flutter, fuss*, lather*, panic*, pother*, state*, stew*, sweat*, tizzy*, to-do*, tumult, turbulence, turmoil, twitter*; SEE CONCEPTS *230,674*

flap [*v*] *flutter*
agitate, beat, dangle, flail, flash, flop, hang, lop, shake, swing, swish, thrash, thresh, vibrate, wag, wave; SEE CONCEPT *149*

flare [*v1*] *erupt, blow*
blaze, boil over, break out, burn, burn up, burst, dart, dazzle, explode, fire up, flash, flicker, flutter, fume, glare, glow, go off, lose control, rant, seethe, shimmer, shoot, waver; SEE CONCEPTS *13,179,249*

flare [*v2*] *spread*
broaden, grow, splay, spread out, widen; SEE CONCEPT *469*

flash [*n1*] *shimmer, flicker*
beam, bedazzlement, blaze, burst, coruscation, dazzle, flame, flare, glance, glare, gleam, glimmer, glint, glisten, glitter, glow, illumination, imprint, impulse, incandescence, luster, phosphorescence, quiver, radiation, ray, reflection, scintillation, shine, spark, sparkle, streak, stream, twinkle, twinkling, vision; SEE CONCEPTS *521,624*

flash [*n2*] *instant, split second*
breathing, burst, jiffy, minute, moment, outburst, second, shake, show, trice, twinkling; SEE CONCEPTS *808,821*

flash [*n3*] *demonstration*
burst, display, manifestation, outburst, show, sign, splash, swank; SEE CONCEPT *261*

flash [*v1*] *shimmer, flicker*
beam, bedazzle, blaze, blink, coruscate, dazzle, flame, flare, glance, glare, gleam, glimmer, glint, glisten, glitter, glow, incandesce, light, phosphoresce, radiate, reflect, scintillate, shine, shoot out, spangle, spark, sparkle, twinkle; SEE CONCEPT *624*

flash [*v2*] *move fast and display*
bolt, brandish, dart, dash, disport, exhibit, expose, flaunt, flit, flourish, fly, parade, race, shoot, show, show off, speed, spring, streak, sweep, trot out, whistle, zoom; SEE CONCEPTS *150,261*

flashy [*adj*] *flamboyant, in poor taste*
blatant, brazen, catchpenny*, cheap, chintzy, flaunting, florid, garish, gaudy, glaring, glittering, glittery, glitzy, jazzy*, loud, meretricious, ornate, ostentatious, showy, snazzy, sparkling, tacky*, tasteless, tawdry, tinsel, vulgar; SEE CONCEPT *589*

flask [*n*] *small container for liquid*
alembic, ampulla, bag, beaker, bottle, canteen, carafe, caster, chalice, crock, cruel, crystal, decanter, demijohn, ewer, fiasco, flacon, flagon, flasket, glass, goblet, gourd, horn, jar, jug, noggin, phial, retort, tumbler, urn, vial; SEE CONCEPT *494*

flat [*n*] *apartment*
chambers, condo, co-op*, crash pad*, floor-through, go-down, joint*, lodging, pad*, railroad apartment, rental, room, rooms, suite, tenement, walk-up; SEE CONCEPT *516*

flat [*adj1*] *level, smooth*
collapsed, complanate, decumbent, deflated, depressed, empty, even, extended, fallen, flush, horizontal, laid low, levelled, low, oblate, on a level, outstretched, pancake*, planar, planate, plane, procumbent, prone, prostrate, punctured, reclining, recumbent, splay, spread out, supine, tabular, unbroken; SEE CONCEPTS *486,490*

flat [*adj2*] *dull, lackluster to the senses*
banal, blah, bland, blind, boring, colorless, dead, dim, drab, draggy, flavorless, ho hum*, inane, innocuous, insipid, jejune, lead balloon*, lifeless, matte, monotonous, muted, pointless, prosaic, prosy, sapless, spiritless, stale, tasteless, tedious, uninteresting, unpalatable, unsavory, unseasoned, vanilla*,

vapid, watery, weak, whitebread*; SEE CONCEPTS *529,537*

flat [*adj3*] *absolute, positive*
categorical, direct, downright, explicit, final, fixed, indubitable, out-and-out*, peremptory, plain, straight, unconditional, unequivocal, unmistakable, unqualified, unquestionable; SEE CONCEPT *535*

flatten [*v*] *level out*
abrade, beat down, compress, crush, debase, deflate, depress, even out, fell, floor, flush, grade, ground, iron out, knock down, lay, lay low, level, mow down, plane, plaster*, prostrate, raze, roll, smash, smooth, spread out, squash, straighten, subdue, trample; SEE CONCEPTS *137,250,469,702*

flatter [*v1*] *compliment excessively*
adulate, beslaver, blandish, bootlick*, brownnose*, build up*, butter up*, cajole, cater to, charm, con, court, fawn*, get next to*, glorify, grovel, humor, inveigle, jolly, lay it on thick*, massage, oil*, overpraise, play up to*, praise, rub the right way*, salve, sell, snow*, soften*, soft-soap*, spread it on*, stroke, suck up to*, sweeten up*, sweet-talk*, toady*, wheedle, work on*, work over*; SEE CONCEPTS *59,69*

flatter [*v2*] *complement, enhance*
adorn, beautify, become, decorate, do something for*, embellish, enrich, finish, go with*, grace, ornament, perfect, put in best light*, set off, show to advantage, suit; SEE CONCEPTS *162,664*

flattery [*n*] *false praise, compliments*
adulation, applause, approbation, blandishment, blarney*, bootlicking*, cajolery, commendation, encomium, eulogy, eyewash*, fawning*, flattering, flummery, fulsomeness, gallantry, gratification, hokum*, honeyed words, incense, ingratiation, jive*, laud, mush*, obsequiousness, palaver, plaudits, pretty speech, puffery*, servility, smoke*, snow*, snow job*, soft-soap*, soft words, stroke*, sweet talk*, sycophancy, toadyism, tribute, truckling, unctuousness; SEE CONCEPTS *59,69*

flatulent [*adj*] *pretentious, long-winded*
bombastic, inflated, oratorical, overblown, pompous, prolix, shallow, superficial, swollen, tedious, tumescent, tumid, turgid, windy, wordy; SEE CONCEPTS *267,404*

flaunt [*v*] *make an exhibition, show off*
advertise, air, boast, brandish, break out, broadcast, declare, disclose, display, disport, divulge, exhibit, expose, fan it*, flash, flash about, flourish, gasconade, grandstand*, hotdog*, let it all hang out*, make a scene*, parade, proclaim, put on an act*, reveal, roll out, show and tell, showcase, show off, smack with*, sport, spring on*, streak, throw weight around*, trot out*, vaunt, wave around, whip out*; SEE CONCEPT *261*

flavor [*n1*] *odor and taste*
acidity, aroma, astringency, bitterness, essence, extract, flavoring, gusto, hotness, piquancy, pungency, relish, saltiness, sapidity, sapor, savor, seasoning, smack, sourness, spiciness, sweetness, tang, tartness, taste, twang, vim, wallop, zest, zing; SEE CONCEPT *614*

flavor [*n2*] *aura, essence*
aspect, character, feel, feeling, property, quality, soupçon, stamp, style, suggestion, tinge, tone, touch; SEE CONCEPT *673*

flavor [*v*] *add seasoning*
add zing, add zip, ginger, hot it up*, imbue, impart, infuse, lace, leaven, pepper, pep up*, salt, season, spice; SEE CONCEPT *170*

flavoring [*n*] *spice, extract added to food*
additive, condiment, distillation, essence, herb, quintessence, relish, sauce, seasoning, spirit, tincture, zest; SEE CONCEPT *428*

flaw [*n*] *imperfection*
blemish, bug, catch*, Catch-22*, defect, disfigurement, failing, fault, foible, glitch*, gremlin*, pitfall, slipup, speck, spot, stain, typo*, vice, wart*, weakness, weak spot; SEE CONCEPTS *580,674*

flawless [*adj*] *spotless, intact*
absolute, entire, faultless, immaculate, impeccable, irreproachable, perfect, sound, unblemished, unbroken, undamaged, unimpaired, unmarred, unsullied, whole; SEE CONCEPTS *574,579*

fleck [*n*] *spot, pinpoint mark*
bit, dot, mite, mote, patch, pinpoint, speck, speckle, stipple, streak, stripe; SEE CONCEPTS *284,831*

fleck [*v*] *mark with spots*
bespeckle, besprinkle, dapple, dot, dust, maculate, mottle, speckle, spot, stipple, streak, variegate; SEE CONCEPT *79*

fledgling [*n*] *beginner in activity*
apprentice, chick, colt, freshman, greenhorn*, learner, neophyte, nestling, newcomer, novice, rookie, tenderfoot*, trainee, tyro*; SEE CONCEPTS *352,366,424*

flee [*v*] *run away to escape*
abscond, avoid, beat a hasty retreat*, blow*, bolt*, break, cut and run*, cut out*, decamp, depart, desert, elude, escape, evade, fly, fly the coop*, get*, get away, get the hell out*, hotfoot*, jump, leave, make a getaway*, make off*, make one's escape*, make oneself scarce*, make quick exit*, make tracks*, retreat, run, scamper, scoot, scram*, skedaddle*, skip*, split*, step on it*, step on the gas*, take a hike*, take flight, take off, vamoose*, vanish; SEE CONCEPTS *102,150,195*

fleece [*v*] *plunder, steal*
bleed*, burn*, cheat*, clip*, con, cozen, defraud, despoil, flimflam*, gouge, gyp*, hustle, jerk around*, milk*, mulct, overcharge, pluck, rifle, rip off*, rob, rook*, rope in*, run a game on*, sell a bill of goods*, shaft*, strip, swindle, take for a ride*, take to the cleaners*; SEE CONCEPTS *59,139,342*

fleecy [*adj*] *downy, woolly; like a lamb's coat*
floccose, flocculent, fluffy, hairy, hirsute, lanose, pileous, pilose, shaggy, soft, whiskered; SEE CONCEPT *606*

fleet [n] *group of ships*
argosy, armada, flotilla, formation, line, naval force, navy, sea power, squadron, tonnage, vessels, warships; SEE CONCEPTS *322,432,506*

fleet [adj] *quick in movement*
agile, barreling, breakneck*, brisk, expeditious, expeditive, fast, flying, hasty, in nothing flat*, like greased lightning*, lively, mercurial, meteoric, nimble, nimble-footed, on the double*, rapid, screaming, speedball*, speedy, swift, winged; SEE CONCEPTS *584,588*

fleeting [adj] *brief, transient*
cursory, ephemeral, evanescent, fading, flash in the pan*, flitting, flying, fugacious, fugitive, impermanent, meteoric, momentary, passing, short, short-lived, sudden, temporary, transitory, vanishing, volatile; SEE CONCEPTS *551,798*

flesh [n1] *body tissue, skin*
beef, body, brawn, cells, corpuscles, fat, fatness, flesh and blood, food, meat, muscle, plasm, plasma, protoplasm, sinews, thews, weight; SEE CONCEPT *392*

flesh [n2] *humankind*
animality, carnality, homo sapiens, humanity, human nature, human race, living creatures, man, mankind, mortality, people, physicality, physical nature, race, sensuality, stock, world; SEE CONCEPTS *407,417*

fleshly [adv1] *lecherous, desiring sex*
animal, animalistic, bodily, carnal, erotic, gross, lascivious, lewd, lustful, profane, sensual, venereal, voluptuous; SEE CONCEPTS *372,529,545*

fleshly [adv2] *bodily*
corporal, corporeal, earthly, human, material, mundane, of this world, physical, secular, somatic, terrestrial, worldly; SEE CONCEPT *536*

fleshy [adj] *overweight*
adipose, ample, beefy*, brawny, chubby*, chunky*, corpulent, fat, gross, heavy, hefty, husky, meaty*, obese, plump, porcine, portly, pudgy*, pulpy, sarcous, stout, tubby*, weighty, well-padded*, zaftig*; SEE CONCEPTS *406,491,773*

flex [v] *bend*
angle, bend, contract, crook, curve, lean, mold, ply, spring, stretch, tighten, tilt, yield; SEE CONCEPTS *147,149*

flexibility [n] *elasticity, adaptability*
adjustability, affability, complaisance, compliance, docility, extensibility, flaccidity, flexibleness, give, limberness, litheness, plasticity, pliability, pliancy, resilience, springiness, suppleness, tensility, tractability; SEE CONCEPTS *652,731*

flexible [adj1] *pliable, bendable*
adjustable, bending, ductile, elastic, extensible, extensile, flexile, formable, formative, impressionable, like putty*, limber, lithe, malleable, moldable, plastic, pliant, soft, spongy, springy, stretch, stretchable, stretchy, supple, tensile, tractable, tractile, whippy*, willowy, yielding; SEE CONCEPTS *485,488*

flexible [adj2] *adaptable, responsive*
acquiescent, adjustable, amenable, biddable, complaisant, compliant, discretionary, docile, gentle, go-ing every which way*, hanging loose*, like putty in hands*, manageable, open, rolling with punches*, tractable, variable; SEE CONCEPTS *401,542*

flicker [n] *spark, glimmer*
beam, flare, flash, gleam, oscillation, quivering, ray, scintillation, twinkle, vibration; SEE CONCEPTS *145, 624,831*

flicker [v] *sparkle, flutter*
blare, blaze, blink, burn, dance, flare, flash, flit, flitter, fluctuate, glance, gleam, glimmer, glint, glitter, glow, hover, oscillate, quaver, quiver, scintillate, shimmer, swing, tremble, twinkle, vibrate, waver; SEE CONCEPTS *152,624*

flight [n1] *flying; journey*
aerial navigation, aeronautics, arrival, aviation, avigation, departure, gliding, hop, jump, mounting, navigation, shuttle, soaring, take-off, transport, trip, volitation, voyage, winging; SEE CONCEPT *224*

flight [n2] *fleeing; departure*
beat*, break*, breakout, escape, escapement, escaping, exfiltration, exit, exodus, fugue, getaway, getaway car*, lam, out*, powder*, retreat, retreating, running away, slip*, spring*; SEE CONCEPTS *102,195*

flightiness [n] *irresponsibility*
airheadedness*, capriciousness, changeability, dizziness, fickleness, flippancy, frivolity, giddiness, inconstancy, instability, levity, lightness, mercurialness, variability, volatility, whimsicality, whimsicalness; SEE CONCEPT *633*

flighty [adj] *fickle, irresponsible*
airheaded*, birdbrained*, bubbleheaded*, capricious, changeable, dingbat*, dingdong*, ditzy*, dizzy*, effervescent, empty-headed, feather-brained*, frivolous, gaga*, giddy, harebrained*, impetuous, impulsive, inconstant, lightheaded, lively, mercurial, popcorn*, scatterbrained, silly, thoughtless, twit, unbalanced, unstable, unsteady, volatile, whimsical, wild; SEE CONCEPT *401*

flimsy [adj1] *not strong; light, thin*
chiffon, cut-rate*, decrepit, defective, delicate, diaphanous, feeble, fragile, frail, gauzy, gossamer, house of cards*, inadequate, infirm, insubstantial, meager, papery, rickety, rinkydink*, shaky, shallow, sheer, slapdash*, sleazy, slight, superficial, tacky, transparent, unsound, unsubstantial, weak, wobbly; SEE CONCEPTS *489,606*

flimsy [adj2] *unconvincing, implausible*
assailable, baseless, contemptible, controvertible, fallacious, false, feeble, frivolous, groundless, illogical, improbable, inadequate, inane, inconceivable, incredible, inept, lame, poor, puerile, superficial, thin, transparent, trifling, trivial, unbelievable, ungrounded, unpersuasive, unreasonable, unsatisfactory, unsubstantial, weak, weakly, wishful; SEE CONCEPT *267*

flinch [v] *shy away, wince*
avoid, balk, blanch, blench, blink, cower, cringe, crouch, draw back, duck, elude, escape, eschew, evade, flee, quail, recede, recoil, retire, retreat,

shirk, shrink, shun, start, swerve, withdraw; SEE
CONCEPTS *102,150*

fling [*n1*] *casual throw*
cast, chuck, firing, heave, hurl, launching, lob, peg,
pitch, shot, slinging, toss; SEE CONCEPT *222*

fling [*n2*] *unrestrained behavior*
affair, attempt, binge, celebration, crack*, essay,
fun, gamble, go*, good time, indulgence, orgy,
party, rampage, shot*, splurge, spree, stab*, trial,
try, venture, whirl; SEE CONCEPT *386*

fling [*v*] *throw with abandon*
cast, catapult, chuck*, dump, fire, heave, hurl, jerk,
launch, let fly*, lob, peg*, pitch, precipitate, propel,
send, shy*, sling, toss; SEE CONCEPT *222*

flip [*n/v*] *throw, jump with abandon*
cast, chuck, flick, jerk, pitch, snap, spin, toss, twist;
SEE CONCEPTS *194,222*

flippancy [*n*] *irreverence*
archness, cheek, cheekiness, cockiness, disrespectfulness, flightiness, freshness, frivolity, impertinence, impishness, impudence, levity, lightness,
mischievousness, pertness, playfulness, roguishness,
rudeness, sauciness, volatility, waggishness; SEE
CONCEPT *633*

flippant [*adj*] *irreverent*
brassy, breezy, cheeky*, cocky, disrespectful,
flighty, flip*, fresh, frivolous, glib, impertinent, impudent, insolent, lippy*, nervy*, offhand, pert, playful, rude, sassy*, smart*, smart-alecky*, superficial;
SEE CONCEPT *401*

flirt [*n*] *person who makes advances*
coquette, cruiser*, gold digger*, heartbreaker, operator*, philanderer, player, seducer, siren, swinger,
tease, trifler, vamp, vixen, wanton, wolf*; SEE CON-
CEPT *423*

flirt [*v*] *make advances toward someone*
banter, bat eyes at*, come hither*, come on*, coquet, dally, disport, eyeball*, fool, gam*, hit on*,
lead on, linger with, make a move*, make a pass*,
ogle, philander, pick up*, pitch*, proposition, tease,
wink at*; SEE CONCEPTS *375,384*

flirtation [*n*] *amorous advance*
amour, coquetry, courting, cruising, dalliance, flirting, intrigue, love, love affair, philandering, pickup*, romance, romancing, tease, teasing, toying*,
trifling*; SEE CONCEPTS *32,375,384*

flirtatious [*adj*] *provocative, teasing*
amorous, arch, come-hither*, come-on*, coquettish,
coy, dallying, enticing, flirty, libidinous, nymphomaniac, philandering, spoony*, sportive, wolfish*;
SEE CONCEPTS *401,404*

flit [*v*] *flutter, move rapidly*
dance, dart, flash, fleet, flicker, float, fly, hover,
hurry, pass, run, rush, sail, scud*, skim, speed,
sweep, whisk, whiz, wing, zip; SEE CONCEPT *150*

float [*v*] *lie on the surface*
be buoyant, bob, drift, glide, hang, hover, move gently, poise, rest on water, ride, sail, skim, slide, slip

along, smooth along, stay afloat, swim, waft, wash;
SEE CONCEPT *153*

flock [*n*] *congregation*
army, assembly, bevy, brood, cloud, collection, colony, company, convoy, crowd, crush, drift, drove,
flight, gaggle, gathering, group, herd, host, legion,
litter, mass, multitude, pack, progeny, rout, scores,
skein, throng; SEE CONCEPTS *391,432*

flock [*v*] *congregate*
collect, converge, crowd, gather, group, herd, huddle, mass, throng, troop; SEE CONCEPTS *109,384*

flog [*v*] *whip, lash*
beat, belt, cane, castigate, chastise, ferule, flagellate,
flax, flay, give the cat o'nine tails*, hide, hit, larrup,
lather, leather*, paddle, scourge, spank, strike,
stripe, tan one's hide*, thrash, trounce, wax*,
whack, whale*, whomp*, whop*; SEE CONCEPT *189*

flood [*n*] *overwhelming flow, quantity*
abundance, alluvion, bore, bounty, cataclysm, cataract, current, deluge, downpour, drencher, drift, ea-
gre, excess, flow, flux, freshet, glut, inundation,
multitude, niagara, outgushing, outpouring, overflow, plenty, pour, profusion, rush, spate, stream,
superabundance, superfluity, surge, surplus, tide,
torrent, tsunami, wave; SEE CONCEPTS *179,524,786*

flood [*v*] *inundate or submerge*
brim over, choke, deluge, drown, engulf, fill, flow,
glut, gush, immerse, overflow, oversupply, overwhelm, pour over, rush, saturate, surge, swamp,
swarm, sweep, whelm; SEE CONCEPTS *179,209,740*

floor [*n*] *bottom of a room; level of a multistory building*
attic, basement, boards, canvas, carpet, cellar, deck,
downstairs, flat, flooring, ground, landing, level,
lowest point, mat, mezzanine, nadir, rug, stage,
story, tier, upstairs; SEE CONCEPT *440*

floor [*v*] *perplex, confound*
baffle, beat, bewilder, bowl over*, bring down*,
bring up short*, conquer, defeat, discomfit, disconcert, down, drop, dumbfound, fell, flatten, ground,
knock down, lay low*, level, nonplus, overthrow,
prostrate, puzzle, stump, throw; SEE CONCEPTS *16,95*

flop [*n*] *miserable failure*
bomb, bust, debacle, disaster, dud*, fiasco, lemon*,
loser, miscarriage, nonstarter, washout*; SEE CON-
CEPTS *674,699*

flop [*v1*] *fall limply, collapse*
dangle, droop, drop, flag, flap, flounder, flutter,
hang, jerk, lop, quiver, sag, slump, stagger, teeter,
topple, toss, totter, tumble, wave, wiggle; SEE CON-
CEPTS *144,181*

flop [*v2*] *fail miserably*
bomb*, close, come apart*, come to nothing*, fall
flat*, fall short*, flummox, fold, founder, miscarry,
misfire, wash out*; SEE CONCEPT *699*

floral [*adj*] *decorated with flowers*
blooming, blossoming, blossomy, botanic, decorative, dendritic, efflorescent, flower-patterned, flow-

ery, herbaceous, sylvan, verdant; SEE CONCEPT *589*

florid [*adj1*] *very elaborate*
aureate, baroque, busy, decorative, embellished, euphuistic, figurative, flamboyant, flowery, fussy, garnished, grandiloquent, high-flown, luscious, magniloquent, ornamental, ornamented, ornate, overblown, overelaborate, pretentious, rhetorical, rich, sonorous; SEE CONCEPTS *267,589*

florid [*adj2*] *flushed, ruddy*
blowzy, flush, glowing, high-colored, pink, reddened, rubicund, sanguine; SEE CONCEPTS *406,618*

flounce [*v*] *bounce; intermittently move*
fling, jerk, mince, nancy, prance, sashay, spring, stamp, storm, strut, swish, throw, toss; SEE CONCEPT *149*

flounder [*v*] *struggle; be in the dark*
blunder, bobble, cast about, come apart at seams*, drop the ball*, fall down, flop, flummox, foul up*, fumble, go at backwards*, go to pieces*, grope, labor, lurch, make a mess of, miss one's cue*, muddle, plunge, pratfall*, screw up*, slip up*, snafu*, strive, stub one's toe*, stumble, thrash, toil, toss, travail, trip up*, tumble, wallow, work at; SEE CONCEPTS *101,699*

flourish [*n*] *curlicue, decoration*
curl, embellishment, furbelow, garnish, ornamentation, plume, quirk, spiral, sweep, twist; SEE CONCEPTS *259,284*

flourish [*v1*] *grow, prosper*
amplify, arrive, augment, batten, bear fruit, be on top of heap*, bloom, blossom, boom, burgeon, come along, develop, do well, expand, flower, get ahead, get on*, go, go great guns*, hit it big*, increase, live high on hog*, make out*, multiply, score, succeed, thrive, wax; SEE CONCEPTS *141,704,706*

flourish [*v2*] *wave about*
brandish, display, flaunt, flutter, shake, sweep, swing, swish, twirl, vaunt, wag, wield; SEE CONCEPTS *147,152*

flourishing [*adj*] *prospering, going well*
blooming, burgeoning, doing well, expanding, exuberant, going strong, growing, in full swing*, in the pink*, in top form*, lush, luxuriant, mushrooming, profuse, prosperous, rampant, rank, rich, roaring, robust, successful, thriving, vigorous; SEE CONCEPT *528*

flout [*v*] *show contempt for*
affront, defy, deride, disregard, gibe, gird, insult, jeer, laugh at, mock, outrage, quip, repudiate, ridicule, scoff, scorn, slight, sneer, spurn, taunt, thumb nose at*; SEE CONCEPT *54*

flow [*n*] *issue, abundance*
breeze, continuance, continuation, continuity, course, current, deluge, discharge, draft, draw, dribble, drift, ebb, effusion, electricity, emanation, flood, flux, gush, juice, leakage, movement, oozing, outflow, outpouring, plenty, plethora, progress, progression, river, run, sequence, series, spate, spout, spurt, stream, succession, tide, train, wind; SEE CONCEPTS *146,179,467,786*

flow [*v*] *issue, surge, run out*
abound, arise, brim, cascade, circulate, continue, course, deluge, discharge, disembogue, dribble, ebb, emanate, emerge, emit, exudate, exude, flood, glide, gurgle, gush, inundate, jet, leak, move, ooze, overflow, pass, percolate, pour, proceed, progress, pullulate, regurgitate, result, ripple, roll, run, rush, slide, sluice, smooth along, spew, spill, splash, spring, spurt, sputter, squirt, stream, sweep, swell, swirl, teem, trickle, tumble, void, well forth; SEE CONCEPTS *146,179*

flower [*n1*] *bloom of a plant*
annual, blossom, bud, cluster, efflorescence, floret, floweret, head, herb, inflorescence, perennial, pompon, posy, shoot, spike, spray, vine; SEE CONCEPTS *425,428*

flower [*n2*] *best, choicest part*
choice, cream, elite, finest point, freshness, greatest point, height, pick, pride, prime, prize, top; SEE CONCEPTS *668,829*

flower [*v*] *bloom, flourish*
batten, blossom, blow, burgeon, effloresce, mature, open, outbloom, prosper, thrive, unfold; SEE CONCEPTS *253,704*

flowery [*adj*] *ornate, especially referring to speech or writing*
aureate, baroque, bombastic, declamatory, diffuse, embellished, euphemistic, euphuistic, fancy, figurative, florid, grandiloquent, high-flown, magniloquent, ornamented, overwrought, prolix, purple, redundant, rhetorical, rococo, sonorous, swollen, verbose, windy, wordy; SEE CONCEPTS *267,589*

flowing [*adj*] *gushing, abounding*
brimming, continuous, cursive, easy, falling, flooded, fluent, fluid, fluidic, full, issuing, liquefied, liquid, overrun, pouring out, prolific, rich, rippling, rolling, running, rushing, sinuous, smooth, spouting, streaming, sweeping, teeming, tidal, unbroken, uninterrupted; SEE CONCEPTS *482,584*

fluctuate [*v*] *vacillate, change*
alter, alternate, be undecided, blow hot and cold*, ebb and flow, flutter, go up and down*, hem and haw*, hesitate, oscillate, rise and fall*, seesaw*, shift, swing, undulate, vary, veer, vibrate, wave, waver, yo-yo*; SEE CONCEPTS *13,469,697*

fluent [*adj*] *articulate*
chatty, cogent, copious, cursive, declamatory, disputatious, easy, effortless, effusive, eloquent, facile, flowing, garrulous, glib, liquid, loquacious, mellifluent, mellifluous, natural, persuasive, prompt, quick, ready, running, silver-tongued*, smooth, smooth-spoken, talkative, verbose, vocal, voluble, well-versed, wordy; SEE CONCEPTS *267,584*

fluffy [*adj*] *soft, furry*
creamy, downy, featherlike, feathery, fleecy, flocculent, flossy, gossamer, linty, pile, silky, velutinous; SEE CONCEPT *606*

fluid [n] *liquid*
agua, broth, chaser, cooler, goo*, goop*, juice, liquor, solution, vapor; SEE CONCEPT *467*

fluid [adj1] *liquid*
aqueous, flowing, fluent, in solution, juicy, liquefied, lymphatic, melted, molten, running, runny, serous, uncongealed, watery; SEE CONCEPTS *603,757*

fluid [adj2] *adaptable, changeable*
adjustable, changeful, flexible, floating, fluctuating, indefinite, malleable, mercurial, mobile, mutable, protean, shifting, unsettled, unstable, unsteady, variable; SEE CONCEPTS *534,542*

fluke [n] *chance occurrence*
accident, blessing, break, contingency, fortuity, fortunate, fortune, good fortune*, good luck, incident, lucky break*, odd chance, quirk, stroke of luck*, windfall; SEE CONCEPTS *4,679,693*

fluky [adj] *chance*
accidental, casual, chancy, coincidental, contingent, fortuitous, incalculable, incidental, lucky, odd, uncertain, variable; SEE CONCEPT *552*

flurry [n] *commotion, burst*
ado*, agitation, brouhaha*, bustle*, confusion, disturbance, excitement, ferment, flap*, flaw, fluster, flutter, furor, fuss, gust, haste, hurry, outbreak, pother, spell, spurt, squall, stir*, to-do*, tumult, turbulence, turmoil, whirl*, whirlwind*; SEE CONCEPTS *230,524*

flurry [v] *agitate, confuse*
bewilder, bother, bustle, discombobulate*, discompose, disconcert, disquiet, distract, disturb, excite, fluster, flutter, frustrate, fuss, galvanize, hassle, hurry, hustle, perplex, perturb, provoke, quicken, rattle, ruffle, stimulate, unhinge, unsettle, upset; SEE CONCEPTS *7,19*

flush [n] *blush*
bloom, color, freshness, glow, pinkness, redness, rosiness, ruddiness; SEE CONCEPT *622*

flush [adj1] *flat*
even, horizontal, level, planate, plane, smooth, square, true; SEE CONCEPTS *486,490*

flush [adj2] *overflowing, abundant*
affluent, close, full, generous, lavish, liberal, opulent, prodigal, rich, wealthy, well-off; SEE CONCEPTS *334,771*

flush [v1] *become or make pink or red*
blush, burn, color, color up, crimson, flame, glow, go red, mantle, pink, pinken, redden, rose, rouge, suffuse; SEE CONCEPTS *250,469*

flush [v2] *inundate with liquid*
cleanse, douche, drench, eject, expel, flood, hose, rinse, swab, wash; SEE CONCEPTS *165,179*

flushed [adj] *pink, glowing*
ablaze, animated, aroused, blushing, burning, crimson, elated, embarrassed, enthused, exhilarated, feverish, florid, full-blooded, high, hot, inspired, intoxicated, red, rosy, rubicund, ruddy, sanguine, thrilled; SEE CONCEPTS *401,403,618*

fluster [n] *perturbation, upset*
agitation, brouhaha*, commotion, disturbance, dither, flap*, flurry, flutter, furor, ruffle, state*, to-do*, turmoil; SEE CONCEPT *410*

fluster [v] *upset, perturb*
addle, agitate, bewilder, bother, confound, confuse, craze*, discombobulate*, discompose, disquiet, distract, disturb, excite, flip*, flurry, frustrate, fuddle*, get to*, hassle, heat*, hurry, make nervous, make waves*, muddle, mystify, nonplus, perplex, psych*, puzzle, rattle, ruffle, spook*, stir up*, throw off balance*, unhinge*, work up*; SEE CONCEPTS *7,16,19*

flutter [v] *wave rapidly, flap*
agitate, bat, beat, dance, drift, flicker, flit, flitter, flop, fluctuate, hover, lop, oscillate, palpitate, pulsate, quaver, quiver, ripple, ruffle, shake, shiver, swing, throb, tremble, vibrate, wiggle, wobble; SEE CONCEPTS *150,152*

flux [n] *state of constant change*
alteration, change, flow, fluctuation, fluidity, instability, modification, motion, mutability, mutation, transition, unrest; SEE CONCEPT *697*

fly [v1] *take to the air, usually employing wings*
aviate, barnstorm*, bend the throttle*, buzz*, circle, circumnavigate, climb, control, cross, dart, dash, dive, drift, flat-hat*, fleet, flit, float, flutter, glide, hop, hover, hurry, jet, jet out, jet over, maneuver, mount, operate, pilot, reach, remain aloft, rush, sail, scud*, seagull*, shoot, skim, skirt, sky out*, soar, speed, swoop, take a hop*, take flight, take off, take wing, travel, whisk*, whiz*, whoosh*, wing*, wing in*, zip*, zoom*; SEE CONCEPTS *148,150,224*

fly [v2] *run or pass swiftly*
barrel, bolt, breeze, career, dart, dash, elapse, flee, flit, glide, go like the wind*, hasten, hurry, hustle, make off*, pass, race, roll, run its course*, rush, scamper, scoot, shoot, slip away*, speed, sprint, tear, whiz*, zoom*; SEE CONCEPTS *150,818*

fly [v3] *escape, flee*
abscond, avoid, bolt, break, clear, clear out*, cut and run*, decamp, disappear, flee, get away, hasten away, hide, hightail*, light out*, make a getaway*, make off, make quick exit*, run*, run for it, run from, skedaddle*, skip, steal away, take flight, take off, withdraw; SEE CONCEPTS *102,195*

fly-by-night [adj] *undependable*
brief, cowboy*, dubious, here-today-gone-tomorrow*, impermanent, questionable, shady, shifty, short-lived, slimy*, slippery*, treacherous, trustless, unreliable, unsure, untrustworthy; SEE CONCEPTS *542,551*

flyer [n] *person who navigates aircraft*
ace*, airman/woman, aviator, birdman/woman*, flier, flyboy*, jet*, navigator, pilot, skyman/woman*; SEE CONCEPT *348*

flying [adj] *in the air, winged*
aerial, aeronautical, airborne, avian, drifting, express, flapping, fleet, floating, fluttering, gliding,

hovering, mercurial, mobile, on the wing, plumed, soaring, speedy, streaming, swooping, volant, volar, volitant, waving, winging, zooming; SEE CONCEPT *584*

foam [n] *bubbles formed from a liquid*
cream, fluff, froth, head, lather, scum, spray, spume, suds, surf, yeast; SEE CONCEPT *260*

foam [v] *become bubbly*
aerate, boil, bubble, burble, effervesce, ferment, fizz, froth, gurgle, hiss, lather, seethe, simmer, sparkle; SEE CONCEPTS *170,469*

foamy [adj] *bubbly*
barmy, boiling, bubbling, burbling, carbonated, creamy, ebullient, effervescent, fermented, fizzy, foaming, frothy, lathery, scummy*, seething, simmering, spumescent, spumous, spumy, sudsy, yeasty; SEE CONCEPT *485*

focus [n] *center of attraction*
bull's eye*, center, core, cynosure, focal point, headquarters*, heart, hub, limelight*, locus, meeting place, nerve center*, point of convergence, polestar, seat, spotlight, target; SEE CONCEPTS *532,826,829*

focus [v] *aim attention at*
adjust, attract, bring out, center, centralize, concenter, concentrate, convene, converge, direct, fasten, fix, fixate, get detail, home in*, home in on*, hone in*, join, key on*, knuckle down*, meet, move in, pinpoint, pour it on*, put, rivet, sharpen, spotlight*, sweat*, zero in*, zoom in*; SEE CONCEPTS *17,623*

foe [n] *person who is opponent*
adversary, antagonist, anti*, bad guy*, enemy, hostile party, rival; SEE CONCEPT *412*

fog [n1] *heavy mist that reduces visibility*
brume, cloud, effluvium, film, gloom, grease, ground clouds, haze, London fog, miasma, murk, murkiness, nebula, obscurity, pea soup*, smaze, smog, smoke, smother, soup*, steam, vapor, visibility zero-zero*, wisp; SEE CONCEPTS *524,627*

fog [n2] *mental unclarity*
befuddlement, blindness, confusion, daze, haze, maze, mist, muddledness, muddlement, obscurity, perplexity, stupor, trance, vagueness; SEE CONCEPT *410*

fog [v] *muddle, obscure*
addle, becloud, bedim, befuddle, bewilder, blind, blur, cloud, confuse, darken, daze, dim, eclipse, mist, muddy, mystify, obfuscate, perplex, puzzle, steam up, stupefy; SEE CONCEPTS *250,526*

foggy [adj] *hazy, obscure*
blurred, ceiling zero*, closed in, clouded, cloudy, dark, dim, filmy, fogged in, fuzzy, gray, indistinct, misty, murky, mushy, nebulous, pea-soupy*, smazy, smoggy, socked in*, soupy*, unclear, vague, vaporous, vapory, zero-zero*; SEE CONCEPTS *403,525*

foible [n] *personal imperfection*
characteristic, defect, eccentricity, failing, fault, frailty, idiosyncrasy, infirmity, kink, mannerism,

oddity, peculiarity, quirk, shortcoming, singularity, vice, weakness, weak point; SEE CONCEPTS *411,644*

foil [n] *contrast*
antithesis, background, complement, counterblow, defense, guard, setting; SEE CONCEPT *665*

foil [v] *circumvent, nip in the bud*
baffle, balk, beat, bilk, bollix*, buffalo*, check, checkmate, counter, crab, cramp, crimp, curb, dash, defeat, disappoint, disconcert, ditch, dodge, duck, elude, faze, foul up*, frustrate, get around*, give the run-around*, give the slip*, hang up*, hinder, juke, nullify, outwit, prevent, rattle, restrain, run circles around*, run rings around*, shake, shake off, shuffle off, skip, stop, stymie, throw monkey wrench in*, thwart, upset apple cart*; SEE CONCEPTS *121,130*

fold [n] *double thickness*
bend, circumvolution, cockle, convolution, corrugation, crease, crimp, crinkle, dog's ear*, flection, flexure, furrow, gather, gathering, groove, knife-edge*, lap, lapel, layer, loop, overlap, plait, pleat, plicate, plication, plicature, ply, pucker, ridge, rimple, rivel, ruche, ruck, ruffle, rumple, shirring, smocking, tuck, turn, wrinkle; SEE CONCEPT *754*

fold [v1] *lay in creases*
bend, cockle, corrugate, crease, crimp, crisp, crumple, curl, dog-ear*, double, double over, furrow, gather, groove, hem, intertwine, knit, lap, overlap, overlay, plait, pleat, plicate, pucker, purse, replicate, ridge, ruche, ruck, ruffle, telescope, tuck, turn under, wrinkle; SEE CONCEPT *184*

fold [v2] *encase, enclose*
do up, enfold, entwine, envelop, involve, wrap, wrap up; SEE CONCEPT *209*

fold [v3] *fail, close*
become insolvent, be ruined, break, bust, collapse, crash, crumple, give, go bankrupt, go bust, go into Chapter 11*, go under*, impoverish, pauper, pauperize, shut down, yield; SEE CONCEPTS *324,699*

folder [n] *paper envelope for holding items*
binder, case, file, pocket, portfolio, sheath, wrapper, wrapping; SEE CONCEPT *260*

foliage [n] *leaves on trees*
frondescence, greenness, growth, herbage, leafage, umbrage, vegetation, verdure; SEE CONCEPT *428*

folk [n] *person's relations, acquaintances*
body politic, clan, community, confederation, culture group, ethnic group, family, general public, group, house, household, inhabitants, kin, kindred, lineage, masses, ménage, nation, nationality, people, population, proletariat, public, race, settlement, society, state, stock, tribe; SEE CONCEPTS *296,379*

folklore [n] *tales from the past*
ballad, custom, fable, folk story, folk tale, legend, myth, mythology, mythos, oral literature, superstition, tradition, wisdom; SEE CONCEPT *282*

follow [v1] *take the place of*
be subsequent to, chase, come after, come from, come next, displace, ensue, go after, go next, post-

date, proceed from, pursue, replace, result, spring from, succeed, supersede, supervene, supplant; SEE CONCEPTS *128,242,813*

follow [*v2*] *trail, pursue physically*
accompany, attend, bring up the rear*, catenate, chase, come with, concatenate, convoy, dog*, dog the footsteps of*, draggle, escort, freeze, give chase, go after, go with, hound*, hunt, onto*, persecute, put a tail on*, run after, run down, schlepp along*, search, seek, shadow, shag*, spook*, stalk, stick to, string along, tag, tag after*, tag along*, tail, tailgate*, take out after, track; SEE CONCEPT *207*

follow [*v3*] *act in accordance with*
abide by, accord, adhere to, adopt, attend, be consistent with, be devoted to, be guided by, be in keeping, be interested in, comply, conform, copy, cultivate, do like, emulate, follow suit, give allegiance to, harmonize, heed, hold fast, imitate, keep, keep abreast of, keep an eye on, live up to, match, mimic, mind, mirror, model on, note, obey, observe, pattern oneself upon, reflect, regard, serve, string along*, support, take after, take as an example, watch; SEE CONCEPTS *8,91,171*

follow [*v4*] *understand*
accept, appreciate, apprehend, catch*, catch on*, comprehend, dig*, fathom, get*, get the picture*, grasp, realize, see, take in*; SEE CONCEPT *15*

follower [*n*] *person who believes, has great interest*
addict, adherent, admirer, advocate, apostle, attendant, backer, believer, bootlicker*, buff, client, cohort, companion, convert, copycat, devotee, disciple, fan, fancier, freak*, habitué, hanger-on*, helper, henchman/woman, imitator, lackey*, member, minion, parasite, participant, partisan, patron, promoter, proselyte, protégé, pupil, representative, satellite, sectary, servant, sidekick, stooge*, supporter, sycophant, toady*, vassal, votary, worshiper, yes man/woman*, zealot; SEE CONCEPTS *352,366,423*

following [*n*] *persons of an interest, belief*
adherents, audience, circle, clientage, clientele, cortege, coterie, dependents, entourage, fans, group, groupies*, hangers-on*, patronage, patrons, public, retinue, rout, suite, support, supporters, train; SEE CONCEPTS *294,387,417*

following [*adj*] *happening, being next or after*
after a while, afterward, afterwards, attendant, a while later, back, by and by, coming, coming after, coming next, consecutive, consequent, consequential, directly after, ensuing, henceforth, hinder, in pursuit, in search of, in the wake of, later, later on, latter, next, next off*, on the scent*, posterior, presently, proximate, pursuing, rear, resulting, sequent, sequential, serial, seriate, specified, subsequent, succeeding, successive, supervenient, then, trailing, when; SEE CONCEPTS *585,811,818,820*

follow through [*v*] *bring to a conclusion*
complete, conclude, consummate, pursue, see through; SEE CONCEPT *91*

follow up [*v*] *make inquiries*
check out, find out about, investigate, look into, make sure, pursue; SEE CONCEPT *103*

folly [*n*] *nonsense, ridiculous idea*
absurdity, craziness, daftness, dottiness, dumb thing to do*, dumb trick*, fatuity, foolishness, idiocy, imbecility, impracticality, imprudence, inadvisability, inanity, indiscretion, irrationality, lunacy, madness, obliquity, preposterousness, rashness, recklessness, senselessness, silliness, stupidity, triviality, unsoundness, vice, witlessness; SEE CONCEPTS *410,633*

foment [*v*] *instigate, provoke*
abet, agitate, arouse, brew, cultivate, encourage, excite, fan the flames*, foster, goad, incite, nurse, nurture, promote, quicken, raise, set, set on, sow the seeds*, spur, start, stimulate, stir up, whip up*; SEE CONCEPTS *14,221*

fond [*adj*] *have a liking or taste for*
addicted, adoring, affectionate, amorous, attached, caring, devoted, doting, enamored, indulgent, keen on, lovesome, lovey-dovey*, loving, mushy*, partial, predisposed, responsive, romantic, sentimental, silly over, sympathetic, tender, warm; SEE CONCEPTS *32,542*

fondle [*v*] *touch lovingly*
bear hug*, caress, clutch, cosset, cuddle, dandle, embrace, feel, fool around*, grab, grope, hug, love, make love to, neck, nestle, nuzzle, pat, paw, pet, play footsie*, snuggle, squeeze, stroke; SEE CONCEPTS *190,375*

fondness [*n*] *liking or taste for*
affection, attachment, devotion, fancy, kindness, love, partiality, penchant, predilection, preference, soft spot, susceptibility, tenderness, weakness; SEE CONCEPT *32*

food [*n*] *edible material*
aliment, bite*, board, bread, cheer, chow*, comestible, cookery, cooking, cuisine, diet, drink, eatable, eats*, edible, entrée, fare, fast food, feed, fodder*, foodstuff, goodies*, grit*, groceries*, grub*, handout*, home cooking, keep, larder, meal, meat, menu, mess*, moveable feast, nourishment, nutriment, nutrition, pabulum, provision, ration, refreshment, slop*, snack, store, subsistence, support, sustenance, table, take out, tuck, viand, victual, vittles*; SEE CONCEPTS *457,460,461*

fool [*n*] *stupid or ridiculous person*
ass, birdbrain*, blockhead*, bonehead*, boob*, bore, buffoon, clod*, clown, cretin*, dimwit*, dolt*, dope*, dumb ox*, dunce, dunderhead*, easy mark*, fair game*, fall guy*, fathead*, goose*, halfwit, idiot, ignoramus, illiterate, imbecile, innocent, jerk*, lamebrain*, lightweight*, loon*, moron, nerd*, nincompoop*, ninny*, nitwit, numskull*, oaf, sap*, schlemiel*, silly, simpleton, stooge*, sucker*, turkey*, twerp*, twit*, victim; SEE CONCEPTS *412,423*

fool [*v*] *trick, mislead*
bamboozle*, bluff, cheat, chicane, con, deceive, delude, diddle, dupe, fake out*, flimflam*, fox*, gull,

hoax, hoodwink*, jive*, juke*, kid, lead on, make believe, outfox, play-act*, play a trick on, pretend, put on, put one over on*, scam*, snow*, spoof*, suck in*, take in*, trifle; SEE CONCEPT *59*

fool around [v] *waste time*
dawdle, hang around*, idle, kill time*, lark, mess around*, play around*; SEE CONCEPT *681*

fooled [adj] *tricked*
bamboozled*, conned, deceived, deluded, duped, flimflammed*, hornswoggled*, misled, outfoxed*, snowed*, sucked in*; SEE CONCEPT *537*

foolhardy [adj] *impetuous, rash*
adventuresome, adventurous, audacious, bold, breakneck*, daredevil, daring, devil-may-care*, harebrained*, headstrong, imprudent, incautious, irresponsible, madcap, off deep end*, out on limb*, precipitate, reckless, temerarious, venturesome, venturous, wide open; SEE CONCEPT *401*

fooling [n] *joking, tricks*
bluffing, buffoonery, clownishness, farce, frolicking, high jinks*, horseplay, jesting, joking, joshing, kidding, making light*, mockery, nonsense, pretense, roughhouse*, roughhousing*, rowdiness, sham*, skylarking*, spoofing, teasing, trifling; SEE CONCEPT *59*

foolish [adj] *nonsensical, idiotic*
absurd, asinine, brainless, cockamamy*, crazy, daffy*, daft, dippy*, doltish*, dotty*, fantastic, fatuous, feebleminded*, half-baked*, half-witted*, harebrained*, ill-advised, ill-considered, imbecilic, imprudent, incautious, indiscreet, injudicious, insane, irrational, jerky*, kooky*, loony*, ludicrous, lunatic, mad, moronic, nerdy*, nutty*, preposterous, ridiculous, senseless, short-sighted, silly, simple, stupid, unintelligent, unreasonable, unwise, wacky*, weak, witless, zany*; SEE CONCEPTS *401,542,544*

foolishly [adv] *idiotic, without due consideration*
absurdly, idiotically, ill-advisedly, imprudently, incautiously, indiscreetly, injudiciously, mistakenly, short-sightedly, stupidly, unwisely; SEE CONCEPTS *401,542,544*

foolishness [n] *idiocy, nonsense*
absurdity, absurdness, bunk*, carrying-on*, claptrap*, craziness, dumb trick*, folly, foolery, fool trick, horse feathers*, impracticality, imprudence, inanity, indiscretion, insanity, insensibility, irrationality, irresponsibility, ludicrousness, lunacy, mistake, poppycock*, preposterousness, rubbish*, senselessness, silliness, stupidity, tommyrot*, twaddle, unreasonableness, unwiseness, weakness, witlessness; SEE CONCEPT *633*

foot [n1] *extremity of animate being*
hoof, pad, paw, pes; SEE CONCEPT *392*

foot [n2] *base of an object*
bottom, footing, foundation, lowest point, nadir, pier; SEE CONCEPT *442*

foot [n3] *twelve inches/30.48 centimeters measured*
cubic, square; SEE CONCEPTS *790,791*

footing [n1] *foundation, basis*
basement, bedrock, bottom, establishment, foot, foothold, ground, groundwork, infrastructure, installation, resting place, seat, seating, settlement, substratum, substructure, underpinning, understructure, warrant; SEE CONCEPTS *442,661*

footing [n2] *social status*
capacity, character, condition, grade, place, position, rank, relations, relationship, situation, standing, state, station, terms; SEE CONCEPT *388*

fop [n] *man who attempts suaveness*
beau, blade*, cavalier, clotheshorse*, dandy*, dasher*, dude*, fashion plate, gallant, ladies' man, man about town*, man of the world*, peacock*, smooth*, snappy dresser, sport*, swell*; SEE CONCEPT *423*

for [conj] *in consequence of the fact that*
as, as long as, because, being, considering, inasmuch as, now, since, whereas; SEE CONCEPT *544*

for [prep] *in consideration of*
after, as, beneficial to, concerning, conducive to, during, for the sake of, in, in contemplation of, in exchange for, in favor of, in furtherance of, in order to, in order to get, in place of, in pursuance of, in spite of, in the direction of, in the interest of, in the name of, notwithstanding, on the part of, on the side of, pro, supposing, to, to counterbalance, to go to, to the amount of, to the extent of, toward, under the authority of, with, with a view to, with regard to, with respect; SEE CONCEPT *544*

forage [v] *search madly for*
beat, cast about, comb, explore, fine-tooth-comb*, grub, hunt, pilfer, plunder, raid, rake, ransack, ravage, rummage, scour, scrounge, search, seek; SEE CONCEPT *216*

foray [n] *incursion, attempt*
attack, depredation, descent, inroad, invasion, irruption, raid, reconnaissance, sally, sortie; SEE CONCEPTS *86,90,159*

forbear [v] *resist the temptation to*
abstain, avoid, bridle, cease, curb, decline, desist, escape, eschew, evade, forgo, go easy*, hold back*, inhibit, keep, keep from, omit, pause, refrain, restrain, sacrifice, shun, stop, withhold; SEE CONCEPTS *35,121,130,681*

forbearance [n] *resisting, avoidance*
abstinence, endurance, fortitude, going easy on*, living with*, longanimity, moderation, patience, patientness, refraining, resignation, restraint, self-control, temperance, tolerance; SEE CONCEPTS *410,633*

forbearing [adj] *tolerant*
being big*, charitable, clement, considerate, easy, forgiving, gentle, going easy on*, going easy with*, humane, humanitarian, indulgent, lenient, living with*, longanimous, long-suffering, merciful, mild, moderate, patient, soft-shell*, thoughtful; SEE CONCEPTS *404,542*

forbid [v] *outlaw, prohibit an action*
ban, block, cancel, censor, check, debar, declare illegal, deny, deprive, disallow, embargo, enjoin, exclude, forestall, forfend, freeze*, halt, hinder, hold up, impede, inhibit, interdict, lock up, nix*, obstruct, obviate, oppose, preclude, prevent, proscribe, put the chill on*, restrain, restrict, rule out, say no*, shut down*, shut out*, spike*, stop, stymie*, taboo*, veto, withhold; SEE CONCEPT *121*

forbidden [adj] *outlawed, prohibited*
banned, closed, closed-down*, closed-up*, contraband, no-no*, off limits, out of bounds, proscribed, refused, taboo*, verboten, vetoed; SEE CONCEPT *548*

forbidding [adj] *ominous, daunting*
abhorrent, disagreeable, dour, foreboding, frightening, glowering, grim, hostile, menacing, odious, offensive, off-putting, repellent, repulsive, sinister, threatening, tough, ugly, unapproachable, unfriendly, unpleasant; SEE CONCEPTS *537,550*

force [n1] *physical energy, power*
arm, brunt, clout, coercion, compulsion, conscription, constrait, draft, duress, dynamism, effort, enforcement, exaction, extortion, full head of steam*, fury, horsepower, impact, impetus, impulse, might, momentum, muscle, pains*, potency, potential, pow*, pressure, punch, push, sinew, sock*, speed, steam, stimulus, strain, strength, stress, strong arm*, stuff*, subjection, tension, trouble, velocity, vigor, violence, what it takes*; SEE CONCEPTS *641,724*

force [n2] *mental power, energy*
ability, authority, bite*, capability, coercion, cogency, competence, determination, dominance, drive, duress, effect, effectiveness, efficacy, emphasis, fierceness, forcefulness, gumption, guts*, impressiveness, influence, intensity, intestinal fortitude, obligation, persistence, persuasiveness, point, pressure, puissance, punch, push, requirement, sapience, stress, validity, validness, vehemence, vigor, willpower; SEE CONCEPTS *410,677*

force [n3] *military organization*
armed forces, army, battalion, body, cell, corps, crew, detachment, division, guard, horses, host, legion, military, patrol, regiment, reserves, servicemen/women, shop, soldiers, squad, squadron, troop, unit; SEE CONCEPTS *322,417*

force [v1] *obligate to do something*
apply, bear down, bear hard on, bind, blackmail, bring pressure to bear upon*, burden, cause, charge, choke, coerce, command, compel, concuss, conscript, constrain, contract, demand, draft, drag, dragoon*, drive, enforce, enjoin, exact, extort, fix, impel, impose, impress, inflict, insist, limit, make, move, necessitate, oblige, obtrude, occasion, order, overcome, pin down, press, pressure, pressurize, put screws to*, put squeeze on*, require, restrict, sandbag*, shotgun*, strong-arm*, urge, wrest, wring; SEE CONCEPT *14*

force [v2] *use push, violence upon*
assault, blast, break in, break open, burst, bust open, crack open, defile, extort, jimmy*, propel, pry, push, rape, ravish, spoil, squeeze, thrust, twist, undo, violate, wrench, wrest, wring; SEE CONCEPTS *156,208*

forced [adj] *compulsory, strained*
affected, artificial, begrudging, binding, bound, coerced, coercive, compelled, conscripted, constrained, contrived, enforced, factitious, false, grudging, inflexible, insincere, involuntary, labored, mandatory, obligatory, peremptory, rigid, slave, stiff, strained, stringent, unnatural, unwilling, wooden*; SEE CONCEPTS *542,548*

forceful [adj] *effective, powerful*
ball of fire*, bullish*, cogent, coming on strong, commanding, compelling, constraining, convincing, dominant, dynamic, electric, elemental, energetic, forcible, gutsy*, manful, mighty, persuasive, pithy, potent, powerhouse, puissant, punch, punchy*, steamroller*, stringent, strong, take-charge, takeover, telling, titanic, vehement, vigorous, violent, virile, weighty; SEE CONCEPTS *267,401,550*

forcible [adj] *powerful, aggressive*
active, armed, assertive, coercive, cogent, compelling, compulsory, drastic, effective, efficient, energetic, forceful, impressive, intense, mighty, militant, persuasive, potent, puissant, strong, telling, valid, vehement, vigorous, violent, weighty; SEE CONCEPTS *267,537*

forcibly [adv] *against one's will*
by force, coercively, compulsorily, effectively, energetically, hard, mightily, powerfully, strongly, under protest, vigorously; SEE CONCEPTS *544,548*

fore [adv] *in the front*
ahead, ante*, antecedently, before, beforehand, forward, in advance, near, nearest, precedently, previous; SEE CONCEPTS *585,820*

forebode [v] *predict, warn*
augur, betoken, bode, divine, forecast, foresee, foreshadow, foretell, foretoken, forewarn, indicate, omen, portend, premonish, presage, prognosticate, promise; SEE CONCEPTS *70,78*

foreboding [n] *misgiving, bad omen*
anxiety, apprehension, apprehensiveness, augury, bad vibes*, chill, dread, fear, foreshadowing, foretoken, forewarning, funny feeling*, handwriting on wall*, portent, prediction, premonition, prenotion, presage, presentiment, prognostic, prophecy, sinking feeling*, vibes*, warning, wind change*; SEE CONCEPTS *78,689,690*

forecast [n] *prediction, often of weather or business*
anticipation, augury, budget, calculation, cast, conjecture, divination, estimate, foreknowledge, foreseeing, foresight, foretelling, forethought, foretoken, guess, outlook, planning, precognition, prescience, prevision, prognosis, prognostication, projection, prophecy; SEE CONCEPTS *28,37,70,78*

forecast [v] *predict, guess*
adumbrate, anticipate, augur, calculate, call the turn*, conclude, conjecture, demonstrate, determine, divine, dope out*, estimate, figure, figure out*, foresee, foretell, gather, gauge, infer, in the cards*, plan, portend, predetermine, presage, prognosticate, prophesy, reason, see it coming*, soothsay, surmise, telegraph; SEE CONCEPTS *28,37,70,78*

forefather [n] *family predecessor*
ancestor, antecedent, ascendant, author, begetter, father, forebear, forerunner, founder, kinsman, originator, parent, paterfamilias, patriarch, precursor, primogenitor, procreator, progenitor, relative, sire; SEE CONCEPT *414*

forefront/foreground [n] *prominence*
beginning, center, cutting-edge*, focus, fore, forepart, front, lead, leading-edge*, limelight*, on the line*, spearhead*, state-of-the-art, vanguard; SEE CONCEPT *668*

foregoing [adj] *come before; previous*
above, aforementioned, aforesaid, aforestated, antecedent, anterior, former, past, precedent, preceding, prior; SEE CONCEPTS *585,820*

foreign [adj1] *from another country, experience*
adopted, alien, alienated, antipodal, barbarian, barbaric, borrowed, derived, different, distant, estranged, exiled, exotic, expatriate, external, extralocal, extraneous, extrinsic, far, faraway, farfetched, far-off, from abroad, immigrant, imported, inaccessible, nonnative, nonresident, not domestic, not native, offshore, outlandish, outside, overseas, remote, strange, transoceanic, unaccustomed, unexplored, unfamiliar, unknown; SEE CONCEPTS *536,549*

foreign [adj2] *irrelevant*
accidental, adventitious, extraneous, extrinsic, heterogeneous, immaterial, impertinent, inapposite, incompatible, incongruous, inconsistent, inconsonant, irrelative, repugnant, unassimilable, uncharacteristic, unrelated; SEE CONCEPTS *267,537*

foreigner [n] *person from another country*
alien, fresh off the boat*, greenhorn*, immigrant, incomer, newcomer, outlander, outsider, stranger; SEE CONCEPT *413*

foreman/woman [n] *person overseeing others work*
boss, boss lady*, boss man*, executive, head, head honcho*, head man/woman, honcho*, manager, overseer, pit boss*, slave driver*, superintendent, supervisor, taskmaster; SEE CONCEPT *347*

foremost [adj] *first in rank, order*
A-1*, A number-1*, arch, at the cutting edge*, at the leading edge*, champion, chief, first, fore, front, head, headmost, heavy, heavy stuff*, heavyweight*, highest, hotdog*, hotshot*, hot stuff*, inaugural, initial, leading, most important, number one*, original, paramount, preeminent, premier, primary, prime, primo*, principal, supreme; SEE CONCEPTS *568, 585,799*

forensic [adj] *judicial, legal*
argumentative, debatable, dialectic, dialectical, disputative, juridical, juristic, moot, polemical, rhetorical; SEE CONCEPTS *267,319*

foreordain [v] *doom, fate*
destinate, destine, foredoom, foreshadow, foretell, prearrange, predestine, predetermine, preform, preordain, reserve; SEE CONCEPT *70*

forerunner [n1] *messenger, herald*
advertiser, advocate, ancestor, announcer, author, envoy, forebear, forefather, foregoer, harbinger, initiator, originator, pioneer, precursor, progenitor, prognostic, prototype; SEE CONCEPTS *414,423*

forerunner [n2] *example, sign*
advertisement, announcement, antecedent, antecessor, augury, exemplar, foregoer, foreshadow, foretoken, forewarning, indication, mark, model, omen, pattern, portent, precursor, predecessor, premonition, presage, prognostic, prototype, sign, token, warning; SEE CONCEPT *529*

foresee [v] *anticipate, predict*
apprehend, call the turn*, crystal ball it*, discern, divine, dope out*, envisage, espy, expect, forebode, forecast, forefeel, foreknow, foretell, have a hunch*, perceive, predict, preknow, presage, previse, prevision, prognosticate, prophesy, psych out*, see, see it coming*, understand, visualize; SEE CONCEPTS *26,70*

foreshadow [v] *indicate*
adumbrate, augur, be in the wind*, betoken, bode, forebode, foretell, hint, imply, omen, portend, predict, prefigure, presage, promise, prophesy, shadow, signal, suggest, telegraph; SEE CONCEPTS *70,75,261*

foresight [n] *mental preparedness*
anticipation, canniness, care, carefulness, caution, circumspection, clairvoyance, discernment, discreetness, discretion, economy, far-sightedness, foreknowledge, forethought, husbandry, insight, longsightedness, perception, precaution, precognition, preconception, premeditation, premonition, prenotion, prescience, prospect, providence, provision, prudence, sagacity; SEE CONCEPTS *409,410*

forest [n] *area with large number of trees*
backwoods, brake, chase, clump, coppice, copse, cover, covert, grove, growth, jungle, park, shelter, stand, thicket, timber, timberland, weald, wildwood, wood, woodland, woodlot, woods; SEE CONCEPTS *509,517*

foretell [v] *predict, warn*
adumbrate, announce, anticipate, apprehend, augur, auspicate, betoken, bode, call, call it*, call the shot*, crystal ball it*, declare, disclose, divine, divulge, dope*, dope out*, figure, figure out*, forebode, forecast, foreknow, foreshadow, forewarn, make book*, portend, prefigure, presage, proclaim, prognosticate, prophesy, psych, read, reveal, see something coming*, signify, soothsay, tell; SEE CONCEPTS *70,78*

forethought [n] *mental preparedness*
anticipation, canniness, caution, deliberation, discreetness, discretion, far-sightedness, foresight,

gumption, judgment, planning, precaution, premed-itation, providence, provision, prudence, sense; SEE CONCEPT *410*

forever [*adj1*] *for all time; everlasting*
always, durably, endlessly, enduringly, eternally, ever, everlastingly, evermore, everything consid-ered*, for always, forevermore, for good*, for keeps*, for life*, immortally, infinitely, in perpetu-ity, in perpetuum, interminably, lastingly, now and forever*, on and on*, permanently, perpetually, till blue in the face*, till the cows come home*, till death do us part*, till Doomsday*, till the end of time*, unchangingly, world without end*; SEE CONCEPTS *551,649,798,799*

forever [*adj2*] *not ceasing, continually*
all the time, constantly, endlessly, eternally, ever-lastingly, incessantly, interminably, perpetually, reg-ularly, unendingly, unremittingly; SEE CONCEPTS *534,798*

forewarn [*v*] *caution that something may happen*
admonish, advise, alarm, alert, apprise, dissuade, flag, forbode, give fair warning*, give the high sign*, portend, premonish, pull one's coat*, put a bug in one's ear*, put one wise*, put on guard*, telegraph, tip, tip off, wave a red flag*; SEE CONCEPT *78*

foreword [*n*] *introduction to document*
exordium, overture, preamble, preface, preliminary, prelude, prelusion, proem, prolegomenon, prologue; SEE CONCEPT *270*

forfeit [*n*] *something given as sacrifice*
cost, damages, fine, forfeiture, loss, mulct, penalty, relinquishment; SEE CONCEPT *123*

forfeit [*v*] *give up something in sacrifice*
abandon, be deprived of, be stripped of, drop, give over, lose, relinquish, renounce, sacrifice, surrender; SEE CONCEPT *116*

forge [*v1*] *counterfeit*
coin, copy, design, duplicate, fabricate, fake, fal-sify, fashion, feign, frame, imitate, invent, make, phony up*, pirate*, produce, reproduce, scratch, trace, transcribe, trump up*; SEE CONCEPTS *59,171*

forge [*v2*] *make something from scratch*
beat, build, construct, contrive, create, devise, fab-ricate, fashion, form, frame, hammer out*, invent, manufacture, mold, pound, put together, shape, turn out, work; SEE CONCEPTS *168,173,175,205,251*

forgery [*n*] *counterfeiting; counterfeit item*
bogus*, carbon*, carbon copy, cheat, coining, copy, fabrication, fake, faking, falsification, fraudulence, imitating, imitation, imposition, imposture, looka-like, phony, pseudo, sham*, twin, workalike*; SEE CONCEPTS *59,171,716*

forget [*v1*] *not be able to remember*
blow, clean forget*, consign to oblivion*, dismiss from mind, disremember, draw a blank*, escape one's memory*, fail to remember, let slip from mem-ory*, lose consciousness of, lose sight of*, misrec-ollect, obliterate, think no more of*; SEE CONCEPT *40*

forget [*v2*] *leave behind*
blink, discount, disregard, drop, fail, ignore, lose sight of*, neglect, omit, overlook, overpass, pass over, skip, slight, transgress, trespass; SEE CONCEPTS *30,116*

forgetful [*adj*] *tending to not remember*
absent, absent-minded, abstracted, airheaded*, am-nemonic, amnesic, asleep on the job*, bemused, careless, distracted, dreamy, heedless, inattentive, lax, like an absent-minded professor*, looking out window*, mooning, moony*, neglectful, negligent, nirvanic, not on the job*, oblivious, out of it*, out to lunch*, pipe dreaming*, preoccupied, remiss, slack, sloppy, unmindful, unwitting, woolgathering*; SEE CONCEPTS *403,550*

forgetfulness [*n*] *consistent inability to remember*
absent-mindedness, abstraction, amnesia, blackout, blank, blockout, carelessness, dreaminess, fugue, heedlessness, hypomnesia, inattention, lapse of memory, laxness, lethe, limbo, loss of memory, neg-ligence, nirvana, oblivion, obliviousness, paramne-sia, repression, short memory, suppression; SEE CONCEPTS *410,644*

forgive [*v*] *stop blame and grant pardon*
absolve, accept apology, acquit, allow for, amnesty, bear no malice*, bear with, bury the hatchet*, clear, commute, condone, dismiss from mind, efface, ex-culpate, excuse, exempt, exonerate, extenuate, for-get, kiss and make up*, laugh off*, let bygones be bygones*, let it go*, let off*, let off easy*, let pass*, let up on*, make allowance, overlook, palliate, par-don, pocket, purge, release, relent, remit, reprieve, respite, spring, think no more of*, turn other cheek*, wink at*, wipe slate clean*; SEE CONCEPTS *12,50,88*

forgiveness [*n*] *pardon; end of blame*
absolution, acquittal, amnesty, charity, clemency, compassion, condonation, dispensation, exculpation, exoneration, extenuation, grace, immunity, impu-nity, indemnity, justification, lenience, lenity, mercy, overlooking, palliation, purgation, quarter, quittance, remission, remittal, reprieve, respite, vindication; SEE CONCEPTS *685,689*

forgo [*v*] *give up, do without*
abandon, abdicate, abjure, abstain, cede, desist, es-chew, forbear, forsake, give in, go on the wagon*, leave alone, leave out, pack in*, pass, pass on, pass up, quit, refrain, relinquish, renounce, resign, resist, sacrifice, sit out*, surrender, swear off*, take the cure*, take the oath*, waive, yield; SEE CONCEPTS *121,130,681*

forgotten [*adj*] *out of one's mind*
abandoned, blanked out*, blotted out*, blown over*, buried, bygone, clean forgot*, consigned to obliv-ion*, disremembered*, drew a blank*, erased, fell between cracks*, gone, lapsed, left behind, left out, lost, obliterated, omitted, past, past recollection, re-pressed, slipped one's mind*, suppressed, unre-

called, unremembered, unretained; SEE CONCEPTS *402,403,529*

fork [v] *go separate ways*
angle, bifurcate, branch, branch off, branch out, divaricate, diverge, divide, part, split; SEE CONCEPTS *98,738*

forked [adj] *going separate ways*
angled, bifid, bifurcate, bifurcated, branched, branching, dichotomous, dichotonic, divaricate, divided, furcate, furcated, pronged, split, tined, tridented, zigzag; SEE CONCEPTS *485,581*

forlorn [adj] *hopeless, inconsolable*
abandoned, alone, bereft, blue*, cheerless, comfortless, cynical, defenseless, depressed, deserted, desolate, despairing, desperate, despondent, destitute, destroyed, disconsolate, down and out*, dragging*, forgotten, forsaken, friendless, fruitless, futile, godforsaken*, helpless, homeless, in the dumps*, lonely, lonesome, lost, miserable, oppressed, pathetic, pessimistic, pitiable, pitiful, solitary, tragic, unhappy, vain, weighed down, woebegone, wretched; SEE CONCEPT *403*

form [n1] *shape; arrangement*
anatomy, appearance, articulation, cast, configuration, conformation, construction, contour, cut, design, die, embodiment, fashion, figure, formation, framework, mode, model, mold, outline, pattern, plan, profile, scheme, silhouette, skeleton, structure, style, system; SEE CONCEPTS *660,754,757*

form [n2] *animate body and its condition*
anatomy, being, build, condition, fettle*, figure, fitness, frame, health, object, outline, person, phenomenon, physique, shape, silhouette, thing, torso, trim*; SEE CONCEPTS *316,389,720*

form [n3] *accepted procedure; ceremony*
behavior, by the book*, by the numbers*, canon, ceremonial, channels*, conduct, convenance, convention, custom, decorum, done thing*, etiquette, fashion, formality, habit, law, layout, manner, manners, method, mode, practice, precept, proceeding, process, propriety, protocol, regulation, rite, ritual, ropes*, rule, setup, style, usage, way; SEE CONCEPT *687*

form [n4] *document that requires answers or information*
application, blank, chart, data sheet, letter, paper, questionnaire, sheet; SEE CONCEPT *271*

form [n5] *type, kind*
arrangement, character, class, description, design, grade, guise, make, manifestation, manner, method, mode, order, practice, rank, semblance, sort, species, stamp, style, system, variety, way; SEE CONCEPTS *6,378*

form [n6] *organization, arrangement*
format, framework, harmony, order, orderliness, placement, plan, proportion, scheme, structure, symmetry; SEE CONCEPT *727*

form [v1] *bring into existence; make, produce*
arrange, assemble, block out, bring about, build, cast, complete, compose, conceive, concoct, constitute, construct, consummate, contrive, cook up*, create, cultivate, cut, design, develop, devise, dream up, erect, establish, fabricate, fashion, finish, fix, forge, found, frame, hammer out*, invent, knock off*, make up, manufacture, model, mold, organize, outline, pattern, perfect, plan, plot, project, put together, scheme, set, set up, shape, structure, throw together, trace, turn out*, work; SEE CONCEPTS *168,173,205,251*

form [v2] *come into being; arise*
accumulate, acquire, appear, become a reality, become visible, condense, crystallize, develop, eventuate, fall into place*, grow, harden, materialize, mature, rise, set, settle, shape up, show up, take on character, take shape*; SEE CONCEPTS *105,704*

form [v3] *educate, discipline*
breed, bring up, give character, instruct, rear, school, teach, train; SEE CONCEPTS *285,295*

form [v4] *comprise, be a part of*
act as, compose, constitute, figure in, make, make up, serve as; SEE CONCEPT *643*

formal [adj1] *established, orderly*
academic, approved, ceremonial, ceremonialistic, ceremonious, confirmed, conventional, decorous, directed, explicit, express, fixed, formalistic, lawful, legal, methodical, official, precise, prescribed, pro forma, proper, punctilious, regular, rigid, ritual, ritualistic, set, solemn, stately, stereotyped, stereotypical, strict, systematic; SEE CONCEPTS *533,547*

formal [adj2] *stiff, affected, correct*
aloof, by the numbers*, ceremonious, conventional, decorous, distant, exact, nominal, playing the game*, polite, precise, prim, punctilious, reserved, seemly, sententious, starched*, stilted*, straight arrow*, stuffy*, unbending; SEE CONCEPT *401*

formality [n1] *convention, custom*
academism, ceremony, convenance, conventionality, form, gesture, liturgy, matter of form*, officialism, procedure, red tape*, rite, ritual, rituality, rubric, rule, service, solemnity, solemnness, stereotype, tradition; SEE CONCEPT *687*

formality [n2] *etiquette, protocol*
ceremoniousness, conventionalism, correctness, decorum, formalism, honors, mummery, p's and q's*, politesse, propriety, punctiliousness; SEE CONCEPT *633*

formation [n] *composition, establishment*
accumulation, architecture, arrangement, compilation, configuration, constitution, construction, creation, crystallization, deposit, design, development, dispersal, disposition, embodiment, evolution, fabrication, figure, forming, generation, genesis, grouping, induction, makeup, manufacture, order, organization, pattern, production, rank, structure, synthesis; SEE CONCEPTS *173,260*

formative [*adj*] *influential, impressionable*
determinative, developmental, immature, impressible, malleable, moldable, pliant, sensitive, shaping, susceptible; SEE CONCEPTS *534,537*

former [*adj*] *previous in time or order*
above, aforementioned, aforesaid, ancient, antecedent, anterior, bygone, departed, earlier, erstwhile, ex-*, first, foregoing, late, long ago*, long gone, of yore*, old, once, one-time, past, preceding, prior, quondam, sometime, whilom; SEE CONCEPTS *585,820*

formerly [*adv*] *previously in time or order*
aforetime, already, anciently, at one time, away back, a while back, back, back when*, before, before now, before this, down memory lane*, earlier, eons ago*, erewhile, erstwhile, heretofore, in former times, in the olden days*, in the past, lately, long ago, of old, of yore, olden days*, once, once upon a time*, radically, some time ago, time was*, used to be*, water under the bridge*; SEE CONCEPTS *585,820*

formidable [*adj1*] *horrible, terrifying*
appalling, awful, dangerous, daunting, dire, dismaying, dreadful, fearful, fierce, frightful, horrific, imposing, impregnable, intimidating, menacing, redoubtable, shocking, terrible, terrific, threatening; SEE CONCEPT *537*

formidable [*adj2*] *difficult, overwhelming*
all-powerful, arduous, awesome, ballbuster, challenging, colossal, dismaying, effortful, great, hard, impressive, indomitable, intimidating, labored, laborious, mammoth, mighty, murder*, onerous, overpowering, powerful, puissant, rough*, rough go*, staggering, strenuous, tall order*, toilsome, tough*, tough proposition*, tremendous, uphill*; SEE CONCEPT *565*

formless [*adj*] *disorganized, vague*
amorphous, baggy*, blobby*, chaotic, crude, inchoate, incoherent, indefinite, indeterminate, indistinct, nebulous, obscure, orderless, raw, rough, rude, shapeless, unclear, undefined, unformed, unorganized; SEE CONCEPTS *485,535,589*

formula [*n*] *set preparation; rule, recipe*
blueprint, canon, code, credo, creed, custom, description, direction, equation, form, formulary, maxim, method, modus operandi, precept, prescription, principle, procedure, rite, ritual, rote, rubric, specifications, theorem, way; SEE CONCEPTS *268,687*

formulate [*v*] *plan, specify systematically*
codify, coin, compose, concoct, contrive, cook up, couch, define, detail, develop, devise, draft, draw up*, dream up*, evolve, express, forge, frame, give form to, hatch, indite, invent, make, make up*, map, originate, particularize, phrase, prepare, put, set down*, systematize, vamp, word, work out; SEE CONCEPTS *36,173,202*

forsake [*v*] *abandon, turn one's back on*
abdicate, cast off, change one's tune*, desert, disclaim, disown, drift away*, forgo, forswear, give up, have done with, jettison, jilt, kiss goodbye*, leave, leave flat*, leave high and dry*, quit, relinquish, renounce, repudiate, resign, run out on*, set aside, show the door*, spurn, surrender, take the oath*, throw over*, walk out on*, wash one's hands of*, yield; SEE CONCEPTS *30,195,384*

forsaken [*adj*] *abandoned*
cast off, derelict, deserted, desolate, destitute, disowned, forlorn, friendless, godforsaken*, ignored, isolated, jilted, left at the altar*, left behind, left in the lurch*, lonely, lorn, marooned, outcast, solitary, thrown over*; SEE CONCEPT *555*

forswear [*v*] *abandon, disavow*
abjure, deny, disclaim, disown, drop, forgo, forsake, give up, recall, recant, reject, renege, renounce, repudiate, retract, swear off, take back, withdraw; SEE CONCEPTS *44,54*

fort/fortress [*n*] *stronghold*
acropolis, blockhouse, camp, castle, citadel, fastness, fortification, garrison, redoubt, station; SEE CONCEPTS *321,439*

forte [*n*] *person's strong point*
ability, ableness, aptitude, competence, effectiveness, efficiency, eminency, faculty, gift*, long suit*, medium, métier, oyster*, speciality, strength, strong suit*, talent, thing*; SEE CONCEPTS *409,411*

forth [*adv*] *outward*
ahead, alee, along, away, first, forward, into, into the open*, on, onward, out; SEE CONCEPT *581*

forthcoming [*adj*] *expected, imminent*
accessible, anticipated, approaching, at hand, available, awaited, coming, destined, expected, fated, future, impending, inescapable, in evidence, inevitable, in preparation, in prospect, in store*, in the cards*, in the wind*, nearing, obtainable, oncoming, on tap*, open, pending, predestined, prospective, ready, resulting, upcoming; SEE CONCEPTS *548,799*

forthright [*adj*] *straightforward, honest*
aboveboard, bald, blunt, call a spade a spade*, candid, categorical, direct, directly, forward, frank, from the hip*, like it is*, no lie*, open, outspoken, plain, plain-spoken, real, simple, sincere, straight, undisguised, up front*; SEE CONCEPT *267*

forthwith [*adv*] *immediately*
abruptly, at once, away, directly, instantly, now, quickly, right away*, right now*, straightaway, suddenly, tout de suite, without delay; SEE CONCEPTS *544,820*

fortification [*n*] *reinforced position*
barricade, barrier, bastion, battlement, block, blockhouse, breastwork, buffer, bulwark, castle, citadel, consolidation, defense, earthwork, embattlement, entrenchment, fastness, fort, fortress, garrison, keep, outpost, parapet, preparation, presidio, protection, reinforcement, stockade, strengthening, stronghold, support, wall; SEE CONCEPTS *439,729*

fortify [*v1*] *make strong and secure; add to*
brace, build up, bulwark, buttress, charge up, consolidate, embattle, entrench, garrison, gird, prepare,

prop, protect, punch up*, ready, reinforce, secure, shore up*, soup up*, steel*, step up, strengthen, support; SEE CONCEPT *202*

fortify [v2] *encourage, reassure*
arouse, brace, buck up*, build up, cheer, confirm, embolden, energize, enliven, hearten, invigorate, pour it on*, punch up*, rally, refresh, reinforce, renew, restore, rouse, stiffen, stir, strengthen, sustain; SEE CONCEPTS *7,22*

fortitude [n] *strength of mind; guts*
backbone*, boldness, braveness, bravery, constancy, courage, courageousness, dauntlessness, determination, endurance, fearlessness, firmness, grit*, gutsiness, hardihood, heart, intrepidity, mettle, moxie, nerve, patience, perseverance, pith, pluck, resoluteness, resolution, spine*, spirit, spunk, stamina, starch, staying power, stick-to-itiveness*, stomach, stoutheartedness, strength, tenacity, true grit*, valiancy, valor, valorousness, what it takes*; SEE CONCEPTS *410,411*

fortuitous [adj] *lucky, accidental*
arbitrary, casual, chance, contingent, fluke*, fluky*, fortunate, haphazard, happy, incidental, luck in*, luck out*, lucky-dog*, odd, providential, random, serendipitous, unforeseen, unplanned; SEE CONCEPTS *548,552*

fortunate [adj] *having good luck*
advantageous, affluent, auspicious, blessed, born with silver spoon*, bright, charmed, convenient, encouraging, favorable, favored, felicitous, flourishing, fortuitous, gaining, get a break*, golden, happy, healthy, helpful, hopeful, in luck*, in the gravy*, lucky, on a roll*, opportune, overcoming, profitable, promising, propitious, prosperous, providential, rosy, sitting pretty, successful, sunny side*, thriving, timely, triumphant, victorious, wealthy, well-off, well-to-do; SEE CONCEPTS *404,542,572*

fortunately [adv] *luckily*
auspiciously, by good luck, by happy chance*, favorably, happily, in good time*, in nick of time*, opportunely, prosperously, providentially, satisfyingly, seasonably, successfully, swimmingly, well; SEE CONCEPTS *537,544,572*

fortune [n1] *wealth, possessions*
affluence, capital, estate, gold mine*, inheritance, opulence, portion, property, prosperity, resources, riches, substance, treasure, worth; SEE CONCEPTS *335,710*

fortune [n2] *fate, lot in life*
accident, break*, certainty, chance, circumstances, contingency, destiny, doom, expectation, experience, fifty-fifty*, fighting chance*, fluke*, fortuity, fortunateness, good break, hazard, history, karma*, kismet*, life, luck, lucked into*, lucked out*, luckiness, lucky break*, lucky hit*, Moira, portion, providence, roll of the dice*, run of luck*, star, streak of luck, success, way ball bounces*, way cookie crumbles*, wheel of fortune*; SEE CONCEPT *679*

fortune-teller/fortuneteller [n] *person attempting to tell the future*
augur, clairvoyant, crystal ball gazer, diviner, medium, mind reader, oracle, palmist, palm reader, predicter, prophet, psychic, seer, soothsayer, spiritualist, tarot reader, tea-leaf reader; SEE CONCEPTS *348,423*

forward [adj1] *advancing, early*
advanced, ahead, forth, forward-looking, in advance, leading, onward, precocious, premature, progressing, progressive, propulsive, well-developed; SEE CONCEPT *528*

forward [adj2] *in front, first*
advance, anterior, facial, fore, foremost, front, head, leading, ventral; SEE CONCEPTS *581,583,585*

forward [adj3] *brash, impertinent*
aggressive, assuming, audacious, bantam, barefaced, bold, brazen, cheeky*, coming on strong*, confident, familiar, fresh, impudent, nervy*, overassertive, overweening, pert, presuming, presumptuous, pushing, pushy*, rude, sassy*, saucy*, self-assertive, smart, smart-alecky*, uppity*, wise; SEE CONCEPTS *401,404*

forward [v1] *aid, expedite*
advance, assist, back, champion, cultivate, encourage, favor, foster, further, hasten, help, hurry, promote, serve, speed, support, uphold; SEE CONCEPTS *68,110*

forward [v2] *send, ship*
address, consign, deliver, dispatch, express, freight, post, remit, route, transmit, transport; SEE CONCEPT *217*

forward [adv] *toward the front in order, time*
ahead, alee, along, ante, antecedently, before, beforehand, fore, forth, in advance, into prominence, into view, on, onward, out, precedently, previous, to the fore, vanward; SEE CONCEPTS *581,585,799*

fossil [n] *organic remains of previous time*
deposit, eolith, impression, neolith, paleolith, petrifaction, reconstruction, relic, skeleton, specimen, trace; SEE CONCEPTS *429,470,509*

foster [v1] *promote, support*
advance, back, champion, cherish, cultivate, encourage, feed, foment, forward, further, harbor, nurse, nurture, serve, stimulate, uphold; SEE CONCEPT *110*

foster [v2] *give care, accommodation to*
accommodate, assist, bring up, care for, cherish, entertain, favor, harbor, help, house, lodge, minister to, mother, nourish, nurse, oblige, raise, rear, serve, shelter, sustain, take care of; SEE CONCEPTS *110,140,295*

foul [adj1] *disgusting, dirty*
abhorrent, abominable, base, contaminated, despicable, detestable, disgraceful, dishonorable, egregious, fetid, filthy, gross*, hateful, heinous, horrid, icky*, impure, infamous, iniquitous, loathsome, malodorous, mucky*, nasty, nauseating, nefarious, noisome, notorious, offensive, pigpen*, polluted, putrid, rank*, raunchy*, repellent, repulsive, revolting, rot-

ten, scandalous, shameful, squalid, stinking*, sullied, tainted, unclean, vicious, vile, wicked, yecchy*, yucky*; SEE CONCEPTS *485,529*

foul [*adj2*] *vulgar, offensive*
abusive, blasphemous, blue*, coarse, dirty, filthy, foul-mouthed, gross*, indecent, lewd, low, nasty, obscene, profane, raunchy, scatological, scurrilous, smutty*; SEE CONCEPT *267*

foul [*adj3*] *corrupt, dishonest*
caitiff, crooked, dirty, fraudulent, inequitable, monstrous, shady, underhand, underhanded, unfair, unjust, unscrupulous, unsportsmanlike, vicious; SEE CONCEPTS *537,548*

foul [*v*] *make or become dirty*
befoul, begrime, besmear, besmirch, block, catch, choke, clog, contaminate, defile, desecrate, dirty, discolor, ensnare, entangle, fill, jam, pollute, profane, smear, smudge, snarl, soil, spot, stain, sully, taint, tarnish, twist; SEE CONCEPTS *250,469*

foul up [*v*] *make a mess of*
botch, bungle, confuse, jumble, mismanage, mix up*, muck up*, muddle, screw up*, snafu*, snarl, tumble; SEE CONCEPTS *16,234*

found [*v1*] *bring into being*
begin, commence, constitute, construct, create, endow, erect, establish, fashion, father, fix, form, get going, inaugurate, initiate, institute, launch, organize, originate, plant, raise, ring in*, settle, settle up, start, start ball rolling*, start up; SEE CONCEPT *221*

found [*v2*] *put on a base*
bottom, build, erect, establish, ground, predicate, raise, rear, rest, root, stay, support, sustain; SEE CONCEPTS *168,221*

foundation [*n1*] *basis for something physical or mental*
ABCs*, authority, base, basics, bed, bedrock, bottom, bottom line*, brass tacks*, foot, footing, ground, groundwork, guts*, heart*, infrastructure, justification, nitty-gritty*, nub*, nuts and bolts*, prop, reason, root, stay, substratum, substructure, support, underpinning, understructure; SEE CONCEPTS *442,826*

foundation [*n2*] *established institution*
association, charity, company, corporation, endowment, establishment, guild, inauguration, institute, organization, plantation, settlement, set-up, society, trusteeship; SEE CONCEPT *381*

founder [*n*] *person who establishes institution*
architect, author, beginner, benefactor, builder, constructor, designer, establisher, father, forefather, framer, generator, initiator, institutor, inventor, maker, matriarch, mother, organizer, originator, patriarch, patron, planner, prime mover*, sire; SEE CONCEPTS *347,423*

founder [*v*] *go under, fail*
abort, be lost, break down, collapse, come to nothing, fall, fall through, go down, go lame, go to bottom, go under, lurch, miscarry, misfire, sink, sprawl,

stagger, stumble, submerge, submerse, trip; SEE CONCEPTS *181,699*

fountain [*n*] *source, often of liquid*
bubbler, cause, font, fount, geyser, gush, inception, inspiration, jet, lode, mainspring, mine, origin, play, provenance, provenience, pump, reservoir, root, spout, spray, spring, stream, well, wellhead, wellspring; SEE CONCEPTS *514,648*

foxy [*adj*] *shrewd*
artful, astute, canny, crafty, cunning, deceitful, deep, devious, dishonest, experienced, guileful, insidious, intelligent, knowing, retiary, sharp, slick, sly, subtle, tricky, vulpine, wily; SEE CONCEPTS *401,404*

foyer [*n*] *receiving area*
antechamber, anteroom, entrance, entrance hall, hall, lobby, reception, vestibule; SEE CONCEPTS *440, 441,448*

fracas [*n*] *disturbance, fight*
affray, altercation, battle, battle royal*, bickering, brawl, broil*, brouhaha*, dispute, donnybrook*, feud, flap*, fray, free-for-all*, hassle, knock-down-drag-out*, melee, mix up*, quarrel, riot, row, ruction, ruffle, rumpus, run-in*, scrimmage, scuffle, set-to*, squabble, stew*, trouble, tumult, uproar, words*; SEE CONCEPTS *46,106*

fraction [*n1*] *part*
bite, chunk, cut, division, end, fragment, half, piece, portion, section, share, slice; SEE CONCEPT *835*

fraction [*n2*] *incomplete number*
bit, division, fragment, part, partial, piece, portion, quotient, ratio, section, segment, slice, subdivision; SEE CONCEPT *765*

fractional [*adj*] *partial*
apportioned, compartmental, compartmented, constituent, dismembered, dispersed, divided, fragmentary, frationary, incomplete, parceled, part, piecemeal, sectional, segmented; SEE CONCEPT *785*

fractious [*adj*] *grouchy, cross*
awkward, captious, crabby*, disorderly, fretful, froward, huffy*, indocile, indomitable, intractable, irritable, mean, ornery*, peevish, perverse, pettish, petulant, querulous, recalcitrant, refractory, restive, scrappy, snappish, testy, thin-skinned, touchy, uncompliant, undisciplined, unmanageable, unruly, wayward, wild; SEE CONCEPTS *267,401*

fracture [*n*] *break, rupture*
breach, cleavage, cleft, crack, discontinuity, disjunction, displacement, fissure, fragmentation, gap, mutilation, opening, rent, rift, schism, severance, splinter, split, wound; SEE CONCEPTS *309,513*

fragile [*adj*] *breakable, dainty*
brittle, crisp, crumbly, decrepit, delicate, feeble, fine, flimsy, fracturable, frail, frangible, friable, infirm, insubstantial, shatterable, shivery, slight, unsound, weak, weakly; SEE CONCEPTS *485,489*

fragment [*n*] *part, chip*
ace, atom, bit, bite, chunk, crumb, cut, end, fraction, gob*, grain, hunk, iota, job*, lump*, minim,

morsel, particle, piece, portion, remnant, scrap, share, shiver, shred, slice, sliver, smithereen*; SEE CONCEPT *835*

fragment [v] *break into pieces*
break, break up, burst, come apart, crumble, disintegrate, disunite, divide, rend, rive, shatter, shiver, smash, splinter, split, split up; SEE CONCEPTS *98,135,137,246,469*

fragmentary [adj] *broken, incomplete*
bitty, disconnected, discrete, disjointed, fractional, incoherent, part, partial, piecemeal, scattered, scrappy, sketchy, unsystematic; SEE CONCEPT *785*

fragrance [n] *pleasant odor*
aroma, aura, balm, bouquet, fragrancy, incense, perfume, redolence, scent, smell, spice; SEE CONCEPT *600*

fragrant [adj] *smelling pleasant*
ambrosial, aromal, aromatic, balmy, delectable, delicious, delightful, odoriferous, odorous, perfumed, perfumy, redolent, savory, spicy, sweet, sweet-scented, sweet-smelling; SEE CONCEPT *598*

frail [adj] *breakable, weak*
brittle, dainty, decrepit, delicate, feeble, fishy, flimsy, fracturable, fragile, frangible, infirm, insubstantial, puny, sad, shatterable, shattery, sickly, slender, slight, slim, tender, tenuous, thin, unsound, unsubstantial, vulnerable, weakly, wimpy*, wishy-washy*, wispy; SEE CONCEPTS *485,489*

frailty [n] *weakness, flaw*
Achilles heel*, blemish, daintiness, debility, decrepitude, defect, deficiency, delicacy, error, failing, fallibility, fault, feebleness, flimsiness, foible, foil, frailness, imperfection, infirmity, peccability, peccadillo, shortcoming, solecism, suscept, weak point*; SEE CONCEPTS *101,230,411,580*

frame [n] *skeleton, casing*
anatomy, architecture, body, build, cage, carcass, construction, enclosure, fabric, flounce, form, framework, fringe, groundwork, hem, mount, mounting, outline, physique, scaffold, scaffolding, scheme, setting, shell, stage, structure, support, system, trim, trimming, truss, valance; SEE CONCEPTS *442,733,757*

frame [v1] *build*
assemble, back, border, constitute, construct, encase, enclose, erect, fabricate, fashion, forge, form, institute, invent, lath, make, manufacture, mat, model, mold, mount, panel, produce, put together, raise, set up, shingle; SEE CONCEPTS *168,758*

frame [v2] *compose, plan*
block out, conceive, concoct, contrive, cook up, design, devise, draft, draw up, dream up*, form, formulate, hatch, indite, invent, make, make up, map out, outline, prepare, shape, sketch, vamp, write; SEE CONCEPTS *36,173*

framework [n] *foundation, core*
bare bones*, cage, fabric, frame, frame of reference*, groundwork, plan, schema, scheme, shell, skeleton, structure; SEE CONCEPTS *439,479,733*

franchise [n] *authority, right*
authorization, ballot, charter, exemption, freedom, immunity, patent, prerogative, privilege, suffrage, vote; SEE CONCEPT *376*

frank [adj] *completely honest*
aboveboard, apparent, artless, bare-faced*, blunt, bold, brazen, call spade a spade*, candid, direct, downright, easy, familiar, flat-out*, forthright, free, from the hip*, guileless, heart-to-heart*, ingenuous, lay it on the line*, like it is*, matter-of-fact, naive, natural, open, outright, outspoken, plain, plain-spoken, real, saying what one thinks*, scrupulous, sincere, straight, straightforward, transparent, truthful, unconcealed, undisguised, uninhibited, unreserved, unrestricted, up front*, upright; SEE CONCEPTS *267,582*

frankfurter [n] *cylindrical meat sausage*
bowwow*, Coney Island*, dog*, footlong*, frank, hot dog, link, sausage, weenie*, wiener, wiener-wurst; SEE CONCEPTS *457,460*

frankly [adv] *very honestly*
bluntly, candidly, dead level*, dead on*, directly, forthrightly, freely, from the hip*, in truth, laid on the line*, level, on the level*, on the line*, openly, plainly, straight, straightforwardly, to be honest, without reserve; SEE CONCEPT *267*

frantic [adj] *distressed, distracted*
agitated, angry, at wits' end*, berserk, beside oneself*, corybantic, crazy, delirious, deranged, distraught, excited, flipped out*, fraught, freaked out*, frenetic, frenzied, furious, hectic, hot and bothered*, hot under the collar*, hyper*, in a stew*, in a tizzy*, insane, keyed up*, mad, out of control, overwrought, rabid, raging, raving, shook up*, spazzed out*, unglued*, unscrewed*, unzipped*, violent, weird, weirded out*, wigged out*, wild, wired*, worked up*, zonkers*; SEE CONCEPTS *403,542*

fraternal [adj] *brotherly*
congenial, friendly, intimate, kind, sympathetic; SEE CONCEPT *401*

fraternity [n] *brotherhood; interest group; male collegiate group*
association, camaraderie, circle, clan, club, companionship, company, comradeship, fellowship, frat*, Greeks*, guild, house, kinship, league, letter society, order, organization, set, society, sodality, union; SEE CONCEPTS *387,439*

fraternize [v] *socialize with*
associate, break the ice*, chum with*, concur, consort, cooperate, get with, go around with, hang out, hobnob*, join, keep company*, league, loosen up, make the rounds*, mingle, mix, open up, pal around*, run with*, unite; SEE CONCEPT *384*

fraud [n1] *trickery, deception*
artifice, bamboozlement*, blackmail, cheat, chicane, chicanery, con, craft*, deceit, double-dealing*, dupery, duping, duplicity, extortion, fake, fast one*, fast shuffle*, flimflam*, fourberie, fraudulence, graft,

guile, hanky-panky*, hoax, hocus-pocus*, hood-winking*, hustle*, imposture, line, misrepresenta-tion, racket, scam, sell, shakedown*, sham*, sharp practice*, skunk*, smoke*, song*, song and dance*, spuriousness, sting, string, swindle, swindling, treachery, trickery; SEE CONCEPTS *59,192,645*

fraud [*n2*] *person who is false, deceitful*
bastard, bluffer, charlatan, cheat, con man, counter-feit, crook, deceiver, double-dealer*, fake, forger, four-flusher*, gyp*, hoaxer, horse trader*, impostor, mechanic*, mountebank, phony, play actor*, pre-tender, quack*, racketeer, sham*, shark*, swindler; SEE CONCEPT *412*

fraudulent [*adj*] *deceptive, false*
bamboozling*, counterfeit, crafty, criminal, crooked, deceitful, devious, dishonest, dishonorable, double-dealing*, duplicitous, fake, forged, knavish, mock, phony, pseudo, sham*, spurious, swindling, treacherous, tricky; SEE CONCEPTS *545,582*

fraught [*adj*] *full of*
abounding, attended, bristling, charged, filled, heavy, laden, replete, stuffed; SEE CONCEPTS *483,771*

fray [*n*] *fight, battle*
affray, battle royal*, brawl, broil*, brouhaha*, clash, combat, conflict, contest, disturbance, donnybrook*, engagement, fracas, melee, quarrel, riot, row, ruckus, rumble, rumpus, scuffle, set-to*; SEE CON-CEPTS *86,106*

fray [*v*] *shred, come apart*
become ragged, become threadbare, chafe, erode, frazzle, fret, ravel, rip, rub, tatter, tear, unravel, wear, wear away, wear thin; SEE CONCEPT *214*

frazzle [*n*] *exhaustion; something very worn*
collapse, enervation, lassitude, prostration, rag, rem-nant, shred; SEE CONCEPTS *410,720*

frazzle [*v*] *wear out*
exhaust, fray, knock out, poop*, prostrate, rip, shred, tear, tire, tucker*, wear; SEE CONCEPTS *156,186*

freak [*n1*] *something, someone very abnormal*
aberration, abnormality, abortion, anomaly, chi-mera, curiosity, geek*, grotesque, malformation, miscreation, misshape, monster, monstrosity, mu-tant, mutation, oddity, queer, rarity, sport, weirdo*; SEE CONCEPTS *424,580*

freak [*n2*] *irregularity, whim*
caprice, conceit, crochet, fad, fancy, folly, humor, megrim, quirk, turn, twist, vagary, whimsy; SEE CONCEPT *679*

freak [*n3*] *person enthused about something*
addict, aficionado, buff, bug*, devotee, enthusiast, fan, fanatic, fiend*, maniac, nut*, zealot; SEE CON-CEPTS *352,366,423*

freak [*v*] *become extraordinarily upset*
flip out*, go beserk, go insane, go mad, lose control, rave, unhinge*, wig out*; SEE CONCEPTS *7,19,80*

freakish [*adj*] *abnormal, unusual*
aberrant, arbitrary, bizarre, capricious, crazy, erratic, fantastic, far-out, freaky, grotesque, malformed,
monstrous, odd, outlandish, outré, preternatural, queer, strange, unconventional, vagarious, wayward, weird, whimsical, wild; SEE CONCEPT *564*

freckle [*n*] *small discoloration on skin*
blemish, blotch, daisy, dot, lentigo, macula, mole, patch, pepper, pigmentation, pit, pock, pockmark, speck, speckle, sprinkle, stipple; SEE CONCEPT *392*

free [*adj1*] *without charge*
chargeless, comp*, complimentary, costless, for love*, for nothing*, freebie*, free of cost, free ride*, gratis, gratuitous, handout, on the cuff*, on the house*, paper*, unpaid, unrecompensed; SEE CON-CEPT *334*

free [*adj2*] *unrestrained personally*
able, allowed, at large, at liberty, casual, clear, dis-engaged, easy, escaped, familiar, fancy-free*, foot-loose*, forward, frank, free-spirited, free-wheeling, independent, informal, lax, liberal, liberated, loose, off the hook*, on one's own*, on the loose*, open, permitted, relaxed, unattached, uncommitted, un-confined, unconstrained, unengaged, unfettered, un-hampered, unimpeded, unobstructed, unregulated, unrestricted, untrammeled; SEE CONCEPTS *401,542*

free [*adj3*] *unrestrained politically*
at liberty, autarchic, autonomic, autonomous, dem-ocratic, emancipated, enfranchised, freed, indepen-dent, individualistic, liberated, self-directing, self-governing, self-ruling, separate, sovereign, sui juris, unconstrained, unenslaved, unregimented; SEE CON-CEPTS *319,536*

free [*adj4*] *not busy; unoccupied*
at leisure, available, clear, empty, extra, idle, loose, not tied down*, spare, unemployed, unengaged, un-hampered, unimpeded, uninhabited, unobstructed, unoccupied, unused, vacant; SEE CONCEPT *485*

free [*adj5*] *generous, unsparing*
big, big-hearted*, bounteous, bountiful, charitable, eager, handsome, hospitable, lavish, liberal, munif-icent, open-handed*, prodigal, unstinging, willing; SEE CONCEPT *404*

free [*v1*] *liberate, let go*
absolve, acquit, bail, bail out*, clear, cut loose*, deliver, demobilize, discharge, disengage, dis-enthrall, disimprison, dismiss, emancipate, enfran-chise, extricate, let loose*, let off*, let off the hook*, let out, loose, loosen, manumit, pardon, parole, put on the street*, ransom, redeem, release, relieve, re-prieve, rescue, save, set free, spring*, turn loose, turn out, unbind, uncage, unchain, undo, unfetter, unfix, unleash, untie; SEE CONCEPT *127*

free [*v2*] *take burden from*
cast off, clear, cut loose, decontaminate, deliver, dis-charge, disembarrass, disencumber, disengage, dis-entangle, empty, excuse, exempt, extricate, put off, ransom, redeem, relieve, rescue, rid, unburden, undo, unlade, unload, unpack, unshackle; SEE CON-CEPTS *110,211*

freedom [n1] *independence, license to do as one wants*
abandon, abandonment, ability, bent, carte blanche, compass, discretion, elbowroom*, exemption, facility, flexibility, free rein*, full play*, full swing*, immunity, indulgence, laissez faire, latitude, laxity, leeway, liberty, licentiousness, margin, opportunity, own accord*, play, plenty of rope*, power, prerogative, privilege, profligacy, rampancy, range, rein, right, rope*, scope, sweep, swing, unrestraint; SEE CONCEPT *693*

freedom [n2] *political independence*
abolition, abolitionism, autarchy, autonomy, citizenship, deliverance, delivery, democracy, discharge, disengagement, disimprisonment, emancipation, enfranchisement, exemption, extriction, franchise, home rule*, immunity, impunity, liberation, liberty, manumission, parole, prerogative, privilege, probation, redemption, release, relief, representative government, rescue, salvage, salvation, self-determination, self-government, sovereignty; SEE CONCEPT *691*

freedom [n3] *easy attitude*
abandon, boldness, brazenness, candor, directness, disrespect, ease, facility, familiarity, forthrightness, forwardness, frankness, impertinence, informality, ingenuousness, lack of reserve, lack of restraint, laxity, license, openness, overfamiliarity, presumption, readiness, spontaneity, unconstraint; SEE CONCEPT *633*

free-for-all [n] *fight*
affray, battle, brawl, broil*, brouhaha*, fracas, fray, knock-down-drag-out*, melee, riot, row, ruction; SEE CONCEPT *106*

freely [adj1] *without restriction*
advisedly, as you please*, at discretion, at pleasure, at will, candidly, deliberately, designedly, fancy-free*, frankly, intentionally, of one's own accord*, of one's own free will*, openly, plainly, purposely, spontaneously, unchallenged, unreservedly, voluntarily, willingly, without hindrance, without prompting, without reserve, without restraint, without urging; SEE CONCEPT *401*

freely [adv2] *easily, smoothly done*
abundantly, amply, as one pleases*, bountifully, cleanly, copiously, effortlessly, extravagantly, facilely, lavishly, liberally, lightly, like water*, loosely, open-handedly, readily, unhindered, unobstructedly, unstintingly, well, with a free hand*, without encumbrance*, without hindrance*, without restraint*, without stint*; SEE CONCEPT *544*

free will [n] *person's full intent and purpose*
assent, choice, consent, desire, determination, discretion, free choice, freedom, inclination, intent, intention, mind, option, own say so*, own sweet way*, pleasure, power, purpose, say so*, velleity, volition, voluntary decision, willingness, wish; SEE CONCEPTS *20,410*

freeze [v1] *make cold enough to become solid*
benumb, bite, chill, chill to bone*, congeal, frost, glaciate, harden, ice over, ice up, nip, pierce, refrigerate, solidify, stiffen; SEE CONCEPTS *255,521*

freeze [v2] *stop*
dampen, depress, discourage, dishearten, fix, hold up, inhibit, peg, suspend; SEE CONCEPTS *14,121*

freezing [adj] *very cold*
arctic, biting, bitter, chill, chilled, chilly, cold, cutting, frigid, frost-bound, frosty, gelid, glacial, hawkish, icy, nippy, numbing, one-dog night*, penetrating, polar, raw, shivery, Siberian*, snappy*, two-dog night*, wintry; SEE CONCEPT *605*

freight [n] *goods being shipped*
bales, ballast, bulk, burden, carriage, consignment, contents, conveyance, encumbrance, fardel, haul, lading, load, merchandise, pack, packages, payload, shipment, shipping, tonnage, transportation, wares, weight; SEE CONCEPT *338*

frenetic [adj] *maniacal*
corybantic, delirious, demented, distraught, excited, fanatical, frantic, frenzied, furibund, furious, hyper*, in a lather*, insane, lost it*, mad, obsessive, overwrought, phrenetic, rabid, unbalanced, unscrewed*, weirded out*, wigged out*, wild, wired*; SEE CONCEPT *403*

frenzied [adj] *uncontrolled*
agitated, berserk, convulsive, corybantic, delirious, distracted, distraught, excited, feverish, frantic, frenetic, furious, hysterical, mad, maniacal, nuts*, rabid, wild; SEE CONCEPTS *542,544*

frenzy [n] *uncontrolled state or situation*
aberration, agitation, blow, blow a fuse*, blow one's cork*, blow one's stack*, blow one's top*, bout, burst, conniption*, convulsion, craze, delirium, derangement, distemper, distraction, dithers*, excitement, ferment, fever, fit, flap*, flip one's lid*, free-for-all*, furor, fury, fuss, hell broke loose*, hysteria, insanity, lather, lunacy, madness, mania, outburst, paroxysm, passion, rage, row, ruckus, ruction, rumble, rumpus, seizure, spasm, stew, stir, to-do*, transport, turmoil, wingding*; SEE CONCEPTS *230,410,674*

frequency [n] *commonness, repetitiveness*
abundance, beat, constancy, density, frequentness, iteration, number, oscillation, periodicity, persistence, prevalence, pulsation, recurrence, regularity, reiteration, repetition, rhythm; SEE CONCEPT *634*

frequent [adj] *common, repeated*
a good many*, commonplace, constant, continual, customary, everyday, expected, familiar, general, habitual, incessant, intermittent, iterated, manifold, many, monotonous, numberless, numerous, periodic, perpetual, persistent, pleonastic, profuse, recurrent, recurring, redundant, reiterated, reiterative, successive, thick, ubiquitous, usual, various; SEE CONCEPT *530*

frequent [v] *be a regular customer of*
affect, attend, attend regularly, be at home in*, be found at, be often in, drop in, go to, hang about*,

hang around*, hang out at*, haunt*, hit*, infest, overrun, patronize, play*, resort, revisit, visit, visit often; SEE CONCEPTS *227,384*

frequently [*adv*] *commonly, repeatedly*
again and again*, as a rule*, at regular intervals, at short intervals, at times, by ordinary, customarily, every now and then*, generally, habitually, in many instances*, in quick succession, intermittently, many a time*, many times, much, not infrequently, not seldom, oft, often, often enough, oftentimes, oft-times, ordinarily, over and over, periodically, recurrently, regularly, spasmodically, successively, thick and fast*, time and again*, usually, very often; SEE CONCEPTS *530,544,799*

fresh [*adj1*] *new, just produced*
beginning, brand-new*, comer, contemporary, crisp, crude, current, different, gleaming, glistening, green*, hot*, hot off the press*, immature, just out*, late, latest, mint*, modern, modernistic, natural, neoteric, newborn, newfangled*, novel, now, original, radical, raw, recent, sparkling, state-of-the-art, the latest*, this season's*, unconventional, unprocessed, unseasoned, untouched, unusual, up-to-date, virginal, what's happening*, young, youthful; SEE CONCEPTS *578,797*

fresh [*adj2*] *additional*
added, another, auxiliary, else, extra, farther, further, increased, more, new, other, renewed, supplementary; SEE CONCEPTS *546,824*

fresh [*adj3*] *refreshing to the senses*
bracing, bright, brisk, clean, clear, colorful, cool, crisp, definite, fair, invigorating, not stale, pure, quick, sharp, spanking, sparkling, stiff, stimulating, sweet, uncontaminated, unpolluted, vivid; SEE CONCEPT *537*

fresh [*adj4*] *energetic, healthy*
active, alert, blooming, bouncing, bright, bright-eyed, bushy-tailed*, chipper*, clear, dewy, fair, florid, freshened, glowing, good, hardy, invigorated, keen, like new, lively, refreshed, rehabilitated, relaxed, relieved, rested, restored, revived, rosy, ruddy, sprightly, spry, stimulated, undimmed, unfaded, unused, unwearied, unwithered, verdant, vigorous, vital, wholesome, young; SEE CONCEPTS *485,542*

fresh [*adj5*] *inexperienced*
artless, callow, green*, natural, new, raw, tenderfooted*, uncultivated, unpracticed, unskilled, untrained, untried, unversed, young, youthful; SEE CONCEPT *404*

fresh [*adj6*] *sassy, brazen*
bold, cheeky*, disrespectful, familiar, flip*, flippant, forward, impertinent, impudent, insolent, nervy*, pert, presumptuous, rude, saucy*, smart*, smart-alecky*, snippy*, wise; SEE CONCEPTS *267,401*

freshen [*v*] *make like new; revitalize*
activate, air, cleanse, enliven, invigorate, purify, refresh, restore, revive, rouse, spruce up, sweeten, titivate, ventilate; SEE CONCEPT *244*

freshman/woman [*n*] *novice at activity*
apprentice, beginner, crab*, dog*, first-year student, fish*, fox*, freshie*, frog*, frosh*, greenhorn*, green pea*, learner, lowerclassman/woman, neophyte, newcomer, novitiate, plebe, probationer, recruit, rookie, tenderfoot*, yearling*; SEE CONCEPTS *286,350,423*

freshness [*n*] *newness*
bloom, brightness, callowness, cleanness, clearness, dew, dewiness, glow, greenness, inexperience, innovativeness, inventiveness, novelty, originality, rawness, shine, sparkle, vigor, viridity, youth; SEE CONCEPT *715*

fret [*v1*] *worry, be annoyed*
affront, agonize, anguish, bleed, bother, brood, carp, carry heavy load*, chafe, chagrin, distress oneself, eat one's heart out*, fume, fuss, get into a dither*, grieve, lose sleep over*, mope*, pother*, stew, sweat it out*, take on, torment, upset oneself; SEE CONCEPT *410*

fret [*v2*] *upset someone*
abrade, agitate, bother, displease, distress, disturb, gall, get on nerves*, goad, harass, irk, irritate, nag, nettle, peeve, pique, provoke, rile, ruffle, torment, trouble, vex; SEE CONCEPTS *7,19*

fret [*v3*] *rub hard*
abrade, chafe, corrode, erode, excoriate, fray, gall, riffle, ripple, wear, wear away, wear threadbare; SEE CONCEPT *215*

fretful [*adj*] *irritable*
captious, carping*, caviling, complaining, contrary, crabby*, cranky*, critical, cross, crotchety*, edgy, faultfinding, fractious, huffy*, mean, ornery*, out of sorts*, peevish, perverse, petulant, querulous, short-tempered, snappish*, splenetic, testy, touchy, uneasy, worried, wreck*; SEE CONCEPTS *401,403*

friction [*n1*] *rubbing*
abrasion, agitation, attrition, chafing, erosion, filing, fretting, grating, grinding, irritation, massage, rasping, resistance, scraping, soreness, traction, trituration, wearing away; SEE CONCEPT *215*

friction [*n2*] *disagreement*
animosity, antagonism, bad blood*, bad feeling*, bickering, bone to pick*, conflict, counteraction, discontent, discord, disharmony, dispute, dissension, faction, factionalism, flak*, hassle, hatred, hostility, impedance, incompatibility, interference, opposition, quarrel, resentment, resistance, rivalry, row*, ruckus*, rumpus*, set-to*, sour note*, strife, trouble, wrangling*; SEE CONCEPTS *46,106,674*

friend [*n1*] *confidant, companion*
acquaintance, ally, alter ego, amigo/amiga, associate, bedfellow, bosom buddy*, brother*, buddy, chum*, classmate, cohort, colleague, companion*, compatriot, comrade, confrere, consort, cousin, crony, familiar, fellow, intimate, little brother*, little sister*, main man/woman*, main squeeze*, mate, other self*, pal, partner, playmate, roommate,

schoolmate, sidekick, sister*, soul mate*, spare*, well-wisher; SEE CONCEPT *423*

friend [*n2*] *benefactor*
accomplice, adherent, advocate, ally, associate, backer, partisan, patron, supporter, well-wisher; SEE CONCEPT *348*

friendless [*adj*] *without companionship or confidant*
abandoned, adrift, alienated, all alone*, all by one's self*, alone, cut off*, deserted, estranged, forlorn, forsaken, isolated, lonely, lonesome, marooned*, ostracized, shunned, solitary, unattached, without ties; SEE CONCEPT *555*

friendliness [*n*] *companionability*
affability, amiability, amity, benevolence, camaraderie, comity, comradery, congeniality, conviviality, cordiality, friendship, geniality, goodwill, kindliness, kindness, neighborliness, open arms*, sociability, warmth; SEE CONCEPT *388*

friendly [*adj*] *intimate, companionable*
affable, affectionate, amiable, amicable, attached, attentive, auspicious, beneficial, benevolent, benign, buddy-buddy*, chummy*, civil, close, clubby, comradely, conciliatory, confiding, convivial, cordial, faithful, familiar, favorable, fond, fraternal, genial, good, helpful, intimate, kind, kindly, loving, loyal, neighborly, on good terms*, outgoing, peaceable, peaceful, propitious, receptive, sociable, solicitous, sympathetic, tender, thick, welcoming, well-disposed*; SEE CONCEPT *555*

friendship [*n*] *companionship*
accord, acquaintanceship, affection, affinity, agreement, alliance, amiability, amicability, amity, association, attachment, attraction, benevolence, brotherhood, brotherly love, closeness, coalition, comity, company, concord, consideration, consonance, devotion, empathy, esteem, familiarity, favor, favoritism, fellow feeling, fondness, friendliness, fusion, good will, harmony, intimacy, league, love, pact, partiality, rapport, regard, sociability, society, sodality, solidarity, understanding; SEE CONCEPTS *388,714*

fright [*n1*] *extreme apprehension*
alarm, cold sweat*, consternation, dismay, dread, fear, horror, panic, quaking, scare, shiver, shock, terror, trepidation, trepidity; SEE CONCEPT *410*

fright [*n2*] *horrifying or unpleasant sight*
bother, eyesore*, frump*, mess, monstrosity, nuisance, scarecrow, sight, ugliness; SEE CONCEPT *718*

frighten [*v*] *shock, scare*
affright, agitate, alarm, appall, astound, awe, browbeat*, bulldoze*, chill, chill to the bone*, cow, curdle the blood*, daunt, demoralize, deter, disturb, discomfort, disconcert, discourage, dishearten, dismay, disquiet, faze, horrify, intimidate, make blood run cold*, make teeth chatter*, panic, perturb, petrify, repel, scare away, scare off, scare stiff, scare to death*, spook, startle, strike terror into*, terrify, terrorize, unhinge*, unman, unnerve; SEE CONCEPTS *14,42*

frightened [*adj*] *very scared*
abashed, affrighted, afraid, aghast, alarmed, anxious, butterflies*, chicken*, chicken-hearted*, cowed*, dismayed, fearful, frozen, have cold feet*, having kittens*, hung up*, in a panic*, in a sweat*, in cold sweat*, jellyfish*, jittery, jumpy, lily-livered*, mousy*, numb, panicky, petrified, pushing the panic button*, rabbity*, running scared*, scared, scared stiff*, shaky, shivery, sissy*, spooked, startled, terrified, terrorized, terror-stricken, unnerved, uptight, yellow*; SEE CONCEPTS *403,690*

frightful/frightening [*adj1*] *scary, shocking*
alarming, appalling, atrocious, awesome, awful, chilling, daunting, dire, direful, dismaying, disquieting, dread, dreadful, fearful, fearsome, formidable, ghastly, grabber, grim, grisly, gruesome, hair-raising, hairy, harrowing, hideous, horrendous, horrible, horrid, horrifying, inconceivable, intimidating, lurid, macabre, menacing, morbid, ominous, petrifying, portentous, repellent, spooky, terrible, terrifying, traumatic, unnerving, unspeakable; SEE CONCEPTS *529,537*

frightful [*adj2*] *offensive*
annoying, awful, bad, calamitous, disagreeable, dreadful, extreme, ghastly, great, hideous, horrible, insufferable, lewd, shocking, terrible, terrific, unpleasant, vile, wicked, wrong; SEE CONCEPTS *529,545*

frigid [*adj1*] *extremely cold*
antarctic, arctic, chill, chilly, cool, freezing, frostbound, frosty, frozen, gelid, glacial, hyperboreal, icebox*, ice-cold, icy, refrigerated, Siberian*, snappy, three-dog night*, wintry; SEE CONCEPT *605*

frigid [*adj2*] *unresponsive*
aloof, austere, chilly, cold, cold-hearted*, cold-shoulder*, cool, forbidding, formal, frosty, icy, impotent, indifferent, lifeless, passionless, passive, repellent, rigid, stiff, unapproachable, unbending, undersexed, unfeeling, unloving; SEE CONCEPT *404*

frill [*n*] *luxury, nice touch*
amenity, decoration, doodad*, extravagance, fandangle, flounce, foppery*, frippery*, fuss, garbage*, garnish, gathering, gimcrack*, gingerbread*, jazz*, lace, ruffle, superfluity, thing*, tuck; SEE CONCEPTS *646,655,824*

fringe [*n*] *border, trimming*
binding, borderline, brim, brink, edge, edging, flounce, hem, limit, mane, march, margin, outside, outskirts, perimeter, periphery, rickrack, ruffle, skirt, tassel, verge; SEE CONCEPTS *484,825*

frippery [*n*] *waste, nonsense*
adornment, bauble, decoration, fanciness, fandangle*, flashiness, frill, fussiness, gaudiness, knick-knack, meretriciousness, ornament, ostentation, pretentiousness, showiness, tawdriness, toy, trinket; SEE CONCEPTS *655,824*

frisk [*v1*] *cavort*
bounce, caper, dance, frolic, gambol, hop, jump, lark, leap, play, prance, rollick, romp, skip, sport, trip; SEE CONCEPT *384*

frisk [*v2*] *search*
check, fan, inspect, run over, shake down; SEE CON-
CEPT *216*

frisky [*adj*] *full of spirit*
active, antic, bouncy, coltish*, dashing, feeling
one's oats*, frolicsome, full of beans*, gamesome,
high-spirited, in high spirits*, jumpy, kittenish*,
larkish, lively, peppy, playful, prankish, rollicking,
romping, spirited, sportive, wicked, zesty, zippy; SEE
CONCEPTS *401,542,555*

fritter [*v*] *waste away*
be wasteful with, blow*, cast away, consume, dally,
diddle away, dissipate, frivol, go through*, idle, lavish, misspend, run through*, spend like water*,
squander, throw away, trifle, waste; SEE CONCEPTS
156,341

frivolity [*n*] *silliness, childishness*
coquetting, dallying, flightiness, flippancy, flirting,
flummery, folly, fribble, frippery, frivolousness, fun,
gaiety, game, giddiness, jest, levity, lightearted-
ness, lightness, nonsense, play, puerility, shallowness, sport, superficiality, toying, trifling, triviality,
volatility, whimsicality, whimsy; SEE CONCEPTS
388,633

frivolous [*adj*] *trivial, silly*
barmy*, childish, ditzy*, dizzy*, empty-headed*, facetious, featherbrained*, flighty, flip, flippant, foolish, gay, giddy*, harebrained*, idiotic, idle, ill-
considered, impractical, juvenile, light, light-
minded, minor, niggling*, nonserious, not serious,
paltry, peripheral, petty, playful, pointless, puerile,
scatterbrained*, senseless, shallow, silly, sportive,
superficial, tongue-in-cheek*, trivial, unimportant,
unprofound, volatile, whimsical; SEE CONCEPTS
401,402,575

frock [*n*] *women's garment*
apron, clothing, dress, gown, habit, muumuu, robe;
SEE CONCEPT *451*

frog [*n*] *jumping amphibian*
bullfrog, croaker*, Dutch nightingale*, polliwog,
toad; SEE CONCEPT *394*

frolic [*n*] *amusement, revel*
antic, drollery, escapade, fun, fun and games*, gaiety, gambol, game, high jinks*, joke, joviality, lark,
merriment, monkeyshines*, play, prank, romp, shenanigan*, skylarking*, sport, spree, tomfoolery*,
trick; SEE CONCEPTS *59,386*

frolic [*v*] *have fun, make merry*
caper, carouse, cavort, cut capers, cut loose*, fool
around*, frisk, gambol, go on a tear*, kick up one's
heels*, lark, let go*, let loose*, play, prance, raise
hell*, revel, riot, rollick, romp, sport, spree, whoop
it up*; SEE CONCEPTS *384,386*

frolicsome [*adj*] *playful*
antic, coltish, frisky, fun, gamesome, gay, gleeful,
happy, impish, jocular, jovial, kittenish, lively,
merry, mischievous, roguish, rollicking, sportive,
sprightly; SEE CONCEPT *542*

from [*prep1*] *outside of, separating*
against, in distinction to, out of possession of, taken
away; SEE CONCEPT *583*

from [*prep2*] *arising out of*
beginning at, coming out of, deriving out of, originating at, out of, starting with; SEE CONCEPT *549*

front [*n1*] *forward, beginning part of something*
anterior, beginning, bow, breast, brow, exterior, facade, face, facing, fore, foreground, forehead,
forepart, frontage, frontal, frontispiece, front line,
head, lead, obverse, proscenium, top, van, vanguard;
SEE CONCEPTS *833,835,836*

front [*n2*] *appearance put on for show*
air, aspect, bearing, blind, carriage, coloring, countenance, cover, cover-up*, demeanor, disguise, display, expression, exterior, facade, face, fake, figure,
manner, mask, mien, phony, port, presence, pretext,
put-on*, show, veil, window dressing*; SEE CON-
CEPT *716*

front [*adj*] *lead, beginning*
advanced, ahead, anterior, facial, first, fore, foremost, forward, frontal, head, headmost, in the foreground, leading, obverse, topmost, vanward, ventral;
SEE CONCEPTS *567,583,585,632*

front [*v*] *look out on to*
border, confront, cover, encounter, face, look over,
meet, overlay, overlook; SEE CONCEPT *746*

frontier [*n1*] *boundary*
borderland, borderline, bound, confines, edge, limit,
march, perimeter, verge; SEE CONCEPTS *513,745*

frontier [*n2*] *unexplored, unoccupied area of land*
backcountry, backwater, backwoods, boondocks*,
boonies*, bush, hinterland, outback, outskirts,
sticks*, unknown*; SEE CONCEPT *509*

frost [*n*] *extreme cold*
blight, dip, drop, freeze, hoarfrost, ice, Jack Frost*,
rime; SEE CONCEPTS *524,610*

frosty [*adj*] *very cold*
antarctic, arctic, chill, chilly, cool, frigid, frozen,
gelid, glacial, hoar, ice-capped, icicled, icy, nippy*,
rimy, shivery, wintry; SEE CONCEPT *605*

froth [*n*] *lather, bubbles*
barm, ebullition, effervescence, fizz, foam, head,
scud, scum, spindrift, spray, spume, suds, yeast; SEE
CONCEPTS *260,467,468*

frothy [*adj*] *bubbly*
barmy, bubbling, fermenting, fizzing, fizzy, foaming, foamy, soapy, spumescent, spumous, spumy,
sudsy, with a head on*, yeasty; SEE CONCEPT *485*

frown [*v1*] *scowl*
cloud up*, do a slow burn*, give dirty look*, give
the evil eye*, glare, gloom, glower, grimace, knit
brows*, look black*, look daggers*, look stern*,
lower, pout, sulk; SEE CONCEPT *185*

frown [*v2*] *disapprove*
deprecate, discommend, discountenance, discourage, disesteem, disfavor, dislike, look askance at*,

not take kindly to*, object, show displeasure, take a dim view of*; SEE CONCEPTS *21,29*

frozen [*adj1*] *very cold*
antarctic, arctic, chilled, frigid, frosted, icebound, ice-cold, ice-covered, iced, icy, numb, Siberian*; SEE CONCEPT *605*

frozen [*adj2*] *stopped*
fixed, pegged, petrified, rooted, stock-still, suspended, turned to stone; SEE CONCEPTS *534,584*

frugal [*adj*] *economical*
abstemious, canny, careful, chary, conserving, discreet, meager, meticulous, mingy*, niggardly*, parsimonious, penny-pinching*, penny-wise*, preserving, provident, prudent, saving, scrimping, sparing, Spartan*, stingy, thrifty, tight, tightwad*, unwasteful, wary; SEE CONCEPT *334*

frugality [*n*] *economizing*
avarice, avariciousness, carefulness, conservation, economy, forehandedness, good management, husbandry, miserliness, moderation, niggardliness, parsimoniousness, parsimony, penuriousness, providence, prudence, saving, scrimping, stinginess, thrift, thriftiness; SEE CONCEPTS *330,335*

fruit [*n1*] *edible part of vegetative growth developed after flowering*
berry, crop, drupe, grain, harvest, nut, pome, produce, product, yield; SEE CONCEPTS *426,428*

fruit [*n2*] *result of labor*
advantage, benefit, consequence, effect, outcome, pay, profit, result, return, reward; SEE CONCEPTS *230,337*

fruitful [*adj*] *productive*
abounding, abundant, advantageous, beneficial, blooming, blossoming, breeding, childing, conducive, copious, effective, fecund, fertile, flourishing, flush, fructiferous, gainful, plenteous, plentiful, profitable, profuse, proliferant, prolific, propagating, reproducing, rewarding, rich, spawning, successful, useful, well-spent, worthwhile; SEE CONCEPTS *528,537,560*

fruition [*n*] *achievement, maturation*
accomplishment, actualization, attainment, completion, consummation, enjoyment, fulfillment, gratification, materialization, maturity, perfection, pleasure, realization, ripeness, satisfaction, success; SEE CONCEPTS *704,706*

fruitless [*adj*] *bringing no advantage, product*
abortive, barren, empty, futile, gainless, idle, ineffective, ineffectual, infertile, in vain, pointless, profitless, spinning one's wheels*, sterile, to no avail*, to no effect*, unavailable, unavailing, unfruitful, unproductive, unprofitable, unprolific, unsuccessful, useless, vain, wild goose chase*; SEE CONCEPTS *528,537,560*

frustrate [*v*] *thwart, disappoint*
annul, arrest, baffle, balk, bar, beat, block, cancel, check, circumvent, confront, conquer, counter, counteract, cramp, cramp one's style*, crimp, dash,

dash one's hope*, defeat, depress, discourage, dishearten, foil, forbid, forestall, foul up*, give the run around*, halt, hang up*, hinder, hold up, impede, inhibit, lick, negate, neutralize, nullify, obstruct, obviate, outwit, overcome, preclude, prevent, prohibit, render null and void*, ruin, stump*, stymie*, upset applecart*; SEE CONCEPTS *7,19,121*

frustrated [*adj*] *disappointed, thwarted*
balked*, crabbed*, cramped, crimped, defeated, discontented, discouraged, disheartened, embittered, foiled, fouled up*, hung up on*, irked, resentful, stonewalled*, stymied*, through the mill*, ungratified, unsated, unslaked, up the wall*; SEE CONCEPT *403*

frustration [*n*] *disappointment, thwarting*
annoyance, bitter pill*, blocking, blow, bummer, chagrin, circumvention, contravention, curbing, defeat, disgruntlement, dissatisfaction, downer*, drag*, failure, fizzle, foiling, grievance, hindrance, impediment, irritation, letdown, nonfulfillment, nonsuccess, obstruction, old one-two*, resentment, setback, unfulfillment, vexation; SEE CONCEPTS *410,674*

fry [*v*] *cook in hot oil*
brown, deep fry, french fry, fricassee, frizzle, pan fry, sauté, sear, singe, sizzle; SEE CONCEPT *170*

fudge [*v*] *fake, misrepresent*
avoid, color, cook up*, dodge, embellish, embroider, equivocate, evade, exaggerate, falsify, hedge, magnify, overstate, pad, patch, shuffle, slant, stall; SEE CONCEPTS *59,63*

fuel [*n*] *something providing energy*
ammunition, combustible, electricity, encouragement, food, gas, incitement, juice, material, means, nourishment, propellant, provocation; SEE CONCEPTS *467,520,523,661*

fuel [*v*] *give energy to*
charge, fan, feed, fill 'er up*, fill up, fire, gas, gas up*, incite, inflame, nourish, service, stoke up*, supply, sustain, tank up*; SEE CONCEPTS *107,140*

fugitive [*n*] *person escaping from law or other pursuer*
bolter, derelict, deserter, displaced person, dodger, émigré, escapee, escaper, evacuee, exile, fly-by-night*, hermit, hunted person, outcast, outlaw, recluse, refugee, runagate, runaway, stray, transient, truant, vagabond, waif, walkout; SEE CONCEPT *412*

fugitive [*adj*] *fleeing, transient*
avoiding, brief, criminal, elusive, ephemeral, errant, erratic, escaping, evading, evanescent, fleeting, flitting, flying*, fugacious, hot*, impermanent, lamster, momentary, moving, on the lam*, passing, planetary, running away*, short*, short-lived, temporary, transitory, unstable, volatile, wandering, wanted; SEE CONCEPTS *551,584,798*

fulfill [*v*] *bring to completion*
accomplish, achieve, answer, be just the ticket*, carry out, complete, comply with, conclude, conform, discharge, do, effect, effectuate, execute, fill, fill the bill*, finish, hit the bull's-eye*, implement,

keep, make it*, make the grade*, meet, obey, observe, perfect, perform, please, realize, render, satisfy, score*, suffice, suit; SEE CONCEPTS *7,22,91,706*

fulfilled [*adj*] *completed*
accomplished, achieved, actualized, attained, brought about, brought to a close, carried out, compassed, concluded, consummated, crowned, delighted, dispatched, effected, effectuated, executed, finished, gratified, made good*, matured, obtained, perfected, performed, pleased, put into effect, reached, realized, satisfied; SEE CONCEPTS *403,531*

fulfillment [*n*] *accomplishment, completion*
achievement, attainment, carrying out, carrying through, consummation, contentedness, contentment, crowning, discharge, discharging, effecting, end, gratification, implementation, just the ticket*, kick*, kicks* observance, perfection, realization, you got it*; SEE CONCEPTS *230,706*

full [*adj1*] *brimming, filled*
abounding, abundant, adequate, awash, big, bounteous, brimful, burdened, bursting, chockablock, chockfull, competent, complete, crammed, crowded, entire, extravagant, glutted, gorged, imbued, impregnated, intact, jammed full*, jam-packed*, laden, lavish, loaded, overflowing, packed, packed like sardines, padded, plenteous, plentiful, plethoric, profuse, replete, running over, sated, satiated, satisfied, saturated, stocked, stuffed, sufficient, suffused, surfeited, teeming, voluminous, weighted; SEE CONCEPTS *481,483,773,774,788*

full [*adj2*] *thorough*
absolute, abundant, adequate, all-inclusive, ample, blow-by-blow*, broad, choate, circumstantial, clocklike, complete, comprehensive, copious, detailed, entire, exhaustive, extensive, generous, integral, itemized, maximum, minute, particular, particularized, perfect, plenary, plenteous, plentiful, unabridged, unlimited, whole; SEE CONCEPT *531*

full [*adj3*] *deep in sound*
clear, distinct, loud, resonant, rich, rounded, throaty; SEE CONCEPT *594*

full [*adj4*] *satiated in hunger*
glutted, gorged, jaded, lousy with*, sated, satiate, stuffed, surfeited, up to here*; SEE CONCEPTS *406,481,774*

full-bodied [*adj*] *robust*
concentrated, fruity, full-flavored, heady*, heavy, lusty, mellow, potent, redolent, rich, strong, well-matured; SEE CONCEPTS *489,613*

full-grown/full-fledged [*adj*] *developed, ripe, ready*
adult, full-blown*, grown, grown-up, in one's prime*, marriageable, mature, nubile, of age, perfected, prime, ripened; SEE CONCEPTS *558,578,797*

fullness [*n*] *abundance, breadth*
adequateness, ampleness, amplitude, broadness, completeness, completion, comprehensiveness, congestion, copiousness, curvaceousness, dilation, distension, enlargement, entirety, extensiveness, fill,

glut, plenitude, plenty, plenum, profusion, repletion, roundness, satiation, satiety, saturation, scope, sufficiency, surfeit, swelling, totality, tumescence, vastness, voluptuousness, wealth, wholeness, wideness; SEE CONCEPTS *635,730*

full-scale [*adj*] *total, all-out*
all-encompassing, comprehensive, exhaustive, extensive, full-blown*, full-dress*, full-out*, in-depth, major, proper, sweeping, thorough, thoroughgoing, total, unlimited, wide-ranging; SEE CONCEPTS *531,772*

fully [*adv1*] *completely, in all respects*
absolutely, all out*, all the way*, altogether*, entirely, every inch*, from A to Z*, from soup to nuts*, heart and soul*, intimately, outright, perfectly, positively, quite, royal*, thoroughly, through and through*, totally, utterly, wholly, without exaggeration; SEE CONCEPTS *531,772*

fully [*adv2*] *sufficiently, adequately*
abundantly, amply, comprehensively, enough, plentifully, satisfactorily, well; SEE CONCEPT *558*

fulminate [*v*] *criticize harshly*
animadvert, berate, blow up, bluster, castigate, censure, condemn, curse, declaim, denounce, denunciate, execrate, explode, fume, intimidate, inveigh against, menace, protest, rage, rail, reprobate, swear at, thunder, upbraid, vilify, vituperate; SEE CONCEPTS *52,54*

fulmination [*n*] *tirade, condemnation*
blast, curse, denunciation, diatribe, discharge, explosion, intimidation, invective, obloquy, outburst, philippic, reprobation, warning; SEE CONCEPTS *52,54,278*

fulsome [*adj*] *sickening or excessive behavior*
adulatory, bombastic, buttery*, canting, cloying, coarse, extravagant, fawning, flattering, glib, grandiloquent, hypocritical, immoderate, ingratiating, inordinate, insincere, magniloquent, mealy-mouthed*, nauseating, offensive, oily*, oleaginous, overdone, saccharine, sanctimonious, slick*, slimy*, smarmy*, smooth, suave, sycophantic, unctuous, wheedling*; SEE CONCEPTS *267,401*

fumble [*v*] *bumble, mess up*
bollix*, botch*, bungle*, err, feel, flounder, flub*, fluff*, goof*, grapple, grope, lose the handle*, louse up*, misfield, mishandle, mismanage, scrabble*, screw up*, spoil, stumble; SEE CONCEPTS *101,181*

fume [*v*] *get very upset about*
anger, blow up*, boil, bristle, burn, chafe, chomp at the bit*, get hot*, get steamed up*, rage, rant, rave, seethe, smoke*, storm*; SEE CONCEPTS *21,29,410*

fumes [*n*] *pollution, gas in air*
effluvium, exhalation, exhaust, haze, miasma, reek, smog, smoke, stench, vapor; SEE CONCEPTS *437,600*

fun [*n*] *amusement, play*
absurdity, ball*, big time*, blast*, buffoonery, celebration, cheer, clowning, distraction, diversion, enjoyment, entertainment, escapade, festivity, foolery, frolic, gaiety, gambol, game*, good time*, grins*,

high jinks*, holiday, horseplay*, jesting, jocularity, joke, joking, jollity, joy, junketing, laughter, living it up*, merriment, merrymaking, mirth, nonsense, pastime, picnic*, playfulness, pleasure, recreation, rejoicing, relaxation, riot, romp, romping, solace, sport, tomfoolery*, treat, whoopee*; SEE CONCEPTS *386,388*

fun [*adj*] *good, happy*
amusing, boisterous, convivial, diverting, enjoyable, entertaining, lively, merry, pleasant, witty; SEE CONCEPTS *537,572*

function [*n1*] *capacity, job*
action, activity, affair, behavior, business, charge, concern, duty, employment, exercise, faculty, goal, mark, mission, object, objective, occupation, office, operation, part, post, power, province, purpose, raison d'être*, responsibility, role, service, situation, target, task, use, utility, work; SEE CONCEPTS *362,659*

function [*n2*] *social occasion*
affair, celebration, do*, gathering, get-together*, meeting, party, reception; SEE CONCEPT *386*

function [*v*] *perform, work*
act, act the part*, behave, be in action, be in commission, be in operation, be running, cook, do, do duty*, do one's thing*, get with it*, go, go to town*, move, officialize, officiate, operate, percolate*, react, run, serve, take, take care of business*; SEE CONCEPTS *87,362*

functional [*adj*] *working*
handy, occupational, operative, practicable, practical, serviceable, useful, utile, utilitarian, utility; SEE CONCEPT *560*

fund [*n*] *repository, reserve*
armamentarium, capital, endowment, foundation, hoard, inventory, kitty*, mine, pool*, reservoir, source, stock, store, storehouse, supply, treasury, trust, vein; SEE CONCEPTS *332,340,710*

fund [*v*] *provide money for*
back, bankroll, capitalize, endow, finance, float, grubstake*, juice*, patronize, pay for, pick up the check*, pick up the tab*, promote, stake, subsidize, support; SEE CONCEPTS *115,341*

fundamental [*n*] *basic, essential part*
ABCs*, axiom, basic, basis, bottom line*, brass tacks*, coal and ice*, component, constituent, cornerstone, element, essential, factor, foundation, guts*, heart, law, nitty-gritty*, principium, principle, rock bottom*, rudiment, rule, sine qua non*, theorem; SEE CONCEPTS *668,687,826,829*

fundamental [*adj*] *basic, important*
axiological, axiomatic, basal, bottom, bottom-line*, cardinal, central, constitutional, constitutive, crucial, elemental, elementary, essential, first, foundational, grass-roots*, indispensable, integral, intrinsic, key, major, meat-and-potatoes*, necessary, organic, original, paramount, primary, prime, primitive, primordial, principal, radical, requisite, rudimentary,

significant, structural, substratal, substrative, supporting, sustaining, theoretical, underived, underlying, vital; SEE CONCEPTS *546,567*

funds [*n*] *cash reserve*
accounts receivable, affluence, assets, backing, bankroll, belongings, bread*, budget, capital, cash, collateral, currency, dough*, earnings, finance, fluid assets, hard cash*, kitty*, lucre, means, money, money in the bank*, money on hand*, nest egg*, nut*, petty cash, pork barrel*, possessions, proceeds, profits, property, ready money*, resources, revenue, savings, scratch*, securities, specie, stakes*, store*, stuff*, substance, treasure, wealth, wherewithal*, winnings*; SEE CONCEPTS *340,710*

funeral [*n*] *ceremony for the dead*
burial, cremation, entombment, exequies, funeration, inhumation, interment, last rites, obit, obsequies, planting, requiem, sepulture, services, solemnities; SEE CONCEPTS *172,386*

funereal [*adj*] *depressing*
black, bleak, dark, deathlike, depressive, dirgelike, disheartening, dismal, doleful, dreary, elegiac, gloomy, grave, grim, lamenting, lugubrious, melancholy, mournful, oppressive, sad, sepulchral, serious, solemn, somber, woeful; SEE CONCEPTS *403, 537,542*

funk [*n*] *fear, depression*
alarm, cold sweat*, despondency, fright, gloom, misery, panic, trembling; SEE CONCEPTS *27,410*

funnel [*v*] *direct down a path*
carry, channel, conduct, convey, filter, move, pass, pipe, pour, siphon, traject, transmit; SEE CONCEPTS *187,217*

funny [*adj1*] *comical, humorous*
absurd, amusing, antic, blithe, capricious, clever, comic, diverting, droll, entertaining, facetious, farcical, for grins*, gas*, gay, gelastic, good-humored, hilarious, humdinger, humorous, hysterical, jocose, jocular, joking, jolly, killing*, knee-slapper*, laughable, ludicrous, merry, mirthful, playful, priceless, rich, ridiculous, riot, riotous, risible, screaming, side-splitting*, silly, slapstick, sportive, waggish, whimsical, witty; SEE CONCEPTS *267,529,537*

funny [*adj2*] *odd, peculiar*
bizarre, curious, dubious, fantastic, mysterious, perplexing, puzzling, queer, remarkable, strange, suspicious, unusual, weird; SEE CONCEPTS *552,564*

fur [*n*] *hair on animal*
brush, coat, down, fluff, fuzz, hide, jacket, lint, pelage, pelt, pile, skin, wool; SEE CONCEPT *399*

furbish [*v*] *polish; renovate*
brighten, buff, burnish, clean, deck out*, fix up, glaze, gloss, gussy up*, improve, recondition, refurbish, rehabilitate, renew, renovate, restore, rub, shine, smarten up*, spruce up*; SEE CONCEPTS *162,165,700*

furious [*adj1*] *extremely angry, very mad*
bent*, bent out of shape*, beside oneself*, boiling*, browned off*, bummed out*, corybantic, crazed, de-

mented, desperate, enraged, fierce, fit to be tied*, frantic, frenetic, frenzied, fuming, hacked, hopping mad*, incensed, infuriated, insane, irrational, livid, maddened, maniac, on the warpath*, rabid, raging, smoking*, steamed, unreasonable, up in arms*, vehement, vicious, violent, wrathful; SEE CONCEPT *403*

furious [*adj2*] *stormy, turbulent*
agitated, blustering, blustery, boisterous, concentrated, excessive, exquisite, extreme, fierce, flaming, impetuous, intense, intensified, raging, rampageous, rough, savage, tempestuous, terrible, tumultous/tumultuous, ungovernable, unrestrained, vehement, vicious, violent, wild; SEE CONCEPTS *525,537,548*

furnace [*n*] *heating mechanism*
boiler, calefactor, cinerator, cremator, forge, Franklin stove, heater, heating system, incinerator, kiln, oil burner, smithy, stove; SEE CONCEPT *463*

furnish [*v1*] *decorate, supply*
accoutre, apparel, appoint, arm, array, clothe, endow, equip, feather a nest*, fit, fit out*, fix up*, gear, line a nest*, make habitable, outfit, provide, provision, purvey, rig, stock, store, turn out; SEE CONCEPTS *140,177,182*

furnish [*v2*] *give, reveal information*
afford, bestow, deliver, dispense, endow, feed, grant, hand, hand over, offer, present, provide, supply, transfer, turn over; SEE CONCEPTS *60,67,108*

furniture [*n*] *household property*
appliance, appointment, bed, bookcase, buffet, bureau, cabinet, chair, chattel, chest, commode, couch, counter, cupboard, davenport, desk, dresser, effect, equipment, fittings, furnishing, goods, highboy, hutch, movables, possession, sideboard, sofa, stool, table, thing, wardrobe; SEE CONCEPT *443*

furor [*n*] *disturbance, excitement*
ado*, agitation, big scene*, big stink*, bustle, commotion, craze, enthusiasm, fad, ferment, flap*, free-for-all*, frenzy, fury, fuss, hell broke loose*, hullabaloo*, hysteria, lunacy, madness*, mania, outburst, outcry, rage, row, ruckus, stir*, to-do*, tumult, uproar, whirl; SEE CONCEPTS *230,388,410*

furrow [*n*] *ditch*
channel, corrugation, crease, crinkle, crow's-foot*, dike, fluting, fold, groove, gutter, hollow, line, plicate, rabbet, ridge, rimple, rivel, ruck, rut, seam, trench, wrinkle; SEE CONCEPT *513*

further [*adj*] *additional*
added, another, else, extra, farther, fresh, in addition, more, new, other, supplementary; SEE CONCEPT *771*

further [*v*] *advance, lend support*
aid, assist, back up, bail out*, ballyhoo*, champion, contribute, encourage, engender, expedite, facilitate, forward, foster, generate, give a boost to*, go with, hasten, help, lend a hand*, open doors*, patronize, plug, promote, propagate, push, serve, speed, succor, take care of, work for; SEE CONCEPTS *69,87,110*

further [*adv*] *additionally*
again, also, as well as, besides, beyond, distant, farther, furthermore, in addition, moreover, on top of*, over and above*, then, to boot, what's more*, yet, yonder; SEE CONCEPT *771*

furtherance [*n*] *advancement*
advocacy, backing, boosting, carrying-out, championship, progress, progression, promotion, prosecution, pursuit; SEE CONCEPTS *110,704*

furthermore [*adv*] *in addition*
additionally, along, as well, besides, further, likewise, moreover, not to mention, to boot, too, what's more*, withal, yet; SEE CONCEPTS *577,824*

furthest [*adj*] *most distant*
extreme, farthest, furthermost, most remote, outermost, outmost, remotest, ultimate, uttermost; SEE CONCEPTS *586,778*

furtive [*adj*] *sneaky, secretive*
artful, calculating, cautious, circumspect, clandestine, cloaked, conspiratorial, covert, crafty*, creepy*, cunning, disguised, elusive, evasive, foxy, guileful, hidden, hush-hush*, insidious, masked, scheming, secret, shifty*, skulking, slinking*, sly, sneaking, stealthy, sub-rosa*, surreptitious, tricky*, undercover, underhand, underhanded, under-the-table*, under wraps*, wily; SEE CONCEPTS *548,576*

fury [*n*] *anger, wrath*
acerbity, acrimony, asperity, boiling point*, conniption, energy, ferocity, fierceness, fire, flare-up, force, frenzy, furor, impetuosity, indignation, intensity, ire, madness, might, passion, power, rabidity, rage, rampancy, rise, savagery, severity, slow burn*, sore, stew*, storm*, tempestuousness, turbulence, vehemence, violence; SEE CONCEPTS *29,410*

fuse [*v*] *meld, intermix*
agglutinate, amalgamate, bind, blend, cement, coalesce, combine, commingle, deliquesce, dissolve, federate, flux, integrate, interblend, interfuse, intermingle, join, liquefy, liquesce, melt, merge, mingle, run, run together, smelt, solder, thaw, unite, weld; SEE CONCEPT *113*

fusion [*n*] *melding; mixture*
admixture, alloy, amalgam, amalgamation, blend, blending, coadunation, coalescence, coalition, commingling, commixture, compound, federation, heating, immixture, integration, intermixture, junction, liquefaction, liquification, melting, merger, merging, smelting, soldering, synthesis, unification, union, uniting, welding; SEE CONCEPTS *113,260,432*

fuss [*n*] *disturbance, trouble*
ado, agitation, altercation, argument, bickering, bother, broil*, bustle, commotion, complaint, confusion, controversy, difficulty, display, dispute, excitement, falling-out*, fight, flap, flurry, flutter, fret, furor, hassle, kick-up*, objection, palaver, perturbation, quarrel, row, ruckus, scene, squabble, stew*, stink*, stir, storm, to-do*, turmoil, unrest, upset, wingding*, worry; SEE CONCEPTS *46,106,388,633*

fussy [*adj*] *meticulous, particular*
careful, choosy, conscientious, conscionable, dainty, difficult, discriminating, exact, exacting, fastidious, finical, finicky, fretful, fuddy-duddy*, hard to please*, heedful, nit-picking*, overfastidious, over-particular, painstaking, persnickety, picky, picky-picky*, punctilious, punctual, querulous, scrupulous, squeamish, stickling; SEE CONCEPTS *401,404*

futile [*adj*] *hopeless, pointless*
abortive, barren, bootless, delusive, empty, exhausted, forlorn, fruitless, hollow, idle, impracticable, impractical, ineffective, ineffectual, insufficient, in vain, no dice*, nugatory, on a treadmill*, otiose, out the window*, profitless, resultless, save one's breath*, sterile, to no avail*, to no effect*, to no purpose*, trifling, trivial, unavailing, unimportant, unneeded, unproductive, unprofitable, unreal, unsatisfactory, unsubstantial, unsuccessful, useless, vain, valueless, worthless; SEE CONCEPTS *528,548,560*

future [*n*] *time to come*
aftertime, afterward, by and by*, destiny, eternity, expectation, fate, futurity, hereafter, infinity, life to come, millennium, morrow, offing, outlook, posterity, prospect, subsequent time, to be*, tomorrow, world to come*; SEE CONCEPTS *679,807,811,818*

future [*adj*] *to come; expected*
approaching, booked, budgeted, close at hand*, coming, coming up, destined, down the line*, down the pike, down the road*, eventual, fated, final, forthcoming, from here in, from here on, from here to eternity*, from now on in*, imminent, impending, inevitable, in the cards*, in the course of time, in the offing*, just around the corner*, later, likely, looked toward, near, next, planned, prospective, scheduled, subsequent, to be*, ulterior, ultimate, unborn, unfolding, up; SEE CONCEPT *820*

fuzz [*n*] *fluff*
down, dust ball*, dust bunnies*, fiber, floss, fur, hair, lanugo, lint, nap, pile; SEE CONCEPT *260*

fuzzy [*adj1*] *fluffy*
down-covered, downy, flossy, frizzy, furry, hairy, linty, napped, pilate, velutinous, woolly; SEE CONCEPT *606*

fuzzy [*adj2*] *out of focus*
bleary, blurred, dim, distorted, faint, foggy, hazy, ill-defined, indefinite, indistinct, misty, muffled, murky, obscure, shadowy, unclear, unfocused, vague; SEE CONCEPT *619*

G

gab [*n*] *conversation*
blab*, blather*, chat, chitchat*, gossip, idle talk*, loquacity*, palaver*, prattle, small talk*, talk, tête-à-tête, tongue-wagging*, yak*, yakety-yak*; SEE CONCEPT *278*

gab [*v*] *talk a lot*
blabber*, blather*, buzz*, chatter, gossip, jabber*, jaw*, prate, prattle, talk, yak*, yakety-yak*; SEE CONCEPT *266*

gabby [*adj*] *talkative*
chattering, chatty, effusive, garrulous, glib, gossiping, gushing, jabbering, long-winded*, loose-lipped*, loquacious, mouthy*, prattling, prolix, talky, verbose, voluble, windy*, wordy; SEE CONCEPT *267*

gad [*v*] *roam about*
cruise, gallivant, hit the road*, hit the trail*, jaunt, knock about*, knock around*, maunder, mooch*, ramble, range, rove, run around*, stray, traipse, wander; SEE CONCEPTS *149,224*

gadget [*n*] *device, novelty*
apparatus, appliance, business, concern, contraption, contrivance, doodad*, doohickey*, gimmick, gizmo*, invention, object, thing*, thingamajig, tool, utensil, whatchamacallit*, widget*; SEE CONCEPTS *463,499*

gaffe [*n*] *mistake, goof*
blooper*, blunder, boner*, boo-boo*, faux pas*, howler*, impropriety, indecorum, indiscretion, putting foot in mouth*, slip*, solecism; SEE CONCEPTS *101,230*

gag [*n*] *practical joke*
crack, drollery, hoax, jest, quip, ruse, trick, wile, wisecrack, witticism; SEE CONCEPT *59*

gag [*v1*] *silence, stop up*
balk, bottle up*, choke, constrain, cork*, cork up*, curb, deaden, demur, garrote, keep the lid on*, muffle, muzzle, obstruct, put the lid on*, quiet, repress, restrain, shut down, shy, squash*, squelch, stifle, still, stumble, suppress, tape up*, throttle*, tongue-tie*; SEE CONCEPTS *121,130*

gag [*v2*] *vomit, choke*
be nauseated, disgorge, gasp, heave, nauseate, pant, puke*, retch, sicken, spew, strain, struggle, throw up; SEE CONCEPTS *179,308*

gaiety [*n*] *happiness, celebration*
animation, blitheness, brightness, brilliance, cheer, color, colorfulness, conviviality, effervescence, elation, entertainment, exhilaration, festivity, frolic, fun, geniality, gladness, glee, glitter, good humor*, grins*, high spirits*, hilarity, joie de vivre, jollity, joviality, joyousness, lightheartedness, liveliness, merriment, merrymaking, mirth, pleasantness, radiance, revel, reveling, revelry, shindig*, show, showiness, sparkle, sport, sprightliness, vivacity, whoopee*, winging*; SEE CONCEPTS *377,388*

gaily [*adv*] *happily, brightly*
blithely, brilliantly, cheerfully, colorfully, flamboyantly, flashily, gleefully, glowingly, joyfully, laughingly, lightheartedly, merrily, showily, sparklingly, spiritedly, splendidly, vivaciously, with élan*, with spirit*; SEE CONCEPTS *542,589*

gain [*n*] *acquisition, winnings*
accretion, accrual, accumulation, achievement, addition, advance, advancement, advantage, attainment, benefit, boost, buildup, cut, dividend, earnings, emolument, gravy*, growth, headway*,

hike*, improvement, income, increase, increment, lucre, payoff, proceeds, produce, profit, progress, receipts, return, rise, share, take, up*, upping*, velvet*, yield; SEE CONCEPTS *337,344,706,710*

gain [*v*] *acquire, win*
accomplish, achieve, advance, ameliorate, annex, attain, augment, benefit, boost, bring in, build up, capture, clear, collect, complete, consummate, earn, enlarge, enlist, expand, fulfill, gather, get, glean, grow, harvest, have, improve, increase, land, make, make a killing*, move forward, net, obtain, overtake, parlay, perfect, pick up, procure, produce, profit, progress, promote, rack up*, reach, realize, reap, score*, secure, succeed, win over; SEE CONCEPTS *120,124,129*

gainful [*adj*] *very productive, profitable*
advantageous, beneficial, fat, fruitful, generous, going, going concern*, good, in the black*, lucrative, lush, moneymaking, paid off, paying, remunerative, rewarding, rich, satisfying, substantial, sweet*, useful, well-paying, worthwhile; SEE CONCEPT *334*

gainsay [*v*] *contradict*
combat, contravene, controvert, cross, deny, disaffirm, disagree, disclaim, disprove, dispute, fight, impugn, negate, negative, oppose, refute, repudiate, resist, traverse, withstand; SEE CONCEPTS *52,54*

gait [*n*] *way an animal or person moves, walks*
amble, bearing, canter, carriage, clip, gallop, get along, lick, march, motion, movement, pace, run, speed, step, stride, tread, trot, walk; SEE CONCEPT *149*

gala [*n*] *festival*
affair, ball, bash, blast*, blowout*, carnival, celebration, clambake, dance, do, festivity, fete, fiesta, function, get-together*, hop, jamboree, moveable feast, pageant, party, prom, roast, shindig*, stag, to-do*, wingding*; SEE CONCEPTS *377,383*

gala [*adj*] *celebratory*
bright, colorful, convivial, festal, festive, gay, happy, jovial, joyful, merry; SEE CONCEPT *548*

gale [*n*] *violent storm*
blast, blow, burst, chinook, cyclone, hurricane, mistral, monsoon, outbreak, outburst, squall, tempest, tornado, typhoon, wind, windstorm; SEE CONCEPTS *524,526*

gall [*n*] *nerve, brashness*
acrimony, animosity, arrogance, bitterness, brass, brazenness, cheek*, chutzpah*, conceit, confidence, crust, cynicism, effrontery, guts*, haughtiness, hostility, impertinence, impudence, insolence, malevolence, malice, overbearance, pomposity, presumption, rancor, sauciness, self-importance, spite, venom; SEE CONCEPTS *411,633*

gall [*v1*] *upset, irritate*
aggravate, annoy, bedevil, bother, burn, chafe, chide, disturb, exasperate, fret, grate, harass, harry, inflame, irk, nag, peeve, pester, plague, provoke, rile, roil, rub, ruffle, scrape, torment, trouble, vex, worry; SEE CONCEPTS *7,19*

gall [*v2*] *rub raw*
abrade, bark, burn, chafe, corrode, erode, excoriate, file, fray, frazzle, fret, grate, graze, irritate, scrape, scratch, scuff, skin, wear; SEE CONCEPT *215*

gallant [*adj*] *brave, gentlemanly*
attentive, bold, chivalrous, considerate, courageous, courteous, courtly, daring, dashing, dauntless, dignified, doughty, fearless, fire-eating*, game*, glorious, gracious, grand, gritty*, hairy*, heroic, honorable, intrepid, knightly, lionhearted*, lofty, magnanimous, manful, manly, noble, plucky*, polite, quixotic, splendid, stately, stouthearted, suave, thoughtful, urbane, valiant, valorous; SEE CONCEPTS *404,542*

gallantry [*n*] *bravery, gentlemanliness*
address, amenity, attentiveness, audacity, boldness, chivalry, courage, courageousness, courteousness, courtesy, courtliness, daring, dauntlessness, deference, derring-do*, duty, elegance, fearlessness, graciousness, heroism, homage, honor, intrepidity, manliness, mettle, nerve, nobility, pluck*, poise, politeness, prowess, resolution, reverence, savoir-faire, spirit, suavity, tact, urbanity, valiance, valor; SEE CONCEPTS *411,657*

gallery [*n1*] *balcony*
arcade, loggia, mezzanine, patio, porch, upstairs, veranda; SEE CONCEPT *440*

gallery [*n2*] *showplace for wares*
exhibit, exhibition room, hall, museum, salon, showroom, studio, wing; SEE CONCEPTS *448,449*

gallery [*n3*] *audience, usually seated high*
attendance, onlookers, peanut gallery*, public, spectators; SEE CONCEPTS *294,417*

galling [*adj*] *very upsetting*
acid, afflictive, aggravating, annoying, bitter, bothersome, distasteful, exasperating, grievous, harassing, humiliating, irksome, irritating, nettlesome, painful, plaguing, provoking, rankling, unpalatable, vexatious, vexing; SEE CONCEPTS *7,19*

gallivant [*v*] *run around, gad about*
cruise, jaunt, meander, mooch, ramble, range, roam, rove, stray, traipse, wander; SEE CONCEPTS *149,224*

gallop [*v*] *bolt, race with slight jumping motion*
amble, canter, career, course, dart, dash, fly, hasten, hurdle, hurry, jump, leap, lope, pace, rack, run, rush, shoot, speed, spring, sprint, stride, tear along, trot, zoom; SEE CONCEPTS *150,194*

galvanize [*v*] *inspire, stimulate*
animate, arouse, astonish, awaken, commove, electrify, energize, excite, fire*, frighten, innervate, invigorate, jolt, motivate, move, pique, prime, provoke, quicken, shock, spur, startle, stir, stun, thrill, vitalize, wake, zap*; SEE CONCEPTS *7,14,22*

gambit [*n*] *plan, plot*
artifice, design, device, gimmick, jig, maneuver, play, ploy, ruse, trick; SEE CONCEPT *660*

gamble [n] *chance, speculation*
action, bet, fling, leap*, long shot*, lottery, outside chance*, raffle, risk, shot in the dark*, spec*, stab*, throw of the dice*, toss up*, uncertainty, venture, wager; SEE CONCEPTS *28,363*

gamble [v] *take a chance on winning*
back, bet, brave, buck the odds*, cast lots*, challenge, chance, cut the cards, dare, defy, endanger, face, flip the coin*, game, go for broke*, hazard, imperil, jeopardize, lay money on*, lot, make a bet, play, plunge, put, put faith in, put trust in, risk, set, shoot the moon*, shoot the works*, speculate, stake, stick one's neck out*, take a flyer*, tempt fortune*, trust to luck, try one's luck, venture, wager; SEE CONCEPTS *28,363*

gambol [v] *tumble playfully*
bound, caper, carry on, cavort, cut, cut a caper*, cut loose*, fool around*, frisk, frolic, hop, horse around*, jump, kibitz around*, kick up one's heels*, lark, leap, play, prance, revel, roister, rollick, romp, skip, sport, spring, whoop it up*; SEE CONCEPTS *149,194,363*

game [n1] *entertainment*
adventure, amusement, athletics, business, distraction, diversion, enterprise, festivity, frolic, fun, jest, joke, lark, line, merriment, merrymaking, occupation, pastime, plan, play, proceeding, pursuit, recreation, romp, scheme, sport, sports, undertaking; SEE CONCEPTS *292,363*

game [n2] *individual sporting event*
competition, contest, match, meeting, round, tournament; SEE CONCEPT *364*

game [n3] *undomesticated animals chased for food*
chase, fish, fowl, kill, meat, prey, quarry, ravin, victim, wild animals; SEE CONCEPTS *394,457,460*

game [n4] *plot, trick*
butt, derision, design, device, hoax, joke, object of ridicule, plan, ploy, practical joke, prank, scheme, stratagem, strategy, tactic; SEE CONCEPTS *59,660*

game [adj1] *brave, willing*
bold, courageous, dauntless, desirous, disposed, dogged, eager, fearless, gallant, hardy, heroic, inclined, interested, intrepid, nervy*, persevering, persistent, plucky*, prepared, ready, resolute, spirited, spunky, unafraid, unflinching, up for*, valiant, valorous; SEE CONCEPT *404*

game [adj2] *debilitated*
ailing, bad, crippled, deformed, disabled, incapacitated, injured, lame, maimed, weak; SEE CONCEPTS *314,485*

gamut [n] *range*
area, catalogue, compass, diapason, extent, field, panorama, scale, scope, series, spectrum, sweep; SEE CONCEPTS *651,787*

gang [n] *group, mob of people*
assemblage, band, bunch, circle, clan, clique, club, cluster, combo*, company, coterie, crew, crowd, herd, horde, knot, lot, organization, outfit, pack, party, posse, ring, set, shift, squad, syndicate, team, tribe, troop, troupe, workers, zoo*; SEE CONCEPT *387*

gangster [n] *person involved in illegal activities*
bandit, bruiser*, cowboy*, criminal, crook, dealer, desperado, godfather, goon*, gunman, hit man/woman, hood, hoodlum, hooligan*, Mafioso*, member of the family*, mobster, pusher, racketeer, robber, ruffian, soldier*, thug, tough; SEE CONCEPT *412*

gap [n] *break, breach*
aperture, arroyo, blank, caesura, canyon, chasm, cleft, clove, crack, cranny, crevice, cut, defile, difference, disagreement, discontinuity, disparity, divergence, divide, division, fracture, gorge, gulch, gully, hiatus, hole, hollow, inconsistency, interlude, intermission, interruption, interspace, interstice, interval, lacuna, lull, notch, opening, orifice, pause, ravine, recess, rent, respite, rest, rift, rupture, separation, slit, slot, space, vacuity, void; SEE CONCEPTS *513,665*

gape [v1] *gawk*
beam, bore, eye, eyeball*, focus, get a load of*, get an eyeful*, give the eye*, glare, gloat, goggle*, look, ogle, peer, rubberneck*, size up*, stare, take in*, wonder, yawp*; SEE CONCEPT *623*

gape [v2] *be wide open*
cleave, crack, dehisce, divide, frondesce, gap, open, part, split, yaw, yawn; SEE CONCEPT *135*

gaping [adj] *wide open*
broad, cavernous, chasmal, great, open, vast, wide, yawning; SEE CONCEPTS *485,490*

garage [n] *storage building for vehicles, workplace*
barn, carport*, car stall*, parking, parking lot, parking space, repair shop, shop, storage; SEE CONCEPTS *439,449*

garb [n] *clothing*
apparel, appearance, array, attire, clothes, costume, dress, duds*, feathers*, form, garment, gear, guise, habiliment, habit, outfit, rags*, raiment, robes*, semblance, things*, threads*, uniform, vestments, wear; SEE CONCEPT *451*

garb [v] *fit with clothes*
apparel, array, attire, clad, clothe, cover, deck, deck out*, drape, dress, dud*, fit out*, garment, raiment, rig out*, rig up*, robe, suit up*, tog*, turn out*; SEE CONCEPT *167*

garbage [n] *refuse, litter*
bits and pieces*, debris, detritus, dreck, dregs, dross, filth, junk, muck, odds and ends*, offal, rubbish, rubble, scrap, scrapings, sewage, slop*, sweepings, swill, trash, waste; SEE CONCEPT *260*

garble [v] *mix up, misrepresent*
belie, color, confuse, corrupt, distort, doctor, falsify, jumble, misinterpret, mislead, misquote, misstate, mutilate, obscure, pervert, slant, tamper with, twist, warp; SEE CONCEPTS *59,63*

garden [n] *cultivated plants, flowers*
back yard, bed, cold frame, conservatory, enclosure, field, greenhouse, hothouse, nursery, oasis, patch, patio, plot, terrace; SEE CONCEPTS *509,517*

gargantuan [adj] very large
big, colossal, elephantine, enormous, giant, gigantic, heavyweight, huge, humongous, immense, jumbo, leviathan, mammoth, massive, monstrous, monumental, mountainous, prodigious, supercolossal*, super-duper*, titanic, towering, tremendous, vast, whopping*; SEE CONCEPTS *491,773*

gargle [v] rinse the mouth with liquid
irrigate, swish, trill, use mouthwash; SEE CONCEPTS *169,308,616*

garish [adj] flashy, tasteless
blatant, brassy, brazen, cheap, chintzy, flaunting, gaudy, glaring, glittering, kitschy*, loud, meretricious, ornate, ostentatious, overdone, overwrought, raffish, screaming*, showy, tawdry, tinsel, vulgar; SEE CONCEPT *589*

garland [n] strand of material, usually hung
bays, chaplet, coronal, crown, festoon, honors, laurel, palm, wreath; SEE CONCEPTS *260,429*

garment [n] article of clothing
apparel, array, attire, costume, covering, drapes*, dress, duds*, feathers*, garb, gear, get-up*, habiliment, habit, outfit, raiment, robe, things*, threads*, togs*, uniform, vestments, wear, weeds*; SEE CONCEPT *451*

garner [v] collect, accumulate
amass, assemble, cull, cumulate, deposit, extract, gather, glean, harvest, hive, hoard, husband, lay in*, lay up*, pick up, put by*, reap, reserve, roll up*, save, stockpile, store, stow away, treasure; SEE CONCEPTS *109,135*

garnish [n] embellishment, improvement
adornment, decoration, enhancement, furbelow, gingerbread*, ornament, ornamentation, tinsel, trim, trimming; SEE CONCEPT *824*

garnish [v] embellish, improve
adorn, beautify, bedeck, deck, decorate, dress up, enhance, fix up, grace, gussy up*, ornament, set off*, spiff up*, spruce up*, trim; SEE CONCEPT *244*

garrulous [adj] talkative
babbling, blabbermouth*, chattering, chatty, effusive, flap jaw*, gabby, glib, gossiping, gushing, long-winded*, loose-lipped*, loose-tongued*, loquacious, motormouth*, mouthy, prating, prattling, prolix, prosy, running on at the mouth*, verbose, voluble, wind-bag*, windy*, wordy, yakkity*, yakky*; SEE CONCEPTS *267,404*

gas [n] something not liquid or solid
effluvium, fumes, miasma, smoke, stream, vapor, volatile substance; SEE CONCEPT *465*

gash [n] cut made by slicing
cleft, furrow, gouge, incision, laceration, mark, nip, notch, rent, slash, slice, slit, split, tear, wound; SEE CONCEPT *309*

gash [v] cut by slicing
carve, cleave, furrow, gouge, incise, injure, lacerate, lance, mark, nip, notch, pierce, rend, slash, slit, split, tear, wound; SEE CONCEPTS *137,176*

gasp [n] sharply drawn breath
blow, ejaculation, exclamation, gulp, heave, pant, puff, wheeze, whoop; SEE CONCEPTS *163,595*

gasp [v] draw breath in sharply
blow, catch one's breath, choke, convulse, fight for breath, gulp, heave, inhale, inspire, pant, puff, respire, sniffle, snort, wheeze, whoop; SEE CONCEPT *163*

gate [n] movable barrier at entrance
access, bar, conduit, door, doorway, egress, entrance, exit, gateway, issue, lock, opening, passage, port, portal, revolving door, slammer*, turnstile, way, weir; SEE CONCEPTS *440,445*

gather [v1] come or bring together
accumulate, aggregate, amass, assemble, associate, bunch up, capture, choose, close with, cluster, collect, concentrate, congregate, convene, converge, corral, crowd, cull, draw, draw in, flock, forgather, gang up, garner, get together, group, hang around*, hang out*, heap, herd, hoard, huddle, make the scene*, marshal, mass, meet, muster, pick, pile up, pluck, poke*, pour in, punch*, rally, reunite, round up*, scare up*, scrape together*, show up, stack up, stockpile, swarm, throng, unite; SEE CONCEPTS *109,114*

gather [v2] be led to believe; infer
assume, believe, conclude, deduce, draw, expect, find, hear, imagine, judge, learn, make, presume, reckon, suppose, surmise, suspect, take, think, understand; SEE CONCEPT *15*

gather [v3] harvest, pick out
crop, cull, draw, extract, garner, glean, heap, ingather, mass, pick, pick up, pile, pluck, reap, select, stack, take in; SEE CONCEPT *257*

gather [v4] gain, increase
build, deepen, enlarge, expand, grow, heighten, intensify, rise, swell, thicken, wax; SEE CONCEPT *780*

gathering [n] assemblage, accumulation
acquisition, affair, aggregate, aggregation, assembly, association, band, body, bunch, caucus, clambake*, collection, company, concentration, conclave, concourse, conference, congregation, congress, convention, convocation, crowd, crush, drove, flock, function, gain, get-together*, group, heap, herd, hoard, huddle, junction, knot, levy, mass, meet, meeting, muster, parley, party, pile, powwow*, rally, roundup, social function, society, stock, stockpile, swarm, throng, turnout, union; SEE CONCEPTS *324,386,417*

gauche [adj] tactless, unsophisticated
awkward, bumbling, clumsy, crude, graceless, green, halting, ham-handed*, heavy-handed, ignorant, ill-bred, ill-mannered, inelegant, inept, insensitive, lacking, maladroit, oafish, uncouth, uncultured, unhappy, unpolished, wooden*; SEE CONCEPT *404*

gaudy [adj] bright and vulgar
blatant, brazen, brilliant, catchpenny*, chichi*, chintzy, coarse, crude, flashy, flaunting, florid, frou-

frou*, garish, gay, glaring, gross, gussied up*, jazzy, kitschy*, loud, meretricious, obtrusive, ostentatious, pizzazz*, pretentious, putting on the ritz*, raffish, ritzy, screaming*, showy, snazzy, splashy, splendiferous, tasteless, tawdry, tinsel; SEE CONCEPTS *589,618*

gauge [n] *measure, standard*
barometer, basis, benchmark, bore, capacity, check, criterion, degree, depth, example, exemplar, extent, guide, guideline, height, indicator, magnitude, mark, meter, model, norm, pattern, rule, sample, scale, scope, size, span, test, thickness, touchstone*, type, width, yardstick; SEE CONCEPTS *647,680,687,792*

gauge [v] *measure, judge*
adjudge, appraise, ascertain, assess, calculate, calibrate, check, check out, compute, count, determine, estimate, evaluate, eye*, figure, figure in, guess, guesstimate, have one's number*, look over, meter, peg*, quantify, quantitate, rate, reckon, scale, size, size up*, take account of, tally, value, weigh; SEE CONCEPTS *37,764*

gaunt [adj] *skinny*
angular, anorexic, attenuated, bare, bleak, bony, cadaverous, desolate, dismal, dreary, emaciated, forbidding, forlorn, grim, haggard, harsh, lank, lean, like a bag of bones*, meager, peaked, peaky, pinched, rawboned, scraggy, scrawny, skeletal, skeleton, skin and bones*, spare, thin, wasted; SEE CONCEPTS *406,490,491*

gauzy [adj] *see-through, gossamer in texture*
delicate, diaphanous, filmy, flimsy, insubstantial, light, lucid, pellucid, sheer, thin, tiffany, translucent, transparent; SEE CONCEPT *606*

gawk [v] *stare at in amazement*
bore*, eyeball*, gape, gawp, gaze, glare, gloat, goggle*, look, ogle, peer, rubberneck*, yawp*; SEE CONCEPT *623*

gawky [adj] *clumsy*
awkward, bumbling, clownish, gauche, loutish*, lumbering, lumpish*, lumpy, maladroit, oafish, rude, rustic, splay, uncouth, ungainly; SEE CONCEPTS *550,584*

gay [adj1] *happy*
alert, animate, animated, blithe, blithesome, bouncy, brash, carefree, cheerful, cheery, chipper*, chirpy, confident, convivial, devil-may-care*, festive, forward, frivolous, frolicsome, fun-loving, gamesome, glad, gleeful, hilarious, insouciant, jocund, jolly, jovial, joyful, joyous, keen, lighthearted, lively, merry, mirthful, playful, pleasure-seeking, presuming, pushy, rollicking, self-assertive, sparkling, spirited, sportive, sprightly, sunny, vivacious, wild, zippy*; SEE CONCEPTS *403,542*

gay [adj2] *colorful, vivid*
brave, bright, brilliant, flamboyant, flashy, fresh, garish, gaudy, intense, rich, showy; SEE CONCEPTS *589,618*

gay [adj3] *homosexual*
homoerotic, homophile, lesbian, Sapphic; SEE CONCEPT *372*

gaze [n] *long, fixed stare*
fish eye*, glaring, gun*, look, looking, ogling, peek, peep, rubbernecking*, scrutiny, seeing, survey, watching; SEE CONCEPT *623*

gaze [v] *stare at*
admire, beam*, bore*, contemplate, eye, eyeball*, gape, gawk, gawp, get a load of*, get an eyeful*, glare, gloat, inspect, lamp*, look, look fixedly, moon*, observe, ogle, peek, peep, peer, pin*, pipe*, regard, rubber*, rubberneck*, scrutinize, see, size up*, survey, take in*, view, watch, wonder; SEE CONCEPTS *623,626*

gear [n1] *equipment*
accessory, accouterment, adjunct, apparatus, appendage, appurtenance, baggage, belongings, contraption, effects, encumbrances, fittings, habiliment, harness, impedimenta, instrument, kit, kit and kaboodle*, luggage, machinery, material, materiel, means, outfit, paraphernalia, possessions, rigging, setup, stuff, supply, tackle, things, tools, trappings; SEE CONCEPT *496*

gear [n2] *toothed part of wheel*
cog, cogwheel, gearwheel, pinion, ragwheel, sprocket, spurwheel; SEE CONCEPT *464*

gear [n3] *clothing*
apparel, array, attire, clothes, costume, drapes*, dress, duds*, feathers*, garb, garments, habit, outfit, rags*, threads*, toggery*, togs*, wear; SEE CONCEPT *451*

gear [v] *prepare, equip*
accouter, adapt, adjust, appoint, arm, blend, fit, fit out*, furnish, harness, match, organize, outfit, ready, regulate, rig*, suit, tailor, turn out; SEE CONCEPTS *182,202*

gelatinous [adj] *coagulated*
gluey, glutinous, gummy, jelled, jellied, jelly-like, mucilaginous, pudding*, sticky, thick, viscid, viscous; SEE CONCEPT *606*

gem [n] *precious stone; treasure*
bauble*, glass*, hardware*, jewel, jewelry, masterpiece, nonpareil, ornament, paragon, pearl, pick, prize, rock*, sparkler*, stone, trump*; SEE CONCEPTS *337,446,474*

genealogy [n] *person's family tree*
ancestry, blood line, derivation, descent, extraction, generation, genetics, heredity, history, line, lineage, parentage, pedigree, progeniture, stemma, stirps, stock, strain; SEE CONCEPT *296*

general [adj1] *common, accepted*
accustomed, broad, commonplace, conventional, customary, everyday, extensive, familiar, generic, habitual, humdrum, inclusive, matter-of-course*, natural, normal, ordinary, popular, prevailing, prevalent, public, regular, routine, run-of-the-mill*,

typic, typical, uneventful, universal, usual, wide, widespread, wonted; SEE CONCEPTS 530,547

general [adj2] *inexact, approximate*
ill-defined, imprecise, inaccurate, indefinite, loose, not partial, not particular, not specific, uncertain, undetailed, unspecific, vague; SEE CONCEPT 557

general [adj3] *comprehensive*
across-the-board*, all-around*, all-embracing*, all-inclusive*, ample, blanket, broad, catholic, collective, comprehending, diffuse, ecumenical, encyclopedic, endless, extensive, far-reaching, generic, global, inclusive, indiscriminate, infinite, limitless, miscellaneous, overall, panoramic, sweeping, taken as a whole, total, ubiquitous, unconfined, universal, unlimited, wide, worldwide; SEE CONCEPTS 537,772

generality [n] *vague notion*
abstraction, abstract principle, generalization, half-truth, law, loose statement, observation, principle, sweeping statement, universality; SEE CONCEPTS 687,689

generalize [v] *make sweeping assumption, statement*
be metaphysical, conclude, derive, discern, discover, establish, hypothesize, induce, observe, philosophize, postulate, speculate, stay in the clouds*, theorize, vapor; SEE CONCEPTS 37,49

generally [adv] *mainly, in most cases*
about, all in all, almost always, altogether, approximately, as a rule, broadly, by and large, chiefly, commonly, conventionally, customarily, en masse, extensively, for the most part, habitually, largely, mostly, normally, on average, on the whole, ordinarily, overall, popularly, practically, predominantly, primarily, principally, publicly, regularly, roughly, roundly, thereabouts, typically, universally, usually, widely; SEE CONCEPTS 530,547,772

generate [v] *produce, create*
accomplish, achieve, bear, beget, breed, bring about, bring to pass, cause, develop, effect, engender, father, form, found, get up, give birth to, give rise to, hatch, impose, inaugurate, induce, initiate, institute, introduce, make, multiply, muster, occasion, originate, parent, perform, procreate, propagate, provoke, reproduce, set up, sire, spawn, whip up*, work up; SEE CONCEPTS 173,205,251,374

generation [n1] *creation, production*
bearing, begetting, breeding, bringing forth, engenderment, formation, fructifying, genesis, multiplying, origination, procreation, propagation, reproduction, spawning; SEE CONCEPTS 173,205,374

generation [n2] *era; age group*
aeon, age, breed, contemporaries, crop, day, days, eon, epoch, peers, period, rank, span, step, time, times; SEE CONCEPTS 807,816

generic [adj] *common, general*
all-encompassing, blanket, collective, comprehensive, inclusive, nonexclusive, sweeping, universal, wide; SEE CONCEPT 530

generosity [n] *spirit of giving*
all heart*, alms-giving, altruism, beneficence, benevolence, bounteousness, bounty, charitableness, charity, free giving, goodness, heart, high-mindedness, hospitality, kindness, largesse, liberality, magnanimity, munificence, nobleness, openhandedness, philanthropy, profusion, readiness, unselfishness; SEE CONCEPTS 411,657

generous [adj1] *giving, big-hearted*
acceptable, altruistic, beneficent, benevolent, big, bounteous, bountiful, charitable, chivalrous, considerate, easy, equitable, excellent, fair, free, good, greathearted, helpful, high-minded, honest, honorable, hospitable, just, kind, kindhearted, kindly, lavish, liberal, lofty, loose, magnanimous, moderate, munificent, noble, open-handed, philanthropic, princely, prodigal, profuse, reasonable, soft-touch*, thoughtful, tolerant, ungrudging, unselfish, unsparing, unstinting, willing; SEE CONCEPTS 404,542

generous [adj2] *plentiful*
abundant, affluent, ample, aplenty, bounteous, bountiful, copious, dime a dozen*, full, galore, handsome, large, lavish, liberal, luxuriant, no end*, no end in sight*, overflowing, plenteous, plenty, rich, stinking with*, unstinting, wealthy; SEE CONCEPTS 334,589,781

genesis [n] *beginning, creation*
alpha, birth, commencement, dawn, dawning, engendering, formation, generation, inception, opening, origin, outset, propagation, provenance, provenience, root, source, start; SEE CONCEPTS 119,832

genetic [adj] *coming from heredity*
abiogenetic, ancestral, digenetic, eugenic, genesiological, genital, hereditary, historical, matriclinous, patrimonial, phytogenetic, sprogenous, xenogenetic; SEE CONCEPTS 314,549

genial [adj] *extremely nice and happy*
affable, agreeable, amiable, amicable, blithe, cheerful, cheering, cheery, chipper*, chirpy*, congenial, convivial, cordial, easygoing, enlivening, favorable, friendly, gentle, glad, good-natured, gracious, hearty, high, jocund, jolly, jovial, joyous, kind, kindly, merry, neighborly, perky, pleasant, sociable, sunny*, sunny side up*, up*, upbeat, upper*, warm, warm-hearted; SEE CONCEPTS 401,404

geniality [n] *extreme niceness*
affability, agreeability, agreeableness, amenity, amiability, cheerfulness, cheeriness, congenialness, conviviality, cordiality, enjoyableness, friendliness, gladness, good cheer, good nature, gratefulness, happiness, heartiness, jollity, joviality, joy, joyousness, kindliness, kindness, mirth, pleasance, pleasantness, sunniness*, sweetness and light*, warmheartedness, warmth; SEE CONCEPTS 411,633

genius [n] *gift of high intellect*
ability, accomplishment, acumen, acuteness, adept, aptitude, aptness, astuteness, bent, brain, brilliance, capability, capacity, creativity, discernment, Ein-

stein*, endowment, expert, faculty, flair, grasp, head, imagination, inclination, ingenuity, inspiration, intelligence, inventiveness, knack, maestro, master, mastermind, mature, originality, percipience, perspicacity, power, precocity, prodigy, propensity, prowess, reach, sagacity, superability, talent, turn, understanding, virtuoso, wisdom; SEE CONCEPTS *350,409,416*

genre/genus [n] *type, class*
brand, category, character, classification, fashion, group, kind, school, sort, species, style; SEE CONCEPTS *378,388,655*

genteel [adj] *sophisticated, cultured*
affected, aristocratic, artificial, chivalrous, civil, confined, courteous, courtly, cultivated, distingué, elegant, fashionable, formal, gentlemanly, graceful, hollow, intolerant, la-di-da*, ladylike, mannerly, noble, ostentatious, polished, polite, pompous, precious, pretentious, priggish, prim, prissy, provincial, prudish, puritanical, refined, respectable, straitlaced, stuffy*, stylish, urbane, well-behaved, well-bred, well-mannered; SEE CONCEPTS *401,404*

gentility [n] *sophistication, cultivation*
aristocracy, blue blood*, civility, courtesy, courtliness, culture, decorum, elegance, elite, etiquette, flower*, formality, gentle birth*, gentlefolk, gentry, good breeding*, good family*, good manners*, high birth*, mannerliness, nobility, optimacy, polish, politeness, propriety, quality, rank, refinement, respectability, ruling class*, society, upper class, upper crust*, urbanity; SEE CONCEPTS *296,388,411*

gentle [adj1] *having a mild or kind nature*
affable, agreeable, amiable, benign, biddable, bland, compassionate, considerate, cool*, cultivated, disciplined, docile, domesticated, dove-like*, easy, educated, genial, humane, kindly, laid back*, lenient, manageable, meek, mellow, merciful, moderate, pacific, peaceful, placid, pleasant, pleasing, pliable, quiet, soft, softhearted, sweet-tempered, sympathetic, tame, taught, temperate, tender, tractable, trained, warmhearted; SEE CONCEPTS *404,542*

gentle [adj2] *mild, temperate in effect on senses*
balmy, bland, calm, clement, delicate, easy, faint, feeble, gradual, halcyon, hushed, imperceptible, lenient, light, low, low-pitched, low-toned, mellow, mild, moderate, muted, peaceful, placid, quiet, sensitive, serene, slight, slow, smooth, soft, soothing, subdued, tender, tranquil, untroubled; SEE CONCEPTS *525,537,594*

gentle [adj3] *of noble birth*
aristocratic, blue-blooded*, Brahmin*, courteous, cultured, elegant, genteel, gentlemanlike, gentlemanly, high-born, highbred, ladylike, noble, polished, polite, refined, upper-class, well-born, well-bred; SEE CONCEPT *555*

gentleman [n] *man who behaves properly; man born to high social standing*
aristocrat, blue blood*, Brahmin*, brick*, cavalier, esquire, fellow, good egg*, good guy*, lord, nice

guy*, nobleman, patrician, pussycat*, scholar, sir, swell*; SEE CONCEPTS *419,423*

gentlemanly [adj] *cultivated, polished*
civil, civilized, courteous, cultured, gallant, genteel, gentlemanlike, honorable, mannerly, noble, obliging, polished, polite, refined, reputable, suave, urbane, well-bred, well-mannered; SEE CONCEPT *401*

genuine [adj1] *authentic, real*
18-carat*, 24-carat*, absolute, accurate, actual, authenticated, bona fide, certain, certified, demonstrable, exact, existent, factual, for real*, good, hard, honest, honest-to-goodness*, indubitable, in the flesh*, kosher*, legit, legitimate, literal, natural, official, original, palpable, plain, positive, precise, proved, pure, real stuff*, sound, sterling, sure-enough*, tested, true, unadulterated, unalloyed, undoubted, unimpeachable, unquestionable, unvarnished, valid, veritable, very, whole; SEE CONCEPT *582*

genuine [adj2] *unaffected; honest*
actual, artless, candid, earnest, frank, heartfelt, known, natural, open, positive, real, reliable, righteous, sincere, true, trustworthy, undesigning, unfeigned, unimpeachable, unpretended, unquestionable, up front*, valid, well-established; SEE CONCEPTS *267,542*

geography [n] *the earth's features; study of land*
cartography, chorography, earth science, geology, geopolitical study, geopolitics, physiographics, physiography, topography, topology; SEE CONCEPTS *349,509*

germ [n1] *microscopic organism, often causing illness*
antibody, bacterium, bug*, disease, microbe, microorganism, parasite, pathogen, plague, virus, what's going around*; SEE CONCEPTS *306,392*

germ [n2] *beginning*
bud, cause, egg, embryo, inception, nucleus, origin, ovule, ovum, root, rudiment, seed, source, spark, spore, sprig, sprout; SEE CONCEPTS *392,648,826,832*

germane [adj] *appropriate*
ad rem, akin, allied, applicable, applicative, applicatory, apposite, apropos, apt, cognate, connected, fitting, kindred, kosher*, legit*, material, on target*, on the button*, on the nose*, pertinent, proper, related, relating, relevant, right on*, suitable, that's the ticket*, to the point, to the purpose; SEE CONCEPT *558*

germinate [v] *grow*
bud, develop, generate, live, originate, pullulate, shoot, sprout, swell, vegetate; SEE CONCEPT *427*

gestation [n] *process of early development*
evolution, fecundation, gravidity, growth, incubation, maturation, pregnancy, reproduction, ripening; SEE CONCEPTS *316,704,809*

gesture [n] *motion as communication*
action, body language, bow, curtsy, expression, genuflection, gesticulation, high sign, indication, intimation, kinesics, mime, nod, pantomime, reminder,

393

salute, shrug, sign, signal, sign language, token, wave, wink; SEE CONCEPT **74**

gesture/gesticulate [v] *make signs, motions to communicate*
act out, flag, indicate, mime, motion, pantomime, sign, signal, signalize, use one's hands, use sign language, wave; SEE CONCEPT **74**

get [v1] *come into possession of; achieve*
access, accomplish, acquire, annex, attain, bag*, bring, bring in, build up, buy into, buy off, buy out, capture, cash in on*, chalk up*, clean up*, clear, come by, compass, cop*, draw, earn, educe, effect, elicit, evoke, extort, extract, fetch, gain, get hands on*, glean, grab, have, hustle*, inherit, land, lock up, make, make a buy, make a killing*, net, obtain, parlay, pick up, procure, pull, rack up*, realize, reap, receive, score, secure, snag*, snap up*, snowball*, succeed to, take, wangle*, win; SEE CONCEPTS **120,706,710**

get [v2] *fall victim to*
accept, be afflicted with, become infected with, be given, be smitten by, catch, come down with*, contract, get sick, receive, sicken, succumb, take; SEE CONCEPT **93**

get [v3] *seize*
apprehend, arrest, bag*, beat, capture, catch, collar*, defeat, grab, lay hold of*, lay one's hands on*, nab*, nail*, occupy, overcome, overpower, secure, take, trap; SEE CONCEPT **90**

get [v4] *come to be*
achieve, attain, become, come over, develop into, effect, go, grow, realize, run, turn, wax*; SEE CONCEPTS **697,706**

get [v5] *understand*
acquire, catch, catch on to, comprehend, fathom, figure out, follow, gain, get into one's head*, hear, know, learn, look at, master, memorize, notice, perceive, pick up*, receive, see, take in, work out; SEE CONCEPTS **15,31**

get [v6] *arrive*
advance, blow in*, come, come to, converge, draw near, land, make it, reach, show, show up, turn up; SEE CONCEPT **159**

get [v7] *contact for communication*
communicate, get in touch, reach; SEE CONCEPT **266**

get [v8] *arrange, manage desired goal*
adjust, contrive, dispose, dress, fit, fix, make, make up, order, prepare, ready, straighten, succeed, wangle*; SEE CONCEPT **202**

get [v9] *convince, induce*
argue into, beg, bring around, coax, compel, draw, influence, persuade, press, pressure, prevail upon, prompt, provoke, sway, talk into, urge, wheedle, win over; SEE CONCEPT **68**

get [v10] *have an effect on*
affect, amuse, arouse, bend, bias, carry, dispose, entertain, excite, gratify, impress, influence, inspire,

move, predispose, prompt, satisfy, stimulate, stir, stir up, strike, sway, touch; SEE CONCEPTS **7,22**

get [v11] *produce offspring*
beget, breed, father, generate, mother, procreate, produce, propagate, sire; SEE CONCEPT **374**

get [v12] *irritate, upset*
aggravate, annoy, bother, bug*, burn, exasperate, gall, get someone's goat*, irk, nettle, peeve, pique, provoke, put out*, rile, rub the wrong way*, try, vex; SEE CONCEPTS **7,19**

get [v13] *confuse*
baffle, beat, bewilder, buffalo*, confound, discomfit, disconcert, distress, disturb, embarrass, mystify, nonplus, perplex, perturb, puzzle, stick*, stump, upset; SEE CONCEPT **16**

get across [v] *communicate an idea*
bring home*, convey, get through to, impart, make clear, make understood, pass on, put over, transmit; SEE CONCEPT **60**

get ahead [v] *excel, succeed*
advance, be successful, climb, do well, flourish, get on, leave behind, make good, outdo, outmaneuver, overtake, progress, prosper, surpass, thrive; SEE CONCEPTS **141,706**

get along [v1] *make progress*
cope, develop, do, fare, flourish, get by*, get on*, make out, manage, muddle through*, progress, prosper, shift, succeed, thrive; SEE CONCEPTS **117,704**

get along [v2] *depart*
advance, be off, go, go away, leave, march, move, move off, move on, proceed, progress, push ahead, take a hike*; SEE CONCEPT **195**

get along [v3] *be compatible*
agree, be friendly, get on*, harmonize, hit it off*; SEE CONCEPT **388**

get at [v1] *attain*
access, achieve, acquire, arrive, ascertain, gain access, get, get hold of, reach; SEE CONCEPT **120**

get at [v2] *mean, intend*
aim, hint, imply, lead up to, purpose, suggest; SEE CONCEPT **75**

getaway [n] *escape*
break, breakout, decampment, escaping, flight, lam, slip; SEE CONCEPT **102**

get back [v1] *regain*
reclaim, recoup, recover, repossess, retrieve, salvage; SEE CONCEPT **120**

get back [v2] *return*
arrive home, come back, come home, reappear, revert, revisit, turn back; SEE CONCEPT **159**

get back at [v] *settle a score*
be avenged, get even, pay back, retaliate, revenge, take vengeance; SEE CONCEPTS **14,246**

get by [v] *manage, survive*
contrive, cope, do, do well enough, exist, fare, flourish, get along, get on, make ends meet*, make out, muddle through*, prosper, shift, subsist, succeed, thrive; SEE CONCEPT **117**

get down [v] *dismount*
alight, bring down, climb down, come down, descend, disembark, get off, lower, step down; SEE CONCEPT *154*

get in [v] *infiltrate; find a way in*
alight, appear, arrive, blow in*, come, embark, enter, gain ingress, get inside, include, insert, interpose, land, mount, penetrate, reach, show, show up, turn up; SEE CONCEPT *159*

get off [v] *depart*
alight, blow*, descend, disembark, dismount, escape, exit, go, go away, leave, light, pull out, quit, retire, withdraw; SEE CONCEPTS *154,195*

get on [v1] *mount*
ascend, board, climb, embark, enplane, entrain, go up, scale; SEE CONCEPTS *159,166*

get on [v2] *cope, progress*
advance, do, do well enough, fare, get along, get by, make out, manage, muddle through*, prosper, shift, succeed; SEE CONCEPTS *117,704*

get on [v3] *be compatible*
agree, be friendly, concur, get along, harmonize, hit it off; SEE CONCEPT *388*

get on [v4] *put clothing on*
assume, attire, don, draw on, dress, slip into, throw on, wear; SEE CONCEPT *167*

get out [v] *escape*
alight, avoid, beat it*, begone, be off, break out, bug off*, buzz off*, clear out, decamp, depart, dodge, duck, egress, evacuate, evade, exit, extricate oneself, flee, fly, free oneself, go, hightail*, kite*, leave, make tracks*, run away, scram*, shirk, shun, skedaddle*, split, take a hike*, take off, vacate, vamoose*, withdraw; SEE CONCEPTS *102,195*

get over [v] *recover*
come round, get better, mend, overcome, pull through, recuperate, shake off, survive; SEE CONCEPT *35*

get together [v] *gather, accumulate*
assemble, collect, congregate, convene, converge, join, meet, muster, rally, unite; SEE CONCEPTS *109,113*

get up [v] *mount; get out of bed*
arise, ascend, awake, awaken, climb, increase, move up, pile out*, rise, rise and shine*, roll out, scale, spring out, stand, turn out, uprise, upspring; SEE CONCEPT *154*

ghastly [adj] *horrifying, dreadful; pale*
abhorrent, anemic, appalling, ashen, awful, bloodless, cadaverous, corpselike, deathlike, dim, disgusting, faint, frightening, frightful, funereal, ghostly, ghoulish, grim, grisly, gruesome, haggard, hideous, horrendous, horrible, horrid, livid, loathsome, lurid, macabre, mortuary, nauseating, offensive, pallid, repellent, repulsive, sepulchral, shocking, sickening, spectral, supernatural, terrible, terrifying, uncanny, unearthly, unnatural, unpleasant, wan, weak, wraithlike; SEE CONCEPTS *485,529,537*

ghost [n] *spirit of the dead*
apparition, appearance, banshee, daemon, demon, devil, eidolon, ethereal being, haunt, incorporeal being, kelpie, manes, phantasm, phantom, poltergeist, revenant, shade, shadow, soul, specter, spirit, spook, vampire, vision, visitor, wraith, zombie; SEE CONCEPT *370*

ghostly [adj] *spooky*
apparitional, cadaverous, corpselike, deathlike, divine, eerie, eidolic, ghastly, ghostlike, haunted, holy, illusory, insubstantial, pale, phantasmal, phantom, scary, shadowy, spectral, spiritual, spookish, supernatural, uncanny, unearthly, vampiric, wan, weird, wraithlike, wraithy; SEE CONCEPTS *485,537*

giant [n] *extremely large person*
behemoth, bulk, colossus, cyclops, elephant*, goliath, Hercules*, hulk, jumbo*, leviathan, mammoth, monster*, mountain*, ogre, polypheme, titan, whale*, whopper*; SEE CONCEPT *424*

giant [adj] *very large*
big, blimp*, brobdingnagian*, colossal, cyclopean, elephantine*, enormous, gargantuan, gigantic, gross*, Herculean*, huge, hulking, humongous*, immense, jumbo*, mammoth, monstrous*, mountainous, prodigious, super-duper*, titanic, vast, whale of a*, whaling*; SEE CONCEPTS *491,773,779,781*

gibberish [n] *nonsense talk*
babble, balderdash*, blah-blah*, blather, chatter, claptrap*, double talk*, drivel, gobbledygook*, hocus-pocus*, jabber*, jargon, mumbo jumbo*, palaver*, prattle, scat*, twaddle*, yammer*; SEE CONCEPT *278*

gibe [n] *ridicule*
comeback, cutting remark, derision, dig*, dump*, jab, jeer, joke, mockery, parting shot*, put-down*, rank-out*, sarcasm, scoffing, slam*, sneer, swipe, taunt; SEE CONCEPT *278*

gibe [v] *ridicule*
deride, dis*, disrespect, flout, jeer, make fun of*, mock, poke fun at*, scoff, scorn, sneer, taunt; SEE CONCEPTS *52,54*

giddy [adj] *silly, impulsive*
bemused, brainless, bubbleheaded*, capricious, careless, changeable, changeful, ditzy*, dizzy, emptyheaded*, erratic, fickle, flighty*, flustered, frivolous, gaga*, heedless, inconstant, irresolute, irresponsible, lightheaded*, punchy*, reckless, reeling, scatterbrained*, skittish*, slaphappy*, swimming*, thoughtless, unbalanced, unsettled, unstable, unsteady, vacillating, volatile, whimsical, whirling, wild, woozy*; SEE CONCEPTS *314,401*

gift [n1] *something given freely, for no recompense*
allowance, alms, award, benefaction, benefit, bequest, bestowal, bonus, boon, bounty, charity, contribution, courtesy, dispensation, donation, endowment, fairing, favor, gifting, giveaway, goodie, grant, gratuity, hand, hand-me-down*, handout, honorarium, lagniappe, largesse, legacy, libation,

oblation, offering, offertory, philanthropy, pittance, premium, present, presentation, provision, ration, relief, remembrance, remittance, reward, souvenir, subscription, subsidy, tip, token, tribute, write-off*; SEE CONCEPT *337*

gift [n2] *talent, aptitude*
ability, accomplishment, acquirement, aptness, attainment, attribute, bent, capability, capacity, endowment, faculty, flair, forte, genius, head*, instinct, knack, leaning, nose*, numen, power, propensity, set, specialty, turn; SEE CONCEPTS *409, 630,706*

gifted [adj] *talented, intelligent*
able, accomplished, adroit, brilliant, capable, class act, clever, expert, got it*, have on the ball*, have smarts*, have the goods*, hot*, hotshot, ingenious, mad, masterly, phenomenal, shining at*, skilled, smart; SEE CONCEPTS *402,527,528*

gigantic [adj] *very large*
blimp, brobdingnagian*, colossal, cyclopean*, elephantine, enormous, gargantuan, giant, gross*, Herculean*, huge, immense, jumbo*, mammoth, massive, Moby*, monster, monstrous, prodigious, stupendous, super-colossal*, titan, tremendous, vast, whopping*; SEE CONCEPTS *491,773,779,781*

giggle [n/v] *snickering laugh*
cackle, chortle, chuckle, guffaw*, hee-haw*, snicker, snigger, teehee*, titter, twitter; SEE CONCEPT *77*

gild [v] *embellish, decorate*
adorn, aureate, aurify, beautify, bedeck, begild, brighten, coat, deck, dress up, embellish, embroider, engild, enhance, enrich, garnish, glitter, grace, ornament, overlay, paint, plate, tinsel, varnish, wash, whitewash*; SEE CONCEPTS *172,177,202*

gimmick [n] *contrived object; scheme*
aid, apparatus, artifice, catch, concern, contrivance, counterfeit, deceit, device, dodge*, fake, feint, fixture, fun, gadget, gambit, game, gizmo*, imposture, instrument, jest, maneuver, means, method, ploy, ruse, secret, shift, sport, stratagem, stunt, trick, widget*, wile; SEE CONCEPTS *59,260,660*

gingerly [adj] *careful*
calculating, cautious, chary, circumspect, considerate, dainty, delicate, discreet, fastidious, guarded, hesitant, reluctant, safe, squeamish, suspicious, timid, wary; SEE CONCEPTS *542,550*

gingerly [adv] *carefully*
cautiously, charily, circumspectly, daintily, delicately, discreetly, fastidiously, guardedly, hesitantly, reluctantly, safely, squeamishly, suspiciously, timidly, warily; SEE CONCEPTS *542,550*

gird [v1] *encircle; strengthen*
band, belt, bind, block, blockade, bolster, brace, buttress, cincture, circle, enclose, encompass, enfold, environ, fasten, fortify, girdle, hem in*, make ready, pen, prepare, ready, reinforce, ring, round, secure, steel, support, surround; SEE CONCEPTS *250,758*

gird [v2] *make fun of*
deride, flout, fun at, gibe, jeer, jest, mock, poke, quip, ridicule, scoff, scorn, sneer, taunt; SEE CONCEPTS *52,54*

girl [n] *female person, usually young*
baby, chick*, coed, cupcake*, cutie*, dame*, damsel, daughter, debutante, female, gal, lady, lassie, mademoiselle, maid, maiden, miss, schoolgirl, she, sis*, spring chicken*, teenybopper*, tomboy*, virgin; SEE CONCEPTS *415,424*

gist [n] *meaning, essence*
basis, bearing, bottom line*, burden, core, drift, force, heart, idea, import, kernel*, keynote, marrow, matter, meat*, name of the game*, nature of the beast*, nitty gritty*, nuts and bolts*, pith*, point, punch line, quintessence, score, sense, short, significance, soul, spirit, stuff*, subject, substance, summary, tenor, theme, thrust, topic, upshot*; SEE CONCEPT *682*

give [v1] *contribute, supply, transfer*
accord, administer, allow, ante up, award, bequeath, bestow, cede, come across, commit, confer, consign, convey, deed, deliver, dish out*, dispense, dispose of, dole out, donate, endow, entrust, fork over*, furnish, gift, grant, hand down, hand out, hand over, heap upon, lavish upon, lay upon, lease, let have, make over*, parcel out, part with, pass down, pass out, permit, pony up*, present, provide, relinquish, remit, sell, shell out*, subsidize, throw in, tip, transmit, turn over, vouchsafe, will; SEE CONCEPTS *108,223,243*

give [v2] *communicate*
air, announce, be a source of, broadcast, carry, deliver, emit, express, furnish, impart, issue, notify, present, pronounce, publish, put, read, render, state, supply, transfer, transmit, utter, vent, ventilate; SEE CONCEPTS *60,266*

give [v3] *demonstrate, proffer*
administer, bestow, confer, dispense, display, evidence, extend, furnish, hold out, indicate, issue, manifest, minister, offer, pose, present, produce, provide, put on, render, return, set forth, show, tender, yield; SEE CONCEPTS *97,118*

give [v4] *yield, collapse*
allow, bend, bow to, break, cave, cede, concede, contract, crumble, crumple, devote, fail, fall, flex, fold, fold up, give way, go, grant, hand over, lend, open, recede, relax, relent, relinquish, retire, retreat, sag, shrink, sink, slacken, surrender, weaken; SEE CONCEPTS *13,469*

give [v5] *perform action*
address, apply, bend, buckle down, cause, devote, direct, do, engender, lead, make, occasion, produce, throw, turn; SEE CONCEPT *100*

give away [v1] *reveal*
betray, blab*, disclose, discover, divulge, expose, inform, leak, let out, let slip, mouth*, spill, tell, uncover; SEE CONCEPT *60*

give away [v2] *unselfishly transfer*
award, bestow, devote, donate, hand out, present; SEE CONCEPT *108*

give in/give up [v] *admit defeat*
abandon, back down*, bail out*, bow out*, buckle under*, capitulate, cave in*, cease, cede, chicken out*, collapse, comply, concede, cry uncle*, cut out, desist, despair, drop, drop like hot potato*, fold, forswear, give up, hand over, leave off, pull out, quit, relinquish, resign, stop, submit, surrender, take the oath*, throw in the towel*, waive, walk out on, wash one's hands of*, yield; SEE CONCEPTS *8,45,119,385*

given to [adj] *likely to*
accustomed, addicted, apt, disposed, habituated, inclined, in the habit of, inured, liable, obsessed, prone; SEE CONCEPT *542*

give off/give out [v] *discharge*
beam, belch, effuse, emanate, emit, exhale, exude, flow, give forth, issue, pour, produce, radiate, release, send out, smell of, throw out, vent, void; SEE CONCEPT *179*

glacial [adj1] *extremely cold*
antarctic, arctic, biting, bitter, chill, chilly, cold, cool, freezing, frigid, frosty, frozen, gelid, icy, nippy, piercing, polar, raw, wintry; SEE CONCEPT *605*

glacial [adj2] *unfriendly*
aloof, antagonistic, chill, cold, cool, distant, emotionless, frigid, hostile, icy, inaccessible, indifferent, inimical, remote, reserved, seclusive, standoffish, unapproachable, unemotional, withdrawn; SEE CONCEPTS *401,404*

glacier [n] *mountain of ice, snow*
berg, floe, glacial mass, iceberg, icecap, ice field, ice floe, snow slide; SEE CONCEPT *509*

glad [adj] *happy, delightful*
animated, beaming, beautiful, blithesome, bright, can't complain*, cheerful, cheering, cheery, contented, delighted, exhilarated, felicitous, floating on air*, gay, genial, gleeful, gratified, gratifying, hilarious, jocund, jovial, joyful, joyous, lighthearted, merry, mirthful, overjoyed, pleasant, pleased, pleased as punch*, pleasing, radiant, rejoicing, sparkling, tickled, tickled pink*, tickled to death*, up, willing; SEE CONCEPTS *403,529*

gladly [adv] *happily*
acquiescently, ardently, beatifically, blissfully, blithely, cheerfully, cheerily, contentedly, cordially, delightedly, delightfully, ecstatically, enchantedly, enthusiastically, felicitously, freely, gaily, genially, gleefully, gratefully, heartily, jocundly, jovially, joyfully, joyously, lovingly, merrily, paradisiacally, passionately, pleasantly, pleasingly, pleasurably, rapturously, readily, sweetly, warmly, willingly, with good grace, with pleasure, with relish, zealously, zestfully; SEE CONCEPTS *403,538,542*

gladness [n] *happiness*
animation, blitheness, cheer, cheerfulness, delight, felicity, gaiety, glee, high spirits*, hilarity, jollity,
joy, joyousness, mirth, pleasure; SEE CONCEPT *410*

glamorous [adj] *sophisticated in style*
alluring, attractive, bewitching, captivating, charismatic, charming, classy, dazzling, drop-dead gorgeous*, elegant, enchanting, entrancing, exciting, fascinating, flashy, foxy*, glittering, glossy, looking like a million*, lovely, magnetic, nifty, prestigious, righteous, seductive, siren, smart; SEE CONCEPTS *579,589*

glamour [n] *sophisticated style*
allure, allurement, animal magnetism, appeal, attraction, beauty, bewitchment, charisma, charm, color, enchantment, fascination, interest, magnetism, prestige, ravishment, razzle-dazzle*, romance, star quality, witchery; SEE CONCEPTS *655,718*

glance [n1] *brief look*
eye*, eyeball*, flash*, fleeting look, gander, glimpse, lamp*, look, look-see*, peek, peep, quick look, sight, slant*, squint, swivel*, view; SEE CONCEPT *623*

glance [n2] *reflection of light*
coruscation, flash, gleam, glimmer, glint, glisten, shimmer, sparkle, twinkle; SEE CONCEPTS *624,628*

glance [v1] *look at briefly*
browse, check out, dip into*, flash*, flip through, gaze, get a load of*, glimpse, leaf through, peek, peep, peer, riffle through*, run over, run through, scan, see, skim through*, take a gander*, take in, thumb through*, view; SEE CONCEPT *623*

glance [v2] *reflect light*
coruscate, flash, gleam, glimmer, glint, glisten, glitter, shimmer, shine, sparkle, twinkle; SEE CONCEPT *624*

glance [v3] *ricochet, hit off of something*
bounce, brush, careen, carom, contact, dart, graze, kiss*, rebound, scrape, shave*, sideswipe, skim, skip, slant, slide, strike, touch; SEE CONCEPT *189*

glare [n1] *very bright light, shine*
blaze, blinding light, brilliance, dazzle, flame, flare, glow; SEE CONCEPT *628*

glare [n2] *dirty look*
angry stare, bad eye*, black look*, evil eye*, frown, glower, lower, scowl; SEE CONCEPTS *623,716*

glare [v1] *give a dirty look*
bore, do a slow burn*, fix, frown, gape, gawk, gaze, glower, look daggers*, lower, menace, peer, pierce, scowl, stare, stare angrily*, stare icily*, wither; SEE CONCEPT *623*

glare [v2] *shine very brightly*
beam, blare, blaze, blind, blur, daze, dazzle, flame, flare, glaze, glow, radiate; SEE CONCEPT *624*

glaring [adj1] *obvious, unconcealed*
audacious, blatant, brazen, capital, conspicuous, crying, egregious, evident, excessive, extreme, flagrant, gross, inordinate, manifest, noticeable, obtrusive, open, outrageous, outstanding, overt, patent, protrusive, rank, visible; SEE CONCEPTS *576,619*

glaring [adj2] *bright, dazzling; flashy*
blatant, blazing, blinding, brazen, chintzy, florid, garish, gaudy, glowing, loud, meretricious, shining, tawdry; SEE CONCEPTS *589,617*

glass [n1] *object that reflects an image*
looking glass, mirror, reflector, seeing glass; SEE CONCEPTS *260,470*

glass [n2] *object used for drinking liquids*
beaker, bottle, chalice, cup, decanter, goblet, highball, jar, jigger, jug, mug, pilsener, pony, snifter, tumbler; SEE CONCEPT *494*

glasses [n] *object worn to correct vision*
bifocals, blinkers*, cheaters*, contact lenses, eyeglasses, four eyes*, frames, goggles, lorgnette, pince nez, rims*, shades*, specs*, spectacles, trifocals; SEE CONCEPT *446*

glassy [adj1] *polished, smooth*
burnished, clear, glazed, glazy, glossy, hyaline, hyaloid, icy, lustrous, shiny, sleek, slick, slippery, transparent, vitreous, vitric; SEE CONCEPT *606*

glassy [adj2] *expressionless, especially referring to eyes*
blank, cold, dazed, dull, empty, fixed, glazed, lifeless, stupid, vacant; SEE CONCEPTS *406,619*

glaze [n] *varnish, lacquer*
coat, enamel, finish, glint, gloss, luster, patina, polish, sheen, shine; SEE CONCEPTS *259,475*

glaze [v] *varnish, lacquer*
buff, burnish, coat, cover, enamel, furbish, glance, glass, gloss, incrust, make lustrous, make vitreous, overlay, polish, rub, shine, vitrify; SEE CONCEPTS *172,202,215*

gleam [n] *brightness, sparkle*
beam, brilliance, coruscation, flash, flicker, glance, glim, glimmer, glint, glitz, gloss, glow, luster, ray, scintillation, sheen, shimmer, splendor, twinkle; SEE CONCEPTS *620,624*

gleam [v] *sparkle*
beam, burn, coruscate, flare, flash, glance, glimmer, glint, glisten, glister, glitter, glow, radiate, scintillate, shimmer, shine, twinkle; SEE CONCEPTS *620,624*

glean [v] *pick out, collect*
accumulate, amass, ascertain, conclude, cull, deduce, extract, garner, gather, harvest, learn, pick, reap, select, sift, winnow; SEE CONCEPTS *31,135*

glee [n] *extreme happiness*
blitheness, cheerfulness, delectation, delight, elation, enjoyment, exhilaration, exuberance, exultation, fun, gaiety, gladness, hilarity, jocularity, jollity, joviality, joy, joyfulness, joyousness, liveliness, merriment, mirth, pleasure, sprightliness, triumph, verve; SEE CONCEPT *410*

gleeful [adj] *very happy*
blithe, blithesome, boon, cheerful, delighted, elated, exalted, exuberant, exultant, frolicsome, gay, gratified, hilarious, jocund, jolly, jovial, joyful, joyous, jubilant, lighthearted, merry, mirthful, overjoyed, pleased, triumphant; SEE CONCEPT *403*

glen [n] *valley*
canyon, combe, dale, dell, glade, gorge, vale; SEE CONCEPT *509*

glib [adj] *slick, smooth-talking*
artful, articulate, easy, eloquent, facile, fast-talking*, flip, fluent, garrulous, hot-air*, insincere, loquacious, plausible, quick, ready, silver-tongued*, slippery*, smooth, smooth operator*, smooth-spoken*, smooth-tongued*, suave, talkative, urbane, vocal, vocative, voluble; SEE CONCEPTS *267,404*

glide [v] *move smoothly and quickly on surface*
coast, decline, descend, drift, flit, float, flow, fly, glissade, roll, run, sail, scud, shoot, skate, skim, skip, skirr, slide, slink, slip, slither, smooth along, soar, spiral, stream, trip, waft, wing; SEE CONCEPT *150*

glimmer [n] *flash, sparkle*
blink, coruscation, flicker, glance, gleam, glint, glow, grain, hint, inkling, ray, scintillation, shimmer, suggestion, trace, twinkle; SEE CONCEPTS *624,831*

glimmer [v] *sparkle*
blink, coruscate, fade, flash, flicker, glance, gleam, glint, glisten, glister, glitter, glow, scintillate, shimmer, shine, twinkle; SEE CONCEPT *624*

glimpse [n] *brief look*
eye, eyeball*, flash*, gander*, glance, glom*, gun*, impression, lamp*, look, look-see*, peek, peep, quick look, sight, sighting, slant, squint, swivel*; SEE CONCEPT *623*

glimpse [v] *look briefly*
catch sight of, check out, descry, espy, eye, flash, get a load of*, get an eyeful*, peek, sight, spot, spy, take a gander*, take in*, view; SEE CONCEPT *623*

glisten [v] *shimmer*
coruscate, flash, flicker, glance, glare, gleam, glimmer, glint, glister, glitter, glow, scintillate, shine, sparkle, twinkle; SEE CONCEPT *624*

glitter [n] *brilliance, sparkle*
beam, brightness, coruscation, display, flash, gaudiness, glamor, glare, gleam, glint, glisten, glister, glitz, luster, pageantry, radiance, scintillation, sheen, shimmer, shine, show, showiness, splendor, tinsel, twinkle, zap*; SEE CONCEPTS *620,655*

glitter [v] *sparkle*
coruscate, flash, glance, glare, gleam, glimmer, glint, glisten, glister, glow, scintillate, shimmer, shine, spangle, twinkle; SEE CONCEPT *624*

gloat [v] *exclaim triumph*
celebrate, crow*, exult, glory, rejoice, relish, rub it in*, triumph, vaunt, whoop*; SEE CONCEPT *49*

global [adj] *worldwide, all-encompassing*
all-around, all-inclusive, all-out, blanket, catholic, comprehensive, cosmic, cosmopolitan, earthly, ecumenical, encyclopedic, exhaustive, general, grand, international, mundane, overall, pandemic, planetary, spherical, sweeping, thorough, total, un-

bounded, universal, unlimited, world; SEE CONCEPTS *536,772*

globe [*n*] *earth, sphere*
apple*, ball, balloon*, big blue marble*, map, Mother Earth*, orb, planet, rondure, round, spaceship Earth*, spheroid, terrene, world; SEE CONCEPTS *436,511*

gloom [*n1*] *melancholy, depression*
anguish, bitterness, blue devils*, blue funk*, blues*, catatonia, chagrin, cheerlessness, dejection, desolation, despair, despondency, disconsolateness, discouragement, dismals, distress, doldrums, dolor, downheartedness, dullness, dumps*, foreboding, grief, heaviness, heavy-heartedness, horror, low spirits*, malaise, melancholia, misery, misgiving, mopes, morbidity, mourning, oppression, pensiveness, pessimism, sadness, saturninity, sorrow, unhappiness, vexation, weariness, woe; SEE CONCEPT *410*

gloom [*n2*] *darkness, blackness*
bleakness, cloud, cloudiness, dark, dimness, dullness, dusk, duskiness, gloominess, murk, murkiness, obscurity, shade, shadow, twilight; SEE CONCEPTS *620,622,810*

gloomy [*adj1*] *dark, black*
bleak, caliginous, cheerless, clouded, cloudy, crepuscular, desolate, dim, dismal, dreary, dull, dusky, forlorn, funereal, lightless, murky, obscure, overcast, overclouded, sepulchral, shadowy, somber, tenebrous, unilluminated, unlit, wintry; SEE CONCEPTS *525,617,618*

gloomy [*adj2*] *feeling down, blue*
blue*, blue funk*, broody, chapfallen, cheerless, crabbed*, crestfallen, dejected, depressed, desolate, despondent, disconsolate, dismal, dispirited, dour, down, downcast, downhearted, down in the dumps*, down in the mouth*, dragged, forlorn, glum, in low spirits*, in the dumps*, joyless, low, melancholy, mirthless, miserable, moody, moping, mopish, morose, mournful, oppressed, pessimistic, sad, saturnine, solemn, sulky, sullen, surly, ugly, unhappy, weary, woebegone, woeful; SEE CONCEPT *403*

gloomy [*adj3*] *sad, depressing*
acheronian, acherontic, bad, black, bleak, cheerless, cold, comfortless, depressing, depressive, desolate, disconsolate, discouraging, disheartening, dismal, dispiriting, drab, dreary, dull, dusky, funereal, joyless, lugubrious, morose, oppressive, saddening, somber, tenebrific; SEE CONCEPTS *537,548*

glorify [*v1*] *praise*
acclaim, bless, boost, build up, celebrate, commend, cry up, eulogize, exalt, extol, hike, honor, hymn, laud, lionize, magnify, panegyrize, put on a pedestal*, put up, sing the praises of*; SEE CONCEPT *69*

glorify [*v2*] *adore, idolize*
adorn, aggrandize, apotheosize, augment, beatify, bless, canonize, deify, dignify, distinguish, elevate, enhance, ennoble, enshrine, erect, exalt, halo*,

honor, illuminate, immortalize, lift up, magnify, pay homage to, raise, revere, sanctify, transfigure, uprear, venerate, worship; SEE CONCEPT *12*

glorious [*adj*] *adored, idolized; divine*
august, beautiful, bright, brilliant, celebrated, dazzling, delightful, distinguished, effulgent, elevated, eminent, enjoyable, esteemed, exalted, excellent, famed, famous, fine, gorgeous, grand, gratifying, great, heavenly, heroic, honored, illustrious, immortal, magnificent, majestic, marvelous, memorable, noble, notable, noted, pleasurable, preeminent, radiant, remarkable, renowned, resplendent, shining, splendid, sublime, superb, time-honored, triumphant, venerable, well-known, wonderful; SEE CONCEPTS *568,574,579*

glory [*n1*] *fame, importance*
celebrity, dignity, distinction, eminence, exaltation, grandeur, greatness, honor, illustriousness, immortality, kudos, magnificence, majesty, nobility, praise, prestige, renown, reputation, splendor, sublimity, triumph; SEE CONCEPTS *388,668*

glory [*n2*] *great beauty*
brightness, brilliance, effulgence, fineness, gorgeousness, grandeur, luster, magnificence, majesty, pageantry, pomp, preciousness, radiance, resplendence, richness, splendor, sublimity, sumptuousness; SEE CONCEPTS *673,718*

glory [*v*] *boast, exult*
crow, gloat, jubilate, pride oneself, relish, revel, take delight, triumph; SEE CONCEPTS *12,49*

gloss [*n1*] *shine, sheen*
appearance, brightness, brilliance, burnish, facade, finish, front, glaze, gleam, glint, glossiness, luster, polish, shimmer, silkiness, sleekness, slickness, surface, varnish, veneer; SEE CONCEPTS *611,620*

gloss [*n2*] *definition*
annotation, comment, commentary, elucidation, explanation, footnote, interpretation, note, translation; SEE CONCEPT *268*

gloss [*v1*] *make shiny*
buff, burnish, finish, furbish, glance, glaze, lacquer, polish, rub, shine, varnish, veneer; SEE CONCEPTS *202,215*

gloss [*v2*] *conceal truth*
belie, camouflage, cover up, deacon, disguise, doctor, explain, extenuate, falsify, hide, justify, mask, misrepresent, palliate, rationalize, smooth over, softpedal, sugarcoat*, varnish, veil, veneer, white, whiten, whitewash*; SEE CONCEPTS *49,63*

gloss [*v3*] *define*
annotate, comment, construe, elucidate, explain, interpret, justify, translate; SEE CONCEPT *57*

glossy [*adj*] *shiny*
bright, brilliant, burnished, glassy, glazed, gleaming, glistening, lustrous, polished, reflecting, shining, silken, silky, sleek, slick, smooth; SEE CONCEPTS *606,617*

glove [n] *hand covering for warmth, protection*
gage, gauntlet, mitt, mitten, muff; SEE CONCEPT *451*

glow [n] *burning, brightness*
afterglow, bloom, blossom, blush, brilliance, effulgence, flush, glare, gleam, glimmer, glitter, gusto, heat, incandescence, intensity, lambency, light, luminosity, passion, phosphorescence, radiance, ray, splendor, vividness, warmth; SEE CONCEPTS *610, 620,622,673*

glow [v] *burn, radiate*
be suffused, blare, blaze, blush, brighten, color, crimson, fill, flame, flare, flush, gleam, glimmer, glisten, glitter, ignite, kindle, light, mantle, pink, pinken, redden, rose, rouge, shine, smolder, thrill, tingle, twinkle; SEE CONCEPTS *249,469,624*

glower [v] *frown*
glare, gloom, look, look daggers*, lower, scowl, stare, sulk, watch; SEE CONCEPT *623*

glowing [adj1] *burning, bright*
aglow, beaming, flaming, florid, flush, flushed, gleaming, lambent, luminous, lustrous, phosphorescent, red, rich, rubicund, ruddy, sanguine, suffused, vibrant, vivid, warm; SEE CONCEPTS *617,618*

glowing [adj2] *very happy, enthusiastic*
adulatory, ardent, avid, blazing, burning, complimentary, desirous, eager, ecstatic, eulogistic, fervent, fervid, fierce, fiery, flaming, heated, hot-blooded, impassioned, keen, laudatory, panegyrical, passionate, rave, rhapsodic, zealous; SEE CONCEPTS *267,401*

glue [n] *adhesive*
cement, gum, gunk*, mucilage, paste, plaster, spit*, stickum*; SEE CONCEPT *475*

glut [n] *overabundance*
excess, nimiety, oversupply, plenitude, saturation, superabundance, superfluity, surfeit, surplus, too much*; SEE CONCEPTS *740,786*

glut [v] *choke; oversupply*
burden, clog, cloy, congest, cram, deluge, devour, feast, fill, flood, gorge, hog*, inundate, jade, load, make a pig of*, overfeed, overload, overstock, overwhelm, pack*, pall, raven, sate, satiate, saturate, stuff, surfeit, wolf*; SEE CONCEPTS *140,169,209,740*

glutton [n] *person who overeats*
epicure, gorger*, gormandizer, gourmand, hefty eater, hog*, pig*, sensualist, stuffer*; SEE CONCEPT *412*

gnarled [adj] *knotted*
bent, contorted, crooked, deformed, distorted, gnarly, knotty, knurled, leathery, out of shape, rough, rugged, tortured, twisted, weather-beaten, wrinkled; SEE CONCEPTS *485,486*

gnaw [v1] *bite, chew*
champ, chaw, chomp, consume, corrode, crunch, devour, eat, eat away, erode, gum, masticate, munch, nibble, wear; SEE CONCEPTS *169,185*

gnaw [v2] *be bothered, worried about*
annoy, bedevil, beleague, bother, distress, eat at*, fret, harass, harry, haunt, irritate, nag, pester, plague, prey on one's mind*, rankle, tease, trouble, wear down, worry; SEE CONCEPTS *17,34*

gnome [n] *troll*
dwarf, elf, fairy, Tom Thumb*, tot; SEE CONCEPT *424*

go [n1] *spirit, vitality*
activity, animation, bang, birr*, drive, energy, force, get-up-and-go*, hardihood, life, moxie*, oomph*, pep, potency, push, snap*, starch*, tuck*, verve, vigor, vivacity, zest; SEE CONCEPT *411*

go [n2] *try, attempt*
bid, crack, effort, essay, fling, pop, shot, slap, stab, turn, whack, whirl; SEE CONCEPTS *87,677*

go [v1] *advance, proceed physically*
abscond, approach, beat it*, bug out*, cruise, decamp, depart, escape, exit, fare, flee, fly, get away, get going*, get lost, get off*, hie, hightail*, hit the road*, journey, lam, leave, light out*, make a break for it*, make for*, make one's way*, mosey*, move, move out, near, pass, progress, pull out, push off, push on, quit, repair, retire, run along, run away, set off, shove off*, skip out*, split*, take a hike*, take a powder*, take flight, take leave*, take off*, travel, vamoose*, wend, withdraw; SEE CONCEPTS *159,195*

go [v2] *operate, function*
act, carry on, click*, continue, flourish, maintain, make out, move, pan out*, perform, persist, prosper, run, score, succeed, thrive, work; SEE CONCEPTS *4,239*

go [v3] *span, stretch*
connect, cover, extend, fit, give access, lead, make, range, reach, run, spread, vary; SEE CONCEPTS *651,756*

go [v4] *contribute, work towards an end*
avail, befall, chance, come, concur, conduce, develop, eventuate, fall out, fare, happen, incline, lead to, occur, persevere, persist, proceed, result, serve, tend, transpire, turn, turn out, wax*, work out; SEE CONCEPTS *87,704*

go [v5] *agree, harmonize*
accord, be adapted for, be designed for, belong, blend, chime, complement, conform, correspond, dovetail*, enjoy, fit, jibe*, like, match, mesh, relish, set, square, suit; SEE CONCEPTS *8,664,714*

go [v6] *die, collapse*
bend, break, cave, conclude, consume, crumble, decease, decline, demise, depart, deplete, devour, dissipate, drop, exhaust, expend, expire, fail, finish, fold up, fritter, give, pass away*, pass on*, perish, run through*, spend, squander, succumb, terminate, use up, waste, weaken, worsen, yield; SEE CONCEPTS *105,698,699*

go [v7] *elapse*
be spent, expire, flow, lapse, pass, pass away, slip away, transpire, waste away; SEE CONCEPT *804*

go [v8] *endure*
abide, allow, bear, brook, consent to, let, permit, put up with*, stand, stomach*, suffer, swallow*, take, tolerate; SEE CONCEPT *23*

go about [v] *undertake*
approach, be employed, begin, devote oneself to, engage in, get busy with, occupy oneself with, set about, tackle, work at; SEE CONCEPT *100*

goad [n] *stimulus*
catalyst, compulsion, desire, drive, impetus, impulse, impulsion, incentive, incitation, incitement, irritation, lash, lust, motivation, passion, pressure, prod, spur, stimulant, stimulation, urge, whip, zeal; SEE CONCEPTS *20,661*

goad [v] *egg on, incite*
animate, annoy, arouse, bully, coerce, drive, encourage, excite, exhort, fire up*, force, goose*, harass, hound, impel, inspirit, instigate, irritate, key up*, lash, move, needle*, press, prick*, prod, prompt, propel, provoke, push, put up to*, rowel, sic*, sound, spark*, spur, stimulate, sting*, tease, thrust, trigger, turn on*, urge, whip*, work up, worry; SEE CONCEPTS *14,68*

go-ahead [n] *authorization*
assent, consent, green light*, leave, okay, permission; SEE CONCEPT *685*

go-ahead [adj] *progressive*
ambitious, enterprising, entrepreneurial, go-getting*, gumptious*, pioneering, up-and-coming*; SEE CONCEPTS *538,542*

go ahead [v] *proceed*
advance, begin, continue, dash ahead, edge forward, go forward, go on, move on, progress, shoot ahead; SEE CONCEPTS *149,159,704*

goal [n] *aim, purpose of an action*
ambition, design, destination, duty, end, ground zero*, intent, intention, limit, mark, mission, object, objective, purpose, target, use, zero*; SEE CONCEPT *659*

go along/go along with [v] *agree, cooperate*
accompany, acquiesce, act jointly, assent, collaborate, concur, conspire, follow, share in, work together; SEE CONCEPTS *8,18*

goat [n1] *hollow-horned mammal*
billy, buck, he-goat, kid, she-goat; SEE CONCEPTS *394,400*

goat [n2] *person who is brunt of joke*
fall guy*, patsy*, scapegoat; SEE CONCEPT *423*

go back/go back on [v] *break promise; change one's mind*
abandon, betray, be unfaithful, desert, forsake, leave in the lurch*, renege, repudiate, retract, return, revert, run out on; SEE CONCEPTS *13,71*

gobble [v] *eat hurriedly*
cram*, devour, gorge, gulp*, guzzle, ingurgitate, scarf*, stuff*, suck up*, swallow, wolf*; SEE CONCEPT *169*

go-between [n] *person acting as agent*
arbitrator, attorney, broker, dealer, delegate, deputy, emissary, entrepreneur, envoy, factor, interagent, interceder, intercessor, intermediary, intermediate, intermediator, liaison, matchmaker, mediator, medium, messenger, middleman/woman, negotiator, proxy, referee, representative; SEE CONCEPTS *348,423*

go by [v1] *elapse*
exceed, flow on, make one's way, move onward, pass, proceed; SEE CONCEPT *141*

go by [v2] *adopt, conform*
abide by, adjust to, agree, be guided by, comply, cooperate, fall in with, follow, heed, judge from, observe, take as guide; SEE CONCEPTS *8,18*

God [n] *supernatural being worshipped by people*
Absolute Being, Allah, All Knowing, All Powerful, Almighty, Creator, daemon, deity, demigod, demon, Divine Being, divinity, Father, god, holiness, Holy Spirit, idol, Infinite Spirit, Jehovah, King of Kings, Lord, Maker, master, numen, omnipotent, power, prime mover, providence, soul, spirit, totem, tutelary, universal life force, world spirit, Yahweh; SEE CONCEPT *370*

godless [adj] *not religious*
agnostic, atheistic, depraved, evil, graceless, heathen, impious, infidel, irreligious, nonreligious, profane, unclean, undevout, ungodly, unholy, unprincipled, unreligious, unrighteous, wicked; SEE CONCEPT *542*

godly [adj] *religious*
angelic, born-again, celestial, charismatic, deific, devout, divine, god-fearing, good, holy, pietistic, pious, prayerful, righteous, saintlike, saintly, virtuous; SEE CONCEPT *542*

go down [v] *lose, fall*
be beaten, be defeated, cave in, collapse, crumple, decline, decrease, descend, droop, drop, fold, founder, go under, keel, lessen, make less, pitch, plunge, reduce, sag, set, sink, slump, submerge, submerse, submit, succumb, suffer defeat, topple, tumble; SEE CONCEPTS *181,698,699*

godsend [n] *gift, benefit*
advantage, benediction, blessing, boon, good, manna*, stroke of luck*, windfall; SEE CONCEPTS *337,679*

go far [v] *be successful*
achieve, advance, do well, get ahead, get on, make a name*, move up in the world*, progress, rise, succeed; SEE CONCEPTS *704,706*

go for [v1] *reach*
clutch at, fetch, obtain, outreach, seek, stretch for; SEE CONCEPT *149*

go for [v2] *like, choose*
accept, admire, approbate, approve, be attracted to, be fond of, care for, countenance, fancy, favor, hold with, prefer; SEE CONCEPTS *10,32*

go for [v3] *attack*
assail, assault, launch at, run at, rush, rush upon, set upon, spring at; SEE CONCEPT *86*

go into [v1] *take an interest in; participate*
be absorbed in, begin, develop, engage in, enter, get involved with, take on*, take up*, take upon oneself*, undertake; SEE CONCEPT *100*

go into [*v2*] *investigate*
analyze, consider, delve into, dig*, dig into*, discuss, examine, explore, inquire, look into, probe, prospect, pursue, review, scrutinize, sift, study; SEE CONCEPTS *24,103*

gold/golden [*adj1*] *dark yellow*
aureate, auric, auriferous, aurous, aurulent, blond, blonde, caramel, dusty, flaxen, honeyed, mellow yellow, ochroid, straw, tan, tawny, wheat; SEE CONCEPT *618*

golden [*adj2*] *beautiful, advantageous*
auspicious, best, blissful, bright, brilliant, delightful, excellent, favorable, flourishing, glorious, happy, joyful, joyous, opportune, precious, promising, propitious, prosperous, resplendent, rich, rosy, shining, successful, valuable; SEE CONCEPTS *529,574*

gone [*adj*] *not present, no longer in existence*
absent, astray, away, AWOL*, burned up*, consumed, dead, decamped, deceased, defunct, departed, disappeared, disintegrated, displaced, dissipated, dissolved, done, down the drain*, dried up, elapsed, ended, extinct, finished, flown, lacking, left, lost, missing, moved, no more, nonexistent, not a sign of*, not here, out the window*, over, passed, past, quit, removed, retired, run-off, shifted, spent, split, taken a powder*, taken leave*, transferred, traveling, turned to dust*, vanished, withdrawn; SEE CONCEPTS *407,586*

good [*n1*] *advantage, benefit*
asset, avail, behalf, benediction, blessing, boon*, commonwealth, favor, gain, godsend, good fortune, interest, nugget*, plum*, prize, profit, prosperity, service, treasure, use, usefulness, welfare, well-being, windfall; SEE CONCEPTS *337,658,679*

good [*n2*] *morality*
class, dignity, excellence, goodness, ideal, merit, prerogative, probity, quality, rectitude, right, righteousness, straight, uprightness, value, virtue, worth; SEE CONCEPT *645*

good [*adj1*] *pleasant, fine*
acceptable, ace*, admirable, agreeable, bad, boss*, bully, capital, choice, commendable, congenial, crack*, deluxe, excellent, exceptional, favorable, first-class, first-rate, gnarly*, gratifying, great, honorable, marvelous, neat*, nice, pleasing, positive, precious, prime, rad*, recherché*, reputable, satisfactory, satisfying, select, shipshape*, sound, spanking*, splendid, sterling, stupendous, super, superb, super-eminent, super-excellent, superior, tip-top*, up to snuff*, valuable, welcome, wonderful, worthy; SEE CONCEPTS *529,572*

good [*adj2*] *moral, virtuous*
admirable, blameless, charitable, dutiful, estimable, ethical, exemplary, guiltless, honest, honorable, incorrupt, inculpable, innocent, irreprehensible, irreproachable, lily-white*, obedient, praiseworthy, pure, reputable, respectable, right, righteous, sound, tractable, uncorrupted, untainted, upright, well-behaved, worthy; SEE CONCEPT *545*

good [*adj3*] *competent, skilled*
able, accomplished, adept, adroit, au fait, capable, clever, dexterous, efficient, expert, first-rate, proficient, proper, qualified, reliable, satisfactory, serviceable, skillful, suitable, suited, talented, thorough, trustworthy, useful; SEE CONCEPT *527*

good [*adj4*] *useful, adequate*
acceptable, advantageous, all right, ample, appropriate, approving, apt, auspicious, becoming, benefic, beneficial, benignant, brave, commendatory, commending, common, conformable, congruous, convenient, decent, desirable, favorable, favoring, fit, fitting, fruitful, healthful, healthy, helpful, hygienic, meet, needed, opportune, profitable, proper, propitious, respectable, right, salubrious, salutary, satisfying, seemly, serviceable, suitable, tolerable, toward, unobjectionable, wholesome; SEE CONCEPTS *537,558,560*

good [*adj5*] *reliable; untainted*
dependable, eatable, fit to eat, flawless, fresh, intact, loyal, normal, perfect, reliable, safe, solid, sound, stable, trustworthy, unblemished, uncontaminated, uncorrupted, undamaged, undecayed, unhurt, unimpaired, unspoiled, vigorous, whole; SEE CONCEPT *485*

good [*adj6*] *kind, giving*
altruistic, approving, beneficent, benevolent, charitable, considerate, friendly, gracious, humane, humanitarian, kindhearted, kindly, merciful, obliging, philanthropic, tolerant, well-disposed; SEE CONCEPTS *404,542*

good [*adj7*] *authentic, real*
bona fide, conforming, dependable, genuine, honest, justified, kosher*, legitimate, loyal, orthodox, proper, regular, reliable, sound, strict, true, trustworthy, valid, well-founded; SEE CONCEPT *582*

good [*adj8*] *well-behaved*
considerate, decorous, dutiful, kindly, mannerly, obedient, orderly, polite, proper, respectful, seemly, thoughtful, tolerant, tractable, well-mannered; SEE CONCEPT *401*

good [*adj9*] *considerable*
adequate, advantageous, ample, big, complete, entire, extensive, full, great, immeasurable, large, long, lucrative, much, paying, profitable, respectable, sizable, solid, substantial, sufficient, whole, worthwhile; SEE CONCEPTS *334,771,781*

goodbye [*n*] *farewell statement*
adieu, adios, bye-bye, cheerio, ciao, farewell, godspeed*, leave-taking, parting, so long*, swan song*, toodle-oo*; SEE CONCEPTS *195,278*

good-for-nothing [*n*] *person who is idle, worthless*
bad lot*, black sheep*, bum, idler, loafer, ne'er-do-well*, no-good*, profligate, rapscallion, scalawag, scamp, tramp, vagabond, waster*, wastrel; SEE CONCEPT *412*

good-humored [*adj*] *funny, happy*
affable, amiable, buoyant, cheerful, cheery, complaisant, congenial, easy, genial, good-natured, good-tempered, lenient, merry, mild, obliging, pleasant, smiling; SEE CONCEPT *404*

good-looking [*adj*] *handsome*
attractive, beauteous, beautiful, clean-cut, comely, fair, impressive, lovely, pretty, pulchritudinous, righteous; SEE CONCEPT *579*

good-natured [*adj*] *easy-going, easily pleased*
acquiescent, agreeable, altruistic, amiable, benevolent, bighearted, boy-scout, breezy, charitable, complaisant, compliant, cordial, easy, even-tempered, friendly, girl-scout*, good-hearted, good-humored, gracious, helpful, kind, kindly, lenient, marshmallow*, mild, moderate, nice, obliging, softie*, tolerant, warmhearted, well-disposed, willing to please; SEE CONCEPT *404*

goodness [*n*] *decency, excellence*
advantage, beneficence, benefit, benevolence, ethicality, friendliness, generosity, good will, grace, graciousness, honesty, honor, humaneness, integrity, kindheartedness, kindliness, kindness, mercy, merit, morality, nourishment, obligingness, probity, quality, rectitude, righteousness, rightness, superiority, uprightness, value, virtue, wholesomeness, worth; SEE CONCEPTS *411,645*

goods [*n1*] *personal possessions*
appurtenances, belongings, chattels, effects, encumbrances, equipment, furnishings, furniture, gear, impedimenta, movables, paraphernalia, personal property, property, stuff, things, trappings; SEE CONCEPT *446*

goods [*n2*] *merchandise*
bolt, cargo, commodities, fabric, freight, line, load, material, materials, seconds, stock, stuff, textile, vendibles, wares; SEE CONCEPT *338*

good will/goodwill [*n*] *kindliness*
altruism, amity, benevolence, brownie points*, charity, comity, cordiality, favor, friendliness, friendship, generosity, good deed, good side of*, helpfulness, kindness, rapport, right side of*, sympathy, tolerance; SEE CONCEPTS *411,645*

gooey [*adj*] *sticky, gummy*
adhesive, gluey, glutinous, mucilaginous, soft, tacky, viscous; SEE CONCEPT *606*

go off [*v1*] *explode*
befall, blow, blow up, burst, detonate, discharge, fire, happen, mushroom, occur, pass, take place; SEE CONCEPT *179*

go off [*v2*] *leave*
decamp, depart, exit, go away, move out, part, quit; SEE CONCEPT *195*

go on [*v*] *continue*
act, advance, bear, behave, carry, carry on, come about, comport, conduct, deport, endure, execute, go ahead, hang on, happen, hold on, keep on, last,

occur, persevere, persist, proceed, ramble, stay, take place; SEE CONCEPTS *100,239*

go out [*v1*] *become extinguished*
become dark, burn out, cease, darken, die, die out, dim, expire, fade out, flicker, stop shining; SEE CONCEPTS *105,469*

go out [*v2*] *leave*
decamp, depart, exit, go on strike, walk out; SEE CONCEPT *195*

go over [*v1*] *review*
analyze, examine, inspect, investigate, look at, peruse, practice, read, rehearse, reiterate, repeat, review, revise, riffle through*, scan, skim, study, thumb through*; SEE CONCEPTS *24,103*

go over [*v2*] *succeed*
be impressive, be successful, click*, come off*, go, pan out*, prove; SEE CONCEPT *706*

gorge [*n*] *valley*
abyss, arroyo, canyon, chasm, cleft, clough, clove, crevasse, fissure, flume, gap, glen, gulch, pass, ravine; SEE CONCEPT *509*

gorge [*v*] *eat voraciously*
blimp out*, bolt*, cloy, congest, cram, devour, eat like a horse*, feed, fill, glut, gobble, gormandize, gulp, guzzle, hoover*, jade, jam, make a pig of*, overeat, overindulge, pack, sate, satiate, stuff*, surfeit, swallow, wolf*; SEE CONCEPT *169*

gorgeous [*adj*] *beautiful, magnificent*
attractive, beaut*, bright, brilliant, centerfold*, colorful, dazzling, delightful, dream, drop-dead*, easy on the eyes*, elegant, enjoyable, exquisite, fine, flamboyant, foxy*, gaudy, glittering, glorious, good-looking, grand, handsome, imposing, impressive, knockout*, lavish, lovely, lulu*, luxuriant, luxurious, opulent, ostentatious, pleasing, plush, pulchritudinous, ravishing, resplendent, showy, splendid, splendiferous, stunning, sublime, sumptuous, superb; SEE CONCEPTS *579,589*

gory [*adj*] *bloody, horrible*
bleeding, blood-soaked, bloodstained, imbrued, murderous, offensive, sanguinary, sanguine; SEE CONCEPTS *314,537*

gospel [*n*] *fact, doctrine*
actuality, authority, belief, certainty, credo, creed, dogma, faith, last word, scripture, testament, truism, truth, veracity, verity; SEE CONCEPT *689*

gossamer [*adj*] *gauzy, thin*
airy, cobweb, delicate, diaphanous, fibrous, fine, flimsy, light, sheer, silky, tiffany, translucent, transparent; SEE CONCEPT *606*

gossip [*n1*] *talk about others; rumor*
account, babble, back-fence talk*, blather, blether, buzz*, calumny, chatter, chitchat*, chronicle, clothesline*, conversation, cry, defamation, dirty laundry*, dirty linen*, dirty wash*, earful*, grapevine*, hearsay, idle talk, injury, malicious talk, meddling, news, prate, prattle, report, scandal, scut-

tlebutt*, slander, small talk*, story, tale, talk, whispering campaign*, wire*; SEE CONCEPTS *274,278*

gossip [*n2*] *person who talks a lot, spreads rumors*
babbler*, blabbermouth*, busybody, chatterbox, chatterer, circulator, flibbertigibbet*, gossipmonger, informer, meddler, newsmonger, parrot*, prattler, rumormonger, scandalizer*, scandalmonger*, snoop*, talebearer, tattler, telltale; SEE CONCEPT *412*

gossip [*v*] *talk about others; spread rumors*
babble, bad-mouth*, bend one's ear*, blab, blather, blether, chat, chatter, cut to pieces*, cut up*, dish, hint, imply, insinuate, intimate, jaw*, prate, prattle, rattle on*, repeat, report, rumor, schmoose*, spill the beans*, spread*, suggest, talk, talk idly, tattle, tell secrets*, tell tales*, wiggle-waggle*; SEE CONCEPTS *56,60*

go through [*v1*] *endure*
bear, brave, experience, suffer, support, survive, swallow, tolerate, undergo, withstand; SEE CONCEPT *23*

go through [*v2*] *use up*
consume, deplete, exhaust, pay out, spend, squander; SEE CONCEPT *169*

go through [*v3*] *search*
audit, check, examine, explore, hunt, inspect, investigate, look, pass through; SEE CONCEPT *103*

go together/go with [*v1*] *agree, match*
accompany, accord, become, befit, be suitable, blend, complement, concur, correspond, fit, go, harmonize, make a pair*, not clash, suit; SEE CONCEPT *664*

go together/go with [*v2*] *accompany socially*
attend, be with, court, date, escort, go out with*, go steady with*, keep company with*; SEE CONCEPT *384*

go under [*v*] *fail, submerge*
bankrupt, default, die, drown, fall, fold, founder, go down, sink, submerse, submit, succumb, suffocate, surrender; SEE CONCEPTS *181,699*

gourmet [*n*] *person who likes, knows about food*
bon vivant, connoisseur, critic, epicure, epicurean, gastronome, gastronomer, gastronomist, gourmand; SEE CONCEPTS *348,423*

govern [*v1*] *take control; rule*
administer, assume command, be in driver's seat*, be in power, call the shots*, call the signals*, captain*, carry out, command, conduct, control, dictate, direct, execute, exercise authority, guide, head, head up, hold dominion, hold office, hold sway, lay down the law*, lead, manage, master, occupy throne, order, overrule, oversee, pilot, pull the strings*, regulate, reign, render, run, serve the people*, steer, superintend, supervise, sway, tyrannize, wear the crown*; SEE CONCEPT *133*

govern [*v2*] *influence; hold in check*
boss, bridle, check, contain, control, curb, decide, determine, direct, directionalize, discipline, dispose, dominate, get the better of*, guide, handle, incline, inhibit, manage, master, predispose, regulate, re-

strain, rule, shepherd, steer, subdue, sway, tame, underlie; SEE CONCEPTS *7,19,22,130*

government [*n*] *management, administration*
authority, Big Brother*, bureaucracy, command, control, direction, domination, dominion, empire, execution, executive, governance, guidance, influence, jurisdiction, law, ministry, patronage, political practice, politics, polity, power, powers-that-be*, predominance, presidency, regency, regime, regimentation, regulation, restraint, rule, sovereignty, state, statecraft, superintendence, superiority, supervision, supremacy, sway, the feds*, Uncle Sam*, union, Washington*; SEE CONCEPT *299*

governor [*n*] *person administrating government*
administrator, Big Brother*, boss, chief, chief of state, commander, comptroller, controller, director, executive, gubernatorial leader, guv*, head, head honcho*, leader, manager, overseer, presiding officer, ruler, superintendent, supervisor; SEE CONCEPT *354*

go without [*adj*] *deny or be denied*
abstain, be deprived of, do without, fall short*, go short*, lack, need, want; SEE CONCEPT *646*

gown [*n*] *robe, dress*
clothes, costume, frock, garb, garment, habit; SEE CONCEPT *451*

grab [*v*] *latch on to*
capture, catch, catch hold of, clutch, collar*, corral*, get one's fingers on*, get one's hands on*, glom*, grapple, grasp, grip, hook, land, lay one's hands on*, nab, nail, pluck, seize, snag, snap up, snatch, take, take hold of; SEE CONCEPTS *90,190*

grace [*n1*] *charm, loveliness*
address, adroitness, agility, allure, attractiveness, balance, beauty, breeding, comeliness, consideration, cultivation, decency, decorum, dexterity, dignity, ease, elegance, etiquette, finesse, finish, form, gracefulness, lissomeness, lithesomeness, mannerliness, manners, nimbleness, pleasantness, pliancy, poise, polish, propriety, refinement, shapeliness, smoothness, style, suppleness, symmetry, tact, tastefulness; SEE CONCEPTS *633,655,718*

grace [*n2*] *mercy, forgiveness*
benefaction, beneficence, benevolence, caritas, charity, clemency, compassion, compassionateness, favor, forbearance, forgiveness, generosity, goodness, good will, indulgence, kindliness, kindness, leniency, lenity, love, pardon, quarter, reprieve, responsiveness, tenderness; SEE CONCEPTS *278,657,685*

grace [*n3*] *prayer*
benediction, blessing, invocation, petition, thanks, thanksgiving; SEE CONCEPTS *278,368*

grace [*v*] *beautify, embellish*
adorn, bedeck, crown, deck, decorate, dignify, distinguish, elevate, enhance, enrich, favor, garnish, glorify, honor, laureate, ornament, set off; SEE CONCEPTS *202,700*

graceful [adj] *agile, charming, lovely*
adroit, aesthetic, artistic, balletic, beautiful, becoming, comely, controlled, curvaceous, dainty, decorative, delicate, dexterous, easy, elastic, elegant, exquisite, fair, fine, flowing, handsome, harmonious, limber, lissome, lithe, natural, neat, nimble, pleasing, pliant, poised, practiced, pretty, refined, rhythmic, seemly, shapely, skilled, slender, smooth, springy, statuesque, supple, symmetrical, tasteful, trim, willowy; SEE CONCEPTS *579,584,589*

graceless [adj] *clumsy, unsophisticated*
awkward, barbarian, barbaric, barbarous, boorish, clunky*, coarse, corrupt, crude*, forced, gauche, gawky*, ill-mannered, improper, indecorous, inelegant, inept, infelicitous, klutzy*, loutish, oafish, outlandish, rough, rude, shameless, tasteless, two left feet*, uncouth, uncultured, unfortunate, ungainly, unhappy, unmannered; SEE CONCEPTS *401,584*

gracious [adj] *kind, giving*
accommodating, affable, amiable, amicable, approachable, beneficent, benevolent, benign, benignant, big-hearted, bland, bonhomous, charitable, chivalrous, civil, compassionate, complaisant, congenial, considerate, cordial, courteous, courtly, easy, forthcoming, friendly, gallant, genial, good-hearted, good-natured, hospitable, indulgent, kindly, lenient, loving, merciful, mild, obliging, pleasing, polite, sociable, stately, suave, tender, unctuous, urbane, well-mannered; SEE CONCEPTS *401,542*

gradation [n] *classification, step*
arrangement, calibration, change, degree, difference, distinction, divergence, grade, grouping, level, mark, measurement, modification, notch, nuance, ordering, place, point, position, progression, rank, scale, sequence, series, shade, sorting, stage, succession, variation; SEE CONCEPTS *378,665,727,744*

grade [n1] *rank, step*
brand, caliber, category, class, classification, condition, degree, division, echelon, estate, form, gradation, group, grouping, league, level, mark, notch, order, pigeonhole*, place, position, quality, rung*, size, stage, standard, station, tier; SEE CONCEPTS *286,378,665,727,744*

grade [n2] *incline, slope*
acclivity, ascent, bank, cant, climb, declivity, descent, downgrade, elevation, embankment, gradient, height, hill, inclination, inclined plane, lean, leaning, level, obliquity, pitch, plane, ramp, rise, slant, tangent, tilt, upgrade; SEE CONCEPTS *738,757*

grade [v] *evaluate, rank*
arrange, assort, brand, class, classify, group, order, range, rate, sort, value; SEE CONCEPTS *103,291*

gradient [n] *slope*
acclivity, angle, bank, cant, declivity, grade, hill, inclination, incline, lean, leaning, pitch, ramp, rise, slant, tilt; SEE CONCEPTS *738,757*

gradual [adj] *happening slowly, evenly*
bit-by-bit*, by degrees, continuous, creeping, even, gentle, graduate, moderate, piecemeal, progressive, regular, slow, steady, step-by-step*, successive, unhurried; SEE CONCEPTS *544,588,799*

gradually [adv] *happening slowly, evenly*
bit by bit*, by degrees, by installments, constantly, continuously, deliberately, gently, imperceptibly, inch by inch*, increasingly, in small doses*, little by little*, moderately, perceptibly, piece by piece*, piecemeal, progressively, regularly, sequentially, serially, steadily, step by step*, successively, unhurriedly; SEE CONCEPTS *544,588,799*

graduate [n] *person who completes education, pursuit*
alum*, alumna, alumnus, baccalaureate, bachelor, collegian, diplomate, doctor, former student, grad, holder, licentiate, master, product, recipient; SEE CONCEPT *350*

graduate [v1] *complete education, pursuit*
be commissioned, certify, confer degree, earn, finish, get a degree, get out*, give sheepskin*, grant diploma, take a degree, win; SEE CONCEPT *234*

graduate [v2] *classify, grade*
arrange, calibrate, class, grade, group, mark off, measure, measure out, order, proportion, range, rank, regulate, sort; SEE CONCEPTS *84,103*

graft [n1] *transplant*
bud*, grafting, hybridization, implant, jointure, scion, shoot, slip, splice, sprout, union; SEE CONCEPTS *113,257*

graft [n2] *payoff for fraud*
bribe, corruption, gain, hat*, hush money*, juice*, money under the table*, pay, payoff money, payola*, peculation, shake*, share, skimming*, squeeze*, thievery; SEE CONCEPTS *192,344*

graft [v] *transplant, splice*
affix, implant, ingraft, insert, join, plant, propagate, unite; SEE CONCEPTS *113,257*

grain [n1] *seed, piece*
atom, bit, cereal, corn, crumb, drop, fragment, granule, grist, iota, jot, kernel, mite, modicum, molecule, morsel, mote, ounce, particle, pellet, scintilla, scrap, scruple, smidgen, spark, speck, tittle, trace, whit; SEE CONCEPTS *428,831*

grain [n2] *texture of fabric*
character, current, direction, fiber, make-up, nap, pattern, staple, striation, surface, tendency, tissue, tooth, warp and woof, weave, weft; SEE CONCEPT *611*

grammar [n] *language rules*
ABCs*, accidence, alphabet, elements, fundaments, linguistics, morphology, principles, rudiments, sentence structure, stratification, structure, syntax, tagmemics; SEE CONCEPTS *275,276,770*

grand [adj1] *impressive, great*
admirable, ambitious, august, awe-inspiring, dignified, dynamite, elevated, eminent, exalted, excellent, fab*, fine, first-class, first-rate, glorious, grandiose, great, haughty, illustrious, imposing, large, lofty, lordly, luxurious, magnificent, majestic, marvelous, monumental, noble, opulent, ostentatious, outstand-

ing, palatial, pompous, pretentious, princely, regal, rich, smashing, something else*, splendid, stately, striking, sublime, sumptuous, super, superb, terrific, unreal, very good; SEE CONCEPTS *574,589,773*

grand [*adj2*] *most important*
chief, dignified, elevated, exalted, grave, head, highest, leading, lofty, main, majestic, mighty, noble, preeminent, principal, regal, supreme, transcendent; SEE CONCEPT *568*

grandeur [*n*] *great importance*
amplitude, augustness, beauty, breadth, brilliance, celebrity, circumstance, dignity, distinction, elevation, eminence, expansiveness, fame, fineness, glory, grandiosity, gravity, greatness, handsomeness, immensity, impressiveness, inclusiveness, loftiness, luxuriousness, magnificence, majesty, might, nobility, opulence, pomp, preeminence, richness, splendor, state, stateliness, sublimity, sumptuousness, superbity, sway, transcendency, vastness; SEE CONCEPT *668*

grandiloquent [*adj*] *pretentious, flowery (communication)*
aureate, big-talking*, bombastic, declamatory, euphistic, fustian, high-flown, histrionic, inflated, magniloquent, oratorical, orotund, overblown, pompous, purple*, rhetorical, sonorous, swollen, tall-talking*, verbose, windbag*, windy*; SEE CONCEPT *267*

grandiose [*adj*] *theatrical, extravagant*
affected, ambitious, august, bombastic, cosmic, egotistic, flamboyant, fustian, grand, high-falutin'*, high-flown, imposing, impressive, lofty, lordly, magnificent, majestic, monumental, noble, ostentatious, overwhelming, pompous, pretentious, princely, purple*, royal, showy, splashy, stately, unfathomable, vast; SEE CONCEPTS *401,542,589*

grange [*n*] *farm*
acreage, farmstead, hacienda, manor, plantation, ranch; SEE CONCEPTS *258,516,517*

grant [*n*] *allowance, gift*
admission, allocation, allotment, alms, appropriation, assistance, award, benefaction, bequest, boon, bounty, charity, concession, contribution, dole, donation, endowment, fellowship, gifting, gratuity, handout, lump, present, privilege, reward, scholarship, stipend, subsidy; SEE CONCEPTS *337,344*

grant [*v*] *authorize, allow*
accede, accept, accord, acknowledge, acquiesce, admit, agree to, allocate, allot, allow, assign, assume, avow, award, bestow, bless, cede, come across, come around, come through, concede, confer, consent to, convey, donate, drop, gift with*, give, give in, give out, give the nod*, give thumbs-up*, go along with*, impart, invest, own, own up*, permit, present, profess, relinquish, shake on*, sign off on*, sign on*, stake, suppose, surrender, transfer, transmit, vouchsafe, yield; SEE CONCEPTS *8,50,82,83,88*

granted [*adv*] *allowed, accepted*
acknowledged, admitted, assumed, indeed, just so, yes; SEE CONCEPT *558*

granulate [*v*] *crush into tiny pieces*
atomize, comminute, crumble, crystallize, disintegrate, grate, grind, make coarse, make grainy, pound, powder, pulverize, triturate; SEE CONCEPT *186*

graphic [*adj1*] *clear, explicit*
clear-cut, cogent, colorful, compelling, comprehensible, concrete, convincing, definite, descriptive, detailed, distinct, eloquent, expressive, figurative, forcible, illustrative, incisive, intelligible, lively, lucid, moving, perspicuous, picturesque, precise, realistic, stirring, striking, strong, telling, unequivocal, vivid; SEE CONCEPTS *267,535,562*

graphic [*adj2*] *pictorial, visible*
blocked-out, delineated, depicted, descriptive, diagrammatic, drawn, engraved, etched, iconographic, illustrated, illustrational, illustrative, marked-out, outlined, painted, photographic, pictorial, pictoric, pictured, portrayed, representational, seen, sketched, traced, visual; SEE CONCEPTS *576,589,619*

grapple [*v*] *grab, wrestle*
attack, battle, catch, clash, clasp, close, clutch, combat, confront, contend, cope, deal with, do battle*, encounter, engage, face, fasten, fight, grasp, grip, hold, hook, hug, nab, nail, scuffle, seize, snatch, struggle, tackle, take, take on*, tussle; SEE CONCEPTS *106,191*

grasp [*n1*] *hold, grip*
butt, cinch, clamp, clasp, clench, clinch, clutches, embrace, grapple, lug, possession, purchase, tenure; SEE CONCEPTS *191,710*

grasp [*n2*] *understanding*
awareness, comprehension, ken, knowledge, mastery, perception, realization; SEE CONCEPT *409*

grasp [*v1*] *grab*
bag*, catch, clasp, clinch, clutch, collar*, corral, enclose, glom*, grapple, grip, hold, hook, land, seize, snatch, take, take hold of; SEE CONCEPTS *90,191*

grasp [*v2*] *understand*
accept, appreciate, apprehend, catch, catch on*, cognize, compass, comprehend, dig*, envisage, fathom, follow, get, get the drift*, get the picture*, have, know, latch on*, make, perceive, pick up*, realize, see, take, take in*; SEE CONCEPT *15*

grasping [*adj*] *greedy*
acquisitive, avaricious, avid, close-fisted, covetous, desirous, extorting, extortionate, grabby*, itchy*, mean, miserly, niggardly*, penny-pinching*, penurious, prehensile, rapacious, selfish, stingy*, tight-fisted*, usurious, venal; SEE CONCEPTS *326,334,542*

grate [*v1*] *shred, grind down*
abrade, bark, bray, file, fray, gall, mince, pound, pulverize, rasp, raze, rub, scrape, scratch, scuff, skin, triturate; SEE CONCEPTS *186,215*

grate [*v2*] *irritate*
aggravate, annoy, burn, chafe, exasperate, fret, gall, get on one's nerves*, irk, nettle, peeve, pique, pro-

voke, rankle, rile, rub the wrong way*, vex; SEE CONCEPTS *7,14,19*

grateful [*adj1*] *appreciative*
beholden, gratified, indebted, much obliged, obliged, pleased, thankful; SEE CONCEPT *403*

grateful [*adj2*] *pleasing, nice*
acceptable, agreeable, comforting, congenial, consoling, delectable, delicious, delightful, desirable, favorable, good, gratifying, pleasant, pleasurable, pleasureful, refreshing, rejuvenating, renewing, restful, restorative, restoring, satisfactory, satisfying, solacing, welcome; SEE CONCEPTS *537,548,572*

gratification [*n*] *satisfaction*
delight, enjoyment, fruition, fulfillment, glee, hit, indulgence, joy, kick*, kicks*, luxury, pleasure, recompense, regalement, relish, reward, sure shock*, thrill; SEE CONCEPT *410*

gratify [*v*] *give pleasure; satisfy*
appease, arride, baby*, cater to, coddle, content, delectate, delight, do one proud*, do the trick*, enchant, favor, fill the bill*, fulfill*, get one's kicks*, gladden, hit the spot*, humor, indulge, make a hit*, make happy, oblige, pamper, please, recompense, requite, thrill; SEE CONCEPTS *7,22*

grating [*adj*] *irritating; scraping*
annoying, disagreeable, discordant, displeasing, dissonant, dry, grinding, harsh, harsh-sounding, hoarse, irksome, jarring, offensive, rasping, raucous, rough, shrill, squeaky, strident, stridulent, stridulous, unpleasant, vexatious; SEE CONCEPTS *529,592,594*

gratis [*adj*] *free*
as a gift, chargeless, complimentary, costless, for love*, for nothing, freebie*, freely given, free of charge, free ride*, gratuitous, on someone*, on the house*, unpaid for, without charge, without recompense; SEE CONCEPT *334*

gratitude [*n*] *appreciation*
acknowledgment, appreciativeness, grace, gratefulness, honor, indebtedness, obligation, praise, recognition, requital, response, responsiveness, sense of obligation, thankfulness, thanks, thanksgiving; SEE CONCEPTS *32,76,278,410*

gratuitous [*adj1*] *free*
chargeless, complimentary, costless, for nothing, gratis, spontaneous, unasked-for, unpaid, voluntary, willing; SEE CONCEPTS *334,542*

gratuitous [*adj2*] *not necessary*
assumed, baseless, bottomless, causeless, groundless, indefensible, inessential, needless, reasonless, supererogatory, superfluous, uncalled-for, unessential, unfounded, unjustified, unmerited, unnecessary, unprovoked, unsupportable, unwarranted, wanton; SEE CONCEPT *546*

gratuity [*n*] *gift, tip*
alms, benefaction, bonus, boon, bounty, contribution, donation, fringe benefit, grease palm*, largesse, little something*, offering, perk*, perquisite,

present, recompense, reward, salve*, sweetener*, token; SEE CONCEPTS *337,344*

grave [*n*] *burial place*
catacomb, crypt, final resting place*, last home*, mausoleum, mound, permanent address*, place of interment, resting place, sepulcher, shrine, six feet under*, tomb, vault; SEE CONCEPT *305*

grave [*adj1*] *serious; gloomy*
cold sober*, deadpan*, dignified, dour, dull, earnest, grim, grim-faced, heavy, leaden, long-faced, meaningful, muted, no-nonsense*, ponderous, quiet, sad, sage, saturnine, sedate, sober, solemn, somber, staid, strictly business*, subdued, thoughtful, unsmiling; SEE CONCEPT *401*

grave [*adj2*] *crucial, dangerous*
acute, afflictive, consequential, critical, deadly, destructive, dire, exigent, fatal, fell, grievous, hazardous, heavy*, important, killing*, life-and-death*, major, momentous, of great consequence, ominous, perilous, pressing, serious, severe, significant, threatening, ugly, urgent, vital, weighty; SEE CONCEPTS *537,548,567*

graveyard [*n*] *burial area*
boneyard*, burial ground, cemetery, charnel house, God's acre*, memorial park, necropolis; SEE CONCEPT *305*

gravitate [*v*] *be drawn towards; fall to*
approach, be attracted, be influenced, be pulled, descend, drift, drop, fall, incline, lean, move, precipitate, settle, sink, tend; SEE CONCEPTS *34,159*

gravity [*n1*] *force of attraction*
force, heaviness, pressure, weight; SEE CONCEPT *641*

gravity [*n2*] *seriousness, importance*
acuteness, concern, consequence, exigency, hazardousness, momentousness, perilousness, severity, significance, solemnity, urgency, weightiness; SEE CONCEPT *668*

gray/grey [*adj*] *muted silver in color*
ash, ashen, battleship*, cinereal, clouded, dingy, dove, drab, dusky, dusty, granite, heather, iron, lead, leaden, livid, mousy, neutral, oyster, pearly, peppery, powder, sere, shaded, silvered, silvery, slate, smoky, somber, stone; SEE CONCEPT *618*

graze [*v1*] *touch*
abrade, brush, carom, chafe, glance off, kiss*, ricochet, rub, scrape, scratch, shave*, skim, skip; SEE CONCEPT *612*

graze [*v2*] *feed on*
bite, browse, champ, crop, crunch, eat, forage, gnaw, masticate, munch, nibble, pasture, ruminate, uproot; SEE CONCEPT *169*

greasy [*adj*] *slippery, oily*
anointed, creamy, daubed, fat, fatty, greased, lubricated, lubricious, oleaginous, pomaded, salved, slick, slimy*, slithery, smeared, swabbed, unctuous; SEE CONCEPT *606*

great [*adj1*] *very large*
abundant, ample, big, big league*, bulky, bull, colossal, considerable, decided, enormous, excessive,

extended, extensive, extravagant, extreme, fat, gigantic, grievous, high, huge, humongous, husky, immense, inordinate, jumbo*, lengthy, long, major league*, mammoth, mondo*, numerous, oversize, prodigious, prolonged, pronounced, protracted, strong, stupendous, terrible, titanic*, towering, tremendous, vast, voluminous; SEE CONCEPTS *773,781*

great [*adj2*] *important, celebrated*
august, capital, chief, commanding, dignified, distinguished, eminent, exalted, excellent, famed, famous, fine, glorious, grand, heroic, highly regarded, high-minded, honorable, idealistic, illustrious, impressive, leading, lofty, lordly, magnanimous, main, major, noble, notable, noted, noteworthy, outstanding, paramount, primary, princely, principal, prominent, puissant, regal, remarkable, renowned, royal, stately, sublime, superior, superlative, talented; SEE CONCEPT *568*

great [*adj3*] *excellent, skillful*
able, absolute, aces*, adept, admirable, adroit, awesome, bad*, best, brutal, cold*, complete, consummate, crack*, downright, dynamite, egregious, exceptional, expert, fab*, fantastic, fine, first-class*, first-rate*, good, heavy*, hellacious*, marvelous, masterly, number one*, out-and-out*, out of sight*, out of this world*, perfect, positive, proficient, skilled, super-duper*, surpassing, terrific, total, tough, transcendent, tremendous, unmitigated, unqualified, utter, wonderful, zero cool*; SEE CONCEPTS *527,528,574*

greatly [*adv*] *considerably*
abundantly, by much, conspicuously, eminently, emphatically, enormously, exceedingly, exceptionally, extremely, famously, glaringly, highly, hugely, immeasurably, immensely, incalculably, incomparably, incredibly, indeed, infinitely, in great meausure, inimitably, intensely, largely, markedly, mightily, most, much, notably, on a large scale, powerfully, remarkably, strikingly, superlatively, supremely, surpassingly, tremendously, vastly, very, very much; SEE CONCEPTS *537,569,772*

greatness [*n1*] *large size*
abundance, amplitude, bigness, bulk, enormity, force, high degree, hugeness, immensity, infinity, intensity, largeness, length, magnitude, mass, might, potency, power, prodigiousness, sizableness, strength, vastness; SEE CONCEPTS *730,767*

greatness [*n2*] *nobleness of character; eminence*
celebrity, chivalry, dignity, distinction, fame, generosity, glory, grandeur, heroism, high-mindedness, idealism, illustriousness, importance, loftiness, magnanimity, majesty, merit, morality, nobility, note, prominence, renown, stateliness, sublimity, worthiness; SEE CONCEPTS *411,645,668*

greed [*n*] *overwhelming desire for more*
acquisitiveness, avarice, avidity, covetousness, craving, cupidity, eagerness, edacity, esurience, excess, gluttony, gormandizing, graspingness, hunger, indulgence, insatiableness, intemperance, longing, piggishness*, rapacity, ravenousness, selfishness, swinishness*, the gimmies*, voracity; SEE CONCEPT *20*

greedy [*adj*] *desiring excessively*
acquisitive, avaricious, avid, carnivorous, close, close-fisted*, covetous, craving, desirous, devouring, eager, edacious, esurient, gluttonous, gobbling, gormandizing, grabby, grasping, grudging, gulping, guzzling, hoggish*, hungry, impatient, insatiable, insatiate, intemperate, itchy*, miserly, niggardly, omnivorous, parsimonious, pennypinching*, penurious, piggish*, prehensile, rapacious, ravening, ravenous, selfish, stingy, swinish, tight*, tight-fisted*, voracious; SEE CONCEPTS *326,403,542*

green [*n*] *square or park in center of town*
common, field, grass, grassplot, lawn, plaza, sward, terrace, turf; SEE CONCEPTS *509,513*

green [*adj1*] *young, new, blooming*
bosky, budding, burgeoning, callow, developing, flourishing, foliate, fresh, grassy, growing, half-formed, immature, infant, juvenile, leafy, lush, maturing, pliable, puerile, pullulating, raw, recent, sprouting, supple, tender, undecayed, undried, unfledged, ungrown, unripe, unseasoned, verdant, verduous, visculent, youthful; SEE CONCEPTS *485, 578,797*

green [*adj2*] *inexperienced*
callow, credulous, fresh, gullible, ignorant, immature, inexpert, ingenuous, innocent, naive, new, raw, tenderfoot*, unconversant, unpolished, unpracticed, unseasoned, unskillful, unsophisticated, untrained, unversed, wet behind ears*, young, youthful; SEE CONCEPT *404*

green [*adj3*] *emerald in color*
apple, aquamarine, beryl, chartreuse, fir, forest, grass, jade, kelly, lime, malachite, moss, olive, pea, peacock, pine, sage, sap, sea, spinach, verdigris, vert, viridian, willow; SEE CONCEPT *618*

greenhorn [*n*] *inexperienced person*
amateur, apprentice, babe*, beginner, colt*, hayseed*, ignoramus, ingénue, learner, naif, neophyte, newcomer, new hand, novice, recruit, rube*, simpleton, tenderfoot*, tyro*, virgin; SEE CONCEPT *423*

greet [*v*] *welcome*
accost, acknowledge, address, approach, attend, bow, call to, compliment, curtsy, embrace, exchange greetings, extend one's hand, flag, hail, herald, highball*, high-five*, meet, move to, nod, pay respects, receive, recognize, roll out red carpet*, salaam*, salute, say hello, say hi*, shake hands, shoulder, speak to, stop, tip one's hat*, usher in*, whistle, whistle for; SEE CONCEPT *51*

greeting [*n*] *welcome; message of kindness*
accosting, acknowledgment, address, aloha*, attention, best wishes*, blow*, card*, ciao*, compellation, compliments, good wishes*, hail, hello, heralding, hi, highball*, high five*, how-do-you-

do*, howdy*, letter*, nod, note, notice, ovation, reception, regards, respects, rumble, salaam*, salutation, salute, speaking to, testimonial, ushering in, what's happening*; SEE CONCEPT *51*

gregarious [*adj*] *friendly*
affable, clubby*, companionable, convivial, cordial, fun, outgoing, sociable, social; SEE CONCEPT *404*

grief [*n*] *mental suffering*
affliction, agony, anguish, bemoaning, bereavement, bewailing, care, dejection, deploring, depression, desolation, despair, despondency, discomfort, disquiet, distress, dole, dolor, gloom, grievance, harassment, heartache, heartbreak, infelicity, lamentation, lamenting, malaise, melancholy, misery, mortification, mournfulness, mourning, pain, purgatory, regret, remorse, repining, rue, sadness, sorrow, suffering, torture, trial, tribulation, trouble, unhappiness, vexation, woe, worry, wretchedness; SEE CONCEPTS *410,728*

grievance [*n*] *complaint, gripe*
affliction, ax to grind*, beef*, bellyache*, big stink*, blast, case, cross*, damage, distress, flack*, grief, grouse*, hardship, holler*, hoo-ha*, howl*, injury, injustice, jeremiad*, kick, knock*, objection, outrage, pain, pain in the neck*, rap*, resentment, rigor, roar, rumble, sorrow, squawk*, stink*, trial, tribulation, trouble, unhappiness, violence, wrong, yell; SEE CONCEPTS *52,278,689*

grieve [*v1*] *mourn, feel deep distress*
ache, bear, bemoan, bewail, carry on, complain, cry, cry a river*, deplore, eat one's heart out*, endure, hang crepe*, keen, lament, regret, rue, sing the blues*, sorrow, suffer, take it hard*, wail, weep; SEE CONCEPTS *17,410*

grieve [*v2*] *upset, distress someone*
afflict, aggrieve, agonize, break the heart of*, constrain, crush, hurt, injure, pain, sadden, wound; SEE CONCEPTS *7,19*

grievous [*adj*] *severe, painful; serious*
afflicting, agonizing, appalling, atrocious, calamitous, damaging, deplorable, dire, dismal, disquieting, distressing, disturbing, dreadful, egregious, flagrant, glaring, grave, harmful, heart-rending, heavy*, heinous, hurtful, injurious, intolerable, lamentable, monstrous, mournful, offensive, onerous, oppressive, outrageous, pathetic, pitiful, sad, shameful, sharp, shocking, sorrowful, taxing, tough, tragic, troublesome, unbearable, upsetting, villainous, weighty*, wounding; SEE CONCEPTS *537, 544,548*

grill [*v1*] *broil food*
barbecue, burn, charcoal-broil, cook, cook over an open pit, roast, rotisserie, sear; SEE CONCEPT *170*

grill [*v2*] *ask questions aggressively*
catechize, cross-examine, give the third degree*, go over*, inquisition, interrogate, interview, put the pressure on*, put the screws to*, question, roast*, third degree*; SEE CONCEPTS *48,53*

grim [*adj*] *hopeless, horrible in manner, appearance*
austere, barbarous, bleak, cantankerous, churlish, crabbed*, cruel, crusty, dogged, ferocious, fierce, forbidding, foreboding, formidable, frightful, funereal, ghastly, gloomy, glowering, glum, grisly, grouchy, gruesome, grumpy*, harsh, hideous, horrid, implacable, inexorable, intractable, merciless, morose, ominous, relentless, resolute, ruthless, scowling, severe, shocking, sinister, somber, sour, splenetic, stern, stubborn, sulky, sullen, surly, terrible, truculent, unrelenting, unyielding; SEE CONCEPTS *534,544,570*

grimace [*n*] *scowling facial expression*
face, frown, moue, mouth, mouthing, mug*, scowl, smile, smirk, sneer, wry face; SEE CONCEPT *716*

grimace [*v*] *make a pained expression*
contort, deform, distort, frown, make a face, make a wry face, misshape, mouth, mug*, scowl, screw up one's face*, smirk, sneer; SEE CONCEPT *185*

grime [*n*] *dirt*
crud*, dust, film, filth, gook*, gunk*, muck*, smudge, smut*, soil, soot, tarnish; SEE CONCEPT *260*

grimy [*adj*] *dirty*
begrimed, besmirched, cruddy*, dingy*, filthy, foul, grubby*, grungy*, messy, mucky*, nasty, scuzzy*, sleazy*, smeared, smutty*, soiled, sooty, sordid, squalid, unclean; SEE CONCEPTS *485,621*

grin [*n/v*] *smile widely*
beam, crack, simper, smirk; SEE CONCEPTS *185,716*

grind [*n*] *tedious job*
chore, drudgery, groove*, grubwork*, hard work, labor, moil, pace, rote, routine, rut*, sweat*, task, toil, travail, treadmill*; SEE CONCEPT *362*

grind [*v1*] *crush, pulverize*
abrade, atomize, attenuate, beat, bray, chop up, comminute, crumble, crumple, disintegrate, file, granulate, grate, kibble*, levigate, mill, pestle, pound, powder, pulverize*, rasp, reduce, roll out*, scrape, shiver, triturate; SEE CONCEPTS *186,204*

grind [*v2*] *sharpen*
abrade, file, give an edge to, gnash, grate, grit, polish, rub, sand, scrape, smooth, whet; SEE CONCEPTS *186,215*

grind [*v3*] *oppress*
afflict, annoy, harass, hold down, hound, persecute, plague, trouble, tyrannize, vex; SEE CONCEPTS *14,130*

grip [*n1*] *clasp, embrace*
anchor, brace, catch, cinch, cincture, clamp, clamping, clench, clinch, clutch, coercion, constraint, crushing, duress, enclosing, enclosure, fastening, fixing, grapnel, grapple, grasp, gripe, handclasp, handgrip, handhold, handshake, hold, hook, ligature, lug, purchase, restraint, snatch, squeeze, strength, tenure, vise, wrench; SEE CONCEPT *191*

grip [*n2*] *perception, understanding*
clutches*, comprehension, control, domination, grasp, hold, influence, keeping, ken, mastery, possession, power, tenure; SEE CONCEPT *409*

grip [*v1*] *hold tightly*
clap a hand on, clasp, clench, clinch, clutch, get one's hands on*, grasp, latch on to*, lay hands on, nab, seize, snag, snatch, take, take hold of; SEE CONCEPT *191*

grip [*v2*] *entrance, enchant*
catch up, compel, engross, enthrall, fascinate, hold, hypnotize, involve, mesmerize, rivet, spellbind; SEE CONCEPTS *7,11,22*

gripe [*n1*] *complaint*
ache, aching, affliction, disorder, distress, grievance, groan, grouse, grumble, illness, indisposition, infirmity, moan, objection, pain, pang; SEE CONCEPTS *52,278,313*

gripe [*n2*] *strong hold*
clamp, clasp, clench, clinch, clutch, crunch, grab, grapple, grasp, grip, tenure; SEE CONCEPT *191*

gripe [*v1*] *complain*
bellyache*, blow off*, carp, crab*, fuss, groan, grouch, grouse, grumble, kvetch*, moan, murmur, mutter, nag, squawk, take on*, whine, yammer*, yawp*; SEE CONCEPTS *44,52*

gripe [*v2*] *pain, annoy*
ache, bother, compress, cramp, disturb, hurt, irritate, pinch, press, squeeze, vex; SEE CONCEPTS *7,19,219,246*

grisly [*adj*] *horrifying*
abominable, appalling, awful, blood-stained, bloody, disgusting, dreadful, eerie, frightful, ghastly, grim, grody*, gross*, gruesome, hideous, horrible, horrid, lurid, macabre, sanguine, shocking, sick, sickening, terrible, terrifying, yucky*; SEE CONCEPTS *537,544,570*

grit [*n1*] *particles of dirt*
dust, foreign matter, gravel, lumps, pebbles, powder, sand; SEE CONCEPTS *260,831*

grit [*n2*] *courage, determination*
backbone, daring, doggedness, fortitude, gameness, guts*, hardihood, intestinal fortitude*, mettle, moxie*, nerve, perseverance, pluck, resolution, spine*, spirit, spunk, steadfastness, tenacity, toughness; SEE CONCEPTS *411,633*

gritty [*adj1*] *granular*
abrasive, branlike, calculous, crumbly, dusty, friable, grainy, gravelly, in particles, loose, lumpy, permeable, porous, powdery, pulverant, rasping, rough, sabulous, sandy, scratchy; SEE CONCEPT *606*

gritty [*adj2*] *brave*
courageous, determined, dogged, game*, hardy, mettlesome, plucky*, resolute, spirited, steadfast, tenacious, tough; SEE CONCEPTS *401,404*

groan [*n*] *moan, complaint*
cry, gripe, grouse, grumble, grunt, objection, sigh, sob, whine; SEE CONCEPTS *278,595*

groan [*v*] *moan, complain*
bemoan, cry, gripe, grouse, grumble, keen, lament, mumble, murmur, object, sigh, whine; SEE CONCEPTS *44,52,77*

groggy [*adj*] *dizzy, stunned*
befuddled, confused, dazed, dopey*, drunken, faint, hazy, out of it*, punch-drunk*, punchy*, reeling, shaky, slaphappy*, staggering, stupefied, swaying, tired, unsteady, weak, whirling, wobbly, woozy*; SEE CONCEPT *314*

groom [*n1*] *man being married*
benedict, bridegroom, fiancé, husband, spouse, suitor; SEE CONCEPT *419*

groom [*n2*] *male servant*
equerry, hostler, stable boy, stable man; SEE CONCEPTS *348,419*

groom [*v*] *make ready, prepare physically*
brush, clean, coach, comb, curry, dress, drill, educate, lick into shape*, make attractive, make presentable, nurture, preen, prep*, pretty up*, prim, prime, primp, put through grind*, put through mill*, ready, refine, refresh, rub down, shape up, sleek, slick up*, smarten up*, spiff up*, spruce up*, tend, tidy, train, turn out; SEE CONCEPTS *162,202,285*

groove [*n1*] *channel, indentation*
canal, corrugation, crease, crimp, cut, cutting, depression, ditch, flute, fluting, furrow, gouge, gutter, hollow, incision, notch, pucker, rabbet, rut, scallop, score, scratch, slit, trench, valley; SEE CONCEPT *513*

groove [*n2*] *daily routine*
daily grind*, grind, pace, rote, rut*, same old stuff*, shtick*, slot*; SEE CONCEPTS *362,677*

grope [*v*] *feel about for*
cast about, examine, explore, feel blindly, finger*, fish*, flounder, fumble, grabble, handle, manipulate, poke, pry, root, scrabble, search, touch; SEE CONCEPTS *34,216,612*

gross [*n*] *total, whole*
aggregate, all, entirety, sum, sum total, totality; SEE CONCEPTS *344,837*

gross [*adj1*] *large, fat*
adipose, big, bulky, chubby*, corpulent, dense, fleshy, great, heavy, hulking, husky, lumpish, massive, obese, overweight, porcine, portly, stout, thick, unwieldy, weighty; SEE CONCEPTS *773,781*

gross [*adj2*] *whole*
aggregate, all, before deductions, before tax, complete, entire, in sum, outright, total, whole ball of wax*, whole enchilada*, whole nine yards*, whole schmear*, whole shebang*; SEE CONCEPT *785*

gross [*adj3*] *crude, vulgar*
barnyard*, boorish, breezy, callous, carnal, cheap, coarse, corporeal, crass, dull, fleshly, foul, ignorant, improper, impure, indecent, indelicate, inelegant, insensitive, in the gutter*, lewd, loudmouthed, low, low-minded, lustful, obscene, offensive, rank, raunchy, raw, ribald, rough, rude, scatological, sensual, sexual, sleazy*, smutty*, swinish*, tasteless, ugly, uncouth, uncultured, undiscriminating, unfeeling, unrefined, unseemly, unsophisticated, voluptuous; SEE CONCEPTS *267,542,545*

gross [adj4] *obvious, apparent*
absolute, arrant, blatant, capital, complete, downright, egregious, excessive, exorbitant, extreme, flagrant, glaring, grievous, heinous, immoderate, inordinate, manifest, out-and-out*, outrageous, outright*, perfect, plain, rank, serious, shameful, sheer, shocking, unmitigated, unqualified, utter; SEE CONCEPTS 535,537

gross [v] *bring in as total*
earn, make, take in; SEE CONCEPTS 330,351

grotesque [adj] *ugly, misshapen*
aberrant, abnormal, absurd, antic, bizarre, deformed, distorted, eerie, extravagant, extreme, fanciful, fantastic, flamboyant, freakish, grody*, gross*, incongruous, ludicrous, malformed, monstrous, odd, outlandish, perverted, preposterous, queer, ridiculous, strange, surrealistic, uncanny, unnatural, weird, whimsical; SEE CONCEPTS 486,537,579

grouch [n] *person who complains a lot*
bear*, bellyacher*, bug*, complainer, crab*, crank, crosspatch*, curmudgeon, faultfinder, griper, grouser, growler, grumbler, grump*, kicker*, malcontent, moaner, sorehead*, sourpuss*, whiner; SEE CONCEPTS 412,423

grouch [v] *complain a lot*
bellyache*, carp, find fault, gripe, grouse, grumble, moan, murmur, mutter, scold, whine; SEE CONCEPT 52

grouchy [adj] *complaining, irritable*
cantankerous*, cross, crusty*, discontented, grumbling, grumpy*, ill-tempered, irascible, peevish, petulant, querulous, snappy, sulky, surly, testy; SEE CONCEPTS 267,401

ground [n] *earth, land*
arena, dirt, dry land, dust, field, landscape, loam, old sod, park, real estate, sand, sod, soil, terra firma, terrain, turf; SEE CONCEPT 509

ground [v1] *base, set; educate*
acquaint, base, bottom, coach, discipline, establish, familiarize, fit, fix, found, indoctrinate, inform, initiate, instruct, introduce, predicate, prepare, prime, qualify, rest, settle, stay, teach, train, tutor; SEE CONCEPTS 18,285

ground [v2] *restrict; drop in place*
bar, beach, bring down, dock, down, fell, floor, knock down, land, level, mow down*, prevent, strand; SEE CONCEPTS 130,181

groundless [adj] *without reason, justification*
baseless, bottomless, causeless, chimerical, empty, false, flimsy, foundationless, gratuitous, idle, illogical, illusory, imaginary, unauthorized, uncalled-for, unfounded, unjustified, unprovoked, unsupported, unwarranted; SEE CONCEPTS 267,552,582

grounds [n1] *estate, domain*
acreage, area, campus, country, district, environs, fields, gardens, habitat, holding, land, lot, premises, property, real estate, realm, sphere, spot, terrace, terrain, territory, tract, zone; SEE CONCEPTS 508,516

grounds [n2] *basis, premise*
account, antecedent, argument, base, bedrock*, call, cause, chapter and verse*, demonstration, determinant, dope*, evidence, excuse, factor, footing, foundation, goods*, groundwork, inducement, info*, information*, infrastructure, justification, motive, numbers, occasion, pretext, proof, rationale, reason, root*, seat, straight stuff*, substratum, test, testimony, trial, underpinning, wherefore, why, whyfor; SEE CONCEPTS 274,661

grounds [n3] *sediment*
deposit, dregs, grouts, leavings, lees, precipitate, precipitation, residue, settlings; SEE CONCEPT 260

groundwork [n] *basis, fundamentals*
ABCs*, background, base, bedrock*, cornerstone*, footing, foundation, ground, infrastructure, origin, preliminaries, preparation, root, substratum, underpinning, understructure; SEE CONCEPTS 274,442, 660,661

group [n] *number of individuals collectively*
accumulation, aggregation, assemblage, assembly, association, assortment, band, batch, battery, bevy, body, bunch, bundle, cartel, category, chain, circle, class, clique, clot, club, clump, cluster, clutch, collection, combination, combine, company, conglomerate, congregation, coterie, covey, crew, crowd, faction, formation, gang, gathering, grade, league, lot, mess, organization, pack, parcel, party, passel, platoon, pool, posse, set, shooting match, society, sort, suite, syndicate, troop, trust; SEE CONCEPTS 391,432

group [v1] *bring together*
arrange, assemble, associate, band together, bracket, bunch, bunch up*, cluster, collect, congregate, consort, corral, crowd, fraternize, gang around*, gang up*, gather, get together, hang out*, harmonize, huddle, link, make the scene*, meet, organize, poke, punch*, round up*, scare up*, systematize; SEE CONCEPTS 109,114

group [v2] *classify, sort*
arrange, assemble, associate, assort, bracket, categorize, class, dispose, file, gather, marshal, order, organize, pigeonhole*, put together, range, rank; SEE CONCEPTS 18,84,158

grove [n] *cluster of trees*
brake, coppice, copse, covert, forest, orchard, plantation, spinney, stand, thicket, wood, woodland; SEE CONCEPTS 429,517

grovel [v] *abase, demean oneself*
apple-polish*, beg, beg for mercy, beseech, blandish, bootlick*, bow and scrape*, brown-nose*, butter up*, cater to, court, cower, crawl, creep, cringe, crouch, eat crow*, eat dirt*, eat humble pie*, fall all over*, fawn*, flatter, humble oneself, humor, implore, kiss one's feet*, kneel, kowtow*, make much of*, make up to*, pamper, play up to*, prostrate, revere, snivel, soft-soap*, stoop, suck up to*, truckle*, wheedle, yes*; SEE CONCEPTS 384,633

grow [v] *become larger, evolve*
abound, advance, age, amplify, arise, augment, become, branch out, breed, build, burgeon, burst forth, come, come to be, cultivate, develop, dilate, enlarge, expand, extend, fill out, flourish, gain, germinate, get, get bigger, get taller, heighten, increase, issue, luxuriate, maturate, mature, mount, multiply, originate, pop up*, produce, propagate, pullulate, raise, ripen, rise, shoot*, spread, spring up, sprout, stem, stretch, swell, thicken, thrive, turn, vegetate, wax*, widen; SEE CONCEPTS *427,469,704,775*

growl [n/v] *animal-like sound*
bark, bellow, gnarl, gnarr, grumble, grunt, howl, moan, roar, roll, rumble, snarl, thunder; SEE CONCEPTS *77,595*

grown-up [n] *adult*
gentleman, grown person, lady, mam, man, Miss, mister, Mr., Mrs., Ms., woman; SEE CONCEPT *424*

growth [n1] *development, progress*
advance, advancement, aggrandizement, augmentation, beefing up*, boost, buildup, crop, cultivation, enlargement, evolution, evolvement, expansion, extension, fleshing out*, flowering, gain, germination, growing, heightening, hike, improvement, increase, maturation, maturing, multiplication, produce, production, proliferation, prosperity, rise, sprouting, stretching, success, surge, swell, thickening, unfolding, up, upping, vegetation, waxing*, widening; SEE CONCEPTS *427,469,703,704,775*

growth [n2] *tumor*
cancer, cancroid, excrescence, fibrousness, fibrous tissue, fungus, lump, mole, outgrowth, parasite, polyp, swelling, thickening, wen; SEE CONCEPT *306*

grub [n1] *larva*
caterpillar, entozoon, maggot, worm; SEE CONCEPT *398*

grub [n2] *food*
chow*, comestibles, eats*, edibles, feed, nosh*, nurture, provisions, rations, sustenance, viands, victuals, vittles*; SEE CONCEPTS *457,460*

grub [v1] *dig, uncover*
beat, break, burrow, clean, clear, comb, delve, excavate, ferret, fine-tooth-comb*, forage, hunt, poke, prepare, probe, pull up, rake, ransack, root, rummage, scour, search, shovel, spade, unearth, uproot; SEE CONCEPTS *178,216*

grub [v2] *work very hard*
drudge, grind, labor, moil, plod, slave, slog, sweat, toil; SEE CONCEPT *100*

grubby [adj] *dirty, disheveled*
besmeared, black, filthy, foul, frowzy*, grimy, grungy*, impure, messy, mucky*, nasty, scruffy, scuzzy*, seedy*, shabby, sloppy, slovenly, smutty*, soiled, sordid, squalid, unclean, uncleanly, unkempt, untidy, unwashed; SEE CONCEPTS *485,621*

grudge [n] *hard feelings*
animosity, animus, antipathy, aversion, bad blood*, bitterness, bone to pick*, dislike, enmity, grievance, hate, hatred, ill will, injury, injustice, malevolence, malice, maliciousness, malignancy, peeve, pet peeve*, pique, rancor, resentment, spite, spitefulness, spleen, venom; SEE CONCEPT *29*

grudge [v] *feel resentful; give unwillingly*
begrudge, be reluctant, be stingy*, complain, covet, deny, envy, hold back, mind, pinch, refuse, resent, stint; SEE CONCEPT *21*

grueling [adj] *difficult, taxing*
arduous, backbreaking, brutal, chastening, crushing, demanding, excruciating, exhausting, fatiguing, fierce, grinding, hairy*, hard, harsh, heavy*, laborious, punishing, racking, severe, stiff, strenuous, tiring, torturous, trying; SEE CONCEPT *565*

gruesome [adj] *horrible, awful*
abominable, appalling, daunting, fearful, frightful, ghastly, grim, grisly, grody*, gross*, hideous, horrendous, horrid, horrific, horrifying, loathsome, lurid, macabre, monstrous, morbid, offensive, repugnant, repulsive, shocking, sick*, spine-tingling*, terrible, terrifying, ugly, weird*; SEE CONCEPTS *485,548*

gruff [adj1] *bad-tempered, rude*
abrupt, bearish, blunt, boisterous, boorish, brusque, churlish, crabbed*, crabby*, crude, crusty*, curt, discourteous, dour, fierce, grouchy*, grumpy*, ill-natured, impolite, morose, nasty, offhand, rough, saturnine, short, snappy*, snippy*, sour, sullen, surly, truculent, uncivil, ungracious, unmannerly; SEE CONCEPTS *267,401*

gruff [adj2] *rasping in sound*
cracked, croaking, croaky, grating, guttural, harsh, hoarse, husky, low, rough, throaty; SEE CONCEPT *594*

grumble [v1] *complain*
bellyache*, carp, find fault, fuss, gripe, groan, grouch*, grouse, kick, kvetch*, moan, protest, pule, repine, scold, snivel*, squawk*, whine; SEE CONCEPTS *44,52*

grumble [v2] *murmur, rumble*
bark, croak, gnarl, gnarr, growl, grunt, gurgle, mumble, mutter, roar, roll, snap, snarl, snuffle, splutter, whine; SEE CONCEPTS *65,77*

grumpy [adj] *in a bad mood*
bad-tempered, cantankerous*, crabby*, cross, crotchety, disgruntled, dissatisfied, griping, grouchy*, grumbling, irritable, peevish, pettish, petulant, querulous, sulky, sullen, surly, testy, truculent; SEE CONCEPTS *401,403*

guarantee [n] *pledge, promise*
agreement, assurance, attestation, bail, bargain, bond, certainty, certificate, certification, charter, collateral, contract, covenant, deposit, earnest, gage, guaranty, insurance, lock, oath, pawn, pipe, recognizance, security, sure thing*, surety, testament, token, undertaking, vow, warrant, warranty, word, word of honor; SEE CONCEPTS *71,271,685*

guarantee [v] *pledge, promise*
affirm, angel, answer for, assure, attest, aver, back, bankroll, be surety for, bind oneself, certify, con-

firm, cosign, endorse, ensure, evidence, evince, get behind*, give bond, grubstake, guaranty, insure, juice*, maintain, make bail*, make certain, make sure, mortgage, pick up the check*, pick up the tab*, protect, prove, reassure, secure, sign for, stake, stand behind*, stand up for*, support, swear, testify, vouch for, wager, warrant, witness; SEE CONCEPTS *71,110*

guaranteed [adj] *made certain*
affirmed, approved, ascertained, assured, attested, bonded, certified, confirmed, endorsed, for a fact, for sure, have a lock on*, insured, on ice*, pledged, plighted, protected, sealed, secured, sure, sure enough*, sure-fire*, warranted; SEE CONCEPT *535*

guard [n1] *protector*
bouncer*, chaperon, chaperone, chaser*, convoyer, custodian, defender, escort, guardian, lookout, picket, sentinel, sentry, shepherd, shield, ward, warden, watch, watchman; SEE CONCEPT *348*

guard [n2] *defense*
aegis, armament, armor, buffer, bulwark, pad, protection, rampart, safeguard, screen, security, shield, ward; SEE CONCEPT *712*

guard [v] *protect, watch*
attend, baby-sit, bulwark, chaperon, chaperone, conduct, convoy, cover, cover up, defend, escort, fend, keep, keep an eye on*, keep in view, keep under surveillance, look after, lookout, mind, observe, oversee, patrol, police*, preserve, ride shotgun for*, safeguard, save, screen, secure, see after, shelter, shepherd, shield, shotgun, stonewall*, superintend, supervise, tend, watch over; SEE CONCEPTS *96,134*

guarded [adj] *suspicious*
attentive, cagey, calculating, canny, careful, cautious, chary, circumspect, discreet, gingerly, leery, noncommittal, on the lookout*, overcautious, prudent, reserved, restrained, reticent, safe, vigilant, wary, watchful, with eyes peeled*; SEE CONCEPT *542*

guardian [n] *keeper, protector*
angel*, attendant, baby-sitter, bird dog*, cerberus, champion, chaperon, chaperone, conservator, cop*, curator, custodian, defender, escort, guard, keeper, nurse, overseer, paladin, patrol, preserver, safeguard, sentinel, shepherd, sitter, sponsor, superintendent, supervisor, trustee, vigilante, warden, watchdog*; SEE CONCEPTS *414,423*

guess [n] *belief, speculation*
assumption, ballpark figure*, conclusion, conjecture, deduction, divination, estimate, fancy, feeling, guesstimate*, guesswork, hunch*, hypothesis, induction, inference, judgment, notion, opinion, postulate, postulation, prediction, presumption, presupposition, reckoning, shot*, shot in the dark*, sneaking suspicion*, stab*, supposal, supposition, surmisal, surmise, suspicion, theory, thesis, view; SEE CONCEPT *689*

guess [v] *try to figure out; imagine*
believe, calculate, chance, conjecture, dare say, deduce, deem, divine, estimate, fancy*, fathom, fig-

ure, go out on a limb*, guesstimate*, happen upon*, hazard*, hypothesize, infer, judge, jump to a conclusion*, lump it*, opine, penetrate, pick, postulate, predicate, predict, presume, pretend, reason, reckon, select, size up*, solve, speculate, suggest, suppose, surmise, survey, suspect, take a shot at*, take a stab at*, theorize, think, think likely, venture, work out*; SEE CONCEPT *28*

guest [n] *person accommodated, given hospitality*
bedfellow, boarder, caller, client, companion, company, confidant, confidante, customer, fellow, frequenter*, habitué, inmate, lodger, mate, out-of-towner*, partaker, patron, recipient, renter, roomer, sharer, sojourner, tenant, transient, vacationer, visitant, visitor; SEE CONCEPT *423*

guidance [n] *counselling*
advice, auspices, conduct, conduction, control, conveyance, counsel, direction, government, help, instruction, intelligence, leadership, management, navigation, supervision, teaching; SEE CONCEPTS *75,274,278*

guide [n1] *something that or someone who leads*
adviser, attendant, captain, chaperon, cicerone, conductor, controller, convoy, counselor, criterion, design, director, docent, escort, example, exemplar, exhibitor, genie, genius, guiding spirit, guru, ideal, inspiration, lead, leader, lodestar, master, mentor, model, monitor, paradigm, pathfinder, pattern, pilot, pioneer, rudder, scout, standard, superintendent, teacher, usher, vanguard; SEE CONCEPTS *348,423,688*

guide [n2] *information, instructions*
ABCs*, beacon*, bellwether*, bible, catalog, chapter and verse*, clue, compendium, directory, enchiridion, guidebook, guiding light*, handbook, hot lead*, key, landmark, lodestar, manual, mark, marker, no-no's*, pointer, print, sign, signal, signpost, telltale, the book*, the numbers*, tip-off*, vade mecum; SEE CONCEPT *274*

guide [v] *direct, lead*
accompany, advise, attend, beacon*, chaperon, command, conduct, contrive, control, convoy, counsel, coxswain, educate, engineer, escort, govern, handle, have a handle on*, influence, instruct, manage, maneuver, marshal, mastermind, navigate, oversee, pilot, quarterback*, regulate, route, rule, see, shepherd, show, show the way, spearhead*, steer, superintend, supervise, sway, teach, trailblaze*, train, usher; SEE CONCEPTS *75,110,117,187*

guild [n] *association, fellowship*
brotherhood, club, company, corporation, federation, fraternity, group, interest group, league, lodge, order, organization, profession, society, sodality, sorority, trade, union; SEE CONCEPTS *381,387*

guile [n] *slyness, cleverness*
artfulness, artifice, chicanery, craft, craftiness, cunning, deceit, deception, dirty dealing*, dirty pool*, dirty trick*, dirty work*, dishonesty, dissemblance, dissimulation, double-cross*, duplicity, foul play*,

gamesmanship*, jive*, knavery*, one-upmanship*, run-around*, ruse, sellout*, sharp practice*, stab in the back*, treachery, trickery, trickiness, wiliness; SEE CONCEPTS *645,657*

guileless [*adj*] *honest*
aboveboard, artless, candid, frank, genuine, ingenuous, innocent, naive, natural, open, simple, simple-minded, sincere, straightforward, truthful, unaffected, undesigning, unsophisticated, unstudied; SEE CONCEPTS *267,542,545*

guilt [*n*] *blame; bad conscience over responsibility*
answerability, blameworthiness, contrition, crime, criminality, culpability, delinquency, dereliction, disgrace, dishonor, error, failing, fault, guiltiness, indiscretion, infamy, iniquity, lapse, liability, malefaction, malfeasance, malpractice, misbehavior, misconduct, misstep, offense, onus, peccability, penitence, regret, remorse, responsibility, self-condemnation, self-reproach, shame, sin, sinfulness, slip, solecism, stigma, transgression, wickedness, wrong; SEE CONCEPTS *101,532,645,690*

guiltless [*adj*] *blameless, not responsible*
clean, clear, crimeless, exemplary, faultless, free, good, immaculate, impeccable, inculpable, innocent, irreproachable, not guilty, pure, righteous, sinless, spotless, unimpeachable, unsullied, untainted, untarnished, virtuous; SEE CONCEPT *545*

guilty [*adj*] *blameworthy; found at fault*
accusable, at fault, caught, censurable, censured, chargeable, condemned, conscience-stricken, contrite, convictable, convicted, criminal, culpable, damned, delinquent, depraved, doomed, erring, evil, felonious, hangdog*, impeached, incriminated, in error, iniquitous, in the wrong, judged, liable, licentious, offending, on one's head*, out of line*, proscribed, regretful, remorseful, reprehensible, responsible, rueful, sentenced, sheepish, sinful, sorry, to blame, wicked, wrong; SEE CONCEPT *545*

guise [*n*] *appearance, pretense*
air, aspect, behavior, cloak, color, cover, demeanor, disguise, disguisement, dress, facade, face, false front*, false show*, fashion, form, front, mask, mien, mode, pose, posture, role, seeming, semblance, shape, show, showing, simulacrum; SEE CONCEPTS *645,716*

gulf [*n1*] *sea inlet*
basin, bay, bayou, bight, cove, firth, harbor, slough, sound, whirlpool; SEE CONCEPTS *509,514*

gulf [*n2*] *deep, gaping hole*
abyss, breach, cave, cavity, chasm, cleft, crevasse, depth, depths, distance, expanse, gap, gulch, hiatus, hollow, opening, pit, ravine, rent, rift, separation, shaft, split, void, well, whirlpool; SEE CONCEPTS *509,513*

gullible [*adj*] *naive, trusting*
being a sucker*, believing, biting, credulous, easily taken in*, easy mark*, falling hook line and sinker*, foolish, green*, innocent, kidding oneself*, mark*, silly, simple, sucker, susceptible, swallowing whole*, taken in*, taking the bait*, trustful, tumbling for*, unskeptical, unsophisticated, unsuspecting, wide-eyed*; SEE CONCEPTS *402,542*

gully [*n*] *ravine, ditch*
channel, chase, chasm, crevasse, culvert, gutter, notch, trench, watercourse; SEE CONCEPTS *509,513*

gulp [*n*] *swallow*
choke, draught, gasp, mouthful, swig, swill; SEE CONCEPT *185*

gulp [*v*] *eat, drink fast*
belt*, choke down*, chugalug*, consume, devour, dispatch, dispose, drop*, eat, englut, gobble*, guzzle*, imbibe, ingurgitate, inhale*, pour, quaff, scarf down*, slop*, slosh*, stuff, swallow*, swig, swill, take in, toss off*, wolf*, wolf down*; SEE CONCEPTS *169,185*

gum [*n*] *sticky substance*
adhesive, amber, cement, cohesive substance, exudate, glue, mucilage, paste, pitch, plaster, resin, rosin, tar, wax; SEE CONCEPT *466*

gumption [*n*] *nerve, initiative*
ability, acumen, astuteness, cleverness, common sense, discernment, enterprise, get-up-and-go*, good sense, horse sense*, industry, judgment, perspicaciousness, perspicacity, resourcefulness, sagaciousness, sagacity, savvy, sense, shrewdness, spirit, wisdom, wit; SEE CONCEPT *411*

gun [*n*] *weapon that shoots*
9mm.*, blaster*, cannon, difference*, equalizer*, flintlock, forty-five*, handgun, hardware*, howitzer, magnum, mortar, musket, ordnance, peashooter*, persuader*, piece*, pistol, revolver, rifle, rod*, Saturday night special*, shotgun, thirty-eight*, Uzi*; SEE CONCEPT *500*

gurgle [*n/v*] *burble, murmur*
babble, bubble, crow, lap, plash, purl, ripple, slosh, splash, wash; SEE CONCEPTS *65,595*

guru [*n*] *mentor, guide*
authority, guiding light*, leader, maharishi, master, sage, swami, teacher, tutor; SEE CONCEPT *350*

gush [*n*] *outpouring*
burst, cascade, flood, flow, flush, issue, jet, run, rush, spate, spout, spring, spurt, stream, surge; SEE CONCEPTS *467,686*

gush [*v1*] *pour out*
burst, cascade, emanate, emerge, flood, flow, flush, issue, jet, pour, roll, run, rush, sluice, spew, spout, spring, spurt, stream, surge, well; SEE CONCEPT *179*

gush [*v2*] *speak with overwhelming enthusiasm*
babble*, blather, carry on about*, chatter, effervesce, effuse, enthuse, fall all over*, go on about*, jabber, make a to-do over*, overstate, prate, prattle, rave; SEE CONCEPT *49*

gust [*n*] *rush, eruption*
access, blast, blow, breeze, burst, explosion, fit, flare-up, flurry, gale, outburst, paroxysm, passion, puff, sally, squall, storm, surge; SEE CONCEPTS *524,786*

gusto [n] *great enthusiasm*
appetite, appreciation, ardor, brio, delectation, delight, enjoyment, exhilaration, fervor, heart, liking, palate, passion, pleasure, relish, savor, taste, verve, zeal, zest; SEE CONCEPTS *411,657*

gusty [adj] *windy*
airy, blowy, blustering, blustery, breezy, hearty, robust, squally, stormy, tempestuous; SEE CONCEPT *525*

gut [n] *stomach and abdomen*
belly, bowels, duodenum, entrails, innards, intestines, paunch, tripes, tummy*, venter, viscera; SEE CONCEPT *393*

gut [adj] *intuitive*
basic, deep-seated, emotional, heartfelt, innate, inner, instinctive, interior, internal, intimate, involuntary, natural, spontaneous, unthinking, visceral, viscerous; SEE CONCEPT *403*

gut [v] *clean out, strip*
bowel, clean, decimate, despoil, dilapidate, disembowel, draw, dress, empty, eviscerate, exenterate, loot, pillage, plunder, ransack, ravage, rifle, sack; SEE CONCEPTS *165,211*

gutless [adj] *timid*
abject, chicken*, chicken-hearted*, coward, cowardly, craven, faint-hearted*, feeble, irresolute, lily-livered*, pusillanimous, spineless*, submissive, unmanly, weak, wimpy*, yellow*, yellow-bellied*; SEE CONCEPTS *404,542*

guts [n] *nerve, boldness*
audacity, backbone*, courage, daring, dauntlessness, effrontery, forcefulness, fortitude, grit*, hardihood, heart*, intestinal fortitude*, mettle, moxie*, pluck, resolution, sand*, spine*, spirit, spunk*, willpower; SEE CONCEPTS *411,657*

gutsy [adj] *bold, brave*
courageous, determined, gallant, game*, indomitable, intrepid, manful, mettlesome, plucky, resolute, spirited, spunky*, staunch, unfearful, valiant; SEE CONCEPTS *404,542*

gutter [n] *ditch*
channel, conduit, culvert, dike, drain, duct, eaves, fosse, funnel, gully, moat, pipe, runnel, sewer, sluice, spout, sulcation, trench, trough, tube, watercourse; SEE CONCEPTS *440,513*

guttural [adj] *deep in sound*
glottal, grating, gravelly, growling, gruff, harsh, hoarse, husky, inarticulate, low, rasping, rough, sepulchral, thick, throaty; SEE CONCEPT *594*

guy [n] *male person (informal)*
bloke, buck, buddy, cat, chap, dude, fellow, gentleman, lad, man, youth; SEE CONCEPT *419*

guzzle [v] *drink down fast*
bolt*, booze*, carouse*, cram, devour, englut, gobble*, gorge, gormandize, imbibe, ingurgitate, knock back*, quaff, slop*, slosh*, soak, swig, swill, tipple; SEE CONCEPT *169*

gymnasium [n] *arena for sports, recreation*
alley, amphitheater, athletic club, center, circus, coliseum, course, exercise room, field house, floor,
gym, health club, hippodrome, pit, recreation center, ring, rink, spa, stadium, sweatshop*, theater; SEE CONCEPTS *364,438,439*

gymnastics [n] *acrobatic exercise*
acrobatics, aerobatics, balance beam, bars, bodybuilding, calisthenics, floor exercise, free exercise, gym, horse, rings, trampoline, trapeze, tumbling, vaulting, workout; SEE CONCEPT *363*

gyp [v] *defraud, cheat*
beat*, bilk, chicane, cozen, deceive, do*, dupe, fake, flimflam*, gull*, hoax, snow*, swindle, trick; SEE CONCEPT *59*

gyrate [v] *revolve*
circle, circulate, circumduct, gyre, pirouette, purl, roll, rotate, spin, spiral, turn, twirl, whirl, whirligig; SEE CONCEPTS *147,149*

H

habit [n1] *tendency, practice*
addiction, bent, bias, constitution, consuetude, convention, custom, dependence, disposition, fashion, fixation, fixed attitude, frame of mind*, gravitation, groove, habitude, hangup, impulsion, inclination, make-up*, manner, mannerism, mode, nature, obsession, pattern, penchant, persuasion, practice, praxis, predisposition, proclivity, proneness, propensity, quirk, routine, rule, rut, second nature*, set, style, susceptibility, tendency, thing*, turn, usage, use, way, weakness, wont; SEE CONCEPT *644*

habit [n2] *dress, clothing, often for a particular purpose*
apparel, costume, garb, garment, habiliment, riding clothes, robe, vestment; SEE CONCEPT *451*

habitat/habitation [n] *place where someone resides*
abode, accommodations, address, apartment, berth, biosphere, cave, commorancy, condo, condominium, co-op, den, digs*, domicile, dwelling, element, environment, fireside, flat, haunt*, haven, hearth, hole*, home, home plate*, homestead, house, housing, locale, locality, lodging, neck of the woods*, nest, nook, occupancy, occupation, pad*, place, quarters, range, residence, residency, roof*, roost*, seat*, settlement, site, stamping ground*, stomping ground*, surroundings, terrain, territory, turf; SEE CONCEPT *515*

habitual [adj] *usual, established*
accepted, accustomed, addicted, addicting, automatic, chronic, common, confirmed, constant, continual, conventional, customary, cyclic, disciplined, familiar, fixed, frequent, hardened, ingrained, inveterate, iterated, iterative, mechanical, methodical, natural, normal, ordinary, perfunctory, permanent, perpetual, persistent, practiced, recurrent, regular, reiterative, repeated, repetitious, rooted, routine, seasoned, set, standard, steady, systematic, traditional, wonted; SEE CONCEPTS *530,547*

habituate [v] *prepare, accustom*
acclimate, acclimatize, addict, adjust, break in, condition, confirm, devote, discipline, endure, familiar-

ize, harden, inure, make used to, school, season, take to, tolerate, train; SEE CONCEPTS *35,202*

hack [*n1*] *person who does easy work for money*
drudge*, greasy grind*, grind*, hireling, lackey*, old pro*, plodder*, pro*, servant, slave, workhorse*; SEE CONCEPT *348*

hack [*n2*] *taxicab*
cab, carriage, coach, hackney, taxi, vehicle; SEE CONCEPT *505*

hack [*n3/v*] *cut without care*
chop, clip, fell, gash, hackle, hew, lacerate, mangle, mutilate, notch, slash, whack; SEE CONCEPTS *137,176*

hackneyed [*adj*] *clichéd, tired*
antiquated, banal, common, commonplace, conventional, corny*, everyday, familiar tune*, hokey*, moth-eaten*, obsolete, old, old-chestnut*, old-hat*, old-saw*, outdated, outmoded, out-of-date, overworked, pedestrian*, played-out*, quotidian, run-of-the-mill*, stale, stereotyped, stock, threadbare*, timeworn, tripe, trite, unoriginal, well-worn, worn-out*; SEE CONCEPTS *267,530*

hag [*n*] *old, unpleasant woman*
biddy, crone, shrew, sorceress; SEE CONCEPTS *415,423*

haggard [*adj*] *worn, weakened*
ashen, careworn, drawn, emaciated, exhausted, faded, fagged, fatigued, fretted, gaunt, ghastly, lank, lean, pale, pallid, pinched, scraggy, scrawny, shrunken, skinny, spare, starved, thin, tired, wan, wasted, weak, wearied, worn-down, wrinkled; SEE CONCEPTS *314,406,491*

haggle [*v*] *bicker, quarrel*
argue, bargain, barter, beat down*, cavil, chaffer, deal, dicker*, dispute, hammer out a deal*, horse-trade*, make a deal*, palter, quibble, squabble, wrangle; SEE CONCEPT *46*

hail [*n*] *torrent*
barrage, bombardment, broadside, cannonade, hailstorm, pelting, rain, salvo, shower, storm, volley; SEE CONCEPTS *189,524*

hail [*v1*] *call to, yell for*
accost, address, flag, flag down*, greet, hello, holler*, salute, shoulder, shout, signal, sing out*, speak to, wave down, welcome, whistle down*, whistle for*, yawp*, yoo-hoo*; SEE CONCEPTS *47,74,77*

hail [*v2*] *honor, salute*
acclaim, acknowledge, applaud, cheer, commend, compliment, exalt, glorify, greet, hear it for*, kudize, praise, recognize, recommend, root for*, welcome; SEE CONCEPT *69*

hail [*v3*] *come from; originate*
be a native of, be born in, begin, claim as birthplace; SEE CONCEPT *648*

hail [*v4*] *rain down on*
barrage, batter, beat down upon, bombard, pelt, rain, shower, storm, volley; SEE CONCEPT *526*

hair [*n*] *threadlike growth on animate being*
beard, bristle, cilium, coiffure, cowlick, cut, down, eyebrow, eyelash, feeler, fiber, filament, fluff, fringe, frizzies*, fur, grass, haircut, hairstyle, lock, mane, mop*, moustache, quill, ruff, shock, sideburn, split ends, strand, thatch, thread, tress, tuft, vibrissa, villus, whiskers, wig, wool; SEE CONCEPT *392*

hairless [*adj*] *without growth on body part*
bald, baldheaded, beardless, clean-shaven, cue ball*, depilated, egghead*, glabrate, glabrescent, glabrous, shaved, shaven, shorn, skinhead*, smooth, smooth-faced, tonsured, whiskerless; SEE CONCEPT *406*

hairstyle [*n*] *cut, style of a head of hair*
afro*, beehive*, blow dry*, bob*, bouffant, braid, brushcut, bubble*, bun, coiffure, crewcut, cut, do*, dreadlocks, ducktail, fade, feather cut, flattop*, flip, haircut, hairdo, headdress, horse tail, mohawk, natural, pageboy, pigtails, pixie, ponytail, razor cut; SEE CONCEPT *718*

hairy [*adj1*] *having much hair*
bearded, bewhiskered, bristly, bushy, downy, fleecy, flocculent, fluffy, furry, fuzzy, hirsute, lanate, pileous, piliferous, pilose, pubescent, rough, shaggy, stubbly, tufted, unshaven, unshorn, villous, whiskered, woolly; SEE CONCEPT *406*

hairy [*adj2*] *dangerous*
chancy, difficult, hazardous, jeopardous, perilous, risky, scary, treacherous, uncertain, unhealthy, unsound, wicked; SEE CONCEPT *548*

hale [*adj*] *strong and healthy*
able-bodied, alive and kicking*, blooming, fit, fit as a fiddle*, flourishing, healthy, hearty, husky, in fine fettle*, in the pink*, right, robust, sane, sound, stout, strapping, strong, trim, vigorous, well, well-conditioned, wholesome; SEE CONCEPTS *314,489*

half [*n*] *one of two equal parts of a whole*
bisection, division, fifty percent, fraction, hemisphere, moiety; SEE CONCEPT *835*

half [*adj*] *partial*
bisected, divided, even-steven*, fifty-fifty*, fractional, halved, incomplete, limited, moderate, partly; SEE CONCEPT *785*

half-baked/half-witted [*adj*] *stupid; not thought through*
backward, batty*, birdbrained*, blockheaded*, bone-headed*, brainless, crazy, dumb, feeble-minded, foolish, harebrained*, idiotic, ignorant, ill-conceived, imbecilic, impractical, indiscreet, moronic, poorly planned, retarded, senseless, short-sighted, silly, slow, sophomoric, underdeveloped, unformed, witless; SEE CONCEPTS *403,529,548*

half-breed [*n*] *mixed creation; offspring of parents of different strains*
bastard, cross, crossbred, cross-breed, half-blood, half-caste, hybrid, mongrel*, mule, mutt*, outcast; SEE CONCEPTS *260,394,414*

halfhearted [*adj*] *without enthusiasm*
apathetic, cool, impassive, indifferent, irresolute, lackluster, listless, lukewarm, neutral, passive, perfunctory, spiritless, tame, tepid, unenthusiastic, uninterested; SEE CONCEPTS *401,542*

halfway [adj] *not complete; in the middle*
betwixt and between*, center, centermost, central, equidistant, imperfect, incomplete, intermediate, medial, median, mid*, middle, middlemost, midway, moderate, part, partial, part-way, smack dab*, smack in the middle*; SEE CONCEPTS *531,586*

halfway [adv] *not complete; in the middle*
comparatively, compromising, conciliatory, half the distance, imperfectly, incompletely, in part, insufficiently, medially, middling, midway, moderately, nearly, partially, partly, pretty*, rather, restrictedly, to a degree, to some extent, to the middle, unsatisfactorily; SEE CONCEPTS *531,586*

hall [n1] *corridor*
anteroom, entrance, entranceway, entry, foyer, gallery, hallway, lobby, pass, passage, passageway, room, rotunda, vestibule; SEE CONCEPT *440*

hall [n2] *room for large affairs*
amphitheater, arena, armory, assembly room, auditorium, ballroom, casino, chamber, church, gallery, gym, gymnasium, lounge, lyceum, mart, meeting place, refectory, salon, stateroom, theater; SEE CONCEPTS *438,439,441,448*

hallmark [n] *symbol, authentication*
badge, certification, device, emblem, endorsement, indication, mark, ratification, seal, sign, signet, stamp, sure sign, telltale sign, trademark; SEE CONCEPTS *284,628*

hallowed [adj] *holy, revered*
anointed, beatified, blessed, consecrated, dedicated, divine, enshrined, holy, honored, inviolable, sacred, sacrosanct, sanctified, unprofane; SEE CONCEPT *568*

hallucinate [v] *imagine vividly*
blow one's mind*, daydream, envision, fantasize, freak out*, have visions, head trip*, hear voices*, trip*, visualize; SEE CONCEPT *34*

hallucination [n] *dream, delusion*
aberration, apparition, fantasy, figment of the imagination*, head trip*, illusion, mirage, phantasm, phantasmagoria, phantom, trip*, vision, wraith; SEE CONCEPTS *529,532,690*

halo [n] *ring of light*
aura, aureola, aureole, aurora, corona, crown of light, glory, halation, nimbus, radiance; SEE CONCEPTS *624,628*

halt [n] *end, stoppage*
arrest, break, break-off*, close, cutoff, freeze*, grinding halt, impasse, interruption, layoff, letup, pause, screaming halt*, screeching halt*, stand, standstill, stop, termination; SEE CONCEPT *119*

halt [v1] *stop, cause to stop*
adjourn, arrest, balk, bar, block, blow the whistle on*, break off*, bring to an end, bring to standstill, call it a day*, cease, cease fire, check, close down, come to an end, cool it*, curb*, cut short, desist, deter, draw up, drop anchor*, end, frustrate, hamper, hold at bay*, hold back, impede, intermit, interrupt, obstruct, pause, pull up*, punctuate, put a cork in*, rest, stall, stand still, stay, stem, stop, suspend, terminate, wait; SEE CONCEPTS *121,234*

halt [v2] *hesitate, stutter*
be defective, dither, falter, hobble, limp, pause, shilly-shally*, stagger, stammer, stumble, vacillate, waver, whiffle*, wiggle-waggle*; SEE CONCEPTS *234,721,804*

halting [adj] *hesitant*
awkward, bumbling, clumsy, doubtful, faltering, gauche, imperfect, indecisive, inept, irresolute, labored, limping, lumbering, maladroit, slow, stammering, stumbling, stuttering, tentative, uncertain, unhandy, vacillating, vacillatory, wavering, wooden*; SEE CONCEPTS *534,550*

halve [v] *cut in half*
bisect, divide equally, reduce by fifty percent, share equally, split in two; SEE CONCEPT *98*

hamburger [n] *ground beef sandwich*
beefburger, burger, cheeseburger, chopped beefsteak, ground beef, ground chuck, ground round, ground sirloin, salisbury steak; SEE CONCEPTS *457,460*

hammer [v] *beat, hit*
bang, batter, bear down, clobber, defeat, drive, drub, fashion, forge, form, knock, make, pound, pummel, shape, strike, tap, thrash, trounce, wallop, whack, whomp; SEE CONCEPT *189*

hammer away/hammer into [v] *work hard at*
continue, drive home*, drub into*, drudge, drum into*, endeavor, grind*, grind into*, impress upon, instruct, keep on, peg away*, persevere, persist, plug away*, pound away*, repeat, stick to*, try hard, try repeatedly, work; SEE CONCEPTS *68,87,239*

hammer out [v] *bring to a conclusion*
accomplish, bring about, build, complete, construct, erect, establish, excogitate, fight through, finish, form, make, negotiate, produce, settle, set up, sort out, thrash out*, work out; SEE CONCEPTS *91,706*

hamper [n] *basket for storage*
bassinet, carton, crate, creel, laundry basket, pannier; SEE CONCEPT *494*

hamper [v] *impede, restrict*
baffle, balk, bar, bind, block, check, clog, cramp, cramp one's style*, cumber, curb, discomfit, drag one's feet*, embarrass, encumber, entangle, fetter, foil, frustrate, get in the way*, hamstring*, handicap, hang up*, hinder, hobble, hog-tie*, hold up*, inconvenience, inhibit, interfere with, leash, obstruct, prevent, restrain, retard, shackle, slow down, stymie, thwart, tie, tie one's hands*, tie up, trammel; SEE CONCEPT *130*

hand [n1] *appendage at end of human arm, including fingers*
duke*, extremity, fin*, fist, grasp, grip, ham*, hold, hook, metacarpus, mitt*, palm, paw*, phalanges, shaker*; SEE CONCEPT *392*

hand [n2] *person who does labor*
aide, artificer, artisan, craftsman/woman, craftsperson, employee, handyman/woman, help, helper,

hired man/woman, laborer, operative, roustabout, worker, workman/woman; SEE CONCEPT *348*

hand [*n3*] *help, aid*
ability, agency, assistance, control, direction, guidance, influence, instruction, knack, lift, part, participation, relief, share, skill, succor, support; SEE CONCEPTS *110,630*

hand [*n4*] *handwriting*
calligraphy, chirography, longhand, penmanship, script; SEE CONCEPT *79*

hand [*n5*] *round of applause*
applause, clap, handclapping, ovation, thunderous reception; SEE CONCEPT *189*

handbag [*n*] *woman's carryall*
backpack, bag, clutch, evening bag, grip, hide, knapsack, leather, pocketbook, portmanteau, purse, reticule; SEE CONCEPT *446*

handbook [*n*] *document giving instruction, information*
bible, compendium, directory, enchiridion, encyclopedia, fundamentals, guide, guidebook, instruction book, manual, text, textbook, vade mecum; SEE CONCEPT *280*

handful [*adj*] *a small quantity*
few, scattering, small number, smattering, some, spattering, sprinkling; SEE CONCEPT *789*

handicap [*n1*] *disadvantage*
affliction, baggage*, barrier, block, burden, detriment, disability, disorder, drawback, embarrassment, encumbrance, hangup*, hindrance, impairment, impediment, injury, limitation, load, millstone, obstacle, psychological baggage*, restriction, shortcoming, stumbling block*; SEE CONCEPTS *666,674*

handicap [*n2*] *advantage*
bulge, edge*, favor, head start*, odds, penalty, points*, start, upper hand*, vantage; SEE CONCEPT *693*

handicap [*v*] *give disadvantage*
burden, cripple, encumber, hamper, hamstring*, hinder, hog-tie*, hold back, impede, limit, put out of commission*, restrict, retard, sideline*, take out*; SEE CONCEPTS *130,246*

handicraft [*n*] *artwork, skill*
achievement, art, artifact, artisanship, calling, craft, craftsmanship, creation, design, handiwork, invention, métier, product, production, profession, result, trade, vocation, workmanship; SEE CONCEPTS *259,630*

handle [*n1*] *something to grip*
arm, bail, crank, ear, grasp, grip, haft, handgrip, helve, hilt, hold, holder, knob, shaft, stem, stock, tiller; SEE CONCEPTS *445,502,831*

handle [*n2*] *nickname*
appellation, byname, byword, cognomen, denomination, designation, moniker, name, nomen, sobriquet, style, title; SEE CONCEPT *683*

handle [*v1*] *touch*
check, examine, feel, finger*, fondle, grasp, hold, manipulate, maul, palpate, paw*, pick up, poke, test, thumb*, try; SEE CONCEPT *612*

handle [*v2*] *manage, take care of*
administer, advise, apply, behave toward, bestow, call the signals*, command, conduct, control, cope with, cut the mustard*, deal with, direct, discuss, dispense, dominate, employ, exercise, exploit, get a handle on*, govern, guide, hack it*, make out*, make the grade*, maneuver, manipulate, operate, play, ply, run, run things, serve, steer, supervise, swing, take, treat, use, utilize, wield, work; SEE CONCEPTS *91,117*

handle [*v3*] *carry as merchandise*
deal in, market, offer, retail, sell, stock, trade, traffic in; SEE CONCEPT *345*

handling [*n*] *management*
administration, approach, care, charge, conduct, direction, manipulation, running, styling, superintendence, supervision, treatment; SEE CONCEPT *117*

hand out [*v*] *give to others*
bestow, deal out, deliver, devote, disburse, dish out, dispense, disseminate, distribute, donate, give away, give out, hand over, mete, present, provide; SEE CONCEPTS *108,140*

hand over [*v*] *give back; release*
abandon, cede, commend, commit, consign, deliver, dispense, donate, entrust, feed, find, fork out*, fork up*, give up, hand, leave, present, provide, relegate, relinquish, supply, surrender, transfer, turn over, waive, yield; SEE CONCEPTS *108,131*

handsome [*adj1*] *attractive*
admirable, Adonis-like*, aristocratic, athletic, august, beautiful, becoming, clean-cut, comely, dapper, elegant, fair, fashionable, fine, good-looking, graceful, impressive, lovely, majestic, muscular, noble, personable, pulchritudinous, robust, sharp, smart, smooth, spruce, stately, strong, stylish, suave, virile, well-dressed, well-proportioned; SEE CONCEPT *579*

handsome [*adj2*] *abundant*
ample, bounteous, bountiful, considerable, extensive, full, generous, gracious, large, lavish, liberal, magnanimous, munificent, openhanded, plentiful, princely, sizable, unsparing; SEE CONCEPT *781*

handsomely [*adv*] *abundantly*
amply, bountifully, generously, lavishly, liberally, magnanimously, munificently, nobly, plentifully, richly; SEE CONCEPT *781*

handwriting [*n*] *the way a person writes*
autography, calligraphy, chicken scratch*, chirography, ductus, griffonage, hand, hieroglyphics, longhand, manuscript, manuscription, mark, pencraft, penmanship, penscript, scratching*, scrawl, scribble, script, scription, scrivenery, scrivening, style, writing; SEE CONCEPTS *284,625,628*

handy [*adj1*] *nearby*
accessible, adjacent, at hand, available, close, close-at-hand, close by, convenient, near, near-at-hand, on hand, ready, within reach; SEE CONCEPT *586*

handy [*adj2*] *easy to use*
adaptable, advantageous, available, beneficial, central, convenient, functional, gainful, helpful, man-

ageable, neat, practicable, practical, profitable, ready, serviceable, useful, utile, wieldy; SEE CONCEPT *560*

handy [*adj3*] *adept physically*
able, adroit, clever, deft, dexterous, expert, fit, ingenious, nimble, proficient, ready, skilled, skillful; SEE CONCEPT *527*

hang [*v1*] *suspend or be suspended*
adhere, attach, beetle, be fastened, be in mid-air, be loose, bend, be pendent, be poised, bow, cling, cover, dangle, deck, decorate, depend, drape, drift, droop, drop, fasten, fix, flap, float, furnish, hold, hover, impend, incline, lean, loll, lop, lower, nail, overhang, pin, project, remain, rest, sag, stay up, stick, suspend, swing, tack, trail, wave; SEE CONCEPTS *144,201,746*

hang [*v2*] *kill by suspension from a rope*
execute, gibbet, hoist, lynch, noose, scrag, send to the gallows, stretch*, string up*, swing*; SEE CONCEPT *252*

hang [*v3*] *depend on future action*
await, be conditional upon, be contingent on, be dependent on, be determined by, be in limbo, be in suspense, cling, hinge, pend, rest, turn on; SEE CONCEPT *681*

hang about/hang around/hang out [*v*] *associate with; be residing in*
abide, affect, dally, frequent, get along with, haunt, have relations with, linger, live, loiter, reside, resort, roam, spend time, stand around, swell, tarry, waste time; SEE CONCEPTS *114,226*

hanger-on [*n*] *person who attends the powerful for status or benefit*
dependent, flunky*, follower, freeloader*, lackey*, leech*, nuisance, parasite, sponger*, sycophant, truckler*; SEE CONCEPT *423*

hang on [*v*] *continue, endure*
be tough, carry on, cling, clutch, go on, grasp, grip, hold fast, hold on, hold out, persevere, persist, remain; SEE CONCEPTS *23,239*

hang-out [*n*] *place for socializing*
bar, den*, dive*, haunt*, home, honky-tonk*, joint*, purlieu, resort, stomping ground*, watering hole*; SEE CONCEPTS *439,447,449*

hangover [*n*] *result of heavy drinking*
aftereffect, big head*, delirium tremens, drunkenness, DTs*, headache, morning after*, shakes*, under the weather*, willies*, withdrawal; SEE CONCEPT *316*

hang-up [*n*] *preoccupation*
block, difficulty, dilemma, disturbance, impasse, inhibition, obsession, predicament, problem, reserve, restraint, thing; SEE CONCEPTS *532,674,690*

hanker after/hanker for [*v*] *desire strongly*
ache, covet, crave, hunger, itch, long, lust, partial to, pine, sigh, thirst, want, wish, yearn, yen; SEE CONCEPT *20*

hankering [*n*] *strong desire*
ache, craving, druthers*, fire in belly*, hunger, itch*, longing, munchies*, pining, thirst, urge, want,

weakness, wish, yearning, yen; SEE CONCEPTS *20,709*

hanky-panky [*n*] *mischief*
chicane, chicanery, deception, devilry, double-dealing, fourberie, fraud, funny business*, knavery, machinations, monkey business*, sharp practice*, shenanigans*, skullduggery*, subterfuge, trickery; SEE CONCEPTS *59,384*

haphazard [*adj*] *without plan or organization*
accidental, aimless, all over the map*, any old way*, any which way*, arbitrary, careless, casual, chance, designless, desultory, devil-may-care*, disorderly, disorganized, erratically, fluke, helter-skelter*, hit-or-miss*, incidental, indiscriminate, irregular, loose, offhand, purposeless, random, reckless, slapdash, slipshod, spontaneous, sudden, unconcerned, unconscious, unconsidered, uncoordinated, unexpected, unmethodical, unorganized, unpremeditated, unsystematic, unthinking, willy-nilly*; SEE CONCEPTS *535,581*

hapless [*adj*] *unfortunate*
behind the eightball*, cursed, hexed, ill-fated, ill-starred, infelicitous, jinxed, jonah*, loser, luckless, miserable, poor fish*, sad sack*, snakebit*, star-crossed*, unhappy, unlucky, untoward, voodooed*, woeful, wretched; SEE CONCEPT *548*

happen [*v*] *come to pass; occur*
appear, arise, arrive, become a fact, become known, become of, befall, be found, betide, bump, chance, come about, come after, come into being, come into existence, come off, crop up*, develop, down, ensue, eventuate, fall, follow, go on, hit, issue, light, luck, materialize, meet, pass, present itself, proceed, recur, result, shake, smoke*, spring, stumble, stumble upon, supervene, take effect, take place, transpire, turn out, turn up, what goes*; SEE CONCEPT *4*

happening [*n*] *occurrence*
accident, adventure, affair, case, chance, circumstance, episode, event, experience, go*, incident, milestone, occasion, phenomenon, proceeding, scene, thing*; SEE CONCEPT *4*

happily [*adv1*] *with joy, pleasure*
agreeably, blissfully, blithely, brightly, buoyantly, cheerfully, contentedly, delightedly, delightfully, devotedly, elatedly, enthusiastically, exhilaratingly, exultantly, freely, gaily, gladly, gleefully, graciously, heartily, hilariously, jovially, joyfully, joyously, laughingly, lightheartedly, lightly, lovingly, merrily, optimistically, peacefully, playfully, sincerely, smilingly, sportively, vivaciously, willingly, with relish, with zeal, zestfully; SEE CONCEPTS *403,542*

happily [*adv2*] *successfully*
appropriately, aptly, auspiciously, favorably, felicitously, fortunately, gracefully, propitiously, prosperously, providentially, satisfyingly, seasonably, swimmingly, well; SEE CONCEPT *548*

happiness [*n*] *high spirits, satisfaction*
beatitude, blessedness, bliss, cheer, cheerfulness, cheeriness, content, contentment, delectation, de-

light, delirium, ecstasy, elation, enchantment, enjoyment, euphoria, exhilaration, exuberance, felicity, gaiety, geniality, gladness, glee, good cheer, good humor, good spirits, hilarity, hopefulness, joviality, joy, jubilation, laughter, lightheartedness*, merriment, mirth, optimism, paradise, peace of mind, playfulness, pleasure, prosperity, rejoicing, sanctity, seventh heaven*, vivacity, well-being; SEE CONCEPT *410*

happy [*adj1*] *in high spirits; satisfied*
blessed, blest, blissful, blithe, can't complain*, captivated, cheerful, chipper, chirpy, content, contented, convivial, delighted, ecstatic, elated, exultant, flying high*, gay, glad, gleeful, gratified, intoxicated, jolly, joyful, joyous, jubilant, laughing, light, lively, looking good*, merry, mirthful, on cloud nine*, overjoyed, peaceful, peppy, perky, playful, pleasant, pleased, sparkling, sunny, thrilled, tickled, tickled pink*, up, upbeat, walking on air*; SEE CONCEPT *403*

happy [*adj2*] *lucky*
accidental, advantageous, appropriate, apt, auspicious, befitting, casual, convenient, correct, effective, efficacious, enviable, favorable, felicitous, fitting, fortunate, incidental, just, lucky, meet, nice, opportune, promising, proper, propitious, providential, right, satisfactory, seasonable, successful, suitable, timely, well-timed; SEE CONCEPT *558*

happy-go-lucky [*adj*] *carefree and untroubled*
blithe, casual, cheerful, cool, devil-may-care*, easy, easygoing, feckless, free-minded, heedless, improvident, insouciant, irresponsible, lackadaisical*, lighthearted, nonchalant, reckless, unconcerned; SEE CONCEPTS *404,542*

harangue [*n*] *long lecture*
address, chewing out*, declamation, diatribe, discourse, exhortation, hassle, jeremiad, oration, philippic, reading out*, screed, sermon, speech, spiel*, spouting, tirade; SEE CONCEPTS *51,278*

harangue [*v*] *give a long lecture*
accost, address, apostrophize, buttonhole*, chew out*, declaim, exhort, get on a soapbox*, go on about*, hold forth, lecture, orate, perorate, rant, rave, soapbox*, spiel*, spout, stump, talk to, yell at; SEE CONCEPT *51*

harass [*v*] *badger*
annoy, attack, bait, bedevil, beleaguer, bother, bug*, burn*, despoil, devil*, distress, disturb, eat*, exasperate, exhaust, fatigue, foray, get to*, give a bad time*, give a hard time*, gnaw*, harry, hassle, heckle, hound*, intimidate, irk, irritate, jerk around*, macerate, maraud, noodge*, pain*, perplex, persecute, pester, plague, raid, rattle one's cage*, ride, strain, stress, tease, tire, torment, trouble, try, vex, weary, work on*, worry; SEE CONCEPTS *7,14,19*

harassment [*n*] *badgering*
aggravation, annoyance, bedevilment, bother, bothering, disturbance, exasperation, hassle, irking, irri-

tation, molestation, nuisance, persecution, perturbation, pestering, provocation, provoking, torment, trouble, vexation, vexing; SEE CONCEPTS *14,313*

harbinger [*n*] *indication*
augury, forerunner, foretoken, herald, messenger, omen, portent, precursor, sign, signal; SEE CONCEPTS *74,284,529*

harbor [*n1*] *place for storing boats in the water*
anchorage, arm, bay, bight, breakwater, chuck, cove, dock, embankment, firth, gulf, haven, inlet, jetty, landing, mooring, pier, port, road, roadstead, wharf; SEE CONCEPTS *439,509,514*

harbor [*n2*] *place for seclusion*
asylum, cover, covert, harborage, haven, port, refuge, retreat, sanctuary, sanctum, security, shelter; SEE CONCEPT *515*

harbor [*v1*] *hide, protect*
accommodate, board, bunk, conceal, defend, domicile, entertain, guard, hold back, house, lodge, nurse, nurture, provide refuge, put up, quarter, relieve, safeguard, screen, secrete, secure, shelter, shield, suppress, withhold; SEE CONCEPTS *134,188*

harbor [*v2*] *hold in imagination*
believe, brood over, cherish, cling to, consider, entertain, foster, hold, imagine, maintain, nurse, nurture, regard, retain; SEE CONCEPT *17*

hard [*adj1*] *rocklike*
adamantine, callous, compact, compacted, compressed, concentrated, consolidated, dense, firm, hardened, impenetrable, indurate, indurated, inflexible, iron*, packed, rigid, rocky, set, solid, stiff, stony, strong, thick, tough, unyielding; SEE CONCEPT *604*

hard [*adj2*] *difficult, exhausting*
arduous, backbreaking, bothersome, burdensome, complicated, demanding, difficile, distressing, effortful, exacting, fatiguing, formidable, grinding, hairy*, heavy*, Herculean*, intricate, involved, irksome, knotty*, labored, laborious, mean, merciless, murder, onerous, operose, rigorous, rough, rugged, scabrous, serious, severe, slavish, sticky, strenuous, terrible, tiring, toilful, toilsome, tough, troublesome, unsparing, uphill*, uphill battle*, wearing, wearisome, wearying; SEE CONCEPTS *529,538,565*

hard [*adj3*] *cruel, ruthless*
acrimonious, angry, antagonistic, austere, bitter, bleak, brutal, callous, cold, cold-blooded*, cold fish*, dark, disagreeable, distressing, dour, exacting, grievous, grim, hard as nails*, hard-boiled*, harsh, hostile, inclement, intemperate, intolerable, obdurate, painful, perverse, pitiless, rancorous, resentful, rigorous, rugged, severe, stern, strict, stringent, stubborn, thick-skinned*, tough, unfeeling, unjust, unkind, unpleasant, unrelenting, unsparing, unsympathetic, vengeful; SEE CONCEPTS *401,542*

hard [*adj4*] *true, indisputable*
absolute, actual, bare, cold, definite, down-to-earth, genuine, plain, positive, practical, pragmatic, realis-

tic, sure, undeniable, unvarnished, verified; SEE CONCEPTS *535,582*

hard [*adv1*] *with great force*
actively, angrily, animatedly, boisterously, briskly, brutally, cruelly, earnestly, energetically, ferociously, fiercely, forcefully, forcibly, frantically, furiously, heavily, intensely, keenly, like fury, madly, meanly, painfully, powerfully, relentlessly, rigorously, roughly, rowdily, savagely, seriously, severely, sharply, spiritedly, sprightly, stormily, strongly, tumultously/tumultuously, turbulently, uproariously, urgently, viciously, vigorously, violently, vivaciously, wildly, with all one's might; SEE CONCEPT *540*

hard [*adv2*] *with determination*
assiduously, closely, determinedly, diligently, doggedly, earnestly, exhaustively, industriously, intensely, intensively, intently, painstakingly, persistently, searchingly, sharply, steadily, strenuously, thoroughly, unremittingly, untiringly; SEE CONCEPT *538*

hard [*adv3*] *with difficulty*
agonizingly, arduously, awkwardly, badly, burdensomely, carefully, cumbersomely, cumbrously, difficultly, distressingly, exhaustingly, gruelingly, hardly, harshly, inconveniently, laboriously, painfully, ponderously, roughly, severely, strenuously, tiredly, toilsomely, unwieldily, vigorously, with great effort; SEE CONCEPT *565*

hard [*adv4*] *with resentment*
bitterly, hardly, keenly, rancorously, reluctantly, resentfully, slowly, sorely; SEE CONCEPT *403*

hard [*adv5*] *in a fixed manner*
close, fast, firm, firmly, fixedly, solidly, steadfastly, tight, tightly; SEE CONCEPTS *488,586*

hard-core [*adj*] *dedicated*
determined, devoted, die-hard*, dyed-in-the-wool*, explicit, extreme, faithful, intransigent, obstinate, resolute, rigid, staunch, steadfast, stubborn, uncompromising, unwavering, unyielding; SEE CONCEPTS *535,542*

harden [*v1*] *make or become solid*
amalgamate, anneal, bake, brace, buttress, cake, calcify, callous, cement, close, clot, coagulate, compact, congeal, consolidate, contract, crystallize, curdle, densify, dry, firm, fix, fortify, fossilize, freeze, gird, indurate, jell, nerve, ossify, petrify, precipitate, press, reinforce, set, settle, solidify, starch, steel, stiffen, strengthen, temper, thicken, toughen, vitrify; SEE CONCEPTS *250,469*

harden [*v2*] *accustom*
acclimate, acclimatize, adapt, adjust, blunt, brutalize, callous, callus, case-harden, climatize, coarsen, conform, deaden, develop, discipline, dull, embitter, habituate, indurate, inure, make callous, numb, paralyze, render insensitive, roughen, season, steel, stiffen, strengthen, stun, stupefy, teach, train; SEE CONCEPTS *35,235*

hardened [*adj*] *unfeeling*
accustomed, benumbed, callous, case-hardened, coldhearted*, contemptuous, cruel, disdainful, habituated, hard-as-nails*, hard-bitten*, hard-boiled*, hardhearted*, heartless, impenetrable, impious, inaccessible, indurated, inured, irreverent, obdurate, obtuse, prepared, resistant, seasoned, steeled, toughened, unashamed, unbending, uncaring, uncompassionate, unemotional, unrepenting, unsubmissive; SEE CONCEPTS *404,542*

hardhearted [*adj*] *cold, cruel*
brutish, callous, cold-blooded*, coldhearted*, hard, hard-boiled*, heartless, indifferent, inhuman, insensitive, intolerant, merciless, obdurate, pitiless, stony, uncaring, uncompassionate, unemotional, unfeeling, unkind, unsympathetic; SEE CONCEPTS *401,404*

hardly [*adv*] *scarcely; with difficulty*
almost inconceivably, almost not, barely, by a hair, by no means, comparatively, detectably, faintly, gradually, imperceptibly, infrequently, just, little, no more than, not a bit, not at all, not by much, not likely, not markedly, not measurably, not much, not notably, not noticeably, not often, not quite, no way, once in a blue moon*, only, only just, perceptibly, practically, pretty near, rarely, scantly, seldom, simply, slightly, somewhat, sparsely, sporadically, with trouble; SEE CONCEPTS *541,552,771*

hard-nosed/hardheaded [*adj*] *stubborn*
astute, bullheaded*, hard*, hard-boiled*, headstrong, intractable, levelheaded, locked-in*, mulish, obstinate, pertinacious, perverse, pigheaded*, practical, pragmatic, rational, realistic, resolute, sensible, shrewd, sober, stand pat, tough, tough-nut*, unsentimental, unyielding, willful; SEE CONCEPTS *404,542*

hardship [*n*] *personal burden*
accident, adversity, affliction, asperity, austerity, calamity, case, catastrophe, curse, danger, destitution, difficulty, disaster, discomfort, distress, drudgery, fatigue, grief, grievance, hard knocks*, hazard, Herculean task*, injury, labor, mischance, misery, misfortune, need, oppression, peril, persecution, privation, rainy day*, rigor, rotten luck*, sorrow, suffering, toil, torment, tough break*, tough luck*, travail, trial, tribulation, trouble, uphill battle*, vicissitude, want, worry; SEE CONCEPTS *674,675*

hardware [*n*] *tools; fittings, especially made of metal*
accouterments, appliances, fasteners, fixtures, household furnishings, housewares, implements, ironware, kitchenware, metalware, plumbing, utensils; SEE CONCEPTS *338,499*

hardy [*adj*] *strong, tough*
able, able-bodied, acclimatized, brawny, burly, capable, enduring, firm, fit, fresh, hale, hardened, healthy, hearty, hefty, Herculean*, indefatigable, in fine fettle*, in good condition, in good shape, inured, lusty, mighty, muscular, physically fit, powerful, resistant, robust, rugged, seasoned, solid, sound, stal-

wart, staunch, stout, sturdy, substantial, tenacious, toughened, unflagging, vigorous, well; SEE CONCEPTS *314,485,489*

harebrained [*adj*] *stupid, unthinking*
absurd, asinine, barmy, bizarre, careless, changeable, crazy, dizzy*, empty-headed*, featherbrained*, flighty, foolish, frivolous, giddy, half-baked*, heedless, inane, irresponsible, loony*, mindless, preposterous, rash, rattlebrained, reckless, scatterbrained*, unstable, unsteady, wacky*, wild; SEE CONCEPTS *402,529*

harm [*n*] *injury, evil*
abuse, banefulness, damage, deleteriousness, detriment, disservice, foul play*, hurt, ill, immorality, impairment, infliction, iniquity, loss, marring, mischance, mischief, misfortune, misuse, noxiousness, outrage, perniciousness, prejudice, ravage, ruin, ruination, sabotage, sin, sinfulness, vandalism, vice, violence, wear and tear*, wickedness, wrong; SEE CONCEPTS *309,674,728*

harm [*v*] *injure; cause evil*
abuse, blemish, bruise, cripple, crush, damage, dilapidate, discommode, disserve, do violence to, dump on*, get, hurt, ill-treat, impair, incommode, inconvenience, louse up*, maim, maltreat, mangle, mar, mess up*, misuse, molest, muck up*, mutilate, nick, outrage, prejudice, put down, ruin, sabotage, sap*, scathe, shatter, shock, spoil, stab, tarnish, total, trample, traumatize, tweak*, undermine, vandalize, vitiate, wing*, wound, wreck, wrench, wrong, zing*; SEE CONCEPTS *7,19,246,313*

harmful [*adj*] *injurious, hurtful*
adverse, bad, baleful, baneful, calamitous, cataclysmic, catastrophic, consumptive, corroding, corrupting, crippling, damaging, deleterious, destructive, detrimental, dire, disadvantageous, disastrous, evil, harassing, incendiary, inimical, internecine, malefic, malicious, malignant, menacing, mischievous, murderous, nocuous, noxious, painful, pernicious, pestiferous, pestilential, risky, ruinous, sinful, sinister, subversive, toxic, undermining, unhealthy, unsafe, unwholesome, virulent; SEE CONCEPT *537*

harmless [*adj*] *not injurious or dangerous*
controllable, disarmed, gentle, guiltless, hurtless, innocent, innocuous, innoxious, inoffensive, inoperative, kind, manageable, naive, nonirritating, nontoxic, painless, paper-tiger*, powerless, pussycat*, reliable, safe, sanitary, simple, soft*, softie*, sound, sure, trustworthy, unobjectionable, unoffensive; SEE CONCEPT *537*

harmonious [*adj*] *agreeable, corresponding; friendly*
accordant, adapted, amicable, balanced, compatible, concordant, congenial, congruous, consonant, coordinated, cordial, correspondent, dulcet, euphonious, fraternal, harmonic, harmonizing, in accord, in chorus, in concert, in harmony, in step, in tune, in unison, like, matching, mellifluous, melodic, melodious, mix, musical, of one mind*, on same wave-

length*, peaceful, rhythmical, silvery, similar, simpatico, sonorous, suitable, sweet-sounding, symmetrical, sympathetic, symphonic, symphonious, tuneful; SEE CONCEPT *563*

harmonize [*v*] *correspond, match*
accord, adapt, adjust, agree, arrange, attune, be in unison, be of one mind*, blend, carol, chime with, cohere, combine, compose, cooperate, coordinate, correlate, correspond, fit in with*, integrate, orchestrate, proportion, reconcile, reconciliate, relate, set, sing, suit, symphonize, synthesize, tune, unify, unite; SEE CONCEPTS *77,664*

harmony [*n1*] *social agreement*
accord, affinity, amicability, amity, compatibility, concord, conformity, consensus, consistency, cooperation, correspondence, empathy, fellow-feeling, friendship, good will, kinship, like-mindedness, meeting of minds*, peace, rapport, sympathy, tranquility, unanimity, understanding, unity; SEE CONCEPT *388*

harmony [*n2*] *correspondence, balance*
accord, agreement, articulation, chime, concord, concordance, conformance, conformity, congruity, consistency, consonance, fitness, form, integration, integrity, oneness, order, parallelism, proportion, regularity, suitability, symmetry, togetherness, tune, unity; SEE CONCEPT *664*

harmony [*n3*] *musical accordance*
accord, arrangement, attunement, blend, blending, chime, chord, chorus, composition, concentus, concert, concinnity, concurrence, consonance, diapason, euphony, harmonics, mellifluousness, melodiousness, melody, music, organum, overtone, piece, polyphony, richness, symphony, triad, tune, tunefulness, unison, unity; SEE CONCEPTS *65,262,595*

harness [*n*] *gear for controlling animal*
belt, equipment, strap, tack, tackle, trappings; SEE CONCEPT *496*

harness [*v*] *rein in; control*
accouter, apply, bind, bridle, channel, check, cinch, collar, constrain, couple, curb, domesticate, employ, equip, exploit, fasten, fetter, fit, furnish, gear, govern, hitch, hold, leash, limit, make productive, mobilize, muzzle, outfit, put in harness, render useful, rig, saddle, secure, strap, tackle, tame, tie, utilize, yoke; SEE CONCEPTS *94,130,191*

harrowing [*adj*] *dangerous, frightening*
agonizing, alarming, chilling, distressing, disturbing, excruciating, heartbreaking, heart-rending, nerve-racking, painful, racking, soaring, tearing, terrifying, tormenting, torturing, torturous, traumatic; SEE CONCEPTS *529,548*

harry [*v*] *pester, annoy*
attack, badger, bedevil, beleaguer, chivy, depredate, devastate, disturb, fret, gnaw, harass, hassle, irk, irritate, lay waste, molest, persecute, perturb, pester, pillage, plague, plunder, ravage, sack, tease, torment, trouble, upset, vex, worry; SEE CONCEPTS *7,19*

harsh [*adj1*] *rough, crude (to the senses)*
acrid, asperous, astringent, bitter, bleak, cacophonous, caterwauling, clashing, coarse, cracked, craggy, creaking, croaking, disagreeing, discordant, dissonant, disturbing, earsplitting, flat, glaring, grating, grim, guttural, hard, hoarse, incompatible, jagged, jangling, jarring, noisy, not smooth, off-key*, out-of-key*, out-of-tune*, rasping, raucous, rigid, rugged, rusty, screeching, severe, sharp, sour, strident, stridulous, tuneless, uneven, unlevel, unmelodious, unmusical, unrelenting; SEE CONCEPTS *537,569*

harsh [*adj2*] *nasty, abusive*
austere, bitter, brutal, comfortless, cruel, cussed, discourteous, dour, grim, gruff, hairy*, hard, hard-boiled, hard-nosed*, hard-shell*, mean, pitiless, punitive, relentless, rude, ruthless, severe, sharp, stern, stringent, tough, uncivil, unfeeling, ungracious, unkind, unpleasant, unrelenting, wicked; SEE CONCEPTS *267,542*

harvest [*n*] *crops; taking in of crops*
autumn, by-product, consequence, cropping, effect, fall, fruitage, fruition, garnering, gathering, harvesting, harvest-time, ingathering, intake, output, produce, reaping, repercussion, result, return, season, storing, summer, yield, yielding; SEE CONCEPTS *257,338,429*

harvest [*v*] *gathering of produce*
accumulate, acquire, amass, bin, cache, collect, crop, cull, cut, garner, gather, get, glean, harrow, hoard, mow, pick, pile up, plow, pluck, reap, squirrel*, stash, store, stow, strip, take in; SEE CONCEPTS *142,257*

hash [*n*] *mess, mix-up*
assortment, clutter, confusion, hodgepodge*, hotchpotch*, jumble, litter, medley, melange, miscellany, mishmash*, muddle*, salmagundi*, shambles*, stew*; SEE CONCEPTS *260,432*

hassle [*n*] *problem, fight*
altercation, argument, bickering, bother, clamor, commotion, difficulty, disagreement, dispute, inconvenience, quarrel, row, run-in*, squabble, struggle, trial, trouble, try, tumult, turmoil, tussle, uproar, upset, whirl, wrangle; SEE CONCEPTS *46,106,674*

hassle [*v*] *bother, harass*
annoy, argue, argufy, badger, bedevil, beleaguer, bicker, dispute, dun, harry, hound, pester, plague, quibble, squabble, worry, wrangle; SEE CONCEPTS *14,16,46*

haste [*n*] *extreme speed, hurry*
alacrity, briskness, bustle, carelessness, celerity, dash, dispatch, drive, expedition, expeditiousness, fleetness, flurry, foolhardiness, hastiness, heedlessness, hurly-burly*, hurriedness, hustle, hustling, impatience, impetuosity, incautiousness, nimbleness, pace, precipitancy, precipitateness, prematureness, press, promptitude, promptness, quickness, rapidity, rapidness, rashness, recklessness, rush, scamper, scramble, scurry, scuttle, swiftness, urgency, velocity; SEE CONCEPTS *755,818*

hasten [*v*] *speed something; hurry*
accelerate, advance, bolt, bound, burn, bustle, clip*, cover ground*, dash, dispatch, expedite, express, flee, fly, gallop, get cracking*, get the lead out*, goad, haste, hie, hurry up, hustle, leap, make haste, make tracks*, move quickly, not lose a minute*, pace, plunge, precipitate, press, push, quicken, race, run, rush, scamper, scoot, scurry, scuttle, shake a leg*, skip, speed, sprint, spurt, step on it*, step up*, take wing*, tear, trot, urge, waste no time*, whip around; SEE CONCEPTS *150,152*

hastily [*adv*] *with great speed*
agilely, apace, carelessly, double-quick, expeditiously, fast, flat-out*, heedlessly, hurriedly, impetuously, impulsively, lickety-split*, nimbly, on spur of the moment*, posthaste, precipitately, prematurely, promptly, quickly, rapidly, rashly, recklessly, speedily, straightaway, subito, suddenly, swiftly, thoughtlessly, too quickly, unpremeditatedly; SEE CONCEPTS *544,588*

hasty [*adj*] *speedy; without much thought*
abrupt, agile, brash, breakneck*, brief, brisk, careless, chop-chop*, cursory, eager, expeditious, fast, fiery, fleet, fleeting, foolhardy, harefooted*, headlong, heedless, hurried, ill-advised, impatient, impetuous, impulsive, incautious, inconsiderate, madcap*, on the double*, passing, PDQ*, perfunctory, precipitate, prompt, pronto*, quick, quickened, quickie, rapid, rash, reckless, rushed, short, slam-bang*, slapdash*, snappy*, sudden, superficial, swift, thoughtless, urgent; SEE CONCEPTS *542, 588,799*

hat [*n*] *covering for the head*
boater, bonnet, bowler, bucket, chapeau, fedora, headgear, headpiece, helmet, lid*, millinery, Panama, sailor*, skimmer, sombrero, Stetson, stove pipe*, straw*, tam, tam o'shanter*, ten-gallon*, topper*; SEE CONCEPT *451*

hatch [*v*] *create, plan*
bear, brainstorm*, breed, bring forth, brood, cause, come up with, conceive, concoct, contrive, cook up*, design, devise, dream up*, engender, father, formulate, generate, get up, give birth, incubate, induce, invent, lay eggs, make, make up, occasion, originate, parent, plot, prepare, procreate, produce, project, provoke, scheme, set, sire, spawn, spitball*, think up*, throw together*, trump up*, whip up*, work up*; SEE CONCEPTS *36,173,251*

hate [*n*] *extreme dislike*
abhorrence, abomination, anathema, animosity, animus, antagonism, antipathy, aversion, bête noire*, black beast*, bother, bugbear*, detestation, disgust, dislike, enmity, execration, frost*, grievance, gripe, hatred, horror, hostility, ill will, irritant, loathing, malevolence, malignity, mislike, nasty look, no love lost*, nuisance, objection, odium, pain, rancor, rank-

ling, repugnance, repulsion, resentment, revenge, revulsion, scorn, spite, trouble, venom; SEE CONCEPT *29*

hate [*v*] *dislike very strongly*
abhor, abominate, allergic to*, anathematize, bear a grudge against, be disgusted with, be hostile to, be loath, be reluctant, be repelled by, be sick of, be sorry, can't stand*, contemn, curse, deprecate, deride, despise, detest, disapprove, disdain, disfavor, dislike, disparage, down on*, execrate, feel malice to, have an aversion to*, have enough of*, have no use for*, loathe, look down on, nauseate*, not care for*, object to, recoil from, scorn, shudder at, shun, spit upon*, spurn; SEE CONCEPT *29*

hateful [*adj*] *nasty, obnoxious*
abhorrent, abominable, accursed, awful, bitter, blasted, catty*, confounded, cursed, cussed, damnable, damned, despicable, despiteful, detestable, disgusting, evil, execrable, forbidding, foul, gross, heinous, horrid, infamous, invidious, loathsome, malevolent, malign, mean, odious, offensive, ornery*, pesky, pestiferous, repellent, repugnant, repulsive, resentful, revolting, shuddersome, spiteful, uncool*, undesirable, vicious, vile; SEE CONCEPTS *267,404*

hatred [*n*] *severe dislike*
abhorrence, abomination, acrimony, alienation, allergy to*, animosity, animus, antagonism, antipathy, aversion, bitterness, coldness, contempt, detestation, disapproval, disfavor, disgust, displeasure, distaste, enmity, envy, execration, grudge, hard feelings*, hate, horror, hostility, ignominy, ill will, invidiousness, loathing, malevolence, malice, malignance, militancy, no use for*, odium, pique, prejudice, rancor, repugnance, repulsion, revenge, revulsion, scorn, spite, spleen, venom; SEE CONCEPT *29*

haughtiness [*n*] *air of supremacy*
airs, aloofness, arrogance, conceit, contempt, contemptuousness, disdain, disdainfulness, hauteur, insolence, loftiness, pomposity, pride, snobbishness, superbity, superciliousness; SEE CONCEPT *633*

haughty [*adj*] *arrogant*
assuming, cavalier*, conceited, contemptuous, detached, disdainful, distant, egotistic, egotistical, high, high and mighty*, hoity-toity*, imperious, indifferent, lofty, lordly, on high horse*, overbearing, overweening, proud, reserved, scornful, sniffy*, snobbish, snooty*, snotty*, stuck-up*, supercilious, superior, uppity*; SEE CONCEPT *401*

haul [*n*] *something obtained or moved*
booty, burden, cargo, catch, find, freight, gain, harvest, lading, load, loot*, payload*, spoils, takings*, yield; SEE CONCEPTS *337,338*

haul [*v*] *move, pull to another spot*
back, boost, bring, buck, carry, cart, convey, drag, draw, elevate, gun, heave, heel, hoist, hump, jag, lift, lug, pack, piggy back*, raise, rake, remove, ride, shift, schlepp*, shoulder, tote, tow, trail, transport, trawl, truck, tug; SEE CONCEPTS *147,148*

haunt [*n*] *place for socializing*
abode, bar, clubhouse, cubbyhole*, den, dwelling, gathering place, habitat, hangout*, headquarters, home, lair, living quarters, locality, meeting place, niche, place, purlieu, range, rendezvous, resort, retreat, site, stomping ground*, trysting place, watering hole*; SEE CONCEPTS *435,516*

haunt [*v1*] *visit as a spirit*
agitate, agonize, annoy, appall, appear, bedevil, be ever present, beset, besiege, come back, disquiet, dwell, float, frighten, harass, harrow, hound*, hover, infest, inhabit, intrude, madden, manifest, materialize, molest, nettle, obsess, overrun, permeate, pervade, pester, plague, possess, prey on, rack*, reappear, recur, return, rise, spook*, stay with, tease, terrify, terrorize, torment, trouble, vex, voodoo*, walk, weigh on, worry; SEE CONCEPT *14*

haunt [*v2*] *spend a lot of time at*
affect, frequent, habituate, hang about*, hang around*, hang out*, infest, repair, resort, tarry at, visit; SEE CONCEPT *384*

have [*v1*] *be in possession*
accept, acquire, admit, annex, bear, carry, chalk up, compass, corner, enjoy, gain, get, get hands on*, get hold of*, have in hand, hog*, hold, include, keep, land, latch on to*, lock up*, obtain, occupy, own, pick up, possess, procure, receive, retain, secure, sit on*, take, take in, teem with; SEE CONCEPTS *124,142,710*

have [*v2*] *endure, bear*
allow, become, be compelled to, be forced to, be one's duty to, be up to, consider, enjoy, entertain*, experience, fall on, feel, know, leave, let, meet with, must, need, ought, permit, put up with*, rest with, see, should, suffer, sustain, think about, tolerate, undergo; SEE CONCEPTS *23,83,646*

have [*v3*] *contain*
comprehend, comprise, embody, embrace, encompass, include, involve, subsume, take in; SEE CONCEPTS *642,742*

have [*v4*] *cheat, trick*
buy off*, deceive, dupe*, fix*, fool, outfox, outmaneuver, outsmart, outwit, overreach, swindle, take in*, tamper with, undo*; SEE CONCEPTS *59,192*

have [*v5*] *bring into the world*
bear, beget, bring forth, deliver, give birth; SEE CONCEPT *374*

haven [*n*] *refuge, port*
anchorage, asylum, cover, covert, harbor, harborage, retreat, roadstead, sanctuary, sanctum, shelter; SEE CONCEPTS *435,515*

havoc [*n*] *chaotic situation*
calamity, cataclysm, catastrophe, chaos, confusion, damage, desolation, despoiling, destruction, devastation, dilapidation, disorder, disruption, loss, mayhem, plunder, rack and ruin*, ravages, ruination, shambles*, vandalism, waste, wreck, wreckage; SEE CONCEPT *674*

hazard [n1] *danger*
double trouble*, dynamite, endangerment, hot potato*, imperilment, jeopardy, peril, risk, risky business*, thin ice*, threat; SEE CONCEPT *675*

hazard [n2] *luck, chance*
accident, adventure, coincidence, dynamite, fling*, fluke*, go*, hundred-to-one*, long shot, luck, lucky break*, lucky hit*, misfortune, mishap, possibility, risk, risky business*, stroke of luck*, toss-up, venture, wager, way cookie crumbles*, way the ball bounces*; SEE CONCEPT *693*

hazard [v] *take a chance; risk*
adventure, chance, conjecture, dare, endanger, gamble, go for broke*, go out on limb*, guess, imperil, jeopardize, presume, proffer, skate on thin ice*, speculate, stake, submit, suppose, take a plunge*, throw out, try, venture, volunteer, wager; SEE CONCEPTS *28,87*

hazardous [adj] *dangerous, unpredictable*
chancy, dicey*, difficult, hairy*, haphazard, hot*, insecure, parlous, perilous, precarious, risky, touchy, uncertain, unhealthy, unsafe, unsound, venturesome, wicked; SEE CONCEPT *548*

haze [n] *cloudy air*
brume, cloud, dimness, film, fog, fumes, ground clouds, haziness, indistinctness, miasma, mist, murk, obscurity, smog, smokiness, smother, soup*, steam, vapor; SEE CONCEPT *524*

hazy [adj1] *cloudy*
bleared, bleary, blurred, blurry, clouded, crepuscular, dim, dull, dusky, faint, foggy, frosty, fuliginous, fumy, fuzzy, gauzy, indefinite, indistinct, misty, murky, mushy*, nebulous, obfuscated, obfuscous, obscure, opaque, overcast, rimy, screened, shadowy, smoggy, smoky, soupy*, steaming, thick, unclear, vague, vaporous, veiled; SEE CONCEPT *525*

hazy [adj2] *confused*
dazed, dizzy, dreamy, groggy, ill-defined, indefinite, indistinct, muddled, murky, nebulous, obscure, stuporous, tranced, uncertain, unclear, unintelligible, unsound, vague, whirling; SEE CONCEPTS *402,529*

head [n1] *top part of animate body*
attic*, belfry*, brain, coconut*, cranium, crown, dome*, gray matter, noggin*, noodle*, pate, scalp, skull, thinker*, think tank*, top story*, upper story*, upstairs*; SEE CONCEPT *392*

head [n2] *leader*
boss, captain, chief, chieftain, commander, commanding officer, director, dominator, executive, headmaster, headmistress, honcho*, kingfish*, lead-off man/woman*, manager, master, officer, president, principal, superintendent, supervisor, top dog*; SEE CONCEPT *347*

head [n3] *top part*
apex, banner, beak, bill, cap, cork, crest, crown, heading, headline, height, peak, pitch, point, promontory, streamer, summit, tip, top, vertex; SEE CONCEPT *836*

head [n4] *front, beginning*
commencement, first place, fore, forefront, fountainhead, origin, rise, source, start, van, vanguard; SEE CONCEPTS *648,727*

head [n5] *ability, intelligence*
aptitude, aptness, bent, brains, capacity, faculty, flair, genius, gift, intellect, knack, mentality, mind, talent, thought, turn, understanding; SEE CONCEPTS *409,630*

head [n6] *turning point*
acme, climax, conclusion, crisis, culmination, end; SEE CONCEPT *832*

head [adj] *most important; chief*
arch, champion, first, foremost, front, highest, leading, main, pioneer, preeminent, premier, prime, principal, stellar, supreme, topmost; SEE CONCEPTS *568,574*

head [v] *manage, oversee*
address, be first, be in charge, command, control, direct, dominate, go first, govern, guide, hold sway over*, lead, lead the way*, pioneer, precede, rule, run, supervise; SEE CONCEPT *117*

headlong [adj] *dangerous, reckless*
abrupt, brash, breakneck, daredevil, daring, foolhardy, hasty, hurried, impetuous, impulsive, inconsiderate, precipitant, precipitate, rash, rough, rushing, sudden, tempestuous, thoughtless; SEE CONCEPTS *542,588*

headstrong [adj] *stubborn*
bullheaded*, contrary, determined, foolhardy, froward, hard-core*, hard-nosed, hard-shell*, heedless, imprudent, impulsive, intractable, locked-in*, mule, mulish, murder, obstinate, perverse, pig-headed*, rash, reckless, refractory, self-willed, strong-minded, uncontrollable, ungovernable, unruly, unyielding, willful; SEE CONCEPTS *401,403*

headway [n] *progress*
advance, advancement, anabasis, ground, improvement, increase, march, proficiency, progression, promotion, way; SEE CONCEPTS *230,704*

heady [adj] *thrilling, intoxicating*
exciting, exhilarating, inebriating, overwhelming, potent, powerful, provocative, spirituous, stimulating, strong; SEE CONCEPT *529*

heal [v] *cure, recover*
alleviate, ameliorate, attend, bring around, compose, conciliate, convalesce, doctor, dress, fix, free, get well, harmonize, improve, knit, make healthy, make sound, make well, make whole, medicate, meliorate, mend, minister to, patch up, physic, put on feet again*, reanimate, rebuild, reconcile, regenerate, rehabilitate, rejuvenate, remedy, renew, renovate, repair, restore, resuscitate, revive, revivify, salve, set, settle, soothe, treat; SEE CONCEPTS *308,310*

health [n] *physical, mental wellness*
bloom*, clean bill*, complexion, constitution, energy, eupepsia, euphoria, fettle, fine feather*, fitness, form, good condition, haleness, hardihood, hardi-

ness, healthfulness, healthiness, lustiness, pink*, prime*, robustness, salubriousness, salubrity, shape, soundness, stamina, state, strength, tone, tonicity, top form, verdure, vigor, well-being, wholeness; SEE CONCEPTS *316,410,720*

healthful/healthy [*adj1*] *good for one's wellness*
advantageous, aiding, aseptic, beneficial, benign, body-building, bracing, cathartic, clean, compensatory, conducive, corrective, desirable, disease-free, energy-giving, fresh, harmless, healing, health-giving, healthy, helpful, hygienic, innocuous, invigorating, mitigative, nourishing, nutritious, nutritive, profitable, pure, restorative, salubrious, salutary, sanatory, sanitary, stimulating, sustaining, tonic, unadulterated, untainted, useful, wholesome; SEE CONCEPT *537*

healthy [*adj2*] *in good condition*
able-bodied, active, all right, athletic, blooming, bright-eyed*, bushy-tailed*, chipper*, firm, fit, flourishing, fresh, full of life*, hale, hardy, healthful, hearty, husky, in fine feather*, in fine fettle*, in good shape, in the pink*, lively, lusty, muscular, normal, physically fit, potent, restored, robust, rosy-cheeked*, safe and sound*, sound, stout, strong, sturdy, tough, trim, unimpaired, vigorous, virile, well, whole; SEE CONCEPTS *314,403*

heap [*n*] *pile, accumulation*
abundance, agglomeration, aggregation, a lot*, amassment, assemblage, bank, batch, bulk, bunch, bundle, cargo, clump, cluster, collection, concentration, congeries, deposit, fullness, gathering, gobs*, great deal, harvest, haul, hill, hoard, jumble, load, lot, lots, lump, mass, million, mint, mound, mountain, much, ocean, oodles*, plenty, pot, profusion, quantity, scad*, stack, stock, stockpile, store, sum, thousand, ton, total, trillion, volume, whole; SEE CONCEPTS *432,786*

heap [*v*] *amass, collect in pile*
accumulate, add, arrange, augment, bank, bunch, concentrate, deposit, dump, fill, fill up, gather, group, hoard, increase, load, lump, mass, mound, pack, pile, stack, stockpile, store, swell; SEE CONCEPT *109*

hear [*v1*] *detect by perceiving sound*
apprehend, attend, auscultate, be all ears*, become aware, catch, descry, devour, eavesdrop, get*, get an earful*, get wind of*, give an audience to*, give attention, give ears*, hark, hearken, heed, listen, make out*, overhear, perceive, pick up*, read, strain, take in*; SEE CONCEPTS *590,596*

hear [*v2*] *become aware of information*
apperceive, ascertain, be advised, be informed, be led to believe, be told of, catch, catch on, descry, determine, discover, find out, gather, get the picture*, get wind of*, get wise to*, glean, have on good authority*, learn, pick up*, receive, see, tumble*, understand, unearth; SEE CONCEPTS *15,31*

hearing [*n1*] *ability to perceive sound*
audition, auditory, auditory range, detecting, distinguishing, ear, earshot, effect, extent, faculty, hear-ing distance, listening, perception, range, reach, recording, sense, sound; SEE CONCEPT *597*

hearing [*n2*] *opportunity to present views, knowledge, or skill*
admittance, attendance, attention, audience, audit, audition, chance, conference, congress, consultation, council, discussion, inquiry, interview, investigation, meeting, negotiation, notice, parley, performance, presentation, reception, review, test, trial, tryout; SEE CONCEPTS *48,103,317,693*

hearsay [*n*] *unsubstantiated information*
clothesline*, comment, cry, gossip, grapevine*, leak*, mere talk*, noise*, report, rumble*, rumor, scandal, scuttlebutt*, talk, talk of the town*, word of mouth*; SEE CONCEPTS *51,278*

heart [*n1*] *person's emotions*
affection, benevolence, character, compassion, concern, disposition, emotion, feeling, gusto, humanity, inclination, love, nature, palate, pity, relish, response, sensitivity, sentiment, soul, sympathy, temperament, tenderness, understanding, zest; SEE CONCEPT *410*

heart [*n2*] *courage*
boldness, bravery, dauntlessness, fortitude, gallantry, guts*, mettle, mind, moxie*, nerve, pluck, purpose, resolution, soul, spirit, spunk*, will; SEE CONCEPT *411*

heart [*n3*] *essence, central part*
basic, bosom, bottom line*, center, coal and ice*, core, crux, focal point, focus, gist, hub, kernel, marrow, middle, nitty-gritty*, nub, nucleus, pith, polestar*, quick*, quintessence, root, seat, soul; SEE CONCEPT *826*

heart [*n4*] *blood-pumping organ in animate being*
cardiac organ, clock*, ticker*, vascular organ; SEE CONCEPTS *393,420*

heartbreak [*n*] *mental or emotional misery*
affliction, agony, anguish, bale, bitterness, broken heart, care, desolation, despair, distress, grief, heartache, heartsickness, heavy heart*, pain, regret, remorse, rue, sorrow, suffering, torment, torture, woe; SEE CONCEPTS *410,728*

heartbreaking [*adj*] *disappointing*
affecting, afflictive, agonizing, bitter, calamitous, cheerless, deplorable, dire, distressing, grievous, heart-rending, joyless, lamentable, moving, pitiful, poignant, regrettable, sad, touching, tragic, unfortunate; SEE CONCEPTS *529,537*

hearten [*v*] *raise someone's spirits*
animate, arouse, assure, buck up, buoy, cheer, comfort, console, embolden, encourage, energize, enliven, incite, inspire, inspirit, rally, reassure, revivify, rouse, steel, stimulate, stir, strengthen; SEE CONCEPTS *7,22*

heartfelt [*adj*] *genuine*
ardent, bona fide, cordial, deep, devout, earnest, fervent, heart-to-heart, hearty, honest, profound, sin-

cere, true, unfeigned, warm, wholehearted; SEE CONCEPTS *267,582*

heartless [adj] *without feeling; cold*
brutal, callous, cold-blooded*, cold fish*, cold-hearted*, cruel, hard, hard as nails*, hard-boiled*, hard-hearted*, harsh, inhuman, insensitive, merciless, obdurate, pitiless, ruthless, savage, thick-skinned*, uncaring, uncompassionate, unemotional, unfeeling, unkind, unsympathetic; SEE CONCEPTS *401,542*

hearty [adj1] *energetic, enthusiastic*
affable, animated, ardent, avid, back-slapping*, brotherly, cheerful, cheery, cordial, deep, deepest, deep-felt, devout, eager, earnest, ebullient, effusive, exuberant, frank, friendly, gay, generous, genial, genuine, glad, gushing, heartfelt, honest, impassioned, intense, jolly, jovial, neighborly, passionate, profuse, real, responsive, sincere, true, unfeigned, unreserved, unrestrained, vivacious, warm, warm-hearted, wholehearted, zealous; SEE CONCEPTS *401,542*

hearty [adj2] *healthy, full*
active, ample, energetic, filling, glowing, good, hale, hardy, nourishing, robust, sizable, solid, sound, square, strong, substantial, vigorous, well; SEE CONCEPTS *314,773*

heat [n1] *high temperature*
calefaction, calidity, dog days*, fever, fieriness, heatwave, hotness, hot spell, hot weather, incalescence, incandescence, sultriness, swelter, temperature, torridity, torridness, warmness, warmth; SEE CONCEPT *610*

heat [n2] *anger, passion*
agitation, ardor, desire, earnestness, excitement, ferocity, fervor, fever, fury, impetuosity, intensity, rage, vehemence, violence, warmth, zeal; SEE CONCEPTS *410,657*

heat [v] *make or become hot*
bake, bask, blaze, boil, broil, calorify, chafe, char, enflame, enkindle, fire, flame, flush, frizzle, fry, glow, grill, grow hot, grow warm, ignite, incandesce, incinerate, inflame, kindle, melt, oxidate, oxidize, perspire, raise the temperature, reheat, roast, scald, scorch, sear, seethe, set on fire, singe, smelt, steam, sun, swelter, tepefy, thaw, toast, warm, warm up; SEE CONCEPTS *255,469*

heated [adj1] *angry*
acrimonious, ardent, avid, bitter, excited, fervent, fervid, feverish, fierce, fiery, frenzied, furious, hectic, impassioned, indignant, intense, irate, ireful, mad, passionate, raging, stormy, tempestuous, vehement, violent, wrathful; SEE CONCEPT *267*

heated [adj2] *warmed*
baked, baking, boiling, broiled, broiling, burned, burning, burnt, cooked, fiery, fired, fried, hot, parched, scalding, scorched, scorching, sizzling, toasted; SEE CONCEPT *605*

heathen [adj] *not believing in Christian god*
agnostic, atheistic, barbarian, godless, idolatrous, infidel, irreligious, nonbeliever, non-Christian, pagan, profane, skeptic; SEE CONCEPT *545*

heave [v1] *lift, throw with effort*
boost, cast, chuck, drag, elevate, fling, haul, heft, hoist, hurl, launch, pitch, pull, raise, send, sling, throw, toss, tug; SEE CONCEPTS *196,222*

heave [v2] *discharge with force; expel from digestive system by mouth*
billow, breathe, cast, dilate, disgorge, exhale, expand, gag, groan, huff, palpitate, pant, puff, puke*, retch, rise, sign, sob, spew, spit up, surge, suspire, swell, throb, throw up, upchuck*, vomit; SEE CONCEPTS *163,179*

heaven [n] *place where god lives; wonderful feeling*
afterworld, Arcadia, atmosphere, azure*, beyond, bliss, Canaan, dreamland, ecstasy, Elysium, empyrean, enchantment, eternal home, eternal rest, eternity, fairyland*, felicity, firmament, glory, great unknown*, happiness, happy hunting ground*, harmony, heights, hereafter, immortality, kingdom, kingdom come, life everlasting, life to come, next world, nirvana, paradise, pearly gates*, promised land*, rapture, Shangri-la*, sky*, the blue*, transport, upstairs*, Utopia, wonderland*, Zion; SEE CONCEPTS *370,410,435*

heavenly [adj] *very pleasant*
adorable, alluring, ambrosial, angelic, beatific, beautiful, blessed, blissful, celestial, cherubic, darling, delectable, delicious, delightful, divine, empyrean, enjoyable, entrancing, excellent, exquisite, extraterrestrial, glorious, godlike, holy, immortal, lovely, luscious, lush, paradisaical, rapturous, ravishing, scrumptious, seraphic, sublime, superhuman, supernal, supernatural, sweet, wonderful, yummy; SEE CONCEPTS *537,572*

heavy [adj1] *having great weight*
abundant, ample, awkward, beefy*, big, built, bulky, burdensome, chunky*, considerable, copious, corpulent, cumbersome, cumbrous, elephantine, enceinte, excessive, expectant, fat, fleshy, gravid, gross*, hefty, huge, laden, large, lead-footed*, loaded, lumbering, massive, obese, oppressed, overweight, parturient, ponderous, porcine, portly, pregnant, stout, substantial, top-heavy, two-ton*, unmanageable, unwieldy, weighted, weighty, zaftig*; SEE CONCEPT *491*

heavy [adj2] *difficult, severe*
abstruse, acroamatic, arduous, boisterous, burdensome, complex, complicated, confused, effortful, esoteric, formidable, grave, grievous, hard, harsh, intolerable, knotty*, labored, laborious, onerous, oppressive, profound, recondite, rough, serious, solemn, stormy, strenuous, tedious, tempestuous, toilsome, tough, troublesome, turbulent, vexatious, violent, wearisome, weighty, wild; SEE CONCEPTS *538,565,569*

heavy [*adj3*] *depressed, gloomy*
close, cloudy, crestfallen, damp, dark, dejected, despondent, disconsolate, dismal, downcast, dull, grieving, leaden, lowering, melancholy, oppressive, overcast, sad, sodden, soggy, sorrowful, stifling, wet; SEE CONCEPTS *403,525,548*

heavy [*adj4*] *listless, slow*
apathetic, comatose, dull, hebetudinous, indifferent, lethargic, sluggish, slumberous, torpid; SEE CONCEPT *584*

heckle [*v*] *jeer*
badger, bait, bother, bully, chivy, dis*, discomfit, disconcert, disrupt, disturb, embarrass, faze, gibe, hound*, interrupt, pester, plague, rattle, ride*, ridicule, shout at, taunt, tease, torment, worry; SEE CONCEPTS *44,47*

hectic [*adj*] *frantic, turbulent*
animated, boisterous, burning, chaotic, confused, disordered, excited, exciting, fervid, fevered, feverish, flurrying, flustering, frenetic, frenzied, furious, hassle, heated, hell broke loose*, jungle*, madhouse*, nutsy*, restless, riotous, rip-roaring, tumultuous, unsettled, wild, woolly*, zoolike*; SEE CONCEPT *548*

hedge [*n*] *boundary, obstacle, especially one made of plants*
barrier, bush, enclosure, fence, guard, hedgerow, hurdle, protection, quickset, screen, shrubbery, thicket, windbreak*; SEE CONCEPTS *429,470*

hedge [*v1*] *avoid, dodge*
beat around the bush*, be noncommittal, blow hot and cold*, cop a plea*, cop out*, duck, equivocate, evade, flip-flop*, fudge*, give the run around*, hem and haw*, jive*, pass the buck*, prevaricate, pussyfoot*, quibble, run around, shilly-shally*, shuck*, shuffle, sidestep, sit on the fence*, stall, stonewall*, temporize, tergiversate, tergiverse, waffle*; SEE CONCEPTS *18,30*

hedge [*v2*] *enclose*
block, border, cage, confine, coop, corral, edge, fence, girdle, hem in, hinder, immure, obstruct, pen, restrict, ring, siege, surround; SEE CONCEPT *758*

hedonist [*n*] *person who seeks pleasure above other values*
bon vivant, debauchee, epicure, epicurean, glutton, gourmand, lecher, libertine, man/woman of pleasure, pleasuremonger, pleasureseeker, profligate, rake, sensualist, sybarite, thrill-seeker, voluptuary; SEE CONCEPT *423*

heed [*n*] *care, thought*
application, attention, carefulness, caution, cognizance, concentration, concern, consideration, debate, deliberation, ear*, heedfulness, interest, listen up*, mark, mind*, note, notice, observance, observation, regard, remark, respect, spotlight*, study, tender loving care*, TLC*, watchfulness; SEE CONCEPTS *17,532*

heed [*v*] *give care, thought to*
attend, baby-sit, bear in mind, be aware, be guided by, catch, consider, dig*, do one's bidding*, follow, follow orders, get a load of*, give ear*, hark, hear, hearken, keep eye peeled*, keep tabs*, listen, mark, mind, mind the store*, note, obey, observe, pay attention, pick up, regard, ride herd on*, see, sit, spot, stay in line*, take notice of, take to heart*, toe the line*, watch, watch one's step*, watch out, watch over, watch the store*; SEE CONCEPTS *17,623*

heedless [*adj*] *careless*
asleep at switch*, daydreaming, disregardful, fast and loose*, feckless, foolhardy, goofing off*, impetuous, imprudent, inadvertent, inattentive, incautious, inconsiderate, irreflective, neglectful, negligent, oblivious, out to lunch*, precipitate, rash, reckless, slapdash*, sloppy, thoughtless, uncaring, unmindful, unobservant, unthinking, unwary; SEE CONCEPT *401*

hefty [*adj*] *big, bulky*
ample, awkward, beefy*, brawny, burly, colossal, cumbersome, extensive, fat, forceful, heavy, hulking, husky, large, large-scale, major, massive, muscular, ponderous, powerful, robust, sizable, strapping*, strong, sturdy, substantial, thumping*, tremendous, unwieldy, vigorous, weighty; SEE CONCEPTS *491,773*

height [*n1*] *altitude, top part*
acme, apex, apogee, brow, ceiling, crest, crown, cusp, elevation, extent, highness, hill, loftiness, mountain, peak, pinnacle, pitch, prominence, rise, solstice, stature, summit, tallness, tip, tiptop, top, vertex, zenith; SEE CONCEPTS *741,743,791,836*

height [*n2*] *climax; importance*
acme, crest, crisis, crowning point, culmination, dignity, eminence, end, exaltation, extremity, grandeur, heyday*, high point, limit, loftiness, maximum, ne plus ultra*, prominence, sublimity, top, ultimate, utmost degree, uttermost; SEE CONCEPTS *388,668,832*

heinous [*adj*] *horrifying, monstrous*
abhorrent, abominable, accursed, atrocious, awful, bad, beastly, crying, cursed, evil, execrable, flagitious, flagrant, frightful, godawful*, grave, gross*, hateful, hideous, horrendous, infamous, iniquitous, nefarious, odious, offensive, outrageous, raunchy, revolting, scandalous, shocking, stinking*, unspeakable, vicious, villainous; SEE CONCEPTS *529,548,570*

heir [*n*] *person who inherits possessions*
beneficiary, crown prince/princess, devisee, grantee, heiress, heritor, inheritor, inheritress, inheritrix, next in line, scion, successor; SEE CONCEPTS *355,414*

heirloom [*n*] *something inherited, often antique*
antique, bequest, birthright, gift, heritage, inheritance, legacy, patrimony, reversion; SEE CONCEPT *337*

hell [*n*] *place where devil lives; bad situation*
Abaddon*, abyss, affliction, agony, anguish, blazes*, bottomless pit*, difficulty, everlasting fire*, fire and brimstone*, Gehenna*, grave, Hades, hellfire, infernal regions, inferno, limbo, lower world,

misery, nether world, nightmare, ordeal, pandemonium, perdition, pit, place of torment, purgatory, suffering, torment, trial, underworld, wretchedness; SEE CONCEPTS *370,435,674*

help [*n1*] *assistance, relief*
advice, aid, assist, avail, balm*, benefit, comfort, cooperation, corrective, cure, guidance, hand, helping hand*, lift*, maintenance, nourishment, remedy, service, succor, support, sustenance, use, utility; SEE CONCEPTS *658,694*

help [*n2*] *employee*
abettor, adjutant, aide, ally, ancilla, assistant, attendant, auxiliary, collaborator, colleague, deputy, domestic, hand, helper, helpmate, mate, partner, representative, right-hand man/woman*, servant, subsidiary, supporter, worker; SEE CONCEPT *348*

help [*v1*] *aid, assist*
abet, accommodate, advocate, back, ballyhoo*, befriend, benefit, be of use, bolster, boost, buck up*, cheer, cooperate, do a favor, do a service, do one's part*, encourage, endorse, further, go to bat for*, go with, hype*, intercede, lend a hand*, maintain, open doors*, patronize, plug*, promote, prop, puff*, push, relieve, root for*, sanction, save, second, see through, serve, stand by, stick up for*, stimulate, stump for*, succor, support, sustain, take under wing*, uphold, work for; SEE CONCEPT *110*

help [*v2*] *improve*
alleviate, ameliorate, amend, attend, better, cure, doctor, ease, facilitate, heal, meliorate, mitigate, nourish, palliate, relieve, remedy, restore, revive, treat; SEE CONCEPT *244*

helpful [*adj*] *beneficial, beneficent*
accessible, accommodating, advantageous, applicable, benevolent, bettering, caring, conducive, considerate, constructive, contributive, convenient, cooperative, crucial, effectual, efficacious, essential, favorable, fortunate, friendly, good for, important, improving, instrumental, invaluable, kind, neighborly, operative, practical, pragmatic, productive, profitable, serendipitous, serviceable, significant, suitable, supportive, symbiotic, sympathetic, timely, usable, useful, utilitarian, valuable; SEE CONCEPTS *537,560*

helping [*n*] *portion of food*
allowance, course, dollop, meal, order, piece, plateful, ration, serving, share; SEE CONCEPT *457*

helpless [*adj*] *incapable, incompetent; vulnerable*
abandoned, basket-case*, debilitated, defenseless, dependent, destitute, disabled, exposed, feeble, forlorn, forsaken, friendless, handcuffed, impotent, inefficient, inexpert, infirm, invalid, over a barrel*, paralyzed, pinned*, powerless, prostrate, shiftless, tapped, tapped out*, unable, unfit, unprotected, up creek without paddle*, weak, with hands tied*; SEE CONCEPTS *401,542*

helter-skelter [*adv*] *carelessly, confused*
about, anyhow, any which way*, anywise, around, at random, cluttered, disorderly, haphazard, hastily,

headlong, higgledy-piggledy*, hit-or-miss*, hotfoot*, hurriedly, impetuously, incautiously, in confusion, incontinently, irregular, jumbled, muddled, pell-mell*, random, randomly, rashly, recklessly, topsy-turvy*, tumultous/tumultuous, unmindfully, wildly; SEE CONCEPT *544*

hem [*n*] *border, edge*
brim, brink, define, edging, fringe, margin, perimeter, periphery, piping, rim, selvage, skirt, skirting, trimming, verge; SEE CONCEPTS *484,513*

hem/hem in [*v*] *enclose, restrict*
begird, beset, border, bound, cage, circle, circumscribe, close in, confine, corral, define, edge, encircle, encompass, envelop, environ, fence, fringe, girdle, hedge in, immure, margin, pen, rim, ring, round, shut, shut in, skirt, surround, verge; SEE CONCEPTS *130,758*

hence [*adv*] *for that reason; therefore*
accordingly, as a deduction, away, consequently, ergo, forward, from here, from now on, henceforth, henceforward, hereinafter, in the future, it follows that, on that account, onward, out, so, then, thence, thereupon, thus, wherefore; SEE CONCEPT *799*

herald [*n*] *omen, messenger*
adviser, bearer, courier, crier, forerunner, harbinger, indication, outrider, precursor, prophet, reporter, runner, sign, signal, token; SEE CONCEPTS *274, 284,423*

herald [*v*] *bring message*
advertise, announce, ballyhoo*, broadcast, declare, forerun, foretoken, harbinger, indicate, pave the way*, portend, precede, preindicate, presage, proclaim, promise, publicize, publish, show, tout, trumpet*, usher in*; SEE CONCEPT *60*

herd [*n*] *large group*
assemblage, bevy, brood, clan, collection, covey, crowd, crush, drift, drove, flight, flock, gaggle, gathering, hoi polloi*, horde, lot, mass, mob, multitude, nest, pack, people, populace, press, rabble, school, swarm, throng; SEE CONCEPTS *397,432*

herd [*v*] *gather; shepherd*
assemble, associate, collect, congregate, corral, drive, flock, force, goad, guide, huddle, lead, muster, poke, punch, rally, round up*, run, scare up*, spur; SEE CONCEPT *109*

here [*adv*] *in this place*
attendant, attending, available, hereabouts, hither, hitherto, in this direction, on board, on deck, on hand, on-the-spot, on this spot, present, within reach; SEE CONCEPT *583*

hereafter [*n*] *life after death*
afterlife, aftertime, afterward, afterworld, by-and-by*, future, future existence, future life, heaven, hell, next world, offing, otherworld, the beyond*, to-be*, underworld, world to come*; SEE CONCEPT *370*

hereafter [*adv*] *from now on*
after this, eventually, hence, henceforth, henceforward, hereupon, in the course of time, in the future, ultimately; SEE CONCEPT *799*

hereditary [*adj*] *inherited; transmitted at birth*
ancestral, bequeathed, family, genealogical, genetic, handed down, heritable, inborn, inbred, inheritable, inherited, lineal, maternal, paternal, patrimonial, traditional, transmissible, transmitted, willed; SEE CONCEPT *549*

heredity [*n*] *transmission of traits from parents to offspring*
ancestry, congenital traits, constitution, eugenics, genesiology, genetic make-up, genetics, inborn character, inheritance; SEE CONCEPT *648*

heresy [*n*] *unorthodox opinion, especially in religious matters*
agnosticism, apostasy, atheism, blasphemy, defection, disbelief, dissent, dissidence, divergence, error, fallacy, heterodoxy, iconoclasm, impiety, infidelity, misbelief, nonconformism, nonconformity, paganism, revisionism, schism, sectarianism, secularism, sin, unorthodoxy; SEE CONCEPT *689*

heretical [*adj*] *unorthodox*
agnostic, apostate, atheistic, differing, disagreeing, dissenting, dissentive, dissident, freethinking, heterodox, iconoclastic, idolatrous, impious, infidel, misbelieving, miscreant, nonconformist, revisionist, schismatic, sectarian, skeptical, unbelieving; SEE CONCEPTS *529,545*

heritage [*n*] *person's background, tradition*
ancestry, bequest, birthright, convention, culture, custom, dowry, endowment, estate, fashion, heirship, heritance, inheritance, legacy, lot, patrimony, portion, right, share, tradition; SEE CONCEPTS *296,648,678*

hermit [*n*] *person who chose to live alone outside of human society*
anchoress, anchoret, anchorite, ascetic, eremite, hermitress, misanthrope, monk, pillarist, recluse, skeptic, solitaire, solitarian, solitary, stylite; SEE CONCEPTS *361,423*

hero/heroine [*n*] *brave person; champion*
ace, adventurer, celebrity, combatant, conqueror, daredevil, demigod, diva, exemplar, gallant, god, goddess, great person, heavy, ideal, idol, lead, leading lady*, leading man*, lion, martyr, master, model, paladin, person of the hour*, popular figure, prima donna*, principal, protagonist, saint, star, superstar, tin god*, victor, worthy; SEE CONCEPTS *352,416*

heroic [*adj*] *brave, champion*
bigger than life*, bold, classic, courageous, daring, dauntless, doughty, elevated, epic, exaggerated, fearless, fire-eating*, gallant, grand, grandiose, gritty, gutsy*, gutty*, high-flown, impavid, inflated, intrepid, lion-hearted, mythological, noble, stand tall*, stouthearted, unafraid, undaunted, valiant, valorous; SEE CONCEPTS *401,404*

heroism [*n*] *bravery*
boldness, chivalry, courage, courageousness, daring, doughtiness, fearlessness, fortitude, gallantry, intre-

pidity, nobility, prowess, spirit, strength, valiance, valiancy, valor, valorousness; SEE CONCEPTS *411,633*

hesitant [*adj*] *uncertain, waiting*
afraid, averse, backward, dawdling, delaying, diffident, disinclined, doubtful, doubting, faltering, half-hearted, halting, hanging back, hesitating, indecisive, irresolute, lacking confidence, lazy, loath, reluctant, shy, skeptical, slow, tentative, timid, uneager, unpredictable, unsure, unwilling, vacillating, wavering; SEE CONCEPTS *534,535,542*

hesitate [*v*] *wait; be uncertain*
alternate, balance, balk, be irresolute, be reluctant, be unwilling, blow hot and cold*, dally, debate, defer, delay, demur, dillydally*, dither, doubt, equivocate, falter, flounder, fluctuate, fumble, hang*, hang back, hedge, hem and haw*, hold back, hold off, hover, linger, oscillate, pause, ponder, pull back, pussyfoot*, scruple, seesaw*, shift, shrink, shy away, sit on fence*, stammer, stop, straddle, stumble, stutter, swerve, tergiversate, think about, think twice*, vacillate, waffle*, waver, weigh; SEE CONCEPTS *21,121,681*

hesitation [*n*] *waiting; uncertainty*
averseness, dawdling, delay, delaying, demurral, doubt, dubiety, equivocation, faltering, fluctuation, fumbling, hemming and hawing*, hesitancy, indecision, indecisiveness, indisposition, irresolution, misgiving, mistrust, oscillation, pause, procrastination, qualm, reluctance, scruple, skepticism, stammering, stumbling, stuttering, unwillingness, vacillation, wavering; SEE CONCEPTS *21,121,410,681*

heterogeneous [*adj*] *assorted, miscellaneous*
amalgamate, composite, confused, conglomerate, contrary, contrasted, different, discordant, discrepant, disparate, dissimilar, divergent, diverse, diversified, incongruous, independent, inharmonious, jumbled, mingled, mixed, mongrel, mosaic, motley, multifarious, multiplex, odd, opposed, unallied, unlike, unrelated, variant, varied, variegated; SEE CONCEPT *564*

hiatus [*n*] *pause, interruption*
aperture, blank, breach, break, chasm, discontinuity, gap, interim, interval, lacuna, lapse, opening, rift, space; SEE CONCEPT *807*

hibernate [*v*] *lie dormant; sleep through cold weather*
hide, hole up, immure, lie torpid, sleep, vegetate, winter; SEE CONCEPT *315*

hidden [*adj*] *unseen, secret*
abstruse, buried, clandestine, cloaked, close, clouded, concealed, covered, covert, cryptic, dark, disguised, eclipsed, esoteric, hermetic, hermetical, imperceivable, indiscernible, in the dark, invisible, latent, masked, mysterious, mystic, mystical, obscure, occult, out of view, private, QT*, recondite, screened, secluded, secreted, sequestered, shadowy, shrouded, surreptitious, ulterior, undercover, underground, undetected, undisclosed, unexposed, un-

known, unrevealed, veiled, withheld; SEE CONCEPT *576*

hide [v] *conceal; remain unseen*
adumbrate, blot out, bury, cache, camouflage, cloak, cover, curtain*, disguise, dissemble, ditch, duck, eclipse, ensconce, go into hiding, go underground, harbor, hold back, hole up*, hush up, keep from, keep secret, lie low*, lock up, mask, not give away, not tell, obscure, plant, protect, put out of the way, reserve, salt away*, screen, secrete, shadow, shelter, shield, shroud, smuggle, squirrel*, stash, stifle, stow away, suppress, take cover, tuck away, veil, withhold; SEE CONCEPTS *17,188*

hideous [adj] *grotesque, horrible*
abominable, animal, appalling, awful, beast, bestial, detestable, disgusting, dreadful, frightful, ghastly, grim, grisly, gross*, gruesome, hateful, horrendous, horrid, loathsome, macabre, monstrous, morbid, nasty, odious, offensive, repellent, repugnant, repulsive, revolting, shocking, sick, sickening, terrible, terrifying, ugly, uncomely, unsightly, weird; SEE CONCEPTS *537,579*

high [adj1] *tall; at a great distance aloft*
aerial, alpine, altitudinous, big, colossal, elevated, eminent, flying, formidable, giant, gigantic, grand, great, high-reaching, high-rise, hovering, huge, immense, large, lofty, long, sky-high, sky-scraping, soaring, steep, towering, tremendous, uplifted, upraised; SEE CONCEPTS *779,782*

high [adj2] *extreme*
costly, dear, excessive, exorbitant, expensive, extraordinary, extravagant, grand, great, high-priced, intensified, lavish, luxurious, precious, rich, sharp, special, steep, stiff, strong, unusual; SEE CONCEPTS *334,569*

high [adj3] *important*
arch, capital, chief, consequential, crucial, distinguished, eminent, essential, exalted, extreme, grave, influential, leading, necessary, noble, powerful, prominent, ruling, serious, significant, superior; SEE CONCEPT *567*

high [adj4] *very happy*
boisterous, bouncy, cheerful, elated, excited, exhilarated, exuberant, joyful, lighthearted, merry, psyched*, pumped*; SEE CONCEPT *403*

high [adj5] *intoxicated, drugged*
delirious, doped, drunk, euphoric, flying*, freaked out*, inebriated, on a trip*, potted*, spaced out*, stoned*, tanked*, tipsy; SEE CONCEPT *314*

high [adj6] *shrill, strong (on the senses)*
acute, high-pitched, loud, malodorous, penetrating, piercing, piping, putrid, rancid, rank, reeking, sharp, smelly, soprano, strident, treble; SEE CONCEPTS *406,594,598*

highlight [n] *memorable part*
best part, climax, feature, focal point, focus, high point, high spot, main feature, peak; SEE CONCEPT *832*

highly [adv] *very, well*
awful, awfully, bloody*, but good*, decidedly, deeply, eminently, exceedingly, exceptionally, extraordinarily, extremely, greatly, hugely, immensely, jolly, mighty, mucho*, notably, parlous, plenty, powerful, profoundly, real, really, remarkably, right, so, so much*, strikingly, supremely, surpassingly, terribly, terrifically, too much*, tremendously, vastly, very much; SEE CONCEPTS *537,569*

high-strung [adj] *nervous*
all shook up*, choked*, easily upset, edgy, excitable, fidgety, hyper*, impatient, irascible, irritable, jittery, jumpy, nervy, neurotic, on pins and needles*, on ragged edge, restless, sensitive, spooked*, stressed, taut, temperamental, tense, tight*, unrestful, uptight*, wired*, zonkers*; SEE CONCEPTS *401,404*

highway [n] *heavily traveled, capacious road*
artery, avenue, boulevard, drag*, four-lane*, freeway, interstate, parking lot*, parkway, path, pike*, roadway, skyway, street, superhighway, super slab*, thoroughfare, toll road, track, turnpike; SEE CONCEPT *501*

hike [n] *journey by foot*
backpack, constitutional, excursion, exploration, march, ramble, tour, traipse, tramp, trek, trip, walk, walkabout; SEE CONCEPTS *149,224,363*

hike [v1] *walk for recreation*
backpack, explore, hit the road*, hoof*, leg it*, ramble, rove, stroll, stump, tour, tramp, travel, tromp; SEE CONCEPTS *149,224,363*

hike [v2] *raise, increase*
advance, boost, jack, jump, lift, pull up, put up, up*, upgrade; SEE CONCEPTS *236,245*

hilarious [adj] *very funny*
amusing, comical, convivial, entertaining, exhilarated, frolicsome, gay, gleeful, gut-busting*, happy, humorous, jocular, jolly, jovial, joyful, joyous, laughable, lively, merry, mirthful, noisy, priceless, riot, rollicking, scream, side-splitting*, uproarious, witty; SEE CONCEPT *529*

hill [n] *uprising of earth's surface; pile*
acclivity, ascent, bluff, butte, cliff, climb, down, drift, dune, elevation, eminence, esker, fell, gradient, headland, heap, height, highland, hillock, hilltop, hummock, inclination, incline, knoll, mesa, mound, mount, precipice, prominence, promontory, protuberance, range, ridge, rise, rising ground, shock, slope, stack, summit, talus, tor, upland; SEE CONCEPT *509*

hinder [v] *prevent, slow down*
arrest, balk, bar, block, bottleneck, box in, burden, check, choke, clog, contravene, counteract, crab, cramp, crimp, cripple, curb, debar, delay, deter, encumber, fetter, frustrate, get in the way*, hamper, hamstring*, handicap, hog-tie*, hold back, hold up, impede, inhibit, interfere, interrupt, louse up*, muzzle, neutralize, obstruct, offset, oppose, preclude,

prevent, prohibit, resist, retard, shut out, snafu*, stay, stop, stymie*, terminate, thwart, trammel; SEE CONCEPTS *121,130*

hindrance [n] *obstruction, difficulty*
albatross*, baggage*, ball and chain*, bar, barrier, catch, Catch-22*, check, clog, crimp, cumbrance, deterrent, drag, drawback, encumbrance, excess baggage*, foot dragging*, glitch*, gridlock, handicap, hang-up*, hitch, impedance, impediment, interference, interruption, intervention, jam-up*, joker, limitation, lock, millstone*, monkey wrench*, obstacle, restraint, restriction, snag, stoppage, stumbling block*, trammel; SEE CONCEPTS *666,674*

hinge [n] *pivot, turning point*
articulation, axis, ball-and-socket, butt, elbow, hook, joint, juncture, knee, link, pin, spring, swivel; SEE CONCEPTS *471,498*

hinge [v] *be contingent on*
be subject to, be undecided, depend, hang, pend, pivot, rest, revolve around, stand on, turn, turn on; SEE CONCEPT *711*

hint [n] *indication; suggestion*
adumbration, advice, allusion, announcement, clue, communication, connotation, denotation, evidence, flea in ear*, glimmering, help, idea, implication, impression, inference, information, inkling, innuendo, insinuation, intimation, iota, lead, mention, notice, notion, observation, omen, pointer, print, reference, reminder, scent, sign, signification, smattering, suggestion, suspicion, symptom, taste, telltale, tinge, tip, tip-off*, token, trace, warning, whiff*, whisper, wink*, word to wise*, wrinkle*; SEE CONCEPT *274*

hint [v] *suggest; indicate*
acquaint, adumbrate, advise, allude to, angle, apprise, bring up, broach, coax, connote, cue, drop, expose, fish*, foreshadow, give an inkling*, impart, imply, infer, inform, insinuate, intimate, jog memory, leak*, let it be known, let out of bag*, make*, mention, point, prefigure, press, prompt, put flea in ear*, recall, refer to, remind, say in passing, shadow, signify, solicit, spring, tip off*, tip one's hand*, touch on*, whisper, wink*; SEE CONCEPTS *60,74,75*

hire [v] *commission for responsibility, use*
add to payroll, appoint, authorize, book, bring in, bring on board, carry, charter, contract for, delegate, draft, employ, empower, engage, enlist, exploit, fill a position, find help, give a break*, give job to, give work, ink*, lease, let, make use of, obtain, occupy, pick, place, pledge, procure, promise, put on*, put to work, rent, retain, secure, select, sign on, sign up*, sublease, sublet, take on, truck with*, use, utilize; SEE CONCEPT *351*

hiss [n] *buzzing sound; jeer*
boo, Bronx cheer*, buzz, catcall, contempt, derision, hissing, hoot, sibilance, sibilation; SEE CONCEPTS *278,595*

hiss [v] *make buzzing sound; ridicule*
blow, boo, catcall, condemn, damn, decry, deride, disapprove, hoot, jeer, mock, rasp, revile, seethe,

shout down, shrill, sibilate, siss, spit, wheeze, whirr, whisper, whistle, whiz; SEE CONCEPTS *52,77*

historic [adj] *momentous, remarkable*
celebrated, consequential, extraordinary, famous, important, memorable, notable, outstanding, red-letter*, significant, well-known; SEE CONCEPTS *548,568*

historical [adj] *recorded as actually having happened*
actual, ancient, archival, attested, authentic, chronicled, classical, commemorated, documented, factual, important, in truth, old, past, real, verifiable; SEE CONCEPTS *548,582,820*

history [n1] *past events, experiences*
ancient times, antiquity, bygone times, days of old*, days of yore*, good old days*, old days*, olden days*, past, yesterday, yesteryear; SEE CONCEPTS *678,807*

history [n2] *chronicle of events*
account, annals, autobiography, biography, diary, epic, journal, memoirs, narration, narrative, prehistory, recapitulation, recital, record, relation, report, saga, story, tale, version; SEE CONCEPTS *268,271*

hit [n1] *strike, bump*
bang, bat, bell-ringer*, belt, blow, bonk, box*, buffet, butt, chop, clash, clip, clout, collision, cuff*, fisticuff, glance, impact, knock, lick*, one-two punch*, paste*, pat, plunk, punch, rap, roundhouse*, shock, shot, slap, slog, smack, smash, sock, spank, stroke, swat, swing, swipe, tap, uppercut, wallop, whammy*, whop, zap*, zinger*; SEE CONCEPTS *189,200*

hit [n2] *entertainment success*
achievement, bang, click, favorite, knockout, masterstroke, sellout, sensation, smash, SRO*, triumph, winner, wow; SEE CONCEPT *706*

hit [v1] *strike*
bang, bash, bat, batter, beat, belt, blast, blitz, box*, brain*, buffet, bump, clap, clip, clobber, clout, club, crack, cudgel, cuff*, dab, ding*, flail, flax, flog, give a black eye*, hammer*, hook, jab, kick, knock, knock around, knock out, KO*, lace, lambaste, larrup, lather, let fly*, let have it*, lob, nail*, pellet, pelt, percuss, pop, pound, punch, rap, ride roughshod*, slap, smack, sock, stone, swat, tap, thrash, thump, thwack, trash, uppercut, wallop, whack*, whang*; SEE CONCEPTS *189,200*

hit [v2] *collide, bump into*
bang into, buffet, butt, carom, clash, crash, glance, jostle, knock, light, meet, meet head-on*, pat, rap, run into, scrape, sideswipe, smash, stumble, tap, thud, thump; SEE CONCEPTS *189,208*

hit [v3] *accomplish*
achieve, affect, arrive at, attain, gain, influence, leave a mark, occur, overwhelm, reach, secure, strike, touch; SEE CONCEPTS *199,706*

hitch [n] *problem, difficulty*
block, bug*, catch, check, delay, discontinuance, drawback, glitch*, hang-up, hindrance, hold-up, im-

pediment, interruption, joker, mishap, snafu*, snag, stoppage, stumbling block, tangle, trouble; SEE CONCEPTS *666,674*

hitch [v] *join, fasten*
attach, chain, connect, couple, harness, hook, lash, make fast, moor, strap, tether, tie, unite, yoke; SEE CONCEPTS *85,113,160*

hoard [n] *stockpile*
abundance, accumulation, agglomeration, aggregation, amassment, backlog, cache, collection, conglomeration, cumulation, fund, garner, heap, inventory, mass, nest egg*, pile, reserve, reservoir, riches, stock, store, supply, treasure, treasure-trove*, trove, wealth; SEE CONCEPT *712*

hoard [v] *put away, accumulate*
acquire, amass, buy up, cache, collect, deposit, garner, gather, hide, keep, lay away, lay up, pile up, put aside for rainy day*, put by, save, scrimp, sock away*, squirrel*, stash, stockpile, store, stow away, treasure; SEE CONCEPTS *135,710*

hoarse [adj] *raspy in voice*
blatant, breathy, cracked, croaking, croaky, croupy, discordant, dry, grating, gravelly, growling, gruff, guttural, harsh, husky, indistinct, jarring, piercing, ragged, raucous, rough, scratching, squawking, stertorous, strident, stridulous, thick, throaty, uneven, whispering; SEE CONCEPT *594*

hoax [n] *trick*
cheat, cock-and-bull story*, con*, con game*, crock*, deceit, deception, dodge, fabrication, fake, falsification, fast one*, fast shuffle*, fib, flimflam*, fraud, gimmick, gyp*, hooey*, humbug*, hustle, imposture, joke, lie, practical joke, prank, put-on, racket, ruse, scam, sell, shift, snow job*, spoof, sting, swindle, whopper*; SEE CONCEPTS *59,63*

hoax [v] *trick*
bamboozle*, bluff, chicane, con, deceive, delude, dupe, fake out, fleece, flimflam*, fool, frame, gammon, gull, hoodwink*, Murphy*, play games with*, pull one's leg*, rook*, run a game on*, set up*, sting*, swindle, take for a ride*, take in*; SEE CONCEPT *59*

hobble [v1] *limp*
clump, dodder, falter, halt, hitch, scuff, shuffle, stagger, stumble, totter; SEE CONCEPT *151*

hobble [v2] *cripple, restrict*
clog, cramp, cramp one's style, crimp, curb, entrammel, fasten, fetter, gimp, hamper, hamstring*, hang up*, hinder, hog-tie*, leash, put a crimp in*, shackle, tie, trammel; SEE CONCEPT *130*

hobby [n] *pleasurable pastime*
amusement, art, avocation, bag*, craft, craze, distraction, diversion, divertissement, fad*, fancy, favorite occupation, fun, game, interest, kick*, labor of love*, leisure activity, leisure pursuit, obsession, occupation, pet topic, play, quest, relaxation, schtick*, shot, sideline, specialty, sport, thing*, va-

gary, weakness, whim, whimsy; SEE CONCEPTS *363,364*

hocus-pocus [n] *deception, magic*
abracadabra*, artifice, cant, chant, charm, cheating, chicanery, conjuring, deceit, deception, delusion, flimflam*, fraud, gibberish, gobbledegook*, hoax, humbug, imposture, incantation, jargon, juggling, legerdemain, mumbo-jumbo*, mummery, nonsense, open-sesame*, rigmarole*, sleight of hand*, spell, swindle, trick, trickery; SEE CONCEPTS *59,278*

hodgepodge [n] *mixture, mess*
collection, combination, goulash*, hash, jumble, medley, mélange, miscellany, mishmash*, mixed bag, olio, patchwork, potpourri, salmagundi*; SEE CONCEPTS *260,432*

hogwash [n] *nonsense*
absurdity, balderdash*, baloney*, bull*, bunk*, debris, drivel*, foolishness, hokum, hooey*, horsefeathers*, poppycock*, refuse, ridiculousness, rot, rubbish, trash, twaddle*; SEE CONCEPT *278*

hoist [v] *lift*
elevate, erect, heave, pick up, raise, rear, take up, uphold, uplift, upraise, uprear; SEE CONCEPT *196*

hold [n] *grasp, possession*
authority, clasp, clench, clinch, clout, clutch, control, dominance, dominion, grip, influence, mastery, occupancy, occupation, ownership, pull, purchase, retention, sway, tenacity, tenure; SEE CONCEPTS *190,343,710*

hold [v1] *have in one's hands, possession; grasp*
adhere, arrest, bind, bottle up, carry, catch, check, cherish, clasp, cleave, clench, clinch, cling, clutch, confine, contain, cork up*, cradle, detain, embrace, enclose, enjoy, fondle, freeze to*, grip, handle, hang on, have, hug, imprison, keep, keep close, keep out, lock up, maintain, not let go, nourish, occupy, own, palm, possess, press, put a lock on, restrain, retain, secure, seize, squeeze, stay put, stick, take, trammel, vise, wield, withhold, wring; SEE CONCEPTS *190,191,200,710*

hold [v2] *believe*
assume, aver, bet bottom dollar*, buy*, consider, credit, cross one's heart*, deem, entertain, esteem, feel, have hunch*, have sneaking suspicion*, judge, lap up, lay money on, maintain, okay, presume, reckon, regard, sense, set store by*, swear by, swear up and down*, take as gospel truth*, take stock in*, think, view; SEE CONCEPT *12*

hold [v3] *continue, endure*
apply, be in effect, be in force, be the case, be valid, exist, have bearing, hold good, hold true, last, operate, persevere, persist, remain, remain true, resist, stand up, stay, stay staunch, wear; SEE CONCEPT *239*

hold [v4] *support*
bear, bolster, brace, buttress, carry, lock, prop, shore up, shoulder, stay, sustain, take, underpin, uphold; SEE CONCEPTS *110,190*

hold [*v5*] *have a capacity for*
accommodate, be equipped for, carry, comprise, contain, include, seat, take; SEE CONCEPTS *719,742*

hold [*v6*] *conduct meeting, function*
assemble, call, carry on, celebrate, convene, have, officiate, preside, run, solemnize; SEE CONCEPTS *324,384*

hold back/hold off [*v*] *repress*
bit, bridle, check, control, curb, defer, delay, deny, forbear, hold down, hold in, inhibit, keep, keep back, keep out, postpone, prevent, put off, refrain, refuse, restrain, stop, suppress, withhold; SEE CONCEPTS *121,130*

holdup [*n1*] *problem*
bottleneck*, delay, difficulty, gridlock*, hitch, obstruction, setback, snag, stoppage, traffic jam*, trouble, wait; SEE CONCEPTS *192,674*

holdup [*n2*] *take goods illegally by force*
burglary, crime, mugging, robbery, stickup, theft; SEE CONCEPT *192*

hold up [*v1*] *postpone*
delay, detain, hinder, hold off, impede, interfere, interrupt, pause, prorogue, retard, set back, slow down, stay, stop, suspend, waive; SEE CONCEPTS *121,130*

hold up [*v2*] *rob*
burglarize, mug, steal from, stick up, waylay; SEE CONCEPTS *139,192*

hole [*n1*] *opening in solid object*
aperture, breach, break, burrow, cave, cavern, cavity, chamber, chasm, chink, cistern, cleft, covert, crack, cranny, crater, cut, den, dent, depression, dimple, dip, excavation, eyelet, fissure, foramen, fracture, gap, gash, gorge, hollow, hovel, keyhole, lacuna, lair, leak, mouth, nest, niche, nick, notch, orifice, outlet, passage, peephole, perforation, pit, pocket, pockmark, puncture, rent, retreat, scoop, shaft, shelter, space, split, tear, tunnel, vacuity, vent, void, window; SEE CONCEPT *513*

hole [*n2*] *predicament*
box*, corner*, difficulty, dilemma, emergency, fix, imbroglio, impasse, jam, mess, pickle*, plight, quandary, scrape, spot, tangle; SEE CONCEPT *674*

holiday [*n*] *celebratory day; time off*
anniversary, break, celebration, day of rest, feast, festival, festivity, fete, few days off*, fiesta, gala, gone fishing*, holy day, jubilee, layoff, leave, liberty, long weekend*, recess, red-letter day*, saint's day, vacation; SEE CONCEPTS *364,802*

holiness [*n*] *religiousness*
asceticism, beatitude, blessedness, consecration, devotion, devoutness, divineness, divinity, faith, godliness, grace, humility, inviolability, piety, purity, religiosity, reverence, righteousness, sacredness, saintliness, sanctity, spirituality, unction, venerableness, virtuousness, worship; SEE CONCEPTS *368,645*

hollow [*n*] *empty or dented area*
basin, bottom, bowl, cave, cavern, cavity, chamber, channel, cleft, concavity, crater, cup, dale, den, dent, depression, dimple, dip, dish, excavation, groove, gulf, hole, indentation, notch, pit, pocket, sag, scoop, sinkage, sinkhole, socket, trough, vacuity, valley, void; SEE CONCEPTS *740,754*

hollow [*adj1*] *empty, hollowed out*
alveolate, arched, carved out, cavernous, cleft, concave, cupped, cup-shaped, curved, deep-set, depressed, dimpled, excavated, incurved, indented, infundibular, notched, not solid, pitted, striated, sunken, troughlike, unfilled, vacant, vaulted, void; SEE CONCEPTS *483,490*

hollow [*adj2*] *deep, resonant in sound*
cavernous, clangorous, dull, echoing, flat, ghostly, low, muffled, mute, muted, resounding, reverberant, ringing, roaring, rumbling, sepulchral, sounding, thunderous, toneless, vibrant, vibrating; SEE CONCEPT *594*

hollow [*adj3*] *meaningless*
empty, fruitless, futile, idle, nugatory, otiose, pointless, specious, unavailing, useless, vain, worthless; SEE CONCEPT *560*

hollow [*adj4*] *false, artificial*
cynical, deceitful, faithless, flimsy, hypocritical, insincere, treacherous, unsound, weak; SEE CONCEPT *267*

hollow [*v*] *empty out; make concave*
channel, chase, corrugate, dent, dig, dish, ditch, excavate, furrow, gorge, groove, indent, notch, pit, rabbet, remove, rut, scoop, shovel, trench; SEE CONCEPTS *178,211*

holy [*adj*] *religious, sacred*
angelic, believing, blessed, chaste, clean, consecrated, dedicated, devoted, devotional, devout, divine, faithful, faultless, glorified, god-fearing, godlike, godly, good, hallowed, humble, immaculate, innocent, just, moral, perfect, pietistic, pious, prayerful, pure, revered, reverent, righteous, sacrosanct, sainted, saintlike, saintly, sanctified, seraphic, spiritual, spotless, sublime, uncorrupt, undefiled, untainted, unworldly, upright, venerable, venerated, virtuous; SEE CONCEPTS *545,567,574*

homage [*n*] *devotion, admiration*
adoration, adulation, allegiance, awe, deference, duty, esteem, faithfulness, fealty, fidelity, genuflection, honor, kneeling, loyalty, obeisance, praise, respect, reverence, service, tribute, worship; SEE CONCEPTS *32,69*

home [*n1*] *place where human lives*
abode, address, apartment, asylum, boarding house, bungalow, cabin, castle, cave*, commorancy, condo, condominium, co-op, cottage, crash pad*, diggings*, digs*, domicile, dormitory, dump*, dwelling, farm, fireside*, flat, habitation, hangout*, haunt, hearth, hideout, hole in the wall*, home plate*, homestead, hospital, house, hut, joint*, living quarters, manor, mansion, nest*, orphanage, pad*, palace, parking place*, place, residence, resort, roof*, rooming house, roost*, shanty, shelter,

trailer, turf, villa, where the hat is*; SEE CONCEPT *516*

home [*n2*] *birthplace, environment*
abode, camping ground*, country, element, family, farm, fatherland, fireside*, habitat, habitation, haunt, haven, hearth, hills, home ground, homeland, homestead, hometown, household, land, locality, motherland, neck of the woods*, neighborhood, range, roof, site, soil, stamping ground*, stomping ground*, territory; SEE CONCEPTS *510,515,648*

home [*adj*] *domestic*
at ease, at rest, central, down home*, familiar, family, homely, homey, household, inland, in one's element*, internal, in the bosom*, local, national, native; SEE CONCEPT *536*

homeless [*adj*] *displaced*
abandoned, banished, deported, derelict, desolate, destitute, disinherited, displaced, dispossessed, down-and-out*, estranged, exiled, forlorn, forsaken, friendless, houseless, itinerant, outcast, refugee, uncared-for, unhoused, unsettled, unwelcome, vagabond, vagrant, wandering, without a roof*; SEE CONCEPT *555*

homely [*adj1*] *ordinary, comfortable*
comfy, cozy, domestic, everyday, familiar, friendly, homelike, homespun, homey, inelaborate, informal, modest, natural, plain, simple, snug, unaffected, unassuming, unostentatious, unpretentious, welcoming; SEE CONCEPTS *579,589*

homely [*adj2*] *unattractive*
animal, disgusting, plain, ugly, unaesthetic, unalluring, uncomely, unhandsome, unpretty; SEE CONCEPT *579*

homicide [*n*] *killing*
assassination, big chill*, bloodshed, bump-off*, butchery, carnage, crime, death, erase*, foul play, hit, manslaughter, murder, offing, ride, rubout*, slaying; SEE CONCEPT *252*

homogenous [*adj*] *similar, comparable*
akin, alike, analogous, cognate, consistent, homologous, identical, kindred, like, uniform, unvarying; SEE CONCEPTS *487,573*

homosexual [*adj*] *sexually attracted to the same sex*
gay, homoerotic, homophile, lesbian; SEE CONCEPT *372*

honest [*adj*] *truthful, candid*
aboveboard, authentic, bona fide*, conscientious, decent, direct, equitable, ethical, fair, fair and square*, forthright, frank, genuine, high-minded*, honorable, impartial, ingenuous, just, law-abiding*, lay it on the line*, like it is*, no lie*, on the level*, on the up and up*, open, outright, plain, proper, real, reliable, reputable, scrupulous, sincere, straight, straightforward, true, true blue*, trustworthy, trusty, truthful, undisguised, unfeigned, upfront*, upright, veracious, virtuous, what you see is what you get*; SEE CONCEPTS *267,545*

honesty [*n*] *truthfulness, candidness*
bluntness, candor, confidence, conscientiousness, equity, evenhandedness, fairness, faithfulness, fidelity, frankness, genuineness, goodness, honor, impeccability, incorruptibility, integrity, justness, loyalty, morality, openness, outspokenness, plainness, principle, probity, rectitude, reputability, responsibility, right, scrupulousness, self-respect, sincerity, soundness, straightforwardness, straightness, trustiness, trustworthiness, truthfulness, uprightness, veracity, virtue; SEE CONCEPTS *633,645*

honor [*n1*] *respect*
account, adoration, adulation, aggrandizement, apotheosis, approbation, attention, canonization, celebration, confidence, consideration, credit, deference, deification, dignity, distinction, elevation, esteem, exaltation, faith, fame, fealty, glorification, glory, greatness, high standing, homage, immortalization, laud, laurel, lionization, notice, obeisance, popularity, praise, prestige, rank, recognition, renown, reputation, repute, reverence, tribute, trust, veneration, worship, wreath; SEE CONCEPTS *668,689*

honor [*n2*] *integrity*
character, chastity, courage, decency, fairness, goodness, honestness, honesty, incorruption, incorruptness, innocence, modesty, morality, morals, principles, probity, purity, rectitude, righteousness, trustworthiness, truthfulness, uprightness, virginity, virtue; SEE CONCEPTS *411,645*

honor [*n3*] *praise, award*
acclaim, accolade, adoration, badge, bays, commendation, compliment, credit, decoration, deference, distinction, favor, homage, kudos, laurels, pleasure, privilege, recognition, regard, respect, reverence, source of pride, tribute, veneration; SEE CONCEPTS *278,337,689*

honor [*v*] *recognize, treat with respect*
acclaim, admire, adore, aggrandize, appreciate, be faithful, be true, celebrate, commemorate, commend, compliment, decorate, dignify, distinguish, ennoble, erect, esteem, exalt, give glad hand*, give key to city*, glorify, hallow, keep, laud, lionize, live up to, look up to, magnify, observe, praise, prize, respect, revere, roll out red carpet*, sanctify, sublime, uprear, value, venerate, worship; SEE CONCEPTS *10,633*

hook [*n*] *curved fastener*
angle, catch, clasp, crook, curve, grapnel, grapple, hasp, holder, link, lock, peg; SEE CONCEPTS *260,498*

hook [*v*] *grab, catch*
angle, bag, clasp, crook, curve, enmesh, ensnare, entrap, fasten, fix, hasp, lasso, net, pin, secure, snare, trap; SEE CONCEPT *190*

hop [*n/v*] *jump on one leg*
bounce, bound, caper, dance, hurdle, leap, lop, lope, skip, skitter, spring, step, trip, vault; SEE CONCEPT *194*

hope [n] *longing; dream*
achievement, ambition, anticipation, aspiration, assumption, belief, bright side*, buoyancy, castles in air*, concern, confidence, daydream, dependence, desire, dream, endurance, expectancy, expectation, faith, fancy, fool's paradise*, fortune, gain, goal, greedy glutton*, hopefulness, light at end of tunnel*, optimism, pipe dream*, promise, promised land*, prospect, reliance, reverie, reward, rosiness, sanguineness, security, stock, thing with feathers*, Utopia, wish; SEE CONCEPTS *20,410,709*

hope [v] *long for, dream about*
anticipate, aspire, assume, await, believe, be sure of, cherish, contemplate, count on, deem likely, depend on, desire, expect, feel confident, foresee, hang in*, have faith, hold, keep fingers crossed*, knock on wood*, look at sunny side*, look forward to, pray, presume, promise oneself, rely, suppose, surmise, suspect, sweat*, sweat it*, sweat it out*, take heart*, think to, trust, watch for, wish; SEE CONCEPT *20*

hopeful [adj1] *optimistic, expectant*
anticipating, anticipative, assured, at ease, blithe, buoyant, calm, cheerful, comfortable, confident, content, eager, elated, emboldened, enthusiastic, expecting, faithful, forward-looking*, high, hoping, inspirited, keeping the faith*, lighthearted, looking forward to, reassured, rose-colored*, rosy*, sanguine, satisfied, serene, trustful, trusting, unflagging, upbeat; SEE CONCEPT *403*

hopeful [adj2] *promising, auspicious*
advantageous, arousing, beneficial, bright, cheerful, cheering, conducive, convenient, elating, encouraging, enlivening, exciting, expeditious, fair, favorable, fine, fit, flattering, fortifying, fortunate, golden, good, gracious, halcyon, heartening, helpful, inspiring, inspiriting, likely, lucky, opportune, pleasant, pleasing, probable, promiseful, propitious, providential, reasonable, reassuring, roseate, rosy*, rousing, stirring, suitable, sunny, timely, uplifting, well-timed; SEE CONCEPT *548*

hopeless [adj] *futile, pessimistic*
bad, beyond recall, cynical, dejected, demoralized, despairing, desperate, despondent, disconsolate, discouraging, downhearted, fatal, forlorn, gone*, goner*, helpless, ill-fated, impossible, impracticable, incurable, in despair, irredeemable, irreparable, irreversible, irrevocable, lost, menacing, no-win, past hope, pointless, sad, shot down*, sinister, sunk, threatening, tragic, unachievable, unavailing, unfortunate, unmitigable, up creek*, useless, vain, woebegone, worsening; SEE CONCEPTS *529,548*

horde [n] *uncontrolled throng, pack*
band, crew, crowd, drove, everybody, gang, gathering, host, jam, mob, multitude, press, push, squash, swarm, troop, turnout, wall-to-wall*; SEE CONCEPTS *397,417*

horizon [n] *skyline, extent*
border, boundary, compass, field of vision, ken, limit, perspective, prospect, purview, range, reach, realm, scope, sphere, stretch, vista; SEE CONCEPTS *484,509,529*

horizontal [adj] *lying flat*
accumbent, aligned, even, flush, level, parallel, plane, recumbent, regular, smooth, straight, uniform; SEE CONCEPTS *581,583*

horrible/horrendous/horrid [adj] *repulsive, very unpleasant*
abhorrent, abominable, appalling, awful, beastly, cruel, detestable, disagreeable, disgusting, dreadful, eerie, execrable, fearful, frightful, ghastly, grim, grisly, gross*, gruesome, heinous, hideous, loathsome, lousy, lurid, mean, nasty, obnoxious, offensive, repellent, revolting, scandalous, scary, shameful, shocking, terrible, terrifying, ungodly, unholy, unkind; SEE CONCEPTS *529,537*

horrify [v] *scare*
affright, alarm, appall, chill off*, consternate, daunt, disgust, dismay, frighten, intimidate, outrage, petrify, scare to death*, shake, shock, sicken, terrify, terrorize; SEE CONCEPTS *7,14,19*

horror [n] *fear, revulsion*
abhorrence, abomination, alarm, antipathy, apprehension, aversion, awe, chiller, consternation, detestation, disgust, dislike, dismay, dread, fright, hate, hatred, loathing, monstrosity, panic, repugnance, terror, trepidation; SEE CONCEPTS *27,29,532,690*

hospitable [adj] *sociable, accommodating*
accessible, amenable, amicable, bountiful, charitable, companionable, convivial, cooperative, cordial, courteous, friendly, generous, genial, gracious, gregarious, kind, liberal, magnanimous, neighborly, obliging, open, open-minded, philanthropic, receptive, red-carpet treatment*, responsive, tolerant, welcoming; SEE CONCEPTS *542,555*

hospital [n] *place where ill, injured are treated*
clinic, emergency room, health service, hospice, infirmary, institution, nursing home, rest home, sanatorium, sanitarium, sick bay*, surgery, ward; SEE CONCEPTS *312,439,449*

hospitality [n] *neighborliness*
accommodation, affability, amiability, cheer, companionship, comradeship, consideration, conviviality, cordiality, entertainment, friendliness, generosity, geniality, good cheer, good fellowship, heartiness, hospitableness, obligingness, reception, sociability, warmth, welcome; SEE CONCEPTS *388,657*

host/hostess [n1] *person who entertains, performs*
anchor man/woman, emcee, entertainer, innkeeper, keeper, landlord/lady, man/woman of the house, manager, master, master of ceremonies, mistress/moderator, owner, presenter, proprietor, toastmaster; SEE CONCEPT *352*

host [n2] *large group*
army, array, cloud, crowd, crush, drove, flock, gathering, horde, legion, multitude, myriad, rout, score, swarm, throng; SEE CONCEPTS *417,432*

host [v] *entertain, accommodate*
do the honors*, introduce, pick up the check*, present, receive, spread oneself*, throw a party, treat, wine and dine*; SEE CONCEPTS *292,384*

hostage [n] *person held captive until captor's demand is met*
captive, earnest, guaranty, pawn, pledge, prisoner, sacrificial lamb*, scapegoat*, security, surety, token, victim; SEE CONCEPTS *359,423*

hostile [adj] *antagonistic, mean*
adverse, alien, allergic, anti*, argumentative, bellicose, belligerent, bitter, catty*, chill*, cold*, competitive, contentious, contrary, disapproving, dour, hateful, ill-disposed, inhospitable, inimical, malevolent, malicious, malignant, militant, nasty, opposed, opposite, oppugnant, ornery*, pugnacious, rancorous, scrappy*, sour*, spiteful, surly, unfavorable, unfriendly, unkind, unpropitious, unsociable, unsympathetic, unwelcoming, viperous, virulent, vitriolic, warlike; SEE CONCEPTS *401,542*

hostility [n] *antagonism, meanness*
abhorrence, aggression, animosity, animus, antipathy, aversion, bad blood*, bellicosity, belligerence, bitterness, detestation, disaffection, enmity, estrangement, grudge, hatred, ill will, inimicality, malevolence, malice, opposition, rancor, resentment, spite, spleen, unfriendliness, venom, virulence, war, warpath; SEE CONCEPTS *633,657*

hot [adj1] *very high in temperature*
baking, blazing, blistering, boiling, broiling, burning, calescent, close, decalescent, febrile, fevered, feverish, feverous, fiery, flaming, heated, humid, igneous, incandescent, like an oven*, on fire, ovenlike, parching, piping, recalescent, red*, roasting, scalding, scorching, searing, sizzling, smoking, steaming, stuffy, sultry, summery, sweltering, sweltry, thermogenic, torrid, tropic, tropical, very warm, warm, white*; SEE CONCEPT *605*

hot [adj2] *spicy to taste*
acrid, biting, peppery, piquant, pungent, racy, sharp, spicy, zestful; SEE CONCEPT *613*

hot [adj3] *passionate, vehement*
angry, animated, ardent, aroused, distracted, eager, enthusiastic, excited, fervent, fervid, fierce, fiery, furious, ill-tempered, impassioned, impetuous, indignant, inflamed, intense, irascible, lustful, raging, stormy, temperamental, touchy, violent; SEE CONCEPTS *401,403*

hot [adj4] *new, in vogue*
approved, cool*, dandy, favored, fresh, glorious, groovy*, in, in demand, just out*, keen, latest*, marvelous, neat*, nifty*, peachy*, popular, recent, sought-after, super, trendy, up-to-the-minute*; SEE CONCEPT *589*

hot [adj5] *sexually excited*
aroused, carnal, concupiscent, erotic, lascivious, lewd, libidinous, lustful, passionate, prurient, salacious, sensual; SEE CONCEPTS *372,555*

hotel [n] *place where one pays for accommodation*
auberge, boarding house, caravansary, dump*, fleabag*, flophouse*, hospice, hostel, hostelry, house, inn, lodging, motel, motor inn, public house, resort, roadhouse, rooming house, spa, tavern; SEE CONCEPTS *439,449,516*

hound [n] *dog*
afghan, airedale, akita, basset, beagle, bowwow*, canine, dachshund, man's best friend*, mongrel, mutt, pointer, pooch, poodle, retriever; SEE CONCEPTS *394,400*

hound [v] *chase, badger*
annoy, bait, be at, beat the bushes*, be on one's back*, be on one's case*, be on one's tail*, birddog*, bother, bug, chivy, curdle, dog*, drive, give chase, goad, harass, harry, hassle, heckle, hector, hunt, hunt down, impel, leave no stone unturned*, look all over hell*, persecute, pester, prod, provoke, pursue, rag*, rag on*, ride, scout, scratch, scratch around, search high heaven*, tail, take out after*, track down, turn inside out, turn upside down, yap at*; SEE CONCEPTS *7,19,207*

house [n1] *human habitat*
abode, apartment, box*, building, bullpen, castle, cave*, commorancy, condo, condominium, co-op, coop, crash pad*, crib*, cubbyhole*, den, diggings*, digs*, domicile, dump*, dwelling, edifice, flat, flophouse*, habitation, hole in the wall*, home, home plate*, homestead, joint, kennel, layout, lean-to*, mansion, pad, pied-à-terre, pigpen*, pigsty*, rack*, residence, residency, roof, roost*, setup, shack, shanty, turf*; SEE CONCEPTS *439,516*

house [n2] *family, ancestry*
clan, dynasty, family tree, folk, folks, household, kin, kindred, line, lineage, ménage, race, stock, tradition, tribe; SEE CONCEPT *296*

house [n3] *business establishment*
business, company, concern, corporation, firm, organization, outfit, partnership; SEE CONCEPT *325*

house [n4] *government body, sometimes elected, responsible for laws*
commons, congress, council, legislative body, legislature, parliament; SEE CONCEPT *299*

household [n] *domestic establishment*
family, family unit, folks, home, house, ménage; SEE CONCEPTS *296,516*

household [adj] *domestic*
domiciliary, everyday, family, home, homely, homey, ordinary, plain; SEE CONCEPT *536*

housework [n] *cleaning, maintaining a home*
administration, bed-making, cooking, domestic art, domestic science, dusting, home economics, home-making, housecraft, housekeeping, housewifery, husbandry, ironing, laundering, management, mopping, sewing, stewardship, sweeping, washing; SEE CONCEPTS *165,170,202*

housing [n] *place of accommodation*
construction, digs*, dwelling, habitation, home, house, lodgment, quarter, quarterage, residence, roof,

shelter, sheltering, stopping place; SEE CONCEPTS *388,516*

hovel [n] *tiny unkempt house*
burrow, cabin, cottage, den, dump*, hole*, hut, hutch, lean-to, pigpen*, pigsty*, rathole*, rattrap*, shack, shanty, shed, stall, sty*; SEE CONCEPT *516*

hover [v] *hang, float over*
be suspended, brood over, dance, drift, flicker, flit, flitter, flutter, fly, hang about, linger, poise, wait nearby, waver; SEE CONCEPT *154*

how [adv] *in what way or manner*
according to what, after what precedent, by means of, by virtue of what, by what means, by what method, by whose help, from what source, through what agency, through what medium, to what degree, whence, whereby, wherewith; SEE CONCEPT *544*

however [adv] *still, nevertheless*
after all, all the same, anyhow, be that as it may, but, despite, for all that, howbeit, in spite of, nonetheless, notwithstanding, on the other hand, per contra, though, withal, without regard to, yet; SEE CONCEPT *544*

howl [n/v] *long, painful cry*
bark, bawl, bay, bellow, blubber, clamor, groan, growl, hoot, keen, lament, moan, outcry, quest, roar, scream, shout, shriek, ululate, wail, weep, whimper, whine, yell, yelp, yip, yowl; SEE CONCEPTS *64,77,595*

hub [n] *center, focal point*
core, focus, heart, middle, nerve center*, pivot, polestar, seat; SEE CONCEPT *826*

hubbub [n] *commotion, disorder*
babel, bedlam, brouhaha*, clamor, confusion, din, disturbance, fuss, hassle, hell broke loose*, hue and cry*, hullabaloo*, hurly-burly*, jangle, noise, pandemonium, racket, riot, rowdydow*, ruckus, ruction, rumpus, to-do*, tumult, turmoil, uproar, whirl; SEE CONCEPTS *230,384,388*

huddle [n] *assemblage, crowd, often disorganized*
bunch, chaos, cluster, clutter, confab*, conference, confusion, disarray, discussion, disorder, gathering, group, heap, jumble, mass, meeting, mess*, muddle; SEE CONCEPTS *230,260,417,432*

huddle [v] *meet, discuss*
bunch, cluster, confer, consult, converge, crouch, crowd, cuddle, curl up, draw together, flock, gather, herd, hug, hunch up*, mass, nestle, parley, powwow*, press, press close, snuggle, throng; SEE CONCEPTS *56,114,154*

hue [n] *color, shade*
aspect, cast, chroma, complexion, dye, tincture, tinge, tint, tone, value; SEE CONCEPT *622*

huff [n] *bad mood*
anger, annoyance, dudgeon, miff, offense, passion, perturbation, pet*, pique, rage, snit*, stew*, temper, tiff, umbrage; SEE CONCEPT *410*

huff [v] *sigh, breathe out forcefully*
blow, expire, gasp, heave, pant, puff; SEE CONCEPT *163*

huffy [adj] *angry, in a bad mood*
angered, angry, annoyed, crabbed, crabby, cross, crotchety, crusty, curt, disgruntled, exasperated, fractious, grumpy, huffish, hurt, insulted, irked, irritable, miffed, moody, moping, nettled, offended, peeved, peevish, pettish, petulant, piqued, provoked, put out*, querulous, resentful, riled, short, snappish, snappy, stewed, sulky, sullen, surly, testy, touchy, vexed, waspish; SEE CONCEPTS *401,403*

hug [n] *embrace*
affection, bear hug*, bunny hug*, caress, clasp, clinch, lock, squeeze, tight grip; SEE CONCEPTS *190,375*

hug [v] *hold close, cling to*
bear hug, be near to, cherish, clasp, clinch, cradle, cuddle, embrace, enbosom, enfold, envelop, fold in arms, follow closely, grasp, hold onto, keep close, lie close, lock, love, nestle, nurse, press, receive, retain, seize, squeeze, stay near, take in one's arms, welcome; SEE CONCEPTS *190,375*

huge [adj] *extremely large*
behemothic, bulky, colossal, cyclopean, elephantine, enormous, extensive, gargantuan, giant, gigantic, great, gross*, humongous, immeasurable, immense, jumbo, king-size, leviathan, lusty, magnificent, mammoth, massive, mighty, mondo*, monster*, monstrous*, monumental, mountainous, outsize, oversize, planetary, prodigious, stupendous, titanic*, towering, tremendous, vast, walloping, whopping*; SEE CONCEPTS *771,773*

hulk [n] *large piece, lump; remains*
blob, body, bulk, chunk, clod, clump, frame, hull, hunk, mass, ruins, shambles, shell, shipwreck, skeleton, wreck; SEE CONCEPT *829*

hull [n] *skeleton, body*
bark, case, casing, cast, covering, frame, framework, husk, mold, peel, peeling, pod, rind, shell, shuck, skin, structure; SEE CONCEPTS *484,829*

hum [v] *buzz, vibrate*
bombilate, bombinate, bum, bumble, croon, drone, moan, mumble, murmur, purr, rustle, sing, sing low, sound, strum, throb, thrum, trill, warble, whir, whisper, zoom; SEE CONCEPTS *65,77*

human [n] *person; animate being who speaks*
being, biped, body, character, child, creature, homo sapien, human being, individual, life, man/woman, mortal, naked ape*, person, personage, soul, wight; SEE CONCEPT *417*

human [adj] *characteristic of people*
animal, anthropoid, anthropological, anthropomorphic, biped, bipedal, civilized, creatural, ethnologic, ethological, fallible, fleshly, forgivable, hominal, homonid, homonine, humanistic, individual, manmade, mortal, personal, vulnerable; SEE CONCEPTS *406,549*

humane [adj] *kind, compassionate*
accommodating, altruistic, amiable, approachable, benevolent, benign, benignant, broad-minded, charitable, clement, considerate, cordial, democratic, for-

bearing, forgiving, friendly, generous, genial, gentle, good, good-natured, gracious, helpful, human, humanitarian, indulgent, kindhearted, kindly, lenient, liberal, magnanimous, merciful, mild, natural, obliging, open-minded, philanthropic, pitying, righteous, sympathetic, tender, tenderhearted, tolerant, understanding, unselfish, warmhearted; SEE CONCEPTS *401,542*

humanitarian [*n*] *person who gives generously*
altruist, benefactor, bleeding heart*, do-gooder*, Good Samaritan*, good scout*, helper, patron, philanthropist, Robin Hood*; SEE CONCEPTS *416,423*

humanitarian [*adj*] *giving, compassionate*
altruistic, beneficent, benevolent, charitable, eleemosynary, generous, good, humane, idealistic, kindly, philanthropic, public-spirited; SEE CONCEPT *542*

humble [*adj1*] *meek, unassuming*
apprehensive, backward, bashful, biddable, blushing, content, courteous, deferential, demure, diffident, docile, fearful, gentle, hesitant, lowly, manageable, mild, modest, obliging, obsequious, ordinary, polite, quiet, reserved, respectful, retiring, reverential, sedate, self-conscious, self-effacing, servile, sheepish, shy, simple, soft-spoken, standoffish, submissive, subservient, supplicatory, tentative, timid, timorous, tractable, unambitious, unobtrusive, unostentatious, unpretentious, withdrawn; SEE CONCEPTS *401,404*

humble [*adj2*] *poor, inferior*
base, beggarly, common, commonplace, contemptible, humdrum, ignoble, inglorious, insignificant, little, low, low-born, lowly, low-ranking, meager, mean, measly, menial, miserable, modest, obscure, ordinary, paltry, petty, pitiful, plebeian, proletarian, puny, rough, scrubby, seemly, servile, severe, shabby, simple, small, sordid, trivial, unassuming, uncouth, underprivileged, undistinguished, unfit, unimportant, unpretentious, unrefined, vulgar, wretched; SEE CONCEPTS *334,549,589*

humble [*v*] *shame, put down*
abase, abash, bemean, break, bring down*, cast down, chagrin, chasten, confound, confuse, crush*, cut to the quick*, debase, deflate, degrade, demean, demote, deny, discomfit, discredit, disgrace, embarrass, hide, humiliate, lower*, make eat dirt*, make one feel small*, mortify, overcome, pop one's balloon*, pull down*, put away*, put one away*, put to shame, reduce, silence, sink, snub, squash*, squelch, strike dumb, subdue, take down*, take down a peg*, upset; SEE CONCEPTS *14,16,44,52*

humdrum [*adj*] *boring, uneventful*
arid, banausic, blah, bromidic, common, commonplace, dim, dime a dozen*, drab, dreary, dull, everyday, garden-variety*, insipid, lifeless, monotone, monotonous, mundane, ordinary, pedestrian, plodding, prosy, repetitious, routine, tedious, tiresome, toneless, treadmill, uninteresting, unvaried, vanilla*, wearisome, white-bread*; SEE CONCEPT *548*

humid [*adj*] *very damp, referring to weather*
boiling, clammy, close, dank, irriguous, moist, mucky, muggy, oppressive, sodden, soggy, steamy,

sticky, stifling, stuffy, sultry, sweaty, sweltering, watery, wet; SEE CONCEPTS *525,603*

humidity [*n*] *very damp weather*
clamminess, damp, dampness, dankness, dew, dewiness, evaporation, fogginess, heaviness, humectation, humidness, moistness, moisture, mugginess, oppressiveness, sogginess, steam, steaminess, stickiness, sultriness, sweatiness, swelter, thickness, vaporization, wet, wetness; SEE CONCEPTS *524,607*

humiliate [*v*] *embarrass, put down*
abase, abash, base, bemean, blister, break, bring down*, bring low*, cast down, chagrin, chasten, confound, confuse, conquer, crush*, cut down to size*, debase, degrade, demean, denigrate, deny, depress, discomfit, discountenance, disgrace, dishonor, downplay, humble, lower, make a fool of*, make ashamed, mortify, pan, play down, put out of countenance*, put to shame, rip*, run down*, shame, shoot down*, slam*, smear, snub, squash*, subdue, take down*, take down a peg*, tear down*, vanquish, wither; SEE CONCEPTS *14,44,52*

humiliation [*n*] *embarrassment*
abasement, affront, chagrin, comedown*, comeuppance, condescension, confusion, degradation, discomfiture, disgrace, dishonor, humbling, ignominy, indignity, loss of face*, mental pain, mortification, put-down, resignation, self-abasement, shame, submission, submissiveness, touché*; SEE CONCEPTS *388,410*

humility [*n*] *humbleness, modesty*
abasement, bashfulness, demureness, diffidence, docility, fawning, inferiority complex, lack of pride, lowliness, meekness, mortification, nonresistance, obedience, obsequiousness, passiveness, reserve, resignation, self-abasement, self-abnegation, servility, sheepishness, shyness, subjection, submissiveness, subservience, timidity, timorousness, unobtrusiveness, unpretentiousness; SEE CONCEPTS *633,657*

humor [*n1*] *comedy, funniness*
amusement, badinage, banter, buffoonery, clowning, comicality, comicalness, drollery, facetiousness, farce, flippancy, fun, funniness, gag, gaiety, happiness, high spirits, jest, jesting, jocoseness, jocularity, joke, joking, joyfulness, kidding, levity, lightness, playfulness, pleasantry, raillery, tomfoolery, whimsy, wisecrack, wit, witticism, wittiness; SEE CONCEPT *293*

humor [*n2*] *mood, temperament*
bee, bent, bias, caprice, character, complexion, conceit, disposition, fancy, frame of mind, individualism, individuality, makeup, mind, nature, notion, personality, propensity, quirk, spirits, strain, temper, tone, vagary, vein, whim; SEE CONCEPTS *9,410,411*

humorous [*adj*] *funny, comical*
amusing, camp*, campy*, comic, droll, entertaining, facetious, farcical, hilarious, jocose, jocular, jokey, joshing, laughable, ludicrous, merry, playful, pleasant, priceless, ribald, screaming*, side-splitting*, too funny for words*, waggish, whimsical, witty; SEE CONCEPTS *267,529*

hump [n] *swelling, projection*
bulge, bump, convexedness, convexity, dune, elevation, eminence, excrescence, gibbosity, hill, hummock, humpback, hunch, hunchback, knap, knob, knurl, kyphosis, mound, prominence, protrusion, protuberance, ridge, swell, tumescence; SEE CONCEPTS *471,513*

hunch [n] *feeling, idea*
anticipation, apprehension, auguration, augury, boding, clue, expectation, feeling in one's bones*, foreboding, forecast, foreknowledge, forewarning, forewisdom, funny feeling*, glimmer, hint, impression, inkling, instinct, intuition, misgiving, notion, omination, portent, preapprehension, precognition, preconceived notion, premonition, prenotation, prenotice, presage, presagement, prescience, presentiment, qualm, suspicion, thought; SEE CONCEPT *689*

hunch [v] *cower, crouch*
arch, bend, bow, curve, draw in, draw together, huddle, hump, lean, scrooch down, squat, stoop, tense; SEE CONCEPT *154*

hunger [n] *appetite for food, other desire*
ache, appetence, appetency, appetition, a stomach for*, big eyes*, bottomless pit*, craving, desire, emptiness, esurience, eyes for*, famine, famishment, gluttony, greed, greediness, hungriness, longing, lust, mania, munchies*, ravenousness, starvation, sweet tooth*, vacancy, void, voracity, want, yearning, yen; SEE CONCEPTS *20,709*

hungry [adj] *starving; desirous*
athirst, avid, carnivorous, could eat a horse*, covetous, craving, eager, edacious, empty, esurient, famished, famishing, flying light*, got the munchies*, greedy, hankering, hoggish, hollow, hungered, insatiate, keen, omnivorous, on empty stomach*, piggish*, rapacious, ravenous, starved, starving, unfilled, unsatisfied, voracious, yearning; SEE CONCEPTS *20,406*

hunk [n] *glob of solid material*
a lot*, batch, bit, block, bulk, bunch, chunk, clod, gob*, large piece, loads*, loaf, lump, mass, morsel, nugget, piece, pile, portion, quantity, slab, slice, wad, wedge; SEE CONCEPTS *470,471*

hunt [n] *search, chase*
coursing, exploration, field sport, following, frisking, game, hounding, hunting, inquest, inquiry, inquisition, interrogation, investigation, look-see*, meddling, probe, prosecution, prying, pursuance, pursuing, pursuit, quest, race, raid, reconnaissance, research, rummage, scrutiny, seeking, sifting, snooping, sporting, steeplechase, study, tracing, trailing; SEE CONCEPTS *207,216*

hunt [v1] *chase for killing*
beat the bushes*, bird-dog*, capture, course, dog, drag, drive, fish, follow, give chase, grouse, gun*, gun for*, hawk, heel, hound, kill, look for, poach, press, pursue, ride, run, scent, scratch, scratch around, seek, shadow, shoot, snare, stalk, start, track, trail; SEE CONCEPTS *207,216,252,363*

hunt [v2] *look, search for*
be on the lookout*, cast about, delve, drag, examine, ferret out, fish for, forage, go after, grope, inquire, interrogate, investigate, look all over hell*, look high and low*, nose around*, probe, prowl, quest, question, ransack, rummage, run down, scour, scratch around*, search high heaven*, seek, sift, trace, trail, try to find, winnow; SEE CONCEPT *216*

hurdle [n] *barrier, obstacle*
bar, barricade, blockade, complication, difficulty, fence, hamper, handicap, hedge, hindrance, impediment, interference, mountain, obstruction, rub, snag, stumbling block, traverse, wall; SEE CONCEPTS *470,674*

hurdle [v] *jump over obstacle*
bounce, bound, clear, conquer, down, hop, jump, jump across, leap over, lick, lop, master, negotiate, over, overcome, saltate, scale, spring, surmount, vault; SEE CONCEPT *194*

hurl [v] *throw forcefully*
bung, cast, chuck, chunk, fire, fling, gun, heave, launch, let fly, lob, peg, pitch, project, propel, send, sling, toss; SEE CONCEPT *222*

hurricane [n] *violent windstorm*
blow, cyclone, gale, line storm, monsoon, storm, tempest, tornado, tropical cyclone, tropical storm, twister, typhoon, whirlwind; SEE CONCEPTS *524,526*

hurried [adj] *quick, rushed*
abrupt, breakneck, brief, cursory, fast, hasty, headlong, hectic, impetuous, perfunctory, precipitant, precipitate, precipitous, rushing, short, slapdash, speedy, subitaneous, sudden, superficial, swift; SEE CONCEPTS *548,588,799*

hurry [n] *speed in action, motion*
bustle, celerity, commotion, dash, dispatch, drive, expedition, expeditiousness, flurry, haste, precipitance, precipitateness, precipitation, promptitude, push, quickness, rush, rustle, scurry, speediness, swiftness, urgency; SEE CONCEPTS *657,748,755*

hurry [v] *act, move speedily*
accelerate, barrel, beeline*, be quick, bestir, breeze, bullet, burst, bustle, dash, dig in, drive, expedite, fleet, flit, fly, get a move on*, goad, go like lightning*, haste, hasten, hurry up, hustle, jog, lose no time, make haste, make short work of*, make time*, make tracks*, move, nip, push, quicken, race, rip, rocket, roll, run, rush, sally, scoot, scurry, shake a leg*, smoke, speed, speed up, spur, step on gas*, step on it*, turn on steam*, urge, whirl, whish, whisk, whiz, zip; SEE CONCEPTS *150,234*

hurt [n] *injury; damage*
ache, black and blue*, blow, boo-boo*, bruise, chop, detriment, disadvantage, disaster, discomfort, disservice, distress, down, gash, harm, ill, ill-treatment, loss, mark, mischief, misfortune, nick, ouch, outrage, pain, pang, persecution, prejudice, ruin,

scratch, sore, soreness, suffering, wound, wrong; SEE CONCEPTS *316,728*

hurt [*adj*] *physically or mentally injured*
aching, aggrieved, agonized, all torn up*, battered, bleeding, bruised, buffeted, burned, busted up*, contused, crushed, cut, damaged, disfigured, distressed, disturbed, grazed, harmed, hit, impaired, indignant, in pain, lacerated, marred, mauled, miffed, mutilated, nicked, offended, pained, piqued, put away, resentful, rueful, sad, scarred, scraped, scratched, shook, shot, sore, stricken, struck, suffering, tender, tortured, umbrageous, unhappy, warped, wounded; SEE CONCEPTS *314,403*

hurt [*v1*] *cause physical pain; experience pain*
abuse, ache, afflict, ail, belt, be sore, be tender, bite, blemish, bruise, burn, cramp, cut, cut up, damage, disable, do violence, flail, flog, harm, impair, injure, kick, lacerate, lash, maltreat, mar, maul, mess up, nip, pain, pierce, pinch, pommel, prick, pummel, punch, puncture, punish, rough up, shake up, slap, slug, smart, spank, spoil, squeeze, stab, sting, tear, throb, torment, torture, total, trouble, wax, whack, whip, wing, wound, wrack up, wring; SEE CONCEPTS *246,313*

hurt [*v2*] *cause mental pain*
abuse, afflict, aggrieve, annoy, burn, chafe, constrain, cut to the quick*, discomfit, discommode, displease, distress, excruciate, faze, give no quarter*, go for jugular*, grieve, hit where one lives*, injure, lambaste, lay a bad trip on*, lean on*, martyr, martyrize, pain, prejudice, punish, put down, put out, sadden, sting*, thumb nose at*, torment, torture, try, upset, vex, vitiate, work over*, wound, zing*; SEE CONCEPTS *7,14,19*

hurtful [*adj*] *injurious, cruel*
aching, afflictive, bad, cutting, damaging, dangerous, deadly, deleterious, destructive, detrimental, disadvantageous, distressing, evil, harmful, hurting, malicious, mean, mischievous, nasty, nocuous, noxious, ominous, pernicious, poisonous, prejudicial, spiteful, unkind, upsetting, wounding; SEE CONCEPTS *537,542*

hurtle [*v*] *plunge, charge*
bump, collide, fly, lunge, push, race, rush, rush headlong, scoot, scramble, shoot, speed, spurt, tear; SEE CONCEPT *150*

husband [*n*] *married man*
bridegroom, companion, consort, groom, helpmate, hubby, mate, monogamist, monogynist, other half, partner, roommate, spouse; SEE CONCEPTS *414,419*

husbandry [*n*] *agricultural pursuits*
agriculture, agronomy, cultivation, economy, farming, geoponics, land management, management, tillage; SEE CONCEPT *257*

hush [*n*] *quiet*
calm, lull, peace, peacefulness, quietude, silence, still, stillness, tranquility; SEE CONCEPT *65*

hush [*v*] *attempt to make quiet*
burke, choke, gag, muffle, mute, muzzle, quiet, quieten, shush*, shut up, silence, stifle, still, stop, suppress; SEE CONCEPTS *65,87*

hush-hush [*adj*] *secret*
clandestine, classified, closet, confidential, covert, dark, private, restricted, sub-rosa*, surreptitious, top-secret, undercover, under-the-table*; SEE CONCEPT *576*

hush up [*v*] *keep secret*
burke, conceal, cover, cover up, keep dark, sit on, smother, squash, stifle, suppress; SEE CONCEPT *266*

husk [*n*] *covering, case*
aril, bark, case, chaff, glume, hull, outside, pod, rind, shell, shuck, skin; SEE CONCEPTS *428,484*

husky [*adj1*] *deep, scratchy in sound*
croaking, croaky, growling, gruff, guttural, harsh, hoarse, loud, rasping, raucous, rough, throaty; SEE CONCEPT *594*

husky [*adj2*] *big, burly*
brawny, gigantic, hefty, Herculean*, mighty, muscular, powerful, rugged, sinewy, stalwart, stocky, stout, strapping, strong, sturdy, thickset, well-built; SEE CONCEPT *773*

hustle [*v*] *hurry; work hurriedly*
apply oneself, be conscientious, bulldoze*, bustle, elbow, fly, force, haste, hasten, hotfoot*, impel, jog, press, push, race, rush, shove, speed, thrust, use elbow grease*; SEE CONCEPTS *91,150*

hut [*n*] *tiny, often roughly built, house*
box*, bungalow, cabana, cabin, camp, chalet, cot, cottage, crib*, den, dugout, dump*, hovel*, hutch, lean-to, lodge, log house, pigeonhole*, rathole*, refuge, shack, shanty, shed, shelter, summer house, tepee, wigwam; SEE CONCEPT *516*

hybrid [*n*] *composite, mixture*
amalgam, bastard, combination, compound, cross, crossbreed, half-blood, half-breed, half-caste, incross, miscegenation, mongrel, mule, outcross; SEE CONCEPTS *260,394,414,429*

hygiene [*n*] *cleanliness*
healthful living, hygienics, preventive medicine, public health, regimen, salutariness, sanitation, wholesomeness; SEE CONCEPTS *316,405*

hygienic [*adj*] *clean*
aseptic, disinfected, germ-free, good, healthful, healthy, pure, salubrious, salutary, salutiferous, sanitary, sterile, uncontaminated, uninfected, wholesome; SEE CONCEPT *621*

hymn [*n*] *religious song*
aria, canticle, carol, chant, choral, chorale, descant, ditty, evensong, hosanna, laud, lay, lied, littany, ode, oratorio, paean, psalm, shout, song of praise, worship song; SEE CONCEPTS *262,595*

hype [*n*] *extensive publicity*
advertising, buildup*, plugging*, promotion; SEE CONCEPTS *292,324*

hyperbole [n] *exaggeration*
amplification, big talk*, coloring*, distortion, embellishment, embroidering, enlargement, hype*, laying it on thick*, magnification, metaphor, mountain out of molehill*, overstatement, PR*, tall talk*; SEE CONCEPT *268*

hypnotic [adj] *spellbinding, sleep-inducing*
anesthetic, anodyne, calmative, lenitive, mesmeric, mesmerizing, narcotic, opiate, sleepy, somniferous, somnolent, soothing, soporific, soporose, trance-inducing; SEE CONCEPTS *529,537*

hypnotize [v] *put in trance; spellbind*
anesthetize, bring under control, captivate, charm, drug, dull the will, entrance, fascinate, hold under a spell, induce, lull to sleep, magnetize, make drowsy, make sleepy, mesmerize, narcotize, put to sleep, soothe, stupefy, subject to suggestion; SEE CONCEPT *250*

hypocrisy [n] *deceitfulness, pretense*
affectation, bad faith*, bigotry, cant, casuistry, deceit, deception, dishonesty, display, dissembling, dissimulation, double-dealing, duplicity, false profession, falsity, fraud, glibness, imposture, insincerity, irreverence, lie, lip service*, mockery, pharisaicalness, pharisaism, phoniness, pietism, quackery, sanctimoniousness, sanctimony, speciousness, unctuousness; SEE CONCEPTS *63,633,657*

hypocrite [n] *person who pretends, is deceitful*
actor, attitudinizer, backslider*, bigot, bluffer, casuist, charlatan, cheat, con man, crook, deceiver, decoy, dissembler, dissimulator, fake, faker, four-flusher*, fraud, hook*, humbug, impostor, informer, lip server*, malingerer, masquerader, mountebank, Pharisee, phony, playactor*, poser, pretender, quack*, smoothie*, sophist, swindler, trickster, two-face*, two-timer*, wolf in sheep's clothing*; SEE CONCEPT *412*

hypocritical [adj] *deceitful, pretending*
affected, artificial, assuming, bland, canting, captious, caviling, deceptive, deluding, dissembling, double, double-dealing, duplicitous, faithless, false, feigning, fishy*, fraudulent, glib, hollow, insincere, jivey, left-handed, lying, moralistic, oily, pharisaical, phony, pietistic, pious, sanctimonious, self-righteous, smooth, smooth-spoken, smooth-tongued*, snide, specious, spurious, two-faced*, unctuous, unnatural, unreliable; SEE CONCEPTS *267,401,542*

hypothesis [n] *theory*
antecedent, apriority, assignment, assumption, attribution, axiom, basis, belief, conclusion, condition, conjecture, data, deduction, demonstration, derivation, explanation, foundation, ground, guess, inference, interpretation, layout, lemma, philosophy, plan, position, postulate, premise, presupposition, principle, proposal, proposition, rationale, reason, scheme, shot in the dark*, speculation, starting point, suggestion, supposition, surmise, system, tentative law, term, theorem, thesis; SEE CONCEPTS *661,689*

hypothetical [adj] *guessed, assumed*
academic, assumptive, casual, concocted, conditional, conjecturable, conjectural, contestable, contingent, debatable, disputable, doubtful, equivocal, imaginary, imagined, indefinite, indeterminate, postulated, presumptive, presupposed, pretending, problematic, provisory, putative, questionable, refutable, speculative, stochastic, supposed, suppositional, suppositious, suspect, theoretic, theoretical, uncertain, unconfirmed, vague; SEE CONCEPTS *529,552,582*

hysteria [n] *state of extreme upset*
agitation, delirium, excitement, feverishness, frenzy, hysterics, madness, mirth, nervousness, panic, unreason; SEE CONCEPT *410*

hysterical [adj] *very upset, excited*
agitated, berserk, beside oneself, blazing, carried away*, convulsive, crazed, crazy, delirious, distracted, distraught, emotional, fiery, frantic, frenzied, fuming, furious, impassioned, impetuous, in a fit, incensed, irrepressible, mad, maddened, nervous, neurotic, overwrought, panic-stricken, passionate, possessed, rabid, raging, rampant, raving, seething, spasmodic, tempestuous, turbulent, uncontrollable, uncontrolled, unnerved, unrestrained, uproarious, vehement, violent, wild, worked up*; SEE CONCEPTS *403,542*

I

ice [n] *frozen water*
chunk, crystal, cube ice, diamonds*, dry ice, floe, glacier, glaze, hail, hailstone, iceberg, ice cube, icicle, permafrost, sleet; SEE CONCEPTS *470,514*

icky [adj] *not pleasant*
disgusting, horrible, loathsome, nasty, noisome, offensive, repellent, revolting, sickening, vile; SEE CONCEPT *570*

icy [adj1] *frozen; slippery when frozen*
antarctic, arctic, biting, bitter, chill, chilled to the bone*, chilling, chilly, cold, freezing, frigid, frostbound, frosty, frozen over, gelid, glacial, glaring, iced, polar, raw, refrigerated, rimy, shivering, shivery, sleeted, smooth as glass*; SEE CONCEPTS *605,606*

icy [adj2] *aloof*
chill, cold, distant, emotionless, forbidding, frigid, frosty, glacial, hostile, indifferent, steely, stony, unemotional, unfriendly, unwelcoming; SEE CONCEPTS *401,404*

idea [n] *something understood, planned, or believed*
abstraction, aim, approximation, belief, brainstorm*, clue, concept, conception, conclusion, conviction, design, doctrine, end, essence, estimate, fancy, feeling, flash*, form, guess, hint, hypothesis, import, impression, inkling, intention, interpretation, intimation, judgment, meaning, notion, object, objective, opinion, pattern, perception, plan, purpose, reason, scheme, sense, significance, solution, suggestion,

suspicion, teaching, theory, thought, understanding, view, viewpoint; SEE CONCEPTS *529,660,661,689*

ideal [n] *model*
archetype, criterion, epitome, example, exemplar, goal, idol, jewel, last word*, mirror, nonesuch, nonpareil, paradigm, paragon, pattern, perfection, prototype, standard; SEE CONCEPTS *671,688*

ideal [adj1] *model, perfect*
absolute, archetypal, classic, classical, complete, consummate, excellent, exemplary, fitting, flawless, have-it-all*, indefectible, optimal, paradigmatic, pie-in-the-sky*, prototypical, quintessential, representative, Shangri-la*, supreme; SEE CONCEPTS *533,574*

ideal [adj2] *conceptual; impractical*
abstract, chimerical, dreamlike, extravagant, fanciful, fictitious, high-flown, hypothetical, imaginary, intellectual, in the clouds*, ivory-tower*, mental, mercurial, notional, out-of-reach*, quixotic, theoretical, transcendent, transcendental, unattainable, unearthly, unreal, Utopian*, visionary; SEE CONCEPTS *529,552*

idealist [n] *person who holds fancies in mind, who believes in perfection*
dreamer, enthusiast, escapist, optimist, Platonist, radical, romancer, romantic, romanticist, seer, stargazer, theorizer, transcendalist, Utopian, visionary; SEE CONCEPTS *359,416,423*

ideals [n] *moral beliefs*
ethics, goals, morals, principles, standards, values; SEE CONCEPTS *645,689*

identical [adj] *alike, equal*
carbon copy*, corresponding, dead ringer*, ditto*, double, duplicate, equivalent, exact, identic, indistinguishable, interchangeable, like, like two peas in a pod*, look-alike, matching, same, same difference*, selfsame, spitting image*, tantamount, twin, very, very same, Xerox*; SEE CONCEPTS *487,566,573*

identification [n] *labelling; means of labelling*
apperception, assimilation, badge, bracelet, cataloging, classifying, credentials, description, dog tag, establishment, ID*, identity bracelet, letter of introduction, letter of recommendation, naming, papers, passport, recognition, tag, testimony; SEE CONCEPTS *268,271*

identify [v] *recognize; label*
analyze, button down*, card, catalog, classify, describe, determinate, determine, diagnose, diagnosticate, distinguish, establish, find, make out, name, peg*, pick out, pinpoint, place, put one's finger on*, select, separate, single out*, spot, tab*, tag*; SEE CONCEPTS *38,62*

identify with [v] *put oneself in the place of another*
ally, associate, empathize, feel for*, put in same category*, put oneself in another's shoes*, relate to, respond to, see through someone's eyes*, sympathize, think of in connection*, understand; SEE CONCEPTS *15,39*

identity [n1] *person's individuality*
character, circumstances, coherence, distinctiveness, existence, identification, integrity, ipseity, name, oneness, particularity, personality, self, selfdom, selfhood, selfness, singleness, singularity, status, uniqueness; SEE CONCEPT *411*

identity [n2] *similarity, correspondence*
accord, agreement, congruence, congruity, empathy, equality, equivalence, identicalness, likeness, oneness, rapport, resemblance, sameness, selfsameness, semblance, similitude, unanimity, uniformity, unity; SEE CONCEPTS *664,670*

ideology [n] *beliefs*
articles of faith*, credo, creed, culture, dogma, ideas, outlook, philosophy, principles, system, tenets, theory, view, Weltanschauung*; SEE CONCEPTS *687,689*

idiocy [n] *utter stupidity*
asininity, cretinism, derangement, fatuity, fatuousness, foolishness, imbecility, inanity, insanity, insipidity, lunacy, madness, senselessness, tomfoolery; SEE CONCEPTS *409,410*

idiom [n] *manner of speaking, turn of phrase*
argot, colloquialism, dialect, expression, idiosyncrasy, jargon, language, lingo*, localism, locution, parlance, patois, phrase, provincialism, set phrase, street talk*, style, talk, tongue, usage, vernacular, vernacularism, word; SEE CONCEPT *275*

idiosyncrasy [n] *oddity, quirk*
affectation, bit, characteristic, distinction, eccentricity, feature, habit, mannerism, peculiarity, singularity, trait, trick; SEE CONCEPTS *411,644*

idiot [n] *very stupid person*
blockhead, bonehead*, cretin, dimwit, dork, dumb bell, dunce, fool, halfwit, ignoramus, imbecile, jerk, kook*, moron, nincompoop, ninny*, nitwit, out to lunch*, pinhead*, simpleton, stupid, tomfool, twit*; SEE CONCEPT *412*

idiotic [adj] *very stupid*
asinine, batty*, birdbrained*, crazy, daffy*, daft, dull, dumb, fatuous, foolhardy, foolish, half-witted*, harebrained*, imbecile, imbecilic, inane, insane, lunatic, moronic, senseless, silly, squirrelly*, thickwitted*, unintelligent; SEE CONCEPT *402*

idle [adj1] *not used; out of action*
abandoned, asleep, barren, closed down, dead, deserted, down, dusty, empty, gathering dust*, inactive, inert, jobless, laid-off, leisured, mothballed, motionless, on the bench*, on the shelf*, out of operation, out of work*, passive, quiet, redundant, resting, rusty, sleepy, stationary, still, uncultivated, unemployed, unoccupied, untouched, unused, vacant, void, waste, workless; SEE CONCEPTS *542,560*

idle [adj2] *lazy*
at rest, indolent, lackadaisical, resting, shiftless, slothful, sluggish, taking it easy*; SEE CONCEPTS *401,538*

idle [*adj3*] *worthless, ineffective*
abortive, bootless, empty, frivolous, fruitless, futile, groundless, hollow, insignificant, irrelevant, not serious, nugatory, of no avail*, otiose, pointless, rambling, superficial, trivial, unavailing, unhelpful, unnecessary, unproductive, unsuccessful, useless, vain; SEE CONCEPTS *267,560*

idleness [*n*] *laziness, inaction*
dawdling, dilly-dallying*, dormancy, droning, goof-off time*, hibernation, inactivity, indolence, inertia, joblessness, laze, lazing, leisure, lethargy, loafing, loitering, otiosity, own sweet time*, pottering, shiftlessness, sloth, slothfulness, slouch, slowness, sluggishness, stupor, time on one's hands*, time to burn*, time to kill*, time-wasting, torpidity, torpor, trifling, truancy, unemployment, vegetating; SEE CONCEPTS *657,677,681*

idol [*n*] *person greatly admired*
beloved, darling, dear, deity, desire, eidolon, false god, favorite, fetish, god, goddess, golden calf*, graven image, hero, icon, image, inamorata, pagan symbol, simulacrum, superstar; SEE CONCEPTS *352, 423*

idolize [*v*] *think of very highly; worship*
admire, adore, apotheosize, bow down, canonize, deify, dote on, exalt, glorify, hero-worship, look up to*, love, put on a pedestal*, revere, reverence, venerate; SEE CONCEPTS *10,32*

idyllic [*adj*] *perfect; extremely pleasant*
arcadian, bucolic, charming, comfortable, halcyon, heavenly, ideal, idealized, out-of-this-world*, pastoral, peaceful, picturesque, pleasing, rustic, unspoiled; SEE CONCEPTS *529,572*

iffy [*adj*] *uncertain*
capricious, chancy, conditional, dicey, doubtful, erratic, fluctuant, incalculable, in lap of gods*, problematic, undecided, unpredictable, unsettled, up in the air*, whimsical; SEE CONCEPT *552*

ignite [*v*] *set on fire*
burn, burst into flames, catch fire, enkindle, fire, flare up, inflame, kindle, light, put match to*, set alight, set fire to, start up, take fire, touch off; SEE CONCEPT *249*

ignoble [*adj*] *lowly, unworthy*
abject, base, baseborn, bastard*, coarse, common, contemptible, corrupt, craven, dastardly, degenerate, degraded, despicable, disgraceful, dishonorable, heinous, humble, infamous, inferior, lewd, low, mean, menial, modest, ordinary, peasant, petty, plain, plebeian, poor, rotten, scurvy, servile, shabby, shameful, simple, sordid, unwashed, vile, vulgar, wicked, wretched, wrong; SEE CONCEPTS *542,545,549*

ignorance [*n*] *unintelligence, inexperience*
benightedness, bewilderment, blindness, callowness, crudeness, darkness, denseness, disregard, dumbness, empty-headedness*, fog*, half-knowledge, illiteracy, incapacity, incomprehension, innocence, inscience, insensitivity, lack of education, mental in-

capacity, naiveté, nescience, oblivion, obtuseness, philistinism, rawness, sciolism, shallowness, simplicity, unawareness, unconsciousness, uncouthness, unenlightenment, unfamiliarity, unscholarliness, vagueness; SEE CONCEPTS *409,678*

ignorant [*adj*] *unaware, unknowing*
apprenticed, benighted, birdbrained*, blind to*, cretinous, dense, green*, illiterate, imbecilic, inexperienced, innocent, insensible, in the dark*, mindless, misinformed, moronic, naive, nescient, oblivious, obtuse, shallow, thick, unconscious, unconversant, uncultivated, uncultured, uneducated, unenlightened, uninformed, uninitiated, unintellectual, unknowledgeable, unlearned, unlettered, unmindful, unread, unschooled, unsuspecting, untaught, untrained, unwitting, witless; SEE CONCEPTS *402,542*

ignore [*v*] *disregard on purpose*
avoid, be oblivious to, blink, brush off*, bury head in sand*, cold-shoulder*, discount, disdain, evade, fail, forget, let it go*, neglect, omit, overlook, overpass, pass over, pay no attention to, pay no mind*, pooh-pooh*, reject, scorn, shut eyes to*, slight, take no notice, tune out*, turn back on*, turn blind eye*, turn deaf ear; SEE CONCEPT *30*

ill [*n*] *misfortune*
abuse, affection, affliction, ailment, badness, complaint, condition, cruelty, damage, depravity, destruction, disease, disorder, evil, harm, hurt, illness, indisposition, infirmity, injury, insult, malady, malaise, malice, mischief, misery, pain, sickness, suffering, syndrome, trial, tribulation, trouble, unpleasantness, wickedness, woe, wrong; SEE CONCEPTS *316,674,675*

ill [*adj1*] *sick*
afflicted, ailing, a wreck*, below par*, bummed*, diseased, down, down with, feeling awful, feeling rotten, feeling terrible, got the bug*, indisposed, infirm, laid low*, off one's feet*, on sick list*, out of sorts*, peaked, poorly, queasy, rotten, run-down, running temperature, sick as dog*, under the weather*, unhealthy, unwell, woozy*; SEE CONCEPT *314*

ill [*adj2*] *bad, evil*
acrimonious, adverse, antagonistic, cantankerous, cross, damaging, deleterious, detrimental, disrespectful, disturbing, foreboding, foul, harmful, harsh, hateful, hostile, hurtful, ill-mannered, impertinent, inauspicious, inimical, iniquitous, injurious, malevolent, malicious, nocent, nocuous, noxious, ominous, ruinous, sinister, sullen, surly, threatening, unfavorable, unfortunate, unfriendly, ungracious, unhealthy, unkind, unlucky, unpromising, unpropitious, unwholesome, vile, wicked, wrong; SEE CONCEPTS *537,545,570*

ill-advised [*adj*] *unwise, not thought out*
brash, confused, foolhardy, foolish, half-baked*, hotheaded*, ill-considered, ill-judged, impolitic, imprudent, inappropriate, incautious, inconsiderate, indiscreet, inexpedient, injudicious, madcap*, mis-

guided, off top of one's head*, overhasty, rash, reckless, short-sighted*, thoughtless, unseemly, wrong; SEE CONCEPTS *544,548*

ill at ease [adj] uncomfortable, nervous
anxious, awkward, discomfited, disquieted, disturbed, doubtful, edgy, faltering, fidgety, hesitant, insecure, on edge*, on pins and needles*, on tenterhooks*, out of place*, restless, self-conscious, shy, suspicious, tense, uneasy, unrelaxed, unsettled, unsure; SEE CONCEPTS *401,403*

illegal [adj] against the law
actionable, banned, black-market*, bootleg*, contraband, criminal, crooked, extralegal, felonious, forbidden, heavy*, hot*, illegitimate, illicit, interdicted, irregular, lawless, not approved, not legal, outlawed, outside the law, prohibited, proscribed, prosecutable, racket, shady, smuggled, sub rosa, taboo, unauthorized, unconstitutional, under the table*, unlawful, unlicensed, unofficial, unwarrantable, unwarranted, verboten, violating, wildcat*, wrongful; SEE CONCEPTS *319,545*

illegible [adj] unreadable
cacographic, crabbed, cramped, difficult to read, faint, hard to make out*, hieroglyphic, indecipherable, indistinct, obscure, scrawled, unclear, undecipherable, unintelligible, unreadable; SEE CONCEPTS *535,576*

illegitimate [adj] not legal; born of unmarried parents
adulterine, baseborn, bastard, born out of wedlock*, contraband, fatherless, illegal, illicit, improper, invalid, love child*, misbegotten, natural, spurious, supposititious, unauthorized, unconstitutional, unfathered, unlawful, unsanctioned, wicked, wrong; SEE CONCEPTS *319,549*

ill-fated/ill-starred [adj] doomed
blighted, catastrophic, destroyed, disastrous, hapless, ill-omened, inauspicious, luckless, misfortunate, ruined, star-crossed*, unfortunate, unhappy, unlucky, untoward; SEE CONCEPTS *537,548*

illicit [adj] not legal; forbidden
adulterous, black-market*, bootleg*, clandestine, contraband, contrary to law, criminal, crooked, dirty*, felonious, furtive, guilty, heavy*, illegal, illegitimate, immoral, improper, in violation of law, lawless, left-handed*, out of line*, prohibited, racket, unauthorized, unlawful, unlicensed, wrong, wrongful; SEE CONCEPTS *319,545*

illiterate [adj] unable to read well; lacking education
benighted, catachrestic, dumb, ignorant, inerudite, know-nothing, solecistic, uncultured, uneducated, unenlightened, ungrammatical, uninstructed, unlearned, unlettered, unread, unschooled, untaught, untutored; SEE CONCEPT *402*

ill-mannered [adj] badly behaved
bad-mannered, boorish, cheap, churlish, coarse, discourteous, disrespectful, ill-behaved, ill-bred, impertinent, impolite, insolent, loud, loud-mouthed, loutish, raunchy*, raw, rough, roughneck*, rude,

tacky*, uncivil, uncouth, ungracious, unmannerly, unrefined, vulgar; SEE CONCEPT *401*

ill-natured [adj] bad-tempered
catty, churlish, crabbed, crabby, cross, crotchety, cussed*, dirty*, disagreeable, disobliging, dyspeptic, hot-tempered, ill-humored, irritable, malevolent, malicious, mean, nasty, ornery*, perverse, petulant, spiteful, sulky, sullen, surly, temperamental, tempersome, touchy, unfriendly, unkind, unpleasant; SEE CONCEPTS *401,404*

illness [n] disease; bad health
affliction, ailing, ailment, attack, breakdown, bug*, collapse, complaint, confinement, convalescence, disability, diseasedness, disorder, disturbance, dose, failing health, fit, flu, ill health, indisposition, infirmity, malady, malaise, poor health, prostration, relapse, seizure, sickness, syndrome, unhealth, virus, what's going around*; SEE CONCEPT *306*

illogical [adj] not making sense
absurd, casuistic, cockeyed*, fallacious, false, fatuous, faulty, groundless, hollow, implausible, inconclusive, incongruous, inconsequent, inconsistent, incorrect, invalid, irrational, irrelevant, mad, meaningless, not following, nutty*, off the wall*, preposterous, screwy*, self-contradictory, senseless, sophistic, sophistical, specious, spurious, unconnected, unproved, unreasonable, unscientific, unsound, unsubstantial, untenable, wacky, without basis, without foundation; SEE CONCEPTS *267,529*

ill-timed [adj] not occurring at suitable time
awkward, badly timed, improper, inappropriate, inconvenient, inept, inopportune, malapropos, mistimed, unbecoming, unbefitting, unfavorable, unseasonable, unseemly, unsuitable, untimely, unwelcome; SEE CONCEPT *548*

illuminate [v1] make light
brighten, fire, flash, floodlight, highlight, hit with a light*, ignite, illume, illumine, irradiate, kindle, light, lighten, light up, limelight*, spot, spotlight; SEE CONCEPT *624*

illuminate [v2] make clear; educate
better, clarify, clear up, construe, define, dramatize, edify, elucidate, enlighten, explain, expound, express, finish, give insight, gloss, illustrate, improve, instruct, interpret, perfect, polish, shed light on*, uplight; SEE CONCEPTS *57,285*

illumination [n1] light; making light
beam, brightening, brightness, brilliance, flame, flash, gleam, lighting, lights, radiance, ray; SEE CONCEPTS *620,624*

illumination [n2] clear understanding
awareness, clarification, edification, education, enlightenment, information, insight, inspiration, instruction, perception, revelation, teaching; SEE CONCEPTS *274,409*

illusion [n] false appearance; false belief
apparition, bubble*, chimera, confusion, daydream, deception, déjà vu*, delusion, error, fallacy, false

impression, fancy, fantasy, figment of imagination*, fool's paradise*, ghost, hallucination, head trip*, hocus-pocus*, idolism, ignus fatuus, image, invention, make-believe, mirage, misapprehension, misbelief, misconception, misimpression, mockery, myth, optical illusion, paramnesia, phantasm, pipe dream*, rainbow*, seeming, semblance, trip*; SEE CONCEPTS 689,716

illusory/illusive [adj] *deceptive, false*
apparent, blue-sky*, chimerical, deceitful, delusive, delusory, fake, fallacious, fanciful, fantastic, fictional, fictitious, fictive, hallucinatory, ideal, illusive, imaginary, misleading, mistaken, ostensible, pseudo*, seeming, semblant, sham*, supposititious, unreal, untrue, visionary, whimsical; SEE CONCEPTS 529,552,582

illustrate [v1] *demonstrate, exemplify*
allegorize, bring home*, clarify, clear, clear up, delineate, depict, disclose, draw a picture*, elucidate, emblematize, embody, emphasize, epitomize, evidence, evince, exhibit, explain, expose, expound, get across*, get over*, highlight, illuminate, imitate, instance, interpret, lay out*, limelight*, make clear, make plain, manifest, mark, mirror, ostend, personify, picture, point up*, portray, proclaim, represent, reveal, show, show and tell*, spotlight*, symbolize, typify, vivify; SEE CONCEPTS 57,97

illustrate [v2] *explain by drawing, decorating*
adorn, decorate, delineate, depict, draw, embellish, illuminate, limn, ornament, paint, picture, portray, represent, sketch; SEE CONCEPTS 57,174

illustration [n1] *demonstration, exemplification*
analogy, case, case history, case in point, clarification, elucidation, example, explanation, for instance, instance, interpretation, model, representative, sample, sampling, specimen; SEE CONCEPTS 268,688

illustration [n2] *drawing, artwork that assists explanation*
adornment, cartoon, decoration, depiction, design, engraving, etching, figure, frontispiece, halftone, image, line drawing, painting, photo, photograph, picture, plate, sketch, snapshot, tailpiece, vignette; SEE CONCEPT 259

illustrative [adj] *explanatory*
allegorical, clarifying, comparative, corroborative, delineative, descriptive, diagrammatic, emblematic, exemplifying, explicatory, expository, figurative, graphic, iconographic, illuminative, illustrational, illustratory, imagistic, indicative, interpretive, metaphoric, pictorial, pictoric, representative, revealing, sample, specifying, symbolic, typical; SEE CONCEPT 267

illustrious [adj] *famous, prominent*
big league*, brilliant, celeb*, celebrated, distinguished, eminent, esteemed, exalted, famed, glorious, great, heavy, lofty, monster*, name*, noble, notable, noted, outstanding, remarkable, renowned,

resplendent, signal, splendid, star, sublime, superstar, well-known; SEE CONCEPT 568

ill will [n] *hatred; hard feelings*
acrimony, animosity, animus, antagonism, antipathy, aversion, bad blood*, bad will, blame, despite, dislike, enmity, envy, feud, grudge, hate, hostility, malevolence, malice, maliciousness, no love lost*, objection, rancor, resentment, spite, spitefulness, spleen, unfriendliness, venom; SEE CONCEPT 29

image [n1] *representation; counterpart*
angel*, appearance, carbon*, carbon copy, carved figure, chip off old block*, copy, dead ringer*, double, drawing, effigy, equal, equivalent, facsimile, figure, form, icon, idol, illustration, likeness, match, model, photocopy, photograph, picture, portrait, reflection, replica, reproduction, similitude, simulacre, simulacrum, spitting image*, statue; SEE CONCEPTS 259,667,716

image [n2] *concept*
apprehension, conceit, conception, construct, figure, idea, impression, intellection, mental picture, notion, perception, phantasm, thought, trope, vision; SEE CONCEPTS 529,689

imaginable [adj] *believable, possible*
apprehensible, calculable, comprehensible, conceivable, conjecturable, convincing, credible, likely, plausible, sensible, supposable, thinkable, under the sun*; SEE CONCEPTS 529,552

imaginary [adj] *fictitious, invented*
abstract, apocryphal, apparitional, assumed, chimerical, deceptive, delusive, dreamed-up*, dreamlike, dreamy, fabulous, fancied, fanciful, fantastic, fictional, figmental, fool's paradise*, hallucinatory, hypothetical, ideal, illusive, illusory, imaginative, imagined, legendary, made-up*, mythological, nonexistent, notional, phantasmal, phantasmic, quixotic, shadowy, spectral, supposed, supposititious, theoretical, trumped up*, unreal, unsubstantial, visionary, whimsical; SEE CONCEPTS 529,582

imagination [n] *power to create in one's mind*
acuteness, artistry, awareness, chimera, cognition, conception, creation, creative thought, creativity, enterprise, fabrication, fancy, fantasy, flight of fancy*, idea, ideality, illusion, image, imagery, ingenuity, insight, inspiration, intelligence, invention, inventiveness, mental agility, notion, originality, perceptibility, realization, resourcefulness, sally, supposition, thought, thoughtfulness, unreality, verve, vision, visualization, wit, wittiness; SEE CONCEPTS 409,410

imaginative [adj] *creative, inventive*
artistic, avant-garde, blue-sky*, brain wave, breaking ground, clever, dreamy, enterprising, extravagant, fanciful, fantastic, fertile, fictive, high-flown*, ingenious, inspired, offbeat, original, originative, pie-in-the-sky*, poetic, poetical, productive, quixotic, romantic, utopian, visionary, vivid, way out*, whimsical; SEE CONCEPTS 529,542

imagine [v1] *dream up, conceive*
brainstorm, build castles in air*, conceptualize, conjure up, cook up*, create, depict, devise, dream, envisage, envision, fabricate, fancy, fantasize, fantasy, feature, figure, form, frame, harbor, image, invent, make up, nurture, perceive, picture, plan, project, realize, scheme, see in one's mind*, spark, think of, think up, vision, visualize; SEE CONCEPT *43*

imagine [v2] *assume, deduce*
apprehend, believe, conjecture, deem, expect, fancy, gather, guess, infer, presume, realize, reckon, suppose, surmise, suspect, take for granted, take it, think, understand; SEE CONCEPTS *12,26*

imbecile [n] *very stupid person*
birdbrain, dimwit, dolt, dummy, dunce, fool, halfwit, idiot, jerk, lamebrain*, moron, pinhead*, simpleton; SEE CONCEPT *412*

imbecile [adj] *stupid, foolish*
asinine, backward, deranged, dim-witted, dull, fatuous, feeble-minded, half-witted, idiotic, imbecilic, inane, ludicrous, moronic, retarded, simple, simpleminded, slow, thick, witless; SEE CONCEPT *402*

imbibe [v] *drink, often heavily*
absorb, assimilate, belt*, consume, down, gorge, guzzle*, ingest, ingurgitate, irrigate, partake, put away*, quaff, raise a few*, sip, swallow, swig*, swill*, toss*; SEE CONCEPT *169*

imbroglio [n] *misunderstanding; fight*
altercation, argument, bickering, brawl, broil*, brouhaha*, complexity, complication, dispute, embarrassment, embroilment, entanglement, falling-out*, flack*, involvement, knock-down-drag-out*, miff*, quandary, quarrel, row, run-in*, soap opera*, spat, squabble; SEE CONCEPTS *46,106*

imbue [v] *infuse, saturate*
bathe, diffuse, impregnate, inculcate, infix, ingrain, inoculate, instill, invest, leaven, permeate, pervade, steep, suffuse; SEE CONCEPTS *209,236,245*

imitate [v] *pretend to be; do an impression of*
act like, affect, ape, assume, be like, borrow, burlesque, carbon*, caricature, clone, copy, counterfeit, ditto*, do, do like*, do likewise, duplicate, echo, emulate, falsify, feign, follow, follow in footsteps*, follow suit*, forge, impersonate, look like, match, mime, mimic, mirror, mock, model after, parallel, parody, pattern after, personate, play a part, pretend, put on*, reduplicate, reflect, repeat, replicate, reproduce, resemble, send up*, sham, simulate, spoof, take off*, travesty, Xerox*; SEE CONCEPTS *87,171*

imitation [n] *simulation, substitution*
apery, aping, carbon copy, clone, copy, counterfeit, counterfeiting, counterpart, ditto*, dupe*, duplicate, duplication, echoing, ersatz*, fake, forgery, image, impersonation, impression, likeness, match, matching, mime, mimicry, mirroring, mockery, parallel, paralleling, paraphrasing, parody, parroting, patterning, phony, picture, reflection, replica, representing, reproduction, resemblance, ringer, semblance,

sham*, simulacrum, takeoff*, transcription, travesty, Xerox*; SEE CONCEPTS *171,260,716*

imitative [adj] *simulated, unoriginal*
artful, copied, copycat, copying, counterfeit, deceptive, derivative, echoic, emulative, emulous, following, forged, mimetic, mimic, mimicking, mock, onomatopoeic, parrot*, plagiarized, pseudo*, put-on*, reflecting, reflective, secondhand, sham*, simulant; SEE CONCEPT *582*

immaculate [adj1] *very clean; unspoiled*
bright, clean, errorless, exquisite, faultless, flawless, impeccable, irreproachable, neat, pure, snowy*, spick-and-span*, spotless, spruce, stainless, taintless, trim, unexceptionable, unsoiled, unsullied; SEE CONCEPT *621*

immaculate [adj2] *innocent, uncorrupted*
above reproach, chaste, clean, decent, faultless, flawless, guiltless, incorrupt, modest, perfect, pure, sinless, spotless, stainless, unblemished, uncontaminated, undefiled, unpolluted, unsullied, untarnished, virtuous; SEE CONCEPTS *404,545*

immaterial [adj1] *irrelevant*
extraneous, foreign, impertinent, inapplicable, inapposite, inappropriate, inconsequential, inconsiderable, inconsiderate, inessential, insignificant, irrelative, matter of indifference, meaningless, no big deal*, no never mind*, of no account*, of no consequence*, of no importance*, trifling, trivial, unimportant, unnecessary; SEE CONCEPT *575*

immaterial [adj2] *not existing in physical form*
aerial, airy, apparitional, asomatous, bodiless, celestial, disbodied, discarnate, disembodied, dreamlike, dreamy, ethereal, ghostly, heavenly, impalpable, imponderable, incorporate, incorporeal, insensible, intangible, metaphysical, nonmaterial, nonphysical, psychic, shadowy, spectral, spiritlike, spiritual, subjective, supernatural, unearthly, unembodied, unfleshly, unsubstantial, unworldly, wraithlike; SEE CONCEPT *539*

immature [adj] *young, inexperienced*
adolescent, baby, babyish, callow, childish, crude, green*, half-grown, imperfect, infantile, infantine, jejune, juvenile, kid, kidstuff*, premature, puerile, raw, sophomoric, tender*, tenderfoot*, underdeveloped, undergrown, undeveloped, unfinished, unfledged, unformed, unripe, unseasonable, unseasoned, unsophisticated, untimely, wet behind ears*, youthful; SEE CONCEPTS *485,578,797*

immeasurable [adj] *infinite, incalculable*
alive with, bottomless, boundless, countless, crawling with, endless, extensive, illimitable, immense, indefinite, inestimable, inexhaustible, jillion*, large, limitless, measureless, no end of*, no end to*, umpteen*, unbounded, uncountable, unfathomable, unlimited, unmeasurable, unreckonable, vast, zillion*; SEE CONCEPTS *762,773,781*

immediate [adj1] *instantaneous; without delay*
actual, at once, at present time, at this moment, critical, current, existing, extant, first, hair-trigger*, in-

stant, live, next, now, on hand*, paramount, present, pressing, prompt, up-to-date*, urgent; SEE CONCEPTS 567,585,812,820

immediate [adj2] *near, next*
adjacent, close, contiguous, direct, firsthand, near-at-hand, nearby, nearest, nigh, primary, proximal, proximate, recent; SEE CONCEPTS 586,778

immediately [adv] *at once, right away*
anon, at short notice, away, directly, double-time*, forthwith, hereupon, in a flash*, in a jiffy*, in a New York minute*, in nothing flat*, instantaneously, in-stanter, instantly, like now*, now, now or never*, on the dot*, on the double*, on the spot*, PDQ*, promptly, pronto*, rapidly, right now, shortly, soon, soon afterward, straight away*, straight off*, summarily, thereupon, this instant, this minute, tout de suite*, unhesitatingly, urgently, without delay, without hesitation; SEE CONCEPTS 544,820

immemorial [adj] *ancient, old*
age-old, archaic, fixed, forever, long-standing, of yore, olden, prehistoric, primeval, rooted, time-honored, traditional; SEE CONCEPTS 578,797,799

immense [adj] *extremely large*
barn door*, boundless, Brobdingnagian*, colossal, elephantine, endless, enormous, eternal, extensive, giant, gigantic, great, gross, huge, humongous, il-limitable, immeasurable, infinite, interminable, jumbo*, king-size*, limitless, mammoth, massive, measureless, mighty, monstrous, monumental, prodigious, stupendous, super, titanic*, tremendous, un-bounded, vast; SEE CONCEPT 773

immerse [adj1] *submerge in liquid*
asperse, baptize, bathe, bury, christen, dip, douse, drench, drown, duck, dunk, merge, plunge, saturate, sink, slop, soak, souse, sprinkle, steep, submerse; SEE CONCEPT 256

immerse [adj2] *become deeply involved*
absorb, busy, engage, engross, interest, involve, occupy, soak, take up; SEE CONCEPTS 17,100

immersed [adj] *deeply involved with*
absorbed, bound-up*, buried*, busy, consumed, deep, eat sleep and breathe*, engaged, engrossed, intent, into*, mesmerized, occupied, preoccupied, rapt, spellbound, taken up*, tied up*, turned on*, wrapped up*; SEE CONCEPT 542

immigrant [n] *person from a foreign land*
adoptive citizen, alien, colonist, documented alien, foreigner, incomer, migrant, naturalized citizen, newcomer, outsider, pioneer, settler, undocumented alien; SEE CONCEPT 413

immigrate [v] *enter a foreign area intending to live there*
arrive, colonize, come in, go in, migrate, settle; SEE CONCEPT 159

imminent [adj] *at hand, on the way*
about to happen, approaching, brewing*, close, coming, expectant, fast-approaching, following, forth-coming, gathering, handwriting-on-the-wall*, immediate, impending, ineluctable, inescapable, in-evasible, inevitable, in store*, in the air*, in the cards*, in the offing*, in the wind*, in view*, likely, looming, menacing, near, nearing, next, nigh, on its way, on the horizon, on the verge, overhanging, possible, probable, see it coming*, threatening, to come, unavoidable, unescapable; SEE CONCEPTS 548,820

immobile [adj] *motionless, fixed*
anchored, at a standstill, at rest, frozen, immobilized, immotile, immovable, nailed, nailed down, pat, quiescent, rigid, riveted, rooted, stable, stagnant, static, stationary, steadfast, stiff, still, stock-still, stolid, un-movable, unmoving; SEE CONCEPTS 488,584

immoderate [adj] *excessive, extreme*
dizzying, egregious, enormous, exaggerated, exorbitant, extravagant, inordinate, intemperate, overindulgent, profligate, steep, too much*, too-too*, towering, unbalanced, unbridled, uncalled-for*, un-conscionable, uncontrolled, undue, unjustified, un-measurable, unreasonable, unrestrained, unwar-ranted, wanton; SEE CONCEPTS 544,569

immoral [adj] *evil, degenerate*
abandoned, bad, corrupt, debauched, depraved, dis-honest, dissipated, dissolute, fast*, graceless, impure, indecent, iniquitous, lewd, licentious, loose*, nefarious, obscene, of easy virtue*, pornographic, profligate, rakish, reprobate, saturnalian, shameless, sinful, speedy, unchaste, unclean*, unethical, un-principled, unscrupulous, vicious, vile, villainous, wicked, wrong, X-rated*; SEE CONCEPT 545

immortal [adj1] *death-defying, imperishable*
abiding, amaranthine, ceaseless, constant, deathless, endless, enduring, eternal, evergreen, everlasting, in-corruptible, indestructible, indissoluble, interminable, lasting, never-ceasing, never-ending, perdurable, perennial, permanent, perpetual, phoenixlike, sempiternal, timeless, undying, unfading; SEE CONCEPTS 539,798

immortal [adj2] *famous*
celebrated, eminent, epic, genius, glorious, heroic, illustrious, laureate, paragon, storied; SEE CONCEPT 568

immovable [adj] *fixed, stubborn*
adamant, constant, dead set on*, dug in, fast, firm, hard-nosed, immobile, immotile, immutable, impassive, inflexible, intransigent, locked in*, motionless, obdurate, quiescent, resolute, rooted, secure, set, set in concrete*, set in stone*, solid, stable, stand pat*, stationary, steadfast, stick to guns*, stuck, tough nut*, unalterable, unchangeable, uncompromising, unmodifiable, unshakable, unwavering, unyielding; SEE CONCEPTS 404,488,534

immune [adj] *invulnerable*
allowed, clear, exempt, favored, free, hardened to, insusceptible, irresponsible, licensed, not affected, not liable, not subject, privileged, protected, resistant, safe, unaffected, unanswerable, unliable, un-susceptible; SEE CONCEPTS 314,552

immunity [*n*] *privilege, exemption*
amnesty, charter, exoneration, franchise, freedom, impunity, indemnity, invulnerability, liberty, license, prerogative, protection, release, resistance, right; SEE CONCEPTS *316,376,388*

immutable [*adj*] *unchangeable*
abiding, ageless, changeless, constant, enduring, fixed, immovable, inflexible, invariable, permanent, perpetual, sacrosanct, stable, steadfast, unalterable, unmodifiable; SEE CONCEPT *534*

imp [*n*] *mischievous child, small person*
brat, demon, devil, deviling, devilkin, elf, fiend, gamin, gnome, gremlin, hellcat, hellion, minx, pixie, puck, rascal, rogue, scamp, sprite, troll, tyke, urchin, villain; SEE CONCEPT *412*

impact [*n1*] *collision, force*
appulse, bang, blow, bounce, brunt, buffet, bump, clash, concussion, contact, crash, crunch, crush, encounter, hit, impingement, jar, jolt, jounce, kick, knock, meeting, percussion, pound, punch, quake, quiver, ram, rap, rock, shake, shock, slap, smash, smashup, strike, stroke, thump, tremble, tremor, wallop; SEE CONCEPTS *189,641*

impact [*n2*] *effect*
brunt, burden, consequences, full force, impression, imprint, influence, mark, meaning, power, repercussion, significance, thrust, weight; SEE CONCEPT *230*

impact [*v*] *hit with force*
bang into, clash, collide, crack up, crash, crush, jolt, kick, register, smash, smash up, strike, wrack up*; SEE CONCEPT *189*

impair [*v*] *harm, hinder*
blemish, blunt, cheapen, damage, debase, debilitate, decrease, destroy, deteriorate, devaluate, devalue, diminish, ding*, disqualify, enervate, enfeeble, hurt, injure, invalidate, lessen, lose strength, make useless, mar, prejudice, queer, reduce, rough up*, spoil, tarnish, total, tweak, undermine, unfit, vitiate, weaken, worsen; SEE CONCEPTS *130,240,246*

impaired [*adj*] *injured, faulty*
broken, busted, damaged, debilitated, defective, down*, flawed, harmed, hurt, imperfect, kaput*, marred, on the blink*, on the fritz*, spoiled, unsound; SEE CONCEPTS *485,560*

impale [*v*] *stab*
lance, perforate, pierce, prick, punch, puncture, run through, skewer, skiver, spear, spike, stick, transfix; SEE CONCEPT *220*

impalpable [*adj*] *intangible, unsubstantial*
airy, delicate, disembodied, fine, imperceptible, imponderable, imprecise, inappreciable, incorporeal, indiscernible, indistinct, insensible, insubstantial, nebulous, shadowy, tenuous, thin, unapparent, unobservable, unperceivable, vague; SEE CONCEPTS *485,529,619*

impart [*v1*] *make known*
admit, announce, break, communicate, convey, disclose, discover, divulge, expose, inform, pass on, publish, relate, reveal, tell, transmit; SEE CONCEPT *60*

impart [*v2*] *give*
accord, afford, allow, bestow, cede, confer, contribute, grant, lead, offer, part with, present, relinquish, render, yield; SEE CONCEPT *108*

impartial [*adj*] *fair, unprejudiced*
candid, detached, disinterested, dispassionate, equal, equitable, evenhanded, fair-minded, impersonal, just, middle-of-the-road*, neutral, nondiscriminating, nondiscriminatory, nonpartisan, objective, on-the-fence, open-minded, unbiased, unbigoted, uncolored, unslanted, without favor; SEE CONCEPTS *403,542*

impasse [*n*] *stalemate*
box*, Catch-22*, cessation, corner*, cul-de-sac*, dead end, deadlock, dilemma, fix, gridlock, jam, mire*, morass*, pause, pickle*, plight, predicament, quandary, rest, scrape*, standoff, standstill; SEE CONCEPT *674*

impassioned [*adj*] *excited, vehement*
animated, ardent, blazing, burning, deep, fervent, fervid, fierce, fiery, fired up*, flaming, furious, glowing, heated*, hot-blooded*, inflamed, inspired, intense, melodramatic, moving, mushy, overemotional, passionate, perfervid, powerful, profound, red-hot*, romantic, rousing, sentimental, starry-eyed*, steamed up*, stirring, torrid, violent, vivid, warm, white-hot*, wild about, worked up*, zealous; SEE CONCEPT *403*

impassive [*adj*] *aloof, cool*
apathetic, callous, cold, cold-blooded*, collected, composed, dispassionate, dry, emotionless, hardened, heartless, imperturbable, indifferent, indurated, inexcitable, inexpressive, inscrutable, insensible, insusceptible, matter-of-fact, nonchalant, passionless, phlegmatic, placid, poker-faced*, reserved, reticent, sedate, self-contained, serene, spiritless, stoic, stoical, stolid, taciturn, unconcerned, unemotional, unexcitable, unfeeling, unflappable, unimpressible, unmoved, unruffled, wooden; SEE CONCEPTS *404,542*

impatience [*n*] *inability, unwillingness to wait*
agitation, anger, annoyance, ants in pants*, anxiety, avidity, disquietude, eagerness, edginess, excitement, expectancy, fretfulness, haste, hastiness, heat*, impetuosity, intolerance, irritability, irritableness, nervousness, quick temper, rashness, restiveness, restlessness, shortness, snappiness, suspense, uneasiness, vehemence, violence; SEE CONCEPTS *633,657*

impatient [*adj*] *unable, unwilling to wait*
abrupt, agog, antsy, anxious, appetent, ardent, athirst, avid, breathless, brusque, chafing, choleric, curt, demanding, dying to*, eager, edgy, feverish, fretful, hasty, having short fuse*, headlong, hot-tempered, hot under collar*, impetuous, indignant, intolerant, irascible, irritable, itchy, keen, on pins and needles*, quick-tempered, racing one's motor*, restless, ripe*, snappy, straining, sudden, testy, thirsty, unforbearing, unindulgent, vehement, violent; SEE CONCEPTS *401,542*

impeach [v] *denounce, censure*
accuse, arraign, blame, bring charges against, call into question, call to account, cast aspersions on, cast doubt on, challenge, charge, criminate, criticize, discredit, disparage, hold at fault, impugn, incriminate, inculpate, indict, query, question, reprehend, reprimand, reprobate, tax, try; SEE CONCEPTS *44,52,317*

impeccable [adj] *above suspicion; flawless*
accurate, aces, A-okay*, apple-pie*, clean, correct, errorless, exact, exquisite, faultless, fleckless, immaculate, incorrupt, infallible, innocent, irreproachable, nice, note-perfect, on target*, perfect, precise, pure, right, sinless, stainless, ten*, unblemished, unerring, unflawed, unimpeachable; SEE CONCEPTS *535,574,621*

impecunious [adj] *poverty-stricken*
beggared, broke*, cleaned out*, destitute, dirt poor*, homeless, impoverished, indigent, insolvent, necessitous, needy, penniless, penurious, poor, strapped*, unprosperous; SEE CONCEPT *334*

impede [v] *obstruct, hinder*
bar, block, blow whistle on*, brake, check, clog, close off, cramp one's style*, curb, cut off, dam, delay, deter, discomfit, disconcert, disrupt, embarrass, faze, flag one*, freeze, hamper, hang up, hold up, interfere, oppose, rattle, restrain, retard, saddle with*, shut down, shut off, slow, slow down, stonewall*, stop, stymie, thwart; SEE CONCEPTS *121,130*

impediment [n] *obstruction, hindrance*
bar, barricade, barrier, block, blockage, bottleneck*, burden, catch*, Catch-22*, chain, check, clog, cramp, curb, dead weight*, defect, delay, deterrent, detriment, difficulty, disadvantage, drag*, drawback, encumbrance, fault, flaw, handicap, hazard, hitch, holdup, hurdle, inhibition, load, manacle, millstone*, obstacle, prohibition, red tape*, restraint, restriction, retardation, retardment, road block*, rub*, setback, shackle, snag, stoppage, stricture, stumbling block*, tie, trammel, wall; SEE CONCEPT *666*

impel [v] *prompt, incite*
actuate, boost, compel, constrain, drive, excite, foment, force, goad, induce, influence, inspire, instigate, jog, lash, mobilize, motivate, move, oblige, poke, power, press, prod, propel, push, require, set in motion, shove, spur, start, stimulate, thrust, urge; SEE CONCEPTS *14,68,221,242*

impending [adj] *forthcoming*
approaching, at hand, brewing, coming, gathering, handwriting-on-the-wall*, hovering, imminent, in the cards*, in the offing*, in the wind*, looking to*, looming, menacing, near, nearing, ominous, on the horizon*, overhanging, portending, proximate, see it coming*, threatening, waiting to; SEE CONCEPTS *548,820*

impenetrable [adj1] *dense*
bulletproof, close, compact, firm, hard, hermetic, impassable, impermeable, impervious, inviolable, solid, substantial, thick, unpiercable; SEE CONCEPTS *483,604*

impenetrable [adj2] *incomprehensible*
arcane, baffling, cabalistic, dark, Delphic, enigmatic, enigmatical, hidden, incognizable, indiscernible, inexplicable, inscrutable, mysterious, mystic, obscure, sibylline, unaccountable, unfathomable, ungraspable, unintelligible, unknowable; SEE CONCEPTS *529,576*

imperative [adj1] *necessary*
acute, burning, clamant, clamorous, compulsory, critical, crucial, crying, essential, exigent, immediate, important, importunate, indispensable, inescapable, insistent, instant, no turning back*, obligatory, pressing, urgent, vital; SEE CONCEPT *546*

imperative [adj2] *authoritative*
aggressive, autocratic, bidding, bossy, commanding, dictatorial, dominant, domineering, harsh, high-handed, imperial, imperious, lordly, magisterial, masterful, ordering, overbearing, peremptory, powerful, stern; SEE CONCEPTS *267,574*

imperceptible [adj] *hard to sense; faint*
ephemeral, evanescent, fine, gradual, impalpable, imponderable, inappreciable, inaudible, inconsiderable, inconspicuous, indiscernible, indistinct, indistinguishable, infinitesimal, insensible, insignificant, invisible, microscopic, minute, momentary, shadowy, slight, small, subtle, tiny, trivial, undetectable, unnoticeable, vague; SEE CONCEPTS *406,537*

imperfect [adj] *flawed*
amiss, below par, bottom-of-barrel*, broken, damaged, defective, deficient, disfigured, dud*, faulty, few bugs*, garbage*, immature, impaired, incomplete, inexact, injured, junk*, lemon*, limited, low, marred, minus, partial, patchy, rudimentary, schlocky*, sick, sketchy, two-bit*, undeveloped, unfinished, unsound, vicious, warped; SEE CONCEPTS *570,574,579*

imperfection [n] *flaw*
blemish, bug*, catch, defect, deficiency, deformity, demerit, disfigurement, failing, fallibility, fault, foible, frailty, glitch*, gremlin*, inadequacy, incompleteness, infirmity, insufficiency, peccadillo, problem, shortcoming, sin, stain, taint, weakness, weak point; SEE CONCEPTS *230,671,718*

imperil [v] *cause to be in danger*
chance it, compromise, endanger, expose, hazard, jeopard, jeopardize, jeopardy, menace, peril, risk; SEE CONCEPT *240*

imperious [adj] *bossy, overbearing*
arrogant, authoritative, autocratic, commanding, compulsatory, compulsory, despotic, dictatorial, domineering, exacting, haughty, high-handed, imperative, imperial, lordly, magisterial, mandatory, obligatory, oppressive, overweening, peremptory, required, tyrannical, tyrannous; SEE CONCEPTS *267, 574*

impersonal [adj] *cold, unfriendly*
abstract, bureaucratic, businesslike, candid, cold-blooded*, cold turkey*, colorless, cool, detached,

disinterested, dispassionate, emotionless, equal, equitable, fair, formal, impartial, indifferent, inhuman, neutral, nondiscriminatory, objective, poker-faced*, remote, straight, strictly business*, unbiased, uncolored, unpassioned; SEE CONCEPTS *401,542,544*

impersonate [*v*] *pretend to be another*
act, act a part, act like, act out, ape, assume character, ditto*, do, do an impression of, double as, dress as, enact, fake, imitate, make like*, masquerade as, mimic, mirror, pass oneself off as*, perform, personate, play, playact, play a role, portray, pose as, put on an act*, represent, take the part of*; SEE CONCEPTS *59,292*

impertinence [*n*] *boldness*
assurance, audacity, backchat, back talk*, brazenness, cheek*, chutzpah*, come-back*, crust*, disrespect, disrespectfulness, effrontery, forwardness, freshness, gall, guff, hardihood, impropriety, impudence, incivility, insolence, insolency, lip*, nerve, pertness, presumption, rudeness, sass*, smart mouth*, wisecrack*, wise guy*; SEE CONCEPT *633*

impertinent [*adj*] *bold, disrespectful*
arrogant, brash, brassy*, brazen, contumelious, discourteous, disgracious, flip*, forward, fresh, ill-mannered, impolite, impudent, inappropriate, incongruous, inquisitive, insolent, interfering, intrusive, lippy*, meddlesome, meddling, nosy*, off base*, offensive, out of line*, pert, presumptuous, procacious, prying, rude, sassy, smart, smart alecky*, uncalled-for*, uncivil, ungracious, unmannerly, unsuitable; SEE CONCEPT *401*

imperturbable [*adj*] *calm, collected*
assured, complacent, composed, cool, cool as cucumber*, disimpassioned, equanimous, hard as nails*, immovable, nerveless, nonchalant, roll with punches*, sedate, self-possessed, self-satisfied, smug, stiff upper lip*, stoical, thick-skinned, tranquil, unaffected, undisturbed, unexcitable, unflappable, unmoved, unruffled, untouched; SEE CONCEPT *404*

impervious [*adj*] *unable to be penetrated*
closed to, hermetic, immune, impassable, impassive, impenetrable, impermeable, imperviable, inaccessible, invulnerable, resistant, sealed, tight, unaffected, unapproachable, unmoved, unpierceable, unreceptive, watertight; SEE CONCEPTS *485,534,604*

impetuous [*adj*] *acting without thinking*
abrupt, ardent, eager, fervid, fierce, furious, going off deep end*, hasty, headlong, hurried, impassioned, impulsive, passionate, precipitant, precipitate, precipitous, rash, restive, rushing, spontaneous, spur-of-the-moment, subitaneous, sudden, swift, unbridled, unexpected, unplanned, unpremeditated, unreflecting, unrestrained, unthinking, vehement, violent; SEE CONCEPTS *404,542*

impetus [*n*] *stimulus, force*
catalyst, energy, goad, impulse, impulsion, incentive, incitation, incitement, momentum, motivation, power, pressure, push, spur, stimulant, urge; SEE CONCEPTS *641,661*

impinge [*v*] *trespass*
affect, bear upon, disturb, encroach, influence, infringe, intrude, invade, make inroads, meddle, obtrude, pry, touch, violate; SEE CONCEPTS *14,156*

impious [*adj*] *not religious*
agnostic, apostate, atheistic, blasphemous, canting, contrary, deceitful, defiling, desecrating, desecrative, diabolic, disobedient, disrespectful, godless, hardened, hypocritical, iconoclastic, immoral, iniquitous, irreligious, irreverent, perverted, pietistical, profane, recusant, reprobate, sacrilegious, sanctimonious, satanic, scandalous, sinful, unctuous, undutiful, unethical, unfaithful, ungodly, unhallowed, unholy, unregenerate, unrighteous, unsanctified, wayward, wicked; SEE CONCEPT *545*

impish [*adj*] *mischievous*
casual, coltish, devilish, devil-may-care*, elfin, elvish, fiendish, flippant, free and easy*, fresh, frolicsome, giddy, jaunty, naughty, offhand, pert, pixieish, playful, prankish, puckish, rascally, roguish, saucy, sportive, waggish; SEE CONCEPT *401*

implacable [*adj*] *merciless, cruel*
grim, inexorable, inflexible, intractable, ironfisted, mortal, pitiless, rancorous, relentless, remorseless, ruthless, unappeasable, unbending, uncompromising, unflinching, unforgiving, unrelenting, unyielding, vindictive; SEE CONCEPT *542*

implausible [*adj*] *not likely*
doubtful, dubious, farfetched, far out*, fishy*, flimsy, for the birds*, full of holes*, impossible, improbable, inconceivable, incredible, obscure, problematic, puzzling, reachy, suspect, thin*, too much*, unbelievable, unconvincing, unreasonable, unsubstantial, weak, won't hold water*, won't wash*; SEE CONCEPT *552*

implement [*n*] *agent, tool*
apparatus, appliance, contraption, contrivance, device, equipment, gadget, instrument, machine, utensil; SEE CONCEPT *499*

implement [*v*] *start, put into action*
achieve, actualize, bring about, carry out, complete, effect, enable, enforce, execute, fulfill, invoke, make good, make possible, materialize, perform, provide the means, put into effect, realize, resolve; SEE CONCEPTS *91,99,221*

implicate [*v*] *imply, involve*
accuse, affect, associate, blame, charge, cite, compromise, concern, connect, embroil, entangle, frame, hint, impute, include, incriminate, inculpate, insinuate, lay at one's door*, link, mean, mire, name, pin on*, point finger at*, relate, stigmatize, suggest, tangle; SEE CONCEPTS *44,112*

implication [*n*] *association, suggestion*
assumption, conclusion, connection, connotation, entanglement, guess, hint, hypothesis, incrimination, indication, inference, innuendo, intimation, involve-

ment, link, meaning, overtone, presumption, ramification, reference, significance, signification, undertone, union; SEE CONCEPTS *28,39,278*

implicit [*adj*] *included without question, inherent, absolute*
accurate, certain, complete, constant, constructive, contained, definite, entire, firm, fixed, full, implicative, implied, inarticulate, inevitable, inferential, inferred, latent, practical, steadfast, tacit, taken for granted, total, undeclared, understood, unexpressed, unhesitating, unqualified, unquestioned, unreserved, unsaid, unshakable, unspoken, unuttered, virtual, wholehearted; SEE CONCEPTS *267,535,549*

implied [*adj*] *hinted at*
adumbrated, alluded to, allusive, connoted, constructive, figured, foreshadowed, hidden, implicit, indicated, indicative, indirect, inferential, inferred, inherent, insinuated, intended, involved, latent, lurking, meant, occult, parallel, perceptible, potential, significative, signified, suggested, symbolized, tacit, tacitly assumed, undeclared, understood, unexpressed, unsaid, unspoken, unuttered, wordless; SEE CONCEPTS *267,535*

implore [*v*] *beg*
appeal, beseech, conjure, crave, entreat, go on bended knee*, importune, plead, pray, solicit, supplicate, urge; SEE CONCEPT *48*

imply [*v*] *indicate, mean*
betoken, connote, denote, designate, entail, evidence, give a hint, hint, import, include, insinuate, intend, intimate, involve, mention, point to, presuppose, refer, signify, suggest; SEE CONCEPTS *75, 97,682*

impolite [*adj*] *having bad manners*
bad-mannered, boorish, churlish, crude, discourteous, disgracious, disrespectful, ill-bred, ill-mannered, indecorous, indelicate, insolent, irritable, loutish, moody, oafish, rough, rude, sullen, uncivil, ungallant, ungentlemanly, ungracious, unladylike, unmannered, unmannerly, unrefined; SEE CONCEPT *401*

impolitic [*adj*] *unwise, careless*
brash, ill-advised, ill-judged, imprudent, inadvisable, inconsiderate, indiscreet, inexpedient, injudicious, maladroit, misguided, rash, stupid, tactless, undiplomatic, untimely; SEE CONCEPTS *401,544*

import [*n1*] *meaning*
acceptation, bearing, bottom line*, construction, drift, gist, heart*, implication, intendment, intention, interpretation, meat*, message, name of the game*, nature of beast*, nuts and bolts*, point, punch line*, purport, score*, sense, significance, significancy, signification, stuff*, thrust, understanding; SEE CONCEPT *682*

import [*n2*] *significance, weight*
consequence, design, emphasis, importance, intent, magnitude, moment, momentousness, object, objective, pith, purpose, signification, stress, substance, value, weightiness, worth; SEE CONCEPTS *346,668*

importance [*n1*] *significance, weight*
accent, attention, bearing, caliber, concern, concernment, consequence, denotation, distinction, drift, effect, emphasis, force, gist, gravity, import, influence, interest, materiality, moment, momentousness, notability, paramountcy, point, precedence, preponderance, preponderancy, priority, purport, relevance, sense, seriousness, signification, standing, stress, substance, tenor, usefulness, value, weightiness; SEE CONCEPTS *346,668,682*

importance [*n2*] *prominence, standing*
consequence, conspicuousness, distinction, eminence, esteem, fame, greatness, influence, lionization, mark, notability, note, noteworthiness, rank, reputation, salience, status, usefulness, worth; SEE CONCEPTS *388,671*

important [*adj1*] *valuable, substantial*
big, big-league*, chief, considerable, conspicuous, critical, crucial, decisive, determining, earnest, essential, esteemed, exceptional, exigent, extensive, far-reaching, foremost, front-page*, grave, great, heavy, imperative, importunate, influential, large, marked, material, mattering much, meaningful, momentous, necessary, of moment, of note, of substance, paramount, ponderous, pressing, primary, principal, relevant, salient, serious, signal, significant, something, standout, urgent, vital, weighty; SEE CONCEPT *567*

important [*adj2*] *eminent, influential, outstanding*
aristocratic, big-time*, distinctive, distinguished, effective, esteemed, extraordinary, famous, first-class*, foremost, four-star*, front-page*, grand, heavy*, high-level, high profile, high-ranking, high-up, honored, illustrious, imposing, incomparable, leading, majestic, major-league*, noble, notable, noted, noteworthy, of note, page-one*, potent, powerful, preeminent, prominent, remarkable, seminal, signal, solid, superior, talented, top-drawer*, top-notch*, upper-class, VIP*, well-known; SEE CONCEPTS *555,574*

imported [*adj*] *brought in from another place*
alien, carried, choice, exotic, ferried, foreign, introduced, produced abroad, rare, sent, shipped, transported, trucked; SEE CONCEPT *549*

importunate [*adj*] *demanding, insistent*
burning, clamant, clamorous, crying, disturbing, dogged, earnest, exigent, harassing, imperative, instant, overly solicitous, persevering, persistent, pertinacious, pressing, solicitous, troublesome, urgent; SEE CONCEPTS *267,401*

importune [*v*] *demand, insist*
appeal, ask, badger, beg, beseech, beset, besiege, con*, crave, dun, egg on*, entreat, goose*, harass, hound*, implore, insist on, invoke, nag, persuade, pester, plague, plead, pray, press, sell, solicit, supplicate, urge, work on*; SEE CONCEPT *53*

impose [v] *set, dictate*
appoint, burden, charge, command, compel, constrain, decree, demand, encroach, enforce, enjoin, establish, exact, fix, foist, force, force upon, horn in, inflict, infringe, institute, introduce, intrude, lade, lay, lay down, lay down the law, levy, move in on, oblige, obtrude, ordain, order, place, prescribe, presume, promulgate, put, put foot down*, read riot act*, require, saddle*, take advantage, trespass, visit, wish, wreak, wreck; SEE CONCEPTS *18,53,133*

imposing [*adj*] *impressive*
arty, august, baronial, big, commanding, dignified, effective, exciting, grand, grandiose, imperial, magnificent, majestic, massive, mega*, mind-blowing, monumental, moving, noble, ominous, one for the book*, overblown, overwhelming, pretentious, princely, regal, royal, something else*, something to write home about*, stately, stirring, striking, towering; SEE CONCEPTS *537,574,773*

imposition [*n1*] *deception*
artifice, cheating, con, craftiness, dissimulation, fraud, hoax, hocus-pocus*, hypocrisy, illusion, imposture, stratagem, trick, trickery; SEE CONCEPTS *59, 645*

imposition [*n2*] *burden*
charge, command, constraint, demand, drag, duty, encroachment, encumbrance, intrusion, levy, pain, pain in the neck*, pressure, presumption, restraint, tax; SEE CONCEPTS *14,130*

impossible [*adj1*] *beyond the bounds of possibility*
absurd, beyond, contrary to reason, cureless, futile, hardly possible, hopeless, hundred-to-one*, impassable, impervious, impracticable, impractical, inaccessible, inconceivable, inexecutable, infeasible, insurmountable, irrealizable, irreparable, no-go*, not a prayer*, no-way*, no-win*, out of the question*, preposterous, too much, unachievable, unattainable, uncorrectable, unfeasible, unimaginable, unobtainable, unreasonable, unrecoverable, unthinkable, unworkable, useless, visionary, way out; SEE CONCEPT *552*

impossible [*adj2*] *intolerable, ungovernable*
absurd, egregious, hopeless, improper, incongruous, ludicrous, objectionable, offensive, outrageous, preposterous, unacceptable, unanswerable, undesirable, unreasonable, unsuitable; SEE CONCEPT *401*

impostor [*n*] *person pretending to be something else*
actor, beguiler, bluffer, charlatan, cheat, con man/woman, deceiver, empiric, fake, faker, four-flusher*, fraud, hypocrite, imitator, impersonator, masquerader, mimic, mocker, mountebank, pettifogger, phony, pretender, pseudo, quack, rogue, scorner, sham, sharper, shyster, trickster, wolf; SEE CONCEPT *412*

imposture [*n*] *fraud, trick*
artifice, cheat, con, copy, counterfeit, deceit, deception, fabrication, fake, feint, fiddle, flimflam*, forgery, gambit, gyp, hoax, hocus-pocus*, illusion, imitation, impersonation, imposition, make-believe, maneuver, masquerade, phony, ploy, pretense, pretension, put-on*, quackery, ruse, sell, sham, sleight, spoof, stratagem, swindle, wile; SEE CONCEPTS *59,192,645,674*

impotent [*adj*] *disabled; unable to perform action*
barren, crippled, dud, effete, emasculate, enervated, enfeebled, feeble, forceless, frail, frigid, gutless, helpless, inadequate, incapable, incapacitated, incompetent, ineffective, ineffectual, inept, infecund, infirm, nerveless, paper tiger*, paralyzed, powerless, prostrate, sterile, unfruitful, unproductive, weak; SEE CONCEPT *485*

impoverished [*adj*] *poor, exhausted*
bankrupt, barren, beggared, broke*, clean, depleted, destitute, distressed, drained, empty, flat*, flat broke*, have-not*, hurting, impecunious, indigent, insolvent, necessitous, needy, penurious, played out*, poverty-stricken, reduced, ruined, spent, sterile, strapped; SEE CONCEPTS *334,560*

impractical/impracticable [*adj*] *unrealistic*
abstract, absurd, chimerical, idealistic, illogical, impossible, impracticable, improbable, inapplicable, inefficacious, infeasible, inoperable, irrealizable, ivory-tower*, no-go*, nonfunctional, nonviable, not a prayer*, otherworldly, out of the question*, quixotic, romantic, speculative, starry-eyed*, theoretical, unattainable, unbusinesslike, unfeasible, unreal, unserviceable, unusable, unwise, unworkable, useless, visionary, wild, won't fly*; SEE CONCEPT *552*

impregnate [*v*] *infuse, fill; make pregnant*
charge, conceive, drench, fecundate, fertilize, imbrue, implant, inoculate, inseminate, leaven, overflow, percolate, permeate, pervade, procreate, produce, reproduce, saturate, seethe, soak, sodden, souse, steep, suffuse, transfuse; SEE CONCEPTS *179,375*

impress [*v1*] *influence*
affect, arouse, awe, be conspicuous, blow away*, buffalo*, bulldoze*, carry, electrify, enforce, enthuse, excite, faze, galvanize, get*, grab, grandstand*, inspire, kill*, knock out*, make a hit*, make an impression, make splash*, move, overawe, pique, provoke, push around*, register, score, show off, slay*, stimulate, stir, strike, sway, thrill, touch*; SEE CONCEPTS *7,19,22,261*

impress [*v2*] *press down to make design*
carve, dent, emboss, engrave, etch, imprint, indent, inscribe, mark, print, stamp; SEE CONCEPT *174*

impress [*v3*] *emphasize*
bring home*, drive home*, establish, fix, get into head*, inculcate, instill, press, set, stress; SEE CONCEPT *49*

impression [*n1*] *influence*
consequence, effect, feeling, impact, reaction, response, result, sway; SEE CONCEPT *230*

impression [*n2*] *feeling, idea*
apprehension, belief, conceit, concept, conception, conjecture, conviction, fancy, feel, hunch, image,

inkling, intellection, memory, notion, opinion, perception, recollection, sensation, sense, supposition, suspicion, theory, thought, view; SEE CONCEPTS *529,689*

impression [*n3*] *design made by pressing*
brand, cast, dent, depression, dint, fingerprint, footprint, form, hollow, impress, imprint, indentation, mark, matrix, mold, outline, pattern, print, sign, spoor, stamp, stamping, trace, track, vestige; SEE CONCEPTS *284,625*

impression [*n4*] *pretending to be somebody*
imitation, impersonation, masquerade, parody, sendup, takeoff; SEE CONCEPT *263*

impressionable [*adj*] *easily taught; gullible*
affectable, affected, feeling, impressible, influenceable, ingenuous, open, perceptive, plastic, receptive, responsive, sensible, sensile, sensitive, sentient, suggestible, susceptible, susceptive, vulnerable, waxlike; SEE CONCEPTS *402,403*

impressive [*adj*] *powerful, influential*
absorbing, affecting, arresting, august, awe-inspiring, consequential, cool*, deep*, dramatic, effective, eloquent, excited, exciting, extraordinary, forcible, grand, impassioned, important, imposing, inspiring, intense, lavish, luxurious, majestic, massive, momentous, monumental, moving, noble, notable, penetrating, prime*, profound, remarkable, rousing, splendid, stately, stirring, striking, sumptuous, superb, thrilling, touching, towering, vital, well-done; SEE CONCEPTS *574,773*

imprint [*n*] *impression; symbol*
banner, dent, design, effect, emblem, heading, impress, indentation, influence, mark, name, print, sign, signature, stamp, trace, trademark; SEE CONCEPTS *284,625*

imprint [*v*] *stamp*
designate, engrave, establish, etch, fix, impress, inscribe, mark, offset, print; SEE CONCEPT *174*

imprison [*v*] *confine; put in jail*
apprehend, bastille, bottle up*, cage, check, circumscribe, closet, commit, constrain, curb, detain, fence in, hold, hold captive, hold hostage, hold in custody, ice*, immure, impound, incarcerate, intern, jail, keep, keep captive, keep in custody, limit, lock in, lock up, nab, occlude, pen, put away, put behind bars, rail in, remand, restrain, send to prison, send up*, shut in, stockade, take prisoner, trammel; SEE CONCEPTS *90,191,317*

improbable [*adj*] *not likely*
doubtful, dubious, fanciful, far-fetched, flimsy*, hundred-to-one*, iffy*, implausible, inconceivable, not expected, outside chance*, questionable, rare, slim, slim and none*, unbelievable, uncertain, unconvincing, unheard of, unimaginable, unlikely, unsubstantial, weak; SEE CONCEPT *552*

impromptu [*adj/adv*] *unrehearsed, improvised*
ad-lib, dashed off, extemporaneous, extempore, extemporized, fake, faked, improv*, improviso, off-

hand, off the cuff*, played by ear*, shot from the hip*, spontaneous, spur-of-the-moment, thrown off*, tossed off*, unpremeditated, unprepared, unscripted, unstudied, vamped, whipped up*, winged*; SEE CONCEPT *267*

improper [*adj1*] *not suitable*
abnormal, at odds, awkward, bad form, discordant, discrepant, erroneous, false, ill-advised, ill-timed, imprudent, inaccurate, inadmissible, inadvisable, inapplicable, inapposite, inappropriate, inapt, incongruous, incorrect, inexpedient, infelicitous, inharmonious, inopportune, irregular, ludicrous, malapropos, odd, off-base*, out-of-place*, out-of-season*, preposterous, unapt, unbefitting, uncalled-for*, uncomely, undue, unfit, unfitting, unseasonable, unsuitable, unsuited, untimely, unwarranted, wrong; SEE CONCEPT *558*

improper [*adj2*] *vulgar, immoral*
blue*, dirty, impolite, indecent, indecorous, indelicate, lewd, malodorous, naughty, risqué, rough, salacious, suggestive, unbecoming, unconventional, unequitable, unethical, ungodly, unjust, unrighteous, unrightful, unseemly, untoward, wrong, wrongful; SEE CONCEPTS *542,545*

impropriety [*n*] *bad taste, mistake*
barbarism, blunder, faux pas, gaffe, gaucherie, goof*, immodesty, impudence, incongruity, incorrectness, indecency, indecorum, inelegance, rudeness, slip*, solecism, unseemliness, unsuitability, vulgarism, vulgarity; SEE CONCEPTS *101,278,674*

improve [*v*] *make or become better*
advance, ameliorate, amend, augment, better, boost, civilize, come around*, convalesce, correct, cultivate, develop, doctor up*, edit, elevate, emend, enhance, gain ground*, help, increase, lift, look up*, make strides, meliorate, mend, perk up*, pick up*, polish, progress, promote, purify, raise, rally, recover, rectify, recuperate, refine, reform, revamp, revise, rise, set right*, shape up*, sharpen, skyrocket*, straighten out*, take off*, touch up*, turn the corner*, update, upgrade; SEE CONCEPTS *244,700*

improvement [*n*] *bettering; something bettered*
advance, advancement, amelioration, amendment, augmentation, betterment, change, civilization, correction, cultivation, development, elevation, enhancement, enrichment, furtherance, gain, growth, increase, preferment, progress, progression, promotion, rally, reclamation, recovery, rectification, reformation, regeneration, renovation, revision, rise, upbeat, upgrade, upswing; SEE CONCEPTS *230,700*

improvident [*adj*] *careless, spendthrift*
extravagant, heedless, imprudent, inconsiderate, lavish, negligent, prodigal, profligate, profuse, reckless, shiftless, shortsighted, thoughtless, thriftless, uneconomical, unthrifty, wasteful; SEE CONCEPTS *334,542*

improvise [*v*] *make up*
ad-lib, brainstorm, coin, concoct, contrive, dash off*, devise, do offhand, do off top of head*, dream

up, extemporize, fake, fake it, improv*, improvisate, invent, jam*, knock off*, make do*, slapdash*, spark, speak off the cuff*, throw together*, wing it*; SEE CONCEPTS *173,266*

improvised [*adj*] *made-up*
ad-lib, autoschediastic, band-aid*, extemporaneous, extempore, extemporized, fly-by-night*, hit-or-miss*, impromptu, improviso, makeshift, offhand, spontaneous, spur-of-the-moment*, unprepared, unrehearsed, unstudied; SEE CONCEPTS *267,589*

imprudent [*adj*] *without much thought*
brash, careless, foolhardy, foolish, heedless, ill-advised, ill-considered, ill-judged, impolitic, improvident, incautious, inconsiderate, indiscreet, inexpedient, injudicious, irresponsible, leaving self wide open*, off the deep end*, overhasty, playing with fire*, rash, reckless, temerarious, thoughtless, unadvisable, unthinking, unwise; SEE CONCEPTS *267,542*

impudent [*adj*] *bold, shameless*
arrant, audacious, barefaced, blatant, boldfaced, brassy, brazen, bumptious, cheeky*, cocky*, contumelious, cool*, flip*, forward, fresh, immodest, impertinent, insolent, nervy*, off-base*, overbold, pert, presumptuous, procacious, rude, sassy*, saucy*, smart*, smart-alecky*, unabashed, unblushing, wise; SEE CONCEPT *401*

impugn [*v*] *criticize, challenge*
assail, attack, blast, break, call into question, cast aspersions upon, cast doubt upon, come down on*, contradict, contravene, cross, cut to shreds*, deny, disaffirm, dispute, gainsay, knock*, negate, negative, oppose, pin something on*, put down*, question, resist, run down, skin alive*, slam*, smear*, stick it to*, swipe at*, tar*, throw doubt on, throw the book at*, thumb nose at*, traduce, trash, traverse, zap*, zing*; SEE CONCEPTS *52,58*

impulse [*n1*] *drive, resolve*
actuation, appeal, bent, caprice, catalyst, desire, disposition, excitant, extemporization, fancy, feeling, flash*, goad, hunch, impellent, impulsion, incitation, incitement, inclination, influence, inspiration, instinct, itch*, lash, lust, mind, motivation, motive, notion, passion, spontaneity, spur, thought, urge, vagary, whim, whimsy, wish, yen; SEE CONCEPTS *20,410*

impulse [*n2*] *throb, stimulus*
augmentation, beat, bump, catalyst, drive, force, impetus, impulsion, lash, momentum, movement, pressure, propulsion, pulsation, pulse, push, rush, shock, shove, stroke, surge, thrust, vibration; SEE CONCEPT *641*

impulsive [*adj*] *tending to act without thought*
abrupt, ad-lib*, automatic, careless, devil-may-care*, emotional, extemporaneous, flaky*, gone off deep end*, hasty, headlong, hot-and-cold*, impetuous, instinctive, intuitive, involuntary, jumping the gun*, mad, offhand, passionate, precipitate, quick,

rash, spontaneous, sudden, swift, unconsidered, unexpected, unmeditated, unpredictable, unpremeditated, unprompted, up-and-down*, violent, winging it*; SEE CONCEPTS *401,542*

impunity [*n*] *freedom*
dispensation, exception, exemption, immunity, liberty, license, nonliability, permission, privilege, security; SEE CONCEPT *376*

impure [*adj*] *not clean mentally, physically; mixed*
admixed, adulterated, alloyed, carnal, coarse, common, contaminated, corrupt, debased, defiled, desecrated, diluted, dirty, doctored*, filthy, foul, gross*, grubby*, immodest, immoral, indecent, infected, lewd, nasty, not pure, obscene, polluted, profaned, smutty*, squalid, sullied, tainted, unchaste, unclean, unrefined, unwholesome, vile, vitiated, weighted, wicked; SEE CONCEPTS *545,621*

impute [*v*] *attribute*
accredit, accuse, adduce, ascribe, assign, blame, brand, censure, charge, credit, hang something on*, hint, indict, insinuate, intimate, lay, pin on*, refer, reference, stigmatize; SEE CONCEPTS *44,49*

inability [*n*] *disabling lack of talent, skill*
disability, disqualification, failure, frailty, impotence, inadequacy, inaptitude, incapability, incapacitation, incapacity, incompetence, ineffectiveness, ineffectualness, inefficacy, inefficiency, ineptitude, ineptness, insufficiency, inutility, lack, necessity, powerlessness, shortcoming, unfitness, weakness; SEE CONCEPT *630*

inaccessible [*adj*] *out of reach*
aloof, away, beyond, distant, elusive, far, faraway, far-off, impassable, impervious, impracticable, insurmountable, not at hand*, out-of-the-way*, remote, unachievable, unapproachable, unattainable, unavailable, unfeasible, ungettable, unobtainable, unreachable, unrealizable, unworkable; SEE CONCEPT *576*

inaccuracy [*n*] *error, erroneousness*
blunder, corrigendum, deception, defect, erratum, exaggeration, fault, howler*, imprecision, incorrectness, inexactness, miscalculation, mistake, slip*, solecism, typo*, unfaithfulness, unreliability, wrong; SEE CONCEPTS *101,230*

inaccurate [*adj*] *erroneous*
all wet*, careless, counterfactual, defective, discrepant, doesn't wash*, fallacious, false, faulty, imprecise, incorrect, in error, inexact, mistaken, off, off base*, out*, specious, unfaithful, unreliable, unsound, untrue, way-off*, wide*, wild*, wrong; SEE CONCEPTS *565,582*

inactive [*adj*] *not engaged in action; inert, lazy*
abeyant, asleep, blah*, disengaged, do-nothing*, dormant, down, draggy, dull, idle, immobile, indolent, in holding pattern*, inoperative, jobless, latent, lax, lethargic, limp, low-key, mothballed*, motionless, on hold, ossified, out of action, out of commission*, out of service, out of work*, passive,

quiescent, quiet, sedentary, slack, sleepy, slothful, slow, sluggish, somnolent, stable, static, still, torpid, unemployed, unoccupied, unused; SEE CONCEPTS *401,560,584*

inadequacy [*n*] *shortage, defect, inability*
blemish, dearth, defalcation, defectiveness, deficiency, deficit, drawback, failing, faultiness, flaw, imperfection, inadequateness, inaptness, incapacity, incompetence, incompetency, incompleteness, ineffectiveness, ineffectualness, inefficacy, inefficiency, ineptitude, insufficiency, lack, meagerness, paucity, poverty, scantiness, shortcoming, skimpiness, underage, unfitness, unsuitableness, weakness; SEE CONCEPTS *335,674,709*

inadequate [*adj*] *defective, insufficient, incompetent*
bare, barren, bush-league*, deficient, depleted, dry, failing, faulty, feeble, found wanting, glitch*, imperfect, impotent, inappreciable, inapt, incapable, incommensurate, incompetent, incomplete, inconsiderable, insubstantial, junk*, lacking, lame*, lemon*, lousy, low, meager, minus, miserly, niggardly, not enough, parsimonious, poor, scanty, scarce, short, shy*, sketchy*, skimpy*, small, spare, sparse, sterile, stinted, stunted*, thin, too little, unequal, unproductive, unqualified, weak; SEE CONCEPTS *546, 570,771*

inadmissible [*adj*] *not appropriate*
exceptionable, ill-favored, ill-timed, immaterial, improper, inappropriate, inapt, incompetent, inept, irrelevant, malapropos, objectionable, unacceptable, unallowable, unbecoming, undesirable, unfit, unqualified, unreasonable, unsatisfactory, unseemly, unsuited, unwanted, unwelcome; SEE CONCEPTS *319,558*

inadvertent [*adj*] *accidental*
careless, chance, feckless, heedless, irreflective, negligent, not on purpose, reckless, thoughtless, uncaring, unconcerned, undesigned, undevised, unheeding, unintended, unintentional, unmindful, unplanned, unpremeditated, unthinking, unthought, unwitting; SEE CONCEPTS *542,544*

inadvisable [*adj*] *not recommended*
careless, foolhardy, foolish, harebrained, ill-advised, impolitic, improper, imprudent, inappropriate, incautious, inconvenient, indiscreet, inexpedient, injudicious, pointless, rash, undesirable, unsensible, unsuitable, unwise, wrong; SEE CONCEPTS *529,558*

inalienable [*adj*] *absolute, inherent*
basic, entailed, inbred, inviolable, natural, nonnegotiable, nontransferable, sacrosanct, unassailable, untransferable; SEE CONCEPT *535*

inane [*adj*] *stupid*
absurd, asinine, daft, ditzy*, empty, fatuous, flat, foolish, frivolous, futile, harebrained*, idiotic, illogical, imbecilic, innocuous, insipid, jejune, laughable, meaningless, mindless, pointless, puerile, ridiculous, sappy*, senseless, silly, trifling, unintelligent, va-

cant, vacuous, vain, vapid, weak, wishy-washy*, worthless; SEE CONCEPTS *542,548*

inanimate [*adj*] *not alive, not organic*
azoic, cold, dead, defunct, dull, exanimate, extinct, idle, inactive, inert, inoperative, insensate, insentient, lifeless, mineral, motionless, nonanimal, nonvegetable, quiescent, soulless, spiritless; SEE CONCEPT *539*

inapplicable [*adj*] *not relevant*
extraneous, foreign, garbage*, immaterial, impertinent, inapposite, inappropriate, inappurtenant, inapropos, inapt, inconsistent, irrelative, irrelevant, remote, unsuitable, unsuited; SEE CONCEPTS *546,558*

inappropriate [*adj*] *not proper, suitable*
bad form, disproportionate, foot-in-mouth*, garbage*, ill-fitted, ill-suited, ill-timed, improper, inapplicable, inapropos, incongruous, inconsonant, incorrect, indecorous, inept, irrelevant, left-field*, malapropos, off*, out of line, out of place, tasteless, unbecoming, unbefitting, undue, unfit, unfitting, unmeet, unseasonable, unseemly, unsuitable, untimely, way off*, wrong, wrong-number*; SEE CONCEPT *558*

inapt [*adj*] *incompetent; not suitable*
awkward, banal, clumsy, dull, flat, gauche, illadapted, ill-fitted, ill-suited, improper, inadept, inapposite, inappropriate, incongruous, inept, inexperienced, inexpert, infelicitous, insipid, jejune, maladroit, malapropos, slow, stupid, unable, undexterous, unfacile, unfit, unhandy, unmeet, unproficient, unskilled, unsuitable, unsuited, untimely; SEE CONCEPTS *527,558*

inarticulate [*adj*] *unable to speak well*
blurred, dumb, faltering, halting, hesitant, hesitating, inaudible, incoherent, incomprehensible, indistinct, maundering, muffled, mum, mumbled, mumbling, mute, obscure, reticent, silent, speechless, stammering, tongue-tied, unclear, unintelligible, unspoken, unuttered, unvocal, unvoiced, vague, voiceless, wordless; SEE CONCEPT *267*

inattentive [*adj*] *negligent, not paying attention*
absent, absentminded, apathetic, blind, bored, careless, deaf*, distracted, distrait, distraught, diverted, dreamy, faraway, heedless, inadvertent, indifferent, inobservant, listless, lost*, musing, neglectful, oblivious, off-guard*, out to lunch*, preoccupied, rapt, regardless, remiss, removed, scatterbrained*, thoughtless, unconscious, undiscerning, unheeding, unmindful, unnoticing, unobservant, unobserving, unperceiving, unthinking, unwatchful, vague; SEE CONCEPTS *403,542*

inaugurate [*v*] *begin; install*
bow, break in, break the ice*, commence, commission, dedicate, get things rolling*, get under way*, induct, initiate, instate, institute, introduce, invest, jump, kick off*, launch, make up, open, ordain, originate, set in motion*, set up, start, usher in; SEE CONCEPT *221*

inauguration [n] *installation of newcomers*
commencement, inaugural, induction, initiation, institution, investiture, launch, launching, opening, setting up; SEE CONCEPT *386*

inauspicious [adj] *ominous, unpromising*
bad, baleful, baneful, black, dire, discouraging, evil, fateful, foreboding, ill-boding, ill-omened, impending, inopportune, sinister, threatening, unfavorable, unfortunate, unlucky, unpromising, unpropitious, untimely, untoward; SEE CONCEPTS *548,570*

inborn/inbred [adj] *coming from birth; natural*
congenital, connate, connatural, constitutional, deep-seated, essential, hereditary, inbred, indigenous, indwelling, ingenerate, ingrained, inherent, inherited, innate, instinctive, intrinsic, intuitive, native, unacquired; SEE CONCEPTS *406,549*

incalculable [adj] *countless, limitless*
boundless, capricious, chancy, enormous, erratic, fluctuant, iffy*, immense, incomputable, inestimable, infinite, innumerable, jillion*, measureless, no end of*, no end to*, numberless, uncertain, uncountable, unfixed, unforeseen, unpredictable, unreckonable, untold, vast, whimsical, without number, zillion*; SEE CONCEPTS *535,773,781*

incandescent [adj] *glowing*
beaming, brilliant, effulgent, fulgent, intense, lambent, lucent, luminous, phosphorescent, radiant, red-hot*, refulgent, shining, white-hot*; SEE CONCEPT *617*

incantation [n] *spell, magic*
abracadabra*, ala kazam*, bewitchment, black magic, chant, charm, conjuration, conjuring, enchantment, formula, hex, hocus-pocus*, hoodoo*, hymn, invocation, mumbo-jumbo*, necromancy, open sesame*, rune, sorcery, voodoo*, witchcraft, wizardry; SEE CONCEPTS *370,689*

incapable [adj] *not adequate; helpless*
butterfingers*, disqualified, feeble, impotent, inadequate, incompetent, ineffective, ineligible, inept, inexperienced, inexpert, inproficient, insufficient, losing, naive, not equal to, not up to*, poor, powerless, unable, uncool*, unequipped, unfit, unqualified, unskilled, unskillful, unsuited, weak; SEE CONCEPT *527*

incapacitate [v] *put out of action*
clip wings*, cripple, damage, disable, disarm, disenable, disqualify, hamstring*, hinder, hog-tie*, hurt, immobilize, lame, lay up*, maim, paralyze, prostrate, put out of commission*, take out, undermine, weaken; SEE CONCEPTS *121,246*

incarcerate [v] *put in jail, confinement*
bastille, book*, cage*, commit, confine, constrain, coop up*, detain, hold, immure, impound, imprison, intern, jail, lock up, put away, put on ice*, put under lock and key*, railroad*, restrain, restrict, send up the river*, settle, slough, take away, throw book at*; SEE CONCEPTS *90,191,317*

incarnate [adj] *in bodily form*
embodied, exteriorized, externalized, human, in human form, in the flesh*, made flesh, manifested, materialized, personified, physical, real, substantiated, tangible, typified; SEE CONCEPTS *490,539*

incautious [adj] *not careful*
any old way*, bold, brash, careless, caught napping*, devil-may-care*, fast-and-loose*, foot-in-mouth*, hasty, heedless, hotheaded*, ill-advised, ill-judged, impetuous, improvident, imprudent, impulsive, inconsiderate, indiscreet, injudicious, madcap*, neglectful, negligent, off guard*, pay no mind*, playing with fire*, precipitate, rash, reckless, regardless, sticking one's neck out*, thoughtless, unalert, unguarded, unmindful, unthinking, unvigilant, unwatchful, wary, wide open*; SEE CONCEPTS *542,544*

incendiary [n] *person who causes fire, trouble*
agitator, arsonist, criminal, demagogue, demonstrator, firebrand*, insurgent, pyromaniac, rabble-rouser*, rebel, revolutionary, rioter; SEE CONCEPT *412*

incendiary [adj] *causing trouble, damage*
dangerous, demagogic, dissentious, inflammatory, malevolent, provocative, rabble-rousing*, seditious, subversive, treacherous, wicked; SEE CONCEPTS *537,570*

incense [n] *strongly fragrant smoke*
aroma, balm, bouquet, burnt offering, essence, flame, frankincense, fuel, myrrh, odor, perfume, punk, redolence, scent, spice; SEE CONCEPTS *599,600*

incense [v] *make very angry*
anger, ask for it*, bother, disgust, egg on*, enrage, exasperate, excite, fire up*, get a rise out of*, get under one's skin*, inflame, infuriate, ire, irritate, mad, madden, make blood boil*, make see red*, provoke, rile, umbrage; SEE CONCEPT *14*

incensed [adj] *very angry*
at end of one's rope*, buffaloed*, bugged*, bummed out*, burned up*, dogged, enraged, exasperated, fuming, furious, hacked, hot and bothered*, huffy*, indignant, infuriated, irate, ireful, mad, maddened, miffed, on the warpath*, peeved, riled, rousted, rubbed the wrong way*, steamed up*, up in arms*, uptight*, wrathful; SEE CONCEPT *403*

incentive [n] *lure, inducement*
allurement, bait, carrot*, catalyst, come-on*, consideration, determinant, drive, encouragement, enticement, excuse, exhortation, goad, ground, impetus, impulse, incitement, influence, insistence, inspiration, instigation, lure, motivation, motive, persuasion, provocation, purpose, rationale, reason, reason why, spring, spur, stimulant, stimulation, stimulus, temptation, urge, whip; SEE CONCEPT *661*

inception [n] *beginning*
birth, commencement, dawn, derivation, fountain, inauguration, initiation, kickoff, origin, outset, prov-

enance, provenience, rise, root, source, start, well, wellspring; SEE CONCEPTS *648,832*

incessant [*adj*] *never-ending, persistent*
ceaseless, constant, continual, continuous, day-and-night*, endless, eternal, everlasting, interminable, interminate, monotonous, nonstop, perpetual, relentless, round-the-clock*, timeless, unbroken, unceasing, unending, unrelenting, unremitting; SEE CONCEPTS *534,798*

inch [*n*] *one-twelfth of a foot/2.54 centimeters measured*
fingerbreadth, one thirty-sixth of a yard, square; SEE CONCEPTS *790,791*

inchoate [*adj*] *undeveloped, beginning*
amorphous, elementary, embryonic, formless, immature, imperfect, inceptive, incipient, just begun, nascent, preliminary, rudimentary, shapeless, unfinished, unformed, unshaped; SEE CONCEPTS *485,578,797*

incident [*n*] *occurrence*
adventure, circumstance, episode, event, fact, happening, matter, milestone, occasion, scene, thing, trip; SEE CONCEPT *2*

incidental [*adj*] *related; minor*
accidental, accompanying, adventitious, ancillary, attendant, by-the-way*, casual, chance, circumstantial, coincidental, concomitant, concurrent, contingent, contributing, contributory, fluke*, fortuitous, irregular, nonessential, occasional, odd, random, secondary, subordinate, subsidiary; SEE CONCEPTS *547,548,577*

incidentally [*adv*] *by chance*
accidentally, as a by-product, as side effect, by the bye*, by the way, casually, fortuitously, in passing, in related manner, not by design, obiter, parenthetically, remotely, subordinately, unexpectedly; SEE CONCEPT *544*

incipient [*adj*] *developing*
basic, beginning, commencing, elementary, embryonic, fundamental, inceptive, inchoate, initial, initiative, initiatory, introductory, nascent, originating, start; SEE CONCEPT *585*

incisive [*adj1*] *very intelligent*
acute, bright, clever, concise, keen, penetrating, perspicacious, piercing, profound, sharp, trenchant; SEE CONCEPT *402*

incisive [*adj2*] *sarcastic*
acerb, acerbic, acid, biting, caustic, clear-cut, concise, crisp, cutting, drilling, laconic, mordant, penetrating, sardonic, satirical, scathing, severe, sharp, slashing, succinct, tart, terse, trenchant; SEE CONCEPT *267*

incite [*v*] *encourage, provoke*
abet, activate, actuate, agitate, animate, arouse, coax, craze, drive, egg on*, encourage, excite, exhort, fan the fire*, foment, force, forward, further, get to*, goad, impel, induce, inflame, influence, inspire, inspirit, instigate, juice*, key up*, motivate,

persuade, prick, promote, prompt, provoke, psych*, push, put up to*, raise, rouse, set, set off*, solicit, spur, stimulate, stir up*, talk into, taunt, trigger, urge, whip up*, work up*; SEE CONCEPTS *14,221,242*

inclement [*adj1*] *bitter, nasty (weather)*
brutal, cold, foul, hard, harsh, intemperate, raw, rigorous, rough, rugged, severe, stormy, tempestuous, violent, wintry; SEE CONCEPT *525*

inclement [*adj2*] *cruel, merciless*
callous, draconian, harsh, intemperate, pitiless, rigorous, ruthless, savage, severe, tyrannical, unfeeling, unkind, unmerciful; SEE CONCEPT *401*

inclination [*n1*] *tendency, bent*
affection, appetite, aptitude, aptness, attachment, attraction, bias, capability, capacity, cup of tea*, desire, disposition, drift, druthers*, fancy, fondness, groove*, idiosyncrasy, impulse, leaning, liking, mind, movement, partiality, penchant, persuasion, pleasure, predilection, predisposition, preference, prejudice, proclivity, proneness, propensity, slant*, soft spot*, stomach*, susceptibility, taste, temperament, thing*, trend, turn*, type, urge, velleity, weakness, whim, will, wish; SEE CONCEPTS *20,411,630*

inclination [*n2*] *slant, angle*
acclivity, bank, bend, bending, bevel, bow, bowing, cant, declivity, deviation, direction, downgrade, grade, gradient, hill, incline, lean, leaning, list, pitch, ramp, slope, tilt; SEE CONCEPT *738*

incline [*n*] *slope*
aclivity, approach, ascent, cant, declivity, descent, dip, grade, gradient, inclination, lean, leaning, plane, ramp, rise, slant, tilt; SEE CONCEPT *738*

incline [*v1*] *tend toward*
affect, be disposed, bend, be partial, be predisposed, be willing, bias, drive, favor, govern, gravitate toward, impel, induce, influence, lean to, look, make willing, move, not mind, persuade, predispose, prefer, prejudice, prompt, sway, turn, verge; SEE CONCEPT *657*

incline [*v2*] *bend, lean*
aim, bevel, bow, cant, cock, deviate, diverge, heel, lay, level, list, lower, nod, point, recline, skew, slant, slope, stoop, tend, tilt, tip, train, turn, veer, yaw; SEE CONCEPT *738*

include [*v*] *contain, involve*
accommodate, add, admit, allow for, append, bear, be composed of, be comprised of, be made up of, build, build in, carry, combine, comprehend, comprise, consist of, constitute, count, cover, cut in on, embody, embrace, encircle, enclose, encompass, entail, enter, have, hold, implicate, incorporate, inject, insert, interject, interpolate, introduce, make allowance for, make room for, number, number among, receive, subsume, take in, take into account, teem with, work in; SEE CONCEPTS *112,532,643*

including [*adj*] *containing*
along with, among other things, as well as, containing, counting, in addition to, inclusive of, in con-

junction with, made up of, not to mention, plus, together with, with; SEE CONCEPT *577*

inclusion [*n*] *addition*
admittance, composition, comprisal, embodiment, embracement, encompassment, formation, incorporation, insertion, involvement, subsumption; SEE CONCEPT *642*

inclusive [*adj*] *all-encompassing, all-embracing*
across-the-board*, all-around, all the options*, all together, ball-of-wax*, blanket*, broad, catchall*, comprehensive, encyclopedic, full, general, global, in toto*, overall, sweeping, umbrella*, wall-to-wall*, whole, without exception; SEE CONCEPT *772*

incognito [*adj*] *in disguise*
anonymous, bearded, camouflaged, concealed, disguised, hidden, incog*, isolated, masked, masquerading, obscure, under assumed name, unknown, unrecognized; SEE CONCEPTS *576,589*

incoherent [*adj*] *unintelligible*
breathless, confused, disconnected, discontinuous, discordant, disjointed, disordered, dumb, faltering, inarticulate, incohesive, incomprehensible, incongruous, inconsistent, indistinct, indistinguishable, irrational, jumbled, maundering, muddled, muffled, mumbling, mute, muttered, puzzling, rambling, stammering, stuttering, tongue-tied*, uncommunicative, unconnected, uncoordinated, uneven, unvocal, wandering, wild; SEE CONCEPT *267*

income [*n*] *money earned by work or investments*
assets, avails, benefits, bottom line*, cash, cash flow, commission, compensation, dividends, drawings, earnings, gains, gravy*, gross, harvest, honorarium, interest, in the black*, livelihood, means, net, pay, payoff, proceeds, profit, receipts, returns, revenue, royalty, salary, take home, wage; SEE CONCEPTS *340,344*

incomparable [*adj*] *superlative*
beyond compare, excellent, exceptional, ideal, inimitable, matchless, paramount, peerless, perfect, preeminent, second to none, sovereign, superior, supreme, surpassing, towering, transcendent, ultimate, unequalled, unmatchable, unmatched, unparalleled, unrivalled, unsurpassable; SEE CONCEPT *574*

incompatible [*adj*] *antagonistic, contradictory*
adverse, antipathetic, antipodal, antithetical, clashing, conflicting, contrary, counter, disagreeing, discordant, discrepant, disparate, factious, inadmissible, inappropriate, incoherent, inconformable, incongruous, inconsistent, inconsonant, inconstant, irreconcilable, jarring, marching to a different drummer*, mismatched, night and day*, offbeat*, opposed, opposite, poles apart*, unadapted, uncongenial, unsuited, warring, whale of difference*; SEE CONCEPT *564*

incompetent [*adj*] *unskillful, unable*
amateur, amateurish, awkward, bungling, bush-league*, clumsy, disqualified, floundering, helpless, inadequate, incapable, incapacitated, ineffectual, in-efficient, ineligible, inept, inexperienced, inexpert, insufficient, maladroit, not cut out for*, not equal to, not have it*, out to lunch*, raw, unadapted, unequipped, unfit, unfitted, unhandy, uninitiated, unproficient, unqualified, unskilled, untrained, useless; SEE CONCEPT *527*

incomplete [*adj*] *unfinished, wanting*
abridged, broken, crude, defective, deficient, expurgated, fractional, fragmentary, garbled, half-done, immature, imperfect, inadequate, incoherent, insufficient, lacking, meager, part, partial, rough, rude, rudimentary, short, sketchy, unaccomplished, unconsummated, under construction, undeveloped, undone, unexecuted, unpolished; SEE CONCEPT *531*

incomprehensible [*adj*] *not understandable*
baffling, beats me*, beyond comprehension, beyond one's grasp*, clear as mud*, cryptic, Delphic*, enigmatic, fathomless, Greek*, impenetrable, incognizable, inconceivable, inscrutable, mysterious, mystifying, obscure, opaque, over one's head*, perplexing, puzzling, sibylline, unclear, unfathomable, ungraspable, unimaginable, unintelligible, unknowable; SEE CONCEPTS *402,529*

inconceivable [*adj*] *beyond reason, belief*
extraordinary, fantastic, imcomprehensible, implausible, impossible, improbable, incogitable, incredible, insupposable, mind-boggling*, phony, rare, reachy, staggering, strange, thin*, unbelievable, unconvincing, unheard-of, unimaginable, unknowable, unlikely, unsubstantial, unthinkable, weak*, won't fly*, won't wash*; SEE CONCEPTS *529,552*

inconclusive [*adj*] *up in the air*
ambiguous, deficient, incomplete, indecisive, indeterminate, lacking, open, uncertain, unconvincing, undecided, uneventful, unfateful, unfinished, unsatisfactory, unsettled, vague; SEE CONCEPTS *537,548*

incongruous [*adj*] *out of place; absurd*
alien, bizarre, conflicting, contradictory, disconsonant, discordant, disparate, distorted, divergent, extraneous, fantastic, fitful, foreign, illogical, improper, inappropriate, inapropos, inapt, incoherent, incompatible, incongruent, inconsistent, irreconcilable, irregular, jumbled, lopsided, mismatched, out of keeping*, rambling, shifting, twisted, unavailing, unbalanced, unbecoming, unconnected, uncoordinated, uneven, unintelligible, unpredictable, unrelated, unsuitable, unsuited; SEE CONCEPTS *547,558*

inconsequential/inconsiderable [*adj*] *of no significance*
casual, dinky*, entry-level*, exiguous, immaterial, inadequate, inappreciable, inconsequent, insignificant, insufficient, light, little, measly, minor, negligible, paltry, petty, picayune, puny, runt, scanty, shoestring*, skimpy, small, small potatoes*, small-time*, trifling, trivial, two-bit*, unconsidered, unimportant, wimpy*, worthless; SEE CONCEPT *575*

inconsiderate [*adj*] *insensitive to others*
boorish, brash, careless, discourteous, hasty, impolite, incautious, indelicate, intolerant, reckless, rude, self-centered, selfish, sharp, short, tactless, thoughtless, unceremonious, uncharitable, ungracious, unkind, unthinking; SEE CONCEPT *401*

inconsistent [*adj*] *contradictory, irregular*
at odds, at variance, capricious, changeable, conflicting, contrary, discordant, discrepant, dissonant, erratic, fickle, illogical, incoherent, incompatible, in conflict, incongruent, incongruous, inconstant, irreconcilable, lubricious, mercurial, out of step*, temperamental, uncertain, unpredictable, unstable, variable, warring; SEE CONCEPTS *534,564*

inconsolable [*adj*] *brokenhearted*
comfortless, dejected, desolate, despairing, disconsolate, discouraged, distressed, forlorn, heartbroken, heartsick, sad, unconsolable; SEE CONCEPT *403*

inconspicuous [*adj*] *hidden, unnoticeable*
camouflaged, concealed, dim, faint, hidden, indistinct, insignificant, low-key*, low-profile*, modest, muted, ordinary, plain, quiet, retiring, secretive, shy, soft-pedalled*, subtle, tenuous, unassuming, unemphatic, unobtrusive, unostentatious; SEE CONCEPTS *485,576*

incontrovertible [*adj*] *beyond dispute*
accurate, authentic, certain, established, incontestable, indisputable, indubitable, irrefutable, nailed down*, no mistake*, no two ways about it*, positive, sure, surefire*, sure thing*, uncontestable, undeniable, unequivocal, unquestionable, unshakable; SEE CONCEPT *535*

inconvenience [*n*] *bother, trouble*
aggravation, annoyance, awkwardness, bothersomeness, cumbersomeness, difficulty, disadvantage, disruption, disturbance, drawback, exasperation, fuss, hindrance, nuisance, pain*, stew*, trial, troublesomeness, uneasiness, unfitness, unhandiness, unsuitableness, untimeliness, unwieldiness, upset, vexation; SEE CONCEPT *674*

inconvenience [*v*] *bother, trouble*
aggravate, discombobulate, discommode, discompose, disoblige, disrupt, disturb, exasperate, give a hard time*, give trouble*, hang up*, interfere, irk, make it tough*, meddle, put on the spot*, put to trouble*, try, upset; SEE CONCEPTS *14,242*

inconvenient [*adj*] *bothersome, troublesome*
annoying, awkward, cumbersome, detrimental, difficult, disadvantageous, discommoding, discommodious, disturbing, embarrassing, incommodious, inexpedient, inopportune, pestiferous, prejudicial, remote, tiresome, troublesome, unhandy, unmanageable, unseasonable, unsuitable, untimely, unwieldy, vexatious; SEE CONCEPTS *537,548*

incorporate [*v*] *include, combine*
absorb, add to, amalgamate, assimilate, associate, blend, charter, coalesce, consolidate, cover, dub, embody, form, fuse, gang up*, hook in*, imbibe, inhaust, integrate, join, link, merge, mix, organize, pool, put together, start, subsume, tie in*, unite; SEE CONCEPTS *112,113,324*

incorrect [*adj*] *wrong*
counterfactual, erroneous, false, faulty, flawed, imprecise, improper, inaccurate, inappropriate, inexact, mistaken, not trustworthy, out*, specious, unfitting, unreliable, unseemly, unsound, unsuitable, untrue, way off*, wide of the mark*, wrong number*; SEE CONCEPTS *558,570*

incorrigible [*adj*] *bad, hopeless*
abandoned, beastly, hardened, incurable, intractable, inveterate, irredeemable, irreparable, loser, recidivous, uncorrectable, unreformed, useless, wicked; SEE CONCEPT *570*

incorruptible [*adj*] *honest, honorable*
above suspicion, imperishable, indestructible, inextinguishable, just, loyal, moral, perpetual, persistent, pure, reliable, straight, trustworthy, unbribable, undestroyable, untouchable, upright; SEE CONCEPTS *485,545*

increase [*n*] *addition, growth*
access, accession, accretion, accrual, accumulation, aggrandizement, augmentation, boost, breakthrough, burgeoning, cumulation, development, elaboration, enlargement, escalation, exaggeration, expansion, extension, gain, hike, incorporation, increment, inflation, intensification, maximization, merger, multiplication, optimization, raise, rise, spread, step-up, surge, swell, swelling, upgrade, upsurge, upturn, waxing; SEE CONCEPTS *763,780*

increase [*v*] *add or grow*
advance, aggrandize, aggravate, amplify, annex, augment, boost, broaden, build, build up, deepen, develop, dilate, distend, double, enhance, enlarge, escalate, exaggerate, expand, extend, further, heighten, inflate, intensify, lengthen, magnify, mark up, mount, multiply, pad*, progress, proliferate, prolong, protract, pullulate, raise, redouble, reinforce, rise, sharpen, slap on*, snowball*, spread, step up, strengthen, supplement, swarm, swell, tack on*, teem, thicken, triple, wax*, widen; SEE CONCEPTS *236,245,780*

increasingly [*adv*] *to a greater extent*
more, more and more, progressively, with acceleration; SEE CONCEPT *772*

incredible [*adj1*] *beyond belief*
absurd, far-fetched, fishy*, flimsy*, implausible, impossible, improbable, incogitable, inconceivable, insupposable, outlandish, out of the question*, preposterous, questionable, ridiculous, rings phony*, suspect, thin*, unbelievable, unconvincing, unimaginable, unsubstantial, untenable, unthinkable; SEE CONCEPT *552*

incredible [*adj2*] *marvellous*
ace*, amazing, astonishing, astounding, awe-inspiring, awesome, extraordinary, fabulous, glori-

ous, great, prodigious, superhuman*, unreal*, wonderful; SEE CONCEPTS *529,572*

incredulous [*adj*] *unbelieving*
aporetic, disbelieving, distrustful, doubtful, doubting, dubious, hesitant, like doubting Thomas*, mistrustful, questioning, quizzical, show-me*, skeptical, suspect, suspicious, uncertain, unconvinced, unsatisfied, wary; SEE CONCEPTS *403,529*

increment [*n*] *small step toward gain*
accession, accretion, accrual, accrument, addition, advancement, augmentation, enlargement, increase, profit, raise, rise, step, supplement; SEE CONCEPTS *763,780*

inculcate [*v*] *implant, infuse information*
brainwash*, break down, communicate, drill, drum into*, educate, hammer into*, impart, impress, indoctrinate, inseminate, instill, instruct, plant, program, shape up, teach, work over*; SEE CONCEPTS *14,285*

incur [*v*] *bring upon oneself*
acquire, arouse, be subjected to, bring down on*, catch, contract, draw, earn, expose oneself to, gain, get, induce, meet with, obtain, provoke; SEE CONCEPT *93*

incurable [*adj*] *unfixable, unchangeable*
cureless, deadly, fatal, hopeless, immedicable, impossible, inoperable, irrecoverable, irremediable, irreparable, nowhere to go*, out of time*, remediless, serious, terminal, uncorrectable, unrecoverable; SEE CONCEPTS *485,548*

incursion [*n*] *invasion*
aggression, attack, foray, infiltration, inroad, intrusion, irruption, penetration, raid; SEE CONCEPTS *86,320*

indebted [*adj*] *under an obligation*
accountable, answerable for, appreciative, beholden, bound, bounden, chargeable, duty-bound, grateful, honor-bound, hooked*, in debt, in hock*, liable, obligated, obliged, owed, owing, responsible, thankful; SEE CONCEPTS *334,546*

indecency [*n*] *obscenity, vulgarity*
bawdiness, coarseness, crudity, drunkenness, evil, foulness, grossness, immodesty, impropriety, impurity, incivility, indecorum, indelicacy, lewdness, licentiousness, offense, outrageousness, pornography, ribaldry, smuttiness, unseemliness, vileness, vulgarity; SEE CONCEPTS *633,645*

indecent [*adj*] *obscene, vulgar; offensive*
blue*, coarse, crude, dirty*, filthy, foul, foulmouthed, gross*, ill-bred, immodest, immoral, improper, impure, in bad taste, indecorous, indelicate, lewd, licentious, malodorous, off-color*, outrageous, pornographic, raunchy*, raw, ridiculous, rough, salacious, scatological, shameless, shocking, smutty*, tasteless, unbecoming, undecorous, unseemly, untoward, vile, vulgar, wicked, X-rated*; SEE CONCEPT *545*

indecisive [*adj*] *uncertain, indefinite*
astraddle, changeable, doubtful, faltering, halting, hemming and hawing*, hesitant, hesitating, hot and cold*, inconclusive, indeterminate, irresolute, of two minds*, on the fence*, tentative, unclear, undecided, undetermined, uneventful, unsettled, unstable, vacillating, waffling, wavering, weak-kneed*, wishy-washy*; SEE CONCEPTS *534,535*

indeed [*adv*] *actually*
absolutely, amen*, certainly, doubtlessly, easily, even, for real, in point of fact, in truth, much, naturally, of course, positively, really, strictly, surely, sure thing*, to be sure, truly, undeniably, undoubtedly, verily, veritably, very, very much, well; SEE CONCEPT *535*

indefatigable [*adj*] *untiring*
active, assiduous, bound and determined*, dead set on*, determined, diligent, dogged, energetic, hellbent*, industrious, inexhaustible, ironclad, nose to grindstone*, painstaking, patient, persevering, persistent, pertinacious, relentless, sedulous, steadfast, stop at nothing*, strenuous, tireless, unfaltering, unflagging, unflinching, unremitting, unwavering, unwearied, unwearying, vigorous; SEE CONCEPT *542*

indefensible [*adj*] *inexcusable*
bad, faulty, inexpiable, insupportable, unforgivable, unjustifiable, unpardonable, untenable, unwarrantable, wrong; SEE CONCEPTS *545,548*

indefinite [*adj*] *ambiguous, vague*
broad, confused, doubtful, dubious, equivocal, evasive, general, ill-defined, imprecise, indeterminable, indeterminate, indistinct, inexact, inexhaustible, infinite, innumerable, intangible, loose, obscure, shadowy, uncertain, unclear, undefined, undependable, undetermined, unfixed, unknown, unlimited, unsettled, unspecific, unsure, wide; SEE CONCEPT *535*

indefinitely [*adv*] *continually*
considerably, endlessly, forever, frequently, regularly, sine die, without end; SEE CONCEPT *798*

indelible [*adj*] *not able to be erased, indestructible*
enduring, ineffaceable, ineradicable, inerasable, inexpungible, inextirpable, ingrained, lasting, memorable, permanent, rememberable, stirring, unforgettable; SEE CONCEPTS *482,529*

indelicate [*adj*] *obscene, vulgar*
base, brash, brutish, callow, coarse, crude, earthy, embarrassing, immodest, improper, indecent, indecorous, lewd, low, lowbred, off-color*, offensive, outrageous, risqué, rude, suggestive, tasteless, unbecoming, unblushing, uncouth, unseemly, untactful, untoward; SEE CONCEPTS *544,545*

indent [*v*] *make a space; push in slightly*
bash, cave in, cut, dent, depress, dint, hollow, jag, mark, nick, notch, pink, pit, rabbet, rut, scallop, score, serrate; SEE CONCEPTS *158,201,208*

independence [*n*] *liberty, freedom*
ability, aptitude, autarchy, autonomy, home rule*, license, qualification, self-determination, self-

government, self-reliance, self-rule, self-sufficiency, separation, skill, sovereignty; SEE CONCEPTS *376,691*

independent [*adj*] *liberated, free*
absolute, autarchic, autarchical, autonomous, free-wheeling, individualistic, nonaligned, nonpartisan, one's own sweet way*, on one's own, self-contained, self-determining, self-governing, self-reliant, self-ruling, self-sufficient, self-supporting, separate, separated, sovereign, unaided, unallied, unconnected, unconstrained, uncontrolled, unregimented; SEE CONCEPT *554*

independently [*adv*] *alone*
all by one's self, apart, autonomously, by oneself, exclusive of, freely, individually, of one's own volition, one at a time, one by one, on one's own, separately, severally, singly, solo, unaided, unrestrictedly, unsupervised, without regard to, without support; SEE CONCEPT *554*

indescribable [*adj*] *beyond words*
impossible, incommunicable, indefinable, ineffable, inexpressible, nondescript, sublime, subtle, unspeakable, untellable, unutterable; SEE CONCEPT *267*

indestructible [*adj*] *lasting, unable to be destroyed*
abiding, deathless, durable, enduring, everlasting, immortal, immutable, imperishable, incorruptible, indelible, indissoluble, inexterminable, inextinguishable, inextirpable, irrefragable, irrefrangible, nonperishable, permanent, perpetual, unalterable, unbreakable, unchangeable, undestroyable, undying, unfading; SEE CONCEPTS *489,534*

indeterminate [*adj*] *uncertain, vague*
borderless, general, imprecise, inconclusive, indefinite, indistinct, inexact, undefined, undetermined, unfixed, unspecified, unstipulated; SEE CONCEPT *535*

index [*n*] *indication*
basis, clue, evidence, formula, guide, hand, indicant, indication, indicator, indicia, mark, model, needle, pointer, ratio, rule, sign, significant, symbol, symptom, token; SEE CONCEPTS *284,290*

index [*v*] *arrange, order*
alphabetize, catalogue, docket, file, list, record, tabulate; SEE CONCEPT *84*

indicate [*v*] *signify, display*
add up to, announce, argue, attest, augur, bespeak, be symptomatic, betoken, button down*, card, connote, demonstrate, denote, designate, evidence, evince, express, finger, hint, illustrate, imply, import, intimate, make, manifest, mark, mean, name, peg*, pin down*, pinpoint*, point out, point to, prove, read, record, register, reveal, show, sign, signal, signify, slot, specify, suggest, symbolize, tab, tag, testify, witness; SEE CONCEPTS *74,118,266*

indication [*n*] *evidence, clue*
adumbration, attestation, augury, auspice, cue, earnest, explanation, expression, forewarning, gesture, hint, implication, index, indicia, inkling, intimation, manifestation, mark, nod, note, notion, omen, pledge, portent, preamble, prefiguration, prognostic,

prolegomenon, proof, reminder, show, sign, signal, significant, signifier, suggestion, symptom, telltale, token, trace, vestige, warning, wind*, wink*; SEE CONCEPTS *74,278,284*

indicative [*adj*] *exhibitive*
apocalyptic, augural, auspicious, characteristic, connotative, demonstrative, denotative, denotive, designative, diagnostic, emblematic, evidential, evincive, expressive, inauspicious, indicatory, indicial, ominous, pointing to, prognostic, significant, significatory, suggestive, symbolic, symptomatic, testatory, testimonial; SEE CONCEPT *267*

indict [*v*] *accuse*
arraign, censure, charge, criminate, face with charges, finger*, frame*, impeach, incriminate, inculpate, prosecute, summon, tax; SEE CONCEPTS *44,317*

indictment [*n*] *accusation*
allegation, arraignment, bill, blame, censure, charge, citation, detention, findings, impeachment, incrimination, presentment, prosecution, statement, summons, warrant, writ; SEE CONCEPTS *44,317,318*

indifference [*n*] *absence of feeling, interest*
alienation, aloofness, apathy, callousness, carelessness, cold-bloodedness, coldness, cold shoulder*, coolness, detachment, disdain, disinterest, disinterestedness, dispassion, disregard, equity, heedlessness, immunity, impartiality, impassiveness, impassivity, inattention, inertia, insensitivity, insouciance, isolationism, lack, lethargy, listlessness, negligence, neutrality, nonchalance, noninterference, objectivity, stoicalness, stoicism, torpor, unconcern, unmindfulness; SEE CONCEPTS *410,657*

indifferent [*adj*] *unfeeling, uninterested*
aloof, apathetic, blasé, callous, cold, cool, detached, diffident, disinterested, dispassionate, distant, equitable, haughty, heartless, heedless, highbrow, impartial, impervious, inattentive, listless, neutral, nonchalant, nonpartisan, objective, passionless, phlegmatic, regardless, scornful, silent, stoical, supercilious, superior, unaroused, unbiased, uncaring, uncommunicative, unconcerned, unemotional, unimpressed, uninvolved, unmoved, unprejudiced, unresponsive, unsocial, unsympathetic; SEE CONCEPTS *403,542*

indigenous [*adj*] *native, inborn*
aboriginal, autochthonous, chthonic, congenital, connate, domestic, endemic, homegrown, inbred, inherent, inherited, innate, natural, original, primitive, unacquired; SEE CONCEPT *549*

indigent [*adj*] *poor*
beggared, busted, destitute, down and out*, flat broke*, hard up*, homeless, impecunious, impoverished, in want, necessitous, needy, penniless, penurious, poverty-stricken; SEE CONCEPT *334*

indigestion [*n*] *upset stomach*
acid indigestion, acidosis, digestive upset, dyspepsia, dyspepsy, flatulence, flu, gas, gaseous stomach, heartburn, nausea, pain; SEE CONCEPT *306*

indignant [*adj*] *very angry*
acrimonious, annoyed, bent out of shape*, boiling*, bugged*, burned up*, disgruntled, displeased, exasperated, fuming, furious, heated, huffy, in a huff*, incensed, irate, livid, mad, miffed, peeved, piqued, p.o.'d*, provoked, resentful, riled, scornful, seeing red*, up in arms*, upset, wrathful; SEE CONCEPTS *403,542*

indignation [*n*] *anger*
animus, boiling point*, danger, displeasure, exasperation, fury, huff*, ire, mad, miff*, pique, rage, resentment, rise, scorn, slow burn*, umbrage, wrath; SEE CONCEPTS *29,657*

indignity [*n*] *embarrassment, humiliation*
abuse, affront, backhanded compliment*, contumely, discourtesy, dishonor, disrespect, grievance, injury, injustice, insult, obloquy, opprobrium, outrage, put-down*, reproach, slap*, slight, slur, snub, take-down*, taunt; SEE CONCEPTS *278,410*

indirect [*adj*] *roundabout; unintended*
ambiguous, ancillary, circuitous, circular, circumlocutory, collateral, complicated, contingent, crooked, devious, discursive, duplicitous, erratic, eventual, implied, incidental, long, long-drawn-out*, long way home*, long-winded*, meandering, oblique, obscure, out-of-the-way, periphrastic, rambling, secondary, serpentine*, sidelong, sinister, sinuous, snaking*, sneaking, sneaky, subsidiary, tortuous, twisting, underhand, vagrant, wandering, winding, zigzag; SEE CONCEPTS *544,581*

indiscretion [*n*] *mistake*
bumble, crudeness, dropping the ball*, dumb move*, error, excitability, faux pas, folly, foolishness, fool mistake*, foul-up, gaffe, gaucherie, goof*, hastiness, imprudence, indiscreetness, ingenuousness, lapse, miscue, misjudgment, misspeak, naiveté, rashness, recklessness, screw-up*, simple-mindedness, slip*, slip of the tongue*, slip-up*, stumble, stupidity, tactlessness, thoughtlessness, unseemliness; SEE CONCEPTS *101,633,674*

indiscriminate [*adj*] *random, chaotic*
aimless, assorted, broad, careless, confused, designless, desultory, extensive, general, haphazard, heterogeneous, hit-or-miss*, imperceptive, jumbled, mingled, miscellaneous, mixed, mongrel, motley*, multifarious, promiscuous, purposeless, shallow, spotty, superficial, sweeping, unconsidered, uncritical, undiscriminating, unmethodical, unplanned, unselective, unsystematic, varied, variegated, wholesale*, wide; SEE CONCEPTS *403,542,585,772*

indispensable [*adj*] *necessary*
basal, basic, cardinal, crucial, essential, fundamental, imperative, key, necessitous, needed, needful, prerequisite, primary, required, requisite, vital; SEE CONCEPT *546*

indisposed [*adj1*] *not well*
ailing, below par, confined, down, down with*, feeling rotten*, got a bug*, ill, infirm, laid up*, on sick list*, out of action*, poorly, sick, sickly, under the weather*, unwell; SEE CONCEPT *314*

indisposed [*adj2*] *unwilling*
afraid, antagonistic, antipathetic, averse, backward, disinclined, hesitant, hostile, inimical, loath, reluctant, uncaring, uneager, uninclined; SEE CONCEPT *542*

indisputable [*adj*] *beyond doubt*
absolute, accurate, actual, certain, double-checked, evident, incontestable, incontrovertible, indubitable, irrefutable, no ifs ands or buts about it*, no mistake*, open and shut*, positive, real, sure, that's a fact*, true, unassailable, undeniable, undoubted, unfabled, unquestionable, veridical; SEE CONCEPTS *535,582*

indistinct [*adj*] *obscure, ambiguous*
bleared, bleary, blurred, confused, dark, dim, doubtful, faint, fuzzy, hazy, ill-defined, inaudible, inconspicuous, indefinite, indeterminate, indiscernible, indistinguishable, inexact, misty, muffled, murky, out of focus, shadowy, unclear, undefined, undetermined, unheard, unintelligible, vague, weak; SEE CONCEPTS *485,535*

indistinguishable [*adj*] *alike*
duplicate, equivalent, identic, identical, like, same, tantamount, twin; SEE CONCEPT *566*

individual [*n*] *singular person, thing*
being, body, character, child, creature, dude*, entity, existence, gal*, guy*, human being, man/woman, material, matter, mortal, number, party, person, personage, self, singleton, somebody, something, soul, stuff, substance, type, unit; SEE CONCEPTS *389,433*

individual [*adj*] *distinctive, exclusive*
alone, characteristic, definite, diacritic, diagnostic, different, discrete, distinct, especial, express, idiosyncratic, indivisible, lone, odd, only, original, own, particular, peculiar, personal, personalized, proper, reserved, respective, secluded, select, separate, several, single, singular, sole, solitary, special, specific, uncommon, unique, unitary, unusual; SEE CONCEPTS *404,564*

individuality [*n*] *personality*
air, character, complexion, difference, discreteness, disposition, dissimilarity, distinction, distinctiveness, eccentricity, habit, humor, identity, idiosyncrasy, independence, individualism, ipseity, make-up, manner, nature, oddity, oneness, originality, particularity, peculiarity, rarity, seity, selfdom, selfhood, selfness, separateness, singleness, singularity, singularness, temper, temperament, uniqueness, unity, unlikeness, way; SEE CONCEPT *411*

individually [*adv*] *separately*
alone, apart, by oneself, distinctively, exclusively, independently, one at a time, one by one, personally, restrictedly, severally, singly, without help; SEE CONCEPT *544*

indoctrinate [v] *brainwash*
break down, convince, drill, ground, imbue, implant, inculcate, influence, initiate, instill, instruct, plant, program, school, teach, train, work over; SEE CONCEPTS *14,285*

indolent [adj] *lazy*
drony, easygoing, faineant, idle, inactive, inert, lackadaisical, languid, lax, lazy, lethargic, listless, resting, shiftless, slothful, slow, slow-going, sluggish, torpid; SEE CONCEPTS *538,542,584*

indomitable [adj] *steadfast, unyielding*
dogged, impassable, impregnable, insuperable, insurmountable, invincible, invulnerable, obstinate, pertinacious, resolute, ruthless, staunch, stubborn, unassailable, unbeatable, unconquerable, undefeatable, unflinching, willful; SEE CONCEPTS *404,489, 534*

induce [v] *cause to happen; encourage*
abet, activate, actuate, argue into, breed, bring about, bring around, bulldoze*, cajole, cause, coax, convince, draw, draw in, effect, engender, generate, get*, get up, give rise to, goose*, impel, incite, influence, instigate, lead to, make, motivate, move, occasion, persuade, press, prevail upon, procure, produce, promote, prompt, sell one on*, set in motion, soft-soap*, squeeze, steamroll*, suck in*, sway, sweet-talk*, talk into*, twist one's arm*, urge, wheedle, win over*; SEE CONCEPTS *14,68,242*

inducement [n] *incentive, motive*
attraction, bait, brainwash*, carrot*, cause, come-on*, con*, consideration, desire, encouragement, hard sell*, hook*, impulse, incitement, influence, leader, lure, reward, snow job*, soft soap*, spur, stimulus, sweet talk*, temptation, twist, urge; SEE CONCEPTS *68,661*

induct [v] *take into an organization*
conscript, draft, enlist, inaugurate, initiate, install, instate, introduce, invest, recruit, sign on, sign up, swear in; SEE CONCEPTS *50,88,320,384*

induction [n1] *taking in, initiation*
consecration, draft, entrance, greetings, inaugural, inauguration, installation, instatement, institution, introduction, investiture, ordination, selection; SEE CONCEPTS *320,384,685*

induction [n2] *inference*
conclusion, conjecture, deducement, generalization, judgment, logical reasoning, ratiocination, rationalization, reason; SEE CONCEPTS *37,689*

indulge [v1] *treat oneself or another to*
allow, baby, cater, coddle, cosset, delight, entertain, favor, foster, give in, give rein to*, go along, go easy on*, gratify, humor, mollycoddle*, nourish, oblige, pamper, pander, pet, please, regale, satiate, satisfy, spoil, spoil rotten*, take care of*, tickle, yield; SEE CONCEPT *110*

indulge [v2] *luxuriate in*
bask in, ego trip*, enjoy, go in for*, live it up*, look out for number one*, revel in, rollick*, take part, wallow in; SEE CONCEPT *20*

indulgence [n] *luxury; gratification*
allowance, appeasement, attention, babying*, coddling*, courtesy, endurance, excess, extravagance, favor, favoring, fondling, fondness, forbearance, fulfillment, goodwill, gratifying, hedonism, immoderation, intemperance, intemperateness, kindness, kowtowing, lenience, leniency, pampering, partiality, patience, permissiveness, petting, placating, pleasing, privilege, profligacy, profligateness, satiation, satisfaction, service, spoiling, toadying*, tolerance, toleration, treating, understanding; SEE CONCEPTS *337,657,712*

indulgent [adj] *lenient, giving*
able to live with*, big*, charitable, clement, compassionate, complaisant, compliant, considerate, easy, easygoing, favorable, fond, forbearing, gentle, going along with*, going easy on*, gratifying, kind, kindly, liberal, merciful, mild, overpermissive, permissive, soft-shelled*, tender, tolerant, understanding; SEE CONCEPTS *404,542*

industrial [adj] *related to manufacturing*
automated, business, factory-made, industrialized, in industry, machine-made, manufactured, manufacturing, mechanical, mechanized, modern, smokestack, streamlined, technical; SEE CONCEPT *536*

industrious [adj] *hardworking*
active, assiduous, ball of fire*, burning, busy, conscientious, diligent, dynamic, eager, energetic, grind*, in full swing*, intent, involved, jumping, laborious, on the go*, operose, perky*, persevering, persistent, plugging, productive, psyched up on*, purposeful, sedulous, spirited, steady, tireless, zealous; SEE CONCEPT *538*

industry [n1] *manufacturing*
big business*, business, commerce, commercial enterprise, corporation, management, manufactory, megacorp*, mob, monopoly, multinational, outfit*, production, trade, traffic; SEE CONCEPTS *323,325*

industry [n2] *hard work*
activity, application, assiduity, attention, care, determination, diligence, dynamism, effort, energy, enterprise, intentness, inventiveness, labor, pains, patience, perseverance, persistence, tirelessness, toil, vigor, zeal; SEE CONCEPT *677*

inebriated [adj] *drunk*
blind drunk*, bombed, boozy, high*, inebriate, intoxicated, loaded*, plastered*, smashed*, tight*, tipsy, under the influence, wasted*; SEE CONCEPT *314*

ineffable [adj] *too great for words*
beyond words, celestial, divine, empyreal, empyrean, ethereal, heavenly, holy, ideal, impossible, incommunicable, incredible, indefinable, indescribable, inexpressible, nameless, sacred, spiritual, too sacred for words*, transcendent, transcendental, unspeakable, untellable, unutterable; SEE CONCEPTS *267,574*

ineffective/ineffectual [adj] *weak, useless*
abortive, anticlimactic, barren, bootless, defeasible, emasculate, feckless, feeble, forceless, fruitless, fu-

tile, idle, impotent, inadequate, incompetent, indecisive, inefficacious, inefficient, inept, inferior,
innocuous, inoperative, invertebrate, lame, limited,
neutralized, not effective, nugatory, null, null and
void*, paltry, powerless, spineless, unable, unavailing, unfruitful, unproductive, unprofitable, unsuccessful, vain, void, withered, worthless; SEE
CONCEPTS *537,560*

inefficient [*adj*] *not working well; wasteful*
can't hack it*, careless, disorganized, extravagant,
faulty, feeble, half-baked*, improficient, improvident, incapable, incompetent, ineffective, ineffectual, inefficacious, inept, inexpert, not cut out for*,
prodigal, shooting blanks*, slack, slipshod, sloppy,
slovenly, unfit, unprepared, unqualified, unskilled,
unskillful, untrained, weak; SEE CONCEPTS
402,527,560

inelegant [*adj*] *clumsy, crude*
awkward, coarse, crass, gauche, graceless, gross, indelicate, labored, oafish, raw, rough, rude, stiff*,
uncouth, uncultivated, uncultured, ungainly, ungraceful, unpolished, unrefined, vulgar, wooden*;
SEE CONCEPTS *267,542,555*

ineligible [*adj*] *not qualified*
disqualified, inappropriate, incompetent, objectionable, ruled out, unacceptable, unavailable, undesirable, unequipped, unfit, unqualified, unsuitable; SEE
CONCEPTS *402,558*

inept [*adj1*] *clumsy, unskilled; incompetent*
all thumbs*, artless, awkward, bumbling, bungling,
butterfingers*, gauche, halting, inadept, incapable,
incompetent, inefficient, inexpert, loser, maladroit,
unapt, undexterous, unfacile, ungraceful, unhandy,
unproficient, unskillful, wooden*; SEE CONCEPTS
402,527

inept [*adj2*] *not suitable; improper*
absurd, ill-timed, inappropriate, inapt, infelicitous,
malapropos, meaningless, not adapted, out of place*,
pointless, ridiculous, undue, unfit, unseasonable, unseemly, unsuitable; SEE CONCEPT *558*

inequality [*n*] *prejudice; lack of balance*
asperity, bias, contrast, difference, discrimination,
disparity, disproportion, dissimilarity, dissimilitude,
diversity, imparity, incommensurateness, injustice,
irregularity, one-sidedness, partisanship, preferenti-
ality, roughness, unequivalence, unevenness, unfairness, unjustness, variation; SEE CONCEPT *665*

inert [*adj*] *not moving; lifeless*
apathetic, asleep, dead, dormant, down, dull, idle,
immobile, impassive, impotent, inactive, inanimate,
indolent, languid, languorous, lazy, leaden, listless,
motionless, numb, paralyzed, passive, phlegmatic,
powerless, quiescent, quiet, slack, sleepy, slothful,
sluggard, sluggish, slumberous, static, still, stolid,
torpid, unmoving, unreactive, unresponsive; SEE
CONCEPTS *542,584*

inertia [*n*] *disinclination to move; lifelessness*
apathy, deadness, drowsiness, dullness, idleness, immobility, immobilization, inactivity, indolence, lan-

guor, lassitude, laziness, lethargy, listlessness,
oscitancy, paralysis, passivity, sloth, sluggishness,
stillness, stupor, torpidity, torpor, unresponsiveness;
SEE CONCEPTS *657,681*

inevitable [*adj*] *certain; cannot be avoided*
all locked up*, assured, binding, compulsory, decided, decreed, destined, determined, doomed, fated,
fateful, fixed, for certain, foreordained, imminent,
impending, ineluctable, ineludible, inescapable, inexorable, inflexible, in the bag*, irresistible, irrevocable, necessary, no ifs ands or buts, obligatory,
ordained, pat*, prescribed, settled, sure, unalterable,
unavoidable, undeniable, unpreventable, without recourse; SEE CONCEPTS *535,552*

inexcusable [*adj*] *not forgivable*
blamable, blameworthy, censurable, criticizable, im-
permissible, indefensible, inexpiable, intolerable,
outrageous, reprehensible, unallowable, unforgivable, unjustifiable, unpardonable, unpermissible, untenable, unwarrantable, wrong; SEE CONCEPTS
545,570

inexorable [*adj*] *unalterable*
adamant, adamantine, bound, bound and determined*, compulsory, dead set on*, dogged, hard,
harsh, hell bent on*, immobile, immovable, implacable, ineluctable, inescapable, inflexible, ironclad,
like death and taxes*, locked in*, mean business*,
merciless, necessary, no going back*, obdurate, obstinate, relentless, remorseless, resolute, rigid, set in
stone*, severe, single-minded, stubborn, unappeasable, unbending, uncompromising, unmovable, unrelenting, unyielding; SEE CONCEPTS *401,534*

inexpensive [*adj*] *not high priced*
bargain, budget, buy, cheap, cost next to nothing*,
cut-rate, dime a dozen*, dirt-cheap*, economical,
for a song*, half-price, low, low-cost, low-priced,
marked down, modest, nominal, popular, popularly
priced, real buy*, real steal*, reasonable, reduced,
steal, thrifty; SEE CONCEPT *334*

inexperienced [*adj*] *unskilled, unfamiliar*
amateur, callow, fresh, green*, ignorant, immature,
inept, inexpert, innocent, kid*, naive, new, prentice,
raw*, rookie, rude, sophomoric, spring chicken*,
tenderfoot*, unaccustomed, unacquainted, unconversant, undisciplined, unfamiliar with, unfledged, unpracticed, unschooled, unseasoned, unsophisticated,
untrained, untried, unused, unversed, unworldly,
verdant, virgin, wet behind ears*, young; SEE CON-
CEPTS *402,404,527*

inexplicable [*adj*] *beyond comprehension, explanation*
baffling, enigmatic, incomprehensible, indecipherable, indescribable, inexplainable, inscrutable, insoluble, mysterious, mystifying, obscure, odd, peculiar,
puzzling, strange, unaccountable, undefinable, unexplainable, unfathomable, unintelligible, unsolvable;
SEE CONCEPTS *267,529*

infallible [adj] unerring, dependable
acceptable, accurate, agreeable, apodictic, authoritative, certain, correct, effective, effectual, efficacious, efficient, exact, faultless, flawless, foolproof, handy, helpful, impeccable, incontrovertible, inerrable, inerrant, omniscient, perfect, positive, reliable, satisfactory, satisfying, sure, surefire, true, trustworthy, unbeatable, undeceivable, unfailing, unimpeachable, unquestionable, useful; SEE CONCEPTS 535,560,574

infamous [adj] shameful, bad in reputation
abominable, atrocious, base, caitiff, contemptible, corrupt, degenerate, despicable, detestable, disgraceful, dishonorable, disreputable, egregious, evil, flagitious, foul, hateful, heinous, ignominious, ill-famed, iniquitous, loathsome, miscreant, monstrous, nefarious, notorious, odious, offensive, opprobrious, outrageous, perverse, questionable, rotten, scandalous, scurvy, shady, shocking, sorry, unhealthy, vicious, vile, villainous, wicked; SEE CONCEPTS 404,545,570

infamy [n] shameful, bad reputation
abomination, atrocity, disapprobation, discredit, disesteem, disgrace, dishonor, disrepute, enormity, evil, ignominy, immorality, impropriety, notoriety, notoriousness, obloquy, odium, opprobrium, outrageousness, scandal, shame, stigma, villainy, wickedness; SEE CONCEPTS 411,645

infant [n] baby
babe, bairn, bambino, bantling, bundle, child, kid, little one, neonate, newborn, small child, suckling, toddler, tot; SEE CONCEPTS 414,424

infant/infantile [adj] very young
baby, babyish, callow, childish, childlike, dawning, developing, early, emergent, green*, growing, immature, infantine, initial, juvenile, kid, naive, nascent, newborn, puerile, tender, unfledged, unripe, weak, youthful; SEE CONCEPTS 542,578,797,820

infatuated [adj] in love with; obsessed
beguiled, besotted, bewitched, captivated, carried away*, charmed, crazy about*, enamored, enraptured, far gone on*, fascinated, foolish, inflamed, intoxicated, possessed, seduced, silly*, smitten, spellbound, under a spell*; SEE CONCEPTS 32,403

infect [v] pollute, contaminate
affect, blight, corrupt, defile, disease, influence, poison, spoil, spread among, spread to, taint, touch, vitiate; SEE CONCEPTS 143,246

infection [n] contamination
bug*, communicability, contagion, contagiousness, corruption, defilement, disease, epidemic, flu, germs, impurity, insanitation, poison, pollution, septicity, virus, what's going around*; SEE CONCEPTS 230,306

infectious [adj] catching, spreading
communicable, contagious, contaminating, corrupting, defiling, diseased, epidemic, infective, mephitic, miasmic, noxious, pestilent, pestilential, poisoning, polluting, toxic, transferable, transmittable, virulent, vitiating; SEE CONCEPTS 314,559

infer [v] conclude
arrive at, ascertain, assume, believe, collect, conjecture, construe, deduce, derive, draw, draw inference, figure, figure out, gather, glean, guess, induce, interpret, intuit, judge, presume, presuppose, reach conclusion, read between lines*, read into*, reason, reckon, speculate, suppose, surmise, think, understand; SEE CONCEPTS 12,15,37

inferior [n] person of lesser rank, importance
adherent, attendant, auxiliary, deputy, disciple, follower, hanger-on, henchman/woman, hireling, junior, menial, minion, minor, peon, satellite, second banana*, serf, slave, subaltern, subject, subordinate, sycophant, underling; SEE CONCEPTS 348,423

inferior [adj1] less in rank, importance
back seat*, bottom, bottom-rung*, entry-level, junior, less, lesser, lower, menial, minor, minus, nether, peon, second, secondary, second-banana*, second-fiddle*, second-string*, slave, smaller, subjacent, subordinate, subsidiary, under, underneath; SEE CONCEPT 567

inferior [adj2] poor, second-rate
average, bad, base, common, déclassé, fair, good-for-nothing*, hack*, imperfect, indifferent, junk*, lemon*, lousy, low-grade, low-rent*, mean, mediocre, middling, ordinary, paltry, poorer, sad, second-class, sorry*, substandard, tawdry, two-bit*, worse, wretched; SEE CONCEPT 574

infernal [adj] damned; underworld
accursed, blamed, blasted, chthonian, confounded, cursed, cussed, damnable, demonic, devilish, diabolical, execrable, fiendish, hellish, lower, malevolent, malicious, monstrous, nether, satanic, subterranean, sulphurous, wicked; SEE CONCEPTS 536,545

infertile [adj] not bearing fruit, young
barren, depleted, drained, effete, exhausted, impotent, impoverished, infecund, nonproductive, sterile, unbearing, unfertile, unfruitful, unproductive; SEE CONCEPTS 406,560

infest [adj] flood, overrun
abound, annoy, assail, beset, crawl, crowd, defile, fill, flock, harass, harry, infect, invade, overspread, overwhelm, pack, penetrate, pester, plague, pollute, press, ravage, swarm, teem, throng, worry; SEE CONCEPTS 14,86,179

infidelity [n] disloyalty, especially sexual
adultery, affair, bad faith, betrayal, cheating, duplicity, extramarital relations, faithlessness, falseness, falsity, fornication, hanky-panky*, inconstancy, lewdness, perfidiousness, perfidy, playing around*, thing*, treacherousness, treachery, treason, two-timing*, unfaithfulness; SEE CONCEPTS 388,645

infiltrate [v] creep in
access, crack*, edge in, filter through, foist, impregnate, insinuate, penetrate, percolate*, permeate, per-

vade, saturate, sneak in, tinge, work into, worm into*; SEE CONCEPTS *159,179*

infinite [*adj*] *limitless, without end*

absolute, all-embracing, bottomless, boundless, enduring, enormous, eternal, everlasting, illimitable, immeasurable, immense, incalculable, incessant, inestimable, inexhaustible, interminable, measureless, million, never-ending, no end of, no end to, numberless, perdurable, perpetual, sempiternal, stupendous, supertemporal, supreme, total, unbounded, uncounted, unending, untold, vast, wide, without limit, without number; SEE CONCEPTS *762,781,798*

infinitesimal [*adj*] *very small*

atomic, imperceptible, inappreciable, inconsiderable, insignificant, little, microscopic, miniature, minuscule, minute, negligible, teeny*, tiny, unnoticeable; SEE CONCEPTS *773,789*

infinity [*n*] *endlessness*

beyond, boundlessness, continuity, continuum, endless time, eternity, expanse, extent, immeasurability, immensity, infinitude, limitlessness, myriad, perpetuity, sempiternity, space, ubiquity, unlimited space, vastitude, vastness; SEE CONCEPTS *730,807*

infirm [*adj*] *sick, weak*

ailing, anemic, anile, debilitated, decrepit, delicate, doddering, enfeebled, failing, faint, faltering, feeble, flimsy, fragile, frail, halting, ill, insecure, irresolute, laid low*, lame, sensile, shaky, unsound, unstable, unsubstantial, vacillating, wavering, weakly, wobbly; SEE CONCEPTS *314,485,489*

infirmity [*n*] *weakness, sickness*

affliction, ailing, ailment, confinement, debilitation, debility, decay, decrepitude, defect, deficiency, disease, diseasedness, disorder, failing, fault, feebleness, flu, frailty, ill health, imperfection, indisposition, malady, malaise, senility, shortcoming, sickliness, unhealth, unhealthiness, unwellness, vulnerability; SEE CONCEPTS *306,674,732*

inflame [*v*] *anger, aggravate*

agitate, annoy, arouse, burn, disturb, embitter, enrage, exacerbate, exasperate, excite, fan, fire, fire up, foment, gall, get*, grate, heat, heat up, ignite, impassion, incense, increase, infuriate, intensify, intoxicate, irritate, kindle, light, madden, provoke, put out*, rile, roil, rouse, steam up, stimulate, vex, worsen; SEE CONCEPTS *7,14,19,22,249*

inflammable [*adj*] *ready to burn*

burnable, combustible, dangerous, flammable, hazardous, ignitable, incendiary, risky, unsafe; SEE CONCEPT *485*

inflammatory [*adj*] *instigative, angering*

anarchic, demagogic, exciting, explosive, fiery, incendiary, incitive, inflaming, insurgent, intemperate, provocative, rabble-rousing*, rabid, rebellious, revolutionary, riotous, seditionary, seditious; SEE CONCEPTS *537,542*

inflate [*v*] *blow up, increase*

aerate, aggrandize, amplify, augment, balloon*, beef up*, bloat, boost, build up, cram*, dilate, distend, enlarge, escalate, exaggerate, exalt, expand, flesh out*, magnify, maximize, overestimate, pad*, puff up*, pump up*, pyramid, raise, spread, stretch, surcharge, swell, up*, widen; SEE CONCEPTS *236, 245,780*

inflated [*adj*] *exaggerated*

aggrandized, amplified, augmented, aureate, bloated, bombastic, diffuse, dilated, distended, dropsical, enlarged, euphuistic, extended, filled, flatulent, flowery, fustian, grandiloquent, grown, magnified, magniloquent, ostentatious, overblown, overestimated, pompous, pretentious, prolix, puffed, pumped up, ranting, rhapsodical, rhetorical, showy, spread, stretched, surcharged, swollen, tumescent, tumid, turgid, verbose, windy, wordy; SEE CONCEPTS *267,773*

inflation [*n*] *increase, swelling*

aggrandizement, blowing up, boom, boost, buildup, distension, enhancement, enlargement, escalation, expansion, extension, hike, intensification, prosperity, puffiness, rise, spread, tumefaction; SEE CONCEPTS *335,763,780*

inflection [*n*] *accent, intonation*

articulation, change, emphasis, enunciation, modulation, pitch, pronunciation, sound, timbre, tonality, tone, tone of voice, variation; SEE CONCEPTS *65,595*

inflexible [*adj1*] *stubborn*

adamant, adamantine, determined, dogged, dyed-in-the-wool*, firm, fixed, hard, hard-and-fast*, immovable, immutable, implacable, indomitable, inexorable, intractable, iron, obdurate, obstinate, relentless, resolute, rigid, rigorous, set, set in one's ways*, single-minded, stand one's ground*, staunch, steadfast, steely, stiff, strict, stringent, unadaptable, unbending, unchangeable, uncompliant, uncompromising, unrelenting, unswayable, unyielding; SEE CONCEPT *404*

inflexible [*adj2*] *hardened, stiff*

hard, immalleable, impliable, inelastic, nonflexible, rigid, set, starched, taut, unbending; SEE CONCEPT *604*

inflict [*v*] *impose something*

administer, apply, bring upon, command, deal out, deliver, dispense, exact, expose, extort, force, force upon, give, give it to*, lay down the law*, levy, mete out, require, stick it to*, strike, subject, visit, wreak; SEE CONCEPTS *50,53,88,242*

influence [*n*] *power, authority*

access, agency, ascendancy, character, clout, command, connections, consequence, control, credit, direction, domination, dominion, drag, effect, esteem, fame, fix, force, grease*, guidance, hold, impact, importance, imprint, in, juice*, leadership, leverage, magnetism, mark, mastery, moment, money, monopoly, network, notoriety, predominance, prerogative, pressure, prestige, prominence, pull, repercussion, reputation, ropes*, rule, significance, spell, supremacy, sway, weight*; SEE CONCEPT *686*

influence [v] *lead to believe, do*

act upon, affect, alter, argue into, arouse, be recognized, bias, brainwash*, bribe, bring to bear, carry weight, change, channel, compel, control, count, determine, direct, dispose, form, get at*, guide, have a part in, impact on, impel, impress, incite, incline, induce, instigate, manipulate, modify, mold, move, persuade, predispose, prejudice, prevail, prompt, pull strings*, regulate, rouse, rule, seduce, sell, shape, snow*, sway, talk into, train, turn, urge, work upon; SEE CONCEPTS *18,68,242*

influential [adj] *effective, powerful*

affecting, authoritative, big-gun*, big-wheel*, controlling, dominant, efficacious, famous, forcible, governing, guiding, hot-dog*, important, impressive, inspiring, instrumental, leading, major-league*, meaningful, momentous, moving, name, persuasive, potent, prominent, significant, strong, substantial, telling, touching, weighty; SEE CONCEPTS *537,568*

influx [n] *flow, rush*

arrival, coming in, convergence, entrance, incursion, inflow, inpouring, inrush, introduction, inundation, invasion, penetration; SEE CONCEPTS *159,179,786*

inform [v] *communicate knowledge, information*

acquaint, advise, apprise, betray, blab*, brief, caution, clue, edify, educate, endow, endue, enlighten, familiarize, fill in, forewarn, give a pointer, give a tip, give away, give two cents*, illuminate, inspire, instruct, invest, leak, let in on*, let know, level, make conversant with, notify, post, relate, send word, show the ropes*, snitch, squeal, tattle, teach, tell, tell on, tip, tout, update, warn, wise; SEE CONCEPT *60*

informal [adj] *casual, simple*

breezy, colloquial, congenial, cool*, democratic, down home*, easy, easygoing, everyday, extempore, familiar, folksy, frank, free, free-and-easy*, homey, improv*, inconspicuous, intimate, laid back*, loose, low-pressure, mellow, mixed, motley, natural, off-the-cuff*, open, ordinary, relaxed, spontaneous, sporty, straightforward, throwaway*, unceremonious, unconstrained, unconventional, unfussy, unofficial, unrestrained, urbane, without ceremony; SEE CONCEPTS *548,589*

informant/informer [n] *person who delivers news*

accuser, adviser, announcer, betrayer, blabbermouth*, canary*, crier, deep throat*, double-crosser, herald, interviewer, journalist, messenger, newsman/woman, notifier, preacher, propagandist, rat*, reporter, sneak, source, stool pigeon*, tattler, tattletale; SEE CONCEPTS *348,354,423*

information [n] *facts, news*

advice, ammo*, break*, chapter and verse*, clue, confidence, counsel, cue, data, dirt*, dope*, dossier, earful*, enlightenment, erudition, illumination, info*, inside story*, instruction, intelligence, knowledge, leak, learning, lore, lowdown*, material,

message, network, notice, notification, orientation, propaganda, report, science, scoop, score, tidings, tip, what's what*, whole story*, wisdom, word*; SEE CONCEPT *274*

informative [adj] *educational*

advisory, chatty, communicative, descriptive, edifying, educative, elucidative, enlightening, explanatory, forthcoming, gossipy, illuminating, informational, instructional, instructive, newsy, revealing, revelatory, significant; SEE CONCEPT *267*

informed [adj] *cognizant, conversant*

abreast, acquainted, apprized, au courant*, au fait*, briefed, enlightened, erudite, expert, familiar, in the know*, into*, knowledgeable, know the score*, know what's what*, learned, on top of*, posted*, primed*, reliable, savvy, tuned in*, up*, up on*, up-to-date, versant, versed, well-read, wise to*; SEE CONCEPT *402*

infraction [n] *violation*

breach, breaking, contravention, crime, error, faux pas, infringement, lapse, offense, sin, slip*, transgression, trespass; SEE CONCEPTS *192,645*

infrequent [adj] *not happening regularly*

exceptional, few, few and far between*, isolated, limited, meager, occasional, odd, rare, scant, scanty, scarce, scattered, seldom, semioccasional, sparse, spasmodic, sporadic, stray, uncommon, unusual; SEE CONCEPT *530*

infringe [v] *violate*

borrow, breach, break, contravene, crash, disobey, encroach, entrench, impose, infract, intrude, invade, lift, meddle, obtrude, offend, pirate, presume, steal, transgress, trespass; SEE CONCEPTS *192,384*

infuriate [v] *make very angry*

aggravate, anger, enrage, exasperate, incense, ire, irritate, madden, make blood boil*, provoke, rile, T-off*, umbrage; SEE CONCEPT *14*

infuse [v] *introduce; soak*

animate, breathe into, imbue, impart, implant, impregnate, inculcate, indoctrinate, ingrain, inoculate, inspire, instill, intersperse, invest, leaven, permeate, pervade, plant, saturate, steep, suffuse; SEE CONCEPTS *140,179,187*

ingenious [adj] *very clever; brilliant*

able, adroit, artistic, bright, canny, crafty, creative, cunning, deviceful, dexterous, fertile, gifted, imaginative, innovational, innovative, innovatory, intelligent, inventive, masterly, original, ready, resourceful, shrewd, skillful, sly, subtle; SEE CONCEPT *402*

ingenuous [adj] *honest, trustful*

artless, candid, childlike, frank, green*, guileless, innocent, like a babe in the woods*, mark, naive, natural, open, outspoken, plain, simple, sincere, square, straightforward, trusting, unaffected, unartful, unartificial, undisguised, unreserved, unschooled, unsophisticated, unstudied, up front*; SEE CONCEPTS *267,542,589*

ingrained [adj] deep-rooted
built-in, chronic, confirmed, congenital, constitutional, deep-seated, fixed, fundamental, hereditary, implanted, inborn, inbred, inbuilt, indelible, indwelling, ineradicable, inherent, innate, in the blood*, intrinsic, inveterate, rooted; SEE CONCEPTS 535,549

ingratiate [v] get on the good side of someone
attract, blandish, brownnose*, captivate, charm, crawl, flatter, get in with*, grovel, hand a line*, insinuate oneself, kowtow*, play up to*, seek favor, truckle; SEE CONCEPTS 7,22,68

ingratiating [adj] fawning, servile
charming, crawling, deferential, disarming, flattering, humble, insinuating, obsequious, saccharine, serving, silken, smarmy*, soft, sycophantic, toadying*, unctuous; SEE CONCEPT 401

ingredient [n] component of concoction
additive, constituent, element, factor, fixing, fundamental, innards, integral, integrant, making, part, part and parcel*, piece; SEE CONCEPT 835

inhabit [v] take up residence in
abide, crash, dwell, indwell, live, locate, lodge, make one's home, occupy, park, people, perch, populate, possess, reside, roost, settle, squat, stay, tenant; SEE CONCEPT 226

inhabitant [n] person who is resident of habitation
aborigine, addressee, autochthon, boarder, citizen, colonist, denizen, dweller, householder, incumbent, indweller, inmate, lessee, lodger, native, neighbor, occupant, occupier, renter, resider, roomer, settler, squatter, suburbanite, tenant, urbanite; SEE CONCEPTS 354,413

inhale [v] breathe in
drag, draw in, gasp, inspire, insufflate, puff, pull, respire, smell, sniff, snort, suck in; SEE CONCEPTS 163,601

inherent [adj] basic, hereditary
built-in, characteristic, congenital, connate, constitutional, deep-rooted, deep-seated, distinctive, elementary, essential, fixed, fundamental, genetic, immanent, implicit, inborn, inbred, inbuilt, indigenous, indispensable, individual, indwelling, ingrained, inherited, innate, inner, instinctive, integral, integrated, internal, in the grain, intimate, intrinsic, inward, latent, native, natural, original, part and parcel*, resident, running in family*, subjective, unalienable; SEE CONCEPTS 404,549

inherit [v] gain as possession from someone's death
accede, acquire, be bequeathed, be granted, be left, come in for, come into, derive, fall heir, get, obtain, receive, succeed, take over; SEE CONCEPTS 124,317

inheritance [n] possession gained through someone's death
bequest, birthright, devise, estate, gift, heirloom, heritage, heritance, legacy, patrimony, primogeniture; SEE CONCEPT 337

inhibit [v] restrict, prevent
arrest, avert, bar, bit, bridle, check, constrain, cramp, curb, discourage, enjoin, faze, forbid, frus-

trate, hang up*, hinder, hog-tie*, hold back, hold down, hold in, impede, interdict, keep in, obstruct, outlaw, prohibit, put on brakes*, repress, restrain, sandbag*, stop, stymie, suppress, taboo*, ward, withhold; SEE CONCEPTS 121,130

inhibited [adj] very shy
bottled up*, cold, constrained, frustrated, guarded, hung up*, passionless, repressed, reserved, reticent, self-conscious, subdued, undemonstrative, undersexed, unresponsive, uptight, withdrawn; SEE CONCEPTS 404,542

inhibition [n] restriction, hindrance
bar, barrier, blockage, check, embargo, hangup, interdict, interference, obstacle, prevention, prohibition, reserve, restraint, reticence, self-consciousness, shyness, sublimation, suppression; SEE CONCEPTS 411,657

inhospitable [adj] unfriendly
brusque, cold, cool, hostile, rude, short, uncongenial, unfavorable, ungenerous, unkind, unreceptive, unsociable, unwelcoming; SEE CONCEPT 401

inhuman/inhumane [adj] animal, savage
barbaric, barbarous, bestial, brutal, cannibalistic, cold-blooded, cruel, devilish, diabolical, fell, ferocious, fiendish, fierce, grim, hateful, heartless, implacable, inhumane, malicious, malign, malignant, mean, merciless, pitiless, relentless, remorseless, ruthless, truculent, uncompassionate, unfeeling, unkind, unrelenting, unsympathetic, vicious, wolfish; SEE CONCEPTS 401,545

inimical [adj] antagonistic, contrary
adverse, antipathetic, destructive, disaffected, harmful, hostile, hurtful, ill, ill-disposed, inimicable, injurious, noxious, opposed, oppugnant, pernicious, repugnant, unfavorable, unfriendly, unwelcoming; SEE CONCEPTS 401,537

inimitable [adj] incomparable
consummate, matchless, nonpareil, peerless, perfect, supreme, unequalled, unexampled, unique, unmatched, unparalleled, unrivalled, unsurpassable; SEE CONCEPT 574

iniquity [n] sin, evil
abomination, baseness, crime, evildoing, heinousness, immorality, infamy, injustice, miscreancy, misdeed, offense, sinfulness, unfairness, unrighteousness, wickedness, wrong, wrongdoing; SEE CONCEPT 645

initial [adj] beginning, primary
antecedent, basic, commencing, earliest, early, elementary, embryonic, first, foremost, fundamental, germinal, headmost, inaugural, inceptive, inchoate, incipient, infant, initiative, initiatory, introductory, leading, maiden, nascent, opening, original, pioneer, virgin; SEE CONCEPTS 585,799,828

initiate [v1] start, introduce
admit, begin, break the ice*, come out with, come up with, commence, dream up, enter, get ball rolling*, get feet wet*, get under way, inaugurate, induct,

install, instate, institute, intro*, invest, kick off*, launch, make up, open, originate, pioneer, set in motion, set up, take in, take up, trigger, usher in; SEE CONCEPT 221

initiate [v2] *teach*
brief, coach, edify, enlighten, familiarize, indoctrinate, induct, inform, instate, instruct, introduce, invest, train; SEE CONCEPT 285

initiation [n] *start, introduction*
admission, baptism, beginning, commencement, debut, enrollment, entrance, inaugural, inauguration, inception, indoctrination, induction, installation, instatement, investiture, preliminaries; SEE CONCEPTS 221,386

initiative [n] *eagerness to do something*
action, ambition, drive, dynamism, energy, enterprise, enthusiasm, get-up-and-go*, gumption*, inventiveness, leadership, moxie*, originality, punch, push, resource, resourcefulness, spunk*, steam*, vigor; SEE CONCEPTS 411,657

inject [v1] *put in, introduce*
add, drag in, force into, imbue, implant, impregnate, include, infuse, insert, instill, interjaculate, interject, place into, squeeze in, stick in, throw in; SEE CONCEPTS 187,208,209

inject [v2] *introduce into bloodstream by use of a needle*
give a shot, inoculate, jab, mainline*, shoot, vaccinate; SEE CONCEPTS 179,310

injection [n] *introduction into bloodstream*
booster, dose, dram, enema, inoculation, needle, vaccine; SEE CONCEPT 311

injunction [n] *decree*
admonition, ban, bar, behest, bidding, charge, command, demand, dictate, embargo, enjoinder, exhortation, instruction, mandate, order, precept, prohibition, ruling, word, writ; SEE CONCEPTS 271,318

injure [v] *hurt, harm*
abuse, aggrieve, batter, blemish, blight, break, contort, cripple, cut up, damage, deface, deform, disable, disfigure, distort, distress, do in*, draw blood*, foul, foul up, grieve, hack up, impair, maim, maltreat, mangle, mar, mutilate, pain, pique, prejudice, queer, ruin, shake up, spoil, sting, tarnish, torment, torture, total, undermine, vitiate, wax, weaken, wound, wrong; SEE CONCEPT 246

injurious [adj] *hurtful*
abusive, adverse, bad, baneful, corrupting, damaging, dangerous, deadly, deleterious, destructive, detrimental, disadvantageous, evil, harmful, iniquitous, insulting, libeling, mischievous, nocent, nocuous, noxious, opprobrious, pernicious, poisonous, prejudicial, ruinous, slanderous, unconducive, unhealthy, unjust, wrongful; SEE CONCEPTS 537,570

injury [n] *hurt, harm*
abrasion, abuse, affliction, affront, agony, bad, bite, blemish, boo-boo*, bruise, burn, chop, cramp, cut, damage, deformation, detriment, discomfiture, dis-

service, distress, evil, fracture, gash, grievance, hemorrhage, ill, impairment, indignity, injustice, insult, laceration, lesion, libel, loss, mischief, misery, mutilation, nick, ouch*, outrage, pang, ruin, scar, scratch, shock, slander, sore, sprain, stab, sting, suffering, swelling, trauma, twinge, wound, wrong; SEE CONCEPTS 309,728

injustice [n] *unfair treatment; bias*
abuse, breach, crime, crying shame*, damage, dirty deal*, discrimination, encroachment, favoritism, grievance, inequality, inequity, infraction, infringement, iniquity, malfeasance, malpractice, maltreatment, miscarriage, mischief, negligence, offense, onesidedness, oppression, outrage, partiality, partisanship, prejudice, railroad*, ruin, sellout*, transgression, trespass, unfairness, unjustness, unlawfulness, villainy, violation, wrong, wrongdoing; SEE CONCEPTS 192,645,674

inkling [n] *idea, clue*
conception, cue, faintest idea*, foggiest idea*, glimmering, hint, hot lead*, hunch*, impression, indication, innuendo, intimation, lead, notion, sneaking suspicion*, suggestion, suspicion, tip, tipoff, whisper; SEE CONCEPT 689

inlet [n] *arm of the sea*
basin, bay, bayou, bight, canal, channel, cove, creek, delta, entrance, estuary, firth, fjord, gulf, harbor, ingress, loch, narrows, passage, slew, slough, sound, strait; SEE CONCEPTS 509,514

inn [n] *accommodation for travellers*
auberge, hospice, hostel, hostelry, hotel, lodge, motel, public house, resort, roadhouse, saloon, tavern; SEE CONCEPTS 439,449,516

innate [adj] *inherited, native*
congenital, connate, connatural, constitutional, deepseated, elemental, essential, hereditary, inborn, inbred, indigenous, ingrained, inherent, instinctive, intrinsic, intuitive, natural, normal, regular, standard, typical, unacquired; SEE CONCEPTS 406,549

inner [adj1] *central, middle physically*
close, constitutional, essential, familiar, focal, inherent, innermore, inside, interior, internal, intestinal, intimate, intrinsic, inward, nuclear; SEE CONCEPTS 826,830

inner [adj2] *mental, private*
central, concealed, deep-rooted, deep-seated, emotional, esoteric, essential, focal, gut*, hidden, individual, inherent, innate, inside, interior, internal, intimate, intrinsic, intuitive, inward, personal, psychological, repressed, secret, spiritual, subconscious, unrevealed, visceral, viscerous; SEE CONCEPTS 529,576

innocence [n1] *blamelessness*
chastity, clean hands*, clear conscience*, guiltlessness, immaculateness, impeccability, incorruptibility, incorruption, inculpability, probity, purity, righteousness, sinlessness, stainlessness, uprightness, virginity, virtue; SEE CONCEPT 645

innocence [n2] *harmlessness, naïveté*
artlessness, candidness, credulousness, forthrightness, frankness, freshness, guilelessness, gullibility, ignorance, inexperience, ingenuousness, innocuousness, innoxiousness, inoffensiveness, lack, nescience, plainness, purity, simplicity, sincerity, unaffectedness, unawareness, unfamiliarity, unknowingness, unsophistication, unworldliness, virginity, virtue; SEE CONCEPTS *409,411*

innocent [adj1] *blameless*
above suspicion, angelic, chaste, clean, cleanhanded, clear, crimeless, exemplary, faultless, free of, good, guilt-free, guiltless, honest, immaculate, impeccable, impeccant, inculpable, in the clear, irreproachable, in the clear, lawful, legal, legitimate, licit, not guilty, pristine, pure, righteous, safe, sinless, spotless, stainless, unblemished, uncensurable, uncorrupt, unguilty, unimpeachable, uninvolved, unoffending, unsullied, untainted, upright, virgin, virginal, virtuous; SEE CONCEPT *545*

innocent [adj2] *harmless, naive*
artless, childlike, credulous, frank, fresh, guileless, gullible, hurtless, ignorant, inexperienced, ingenuous, innocuous, innoxious, inobnoxious, inoffensive, offenseless, open, raw, safe, simple, soft, square, unacquainted, unartificial, uncool, unfamiliar, unhurtful, uninjurious, unmalicious, unobjectionable, unoffensive, unschooled, unsophisticated, unstudied, unsuspicious, unworldly, well-intentioned, well-meant, wide-eyed, youthful; SEE CONCEPTS *404,542*

innocuous [adj] *harmless*
banal, bland, flat, inane, innocent, innoxious, inobnoxious, inoffensive, insipid, jejune, kind, painless, safe, sapless, unobjectionable, unoffending, weak; SEE CONCEPTS *401,572*

innovation [n] *change, novelty*
addition, alteration, contraption, cutting edge*, departure, deviation, introduction, last word*, latest thing*, leading edge*, modernism, modernization, modification, mutation, newness, notion, permutation, shift, variation, vicissitude, wrinkle*; SEE CONCEPTS *260,529,660,665*

innovative [adj] *creative*
avant-garde, breaking new ground*, contemporary, cutting-edge*, deviceful, ingenious, innovational, innovatory, inventive, just out*, leading-edge*, new, newfangled*, original, originative, state-of-the-art; SEE CONCEPTS *529,578,589,797*

innuendo [n] *suggestion*
allusion, aside, aspersion, hint, implication, imputation, insinuation, intimation, overtone, reference, whisper; SEE CONCEPTS *75,278*

innumerable [adj] *many, infinite*
alive with*, beyond number, countless, frequent, incalculable, multitudinous, myriad, numberless, numerous, uncountable, unnumbered, untold; SEE CONCEPT *762*

inoffensive [adj] *not obnoxious; harmless*
calm, clean, friendly, humble, innocent, innocuous, innoxious, mild, neutral, nonprovocative, peaceable, pleasant, quiet, retiring, safe, unobjectionable, unobtrusive, unoffending, white; SEE CONCEPTS *267,542*

inopportune [adj] *not appropriate or suitable*
contrary, disadvantageous, disturbing, ill-chosen, ill-timed, inappropriate, inauspicious, inconvenient, malapropos, mistimed, troublesome, unfavorable, unfortunate, unpropitious, unseasonable, unsuitable, untimely; SEE CONCEPT *558*

inordinate [adj] *excessive, extravagant*
disproportionate, dizzying, exorbitant, extortionate, extravagant, extreme, gratuitous, immoderate, intemperate, irrational, outrageous, overindulgent, overmuch, preposterous, supererogatory, superfluous, surplus, too much, towering, uncalled-for, unconscionable, uncurbed, undue, unmeasurable, unreasonable, unrestrained, untempered, unwarranted, wanton, wasteful; SEE CONCEPTS *570,781*

inquest [n] *investigation*
delving, examination, hearing, inquiry, inquisition, probe, probing, quest, research, trial; SEE CONCEPTS *48,290,318*

inquire [v] *ask; look into*
analyze, catechize, examine, explore, feel out, go over, grill, hit, hit up, inspect, interrogate, investigate, knock, probe, prospect, pry, query, question, request information, roast, scrutinize, search, seek, seek information, sift, study, test the waters*; SEE CONCEPTS *24,48*

inquiring [adj] *wondering, curious*
analytical, catechistic, doubtful, examining, fact-finding, heuristic, inquisitive, interested, interrogative, investigative, investigatory, nosy, outward-looking, probing, prying, questioning, quizzical, searching, Socratic, speculative, studious; SEE CONCEPTS *402,542*

inquiry [n] *asking; looking into*
analysis, audit, catechizing, check, cross-examination, delving, disquisition, examination, exploration, fishing expedition*, grilling, hearing, inquest, inquisition, inspection, interrogation, interrogatory, investigation, legwork*, poll, probe, probing, pursuit, Q and A*, query, quest, question, questioning, quizzing, request, research, scrutiny, search, study, survey, third degree*, trial balloon*, witch hunt*; SEE CONCEPTS *24,48,290*

inquisitive [adj] *curious*
analytical, big-eyed*, challenging, forward, impertinent, inquiring, inquisitorial, interested, intrusive, investigative, meddlesome, meddling, nosy, peering, personal, poking, presumptuous, probing, prying, questioning, scrutinizing, searching, sifting, snooping, speculative; SEE CONCEPT *402*

inroad [n] *advance, foray*
encroachment, impingement, incursion, intrusion, invasion, irruption, onslaught, raid, trespass; SEE CONCEPTS *86,704*

insane [adj] *mentally ill; foolish*
batty*, bizarre, cracked*, crazed, crazy, cuckoo*, daft, demented, derailed, deranged, fatuous, fren-

zied, idiotic, impractical, irrational, irresponsible, loony*, lunatic, mad, maniacal, mental, moonstruck*, nuts*, nutty*, off one's rocker*, of unsound mind, out of one's mind*, paranoid, preposterous, psychopathic, psychotic, rabid, raging, raving, schizophrenic, screwy, senseless, stupid, touched, unhinged, unsettled, wild; SEE CONCEPTS *314, 403,548*

insanely [*adv*] *extremely*
crazily, ferociously, fiercely, furiously, idiotically, irrationally, stupidly, violently, wildly; SEE CONCEPT *569*

insanity [*n*] *mental illness; foolishness*
aberration, absurdity, alienation, craziness, delirium, delusion, dementia, derangement, distraction, dotage, folly, frenzy, hallucination, hysteria, illusion, inanity, irrationality, irresponsibility, lunacy, madness, mania, mental disorder, neurosis, phobia, preposterousness, psychopathy, psychosis, senselessness, stupidity, unbalance, unreasonableness, witlessness; SEE CONCEPTS *316,410*

insatiable [*adj*] *voracious, wanting*
clamorous, crying, demanding, desiring, exigent, gluttonous, greedy, importunate, insatiate, insistent, intemperate, pressing, quenchless, rapacious, ravenous, unappeasable, unquenchable, unsatisfiable, unsatisfied, urgent, yearning; SEE CONCEPTS *20,403,546*

inscribe [*v*] *imprint, write*
book, carve, cut, engrave, engross, etch, impress, indite, list, record, register, scribe; SEE CONCEPT *79*

inscrutable [*adj*] *hidden, mysterious; blank*
ambiguous, arcane, cabalistic, deadpan*, difficult, enigmatic, impenetrable, incomprehensible, inexplicable, mysterial, mystic, poker-faced*, secret, sphinxlike, unaccountable, undiscoverable, unexplainable, unfathomable, unintelligible, unknowable, unreadable; SEE CONCEPTS *529,576*

insecure [*adj1*] *uncertain, worried*
afraid, anxious, apprehensive, choked, diffident, hanging by thread*, hesitant, jumpy, on thin ice*, questioning, shaky, touch and go*, touchy*, troubled, unassured, unconfident, unpoised, unsure, up in the air*, uptight*, vague; SEE CONCEPTS *403,542*

insecure [*adj2*] *dangerous, precarious*
defenseless, exposed, fluctuant, frail, hazardous, immature, insubstantial, loose, open to attack*, perilous, precarious, rickety, rocky, rootless, shaky, unguarded, unprotected, unreliable, unsafe, unshielded, unsound, unstable, unsteady, vacillating, vulnerable, wavering, weak, wobbly; SEE CONCEPTS *488,570*

insensitive [*adj1*] *indifferent, callous*
aloof, bloodless*, coldhearted*, crass, feelingless, hard, hard as nails*, hard-boiled*, hardened, hard hearted*, heartless, imperceptive, incurious, obtuse, stony, tactless, thick-skinned*, tough, uncaring, unconcerned, unfeeling, unkind, unresponsive, unsusceptible; SEE CONCEPT *401*

insensitive [*adj2*] *numb*
anesthetized, asleep, benumbed, dead, deadened, immune to, impervious to, insensible, nonreactive, senseless, unfeeling; SEE CONCEPT *406*

inseparable [*adj*] *unable to be divided*
as one, attached, conjoined, connected, entwined, inalienable, indissoluble, indivisible, inseverable, integral, integrated, intertwined, interwoven, molded, secure, tied up, unified, united, whole; SEE CONCEPT *531*

insert [*v*] *put, tuck in*
admit, drag in, embed, enter, fill in, imbed, implant, include, infix, infuse, inject, inlay, insinuate, instill, intercalate, interject, interlope, interpolate, interpose, introduce, intrude, lug in, obtrude, place, pop in*, root, set, shoehorn*, shove in, squeeze in, stick, work in; SEE CONCEPTS *201,209*

inside [*n*] *middle, lining*
belly, bowels, breast, center, contents, gut, heart, innards, innermost, inner portion, interior, recess, soul, stuffing, womb; SEE CONCEPT *830*

inside [*adj1*] *in the middle; interior*
central, indoors, inner, innermost, internal, intramural, inward, surrounded, under a roof; SEE CONCEPTS *583,830*

inside [*adj2*] *secret*
classified, closet, confidential, esoteric, exclusive, hushed, internal, limited, private, restricted; SEE CONCEPTS *529,576*

inside [*adv*] *within*
indoors, under a roof, under cover, within doors, within walls; SEE CONCEPT *583*

insidious [*adj*] *sneaky, tricky*
artful, astute, corrupt, crafty, crooked, cunning, dangerous, deceitful, deceptive, deep, designing, dishonest, disingenuous, duplicitous, ensnaring, false, foxy, guileful, intriguing, like a snake in the grass*, Machiavellian, perfidious, perilous, secret, slick, sly, smooth, snaky*, sneaking, stealthy, subtle, surreptitious, treacherous, tricky, wily, wormlike*; SEE CONCEPTS *401,542,545*

insight [*n*] *intuitiveness, awareness*
acumen, click*, comprehension, discernment, divination, drift*, intuition, judgment, observation, penetration, perception, perceptivity, perspicacity, sagaciousness, sagacity, sageness, sapience, shrewdness, understanding, vision, wavelength*, wisdom; SEE CONCEPTS *409,410*

insignia [*n*] *emblem*
badge, coat of arms, crest, decoration, earmark, ensign, mark, paraphernalia, regalia, symbol; SEE CONCEPTS *259,284*

insignificant [*adj*] *not important; of no consequence*
casual, immaterial, inappreciable, inconsequential, inconsiderable, infinitesimal, irrelevant, lesser, light, lightweight*, little, meager, meaningless, minim, minimal, minor, minuscule, minute, negligible, nondescript, nonessential, not worth mentioning*, nuga-

tory, paltry, petty, pointless, purportless, scanty, secondary, senseless, small, trifling, trivial, unimportant, unsubstantial; SEE CONCEPT *575*

insincere [*adj*] *dishonest, pretended*
ambidextrous, backhanded, deceitful, deceptive, devious, disingenuous, dissembling, dissimulating, double, double-dealing, duplicitous, evasive, faithless, fake, false, hollow, hypocritical, lying, mendacious, perfidious, phony, pretentious, put-on*, shifty, slick, sly, snide, two-faced*, unfaithful, untrue, untruthful; SEE CONCEPTS *267,542,545*

insinuate [*v1*] *hint, suggest*
allude, ascribe, connote, imply, impute, indicate, intimate, mention, propose, purport, refer, signify; SEE CONCEPTS *49,75*

insinuate [*v2*] *force one's way into*
curry favor*, edge in, fill in, foist, get in with*, horn in*, infiltrate, infuse, ingratiate, inject, insert, instill, intercalate, interject, interpose, introduce, muscle in*, slip in, wedge in, work in, worm in*; SEE CONCEPTS *159,208,384*

insipid [*adj1*] *dull, uninteresting*
anemic, arid, banal, beige, blah*, bland, characterless, colorless, commonplace, dead*, drab, driveling, dry, feeble, flat, ho-hum*, inane, innocuous, jejune, lifeless, limp, mild, mundane, nebbish, nothing, ordinary, plain, pointless, prosaic, prosy, slight, soft*, spiritless, stale, stupid, subdued, tame, tedious, tenuous, thin, tired, trite, unimaginative, vapid, watery, weak, weariful, wearisome, wishywashy*; SEE CONCEPTS *402,404,537*

insipid [*adj2*] *tasteless*
bland, distasteful, flat, flavorless, jejune, mild, savorless, stale, unappetizing, unpalatable, unsavory, vapid, watered-down, watery; SEE CONCEPT *613*

insist [*v*] *order and expect; claim*
assert, asseverate, aver, be firm, contend, demand, hold, importune, lay down the law*, maintain, persist, press, reiterate, repeat, request, require, stand firm, swear, take a stand*, urge, vow; SEE CONCEPTS *49,53*

insistent [*adj*] *demanding*
assertive, burning, clamant, clamorous, continuous, crying, dire, dogged, emphatic, exigent, forceful, imperative, imperious, importunate, incessant, obstinate, peremptory, perseverant, persevering, persistent, pressing, reiterative, resolute, resounding, unrelenting, urgent; SEE CONCEPTS *267,534,540*

insolence [*n*] *boldness, disrespect*
abuse, arrogance, audacity, back talk, brass*, brazenness, cheek*, chutzpah*, contempt, contemptuousness, contumely, effrontery, gall, guff*, hardihood, impertinence, impudence, incivility, insubordination, lip*, offensiveness, pertness, presumption, rudeness, sass*, sauce*, uncivility; SEE CONCEPT *633*

insolent [*adj*] *bold, disrespectful*
abusive, arrogant, barefaced, brassy*, brazen, breezy, contemptuous, contumelious, dictatorial, discourte-

ous, disdainful, flip*, fresh, imperative, impertinent, impolite, impudent, insubordinate, insulting, magisterial, nervy, off-base*, offensive, out-of-line*, overbearing, peremptory, pert, procacious, put down, rude, sassy*, saucy*, smart, smart-alecky*, uncivil, ungracious, wise guy*; SEE CONCEPTS *267,401*

insoluble [*adj*] *mysterious, unable to be solved or answered*
baffling, difficult, impenetrable, indecipherable, inexplicable, inextricable, irresolvable, mystifying, obscure, unaccountable, unconcluded, unfathomable, unresolved, unsolvable, unsolved; SEE CONCEPTS *529,576*

insolvent [*adj*] *financially ruined*
bankrupt, broke*, broken, busted*, failed, foreclosed, in Chapter 11*, in Chapter 13*, indebted, in receivership, in the red*, lost, on the rocks*, out of money, strapped*, taken to the cleaners*, unbalanced, undone, wiped out*; SEE CONCEPT *334*

insomnia [*n*] *inability to sleep soundly*
indisposition, insomnolence, restlessness, sleeplessness, stress, tension, vigil, vigilance, wakefulness; SEE CONCEPT *315*

insouciant [*adj*] *easygoing, casual*
airy, breezy, buoyant, carefree, careless, free and easy*, gay, happy-go-lucky*, heedless, jaunty, lighthearted, nonchalant, sunny, thoughtless, unconcerned, untroubled, unworried; SEE CONCEPTS *404,542*

inspect [*v*] *examine, check*
audit, canvass, case, catechize, check out, clock*, eye*, give the once-over*, go over, go through, inquire, interrogate, investigate, kick the tires*, look over, notice, observe, oversee, probe, question, review, scan, scope, scout, scrutinize, search, study, superintend, supervise, survey, vet, view, watch; SEE CONCEPTS *103,623*

inspection [*n*] *examination, check*
analysis, checkup, frisk, inquest, inquiry, inquisition, inventory, investigation, look-over, maneuvers, once-over*, pageant, parade, perlustration, probe, read, research, review, scan, scrutiny, search, superintendence, supervision, surveillance, survey, view; SEE CONCEPTS *103,290*

inspiration [*n*] *idea, stimulus*
afflatus, animus, approach, arousal, awakening, brainchild*, brainstorm*, creativity, deep think*, elevation, encouragement, enthusiasm, exaltation, fancy, flash*, genius, hunch*, illumination, impulse, incentive, inflatus, influence, insight, motivation, motive, muse, notion, revelation, rumble, spark, spur, stimulation, thought, vision, whim; SEE CONCEPTS *529,661*

inspire [*v*] *encourage, stimulate*
affect, animate, arouse, be responsible for, carry, cause, commove, elate, embolden, endue, enkindle, enliven, exalt, excite, exhilarate, fire up*, galvanize, get*, give impetus, give one an idea*, give rise to*,

hearten, imbue, impress, infect, inflame, influence, inform, infuse, inspirit, instill, invigorate, motivate, occasion, produce, provoke, quicken, reassure, set up, spark, spur, start off, stimulate, stir, strike, sway, touch, trigger, urge, work up; SEE CONCEPTS *7,22, 221,242*

instability [*n*] *imbalance, inconstancy*
alternation, anxiety, capriciousness, changeability, changeableness, disequilibrium, disquiet, fickleness, fitfulness, flightiness, fluctuation, fluidity, frailty, hesitation, immaturity, impermanence, inconsistency, inquietude, insecurity, irregularity, irresolution, mutability, oscillation, pliancy, precariousness, restlessness, shakiness, transience, uncertainty, unfixedness, unpredictability, unreliability, unsteadiness, vacillation, variability, volatility, vulnerability, wavering, weakness; SEE CONCEPTS *410,637,731*

install [*v*] *set up, establish*
build in, ensconce, fix, fix up, furnish, inaugurate, induct, instate, institute, introduce, invest, lay, line, lodge, place, plant, position, put in, settle, station; SEE CONCEPTS *201,221*

installation [*n1*] *establishment, inauguration*
accession, coronation, fitting, furnishing, inaugural, induction, installment, instatement, investiture, investment, launching, ordination, placing, positioning, setting up; SEE CONCEPTS *201,221,832*

installation [*n2*] *equipment*
base, establishment, fort, fortification, furnishings, lighting, machinery, plant, post, power, station, system, wiring; SEE CONCEPTS *439,463,496*

installment [*n*] *part, section*
chapter, division, earnest, episode, partial payment, payment, portion, repayment, token; SEE CONCEPTS *344,835*

instance [*n*] *case, situation*
case history, case in point, detail, example, exemplification, exponent, ground, illustration, item, occasion, occurrence, particular, precedent, proof, reason, representative, sample, sampling, situation, specimen, time; SEE CONCEPTS *688,696,815*

instance [*v*] *name*
adduce, cite, exemplify, illustrate, mention, quote, refer, show, specify; SEE CONCEPT *73*

instant [*n*] *moment*
bat of the eye*, breath, breathing, crack, flash, jiffy*, juncture, minute, nothing flat*, occasion, point, sec*, second, shake*, short while, split second*, tick, time, trice, twinkling*, while, wink*; SEE CONCEPTS *802,808*

instant [*adj*] *immediate, urgent*
burning*, clamant, contemporary, crying*, current, dire, direct, exigent, existent, extant, fast, imperative, importunate, insistent, instantaneous, on-the-spot*, present, present-day, pressing, prompt, quick, split-second*; SEE CONCEPTS *544,588,799*

instantaneous [*adj*] *immediate*
direct, fast, hair-trigger*, in a flash*, instant, momentary, quick, rapid, spontaneous, transitory; SEE CONCEPT *820*

instantly [*adv*] *right now*
at once, away, directly, double-time*, first off*, forthwith, immediately, in a flash*, instantaneously, instanter, now, on a dime*, PDQ*, pronto*, right, right away, spontaneously, straight away*, there and then*, this minute, tout de suite*, without delay; SEE CONCEPTS *544,588,799*

instead [*adv*] *alternatively*
alternately, alternative, as a substitute, in lieu, in place of, in preference, on behalf of, on second thought, preferably, rather, rather than; SEE CONCEPT *560*

instigate [*v*] *influence, provoke*
abet, actuate, add fuel, bring about, egg on*, encourage, fire up*, foment, goad, hint, impel, incite, inflame, initiate, insinuate, kindle, make waves*, move, needle*, persuade, plan, plot, prompt, put up to, rabble-rouse*, raise, rouse, scheme, set on, spur, start, steam up, stimulate, stir up, suggest, turn on, urge, whip up*, work up; SEE CONCEPTS *7,19,22, 221,242*

instill [*v*] *implant, introduce*
brainwash*, catechize, diffuse, disseminate, engender, engraft, force in, imbue, impart, impregnate, impress, inculcate, indoctrinate, infiltrate, infix, infuse, inject, inoculate, inseminate, insert, insinuate, inspire, interject, intermix, program, propagandize, put in head*, suffuse, transfuse; SEE CONCEPTS *14,221,285*

instinct [*n*] *gut feeling, idea*
aptitude, faculty, feeling, funny feeling*, gift, gut reaction*, hunch, impulse, inclination, intuition, knack, know-how*, nose*, predisposition, proclivity, savvy*, sense, sentiment, sixth sense*, talent, tendency, urge; SEE CONCEPTS *529,689*

instinctive [*adj*] *reflex, automatic*
accustomed, by seat of one's pants*, congenital, habitual, impulsive, inborn, ingrained, inherent, innate, instinctual, intrinsic, intuitional, intuitive, involuntary, knee-jerk*, mechanical, native, natural, normal, regular, rooted, second-nature*, spontaneous, typical, unlearned, unmeditated, unpremeditated, unprompted, unthinking, visceral; SEE CONCEPT *544*

institute/institution [*n1*] *organization, usually educational*
academy, association, asylum, business, clinic, college, company, conservatory, establishment, fixture, foundation, guild, hospital, institution, orphanage, school, seminar, seminary, society, system, think tank, university; SEE CONCEPTS *288,381,439*

institute [*n2*] *law; custom*
convention, decree, decretum, doctrine, dogma, edict, establishment, fixture, habit, maxim, ordinance, practice, precedent, precept, prescript, principle, regulation, rite, ritual, rule, statute, tenet, tradition; SEE CONCEPTS *318,687*

institute [*v*] *begin; put into operation*
appoint, bow, break in, bring into being, come out with, come up with, commence, constitute, create,

enact, establish, fix, found, inaugurate, induct, initiate, install, introduce, invest, launch, make up, open, open up, ordain, organize, originate, pioneer, rev, set in motion, settle, set up, start, usher in*; SEE CONCEPTS *173,221,242*

instruct [*v1*] *inform, teach*
acquaint, advise, apprise, brainwash*, break in, break it to, brief, clue in, coach, counsel, discipline, disclose, drill, drum into*, educate, engineer, enlighten, give lessons, ground, guide, keep posted*, lead, lecture, level, notify, pilot, reveal, school, steer, tell, train, tutor, update, wise up*; SEE CONCEPTS *60,285*

instruct [*v2*] *order, command*
assign, bid, charge, define, direct, enjoin, prescribe, tell, warn; SEE CONCEPTS *53,61*

instruction [*n1*] *education*
apprenticeship, chalk talk, coaching, direction, discipline, drilling, edification, enlightenment, grounding, guidance, information, lesson, preparation, schooling, teaching, training, tuition, tutelage; SEE CONCEPTS *274,285*

instruction [*n2*] *demand, command*
advice, briefing, direction, directive, information, injunction, mandate, order, plan, ruling; SEE CONCEPTS *274,278*

instructor [*n*] *person who educates*
adviser, coach, demonstrator, exponent, guide, lecturer, master, mentor, pedagogue, preceptor, professor, schoolmaster, teacher, trainer, tutor; SEE CONCEPT *350*

instrument [*n1*] *tool, implement*
apparatus, appliance, contraption, contrivance, device, doodad*, equipment, gadget, gear, gizmo*, machine, machinery, mechanism, paraphernalia, tackle, utensil; SEE CONCEPTS *463,499*

instrument [*n2*] *means, agent*
agency, channel, factor, force, instrumentality, material, mechanism, medium, ministry, organ, vehicle, wherewithal; SEE CONCEPTS *6,686*

instrumental [*adj*] *influential, assisting*
active, auxiliary, conducive, contributory, helpful, helping, involved, of help, of service, partly responsible, serviceable, subsidiary, useful; SEE CONCEPT *560*

insubordinate [*adj*] *rebellious*
contrary, contumacious, defiant, disaffected, disobedient, disorderly, dissentious, factious, fractious, insurgent, intractable, mutinous, naughty, perverse, recalcitrant, refractory, riotous, seditious, treacherous, turbulent, uncompliant, uncomplying, undisciplined, ungovernable, unruly; SEE CONCEPT *401*

insubstantial [*adj*] *weak, imaginary*
aerial, airy, chimerical, decrepit, ephemeral, false, fanciful, feeble, flimsy, fly-by-night*, fragile, frail, idle, illusory, immaterial, imponderable, incorporeal, infirm, intangible, metaphysical, petty, poor, puny, slender, slight, tenuous, thin, unreal, unsound, unsubstantial; SEE CONCEPT *485*

insufferable [*adj*] *horrible, intolerable*
detestable, distressing, dreadful, impossible, insupportable, outrageous, painful, unacceptable, unbearable, unendurable, unspeakable; SEE CONCEPTS *529,537*

insufficient [*adj*] *not enough; lacking*
bereft, defective, deficient, destitute, devoid, drained, dry, failing, faulty, imperfect, inadequate, incapable, incommensurate, incompetent, incomplete, infrequent, meager, minus, out of, poor, rare, scant, scarce, short, short of, shy, thin, too little too late*, unample, unfinished, unfitted, unqualified, unsatisfactory, wanting; SEE CONCEPTS *546,771*

insular [*adj*] *narrow-minded*
bigoted, circumscribed, closed, confined, contracted, cut off, detached, illiberal, inward-looking, isolated, limited, narrow, parochial, petty, prejudiced, provincial, restricted, secluded, separate, separated, sequestered; SEE CONCEPTS *403,583*

insulate [*v*] *protect; close off*
coat, cocoon, cushion, cut off, inlay, island, isolate, keep apart, line, seclude, separate, sequester, set apart, shield, tape, treat, wrap; SEE CONCEPT *172*

insult [*n*] *hateful communication*
abuse, affront, aspersion, black eye*, blasphemy, cheap shot*, contempt, contumely, derision, despite, discourtesy, disdainfulness, disgrace, disrespect, ignominy, impertinence, impudence, incivility, indignity, insolence, invective, libel, mockery, obloquy, offense, opprobrium, outrage, put-down, rudeness, scorn, scurrility, shame, slam, slander, slap, slap in the face*, slight, snub, superciliousness, taunt, unpleasantry, vilification, vituperation; SEE CONCEPTS *52,54,278*

insult [*v*] *abuse, offend*
abase, affront, aggravate, annoy, blister, curse, cut to the quick*, debase, degrade, deride, dishonor, disoblige, dump on*, flout, gird, humiliate, injure, irritate, jeer, libel, mock, outrage, pan*, provoke, put down*, revile, ridicule, roast*, scoff, slam*, slander, slight, sneer, snub, step on one's toes*, taunt, tease, underestimate, vex; SEE CONCEPTS *52,54*

insurance [*n*] *protection, security*
allowance, assurance, backing, cover, coverage, guarantee, indemnification, indemnity, provision, safeguard, support, warrant, warranty; SEE CONCEPTS *318,332*

insure [*v*] *protect, secure*
assure, cinch, cover, guarantee, guard, hedge, indemnify, register, safeguard, shield, underwrite, warrant; SEE CONCEPTS *317,330*

insurgent [*n*] *rebel*
agitator, anarch, anarchist, demonstrator, frondeur, insurrectionist, malcontent, mutineer, radical, resister, revolter, revolutionary, revolutionist, rioter; SEE CONCEPTS *359,412*

insurgent [*adj*] *rebellious*
anarchical, contumacious, disobedient, factious, insubordinate, insurrectionary, mutinous, revolting,

revolutionary, riotous, seditious; SEE CONCEPT *401*

insurmountable [*adj*] *impossible*
forget it, hopeless, impassable, impregnable, inaccessible, indomitable, ineluctable, insuperable, invincible, not a prayer*, no way*, no-win*, overwhelming, unbeatable, unconquerable, unmasterable; SEE CONCEPTS *552,565*

insurrection [*n*] *rebellion*
coup, disorder, golpe, insurgence, insurgency, mutiny, revolt, revolution, riot, rising, sedition, uprising; SEE CONCEPTS *86,320*

intact [*adj*] *undamaged; all in one piece*
complete, entire, flawless, imperforate, indiscrete, maiden, perfect, scatheless, sound, together, unblemished, unbroken, uncut, undefiled, undeflowered, unharmed, unhurt, unimpaired, uninjured, unmarred, unscathed, untouched, unviolated, virgin, virginal, whole; SEE CONCEPTS *485,531*

intangible [*adj*] *indefinite, obscured*
abstract, abstruse, airy, dim, eluding, elusive, ethereal, evading, evanescent, evasive, hypothetical, impalpable, imperceptible, imponderable, inappreciable, incorporeal, indeterminate, insensible, invisible, rare, shadowy, slender, slight, unapparent, uncertain, unobservable, unreal, unsubstantial, unsure, vague; SEE CONCEPTS *535,582*

integral [*adj1*] *necessary, basic*
component, constituent, elemental, essential, fundamental, indispensable, intrinsic, requisite; SEE CONCEPT *546*

integral [*adj2*] *complete*
aggregate, choate, elemental, entire, full, indivisible, intact, part-and-parcel*, perfect, unbroken, undivided, whole; SEE CONCEPT *531*

integrate [*v*] *mix, merge*
accommodate, amalgamate, arrange, articulate, assimilate, associate, attune, blend, coalesce, combine, come together, compact, concatenate, concentrate, conform, conjoin, consolidate, coordinate, desegregate, embody, fuse, get together, harmonize, incorporate, interface, intermix, join, knit, link, meld with, mesh, orchestrate, organize, proportion, reconcile, reconciliate, symphonize, synthesize, systematize, throw in together, tune, unify, unite, wed; SEE CONCEPTS *113,114*

integrity [*n1*] *honor, uprightness*
candor, forthrightness, goodness, honestness, honesty, honorableness, incorruptibility, incorruption, principle, probity, purity, rectitude, rectitude, righteousness, sincerity, straightforwardness, virtue; SEE CONCEPT *411*

integrity [*n2*] *completeness*
absoluteness, coherence, cohesion, entireness, perfection, purity, simplicity, soundness, stability, totality, unity, wholeness; SEE CONCEPT *635*

intellect [*n*] *capability of the mind; someone with capable mind*
ability, acumen, brains*, cerebration, comprehension, egghead*, genius, intellectual, intellectuality, intelligence, intuition, judgment, mentality, mind, psyche, pundit, reason, savvy*, sense, smarts, thinker, understanding, what it takes*, wits; SEE CONCEPTS *409,416*

intellectual [*n*] *very smart person*
academic, academician, avant-garde, brain*, braintruster*, doctor, egghead*, Einstein*, genius, highbrow*, illuminato, intelligentsia, literato, philosopher, pundit, sage, scholar, thinker, whiz*, wizard; SEE CONCEPTS *350,416*

intellectual [*adj*] *very smart*
bookish, brainy*, cerebral, creative, highbrow*, highbrowed*, intellective, intelligent, inventive, learned, mental, phrenic, psychological, rational, scholarly, studious, subjective, thoughtful; SEE CONCEPT *402*

intelligence [*n1*] *ability to perceive, understand*
acuity, acumen, agility, alertness, aptitude, brainpower, brains*, brightness, brilliance, capacity, cleverness, comprehension, coruscation, discernment, gray matter*, intellect, IQ*, judgment, luminosity, mentality, mind, penetration, perception, perspicacity, precocity, quickness, quotient, reason, sagacity, savvy, sense, skill, smarts, subtlety, the right stuff*, trenchancy, understanding, what it takes*, wit; SEE CONCEPT *409*

intelligence [*n2*] *secret information*
advice, clue, data, dirt, disclosure, facts, findings, hot tip*, info*, inside story*, knowledge, leak, lowdown*, news, notice, notification, picture, report, rumor, tidings, tip-off*, word*; SEE CONCEPT *274*

intelligent [*adj*] *very smart*
able, acute, alert, alive, all there*, apt, astute, brainy*, bright, brilliant, calculating, capable, clever, comprehending, creative, deep*, discerning, enlightened, exceptional, highbrow*, imaginative, ingenious, instructed, inventive, keen, knowing, knowledgeable, original, penetrating, perceptive, perspicacious, profound, quick, quick-witted, rational, ready, reasonable, resourceful, responsible, sage, sharp, smart, thinking, together*, understanding, well-informed, whiz*, wise, witty; SEE CONCEPT *402*

intelligible [*adj*] *understandable*
apprehensible, clear, comprehensible, distinct, fathomable, graspable, knowable, lucid, luminous, obvious, open, plain, unambiguous, unequivocal, unmistakable; SEE CONCEPT *529*

intend [*v*] *have in mind; determine*
add up, aim, appoint, aspire to, attempt, be determined, be resolved, connote, contemplate, decree, dedicate, denote, design, designate, destine, devote, endeavor, essay, expect, express, figure on, have in mind, hope to, import, indicate, look forward, mean, meditate, ordain, plan, plot, propose, purpose, reserve, resolve, scheme, set apart, set aside, signify, spell, strive, think, try; SEE CONCEPTS *18,36,73,129*

intended [adj] engaged; destined
accidentally on purpose, advised, affianced, afore-thought, asked for, betrothed, calculated, contem-plated, contracted, designed, expected, future, intentional, meant, pinned, planned, plighted, prear-ranged, predestined, predetermined, promised, pro-posed, set, setup, steady; SEE CONCEPT 552

intense [adj] forceful, severe; passionate
acute, agonizing, all-consuming, ardent, biting, bit-ter, burning, close, concentrated, consuming, cut-ting, deep, diligent, eager, earnest, energetic, exaggerated, exceptional, excessive, exquisite, ex-traordinary, extreme, fanatical, fervent, fervid, fierce, forcible, full, great, hard, harsh, heightened, impassioned, intensified, intensive, keen, marked, piercing, powerful, profound, protracted, pungent, sharp, shrill, stinging, strained, strong, supreme, un-due, vehement, violent, vivid, zealous; SEE CONCEPT 569

intensify [v] make more forceful, severe
accent, accentuate, add fuel*, add to, aggrandize, aggravate, augment, beef up*, boost, brighten, build up, concentrate, darken, deepen, emphasize, en-hance, escalate, exacerbate, exalt, heat up*, heighten, increase, intensate, lighten, magnify, point, pour it on*, quicken, raise, redouble, rein-force, rise, rouse, set off, sharpen, spike*, step up, strengthen, stress, tone up, whet; SEE CONCEPTS 233,250

intensity [n] passion, force
acuteness, anxiety, ardor, concentration, deepness, depth, earnestness, emotion, emphasis, energy, ex-cess, excitement, extreme, extremity, fanaticism, ferment, ferociousness, ferocity, fervency, fervor, fierceness, fire, force, forcefulness, fury, high pitch*, intenseness, keenness, magnitude, might, nervousness, potency, power, severity, sharpness, strain, strength, tenseness, tension, vehemence, vigor, violence, volume, weightiness, wildness; SEE CONCEPTS 641,669

intensive [adj] exhaustive
accelerated, all-out*, complete, comprehensive, con-centrated, deep, demanding, fast, hard, in-depth, out-and-out*, profound, radical, severe, speeded-up*, thorough, thoroughgoing; SEE CONCEPT 531

intent/intention [n] aim, purpose
acceptation, animus, bottom line*, conation, design, desire, drift, end, goal, heart, hope, idea, import, intendment, intention, meaning, meat*, name of the game*, nature, notion, nub, nuts and bolts*, object, objective, plan, point, project, purport, scheme, score, sense, significance, significancy, significa-tion, target, understanding, volition, will, wish; SEE CONCEPT 659

intent [adj] determined, resolute
absorbed, alert, attending, attentive, bent, bound, committed, concentrated, concentrating, decided, decisive, deep, eager, earnest, engaged, engrossed,

enthusiastic, firm, fixed, hell-bent*, immersed, in-dustrious, intense, minding, occupied, piercing, pre-occupied, rapt, resolved, riveted*, set, settled, steadfast, steady, watchful, watching, wrapped up*; SEE CONCEPTS 403,542

intentional [adj] deliberate
advised, aforethought, calculated, considered, de-signed, designful, done on purpose, intended, meant, meditated, planned, prearranged, premeditated, pro-posed, purposed, studied, unforced, voluntary, will-ful, willing, witting; SEE CONCEPT 544

intently [adv] with concentration
attentively, closely, fixedly, hard, keenly, search-ingly, sharply, steadily, watchfully; SEE CONCEPTS 403,544

inter [v] bury
cover up, entomb, inhume, inurn, lay to rest, plant, put away, sepulcher, sepulture, tomb; SEE CONCEPTS 172,178,367

interact [v] communicate
collaborate, combine, connect, contact, cooperate, get across*, get the message*, interface, interplay, interreact, join, keep in touch, merge, mesh, net-work, reach out, relate, touch, touch base*, unite; SEE CONCEPT 266

intercede [v] mediate
advocate, arbitrate, barge in, butt in*, intermediate, interpose, intervene, intrude, mix in, monkey with*, negotiate, plead, reconcile, speak, step in; SEE CON-CEPTS 56,110

intercept [v] head off; interrupt
ambush, appropriate, arrest, block, catch, check, curb, cut in, cut off, deflect, head off at pass*, hi-jack, hinder, interlope, interpose, make off with, ob-struct, prevent, seize, shortstop*, stop, take, take away; SEE CONCEPTS 121,164

interchange [n] switch, exchange
altering, alternation, barter, change, crossfire, give-and-take*, intersection, junction, mesh, networking, reciprocation, shift, trade, transposition, variation, varying; SEE CONCEPTS 104,697

interchange [v] switch, exchange
alternate, bandy, barter, commute, connect, contact, convert, interact, interface, mesh, network, recipro-cate, relate, reverse, substitute, swap, trade, trans-pose; SEE CONCEPTS 56,104

interchangeable [adj] identical, transposable
changeable, commutable, compatible, converse, convertible, correspondent, equivalent, exchange-able, fungible, interconvertible, mutual, reciprocal, reciprocative, same, substitutable, synonymous, workalike; SEE CONCEPTS 487,573

intercourse [n1] sexual act
carnal knowledge, coition, coitus, copulation, forni-cation, intimacy, love-making, relations, sex, sexual relations; SEE CONCEPT 375

intercourse [n2] communication; business exchange
association, commerce, communion, connection, contact, converse, correspondence, dealings, give-

and-take, interchange, intercommunication, mesh, networking, team play, teamwork, trade, traffic, transactions; SEE CONCEPTS *266,324*

interest [*n1*] *attraction, curiosity*
absorption, activity, affection, attentiveness, care, case, concern, concernment, consequence, diversion, engrossment, enthusiasm, excitement, game, hobby, importance, interestedness, into, leisure activity, matter, moment, note, notice, passion, pastime, preoccupation, pursuit, racket, recreation, regard, relaxation, relevance, significance, sport, suspicion, sympathy, thing; SEE CONCEPTS *20, 532,690*

interest [*n2*] *advantage*
benefit, gain, good, profit, prosperity, welfare, well-being; SEE CONCEPT *693*

interest [*n3*] *share, investment*
accrual, authority, bonus, claim, commitment, credit, discount, due, earnings, gain, influence, involvement, participation, percentage, piece, points, portion, premium, right, stake, title; SEE CONCEPTS *332,344,835*

interest [*v*] *hold the attention of*
affect, amuse, appeal, appeal to, arouse, attract, be interesting to, concern, divert, engage, engross, entertain, enthrall, excite, fascinate, grab, hook, intrigue, involve, lure, move, perk up, pique, please, pull, sit up, snare, tantalize, tempt, titillate, touch, turn on; SEE CONCEPTS *7,11,22*

interested [*adj*] *concerned, curious*
absorbed, affected, attentive, attracted, awakened, biased, caught, concerned, drawn, eat sleep and breathe*, engrossed, enticed, excited, fascinated, fired*, gone*, hooked*, implicated, impressed, inspired, inspirited, intent, into*, involved, keen, lured, moved, obsessed, occupied, on the case*, open, partial, partisan, predisposed, prejudiced, responsive, roused, sold, stimulated, stirred, struck, sympathetic, taken, touched; SEE CONCEPT *403*

interesting [*adj*] *appealing, entertaining*
absorbing, affecting, alluring, amusing, arresting, attractive, beautiful, captivating, charismatic, compelling, curious, delightful, elegant, enchanting, engaging, engrossing, enthralling, entrancing, exceptional, exotic, fascinating, fine, gracious, gripping, impressive, intriguing, inviting, lovely, magnetic, pleasing, pleasurable, prepossessing, provocative, readable, refreshing, riveting, stimulating, stirring, striking, suspicious, thought-provoking, unusual, winning; SEE CONCEPTS *529,572*

interfere [*v*] *meddle, intervene*
baffle, balk, barge in, busybody*, butt in*, conflict, discommode, foil, fool with, frustrate, get in the way*, get involved, hamper, handicap, hang up*, hinder, hold up, horn in*, impede, incommode, inconvenience, inhibit, intercede, interlope, intermeddle, intermediate, intermit, interpose, intrude, jam, make*, mix in, obstruct, obtrude, oppose, poke nose

in*, prevent, remit, step in, stop, suspend, tamper, thwart, trammel, trouble; SEE CONCEPTS *121,384*

interference [*n*] *meddling, impedance*
arrest, background, backseat driving*, barging in*, barring, blocking, checking, choking, clashing, clogging, conflict, hampering, hindrance, intermeddling, interposition, intervention, intrusion, meddlesomeness, obstruction, opposition, prying, resistance, retardation, tackling, tampering, trespassing; SEE CONCEPTS *121,384*

interim [*n*] *interval*
breach, break, breather, breathing spell, coffee break, cutoff, downtime*, gap, hiatus, interlude, interregnum, interruption, lacuna, layoff, letup, meantime, meanwhile, pause, take*, ten*, time*, timeout; SEE CONCEPTS *807,822*

interim [*adj*] *temporary*
acting, ad interim, caretaker*, improvised, intervening, makeshift, pro tem, pro tempore, provisional, stopgap, thrown-together*; SEE CONCEPT *560*

interior [*n*] *center, core*
belly, bosom, contents, heart, heartland, innards, inner parts, inside, internals, intrinsicality, lining, marrow, midst, pith, pulp, soul, substance, viscera, within; SEE CONCEPTS *742,826,830*

interior [*adj*] *inside, central*
autogenous, domestic, endogenous, gut, home, in-house, inland, inner, innermost, internal, intimate, inward, private, remote, secret, visceral, viscerous, within; SEE CONCEPTS *583,826,830*

interject [*v*] *throw in; interrupt*
add, fill in, force in, implant, import, include, infiltrate, infuse, ingrain, inject, insert, insinuate, intercalate, interpolate, interpose, intersperse, introduce, intrude, parenthesize, put in, splice, squeeze in; SEE CONCEPTS *14,51*

interloper [*n*] *person who intrudes, meddles*
alien, busybody, intermeddler, intruder, meddler, obtruder, trespasser, uninvited guest, unwanted visitor; SEE CONCEPTS *412,423*

interlude [*n*] *pause, break*
breathing space*, delay, episode, halt, hiatus, idyll, interim, intermission, interregnum, interruption, interval, lull, meantime, meanwhile, parenthesis, recess, respite, rest, spell, stop, stoppage, wait; SEE CONCEPT *807*

intermediary [*n*] *person who negotiates*
agent, broker, channel, connection, cutout, delegate, emissary, entrepreneur, fixer, go-between*, influence, instrument, interagent, interceder, intercessor, intermediate, mediator, medium, middleman/woman, negotiator, organ, vehicle; SEE CONCEPTS *348,354*

intermediate [*adj*] *middle, in-between*
average, between, center, central, common, compromising, fair, halfway, indifferent, intermediary, interposed, intervening, mean, medial, median, mediocre, medium, mid, middling, midway, moder-

ate, neutral, so-so*, standard, transitional; SEE CON-
CEPTS *585,830*

interminable [*adj*] *infinite*
boring, boundless, ceaseless, constant, continuous,
day-and-night*, dragged out*, dull, endless, eternal,
everlasting, immeasurable, incessant, interminate,
limitless, long, long-drawn-out*, long-winded,
looped, never-ending, no end of*, no end to*, on a
treadmill*, permanent, perpetual, protracted, spun
out*, strung out*, timeless, unbound, unceasing, uninterrupted, unlimited, wearisome; SEE CONCEPT *798*

intermingle [*v*] *blend, mix*
amalgamate, associate, combine, come together,
commingle, commix, fuse, immingle, interblend, interfuse, interlace, intermix, interweave, join, merge,
mesh, network, pool, throw in with, throw together,
wed; SEE CONCEPTS *113,114*

intermission [*n*] *break, recess*
abeyance, abeyancy, break-off, breather, breathing
spell, cessation, doldrums, dormancy, downtime*,
interim, interlude, interregnum, interruption, interval, latency, layoff, let-up*, lull, parenthesis, pause,
quiescence, quiescency, respite, rest, spell, stop,
stoppage, suspense, suspension, time, time-out, wait;
SEE CONCEPT *807*

intermittent [*adj*] *irregular, sporadic*
alternate, arrested, broken, by bits and pieces*,
checked, cyclic, cyclical, discontinuing, discontinuous, epochal, every other, fitful, here and there*,
hit-or-miss*, infrequent, interrupted, isochronal,
isochronous, iterant, iterative, metrical, now and
then*, occasional, on and off*, periodic, periodical,
punctuated, recurrent, recurring, rhythmic, rhythmical, seasonal, serial, shifting, spasmodic, stop-and-
go*; SEE CONCEPTS *482,534,799*

internal [*adj*] *within*
centralized, circumscribed, civic, constitutional, domestic, enclosed, gut, home, indigenous, inherent,
in-house, innate, inner, innermore, inside, interior,
intestine, intimate, intramural, intrinsic, inward, municipal, national, native, private, subjective, visceral,
viscerous; SEE CONCEPTS *536,585,826,830*

international [*adj*] *worldwide*
all-embracing, cosmopolitan, ecumenical, foreign,
global, intercontinental, universal, world; SEE CON-
CEPTS *536,772*

interplay [*n*] *interaction*
coaction, exchange, give-and-take*, mesh, meshing,
networking, reciprocation, reciprocity, team play*,
teamwork, tit for tat*, transaction; SEE CONCEPT *266*

interpolate [*v*] *add*
admit, annex, append, enter, fill in, include, inject,
insert, insinuate, intercalate, interjaculate, interject,
interlope, interpose, introduce, intrude, throw in; SEE
CONCEPTS *112,201,209*

interpret [*v*] *make sense of; define*
adapt, annotate, clarify, comment, commentate, construe, decipher, decode, delineate, depict, describe,

elucidate, enact, exemplify, explain, explicate, expound, gather, gloss, illustrate, image, improvise,
limn, make of, mimic, paraphrase, perform, picture,
play, portray, read, reenact, render, represent, solve,
spell out, take*, throw light on*, translate, understand, view; SEE CONCEPTS *57,292*

interrogate [*v*] *ask pointed questions*
catechize, cross-examine, cross-question, examine,
give the third degree*, go over*, grill, inquire, investigate, pump, put the screws to*, put through the
wringer*, query, question, quiz, roast*, sweat out*,
work over*; SEE CONCEPTS *48,53*

interrupt [*v*] *bother, interfere*
arrest, barge in, break, break in, break off, break
train of thought*, bust in*, butt in*, check, chime
in*, come between, crash, crowd in, cut, cut in on*,
cut off*, cut short*, defer, delay, disconnect, discontinue, disjoin, disturb, disunite, divide, edge in, get
in the way, halt, heckle, hinder, hold up, horn in,
impede, in, infringe, inject, insinuate, intrude, lay
aside, obstruct, prevent, punctuate, put in, separate,
sever, shortstop*, stay, stop, suspend, work in; SEE
CONCEPTS *51,121,384*

interruption [*n*] *break; interference*
abeyance, abeyancy, arrest, blackout, breach, break,
break-off, cessation, check, cutoff, delay, disconnection, discontinuance, disruption, dissolution, disturbance, disuniting, division, doldrums, dormancy,
gap, halt, hiatus, hindrance, hitch, impediment, interim, intermission, interval, intrusion, lacuna, latency, layoff, let-up*, obstacle, obstruction,
parenthesis, pause, quiescence, rift, rupture, separation, severance, split, stop, stoppage, suspension;
SEE CONCEPTS *807,832*

intersect [*v*] *cut across*
bisect, break in two, come together, converge, crisscross, cross, crosscut, cut, decussate, divide, intercross, join, meet, separate, touch, traverse; SEE
CONCEPTS *113,738,749*

intersection [*n*] *crossroads*
circle, cloverleaf, crossing, crosswalk, crossway, interchange, junction, stop; SEE CONCEPT *501*

intersperse [*v*] *scatter*
bestrew, diffuse, distribute, infuse, interfuse, inter-
lard, intermix, intersow, intersprinkle, pepper, sprinkle; SEE CONCEPTS *201,222*

interstice [*n*] *opening, crack*
aperture, chink, cleft, cranny, crevice, fissure, gap,
hole, interval, slit, space; SEE CONCEPT *513*

intertwine/interweave [*v*] *twist around*
associate, braid, connect, convolute, crisscross,
cross, entwine, interknit, interlace, intertwist, intervolve, interwind, interwreathe, link, mesh, network,
relate, reticulate, tangle, tat, weave; SEE CONCEPTS
113,114

interval [*n*] *break, pause*
breach, breathing space*, comma, delay, distance,
downtime, five*, gap, hiatus, interim, interlude, in-

termission, interregnum, interruption, lacuna, layoff, let-up, lull, meantime, opening, parenthesis, pausation, period, playtime, rest, season, space, spell, ten*, term, time, time-out, wait, while; SEE CONCEPTS *807,822*

intervene [*v1*] *mediate*
arbitrate, barge in, butt in*, come between, divide, horn in*, intercede, interfere, intermediate, interpose, interrupt, intrude, involve, meddle, mix in, muscle in*, negotiate, obtrude, part, put in two cents*, reconcile, separate, settle, sever, step in, take a hand*; SEE CONCEPTS *110,234,266*

intervene [*v2*] *happen*
bedevil, befall, come to pass, ensue, occur, succeed, supervene, take place; SEE CONCEPTS *4,242*

interview [*n*] *questioning and evaluation*
account, audience, call, call back, cattle call*, communication, conference, consultation, conversation, dialogue, examination, hearing, meeting, oral, parley, press conference, record, statement, talk; SEE CONCEPTS *48,351*

interview [*v*] *ask questions and evaluate*
consult, converse, examine, get for the record, get opinion, give oral examination, hold inquiry, interrogate, question, quiz, sound out, talk, talk to; SEE CONCEPTS *48,351*

intestinal/intestine [*adj*] *pertaining to digestive organs*
abdominal, alimentary, bowel, celiac, duodenal, gut, innards, inner, inside, interior, internal, inward, rectal, stomachic, ventral, visceral; SEE CONCEPT *406*

intimacy [*n*] *closeness between people*
acquaintance, affection, affinity, close relationship, communion, confidence, confidentiality, experience, familiarity, fraternization, friendship, inwardness, understanding; SEE CONCEPT *388*

intimate [*n*] *person who is friend*
acquaintance, associate, bosom buddy*, brother, chum, close friend, companion, comrade, confidant, confidante, crony, familiar, family, fiancé, lover, mate, pal, sister; SEE CONCEPTS *416,423*

intimate [*adj1*] *friendly, devoted*
affectionate, bosom, buddy-buddy*, cherished, chummy*, close, clubby*, comfy, confidential, cozy, dear, dearest, faithful, fast, fond, loving, mellow, mix, near, nearest, next, nice, regular, roommate, snug, warm; SEE CONCEPT *555*

intimate [*adj2*] *private, personal*
confidential, deep, deep-seated, detailed, elemental, essential, exhaustive, experienced, firsthand, guarded, gut*, immediate, inborn, inbred, in-depth, indwelling, ingrained, inherent, inmost, innate, innermost, interior, internal, intrinsic, penetrating, privy, profound, secret, special, thorough, trusted, uptight, visceral, viscerous; SEE CONCEPTS *529,549*

intimate [*v*] *suggest; tip off*
affirm, air, allude, announce, assert, aver, avouch, communicate, connote, declare, drop a hint*, expose, express, hint, impart, imply, indicate, infer, insinuate, leak, let cat out of bag*, let it be known, make known, make noise*, profess, remind, spill the beans*, spring, state, utter, vent, voice, warn; SEE CONCEPTS *49,60,75*

intimation [*n*] *clue, hint*
allusion, announcement, breath, communication, cue, declaration, implication, indication, inkling, innuendo, insinuation, notice, notion, reminder, shade, shadow, strain, streak, suggestion, suspicion, telltale, tinge, tip, trace, warning, wind; SEE CONCEPTS *274,689*

intimidate [*v*] *frighten, threaten*
alarm, appall, awe, badger, bait, bludgeon, bluster, bowl over*, browbeat*, buffalo*, bulldoze*, bully, chill, coerce, compel, constrain, cow*, daunt, dishearten, dismay, dispirit, disquiet, dragoon, enforce, force, hound*, lean on*, oblige, overawe, push around*, ride*, ruffle, scare, showboat, spook, strong-arm, subdue, terrify, terrorize, threaten, twist someone's arm*; SEE CONCEPTS *7,14,19*

intolerable [*adj*] *unacceptable; beyond bearing*
a bit much, enough already*, excruciating, extreme, impossible, insufferable, insupportable, last straw*, offensive, painful, unbearable, undesirable, unendurable; SEE CONCEPT *529*

intolerant [*adj*] *impatient, prejudiced*
antipathetic, averse, biased, bigoted, chauvinistic, communist, conservative, contemptuous, dictatorial, disdainful, dogmatic, fanatical, fractious, hateful, illiberal, indignant, individualistic, inflexible, irate, irritable, jaundiced, narrow, narrow-minded, obdurate, one-sided, outraged, racialist, racist, short-fuse*, small-minded*, snappy, stuffy, stupid, tilted, uncharitable, unfair, unforbearing, unindulgent, unsympathetic, unwilling, upset, waspish, worked-up*, xenophobic; SEE CONCEPTS *403,404,542*

intoxicated [*adj1*] *drunk*
blind*, bombed*, boozed, buzzed*, drunken, high*, inebriated, loaded*, looped*, muddled, potted*, sloppy, smashed*, tanked*, three sheets to wind*, tied one on*, tight*, tipsy, under the influence, unsober; SEE CONCEPT *406*

intoxicated [*adj2*] *extremely happy*
absorbed, affected, beside oneself, captivated, concerned, delirious, dizzy, drunk, ecstatic, elated, enraptured, euphoric, excited, exhilarated, galvanized, high*, infatuated, interested, moved, piqued, quickened, sent*, stimulated, turned-on*; SEE CONCEPT *403*

intoxicating [*adj*] *causing great happiness*
exciting, exhilarant, exhilarating, exhilarative, eye-popping, heady, inspiring, provocative, rousing, stimulating, stirring, thrilling; SEE CONCEPT *537*

intractable/intransigent [*adj*] *difficult, stubborn*
awkward, bullheaded*, cantankerous, contrary, hang tough*, hard-line*, headstrong, immovable, incompliant, incurable, indocile, indomitable, insoluble,

locked in*, mulish, obdurate, obstinate, pat, pertinacious, perverse, pigheaded*, recalcitrant, refractory, resolute, self-willed, set in stone, tenacious, tough, tough-nut*, tractious, unbending, uncompromising, uncooperative, undisciplined, ungovernable, unmanageable, unpliable, unruly, unyielding, wayward, wild, willful; SEE CONCEPTS *401,534,542*

intrepid [*adj*] *brave, nervy*
audacious, bodacious*, bold, courageous, daring, dauntless, doughty, fearless, gallant, game, gritty, gutsy*, heroic, impavid, lionhearted, nerveless, plucky, resolute, spunky*, stalwart, unafraid, undaunted, unflinching, valiant, valorous; SEE CONCEPT *401*

intricate [*adj*] *complicated, elaborate*
abstruse, baroque, Byzantine*, can of worms*, complex, convoluted, Daedal*, difficult, entangled, fancy, hard, high-tech*, involved, labyrinthine, obscure, perplexing, rococo, sophisticated, tangled, tortuous, tricky; SEE CONCEPT *562*

intrigue [*n1*] *scheme*
artifice, cabal, chicanery, collusion, complication, conspiracy, contrivance, deal, design, dodge, double-dealing*, fix, frame-up*, fraud, game, graft, hookup, knavery, little game*, machination, maneuver, manipulation, plan, plot, ruse, stratagem, trickery, wile; SEE CONCEPTS *192,660*

intrigue [*n2*] *love affair*
affair, amour, attachment, case, flirtation, infatuation, interlude, intimacy, liaison, romance; SEE CONCEPT *388*

intrigue [*v1*] *arouse curiosity*
appeal, attract, bait, captivate, charm, con, delight, draw, enchant, entertain, excite, fascinate, grab, hook, interest, lead on*, mousetrap*, pique, please, pull, rivet, tickle, titillate, tout; SEE CONCEPTS *7,11,22*

intrigue [*v2*] *plot*
angle, be in cahoots*, cogitate, collude, connive, conspire, contrive, cook up*, devise, finagle, frame up*, machinate, maneuver, operate, plan, promote, scheme, set up*, work hand in glove*; SEE CONCEPT *36*

intrinsic [*adj*] *basic, inborn*
built-in, central, congenital, connate, constitutional, constitutive, deep-seated, elemental, essential, fundamental, genuine, hereditary, inbred, indwelling, inherent, inmost, innate, intimate, material, native, natural, particular, peculiar, real, true, underlying; SEE CONCEPTS *404,406,546*

introduce [*v1*] *make known; present*
acquaint, advance, air, announce, bring out, bring up, broach, come out with, do the honors*, familiarize, fix up, get things rolling*, get together, give introduction, harbinger*, herald, kick off, knock down, lead into, lead off, moot, offer, open, open up, originate, pave the way*, precede, preface, pro-

pose, put forward, recommend, set forth, spring with, start ball rolling*, submit, suggest, usher, ventilate; SEE CONCEPTS *60,384*

introduce [*v2*] *begin, institute*
admit, bring forward, bring in, commence, enter, establish, found, inaugurate, induct, initiate, innovate, install, invent, kick off*, launch, organize, pioneer, plan, preface, present, set up, start, unveil, usher in; SEE CONCEPT *221*

introduce [*v3*] *add, insert*
carry, enter, fill in, freight, import, include, infix, inject, inlay, inlet, inset, insinuate, instill, intercalate, interject, interpolate, interpose, put in, send, ship, throw in, transport, work in; SEE CONCEPTS *112,113,209*

introduction [*n*] *something new; something that begins*
addition, admittance, awakening, baptism, basic principles, basic text, beginning, blind date*, commencement, debut, essentials, establishment, exordium, first acquaintance, first taste, foreword, inauguration, inception, induction, influx, ingress, initiation, insertion, installation, institution, interpolation, intro*, launch, lead, lead-in, opening, opening remarks, overture, pioneering, preamble, preface, preliminaries, prelude, presentation, primer, proem, prolegomenon, prologue, survey; SEE CONCEPTS *270,727,828*

introductory [*adj*] *preliminary, first*
anterior, basic, beginning, early, elementary, inaugural, incipient, inductive, initial, initiatory, opening, original, precursory, prefatory, prelusive, preparative, preparatory, primary, prior, proemial, provisional, rudimentary, starting; SEE CONCEPTS *546,585*

introspection [*n*] *self-analysis*
brooding, contemplation, deep thought, egoism, heart-searching, introversion, meditation, reflection, rumination, scrutiny, self-absorption, self-examination, self-observation, self-questioning, soul-searching; SEE CONCEPTS *24,410*

introvert [*n*] *person who retreats mentally*
autist, brooder, egoist, egotist, loner*, narcissist, self-observer, solitary, wallflower*; SEE CONCEPT *423*

intrude [*v*] *trespass, interrupt*
barge in, bother, butt in*, chisel in*, cut in, disturb, encroach, entrench, go beyond, hold up, horn in*, infringe, insinuate, intercalate, interfere, interject, interlope, intermeddle, interpolate, interpose, introduce, invade, meddle, obtrude, overstep, pester, push in, thrust, violate; SEE CONCEPTS *14, 159,208,266*

intruder [*n*] *person who trespasses*
burglar, criminal, gate-crasher*, infiltrator, interferer, interloper, interrupter, invader, meddler, nuisance, obtruder, prowler, raider, snooper, squatter, thief, trespasser; SEE CONCEPTS *412,423*

intuition [*n*] *insight*
clairvoyance, discernment, divination, ESP*, feeling*, foreknowledge, gut reaction*, hunch*, innate knowledge, inspiration, instinct, intuitiveness, nose*, penetration, perception, perceptivity, premonition, presentiment, second sight*, sixth sense*; SEE CONCEPTS *409,689*

intuitive [*adj*] *instinctive*
automatic, direct, emotional, habitual, immediate, inherent, innate, instinctual, involuntary, natural, perceptive, spontaneous, understood, unreflecting, untaught, visceral; SEE CONCEPT *402*

inundate [*v*] *drown, overwhelm*
deluge, dunk, engulf, flood, glut, immerse, overflow, overrun, pour down on, snow*, submerge, swamp, whelm; SEE CONCEPTS *172,179*

invade [*v*] *attack and encroach*
access, assail, assault, breach, burglarize, burst in, crash, descend upon, entrench, fall on, foray, go in, infect, infest, infringe, inroad, interfere, loot, make inroads*, maraud, meddle, muscle in*, occupy, overrun, overspread, overswarm, penetrate, permeate, pervade, pillage, plunder, raid, ravage, storm, swarm over, trespass, violate; SEE CONCEPTS *86,159,320*

invalid [*n*] *sick person*
consumptive, convalescent, cripple, disabled person, incurable, inmate, paralytic, patient, shut-in, weakling; SEE CONCEPT *424*

invalid [*adj1*] *worthless; unfounded*
bad, baseless, fallacious, false, ill-founded, illogical, inoperative, irrational, mad, not binding, not working, nugatory, null, null and void*, reasonless, sophistic, unreasonable, unreasoned, unscientific, unsound, untrue, void, wrong; SEE CONCEPTS *552,560*

invalid [*adj2*] *sickly*
ailing, bedridden, below par, debilitated, disabled, down, feeble, frail, ill, infirm, laid low*, on the sick list*, out of action*, peaked, poorly, run-down, sick, weak; SEE CONCEPT *314*

invalidate [*v*] *render null and void*
abate, abolish, abrogate, annihilate, annul, blow sky-high*, cancel, circumduct, counteract, counterbalance, disannul, discredit, disqualify, impair, negate, negative, neutralize, nix, nullify, offset, overrule, overthrow, quash, refute, revoke, shoot full of holes*, undermine, undo, unfit, weaken, X-out*; SEE CONCEPTS *121,234*

invaluable [*adj*] *priceless*
beyond price, costly, dear, expensive, helpful, inestimable, precious, serviceable, valuable; SEE CONCEPTS *334,568*

invariable [*adj*] *not changing*
changeless, consistent, constant, fixed, immovable, immutable, inalterable, inflexible, monotonous, perpetual, regular, rigid, same, set, static, unalterable, unchangeable, unchanging, undiversified, unfailing, uniform, unmodifiable, unrelieved, unvarying, unwavering; SEE CONCEPT *534*

invasion [*n*] *attack, encroachment*
aggression, assault, breach, entrenchment, foray, forced entrance, incursion, infiltration, infraction, infringement, inroad, intrusion, irruption, maraud, offense, offensive, onslaught, overstepping, raid, transgression, trespass, usurpation, violation; SEE CONCEPTS *86,159,320*

invective [*n*] *verbal abuse*
accusation, berating, billingsgate, blame, blasphemy, castigation, censure, condemnation, contumely, denunciation, diatribe, epithet, jeremiad, obloquy, philippic, reproach, revilement, sarcasm, scurrility, tirade, tongue-lashing*, vilification, vituperation; SEE CONCEPTS *44,52,54,278*

inveigh [*v*] *blame, denounce*
admonish, berate, blast, castigate, censure, condemn, crack down on*, denounce, except, expostulate, go after*, have at*, jump down one's throat*, kick, lambaste, lay into, lay out, let have it, object, protest, rail, read out*, recriminate, remonstrate, reproach, rip into, roast, scold, scorch, sound off, tongue-lash, trash*, upbraid, vituperate, work over*; SEE CONCEPTS *44,52,54*

inveigle [*v*] *entice, manipulate*
allure, bait, bamboozle, beguile, blandish, butter*, cajole, charm, coax, con*, decoy, egg on*, ensnare, entrap, get around*, honey*, hook, influence, jolly, lay it on thick*, lead on*, lure, maneuver, massage, oil*, overdo it, persuade, play up to, rope in*, seduce, snow*, soap*, soften up*, string along*, stroke*, sweet talk*, tempt, toll, urge, wheedle, work over*; SEE CONCEPTS *11,14,59*

invent [*v1*] *create, think up*
ad-lib, author, bear, bring into being, coin, come upon, come up with, compose, conceive, contrive, cook up*, design, devise, discover, dream up, envision, execute, fake, fashion, find, forge, form, formulate, frame, hatch, imagine, improve, improvise, inaugurate, initiate, jam*, knock off*, make, make up, mint, off-the-cuff*, originate, plan, produce, project, toss off*, turn out, wing*; SEE CONCEPTS *36,173*

invent [*v2*] *fabricate*
concoct, conjure up, create out of thin air*, equivocate, fake, falsify, feign, fib, forge, lie, make believe, make up, misrepresent, misstate, pretend, prevaricate, simulate, tell a white lie*, tell untruth, think up, trump up*, vamp; SEE CONCEPTS *59,63*

invention [*n1*] *creation, creativeness*
apparatus, black box*, brainchild*, coinage, concoction, contraption, contrivance, creativity, design, development, device, discovery, doodad*, gadget, genius, gimmick, gizmo*, imagination, ingenuity, innovation, inspiration, inventiveness, novelty, opus, original, originality, resourcefulness; SEE CONCEPTS *260,409,660*

invention [n2] *fabrication, lie*
deceit, fake, falsehood, fancy, fantasy, fib, fiction, figment, forgery, prevarication, sham*, story, tall story*, untruth, yarn*; SEE CONCEPTS **63,278**

inventive [adj] *creative*
adroit, artistic, avant-garde, breaking new ground, causative, constructive, demiurgic, deviceful, fertile, forgetive, formative, fruitful, gifted, imaginative, ingenious, innovational, innovative, innovatory, inspired, original, originative, poetical, productive, resourceful, teeming; SEE CONCEPTS **402,542**

inventory [n] *list of stock; stock*
account, backlog, catalogue, file, fund, hoard, index, itemization, record, register, reserve, reservoir, roll, roster, schedule, stock book, stockpile, store, summary, supply, table, tabulation; SEE CONCEPTS **283,338**

inverse [adj] *opposite*
changed, contrary, converse, flipped, inverted, reverse, reversed, reverted, transposed, turned, turned over; SEE CONCEPT **564**

invert [v] *reverse; turn upside down*
alter, backtrack, capsize, change, convert, double back, evert, flip, flip-flop*, introvert, inverse, modify, overturn, renege, revert, tip, transplace, transpose, turn, turn down, turn inside out, turn over, turn the tables*, upend, upset, upturn; SEE CONCEPTS **213,232**

invest [v1] *contribute money to make money*
advance, back, bankroll, buy into, buy stock, devote, endow, endue, get into, go in for, imbue, infuse, intrust, lay out, lend, loan, pick up the tab*, plow back into*, plunge, provide, put in, put up dough*, salt away*, sink, spend, stake, supply; SEE CONCEPTS **115,330,341**

invest [v2] *give power or authority*
adopt, authorize, bequeath, charge, consecrate, empower, endow, endue, enthrone, establish, honor, inaugurate, induct, initiate, install, instate, license, ordain, sanction, vest; SEE CONCEPTS **50,88**

investigate [v] *check into thoroughly*
be all ears*, bug, case*, check out, check over, check up, consider, delve, dig, examine, explore, eyeball*, feel out, frisk, give the once over*, go into, inquire, inquisite, inspect, interrogate, listen in, look into, look over, look-see, make inquiry, muckrake, nose around*, poke, probe, prospect, pry, put to the test*, question, read, reconnoiter, research, review, run down, scout, scrutinize, search, sift, spy, stake out, study, tap, wiretap; SEE CONCEPTS **48,103,216**

investigation [n] *thorough check*
analysis, case, delving, examination, exploration, fact-finding, gander, hearing, hustle, inquest, inquiry, inquisition, inspection, legwork, observation, observing, pike, probe, probing, quest, quiz, research, review, scrutiny, search, sounding, study, survey, surveying; SEE CONCEPTS **48,103,216,290**

investigator [n] *person who checks thoroughly*
agent, analyst, attorney, auditor, detective, examiner, gumshoe*, hound*, inquirer, inspector, plainclothesman/woman, police, private detective, private eye, prosecutor, researcher, reviewer, Sherlock Holmes*, sleuth, snooper, spy, tester, undercover cop; SEE CONCEPTS **348,355**

investment [n] *something given, lent for a return*
advance, ante, asset, backing, bail, contribution, endowment, expenditure, expense, finance, financing, flutter, grant, hunch, inside, interests, investing, loan, money, piece, plunge, property, purchase, smart money*, spec*, speculation, stab*, stake, transaction, venture, vested interests; SEE CONCEPTS **330,332,340**

inveterate [adj] *long-standing, established*
abiding, accustomed, addicted, chronic, confirmed, continuing, customary, deep-rooted, deep-seated, dyed-in-the-wool*, enduring, entrenched, fixed, habitual, habituated, hard-core*, hardened, inbred, incorrigible, incurable, indurated, ineradicable, ingrained, innate, lifelong, long-lasting, long-lived, obstinate, old, perennial, permanent, persistent, persisting, set, settled, stubborn, sworn, usual; SEE CONCEPTS **404,534,798**

invidious [adj] *hateful*
abominable, calumnious, defamatory, detestable, detracting, detractive, detractory, discriminatory, envious, envying, green-eyed*, jealous, libelous, maligning, obnoxious, odious, offensive, repugnant, scandalous, slanderous, slighting, undesirable, vilifying; SEE CONCEPTS **401,403**

invigorate [v] *stimulate*
activate, animate, brace, buck up, energize, enliven, excite, exhilarate, fortify, freshen, galvanize, harden, inspirit, liven up, nerve, pep up, perk up, pick up, quicken, rally, refresh, reinforce, rejuvenate, renew, restore, revitalize, rouse, snap up*, stir, strengthen, trigger, turn on*, vitalize, vivify, zap; SEE CONCEPTS **7,14,22,110**

invigorating [adj] *stimulating*
aesthetic, bracing, brisk, charged, energizing, exhilarating, exhilarative, fascinating, fresh, healthful, high*, hyper*, interesting, lively, quickening, refreshing, rejuvenating, rejuvenative, restorative, salubrious, tonic, uplifting, vitalizing; SEE CONCEPT **537**

invincible [adj] *indestructible*
bulletproof, impassable, impregnable, indomitable, insuperable, inviolable, invulnerable, irresistible, powerful, strong, unassailable, unattackable, unbeatable, unconquerable, undefeatable, unsurmountable, untouchable, unyielding; SEE CONCEPTS **489,540,551**

invisible [adj] *unable to be seen; hidden*
concealed, covert, deceptive, disguised, ethereal, gaseous, ghostly, ideal, impalpable, imperceptible, imponderable, inappreciable, inconspicuous, indiscernible, infinitesimal, insensible, intangible,

masked, microscopic, not in sight, obliterated, obscured, occult, out of sight, perdu, screened, supernatural, ulterior, unapparent, undisclosed, ungraspable, unnoticeable, unobservable, unperceivable, unreal, unseeable, unseen, unviewable, vaporous, veiled, wraithlike; SEE CONCEPTS *485,582,619*

invitation [*n*] *proposal; asking*
allurement, appeal, attraction, begging, bid, bidding, call, challenge, compliments, coquetry, date, encouragement, enticement, feeler*, ground, hit, incitement, inducement, invite, lure, motive, offer, open door*, overture, paper, pass, petition, pressure, proffer, prompting, proposition, provocation, rain check*, reason, request, solicitation, suggestion, summons, supplication, temptation, urge; SEE CONCEPTS *48,384*

invite [*v*] *ask to do something socially*
allure, appeal to, attract, beg, bid, bring on, call, command, countenance, court, draw, encourage, entice, entreat, give invitation, have in, have over, include as guest, insist, inveigle, invitation, issue, lead, lure, persuade, petition, ply, pray, press, prevail on, propose, provoke, request, send invitation, solicit, suggest, summon, supplicate, tempt, toll, urge, vamp, welcome, woo; SEE CONCEPTS *48, 68,384*

inviting [*adj*] *alluring, captivating*
agreeable, appealing, attractive, beguiling, bewitching, charming, cordial, delightful, encouraging, engaging, enticing, fascinating, intriguing, magnetic, mouthwatering, open, persuasive, pleasing, provocative, seductive, tempting, warm, welcoming, winning, winsome; SEE CONCEPTS *404,529,537*

invocation [*n*] *prayer*
abracadabra*, appeal, beseeching, calling, command, conjuration, entreaty, hocus-pocus*, hoodoo*, mumbo-jumbo*, petition, rune, summons, supplication, voodoo*; SEE CONCEPTS *48,278,368*

invoke [*v1*] *call upon*
adjure, appeal to, beg, beseech, call forth, conjure, crave, entreat, implore, importune, petition, plead, pray, request, send for, solicit, summon, supplicate; SEE CONCEPT *48*

invoke [*v2*] *put into effect*
apply, call in, effect, enforce, have recourse to, implement, initiate, resort to, use; SEE CONCEPTS *50,88*

involuntary [*adj*] *automatic; not done willingly*
automatic, begrudging, blind, compulsory, conditioned, forced, grudging, habitual, impulsive, instinctive, instinctual, knee-jerk*, obligatory, reflex, reflexive, reluctant, spontaneous, uncalculated, unconscious, uncontrolled, unintended, unintentional, unmeditated, unpremeditated, unprompted, unthinking, unwilling, unwitting, will-less; SEE CONCEPT *544*

involve [*v*] *draw in; include*
absorb, affect, argue, associate, bind, catch, commit, complicate, comprehend, comprise, compromise, concern, connect, contain, cover, denote, embrace, embroil, engage, engross, enmesh, entail, entangle, grip, hold, hook, implicate, imply, include, incorporate, incriminate, inculpate, link, mean, mire, mix up*, necessitate, number, point to, preoccupy, presuppose, prove, relate, require, rivet, rope in, snarl up, suggest, take in, tangle, touch, wrap up in*; SEE CONCEPT *112*

involved [*adj1*] *complicated*
Byzantine*, complex, confusing, convoluted, difficult, elaborate, Gordian*, high-tech*, intricate, knotty*, labyrinthine, mazy, muddled, ramified, sophisticated, tangled, tortuous, winding; SEE CONCEPT *562*

involved [*adj2*] *implicated in action*
affected, caught, concerned, eat sleep and breathe*, embarrassed, embroiled, enmeshed, entangled, hooked, immersed in, incriminated, interested, into, knee-deep in*, mixed up in*, mixed up with*, occupied, participating, taking part in, tangled, up to here in*, up to one's neck in*; SEE CONCEPTS *542,545*

inward [*adj1*] *ingoing*
entering, inbound, incoming, infiltrating, inflowing, inpouring, penetrating, through; SEE CONCEPT *581*

inward [*adj2*] *private*
confidential, hidden, inmost, inner, innermost, inside, intellectual, interior, internal, intimate, personal, privy, psychological, religious, secret, spiritual; SEE CONCEPT *529*

iota [*n*] *small bit*
atom, crumb, grain, hint, infinitesimal, jot, mite, molecule, nucleus, ounce, particle, ray, scintilla, scrap, smidgen, speck, trace, whit; SEE CONCEPT *831*

irascible [*adj*] *crabby*
angry, bearish, bitchy*, bristly, cantankerous, choleric, crabbed, cranky, cross, feisty, fractious, grouchy, hasty, hot-tempered, huffy, ireful, irritable, ogre, passionate, peevish, petulant, querulous, quick-tempered, short-tempered, snappish, surly, testy, thin-skinned*, touchy, uptight; SEE CONCEPT *401*

irate [*adj*] *angry*
angered, annoyed, blown a gasket*, enraged, exasperated, fuming, furious, incensed, indignant, infuriated, irritated, livid, mad, piqued, provoked, riled, steamed*, ticked off*, up in arms*, worked up*, wrathful, wroth; SEE CONCEPTS *403,542*

ire [*n*] *anger*
annoyance, boiling point*, conniption, conniption fit*, displeasure, exasperation, fury, indignation, more heat than light*, passion, rage, slow burn*, wrath; SEE CONCEPT *410*

iridescent [*adj*] *rainbow-colored*
irised, lustrous, many-colored, nacreous, opalescent, opaline, pearly, polychromatic, prismatic, rainbowlike, shimmering; SEE CONCEPT *618*

irk [*v*] *aggravate; rub the wrong way*
abrade, annoy, bother, bug*, discommode, disturb, eat*, fret, gall, get on nerves*, get to*, give a hard time*, harass, incommode, inconvenience, irritate, make waves*, miff, nettle, peeve, provoke, put out*, rasp, rile, ruffle, trouble, vex; SEE CONCEPTS *7,19*

iron [*n1*] *hard, ferrous metal*
cast, coke, pig; SEE CONCEPT *476*

iron [*n2*] *restraint made of metal*
bond, chain, cuffs, fetter, handcuffs, leg irons, manacles, shackles; SEE CONCEPT *476*

iron [*adj*] *hard, tough; inflexible*
adamant, adamantine, cruel, dense, ferric, ferrous, firm, heavy, immovable, implacable, indomitable, inexorable, insensible, obdurate, relentless, rigid, robust, steel, steely, strong, stubborn, thick, unbending, unyielding; SEE CONCEPTS *534,604*

ironic/ironical [*adj*] *sarcastic*
acrid, alert, arrogant, backbiting, biting, bitter, burlesque, caustic, chaffing, clever, contemptuous, contradictory, critical, cutting, cynical, defiant, derisive, disparaging, double-edged, exaggerated, implausible, incisive, incongruous, jibing, keen, mocking, mordant, paradoxical, pungent, quick-witted, ridiculous, sardonic, satiric, satirical, scathing, scoffing, sharp, sneering, spicy, trenchant, twisted, uncomplimentary, unexpected, witty, wry; SEE CONCEPTS *267,548*

iron out [*v*] *reconcile a situation*
agree, arbitrate, clear up*, compromise, eliminate, eradicate, erase, expedite, get rid of*, harmonize, negotiate, put right*, reach agreement, resolve, settle, settle differences, simplify, smooth over*, sort out*, straighten out*, unravel; SEE CONCEPT *126*

irony [*n*] *sarcasm*
banter, burlesque, contempt, contrariness, criticism, derision, humor, incongruity, jibe, mockery, mordancy, paradox, quip, raillery, repartee, reproach, ridicule, sardonicism, satire, taunt, twist, wit; SEE CONCEPTS *230,278*

irrational [*adj*] *illogical, senseless*
aberrant, absurd, brainless, cockamamie*, crazy, delirious, demented, disconnected, disjointed, distraught, fallacious, flaky*, foolish, freaky, incoherent, injudicious, insane, invalid, kooky*, loony*, mad, mindless, nonsensical, nutty*, off-the-wall*, preposterous, raving, reasonless, ridiculous, silly, sophistic, specious, stupid, unreasonable, unreasoning, unsound, unstable, unthinking, unwise, wacky*, wild, wrong; SEE CONCEPTS *402,403,529*

irreconcilable [*adj*] *hostile, conflicting*
clashing, diametrically opposed, discordant, discrepant, dissonant, hard-line, implacable, incompatible, incongruous, inconsistent, inexorable, inflexible, inharmonious, intransigent, opposed, reluctant, unappeasable, uncompromising, unfriendly; SEE CONCEPTS *401,564*

irrefutable [*adj*] *beyond question*
accurate, apodictic, can bet on it*, certain, double-checked, evident, final, inarguable, incontestable, incontrovertible, indisputable, indubitable, invincible, ironclad, irrebuttable, irrefragable, irresistible, no ifs ands or buts*, obvious, odds-on*, positive, proven, set, sure, unanswerable, unassailable, undeniable, un-

impeachable, unquestionable; SEE CONCEPTS *529, 535,582*

irregular [*adj1*] *random, variable*
aberrant, aimless, capricious, casual, changeable, designless, desultory, disconnected, discontinuous, eccentric, erratic, faltering, fitful, fluctuating, fragmentary, haphazard, hit-or-miss*, inconstant, indiscriminate, infrequent, intermittent, jerky, nonuniform, occasional, out of order, patchy, purposeless, random, recurrent, shaky, shifting, spasmodic, sporadic, uncertain, unconsidered, uneven, unmethodical, unpunctual, unreliable, unsettled, unsteady, unsystematic, up and down*, weaving; SEE CONCEPTS *534,799*

irregular [*adj2*] *abnormal, peculiar*
aberrant, anomalous, atypical, capricious, deviant, different, disorderly, divergent, eccentric, exceptional, extraordinary, immoderate, improper, inappropriate, inordinate, odd, off-key*, queer, quirky, singular, strange, unconventional, unique, unnatural, unofficial, unorthodox, unsuitable, unusual; SEE CONCEPT *547*

irregular [*adj3*] *bumpy, uneven*
aberrant, amorphous, asymmetrical, bent, broken, cockeyed*, craggy, crooked, devious, disproportionate, eccentric, elliptic, elliptical, hilly, jagged, lopsided, lumpy, meandering, notched, not uniform, off-balance, off-center, out of proportion, pitted, protuberant, rough, scarred, serrate, serrated, unaligned, unbalanced, unequal, unsymmetrical, variable, wobbly, zigzagged; SEE CONCEPTS *490,606*

irregularly [*adv*] *intermittently*
anyhow, any which way*, at intervals, by fits and starts*, by turns, disconnectedly, eccentrically, erratically, fitfully, haphazardly, helter-skelter*, infrequently, in snatches*, jerkily, now and again, occasionally, off and on*, out of sequence, periodically, slapdash, spasmodically, sporadically, uncertainly, uncommonly, unevenly, unmethodically, unpunctually, willy-nilly*; SEE CONCEPTS *544, 548,799*

irrelevant [*adj*] *beside the point*
extraneous, foreign, garbage, immaterial, impertinent, inapplicable, inapposite, inappropriate, inappurtenant, inapropos, inapt, inconsequent, inconsequential, insignificant, not connected with, not germane, not pertaining to, off the point, off the topic, out of order, out of place, outside, pointless, remote, trivial, unapt, unconnected, unimportant, unnecessary, unrelated, without reference; SEE CONCEPTS *560,575*

irreparable [*adj*] *unable to be fixed*
beyond repair, broken, cureless, destroyed, hopeless, impossible, incorrigible, incurable, irrecoverable, irredeemable, irremediable, irremedial, irreplaceable, irretrievable, irreversible, ruined, uncorrectable, unrecoverable; SEE CONCEPTS *314,485*

irrepressible [*adj*] *effervescent, vivacious*
boisterous, bubbling, buoyant, ebullient, enthusiastic, insuppressible, rebellious, rhapsodical, tumultous/

tumultuous, unconstrained, uncontainable, uncontrollable, unmanageable, unquenchable, unrestrainable, unrestrained, unruly, unstoppable; SEE CONCEPT *401*

irreproachable [*adj*] *innocent*
beyond reproach, blameless, exemplary, faultless, good, guiltless, impeccable, inculpable, innocent, irreprehensible, irreprovable, perfect, pure, reproachless, righteous, unblamable, unblemished, unimpeachable, virtuous; SEE CONCEPTS *545,574*

irresistible [*adj*] *compelling; inescapable*
alluring, beautiful, beckoning, charming, enchanting, fascinating, glamorous, imperative, indomitable, ineluctable, inevitable, inexorable, invincible, lovable, overpowering, overwhelming, potent, powerful, ravishing, scrumptious, seductive, sexy, stunning, tempting, unavoidable, unconquerable, urgent; SEE CONCEPTS *529,574,579*

irresolute [*adj*] *indecisive*
changing, doubtful, doubting, faltering, fearful, fickle, fluctuating, halfhearted*, halting, hesitant, hesitating, hot-and-cold*, infirm, on-the-fence*, shaky, tentative, timid, uncertain, undecided, undetermined, unsettled, unstable, unsteady, vacillating, waffling*, wavering, weak, weak-kneed*, wimpy*, wishy-washy*, wobbly; SEE CONCEPTS *403,535*

irresponsible [*adj*] *careless, reckless*
capricious, carefree, devil-may-care*, feckless, fickle, flighty, fly-by-night*, giddy, harebrained, ill-considered, immature, immoral, incautious, lax, loose*, no-account*, rash, reckless, scatterbrained*, shiftless, thoughtless, unaccountable, unanswerable, uncareful, undependable, unpredictable, unreliable, unstable, untrustworthy, wild; SEE CONCEPTS *404,544*

irreverence [*n*] *disrespect*
blasphemy, cheek, derision, discourtesy, flippancy, heresy, impertinence, impiety, impudence, insult, mockery, profanity, ridicule, rudeness, sauciness, sin, sinfulness; SEE CONCEPT *633*

irreverent [*adj*] *disrespectful*
aweless, cheeky*, cocky*, contemptuous, crusty*, derisive, flip*, flippant, fresh, iconoclastic, impertinent, impious, impudent, insolent, irreverential, mocking, out-of-line*, profane, rude, sacrilegious, sassy*, saucy*, tongue-in-cheek*, ungodly, unhallowed, unholy; SEE CONCEPT *401*

irrevocable [*adj*] *fixed, unchangeable*
certain, changeless, constant, doomed, established, fated, final, immutable, indelible, inevitable, invariable, irremediable, irretrievable, irreversible, lost, permanent, predestined, predetermined, settled, unalterable, unrepealable, unreversible; SEE CONCEPTS *534,551*

irritable [*adj*] *bad-tempered, crabby*
annoyed, bearish, brooding, cantankerous, carping, choleric, complaining, contentious, crabbed, cross, crotchety, disputatious, dissatisfied, dyspeptic, easily offended, exasperated, fiery, fractious, fretful, fretting, gloomy, grouchy, grumbling, hasty, hot, huffy, hypercritical, ill-humored, irascible, moody, morose, out of humor, oversensitive, peevish, petulant, plaintive, prickly, querulous, quick-tempered, resentful, sensitive, shrewish, snappy, snarling, surly, tense, testy, touchy; SEE CONCEPTS *401,403*

irritate [*v1*] *upset, anger*
abrade, affront, aggravate, annoy, bother, bug*, burn*, chafe, confuse, distemper, disturb, drive up the wall*, enrage, exasperate, fret, gall, get, get on nerves*, get under skin*, grate, harass, incense, inflame, infuriate, irk, madden, needle*, nettle, offend, pain, peeve, pester, pique, provoke, put out, rankle, rasp, rattle, rile, roil, rub the wrong way*, ruffle, sour, try, vex; SEE CONCEPTS *7,19*

irritate [*v2*] *hurt, chafe*
aggravate, burn, erupt, fret, inflame, intensify, itch, pain, redden, rub, sensitize, sharpen, sting, swell; SEE CONCEPT *246*

island [*n*] *land surrounded by body of water*
archipelago, atoll, bar, cay, enclave, haven, isle, islet, key, peninsula, reef, refuge, retreat, sanctuary, shelter; SEE CONCEPT *509*

isolate [*v*] *cut off, set apart*
abstract, block off, close off, confine, detach, disconnect, disengage, divide, divorce, insulate, island, keep apart, part, quarantine, remove, seclude, segregate, separate, sequester, sever, sunder; SEE CONCEPTS *188,201*

isolated [*adj*] *unique; private*
abandoned, abnormal, alone, anomalous, apart, backwoods*, confined, deserted, detached, exceptional, far-out, forsaken, hidden, incommunicado*, lonely, lonesome, off beaten track*, outlying, out-of-the-way*, random, remote, retired, screened, secluded, segregated, sequestered, single, solitary, special, stranded, unaccompanied, unfrequented, unrelated, untypical, unusual, withdrawn; SEE CONCEPTS *577,583*

issue [*n1*] *point in question*
affair, argument, concern, contention, controversy, matter, matter of contention, point, point of departure, problem, puzzle, question, subject, topic; SEE CONCEPTS *278,532*

issue [*n2*] *result*
causatum, conclusion, consequence, culmination, effect, end, end product, eventuality, finale, fruit, outcome, payoff, result, sequel, termination, upshot; SEE CONCEPT *230*

issue [*n3*] *edition of publication*
copy, impression, installment, number, printing; SEE CONCEPT *280*

issue [*n4*] *distribution*
circulation, delivery, dispersion, dissemination, granting, issuance, issuing, publication, sending out, supply, supplying; SEE CONCEPT *140*

issue [*n5*] *children*
brood, descendants, get, heirs, offspring, posterity, progeniture, progeny, scions, seed; SEE CONCEPTS *296,414*

issue [v1] *distribute*
air, allot, announce, assign, bring out, broadcast, circulate, consign, declare, deliver, dispatch, dispense, emit, get out, give out, promulgate, publish, put in circulation, put out, release, send, send out, transmit; SEE CONCEPTS *60,140,292*

issue [v2] *emit, emerge; come from*
appear, arise, be a consequence, birth, come forth, derive from, emanate, exude, flow, give off, give out, ooze, originate, proceed, release, rise, send forth, spring, spurt, stem, throw off, vent, well; SEE CONCEPTS *179,648*

itch [n1] *scratching; tingling*
crawling, creeping, irritation, itchiness, prickling, psoriasis, rawness, tickle; SEE CONCEPTS *608,728*

itch [n2] *strong desire*
aphrodisia, appetite, appetition, concupiscence, craving, eroticism, hankering, hunger, impulse, longing, lust, lustfulness, motive, passion, prurience, pruriency, restlessness, urge, yearning, yen; SEE CONCEPTS *20,529*

itch [v1] *scratch; tingle*
crawl, creep, irritate, prick, prickle, sting, tickle, titillate; SEE CONCEPTS *185,313,612*

itch [v2] *desire strongly*
ache, be impatient, burn, chafe, crave, hanker, have a yen for, hunger, long, lust, pant, pine, sigh, thirst, want, yearn; SEE CONCEPT *20*

item [n] *part, article*
account, aspect, bit, blurb*, bulletin, column, component, consideration, conversation piece, detail, dispatch, element, entry, feature, incidental, information, matter, minor point, minutia, news, note, notice, novelty, paragraph, particular, piece, point, report, scoop*, scrap, specific, story, thing, write-up; SEE CONCEPTS *270,831,835*

itemize [v] *keep detailed record*
catalog, circumstantiate, cite, count, detail, document, enumerate, individualize, instance, inventory, lay out, list, mention, number, particularize, quote, recite, record, recount, rehearse, relate, set out, specify, spell out, tally; SEE CONCEPTS *57,125*

itinerant [adj] *roaming*
afoot, ambulant, ambulatory, floating, gypsy, journeying, migratory, moving, nomadic, on foot, peripatetic, ranging, riding the rails*, roving, shifting, travelling, unsettled, vagabond, vagrant, wandering, wayfaring; SEE CONCEPTS *536,584*

itinerary [n] *plan of travel*
beat, circuit, course, guide, guidebook, journey, line, outline, path, program, route, run, schedule, tour, way; SEE CONCEPTS *281,660*

J

jab [n/v] *poke*
blow, buck, bump, bunt, dig, hit, jog, lunge, nudge, prod, punch, push, stab, tap, thrust; SEE CONCEPT *189*

jabber [v] *talk incessantly and trivially*
babble, blather*, chatter, drivel, gab, go on and on*, jaw, mumble, murmur, mutter, prate, ramble, run off at mouth*, shoot the breeze*, talk, tattle, utter, yak, yap; SEE CONCEPTS *51,56*

jacket [n] *covering*
case, casing, coat, envelope, folder, fur, hide, parka, pelt, sheath, skin, threads, tunic, wrapper, wrapping; SEE CONCEPTS *451,484*

jaded [adj] *exhausted, indifferent*
been around, blah*, blasé, bored, cool*, done it all*, dulled, fagged, fatigued, fed up*, had it*, mellow, sated, satiated, sick of*, spent, surfeited, tired, tired-out*, up to here*, wearied, weary, worn, worn-down, worn-out; SEE CONCEPTS *401,406*

jagged [adj] *ragged, notched*
asperous, barbed, broken, cleft, craggy, denticulate, harsh, indented, irregular, pointed, ridged, rough, rugged, scabrous, serrated, snaggy, spiked, toothed, uneven, unlevel, unsmooth; SEE CONCEPTS *490,606*

jail [n] *place for incarceration*
bastille, black hole*, brig, bullpen*, can*, cell, clink*, concentration camp, cooler*, detention camp, dungeon, house of correction, inside*, jailhouse, joint*, lockup, pen, penal institution, penitentiary, pound, prison, rack*, reformatory, slammer*, solitary*, stir*, stockade, up the river*; SEE CONCEPTS *439,449,516*

jail [v] *incarcerate*
bastille, book, cage, can*, confine, constrain, detain, hold, immure, impound, imprison, lock up, prison, put away*, put behind bars*, put on ice*, railroad*, send up*, sentence, take away*, throw away the keys*, throw in dungeon, throw the book at*; SEE CONCEPT *317*

jam [n] *troublesome situation*
bind, box, corner, difficulty, dilemma, fix, hole, hot water*, pickle*, plight, predicament, problem, quandary, scrape, spot, strait, trouble; SEE CONCEPT *674*

jam [v] *squeeze in; compress*
bear, bind, block, cease, clog, congest, cram, crowd, crush, elbow, force, halt, jam-pack, jostle, obstruct, pack, press, push, ram, squash, squish, stall, stick, stuff, tamp, throng, wad, wedge; SEE CONCEPTS *121,208*

jangle [n] *cacophony of noises*
babel, clang, clangor, clash, din, dissonance, hubbub*, hullabaloo*, jar, pandemonium, racket, rattle, reverberation, roar, tintamarre, tumult, uproar; SEE CONCEPT *595*

jangle [v] *make clinking noises*
chime, clank, clash, clatter, conflict, disaccord, discord, disharmonize, hit a sour note*, jar, jingle, mismatch, rattle, vibrate; SEE CONCEPT *65*

janitor [n] *person who cleans and maintains*
attendant, caretaker, cleaning person, concierge, custodian, doorkeeper, doorman/woman, doorperson, gatekeeper, house sitter, porter, sitter, super, super-

intendent, sweeper, watchman/woman; SEE CONCEPT *348*

jar [*n1*] *container*
basin, beaker, bottle, burette, can, chalice, crock, cruet, decanter, ewer, flagon, flask, jug, pitcher, pot, tun, urn, vase, vat, vessel; SEE CONCEPT *494*

jar [*n2*] *shocking hit*
bump, clash, collision, concussion, crash, impact, jolt, jounce, rock, smash, succussion, thud, thump; SEE CONCEPT *189*

jar [*v1*] *shock, jolt*
agitate, bang, bounce, bump, clash, convulse, crash, disturb, grate, grind, hit, irritate, jerk, jiggle, jolt, jounce, jump, offend, quake, rasp, rattle, rock, shake, slam, thump, tremor, vibrate, wiggle, wobble; SEE CONCEPTS *65,189*

jar [*v2*] *clash, disharmonize*
annoy, bicker, clash, contend, disaccord, disagree, discompose, discord, grate, grind, interfere, irk, irritate, jangle, mismatch, nettle, oppose, outrage, quarrel, shock, wrangle; SEE CONCEPTS *7,19*

jargon [*n*] *specialized language; dialect*
abracadabra*, argot, balderdash*, banality, bombast, bunk*, buzzwords*, cant, cliché, colloquialism, commonplace term, doublespeak, drivel, fustian, gibberish, hackneyed term, idiom, insipidity, lexicon, lingo*, mumbo jumbo*, neologism, newspeak, nonsense, overused term, palaver, parlance, patois, patter, rigmarole, shoptalk, slang, slanguage*, speech, stale language, street talk*, tongue, trite language, twaddle, usage, vernacular, vocabulary; SEE CONCEPTS *275,276*

jaundiced [*adj*] *tainted, prejudiced*
biased, bigoted, bitter, colored, cynical, disapproving, distorted, envious, grudging, hostile, intolerant, jealous, one-sided, opprobrious, partial, partisan, preconceived, prepossessed, resentful, skeptical, spiteful, suspicious, tendentious, unfair, unfriendly, unindifferent, warped, yellow; SEE CONCEPTS *401,403,542*

jaunt [*n*] *expedition*
adventure, airing, amble, beat, canter, circuit, constitutional, course, cruise, drive, excursion, frolic, gallop, hike, jog, journey, junket, march, outing, patrol, peregrination, picnic, promenade, prowl, ramble, ride, round, roundabout, run, safari, sally, saunter, stroll, tour, tramp, travel, trek, trip, turn, voyage, walk; SEE CONCEPTS *159,195,224*

jaunty [*adj*] *lively*
airy, animated, bold, brash, breezy, buoyant, carefree, careless, cocky, dapper, dashing, debonair, devilish, devil-may-care*, easy, exhilarated, flip*, flippant, forward, free, fresh, frisky, frolicsome, gamesome, gay, high-spirited, hilarious, impetuous, impish, impudent, jocose, joking, jolly, jovial, light, natty, nervy, perky, playful, prankish, provocative, reckless, rollicking, self-confident, showy, smart,

sportive, sporty, sprightly, spruce, swaggering, trim, venturesome, vivacious; SEE CONCEPTS *401,404*

jaw [*n*] *bones of chin*
bone, chops*, jowl, mandible, maxilla, mouth, muzzle*, orifice; SEE CONCEPT *392*

jaw [*v1*] *talk a lot*
babble, chat, chatter, gab*, gossip, jabber, lecture, orate, prate, prattle, yak; SEE CONCEPTS *51,56*

jaw [*v2*] *criticize*
abuse, baste, berate, blame, call on the carpet*, censure, rail, rate, revile, scold, tongue-lash*, upbraid, vituperate; SEE CONCEPT *52*

jazzy [*adj*] *fancy*
animated, exciting, flashy, gaudy, lively, salacious, sexy, smart, snazzy*, spirited, vivacious, wild, zestful, zippy*; SEE CONCEPTS *537,589*

jealous [*adj*] *desirious; wary*
anxious, apprehensive, attentive, begrudging, covetous, demanding, doubting, emulous, envious, envying, grabby, grasping, green-eyed, grudging, guarded, intolerant, invidious, jaundiced, mistrustful, monopolizing, possessive, possessory, protective, questioning, resentful, rival, skeptical, solicitous, suspicious, vigilant, watchful, zealous; SEE CONCEPTS *403,542*

jeer [*v*] *heckle*
banter, comeback, contemn, deride, dig*, fleer, flout, gibe, hector, hoot, jab, jest, laugh at, make a crack*, mock, poke fun, put down, put on, quip, ridicule, scoff, sneer, snipe, taunt; SEE CONCEPT *54*

jell [*v*] *coagulate*
clot, cohere, come together, condense, congeal, crystallize, finalize, form, freeze, gel, gelate, gelatinize, harden, jellify, jelly, materialize, set, solidify, stick, stiffen, take shape, thicken; SEE CONCEPTS *250,469*

jeopardy [*n*] *danger, trouble*
accident, chance, double-trouble*, endangerment, exposure, hazard, insecurity, liability, on the line*, on the spot*, out on a limb*, peril, precariousness, risk, venture, vulnerability; SEE CONCEPT *675*

jerk [*n1*] *a lurching move*
bounce, bump, flick, flop, jolt, pull, quake, quiver, shiver, snag, thrust, tug, tweak, twitch, wiggle, wrench, wriggle, yank; SEE CONCEPTS *80,149,150*

jerk [*n2*] *stupid, bumbling person*
brute, fool, idiot, nincompoop, ninny, oaf, rascal; SEE CONCEPT *423*

jerk [*v*] *move with lurch*
bounce, bump, dance, flick, fling, flip, flop, grab, hook, hurtle, jolt, lug, pluck, pull, quake, quiver, seize, shiver, shrug, sling, snag, snatch, throw, thrust, tug, tweak, twitch, vellicate, whisk, wiggle, wrench, wrest, wriggle, wring, yank; SEE CONCEPTS *150,152*

jest [*n*] *joke*
banter, bon mot, crack, fun, funny, gag, game, hoax, jive, jolly, laugh, one-liner*, play, pleasantry, prank,

quip, rib, rib-tickler*, ridicule, sally, spoof, sport, wisecrack, witticism; SEE CONCEPT *273*

jest [*v*] *joke*
banter, chaff, deride, flout, fool, fun*, gibe*, gird*, jeer, jive*, jolly*, josh*, kid, mock, needle*, put on, quip, rag*, razz*, rib*, roast*, scoff, sneer, spoof, tease; SEE CONCEPT *273*

jester [*n*] *person who jokes, plays jokes*
actor, antic, banterer, buffoon, card*, clown, comedian, comic, cutup*, droll, fool, funnyman/woman, harlequin, humorist, japer, joker, jokester, larker, life of the party*, madcap*, pantaloon, practical joker, prankster, quipster, standup comic, trickster, wag*, wisecracker, wit; SEE CONCEPT *423*

jet [*n1*] *rush, gush of substance*
flow, fountain, spout, spray, spring, spritz, spurt, squirt, stream; SEE CONCEPTS *465,467*

jet [*n2*] *vehicle propelled by ejection of pressurized gas or liquid*
airbus, airplane, plane, supersonic, supersonic transport, turbo; SEE CONCEPTS *463,503*

jet [*adj*] *black*
atramentous, coal-black, dark, ebon, ebony, inky, midnight, obsidian, pitch-black, pitch-dark, raven, sable; SEE CONCEPT *618*

jet [*v*] *spurt, gush*
flow, fly, issue, pour, roll, rush, shoot, soar, spew, spout, spritz, squirt, stream, surge, travel, zoom; SEE CONCEPT *179*

jettison [*v*] *eject; throw overboard*
abandon, abdicate, cashier*, cast, cast off, deep-six*, discard, dump, expel, heave, hurl, junk*, maroon, reject, scrap*, shed, slough, throw away, unload*; SEE CONCEPTS *180,222*

jewel [*n1*] *precious stone*
baguette, bauble, bead, bijou, birthstone, brilliant, gem, gemstone, glass, gullion, hardware*, ornament, rock*, sparkler*, stone, trinket; SEE CONCEPTS *446,474,478*

jewel [*n2*] *something, someone precious*
charm, find, gem, genius, ideal, masterpiece, nonesuch, nonpareil, paragon, pearl*, phenomenon, phoenix*, prize, prodigy, rarity, specialty, treasure, wonder; SEE CONCEPT *671*

jewelry [*n*] *precious stones, metals worn as decoration*
adornment, anklet, band, bangle, bauble, beads, bijou, bracelet, brass, brooch, cameo, chain, charm, choker, costume, cross, crown, diamonds, earring, finery, frippery, gem, glass*, gold, ice*, jewel, junk*, knickknack, lavaliere, locket, necklace, ornament, pendant, pin, regalia, ring, rock, rosary, silver, solitaire, sparkler, stickpin, stone, tiara, tie pin, treasure, trinket; SEE CONCEPT *446*

jibe [*v*] *agree*
accord, conform, correspond, dovetail, fit, fit in, go, harmonize, match, resemble, square, tally; SEE CONCEPT *664*

jiffy [*n*] *instant*
breath, crack, flash, jiff*, minute, moment, second, shake*, split second*, trice, twinkling*; SEE CONCEPT *808*

jiggle [*v*] *bounce up and down*
agitate, bob, fidget, jerk, jig, jigger, jog, joggle, shake, shimmer, shimmy, twitch, vellicate, wiggle; SEE CONCEPTS *150,152*

jilt [*v*] *abandon, betray*
break off*, coquette, deceive, desert, disappoint, discard, ditch*, drop*, dump*, forsake, get rid of, leave, leave at the altar*, leave flat*, reject, throw over*; SEE CONCEPTS *195,297,384*

jingle [*v*] *make metallic clinking noise*
chime, chink, chinkle, clamor, clang, clatter, clink, ding, jangle, rattle, reverberate, ring, sound, tingle, tinkle, tintannabulate; SEE CONCEPT *65*

jinx [*n*] *curse*
black magic, charm, enchantment, evil eye*, hex, hoodoo*, kiss of death*, nemesis, plague, spell, voodoo*; SEE CONCEPTS *230,679*

jinx [*v*] *curse*
bedevil, bewitch, cast a spell on, charm, condemn, damn*, enchant, give the evil eye*, hex, witch; SEE CONCEPTS *14,192*

jitters [*n*] *nervousness*
anxiety, dither, fidgets, heebie-jeebies*, jumps, nerves, shakes, shivers, tenseness, willies*; SEE CONCEPTS *230,410,690*

job [*n1*] *employment*
activity, appointment, assignment, berth, billet, business, calling, capacity, career, chore, connection, craft, daily grind*, engagement, faculty, function, gig*, grind*, handicraft, line, livelihood, means, métier, niche, nine-to-five*, occupation, office, opening, operation, place, position, post, posting, profession, pursuit, racket*, rat race*, situation, spot, stint, swindle*, task, trade, vocation, work; SEE CONCEPTS *351,360*

job [*n2*] *task*
act, action, affair, assignment, burden, business, care, charge, chore, commission, concern, contribution, deed, devoir, duty, effort, enterprise, errand, function, matter, mission, obligation, office, operation, project, province, pursuit, responsibility, role, stint, task, taskwork, thing*, tour of duty, undertaking, venture, work; SEE CONCEPT *362*

jocular/jocose/jocund [*adj*] *funny, playful*
amusing, blithe, camp, cheerful, comic, comical, crazy, daffy, droll, facetious, flaky*, frolicsome, gay, gleeful, happy, humorous, jesting, jokey, joking, jolly, joshing, jovial, joyous, laughable, lighthearted, lively, ludicrous, merry, mischievous, pleasant, roguish, sportive, teasing, wacky, waggish, whimsical, witty; SEE CONCEPTS *267,529*

jog [*v1*] *activate, push*
agitate, arouse, bounce, dig, hit, jab, jar, jerk, jiggle, joggle, jolt, jostle, jounce, nudge, press, prod,

prompt, punch, remind, rock, shake, shove, stimulate, stir, suggest, whack; SEE CONCEPTS *14,208*

jog [*v2*] *run for recreation*
amble, canter, dash, dogtrot, lope, pace, sprint, trot; SEE CONCEPT *151*

join [*v1*] *unite*
accompany, add, adhere, affix, agglutinate, annex, append, assemble, associate, attach, blend, bracket, cement, clamp, clasp, clip, coadunate, coalesce, combine, compound, concrete, conjoin, conjugate, connect, copulate, couple, entwine, fasten, fuse, grapple, hitch on, incorporate, interlace, intermix, juxtapose, knit, leash, link, lock, lump together, marry, mate, melt, mix, pair, put together, slap on, span, splice, stick together, tack on, tag on, tie, tie up, touch, weave, wed, weld, yoke; SEE CONCEPT *113*

join [*v2*] *affiliate with organization*
align, associate with, be in, come aboard*, consort, cooperate, enlist, enroll, enter, fall in with*, follow, fraternize, go to, mingle with, pair with, plug into*, side with, sign on, sign up, take part in, take up with, team up with, throw in with*, tie up with; SEE CONCEPT *114*

join [*v3*] *touch; border on*
abut, adjoin, be adjacent to, be at hand, be close to, be contiguous to, border, bound, butt, communicate, conjoin, extend, fringe, hem, lie beside, lie near, lie next to, line, march, meet, neighbor, open into, parallel, reach, rim, skirt, trench on, verge on; SEE CONCEPT *747*

joint [*n1*] *intersection, juncture*
abutment, articulation, bend, bond, bracket, bridge, concourse, confluence, conjuncture, connection, copula, coupling, crux, elbow, hinge, hyphen, impingement, interconnection, junction, knot, link, meeting, nexus, node, point, seam, splice, suture, swivel, tangency, tie, union, vinculum; SEE CONCEPTS *393,830,831*

joint [*n2*] *cheap hangout*
bar, club, dive*, hole in the wall*, honky-tonk*, juke joint*, roadhouse, tavern; SEE CONCEPTS *439,449*

joint [*adj*] *shared, combined*
collective, common, communal, concerted, conjoint, conjunct, consolidated, cooperative, hand in hand, intermutual, joined, mutual, public, united; SEE CONCEPTS *577,708*

jointly [*adv*] *as one*
accordingly, agreeably, alike, arm in arm*, coincidentally, collectively, combined, companionably, concomitantly, concurrently, conjointly, connectedly, cooperatively, en masse, hand in glove*, hand in hand*, harmoniously, in a group, in common, in company with, in concert, in conjunction, inextricably, in league, in partnership, inseparably, intimately, in unison, mutually, reciprocally, side by side*, similarly, simultaneously, synchronically, together, unitedly, with one another; SEE CONCEPT *577*

joke [*n1*] *fun, quip*
antic, bon mot, buffoonery, burlesque, caper, caprice, chestnut*, clowning, drollery, epigram, escapade, farce, frolic, gag, gambol, game, ha-ha*, hoodwinking*, horseplay*, humor, jape, jest, lark, laugh, mischief, monkeyshine*, mummery, one-liner*, parody, payoff, play, pleasantry, prank, pun, put-on, quirk, raillery, repartee, revel, rib, sally, saw, shaggy-dog story*, shenanigan*, snow job*, sport, spree, stunt, tomfoolery, trick, vagary, whimsy, wisecrack, witticism, yarn; SEE CONCEPT *273*

joke [*n2*] *person that is made fun of*
buffoon, butt, clown, derision, fool, goat, jackass, jestee, laughingstock, mockery, simpleton, sport, target; SEE CONCEPTS *412,423*

joke [*v*] *kid, tease*
banter, chaff, deceive, deride, fool, frolic, fun, gambol, horse around*, jape, jest, jive*, jolly, josh, kid around, laugh, make merry, mock, needle, play, play the clown, play tricks, poke fun*, pull one's leg*, pun, put on, quip, rag, revel, rib, ridicule, roast*, spoof, sport, taunt, trick, wisecrack; SEE CONCEPT *273*

joker [*n*] *person who kids, teases*
actor, banana*, buffoon, card*, clown, comedian, comic, cutup*, droll, farceur, fool, funnyman/woman, funster*, gagster*, humorist, jester, joke-smith, jokester, josher*, kidder, life of the party*, prankster*, punster*, quipster*, second banana*, stand-up comic, stooge, straight man/woman, top banana*, trickster*, wag, wisecracker, wit; SEE CONCEPTS *352,423*

jolly [*adj*] *laughing, joyful*
blithe, blithesome, bouncy, carefree, cheerful, chipper, chirpy, convivial, daffy, delightful, enjoyable, entertaining, festive, frolicsome, funny, gay, gladsome, gleeful, happy, hilarious, jocund, jokey, joshing, jovial, joyous, jubilant, larking, lighthearted, lots of laughs, merry, mirthful, playful, pleasant, sportive, sprightly, zippy*; SEE CONCEPTS *267,542,548*

jolt [*n*] *surprise; sudden push*
blow, bombshell*, bounce, bump, clash, collision, concussion, double whammy*, impact, jar, jerk, jog, jounce, jump, kick, lurch, percussion, punch, quiver, reversal, setback, shake, shock, shot, start, surprise, thunderbolt; SEE CONCEPTS *42,208*

jolt [*v*] *surprise; push suddenly*
astonish, bowl over*, bump, churn, convulse, discompose, disturb, floor, jar, jerk, jog, jostle, knock, knock over*, lay out*, perturb, rock, shake, shake up*, shock, shove, spring something on*, stagger, start, startle, stun, throw a curve*, upset; SEE CONCEPTS *42,208*

jostle [*v*] *bump, shake*
bang into, bulldoze*, bump heads*, butt*, crash, crowd, elbow, hustle, jab, jog, joggle, jolt, nudge, press, push, push around, push aside, rough and tumble*, scramble, shake, shoulder, shove, squeeze, thrust; SEE CONCEPTS *152,189,208*

journal [n] *chronicle*
account, almanac, annals, annual, calendar, chronology, comic book, daily, daybook, diary, gazette, ledger, log, magazine, memento, memoir, minutes, monthly, newspaper, note, observation, organ, paper, periodical, publication, rag, record, register, reminder, reminiscence, review, scandal sheet*, statement, tabloid, weekly; SEE CONCEPTS *271, 280,801*

journalist [n] *person who writes about factual events for a living*
announcer, broadcaster, columnist, commentator, contributor, correspondent, cub, editor, hack, media person, newsman/woman, newspaperman/woman, newspaper person, newsperson, pencil pusher*, pressman/woman, publicist, reporter, scribe, scrivener, stringer*, television commentator, writer; SEE CONCEPTS *348,356*

journey [n] *excursion*
adventure, airing, beat, campaign, caravan, circuit, constitutional, course, crossing, drive, expedition, exploration, hike, itinerary, jaunt, junket, march, migration, odyssey, outing, passage, patrol, peregrination, pilgrimage, progress, promenade, quest, ramble, range, roaming, round, route, run, safari, sally, saunter, sojourn, stroll, survey, tour, tramp, transit, transmigration, travel, traveling, traverse, trek, trip, vagabondage, vagrancy, venture, visit, voyage, wandering, wayfaring; SEE CONCEPT *224*

journey [v] *travel*
circuit, cruise, fare, fly, globe trot*, go, go places, hie, hop, jaunt, jet, junket, knock about*, pass, peregrinate, proceed, process, push on, ramble, range, repair, roam, rove, safari, take a trip, tour, traverse, trek, voyage, wander, wend; SEE CONCEPT *224*

jovial [adj] *very happy*
affable, airy, amiable, animated, bantering, blithe, blithesome, bouncy, buoyant, chaffing, cheery, chipper, chirpy, companionable, conversable, convivial, cordial, daffy*, delightful, dizzy*, enjoyable, facetious, festal, festive, gay, glad, gleeful, good-natured, hilarious, humorous, jocose, jocund, jokey, jolly, jollying, joshing, jubilant, larking, lighthearted, loony, lots of laughs*, merry, mirthful, nutty*, off-the-wall*, pleasant, sociable; SEE CONCEPTS *401,403*

joy [n] *great happiness, pleasure*
alleviation, amusement, animation, bliss, charm, cheer, comfort, delectation, delight, diversion, ecstasy, elation, exultation, exulting, felicity, festivity, frolic, fruition, gaiety, gem, gladness, glee, good humor, gratification, hilarity, humor, indulgence, jewel, jubilance, liveliness, luxury, merriment, mirth, pride, pride and joy, prize, rapture, ravishment, refreshment, regalement, rejoicing, revelry, satisfaction, solace, sport, transport, treasure, treat, wonder; SEE CONCEPTS *410,529*

joyful/joyous [adj] *very happy*
blithesome, cheerful, cheery, delighted, ecstatic, effervescent, elated, enjoyable, enraptured, expansive, festive, flying*, gay, glad, gladsome, gratified, heartening, high*, high as a kite*, jocund, jolly, jovial, joyous, jubilant, lighthearted, merry, overjoyed, pleased, pleasurable, popping, rapturous, satisfied, sunny*, sunny-side up*, transported, upbeat; SEE CONCEPTS *403,542,548*

joyless [adj] *very unhappy*
black, bleak, blue, cheerless, dejected, depressant, depressed, depressing, dismal, dispirited, dispiriting, doleful, downcast, down in the mouth*, dragged, dreary, droopy, gloomy, have the blahs*, heavy*, low, melancholic, melancholy, miserable, mopey, mournful, sad, saddening, somber; SEE CONCEPTS *403,542,548*

jubilant [adj] *very happy*
celebrating, doing handsprings*, elated, enraptured, euphoric, excited, exuberant, exultant, exulting, flipping, flying*, glad, gleeful, joyous, overjoyed, pleased, rejoicing, rhapsodic, thrilled, tickled*, triumphal, triumphant; SEE CONCEPTS *401,403*

judge [n] *person who arbitrates*
adjudicator, appraiser, arbiter, assessor, authority, bench, chancellor, conciliator, court, critic, evaluator, expert, honor, inspector, intercessor, intermediary, interpreter, judiciary, justice, justice of peace, legal official, lordship, magister, magistrate, marshal, moderator, negotiator, peacemaker, reconciler, referee, umpire, warden; SEE CONCEPT *355*

judge [v] *make decision from evidence; deduce*
act on, adjudge, adjudicate, appraise, appreciate, approximate, arbitrate, arrive, ascertain, assess, check, collect, conclude, condemn, consider, criticize, decide, decree, deduct, derive, determine, discern, distinguish, doom, draw, esteem, estimate, evaluate, examine, find, gather, give a hearing, make, make out, mediate, pass sentence, place, pronounce sentence, put, rate, reckon, referee, resolve, review, rule, sentence, settle, sit, size up, suppose, test, try, umpire, value; SEE CONCEPTS *18,317*

judgment [n1] *common sense*
acumen, acuteness, apprehension, astuteness, awareness, brains, capacity, comprehension, discernment, discrimination, experience, genius, grasp, incisiveness, ingenuity, intelligence, intuition, keenness, knowledge, mentality, penetration, perception, percipience, perspicacity, prudence, quickness, range, rationality, reach, readiness, reason, reasoning, sagacity, sanity, sapience, savvy, sense, sharpness, shrewdness, sophistication, soundness, taste, understanding, wisdom, wit; SEE CONCEPTS *37,409*

judgment [n2] *decision about blame*
analysis, appraisal, appreciation, arbitration, assaying, assessment, award, belief, close study, conclusion, contemplation, conviction, decree, deduction, determination, estimate, estimation, evaluation, examination, exploration, finding, idea, inference, inquest, inquiry, inquisition, inspection, observation, opinion, order, probing, pursuit, quest, reconnais-

sance, regard, report, research, resolution, result, review, ruling, scrutiny, search, sentence, sifting, summary, verdict, view, weigh-in; SEE CONCEPTS *103,689*

judgment [*n3*] *doom, fate*
affliction, castigation, chastisement, correction, damnation, infliction, manifestation, misfortune, mortification, punishment, retribution, visitation; SEE CONCEPT *679*

judicial [*adj*] *legal*
administrative, authoritative, constitutional, discriminating, distinguished, equitable, forensic, impartial, judgelike, judiciary, juridical, jurisdictional, juristic, lawful, legalistic, magisterial, official, pontifical, principled, regular, statutory; SEE CONCEPT *319*

judicious [*adj*] *wise, thoughtful*
accurate, acute, astute, calculating, careful, cautious, circumspect, clear-sighted, considerate, considered, diplomatic, discerning, discreet, discriminating, efficacious, enlightened, expedient, far-sighted, informed, judicial, keen, perceptive, perspicacious, politic, profound, prudent, quick-witted, rational, reasonable, sagacious, sage, sane, sapient, seasonable, seemly, sensible, sharp, shrewd, skillful, sober, sophisticated, sound, thorough, wary, well-advised, well-judged, worldly-wise; SEE CONCEPTS *402,403,542*

jug [*n*] *container for liquid*
amphora, beaker, bottle, bucket, canteen, carafe, crock, cruet, decanter, ewer, flagon, flask, growler, hooker, jar, pitcher, pot, tub, urn, vase, vessel; SEE CONCEPT *494*

juggle [*v*] *mislead, falsify; handle several things at once*
alter, beguile, betray, bluff, change, conjure, delude, disguise, doctor*, double-cross, fix, humbug*, illude, maneuver, manipulate, misrepresent, modify, perform magic, prestidigitate, shuffle, take in, tamper with, trim; SEE CONCEPTS *59,63*

juice [*n*] *liquid squeezed from fruit, plant*
abstract, alcohol, aqua vitae, distillation, drink, essence, extract, fluid, liquor, milk, nectar, oil, sap, sauce, secretion, serum, spirit, syrup, water; SEE CONCEPTS *428,467*

juicy [*adj1*] *moist*
dank, dewy, dripping, humid, liquid, luscious, lush, mellow, oily, oozy, pulpy, sappy, saturated, sauced, slippery, slushy, soaked, sodden, succulent, syrupy, viscid, watery, wet; SEE CONCEPT *603*

juicy [*adj2*] *exciting, interesting*
colorful, fascinating, intriguing, piquant, provocative, racy, risqué, sensational, spicy, suggestive, tantalizing, vivid; SEE CONCEPTS *537,548*

jumble [*n*] *hodgepodge*
assortment, chaos, clutter, confusion, derangement, disarrangement, disarray, disorder, farrago, gallimaufry, garbage, goulash, hash*, hodgepodge, litter, medley, mélange, mess, miscellany, mishmash, mixture, muddle, olio, pastiche, patchwork, potpourri, salmagundi, scramble, shuffle, snarl, tangle, tumble; SEE CONCEPT *432*

jumble [*v*] *mix up, confuse*
clutter, confound, derange, disarrange, disarray, dishevel, disorder, disorganize, disturb, entangle, foul up, mess up, mistake, mix, muddle, rummage, shuffle, snarl, tangle, tumble; SEE CONCEPTS *16,84*

jumbo [*adj*] *gigantic*
colossal, cyclopean, elephantine, giant, huge, immense, large, mammoth, mighty, oversized, prodigious; SEE CONCEPT *781*

jump [*n1*] *leap*
bob, bounce, bound, buck, canter, caper, capriole, dance, dive, drop, fall, gambade, gambol, hop, hopping, hurdle, jar, jerk, jolt, leapfrog, leapfrogging, leaping, lurch, nosedive, plummet, plunge, pounce, rise, saltation, shock, skip, skipping, spring, start, swerve, twitch, upspring, upsurge, vault, wrench; SEE CONCEPT *194*

jump [*n2*] *increase, advantage*
advance, ascent, augmentation, boost, handicap, head start, increment, inflation, rise, spurt, start, upper hand, upsurge, upturn; SEE CONCEPTS *704,763*

jump [*n3*] *obstacle*
bar, barricade, barrier, fence, hurdle, impediment, rail, stretch; SEE CONCEPTS *470,674*

jump [*v1*] *leap, spring*
bail out, barge, bob, bounce, bound, buck, canter, caper, clear, curvet, dive, drop, fall, gambol, hop, hurdle, hurtle, jerk, jiggle, jounce, lollop, lop, lunge, lurch, parachute, plummet, pop, quiver, rattle, ricochet, saltate, shake, skip, sky, somersault, surge, take, top, trip, vault, waver, wobble; SEE CONCEPT *194*

jump [*v2*] *recoil*
bob, bolt, bounce, carom, flinch, jerk, jounce, rebound, ricochet, spring, start, startle, wince; SEE CONCEPT *213*

jump [*v3*] *omit, avoid*
abandon, cancel, clear out, cover, cross out, digress, evade, leave, miss, nullify, overshoot, pass over, skip, switch; SEE CONCEPT *25*

jump [*v4*] *increase*
advance, ascend, boost, escalate, gain, hike, jack up, mount, put up, raise, rise, surge, up; SEE CONCEPTS *236,245,763*

jumpy [*adj*] *nervous*
agitated, antsy*, anxious, apprehensive, creepy*, excitable, excited, fidgety, frisky, high-strung*, jittery, on edge*, on pins and needles*, restless, sensitive, shaky, skittish, spooked, tense, timorous, unrestful; SEE CONCEPTS *401,690*

junction/juncture [*n1*] *link, connection*
alliance, annexation, articulation, assemblage, attachment, bond, coalition, coherence, collocation, combination, combine, concatenation, concourse, concursion, confluence, conjugation, consolidation, convergence, coupling, crossing, crossroads, dovetail, elbow, gathering, gore, hinge, hookup, inter-

face, intersection, joining, joint, juncture, knee, linking, meeting, miter, mortise, node, pivot, plug-in, reunion, seam, splice, terminal, tie-in, tie-up, union, weld; SEE CONCEPTS *746,830*

juncture [n2] *turning point*
choice, circumstance, condition, contingency, crisis, crossroad, crux, emergency, exigency, instant, meeting point, moment, occasion, pass, pinch, plight, point, position, posture, predicament, quandary, state, status, strait, time, zero hour*; SEE CONCEPTS *388,693,815*

jungle [n] *wilderness full of plant and animal life*
boscage, bush, chaparral, forest, labyrinth, maze, morass, primeval forest, tangle, undergrowth, wasteland, web, wood, zoo; SEE CONCEPT *517*

junior [adj] *subordinate, younger*
inferior, lesser, lower, minor, second, secondary, second-string*; SEE CONCEPTS *574,578,797*

junk [n] *odds and ends; garbage*
clutter, collateral, debris, filth, hogwash*, litter, miscellany, offal, refuse, rubbish, rubble, rummage, salvage, scrap, trash, waste; SEE CONCEPTS *260,432*

jurisdiction [n] *area of authority*
administration, arbitration, area, authority, bailiwick, bounds, circuit, command, commission, compass, confines, control, discretion, district, domination, dominion, empire, extent, field, hegemony, influence, inquisition, judicature, limits, magistracy, mastery, might, orbit, power, prerogative, province, purview, range, reach, reign, right, rule, say, scope, slot, sovereignty, sphere, stomping grounds*, supervision, sway, territory, turf*, wing, zone; SEE CONCEPTS *198,376,651*

jury [n] *panel that hears legal matter*
board, judges, peers, tribunal; SEE CONCEPTS *299,318*

just [adj1] *fair, impartial*
aloof, blameless, condign, conscientious, decent, dependable, dispassionate, due, equal, equitable, ethical, evenhanded, fair-minded, good, honest, honorable, lawful, nondiscriminatory, nonpartisan, objective, pure, reliable, right, righteous, rightful, rigid, scrupulous, strict, tried, true, trustworthy, unbiased, uncolored, upright, virtuous; SEE CONCEPTS *319,545*

just [adj2] *accurate, precise*
cogent, correct, exact, faithful, good, justified, normal, proper, regular, right, sound, strict, true, undistorted, veracious, veridical, well-founded, well-grounded; SEE CONCEPTS *535,582*

just [adj3] *suitable, appropriate*
apt, befitting, condign, deserved, due, felicitous, fit, fitting, happy, justified, legitimate, meet, merited, proper, reasonable, requisite, right, rightful, well-deserved; SEE CONCEPT *558*

just [adv1] *definitely*
absolutely, accurately, completely, directly, entirely, exactly, expressly, perfectly, precisely, right, sharp,

smack-dab*, square, squarely, unmistakably; SEE CONCEPT *535*

just [adv2] *only now*
almost, a moment ago, approximately, at this moment, barely, by very little, hardly, just a while ago, just now, lately, nearly, now, presently, recently, right now, scarce, scarcely; SEE CONCEPTS *544,820*

just [adv3] *merely*
at most, but, no more than, nothing but, only, plainly, simply, solely; SEE CONCEPT *557*

just about [adv] *almost*
about, all but, approximately, around, as good as, close to, nearly, nigh, not quite, practically, well-nigh; SEE CONCEPTS *762,771,799*

justice [n1] *lawfulness, fairness*
amends, appeal, authority, authorization, charter, code, compensation, consideration, constitutionality, correction, credo, creed, decree, due process, equity, evenness, fair play, fair treatment, hearing, honesty, impartiality, integrity, judicatory, judicature, justness, law, legality, legalization, legal process, legitimacy, litigation, penalty, reasonableness, recompense, rectitude, redress, reparation, review, right, rule, sanction, sentence, square deal*, truth; SEE CONCEPTS *376,645,691*

justice [n2] *person who oversees court of law*
chancellor, court, judge, magistrate, umpire; SEE CONCEPT *354*

justifiable [adj] *reasonable, well-founded*
acceptable, admissible, allowable, condonable, defensible, excusable, fair, fit, forgivable, lawful, legit*, legitimate, licit, logical, pardonable, probable, proper, reasonable, remissible, right, rightful, sound, suitable, tenable, understandable, valid, vindicable, warrantable; SEE CONCEPTS *545,558*

justification [n] *reason, excuse*
absolution, account, acquittal, advocacy, answer, apologia, apology, approval, argument, basis, confirmation, defense, exculpation, exoneration, explanation, extenuation, grounds, idea, mitigation, palliation, palliative, plea, pretext, raison d'être, rationale, rationalization, rebuttal, redemption, reply, response, salvation, sanctification, song and dance*, story, support, validation, vindication, warrant, whatfor*, wherefore*, whitewashing*, whole idea*, why and wherefore*; SEE CONCEPT *661*

justify [v] *legitimize, substantiate*
absolve, acquit, advocate, alibi*, answer for, apologize for, approve, argue for, assert, be answerable for, bear out, brief, claim, clear, condone, confirm, contend, cop a plea*, countenance, crawl, defend, do justice to, establish, exculpate, excuse, exonerate, explain, favor, legalize, maintain, make allowances, make good*, palliate, pardon, plead, rationalize, rebut, show cause, speak in favor, square, stand up for, support, sustain, uphold, validate, verify, vindicate, warrant; SEE CONCEPTS *49,57*

justly [adv] fairly
accurately, befittingly, beneficently, benevolently, benignly, candidly, charitably, correctly, decently, decorously, duly, duteously, dutifully, equally, equitably, evenhandedly, fitly, fittingly, frankly, helpfully, honestly, honorably, impartially, lawfully, legally, legitimately, moderately, nicely, piously, properly, reasonably, respectably, righteously, rightfully, rightly, straightforwardly, temperately, tolerantly, unreservedly, uprightly, virtuously, well; SEE CONCEPTS *544,545*

jut [v] extend
beetle, bulge, elongate, impend, lengthen, overhang, poke, pop, pouch, project, protrude, protuberate, stand out, stick out; SEE CONCEPT *201*

juvenile [n] young person
adolescent, boy, child, girl, infant, kid*, minor, youngster, youth; SEE CONCEPT *424*

juvenile [adj] childish
adolescent, babyish, beardless, blooming, boyish, budding, callow, childlike, developing, formative, fresh, girlish, green, growing, immature, inexperienced, infant, infantile, jejune, junior, kid stuff*, milk-fed*, naive, pubescent, puerile, teenage, tender, undeveloped, unfledged, unripe, unsophisticated, unweaned, vernal, young, younger, youthful; SEE CONCEPTS *401,578,797*

K

keel over [v] fall, faint
black out, capsize, collapse, drop, founder, go down, overturn, pass out, pitch, plunge, slump, swoon, topple, tumble, upset; SEE CONCEPTS *152,181*

keen [adj1] enthusiastic
agog, alert, animate, animated, anxious, appetent, ardent, athirst, avid, breathless, devoted, dying to*, eager, earnest, ebullient, fervent, fervid, fierce, fond of, gung ho*, impassioned, impatient, intense, intent, interested, lively, perfervid, spirited, sprightly, thirsty, vehement, vivacious, warm, zealous; SEE CONCEPTS *401,403*

keen [adj2] sharp, piercing
acid, acute, caustic, cutting, edged, extreme, fine, honed, incisive, intense, observant, penetrating, perceptive, pointed, quick-witted, razor-sharp*, sardonic, satirical, strong, tart, trenchant, unblunted; SEE CONCEPT *267*

keen [adj3] very intelligent
astute, bright, brilliant, canny, clever, discerning, discriminating, Einstein*, nobody's fool*, perceptive, perspicacious, quick, sagacious, sapient, sensitive, sharp, sharp as a tack*, shrewd, whiz, wise; SEE CONCEPT *402*

keep [v1] hold, maintain
accumulate, amass, cache, care for, carry, conduct, conserve, control, deal in, deposit, detain, direct, enjoy, garner, grasp, grip, have, heap, hold back, manage, own, pile, place, possess, preserve, put, put up, reserve, retain, save, season, stack, stock, store, trade in, withhold; SEE CONCEPT *710*

keep [v2] tend; provide for
administer, attend, board, care for, carry on, command, conduct, continue, defend, direct, endure, feed, foster, guard, look after, maintain, manage, mind, minister to, nourish, nurture, operate, ordain, protect, provide for, provision, run, safeguard, shelter, shield, subsidize, support, sustain, victual, watch over; SEE CONCEPTS *110,140*

keep [v3] prevent
arrest, avert, block, check, constrain, control, curb, delay, detain, deter, hamper, hamstring, hinder, hold back, impede, inhibit, limit, obstruct, restrain, retard, shackle, stall, stop, withhold; SEE CONCEPT *121*

keep [v4] commemorate; pay attention to
adhere to, bless, celebrate, comply with, consecrate, fulfill, hold, honor, laud, obey, observe, perform, praise, regard, respect, ritualize, sanctify, solemnize; SEE CONCEPT *377*

keep at [v] continue, endure
be steadfast, carry on, complete, drudge, finish, grind, labor, last, maintain, persevere, persist, remain, slave, stay, stick, toil; SEE CONCEPTS *23,87*

keepsake [n] something precious
emblem, favor, memento, memorial, relic, remembrance, reminder, souvenir, symbol, token, trophy; SEE CONCEPT *446*

keep up [v] maintain, sustain
balance, compete, contend, continue, emulate, go on, hold on, keep pace, keep step, match, pace, persevere, preserve, rival, run with, vie; SEE CONCEPTS *23,87,363*

keg [n] barrel
butt, cask, container, drum, firkin, hogshead, pipe, tub, tun, vat; SEE CONCEPT *494*

kernel [n] seed, essence
atom, bit, center, core, crux, fruit, germ, gist, grain, heart, hub, keynote, marrow, matter, meat, morsel, nub, nubbin, nut, part, piece, pith, root, substance, upshot; SEE CONCEPTS *668,826*

key [n1] item that unlocks
latchkey, master, opener, passkey, screw*, skeleton; SEE CONCEPT *499*

key [n2] answer, solution
blueprint, brand, cipher, clue, code, core, crux, cue, earmark, explanation, fulcrum, guide, hinge, index, indicator, interpretation, lead, lever, marker, means, nexus, nucleus, passport, password, pivot, pointer, root, sign, symptom, ticket, translation; SEE CONCEPTS *274,668*

key [adj] essential, important
basic, chief, crucial, decisive, fundamental, indispensable, leading, main, major, material, pivotal, primary, principal, vital; SEE CONCEPT *568*

keynote/keystone [n] *essence, theme*
basic idea, basis, center, core, cornerstone, criterion, crux, gist, heart, idea, kernel, linchpin, mainspring, marrow, measure, motive, nub, pith, principle, root, source, spring, standard, substance; SEE CONCEPTS *532,661,687*

kick [n1] *thrill, enjoyment*
bang*, buzz*, excitement, fun, gratification, hoot*, joy, pleasure, refreshment, sensation, stimulation, wallop*; SEE CONCEPTS *388,410*

kick [n2] *power, strength*
backlash, blow, boot*, force, intensity, jar, jolt, pep, punch, pungency, snap, sparkle, tang, verve, vitality, zest, zing*; SEE CONCEPTS *641,732*

kick [v1] *hit with foot*
boot, calcitrate, dropkick, give the foot, jolt, punt; SEE CONCEPT *189*

kick [v2] *complain*
anathematize, carp, combat, condemn, criticize, curse, damn, except, execrate, expostulate, fight, fuss, gripe, grumble, inveigh, mumble, object, oppose, protest, rebel, remonstrate, repine, resist, spurn, wail, whine, withstand; SEE CONCEPT *52*

kick [v3] *quit a habit*
abandon, desist, give up, go cold turkey*, leave off, stop; SEE CONCEPT *234*

kickback [n] *bribe*
cut, gift, graft, money under the table*, oil*, payment, payoff, payola, percentage, recompense, reward, share; SEE CONCEPTS *192,344*

kick out [v] *get rid of*
ax, boot*, bounce*, can*, cashier*, chase, chuck, discharge, dismiss, drop, eject, evict, expel, extrude, fire, oust, out, reject, remove, sack*, throw out, toss out; SEE CONCEPTS *180,351,384*

kid [n] *young person*
baby, bairn, boy, child, daughter, girl, infant, juvenile, lad, little one*, son, teenager, tot, youngster, youth; SEE CONCEPTS *414,424*

kid [v] *fool, ridicule*
bamboozle*, banter, beguile, bother, cozen, delude, dupe, flimflam*, fun*, gull, hoax, hoodwink, jape, jest, joke, jolly, josh, make fun of, make sport of, mock, pretend, rag*, razz, rib, roast, spoof, tease, trick; SEE CONCEPTS *59,273*

kidnap [v] *abduct; hold for ransom*
bodysnatch*, bundle off, capture, carry away, carry off, coax, decoy, entice, grab, hijack, impress, inveigh, lay hands on, lure, make off with*, pirate, ravish, remove, run away with, seduce, seize, shanghai*, skyjack, snatch, spirit away*, steal, waylay; SEE CONCEPTS *90,139*

kill [v1] *deprive of existence; destroy*
annihilate, asphyxiate, assassinate, crucify, dispatch, do away with*, do in*, drown, dump, electrocute, eradicate, erase*, execute, exterminate, extirpate, finish, garrote, get*, guillotine, hang, hit*, immolate, liquidate, lynch, massacre, murder, neutralize,

obliterate, off*, poison, polish off*, put away*, put to death, rub out*, sacrifice, slaughter, slay, smother, snuff, strangle, suffocate, waste*, wipe out*, X-out*, zap*; SEE CONCEPT *252*

kill [v2] *turn off; cancel*
annul, cease, counteract, deaden, defeat, extinguish, forbid, halt, negative, neutralize, nix*, nullify, prohibit, quash, quell, recant, refuse, revoke, ruin, scotch*, shut off, smother, stifle, still, stop, suppress, turn out, veto; SEE CONCEPTS *121,239*

kin [n] *blood relative*
affinity, blood, clan, connection, consanguinity, cousin, extraction, family, folk, house, kindred, kinsfolk, kinship, kinsman/woman, kith, lineage, member, people, race, relation, relationship, sibling, stock, tribe, woman; SEE CONCEPTS *296,414,421*

kind [n1] *class, species*
brand, breed, classification, family, genus, ilk, kin, order, race, set, sort, type, variety; SEE CONCEPT *378*

kind [n2] *type, character*
breed, complexion, connection, denomination, description, designation, essence, fiber, gender, habit, ilk, likes, lot, manner, mold, nature, number, persuasion, set, sort, stamp, stripe, style, temperament, tendency, tribe, variety, way; SEE CONCEPTS *411,673*

kind [adj] *generous, good*
affectionate, all heart*, altruistic, amiable, amicable, beneficent, benevolent, benign, big, bleeding-heart*, bounteous, charitable, clement, compassionate, congenial, considerate, cordial, courteous, eleemosynary, friendly, gentle, good-hearted, gracious, heart in right place*, humane, humanitarian, indulgent, kindhearted, kindly, lenient, loving, mild, neighborly, obliging, philanthropic, propitious, softhearted, soft touch, sympathetic, tenderhearted, thoughtful, tolerant, understanding; SEE CONCEPTS *401,404,542*

kindhearted [adj] *compassionate, helpful*
altruistic, amiable, amicable, considerate, generous, good, good-natured, gracious, humane, kind, merciful, responsive, softhearted, sympathetic, tender, tenderhearted, warm, warmhearted; SEE CONCEPTS *404,542*

kindle [v1] *start a fire*
blaze, burn, fire, flame, flare, glow, ignite, inflame, light, set alight, set fire; SEE CONCEPT *249*

kindle [v2] *excite, incite*
agitate, animate, arouse, awaken, bestir, burn up*, challenge, egg on*, enkindle, exasperate, fire up*, foment, get smoking*, induce, inflame, inspire, key up*, provoke, rally, rouse, sharpen, stimulate, stir, thrill, turn on*, wake, waken, whet, work up*; SEE CONCEPTS *7,14,22,221*

kindly [adj] *compassionate, helpful*
attentive, beneficial, benevolent, benign, benignant, cool, cordial, favorable, friendly, generous, genial, gentle, good, good-hearted, good-natured, gracious,

hearty, humane, kind, kindhearted, mellow, merciful, mild, neighborly, pleasant, polite, sociable, sympathetic, thoughtful, warm; SEE CONCEPTS *404,542*

kindly [*adv*] *with compassion*
affectionately, agreeably, benevolently, benignly, carefully, charitably, compassionately, considerately, cordially, courteously, delicately, generously, genially, good-naturedly, graciously, heedfully, helpfully, humanely, politely, solicitously, sympathetically, tenderly, thoughtfully, tolerantly, understandingly, well; SEE CONCEPTS *542,544*

kindness [*n1*] *compassion, generosity*
affection, altruism, amiability, beneficence, benevolence, charity, clemency, consideration, cordiality, courtesy, decency, delicacy, fellow feeling, forbearance, gentleness, good intention, goodness, good will, grace, graciousness, heart, helpfulness, hospitality, humanity, indulgence, kindliness, magnanimity, mildness, patience, philanthropy, serviceability, solicitousness, solicitude, sweetness, sympathy, tact, tenderness, thoughtfulness, tolerance, understanding, unselfishness; SEE CONCEPTS *633,657*

kindness [*n2*] *helping act; service*
accommodation, aid, alms, assistance, benediction, benefaction, benevolence, benison, blessing, boon, boost, bounty, charity, dispensation, favor, generosity, good deed, good turn, help, indulgence, lift, mercy, philanthropy, relief, succor; SEE CONCEPTS *110,657*

kindred [*n*] *blood relative*
affinity, blood, clan, connection, consanguinity, cousin, family, flesh, folk, homefolk, house, kin, kinsfolk, kinsman/woman, lineage, race, relation, relationship, stock, tribe, woman; SEE CONCEPTS *296,414,421*

kindred [*adj*] *corresponding, matching*
affiliated, agnate, akin, alike, allied, analogous, cognate, congeneric, congenial, connate, connatural, consanguine, germane, homogeneous, incident, kin, likable, parallel, related, similar; SEE CONCEPT *563*

king [*n*] *male royal ruler*
baron, Caesar, caliph, crowned head, czar, emperor, gerent, imperator, kaiser, khan, magnate, maharajah, majesty, mikado, mogul, monarch, overlord, pasha, potentate, prince, rajah, rex, shah, sovereign, sultan, tycoon; SEE CONCEPTS *354,422*

kingdom [*n*] *area ruled by monarch*
commonwealth, country, county, crown, division, domain, dominion, dynasty, empire, field, lands, monarchy, nation, possessions, principality, province, realm, reign, rule, scepter, sovereignty, sphere, state, suzerainty, sway, territory, throne, tract; SEE CONCEPTS *508,510*

kink [*n1*] *bend, twist*
coil, corkscrew, crimp, crinkle, curl, curve, entanglement, frizz, knot, loop, tangle, wrinkle; SEE CONCEPT *436*

kink [*n2*] *spasm of muscular tissue*
charley horse*, cramp, crick, knot, muscle spasm, pain, pang, pinch, stab, stitch, tweak, twinge; SEE CONCEPTS *185,728*

kink [*n3*] *complication*
defect, difficulty, flaw, hitch, impediment, imperfection, knot, tangle; SEE CONCEPT *674*

kink [*n4*] *person's idiosyncrasy*
eccentricity, fetish, foible, notion, peculiarity, quirk, singularity, vagary, whim; SEE CONCEPT *411*

kinky [*adj1*] *twisted*
coiled, crimped, curled, curly, frizzled, frizzy, knotted, matted, matty, rolled, tangled; SEE CONCEPT *486*

kinky [*adj2*] *bizarre, perverted*
degenerated, depraved, deviant, eccentric, far-out, licentious, odd, outlandish, outré, peculiar, perverted, queer, quirky, sick, strange, unconventional, unnatural, unusual, warped, weird; SEE CONCEPTS *372,542,589*

kiss [*n*] *touching lips to another*
butterfly*, caress, embrace, endearment, osculation, peck, salutation, salute, smack*, smooch; SEE CONCEPTS *185,375*

kiss [*v*] *touch one's lips to another's*
blow, brush, butterfly*, French*, glance, graze, greet, lip, make out*, mush*, neck*, osculate, peck, pucker up*, salute, smack, smooch*; SEE CONCEPTS *185,375*

kit [*n*] *provisions, equipment*
accoutrements, apparatus, assortment, bag, collection, container, effects, gear, impedimenta, implements, material, outfit, pack, paraphernalia, rig, satchel, selection, set, stock, stuff, suitcase, supplies, tackle, things, tools, trappings, utensils; SEE CONCEPTS *494,496*

kitchen [*n*] *room for cooking food*
canteen, cookery, cookhouse, cook's room, cuisine, eat-in, gallery, galley, kitchenette, mess, scullery; SEE CONCEPT *448*

kittenish [*adj*] *frisky, playful*
childish, coquettish, coy, elvish, flirtatious, frolicsome, fun-loving, impish, jaunty, mischievous, roguish, sportive; SEE CONCEPT *401*

knack [*n*] *ability, talent*
adroitness, aptitude, aptness, bent, capacity, command, dexterity, expertise, expertism, expertness, facility, faculty, flair, forte, genius, gift, handiness, hang of it*, head*, ingenuity, know-how, mastership, mastery, nose*, propensity, quickness, readiness, savvy, set, skill, skillfulness, trick, turn; SEE CONCEPTS *409,630*

knave [*n*] *rascal, villain*
bastard, blackguard, cad, fraud, heel*, lowlife*, miscreant, rapscallion, reprobate, rogue, scamp, scoundrel, swindler; SEE CONCEPT *412*

knead [*v*] *mix by pressing*
aerate, alter, blend, form, manipulate, massage, mold, ply, press, push, rub, shape, squeeze, stroke, twist, work; SEE CONCEPTS *170,208*

kneel [*v*] *get down on one's knees*
bow, bow down, curtsey, do obeisance, genuflect, kowtow*, prostrate oneself, stoop; SEE CONCEPT *154*

knickknack [*n*] *trinket; decorative piece*
bagatelle, bauble, bibelot, bric-a-brac, conversation piece, curio, curiosity, device, embellishment, flummery, frill, furbelow, gadget*, miniature, notion, novelty, objet d'art, ornament, plaything*, showpiece, souvenir, thingamajig*, toy, trapping, trifle, whatnot*, whimsy; SEE CONCEPTS *259, 260,445*

knife [*n*] *cutting tool*
bayonet, blade, bolo, cutlass, cutter, cutting edge, dagger, edge, lance, lancet, machete, point, ripper, sabre, scalpel, scimitar, scythe, shank, shiv, sickle, skewer, skiver, steel, stiletto, switchblade, sword, tickler; SEE CONCEPTS *495,499*

knife [*v*] *stab with pointed tool*
brand, carve, chop down, clip, cut, hurt, impale, jag, kill, lacerate, lance, open up, pierce, shank, shiv, slash, slice, spit, stick, thrust, wound; SEE CONCEPTS *176,220,246*

knit [*v*] *intertwine*
affiliate, affix, ally, bind, cable, connect, contract, crochet, fasten, heal, interlace, intermingle, join, link, loop, mend, net, purl, repair, secure, sew, spin, tie, unite, weave, web; SEE CONCEPTS *113,202,218*

knob [*n*] *lump, handle*
bulge, bulk, bump, bunch, doorknob, hump, knot, knurl, latch, lever, nub, opener, projection, protrusion, protuberance, snag, stud, swell, swelling, trigger, tumor; SEE CONCEPTS *445,471*

knock [*n1*] *pushing, striking*
beating, blow, box, clip, conk, cuff, hammering, hit, injury, lick, rap, slap, smack, swat, swipe, thump, whack; SEE CONCEPT *189*

knock [*n2*] *strong criticism*
blame, censure, condemnation, criticism, defeat, failure, flak, pan, rap, rebuff, rejection, reversal, setback, stricture, swipe; SEE CONCEPTS *52,278*

knock [*v1*] *push over; strike*
abuse, bash, batter, beat, beat up, bob, bruise, buffet, clap, clout, cuff, damage, deck, drub*, fell, flatten, floor, hit, hurt, KO*, level, maltreat, manhandle, maul, mistreat, pound, punch, rap, roughhouse, slap, smack, tap, thrash, thump, thwack*, total, wallop, whack*, wound; SEE CONCEPT *189*

knock [*v2*] *criticize harshly*
abuse, alive*, belittle, blame, carp, cavil, censure, condemn, denounce, denunciate, deprecate, disparage, find fault, lambaste, reprehend, reprobate, run down*, skin alive*, slam; SEE CONCEPT *52*

knock about/knock around [*v*] *roam, wander*
drift, ramble, range, rove, traipse, travel, walk; SEE CONCEPTS *151,224*

knock off [*v1*] *kill*
assassinate, do away with*, do in*, dust*, eliminate, execute, finish, liquidate, murder, rub out*, shoot, slay, stab, waste; SEE CONCEPT *252*

knock off [*v2*] *steal*
filch, knock over, loot, pilfer, pinch, plunder, purloin, ransack, relieve, rifle, rip off*, rob, thieve; SEE CONCEPTS *139,192*

knock off [*v3*] *stop action; accomplish*
achieve, cease, complete, conclude, desist, discontinue, eliminate, finish, give over, halt, leave off, quit, stop work, succeed, surcease, terminate; SEE CONCEPTS *119,234*

knot [*n1*] *bow, loop*
bond, braid, bunch, coil, connection, contortion, entanglement, gnarl, helix, hitch, joint, kink, ligament, ligature, link, mat, nexus, perplexity, rosette, screw, snag, snarl, spiral, splice, tangle, tie, twirl, twist, vinculum, warp, whirl, whorl, yoke; SEE CONCEPTS *436,471*

knot [*n2*] *lump; crowd*
aggregation, assemblage, assortment, band, bunch, circle, clique, clump, cluster, collection, company, crew, gang, gathering, group, heap, mass, mob, pack, pile, set, squad, swarm, tuft; SEE CONCEPT *432*

knot [*v*] *weave, complicate*
bind, cord, entangle, knit, loop, secure, tat, tether, tie; SEE CONCEPTS *85,113,160*

knotty [*adj*] *troublesome*
baffling, complex, complicated, difficult, effortful, elaborate, formidable, Gordian*, hard, intricate, involved, labyrinthine, mazy, mystifying, perplexing, problematical, puzzling, ramified, reticular, rough, rugged, sophisticated, sticky*, terrible, thorny*, tough, tricky, uphill*; SEE CONCEPTS *529,565*

know [*v1*] *understand information*
apperceive, appreciate, apprehend, be acquainted, be cognizant, be conversant in, be informed, be learned, be master of, be read, be schooled, be versed, cognize, comprehend, differentiate, discern, discriminate, distinguish, experience, fathom, feel certain, get the idea*, grasp, have, have down pat*, have information, have knowledge of, ken, learn, notice, on top of*, perceive, prize, realize, recognize, see, undergo; SEE CONCEPTS *15,38*

know [*v2*] *be familiar with*
associate, be acquainted with, be friends with, experience, feel, fraternize, get acquainted, have dealings with, identify, savor, see, sustain, taste, undergo; SEE CONCEPT *384*

know-how [*n*] *skill, talent*
ability, adroitness, aptitude, art, background, capability, command, craft, cunning, dexterity, experience, expertise, expertness, faculty, flair, ingenuity, knack, knowledge, mastery, proficiency, savoir-faire, wisdom; SEE CONCEPTS *409,630*

knowing [*adj*] *experienced, aware*
alive, apprehensive, astute, awake, brainy, bright, brilliant, canny, clever, cognizant, competent, conscious, conversant, cool*, crack*, deliberate, discerning, expert, insightful, intelligent, intended, intentional, judicious, knowledgeable, observant, perceptive, percipient, qualified, quick, quick-witted, sagacious, sage, sensible, sentient, sharp, skillful, slick*, smart, sophic, sophisticated, tuned-in, vigilant, watchful, well-informed, wise, with-it, witting, worldly, worldly-wise; SEE CONCEPT *402*

knowledge [n] *person's understanding; information*
ability, accomplishments, acquaintance, apprehension, attainments, awareness, cognition, comprehension, consciousness, dirt*, discernment, doctrine, dogma, dope*, education, enlightenment, erudition, expertise, facts, familiarity, goods*, grasp, inside story*, insight, instruction, intelligence, judgment, know-how*, learning, light*, lore, observation, philosophy, picture, power*, principles, proficiency, recognition, scholarship, schooling, science, scoop*, substance, theory, tuition, wisdom; SEE CONCEPTS *274,409,529*

knowledgeable [adj] *aware, educated*
abreast, acquainted, alert, appreciative, apprised, au courant, au fait, brainy, bright, brilliant, clever, cognizant, conscious, conversant, discerning, erudite, experienced, familiar, informed, insightful, intelligent, in the know, knowing, learned, lettered, omniscient, perceptive, plugged in*, posted, prescient, privy, quick-witted, sagacious, sage, savvy, scholarly, sensible, sharp, smart, sophic, sophisticated, tuned-in*, understanding, versed, well-informed, well-rounded, wise, with-it; SEE CONCEPT *402*

known [adj] *famous, popular*
accepted, acknowledged, admitted, avowed, celebrated, certified, common, confessed, conscious, down pat*, established, familiar, hackneyed, manifest, noted, notorious, obvious, patent, plain, proverbial, published, received, recognized, well-known; SEE CONCEPTS *529,567,576*

kook [n] *eccentric person*
crackpot, crank, crazy*, dingbat*, flake*, fruitcake*, lamebrain, lunatic, nut, screwball*, wacko*, weirdo; SEE CONCEPTS *412,423*

kowtow [v] *grovel*
bow, brownnose*, cave in*, court, cower, cringe, fawn, flatter, fold, genuflect, give in, go along with, kneel, knuckle under, lie down and roll over*, pander, prostrate, say uncle*, stoop, toe the mark*; SEE CONCEPT *384*

kudos [n] *praise, acclaim*
applause, credit, distinction, eminence, esteem, fame, flattery, glory, honor, illustriousness, laudation, notability, pat on the back*, plaudits, plum*, PR*, preeminence, prestige, prominence, puff*, pumping up*, raves*, regard, renown, repute, strokes*; SEE CONCEPTS *69,268*

L

label [n] *marker, description; brand*
characterization, classification, company, design, epithet, hallmark, identification, insignia, logo, mark, number, price mark, stamp, sticker, tag, tally, ticket, trademark; SEE CONCEPTS *268,270,284*

label [v] *mark, describe; brand*
call, characterize, class, classify, define, designate, identify, name, specify, stamp, sticker, tag, tally; SEE CONCEPTS *62,79*

labor [n1] *work, undertaking*
activity, chore, daily grind, diligence, drudgery, effort, employment, endeavor, energy, exercise, exertion, grind*, gruntwork*, industry, job, moonlight*, operation, pains*, pull, push, strain, stress, struggle, sweat, toil, travail; SEE CONCEPTS *87,100, 351,360,362*

labor [n2] *person(s) performing service*
apprentice, blue collar, breadwinner, employee, hack*, hand, hard hat*, help, helper, hireling, instrument, laborer, learner, operative, prentice, proletariat, rank and file*, toiler, worker, work force, working people, workmen/women; SEE CONCEPTS *325,348*

labor [n3] *childbirth process*
birth, birth pangs, childbearing, contractions, delivery, giving birth, pains, parturition, throes, travail; SEE CONCEPT *374*

labor [v] *work very hard*
bear down, cultivate, drive, drudge, endeavor, exert oneself, grind, plod, plug away*, pour it on*, slave, strain, strive, struggle, sweat, tend, toil, travail, work oneself to the bone*; SEE CONCEPTS *87,100*

labored [adj] *difficult to understand, unclear*
affected, arduous, awkward, clumsy, contrived, effortful, far-fetched, forced, hard, heavy, inept, maladroit, operose, overdone, overwrought, ponderous, stiff, strained, strenuous, studied, toilsome, unnatural, uphill*, weighty; SEE CONCEPT *538*

laborious [adj1] *hard, difficult*
arduous, backbreaking, burdensome, effortful, fatiguing, forced, heavy, herculean*, labored, onerous, operose, ponderous, rough go*, stiff, strained, strenuous, tiresome, toilsome, tough, tough job*, wearing, wearisome, wicked*; SEE CONCEPTS *538,565*

laborious [adj2] *hardworking*
active, assiduous, diligent, indefatigable, industrious, operose, painstaking, persevering, sedulous, tireless, unflagging; SEE CONCEPTS *538,550*

labyrinth [n] *maze, complexity*
coil, complication, convolution, entanglement, intricacy, jungle, knot, mesh, morass, perplexity, problem, puzzle, riddle, skein, snarl, tangle, web; SEE CONCEPTS *436,663,666*

lace [n1] *netted material*
appliqué, banding, border, crochet, edging, filigree, mesh, net, netting, openwork, ornament, tatting, threadwork, tissue, trim, trimming; SEE CONCEPT *473*

lace [n2] *string used to connect*
band, cord, rope, shoelace, thong, thread, tie; SEE CONCEPT *475*

lace [v] *fasten, intertwine*
add, attach, bind, close, do up, fortify, interlace, interweave, mix, plat, spike, strap, thread, tie, twine; SEE CONCEPT *113*

lacerate [v] *tear, cut; wound*
claw, gash, harm, hurt, injure, jag, lance, maim, mangle, mutilate, puncture, rend, rip, score, serrate,

slash, stab, torment, torture; SEE CONCEPTS *137,176, 214,220,246*

lack [n] *deficiency, need*
abridgement, absence, curtailment, dearth, decrease, default, defect, deficit, depletion, deprivation, destitution, distress, exigency, exiguity, inadequacy, inferiority, insufficience, insufficiency, loss, meagerness, miss, necessity, paucity, poverty, privation, reduction, retrenchment, scantiness, scarcity, shortage, shortcoming, shortfall, shortness, shrinkage, shrinking, slightness, stint, want; SEE CONCEPTS *707,709*

lack [v] *do not have*
be deficient in, be short of, be without, have need of, hurting for*, minus, miss, need, not got, out, require, too little too late*, want; SEE CONCEPTS *20,646*

lackadaisical [adj] *careless, indifferent*
abstracted, apathetic, daydreaming, disinterested, dreamy, dull, emasculated, energyless, enervated, faineant, halfhearted, having spring fever*, idle, inattentive, incurious, indolent, inert, laid-back, languid, languishing, languorous, lazy, lethargic, limp, listless, moony*, passive, romantic, sentimental, slothful, spiritless, spring fever*, unconcerned; SEE CONCEPTS *403,542,544*

lacking [adj] *wanting, deficient*
can't cut it*, coming up short*, defective, deprived of, flawed, impaired, inadequate, incomplete, minus, missing, needed, needing, not hacking it*, not making it*, sans, short, without; SEE CONCEPTS *546,771*

lackluster [adj] *dull, lifeless*
blah*, blind, boring, colorless, dark, dead, dim, drab, draggy*, dry, dull, flat*, ho-hum*, laid-back*, leaden, lusterless, matte, muted, nothing*, obscure, pabulum*, prosaic, sombre, unimaginative, uninspired, vanilla*, vapid, zero*; SEE CONCEPTS *542, 548,617*

laconic [adj] *short, to the point*
breviloquent, brief, brusque, compact, compendiary, compendious, concise, crisp, curt, pithy, sententious, short and sweet*, succinct, terse; SEE CONCEPTS *267,773,798*

lacy [adj] *delicate, netlike*
elegant, fancy, filigree, fine, frilly, gauzy, gossamer, lacelike, meshy, open, ornate, patterned, sheer, thin, transparent; SEE CONCEPT *606*

lad [n] *young man*
boy, buddy, child, fellow, guy, half-pint*, juvenile, kid*, runt*, schoolboy, son, stripling, youngster, youth; SEE CONCEPTS *419,424*

laden [adj] *loaded down*
burdened, charged, encumbered, fraught, full, hampered, loaded, oppressed, taxed, weighed down, weighted; SEE CONCEPTS *485,538*

lady [n] *woman; well-bred woman*
adult, baroness, contessa, countess, czarina, dame, duchess, empress, female, gal*, gentlewoman, girl, madam, matron, mistress, noblewoman, princess, queen, rani, squaw, sultana, woman; SEE CONCEPT *415*

ladylike [adj] *feminine, well-mannered*
courtly, cultured, decorous, elegant, genteel, gentle, matronly, modest, polite, proper, refined, respectable, well-bred, womanly; SEE CONCEPT *401*

lag [v] *move slowly; delay*
be behind, dally, dawdle, decrease, dillydally*, diminish, drag, drag one's feet*, ebb, fail, fall off, falter, flag, get no place fast*, hang back, hobble, idle, inch, inch along*, jelly, limp, linger, loiter, lose strength, lounge, plod, poke, procrastinate, put off, retard, saunter, shuffle, slacken, slouch, slow, slow up, stagger, stay, straggle, tail, tarry, tool, trail, trudge, wane; SEE CONCEPTS *151,153*

lair [n] *hideout, habitat*
burrow, cave, den, earth, form, hideaway, hole, nest, pen, refuge, resting place, retreat, sanctuary; SEE CONCEPT *515*

laissez-faire [n] *free enterprise, for the most part unrestrained by law*
free trade, indifference, individualism, live and let live*, neutrality, nonintervention; SEE CONCEPTS *388,691*

lake [n] *inland body of water*
basin, creek, inland sea, lagoon, lakelet, loch, mere, millpond, mouth, pond, pool, reservoir, sluice, spring, tarn; SEE CONCEPT *514*

lambaste [v] *punish, beat*
assail, attack, berate, blister, bludgeon, castigate, censure, criticize, cudgel, denounce, excoriate, flay, flog, hammer, hit, lash into*, pan, pelt, pound, pummel, rake over the coals*, read the riot act*, rebuke, reprimand, rip into, roast, scathe, scold, scorch, scourge, shellac, slam, slap, slash, smear, smother, strike, thrash, trim, upbraid, wallop, whip; SEE CONCEPTS *52,54,86*

lame [adj1] *unable to walk properly*
bruised, crip, crippled, defective, deformed, disabled, game, gimp, gimpy, halt, handicapped, hobbling, limping, pained, raw, sidelined, sore, stiff; SEE CONCEPTS *314,489*

lame [adj2] *feeble, weak*
faltering, faulty, flabby, flimsy, inadequate, ineffective, inefficient, insufficient, poor, thin, unconvincing, unpersuasive, unpleasing, unsatisfactory, unsuitable; SEE CONCEPTS *558,570*

lament/lamentation [n] *grief, complaint*
complaining, dirge, elegy, grieving, jeremiad, keen, keening, lament, moan, moaning, mourning, plaint, requiem, sob, sobbing, sorrow, tears, threnody, ululation, wail, wailing, weeping; SEE CONCEPTS *29,278,410*

lament [v] *to mourn or grieve deeply*
bawl, beat one's breast*, bemoan, bewail, bleed, cry, deplore, eat one's heart out*, grieve, howl, hurt, kick self*, moan, mourn, rain, regret, repine, rue,

sing, sob, sorrow, take it hard*, wail, weep; SEE CONCEPTS *52,54*

lamentable [*adj*] *upsetting, miserable*
afflictive, awful, bad, calamitous, deplorable, dire, dirty, distressing, doleful, dolorous, god-awful, grievous, grim, heartbreaking, hurting, lousy, low, lugubrious, meager, mean, melancholy, mournful, pitiful, plaintive, poor, regret, rotten, rueful, sad, sorrowful, stinking, tragic, unfavorable, unfortunate, unsatisfactory, woeful, wretched; SEE CONCEPTS *529,537*

laminate [*v*] *cover with veneer*
coat, exfoliate, face, flake, foil, foliate, layer, overlayer, plate, separate, split, stratify, veneer; SEE CONCEPT *172*

lampoon [*n*] *parody, satire*
burlesque, caricature, invective, pasquil, pasquinade, pastiche, ridicule, roast*, send-up*, skit, squib, takedown, takeoff*; SEE CONCEPTS *263,273*

lampoon [*v*] *ridicule, make fun of*
burlesque, caricature, jape, mock, parody, pasquinade, put on*, rail, roast*, satirize, send up*, squib, take off*, travesty; SEE CONCEPT *273*

land [*n*] *earth's surface; ownable property*
acreage, acres, area, beach, continent, country, countryside, dirt, district, earth, estate, expanse, extent, farming, farmland, fatherland, field, ground, grounds, holding, home, homeland, loam, mainland, manor, motherland, nation, parcel, plot, province, purlieu, quarry, quinta, ranch, real estate, realty, region, shore, sod, soil, stretch, sweep, terra firma, terrain, territory, tillage, tract; SEE CONCEPTS *508,509,510,515*

land [*v1*] *arrive, come to rest on*
alight, berth, bring in, check in, come ashore, come down, come in, come to berth, debark, descend upon, disembark, ditch, dock, drop anchor, flatten out, get down, ground, level off, light on, make land, pilot, put down, put in, set down, set on deck, settle, sit down, splash down, steer, take down, thump, touch down; SEE CONCEPTS *159,181*

land [*v2*] *achieve, acquire*
annex, bring in, gain, get, have, obtain, pick up, procure, secure, win; SEE CONCEPTS *120,706*

landlord [*n*] *owner of property leased*
freeholder, host/hostess, hotelier, hotelkeeper, innkeeper, lessor, property owner, proprietor, saw, slumlord, squire; SEE CONCEPT *347*

landmark [*n1*] *historical or notable sight*
battleground, benchmark, bend, blaze, feature, fragment, guide, hill, mark, marker, memorial, milepost, milestone, monument, mountain, museum, promontory, remnant, ruins, souvenir, specimen, stone, survival, trace, tree, vantage point, vestige, waypost; SEE CONCEPTS *198,284,447*

landmark [*n2*] *turning point*
crisis, event, milepost, milestone, stage, watershed, waypost; SEE CONCEPTS *696,817*

landscape [*n*] *countryside; picture of countryside*
mural, outlook, painting, panorama, photograph, prospect, scene, scenery, sketch, view, vista; SEE CONCEPTS *259,509*

language [*n*] *system of words for communication*
accent, argot, articulation, brogue, cant, communication, conversation, dialect, diction, dictionary, discourse, doublespeak*, expression, gibberish, idiom, interchange, jargon, lexicon, lingua franca, mother tongue, palaver, parlance, patois, phraseology, prose, signal, slang, sound, speech, style, talk, terminology, tongue, utterance, verbalization, vernacular, vocabulary, vocalization, voice, word, wording; SEE CONCEPT *276*

languid [*adj*] *drooping, dull, listless*
apathetic, blah*, blahs*, comatose, dopey, easy, energyless, enervated, faint, feeble, heavy, impassive, inactive, indifferent, inert, infirm, lackadaisical, laidback, languishing, languorous, lazy, leaden, leisurely, lethargic, limp, moony*, nebbish, phlegmatic, pining, sickly, sleepyhead*, slow, sluggish, snoozy*, spiritless, supine, torpid, unconcerned, unenthusiastic, unhurried, uninterested, weak, weary, wimpy*; SEE CONCEPTS *403,542,584*

languish [*v*] *droop; become dull, listless*
be disregarded, be neglected, brood, conk out*, decline, desire, despond, deteriorate, die on vine*, dwindle, ebb, fade, fag, fag out, fail, faint, fizzle out, flag, go soft*, go to pieces*, grieve, hanker, hunger, knock out, long, pine, repine, rot, sicken, sigh, snivel, sorrow, suffer, tucker, waste, waste away, weaken, wilt, wither, yearn; SEE CONCEPTS *20,105,469*

lanky [*adj*] *tall and thin*
angular, attenuated, beanpole*, beanstalk*, bony, broomstick*, extenuated, gangling, gangly, gaunt, lean, meager, rangy, rawboned, scraggy, scrawny, slender, spare, spindling, spindly, stilt, stringy, twiggy*, weedy; SEE CONCEPTS *491,779*

lap [*n*] *orbit, circuit*
circle, course, distance, loop, round, tour; SEE CONCEPTS *364,436*

lap [*v1*] *slosh, wash against*
bathe, bubble, burble, drink, gurgle, lave, lick, lip, plash, purl, ripple, sip, slap, splash, sup, swish; SEE CONCEPT *144*

lap [*v2*] *overlap*
cover, enfold, envelop, fold, imbricate, overlie, override, ride, shingle, swaddle, swathe, turn, twist, wrap; SEE CONCEPTS *172,201*

lapse [*n1*] *mistake*
blunder, breach, bungle, crime, error, failing, failure, fault, flub, foible, frailty, gaff, goof, goof-up*, indiscretion, miscue, negligence, offense, omission, oversight, screw-up*, sin, slip, slip-up, transgression, trespass, trip*, vice, violation; SEE CONCEPTS *101,674*

lapse [n2] *break in action*
gap, intermission, interruption, interval, lacuna, lull, passage, pause; SEE CONCEPT *807*

lapse [n3] *backsliding*
decadence, declension, decline, degeneration, descent, deterioration, devolution, drop, fall, recession, regression, relapse, retrogradation, retrogression; SEE CONCEPTS *230,316,388*

lapse [v] *become void; fall back into previous pattern*
apostatize, backslide, become obsolete, cease, decline, degenerate, descend, deteriorate, die, elapse, end, expire, go by, pass, recede, recidivate, relapse, retrograde, return, revert, run out, slide, slip, subside, terminate, weaken; SEE CONCEPTS *119,698*

larceny [n] *theft*
burglary, crime, lift, misappropriation, pilfering, pinch, purloining, robbery, steal, stealing, thievery, thieving, touch; SEE CONCEPTS *139,192*

large [adj] *big, abundant*
ample, barn door*, blimp*, booming, broad, bulky, capacious, colossal, comprehensive, considerable, copious, enormous, excessive, exorbitant, extensive, extravagant, full, generous, giant, gigantic, goodly, grand, grandiose, great, gross, hefty, huge, humongous*, immeasurable, immense, jumbo*, king-size, liberal, massive, monumental, mountainous, plentiful, populous, roomy, sizable, spacious, stupendous, substantial, super, sweeping, thumping, tidy, vast, voluminous, whopping*, wide; SEE CONCEPTS *773,781*

largely [adv] *to a great extent*
abundantly, as a rule, broadly, by and large, chiefly, commodiously, comprehensively, considerably, copiously, expansively, extensively, extravagantly, generally, generously, grandly, immoderately, imposingly, in a big way, in a grand manner, lavishly, liberally, magnificently, mainly, mostly, on a large scale, overall, predominantly, primarily, principally, prodigally, prodigiously, voluminously, widely; SEE CONCEPTS *544,772*

lascivious [adj] *sexually aroused; displaying excessive interest in sex*
bawdy, blue, bodily, carnal, coarse, crude, evil-minded, fast*, fleshly, gross*, hard-core*, hot*, immoral, incontinent, indecent, lecherous, lewd, libertine, libidinous, licentious, low-down*, lustful, nasty, obscene, off-color*, offensive, orgiastic, pornographic, prurient, randy, raunchy*, raw, ribald, rough, salacious, scurrilous, sensual, smutty*, softcore*, steamy, suggestive, unchaste, voluptuous, vulgar, wanton, X-rated*; SEE CONCEPTS *372,403*

lash [v1] *beat, whip*
baste, batter, buffet, chastise, dash, drum, flagellate, flay, flog, hammer, hide, hit, horsewhip, knock, lam, lather, pound, pummel, scourge, smack, strap, strike, thrash, wear out, whale*, whip; SEE CONCEPT *189*

lash [v2] *criticize harshly*
abuse, attack, baste, bawl out*, belabor, berate, blister, castigate, censure, chew out*, exprobate, flay, fulminate, jaw, lambaste, lampoon, ridicule, satirize, scold, tear into*, tell off*, tongue-lash*, upbraid; SEE CONCEPT *52*

last [n] *end*
close, completion, conclusion, ending, finale, finis, finish, omega, termination; SEE CONCEPT *832*

last [adj] *final; newest*
aftermost, antipodal, at the end, bitter end, climactic, closing, concluding, conclusive, crowning, curtains*, definitive, determinate, determinative, end, ending, eventual, extreme, far, far-off, farthest, finishing, furthest, hindmost, lag, latest, least, lowest, meanest, most recent, once and for all*, outermost, rearmost, remotest, supreme, swan song*, terminal, ulterior, ultimate, utmost, uttermost; SEE CONCEPTS *585,778,799*

lasting [adj] *enduring, unending*
abiding, constant, continual, continuing, deep-rooted, durable, endless, eternal, everlasting, forever, incessant, indelible, indissoluble, inexhaustible, inexpungible, in for long haul*, lifelong, long-standing, long-term, old, perdurable, perennial, permanent, perpetual, persisting, stable, till the cows come home*, unceasing, undying, unremitting; SEE CONCEPTS *551,798*

lastly/last [adv] *in the end*
after, after all, all in all, at last, at the end, behind, bringing up rear*, finally, in conclusion, in the rear, to conclude, to sum up, ultimately; SEE CONCEPTS *585,799*

latch [n] *lock*
bar, bolt, catch, clamp, fastening, hasp, hook, padlock; SEE CONCEPTS *445,499*

latch [v] *fasten with lock*
bar, bolt, cinch, close, close up, lock, make fast, secure; SEE CONCEPTS *85,160*

late [adj1] *not on time*
backward, behind, behindhand, behind time, belated, blown*, delayed, dilatory, eleventh-hour*, gone, held up, hung up*, in a bind*, in the lurch*, jammed*, lagging, last-minute, missed the boat*, not in time, out of luck*, overdue, postponed, put off, remiss, slow, stayed, strapped*, tardy, too late, unpunctual; SEE CONCEPTS *548,799*

late [adj2] *new*
advanced, fresh, just out, modern, recent; SEE CONCEPTS *578,797*

late [adj3] *dead*
asleep, bygone, cold, deceased, defunct, departed, erstwhile, ex-*, exanimate, extinct, former, inanimate, lifeless, old, once, onetime, past, preceding, previous, quondam, sometime; SEE CONCEPT *539*

late [adv] *at the last minute*
backward, behind, behindhand, behind time, belatedly, dilatorily, slowly, tardily, unpunctual; SEE CONCEPT *799*

lately [adv] new, recently
afresh, anew, a short time ago, in recent times, just now, latterly, new, newly, not long ago, of late; SEE CONCEPT 820

latent [adj] dormant, hidden
abeyant, between the lines, concealed, contained, covert, idle, immature, implied, in abeyance, inactive, inert, inferential, inferred, inherent, inoperative, intrinsic, invisible, involved, lurking, passive, possible, potential, quiescent, rudimentary, secret, sleeping, smoldering, suppressed, suspended, tacit, torpid, underdeveloped, underlying, undeveloped, unexposed, unexpressed, unrealized, unripe, unseen, veiled, vestigial; SEE CONCEPTS 404,576

later [adj] coming after
after, downstream, ensuing, following, more recent, next, posterior, postliminary, proximate, subsequent, subsequential, succeeding, ulterior; SEE CONCEPT 799

later [adv] happening after
after, afterward, again, at another time, behind, by and by*, come Sunday*, down the line*, down the road*, in a while, infra, in time, later on, latterly, more recent, next, subsequently, succeeding, thereafter; SEE CONCEPT 799

lateral [adj] sideways
crabwise, edgeways, flanking, oblique, side, side-by-side, sidelong, sideward, sidewise, skirting; SEE CONCEPTS 581,583

lather [n1] bubbles
cream, foam, froth, head, soap, soapsuds, spume, suds, yeast; SEE CONCEPTS 260,437

lather [n2] commotion, fuss
agitation, bustle, clamor, confusion, dither, fever, flap*, fluster, hassle, hoopla*, hubbub*, hullabaloo*, sweat*, tizzy*, tsimmes*, tumult, turbulence, turmoil, twitter*; SEE CONCEPTS 230,388

lather [v] cause to bubble
beat, foam, froth, scrub, soap, wash, whip; SEE CONCEPT 165

latitude [n] freedom, room to move; scope
breadth, compass, elbow room, extent, independence, indulgence, laxity, leeway, liberty, license, margin, play, range, reach, room, run, run of, space, span, spread, sweep, swing, unrestrictedness, width; SEE CONCEPTS 651,739,756,787

latter [adj] latest, concluding
closing, eventual, final, following, hindmost, lag, last, last-mentioned, later, modern, rearmost, recent, second, terminal; SEE CONCEPTS 585,799

lattice [n] mesh, trellis
filigree, frame, fretwork, grating, grid, grill, latticework, net, network, openwork, reticulation, screen, structure, tracery, web; SEE CONCEPT 259

laud [v] acclaim, praise
admire, adore, approve, bless, boost, build up, celebrate, commend, compliment, cry up, eulogize, extol, flatter, glorify, hand it to*, honor, hymn, magnify, panegyrize, pat on the back*, revere, rev-

erence, sing the praises of*, stroke, toss a bouquet*, venerate, worship; SEE CONCEPT 69

laudable [adj] admirable
commendable, creditable, deserving, estimable, excellent, mean, meritable, meritorious, of note, praisable, praiseworthy, stellar, terrific, thankworthy, worthy; SEE CONCEPT 574

laudatory [adj] complimentary
acclamatory, adulatory, approbative, approbatory, approving, commendatory, encomiastic, eulogistic, flattering, laudative, panegyrical, praiseful; SEE CONCEPT 267

laugh/laughter [n] audible expression of amusement
amusement, cachinnation, cackle, chortle, chuckle, chuckling, crack-up*, crow, fit, gesture, giggle, giggling, glee, guffaw, hilarity, howling, merriment, mirth, peal, rejoicing, roar, shout, shriek, snicker, snigger, snort, sound, titter, yuck*; SEE CONCEPTS 77,185

laugh [v] expressing amusement, happiness with sound
be convulsed*, be in stitches*, break up*, burst*, cachinnate, chortle, chuckle, crack up*, crow, die laughing*, fracture*, giggle, grin, guffaw, howl, roar, roll in the aisles*, scream, shriek, snicker, snort, split one's sides*, titter, whoop*; SEE CONCEPTS 77,185

laughable [adj] easily made fun of
absurd, amusing, asinine, bizarre, camp, campy, comic, comical, derisive, derisory, diverting, droll, eccentric, entertaining, facetious, fantastic, farcical, funny, gelastic, har-har*, hilarious, humorous, inane, jocose, jocular, jokey, joshing, ludicrous, mirthful, mocking, nonsensical, preposterous, rich, ridiculous, riot, risible, scream, unusual, witty; SEE CONCEPTS 267,550

laugh at [v] ridicule
belittle, deride, hoot, jeer, lampoon, make fun of, mock, scoff, taunt; SEE CONCEPT 54

launch [v1] send off
barrage, bombard, bung, cast, catapult, discharge, dispatch, drive, eject, fire, fling, heave, hurl, lance, pitch, project, propel, send forth, set afloat, set in motion, shoot, sling, throw, toss; SEE CONCEPTS 179,222

launch [v2] begin, initiate
bow, break the ice*, break the seal*, commence, embark upon, get show on road*, inaugurate, instigate, institute, introduce, jump, kick off*, open, originate, set going, start, start ball rolling*, usher in*; SEE CONCEPT 221

laurels [n] credit, praise
acclaim, accolade, award, badge, bays, blue ribbon, commendation, crown, decoration, distinction, fame, feather in cap*, glory, gold, gold star*, kudos, prestige, recognition, renown, reward; SEE CONCEPTS 69,278,337

lavish [adj] profuse; splendid
abundant, bountiful, copious, effusive, exaggerated, excessive, extravagant, exuberant, first-class, free,

generous, gorgeous, grand, immoderate, impressive, improvident, inordinate, intemperate, liberal, lush, luxuriant, luxuriant, luxurious, munificent, open-handed, opulent, plentiful, plush, posh, prodigal, profligate, profusive, prolific, riotous, ritzy, sumptuous, swanky, thriftless, unreasonable, unrestrained, unsparing, unstinging, wasteful, wild; SEE CONCEPTS *334,589,781*

lavish [*v*] *pamper, shower*
be generous, be wasteful, deluge, dissipate, expend, fritter, give, go through, heap, pour, run through*, scatter, spend, spend money like water*, squander, thrust upon, waste; SEE CONCEPTS *110,327,341*

law [*n1*] *rules of a government, society*
act, assize, behest, bidding, bylaw, canon, case, caveat, charge, charter, code, command, commandment, constitution, covenant, decision, decree, decretum, demand, dictate, divestiture, due process, edict, enactment, equity, garnishment, injunction, institute, instruction, jurisprudence, legislation, mandate, measure, notice, order, ordinance, precedent, precept, prescript, prescription, reg*, regulation, requirement, ruling, statute, subpoena, summons, warrant, writ; SEE CONCEPT *318*

law [*n2*] *standard, principle of behavior*
assumption, axiom, base, canon, cause, criterion, exigency, formula, foundation, fundamental, generalization, ground, guide, maxim, origin, postulate, precept, principium, proposal, proposition, reason, regulation, rule, source, theorem, truth, usage; SEE CONCEPT *687*

lawful [*adj*] *allowable, legitimate*
authorized, bona fide, canonical, card-carrying*, commanded, condign, constitutional, decreed, due, enacted, enforced, enjoined, established, innocent, judged, judicial, jural, juridical, jurisprudent, just, justifiable, kosher*, legal, legalized, legislated, legit*, legitimate, legitimatized, licit, mandated, official, of right, on the level*, on the up and up*, ordained, ordered, passed, permissible, proper, protected, rightful, ruled, statutory, valid, vested, warrantable, warranted; SEE CONCEPTS *319,545*

lawless [*adj*] *reckless, ungoverned*
anarchic, anarchical, anarchistic, bad, barbarous, chaotic, contumacious, criminal, despotic, disobedient, disordered, disorderly, evil, fierce, heterodox, infringing, insubordinate, insurgent, mutinous, nihilistic, noncompliant, nonconformist, piratical, rebellious, recusant, revolutionary, riotous, savage, seditious, tempestuous, terrorizing, traitorous, turbulent, tyrannous, uncivilized, uncultivated, unorthodox, unpeaceful, unrestrained, unruly, untamed, violent, warlike, wild; SEE CONCEPTS *319,545*

lawn [*n*] *cultivated area of green grass*
backyard, garden, grass, grassplot, green, park, plot, terrace, yard; SEE CONCEPTS *509,513,517*

lawsuit [*n*] *case brought to court*
accusation, action, argument, arraignment, assumpsit, bill, cause, claim, contest, dispute, impeachment, indictment, litigation, presentment, proceedings, prosecution, replevin, suit, trial; SEE CONCEPT *318*

lawyer [*n*] *person who is trained to counsel or argue in cases of law*
advocate, attorney, attorney-at-law, barrister, counsel, counsellor, counselor, defender, jurisprudent, jurist, legal adviser, legal eagle*, legist, member of the bar, mouthpiece*, pleader, practitioner, proctor, procurator, solicitor; SEE CONCEPT *355*

lax [*adj*] *slack, remiss*
any way*, asleep on job*, behindhand, broad, careless, casual, delinquent, derelict, devil-may-care*, disregardful, easygoing, flaccid, forgetful, general, imprecise, inaccurate, indefinite, indifferent, inexact, lenient, neglectful, negligent, nonspecific, oblivious, overindulgent, paying no mind*, regardless, shapeless, slipshod, sloppy, soft, unmindful, vague, yielding; SEE CONCEPTS *401,542,557*

lay [*adj*] *amateur, not trained in a religious or other profession*
inexpert, nonclerical, nonprofessional, nonspecialist, ordinary, secular, temporal, unsacred; SEE CONCEPT *574*

lay [*v1*] *put, place*
arrange, deposit, dispose, establish, fix, leave, locate, order, organize, plant, posit, position, repose, rest, set, set down, set out, settle, spread, stick, systematize; SEE CONCEPTS *158,201*

lay [*v2*] *produce, advance*
adduce, allege, bear, bring forth, bring forward, cite, deposit, generate, lodge, offer, present, put forward, submit, yield; SEE CONCEPTS *66,205*

lay [*v3*] *credit, allocate*
accredit, address, aim, allot, apply, ascribe, assess, assign, attribute, burden, cast, charge, direct, encumber, impose, impute, incline, level, point, refer, saddle, tax, train, turn, zero in*; SEE CONCEPTS *49,50,88,187*

lay [*v4*] *design, plan*
concoct, contrive, devise, hatch, plot, prepare, work out; SEE CONCEPT *36*

lay [*v5*] *make smooth*
allay, alleviate, appease, assuage, calm, even, flatten, flush, iron, level, plane, press, quiet, relieve, smooth, steam, still, suppress; SEE CONCEPTS *235,250*

lay [*v6*] *bet, wager*
gamble, game, give odds, hazard, play, risk, stake; SEE CONCEPT *363*

layer [*n*] *coating, tier*
band, bed, blanket, coat, coping, couch, course, cover, covering, film, flag, flap, floor, fold, girdle, lamina, lamination, lap, mantle, overlap, overlay, panel, ply, row, seam, sheet, slab, story, stratum, stripe, substratum, thickness, zone; SEE CONCEPTS *744,835*

lay into [*v*] *criticize, attack*
assail, battle, belabor, fire at*, invade, lambaste, let fly at*, set about; SEE CONCEPTS *52,86*

layman/woman [n] *amateur person, not trained in religious or other profession*
believer, dilettante, follower, laic, lay person, member, neophyte, nonprofessional, novice, outsider, parishioner, proselyte, recruit, secular; SEE CONCEPTS *361,423*

layoff [n] *dismissal from job or responsibility*
cutback, discharge, early retirement, respite, unemployment; SEE CONCEPT *351*

lay off [v1] *stop doing*
cease, desist, end, give a rest, give up, halt, leave alone, leave off, let up, lie by, quit, rest, spell; SEE CONCEPTS *119,234*

lay off [v2] *relieve of responsibility*
discharge, dismiss, drop, fire, let go, oust, pay off, retire early; SEE CONCEPT *351*

layout [n] *physical arrangement*
blueprint, chart, design, diagram, draft, formation, geography, map, organization, outline, plan, purpose; SEE CONCEPTS *625,660*

lay out [v1] *spend money*
disburse, expend, give, invest, lend, outlay, pay, put out, put up, shell out*; SEE CONCEPTS *327,341*

lay out [v2] *design, plan*
arrange, chart, diagram, display, exhibit, map, outline, set out, spread out; SEE CONCEPTS *36,158,174*

lay up/lay by [v1] *set aside, store*
accumulate, amass, build up, bury, conserve, cumulate, garner, hoard, keep, lay in, preserve, put away, roll up, salt away, save, spare, store up, treasure; SEE CONCEPTS *120,134*

lay up [v2] *hurt, incapacitate*
beat up, confine, disable, harm, hospitalize, injure; SEE CONCEPT *246*

laziness [n] *unwillingness to work, be active*
apathy, dilatoriness, do-nothingness, dormancy, dreaminess, drowsiness, dullness, faineance, faineancy, heaviness, idleness, inactivity, indolence, inertia, inertness, lackadaisicalness, languidness, languorousness, laxness, leadenness, leisureliness, lethargy, listlessness, neglectfulness, negligence, otioseness, otiosity, passivity, remissness, slackness, sleepiness, sloth, slothfulness, slowness, sluggishness, stolidity, supineness, tardiness, torpescence, torpidness, weariness; SEE CONCEPTS *411,633*

lazy [adj] *inactive, sluggish*
apathetic, asleep on the job*, careless, comatose, dallying, dilatory, drowsy, dull, flagging, idle, inattentive, indifferent, indolent, inert, lackadaisical, laggard, lagging, languid, languorous, lethargic, lifeless, loafing, neglectful, out of it*, passive, procrastinating, remiss, shiftless, slack, sleepy, slothful, slow, slow-moving, snoozy*, somnolent, supine, tardy, tired, torpid, trifling, unconcerned, unenergetic, unindustrious, unpersevering, unready, weary; SEE CONCEPTS *401,404*

lead [n1] *first place, supremacy*
advance, advantage, ahead, bulge, cutting edge*, direction, edge, example, facade, front rank, guidance,

head, heavy, leadership, margin, model, over, pilot, point, precedence, primacy, principal, priority, protagonist, spark, star, start, title role, top, top spot, vanguard; SEE CONCEPTS *668,693,828*

lead [n2] *clue*
evidence, guide, hint, indication, proof, sign, suggestion, tip, trace; SEE CONCEPTS *274,284*

lead [v1] *guide physically*
accompany, attend, be responsible for, chaperone, coerce, compel, conduct, convey, convoy, direct, drive, escort, find a way, force, get, go along with, guard, impel, induce, manage, pass along, persuade, pilot, point out, point the way, precede, prevail, protect, quarterback*, route, safeguard, see, shepherd, show, show around, show in, show the way, span, squire, steer, traverse, usher, watch over; SEE CONCEPT *187*

lead [v2] *guide mentally; influence*
affect, bring, bring on, call the shots*, cause, command, conduce, contribute, convert, direct, dispose, draw, get the jump on*, go out in front*, govern, head, helm, incline, induce, introduce, manage, mastermind, motivate, move, persuade, preside over, prevail, produce, prompt, quarterback*, result in, run things*, serve, shepherd, spearhead*, spur, supervise, tend, trail-blaze*; SEE CONCEPTS *68,117,221*

lead [v3] *surpass*
be ahead, blaze a trail*, come first*, exceed, excel, mastermind, outdo, outstrip, precede, preface, transcend, usher; SEE CONCEPT *141*

lead (a life) [v4] *experience*
have, live, pass, spend, undergo; SEE CONCEPT *678*

leader [n] *person who guides*
boss, captain, chief, chieftain, commander, conductor, controller, counsellor, dean, dignitary, director, doyen, eminence, exec, foreman/woman, forerunner, general, governor, guide, harbinger, head, herald, lead, lion*, luminary, maestro, manager, master, maven, mistress, notability, notable, officer, pacesetter, pilot, pioneer, precursor, president, principal, rector, ringleader, ruler, shepherd, skipper, superintendent, superior; SEE CONCEPTS *347,354*

leadership [n] *guidance*
administration, authority, capacity, command, conduction, control, conveyance, direction, directorship, domination, foresight, hegemony, influence, initiative, management, pilotage, power, preeminence, primacy, skill, superintendency, superiority, supremacy, sway; SEE CONCEPTS *376,686*

leading [adj] *chief, superior*
arch, best, champion, dominant, dominating, famous, first, foremost, governing, greatest, headmost, highest, inaugural, initial, main, noted, notorious, number one*, outstanding, popular, preeminent, premier, primary, principal, prominent, ruling, stellar, top, well-known; SEE CONCEPTS *574,585*

leaf [n1] *green foliage of plant*
blade, bract, flag, foliole, frond, leaflet, needle, pad, petal, petiole, scale, stalk, stipule; SEE CONCEPT *428*

leaf [n2] *page of document*
folio, paper, sheet; SEE CONCEPT *270*

leaf [v] *flip through*
browse, dip into, glance, riff, riffle, run through, scan, skim, thumb; SEE CONCEPTS *72,623*

leafy [adj] *abundant in foliage*
abounding, abundant, covered, green, hidden, leafed, leaved, shaded, shady, umbrageous, verdant, wooded; SEE CONCEPTS *485,583*

league [n1] *association, federation*
alliance, band, brotherhood, bunch, circle, circuit, club, coalition, combination, combine, compact, company, confederacy, confederation, conference, consortium, crew, fellowship, fraternity, gang, group, guild, loop, mob, order, organization, outfit, partnership, pool, ring, sisterhood, society, sodality, sorority, union, unit; SEE CONCEPTS *365,381,387*

league [n2] *group of a certain ability*
category, circle, class, grade, grouping, level, pigeonhole*, rank, status, tier; SEE CONCEPTS *388,630*

league [v] *associate*
ally, amalgamate, band, coadjute, collaborate, combine, concur, confederate, conjoin, consolidate, cooperate, federate, join forces, unite; SEE CONCEPTS *8,10,114*

leak [n] *opening; seepage through opening*
aperture, chink, crack, crevice, decrease, destruction, detriment, drip, drop, escape, expenditure, exposure, fissure, flow, hole, leakage, leaking, loss, outgoing, percolation, pit, puncture, short circuit, slip; SEE CONCEPTS *116,513*

leak [v] *seep; make known*
break, come out, discharge, disclose, divulge, drip, drool, escape, exude, get out, give away, let slip*, make public, ooze, out, pass, pass on, percolate, reveal, slip, spill, spill the beans, tell, transpire, trickle; SEE CONCEPTS *60,116,179*

lean [adj] *bare, thin*
angular, anorexic, barren, beanpole*, bony, emaciated, gangling, gangly, gaunt, haggard, inadequate, infertile, lank, lanky, meager, no fat, pitiful, poor, rangy, rawboned, scanty, scraggy, scrawny, shadow*, sinewy, skinny, slender, slim, spare, sparse, stick, stilt, stringy, svelte, sylphlike, twiggy*, unfruitful, unproductive, wasted, wiry, wizened, worn; SEE CONCEPTS *485,491*

lean [v1] *bend, angle toward*
bear on, beetle, be off, be slanted, bow, cant, careen, cock, curve, decline, deflect, dip, divert, drift, droop, fasten on, hang on, heel, incline, jut, list, nod, overhang, pitch, place, prop, put weight on, recline, repose, rest, rest on, roll, sag, sheer, sink, slant, slope, tilt, tip, turn, twist, veer; SEE CONCEPTS *147,201,738*

lean [v2] *be disposed*
be prone, be willing, favor, gravitate toward, have propensity, incline, look, not mind, prefer, tend; SEE CONCEPT *20*

lean [v3] *count, depend on*
bank on*, believe in, bet bottom dollar*, bet on*, confide, gamble on*, have faith, hinge on*, lay money on*, put faith in, rely, trust; SEE CONCEPTS *12,26*

leaning [n] *tendency, bias*
aptitude, bent*, cup of tea*, disposition, drift, favor, favoritism, inclination, inclining, liking, mindset, partiality, penchant, predilection, predisposition, proclivity, proneness, propensity, sentiment, taste, thing, weakness; SEE CONCEPTS *20,32,689*

leap [n] *jump; increase*
bound, caper, escalation, frisk, hop, rise, skip, spring, surge, upsurge, upswing, vault; SEE CONCEPTS *194,780*

leap [v] *jump, jump over; increase*
advance, arise, ascend, bounce, bound, caper, cavort, clear, escalate, frisk, hop, hurdle, lop, mount, rise, rocket, saltate, skip, soar, spring, surge, vault; SEE CONCEPTS *194,780*

learn [v1] *acquire information*
apprentice, attain, become able, become versed, be taught, be trained, brush up on*, burn midnight oil*, commit to memory, con, crack the books*, cram*, determine, drink in*, enroll, gain, get, get down pat*, get the hang of*, get the knack of*, grasp, grind, imbibe, improve mind, lucubrate, major in, master, matriculate, memorize, minor in, peruse, pick up*, pore over, prepare, read, receive, review, soak up*, specialize in, study, take course*, take in, train in, wade through*; SEE CONCEPTS *31,33*

learn [v2] *discover, find out*
ascertain, catch on, detect, determine, dig up*, discern, gain, gather, hear, see, smoke out*, stumble upon*, trip over, tumble, uncover, understand, unearth; SEE CONCEPTS *34,183*

learned [adj] *well-informed*
abstruse, academic, accomplished, bookish, brainy*, conversant, cultivated, cultured, deep*, educated, erudite, esoteric, experienced, expert, grave, grounded, highbrow*, intellectual, in the know*, judicious, lettered, literary, literate, omniscient, pansophic, pedantic, philosophic, philosopical, polymath, posted, professorial, recondite, sage, sapient, scholarly, scientific, sharp, skilled, solemn, solid, sound, studied, studious, versed, well-educated, well-grounded, well-read, well-rounded; SEE CONCEPT *402*

learner [n] *person who receives education*
abecedarian, apprentice, beginner, bookworm, catechumen, disciple, freshman, initiate, neophyte, novice, probationer, pupil, scholar, schoolboy, student, trainee; SEE CONCEPT *350*

learning [n] *education, knowledge*
acquirements, attainments, culture, erudition, information, letters, literature, lore, research, scholarship, schooling, science, study, training, tuition, wisdom; SEE CONCEPTS *274,409*

lease [v] *rent object, residence*
charter, hire, let, loan, rent out, sublease, sublet; SEE CONCEPTS *89,115*

leash [n] *rein*
bridle, chain, check, control, cord, curb, deterrent, hold, lead, restraint, rope, strap, tether; SEE CONCEPT *475*

leash [v] *rein, hold*
bridle, check, clog, control, curb, entrammel, fasten, fetter, hamper, hobble, hog-tie*, hold back, restrain, secure, shackle, suppress, tether, tie, tie up, trammel; SEE CONCEPT *191*

least [adj] *slightest, smallest*
atomic, bottom, entry-level, feeblest, fewest, finical, first, gutter, infinitesimal, last, lowest, meanest, microcosmic, microscopic, minimal, minimum, minute, minutest, molecular, most trivial, nadir, next to nothing*, niggling*, piddling*, poorest, second, short-end*, third*, tiniest, trivial, unimportant; SEE CONCEPTS *585,789*

leathery [adj] *hard, durable*
coriaceous, hard, hardened, leatherlike, rough, rugged, strong, tough, wrinkled; SEE CONCEPTS *489,606*

leave [n1] *permission*
allowance, assent, authorization, concession, consent, dispensation, freedom, go-ahead*, green light*, liberty, okay, permit, sanction, sufferance, tolerance; SEE CONCEPTS *376,685*

leave [n2] *holiday, time off*
adieu, departure, farewell, furlough, goodbye, leave of absence, leave-taking, liberty, parting, retirement, sabbatical, vacation, withdrawal; SEE CONCEPTS *802,807*

leave [v1] *depart, abandon physically*
abscond, beat it*, break away, clear out*, come away, cut out, decamp, defect, desert, disappear, ditch*, elope, embark, emigrate, escape, exit, flee, flit, fly, forsake, give the slip*, go, go away, go forth, head out*, issue, migrate, move, move out, part, pull out*, push off*, quit, relinquish, remove oneself, retire, ride off*, run along*, sally, say goodbye*, scram, set out, slip out, split*, start, step down, take a hike*, take leave, take off, vacate, vamoose*, vanish, walk out, withdraw; SEE CONCEPT *195*

leave [v2] *abandon, renounce*
back out*, cease, cede, desert, desist, drop, drop out*, evacuate, forbear, forsake, give notice, give up*, hand over, knock off, maroon, quit, refrain, relinquish, resign, stop, surrender, terminate, waive, yield; SEE CONCEPT *234*

leave [v3] *forget, neglect*
allow, drop, have, lay down, leave behind, let, let be, let continue, let go, let stay, mislay, omit, permit, suffer; SEE CONCEPTS *30,83*

leave [v4] *give, especially after death*
allot, apportion, assign, bequeath, bequest, cede, commit, confide, consign, demise, devise, entrust, give over, hand down, leave behind, legate, refer, transmit, will; SEE CONCEPTS *108,317*

leave off [v] *stop*
abstain, break off, cease, desist, discontinue, end, give over, give up, halt, knock off*, quit, refrain, surcease; SEE CONCEPT *234*

lecherous [adj] *lustful, lewd*
carnal, concupiscent, corrupt, fast*, hot and heavy*, incontinent, lascivious, libertine, libidinous, licentious, low-down*, lubricous, prurient, raunchy*, salacious, satyric, sensual, unchaste, wanton; SEE CONCEPTS *372,401*

lecture [n1] *lesson, speech*
address, allocution, chalk talk*, discourse, disquisition, harangue, instruction, oration, pep talk*, pitch*, soapbox*, spiel*, talk; SEE CONCEPTS *60, 278*

lecture [n2] *speech of criticism*
castigation, censure, chiding, dressing-down*, going-over*, harangue, moralism, preaching, preachment, rebuke, reprimand, reproof, scolding, sermon, talking-to*, telling off*; SEE CONCEPTS *52,54*

lecture [v1] *give a lesson, speech*
address, declaim, deliver, discourse, expound, get on a soapbox*, give a talk, harangue, hold forth, orate, prelect, recite, speak, spiel*, spout, talk, teach; SEE CONCEPTS *60,266*

lecture [v2] *criticize lengthily*
admonish, berate, chide, exprobate, flay, give going-over*, give piece of mind*, moralize, preach, rank on, rate, reprimand, reprove, scold, sermonize, tell off; SEE CONCEPT *52*

ledge [n] *shelf*
bar, bench, berm, bracket, console, edge, jut, mantle, offset, path, projection, reef, ridge, rim, route, sill, step, strip, tier, track, trail, walk, way; SEE CONCEPTS *445,513*

leer [n/v] *look at longingly*
eye, eyeball*, gloat, goggle*, ogle, smirk, sneer, squint, stare, wink; SEE CONCEPT *623*

leery [adj] *suspicious*
careful, cautious, chary, distrustful, doubting, dubious, on one's guard*, shy, skeptical, uncertain, unsure, wary; SEE CONCEPT *529*

leeway [n] *room to move, grow*
elbow room*, extent, headway, latitude, margin, play, scope, space; SEE CONCEPT *739*

left [adj1] *on west side when facing north*
hard to left, larboard, near, nigh side, port, portside, sinister, sinistral, south; SEE CONCEPTS *581,583*

left [adj2] *politically radical*
leftist, left-wing, liberal, progressive, revolutionary, socialist; SEE CONCEPT *529*

left [adj3] *abandoned*
continuing, departed, extra, forsaken, gone out, leftover, marooned, over, remaining, residual, split, staying; SEE CONCEPT *577*

left-handed [*adj1*] *clumsy*
awkward, backhanded, careless, fumbling, gauche, heavy-handed, maladroit; SEE CONCEPT *584*

left-handed [*adj2*] *insincere, ironic*
ambidextrous, ambiguous, backhanded*, double, enigmatic, equivocal, hypocritical, indirect, sardonic; SEE CONCEPT *267*

leftover [*n*] *remainder, remains*
debris, leavings, legacy, oddments, odds and ends*, orts, remnants, residue, scraps, surplus, survivor, trash; SEE CONCEPTS *260,457*

leftover [*adj*] *remaining, excess*
extra, residual, surplus, unconsumed, uneaten, untouched, unused, unwanted; SEE CONCEPTS *560,771*

leg [*n*] *appendage used for support*
brace, column, lap, limb, member, part, pile, pole, portion, post, prop, section, segment, shank, stage, stake, stilt, stretch, stump, support, upright; SEE CONCEPTS *392,471,832*

legacy [*n*] *inheritance, heritage*
bequest, birthright, devise, endowment, estate, gift, heirloom, patrimony, throwback, tradition; SEE CONCEPTS *337,710*

legal [*adj*] *allowable, permissible*
acknowledged, allowed, authorized, card-carrying*, chartered, clean*, condign, constitutional, contractual, decreed, due, enforced, enforcible, enjoined, fair, forensic, granted, innocent, judged, judicial, juridical, just, justifiable, justified, lawful, legalized, legit*, legitimate, licit, on the level*, on up and up*, ordained, passed, precedented, prescribed, proper, protected, right, rightful, sanctioned, sound, statutory, straight, sure enough, valid, warranted, within the law; SEE CONCEPT *319*

legalize [*v*] *allow, validate*
approve, authorize, clean up, codify, constitute, decree, decriminalize, enact, formulate, launder, legislate, legitimate, legitimatize, license, ordain, permit, regulate, sanction; SEE CONCEPTS *298, 317*

legend [*n1*] *story of the past, often fictitious*
fable, fiction, folklore, folk story, folk tale, lore, myth, mythology, mythos, narrative, saga, tale, tradition; SEE CONCEPT *282*

legend [*n2*] *brief description in document*
cipher, code, device, epigraph, epitaph, head, heading, inscription, key, motto, rubric, table, underline; SEE CONCEPTS *268,270*

legendary [*adj1*] *fictitious but well known*
allegorical, apocryphal, created, customary, doubtful, dubious, fabled, fabricated, fabulous, fanciful, figmental, handed-down, imaginary, imaginative, improbable, invented, mythical, mythological, related, romantic, storied, told, traditional, unhistoric, unhistorical, unreal, unverifiable; SEE CONCEPTS *267,552*

legendary [*adj2*] *famous*
celebrated, famed, illustrious, immortal, renowned, well-known; SEE CONCEPT *568*

legible [*adj*] *easy to read*
clear, coherent, decipherable, distinct, easily read, intelligible, lucid, neat, plain, readable, sharp, understandable; SEE CONCEPTS *267,535,576*

legion [*n*] *mass, force of people*
army, body, brigade, cloud, company, division, drove, flock, group, horde, host, multitude, myriad, number, phalanx, rout, scores, throng, troop; SEE CONCEPTS *322,387,417*

legion [*adj*] *numerous*
countless, many, multifarious, multitudinal, multitudinous, myriad, numberless, populous, several, sundry, various, very many, voluminous; SEE CONCEPTS *762,781*

legislation [*n*] *law of a government*
act, bill, charter, codification, constitution, enactment, lawmaking, measure, prescription, regulation, ruling, statute; SEE CONCEPT *318*

legislative [*adj*] *lawmaking*
aldermanic, congressional, decreeing, enacting, jurisdictive, lawgiving, legislational, legislatorial, ordaining, parliamentarian, parliamentary, senatorial, statute-making, synodical; SEE CONCEPT *319*

legislator [*n*] *person in government who makes laws*
administrator, alderman/woman, assemblyman/woman, congressman/woman, councilman/woman, deputy, lawgiver, lawmaker, leader, member, parliamentarian, representative, senator; SEE CONCEPT *354*

legislature [*n*] *governmental body, most often elected, that makes laws*
assembly, body, chamber, congress, council, diet, house, house of representatives, lawmakers, parliament, plenum, senate, voice of people; SEE CONCEPT *299*

legitimate [*adj*] *authentic, valid, legal*
accepted, accredited, acknowledged, admissible, appropriate, authorized, canonical, certain, cogent, consistent, correct, customary, fair, genuine, innocent, just, justifiable, lawful, licit, logical, natural, normal, official, on the level, on the up and up, orthodox, probable, proper, real, reasonable, received, recognized, regular, reliable, rightful, sanctioned, sensible, sound, statutory, sure, true, typical, usual, verifiable, warranted, well-founded; SEE CONCEPTS *319,558,582*

leisure [*n*] *free time and its activities*
chance, convenience, ease, freedom, holiday, idle hours, intermission, leave of absence, liberty, one's own sweet time*, opportunity, pause, quiet, range, recess, recreation, relaxation, repose, requiescence, respite, rest, retirement, sabbatical, scope, spare moments*, spare time, time, time off*, unemployment, vacant hour*, vacation; SEE CONCEPTS *363,681,807*

leisurely [*adj*] *casual, unhurried*
comfortable, delayed, deliberate, dilatory, easy, free, gentle, laggard, laid-back*, languid, lax, lazy, relaxed, restful, retarded, slack, slackened, slow, slow-moving, unhasty; SEE CONCEPTS *550,584,799*

leisurely [*adv*] *casually, unhurriedly*
at one's convenience*, at one's leisure, calmly, comfortably, composedly, deliberately, dilatorily, easily, gradually, inactively, indolently, laggardly, langorously, languidly, lazily, lethargically, lingeringly, listlessly, slowly, sluggishly, taking one's time*, tardily, torpidly, with delay, without haste; SEE CONCEPTS *544,584,799*

lend [*v*] *loan, accommodate*
add, advance, afford, allow, bestow, confer, contribute, entrust, extend, furnish, give, grant, impart, lay on one, lend-lease, let, loan shark, oblige, permit, present, provide, shark, stake, supply, trust; SEE CONCEPTS *115,140*

length [*n*] *extent of object, distance, time*
breadth, compass, continuance, diameter, dimension, duration, elongation, endlessness, expanse, expansion, extensiveness, height, interval, lastingness, lengthiness, limit, linearity, loftiness, longitude, longness, magnitude, measure, mileage, orbit, panorama, period, piece, portion, protractedness, purview, quantity, radius, range, ranginess, reach, realm, remoteness, season, section, segment, space, spaciousness, span, stretch, stride, tallness, term, unit, width, year; SEE CONCEPTS *651,721,743, 787,804*

lengthen [*v*] *extend*
amplify, augment, continue, dilate, distend, drag out, draw, draw out*, elongate, expand, increase, let out, make longer, pad, proceed, prolong, prolongate, protract, reach, spin out*, stretch, string out*; SEE CONCEPTS *236,239,245*

lengthy [*adj*] *extended*
diffuse, dragging, drawn-out, elongate, elongated, interminable, lengthened, long, longish, long-winded, overlong, padded, prolix, prolonged, protracted, tedious, tiresome, verbose, very long, wearisome, windy, wordy; SEE CONCEPTS *267, 482,782*

lenient [*adj*] *permissive*
allowing, amiable, assuaging, assuasive, being big*, benign, benignant, charitable, clement, compassionate, complaisant, compliant, condoning, easy, easygoing, emollient, excusing, favoring, forbearing, forgiving, gentle, going easy on*, good-natured, humoring, indulgent, kind, kindly, letting, live with*, loving, merciful, mild, mollycoddling*, obliging, pampering, pardoning, permitting, soft, softhearted, soft-shell*, sparing, spoiling, sympathetic, tender, tolerant, yielding; SEE CONCEPTS *401,542*

less [*adj*] *smaller, inferior*
beneath, declined, deficient, depressed, diminished, excepting, fewer, lacking, lesser, limited, lower, minor, minus, negative, not as great, reduced, secondary, shortened, shorter, slighter, subordinate, subtracting, unsubstantial, without; SEE CONCEPTS *574,762,789*

less [*adv*] *little*
barely, in a lower degree, meagerly, to a smaller extent; SEE CONCEPTS *530,544*

lessen [*v*] *lower, reduce*
abate, abridge, amputate, attenuate, become smaller, clip, close, contract, crop, curtail, cut, cut back, decline, decrease, de-escalate, degrade, die down, dilute, diminish, downsize, drain, dwindle, ease, erode, grow less, impair, lighten, minify, minimize, mitigate, moderate, narrow, roll back, shrink, slacken, slack up, slow down, soft-pedal*, take the bite out*, take the edge off*, take the sting out*, taper, taper off, thin, truncate, weaken, wind down; SEE CONCEPTS *247,698,776*

lesser [*adj*] *inferior, secondary*
a notch under*, bottom, bush, bush-league*, dinky*, insignificant, less important, low, lower, minor, minor-league*, nether, second-fiddle*, second-string*, slighter, small, small-fry*, small-time*, subjacent, subordinate, third-string*, undersized; SEE CONCEPTS *575,793*

lesson [*n1*] *information taught*
assignment, chalk talk*, class, coaching, drill, education, exercise, homework, instruction, lecture, period, practice, quiz, reading, recitation, schooling, study, task, teaching, test, tutoring; SEE CONCEPTS *274,285,287*

lesson [*n2*] *helpful example, communication*
admonition, censure, chiding, deterrent, exemplar, helpful word, message, model, moral, noble action, notice, precept, punishment, rebuke, reprimand, reproof, scolding, warning; SEE CONCEPTS *123,661,688*

let [*v1*] *allow*
accredit, approve, authorize, be big*, cause, certify, commission, concede, enable, endorse, free up, give, give leave, give okay, give permission, grant, have, hear of, leave, license, live with, make, permit, sanction, sit still for*, suffer, tolerate, warrant; SEE CONCEPTS *50,83,88*

let [*v2*] *rent out object, property*
charter, hire, lease, sublease, sublet; SEE CONCEPTS *89,115*

letdown [*n*] *disappointment*
anticlimax, balk, bitter pill*, blow, chagrin, comedown, disgruntlement, disillusionment, frustration, setback, washout*; SEE CONCEPTS *410,728*

let down [*v*] *disappoint*
abandon, depress, disenchant, disillusion, dissatisfy, fail, fall short, leave in lurch*, leave stranded*, lower, pull down, take down; SEE CONCEPTS *7,19*

lethal [*adj*] *deadly*
baleful, dangerous, deathly, destructive, devastating, fatal, harmful, hurtful, malignant, mortal, mortiferous, mortuary, murderous, necrotic, noxious, perni-

cious, pestilent, pestilential, poisonous, virulent; SEE CONCEPT 537

lethargic [adj] *lazy, sluggish*
apathetic, blah*, comatose, debilitated, dilatory, dopey, dormant, draggy*, drippy*, drowsy, dull, enervated, having spring fever*, heavy, idle, impassive, inactive, indifferent, inert, lackadaisical, laggard, laid-back*, languid, languorous, listless, moony*, nebbish, out of it*, passive, phlegmatic, sleepy, sleepyhead*, slothful, slow, slumberous, snoozy, somnolent, spiritless, stolid, stretchy, stupefied, stupid, supine, torpid, wimpy*; SEE CONCEPTS 401,403,584

lethargy [n] *laziness, sluggishness*
apathy, coma, disinterest, disregard, drowsiness, dullness, hebetude, heedlessness, idleness, impassivity, inaction, inactivity, inanition, indifference, indolence, inertia, inertness, insouciance, languor, lassitude, listlessness, passiveness, phlegm, sleep, sleepiness, sloth, slowness, slumber, stupor, supineness, torpidity, torpidness, torpor, unconcern, unmindfulness; SEE CONCEPTS 315,410,633,748

let off [v] *make not subject to punishment or action*
abandon, absolve, discharge, dispense, drop, excuse, exempt, exonerate, forgive, let go, pardon, privilege from, release, relieve, remove, spare; SEE CONCEPTS 50,83,88,317

let on [v] *acknowledge, admit*
allow, avow, betray, concede, confess, disclose, divulge, give away, grant, hint, imply, indicate, let out, make known, mouth*, own, own up*, reveal, say, spill*, suggest, tell, uncover, unveil; SEE CONCEPTS 57,60

letter [n1] *symbol of an alphabet*
ABCs*, alphabet, cap, capital, character, majuscule, minuscule, rune, sign, small letter, type, uncial; SEE CONCEPT 284

letter [n2] *written communication*
acknowledgment, answer, billet, dispatch, epistle, junk mail*, kite, line, memo, memorandum, message, missive, note, postcard, reply, report, thank you; SEE CONCEPTS 271,278

let up [v] *pause*
abate, cease, decrease, die down, die out, diminish, ease, ease off, ease up, ebb, fall, moderate, release, relent, slacken, slow down, stop, subside, wane; SEE CONCEPTS 240,698

let-up [n] *pause*
abatement, break, cessation, interval, lapse, lessening, lull, recess, remission, respite, slackening; SEE CONCEPT 807

level [n1] *horizontal position or thing*
altitude, elevation, floor, height, layer, plain, plane, story, stratum, surface, zone; SEE CONCEPTS 738,744

level [n2] *rank, position*
achievement, degree, grade, stage, standard, standing, status; SEE CONCEPTS 286,388

level [adj] *smooth, balanced*
akin, aligned, alike, calm, commensurate, common, comparable, consistent, constant, continuous, equable, equivalent, even, exact, flat, flush, horizontal, identical, in line, leveled, like, lined up, matched, matching, of same height, on a line, on a par, on one plane, parallel, plain, planate, plane, planed, polished, precise, proportionate, regular, rolled, same, stable, steady, straight, trim, trimmed, unbroken, unfluctuating, uniform, uninterrupted; SEE CONCEPTS 401,490,566

level [v1] *make even*
equalize, equate, even, even off, even out, flatten, flush, grade, lay, make equal, make flat, mow, plane, press, roll, smooth, smoothen, straighten, surface; SEE CONCEPT 250

level [v2] *destroy, demolish*
bring down, bulldoze*, devastate, down*, drop, equalize, fell, flatten, floor, ground, knock down, knock over, lay low, mow*, pull down, raze, ruin, smooth, tear down, waste*, wreck; SEE CONCEPTS 208,252

level [v3] *be honest*
be aboveboard, be frank, be on the up and up*, be open, be straight, be straightforward, be up-front*, come clean*, come to terms*, keep nothing back*, talk straight*, tell the truth; SEE CONCEPT 49

level [v4] *aim, direct*
address, beam, cast, focus, incline, lay, point, slant, train, turn, zero in on; SEE CONCEPT 187

levelheaded [adj] *reasonable, calm*
all there*, balanced, collected, commonsensical, composed, cool, cool as cucumber*, coolheaded*, dependable, discreet, even-tempered, far-sighted, in one's right mind*, judicious, practical, prudent, rational, sane, self-possessed, sensible, steady, together, unflappable, wise, with all marbles*; SEE CONCEPTS 403,542

leverage [n] *influence*
advantage, ascendancy, authority, bargaining chip*, break, clout, drag, edge, grease*, jump on*, power, pull, rank, ropes*, suction, weight; SEE CONCEPTS 686,693

levity [n] *funniness, silliness*
absurdity, amusement, buoyancy, facetiousness, festivity, fickleness, flightiness, flippancy, folly, foolishness, frivolity, giddiness, happiness, high spirits, hilarity, jocularity, laughs, lightheartedness, mirth, picnic*, pleasantry, repartee, trifling, triviality, volatility, wit; SEE CONCEPTS 273,410

levy [n] *assessment, tax*
burden, collection, custom, duty, exaction, excise, fee, gathering, imposition, impost, muster, tariff, toll; SEE CONCEPT 329

levy [v] *assess, impose*
call, call up, charge, collect, demand, exact, extort, gather, lay on, place, put on, raise, set, summon, tax, wrest, wring; SEE CONCEPT 330

lewd [*adj*] *vulgar, indecent*
bawdy, blue, coarse, erotic, fast*, filthy*, foul-mouthed, gross*, hard-core*, immodest, immoral, improper, impure, in bad taste, incontinent, indelicate, lascivious, lecherous, libertine, libidinous, licentious, loose*, lustful, naughty, obscene, off-color*, pornographic, profligate, questionable, racy*, rakish, ribald, risque, salacious, scandalous, scurrilous, shameless, smutty, suggestive, taboo, unchaste, unclean, unconventional, unvirtuous, vile, wanton, wicked, X-rated*; SEE CONCEPTS *372,542,545*

lexicon [*n*] *collection of word meanings, usage*
dictionary, glossary, terminology, thesaurus, vocabulary, wordbook, wordlist, word stock; SEE CONCEPTS *276,280*

liability [*n1*] *answerability, responsibility*
accountability, accountableness, amenability, amenableness, arrearage, blame, burden, compulsion, culpability, debt, duty, indebtedness, obligation, onus, owing, subjection, susceptibility; SEE CONCEPT *645*

liability [*n2*] *burden, debt*
account, arrear, arrearage, bad news*, baggage*, balance, bite*, chance, chit*, contingency, contract, damage, debit, disadvantage, drag*, drawback, due*, encumbrance, handicap, hindrance, impediment, inconvenience, indebtedness, indebtment, involvement, IOU*, lease, loan, millstone*, minus, misfortune, mortgage, nuisance, obligation, onus, pledge, possibility, remainder, responsibility, tab; SEE CONCEPTS *332,674*

liability [*n3*] *chance, probability*
exposure, likelihood, openness, proneness, susceptibility, tendency, vulnerability, vulnerableness; SEE CONCEPTS *650,657*

liable [*adj1*] *answerable, responsible*
accountable, amenable, bound, chargeable, obligated, subject, tied; SEE CONCEPT *545*

liable [*adj2*] *open, likely*
apt, assailable, attackable, beatable, conquerable, disposed, exposed, given, inclined, in danger, penetrable, prone, sensitive, subject, susceptible, tending, verisimilar, vincible, vulnerable; SEE CONCEPTS *542,552*

liaison [*n1*] *person who acts as go-between*
communication, connection, contact, fixer, hookup, in, interchange, interface, intermediary, link; SEE CONCEPTS *348,354,423*

liaison [*n2*] *love affair*
amour, encounter, entanglement, fling, illicit romance, interlude, intrigue, romance; SEE CONCEPTS *32,388*

liar [*n*] *person who tells falsehood*
cheat, con artist, con man/woman, deceiver, deluder, dissimulator, equivocator, fabler, fabricator, fabulist, false witness, falsifier, fibber, maligner, misleader, perjurer, phony, prevaricator, promoter, storyteller, trickster*; SEE CONCEPT *412*

libel [*n*] *purposeful lie about someone, often malicious*
aspersion, calumny, defamation, denigration, lying, malicious, obloquy, smear, vituperation; SEE CONCEPTS *63,318*

libel [*v*] *purposefully lie about someone*
asperse, bad-mouth*, blacken, blister, burlesque, calumniate, caricature, crack, defame, denigrate, derogate, drag name through mud*, give a black eye*, knock, malign, mark*, mark wrong, revile, roast, scandalize, scorch, sizzle, slur, smear, tear down, traduce, travesty, vilify; SEE CONCEPTS *63,192*

libelous [*adj*] *derogatory*
aspersive, backbiting, calumniatory, calumnious, contumelious, debasing, defamatory, depreciative, detracting, detractory, disparaging, false, injurious, invidious, malevolent, malicious, maligning, opprobrious, pejorative, sarcastic, scurrilous, traducing, untrue, vilifying, vituperative; SEE CONCEPT *267*

liberal [*adj1*] *progressive*
advanced, avant-garde, broad, broad-minded, catholic, enlightened, flexible, free, general, high-minded, humanistic, humanitarian, indulgent, intelligent, interested, latitudinarian, left, lenient, libertarian, loose, magnanimous, permissive, radical, rational, reasonable, receiving, receptive, reformist, tolerant, unbiased, unbigoted, unconventional, understanding, unorthodox, unprejudiced; SEE CONCEPTS *529,542*

liberal [*adj2*] *giving, generous*
altruistic, beneficent, benevolent, bighearted*, bounteous, bountiful, casual, charitable, eleemosynary, exuberant, free, free-and-easy, handsome, kind, lavish, loose, munificent, openhanded, openhearted, philanthropic, princely, prodigal, profuse, Santa Claus*, soft-touch, unselfish, unsparing, unstinging; SEE CONCEPTS *334,401,404*

liberal [*adj3*] *abundant, profuse*
ample, aplenty, bounteous, bountiful, copious, dime a dozen*, galore, generous, handsome, lavish, munificent, no end, plentiful, plenty, rich; SEE CONCEPT *771*

liberate [*v*] *give freedom*
bail one out*, deliver, detach, discharge, disembarrass, emancipate, free, free up*, get out from under*, let loose*, let out*, loose, loosen, manumit, redeem, release, rescue, save, save one's neck*, set free, unbind, unchain, unhook, unshackle; SEE CONCEPTS *83,110*

liberty [*n*] *freedom*
autarchy, authorization, autonomy, birthright, carte blanche, choice, convenience, decision, deliverance, delivery, dispensation, emancipation, enfranchisement, enlightenment, exemption, franchise, free speech, immunity, independence, leave, leisure, liberation, license, opportunity, permission, power of choice, prerogative, privilege, relaxation, release, rest, right, sanction, self-determination, self-government, sovereignty, suffrage, unconstraint; SEE CONCEPTS *388,691*

libidinous [adj] *lustful*
carnal, coarse, concupiscent, debauched, fast, hot*, impure, incontinent, lascivious, lecherous, libertine, loose*, obscene, passionate, prurient, salacious, satyric, sensual, unchaste, wanton, wicked; SEE CONCEPTS 372,545

license [n1] *authority, permission*
authorization, carte blanche*, certificate, charter, consent, dispensation, entitlement, exemption, freedom, go-ahead*, grant, green light*, immunity, independence, latitude, leave, liberty, okay*, permit, privilege, right, self-determination, ticket, unconstraint, warrant; SEE CONCEPT 685

license [n2] *abandon, indulgence*
anarchy, animalism, arrogance, audacity, boldness, complacency, debauchery, disorder, effrontery, excess, forwardness, gluttony, immoderation, impropriety, irresponsibility, lawlessness, laxity, looseness, presumptuousness, prodigality, profligacy, refractoriness, relaxation, relaxedness, sauciness, self-indulgence, sensuality, slackness, temerity, unrestraint, unruliness, wantonness, wildness; SEE CONCEPTS 633,645

license [v] *authorize*
accredit, allow, certify, commission, empower, enable, let, permit, privilege, sanction, suffer, warrant; SEE CONCEPTS 50,83,88

licentious [adj] *immoral, uncontrolled*
abandoned, amoral, animal, carnal, corrupt, debauched, depraved, desirous, disorderly, dissolute, fast, fast and loose*, fleshly, impure, incontinent, in the fast lane*, lascivious, lax, lecherous, lewd, libertine, libidinous, lickerish, loose*, lubricous, lustful, oversexed, profligate, promiscuous, relaxed, reprobate, salacious, satyric, scabrous, sensual, swinging, unconstrained, uncontrollable, uncurbed, unmoral, unprincipled, unruly, wanton; SEE CONCEPTS 372,401,545

lick [n] *light touch; little amount*
bit, brush, cast, dab, dash, hint, sample, smack, speck, stroke, suggestion, taste, tinge, trace, whiff; SEE CONCEPTS 612,831

lick [v1] *touch with tongue*
brush, calm, caress, fondle, glance, gloss, graze, lap, lap against, move over, osculate, pass over, play, quiet, ripple, rub, soothe, stroke, sweep, taste, tongue, touch, tranquilize, wash; SEE CONCEPTS 185,612

lick [v2] *play over with fire*
blaze, burn, dart, flick, flicker, fluctuate, flutter, ignite, kindle, leap, palpitate, quiver, ripple, run over, shoot, touch, tremble, vacillate, vibrate, waver; SEE CONCEPTS 249,612

lick [v3] *defeat, sometimes by hitting*
beat, best, clobber, conquer, down, excel, flog, hit, hurdle, lambaste, master, outdo, outstrip, overcome, overwhelm, rout, slap, smear, smother, spank, strike, surmount, surpass, thrash, throw, top, trim, trounce, vanquish, wallop, whip; SEE CONCEPTS 95,141,189

lid [n] *top covering*
cap, cover, hood, roof, top; SEE CONCEPT 836

lie [n] *untruth*
aspersion, backbiting, calumniation, calumny, deceit, deception, defamation, detraction, dishonesty, disinformation, distortion, evasion, fable, fabrication, falsehood, falseness, falsification, falsity, fib, fiction, forgery, fraudulence, guile, hyperbole, inaccuracy, invention, libel, mendacity, misrepresentation, misstatement, myth, obloquy, perjury, prevarication, revilement, reviling, slander, subterfuge, tale, tall story*, vilification, white lie*, whopper; SEE CONCEPTS 63,278

lie [v1] *tell an untruth*
bear false witness, beguile, be untruthful, break promise, bull*, con, concoct, deceive, delude, dissemble, dissimulate, distort, dupe*, equivocate, exaggerate, fabricate, fake, falsify, fib, forswear, frame, fudge, go back on*, invent, make believe, malign, misguide, misinform, misinstruct, mislead, misrepresent, misspeak, misstate, overdraw, palter, perjure, pervert, phony, plant*, prevaricate, promote, put on*, put up a front*, queer*, snow*, softsoap*, string along*, victimize; SEE CONCEPT 63

lie [v2] *be prostrate, flat*
be prone, be recumbent, be supine, couch, go to bed*, laze, lie down, loll, lounge, nap, recline, repose, rest, retire, siesta, sleep, sprawl, stretch out, turn in; SEE CONCEPTS 154,201

lie [v3] *be situated*
be, be beside, be buried, be established, be even, be fixed, be found, be interred, be level, be located, belong, be on, be placed, be seated, beset, be smooth, exist, extend, have its seat in, occupy, prevail, reach, remain, spread, stretch; SEE CONCEPT 746

life [n1] *animation, spirit*
activity, being, breath, brio, dash, élan*, élan vital*, energy, enthusiasm, entity, esprit, essence, excitement, get-up-and-go*, go*, growth, heart, high spirits, impulse, lifeblood, liveliness, oomph*, sentience, soul, sparkle, verve, viability, vigor, vitality, vivacity, zest*, zing*; SEE CONCEPT 411

life [n2] *existence, duration*
being, career, continuance, course, cycle, days, endurance, epoch, era, expectancy, extent, generation, history, length, life span, lifetime, longevity, orbit, period, pilgrimage, record, season, span, survival, time; SEE CONCEPTS 816,817

life [n3] *being*
animal, animateness, animation, body, breath, consciousness, continuance, creature, endurance, entity, essence, existence, flesh, flesh and blood*, growth, human, human being, individual, living, living being, living thing, man, metabolism, mortal, mortal being, organism, person, personage, presence, soul, subsistence, substantiality, survival, symbiosis, via-

bility, vitality, vital spark*, wildlife, woman; SEE
CONCEPT *389*

life [n4] *history, biography*
autobiography, bio, career, confession, curriculum
vitae, journal, life story, memoir, memorial, story;
SEE CONCEPT *271*

life [n5] *person's experiences*
attainment, behavior, circumstances, conduct, development, enjoyment, enlightenment, growth, hand
one is dealt*, happiness, human condition, journey,
knowledge, lifestyle, participation, personality, realization, suffering, trials and tribulations*, vicissi-
tudes, way of life*, world; SEE CONCEPT *678*

lifeless [adj1] *not living, not containing living things*
asleep, bare, barren, brute, cold, comatose, dead,
deceased, defunct, departed, desert, empty, exanimate, extinct, faint, inanimate, inert, inorganic, insensate, insensible, late, out cold*, sterile,
unconscious, uninhabited, waste; SEE CONCEPTS
485,539

lifeless [adj2] *dull, spiritless*
blah*, cold, colorless, drab, draggy*, dull, flat, hollow, insipid, lackluster, lethargic, listless, lusterless,
nothing*, pabulum*, passive, prosaic, prosy, slothful, slow*, sluggish, spent, static, stiff*, torpid,
wooden*, zero*; SEE CONCEPTS *401,542,584*

lifelong [adj] *lasting*
constant, continuing, deep-rooted, enduring, for life,
inveterate, lifetime, livelong, long-lasting, long-
lived, long-standing, old, perennial, permanent, persistent; SEE CONCEPT *798*

lifetime [n] *span of animate being's existence*
all one's born days*, career, continuance, course,
cradle to grave*, days, endurance, existence, life,
life span, natural life, period, time; SEE CONCEPT *817*

lifework [n] *person's calling*
business, career, interest, mission, occupation, profession, purpose, pursuit, vocation, work; SEE CON-
CEPTS *349,360*

lift [n1] *transportation*
car ride, drive, journey, passage, ride, run, transport;
SEE CONCEPT *155*

lift [n2] *help, aid*
assist, assistance, boost, comfort, encouragement,
hand, leg up*, pick-me-up*, reassurance, relief,
secours, shot in the arm*, succor, support; SEE CON-
CEPTS *110,700*

lift [v1] *move upwards; ascend*
arise, aspire, bear aloft, boost, bring up, build up,
buoy up, climb, come up, disappear, disperse, dissipate, draw up, elevate, erect, goose*, heft, hike,
hike up, hoist, jack up, jump up, mount, move up,
pick up, put up, raise, raise high, rear, rise, soar,
take up, up, upheave, uphold, uplift, upraise, uprear,
vanish; SEE CONCEPTS *196,200,236,245*

lift [v2] *repeal, revoke*
annul, cancel, countermand, dismantle, end, recall,
relax, remove, rescind, reverse, stop, terminate; SEE
CONCEPTS *234,317*

lift [v3] *steal*
abstract, appropriate, cop, copy, crib, filch, hook,
nip, pilfer, pinch, pirate, plagiarize, pocket, purloin,
snitch, swipe, take, thieve; SEE CONCEPTS *139,200*

lift [v4] *promote, improve*
advance, ameliorate, boost, build up, dignify, elevate, enhance, exalt, hike, jack up, raise, support,
upgrade; SEE CONCEPTS *110,244*

ligature [n] *link*
band, bandage, binding, bond, connection, knot, ligament, nexus, rope, tie, yoke; SEE CONCEPTS *471,831*

light [n1] *luminescence from sun or other source*
aurora, beacon, blaze, brightness, brilliance, brilliancy, bulb, candle, coruscation, dawn, daybreak,
daylight, daytime, effulgence, emanation, flare,
flash, fulgor, glare, gleam, glimmer, glint, glitter,
glow, illumination, incandescence, irradiation, lambency, lamp, lantern, lighthouse, luminosity, luster,
morn, morning, phosphorescence, radiance, radiation, ray, refulgence, scintillation, sheen, shine,
sparkle, splendor, star, sun, sunbeam, sunrise, sunshine, taper, torch, window; SEE CONCEPTS
620,624,628,810

light [n2] *context, point of view; understanding*
angle, approach, aspect, attitude, awareness, comprehension, condition, education, elucidation, enlightenment, example, exemplar, explanation,
illustration, information, insight, interpretation,
knowledge, model, paragon, slant, standing, vantage
point, viewpoint; SEE CONCEPTS *274,409,682,688*

light [adj1] *illuminated*
ablaze, aglow, bright, brilliant, burnished, clear,
cloudless, flashing, fluorescent, glossy, glowing,
lambent, lucent, luminous, lustrous, phosphorescent,
polished, radiant, refulgent, resplendent, rich, scin-
tillant, shining, shiny, sunny, unclouded, unob-
scured, vivid, well-lighted, well-lit; SEE CONCEPTS
617,618

light [adj2] *blond, fair*
bleached, faded, fair-skinned, light-hued, light-
skinned, light-toned, pale, pastel, tow-headed; SEE
CONCEPTS *406,618*

light [adj3] *not heavy*
agile, airy, atmospheric, buoyant, crumbly, dainty,
delicate, downy, easy, effervescent, ethereal, featherweight, feathery, filmy, flimsy, floatable, floating,
fluffy, friable, frothy, gossamery, graceful, imponderous, inconsequential, insubstantial, light-footed,
lightweight, lithe, little, loose, meager, nimble,
petty, porous, portable, sandy, sheer, slender, slight,
small, spongy, sprightly, sylphlike, thin, tissuelike,
trifling, trivial, unheavy, unsubstantial, weightless;
SEE CONCEPT *491*

light [adj4] *small in amount, content*
casual, digestible, faint, fractional, fragmentary,
frivolous, frugal, gentle, hardly any, hardly enough,
inadequate, inconsequential, inconsiderable, indistinct, insignificant, insufficient, mild, minor, minus-

cule, minute, moderate, modest, not many, not much, not rich, puny, restricted, scanty, shoestring*, slight, soft, sparse, superficial, thin, tiny, trifling, trivial, unimportant, unsubstantial, weak, wee; SEE CONCEPTS *762,789*

light [*adj5*] *simple, easy*
effortless, facile, manageable, moderate, smooth, undemanding, unexacting, untaxing, untroublesome; SEE CONCEPT *538*

light [*adj6*] *funny, cheery*
airy, amusing, animated, blithe, carefree, cheerful, chipper*, chirpy, diverting, dizzy, entertaining, fickle, flighty, frivolous, gay, giddy, high, humorous, lighthearted, lively, merry, perky, pleasing, sunny, sunny-side up*, superficial, trifling, trivial, up, upbeat, witty; SEE CONCEPTS *401,542*

light [*v1*] *illuminate*
animate, brighten, cast, fire, flood, floodlight, furnish with light, highlight, ignite, illume, illumine, inflame, irradiate, kindle, lighten, light up, limelight, make bright, make visible, put on, shine, spot, spotlight, switch on, turn on; SEE CONCEPTS *250,624*

light [*v2*] *start on fire*
burn, enkindle, fire, flame, ignite, inflame, kindle, set fire to, set on fire, spark, strike a match; SEE CONCEPT *249*

light [*v3*] *step down; land*
alight, arrive, come down, deplane, detrain, disembark, drop, fly down, get down, perch, rest, roost, set down, settle, settle down, sit, sit down, stop, touch down; SEE CONCEPTS *159,181*

lighten [*v1*] *illuminate*
become light, brighten, flash, gleam, illume, irradiate, light, light up, make bright, shine; SEE CONCEPT *624*

lighten [*v2*] *reduce weight, load*
allay, alleviate, ameliorate, assuage, attenuate, buoy, change, comfort, cut down, decrease, dilute, disburden, disencumber, ease, empty, eradicate, extenuate, facilitate, free, jettison, lessen, levitate, make less, make lighter, mitigate, mollify, pour out, put off, reduce, relieve, remove, shift, take, take a load off*, thin, throw out, unburden, unload, uplight, upraise; SEE CONCEPTS *110,244,250*

lighten [*v3*] *cheer up; inspire*
brighten, buoy up, cheer, elate, encourage, gladden, hearten, lift, perk up, revive, take a load off; SEE CONCEPTS *7,22*

light-headed [*adj*] *silly; feeling faint*
changeable, delirious, dizzy, empty, faint, featherbrained*, fickle, flighty, flippant, foolish, frivolous, gaga*, giddy, harebrained*, hazy, punchy*, reeling, rocky, scatterbrained*, shallow, superficial, swimming, swimmy, tired, trifling, vertiginous, whirling, woozy*; SEE CONCEPTS *314,401*

lighthearted [*adj*] *carefree, untroubled*
blithe, blithesome, bright, buoyant, cheerful, effervescent, expansive, feelgood*, frolicsome, gay,

glad, gleeful, happy, happy-go-lucky*, high-spirited, insouciant, jocund, jolly, jovial, joyful, joyous, laid-back, lightsome, lively, merry, playful, resilient, spirited, sprightly, sunny, upbeat, vivacious, volatile; SEE CONCEPTS *404,542*

lightly [*adv*] *gently, effortlessly*
agilely, airily, breezily, carelessly, casually, daintily, delicately, easily, ethereally, faintly, flippantly, freely, frivolously, gingerly, heedlessly, indifferently, leniently, mildly, moderately, nimbly, peacefully, quietly, readily, simply, slightingly, slightly, smoothly, softly, sparingly, sparsely, subtly, tenderly, tenuously, thinly, thoughtlessly, timidly, unsubstantially, well; SEE CONCEPTS *538,544,584*

light out [*v*] *run away*
abscond, depart, escape, head, leave, make, make off, quit, set out, strike out, take a hike, take off; SEE CONCEPT *195*

lightweight [*adj*] *inconsequential*
failing, featherweight, foolish, imponderous, incompetent, insignificant, of no account, paltry, petty, slight, trifling, trivial, unimportant, weightless, worthless; SEE CONCEPTS *491,575*

likable [*adj*] *nice, pleasant*
agreeable, amiable, appealing, attractive, charismatic, charming, engaging, enjoyable, friendly, genial, good, good-natured, pleasing, preferable, relishable, sweet, sweet-natured, sympathetic, winning, winsome; SEE CONCEPT *404*

like [*adj*] *similar*
according to, agnate, akin, alike, allied, allying, analogous, approximating, approximative, close, coextensive, cognate, commensurate, comparable, compatible, conforming, congeneric, congenerous, consistent, consonant, corresponding, double, equal, equaling, equivalent, homologous, identical, in the manner of, jibing, matching, much the same, near, not far from, not unlike, on the order of, parallel, related, relating, resembling, same, selfsame, such, twin, undifferentiated, uniform; SEE CONCEPTS *487,573*

like [*v1*] *enjoy, be fond of*
admire, adore, appreciate, approve, be gratified by, be keen on, be partial to, be pleased by, be sweet on, care for, care to, cherish, delight in, derive pleasure from, dig, dote on, esteem, exclaim, fancy, feast on, find appealing, get a kick out of*, go for*, hanker for, hold dear, indulge in, love, luxuriate in, prize, rejoice in, relish, revel in, savor, stuck on*, take an interest in, take delight in, take satisfaction in, take to; SEE CONCEPT *32*

like [*v2*] *choose, feel inclined*
care to, choose to, desire, elect, fancy, feel disposed, feel like, have a preference for, incline toward, please, prefer, select, want, will, wish; SEE CONCEPTS *20,41*

likelihood [*n*] *chance of something happening*
coin flip*, direction, even break, fair shake, fifty-fifty*, fighting chance*, good chance*, liability, like-

liness, long shot*, outside chance*, plausibility, possibility, presumption, probability, prospect, reasonableness, shot at*, strong possibility, tendency, toss-up*, trend; SEE CONCEPT *650*

likely [*adj*] *probable, apt, hopeful*
acceptable, achievable, anticipated, assuring, attainable, believeable, conceivable, conjecturable, credible, destined, disposed, expected, fair, favorite, feasible, given to, imaginable, inclined, in favor of, inferable, in the cards*, in the habit of*, liable, odds-on*, on the verge of, ostensible, plausible, possible, practicable, predisposed, presumable, promising, prone, rational, reasonable, seeming, subject to, supposable, tending, thinkable, true, up-and-coming*, verisimilar, workable; SEE CONCEPT *552*

likely [*adv*] *probably*
assumably, doubtless, doubtlessly, in all likelihood, in all probability, like as not, most likely, no doubt, presumably, presumptively, prima facie, seemingly, to all appearances; SEE CONCEPT *552*

likeness [*n*] *correspondence in appearance; something that corresponds*
affinity, agreement, alikeness, analogousness, analogy, appearance, carbon, clone, comparableness, comparison, conformity, copy, counterpart, dead ringer*, delineation, depiction, ditto*, double, effigy, equality, equivalence, facsimile, form, guise, identicalness, identity, image, knock-off*, lookalike*, model, parallelism, photocopy, photograph, picture, portrait, replica, representation, reproduction, resemblance, sameness, semblance, similarity, simile, similitude, study, uniformity, Xerox; SEE CONCEPTS *664,670,716*

likewise [*adj*] *also, similarly*
additionally, along, as well, besides, correspondingly, further, furthermore, in addition, in like manner, in the same way, more, moreover, so, too, withal; SEE CONCEPT *563*

liking [*n*] *fondness, taste*
affection, affinity, appetite, appreciation, attachment, attraction, bent, bias, desire, devotion, fancy, favoritism, inclination, love, mind, palate, partiality, passion, penchant, pleasure, predilection, preference, proneness, propensity, relish, soft spot*, stomach, sympathy, tendency, tooth, velleity, weakness, will; SEE CONCEPTS *20,32,529*

limb [*n*] *appendage*
arm, bough, branch, extension, extremity, fin, gam*, leg, lobe, member, offshoot, part, pin, pinion, process, projection, spray, sprig, spur, stem, switch, unit, wheel, wing; SEE CONCEPTS *392,428*

limber [*adj*] *flexible*
agile, deft, elastic, graceful, lissome, lithe, lithesome, loose, nimble, plastic, pliable, pliant, resilient, springy, spry, supple; SEE CONCEPTS *406,488*

limbo [*n*] *state of uncertainty*
demilitarized zone, left field*, no-man's-land*, nothingness, nowhere, oblivion, out there*, Siberia*; SEE CONCEPTS *679,705*

limit [*n1*] *greatest extent*
absolute, bitter end*, border, bottom line*, bound, bourne, breaking point*, brim, brink, cap, ceiling, check, circumscription, conclusion, confinement, confines, curb, cutoff point*, deadline, destination, edge, end, end point, extremity, far out, farthest point, farthest reach, fence, finality, goal, limitation, margin, maximum, obstruction, restraint, restriction, rim, termination, the max*, the most*, tops*, ultimate, utmost, verge; SEE CONCEPTS *5,529,548,832*

limit [*n2*] *physical boundary*
border, borderland, compass, confines, edge, end, extent, extreme, extremity, frontier, perimeter, periphery, precinct, purlieu; SEE CONCEPTS *513,745*

limit [*v*] *confine, restrict*
appoint, assign, bar, bottle up, bound, cap, check, circumscribe, constrict, contract, cork, cramp, curb, define, delimit, delimitate, demarcate, draw the line, fix, hem in, hinder, inhibit, keep the lid on*, lessen, narrow, prescribe, ration, reduce, restrain, set, specify; SEE CONCEPTS *5,130*

limitation [*n*] *restraint, disadvantage*
bar, block, check, circumspection, condition, constraint, control, cramp, curb, definition, drawback, impediment, inhibition, injunction, modification, obstruction, qualification, reservation, restriction, snag, stint, stricture, taboo; SEE CONCEPTS *666,674*

limited [*adj1*] *restricted, definite*
bound, bounded, checked, circumscribed, confined, constrained, controlled, curbed, defined, delimited, determinate, finite, fixed, hampered, hemmed in, local, modified, narrow, particular, precise, qualified, reserved, restrained, sectional, topical; SEE CONCEPTS *554,557*

limited [*adj2*] *inadequate, short*
cramped, diminished, faulty, ineffectual, insufficient, little, mean, minimal, narrow, paltry, poor, reduced, restricted, set, small, unsatisfactory; SEE CONCEPT *771*

limitless [*adj*] *never-ending, infinite*
bottomless, boundless, countless, endless, illimitable, immeasurable, immense, incomprehensible, indefinite, inexhaustible, innumerable, measureless, no end of*, no end to*, no holds barred*, no ifs ands or buts*, no strings*, numberless, unbounded, uncalculable, undefined, unending, unfathomable, unlimited, untold, vast, wide-open; SEE CONCEPTS *762,771,798*

limp [*n*] *faltering walk*
bad wheel, falter, flat wheel, floppy, gimp, halt, hitch, hobble, lameness; SEE CONCEPT *151*

limp [*adj*] *not stiff; weak*
bending, debilitated, drooping, droopy, ductile, enervated, exhausted, feeble, flabby, flaccid, flexible, flexuous, flimsy, floppy, impressible, infirm, languid, languishing, lax, lethargic, limber, listless, loose, plastic, pliable, pliant, relaxed, slack, soft, spent, spiritless, supple, tired, unsubstantial, weak-

ened, wearied, worn out, yielding; SEE CONCEPTS *490,604*

limp [*v*] *walk with faltering step*
clump, dodder, falter, flag, gimp, halt, hitch, hobble, hop, lag, scuff, shamble, shuffle, stagger, stumble, teeter, totter, waddle, walk lamely; SEE CONCEPT *151*

limpid [*adj*] *clear, comprehensible*
bright, comprehensible, crystal-clear, crystalline, definite, distinct, filmy, intelligible, lucid, luculent, obvious, pellucid, perspicuous, pure, see-through, thin, translucent, transparent, transpicuous, unambiguous; SEE CONCEPT *535*

line [*n1*] *mark, stroke; border*
band, bar, borderline, boundary, channel, configuration, contour, crease, dash, delineation, demarcation, edge, figuration, figure, frontier, furrow, groove, limit, lineament, lineation, outline, profile, rule, score, scratch, silhouette, streak, stripe, tracing, underline, wrinkle; SEE CONCEPTS *284,436*

line [*n2*] *row, succession; course*
arrangement, array, axis, band, block, border, catalogue, channel, column, concatenation, crack, direction, division, drain, echelon, file, fissure, formation, furrow, groove, group, lane, length, list, magazine, mark, order, path, progression, queue, rank, ridge, road, route, row, scar, seam, sequence, series, street, string, thread, tier, track, train, trajectory, trench, way; SEE CONCEPTS *501,727,738,744*

line [*n3*] *cord, rope*
cable, filament, strand, string, thread, wire; SEE CONCEPT *475*

line [*n4*] *belief, policy*
approach, avenue, course, course of action, ideology, method, polity, position, practice, principle, procedure, program, route, scheme, system; SEE CONCEPTS *687,689*

line [*n5*] *person's calling, interest*
activity, area, business, department, employment, field, forte, job, occupation, profession, province, pursuit, racket*, specialization, trade, vocation, work; SEE CONCEPTS *349,360*

line [*n6*] *ancestry*
breed, descent, family, heredity, lineage, pedigree, race, stock, strain, succession; SEE CONCEPT *296*

line [*n7*] *written communication*
card, letter, message, note, postcard, report, word; SEE CONCEPT *271*

line [*n8*] *hint; influential communication*
clue, indication, information, lead, patter, persuasion, pitch, prepared speech, song and dance*, spiel*; SEE CONCEPT *278*

line [*n9*] *merchandise carried by store*
commodity, goods, involvement, materials, produce, trade, vendibles, wares; SEE CONCEPT *338*

line [*v1*] *border, mark*
abut, adjoin, align, allineate, array, bound, butt against, communicate, crease, cut, delineate, draw,
edge, fix, follow, fringe, furrow, group, inscribe, join, line up, march, marshal, neighbor, order, ordinate, outline, place, queue, range, rank, rim, rule, score, skirt, touch, trace, underline, verge; SEE CONCEPTS *79,84,753*

line [*v2*] *put covering inside object*
bush, ceil, cover, encrust, face, fill, incrust, interline, overlay, panel, quilt, reinforce, sheath, stuff, wad, wainscot; SEE CONCEPTS *172,218*

lineage [*n*] *ancestry*
birth, blood, breed, clan, descendants, descent, extraction, family, folk, forbears, forefathers, genealogy, heredity, house, kin, kindred, line, offspring, origin, pedigree, progenitors, progeny, race, stirps, stock, succession, tribe; SEE CONCEPT *296*

linger [*v1*] *loiter, delay*
amble, be dilatory, be long, be tardy, crawl, dally, dawdle, dillydally*, drift, falter, fool around*, fritter away*, goof off*, hang around*, hang out*, hesitate, hobble, idle, lag, loll, lumber, mope, mosey, plod, poke, procrastinate, put off, putter, remain, saunter, shuffle, sit around, slouch*, stagger, stay, stick around, stop, stroll, take one's time*, tarry, tool, totter, trail, traipse, trifle, trudge, vacillate, wait, wait around; SEE CONCEPTS *151,681*

linger [*v2*] *continue, endure*
abide, bide, cling, hang on, last, persist, remain, stand, stay, stick around, survive, wait; SEE CONCEPTS *23,239*

lingo [*n*] *dialect spoken by a group*
argot, cant, idiom, jargon, language, patois, patter, slang, speech, talk, tongue, vernacular, vocabulary; SEE CONCEPT *276*

link [*n*] *component, connection*
articulation, association, attachment, bond, channel, connective, constituent, contact, copula, coupler, coupling, division, element, fastening, hitch, hookup, in, interconnection, interface, intersection, joining, joint, junction, knot, ligament, ligation, ligature, loop, member, network, nexus, part, piece, relationship, ring, seam, section, splice, tie, tie-up, vinculum, weld, yoke; SEE CONCEPTS *471,835*

link [*v*] *connect*
associate, attach, bind, bracket, combine, conjoin, conjugate, couple, fasten, group, hitch on, hook up, identify, incorporate, interface, join, meld with, network, plug into, relate, slap on, tack on, tag along, tag on, team up with, throw in with*, tie, tie in with, unite, yoke; SEE CONCEPTS *113,114,193*

lip [*n1*] *edge, brink*
border, brim, chops, flange, flare, labium, labrum, margin, nozzle, overlap, portal, projection, rim, spout; SEE CONCEPTS *392,484,513*

lip [*n2*] *insolence*
back talk, cheek*, effrontery, guff*, impertinence, jaw*, mouth*, rudeness, sass*, sauce*, sauciness; SEE CONCEPTS *54,278*

liquid [n] *fluid*

aqua, aqueous material, broth, elixir, extract, flow, flux, goo*, goop*, juice, liquor, melted material, nectar, sap, secretion, slop*, solution, swill*; SEE CONCEPT *467*

liquid [adj1] *fluid, flowing, melting*

aqueous, damp, deliquescent, dissolvable, dissolved, dulcet, fluent, fluidic, fusible, ichorous, juicy, liquefied, liquescent, liquiform, luscious, mellifluent, mellifluous, mellow, meltable, melted, moist, molten, moving, pulpy, running, runny, sappy, serous, smooth, soft, solvent, splashing, succulent, thawed, thin, uncongealed, viscous, watery, wet; SEE CONCEPTS *485,584,603*

liquid [adj2] *readily available*

convertible, fluid, free, marketable, negotiable, quick, ready, realizable, usable; SEE CONCEPT *334*

liquidate [v1] *pay; change into cash*

cash, cash in, cash out, clear, convert, discharge, exchange, honor, pay off, quit, realize, reimburse, repay, satisfy, sell off, sell up, settle, square; SEE CONCEPT *330*

liquidate [v2] *destroy, dissolve*

abolish, annihilate, annul, cancel, dispatch, do away with*, do in*, eliminate, exterminate, finish off*, get rid of*, kill, murder, purge, remove, rub out*, silence, terminate, vaporize, wipe out*; SEE CONCEPT *252*

liquor [n] *drink; alcoholic beverage*

alcohol, aqua vitae, booze*, broth, decoction, drinkable, elixir, extract, firewater*, fluid, hard stuff*, inebriant, infusion, intoxicant, liquid, moonshine*, poison*, potable, sauce*, solvent, spirits, stock, the bottle*, whiskey; SEE CONCEPT *455*

list [n] *record, tabulation*

account, agenda, archive, arrangement, ballot, bill, brief, bulletin, calendar, canon, catalog, catalogue, census, checklist, contents, dictionary, directory, docket, draft, enumeration, file, gazette, index, inventory, invoice, lexicon, lineup, listing, loop, manifest, memorandum, menu, outline, panel, poll, program, prospectus, register, roll, roll call, row, schedule, screed, scroll, series, slate, statistics, syllabus, table, tally, thesaurus, ticket, timetable, vocabulary; SEE CONCEPT *281*

list [v1] *keep a record; tabulate*

arrange, bill, book, button down, calender, catalogue, census, chart, chronicle, classify, detail, docket, enroll, enter, enumerate, file, index, inscribe, insert, inventory, invoice, itemize, keep count, manifest, note, numerate, particularize, peg, place, poll, post, put down as, put down for, record, register, run down, schedule, set down, specialize, specify, spell out, tab, tally, tick off, write down; SEE CONCEPTS *79,125*

list [v2] *lean, slant*

cant, careen, heel, incline, pitch, recline, slope, tilt, tip; SEE CONCEPTS *154,201,738*

listen [v] *hear and pay attention*

accept, admit, adopt, attend, audit, auscult, auscultate, be all ears*, be attentive, catch, concentrate, eavesdrop, entertain, get, get a load of*, give an audience to, give attention, give heed to, hang on words*, hark, harken, hearken, hear out, hear tell, lend an ear*, mind, monitor, obey, observe, overhear, pay attention, pick up on*, prick up ears*, receive, take advice*, take into consideration*, take notice, take under advisement*, tune in, tune in on*, welcome; SEE CONCEPT *596*

listless [adj] *spiritless, without energy*

absent, abstracted, apathetic, blah*, bored, careless, dormant, dreamy, drowsy, dull, easygoing, energyless, enervated, faint, heavy, heedless, impassive, inanimate, inattentive, indifferent, indolent, inert, insouciant, lackadaisical, lagging, laid-back*, languid, languishing, languorous, leaden, lethargic, lifeless, limp, lukewarm, lymphatic, mopish, neutral, out of it*, passive, phlegmatic, slack, sleepy, slow, sluggish, stupid, supine, thoughtless, torpid, uninterested, vacant; SEE CONCEPTS *401,584*

litany [n] *recital of items, often part of religious services*

account, catalogue, enumeration, invocation, list, petition, prayer, recitation, refrain, repetition, supplication, tale; SEE CONCEPTS *278,368*

literacy [n] *ability to read*

articulacy, articulateness, background, cultivation, education, knowledge, learning, proficiency, refinement, scholarship; SEE CONCEPTS *409,630*

literal [adj] *word for word; exact, real*

accurate, actual, apparent, authentic, bona fide, close, critical, faithful, genuine, gospel, methodical, natural, not figurative, ordinary, plain, scrupulous, simple, strict, to the letter*, true, undeviating, unerring, unexaggerated, unvarnished, usual, veracious, verbal, verbatim, veritable, written; SEE CONCEPTS *267,557*

literally [adv] *word for word; exactly*

actually, completely, correctly, direct, directly, faithfully, indisputably, letter by letter*, literatim, not figuratively, plainly, precisely, really, rightly, rigorously, sic*, simply, straight, strictly, to the letter*, truly, undeviatingly, undisputably, unerringly, unmistakably, verbatim, veritably; SEE CONCEPTS *267,557*

literary [adj] *concerning books*

belletristic, bookish, classical, erudite, formal, learned, lettered, literate, scholarly, well-read; SEE CONCEPTS *267,536*

literature [n] *written matter, both fictional and non-fictional*

abstract, article, belles-lettres, biography, books, brochure, classics, comment, composition, critique, discourse, discussion, disquisition, dissertation, drama, essay, exposition, findings, history, humanities, information, leaflet, letters, lit*, literary works, lore, novel, observation, pamphlet, paper, poetry, precis, prose, report, research, story, summary, theme, thesis, tract, treatise, treatment, writings, written work; SEE CONCEPT *280*

lithe [*adj*] *flexible, graceful and slender*
agile, lean, lightsome, limber, lissome, loose, nimble, pliable, pliant, slight, slim, spare, supple, thin; SEE CONCEPTS *488,491,584*

litigate [*v*] *bring matter before court of law*
appeal, contest, dispute, drag into court*, file suit, go to court, go to law, institute legal proceedings, press charges, prosecute, see one in court*, sue, take the law on*; SEE CONCEPT *317*

litigation [*n*] *matter coming before court of law*
action, case, cause, contention, dispute, lawsuit, process, prosecution, suit, trial; SEE CONCEPT *318*

litter [*n1*] *mess, debris*
clutter, collateral, confusion, detritus, disarray, disorder, garbage, hash, hodgepodge, jumble, jungle, junk, mishmash, muck, muddle, offal, rash, refuse, rubbish, rummage, scattering, scramble, shuffle, trash, untidiness, waste; SEE CONCEPTS *260,432*

litter [*n2*] *animal offspring*
brood, cubs, family, kittens, offspring, piglets, progeny, puppies, school, young; SEE CONCEPTS *394,397*

litter [*v*] *make a mess*
clutter, confuse, derange, dirty, disarrange, disarray, disorder, jumble, mess up, scatter, strew; SEE CONCEPT *254*

little [*n*] *small amount of something*
bit, dab, dash, fragment, hint, modicum, particle, pinch, snippet, soupçon, speck, spot, taste, touch, trace, trifle, whit; SEE CONCEPT *835*

little [*adj1*] *small in size, amount*
babyish, bantam, brief, cramped, diminutive, dinky, dwarf, elfin, embryonic, fleeting, hardly any, hasty, immature, imperceptible, inappreciable, inconsiderable, infant, infinitesimal, insufficient, junior, light, Lilliputian*, limited, meager, microscopic, mini, miniature, minute, not big, not large, peanut, petite, pygmy, scant, short, short-lived, shrimpy, shriveled, skimpy, slight, snub, sparse, stubby, stunted, teeny, tiny, toy, truncated, undersized, undeveloped, wee, wizened, young; SEE CONCEPTS *773,789*

little [*adj2*] *not important*
casual, inconsiderable, insignificant, light, minor, minute, negligible, paltry, petty, shoestring*, small, trifling, trivial, unimportant; SEE CONCEPT *575*

little [*adj3*] *narrow-minded*
base, bigoted, cheap, contemptible, hidebound, illiberal, ineffectual, limited, mean, narrow, niggardly, paltry, petty, provincial, self-centered, selfish, set, small, small-minded, vulgar, wicked; SEE CONCEPT *404*

little [*adv*] *infrequently, not much*
a little, barely, hardly, hardly ever, not many, not often, not quite, only just, rarely, scarcely, seldom, somewhat; SEE CONCEPTS *530,544*

liturgy [*n*] *worship, ceremony*
celebration, ceremonial, form, formality, formula, observance, rite, ritual, sacrament, service, services; SEE CONCEPT *368*

livable [*adj*] *adequate, acceptable*
bearable, comfortable, cozy, endurable, fit, habitable, homey, inhabitable, lodgeable, passable, satisfactory, snug, sufferable, supportable, sustainable, tenantable, tolerable, worthwhile; SEE CONCEPTS *485,558*

live [*adj1*] *existent*
alive, animate, aware, breathing, conscious, living, vital; SEE CONCEPT *539*

live [*adj2*] *energetic, vigorous*
active, alert, brisk, burning, controversial, current, dynamic, earnest, effective, effectual, efficacious, efficient, functioning, hot, lively, operative, pertinent, pressing, prevalent, running, topical, unsettled, vital, vivid, working; SEE CONCEPTS *542,560*

live [*v1*] *exist*
abide, be, be alive, breathe, continue, draw breath, endure, get along, get by, have life, last, lead, maintain, make it, move, pass, persist, prevail, remain, remain alive, subsist, survive; SEE CONCEPT *407*

live [*v2*] *inhabit a dwelling*
abide, bide, bunk*, crash*, dwell, hang one's hat*, hang out*, locate, lodge, nest, occupy, perch, reside, roost, settle; SEE CONCEPT *226*

live [*v3*] *enjoy being alive*
be happy, delight, experience, flourish, love, luxuriate, make the most of, prosper, relish, savor, take pleasure, thrive; SEE CONCEPT *678*

live [*v4*] *make money to support living*
acquire a livelihood, earn a living, earn money, fare, feed, get along*, get by*, maintain, make ends meet*, make it, profit, subsist, support; SEE CONCEPT *351*

livelihood [*n*] *occupation*
alimentation, art, bread and butter*, business, circumstances, craft, employment, game*, grind*, income, job, keep*, living, maintenance, means, nine-to-five*, profession, racket*, rat race*, resources, slot, source of income, subsistence, support, sustenance, thing*, trade, vocation, what one is into*, work; SEE CONCEPTS *349,351,360*

lively [*adj*] *energetic, active, busy*
agile, alert, animate, animated, astir, blithe, blithesome, bouncy, bright, brisk, buoyant, bustling, buzzing, cheerful, chipper*, chirpy*, complex, dashing, driving, effervescent, enjoyable, enterprising, entertaining, festive, frisky, frolicsome, full of pep*, gay, go-go*, happy, hyper*, industrious, involved, jocund, jumping, keen, merry, nimble, peppy*, perky, pert, provocative, quick, refreshing, rousing, snappy, sparkling, spirited, sprightly, spry, stimulating, stirring, vigorous, vivacious, zippy*; SEE CONCEPTS *401,542,548*

livid [*adj1*] *pale, ashen*
ashy, blanched, bloodless, colorless, discolored, dusky, gloomy, greyish, grisly, leaden, lurid, murky, pallid, pasty, wan, waxen; SEE CONCEPT *618*

livid [*adj2*] *bruised*
black-and-blue, contused, purple; SEE CONCEPT *618*

livid [*adj3*] *extremely angry*
beside oneself, black*, boiling, enraged, exasperated, flaming, fuming, furious, hot*, incensed, indignant, infuriated, mad, offended, outraged; SEE CONCEPTS *403,542*

living [*n*] *lifestyle; source of income*
alimentation, bread and butter*, existence, income, job, keep*, livelihood, maintenance, means, mode, occupation, salt*, subsistence, support, sustainment, sustenance, sustentation, way, work; SEE CONCEPTS *335,351*

living [*adj*] *existing, active*
alert, alive, animated, around, awake, breathing, brisk, contemporary, continuing, current, developing, dynamic, existent, extant, in use, live, lively, ongoing, operative, persisting, strong, subsisting, ticking, vigorous, vital, warm; SEE CONCEPTS *539,560*

load [*n1*] *cargo, freight*
amount, bale, bundle, capacity, charge, consignment, contents, encumbrance, goods, haul, heft, hindrance, lading, mass, pack, parcel, part, payload, shipment, shot, weight; SEE CONCEPTS *338,432*

load [*n2*] *burden, pressure*
affliction, albatross, care, charge, cumber, deadweight*, drag, drain, duty, encumbrance, excess baggage*, incubus, liability, millstone*, obligation, onus, oppression, responsibility, task, tax, trouble, trust, weight, worry; SEE CONCEPT *674*

load [*v1*] *burden, saddle*
arrange, ballast, bear, carry, charge, chock, choke, containerize, cram, fill, flood, freight, glut, gorge, heap, heap up, jam*, lade, lumber, mass, oversupply, pack, pile, pile it on, pile up, place, pour in, put aboard, ram in, stack, store, stow, stuff, surfeit, swamp, top, top off, weigh, weigh down, weight; SEE CONCEPT *209*

load [*v2*] *overburden, pressure*
burden, charge, encumber, hamper, lade, oppress, saddle, task, tax, trouble, weigh down, weight, worry; SEE CONCEPT *14*

loaf [*n*] *block of something*
bun, cake, cube, dough, lump, mass, pastry, roll, slab, twist; SEE CONCEPTS *436,457,460,461*

loaf [*v*] *be idle, lazy*
be inactive, be indolent, be slothful, be unoccupied, bum*, bum around*, dally, dillydally*, dream, drift, evade, fool around*, fritter away*, goldbrick, hang out*, idle, kill time*, knock around*, laze, let down, lie, loiter, loll, lounge, lounge around, malinger, not lift a finger*, pass time, piddle, relax, saunter, shirk, sit around, slack, slow down, stall, stand around,

stroll, take it easy, trifle, twiddle thumbs*, vegetate, waste time, while away hours*; SEE CONCEPTS *210,681*

loafer [*n*] *person who is idle, lazy*
beachcomber, deadbeat, do-nothing, good-for-nothing*, goof-off*, idler, lazybones*, lounger, malingerer, ne'er-do-well*, shirker, slacker, slouch, sluggard, sponger, wanderer, waster, wastrel; SEE CONCEPT *412*

loan [*n*] *money given temporarily*
accommodation, advance, allowance, credit, extension, floater, investment, mortgage, time payment, trust; SEE CONCEPT *332*

loan [*v*] *give money, possession temporarily*
accommodate, advance, allow, credit, lay on one, lend, let out, provide, score, scratch, stake, touch; SEE CONCEPT *115*

loath [*adj*] *against, averse*
afraid, counter, disinclined, hesitant, indisposed, opposed, reluctant, remiss, resisting, uneager, unwilling; SEE CONCEPTS *29,542*

loathe [*v*] *dislike very strongly*
abhor, abominate, be allergic to*, be down on, decline, despise, detest, execrate, feel repugnance, find disgusting, hate, have aversion to, have no use for*, refuse, reject, repudiate, revolt, spurn; SEE CONCEPT *29*

loathsome [*adj*] *hateful*
abhorrent, abominable, beastly, creepy, deplorable, detestable, disgusting, execrable, gross, hideous, horrible, invidious, lousy, nasty, nauseating, obnoxious, odious, offensive, pesky, pestiferous, repellent, repugnant, repulsive, revolting, sleazy*, slimy*, uncool*, vile; SEE CONCEPTS *485,529,570*

lobby [*n*] *entrance hall*
antechamber, corridor, doorway, foyer, gateway, hall, hallway, passage, passageway, porch, vestibule, waiting room; SEE CONCEPTS *441,448*

lobby [*v*] *press for political action*
advance, affect, alter, bill, billboard*, boost, bring pressure to bear*, build up, campaign for, change, drum, exert influence, further, hard sell*, high pressure, hype*, induce, influence, make a pitch for*, modify, persuade, pitch, plug, politick, press, pressure, procure, promote, pull strings*, push, put pressure on, request, sell, sell on*, soft-sell*, soft-soap*, solicit, solicit votes, splash, spot, sway, sweet-talk*, thump, urge; SEE CONCEPTS *68,300*

local [*n*] *person deeply rooted in community*
character, inhabitant, native, resident; SEE CONCEPTS *413,423*

local [*adj*] *of a community, restricted to immediate area*
bounded, civic, confined, district, divisional, geographical, insular, legendary, limited, narrow, neighborhood, parish, parochial, provincial, regional, sectarian, sectional, small-town, territorial, town, vernacular; SEE CONCEPT *536*

locale/locality [n] *physical setting*
area, bailiwick, belt, district, domain, haunt, hole, home, locality, location, locus, neck of the woods*, neighborhood, place, position, region, scene, sector, site, sphere, spot, stage, stomping ground*, territory, theater, tract, turf, venue, vicinity, zone; SEE CONCEPT *198*

locate [v1] *find*
come across, come upon, detect, determine, discover, establish, ferret out*, get at, happen upon, hit upon, hook*, lay one's hands on*, light upon*, meet with, pick up on, pin down, pinpoint, place, position, read, search out, smell out, smoke out*, spot, station, strike, stumble on, track down, trip over*, uncover, unearth, zero in on*; SEE CONCEPT *183*

locate [v2] *settle*
dig in, dispose, dwell, establish, fix, hang one's hat*, inhabit, park, place, put, reside, seat, set, situate, squat, stand; SEE CONCEPT *226*

location [n] *place of residence or activity*
area, bearings, district, fix*, hole, locale, locality, locus, neck of the woods*, neighborhood, part, point, position, post, region, scene, section, site, situation, spot, station, tract, turf, venue, whereabouts; SEE CONCEPT *198*

lock [n] *device that fastens and bars free passage*
bar, bolt, bond, catch, clamp, clasp, clinch, connection, fastening, fixture, grapple, grip, hasp, hook, junction, latch, link, padlock; SEE CONCEPT *499*

lock [v] *fasten, clasp*
bar, bolt, button, button up, clench, close, clutch, embrace, encircle, enclose, engage, entwine, grapple, grasp, hug, join, latch, link, mesh, press, seal, secure, shut, turn the key, unite; SEE CONCEPTS *85,160*

lodge [n] *cabin; vacation residence*
abode, auberge, burrow, camp, chalet, cottage, couch, country house, den, dormitory, dwelling, gatehouse, haunt, home, hospice, hostel, hostelry, hotel, house, hut, inn, motel, public house, retreat, roadhouse, shack, shanty, shelter, stopover, tavern, villa; SEE CONCEPT *516*

lodge [v1] *become fixed or wedged*
abide, catch, come to rest, embed, entrench, fix, imbed, implant, infix, ingrain, install, plant, remain, root, stay, stick; SEE CONCEPT *201*

lodge [v2] *stay at temporary residence*
abide, accommodate, bestow, board, bunk, canton, crash, domicile, dwell, entertain, harbor, hole up*, hostel, house, locate, nest, park*, perch*, put up, quarter, rent, reside, room, roost*, shelter, sojourn, squat, station, stay, stay over, stop*; SEE CONCEPT *226*

lodging [n] *accommodation for rent*
abode, address, apartment, bed and breakfast, boarding house, camp, castle, chambers, cover, domicile, dorm, dwelling, habitation, harbor, home, hostel, hotel, inn, lodge, lodgment, motel, palace, pied-à-terre, place, port, protection, quarters, residence, resort, roof, room, room and board, rooming house, shelter; SEE CONCEPT *516*

loft [n] *room on upper floor*
apartment, attic, dormer, garret, storage, studio; SEE CONCEPT *448*

lofty [adj1] *high, elevated*
aerial, airy, high-rise, lifted, raised, sky-high, sky-scraping, skyward, soaring, spiring, tall, towering; SEE CONCEPT *779*

lofty [adj2] *grand, stately*
arresting, benevolent, big, chivalrous, commanding, considerate, dignified, distinguished, elevated, exalted, generous, great, illustrious, imposing, magnanimous, majestic, noble, renowned, striking, sublime, superb, superior, utopian, visionary; SEE CONCEPT *574*

lofty [adj3] *arrogant, high and mighty*
ambitious, cavalier, condescending, disdainful, grandiose, haughty, high-minded, immodest, insolent, lordly, overbearing, patronizing, pretentious, proud, snooty, supercilious; SEE CONCEPT *401*

log [n1] *stump of tree*
block, bole, chunk, length, piece, stick, timber, trunk, wood; SEE CONCEPTS *428,479*

log [n2] *record*
account, book, chart, daybook, diary, journal, listing, logbook, register, tally; SEE CONCEPT *271*

logic [n] *science of reasoning*
antithesis and synthesis, argumentation, coherence, connection, course of thought, deduction, dialectic, good sense, induction, inference, linkage, philosophy, ratiocination, rationale, relationship, sanity, sense, sound judgment, syllogism, syllogistics, thesis, train of thought; SEE CONCEPTS *37,349,689*

logical [adj1] *probable, reasonable*
analytic, analytical, clear, cogent, coherent, commonsensical, compelling, congruent, consequent, consistent, convincing, deducible, discerning, discriminating, extensional, fair, germane, holding together, holding water*, inferential, intelligent, judicious, juridicious, justifiable, kosher*, legit*, legitimate, lucid, most likely, necessary, obvious, perceptive, perspicuous, pertinent, plausible, rational, relevant, sensible, sound, subtle, telling, valid, well-organized, wise; SEE CONCEPTS *402,529,552*

loiter [v] *hang around; stroll*
amble, dabble, dally*, dawdle, delay, diddle, drag, flag, fritter away, get no place fast*, halt, hover, idle, lag, linger, loaf, loll, lounge, pass time, pause, poke, procrastinate, put off, ramble, saunter, shamble, shuffle, slacken, slough, tarry, trail, traipse, wait, waste time; SEE CONCEPTS *151,210,681*

loll [v] *lay sprawled*
bum, dangle, dawdle, droop, drop, flap, flop, goof off, hang, hang loose, idle, laze, lean, loaf, loiter, lounge, recline, relax, rest, sag, slouch, slump, sprawl; SEE CONCEPTS *154,210*

lone [*adj*] *by oneself; only*
abandoned, alone, deserted, forsaken, isolated, lonely, lonesome, one, onliest, particular, secluded, separate, separated, single, singular, sole, solitary, solo, stag, unaccompanied, unique; SEE CONCEPT *577*

lonely [*adj1*] *feeling friendless, forlorn*
abandoned, alone, apart, by oneself, comfortless, companionless, deserted, desolate, destitute, disconsolate, down, empty, estranged, forsaken, godforsaken, homeless, isolated, left, lone, lonesome, outcast, reclusive, rejected, renounced, secluded, single, solitary, troglodytic, unattended, unbefriended, uncherished, unsocial, withdrawn; SEE CONCEPTS *403,555*

lonely [*adj2*] *out-of-the-way*
alone, deserted, desolate, godforsaken, isolated, obscure, off the beaten track*, private, quiet, remote, removed, retired, secluded, secret, sequestered, solitary, unfrequented, uninhabited; SEE CONCEPT *583*

lonesome [*adj*] *forlorn, friendless*
alone, cheerless, companionless, deserted, desolate, dreary, gloomy, homesick, isolated, lone, lonely, solitary; SEE CONCEPTS *403,555*

long [*adj1*] *extended in space or time*
continued, deep, distant, drawn out, elongate, elongated, enduring, enlarged, expanded, extensive, faraway, far-off, far-reaching, gangling, great, high, king-size*, lanky, lasting, lengthened, lengthy, lingering, lofty, longish, outstretched, prolonged, protracted, rangy, remote, running, spread out, spun out, stretch, stretched, stretching, stringy, sustained, tall, towering; SEE CONCEPTS *482,779,798*

long [*adj2*] *interminable, excessive in length*
boundless, delayed, diffuse, diffusive, dilatory, dragging, drawn-out, for ages*, forever and a day*, late, lengthy, limitless, lingering, long-drawn-out*, long-winded*, overlong, prolix, prolonged, protracted, slow, sustained, tardy, unending, verbose, without end, wordy; SEE CONCEPTS *544,798*

long [*v*] *desire, crave*
ache, aim, aspire, covet, dream of, hanker, have a yen for, hunger, itch, lust, miss, pine, sigh, spoil for, suspire, thirst, want, wish, yearn; SEE CONCEPT *20*

longing [*n*] *strong desire*
ambition, aspiration, coveting, craving, fire in the belly*, hankering, hunger, hungering, itch, pining, thirst, urge, wish, yearning, yen; SEE CONCEPTS *20,709*

longing [*adj*] *desirous*
anxious, ardent, avid, craving, eager, hungry, languishing, pining, ravenous, wishful, wistful, yearning; SEE CONCEPT *403*

look [*n1*] *visual examination*
attention, beholding, case, cast, contemplation, evil eye, eye, flash, gander, gaze, glance, glimpse, gun, inspection, introspection, keeping watch, leer, looksee*, marking, noticing, observation, once-over, peek, reconnaissance, regard, regarding, review,

scrutiny, sight, slant, speculation, squint, stare, surveillance, survey, swivel, view, viewing; SEE CONCEPT *623*

look [*n2*] *characteristic, stylish appearance*
air, aspect, bearing, cast, complexion, countenance, demeanor, effect, expression, face, fashion, guise, manner, mien, mug*, physiognomy, presence, seeming, semblance, visage; SEE CONCEPTS *655,673,716*

look [*v1*] *examine visually*
admire, attend, behold, beware, consider, contemplate, eye, feast one's eyes*, flash, focus, gape, gawk, gaze, get a load of, glance, glower, goggle, heed, inspect, mark, mind, note, notice, observe, ogle, peep, peer, pore over, read, regard, rubberneck*, scan, scout, scrutinize, see, spot, spy, stare, study, survey, take a gander*, take in the sights*, tend, view, watch; SEE CONCEPT *623*

look [*v2*] *appear, seem to be*
display, evidence, exhibit, express, indicate, look like, make clear, manifest, present, resemble, seem, show, sound, strike as; SEE CONCEPTS *261,716*

look [*v3*] *expect, anticipate*
await, await, count on, divine, forecast, foretell, hope, hunt, reckon on, search, seek; SEE CONCEPT *26*

look [*v4*] *face*
front, front on, give onto, overlook; SEE CONCEPT *746*

look down on [*v*] *hold in contempt*
abhor, contemn, despise, disdain, scorn, scout, sneer, spurn, turn nose up at; SEE CONCEPT *29*

look into [*v*] *check, research*
audit, check out, delve into, dig, examine, explore, follow up, go into, inquire, inspect, investigate, look over, make inquiry, probe, prospect, scrutinize, sift, study; SEE CONCEPT *103*

lookout [*n*] *guard; place from which to guard*
anchor, beacon, belvedere, case, catbird seat*, citadel, crow's nest*, cupola, eagle eye*, hawk, observance, observation, observatory, outlook, overlook, panorama, patrol, post, scene, scout, sentinel, sentry, spotter, station, surveillance, tip, tower, view, vigil, vigilance, ward, watch, watcher, watchman/woman, watchtower*, weather eye*, widow's walk*; SEE CONCEPTS *198,358,623*

look out [*v*] *be wary*
be alert, be careful, be on guard, beware, check out, have a care, heads up*, hearken, keep an eye out*, keep tabs*, listen, mind, notice, pay attention, peg*, pick up on*, scope, shotgun*, size up, spot, spy, watch out; SEE CONCEPTS *35,623*

look up [*v1*] *research*
come upon, confirm, discover, find, hunt for, peruse, scan, search for, seek, seek out, track down; SEE CONCEPTS *72,216*

look up [*v2*] *improve*
advance, ameliorate, come along, convalesce, gain, get better, mend, perk up, pick up, progress, recu-

perate, shape up, show improvement; SEE CONCEPTS *303,700*

loom [*v*] *appear, often imposingly*
approach, await, be at hand*, become visible, be coming, be forthcoming, be imminent, be in the cards*, be in the wind*, be near, break through, brew, bulk, come forth, come into view, come on, come on the scene*, dawn, dominate, emanate, emerge, figure, gather, hang over, hover, impend, impress, issue, lower, make up, menace, mount, near, overhang, overshadow, overtop, portend, rear, rise, seem huge, seem large, show, soar, stand out, take shape, threaten, top, tower; SEE CONCEPTS *118,159,261*

loop [*n*] *circle, spiral*
bend, circuit, circumference, coil, convolution, curl, curve, eyelet, hoop, kink, knot, loophole, noose, ring, twirl, twist, whorl, wreath; SEE CONCEPT *436*

loop [*v*] *circle, spiral*
arc, arch, begird, bend, bow, braid, coil, compass, connect, crook, curl, curve, curve around, encircle, encompass, fold, gird, girdle, join, knot, ring, roll, surround, tie together, turn, twist, wind around; SEE CONCEPTS *147,201,754*

loose [*adj1*] *not tight; unconstrained*
apart, asunder, at large, baggy, clear, detached, disconnected, easy, escaped, flabby, flaccid, floating, free, hanging, insecure, lax, liberated, limp, loosened, movable, not fitting, relaxed, released, separate, slack, slackened, sloppy, unattached, unbolted, unbound, unbuttoned, uncaged, unclasped, unconfined, unconnected, undone, unfastened, unfettered, unhinged, unhooked, unlatched, unlocked, unpinned, unrestrained, unrestricted, unsecured, unshackled, untied, wobbly; SEE CONCEPT *485*

loose [*adj2*] *indefinite, vague*
detached, diffuse, disconnected, disordered, illdefined, imprecise, inaccurate, indistinct, negligent, obscure, rambling, random, remiss; SEE CONCEPTS *267,529*

loose [*adj3*] *promiscuous*
abandoned, capricious, careless, corrupt, debauched, disreputable, dissipated, dissolute, easy, fast, heedless, high living*, immoral, imprudent, inconstant, lax, lewd, libertine, licentious, light, negligent, out of control*, playing, profligate, rash, reckless, speeding, swinging, thoughtless, unchaste, unmindful, unrestrained, wanton; SEE CONCEPTS *372, 401,545*

loose/loosen [*v*] *set free; unbind*
alleviate, become unfastened, break up, deliver, detach, discharge, disconnect, disengage, disenthrall, disjoin, ease, ease off, emancipate, extricate, free, let go, let out, liberate, loosen, manumit, mitigate, relax, release, separate, slacken, unbar, unbolt, unbuckle, unbutton, unchain, unclasp, undo, unfasten, unfix, unhitch, unhook, unlace, unlash, unlatch, unleash, unlock, unloose, unpin, unscrew, unsnap, un-

stick, unstrap, untie, untighten, work free, work loose; SEE CONCEPTS *127,250*

loot [*n*] *stolen goods*
booty, dough*, graft, haul, hot goods*, lift*, make*, money, pickings*, pillage, plunder, plunderage, prize, seizure, spoils, squeeze, take*; SEE CONCEPTS *337,340*

loot [*v*] *steal goods*
appropriate, boost, burglarize, despoil, grab, gut, liberate, lift, loft, make, moonlight requisition*, pillage, plunder, raid, ransack, ravage, relieve, requisition, rifle, rip off*, rob, sack, salvage, smash and grab*, snatch, snitch*, stick up, swipe, take, thieve, tip over; SEE CONCEPTS *139,192*

lopsided [*adj*] *leaning, falling to one side; larger on one side*
askew, asymmetrical, awry, cockeyed, crooked, disproportional, disproportionate, inclinatory, irregular, nonsymmetrical, off-balance, one-sided, out of shape, overbalanced, squint, tilting, top-heavy, unbalanced, unequal, uneven, unsteady, warped; SEE CONCEPT *480*

loquacious [*adj*] *talkative*
babbling, chattering, chatty, fluent, gabby*, garrulous, gossipy, jabbering, long-winded*, looselipped*, motormouth*, multiloquent, prolix, verbose, voluble, wordy, yacking*; SEE CONCEPTS *267,401*

lord [*n*] *male person who is master, member of the nobility*
aristocrat, baron, bishop, captain, commandant, commander, count, don, duke, earl, governor, king, leader, liege, magnate, marquis, monarch, noble, nobleman, overlord, parliamentarian, patrician, peer, potentate, prince, royalty, ruler, seigneur, sovereign, superior, viscount; SEE CONCEPTS *354,422*

lordly [*adj1*] *arrogant, disdainful*
affected, authoritarian, bossy, cavalier, condescending, despotic, dictatorial, domineering, egotistic, haughty, high and mighty*, high-handed, imperious, insolent, lofty, magisterial, on one's high horse*, overbearing, patronizing, pompous, proud, puffed, snobbish, stuck-up, supercilious, superior, tyrannical; SEE CONCEPT *401*

lordly [*adj2*] *grand, majestic*
aristocratic, august, dignified, exalted, gracious, grandiose, honorable, imperial, imposing, lofty, magnificent, noble, princely, regal, stately; SEE CONCEPT *574*

lore [*n*] *myths, traditional wisdom*
adage, belief, custom, doctrine, enlightenment, erudition, experience, fable, folklore, information, knowledge, learning, legend, letters, mythology, mythos, saga, saw, saying, scholarship, science, superstition, tale, teaching, tradition; SEE CONCEPTS *274,282,287*

lose [*v1*] *be deprived of; mislay*
be careless, become poorer, be impoverished, bereave, be reduced, capitulate, consume, default, de-

plete, disinherit, displace, dispossess, dissipate, divest, drain, drop, exhaust, expend, fail, fail to keep, fall short, forfeit, forget, give up, lavish, misplace, miss, misspend, oust, pass up, relinquish, rob, sacrifice, squander, suffer, suffer loss, surrender, use up, waste, yield; SEE CONCEPTS *116,156*

lose [*v2*] *be defeated*
be humbled, be outdistanced, be sunk, be taken to cleaners*, be the loser, be worsted*, come up short, decline, drop, drop a bundle*, fall, kiss goodbye*, lose out, miss, succumb, suffer defeat, take a beating*, take the count*, take the heat*, yield; SEE CONCEPTS *384,674*

lose [*v3*] *escape, avoid*
clear, dodge, duck, elude, evade, give the slip*, leave behind, outrun, rid, shake, shake off*, slip away, stray, throw off*, unburden, wander from; SEE CONCEPTS *30,102*

loser [*n*] *person, thing that fails*
also-ran*, deadbeat*, defeated, disadvantaged, down-and-outer*, dud*, failure, fall guy*, flop*, flunkee*, has-been, underdog, underprivileged; SEE CONCEPTS *412,423,433*

loss [*n*] *misfortune, deficit; something misplaced or lost*
accident, bad luck, bereavement, calamity, casualty, cataclysm, catastrophe, cost, damage, death, debit, debt, defeat, deficiency, depletion, deprivation, destitution, destruction, detriment, disadvantage, disappearance, disaster, dispossession, failure, fall, fatality, forfeiture, harm, hurt, impairment, injury, losing, misadventure, mishap, mislaying, misplacing, need, perdition, privation, retardation, ruin, sacrifice, shrinkage, squandering, trial, trouble, undoing, want, waste, wreckage; SEE CONCEPTS *407,674,707*

lost [*adj1*] *missing, off-track*
absent, adrift, astray, at sea, cast away, disappeared, disoriented, down the drain*, fallen between cracks*, forfeit, forfeited, gone, gone astray, hidden, invisible, irrecoverable, irretrievable, irrevocable, kiss goodbye*, lacking, minus, mislaid, misplaced, missed, nowhere to be found*, obscured, off-course, out the window*, strayed, unredeemed, vanished, wandering, wayward, without; SEE CONCEPT *576*

lost [*adj2*] *extinct, destroyed*
abolished, annihilated, bygone, consumed, dead, demolished, devastated, dissipated, eradicated, exterminated, forgotten, frittered, gone, lapsed, misspent, misused, obliterated, obsolete, out-of-date, past, perished, ruined, squandered, unremembered, wasted, wiped out*, wrecked; SEE CONCEPTS *539,560*

lost [*adj3*] *distracted, dreaming*
absent, absentminded, absorbed, abstracted, bemused, bewildered, distrait, dreamy, engrossed, entranced, faraway, feeble, going in circles*, ignorant, inconscient, musing, perplexed, preoccupied, rapt,

spellbound, taken in*, taken up*, unconscious, wasted; SEE CONCEPT *403*

lot [*n1*] *piece of property*
acreage, allotment, apportionment, area, block, clearing, division, field, frontage, parcel, part, patch, percentage, piece, plat, plot, plottage, portion, property, real estate, tract; SEE CONCEPTS *509,710*

lot [*n2*] *quantity, often large*
abundance, aggregate, aggregation, amplitude, assortment, barrel, batch, body, bunch, bundle, circle, clump, cluster, clutch, collection, conglomerate, conglomeration, consignment, crowd, great deal, group, heap, load, mass, mess, much, multiplicity, number, ocean, oodles, order, pack, pile, plenitude, plenty, push, reams, requisition, scores, set, stack, stacks; SEE CONCEPTS *432,786*

lot [*n3*] *portion, share*
allotment, allowance, bite, cut, parcel, part, percentage, piece, quota, ration, slice, take; SEE CONCEPTS *710,835*

lot [*n4*] *fate, destiny*
accident, break, breaks, chance, circumstance, decree, doom, foreordination, fortune, hand one is dealt*, hazard, karma, kismet, Moira*, plight, portion, predestination, run of luck*, way cookie crumbles*, wheel of fortune*; SEE CONCEPT *679*

lotion [*n*] *creamy solution*
balm, cosmetic, cream, demulcent, embrocation, lenitive, liniment, medicine, ointment, palliative, preparation, salve, unguent, wash; SEE CONCEPTS *311,446,466*

loud [*adj1*] *blaring, noisy*
big, blatant, blustering, boisterous, booming, cacophonous, clamorous, crashing, deafening, deep, ear-piercing, ear-splitting, emphatic, forte, full, full-mouthed, fulminating, heavy, high-sounding, intense, loud-voiced, lusty, obstreperous, pealing, piercing, powerful, rambunctious, raucous, resonant, resounding, ringing, roaring, rowdy, sonorous, stentorian, strident, strong, thundering, tumultuous, turbulent, turned up, uproarious, vehement, vehement, vociferous, wakes the dead*; SEE CONCEPTS *592,594*

loud [*adj2*] *offensive, gaudy*
brash, brassy, brazen, chintzy, coarse, crass, crude, flamboyant, flashy, garish, glaring, gross, lurid, meretricious, obnoxious, obtrusive, ostentatious, raucous, rude, showy, tasteless, tawdry, vulgar; SEE CONCEPTS *401,542,589*

lounge [*n*] *club, socializing place*
bar, barroom, club room, cocktail lounge, dive*, drinkery, hideaway, lobby, mezzanine, parlor, pub, reception, saloon, spot, tap, taproom, watering hole*; SEE CONCEPTS *293,449*

lounge [*v*] *lie about, waste time*
bum*, dawdle, fritter away, goldbrick*, goof off*, idle, kill time*, laze, loaf, loiter, loll*, pass time, recline, relax, repose, saunter, sprawl, take it easy*; SEE CONCEPTS *154,210,681*

lousy [*adj*] *very bad*
awful, base, contemptible, despicable, dirty, disliked, execrable, faulty, harmful, hateful, horrible, inferior, low, mean, miserable, no good*, outrageous, poor, rotten, second-rate*, shoddy, slovenly, terrible, unpopular, unwelcome, vicious, vile; SEE CONCEPT *571*

lovable [*adj*] *very likable; endearing*
adorable, agreeable, alluring, amiable, angelic, appealing, attractive, bewitching, captivating, charming, cuddly, delightful, desirable, enchanting, engaging, enthralling, entrancing, fascinating, fetching, friendly, genial, lovely, lovesome, pleasing, ravishing, seductive, sweet, winning, winsome; SEE CONCEPT *404*

love [*n1*] *adoration; very strong liking*
adulation, affection, allegiance, amity, amorousness, amour, appreciation, ardency, ardor, attachment, case, cherishing, crush, delight, devotedness, devotion, emotion, enchantment, enjoyment, fervor, fidelity, flame, fondness, friendship, hankering, idolatry, inclination, infatuation, involvement, lust, mad for, partiality, passion, piety, rapture, regard, relish, respect, sentiment, soft spot*, taste, tenderness, weakness, worship, yearning, zeal; SEE CONCEPT *32*

love [*n2*] *person who is loved by another*
admirer, angel, beau, beloved, boyfriend, courter, darling, dear, dearest, dear one, flame, girlfriend, honey, inamorata, inamorato, Juliet*, loved one, lover, paramour, passion, Romeo*, spark, squire, suitor, swain, sweet, sweetheart, truelove, valentine; SEE CONCEPT *423*

love [*v1*] *adore, like very much*
admire, adulate, be attached to, be captivated by, be crazy about, be enamored of, be enchanted by, be fascinated with, be fond of, be in love with, canonize, care for, cherish, choose, deify, delight in, dote on, esteem, exalt, fall for, fancy, glorify, go for*, gone on*, have affection for, have it bad*, hold dear, hold high, idolize, long for, lose one's heart to*, prefer, prize, put on pedestal*, think the world of*, thrive with, treasure, venerate, wild for*, worship; SEE CONCEPT *32*

love [*v2*] *have sexual relations*
canoodle, caress, clasp, cling, cosset, court, cuddle, dandle, draw close, embrace, feel, fondle, hold, hug, kiss, lick, look tenderly, make love, neck*, pet*, press, shine, soothe, stroke, take into arms, tryst, WOO; SEE CONCEPTS *375,384*

love affair [*n*] *sexual relationship outside of marriage*
adultery, affair, amour, devotion, enthusiasm, extracurricular activity, flirtation, intrigue, liaison, love, menage à trois, passion, romance, triangle; SEE CONCEPTS *375,388*

lovely [*adj*] *beautiful, charming; agreeable*
admirable, adorable, alluring, amiable, attractive, beauteous, bewitching, captivating, comely, dainty, delectable, delicate, delicious, delightful, enchanting, engaging, enjoyable, exquisite, exquisite, fair, good-looking, gorgeous, graceful, gratifying, handsome, knockout, lovesome, nice, picture, pleasant, pleasing, pretty, pulchritudinous, rare, scrumptious, splendid, stunning, sweet, winning; SEE CONCEPTS *537,579,589*

lover [*n*] *person having sexual relationship*
admirer, beau, beloved, boyfriend, courter, darling, dear, dearest, escort, fiancé, fiancée, flame, gentleman friend, girlfriend, idolizer, inamorata, inamorato, infatuate, Juliet*, master, mistress, paramour, petitioner, Romeo*, significant other, solicitor, steady, suitor, suppliant, swain, sweetheart, truelove, valentine, wooer; SEE CONCEPT *423*

loving [*adj*] *expressing adoration*
admiring, affectionate, amatory, amiable, amorous, anxious, appreciative, ardent, attached, attentive, benevolent, bound up, caring, concerned, considerate, cordial, dear, demonstrative, devoted, doting, earnest, enamored, erotic, expressive, faithful, fervent, fond, friendly, generous, idolatrous, impassioned, infatuated, kind, liking, loyal, passionate, respecting, reverent, reverential, romantic, sentimental, solicitous, tender, thoughtful, valuing, warm, warmhearted, worshipful, zealous; SEE CONCEPTS *372,401,542*

low [*adj1*] *close to the ground; short*
below, beneath, bottom, bottommost, crouched, decumbent, deep, depressed, flat, ground-level, inferior, junior, lesser, level, little, lowering, low-hanging, low-lying, low-set, minor, nether, not high, profound, prostrate, rock-bottom, shallow, small, squat, squatty, stunted, subjacent, subsided, sunken, under, unelevated; SEE CONCEPTS *583,779,782,793*

low [*adj2*] *reduced; mediocre*
cheap, cut, cut-rate*, deficient, depleted, economical, inadequate, inexpensive, inferior, insignificant, little, low-grade, marked down, meager, moderate, modest, nominal, paltry, poor, puny, reasonable, scant, second-rate*, shoddy, slashed, small, sparse, substandard, trifling, uncostly, worthless; SEE CONCEPTS *334,574,789*

low [*adj3*] *crude, vulgar*
abject, base, blue, coarse, common, contemptible, crass, crumby, dastardly, degraded, depraved, despicable, disgraceful, dishonorable, disreputable, gross*, ignoble, ill-bred, inelegant, mean, menial, miserable, nasty, obscene, off-color, offensive, raw, rough, rude, scrubby, scruffy*, scurvy, servile, sordid, unbecoming, uncouth, undignified, unrefined, unworthy, vile, woebegone, woeful, wretched; SEE CONCEPTS *404,542*

low [*adj4*] *living in, coming from poor circumstances*
base, baseborn, humble, ignoble, lowborn, lowly, mean, meek, obscure, plain, plebeian, poor, rude, simple, unpretentious, unwashed; SEE CONCEPT *549*

low [*adj5*] *depressed*
bad, blue*, crestfallen, dejected, despondent, disheartened, down, down and out*, downcast, downhearted, down in the dumps*, down in the mouth*, dragged, fed up, forlorn, gloomy, glum, in the pits*, low-down*, miserable, moody, morose, sad, singing the blues*, spiritless, unhappy; SEE CONCEPT *403*

low [*adj6*] *not feeling well*
ailing, debilitated, dizzy, dying, exhausted, faint, feeble, frail, ill, indisposed, poorly, prostrate, reduced, sick, sickly, sinking, stricken, unwell, weak; SEE CONCEPT *314*

low [*adj7*] *not loud*
faint, gentle, hushed, muffled, muted, quiet, soft, subdued, whispered; SEE CONCEPT *594*

lower [*adj*] *under, inferior*
bush-league*, curtailed, decreased, diminished, junior, lessened, lesser, low, lower rung, minor, nether, pared down, reduced, secondary, second-class, second-fiddle*, second-string*, smaller, subjacent, subordinate, under; SEE CONCEPTS *586,772*

lower [*v1*] *let down; fall*
bring low, cast down, couch, demit, depress, descend, detrude, droop, drop, ground, let down, make lower, push down, reduce, set down, sink, submerge, take down; SEE CONCEPT *181*

lower [*v2*] *reduce, minimize*
abate, clip, curtail, cut, cut back, cut down, decrease, decry, de-escalate, deflate, demote, depreciate, devaluate, devalue, diminish, downgrade, downsize, lessen, mark down, moderate, pare, prune, roll back, scale down, shave, slash, soften, tone down, undervalue, write off; SEE CONCEPTS *236,240,247*

lower [*v3*] *belittle, disgrace*
abase, bemean, cast down, condescend, debase, degrade, deign, demean, depress, devalue, downgrade, humble, humiliate, stoop; SEE CONCEPTS *7,19*

low-key [*adj*] *subdued*
easygoing, laid-back*, loose, low-pitched, muffled, muted, played down, quiet, relaxed, restrained, sober, softened, soft-sell*, subtle, toned down, understated; SEE CONCEPTS *542,544,548*

lowly [*adj*] *inferior, plain*
average, base, baseborn, cast down, common, commonplace, docile, dutiful, everyday, gentle, humble, ignoble, low, lowborn, mean, meek, menial, mild, modest, mundane, obscure, obsequious, ordinary, plebeian, poor, proletarian, prosaic, retiring, reverential, servile, simple, submissive, subordinate, unassuming, unpretentious, withdrawing; SEE CONCEPTS *404,547,549*

loyal [*adj*] *faithful, dependable*
allegiant, ardent, attached, behind one, believing, coming through, constant, devoted, dutiful, dyed-in-the-wool*, firm, on one's side*, patriotic, resolute, staunch, steadfast, steady, tried-and-true*, true, true-blue*, trustworthy, trusty, unfailing, unswerving, unwavering; SEE CONCEPTS *404,545*

loyalty [*n*] *faithfulness, dependability*
adherence, allegiance, ardor, attachment, bond, conscientiousness, constancy, devotedness, devotion, duty, earnestness, faith, fealty, fidelity, homage, honesty, honor, incorruptibility, integrity, inviolability, obedience, patriotism, probity, reliability, resolution, scrupulousness, sincerity, single-mindedness, singleness, staunchness, steadfastness, subjection, submission, support, tie, troth, trueheartedness, trueness, trustiness, trustworthiness, truth, truthfulness, uprightness, zeal; SEE CONCEPTS *411,645*

lubricate [*v*] *make slippery*
anoint, cream, grease, lard, lube, make, oil, oil the wheels*, slick, smear, smooth, tallow, wax; SEE CONCEPT *202*

lucid [*adj1*] *evident, obvious*
apprehensible, clear, clear-cut, comprehendible, comprehensible, crystal clear, distinct, explicit, fathomable, graspable, intelligible, knowable, limpid, luminous, pellucid, plain, translucent, transparent, transpicuous, unambiguous, unblurred, understandable; SEE CONCEPT *529*

lucid [*adj2*] *brilliant, shining*
beaming, bright, effulgent, gleaming, incandescent, lambent, luminous, lustrous, radiant, refulgent, resplendent; SEE CONCEPT *617*

lucid [*adj3*] *clear, transparent*
clear, crystalline, diaphanous, gauzy, glassy, limpid, obvious, pellucid, pure, sheer, translucent, transpicuous, unblurred; SEE CONCEPTS *606,619*

lucid [*adj4*] *clearheaded, sensible*
all there, compos mentis, cool, got head together*, in right mind, normal, rational, reasonable, right, sane, sober, sound, together; SEE CONCEPTS *402,403*

luck [*n1*] *good fortune*
advantage, big break*, blessing, break*, fluke*, fortunateness, godsend*, good luck, happiness, health, in the cards*, karma*, kismet*, Lady Luck*, luckiness, lucky break*, mazel tov*, occasion, opportunity, profit, prosperity, run of luck*, serendipity, smile*, streak of luck, stroke, success, triumph, victory, weal, wealth, win, windfall; SEE CONCEPT *693*

luck [*n2*] *chance*
accident, break, destiny, fate, fifty-fifty*, fortuity, fortune, happenstance, hazard, occasion, occurrence, toss-up*, unforeseen event; SEE CONCEPT *679*

luckily [*adv*] *happily*
by chance, favorably, fortuitously, fortunately, opportunely, propitiously, providentially; SEE CONCEPTS *544,572*

lucky [*adj*] *fortunate, opportune*
advantageous, adventitious, all systems go*, auspicious, beneficial, benign, blessed, charmed, coming up roses*, everything going*, favored, felicitous, fortuitous, getting a break*, golden, happy, hit it big*, holding aces*, hopeful, hot, in the groove*, into something, on a roll, on a streak, promising, propitious, prosperous, providential, serendipitous,

striking it rich*, successful, timely, well; SEE CONCEPTS *537,572*

lucrative [*adj*] *productive, well-paid*
advantageous, cost effective, fatness, fruitful, gainful, good, high-income*, in the black*, money-making, paying, profitable, remunerative, sweet, worthwhile; SEE CONCEPT *334*

ludicrous [*adj*] *absurd, ridiculous*
antic, bizarre, burlesque, comic, comical, crazy, droll, fantastic, farcical, foolish, funny, gelastic, grotesque, incongruous, laughable, nonsensical, odd, outlandish, preposterous, risible, silly, zany; SEE CONCEPT *548*

lug [*v*] *drag something around*
bear, buck, carry, convey, draw, ferry, haul, heave, hump, jerk, lift, lurch, pack, pull, rake, schlepp,snap, tote, tow, transport, trawl, tug, vellicate, yank; SEE CONCEPT *206*

luggage [*n*] *bag, suitcase*
baggage, carry-on, case, fortnighter, gear, impedimenta, paraphernalia, suit bag, things*, tote bag, trunk, valise; SEE CONCEPTS *446,494*

lukewarm [*adj1*] *slightly heated*
blood-warm, milk-warm, tepid, warm, warmish; SEE CONCEPT *605*

lukewarm [*adj2*] *indifferent, unenthusiastic*
apathetic, chilly, cold, cool, halfhearted, hesitant, indecisive, irresolute, phlegmatic, tepid, uncertain, uncommitted, unconcerned, undecided, uninterested, unresolved, unresponsive, wishy-washy*; SEE CONCEPTS *403,542*

lull [*n*] *pause, calm*
abeyance, break, breather, breathing spell, calmness, coffee break, comma*, downtime*, hiatus, hush, lay-off, letup, pausation, quiescence, quiet, respite, silence, stillness, stop, time-out*, tranquility; SEE CONCEPT *807*

lull [*v*] *calm, ease off*
abate, allay, balm, becalm, cease, chill out*, compose, cool*, cool off*, decrease, die down, diminish, dwindle, ebb, fall, hush, lay back, let up, lullaby, moderate, pacify, put a lid on*, qualify, quell, quiet, quiet down, settle, slacken, soft-pedal*, soothe, still, stroke, subdue, subside, take it easy*, take the edge off*, take the sting out*, temper, tranquilize, wane; SEE CONCEPTS *7,22,210,698*

lumber [*v1*] *walk heavily, clumsily*
barge, clump, galumph, lump, plod, shamble, shuffle, slog, stump, trudge, trundle, waddle; SEE CONCEPT *151*

lumber [*v2*] *burden*
charge, cumber, encumber, impose upon, lade, land, load, saddle, tax, weigh; SEE CONCEPT *14*

lumbering [*adj*] *clumsy, awkward*
blundering, bovine, bumbling, clodhopping*, clunking, elephantine, gauche, gawky, halting, heavy, heavy-footed, hulking, inept, klutzy*, lead-footed*, lumpish, maladroit, overgrown, ponderous, splay,

two left feet*, ungainly, unhandy, unwieldy, wooden; SEE CONCEPTS *406,584*

luminary [*n*] *very important person*
big name*, celeb*, celebrity, dignitary, eminence, leader, lion*, name, notability, notable, personage, personality, somebody*, star, superstar, VIP*, worthy; SEE CONCEPTS *352,423*

luminescent [*adj*] *glowing, shining*
bright, effulgent, fluorescent, luminous, phosphorescent, radiant; SEE CONCEPT *617*

luminous [*adj1*] *bright, glowing*
beaming, brilliant, clear, crystal, effulgent, fulgent, illuminated, incandescent, lambent, lighted, lit, lucent, lucid, luminescent, lustrous, radiant, refulgent, resplendent, shining, translucent, transparent, vivid; SEE CONCEPT *617*

luminous [*adj2*] *obvious, understandable*
apprehensible, bright, brilliant, clear, comprehendible, comprehensible, evident, fathomable, graspable, intelligible, knowable, lucid, perspicacious, perspicuous; SEE CONCEPT *529*

lump [*n*] *clump, mass*
agglomeration, ball, bit, block, bulge, bulk, bump, bunch, cake, chip, chunk, cluster, crumb, dab, gob, group, growth, handful, hunk, knot, knurl, lot, morsel, mountain, much, nugget, part, peck, piece, pile, portion, protrusion, protuberance, scrap, section, solid, spot, swelling, tumescence, tumor, wad, wedge; SEE CONCEPTS *432,470,471*

lump [*v*] *tolerate, withstand*
abide, bear, brook, digest, endure, put up with, stand, stomach, suffer, swallow, take; SEE CONCEPT *23*

lunacy [*n*] *craziness, madness*
aberration, absurdity, alienation, asininity, dementia, derangement, distraction, fatuity, folly, foolhardiness, foolishness, idiocy, imbalance, imbecility, inanity, ineptitude, insanity, mania, psychopathy, psychosis, senselessness, silliness, stupidity; SEE CONCEPTS *410,633*

lunatic [*n*] *person who is crazy, mad*
crackpot*, crank, cuckoo*, demoniac, ding-a-ling*, flake*, fruitcake*, kook*, lamebrain*, loon*, madman/woman, maniac, neurotic, nut*, paranoid, psycho*, psychopath, psychotic, scatterbrain, schizo*; SEE CONCEPTS *412,809*

lunatic [*adj*] *crazy, mad*
absurd, baked*, balmy*, bananas*, bonkers*, cracked, crazed, daft, demented, deranged, dippy*, flaky*, flipped out*, foolish, freaked out*, fried*, idiotic, insane, irrational, kooky*, loco, maniac, maniacal, nonsensical, nutty*, preposterous, psyched out*, psychotic, schizoid*, screwy*, stupid, unsound, whacko*, zany; SEE CONCEPTS *401,403*

lunge [*n*] *pounce*
charge, cut, jab, jump, pass, spring, stab, swing, swipe, thrust; SEE CONCEPTS *159,194*

lunge [*v*] *pounce, dive for*
bound, burst, charge, cut, dash, drive, fall upon, hit, jab, jump, leap, lurch, pitch, plunge, poke, push, set

upon, stab, strike, surge, thrust; SEE CONCEPTS *159,194*

lurch [v] *move toward with jerk*
blunder, bumble, careen, dodge, duck, falter, flounder, heave, jerk, lean, list, move to the side, pitch, reel, rock, roll, seesaw, slide, slip, stagger, stumble, sway, swing, teeter, tilt, toss, totter, wallow, weave, wobble, yaw; SEE CONCEPTS *80,150,152,194*

lure [n] *bait*
allurement, ambush, appeal, attraction, bribe, call, camouflage, carrot*, come-on*, con game*, decoy, delusion, draw, enticement, fake, gimmick, hook, illusion, incentive, inducement, inveiglement, invitation, magnet*, mousetrap*, pull, seducement, seduction, siren song*, sitting duck*, snare, sweetener*, temptation, tout, trap, trick; SEE CONCEPTS *32,529*

lure [v] *attract, seduce*
allure, bag, bait, beckon, beguile, bewitch, cajole, captivate, capture, catch, charm, come on*, decoy, drag, draw, enchant, ensnare, entice, fascinate, grab, haul, hit on*, hook, inveigle, invite, lead on, pull, rope, steer, suck in*, sweep off one's feet*, tempt, train, turn on, vamp; SEE CONCEPT *11*

lurid [adj] *shocking, gruesome*
ashen, bloody, deep, disgusting, distinct, exaggerated, extreme, fiery, ghastly, gory*, graphic, grim, grisly, hideous, horrible, horrid, horrifying, livid, low-down, macabre, melodramatic, obscene, off-color, offensive, purple*, racy, raunchy, revolting, rough, salty, sanguine*, savage, sensational, sinister, startling, terrible, terrifying, violent, vivid, yellow*; SEE CONCEPTS *267,537*

lurk [v] *hide; move stealthily*
conceal oneself, creep, crouch, go furtively, gumshoe, lie in wait, prowl, skulk, slide, slink, slip, snake, sneak, snoop, stay hidden, steal, wait; SEE CONCEPTS *151,188*

luscious [adj] *delicious, delectable*
adorable, ambrosial, appetizing, choice, darling, delish, deluxe, distinctive, divine, exquisite, flamboyant, flavorsome, heavenly, honeyed, juicy, lush, luxurious, mellow, mouth-watering, nectarious, opulent, ornate, palatable, palatial, piquant, rare, rich, savory, scrumptious, succulent, sumptuous, sweet, toothsome, voluptuous, yummy*; SEE CONCEPTS *574,613*

lush [adj] *profuse and delightful*
abundant, ambrosial, delectable, delicious, deluxe, dense, elaborate, extensive, extravagant, exuberant, flourishing, fresh, grand, green, heavenly, juicy, lavish, luscious, luxuriant, luxurious, opulent, ornate, overgrown, palatial, plush, prodigal, prolific, rank, rich, riotous, ripe, ritzy, scrumptious, sensuous, succulent, sumptuous, teeming, tender, verdant, voluptuous; SEE CONCEPTS *574,589,771*

lust [n] *appetite, passion*
animalism, aphrodisia, appetence, appetition, avidity, carnality, concupiscence, covetousness, craving, cupidity, desire, eroticism, excitement, fervor, greed, hunger, itch, lasciviousness, lechery, lewdness, libido, licentiousness, longing, prurience, pruriency, salaciousness, salacity, sensualism, sensuality, thirst, urge, wantonness, weakness, yen; SEE CONCEPTS *20,709*

lust [v] *desire strongly*
ache, be consumed with desire, be hot for*, covet, crave, hanker, hunger for, itch, long, need, pine, thirst, want, wish, yearn, yen; SEE CONCEPT *20*

luster [n] *gloss, shine*
afterglow, brightness, brilliance, brilliancy, burnish, candescence, dazzle, effulgence, glaze, gleam, glint, glitter, glow, incandescence, iridescence, lambency, luminousness, opalescence, polish, radiance, refulgence, resplendence, sheen, shimmer, sparkle; SEE CONCEPT *620*

lustrous [adj] *glossy, shining*
bright, burnished, dazzling, effulgent, fulgent, glace, gleaming, glinting, glistening, glorious, glowing, incandescent, lambent, lucent, luminous, polished, radiant, refulgent, shimmering, shiny, sparkling, splendid, waxy; SEE CONCEPT *617*

lusty [adj] *energetic, healthy*
brawny, dynamic, hale, hearty, potent, powerful, red-blooded, robust, rugged, stalwart, stout, strapping, strenuous, strong, sturdy, tough, vigorous, virile, vital; SEE CONCEPTS *314,485,489*

luxuriant [adj] *profuse, plush*
abundant, ample, copious, deluxe, dense, elaborate, excessive, extravagant, exuberant, fancy, fecund, fertile, flamboyant, flourishing, fruitful, lavish, luscious, lush, opulent, overflowing, palatial, plenteous, plentiful, prodigal, productive, profusive, prolific, rampant, rank, rich, riotous, sumptuous, superabundant, teeming, thriving; SEE CONCEPTS *574,771*

luxuriate [adj] *indulge, prosper*
abound, bask, be in clover*, bloom, burgeon, delight, eat up*, enjoy, feast, flourish, grow, increase, live extravagantly, live high on hog*, live in luxury*, live it up*, love, overdo, relish, revel, riot, roll, rollick, take it easy*, thrive, wallow, wanton; SEE CONCEPTS *539,544,589*

luxurious [adj] *affluent, indulgent*
comfortable, costly, deluxe, easy, elaborate, epicurean, expensive, extravagant, fancy, fit for a king/queen*, gorgeous, grand, grandiose, gratifying, hedonistic, immoderate, imposing, impressive, in lap of luxury, lavish, luscious, lush, magnificent, majestic, opulent, ostentatious, palatial, pampered, pleasurable, pleasure-loving, plush, plushy, posh, pretentious, rich, ritzy*, self-indulgent, sensual, sensuous, splendid, stately, sumptuous, sybaritic, upscale, voluptuous, well-appointed; SEE CONCEPTS *544,574,589*

luxury [n] *great pleasure, indulgence*
affluence, bliss, comfort, delight, enjoyment, exorbitance, extravagance, extravagant, frill, gratifica-

tion, hedonism, high living, immoderation, intemperance, leisure, luxuriousness, opulence, rarity, richness, satisfaction, splendor, sumptuousness, treat, well-being; SEE CONCEPTS *337,388,712*

lying [*adj*] *dishonest*
committing perjury, deceitful, deceptive, delusive, delusory, dissembling, dissimulating, double-crossing*, double-dealing*, equivocating, false, falsifying, fibbing, guileful, inventing, knavish, mendacious, misleading, misrepresenting, misstating, perfidious, prevaricating, roguish, shifty, treacherous, tricky, two-faced*, two-timing*, unreliable, untruthful, wrong; SEE CONCEPT *267*

M

macabre [*adj*] *very eerie; deathlike*
cadaverous, deathly, dreadful, frightening, frightful, ghastly, ghostly, ghoulish, grim, grisly, gruesome, hideous, horrible, horrid, lurid, morbid, offensive, scary, spookish, spooky, terrible, unearthly, weird; SEE CONCEPTS *537,547*

machinate [*v*] *maneuver, plot*
cogitate, collude, come up with, connive, conspire, contrive, design, devise, engineer, finagle, hatch, intrigue, invent, mastermind, plan, play games*, promote, pull strings*, scheme, trump up*, wangle; SEE CONCEPT *36*

machination [*n*] *maneuver, plot*
artifice, cabal, conspiracy, design, device, dirty work*, dodge*, gamesmanship, intrigue, monkey business*, on the make*, ploy, practice, ruse, scheme, sellout, skullduggery, song and dance*, stratagem, trick; SEE CONCEPT *660*

machine [*n1*] *device that performs a task*
apparatus, appliance, automaton, automobile, computer, contraption, contrivance, engine, gadget, implement, instrument, mechanism, motor, robot, thingamabob*, tool, vehicle, widget*; SEE CONCEPT *463*

machine [*n2*] *well-run political organization*
agency, lineup, machinery, movement, party, ring, setup, structure, system; SEE CONCEPT *301*

machine [*n3*] *person who acts automatically*
agent, automaton, clone, drudge, grind, laborer, mechanical, puppet, robot, zombie*; SEE CONCEPTS *348,423*

machinery [*n*] *devices performing work*
accouterment, agency, agent, apparatus, appliance, channel, contraption, contrivance, engine, equipment, gadget, gear, habiliments, implement, instrument, materiel, means, mechanism, medium, method, motor, organ, outfit, paraphernalia, shifts, structure, system, tackle, tool, utensil, vehicle, works; SEE CONCEPTS *463,770*

mad [*adj1*] *crazy, insane*
aberrant, absurd, bananas*, batty, crazed, cuckoo*, daft, delirious, demented, deranged, distracted, fan-

tastic, foolhardy, foolish, frantic, frenetic, frenzied, illogical, imprudent, invalid, irrational, kooky*, loony*, ludicrous, lunatic, mental, non compos mentis, nonsensical, nutty*, off one's rocker*, of unsound mind, out of one's mind*, preposterous, psychotic, rabid, raving, senseless, unbalanced, unhinged, unreasonable, unsafe, unsound, unstable, wacky*; SEE CONCEPTS *403,529*

mad [*adj2*] *very angry*
abandoned, agitated, berserk, distracted, distraught, enraged, exasperated, excited, frantic, frenetic, fuming, furious, incensed, infuriated, irritated, livid, provoked, raging, resentful, seeing red*, uncontrolled, very upset, wild, wrathful; SEE CONCEPT *403*

mad [*adj3*] *enthusiastic; in love*
ardent, avid, crazy, daft, devoted, enamoured, enthused, fanatical, fond, hooked*, impassioned, infatuated, keen, nuts*, wild, zealous; SEE CONCEPTS *32,403*

madcap [*adj*] *crazy, impulsive*
brash, foolhardy, foolish, frivolous, harebrained, heedless, hotheaded, ill-advised, imprudent, incautious, inconsiderate, lively, rash, reckless, stupid, thoughtless, wild; SEE CONCEPT *548*

madden [*v*] *make very angry*
anger, annoy, bother, craze, derange, distract, drive crazy, drive insane, drive out of mind*, drive to distraction*, enrage, exasperate, frenzy, incense, inflame, infuriate, ire, irritate, make see red*, pester, possess, provoke, shatter, steam up*, umbrage, unbalance, unhinge*, upset, vex; SEE CONCEPTS *7,19*

made-up [*adj*] *invented mentally*
fabricated, false, fictional, imaginary, make-believe, mythical, prepared, specious, trumped-up, unreal, untrue; SEE CONCEPT *582*

madhouse [*n*] *place where mentally ill live; place full of commotion*
asylum, bedlam, chaos, insane asylum, loony bin*, mental hospital, mental institution, pandemonium, psychiatric hospital, sanitarium, turmoil, uproar; SEE CONCEPTS *312,449,516,674*

madly [*adj*] *wildly, fiercely*
absurdly, crazily, deliriously, dementedly, desperately, devotedly, distractedly, energetically, exceedingly, excessively, excitedly, extremely, foolishly, frantically, frenziedly, furiously, hard, hastily, hurriedly, hysterically, insanely, intensely, irrationally, like mad, ludicrously, nonsensically, passionately, psychotically, quickly, rabidly, rapidly, rashly, recklessly, senselessly, something fierce, speedily, stormily, to distraction, tumultously/tumultuously, turbulently, unreasonably, violently; SEE CONCEPTS *537,540,544*

madman/madwoman [*n*] *person who is considered mentally ill*
bedlamite, crazy person, demented, deranged, idiot, imbecile, loon, lunatic, maniac, mental case*, pa-

tient, psycho*, psychopath, psychotic, raver*, schizophrenic; sociopath; SEE CONCEPTS *412,423*

magazine [*n1*] *periodic publication*
annual, bimonthly, biweekly, booklet, broadside, brochure, circular, daily, digest, gazette, glossy, joint, journal, manual, monthly, newsletter, newspaper, organ, pamphlet, paper, periodical, pulp*, quarterly, rag*, review, semiweekly, sheet*, slick, throwaway*, weekly; SEE CONCEPT *280*

magazine [*n2*] *arsenal of weapons*
ammunition dump, armory, cache, depository, depot, munitions dump, repertory, repository, store, storehouse, warehouse; SEE CONCEPTS *321,500*

magic [*n*] *supernatural power; appearance of impossible feats by tricks*
abracadabra*, alchemy, allurement, astrology, augury, bewitchment, black art, conjuring, conjury, devilry, diabolism, divination, enchantment, exorcism, fascination, foreboding, fortune-telling, hocus-pocus*, horoscopy, illusion, incantation, legerdemain, magnetism, necromancy, occultism, power, prediction, presage, prestidigitation, prophecy, rune, sleight of hand, soothsaying, sorcery, sortilege, spell, superstition, taboo, thaumaturgy, trickery, voodoo, voodooism, witchcraft, wizardry; SEE CONCEPTS *370,689*

magic/magical [*adj*] *bewitching, charming*
bewitched, charismatic, clairvoyant, conjuring, demoniac, diabolic, eerie, enchanted, enchanting, ensorcelled, entranced, entrancing, extraordinary, fascinating, fiendish, ghostly, haunted, imaginary, magnetic, marvelous, miraculous, mysterious, mystic, mythical, necromantic, occult, otherworldly, parapsychological, runic, sorcerous, spectral, spellbinding, spellbound, spiritualistic, spooky, telekinetic, thaumaturgic, tranced, uncanny, unusual, weird, witching, witchlike, wizardly, wonderful; SEE CONCEPTS *537,548,582*

magician [*n*] *person who performs supernatural feats or tricks*
archimage, charmer, conjurer, diabolist, diviner, enchanter, enchantress, exorciser, exorcist, fortune-teller, genie, genius, illusionist, marvel, medicine man/woman, medium, miracle worker, necromancer, prophet, satanist; seer, shaman, siren, soothsayer, sorcerer, spellbinder, thaumaturge, theurgist, trickster, virtuoso, voodoo, warlock, witch, witch doctor, wizard; SEE CONCEPTS *352,361*

magnanimous [*adj*] *very giving and kind*
all heart, altruistic, beneficent, benevolent, big, big-hearted, bountiful, charitable, chivalrous, considerate, forgiving, free, generous, great, greathearted, handsome, has heart in right place*, high-minded, kindly, knightly, liberal, lofty, loose, munificent, noble, openhanded, princely, Santa Claus*, selfless, soft*, soft-touch*, ungrudging, unselfish, unstinting; SEE CONCEPTS *404,542*

magnate [*n*] *very important person, usually in business*
aristocrat, baron, bigwig*, businessman/woman, capitalist, captain of industry, chief, czar, figure, financier, industrialist, leader, lion*, magnifico*, merchant, mogul, name, noble, notable, peer, personage, plutocrat, tycoon, VIP*; SEE CONCEPT *347*

magnetic [*adj*] *drawing, attractive*
alluring, appealing, arresting, attractive, bewitching, captivating, charismatic, charming, enchanting, entrancing, fascinating, hypnotic, inviting, irresistible, mesmerizing, pulling, seductive; SEE CONCEPTS *404,537*

magnetism [*n*] *charm, attractiveness*
allure, appeal, attraction, captivatingness, charisma, draw, drawing power, enchantment, fascination, glamour, hypnotism, influence, lure, magic, mesmerism, power, pull, seductiveness, spell, witchcraft, witchery; SEE CONCEPTS *411,676*

magnificent [*adj*] *glorious, wonderful*
arresting, august, brilliant, chivalric, commanding, elegant, elevated, exalted, excellent, fine, glittering, gorgeous, grand, grandiose, high-minded, imperial, imposing, impressive, lavish, lofty, lordly, luxurious, magnanimous, magnific, majestic, noble, opulent, outstanding, palatial, plush, pompous, posh, princely, proud, radiant, regal, resplendent, rich, royal, smashing, splendid, standout, stately, striking, sublime, sumptuous, superb, superior, superlative, swanky, towering, transcendent; SEE CONCEPTS *485,572*

magnify [*v1*] *enlarge, intensify*
aggrandize, aggravate, amplify, augment, bless, blow up, boost, build up, deepen, dignify, dilate, distend, enhance, ennoble, eulogize, exalt, expand, extend, glorify, heighten, hike, hike up, increase, inflate, intensate, jack up, jump up, mount, multiply, pad, pyramid, redouble, rise, rouse, run up, step up, sweeten, swell; SEE CONCEPTS *236,244,245*

magnify [*v2*] *exaggerate, blow out of proportion*
aggravate, blow up*, boost, color, dramatize, embellish, embroider, enhance, fudge*, inflate, make mountain of molehill*, overcharge, overdo, overdraw, overemphasize, overestimate, overplay, overrate, overstate, overstress, pad*, puff up*, pyramid; SEE CONCEPTS *49,69,266*

magnitude [*n1*] *importance*
consequence, degree, eminence, grandeur, greatness, import, mark, moment, momentousness, note, pith, significance, signification, weight, weightiness; SEE CONCEPT *668*

magnitude [*n2*] *size*
admeasurement, amount, amplitude, bigness, breadth, bulk, capacity, compass, dimension, dimensions, enormity, enormousness, expanse, extent, greatness, hugeness, immensity, intensity, largeness, mass, measure, measurement, proportion, propor-

tions, quantity, range, reach, sizableness, space, strength, tremendousness, vastness, volume; SEE CONCEPT *730*

maid [*n*] *housekeeper, cleaning person*
aide, au pair, chambermaid, cleaning lady, cleaning woman, domestic, help, housemaid, live-in, nurse; SEE CONCEPTS *348,415*

maiden [*adj*] *earliest*
beginning, first, fresh, inaugural, initial, initiatory, intact, introductory, new, original, pioneer, primary, prime, unbroached, untapped, untried, unused, virgin; SEE CONCEPTS *548,585*

mail [*n*] *written correspondence; system for sending correspondence*
air mail, communication, junk mail, letter, package, parcel, post, postal service, postcard, post office; SEE CONCEPTS *271,770*

mail [*v*] *send through the postal system*
dispatch, drop, express, forward, post, send by mail, send by post, transmit; SEE CONCEPT *217*

maim [*v*] *cripple, put out of action*
batter, blemish, break, castrate, crush, damage, deface, disable, disfigure, dismember, disqualify, gimp*, hack, hamstring*, harm, hog-tie*, hurt, impair, incapacitate, injure, lame, mangle, mar, massacre, maul, mayhem, mutilate, spoil, truncate, warp, wound; SEE CONCEPT *246*

main [*n*] *pipe for system*
cable, channel, conduit, duct, line, trough, trunk; SEE CONCEPT *494*

main [*adj1*] *principal, predominant*
capital, cardinal, central, chief, controlling, critical, crucial, essential, foremost, fundamental, head, leading, major, necessary, outstanding, paramount, particular, preeminent, premier, prevailing, primary, prime, special, star, stellar, supreme, vital; SEE CONCEPTS *546,567,829*

main [*adj2*] *absolute, utter*
brute, direct, downright, entire, mere, only, pure, sheer, simple, undisguised, utmost; SEE CONCEPT *535*

mainly [*adv*] *for the most part*
above all, chiefly, essentially, first and foremost, generally, in general, in the main, largely, mostly, most of all, on the whole, overall, predominantly, primarily, principally, substantially, to the greatest extent, usually; SEE CONCEPTS *530,544,772*

mainstay [*n*] *chief support*
anchor, backbone, brace, bulwark, buttress, crutch*, good right arm*, linchpin*, maintainer, pillar, prop, right-hand man/woman*, sinew, staff, standby, stay, strength, supporter, sustainer, upholder; SEE CONCEPTS *646,712*

maintain [*v1*] *care for, keep up*
advance, carry on, conserve, continue, control, cultivate, finance, go on with, guard, husband, keep, keep going, look after, manage, nurture, perpetuate, persevere, preserve, prolong, protect, provide, re-

new, repair, retain, save, supply, support, sustain, take care of, uphold; SEE CONCEPTS *134,140*

maintain [*v2*] *assert, claim; argue for*
advocate, affirm, allege, asseverate, attest, aver, avow, back, champion, contend, correct, declare, defend, emphasize, fight for, hold, insist, justify, persist, plead for, profess, protest, rectify, report, right, say, stand by, state, stress, uphold, vindicate; SEE CONCEPTS *46,49,68*

maintenance [*n*] *perpetuation, support; sustenance*
aliment, alimentation, alimony, allowance, bacon, bread, bread and butter*, care, carrying, conservation, continuance, continuation, food, keep, keeping, livelihood, living, nurture, preservation, prolongation, provision, repairs, resources, retainment, salt*, subsistence, supply, support, sustaining, sustainment, sustention, upkeep, wherewithal; SEE CONCEPTS *134,340,457,712*

majestic [*adj*] *impressive, splendid*
august, awesome, ceremonious, cool, courtly, dignified, elevated, exalted, fab*, grand, grandiose, imperial, imposing, kinglike, kingly, lofty, magnific, magnificent, marvelous, mind-blowing, monumental, noble, out of this world*, pompous, princely, regal, royal, smashing, sovereign, stately, stunning, sublime, sumptuous, superb; SEE CONCEPTS *567,572,574*

major [*adj1*] *bigger*
above, better, big, chief, considerable, dominant, elder, exceeding, extensive, extreme, greater, hefty, higher, large, larger, large-scale, leading, main, most, oversized, primary, senior, sizable, superior, supreme, ultra, upper, uppermost; SEE CONCEPTS *574,773*

major [*adj2*] *important*
big, chief, critical, crucial, dangerous, grave, great, grievous, heavyweight, influential, life and death*, main, major-league, meaningful, notable, outstanding, overshadowing, preeminent, principal, radical, serious, significant, star, stellar, top, vital, weighty; SEE CONCEPT *568*

majority [*n1*] *plurality, most*
best part*, bulk, greater number, greater part, larger part, lion's share*, mass, max*, more, more than half*, preponderance, superiority; SEE CONCEPTS *766,829,835*

majority [*n2*] *adulthood*
age of consent, drinking age, estate, full age, legal maturity, manhood, maturity, prime, prime of life*, ripe age*, seniority, voting age, womanhood; SEE CONCEPTS *715,817*

make [*v1*] *create, build*
accomplish, adjust, arrange, assemble, beget, brew, bring about, cause, compose, conceive, constitute, construct, cook, cook up*, dash off*, draw on, dream up, effect, engender, fabricate, fashion, father, forge, form, frame, generate, get ready, give rise to, hatch, initiate, invent, knock off*, lead to, manufacture,

mold, occasion, originate, parent, prepare, procreate, produce, put together, secure, shape, sire, spawn, synthesize, tear off, throw together*, whip, whip out*; SEE CONCEPTS *168,173,205,221*

make [*v2*] *induce, compel*
bring about, cause, coerce, concuss, constrain, dragoon, drive, effect, force, horn in*, impel, impress, initiate, interfere, meddle, oblige, press, pressurize, prevail upon, require, secure, shotgun, start, tamper; SEE CONCEPTS *14,221*

make [*v3*] *designate, appoint*
advance, assign, constitute, create, delegate, elect, finger, install, invest, name, nominate, ordain, proffer, select, tap, tender; SEE CONCEPTS *50,88*

make [*v4*] *enact, execute*
act, carry on, carry out, carry through, conduct, declare, decree, do, draft, draw up, effect, engage in, establish, fix, form, formulate, frame, legislate, pass, perform, practice, prepare, prosecute, wage; SEE CONCEPTS *91,100,242*

make [*v5*] *add up to; constitute*
amount to, come to, compose, compound, comprise, construct, embody, equal, fabricate, form, make up, mix, organize, put together, represent, structure, synthesize, texture; SEE CONCEPTS *664,667*

make [*v6*] *estimate, infer*
calculate, collect, conclude, deduce, deduct, derive, dope out, draw, figure, gather, gauge, judge, reckon, suppose, think; SEE CONCEPTS *15,37*

make [*v7*] *earn, acquire*
bring home bacon*, bring in, clean up*, clear, gain, get, harvest, hustle, net, obtain, pull, pull down*, rate, realize, reap, receive, secure, sock*, take in; SEE CONCEPTS *120,124,351*

make [*v8*] *arrive, aim at*
advance, arrive at, arrive in time, attain, bear, break for, catch, get to, go, head, light out, meet, move, proceed, progress, reach, set out, strike out, take off; SEE CONCEPTS *159,224*

make-believe [*n*] *unreality*
charade, disguise, dissimulation, dream, fairy tale, fakery, fantasy, imagination, pageant, playacting, pretense, pretension, pretentiousness, sham; SEE CONCEPTS *689,725*

make-believe [*adj*] *imagined, unreal*
acted, dream, false, fantasized, fantasy, fictional, fraudulent, imaginary, made-up, mock, pretend, pretended, sham, simulated; SEE CONCEPTS *529,582*

make believe [*v*] *pretend, dream*
act as if, act as though, counterfeit, enact, fantasize, feign, fool, imagine, play, playact*, simulate; SEE CONCEPTS *12,59*

make off [*v*] *flee, run away*
abscond, bolt*, clear, cut and run, decamp, depart, escape, fly*, go, leave, make away, quit, retire, run, run for it, run off, scamper, scoot, skedaddle*, skip*, withdraw; SEE CONCEPTS *102,150,195*

make out [*v1*] *see, recognize*
detect, discern, discover, distinguish, espy, notice, observe, perceive, remark; SEE CONCEPT *626*

make out [*v2*] *understand*
accept, catch, collect, compass, comprehend, conclude, decipher, deduce, deduct, derive, dig, fathom, follow, gather, grasp, infer, judge, perceive, realize, recognize, see, take in, work out; SEE CONCEPTS *15,18*

make out [*v3*] *get by, succeed*
accomplish, achieve, do, do well enough, do with, endure, fare, flourish, get along, get on, manage, muddle through, prosper, score, thrive; SEE CONCEPTS *23,91,140*

makeshift [*n*] *temporary help*
expediency, expedient, last resort, pis aller, recourse, refuge, replacement, resort, resource, shift, stopgap, substitute; SEE CONCEPTS *658,712*

makeshift [*adj*] *temporary*
alternative, band-aid*, expedient, hit-or-miss*, make-do*, provisional, quick-and-dirty*, slapdash*, stopgap, substitute, temp, throwaway*; SEE CONCEPTS *551,560*

makeup [*n1*] *cosmetics*
blush, face*, foundation, greasepaint, lipstick, maquillage, paint, pancake, powder*; SEE CONCEPT *446*

makeup [*n2*] *structure, composition*
architecture, arrangement, assembly, configuration, constitution, construction, content, contents, design, form, format, formation, layout, order, ordering, organization, plan, scheme, setup, shape, spread, style; SEE CONCEPT *757*

makeup [*n3*] *person's character*
build, cast, complexion, constitution, disposition, fiber, figure, frame of mind, grain, humor, individualism, individuality, make, mold, nature, personality, stamp, stripe, temper, temperament, vein; SEE CONCEPT *411*

make up [*v1*] *create*
ad-lib*, blend, coin, combine, compose, compound, concoct, construct, contrive, cook up*, devise, dream up, fabricate, fake it, fashion, fix, formulate, frame, fuse, hatch, improv*, improvise, invent, join, knock off, make, meld, merge, mingle, mix, originate, play by ear*, prepare, pretend, put together, ready, trump up, vamp, whip up*, wing it*, write; SEE CONCEPTS *173,202*

make up [*v2*] *comprise, constitute*
complete, compose, consist, fill, form, furnish, include, make, meet, provide, supply; SEE CONCEPT *643*

make up [*v3*] *compensate, reconcile*
accommodate, atone, balance, bury the hatchet*, come to terms, compose, conciliate, counterbalance, counterpoise, countervail, forgive and forget, make amends, make peace, mend, offset, outweigh, pacify, recompense, redeem, redress, requite, set off, settle, shake hands; SEE CONCEPTS *126,384*

maladroit [*adj1*] *awkward, clumsy*
all thumbs*, blundering, bumbling, bungling, clunky, floundering, gauche, halting, heavy-handed, inept, inexpert, klutzy*, lumbering, stumbling, two left feet*, two left hands*, ungraceful, unhandy, unskillful; SEE CONCEPTS *401,584*

maladroit [*adj2*] *tactless*
brash, gauche, impolitic, inconsiderate, inelegant, insensitive, thoughtless, undiplomatic, untactful, untoward; SEE CONCEPT *401*

malaise [*n*] *depression, sickness*
angst, anxiety, debility, decrepitude, despair, discomfort, disquiet, distress, doldrums, enervation, feebleness, illness, infirmity, infirmness, lassitude, melancholy, pain, sickliness, unease, uneasiness, unhealthiness, weakness; SEE CONCEPTS *316,410*

male [*n*] *man*
boy, brother, dude*, father, fellow, gent*, gentleman, guy, he, husband, jock*, sir, son; SEE CONCEPT *419*

male [*adj*] *masculine*
macho*, manful, manlike, manly, paternal, potent, virile; SEE CONCEPTS *371,408*

malediction [*n*] *curse*
anathema, commination, curse word, cuss, cuss word, damn, damnation, damning, darn, denunciation, dirty name*, dirty word*, execration, expletive, four-letter word*, imprecation, jinx, no-no*, oath, swear word, whammy*; SEE CONCEPT *278*

malevolent [*adj*] *hateful*
bad-natured, baleful, catty*, despiteful, dirty, evil, evil-minded, hellish, hostile, lousy, malicious, malign, malignant, murder, murderous, pernicious, poison, rancorous, rough, sinister, spiteful, tough, vengeful, vicious, vindictive, waspish, wicked; SEE CONCEPTS *401,542*

malformed [*adj*] *distorted*
abnormal, contorted, crooked, deformed, distorted, grotesque, irregular, misshapen, twisted, warped; SEE CONCEPT *486*

malfunction [*n*] *breakdown, failure*
bug*, defect, fault, flaw, glitch*, gremlin*, impairment, slip; SEE CONCEPTS *658,674*

malice [*n*] *hate, vengefulness*
acerbity, animosity, animus, antipathy, bad blood, bane, bile, bitterness, despite, despitefulness, dirt, dislike, down, enmity, evil, grudge, hatefulness, hatred, hostility, ill will, implacability, malevolence, maliciousness, malignance, malignity, meanness, mordacity, poison, rancor, repugnance, resentment, spite, spitefulness, spleen, umbrage, venom, viciousness, vindictiveness; SEE CONCEPT *29*

malicious [*adj*] *hateful*
awful, bad-natured, baleful, beastly, bitter, catty*, cussed, deleterious, despiteful, detrimental, envious, evil, evil-minded, green*, green-eyed*, gross*, ill-disposed, injurious, jealous, low, malevolent, malign, malignant, mean, mischievous, nasty, noxious,

ornery, pernicious, petty, poisonous, rancorous, resentful, spiteful, uncool, vengeful, venomous, vicious, virulent, wicked; SEE CONCEPTS *267,401,542*

malign [*adj*] *hurtful, injurious*
antagonistic, antipathetic, bad, baleful, baneful, deleterious, despiteful, destructive, detrimental, evil, harmful, hateful, hostile, inimical, injurious, malefic, maleficent, malevolent, malignant, noxious, pernicious, rancorous, sinister, spiteful, vicious, wicked; SEE CONCEPTS *267,537,542*

malign [*v*] *slander, defame*
abuse, accuse, asperse, backbite*, bad-mouth*, befoul, besmirch, bespatter, blacken, calumniate, cast aspersion, curse, decry, defile, denigrate, depreciate, derogate, detract, dirty*, disparage, harm, injure, insult, misrepresent, mudsling, opprobriate, pollute, rap, revile, roast*, run down*, scandalize, slur, smear, soil, spatter, speak ill of, stain, sully, taint, take a swipe at*, tarnish, tear down, traduce, vilify, villainize, vituperate; SEE CONCEPTS *44,52,54,63*

malignant [*adj*] *diseased*
cancerous, deadly, destructive, fatal, internecine, lethal, mortal, pestilential, poisonous; SEE CONCEPT *314*

malleable [*adj*] *pliable*
adaptable, compliant, ductile, flexible, governable, go-with-the-flow*, impressionable, manageable, moldable, plastic, pliant, putty in hands*, rolls with punches*, soft, submissive, supple, tractable, tractile, transformable, workable, yielding; SEE CONCEPTS *403,485*

malodorous [*adj*] *foul-smelling*
bad, decayed, decomposed, fetid, foul, frowzy, funky*, fusty, gamy*, high*, infested, lousy, mephitic, musty, nasty, nauseating, noisome, noxious, off*, offensive, pestilential, poisonous, polluted, putrid, rancid, rank, reeking, rotten, smelly, stale, stenchful, stinking, strong, tainted, vile; SEE CONCEPT *598*

malpractice [*n*] *abuse, misconduct*
carelessness, dereliction, malefaction, misbehavior, misdeed, mismanagement, negligence, offense, transgression, violation; SEE CONCEPTS *101,156, 310,324*

mammoth [*adj*] *huge*
behemothic, colossal, elephantine, enormous, gargantuan, giant, gigantic, high, immense, jumbo, large, leviathan, long, massive, mighty, monstrous, monumental, mountainous, prodigious, stupendous, titanic, vast; SEE CONCEPT *773*

man [*n1*] *human race; member of the human race*
being, body, character, creature, earthling, fellow creature, flesh, folk, Homo sapiens, human, human being, humanity, humankind, individual, mortal, mortality, person, personage, populace, somebody, soul, species; SEE CONCEPT *417*

man [*n2*] *male human*
beau, bloke*, boy, boyfriend, brother, chap*, daddy, dude*, fellow, gent*, gentleman, grandfather, guy,

he, husband, jock*, macho*, mister, nephew, papa, sir, son, swain*, uncle; SEE CONCEPTS *414,419*

manage [v1] *be in charge, control*
administer, advocate, boss, call the shots*, call upon, captain, care for, carry on, command, concert, conduct, counsel, designate, direct, disburse, dominate, engage in, engineer, execute, govern, guide, handle, head, hold down*, influence, instruct, maintain, manipulate, mastermind, minister, officiate, operate, oversee, pilot, ply, preside, regulate, request, rule, run, run the show, steer, superintend, supervise, take care of, take over, take the helm*, train, use, watch, watch over, wield; SEE CONCEPTS *94,117*

manage [v2] *accomplish*
achieve, arrange, bring about, bring off, carry out, con, contrive, cook*, cope with, deal with, doctor*, effect, engineer, execute, finagle, fix, jockey*, plant*, play games*, pull strings*, push around, put one over*, rig*, scam*, succeed, swing, upstage, wangle*, work; SEE CONCEPTS *91,706*

manage [v3] *survive, get by*
bear up, carry on, cope, endure, fare, get along*, get on*, make do*, make out*, muddle, scrape by*, shift, stagger; SEE CONCEPTS *23,407*

management [n1] *persons running an organization*
administration, authority, board, bosses, brass, directorate, directors, employers, execs*, executive, executives, executive suite, front office*, head, mainframe*, man/woman upstairs*, management, micro management*, top brass*, upstairs*; SEE CONCEPT *325*

management [n2] *running an organization*
administration, care, charge, command, conduct, control, direction, governance, government, guidance, handling, intendance, manipulation, operation, oversight, rule, superintendence, superintendency, supervision; SEE CONCEPTS *117,324*

manager [n] *person who runs organization*
administrator, boss, boss lady*, comptroller, conductor, controller, director, exec*, executive, foreman/woman, governor, handler, head, head man/woman, impresario, man*, officer, official, organizer, overseer, producer, proprietor, slave driver*, straw boss*, superintendent, supervisor, top dog*, zookeeper*; SEE CONCEPT *347*

mandate [n] *authority, order*
authorization, behest, bidding, blank check*, carte blanche*, charge, command, commission, decree, dictate, directive, edict, fiat, go-ahead*, green light*, imperative, injunction, instruction, okay*, precept, sanction, warrant, word*; SEE CONCEPTS *318,685*

mandatory [adj] *required, necessary*
binding, commanding, compelling, compulsatory, compulsory, de rigueur, essential, forced, imperative, imperious, indispensable, involuntary, irremissible, needful, obligatory, requisite; SEE CONCEPT *546*

maneuver [n1] *move, tactic*
action, angle, artifice, contrivance, curveball, demarche, device, dodge, fancy footwork*, feint, finesse, gambit, game, gimmick, intrigue, jig*, machination, manipulation, measure, movement, one-upmanship, plan, play, plot, ploy, procedure, proceeding, ruse, scheme, shenanigans*, shuffle*, step, stratagem, stunt, subterfuge, trick; SEE CONCEPTS *6,660*

maneuver [n2] *military practice, operation*
battle, deployment, drill, evolution, exercise, measure, movement, parade, plan, procedure, proceeding, stratagem, tactics, war games; SEE CONCEPT *320*

maneuver [v1] *plan, scheme*
angle, beguile, cheat, come up with, con, conspire, contrive, cook, design, devise, doctor, engineer, exploit, fence, finagle, finesse, go around, intrigue, jockey, leave holding the bag*, machinate, manage, manipulate, move, navigate, operate, plan, play, play games*, plot, proceed, pull strings*, push around, put one over*, rig, scam, scheme, sham, shift, trick, upstage, wangle, work; SEE CONCEPTS *36,59*

maneuver [v2] *direct physically*
deploy, dispense, drive, exercise, guide, handle, manipulate, move, navigate, negotiate, pilot, ply, steer, swing, wield; SEE CONCEPTS *187,225*

mangle [v] *mutilate, deform*
batter, break, bruise, butcher, carve, contort, crush, cut, damage, deface, destroy, disfigure, distort, flay, hack, hash, impair, injure, injure, lacerate, maim, mar, maul, rend, ruin, separate, slash, slay, slice, slit, spoil, tear, wound, wreck; SEE CONCEPTS *176,246,252*

mangy [adj] *scruffy*
decrepit, dirty, impoverished, indigent, mean, motheaten*, poor, ragtag*, shabby, shoddy, sick, sleazy*, squalid, tattered; SEE CONCEPTS *485,621*

manhandle [v] *push around, handle roughly*
abuse, batter, beat, bully*, damage, knock about*, maltreat, mangle, maul, mistreat, paw, pull, push, roughhouse*, rough up*, slap; SEE CONCEPTS *189,208,246*

manhood/womanhood [n] *physical maturity and strength of adult male or female*
adulthood, coming of age*, fecund, femininity, fertility, honor, manfulness, manliness, masculinity, mettle, nobility, potency, virility, womanness, womanliness; SEE CONCEPTS *633,715*

mania [n] *fixation, madness*
aberration, ax to grind*, bee*, bee in bonnet*, bug*, bug in ear*, compulsion, craving, craze, craziness, delirium, dementia, derangement, desire, disorder, enthusiasm, fad, fancy, fascination, fetish, fixed idea, frenzy, furor, grabber*, hang-up*, idée fixe, infatuation, insanity, lunacy, monomania, obsession, on the brain*, partiality, passion, preoccupation, rage, thing, tiger*, tiger by the tail*; SEE CONCEPTS *20,32,410,529*

maniac [n] *person who is crazy, overenthusiastic*
bedlamite, bigot, crackpot*, enthusiast, fan, fanatic, fiend, flake*, freak, fruitcake*, kook*, loon, loony*, lunatic, madman/woman, nut*, nutcase*, psycho*, psychopath, schizoid*, screwball*, Section 8*, zealot; SEE CONCEPT *412*

manic/maniacal [adj] *overexcited, crazy*
berserk, crazed, demented, deranged, excited, flipped*, flipped out*, freaked out*, freaky*, frenzied, high*, insane, lunatic, mad, nutty*, psychotic, rabid, raving, turned-out, unbalanced, up*, wild; SEE CONCEPT *403*

manifest [adj] *clear, obvious*
apparent, big as life*, bold, clear-cut*, conspicuous, crystal clear*, disclosed, distinct, divulged, evidenced, evident, evinced, glaring, noticeable, open, palpable, patent, plain, prominent, revealed, shown, straightforward, told, unambiguous, unmistakable, visible; SEE CONCEPTS *529,576*

manifest [v] *exhibit, make plain*
confirm, declare, demonstrate, display, embody, establish, evidence, evince, expose, express, exteriorize, externalize, flash, illustrate, incarnate, let it all hang out*, mark, materialize, objectify, ostend, parade, personalize, personify, personize, proclaim, prove, reveal, set forth, show, show and tell*, showcase, signify, sport, strut, substantiate, suggest, utter, vent, voice, wave around*; SEE CONCEPTS *118,261*

manifestation [n] *exhibition, proof*
appearance, demonstration, disclosure, display, explanation, exposure, expression, indication, instance, mark, materialization, meaning, phenomenon, revelation, show, sign, symptom, token; SEE CONCEPTS *642,672*

manifold [adj] *abundant, many*
assorted, complex, copious, different, diverse, diversified, diversiform, multifarious, multifold, multiform, multiple, multiplied, multitudinous, multivarious, numerous, sundry, varied, various; SEE CONCEPTS *564,762,781*

manipulate [v1] *maneuver, handle physically*
employ, feel, finger*, form, manage, mold, operate, ply, shape, swing, thumb*, use, wield, work; SEE CONCEPTS *225,612*

manipulate [v2] *change to suit one's desire*
beguile, conduct, control, direct, engineer, exploit, finagle, finesse, guide, handle, influence, jockey, machinate, maneuver, massage, mold, negotiate, play, play games*, pull strings*, pull wires*, push around, shape, steer, upstage, use; SEE CONCEPTS *14,234*

mankind [n] *the human race*
community, flesh, Homo sapiens, humanity, humankind, human species, mortality, mortals, people, society; SEE CONCEPT *417*

manly [adj] *courageous, strong*
audacious, bold, brave, confident, daring, dauntless, dignified, fearless, firm, gallant, hardy, heroic, intrepid, lionhearted, male, manful, manlike, masculine, muscular, noble, powerful, red-blooded*, resolute, robust, self-reliant, stately, staunch, stouthearted, strapping, two-fisted*, undaunted, valiant, valorous, vigorous, virile; SEE CONCEPT *401*

man-made [adj] *artificial*
counterfeit, ersatz, factitious, false, manufactured, not genuine, plastic, synthetic, unnatural; SEE CONCEPTS *549,582*

manner [n1] *person's behavior, conduct*
address, affectation, affectedness, air, appearance, aspect, bearing, comportment, demeanor, deportment, idiosyncrasy, look, mannerism, mien, peculiarity, presence, style, tone, turn, way; SEE CONCEPTS *411,633,644*

manner [n2] *method, approach*
consuetude, custom, fashion, form, genre, habit, habitude, line, means, mode, modus, practice, procedure, process, routine, style, system, tack, technique, tenor, tone, trick, usage, use, vein, way, wise, wont; SEE CONCEPTS *6,660*

manner [n3] *class, category*
brand, breed, form, kind, nature, sort, type, variety; SEE CONCEPT *378*

mannered [adj] *affected, put-on*
airish*, apish*, artificial, artsy, campy*, chichi*, conscious, gone Hollywood*, highfaluting*, posed, pretentious, self-conscious, stilted, stuck up*, unnatural; SEE CONCEPT *401*

mannerism [n] *peculiarity of how someone behaves, acts*
affectation, air, characteristic, eccentricity, foible, habit, idiosyncrasy, oddness, pose, pretension, queerness, quirk, singularity, trait, trick; SEE CONCEPT *644*

mannerly [adj] *polite, well-behaved*
charming, civil, civilized, considerate, courteous, decorous, genteel, gentlemanly, gracious, ladylike, polished, refined, respectful, well-bred, well-mannered; SEE CONCEPT *401*

manners [n] *polite, refined social behavior*
amenities, bearing, behavior, breeding, carriage, ceremony, civilities, comportment, conduct, courtesy, culture, decorum, demeanor, deportment, dignity, elegance, etiquette, formalities, good breeding, good form, mien, mores, polish, politeness, politesse, propriety, protocol, p's and q's*, refinement, social graces, sophistication, taste, urbanity; SEE CONCEPT *633*

mansion [n] *very large house*
abode, building, castle, chateau, dwelling, estate, habitation, hall, home, manor, palace, residence, seat, villa; SEE CONCEPTS *439,516*

manslaughter [n] *killing without malice aforethought*
assassination, crime, foul play*, hit*, homicide, killing, murder, rubout*; SEE CONCEPT *252*

manual [n] *book giving instruction*
bible, compendium, cookbook, enchiridion, guide, guidebook, handbook, primer, reference book,

schoolbook, text, textbook, workbook; SEE CONCEPT *280*

manual [*adj*] *done by hand*
chiral, hand-operated, human, not automatic, physical, standard; SEE CONCEPT *544*

manufacture/manufacturing [*n*] *production of processed goods*
accomplishment, assembling, assembly, casting, completion, composing, composition, construction, creation, doing, erection, fabrication, finishing, forging, formation, making, mass-production, preparing, produce, tooling; SEE CONCEPT *324*

manufacture [*v1*] *build, produce*
accomplish, assemble, carve, cast, cobble*, complete, compose, construct, create, execute, fabricate, fashion, forge, form, frame, fudge together*, machine, make, make up, mass-produce, mill, mold, prefab, process, put together, shape, synthesize, throw together, tool, turn out; SEE CONCEPT *205*

manufacture [*v2*] *concoct, invent*
contrive, cook up*, create, devise, fabricate, hatch, make up, produce, think up, trump up*; SEE CONCEPTS *35,36*

many [*n*] *abundance; a lot*
gobs*, heaps*, horde, jillion*, large numbers, mass, multitude, oodles*, piles*, plenty, scads*, scores, thousands, throng, tons, umpteen*, whole slew*; SEE CONCEPTS *432,786*

many [*adj*] *profuse, abundant*
abounding, alive with, bounteous, bountiful, copious, countless, crowded, divers, frequent, innumerable, legion, lousy with*, manifold, multifarious, multifold, multiplied, multitudinous, myriad, no end of*, numberless, numerous, plentiful, populous, prevalent, profuse, rife, several, sundry, teeming, umpteen, uncounted, varied, various; SEE CONCEPTS *762,771*

map [*n*] *chart of geographic area*
atlas, delineation, design, diagram, draft, drawing, elevation, globe, graph, ground plan, outline, picture, plan, plat, portrayal, print, projection, sketch, topographical depiction, tracing; SEE CONCEPT *625*

mar [*v*] *hurt, damage*
bend, blemish, blight, blot, break, bruise, deface, deform, detract, ding*, disfigure, foul up, harm, impair, injure, louse up, maim, mangle, mess up*, mutilate, queer*, rough up, ruin, scar, scratch, shake up, spoil, stain, sully, taint, tarnish, tweak, vitiate, warp, wreck; SEE CONCEPT *246*

maraud [*v*] *pillage and plunder*
despoil, forage, foray, harass, harry, loot, raid, ransack, ravage, sack; SEE CONCEPTS *86,139*

march [*v*] *walk with deliberation*
advance, boot, debouch, drill, file, forge ahead, go on, hoof it*, journey, mount, move, move out, pace, parade, patrol, pound, pound the pavement*, proceed, progress, promenade, range, space, stalk, step,

step out, stomp, stride, strut, traipse, tramp, tread; SEE CONCEPT *150*

margin [*n*] *border; room around something*
allowance, bound, boundary, brim, brink, compass, confine, edge, elbowroom*, extra, field, frame, hem, latitude, leeway, limit, lip, perimeter, periphery, play, rim, scope, selvage, shore, side, skirt, space, surplus, trimming, verge; SEE CONCEPTS *270,484,513*

marginal [*adj*] *borderline; slight*
bordering, insignificant, low, minimal, minor, negligible, on the edge, peripheral, rimming, small, verging; SEE CONCEPTS *513,789*

marine/maritime [*adj*] *concerning the sea*
abyssal, aquatic, coastal, deep-sea, hydrographic, littoral, maritime, natatorial, nautical, naval, navigational, Neptunian, oceangoing, oceanic, oceanographic, of the sea, pelagic, saltwater, sea, seafaring, seagoing, seashore, seaside, shore; SEE CONCEPT *536*

mariner [*n*] *person who makes living on the sea*
bluejacket*, captain, crew, mate, navigator, sailor, salt*, sea dog*, seafarer, seaman/woman, shipmate, swab*, yachtie*; SEE CONCEPTS *348,366*

marital [*adj*] *concerning marriage*
conjugal, connubial, married, matrimonial, nuptial, spousal, wedded; SEE CONCEPT *555*

mark [*n1*] *blemish; character*
autograph, blaze, blot, blotch, brand, brand name, bruise, check, cross, dent, dot, impression, imprint, ink, John Hancock*, John Henry*, label, line, logo, nick, pock, point, record, register, representation, scar, score, scratch, sign, signature, smudge, splotch, spot, stain, stamp, streak, stroke, symbol, tag, ticket, trace, trademark, underlining, X*; SEE CONCEPTS *79,284*

mark [*n2*] *characteristic, symptom*
affection, attribute, badge, blaze, brand, character, device, distinction, earmark, emblem, evidence, feature, hallmark, idiosyncrasy, image, impression, incision, index, indication, indicia, label, marking, note, particularity, peculiarity, print, proof, property, quality, seal, sign, significant, stamp, symbol, symptom, token, trait, type, virtue; SEE CONCEPTS *411,644,716*

mark [*n3*] *criterion, standard*
gauge, level, measure, norm, yardstick; SEE CONCEPTS *561,783*

mark [*n4*] *goal, target*
aim, ambition, bull's eye*, duty, end, function, object, objective, prey, purpose, use; SEE CONCEPT *659*

mark [*n5*] *importance*
consequence, dignity, distinction, effect, eminence, fame, influence, manifestation, notability, note, notice, prestige, quality, regard, result, standing, value; SEE CONCEPTS *346,668*

mark [*v1*] *blemish, stain*
autograph, blaze, blot, blotch, brand, bruise, chalk, check, dent, dot, impress, imprint, initial, ink, inscribe, label, letter, nick, pinpoint, point, print, scar,

score, scratch, seal, sign, smudge, splotch, stamp, streak, stroke, trace, underline, write, X*; SEE CONCEPTS *79,250*

mark [v2] *characterize*
bespeak, betoken, brand, check off, demonstrate, denote, designate, distinguish, earmark, evidence, evince, exemplify, exhibit, feature, identify, illustrate, indicate, individualize, individuate, label, manifest, mark off, ostend, point out, point up*, proclaim, qualify, remark, set apart, show, show up, signalize, signify, singularize, stake out*, stamp; SEE CONCEPT *261*

mark [v3] *see, notice*
attend, behold, chronicle, discern, distinguish, eye, hearken, mind, note, observe, pay attention, pay heed, perceive, regard, register, remark, take notice of, view, watch, write down; SEE CONCEPTS *38,626*

marked [adj] *apparent, obvious*
arresting, clear, considerable, conspicuous, decided, distinct, evident, manifest, notable, noted, noticeable, outstanding, patent, pointed, prominent, pronounced, remarkable, salient, signal, striking; SEE CONCEPTS *485,535,589*

markedly [adv] *distinctly*
clearly, considerably, conspicuously, decidedly, especially, evidently, greatly, manifestly, notably, noticeably, obviously, outstandingly, particularly, patently, remarkably, signally, strikingly, to a great extent; SEE CONCEPTS *535,544*

market/mart [n] *place, venue for selling goods*
bazaar, booth, business, chain store, co-op, corner store, deli, delicatessen, department store, dimestore, drugstore, emporium, exchange, fair, general store, grocery store, mall, mart, outlet, shop, shopping mall, showroom, souk, square, stall, stock exchange, store, supermarket, trading post, truck, variety store, warehouse; SEE CONCEPTS *323,333,449*

market [v] *package and sell goods*
advertise, barter, display, exchange, merchandise, offer for sale, retail, vend, wholesale; SEE CONCEPTS *324,345*

marketable [adj] *easily sold; in demand*
bankable, commercial, fit, for sale, good, hot*, merchandisable, merchantable, profitable, salable, sellable, selling, sought after, sound, traficable, vendible, wanted; SEE CONCEPTS *334,546*

maroon [v] *abandon*
beach, cast ashore, cast away, desert, forsake, isolate, leave, leave high and dry*, strand; SEE CONCEPTS *195,384*

marriage [n] *legal joining of two people; a union*
alliance, amalgamation, association, confederation, conjugality, connubiality, consortium, coupling, espousal, holy matrimony, link, match, mating, matrimony, merger, monogamy, nuptials, pledging, sacrament, spousal, tie, tie that binds*, wedded bliss*, wedded state, wedding, wedding bells*, wedding ceremony, wedlock; SEE CONCEPTS *297,388*

marrow [n] *heart, essence*
bottom, core, cream, essentiality, gist, kernel, meat, pith, quick, quintessence, quintessential, soul, spirit, stuff, substance, virtuality; SEE CONCEPT *826*

marry [v] *become husband and wife in legal ceremony*
ally, associate, become one, bond, catch*, combine, conjoin, conjugate, contract, couple, drop anchor*, espouse, get hitched*, get married, join, knit, land*, lead to altar, link, match, mate, merge, one, pledge, plight one's troth, promise, relate, settle down*, take vows, tie, tie the knot*, unify, unite, walk down aisle*, wed, wive, yoke; SEE CONCEPT *297*

marsh [n] *swamp*
bog, estuary, everglade, fen, mire, morass, moss, quag, quagmire, slough, swampland, wetland; SEE CONCEPT *509*

marshal [v] *organize, guide*
align, arrange, array, assemble, collect, conduct, deploy, direct, dispose, distribute, draw up, escort, gather, group, lead, line up, methodize, mobilize, muster, order, rally, rank, shepherd, space, systematize, usher; SEE CONCEPTS *84,117,187*

martial [adj] *having to do with armed hostilities*
aggressive, bellicose, belligerent, combative, hostile, military, pugnacious, soldierly, warlike; SEE CONCEPT *401*

martyrdom [n] *suffering endured for sake of a cause*
affliction, agonizing, agony, anguish, crucifixion, devotion, distress, mortification, ordeal, pain, persecution, sacrifice, self-immolation, self-sacrifice, torment, torture, unselfishness; SEE CONCEPTS *410,411*

marvel [n] *wonder*
curiosity, genius, miracle, one for the books*, phenomenon, portent, prodigy, sensation, something else*, stunner, whiz; SEE CONCEPTS *529,671*

marvel [v] *be amazed*
be awed, be surprised, feel surprise, gape, gaze, goggle, stand in awe, stare, wonder; SEE CONCEPT *17*

marvelous [adj1] *hard to believe; amazing*
astonishing, astounding, awe-inspiring, awesome, awful, bewildering, breathtaking, confounding, difficult to believe, extraordinary, fabulous, fantastic, implausible, improbable, incomprehensible, inconceivable, incredible, miraculous, phenomenal, prodigious, remarkable, singular, spectacular, staggering, strange, striking, stunning, stupendous, supernatural, surprising, unbelievable, unimaginable, unlikely, unusual, wonderful, wondrous; SEE CONCEPTS *529,552*

marvelous [adj2] *superb, great*
agreeable, astonishing, bad*, boss*, colossal, cool*, divine, dreamy*, enjoyable, excellent, fab*, fabulous, fantastic, glorious, greatest, groovy*, hot*, keen, magnificent, neat*, out of this world*, outrageous, peachy, pleasant, pleasurable, prime*, rewarding, satisfying, sensational, smashing, solid*, solid gold*, spectacular, splendid, stupendous, super, supreme, swell, terrific, wonderful; SEE CONCEPT *574*

masculinity/masculine [n/adj] *manly*
butch, macho*, male, manful, mannish, muscular, potent, virile; SEE CONCEPTS *371,408,648*

mash [v] *smash, squash*
brew, bruise, chew, crush, decoct, grind, hash, infuse, macerate, masticate, mush up, pound, press, pulp, pulverize, push, reduce, scrunch, squeeze, squish, steep, triturate; SEE CONCEPTS *170,186,208*

mask [n] *false face, cover*
affectation, air*, appearance, aspect, beard*, blind, camouflage, cloak*, concealment, cover-up, disguise, disguisement, dissembling, dissimulation, domino*, facade, fig leaf*, front, guise, hood, masquerade, pose, posture, pretense, pretext, put-on*, screen, semblance, show*, simulation, veil*, veneer, visage, visor, window dressing*; SEE CONCEPTS *450,716*

mask [v] *disguise*
beard, camouflage, cloak, conceal, cover, cover up, defend, dissemble, dissimulate, dress up, front, guard, hide, obscure, protect, safeguard, screen, secrete, shield, veil; SEE CONCEPTS *172,188,384*

masquerade [n] *disguise; social occasion for disguises*
carnival, circus, cloak, color, costume, costume ball, cover, cover-up, deception, dissimulation, domino*, facade, festivity, front, guise, impersonation, imposture, Mardi Gras*, mask, masked ball, masking, mummery, personation, pose, pretense, put-on, revel, screen, show, subterfuge, veil; SEE CONCEPTS *172,188,383,451*

masquerade [v] *disguise*
attitudinize, dissemble, dissimulate, frolic, impersonate, mask, pass as, pass for, pass off, pose, posture, pretend, revel; SEE CONCEPT *59*

mass [n1] *body of matter; considerable portion*
accumulation, aggregate, assemblage, band, batch, block, bulk, bunch, chunk, clot, coagulation, collection, combination, concretion, conglomeration, core, corpus, crowd, entirety, gob, great deal, greater part, group, heap, horde, host, hunk, knot, lion's share*, load, lot, lump, majority, mob, mound, mountain, much, number, object, peck, piece, pile, plurality, preponderance, pyramid, quantity, shock, stack, staple, stockpile, sum, sum total, throng, totality, troop, volume, wad, whole; SEE CONCEPTS *432,786,835*

mass [n2] *bulk, measurement*
dimension, extent, greatness, magnitude, size, span, volume; SEE CONCEPT *792*

massacre [n] *killing of many*
annihilation, assassination, bloodbath, bloodshed, butchery, carnage, decimation, extermination, genocide, internecion, murder, slaughter, slaying; SEE CONCEPT *252*

massacre [v] *kill, often in great numbers*
annihilate, butcher, decimate, depopulate, exterminate, kill, mass murder, murder, slaughter, slay; SEE CONCEPT *252*

massage [n] *kneading of body parts*
back rub, beating, chirapsia, manipulation, rolfing*, rubbing, rubbing-down, stroking; SEE CONCEPTS *308,310*

massage [v] *knead body parts*
caress, manipulate, pat, press, push, rolf*, rub, rub down, stimulate, stroke; SEE CONCEPTS *208,308,310*

masses [n] *public, crowd*
commonalty, common people, great unwashed*, hoi polloi*, lower class, mob, multitude, proletariat, rabble, rank and file*, riffraff*, trash*; SEE CONCEPT *417*

massive [adj] *very large*
big, bulky, colossal, cracking, cumbersome, cumbrous, elephantine, enormous, extensive, gargantuan, gigantic, grand, great, gross, heavy, hefty, huge, hulking, immense, imposing, impressive, mammoth, mighty, monster, monumental, mountainous, ponderous, prodigious, solid, stately, substantial, titanic, towering, tremendous, unwieldy, vast, walloping, weighty, whopping*; SEE CONCEPTS *773,781*

master [n1] *person in charge*
administrator, boss, captain, chief, chieftain, commandant, commander, commanding officer, conqueror, controller, director, employer, general, governor, guide, guru, head, head man/woman, instructor, judge, lord, manager, matriarch, overlord, overseer, owner, patriarch, pedagogue, preceptor, principal, pro, ruler, schoolmaster, skipper, slave driver*, spiritual leader, superintendent, supervisor, swami*, taskmaster, teacher, top dog*, tutor, wheel*; SEE CONCEPTS *347,350,354*

master [n2] *expert, skilled person*
ace*, adept, artist, artiste, authority, buff*, champion, connoisseur, conqueror, doctor, doyen, doyenne, expert, genius, guru, maestro, maven, old hand*, old pro*, past master, prima donna*, pro, professional, proficient, protagonist, pundit, real pro*, sage, savant, scientist, shark, victor, virtuoso, whiz*, whiz-bang*, winner, wizard; SEE CONCEPTS *350,366,423*

master [adj1] *expert*
ace*, adept, crack*, crackerjack*, experienced, masterly, proficient, skilled, skillful; SEE CONCEPT *527*

master [adj2] *dominant, main*
ascendant, chief, controlling, foremost, grand, great, leading, major, overbearing, paramount, predominant, predominate, preponderant, prevalant, prime, principal, regnant, sovereign, supreme; SEE CONCEPT *568*

master [v1] *learn; become proficient*
acquire, beat the game*, beat the system*, bone up*, bury yourself in*, comprehend, cram, excel in, gain mastery, get down cold*, get down pat*, get hold of*, get the hang of*, get the knack of*, grasp, grind, hit the books*, learn the ropes*, megastudy*, pick

up, study, swamp*, understand; SEE CONCEPTS *31,630*

master [*v2*] *conquer, dominate*
be on top of*, best, break, break in, bridle, call the shots*, check, command, control, curb, defeat, direct, domesticate, down, gentle, govern, have the upper hand*, humble, hurdle, keep under thumb*, lead by the nose*, lick, manage, overcome, overpower, prevail, quash, quell, regulate, rule, rule the roost*, run the show, subdue, subjugate, suppress, surmount, tame, throw, triumph, vanquish; SEE CONCEPTS *95,117*

masterful [*adj1*] *expert, skilled*
adept, adroit, clever, consummate, crack, crackerjack*, deft, dexterous, excellent, exquisite, fine, finished, first-rate, master, masterly, preeminent, proficient, skillful, superior, superlative, supreme, transcendent; SEE CONCEPT *527*

masterful [*adj2*] *domineering, bossy*
absolute, arbitrary, arrogant, authoritarian, authoritative, autocratic, commanding, cracking the whip*, despotic, dictative, dictatorial, doctrinaire, dogmatic, high-and-mighty*, high-handed*, imperative, imperious, in charge, in driver's seat*, magisterial, on high horse*, overbearing, overweening, peremptory, powerful, self-willed, tyrannical; SEE CONCEPTS *401,542*

mastermind [*n*] *person who devises a great idea*
administrator, architect, artist, author, authority, brain, brains, director, doctor, engineer, expert, genius, intellect, leader, manager, organizer, philosopher, planner, virtuoso; SEE CONCEPTS *348,350*

mastermind [*v*] *be the brains behind an idea*
conceive, cook up*, devise, direct, engineer, manage, organize, plan, supervise, think up; SEE CONCEPTS *36,173*

masterpiece [*n*] *respected work of art*
chef d'oeuvre, classic, cream*, cream of the crop*, flower, gem, jewel, magnum opus, masterstroke, master work, model, monument, perfection, pièce de résistance*, prize, showpiece, standard, tour de force*, treasure; SEE CONCEPT *259*

mastery [*n1*] *command, expertise*
ability, acquirement, adeptness, adroitness, attainment, capacity, cleverness, comprehension, cunning, deftness, dexterity, expertism, expertness, familiarity, finesse, genius, grasp, grip, ken, knack, knowhow, knowledge, mastership, power, proficiency, prowess, skill, understanding, virtuosity, wizardry; SEE CONCEPT *630*

mastery [*n2*] *domination, rule*
ascendancy, authority, command, conquest, control, dominion, government, jurisdiction, might, power, preeminence, sovereignty, superiority, supremacy, sway, swing, triumph, upper hand*, victory, whip hand*; SEE CONCEPT *376*

match [*n1*] *competition*
bout, contest, engagement, event, game, meet, race, rivalry, sport, test, trial; SEE CONCEPT *363*

match [*n2*] *counterpart, equal*
adversary, analogue, antagonist, approximation, companion, competitor, complement, copy, correlate, countertype, dead ringer*, double, duplicate, equivalent, fellow, like, lookalike, mate, opponent, parallel, peer, replica, ringer*, rival, spitting image*, twin; SEE CONCEPTS *664,667,716*

match [*n3*] *couple*
affiliation, alliance, combination, duet, espousal, marriage, mating, pair, pairing, partnership, union; SEE CONCEPTS *297,388*

matching [*adj*] *corresponding, equal*
analogous, comparable, coordinating, double, duplicate, equivalent, identical, like, paired, parallel, same, twin; SEE CONCEPT *566*

matchless [*adj*] *unequalled, unique*
alone, consummate, excellent, exquisite, incomparable, inimitable, nonpareil, only, peerless, perfect, superior, superlative, supreme, unapproached, unmatched, unparalleled, unrivaled; SEE CONCEPT *574*

mate [*n*] *one of a pair; partner*
acquaintance, alter ego, amigo, analog, assistant, associate, bedmate, bride, buddy*, chum*, classmate, cohort, colleague, companion, compeer, complement, comrade, concomitant, confidant, confrere, consort, coordinate, counterpart, coworker, crony, double, duplicate, familiar, fellow, fellow worker, friend, groom, helper, helpmate, husband, intimate, match, pal*, peer, playmate, reciprocal, roommate, schoolmate, sidekick*, spouse, subordinate, twin; SEE CONCEPTS *296,423,664*

mate [*v*] *marry and breed*
cohabit, copulate, couple, crossbreed, generate, join, land, match, merge, pair, procreate, serve, tie, tie the knot*, wed, yoke; SEE CONCEPTS *297,375*

material [*n1*] *matter, fabric*
being, body, bolt, cloth, component, constituent, crop, element, entity, equipment, gear, goods, habiliments, individual, ingredient, machinery, materiel, object, outfit, paraphernalia, staple, stock, stuff, substance, supply, tackle, textile, thing; SEE CONCEPTS *475,523*

material [*n2*] *written matter*
data, evidence, facts, information, notes, reading, text, work; SEE CONCEPTS *271,274*

material [*adj1*] *bodily, tangible*
actual, animal, appreciable, carnal, concrete, corporeal, earthly, fleshly, incarnate, nonspiritual, objective, palpable, perceptible, phenomenal, physical, real, sensible, sensual, substantial, true, worldly; SEE CONCEPT *485*

material [*adj2*] *important, relevant*
ad rem, applicable, applicative, apposite, apropos, big, cardinal, consequential, considerable, essential, fundamental, germane, grave, indispensable, intrinsic, key, meaningful, momentous, pertinent, pointful, primary, serious, significant, substantial, vital, weighty; SEE CONCEPT *567*

materialistic [adj] *thinking mainly about physical things*
acquisitive, banausic, carnal, earthly-minded, earthy, greedy, material, mundane, object-oriented, possessive, profane, secular, sensual, temporal, terrestrial, unspiritual; SEE CONCEPT *542*

materialize [v] *come into being*
actualize, appear, become concrete, become real, become visual, be incarnate, be realized, coalesce, come about, come to pass, corporealize, develop, embody, emerge, entify, evolve, exteriorize, externalize, happen, hypostatize, make real, manifest, metamorphose, objectify, occur, personalize, personify, personize, pragmatize, realize, reify, substantialize, substantiate, symbolize, take form, take place, take shape, turn up, typify, unfold, visualize; SEE CONCEPTS *105,173,184,231,251*

maternal [adj] *motherly*
affectionate, kind, parental, protective, sympathetic, warm; SEE CONCEPT *401*

maternity [n] *period of being pregnant with child*
gestation, maternology, motherhood, motherliness, mothership, parenthood; SEE CONCEPTS *316,817*

mathematical [adj] *concerning manipulation of numbers*
algebraic, algorithmic, analytical, arithmetical, computative, geometrical, math, measurable, numerical, scientific, trigonometric; SEE CONCEPT *762*

matriarch [n] *woman who heads family, organization*
author, creator, dame, dowager, fountainhead, grande dame, grandmother, matron, mistress, mother, queen, ruler, senior; SEE CONCEPTS *414,415*

matriculate [v] *begin, enroll*
enter, join, register, sign up for; SEE CONCEPTS *114,119*

matrimonial [adj] *married*
betrothed, bridal, conjugal, connubial, engaged, epithalamic, espoused, hymeneal, marital, nuptial, spousal, wedded, wedding; SEE CONCEPT *555*

matrimony [n] *being joined in marriage*
alliance, bells*, conjugality, connubiality, marital rites, marriage, match, nuptials, shotgun wedding*, union, wedding, wedding bells*, wedding ceremony, wedlock; SEE CONCEPT *297*

matrix [n] *something from which another originates*
cast, forge, form, grid, model, mold, origin, pattern, source, womb; SEE CONCEPT *648*

matron [n] *older woman, often one who oversees*
administrator, dame, dowager, grande dame, housekeeper, housemother, lady, matriarch, mother, superintendent, wife; SEE CONCEPTS *348,415*

matted [adj] *tangled*
disordered, kinky, knotted, rumpled, snarled, tousled, twisted, uncombed; SEE CONCEPT *606*

matter [n1] *substance*
amount, being, body, constituents, corporeality, corporeity, element, entity, individual, material, materialness, object, phenomenon, physical world, protoplasm, quantity, stuff, substantiality, sum, thing; SEE CONCEPTS *407,433,470*

matter [n2] *concern, issue*
affair, bag, business, circumstance, episode, event, goings-on*, incident, job, lookout, nub, occurrence, proceeding, question, shooting match*, situation, subject, thing, topic, transaction, undertaking; SEE CONCEPTS *532,696*

matter [n3] *subject, thesis*
argument, context, focus, head, interest, motif, motive, point, purport, resolution, sense, subject matter, substance, text, theme, topic; SEE CONCEPTS *349,529*

matter [n4] *significance, meaning*
amount, body, burden, consequence, content, core, extent, gist, import, importance, magnitude, meat, moment, neighborhood, note, order, pith, range, sense, substance, text, tune, upshot, vicinity, weight; SEE CONCEPTS *651,668*

matter [n5] *difficulty, problem*
circumstance, complication, distress, grievance, perplexity, predicament, to-do*, trouble, upset, worry; SEE CONCEPTS *666,674*

matter [n6] *secretion of a sore*
discharge, infection, maturation, purulence, pus, suppuration, ulceration; SEE CONCEPTS *311,467*

matter [v] *be of consequence, importance*
affect, be important, be of value, be substantive, carry weight, count, cut ice*, express, have influence, imply, import, involve, make a difference, mean, mean something, signify, value, weigh; SEE CONCEPTS *7,19,22,130,682*

matter-of-fact [adj] *realistic, unembellished*
apathetic, calm, cold, cold-blooded*, deadpan, down-to-earth*, dry, dull, earthy, emotionless, factual, feasible, flat, hard-boiled*, impassive, impersonal, lifeless, mundane, naked*, objective, phlegmatic, plain, practical, pragmatic, prosaic, prosy, serious, sober, stoic, stolid, unaffected, unidealistic, unimaginative, unimpassioned, unsentimental, unvarnished; SEE CONCEPTS *267,582*

mature [adj] *adult, grown-up*
complete, cultivated, cultured, developed, fit, full-blown, full-fledged, full-grown, fully grown, grown, in full bloom, in one's prime, manly, matured, mellow, mellowed, of age, perfected, prepared, prime, ready, ripe, ripened, seasoned, settled, sophisticated, womanly; SEE CONCEPTS *485,578,797*

mature [v] *become adult, fully grown*
advance, age, arrive, attain majority, become experienced, become wise, bloom, blossom, come of age, culminate, develop, evolve, fill out, flower*, grow, grow up, maturate, mellow*, mushroom*, perfect, prime, progress, reach adulthood, reach majority, ripen, round, season, settle down*, shoot up*; SEE CONCEPT *704*

maturity [n] *adulthood, full growth*
ability, advancement, capability, civilization, completion, cultivation, culture, development, experi-

ence, fitness, full bloom, fullness, majority, manhood, maturation, matureness, maturescence, mellowness, mentality, perfection, postpubescence, prime, prime of life, readiness, ripeness, sophistication, wisdom, womanhood; SEE CONCEPTS *678, 715,720*

maudlin [*adj*] *teary, overemotional*
bathetic, befuddled, confused, cornball*, drippy*, emotional, gushing, insipid, lachrymose, mawkish, mushy*, romantic, schmaltzy*, sentimental, slush*, soap*, soapy*, soppy*, syrupy*, tearful, tear-jerking*, weak, weepy; SEE CONCEPTS *529,542*

maul [*v*] *mangle, abuse*
bang, bash, batter, beat, beat up, bludgeon, break face, buffet, claw, clean, drub, flagellate, flail, handle roughly, hit, hurt, ill-treat, knock about*, knock around*, lacerate, lash, lean on*, let have it*, maltreat, manhandle, molest, mug, muscle, paste*, paw, pelt, pound, pummel, put in the hospital*, rough up, skin, take care of*, thrash, trample, wax, whip, work over*; SEE CONCEPTS *189,246*

mauve [*adj*] *purplish color*
lavender, lilac, plum, purple, violaceous, violet; SEE CONCEPT *618*

maverick [*n*] *person who takes chances, departs from accepted course*
bohemian, dissenter, extremist, malcontent, nonconformist, radical; SEE CONCEPTS *348,423*

mawkish [*adj*] *sentimental, emotional*
bathetic, cloying, feeble, gooey*, gushing, gushy*, lovey-dovey*, maudlin, mushy*, nauseating, romantic, sappy*, schmaltzy*, sickening, sloppy, tear-jerking*, teary; SEE CONCEPTS *401,542*

maxim [*n*] *saying*
adage, aphorism, apophthegm, axiom, belief, brocard, byword, canon, commonplace, device, dictum, epithet, formula, law, moral, motto, platitude, precept, prescript, proverb, rule, saw, tenet, theorem, truism; SEE CONCEPTS *278,689*

maximum [*n*] *upper limit, greatest amount*
apex, apogee, ceiling, climax, crest, culmination, extremity, height, max*, maxi*, most, nonpareil, peak, pinnacle, preeminence, record, summit, supremacy, the end*, top, utmost, uttermost, zenith; SEE CONCEPTS *706,766,836*

maximum [*adj*] *highest, utmost*
best, biggest, greatest, largest, maximal, most, mostest, outside, paramount, superlative, supreme, top, topmost, ultimate; SEE CONCEPTS *574,762,781*

maybe [*adv*] *possibly*
as it may be, can be, conceivable, conceivably, could be, credible, feasible, imaginably, it could be, might be, obtainable, perchance, perhaps, weather permitting; SEE CONCEPT *552*

mayhem [*n*] *chaos, confusion*
anarchy, commotion, destruction, disorder, fracas, havoc, pandemonium, trouble, violence; SEE CONCEPTS *106,675*

maze [*n*] *labyrinth; confusion*
bewilderment, convolution, entanglement, hodge-podge, imbroglio, intricacy, jungle, knot, meander, meandering, mesh, miscellany, morass, muddle, network, perplexity, puzzle, quandary, skein, snarl, tangle, torsion, twist, uncertainty, web, winding; SEE CONCEPTS *436,529,674*

meadow [*n*] *grassy field*
bottoms*, carpet*, grassland, heath, lea, mead, pasturage, pasture, plain, prairie, rug*, steppe, veldt; SEE CONCEPT *509*

meager [*adj1*] *small, inadequate; poor*
bare, barren, deficient, exiguous, flimsy, inappreciable, inconsiderable, infertile, insubstantial, insufficient, little, mere, minimum, miserable, paltry, puny, scant, scanty, scrimp, scrimpy, shabby, short, skimp, skimpy, slender, slight, spare, sparse, subtle, tenuous, too little too late*, unfinished, unfruitful, unproductive, wanting, weak; SEE CONCEPTS *546,789*

meager [*adj2*] *very thin*
angular, anorexic, bare, beanpole*, beanstalk*, bony, broomstick*, emaciated, gangling, gangly, gaunt, hungry, lacking, lank, lanky, lean, lithe, little, narrow, rawboned, scrawny, skin and bones*, skinny, slender, slim, spare, starved, stinted, stunted, tenuous, underfed, wanting, willowy, withered; SEE CONCEPT *491*

meal [*n*] *food, often taken by several individuals together*
banquet, blue plate*, board, breakfast, brunch, carryout, chow*, chow time*, collation, cookout, dessert, din-din, dinner, eats*, fare, feast, feed, grub*, lunch, luncheon, mess, munchies*, picnic, potluck, refection, refreshment, regalement, repast, snack, special*, spread, square meal*, supper, table, tea; SEE CONCEPT *459*

mean [*n*] *average*
balance, center, compromise, happy medium, median, middle, middle course, midpoint, norm, par; SEE CONCEPTS *727,830*

mean [*adj1*] *ungenerous*
beggarly, close, greedy, mercenary, mingy, miserly, niggard, niggardly, parsimonious, penny-pinching*, penurious, rapacious, scrimpy, selfish, stingy, tight, tight-fisted*; SEE CONCEPT *334*

mean [*adj2*] *hostile, rude*
bad-tempered, callous, cantankerous, churlish, contemptible, dangerous, despicable, difficult, dirty*, disagreeable, dishonorable, down*, evil, formidable, hard, hard-nosed*, ignoble, ill-tempered, infamous, knavish, liverish, lousy*, low-down and dirty*, malicious, malign, nasty, perfidious, pesky, rotten, rough, rugged, scurrilous, shameless, sinking, snide, sour, the lowest*, touch, treacherous, troublesome, ugly, unfriendly, unpleasant, unscrupulous, vexatious, vicious, vile; SEE CONCEPTS *267,401,542*

mean [*adj3*] *poor; of or in inferior circumstances*
base, beggarly, common, contemptible, déclassé, down-at-heel*, hack, humble, ignoble, ineffectual,

inferior, insignificant, limited, low, lowborn, lowly, mediocre, menial, miserable, modest, narrow, obscure, ordinary, paltry, petty, pitiful, plebeian, proletarian, run-down*, scruffy*, second-class*, second-rate, seedy*, servile, shabby*, sordid, squalid, tawdry, undistinguished, unwashed, vulgar, wretched; SEE CONCEPTS *334,485,589*

mean [*adj4*] *average*
common, conventional, halfway, intermediate, medial, median, mediocre, medium, middle, middling, normal, popular, standard, traditional; SEE CONCEPTS *547,585*

mean [*v1*] *signify, convey*
add up, adumbrate, allude, allude to, argue, attest, augur, betoken, connote, denote, designate, determine, drive at*, express, foreshadow, foretell, herald, hint at, imply, import, indicate, intimate, involve, name, point to, portend, presage, promise, purport, represent, say, speak of, spell, stand for, suggest, symbolize, tell the meaning of, touch on; SEE CONCEPTS *55,73,682*

mean [*v2*] *have in mind; intend*
aim, anticipate, aspire, contemplate, design, desire, destine, direct, expect, fate, fit, make, match, plan, predestine, preordain, propose, purpose, resolve, set out, suit, want, wish; SEE CONCEPTS *26,36*

meander [*v*] *wander, zigzag*
be all over the map*, change, drift, extravagate, gallivant, get sidetracked, peregrinate, ramble, range, recoil, roam, rove, snake, stray, stroll, traipse, turn, twine, twist, vagabond, wind; SEE CONCEPTS *151,738*

meaning [*n1*] *message, signification*
acceptation, allusion, bearing, bottom line*, connotation, content, context, definition, denotation, drift, effect, essence, explanation, force, gist, heart*, hint, implication, import, interpretation, intimation, meat, name of the game*, nature of beast*, nitty-gritty*, nuance, nuts and bolts*, pith, point, purport, sense, significance, spirit, stuff, subject, subject matter, substance, suggestion, symbolization, tenor, thrust, understanding, upshot, use, value, worth; SEE CONCEPTS *278,661,682*

meaning [*n2*] *intention, aim*
animus, design, end, goal, idea, intentness, interest, object, plan, point, purpose, trend; SEE CONCEPT *659*

meaningful [*adj*] *significant*
allusive, big, clear, concise, consequential, considerable, deep, eloquent, essential, exact, explicit, expressive, heavy, important, indicative, intelligible, material, momentous, pointed, pregnant, purposeful, relevant, sententious, serious, substantial, succinct, suggestive, useful, valid, weighty, worthwhile; SEE CONCEPTS *267,567*

meaningless [*adj*] *without use, value, worth*
absurd, aimless, blank, doesn't cut it*, doublespeak*, double-talk*, empty, feckless, fustian, futile, good-for-nothing, hollow, hot air*, inane, inconsequential, insignificant, insubstantial, nonsen-

sical, nothing, nugatory, pointless, purportless, purposeless, senseless, trifling, trivial, unimportant, unmeaning, unpurposed, useless, vacant, vague, vain, valueless, vapid, worthless; SEE CONCEPT *575*

means [*n1*] *way, method*
agency, agent, aid, apparatus, auspices, avenue, channel, course, dodge*, equipment, expedient, factor, fashion, gimmick*, instrument, instrumentality, instrumentation, intermediary, machinery, manner, measure, mechanism, medium, ministry, mode, modus operandi, organ, organization, paraphernalia, path, power, process, road, route, step, stepping-stone, system, tactic, technique, trick, vehicle, ways and means*; SEE CONCEPT *6*

means [*n2*] *wealth, resources*
ace in the hole*, affluence, assets, backing, bankroll, budget, bundle, capital, dough*, estate, finances, fortune, funds, holdings, income, intangibles, kitty*, money, nest egg*, nut*, pocket, possessions, property, purse, rainy day*, reserves, revenue, riches, savings, securities, sock*, stake, stuff, substance, ways and means*, wherewithal; SEE CONCEPTS *332,340*

meantime [*n/adv*] *in the intervening time*
at the same time, concurrently, for now, for the duration, for the moment, for then, interim, interregnum, interruption, interval, in the meantime, in the interval, in the meanwhile, meanwhile, recess, simultaneously, while; SEE CONCEPTS *799,807*

meanwhile [*adv*] *at the same time*
ad interim, concurrently, during the interval, for now, for the duration, for the moment, for then, for the time being, in the interim, in the interval, in the intervening time, in the meantime, meantime, simultaneously, till, until, up to, when; SEE CONCEPT *799*

measly [*adj*] *skimpy*
beggarly, contemptible, insignificant, meager, mean, miserable, miserly, niggardly*, niggling*, paltry, pathetic, petty, picayune, piddling*, pitiful, poor, puny, scanty, stingy, trifling, trivial, ungenerous, unimportant, valueless, worthless; SEE CONCEPT *789*

measurable [*adj*] *determinable*
assessable, calculable, commensurate, computable, fathomable, gaugeable, material, mensurable, perceptible, quantifiable, quantitative, significant, surveyable, weighable; SEE CONCEPT *529*

measure [*n1*] *portion, scope*
admeasurement, admensuration, allotment, allowance, amount, amplification, amplitude, area, bang, breadth, bulk, capacity, degree, depth, dimension, distance, duration, extent, fix, frequency, height, hit, magnitude, mass, meed, mensuration, nip, part, pitch, proportion, quantity, quantum, quota, range, ratio, ration, reach, share, shot, size, slug, span, strength, sum, volume, weight; SEE CONCEPTS *786,792,835*

measure [*n2*] *standard, rule*
benchmark*, canon, criterion, example, gauge, meter, method, model, norm, pattern, scale, system,

test, touchstone*, trial, type, yardstick; SEE CON-CEPTS *687,688*

measure [*n3*] *preventive or institutive action*
act, action, agency, bounds, control, course, deed, device, effort, expedient, limit, limitation, makeshift, maneuver, means, moderation, move, procedure, proceeding, project, proposal, proposition, resort, resource, restraint, shift, step, stopgap*, stratagem; SEE CONCEPT *5*

measure [*n4*] *bill, law*
act, enactment, project, proposal, proposition, resolution, statute; SEE CONCEPT *318*

measure [*n5*] *beat, rhythm*
accent, cadence, cadency, division, melody, meter, rhyme, step, stress, stroke, swing, tempo, throb, time, tune, verse, vibration; SEE CONCEPTS *65,262*

measure [*v*] *calculate, judge*
adapt, adjust, align, appraise, assess, average, beat, blend, bound, calibrate, caliper, check, check out, choose, compute, delimit, demarcate, determine, dope out*, estimate, evaluate, even, eye*, figure, fit, gauge, gradate, grade, graduate, level, limit, line, look over, mark, mark out, mete, pace off, peg*, plumb, portion, quantify, rank, rate, read, reckon, regulate, rhyme, rule, scale, shade, size, size up, sound, square, stroke, survey, tailor, take account, time, value, weigh; SEE CONCEPTS *103,197,764*

measurement [*n*] *calculation*
altitude, amount, amplitude, analysis, appraisal, area, assessment, calibration, capacity, computation, degree, density, depth, determination, dimension, distance, estimation, evaluation, extent, frequency, height, judgment, length, magnitude, mass, measure, mensuration, metage, pitch, quantification, quantity, range, reach, scope, size, survey, thickness, time, valuation, volume, weight, width; SEE CONCEPTS *730,792*

meat [*n1*] *flesh of animal consumed as food*
aliment, brawn, chow, comestible, eats*, edible, fare, food, foodstuff, grub*, muscle, nourishment, nutriment, provision, ration, subsistence, sustenance, victual; SEE CONCEPTS *399,457,460*

meat [*n2*] *core, gist*
burden, essence, heart, kernel, marrow, matter, nub, nucleus, pith, point, sense, short, substance, thrust, upshot; SEE CONCEPTS *682,826*

meaty [*adj*] *significant*
compact, epigrammatic, factual, full of content, interesting, meaningful, pithy, pointed, profound, rich, substantial, weighty; SEE CONCEPT *267*

mechanical [*adj*] *done by machine; machinelike*
automated, automatic, cold, cursory, emotionless, fixed, habitual, impersonal, instinctive, involuntary, laborsaving, lifeless, machine-driven, matter-of-fact, monotonous, perfunctory, programmed, routine, spiritless, standardized, stereotyped, unchanging, unconscious, unfeeling, unthinking, useful; SEE CONCEPT *544*

mechanism [*n1*] *machine, device*
apparatus, appliance, black box*, components, contrivance, doohickey*, gadget, gears, gimmick, innards, instrument, machinery, motor, structure, system, tool, workings, works; SEE CONCEPT *463*

mechanism [*n2*] *means, method*
agency, execution, functioning, medium, operation, performance, procedure, process, system, technique, workings; SEE CONCEPT *6*

medal [*n*] *decoration of honor*
badge, commemoration, gold, hardware*, laurel, medallion, reward, ribbon, wreath; SEE CONCEPTS *337,476*

meddle [*v*] *intervene, interfere*
abuse rights, advance, barge in, break in on, busybody*, butt in*, chime in, come uninvited, crash the gates*, dabble in, encroach, encumber, fool with, hinder, horn in*, impede, impose, infringe, inquire, interlope, intermeddle, interpose, intervene, intrude, invade, kibitz*, mess around, mix in, molest, obtrude, pry, push in, put two cents in*, sidewalk-superintend*, snoop, stick nose in*, tamper, trespass, worm in*; SEE CONCEPTS *14,384*

meddlesome [*adj*] *interfereing*
busy, busybody*, chiseling*, curious, encumbering, hindering, impeding, impertinent, intermeddling, interposing, interrupting, intruding, intrusive, kibitzing*, meddling, mischievous, nosy, obstructive, officious, prying, pushy, snooping*, snoopy*, tampering, troublesome; SEE CONCEPT *555*

media [*n*] *communication by publication or broadcast*
announcement, announcing, cable, communications, correspondence, disclosure, expression, intelligence, news, publishing, radio, television; SEE CONCEPT *279*

median [*n/adj*] *middle*
average, center, centermost, central, equidistant, halfway, intermediary, intermediate, mean, medial, mid, middlemost, midmost, midpoint, midway, par; SEE CONCEPTS *585,727,746,830*

mediate [*v*] *try to bring to an agreement*
act as middle*, arbitrate, bring to terms, conciliate, deal, go fifty-fifty*, intercede, interfere, intermediate, interpose, intervene, make a deal, make peace, meet halfway*, moderate, negotiate, propitiate, reconcile, referee, resolve, restore harmony, settle, step in, strike happy medium*, trade off, umpire; SEE CONCEPTS *126,324,384*

mediation [*n*] *attempt to bring to agreement*
arbitration, conciliation, intercession, interposition, intervention, negotiation, reconciliation; SEE CONCEPTS *126,324,384*

mediator [*n*] *person who negotiates agreement*
advocate, arbiter, arbitrator, broker, conciliator, fixer, go-between*, interagent, interceder, intermediary, intermediator, judge, medium, middleman/woman, moderator, negotiator, peacemaker, ref*, referee, rent-a-judge*, troubleshooter*, umpire; SEE CONCEPTS *348,423*

medicine/medication [n] *substance that helps cure, alleviate, or prevent illness*
anesthetic, antibiotic, antidote, antiseptic, antitoxin, balm, biologic, capsule, cure, dose, drug, elixir, injection, inoculation, liniment, lotion, medicament, ointment, pharmaceutical, pharmacon, physic, pill, potion, prescription, remedy, salve, sedative, serum, tablet, tincture, tonic, vaccination, vaccine; SEE CONCEPT 307

medieval [adj] *having to do with the Middle Ages; very old*
antediluvian, antiquated, antique, archaic, feudal, Gothic, old, old-fashioned, primitive, unenlightened; SEE CONCEPTS 549,578,797

mediocre [adj] *average, commonplace*
characterless, colorless, common, conventional, decent, dull, fair, fairish, fair to middling*, humdrum*, indifferent, inferior, insignificant, intermediate, mainstream, mean, medium, middling, moderate, no great shakes*, of poor quality, ordinary, passable, pedestrian, run-of-the-mill*, second-rate, so-so*, standard, tolerable, undistinguished, unexceptional, uninspired, vanilla*; SEE CONCEPTS 533,547

meditate [v] *think deeply about*
brood over, cogitate, consider, contemplate, deliberate, design, devise, dream, entertain idea*, figure, have in mind*, intend, moon*, mull over, muse, plan, ponder, purpose, put on thinking cap*, puzzle over, reflect, revolve, roll, ruminate, say to oneself, scheme, speculate, study, think, think over, track, view, weigh; SEE CONCEPT 17

medium [n1] *means, mode*
agency, agent, avenue, channel, clairvoyant, factor, form, instrument, instrumentality, intermediate, measure, mechanism, ministry, organ, psychic, seer, tool, vehicle, way; SEE CONCEPTS 658,712

medium [n2] *atmosphere, setting*
ambience, ambient, climate, conditions, element, habitat, influences, milieu, surroundings; SEE CONCEPTS 673,696

medium [n3] *area of artistic expression*
art, drama, interpretation, manifestation, mark, music, painting, revelation, sculpture, speech, writing; SEE CONCEPTS 259,263,293

medium [adj] *midway, average*
common, commonplace, fair, fairish, intermediate, mean, medial, median, mediocre, middle, middling, moderate, neutral, normal, ordinary, par, passable, popular, run-of-the-mill*, so-so*, standard, tolerable; SEE CONCEPTS 533,547

medley [n] *miscellany*
assortment, brew, collection, combo, composition, confusion, conglomeration, farrago, hodgepodge, jumble, mélange, melee, mingling, mishmash, mixed bag, mixture, pasticcio, pastiche, patchwork, potpourri, salmagundi, variety; SEE CONCEPTS 262,432

meek [adj] *very shy; compliant*
acquiescent, deferential, docile, forbearing, gentle, humble, lenient, longanimous, long-suffering, lowly, manageable, mild, milquetoast*, modest, nothing, orderly, pabulum*, passive, patient, peaceful, plain, resigned, serene, soft, spineless, spiritless, subdued, submissive, tame, timid, tolerant, unassuming, unpretentious, unresisting, weak, weak-kneed*, wishy-washy*, yielding, zero*; SEE CONCEPT 401

meet [n] *sporting event involving several participants*
athletic event, competition, conflict, contest, event, match, meeting, tournament, tourney; SEE CONCEPT 363

meet [adj] *fitting*
accommodated, applicable, appropriate, apt, conformed, equitable, expedient, fair, felicitous, fit, good, happy, just, proper, reconciled, right, suitable, timely; SEE CONCEPT 558

meet [v1] *happen on*
accost, affront, brush against, bump into, chance on, clash, collide, come across, come up against, confront, contact, cross, dig up*, encounter, engage, experience, face, fall in with*, find, front, get together, grapple, greet, hit, light, luck*, make a meet, meet face to face, rendezvous with, rub eyeballs*, run across, run into, run up against, salute, see, strike, stumble, touch shoulders*, tumble, tussle, wrestle; SEE CONCEPTS 183,384,626

meet [v2] *connect, join*
abut, adhere, adjoin, border, coincide, connect, converge, cross, intersect, link, link up, reach, touch, unite; SEE CONCEPTS 612,759

meet [v3] *perform, carry out*
answer, approach, come up to, comply, cope with, discharge, equal, execute, fit, fulfill, gratify, handle, match, measure up, rival, satisfy, suffice, tie, touch; SEE CONCEPT 91

meet [v4] *come together, convene*
appear, assemble, be introduced, be present, be presented, collect, congregate, converge, enter in, flock, foregather, gather, get together, get to know, join, make acquaintance, muster, open, rally, rendezvous, show, sit; SEE CONCEPTS 114,324

meeting [n1] *gathering, conference*
affair, assemblage, assembly, assignation, audience, bunch, call, cattle call*, company, competition, conclave, concourse, concursion, confab*, conflict, confrontation, congregation, congress, contest, convention, convocation, date, encounter, engagement, gang, get-together, huddle, introduction, meet, one on one*, parley, powwow*, rally, rendezvous, reunion, session, showdown, talk, tryst, turnout*; SEE CONCEPTS 324,363,384

meeting [n2] *convergence, intersection*
abutment, agreement, apposition, concourse, confluence, conjunction, connection, contact, crossing, joining, junction, juxtaposition, unification, union; SEE CONCEPTS 113,684

melancholy [n] *depression, sadness*
blahs*, blue devils*, blue funk*, blues*, boredom, bummer*, dejection, despair, desperation, despondency, dismals, dolefuls, dolor, downer*, down trip*, dumps, ennui, funk, gloom, gloominess, grief, letdown, low spirits, miserableness, misery, mopes*, mournfulness, pensiveness, sorrow, tedium, unhappiness, wistfulness, woe, wretchedness; SEE CONCEPT *410*

melancholy [adj] *sad, depressed*
blue*, dejected, despondent, destroyed, disconsolate, dismal, dispirited, doleful, dolorous, down*, down and out*, downbeat, downcast, downhearted, down in the dumps*, down in the mouth*, dragged, droopy, funereal, gloomy, glum, grim, heavyhearted, in blue funk*, joyless, lachrymose, low, low-spirited, lugubrious, mirthless, miserable, moody, moony*, mournful, pensive, saddened, saddening, somber, sorrowful, sorry, torn up, trite, unhappy, wet blanket*, wistful, woebegone, woeful; SEE CONCEPT *403*

mélange [n] *mixture*
assortment, combo, confusion, farrago, gallimaufry, hodgepodge, jumble, medley, miscellany, mishmash, mix, mixed bag, pasticcio, pastiche, patchwork, potpourri, salmagundi, soup, stew; SEE CONCEPT *432*

meld [v] *blend, bring together*
amalgamate, associate, compound, dissolve, feather in, fuse, interblend, interface, interfuse, intermingle, marry, merge, mingle, mix, unite; SEE CONCEPTS *113,193*

melee [n] *battle, fight*
affray, battle royal*, brawl, broil, brouhaha*, brush, clash, donnybrook*, fracas, fray, free-for-all*, knock-down-drag-out*, row, ruckus, ruction, rumpus, scrimmage, scuffle, set-to*, skirmish, to-do*, tussle, words; SEE CONCEPT *106*

mellow [adj] *ripe, mature; softened*
aged, cultured, cured, delicate, developed, dulcet, flavorful, full, full-flavored, fully developed, juicy, matured, mellifluent, mellifluous, melodious, perfect, perfected, rich, ripened, rounded, sapid, savory, seasoned, smooth, soft, soothing, sweet, tuneful; SEE CONCEPTS *462,578,594,797*

mellow [v] *ripen, mature*
age, arrive, develop, grow, grow up, improve, maturate, milden, mollify, perfect, ripe, season, settle down, soften, sweeten; SEE CONCEPTS *678,704*

melodious/melodic [adj] *harmonious, musical*
accordant, agreeable, assonant, canorous, clear, concordant, dulcet, euphonic, euphonious, harmonic, in tune, mellifluous, mellow, pleasing, resonant, silvery, soft, songful, sweet, sweet-sounding, symphonic, symphonious, tuned, tuneful, well-tuned; SEE CONCEPT *594*

melodramatic [adj] *extravagant in speech, behavior*
artificial, blood-and-thunder*, cliff-hanging*, cloak-and-dagger*, exaggerated, ham*, hammy*, histri-

onic, hokey*, overdramatic, overemotional, sensational, spectacular, stagy, theatrical; SEE CONCEPT *542*

melody [n] *harmony, tune*
air, aria, assonance, carillon, chant, chime, concord, consonance, descant, diapason, euphony, inflection, lay, lyric, measure, melodiousness, music, musicality, refrain, resonance, run, song, strain, theme, tunefulness, unison; SEE CONCEPTS *262,595*

melt [v1] *liquefy; dissolve*
cook, deliquesce, diffuse, disappear, disintegrate, disperse, evanesce, evaporate, fade, flow, flux, fuse, go, heat, merge, pass away, render, run, smelt, soften, thaw, vanish, warm, waste away; SEE CONCEPTS *250,255*

melt [v2] *give in, yield*
become lenient, disarm, forgive, mollify, relax, relent, show mercy, soften, touch; SEE CONCEPT *35*

member [n1] *part of a group*
affiliate, associate, branch, brother, chapter, component, comrade, constituent, cut, division, fellow, joiner, offshoot, parcel, piece, portion, post, representative, section, segment, sister, unit; SEE CONCEPTS *417,834,835*

member [n2] *appendage*
arm, component, constituent, element, extremity, feature, fragment, leg, limb, organ, part, portion, segment; SEE CONCEPT *392*

membership [n] *belonging to organization; those belonging to a group*
associates, association, body, brotherhood, club, company, enrollment, fellows, fellowship, group, members, participation, sisterhood, society; SEE CONCEPTS *381,417*

membrane [n] *covering layer*
film, lamina, leaf, mucosa, sheath, sheet; SEE CONCEPT *484*

memento [n] *souvenir*
keepsake, memorial, relic, remembrance, remembrancer, reminder, token, trace, trophy, vestige; SEE CONCEPTS *337,446*

memoir [n] *record of experiences*
account, anecdote, annal, autobiography, bio*, biography, chronicle, confessions, diary, discourse, dissertation, essay, journal, life, life story, memory, monograph, narrative, note, recollection, register, reminiscence, thesis, tractate, transactions, treatise, vita; SEE CONCEPTS *271,280,282*

memorable [adj] *noteworthy, significant*
A-1*, big-league*, bodacious, catchy, celebrated, critical, crucial, decisive, distinguished, doozie*, enduring, eventful, extraordinary, famous, great, heavy*, heavyweight*, historic, hot*, illustrious, important, impressive, indelible, interesting, lasting, major-league, meaningful, mind-blowing*, momentous, monumental, notable, observable, red-letter*, remarkable, rememberable, rubric, serious, signal, something, standout, striking, super, surpassing, ter-

rible, terrific, top-drawer, unforgettable; SEE CONCEPTS *529,548*

memorandum/memo [n] *written note*
announcement, chit, diary, directive, dispatch, epistle, jotting, letter, message, minute, missive, notation, notice, record, reminder, tickler; SEE CONCEPTS *271,277,278*

memorial [n] *monument, testimonial in honor, praise*
cairn, ceremony, column, headstone, inscription, keepsake, mausoleum, memento, monolith, obelisk, pillar, plaque, record, relic, remembrance, reminder, shaft, slab, souvenir, statue, stele, tablet, token, tombstone, trophy; SEE CONCEPTS *337,386*

memorial [adj] *commemorative*
canonizing, celebrative, commemoratory, consecrating, consecrative, dedicatory, deifying, enshrining, in tribute, memorializing, monumental, remembering; SEE CONCEPT *537*

memory [n1] *ability to hold in the mind*
anamnesis, awareness, camera-eye*, cognizance, consciousness, dead-eye*, flashback, memorization, mind, mindfulness, mind's eye*, recall, recapture, recognition, recollection, reflection, remembrance, reminiscence, retention, retentiveness, retrospection, subconsciousness, thought; SEE CONCEPT *409*

memory [n2] *specific thing remembered*
concept, cue, fantasy, hint, image, jog, memo, memoir, mnemonic*, picture, prod, prompt, reminder, representation, suggestion, thought, vision; SEE CONCEPTS *529,678*

menace [n] *danger; pest*
annoyance, caution, commination, hazard, intimidation, jeopardy, nuisance, peril, plague, risk, scare, threat, thunder, trouble, troublemaker, warning; SEE CONCEPTS *412,675*

menace [v] *bother, frighten*
alarm, bad-eye*, browbeat, bully, chill, compromise, endanger, hazard, impend, imperil, intimidate, jeopardize, lean on, loom, lower, overhang, peril, portend, push around, put heat on*, risk, scare, scare hell out of*, spook, terrorize, threaten, torment, whip around*; SEE CONCEPTS *7,19*

menacing [adj] *intimidating, ominous*
alarming, approaching, dangerous, frightening, imminent, impending, intimidatory, looming, louring, lowering, minacious, minatory, overhanging, threatening; SEE CONCEPTS *401,537,548*

mend [v] *correct, improve, fix*
aid, ameliorate, amend, better, condition, convalesce, correct, cure, darn, doctor, emend, fiddle with, gain, get better, get well, heal, knit, look up, overhaul, patch, perk up, ready, rebuild, recondition, reconstruct, recover, rectify, recuperate, redress, refit, reform, refurbish, rejuvenate, remedy, renew, renovate, repair, restore, retouch, revamp, revise, right, service, sew; SEE CONCEPTS *126,244,303,700*

mendacious [adj] *dishonest*
deceitful, deceptive, duplicitous, equivocating, erroneous, fallacious, false, fibbing, fraudulent, insin-

cere, knavish, lying, paltering, perfidious, perjured, prevaricating, shifty, spurious, untrue, untruthful, wrong; SEE CONCEPT *267*

menial [adj] *lowly, low-status*
abject, base, baseborn, boring, common, degrading, demeaning, dull, fawning, grovelling, humble, humdrum, ignoble, ignominious, low, mean, obeisant, obsequious, routine, servile, slavish, sorry, subservient, sycophantic, unskilled, vile; SEE CONCEPTS *574,575*

mental [adj1] *concerning the mind*
brainy, cerebral, clairvoyant, deep, heavy, ideological, imaginative, immaterial, inner, intellective, intellectual, mysterious, phrenic, psychic, psychical, psychological, rational, reasoning, spiritual, subconscious, subjective, subliminal, telepathic, thinking, thoughtful, unreal; SEE CONCEPTS *402,403*

mental [adj2] *insane*
deranged, disturbed, fruity, loco*, lunatic, mad, maniac, mentally ill, mindless, non compos mentis, nuts*, nutsy*, psychiatric, psychotic, unbalanced, unstable; SEE CONCEPTS *314,403*

mentality [n] *state of mind; intelligence*
attitude, brainpower, brains, cast, character, comprehension, disposition, frame of mind*, headset*, intellect, intelligence quotient, IQ, makeup, mental age, mind, mindset*, outlook, personality, psychology, rationality, reasoning, routine, sense, turn of mind*, understanding, way of thinking*, wit; SEE CONCEPTS *409,411*

mention [n] *referral, observation*
acknowledgment, allusion, citation, comment, footnote, indication, naming, note, notice, notification, recognition, reference, remark, specifying, tribute, utterance; SEE CONCEPTS *73,278*

mention [v] *refer to*
acknowledge, acquaint, adduce, advert, allude to, bring up, broach, call attention to, cite, communicate, declare, designate, detail, disclose, discuss, divulge, enumerate, hint at, impart, infer, instance, intimate, introduce, make known, name, notice, notify, observe, point out, point to, quote, recount, remark, report, reveal, speak about, speak of, specify, state, suggest, tell, throw out, touch on; SEE CONCEPT *73*

mentor [n] *person who advises*
adviser, coach, counsellor, guide, guru, instructor, teacher, trainer, tutor; SEE CONCEPT *350*

menu [n] *list from which to choose, often to choose food*
bill of fare, card, carte, carte du jour, cuisine, food, spread, table; SEE CONCEPT *283*

mercenary [n] *person who fights, kills for money*
hireling, legionnaire, merc, professional soldier, slave, soldier of fortune, warrior; SEE CONCEPTS *358,412*

mercenary [adj] *greedy for money*
acquisitive, avaricious, bribable, corrupt, covetous, grabby, grasping, miserly, money-grubbing, selfish,

sordid, stingy, unethical, unprincipled, unscrupulous, venal; SEE CONCEPT *401*

merchandise [*n*] *goods for sale*
commodity, effects, job lot, line, material, number, produce, product, seconds, staple, stock, stuff, truck, vendible, wares; SEE CONCEPT *338*

merchandise [*v*] *sell goods*
advertise, buy and sell, deal in, distribute, do business in, market, promote, publicize, retail, trade, traffic in, vend, wholesale; SEE CONCEPT *345*

merchant [*n*] *person who sells goods*
broker, businessman/woman, consigner, dealer, exporter, handler, jobber, marketer, operator, retailer, robber baron, salesman/woman, seller, sender, shipper, shopkeeper, storekeeper, trader, tradesman/woman, trafficker, tycoon, vendor, wholesaler; SEE CONCEPT *347*

merciful [*adj*] *kind, sparing*
all heart*, beneficent, benign, benignant, bleeding heart*, charitable, clement, compassionate, condoning, easygoing, feeling, forbearing, forgiving, generous, gentle, gracious, heart in right place*, humane, humanitarian, indulgent, kindly, lenient, liberal, mild, pardoning, pitiful, pitying, soft*, softhearted*, sympathetic, tender, tenderhearted, tolerant; SEE CONCEPTS *401,542*

merciless [*adj*] *mean, heartless*
barbarous, callous, compassionless, cruel, cutthroat, dog-eat-dog*, fierce, going for jugular*, gratuitous, grim, hard, hard hearted, harsh, hatchet job*, having a killer instinct*, implacable, inexorable, inhumane, iron-fisted, mean machine*, mortal, pitiless, relentless, ruthless, severe, taking no prisoners*, unappeasable, uncalled-for, unfeeling, unflinching, unforgiving, unmerciful, unpitying, unrelenting, unsparing, unsympathetic, unyielding, wanton; SEE CONCEPTS *401,542*

mercurial [*adj*] *flighty, temperamental*
blowing hot and cold*, bubbleheaded*, buoyant, capricious, changeable, effervescent, elastic, erratic, expansive, fickle, flaky, flighty, flip*, fluctuating, gaga*, gay, impulsive, inconstant, irregular, irrepressible, lighthearted, lively, lubricious, mad, mobile, movable, quicksilver, resilient, short-fuse*, spirited, sprightly, ticklish, unpredictable, unstable, up-and-down*, variable, volatile, yo-yo*; SEE CONCEPTS *401,404*

mercy [*n*] *kindness, compassion*
benevolence, benignancy, blessing, boon, charity, clemency, commiseration, favor, forbearance, forgiveness, generosity, gentleness, godsend, goodwill, grace, humanity, kindliness, lenience, leniency, lenity, lifesaver, luck, mildness, pity, quarter, relief, ruth, softheartedness, sympathy, tenderness, tolerance; SEE CONCEPTS *32,633*

mere [*adj*] *nothing more; absolute*
bald, bare, blunt, common, complete, entire, insignificant, little, minor, plain, poor, pure, pure and simple, sheer, simple, small, stark, unadorned, un-

adulterated, unmitigated, unmixed, utter, very; SEE CONCEPTS *535,589*

meretricious [*adj*] *gaudy, flashy*
blatant, bogus, brazen, chintzy, counterfeit, garish, glaring, insincere, loud, misleading, ornate, phony, plastic*, put-on*, sham, showy, spurious, superficial, tawdry, tinsel, trashy; SEE CONCEPTS *542, 589*

merge [*v*] *bring or come together*
absorb, amalgamate, assimilate, become lost in, become partners, be swallowed up*, blend, cement, centralize, coalesce, combine, come aboard*, compound, conglomerate, consolidate, converge, deal one in, fuse, hitch on*, hook up*, immerge, incorporate, interface, intermingle, intermix, join, join up, line up, marry, meet, meld, melt into, mingle, mix, network, plug into, pool, slap on, submerge, synthesize, tack on*, tag, team up*, throw in together*, tie in, unite; SEE CONCEPTS *113,193,324*

merger [*n*] *consolidation*
alliance, amalgamation, cahoots*, coadunation, coalition, combination, fusion, hookup, incorporation, lineup, melding, mergence, merging, organization, pool, takeover, tie-in, tie-up, unification, union; SEE CONCEPTS *323,324,703*

meridian [*n*] *summit, climax*
acme, apex, apogee, crest, culmination, extremity, high noon, high-water mark, peak, pinnacle, zenith; SEE CONCEPTS *832,836*

merit [*n*] *advantage*
arete, asset, benefit, caliber, credit, desert, dignity, excellence, excellency, good, goodness, honor, integrity, perfection, quality, stature, strong point, talent, value, virtue, worth, worthiness; SEE CONCEPT *693*

merit [*v*] *be entitled to*
be in line for, be worthy, deserve, earn, get one's comeuppance*, get one's due*, get one's just desserts*, get what is coming*, have a claim, have a right, have coming, incur, justify, rate, warrant; SEE CONCEPT *129*

meritorious [*adj*] *honorable, commendable*
admirable, boss*, choice, creditable, deserving, estimable, excellent, exemplary, golden, good, laudable, meritable, noble, praisable, praiseworthy, right, righteous, thankworthy, top drawer*, virtuous, winner, world-beating*, worthy; SEE CONCEPTS *404,548,572*

merriment/merrymaking [*n*] *enjoyment, amusement*
brawl, buffoonery, cheerfulness, conviviality, festivity, frolic, fun, fun and games*, gaiety, glee, happiness, hilarity, hoopla*, indulgence, jocularity, jocundity, jollity, joviality, joy, laughs, laughter, levity, liveliness, mirth, picnic, recreation, revel, revelry, self-indulgence, shindig, sport, whoopee*, wingding*; SEE CONCEPTS *386,410*

merry [*adj*] *very happy; festive*
amusing, blithe, blithesome, boisterous, boon, carefree, cheerful, comic, comical, convivial, enjoyable,

entertaining, facetious, festive, frolicsome, fun-loving, funny, gay, glad, gleeful, grooving*, hilarious, humorous, jocund, jolly, joyful, joyous, jumping, larking, lighthearted, lively, mad, mirthful, perky, pleasant, riotous, rip-roaring*, rocking, rollicking, saturnalian, sportive, sunny, unconstrained, uproarious, vivacious, wild, winsome, zappy*, zingy*, zippy*; SEE CONCEPTS *403,548, 572*

mesh [n] *netting, entanglement*
cobweb, jungle, knot, labyrinth, maze, morass, net, network, plexus, reticulation, screen, skein, snare, snarl, tangle, toils, tracery, trap, web; SEE CONCEPTS *611,733*

mesh [v] *entangle, connect*
agree, catch, coincide, combine, come together, co-ordinate, dovetail, engage, enmesh, ensnare, fit, fit together, harmonize, interlock, knit, net, snare, tangle, trap; SEE CONCEPTS *113,193*

mesmerize [v] *captivate*
catch up, control, deaden, drug, ensorcell, enthrall, entrance, fascinate, grip, hold spellbound, hypnotize, magnetize, numb, render unconscious, spellbind, stupefy; SEE CONCEPTS *11,14*

mess [n1] *disorder, litter*
botch, chaos, clutter, combination, compound, confusion, debris, dirtiness, disarray, discombobulation*, disorganization, every which way*, eyesore, fright, hash, hodgepodge, jumble, mayhem, mishmash, monstrosity, salmagundi*, shambles, sight, turmoil, untidiness, wreck, wreckage; SEE CONCEPTS *230,260*

mess [n2] *difficulty, predicament*
dilemma, fix, imbroglio, jam, mix-up, muddle, perplexity, pickle*, plight, stew; SEE CONCEPT *674*

message [n1] *communication, often written*
bulletin, cannonball, communiqué, directive, dispatch, dope, earful, epistle, information, intelligence, intimation, letter, memo, memorandum, missive, news, note, notice, paper, report, tidings, wire, word; SEE CONCEPTS *271,274*

message [n2] *meaning, idea*
acceptation, import, intendment, moral, point, purport, sense, significance, significancy, signification, theme, understanding; SEE CONCEPTS *661,682*

mess around [v] *fiddle; goof off*
amuse oneself, dabble, dawdle, doodle, fool around, loiter, muck around*, play, play around, play the fool*, potter, puddle, putter, tinker, trifle; SEE CONCEPTS *87,363*

messenger [n] *person carrying information to another*
agent, ambassador, bearer, carrier, commissionaire, courier, crier, delegate, delivery boy, delivery person, detachment, detail, dispatcher, emissary, envoy, errand boy*, flag-bearer, forerunner, go-between*, gofer*, harbinger, herald, intermediary, internuncio, mediator, minister, post, precursor, prophet, runner, schlepper*; SEE CONCEPT *348*

mess up [v] *disorder, dirty*
befoul, besmirch, bobble, bollix*, botch, bungle, clutter, confuse, damage, derange, destroy, disarrange, discompose, dishevel, disorganize, disturb, foul, goof up*, gum up*, jumble, litter, louse up, muddle, pollute, ruin, rummage, scramble, screw up*, smear, soil, spoil, unsettle, upset; SEE CONCEPTS *158,252,254*

messy [adj] *cluttered, dirty*
blotchy*, careless, chaotic, confused, disheveled, disordered, disorganized, grimy, grubby*, littered, muddled, raunchy*, rumpled, slapdash*, slipshod*, sloppy, slovenly, unfastidious, unkempt, unneat, unthorough, untidy; SEE CONCEPTS *485,621*

metal [n] *lustrous chemical element*
alloy, casting, deposit, foil, hardware, ingot, leaf, load, mail, mineral, native rock, ore, plate, solder, vein; SEE CONCEPT *476*

metamorphose [v] *convert, transform*
age, alter, be reborn, change, commute, develop, diverge, mature, mutate, remake, remodel, reshape, ripen, transfigure, translate, transmogrify, transmute, transmute, transubstantiate, vary; SEE CONCEPTS *469,697,701*

metamorphosis [n] *conversion, transformation*
alteration, change, changeover, evolution, mutation, rebirth, transfiguration, transfigurement, translation, transmogrification, transmutation, transubstantiation; SEE CONCEPTS *469,697,701*

metaphor [n] *figure of speech, implied comparison*
allegory, analogy, emblem, hope, image, metonymy, personification, similitude, symbol, trope; SEE CONCEPT *275*

metaphysical [adj] *not physical; without physical presence*
abstract, abstruse, bodiless, deep, difficult, discarnate, esoteric, eternal, fundamental, high-flown, ideal, immaterial, impalpable, incorporeal, insubstantial, intangible, intellectual, jesuitic, mystical, nonmaterial, nonphysical, numinous, oversubtle, philosophical, preternatural, profound, recondite, spiritual, superhuman, superior, supermundane, supernatural, suprahuman, supramundane, supranatural, theoretical, transcendental, unearthly, unfleshly, universal, unphysical, unreal, unsubstantial; SEE CONCEPTS *529,582*

mete [v] *administer, distribute*
admeasure, allocate, allot, allow, apportion, assign, deal, dispense, divide, dole, give, lot, measure, parcel, portion, ration, share; SEE CONCEPTS *98,108*

meteoric [adj] *brief, sudden*
dazzling, ephemeral, flashing, fleeting, momentary, overnight, rapid, spectacular, speedy, swift, transient; SEE CONCEPTS *548,798,799*

meter [n] *rhythm, beat*
cadence, cadency, feet, lilt, measure, mora, music, pattern, poetry, rhyme, rhythmus, structure, swing; SEE CONCEPTS *65,262*

method [*n1*] *means, procedure*
adjustment, approach, arrangement, channels, course, custom, design, disposal, disposition, fashion, form, formula, habit, line, manner, mechanism, method, mode, modus, modus operandi, nuts and bolts*, plan, practice, proceeding, process, program, receipt, recipe, red tape*, ritual, rote, routine, rubric, rule, rut, schema, scheme, shortcut, style, system, tack, tactics, technic, technique, tenor, the book*, usage, way, ways and means*, wise, wrinkle*; SEE CONCEPTS *6,660*

method [*n2*] *order, pattern*
arrangement, classification, design, form, orderliness, organization, plan, planning, purpose, regularity, structure, system; SEE CONCEPTS *727,770*

methodical/methodic [*adj*] *organized, precise*
all together, analytical, businesslike, by the book*, by the numbers, careful, cut-and-dried*, deliberate, disciplined, efficient, exact, fixed, framed, in a groove*, logical, methodized, meticulous, neat, ordered, orderly, painstaking, planned, regular, scrupulous, set-up*, structured, systematic, tidy, together, well-regulated; SEE CONCEPTS *326,542, 544,585*

meticulous [*adj*] *detailed, perfectionist*
accurate, cautious, conscientious, conscionable, crossing the t's*, dotting the i's*, exact, fastidious, fussy, heedful, microscopic, nitpicking*, painstaking, particular, persnickety*, picky, precise, punctilious, punctual, scrupulous, stickling, strict, thorough; SEE CONCEPTS *542,544,557*

metropolitan [*adj*] *concerning a city*
city, cosmopolitan, modern, municipal, urban, urbane; SEE CONCEPT *536*

mettle [*n*] *boldness, strength of character*
animation, ardor, backbone, bravery, caliber, courage, daring, dauntlessness, disposition, energy, fire, force, fortitude, gallantry, gameness, grit*, guts*, hardihood, heart*, indomitability, kidney*, life*, makeup, moxie, nature, nerve, pluck, quality, resolution, resolve, spirit, spunk, stamina, stamp*, starch, temper, temperament, valor, vigor, vitality; SEE CONCEPT *411*

microbe [*n*] *bacteria*
bacillus, bacterium, bug*, crud, germ, microorganism, pathogen, plague, virus, what's going around*; SEE CONCEPT *306*

microscopic [*adj*] *very tiny, almost undetectable*
atomic, diminutive, imperceptible, infinitesimal, invisible, little, minuscule, minute, negligible, teeny*, wee*; SEE CONCEPTS *773,789*

middle [*n*] *center*
core, deep, focus, halfway, halfway point, heart, inside, marrow, mean, media, midpoint, midriff, midsection, midst, thick, waist; SEE CONCEPTS *746, 761,830,833*

middle [*adj*] *central*
average, between, betwixt and between*, center, centermost, equidistant, halfway, inner, inside, intermediate, intervening, mainstream, mean, medial, median, medium, mezzo*, middlemost, middle of the road*, midmost, smack in the middle, straddling the fence*; SEE CONCEPTS *547,583,830*

middleman/woman [*n*] *person who acts as intermediary*
agent, broker, connection, distributor, entrepreneur, fixer, go-between*, influence, interagent, interceder, intercessor, intermediate, intermediator, jobber*, mediator, representative, salesman/woman, salesperson, wholesaler; SEE CONCEPT *348*

middling [*adj*] *adequate, okay*
all right, average, common, conventional, decent, fair, fairish, good, indifferent, intermediate, mean, mediocre, medium, moderate, modest, okay, ordinary, passable, run-of-the-mill*, so-so*, tolerable, traditional, unexceptional, unremarkable; SEE CONCEPT *547*

midget [*n*] *very small person*
bantam, dwarf, gnome, homuncule, homunculus, Lilliputian*, little person, manikin, midge, pygmy, runt*; SEE CONCEPT *424*

midget [*adj*] *very short, small*
baby, diminutive, dwarf, dwarfish, knee-high*, Lilliputian, miniature, minikin, pocket, pygmy, teensy*, teeny*, tiny; SEE CONCEPTS *773,779*

midst [*n*] *middle, core*
betwixt and between*, bosom, center, deep, depths, halfway, heart, hub, interior, mean, medium, midpoint, nucleus, thick; SEE CONCEPT *830*

mien [*n*] *person's presence, manner*
act, address, air, appearance, aspect, aura, bearing, carriage, countenance, demeanor, deportment, expression, front, image, look, mannerism, port, set, style; SEE CONCEPTS *411,644*

miff [*v*] *annoy*
aggrieve, bother, displease, hurt, irk, irritate, nettle, offend, pester, pique, provoke, put out, resent, upset, vex; SEE CONCEPTS *7,19*

might [*n*] *ability, power*
adequacy, arm, authority, capability, capacity, clout, command, competence, control, domination, efficacy, efficiency, energy, force, forcefulness, forcibleness, get-up-and-go*, jurisdiction, lustiness, mastery, moxie*, muscle*, potency, powerfulness, prowess, puissance, punch, qualification, qualifiedness, sinew*, steam, strength, strenuousness, strong arm*, sway, valor, vigor, vigorousness; SEE CONCEPTS *411,641,732*

mightily [*adv1*] *very much, extremely*
decidedly, exceedingly, greatly, highly, hugely, intensely, mighty, much, notably, surpassingly, very; SEE CONCEPT *569*

mightily [*adv2*] *forcefully*
arduously, energetically, forcibly, hard, hardly, laboriously, lustily, manfully, might and main*, powerfully, strenuously, strongly, vigorously, with all one's strength; SEE CONCEPTS *540,544*

mighty [*adj1*] *forceful, powerful*
boss*, doughty, hardy, indomitable, lusty, manful, muscular, omnipotent, potent, powerhouse, puissant, robust, stalwart, steamroller*, stout, strapping, strengthy, strong, strong as ox*, sturdy, vigorous, wieldy; SEE CONCEPTS *489,540*

mighty [*adj2*] *gigantic, monumental*
august, bulky, colossal, considerable, dynamic, eminent, enormous, extensive, extraordinary, grand, great, heroic, high, huge, illustrious, immense, imposing, impressive, intense, irresistible, large, magnificent, majestic, massive, moving, notable, prodigious, renowned, stupendous, titanic, towering, tremendous, vast; SEE CONCEPTS *537,773,781*

migrant [*n*] *person who moves to a foreign place*
departer, drifter, emigrant, evacuee, expatriate, gypsy, immigrant, itinerant, migrator, mover, nomad, rover, tinker, transient, traveler, vagrant, wanderer; SEE CONCEPT *413*

migrant/migratory [*adj*] *moving, traveling*
casual, changing, drifting, emigrating, errant, gypsy, immigrant, immigrating, impermanent, itinerant, migrative, migratorial, mobile, nomad, nomadic, on the move, passing over, passing through, peripatetic, ranging, roving, seasonal, shifting, temporary, tramp, transient, transmigratory, unsettled, vagabond, vagrant, wandering; SEE CONCEPT *584*

migrate [*v*] *move, travel to another place*
drift, emigrate, immigrate, journey, leave, nomadize, range, roam, rove, shift, transmigrate, trek, voyage, wander; SEE CONCEPTS *198,224*

mild [*adj1*] *gentle, temperate, nonirritating*
balmy, benign, benignant, blah*, bland, breezy, calm, choice, clear, clement, cool, dainty, delicate, demulcent, easy, emollient, exquisite, faint, fine, flat, genial, ho-hum*, lenient, lenitive, light, lukewarm, medium, mellow, moderate, mollifying, nothing, nothing much*, pabulum, pacific, peaceful, placid, smooth, soft, soothing, sunny, tempered, tepid, untroubled, vanilla*, warm, weak, wimpy*; SEE CONCEPTS *485,525,537*

mild [*adj2*] *easygoing, pleasant in personality*
amiable, balmy, bland, calm, clement, compassionate, complaisant, deferential, docile, dull, easy, equable, feeble, flat, forbearant, forbearing, forgiving, gentle, good-humored, good-natured, goodtempered, humane, indulgent, insipid, jejune, kind, lenient, meek, mellow, merciful, mild-mannered, moderate, obeisant, obliging, pacific, patient, peaceable, placid, serene, smooth, soft, spiritless, subdued, submissive, subservient, tame, temperate, tender, tranquil, unassuming, vapid, warm; SEE CONCEPTS *401,404*

mile [*n*] *5,280 feet/1.609 kilometers measured*
nautical, square, statute; SEE CONCEPTS *790,791*

milestone [*n*] *achievement*
anniversary, breakthrough, discovery, event, landmark, milepost, occasion, turning point, waypost; SEE CONCEPTS *2,706*

milieu [*n*] *environment, atmosphere*
ambience, ambient, background, bag, climate, element, locale, location, medium, mise-en-scène, nabe, neighborhood, place, scene, setting, space, sphere, surroundings, thing, turf; SEE CONCEPT *673*

militant [*n*] *person who fights, is aggressive*
activist, belligerent, combatant, demonstrator, fighter, objector, partisan, protester, rioter, warrior; SEE CONCEPTS *358,359*

militant [*adj*] *aggressive, combative*
active, assertive, assertory, bellicose, belligerent, combating, contending, contentious, embattled, fighting, gladiatorial, in arms, martial, militaristic, military, offensive, pugnacious, pushy, quarrelsome, scrappy, self-assertive, truculent, up in arms, vigorous, warlike, warring; SEE CONCEPT *401*

military [*n*] *armed force*
air force, army, force, marines, navy, service, servicemen/women, servicepeople, soldiery, troop; SEE CONCEPT *322*

military [*adj*] *soldierlike; concerning the armed forces*
aggressive, armed, army, chauvinistic, combatant, combative, fighting, for war, martial, militant, militaristic, noncivil, soldierly, warlike, warmongering; SEE CONCEPT *536*

milk [*n*] *liquid produced by mammals*
buttermilk, chalk*, condensed, cream, evaporated, formula, goat, half-and-half, homogenized, laiche, low fat, moo juice*, pasteurized, powdered, raw, skim, two-percent, whole; SEE CONCEPT *467*

milk [*v*] *tap; exploit*
bleed, drain, draw off, elicit, empty, evince, evoke, exhaust, express, extort, extract, fleece, impose on, let out, press, pump, siphon, suck, take advantage, take out, use, wring; SEE CONCEPTS *139,142,156,225*

milky [*adj*] *white, cloudy*
alabaster, clouded, frosted, lacteal, lacteous, lactescent, milk-white, opalescent, opaline, opaque, pearly, whitish; SEE CONCEPT *618*

mill [*n*] *factory*
foundry, manufactory, plant, shop, sweatshop, works; SEE CONCEPTS *439,449*

mill [*v*] *grind*
comminute, crush, granulate, grate, pound, powder, press, pulverize; SEE CONCEPT *186*

mimic [*n*] *person who imitates*
actor, caricaturist, comedian, copycat, imitator, impersonator, impressionist, mime, mummer, parodist, parrot, performer, playactor, player, thespian, trouper; SEE CONCEPT *352*

mimic [*v*] *imitate, mock*
act, ape, burlesque, caricature, copy, copycat, ditto*, do, do like*, echo, enact, fake, go like*, impersonate, look like*, make believe, make fun of, make like*, mime, mirror, pantomime, parody, parrot, perform, personate, play, resemble, ridicule, sham, simulate, take off*, travesty; SEE CONCEPTS *54,59,111,171*

mince [v1] *chop up*
chip, crumble, cut, dice, divide, grind, hack, hash, whack; SEE CONCEPT *176*

mince [v2] *pose, put on airs*
attitudinize, flounce, posture, prance, sashay, strut; SEE CONCEPT *59*

mince [v3] *euphemize, hold back in communication*
alleviate, decrease, diminish, extenuate, lessen, minimize, moderate, palliate, soften, spare, tone down, weaken; SEE CONCEPT *266*

mincing [adj] *affected, pretentious*
artificial, dainty, delicate, effeminate, fastidious, finical, finicky, fussy, genteel, insincere, la-di-da*, nice, particular, persnickety, precious, sissy, squeamish, stilted, too-too*, unnatural; SEE CONCEPTS *401,404*

mind [n1] *intelligence*
apperception, attention, brain, brainpower, brains, capacity, cognizance, conception, consciousness, creativity, faculty, function, genius, head, imagination, ingenuity, instinct, intellect, intellectual, intelectuality, intuition, judgment, lucidity, marbles*, mentality, observation, perception, percipience, power, psyche, ratiocination, reason, reasoning, regard, sanity, sense, soul, soundness, spirit, talent, thinker, thought, understanding, wisdom, wits; SEE CONCEPTS *393,409*

mind [n2] *memory*
attention, cognizance, concentration, head, mark, note, notice, observance, observation, recollection, regard, remark, remembrance, subconscious, thinking, thoughts; SEE CONCEPTS *409,630*

mind [n3] *inclination, tendency; belief*
attitude, bent, conviction, desire, determination, disposition, eye, fancy, feeling, humor, impulse, intention, judgment, leaning, liking, mood, notion, opinion, outlook, persuasion, pleasure, point of view, purpose, sentiment, strain, temper, temperament, thoughts, tone, urge, vein, view, way of thinking, will, wish; SEE CONCEPTS *20,657,689*

mind [v1] *be bothered; care*
be affronted, be opposed, complain, deplore, disapprove, dislike, look askance at, object, resent, take offense; SEE CONCEPTS *21,29*

mind [v2] *comply, obey*
adhere to, attend, behave, do as told, follow, follow orders, heed, keep, listen, mark, note, notice, observe, pay attention, pay heed, regard, respect, take heed, watch; SEE CONCEPTS *23,91*

mind [v3] *attend, tend*
baby-sit, be attentive, behold, care for, discern, discipline, ensure, give heed to, govern, guard, have charge of, keep an eye on*, listen up, look, make certain, mark, mind the store*, note, notice, observe, oversee, perceive, regard, ride herd on*, see, sit, superintend, supervise, watch; SEE CONCEPTS *110,295,596,623*

mind [v4] *be careful*
be cautious, be concerned, be on guard, be solicitous, be wary, have a care, mind p's and q's*, take care, tend, toe the line*, trouble, watch, watch one's step*, watch out*; SEE CONCEPT *34*

mind [v5] *remember*
bethink, bring to mind, cite, recall, recollect, remind, reminisce, retain; SEE CONCEPT *40*

mindful [adj] *attentive, aware*
alert, alive to, apprehensive, au courant, be up on*, cagey, careful, cautious, chary, cognizant, conscientious, conscious, conversant, heedful, in the know, know all the answers*, knowing, know ins and outs*, knowledgeable, observant, observative, observing, on one's toes*, on the ball*, on the job*, on to*, plugged in*, regardful, respectful, sensible, solicitous, thoughtful, tuned in*, vigilant, wary, watchful, with eyes peeled*; SEE CONCEPTS *402,403,542*

mindless [adj] *oblivious, stupid; automatic*
asinine, brutish, careless, daydreaming, foolish, forgetful, gratuitous, heedless, idiotic, imbecilic, inattentive, mooning, moony, moronic, neglectful, negligent, nitwitted, obtuse, out, out of it*, rash, senseless, silly, simple, spaced-out*, thoughtless, unaware, unintelligent, unmindful, unthinking, witless; SEE CONCEPTS *403,538*

mine [n] *deposit, supply*
abundance, bed, bonanza, ditch, excavation, field, fount, fountain, fund, gold mine, hoard, lode, pit, quarry, reserve, shaft, source, spring, stock, store, treasure trove, treasury, trench, vein, wealth, well, wellspring; SEE CONCEPTS *449,509,712*

mine [v] *dig up*
burrow, delve, dig for, drill, excavate, extract, hew, pan, quarry, sap, scoop, shovel, unearth, work; SEE CONCEPT *178*

mingle [v1] *physically join*
admix, alloy, blend, coalesce, commingle, compound, intermingle, intermix, interweave, make up, marry, meld, merge, mix, unite, wed; SEE CONCEPT *193*

mingle [v2] *socialize*
associate, circulate, consort, fraternize, gang up*, hang out*, hobnob, mix, network, pool, rub shoulders*, tie in, work the room*; SEE CONCEPT *384*

miniature [n] *tiny thing*
baby, dwarf, insignificancy, midget, model, pocket edition, pygmy, toy; SEE CONCEPT *730*

miniature [adj] *tiny*
baby, diminutive, dwarf, dwarfish, itsy-bitsy*, itty-bitty*, Lilliputian, little, midget, mini, minikin, minuscule, minute, mite, model, petite, pint-sized, pocket, pygmy, reduced, scaled-down, small, small-scale, teensy*, teeny*, toy, wee; SEE CONCEPTS *773,789*

minimal [adj] *littlest, slightest*
basal, basic, essential, fundamental, least, least possible, lowest, minimum, nominal, smallest, token; SEE CONCEPTS *762,773,789*

minimize [v] *make smaller; underrate*
abbreviate, attenuate, belittle, cheapen, curtail, cut down to size, cut rate, decrease, decry, deprecate, depreciate, derogate, detract, diminish, discount, disparage, downplay*, dwarf*, knock*, knock down*, lessen, make light of*, make little of, miniaturize, pan, play down, pooh-pooh*, poor-mouth*, prune, put down, reduce, run down, shrink, underestimate, underplay; SEE CONCEPTS *54,240,247*

minimum [n] *lowest amount*
atom, bottom, dab, depth, dot, gleam, grain, hair, iota, jot, least, lowest, margin, modicum, molecule, nadir, narrowest, particle, pittance, point, scintilla, scruple, shadow, slightest, smallest, smidgen, soupçon, spark, speck, trifle, whit; SEE CONCEPTS *786,831*

minimum [adj] *least, lowest*
least possible, littlest, merest, minimal, slightest, smallest, tiniest; SEE CONCEPTS *762,789*

minister [n1] *person in charge of church*
abbot, archbishop, archdeacon, bishop, chaplain, churchman/woman, clergy, clergyman/woman, cleric, clerical, clerk, confessor, curate, deacon, dean, diocesan, divine, ecclesiastic, lecturer, missionary, monk, padre, parson, pastor, preacher, preacher man/woman*, prelate, priest, pulpiteer, rector, reverend, shepherd, vicar; SEE CONCEPT *361*

minister [n2] *person high in government*
administrator, agent, aide, ambassador, assistant, cabinet member, consul, delegate, diplomat, envoy, executive, legate, liaison, lieutenant, officeholder, official, plenipotentiary, premier, prime minister, secretary, statesman/woman; SEE CONCEPT *354*

minister [v] *help, serve*
accommodate, administer, aid, answer, attend, be solicitous of, cater to, cure, doctor, do for, foster, heal, mother, nurse, pander, pander to, remedy, succor, take care of, tend, treat, wait on, watch over; SEE CONCEPT *110*

minor [n] *person under legal age of maturity*
adolescent, baby, boy, child, girl, infant, junior, juvenile, lad, little one, schoolboy, schoolgirl, teenager, underage, youngster, youth; SEE CONCEPT *424*

minor [adj] *insignificant, small*
accessory, below the mark, bush-league*, casual, dependent, dinky*, inconsequential, inconsiderable, inferior, junior, lesser, light, low, minus, negligible, paltry, petty, piddling, secondary, second-string*, slight, smaller, small-fry*, small-time, subordinate, subsidiary, tacky, trifling, trivial, two-bit*, unimportant, younger; SEE CONCEPTS *575,773,789*

mint [n] *a lot of money*
boodle, bundle, fortune, heap, king's ransom*, million, packet, pile, pot, roll, wad; SEE CONCEPTS *340, 786*

mint [adj] *brand-new*
excellent, first-class, fresh, intact, original, perfect, spanking-new*, spick-and-span*, unblemished, un-damaged, unmarred, untarnished, virgin; SEE CONCEPTS *574,578,797*

mint [v] *create, coin*
cast, construct, devise, fabricate, fashion, forge, invent, issue, make, make up, mold, monetize, produce, provide, punch, stamp, strike, think up; SEE CONCEPTS *43,173,205,251*

minute [n] *very brief time period*
bat of an eye*, breath, breathing, crack, flash, instant, jiffy*, min*, mo*, moment, nothing flat*, sec*, second, shake, short time*, sixtieth of hour, sixty seconds, split second, twinkling*; SEE CONCEPTS *803,807,821*

minute [adj1] *very small*
atomic, diminutive, exact, exiguous, fine, inconsiderable, infinitesimal, insignificant, invisible, little, microbic, microscopic, miniature, minim, minimal, minuscule, molecular, peewee*, piddling, precise, puny, slender, teeny-weeny*, tiny, wee; SEE CONCEPTS *773,789*

minute [adj2] *unimportant*
immaterial, inconsiderable, insignificant, light, little, minor, negligible, nonessential, paltry, petty, picayune, piddling, puny, slight, small, trifling, trivial; SEE CONCEPT *575*

minute [adj3] *exact, precise*
blow-by-blow*, careful, circumstantial, clocklike, close, critical, detailed, elaborate, exhaustive, full, itemized, meticulous, painstaking, particular, particularized, punctilious, scrupulous, specialized, thorough; SEE CONCEPT *557*

miracle [n] *wonderful, surprising event or thing*
marvel, phenomenon, portent, prodigy, rarity, revelation, sensation, stunner, supernatural occurrence, surprise, thaumaturgy, unusualness, wonder; SEE CONCEPTS *671,689,693*

miraculous [adj] *surprisingly wonderful*
amazing, anomalous, astonishing, astounding, awesome, extraordinary, fabulous, freakish, heavy, incredible, inexplicable, magical, marvelous, monstrous, numinous, phenomenal, preternatural, prodigious, spectacular, staggering, strange, stupefying, stupendous, superhuman, superior, supermundane, supernatural, supranatural, thaumaturgic, the utmost, unaccountable, unbelievable, unearthly, unimaginable, unreal, wonderworking, wondrous; SEE CONCEPTS *529,548,572*

mirage [n] *imaginary vision*
delusion, fantasy, hallucination, ignis fatuus, illusion, optical illusion, phantasm; SEE CONCEPTS *529,628*

mire [n] *muck, morass*
bog, dirt, fen, glop*, goo*, gunk*, marsh, moss, mud, ooze*, quagmire, quicksand, slime*, swamp; SEE CONCEPTS *509,674*

mire [v] *delay, catch up in*
bog down, cling, decelerate, detain, dirty, embroil, enmesh, ensnare, entangle, entrap, flounder, hang

up, implicate, involve, retard, set back, sink, slow down, slow up, snare, soil, stick, tangle, trap; SEE CONCEPTS *112,121*

mirror [*n*] *glass that reflects image*
cheval glass, gaper, hand glass, imager, looking glass, pier glass, polished metal, reflector, seeing glass, speculum; SEE CONCEPTS *443,470*

mirror [*v*] *copy, reflect*
act like, depict, double, echo, embody, emulate, epitomize, exemplify, follow, glass, illustrate, image, imitate, make like, mimic, personify, represent, show, simulate, symbolize, take off*, typify; SEE CONCEPTS *111,118,171*

mirth [*n*] *great joy*
amusement, cheer, cheerfulness, convulsions, entertainment, festivity, frivolity, frolic, fun, gaiety, gladness, glee, happiness, hilarity, hysteria, hysterics, jocularity, jocundity, jollity, joviality, joyousness, kicks*, laughs, laughter, levity, lightheartedness, merriment, merrymaking, pleasure, rejoicing, revelry, sport, whoopee*; SEE CONCEPTS *388,410*

misadventure [*n*] *bad luck, mishap*
accident, adversity, bad break*, blunder, calamity, casualty, cataclysm, catastrophe, debacle, disaster, error, failure, faux pas*, ill fortune, lapse, mischance, misfortune, reverse, setback, slip, tragedy, woe; SEE CONCEPT *674*

misanthrope [*n*] *person who hates others*
cynic, doubter, egoist, egotist, hater, isolate, loner, misanthropist, misogynist, recluse, skeptic; SEE CONCEPT *412*

misanthropic [*adj*] *unsociable, cynical*
antisocial, egoistic, egotistical, eremitic, hating, inhumane, malevolent, misanthropical, misogynic, misogynist, reclusive, reserved, sarcastic, selfish, solitary, standoffish, unfriendly; SEE CONCEPT *404*

misapprehend [*v*] *get the wrong idea, impression*
blunder, confuse, err, misconceive, misconstrue, misinterpret, misread, miss, mistake, misunderstand; SEE CONCEPT *15*

misappropriate [*v*] *use wrongly; steal*
abuse, appropriate, defalcate, embezzle, misapply, misspend, misuse, peculate, plunder, pocket, rob, swindle; SEE CONCEPTS *139,156,341*

misbegotten [*adj*] *illegitimate, illicit*
baseborn, bastard, dishonest, disreputable, fatherless, illegal, natural, poor, shady, spurious, stolen, suppositious, unlawful, unrespectable; SEE CONCEPTS *319,549*

misbehave [*v*] *act in inappropriate manner*
act up, be at fault, be bad, be dissolute, be guilty, be immoral, be indecorous, be insubordinate, be mischievous, bend the law*, be out of line*, be out of order*, be reprehensible, carry on, cut up, deviate, do evil, do wrong, fail, fool around*, get into mischief, go astray, go wrong, make trouble, misconduct, offend, roughhouse*, sin, sow wild oats*, take

a wrong turn*, transgress, trespass; SEE CONCEPTS *633,645*

misbehavior [*n*] *naughty act, conduct*
acting up*, fault, immorality, impropriety, incivility, indiscipline, insubordination, mischief, misconduct, misdeed, misdemeanor, misdoing, monkey business*, naughtiness, rudeness, shenanigans*, transgression, wrongdoing; SEE CONCEPTS *633,645*

miscalculate [*v*] *make a mistake*
blow*, blunder, discount, disregard, drop the ball*, err, get signals crossed*, get wrong, go wrong, mess up*, misconstrue, miscount, misinterpret, misjudge, misread, misreckon, miss by a mile*, misunderstand, mix up, overestimate, overlook, overrate, overvalue, slip up, stumble, underestimate, underrate, undervalue; SEE CONCEPT *101*

miscarriage [*n*] *failure*
abortion, botch, breakdown, defeat, error, interruption, malfunction, misadventure, mischance, misfire, mishap, miss, mistake, nonsuccess, perversion, undoing; SEE CONCEPTS *230,699*

miscellaneous [*adj*] *diversified, various*
assorted, confused, conglomerate, different, disordered, disparate, divergent, divers, diverse, heterogeneous, indiscriminate, jumbled, many, mingled, mixed, motley, muddled, multifarious, multiform, odd, promiscuous, scattered, scrambled, sundry, unmatched, unsorted, varied, variegated; SEE CONCEPT *564*

miscellany [*n*] *varied collection*
accumulation, aggregation, anthology, assortment, brew, collectanea, combination, combo, compilation, conglomeration, cumulation, diversity, farrago, gallimaufry, garbage*, hash, hodgepodge, jumble, medley, mélange, melee, mess, mishmash, mix, mixed bag, mixture, muddle, odds and ends*, olio, pasticcio, pastiche, patchwork, potpourri, salad, salmagundi, smorgasbord, stew, variety; SEE CONCEPTS *432,665*

mischief [*n*] *trouble, damage*
atrocity, catastrophe, devilment, devilry, dirty trick*, evil, fault, friskiness, frolicsomeness, funny business*, gag, harm, high jinks*, hurt, ill, impishness, injury, misbehavior, mischievousness, misconduct, misdoing, misfortune, monkey business*, naughtiness, outrage, playfulness, prank, rascality, roguery, roguishness, sabotage, shenanigans, sportiveness, transgression, vandalism, waggery, waggishness, waywardness, wrong, wrongdoing; SEE CONCEPTS *192,633,645*

mischievous [*adj*] *devilish, wicked*
arch, artful, bad, bothersome, damaging, dangerous, deleterious, destructive, detrimental, dickens*, evil, exasperating, foxy*, frolicsome, harmful, hazardous, holy terror*, hurtful, ill, ill-behaved, impish, injurious, insidious, irksome, malicious, malignant, misbehaving, naughty, nocuous, perilous, pernicious, playful, precarious, puckish, rascal, rascally,

risky, roguish, rude, sinful, sly, spiteful, sportive, teasing, tricky, troublesome, vexatious, vexing, vicious, wayward; SEE CONCEPTS *401,545*

misconception [*n*] *wrong idea, impression*
delusion, error, fallacy, fault, misapprehension, misconstruction, misinterpretation, mistake, mistaken belief, misunderstanding; SEE CONCEPTS *409,689*

misconduct [*n*] *bad or unethical behavior*
delinquency, dereliction, evil, immorality, impropriety, malfeasance, malpractice, malversation, misbehavior, mischief, misdemeanor, misdoing, mismanagement, naughtiness, offense, rudeness, transgression, wrongdoing; SEE CONCEPTS *192,633,645*

misconstrue [*v*] *get a wrong or false impression*
distort, exaggerate, misapprehend, misconceive, misinterpret, misjudge, misread, mistake, mistranslate, misunderstand, pervert, take the wrong way; SEE CONCEPT *15*

miscreant [*n*] *person who is very bad, immoral*
blackguard, black sheep*, bootlegger, bully, cad, caitift, convict, criminal, culprit, delinquent, drunkard, evildoer, felon, fink*, heel*, hoodlum, jailbird, knave, loafer, louse*, lowlife*, malefactor, outcast, outlaw, pickpocket, racketeer, rapscallion, rascal, rat*, reprobate, rogue, rowdy, ruffian, scalawag, scamp, scoundrel, scum*, sinner, sneak, vagabond, villain, wretch, wrongdoer; SEE CONCEPT *412*

miscreant [*adj*] *evil, immoral*
corrupt, criminal, degenerate, depraved, flagitious, infamous, iniquitous, nefarious, perverse, rascally, reprehensible, reprobate, unhealthy, unprincipled, vicious, villainous, wicked; SEE CONCEPTS *401,545*

misdeed/misdemeanor [*n*] *sin, crime*
breach of law, criminality, dirt*, dirty deed*, dirty pool*, fault, infringement, malefaction, misbehavior, misconduct, miscue, offense, peccadillo, slipup, transgression, trespass, villainy, violation, wrong, wrongdoing; SEE CONCEPTS *192,633,645*

miser [*n*] *person who hoards money, possessions*
cheapskate*, churl, curmudgeon, harpy*, hoarder, misanthrope, misanthropist, moneygrubber*, niggard, penny-pincher*, pinchfist*, pinchpenny*, Scrooge*, stiff*, tightwad*; SEE CONCEPTS *348, 412,423*

miserable [*adj1*] *unhappy, depressed*
afflicted, agonized, ailing, anguished, brokenhearted, crestfallen, dejected, desolate, despairing, despondent, destroyed, disconsolate, discontented, distressed, doleful, dolorous, down, downcast, down in the mouth*, forlorn, gloomy, heartbroken, hopeless, hurt, hurting, ill, injured, in pain, melancholy, mournful, on a downer*, pained, pathetic, pitiable, racked, rueful, ruthful, sad, sick, sickly, sorrowful, strained, suffering, tormented, tortured, tragic, troubled, woebegone, wounded, wretched; SEE CONCEPT *403*

miserable [*adj2*] *destitute, shabby*
abject, bad, contemptible, deplorable, despicable, detestable, disgraceful, godforsaken, impoverished, indigent, inferior, lamentable, low, meager, mean, needy, paltry, pathetic, penniless, piteous, pitiable, poor, poverty-stricken, sad, scanty, scurvy, shameful, sordid, sorry, squalid, tragic, vile, worthless, wretched; SEE CONCEPTS *485,570*

miserly [*adj*] *greedy, stingy*
abject, avaricious, beggarly, cheapskate*, churlish, close, close-fisted, covetous, grasping, ignoble, illiberal, last of big spenders*, mean, niggardly, parsimonious, penny-pinching*, penurious, skinflint*, sordid, tightfisted*, ungenerous; SEE CONCEPTS *326,334,401,404*

misery [*n1*] *pain, mental or physical*
ache, agony, anguish, anvil chorus, bad news*, blues*, depression, desolation, despair, despondency, discomfort, distress, dolor, gloom, grief, hardship, headache, heartache, hurting, melancholy, pang, passion, sadness, sorrow, squalor, stitch, suffering, throe, torment, torture, twinge, unhappiness, woe, worriment, worry, wretchedness; SEE CONCEPT *728*

misery [*n2*] *trouble, disaster*
adversity, affliction, anxiety, bitter pill*, burden, calamity, catastrophe, curse, destitution, difficulty, grief, indigence, load, misfortune, need, ordeal, penury, poverty, privation, problem, sordidness, sorrow, squalor, trial, tribulation, want, woe; SEE CONCEPTS *335,666,674*

misfortune/mishap [*n*] *bad luck; disaster*
accident, adversity, affliction, annoyance, anxiety, bad break*, bad news*, blow*, burden, calamity, casuality, cataclysm, catastrophe, contretemps, cross, crunch, debacle, disadvantage, disappointment, discomfort, dole, failure, hard luck*, hardship, harm, inconvenience, infelicity, loss, misadventure, mischance, misery, nuisance, reverse, rotten luck, setback, stroke of bad luck*, tough luck*, tragedy, trial, tribulation, trouble, unpleasantness, visitation, worry; SEE CONCEPTS *674,679*

misgiving [*n*] *uncertainty*
anxiety, apprehension, apprehensiveness, distrust, doubt, fear, foreboding, hesitation, mistrust, premonition, prenotion, presage, presentiment, qualm, reservation, scruple, suspicion, unbelief, unease, worry; SEE CONCEPTS *21,689,690*

misguided [*adj*] *ill-advised, deluded*
bearded, bum-steer*, confused, deceived, disinformed, erroneous, faked-out*, foolish, imprudent, indiscreet, inexpedient, injudicious, led up garden path*, misled, misplaced, mistaken, stonewalled*, uncalled for, unreasonable, unwarranted, unwise, wrong; SEE CONCEPTS *544,548,570*

mishandle/mismanage [*v*] *mess up*
abuse, be incompetent, be inefficient, blow, blunder, botch*, bungle, confound, err, flub*, foul up, fumble, goof*, goof up*, gum up*, harm, make a hash of*, make a mess of*, maladminister, misapply, misconduct, misdirect, misemploy, misgovern, mistreat,

misuse, muff*, overlook, pervert, prostitute, put foot in*, screw up*, shoot oneself in foot*; SEE CONCEPTS *101,156,384*

misinform [v] *give wrong information intentionally*
bait and switch*, cover up, deceive, disinform, doublespeak*, double-talk*, lead astray, lie, misdirect, misguide, mislead, misstate, mousetrap*, pervert, prevaricate, put on*, put on an act*, put on false front*, put up smoke screen*, signify, string along*, wrong steer*; SEE CONCEPT *63*

misjudge [v] *get the wrong idea*
bark up wrong tree*, be misled, be overcritical, be partial, be unfair, be wrong, come to hasty conclusion, dogmatize, drop the ball*, err, misapprehend, miscalculate, miscomprehend, misconceive, misconjecture, misconstrue, misdeem, misreckon, miss by a mile*, mistake, misthink, misunderstand, overestimate, overrate, prejudge, presume, presuppose, put foot in*, stumble, suppose, underestimate, underrate; SEE CONCEPTS *12,18,101*

mislead [v] *give someone the wrong idea, information*
bait, beguile, betray, bilk, bluff, bunk, cheat, cozen, deceive, defraud, delude, double-cross*, dupe, enmesh, ensnare, entangle, entice, fool, fudge*, gull, hoax, hoodwink*, hose*, illude, inveigle, juggle, lead astray, lead on*, lie, lure, misdirect, misguide, misinform, misrepresent, outwit, overreach, pervert, pull wool over eyes*, put on*, rip off*, rook, rope in*, scam, seduce, shaft, snow*, take in, tempt, trick, victimize; SEE CONCEPTS *59,63*

misleading [adj] *deceptive, confusing*
ambiguous, beguiling, bewildering, casuistical, catchy, confounding, deceitful, deceiving, deluding, delusive, delusory, demagogic, disingenuous, distracting, evasive, fallacious, false, inaccurate, perplexing, puzzling, sophistical, specious, spurious, tricky, wrong; SEE CONCEPTS *267,548*

misplace [v] *lose; be unable to find*
be unable to lay hands on*, confuse, disarrange, dishevel, disorder, disorganize, displace, disturb, forget whereabouts of, lose track of, misfile, mislay, miss, mix, muss, place unwisely, place wrongly, put in wrong place, remove, scatter, unsettle; SEE CONCEPTS *116,201*

misrepresent/misquote [v] *lie, distort*
adulterate, angle, beard*, belie, build up, cloak, color, con, confuse, cover up, disguise, distort, dress, embellish, embroider, equivocate, exaggerate, falsify, garble, give snow job*, mangle, mask, miscolor, misinterpret, misreport, misstate, overdraw, overstate, palter, pervert, phony up*, pirate*, prevaricate, promote, puff*, skew, slant, snow*, spread it on*, stretch, take out of context*, throw a curve*, trump up*, twist, warp; SEE CONCEPT *63*

miss [n1] *failure*
absence, blunder, default, defect, error, fault, loss, mishap, mistake, omission, oversight, slip, want; SEE CONCEPTS *101,699*

miss [n2] *young girl*
damsel, female, gal, lass, lassie, maid, maiden, schoolgirl, unmarried woman, virgin, young lady; SEE CONCEPT *415*

miss [v1] *fail, make a mistake*
be late for, blow, blunder, botch, disregard, drop, drop the ball*, err, fall flat on face*, fall short, flub*, forget, fumble, ignore, juggle, let go, let slip, lose, miscarry, misfire, mislay, misplace, mistake, muff, neglect, omit, overlook, overshoot, pass over, pass up, skip, slight, slip, trip, trip up, undershoot; SEE CONCEPTS *101,699*

miss [v2] *want; feel a loss*
crave, desire, long, need, pine, wish, yearn; SEE CONCEPT *20*

missile [n] *projectile weapon*
ammunition, arrow, bat, bird*, bolt, bomb, bullet, cartridge, dart, MX*, pellet, projectile, rocket, shot, stealth, trajectile; SEE CONCEPT *500*

missing [adj] *gone, absent*
astray, away, AWOL*, disappeared, lacking, left behind, left out, lost, mislaid, misplaced, not present, nowhere to be found*, omitted, removed, short, unaccounted for, wanting; SEE CONCEPTS *539,576*

mission [n] *person's task, responsibility*
aim, assignment, business, calling, charge, commission, duty, end, errand, goal, job, lifework, object, objective, office, operation, profession, purpose, pursuit, quest, sortie, trade, trust, undertaking, vocation, work; SEE CONCEPTS *360,362,659*

missionary [n] *person who aids, does religious work*
apostle, clergy, clergyman/woman, converter, evangelist, herald, messenger, minister, missioner, padre, pastor, preacher, preacher man/woman*, promoter, propagandist, proselytizer, revivalist, teacher; SEE CONCEPTS *361,416*

missive [n] *written communication*
dispatch, epistle, letter, line, memo, memorandum, message, note, report, word; SEE CONCEPTS *271,278*

misspent [adj] *wasted*
blown*, dissipated, down the drain*, idle, imprudent, misapplied, prodigal, profitless, squandered, thrown away; SEE CONCEPTS *544,560,570*

misstep [n] *mistake, wrong move*
bad move*, blunder, bungle, error, failure, false step, faux pas*, fluff*, gaffe, indiscretion, lapse, miscue, miss, slip, slipup*, stumble, trip; SEE CONCEPTS *101,674,699*

mist [n] *film, vapor*
brume, cloud, condensation, dew, drizzle, fog, ground clouds, haze, moisture, rain, smog, soup*, spray, steam, visibility zero*; SEE CONCEPT *524*

mist [v] *cloud, steam up*
becloud, befog, blur, dim, drizzle, film, fog, haze, mizzle, murk, obscure, overcast, overcloud, rain, shower, sprinkle, steam; SEE CONCEPT *526*

mistake [n] *error, misunderstanding*
aberration, blooper*, blunder, boo-boo*, bungle, confusion, delusion, erratum, false move, false step,

fault, faux pas*, flub*, fluff*, gaffe, illusion, inaccuracy, inadvertence, lapse, misapplication, misapprehension, miscalculation, misconception, misinterpretation, misjudgment, misprint, misstatement, misstep, muddle, neglect, omission, overestimation, oversight, slight, slip, slip of tongue*, slipup*, snafu*, solecism, trip*, typographical error, underestimation; SEE CONCEPTS *101,230,410*

mistake [*v*] *mix up, misunderstand*
addle, be off the mark*, be wrong, blunder, botch*, bungle, confound, confuse, deceive oneself, err, fail, get wrong, goof*, have wrong impression, jumble, lapse, make a mess*, misapprehend, miscalculate, misconceive, misconstrue, miscount, misdeem, misinterpret, misjudge, misknow, misread, miss, miss the boat*, not know, omit, overestimate, overlook, put foot in*, slip*, slip up*, snarl, take for*, tangle, underestimate; SEE CONCEPTS *15,101*

mistaken [*adj*] *wrong, incorrect*
all wet*, at fault, barking up wrong tree*, confounded, confused, confused with, deceived, deluded, duped, erroneous, fallacious, false, faulty, fooled, ill-advised, illogical, inaccurate, inappropriate, misconstrued, misguided, misinformed, misinterpreting, misjudging, misled, misunderstanding, off base*, off track*, tricked, unadvised, under wrong impression, unfounded, unreal, unsound, untrue, warranted, way off*, wide of mark*, wrongly identified, wrong number*; SEE CONCEPTS *402,529*

mistreat [*v*] *treat badly or wrongly*
abuse, backbite, bash, brutalize, bung up*, chop, do wrong, dump on*, give black eye*, handle roughly, harm, injure, kick around, knock around, maltreat, manhandle, maul, mess up, misuse, molest, outrage, push around, rip, roughhouse*, rough up, shake up, total*, trash*, wax*, wound, wrong; SEE CONCEPTS *14,156,246*

mistress [*n1*] *woman who has authority*
career woman, chairwoman, connoisseur, dame, doyenne, expert, hostess, housekeeper, manager, matriarch, maven, mother, president, teacher, wife; SEE CONCEPTS *296,347,350,527*

mistress [*n2*] *woman who is lover of man to whom she is not married*
bedmate, concubine, courtesan, doxy, girlfriend, inamorata, ladylove, other woman*, paramour, roommate, sweetheart; SEE CONCEPTS *415,423*

mistrust [*n*] *doubtfulness*
apprehension, chariness, concern, distrust, doubt, dubiety, dubiosity, fear, foreboding, incertitude, misgiving, presentiment, scruple, skepticism, suspicion, uncertainty, wariness, wonder; SEE CONCEPTS *21,27,690*

mistrust [*v*] *doubt*
apprehend, beware, be wary, challenge, disbelieve, dispute, distrust, fear, have doubts, question, scruple, suspect, suspicion; SEE CONCEPT *21*

misty [*adj*] *filmy, obscure*
bleary, blurred, closed in, clouded, cloudy, dark, dewy, dim, enveloped, foggy, fuzzy, hazy, indistinct, murky, mushy, nebulous, opaque, overcast, shrouded, socked in, soupy*, unclear, vague, vaporous; SEE CONCEPTS *525,603,617*

misunderstand [*v*] *get the wrong idea*
be at cross purposes*, be bewildered, be confused, be perplexed, confound, confuse, fail, get signals crossed*, get signals mixed*, get wrong, get wrong impression*, misapply, misapprehend, miscalculate, miscomprehend, misconceive, misconstrue, misinterpret, misjudge, misknow, misread, misreckon, miss*, miss the point*, mistake, not register*, take amiss, take wrongly; SEE CONCEPT *15*

misunderstanding [*n1*] *instance of having the wrong idea*
confounding, confusion, delusion, error, false impression, misapprehension, misconception, misconstruction, misinterpretation, misjudgment, misreckoning, mistake, mix-up, wrong idea*; SEE CONCEPT *409*

misunderstanding [*n2*] *argument, fight*
bad vibes*, blowup*, breach, break, clash, conflict, crossed wires*, debate, difference, difficulty, disagreement, discord, dissension, falling-out*, feud, fuss, quarrel, rift, row, run-in*, rupture, set-to, sour note*, spat, squabble, tiff*, variance, words*; SEE CONCEPTS *46,106*

misuse [*n*] *abuse; wrong application*
abusage, barbarism, catachresis, corruption, cruel treatment, desecration, dissipation, exploitation, harm, ill-treatment, injury, malapropism, maltreatment, manhandling, misapplication, misemployment, mistreatment, misusage, perversion, profanation, prostitution, rough handling, solecism, squandering, waste; SEE CONCEPT *156*

misuse [*v*] *abuse; apply wrongly*
blow*, brutalize, corrupt, cut up, desecrate, dissipate, exploit, go through, handle roughly, ill-treat, maltreat, manhandle, maul, mess up, misapply, misemploy, mistreat, molest, outrage, pervert, profane, prostitute, run through*, shake up, squander, waste, wrong; SEE CONCEPT *156*

mitigate [*v*] *check, diminish, lighten*
abate, allay, alleviate, appease, assuage, blunt, calm, come together, cool*, dull, ease, extenuate, lessen, meet halfway*, moderate, modify, mollify, pacify, palliate, placate, quiet, reduce, relieve, remit, soften, soothe, subdue, take the edge off*, temper, tone down, tranquilize, weaken; SEE CONCEPTS *233,240*

mix/mixture [*n*] *assortment, combination*
admixture, adulteration, alloy, amalgam, amalgamation, assimilation, association, batter, blend, brew, combine, combo, commixture, composite, compound, concoction, confection, conglomeration, cross, crossing, dough, fusion, goulash, grab bag*, hodgepodge, hybrid, hybridization, incorporation,

infiltration, interfusion, jumble, mash, medley, melange, merger, mingling, miscellany, mishmash, mixed bag, mosaic, package, patchwork, potpourri, salmagundi, saturation, soup*, stew*, transfusion, union, variety; SEE CONCEPTS *260,432*

mix [*v1*] *combine, join*
admix, adulterate, alloy, amalgamate, associate, blend, braid, coalesce, commingle, commix, compound, conjoin, cross, embody, fuse, hybridize, incorporate, infiltrate, infuse, instill, interbreed, intermingle, interweave, jumble, knead, link, lump, make up, merge, mingle, mix up, put together, saturate, stir, suffuse, synthesize, tangle, transfuse, unite, weave, work in; SEE CONCEPTS *113,193*

mix [*v2*] *socialize*
associate, come together, consort, fraternize, get along, hang out, hobnob, join, mingle; SEE CONCEPT *114*

mixed [*adj*] *assorted, combined*
alloyed, amalgamated, assimilated, assorted, blended, brewed, composite, compound, conglomerate, crossbred, crossed, different, disordered, diverse, diversified, embodied, fused, heterogeneous, hybrid, hybridized, incorporated, infused, interbred, interdenominational, joint, kneaded, married, merged, mingled, miscellaneous, mongrel, motley, multifarious, tied, transfused, united, varied, woven; SEE CONCEPTS *485,564,772*

mix up [*v*] *confuse*
addle, befuddle, bewilder, confound, derange, disorder, disorganize, disrupt, distract, disturb, dizzy, fluster, foul up*, jumble, mess up*, mistake, muddle, perplex, puzzle, snafu*, upset; SEE CONCEPTS *16,158*

mix-up [*n*] *confusion, misunderstanding*
botch*, chaos, commotion, disorder, jumble, mess, mistake, muddle, shambles*, tangle, turmoil; SEE CONCEPTS *230,674*

moan [*n*] *groan, complaint*
beef, cry, gripe, grouse, grumble, lament, lamentation, plaint, sigh, sob, wail, whine; SEE CONCEPTS *52,77*

moan [*v*] *groan, complain*
bemoan, bewail, carp, deplore, grieve, gripe, grouse, grumble, keen, lament, mourn, sigh, sob, wail, whine; SEE CONCEPTS *52,77*

mob [*n*] *large group of people*
assemblage, body, cabal, camp, canaille, cattle, circle, clan, class, clique, collection, commonality, company, coterie, crew, crowd, crush, drove, flock, gang, gathering, herd, horde, host, jam, lot, mass, masses, multitude, pack, populace, posse, press, proletariat, rabble, riffraff, ring, riot, scum, set, swarm, throng, troop; SEE CONCEPTS *378,417,432*

mob [*v*] *come upon by pushing; surround*
attack, cram, crowd, fill, hustle, jam, jostle, overrun, pack, riot, set upon, swarm, throng; SEE CONCEPTS *208,758*

mobile [*adj*] *movable, travelling*
adaptable, ambulatory, changeable, fluid, free, itinerant, liquid, locomotive, loose, migrant, migratory, motile, motorized, moving, mutable, nomadic, peripatetic, portable, roaming, roving, unsettled, unstable, unstationary, unsteadfast, unsteady, versatile, wandering; SEE CONCEPTS *576,584*

mobilize [*v*] *ready for action, movement*
activate, actuate, animate, assemble, call to arms, call up, catalyze, circulate, drive, gather, get ready, impel, make ready, marshal, muster, organize, prepare, propel, put in motion, rally, ready, set in motion, set off; SEE CONCEPTS *148,187,221,320*

mock [*adj*] *artificial, fake*
apish*, bogus*, counterfeit, dummy, ersatz*, faked, false, feigned, forged, fraudulent, hokey*, imitation, imitative, make-believe, mimic, phony, pretended, pseudo*, put-on*, quasi*, sham*, simulated, so-called*, spurious, substitute, unreal; SEE CONCEPTS *566,582*

mock [*v1*] *ridicule*
buffoon, burlesque, caricature, chaff, deride, flout, hoot, insult, jape, jeer, kid, laugh at, make fun of, needle, parody, poke fun at*, rally, rib*, scoff, scorn, show contempt, sneer, taunt, tease, thumb nose at*, travesty; SEE CONCEPTS *7,19,49*

mock [*v2*] *mimic*
affect, ape, assume, burlesque, caricature, counterfeit, ditto*, do, fake, feign, hoke, imitate, lampoon, mime, mirror, parody, satirize, send up*, simulate, take off*, travesty; SEE CONCEPT *111*

mock [*v3*] *deceive*
beguile, belie, betray, challenge, cheat, defeat, defy, delude, disappoint, double-cross*, dupe, elude, foil, fool, frustrate, juggle, let down*, mislead, sell out*, thwart; SEE CONCEPTS *59,63*

mockery [*n1*] *joke, parody*
apology, burlesque, butt*, caricature, deception, farce, imitation, jest, lampoon, laughingstock, mimicry, mock, pretense, send-up*, sham*, spoof, sport*, take-off*, travesty; SEE CONCEPTS *111,278*

mockery [*n2*] *insult, disrespect*
contempt, contumely, derision, disdain, disparagement, gibe, jeer, ridicule, scoffing, scorn, sport; SEE CONCEPTS *49,278*

mode [*n1*] *manner, way*
approach, book, channels, condition, course, custom, fashion, form, mechanism, method, modus, nuts and bolts*, plan, posture, practice, procedure, process, quality, rule, situation, state, status, style, system, technique, tone, vein, wise; SEE CONCEPTS *6,644*

mode [*n2*] *trend, fad*
chic, convention, craze, cry, dernier cri*, fashion, furor, last word*, latest thing*, latest wrinkle*, look, mainstream, now*, rage*, style, thing*, vogue; SEE CONCEPTS *529,655*

model [*n1*] *imitation, replica*
cartoon, clone, copy, copycat, dead ringer*, ditto*, dummy, duplicate, effigy, engraving, facsimile, figure, figurine, game plan, illustration, image, knock-off, layout, look-alike, miniature, mock-up, painting, paste-up, photograph, picture, pocket, portrait, print, relief, representation, ringer*, setup, sketch, spitting image*, statue, statuette, tracing, visual; SEE CONCEPTS *259,625,628,667*

model [*n2*] *example, standard*
apotheosis, archetype, beau ideal, criterion, design, emblem, embodiment, epitome, exemplar, gauge, hero, ideal, lodestar, mirror, mold, nonesuch, nonpareil, original, paradigm, paragon, pattern, prototype, quintessence, role model, saint, symbol, touchstone, type; SEE CONCEPTS *687,688*

model [*n3*] *person, thing which poses*
dummy, manikin, mannequin, nude, sitter, subject; SEE CONCEPT *348*

model [*n4*] *type, version*
configuration, design, form, kind, mark, mode, style, variety; SEE CONCEPTS *378,463,505,654*

model [*adj*] *typical, ideal*
archetypal, classic, classical, commendable, copy, dummy, exemplary, facsimile, flawless, illustrative, imitation, miniature, paradigmatic, perfect, prototypical, quintessential, representative, standard, typical, very; SEE CONCEPTS *566,574*

model [*v1*] *form, shape*
base, carve, cast, create, design, fashion, mold, pattern, plan, sculpt; SEE CONCEPT *184*

model [*v2*] *display, pose*
parade, represent, set example, show off, sit, sport, wear; SEE CONCEPT *138*

moderate [*adj1*] *calm, temperate*
abstinent, balanced, bearable, careful, cautious, compromising, conservative, considerate, considered, controlled, cool, deliberate, disciplined, dispassionate, equable, even, gentle, impartial, inconsiderable, inexpensive, judicious, limited, low-key, measured, middle-of-the-road*, midway, mild, modest, monotonous, neutral, nonpartisan, not excessive, pacific, peaceable, pleasant, reasonable, reserved, restrained, sober, soft, steady, straight, tame, tolerable, tolerant, tranquil, untroubled; SEE CONCEPTS *533,563*

moderate [*adj2*] *fair, average, so-so*
bland, fairish*, fair to middling*, inconsequential, inconsiderable, indifferent, intermediate, mean, mediocre, medium, middling*, ordinary, paltry, passable, piddling*, trifling, trivial, unexceptional; SEE CONCEPTS *547,575*

moderate [*v1*] *restrain, control*
abate, allay, alleviate, appease, assuage, calm, chasten, check, constrain, cool*, cool out*, curb, decline, decrease, die down, diminish, ease off, fall, lessen, let up, meet halfway, mitigate, modify, modulate, mollify, pacify, play down, qualify, quiet, re-

duce, regulate, relent, relieve, repress, slacken, slow, soften, soft-pedal, subdue, subside, tame, temper, tone down, wane; SEE CONCEPTS *94,130,240*

moderate [*v2*] *mediate, arbitrate*
chair, judge, make peace*, negotiate, preside, referee, take the chair*, umpire; SEE CONCEPTS *18, 317*

moderately [*adv*] *to a degree, to some extent*
a little, averagely, enough, fairly, gently, in moderation, in reason, kind of, more or less*, more than not*, not exactly, passably, pretty, quite, quite a bit, rather, reasonably, slightly, some, something, somewhat, sort of, so-so*, temperately, tolerable, tolerably, tolerantly, within limits*, within reason*; SEE CONCEPTS *544,772*

moderation [*n*] *temperance*
balance, calmness, composure, constraint, coolness, dispassionateness, equanimity, fairness, forbearance, golden mean, judiciousness, justice, justness, lenity, measure, mildness, moderateness, patience, poise, quiet, reasonableness, restraint, sedateness, sedation, sobriety, steadiness, toleration; SEE CONCEPTS *633,657*

modern [*adj*] *new, up-to-date*
avant-garde, coincident, concomitant, concurrent, contempo, contemporary, current, cutting-edge*, fresh, last word*, late, latest, latter-day*, leading-edge*, modernistic, modernized, modish, neoteric, newfangled*, new-fashioned, novel, now, present, present-day, prevailing, prevalent, recent, state-of-the-art*, stylish, today, twenty-first century*, up-to-the-minute, with-it*; SEE CONCEPTS *578,589, 797*

modernize [*v*] *bring up-to-date; remodel*
improve, refresh, regenerate, rejuvenate, remake, renew, renovate, restore, revamp, revive, update; SEE CONCEPTS *168,177,202*

modest [*adj1*] *shy*
bashful, blushing, chaste, coy, demure, diffident, discreet, humble, lowly, meek, moderate, nice, proper, prudent, quiet, reserved, resigned, reticent, retiring, seemly, self-conscious, self-effacing, sheepish, silent, simple, temperate, timid, unassertive, unassuming, unassured, unboastful, unobtrusive, unpresuming, unpretending, unpretentious, withdrawing; SEE CONCEPTS *401,404*

modest [*adj2*] *limited, ordinary*
average, cheap, discreet, dry, economical, fair, humble, inelaborate, inexpensive, middling, moderate, natural, plain, reasonable, simple, small, unadorned, unaffected, unembellished, unembroidered, unexceptional, unexcessive, unextravagant, unextreme, unobtrusive, unornamented, unostentatious, unpretentious, unradical, unstudied; SEE CONCEPTS *334,547,562*

modesty [*n*] *shyness*
bashfulness, celibacy, chastity, constraint, coyness, decency, delicacy, demureness, diffidence, discreetness, humbleness, humility, inhibition, innocence,

lack of pretension, meekness, propriety, prudery, purity, quietness, reserve, reticence, self-effacement, simplicity, timidity, unobtrusiveness, unostentatiousness, unpretentiousness, virtue; SEE CONCEPT *633*

modicum [*n*] *bit, small amount*

atom, crumb, dash, drop, fraction, fragment, grain, inch, iota, jot, little, minim, mite, molecule, ounce, particle, pinch, scrap, shred, smidge, speck, tinge, touch, trifle, whit; SEE CONCEPT *831*

modify [*v1*] *alter, change*

adapt, adjust, become, convert, correct, customize, doctor, mutate, recast, redo, refashion, reform, remodel, reorganize, repair, reshape, revise, rework, shift gears*, switch over, transfigure, transform, transmogrify, transmute, turn, turn one around*, turn over new leaf*, turn the corner*, turn the tables*, tweak*, vary; SEE CONCEPT *232*

modify [*v2*] *lessen, reduce*

abate, curb, decrease, limit, lower, mitigate, moderate, modulate, qualify, relax, remit, restrain, restrict, slacken, soften, temper, tone down; SEE CONCEPTS *236,240,247*

modish [*adj*] *very fashionable*

a la mode*, all the rage*, chic, contemporary, current, dashing, exclusive, faddy, fresh, happening, hip*, in*, in*, in-thing*, last-word, latest, mod*, now*, smart, stylish, swank, swish*, trendy, up-to-date, up-to-the-minute, vogue, voguish, with-it*; SEE CONCEPTS *578,589,797*

modulate [*v*] *adjust, harmonize*

attune, balance, fine-tune, inflect, regulate, restrain, revamp, switch, temper, tone, transmogrify, tune, tweak, vary; SEE CONCEPT *202*

mogul [*n*] *person who has great power, many possessions*

baron, czar, executive, key player*, king, magnate, notable, personage, potentate, prince, princess queen, royalty, top brass*, tycoon, VIP*; SEE CONCEPTS *347,354*

moist [*adj*] *wet, wettish*

clammy, damp, dampish, dank, dewy, dripping, drippy, drizzly, humid, irriguous, muggy, not dry, oozy*, rainy, soggy, teary, watery; SEE CONCEPT *603*

moisten [*v*] *make wet, damp*

bathe, bedew, damp, dampen, dip, drench, humidify, lick, mist, moisturize, rain on, rinse, saturate, shower, soak, sog, sop, splash, splatter, spray, sprinkle, squirt, steam, steep, wash, water, water down, waterlog, wet; SEE CONCEPT *256*

moisture [*n*] *dampness; liquid*

damp, dankness, dew, drizzle, fog, humidity, mist, perspiration, precipitation, rain, sweat, water, wateriness, wet, wetness; SEE CONCEPTS *467,524*

mold [*n*] *form, pattern*

cast, cavity, character, class, depression, description, design, die, frame, image, impression, kind, lot, matrix, model, nature, shape, sort, stamp, type, womb; SEE CONCEPTS *378,411,436*

mold [*v*] *form, give shape*

build, construct, devise, erect, fashion, forge, form, frame, make, pat, plan, plant, plot, put together, round, scheme, sculpt, shape, whittle; SEE CONCEPTS *173,175,184,251*

molecule [*n*] *smallest part*

bit, fragment, iota, jot, minim, mite, modicum, mote, ounce, particle, ray, speck, unit; SEE CONCEPTS *393,831*

molest [*v1*] *physically abuse*

accost, assail, attack, disorganize, displace, disturb, encroach, fondle, harm, hinder, hurt, illtreat, injure, interfere, intrude, maltreat, manhandle, meddle, misuse, rape; SEE CONCEPTS *246,375*

molest [*v2*] *bother, annoy*

abuse, afflict, badger, bait, bedevil, beset, break in, bug*, confuse, discommode, discompose, disquiet, disturb, encroach, frighten, harass, harry, heckle, hector, interrupt, intrude, irk, irritate, obtrude, persecute, perturb, pester, plague, pother, pursue, scare, tease, terrify, torment, trouble, upset, vex, worry; SEE CONCEPTS *7,14,19*

mollify [*v*] *pacify, soothe*

abate, allay, alleviate, ameliorate, appease, assuage, blunt, calm, compose, conciliate, cool, cushion, decrease, diminish, dulcify, ease, fix up, lessen, lighten, lull, mellow, mitigate, moderate, modify, pacify, patch things up*, placate, propitiate, quell, quiet, reduce, relieve, soften, sweeten, take sting out*, temper, tranquilize; SEE CONCEPTS *7,22,244,698*

moment [*n1*] *very brief time period*

bit, breathing, crack, date, flash, hour, instant, jiff*, jiffy*, juncture, minute, nothing flat*, no time*, occasion, point, point in time, sec*, second, shake, split second*, stage, three winks*, tick*, time, trice*, twinkle*, twinkling*, while, wink*; SEE CONCEPTS *807,808*

moment [*n2*] *importance*

advantage, avail, concern, consequence, gravity, import, magnitude, momentousness, note, pith, profit, seriousness, significance, signification, substance, use, value, weight, weightiness, worth; SEE CONCEPT *668*

momentarily [*adv*] *for a very short time*

briefly, for a little while, for a minute, for a moment, for an instant, for a second, for a short time, for a short while, immediately, instantly, now, right now, temporarily; SEE CONCEPT *820*

momentary [*adj*] *brief, fleeting*

cursory, dreamlike, ephemeral, evanescent, flashing, flitting*, flying, fugacious, fugitive, gone in flash*, hasty, impermanent, impulsive, instantaneous, in wink of an eye*, like lightning, passing, quick, shifting, short, short-lived, spasmodic, summary, temporary, transient, transitory, vanishing, volatile; SEE CONCEPT *798*

momentous [adj] very important; serious
big, chips are down*, consequential, considerable, critical, crucial, decisive, earth-shaking, earth-shattering, epochal, eventful, far-reaching, fateful, grave, heavy, heavy number, historic, material, meaningful, memorable, notable, of moment, outstanding, pivotal, significant, substantial, vital, weighty; SEE CONCEPT 568

momentum [n] impetus, push
drive, energy, force, impulse, power, propulsion, strength, thrust; SEE CONCEPTS 641,712

monarch [n] ruler
autocrat, crowned head, despot, emperor, empress, king, majesty, potentate, prince, princess, queen, sovereign; SEE CONCEPTS 354,422

monastery [n] place where monks live
abbey, cloister, friary, house, lamasery, priory, religious community; SEE CONCEPTS 368,439,516

monetary [adj] concerning money, finances
budgetary, capital, cash, commercial, financial, fiscal, pecuniary, pocket; SEE CONCEPT 334

money [n] currency accepted as exchange for goods, services
Almighty Dollar*, banknote, bankroll, bill, bread*, bucks*, capital, cash, check, chips, coin, coinage, dough*, finances, fund, funds, gold, gravy*, greenback*, hard cash*, legal tender, loot*, medium of exchange, pay, payment, pesos*, property, resources, riches, roll, salary, silver, specie, treasure, wad*, wage, wealth, wherewithal*; SEE CONCEPT 340

moneyed [adj] rich
affluent, fat-cat*, flush*, leisure-class*, loaded*, opulent, prosperous, upper-class, upscale, uptown, wealthy, well-heeled*, well-off*, well-to-do*; SEE CONCEPT 334

moneymaking [adj] producing profit
advantageous, gainful, going, good, lucrative, paying, profitable, remunerative, successful, thriving, well-paying; SEE CONCEPT 334

mongrel [n] animal of mixed background
bastard, cross, crossbreed, cur, half-blood, half-breed, hybrid, mixed breed, mixture, mule, mutt; SEE CONCEPT 394

monitor [n] person who watches, oversees
adviser, auditor, counselor, director, eavesdropper, guide, informant, invigilator, listener, overseer, supervisor, watchdog; SEE CONCEPTS 348,350

monitor [v] listen, watch carefully
advise, audit, check, control, counsel, follow, keep an eye on*, keep track of*, observe, oversee, record, scan, supervise, survey, track; SEE CONCEPTS 117,596,623

monk [n] man who devotes life to contemplation of god
abbot, anchorite, ascetic, brother, cenobite, eremite, friar, hermit, monastic, priest, recluse, religious, solitary; SEE CONCEPT 361

monkey [n] primate animal; person who acts like monkey
anthropoid, ape, baboon, chimpanzee, gorilla, imp, lemur, monk, orangutan, rascal, scamp, simian; SEE CONCEPT 394

monkey [v] fiddle, tamper with
busybody, butt in*, fool, fool around*, fool with*, horn in*, interfere, interlope, intermeddle, make*, meddle, mess, play, pry, tinker, trifle; SEE CONCEPTS 87,612

monologue [n] speech by one person
address, descant, discourse, disquisition, harangue, lecture, one-man/woman show*, sermon, soliloquy, speech, stand-up bit*, talk; SEE CONCEPTS 266,278

monopolize [v] dominate, control
absorb, acquire, bogart, consume, copyright, corner, corner the market*, devour, employ, engross, exclude, exercise control, have, hog*, hold, keep to oneself, lock up*, manage, own, own exclusively, patent, possess, restrain, sew up*, sit on*, syndicate, take over, take up, use, utilize; SEE CONCEPTS 94,324,710

monopoly [n] something held, owned exclusively
cartel, consortium, copyright, corner, holding, oligopoly, ownership, patent, pool, possessorship, proprietorship, syndicate, trust; SEE CONCEPT 710

monotonous [adj] all the same, remaining the same
banausic, blah*, boring, colorless, dreary, droning, dull, dull as dishwater*, flat, flat as pancake*, ho-hum*, humdrum*, monotone, nothing, pedestrian, plodding, prosaic, puts one to sleep*, recurrent, reiterated, repetitious, repetitive, same, samely, sing-song*, soporific, tedious, tiresome, toneless, treadmill, unchanged, unchanging, uniform, uninflected, uninteresting, unrelieved, unvaried, unvarying, wearisome, wearying; SEE CONCEPTS 529,534,544

monotony [n] boredom; sameness
colorlessness, continuance, continuity, dreariness, dryness, dullness, ennui, equability, evenness, flatness, humdrum*, identicalness, invariability, levelness, likeness, monotone, monotonousness, oneness, repetitiousness, repetitiveness, routine, same old thing*, similarity, tediousness, tedium, tiresomeness, unchangeableness, uniformity, wearisomeness; SEE CONCEPTS 410,637,673

monster [n] giant animal; supernatural being
abnormality, barbarian, beast, behemoth, bogeyman, brute, centaur, colossus, demon, devil, dragon, fiend, Frankenstein, freak, giant, hellion, horror, leviathan, lusus, mammoth, miscreation, monstrosity, mutant, naturae, ogre, phoenix, savage, titan, villain, werewolf, whale; SEE CONCEPTS 370,394,412

monstrous [adj1] unnatural, shocking
aberrant, abnormal, atrocious, cruel, desperate, devilish, diabolical, disgraceful, dreadful, egregious, evil, fiendish, flagitious, foul, freakish, frightful, grotesque, gruesome, heinous, hellish, hideous, hor-

rendous, horrible, horrifying, infamous, inhuman, intolerable, loathsome, macabre, miscreated, morbid, obscene, odious, ominous, outrageous, preposterous, rank, satanic, scandalous, teratoid, terrible, uncanny, unusual, vicious, villainous; SEE CONCEPTS *537,564,582*

monstrous [*adj2*] *very large*
colossal, cracking, elephantine, enormous, fantastic, gargantuan, giant, gigantic, grandiose, great, huge, immense, impressive, magnificent, mammoth, massive, monumental, prodigious, stupendous, titanic, towering, tremendous, vast, whopping; SEE CONCEPTS *773,781*

monument [*n*] *memorial, remembrance*
cairn, cenotaph, column, commemoration, erection, footstone, gravestone, headstone, ledger, magnum opus, marker, masterpiece, mausoleum, memento, monolith, obelisk, pile, pillar, record, reminder, shrine, slab, statue, stele, stone, tablet, testament, token, tomb, tombstone, tower, tribute, witness; SEE CONCEPTS *259,271,305,470*

monumental [*adj*] *impressive, overwhelming*
awe-inspiring, awesome, classic, enduring, enormous, fantastic, gigantic, grand, great, historic, huge, immense, immortal, important, lasting, lofty, majestic, mammoth, massive, memorable, mighty, mortal, mountainous, outstanding, prodigious, significant, stupendous, towering, tremendous, unforgettable, vast; SEE CONCEPTS *568,773*

mood [*n*] *state of mind*
affection, air, atmosphere, attitude, aura, bent*, blues*, caprice, character, color*, condition, crotchet, cue, depression, desire, disposition, doldrums, dumps*, emotion, fancy, feel*, feeling, frame of mind*, high spirits, humor, inclination, individuality, low spirits, melancholy, mind, personality, pleasure, propensity, response, scene, semblance, soul, spirit, strain, temper, temperament, tendency, tenor, timbre, vagary, vein, whim, wish; SEE CONCEPTS *410,411,673*

moody [*adj*] *crabby, temperamental*
angry, cantankerous, capricious, changeable, crabbed*, crestfallen, cross, dismal, doleful, dour, downcast, down in the dumps*, down in the mouth*, erratic, fickle, fitful, flighty, frowning, gloomy, glum, huffy, ill-humored, ill-tempered, impulsive, in a huff*, in the doldrums, introspective, irascible, irritable, lugubrious, melancholy, mercurial, miserable, moping, morose, offended, out of sorts*, pensive, petulant, piqued, sad, saturnine, short-tempered, splenetic, sulky, sullen, testy, touchy; SEE CONCEPT *403*

moon [*n*] *earth's satellite*
celestial body, crescent, full moon, half-moon, heavenly body, man in the moon*, new moon, old moon, orb of night*, planetoid, pumpkin*, quarter-moon, satellite; SEE CONCEPTS *511,809*

moon [*v*] *dream about; desire*
daydream, idle, languish, mope, pine, waste time, yearn; SEE CONCEPT *20*

moor [*v*] *anchor, fasten securely*
berth, catch, chain, dock, fix, lash, make fast, picket, secure, tether, tie, tie up; SEE CONCEPTS *85,160*

moot [*adj*] *doubtful, arguable*
at issue, contestable, controversial, debatable, disputable, dubious, open, open to debate, problematic, questionable, suspect, uncertain, undecided, unresolved, unsettled; SEE CONCEPT *535*

mop [*n1*] *tangle of material, often used to absorb liquid*
duster, sponge, squeegee, swab, sweeper, towel; SEE CONCEPTS *392,499*

mop [*n2*] *thick mass of hair*
mane, shock, tangle, thatch, tresses; SEE CONCEPT *399*

mop [*v*] *clean by using water and cloth*
dab, dust, pat, polish, rub, soak up, sponge, squeegee, swab, towel off, wash, wipe; SEE CONCEPT *165*

mope [*v*] *pout, be dejected*
ache, be apathetic, be down in the mouth*, be gloomy, be in a funk*, bleed*, brood, chafe, despair, despond, droop, eat one's heart out, fret, grieve, grumble, grump, idle, lament, languish, lose heart, moon, pine, pine away*, regret, repine, sink, stew over*, sulk, sweat over*, waste time*, wear a long face*, yearn; SEE CONCEPTS *20,410*

moral [*n*] *lesson, proverb*
adage, aphorism, apophthegm, axiom, dictum, epigram, gnome, maxim, meaning, message, moralism, motto, point, precept, rule, saw, saying, sermon, significance, truism; SEE CONCEPTS *278,283*

moral [*adj*] *ethical, honest*
aboveboard, blameless, chaste, conscientious, correct, courteous, decent, decorous, dutiful, elevated, exemplary, good, high-minded, honorable, immaculate, incorruptible, innocent, just, kindly, kosher*, laudable, meet, meritorious, modest, moralistic, noble, praiseworthy, principled, proper, pure, respectable, right, righteous, saintly, salt of the earth*, scrupulous, seemly, square, straight, true-blue*, trustworthy, truthful, upright, upstanding, virtuous, worthy; SEE CONCEPT *545*

morale [*n*] *confidence, self-esteem*
assurance, attitude, disposition, drive, esprit, esprit de corps, heart, humor, mettle, mood, outlook, resolve, self-confidence, self-possession, spirit, temper, temperament, turn, vigor; SEE CONCEPTS *410,411*

morality [*n*] *ethics, honesty*
chastity, conduct, decency, ethicality, ethicalness, gentleness, godliness, good habits, goodness, honor, ideals, incorruptibility, incorruption, integrity, justice, manners, moral code, morals, mores, philosophy, principle, principles, probity, purity, rectitude,

righteousness, rightness, saintliness, standards, uprightness, virtue, worthiness; SEE CONCEPT 645

morals [n] *personal principles, standards*
behavior, beliefs, conduct, customs, dogmas, ethic, ethics, habits, ideals, integrity, manners, morality, mores, policies, scruples; SEE CONCEPTS 411,645,687

morass [n] *bog; mess*
chaos, confusion, fen, jam, jungle, knot, labyrinth, marsh, maze, mesh, mix-up, muddle, quagmire, skein, snarl, swamp, tangle, web; SEE CONCEPTS 230,509

morbid [adj] *gloomy, nasty, sickly*
aberrant, abnormal, ailing, brooding, dark, deadly, depressed, despondent, diseased, dreadful, frightful, ghastly, ghoulish, grim, grisly, gruesome, hideous, horrid, infected, irascible, macabre, malignant, melancholy, monstrous, moody, pathological, pessimistic, psychotic, saturnine, sick, sickly, somber, sullen, unhealthy, unnatural, unsound, unusual, unwholesome; SEE CONCEPTS 314,403,537

more [adj] *additional, greater*
added, aggrandized, also, amassed, and, another, augmented, besides, bounteous, deeper, else, enhanced, exceeding, expanded, extended, extravagant, farther, fresh, further, heavier, higher, in addition, increased, innumerable, larger, likewise, major, massed, more than that, new, numerous, other, over and above, spare, supplementary, too many, wider; SEE CONCEPTS 762,771

more [adv] *to a greater extent*
additionally, along with, also, as well, besides, better, beyond, further, furthermore, in addition, likewise, longer, moreover, over, too, withal; SEE CONCEPTS 544,772

moreover [adv] *additionally*
also, as well, besides, by the same token*, further, furthermore, in addition, likewise, more, to boot*, too, what is more*, withal, yet; SEE CONCEPTS 544,772

morning [n] *first part of the day*
after midnight, AM, ante meridiem, aurora, before lunch, before noon, breakfast time*, break of day, cockcrow*, crack of dawn*, dawn, daybreak, daylight, dayspring, early bright*, first blush*, foreday, forenoon, morn*, morningtide, morrow, prime*, sunrise, sunup, wee hours*; SEE CONCEPTS 801,802,806,810

moron [n] *very stupid person*
addlepate, blockhead*, boob*, cretin, dimwit, dingbat*, dolt, dope*, dork*, dumbbell*, dummy*, dunce, fool, halfwit, idiot, ignoramus, imbecile, lamebrain*, loony*, loser*, mental defective*, nerd*, retard*, simpleton, stupid; SEE CONCEPTS 350,423

morose [adj] *very depressed, pessimistic*
acrimonious, blue*, brusque, cantankerous, choleric, churlish, crabbed*, crabby*, cranky*, cross, dolorous, dour, down, down in the dumps*, down in the mouth*, frowning, gloomy, glum, grouchy, gruff,

harsh, having blue devils*, having the blahs*, ill-humored, ill-tempered, in a bad mood*, in a blue funk*, irritable, low, melancholy, moody, moping, mournful, perverse, perversive, sad, saturnine, singing the blues*, snappish, sour, splenetic, sulky, sullen, surly, taciturn, testy, troubled, ugly; SEE CONCEPT 403

morsel [n] *tiny piece*
bait, bit, bite, chunk, crumb, cut, delicacy, drop, fraction, fragment, grain, hunk, lump, mouthful, nibble, nosh, part, sample, scrap, segment, slice, snack, soupçon, taste, tidbit, treat; SEE CONCEPTS 457, 458,831,835

mortal [n] *human being*
animal, being, body, character, creature, earthling, human, individual, living soul, man, naked ape, party, person, personage, soul, woman; SEE CONCEPT 417

mortal [adj1] *deadly*
bitter, death-dealing, deathly, destructive, dire, ending, extreme, fatal, grave, great, grievous, grim, intense, killing, last, lethal, malignant, merciless, monstrous, mortiferous, murderous, noxious, pestilent, pestilential, poisonous, relentless, remorseless, ruthless, severe, terminal, terrible, unrelenting; SEE CONCEPT 537

mortal [adj2] *human*
animate, bipedal, corporeal, creatural, earthly, ecce homo, ephemeral, evanescent, fading, finite, frail, fugacious, impermanent, momentary, passing, perishable, precarious, sublunary, temporal, transient, weak, worldly; SEE CONCEPT 549

mortality [n1] *death*
bloodshed, carnage, deadliness, destruction, dying, extinction, fatality, killing, lethality, loss of life; SEE CONCEPT 407

mortality [n2] *humanness*
being, ephemerality, flesh, Homo sapiens, humanity, humankind, human race, impermanence, temporality, transience; SEE CONCEPTS 417,648

mortify [v] *embarrass*
abase, abash, affront, annoy, belittle, chagrin, chasten, confound, control, crush, deflate, deny, disappoint, discipline, discomfit, disgrace, displease, get one's comeuppance*, harass, humble, humiliate, put to shame, ridicule, shame, subdue, take down a peg*, take the wind out*, vex, worry; SEE CONCEPTS 7,19,52,54

most [adj] *best, greatest*
better, biggest, greater, highest, largest, lion's share*, max*, maximum, ultimate, utmost, uttermost; SEE CONCEPTS 771,772

most [adv] *nearly all; extremely*
about, all but, almost, approximately, close, eminently, exceedingly, in the majority, mightily, much, nearly, nigh, practically, remarkably, super, surpassingly, too, very, well-nigh; SEE CONCEPTS 544, 569,771

mostly [*adv*] *generally, mainly*
above all, almost entirely, as a rule*, chiefly, customarily, essentially, for the most part*, frequently, in many instances*, largely, many times, most often, often, on the whole*, overall, particularly, predominantly, primarily, principally, regularly, usually; SEE CONCEPTS *544,548,772*

motel [*n*] *temporary, short-term residence, often for travelers*
cabin, court, hotel, inn, lodge, motor court, resort, roadhouse; SEE CONCEPTS *439,449,516*

mother [*n*] *female person who has borne children; originator*
child-bearer, creator, grandmother, mammalian, matriarch, matron, mom*, mommy*, nurse, nurturer, origin, parent, source; SEE CONCEPTS *394,400,414, 415,423*

mother [*v*] *produce; care for, spoil*
baby, bear, bring forth, cherish, fuss over, give birth to, indulge, minister to, nurse, nurture, pamper, protect, raise, rear, serve, spoil, tend, wait on; SEE CONCEPT *295*

motherly [*adj*] *caring, nurturing*
affectionate, careful, caretaking, comforting, devoted, fond, gentle, kind, loving, maternal, protecting, protective, sheltering, supporting, sympathetic, tender, warm, watchful; SEE CONCEPT *401*

motion [*n1*] *movement, action*
act, advance, agitation, ambulation, body English*, change, changing, direction, drift, dynamics, flow, fluctuation, flux, full swing*, gesticulation, gesture, high sign*, inclination, kinetics, locomotion, mobility, motility, move, oscillation, passage, passing, progress, sign, signal, stir, stirring, stream, sway, sweep, swing, tendency, travel, wave, wavering; SEE CONCEPT *145*

motion [*n2*] *formal suggestion in a meeting*
plan, proposal, proposition, recommendation, submission; SEE CONCEPTS *75,278*

motion [*v*] *gesture, direct*
beckon, flag, gesticulate, guide, invite, move, nod, sign, signal, signalize, wave; SEE CONCEPT *149*

motionless [*adj*] *calm, not moving*
apoplectic, at a standstill, at rest, becalmed, dead, deadlocked, deathly, firm, fixed, frozen, halted, immobile, immotile, inanimate, inert, lifeless, numb, palsied, paralyzed, petrified, quiescent, quiet, spellbound, stable, stagnant, stalled, standing, static, stationary, steadfast, still, stock-still, torpid, transfixed, unmovable, unmoved, unmoving; SEE CONCEPTS *488,584*

motivate [*v*] *stimulate, instigate*
actuate, arouse, bring, cause, dispose, draw, drive, egg on*, excite, fire, galvanize, give incentive, goad, goose*, impel, incite, incline, induce, innervate, innerve, inspire, inspirit, lead, move, persuade, pique, predetermine, predispose, prevail upon, prompt, propel, provoke, quicken, rouse, set afoot, set astir,

sound, spark, spur, suggest, sway, touch off, trigger, whet; SEE CONCEPTS *14,68,242*

motivation [*n*] *ambition, inspiration*
action, actuation, angle, catalyst, desire, disposition, drive, encouragement, fire, get up and go*, gimmick, goose*, hunger, impetus, impulse, impulsion, incentive, incitation, incitement, inclination, inducement, instigation, interest, kick*, motive, persuasion, predetermination, predisposition, provocation, push, reason, right stuff*, spur, stimulus, suggestion, wish; SEE CONCEPTS *20,411,689*

motive [*n*] *reason, purpose*
aim, antecedent, basis, cause, consideration, design, determinant, drive, emotion, end, feeling, grounds, idea, impulse, incentive, incitement, inducement, influence, inspiration, intent, intention, mainspring, motivation, object, occasion, passion, rationale, root, spring, spur, stimulus, thinking; SEE CONCEPTS *20,661,689*

motley [*adj*] *mixed, varied*
assorted, conglomerate, dappled, discrepant, disparate, dissimilar, diversified, heterogeneous, indiscriminate, kaleidoscopic, mingled, miscellaneous, mixed, mottled, multicolor, multicolored, multiform, multihued, polychromatic, prismatic, rainbow, unlike, varicolored, variegated, various, versicolor; SEE CONCEPTS *564,618,772*

mottled [*adj*] *speckled*
blotchy, checkered, dappled, flecked, freckled, maculate, marbled, motley, piebald, pied, skewbald, spotted, streaked, tabby, variegated; SEE CONCEPTS *606,618*

motto [*n*] *saying, slogan*
adage, aphorism, apothegm, battle cry, byword, catchphrase, cry, epigram, formula, maxim, precept, proverb, rallying cry, rule, saw, sentiment, shibboleth, war cry, watchword, word; SEE CONCEPT *278*

mound [*n*] *heap, hill*
anthill, bank, drift, dune, embankment, hillock, knoll, mass, molehill, mountain, pile, rise, shock, stack, tumulus; SEE CONCEPTS *432,509*

mount [*v1*] *climb*
arise, ascend, back, bestride, clamber up, climb onto, climb up on, escalade, escalate, get astride, get up on, go up, jump on, lift, rise, scale, soar, tower, up, vault; SEE CONCEPTS *149,154,166*

mount [*v2*] *increase, grow*
accumulate, aggravate, augment, build, deepen, enhance, enlarge, escalate, expand, heighten, intensate, intensify, multiply, pile up, redouble, rise, rouse, swell, upsurge, wax; SEE CONCEPTS *704,780*

mount [*v3*] *affix, frame*
emplace, exhibit, fit, install, place, position, prepare, produce, put in place, put on, set up, show, stage; SEE CONCEPTS *174,261*

mountain [*n*] *very large hill*
abundance, alp, bank, bluff, butte, cliff, crag, dome, drift, elevation, eminence, glob, heap, height, hump, mass, mesa, mound, mount, palisade, peak, pike,

pile, precipice, pyramid, range, ridge, shock, sierra, stack, ton, tor, volcano; SEE CONCEPTS *432,509*

mourn [*v*] *be sad over loss*
ache, agonize, anguish, be brokenhearted*, bemoan, be sad, bewail, bleed, blubber, carry on, complain, cry, deplore, fret, grieve, hang crepe*, hurt, keen, lament, languish, long for, miss, moan, pine, rain, regret, repine, rue, sigh, sob, sorrow, suffer, take it hard*, wail, wear black*, weep, wring hands*, yearn; SEE CONCEPTS *23,410*

mourning [*n*] *sadness, time of sadness*
aching, bereavement, blackness, crying, darkness, grief, grieving, keening, lamentation, lamenting, languishing, moaning, pining, repining, sorrowing, wailing, weeping, woe; SEE CONCEPTS *388,410*

mousy [*adj*] *drab; quiet*
bashful, colorless, diffident, dull, indeterminate, ineffectual, pale, plain, self-effacing, shy, timid, timorous, unassertive, unassuming; SEE CONCEPTS *401,618*

mouth [*n1*] *opening*
aperture, beak, box, cavity, chops, clam, crevice, delta, door, embouchement, entrance, estuary, firth, fly trap, funnel, gate, gills, gob, harbor, inlet, jaws, kisser, lips, mush, orifice, portal, rim, trap, yap; SEE CONCEPTS *392,513*

mouth [*n2*] *backtalk*
boasting, braggadocio, bragging, cheek, empty talk*, freshness, gas*, guff*, hot air*, idle talk, impudence, insolence, lip, rudeness, sass, sauce*; SEE CONCEPTS *54,278*

movable [*adj*] *transportable*
adaptable, adjustable, ambulatory, conveyable, deployable, detachable, in parts, liftable, loose, mobile, motile, moving, not fastened, not fixed, on wheels, portable, portative, removable, separable, shiftable, transferable, turnable, unattached, unfastened, unstationary, unsteady; SEE CONCEPTS *488,584*

move [*n*] *progress, deed*
act, action, alteration, change, maneuver, measure, modification, motion, movement, ploy, procedure, proceeding, shift, step, stir, stirring, stratagem, stroke, turn, variation; SEE CONCEPTS *2,660*

move [*v1*] *be in motion, put in motion*
actuate, advance, blow, budge, bustle, carry, change, climb, crawl, cross, depart, dislocate, disturb, drift, drive, exit, flow, fly, get away, get going, get off, glide, go, go away, head for, hurry, impel, jump, leap, leave, locomote, march, migrate, offload, position, proceed, progress, propel, pull out, push, quit, relocate, remove, roll, run, scram, shift, ship, shove, skip out, split, stir, switch, take off, transfer, transport, transpose, travel, traverse, walk, withdraw; SEE CONCEPTS *147,149,198*

move [*v2*] *motivate, influence*
activate, actuate, advocate, affect, agitate, bring, bring up, budge, carry, cause, convert, draw up, drive, excite, get going, give rise to, impel, impress,

incite, induce, inspire, inspirit, instigate, introduce, lead, operate, persuade, play on, prevail upon, prompt, propel, propose, push, put forward, quicken, recommend, rouse, shift, shove, start, stimulate, stir, strike, submit, suggest, sway, touch, tug at, turn, urge, work on; SEE CONCEPTS *7,19,22,75,242*

movement [*n1*] *motion, activity*
act, action, advance, agitation, alteration, change, changing, deed, development, displacement, dynamism, evolution, evolving, exercise, flight, flow, flux, gesture, journey, journeying, locomotion, maneuver, migration, mobility, motility, movableness, move, moving, operation, operativeness, passage, progress, progression, regression, roaming, shift, shifting, steps, stir, stirring, transferal, transit, translating, transplanting, undertaking, velocity, voyaging, wandering; SEE CONCEPTS *2,145,697*

movement [*n2*] *drive, campaign*
change, crusade, current, demonstration, displacement, drift, evolution, faction, flight, flow, front, group, grouping, march, mobilization, organization, party, patrol, shift, sweep, swing, tendency, transfer, transition, trend, unrest, withdrawal; SEE CONCEPTS *381,697*

movie [*n*] *presentation of action on continuous film*
cine, cinema, cinematics, cinematograph, feature, film, flick*, motion picture, moving picture, photoplay, picture, screenplay, show, silent*, silver screen*, talkie*, talking picture, videotape; SEE CONCEPTS *263,293*

moving [*adj1*] *affecting, exciting*
affective, arousing, awakening, breathless, dynamic, eloquent, emotional, emotive, expressive, facund, far-out*, felt in gut*, grabbed by*, gripping, hairy*, heartbreaking, heartrending, impelling, impressive, inspirational, inspiring, meaningful, mind-bending*, mind-blowing*, motivating, persuasive, poignant, propelling, provoking, quickening, rallying, rousing, sententious, significant, something*, stimulating, stimulating, stimulative, stirring, stunning, touching, turned on by*; SEE CONCEPTS *529,537*

moving [*adj2*] *mobile*
advancing, changing, climbing, evolving, flying, going, jumping, motile, movable, nomadic, portable, progressing, roaming, roving, running, shifting, traversing, unfixed, unstable, unsteadfast, unsteady, walking; SEE CONCEPTS *488,584*

much [*n*] *a great deal*
abundance, a good deal*, all kinds of*, a lot*, amplitude, appreciable amount, barrel, breadth, completeness, copiousness, excess, exuberance, fullness, gobs*, great quantity, heaps*, loads*, lots*, lump, mass, mess*, mountain, multiplicity, oodles*, overage, oversupply, pack, peck, pile, plentifulness, plenty, plethora, profuseness, riches, scads*, sufficiency, superabundance, superfluity, thousands, tons*, very much, volume, wealth; SEE CONCEPT *771*

much [adj] *plenty*
abundant, adequate, a lot of*, ample, complete, considerable, copious, countless, endless, enough, everywhere, extravagant, full, galore, generous, great, heaps*, immeasurable, jam-packed*, lavish, loads*, lotsa*, many, mega*, mucho*, no end*, plenteous, plentiful, profuse, satisfying, scads*, sizable, substantial, sufficient, very many, voluminous; SEE CONCEPTS *772,781*

much [adv] *greatly, a lot*
again and again, a great deal*, considerably, decidedly, eminently, exceedingly, exceptionally, extremely, frequently, highly, hugely, indeed, notably, oft, often, over and over*, regularly, repeatedly, surpassingly, time and time again*, very; SEE CONCEPTS *530,544,548*

muddle [n] *confused state*
ataxia, awkwardness, botch, chaos, clutter, complexity, complication, confusion, daze, difficulty, dilemma, disarrangement, disarray, disorder, disorganization, emergency, encumbrance, fog, foul-up*, hash, haze, intricacy, involvement, jumble, mess, mess and a half*, mix-up*, muss*, perplexity, plight, predicament, quandary, rat's nest*, screw-up*, shambles*, snarl, struggle, tangle, trouble; SEE CONCEPTS *230,410,666*

muddle [v] *confuse, disorganize*
addle, befuddle, bewilder, blunder, botch, bungle, clutter, complicate, confound, confuse, daze, derange, disarrange, discombobulate*, disorder, disorient, disturb, entangle, fluster, foul, foul up, jumble, louse up, make a mess of*, mess, misarrange, mix, mix up, muck, mumble, murmur, nonplus, perplex, perturb, psych out*, rattle, ravel, ruffle, scramble, shuffle, snafu*, snarl, spoil, stir up, stupefy, tangle, throw, throw off, tumble; SEE CONCEPTS *16,84,242*

muddy [adj] *dark and cloudy*
addled, bemired, bespattered, black, blurred, boggy*, caked, confused, dingy, dirty, dull, filthy, flat, foul, fuzzy, gloomy, greasy, grimy, grubby*, gummy*, gunky*, hazy, impure, indistinct, marshy, miry, mucky*, obscure, opaque, roily, sloppy, slushy, smoky, sodden, soggy, soiled, subfuse, swampy, turbid, unclean, unclear; SEE CONCEPTS *485,606,618*

muffle [v] *suppress, make quiet*
conceal, cover, cushion, dampen, deaden, decrease, drown, dull, envelop, gag, hide, hush, mellow, mute, muzzle, put the lid on*, quieten, shut down, silence, sit down on*, smother, soften, soft-pedal*, squelch, stifle, subdue, tone down*, wrap*; SEE CONCEPTS *65,121,240*

muffled [adj] *quietened*
deadened, dim, dull, faint, flat, indistinct, mute, muted, obscure, silenced, stifled, strangled, subdued, suppressed; SEE CONCEPT *594*

muggy [adj] *humid*
clammy*, close, damp, dampish, dank, moist, mucky*, oppressive, soggy, sticky, stuffy, sultry, wettish; SEE CONCEPTS *525,603*

mull [v] *think about seriously*
brood over, chaw, consider, contemplate, delay, deliberate, examine, figure, hammer away at*, linger, meditate, moon*, muse on, ponder, pore over, procrastinate, rack one's brains*, reflect, review, revolve, ruminate, stew over*, study, sweat over*, think over, turn over, weigh, woolgather*; SEE CONCEPT *17*

multicolored [adj] *having various hues*
checkered, dappled, flecked, kaleidoscopic, marbled, motley, mottled, multicolor, particolored, piebald, pied, polychrome, prismatic, speckled, spotted, streaked, varicolored, veined, versicolor; SEE CONCEPT *618*

multiple/multifarious [adj] *diversified, miscellaneous*
assorted, collective, conglomerate, different, diverse, diversiform, heterogeneous, indiscriminate, legion, manifold, many, mixed, motley, multiform, multiplex, multitudinal, multitudinous, numerous, populous, several, sundry, varied, variegated, various, voluminous; SEE CONCEPTS *564,762,772*

multiply [v] *increase; reproduce*
accumulate, add, aggrandize, aggregate, augment, boost, breed, build up, compound, cube, double, enlarge, expand, extend, generate, heighten, magnify, manifold, mount, populate, procreate, produce, proliferate, propagate, raise, repeat, rise, spread, square; SEE CONCEPTS *171,374*

multitude [n] *large group*
aggregation, army, assemblage, assembly, collection, commonalty, concourse, congregation, crowd, crush, drove, great number, heap, herd, horde, host, infinitude, infinity, jam*, legion, loads, lot, lots*, majority, mass, mob, much, myriad, number, numbers, ocean*, oodles*, people, plenitude, plurality, populace, proletariat, public, push*, quantity, scores*, sea, slew*, swarm, throng, turnout; SEE CONCEPTS *417,432*

multitudinous [adj] *many, considerable*
abounding, abundant, copious, countless, great, heaps*, infinite, innumerable, innumerous, legion, manifold, multifarious, myriad, numberless, numerous, populous, profuse, several, sundry, teeming, uncountable, uncounted, unnumbered, untold, various, voluminous; SEE CONCEPTS *762,781*

mumble [v] *say low and inarticulately*
grumble, maunder, murmur, mutter, ramble, rumble, say to oneself, speak, stammer, stutter, swallow, talk, utter, verbalize, vocalize, voice, whimper, whine, whisper; SEE CONCEPTS *47,77*

munch [v] *chew, eat*
bite, break up, champ, chomp, crunch, crush, grind, mash, masticate, press, reduce, ruminate, scrunch, smash, soften; SEE CONCEPTS *169,185*

mundane [*adj*] *ordinary*
banal, commonplace, day-to-day, earthly, everyday, humdrum*, lowly, normal, prosaic, routine, workaday*, workday, worldly; SEE CONCEPT *547*

municipal [*adj*] *concerning cities*
borough, burghal, city, civic, civil, community, corporate, domestic, home, incorporated, internal, local, metropolitan, native, public, town, urban; SEE CONCEPT *536*

munificent [*adj*] *giving, generous*
beneficent, benevolent, big, big-hearted, bounteous, bountiful, charitable, free, handsome, kind, lavish, liberal, loose, magnanimous, openhanded, philanthropic, prince, princely, rich, unsparing, unstinting; SEE CONCEPTS *334,401*

murder [*n*] *killing*
annihilation, assassination, blood, bloodshed, butchery, carnage, crime, death, destruction, dispatching, felony, foul play*, hit*, homicide, knifing, liquidation, lynching, manslaughter, massacre, off*, offing*, one-way ticket*, rub out*, shooting, slaying, taking out*, terrorism, the business*, the works*; SEE CONCEPTS *192,252*

murder [*v*] *kill*
abolish, asphyxiate, assassinate, behead, blot out*, bump off*, butcher, chill*, cool*, decapitate, defeat, destroy, dispatch, do in*, drub*, dust off*, electrocute, eliminate, eradicate, execute, exterminate, extinguish, finish, garotte, guillotine, hang, hit*, knife, knock off*, liquidate, lynch, mangle, mar, massacre, misuse, off*, put away*, rub out*, ruin, shoot, slaughter, slay, smother, snuff, spoil, strangle, take a life, take for a ride*, take out*, thrash*, waste*; SEE CONCEPTS *192,252*

murderer [*n*] *person who kills*
assassin, butcher, criminal, cutthroat, enforcer, executioner, gunman/woman, hit-and-run*, hit man/woman*, homicide, killer, manslaughterer, perpetrator, slaughterer, slayer, soldier, trigger man/woman*; SEE CONCEPT *412*

murderous [*adj*] *very difficult*
arduous, brutal, criminal, cruel, dangerous, deadly, destroying, destructive, devastating, exhausting, fell, ferocious, harrowing, hellish, killing, lethal, ruinous, sapping, savage, strenuous, unpleasant; SEE CONCEPTS *538,548,565*

murky [*adj*] *gloomy, obscure*
black, caliginous, cheerless, cloudy, dark, darkened, dim, dingy, dirty, dismal, drab, dreary, dull, dun*, dusk, dusky, filthy, foggy, foul, fuzzy, glowering, gray, grubby*, impenetrable, lowering, misty, mucky, muddy, nasty, nebulous, nubilous, overcast, roily, sad, smoky, somber, squalid, stormy, tenebrous, turbid, unclean; SEE CONCEPTS *617,618*

murmur [*n*] *low, continuous sound*
babble, buzz, buzzing, drone, grumble, hum, humming, mumble, murmuration, mutter, muttering, purr, rumble, rumor, undertone, whisper, whispering; SEE CONCEPTS *65,595*

murmur [*v*] *make low, continuous sound*
babble, burble, buzz, drip, drone, flow, growl, gurgle, hum, meander, moan, mumble, mutter, purl, purr, ripple, rumble, stage-whisper, stammer, stutter, susurrate, tinkle, trickle, utter, verbalize, vocalize, voice, whisper; SEE CONCEPTS *65,77*

muscle [*n1*] *large fibers of animal body*
beef, brawn, flesh, meat, might, sinew, tendon, thew, tissue; SEE CONCEPTS *393,420*

muscle [*n2*] *power, influence*
brawn, clout, energy, force, forcefulness, might, potency, sinew, stamina, strength, strong arm*, sturdiness, weight; SEE CONCEPTS *641,686*

muscular [*adj*] *powerfully built*
able-bodied, athletic, brawny, bruising, burly, fibrous, hefty, Herculean*, hulky, husky, lusty, mighty, muscled, powerful, powerhouse*, pumped up*, ripped*, robust, ropy, sinewy, stalwart, stout, strapping, stringy, strong, sturdy, tiger*, tough, vigorous, well-built, wicked, wiry; SEE CONCEPTS *485,489*

muse [*v*] *think about, dream*
be lost in thought*, brood, build castles in air*, chew over*, cogitate, consider, contemplate, deliberate, feel, meditate, moon*, mull over, percolate, ponder, puzzle over, reflect, revolve, roll, ruminate, speculate, think, think over, turn over, weigh; SEE CONCEPT *17*

museum [*n*] *place for viewing artifacts or exhibits*
archive, building, depository, exhibition, foundation, gallery, hall, institution, library, menagerie, repository, salon, storehouse, treasury, vault; SEE CONCEPTS *439,449*

mushroom [*v*] *sprout; grow quickly*
augment, blow up, boom, burgeon, burst, detonate, expand, explode, flourish, go off, grow, grow rapidly, increase, luxuriate, proliferate, shoot up, spread, spring up; SEE CONCEPTS *179,704*

mushy [*adj1*] *doughy, soft*
gelatinous, jelled, mashy*, muddy, pap*, pastelike, pulpous, pulpy, quaggy, semiliquid, semisolid, slushy, spongy, squashy*, squishy*; SEE CONCEPTS *604,606*

mushy [*adj2*] *romantic, corny*
bathetic, effusive, emotional, lovey-dovey*, maudlin, mawkish, saccharine, schmaltzy*, sentimental, sloppy*, slushy*, soppy*, sugary, syrupy, tearjerking, weepy, wet; SEE CONCEPTS *267,542*

music [*n*] *sounds that are pleasant, harmonized*
a cappella, acoustic, air, bebop, bop, chamber, classical, folk, fusion, hard rock, harmony, heavy metal, hymn, instrumental, jazz, measure, melody, modern, opera, piece, plainsong, popular, ragtime, rap, refrain, rock, rock and roll, singing, song, soul, strain, swing, tune; SEE CONCEPTS *263, 595*

musical [*adj*] *harmonic, lyrical*
agreeable, blending, chiming, choral, consonant, dulcet, euphonious, harmonious, lilting, mellow, melodic, melodious, operatic, orchestral, pleasing, rhythmic, silvery, songful, sweet, sweet-sounding, symphonic, symphonious, tuned, tuneful, vocal; SEE CONCEPT *594*

musician [*n*] *person who performs music*
artist, artiste, composer, conductor, diva, entertainer, instrumentalist, maestro, performer, player, session man/woman, soloist, virtuoso, vocalist; SEE CONCEPT *352*

muss [*n*] *disorder*
chaos, confusion, disarrangement, hash, mess, mess-up, mix-up, muddle, shambles, turmoil; SEE CONCEPTS *230,674*

muss [*v*] *dishevel, disorder*
clutter, crumple, disarrange, disarray, disorganize, disrupt, disturb, jumble, mess up, mix up, muddle, ruffle, rummage, rumple, tangle, tousle, upset, wrinkle; SEE CONCEPT *158*

must [*n*] *necessity, essential*
charge, commitment, committal, condition, devoir, duty, fundamental, imperative, necessary, need, obligation, ought, precondition, prerequisite, requirement, requisite, right, sine qua non; SEE CONCEPTS *646,709*

must [*v*] *ought, should*
be compelled, be destined, be directed, be doomed*, be driven*, be made, be necessitated, be obliged, be one's fate, be ordered, be required, got to, have, have got to*, have no choice, have to, must needs*, need, pushed to the wall*; SEE CONCEPT *650*

muster [*n*] *gathering*
aggregation, assemblage, assembly, call-up*, collection, company, congeries, convocation, crowd, draft, group, head count*, meeting, mobilization, nose count*, rally, roll, roll call*, roster, roundup*; SEE CONCEPTS *417,432*

muster [*v*] *gather, come together*
assemble, call together, call up, collect, congregate, congress, convene, convoke, enroll, enter, group, join up, marshal, meet, mobilize, organize, raise, rally, rendezvous, round up, sign on, sign up, summon; SEE CONCEPT *109*

musty [*adj1*] *stuffy, aged*
airless, ancient, antediluvian, antique, crumbling, dank, decayed, decrepit, dirty, dried-out*, dry, fetid, filthy, frowzy*, malodorous, mildewed, mildewy, moldy, moth-eaten*, noisome, old, putrid, rotten, smelly, spoiled, squalid, stale, stuffy; SEE CONCEPTS *578,598,603,797*

musty [*adj2*] *worn-out, cliché*
ancient, antiquated, banal, common, commonplace, dull, hackneyed, hoary, obsolete, old-fashioned, old hat*, shopworn*, stale, stereotypical, threadbare, timeworn*, tired, trite, warmed-over*, worn; SEE CONCEPTS *267,530,578,797*

mutation [*n*] *metamorphosis*
alteration, anomaly, change, deviant, deviation, evolution, innovation, modification, mutant, novelty, permutation, transfiguration, transformation, variation, vicissitude; SEE CONCEPTS *665,697*

mute [*adj*] *unable to speak*
aphasiac, aphasic, aphonic, deaf and dumb*, dumb, inarticulate, muffled, mum, quiet, silenced, silent, speechless, tongueless, tongue-tied, unexpressed, unpronounced, unsounded, unspeaking, unspoken, voiceless, wordless; SEE CONCEPT *593*

mute [*v*] *muffle, tone down sound*
benumb, bottle up*, cork up*, dampen, deaden, decrease the volume, drown, gag, hush, keep it down*, lower, moderate, muzzle, pipe down*, put damper on*, put the lid on*, reduce, silence, soften, soft-pedal*, subdue, turn down; SEE CONCEPTS *65,240*

mutilate [*v*] *maim, damage*
adulterate, amputate, batter, bowdlerize, butcher, cripple, crush, cut to pieces, cut up, damage, deface, disable, disfigure, dismember, distort, expurgate, hack*, hash up*, hurt, injure, lacerate, lame, mangle, mar, mess up*, ravage, scratch, spoil, weaken; SEE CONCEPTS *176,246*

mutiny [*n*] *defiance, resistance*
disobedience, insubordination, insurrection, refusal to obey, revolt, revolution, riot, rising, strike, uprising; SEE CONCEPTS *300,388,633*

mutiny [*v*] *defy, revolt*
be insubordinate, disobey, insurrect, kick over, rebel, refuse to obey, resist, rise against, rise up, strike; SEE CONCEPTS *300,384*

mutter [*v*] *grumble, mumble*
complain, croak, groan, grouch*, grouse, growl, grunt, moan, muddle, murmur, rumble, snarl, sputter, swallow, whisper; SEE CONCEPTS *52,77*

mutual [*adj*] *shared, common*
associated, bilateral, collective, communal, conjoint, conjunct, connected, convertible, correlative, dependent, give-and-take*, given and taken*, interactive, interchangeable, interchanged, interdependent, intermutual, joint, partaken, participated, public, reciprocal, reciprocated, related, requited, respective, returned, two-sided*, united; SEE CONCEPTS *563,708*

mutually [*adv*] *together*
all at once, as a group, by agreement, by contract, commonly, conjointly, cooperatively, en masse, in collaboration, in combination, in conjunction, jointly, reciprocally, respectively; SEE CONCEPTS *544,577*

muzzle [*n*] *covering for control*
cage, cover, envelope, gag, guard, sheath, wrap; SEE CONCEPT *172*

muzzle [*v*] *gag, quiet*
bottle up*, censor, check, choke, clamp down on*, cork, crack down on*, curb, dry up*, dummy up*, hush, ice*, muffle, prevent, quieten, repress, re-

strain, restrict, shush, shut down, silence, squash, squelch, stifle, still, stop, suppress, tongue-tie*, trammel; SEE CONCEPTS *121,250*

myopic [*adj*] *able only to see things near at hand*
astigmatic, biased, blind, halfsighted, nearsighted, presbyopic, shortsighted; SEE CONCEPT *619*

myriad [*n*] *a lot*
army, flood, heap, horde, host, loads*, mint, mountain*, multitude, oodles*, scores, slew, stacks*, swarm, thousands*; SEE CONCEPT *786*

myriad [*adj*] *innumerable*
countless, endless, gobs*, heaping, immeasurable, incalculable, infinite, multiple, multitudinous, no end of*, numberless, thousand-and-one*, uncounted, untold, variable; SEE CONCEPTS *762,781*

mysterious [*adj*] *secret, concealed*
abstruse, alchemistic, arcane, astrological, baffling, cabalistic, covert, cryptic, curious, dark, difficult, enigmatic, enigmatical, equivocal, esoteric, furtive, hidden, impenetrable, incomprehensible, inexplicable, inscrutable, insoluble, magical, mystical, mystifying, necromantic, obscure, occult, oracular, perplexing, puzzling, recondite, secretive, sphinxlike, spiritual, strange, subjective, symbolic, transcendental, uncanny, unfathomable, unknowable, unknown, unnatural, veiled, weird; SEE CONCEPTS *529,576*

mystery [*n*] *puzzle, secret*
abstruseness, brainteaser*, braintwister*, charade, chiller, cliffhanger*, closed book*, conundrum, crux, cryptogram, difficulty, enigma, grabber, inscrutability, inscrutableness, mindboggler*, mystification, occult, oracle, perplexity, poser, problem, puzzlement, question, rebus, riddle, rune, secrecy, sixty-four-thousand-dollar question*, sphinx, stickler, stumper, subtlety, teaser, thriller, tough nut to crack*, twister, unfathomableness, whodunit*, why*; SEE CONCEPTS *282,532,696*

mystic/mystical [*adj*] *secret, esoteric*
abstruse, anagogic, arcane, cabalistic, cryptic, enigmatical, esoteric, hidden, imaginary, impenetrable, inscrutable, magic, magical, metaphysical, mysterial, mysterious, necromantic, nonrational, numinous, occult, otherworldly, paranormal, preternatural, quixotic, sorcerous, spiritual, supernatural, telestic, thaumaturgic, transcendental, unaccountable, unknowable, visionary, witchlike, wizardly; SEE CONCEPTS *529,549,582*

mystify [*v*] *bewilder, confuse*
baffle, bamboozle*, beat*, befog*, buffalo*, confound, deceive, elude, escape, floor*, fog in*, hoodwink*, lick*, lie, perplex, puzzle, stump*, throw*, trick; SEE CONCEPT *16*

mystique [*n*] *person's strong impression*
attitude, awe, character, charisma, charm, complex, fascination, glamour, magic, nature, spell, temperament; SEE CONCEPT *411*

myth [*n*] *fictitious story, often ancient*
allegory, apologue, creation, delusion, fable, fabrication, fairy story, fancy, fantasy, fiction, figment, folk ballad, folk tale, illusion, imagination, invention, legend, lore, mythos, parable, saga, superstition, tale, tall story*, tradition; SEE CONCEPT *282*

mythical/mythological [*adj*] *make-believe, fairy-tale*
allegorical, chimerical, created, fabled, fabricated, fabulous, false, fanciful, fantasy, fictitious, fictive, folkloric, imaginary, invented, legendary, made-up, mythic, nonexistent, pretended, storied, supposititious, traditional, unreal, untrue, visionary, whimsical; SEE CONCEPTS *267,582*

mythology [*n*] *folklore*
belief, conviction, folk tales, legend, lore, mythicism, mythos, myths, stories, tradition; SEE CONCEPT *282*

N

nab [*v*] *seize*
apprehend, arrest, capture, catch, clutch, cop*, detain, grab, nail*, pick up*, run in*, snatch*, take*, take into custody; SEE CONCEPTS *90,317*

nag [*v*] *harass, bother*
annoy, badger, bait, berate, bug*, carp at, dog*, eat*, egg*, find fault, fuss, give a hard time*, goad, harry, heckle, hector, henpeck, hound, importune, irk, irritate, needle, nudge*, pester, pick at, plague, prod, provoke, ride, scold, take it out on*, tease, torment, upbraid, urge, vex, work on*, worry; SEE CONCEPTS *7,19,52*

nail [*v1*] *fasten, fix with pointed object*
attach, beat, bind, drive, hammer, hit, hold, join, pin, pound, secure, sock*, spike, strike, tack, whack*; SEE CONCEPTS *85,160,189*

nail [*v2*] *capture, arrest*
apprehend, bag, catch, collar*, detain, get*, hook*, nab, pinch*, prehend, secure, seize, take*; SEE CONCEPTS *90,317*

naive [*adj*] *childlike, trusting*
aboveboard, artless, callow, candid, confiding, countrified, credulous, forthright, frank, fresh, green*, guileless, gullible, harmless, ignorant, impulsive, ingenuous, innocent, innocuous, instinctive, jejune, lamb*, like a babe in the woods*, natural, open, original, patsy*, plain, simple, simple-minded, sincere, spontaneous, square, sucker*, trusting, unaffected, unjaded, unpretentious, unschooled, unsophisticated, unsuspecting, unsuspicious, untaught, unworldly, virgin, wide-eyed*; SEE CONCEPTS *401,542,678*

naiveté [*n*] *innocence, gullibility*
artlessness, callowness, candor, childishness, credulity, frankness, guilelessness, inexperience, ingenuousness, naturalness, openness, simplicity; SEE CONCEPTS *633,657,678*

naked [*adj1*] *without covering*
au naturel, bald, bare, bared, bare-skinned, barren, defenseless, denuded, disrobed, divested, exposed,

helpless, in birthday suit*, in dishabille*, in the altogether*, in the buff*, in the raw*, leafless, natural, nude, open, peeled*, raw, stark-naked*, stripped, threadbare, unclad, unclothed, unconcealed, uncovered, undraped, undressed, unprotected, unveiled, vulnerable, without a stitch*; SEE CONCEPTS *485,589*

naked [*adj2*] *manifest, evident*
artless, blatant, disclosed, discovered, dry, matter-of-fact, obvious, open, overt, palpable, patent, plain, pure, revealed, sheer, simple, stark, unadorned, undisguised, unexaggerated, unmistakable, unqualified, unvarnished; SEE CONCEPTS *267,529*

name [*n1*] *title given to something, someone*
agname, agnomen, alias, appellation, autograph, autonym, brand, cognomen, compellation, denomination, designation, epithet, eponym, flag*, handle*, head, heading, Jane/John Doe*, John Hancock*, John Henry*, label, matronymic, moniker, monogram, nickname, nomen, patronymic, pen name, pet name, place name, prenomen, proper name, pseudonym, rubric, sign, signature, sobriquet, stage name, style, surname, tag, term, trade name; SEE CONCEPTS *268,683*

name [*n2*] *fame, distinction*
character, credit, eminence, esteem, honor, note, praise, renown, rep*, report, reputation, repute; SEE CONCEPTS *388,668*

name [*n3*] *celebrity*
big name*, celeb*, entertainer, headliner, hero, lion*, luminary, notability, notable, personality, somebody*, star, superstar; SEE CONCEPTS *352,366*

name [*v1*] *give a title*
baptize, call, characterize, christen, classify, cognominate, define, denominate, designate, dub, entitle, give a handle*, identify, label, nickname, nomenclature, put tag on, style, tag, term, ticket, title; SEE CONCEPT *62*

name [*v2*] *choose, designate*
announce, appoint, cite, classify, commission, connote, declare, delegate, denote, elect, identify, index, instance, list, make, mark, mention, nominate, peg*, pin down*, point to, put down for, put finger on*, recognize, refer to, remark, select, signify, single out, slot, specify, suggest, tab, tag, tap; SEE CONCEPTS *41,50,88*

nameless [*adj*] *unknown, anonymous*
incognito, inconspicuous, innominate, Jane/John Doe*, obscure, pseudonymous, unacknowledged, uncelebrated, undesignated, undistinguished, unfamed, unheard-of, unnamed, unnoted, unsung, untitled, whatchamacallit*, X*; SEE CONCEPTS *267,576*

namely [*adv*] *that is to say*
by way of explanation, especially, expressly, id est*, i.e., in other words, in plain English*, particularly, scilicet, specially, specifically, strictly speaking, that is, to wit, videlicet, viz.; SEE CONCEPT *557*

nap [*n1*] *short, light sleep*
break, catnap, doze, few z's*, forty winks*, interlude, intermission, microsleep*, nod, pause, respite, rest, shuteye*, siesta, snooze*, spot; SEE CONCEPT *315*

nap [*n2*] *grain of material*
down, feel, fiber, grit, outside, pile, roughness, shag, smoothness, surface, tooth, wale, warp, weave, weft, woof; SEE CONCEPTS *473,611*

nap [*v*] *take a short, light sleep*
catch forty winks*, catnap, doze, drop off*, drowse, get some shut-eye*, grab some z's*, nod, nod off, rack*, relax, rest, sleep, snooze, take a siesta*, take a snooze*; SEE CONCEPTS *210,315*

narcissistic [*adj*] *concerned only with oneself*
conceited, egotistic, egotistical, self-centered, self-involved, self-loving, stuck-up, vain, vainglorious; SEE CONCEPTS *401,404*

narcotic [*n*] *powerful drug inducing anesthesia or sleep*
analgesic, anesthetic, anodyne, dope*, downer*, fix*, hard drug, hard stuff*, heroin, hypnotic, junk*, laudanum, lenitive, merchandise*, nepenthe, opiate, opium, painkiller, sedative, somnifacient, soporific, stuff*, stupefacient, tranquilizer; SEE CONCEPT *307*

narcotic [*adj*] *dulling, painkilling*
analgesic, anesthetic, calming, deadening, dulling, hypnotic, numbing, opiate, sedative, somnifacient, somnific, somnolent, somnorific, soporiferous, soporific, stupefacient, stupefactive, stupefying; SEE CONCEPT *537*

narrate [*v*] *describe, detail*
characterize, chronicle, delineate, depict, descant, disclose, discourse, enumerate, expatiate, give an account of, hold forth, make known, paint, picture, portray, proclaim, recite, recount, rehearse, relate, repeat, report, reveal, set forth, spin, state, tell, tell a story, unfold; SEE CONCEPTS *55,72*

narration [*n*] *description, reading*
account, anecdote, explanation, narrative, recital, recountal, recounting, rehearsal, relation, report, story, storytelling, tale, telling, voice-over*, yarn*; SEE CONCEPTS *55,72,282*

narrative [*n*] *story, tale*
account, anecdote, book, chronicle, chronology, description, detail, fiction, history, line, long and short of it*, narration, old wives' tale*, plot, potboiler*, recount, report, statement, version, yarn*; SEE CONCEPTS *271,282*

narrative [*adj*] *storylike, chronological*
anecdotal, fictional, fictive, historical, narrated, recounted, reported, retold, sequential; SEE CONCEPT *267*

narrow [*adj1*] *confined, restricted*
attenuated, circumscribed, close, compressed, confining, constricted, contracted, cramped, definite, determinate, exclusive, exiguous, fine, fixed, incapacious, limited, linear, meager, near, paltry, pent, pinched, precarious, precise, scant, scanty, select, set, shrunken, slender, slim, small, spare, strait,

taper, tapered, tapering, thin, threadlike, tight; SEE CONCEPTS *554,773*

narrow [*adj2*] *intolerant, small-minded*
biased, bigoted, conservative, conventional, dogmatic, hidebound, illiberal, inexorable, inflexible, narrow-minded, obdurate, parochial, partial, prejudiced, reactionary, stupid; SEE CONCEPTS *403,542*

narrow [*adj3*] *cheap, stingy*
avaricious, close, mean, mercenary, niggardly*, scrimpy*, tight*, ungenerous; SEE CONCEPT *334*

narrow [*v*] *reduce, simplify*
circumscribe, constrict, contract, diminish, limit, taper, tighten; SEE CONCEPTS *130,236,247*

narrowly [*adv*] *just, closely*
almost, barely, by a hair*, by a whisker*, by narrow margin, carefully, close, nearly, only just, painstakingly, scarcely, scrutinizingly; SEE CONCEPTS *544,799*

narrow-minded [*adj*] *biased, intolerant*
bigoted, conservative, conventional, hidebound, illiberal, insular, narrow, opinionated, parochial, petty, prejudiced, provincial, reactionary, short-sighted, small-minded, strait-laced, unenlarged; SEE CONCEPTS *403,542*

nasty [*adj1*] *disgusting, offensive*
awful, beastly, bum*, dirty, disagreeable, fierce, filthy, foul, gross, grubby, hellish, horrible, horrid, icky*, impure, loathsome, lousy, malodorous, mephitic, murderous*, nauseating, noisome, noxious, objectionable, obnoxious, obscene, odious, ornery, outrageous, poison, polluted, raunchy*, repellent, repugnant, repulsive, revolting, rough, sickening, soiled, squalid, stinking, tough, unappetizing, unclean, uncleanly, ungodly, unholy, unpleasant, vile, vulgar, yucky*; SEE CONCEPTS *485,548,571*

nasty [*adj2*] *indecent, smutty*
blue*, coarse, dirty, filthy, foul, gross, immodest, immoral, improper, impure, indecorous, indelicate, lascivious, lewd, licentious, obscene, pornographic, raunchy*, ribald, scatological, shameful, unseemly, vulgar, wicked, X-rated*; SEE CONCEPTS *372,545*

nasty [*adj3*] *bad-tempered, mean*
abusive, annoying, beastly, critical, cruel, despicable, disagreeable, distasteful, evil, fierce, hateful, malevolent, malicious, malign, malignant, ornery, ruthless, sarcastic, sordid, spiteful, squalid, unkind, unpleasant, vicious, vile, wicked; SEE CONCEPT *401*

nasty [*adj4*] *injurious, dangerous*
bad, critical, damaging, harmful, noxious, painful, poisonous, serious, severe, ugly; SEE CONCEPT *537*

nation [*n*] *country with its own government*
body politic, commonwealth, community, democracy, domain, dominion, empire, fatherland, kingdom, land, monarchy, motherland, people, populace, population, principality, public, race, realm, republic, society, sovereignty, state, tribe, union; SEE CONCEPT *510*

national [*adj*] *concerning a country with a government*
civic, civil, communal, countrywide, domestic, ethnic, federal, general, governmental, home, imperial, inland, internal, interstate, nationwide, native, politic, political, public, royal, social, societal, sovereign, state, sweeping, vernacular, widespread; SEE CONCEPT *536*

nationality [*n*] *place of birth*
allegiance, birth, body politic, citizenship, community, country, ethnic group, nation, native land, origin, political home, race, society; SEE CONCEPTS *380,510*

native [*n*] *person born in the country in which he/she dwells*
aboriginal, aborigine, ancient, autochthon, citizen, countryman/woman, dweller, home towner, indigene, inhabitant, landsman/woman, local, national; SEE CONCEPT *413*

native [*adj1*] *innate, inherent*
built-in, congenital, connate, connatural, constitutional, endemic, essential, fundamental, genuine, hereditary, implanted, inborn, inbred, indigenous, ingrained, inherited, instinctive, intrinsic, inveterate, inwrought, natal, natural, original, real, unacquired, wild; SEE CONCEPTS *404,549*

native [*adj2*] *domestic, home*
aboriginal, autochthonous, belonging, endemic, from, homegrown, homemade, indigenous, inland, internal, local, mother, municipal, national, original, primary, primeval, primitive, regional, related, vernacular; SEE CONCEPT *536*

natural [*adj1*] *normal, everyday*
accustomed, anticipated, characteristic, common, commonplace, congenital, connatural, consistent, constant, counted on, customary, essential, familiar, general, habitual, inborn, indigenous, ingenerate, inherent, innate, instinctive, intuitive, involuntary, legitimate, logical, looked for, matter-of-course, natal, native, ordinary, prevailing, prevalent, probable, reasonable, regular, relied on, spontaneous, typic, typical, unacquired, uncontrolled, uniform, universal, usual; SEE CONCEPTS *530,547*

natural [*adj2*] *open, unaffected*
artless, being oneself, candid, childlike, credulous, direct, easy, folksy, forthright, frank, genuine, homey*, ignorant, impulsive, inartificial, ingenuous, innocent, instinctive, laid-back*, naive, plain, primitive, provincial, real, rustic, simple, simplehearted, sincere, spontaneous, straightforward, trusting, unassumed, uncontrived, undesigning, unembarrassed, unfeigned, unforced, unlabored, unpolished, unpretentious, unschooled, unsophisticated, unstudied, unworldly, up-front*; SEE CONCEPTS *267,401,404*

natural [*adj3*] *organic, unrefined*
agrarian, agrestal, crude, native, plain, pure, raw, unbleached, uncultivated, undomesticated, unmixed,

unpolished, unprocessed, whole, wild; SEE CONCEPTS *462,485*

naturally [*adv*] *as anticipated*
artlessly, but of course*, by birth, by nature, candidly, casually, characteristically, commonly, consistently, customarily, easily, freely, generally, genuinely, habitually, impulsively, informally, innocently, instinctively, normally, openly, ordinarily, readily, simply, spontaneously, typically, unaffectedly, uniformly, unpretentiously, usually; SEE CONCEPT *544*

nature [*n1*] *character, disposition*
attributes, being, bottom line*, complexion, constitution, description, drift, essence, essentiality, features, heart*, humor, individualism, individuality, like, makeup, meat*, mood, name of game*, name of tune*, nature of beast*, outlook, personality, point, quality, score, stuff, temper, temperament, texture, traits, type; SEE CONCEPTS *411,682*

nature [*n2*] *type, kind*
anatomy, brand, cast, category, character, color, conformation, description, figure, framework, ilk, shape, sort, species, stripe*, structure, style, variety, way; SEE CONCEPT *378*

nature [*n3*] *earth, creation*
birds and bees*, cosmos, country, countryside, environment, forest, generation, landscape, macrocosm, megacosm, natural history, outdoors, scenery, seascape, setting, universe, view, world; SEE CONCEPTS *407,429,509,511*

naughty [*adj1*] *bad, misbehaved*
annoying, badly behaved*, contrary, disobedient, disorderly, evil, exasperating, fiendish, fractious, froward, headstrong, impish, indecorous, insubordinate, intractable, mischievous, obstreperous, perverse, playful, rascally, raunchy, recalcitrant, refractory, roguish, rough, rowdy, sinful, teasing, tough, ungovernable, unmanageable, unruly, wanton, wayward, wicked, willful, worthless, wrong; SEE CONCEPT *401*

naughty [*adj2*] *obscene, vulgar*
adult, bawdy, blue*, dirty*, hot*, improper, lascivious, lewd, loose*, off-color*, pornographic, purple*, ribald, risqué, steamy*; SEE CONCEPTS *372,545*

nausea [*n*] *sickness in stomach; revulsion*
abhorrence, aversion, biliousness, disgust, hatred, loathing, offense, qualm, qualms, queasiness, regurgitation, rejection, repugnance, retching, squeamishness, vomiting; SEE CONCEPTS *316,410*

nauseate [*v*] *make sick; disgust*
bother, disturb, horrify, offend, reluct, repel, repulse, revolt, sicken; SEE CONCEPTS *14,308*

nauseous [*adj*] *disgusting*
abhorrent, brackish, detestable, distasteful, ill, loathsome, nauseated, nauseating, offensive, queasy, repugnant, repulsive, revolting, rocky*, seasick, sick, sick as dog*, sickening, squeamish; SEE CONCEPTS *314,529*

nautical/naval [*adj*] *concerning ships, sea*
abyssal, aquatic, boating, cruising, deep-sea, marine, maritime, navigating, navigational, oceangoing, oceanic, oceanographic, pelagic, rowing, sailing, sailorly, salty, seafaring, seagoing, sea-loving, thalassic, yachting; SEE CONCEPT *536*

navigate [*v*] *guide along route, often over water*
captain*, cross, cruise, direct, drive, handle, head out for*, helm, journey, lay the course*, maneuver, operate, pilot, plan, plot, ride out, sail, skipper*, steer, voyage; SEE CONCEPTS *148,187,224*

navigation [*n*] *traveling, guiding along route, often over water*
aeronautics, boating, cruising, exploration, flying, helmsmanship, nautics, navigating, ocean travel, pilotage, piloting, plotting a course, sailing, seafaring, seamanship, shipping, steerage, steering, voyage, voyaging, yachting; SEE CONCEPTS *155,187,224*

near [*adj1*] *close by physically*
abreast, abutting, adjacent, adjoining, alongside, along toward, approximal, around, at close quarters, available, beside, bordering, burning, close, close-at-hand, close-by, close shave*, conterminous, contiguous, convenient, hair's breadth*, handy, immediate, in close proximity*, near-at-hand*, nearby, neighboring, next door*, nigh*, not remote, practically, proximal, proximate, ready, side-by-side, touching, vincinal, warm*, within stone's throw*; SEE CONCEPTS *586,778*

near [*adj2*] *close in time; forthcoming*
approaching, approximate, at hand, coming, comparative, expected, imminent, impending, in the offing*, looming, near-at-hand*, next, relative; SEE CONCEPTS *812,820*

near [*adj3*] *familiar*
affecting, akin, allied, attached, close, connected, dear, friendly, intimate, related, touching; SEE CONCEPT *555*

nearby [*adj*] *adjoining*
adjacent, close, close-at-hand, close-by, contiguous, convenient, handy, immediate, neighboring, proximate, ready; SEE CONCEPTS *586,778*

nearby [*adv*] *within reach*
about, at close quarters, close, close at hand, hard, near, near-at-hand*, nigh*, not far away; SEE CONCEPTS *586,778*

nearing [*adj*] *approaching*
advancing, approximating, coming, forthcoming, imminent, impending, oncoming, threatening, upcoming; SEE CONCEPTS *548,820*

nearly [*adv*] *almost*
about, all but*, approaching, approximately, as good as*, circa*, close but no cigar*, closely, give or take a little*, in effect, in essence, in substance, in the ballpark*, in the neighborhood*, just about, more or less, most, much, nearabout, not quite, practically, pretty near, roughly, round, roundly, some, some-

where, upwards of*, virtually, well-nigh*, within a little*; SEE CONCEPT **566**

neat [*adj1*] *arranged well, uncluttered*
accurate, apple-pie order*, chic*, correct, dainty, dapper, elegant, exact, fastidious, finical, finicky, immaculate, in good order, in good shape, methodical, natty, neat as a pin*, nice, orderly, precise, prim, proper, regular, shipshape*, sleek, slick, smart, spick-and-span*, spotless, spruce, systematic, tidy, trim, well-groomed, well-kept; SEE CONCEPTS **485,589,621**

neat [*adj2*] *clever, practiced*
able, adept, adroit, agile, apt, artful, deft, dexterous, efficient, effortless, elegant, expert, finished, graceful, handy, nimble, precise, proficient, quick, ready, skillful, speedy, stylish, well-judged; SEE CONCEPTS **527,542**

nebulous [*adj*] *confused, obscure*
ambiguous, amorphous, cloudy, dark, dim, hazy, imprecise, indefinite, indeterminate, indistinct, misty, murky, shadowy, shapeless, uncertain, unclear, unformed, vague; SEE CONCEPTS **535,617**

necessarily [*adv*] *inevitably, certainly*
accordingly, as a matter of course*, automatically, axiomatically, beyond one's control*, by definition, by its own nature*, cardinally, come what may*, compulsorily, consequently, exigently, from within*, fundamentally, incontrovertibly, indubitably, ineluctably, inescapably, inexorably, irresistibly, naturally, no doubt, of course, of necessity, perforce, positively, pressingly, significantly, undoubtedly, unpreventably, unquestionably, vitally, willy-nilly*, without fail*; SEE CONCEPTS **535,544**

necessary [*adj1*] *essential*
all-important, basic, binding, bottom-line*, cardinal, chief, compelling, compulsory, crucial, decisive, de rigueur*, elementary, exigent, expedient, fundamental, imperative, incumbent on, indispensable, mandatory, momentous, name of game*, needed, needful, obligatory, paramount, prerequisite, pressing, prime, principal, quintessential, required, requisite, significant, specified, unavoidable, urgent, vital, wanted; SEE CONCEPTS **546,568**

necessary [*adj2*] *inevitable*
assured, certain, fated, imminent, ineluctable, ineludible, inerrant, inescapable, inevasible, inexorable, infallible, returnless, unavoidable, undeniable, unescapable; SEE CONCEPTS **535,548**

necessitate [*v*] *call for, make necessary*
ask, behoove, cause, coerce, command, compel, constrain, crave, demand, drive, entail, force, impel, make, oblige, postulate, require, take; SEE CONCEPTS **53,242,646**

necessity [*n*] *need, essentiality*
call, cause, claim, compulsion, demand, desideratum, duress, essence, essential, exaction, exigency, fundamental, godsend*, imperative, indispensability, inevitability, inexorableness, life or death*,

must, necessary, needfulness, no alternative, no choice, obligation, pinch, precondition, prerequisite, privation, requirement, requisite, sine qua non, stress, undeniability, urgency, vital part, vitals, want; SEE CONCEPTS **646,709**

need [*n1*] *want, requirement*
charge, commitment, committal, compulsion, demand, desideratum, devoir, duty, essential, exigency, extremity, longing, must, obligation, occasion, ought, requisite, right, the urge, urgency, use, weakness, wish; SEE CONCEPTS **20,709**

need [*n2*] *poverty*
deprivation, destitution, distress, extremity, impecuniousness, impoverishment, inadequacy, indigence, insufficiency, lack, neediness, paucity, pennilessness, penury, poorness, privation, shortage, want; SEE CONCEPTS **335,709**

need [*n3*] *emergency; pressing lack*
deficiency, exigency, inadequacy, insufficiency, necessity, obligation, shortage, urgency, want; SEE CONCEPTS **646,709**

need [*v*] *want something*
be deficient, be deprived, be down and out*, be hard up*, be inadequate, be in need of, be in want, be needy, be poor, be short, be without, call for, claim, covet, crave, demand, desire, die for*, do without, drive for*, exact, feel a dearth of*, feel the necessity for, feel the pinch*, go hungry*, hanker, have occasion for, have occasion to, have use for*, hunger, hurt for, lack, long, lust, miss, necessitate, pine, require, suffer privation, thirst, wish, yearn, yen for; SEE CONCEPTS **20,646**

needle [*v*] *tease, annoy*
aggravate, badger, bait, bedevil, bother, examine, gnaw, goad, harass, hector, irk, irritate, nag, nettle, pester, plague, prick, prod, provoke, question, quiz, ride*, rile, ruffle, spur, sting, taunt, tweak*, worry; SEE CONCEPTS **7,19,54**

needless [*adj*] *unnecessary, groundless*
causeless, dispensable, excessive, expendable, gratuitous, inessential, nonessential, pointless, redundant, superfluous, uncalled-for, undesired, unrequired, unwanted, useless; SEE CONCEPTS **546,575**

needy [*adj*] *deprived, impoverished*
beggared, dead broke*, destitute, dirt poor*, disadvantaged, down-and-out*, down at heel*, down to last cent*, flat*, impecunious, indigent, necessitous, penniless, penurious, poor, poverty-stricken, underprivileged, unprosperous; SEE CONCEPT **334**

nefarious [*adj*] *bad, sinful*
abominable, atrocious, base, corrupt, criminal, degenerate, depraved, detestable, dreadful, evil, execrable, flagitious, flagrant, foul, glaring, gross, heinous, horrible, infamous, infernal, iniquitous, miscreant, monstrous, odious, opprobrious, outrageous, perverse, putrid, rank, rotten, shameful, treacherous, vicious, vile, villainous, wicked; SEE CONCEPTS **401,545,548**

negate [v] *contradict, countermand*
abate, abolish, abrogate, annihilate, annul, belie, blackball*, break with*, cancel, cancel out, controvert, countercheck, cross*, deny, ding*, disaffirm, disallow, disprove, dump*, fly in the face of*, frustrate, gainsay, impugn, invalidate, kill, negative, neutralize, nullify, oppose, put down, quash*, rebut, redress, refute, repeal, rescind, retract, reverse, revoke, stonewall*, traverse, turn down, turn thumbs down*, undo, vitiate, void; SEE CONCEPTS *46,50, 88,121*

negation [n] *contradiction, denial*
antithesis, antonym, blank, cancellation, contrary, converse, counterpart, disavowal, disclaimer, forget it*, gainsaying, inverse, like hell*, negatory, neutralization, no, nonexistence, nothingness, nullification, nullity, opposite, opposition, proscription, refusal, rejection, renunciation, repudiation, reverse, vacuity, veto, void; SEE CONCEPTS *121,278,685*

negative [n] *contradiction*
denial, disavowal, nay, refusal, refutation; SEE CONCEPT *278*

negative [adj] *bad, contradictory*
abrogating, adverse, against, annulling, antagonistic, anti, balky, colorless, con, contrary, contravening, counteractive, cynical, denying, detrimental, disallowing, disavowing, dissentient, dissenting, gainsaying, gloomy, impugning, invalidating, jaundiced, naysaying, neutralizing, nugatory, nullifying, opposing, pessimistic, privative, recusant, refusing, rejecting, removed, repugnant, resisting, resistive, unaffirmative, unenthusiastic, unfavorable, uninterested, unwilling, weak; SEE CONCEPTS *267,403,570*

neglect [n1] *disregard*
carelessness, coolness, delinquency, disdain, disregardance, disrespect, heedlessness, inadvertence, inattention, inconsideration, indifference, laxity, laxness, oversight, scorn, slight, thoughtlessness, unconcern; SEE CONCEPTS *410,657*

neglect [n2] *failure, default*
carelessness, chaos, delay, delinquency, dereliction, dilapidation, forgetfulness, lapse, laxity, laxness, limbo, neglectfulness, negligence, omission, oversight, pretermission, remissness, slackness, slovenliness; SEE CONCEPTS *674,699*

neglect [v1] *be indifferent, leave alone*
affront, brush aside, brush off, contemn, depreciate, despise, detest, discount, disdain, dismiss, disregard, have nothing to do with*, ignore, keep at arm's length*, keep one's distance*, laugh off*, let go*, live with*, make light of*, not care for*, overlook, pass by, pass over, pass up, pay no attention to, pay no mind*, pretermit, rebuff, reject, scant, scorn, shrug off*, slight, slur, spurn, tune out*, underestimate; SEE CONCEPTS *30,681*

neglect [v2] *fail to do; forget*
be careless, be derelict, be irresponsible, be negligent, be remiss, bypass, defer, discard, dismiss, dis-

regard, elide, evade, gloss over*, let pass*, let slide*, look the other way*, lose sight of*, miss, not trouble oneself*, omit, overleap, overlook, overpass, pass over, postpone, procrastinate, shirk, skimp, skip, suspend, think little of*, trifle; SEE CONCEPTS *101,699*

neglectful [adj] *careless, failing*
behindhand, delinquent, derelict, disregardful, heedless, inattentive, indifferent, lax, lazy, negligent, regardless, remiss, slack, thoughtless, uncaring, unmindful; SEE CONCEPTS *401,542*

negligent [adj] *careless, indifferent*
asleep at switch*, behindhand, cursory, delinquent, derelict, discinct, disregardful, forgetful, heedless, inadvertent, inattentive, inconsiderate, incurious, lax, neglectful, nonchalant, offhand, regardless, remiss, slack, slapdash*, slipshod*, sloppy*, slovenly, thoughtless, unconcerned, unheedful, unmindful, unthinking; SEE CONCEPTS *401,542*

negligible [adj] *insignificant*
imperceptible, inconsequential, minor, minute, off*, outside, petty, remote, slender, slight, slim, small, trifling, trivial, unimportant; SEE CONCEPTS *552,575,789*

negotiate [v1] *bargain, discuss*
accommodate, adjudicate, adjust, agree, arbitrate, arrange, bring to terms*, bury the hatchet*, come across with*, compose, concert, conciliate, confer, connect, consult, contract, covenant, cut a deal*, deal, debate, dicker*, haggle, hammer out a deal*, handle, horse trade*, intercede, make a deal, make peace*, make terms*, manage, mediate, moderate, network, parley*, referee, settle, step in*, stipulate, swap, transact, treat, umpire*, work out*, work out a deal; SEE CONCEPTS *8,56,68*

negotiate [v2] *traverse, cross*
clear, get around, get over, get past, hurdle, leap over, overleap, pass, pass through, surmount, vault; SEE CONCEPTS *149,224*

negotiation [n] *bargaining*
agreement, arbitration, colloquy, compromise, conference, consultation, debate, diplomacy, discussion, intervention, mediation, meeting, transaction; SEE CONCEPTS *56,68,684*

negotiator [n] *person who bargains, controls discussion*
adjudicator, ambassador, arbitrator, broker, delegate, diplomat, fixer*, go-between*, interagent, intermediary, intermedium, judge, mediator, middleman/woman, middleperson, moderator; SEE CONCEPTS *348,354,423*

neighbor [n] *person who lives close by*
acquaintance, bystander, friend, homebody*, nearby resident, next-door neighbor; SEE CONCEPT *423*

neighbor [v] *be next to*
abut, adjoin, be adjacent, be contiguous, be near, be nearby, border, butt against, communicate, connect,

join, line, march, surround, touch, verge; SEE CONCEPT *759*

neighborhood [*n*] *community, surroundings*
adjacency, area, block, closeness, confines, contiguity, district, environs, ghetto, jungle*, locale, locality, nearness, neck of the woods*, parish, part, precinct, propinquity, proximity, purlieus, quarter, region, section, slum, stomping ground*, street, suburb, territory, tract, turf, vicinage, vicinity, ward, zone, ZOO*; SEE CONCEPTS *198,379,516*

neighborly [*adj*] *friendly*
amiable, civil, companionable, considerate, cooperative, cordial, genial, gracious, gregarious, harmonious, helpful, hospitable, kind, obliging, sociable, social, well-disposed; SEE CONCEPT *401*

neologism [*n*] *new word*
buzz word*, coinage, neology, new phrase, slang, synthetic word*, vogue word*; SEE CONCEPT *275*

nerve [*n*] *daring, boldness*
assumption, assurance, audacity, backbone, brass*, bravery, brazenness, cheek*, chutzpah*, confidence, coolness, courage, crust*, determination, effrontery, endurance, energy, face*, fearlessness, firmness, force, fortitude, gall*, gameness, grit*, guts*, hardihood, hardiness, heart*, impertinence, impudence, insolence, intestinal fortitude, intrepidity, mettle, might, moxie*, pluck*, presumption, resolution, sauce*, spirit, spunk*, starch, steadfastness, stomach*, temerity, vigor, will; SEE CONCEPT *411*

nerve [*v*] *strengthen, hearten*
animate, brace, cheer, embolden, encourage, enhearten, fortify, inspirit, invigorate, steel; SEE CONCEPTS *7,14,22*

nerveless [*adj1*] *calm, cool*
collected, composed, controlled, impassive, imperturbable, intrepid, patient, self-possessed, tranquil, unemotional; SEE CONCEPT *542*

nerveless [*adj2*] *scared to death*
afraid, cowardly, debilitated, enervated, fearful, feeble, nervous, petrified, spineless*, timid, weak, yellow-bellied*; SEE CONCEPTS *401,403*

nerves [*n*] *extreme anxiety*
fretfulness, hysteria, imbalance, irritation, nervousness, neurasthenia, sleeplessness, strain, stress, tenseness, tension; SEE CONCEPT *410*

nervous [*adj*] *anxious, fearful*
afraid, agitated, annoyed, apprehensive, basket case*, bothered, concerned, distressed, disturbed, edgy, excitable, fidgety, fitful, flustered, fussy*, hesitant, high-strung*, hysterical, irritable, jittery*, jumpy*, nervy*, neurotic, on edge*, overwrought, querulous, restive, ruffled, sensitive, shaky*, shrinking, shy, skittish, snappish, solicitous, spooked*, taut, tense, timid, timorous, troubled, twitchy*, uneasy, unrestful, unstrung*, upset, uptight, volatile, weak, wired*, worried; SEE CONCEPTS *403,542*

nervousness [*n*] *anxious state*
agitation, all-overs*, anger, animation, butterflies*, cold sweat*, creeps*, delirium, discomfiture, dis-

quiet, disquietude, dithers*, excitability, feverishness, fidgets*, flap*, fluster*, fuss*, impatience, jitters*, jumps*, moodiness, neurasthenia, neuroticism, perturbation, quivers, sensitivity, shakes, stage fright, stimulation, stress, tension, timidity, tizzy*, to-do*, touchiness, trembles*, tremulousness, turbulence, uneasiness, willies*, worry; SEE CONCEPTS *410,657*

nervy [*adj*] *bold, pushy*
cheeky*, crass, crude, forward, fresh*, impudent, inconsiderate, pert, plucky*, rude, sassy*, smart, smart-alecky*, wise; SEE CONCEPT *401*

nestle [*v*] *curl up*
bundle, burrow, cuddle, huddle, lie against, lie close, make snug*, move close, nuzzle, settle down, snug*, snuggle, take shelter; SEE CONCEPTS *154,612*

net [*n*] *mesh, web*
cloth, fabric, lace, lacework, lattice, netting, network, openwork, reticulum, screen, tracery; SEE CONCEPTS *473,770*

net [*adj*] *profiting*
after deductions, after taxes, clear, excluding, exclusive, final, irreducible, pure, remaining, take-home, undeductible; SEE CONCEPT *334*

net [*v1*] *capture*
bag*, catch, enmesh, ensnare, entangle, hook*, lasso*, nab*, trap; SEE CONCEPT *90*

net [*v2*] *gain after expenses*
accumulate, bring in, clean up, clear, earn, make, profit, realize, reap; SEE CONCEPT *330*

nettle [*v*] *provoke, upset*
annoy, chafe, disgust, disturb, exasperate, fret, get*, goad, harass, huff, incense, insult, irritate, miff, peeve*, pester, pet, pique, put out*, rile, roil, ruffle, snit*, stew, sting*, tease, tiff, vex; SEE CONCEPTS *7,14,19*

network [*n*] *system of connections*
arrangement, artery, chain, checkerboard*, circuitry, complex, convolution, crisscross*, fabric, fiber, grid, grill*, grillwork, hookup, interconnections, jungle, labyrinth, maze, mesh, net, netting, nexus, organization, patchwork*, plexus, reticulation, reticule, screening, structure, system, tessellation, tracks, waffle, weave, web, wiring; SEE CONCEPTS *381,388,770*

neurosis [*n*] *mental disturbance, disorder*
aberration, abnormality, affliction, breakdown, compulsion, crack-up*, derangement, deviation, hysteria, inhibition, insanity, instability, madness, maladjustment, mental illness, neurasthenia, obsession, personality disorder, phobia, psychological disorder, psychopathy; SEE CONCEPTS *316,410*

neurotic [*adj*] *mentally maladjusted*
aberrant, abnormal, anxious, basket case*, bundle of nerves*, choked*, clutched, compulsive, deviant, disordered, disoriented, distraught, disturbed, erratic, hung up*, hysteric, inhibited, manic, nervous, nervous wreck*, obsessive, overwrought, psycho-

neurotic, unhealthy, unstable, upset, uptight, wired*; SEE CONCEPTS *314,403*

neuter [*v*] *remove sex organs*
alter, castrate, change, desexualize, doctor, dress, emasculate, fix, geld, make barren, make impotent, make infertile, make sexless, mutilate, spay, sterilize, unsex; SEE CONCEPTS *157,250*

neutral [*adj1*] *impartial, noncommittal*
aloof, bystanding, calm, clinical, collected, cool, detached, disengaged, disinterested, dispassionate, easy, evenhanded, fair-minded, impersonal, inactive, indifferent, inert, middle-of-road*, nonaligned, nonbelligerent, nonchalant, noncombatant, noncommittal, nonparticipating, nonpartisan, on sidelines*, on the fence*, pacifistic, poker-faced*, relaxed, unaligned, unbiased, uncommitted, unconcerned, undecided, uninvolved, unprejudiced; SEE CONCEPTS *403,542*

neutral [*adj2*] *flat, dull to senses*
abstract, achromatic, colorless, drab, expressionless, indeterminate, indistinct, indistinguishable, intermediate, toneless, undefined, vague, vanilla; SEE CONCEPTS *485,537,618*

neutralize [*v*] *counteract*
abrogate, annul, balance, cancel, compensate for, conquer, counterbalance, countercheck, counterpoise, countervail, defeat, frustrate, invalidate, negate, negative, nullify, offset, overcome, override, overrule, redress, subdue, undo; SEE CONCEPTS *121,232*

never [*adv*] *not at any time*
at no time, don't hold your breath*, forget it, nevermore, not at all, not ever, not in any way, not in the least, not on your life*, not under any condition, no way*; SEE CONCEPT *799*

never-ending [*adj*] *continual, unceasing*
amaranthine, boundless, ceaseless, constant, continuous, endless, eternal, everlasting, immortal, incessant, interminable, nonstop, perpetual, persistent, relentless, timeless, unbroken, unchanging, uninterrupted, unremitting; SEE CONCEPTS *482,798*

nevertheless [*adv*] *however*
after all, although, but, even so, even though, howbeit, nonetheless, not the less, notwithstanding, regardless, still, still and all, though, withal, yet; SEE CONCEPT *544*

new [*adj1*] *recent, fresh*
advanced, au courant, brand-new, contemporary, current, cutting-edge*, dewy, different, dissimilar, distinct, fashionable, inexperienced, just out*, late, latest, modern, modernistic, modish*, neoteric, newfangled*, novel, now*, original, recent, spick-and-span*, state-of-the-art*, strange, topical, ultramodern, unaccustomed, uncontaminated, unfamiliar, unique, unknown, unlike, unseasoned, unskilled, unspoiled, untouched, untrained, untried, untrodden, unused, unusual, up-to-date, virgin, youthful; SEE CONCEPTS *564,578,797*

new [*adj2*] *additional*
added, another, else, extra, farther, fresh, further, increased, more, other, supplementary; SEE CONCEPTS *771,824*

new [*adj3*] *modernized, restored*
altered, changed, improved, redesigned, refreshed, regenerated, renewed, revived; SEE CONCEPT *589*

new [*adv*] *recently*
afresh, anew, freshly, lately, newly, of late; SEE CONCEPT *820*

newcomer [*n*] *person who has just arrived in area*
alien, arrival, beginner, blow-in*, colt*, foreigner, freshman/woman, greenhorn*, immigrant, incomer, Johnny-come-lately*, late arrival, latecomer, maverick, neophyte, new kid on the block*, novice, novitiate, outsider, rookie, settler, stranger, tenderfoot*; SEE CONCEPTS *413,423*

newfangled [*adj*] *quite recent*
contemporary, fashionable, fresh, gimmicky*, in vogue, modern, modernistic, neoteric, new, new-fashioned, novel, popular, unique; SEE CONCEPTS *578,589,797*

newly [*adv*] *very recently*
anew, freshly, just, lately, latterly, of late; SEE CONCEPT *820*

news [*n*] *information, revelation*
account, advice, announcement, broadcast, bulletin, cable, cognizance, communication, communiqué, copy, data, description, disclosure, discovery, dispatch, enlightenment, exposé, eye-opener*, front-page news*, headlines, hearsay, intelligence, itemization, knowledge, leak, lowdown, message, narration, news flash, particularization, recital, recognition, release, report, rumor, scandal, scoop*, specification, statement, story, telecast, telegram, telling, the goods*, tidings*, word*; SEE CONCEPTS *268,274,293*

newspaper [*n*] *regular, continuous publication containing information*
biweekly, bulldog*, community, daily, extra, gazette, journal, magazine, metropolitan, organ, paper, periodical, press, rag*, record, review, scandal sheet*, sheet, tabloid, trade, weekly; SEE CONCEPTS *279,280*

next [*adj*] *coming immediately after in space, time, order*
abutting, adjacent, adjoining, after, alongside, attached, back-to-back, beside, close, closest, coming, consequent, conterminous, ensuing, following, hard by*, later, meeting, nearest, neighboring, on the side, proximate, side-by-side, subsequent, succeeding, touching; SEE CONCEPTS *585,586,799*

next [*adv*] *immediately after in time, space, order*
after, afterward, afterwhile, behind, by and by, closely, coming up, following, later, latterly, next off, subsequently, thereafter; SEE CONCEPTS *585,586,799*

nibble [n] *morsel, bite*
crumb, peck, snack, soupçon, taste, tidbit; SEE CON-
CEPTS *458,831*

nibble [v] *bite, pick at*
crop, eat, eat like a bird*, gnaw, munch, nip*, nosh
on*, peck*, snack; SEE CONCEPT *169*

nice [adj1] *likable, agreeable*
admirable, amiable, approved, attractive, becoming,
charming, commendable, considerate, copacetic,
cordial, courteous, cultured, decorous, delightful,
ducky, fair, favorable, fine and dandy*, friendly, genial, gentle, good, gracious, helpful, ingratiating, inviting, kind, kindly, lovely, nifty*, obliging, okay*,
peachy*, pleasant, pleasurable, polite, prepossessing, seemly, simpatico, superior, swell, unpresumptuous, welcome, well-mannered, winning, winsome;
SEE CONCEPTS *404,548,572*

nice [adj2] *precise, neat, refined*
accurate, becoming, befitting, careful, choosy, conforming, correct, critical, cultured, dainty, decent,
delicate, discerning, discriminating, distinguishing,
exact, exacting, fastidious, fine, finespun, finical,
finicking, finicky*, fussy*, genteel, hairline*, hairsplitting*, meticulous, minute, particular, persnickety*, picky*, proper, refined, respectable, right,
rigorous, scrupulous, seemly, squeamish, strict, subtle, tidy, trim, trivial*, virtuous, well-bred; SEE CON-
CEPTS *542,557,558*

niche [n] *place all one's own*
alcove, byplace, calling, compartment, corner, cranny*, cubbyhole*, hole, hollow, indentation, nook,
opening, pigeonhole*, position, recess, slot, vocation; SEE CONCEPTS *440,513,630*

nick [n/v] *chip, scratch*
cut, damage, dent, dint, indent, jag, knock, mark,
mill, notch, scar, score, slit; SEE CONCEPTS
137,176,208

nickname [n] *informal title*
appellation, byname, byword, denomination, diminutive, epithet, familiar name, handle*, label, moniker, pet name*, sobriquet, style, tag*; SEE CONCEPTS
268,683

nifty [adj] *marvelous*
chic, clever, cool*, dandy, enjoyable, excellent,
groovy*, keen, neat, peachy*, pleasing, quick,
sharp, smart, spruce, stylish, super, swell, terrific;
SEE CONCEPT *572*

night [n] *part of day after sundown and before sunrise*
after dark, after hours*, bedtime, before dawn,
black*, blackness, dark, dark hours, darkness, dead
of night*, dim, duskiness, dusk to dawn, evening,
eventide, gloom, midnight, nightfall, nighttide,
nighttime, nite, obscurity*, pitch dark, twilight,
witching hour*; SEE CONCEPTS *620,801,806,810*

nightclub [n] *place for evening entertainment*
bar, bistro, cabaret, café, casino, disco*, disco-
theque, dive*, hideaway*, honky-tonk*, joint*,
nightery, night spot, nitery, restaurant, roadhouse,
saloon, speakeasy*, spot, supper club, tavern, theatre, watering hole*; SEE CONCEPTS *293,439,449*

nightfall [n] *beginning of darkness*
black*, crepuscule, dim, dusk, eve, eventide, sundown, sunset, twilight, vespers*; SEE CONCEPT *810*

nightgown [n] *dress in which to sleep*
bedgown, lingerie, negligee, nightdress, nightie*,
nightrobe, nightshirt, pajamas, PJs*, sleeper*; SEE
CONCEPT *451*

nightly [adj/adv] *each evening; after dark*
at night, by night, every night, in the night, night
after night, nights, nighttime, nocturnal, nocturnally;
SEE CONCEPTS *541,799,801*

nightmare [n] *bad dream or experience*
dream, fancy, fantasy, hallucination, horror, illusion,
incubus, ordeal, phantasm, succubus, torment, trial,
tribulation, vision; SEE CONCEPTS *315,674*

nihilism [n] *refusal to believe*
abnegation, agnosticism, anarchy, atheism, denial,
disbelief, disorder, lawlessness, mob rule*, nonbelief, rejection, renunciation, repudiation, skepticism,
terrorism; SEE CONCEPT *689*

nil [adj] *nonexistent*
naught, nihil, nix*, none, nothing, nought, zero; SEE
CONCEPTS *539,762,771*

nimble [adj] *dexterous, smart*
active, adept, adroit, agile, alert, bright, brisk,
clever, deft, handy, light, lissome, lithe, lively, proficient, prompt, quick, quick-witted, ready, skillful,
sprightly, spry, swift, vigilant, wide-awake; SEE
CONCEPTS *402,527,584*

nip [n] *swallow, taste*
bite, catch, dram, drop, finger, jolt, morsel, mouthful, nibble, pinch, portion, shot*, sip, slug*, snifter,
soupçon, toothful; SEE CONCEPTS *458,831*

nip [v1] *bite; take small part*
catch, clip, compress, grip, munch, nab at*, nibble,
pinch, sink teeth into*, snag, snap*, snip*, squeeze*,
take a chunk out of*, tweak, twinge, twitch; SEE
CONCEPTS *142,169,190*

nip [v2] *stop, thwart*
arrest, balk, blight, check, dash, end, frustrate; SEE
CONCEPTS *121,234*

nobility [n] *aristocracy; eminence*
dignity, elevation, elite, ennoblement, exaltation, excellence, generosity, gentry, glorification, grandeur,
greatness, high society, honor, illustriousness, incorruptibility, integrity, loftiness, magnanimity, magnificence, majesty, nobleness, patricians, peerage,
royalty, ruling class, society, stateliness, sublimity,
superiority, upper class, uprightness, virtue, worthiness; SEE CONCEPTS *378,388,668*

noble/nobleman/noblewoman [n] *member of royal or
important family*
archduchess, archduke, aristocrat, blue blood*,
count, countess, duchess, duke, emperor, empress,
gentleman, gentlewoman, lady, lord, patrician, peer,

prince, princess, royalty, silk stocking*; SEE CONCEPTS *422,423*

noble [*adj1*] *aristocratic*
gentle, highborn, imperial, kingly, lordly, nobiliary, patrician, princely, queenly, titled, wellborn; SEE CONCEPTS *549,555*

noble [*adj2*] *dignified, excellent*
august, beneficent, benevolent, benign, big, bounteous, brilliant, charitable, courtly, cultivated, dignified, distinguished, elevated, eminent, extraordinary, first-rate, generous, gracious, grand, great, greathearted, high-minded, honorable, humane, imposing, impressive, liberal, lofty, lordly, magnanimous, magnificent, meritorious, preeminent, princely, refined, remarkable, reputable, splendid, stately, sublime, supreme, sympathetic, tolerant, upright, virtuous, worthy; SEE CONCEPTS *401,404,572*

nobody/nonentity [*n*] *person of little importance*
cipher, insignificancy, lightweight*, little guy*, menial, nix*, nothing, parvenu*, small potato*, squirt*, upstart, wimp*, zero*, zip; SEE CONCEPT *423*

nocturnal [*adj*] *happening at night*
after dark, late, night, night-loving, nightly, nighttime; SEE CONCEPTS *799,801*

nod [*n*] *gesture of the head*
acceptance, acknowledgment, affirmative, beckon, bow, dip, greeting, inclination, indication, permission, salute, sign, signal, yes*; SEE CONCEPTS *74,185,685*

nod [*v1*] *gesture with head*
acknowledge, acquiesce, agree, approve, assent, beckon, bend, bow, concur, consent, curtsy, dip, duck, greet, indicate, recognize, respond, salute, say yes, sign, signal; SEE CONCEPTS *10,50,74,88,185*

nod [*v2*] *fall asleep*
become inattentive, be sleepy, doze, drift, drift off, droop, drowse, nap, sleep, slump; SEE CONCEPTS *210,315,681*

node/nodule [*n*] *knot, growth*
bud, bulge, bump, burl, clot, knob, lump, protuberance, swelling, tumor; SEE CONCEPTS *471,831*

noise [*n*] *sound that is loud or not harmonious*
babble, babel, bang, bedlam, bellow, bewailing, blare, blast, boisterousness, boom, buzz, cacophony, caterwauling, clamor, clang, clatter, commotion, crash, cry, detonation, din, discord, disquiet, disquietude, drumming, eruption, explosion, fanfare, fireworks, fracas*, fuss, hoo-ha*, hubbub*, hullabaloo*, jangle, lamentation, outcry, pandemonium, peal, racket, ring, roar, row, shot, shouting, sonance, squawk, stridency, talk, thud, tumult, turbulence, uproar, uproariousness, yelling, yelp; SEE CONCEPTS *521,595*

noiseless [*adj*] *quiet*
hushed, hushful, inaudible, mute, muted, silent, soundless, speechless, still, voiceless, wordless; SEE CONCEPT *594*

noisome [*adj*] *immoral, bad, offensive*
baneful, dangerous, deadly, deleterious, disgusting, fetid, foul, harmful, horrid, hurtful, injurious, insalubrious, insalutary, loathsome, malodorous, mephitic, mischievous, nauseating, noxious, pernicious, pestiferous, pestilential, poisonous, putrid, rank, reeking, repulsive, sickening, sickly, smelly, stinking, unhealthful, unhealthy, unwholesome, vile, yucky*; SEE CONCEPTS *537,571,598*

noisy [*adj*] *very loud and unharmonious in sound*
blatant, blusterous, boisterous, booming, cacophonous, chattering, clamorous, clangorous, clattery, deafening, disorderly, ear-popping, ear-splitting, jumping, loudmouth, obstreperous, piercing, rackety, raising Cain*, raising the roof*, rambunctious, raspy, riotous, rowdy, screaming, strepitous, strident, tumultous/tumultuous, turbulent, turned up, uproarious, vociferous; SEE CONCEPTS *592,594*

nomad [*n*] *person who wanders from place to place*
hobo, itinerant, migrant, pilgrim, rambler, roamer, rover, vagabond, wanderer, wayfarer; SEE CONCEPT *413*

nomadic [*adj*] *itinerant*
drifting, gypsy, itinerate, migrant, migratory, pastoral, perambulant, perambulatory, peripatetic, roaming, roving, traveling, vagabond, vagrant, wandering, wayfaring; SEE CONCEPTS *401,536,584*

nomenclature [*n*] *vocabulary*
classification, codification, glossary, locution, phraseology, taxonomy, terminology; SEE CONCEPTS *275,276,683*

nominal [*adj1*] *supposed, theoretical*
alleged, apparent, as advertised, formal, given, honorary, in effect only, in name only, mentioned, named, ostensible, pretended, professed, puppet, purported, seeming, self-styled, simple, so-called, stated, suggested, titular; SEE CONCEPT *582*

nominal [*adj2*] *insignificant*
cheap, inconsiderable, inexpensive, low, low-priced, meaningless, minimal, small, symbolic, token, trifling, trivial, unnecessary; SEE CONCEPTS *334,575,789*

nominate [*v*] *designate, select*
appoint, assign, call, choose, cognominate, commission, decide, denominate, draft, elect, elevate, empower, intend, make, mean, name, offer, present, proffer, propose, purpose, put down for, put up, recommend, slate, slot, specify, submit, suggest, tab, tap, tender, term; SEE CONCEPTS *41,50,75,88,300*

nomination [*n*] *appointment for responsibility*
choice, designation, election, naming, proposal, recommendation, selection, suggestion; SEE CONCEPTS *41,50,75,88,300*

nonchalant [*adj*] *easygoing, laid back*
airy, aloof, apathetic, blasé, calm, careless, casual, cold, collected, composed, cool, detached, disimpassioned, disinterested, dispassionate, easy, effortless, happy, impassive, imperturbable, incurious, indiffer-

ent, insouciant, lackadaisical, light, listless, loose, lukewarm, mellow, neglectful, negligent, neutral, offhand, placid, serene, smooth, trifling, uncaring, unconcerned, unemotional, unexcited, unfeeling, unflappable, unimpressible, unperturbed, unruffled, untroubled; SEE CONCEPTS 401,404,542

noncommittal [adj] *unwilling to decide*
ambiguous, buttoned up*, careful, cautious, circumspect, clammed up*, constrained, discreet, equivocal, evasive, even-steven*, guarded, hush-hush, incommunicable, indefinite, judicious, middleground*, middle-of-the-road*, neutral, no-man's land*, on-the-fence*, playing-it-cool, politic, reserved, restrained, tactful, temporizing, tentative, unrevealing, vague, wary, zipped*; SEE CONCEPTS 267,403,542

noncompliant [adj] *unwilling to go along with something*
belligerent, contumacious, declinatory, declining, divergent, impatient, irregular, negative, objecting, rebellious, recalcitrant, refractory, refusing, restive, truculent; SEE CONCEPTS 401,542

nonconformist [n] *person who goes against normal behavior, beliefs*
beatnik*, bohemian*, demonstrator, different breed*, dissenter, dissentient, dissident, dropout, eccentric, fish out of water*, freak*, heretic, iconoclast, individualist, liberal, malcontent, maverick, misbeliever, night person, oddball, offbeat, original, protester, radical, rebel, sectary, separatist, swinger, weirdo*; SEE CONCEPTS 359,423

nonconformist [adj] *unwilling to behave, believe as most do*
beatnik*, bohemian*, dissident, dropout, freak*, heretical, heterodox, hippie*, iconoclastic, maverick, oddball, offbeat, original, rebel, schismatic*, sectarian, swinger, unorthodox, weird*; SEE CONCEPTS 401,542

nonconformity [n] *belief, behavior different from most*
bohemianism, breach, contumaciousness, denial, disaffection, disagreement, disapprobation, disapproval, discordance, disobedience, dissent, eccentricity, exception, heresy, heterodoxy, iconoclasm, insubordination, lawlessness, mutinousness, negation, nonacceptance, nonagreement, noncompliance, nonconsent, objection, opposition, originality, recalcitrance, recusance, recusancy, rejection, strangeness, transgressiveness, unconventionality, uniqueness, unorthodoxy, unruliness, veto, violation; SEE CONCEPTS 633,657,689

nondescript [adj] *undistinguished, commonplace*
characterless, colorless, common, dull, empty, featureless, garden*, indescribable, indeterminate, mousy*, ordinary, unclassifiable, unclassified, unexceptional, uninspiring, uninteresting, unmemorable, unremarkable, vague; SEE CONCEPTS 529,537,547

none [prep] *not one thing*
nil, nobody, no one, no one at all, no part, not a bit, not any, not anyone, not anything, not a soul, not a

thing, nothing, not one, zero, zilch*; SEE CONCEPT 407

nonessential [adj] *not needed or important*
deadwood*, dispensable, excess baggage*, excessive, expendable, extraneous, inessential, insignificant, peripheral, petty, superfluous, trivial, unimportant, unnecessary; SEE CONCEPTS 546,575

nonexistent [adj] *fictional, not real*
absent, airy, baseless, blank, chimerical, dead, defunct, departed, dreamlike, dreamy, empty, ethereal, extinct, extinguished, fancied, flimsy, gone, gossamery, groundless, hallucinatory, hypothetical, illusory, imaginary, imagined, immaterial, imponderable, insubstantial, legendary, lost, missing, mythical, negative, null, null and void*, passed away, passed on, perished, shadowy, tenuous, ungrounded, unreal, unsubstantial, vacant, vague, vaporous, void, without foundation; SEE CONCEPTS 539,582

nonpartisan [adj] *impartial; not political*
detached, equitable, fair, free-wheeling*, independent, indifferent, just, middle-of-the-road*, neutral, nonaligned, nondiscriminatory, objective, on one's own*, on-the-fence*, playing it cool*, unaffected, unaffiliated, unbiased, unbigoted, uncolored, unimplicated, uninfluenced, uninvolved, unprejudiced; SEE CONCEPT 542

nonplus [v] *confuse, perplex*
astonish, astound, baffle, balk, beat, bewilder, boggle, buffalo*, confound, daze, discomfit, disconcert, discountenance, dismay, dumbfound, embarrass, faze, floor*, flurry, fluster, frustrate, get*, mess with one's head*, muddle, mystify, overcome, paralyze, puzzle, rattle, rattle one's cage*, stagger, stick, stump, stun, stymie*, take aback, throw*, throw into tizzy*, thwart; SEE CONCEPTS 14,16

nonsense [n] *craziness, ridiculousness*
absurdity, babble, balderdash*, baloney*, bananas*, bombast, bull*, bunk*, claptrap*, drivel, fatuity, flightiness, folly, foolishness, fun, gibberish, giddiness, hogwash*, hooey*, hot air*, imprudence, inanity, irrationality, jazz, jest, jive*, joke, ludicrousness, madness, mumbo jumbo*, palaver, poppycock*, prattle, pretense, ranting, rashness, rot, rubbish, scrawl, scribble, senselessness, silliness, soft soap*, stupidity, thoughtlessness, trash*, tripe*; SEE CONCEPTS 230,388,633

nonstop [adj] *continuous, direct*
ceaseless, constant, endless, incessant, interminable, relentless, round-the-clock*, steady, unbroken, unending, unfaltering, uninterrupted, unremitting; SEE CONCEPTS 482,584,798

nonviolent [adj] *peaceful*
irenic, nonbelligerent, pacifist, passive, peaceable, quiet, resistant, without violence; SEE CONCEPT 401

nook [n] *corner, cubbyhole*
alcove, byplace, cavity, compartment, cranny, crevice, den, hideout, hole, inglenook, niche, opening, quoin, recess, retreat; SEE CONCEPTS 440,513

noon [n] *the middle of a day*
apex, high noon, meridian, midday, noonday, noontide, noontime, twelve noon, twelve o'clock; SEE CONCEPTS *801,802,806*

norm [n] *average, standard*
barometer, benchmark*, criterion, gauge, mean, measure, median, medium, model, par, pattern, rule, scale, touchstone*, type, yardstick; SEE CONCEPTS *647,687,688*

normal [adj1] *common, usual*
accustomed, acknowledged, average, commonplace, conventional, customary, general, habitual, mean, median, methodical, natural, orderly, ordinary, popular, prevalent, regular, routine, run-of-the-mill*, standard, traditional, typic, typical, unexceptional; SEE CONCEPT *547*

normal [adj2] *sane, rational*
all there*, compos mentis*, cool*, healthy, in good health, in one's right mind*, lucid, reasonable, right, right-minded, sound, together, well-adjusted, whole, wholesome; SEE CONCEPTS *314,403*

normally [adv] *usually*
as a rule, commonly, habitually, in accordance with, ordinarily, regularly, typically; SEE CONCEPT *547*

north [adj/adv] *toward the top pole of the earth*
arctic, boreal, cold, frozen, hyperborean, northbound, northerly, northern, northmost, northward, polar, septentrional, toward North Pole, tundra; SEE CONCEPTS *581,583*

nose [n] *smelling organ of animate being*
adenoids, beak*, bill*, horn*, muzzle*, nares, nostrils, olfactory nerves, proboscis, schnoz*, smeller*, sneezer*, sniffer*, snoot*, snout*, snuffer*, whiffer*; SEE CONCEPTS *392,601*

nose [v] *detect, search*
busybody*, examine, inspect, meddle, mouse*, pry, scent, smell, sniff, snoop*; SEE CONCEPTS *103,216*

nostalgia [n] *pleasant remembrances*
fond memories*, hearts and flowers*, homesickness, loneliness, longing, pining, reminiscence, remorse, schmaltz*, sentimentality, tear-jerker*, wistfulness, yearning; SEE CONCEPTS *20,410*

nostalgic [adj] *longingly remembering*
cornball*, down memory lane*, drippy*, homesick, like yesterday*, lonely, lonesome, longing, mushy*, old-hat, regretful, sappy*, sentimental, sloppy, syrupy*, wistful, yearning; SEE CONCEPTS *403,529*

nostrum [n] *cure-all, often ineffective*
catholicon, cure, drug, elixir, fix, formula, home remedy, medicine, panacea, patent medicine, potion, quack medicine*, quick fix*, remedy, treatment; SEE CONCEPTS *307,311*

nosy [adj] *very curious; prying*
eavesdropping, inquisitive, inquisitorial, inquisitory, interested, interfering, intermeddling, intrusive, meddlesome, personal, searching, snooping, snoopy; SEE CONCEPT *401*

notable [n] *person who is famous, very important*
baron, big man/woman on campus*, big name*, big shot*, big-time operator*, big wheel*, celebrity, chief, czar, dignitary, eminence, executive, figure*, heavyweight*, high-up, hotdog*, king, kingpin*, leader, lion*, luminary, magnate, mogul, name, notability, personage, personality, pooh-bah*, power, prince, queen, somebody*, star, superstar, VIP*, worthy; SEE CONCEPTS *347,352,423*

notable [adj] *very important; famous*
big-league*, bodacious*, celebrated, celebrious, conspicuous, distingué, distinguished, eminent, eventful, evident, extraordinary, famed, great, heavy*, high-profile*, illustrious, major-league*, manifest, marked, memorable, momentous, nameable, noteworthy, noticeable, notorious, observable, outstanding, preeminent, prominent, pronounced, rare, red-letter*, remarkable, renowned, rubric, serious, something else*, striking, top-drawer*, uncommon, unusual, well-known; SEE CONCEPT *568*

notably [adv] *especially*
conspicuously, distinctly, exceedingly, exceptionally, extremely, greatly, highly, hugely, markedly, noticeably, outstandingly, particularly, prominently, remarkably, reputably, signally, strikingly, uncommonly, very; SEE CONCEPT *569*

notation [n] *written remarks*
characters, chit, code, figures, jotting, memo, memorandum, note, noting, record, representation, script, signs, symbols, system; SEE CONCEPTS *268,284*

notch [n1] *indentation*
cleft, cut, gap, gash, groove, incision, indent, indenture, mark, mill, nick, nock, rabbet, rut, score, scratch; SEE CONCEPT *513*

notch [n2] *level within classification*
cut, degree, grade, rung, stage, step; SEE CONCEPTS *388,744*

notch [v] *indent*
chisel, cleave, crenelate, crimp, cut, dent, gash, incise, jag, mark, mill, nick, scallop, score, scratch; SEE CONCEPTS *137,176,208*

note/notes [n1] *written communication*
agenda, annotation, calendar, comment, commentary, datum, definition, diary, dispatch, entry, epistle, gloss, inscription, jotting, journal, letter, line, marginalia, mark, memo, memorandum, message, minute, missive, obiter dictum, observation, record, remark, reminder, scratch, scrawl, scribble, summary, thank-you, word; SEE CONCEPT *271*

note [n2] *symbol, often used in reference to music*
character, degree, figure, flat, indication, interval, key, lick*, mark, natural, pitch, representation, scale, sharp, sign, step, token, tone; SEE CONCEPTS *262,284*

note [n3] *attention, heed*
cognizance, mark, mind, notice, observance, observation, regard, remark; SEE CONCEPT *529*

note [v] *observe, perceive*
catch, clock, denote, descry, designate, dig, discern, discover, distinguish, enter, get a load of*, get an eyeful*, heed, indicate, jot down, mark, mention, notice, pick up on*, put down, record, register, re-

mark, see, set down, spot, take in*, transcribe, view, write, write down; SEE CONCEPTS *34,626*

noted [*adj*] *famous, eminent*
acclaimed, celeb*, celebrated, conspicuous, distinguished, esteemed, illustrious, leading, name, notable, notorious, of note, popular, prominent, recognized, redoubted, renowned, somebody, star, well-known; SEE CONCEPT *568*

noteworthy [*adj*] *important*
boss*, conspicuous, cool*, evident, exceptional, extraordinary, heavy*, high-profile*, hot*, major-league, manifest, meaningful, memorable, mindblowing, murder, nameable, notable, noticeable, observable, outstanding, patent, prominent, red-letter*, remarkable, serious, significant, something-else*, splash*, stand-out*, super, terrific, the end*, underlined*, unique, unusual, utmost; SEE CONCEPTS *567,568*

nothing/nothingness [*n*] *emptiness, nonexistence*
annihilation, aught, blank, cipher, extinction, fly speck*, insignificancy, naught, nihility, nobody, nonbeing, nonentity, not anything, no thing*, nought, nullity, obliteration, oblivion, shutout*, trifle, void, wind*, zero*, zilch*, zip; SEE CONCEPTS *407,707*

nothingness [*n2*] *insignificance*
pettiness, smallness, unimportance, worthlessness; SEE CONCEPT *668*

notice [*n1*] *observation*
apprehension, attention, care, civility, cognizance, concern, consideration, ear, grasp, heed, mark, mind, note, observance, regard, remark, respect, thought, understanding; SEE CONCEPTS *34,532*

notice [*n2*] *announcement, information*
admonition, advertisement, advice, caution, caveat, circular, clue, comment, comments, communication, criticism, critique, cue, declaration, directive, enlightenment, goods*, handbill, info*, instruction, intelligence, intimation, know*, lowdown*, manifesto, memo, memorandum, news, note, notification, order, picture, poster, proclamation, remark, review, score, sign, squib*, story, tip, warning, whole story*, write-up; SEE CONCEPTS *271,274,278*

notice [*v*] *observe, perceive*
acknowledge, advert, allude, catch, clock, descry, detect, dig*, discern, distinguish, espy, flash on*, get a load of*, heed, look at, make out*, mark, mind, note, pick up on, recognize, refer, regard, remark, see, spot, take in; SEE CONCEPTS *34,626*

noticeable [*adj*] *conspicuous, evident*
apparent, appreciable, arresting, arrestive, big as life*, can't miss it*, clear, distinct, eye-catching, manifest, marked, notable, noteworthy, observable, obvious, open and shut*, outstanding, palpable, patent, perceptible, plain, pointed, prominent, remarkable, salient, sensational, signal, spectacular, striking, under one's nose*, unmistakable; SEE CONCEPTS *529,537,567*

notify [*v*] *inform*
acquaint, advise, air, alert, announce, apprise, assert, blazon, brief, broadcast, cable, caution, circulate, clue in, convey, cue, debrief, declare, disclose, disseminate, divulge, enlighten, express, fill in, give, herald, hint, let in on, let know, make known, mention, pass out, post, proclaim, promulgate, publish, radio, report, reveal, send word, speak, spread, state, suggest, talk, teach, telephone, tell, tip off, vent, warn, wire, wise up*, write; SEE CONCEPTS *60,79*

notion [*n1*] *belief, idea*
angle, apprehension, approach, assumption, awareness, clue, comprehension, conceit, concept, conception, consciousness, consideration, cue, discernment, flash, hint, image, imagination, impression, inclination, indication, inkling, insight, intellection, intimation, intuition, judgment, knowledge, opinion, penetration, perception, sentiment, slant, spark, suggestion, telltale, thought, twist, understanding, view, wind, wrinkle; SEE CONCEPTS *529,532,689*

notion [*n2*] *whim, desire*
caprice, conceit, fancy, humor, imagination, impulse, inclination, wish; SEE CONCEPT *20*

notoriety [*n*] *reputation*
ballyhoo*, celebrity, center stage*, dishonor, disrepute, éclat*, fame, flak*, infamy, ink*, name*, obloquy, opprobrium, renown, rep*, scandal, splash*, spotlight*, wise*; SEE CONCEPTS *388,411*

notorious [*adj*] *known for a trait, often an unadmirable one*
belled, blatant, crying, dishonorable, disreputable, flagrant, glaring, ill-famed, infamous, leading, noted, obvious, open, opprobrious, overt, patent, popular, prominent, questionable, scandalous, shady, shameful, undisputed, wanted, well-known, wicked; SEE CONCEPT *404*

notwithstanding [*adv/prep*] *although, however*
after all, against, at any rate, but, despite, for all that, howbeit, in any case, in any event, in spite of, nevertheless, nonetheless, on the other hand, regardless of, though, to the contrary, withal, yet; SEE CONCEPT *544*

nourish [*v*] *feed, care for*
attend, cherish, comfort, cultivate, encourage, foster, furnish, maintain, nurse, nurture, promote, provide, supply, support, sustain, tend; SEE CONCEPTS *140,295*

nourishing [*adj*] *healthful*
alimentative, beneficial, health-giving, healthy, nutrient, nutrimental, nutritious, nutritive, wholesome; SEE CONCEPTS *462,537*

nourishment [*n*] *food*
aliment, diet, feed, foodstuff, home cooking*, maintenance, nutriment, nutrition, pabulum, pap*, provender, support, sustenance, viands, victuals, vittles*; SEE CONCEPT *457*

novel [n] *fictional book*
best-seller, cliff-hanger, fiction, narrative, novelette, novella, paperback, potboiler*, prose, romance, story, tale, yarn*; SEE CONCEPT **280**

novel [adj] *new, original*
at cutting edge*, atypical, avant-garde, breaking new ground*, contemporary, different, far cry*, fresh, funky*, innovative, just out*, modernistic, neoteric, newfangled, new-fashioned, now*, odd, offbeat, peculiar, rare, recent, singular, strange, uncommon, unfamiliar, unique, unusual; SEE CONCEPTS **564,578,797**

novelty [n1] *newness, originality*
change, crazy*, creation, dernier cri*, freshness, innovation, last word*, modernity, mutation, newfangled contraption, oddball, oddity, original, origination, permutation, recentness, sport*, strangeness, surprise, unfamiliarity, uniqueness, vicissitude, weird*; SEE CONCEPTS **665,697,715**

novelty [n2] *trinket, gadget*
bagatelle*, bauble, bibelot*, conversation piece, curio, curiosity, gewgaw*, gimcrack*, gimmick, item, knick-knack, memento, objet d'art*, oddity, souvenir, trifle, whatnot*; SEE CONCEPTS **260,445,446**

novice [n] *person just learning something*
amateur, apprentice, beginner, colt*, convert*, cub*, first of May*, fledgling, freshman/woman, greenhorn, gremlin, know from nothing*, learner, mark*, neophyte, new boy/girl, newcomer, new kid on the block*, novitiate, postulant, prentice, probationer, proselyte, punk*, pupil, recruit, rookie, starter, student, tenderfoot*, trainee, undergraduate; SEE CONCEPTS **348,350,423**

now [adv] *presently*
any more, at once, at the moment, at this moment, at this time, away, directly, first off, forthwith, here and now, immediately, in a minute, in a moment, in nothing flat, instanter, instantly, just now, like now*, momentarily, nowadays, on the double*, PDQ*, promptly, pronto*, right away, right now, soon, straightaway, these days, this day, today; SEE CONCEPTS **812,820**

noxious [adj] *deadly, injurious*
baneful, corrupting, dangerous, deleterious, destructive, detrimental, fetid, foul, harmful, hurtful, injurious, insalubrious, insalutary, noisome, pernicious, pestiferous, pestilent, pestilential, poisonous, putrid, sickly, spoiled, stinking, toxic, unhealthful, unhealthy, unwholesome, venomous, virulent; SEE CONCEPTS **485,537**

nuance [n] *slight difference; shading*
dash, degree, distinction, gradation, hint, implication, nicety, refinement, shade, shadow, soupçon, subtlety, suggestion, suspicion, tinge, touch, trace; SEE CONCEPT **665**

nub [n1] *core, gist*
basic, bottom line*, crux, essence, heart*, kernel, meat*, meat and potatoes*, nitty-gritty*, nubbin, nucleus, pith, point, short, substance, upshot; SEE CONCEPTS **661,682,826**

nub [n2] *bump, knot*
bulge, knob, lump, node, protuberance, swelling; SEE CONCEPT **471**

nuclear weapon [n] *explosive driven by nuclear energy*
A-bomb, atomic bomb, atomic weapon, doomsday machine*, H-bomb, hydrogen bomb, mininuke*, mirv*, MX*, neutron bomb, nuke*; SEE CONCEPT **500**

nucleus [n] *core; basis for something's beginning*
budding, center, crux, embryo, focus, foundation, germ, heart, hub, kernel, matter, nub, pivot, premise, principle, seed, spark; SEE CONCEPTS **393,826,828**

nude [adj] *without clothes, covering*
au naturel*, bald, bare, bare-skinned, buck naked*, dishabille*, disrobed, exposed, garmentless, in birthday suit, in one's skin*, in the altogether*, naked, peeled*, raw, skin, stark, stark-naked*, stripped, unattired, unclad, unclothed, uncovered, undraped, undressed, wearing only a smile*, without a stitch*; SEE CONCEPT **485**

nudge [n/v] *bump, elbow*
dig, jab, jog, poke, prod, punch, push, shove, tap, touch; SEE CONCEPTS **208,612**

nugget [n] *lump, solid piece; often of metal ore*
asset, bullion, chunk, clod, clump, gold, hunk, ingot, mass, plum, rock, treasure, wad*; SEE CONCEPT **471**

nuisance [n] *annoyance; annoying person*
besetment, blister, bore, bother, botheration, botherment, bum*, creep, drag*, drip*, exasperation, frump, gadfly, headache*, inconvenience, infliction, insect*, irritant, irritation, louse, nag*, nudge*, offense, pain, pain in the neck*, pest, pester, pesterer, pill*, plague, poor excuse*, problem, terror, trouble, vexation; SEE CONCEPTS **412,674**

null [adj] *ineffectual, valueless*
absent, bad, barren, characterless, imaginary, ineffective, inefficacious, inoperative, invalid, negative, nonexistent, nothing, null and void*, powerless, unavailing, unreal, unsanctioned, useless, vain, void, worthless; SEE CONCEPTS **560,570**

nullify [v] *cancel, revoke*
abate, abolish, abrogate, annihilate, annul, ax, blue pencil*, bring to naught*, call all bets off*, compensate, confine, counteract, counterbalance, countervail, disannul, forget it*, invalidate, kill*, limit, negate, neutralize, nig*, offset, quash*, render null and void*, renege, renig*, repeal, rescind, restrict, scratch*, scrub*, squash*, stamp out*, take out*, torpedo*, trash*, undo, veto, vitiate, void, wash out*, wipe out*, zap*; SEE CONCEPTS **50,88,121,234**

numb [adj] *deadened, insensitive*
aloof, anesthetized, apathetic, asleep, benumbed, callous, casual, comatose, dazed, dead, detached, disinterested, frozen, immobilized, incurious, indif-

ferent, insensate, insensible, insentient, lethargic, listless, numbed, paralyzed, phlegmatic, remote, senseless, stupefied, stuporous, torpid, unconcerned, unconscious, uncurious, unfeeling, uninterested; SEE CONCEPTS *403,609*

numb [*v*] *deaden*
anesthetize, benumb, blunt, chill, desensitize, dull, freeze, frost, immobilize, obtund, paralyze, stun, stupefy; SEE CONCEPTS *250,255*

number [*n1*] *unit of the mathematical system*
cardinal, character, chiffer, cipher, count, decimal, denominator, digit, emblem, figure, folio, fraction, googol, integer, numeral, numerator, ordinal, prime, representation, sign, statistic, sum, symbol, total, whole number; SEE CONCEPTS *765,784*

number [*n2*] *aggregate, bunch*
abundance, amount, caboodle*, collection, company, conglomeration, crowd, estimate, flock, horde, jillion*, lot, manifoldness, many, multitide, plenitude, plenty, product, quantity, slew*, sum, throng, total, totality, umpteen*, volume, whole, zillion*; SEE CONCEPTS *432,786*

number [*v*] *count, calculate*
account, add, add up, aggregate, amount, come, computer, count heads*, count noses*, count off, enumerate, estimate, figure in, figure out, include, keep tabs, numerate, reckon, run, run down, run into, run to, sum, take account of, tale, tally, tell, tick off*, total, tote*, tote up*; SEE CONCEPT *764*

numbered [*adj*] *limited in number*
categorized, checked, contained, counted, designated, doomed, enumerated, fated, fixed, included, indicated, marked, specified, told, totalled; SEE CONCEPT *554*

numberless [*adj*] *infinite*
countless, endless, heaps*, incalculable, innumerable, jillion, many, multitudinous, myriad, no end of*, no end to*, numerous, umpteen, uncountable, uncounted, unnumbered, untold, zillion*; SEE CONCEPTS *482,762,781*

numeral [*n*] *symbol of mathematical system*
character, chiffer, cipher, digit, figure, integer, number; SEE CONCEPTS *284,784*

numeric/numerical [*adj*] *concerning mathematics*
algebraic, algorithmic, arithmetic, arithmetical, binary, differential, digital, exponent, exponential, fraction, fractional, integral, logarithm, logarithmic, mathematical, numeral, numerary, statistical; SEE CONCEPT *762*

numerous [*adj*] *many, abundant*
big, copious, diverse, great, infinite, large, legion, lousy with*, multifarious, multitudinal, multitudinous, plentiful, populous, profuse, rife, scads*, several, sundry, thick, umpteen*, various, voluminous, zillion*; SEE CONCEPTS *762,781*

nun [*n*] *woman in religious order*
abbess, anchorite, canoness, mother superior, postulant, prioress, religious woman, sister, vestal, vestal virgin; SEE CONCEPT *361*

nuptial [*adj*] *concerning marriage*
bridal, conjugal, connubial, espousal, hymeneal, marital, married, matrimonial, spousal, wedded, wedding; SEE CONCEPT *555*

nuptials [*n*] *marriage ceremony*
bridal, espousal, marriage, matrimony, spousal, wedding; SEE CONCEPT *297*

nurse [*n*] *person who tends to sick, cares for someone*
assistant, attendant, baby sitter, caretaker, foster parent, medic, minder, nursemaid, nurse practitioner, nurserymaid, practical nurse, registered nurse, RN, sitter, therapist, wet nurse; SEE CONCEPTS *357,414*

nurse [*v1*] *care for, tend*
advance, aid, attend, baby-sit*, cherish, cradle, cultivate, encourage, father, feed, forward, foster, further, harbor, humor, immunize, indulge, inoculate, irradiate, keep alive, keep an eye on*, keep tabs on*, look after, medicate, minister to, mother, nourish, nurture, pamper, preserve, promote, see to, serve, sit, succor, support, take care of, take charge of, treat, vaccinate, wait on, watch out for, watch over, X-ray*; SEE CONCEPTS *110,140*

nurse [*v2*] *give milk, usually from breast*
bottle-feed, breast-feed, cradle, dry-nurse, feed, give suck, lactate, mother, nourish, nurture, suck, suckle, wet-nurse; SEE CONCEPTS *140,295*

nurture [*n*] *development, nourishment*
breeding, care, diet, discipline, edibles, education, feed, food, instruction, nutriment, provender, provisions, rearing, subsistence, sustenance, training, upbringing, viands, victuals; SEE CONCEPTS *457,712*

nurture [*v*] *feed, care for*
back, bolster, bring up, cherish, cultivate, develop, discipline, educate, foster, instruct, nourish, nurse, nursle, provide, raise, rear, school, support, sustain, tend, train, uphold; SEE CONCEPTS *110,140,295*

nut [*n1*] *seed of fruit, vegetable*
achene, caryopsis, kernel, stone, utricle; SEE CONCEPT *428*

nut [*n2*] *crazy, overenthusiastic person*
bedlamite, bigot, crackpot, crank, dement, eccentric, fanatic, fiend, freak, harebrain, loony*, lunatic, madman/woman, maniac, non compos mentis, screwball*, zealot; SEE CONCEPTS *412,423*

nutrition [*n*] *food*
diet, menu, nourishment, nutriment, subsistence, sustenance, victuals; SEE CONCEPT *457*

nutritious [*adj*] *healthy*
alimental, alimentative, balanced, beneficial, good, healthful, health-giving, invigorating, nourishing, nutrient, nutrimental, nutritive, salubrious, salutary, strengthening, wholesome; SEE CONCEPT *462*

nuts/nutty [*adj*] *mentally deranged*
absurd, batty*, bedlamite, cracked*, crazy, daffy, daft, demented, eccentric, enthusiastic, foolish, gung ho*, harebrained, insane, irrational, keen, kooky, loony, lunatic, mad, out of one's mind*, ridiculous,

touched, unusual, wacky*, warm, zealous; SEE CONCEPT *403*

nuzzle [*v*] *cuddle*
bundle, burrow, caress, fondle, nestle, nudge, pet, snug, snuggle; SEE CONCEPTS *190,612*

nymph [*n*] *young, naive woman; female nature spirit*
damsel, dryad, fairy, girl, goddess, lass, maid, maiden, mermaid, naiad, nymphet, spirit, sprite, sylph; SEE CONCEPTS *415,424*

O

oaf [*n*] *person who is clumsy, stupid*
beast, blunderer, bruiser, brute, chump*, clod, clown, dolt, dumb ox*, dunce, fool, goon*, half-wit*, idiot, imbecile, klutz*, loser, lout*, moron, nincompoop*, ox*, sap*, simpleton*; SEE CONCEPT *412*

oasis [*n*] *refuge*
haven, resting place, retreat, sanctuary, sanctum, spot, tract; SEE CONCEPT *515*

oath [*n1*] *promise*
adjuration, affidavit, affirmation, avowal, bond, contract, deposition, pledge, profession, sworn declaration, sworn statement, testimony, vow, word, word of honor; SEE CONCEPTS *71,278*

oath [*n2*] *curse*
blasphemy, cuss*, cuss word*, dirty name*, dirty word*, expletive, four-letter word*, imprecation, malediction, no-no*, profanity, strong language, swearword; SEE CONCEPTS *54,278*

obdurate [*adj*] *pigheaded, stubborn*
adamant, bullhead*, callous, cold fish*, dogged, firm, fixed, hanging tough*, hard, hard-boiled*, hard-hearted*, hard-nosed*, harsh, heartless, immovable, implacable, indurate, inexorable, inflexible, iron*, mean, mulish*, obstinate, perverse, relentless, rigid, set in stone*, stiff-necked*, thick-skinned*, tough, tough nut to crack*, unbending, uncompassionate, uncompromising, uncooperative, unemotional, unfeeling, unimpressible, unrelenting, unshakable, unsympathetic, unyielding; SEE CONCEPTS *401,542*

obedience [*n*] *good behavior; submissiveness*
accordance, acquiescence, agreement, compliance, conformability, conformity, deference, docility, duteousness, dutifulness, duty, manageability, meekness, observance, orderliness, quietness, respect, reverence, servility, submission, subservience, tameness, tractability, willingness; SEE CONCEPTS *411,633*

obedient [*adj*] *well-behaved; submissive*
acquiescent, amenable, at one's beck and call*, attentive, biddable, complaisant, compliant, controllable, deferential, devoted, docile, docious, duteous, dutiful, faithful, governable, honoring, in one's clutches*, in one's pocket*, in one's power*, law-abiding, loyal, obeisant, obliging, observant, on a string*, pliant, regardful, resigned, respectful, rev-erential, sheeplike*, subservient, tame, tractable, under control, venerating, well-trained, willing, wrapped around finger*, yielding; SEE CONCEPTS *401,404*

obeisance [*n*] *salutation*
allegiance, bending of the knee*, bow, curtsy, deference, fealty, genuflection, homage, honor, kow-tow*, loyalty, praise, respect, reverence, salaam*; SEE CONCEPTS *154,384*

obese [*adj*] *very overweight*
adipose, avoirdupois, corpulent, fat, fleshy, gross, heavy, outsize, paunchy, plump, porcine, portly, pudgy, rotund, stout; SEE CONCEPT *491*

obey [*v*] *conform, give in*
abide by, accede, accept, accord, acquiesce, act upon, adhere to, agree, answer, assent, be loyal to, be ruled by, bow to*, carry out, comply, concur, discharge, do as one says, do one's bidding, do one's duty, do what is expected, do what one is told, embrace, execute, follow, fulfill, get in line*, give way*, heed, hold fast*, keep, knuckle under*, live by, mind, observe, perform, play second fiddle*, respond, serve, submit, surrender, take orders, toe the line*; SEE CONCEPTS *91,136*

obituary [*n*] *notice of person's death*
announcement, death notice, eulogy, mortuary tribute, necrology, obit, register; SEE CONCEPTS *268,270*

object [*n1*] *thing able to be seen/felt/perceived*
article, body, bulk, commodity, doodad*, doohickey*, entity, fact, gadget, gizmo*, item, mass, matter, phenomenon, reality, something, substance, thingamajig*, volume, whatchamacallit*, widget*; SEE CONCEPT *433*

object [*n2*] *purpose, use*
aim, design, duty, end, end in view, end purpose, function, goal, idea, intent, intention, mark, mission, motive, objective, point, reason, target, view, wish; SEE CONCEPT *659*

object [*n3*] *aim, recipient*
butt*, focus, ground zero*, receiver, target, victim, zero*; SEE CONCEPTS *124,532*

object [*v*] *disagree, argue against*
balk, be displeased, challenge, complain, crab*, criticize, cross, demur, deprecate, disapprove, disavow, discommend, discountenance, disesteem, dispute, dissent, except, expostulate, frown, go one-on-one*, gripe, grouse, inveigh, kick*, make a stink*, mix it up with*, oppose, protest, rail, raise objection, rant, rave, remonstrate, sound off*, spurn, squawk*, storm, take exception, take on, tangle; SEE CONCEPTS *12,21,46*

objection [*n*] *argument, disagreement*
cavil, censure, challenge, counter-argument, criticism, declination, demur, demurral, demurring, difficulty, disapprobation, disapproval, discontent, disesteem, disinclination, dislike, displeasure, dissatisfaction, doubt, exception, grievance, gripe, hesitation, kick, niggle*, odium, opposition, protest,

protestation, question, rejection, reluctance, remonstrance, remonstration, repugnancy, revilement, scruple, shrinking, squawk*, stink*, unwillingness; SEE CONCEPTS *21,46,410,689*

objectionable [*adj*] *not nice; unpleasant*
abhorrent, censurable, deplorable, disagreeable, dislikable, displeasing, distasteful, exceptionable, ill-favored, inadmissible, indecorous, inexpedient, insufferable, intolerable, invidious, loathsome, lousy, murder, noxious, obnoxious, offensive, opprobrious, poison, regrettable, repellent, reprehensible, repugnant, repulsive, revolting, unacceptable, undesirable, unfit, unpalatable, unsatisfactory, unseemly, unsuitable, unwanted, unwelcome; SEE CONCEPTS *548,558,570*

objective [*n*] *aim, goal*
ambition, aspiration, design, end, end in view*, goal, ground zero*, intention, mark, mission, object, purpose, target, zero*; SEE CONCEPT *659*

objective [*adj*] *fair, impartial*
cold, cool, detached, disinterested, dispassionate, equitable, evenhanded, impersonal, judicial, just, like it is*, nondiscriminatory, nonpartisan, open-minded*, straight, strictly business*, unbiased, uncolored, unemotional, uninvolved, unprejudiced, unprepossessed; SEE CONCEPTS *403,542*

objectively [*adv*] *impartially*
considerately, detachedly, disinterestedly, dispassionately, equitably, evenhandedly, indifferently, justly, neutrally, on the up and up*, open-mindedly*, soberly, squarely, with an open mind*, with impartiality, with objectivity, without favor, without prejudice; SEE CONCEPTS *542,544*

obligate [*v*] *require*
astrict, bind, constrain, force, indebt, make indebted, oblige, restrain, restrict; SEE CONCEPTS *53,130,646*

obligation [*n*] *responsibility*
accountability, accountableness, agreement, bond, burden, business, call, cause, charge, chit*, commitment, committal, compulsion, conscience, constraint, contract, debit, debt, devoir, due bill, dues, duty, engagement, IOU*, liability, must, necessity, need, occasion, onus, ought, part, place, promise, requirement, restraint, right, trust, understanding; SEE CONCEPTS *329,335,388,645*

obligatory [*adj*] *essential, required*
binding, coercive, compulsatory, compulsory, de rigueur, enforced, imperative, imperious, mandatory, necessary, requisite, unavoidable; SEE CONCEPT *546*

oblige [*v1*] *require*
bind, coerce, command, compel, constrain, force, impel, make, necessitate, obligate, shotgun*; SEE CONCEPTS *14,242,646*

oblige [*v2*] *do a favor or kindness*
accommodate, aid, assist, avail, bend over backward*, benefit, come around, contribute, convenience, don't make waves*, favor, fill the bill*, fit in, go fifty-fifty*, gratify, grin and bear it*, help, indulge, make a deal*, make room*, meet halfway*, please, profit, put oneself out*, roll with it*, serve, swim with the tide*, take it*, toe the mark*; SEE CONCEPTS *110,136,384*

obliging [*adj*] *friendly, helpful*
accommodating, agreeable, amiable, cheerful, civil, complaisant, considerate, cooperative, courteous, eager to please, easy, easygoing, good-humored, good-natured, hospitable, kind, lenient, mild, polite, willing; SEE CONCEPTS *401,404*

oblique [*adj1*] *slanting; at an angle*
angled, askance, askew, aslant, asymmetrical, awry, bent, cater-cornered, crooked, diagonal, distorted, diverging, inclined, inclining, leaning, on the bias, pitched, pitching, sideways, skew, slanted, sloped, sloping, strained, tilted, tilting, tipped, tipping, turned, twisted; SEE CONCEPTS *485,490*

oblique [*adj2*] *indirect, evasive*
backhanded, circuitous, circular, circumlocutory, collateral, devious, implied, obliquitous, obscure, roundabout, sidelong, vague; SEE CONCEPT *267*

obliterate [*v*] *destroy*
annihilate, ax*, black out*, blot out*, blue pencil*, bog, cancel, cover, cut, defeat, delete, do in*, efface, eliminate, eradicate, erase, expunge, exterminate, extirpate, finish, finish off*, kill, knock off*, knock out*, KO*, level*, liquidate, mark out, nix*, obscure, off, ravage, root out*, rub off*, rub out*, scratch, scrub, shoot down, sink, smash, squash, take apart, take out*, torpedo*, total*, trash*, wash out*, waste, wipe off face of earth*, wipe out*, X-out*, zap*; SEE CONCEPT *252*

oblivion [*n1*] *mental blankness*
abeyance, amnesia, carelessness, disregard, forgetfulness, inadvertence, indifference, insensibility, insensibleness, Lethe*, neglect, nirvana*, obliviousness, unawareness, unconcern, unconsciousness, unmindfulness; SEE CONCEPTS *410,633*

oblivion [*n2*] *nothingness, obscurity*
blackness, darkness, eclipse, emptiness, extinction, limbo, nihility, nirvana*, no-man's-land*, nonexistence, nothing, nowhere*, nullity, out there*, void; SEE CONCEPTS *407,672,679*

oblivious [*adj*] *unaware, ignorant*
absent, absentminded, absorbed, abstracted, amnesic, blind*, blundering, careless, deaf*, disregardful, distracted, dreamy, forgetful, forgetting, gone, heedless, inattentive, incognizant, inconversant, insensible, neglectful, negligent, not all there*, out to lunch*, overlooking, preoccupied, regardless, spacey*, strung out*, unacquainted, unconcerned, unconscious, undiscerning, unfamiliar, uninformed, uninstructed, unknowing, unmindful, unnoticing, unobservant, unrecognizing, unwitting, zonked*; SEE CONCEPTS *402, 403,542*

oblong [*adj*] *elongated and rounded*
egg-shaped, ellipsoidal, elliptical, elongate, long, oval, ovaliform, ovaloid, ovate, ovated, ovoid, rectangular; SEE CONCEPT *486*

obnoxious [*adj*] *offensive, repulsive*
abhorrent, abominable, annoying, awful, beastly*, big mouth*, detestable, disagreeable, disgusting, dislikable, displeasing, foul, gross*, hatable, hateful, heel, horrid, insufferable, invidious, loathsome, mean, nasty, nauseating, objectionable, odious, off-color*, ornery, pain in the neck*, pesky*, pestiferous, pill*, repellent, reprehensible, repugnant, revolting, rotten, sickening, stinking, unpleasant; SEE CONCEPTS *267,401,542*

obscene [*adj*] *indecent, offensive, immoral*
atrocious, barnyard*, bawdy, blue*, coarse, crude, dirty*, disgusting, evil, filthy, foul, gross, heinous, hideous, horrible, immodest, improper, impure, lascivious, lewd, licentious, loathsome, loose*, lustful, nasty, noisome, outrageous, porno*, pornographic, profane, prurient, rank*, raunchy*, raw, repellent, repugnant, ribald, salacious, scabrous, scatological, scurrilous, shameless, shocking, sickening, smutty*, suggestive, unchaste, unclean, unwholesome, vile, wanton, wicked, X-rated*; SEE CONCEPTS *267, 372,545*

obscenity [*n*] *indecency, immorality; vulgarism*
abomination, affront, atrocity, bawdiness, blight, blueness*, coarseness, curse, dirtiness, dirty name*, dirty word*, evil, filthiness, foulness, four-letter word*, immodesty, impropriety, impurity, indecency, indelicacy, lewdness, licentiousness, lubricity, offense, outrage, porn*, pornography, profanity, prurience, salacity, scatology, scurrility, sleaze*, smut*, smuttiness, suggestiveness, swearword, vileness, vulgarity, wrong, X-rating*; SEE CONCEPTS *278,645*

obscure [*adj1*] *not easily understood*
abstruse, ambiguous, arcane, clear as mud*, complicated, concealed, confusing, cryptic, dark, deep, dim, doubtful, enigmatic, enigmatical, esoteric, far-out, hazy, hidden, illegible, illogical, impenetrable, incomprehensible, inconceivable, incredible, indecisive, indefinite, indeterminate, indistinct, inexplicable, inscrutable, insoluble, intricate, involved, mysterious, occult, opaque, recondite, unaccountable, unbelievable, unclear, undefined, unfathomable, unintelligible, vague; SEE CONCEPT *529*

obscure [*adj2*] *cloudy, shadowy*
blurred, caliginous, clouded, dark, dense, dim, dusk, dusky, faint, fuliginous, gloomy, indistinct, lightless, murky, obfuscated, shady, somber, tenebrous, umbrageous, unilluminated, unlit, veiled; SEE CONCEPT *617*

obscure [*adj3*] *out-of-the-way, little-known*
abstruse, arcane, blind, cabalistic, close, covered, cryptic, dark, deep, devious, distant, enigmatic, esoteric, far, far-off, hidden, humble, inaccessible, inconspicuous, inglorious, invisible, irrelevant, lonesome, lowly, minor, mysterious, nameless, odd, oracular, orphic, rare, recondite, remote, removed, reticent, retired, secluded, secret, secretive, seldom seen, sequestered, solitary, undisclosed, undistin-

guished, unheard-of, unhonored, unimportant, unknown, unnoted, unseen, unsung; SEE CONCEPT *576*

obscure [*v*] *conceal, hide*
adumbrate, becloud, bedim, befog, belie, blear, blind, block, block out, blur, camouflage, cloak, cloud, cloud the issue*, con, conceal, confuse, cover, cover up, darken, dim, disguise, double-talk*, eclipse, equivocate, falsify, fog, fuzz, gloom, gray, haze, mask, misrepresent, mist, muddy, muddy the waters*, murk, obfuscate, overcast, overcloud, overshadow, pettifog*, screen, shade, shadow, shroud, stonewall*, throw up smoke screen*, veil, wrap; SEE CONCEPTS *16,63,172,188*

obsequious [*adj*] *groveling, submissive*
abject, beggarly, brownnosing*, complacent, compliable, compliant, cringing, crouching, deferential, enslaved, fawning, flattering, ingratiating, kowtowing*, menial, obeisant, oily*, parasitic, parasitical, prostrate, respectful, servile, slavish, sneaking, sniveling, spineless*, stipendiary, subject, submissive, subordinate, subservient, sycophantic, toadying*, unctuous; SEE CONCEPTS *401,404*

observable [*adj*] *apparent*
appreciable, clear, detectable, discernible, discoverable, evident, noticeable, obvious, open, palpable, patent, perceivable, perceptible, recognizable, sensible, tangible, visible; SEE CONCEPTS *529,576*

observance [*n1*] *attention to, knowledge of something*
acknowledgment, acquittal, acquittance, adherence, awareness, carrying out, celebration, cognizance, compliance, discharge, fidelity, fulfillment, heed, heeding, honoring, keeping, mark, mind, note, notice, obedience, observation, performance, regard, remark, satisfaction; SEE CONCEPTS *409,410,633*

observance [*n2*] *ceremony, rite*
celebration, ceremonial, custom, fashion, form, formality, liturgy, performance, practice, ritual, rule, service, tradition; SEE CONCEPTS *377,384,687*

observant [*adj*] *alert, watchful*
advertent, alive, attentive, bright, clear-sighted*, comprehending, considering, contemplating, correct, deducing, detecting, discerning, discovering, discriminating, eager, eagle-eyed*, heedful, intelligent, intentive, interested, keen, mindful, not missing a trick*, obedient, observative, on one's toes*, on the ball*, penetrating, perceptive, questioning, quick, regardful, searching, sensitive, sharp, sharp-eyed*, surveying, understanding, vigilant, wide-awake*; SEE CONCEPTS *402,403*

observation [*n1*] *attention, scrutiny*
ascertainment, check, cognition, cognizance, conclusion, consideration, detection, estimation, examination, experience, heedfulness, information, inspection, investigation, knowledge, mark, measurement, mind, monitoring, note, notice, noticing, once-over*, overlook, perception, probe, recognizing, regard, remark, research, review, search, study, supervision, surveillance, view, watching; SEE CONCEPTS *409,410*

observation [n2] *comment on something scrutinized*
annotation, catch phrase, comeback, commentary, crack*, finding, mention, mouthful*, note, obiter dictum, opinion, pronouncement, reflection, remark, saying, say so*, thought, utterance, wisecrack; SEE CONCEPTS *51,278*

observe [v1] *see, notice*
beam, behold, catch, contemplate, detect, dig, discern, discover, distinguish, eagle-eye*, espy, examine, eyeball*, flash*, get a load of*, get an eyeful of*, inspect, keep one's eye on*, lamp*, look at, make out*, mark, mind, monitor, note, pay attention to, perceive, pick up on*, read, recognize, regard, scrutinize, spot, spy, study, survey, take in*, view, watch, witness; SEE CONCEPTS *24,34,103,265,626*

observe [v2] *comment, remark*
animadvert, commentate, declare, mention, mouth off*, note, opine, say, state, wisecrack; SEE CONCEPT *51*

observe [v3] *celebrate, commemorate*
dedicate, hold, honor, keep, remember, respect, revere, reverence, solemnize, venerate; SEE CONCEPT *377*

observe [v4] *abide by, obey*
adhere, adopt, comply, comply with, conform, follow, fulfill, heed, honor, keep, mind, perform, respect; SEE CONCEPTS *91,384*

obsessed [adj] *consumed, driven about belief, desire*
bedeviled, beset, bewitched, captivated, controlled, dogged*, dominated, eat sleep and breathe*, engrossed, fiendish, fixated, gripped, harassed, haunted, have on the brain*, held, hooked, hung up on*, immersed in, infatuated, into*, overpowered, plagued*, possessed, preoccupied, prepossessed, really into*, seized, taken over, tied up*, tormented, troubled, turned on, up to here in*, wound up with*, wrapped up in*; SEE CONCEPTS *403,404*

obsession [n] *fixation; consumption with belief, desire*
attraction, ax to grind*, bug in ear*, case*, complex, compulsion, concrete idea, craze*, crush, delusion, enthusiasm, fancy, fascination, fetish, hang-up*, idée fixe, infatuation, mania, monkey*, must, neurosis, one-track mind*, passion, phantom, phobia, preoccupation, something on the brain*, thing*, tiger by the tail*; SEE CONCEPTS *20,410,529,689,690*

obsolete [adj] *no longer in use, in vogue*
anachronistic, ancient, antediluvian, antiquated, antique, archaic, bygone, dated, dead, dead and gone*, dinosaur*, discarded, disused, done for*, dusty, extinct, fossil, gone, had it*, has-been*, horse and buggy*, kaput*, moldy*, moth-eaten*, old, old-fashioned, old-hat, old-school, out*, outmoded, out-of-date, out-of-fashion, outworn, passé, stale, superannuated, superseded, timeworn, unfashionable; SEE CONCEPTS *539,560,589*

obstacle [n] *impediment, barrier*
bar, block, booby trap*, bump*, catch, Catch-22*, check, clog*, crimp*, difficulty, disincentive, encumbrance, hamper, handicap, hang-up*, hardship, hindrance, hitch*, hurdle, interference, interruption, joker*, monkey wrench*, mountain, obstruction, restriction, rub*, snag, stumbling block*, traverse, vicissitude; SEE CONCEPTS *470,532,666,674*

obstinate [adj] *stubborn, determined*
adamant, cantankerous, contradictory, contrary, contumacious, convinced, dead set on*, dogged, dogmatic, firm, hard, hardened, headstrong, heady, immovable, indomitable, inflexible, intractable, intransigent, locked in*, mulish*, obdurate, opinionated, opinionative, persistent, pertinacious, perverse, pigheaded*, recalcitrant, refractory, relentless, resolved, restive, self-willed, steadfast, strong-minded, tenacious, unalterable, unflinching, unmanageable, unyielding, willful; SEE CONCEPTS *401,542*

obstruct [v] *prevent, restrict*
arrest, bar, barricade, block, check, choke, clog, close, congest, crab, curb, cut off, drag one's feet*, fill, foul up, frustrate, get in the way*, hamper, hamstring*, hang up*, hide, hinder, hold up, impede, inhibit, interfere, interrupt, mask, monkey with*, obscure, occlude, plug, restrain, retard, sandbag*, shield, shut off, slow down, stall, stonewall*, stop, stopper, stymie*, terminate, throttle, thwart, trammel, weigh down; SEE CONCEPTS *5,121,130*

obstruction [n] *obstacle, impediment*
bar, barricade, barrier, block, blockage, blocking, booby trap*, check, checkmate*, circumvention, difficulty, gridlock*, hamper, hindrance, hurdle, interference, jam*, lock, monkey wrench*, mountain*, restraint, roadblock*, snag, stop, stoppage, stumbling block*, trammel, trouble, wall; SEE CONCEPTS *470,532,666,674*

obtain [v] *get, acquire*
access, accomplish, achieve, annex, attain, beg borrow or steal*, capture, chalk up*, collect, come by, compass, cop*, corral, drum up*, earn, effect, fetch, gain, gather, get at, get hold of*, get one's hands on*, glean, gobble up*, grab, have, hoard, inherit, invade, lay up, make use of, nab*, occupy, pick up, pocket*, procure, purchase, reach, realize, reap, receive, recover, retrieve, salvage, save, score, scrape together, scrape up, secure, seize, snag, take, wangle, win; SEE CONCEPT *120*

obtainable [adj] *achievable, available*
at hand*, attainable, derivable, duck soup*, gettable, in stock, no problem*, no sweat*, on deck*, on offer*, on tap*, piece of cake*, procurable, purchasable, pushover, ready, realizable, securable, there for the taking*, to be had*; SEE CONCEPTS *528,576*

obtrusive [adj] *pushy, obvious*
bulging, busy, forward, impertinent, importunate, interfering, intrusive, jutting, meddlesome, meddling, nosy, noticeable, officious, presumptuous, projecting, prominent, protruding, protuberant, prying, sticking out; SEE CONCEPTS *401,542*

obtuse [*adj1*] *stupid*
dense, dopey*, dull*, dumb, imperceptive, insensitive, opaque, retarded, slow on uptake*, stolid, thick, uncomprehending, unintelligent; SEE CONCEPT *402*

obtuse [*adj2*] *blunt, not sharp*
round, rounded; SEE CONCEPTS *485,486*

obviate [*v*] *make unnecessary*
anticipate, avert, block, counter, counteract, deter, do away with, forestall, forfend, hinder, interfere, interpose, intervene, preclude, prevent, remove, restrain, rule out, stave off, ward; SEE CONCEPT *121*

obvious [*adj*] *apparent, understandable*
accessible, barefaced, bright, clear, clear as a bell*, conclusive, conspicuous, discernible, distinct, distinguishable, evident, explicit, exposed, glaring, indisputable, in evidence, lucid, manifest, noticeable, observable, open, overt, palpable, patent, perceivable, perceptible, plain, precise, prominent, pronounced, public, recognizable, self-evident, self-explanatory, standing out, straightforward, transparent, unconcealed, undeniable, undisguised, unmistakable, unsubtle, visible; SEE CONCEPTS *485,529*

occasion [*n1*] *chance*
break*, convenience, demand, excuse, incident, instant, moment, need, occurrence, opening, opportunity, possibility, season, shot*, show, time, use; SEE CONCEPT *693*

occasion [*n2*] *reason, cause*
antecedent, basis, call, circumstance, determinant, excuse, foundation, ground, grounds, incident, inducement, influence, justification, motivation, motive, necessity, obligation, prompting, provocation, purpose, right, warrant; SEE CONCEPT *661*

occasion [*n3*] *event, happening*
affair, celebration, circumstance, episode, experience, go*, goings-on*, happening, incident, instant, milepost*, milestone*, moment, occurrence, scene, thing*, time, while; SEE CONCEPTS *2,386*

occasion [*v*] *make happen, bring about*
breed, cause, create, do, effect, elicit, engender, evoke, generate, give rise to, hatch, induce, influence, inspire, lead to, move, muster, originate, persuade, produce, prompt, provoke, work up; SEE CONCEPTS *68,242*

occasional [*adj*] *irregular, sporadic*
casual, desultory, especial, exceptional, exclusive, few, incidental, infrequent, intermittent, not habitual, odd, off and on*, particular, random, rare, scarce, seldom, semioccasional, special, specific, sporadic, uncommon, unfrequent, unusual; SEE CONCEPTS *530,541*

occasionally [*adv*] *every now and then*
at intervals, at random, at times, every so often, from time to time, hardly, infrequently, irregularly, now and again, once in a blue moon*, once in a while, once or twice*, on occasion, periodically, seldom, sometimes, sporadically, uncommonly; SEE CONCEPTS *530,541*

occlude [*v*] *block, prevent*
choke, clog, close, close out, congest, curb, fill, hinder, impede, leave out, lock out, obstruct, plug, seal, shut, stopper, stop up, throttle; SEE CONCEPTS *121,201*

occult [*adj*] *mysterious, secret; supernatural*
abstruse, acroamatic, arcane, cabalistic, concealed, deep, eerie, esoteric, hermetic, hidden, invisible, magic, magical, mystic, mystical, obscure, orphic, preternatural, profound, psychic, recondite, transmundane, unearthly, unknown, unrevealed, veiled, weird; SEE CONCEPTS *576,582*

occupancy [*n*] *residence of place*
control, deed, habitation, holding, inhabitance, inhabitancy, occupation, ownership, possession, retention, settlement, tenancy, tenure, term, title, use; SEE CONCEPTS *518,710*

occupant [*n*] *person who resides in a place*
addressee, denizen, dweller, holder, householder, incumbent, indweller, inhabitant, inmate, lessee, occupier, possessor, renter, resident, resider, tenant, user; SEE CONCEPT *414*

occupation [*n1*] *profession, business*
activity, affair, calling, chosen work, craft, daily grind*, day gig*, do, dodge*, employment, game*, grindstone*, hang*, job, lick*, line, line of work, métier, moonlight*, nine-to-five*, play*, post, pursuit, racket*, rat race*, slot*, thing*, trade, vocation, walk of life*, what one is into*, work; SEE CONCEPTS *349,351,360*

occupation [*n2*] *control, possession*
habitation, holding, inhabitancy, inhabitation, occupancy, ownership, residence, settlement, tenancy, tenure, title, use; SEE CONCEPTS *518,710*

occupation [*n3*] *seizure, takeover*
attack, capture, conquest, entering, foreign rule, invasion, subjugation; SEE CONCEPTS *86,90,320*

occupied [*adj1*] *busy*
active, clocked up*, employed, engaged, engrossed, head over heels*, tied up*, too much on plate*, working; SEE CONCEPT *542*

occupied [*adj2*] *inhabited; in use*
busy, engaged, full, leased, lived-in*, peopled*, populated, populous, rented, settled, taken, unavailable, utilized; SEE CONCEPT *560*

occupy [*v1*] *be busy with*
absorb, amuse, attend, be active with, be concerned with, busy, divert, employ, engage, engross, entertain, fill, hold attention, immerse, interest, involve, keep busy, keep occupied, monopolize, preoccupy, soak, take up, tie up, utilize; SEE CONCEPTS *7,17,19,22*

occupy [*v2*] *reside; use*
be established, be in command, be in residence, cover, dwell, ensconce, establish, fill, hold, inhabit, involve, keep, live in, maintain, own, people, per-

meate, pervade, populate, possess, remain, sit, stay, take up, tenant, utilize; SEE CONCEPTS *225,226*

occupy [*v3*] *seize, take over*
capture, conquer, garrison, hold, invade, keep, obtain, overrun, take possession; SEE CONCEPTS *86,90,320*

occur [*v1*] *take place, happen*
action, appear, arise, befall, be found, be present, betide, chance, come about, come off*, come to pass, cook*, crop up, develop, ensue, eventualize, eventuate, exist, follow, go, jell*, manifest, materialize, obtain, present itself, result, shake*, show, smoke*, take place, transpire, turn out, turn up; SEE CONCEPTS *4,242*

occur [*v2*] *come to mind*
come to one*, cross one's mind*, dawn on*, expose, flash*, go through one's head*, hit, offer itself, present itself, reveal, spring to mind*, strike, suggest itself; SEE CONCEPTS *34,43*

occurrence [*n*] *happening, development*
accident, adventure, affair, appearance, circumstance, condition, contingency, emergency, episode, event, exigency, existence, incidence, incident, instance, juncture, manifestation, materialization, occasion, pass, piece, proceeding, routine, scene, situation, state, thing*, transaction, transpiration; SEE CONCEPTS *4,230,696*

ocean [*n*] *very large body of water*
blue*, bounding main*, brine, briny*, briny deep*, Davy Jones's locker*, deep, drink*, high seas*, main, pond, puddle, salt water, sea, seaway, Seven Seas, sink, tide; SEE CONCEPT *514*

odd/oddball [*adj1*] *unusual, abnormal*
atypical, avant-garde, bizarre, character, crazy, curious, deviant, different, eccentric, erratic, exceptional, extraordinary, fantastic, flaky*, freak*, freakish*, freaky*, funny, idiosyncratic, irregular, kinky*, kooky*, offbeat, off-the-wall*, outlandish, out of the ordinary, peculiar, quaint, queer, rare, remarkable, singular, spacey*, strange, uncanny, uncommon, unconventional, unique, unusual, way out*, weird, weirdo*, whimsical; SEE CONCEPTS *404,542,564*

odd [*adj2*] *miscellaneous, various*
accidental, casual, chance, contingent, different, fluky*, fortuitous, fragmentary, incidental, irregular, occasional, odd-lot*, periodic, random, seasonal, sundry, varied; SEE CONCEPT *552*

odd [*adj3*] *single, unmatched; uneven*
additional, alone, exceeding, individual, irregular, left, leftover, lone, lonely, over, over and above, remaining, singular, sole, solitary, spare, surplus, unconsumed, unitary, unpaired; SEE CONCEPTS *480,577*

oddity [*n1*] *abnormality*
anomaly, bizarreness, characteristic, conversation piece, curiosity, eccentricity, extraordinariness, freak, freakishness, idiosyncrasy, incongruity, irreg-

ularity, kink, oddness, outlandishness, peculiarity, phenomenon, queerness, quirk, rarity, singularity, strangeness, unconventionality, unnaturalness; SEE CONCEPTS *260,411,665*

oddity/oddball [*n2*] *person who is very different*
case*, character, duck*, eccentric, fish out of water*, maverick, misfit, odd bird*, original*, rara avis*, screwball*, weirdo*; SEE CONCEPT *423*

odds [*n1*] *advantage*
allowance, benefit, bulge, difference, disparity, dissimilarity, distinction, draw, edge, handicap, head start, lead, overlay, start, superiority, vantage; SEE CONCEPT *693*

odds [*n2*] *probability*
balance, chances, favor, likelihood, superiority, tossup; SEE CONCEPT *650*

odds and ends [*n*] *miscellaneous paraphernalia*
assortment, bits, bits and pieces*, debris, et cetera*, hodgepodge, jumble, leavings, litter, medley, mélange, melee, miscellany, motley, oddments, olio, particles, potpourri, remnants, rest, rubbish, rummage, scraps, sundry items, this and that*; SEE CONCEPTS *260,432,446*

odious [*adj*] *hateful, horrible*
abhorrent, abominable, creepy*, detestable, disgusting, execrable, foul, hatable, horrid, loathsome, mean, obnoxious, offensive, ornery, pain in the neck*, repellent, repugnant, repulsive, revolting, unpleasant, vile; SEE CONCEPTS *401,404*

odium [*n*] *shame, dishonor*
abhorrence, antipathy, aversion, bar sinister*, black eye*, blame, blot, blur, brand, censure, condemnation, detestation, disapproval, discredit, disesteem, disfavor, disgrace, dislike, disspprobation, disrepute, enmity, execration, hate, hatred, ignominy, infamy, malice, obloquy, onus, opprobrium, rebuke, reprobation, resentment, shame, slur, spot, stain, stigma; SEE CONCEPTS *29,388*

odor [*n*] *scent*
air, aroma, bouquet, effluvium, efflux, emanation, essence, exhalation, flavor, fragrance, musk, perfume, pungence, pungency, redolence, smell, snuff, stench, stink, tang, tincture, trail, whiff; SEE CONCEPT *599*

odorless [*adj*] *without fragrance*
deodorant, deodorizing, flat, inodorous, odor-free, unaromatic, unfragrant, unperfumed, unscented, unsmelling; SEE CONCEPT *598*

odorous [*adj*] *having fragrance*
aromatic, balmy, dank, effluvious, fetid, flavorsome, flowery, foul, fragrant, heady, honeyed, loud, malodorous, mephitic, miasmic, moldy, musty, nauseous, odoriferant, odoriferous, offensive, olfactive, olfactory, perfumatory, perfumed, perfumy, pungent, putrid, redolent, reeking, rotten, savorous, savory, scented, scentful, scent-laden, skunky*, smelly, spicy, stagnant, stale, stinking, strong,

sweet, sweet-scented, sweet-smelling, tumaceous, unsavory, whiffy*; SEE CONCEPT *598*

of course [*adv*] *as expected*
by all means, certainly, definitely, indeed, indubitably, naturally, obviously, surely, undoubtedly, without a doubt; *see concept 544*

off [*adj1*] *gone; remote*
absent, canceled, finished, inoperative, negligible, not employed, not on duty, on vacation, outside, postponed, slender, slight, slim, small, unavailable; SEE CONCEPT *552*

off [*adj2*] *below par*
bad, decomposed, disappointing, disheartening, displeasing, low-quality, mortifying, not up to par*, not up to snuff*, poor, quiet, rancid, rotten, slack, sour, substandard, turned, unrewarding, unsatisfactory; SEE CONCEPT *570*

off [*adv*] *apart, away*
above, absent, afar, ahead, aside, away from, behind, below, beneath, beside, disappearing, divergent, elsewhere, far, farther away, gone away, in the distance, not here, out, over, removed, to one side, turning aside, up front, vanishing; SEE CONCEPTS *583,778*

offbeat [*adj*] *strange, very different*
bizarre, bohemian*, eccentric, far-out, freaky, fresh, idiosyncratic, novel, oddball, outré, uncommon, unconventional, unique, unorthodox, unusual, way-out*, weird; SEE CONCEPT *564*

off-color [*adj*] *risqué*
blue*, indelicate, purple*, racy*, salty*, shady, suggestive, vulgar, wicked; SEE CONCEPT *545*

offend [*v*] *displease, insult*
affront, aggrieve, anger, annoy, antagonize, be disagreeable, disgruntle, disgust, disoblige, distress, disturb, exasperate, fret, gall, horrify, hurt, irritate, jar, miff, nauseate, nettle, outrage, pain, pique, provoke, repel, repulse, rile, shock, sicken, sin, slight, slur, snub, sting, transgress, trespass, turn one off*, upset, vex, wound, zing*; SEE CONCEPTS *7,14,19*

offense [*n1*] *violation, trespass*
breach, crime, delinquency, fault, infraction, lapse, malfeasance, misdeed, misdemeanor, peccadillo, sin, transgression, wrong, wrongdoing; SEE CONCEPTS *192,691*

offense [*n2*] *insult, displeasure*
affront, aggression, assailment, assault, attack, battery, black eye*, blitz*, blitzkrieg*, dig*, dirty dig*, harm, hit*, hurt, indignation, indignity, injury, injustice, left-handed compliment*, mugging, offensive, onset, onslaught, outrage, push*, put-down*, slam*, slap in the face*, slight, snub, zinger*; SEE CONCEPTS *52,278*

offense [*n3*] *anger, hard feelings*
annoyance, conniption*, displeasure, explosion, fit, flare-up*, huff, indignation, ire, miff, needle*, outburst, pique, resentment, scene, tantrum, tizzy*, umbrage, wounded feelings, wrath; SEE CONCEPT *410*

offensive [*n*] *attack*
aggression, assailment, assault, drive, invasion, onset, onslaught, push; SEE CONCEPTS *86,320*

offensive [*adj1*] *disrespectful, insulting; displeasing*
abhorrent, abusive, annoying, biting, cutting, detestable, disagreeable, discourteous, distasteful, dreadful, embarrassing, evil, foul, ghastly, grisly, gross, hideous, horrible, horrid, impertinent, insolent, invidious, irritating, nauseating, objectionable, obnoxious, odious, off-color*, offending, opprobrious, outrageous, repellent, reprehensible, repugnant, repulsive, revolting, rotten, rude, shocking, stinking*, terrible, uncivil, unmannerly; SEE CONCEPTS *267,529,537*

offensive [*adj2*] *attacking*
aggressive, assailing, assaulting, belligerent, invading; SEE CONCEPT *548*

offer [*n*] *proposal, suggestion*
action, attempt, bid, endeavor, essay, feeler*, hit*, overture, pass*, pitch*, presentation, proposition, propoundment, rendition, submission, tender; SEE CONCEPTS *66,67,278*

offer [*v1*] *present, propose for acceptance*
accord, advance, afford, allow, award, be at service, bid, come forward, display, donate, exhibit, extend, furnish, give, grant, hold out, lay at one's feet*, make available, move, place at disposal*, ply, pose, press, proffer, propound, provide, put forth, put forward, put on the market, put up, put up for sale, sacrifice, show, submit, suggest, tender, volunteer; SEE CONCEPT *67*

offer [*v2*] *propose*
adduce, advance, advise, allege, cite, make a motion, make a pitch*, present, proposition, submit, suggest; SEE CONCEPT *66*

offer [*v3*] *try*
assay, attempt, endeavor, essay, seek, strive, struggle, undertake; SEE CONCEPT *87*

offering [*n*] *donation*
alms, atonement, benefaction, beneficence, charity, contribution, expiation, gift, oblation, present, sacrifice, subscription; SEE CONCEPTS *337,340*

offhand [*adj1*] *abrupt, careless*
aloof, breezy, brusque, casual, cavalier, cool*, curt, easygoing, folksy, glib, informal, laid-back, mellow, perfunctory, unceremonious, unconcerned, uninterested; SEE CONCEPTS *267,401,542*

offhand [*adj2/adv*] *ad-lib, extemporaneous*
extemporary, extempore, impromptu, improvised, informal, off the cuff*, off the hip*, off the top of head*, spontaneous, spur-of-the-moment*, throwaway*, unpremeditated, unprepared, unrehearsed, unstudied, without preparation; SEE CONCEPT *267*

office [*n1*] *business, responsibility*
appointment, berth, billet, capacity, charge, commission, connection, duty, employment, function, job, obligation, occupation, performance, place, post, province, responsibility, role, service, situation,

spot, station, trust, work; SEE CONCEPTS *351,362,376*

office [*n2*] *place of business*
agency, building, bureau, cave, center, department, facility, factory, foundry, room, salt mines*, setup, shop, store, suite, warehouse, workstation; SEE CONCEPTS *312,439,441,448,449*

officer [*n1*] *person who has high position in organization*
administrator, agent, appointee, bureaucrat, chief, civil servant, deputy, dignitary, director, executive, functionary, head, leader, magistrate, manager, officeholder, official, president, public servant, representative; SEE CONCEPT *347*

officer [*n2*] *person in law enforcement*
arm*, badge*, black and white*, captain, cop*, deputy, detective, flatfoot*, mounty, police, policeman/woman, sergeant, sheriff; SEE CONCEPTS *354, 355,358*

official [*n*] *person representing organization*
administrator, agent, big shot*, boss, brains*, brass*, bureaucrat, CEO*, chancellor, civil servant, commissioner, comptroller, dignitary, director, exec*, executive, front office*, functionary, governor, head man/woman, higher-up*, incumbent, leader, magistrate, manager, marshal, mayor, minister, officeholder, officer, panjandrum, premier, president, representative, secretary, top*, top brass*, top dog*, top drawer*, treasurer; SEE CONCEPTS *347,354*

official [*adj*] *authorized, legitimate*
accredited, approved, authentic, authenticated, authoritative, bona fide*, canonical, cathedral, ceremonious, certified, cleared, conclusive, correct, customary, decided, decisive, definite, endorsed, established, ex cathedra*, ex officio*, fitting, formal, legitimate, licensed, okay*, ordered, orthodox, positive, precise, proper, real, recognized, rightful, sanctioned, suitable, true, valid; SEE CONCEPT *535*

officiate [*v*] *oversee, manage*
act, boss, chair, command, conduct, direct, do the honors*, emcee, function, govern, handle, preside, run, serve, superintend, umpire; SEE CONCEPT *117*

officious [*adj*] *self-important, dictatorial*
busy, forward, impertinent, inquisitive, interfering, intrusive, meddlesome, meddling, obtrusive, opinionated, overzealous, pragmatic, pushy, rude; SEE CONCEPT *404*

off-key [*adj*] *not harmonious*
abnormal, anomalous, clinker*, deviant, discordant, dissonant, divergent, inharmonious, irregular, jarring, out of keeping*, out of tune*, sour*, sour note*, unnatural; SEE CONCEPT *594*

offset [*v*] *counterbalance, compensate*
account, allow for, atone for, balance, be equivalent, cancel out, charge, counteract, counterpoise, counterpose, countervail, equal, equalize, equipoise, make amends, make up for, negate, neutralize, outweigh, recompense, redeem, requite, set off; SEE CONCEPTS *126,232*

offshoot [*n*] *development, product*
adjunct, appendage, branch, by-product, derivative, descendant, limb, outgrowth, spin-off, sprout; SEE CONCEPTS *260,824*

offspring [*n*] *child, children*
baby, bambino*, brood, chip off old block*, cub, descendant, family, generation, heir, heredity, issue, kid*, lineage, offshoot, posterity, produce, progeniture, progeny, pup*, scion, seed, spawn, succession, successor, young; SEE CONCEPTS *296,414*

often [*adv*] *frequently*
again and again, a number of times, generally, many a time, much, oftentimes, ofttimes, over and over, recurrently, regularly, repeatedly, time after time, time and again, usually; SEE CONCEPT *541*

ogre [*n*] *nasty person*
bogeyman*, demon, devil, fiend, giant, monster, monstrosity, specter, troll; SEE CONCEPT *412*

oil [*v*] *lubricate*
anoint, coat, grease, lard, lube, pomade, slick, smear; SEE CONCEPTS *172,256*

oily [*adj1*] *fatty, greasy*
adipose, buttery, creamy, lardy, lubricant, lubricative, lubricous, lustrous, oiled, oil-soaked, oleaginous, polished, rich, saponaceous, sleek, slippery, smeary, smooth, soapy, soothing, swimming, unctuous, waxy; SEE CONCEPTS *603,606*

oily [*adj2*] *flattering*
bland*, cajoling, coaxing, compliant, fulsome, glib, gushing*, hypocritical, ingratiating, insinuating, obsequious, plausible, servile, slick, smarmy*, smooth, smooth-tongued*, suave, supple, unctuous; SEE CONCEPTS *267,401*

ointment [*n*] *cream for treatment*
balm, cerate, demulcent, dressing, embrocation, emollient, lenitive, liniment, lotion, medicine, salve, unguent; SEE CONCEPTS *311,466*

okay [*n*] *agreement*
acceptance, affirmation, approbation, approval, assent, authorization, benediction, blessing, consent, endorsement, favor, go-ahead*, green light*, permission, sanction, say-so*, seal of approval*, yes; SEE CONCEPT *684*

okay [*adj*] *acceptable, satisfactory*
accurate, adequate, all right, approved, convenient, correct, fair, fine, good, in order, middling, not bad, passable, permitted, so-so*, surely, tolerable; SEE CONCEPT *558*

okay [*v*] *agree to*
accept, accredit, approve, authorize, certify, condone, confirm, consent to, endorse, give one's consent, give the go-ahead*, give the green light*, notarize, pass, rubber-stamp*, sanction, say yes to; SEE CONCEPTS *10,50,88*

old [*adj1*] *advanced in age*
aged, along in years*, ancient, broken down*, debilitated, decrepit, deficient, doddering, elderly, enfeebled, exhausted, experienced, fossil*, geriatric,

getting on*, gray, gray-haired*, grizzled*, hoary*, impaired, inactive, infirm, mature, matured, not young, olden, oldish, over the hill*, past one's prime*, patriarchal, seasoned, senile, senior, skilled, superannuated, tired, venerable, versed, veteran, wasted*; SEE CONCEPTS *578,797*

old [*adj2*] *obsolete, outdated*
aboriginal, age-old, antediluvian, antiquated, antique, archaic, bygone, cast-off, crumbling, dated, decayed, demode, done, early, erstwhile, former, hackneyed*, immemorial, late, moth-eaten*, of old, of yore, olden, oldfangled, old-fashioned, old-time, once, onetime, original, outmoded, out-of-date, passé, past, primeval, primitive, primordial, pristine, quondam, relic, remote, rusty, sometime, stale, superannuated, time-worn, traditional, unfashionable, unoriginal, venerable, worn-out; SEE CONCEPTS *558,560,799*

old [*adj3*] *traditional, long-established*
age-old, constant, continuing, enduring, established, experienced, familiar, firm, hardened, inveterate, lifelong, long-lasting, long-lived, of long standing, perennial, perpetual, practiced, skilled, solid, staying, steady, time-honored, versed, veteran, vintage; SEE CONCEPTS *482,530,798*

old age [*n*] *latter part of animate life*
advancing years*, age, agedness, autumn of life*, caducity, debility, declining years*, decrepitude, dotage, elderliness, evening of life*, feebleness, golden age*, golden years*, infirmity, second childhood*, senectitude, senescence, senility, years; SEE CONCEPTS *715,817*

older [*adj*] *most senior*
earlier, elder, eldest, first, first-born, former, lower, of a former period, of an earlier time, preceding, prior, senior; SEE CONCEPTS *578,585,797*

old-fashioned [*adj*] *outmoded, obsolete*
ancient, antiquated, antique, archaic, behind the times*, bygone, corny*, dated, dead*, demode, demoded, disapproved, dowdy*, extinct, grown old, moldy*, musty, neglected, not current, not modern, not with it*, obsolescent, odd*, of old, of olden days*, of the old school*, olden, old-fangled*, old-hat*, old-time, out*, outdated, out-of-date, out of it*, out-of-style, outworn, passé*, past, primitive, rococo*, superannuated, unfashionable, unstylish, vintage; SEE CONCEPTS *578,589,797,799*

old hand [*n*] *person very experienced in something*
expert, longtimer, master, mistress, old guard*, old school*, old-timer*, past master, vet*, veteran; SEE CONCEPT *423*

omen [*n*] *sign of something to come*
augury, auspice, bodement, boding, foreboding, foretoken, harbinger, indication, portent, premonition, presage, prognostic, prognostication, prophecy, straw, warning, writing on the wall*; SEE CONCEPTS *74,278,689*

ominous [*adj*] *menacing, foreboding*
apocalyptic, augural, baleful, baneful, clouded, dangerous, dark, dire, direful, dismal, doomed, doomful, fateful, fearful, forbidding, gloomy, grim, haunting, hostile, ill-boding, ill-fated, impending, inauspicious, inhospitable, lowering, malefic, malificent, malign, minatory, perilous, portentous, precursive, premonitory, presaging, prescient, prophetic, sinister, suggestive, threatening, unfriendly, unlucky, unpromising, unpropitious; SEE CONCEPT *548*

omission [*n*] *something forgotten or excluded*
blank, breach, break, cancellation, carelessness, chasm, cutting out, default, disregard, disregardance, elimination, elision, excluding, exclusion, failing, failure, forgetfulness, gap, hiatus, ignoring, inadvertence, inadvertency, lack, lacuna, lapse, leaving out, missing, neglect, noninclusion, overlook, overlooking, oversight, passing over, preclusion, preterition, pretermission, prohibition, repudiation, skip, slighting, slip, withholding; SEE CONCEPTS *25,116,699*

omit [*v*] *exclude, forget*
bar, blink at*, bypass, cancel, cast aside, count out, cut, cut out, delete, discard, dismiss, disregard, drop, edit, eliminate, evade, except, exclude, fail, ignore, knock off, leave out, leave undone, let go, let slide*, miss, miss out, neglect, overlook, overpass, pass by, pass over, preclude, prohibit, reject, repudiate, skip, slight, snip, trim, void, withhold, X-out*; SEE CONCEPTS *25,121,211*

omnipotent [*adj*] *all-powerful*
almighty, divine, godlike, mighty, supreme, unlimited, unrestricted; SEE CONCEPT *574*

omniscient [*adj*] *all-knowing*
all-seeing, almighty, infinite, knowledgeable, pansophical, preeminent, wise; SEE CONCEPT *402*

on [*adv*] *in contact; ahead of*
about, above, adjacent, against, approaching, at, beside, close to, covering, forth, forward, held, leaning on, near, next, on top of, onward, over, resting on, situated on, supported, touching, toward, upon, with; SEE CONCEPTS *585,586,750*

once [*adj/adv*] *in the past; occurred one time only*
already, a single time, at one time, away back, back, back when, before, but once, bygone, earlier, erstwhile, formerly, heretofore, in the old days, in the olden days, in times gone by, in times past, late, long ago, old, once only, once upon a time, one, one time before, one time previously, only one time, on one occasion, previously, quondam, sometime, this time, time was, whilom; SEE CONCEPTS *799,820*

oncoming [*adj*] *impending*
advancing, approaching, coming, expected, forthcoming, imminent, looming, nearing, onrushing, upcoming; SEE CONCEPTS *548,799*

one [*adj*] *individual*
alone, definite, different, lone, odd, one and only, only, particular, peculiar, precise, separate, single,

singular, sole, solitary, special, specific, uncommon, unique; SEE CONCEPTS *577,762,789*

onerous [*adj*] *very difficult; requiring hard labor*
arduous, austere, backbreaking, burdensome, crushing, cumbersome, demanding, difficult, distressing, embittering, exacting, excessive, exhausting, exigent, fatiguing, formidable, galling, grave, grinding, grueling, hard*, harsh, headache, heavy*, intolerable, irksome, laborious, merciless, oppressive, overpowering, overtaxing, painful, plodding, ponderous, pressing, responsible, rigorous, serious, severe, strenuous, taxing, tiresome, tiring, toilsome, troublesome, vexatious, weighty; SEE CONCEPTS *538,565*

ongoing [*adj*] *continuous*
advancing, continuing, current, developing, evolving, extant, growing, heading, in process, in progress, marching, open-ended, progressing, successful, unfinished, unfolding; SEE CONCEPTS *482,798*

onlooker [*n*] *person observing an event*
beholder, bystander, eyewitness, looker-on, observer, sightseer, spectator, viewer, watcher, witness; SEE CONCEPT *423*

only [*adj*] *singular*
alone, apart, by oneself, exclusive, individual, isolated, lone, matchless, once in a lifetime, one, one and only, one shot, onliest, particular, peerless, single, sole, solitary, solo, unaccompanied, unequaled, unique, unparalleled, unrivaled; SEE CONCEPT *577*

only [*adv*] *barely; exclusively*
alone, at most, but, entirely, hardly, just, merely, nothing but, particularly, plainly, purely, simply, solely, totally, uniquely, utterly, wholly; SEE CONCEPTS *535,772*

onset [*n*] *beginning; attack*
access, aggression, assailment, assault, birth, charge, commencement, dawn, dawning, encounter, inception, incipience, kickoff*, offense, offensive, onfall, onrush, onslaught, opening, origin, outbreak, outset, outstart, rush, seizure, start; SEE CONCEPTS *86, 221,832*

onslaught [*n*] *attack*
aggression, assailment, assault, blitz, charge, incursion, invasion, offense, offensive, onfall, onrush, onset; SEE CONCEPT *86*

onus [*n*] *burden*
bar sinister*, black eye*, blame, blot, blur, brand, charge, culpability, deadweight*, duty, encumbrance, fault, guilt, incubus, liability, load, millstone*, obligation, odium, oppression, responsibility, slur, spot, stain, stigma, task, tax, weight; SEE CONCEPTS *388,674*

onward/onwards [*adv*] *ahead, beyond*
alee, along, forth, forward, in front, in front of, moving, on, on ahead; SEE CONCEPTS *585,778*

ooze [*n*] *liquid emitted*
alluvium, fluid, glop*, goo*, gook*, gunk*, mire, muck*, mud, silt, slime*, sludge; SEE CONCEPTS *466,467*

ooze [*v*] *emit liquid*
bleed, discharge, drain, dribble, drip, drop, escape, exude, filter, flow, issue, leach, leak, overflow, percolate, perspire, seep, spurt, strain, sweat, swelter, trickle, weep, well; SEE CONCEPT *179*

opaque [*adj1*] *clouded, muddy*
blurred, cloudy, dark, darkened, dim, dirty, dull, dusky, filmy, foggy, frosty, fuliginous, gloomy, hazy, impenetrable, lusterless, misty, muddied, murky, nontranslucent, nontransparent, nubilous, obfuscated, shady, smoky, sooty, thick, turbid; SEE CONCEPTS *606,617,618*

opaque [*adj2*] *hard to understand*
abstruse, amphibological, arcane, baffling, concealed, cryptic, difficult, enigmatic, equivocal, imperceptive, incomprehensible, nubilous, obscure, obtuse, perplexing, purblind, tenebrous, uncertain, unclear, unfathomable, unintelligible, vague; SEE CONCEPT *529*

open [*adj1*] *unfastened, unclosed*
accessible, agape, airy, ajar, bare, clear, cleared, dehiscent, disclosed, emptied, expanded, expansive, exposed, extended, extensive, free, gaping, made passable, naked, navigable, passable, patent, patulous, peeled, removed, rent, revealed, ringent, rolling, spacious, spread out, stripped, susceptible, unbarred, unblocked, unbolted, unburdened, uncluttered, uncovered, unfolded, unfurled, unimpeded, unlocked, unobstructed, unplugged, unsealed, unshut, unstopped, vacated, wide, yawning; SEE CONCEPTS *485,576*

open [*adj2*] *accessible; not forbidden*
admissible, agreeable, allowable, approachable, appropriate, attainable, available, employable, fit, free, general, getable*, nondiscriminatory, not posted, obtainable, on deck*, on tap*, open-door*, operative, permitted, practicable, proper, public, reachable, securable, suitable, to be had*, unconditional, unoccupied, unqualified, unrestricted, usable, vacant, welcoming, within reach; SEE CONCEPTS *560,576*

open [*adj3*] *clear, obvious*
apparent, avowed, barefaced, blatant, conspicuous, downright, evident, flagrant, frank, manifest, noticeable, overt, plain, unconcealed, undisguised, visible, well-known; SEE CONCEPTS *267,535*

open [*adj4*] *undecided*
ambiguous, arguable, controversial, debatable, doubtful, dubious, dubitable, equivocal, indecisive, in question, moot, problematic, questionable, uncertain, unresolved, unsettled, up for discussion*, up in the air*, yet to be decided*; SEE CONCEPTS *267,529*

open [*adj5*] *honest, objective*
artless, candid, disinterested, fair, frank, free, guileless, impartial, ingenuous, innocent, lay it on the line*, mellow, natural, objective, on the level*, open-and-shut*, openhearted*, plain, receptive, sincere, straightforward, talking turkey*, transparent, unbiased, uncommitted, unconcealed, undisguised,

undissembled, unprejudiced, unreserved, up-front*;
SEE CONCEPTS *267,542*

open [*v1*] *begin*
begin business, bow, commence, convene, embark, get things rolling*, inaugurate, initiate, jump, kick off, launch, meet, raise the curtain*, ring in*, set in motion, set up shop*, sit, start, start the ball rolling*; SEE CONCEPT *221*

open [*v2*] *clear, breach, expose; spread*
bare, break in, break out, broach, burst, bust in, come apart, crack, disclose, display, disrupt, expand, fissure, free, gap, gape, hole, jimmy, kick in, lacerate, lance, penetrate, perforate, pierce, pop, puncture, release, reveal, rupture, separate, sever, slit, slot, split, tap, throw wide, unbar, unblock, unbolt, unclose, unclothe, uncork, uncover, undo, unfasten, unfold, unfurl, unlatch, unlock, unroll, unseal, unshut, unstop, untie, unwrap, vent, ventilate, yawn, yawp; SEE CONCEPTS *135,250,469*

opening [*n1*] *gap, hole*
aperture, breach, break, cavity, chink, cleft, crack, cranny, crevice, cut, discontinuity, door, fissure, hatch, interstice, mouth, orifice, outlet, perforation, recess, rent, rift, rupture, scuttle, slit, slot, space, split, spout, tear, vent, window; SEE CONCEPT *513*

opening [*n2*] *chance*
availability, big break*, connection, cut*, fling*, go*, go-at*, in the running*, iron in the fire*, look-in*, occasion, opportunity, place, possibility, run, scope, shot*, show, squeak*, time, vacancy, whack*; SEE CONCEPT *693*

opening [*n3*] *beginning*
birth, coming out, commencement, curtain-raiser*, dawn, inauguration, inception, initiation, kickoff, launch, launching, onset, opener, outset, start; SEE CONCEPT *832*

openly [*adv*] *honestly*
aboveboard, artlessly, blatantly, brazenly, candidly, face to face, flagrantly, forthrightly, frankly, fully, honestly, in broad daylight, in full view, ingenuously, in public, in the open, naively, naturally, plainly, publicly, readily, shamelessly, simply, straight, unabashedly, unashamedly, under one's nose*, unhesitatingly, unreservedly, wantonly, warts and all*, willingly, without pretense, without reserve; SEE CONCEPTS *267,544*

operate [*v1*] *perform, function*
accomplish, achieve, act, act on, advance, behave, be in action, bend, benefit, bring about, burn, carry on, click*, compel, complete, concern, conduct, contact, contrive, convey, cook*, determine, direct, do, enforce, engage, exert, finish, fulfill, get results, go, hit*, hum, influence, keep, lift, move, ordain, percolate, proceed, produce, produce a result, progress, promote, react, revolve, roll, run, serve, spin, take, tick, transport, turn, work; SEE CONCEPTS *91,680,706*

operate [*v2*] *manage, use*
administer, be in charge, be in driver's seat*, be in saddle*, call the play*, call the shots*, call the signals*, carry on, command, conduct, drive, handle, hold the reins*, keep, make go*, maneuver, manipulate, ordain, pilot, play, ply, pull the strings*, pull the wires*, run, run the show*, run things*, sit on top of*, steer, wield, work; SEE CONCEPTS *94, 117,148*

operate [*v3*] *perform surgery*
amputate, carve up, cut, excise, explore, open up, remove, set, transplant, treat; SEE CONCEPT *310*

operation [*n1*] *movement, working*
act, action, activity, affair, agency, application, ballgame*, bit, carrying on, conveyance, course, deal, deed, doing, effect, effort, employment, engagement, enterprise, exercise, exercising, exertion, exploitation, force, handiwork, happening, influence, instrumentality, labor, manipulation, motion, movement, performance, play, procedure, proceeding, process, progress, progression, scene, service, transaction, transference, trip, undertaking, use, work, workmanship; SEE CONCEPTS *658,680*

operation [*n2*] *business concern*
affair, deal, enterprise, going concern, proceeding, transaction, undertaking; SEE CONCEPTS *324,325*

operation [*n3*] *surgical procedure*
biopsy, excision, surgery; SEE CONCEPT *310*

operative [*adj*] *active, functioning; influential*
accessible, alive, crucial, current, dynamic, effective, efficient, employable, functional, important, indicative, in force, in operation, key, live, open, operational, practicable, relevant, running, serviceable, significant, standing, usable, workable, working; SEE CONCEPTS *560,567*

opinion [*n*] *belief*
assessment, assumption, attitude, conception, conclusion, conjecture, estimate, estimation, eye*, fancy, feeling, guess, hypothesis, idea, imagining, impression, inclination, inference, judgment, mind, notion, persuasion, point of view, postulate, presumption, presupposition, reaction, say-so*, sentiment, slant, speculation, supposition, surmise, suspicion, take*, theorem, theory, thesis, think*, thought, view, viewpoint; SEE CONCEPT *689*

opinionated [*adj*] *believing very strongly and conveying it*
adamant, arbitrary, assertive, biased, bigoted, bossy, bullheaded*, cocksure*, cocky*, conceited, dictatorial, doctrinaire, dogmatic, hard-line*, high-handed, inflexible, intransigent, locked in*, obdurate, obstinate, one-sided, oracular, overbearing, pigheaded*, positive, pragmatic, pragmatical, prejudiced, self-assertive, set in stone*, set-on, single-minded, stubborn, tilted, uncompromising, unyielding, weighted; SEE CONCEPTS *267,404*

opponent [*n*] *person with whom one competes*
adversary, antagonist, anti*, aspirant, assailant, bad guy*, bandit*, bidder, candidate, challenger, com-

petitor, con, contestant, counteragent, dark horse*, disputant, dissentient, enemy, entrant, foe, litigant, match, opposer, opposition, oppugnant, player, rival; SEE CONCEPT *366*

opportune [*adj*] *advantageous, lucky*
appropriate, apt, auspicious, convenient, favorable, felicitous, fit, fitting, fortuitous, fortunate, happy, helpful, pat, proper, propitious, seasonable, suitable, timely, timeous, well-timed; SEE CONCEPTS *548,572*

opportunity [*n*] *lucky chance; favorable circumstances*
befalling, break*, connection, contingency, convenience, cut*, event, excuse, fair shake*, fighting chance*, fitness, fling*, fortuity, freedom, go*, go at*, good fortune, good luck, happening, hope, hour, iron in the fire*, juncture, leisure, liberty, moment, occasion, one's move*, one's say*, one's turn*, opening, pass, prayer*, probability, relief, room, run, scope, shot*, show, space, spell, squeak, stab, the hunt*, the running*, time, turn, whack*; SEE CONCEPT *693*

oppose [*v1*] *fight, obstruct*
argue, assail, assault, attack, bar, battle, bombard, call in question, check, combat, confront, contradict, controvert, counter, counterattack, cross, debate, defy, deny, disagree, disapprove, dispute, encounter, expose, face, face down*, fight, fly in the face of*, frown at, gainsay, hinder, neutralize, not countenance, prevent, protest, resist, reverse, run counter to, search out, speak against, stand up to, take a stand, take issue, take on, taunt, thwart, turn the tables*, withstand; SEE CONCEPTS *21,54,106*

oppose [*v2*] *compare, play off*
array, confront, contrast, counter, counterbalance, face, match, pit, set against, vie; SEE CONCEPTS *73,363*

opposed/opposing [*adj*] *antagonistic, against*
against the grain*, allergic*, anti*, antipathetic, antithetical, antonymous, at cross-purposes, at odds, averse, battling, clashing, combating, conflicting, confronting, contrary, controverting, counter, crossing, defending, defensive, denying, disagreeing, disputed, disputing, dissentient, enemy, exposing, facing, gainsaying, hostile, incompatible, inimical, in opposition, irreconcilable, objecting, obstructive, opposite, protesting, repelling, restrictive, rival, up against, warring; SEE CONCEPTS *403,542,564*

opposite [*n*] *something completely unlike another*
adverse, antilogy, antipode, antipole, antithesis, antonym, contra*, contradiction, contrary, contrast, converse, counterpart, foil, inverse, obverse, opposition, other extreme*, other side*, other side of coin*, paradox, reverse, vice versa; SEE CONCEPT *665*

opposite [*adj*] *unlike, conflicting; completely different*
adverse, antagonistic, antipodal, antipodean, antithetical, contradictory, contrapositive, contrary, contrasted, corresponding, counter, crosswise, diametric, diametrically opposed, different, differing, dissimilar,

diverse, facing, flip-side*, fronting, hostile, inconsistent, independent, inimical, inverse, irreconcilable, obverse, opposed, ornery*, paradoxical, polar, repugnant, retrograde, reverse, reversed, separate, unalike, unconnected, unrelated, unsimilar, violative, vis-à-vis; SEE CONCEPT *564*

opposition [*n1*] *obstruction, antagonism*
action, antinomy, antithesis, aversion, brush, civil disobedience, clash, combat, competition, con, conflict, confronting, contention, contest, contradistinction, contraposition, contrariety, counteraction, counterattack, defense, defiance, disapproval, duel, encounter, engagement, fray, grapple, hostility, negativism, obstructiveness, opposure, oppugnancy, prevention, repugnance, repulsion, resistance, rivalry, skirmish, strife, struggle, unfriendliness, violation, war, warfare; SEE CONCEPTS *29,92,106,665*

opposition [*n2*] *person, people competing*
adversary, antagonist, bad guys*, disputant, enemy, foe, iconoclast, opponent, other side, rebel, rival; SEE CONCEPTS *348,366*

oppress [*v*] *depress, subdue*
abuse, afflict, aggrieve, annoy, beat down*, burden, crush, despotize, dishearten, dispirit, distress, encumber, force, handicap, harass, harry, hound*, keep down, maltreat, outrage, overcome, overload, overpower, overthrow, overwhelm, persecute, pick on, plague, press, prey on, put down, put screws to*, put the squeeze on*, put upon, ride, rule, sadden, saddle*, smother, strain, subjugate, suppress, tax, torment, torture, trample, trouble, tyrannize, vex, weigh heavy upon, worry, wrong; SEE CONCEPTS *7,14,19,133*

oppression [*n*] *misery, hardship*
abuse, abusiveness, autocracy, brutality, calamity, coercion, compulsion, conquering, control, cruelty, despotism, dictatorship, domination, fascism, force, forcibleness, hardness, harshness, injury, injustice, iron hand*, maltreatment, martial law, overthrowing, persecution, severity, subduing, subjection, suffering, torment, tyrany; SEE CONCEPTS *14,320,674*

oppressive [*adj1*] *overwhelming, repressive*
backbreaking*, bleak, brutal, burdensome, confining, cruel, demanding, depressing, depressive, despotic, dictatorial, discouraging, disheartening, dismal, dispiriting, exacting, exigent, gloomy, grievous, grinding, harsh, headache*, heavy, heavy-handed*, hefty, inhuman, ironhanded*, mean, onerous, overbearing, rough going*, severe, somber, superincumbent, taxing, tough, troublesome, tyrannical, unjust, weighty; SEE CONCEPTS *537,548*

oppressive [*adj2*] *hot and humid*
airless, close, heavy, muggy, overpowering, steam bath*, steamy, sticky, stifling, stuffy, suffocating, sultry, sweat box*, torrid; SEE CONCEPT *525*

opprobrious [*adj*] *abusive, hateful*
abasing, calumniatory, contemptuous, contumelious, damaging, debasing, defamatory, defaming, denigrat-

ing, depreciative, derogative, despicable, despiteful, detractive, disgracing, dishonoring, disparaging, humiliating, hurting, injuring, injurious, insolent, insulting, invective, libeling, malevolent, malign, malignant, maligning, notorious, offending, offensive, pejorative, reproaching, reviling, scandalous, scurrilous, shaming, spiteful, truculent, vile, vitriolic, vituperative, vulgar; SEE CONCEPTS *267,404,542*

opt [*v*] *choose*
cull, decide, elect, exercise choice, go for, make a selection, mark, pick, prefer, select, single out*, take; SEE CONCEPT *41*

optimism [*n*] *state of having positive beliefs*
anticipation, assurance, brightness, buoyancy, calmness, certainty, cheer, cheerfulness, confidence, easiness, elation, encouragement, enthusiasm, exhilaration, expectation, good cheer, happiness, hopefulness, idealism, looking on bright side*, positivism, rose-colored glasses*, sanguineness, sureness, trust; SEE CONCEPTS *410,689*

optimistic [*adj*] *believing positively*
assured, bright, buoyant, cheerful, cheering, confident, encouraged, expectant, happy, high, hopeful, hoping, idealistic, keeping the faith, merry, on cloud nine*, on top of world*, positive, promising, ray of sunshine*, rose-colored*, rosy, sanguine, sunny*, trusting, upbeat, Utopian; SEE CONCEPTS *404,542*

optimum [*adj*] *best*
24-carat*, A1*, ace, capital, choice, choicest, excellent, flawless, gilt-edge*, greatest, highest, ideal, matchless, maximum, most advantageous, most favorable, optimal, peak, peerless, perfect, select, solid gold*, superlative, world class*; SEE CONCEPT *574*

option [*n*] *alternative*
advantage, benefit, choice, claim, dibs*, dilemma, discretion, druthers, election, flipside*, franchise, free will*, grant, license, opportunity, other side of coin*, pickup, preference, prerogative, privilege, right, selection, take it or leave it*; SEE CONCEPTS *376,712*

optional [*adj*] *possible; available as choice*
alternative, arbitrary, discretional, discretionary, elective, extra, facultative, free, noncompulsory, nonobligatory, no strings attached*, not required, open, unforced, unrestricted, up to the individual, volitional, voluntary; SEE CONCEPTS *552,576*

opulent [*adj*] *rich, luxurious, profuse*
abundant, affluent, copious, deluxe, extravagant, exuberant, frilly*, lavish, luscious, luxuriant, moneyed, ostentatious, palatial, plentiful, plush, pretentious, prodigal, profusive, prolific, prosperous, rich, riotous, showy, sumptuous, swank, upholstered*, velvet*, wealthy, well-heeled*, well-off*, well-to-do*; SEE CONCEPTS *334,589,781*

opus [*n*] *great work of writing or music*
composition, creation, magnum opus, masterpiece, music, oeuvre, piece, product, production; SEE CONCEPTS *263,271*

oracle [*n*] *prophecy*
answer, apocalypse, augury, canon, commandment, divination, edict, fortune, law, prediction, prognostication, revelation, vision; SEE CONCEPTS *70, 278,689*

oracular [*adj*] *prophetic*
ambiguous, anticipating, apocalyptic, arcane, auguring, auspicious, authoritative, cabalistic, clairvoyant, cryptic, Delphian, discovering, divining, divulging, dogmatic, fatidic, foreboding, forecasting, foretelling, imperious, interpretive, mantic, mysterious, mystical, obscure, occult, ominous, peremptory, portending, portentous, positive, predicting, presaging, prescient, proclaiming, prognosticating, prophesying, sage, secret, sibylline, significant, soothsaying, vague, vatic, venerable, wise; SEE CONCEPT *267*

oral [*adj*] *spoken*
articulate, ejaculatory, lingual, narrated, phonated, phonetic, phonic, recounted, related, said, sonant, sounded, told, unwritten, uttered, verbal, viva voce, vocal, voiced, word-of-mouth; SEE CONCEPT *267*

orange [*n/adj*] *combination of red and yellow*
apricot, bittersweet, carrot, coral, peach, red-yellow, salmon, tangerine, titian; SEE CONCEPTS *618,622*

oration [*n*] *speech*
address, chalk talk*, declamation, discourse, harangue, homily, lecture, pep talk*, pitch*, sermon, soapbox*, spiel*; SEE CONCEPTS *266,278*

orb [*n*] *globe*
ball, circle, eye*, lamp, ring, rondure, round, sphere; SEE CONCEPT *436*

orbit [*n1*] *circuit, revolution*
apogee, circle, circumgyration, course, curve, cycle, ellipse, lap, locus, path, pattern, perigee, rotation, round, track, trajectory; SEE CONCEPTS *436,738*

orbit [*n2*] *influence, domain*
ambit, area, arena, boundary, bounds, career, circle, circumference, compass, course, department, dominion, extension, extent, field, jurisdiction, limit, pilgrimage, precinct, province, purview, radius, range, reach, realm, scope, sphere, sweep; SEE CONCEPTS *349,673,686*

orchestrate [*v*] *organize; cause to happen*
arrange, blend, compose, concert, coordinate, harmonize, integrate, manage, present, put together, score, set up, symphonize, synthesize, unify; SEE CONCEPTS *117,242*

ordain [*v*] *establish, install*
anoint, appoint, bless, call, commission, consecrate, constitute, deal, deal with, decree, delegate, destine, dictate, elect, enact, enjoin, fix, frock, impose, institute, invest, lay down the law*, legislate, nominate, order, prescribe, pronounce, put foot down*, rule, set, walk heavy*, will; SEE CONCEPTS *18, 50,88,317*

ordeal [*n*] *trouble, suffering*
affliction, agony, anguish, calamity, calvary, cross, crucible, difficulty, distress, nightmare, test, tor-

ment, torture, trial, tribulation, visitation; SEE CONCEPTS *674,728*

order [*n1*] *arrangement, organization*
adjustment, aligning, array, assortment, cast, categorization, classification, codification, composition, computation, disposal, disposition, distribution, establishment, form, grouping, harmony, layout, line, lineup, management, method, neatness, ordering, orderliness, pattern, placement, plan, procedure, procession, progression, propriety, regularity, regulation, rule, scale, scheme, sequence, series, setup, standardization, structure, succession, symmetry, system, tidiness, uniformity; SEE CONCEPT *727*

order [*n2*] *lawfulness*
calm, control, decorousness, decorum, discipline, goodness, integrity, law, law and order, niceness, orderliness, peace, peacefulness, probity, properness, propriety, quiet, rectitude, rightness, seemliness, suitability, tranquility, uprightness; SEE CONCEPTS *633,691*

order [*n3*] *class, status*
bracket, branch, breed, cast, caste, degree, description, estate, family, feather, genre, genus, grade, hierarchy, ilk, kidney, kind, line, nature, pecking order*, pigeonhole*, place, position, rank, set, slot, sort, species, station, stripe, subclass, taxonomic group, type; SEE CONCEPT *378*

order [*n4*] *command*
authorization, behest, bidding, charge, commandment, decree, dictate, direction, directive, injunction, instruction, law, mandate, ordinance, permission, precept, regulation, rule, say-so*, stipulation, ukase, word*; SEE CONCEPTS *53,278,685*

order [*n5*] *request; purchase agreement*
amount, application, booking, bulk, commission, engagement, goods, materials, purchase, quantity, requisition, reservation, reserve, shipment, stipulation; SEE CONCEPTS *332,338,684*

order [*n6*] *organization*
association, brotherhood, club, community, company, fellowship, fraternity, guild, league, lodge, sect, sisterhood, society, sodality, sorority, union; SEE CONCEPT *387*

order [*v1*] *command, authorize*
adjure, apply for, bid, book, buy, call for, call the shots*, call the signals*, charge, contract for, decree, dictate, direct, enact, engage, enjoin, hire, instruct, obtain, ordain, prescribe, pull strings*, request, require, reserve, rule the roost*, secure, send away for, tell, warn; SEE CONCEPTS *50, 53,88,327*

order [*v2*] *arrange, organize*
adapt, adjust, align, alphabetize, array, assign, catalogue, class, classify, codify, conduct, control, dispose, distribute, establish, file, fix, formalize, furnish, group, hierarchize, index, lay out, line, line up, locate, manage, marshal, methodize, neaten, normalize, pattern, place, plan, put away, put to rights,

range, regiment, regularize, regulate, right, routine, set guidelines, set in order, settle, sort out, space, standardize, streamline, systematize, tabulate, tidy; SEE CONCEPTS *84,158*

orderly [*adj1*] *methodical, organized*
alike, all together, arranged, businesslike, careful, clean, conventional, correct, exact, fixed, formal, framed, in apple-pie order*, in good shape, in order, in shape, methodic, neat, neat as button*, neat as pin*, precise, regular, regulated, scientific, set-up, shipshape*, slick, spick-and-span*, systematic, systematized, thorough, tidy, together, to rights*, trim, uncluttered, uniform; SEE CONCEPTS *326,485, 585,589*

orderly [*adj2*] *well-behaved*
at peace, calm, controlled, decorous, disciplined, docile, law-abiding, manageable, nonviolent, obedient, peaceable, quiet, restrained, submissive, tranquil, well-mannered; SEE CONCEPT *401*

ordinance [*n*] *law, rule*
authorization, canon, code, command, decree, dictum, direction, edict, enactment, fiat, mandate, order, precept, prescript, reg, regulation, ruling, statute, ukase; SEE CONCEPT *318*

ordinarily [*adv*] *usually*
as a rule, commonly, customarily, frequently, generally, habitually, in general, normally, regularly; SEE CONCEPT *530*

ordinary [*adj1*] *common, regular*
accustomed, customary, established, everyday, familiar, frequent, general, habitual, humdrum*, natural, normal, popular, prevailing, public, quotidian, routine, run-of-the-mill*, settled, standard, stock, traditional, typical, usual, wonted; SEE CONCEPTS *533,547*

ordinary [*adj2*] *average; not distinctive*
characterless, common, commonplace, conventional, dull, fair, familiar, garden*, garden variety*, generic, habitual, homespun, household, humble, indifferent, inferior, mean, mediocre, modest, no great shakes*, normal, pedestrian, plain, plastic, prosaic, quotidian, routine, run-of-the-mill*, second-rate, simple, so-so*, stereotyped, undistinguished, uneventful, unexceptional, uninspired, unmemorable, unnoteworthy, unpretentious, unremarkable, usual, vanilla*, white-bread*, workaday; SEE CONCEPTS *530,575*

organ [*n*] *means, tool*
agency, agent, channel, device, element, forum, implement, instrument, journal, magazine, medium, member, ministry, mouthpiece, newspaper, paper, part, periodical, process, publication, review, structure, unit, vehicle, voice, way; SEE CONCEPTS *280,499,712*

organic [*adj*] *basic, natural*
amoebic, anatomical, animate, basal, biological, biotic, cellular, constitutional, elemental, essential, fundamental, inherent, innate, integral, live, living,

necessary, nuclear, original, plasmic, primary, prime, primitive, principal, structural, vital; SEE CONCEPT *549*

organism [*n*] *living thing*
animal, being, body, creature, entity, morphon, person, plant, structure; SEE CONCEPTS *389,429*

organization [*n1*] *arrangement, arranging*
alignment, assembling, assembly, chemistry, composition, configuration, conformation, constitution, construction, coordination, design, disposal, format, formation, forming, formulation, framework, grouping, harmony, institution, make-up, making, management, method, methodology, organism, organizing, pattern, plan, planning, regulation, running, situation, standard, standardization, structure, structuring, symmetry, system, unity, whole; SEE CONCEPTS *84,117,727*

organization [*n2*] *group bound by interest/work/goal*
affiliation, aggregation, alliance, association, band, body, brotherhood, business, cartel, circle, clique, club, coalition, combination, combine, company, concern, concord, confederation, consortium, cooperative, corporation, coterie, crew, establishment, federation, fellowship, fraternity, guild, house, industry, institute, institution, league, lodge, machine, monopoly, order, outfit, party, profession, set, society, sodality, sorority, squad, syndicate, team, trade, troupe, trust, union; SEE CONCEPT *381*

organize [*v*] *arrange, systematize*
adapt, adjust, be responsible for, catalogue, classify, codify, combine, compose, constitute, construct, coordinate, correlate, create, dispose, establish, fashion, fit, form, formulate, frame, get going*, get together, group, harmonize, lick into shape*, line up, look after, marshal, mastermind, methodize, mold, pigeonhole*, put in order, put together, range, regulate, run, see to, settle, set up, shape, standardize, straighten, straighten out, tabulate, tailor, take care of, whip into shape*; SEE CONCEPTS *36,84,158*

orgy [*n*] *celebration devoted to sensual enjoyment*
bacchanal, bacchanalia, bender*, binge*, blowout*, bout*, carousal, circus*, debauch, dissipation, excess, feast, fling*, indulgence, jag*, merrymaking, overindulgence, party, rampage*, revel, revelry, saturnalia, splurge, spree, surfeit, tear*; SEE CONCEPTS *377,383*

orient [*v*] *familiarize*
acclimatize, adapt, adjust, align, conform, determine, direct, get one's bearings*, locate, orientate, turn; SEE CONCEPTS *35,202*

orientation [*n*] *introduction, adjustment*
acclimatization, adaptation, assimilation, bearings, breaking in*, coordination, direction, familiarization, fix*, lay of the land*, location, position, sense of direction, settling in*; SEE CONCEPTS *31,832*

origin [*n1*] *cause, basis*
agent, ancestor, ancestry, antecedent, author, base, causality, causation, connection, creator, derivation,

determinant, egg*, element, embryo, fountain, generator, germ, horse's mouth*, impulse, inception, inducement, influence, inspiration, mainspring, motive, nucleus, occasion, parent, parentage, principle, producer, progenitor, provenance, provenience, root, roots, seed, source, sperm, spring, stock, well, wellspring; SEE CONCEPTS *229,648,661*

origin [*n2*] *beginning, inception*
alpha, birth, blast off, commencement, creation, dawn, dawning, day one*, early stage, embarkation, emergence, entrance, entry, forging, foundation, genesis, git go*, inauguration, ingress, initiation, introduction, launch, nativity, opener, origination, outbreak, outset, rise, square one*, start, starting point*; SEE CONCEPT *832*

origin [*n3*] *family, heritage*
ancestry, beginnings, birth, blood, descent, extraction, lineage, maternity, parentage, paternity, pedigree, stock; SEE CONCEPT *296*

original [*n1*] *standard, prototype*
archetype, coinage, creation, exemplar, forerunner, invention, master, model, mother, novelty, paradigm, pattern, precedent, precursor, type; SEE CONCEPTS *260,688*

original [*n2*] *person who is eccentric*
anomaly, card*, case*, character, eccentric, nonconformist, oddball, oddity, queer, weirdo; SEE CONCEPT *423*

original [*adj1*] *earliest*
aboriginal, archetypal, authentic, autochthonous, beginning, commencing, early, elementary, embryonic, first, first-hand, genuine, inceptive, infant, initial, introductory, maiden, master, opening, pioneer, primary, prime, primeval, primitive, primordial, pristine, prototypal, rudimental, rudimentary, start, underivative, underived; SEE CONCEPTS *549,585*

original [*adj2*] *fresh, new*
avant garde, breaking new ground*, causal, causative, conceiving, creative, demiurgic, devising, envisioning, fertile, formative, generative, imaginative, ingenious, innovational, innovative, innovatory, inspiring, inventive, new, novel, originative, productive, quick, ready, resourceful, seminal, sensitive, unconventional, unprecedented, untried, unusual; SEE CONCEPTS *578,589,797*

originality [*n*] *creativeness*
boldness, brilliance, cleverness, creative spirit, creativity, daring, freshness, imagination, imaginativeness, individuality, ingeniousness, ingenuity, innovation, innovativeness, invention, inventiveness, modernity, new idea, newness, nonconformity, novelty, resourcefulness, spirit, unconventionality, unorthodoxy; SEE CONCEPTS *409,410*

originally [*adv*] *initially*
at first, at the outset, at the start, basically, by birth, by origin, first, formerly, incipiently, in the beginning, in the first place, incipiently, primarily, prim-

itively, to begin with; SEE CONCEPTS *578,585,797,799*

originate [*v1*] *begin; spring*

arise, be born, begin, birth, come, come from, come into existence, commence, dawn, derive, emanate, emerge, flow, hail from, issue, proceed, result, rise, start, stem; SEE CONCEPTS *105,221*

originate [*v2*] *create, introduce*

break the ice*, bring about, cause, coin, come up with, compose, conceive, develop, discover, evolve, father, form, formulate, found, generate, give birth to, hatch, inaugurate, initiate, innovate, institute, invent, launch, make, mother, open up, parent, pioneer, procreate, produce, set in motion, set up, sire, spark, spawn, start, think up, usher in; SEE CONCEPTS *43,173,251*

ornament [*n*] *decoration*

accessory, adornment, art, bauble, beautification, design, doodad*, embellishment, embroidery, flower, frill, frou frou*, garnish, gewgaw*, gimcrack*, gingerbread*, honor, jewel, knickknack*, pride, treasure, trimming, trinket; SEE CONCEPTS *259,476*

ornament [*v*] *decorate*

adorn, array, beautify, bedeck, bedizen, brighten, deck, dress, dress up*, embellish, embroider, enrich, festoon, fix up*, garnish, gild, grace, ornamentalize, polish, prank, prettify, primp, smarten*, spruce up*, trim; SEE CONCEPTS *162,167,177*

ornamental [*adj*] *decorative*

accessory, adorning, attractive, beautiful, beautifying, decking, decorating, delicate, dressy, elaborate, embellishing, enhancing, exquisite, fancy, festooned, florid, for show*, furbishing, garnishing, heightening, luxurious, ornate, setting off*, showy; SEE CONCEPTS *579,589*

ornate [*adj*] *fancily decorated*

adorned, aureate, baroque, beautiful, bedecked, bright, brilliant, busy, colored, convoluted, dazzling, elaborate, elegant, embroidered, fancy, fine, flamboyant, flashy, flaunting, florid, flowery, fussy, gaudy, gilded, glamorous, glitzy, glossy, high-wrought, jeweled, lavish, luscious, magnificent, meretricious, opulent, ornamented, ostentatious, overdone, overelaborate, pretentious, resplendent, rich, rococo, showy, sparkling, splashy, sumptuous, superficial, tawdry, variegated; SEE CONCEPTS *579,589*

orphan [*n*] *child without parents*

foundling, ragamuffin*, stray, waif; SEE CONCEPT *414*

orthodox [*adj*] *accepted, traditional*

according to the book*, acknowledged, admitted, approved, authoritative, buttoned-down*, by the numbers*, canonical, conformist, conservative, conventional, correct, customary, devout, die-hard, doctrinal, established, in line*, legitimate, official, old-line*, pious, proper, punctilious, reactionary, received, recognized, religious, right, rightful, sanctioned, sound, square, standard, straight, straight ar-

row, traditional, traditionalistic, true, well-established; SEE CONCEPTS *533,558*

oscillate [*v*] *change back and forth*

be unsteady, dangle, fishtail, flicker, fluctuate, librate, lurch, palpitate, pendulate, pitch, pivot, reel, ripple, rock, roll, seesaw, stagger, sway, swing, switch, swivel, teeter, teeter-totter*, thrash, toss, totter, undulate, vacillate, vary, vibrate, waddle, wag, waggle, waltz, wave, waver, whirl, wiggle, wobble; SEE CONCEPTS *13,147,697*

ossify [*v*] *become very hard from aging*

congeal, fossilize, freeze, harden, indurate, petrify, solidify, stiffen, thicken, turn to bone; SEE CONCEPT *469*

ostensible [*adj*] *alleged, supposed*

apparent, avowed, colorable, demonstrative, exhibited, illusive, illusory, likely, manifest, notable, outward, plausible, pretended, professed, purported, quasi, seeming, semblant, so-called*, specious, superficial; SEE CONCEPTS *552,582*

ostensibly [*adv*] *apparently*

at first blush*, evidently, externally, for all intents and purposes*, for show*, officially, on the face*, on the surface*, outwardly, professedly, seemingly, sensibly, superficially, supposedly, to the eye*; SEE CONCEPT *582*

ostentation [*n*] *exhibitionism, flashiness*

affectation, array, boast, boasting, brag, braggadocio*, bragging, bravado, demonstration, display, exhibition, false front*, flamboyance, flash*, flaunting, flourish, fuss, garishness, grandstand play*, magnificence, pageant, pageantry, parade, parading, pomp, pomposity, pompousness, pretending, pretension, pretentiousness, put-on, shine*, show, showiness, showing off*, showoff*, spectacle, splendor, splurge, swagger*, swaggering, swank*, vainglory, vaunt*, vaunting*, window-dressing; SEE CONCEPTS *633,655*

ostentatious [*adj*] *flashy, showy*

boastful, chichi*, classy, conspicuous, crass*, dashing, egotistic, exhibitionistic, extravagant, flamboyant, flatulent, flaunted, fussy, garish, gaudy, gay, glittery, grandiose, highfaluting*, jaunty, loud, obtrusive, peacocky, pompous, pretentious, spectacular, splashy, splurgy, sporty, swank, swanky*, theatrical, tinsel*, tony*, uptown*, vain, vulgar; SEE CONCEPTS *401,589*

ostracize [*v*] *exile, banish*

avoid, blackball*, blacklist*, boycott, cast out, cold-shoulder*, cut, deport, displace, drop, exclude, excommunicate, expatriate, expel, expulse, leave in the cold, oust, reject, shun, shut out, snub, throw out; SEE CONCEPTS *25,384*

other [*adj1*] *additional, added*

alternative, another, auxiliary, else, extra, farther, fresh, further, more, new, spare, supplementary; SEE CONCEPT *771*

other [adj2] *different*

contrasting, disparate, dissimilar, distant, distinct, divergent, diverse, opposite, otherwise, remaining, separate, unalike, unequal, unlike, unrelated, variant; SEE CONCEPT *564*

otherwise [adv] *in another way; alternatively*

any other way, contrarily, differently, diversely, elseways, if not, in different circumstances, on the other hand, or else, or then, under other conditions, variously; SEE CONCEPT *544*

ounce [n] *one-sixteenth of a pound/28.35 grams of weight*

avoirdupois, Troy, uncia; SEE CONCEPT *795*

oust [v] *expel, get rid of*

banish, bereave, boot out*, bounce*, bundle off*, cast out, chase, depose, deprive, dethrone, discharge, disinherit, dislodge, displace, dispossess, divest, drive out, eject, evict, expulse, fire, force out, give the 1-2-3*, kick out, lay off, let go, lose, ostracize, pack off, pink slip*, relegate, remove, rob, sack, send packing*, show the door*, throw out, topple, transport, turn out, unseat; SEE CONCEPTS *25,211,351*

out [adj] *not possible; gone*

absent, antiquated, at an end, away, behind the times*, cold, dated, dead, demode, doused, ended, exhausted, expired, extinguished, finished, impossible, not allowed, not on, old-fashioned, old-hat*, outmoded, outside, passé, ruled out, unacceptable, unfashionable, used up; SEE CONCEPTS *539,552,576*

out [adv] *outside, outdoors*

out of doors, outward, without; SEE CONCEPT *583*

outbreak [n] *very sudden happening*

beginning, blowup, brawl, break, breaking, burst, bursting, commencement, commotion, convulsion, crack, crash, dawn, detonation, discharge, disorder, disruption, ebullition, effervescence, epidemic, eruption, explosion, fit, flare-up, flash, fury, gush, gushing, insurrection, irruption, mutiny, onset, outburst, outpouring, paroxysm, plague, rebellion, rending, revolution, roar, sally, sortie, spasm, spurt, storm, sundering, surge, thunder, tumult, uprising, volley; SEE CONCEPTS *2,86,179,832*

outburst [n] *fit of temper*

access, attack, blow, burst, conniption*, discharge, eruption, explosion, flare, flare-up, frenzy, gush, gust, outbreak, outpouring, paroxysm, rapture, scene, spasm, storm, surge, tantrum, transport, upheaval; SEE CONCEPT *633*

outcast [n] *person who is unwanted, not accepted*

bum*, castaway, deportee, derelict, displaced person, exile, expatriate, fugitive, gypsy, hobo*, persona non grata*, rascal, refugee, reprobate, tramp, untouchable, vagabond, vagrant, wretch; SEE CONCEPT *423*

outcome [n] *consequence, effect*

aftereffect, aftermath, blowoff, causatum, chain reaction*, conclusion, end, end result*, event, fallout, issue, payback*, payoff*, reaction, result, score, sequel, upshot*; SEE CONCEPT *230*

outcry [n] *scream, exclamation*

clamor, commotion, complaint, convulsion, cry, ferment, flak*, hoo-ha*, howl, hubba-hubba*, hullabaloo*, noise, objection, outburst, protest, screech, tumult, uproar, upturn, yell; SEE CONCEPTS *77,278*

outdated/out-of-date [adj] *old-fashioned*

anachronous, antiquated, antique, archaic, back number*, behind the times*, dated, demode, dusty, has-been*, moth-eaten*, musty, not with it*, obsolete, old, old-hat*, out, outmoded, out-of-style*, passé*, square, tired, unfashionable, vintage; SEE CONCEPTS *578,589,797*

outdo [v] *better, overcome*

beat, best, blow out of water*, bulldoze*, bury*, cook*, cream*, defeat, do in*, down*, eclipse, exceed, excel, fake out*, go one better*, leave behind*, lick, outclass, outdistance, outfox, outgun, outjockey, outmaneuver, outrival, outshine, outsmart, outstrip, pull a fast one*, shake off*, shoot ahead*, snow*, surpass, top, transcend, trash*; SEE CONCEPTS *95,141*

outdoor [adj/adv] *in the open air*

alfresco, casual, free, garden, healthful, hilltop, informal, in the open, invigorating, mountain, natural, nature-loving, open-air, out-of-doors, out of the house, outside, patio, picnic, rustic, unrestricted, woods, yard; SEE CONCEPT *583*

outdoors [n] *open air; nature*

bucolic surroundings, country, countryside, environment, fresh air, garden, green earth*, hill, Mother Nature*, mountain, open, out-of-doors, patio, without, woods, yard; SEE CONCEPT *198*

outer [adj] *external, exposed*

alien, beyond, exoteric, exterior, extraneous, extrinsic, outermost, outlying, outmost, outside, outward, over, peripheral, remote, superficial, surface, without; SEE CONCEPTS *484,583*

outfit [n1] *set of clothes or equipment*

accoutrements, apparatus, appliances, clothing, costume, ensemble, equipment, garb, gear, get-up*, guise, kit, machinery, materiel, outlay, paraphernalia, provisions, rig, rigging, suit, supplies, tackle, togs, trappings*, wardrobe; SEE CONCEPTS *451,496*

outfit [n2] *large group; business*

band, clique, company, concern, corps, coterie, crew, enterprise, establishment, firm, house, organization, party, set, squad, team, troop, troupe, unit; SEE CONCEPTS *325,417*

outfit [v] *clothe, equip*

accoutre, appoint, arm, deck out*, drape, fit out*, furnish, gear, prepare, provide, provision, rig up*, stock, suit, supply, tog*, turn out*; SEE CONCEPTS *167,182*

outgoing [adj1] *demonstrative, extroverted*

approachable, civil, communicative, cordial, easy, expansive, extrovert, friendly, genial, gregarious, informal, kind, open, sociable, sympathetic, unconstrained, unreserved, unrestrained, warm; SEE CONCEPT **404**

outgoing [adj2] *leaving*
departing, ex-*, former, last, migratory, outbound, outward-bound, past, retiring, withdrawing; SEE CONCEPTS **581,584**

outgrowth [n1] *projection*
bulge, enlargement, excrescence, jut, node, offshoot, outcrop, process, prolongation, prominence, protuberance, shoot, sprout, swelling; SEE CONCEPTS **471,824**

outgrowth [n2] *product, consequence*
aftereffect, branch, by-product*, child, derivative, descendant, development, effect, emergence, end, end result*, issue, member, offshoot, offspring, outcome, result, spin-off*, yield; SEE CONCEPTS **230,260**

outing [n] *short trip*
airing, drive, excursion, expedition, jaunt, junket, long weekend, picnic, pleasure trip, roundabout, spin*, vacation, weekend; SEE CONCEPTS **224,386**

outlandish [adj] *bizarre, very strange*
alien, awkward, barbaric, barbarous, boorish, clumsy, curious, droll, eccentric, erratic, exotic, extravagant, fantastic, far-out*, foreign, freakish, gauche, graceless, grotesque, kinky*, odd, outrageous, outré*, peculiar, preposterous, quaint, queer, ridiculous, rude, singular, tasteless, ultra, unconventional, uncouth, unheard-of*, unorthodox, unusual, weird, whimsical, wild; SEE CONCEPTS **401,548**

outlast [v] *endure beyond another*
hang on, outlive, outstay, outwear, remain, survive; SEE CONCEPT **407**

outlaw [n] *person who is running from the law*
bad guy*, badman/woman*, bandit, brigand, con, criminal, crook, desperado, drifter, ex-con, fugitive, gangster, gunman/woman, gunslinger*, highwayman*, hood*, hoodlum, hooligan*, jailbird, marauder, mobster, mug*, outcast, pariah, racketeer, robber, wrong number*; SEE CONCEPT **412**

outlaw [v] *prohibit; make illegal*
ban, banish, bar, condemn, damn, disallow, embargo, enjoin, exclude, forbid, illegalize, inhibit, interdict, prevent, proscribe, stop, taboo; SEE CONCEPTS **121,317**

outlay [n] *expenses*
bite*, bottom line*, charge, cost, damage, disbursement, expenditure, expense, highway robbery*, investment, price tag, score*, setback*, spending, tab*, throw*, tune*; SEE CONCEPT **344**

outlet [n1] *place where one can enter, leave*
aperture, avenue, break, channel, crack, duct, egress, escape, exit, hole, nozzle, opening, orifice, porthole, release, safety valve, spout, tear, vent, way out; SEE CONCEPTS **513,693**

outlet [n2] *store that sells discounted items*
factory store, market, mill store, seconds store, shop, showroom; SEE CONCEPTS **439,448,449**

outline [n1] *plan, sketch*
bare facts*, blueprint, diagram, draft, drawing, floor plan, frame, framework, ground plan, layout, main features, recapitulation, résumé, rough draft, rough idea, rundown, skeleton, summary, synopsis, thumbnail sketch*, tracing; SEE CONCEPT **268**

outline [n2] *form, tracing of an object*
configuration, conformation, contour, delineation, figuration, figure, profile, shape, silhouette; SEE CONCEPTS **436,625**

outline [v] *sketch out; plan*
adumbrate, block out, characterize, chart, delineate, describe, draft, lay out, paint, plot, recapitulate, rough out, skeleton, skeletonize, summarize, tell about, trace; SEE CONCEPTS **36,55,174**

outlook [n1] *point of view*
angle*, attitude, direction, frame of mind*, headset*, mind-set*, perspective, routine, scope, side, size of it*, slant*, standpoint, viewpoint, views, vision; SEE CONCEPTS **410,689**

outlook [n2] *probable future*
appearances, chance, expectation, forecast, law of averages*, likelihood, normal course, opening, opportunity, possibility, probability, prospect, prospects, risk; SEE CONCEPT **679**

outlook [n3] *scene, view*
aspect, lookout, panorama, perspective, prospect, scape, sight, vista; SEE CONCEPTS **509,628**

outlying [adj] *in rural area; remote*
afar, backwoods, distant, external, faraway, far-flung*, far-off, off-lying, outer, out-of-the-way*, peripheral, provincial, removed; SEE CONCEPT **583**

outmoded [adj] *obsolete, old-fashioned*
anachronistic, antediluvian, antiquated, antique, archaic, behind the times*, bent, bygone, dated, dead, demode, dinosaur*, disused, extinct, fossilized, has-been*, horse and buggy*, moldy*, moth-eaten*, musty*, obsolescent, obsolete, olden, old-hat*, old-time, out, out-of-date, out-of-style, outworn, passé*, superannuated, superseded, tired, unfashionable, unstylish, unusable, vintage; SEE CONCEPTS **560,578, 589,797**

output [n] *something produced*
achievement, amount, crop, gain, harvest, making, manufacture, manufacturing, producing, product, production, productivity, profit, take, turnout, yield; SEE CONCEPTS **205,260**

outrage [n1] *atrocity, evil*
abuse, affront, barbarism, damage, desecration, enormity, evildoing, harm, hurt, indignity, inhumanity, injury, insult, mischief, misdoing, offense, profanation, rape, rapine, ravishing, ruin, shock, violation, violence, wrongdoing; SEE CONCEPTS **192,645,674**

outrage [n2] *anger*
blowup, flare-up*, fury, huff*, hurt, indignation, resentment, ruckus*, shock*, stew*, storm*, wrath; SEE CONCEPT **29**

outrage [v] *wrong, offend, abuse*
affront, aggrieve, boil over*, burn up*, defile, deflower, desecrate, do violence to, fire up*, force, ill-treat, incense, infuriate, injure, insult, jar*, kick up a row*, madden, make hit the ceiling*, maltreat, mistreat, misuse, oppress, persecute, raise Cain*, rape, ravage, ravish, reach boiling point*, scandalize, shock, spoil, violate, whip up*; SEE CONCEPTS *7,19,29,246*

outrageous [adj1] *very bad*
abominable, atrocious, barbaric, beastly, brazen, contemptible, contumelious, corrupt, criminal, debasing, debauching, degenerate, depraving, disgraceful, disgracing, egregious, flagitious, flagrant, gross, heinous, horrendous, horrible, ignoble, infamous, inhuman, iniquitous, malevolent, monstrous, nefarious, notorious, odious, opprobrious, scandalous, scurrilous, shameless, shaming, shocking, sinful, unbearable, ungodly, unspeakable, villainous, violent, wanton, wicked; SEE CONCEPT *571*

outrageous [adj2] *beyond reasonable limits*
barbarous, crazy*, excessive, exorbitant, extortionate, extravagant, immoderate, inordinate, last straw*, offensive, out of bounds*, preposterous, scandalous, shocking, steep*, too much*, uncivilized, unconscionable, unreasonable; SEE CONCEPTS *569,771*

outright [adj] *complete, unconditional*
absolute, all, arrant, consummate, definite, direct, downright, entire, flat, gross, out-and-out*, perfect, positive, pure, straightforward, thorough, thoroughgoing, total, undeniable, unequivocal, unmitigated, unqualified, utter, whole, wholesale; SEE CONCEPTS *531,535*

outside [n] *exterior; out-of-doors*
appearance, covering, facade, face, front, integument, open, open air, outdoors, seeming, sheath, skin, surface, topside, without; SEE CONCEPTS *198,484*

outside [adj1] *external*
alfresco, alien, apart from, away from, exterior, external, extramural, extraneous, extreme, farther, farthest, foreign, furthest, open-air, out, outdoor, outer, outermost, outward, over, surface; SEE CONCEPTS *484,583*

outside [adj2] *slight, slim*
distant, faint, far, marginal, negligible, off, remote, slender, small, unlikely; SEE CONCEPTS *552,789*

outsider [n] *person who is foreign to something*
alien, floater*, foreigner, incomer*, interloper, intruder, newcomer, odd one out*, outlander, refugee, stranger; SEE CONCEPTS *413,423*

outskirts [n] *edge of a geographic area*
bedroom community*, border, boundary, edge, environs, limit, outpost, periphery, purlieu, purlieus, sticks*, suburb, suburbia, vicinity; SEE CONCEPTS *508,513*

outspoken [adj] *explicit, unreserved*
abrupt, artless, blunt, calling spade a spade*, candid, direct, forthright, frank, free, laying it on the line*,
open, plain, plain-spoken, point-blank*, round, square, straightforward, strident, talking turkey*, unceremonious, unequivocal, unreticent, up front*, vocal; SEE CONCEPTS *267,404*

outstanding [adj1] *superior, excellent*
A-1*, ace*, A-number 1*, bad*, boss*, capital*, celebrated, chief, cool*, crack*, distinguished, dominant, eminent, eventful, exceptional, famous, far-out*, great, greatest, hundred-proof*, important, impressive, magnificent, main, major, meritorious, momentous, mostest, murder*, number one*, out-of-sight*, out-of-this-world*, phenomenal, predominant, preeminent, primo*, principal, special, standout, star, stellar, super, superior, superlative, tops*, well-known, world-class; SEE CONCEPTS *568,574*

outstanding [adj2] *noticeable, striking*
arresting, arrestive, conspicuous, distinguished, eye-catching, important, leading, marked, memorable, notable, noteworthy, prominent, pronounced, remarkable, salient, signal; SEE CONCEPTS *485,537*

outstanding [adj3] *referring to an unpaid debt*
due, mature, ongoing, open, overdue, owing, payable, pending, remaining, uncollected, unresolved, unsettled; SEE CONCEPT *334*

outward [adj] *visible; for appearances*
apparent, evident, exterior, external, from within, noticeable, observable, obvious, on the surface, open, ostensible, out, outer, outside, over, perceptible, superficial, surface, to the eye, toward the edge; SEE CONCEPTS *576,581,583*

outwardly [adv] *to all appearances*
apparently, as far as one can see, evidently, externally, for all intents and purposes, in appearance, officially, on the face of it, on the surface, ostensibly, professedly, seemingly, superficially, to the eye; SEE CONCEPTS *544,576*

outweigh [v] *override, dominate*
atone for, balance, cancel out, compensate, counterbalance, counterpoise, countervail, eclipse, exceed, excel, make up for, offset, outbalance, outrival, outrun, overcome, overshadow, predominate, preponderate, prevail, set off, surpass, take precedence, tip the scales; SEE CONCEPT *141*

outwit/outsmart [v] *get the better of; figure out before another*
baffle, bamboozle*, beat*, bewilder, cap, cheat, circumvent, con, confuse, deceive, defeat, defraud, dupe, end-run*, fake out*, finagle*, fox*, goose*, gull*, gyp*, have*, hoax, hoodwink, lead astray*, make a fool of*, make a monkey of*, mislead, outdo, outfox, outgeneral, outguess, outjockey, outmaneuver, outthink, overreach, pull a fast one on*, put one over on*, run circles around*, swindle, take in*, top*, trick, worst*; SEE CONCEPTS *15,59*

oval [adj] *long and rounded in shape*
egg-shaped, ellipsoidal, elliptic, elliptical, oblong, ooid, ovaloid, ovate, oviform, ovoid; SEE CONCEPT *486*

ovation [n] *clapping and cheers*
acclaim, acclamation, applause, big hand*, bravos, cheering, hand, laudation, plaudits, praise, salvo, testimonial, tribute; SEE CONCEPTS *69,264*

over [adj1] *accomplished*
ancient history, at an end, by, bygone, closed, completed, concluded, done, done with, ended, finished, gone, past, settled, up; SEE CONCEPTS *531,548*

over [adj2/adv1] *in addition*
additionally, beyond, ever, excessively, extra, extremely, immensely, in excess, inordinately, left over, more, over and above, overly, overmuch, remaining, superfluous, surplus, too, unduly, unused; SEE CONCEPTS *544,771*

over [adv2] *above*
aloft, beyond, covering, farther up, higher than, in heaven, in the sky, off, on high, on top of, overhead, overtop, straight up, traversely, uphigh, upstairs; SEE CONCEPTS *583,793*

overabundance [n] *excess*
embarrassment of riches*, glut, nimiety, overflow, overkill, overmuch, oversupply, plethora, profusion, superabundance, superfluity, surfeit, surplus, surplusage, too much*; SEE CONCEPTS *767,786*

overall [adj] *complete, general*
all-embracing, blanket, comprehensive, global, inclusive, long-range, long-term, sweeping, thorough, total, umbrella; SEE CONCEPT *772*

overall [adv] *in general*
all over, chiefly, everyplace, everywhere, generally speaking, in the long run, largely, mainly, mostly, on the whole, predominantly, primarily, principally, throughout; SEE CONCEPTS *548,772*

overbearing [adj] *arrogant, domineering*
ascendant, autocratic, bossy, cavalier, cocky*, despotic, dictatorial, disdainful, dogmatic, domineering, egotistic, haughty, high-and-mighty*, high-handed*, imperative, imperial, imperious, insolent, lordly, magisterial, master, masterful, officious, oppressive, overweening, paramount, peremptory, predominant, preponderant, prevalent, proud, regnant, sniffy*, snotty*, sovereign, stuffy, supercilious, superior, tyrannical, uppity*; SEE CONCEPTS *401,404*

overblown [adj] *excessive, too much*
aureate, bombastic, disproportionate, euphuistic, flowery, fulsome, grandiloquent, hyped up*, immoderate, inflated, magniloquent, oratorical, overdone, pompous, pretentious, profuse, rhetorical, sonorous, superfluous, turgid, undue, verbose, windy; SEE CONCEPTS *267,548*

overcast [adj] *cloudy, darkened*
clouded, clouded over, dark, dismal, dreary, dull, gray, hazy, leaden, lowering, murky, nebulous, not clear, not fair, oppressive, somber, sunless, threatening; SEE CONCEPT *525*

overcome [adj] *overwhelmed; visibly moved*
affected, at a loss for words, beaten, blown-away*, bowled-over*, buried*, conquered, defeated, over-

thrown, run-over*, speechless, swamped, swept off one's feet*, taken*, unable to continue; SEE CONCEPT *403*

overcome [v] *beat, defeat*
best*, be victorious, come out on top*, conquer, crush, down*, drown, get around*, get the better of*, hurdle, knock over*, knock socks off*, lick*, master, outlive, overpower, overthrow, overwhelm, prevail, prostrate, reduce, render, rise above*, shock, stun, subdue, subjugate, surmount, survive, throw*, triumph over, vanquish, weather*, whelm*, win, worst*; SEE CONCEPT *95*

overconfident [adj] *overly sure of oneself*
brash, careless, cocksure*, cocky*, foolhardy, heading for a fall*, heedless, hubristic, impudent, overweening, presuming, presumptuous, pushy*, rash, reckless, self-assertive; SEE CONCEPTS *401,542*

overdo [v] *go to extremes; carry too far*
amplify, be intemperate, belabor, bite off too much*, do to death, drive oneself, exaggerate, fatigue, go overboard*, go too far*, hype, lay it on*, magnify, make federal case*, not know when to stop*, overburden, overestimate, overindulge, overload, overplay, overrate, overreach, overstate, overtax, overtire, overuse, overvalue, overwork, pile on*, pressure, puff*, run into the ground*, run riot*, strain oneself, stretch, talk big*, wear down*, wear oneself out*; SEE CONCEPTS *87,112,156*

overdue [adj] *late, behind schedule*
behindhand, behind time, belated, delinquent, due, held up*, hung up*, jammed*, long delayed, mature, not punctual, outstanding, owing, payable, tardy, unpaid, unpunctual, unsettled; SEE CONCEPTS *334, 548,799*

overflow [n] *flood, inundation*
advance, cataclysm, cataract, congestion, deluge, discharge, encroachment, enforcement, engorgement, excess, exuberance, flash flood, flooding, infringement, niagara, overabundance, overcrowding, overkill, overmuch, overproduction, plethora, pour, propulsion, push, redundancy, spate, spill, spillover, submergence, submersion, superfluity, surfeit, surplus, torrent; SEE CONCEPT *740*

overflow [v] *pour out, flood*
brim, bubble over, cascade, cover, deluge, discharge, drain, drown, engulf, fall over, gush, inundate, irrupt, issue, jet, leak, overbrim, overrun, overtop, pour, run over, rush, shed, shower, slop, slosh, soak, spill, spill over, spout, spray, spurt, squirt, submerge, surge, swamp, water, wave, well, well over, wet, whelm; SEE CONCEPTS *179,256,740*

overhang [v] *bulge, hang over*
beetle, be imminent, be suspended, cast a shadow, command, dangle over, droop over, endanger, extend, flap over, impend, jut, loom, menace, overtop, poke, portend, pouch, project, protrude, rise above,

stand out, stick out, swing over, threaten, tower above; SEE CONCEPT *752*

overhaul [v] *redo, restore*
check, debug, doctor*, do up*, examine, fiddle with*, fix, give facelift*, improve, inspect, mend, modernize, patch, rebuild, recondition, reconstruct, reexamine, renew, repair, retread, revamp, service, survey; SEE CONCEPTS *126,202,212*

overhead [n] *general, continuing costs of operation*
budget, burden, cost, depreciation, expense, expenses, insurance, outlay, rent, upkeep, utilities; SEE CONCEPTS *329,332*

overhead [adj/adv] *up above*
above, aerial, aloft, atop, hanging, in the sky, on high, over, overhanging, roof, skyward, upper, upward; SEE CONCEPT *586*

overjoyed [adj] *extremely happy*
charmed, delighted, deliriously happy, elated, euphoric, happy as a clam*, happy as a lark*, joyful, jubilant, on cloud nine*, only too happy*, over the moon*, rapturous, ravished, thrilled, tickled pink*, transported; SEE CONCEPT *403*

overlap [v] *lie over something else*
extend along, flap, fold over, go beyond, imbricate, lap over, overhang, overlay, overlie, overrun-,project, protrude, ride, run over, shingle; SEE CONCEPT *759*

overlook [v1] *disregard, neglect*
discount, disdain, fail to notice, forget, ignore, leave out, leave undone, let fall between the cracks*, let go, let slide*, make light of*, miss, omit, overpass, pass, pass by, pay no attention, slight, slip up*; SEE CONCEPTS *30,101,699*

overlook [v2] *make allowances for*
bear with*, blink at*, condone, disregard, excuse, forgive, go along with, grin and bear it*, handle, ignore, let bygones be bygones*, let go, let pass*, live with*, look the other way, pay no mind*, play past*, put up with*, roll with punches*, stand for, stomach, swim with the tide*, take, tune out*, turn blind eye to*, whitewash*, wink at*, wipe slate clean*; SEE CONCEPTS *10,83*

overlook [v3] *have a view of something*
afford a view, command, command a view, dominate, front on, give on, give upon, have a prospect of, inspect, look down, look out, look out on, look over, mount, oversee, overtop, soar above, surmount, survey, top, tower over, view, watch over; SEE CONCEPT *752*

overlook [v4] *supervise*
boss, chaperon, control, oversee, quarterback*, superintend, survey; SEE CONCEPTS *94,117*

overly [adv] *excessively*
ever, exceedingly, extremely, immensely, immoderately, inordinately, over, overfull, overmuch, too, too much, too-too*, unduly, very much; SEE CONCEPT *544*

overplay [v] *be very dramatic*
accent, accentuate, blow out of proportion*, dramatize, exaggerate, get carried away*, ham it up*, hyperbolize, labor at, lay it on thick*, magnify, maximize, mug*, overact, overdo, overdraw, overemphasize, overstate, overstress, overuse, overwork, point up*, show off*, stretch; SEE CONCEPTS *59,87,292*

overpower [v] *beat; get the upper hand*
bear down, beat down, blank, blow away*, bulldoze*, bury, clobber, conquer, cream*, crush, defeat, drown, drub*, immobilize, knock out*, lay one out*, make say uncle*, master, murder*, overthrow, overwhelm, prostrate, put away*, quell, reduce, roll over*, rout, shellack*, shut off*, smash*, subdue, subjugate, swamp*, take care of*, take out*, torpedo*, total*, trash*, trounce, vanquish, waste*, wax*, whelm*; SEE CONCEPTS *95,191*

overrate [v] *assign too much value, importance*
assess too highly, build up, exaggerate, exceed, expect too much of, magnify, make too much of*, overassess, overesteem, overestimate, overpraise, overprize, overreckon, oversell, overvalue, rate too highly, think too highly of*, think too much of*; SEE CONCEPTS *12,49*

override/overrule [v] *cancel, reverse a decision*
alter, annul, bend to one's will*, control, countermand, direct, disallow, disregard, dominate, govern, ignore, influence, invalidate, make null and void*, make void, not heed, nullify, outvote, outweigh, overturn, prevail over, quash, recall, repeal, rescind, revoke, ride roughshod*, rule against, set aside, supersede, sway, take no account of, thwart, trample, upset, vanquish, veto; SEE CONCEPTS *50,88,121,298,317*

overriding [adj] *central, most important*
cardinal, compelling, determining, dominant, final, main, major, number one*, overruling, paramount, pivotal, predominant, prevailing, primary, prime, principal, ruling, supreme, ultimate; SEE CONCEPT *568*

overrun [v1] *defeat, invade*
beat, clobber, drub*, foray, inroad, lambaste, lick, massacre, occupy, overwhelm, put to flight, raid, rout, swamp*, thrash, trim, whip; SEE CONCEPTS *86,95*

overrun [v2] *infest, spread over; exceed*
beset, choke, deluge, go beyond, inundate, invade, overflow, overgrow, overshoot, overspread, overstep, overwhelm, permeate, ravage, run on, run over, spill, spread like wildfire*, surge, surpass, swarm, well over; SEE CONCEPTS *172,179,651*

overseas [adj] *across an ocean*
abroad, across, away, foreign, in foreign land, transatlantic, transoceanic, transpacific; SEE CONCEPT *583*

oversee [v] *manage, supervise*
baby-sit*, be in driver's seat*, boss, call the shots*, captain, chaperon, command, eye*, herd, inspect,

keep one's eye on*, look after, overlook, quarter-back*, ride herd on*, run the show*, shepherd, sit on top of*, skipper, superintend, survey, watch; SEE CONCEPT *117*

overshadow [v] *make obscure, dim, vague*
adumbrate, becloud, bedim, cloud, command, darken, dim, dominate, dwarf, eclipse, excel, govern, haze, leave in the shade*, manage, obfuscate, outshine, outweigh, overcast, overcloud, overweigh, preponderate, rise above*, rule, shadow, steal spotlight*, surpass, take precedence, tower above*, veil; SEE CONCEPTS *620,668*

oversight [n1] *failure, omission*
blank*, blunder, carelessness, chasm, default, delinquency, dereliction, disregard, error, fault, inattention, lapse, laxity, miscue, mistake, neglect, overlook, overlooking, preterition, pretermission, skip, slip, slipup*; SEE CONCEPT *101*

oversight [n2] *care, supervision*
administration, aegis, charge, check, control, custody, direction, guard, guardianship, handling, inspection, intendance, keep, keeping, maintenance, management, superintendence, surveillance, tutelage; SEE CONCEPT *117*

overt [adj] *obvious, unconcealed*
apparent, clear, definite, manifest, observable, open, patent, plain, public, undisguised, visible; SEE CONCEPT *535*

overtake [v] *catch; pass*
beat, befall, better, catch up with, come upon, engulf, gain on, get past, get to, happen, hit, leave behind, outdistance, outdo, outstrip, overhaul, overwhelm, reach, strike, take by surprise; SEE CONCEPTS *95,141*

overthrow [v] *defeat, destroy*
abolish, beat, bring down, bring to ruin, conquer, crush, demolish, depose, dethrone, do away with, eradicate, exterminate, knock down, knock over, level, liquidate, master, oust, overcome, overpower, overrun, overturn, overwhelm, purge, put an end to, raze, ruin, subdue, subjugate, subvert, terminate, tip, topple, tumble, unseat, upend, upset, vanquish; SEE CONCEPTS *95,252,320*

overtone [n] *implication, hint*
association, connotation, flavor, inference, innuendo, intimation, meaning, nuance, sense, suggestion, tone, undercurrent, undertone; SEE CONCEPT *278*

overture [n] *introduction, approach*
advance, bid, conciliatory move, exordium, foreword, invitation, offer, opening, preamble, preface, prelude, prelusion, presentation, proem, prologue, proposal, proposition, signal, suggestion, tender; SEE CONCEPTS *278,384,828,832*

overturn [v] *flip over*
annul, bring down, capsize, countermand, down, invalidate, invert, keel over, knock down, knock over, nullify, overbalance, prostrate, repeal, rescind, reverse, roll, set aside, spill, tip over, topple, tumble,

turn over, turn upside down, upend, upset, upturn, void; SEE CONCEPTS *147,232*

overweight [adj] *heavier than average*
ample, bulky, corpulent, fat, fleshy, gross, heavy, hefty, huge, massive, obese, outsize, overfed, overstuffed, plump, portly, pudgy, rotund, stout, upholstered, weighty; SEE CONCEPT *491*

overwhelm [v1] *flood, beat physically*
bury, conquer, crush, defeat, deluge, destroy, drown, drub*, engulf, inundate, massacre, overcome, overflow, overpower, overrun, overthrow, rout, smother, submerge, swamp, thrash, total*, whip*, win*; SEE CONCEPTS *86,95*

overwhelm [v2] *astonish, devastate*
bewilder, blow out of the water*, bowl over*, confound, confuse, demoralize, destroy, disturb, do in*, downgrade*, drown, dumbfound, floor*, kill*, overcome, overpower, prostrate, puzzle, render speechless*, run circles around, shatter, shock, stagger, steamroller*, stun, subordinate, surprise, swamp, upset, wreck; SEE CONCEPTS *16,42*

overwrought [adj] *exhausted and excited*
affected, agitated, all shook up*, beside oneself*, crazy, distracted, emotional, excitable, fired-up*, flipped out*, frantic, freaked-out*, high*, hot-and-bothered*, hot under collar*, hyper*, in a state*, keyed-up*, nervous, neurotic, on edge*, overexcited, overstrung, overworked, spent, steamed up*, stirred*, strung-out*, tense, tired, uneasy, unstrung*, uptight*, weary, wired, worked-up, worn, wound-up; SEE CONCEPTS *401,403,542*

owe [v] *have an obligation*
be behind, be beholden, be bound, be contracted, be in arrears, be in debt, be indebted, be into one for, be obligated, be under obligation, feel bound, get on credit, have borrowed, incur, in hock*, lost, on the tab*, ought to, run up a bill*; SEE CONCEPT *335*

owing [adj] *unpaid*
attributable, comeuppance, due, in debt, mature, matured, outstanding, overdue, owed, payable, unsettled; SEE CONCEPT *334*

own [adj] *belonging to individual*
endemic, hers, his, individual, inherent, intrinsic, its, mine, owned, particular, peculiar, personal, private, resident, theirs, very own, yours; SEE CONCEPT *710*

own [v1] *possess; be responsible for*
be in possession of, be master/mistress of, be possessed of, boast, control, dominate, enjoy, fall heir to, have, have in hand, have rights, have title, hold, inherit, keep, occupy, reserve, retain; SEE CONCEPT *710*

own [v2] *acknowledge, admit*
allow, assent to, avow, come clean*, concede, confess, declare, disclose, grant, let on*, make clean breast of*, own up, recognize, tell the truth; SEE CONCEPT *57*

owner [n] *person who has possession of something*
buyer, governor, heir, heir-apparent, heiress, heritor, holder, keeper, landlady, landlord, landowner, legatee, lord, master, mistress, partner, possessor, proprietor, proprietress, proprietrix, purchaser, sharer, slumlord, squire, titleholder; SEE CONCEPTS *343,347,414*

ownership [n] *possession of property*
buying, claim, control, cut, deed, dominion, end, hand, having, holding, occupancy, partnership, piece, possessorship, property, proprietary rights, proprietorship, purchase, purchasing, residence, slice, takeover, tenancy, tenure, title, use; SEE CONCEPT *710*

P

pace [n1] *steps in walking*
clip, footstep, gait, getalong, lick, measure, step, stride, tread, walk; SEE CONCEPT *149*

pace [n2] *speed, tempo of motion*
beat, bounce, celerity, clip, downbeat, lick, momentum, motion, movement, progress, quickness, rapidity, rapidness, rate, swiftness, time, velocity; SEE CONCEPTS *755,818*

pace [v1] *walk back and forth*
ambulate, canter, foot it*, gallop, hoof*, march, patrol, pound*, step, stride, traipse, tread, troop, trot, walk back and forth, walk up and down; SEE CONCEPT *149*

pace [v2] *measure by footsteps*
count, determine, mark out, step, step off; SEE CONCEPTS *291,764*

pacify [v] *make peaceful; appease*
allay, ameliorate, assuage, bury the hatchet*, butter up*, calm, chasten, compose, con, conciliate, cool, dulcify, fix up, grease*, kiss and make up*, lay back, lull, make peace, mitigate, moderate, mollify, pacificate, placate, propitiate, put the lid on*, qualify, quell, quiet, relieve, repress, silence, smooth over, soften, soft-pedal*, soothe, square, still, stroke, subdue, sweeten*, take the edge off*, tame, temper, tranquilize; SEE CONCEPTS *7,22,250*

pack [n1] *kit, package*
backpack, baggage, bale, bundle, burden, equipment, haversack, knapsack, load, luggage, outfit, parcel, rucksack, truss; SEE CONCEPTS *260,446,496*

pack [n2] *group, bunch*
assemblage, band, barrel, bundle, circle, collection, company, crew, crowd, deck, drove, flock, gang, great deal, heap, herd, horde, lot, lump, mess, mob, much, multiplicity, number, peck, pile, press, set, swarm, throng, troop; SEE CONCEPTS *397,417,432*

pack [v1] *make ready for transport*
batch, bind, brace, bunch, bundle, burden, collect, dispose, fasten, gather, get ready, load, package, put in order, store, stow, tie, warehouse; SEE CONCEPT *202*

pack [v2] *fill, compact*
arrange, bind, charge, charge, chock, choke, compress, condense, contract, cram, crowd, drive in, heap, insert, jam, jam-pack*, lade, load, mob, pile, press, push, put away, ram, ram in*, sardine*, squeeze, stuff, tamp, throng, thrust in, top off, wedge; SEE CONCEPT *209*

pack [v3] *transport, carry*
bear, buck, convey, ferry, freight, gun, haul, heel, hump, jag, journey, lug, piggyback*, ride, schlepp*, shoulder, tote, trek, truck; SEE CONCEPTS *148,217*

package [n] *bundle; whole*
amalgamation, assortment, bag, baggage, bale, batch, biddle, bottle, box, bunch, burden, can, carton, combination, container, crate, entity, kit, load, lot, luggage, pack, packet, parcel, pile, sack, sheaf, stack, suitcase, tin, trunk, unit; SEE CONCEPTS *432,494*

packed [adj] *very full*
arranged, awash, brimful, brimming, bundled, chock, chock-full*, compact, compressed, congested, consigned, crammed, crowded, filled, full to the gills*, jammed, jam-packed*, loaded, mobbed, overflowing, overloaded, packed like sardines*, seething, serried, stuffed, swarming, to the roof*, tumid, up to the hilt*, up to the rafters*, wall-to-wall*, wrapped; SEE CONCEPTS *481,483,740,774*

packet [n] *small, often flat, bundle*
bag, carton, container, envelope, file, folder, package, parcel, wrapper, wrapping; SEE CONCEPT *494*

pact [n] *agreement*
alliance, arrangement, bargain, bond, compact, concord, concordat, contract, convention, covenant, deal, league, paper, piece of paper, protocol, settlement, transaction, treaty, understanding; SEE CONCEPTS *271,684*

pad/padding [n1] *protection*
buffer, cushion, filling, packing, stuffing, wad, wadding, waste; SEE CONCEPTS *473,475*

pad [n2] *tablet of paper*
block, jotter, memorandum, notebook, notepad, paper, parchment, quire, ream, scratch, scratch pad, slips; SEE CONCEPTS *260,475*

pad [v1] *protect with cushioning*
cushion, fill, fill out, line, pack, protect, shape, stuff; SEE CONCEPTS *134,202*

pad [v2] *elaborate, amplify*
augment, bulk, embellish, embroider, enlarge, exaggerate, expand, fill out, flesh out*, fudge, increase, inflate, lengthen, magnify, overdraw, overstate, protract, spin, stretch; SEE CONCEPTS *63,244*

pad [v3] *walk quietly; walk ploddingly*
creep, go barefoot, hike, march, patter*, pitter-patter*, plod, pussyfoot*, sneak, steal, traipse, tramp, trek, trudge; SEE CONCEPT *149*

paddle [n] *item used for propelling object*
oar, paddlewheel, pole, propeller, pull, scull, sweep; SEE CONCEPTS *479,499*

paddle [v] *propel with arms or tool*
boat, cruise, cut water*, drift, drive, navigate, oar, pull, row, run rapids*, scull, sky an oar*, slop, splash, stir, sweep, thrash, wade; SEE CONCEPT *147*

pagan [n] *person who does not believe in orthodox Christianity*
agnostic, atheist, doubter, freethinker, heathen, heretic, idolator, idolist, infidel, paganist, pantheist, polytheist, scoffer, skeptic, unbeliever; SEE CONCEPTS *361,423*

pagan [adj] *irreligious*
agnostic, atheistic, heathen, heathenish, idolatrous, impious, infidel, polytheistic, profane, unchristian; SEE CONCEPT *542*

page [n1] *sheet of paper*
folio, leaf, recto, side, signature, surface, verso; SEE CONCEPT *475*

page [n2] *person who serves others*
attendant, bellboy, bellhop, equerry, errand runner, footboy, servant, squire, youth; SEE CONCEPTS *348,354*

page [v1] *call for over communications system*
announce, beep, call, call out, call the name of, hunt for, preconize, seek, send for, summon; SEE CONCEPTS *74,78*

page [v2] *mark sheets of document*
check, count, foliate, number, paginate; SEE CONCEPTS *79,764*

pageant [n] *spectacle or contest*
celebration, charade, display, exhibition, exposition, extravaganza, fair, make-believe, motorcade, parade, pomp, procession, ritual, show, tableau; SEE CONCEPTS *292,377*

pain [n1] *physical suffering*
ache, affliction, agony, burn, catch, convulsion, cramp, crick, discomfort, distress, fever, gripe, hurt, illness, injury, irritation, laceration, malady, misery, pang, paroxysm, prick, sickness, smarting, soreness, spasm, sting, stitch, strain, tenderness, throb, throe, tingle, torment, torture, trouble, twinge, wound; SEE CONCEPTS *316,728*

pain [n2] *mental suffering*
affliction, agony, anguish, anxiety, bitterness, despondency, distress, grief, heartache, hurt, malaise, martyrdom, misery, rack, sadness, shock, suffering, torment, torture, travail, tribulation, woe, worry, wretchedness; SEE CONCEPTS *410,728*

pain [n3] *big problem*
aggravation, annoyance, bore, bother, drag*, effort, exertion, irritation, nuisance, pest, trouble, vexation; SEE CONCEPT *532*

pain [v] *bother, trouble*
ache, afflict, aggrieve, agonize, ail, anguish, annoy, bite, chafe, chasten, constrain, convulse, cut to the quick*, discomfort, disquiet, distress, exasperate, excruciate, gall, grieve, gripe, harass, harm, harrow, hit where one lives*, hurt, inflame, injure, irk, irritate, nick, prick, punish, rack, rile, sadden, smart,

sting, strain, stress, suffer, throb, tingle, torment, torture, upset, vex, worry, wound; SEE CONCEPTS *7,19,246*

painful [adj] *physically or mentally agonizing*
aching, afflictive, agonizing, arduous, awful, biting, burning, caustic, difficult, dire, disagreeable, distasteful, distressing, dreadful, excruciating, extreme, extremely bad, grievous, hard, harrowing, hurtful, hurting, inflamed, irritated, laborious, piercing, raw, saddening, sensitive, severe, sharp, smarting, sore, stinging, tedious, tender, terrible, throbbing, tormenting, troublesome, trying, uncomfortable, unpleasant, vexatious; SEE CONCEPTS *529,537*

painstaking [adj] *meticulous, thorough*
assiduous, by the book*, by the numbers*, careful, conscientious, conscionable, diligent, earnest, exact, exacting, finicky, fussbudget*, fussy, hard-working, heedful, industrious, particular, persevering, persnickety*, picky, punctilious, punctual, scrupulous, sedulous, stickler*, strenuous, thoroughgoing; SEE CONCEPTS *326,538*

paint [n] *tinted covering*
acrylic, chroma, color, coloring, cosmetic, dye, emulsion, enamel, flat, gloss, greasepaint, latex, makeup, oil, overlay, pigment, rouge, stain, tempera, varnish, veneer, wax; SEE CONCEPTS *467,475*

paint [v] *apply colored tint, often to make design*
brush, catch a likeness, coat, color, compose, cover, cover up, daub, decorate, delineate, depict, design, draft, draw, dye, figure, fresco, gloss over, limn, ornament, outline, picture, portray, put on coats*, represent, shade, sketch, slap on*, slather, stipple, swab, tint, touch up, wash; SEE CONCEPTS *172,174*

pair [n] *two of something*
brace, combination, combine, combo, couple, deuce, doublet, duality, duo, dyad, match, mates, span, team, twins, two, two of a kind, twosome, yoke; SEE CONCEPTS *432,784*

pair [v] *make, become a twosome*
balance, bracket, combine, couple, join, marry, match, match up, mate, pair off, put together, team, twin, unite, wed, yoke; SEE CONCEPT *113*

pajamas [n] *sleeping clothes*
jamas*, jammies*, jams*, loungewear, lounging robe, nightdress, nightie*, nightshirt, nightwear, PJ's*, sleeper, sleeping suit; SEE CONCEPT *451*

pal [n] *person's friend*
amiga, amigo, associate, boon companion*, bosom buddy*, bro*, brother, buddy, chum, companion, comrade, connate, crony, good buddy*, homeboy, homegirl, mate, sidekick, sis*, sister; SEE CONCEPT *423*

palace [n] *royal or enormous home*
alcazar, castle, chateau, dwelling, hall, manor, mansion, official residence, royal residence; SEE CONCEPT *516*

palatable [adj] *delicious, agreeable*
acceptable, A-OK*, aperitive, appetizing, attractive, cool, copacetic, delectable, delightful, divine, enjoy-

able, fair, flavorsome, good-tasting, heavenly, home-cooking*, luscious, mellow, mouthwatering, peachy, pleasant, relishing, sapid, saporific, saporous, satisfactory, savory, scrumptious, sugar-coated*, sweetened, tasteful, tasty, tempting, toothsome, toothy*, yummy*; SEE CONCEPTS *529,613*

palatial [*adj*] *grand, opulent*
deluxe, grandiose, illustrious, imposing, impressive, lush, luxuriant, luxurious, magnificent, majestic, monumental, noble, plush, regal, rich, silken, spacious, splendid, stately, sumptuous, upholstered; SEE CONCEPTS *334,485,589*

pale [*adj*] *very light in color or effect*
anemic, ashen, ashy, blanched, bleached, bloodless, cadaverous, colorless, deathlike, dim, doughy, dull, faded, faint, feeble, ghastly, gray, haggard, inadequate, ineffective, ineffectual, insubstantial, livid, lurid, pallid, pasty, poor, sallow, sick, sickly, spectral, thin, unsubstantial, wan, washed-out, waxen, waxlike, weak, white, whitish; SEE CONCEPTS *537,618*

pale [*v*] *become, make lighter or weakened*
blanch, decrease, dim, diminish, dull, fade, faint, go white, grow dull, lessen, lose color, lose luster, muddy, tarnish, whiten; SEE CONCEPTS *240,250*

pall [*n*] *cloud, gloom*
cloak, cloth, covering, damp, damper, dismay, mantle, melancholy, shadow, shroud, veil; SEE CONCEPTS *620,674*

pall [*v*] *bore, tire*
become dull, become tedious, cloy, disgust, fill, glut, gorge, jade, sate, satiate, sicken, surfeit, weary; SEE CONCEPTS *7,19*

palliate [*v*] *gloss over; cover up*
abate, allay, alleviate, apologize for, assuage, camouflage, cloak, conceal, condone, cover, diminish, disguise, dissemble, ease, exculpate, excuse, extenuate, gloze, hide, hush up*, justify, lessen, lighten, make light of*, mask, minimize, mitigate, moderate, mollify, prettify, put on band-aid*, qualify, quick fix*, relieve, screen, soften, soothe, sugarcoat*, temper, varnish, veil, veneer, vindicate, white, whiten, whitewash*; SEE CONCEPTS *57,59,172,188*

palpable [*adj1*] *clear, obvious*
apparent, appreciable, arresting, believable, blatant, certain, colorable, conspicuous, credible, detectable, discernible, distinct, evident, manifest, noticeable, observable, open, ostensible, patent, perceivable, perceptible, plain, plausible, positive, remarkable, seeming, sensible, straightforward, striking, sure, tangible, unequivocal, unmistakable, visible; SEE CONCEPTS *529,535*

palpable [*adj2*] *concrete, real*
material, sensible, solid, substantial, tactile, tangible, touchable; SEE CONCEPTS *485,582*

palpitate [*v*] *beat at a rapid pace, like a heart*
flutter, pitpat*, pitter-patter*, pound, pulsate, pulse, quiver, shiver, throb, tremble, vibrate; SEE CONCEPTS *152,308*

palsied [*adj*] *crippled*
arthritic, atonic, debilitated, disabled, diseased, helpless, neurasthenic, paralytic, paralyzed, rheumatic, sclerotic, shaking, shaky, sick, spastic, trembling, tremorous, weak; SEE CONCEPTS *314,485*

paltry [*adj*] *very poor; worthless*
base, beggarly, cheap, common, contemptible, derisory, despicable, inconsiderable, ineffectual, insignificant, limited, low, low-down*, meager, mean, measly, minor, miserable, narrow, petty, picayune*, piddling, pitiful, puny, set, shabby, shoddy, sleazy*, slight, small, sorry, trashy, trifling, trivial, unconsequential, unimportant, vile, wretched; SEE CONCEPTS *334,485*

pamper [*v*] *serve one's every need, whim*
baby, caress, cater to, coddle, cosset, dandle*, fondle, gratify, humor, indulge, mollycoddle*, overindulge, pet, please, regale, satisfy, spare the rod*, spoil, spoil rotten*, tickle, yield; SEE CONCEPTS *136,295*

pamphlet [*n*] *booklet*
announcement, broadside, brochure, bulletin, circular, compilation, flyer*, folder, handout, leaflet, throwaway*, tract, tractate; SEE CONCEPTS *271,280*

pan [*n*] *container for cooking food*
bucket, casserole, double boiler, frying pan, kettle, pail, pannikin, pot, roaster, saucepan, sheet, skillet, vessel; SEE CONCEPTS *493,494*

pan [*v1*] *look, search for over a wide area*
follow, move, scan, separate, sift, sweep, swing, track, traverse, wash; SEE CONCEPT *216*

pan [*v2*] *criticize strongly*
blame, censure, condemn, cut up, denounce, denunciate, disparage, flay, hammer, jeer at, knock, rap, reprehend, review unfavorably, roast, slam; SEE CONCEPT *52*

panacea [*n*] *cure-all*
catholicon, cure, elixir, nostrum, patent medicine, relief, remedy; SEE CONCEPTS *307,311*

panache [*n*] *person's flamboyant spirit*
brio, charisma, dash, élan, flair, flamboyance, flourish, style, swagger, verve, vigor; SEE CONCEPT *411*

pancake [*n*] *flat, round breakfast cake*
batter cake, blanket*, cake, crepe, flapjack, griddlecake, hot cake, johnnycake, jonnycake, sourdough, waffle, wheat*, wheat cake; SEE CONCEPTS *457,461*

pandemonium [*n*] *craziness, commotion*
anarchy, babel, bedlam, bluster, brouhaha*, chaos, clamor, clatter, confusion, din, hassle, hubbub*, hue and cry*, hullaballoo*, jangle, noise, racket, riot, ruckus, rumpus, tumult, turbulence, turmoil, uproar; SEE CONCEPTS *388,674*

pander [*v*] *cater to, indulge*
brownnose*, cajole, fall all over*, gratify, lay it on*, massage, play the game*, play up to*, please, politic, satisfy, snow*, soap*, soften up, stroke, suck up to*; SEE CONCEPTS *59,136,384*

pang [n] *ache, twinge*
agony, anguish, bite, discomfort, distress, gripe, misery, pain, prick, spasm, stab, sting, stitch, throb, throe, wrench; SEE CONCEPT *728*

panic [n1] *extreme fright*
agitation, alarm, cold feet*, confusion, consternation, crush, dismay, dread, fear, frenzy, fright, horror, hysteria, jam, rush, scare, stampede, terror, trepidation; SEE CONCEPTS *27,410,690*

panic [n2] *sudden drop in value in financial markets*
Black Monday*, bust, crash, depression, rainy day*, slump; SEE CONCEPT *335*

panic [v] *become, make afraid or distressed*
alarm, become hysterical, be terror-stricken, chicken out*, clutch, come apart, freeze up*, go to pieces*, have a fit*, lose it*, lose nerve*, overreact, push panic button*, run scared*, scare, shake in boots*, stampede, startle, terrify, unnerve; SEE CONCEPTS *14,27*

panorama [n] *scene, horizon*
bird's-eye view*, compass, dimension, diorama, extent, orbit, overview, perspective, picture, prospect, purview, radius, range, reach, scenery, scenic view, scope, spectacle, survey, sweep, view, vista; SEE CONCEPTS *529,628,651*

pan out [v] *come to pass; succeed*
click*, come out*, culminate, eventuate, go, go over*, happen, net*, prove out, result, turn out, work out, yield; SEE CONCEPT *706*

pant [v1] *gasp for air*
be out of breath, blow, breathe, chuff, gulp, heave, huff, palpitate, puff, snort, throb, wheeze, whiff, wind; SEE CONCEPT *163*

pant [v2] *long for*
ache, aim, aspire, covet, crave, desire, hunger, lust, pine, sigh, thirst, want, wish, yearn; SEE CONCEPT *20*

pants [n] *clothing for legs, lower half of body*
Bermudas, bloomers, blue jeans, boxer shorts, breeches, briefs, britches*, chaps*, chinos, clam diggers*, cords*, corduroys, denims, drawers, dungarees, jeans, jodhpurs, knickers, overalls, pantaloons*, panties*, pedal pushers, shorts, slacks, trousers, underpants; SEE CONCEPT *451*

paper/papers [n1] *legal document*
affidavit, archive, bill, certificate, certification, citation, contract, credentials, data, deed, diaries, diploma, documentation, dossier, file, grant, ID*, identification papers, indictment, instrument, letter, letters, order, passport, plea, record, subpoena, summons, testimony, token, visa, voucher, warrant, will, writ, writings; SEE CONCEPTS *271,318*

paper [n2] *newspaper*
daily, gazette, journal, news, organ, rag*, weekly; SEE CONCEPT *280*

paper [n3] *thesis, article*
analysis, assignment, composition, critique, dissertation, essay, examination, monograph, report, script, study, theme, treatise; SEE CONCEPTS *271,280*

paper [n4] *material upon which one writes*
card, filing card, letterhead, newsprint, note, note card, note pad, onion skin, pad, papyrus, parchment, poster, rag, sheet, stationery, tissue, vellum; SEE CONCEPTS *260,475*

paper [adj] *thin, flimsy*
cardboard, disposable, insubstantial, paper-thin, papery, wafer-thin; SEE CONCEPT *606*

paper [v] *line with material*
cover, hang, paste up, plaster, wallpaper; SEE CONCEPTS *172,177*

par [n] *average, equilibrium*
adequation, balance, coequality, criterion, equal footing, equality, equatability, equivalence, equivalency, level, mean, median, model, norm, parity, sameness, standard, usual; SEE CONCEPTS *636,667*

parade [n] *pageant, display*
array, autocade, cavalcade, ceremony, column, demonstration, exhibition, fanfare, flaunting, line, march, ostentation, panoply, pomp, procession, review, ritual, shine, show, spectacle, train, vaunting; SEE CONCEPTS *377,386*

parade [v] *show off; march*
advertise, air, boast, brag, brandish, declare, demonstrate, disclose, display, disport, divulge, exhibit, expose, flash, flaunt, march in review, prance, proclaim, publish, reveal, sport, strut, swagger, trot out*, vaunt; SEE CONCEPT *261*

paradigm [n] *example*
archetype, beau ideal*, chart, criterion, ensample, exemplar, ideal, mirror, model, original, pattern, prototype, sample, standard; SEE CONCEPT *688*

paradise [n] *land, feeling of great pleasure; absence of evil*
Arcadia*, ballpark, bliss, City of God*, cloud nine*, delight, divine abode*, Eden*, felicity, happy hunting ground*, heaven, heavenly kingdom, kingdom come*, next world*, pearly gates*, promised land, Shangri-la*, Utopia, wonderland, Zion*; SEE CONCEPTS *370,410,515*

paradox [n] *contradiction, puzzle*
absurdity, ambiguity, anomaly, catch, Catch-22*, enigma, error, inconsistency, mistake, mystery, nonsense, oddity, opposite, reverse; SEE CONCEPT *532*

paragon [n] *outstanding example*
apotheosis, archetype, beau ideal*, beauty, best, champ, champion, crackerjack*, cream*, criterion, cynosure, epitome, essence, exemplar, gem, ideal, jewel*, love, lovely, masterpiece, model, nonesuch, nonpareil, original, paradigm, pattern, peach*, perfection, pick, prototype, quintessence, standard, sublimation, tops*, trump*, ultimate; SEE CONCEPTS *671,688*

parallel [n] *complement, correlation*
analogue, analogy, comparison, corollary, correlate, correspondence, correspondent, counterpart, countertype, double, duplicate, duplication, equal, equivalent, homologue, kin, likeness, match, parallelism,

resemblance, similarity, twin; SEE CONCEPTS *667,670*

parallel [*adj1*] *aligned, side-by-side*
alongside, coextending, coextensive, coordinate, equidistant, extending equally, in the same direction, lateral, laterally, never meeting, running alongside; SEE CONCEPTS *581,586*

parallel [*adj2*] *akin, similar*
agnate, alike, analogous, comparable, complementary, conforming, consonant, correspondent, corresponding, equal, identical, like, matching, resembling, uniform; SEE CONCEPTS *487,573*

parallel [*v*] *be alike*
agree, assimilate, chime, collimate, collocate, compare, complement, conform, copy, correlate, correspond, equal, equate, imitate, keep pace, liken, match, paragon, parallelize; SEE CONCEPTS *111,171,667*

paralytic [*adj*] *crippled*
diplegic, disabled, immobile, immobilized, inactive, incapacitated, insensible, lame, numb, palsied, palsified, paralyzed, paraplegic, powerless, quadriplegic; SEE CONCEPTS *314,485*

paralyze [*v*] *immobilize, cripple*
anesthetize, appall, arrest, astound, bemuse, benumb, bring to grinding halt*, close, daunt, daze, deaden, debilitate, demolish, destroy, disable, disarm, enfeeble, freeze, halt, incapacitate, knock out, lame, make inert, make nerveless, nonplus, numb, palsy, petrify, prostrate, shut down*, stop dead*, stun, stupefy, transfix, weaken; SEE CONCEPTS *14,121,246,252*

parameter [*n*] *limit*
constant, criterion, framework, guideline, limitation, restriction, specification; SEE CONCEPT *687*

paramount [*adj*] *principal, superior*
ascendant, capital, cardinal, chief, commanding, controlling, crowning, dominant, eminent, first, foremost, headmost, leading, main, master, outstanding, overbearing, predominant, predominate, preeminent, premier, preponderant, prevalent, primary, prime, regnant, sovereign, supreme; SEE CONCEPTS *568,574*

paraphernalia [*n*] *equipment, belongings*
accoutrements, apparatus, appurtenances, baggage, effects, equipage, gear, habiliments, impedimenta, impediments, machinery, material, materiel, outfit, regalia, stuff, tackle, things, trappings; SEE CONCEPTS *446,496*

paraphrase [*n*] *translation, interpretation*
digest, explanation, rehash, rendering, rendition, rephrasing, restatement, rewording, summary, version; SEE CONCEPTS *55,57,268*

paraphrase [*v*] *interpret, translate*
express in other words, express in own words, recapitulate, rehash, render, rephrase, restate, reword, summarize, transcribe; SEE CONCEPTS *55,57*

parasite [*n*] *something that exists by taking from or depending on another*
barnacle, bloodsucker*, bootlicker*, brownnose*, deadbeat*, dependent, flunky, freeloader*, groupie*, hanger-on*, idler, leech, scrounger, sponge*, stooge*, sucker*, sycophant, taker*, yes-man/woman*; SEE CONCEPTS *394,412*

parcel [*n1*] *container prepared to be sent*
bindle, bundle, carton, load, pack, package, packet; SEE CONCEPT *494*

parcel [*n2*] *group, bunch*
array, band, batch, body, clot, clump, cluster, clutch, collection, company, crew, crowd, gang, lot, pack; SEE CONCEPT *432*

parcel [*n3*] *piece of land*
acreage, plat, plot, property, tract; SEE CONCEPTS *509,513*

parcel [*n4*] *part, piece*
bite, chunk, cut, division, lion's share*, member, moiety, piece of the action*, portion, rake-off*, section, segment, slice; SEE CONCEPTS *829,835*

parch [*v*] *dry, burn*
blister, brown, dehydrate, desiccate, dry up, evaporate, exsiccate, make thirsty, scorch, sear, shrivel, stale, wither; SEE CONCEPTS *249,255*

parched [*adj*] *very dry*
arid, burned, cotton-mouth*, dehydrated, dried out, dried up*, dry as dust*, scorched, shriveled, thirsty, waterless, withered; SEE CONCEPT *603*

pardon [*n*] *forgiveness*
absolution, acquittal, allowance, amnesty, anchor, clemency, commute, conciliation, condonation, discharge, exculpation, excuse, exoneration, forbearance, freeing, grace, indemnification, indemnity, indulgence, justification, kindness, lifeboat*, lifesaver*, mercy, release, remission, reprieve, vindication; SEE CONCEPTS *10,318,685*

pardon [*v*] *forgive*
absolve, accept, acquit, amnesty, blink at*, bury the hatchet*, clear, condone, discharge, exculpate, excuse, exonerate, free, give absolution, grant amnesty, justify, let off*, let off easy*, liberate, lifeboat*, overlook, release, remit, reprieve, rescue, spring*, suspend charges, tolerate, wink at*, wipe slate clean*, write off*; SEE CONCEPTS *10,50,88,317*

pare [*v*] *peel, trim*
carve, clip, crop, cut, cut back, cut down, decorticate, decrease, dock, flay, knock off, lop, lower, mark down, prune, reduce, scalp, scrape, shave, shear, skin, skive, slash, strip, thin, uncover; SEE CONCEPTS *176,202,236,247*

parent [*n*] *person, source of product*
ancestor, architect, author, begetter, cause, creator, father, folks, forerunner, fountainhead, guardian, mother, origin, originator, procreator, progenitor, prototype, root, sire, wellspring; SEE CONCEPTS *414,648*

parenthetical [*adj*] *incidental*
bracketed, by the way, episodic, explanatory, extraneous, extrinsic, incidental, in parenthesis, inserted, intermediate, interposed, qualifying, related, subordinate; SEE CONCEPTS *544,577*

parish [n] *congregation of a church*
archdiocese, bethel, church, churchgoers, community, flock*, fold*, parishioners, territory; SEE CONCEPT *369*

parity [n] *equality, balance*
adequation, affinity, agreement, analogy, approximation, closeness, coequality, conformity, congruity, consistency, correspondence, equal terms, equivalence, equivalency, likeness, nearness, par, parallelism, paraphernalia, resemblance, sameness, similarity, similitude, terms, uniformity, unity; SEE CONCEPTS *667,670*

park [n] *land that is reserved for pleasure, recreation*
esplanade, estate, forest, garden, grass, green, grounds, lawn, lot, meadow, parkland, place, playground, plaza, pleasure garden, recreation area, square, tract, village green, woodland; SEE CONCEPTS *509,513*

park [v] *place vehicle in a position*
deposit, leave, line up, maneuver, order, position, put, seat, stand, station, store; SEE CONCEPTS *148,201*

parlor [n] *sitting room*
drawing room, front room, guest room, living room, lounge, reception, salon, waiting room; SEE CONCEPT *448*

parochial [adj] *narrow-minded, restricted*
biased, bigoted, conservative, conventional, insular, inward-looking, limited, local, narrow, petty, prejudiced, provincial, regional, sectarian, sectional, shallow, small-minded, small-town; SEE CONCEPT *542*

parody [n] *imitation, spoof*
apology, burlesque, caricature, cartoon, copy, derision, farce, irony, jest, joke, lampoon, mime, mimicry, misrepresentation, mockery, mock-heroic*, pastiche, play-on*, raillery, rib*, ridicule, roast*, satire, send-up*, skit, takeoff*, travesty; SEE CONCEPTS *59,273,292*

parody [v] *imitate, spoof*
ape, burlesque, caricature, copy, deride, disparage, distort, do a takeoff of*, exaggerate, impersonate, jeer, jest, joke, lampoon, laugh at, mime, mimic, mock, poke fun at, put on*, ridicule, roast, satirize, send up, sheik*, take off*, travesty; SEE CONCEPTS *59,111,273*

paroxysm [n] *seizure, spasm*
agitation, anger, attack, convulsion, eruption, excitement, explosion, fit, flare-up*, frenzy, frothing, fuming, furor, fury, hysterics, outbreak, outburst, passion, rage, violence; SEE CONCEPTS *308,316,410*

parrot [v] *repeat*
ape, chant, copy, copycat, echo, imitate, mime, mimic, quote, recite, reiterate; SEE CONCEPTS *47,77,171*

parry [v] *ward off, circumvent*
anticipate, avoid, block, bypass, deflect, dodge, duck*, elude, evade, fence*, fend off, forestall, hold at bay*, preclude, prevent, rebuff, rebuke, repel, re-

pulse, resist, shirk, shun, sidestep, stave off; SEE CONCEPTS *25,30,121*

parsimonious [adj] *penny-pinching*
avaricious, chintzy*, close, frugal, greedy, illiberal, mean, miserly, niggardly*, penurious, prudent, saving, scrimpy, selfish, skinflint*, sparing, stingy*, tight*, tightfisted*, tightwad*; SEE CONCEPTS *334,401*

part [n1] *piece, portion of something*
allotment, any, apportionment, articulation, atom, bit, bite, branch, chip, chunk, component, constituent, cut, department, detail, division, element, extra, factor, fraction, fragment, helping, hunk, ingredient, installment, item, limb, lot, lump, measure, meed, member, module, moiety, molecule, organ, parcel, particle, partition, piece, quantum, quota, ration, scrap, section, sector, segment, share, side, slab, slice, sliver, splinter, subdivision, unit; SEE CONCEPT *834*

part [n2] *person or group's interest, concern*
behalf, bit, business, capacity, cause, charge, duty, faction, function, involvement, office, party, place, responsibility, role, say, share, side, task, work; SEE CONCEPTS *362,532*

part [n3] *theatrical role*
bit, character, hero, heroine, ingenue, lead, lines, supporting role, walk-on; SEE CONCEPT *263*

part [v1] *break, disconnect*
articulate, break up, cleave, come apart, detach, dichotomize, disjoin, dismantle, dissever, disunite, divide, factor, itemize, particularize, partition, portion, rend, section, segment, separate, sever, slice, split, strip, subdivide, sunder, tear; SEE CONCEPTS *98,135*

part [v2] *leave, go away from someone*
break, break off, break up, clear out*, cut and run*, dedomicile, depart, ease out, go, go separate ways*, hit the road*, leave flat*, part company, pull out*, push off, quit, quit the scene*, say goodbye, separate, ship out*, shove off*, split, split up*, take a hike*, take leave, take off, walk out on, withdraw; SEE CONCEPTS *195,297,384*

partake [v] *eat, share*
be a party to, be in on, be into, consume, devour, divide, engage, enter into, feed, get in the act, have a hand in, ingest, participate, receive, sample, savor, sip, sit in, sit in on, take, take part, tune in; SEE CONCEPTS *169,225*

partial [adj1] *incomplete*
fractional, fragmentary, half done, halfway, imperfect, limited, part, sectional, uncompleted, unfinished, unperformed; SEE CONCEPT *531*

partial [adj2] *biased, prejudiced*
colored, discriminatory, disposed, favorably inclined, influenced, interested, jaundiced, minded, one-sided, partisan, predisposed, prepossessed, tendentious, unfair, unindifferent, unjust, warped; SEE CONCEPTS *403,542*

partiality [n] *favoritism, fondness*
affinity, bias, cup of tea*, dish, druthers*, flash, inclination, inclining, leaning, liking, love, partisanship, penchant, predilection, predisposition, preference, prejudice, proclivity, propensity, taste, tendency, thing*, type, weakness; SEE CONCEPTS *32,709*

partially [adv] *incompletely*
by degrees, by installments, fractionally, halfway, in part, in some measure, little by little, moderately, not wholly, partly, piece by piece, piecemeal, somewhat, to a certain degree, to a certain extent; SEE CONCEPTS *531,544*

participant [n] *person who takes part in activity*
actor, aide, a party to, assistant, associate, attendant, colleague, confrere, contributor, fellow, helper, member, partaker, participator, partner, party, player, shareholder, sharer; SEE CONCEPTS *352,366,423*

participate [v] *take part in activity*
aid, associate with, be a participant, be a party to, be into*, chip in*, come in, compete, concur, cooperate, engage, engage in, enter into, get in on*, get in on the act*, go into, have a hand in*, have to do with, join in, latch on*, lend a hand, partake, perform, play, share, sit in*, sit in on*, strive, take an interest in, tune in*; SEE CONCEPT *100*

particle [n] *atom, piece*
bit, crumb, dot, dribble, drop, fleck, fragment, grain, hoot, iota, jot, minim, mite, modicum, molecule, morsel, mote, ounce, ray, scrap, scruple, seed, shred, smidgen, smithereen, speck, spot, stitch, whit; SEE CONCEPT *831*

particular [n] *detail*
ABC's*, article, bottom line*, brass tacks*, case, chapter and verse*, circumstance, clue, cue, element, fact, facts of life, feature, gospel, item, know*, lowdown*, nitty-gritty*, nuts and bolts*, picture, point, rundown*, scoop*, score*, speciality, specific, specification, story, thing*, what's what*, whole story*; SEE CONCEPTS *274,532,832*

particular [adj1] *exact, specific*
accurate, appropriate, blow-by-blow*, circumstantial, clocklike, detailed, distinct, especial, express, full, individual, intrinsic, itemized, limited, local, meticulous, minute, painstaking, particularized, peculiar, precise, scrupulous, selective, singular, special, thorough, topical; SEE CONCEPT *557*

particular [adj2] *notable, uncommon*
especial, exceptional, exclusive, lone, marked, noteworthy, odd, one, only, peculiar, personal, remarkable, respective, separate, single, singular, sole, solitary, unique, unusual; SEE CONCEPT *564*

particular [adj3] *finicky, demanding*
careful, choicy, choosy, critical, dainty, discriminating, exacting, fastidious, finical, fussbudget*, fussy, hard to please, meticulous, nice, nit-picking*, persnickety*, picky*, rough, stickler*, tough; SEE CONCEPTS *404,542*

particularly [adv] *specifically*
decidedly, distinctly, especially, exceptionally, explicitly, expressly, individually, in particular, markedly, notably, outstandingly, peculiarly, principally, singularly, specially, surprisingly, uncommonly, unusually; SEE CONCEPT *557*

parting [n] *goodbye, separation*
adieu, bisection, break, breaking, breakup, crossroads*, departure, detachment, divergence, division, farewell, going, leave-taking, on the rocks*, partition, rift, rupture, severance, split, split-up, valediction; SEE CONCEPTS *195,297,384*

parting [adj] *farewell*
departing, final, goodbye, last, valedictory; SEE CONCEPT *267*

partisan [n] *person devoted to another or cause*
accessory, adherent, backer, champion, cohort, defender, devotee, disciple, follower, henchman/woman, satellite, stalwart, supporter, sycophant, sympathizer, upholder, votary, zealot; SEE CONCEPTS *359,423*

partisan [adj] *interested, factional*
accessory, adhering, biased, bigoted, blind, cliquish, colored, conspiratorial, denominational, devoted, diehard*, exclusive, fanatic, jaundiced, one-sided, overzealous, partial, prejudiced, prepossessed, sectarian, sympathetic, tendentious, unjust, unreasoning, warped, zealous; SEE CONCEPTS *401,542,548*

partition [n] *divider, division*
allotment, apportionment, barrier, detachment, disconnection, dissolution, distribution, disunion, dividing, hindrance, obstruction, parting, portion, rationing, rupture, screen, segregation, separation, severance, share, splitting, wall; SEE CONCEPTS *98,440,443,470*

partition [v] *divide, separate*
apportion, cut, cut in, cut into, cut up, deal, disburse, dispense, disperse, distribute, divvy up*, dole out*, fence off*, measure out, parcel out, portion, screen, section, segment, separate, share, size into, slice, split, split up, subdivide, wall off*; SEE CONCEPTS *98,135*

partly [adv] *not completely*
at best, at least, at most, at worst, bit by bit, by degrees, carelessly, halfway, inadequately, in a general way, in bits and pieces*, incompletely, in part, in some measure, in some ways, insufficiently, little by little, measurably, notably, not entirely, not fully, noticeably, not strictly speaking, not wholly, partially, piece by piece, piecemeal, relatively, slightly, so far as possible, somewhat, to a certain degree, to a certain extent, up to a certain point, within limits*; SEE CONCEPT *531*

partner [n] *person who takes part with another*
accomplice, ally, assistant, associate, bedfellow, buddy, chum*, cohort, collaborator, colleague, companion, comrade, confederate, confrere, consort, coworker, crony*, date, friend, helper, helpmate,

husband, mate, pal*, participant, playmate, side-kick*, spouse, teammate, wife; SEE CONCEPTS *348,414,423*

partnership [*n*] *alliance; participation*
affiliation, assistance, association, band, body, brotherhood, business, cahoots*, cartel, chumminess, clique, club, combination, combine, community, companionship, company, conglomerate, conjunction, connection, consociation, cooperation, cooperative, corporation, coterie, crew, faction, fellowship, firm, fraternity, friendship, gang, help, hookup, house, interest, joining, lodge, mob, organization, ownership, party, ring, sharing, society, sorority, tie-up, togetherness, union; SEE CONCEPTS *325,381,388*

party [*n1*] *social gathering*
affair, amusement, at-home*, ball, banquet, barbecue, bash*, blowout*, carousal, carousing*, celebration, cocktails, coffee klatch, coming-out, dinner, diversion*, do*, entertainment, feast, festive occasion, festivity, fete, fun, function, gala, get-together, luncheon, mingle*, movable feast*, orgy*, prom, reception, riot, shindig*, social, soiree, splurge*, spree*, tea; SEE CONCEPT *383*

party [*n2*] *gang, group*
assembly, band, bevy, body, bunch, cluster, company, corps, covey, crew, crowd, detachment, force, gathering, mob, multitude, outfit, squad, team, troop, troupe, unit; SEE CONCEPTS *417,432*

party [*n3*] *group supporting certain beliefs*
alliance, association, bloc, body, cabal, clique, coalition, combination, combine, confederacy, coterie, electorate, faction, grouping, junta, league, ring, sect, set, side, union; SEE CONCEPTS *301,381*

party [*n4*] *individual*
being, body, character, creature, human, man, mortal, part, person, personage, somebody, someone, woman; SEE CONCEPT *417*

party [*n5*] *person(s) involved in legal action*
actor, agent, cojuror, compurgator, confederate, contractor, defendant, litigant, partaker, participant, participator, plaintiff, plotter, sharer; SEE CONCEPT *355*

pass [*n1*] *opening through solid*
canyon, cut, gap, gorge, passage, passageway, path, ravine; SEE CONCEPTS *509,513*

pass [*n2*] *authorization, permission*
admission, chit*, comp, free ride*, furlough, identification, license, order, paper, passport, permit, safeconduct*, ticket, visa, warrant; SEE CONCEPTS *271,685*

pass [*n3*] *sexual proposition*
advance, approach, overture, play, suggestion; SEE CONCEPTS *375,384*

pass [*n4*] *predicament*
condition, contingency, crisis, crossroads*, emergency, exigency, juncture, pinch, plight, situation, stage, state, strait, turning point*, zero hour*; SEE CONCEPT *674*

pass [*v1*] *go by, elapse; move onwards*
befall, blow past, catch, come off, come to pass, come up, crawl, cross, cruise, depart, develop, drag, fall out, fare, flow, fly, fly by, get ahead, give, glide, glide by, go, go past, happen, hie, journey, lapse, leave, linger, move, occur, pass away, pass by, proceed, progress, push on, reach, repair, rise, roll, run, run by, run out, slip away, take place, transpire, travel, wend; SEE CONCEPTS *2,149,242*

pass [*v2*] *surpass, beat*
exceed, excel, go beyond, go by, leave behind, outdistance, outdo, outgo, outrace, outshine, outstrip, shoot ahead of, surmount, top, transcend; SEE CONCEPT *141*

pass [*v3*] *succeed, graduate*
answer, do, get through, matriculate, pass muster, qualify, suffice, suit; SEE CONCEPT *706*

pass [*v4*] *give, transfer*
buck, convey, deliver, exchange, hand, hand over, kick, let have, reach, relinquish, send, shoot, throw, transmit; SEE CONCEPTS *108,217*

pass [*v5*] *cease*
blow over*, cash in*, close, decease, demise, depart, die, disappear, discontinue, dissolve, drop, dwindle, ebb, end, evaporate, expire, fade, go, melt away, pass away, perish, peter out*, stop, succumb, terminate, vanish, wane; SEE CONCEPTS *105,119*

pass [*v6*] *enact, legislate*
accept, adopt, approve, authorize, become law, become ratified, become valid, be established, be ordained, be sanctioned, carry, decree, engage, establish, ordain, pledge, promise, ratify, sanction, undertake, validate, vote in; SEE CONCEPTS *298, 317*

pass [*v7*] *express formally*
claim, declare, deliver, pronounce, state, utter; SEE CONCEPTS *49,60*

pass [*v8*] *decide not to do*
decline, discount, disregard, fail, forget, ignore, masquerade, miss, neglect, not heed, omit, overlook, pass on, pass up, refuse, skip, slight; SEE CONCEPTS *25,30*

pass [*v9*] *rid of waste*
defecate, discharge, eliminate, emit, empty, evacuate, excrete, expel, exude, give off, send forth, void; SEE CONCEPT *179*

passable [*adj1*] *acceptable, admissible*
adequate, allowable, all right, average, common, fair, fair enough, mediocre, middling*, moderate, not too bad*, ordinary, presentable, respectable, so-so*, tolerable, unexceptional; SEE CONCEPT *558*

passable [*adj2*] *clear and able to be traveled*
accessible, attainable, beaten, broad, crossable, easy, fair, graded, motorable, navigable, open, penetrable, reachable, travelable, traveled, traversable, unblocked, unobstructed; SEE CONCEPTS *559,576*

passage/passageway [*n*] *path for travel*
access, alley, alleyway, avenue, channel, corridor, course, doorway, entrance, entrance hall, exit, gap, hall, hallway, lane, line, lobby, opening, pathway, road, route, shaft, subway, thoroughfare, tunnel, vestibule, way; SEE CONCEPTS *440,501*

passage [*n2*] *excerpt from document*
clause, extract, paragraph, piece, portion, quotation, reading, section, sentence, text, transition, verse; SEE CONCEPT *270*

passage [*n3*] *travel*
advance, change, conversion, crossing, flow, journey, motion, movement, passing, progress, progression, tour, traject, transfer, transference, transit, transition, transmission, transmittal, transmittance, traverse, traversing, trek, trip, voyage; SEE CONCEPTS *145,217,224,704*

passage [*n4*] *authorization; enactment*
acceptance, allowance, establishment, freedom, legalization, legislation, passing, passport, permission, ratification, right, safe-conduct, visa, warrant; SEE CONCEPTS *318,685*

pass away [*v*] *die*
decease, demise, depart, drop, expire, pass on, perish, succumb; SEE CONCEPT *304*

pass by [*v*] *neglect, forget*
abandon, disregard, fail, ignore, leave, miss, not choose, omit, overlook, overpass, pass over; SEE CONCEPTS *25,30*

passé [*adj*] *old-fashioned*
antiquated, belated, dated, dead, démodé, disused, extinct, has-been, obsolete, outdated, outmoded, out-of-date, outworn, superseded, unfashionable, yesterday; SEE CONCEPTS *578,589,797*

passenger [*n*] *person who rides in vehicle conducted by another*
commuter, customer, excursionist, fare*, hitchhiker, patron, pilgrim, rider, tourist, traveler, voyager, wanderer, wayfarer; SEE CONCEPT *423*

passing [*n*] *death*
decease, defunction, demise, dissolution, end, finish, loss, silence, sleep, termination; SEE CONCEPT *304*

passing [*adj*] *brief, casual*
cursory, ephemeral, evanescent, fleeting, fugacious, fugitive, glancing, hasty, impermanent, momentary, quick, shallow, short, short-lived, slight, superficial, temporary, transient, transitory; SEE CONCEPTS *551,798*

passion [*n1*] *strong emotion*
affection, affectivity, agony, anger, animation, ardor, dedication, devotion, distress, dolor, eagerness, ecstasy, excitement, feeling, fervor, fire, fit, flare-up, frenzy, fury, heat, hurrah, indignation, intensity, ire, joy, misery, outbreak, outburst, paroxysm, rage, rapture, resentment, sentiment, spirit, storm, suffering, temper, transport, vehemence, warmth, wrath, zeal, zest; SEE CONCEPT *410*

passion [*n2*] *adoration, love*
affection, amorousness, amour, appetite, ardor, attachment, concupiscence, craving, crush*, desire, emoting, eroticism, excitement, fondness, infatuation, keenness, lust, prurience, urge, weakness, yen; SEE CONCEPTS *32,372*

passion [*n3*] *very strong interest*
craving, craze, drive, enthusiasm, fad*, fancy, fascination, idol, infatuation, jazz*, mania, obsession; SEE CONCEPTS *349,532,690*

passionate [*adj1*] *sensual, desirous*
amorous, ardent, aroused, concupiscent, desirous, erotic, heavy*, hot*, lascivious, libidinous, loving, lustful, prurient, romantic, sexy, steamy*, stimulated, sultry, turned-on*, wanton, wistful; SEE CONCEPT *372*

passionate [*adj2*] *very excited; enthusiastic*
affecting, animated, ardent, blazing, burning, deep, dramatic, eager, eloquent, emotional, expressive, fervent, fervid, fierce, fiery, flaming, forceful, frenzied, glowing, headlong, heartfelt, heated, high-powered, high-pressure, hot*, hotblooded*, impassioned, impetuous, impulsive, inspiring, intense, melodramatic, moving, poignant, precipitate, quickened, spirited, steamed up*, stimulated, stirring, strong, thrilling, vehement, violent, warm, warm, wild, zealous; SEE CONCEPTS *401,542*

passionate [*adj3*] *very angry*
all shook up*, choleric, enraged, fiery, frantic, furious, hotheaded*, hot-tempered*, inflamed, irascible, irritable, mean, peppery, quick-tempered, shaken, steamed-up*, stormy, tempestuous, testy, touchy*, vehement, violent; SEE CONCEPTS *401,542*

passive [*adj*] *lifeless, inactive*
acquiescent, apathetic, asleep, bearing, compliant, cool, docile, enduring, flat, forbearing, going through motions*, hands off*, idle, indifferent, inert, laid-back*, latent, long-suffering, moony, motionless, nonresistant, nonviolent, patient, phlegmatic, poker-faced*, quiescent, quiet, receptive, resigned, sleepy, static, stolid, submissive, tractable, unassertive, unflappable, uninvolved, unresisting, walking through it*, yielding; SEE CONCEPTS *542,584*

pass off [*v*] *give because one does not want it*
eject, foist, make a pretense of*, palm, palm off*, send forth, work off; SEE CONCEPT *108*

pass out [*v*] *become unconscious, usually from abusing a substance*
black out*, drop, faint, keel over*, lose consciousness, swoon; SEE CONCEPT *308*

pass over [*v*] *ignore, disregard*
dismiss, fail, forget, miss, neglect, not dwell on, omit, overlook, overpass, pass, pass by, skip, take no notice of*; SEE CONCEPTS *25,30*

passport [*n*] *identification of origin, country*
authorization, credentials, key, license, pass, permit, safe-conduct*, ticket, travel permit, visa, warrant; SEE CONCEPTS *271,685*

password [*n*] *secret word given for entry*
countersign, identification, key, key word, open sesame*, parole, phrase, signal, ticket, watchword, word; SEE CONCEPT *278*

past [*n1*] *time gone by*
antiquity, days gone by*, former times, good old days*, history, long ago, olden days*, old lang syne, old times*, time immemorial*, times past*, years ago*, yesterday, yesteryear, yore; SEE CONCEPTS *807,811,816,818*

past [*adj1*] *preceding, done*
accomplished, ago, antecedent, anterior, completed, elapsed, ended, extinct, finished, foregoing, forgotten, former, gone, gone by, over, over and done, precedent, previous, prior, spent; SEE CONCEPTS *531,585*

past [*adj2*] *olden, former*
ages ago*, ancient, ancient history*, back when*, behind one*, bygone, bypast, down memory lane*, earlier, early, erstwhile, ex-*, foregoing, gone-by*, good old days*, late, latter, latter-day, long-ago, old, olden days*, once, one-time, over, preceding, previous, prior, quondam, recent, retired, sometime, time was*, way back*, way back when*; SEE CONCEPT *820*

paste [*n/v*] *glue, adhesive*
cement, fasten, fix, gum, mucilage, patch, plaster, spit, stick, stickum*; SEE CONCEPTS *85,160,466*

pastel [*adj*] *muted in color*
delicate, light, pale, soft-hued, toned; SEE CONCEPT *618*

pastime [*n*] *leisure activity*
amusement, distraction, diversion, entertainment, fun, fun and games*, game, hobby, leisure, play, recreation, relaxation, sport; SEE CONCEPT *363*

pastor [*n*] *person who conducts church services*
churchman/woman, clergyman/woman, divine, ecclesiastic, minister, padre, parson, preacher man/woman*, priest, rector, reverend, shepherd, vicar; SEE CONCEPT *361*

pastoral [*adj*] *peaceful, especially referring to the countryside*
agrarian, agrestic, Arcadian, bucolic, countrified, country, idyllic, outland, provincial, rural, rustic, simple, sylvan; SEE CONCEPT *583*

pastry [*n*] *baked product made with flour*
bread, cake, croissant, dainty, Danish, delicacy, doughnut, éclair, panettone, patisserie, phyllo, pie, strudel, sweet roll, tart, turnover; SEE CONCEPTS *457,461*

pasty [*adj1*] *sticky*
adhesive, doughy, gelatinous, gluelike, gluey, glutinous, gooey, mucilaginous, starchy; SEE CONCEPT *606*

pasty [*adj2*] *very pale*
anemic, ashen, bloodless, dull, pallid, sallow, sickly, unhealthy, wan, waxen; SEE CONCEPT *618*

pat [*n1/v*] *tap, touch*
beat, caress, dab, fondle, form, hit, massage, mold, pet, punch, rub, slap, stroke, tip, whittle; SEE CONCEPTS *184,189,612*

pat [*n2*] *small slice or slab*
cake, dab, lump, piece, portion; SEE CONCEPTS *458,835*

pat [*adj*] *relevant, suitable*
apposite, apropos, apt, auspicious, felicitous, fitting, happy, neat, opportune, pertinent, propitious, rehearsed, suitable, timely, to the point; SEE CONCEPT *558*

pat [*adv*] *exactly, fittingly*
aptly, faultlessly, flawlessly, just right, opportunely, perfectly, plumb, precisely, relevantly, seasonably; SEE CONCEPTS *535,557*

patch [*n1*] *piece, spot, area*
bit, blob, chunk, fix, ground, hunk, land, lot, plat, plot, scrap, shred, spot, stretch, strip, tract; SEE CONCEPTS *452,471,513*

patch [*n2*] *piece applied to cover a gap or lack*
application, appliqué, band-aid*, mend, reinforcement; SEE CONCEPTS *452,831*

patch [*v*] *fix, mend*
cobble, cover, darn, do up, fiddle with, overhaul, rebuild, recondition, reconstruct, reinforce, repair, retread, revamp, sew; SEE CONCEPTS *212,218*

patch up [*v*] *settle differences*
adjust, appease, bury the hatchet*, compensate, conciliate, make friends*, mediate, negotiate, placate, restore, settle, smooth; SEE CONCEPT *384*

patchwork [*n*] *mixture, hodgepodge*
check, confusion, disorder, hash, jumble, medley, miscellany, mishmash, muddle, olio, pastiche, plaid, salad, salmagundi, stew, tartan; SEE CONCEPTS *260,432,475*

patchy [*adj*] *spotty, not consistent*
erratic, fitful, irregular, random, sketchy, uneven, variable, varying; SEE CONCEPT *482*

patent [*n*] *copyright on an invention*
charter, concession, control, franchise, license, limitation, privilege, protection; SEE CONCEPTS *271,318,685*

patent [*adj*] *unconcealed, conspicuous*
apparent, barefaced*, blatant, clear, clear-cut, controlled, crystal clear*, distinct, downright, evident, exclusive, flagrant, glaring, gross*, indisputable, limited, manifest, obvious, open, open and shut*, palpable, plain, prominent, rank, straightforward, transparent, unequivocal, unmistakable; SEE CONCEPT *576*

paternal [*adj*] *fatherly*
benevolent, concerned, fatherlike, patrilineal, patrimonial, protective, solicitous; SEE CONCEPTS *401,542*

path [*n*] *course, way*
aisle, artery, avenue, beat, beaten path, boulevard, byway, crosscut, direction, drag, footpath, groove, highway, lane, line, pass, passage, pathway, procedure, rail, road, roadway, route, rut, shortcut, street, stroll, terrace, thoroughfare, track, trail, walk, walkway; SEE CONCEPTS *6,501*

pathetic [*adj*] *sad, affecting*
commiserable, deplorable, distressing, feeble, heartbreaking, heartrending*, inadequate, lamentable,

meager, melting, miserable, moving, paltry, petty, piteous, pitiable, pitiful, plaintive, poignant, poor, puny, rueful, sorry, tender, touching, useless, woeful, worthless, wretched; SEE CONCEPTS *485,529*

pathos [n] *deep sadness*
desolation, emotion, feeling, passion, pitiableness, pitifulness, plaintiveness, poignance, poignancy, sentiment; SEE CONCEPT *410*

patience [n] *capacity, willingness to endure*
backbone*, bearing, calmness, composure, constancy, cool*, diligence, endurance, equanimity, even temper, forbearance, fortitude, grit*, guts*, gutsiness, heart, humility, imperturbability, intestinal fortitude*, legs*, leniency, longanimity, long-suffering, moderation, moxie*, nonresistance, passiveness, passivity, perseverance, persistence, poise, resignation, restraint, self-control, serenity, starch*, staying power*, stoicism, submission, sufferance, tolerance, toleration, yielding; SEE CONCEPTS *411,657*

patient [n] *person being treated for medical problem*
case, convalescent, emergency, inmate, invalid, outpatient, shut-in, sick person, subject, sufferer, victim; SEE CONCEPT *357*

patient [adj] *capable, willing to endure*
accommodating, calm, composed, easy-going, enduring, even-tempered, forbearing, forgiving, gentle, imperturbable, indulgent, lenient, long-suffering, meek, mild, mild-tempered, persevering, persistent, philosophic, philosophical, quiet, resigned, self-possessed, serene, stoical, submissive, tolerant, tranquil, uncomplaining, understanding, unruffled, untiring; SEE CONCEPTS *404,542*

patriarch [n] *man who heads family, organization*
ancestor, architect, author, chief, creator, elder, father, founder, generator, grandfather, head, inventor, maker, master, originator, paterfamilias, ruler, senior, sire; SEE CONCEPTS *348,414,419*

patrician [n] *person born to upper-class*
aristocrat, blue blood*, gentleman/woman, noble, nobleman/woman, peer, silk stocking*, upper cruster*; SEE CONCEPT *423*

patrician [adj] *upper-class*
aristocratic, blue-blooded*, gentle, grand, highborn, high-class, noble, royal, well-born; SEE CONCEPTS *334,549*

patriot [n] *person who loves his or her country*
flag-waver*, good citizen, jingoist*, loyalist, nationalist, partisan, patrioteer, statesman/woman, ultranationalist, volunteer; SEE CONCEPT *413*

patrol [n] *guarding; guard*
convoying, defending, escorting, garrison, lookout, patrolman/woman, policing, protecting, protection, rounds, safeguarding, scouting, sentinel, spy, vigilance, watch, watching, watchman/woman; SEE CONCEPTS *134,354,358*

patrol [v] *guard, protect*
cruise, inspect, keep guard, keep watch, make the rounds*, mount, police, pound, range, ride shotgun,

safeguard, shotgun, walk the beat*, watch; SEE CONCEPTS *134,623*

patron [n1] *person who supports a cause*
advocate, angel*, backer, benefactor, benefactress, booster, champion, defender, encourager, fairy godmother/father*, fan, financer, friend, front*, guarantor, guardian, guide, head, helper, leader, partisan, patron saint*, philanthropist, protector, sponsor, supporter, surety, sympathizer, well-wisher; SEE CONCEPTS *348,359,423*

patron [n2] *person who does business at establishment*
buyer, client, customer, frequenter, habitué, purchaser, shopper; SEE CONCEPT *348*

patronage [n1] *support of a cause*
advocacy, aegis, aid, assistance, auspices, backing, benefaction, championship, encouragement, financing, grant, guardianship, help, promotion, protection, recommendation, sponsorship, subsidy, support; SEE CONCEPTS *110,332,341*

patronage [n2] *business done at an establishment*
buying, clientage, clientele, commerce, custom, shopping, trade, trading, traffic; SEE CONCEPTS *323,324*

patronage [n3] *condescension*
civility, cronyism, deference, deigning, disdain, insolence, patronization, patronizing, stooping, sufferance, toleration; SEE CONCEPTS *83,300*

patronize [v1] *condescend*
be gracious to, be lofty, be overbearing, deign, favor, indulge, look down on*, lord it over*, pat on the back*, snub, stoop, talk down to*, toss a few crumbs*, treat as inferior, treat badly, treat like a child*; SEE CONCEPT *384*

patronize [v2] *support a cause*
assist, back, befriend, foster, fund, help, maintain, promote, sponsor, subscribe to; SEE CONCEPTS *110,341*

patronize [v3] *do business at an establishment*
be a client, be a customer, buy, buy from, deal with, frequent, give business to, habituate, purchase from, shop at, shop with, trade with; SEE CONCEPTS *324,327*

patter [n1/v1] *light walk; soft beat*
chatter, pad, pat, pelt, pitapat*, pitter-patter*, rat-a-tat*, rattle, scurry, scuttle, skip, tap, tiptoe, trip; SEE CONCEPTS *65,149*

patter [n2] *casual talk*
argot, cant, chatter, dialect, jabber*, jargon, jive*, line*, lingo, monologue, patois, pitch*, prattle*, slant*, spiel*, vernacular; SEE CONCEPTS *276,278*

patter [v2] *gab, chatter*
babble, blab*, clack*, hold forth*, jabber, jaw*, prate, prattle, rattle, spiel*, spout, tattle, yak, yakety-yak*; SEE CONCEPT *266*

pattern [n1] *design, motif*
arrangement, decoration, device, diagram, figure, guide, impression, instruction, markings, mold, motive, original, ornament, patterning, plan, stencil, template, trim; SEE CONCEPTS *259,625*

pattern [n2] *arrangement, order*
constellation, kind, method, orderliness, plan, sequence, shape, sort, style, system, type, variety; SEE CONCEPTS *6,727,770*

pattern [n3] *model, example*
archetype, beau ideal*, copy, criterion, cynosure, ensample, exemplar, guide, mirror, norm, original, paradigm, paragon, prototype, sample, specimen, standard; SEE CONCEPT *688*

pattern [v] *copy, imitate; decorate*
design, emulate, follow, form, model, mold, order, shape, style, trim; SEE CONCEPTS *111,171*

paucity [n] *lack, scarcity*
absence, dearth, deficiency, famine, fewness, insufficience, insufficiency, meagerness, paltriness, poverty, rarity, scantiness, scarceness, shortage, slenderness, slightness, smallness, sparseness, sparsity; SEE CONCEPTS *335,646,767*

paunch [n] *large stomach*
abdomen, belly, bulge, epigastrium, fat, gut, potbelly*, spare tire*, tummy*; SEE CONCEPT *399*

pauper [n] *person who is poor*
almsman, bankrupt, beggar, bum, dependent, destitute, down-and-out*, have-not*, homeless, indigent, insolvent, in the gutter*, lazarus*, mendicant, poor person, supplicant; SEE CONCEPT *423*

pause [n] *wait, delay*
abeyance, break, break-off*, breathing space*, breathing spell*, caesura, cessation, coffee break*, comma*, cutoff, deadlock, discontinuance, downtime*, freeze*, gap, gridlock*, halt, happy hour*, hesitancy, hesitation, hiatus, hitch*, hush*, interim, interlude, intermission, interregnum, interruption, interval, lacuna, lapse, layoff, let-up*, lull, pausation, recess, respite, rest, rest period, stand, standstill, stay, stillness, stopover, stoppage, suspension, time out*; SEE CONCEPT *807*

pause [v] *wait, delay*
break it up*, call time*, catch one's breath*, cease, come to standstill*, deliberate, desist, discontinue, drop, halt, hesitate, hold back, interrupt, put on hold, reflect, rest, shake, sideline, stop briefly, suspend, take a break*, take a breather*, take five*, take ten*, think twice*, waver; SEE CONCEPTS *119,121, 234*

pave [v] *cover with asphalt, concrete*
brick, cobblestone, flagstone, gravel, lay asphalt, lay concrete, macadamize, surface, tar, tile; SEE CONCEPTS *168,172*

pavilion [n] *domed building or tent*
awning, canopy, cover, covering, dome, structure; SEE CONCEPT *439*

paw [v] *touch roughly*
clap, claw, clutch, dig, feel, finger, fondle, grab, grate, grope, handle, hit, manhandle, maul, molest, palpate, pat, rake, rasp, rub, scratch, search, slap, smite, stroke; SEE CONCEPTS *375,612*

pawn [n1] *security for a loan*
.assurance, bond, collateral, earnest, forfeit, gage, gambit, guarantee, guaranty, pledge, security, token, warrant; SEE CONCEPT *332*

pawn [n2] *person who is a fool*
creature, dupe*, instrument, mark*, patsy*, pigeon*, puppet, stooge*, sucker*, tool, toy, victim; SEE CONCEPT *412*

pawn [v] *give as security for a loan*
deposit, give in earnest, hazard, hock*, hook*, mortgage, pledge; SEE CONCEPTS *115,330*

pay [n] *earnings from employment*
allowance, bacon*, bread*, commission, compensation, consideration, defrayment, emoluments, fee, hire*, honorarium, income, indemnity, meed, payment, perquisite, pittance, proceeds, profit, reckoning, recompensation, recompense, redress, reimbursement, remuneration, reparation, requital, return, reward, salary, satisfaction, scale, settlement, stipend, stipendium, take-home*, takings*, wage, wages; SEE CONCEPTS *329,332,340,344*

pay [v1] *give money for goods, services*
adjust, bear the cost, bear the expense, bequeath, bestow, chip in*, clear, come through, compensate, confer, cough up*, defray, dig up*, disburse, discharge, extend, foot*, foot the bill*, grant, handle, hand over*, honor, kick in*, liquidate, make payment, meet, offer, plunk down*, prepay, present, proffer, put up*, recompense, recoup, refund, reimburse, remit, remunerate, render, repay, requite, reward, satisfy, settle, stake, take care of*; SEE CONCEPTS *327,341,351*

pay [v2] *be advantageous*
benefit, be worthwhile, repay, serve; SEE CONCEPT *700*

pay [v3] *make amends*
answer, atone, be punished, compensate, get just desserts, suffer, suffer consequences; SEE CONCEPT *23*

pay [v4] *profit, yield*
be profitable, be remunerative, bring in, kick back*, make a return, make money, pay dividends, pay off*, pay out*, produce, provide a living, return, show gain, show profit, sweeten*, yield profit; SEE CONCEPT *330*

pay [v5] *get revenge*
avenge oneself, get even, make up for, pay back*, pay one's dues*, punish, reciprocate, recompense, repay, requite, retaliate, settle a score*, square, square things*; SEE CONCEPT *122*

payable [adj] *to be paid*
due, mature, maturing, obligatory, outstanding, overdue, owed, owing, receivable, unpaid, unsettled; SEE CONCEPT *334*

payment [n] *fee; installment of fee*
acquittal, advance, alimony, amends, amortization, amount, annuity, award, bounty, cash, defrayal, defrayment, deposit, disbursement, discharge, down,

fee, hire, indemnification, outlay, part, paying, pay-off, pension, portion, premium, quittance, reckoning, recompense, redress, refund, reimbursement, remittance, remuneration, reparation, repayment, requital, restitution, retaliation, return, reward, salary, settlement, subsidy, sum, support, wage; SEE CONCEPT *344*

payoff [n] *conclusion, climax*
adjustment, clincher*, consequence, culmination, day of reckoning*, finale, final reckoning*, judgment, moment of truth*, outcome, pay, payment, punch line*, result, retribution, reward, settlement, upshot*; SEE CONCEPTS *230,679*

peace [n1] *harmony, agreement*
accord, amity, armistice, brotherhood, cessation, conciliation, concord, fraternalism, fraternization, friendship, love, neutrality, order, pacification, pacifism, reconciliation, treaty, truce, unanimity, union, unity; SEE CONCEPTS *388,691*

peace [n2] *calm, serenity*
amity, calmness, composure, concord, congeniality, contentment, equanimity, harmony, hush, lull, peacefulness, placidity, quiet, quietude, relaxation, repose, reserve, rest, silence, stillness, sympathy, tranquility; SEE CONCEPTS *410,705,720*

peaceable [adj] *friendly, serene*
amiable, amicable, calm, complacent, conciliatory, gentle, irenic, mild, neighborly, nonviolent, pacific, pacificatory, pacifist, peaceful, peace-loving, placid, quiet, restful, still, tranquil; SEE CONCEPT *548*

peaceful [adj] *friendly, serene*
all quiet, amicable, at peace, bloodless, calm, collected, composed, constant, easeful, equable, free from strife*, gentle, halcyon, harmonious, irenic, level, mellow, neutral, neutralist, nonbelligerent, nonviolent, on friendly terms*, on good terms*, pacifistic, peaceable, peace-loving, placatory, placid, quiet, restful, smooth, sociable, steady, still, tranquil, undisturbed, unruffled, untroubled, without hostility; SEE CONCEPTS *485,542*

peacemaker [n] *person who settles problem*
appeaser, arbitrator, conciliator, diplomat, makepeace, mediator, negotiator, pacificator, pacifier, pacifist, peacekeeper, peacemonger*, placater, statesman/woman, statesperson; SEE CONCEPTS *354,416*

peak [n1] *top of something*
aiguille, alp, apex, brow, bump, cope, crest, crown, hill, mount, mountain, pinnacle, point, roof, spike, summit, tip, vertex; SEE CONCEPTS *509,836*

peak [n2] *maximum, zenith*
acme, apex, apogee, capstone, climax, crown, culmination, greatest, height, high point, meridian, ne plus ultra, pinnacle, summit, tip, top; SEE CONCEPTS *668,766,767,832*

peak [v] *reach highest point*
be at height, climax, come to a head*, crest, culminate, reach the top, reach the zenith, top out*; SEE CONCEPTS *763,780*

peaked [adj] *pale, sick*
ailing, bilious, emaciated, ill, in bad shape*, peaky, poorly, sickly, under the weather*, wan; SEE CONCEPTS *314,618*

peal [n] *chime, clang*
blast, carillon, clamor, clap, crash, resounding, reverberation, ring, ringing, roar, rumble, sound, thunder, tintinnabulation; SEE CONCEPT *595*

peal [v] *chime, clang*
bell, bong, crack, crash, knell, resonate, resound, reverberate, ring, ring out, roar, roll, rumble, sound, strike, thunder, tintinnabulate, toll; SEE CONCEPT *65*

pearly [adj] *opalescent*
fair, frosted, iridescent, ivory, milky, nacreous, off-white, opaline, pearl, silver; SEE CONCEPT *618*

peck [n/v] *bite*
beak, dig, hit, jab, kiss, mark, nibble, pick, pinch, poke, prick, rap, strike, tap; SEE CONCEPTS *169,189*

peculiar [adj1] *characteristic, distinguishing*
appropriate, diacritic, diagnostic, distinct, distinctive, endemic, exclusive, idiosyncratic, individual, intrinsic, local, particular, personal, private, proper, restricted, special, specific, typical, unique; SEE CONCEPTS *404,557*

peculiar [adj2] *bizarre, odd*
abnormal, bent*, creepy*, curious, eccentric, exceptional, extraordinary, flaky*, freakish, freaky, funny, idiosyncratic, kinky*, kooky*, oddball, offbeat, off-the-wall*, outlandish, quaint, queer, singular, strange, uncommon, unconventional, uncustomary, unusual, wacky*, way-out*, weird, wonderful; SEE CONCEPTS *404,564*

peculiarity [n] *characteristic; oddity*
abnormality, affectation, attribute, bizarreness, character, distinctiveness, eccentricity, feature, foible, freakishness, gimmick, idiosyncrasy, kink*, mannerism, mark, odd trait, particularity, property, quality, queerness, quirk, savor, schtick*, singularity, slant*, specialty, trait, twist*, unusualness; SEE CONCEPTS *411,665*

pedagogic [adj] *educational*
academic, dogmatic, instructive, learned, professorial, profound, scholastic, teaching; SEE CONCEPTS *529,536*

pedantic [adj] *bookish, precise*
abstruse, academic, arid, didactic, doctrinaire, donnish, dry, dull, egotistic, erudite, formal, fussy, hair-splitting*, learned, nit-picking, ostentatious, over-nice, particular, pedagogic, pompous, priggish*, punctilious, scholastic, schoolish, sententious, stilted; SEE CONCEPTS *401,529*

peddle [v] *sell door to door*
canvas*, hawk*, huckster*, market, monger*, push, sell, shove, solicit, trade, vend; SEE CONCEPT *345*

pedestrian [n] *person traveling on foot*
ambler, hiker, jaywalker*, passerby, stroller, walker; SEE CONCEPT *366*

pedestrian [*adj*] *everyday, dull*
banal, banausic, blah*, boring, commonplace, dim, dreary, flat, humdrum*, inane, jejune, mediocre, monotone, monotonous, mundane, ordinary, platitudinous, plodding, prosaic, run-of-the-mill*, stodgy, truistic, unimaginative, uninspired, uninteresting, wishy-washy*; SEE CONCEPTS *530,547*

pedigree [*n*] *ancestry, heritage*
blood, breed, clan, derivation, descent, extraction, family, family tree, genealogy, heredity, line, lineage, origin, race, stirps, stock; SEE CONCEPT *296*

pedigree [*adj*] *purebred*
full-blooded, pedigreed, pure-blood, thoroughbred; SEE CONCEPT *549*

peek/peep [*n*] *sneaked look*
blink, gander*, glance, glimpse, look-see, sight; SEE CONCEPT *623*

peek/peep [*v*] *sneak a look*
blink, glance, glimpse, have a gander, look, peer, snatch, snoop, spy, squint, stare, take a look; SEE CONCEPT *623*

peel [*n*] *skin, covering*
bark, cover, epicarp, exocarp, husk, peeling, pellicle, rind, shell, shuck; SEE CONCEPTS *428,484*

peel [*v*] *take off outer covering*
decorticate, delaminate, desquamate, excorticate, exfoliate, flake, flay, pare, pull off, scale, shave, skin, strip, tear off, uncover; SEE CONCEPTS *142,176,211*

peep [*n2/v2*] *chirp*
chatter, cheep, chirrup, chuck, churr, coo, cry, hoot, pipe, squeak, tweet, twitter; SEE CONCEPT *64*

peep/peer [*v3/v2*] *appear briefly*
become visible, crop up, emerge, open to view, peep out, peer out, show partially; SEE CONCEPT *261*

peer [*n*] *person who is another's equal*
associate, coequal, companion, compeer, fellow, like, match, rival; SEE CONCEPT *423*

peer [*v1*] *scan, scrutinize*
bore, eagle eye*, eye*, eyeball*, focus, gape, gawk, gaze, get a load of, glare, glim, gloat, inspect, look, peep, pin*, pry, rubberneck*, snoop, spy, squint, stare; SEE CONCEPTS *103,623*

peerless [*adj*] *having no equal; superior*
aces*, all-time, alone, best, beyond compare, champion, excellent, faultless, gilt-edge*, greatest, incomparable, matchless, most, nonpareil*, only, outstanding, perfect, second to none*, solid-gold*, super, superlative, supreme, tops*, unequaled, unexampled, unique, unmatched, unparagoned, unparalleled, unrivaled, unsurpassed, world class*; SEE CONCEPT *574*

peeve [*n*] *something strongly disliked*
annoyance, bother, gripe, nuisance, pest, sore point*, vexation; SEE CONCEPTS *532,690*

peeve [*v*] *bother, annoy*
aggravate, anger, bug*, bum*, burn*, disturb, drive up the wall*, exasperate, gall, get, get one's goat*, hack*, irk, irritate, miff*, nettle, pique, provoke, put out, rile, roil, rub the wrong way*, steam*, T-off*, vex; SEE CONCEPTS *7,19*

peevish [*adj*] *irritable, testy*
acrimonious, angry, bad-tempered, cantankerous, captious, carping, caviling, childish, churlish, complaining, crabbed*, cranky, critical, cross, crotchety*, crusty*, cussed, fault-finding, fractious, fretful, fretting, grouchy, grousing, growling, grumpy, huffy, ill-natured, mean, morose, obstinate, ogre, ornery, out-of-sorts*, pertinacious, petulant, querulous, short-tempered, snappy, splenetic, sulky, sullen, surly, tetchy, touchy, ugly, waspish, waspy, whining; SEE CONCEPTS *401,542*

peg [*v*] *attach*
clinch, fasten, fix, join, make fast, pin, secure, tighten; SEE CONCEPTS *85,160*

pejorative [*adj*] *negative, belittling*
debasing, deprecatory, depreciatory, derisive, derogatory, detracting, detractive, detractory, disadvantageous, disparaging, irreverent, rude, slighting, uncomplimentary, unpleasant; SEE CONCEPT *267*

pell-mell [*n*] *disorder*
anarchy, ataxia, chaos, clutter, confusion, disarray, ferment, helter-skelter, huddle, muddle, pandemonium, snarl, tumult, turmoil, upheaval; SEE CONCEPT *674*

pell-mell [*adj*] *disordered*
chaotic, confused, disarrayed, disorganized, haphazard, muddled, tumultous/tumultuous; SEE CONCEPTS *562,585*

pell-mell [*adv*] *hurriedly and carelessly*
foolishly, full tilt*, hastily, headlong, heedlessly, helter-skelter, impetuously, incontinently, indiscreetly, posthaste, precipitiously, rashly, recklessly, thoughtlessly; SEE CONCEPTS *544,799*

pelt [*n*] *animal fur*
coat, epidermis, fell, hair, hide, jacket, skin, slough, wool; SEE CONCEPT *399*

pelt [*v*] *beat; throw hard*
assail, batter, belabor, belt, bombard, career, cast, charge, dash, hammer, hurl, knock, lapidate, pepper, pound, pour, pummel, rain, rush, shoot, shower, sling, speed, stone, strike, swat, tear, thrash, wallop; SEE CONCEPTS *189,222*

pen [*n1*] *enclosure*
cage, coop, corral, fence, fold, hedge, hutch, jail, penitentiary, prison, sty, wall*; SEE CONCEPTS *439,443*

pen [*n2*] *writing instrument*
ball point, felt-tip, fountain pen, marker, nib, quill, reed, stick, stylograph; SEE CONCEPTS *277,499*

pen [*v1*] *enclose*
box, cage, case, close in, confine, coop, corral, fence in, hedge, hem in, mew*, shut in; SEE CONCEPTS *191,758*

pen [*v2*] *write*
autograph, commit to paper, compose, draft, draw up, engross, indict, jot down; SEE CONCEPT *79*

penal [adj] *disciplinary*
chastening, corrective, penalizing, punishing, punitive, punitory, reformatory, retributive; SEE CONCEPTS *548,583*

penalize [v] *punish*
amerce, castigate, chasten, chastise, condemn, correct, discipline, dock*, fine, handicap, hit with*, impose penalty, inflict handicap, judge, mulct, put at disadvantage, scold, slap with*, throw the book at*; SEE CONCEPT *122*

penalty [n] *punishment*
amends, amercement, cost, damages, disadvantage, discipline, dues, fall, fine, forfeit, forfeiture, handicap, mortification, mulct, price, rap*, retribution; SEE CONCEPTS *344,679*

penance [n] *reparation for wrong*
absolution, atonement, attrition, compensation, compunction, confession, contrition, expiation, forgiveness, hair shirt*, mortification, penalty, penitence, punishment, purgation, remorse, remorsefulness, repentance, retribution, rue, ruth, sackcloth and ashes*, self-flagellation*, shrift, sorrow, suffering; SEE CONCEPTS *126,367,384,410*

penchant [n] *fondness, inclination*
affection, affinity, attachment, bias, disposition, druthers*, inclining, itch*, leaning, liking, partiality, predilection, predisposition, proclivity, proneness, propensity, taste, tendency, tilt*, turn*, weakness, yen; SEE CONCEPTS *20,32,411,709*

pending [adj] *about to happen*
awaiting, continuing, dependent, forthcoming, hanging, imminent, impending, indeterminate, in line*, in the balance*, in the offing*, in the works*, ominous, on board*, on line*, pensile, undecided, undetermined, unsettled, up in the air*; SEE CONCEPT *548*

pendulous/pendent [adj] *hanging*
dangling, dependent, drooping, pending, pendulant, pensile, suspended, swinging; SEE CONCEPTS *485,584*

penetrate [v1] *pierce; get through physically*
access, barge in, bayonet, blow in, bore, break in, breeze in, bust in, charge, come, crack, diffuse, drill, drive, eat through, encroach, enter, filter in, force, get in, gore, go through, impale, infiltrate, ingress, insert, insinuate, introduce, invade, jab, knife, make a hole, make an entrance, pass through, percolate, perforate, permeate, pervade, pop in, prick, probe, puncture, ream, run into, saturate, seep, sink into, spear, stab, stick into, suffuse, thrust, trespass; SEE CONCEPTS *159,179,220*

penetrate [v2] *understand or be understood*
affect, become clear, come across*, comprehend, decipher, discern, fathom, figure out, get across*, get over*, get through*, get to the bottom*, grasp, impress, perceive, put over*, see through*, sink in*, soak in*, touch, unravel, work out; SEE CONCEPT *15*

penetrating [adj1] *stinging, harsh*
biting, carrying, clear-cut, crisp, cutting, edged, entering, forcing, going through, infiltrating, ingoing, intrusive, passing through, penetrant, permeating, pervasive, piercing, pointed, puncturing, pungent, sharp, shrill, strong, trenchant; SEE CONCEPTS *267,537*

penetrating [adj2] *very intelligent*
acute, astute, critical, discerning, discriminating, incisive, keen, penetrative, perceptive, perspicacious, profound, quick, quick-witted, sagacious, searching, sharp, sharp-witted, shrewd; SEE CONCEPT *402*

penitence [n] *shame, sorrow*
anguish, attrition, compunction, contriteness, contrition, debasement, degradation, distress, grief, humbling, humiliation, penance, qualm, regret, remorse, remorsefulness, repentance, rue, ruefulness, ruth, sadness, scruple, self-castigation, self-condemnation, self-flagellation, self-punishment, self-reproach; SEE CONCEPT *410*

penitent [adj] *shamed, sorrowful*
abject, apologetic, atoning, attritional, compunctious, conscience-stricken, contrite, penitential, regretful, remorseful, repentant, rueful, sorry; SEE CONCEPTS *403,542*

penitentiary [n] *jail*
big house*, campus*, can*, college, cooler*, correctional institution, inside*, joint*, lockup*, pen*, penal institution, prison, reformatory, slammer*, stockade; SEE CONCEPTS *439,449,516*

pennant [n] *flag, banner*
banderole, bunting, burgee, color, decoration, emblem, ensign, jack, pennon, screamer, standard, streamer; SEE CONCEPTS *260,473*

penniless [adj] *without any money*
bankrupt, broke*, clean*, cleaned out*, dead broke*, destitute, dirt poor*, down to last penny*, flat*, flat broke*, impecunious, impoverished, indigent, in the gutter*, lacking, moneyless, necessitous, needy, on last leg*, over a barrel*, penurious, poor, poverty-stricken, ruined, strapped*, tapped out*, without one dime*; SEE CONCEPT *334*

pension [n] *benefits paid after retirement*
allowance, annuity, gift, grant, IRA*, payment, premium, retirement account, reward, social security, subsidy, subvention, superannuation, support; SEE CONCEPTS *332,344*

pensive [adj] *meditative, solemn*
absorbed, abstracted, attentive, cogitative, contemplative, dreamy, grave, melancholy, mournful, musing, pondering, preoccupied, reflecting, reflective, ruminating, ruminative, sad, saddened, serious, sober, sorrowful, speculative, thinking, thoughtful, wistful, withdrawn; SEE CONCEPT *403*

pent-up [adj] *held within*
bottled-up, bridled, checked, constrained, curbed, held-back, held in check, inhibited, repressed, restrained, restricted, smothered, stifled, suppressed; SEE CONCEPTS *401,403*

people [n] *human beings*
bodies, body politic*, bourgeois, cats*, citizens, clan, commonality, common people, community,

crowd, family, folk, folks, general public, heads*, herd, hoi polloi*, horde, humanity, humankind, human race, humans, inhabitants, John/Jane Q. Public*, kinsmen, man/woman in the street*, masses, mob, mortals, multitude, nation, nationality, persons, plebeians, populace, population, proletariat, public, rabble, race, rank and file*, riffraff, society, tribe; SEE CONCEPTS *296,379,380,417*

pep [*n*] *vim, vigor*
animation, bang, birr, energy, get-up-and-go*, go, gusto, hardihood, high spirits, life, liveliness, moxie*, potency, punch*, push, snap*, spirit, starch*, tuck*, verve, vitality, vivacity, zip*; SEE CONCEPTS *411,633*

peppery [*adj1*] *highly seasoned*
fiery, hot, piquant, poignant, pungent, racy, snappy, spicy, zestful, zesty; SEE CONCEPT *613*

peppery [*adj2*] *irritable; sarcastic*
acute, angry, astringent, biting, caustic, choleric, cranky, cross, fiery, hot-tempered, incisive, irascible, keen, lively, passionate, quick-tempered, sharp, sharp-tempered, snappish, spirited, spunky, stinging, testy, touchy, trenchant, waspish; SEE CONCEPTS *267,401,542*

peppy [*adj*] *lively, vigorous*
active, alert, animate, animated, bright, gay, keen, perky, sparkling, spirited, sprightly, vivacious; SEE CONCEPTS *401,404*

pep up [*v*] *invigorate, inspire*
animate, enliven, exhilarate, jazz up*, quicken, stimulate, vitalize, vivify; SEE CONCEPTS *7,22*

perceive [*v1*] *notice, see*
apperceive, apprehend, be aware of, behold, descry, discern, discover, distinguish, divine, espy, feel, grasp, identify, look, make out, mark, mind, note, observe, realize, recognize, regard, remark, seize, sense, spot, spy, take; SEE CONCEPTS *38,626*

perceive [*v2*] *understand*
appreciate, apprehend, comprehend, conclude, copy, deduce, distinguish, feature, feel, flash*, gather, get, get the message*, get the picture*, grasp, know, learn, pin*, read, realize, recognize, see, sense, track; SEE CONCEPT *15*

percentage [*n*] *portion, allotment*
allowance, bite, bonus, chunk, commission, corner*, cut, discount, division, duty, fee, holdout, interest, juice*, payoff, percent, piece, piece of the action*, points*, proportion, quota, rate, ratio, section, slice*, split*, taste*, winnings; SEE CONCEPTS *766,784,835*

perceptible [*adj*] *noticeable, obvious*
apparent, appreciable, audible, clear, cognizable, conspicuous, detectable, discernible, distinct, distinguishable, evident, lucid, observable, palpable, perceivable, perspicuous, recognizable, sensible, signal, tangible, understandable, visible; SEE CONCEPTS *529,576*

perception [*n*] *understanding, idea*
acumen, apprehending, apprehension, approach, attention, attitude, awareness, big idea*, brainchild*, brain wave*, conceit, concept, conception, consciousness, discernment, feeling, flash, grasp, image, impression, insight, intellection, judgment, knowledge, light, notion, observation, opinion, perspicacity, picture, plan, realizing, recognition, sagacity, sensation, sense, study, taste, thought, viewpoint; SEE CONCEPTS *409,410,689*

perceptive [*adj*] *alert, sensitive*
acute, astute, awake, aware, brainy, conscious, discerning, discreet, ear to the ground*, gnostic, incisive, insighted, insightful, intuitive, judicious, keen, knowing, knowledgeable, knows what's what*, observant, penetrating, penetrative, percipient, perspicacious, quick, rational, responsive, sagacious, sage, savvy, sharp, sophic, tuned in*, wise, wise to*; SEE CONCEPTS *402,542*

perch [*n*] *object placed high for sitting on*
branch, landing place, lounge, pole, post, resting place, roost, seat; SEE CONCEPTS *443,479*

perch [*v*] *sit atop of*
alight, balance, land, light, rest, roost, set down, settle, sit on, squat, touch down; SEE CONCEPT *154*

percolate [*v*] *seep, drip (liquid)*
bleed, bubble, charge, drain, exude, filter, filtrate, impregnate, leach, ooze, pass through, penetrate, perk, permeate, pervade, saturate, strain, sweat, transfuse, transude, weep; SEE CONCEPTS *179,181*

peremptory [*adj*] *overbearing, authoritative*
absolute, arbitrary, assertive, autocratic, binding, bossy, categorical, certain, commanding, compelling, decided, decisive, dictatorial, dogmatic, domineering, final, finished, firm, fixed, high-handed, imperative, imperial, imperious, incontrovertible, intolerant, irrefutable, magisterial, masterful, obligatory, obstinate, positive, rigorous, severe, stringent, tyrannical, uncompromising, undeniable; SEE CONCEPTS *535,537,542*

perennial [*adj*] *enduring, perpetual*
abiding, annual, ceaseless, chronic, constant, continual, continuing, deathless, durable, eternal, everlasting, immortal, imperishable, incessant, inveterate, lasting, lifelong, long-lasting, long-lived, longstanding, never-ending, old, perdurable, permanent, persistent, recurrent, seasonal, sustained, unceasing, unchanging, undying, unfailing, uninterrupted, yearlong, yearly; SEE CONCEPTS *539,798*

perfect [*adj1*] *flawless, superlative*
absolute, accomplished, aces*, adept, A-OK*, beyond compare, blameless, classical, consummate, crowning, culminating, defectless, excellent, excelling, experienced, expert, faultless, finished, foolproof, ideal, immaculate, impeccable, indefectible, masterful, masterly, matchless, out-of-this-world*, paradisiac, paradisiacal, peerless, pure, skilled, skillful, sound, splendid, spotless, stainless, sublime, superb, supreme, ten*, unblemished, unequaled, unmarred, untainted, untarnished, utopian; SEE CONCEPT *574*

perfect [adj2] *whole, intact*
absolute, choate, complete, completed, consummate, downright, entire, finished, flawless, full, gross, integral, out-and-out*, outright, positive, rank, sheer, simple, sound, unadulterated, unalloyed, unblemished, unbroken, undamaged, unimpaired, unmitigated, unmixed, unqualified, utter; SEE CONCEPTS 482,485

perfect [adj3] *accurate, correct*
appropriate, bull's-eye*, certain, close, dead-on*, definite, distinct, exact, express, faithful, fit, ideal, model, needed, on target*, on the button*, on the money*, precise, proper, required, requisite, right, sharp, strict, suitable, textbook, to a T*, to a turn*, true, unerring, very; SEE CONCEPTS 535,557,558

perfect [v] *polish; achieve*
accomplish, ameliorate, carry out, complete, consummate, crown, cultivate, develop, effect, elaborate, finish, fulfill, hone, idealize, improve, perform, put finishing touch on, realize, refine, round, slick, smooth; SEE CONCEPTS 91,244,706

perfection [n] *achievement, completeness*
accomplishment, achieving, acme, arete, completion, consummation, crown, ending, entireness, evolution, exactness, excellence, excellency, exquisiteness, faultlessness, finish, finishing, fulfillment, ideal, idealism, impeccability, integrity, maturity, merit, paragon, perfectness, phoenix, precision, purity, quality, realization, ripeness, sublimity, superiority, supremacy, transcendence, virtue, wholeness; SEE CONCEPTS 671,706

perfectly [adv1] *absolutely*
altogether, completely, consummately, entirely, fully, quite, thoroughly, totally, utterly, well, wholly; SEE CONCEPTS 531,544

perfectly [adv2] *without flaw*
admirably, correctly, excellently, exquisitely, faultlessly, fitly, flawlessly, ideally, impeccably, superbly, superlatively, supremely, to perfection, wonderfully; SEE CONCEPT 574

perforate [v] *make a hole in*
bore, drill, drive, hole, honeycomb*, penetrate, permeate, pierce, pit, poke full of holes*, probe, punch, puncture, shoot full of holes*, slit, stab; SEE CONCEPT 220

perform [v1] *carry out, accomplish*
achieve, act, be engaged in, behave, bring about, bring off, carry through, carry to completion, complete, comply, deliver the goods*, discharge, dispose of, do, do justice to*, do to a turn*, effect, end, enforce, execute, finish, fulfill, function, go that route*, implement, meet, move, observe, operate, percolate, perk, pull off, pull off*, put through, react, realize, run with the ball*, satisfy, take, take care of business*, tick, transact, wind up, work; SEE CONCEPTS 91,199

perform [v2] *act, depict as entertainment*
act out, appear as, be on, bring down the house*, discourse, display, do a number*, do a turn*, drama-

tize, emote, enact, execute, exhibit, give, go on, ham*, ham it up*, impersonate, offer, personate, play, playact, present, produce, put on, render, represent, show, stage, tread the boards*; SEE CONCEPT 292

performance [n1] *accomplishment*
achievement, act, administration, attainment, carrying out, completion, conduct, consummation, discharge, doing, enforcement, execution, exploit, feat, fruition, fulfillment, pursuance, realization, work; SEE CONCEPT 706

performance [n2] *acting, depiction*
act, appearance, ballet, behavior, burlesque, business, ceremony, concert, custom, dance, display, drama, exhibition, gig*, interpretation, matinee, offering, opera, pageant, play, portrayal, presentation, production, recital, rehearsal, representation, review, revue, rigmarole, rite, set, show, special, spectacle, stage show, stunt, to-do*; SEE CONCEPT 263

performance [n3] *efficiency*
action, conduct, effectiveness, efficacy, exercise, functioning, operation, practice, pursuit, running, working; SEE CONCEPT 630

perfume [n] *scent, often manufactured and packaged for personal use*
aroma, attar, balm, balminess, bouquet, cologne, eau de cologne, essence, fragrance, incense, odor, oil, redolence, sachet, smell, spice, sweetness; SEE CONCEPTS 599,600

perfunctory [adj] *automatic, unthinking*
apathetic, careless, cool, cursory, disinterested, going through the motions*, heedless, impersonal, inattentive, indifferent, involuntary, lackadaisical, laid-back*, mechanical, negligent, offhand, phoning it in*, routine, sketchy, slipshod*, slovenly, standard, stereotyped, stock, superficial, unaware, unconcerned, uninterested, usual, walking through it*, wooden*; SEE CONCEPTS 542,544

perhaps [adv] *possibly*
as it may be, as the case may be, conceivably, feasibly, for all one knows, imaginably, it may be, maybe, perchance, reasonably; SEE CONCEPT 552

peril [n] *danger, risk*
cause for alarm*, double trouble*, endangerment, exposure, hazard, insecurity, jeopardy, liability, menace, openness, pitfall, risky business*, uncertainty, vulnerability; SEE CONCEPT 675

perilous [adj] *very dangerous*
chancy, delicate, dicey*, dynamite, exposed, hairy*, hazardous, insecure, loaded*, on thin ice*, playing with fire*, precarious, risky, rugged, Russian roulette*, shaky, threatening, ticklish, touch and go*, touchy, treacherous, uncertain, unhealthy, unsafe, unsound, unstable, unsteady, unsure, vulnerable, wicked*; SEE CONCEPTS 548,587

perimeter [n] *circumference, border*
ambit, borderline, boundary, bounds, brim, brink, circuit, compass, confines, edge, fringe, hem, limit, margin, outline, periphery, skirt, verge; SEE CONCEPTS 484,745,792

period [*n1*] *extent of time*
aeon, age, course, cycle, date, days, duration, epoch, era, generation, interval, measure, season, space, span, spell, stage, stretch, term, time, while, years; SEE CONCEPTS *807,822*

period [*n2*] *ending*
cessation, close, closing, closure, conclusion, discontinuance, end, limit, stop, termination; SEE CONCEPT *832*

periodic [*adj*] *at fixed intervals*
alternate, annual, at various times, centennial, cyclic, cyclical, daily, epochal, every once in a while, every so often, fluctuating, hourly, infrequent, intermittent, isochronal, isochronous, monthly, occasional, on-again-off-again*, on certain occasions, orbital, perennial, periodical, recurrent, recurring, regular, repeated, rhythmic, routine, seasonal, serial, spasmodic, sporadic, weekly, yearly; SEE CONCEPTS *541,799*

periodical [*n*] *regular publication*
journal, mag*, magazine, monthly, newspaper, number, paper, quarterly, rag*, review, serial, sheet*, slick*, throwaway*, weekly; SEE CONCEPT *280*

peripatetic [*adj*] *constantly traveling*
ambulant, itinerant, itinerate, migrant, mobile, nomadic, perambulant, roaming, roving, vagabond, vagrant, wandering, wayfaring; SEE CONCEPTS *401,584*

peripheral [*adj*] *minor, outside*
beside the point, borderline, exterior, external, incidental, inessential, irrelevant, minor, outer, outermost, perimetric, secondary, superficial, surface, tangential, unimportant; SEE CONCEPTS *575,583,831*

periphery [*n*] *outskirts, outer edge*
ambit, border, boundary, brim, brink, circuit, circumference, compass, covering, edge, fringe, hem, margin, outside, perimeter, rim, skirt, verge; SEE CONCEPTS *484,745*

perish [*v*] *die, decline, decay*
be destroyed, be killed, be lost, bite the dust*, break down, buy the farm*, cease, check out*, collapse, corrupt, croak, crumble, decease, decompose, demise, depart, disappear, disintegrate, end, expire, fall, give up the ghost*, go, go under, kick the bucket*, lose life, OD*, pass, pass away, pass on, rot, succumb, vanish, waste*, wither; SEE CONCEPTS *13,105,304*

perishable [*adj*] *liable to spoil, rot*
decaying, decomposable, destructible, easily spoiled, short-lived, unstable; SEE CONCEPTS *462,485*

perjure [*v*] *give false testimony*
bear false witness*, commit perjury, deceive, delude, equivocate, falsify, forswear, lie, lie under oath, mislead, prevaricate, swear falsely, trick; SEE CONCEPTS *63,317*

perk [*n*] *benefit*
advantage, bonus, dividend, extra, fringe benefit, gratuity, gravy*, lagniappe, largess, perquisite, plus, tip; SEE CONCEPT *344*

perk up [*v*] *cheer*
ameliorate, be refreshed, brighten, buck up*, cheer up, convalesce, gain, improve, invigorate, liven up, look up, mend, pep up, rally, recover, recuperate, refresh, renew, revive, shake, take heart*; SEE CONCEPTS *7,22,244,308*

perky [*adj*] *animated, happy*
active, alert, aware, bouncy, bright, bright-eyed and bushy-tailed*, brisk, bubbly, buoyant, cheerful, cheery, gay, in fine fettle*, jaunty, lively, spirited, sprightly, sunny, vivacious; SEE CONCEPTS *401,404*

permanent [*adj*] *constant, lasting*
abiding, changeless, continual, diurnal, durable, enduring, everlasting, fixed, forever, forever and a day*, for keeps*, immutable, imperishable, indestructible, in for the long haul*, invariable, long-lasting, perdurable, perduring, perennial, perpetual, persistent, set, set in concrete*, set in stone*, stable, steadfast, unchanging, unfading; SEE CONCEPTS *551,649,798*

permeable [*adj*] *absorbent, penetrable*
absorptive, accessible, enterable, passable, pervious, porose, porous, spongelike, spongy; SEE CONCEPTS *576,604,606*

permeate [*v*] *filter, spread throughout*
charge, diffuse, drench, fill, go through, imbue, impregnate, infiltrate, infuse, ingrain, interfuse, invade, pass through, penetrate, percolate, pervade, pierce, saturate, seep, soak, stab, stalk, steep, suffuse, transfuse; SEE CONCEPTS *159,179,256*

permissible [*adj*] *allowable, legal*
acceptable, admissible, all right, approved, authorized, bearable, endorsed, kosher*, lawful, legalized, legit*, legitimate, licit, okay*, on the up and up*, permitted, proper, sanctioned, tolerable, tolerated, unforbidden, unprohibited; SEE CONCEPTS *319, 548,554*

permission [*n*] *authorization, consent*
acceptance, acknowledgment, acquiescence, admission, agreement, allowance, approbation, approval, assent, avowal, canonization, carte blanche*, concession, concurrence, condonance, condonation, dispensation, empowerment, endorsement, freedom, imprimatur, indulgence, leave, letting, liberty, license, okay, permit, privilege, promise, recognition, rubber stamp*, sanctification, sanction, stamp of approval*, sufferance, tolerance, toleration, verification, warrant; SEE CONCEPTS *50,83,88,376,685*

permissive [*adj*] *very lenient*
acquiescent, agreeable, allowing, approving, easygoing, forbearing, free, indulgent, latitudinarian, lax, liberal, open-minded, permitting, susceptible, tolerant; SEE CONCEPT *401*

permit [*n*] *authorization*
admittance, allowance, charter, concession, consent, empowering, favor, franchise, go-ahead*, grant, green light*, indulgence, leave, legalization, liberty, license, pass, passport, patent, permission, privilege,

safe-conduct, sanction, sufferance, toleration, visa, warrant; SEE CONCEPTS *271,376,685*

permit [v] *allow participation*
abet, accede, accept, acquiesce, admit, agree, authorize, bless, blink at*, boost, buy, charter, concede, concur, condone, consent, empower, enable, endorse, endure, franchise, give leave, give permission, go for, grant, have, humor, indulge, leave, let, let pass, license, okay, pass, privilege, sanctify, sanction, say yes, shake on*, sign, sign off on*, suffer, take kindly to*, thumbs up*, tolerate, warrant, wink at*; SEE CONCEPTS *50,83,88*

pernicious [adj] *bad, hurtful*
baleful, damaging, dangerous, deadly, deleterious, destructive, detrimental, devastating, evil, fatal, harmful, iniquitous, injurious, killing, lethal, maleficent, malevolent, malicious, malign, malignant, miasmatic, miasmic, mortal, nefarious, noisome, noxious, offensive, pestiferous, pestilent, pestilential, poisonous, prejudicial, ruinous, sinister, toxic, venomous, virulent, wicked; SEE CONCEPTS *537, 548,571*

perpendicular [adj] *at right angles to*
erect, horizontal, on end, plumb, sheer, standing, stand-up, steep, straight, straight-up, upright, vertical; SEE CONCEPTS *581,583*

perpetrate [v] *be responsible for*
act, bring about, carry out, commit, do, effect, enact, execute, inflict, perform, pull, up and do*, wreak; SEE CONCEPT *91*

perpetual [adj] *continual, lasting*
abiding, ceaseless, constant, continued, continuous, endless, enduring, eternal, everlasting, going on, immortal, imperishable, incessant, infinite, interminable, intermittent, never-ceasing, never-ending, perdurable, perennial, permanent, persistent, recurrent, recurring, reoccuring, repeated, repeating, repetitious, returning, sempiternal, unceasing, unchanging, undying, unending, unfailing, uninterrupted, unremitting, without end; SEE CONCEPTS *551,649,798,799*

perpetuate [v] *keep going*
bolster, conserve, continue, eternalize, eternize, immortalize, keep, keep alive, keep in existence, keep up, maintain, preserve, secure, support, sustain; SEE CONCEPT *239*

perplex [v] *confuse, mix up*
astonish, astound, baffle, balk, befuddle, beset, bewilder, buffalo*, complicate, confound, discombobulate*, discompose, dumbfound, encumber, entangle, fog, get to*, involve, jumble, muck, muddle, muddy the waters*, mystify, nonplus, perturb, pose, puzzle, rattle, ravel, snarl up, stumble, stump, surprise, tangle, thicken, thwart; SEE CONCEPTS *16,84*

per se [adv] *essentially*
alone, as such, by and of itself, by definition, by itself, by its very nature, fundamentally, independently, in essence, in itself, intrinsically, of itself,

singularly, solely, virtually; SEE CONCEPTS *544,577*

persecute [v] *wrong, torment*
afflict, aggrieve, annoy, badger, bait, beat, be on one's case*, bother, crucify, distress, dog*, dragoon, drive up the wall*, exile, expel, harass, hector, hound*, hunt, ill-treat, injure, maltreat, martyr, molest, oppress, outrage, pester, pick on, plague, pursue, tease, torture, tyrannize, vex, victimize, worry; SEE CONCEPTS *7,19,44,246*

perseverance [n] *diligence, hard work*
backbone*, constancy, continuance, cool, dedication, determination, doggedness, drive, endurance, grit*, guts*, immovability, indefatigability, moxie*, never say die*, persistence, pertinacity, pluck, prolonging, purposefulness, pursuance, resolution, sedulity, spunk, stamina, steadfastness, stick-to-itiveness*, tenacity; SEE CONCEPTS *411,633*

persevere [v] *keep at; work hard*
be determined, be resolved, be stubborn, carry on, continue, endure, go for broke*, go for it*, go on, hang in*, hang tough*, hold fast*, hold on, keep driving*, keep going, keep on, leave no stone unturned*, maintain, never say die*, persist, plug away*, press on, proceed, pursue, remain, see it through*, stand firm*, stay the course*, stick with it*; SEE CONCEPTS *87,239*

persist [v] *carry on, carry through*
abide, be resolute, be stubborn, continue, endure, follow through*, follow up*, go all the way*, go on, go the limit*, grind, hold on, insist, keep up*, last, leave no stone unturned*, linger, obtain, perdure, perseverate, persevere, prevail, pursue, recur, remain, repeat, see through, stick it out*, stick to guns*, strive, tough it out*; SEE CONCEPTS *23,87,91,239*

persistent [adj] *determined; continuous*
assiduous, bound, bound and determined*, bulldogged*, constant, continual, dogged, endless, enduring, firm, fixed, immovable, incessant, indefatigable, in for long haul*, insistent, interminable, like bad penny*, never-ending, obdurate, obstinate, perpetual, perseverant, persevering, persisting, pertinacious, relentless, repeated, resolute, steadfast, steady, stick-to-itive*, sticky, stubborn, tenacious, tireless, unflagging, unrelenting, unremitting, unshakable; SEE CONCEPTS *326,401,404,538*

persnickety [adj] *fussy, particular*
careful, choosy, fastidious, finicky, nice, picky; SEE CONCEPT *404*

person [n] *human being*
being, bird*, body, cat*, chap*, character, creature, customer, dude*, fellow, gal, guy, head*, human, identity, individual, individuality, joker*, lad*, lady, lass, life, living soul, man, mortal, party, personage, personality, self, somebody, soul, specimen, spirit, unit*, woman; SEE CONCEPT *417*

personable [adj] *friendly, sociable*
aces*, affable, agreeable, all heart*, all right*, amiable, attractive, charming, easygoing, good egg*,

gregarious, likable, nice, okay, pleasant, pleasing, presentable, sweetheart*, white-hat*, winning; SEE CONCEPT *404*

personage/personality [*n/n2*] *celebrity, notable*
big shot*, bigwig*, brass*, celeb*, chief, cynosure, dignitary, distinguished person, eminence, face*, hot shot*, individual, luminary, monster*, name*, public figure, somebody, star, superstar, top dog*, VIP*, worthy; SEE CONCEPTS *352,354,423*

personal [*adj*] *private, individual*
claimed, exclusive, intimate, own, particular, peculiar, privy, retired, secluded, secret, special; SEE CONCEPT *536*

personality [*n1*] *person's character, traits*
charisma, charm, complexion, disposition, dynamism, emotions, identity, individuality, likableness, magnetism, makeup, nature, psyche, selfdom, selfhood, singularity, temper, temperament; SEE CONCEPT *411*

personally [*adv*] *independently*
alone, by oneself, directly, for oneself, for one's part, individualistically, individually, in one's own view, in person, in the flesh, narrowly, on one's own, privately, solely, specially, subjectively; SEE CONCEPTS *544,577*

personify [*v*] *represent some other being, character*
act out, body forth, contain, copy, emblematize, embody, epitomize, exemplify, express, exteriorize, externalize, hominify, humanize, illustrate, image, imitate, impersonate, incarnate, live as, make human, manifest, materialize, mirror, objectify, personize, substantiate, symbolize, typify; SEE CONCEPTS *261,716*

personnel [*n*] *employees of business or other enterprise*
cadre, corps, crew, faculty, group, helpers, human resources, members, men and women, office, organization, people, shop, staff, troop, troops, workers, work force; SEE CONCEPTS *325,417*

perspective [*n*] *view, outlook*
angle, aspect, attitude, broad view, context, frame of reference*, headset*, landscape, mindset*, objectivity, overview, panorama, proportion, prospect, relation, relative importance, relativity, scene, size of it*, viewpoint, vista, way of looking; SEE CONCEPTS *410,629,689*

perspicacious [*adj*] *observant, perceptive*
acute, alert, astute, aware, clear-sighted, clever, discerning, heady*, judicious, keen, penetrating, percipient, sagacious, savvy, sharp, sharp-witted, shrewd; SEE CONCEPT *402*

perspicuous [*adj*] *clear, obvious*
apparent, clear-cut, comprehensible, crystal*, crystal-clear*, distinct, easily understood, explicit, intelligible, limpid, lucent, lucid, luminous, pellucid, plain, self-evident, straightforward, transparent, unambiguous, unblurred, understandable; SEE CONCEPT *529*

perspire [*v*] *become wet with sweat*
be damp, be wet, break a sweat*, drip, exude, get in a lather*, glow, lather, pour, secrete, sweat, swelter; SEE CONCEPTS *185,469*

persuade [*v*] *cause to believe; convince to do*
actuate, advise, affect, allure, argue into, assure, blandish, brainwash, bring around, bring to senses, cajole, coax, convert, counsel, draw, enlist, entice, exhort, gain confidence of, get, impel, impress, incite, incline, induce, influence, inveigle, lead, lead to believe, lead to do, move, prevail upon, prompt, propagandize, proselyte, proselytize, reason, satisfy, seduce, sell, stroke, sway, talk into, touch, turn on to, urge, wear down*, wheedle, win argument, win over, woo, work over; SEE CONCEPT *68*

persuasion [*n1*] *influencing to do, believe*
alignment, alluring, arm-twist*, blandishment, brainwash, brainwashing, cajolery, cogency, con, conversion, enticement, exhortation, force, goose*, hard sell*, hook*, inducement, inveiglement, persuasiveness, potency, power, promote, pull*, seduction, sell*, snow job*, soft soap*, squeeze*, sweet talk*, wheedling, winning over, working over; SEE CONCEPTS *68,686*

persuasion [*n2*] *belief, religion*
bias, camp, certitude, church, communion, connection, conviction, credo, creed, cult, denomination, eye, faction, faith, feeling, mind*, opinion, partiality, party, predilection, prejudice, school, school of thought*, sect, sentiment, side, tenet, view; SEE CONCEPT *689*

persuasive [*adj*] *effective, influential*
actuating, alluring, cogent, compelling, conclusive, convictive, convincing, credible, effectual, efficacious, efficient, eloquent, energetic, enticing, forceful, forcible, impelling, impressive, inducing, inspiring, inveigling, logical, luring, moving, plausible, pointed, potent, powerful, seductive, slick, smooth, sound, stimulating, stringent, strong, swaying, telling, touching, unctuous, valid, weighty, wheedling, winning; SEE CONCEPTS *267,537,542*

pert [*adj*] *lively, bold*
animated, audacious, brash, brazen, breezy, bright, brisk, cheeky*, dapper, daring, dashing, disrespectful, flip*, flippant, forward, fresh, gay, impertinent, impudent, insolent, jaunty, keen, nervy, perky, presumptuous, sassy, saucy, smart, smart-alecky*, spirited, sprightly, vivacious, wise; SEE CONCEPTS *401,404*

pertain [*v*] *be relevant to*
affect, appertain, apply, associate, be appropriate, bear on, befit, belong, be part of, be pertinent, combine, concern, connect, inhere with, join, refer, regard, relate, touch, vest; SEE CONCEPT *532*

pertinent [*adj*] *relevant, suitable*
admissible, ad rem, applicable, apposite, appropriate, apropos, apt, connected, fit, fitting, germane, kosher*, legit*, material, on target*, on the button*, on the nose*, opportune, pat*, pertaining, proper,

related, right on, to the point, to the purpose; SEE CONCEPT *558*

perturb [v] *upset, unsettle*
agitate, alarm, annoy, bewilder, bother, bug*, confound, confuse, disarrange, discompose, disconcert, discountenance, dismay, disorder, disquiet, disturb, flurry, fluster, irritate, make a scene*, make waves*, muddle, needle, perplex, pester, ruffle, stir up*, trouble, vex, worry; SEE CONCEPTS *7,16,19*

peruse [v] *check out; examine*
analyze, browse, check, glance over, inspect, look through, pore over, read, scan, scrutinize, skim, study; SEE CONCEPTS *72,103*

pervade [v] *affect strongly; spread through*
charge, diffuse, extend, fill, imbue, impregnate, infuse, overspread, penetrate, percolate, permeate, suffuse, transfuse; SEE CONCEPTS *172,179*

pervasive [adj] *extensive*
all over the place*, can't get away from*, common, general, inescapable, omnipresent, permeating, pervading, prevalent, rife, ubiquitous, universal, wall-to-wall*, widespread; SEE CONCEPT *772*

perverse [adj] *mean, ornery; troublesome*
abnormal, bad-tempered, cantankerous, capricious, contradictory, contrary, contumacious, corrupt, crabby*, cross, degenerate, delinquent, depraved, deviant, disobedient, dogged*, erring, fractious, hard-nosed*, headstrong, intractable, intransigent, irritable, miscreant, mulish*, nefarious, obdurate, obstinate, petulant, pigheaded*, rebellious, refractory, rotten*, self-willed, spiteful, stubborn, unhealthy, unmanageable, unreasonable, unyielding, villainous, wayward, wicked, willful; SEE CONCEPTS *401,542,571*

pervert [n] *person who lacks morals*
debauchee, degenerate, deviant, deviate, freak, weirdo; SEE CONCEPT *412*

pervert [v] *twist, turn away from what is acceptable or correct*
abuse, adulterate, alloy, animalize, bastardize*, brainwash, color, corrupt, cut*, debase, debauch, demoralize, deprave, desecrate, distort, divert, doctor, doctor up*, fake, falsify, fudge*, garble, misconstrue, misinterpret, misrepresent, misstate, mistreat, misuse, outrage, phony up*, prostitute, queer, ruin, salt*, seduce, spike, vitiate, warp, water*; SEE CONCEPTS *14,63,156,252*

perverted [adj] *immoral, evil*
abandoned, aberrant, abnormal, abused, contorted, corrupt, corrupted, debased, debauched, defiled, depraved, deviant, deviating, distorted, foreign, grotesque, impaired, kinky, misguided, misused, monstrous, outraged, polluted, queer, sick, tainted, twisted, unhealthy, unnatural, vicious, vitiate, vitiated, warped, wicked; SEE CONCEPTS *485,545*

pesky [adj] *bothersome*
annoying, disturbing, irksome, mean, nettlesome, peeving, provoking, troublesome, ugly, vexatious, vexing, wicked; SEE CONCEPTS *529,537*

pessimism [n] *belief in bad outcome*
cynicism, dark side*, dejection, depression, despair, despondency, dim view*, distrust, dyspepsia, expectation of worst, gloom, gloominess, gloomy outlook, glumness, grief, hopelessness, low spirits, melancholy, sadness, unhappiness; SEE CONCEPTS *410,689*

pessimist [n] *person who expects bad outcome*
complainer, crepehanger*, cynic, defeatist, depreciator, downer, gloomy, killjoy*, misanthrope, party pooper*, prophet of doom*, sourpuss*, wet blanket*, worrier, worrywart*; SEE CONCEPTS *412,423*

pessimistic [adj] *expecting bad outcome*
bleak, cynical, dark, dejected, depressed, despairing, despondent, discouraged, distrustful, downhearted, fatalistic, foreboding, gloomy, glum, hopeless, melancholy, misanthropic, morbid, morose, realistic, resigned, sad, sullen, troubled, worried; SEE CONCEPTS *403,548*

pest [n] *person or thing that presents problem*
annoyance, badgerer, bane, besetment, blight, blister, bore, bother, botheration, bug*, contagion, crashing bore*, creep, curse, drag, drip, epidemic, exasperation, headache*, infection, irritant, irritation, nag, nudge, nuisance, pain*, pain in the neck*, pesterer, pestilence, pill*, plague*, scourge*, tease*, thorn in side*, tormentor, trial*, trouble, vexation, virus*; SEE CONCEPTS *306,398,412,674*

pester [v] *bother, harass*
annoy, badger, be at, bedevil, beleaguer, bug*, disturb, dog*, drive crazy, drive up the wall*, fret, get at*, get in one's hair*, get on one's nerves*, get to*, harry, hassle, hector, hound, importune, insist, irk, mess with*, nag, nudge, pick at*, plague, provoke, remind, ride*, tantalize, tease, torment, work on*, worry; SEE CONCEPTS *7,19,48*

pestilent/pestilential [adj] *dangerous, harmful*
baneful, contagious, contaminating, corrupting, deadly, deleterious, destructive, detrimental, diseased, evil, fatal, infectious, injurious, lethal, mortal, noxious, pernicious, pestiferous, ruinous, tainting, troublesome, vicious; SEE CONCEPTS *314,537*

pet [n] *favorite thing, person*
apple of eye*, beloved, blue-eyed one*, cat, darling, dear, dog, evergreen*, fair-haired*, favorite, idol, jewel*, love, lover, persona grata*, treasure*; SEE CONCEPTS *394,416*

pet [adj] *favorite*
affectionate, blue-eyed*, cherished, darling, dear, dearest, endearing, fair-haired*, favored, loved, precious, preferred, special; SEE CONCEPTS *568,574*

pet [v] *stroke, kiss*
baby, caress, coddle, cosset, cuddle, dandle, embrace, fondle, grab, hug, love, make love, neck*, pamper, pat, smooch*, spoil, spoon*, touch; SEE CONCEPTS *375,612*

peter out [v] *dwindle, decrease*
abate, come to nothing*, die out*, diminish, drain, ebb, evaporate, fade, fail, give out, lessen, miscarry,

rebate, recede, run dry, run out, stop, taper off, wane; SEE CONCEPTS *105,698*

petite [*adj*] *very small*
baby, bantam, dainty, delicate, diminutive, dwarf, elfin, little, miniature, minikin*, slight, smallish, tiny, wee*; SEE CONCEPTS *773,779,789*

petition [*n*] *appeal, plea*
address, application, entreaty, imploration, imprecation, invocation, memorial, prayer, request, round robin, solicitation, suit, supplication; SEE CONCEPTS *271,662*

petition [*v*] *plead, appeal for*
adjure, ask, beg, beseech, call upon, entreat, impetrate, implore, pray, press, put in for, request, seek, solicit, sue, supplicate, urge; SEE CONCEPTS *48,53*

petrify [*v1*] *make hard*
calcify, clarify, fossilize, harden, lapidify, mineralize, set, solidify, turn to stone; SEE CONCEPT *250*

petrify [*v2*] *frighten*
alarm, amaze, appall, astonish, astound, benumb, chill, confound, daze, dismay, dumbfound, horrify, immobilize, numb, paralyze, put chill on*, scare, scare silly*, scare stiff*, spook*, startle, stun, stupefy, terrify, transfix; SEE CONCEPTS *7,14,19,42*

petty [*adj*] *trivial, insignificant*
base, casual, cheap, contemptible, frivolous, inconsequent, inconsiderable, inessential, inferior, irrelevant, junior, lesser, light, little, lower, measly, minor, narrow-minded, negligible, nickel-and-dime*, niggling*, paltry, peanut*, penny-ante*, pettifogging*, picayune*, piddling*, scratch, secondary, shabby, shallow, shoestring*, slight, small, small-minded, subordinate, trifling, two-bit*, unimportant; SEE CONCEPTS *403,575*

petulant [*adj*] *crabby, moody*
bad-tempered, captious, caviling, complaining, cranky*, cross, crybaby*, displeased, fault-finding, fractious, fretful, grouchy, grumbling, huffy, ill-humored, impatient, irritable, mean, peevish, perverse, pouting, querulous, snappish, sour, sulky, sullen, testy, touchy, ungracious, uptight*, waspish, whining, whiny; SEE CONCEPTS *401,542*

phantom [*n*] *ghost; figment of the imagination*
apparition, chimera, daydream, delusion, dream, eidolon, figment, hallucination, haunt, ignis fatuus, illusion, mirage, nightmare, phantasm, revenant, shade, shadow, specter, spirit, spook, vision, wraith; SEE CONCEPTS *370,529*

phase [*n*] *period in life of something*
appearance, aspect, chapter, condition, development, facet, juncture, point, position, posture, stage, state, step, time; SEE CONCEPTS *816,834*

phenomenal [*adj*] *astounding, exceptional*
extraordinary, fantastic, marvelous, miraculous, outstanding, preternatural, prodigious, rare, remarkable, sensational, singular, substantial, uncommon, unique, unparalleled, unusual, unwonted, wondrous; SEE CONCEPTS *564,574*

phenomenon [*n*] *rare occurrence; wonder*
abnormality, actuality, anomaly, appearance, aspect, circumstance, curiosity, episode, event, exception, experience, fact, happening, incident, marvel, miracle, nonpareil, one for the books*, paradox, peculiarity, portent, prodigy, rara avis*, rarity, reality, sensation, sight, something else*, spectacle, stunner*, uniqueness; SEE CONCEPTS *230,529,678*

philanderer [*n*] *person who has many love affairs*
adulterer, chaser, cruiser, dallier, debaucher, Don Juan*, flirt, gallant, Jezebel*, lover, operator*, playboy/girl, swinger, womanizer; SEE CONCEPTS *419,423*

philanthropic [*adj*] *charitable, giving*
altruistic, beneficent, benevolent, benignant, big-hearted, bountiful, contributing, donating, eleemosynary, generous, good, gracious, helpful, humane, humanitarian, kind, kindhearted, liberal, magnanimous, munificent, openhanded, patriotic, public-spirited; SEE CONCEPTS *404,542*

philosophical/philosophic [*adj1*] *thinking deeply, rationally*
abstract, cogitative, deep, erudite, judicious, learned, logical, pensive, profound, rational, reflective, sagacious, sapient, theoretical, thoughtful, wise; SEE CONCEPT *402*

philosophical/philosophic [*adj2*] *calm, serene*
collected, commonsensical, composed, cool*, cool as cucumber*, enduring, impassive, imperturbable, patient, resigned, stoical, tranquil, unagitated, unflappable, unmoved, unruffled; SEE CONCEPT *401*

philosophy [*n*] *principles, knowledge*
aesthetics, attitude, axiom, beliefs, conception, convictions, doctrine, idea, ideology, logic, metaphysics, ontology, outlook, rationalism, reason, reasoning, system, tenet, theory, thinking, thought, truth, values, view, viewpoint, wisdom; SEE CONCEPTS *349,687,689*

phobia [*n*] *fear*
anxiety, aversion, avoidance, awe, detestation, disgust, dislike, distaste, dread, fear, hang-up*, hatred, horror, irrationality, loathing, neurosis, obsession, repulsion, resentment, revulsion, terror, thing*, thing about*, tiger*; SEE CONCEPTS *27,29,529*

phony [*adj*] *fake, false*
affected, artificial, assumed, bastard, bogus, counterfeit, forged, imitation, pseudo*, put-on*, sham*, spurious, trick; SEE CONCEPT *582*

photocopy [*n/v*] *mechanical image produced from a copier; making the image*
copy, duplicate, reproduce, stat, velox, Xerox; SEE CONCEPT *269*

photograph [*n*] *a still picture taken with a camera*
blowup, close-up, image, Kodachrome*, Kodak*, likeness, microfilm, mug*, negative, photo, photostat, pic*, picture, pinup*, pix*, Polaroid*, portrait, positive, print, shot*, slide, snap, snapshot, transparency; SEE CONCEPT *265*

photograph [v] *take a picture with a camera*
capture*, capture on film*, cinematize, close-up*, copy, film, get, get a likeness*, get a shot*, illustrate, lens*, make a picture*, microfilm, mug*, photo, photoengrave, photostat, picture, print, record, reproduce, roll, shoot, snap*, snapshot, take*, turn*, X-ray*; SEE CONCEPT *174*

photographic [adj] *exact, retentive in detail*
accurate, cinematic, detailed, faithful, filmic, graphic, lifelike, minute, natural, pictorial, picturesque, precise, realistic, true-to-life*, visual, vivid; SEE CONCEPT *557*

phrase [n] *group of words; way of speaking*
byword, catchphrase, catchword, diction, expression, idiom, locution, maxim, motto, parlance, phraseology, phrasing, remark, saying, shibboleth, slogan, styling, tag, terminology, utterance, verbalism, verbiage, watchword, wordage, wording; SEE CONCEPTS *275,278*

phrase [v] *express in words carefully*
couch, formulate, frame, present, put, put into words, say, term, utter, voice, word; SEE CONCEPT *55*

physical [adj1] *tangible, material*
concrete, corporeal, environmental, gross, materialistic, natural, objective, palpable, phenomenal, ponderable, real, sensible, solid, somatic, substantial, visible; SEE CONCEPT *582*

physical [adj2] *concerning the body*
bodily, brute, carnal, corporal, corporeal, earthly, fleshly, incarnate, mortal, personal, somatic, unspiritual, visceral; SEE CONCEPT *485*

physician [n] *person trained in medical science*
bones*, doc*, doctor, general practitioner, healer, intern, MD*, medic, medical practitioner, medico, quack*, sawbones*, specialist, surgeon; SEE CONCEPT *357*

physique [n] *build of human body*
anatomy, body, built, character, configuration, constitution, corpus, figure, form, frame, habit, habitus, makeup, muscles, nature, shape, structure, type; SEE CONCEPTS *405,757*

pick [n] *a chosen option, usually the choicest*
aces, bag, best, choice, choosing, cream*, crème de la crème*, cup of tea*, decision, druthers*, elect, elite, fat, flower*, preference, pride, prime, prize, select, selection, top, tops; SEE CONCEPTS *529,671*

pick [v1] *choose, select*
cull, decide upon, elect, finger*, fix upon, go down the line*, hand-pick, mark, name, optate, opt for, pick and choose, pick out, prefer, say so, separate, settle on, sift out*, single out, slot, sort out, tab, tag, take, take it or leave it*, tap, winnow; SEE CONCEPT *41*

pick [v2] *gather, harvest*
accumulate, choose, collect, cull, cut, draw, pluck, pull; SEE CONCEPTS *41,109,206*

pick [v3] *break into something closed, locked*
break open, crack, dent, force, hit, indent, jimmy, open, pry, strike; SEE CONCEPT *192*

pick at/pick on [v] *nag, provoke*
badger, bait, blame, bully, carp, cavil, criticize, find fault, foment, get at*, get to*, goad, hector, incite, instigate, quibble, start, tease, torment; SEE CONCEPTS *7,19,52*

picket [n1] *post of structure*
pale, paling, palisade, panel, peg, pillar, rail, stake, stanchion, upright; SEE CONCEPTS *445,479*

picket [n2] *person who demonstrates for cause*
demonstrator, picketer, protester, striker; SEE CONCEPTS *348,359*

picket [n3] *person acting as guard*
guard, lookout, patrol, patrolman/woman, scout, sentinel, sentry, spotter, vedette, ward, watch, watchman/woman; SEE CONCEPT *348*

picket [v] *protest against, for cause*
blockade, boycott, demonstrate, hit the bricks*, strike, walk out; SEE CONCEPTS *300,351*

pickle [n] *sticky situation*
bind, box*, corner*, difficulty, dilemma, disorder, fix, hole*, hot water*, jam*, plight, predicament, quandary, scrape, spot*, tight spot*; SEE CONCEPT *674*

pickle [v] *preserve fruit or vegetable*
can, cure, keep, marinade, salt, souse, steep; SEE CONCEPT *170*

pick up [v1] *lift, raise*
elevate, gather, grasp, hoist, rear, take up, uphold, uplift, upraise, uprear; SEE CONCEPT *196*

pick up [v2] *obtain, find*
acquire, annex, buy, chalk up*, come across, compass, cull, extract, gain, garner, gather, get, get the hang of*, glean, happen upon*, have, learn, master, procure, purchase, score, secure, take; SEE CONCEPTS *31,120,183*

pick up [v3] *improve*
continue, gain, gain ground*, get better, get well, increase, make a comeback*, mend, perk up*, rally, recommence, recover, renew, reopen, restart, resume, swell, take up; SEE CONCEPTS *234,700*

pick up [v4] *call for socially*
accompany, apprehend, collect, drop in for*, get*, give a lift*, go for*, go to get*, invite, offer, proposition, stop for*; SEE CONCEPTS *224,384*

pick up [v5] *arrest for crime*
apprehend, book*, bust*, collar*, detain, nab, pinch*, pull in*, run in*, take into custody; SEE CONCEPT *317*

picky [adj] *choosy, finicky*
captious, carping, critical, dainty, fastidious, fault-finding, fussy, nice, particular, persnickety; SEE CONCEPT *404*

picnic [n1] *outdoor meal*
barbecue, clambake, cookout, dining alfresco, excursion, fish fry, outing, weiner roast; SEE CONCEPTS *386,459*

picnic [n2] *very easy undertaking*
breeze*, child's play*, cinch, duck soup*, kid stuff*, lark*, light work, no trouble, piece of cake*, push-over*, setup*, smooth sailing*, snap, sure thing, walkover*; SEE CONCEPTS *362,693*

picture [n1] *illustration, likeness of something*
account, art, blueprint, canvas, cartoon, copy, delineation, depiction, description, doodle, double, draft, drawing, duplicate, effigy, engraving, figure, icon, image, impression, lookalike, outline, painting, panorama, photo, photograph, piece, portrait, portraiture, portrayal, presentment, print, re-creation, replica, report, representation, ringer*, similitude, simulacrum, sketch, spectacle, spitting image*, statue, tableau, twin; SEE CONCEPTS *259,625*

picture [n2] *perfect example*
archetype, embodiment, epitome, essence, idea, personification; SEE CONCEPT *688*

picture [n3] *entertainment film*
cartoon, cinema, flick*, motion picture, movie, moving picture, photoplay, picture show, show; SEE CONCEPT *293*

picture [v1] *depict, describe*
delineate, draw, illustrate, image, interpret, limn, paint, photograph, portray, render, represent, show, sketch; SEE CONCEPTS *79,174*

picture [v2] *form vision in one's mind*
conceive of, create, daydream, dream, envision, fancy, fantasy, image, imagine, portray, see, see in the mind's eye*, visualize; SEE CONCEPTS *17,43*

picturesque [adj] *very attractive, referring to scenery*
arresting, artistic, beautiful, charming, colorful, graphic, photographic, pictorial, pleasant, pretty, quaint, scenic, striking, unusual, vivid; SEE CONCEPTS *579,589*

piddling [adj] *insignificant*
derisory, little, measly*, niggling*, paltry, peanut*, pettifogging*, petty, picayune, puny, trifling, trivial, unimportant, useless, worthless; SEE CONCEPTS *575,789*

piece [n1] *part*
allotment, bit, bite, case, chomp, chunk, cut, division, dole, end, example, fraction, fragment, gob, half, hunk, instance, interest, iota, item, length, lot, lump, member, moiety, morsel, mouthful, parcel, percentage, portion, quantity, quota, sample, scrap, section, segment, share, shred, slice, smithereen*, snack, specimen; SEE CONCEPTS *834,835*

piece [n2] *work of art, music, writing*
arrangement, article, bit, composition, creation, discourse, dissertation, engraving, exposition, icon, item, lines, painting, paper, part, photograph, print, production, sketch, song, statue, study, theme, thesis, treatise, treatment, vignette, work; SEE CONCEPTS *259,262,263,271*

piece [v] *put together*
assemble, combine, compose, create, fix, join, make, mend, patch, repair, restore, unite; SEE CONCEPTS *113,173,193,251*

piecemeal [adj/adv] *bit by bit*
at intervals, by degrees, by fits and starts*, fitfully, fragmentary, gradual, gradually, intermittent, intermittently, interrupted, little by little*, partial, partially, patchy, spotty, step by step*, unsystematic; SEE CONCEPTS *531,544*

pier [n] *support; place for boats*
berth, buttress, column, dam, dock, jetty, landing, levee, mole, pierage, pilaster, pile, piling, pillar, post, promenade, quay, slip, upright, wharf, wharfage; SEE CONCEPTS *439,443,479*

pierce [v] *cut, penetrate*
bore, break, break in, break through, cleave, crack, crack open, drill, enter, gash, go through, incise, intrude, jimmy, pass through, perforate, plow, prick, probe, puncture, run through, slash, slice, slit, spike, stab, stick into, transfix; SEE CONCEPTS *137, 159,176,220*

piercing [adj] *intense to the senses*
acute, agonizing, arctic, biting, bitter, blaring, cold, deafening, earsplitting, excruciating, exquisite, fierce, freezing, frosty, high, high-pitched, keen, knifelike, loud, nippy, numbing, painful, penetrating, powerful, racking, raw, roaring, severe, sharp, shattering, shooting, shrill, stabbing, stentorian, stentorious, thin, treble, wintry; SEE CONCEPTS *406,537,592,594*

piety [n] *devotion, religiousness*
allegiance, application, ardor, belief, devoutness, docility, dutifulness, duty, faith, fealty, fervor, fidelity, godliness, grace, holiness, loyalty, obedience, passion, piousness, religion, religiosity, reverence, sanctity, veneration, zeal; SEE CONCEPTS *633,689*

pig [n] *animal of swine family*
boar, cob roller*, hog, piggy*, piglet, porker*, porky, shoat, sow, swine; SEE CONCEPTS *394,400*

pigheaded [adj] *stubborn*
bullheaded, contrary, dense*, froward, headstrong, inflexible, insistent, intractable, mulish*, obstinate, perverse, recalcitrant, self-willed, stiff-necked, stupid*, unyielding, willful; SEE CONCEPTS *404,542*

pigment [n] *color, shade*
colorant, coloring, coloring matter, dye, dyestuff, oil, paint, stain, tincture, tint; SEE CONCEPTS *259,622*

pile [n1] *heap, collection*
accumulation, aggregate, aggregation, amassment, assemblage, assortment, bank, barrel, buildup, chunk, conglomeration, drift, gob, great deal, hill, hoard, hunk, jumble, lump, mass, mound, mountain, much, ocean, oodles*, pack, peck, pyramid, quantity, shock, stack, stockpile; SEE CONCEPTS *432,786*

pile [n2] *wealth*
affluence, boodle*, bundle*, dough*, fortune, mint*, money, pot*, riches, wad*; SEE CONCEPTS *335,340*

pile [v] *gather, pack; put on top of another*
accumulate, amass, assemble, bank, bunch, charge, choke, collect, crowd, crush, fill, flock, heap, hill,

hoard, jam, load, mass, mound, rush, stack, store; SEE CONCEPTS *84,109,201,750*

pilfer [v] *steal, embezzle*
annex, appropriate, borrow, cop*, crib*, filch*, liberate*, lift*, moonlight*, palm*, pinch*, pluck*, purloin, requisition, rip off*, rob, scrounge, snare, snatch, swipe, take, thieve, walk off with*; SEE CONCEPTS *139,142,192*

pilgrimage [n] *long journey*
crusade, excursion, expedition, mission, tour, travel, trip, wayfaring; SEE CONCEPT *224*

pill [n1] *capsule of medicine*
bolus, dose, lozenge, medicine, pellet, pilule, tablet, troche; SEE CONCEPTS *307,470*

pill [n2] *person who is very annoying*
bore, drag*, nuisance, pain*, pain in the neck*, pest, trial*; SEE CONCEPTS *412,423*

pillage [v] *plunder, destroy*
appropriate, arrogate, confiscate, depredate, desecrate, desolate, despoil, devastate, devour, encroach, gut, invade, lay waste*, lift*, loot, maraud, nab*, pilfer, pinch*, purloin, raid, ransack, ravage, rifle*, rob, ruin, sack, spoil, spoliate, steal, strip, swipe, thieve, trespass, usurp, waste; SEE CONCEPTS *86,139,252*

pillar [n1] *column of building, or freestanding column*
colonnade, mast, obelisk, pedestal, pier, pilaster, piling, post, prop, shaft, stanchion, support, tower, upright; SEE CONCEPT *440*

pillar [n2] *mainstay; source of strength*
backbone*, guider, leader, light*, rock*, sinew, supporter, tower of strength*, upholder, worthy; SEE CONCEPTS *423,712*

pilot [n] *person who guides aircraft, ship, or other vehicle*
ace*, aerialist, aeronaut, aviator, bellwether*, birdman/woman*, captain, conductor, coxswain, dean, director, doyen/doyenne, eagle*, flier*, flyboy*, flyer, fly-gal*, guide, helmsman/woman, jockey*, lead, leader, navigator, one at the controls, one at the wheel, scout*, steerer, steersman/woman, wheelman/woman; SEE CONCEPT *348*

pimple [n] *small swelling on the skin*
abscess, acne, beauty spot, blackhead, blemish, blister, boil, bump, carbuncle, caruncle, excrescence, furuncle, hickey*, inflammation, lump, papula, papule, pustule, spot, whitehead, zit*; SEE CONCEPT *306*

pin [v] *attach, hold in place*
affix, bind, clasp, close, fasten, fix, hold down, hold fast, immobilize, join, pinion, press, restrain, secure; SEE CONCEPTS *85,160,190*

pinch [n1] *tight pressing*
compression, confinement, contraction, cramp, grasp, grasping, hurt, limitation, nip, nipping, pressure, squeeze, torment, tweak, twinge; SEE CONCEPT *728*

pinch [n2] *very small amount*
bit, dash, drop, jot, mite, small quantity, soupçon, speck, splash, splatter, taste; SEE CONCEPT *831*

pinch [n3] *predicament*
box*, clutch, contingency, crisis, crunch*, difficulty, emergency, exigency, hardship, juncture, necessity, oppression, pass, plight, pressure, strait, stress, tight spot*, tight squeeze*, turning point*, zero hour*; SEE CONCEPT *674*

pinch [v1] *press tightly*
chafe, compress, confine, cramp, crush, grasp, hurt, nip, pain, squeeze, tweak, twinge, wrench, wrest, wring; SEE CONCEPTS *219,313*

pinch [v2] *be stingy*
afflict, distress, economize, oppress, pinch pennies*, press, scrape, scrimp, skimp, spare, stint; SEE CONCEPT *330*

pinch [v3] *steal*
cop*, crib*, filch*, knock off*, lift*, nab*, pilfer, purloin, rob, snatch, swipe, take; SEE CONCEPT *139*

pinch [v4] *arrest*
apprehend, bust*, collar*, detain, hold, nab*, pick up*, pull in*, run in*, take into custody; SEE CONCEPTS *90,317*

pine [v] *long for*
ache, agonize, brood, carry a torch*, covet, crave, desire, dream, fret, grieve, hanker, languish for, lust after, mope*, mourn, sigh, spoil for*, thirst for, want, wish, yearn, yen for; SEE CONCEPT *20*

pink [n1/adj] *rose color*
blush, coral, flush, fuchsia, rose, roseate, salmon; SEE CONCEPT *622*

pink [n2] *best condition*
acme*, best, bloom*, fitness, good health, height*, peak, perfection, prime, summit, trim*, verdure; SEE CONCEPTS *316,388*

pink [v] *cut in zigzag*
incise, notch, perforate, prick, punch, scallop, score; SEE CONCEPT *176*

pinnacle [n] *top, crest*
acme, apex, apogee, belfry, climax, cone, crown, culmination, eminence, greatest, height, max*, meridian, most*, needle*, obelisk, peak, pyramid, spire, steeple, summit, tops, tower, vertex, zenith; SEE CONCEPTS *706,836*

pinpoint [v] *define, locate*
determinate, diagnose, distinguish, finger*, get a fix on*, home in on*, identify, place, recognize, spot; SEE CONCEPTS *38,183*

pioneer [n] *person who finds a new place, founds something*
colonist, colonizer, developer, explorer, founder, founding father/mother, frontiersman/woman, guide, homesteader, immigrant, innovator, leader, pathfinder, pilgrim, scout, settler, squatter, trailblazer; SEE CONCEPTS *348,413*

pioneer [adj] *early, first*
avant-garde, brave, experimental, head, initial, lead, maiden, original, pioneering, primary, prime, untried; SEE CONCEPT *585*

pioneer [v] *invent; lay the groundwork*
begin, colonize, create, develop, discover, establish, explore, found, get the jump on*, go out in front*, initiate, instigate, institute, launch, map out, open up, originate, prepare, show the way, spearhead*, start, take the lead, trailblaze*; SEE CONCEPTS *173,221,324*

pious [adj] *dedicated, religious*
born-again*, clerical, devoted, devout, divine, ecclesiastical, God-fearing, godly, goody-goody*, hallowed, orthodox, prayerful, priestlike, priestly, reverent, righteous, sacred, saintly, sanctimonious, spiritual; SEE CONCEPT *401*

pipe [n] *passage, tube*
aqueduct, canal, channel, conduit, conveyer, duct, hose, line, main, pipeline, sewer, spout, trough, vent, vessel; SEE CONCEPTS *475,499*

pipe [v1] *conduct through tube, passage*
bring in, carry, channel, convey, funnel, siphon, supply, traject, transmit; SEE CONCEPT *217*

pipe [v2] *make a sound; peep*
blubber*, boohoo*, cheep*, cry, play, say, shout, sing, sob, sound, speak, talk, toot*, trill, tweet, twitter, wail, warble, weep, whistle; SEE CONCEPTS *47,65,77*

piquant [adj] *flavorful, biting*
appealing, appetizing, delicious, highly-seasoned, interesting, lively, peppery, poignant, provocative, pungent, racy, savory, sharp, snappy, sparkling, spicy, spirited, stimulating, stinging, tangy, tart, well-flavored, with a kick*, zestful, zesty; SEE CONCEPTS *529,613*

pique [n] *anger, irritation*
annoyance, blowup*, conniption*, dander*, displeasure, flare-up, grudge, huff, hurt, irk, miff, offense, peeve, pet*, pet peeve*, provocation, resentment, rise, ruckus, slow burn*, snit, sore*, stew*, storm*, tiff*, umbrage, vexation, wingding*; SEE CONCEPTS *29,410*

pique [v] *offend, provoke*
absorb, affront, annoy, arouse, bother, bug*, displease, egg on*, exasperate, excite, fire up*, gall, galvanize, get*, get a rise out of*, get dander up*, get under skin*, give a hard time*, give the business*, goad, goose*, grab, ignite, incense, innervate, irk, irritate, kindle, make waves*, miff, mortify, motivate, move, nettle, offend, peeve, prick, provoke, put out*, quicken, rile, rouse, spur, stimulate, sting*, stir, turn off*, vex, whet, work up*, wound; SEE CONCEPTS *7,14,19,22*

pit [n] *hole, cavity*
abyss, chasm, crater, dent, depression, dimple, excavation, grave, gulf, hell, hollow, indentation, mine, perforation, pockmark, pothole, puncture, shaft, tomb, trench, well; SEE CONCEPTS *509,513*

pit [v] *oppose, play off*
contend, counter, match, put in opposition, set against, vie; SEE CONCEPTS *92,363*

pitch [n1] *tilt*
angle, cant, degree, dip, gradient, height, incline, level, point, slant, slope, steepness; SEE CONCEPTS *692,738*

pitch [n2] *tone of sound*
frequency, harmonic, modulation, rate, sound, timbre; SEE CONCEPT *65*

pitch [n3] *talk to convince*
patter*, persuasion, sales talk, song and dance*, spiel*; SEE CONCEPTS *68,278*

pitch [v1] *throw, hurl*
bung, cast, chuck, chunk, fire, fling, gun, heave, launch, lob, peg, sling, toss, unseat; SEE CONCEPT *222*

pitch [v2] *put up, erect*
fix, locate, place, plant, raise, settle, set up, station; SEE CONCEPT *168*

pitch [v3] *dive, roll*
ascend, bend, bicker, careen, descend, dip, drive, drop, fall, flounder, go down, heave, lean, lunge, lurch, plunge, rise, rock, seesaw, slope, slump, stagger, tilt, topple, toss, tumble, vault, wallow, welter, yaw; SEE CONCEPTS *147,181,201*

pitch in [v] *help; get busy*
aid, attack, begin, buckle down*, chip in*, come through, commence, contribute, cooperate, do, do one's bit*, fall to*, get cracking*, get going, go to it*, hop to it*, join in, jump in*, launch, lend a hand*, participate, plunge into*, set about, set to, subscribe, tackle, tee off*, volunteer, wade in; SEE CONCEPTS *100,110*

piteous [adj] *miserable, pathetic*
affecting, beseeching, commiserable, deplorable, distressing, doleful, dolorous, entreating, grievous, heartbreaking, heart-rending, imploring, lamentable, melancholy, mournful, moving, pitiable, pitiful, plaintive, poignant, poor, rueful, ruined, sad, sorrowful, supplicating, woeful, wretched; SEE CONCEPTS *485,529*

pitfall [n] *hazard, trap*
booby trap*, catch*, danger, deadfall*, difficulty, downfall, drawback, entanglement, hook*, mesh*, mousetrap*, peril, pit*, quicksand*, risk, setup*, snag*, snare, swindle*, toil, web; SEE CONCEPTS *674,679*

pithy [adj] *brief, to the point*
cogent, compact, concise, crisp, curt, down to brass tacks*, effective, epigrammatic, expressive, forceful, honed, laconic, lean, meaningful, meaty*, pointed, pregnant, short, short-and-sweet*, significant, substantial, succinct, terse, trenchant, useful; SEE CONCEPT *267*

pitiful [adj] *in bad shape; poor*
abject, affecting, afflicted, arousing, base, beggarly, cheap, cheerless, comfortless, commiserative, compassionate, contemptible, deplorable, despicable, dismal, distressed, distressing, grievous, heartbreaking, heart-rending, inadequate, insignificant, joyless,

lamentable, low, mean, miserable, mournful, moving, paltry, pathetic, piteous, pitiable, sad, scummy, scurvy, shabby, sorrowful, sorry, stirring, suffering, tearful, touching, unhappy, vile, wimpy, woeful, worthless, wretched; SEE CONCEPTS *485,529*

pitiless [adj] *without mercy or care*
austere, barbarous, brutal, callous, cold*, coldblooded*, coldhearted*, cruel, cutthroat*, dog-eat-dog*, frigid, goes for jugular*, hardhearted*, harsh, hatchet-job*, heartless, implacable, indifferent, inexorable, inhuman, inhumane, insensible, killer instinct*, mean, merciless, obdurate, relentless, remorseless, ruthless, satanic, savage, soulless*, stony*, take no prisoners*, uncaring, uncompassionate, unconcerned, unfeeling, unmerciful, unrelenting, unsympathetic; SEE CONCEPT *401*

pittance [n] *small amount*
allowance, bit, chicken feed*, dole*, dribble*, driblet*, drop*, drop in the bucket*, inadequacy, insufficiency, mite, modicum, pay, peanuts*, pension, portion, ration, scrap*, slave wages*, smidgen, trace, trifle, wage; SEE CONCEPTS *344,786*

pity [n1] *feeling of mercy toward another*
benevolence, brotherly love, charity, clemency, comfort, commiseration, compassion, compunction, condolement, condolence, dejection, distress, empathy, favor, fellow feeling, forbearance, goodness, grace, humanity, identification, kindliness, kindness, lenity, melancholy, mercy, philanthropy, quarter, rue, ruth, sadness, solace, sorrow, sympathy, tenderness, understanding, unselfishness, warmth, yearning; SEE CONCEPTS *410,657*

pity [n2] *sad situation*
bad luck, catastrophe, crime, crisis, crying shame*, disaster, mischance, misfortune, mishap, regret, shame, sin; SEE CONCEPT *674*

pity [v] *feel sorry for; spare*
ache*, be sorry for, be sympathetic, bleed for*, comfort, commiserate, condole, console, feel for, feel with, forgive, give quarter*, grant amnesty, grieve with, have compassion, have mercy on, identify with, lament with, pardon, put out of one's misery*, relent, reprieve, show forgiveness*, show sympathy*, solace, soothe, sympathize, take pity on*, understand, weep for*; SEE CONCEPTS *10,34,83*

pivot [n] *center point about which something revolves*
axis, axle, center, focal point, fulcrum, heart, hinge, hub, kingpin, shaft, spindle, swivel, turning point; SEE CONCEPTS *445,464,498,830*

pivot [v] *revolve around center point*
be contingent, depend, hang, hinge, rely, rotate, sheer, spin, swivel, turn, twirl, veer, volte-face, wheel, whip, whirl; SEE CONCEPTS *147,532*

pivotal [adj] *very important*
cardinal, central, climactic, critical, crucial, decisive, determining, essential, focal, middle, momentous, overriding, overruling, principal, ruling, vital; SEE CONCEPT *568*

placate [v] *soothe, pacify*
appease, assuage, calm, cheer, comfort, conciliate, humor, make nice*, make peace*, make up*, mollify, pacify, play up to*, pour oil on*, propitiate, reconcile, satisfy, soft-pedal*, soothe, stroke*, sweeten, take the edge off*, tranquilize, win over*; SEE CONCEPTS *7,22,126*

place [n1] *location with purpose, function*
abode, accommodation, apartment, area, berth, city, community, compass, corner, country, distance, district, domicile, dwelling, field, habitat, hamlet, hangout, hole, home, house, joint, latitude, lay, locale, locality, locus, longitude, neighborhood, niche, nook, pad, part, plant, point, position, property, quarter, region, reservation, residence, room, seat, section, site, situation, spot, station, stead, suburb, town, venue, vicinity, village, volume, whereabouts, zone; SEE CONCEPTS *435,515*

place [n2] *position, rank*
capacity, character, footing, grade, pecking order*, slot, standing, state, station, status; SEE CONCEPT *388*

place [n3] *job, employment*
appointment, berth, connection, occupation, office, position, post, profession, situation, spot, trade; SEE CONCEPT *360*

place [n4] *duty, role*
affair, charge, concern, function, prerogative, responsibility, right; SEE CONCEPT *532*

place [v1] *locate, situate*
allocate, allot, assign, deposit, dispose, distribute, establish, finger, fix, install, lay, locate, lodge, nail, park, peg, plank, plant, plop, plunk, position, put, put in place, quarter, repose, rest, set, settle, situate, spot, stand, station, stick, store, stow; SEE CONCEPT *201*

place [v2] *order, sort*
allocate, appoint, approximate, arrange, assign, call, charge, class, classify, commission, constitute, delegate, deputize, designate, entrust, estimate, fix, give, grade, group, judge, name, nominate, ordain, put, rank, reckon; SEE CONCEPTS *50,84,88,98*

place [v3] *identify, recognize*
associate, determinate, determine, diagnose, distinguish, figure out*, finger*, identify, indicate, know, nail*, peg*, pinpoint, put one's finger on*, recognize, remember, set in context, spot, tell; SEE CONCEPT *38*

placid [adj] *calm, mild*
collected, composed, cool*, cool as cucumber*, detached, easy, easygoing, equable, even, even-tempered, gentle, halcyon, hushed, imperturbable, inexcitable, irenic, peaceful, poised, quiet, restful, self-possessed, serene, still, tranquil, unagitated, undisturbed, unexcitable, unflappable, unmoved, unruffled, untroubled; SEE CONCEPTS *401,485*

plagiarism [n] *copying of another's written work*
appropriation, borrowing, counterfeiting, cribbing, falsification, fraud, infringement, lifting, literary theft, piracy, stealing, theft; SEE CONCEPTS *139,192*

plague [n1] *disease that is widespread*
affliction, contagion, curse, epidemic, hydra, infection, infestation, influenza, invasion, outbreak, pandemic, pestilence, rash, ravage, scourge; SEE CONCEPT *306*

plague [n2] *annoyance, curse*
affliction, aggravation, bane, besetment, blast, blight, bother, botheration, calamity, cancer, evil, exasperation, hydra, irritant, nuisance, pain, pest, problem, scourge, thorn in side, torment, trial, vexation; SEE CONCEPTS *674,679*

plague [v] *annoy, disturb*
afflict, badger, bedevil, beleaguer, bother, chafe, fret, gall, gnaw, harass, harry, hassle, haunt, hector, hound, infest, irk, molest, pain, persecute, pester, pursue, ride, tease, torment, torture, trouble, vex, worry; SEE CONCEPTS *7,14,19*

plain [n] *level land*
champaign, expanse, field, flat, flatland, grassland, heath, level, meadow, moor, moorland, open country, plateau, prairie, steppe, tundra; SEE CONCEPT *509*

plain [adj1] *clear, obvious*
apparent, audible, big as life*, broad, calling a spade a spade*, comprehensible, definite, distinct, evident, legible, lucid, manifest, open, open-and-shut*, palpable, patent, talking turkey*, transparent, unambiguous, understandable, unequivocal, unmistakable, visible; SEE CONCEPTS *529,535,576*

plain [adj2] *straightforward in speech*
abrupt, artless, blunt, candid, direct, downright, forthright, frank, guileless, honest, impolite, ingenuous, open, outspoken, rude, sincere, straightforward, unconcealed, undisguised, undissembled, unfeigned, unvarnished; SEE CONCEPT *267*

plain [adj3] *normal, everyday*
average, common, commonplace, conventional, dull, frugal, homely, lowly, modest, ordinary, plain Jane*, quotidian, routine, simple, traditional, unaffected, unassuming, unpretentious, unremarkable, usual, vanilla*, white-bread*, workaday; SEE CONCEPT *547*

plain [adj4] *unembellished, basic*
austere, bare, bare bones*, clean, discreet, dry, inelaborate, modest, muted, pure, restrained, severe, simple, spartan, stark, stripped down, unadorned, unaesthetic, unbeautified, undecorated, unornamented, unostentatious, unpatterned, unpretentious, unvarnished, vanilla*; SEE CONCEPTS *485,589*

plain [adj5] *ugly*
deformed, hard on the eyes*, homely, inelegant, not beautiful, ordinary, plain-featured, ugly, unalluring, unattractive, uncomely, unlovely, unpretty; SEE CONCEPT *579*

plaintive [adj] *pathetic, woebegone*
beefing*, bellyaching*, cantankerous, crabby*, cranky*, deploring, disconsolate, doleful, grief-stricken, grievous, grousing, grumpy*, heart-rending, lamentatory, lamenting, lugubrious, melancholy, mournful, out of sorts*, pathetic, piteous, pitiful, rueful, sad, saddening, sorrowful, wailing, wistful, woeful; SEE CONCEPTS *401,529*

plan [n1] *scheme, design, way of doing things*
aim, angle, animus, arrangement, big picture*, contrivance, course of action, deal, device, disposition, expedient, game plan, gimmick, ground plan, idea, intendment, intent, intention, layout, machination, meaning, means, method, orderliness, outline, pattern, picture, platform, plot, policy, procedure, program, project, projection, proposal, proposition, purpose, scenario, scheme, stratagem, strategics, strategy, suggestion, system, tactics, treatment, trick, undertaking; SEE CONCEPT *660*

plan [n2] *written description; diagram*
agenda, agendum, blueprint, chart, delineation, draft, drawing, form, illustration, layout, map, projection, prospectus, representation, road map, rough draft, scale drawing, sketch, time line, view; SEE CONCEPTS *268,271,625*

plan [v1] *think out; prepare in advance*
arrange, bargain for, block out, blueprint, brainstorm*, calculate, concoct, conspire, contemplate, contrive, cook up*, craft, design, devise, draft, engineer, figure on, figure out, fix to, form, formulate, frame, hatch*, intrigue, invent, lay in provisions, line up*, make arrangements, map, mastermind, meditate, organize, outline, plot, prepare, project, quarterback*, ready, reckon on, represent, rough in*, scheme, set out, shape, sketch, steer, trace, work out; SEE CONCEPT *36*

plan [v2] *intend, mean*
aim, bargain for*, contemplate, count on, design, envisage, foresee, have every intention*, mind, propose, purpose, reckon on*; SEE CONCEPTS *26,35*

plane [n1] *flat surface; level*
condition, degree, extension, face, facet, flat, footing, grade, horizontal, level surface, obverse, position, sphere, stratum; SEE CONCEPTS *744,757*

plane [n2] *aircraft*
airbus, airplane, airship, bird*, craft, crate, jet, ship, twin-engine; SEE CONCEPT *504*

plane [adj] *level, horizontal*
even, flat, flush, plain, planate, regular, smooth, uniform; SEE CONCEPTS *490,581*

planet [n] *celestial body orbiting a star*
apple*, asteroid, earth, globe, heavenly body, luminous body, marble, planetoid, spaceship Earth*, sphere, terrene, wandering star*, world; SEE CONCEPT *511*

plant [n1] *organism belonging to the vegetable kingdom*
annual, biennial, bush, creeper*, cutting*, flower, grass, greenery, herb, perennial, seedling, shoot, shrub, slip, sprout, tree, vine, weed; SEE CONCEPT *429*

plant [n2] *factory and its buildings, equipment*
apparatus, forge, foundry, gear, machinery, manufactory, mill, shop, works, yard; SEE CONCEPTS *439,449,463,496*

plant [*v1*] *put in the ground for growing*
bury, cover, farm, grow, implant, pitch, pot, raise, scatter, seed, seed down, set out, sow, start, stock, transplant; SEE CONCEPTS *178,253*

plant [*v2*] *establish, set*
deposit, fix, found, imbed, insert, install, institute, lodge, park, plank, plank down, plop, plunk, root, settle, station; SEE CONCEPTS *18,201,221*

plaster [*n*] *thick, gooey material that hardens*
adhesive, binding, cement, coat, dressing, glue, gum, gypsum, lime, mortar, mucilage, paste, plaster of Paris, stucco; SEE CONCEPTS *466,475*

plaster [*v*] *spread, smear*
adhere, bedaub, besmear, bind, cement, coat, cover, daub, glue, gum, overlay, paste, smudge; SEE CONCEPT *202*

plastic [*adj1*] *flexible, soft; made of manufactured, treated compounds*
artificial, bending, cast, cellulose, chemical, ductile, elastic, fictile, formable, moldable, molded, pliable, pliant, pseudo, resilient, shapeable, substitute, supple, synthetic, workable; SEE CONCEPTS *582,604*

plastic [*adj2*] *easily influenced*
amenable, bending, compliant, docile, ductile, flexible, giving, impressionable, influenceable, malleable, manageable, moldable, pliable, pliant, receptive, responsive, suggestible, supple, susceptible, tractable, yielding; SEE CONCEPT *542*

plate [*n1*] *dish or meal served*
bowl, casserole, course, helping, platter, portion, service, serving, trencher; SEE CONCEPTS *459,493*

plate [*n2*] *sheet, panel*
coat, disc, flake, foil, lamella, lamina, layer, leaf, plane, print, scale, slab, slice, spangle, stratum; SEE CONCEPT *475*

plate [*v*] *coat with metallic material*
anodize, bronze, chrome, cover, electroplate, enamel, encrust, face, flake, foil, gild, laminate, layer, nickel, overlay, platinize, scale, silver, stratify; SEE CONCEPTS *172,202*

plateau [*n*] *level; flat, often high, land*
elevation, highland, mesa, plain, stage, table, tableland, upland; SEE CONCEPTS *509,744*

platform [*n1*] *stand or stage*
belvedere, dais, floor, podium, pulpit, rostrum, scaffold, scaffolding, staging, terrace; SEE CONCEPTS *440,443*

platform [*n2*] *political stance, promises*
manifesto, objectives, party line*, plank, policy, principle, program, soapbox*, stump*, tenets; SEE CONCEPTS *278,689*

platitude [*n*] *dull, overused saying*
banality, boiler plate*, bromide*, buzzword, chestnut*, cliché, commonplace, corn*, evenness, familiar tune*, flatness, hackneyed saying, high camp*, hokum*, inanity, insipidity, monotony, motto, old chestnut*, old story*, potboiler*, prosaicism, proverb, saw*, shibboleth*, stereotype, tag*, triteness, trite remark, triviality, truism, vapidity, verbiage; SEE CONCEPTS *278,388*

platonic [*adj*] *expressing nonphysical love*
ideal, idealistic, intellectual, quixotic, spiritual, transcendent, Utopian, visionary; SEE CONCEPTS *403,555*

platoon [*n*] *group of military people*
army, array, batch, battery, bunch, clump, cluster, company, detachment, lot, outfit, parcel, patrol, set, squad, squadron, team, troop, unit; SEE CONCEPTS *322,417*

plausible [*adj*] *reasonable, believable*
colorable, conceivable, credible, creditable, like as not, like enough, likely, logical, persuasive, possible, presumable, probable, smooth, sound, specious, supposable, tenable, valid, very likely; SEE CONCEPT *552*

play [*n1*] *theater piece*
comedy, curtain-raiser*, drama, entertainment, farce, flop*, hit*, mask*, musical, one-act*, opera, performance, potboiler*, show, smash*, smash hit*, stage show, theatrical, tragedy, turkey*; SEE CONCEPT *263*

play [*n2*] *amusement, entertainment*
caper, dalliance, delectation, delight, disport, diversion, foolery, frisk, frolic, fun, gambling, gambol, game, gaming, happiness, humor, jest, joking, lark, match, pastime, pleasure, prank, recreation, relaxation, romp, sport, sportiveness, teasing; SEE CONCEPTS *292,363*

play [*n3*] *latitude, range*
action, activity, elbowroom*, exercise, give, leeway, margin, motion, movement, operation, room, scope, space, sweep, swing, working*; SEE CONCEPTS *651,745*

play [*v1*] *have fun*
amuse oneself, be life of party*, caper, carouse, carry on, cavort, clown, cut capers, cut up*, dally, dance, disport, divert, entertain, entertain oneself, frisk, frolic, gambol, go on a spree*, horse around*, idle away, joke, jump, kibitz*, kick up heels*, let go*, let loose*, make merry, mess around*, rejoice, revel, romp, show off, skip, sport, toy, trifle; SEE CONCEPTS *292,384*

play [*v2*] *compete in sport*
be on a team, challenge, compete, contend, contest, disport, engage in, participate, recreate, rival, sport, take on, take part, vie; SEE CONCEPTS *92,363*

play [*v3*] *act; take the part of*
act the part of, discourse, do*, enact, execute, ham*, ham it up*, impersonate, lay an egg*, perform, personate, playact, play a gig*, portray, present, read a part, represent, take the role of, tread the boards*; SEE CONCEPT *292*

play [*v4*] *gamble, risk*
bet, chance, exploit, finesse, game, hazard, jockey*, lay money on*, maneuver, manipulate, put, set, speculate, stake, take, wager; SEE CONCEPTS *341,363*

631

play [v5] *produce music*
blow, bow, drum, execute, fiddle, fidget, finger, operate, pedal, perform, render, tickle, work; SEE CONCEPT 65

play around [v] *have love affair*
dally, flirt, fool around*, philander, take lightly, trifle*, womanize; SEE CONCEPTS 375,384

playboy/playgirl [n] *person who engages in sexual exploits*
chaser, flirt, lover boy/girl*, man/woman about town*, night owl*, operator*, philanderer, pleasure seeker, rake, scoundrel, seducer, seductress, swinger*, womanizer; SEE CONCEPTS 412,415,419,423

play down [v] *pretend as if something were unimportant*
belittle, de-emphasize, gloss over*, hold back*, make light of*, make little of*, minimize, mute, restrain, soften, soft-pedal*, underplay, underrate; SEE CONCEPTS 49,59,63

player [n1] *person participating in sport*
amateur, athlete, champ, competitor, contestant, jock*, member, opponent, participant, pro, professional, rookie, sportsman/woman, superjock*, sweat*, team player; SEE CONCEPT 366

player [n2] *person who acts in performance*
actor, actress, bit player, entertainer, extra, ham*, hambone*, impersonator, lead, mime, mimic, performer, playactor, scene stealer*, spear carrier*, stand-in, star, thespian, trouper, understudy, walk-on; SEE CONCEPT 352

player [n3] *person who produces music*
artist, cat*, instrumentalist, musician, music maker, performer, rocker, soloist, virtuoso; SEE CONCEPT 352

playful [adj] *funny, fun-loving*
antic, blithe, cheerful, coltish*, comical, elfish*, feeling one's oats*, flirtatious, frisky, frolicsome, full of pep*, gamesome, gay, good-natured, happy, hilarious, humorous, impish, jaunty, jesting, jocund, joking, joyous, kittenish*, lighthearted, lively, merry, mirthful, mischievous, peppy, pixie, prankish, puckish, roguish, rollicking, snappy, spirited, sportive, sprightly, teasing, tongue-in-cheek*, vivacious, waggish, whimsical, zippy*; SEE CONCEPTS 401,542

plaything [n] *toy*
amusement, bauble, doll, gadget, game, gimcrack, pastime, trifle, trinket; SEE CONCEPT 446

play up [v] *emphasize*
accentuate, bring to the fore*, call attention to, feature, highlight, italicize*, magnify, make a big thing of*, make a production of*, point up, stress, turn spotlight on*, underline, underscore; SEE CONCEPT 49

playwright [n] *person who writes for the theater*
author, dramatist, dramaturge, dramaturgist, librettist, scenarist, scripter, tragedian, writer; SEE CONCEPT 348

plaza [n] *central location, spot*
common, court, green, park, square, village green; SEE CONCEPTS 509,513

plea [n1] *begging request*
appeal, application, begging, entreaty, imploration, imprecation, intercession, orison, overture, petition, prayer, round robin*, solicitation, suit, supplication; SEE CONCEPT 662

plea [n2] *excuse, defense*
action, alibi, allegation, apology, argument, cause, claim, cop-out*, explanation, extenuation, fish tale*, justification, mitigation, out, palliation, pleading, pretext, rationalization, right, song and dance*, story, vindication, whitewash*; SEE CONCEPTS 57,278,318

plead [v1] *beg, request*
appeal, ask, beseech, cop a plea*, crave, crawl, entreat, entreaty, implore, importune, make up for, petition, pray, solicit, square things*, supplicate; SEE CONCEPT 48

plead [v2] *present a defense*
adduce, advocate, allege, answer charges, argue, assert, avouch, cite, cop a plea*, declare, give evidence, maintain, plea bargain, present, put forward, respond, use as excuse, vouch; SEE CONCEPTS 49,317

pleasant [adj] *acceptable; friendly*
affable, agreeable, amiable, amusing, bland, charming, cheerful, cheering, cheery, civil, civilized, congenial, convivial, cool*, copacetic, cordial, delectable, delightful, diplomatic, enchanting, engaging, enjoyable, fine, fine and dandy*, fun, genial, genteel, good-humored, gracious, gratifying, homey, jolly, jovial, kindly, likable, lovely, mild, mild-mannered, nice, obliging, pleasing, pleasurable, polite, refreshing, satisfying, social, soft, sweet, sympathetic, urbane, welcome; SEE CONCEPTS 542,548,572

pleasantry [n] *nice remark*
badinage, banter, bon mot*, humor, jest, joke, joking, levity, merriment, quip, quirk, repartee, sally*, squib*, wit, witticism; SEE CONCEPTS 273,278

please [v1] *delight, make happy*
amuse, charm, cheer, content, delectate, enchant, entertain, fill the bill*, give pleasure, gladden, go over big*, grab, gratify, hit the spot*, humor, indulge, kill*, make the grade*, overjoy, pleasure, regale, rejoice, satisfy, score, suit, sweep off feet*, tickle, tickle pink*, titillate, turn on*, wow*; SEE CONCEPTS 7,22

please [v2] *will, elect to do*
be inclined, choose, command, demand, desire, like, opt, prefer, see fit, want, wish; SEE CONCEPT 20

pleasing/pleasurable [adj] *welcome, nice*
adorable, agreeable, amiable, amusing, attractive, charming, congenial, darling, delicious, delightful, enchanting, engaging, enjoyable, entertaining, favorable, good, grateful, gratifying, likable, luscious, mellow, musical, palatable, pleasant, polite, satis-

factory, satisfying, savory, suitable, sweet, winning; SEE CONCEPTS *537,572*

pleasure [*n1*] *delight, happiness*
amusement, bliss, buzz*, comfort, contentment, delectation, diversion, ease, enjoyment, entertainment, felicity, flash*, fruition, game, gladness, gluttony, gratification, gusto, hobby, indulgence, joie de vivre, joy, joyride*, kick*, kicks*, luxury, primrose path*, recreation, relish, revelry, satisfaction, seasoning, self-indulgence, solace, spice, thrill, titillation, turn-on*, velvet*, zest; SEE CONCEPTS *388,410*

pleasure [*n2*] *will, inclination*
choice, command, desire, fancy, liking, mind, option, preference, purpose, velleity, want, wish; SEE CONCEPTS *20,659*

plebeian [*n*] *person of lower class*
commonalty, commoner, common man, common people, John/Jane Q. Public*, man/woman in the street*, peasant, pleb*, plebe*, proletarian, rank and file*; SEE CONCEPTS *413,423*

plebeian [*adj*] *base, lower-class*
banal, coarse, common, conventional, humble, ignoble, low, lowborn, lowly, mean, ordinary, pedestrian, popular, proletarian, traditional, uncultivated, unrefined, unsophisticated, unwashed, vulgar, working-class; SEE CONCEPT *549*

pledge [*n1*] *word of honor*
agreement, assurance, covenant, guarantee, health, oath, promise, toast, undertaking, vow, warrant, word; SEE CONCEPTS *71,278*

pledge [*n2*] *sign of good faith*
bail, bond, collateral, deposit, earnest, gage, guarantee, guaranty, pawn, security, surety, token, warrant, warranty; SEE CONCEPTS *318,332,446*

pledge [*v*] *guarantee; give word of honor*
contract, covenant, engage, give word*, hock*, hook*, mortgage, pawn, plight, promise, sign for, soak*, swear, undertake, vouch, vow; SEE CONCEPT *71*

plenary [*adj*] *entire, whole*
absolute, complete, full, general, inclusive, open, sweeping, thorough, unconditional, unlimited, unqualified, unrestricted; SEE CONCEPT *531*

plentiful/plenty [*adj*] *abundant, productive*
abounding, ample, appreciable, bounteous, bountiful, bumper*, chock-full*, competent, complete, copious, enough, excessive, extravagant, exuberant, fertile, flowing, flush*, fruitful, full, fulsome, generous, improvident, inexhaustible, infinite, large, lavish, liberal, lousy with*, lush, luxuriant, no end*, overflowing, plenteous, prodigal, profuse, prolific, replete, rife, sufficient, superabundant, superfluous, swarming, swimming, teeming, unlimited, well-provided; SEE CONCEPTS *762,781*

plenty [*n*] *much, abundance*
affluence, avalanche*, bunch*, capacity, copiousness, cornucopia, deluge*, enough, fertility, flood*, fruitfulness, full house*, fund, good deal*, great

deal*, heaps*, loads*, lots, luxury, mass, masses*, mine*, mountains*, oodles*, opulence, peck*, piles*, plenitude, plenteousness, plentifulness, plethora, profuseness, profusion, prosperity, quantity, stacks*, store, sufficiency, torrent*, volume, wealth; SEE CONCEPTS *767,786*

plethora [*n*] *excess*
deluge, flood, glut, many, much, overabundance, overflow, overkill, overmuch, plenty, profusion, superabundance, superfluity, surfeit, surplus; SEE CONCEPTS *767,786*

pliable [*adj*] *bendable, adaptable*
compliant, docile, ductile, easily led, easy, flexible, go with the flow*, hanging loose*, impressionable, limber, lithe, malleable, manageable, manipulable, moldable, obedient, plastic, pliant, putty*, receptive, responsive, rolling with punches*, spongy, submissive, supple, susceptible, tractable, yielding; SEE CONCEPTS *404,488*

plight [*n*] *dilemma, difficulty; situation*
bad news*, circumstances, condition, corner*, double trouble*, extremity, fix*, hole*, impasse, jam, perplexity, pickle*, pinch*, predicament, quandary, scrape*, spot*, state*, straits, tight situation, trouble; SEE CONCEPTS *666,674*

plod [*v1*] *walk heavily*
clump*, drag, flounder, hike, lumber*, plug, schlepp*, slog*, stamp, stomp, toil, tramp, trample, tread, tromp, trudge, wallow; SEE CONCEPT *151*

plod [*v2*] *work slowly and under duress*
bear down*, buckle down*, drudge, grind, knuckle down*, labor, persevere, plough through*, plug away*, scratch*, slave, sweat*, toil; SEE CONCEPTS *87,677*

plot [*n1*] *plan, scheme*
artifice, booby trap*, cabal, collusion, complicity, connivance, conniving, conspiracy, contrivance, covin, design, device, fix, frame, frame-up*, game, intrigue, little game*, machination, maneuver, practice, ruse, scam, setup, stratagem, trick; SEE CONCEPT *660*

plot [*n2*] *story line*
action, design, development, enactment, events, incidents, movement, narrative, outline, picture, progress, scenario, scene, scheme, story, structure, subject, suspense, theme, thread, unfolding; SEE CONCEPTS *264,282*

plot [*n3*] *tract of land*
acreage, allotment, area, division, ground, land, lot, parcel, patch, piece, plat, spread; SEE CONCEPTS *509,513*

plot [*v1*] *plan, scheme*
angle, brew*, cabal, cogitate, collude, conceive, concoct, connive, conspire, contrive, cook up*, design, devise, draft, finagle, frame, hatch*, imagine, intrigue, lay*, machinate, maneuver, operate, outline, project, promote, rough out*, set up, sketch, wangle; SEE CONCEPT *36*

plot [*v2*] *map out; draw*
calculate, chart, compute, draft, lay out, locate, mark, outline, put forward; SEE CONCEPTS *36,79,174*

plow [*v*] *dig up ground for cultivation*
break, break ground, bulldoze, cultivate, farm, furrow, harrow, harvest, list, push, rake, reap, ridge, rush, shove, smash, till, trench, turn, turn over; SEE CONCEPT *178*

ploy [*n*] *game, trick*
artifice, contrivance, device, dodge, feint, gambit, maneuver, move, play, ruse, scheme, stratagem, subterfuge, tactic, trick, wile; SEE CONCEPT *59*

pluck [*n*] *person's resolution, courage*
backbone*, boldness, bravery, dauntlessness, determination, grit, guts*, hardihood, heart*, intestinal fortitude*, intrepidity, mettle, moxie*, nerve, resolution, spirit, spunk; SEE CONCEPT *411*

pluck [*v*] *grab, pull out; pick at*
catch, clutch, collect, cull, draw, finger, gather, harvest, jerk, pick, plunk, pull at, snatch, strum, tug, tweak, yank; SEE CONCEPT *206*

plug [*n1*] *stopper*
bung, connection, cork, filling, fitting, occlusion, river, spigot, stopple, tampon, wedge; SEE CONCEPTS *471,836*

plug [*n2*] *publicity*
advertisement, blurb*, good word*, hype*, mention, push*, write-up; SEE CONCEPT *274*

plug [*v1*] *stop up*
block, bung, choke, clog, close, congest, cork, cover, drive in, fill, obstruct, occlude, pack, ram, seal, secure, stop, stopper, stopple, stuff; SEE CONCEPT *209*

plug [*v2*] *publicize*
advertise, boost*, build up*, hype*, mention, promote, push*, write up; SEE CONCEPTS *49,60*

plum [*n*] *reward, prize*
asset, bonus, carrot*, catch*, cream*, dividend, find, meed, nugget*, pick, premium, treasure; SEE CONCEPTS *337,712*

plumb [*adj*] *vertical*
erect, perpendicular, sheer, straight, straight up, up and down, upright; SEE CONCEPT *581*

plumb [*v*] *probe, go into*
delve, explore, fathom, gauge, get to the bottom of*, measure, penetrate, search, sound, take soundings, unravel; SEE CONCEPTS *181,216,291*

plummet [*v*] *fall hard and fast*
collapse, crash, decline, decrease, descend, dip, dive, downturn, drop, drop down, dump, fall, nose-dive, plunge, precipitate, sink, skid, stoop, swoop, tumble; SEE CONCEPTS *181,698,763*

plump [*adj*] *chubby, fat*
beefy*, burly, buxom, chunky*, corpulent, filled, fleshy, full, obese, portly, pudgy*, rotund, round, stout, tubby*; SEE CONCEPT *491*

plunder [*n*] *something stolen*
booty, goods*, graft, hot goods*, loot, make*, pickings*, pillage, plunderage, prey, prize, quarry, rapine, raven, spoil, stuff*, take*, trappings*, winnings*; SEE CONCEPT *710*

plunder [*v*] *ravage, steal*
appropriate, burn, depredate, despoil, devastate, fleece, forage, foray, grab, gut, kip, knock off*, knock over*, lay waste, liberate, lift, loft, loot, maraud, moonlight requisition*, pillage, prey, prowl, raid, ransack, relieve, requisition, rifle, rip off*, rob, sack, salvage, smash and grab*, snatch, spoil, stick up*, strip; SEE CONCEPTS *86,139,252*

plunge [*n*] *quick drop; enthusiastic attempt*
belly flop*, descent, dive, duck, dunk, fall, high dive, immersion, investment, jump, nose-dive, spree, submergence, submersion, swoop, venture; SEE CONCEPTS *100,150,152,181,194*

plunge [*v*] *dive or fall fast*
belly-flop*, career, cast, charge, dash, descend, dip, drive, drop, duck, fling, go down, go the limit, go whole hog*, hurtle, immerge, immerse, jump, keel, lunge, lurch, nose-dive, pitch, plummet, plunk, propel, rush, shoot the works*, sink, sound, submerge, submerse, swoop, take a flyer*, take a header*, tear, throw, throw oneself, thrust, topple, tumble; SEE CONCEPTS *100,150,152,181,194*

plurality [*n*] *large part of a group*
advantage, bulk, greater part, lead, majority, mass, most, multiplicity, nearly all, numerousness, preponderance, profusion, variety; SEE CONCEPTS *382,829*

plus [*n*] *asset; something added*
advantage, benefit, bonus, extra, gain, good point, overage, overstock, oversupply, perk, surplus; SEE CONCEPT *693*

plus [*adj*] *added, extra*
additional, augmented, boosted, enlarged, expanded, increased, positive, supplementary, surplus; SEE CONCEPTS *762,771*

plush [*adj*] *luxurious, rich*
costly, deluxe, elegant, lavish, luscious, lush, luxury, opulent, palatial, ritzy, silken, sumptuous; SEE CONCEPTS *334,589*

ply [*v*] *use, work at*
carry on, dispense, employ, exercise, exert, follow, function, handle, maneuver, manipulate, practice, pursue, put out, swing, throw, utilize, wield; SEE CONCEPTS *100,225*

poach [*v*] *infringe upon; trespass*
appropriate, encroach, filch, fish illegally, hunt illegally, intrude, pilfer, plunder, rob, smuggle, steal; SEE CONCEPTS *139,192*

pocket [*n*] *cavity, pouch*
bag, chamber, compartment, hole, hollow, opening, receptacle, sack, socket; SEE CONCEPTS *452,513*

pocket [*adj*] *small, portable*
abridged, canned, capsule, compact, concise, condensed, diminutive, dwarfish, epitomized, itsy-bitsy*, little, midget, miniature, minute, peewee*, pint-sized*, potted, tiny, wee; SEE CONCEPT *773*

pocket [v] *help oneself to something*
abstract, appropriate, conceal, enclose, filch, hide, lift, nab, pilfer, pinch, purloin, shoplift, steal, swipe, take; SEE CONCEPTS *139,142*

pocketbook [n] *accessory for carrying personal items*
bag, clutch, frame, handbag, hide, leather, pouch, purse, reticule, suitcase, wallet; SEE CONCEPTS *446,450*

pod [n/v] *encasement of vegetable seeds*
capsule, case, covering, hull, husk, sheath, sheathing, shell, shuck, skin, vessel; SEE CONCEPTS *428,484*

podium [n] *structure from which speakers orate*
dais, platform, pulpit, rostrum, soapbox*, stage, stump*; SEE CONCEPT *443*

poem [n] *highly expressive, rhythmical literary piece*
ballad, beat, blank verse, composition, creation, epic, free verse, haiku, limerick, lines, lyric, ode, poesy, poetry, quatrain, rhyme, rime, rune, sestina, song, sonnet, verse, villanelle, words, writing; SEE CONCEPTS *268,282*

poet [n] *person who writes expressive, rhythmic verse*
artist, author, balladist, bard, dilettante, dramatist, librettist, lyricist, lyrist, maker, metrist, odist, parodist, poetaster, rhapsodist, rhymer, rimer, sonnetist, versifier, writer; SEE CONCEPTS *348,423*

poetic [adj] *with rhythm and beauty; related to poetic composition*
anapestic, dactylic, dramatic, elegiac, epic, epical, epodic, iambic, idyllic, imaginative, lyric, lyrical, melodious, metrical, odic, rhythmical, romantic, songlike, tuneful; SEE CONCEPT *267*

poetry [n] *expressive, rhythmic literary work*
balladry, doggerel, metrical composition, paean, poems, poesy, rhyme, rhyming, rime, rune, song, stanza, verse, versification; SEE CONCEPTS *268,282,349*

poignant [adj1] *affecting, painful*
agitating, agonizing, bitter, distressing, disturbing, emotional, heartbreaking, heart-rending, impressive, intense, moving, passionate, pathetic, perturbing, piteous, pitiful, sad, sentimental, sorrowful, touching, upsetting; SEE CONCEPTS *529,548*

poignant [adj2] *sharp, bitter*
acrid, acute, biting, caustic, keen, penetrating, peppery, piercing, piquant, pointed, pungent, racy, sarcastic, severe, sharp, snappy, spicy, stinging, tangy, zesty; SEE CONCEPTS *267,613*

point [n1] *speck*
bit, count, dot, fleck, flyspeck, full stop, iota, mark, minim, mite, mote, notch, particle, period, scrap, stop, tittle, trace; SEE CONCEPTS *79,831*

point [n2] *specific location*
locality, locus, place, position, site, situation, spot, stage, station, where; SEE CONCEPT *198*

point [n3] *sharp end, top, end of extension*
apex, awn, barb, beak, bill, cape, claw, cusp, dagger, end, foreland, head, headland, jag, nib, pin point, prick, prickler, promontory, prong, snag,

spike, spine, spire, spur, sticker, stiletto, summit, sword, thorn, tine, tip, tooth; SEE CONCEPTS *827,836*

point [n4] *circumstance, stage; limited time*
brink, condition, date, degree, duration, edge, extent, instant, juncture, limit, moment, period, point in time, position, threshold, time, verge, very minute; SEE CONCEPTS *696,815*

point [n5] *goal, aim*
appeal, attraction, bottom line*, charm, cogency, design, effectiveness, end, fascination, intent, intention, interest, motive, name of the game*, nitty-gritty*, nub, nuts and bolts*, object, objective, punch*, purpose, reason, significance, use, usefulness, utility, validity, validness; SEE CONCEPT *659*

point [n6] *meaning, essence*
argument, bottom line*, burden, core, crux, drift, force, gist, head, heart, idea, import, kicker*, main idea, marrow, matter, meat*, motif, motive, name of the game*, nitty-gritty*, nub, nuts and bolts*, pith, pointer, proposition, punch line*, question, score, stuff, subject, subject matter, text, theme, thrust, tip, tip-off*, topic; SEE CONCEPTS *274,682*

point [n7] *aspect, characteristic*
attribute, case, circumstance, circumstantial, constituent, detail, element, facet, feature, instance, item, material, nicety, part, particular, peculiarity, property, quality, respect, side, thing, trait; SEE CONCEPTS *274,411,654*

point [n8] *scoring unit of sport competition*
count, mark, notch, score, tally; SEE CONCEPTS *364,784*

point [v1] *show as probable; call attention*
bespeak, button down*, denote, designate, direct, finger*, hint, imply, indicate, lead, make*, name, offer, peg*, pin down*, put down for*, put finger on*, signify, suggest, tab*, tag*; SEE CONCEPTS *118,138*

point [v2] *direct, lead*
aim, beam*, bring to bear, cast, face, guide, head, influence, lay, level, look, slant, steer, tend, train, turn, zero in*; SEE CONCEPTS *187,201,623*

pointed [adj1] *having a sharp end or part*
acicular, aciculate, acuminate, acuminous, acute, barbed, cornered, cuspidate, edged, fine, keen, mucronate, peaked, piked, pointy, pronged, sharp, sharp-cornered, spiked; SEE CONCEPTS *490,606*

pointed [adj2] *penetrating, biting*
accurate, acid, acute, barbed, boiled down, calling a spade a spade*, cutting, in a nutshell*, incisive, insinuating, keen, laid on the line*, legit, meaty*, on the button*, on the nose*, pertinent, pregnant, right-on*, right to it*, sarcastic, sharp, short-and-sweet*, tart, telling, trenchant; SEE CONCEPT *267*

pointer [n1] *indicator*
arrow, dial, director, gauge, guide, hand, index, mark, needle, register, rod, signal; SEE CONCEPTS *464,498*

pointer [n2] *hint, suggestion*
advice, caution, clue, information, recommendation, steer, tip, tip-off, warning; SEE CONCEPTS *75,274*

pointless [*adj*] *ridiculous, senseless*
absurd, aimless, around in circles*, fruitless, futile, going nowhere*, impotent, inane, inconsequential, ineffective, ineffectual, insignificant, in vicious circle*, irrelevant, meaningless, needle in haystack*, nongermane, nonsensical, not pertinent, on treadmill*, powerless, purportless, remote, silly, stupid, trivial, unavailing, uninteresting, unnecessary, unproductive, unprofitable, useless, vague, vain, worthless; SEE CONCEPTS *529,548*

point out [*v*] *call attention to*
advert, allude, bring up, denote, designate, identify, indicate, mention, refer, remind, reveal, show, specify; SEE CONCEPTS *49,73,261*

poise [*n*] *self composure, dignity*
address, aplomb, assurance, balance, bearing, calmness, confidence, cool, coolness, delicatesse, diplomacy, elegance, equability, equanimity, equilibrium, grace, gravity, polish, presence, presence of mind, sangfroid, savoir-faire, self-assurance, self-possession, serenity, stasis, tact, tactfulness, tranquility; SEE CONCEPTS *633,717*

poise [*v*] *balance, suspend*
ballast, be ready, brood, float, hang, hold, hover, position, stabilize, stand, steady, support, wait; SEE CONCEPT *154*

poison [*n*] *substance that causes harm, death*
adulteration, bacteria, bane, blight, cancer, contagion, contamination, corruption, germ, infection, malignancy, miasma, toxicant, toxin, toxoid, venin, venom, virus; SEE CONCEPTS *307,475,674,675*

poison/poisonous [*adj*] *very harmful*
bad, baleful, baneful, corrupt, corruptive, dangerous, deadly, deleterious, destructive, detrimental, evil, fatal, hurtful, infective, lethal, malicious, malignant, mephitic, miasmatic, morbid, mortal, nocuous, noisome, noxious, peccant, pernicious, pestiferous, pestilential, septic, toxic, toxicant, toxiferous, venomous, vicious, viperous, virulent; SEE CONCEPT *537*

poison [*v*] *contaminate, pollute*
adulterate, corrupt, debase, defile, deprave, destroy, envenom, fester, harm, infect, injure, kill, make ill, murder, pervert, stain, subvert, taint, undermine, vitiate, warp; SEE CONCEPTS *14,246,252*

poke [*n*] *push, thrust*
blow, boost, bunt, butt, dig, hit, jab, nudge, prod, punch, shove, stab; SEE CONCEPTS *189,208*

poke [*v1*] *push at; thrust*
arouse, awaken, bulge, butt*, crowd, dig, elbow*, goose*, hit, jab, jostle, jut, nudge*, overhang, prod, project, protrude, provoke, punch, ram, rouse, shoulder*, shove, stab, stand out, stick, stick out, stimulate, stir; SEE CONCEPTS *189,208,723*

poke [*v2*] *interfere, snoop*
busybody*, butt in*, intrude, meddle, nose*, peek, pry, tamper; SEE CONCEPT *384*

poke [*v3*] *move along slowly*
dally, dawdle, delay, drag, get no place fast*, idle, lag, loiter, mosey*, procrastinate, put off*, schlepp along*, tarry, toddle*, trail; SEE CONCEPT *151*

polar [*adj1*] *very cold*
arctic, extreme, farthest, freezing, frigid, frozen, glacial, icy, north, south, terminal; SEE CONCEPTS *583,605*

polar [*adj2*] *opposite, opposed*
antagonistic, antipodal, antipodean, antithetical, contradictory, contrary, converse, counter, diametric, reverse; SEE CONCEPT *564*

pole [*n*] *bar, post*
beam, extremity, flagpole, flagstaff, leg, mast, pile, plank, rod, shaft, spar, staff, stake, standard, stave, stick, stilt, stud, terminus; SEE CONCEPTS *440, 470,475,479*

police/police officer [*n*] *person, people hired to uphold the laws*
arm of the law*, badge*, bear*, beat cop, black and white*, blue*, bluecoat*, bobby, constable, constabulary, cop*, copper*, corps*, detective, fed*, flatfoot*, force, gendarme, heat*, law, law enforcement, narc*, patrolman/woman; SEE CONCEPTS *299,354*

policy [*n*] *procedure, tactics*
action, administration, approach, arrangement, behavior, channels, code, course, custom, design, guideline, line, management, method, order, organization, plan, polity, practice, program, protocol, red tape*, rule, scheme, stratagem, strategy, tenet, the book*, the numbers*, theory; SEE CONCEPTS *6,271,660,687*

polish [*n1*] *shine, brightness*
brilliance, burnish, finish, glaze, glint, gloss, luster, sheen, smoothness, sparkle, varnish, veneer, wax; SEE CONCEPTS *492,611,620*

polish [*n2*] *cultivated look, performance*
breeding, class, cultivation, culture, elegance, finesse, finish, grace, politesse, refinement, style, suavity, urbanity; SEE CONCEPTS *388,633,655*

polish [*v1*] *shine, buff*
brighten, burnish, clean, finish, furbish, glaze, gloss, rub, scour, scrub, sleek, slick, smooth, wax; SEE CONCEPTS *202,215*

polish [*v2*] *improve performance, look*
amend, better, brush up, correct, cultivate, emend, enhance, finish, furbish, make improvement, mature, mend, perfect, refine, round, sleek, slick, smooth, touch up; SEE CONCEPT *244*

polish off [*v*] *finish using*
consume, devour, dispatch, dispose of, do away with*, down*, eat, eat up, eliminate, get rid of*, liquidate, put away*, swill*, use up, wolf*; SEE CONCEPTS *169,225*

polite [*adj*] *mannerly, civilized*
affable, amenable, amiable, attentive, bland, civil, complaisant, concerned, conciliatory, condescend-

ing, considerate, cordial, courteous, courtly, cultured, deferential, diplomatic, elegant, friendly, genteel, gentle, gentlemanly, good-natured, gracious, mild, neighborly, nice, obliging, obsequious, pleasant, polished, politic, punctilious, refined, respectful, smooth, sociable, solicitous, sympathetic, thoughtful, urbane, well-behaved, well-bred, well-mannered; SEE CONCEPT *401*

politic [*adj*] *wise, tactful*
adroit, advisable, canny*, cool, delicate, diplomatic, discreet, expedient, in one's best interests*, judicious, on the lookout*, perspicacious, prudent, sagacious, sensible, sharp, shrewd, smooth, tactical, tuned in*, urbane; SEE CONCEPT *401*

politician [*n*] *person pursuing or occupying elective office*
baby-kisser*, boss, chieftain, congressman/woman, congressperson, democrat, grandstander*, handshaker*, lawmaker, leader, legislator, member of parliament, officeholder, office seeker, orator, partisan, party member, politico*, president, public servant, republican, senator, speaker, statesman/woman, statesperson, whistle-stopper*; SEE CONCEPT *359*

politics [*n*] *art and science of administration of government*
affairs of state, backroom*, campaigning, civics, domestic affairs, electioneering, foreign affairs, government, government policy, hat in the ring*, internal affairs, jungle*, legislature, matters of state, political science, polity, smoke-filled room*, statecraft, statesmanship, zoo*; SEE CONCEPTS *300,301*

poll [*n*] *census; tally of answers to questions of opinion*
ballot, canvas, count, figures, opinion, returns, sampling, survey, vote, voting; SEE CONCEPTS *48,300*

poll [*v*] *take census; question*
ballot, canvas, enroll, examine, interview, list, register, sample, send up a balloon*, survey, tally, test the waters*, vote; SEE CONCEPTS *48,300*

pollute [*v*] *make dirty; corrupt*
adulterate, alloy, befoul, besmirch, contaminate, corrupt, debase, debauch, defile, deprave, desecrate, dirty, dishonor, foul, infect, make filthy, mar, poison, profane, soil, spoil, stain, sully, taint, violate; SEE CONCEPTS *246,254*

pollution [*n*] *dirtiness, contamination*
abuse, adulteration, besmearing, besmirching, blight, corruption, decomposition, defilement, desecration, deterioration, dirtying, fouling, foulness, impairment, impurity, infection, misuse, polluting, profanation, rottenness, soiling, spoliation, taint, tainting, uncleanness, vitiation; SEE CONCEPT *720*

pomp [*n*] *pageantry, display*
affectation, array, ceremonial, ceremony, fanfare, flourish, formality, grandeur, grandiosity, magnificence, ostentation, pageant, panoply, parade, pomposity, ritual, shine, show, solemnity, splendor, state, vainglory; SEE CONCEPTS *335,377,655*

pompous [*adj*] *arrogant, egotistic*
affected, bloated, boastful, bombastic, conceited, flatulent, flaunting, flowery, fustian, grandiloquent, grandiose, high and mighty*, highfaluting*, high-flown*, imperious, important, inflated, magisterial, magniloquent, narcissistic, orotund, ostentatious, overbearing, overblown, pontifical, portentous, presumptuous, pretentious, puffed up*, puffy*, rhetorical, self-centered, self-important, selfish, showy, sonorous, stuck-up*, supercilious, turgid, uppity*, vain, vainglorious, windy*; SEE CONCEPTS *267, 401,542*

pond [*n*] *small body of water*
basin, dew, duck pond, lagoon, lily pond, millpond, pool, puddle, small lake, splash; SEE CONCEPT *514*

ponder [*v*] *think about seriously*
appraise, brood, build castles in air*, cerebrate, cogitate, consider, contemplate, daydream, debate, deliberate, dwell, evaluate, examine, excogitate, figure, give thought to, meditate, mind, moon*, mull, mull over, muse, noodle around*, perpend, pipe dream*, put on thinking cap*, puzzle over, reason, reflect, revolve, roll, ruminate, speculate, study, think out, think over, turn over, weigh, woolgather*; SEE CONCEPTS *17,24*

ponderous [*adj1*] *heavy, cumbersome*
awkward, bulky, burdensome, clumsy, cumbrous, dull, elephantine, graceless, hefty, huge, laborious, lifeless, lumbering, massive, onerous, oppressive, substantial, troublesome, unhandy, unwieldy, weighty; SEE CONCEPTS *491,565*

ponderous [*adj2*] *dreary, tedious*
arid, barren, cardboard*, dry, dull, heavy, humdrum*, labored, lifeless, long-winded*, monotonous, pedantic, pedestrian, plodding, prolix, stiff*, stilted, stodgy, stuffy*, vapid, verbose, wooden*; SEE CONCEPTS *267,529,542*

pool [*n1*] *collection of liquid*
basin, bath, lagoon, lake, mere, millpond, mud puddle, natatorium, pond, puddle, splash, swimming pool, tank, tarn; SEE CONCEPTS *364,514*

pool [*n2*] *supply of money, goods*
bank, combine, conglomerate, equipment, funds, group, jackpot, kitty*, pot, provisions, stakes; SEE CONCEPTS *340,432*

pool [*v*] *combine*
amalgamate, blend, join forces, league, merge, put together, share; SEE CONCEPTS *113,193*

poor [*adj1*] *lacking sufficient money*
bad off*, bankrupt, beggared, beggarly, behind eight ball*, broke*, destitute, dirt poor*, down-and-out*, empty-handed*, flat*, flat broke*, fortuneless, hard up*, impecunious, impoverished, indigent, in need, insolvent, in want, low, meager, moneyless, necessitous, needy, pauperized, penniless, penurious, pinched*, poverty-stricken, reduced*, scanty*, stone broke*, strapped*, suffering, truly needy, underprivileged, unprosperous; SEE CONCEPT *334*

poor [adj2] *deficient, inadequate*
base, below par, common, contemptible, crude, diminutive, dwarfed, exiguous, faulty, feeble, humble, imperfect, incomplete, inferior, insignificant, insufficient, lacking, low-grade, lowly, meager, mean, mediocre, miserable, modest, niggardly*, ordinary, paltry, pitiable, pitiful, plain, reduced, rotten, scanty, second-rate*, shabby, shoddy, skimpy, slight, sorry*, sparse, subnormal, subpar, substandard, trifling, trivial, unsatisfactory, valueless, weak, worthless; SEE CONCEPTS *570,574*

poor [adj3] *weak, unfertile*
bare, barren, depleted, exhausted, feeble, fruitless, impaired, imperfect, impoverished, indisposed, infertile, infirm, puny, sick, sterile, unfruitful, unproductive, worthless; SEE CONCEPT *314*

poor [adj4] *unfortunate, unhappy*
commiserable, hapless, ill-fated, luckless, miserable, pathetic, piteous, pitiable, pitiful, rueful, unlucky, wretched; SEE CONCEPTS *542,548*

poorly [adj] *not well*
ailing, below par, failing, ill, indisposed, low, mean, out of sorts*, rotten*, sick, sickly, under the weather*, unwell; SEE CONCEPT *314*

poorly [adv] *unsatisfactorily*
badly, crudely, defectively, inadequately, incompetently, inexpertly, inferiorly, insufficiently, meanly, shabbily, unsuccessfully; SEE CONCEPTS *544,571,574*

pop [n] *bang*
burst, crack, explosion, jump, leap, report, snap, strike, thrust, whack; SEE CONCEPT *595*

pop [v] *jump, burst*
appear, bang, blow, crack, dart, explode, go, go off, hit, insert, jump, leap, protrude, push, put, report, rise, shove, snap, sock, stick, strike, thrust, whack; SEE CONCEPT *145*

popular [adj1] *well-known, favorite*
accepted, approved, attractive, beloved, caught on*, celebrated, crowd-pleasing*, faddish*, famous, fashionable, favored, in*, in demand, in favor, in the mainstream*, in vogue, leading, likable, liked, lovable, noted, notorious, now*, okay*, pleasing, praised, preferred, prevailing, prominent, promoted, right stuff*, run-after*, selling, social, societal, sought, sought-after, stylish, suitable, the rage*, thing*, trendy, well-liked, well-received; SEE CONCEPTS *555,589*

popular [adj2] *common, standard*
accepted, accessible, adopted, approved, conventional, current, demanded, embraced, familiar, general, in demand, in use, ordinary, prevailing, prevalent, proletarian, public, rampant, regnant, rife, ruling, stock, ubiquitous, universal, widespread; SEE CONCEPT *530*

popularity [n] *recognition, celebrity*
acceptance, acclaim, adoration, approval, currency, demand, esteem, fame, fashion, fashionableness, favor, following, heyday, idolization, lionization, prevalence, regard, renown, reputation, repute, universality, vogue; SEE CONCEPTS *388,655*

popularize [v] *make widely popular, accessible*
catch on, disseminate, familiarize, generalize, give currency, make available, promote, restore, resurrect, revive, simplify, spread, universalize; SEE CONCEPTS *324,384*

population [n] *inhabitants of a place*
citizenry, community, culture, denizens, dwellers, folk, natives, people, populace, public, residents, society, state; SEE CONCEPT *379*

populous [adj] *packed with inhabitants*
crawling, crowded, dense, heavily populated, jammed, legion, many, multifarious, multitudinal, multitudinous, numerous, occupied, overpopulated, peopled, populated, settled, several, swarming, teeming, thick, thronged, various, voluminous; SEE CONCEPT *583*

pore [n] *small aperture in skin*
foramen, opening, orifice, outlet, stoma, sweat gland, vesicle; SEE CONCEPT *418*

pore [v] *go over carefully*
brood, contemplate, dwell on, examine, look over, muse, peruse, ponder, read, regard, scan, scrutinize, study; SEE CONCEPTS *24,72,103*

pornographic [adj] *obscene*
adult, immoral, indecent, lewd, off-color, offensive, porn*, porno*, prurient, purple*, raunchy*, rough, salacious, sexy, smutty*, steamy*, X-rated*; SEE CONCEPTS *267,372,545*

porous [adj] *having holes; absorbent*
absorptive, penetrable, permeable, pervious, spongelike, spongy; SEE CONCEPT *606*

port [n] *place for boat docking, traffic, and storage*
anchorage, boatyard, dockage, docks, dockyard, gate, harbor, harborage, haven, landing, piers, refuge, retreat, roads, roadstead, sanctuary, seaport, shelter, wharf; SEE CONCEPTS *449,509*

portable [adj] *easily transported*
carriageable, cartable, compact, convenient, conveyable, easily carried, handy, haulable, light, lightweight, manageable, movable, portative, transportable, wieldy; SEE CONCEPTS *491,584,773*

portal [n] *hole or door in vessel*
doorway, entrance, entry, entryway, gate, gateway, ingress, opening, way in; SEE CONCEPT *502*

portend [v] *foreshadow, indicate*
adumbrate, augur, be in the cards*, bespeak, betoken, bode, call*, crystal-ball*, forebode, forecast, foreshow, foretell, foretoken, forewarn, harbinger, have a hunch, herald, hint, omen, point to, predict, premonish, presage, prognosticate, promise, prophesy, read, see coming*, threaten, warn of; SEE CONCEPTS *71,78,261*

portent [n1] *indication, forewarning*
augury, bodement, boding, caution, clue, foreboding, foreshadowing, foretoken, funny feeling*, handwriting on the wall*, harbinger, hunch, omen, premonition, presage, presentiment, prognostic, prognostication, sign, sinking feeling*, threat, vibes*, warning; SEE CONCEPT *278*

portent [*n2*] *miracle*
marvel, phenomenon, prodigy, sensation, stunner, wonder; SEE CONCEPTS *230,529*

porter [*n*] *person who serves as attendant, caretaker*
baggage carrier, bearer, bellhop, carrier, concierge, doorkeeper, doorman/woman, doorperson, gate-keeper, janitor, red cap*, sky cap*, transporter; SEE CONCEPT *348*

portfolio [*n*] *flat case for transporting papers*
attaché case, bag, brief bag, briefcase, case, container, envelope, folder, notebook, valise; SEE CONCEPT *494*

portion [*n1*] *share, cut, ration*
allocation, allotment, allowance, apportionment, bang, bit, chunk, division, divvy*, drag*, dram, excerpt, extract, fix, fraction, fragment, gob, helping, hit, hunk, lagniappe, lion's share*, lot, lump, measure, meed, member, moiety, morsel, parcel, part, piece, piece of action*, plum, quantity, quantum, quota, scrap, section, segment, serving, share, shot*, slug*, smithereen*, taste; SEE CONCEPT *835*

portion [*n2*] *fate, destiny*
circumstance, cup*, doom, fortune, kismet*, lot*, luck; SEE CONCEPT *679*

portion [*v*] *divide into pieces*
administer, allocate, allot, apportion, assign, deal, dispense, distribute, divvy up*, dole out*, mete out*, parcel, part, partition, piece, prorate, quota, ration, section, share, shift; SEE CONCEPTS *98,140*

portly [*adv*] *bulky, fat*
ample, avoirdupois, beefy*, broad, burly, corpulent, fleshy, heavy, hefty, husky, large, obese, overweight, plump, rotund, stout; SEE CONCEPT *491*

portrait [*n*] *drawn representation; description*
account, characterization, depiction, figure, image, likeness, model, painting, photograph, picture, portraiture, portrayal, profile, silhouette, simulacrum, sketch, snapshot, spitting image*, vignette; SEE CONCEPTS *259,268,625*

portray [*v*] *represent, imitate*
act like, characterize, copy, delineate, depict, describe, draw, duplicate, figure, illustrate, image, impersonate, interpret, limn, mimic, paint, parody, photograph, picture, render, reproduce, simulate, sketch; SEE CONCEPTS *55,174,265*

pose [*n*] *artificial position*
act, affectation, air, attitude, attitudinizing, bearing, carriage, facade, fake, false show, front, guise, mannerism, masquerade, mien, positure, posture, posturing, pretense, pretension, role, stance, stand; SEE CONCEPTS *633,716*

pose [*v1*] *sit, stand in place*
arrange, model, peacock, poise, position, posture, sit for, strike a pose, strut; SEE CONCEPTS *154,174*

pose [*v2*] *pretend, fake*
act, affect, attitudinize, feign, grandstand*, impersonate, make believe, make out like*, masquerade, pass off*, peacock*, playact, posture, profess, purport, put on airs*, put up a front*, sham*, show off*, strike an attitude*, take off as*; SEE CONCEPTS *59,63,633*

pose [*v3*] *offer, put forward idea*
advance, ask, extend, give, hold out, posit, prefer, present, proffer, propose, proposition, propound, put, query, question, set, state, submit, suggest, tender; SEE CONCEPTS *66,67,75*

posh [*adj*] *luxurious, upper-class*
chic, classy, deluxe, elegant, exclusive, fashionable, grand, high-class, la-di-da*, luxury, modish*, opulent, rich, ritzy*, smart, swank, swanky*, swish*, trendy; SEE CONCEPTS *334,589*

position [*n1*] *physical place*
area, bearings, district, environment, fix, geography, ground, locale, locality, location, locus, point, post, reference, region, scene, seat, setting, site, situation, space, spot, stand, station, surroundings, topography, tract, whereabouts*; SEE CONCEPT *198*

position [*n2*] *posture, stance*
arrangement, attitude, ballgame*, bearing, carriage, circumstances, condition, deportment, disposition, form, habit, how things stack up*, like it is*, manner, mien, pass, plight, port, pose, predicament, situation, spot, stand, state, status, strait, the size of it*; SEE CONCEPT *696*

position [*n3*] *belief, point of view*
angle, attitude, color, judgment, opinion, outlook, slant, stance, stand, standpoint, view, viewpoint; SEE CONCEPT *689*

position [*n4*] *class, stature*
cachet, capacity, caste, character, consequence, dignity, footing, importance, place, prestige, rank, reputation, situation, sphere, standing, station, status; SEE CONCEPTS *378,388*

position [*n5*] *responsibility in business or other enterprise*
berth, billet, capacity, connection, do*, duty, employment, function, job, nine-to-five*, occupation, office, place, post, profession, role, situation, slot*, spot*, trade; SEE CONCEPTS *324,349,360*

position [*v*] *place physically in location*
arrange, array, dispose, fix, lay out, locate, put, set, settle, stand, stick; SEE CONCEPTS *158,201*

positive [*adj1*] *definite, certain*
absolute, actual, affirmative, assured, categorical, clear, clear-cut, cocksure*, cold*, complete, conclusive, concrete, confident, consummate, convinced, decided, decisive, direct, downright, explicit, express, factual, firm, forceful, forcible, genuine, hard, inarguable, incontestable, incontrovertible, indisputable, indubitable, irrefutable, out-and-out*, outright, perfect, rank, real, specific, sure, thorough, thoroughgoing, unambiguous, undeniable, unequivocal, unmistakable, unmitigated; SEE CONCEPTS *535,582*

positive [*adj2*] *beneficial, helpful*
affirmative, constructive, effective, efficacious, forward-looking, good, practical, productive, progressive, reasonable, sound, useful; SEE CONCEPT *572*

positively [*adv*] *absolutely, definitely*
amen*, assuredly, categorically, certainly, doubtless, doubtlessly, easily, emphatically, firmly, flat*, flat out*, for a fact*, indubitably, no catch*, no holds barred*, no ifs ands or buts*, no kicker*, no strings attached*, on the money*, on the nose*, really truly*, right on*, sure, surely, the ticket*, to a tee*, undeniably, undoubtedly, unequivocally, unmistakably, unquestionably, with certainty, without qualification; SEE CONCEPTS *535,544,582*

possess [*v*] *have or obtain*
acquire, bear, be blessed with, be born with, be endowed with, carry, control, corner*, corner the market*, dominate, enjoy, get hands on*, get hold of*, grab, have to name*, hog*, hold, latch on to, lock up, maintain, occupy, own, retain, seize, sit on, take over, take possession; SEE CONCEPTS *120,710*

possessed [*adj*] *bewitched; under a spell*
bedeviled, berserk*, consumed, crazed*, cursed, demented, enchanted, enthralled, fiendish, frenetic, frenzied, gone*, haunted, hooked*, insane, into*, mad*, obsessed, raving*, taken over*, violent; SEE CONCEPT *401*

possession [*n1*] *control, ownership*
custody, dominion, hold, mastery, occupancy, occupation, possessorship, proprietary, proprietary rights, proprietorship, retention, tenancy, tenure, title; SEE CONCEPTS *343,710*

possession [*n2*] *something owned; property*
accessories, appointments, appurtenances, assets, baggage, belongings, chattels, effects, equipment, estate, fixtures, furnishings, furniture, goods, impedimenta, paraphernalia, province, real estate, settlement, tangibles, territory, things, trappings, tricks, wealth; SEE CONCEPTS *446,710*

possibilities [*n*] *potential*
capabilities, potentiality, promise, prospects, talent; SEE CONCEPTS *411,650*

possibility [*n*] *feasibility, likelihood; chance*
achievability, action, attainableness, break, circumstance, contingency, fair shake*, fifty-fifty*, fling*, fluke*, fortuity, happening, hazard, hope, incident, instance, liability, likeliness, occasion, occurrence, odds*, opportunity, outside chance*, plausibility, play*, potentiality, practicability, prayer*, probability, prospect, risk*, shot*, stab*, toss-up*, workableness; SEE CONCEPTS *650,693*

possible [*adj*] *likely, attainable*
accessible, achievable, adventitious, advisable, available, breeze*, can do*, cinch, conceivable, credible, dependent, desirable, doable, dormant, duck soup*, easy as pie*, expedient, feasible, fortuitous, hopeful, hypothetical, imaginable, indeterminate, latent, no sweat*, obtainable, piece of cake*, potential, practicable, probable, promising, pushover*, realizable, setup, simple as ABC*, snap, thinkable, uncertain, viable, welcome, within reach, workable; SEE CONCEPTS *528,552,576*

possibly [*adv*] *by chance; in some way*
at all, by any chance, by any means, conceivably, could be, God willing*, if possible, in any way, likely, maybe, not impossibly, peradventure, perchance, perhaps, probably, within realm of possibility; SEE CONCEPTS *544,552*

post [*n1*] *upright support*
column, doorpost, leg, mast, newel, pale, palisade, panel, pedestal, picket, pile, pillar, pole, prop, rail, shaft, stake, standard, stilt, stock, stud, upright; SEE CONCEPTS *440,445,470,479*

post [*n2*] *job, employment*
appointment, assignment, berth, billet, office, place, position, situation; SEE CONCEPTS *351,362*

post [*n3*] *lookout, station*
beat, locus, place, position, whereabouts; SEE CONCEPTS *198,321,439*

post [*n4*] *mail service*
collection, delivery, mail, PO*, postal service, post office; SEE CONCEPTS *299,770*

post [*v1*] *situate, position*
assign, establish, locate, place, put, set, station; SEE CONCEPT *201*

post [*v2*] *advise, inform*
acquaint, apprive, brief, clue, fill in, notify, put wise to, report, tell, warn, wise up; SEE CONCEPT *60*

poster [*n*] *large paper advertisement*
affiche, announcement, banner, bill, billboard, broadside, handbill, notice, placard, public notice, sheet, sign, signboard, sticker; SEE CONCEPT *271*

posterior [*n*] *behind of animate being*
back, backside, bottom, butt*, buttocks, can*, cheeks*, derriere, duff*, fanny*, hind part, keester*, moon*, rear, rear end, rump, seat, tail, tail end, tuchis*, tush*; SEE CONCEPT *392*

posterior [*adj1*] *rear*
after, back, behind, dorsal, hind, hinder, hindmost, in back of, last, retral; SEE CONCEPTS *583,827*

posterior [*adj2*] *subsequent*
after, coming after, ensuing, following, later, latter, next, postliminary, subsequential, succeeding; SEE CONCEPTS *585,799*

posterity [*n*] *future generations*
breed, brood, children, descendants, family, heirs, issue, lineage, next generation, offspring, progeniture, progeny, scions, seed, stock, succeeding generations, successors, unborn; SEE CONCEPT *296*

posthaste [*adj/adv*] *very fast*
at once, breakneck*, directly, double-quick*, expeditious, fast, flat-out*, fleet, fleetly, full tilt*, hastily, hasty, headlong, lickety-split*, pell-mell*, promptly, pronto, quick, quickly, rapid, rapidly, speedily, speedy, straightaway, swift, swiftly; SEE CONCEPTS *544,588,799*

postmortem [*n*] *analysis after death*
autopsy, coroner's report, dissection, examination, necropsy, post*; SEE CONCEPTS *103,310*

postmortem [adj] *following death*
future, later, posthumous, postmundane, post-obit, post-obituary; SEE CONCEPT *799*

postpone [v] *put off till later time*
adjourn, cool it*, defer, delay, give a rain check*, hang fire*, hold off, hold over, hold up, lay over, pigeonhole*, prorogue, put back, put on back burner*, put on hold, shelve, suspend, table; SEE CONCEPT *130*

postulate [v] *suppose, figure*
advance, affirm, assert, assume, aver, estimate, guess, hypothesize, posit, predicate, premise, presuppose, propose, put forward, speculate, suppose, take for granted, theorize; SEE CONCEPTS *12,26*

posture [n1] *stance, circumstance*
aspect, attitude, bearing, brace, carriage, condition, demeanor, deportment, disposition, mien, mode, phase, port, pose, position, positure, presence, set, situation, state; SEE CONCEPTS *657,723*

posture [n2] *beliefs*
attitude, disposition, feeling, frame of mind, inclination, mood, outlook, point of view, sentiment, stance, standpoint; SEE CONCEPT *410*

posture [v] *display an attitude*
affect, attitudinize, display, do a bit*, do for effect*, fake, fake it, make a show*, masquerade, pass for, pass off, playact, pose, put on airs*, put up a front*, show off*; SEE CONCEPTS *59,261*

pot [n1] *container, cauldron*
basin, bowl, bucket, can, canister, crock, crucible, cup, jar, jug, kettle, mug, pan, pitcher, receptacle, saucepan, tankard, urn, vessel; SEE CONCEPT *494*

pot [n2] *marijuana*
cannabis, grass*, hashish, maryjane*, weed*; SEE CONCEPT *307*

potency [n] *effectiveness*
authority, birr, capability, capacity, command, control, dominion, efficacy, efficiency, energy, force, go*, hardihood, influence, juice*, kick*, might, moxie*, muscle*, pep, potential, power, puissance, punch, sinew*, snap, sock*, steam*, strength, sway, vigor, virility, virtue, what it takes*, zap*, zing*, zip*; SEE CONCEPTS *411,676,732*

potent [adj] *effective, powerful, forceful*
almighty, authoritative, ball of fire*, cogent, commanding, compelling, convincing, dominant, dynamic, efficacious, forcible, full-bodied, go-getter*, great, gutsy*, impressive, influential, lusty, mighty, persuasive, powerhouse, puissant, punchy, robust, spanking, stiff, strong, sturdy, telling, trenchant, useful, vigorous, virile; SEE CONCEPTS *372,489,540*

potential [n] *possibility for achievement*
ability, aptitude, capability, capacity, potentiality, power, the makings*, what it takes*, wherewithal; SEE CONCEPTS *650,706*

potential [adj] *promising*
abeyant, budding, conceivable, dormant, embryonic, future, hidden, imaginable, implied, inherent, latent, likely, lurking, plausible, possible, prepatent, probable, quiescent, thinkable, undeveloped, unrealized, within realm of possibility; SEE CONCEPTS *528,552*

potion [n] *concoction prepared for mental or physical effect*
aromatic, brew, cordial, cup, dose, draft, dram, draught, drink, elixir, libation, liquid, liquor, medicine, mixture, nip, philter, remedy, restorative, spirits, stimulant, tonic; SEE CONCEPTS *307,467*

potpourri [n] *miscellany*
assortment, blend, collection, combination, combo, gallimaufry, goulash, hash, hodgepodge, medley, mélange, mishmash, mixed bag, mixture, motley, olio*, pastiche*, patchwork, salmagundi*, soup, stew; SEE CONCEPTS *260,432*

pottery [n] *containers made from clay; clay art*
ceramics, crockery, earthenware, firing, glazing, porcelain, porcelainware, stoneware, terra cotta; SEE CONCEPTS *174,259,494*

pouch [n] *soft container, often made of cloth or skin*
bag, pocket, poke, purse, receptacle, sac, sack; SEE CONCEPTS *446,450,494*

pounce [n/v] *leap at; take by surprise*
ambush, attack, bound, dart, dash, dive, drop, fall upon, jump, snatch, spring, strike, surge, swoop, take unawares; SEE CONCEPTS *86,159,194*

pound [n] *sixteen ounces/.454 kilograms of weight*
avoirdupois, pint, Troy; SEE CONCEPT *795*

pound [v1] *crush; beat rhythmically*
batter, belabor, bruise, buffet, clobber, comminute, drub, hammer, hit, malleate, palpitate, pelt, pestle, powder, pulsate, pulse, pulverize, pummel, stomp, strike, thrash, throb, thump, tramp, triturate, wallop; SEE CONCEPTS *150,186,189*

pound [v2] *impress; make someone listen*
din, drive, drub, drum, grave, hammer, stamp; SEE CONCEPTS *14,49*

pour [v] *be or make flowing*
cascade, cataract, course, crowd, decant, deluge, discharge, drain, drench, emit, flood, flow, give off, gush, inundate, issue, jet, let flow, proceed, rain, rill, roll, run, rush, sheet, shower, sluice, spew, spill, splash, spout, spring, stream, surge, swarm, teem, throng; SEE CONCEPTS *146,179,209*

pout [n] *sad face*
frown, glower, long face, moue, sullen look; SEE CONCEPT *716*

pout [v] *make a sad face; be sad*
be cross, be in bad mood*, be moody, be petulant, be sullen, frown, grouch, grump*, make a long face*, make a moue, mope, stick one's lip out*, sulk; SEE CONCEPTS *261,410*

poverty [n] *want; extreme need, often financial*
abjection, aridity, bankruptcy, barrenness, beggary, dearth, debt, deficiency, deficit, depletion, destitution, difficulty, distress, emptiness, exiguity, famine, hardship, impecuniousness, impoverishment, inadequacy, indigence, insolvency, insufficiency,

lack, meagerness, necessitousness, necessity, pass, paucity, pauperism, pennilessness, penury, pinch, poorness, privation, reduction, scarcity, shortage, starvation, straits, underdevelopment, vacancy; SEE CONCEPTS *335,709*

poverty-stricken [*adj*] *in great need; financially poor*
bad off*, bankrupt, beggared, beggarly, broke*, destitute, dirt poor*, distressed, down-and-out*, hard up*, impecunious, impoverished, indigent, in dire circumstances*, in want, moneyless, necessitous, needful, needy, penniless, penurious, short*, stone broke*, stranded*, strapped*, unmoneyed, wanting; SEE CONCEPT *334*

powder [*n*] *fine, loose grains made by crushing a solid*
crumb, dust, film, grain, grit, meal, particle, pounce, pulverulence, seed, talc; SEE CONCEPTS *471,831*

powder [*v*] *crush into fine grains; sprinkle fine grains*
abrade, bray, comminute, cover, crumble, crunch, dredge, dust, file, flour, granulate, grate, grind, pestle, pound, pulverize, rasp, reduce, scatter, scrape, smash, strew, triturate; SEE CONCEPTS *186,222*

powdery [*adj*] *consisting of fine, loose grains*
arenaceous, arenose, branny, chalky, crumbling, crumbly, dry, dusty, fine, floury, friable, grainy, granular, gravelly, gritty, impalpable, loose, mealy, pulverized, pulverulent, sandy; SEE CONCEPT *606*

power [*n1*] *ability, competence*
aptitude, bent, capability, capacity, competency, dynamism, effectiveness, efficacy, endowment, faculty, function, gift, influence, potential, potentiality, qualification, skill, talent, turn, virtue; SEE CONCEPT *630*

power [*n2*] *physical ability, capacity*
applied force, arm*, brawn, dynamism, energy, force, forcefulness, horsepower, intensity, mechanical energy, might, muscle*, omnipotence, potency, potential, powder, puissance, sinew*, strength, vigor, vim, virtue, voltage, weight; SEE CONCEPTS *520,641,732*

power [*n3*] *control, dominance*
ascendancy, authority, authorization, birthright, clout, command, connection, diadem, direction, domination, dominion, hegemony, imperium, influence, inside track*, jurisdiction, law, leadership, license, management, masterdom, mastery, might, moxie*, omnipotence, paramountcy, predominance, prerogative, prestige, privilege, regency, right, rule, say-so*, sovereignty, steam, strength, strings*, superiority, supremacy, sway, warrant, weight*, wire*; SEE CONCEPTS *376,671*

powerful [*adj*] *strong, effective*
able, all-powerful, almighty, authoritarian, authoritative, capable, cogent, commanding, compelling, competent, controlling, convincing, dominant, dynamic, effectual, efficacious, energetic, forceful, forcible, impressive, in control, influential, in the saddle*, mighty, omnipotent, overruling, paramount, persuasive, potent, preeminent, prevailing, puissant, robust, ruling, sovereign, stalwart, strap-

ping*, strengthy, sturdy, supreme, telling, upper hand*, vigorous, weighty, wicked*, wieldy; SEE CONCEPTS *489,527,540,574*

powerfully [*adv*] *with energy, authority*
effectively, energetically, forcefully, forcibly, hard, intensely, mightily, severely, strongly, vigorously, with might and main; SEE CONCEPTS *540,544,569*

powerless [*adj*] *weak; unable*
blank, chicken*, debilitated, defenseless, dependent, disabled, disenfranchised, etiolated, feeble, frail, gutless, helpless, impotent, incapable, incapacitated, ineffective, ineffectual, inert, infirm, out of gas*, paralyzed, passive, prostrate, subject, supine, tied, unarmed, unfit, vulnerable, wimp*, wishy-washy*; SEE CONCEPTS *489,527*

powwow [*n*] *discussion*
confab*, confabulation, conference, consultation, council, get-together, huddle, meeting, palaver, parley, talk; SEE CONCEPTS *56,324,384*

powwow [*v*] *discuss*
advise, confab*, confabulate, confer, consult, get together, go into a huddle*, huddle, meet, palaver, parley, talk, treat; SEE CONCEPT *56*

practicable [*adj*] *within the realm of possibility*
accessible, achievable, applicable, attainable, doable, employable, feasible, functional, handy, open, operative, performable, possible, practical, serviceable, usable, useful, utile, utilizable, viable, workable; SEE CONCEPT *560*

practical [*adj1*] *realistic, useful*
applied, both feet on the ground*, businesslike, commonsensical, constructive, doable, down-to-earth, efficient, empirical, experimental, factual, feasible, functional, handy, hard-boiled*, implicit, in action, in operation, matter-of-fact*, nuts and bolts*, operative, orderly, possible, practicable, pragmatic, rational, reasonable, sane, sensible, serviceable, sober, solid, sound, systematic, unidealistic, unromantic, usable, useful, utile, utilitarian, virtual, workable, workaday, working; SEE CONCEPTS *533,542,560*

practical [*adj2*] *experienced, proficient*
accomplished, cosmopolitan, effective, efficient, qualified, seasoned, skilled, sophisticated, trained, versed, vet*, veteran, working, worldly, worldly-wise; SEE CONCEPTS *326,527,528,678*

practically [*adj*] *almost; very nearly*
about, all but, approximately, as good as, as much as, basically, close to, essentially, for all intents and purposes*, fundamentally, in effect, in essence, morally, most, much, nearly, nigh, virtually, well-nigh; SEE CONCEPTS *531,772*

practice [*n1*] *routine, usual procedure*
convenance, convention, custom, fashion, form, habit, habitude, manner, method, mode, praxis, proceeding, process, rule, system, tradition, trick, usage, use, usefulness, utility, way, wont; SEE CONCEPT *687*

practice [*n2*] *exercise, application*
action, assignment, background, discipline, drill, drilling, effect, experience, homework, iteration, op-

eration, preparation, prepping, recitation, recounting, rehearsal, relating, repetition, seasoning, study, training, tune-up, use, work-out; SEE CONCEPTS *87,100,658*

practice [*n3*] *business; clientele of business*
career, clients, patients, profession, vocation, work; SEE CONCEPTS *325,417*

practice [*v1*] *repeat action to improve*
become seasoned, build up, discipline, do again, dress, dress rehearse*, drill, dry run*, exercise, go over, habituate, hone, iterate, polish, prepare, recite, rehearse, run through, shake-down*, sharpen, study, train, try out, tune up, walk through, warm up, work, work out; SEE CONCEPTS *87,100*

practice [*v2*] *carry out; undertake*
apply, carry on, do, engage in, execute, follow, fulfill, function, live up to, observe, perform, ply, pursue, put into effect, specialize in, work at; SEE CONCEPTS *91,310,317,324*

pragmatic [*adj*] *sensible*
businesslike, commonsensical, down-to-earth, efficient, hard, hard-boiled*, hard headed*, logical, matter-of-fact, practical, realistic, sober, unidealistic, utilitarian; SEE CONCEPTS *401,542*

praise [*n*] *congratulations; adoration*
acclaim, acclamation, accolade, applause, appreciation, approbation, approval, big hand*, boost, bravo, celebration, cheer, cheering, citation, commendation, compliment, cry, devotion, encomium, esteem, eulogy, exaltation, extolment, flattery, glorification, glory, good word*, homage, hurrah, hymn, kudos*, laudation, obeisance, ovation, panegyric, pat on the back*, plaudit, puff*, rave, recognition, recommendation, regard, sycophancy, thanks, tribute, worship; SEE CONCEPTS *69,278*

praise [*v*] *congratulate; adore*
acclaim, admire, adulate, advocate, aggrandize, applaud, appreciate, approve, bless, boost, bow down*, build up*, cajole, celebrate, cheer, cite, clap, commend, compliment, cry up*, dignify, distinguish, elevate, endorse, ennoble, eulogize, exalt, extol, flatter, give thanks, glorify, hail, honor, laud, make much of*, panegyrize, pay homage, pay tribute, proclaim, puff*, rave over, recommend, resound, reverence, root*, sanction, sing the praises*, smile on*, stroke*, tout, worship; SEE CONCEPT *69*

praiseworthy [*adj*] *deserving congratulations, adoration*
admirable, commendable, creditable, estimable, excellent, exemplary, fine, gnarly, gone, honorable, keen, laudable, meritable, meritorious, pillar, salt of earth*, select, slick, stellar, swell, thankworthy, tough, worthy; SEE CONCEPTS *568,574*

prance [*v*] *cavort; show off*
bound, caper, dance, flounce, foot it*, frisk, gambol, hoof it*, jump, leap, mince, parade, romp, sashay, skip, spring, stalk, step, strut, swagger, sweep, tread; SEE CONCEPTS *150,292,384*

prank [*n*] *practical joke; frivolity*
antic, caper, caprice, escapade, fancy, fooling, frolic, gag, gambol, high jinks*, horseplay*, hotfoot*, lark, levity, lightness, monkeyshines*, play, put-on, rib*, rollick, roughhouse*, roughhousing*, rowdiness, shenanigans, shine*, skylarking*, spoof, sport, tomfoolery, trick, whim; SEE CONCEPTS *59,384*

pray [*v*] *plead; call upon for help, answer*
adjure, appeal, ask, beseech, brace, commune with, crave, cry for, entreat, implore, importune, invocate, invoke, petition, recite, request, say, solicit, sue, supplicate, urge; SEE CONCEPTS *48,367*

prayer [*n*] *pleading, especially with a deity; request for help, answer*
adoration, appeal, application, begging, benediction, beseeching, communion, devotion, entreaty, grace, imploration, imploring, imprecation, invocation, litany, orison, petition, plea, pleading, request, rogation, service, suit, supplication, worship; SEE CONCEPTS *48,367,662*

preach [*v1*] *speak publicly about beliefs*
address, deliver, deliver sermon, evangelize, exhort, give sermon, homilize, inform, minister, mission, missionary, orate, prophesy, pulpiteer, sermonize, talk, teach; SEE CONCEPTS *51,285,367*

preach [*v2*] *lecture, moralize*
admonish, advocate, blow, exhort, get on a soapbox*, harangue, pile it on*, preachify, sermonize, talk big*, urge; SEE CONCEPTS *51,75*

preacher [*n*] *person who gives religious instruction*
churchman/woman, clergyman/woman, cleric, clerical, divine, ecclesiastic, evangelist, evangelizer, minister, missionary, padre, parson, pulpiter, reverend, revivalist, sermonizer; SEE CONCEPT *361*

precarious [*adj*] *tricky, doubtful*
ambiguous, borderline, chancy, contingent, dangerous, delicate, dicey*, dubious, dynamite, equivocal, hairy*, hanging by a thread*, hazardous, iffy*, impugnable, indecisive, insecure, loaded, on thin ice*, open, out on a limb*, perilous, problematic, risky, rocky, rugged*, sensitive, shaky, slippery, ticklish, touch and go*, touchy, uncertain, unhealthy, unreliable, unsafe, unsettled, unstable, unsteady, unsure; SEE CONCEPTS *535,587*

precaution [*n*] *carefulness; preventative measure*
anticipation, canniness, care, caution, circumspection, discreetness, discretion, foresight, forethought, insurance, protection, providence, provision, prudence, regard, safeguard, safety measure, wariness; SEE CONCEPTS *410,633,729*

precede [*v*] *go ahead of in space, time, order*
announce, antecede, antedate, anticipate, be ahead of, come first, forerun, foreshadow, go before, go in advance, guide, harbinger, have a head start*, head, head up, herald, introduce, lead, light the way*, outrank, pace, pave the way*, pioneer, predate, preexist, preface, presage, rank, ring in*, run ahead, scout, take precedence, usher; SEE CONCEPTS *727,747,813,818*

precedence [n] *highest in rank; first in order*
antecedence, anteposition, earliness, lead, precedency, precession, preeminence, preexistence, preference, prevenience, previousness, primary, priority, rank, seniority, superiority, supremacy; SEE CONCEPTS *671,727,747,818*

precedent [n] *authoritative example*
antecedent, authority, criterion, exemplar, instance, model, paradigm; SEE CONCEPT *688*

preceding [adj] *earlier, above*
above-mentioned, above-named, aforeknown, aforementioned, aforesaid, ahead of, antecedent, anterior, before, erstwhile, foregoing, forerunning, former, forward, front, head, heretofore, introductory, lead, leading, one time, other, past, pioneer, pioneering, precedent, precursive, precursory, preexistent, prefatory, preliminary, preparatory, prevenient, previous, prior, supra; SEE CONCEPTS *585,586,799,811,818*

precept [n] *law, rule of behavior, action*
axiom, behest, bidding, byword, canon, command, commandment, decree, decretum, direction, doctrine, dogma, edict, formula, fundamental, guideline, injunction, instruction, law, mandate, maxim, motto, order, ordinance, prescript, principle, regulation, rule, saying, statute, tenet; SEE CONCEPTS *318,687*

precious [adj1] *favorite, valued*
adored, beloved, blue-eyed*, cherished, darling, dear, dearest, fair-haired*, idolized, inestimable, loved, pet, prized, treasured; SEE CONCEPTS *529,567*

precious [adj2] *expensive; rare*
choice, costly, dear, exquisite, fine, high-priced, inestimable, invaluable, priceless, prizable, prized, recherché, rich, treasurable, valuable, worth eyeteeth*, worth king's ransom*, worth weight in gold*; SEE CONCEPT *334*

precious [adj3] *extremely sophisticated and picky*
affected, alembicated, artful, artificial, chichi*, choosy, dainty, delicate, fastidious, finicky, fragile, fussy, la-di-da*, nice, ostentatious, overnice, overrefined, particular, persnickety*, precieux, pretentious, refined, showy, sophisticated, stagy, studied; SEE CONCEPT *401*

precipice [n] *face or brink of a rock, mountain*
bluff, cliff, crag, height, sheer drop, steep; SEE CONCEPTS *509,513*

precipitate [v] *hurry, speed*
accelerate, advance, bring on, cast, discharge, dispatch, expedite, fling, further, hasten, hurl, launch, let fly, press, push forward, quicken, send forth, speed up, throw, trigger; SEE CONCEPTS *152,242,704*

precipitation [n] *moisture in air or falling from sky*
cloudburst, condensation, drizzle, hail, hailstorm, heavy dew, precip*, rain, rainfall, rainstorm, sleet, snow, storm, wetness; SEE CONCEPTS *467,524,526*

precipitous/precipitate [adj1] *very fast, sudden; impulsive; initial*
abrupt, breakneck*, brief, frantic, gone off half-cocked*, harum-scarum*, hasty, headlong, heedless, hurried, ill-advised, impatient, impetuous, indis-

creet, jump the gun*, madcap, off the hip*, off the top of head*, plunging, precipitant, quick, rapid, rash, reckless, refractory, rushing, subitaneous, swift, unanticipated, uncontrolled, unexpected, unforeseen, violent, willful, without warning; SEE CONCEPTS *229,401,542,588,799*

precipitous [adj2] *steep, falling sharply*
abrupt, arduous, craggy, dizzy, dizzying, high, perpendicular, precipitate, sharp, sheer; SEE CONCEPTS *490,583,779*

precis [n] *abridgment*
abstract, aperçu, compendium, condensation, digest, outline, pandect, résumé, rundown, sketch, summary, survey, syllabus, synopsis; SEE CONCEPT *283*

precise [adj1] *exact, accurate*
absolute, actual, categorical, circumscribed, clear-cut, correct, decisive, definite, determinate, explicit, express, fixed, individual, limited, literal, narrow, nice, on the button*, on the money*, on the nose*, particular, proper, restricted, right, rigid, rigorous, specific, strict, stringent, unequivocal, very, well-defined; SEE CONCEPTS *535,557,653*

precise [adj2] *meticulous, fastidious*
careful, ceremonious, choosy, exact, finicky, formal, fussy, genteel, inflexible, nice, particular, persnickety*, picky, priggish, prim, prissy, prudish, punctilious, puritanical, rigid, scrupulous, stickling, stiff*, strait-laced, strict, stuffy, uncompromising; SEE CONCEPTS *401,542*

precisely [adv] *exactly, just*
absolutely, accurately, as well, correctly, definitely, even, expressly, for a fact, for sure, just so, literally, no ifs ands or buts*, no mistake*, on the button*, on the money*, on the nose*, plumb, right, sharp, smack*, smack-dab*, specifically, square, squarely, strictly, sure, sure thing*, the ticket*, the very thing*, to a tee*, yes; SEE CONCEPTS *535,557*

precision [n] *accuracy*
attention, care, carefulness, correctness, definiteness, definitiveness, definitude, exactitude, exactness, fidelity, heed, meticulousness, nicety, particularity, preciseness, rigor, sureness; SEE CONCEPTS *638,654*

preclude [v] *inhibit; make impossible*
avert, cease, check, debar, deter, discontinue, exclude, forestall, forfend, hinder, impede, interrupt, make impracticable, obviate, prevent, prohibit, put a stop to, quit, restrain, rule out, stave off, stop, ward; SEE CONCEPTS *121,234*

precocious [adj] *exceptionally smart, ahead of age in understanding*
advanced, aggressive, ahead of time*, beforehand, bold, brassy*, bright, cheeky*, cocky*, developed, early, flip*, flippant, forward, fresh, intelligent, mature, nervy, premature, presumptuous, pushy, quick, sassy, smart-alecky*; SEE CONCEPT *402*

preconception [n] *idea formed before event occurs or facts are received*
assumption, bias, delusion, illusion, inclination, notion, preconceived idea, predisposition, prejudgment,

prejudice, prepossession, presumption, presupposition; SEE CONCEPT *689*

precursor [*n1*] *something that indicates outcome or event beforehand*
forerunner, harbinger, herald, messenger, outrider, usher, vanguard; SEE CONCEPTS *70,278*

precursor [*n2*] *something that precedes another*
ancestor, antecedent, antecessor, forebear, forefather, foregoer, foremother, forerunner, original, originator, parent, pioneer, predecessor, prototype; SEE CONCEPTS *648,727,828*

predatory [*adj*] *eating, destroying for sustenance or without conscience*
bloodthirsty, carnivorous, depredatory, despoiling, greedy, hungry, hunting, marauding, pillaging, plundering, predacious, predative, preying, rapacious, raptorial, ravaging, ravening, thieving, voracious, vulturine, vulturous, wolfish; SEE CONCEPTS *401,406*

predecessor [*n*] *something, someone that comes before*
ancestor, antecedent, antecessor, forebear, forefather, foregoer, foremother, forerunner, former, precursor, previous, prior, prototype; SEE CONCEPTS *414,828*

predetermined [*adj*] *decided in advance*
agreed, arranged, calculated, cut and dried*, deliberate, destined, determined, doomed, fated, fixed, foredestined, foreordained, forethought, planned, prearranged, precogitated, predestined, premeditated, preordained, preplanned, proposed, set, settled, set up; SEE CONCEPT *548*

predicament [*n*] *difficult situation*
asperity, bad news*, bind*, Catch-22*, circumstance, clutch, condition, corner*, crisis, deadlock, deep water*, dilemma, drag*, emergency, exigency, fix*, hang-up*, hardship, hole, hot water*, imbroglio, impasse, jam*, juncture, large order*, lot, mess*, muddle, pass, perplexity, pickle*, pinch, plight, position, posture, puzzle, quagmire, quandary, rigor, rough go*, scrape*, soup*, spot*, state*, strait, tall order* ticklish spot* tight situation* trouble, vicissitude; SEE CONCEPTS *388,674*

predict [*v*] *express an outcome in advance*
adumbrate, anticipate, augur, be afraid, call, call it, conclude, conjecture, croak, crystal-ball* divine, envision, figure, figure out, forebode, forecast, foresee, forespeak, foretell, gather, guess, have a hunch*, hazard a guess*, infer, judge, make book*, omen, portend, presage, presume, prognosticate, prophesy, psych out*, read, see coming*, see handwriting on wall*, size up*, soothsay, suppose, surmise, telegraph*, think, vaticinate; SEE CONCEPT *70*

predictable [*adj*] *very easy to foretell*
anticipated, calculable, certain, expected, foreseeable, foreseen, likely, prepared, sure, sure-fire*; SEE CONCEPTS *404,542,548*

prediction [*n*] *declaration made in advance of event*
anticipation, augury, cast, conjecture, crystal gazing*, divination, dope, forecast, forecasting, foresight, foretelling, fortune-telling, guess, horoscope, hunch*, indicator, omen, palmistry, presage, prevision, prognosis, prognostication, prophecy, soothsaying, surmising, tip, vaticination, zodiac; SEE CONCEPTS *70,278,689*

predilection [*n*] *inclination, preference toward something*
bent*, bias, cup of tea*, dish*, druthers*, fancy, flash, fondness, groove, inclining, leaning, liking, love, mindset*, partiality, penchant, predisposition, proclivity, proneness, propensity, taste*, tendency, thing*, type, weakness; SEE CONCEPTS *20,32,709*

predispose [*v*] *influence to believe something*
activate, affect, animate, bend*, bias, cultivate, dispose, govern, impress, incline, indoctrinate, induce, inspire, lead, make expectant, make of a mind to*, prejudice, prepare, prime, prompt, stimulate, strike, sway, teach, urge; SEE CONCEPTS *12,14,26,68*

predisposed [*adj*] *willing, inclined*
agreeable, amenable, biased, eager, enthusiastic, fain, given to, liable, likely, minded, partial, prone, ready, subject, susceptible; SEE CONCEPT *403*

predisposition [*n*] *willingness, inclination*
bent*, bias, choice, cup of tea*, dish*, disposition, druthers*, flash, groove, leaning, likelihood, liking, option, partiality, penchant, potentiality, predilection, preference, proclivity, proneness, propensity, susceptibility, tendency, thing*, type, weakness; SEE CONCEPTS *20,32,410,709*

predominant [*adj*] *ruling; most important*
absolute, all-powerful, almighty, arbitrary, ascendant, authoritative, capital, chief, controlling, directing, dominant, dominating, effective, efficacious, governing, holding the reins*, imperious, influential, leading, main, master, mighty, official, omnipotent, overbearing, overpowering, paramount, potent, predominate, preponderant, prevailing, prevalent, primary, prime, principal, prominent, reigning, sovereign, superior, superlative, supervisory, supreme, surpassing, transcendent, weighty; SEE CONCEPTS *568,574*

predominate [*v*] *be the most important, noticeable*
carry weight*, command, dominate, domineer, get the upper hand*, govern, hold sway*, manage, outweigh, overrule, overshadow, preponderate, prevail, reign, rule, tell; SEE CONCEPTS *94,117,141*

preeminent [*adj*] *most important; superior*
capital, chief, consummate, distinguished, dominant, excellent, foremost, incomparable, main, major, matchless, number one*, outstanding, paramount, peerless, predominant, principal, renowned, stellar, supreme, surpassing, towering, transcendent, ultimate, unequalled, unmatchable, unrivalled, unsurpassable, unsurpassed; SEE CONCEPTS *568,574*

preempt [*v*] *take over in place of another*
accroach, acquire, annex, anticipate, appropriate, arrogate, assume, bump, commandeer, confiscate, expropriate, obtain, seize, sequester, take, usurp; SEE CONCEPTS *121,142,234*

preface [n] *introduction*
beginning, exordium, explanation, foreword, overture, preamble, preliminary, prelude, prelusion, proem, prolegomenon, prologue; SEE CONCEPT *270*

preface [v] *introduce*
begin, commence, launch, lead, lead up to, open, precede, prefix, usher; SEE CONCEPTS *57,221*

prefer [v] *favor; single out*
adopt, advance, aggrandize, be partial to, be turned on to, choose, cull, desire, elect, elevate, fancy, finger, fix upon, go for, incline, like better, mark, optate, opt for, pick, place, pose, present, promote, propone, proposition, propound, put, put forward, raise, select, suggest, tag, take, tap, upgrade, wish, would rather*, would sooner*; SEE CONCEPTS *20,41*

preference [n1] *first choice*
alternative, choice, cup of tea*, desire, druthers*, election, favorite, flash*, groove, inclination, option, partiality, pick, predilection, prepossession, propensity, say, say so*, selection, top, weakness; SEE CONCEPTS *20,529,709*

preference [n2] *favorable treatment*
advancement, advantage, elevation, favoritism, first place, precedence, preferment, prelation, pride of place, priority, promotion, upgrading; SEE CONCEPT *693*

preferred [adj] *favorite, chosen*
adopted, approved, culled, decided upon, elected, endorsed, fancied, favored, handpicked, liked, named, picked, popular, sanctioned, selected, set apart, settled upon, singled out, taken, well-liked; SEE CONCEPTS *555,574*

pregnant [adj1] *expecting a child*
abundant, anticipating, enceinte, expectant, expecting*, fecund, fertile, fraught, fruitful, gestating, gravid, heavy, hopeful, in delicate condition*, in family way*, parous, parturient, productive, prolific, replete, teeming, with child*; SEE CONCEPTS *406,485*

pregnant [adj2] *significant, meaningful*
charged, consequential, creative, eloquent, expressive, fecund, imaginative, important, inventive, loaded, momentous, original, pointed, redolent, rich, seminal, sententious, suggestive, telling, weighty; SEE CONCEPTS *267,567*

prejudice [n] *belief without basis, information; intolerance*
ageism, animosity, antipathy, apartheid, aversion, bad opinion, bias, bigotry, chauvinism, contemptuousness, detriment, discrimination, disgust, dislike, displeasure, disrelish, enmity, foregone conclusion, illiberality, injustice, jaundiced eye, mindset*, misjudgment, narrow-mindedness, one-sidedness, partiality, pique, preconceived notion, preconception, prejudgment, prepossession, racism, repugnance, revulsion, sexism, slant, spleen, tilt, twist, umbrage, unfairness, warp, xenophobia; SEE CONCEPT *689*

prejudice [v] *influence another's beliefs without basis, information*
angle*, bend*, bias, blemish*, color*, damage, dispose, distort, harm, hinder, hurt, impair, incline, indoctrinate, injure, jaundice, mar, poison*, predispose, prejudge, prepossess, skew*, slant*, spoil, sway*, twist*, undermine, vitiate, warp*; SEE CONCEPTS *7,14,19*

prejudicial [adj] *harmful, undermining*
bad, biased, bigoted, counterproductive, damaging, deleterious, detrimental, differential, disadvantageous, discriminatory, evil, hurtful, inimical, injurious, mischievous, nocuous, unfavorable, unjust; SEE CONCEPTS *537,545,570*

preliminary [n] *introductory event; beginning*
first round, foundation, groundwork, initiation, introduction, opening, preamble, preface, prelims*, prelude, preparation, start; SEE CONCEPTS *828,832*

preliminary [adj] *introductory, initial*
basic, elemental, elementary, exploratory, first, fundamental, inductive, initiatory, opening, pilot, preceding, precursory, prefatory, preparatory, preparing, primal, primary, prior, qualifying, readying, test, trial; SEE CONCEPTS *549,585,799*

prelude [n] *beginning of event*
commencement, curtain-raiser*, exordium, foreword, intro*, introduction, overture, preamble, preface, preliminary, prelusion, preparation, proem, prolegomenon, prologue, start; SEE CONCEPTS *264,832*

premature [adj1] *earlier in occurrence than anticipated*
a bit previous, abortive, early on, embryonic, forward, green*, immature, incomplete, inopportune, overearly, oversoon, precipitate, predeveloped, previous, raw*, soon, unanticipated, undeveloped, unfledged, unripe, untimely; SEE CONCEPTS *485,549*

premature [adj2] *rash, impulsive*
half-baked*, half-cocked*, hasty, ill-considered, inopportune, jumping the gun*, overhasty, precipitate, previous, too soon, untimely; SEE CONCEPTS *401,542*

premeditated [adj] *planned, intended*
advised, aforethought, calculated, conscious, considered, contrived, deliberate, designed, fixed, framed up, intentional, laid-out*, prepense, purposed, rigged*, set-up*, sewn-up*, stacked deck*, studied, thought-out, willful; SEE CONCEPTS *542,548*

premier [adj] *leading; original*
arch, beginning, champion, chief, earliest, first, foremost, head, highest, inaugural, initial, main, opening, primary, prime, principal; SEE CONCEPTS *568,585*

premiere [n] *original production*
beginning, debut, first night, first performance, first showing, opening, opening night; SEE CONCEPTS *263,832*

premise [n] *hypothesis, argument*
apriorism, assertion, assumption, basis, evidence, ground, posit, postulate, postulation, presumption, presupposition, proof, proposition, supposition, thesis; SEE CONCEPTS *529,689*

premise [v] *hypothesize*
announce, assume, begin, commence, introduce, posit, postulate, predicate, presume, presuppose, start, state, suppose; SEE CONCEPTS *18,37*

premises [n] *grounds and buildings*
bounds, campus, digs, establishment, fix, flat, hangout*, home, house, joint*, land, lay, layout, limits, neck of the woods*, office, pad, place, plant, property, real estate*, roof, scene, site, spot, terrace, turf, zone; SEE CONCEPTS *198,515*

premium [n] *bonus, prize*
appreciation, boon, bounty, carrot*, dividend, extra, fee*, gravy*, guerdon, meed, percentage, perk*, perquisite, plum*, recompense, regard, remuneration, reward, spiff*, stock, store, value; SEE CONCEPTS *337,344*

premium [adj] *excellent*
choice, exceptional, prime, select, selected, superior; SEE CONCEPT *574*

premonition [n] *feeling that an event is about to occur*
apprehension, apprehensiveness, feeling, feeling in bones*, foreboding, forewarning, funny feeling, handwriting on wall*, hunch, idea, intuition, misgiving, omen, portent, prenotion, presage, presentiment, sign, sinking feeling, suspicion, vibes, vibrations, warning, wind change*, winds*, winds of change*, worriment; SEE CONCEPTS *410, 529,689,690*

preoccupied [adj] *busy; mentally caught up in something*
absent, absentminded, absorbed, abstracted, airheaded*, asleep*, bemused, bugged*, daydreaming, deep*, distracted, distrait, engaged, engrossed, faraway, fascinated, forgetful, have on the brain*, heedless, hung up*, immersed, inconscient, intent, lost, lost in thought*, mooning*, moony*, oblivious, obsessed, rapt, removed, spellbound, spread out*, taken up, unaware, woolgathering*, wrapped-up*; SEE CONCEPT *403*

preparation [n1] *development, readiness*
alertness, anticipation, arrangement, background, base, basis, build-up*, construction, dry run*, education, establishment, evolution, expectation, fitting, foresight, formation, foundation, gestation, getting ready, groundwork, homework, incubation, lead time*, making ready, manufacture, measure, plan, precaution, preparedness, preparing, provision, putting in order, qualification, readying, rehearsal, rundown, safeguard, schoolwork, study, substructure, training, tryout, workout; SEE CONCEPTS *35,202,285*

preparation [n2] *something concocted, put together*
arrangement, blend, brew, composition, compound, concoction, confection, decoction, medicine, mixture, product, tincture; SEE CONCEPT *260*

preparatory [adj] *introductory, basic*
before, elementary, in advance of, in anticipation of, inductive, opening, precautionary, prefatory, preliminary, prelusive, prep*, preparative, previous, primary, prior to; SEE CONCEPTS *546,585*

prepare [v] *make or get ready*
adapt, adjust, anticipate, appoint, arrange, assemble, brace, build up, coach, concoct, construct, contrive, cook, develop, dispose, draw up, endow, equip, fabricate, fashion, fill in, fit, fit out, fix, form, formulate, fortify, furnish, gird, groom, lay the groundwork, make, make provision, make up, outfit, perfect, plan, practice, prime, produce, provide, put in order, put together, qualify, ready, settle, smooth the way*, steel*, strengthen, supply, train, turn out, warm up; SEE CONCEPTS *35,202*

prepared [adj] *ready in body or mind*
able, adapted, adjusted, all bases covered*, all set*, all systems go*, arranged, available, disposed, fit, fixed, framed, gaffed, groomed, handy, inclined, in order, in readiness, minded, of a mind, on guard*, planned, predisposed, prepped, primed, processed, psyched-up*, put up, qualified, rehearsed, rigged*, set, set-up, sewed-up, stacked, up*, up on*, willing, wired; SEE CONCEPTS *403,485,560*

preponderance [n] *great numbers; supremacy*
advantage, ascendancy, bigger half*, bulk, command, dominance, domination, dominion, extensiveness, greater part, lion's share*, mass, masterdom, max*, most, power, predominance, prevalence, superiority, sway, weight; SEE CONCEPTS *671,686,767*

prepossessed [adj] *made partial by initial impression*
biased, colored, inclined, jaundiced, one-sided, opinionated, partisan, predisposed, prejudiced, tendentious, unindifferent, warped; SEE CONCEPTS *403,542*

prepossessing [adj] *attractive, handsome*
alluring, amiable, appealing, attracting, beautiful, bewitching, captivating, charming, drawing, enchanting, engaging, fair, fascinating, fetching, good-looking, inviting, likable, lovable, magnetic, pleasant, pleasing, striking, taking, winning; SEE CONCEPTS *404,537*

preposterous [adj] *ridiculous, bizarre*
absurd, asinine, crazy, excessive, exorbitant, extravagant, extreme, fantastic, far-out*, foolish, harebrained*, impossible, incredible, insane, irrational, laughable, ludicrous, monstrous, nonsensical, out of the question*, outrageous, senseless, shocking, silly, stupid, taking the cake*, thick*, too much*, unbelievable, unreasonable, unthinkable, unusual, wacky*, wild; SEE CONCEPTS *529,548,552*

prerequisite [n] *condition, necessity*
essential, imperative, must, need, postulate, precondition, qualification, requirement, requisite, sine qua non; SEE CONCEPTS *646,709*

prerequisite [adj] *necessary*
called for, essential, expedient, imperative, important, indispensable, mandatory, necessitous, needful, obligatory, of the essence, required, requisite, vital; SEE CONCEPT *546*

prerogative [n] *right, privilege*
advantage, appanage, authority, birthright, choice, claim, droit, due, exemption, immunity, liberty, perquisite, sanction, title; SEE CONCEPT *376*

presage [n] *prediction, indication*
apprehension, apprehensiveness, augury, auspice, bodement, boding, forecast, foretoken, forewarning, harbinger, intimation, misgiving, omen, portent, pre-

monition, prenotion, presentiment, prognostic, prognostication, prophecy, sign, warning; SEE CONCEPTS *410,529,689*

presage [*v*] *predict or have a feeling*
adumbrate, announce, augur, betoken, bode, divine, feel, forebode, forecast, forerun, foresee, foreshadow, foreshow, foretell, foretoken, forewarn, harbinger, herald, intuit, omen, point to, portend, preindicate, prognosticate, promise, prophesy, sense, signify, soothsay, vaticinate, warn; SEE CONCEPTS *34,70,118*

prescribe [*v*] *stipulate action to be taken*
appoint, assign, choose, command, decide, decree, define, designate, determine, dictate, direct, enjoin, establish, fix, guide, impose, lay down, ordain, order, pick out, require, rule, select, set, settle, specify, write prescription; SEE CONCEPTS *50,60,61,88*

prescription [*n*] *formula, medicine*
decree, direction, drug, edict, instruction, law, mixture, ordinance, preparation, prescript, recipe, regulation, remedy, rule; SEE CONCEPTS *274,307,311,318*

presence [*n1*] *occupancy, attendance*
being, companionship, company, existence, habitation, inhabitance, latency, occupation, omnipresence, potentiality, residence, subsistence, ubiety, ubiquity, whereabouts; SEE CONCEPTS *407,518,710*

presence [*n2*] *appearance, demeanor*
address, air, aspect, aura, bearing, behavior, carriage, comportment, deportment, ease, look, mien, personality, poise, port, seeming, self-assurance, set; SEE CONCEPTS *411,673,716*

presence [*n3*] *closeness, vicinity*
immediate circle, nearness, neighborhood, propinquity, proximity; SEE CONCEPT *747*

presence [*n4*] *ghost*
apparition, manifestation, shade, specter, spirit, supernatural being, wraith; SEE CONCEPT *370*

presence [*n5*] *composure of mind*
acumen, alertness, aplomb, calmness, cool, coolness, imperturbability, levelheadedness, quickness, sangfroid, self-assurance, self-command, self-composure, self-possession, sensibility, sobriety, watchfulness, wits; SEE CONCEPTS *410,657*

present [*n1*] *existing time*
here and now, instant, nonce, now, present moment, the time being, this day, this time, today; SEE CONCEPTS *802,807,815*

present [*n2*] *gift*
benefaction, benevolence, boon, bounty, compliment, donation, endowment, favor, gifting, giveaway, goodie*, grant, gratuity, handout, largess, lump, offering, stake, write-off; SEE CONCEPT *337*

present [*adj1*] *existing; at this time*
ad hoc, already, at this moment, begun, being, coeval, commenced, contemporaneous, contemporary, current, even now, existent, extant, for the time being, going on, immediate, in duration, in process, instant, just now, modern, nowadays, present-day,

prompt, started, today, topical, under consideration, up-to-date; SEE CONCEPT *820*

present [*adj2*] *nearby, here*
accounted for, at hand, attendant, available, existent, in attendance, in view, made the scene*, near, on board, on deck, on hand, on-the-spot, ready, show up, there, there with bells on*, within reach; SEE CONCEPTS *539,583*

present [*v1*] *introduce; demonstrate*
acquaint, adduce, advance, allege, cite, declare, display, do, do the honors, exhibit, expose, expound, extend, fix up, get together, give, give an introduction, hold out, imply, infer, intimate, lay, make a pitch*, make known, manifest, mount, offer, open to view, perform, pitch, pose, produce, proffer, proposition, put forward, put on, raise, recount, relate, roll out, show, stage, state, submit, suggest, tender, trot out; SEE CONCEPTS *66,261*

present [*v2*] *give, hand over*
award, bestow, come up with, confer, devote, donate, entrust, furnish, gift, give away, grant, hand out, kick in*, lay on*, offer, proffer, put at disposal, put forth; SEE CONCEPTS *67,108*

presentable [*adj*] *respectable; fit to be seen*
acceptable, attractive, becoming, decent, fit, good enough*, not bad*, okay*, passable, prepared, proper, satisfactory, suitable, tolerable; SEE CONCEPTS *558,579*

presentation [*n*] *performance; something given, displayed*
act, appearance, arrangement, award, bestowal, coming out, conferral, debut, delivering, delivery, demonstration, display, dog and pony show*, donation, exhibition, exposition, giving, introduction, investiture, knockdown*, launch, launching, offering, overture, pitch, present, production, proposal, proposition, reception, remembrance, rendition, representation, sales pitch*, show, staging, submission; SEE CONCEPTS *261,263,337*

presentiment [*n*] *anticipation, expectation*
apprehension, apprehensiveness, discomposure, disquietude, disturbance, fear, feeling, feeling in bones*, foreboding, forecast, forethought, funny feeling*, handwriting on wall*, hunch, intuition, misgiving, perturbation, premonition, prenotion, presage, sinking feeling, vibes, worriment; SEE CONCEPTS *410,532,689*

presently [*adv*] *in a short while*
anon, before long, before you know it, by and by, directly, down the line*, down the pike*, down the road*, immediately, in a minute, in a moment, in a short time, now, nowadays, pretty soon, shortly, soon, today, without delay; SEE CONCEPT *820*

preservation [*n*] *maintenance, protection*
canning, care, conservancy, conservation, curing, defense, evaporation, freezing, guard, guardianship, husbanding, keeping, perpetuation, pickling, preserval, refrigeration, safeguard, safeguarding, safekeep-

ing, safety, salvation, saving, security, shield, storage, support, sustentation, tanning, upholding, ward; SEE CONCEPTS *134,170,202,257*

preserve [*v*] *care for, maintain; continue*
bottle, can, conserve, cure, defend, evaporate, freeze, guard, keep, keep up, mothball*, mummify, perpetuate, pickle, process, protect, put up, refrigerate, retain, safeguard, save, season, secure, shelter, shield, store, sustain, uphold; SEE CONCEPTS *134,170,202*

preserves [*n*] *thickened fruit prepared for storage and use as a condiment*
confection, confiture, conserve, extract, gelatin, jam, jell, jelly, marmalade, pectin, spread, sweet; SEE CONCEPTS *457,461*

preside [*v*] *be in authority*
administer, advise, be at the head of*, be in driver's seat*, call the signals*, carry on, chair, conduct, control, direct, do the honors, govern, handle, head, head up, keep, lead, manage, officiate, operate, ordain, oversee, pull the strings*, run, run the show*, sit on top of*, supervise; SEE CONCEPTS *94,117*

press [*n1*] *people or person working in communications*
columnist, correspondent, editor, fourth estate*, interviewer, journalism, journalist, magazine, media, newsman/woman, newspaper, paper, periodical, photographer, publicist, publisher, reporter, writer; SEE CONCEPTS *280,349,356*

press [*n2*] *horde, large group*
bunch, crowd, crush, drove, flock, herd, host, mob, multitude, pack, push, swarm, throng; SEE CONCEPT *432*

press [*n3*] *strain, pressure*
bustle, confusion, demand, hassle, haste, hurry, rush, stress, urgency; SEE CONCEPTS *230,674*

press [*v1*] *push on with force*
bear down, bear heavily, bulldoze*, clasp, compress, condense, constrain, crowd, crush, cumber, depress, embrace, enfold, express, finish, flatten, force down, hold, hug, impel, iron, jam, level, mangle, mash, mass, move, pack, pile, pin down, ram, reduce, scrunch, shove, smooth, squash, squeeze, squish, steam, stuff, thrust, unwrinkle, weigh; SEE CONCEPTS *191,208*

press [*v2*] *pressure, trouble*
afflict, assail, beg, beset, besiege, buttonhole*, come at, compel, constrain, demand, depress, disquiet, enjoin, entreat, exhort, force, harass, implore, importune, insist on, lean on, oppress, petition, plague, plead, pressurize, push, railroad*, sadden, sell, squeeze, sue, supplicate, torment, urge, vex, weigh down, work on, worry; SEE CONCEPT *14*

pressing [*adj*] *very important; urgent*
acute, burning, claiming, clamant, clamorous, compelling, constraining, critical, crucial, crying, demanding, dire, distressing, exacting, exigent, forcing, heat-on*, high-priority, hurry-up*, immedi-

ate, imperative, importunate, insistent, instant, life-and-death*, obliging, requiring, serious, urgent, vital; SEE CONCEPTS *548,568*

pressure [*n1*] *physical force, weight*
burden, compressing, compression, crushing, encumbrance, heaviness, load, mass, shear, squeeze, squeezing, strain, strength, stress, tension, thrust; SEE CONCEPTS *641,734*

pressure [*n2*] *demand, difficulty*
adversity, affliction, albatross*, burden, choke, clout, coercion, compulsion, confinement, constraint, crunch, discipline, distress, drag, duress, exigency, force, full court press*, hardship, hassle, heat, hurry, influence, inside track*, load, misfortune, necessity, obligation, persuasion, power, press, pressure cooker*, pull, requirement, strain, stress, sway, tension, trouble, unnaturalness, urgency, weight; SEE CONCEPTS *14,666,674,686*

pressure [*v*] *bother, urge*
come at, compel, constrain, drive, impel, insist, lean on*, politick, press, push, push around*, rush, sell, squeeze, twist arm*, work over*; SEE CONCEPTS *7,14,19,22*

prestige [*n*] *fame, influence*
authority, cachet, celebrity, consequence, control, credit, dignity, distinction, éclat*, eminence, esteem, fame, illustriousness, importance, kudos*, position, power, preeminence, prominence, prominency, rank, regard, renown, reputation, repute, standing, state, stature, status, sway, weight; SEE CONCEPTS *388,668*

prestigious [*adj*] *famous, influential*
celebrated, distinguished, eminent, esteemed, exalted, famed, great, illustrious, important, imposing, impressive, notable, prominent, renowned, reputable, respected; SEE CONCEPTS *555,568*

presumably [*adv*] *likely, reasonably*
apparently, assumably, credible, doubtless, doubtlessly, hypothetically, in all likelihood, in all probability, indubitably, it would seem, most likely, on the face of it, presumptively, probably, seemingly, supposedly, surely, theoretically, unquestionably; SEE CONCEPTS *544,552*

presume [*v1*] *make assumption; believe*
assume, bank on*, be afraid, conclude, conjecture, consider, count on, depend, figure, gather, guess, infer, jump the gun*, posit, postulate, predicate, premise, presuppose, pretend, rely, speculate, suppose, surmise, take for granted, take it, think, trust; SEE CONCEPTS *12,26,28*

presume [*v2*] *dare; take the liberty*
go so far, have the audacity, impose, infringe, intrude, make bold, undertake, venture; SEE CONCEPT *87*

presumption [*n1*] *belief, hypothesis*
anticipation, apriorism, assumption, basis, chance, conjecture, grounds, guess, likelihood, opinion, plausibility, posit, postulate, postulation, premise, presupposition, probability, reason, shot, shot in the

dark*, sneaking suspicion*, stab, supposition, surmise, suspicion, thesis; SEE CONCEPT *689*

presumption [*n2*] *forwardness, daring*
arrogance, assurance, audacity, boldness, brashness, brass, cheek*, chutzpah*, confidence, contumely, effrontery, gall, impudence, insolence, nerve, presumptuousness, rudeness, temerity; SEE CONCEPT *633*

presumptuous [*adj*] *very self-confident*
arrogant, audacious, bold, cheeky*, conceited, confident, contumelious, egotistic, foolhardy, forward, fresh, insolent, overconfident, overfamiliar, overweening, pompous, presuming, pretentious, pushy, rash, rude, self-assertive, self-assured, self-satisfied, smug, supercilious, uppity*; SEE CONCEPTS *401,542*

pretend [*v1*] *fake, falsify*
act, affect, allege, assume, be deceitful, beguile, be hypocritical, bluff, cheat, claim, claim falsely, counterfeit, cozen, deceive, delude, dissemble, dissimulate, dupe, fake out*, feign, fish*, fool, fudge*, hoodwink*, impersonate, jazz*, jive*, lay claim*, let on*, make out*, malinger, masquerade, mislead, pass off*, pass oneself off as*, profess, purport, put on*, put up a front*, sham*, shuck and jive*, simulate, stonewall*, sucker*, whitewash*; SEE CONCEPTS *59,63*

pretend [*v2*] *play the part of*
act, assume the role, imagine, imitate, impersonate, make as if, make believe, make out like, make up, masquerade, mimic, play, playact, portray, pose, purport, put on a front*, put on airs*, put on an act*, represent, reproduce, suppose; SEE CONCEPTS *111, 171,292,384*

pretended [*adj*] *alleged; imaginary*
affected, artificial, assumed, avowed, bluffing, bogus, charlatan, cheating, concealed, counterfeit, covered, dissimulated, factitious, fake, false, falsified, feigned, fictitious, impostrous, imposturous, lying, make-believe, masked, mock, ostensible, phony, pretend, professed, pseudo*, purported, put-on*, quack*, sham*, shammed*, simulated, so-called, spurious, supposed; SEE CONCEPTS *545,582*

pretense [*n*] *falsehood, affected show; cover*
act, acting, affectation, appearance, artifice, charade, claim, cloak, deceit, deception, display, dissimulation, double-dealing*, dumb act*, evasion, excuse, fabrication, facade, fakery, faking, falsification, feigning, gag, guise, insincerity, invention, make-believe, mask, masquerade, misrepresentation, misstatement, ostentation, posing, posturing, pretentiousness, pretext, routine, ruse, semblance, schtick*, sham*, shuffling, simulation, stall, stunt, subterfuge, trickery, veil, veneer, wile; SEE CONCEPTS *59,63, 633,716*

pretension [*n1*] *airs, snobbishness*
affectation, big talk*, charade, conceit, disguise, fake*, false front*, front, hypocrisy, ostentation, phony, pomposity, pretentiousness, put-on*, self-importance, show, showboat*, showiness, showoff, snobbery, splash*, vainglory, vanity; SEE CONCEPT *633*

pretension [*n2*] *false claim, assertion of importance*
allegation, ambition, ambitiousness, aspiration, assumption, charade, declaration, demand, disguise, maintenance, make-believe, pageant, pretense, pretext, profession, title; SEE CONCEPTS *278,657*

pretentious [*adj*] *snobbish, conceited*
affected, arty, assuming, aureate, big*, bombastic, chichi*, conspicuous, euphuistic, exaggerated, extravagant, feigned, flamboyant, flashy, flaunting, flowery, gaudy, grandiloquent, grandiose, highfaluting*, high-flown*, high-sounding*, hollow, imposing, inflated, jazzy*, la-di-da*, lofty, magniloquent, mincing, ornate, ostentatious, overambitious, overblown, pompous, puffed up*, put-on*, rhetorical, showy, snobbish, specious, splashy, stilted, swank, too-too*, tumid, turgid, utopian, vainglorious; SEE CONCEPTS *401,542,589*

preternatural [*adj*] *unusual, abnormal*
aberrant, anomalous, atypical, deviant, deviative, extraordinary, ghostly, inexplicable, irregular, marvelous, miraculous, mysterious, odd, peculiar, strange, superhuman, superior, supermundane, supernatural, unaccountable, unearthly, unnatural, unrepresentative, untypical; SEE CONCEPT *564*

pretext [*n*] *disguise; alleged reason*
affectation, alibi, appearance, bluff, cleanup, cloak, color*, coloring*, copout*, cover, cover story*, cover-up*, device, excuse, face, feint, fig leaf*, front, guise, mask, masquerade, plea, ploy, pretense, red herring*, routine, ruse, semblance, show, simulation, song and dance*, stall, stratagem, subterfuge, veil*; SEE CONCEPTS *59,661,716*

pretty [*adj*] *attractive*
appealing, beauteous, beautiful, boss*, charming, cheerful, cher*, comely, cute, dainty, darling, delicate, delightful, dishy*, dreamboat*, elegant, eyeful*, fair, fine, foxy, good-looking, graceful, handsome, looker, lovely, neat, nice, picture, pleasant, pleasing, pulchritudinous, tasteful; SEE CONCEPT *579*

pretty [*adv*] *considerable; somewhat*
a little, ample, fairly, kind of, large, moderately, more or less, much, notable, pretty much, quite, rather, reasonably, sizable, some, something, sort of, tolerably; SEE CONCEPTS *531,569*

prevail [*v*] *dominate, control*
abound, beat, be common, be current, be prevalent, best, be usual, be victorious, be widespread, carry, come out on top*, command, conquer, domineer, exist generally, gain, get there, go great guns*, go places*, hit pay dirt*, luck out*, make it, make out, master, move out, obtain, overcome, overrule, predominate, preponderate, prove, reign, succeed, take off, triumph, win; SEE CONCEPTS *94,95,141*

prevailing [*adj*] *general, dominant*
all-embracing, by the numbers*, catholic, common, comprehensive, current, customary, ecumenical, established, familiar, fashionable, influential, in style, in vogue, main, operative, ordinary, popular, pre-

dominant, predominating, preponderating, prevalent, principal, rampant, regnant, regular, rife, ruling, set, steady, sweeping, universal, usual, widespread, worldwide; SEE CONCEPT *530*

prevail upon/prevail on [v] *persuade, influence*
affect, argue into, bring around, convince, crack, dispose, draw, get, get around, impress, incline, induce, promote, prompt, put across, ram down throat*, sell*, suck in*, sway, talk into, win over; SEE CONCEPT *68*

prevalent [adj1] *accepted, widespread*
accustomed, common, commonplace, current, customary, established, everyday, extensive, faddy, frequent, general, habitual, in use, latest*, latest word*, leading edge*, natural, new, normal, now*, ongoing, popular, prevailing, rampant, regnant, regular, rife, run-of-the-mill*, state-of-the-art*, stylish, swinging, trendy, typic, typical, ubiquitous, universal, up-to-date, usual, with it*, wonted; SEE CONCEPTS *530,547,589*

prevalent [adj2] *governing, superior*
ascendant, compelling, dominant, master, overbearing, paramount, powerful, predominant, predominate, preponderant, prevailing, regnant, ruling, sovereign, successful; SEE CONCEPTS *536,574*

prevaricate [v] *deceive; stretch the truth*
beat around the bush*, beg the question*, belie, cavil, con, distort, dodge, equivocate, evade, exaggerate, fabricate, falsify, fib, garble, hedge, invent, jive*, lie*, misrepresent, misspeak, palter, phony up*, put on*, quibble, shift, shuffle, tergiversate; SEE CONCEPT *63*

prevent [v] *keep from happening or continuing*
anticipate, arrest, avert, avoid, baffle, balk, bar, block, check, chill*, cool, cork, counter, counteract, dam, debar, defend against, foil, forbid, forestall, forfend, frustrate, halt, hamper, head off, hinder, hold back, hold off, impede, inhibit, intercept, interdict, interrupt, keep lid on*, limit, nip in the bud*, obstruct, obviate, preclude, prohibit, put an end to, put a stop to, repress, restrain, restrict, retard, rule out, shut out, stave off, stop, thwart, turn aside, ward off; SEE CONCEPT *121*

preview [n] *preliminary showing*
examination, preliminary study, research, show, sneak, sneak peek*, survey, viewing; SEE CONCEPTS *263,292,832*

previous [adj1] *former, prior*
antecedent, anterior, earlier, erstwhile, ex, foregoing, one-time, past, precedent, preceding, quondam, sometime; SEE CONCEPTS *585,811,818,820*

previous [adj2] *premature*
ahead of, early, inopportune, overearly, oversoon, precipitate, soon, too early, too soon, unfounded, untimely, unwarranted; SEE CONCEPTS *558,799*

previously [adv] *earlier*
ahead, already, ante, antecedently, at one time, away back, a while ago, back, back when, before, beforehand, erstwhile, fore, formerly, forward, heretofore, hitherto, in advance, in anticipation, in days gone by, in the past, long ago, once, one-shot, precedently, then, time was, until now; SEE CONCEPT *820*

prey [n] *target of attack*
casualty, chased*, dupe*, fall guy*, game, kill, loot, mark, martyr, mug*, pillage, quarry, quest, raven, spoil, sufferer, underdog, victim; SEE CONCEPTS *394,423*

prey on [v] *attack, terrorize*
blackmail, bleed, bully, burden, consume, depredate, devour, distress, eat, exploit, feed on, fleece, haunt, hunt, intimidate, live off, load, oppress, plunder, raid, seize, take advantage of, tax, trouble, victimize, weigh, worry; SEE CONCEPTS *14,86,169*

price [n1] *financial value*
amount, appraisal, appraisement, asking price, assessment, barter, bill, bounty, ceiling, charge, compensation, consideration, cost, damage, demand, disbursement, discount, dues, estimate, exaction, expenditure, expense, face value, fare, fee, figure, hire, outlay, output, pay, payment, premium, prize, quotation, ransom, rate, reckoning, retail, return, reward, score, sticker*, tab, tariff, ticket, toll, tune*, valuation, wages, wholesale, worth; SEE CONCEPT *329*

price [n2] *consequences of action*
cost, expense, penalty, sacrifice, toll; SEE CONCEPT *230*

price [v] *assess financial value*
appraise, cost, estimate, evaluate, fix, mark down, mark up, put a price on, rate, reduce, sticker, value; SEE CONCEPT *330*

priceless [adj1] *precious, irreplaceable*
beyond price, cherished, collectible, costly, dear, expensive, incalculable, incomparable, inestimable, invaluable, out-of-bounds*, out-of-sight*, prized, rare, rich, treasured, valuable, valued, without price, worth a king's ransom*, worth its weight in gold*; SEE CONCEPTS *334,568*

priceless [adj2] *extremely funny*
absurd, amusing, comic, droll, hilarious, humorous, killing, rib-tickling*, ridiculous, riotous, scream, sidesplitting; SEE CONCEPT *267*

prick [n] *small hole made by stab*
cut, gash, jab, jag, perforation, pinhole, prickle, puncture, stab, wound; SEE CONCEPT *309*

prick [v] *stab, perforate*
bore, cut, drill, enter, hurt, jab, lance, pierce, pink, punch, puncture, slash, slit, smart, spur, sting; SEE CONCEPT *220*

prickly [adj1] *thorny or difficult*
annoying, barbed, bothersome, brambly, briery, bristly, complicated, echinated, intricate, involved, knotty, nettlesome, pointed, sharp, spiny, stimulating, ticklish, tricky, troublesome, trying; SEE CONCEPTS *485,565*

prickly [adj2] *irritable, bad-tempered*
cantankerous, edgy, fractious, fretful, grumpy, irritable, peevish, petulant, snappish, touchy, waspish; SEE CONCEPT *401*

pride [*n1*] *self-esteem*
amour-propre, delight, dignity, ego, egoism, egotism, ego trip, face, gratification, happiness, honor, joy, pleasure, pridefulness, repletion, satisfaction, self-admiration, self-confidence, self-glorification, self-love, self-regard, self-respect, self-satisfaction, self-sufficiency, self-trust, self-worth, sufficiency; SEE CONCEPT *411*

pride [*n2*] *arrogance, self-importance*
airs, assumption, big-headedness*, cockiness*, conceit, condescension, contumely, disdain, disdainfulness, egoism, egotism, haughtiness, hauteur, hubris, huff, immodesty, insolence, loftiness, narcissism, overconfidence, patronage, pragmatism, presumption, pretension, pretentiousness, proud flesh*, self-exaltation, self-importance, self-love, smugness, snobbery, superbity, superciliousness, swagger, swelled head*, vainglory, vanity; SEE CONCEPT *633*

pride [*n3*] *treasure; best*
boast, choice, cream, elite, fat, flower*, gem*, glory, jewel*, pick, pride and joy*, prime, prize, top*; SEE CONCEPTS *446,668,689*

pride [*v*] *take pleasure in accomplishment*
be proud, boast, brag, congratulate, crow, exult, felicitate, flatter oneself, gasconade, glory in, hold head high, overbear, pique*, plume*, prance, preen, presume, puff up*, revel in, strut, swagger, swell, vaunt; SEE CONCEPTS *10,633*

priest [*n*] *man who is minister in Roman or Orthodox Catholic church*
churchman, clergyman, cleric, curate, divine, ecclesiastic, elder, father, father confessor, friar, holy man, lama, man of God, man of the cloth*, monk, padre, pontiff, preacher, rector, vicar; SEE CONCEPT *361*

prim [*adj*] *particular, fussy*
blue-nose*, ceremonial, ceremonious, choosy, cleanly, conventional, correct, dapper*, decorous, demure, fastidious, formal, genteel, good, goody-goody*, nice, nit-picking*, orderly, overmodest, polite, precise, priggish, prissy, proper, prudish, puritanical, rigid, shipshape*, spic-and-span*, spruce, stickling, stiff, straight, strait-laced, stuffy*, tidy, uncluttered, upright, Victorian, well-groomed, wooden*; SEE CONCEPTS *401,404*

primarily [*adv1*] *generally; for the most part*
above all, basically, chiefly, especially, essentially, fundamentally, generally, largely, mainly, mostly, on the whole, overall, predominantly, principally; SEE CONCEPTS *531,544,772*

primarily [*adv2*] *in the beginning*
at first, at the start, first and foremost, from the start, initially, in the first place, originally, primitively; SEE CONCEPTS *548,799*

primary/prime [*adj1*] *best, principal*
capital, cardinal, chief, crackerjack*, dominant, excellent, fab*, first, first-class*, greatest, heavy, highest, hot*, leading, main, number one*, paramount,

primo*, state-of-the-art*, stellar, top, top-of-the-line*, tough*, world-class*; SEE CONCEPTS *567,574*

primary/prime [*adj2*] *earliest*
aboriginal, beginning, direct, first, firsthand, immediate, initial, maiden, original, pioneer, primal, primeval, primitive, primordial, pristine; SEE CONCEPTS *585,799*

primary/prime [*adj3*] *basic, fundamental*
basal, beginning, bottom, central, elemental, elementary, essential, first, foundational, introductory, meat-and-potatoes*, original, primitive, principal, radical, rudimentary, simple, three Rs*, ultimate, underivative, underived, underlying; SEE CONCEPTS *549,585*

prime [*n1*] *best part of existence*
best, best days*, bloom, choice, cream*, elite, fat, flower*, flowering*, height, heyday, maturity, peak, perfection, pink*, prize, spring, springtime, top, verdure, virility, vitality, zenith; SEE CONCEPT *816*

prime [*n2*] *beginning; spring*
adolescence, aurora, dawn, daybreak, dew, greenness*, juvenility, morn*, morning, opening, puberty, pubescence, springtime, start, sunrise, sunup, tender years*, vitality, youth, youthfulness; SEE CONCEPTS *817,832*

prime [*v*] *get ready; prepare*
break in, brief, clue*, coach, cram, excite, fill in, fit, galvanize, groom, inform, innervate, make ready, motivate, move, notify, prep*, provoke, rehearse, stimulate, tell, train; SEE CONCEPTS *7,19,22,35,202*

primeval [*adj*] *ancient*
earliest, early, first, old, original, prehistoric, primal, primary, primitive, primordial, pristine; SEE CONCEPT *799*

primitive [*adj1*] *ancient, original*
archaic, basic, earliest, early, elementary, essential, first, fundamental, old, primal, primary, primeval, primordial, pristine, substratal, underivative, underived, underlying, undeveloped, unevolved; SEE CONCEPT *799*

primitive [*adj2*] *barbaric, crude*
animal, atavistic, austere, barbarian, barbarous, brutish, childlike, fierce, ignorant, naive, natural, nonliterate, preliterate, raw, rough, rude, rudimentary, savage, simple, uncivilized, uncultivated, uncultured, underdeveloped, undeveloped, undomesticated, unlearned, unrefined, unsophisticated, untamed, untaught, untrained, untutored, vestigial, wild; SEE CONCEPTS *406,485*

primordial [*adj*] *earliest*
basic, early, elemental, first, fundamental, original, prehistoric, primal, primary, prime, primeval, primitive, pristine, radical; SEE CONCEPT *799*

primp [*v*] *beautify and dress nicely*
deck out*, dress up, fix up, get dressed up, groom, gussy up*, preen, prepare, slick*, smarten, spiff, spruce, titivate; SEE CONCEPTS *162,167,202*

principal [*n1*] *person in charge of organization, often an educational one*
administrator, boss, chief, dean, director, exec*, guru, head, head man/woman*, headmaster/mistress, high priest, lead, leader, master, preceptor, protagonist, rector, ruler, star, superintendent; SEE CONCEPTS *347,350*

principal [*n2*] *original amount of property either owned or owed*
assets, capital, capital funds, money; SEE CONCEPT *332*

principal [*adj*] *most important*
arch, capital, cardinal, champion, chief, controlling, crowning, dominant, essential, first, foremost, greatest, head, highest, incomparable, key, leading, main, mainline, major, matchless, maximum, outstanding, paramount, peerless, predominant, preeminent, premier, prevailing, primary, prime, prominent, second-to-none, sovereign, star, stellar, strongest, supereminent, superior, supreme, transcendent, unapproachable, unequaled, unparalleled, unrivaled; SEE CONCEPTS *568,574*

principally [*adv*] *mainly*
above all, basically, before anything else, cardinally, chiefly, dominantly, eminently, especially, essentially, first and foremost, first of all, for the most part, fundamentally, generally, importantly, in the first place, in the main, largely, materially, mostly, notably, particularly, peculiarly, predominantly, preeminently, prevailingly, prevalently, primarily, substantially, superlatively, supremely, to a great degree, universally, vitally; SEE CONCEPTS *531, 544,772*

principle [*n1*] *law, standard*
assumption, axiom, basis, canon, convention, criterion, dictum, doctrine, dogma, ethic, form, formula, foundation, fundamental, golden rule*, ground, maxim, origin, postulate, precept, prescript, principium, proposition, regulation, rule, source, theorem, truth, usage, verity; SEE CONCEPTS *318,687*

principle/principles [*n2*] *belief, morality; morals*
attitude, character, code, conduct, conscience, credo, ethic, ethics, faith, ideals, integrity, opinion, policy, probity, rectitude, scruples, sense of duty, sense of honor, system, teaching, tenet, uprightness; SEE CONCEPTS *645,689*

print [*n*] *publication; something impressed*
black-and-white*, book, characters, composition, copy, edition, engraving, face, font, impress, impression, imprint, indentation, issue, lettering, letters, lithograph, magazine, newspaper, newsprint, periodical, photograph, printed matter, stamp, type, typeface, typescript, typesetting, writing; SEE CONCEPTS *259,265,280*

print [*v*] *produce writing, impression; reproduce publication*
calligraph, compose, disseminate, engrave, go to press, impress, imprint, issue, let roll, letter, mark,

offset, publish, put to bed*, reissue, reprint, run off, set, set type, stamp, strike off; SEE CONCEPTS *174,203,205*

prior [*adj*] *earlier*
above-mentioned, aforementioned, ahead, antecedent, anterior, before, foregoing, former, forward, past, precedent, preceding, preexistent, preexisting, previous; SEE CONCEPTS *811,812,818,820*

priority [*n*] *first concern*
antecedence, arrangement, crash project*, greatest importance, lead, order, precedence, preeminence, preference, prerogative, previousness, rank, right of way*, seniority, superiority, supremacy, transcendence; SEE CONCEPTS *532,668,727*

prison [*n*] *residence for incarcerating criminals*
bastille, can*, clink*, confinement, cooler*, dungeon, G*, guardhouse, jail, keep, lockup, pen*, penal institution, penitentiary, reformatory, slammer*, statesville*, stockade, up the river*; SEE CONCEPTS *439,449,516*

prisoner [*n*] *person jailed for crime; person kept against their will*
captive, chain gang member, con, convict, culprit, detainee, hostage, internee, jailbird*, lag*, lifer*, loser*, tough*, yardbird*; SEE CONCEPT *412*

prissy [*adj*] *particular and fussy*
effeminate, epicene, fastidious, finicky, genteel, goody-goody*, goody-two-shoes*, overnice, pansified, persnickety, picky, precious, prim, prim and proper*, prudish, puritanical, sissified, sissy, squeamish, stickling, strait-laced, stuffy*, tight-laced*, Victorian; SEE CONCEPTS *401,404*

privacy [*n*] *solitude, secrecy*
aloofness, clandestineness, concealment, confidentiality, isolation, one's space, penetralia, privateness, quiet, retirement, retreat, seclusion, separateness, separation, sequestration, solitude; SEE CONCEPTS *388,631,714*

private [*n*] *lowest rank of person enlisted in armed service*
doughboy*, enlisted man/woman, enlisted person, first-class*, GI, infantry, private soldier, sailor, second-class*, soldier; SEE CONCEPT *358*

private [*adj1*] *personal, intimate*
behind the scenes*, clandestine, closet*, close to one's chest*, confidential, discreet, exclusive, hushed, hush-hush*, independent, individual, inside, nonpublic, not open, off the record*, own, particular, privy*, reserved, secret, separate, special, under one's hat*, unofficial; SEE CONCEPTS *267,406*

private [*adj2*] *hidden, isolated*
concealed, discreet, quiet, removed, retired, secluded, secret, separate, sequestered, solitary, withdrawn; SEE CONCEPTS *576,583*

privilege [*n*] *right, due*
advantage, allowance, appanage, appurtenance, authority, authorization, benefit, birthright, boon, chance, charter, claim, concession, entitlement,

event, exemption, favor, franchise, freedom, grant, immunity, liberty, license, opportunity, perquisite, prerogative, right, sanction; SEE CONCEPT *376*

privileged [*adj1*] *favored, elite*
advantaged, entitled, honored, indulged, powerful, ruling, special; SEE CONCEPTS *334,574*

privileged [*adj2*] *allowed, exempt*
authorized, chartered, eligible, empowered, entitled, excused, franchised, free, furnished, granted, immune, kosher*, legit*, licensed, okay*, okayed*, palatine, qualified, sanctioned, special, vested; SEE CONCEPT *548*

privileged [*adj3*] *confidential, secret*
exceptional, for eyes only*, inside, not for publication, off the record*, on the QT*, privy, special, top secret, under one's hat*; SEE CONCEPT *267*

privy [*adj1*] *secret*
buried, concealed, confidential, covert, hidden, hush-hush*, obscured, off the record*, personal, private, separate, shrouded, ulterior; SEE CONCEPTS *267,576*

privy [*adj2*] *aware*
acquainted, apprised, cognizant, conscious, informed, in on*, in the know*, private, privileged, wise; SEE CONCEPT *402*

prize [*n1*] *award, winnings*
accolade, acquirement, acquisition, advantage, blue ribbon*, bonus, bounty, cake*, capture, carrot*, championship, citation, crown, decoration, dividend, feather in cap*, first place*, gold*, gold star*, gravy*, guerdon, haul, honor, inducement, jackpot, laurel, loot*, medal, meed, payoff, pickings*, pillage, plum*, plunder*, possession, premium, privilege, purse, recompense, requital, reward, scholarship, spoil, spoils, stakes, strokes*, swag*, title, trophy, windfall; SEE CONCEPTS *337,344,693,710*

prize [*n2*] *goal; best*
aim, ambition, choice, conquest, cream*, desire, elite, fat, flower*, gain, gold*, hope, pick, pride, prime, top*; SEE CONCEPTS *659,709*

prize [*adj*] *best*
award-winning, champion, choice, cream*, elite, fat, first-class*, first-rate*, outstanding, pick, prime, top, topnotch, winning; SEE CONCEPT *574*

prize [*v*] *value highly*
appreciate, apprize, cherish, count, enshrine, esteem, guard, hold dear, rate, regard highly, set store by*, treasure; SEE CONCEPTS *10,32*

probability [*n*] *likelihood of something happening*
anticipation, chance, chances, conceivability, contingency, credibility, expectation, feasibility, hazard, liability, likeliness, odds, outside chance*, plausibility, possibility, practicability, prayer, presumption, promise, prospect, reasonableness, shot, snowball chance*, toss-up*; SEE CONCEPT *650*

probable [*adj*] *likely to happen*
apparent, believable, credible, earthly, feasible, illusory, in the cards*, mortal, most likely, odds-on*,

ostensible, plausible, possible, presumable, presumed, rational, reasonable, seeming; SEE CONCEPT *552*

probably [*adv*] *likely to happen*
apparently, as likely as not, assumably, as the case may be, believably, dollars to doughnuts*, doubtless, expediently, feasibly, imaginably, in all likelihood, in all probability, like enough, maybe, most likely, no doubt, one can assume, perchance, perhaps, plausibly, possibly, practicably, presumably, presumptively, reasonably, seemingly, to all appearances; SEE CONCEPT *552*

probe [*n*] *investigation*
delving, detection, examination, exploration, fishing expedition*, inquest, inquiry, inquisition, legwork*, probing, quest, research, scrutiny, study, third degree*; SEE CONCEPTS *31,103,216,290*

probe [*v*] *explore, investigate*
ask, catechize, check, check out, check over, check up, delve into, dig, examine, eye, feel around, feel out, go into, inquire, interrogate, look into, look-see, penetrate, pierce, poke, prod, prospect, put out a feeler*, query, quiz, scrutinize, search, sift, sound, sound out, study, test, test the waters*, verify; SEE CONCEPTS *31,103,216*

probity [*n*] *fairness, honesty*
equity, fidelity, goodness, honor, integrity, justice, morality, rectitude, righteousness, rightness, sincerity, trustworthiness, truthfulness, uprightness, virtue, worth; SEE CONCEPTS *411,645*

problem [*n1*] *difficulty; bad situation*
botheration, box*, can of worms*, complication, count*, crunch*, dilemma, disagreement, dispute, disputed point, doubt, headache*, hitch*, hot water*, issue, mess*, obstacle, pickle*, point at issue*, predicament, quandary, question, scrape*, squeeze*, trouble, worriment; SEE CONCEPTS *666,674*

problem [*n2*] *puzzle, question*
brainteaser*, bugaboo*, cliff-hanger*, conundrum, enigma, example, grabber*, illustration, intricacy, mind-boggler*, mystery, poser*, puzzler, query, riddle, sixty-four dollar question*, stickler, stumper, teaser, twister; SEE CONCEPTS *529,532*

problematic [*adj*] *open to doubt*
ambiguous, arguable, chancy, debatable, disputable, doubtful, dubious, dubitable, enigmatic, iffy*, indecisive, moot, open, precarious, problematical, puzzling, questionable, suspect, tricky, uncertain, unsettled, up for grabs*; SEE CONCEPT *529*

procedure [*n*] *process, system for accomplishing something*
action, agenda, agendum, channels, conduct, course, custom, daily grind*, fashion, form, formula, game plan*, gimmick, grind, idea, layout, line, maneuver, measure, method, mode, modus operandi, move, nuts and bolts*, operation, performance, plan, policy, polity, practice, proceeding, program, red tape*, routine, scheme, setup, step, strategy, style, the book*, the numbers*, transaction; SEE CONCEPT *6*

proceed [v1] *physically or mentally carry on, carry out*
advance, continue, fare, get, get going, get on with, get under way*, go ahead, go on, hie, journey, make a start, march, move on, move out, pass, press on, progress, push on, repair, set in motion, travel, wend; SEE CONCEPTS *43,91*

proceed [v2] *flow from; originate*
arise, come, derive, emanate, ensue, extend, follow, head, issue, pass, result, rise, spring, stem; SEE CONCEPTS *179,230,676*

proceeding [n] *undertaking, course of action*
act, action, adventure, casualty, circumstance, come off, deed, exercise, experiment, go-down*, goings-on*, happening, incident, maneuver, measure, move, movement, occurrence, operation, performance, procedure, process, step, transaction, venture; SEE CONCEPTS *2,3*

proceedings [n] *account, report of event*
affairs, annals, archives, business, dealings, documents, doings*, matters, minutes, records, transactions; SEE CONCEPT *271*

proceeds [n] *earnings from business*
gain, gate, handle, income, interest, lucre, produce, product, profit, receipts, result, returns, revenue, reward, split, take, takings, till, yield; SEE CONCEPT *344*

process [n] *method; series of actions to achieve result*
action, advance, case, channels*, course, course of action*, development, evolution, fashion, formation, growth, manner, means, measure, mechanism, mode, modus operandi, movement, operation, outgrowth, performance, practice, procedure, proceeding, progress, progression, red tape*, routine, rule, stage, step, suit, system, technique, transaction, trial, unfolding, way, wise, working; SEE CONCEPT *6*

process [v] *subject to series of action to achieve result*
alter, concoct, convert, deal with, dispose of, fulfill, handle, make ready, prepare, refine, take care of, transform, treat; SEE CONCEPT *204*

procession [n] *parade, sequence*
advance, autocade, cavalcade, column, consecution, cortege, course, cycle, file, march, motorcade, movement, order, process, run, series, string, succession, train; SEE CONCEPTS *155,727*

proclaim [v] *advertise, make known*
affirm, announce, annunciate, blast, blaze, blazon, broadcast, call, circulate, declare, demonstrate, disseminate, enunciate, evidence, evince, exhibit, expound, get on a soapbox*, give out, herald, illustrate, indicate, manifest, mark, ostend, pass the word*, profess, promulgate, publish, shoot off mouth*, shout out, show, sound off, spiel*, spout, spread it around*, stump*, trumpet*, utter, vent, ventilate, voice; SEE CONCEPTS *49,60*

proclamation [n] *advertisement, announcement*
broadcast, declaration, decree, edict, manifesto, notice, notification, promulgation, pronouncement, pronunciamento*, publication; SEE CONCEPTS *271,278*

proclivity [n] *inclination, tendency*
bent*, bias, cup of tea*, disposition, druthers*, facility, flash*, groove*, inclining, leaning, liableness, penchant, predilection, predisposition, proneness, propensity, thing for*, type, weakness; SEE CONCEPTS *20,32,411*

procrastinate [v] *delay, put off doing*
adjourn, be dilatory, cool*, dally, dawdle, defer, drag, drag one's feet*, give the run around*, goldbrick*, hang fire*, hesitate, hold off, lag*, let slide, linger, loiter, pause, play a waiting game*, play for time*, poke*, postpone, prolong, protract, retard, shilly-shally*, stall, stay, suspend, tarry, temporize, wait; SEE CONCEPTS *121,237,681*

procreate [v] *reproduce*
beget, breed, conceive, create, engender, father, generate, get, give birth to, hatch, impregnate, make, mother, multiply, originate, parent, produce, progenerate, proliferate, propagate, sire, spawn; SEE CONCEPTS *173,251,374*

procure [v] *acquire, obtain*
annex, appropriate, bring around, buy, buy out, buy up, come by, compass, cop*, corral, draw, earn, effect, find, gain, get, get hold of, grab, have, induce, land*, latch on to, lay hands on, make a haul*, manage to get*, persuade, pick up, prevail upon, promote, purchase, score, secure, solicit, wangle, win; SEE CONCEPTS *68,120,327*

prod [v1] *poke at*
crowd, dig, drive, elbow, goose, jab, jog, nudge, press, prick, punch, push, shove; SEE CONCEPT *208*

prod [v2] *urge, incite*
crowd*, egg on*, excite, exhort, goad, goose*, impel, instigate, jog memory, motivate, move, pique, prick, prompt, propel, provoke, push, remind, rouse, sic*, sound, spark, spur, stimulate, stir up, trigger, turn on; SEE CONCEPTS *7,19,22,242*

prodigal [n] *person who spends a lot*
big spender*, compulsive shopper*, deep pockets*, dissipator, high roller*, profligate, spender, spendthrift, sport, squanderer, waster, wastrel; SEE CONCEPTS *348,412*

prodigal [adj1] *wasteful*
dissipated, excessive, extravagant, immoderate, improvident, intemperate, lavish, profligate, reckless, spendthrift, squandering, wanton; SEE CONCEPTS *401,560*

prodigal [adj2] *luxurious, profuse*
abundant, bounteous, bountiful, copious, exuberant, lavish, lush, luxuriant, moneyed, munificent, opulent, profusive, riotous, sumptuous, superabundant, teeming; SEE CONCEPTS *334,781*

prodigious [adj1] *huge, enormous*
big, colossal*, fantastic, giant, gigantic, gross, Herculean*, immeasurable, immense, inordinate, jumbo*, king-size*, large, mammoth, massive, mighty, monstrous, monumental, mortal, stupendous, towering, tremendous, vast; SEE CONCEPTS *773,781*

prodigious [*adj2*] *extraordinary, fabulous*
abnormal, amazing, astonishing, astounding, bad, exceptional, fab, fantastic, heavy, impressive, marvelous, miraculous, out-of-this-world*, phenomenal, preternatural, remarkable, spectacular, staggering, startling, state-of-the-art*, striking, stupendous, surprising, unreal, unusual, utmost, wonderful; SEE CONCEPTS *567,572,574*

prodigy [*n*] *person or thing that is extraordinary*
boy/girl wonder*, brain*, child genius, curiosity, enormity, freak*, genius, intellect, marvel, mastermind, miracle, monster, natural, one in a million*, phenomenon, portent, rare bird*, rarity, sensation, spectacle, stunner, talent, whiz*, whiz kid*, wizard, wonder, wonder child, wunderkind; SEE CONCEPTS *416,671,706*

produce [*n*] *fruit and vegetables*
crop, fruitage, goods, greengrocery, harvest, outcome, outgrowth, outturn, production, yield; SEE CONCEPTS *426,429,431,457,461*

produce [*v1*] *generate, create*
afford, assemble, author, bear, beget, blossom, breed, bring forth, bring out, build, come through, compose, conceive, construct, contribute, cultivate, deliver, design, develop, devise, effectuate, engender, erect, fabricate, fetch, flower, form, frame, furnish, give, give birth, give forth, imagine, invent, make, manufacture, multiply, offer, originate, parent, present, procreate, propagate, provide, put together, render, reproduce, return, show fruit, supply, turn out, write, yield; SEE CONCEPTS *205,374*

produce [*v2*] *cause, effect*
beget, breed, bring about, draw on, engender, generate, get up, give rise to, hatch, induce, make, make for, muster, occasion, provoke, result in, secure, set off, work up; SEE CONCEPT *242*

produce [*v3*] *demonstrate, show*
advance, bring forward, bring to light, display, exhibit, offer, present, put forward, set forth, unfold; SEE CONCEPT *261*

produce [*v4*] *put on a public performance*
act, come through, direct, do, exhibit, make, mount, percolate, perform, perk, play, present, pull off*, show, stage; SEE CONCEPTS *292,324*

product [*n*] *result or goods created*
aftermath, amount, artifact, blend, brand, brew, by-product, commodity, compound, concoction, confection, consequence, contrivance, creation, crop, decoction, device, effect, emolument, fabrication, fruit, gain, handiwork, invention, issue, legacy, line, manufacture, merchandise, offshoot, outcome, outgrowth, output, preparation, produce, production, profit, realization, result, returns, spinoff, stock, synthetic, upshot, work, yield; SEE CONCEPTS *230,338*

production [*n*] *creating of goods, result*
assembly, authoring, bearing, blossoming, construction, creation, direction, elongation, engendering, extention, fabrication, formulation, fructification, generation, giving, lengthening, making, manage-ment, manufacture, manufacturing, origination, preparation, presentation, producing, prolongation, protraction, provision, rendering, reproduction, return, staging, yielding; SEE CONCEPT *205*

productive [*adj*] *fruitful, creative*
advantageous, beneficial, constructive, dynamic, effective, energetic, fecund, fertile, gainful, generative, gratifying, inventive, plentiful, producing, profitable, prolific, rewarding, rich, teeming, useful, valuable, vigorous, worthwhile; SEE CONCEPTS *537,542,560*

productivity [*n*] *output, work rate*
abundance, capacity, fecundity, fertility, mass production, potency, production, productiveness, richness, yield; SEE CONCEPT *630*

profane [*adj*] *immoral, crude, disrespectful of religion*
abusive, atheistic, blasphemous, coarse, dirty*, filthy*, foul, godless, heathen, idolatrous, impious, impure, indecent, infidel, irreligious, irreverent, irreverential, mundane, nasty, obscene, pagan, profanatory, raunchy, sacrilegious, sinful, smutty*, temporal, transient, transitory, unconsecrated, ungodly, unhallowed, unholy, unsanctified, vulgar, wicked, worldly; SEE CONCEPTS *267,401,545*

profane [*v*] *defile, desecrate*
abuse, be evil, befoul, blaspheme, commit sacrilege, commit sin, contaminate, curse, cuss, damn, darn, debase, despoil, do wrong, flame, hoodoo*, misuse, mock, mudsling*, pervert, pollute, prostitute, put double whammy on*, revile, scorn, swear, talk dirty*, tar, trash, vice, violate, vitiate, voodoo*; SEE CONCEPTS *44,52,58,63*

profanity [*n*] *foul language*
abuse, blasphemy, curse, cursing, cuss, cuss word, dirty language*, dirty name*, dirty word*, execration, four-letter word*, impiety, imprecation, irreverence, malediction, no-no*, obscenity, profaneness, sacrilege, swearing, swearword, taboo; SEE CONCEPTS *278,645*

profess [*v*] *declare, assert*
acknowledge, act as if, admit, affirm, allege, announce, asseverate, aver, avouch, avow, blow hot air*, certify, claim, come out*, confess, confirm, constate, croon, cross heart*, depose, dissemble, fake, feign, get off chest*, get on soapbox*, maintain, make out, open up*, own, own up*, predicate, pretend, proclaim, purport, purport, say so*, sing*, soapbox*, spiel*, spout*, state, stump*, swear on bible*, swear up and down*, talk big*, vouch; SEE CONCEPTS *49,63*

profession [*n1*] *line of work requiring academic or practical preparation*
art, avocation, berth, billet, biz*, business, calling, career, chosen work, concern, craft, dodge*, employment, engagement, field, game*, handicraft, lifework, line*, line of work*, métier, occupation, office, position, post, pursuit, rat race*, role, service, situation, slot*, specialty, sphere, thing*, trade,

undertaking, vocation, walk of life*; SEE CONCEPT *360*

profession [n2] *declaration*
acknowledgment, affirmation, assertion, attestation, avowal, claim, confession, pretense, statement, testimony, vow; SEE CONCEPT *278*

professional [n] *person prepared for work by extended study or practice*
adept, artist, artiste, authority, brain*, egghead*, expert, hotshot*, maestro, master, maven, old hand*, old pro*, old war-horse*, past master, phenom, powerhouse, pro, proficient, pundit, shark, specialist, star, superstar, virtuoso, whiz*, whiz kid*, wizard; SEE CONCEPTS *347,348*

professional [adj] *skilled, trained*
able, ace, acknowledged, adept, competent, crackerjack*, efficient, experienced, expert, finished, knowing one's stuff*, known, learned, licensed, masterly, on the ball*, polished, practiced, proficient, qualified, sharp, skillful, slick*, there*, up to speed*, well-qualified; SEE CONCEPTS *326,402, 527,528*

professor [n] *person who teaches college courses*
assistant, brain*, don, educator, egghead*, faculty member, fellow, guru*, instructor, lecturer, maven, pedagogue, principal, prof*, pundit, quant*, rocket scientist*, sage, savant, schoolmaster/mistress, teacher, tutor; SEE CONCEPT *350*

proffer [v] *suggest, offer*
extend, gift, give, hand, hit on, hold out, make a pitch*, pose, present, propose, proposition, propound, submit, tender, volunteer; SEE CONCEPTS *66,67,75*

proficiency [n] *ability, skillfulness*
accomplishment, advance, advancement, aptitude, chops, competence, dexterity, efficiency, expertise, expertness, facility, formula, green thumb*, headway*, knack*, know-how*, knowledge, learning, makings, mastery, moxie*, oil*, progress, right stuff*, savvy, skill, stuff, talent, what it takes*; SEE CONCEPTS *409,630,706*

proficient [adj] *able, skilled*
accomplished, adept, apt, capable, clever, competent, consummate, conversant, crack*, crackerjack*, drilled, effective, effectual, efficient, exercised, experienced, expert, finished, gifted, master, masterful, masterly, on the beam*, phenom, pro, qualified, savvy, sharp, skillful, slick*, talented, trained, up to speed*, versed, whiz*, with it*; SEE CONCEPTS *402,527,528*

profile [n1] *drawing of outline*
contour, delineation, figuration, figure, form, likeness, line, lineament, lineation, portrait, shadow, shape, side view, silhouette, sketch; SEE CONCEPTS *259,625*

profile [n2] *description, characterization*
analysis, biography, character sketch, chart, diagram, review, sketch, study, survey, thumbnail sketch, vignette, vita; SEE CONCEPTS *268,283*

profit [n] *gain*
accumulation, acquisition, advancement, advantage, aggrandizement, augmentation, avail, benefit, bottom line*, cleanup, earnings, emoluments, gate*, goods*, gravy*, gross, harvest, income, interest, killing, lucre, net, output, outturn, percentage, proceeds, product, production, receipt, receipts, remuneration, return, revenue, saving, skim*, split*, surplus, take*, takings*, turnout, use, value, velvet*, winnings, yield; SEE CONCEPTS *332,344,693*

profit [v] *gain; get or give an advantage*
aid, avail, benefit, be of advantage, better, capitalize on, cash in on, clean up, clear, contribute, earn, exploit, help, improve, learn from, make a haul*, make a killing*, make capital, make good use of*, make it big*, make money, make the most of*, pay, pay off, promote, prosper, put to good use*, realize, reap the benefit*, recover, score, serve*, stand in good stead*, take advantage of, thrive, turn to advantage, use, utilize, work for; SEE CONCEPTS *110,124,330,693*

profitable [adj] *advantageous; money-making*
assisting, beneficial, commercial, conducive, contributive, cost-effective, effective, effectual, favorable, fruitful, gainful, going*, good, instrumental, in the black*, lucrative, paid off, paying, paying well, practical, pragmatic, productive, remunerative, rewarding, self-sustaining, serviceable, successful, sustaining, sweet, useful, valuable, well-paying, worthwhile; SEE CONCEPTS *334,537,572*

profligate [n] *person who is immoral*
debauchee, degenerate, dissipater, good-for-nothing*, lecher, libertine, nighthawk*, no-good*, old goat*, operator*, playboy/girl, prodigal, rake, reprobate, roué, swinger, waster, wastrel; SEE CONCEPT *412*

profligate [adj1] *immoral, corrupt*
abandoned, debauched, degenerate, depraved, dissipated, dissolute, iniquitous, lax, lewd, libertine, licentious, loose, promiscuous, reprobate, shameless, unprincipled, vicious, vitiated, wanton, wicked, wild; SEE CONCEPT *545*

profligate [adj2] *wasteful*
extravagant, immoderate, improvident, lavish, prodigal, reckless, spendthrift, squandering; SEE CONCEPTS *334,401*

profound [adj1] *intellectual, thoughtful*
abstruse, acroamatic, deep, difficult, discerning, enlightened, erudite, esoteric, heavy, hermetic, informed, intellectual, intelligent, knowing, knowledgeable, learned, mysterious, occult, Orphic, penetrating, philosophical, recondite, reflective, sagacious, sage, scholarly, secret, serious, shrewd, skilled, subtle, thorough, weighty, wise; SEE CONCEPTS *402,529*

profound [adj2] *bottomless*
abysmal, buried, cavernous, deep, fathomless, subterranean, yawning; SEE CONCEPT *777*

profound [*adj3*] *intense; emotional*
abject, absolute, acute, consummate, deep, deeply felt, deep-seated, exhaustive, extensive, extreme, far-reaching, great, hard, heartfelt, heartrending, hearty, intense, keen, out-and-out, pronounced, sincere, thorough, total, utter; SEE CONCEPTS *403, 531,569*

profuse [*adj*] *abundant, excessive*
abounding, alive with*, ample, aplenty, bounteous, bountiful, copious, crawling with*, dime a dozen*, extravagant, extreme, exuberant, fulsome, galore, generous, immoderate, lavish, liberal, lush, luxuriant, no end*, openhanded, opulent, overflowing, plentiful, plenty, prodigal, profusive, prolific, riotous, sumptuous, superfluous, swarming, teeming, thick with*, unstinting; SEE CONCEPTS *762,781*

progeny [*n*] *offspring*
begats, breed, children, descendants, family, get*, issue, kids*, lineage, posterity, progeniture, race, scions, seed, stock, young; SEE CONCEPTS *296,414*

prognosis [*n*] *forecast*
cast, diagnosis, expectation, foretelling, guess, prediction, prevision, prognostication, projection, prophecy, speculation, surmise; SEE CONCEPTS *274,689*

prognosticate [*v*] *predict, foretell*
adumbrate, augur, betoken, call it*, crystal-ball*, divine, forebode, forecast, foreshadow, harbinger, have a hunch*, herald, make book*, point to, portend, presage, prophesy, read, see coming*, soothsay, vaticinate; SEE CONCEPT *70*

program [*n1*] *agenda, list*
affairs, appointments, arrangements, bill, bulletin, business, calendar, card, catalog, chores, curriculum, details, docket, happenings, index, lineup, listing, meetings, memoranda, necessary acts*, order of business*, order of events*, order of the day*, plan, plans, preparations, record, schedule, series of events, slate, syllabus, things to do*, timetable; SEE CONCEPTS *281,283*

program [*n2*] *scheme, plan*
course, design, instructions, line, order, plan of action, policy, polity, procedure, project, sequence; SEE CONCEPTS *274,660*

program [*n3*] *performance in medium*
broadcast, presentation, production, show; SEE CONCEPT *263*

program [*v*] *plan out; supply instructions*
arrange, bill, book, budget, calculate, compile, compute, design, draft, edit, engage, enter, estimate, feed, figure, formulate, get on line*, itemize, lay on, lay out, line up, list, map out, pencil in*, poll, prearrange, prioritize, process, register, schedule, set, set up, slate, work out; SEE CONCEPTS *36,60,84,384*

progress [*n*] *advancement, gain*
advance, amelioration, anabasis, betterment, boost, break, breakthrough, buildup, course, dash, development, evolution, evolvement, expedition, flowering, growth, headway, hike, impetus, improvement, increase, journey, lunge, march, momentum, motion, movement, ongoing, pace, passage, process, procession, proficiency, progression, promotion, rate, rise, step forward, stride, tour, unfolding, voyage, way; SEE CONCEPTS *704,706*

progress [*v1*] *move forward*
advance, continue, cover ground*, dash, edge, forge ahead, gain ground, get along, get on, go forward, keep going, lunge, make headway*, make strides*, move on, proceed, shoot, speed, travel; SEE CONCEPTS *149,159*

progress [*v2*] *improve, advance*
ameliorate, become better, better, blossom, boost, develop, gain, grow, increase, make first rate, mature, shape up, straighten up, truck, turn over new leaf*, upgrade; SEE CONCEPT *700*

progressive [*adj*] *liberal; growing*
accelerating, advanced, advancing, avant-garde*, bleeding-heart*, broad, broad-minded, continuing, continuous, developing, dynamic, enlightened, enterprising, escalating, forward-looking, go-ahead*, gradual, graduated, increasing, intensifying, left*, left of center*, lenient, modern, ongoing, onward, open-minded, radical, reformist, revolutionary, tolerant, up-and-coming*, up-to-date, wide; SEE CONCEPTS *542,544*

prohibit [*v*] *make impossible; stop*
ban, block, bottle up*, box in*, bring to screeching halt*, constrain, cool*, cork*, debar, disallow, enjoin, forbid, forfend, freeze*, gridlock, halt, hamper, hang up*, hinder, hold up, impede, inhibit, interdict, jam up*, keep lid on*, kill, lock up, nix, obstruct, outlaw, pass on*, preclude, prevent, proscribe, put a lock on*, put a stopper in*, put chill on*, put down, put half nelson on*, restrain, restrict, rule out, shut out, spike*, stymie*, taboo*, throw cold water on*, tie up*, veto, zing*; SEE CONCEPTS *50,88,121,130,317*

prohibited [*adj*] *forbidden*
banned, barred, closed down, contraband, crooked*, illegal, illicit, no-no*, not allowed, not approved, off limits*, out of bounds*, out of line*, proscribed, refused, restricted, shady*, taboo, verboten, vetoed, wildcat*; SEE CONCEPTS *554,576*

prohibition [*n*] *ban, forbiddance*
bar, constraint, disallowance, don't*, embargo, exclusion, injunction, interdict, interdiction, negation, no-no*, obstruction, off limits*, out of bounds*, prevention, proscription, refusal, repudiation, restriction, taboo, temperance, veto; SEE CONCEPTS *121,130,652,691*

prohibitive [*adj*] *restrictive; beyond one's financial means*
conditional, excessive, exorbitant, expensive, extortionate, forbidding, high-priced, limiting, preposterous, preventing, prohibiting, proscriptive, repressive, restraining, sky-high*, steep*, suppressive; SEE CONCEPTS *334,554*

project [n] *undertaking, work*
activity, adventure, affair, aim, assignment, baby*, blueprint*, business, concern, deal, design, enterprise, exploit, feat, game plan, intention, job, matter, occupation, outline, pet*, plan, program, proposal, proposition, scheme, setup, strategy, task, thing*, venture; SEE CONCEPTS *324,349,362*

project [v1] *plan*
arrange, blueprint, calculate, cast, chart, conceive, contemplate, contrive, delineate, design, devise, diagram, draft, envisage, envision, estimate, extrapolate, feature, forecast, frame, gauge, image, imagine, intend, map out, outline, predetermine, predict, propose, purpose, reckon, scheme, see, think, vision, visualize; SEE CONCEPTS *28,36,37,70*

project [v2] *bulge, hang out*
be conspicuous, beetle, be prominent, extend, hang over, jut, lengthen, overhang, poke, pop out, pout, prolong, protrude, protuberate, push out, stand out, stick out, stretch out, thrust out; SEE CONCEPT *747*

project [v3] *throw, discharge*
cast, fling, heave, hurl, launch, pitch, propel, shoot, transmit; SEE CONCEPTS *179,222*

projection [n1] *bulge, overhang*
bump, bunch, eaves, extension, hook, jut, knob, ledge, outthrust, point, prolongation, prominence, protrusion, protuberance, ridge, rim, shelf, sill, spine, spur, step, swelling; SEE CONCEPTS *471, 509,513*

projection [n2] *prediction*
calculation, computation, estimate, estimation, extrapolation, forecast, guess, prognostication, reckoning; SEE CONCEPTS *28,278*

proliferate [v] *increase quickly*
breed, burgeon, engender, escalate, expand, generate, grow rapidly, multiply, mushroom*, procreate, propagate, reproduce, run riot*, snowball*; SEE CONCEPT *780*

prolific [adj] *fruitful, productive*
abounding, abundant, bountiful, breeding, copious, creative, fecund, fertile, generating, generative, luxuriant, profuse, proliferant, rank, reproducing, reproductive, rich, spawning, swarming, teeming, yielding; SEE CONCEPTS *485,542*

prolong [v] *extend, draw out*
carry on, continue, delay, drag one's feet*, drag out*, hold, hold up, increase, lengthen, let it ride*, make longer, pad*, perpetuate, protract, spin out*, stall, stretch, stretch out; SEE CONCEPTS *239,250*

prominence [n1] *something that sticks out*
bulge, bump, cliff, conspicuousness, crag, crest, elevation, eminence, headland, height, high point, jutting, markedness, mound, pinnacle, projection, promontory, protrusion, protuberance, rise, spur, swelling, tor; SEE CONCEPTS *513,836*

prominence [n2] *distinction, outstandingness*
celebrity, eminence, fame, greatness, illustriousness, importance, influence, kudos*, name, notability, precedence, preeminence, prestige, rank, renown, reputation, salience, specialness, standing, top billing*, weight; SEE CONCEPT *668*

prominent [adj1] *sticking out; conspicuous*
arresting, beetling, bulging, easily seen, embossed, extended, extrusive, eye-catching, flashy, hanging out, hilly, in the foreground, jutting, marked, noticeable, obtrusive, obvious, outstanding, projecting, pronounced, protruding, protrusive, protuberant, raised, relieved, remarkable, rough, rugged, salient, shooting out, signal, standing out, striking, to the fore, unmistakable; SEE CONCEPTS *485,583,619*

prominent [adj2] *very important; famous*
big-league*, big-name*, big-shot*, celebrated, chief, distinguished, eminent, famed, foremost, great, high-profile*, leading, main, notable, noted, notorious, outstanding, popular, preeminent, renowned, respected, top, underlined, VIP*, well-known, well-thought-of, world-class*; SEE CONCEPT *568*

promiscuous [adj] *very sexually active*
abandoned, debauched, dissipated, dissolute, easy*, fast*, immoral, indiscriminate, lax, libertine, licentious, loose*, of easy virtue, oversexed, profligate, pushover, run around*, unbridled, unchaste, undiscriminating, unrestricted, wanton, wild; SEE CONCEPTS *372,545*

promise [n1] *one's word that something will be done*
affiance, affirmation, agreement, asseveration, assurance, avowal, betrothal, bond, commitment, compact, consent, contract, covenant, earnest, engagement, espousal, guarantee, insurance, marriage, oath, obligation, pact, parole, pawn, pledge, plight, profession, promissory note, sacred word, security, stipulation, swear, swearing, token, troth, undertaking, vow, warrant, warranty, word, word of honor; SEE CONCEPTS *71,278*

promise [n2] *hope, possibility*
ability, aptitude, capability, capacity, encouragement, flair, good omen, outlook, potential, talent; SEE CONCEPTS *630,650*

promise [v1] *give word that something will be done*
accede, affiance, affirm, agree, answer for, assent, asservate, assure, bargain, betroth, bind, commit, compact, consent, contract, covenant, cross heart*, declare, engage, ensure, espouse, guarantee, hock*, insure, live up to*, mortgage, obligate, pass, pawn*, pledge, plight, profess, say so*, secure, stipulate, string along*, subscribe, swear, swear on bible*, swear up and down*, take an oath, undertake, underwrite, vouch, vow, warrant; SEE CONCEPT *71*

promise [v2] *bring hope, possibility*
augur, bespeak, betoken, bode, denote, encourage, forebode, foreshadow, foretoken, give hope, hint, hold out hope*, hold probability, indicate, lead to expect, like, look, omen, portend, presage, seem likely, show signs of*, suggest; SEE CONCEPTS *118,650*

promising [adj] hopeful
able, assuring, auspicious, bright, encouraging, favorable, gifted, happy, likely, lucky, propitious, reassuring, rising, roseate, rosy, talented, up-and-coming; SEE CONCEPTS *406,548*

promote [v1] help, advance
advertise, advocate, aid, assist, avail, back, befriend, benefit, bolster, boost, build up*, call attention to, champion, contribute, cooperate, cry*, develop, encourage, endorse, espouse, forward, foster, further, get behind, hype*, improve, nourish, nurture, patronize, plug*, popularize, propagandize, publicize, puff*, push, push for, recommend, sell, serve, speak for, speed, sponsor, stimulate, subsidize, succor, support, uphold, urge, work for; SEE CONCEPTS *49,110,324*

promote [v2] give a higher position in organization
advance, aggrandize, ascend, better, dignify, elevate, ennoble, exalt, favor, graduate, honor, increase, kick upstairs*, magnify, move up, prefer, raise, skip, up*, upgrade; SEE CONCEPT *351*

promotion [n1] higher position in organization
advance, advancement, advocacy, aggrandizement, backing, betterment, boost, break, breakthrough, buildup, bump, elevation, encouragement, ennoblement, exaltation, favoring, furtherance, go-ahead*, hike, honor, improvement, jump, jump up, lift, move up, preference, preferment, prelation, progress, raise, rise, step up, support, upgrade, upgrading; SEE CONCEPT *351*

promotion [n2] publicity
advertising, advertising campaign, ballyhoo*, blurb*, buildup*, hard sell*, hoopla*, hype*, notice, pitch, pizzazz*, plug*, PR*, press*, press-agentry, promo*, propaganda, publicity, public relations, puff*, puffery*, pushing, squib*; SEE CONCEPTS *49,110,271,324*

prompt [n] hint
cue, help, jog, jolt, mnemonic, prod, reminder, spur, stimulus, twit; SEE CONCEPT *274*

prompt [adj] early, responsive
alert, apt, brisk, eager, efficient, expeditious, immediate, instant, instantaneous, on the ball*, on the button*, on the dot*, on the nose*, on time, precise, punctual, quick, rapid, ready, smart, speedy, swift, timely, unhesitating, vigilant, watchful, wide-awake, willing; SEE CONCEPTS *401,799*

prompt [v] incite, cue
advise, aid, arouse, assist, bring up, call forth, cause, convince, draw, egg on*, elicit, evoke, exhort, get, give rise to, goad, help, help out, hint, impel, imply, indicate, induce, inspire, instigate, jog, mention, motivate, move, occasion, persuade, prick*, prod, propel, propose, provoke, refresh, remind, sic*, spur, stimulate, suggest, talk into, urge, win over; SEE CONCEPTS *68,242*

promptly [adv] immediately
at once, directly, expeditiously, fast, flat-out*, fleetly, hastily, in nothing flat*, instantly, lickety-split*, like a shot*, now, on the dot*, on the double*, on time, PDQ*, posthaste, pronto, punctually, quickly, rapidly, right away, sharp, speedily, straightaway, swiftly, unhesitatingly; SEE CONCEPTS *544,799*

promulgate [v] make known
advertise, announce, annunciate, broadcast, call, circulate, communicate, declare, decree, disseminate, drum, issue, make public, notify, pass the word, proclaim, promote, publish, sound, spread, toot, trumpet; SEE CONCEPT *60*

prone [adj1] lying down
decumbent, face down, flat, horizontal, level, procumbent, prostrate, reclining, recumbent, resupine, supine; SEE CONCEPT *583*

prone [adj2] liable, likely
apt, bent, devoted, disposed, exposed, fain, given, inclined, minded, open, predisposed, ready, sensitive, subject, susceptible, tending, willing; SEE CONCEPTS *542,552*

pronounce [v1] produce words vocally
accent, articulate, enunciate, phonate, say, sound, speak, stress, utter, verbalize, vocalize, voice; SEE CONCEPT *47*

pronounce [v2] announce, declare
affirm, assert, blast, call, decree, deliver, drum, judge, mouth, proclaim, say, sound off, spread around, trumpet, verbalize; SEE CONCEPT *49*

pronounced [adj] distinct, evident
arresting, assured, broad, clear, clear-cut, conspicuous, decided, definite, marked, notable, noticeable, obvious, outstanding, striking, strong, unmistakable; SEE CONCEPTS *535,576,619*

pronouncement [n] declaration, statement
advertisement, announcement, broadcast, decree, dictum, edict, judgment, manifesto, notification, proclamation, promulgation, pronunciamento, publication, report, statement, ukase; SEE CONCEPTS *271,274,278*

proof [n1] evidence, authentication
affidavit, argument, attestation, averment, case, certification, chapter and verse*, cincher*, clue, confirmation, corroboration, credentials, criterion, cue*, data, demonstration, deposition, documents, establishment, exhibit, facts, goods*, grabber*, grounds, information, lowdown*, nitty-gritty*, paper trail*, picture, reason, reasons, record, scoop*, score*, skinny*, smoking gun*, straight stuff*, substantiation, testament, testimony, trace, validation, verification, warrant, wherefore*, why*, whyfor*, witness; SEE CONCEPT *274*

proof [n2] photographic print
galley, galley proof, impression, page proof, pass, pull, repro, revise, slip, stereo, trial, trial print, trial proof; SEE CONCEPT *265*

prop [n] support
aid, assistance, brace, buttress, column, mainstay, post, shore, stanchion, stay, strengthener, strut, truss, underpinning; SEE CONCEPTS *440,470*

prop [v] *hold up or lean against*
bear up, bolster, brace, buoy, buttress, carry, maintain, rest, set, shore, stand, stay, strengthen, support, sustain, truss, underprop, uphold; SEE CONCEPTS *190,201*

propaganda [n] *information that is designed to mislead or persuade*
advertising, agitprop, announcement, brainwashing, disinformation, doctrine, evangelism, handout, hogwash*, hype*, implantation, inculcation, indoctrination, newspeak, promotion, promulgation, proselytism, publication, publicity; SEE CONCEPT *278*

propagate [v1] *breed, reproduce*
bear, beget, engender, father, fecundate, fertilize, generate, grow, impregnate, increase, inseminate, make pregnant, mother, multiply, originate, procreate, produce, proliferate, raise, sire; SEE CONCEPT *374*

propagate [v2] *spread, make known*
broadcast, circulate, develop, diffuse, disperse, disseminate, distribute, proclaim, promulgate, publicize, publish, radiate, scatter, strew, transmit; SEE CONCEPTS *60,222*

propel [v] *throw; release into air*
actuate, drive, force, impel, launch, mobilize, move, press, push, send, set going, set in motion, shoot, shove, start, thrust; SEE CONCEPTS *208,221,222*

propensity [n] *inclination, weakness*
ability, aptness, bent*, bias, capacity, competence, disposition, flash, inclining, leaning, liability, partiality, penchant, predilection, predisposition, proclivity, proneness, susceptibility, sweet tooth*, talent, tendency, thing*, tilt*, yen; SEE CONCEPTS *20,411,630,709*

proper [adj1] *suitable*
able, applicable, appropriate, apt, au fait, becoming, befitting, capable, competent, convenient, decent, desired, felicitous, fit, fitting, good, happy, just, legitimate, meet, qualified, right, suited, true, useful; SEE CONCEPT *558*

proper [adj2] *mannerly, decent*
becoming, befitting, by the book*, by the numbers*, comely, comme il faut*, conforming, correct, decorous, demure, de rigueur*, genteel, gentlemanly, in line, kosher*, ladylike, moral, nice, polite, precise, priggish, prim, prissy, prudish, punctilious, puritanical, refined, respectable, right, seemly, solid, square*, stone, straight*, strait-laced, stuffy*; SEE CONCEPTS *401,404*

proper [adj3] *conventional, correct*
absolute, accepted, accurate, arrant, complete, consummate, customary, decorous, established, exact, formal, free of error, on target*, on the button*, on the nose*, on the right track*, orthodox, out-and-out*, precise, right, unmistaken, usual, utter; SEE CONCEPTS *326,533*

proper [adj4] *individual, personal*
characteristic, distinctive, idiosyncratic, own, particular, peculiar, private, respective, special, specific; SEE CONCEPTS *549,557*

property [n1] *possessions, real estate*
acreage, acres, assets, belongings, buildings, capital, chattels, claim, dominion, effects, equity, estate, farm, freehold, goods, holdings, home, house, inheritance, land, means, ownership, plot, possessorship, premises, proprietary, proprietorship, realty, resources, riches, substance, title, tract, wealth, worth; SEE CONCEPTS *446,509,515,710*

property [n2] *characteristic, feature*
ability, affection, attribute, character, hallmark, idiosyncrasy, mark, peculiarity, quality, trait, virtue; SEE CONCEPTS *411,654*

prophecy [n] *prediction*
apocalypse, augury, cast, divination, forecast, foretelling, oracle, presage, prevision, prognosis, prognostication, revelation, second sight, soothsaying, vision; SEE CONCEPTS *70,278,689*

prophesy [v] *predict, warn*
adumbrate, augur, call*, call the turn*, crystal-ball*, divine, forecast, foresee, foretell, forewarn, have a hunch*, make book*, portend, predict, presage, prognosticate, psych it out*, see coming*, soothsay, vaticinate; SEE CONCEPT *70*

prophet [n] *person, thing that predicts future*
astrologer, augur, auspex, bard, clairvoyant, diviner, druid, evocator, forecaster, fortuneteller, haruspex, horoscopist, magus, medium, meteorologist, oracle, ovate, palmist, predictor, prognosticator, prophesier, reader, seer, seeress, sibyl, soothsayer, sorcerer, tea-leaf reader, witch, wizard; SEE CONCEPTS *361,423*

prophetic [adj] *telling of the future*
apocalyptic, augural, Delphian*, divinatory, fatidic, foreshadowing, mantic, occult, oracular, predictive, presaging, prescient, prognostic, prophetical, pythonic, sibylline, vaticinal, veiled; SEE CONCEPT *267*

propitious [adj1] *full of promise; good, favorable*
advantageous, auspicious, beneficial, benign, brave, bright, dexter, encouraging, favoring, fortunate, happy, hopeful, lucky, opportune, pat, promising, prosperous, rosy, seasonable, timely, toward, useful, well-timed; SEE CONCEPTS *548,560,572*

propitious [adj2] *friendly*
benevolent, benign, favorably inclined, gracious, kind, nice, well-disposed; SEE CONCEPT *401*

proponent [n] *person who advocates, supports cause*
advocate, backer, champion, defender, enthusiast, exponent, expounder, friend, partisan, patron, protector, second, seconder, spokesman/woman, spokesperson, subscriber, supporter, upholder, vindicator; SEE CONCEPTS *355,359,423*

proportion [n1] *relative amount, size of part to whole*
admeasurement, amplitude, apportionment, breadth, bulk, capacity, cut, degree, dimension, distribution, division, equation, expanse, extent, fraction, magnitude, measure, measurement, part, percentage, portion, quota, rate, ratio, relationship, scale, scope, segment, share, volume; SEE CONCEPTS *730,783*

proportion [n2] *balance between parts of whole*
agreement, congruity, correspondence, harmony, symmetry; SEE CONCEPTS *664,717*

proportionate/proportional [adj] *balanced, corresponding*
commensurable, commensurate, comparable, comparative, compatible, consistent, contingent, correlative, correspondent, corresponding, dependent, equal, equitable, equivalent, even, in proportion, just, reciprocal, relative, symmetrical, uniform; SEE CONCEPTS *480,563*

proposal [n] *suggestion, presentation for action*
angle, bid, big idea*, brain child*, design, feeler*, game plan*, idea, layout, motion, offer, outline, overture, pass, picture, pitch, plan, proffer, program, project, proposition, recommendation, scenario, scheme, setup, tender, terms; SEE CONCEPTS *271,324,662*

propose [v1] *suggest, present for action*
adduce, advance, advise, affirm, ask, assert, broach, come up with*, contend, counsel, hit on*, hold out, introduce, invite, kibitz*, lay before*, lay on the line*, make a motion, make a pitch*, move for, name, nominate, offer, pose, prefer, press, proffer, propone, proposition, propound, put forward, put to, put up, recommend, request, set forth, solicit, speak one's piece*, spitball*, state, submit, tender, urge, volunteer; SEE CONCEPTS *66,75*

propose [v2] *intend; have in mind*
aim, contemplate, design, have every intention, mean, mind, plan, purpose, scheme; SEE CONCEPTS *26,36*

propose [v3] *ask for hand in marriage*
ask in marriage, fire the question*, get down on one knee*, make a proposal, offer marriage, pop the question*, press one's suit*; SEE CONCEPTS *48,297*

proposition [n] *suggestion; scheme*
hypothesis, invitation, motion, overture, plan, premise, presentation, proffer, program, project, proposal, recommendation; SEE CONCEPTS *384,662*

proposition [v] *make suggestion, often improper*
accost, approach, ask, pose, prefer, propose, propound, put, solicit, suggest; SEE CONCEPTS *48,375*

proprietor [n] *person who owns something*
freeholder*, front office, holder, landlady, landlord, land owner, master, meal ticket*, owner, possessor, proprietary, proprietress, slumlord, titleholder; SEE CONCEPTS *343,347*

propriety [n1] *suitableness, appropriateness*
accordance, advisability, agreeableness, appositeness, aptness, becomingness, compatibility, concord, congruity, consonance, convenience, correctness, correspondence, decorum, ethicality, expedience, fitness, harmony, justice, legitimacy, meetness, morality, order, pleasantness, properness, recommendability, rectitude, respectability, rightness, seemliness, suitability; SEE CONCEPT *656*

propriety [n2] *good manners*
accepted conduct, amenities, breeding, civilities, correctness, courtesy, decency, decorum, delicacy, dignity, etiquette, good behavior, good form, manners, modesty, mores*, niceties, politeness, politesse, protocol, punctilio, rectitude, refinement, respectability, rules of conduct, seemliness, social conventions, social grace, the done thing*; SEE CONCEPTS *633,644*

prosaic [adj] *unimaginative*
actual, banal, blah*, boring, clean, colorless, common, commonplace, dead*, diddly*, drab, dry, dull, everyday, factual, flat*, garden-variety*, hackneyed, ho-hum*, humdrum*, irksome, lackluster, lifeless, literal, lowly, lusterless, matter-of-fact, monotonous, mundane, nothing, nowhere, ordinary, pabulum*, pedestrian, platitudinous, plebeian, practicable, practical, prose, prosy, routine, square, stale, tame, tedious, trite, uneventful, unexceptional, uninspiring, vanilla*, vapid, workaday, yawn*, zero*; SEE CONCEPTS *267,537,547*

proscribe [v] *condemn, exclude*
ban, banish, blackball*, boycott, censure, damn, denounce, deport, doom*, embargo, excommunicate, exile, expatriate, expel, forbid, interdict, ostracize, outlaw, prohibit, reject, sentence; SEE CONCEPTS *25,121,317*

prose [n] *written, nonrhythmic literature*
book, composition, essay, exposition, fiction, nonfiction, speech, story, talk, text, tongue*, writing; SEE CONCEPTS *268,271*

prosecute [v1] *bring action against in court*
arraign, bring suit, bring to trial, contest, do, haul into court*, indict, involve in litigation, law, litigate, prefer charges, pull up, put away, put on docket, put on trial, see in court*, seek redress, sue, summon, take to court, try, turn on the heat*; SEE CONCEPT *317*

prosecute [v2] *follow through, persevere*
carry on, carry through, conduct, continue, direct, discharge, engage in, execute, follow through, follow up, manage, perform, persist, practice, pursue, put through, see through, wage, work at; SEE CONCEPT *91*

prospect [n1] *outlook for future*
anticipation, calculation, chance, contemplation, expectancy, expectation, forecast, future, hope, in the cards*, irons in the fire*, likelihood, odds, opening, plan, possibility, presumption, probability, promise, proposal, thought; SEE CONCEPTS *689,693*

prospect [n2] *landscape, vista*
aspect, lookout, outlook, overlook, panorama, perspective, scape, scene, sight, spectacle, view, vision; SEE CONCEPTS *509,628*

prospect [v] *look for; seek*
delve, dig, explore, go after, go into, inquire, investigate, look, look into, probe, search, sift, survey; SEE CONCEPT *216*

prospective [adj] anticipated, potential
about to be, approaching, awaited, coming, considered, destined, eventual, expected, forthcoming, future, hoped-for, imminent, impending, intended, likely, looked-for, planned, possible, promised, proposed, soon-to-be, to be*, to come; SEE CONCEPTS 548,552

prospectus [n] details, outline of event
announcement, catalogue, conspectus, design, list, plan, program, scheme, syllabus, synopsis; SEE CONCEPT 283

prosper [v] be fortunate; succeed
advance, arrive, augment, batten, bear, bear fruit, become rich, become wealthy, be enriched, benefit, bloom, blossom, catch on*, do well, do wonders*, fare well, fatten*, feather nest*, flourish, flower, gain, get on*, get there*, go places*, go to town*, grow rich, hit it big, hit the jackpot*, increase, make a killing*, make good*, make it*, make mark*, make money, make out*, multiply, produce, progress, rise, score*, strike it rich*, thrive, turn out well, yield; SEE CONCEPT 706

prosperity [n] affluence, good fortune
abundance, accomplishment, advantage, arrival, bed of roses*, benefit, boom, clover, do, ease*, easy street*, exorbitance, expansion, flying colors*, fortune, good, good times, gravy train*, growth, high on the hog*, increase, inflation, interest, life of luxury*, luxury, opulence, plenteousness, plenty, prosperousness, riches, success, successfulness, the good life*, thriving, velvet, victory, wealth, welfare, well-being; SEE CONCEPTS 335,706

prosperous [adj1] successful, thriving
affluent, blooming, booming, comfortable, doing well, easy, flourishing, fortunate, halcyon, in clover*, in the money*, lousy rich, lucky, main-line*, moneyed, money to burn*, on top of heap*, opulent, palmy, prospering, rich, roaring, robust, sitting pretty*, snug, substantial, upper-class*, uptown, wealthy, well, well-heeled*, well-off, well-to-do; SEE CONCEPTS 334,528

prosperous [adj2] promising, advantageous
appropriate, auspicious, bright, convenient, desirable, favorable, felicitous, fortunate, good, happy, lucky, opportune, profitable, propitious, seasonable, timely, well-timed; SEE CONCEPTS 548,572

prostitute [n] person who sells sex
bawd, call girl, concubine, courtesan, fallen woman*, floozy*, gigolo, harlot, hooker, host/hostess, hustler, nymphomaniac*, painted*, pickup*, pro*, streetwalker, whore; SEE CONCEPTS 348,412,415,419

prostitute [v] degrade oneself
abuse, cheapen, corrupt, debase, debauch, demean, deprave, devalue, misapply, misemploy, misuse, pervert, profane, vitiate, wench, whore; SEE CONCEPTS 156,645

prostrate [adj1] flat, horizontal
abject, bowed low, procumbent, prone, reclining, recumbent, supine; SEE CONCEPT 583

prostrate [adj2] helpless
beaten, defenseless, disarmed, impotent, open, overcome, overpowered, overwhelmed, paralyzed, powerless, reduced, weak; SEE CONCEPT 542

prostrate [adj3] tired, worn
crippled, dejected, depressed, disarmed, drained, drowned, exhausted, fagged*, fallen, frazzled*, immobilized, incapacitated, inconsolable, knocked over*, obedient, overcome, paralyzed, pooped*, spent*, submissive, subservient, tuckered*, wearied, worn out; SEE CONCEPTS 406,485

prostrate [v1] fall on knees; submit
abase, bow, bow down, cast before, cringe, fall at feet, give in, grovel, kneel, kowtow*, obey, surrender; SEE CONCEPT 384

prostrate [v2] overwhelm; wear out
bring low, cripple, debilitate, defeat, destroy, disable, disarm, drain, drown, exhaust, fatigue, fell, floor, frazzle*, immobilize, impair, incapacitate, knock over, level, mow*, overcome, overpower, overthrow, overtire, overturn, paralyze, reduce, ruin, sap, tire, tucker out*, weary, whelm, wreck; SEE CONCEPTS 95,250,252

protagonist [n] person who takes the lead; central figure of narrative
advocate, central character, champion, combatant, exemplar, exponent, hero, heroine, idol, lead, lead character, leader, mainstay, prime mover, principal, standard-bearer, warrior; SEE CONCEPTS 352,359,423

protect [v] take care of; guard from harm
assure, bulwark, care for, champion, chaperon, conserve, cover, cover all bases*, cover up, cushion, defend, fend, foster, give refuge, give sanctuary*, go to bat for*, harbor, hedge, insulate, keep, keep safe, look after, preserve, ride shotgun for*, safeguard, save, screen, secure, sentinel, shade, shelter, shield, shotgun*, stand guard, stonewall*, support, take under wing*, watch, watch over; SEE CONCEPTS 96,134

protection [n] care, guardianship
aegis, armament, armor, assurance, barrier, buffer, bulwark, camouflage, certainty, charge, conservation, cover, custody, defense, fix, guard, guarding, insurance, invulnerability, preservation, protecting, reassurance, refuge, safeguard, safekeeping, safety, salvation, screen, security, self-defense, shelter, shield, stability, strength, surety, tutelage, umbrella*, ward, wardship; SEE CONCEPTS 712,729

protective [adj] guarding, securing
careful, conservational, conservative, covering, custodial, defensive, emergency, fatherly, guardian, insulating, jealous, maternal, motherly, paternal, possessive, preservative, protecting, safeguarding, sheltering, shielding, vigilant, warm, watchful; SEE CONCEPTS 542,550

protest [n] complaint, disapproval
bellyache*, big stink*, blackball*, challenge, clamor, declaration, demonstration, demur, demurral, difficulty, dissent, flak*, formal complaint, grievance,

gripe, grouse*, holler*, howl, kick*, knock*, march, moratorium, nix, objection, outcry, protestation, question, rally, remonstrance, remonstration, revolt, riot, stink*, tumult, turmoil; SEE CONCEPTS 52,54,300

protest [v] *complain, disapprove; argue against*
affirm, assert, asseverate, attest, avouch, avow, back-talk*, be against, be displeased by, blast*, buck, combat, constate, contend, cry out, declare, demonstrate, demur, disagree, except, expostulate, fight, holler, howl, insist, inveigh against, kick*, maintain, make a stink*, object, oppose, predicate, profess, put up a fight*, rebel, remonstrate, resist, revolt, say no*, sound off*, squawk*, take exception*, testify, thumbs down*; SEE CONCEPTS 46, 52,54,300

protocol [n] *rules of conduct, behavior in certain situation*
agreement, code, compact, concordat, contract, conventions, courtesy, covenant, custom, decorum, etiquette, formalities, good form, manners, obligation, order, pact, politesse, propriety, p's and q's*, treaty; SEE CONCEPTS 684,687

prototype [n] *original, example*
ancestor, antecedent, antecessor, archetype, criterion, first, forerunner, ideal, mock-up*, model, norm, paradigm, pattern, precedent, precursor, predecessor, standard, type; SEE CONCEPT 688

protract [v] *extend, draw out*
continue, cool*, defer, delay, drag on*, drag out*, draw, elongate, hold off, hold up, keep going, lengthen, pad*, postpone, procrastinate, prolong, prolongate, put off, put on hold, spin out*, stall, stretch, stretch out; SEE CONCEPTS 237,239,250

protrude [v] *stick out*
beetle, bulge, butt out, come through, distend, extend, extrude, jut, jut out, obtrude, overhang, point, poke, pop, pouch, pout, project, shoot out, stand out, start, stick up, swell; SEE CONCEPTS 208,746

protuberance [n] *lump, outgrowth*
bulge, bump, excrescence, jut, jutting, knob, outthrust, process, projection, prominence, protrusion, swelling, tumor; SEE CONCEPTS 471,824

proud [adj1] *pleased, pleasing*
appreciative, august, content, contented, dignified, eminent, fiery, fine, glad, glorious, gorgeous, grand, gratified, gratifying, great, great-hearted, honored, illustrious, imposing, impressive, magnificent, majestic, memorable, noble, red-letter*, rewarding, satisfied, satisfying, self-respecting, spirited, splendid, stately, sublime, superb, valiant, vigorous, well-pleased; SEE CONCEPTS 403,572,574

proud [adj2] *arrogant, self-important*
bloated, boastful, cavalier, cocky*, conceited, contemptuous, cool*, disdainful, dismissive, domineering, egotistic, egotistical, haughty, high-and-mighty*, high-handed*, huffy*, imperious, insolent, lofty, lordly, masterful, narcissistic, ostentatious, overbearing, pompous, presumptuous, pretentious,

puffed up*, scornful, self-satisfied, sniffy*, snobbish, snooty*, stuck-up*, supercilious, superior, vain, vainglorious; SEE CONCEPTS 401,542

prove [v] *establish facts; put to a test*
add up, affirm, analyze, ascertain, assay, attest, authenticate, back, bear out, certify, check, confirm, convince, corroborate, declare, demonstrate, determine, document, end up, establish, evidence, evince, examine, experiment, explain, find, fix, have a case*, justify, make evident, manifest, pan out*, put to the test*, result, settle, show, show clearly, show once and for all*, substantiate, sustain, test, testify, trial, try, turn out, uphold, validate, verify, warrant, witness; SEE CONCEPTS 57,118,138

proverb [n] *saying referring to common fact, knowledge*
adage, aphorism, apophthegm, axiom, byword, catch phrase, daffodil*, dictum, epigram, folk wisdom, gnome, maxim, moral, motto, platitude, precept, repartee, saw*, saying, text, truism, witticism, word; SEE CONCEPTS 275,278

proverbial [adj] *conventional, traditional*
accepted, acknowledged, archetypal, axiomatic, current, customary, famed, familiar, famous, general, legendary, notorious, self-evident, time-honored, typical, unquestioned, well-known; SEE CONCEPT 530

provide [v1] *supply, support*
accommodate, add, administer, afford, arrange, bestow, bring, care, cater, contribute, dispense, equip, favor, feather*, feed, fit, fit out, fix up, fix up with, furnish, give, grant, hand over, heel*, impart, implement, indulge, keep, lend, line, look after, maintain, minister, outfit, prepare, present, procure, produce, proffer, provision, ration, ready, render, replenish, serve, stake, stock, stock up*, store, supply, sustain, take care of, transfer, turn out, yield; SEE CONCEPTS 108,110,136,140

provide [v2] *determine, specify*
condition, lay down, postulate, require, state, stipulate; SEE CONCEPTS 18,646

provident [adj] *careful, frugal*
canny, cautious, discreet, economical, expedient, far-sighted, foresighted, judicious, penny-pinching*, politic, prepared, prudent, sagacious, saving, shrewd, sparing, thrifty, tight, unwasteful, vigilant, well-prepared, wise; SEE CONCEPTS 334,401

providing/provided [conj] *as long as; with the understanding*
contingent upon, given, if, if and only if, in case, in the case that, in the event, on condition, on the assumption, on these terms, subject to, supposing, with the proviso; SEE CONCEPTS 544,546

province [n] *area of rule, responsibility*
arena, bailiwick, business, calling, canton, capacity, champaign, charge, colony, concern, county, demesne, department, dependency, district, division, domain, dominion, duty, employment, field, function, jurisdiction, line, office, orbit, part, post, pur-

suit, realm, region, role, section, shire, sphere, terrain, territory, tract, walk, work, zone; SEE CONCEPTS *198,349,362,508,532*

provincial [*adj*] *countrified; limited*
bigoted, bucolic, country, hidebound, homegrown, homespun, insular, inward-looking, local, narrow, narrow-minded, parochial, pastoral, petty, rude, rural, rustic, sectarian, small-minded, small-town, uninformed, unpolished, unsophisticated; SEE CONCEPTS *403,549,589*

provision [*n1*] *supplies, supplying*
accouterment, arrangement, catering, emergency, equipping, fitting out, foundation, furnishing, groundwork, outline, plan, prearrangement, precaution, preparation, procurement, providing, stock, store, supplying; SEE CONCEPTS *140,712*

provision/proviso [*n2*] *stipulation, condition of agreement*
agreement, catch*, Catch-22*, clause, demand, fine print*, joker*, kicker*, limitation, prerequisite, qualification, requirement, reservation, restriction, rider, small print*, specification, stipulation, strings*, term, terms; SEE CONCEPTS *270,684,711*

provisional [*adj*] *contingent, tentative*
conditional, dependent, ephemeral, experimental, interim, limited, makeshift, passing, pro tem, provisionary, provisory, qualified, rough-and-ready*, stopgap*, temporary, test, transient, transitional; SEE CONCEPTS *546,554,711*

provocation [*n*] *incitement, stimulus*
affront, annoyance, bothering, brickbat*, casus belli, cause, challenge, dare, defy, grabber*, grievance, grounds, harassment, incentive, indignity, inducement, injury, instigation, insult, irking, justification, motivation, offense, provoking, reason, taunt, vexation, vexing; SEE CONCEPTS *14,240,532*

provocative [*adj1*] *aggravating*
annoying, challenging, disturbing, exciting, galling, goading, heady, incensing, inciting, influential, inspirational, insulting, intoxicating, offensive, outrageous, provoking, pushing, spurring, stimulant, stimulating; SEE CONCEPT *529*

provocative [*adj2*] *sexually stimulating*
alluring, arousing, enchanting, erotic, exciting, heady, interesting, intoxicating, intriguing, inviting, seductive, sexy, stimulating, suggestive, tantalizing, tempting; SEE CONCEPTS *372,537*

provoke [*v1*] *make angry*
abet, abrade, affront, aggravate, anger, annoy, bother, bug*, chafe, enrage, exasperate, exercise, foment, fret, gall*, get*, get on one's nerves*, get under one's skin*, grate, hit where one lives*, incense, incite, inflame, infuriate, insult, irk, irritate, madden, make blood boil*, make waves*, nag, offend, perturb, pique, put out, raise, rile, roil, ruffle, set*, set on*, try one's patience*, upset, vex, whip up*, work into lather*, work up*; SEE CONCEPTS *7,19*

provoke [*v2*] *start, evoke; stimulate*
animate, arouse, awaken, begin, bestir, bring about, bring down, bring on, bring to one's feet*, build up, call forth, cause, challenge, draw forth, electrify, elicit, enthuse, excite, fire, fire up*, galvanize, generate, give rise to, incite, induce, inflame, innervate, innerve, inspire, instigate, kindle, lead to, make, motivate, move, occasion, pique, precipitate, prime, produce, promote, prompt, quicken, rally, rouse, roust, stir, suscitate, thrill, titillate, titivate, waken, whet; SEE CONCEPTS *7,19,22,221,242*

prowess [*n1*] *ability, skill*
accomplishment, address, adeptness, adroitness, aptitude, attainment, command, deftness, dexterity, excellence, expertise, expertness, facility, genius, mastery, readiness, sleight, talent; SEE CONCEPT *630*

prowess [*n2*] *bravery*
backbone*, boldness, courage, daring, dauntlessness, fearlessness, gallantry, grit*, guts*, heart*, heroism, intrepidity, mettle, moxie*, nerve, pluck, right stuff*, spunk, starch*, stomach*, stuff*, true grit*, valiance, valiancy, valor, valorousness, what it takes*; SEE CONCEPTS *411,633*

prowl [*v*] *move stealthily*
cruise, hunt, lurk, nose around*, patrol, range, roam, rove, scavenge, skulk, slink, snake, sneak, stalk, steal, stroll, tramp; SEE CONCEPT *151*

proximity [*n*] *nearness to something*
adjacency, appropinquity, closeness, concurrence, contiguity, contiguousness, immediacy, juxtaposition, propinquity, togetherness; SEE CONCEPT *747*

prudent [*adj*] *wise, sensible in action and thought*
advisable, canny, careful, cautious, circumspect, discerning, discreet, economical, far-sighted, frugal, hedging one's bets*, judgmatic, judicious, leery, playing safe*, politic, provident, reasonable, sagacious, sage, sane, sapient, shrewd, sound, sparing, tactical, thinking twice*, thrifty, vigilant, wary; SEE CONCEPTS *401,542*

prudish [*adj*] *shy and strict in behavior*
affected, artificial, austere, bigoted, conventional, demure, fastidious, finicky*, genteel, illiberal, mincing, narrow, narrow-minded, offish, old-maid, overexact, overmodest, overnice, precise, pretentious, priggish*, prim, prissy*, proper, puritanical, rigid, rigorous, scrupulous, severe, simpering, square, squeamish*, starchy*, stern, stiff*, stilted, straitlaced, strict, stuffy, uptight*, Victorian*; SEE CONCEPT *401*

prune [*v*] *trim; cut short*
clip, cut back, dock, eliminate, exclude, gut, knock off, lop, pare down, reduce, shape, shave, shear, shorten, skive, snip, thin; SEE CONCEPTS *137, 176,236,247*

pry [*v1*] *interfere in someone else's business*
be a busybody*, be all ears*, be curious, be inquisitive, be nosy, bug*, ferret out, gape, gaze, hunt, inquire, intrude, investigate, listen in, meddle, nose,

peek, peep, peer, poke, poke nose into*, ransack, reconnoiter, rubberneck*, search, snoop, spy, stare, tap, tune in on*, wiretap; SEE CONCEPTS *216,384,623*

pry [*v2*] *force or break open*
disengage, disjoin, divide, elevate, elicit, extort, extract, heave, hoist, jimmy, lever, lift, move, pick up, press, prize, pull, push, raise, rear, separate, take up, tear, tilt, turn, turn out, twist, uplift, upraise, uprear, wrest, wring; SEE CONCEPTS *196,206,211*

psalm [*n*] *song of praise*
canticle, celebration, chant, chorale, eulogy, hymn, paean, shout, verse; SEE CONCEPT *595*

pseudo [*adj*] *artificial, fake*
bogus, counterfeit, ersatz, false, imitation, mock, not genuine, not kosher*, not legit*, not real, phony, pirate, pretend, pretended, quasi*, queer*, sham*, simulated, spurious, wrong; SEE CONCEPT *582*

pseudonym [*n*] *false name*
AKA*, alias, ananym, anonym, assumed name, handle*, incognito*, nickname, nom de guerre, nom de plume, pen name, professional name, stage name, summer name*; SEE CONCEPTS *268,683*

psyche [*n*] *innermost self; personality*
anima, animus, character, ego, élan vital, essential nature, individuality, inner child, inner man/woman, mind, pneuma, self, soul, spirit, spirituality, subconscious, true being; SEE CONCEPTS *410,411*

psychedelic [*adj*] *affecting the mind so as to produce vivid visions*
consciousness-expanding, crazy*, experimental, freaky*, hallucinatory, hallucinogenic, kaleidoscopic, mind-bending*, mind-blowing*, mind-changing, mind-expanding*, multicolored*, psychoactive, psychotomimetic, psychotropic, trip*; SEE CONCEPTS *529,537*

psychiatrist [*n*] *person who treats mental disorders*
analyst, clinician, doctor, guru, psychoanalyst, psychologist, psychotherapist, shrink*, therapist; SEE CONCEPT *357*

psychic [*adj*] *extrasensory in perception*
analytic, cerebral, clairvoyant, immaterial, impressible, impressionable, intellective, intellectual, mental, metaphysical, mystic, occult, preternatural, psychal, psychical, psychogenic, psychological, responsive, sensible, sensile, sensitive, sentient, spiritual, supernatural, supersensible, supersensitive, supersensory, supersensual, susceptible, susceptive, telekinetic, telepathic, transmundane, unworldly; SEE CONCEPTS *402,403*

psychological [*adj*] *concerning the mind*
cerebral, cognitive, emotional, experimental, imaginary, intellective, intellectual, in the mind, irrational, mental, psychical, psychosomatic, subconscious, subjective, unconscious, unreal; SEE CONCEPTS *403,536*

psychology [*n*] *study of the mind; emotional and mental constitution*
attitude, behaviorism, medicine, mental make-up, mental processes, personality study, psych*, science

of the mind, therapy, way of thinking*, where head is at*; SEE CONCEPTS *349,360,410*

psychopath [*n*] *person who is mentally deranged, often prone to hurt others*
antisocial personality, insane person, lunatic, madman/woman, maniac, mental case*, nutcase*, psycho*, psychotic, schizoid*, sociopath, unstable personality; SEE CONCEPT *412*

psychotic [*adj*] *mentally deranged*
certifiable*, crazy, demented, distracted, flipped-out*, insane, lunatic, mad, manic-depressive, mental, non compos mentis, nuts*, off one's rocker*, over the edge*, psycho*, psychopathic, schizophrenic, sick, unbalanced, unhinged*; SEE CONCEPT *403*

pub [*n*] *business where liquor and food are served*
after-hours joint*, ale house*, bar, barroom, beer joint*, drinkery, drinking establishment, gin mill*, inn, joint*, lounge, public house, roadhouse, saloon, taproom, tavern; SEE CONCEPTS *439,448,449*

puberty [*n*] *young adulthood*
adolescence, awkward stage*, boyhood, girlhood, greenness*, high-school years, juvenescence, juvenility, potency, preadolescence, pubescence, spring*, springtide*, springtime*, teenage years, teens, youth, youthfulness; SEE CONCEPT *817*

public [*n*] *people of community; people interested in something*
audience, bodies*, buyers, citizens, clientele, commonalty, community, country, electorate, everyone, followers, following, heads, masses, men and women, mob, multitude, nation, patrons, people, populace, population, society, suite, supporters, voters; SEE CONCEPTS *379,417*

public [*adj1*] *community, general*
accessible, city, civic, civil, common, communal, conjoint, conjunct, country, federal, free, free to all, government, governmental, intermutual, metropolitan, municipal, mutual, national, not private, open, open-door, popular, social, state, universal, unrestricted, urban, widespread, without charge; SEE CONCEPTS *536,576*

public [*adj2*] *known, acknowledged*
exposed, general, in circulation, notorious, obvious, open, overt, patent, plain, popular, prevalent, published, recognized, social, societal, usual, vulgar, widespread; SEE CONCEPTS *267,530*

publication [*n1*] *printing of written or visual material*
advertisement, airing, announcement, appearance, broadcast, broadcasting, communication, declaration, disclosure, discovery, dissemination, divulgation, issuance, issuing, notification, proclamation, promulgation, pronunciamento, publicity, public relations, publishing, reporting, revelation, statement, ventilation, writing; SEE CONCEPTS *60,274,292*

publication [*n2*] *something printed for reading*
annual, book, booklet, brochure, handbill, information, issue, leaflet, magazine, news, newsletter, newspaper, pamphlet, periodical; SEE CONCEPT *280*

publicity [n] *promotion of something, someone*
advertising, announcement, announcing, attention, ballyhoo*, big noise*, billing, blurb*, boost*, broadcasting, build-up*, clout*, commercial, currency, distribution, fame, handout, hoopla*, hype*, ink*, limelight*, noise*, notoriety, pitch, plug*, PR*, press, press-agentry, promo*, promulgation, propaganda, public notice, public relations, puff*, puffery*, pushing, réclame, release, report, scratch*, spotlight*, spread, write-up; SEE CONCEPTS *274,280,293*

publicize [v] *make widely known; promote*
advance, advertise, announce, bill, billboard, boost*, broadcast, build up*, cry, drum*, extol, hard sell*, headline, hype*, immortalize, make a pitch for, pitch, play up*, plug*, press-agent, promulgate, propagandize, puff*, push, put on the map*, skywrite*, soft-sell*, splash, spot*, spotlight*, spread, tout, trumpet*, write up; SEE CONCEPTS *60,292,324*

pucker [n] *wrinkle*
crease, crinkle, crumple, fold, furrow, plait, ruck, ruckle; SEE CONCEPT *754*

pucker [v] *draw together; wrinkle*
cockle, compress, condense, contract, crease, crinkle, crumple, fold, furrow, gather, knit, purse, ruckle, ruck up, ruffle, screw up, squeeze, tighten; SEE CONCEPTS *185,219*

pudgy [adj] *slightly fat*
chubby*, hefty, plump, plumpish, rotund, round, stout, thick-bodied, tubby*; SEE CONCEPTS *491,773*

puerile [adj] *childish*
babyish, babylike, boyish, callow, foolish, girlish, green*, immature, inane, inexperienced, infantile, irresponsible, jejune, juvenile, naive, petty, ridiculous, silly, trivial, unfledged, ungrown, weak, young; SEE CONCEPTS *401,578,797*

puff [n1] *blast of air*
breath, draft, drag, draught, draw, emanation, flatus, flurry, gust, pull, smoke, waft, whiff, wind, wisp; SEE CONCEPTS *437,524*

puff [n2] *advertisement*
advertising, blurb*, boost*, buildup*, commendation, favorable mention, good word, hype*, laudation, plug*, praise, press-agentry, promo*, promotion, publicity, puffery*, push*, sales talk, write-up; SEE CONCEPTS *69,278,324*

puff [v1] *inhale or exhale air*
blow, breathe, distend, drag, draw, enlarge, fill, gasp, gulp, heave, huff, huff and puff*, inflate, pant, pull at, pull on, smoke, suck, swell, wheeze, whiff; SEE CONCEPTS *163,185,526*

puff [v2] *publicize*
admire, advertise, ballyhoo*, blow up*, build, commend, congratulate, cry*, flatter, hype*, overpraise, plug*, praise, press-agent*, promote, push; SEE CONCEPTS *49,69*

puffy [adj] *swollen*
billowy, bloated, blown, bulgy, distended, distent, enlarged, expanded, full, increased, inflamed, inflated, puffed up; SEE CONCEPT *485*

pugnacious [adj] *belligerent*
aggressive, antagonistic, argumentative, bellicose, brawling, cantankerous, chip on shoulder*, choleric, combative, contentious, defiant, disputatious, have a bone to pick*, hot-tempered, irascible, irritable, itching to fight*, militant, petulant, pushing, pushy*, quarrelsome, ready to fight, rebellious, salty*, scrappy*, self-assertive, truculent, warlike; SEE CONCEPTS *401,542*

pull [v1] *drawing something with force*
cull, dislocate, drag, evolve, extract, gather, haul, heave, jerk, lug, paddle, pick, pluck, remove, rend, rip, row, schlepp*, sprain, strain, stretch, take out, tear, tow, trail, truck, tug, twitch, uproot, weed, wrench, yank; SEE CONCEPT *206*

pull [v2] *attract*
draw, entice, get, lure, magnetize, obtain, pick up, secure, win; SEE CONCEPT *11*

pull down [v] *destroy; knock over*
annihilate, bulldoze, decimate, demolish, destruct, dismantle, let down, lower, raze, remove, ruin, take down, tear down, wreck; SEE CONCEPT *252*

pull in [v1] *arrest*
apprehend, bust, collar, detain, nab, nail, pick up, pinch, run in, take into custody; SEE CONCEPTS *90,317*

pull in [v2] *attract, obtain*
absorb, bring in, clear, draw, draw in, earn, gain, gross, make, net, pocket, suck, take home*; SEE CONCEPT *120*

pull off [v] *accomplish*
achieve, bring off, carry out, manage, score, score a success, secure, succeed, win; SEE CONCEPTS *91,706*

pull out [v] *quit*
abandon, depart, evacuate, exit, get off, go, leave, retire, retreat, shove off, stop, stop participating, take off, withdraw; SEE CONCEPTS *119,121,195*

pull through [v] *recover*
come through, get better, get over, improve, rally, ride out*, survive, triumph, weather*; SEE CONCEPTS *303,700,706*

pull up [v] *stop, halt*
arrive, brake, bring up, come to a halt, come to a stop, draw up, fetch up, get there, haul up, pause, reach a standstill; SEE CONCEPTS *119,121,159*

pulp [n] *flesh of plant, animal*
batter, curd, dough, grume, jam, marrow, mash, mush, pap, paste, pomace, poultice, sarcocarp, semisolid, soft part, sponge, triturate; SEE CONCEPTS *399,428*

pulp [adj] *cheap, vulgar, especially regarding reading material*
lurid, mushy, rubbish, sensational, trash, trashy; SEE CONCEPT *267*

pulp [v] *mash, pulverize*
bruise, coagulate, crush, gelatinate, macerate, squash, triturate; SEE CONCEPTS *208,219*

pulpit [n] *structure from which sermon is given*
desk, lectern, platform, podium, rostrum, soapbox*, stage, stump*; SEE CONCEPTS *368,443*

pulsate/pulse [v] *quiver, beat*
drum, fluctuate, hammer, oscillate, palpitate, pound, pump, roar, throb, thrum, thud, thump, tick, vibrate; SEE CONCEPTS *147,185*

pulse [n] *rhythm, beat*
beating, oscillation, pulsation, stroke, throb, throbbing, vibration; SEE CONCEPTS *147,185*

pulverize [v1] *smash by beating, crushing*
abrade, atomize, beat, bray, break up, buck, comminute, contriturate, crumble, crunch, crush, flour, fragment, fragmentalize, fragmentize, granulate, grate, grind, levigate, micronize, mill, mull, pestle, pound, powder, shatter, splinter, triturate; SEE CONCEPTS *186,219*

pulverize [v2] *destroy*
annihilate, crush, decimate, defeat, demolish, destruct, dynamite, flatten, rub out*, ruin, shatter, smash, tear down*, vanquish, vaporize, wax, wreck; SEE CONCEPT *252*

pump [v1] *draw or push out*
bail out, blow up, dilate, distend, draft, drain, draw, draw off, drive, drive out, elevate, empty, force, force out, inflate, inject, pour, push, send, siphon, supply, swell, tap; SEE CONCEPTS *142,206,208*

pump [v2] *question relentlessly*
cross-examine, draw out, give the third degree*, grill, interrogate, probe, query, question, quiz, worm out of*; SEE CONCEPTS *48,53*

pun [n] *play on words*
ambiguity, calembour, conceit, double entendre, double meaning, equivoque, joke, paronomasia, quibble, quip, witticism; SEE CONCEPTS *273,278*

punch [n1/v1] *hit*
bash, belt, biff, blow, bop, box, buffet, clip, clout, cuff, dig, jab, jog, knock, lollop, nudge, one-two*, plug, plunk*, poke, prod, pummel, rap, shot, slam, slap, slug, smack, smash, sock, strike, stroke, thrust, thump, wallop; SEE CONCEPT *189*

punch [n2] *energy, vigor*
bite, cogency, drive, effectiveness, force, forcefulness, impact, point, validity, validness, verve; SEE CONCEPTS *676,682*

punch [v2] *perforate, prick*
bore, cut, drill, jab, pierce, poke, puncture, stab, stamp; SEE CONCEPT *220*

punctilious [adj] *careful, finicky*
ceremonious, conscientious, conscionable, conventional, exact, formal, formalistic, fussy, good eye*, heedful, meticulous, nice, observant, overconscientious, overscrupulous, painstaking, particular, persnickety, precise, proper, punctual, right on*, scrupulous, strict; SEE CONCEPTS *401,542,557*

punctual [adj] *on time*
accurate, careful, conscientious, conscionable, constant, cyclic, dependable, early, exact, expeditious, fussy, heedful, in good time*, meticulous, on schedule, on the button*, on the dot*, on the nose*, painstaking, particular, periodic, precise, prompt, punctilious, quick, ready, recurrent, regular, reliable, scrupulous, seasonable, steady, strict, timely, under the wire*; SEE CONCEPTS *544,550,799*

punctuate [v] *lay stress on*
accent, accentuate, break, divide, emphasize, interject, interrupt, intersect, intersperse, mark, pepper*, point, point up*, separate, sprinkle, stress, underline; SEE CONCEPTS *49,79,98,266*

puncture [n] *hole, rupture*
break, cut, damage, flat, flat tire*, jab, leak, nick, opening, perforation, prick, slit, stab; SEE CONCEPTS *309,513,674*

puncture [v1] *poke hole in*
bore, cut, cut through, deflate, drill, go down, go flat, knife, lacerate, lance, nick, open, penetrate, perforate, pierce, prick, punch, riddle, rupture; SEE CONCEPTS *137,220*

puncture [v2] *deflate someone's idea, feelings*
blow sky high*, discourage, discredit, disillusion, disprove, explode, flatten*, humble, knock bottom out*, knock props from under*, poke full of holes*, shoot full of holes*, take down a peg*; SEE CONCEPTS *7,19,54*

pundit [n] *person who is authority*
auger, bookworm, brain*, buff, cereb*, cognoscenti, egghead*, expert, guru*, intellectual, learned one, maestro, maven, philosopher, professor, savant, scholar, solon, teacher, thinker; SEE CONCEPTS *416,423*

pungent [adj1] *highly flavored*
acid, acrid, aromatic, bitter, effluvious, hot, nosey*, odoriferous, peppery, piquant, poignant, racy, rich, salty, seasoned, sharp, snappy, sour, spicy, stinging, stinking*, strong, tangy, tart, whiffy*, zesty; SEE CONCEPT *613*

pungent [adj2] *sharp, stinging in speech*
acrimonious, acute, barbed, biting, bitter, caustic, cutting, exciting, hot, incisive, keen, mordant, penetrating, peppery, piercing, poignant, pointed, provocative, racy, salt, salty, sarcastic, scathing, snappy, spicy, stimulating, stringent, telling, trenchant, zesty; SEE CONCEPT *267*

punish [v] *penalize for wrongdoing*
abuse, attend to, batter, beat, beat up, blacklist, castigate, chasten, chastise, correct, crack down on*, cuff, debar, defrock, discipline, dismiss, do in, execute, exile, expel, fine, flog, give a going over*, give the works*, harm, hurt, immure, incarcerate, injure, knock about, lash, lecture, maltreat, manhandle, misuse, oppress, paddle, rap knuckles*, reprove, rough up, scourge, sentence, slap wrist, spank, switch, teach a lesson, throw the book at*, train, whip; SEE CONCEPT *122*

punishment [n] *penalty*
abuse, amercement, beating, castigation, chastening, chastisement, comeuppance, confiscation, correc-

tion, deprivation, disciplinary action, discipline, forfeit, forfeiture, gallows, hard work, infliction, just desserts*, lumps, maltreatment, manhandling, mortification, mulct, ostracism, pain, penance, proof, punitive measures, purgatory, reparation, retribution, rod, rough treatment, sanction, sequestration, short shrift*, slave labor*, suffering, torture, trial, unhappiness, victimization, what for*; SEE CONCEPT *123*

punitive [*adj*] *concerning punishment*
castigating, correctional, disciplinary, in reprisal, in retaliation, penal, punishing, punitory, retaliative, retaliatory, revengeful, vindictive; SEE CONCEPT *319*

puny [*adj*] *small, insignificant*
diminutive, dwarfish, feeble, fragile, frail, half-pint*, inconsequential, inferior, infirm, little, measly*, minor, niggling*, nothing, paltry, peanut*, peewee*, petty, picayune, piddling*, pint-sized*, pygmy, runt, shrimp*, small-fry*, small time*, stunted, tiny, trifling, trivial, two-bit*, unconsequential, underfed, undersized, undeveloped, unsound, unsubstantial, weak, weakly, wee*, worthless, zero*, zilch*; SEE CONCEPTS *489,575,773*

pupil [*n*] *person who is learning something*
adherent, attendant, beginner, bookworm*, brain*, catechumen, disciple, follower, freshman, graduate student, junior, learner, neophyte, novice, satellite, scholar, schoolboy/girl, senior, sophomore, student, tenderfoot*, undergraduate; SEE CONCEPT *350*

puppet [*n*] *person or toy manipulated by another*
creature, doll, dupe*, figurehead, figurine, instrument, jerk*, manikin, marionette, moppet, mouthpiece*, patsy*, pawn, pushover, schlemiel*, servant, soft touch*, stooge*, tool*, victim; SEE CONCEPTS *423,446*

purchase [*n*] *possession obtained with money*
acquirement, acquisition, asset, bargain, booty*, buy, gain, investment, property, steal; SEE CONCEPTS *446,710*

purchase [*v*] *buy, obtain*
achieve, acquire, attain, come by, cop*, deal in, earn, gain, get hold of, go shopping, invest, make a buy, make a purchase, market, patronize, pay for, pick up, procure, realize, redeem, secure, shop, shop for, take, take up, truck*, win; SEE CONCEPT *327*

pure [*adj1*] *unmixed, genuine*
authentic, bright, classic, clear, complete, fair, flawless, kosher*, limpid, lucid, natural, neat, out-and-out*, pellucid, perfect, plain, plenary, pure and simple, real, simple, straight, total, transparent, true, twenty-four carat*, unadulterated, unalloyed, unclouded, undiluted, unmingled; SEE CONCEPT *485*

pure [*adj2*] *clean, uncontaminated*
disinfected, germ-free, immaculate, intemerate, pasteurized, pristine, purified, refined, sanitary, snowy, spotless, stainless, sterile, sterilized, taintless, unadulterated, unblemished, undebased, unpolluted, unsoiled, unspotted, unstained, unsullied, untainted, untarnished, wholesome; SEE CONCEPT *621*

pure [*adj3*] *virginal, chaste*
babe in woods*, Bambi*, blameless, blue-eyed*, celibate, clean, continent, decent, exemplary, fresh, good, guileless, honest, immaculate, inculpable, innocent, inviolate, irreproachable, kid, lily white*, maidenly, modest, pure as driven snow*, righteous, sinless, spotless, stainless, true, unblemished, unblighted, uncorrupted, undefiled, unprofaned, unspotted, unstained, unsullied, upright, virgin, virtuous, wet behind ears*, wide-eyed*; SEE CONCEPT *372*

pure [*adj4*] *absolute, utter*
blasted*, blessed*, complete, confounded, infernal*, mere, out-and-out, sheer, thorough, unmitigated, unqualified; SEE CONCEPTS *531,535*

pure [*adj5*] *theoretical*
abstract, academic, philosophical, speculative, tentative, unproved; SEE CONCEPT *529*

purely [*adv*] *simply, absolutely*
all, all in all, altogether, barely, completely, entirely, essentially, exactly, exclusively, in toto*, just, merely, only, plainly, quite, solely, totally, utterly, wholly; SEE CONCEPTS *531,544*

purge [*n*] *elimination, removal*
abolition, abstersion, catharsis, clarification, cleaning, cleanup, coup, crushing, disposal, disposition, ejection, eradication, evacuation, excretion, expulsion, expurgation, extermination, extirpation, liquidation, murder, purification, reign of terror*, suppression, witch hunt; SEE CONCEPTS *165,211,252*

purge [*v*] *rid of; clean out*
abolish, absolve, clarify, clean out, cleanse, clear, depurate, disabuse, dismiss, dispose of, do away with*, eject, eradicate, erase, excrete, exonerate, expel, expiate, expunge, exterminate, forgive, get rid of*, kill, liquidate, oust, pardon, prevent, purify, remove, rout out, shake out*, sweep out, unload, wash, wipe off map*, wipe out; SEE CONCEPTS *165,211,252*

purification [*n*] *freeing, cleansing*
ablution, absolution, atonement, baptism, bathing, catharsis, depuration, disinfection, distillation, expiation, expurgation, forgiveness, grace, lavation, laving, lustration, purgation, purge, purifying, rarefaction, rebirth, redemption, refinement, regeneration, salvation, sanctification, washing; SEE CONCEPTS *165,367*

purify [*v*] *free; make clean*
absolve, aerate, aerify, atone, chasten, clarify, clean, cleanse, clear, decontaminate, deodorize, depurate, deterge, disinfect, edulcorate, elutriate, exculpate, exonerate, expiate, filter, fumigate, lustrate, oxygenate, purge, rarify, redeem, refine, remit, sanctify, sanitize, shrive, sublimate, wash; SEE CONCEPTS *165,367*

purple [*n/adj*] *blue and red colors mixed together*
amethyst, bluish red, color, heliotrope, lavender, lilac, magenta, mauve, mulberry, orchid, perse, plum, pomegranate, reddish blue, violaceous, violet, wine; SEE CONCEPTS *618,622*

purport [n] *meaning, implication*
acceptation, aim, bearing, burden, connotation, core, design, drift, gist, heart, idea, import, intendment, intent, intention, matter, meat, message, nub, object, objective, pith, plan, point, purpose, score, sense, significance, significancy, signification, spirit, stuff, substance, tendency, tenor, thrust, understanding, upshot; SEE CONCEPTS *20,659,660,689*

purport [v] *assert, mean*
allege, betoken, claim, convey, declare, denote, express, imply, import, indicate, intend, maintain, point to, pose as, pretend, proclaim, profess, signify, suggest; SEE CONCEPTS *49,682*

purpose [n1] *intention, meaning, aim*
ambition, animus, aspiration, big idea*, bourn, calculation, design, desire, destination, determination, direction, dream, drift, end, expectation, function, goal, hope, idea, intendment, intent, mecca, mission, object, objective, plan, point, premeditation, principle, project, proposal, proposition, prospect, reason, resolve, scheme, scope, target, ulterior motive, view, whatfor*, where one's headed*, whole idea*, why and wherefore*, whyfor*, will, wish; SEE CONCEPTS *20,659,660,689*

purpose [n2] *persistence, resolve*
confidence, constancy, determination, faith, firmness, resolution, single-mindedness, steadfastness, tenacity, will; SEE CONCEPTS *633,644*

purpose [n3] *use*
advantage, avail, benefit, duty, effect, function, gain, goal, good, mark, mission, object, objective, outcome, profit, result, return, target, utility; SEE CONCEPTS *658,694*

purpose [v] *intend, set sights on*
aim, aspire, bid for, commit, conclude, consider, contemplate, decide, design, determine, have a mind to*, have in view, intend, make up one's mind*, mean, meditate, mind, plan, ponder, propose, pursue, resolve, think to, work for, work toward; SEE CONCEPTS *18,36,87*

purposeful [adj] *resolved to do something*
bent, be out for blood*, bound, calculated, dead set on*, decided, deliberate, determined, firm, fixed, intense, intent, mean business*, obstinate, persistent, playing hard ball*, positive, purposive, resolute, settled, single-minded, stalwart, staunch, steadfast, steady, strong-willed, stubborn, telological, tenacious, undeviating, unfaltering, unwavering; SEE CONCEPTS *326,403,542*

purposeless [adj] *useless, insignificant*
aimless, designless, desultory, drifting, empty, feckless, floundering, fustian, goalless, good-for-nothing*, haphazard, hit-or-miss*, indiscriminate, irregular, meaningless, motiveless, needless, nonsensical, pointless, purportless, random, senseless, uncalled for, undirected, unhelpful, unnecessary, unplanned, unprofitable, unpurposed, vacuous, wanton, worthless; SEE CONCEPTS *544,560*

purposely [adv] *intentionally*
advisedly, by design, calculatedly, consciously, deliberately, designedly, explicitly, expressly, knowingly, on purpose, prepensely, purposedly, willfully, with intent; SEE CONCEPTS *529,544*

purse [n1] *tote for carrying personal items*
bag, billfold, bursa, carryall, clutch, frame, handbag, hide, leather, lizard, moneybag, pocket, pocketbook, poke, pouch, receptacle, reticule, sack, wallet; SEE CONCEPTS *339,446,450,494*

purse [n2] *award; winnings*
coffers, exchequer, funds, gift, means, money, present, prize, resources, reward, stake, treasury, wealth, wherewithal; SEE CONCEPTS *337,344*

purse [v] *press together*
close, cockle, contract, crease, knit, pucker, ruffle, tighten, wrinkle; SEE CONCEPTS *185,208*

pursue [v1] *chase, follow*
accompany, attend, badger, bait, bird-dog*, bug, camp on the doorstep of*, chivy, dog*, fish*, give chase, go after, harass, harry, haunt, hound, hunt, hunt down, move behind, nose around*, oppress, persevere, persist, plague, play catch up*, poke around, prowl after, ride, run after, run down, scout out, search for, search high heaven*, search out, seek, shadow, stalk, tag, tail*, take out after, trace, track, track down, trail; SEE CONCEPT *207*

pursue [v2] *have as one's goal*
aim for, aspire to, attempt, desire, go in for, go out for, have a go at, purpose, seek, strive for, try for, work for, work toward; SEE CONCEPTS *20,36*

pursue [v3] *persist, persevere*
adhere, apply oneself, carry on, conduct, continue, cultivate, engage in, hold to, keep on, maintain, perform, ply, practice, proceed, prosecute, see through, tackle, wage, work at; SEE CONCEPTS *87,100,239*

pursue [v4] *seek social alliance with*
address, call, chase, chase after, court, date, go after, go for, pay attention, pay court*, play up to, rush*, spark, sue, sweetheart*, WOO; SEE CONCEPT *384*

pursuit [n1] *chase, search*
following, going all out, hunt, hunting, inquiry, pursual, pursuance, pursuing, quest, reaching, seeking, stalk, tracking, trail, trailing; SEE CONCEPT *207*

pursuit [n2] *occupation, interest of person*
accomplishing, accomplishment, activity, biz*, business, calling, career, do*, employment, game*, go*, hang*, hobby, job, line*, occupation, pastime, pleasure, racket, swindle, thing*, undertaking, venture, vocation, work; SEE CONCEPT *349*

push [n1] *physical force*
advance, assault, attack, bearing, blow, butt, charge, drive, driving, effort, energy, exerting, exertion, forcing, impact, jolt, lean, mass, nudge, offensive, onset, poke, prod, propulsion, shove, shoving, straining, thrust, thrusting, weight; SEE CONCEPTS *200,208,641,724*

push [*n2*] *mental determination*
ambition, drive, dynamism, energy, enterprise, get-up-and-go*, go*, gumption*, guts*, initiative, pep, punch, snap, spunk, starch, vigor, vitality; SEE CONCEPTS *410,411*

push [*v1*] *thrust, press with force*
accelerate, bear down, budge, bulldoze*, bump, butt, crowd, crush against, depress, dig, drive, elbow, exert, force, gore, high pressure*, hustle, impel, jam, jostle, launch, lie on, make one's way*, move, muscle, nudge, poke, pour it on*, pressure, propel, put the arm on*, railroad*, ram*, rest on, shift, shoulder, shove, squash, squeeze, squish, steamroll*, stir, strain, strong-arm*; SEE CONCEPTS *200,208,243*

push [*v2*] *incite, urge*
bear down, browbeat, bulldoze*, coerce, constrain, dragoon, egg on*, encourage, exert influence, expedite, fire up*, goad, goose*, go to town on*, hurry, impel, influence, inspire, jolly, key up*, kid, lean on*, motivate, oblige, overpress, persuade, pour it on*, press, pressure, prod, push around, put the screws to*, put up to*, railroad*, sell on*, speed, speed up, spur, squeeze, steamroll*, strong-arm*, turn on*; SEE CONCEPTS *14,68,243*

push [*v3*] *advertise, promote*
advance, boost, cry up*, hype*, make known, plug*, propagandize, publicize, puff*; SEE CONCEPTS *49,324*

push off/push on [*v*] *leave; go to another place*
beat it*, continue, depart, exit, fare, get away, get lost*, go, go away, hie, hit the road*, journey, keep going, launch, light out, make oneself scarce*, make progress, pass, proceed, process, pull out, quit, repair, shove off, start, take off, travel, wend, withdraw; SEE CONCEPTS *195,704*

pushover [*n*] *something or someone easily influenced*
breeze, child's play*, chump*, cinch, duck soup*, easy game*, easy mark*, easy pickings*, fool, kid stuff*, picnic*, piece of cake*, setup, snap, soft touch*, stooge*, sucker, victim, walkover; SEE CONCEPTS *423,693*

pushy [*adj*] *aggressive, offensive*
ambitious, assertive, bold, brash, bumptious, forceful, loud, militant, obnoxious, obtrusive, officious, presumptuous, pushful, pushing, self-assertive; SEE CONCEPTS *401,404*

pussyfoot [*v*] *walk or act very carefully*
avoid, beat around the bush*, be noncommittal, creep, dodge, equivocate, evade, glide, hedge, hem and haw*, lurk, prevaricate, prowl, shuffle, sidestep, sit on the fence*, skulk, slide, slink, slip, sneak, steal, tergiversate, tergiverse, tiptoe, tread warily, weasel*; SEE CONCEPTS *151,410*

put [*v1*] *position*
bring, concenter, concentrate, deposit, embed, establish, fasten, fix, fixate, focus, insert, install, invest, lay, nail, park, peg, place, plank, plank down, plant, plop, plunk, plunk down, quarter, repose, rest, rivet, seat, set, settle, situate, stick; SEE CONCEPT *201*

put [*v2*] *propose; express in words*
advance, air, bring forward, couch, express, formulate, forward, give, offer, phrase, pose, posit, prefer, present, propone, proposition, propound, render, set, set before, state, submit, suggest, tender, translate, transpose, turn, utter, vent, ventilate, word; SEE CONCEPTS *47,66,67*

put [*v3*] *commit, assign*
condemn, consign, constrain, doom, employ, enjoin, force, impose, induce, inflict, levy, make, oblige, require, set, subject, subject to; SEE CONCEPTS *14,242*

putative [*adj*] *commonly believed*
accepted, alleged, assumed, conjectural, hypothetical, imputed, presumed, presumptive, reported, reputed, supposed, suppositional, suppositious; SEE CONCEPT *529*

put away/put aside/put by [*v1/v*] *keep in reserve*
cache, deposit, keep, lay aside, lay away, lay by, lay in, put by, put out of the way, salt away*, save, set aside, squirrel away*, stockpile, store, store away*, stow away; SEE CONCEPTS *129,134*

put away [*v2*] *incarcerate*
certify, commit, confine, institutionalize, jail, lock up; SEE CONCEPT *317*

put away [*v3*] *consume*
devour, eat up, gobble*, gulp down, polish off*, punish, put down, shift, swill, wolf down*; SEE CONCEPT *169*

put away [*v4*] *kill*
assassinate, bury, cool*, cut off, destroy, dispatch, do away with, do in*, dust off*, execute, finish, inter, knock off*, liquidate, murder, plant, put down*, put out of its misery*, put to sleep*, slay, tomb; SEE CONCEPT *252*

put-down [*n*] *nasty commentary*
cut*, dig*, disparagement, gibe*, humiliation, indignity, insult, jibe*, knock*, pan*, rebuff, sarcasm, slight, sneer*, snub, suppression; SEE CONCEPTS *54,278*

put down [*v1*] *write into record*
enter, inscribe, jot down, log, record, set down, take down, transcribe, write down; SEE CONCEPT *79*

put down [*v2*] *subdue*
annihilate, crush, defeat, dismiss, extinguish, quash*, quell, reject, repress, silence, squash*, stamp out*, suppress; SEE CONCEPTS *95,252*

put down [*v3*] *comment negatively*
belittle, condemn, crush, decry, deflate, derogate, discount, dismiss, disparage, downcry, humiliate, minimize, mortify, opprobriate, reject, run down, shame, slight, snub, write off; SEE CONCEPT *54*

put off [*v*] *defer, delay*
adjourn, dally, dawdle, dillydally*, drag one's feet*, hold off, hold over, lag*, lay over, linger, loiter, poke*, postpone, prorogue, put back, reschedule, retard, shelve, stay, suspend, tarry, trail; SEE CONCEPTS *121,234*

put on [v1] *pretend*
act, affect, assume, bluff, confound, confuse, counterfeit, deceive, don, fake, feign, make believe, masquerade, playact, pose, pull, put on a front, put on an act, sham, simulate, strike, take on, trick; SEE CONCEPT 59

put on [v2] *stage a performance*
do, mount, present, produce, show; SEE CONCEPT 292

put out [v1] *upset, irritate; inconvenience*
aggravate, anger, annoy, bother, burn, confound, discomfit, discommode, discompose, disconcert, discountenance, disoblige, displease, dissatisfy, disturb, embarrass, exasperate, gall, get*, grate, harass, impose upon, incommode, inflame, irk, nettle, perturb, provoke, put on the spot*, rile, roil, trouble, vex; SEE CONCEPTS 7,14,19

put out [v2] *extinguish fire*
blow out, douse, out, quench, smother, snuff out, stamp out; SEE CONCEPT 252

putrefy [v] *rot*
break down, corrupt, crumble, decay, decompose, deteriorate, disintegrate, go bad*, molder, putresce, spoil, stink, taint, turn; SEE CONCEPT 469

putrid [adj] *rotten, stinking*
bad, contaminated, corrupt, decayed, decomposed, fetid, foul, high, malodorous, moldered, nidorous, noisome, off, putrefied, rancid, rank, reeking, rotting, smelly, spoiled, strong, tainted, whiffy*; SEE CONCEPTS 485,598

putter [v] *dawdle*
doodle, fiddle, fritter, goof around*, loiter, mess, mess around*, niggle, poke*, potter*, puddle*, shuffle around, tinker*; SEE CONCEPTS 87,210

put up [v1] *accommodate guest*
bestow, billet, board, bunk, domicile, entertain, give lodging, harbor, house, lodge, make welcome, provide, quarter, take in; SEE CONCEPTS 324,384

put up [v2] *build, erect*
construct, fabricate, forge, make, put together, raise, rear, shape, uprear; SEE CONCEPT 168

puzzle [v1] *baffle, confuse*
addle, amaze, bamboozle*, beat, befog, befuddle, bemuse, bewilder, buffalo*, complicate, confound, discombobulate*, disconcert, distract, disturb, dumbfound, flabbergast, floor*, flummox, foil, frustrate, get to*, mystify, nonplus, obscure, perplex, pose, profundicate, psych out*, put off, rattle, snow*, stir, stumble, stump, throw; SEE CONCEPT 16

puzzle [v2] *wonder about*
ask oneself, brood, cudgel, marvel, mull over, muse, ponder, rack one's brains*, study, think about, think hard; SEE CONCEPT 17

puzzled [adj] *confused*
at a loss*, at sea*, baffled, bewildered, bollixed, clueless, come apart, come unzipped*, discombobulated*, dopey*, doubtful, floored*, foggy, fouled up*, hung up*, in a fog*, lost, loused up*, messed up*, mind-blown*, mixed up*, mucked up*, mystified, nonplussed, perplexed, rattled, screwed up*, shook, shook up, spaced out*, stuck, stumped, thrown, unglued*, without a clue; SEE CONCEPTS 403,690

puzzling [adj] *very confusing*
abstruse, ambiguous, baffling, bewildering, beyond one, difficult, enigmatic, hard, incomprehensible, inexplicable, involved, knotty, labyrinthine, misleading, mystifying, obscure, perplexing, surprising, unaccountable, unclear, unfathomable; SEE CONCEPT 529

Q

quack [n] *person who pretends to be an expert*
actor, bum*, bunco artist, charlatan, cheat, con artist, con man, counterfeit, counterfeiter, fake, faker, flimflammer*, four-flusher*, fraud, hoser*, humbug, impostor, mountebank, phony, playactor, pretender, pseudo*, put-on*, quacksalver*, rogue, sham, shammer*, shark*, sharp*, simulator, slicker*, whip*; SEE CONCEPT 412

quack [adj] *counterfeit*
bum*, dishonest, dissembling, fake, false, fraudulent, phony, pretended, pretentious, pseudo*, sham*, simulated, unprincipled; SEE CONCEPT 582

quaff [v] *drink down*
down, gulp, guzzle, imbibe, ingurgitate, partake, sip, sup, swallow, swig, swill, toss; SEE CONCEPT 169

quagmire [n1] *bad situation*
box*, corner*, difficulty, dilemma, entanglement, fix, hole*, imbroglio, impasse, involvement, jam, mire, morass, muddle, pass, perplexity, pickle*, pinch*, plight, predicament, quandary, scrape, trouble; SEE CONCEPTS 666,674

quagmire [n2] *bog*
fen, marsh, marshland, mire, morass, moss, quag, quicksand, slough, swamp; SEE CONCEPT 509

quail [v] *cower, shrink*
blanch, blench, cringe, droop, faint, falter, flinch, have cold feet*, quake, recoil, shake, shudder, start, tremble, wince; SEE CONCEPTS 35,149,195

quaint [adj1] *strange, odd*
bizarre, curious, droll, eccentric, erratic, fanciful, fantastic, freakish, freaky*, funny, idiosyncratic, laughable, oddball, offbeat, off the beaten track*, original, outlandish, peculiar, queer*, singular, special, unusual, weird*, whimsical; SEE CONCEPTS 564,589

quaint [adj2] *old-fashioned; nostalgically attractive*
affected, ancient, antiquated, antique, archaic, artful, baroque, captivating, charming, colonial, curious, cute, enchanting, fanciful, Gothic*, ingenious, old-world, picturesque, pleasing, Victorian*, whimsical; SEE CONCEPTS 578,589,797

quake [n] *earthquake*
aftershock, convulsion, quaker, seism, shake, shock, temblor, tremblor, tremor; SEE CONCEPT 526

quake [v] *shake, vibrate*
convulse, cower, fluctuate, jar, jitter, move, pulsate, quail, quiver, rock, shiver, shrink, shudder, throb, totter, tremble, tremor, twitter, waver, wobble; SEE CONCEPT *152*

qualification [n1] *ability, aptitude*
accomplishment, adequacy, attainment, attribute, capability, capacity, competence, eligibility, endowment, experience, fitness, goods, makings, might, qualifiedness, quality, skill, stuff, suitability, suitableness, what it takes*; SEE CONCEPT *630*

qualification [n2] *requirement, restriction*
allowance, caveat, condition, contingency, criterion, essential, exception, exemption, limitation, modification, need, objection, postulate, prerequisite, provision, proviso, requisite, reservation, stipulation; SEE CONCEPTS *646,652*

qualified [adj1] *able, skillful*
accomplished, adept, adequate, all around, au fait, capable, catechized, certified, competent, disciplined, efficient, equipped, examined, experienced, expert, fit, fitted, good, instructed, knowledgeable, licensed, practiced, pro*, proficient, proper, proved, quizzed, talented, tested, trained, tried, up to snuff*, up to speed*, vet*, veteran, war-horse*, wicked; SEE CONCEPT *527*

qualified [adj2] *limited, restricted*
bounded, circumscribed, conditional, confined, contingent, definite, determined, equivocal, fixed, guarded, modified, partial, provisional, reserved; SEE CONCEPT *554*

qualify [v1] *make or become ready, prepared*
authorize, capacitate, certify, check out, come up to snuff*, commission, condition, cut it*, earn one's wings*, empower, enable, endow, entitle, equip, fill the bill*, fit, get by*, ground, hack it*, make it*, make the cut*, make the grade*, measure up, meet, pass, pass muster*, permit, prepare, ready, sanction, score, suffice, suit, train; SEE CONCEPTS *99,630*

qualify [v2] *lessen, restrict*
abate, adapt, alter, assuage, change, circumscribe, diminish, ease, lessen, limit, mitigate, moderate, modify, modulate, reduce, regulate, restrain, soften, temper, vary, weaken; SEE CONCEPTS *240,698*

qualify [v3] *characterize, distinguish*
ascribe, assign, attribute, describe, designate, impute, individualize, individuate, mark, name, predicate, signalize, singularize; SEE CONCEPT *411*

quality [n1] *characteristic, feature*
affection, affirmation, aspect, attribute, character, condition, constitution, description, element, endowment, essence, factor, genius, individuality, kind, make, mark, name of tune*, nature, nature of beast*, parameter, peculiarity, predication, property, savor, sort, trait, virtue, way of it*; SEE CONCEPT *543*

quality [n2] *value, status*
arete, caliber, capacity, character, class, condition, distinction, excellence, excellency, footing, grade,

group, kind, merit, perfection, place, position, preeminence, rank, repute, standing, state, station, stature, step, superbness, superiority, value, variety, virtue, worth; SEE CONCEPTS *346,378,668*

qualm [n] *nagging doubt*
agitation, anxiety, apprehension, compunction, conscience, demur, disquiet, doubt, foreboding, hesitation, indecision, insecurity, misdoubt, misgiving, mistrust, nervousness, objection, pang, perturbation, presentiment, regret, reluctance, remonstrance, remorse, scruple, suspicion, twinge, uncertainty, unease, uneasiness; SEE CONCEPTS *410,532*

quandary [n] *delicate situation*
bewilderment, bind, Catch-22*, clutch, corner*, difficulty, dilemma, double trouble*, doubt, embarrassment, hang-up*, impasse, mire, perplexity, pickle*, plight, predicament, puzzle, spot*, strait, uncertainty, up a tree*; SEE CONCEPTS *532,674,690*

quantity [n] *number or amount*
abundance, aggregate, allotment, amplitude, batch, body, budget, bulk, capacity, deal, expanse, extent, figure, greatness, length, load, lot, magnitude, mass, measure, multitude, part, pile, portion, profusion, quota, size, sum, total, variety, volume; SEE CONCEPT *787*

quarrel [n] *disagreement*
affray, altercation, argument, battle royal*, beef*, bickering*, brannigan*, brawl, breach, broil*, catfight*, combat, commotion, complaint, contention, controversy, difference, difference of opinion, difficulty, disapproval, discord, disputation, dispute, dissension, dissidence, disturbance, dust*, falling-out*, feud, fight, fisticuffs*, fracas, fray, fuss, hassle, misunderstanding, objection, rhubarb*, row, ruckus*, run-in, scrap, set-to*, spat, squabble, strife, struggle, tiff, tumult, vendetta, wrangle; SEE CONCEPTS *46,106*

quarrel [v] *disagree*
altercate, argue, battle, be at loggerheads*, bicker, brawl, break with, bump, carp, caterwaul, cavil, charge, clash, collide, complain, contend, contest, cross swords*, differ, disapprove, dispute, dissent, divide, embroil, fall out*, feud, fight, find fault, get tough with*, hassle, have it out*, have words*, lock horns*, mix it up*, object to, row, scrap, set to, spar, spat, squabble, strive, struggle, take exception, take on, tangle, vary, war, wrangle; SEE CONCEPTS *46,106*

quarrelsome [adj] *being disagreeable*
argumentative, bad-tempered, bellicose, belligerent, brawling, cantankerous, cat-and-dog*, choleric, churlish, combative, contentious, crabby*, cross, disputatious, dissentious, excitable, fiery, fractious, gladiatorial, hasty, have chip on shoulder*, hotheaded*, huffy, impassioned, irascible, irritable, litigious, ornery, passionate, peevish, pettish, petulant, pugnacious, querulous, ructious, snappy, tempestuous, thin-skinned*, touchy, truculent, turbulent, unruly, violent, war; SEE CONCEPTS *401,542*

quarry [n] *goal*
aim, chase, game, objective, prey, prize, quest, raven, victim; SEE CONCEPT **659**

quarter [n1] *one of four equal parts*
division, farthing, fourth, one-fourth, part, portion, quad, quadrant, quartern, section, semester, span, term, two bits*; SEE CONCEPT **835**

quarter [n2] *area, neighborhood*
barrio, bearing, direction, district, division, domain, ghetto, inner city, locality, location, neck of the woods*, old town, part, place, point, position, precinct, province, region, section, sector, side, skid row, slum, spot, station, stomping ground*, territory, turf, zone, zoo*; SEE CONCEPTS **508,512**

quarter [n3] *forgiveness*
clemency, compassion, favor, grace, leniency, lenity, mercy, pity; SEE CONCEPTS **410,633**

quarter [v1] *divide into four equal parts*
cleave, cut, cut up, dismember, fourth; SEE CONCEPT **98**

quarter [v2] *provide lodging*
accommodate, billet, board, bunk, canton, domicile, domiciliate, entertain, establish, harbor, house, install, lodge, place, post, put up, settle, shelter, station; SEE CONCEPT **140**

quarters [n] *place to live or sleep*
abode, accommodation, apartment, barracks, billet, cabin, cantonment, chambers, condo, cottage, digs*, domicile, dorm, dwelling, flat, fraternity, habitat, habitation, home, house, lodge, lodging, place, post, ranch, residence, room, roost*, shelter, sorority, station, tent; SEE CONCEPT **516**

quash [v1] *destroy, defeat*
annihilate, beat, crush, extinguish, extirpate, overcome, overthrow, put down, quell, quench, repress, scrunch*, snow under*, squash*, squish*, subdue, suppress, trash; SEE CONCEPTS **95,252**

quash [v2] *nullify, cancel*
abrogate, annul, black out*, bottle up*, clamp down on, cork up*, crack down on*, declare null and void*, discharge, dissolve, hush up*, invalidate, kill, negate, overrule, overthrow, put damper on*, put the lid on*, queer, repeal, rescind, reverse, revoke, set aside, shut down, squelch, undo, vacate, veto, vitiate, void, watergate*; SEE CONCEPTS **121,234,266**

quasi [adj] *almost; to a certain extent*
apparent, apparently, fake, mock, near, nominal, partly, pretended, pseudo-*, seeming, seemingly, semi-, sham*, so-called, supposedly, synthetic, virtual, would-be*; SEE CONCEPT **582**

queasy [adj] *not feeling well; not comfortable*
anxious, bilious, concerned, fidgety, green around gills*, groggy, ill, ill at ease, indisposed, nauseated, pukish, qualmish, queer, restless, rocky*, sick, sick as a dog*, sickly, squeamish, troubled, uncertain, uncomfortable, under the weather*, uneasy, unwell, upset, worried; SEE CONCEPTS **314,403**

queer [adj1] *very odd; abnormal*
anomalous, atypical, bizarre, crazy, curious, demented, disquieting, doubtful, droll, dubious, eccentric, eerie, erratic, extraordinary, fishy*, flaky*, fly ball*, freaky*, funny, idiosyncratic, irrational, irregular, kinky*, kooky*, mad, mysterious, oddball, off the wall*, outlandish, outré, peculiar, puzzling, quaint, questionable, remarkable, shady, singular, strange, suspicious, touched, unbalanced, uncanny, uncommon, unconventional, unhinged, unnatural, unorthodox, unusual, wacky*, weird; SEE CONCEPTS **404,548,564**

queer [adj2] *not feeling well*
dizzy, faint, giddy, green*, ill, lightheaded, pukish*, qualmish, qualmy*, queasy*, reeling, sick, squeamish*, uneasy; SEE CONCEPT **314**

quell [v1] *defeat, suppress*
annihilate, conquer, crush, extinguish, hush up*, kill, overcome, overpower, put down, put the lid on*, queer, quench, shut down, silence, sit on, stamp out*, stifle, stop, subdue, subjugate, vanquish; SEE CONCEPTS **95,121,234**

quell [v2] *alleviate, calm*
allay, appease, assuage, check, compose, deaden, dull, ease, mitigate, moderate, mollify, pacify, quiet, reduce, silence, soothe, still; SEE CONCEPTS **7,22,110**

quench [v1] *destroy, extinguish*
annihilate, check, choke, crush, dampen, decimate, demolish, destruct, dismantle, douse, end, kill, knock down, moisten, put down, put out, quash*, quell, raze, ruin, shatter, smother, snuff out*, stifle, suppress, wreck; SEE CONCEPTS **234,252**

quench [v2] *satisfy, especially thirst*
allay, alleviate, appease, assuage, content, cool*, glut, gorge, gratify, lighten, mitigate, moisten, relieve, sate, satiate, slake; SEE CONCEPTS **136,244**

querulous [adj] *grouchy, hard to please*
bearish, bemoaning, cantankerous, captious, carping, censorious, complaining, critical, cross, crying, deploring, discontented, dissatisfied, edgy, faultfinding, fretful, grousing, grumbling, grumbly, huffy* irascible, irritable, lamenting, out of sorts* peevish, petulant, plaintive, scrappy, snappy, sour, testy, thin-skinned* touchy, uptight, wailing, waspish, waspy, whimpering, whining, whiny; SEE CONCEPTS **401,542**

query [n] *demand for answers*
concern, doubt, dubiety, inquiry, interrogation, interrogatory, mistrust, objection, problem, question, questioning, reservation, skepticism, suspicion, uncertainty; SEE CONCEPTS **21,48,53,662**

query [v] *ask*
catechize, challenge, disbelieve, dispute, distrust, doubt, enquire, examine, hit up, impeach, impugn, inquire, interrogate, knock, mistrust, put out a feeler* question, quiz, suspect, test the waters*; SEE CONCEPTS **21,48,53**

quest [*n*] *search, exploration*
adventure, chase, crusade, delving, enterprise, examination, expedition, hunt, inquest, inquiry, inquisition, investigation, journey, mission, pilgrimmage, prey, probe, probing, pursual, pursuit, quarry, research, seeking, voyage; SEE CONCEPTS *48,103,216*

question [*n1*] *asking for answer*
catechism, examination, inquest, inquiring, inquiry, inquisition, interrogation, interrogatory, investigation, poll, Q and A*, query, questioning, third degree*, wringer*; SEE CONCEPTS *48,53*

question [*n2*] *controversy, doubt*
argument, challenge, confusion, contention, debate, demur, demurral, difficulty, dispute, dubiety, enigma, misgiving, mystery, objection, problem, protest, puzzle, query, remonstrance, remonstration, uncertainty; SEE CONCEPTS *666,674*

question [*n3*] *issue, point at issue*
discussion, motion, point, problem, proposal, proposition, subject, theme, topic; SEE CONCEPTS *532,690*

question [*v1*] *ask for answer*
ask about, catechize, challenge, cross-examine, enquire, examine, give the third degree*, go over, grill, hit*, hit up*, hold out for, inquire, interrogate, interview, investigate, knock*, make inquiry, petition, pick one's brains*, probe, pry, pump, put through the wringer*, put to the question*, query, quest, quiz, raise question, roast*, search, seek, show curiosity, solicit, sound out*, sweat it out of*, work over*; SEE CONCEPTS *48,53*

question [*v2*] *doubt*
call into question, cast doubt upon, challenge, controvert, disbelieve, dispute, distrust, hesitate, impeach, impugn, mistrust, oppose, puzzle over, query, suspect, suspicion, wonder about; SEE CONCEPT *21*

questionable [*adj*] *doubtful, uncertain*
ambiguous, apocryphal, arguable, contingent, controversial, controvertible, cryptic, debatable, disputable, dubious, dubitable, enigmatic, equivocal, fishy*, hard to believe, hypothetical, iffy*, indecisive, indefinite, indeterminate, moot, mysterious, obscure, occult, open to doubt, open to question, oracular, paradoxical, problematic, problematical, provisional, shady, suspect, suspicious, unconfirmed, undefined, under advisement, under examination, unproven, unreliable, unsettled, vague; SEE CONCEPTS *529,535*

queue [*n*] *sequence*
chain, concatenation, echelon, file, line, order, progression, rank, row, series, string, succession, tail, tier, train; SEE CONCEPTS *432,727*

quibble [*n*] *objection, complaint*
artifice, cavil, criticism, dodge, duplicity, equivocation, evasion, hair-splitter*, nicety, niggle*, nitpicker*, pretense, prevarication, protest, quiddity, quirk, shift, sophism, subterfuge, subtlety; SEE CONCEPTS *46,52*

quibble [*v*] *disagree over minor issues*
altercate, argue over, argufy, avoid, bicker, blow hot and cold*, carp, catch at straws*, cavil, chicane, criticize, dispute, equivocate, evade, fence*, flipflop*, hassle, have at it*, hem and haw*, hypercriticize*, make a big thing about*, nit-pick*, paralogize, pettifog*, pretend, prevaricate, put up an argument, set to, shift, spar, split hairs*, squabble, talk back, waffle, wrangle; SEE CONCEPTS *46,52*

quick [*adj1*] *fast, speedy*
abrupt, accelerated, active, agile, alert, a move on*, animated, ASAP*, breakneck*, brief, brisk, cursory, curt, double time*, energetic, expeditious, expeditive, express, fleet, flying, going, harefooted*, hasty, headlong, hurried, immediate, impatient, impetuous, instantaneous, keen, lively, mercurial, move it, nimble, on the double*, perfunctory, posthaste, prompt, pronto*, rapid, snappy, spirited, sprightly, spry, sudden, swift, the lead out*, winged*; SEE CONCEPTS *544,588*

quick [*adj2*] *very smart*
able, active, acute, adept, adroit, all there, apt, astute, bright, canny, capable, clever, competent, deft, dexterous, discerning, effective, effectual, intelligent, keen, knowing, nimble-witted, on the ball*, perceptive, perspicacious, prompt, quick on the draw, quick on the trigger*, quick on the uptake*, quick-witted, ready, receptive, savvy, sharp, sharp as a tack*, shrewd, skillful, slick, smart as a whip*, vigorous, whiz*, wired*, wise; SEE CONCEPT *402*

quicken [*v*] *make faster; invigorate*
accelerate, activate, actuate, animate, arouse, awaken, dispatch, energize, excite, expedite, galvanize, goad, grow, hasten, hurry, impel, incite, increase, innervate, innerve, inspire, kindle, liven, make haste, motivate, move, pique, precipitate, promote, refresh, revitalize, revive, rouse, shake up, speed, spring, spur, step up, stimulate, stir, strengthen, urge, vitalize, vivificate, vivify; SEE CONCEPTS *7,19,22,250*

quick-tempered [*adj*] *easily upset, angered*
choleric, cranky, cross, excitable, fiery, hot-tempered, impatient, impulsive, inflammable, irascible, irritable, passionate, peppery, petulant, quarrelsome, ratty, sensitive, short-tempered, shrewish, splenetic, temperamental, testy, waspish; SEE CONCEPTS *401,404*

quick-witted [*adj*] *very smart*
acute, agile, alert, apt, astute, brainy, bright, brilliant, canny, clever, facetious, humorous, intelligent, keen, knowing, nimble-witted, on the ball*, penetrating, penetrative, perceptive, prompt, quick, quick on the draw*, quick on the uptake*, ready, savvy, sharp, sharp as a tack*, sharp-sighted, sharp-witted, shrewd, slick*, whiz*, wired*, wise, witty; SEE CONCEPTS *267,402*

quiet [*n*] *calmness, silence*
calm, cessation, dead air*, ease, hush, lull, noiselessness, peace, quietness, quietude, relaxation, re-

pose, rest, serenity, soundlessness, speechlessness, still, stillness, stop, termination, tranquillity; SEE CONCEPTS *65,315,592,673,705*

quiet [*adj1*] *without or with little sound*
buttoned up*, clammed up*, close, close-mouthed, could hear a pin drop*, dumb, Garbo*, hushed, hushful, inaudible, low, low-pitched, muffled, mute, muted, noiseless, not saying boo*, peaceful, quiescent, quieted, reserved, reticent, secretive, silent, soft, soundless, speechless, still, stilled, taciturn, tight-lipped*, uncommunicative, unexpressed, unspeaking, unuttered, whist; SEE CONCEPTS *592,594*

quiet [*adj2*] *calm, peaceful*
collected, contented, docile, fixed, gentle, halcyon, hushed, inactive, isolated, level, meek, mild, motionless, pacific, placid, private, remote, reserved, restful, retired, secluded, secret, sedate, sequestered, serene, shy, smooth, stable, stagnant, still, tranquil, unanxious, undisturbed, unexcited, unfrequented, unruffled, untroubled; SEE CONCEPTS *401, 583,584,705*

quiet [*adj3*] *simple, unobtrusive*
conservative, homely, inobtrusive, modest, plain, restrained, sober, subdued, tasteful, unassuming, unobtrusive, unpretentious; SEE CONCEPT *589*

quiet [*v*] *make silent, calm*
allay, ameliorate, appease, assuage, becalm, button one's lip*, calm, calm down, can it, choke, clam up*, compose, console, cool it*, cool out*, dummy up*, fix up, gag, gratify, hold it down, hush, ice*, inactivate, lull, moderate, mollify, muffle, muzzle, pacify, palliate, patch things up*, please, quieten, reconcile, relax, satisfy, settle, shush, shut up, silence, slack, smooth, soften, soft-pedal*, soothe, square, squash, squelch, still, stroke, subdue, take the bite out of*, tranquilize; SEE CONCEPTS *126,244,266*

quilt [*n*] *thick bedcovering made of patches*
batt, bedspread, blanket, comforter, counterpane, cover, coverlet, down, duvet, eiderdown, pad, patchwork, pouf, puff; SEE CONCEPTS *445,451,473*

quintessence [*n*] *essence, core*
apotheosis, bottom, distillation, epitome, essentiality, extract, gist, heart, kernel, last word, lifeblood, marrow, pith, quiddity, soul, spirit, stuff, substance, ultimate, virtuality; SEE CONCEPTS *682,826*

quip [*n*] *witty communication, often verbal*
badinage, banter, bon mot, crack, drollery, gag, gibe, insult, jeer, jest, joke, mockery, offense, pleasantry, pun, repartee, retort, riposte, sally, satire, spoof, wisecrack, witticism; SEE CONCEPTS *273,278*

quirk [*n*] *oddity of personality, way of doing something*
aberration, caprice, characteristic, conceit, crotchet, eccentricity, equivocation, fancy, fetish, foible, habit, humor, idée fixe, idiosyncrasy, irregularity, kink, knack, mannerism, peculiarity, quibble, singularity, subterfuge, trait, turn, twist, vagary, whim, whimsy; SEE CONCEPTS *411,644*

quit [*v1*] *abandon, leave*
abdicate, blow*, book*, bow out, check out, cut out*, decamp, depart, desert, drop, drop out, evacuate, exit, forsake, get off, give up, go, go away from, hang it up*, leave flat*, leave hanging*, pull out, push off*, relinquish, renounce, resign, retire, run out on, surrender, take a walk*, take off, throw over*, vacate, walk out on, withdraw, yield; SEE CONCEPT *195*

quit [*v2*] *stop doing something*
abandon, break off, call it a day*, call it quits*, cease, conclude, cut it out*, desist, discontinue, drop, end, get on the wagon*, give notice, give over*, give up, halt, hang it up*, kick over*, kick the habit*, knock off*, leave, leave off*, pack in*, quit cold, resign, retire, secede, sew up*, surcease, suspend, take the cure*, terminate, wind up*, withdraw, wrap up*; SEE CONCEPTS *119,234*

quite [*adv1*] *completely*
absolutely, actually, all, all in all, all told, altogether, considerably, entirely, fully, in all respects, in fact, in reality, in toto, in truth, just, largely, perfectly, positively, precisely, purely, really, thoroughly, totally, truly, utterly, well, wholly, without reservation; SEE CONCEPTS *531,582*

quite [*adv2*] *to a certain extent*
considerably, fairly, far, moderately, more or less, pretty, rather, reasonably, relatively, significantly, somewhat, to some degree, very; SEE CONCEPTS *569,772*

quiver [*n*] *shaking, vibration*
convulsion, flash, glimmer, glitter, oscillation, palpitation, pulsation, shake, shimmer, shiver, shudder, sparkle, spasm, throb, tic, tremble, tremor, twinkle; SEE CONCEPT *152*

quiver [*v*] *shake, vibrate*
agitate, beat, convulse, dither, jitter, oscillate, palpitate, pulsate, pulse, quake, quaver, shiver, shudder, thrill, throb, tremble, tremor, twitter; SEE CONCEPT *152*

quiz [*n*] *questioning, often in an organized academic setting*
blue book*, check, exam, examination, investigation, pop quiz, query, shotgun*, test; SEE CONCEPT *290*

quiz [*v*] *question*
ask, catechize, check, cross-examine, examine, give the third degree*, grill*, inquire, interrogate, investigate, pick one's brains*, pump*, query, test; SEE CONCEPT *48*

quizzical [*adj*] *appearing confused or curious*
amusing, aporetic, arch, bantering, curious, derisive, disbelieving, eccentric, incredulous, inquiring, inquisitive, mocking, odd, probing, quaint, queer, questioning, sardonic, searching, show-me*, skeptical, supercilious, suspicious, teasing, unbelieving, unusual; SEE CONCEPTS *267,485*

quota [*n*] *portion allotted to something*
allocation, allotment, allowance, apportionment, assignment, bite, chunk, cut, division, divvy*, end,

lot, measure, meed, part, partage, percentage, piece, piece of action*, proportion, quantum, ration, share, slice, split; SEE CONCEPTS *768,835*

quotation/quote [*n1*] *repetition of something spoken or written by someone*
citation, citing, cutting, excerpt, extract, passage, quote, recitation, reference, repetition, saying, selection; SEE CONCEPTS *274,278*

quotation/quote [*n2*] *financial estimate*
bid, bid price, charge, cost, current price, figure, market price, price, price named, published price, quote, rate, stated price, tender; SEE CONCEPTS *274,332,784*

quote [*v*] *repeat something spoken, written by another*
adduce, attest, cite, detail, excerpt, extract, instance, name, paraphrase, parrot, proclaim, recall, recite, recollect, reference, refer to, retell; SEE CONCEPTS *79,171*

R

rabid [*adj*] *very angry; maniacal*
berserk, bigoted, bitten, corybantic, crazed*, crazy, delirious, deranged, enthusiastic, extreme, extremist, fanatical, fervent, flipped*, foaming at the mouth*, frantic, freaked out*, frenetic, frenzied, furious, hot*, hydrophobic, infuriated, insane, intemperate, intolerant, irrational, keen, mad, mad-dog*, narrow-minded, nutty*, obsessed, overboard, poisoned, radical, raging, revolutionary, sick*, sizzling, smoking*, steamed up*, ultra, ultraist, violent, virulent, wild, zealous; SEE CONCEPT *403*

race [*n1*] *pursuit; running, speeding*
chase, clash, clip, competition, contention, contest, course, dash, engagement, event, go, marathon, match, meet, relay, rivalry, run, rush, scurry, sprint, spurt; SEE CONCEPT *363*

race [*n2*] *ethnic group*
blood, breed, clan, color, cultural group, culture, family, folk, house, issue, kin, kind, kindred, line, lineage, nation, nationality, offspring, people, progeny, seed, species, stock, strain, tribe, type, variety; SEE CONCEPT *380*

race [*n3*] *stream, river*
branch, brook, creek, duct, gill, raceway, rill, rindle, rivulet, run, runnel, sluice, tide; SEE CONCEPT *514*

race [*v*] *run, speed in competition*
boil, bolt, bustle, career, chase, compete, contest, course, dart, dash, fling, fly, gallop, haste, hasten, hie, hurry, hustle, lash, outstrip, plunge ahead, post, pursue, rush, scamper, scramble, scud, scuttle, shoot, skim, sprint, spurt, swoop, tear, whisk, wing; SEE CONCEPTS *150,363*

racial [*adj*] *ethnic*
ancestral, ethnological, folk, genealogical, genetic, hereditary, lineal, maternal, matriarchal, national, paternal, patriarchal, phyletic, phylogenetic, tribal; SEE CONCEPT *549*

racism [*n*] *prejudice against an ethnic group*
apartheid, bias, bigotry, discrimination, illiberality, one-sidedness, partiality, racialism, sectarianism, segregation, unfairness; SEE CONCEPT *689*

rack [*n*] *frame, framework*
arbor, bed, box, bracket, counter, furniture, holder, ledge, perch, receptacle, shelf, stand, structure, trestle; SEE CONCEPTS *443,479*

rack [*v*] *torture; strain*
afflict, agonize, crucify, distress, excruciate, force, harass, harrow, martyr, oppress, pain, persecute, pull, shake, stress, stretch, tear, torment, try, wrench, wring; SEE CONCEPTS *7,19,246*

racket [*n1*] *commotion; fight*
agitation, babel, battle, blare, brawl, clamor, clangor, clash, clatter, commotion, din, disturbance, fracas, free-for-all*, fuss, hoo-ha*, hubbub*, jangle, noise, outcry, pandemonium, riot, roar, row, ruction, rumpus*, shouting, shuffle, squabble, squall, stir, to-do*, tumult, turbulence, turmoil, uproar, vociferation, wrangle; SEE CONCEPTS *65,106,230*

racket [*n2*] *criminal activity*
cheating, confidence game, con game, conspiracy, corruption, crime, dirty pool*, dishonesty, dodge, extortion, fraud, game, graft, illegality, illicit scheme, intrigue, lawlessness, lay, plot, push, scheme, shakedown, squeeze*, swindle, swindling, theft, trick, underworld; SEE CONCEPT *192*

racy [*adj1*] *energetic, zestful*
animated, bright, buoyant, clever, distinctive, entertaining, exciting, exhilarating, fiery, forceful, forcible, gingery, heady, keen, lively, mettlesome, peppery, piquant, playful, poignant, pungent, rich, salty, saucy, sharp, snappy, sparkling, spicy, spirited, sportive, sprightly, stimulating, strong, tangy, tart, tasty, vigorous, vivacious, witty, zesty; SEE CONCEPTS *401,613*

racy [*adj2*] *risqué, vulgar*
bawdy, blue*, broad, erotic, immodest, indecent, indelicate, lewd, lurid, naughty, off-color*, purple*, shady*, smutty*, spicy*, suggestive, wicked; SEE CONCEPTS *267,545*

radiance [*n1*] *brightness, luminescence*
brilliance, effulgence, glare, gleam, glitter, glow, incandescence, light, luminosity, luster, resplendence, shine; SEE CONCEPT *620*

radiance [*n2*] *happiness*
delight, gaiety, joy, pleasure, rapture, warmth; SEE CONCEPT *633*

radiant [*adj1*] *bright, luminous*
beaming, brilliant, effulgent, gleaming, glittering, glorious, glowing, incandescent, lambent, lucent, lustrous, radiating, refulgent, resplendent, shining, sparkling, sunny; SEE CONCEPT *617*

radiant [*adj2*] *happy in appearance*
beaming, beatific, blissful, bright, cheerful, cheery, delighted, ecstatic, gay, glad, glowing, joyful, joyous, rapturous; SEE CONCEPT *401*

radiate [v] *give off; scatter*
afford, beam, branch out, broadcast, circulate, diffuse, disseminate, distribute, diverge, emanate, emit, expand, give out, gleam, glitter, illumine, irradiate, issue, light up, pour, proliferate, propagate, ramble, ramify, send out, shed, shine, shoot out, spread, spread out, sprinkle, strew, throw out, transmit, yield; SEE CONCEPTS *118,217,620,716*

radical [n] *person who advocates significant, often extreme change*
agitator, anarchist, avant-garde, extremist, fanatic, firebrand, freethinker, iconoclast, insurgent, insurrectionist, leftist, left-winger, militant, mutineer, nihilist, nonconformist, objector, pacifist, progressive, rebel, reformer, renegade, revolter, revolutionary, rioter, secessionist, subversive, ultraist; SEE CONCEPT *359*

radical [adj1] *fundamental, basic*
basal, bottom, cardinal, constitutional, deep-seated, essential, foundational, inherent, innate, intrinsic, meat-and-potatoes*, native, natural, organic, original, primal, primary, primitive, profound, thoroughgoing, underlying, vital; SEE CONCEPTS *546,549*

radical [adj2] *deviating by extremes*
advanced, anarchistic, complete, entire, excessive, extremist, fanatical, far-out*, freethinking, iconoclastic, immoderate, insubordinate, insurgent, insurrectionary, intransigent, lawless, leftist, militant, mutinous, nihilistic, progressive, rabid, rebellious, recalcitrant, recusant, refractory, restive, revolutionary, riotous, seditious, severe, sweeping, thorough, ultra, ultraist, uncompromising, violent, way out*; SEE CONCEPTS *403,529,542*

radio [n] *communication by electronic air waves*
AM-FM, CB, Marconi, radionics, radiotelegraph, radiotelegraphy, radiotelephone, radio-telephonics, receiver, shortwave, telegraphy, telephony, transmission, walkman, wireless; SEE CONCEPT *279*

radius [n] *range, sweep*
ambit, boundary, compass, expanse, extension, extent, interval, limit, orbit, purview, reach, semidiameter, space, span, spoke; SEE CONCEPT *651*

raffish [adj] *unmindful of social conventions*
bohemian*, careless, casual, coarse, dashing, devil-may-care*, disreputable, fast*, gay, jaunty, rakish, sporty, tasteless, tawdry, unconventional, uncouth, vulgar, wild; SEE CONCEPT *401*

raffle [n] *lottery for a prize*
bet, betting, disposition, draw, drawing, flier*, gambling, game of chance, gaming, long odds*, lots*, numbers*, numbers game*, pool, random shot, speculation, stake, sweep, sweepstake, tossup*, wager, wagering; SEE CONCEPTS *363,364*

ragamuffin [n] *person who is poor, tattered*
beggar, bum*, gamin, guttersnipe*, hobo, loafer, orphan, scarecrow, street person, tatterdemalion*, tramp, urchin, vagabond, vagrant, waif, wastrel; SEE CONCEPTS *412,423*

rage [n1] *extreme anger*
acerbity, acrimony, agitation, animosity, apoplexy, asperity, bitterness, blowup*, bluster, choler, convulsion, dander, eruption, exasperation, excitement, explosion, ferment, ferocity, fireworks, frenzy, furor, fury, gall, heat*, hemorrhage, huff*, hysterics, indignation, ire, irritation, madness, mania, obsession, outburst, paroxysm, passion, rampage, raving, resentment, spasm, spleen, squall, storm, tantrum, temper, umbrage, uproar, upset, vehemence, violence, wingding*, wrath; SEE CONCEPTS *410,657*

rage [n2] *something in vogue; popular notion*
caprice, chic, conceit, craze, crotchet, cry, dernier cri, enthusiasm, fad, fancy, fashion, freak, furor, happening, hot spot*, in*, in-spot*, in-thing*, last word*, latest*, latest thing*, latest wrinkle*, mania, mode, newest wrinkle*, now*, passion, style, thing*, up to the minute*, vagary, vogue, whim; SEE CONCEPTS *388,655*

rage [v] *be very angry*
be beside oneself*, be furious, be uncontrollable, blow a fuse*, blow one's top*, blow up*, boil over*, bristle, chafe, champ at bit*, erupt, fly off the handle*, foam at the mouth*, fret, fulminate, fume, go berserk, have a fit, have a tantrum, let off steam*, look daggers*, make a fuss over, overflow, rail at, rampage, rant, rant and rave*, rave, roar, scold, scream, seethe, snap at, splutter, steam, storm, surge, tear, throw a fit*, work oneself into sweat*, yell; SEE CONCEPTS *29,410*

ragged [adj] *worn-out; in shreds*
badly dressed, badly worn, battered, broken, contemptible, crude, desultory, dilapidated, dingy, disorganized, down at the heel*, fragmented, frayed, frazzled, full of holes*, in holes*, in rags, in tatters*, irregular, jagged, mean, moth-eaten, notched, patched, poor, poorly made, rent, rough, rugged, scraggy, seedy, serrated, shabby, shaggy, shoddy, shredded, tacky*, tattered, tatty*, threadbare, torn, uneven, unfinished, unkempt, unpressed, worse for wear*; SEE CONCEPT *485*

raging [adj] *violent; very mad*
angry, at boiling point*, bent*, bent out of shape*, beside oneself*, blowing a gasket*, blowing one's top*, blustering, blustery, boiling mad*, boiling over*, enraged, fit to be tied*, frenzied, fuming, furious, going ape*, incensed, infuriated, irate, mad as a hornet*, on the warpath*, rabid*, ranting and raving*, raving, raving mad, rough, seeing red*, seething, stormy, tempestuous, throwing a fit, turbulent, wild; SEE CONCEPTS *403,542*

raid [n] *attack, seizure*
arrest, assault, break-in, bust, capture, descent, foray, forced entrance, hit-and-run*, incursion, inroad, invasion, irruption, onset, onslaught, pull, reconnaissance, roundup, sally*, shootup*, sortie*, surprise attack, sweep, tipover*; SEE CONCEPTS *86,317*

raid [v] *attack, pillage*
assail, assault, blockade, bomb, bombard, breach, break in, charge, descend on, despoil, devastate, fall upon, fire on, forage, foray, harass, harry, heat, inroad, invade, knock off*, knock over*, lean against, lean on, loot, maraud, march on, overrun, pirate, plunder, rake, ransack, rifle, rob, sack, sally, sally forth, shell, slough, spoliate, storm, strafe, strike, sweep, swoop, tip over*, torpedo, waste; SEE CONCEPT 86

rail/railing [n] *post, pole along an edge*
balustrade, banister, bar, barrier, fence, paling, rails, rest, siding; SEE CONCEPTS 443,479

rail [v] *criticize harshly*
abuse, attack, bawl out*, berate, blast, castigate, censure, chew out*, complain, fulminate, fume, inveigh, jaw, objurate, rant, rate, revile, scold, thunder, tongue-lash*, upbraid, vituperate, vociferate, whip; SEE CONCEPT 52

rain [n] *downpour of water or other substance*
cat-and-dog weather*, cloudburst, condensation, deluge, drencher, drizzle, fall, flood, flurry, hail, heavy dew, liquid sunshine*, mist, monsoon, pour, pouring, precip*, precipitation, raindrops, rainfall, rainstorm, sheets, shower, showers, sleet, spate, spit, sprinkle, sprinkling, stream, sun shower*, torrent, volley*, wet stuff*, window washer*; SEE CONCEPT 526

rain [v] *drop water or other substance*
bestow, bucket, come down in buckets*, deposit, drizzle, fall, hail, lavish, mist, patter, pour, shower, sleet, sprinkle, storm; SEE CONCEPT 526

raise [n] *increase in salary or position*
accession, accretion, addition, advance, augmentation, boost, bump, hike, hold-up*, increment, jump, jump-up*, leg*, leg-up*, move-up*, promotion, raising, rise, step-up*; SEE CONCEPTS 344,351,763

raise [v1] *lift; build from the ground*
boost, bring up, construct, elevate, erect, establish, exalt, heave, hoist, hold up, lever, lift, lift up, mount, move up, place up, prise, promote, pry, pull up, put on its end, put up, rear, run up, set up, set upright, shove, stand up, take up, throw up, upcast, upheave, uplift, upraise, uprear; SEE CONCEPTS 168,196

raise [v2] *increase, augment*
advance, aggravate, amplify, assemble, boost, build up, collect, congregate, congress, dignify, enhance, enlarge, escalate, exaggerate, exalt, fetch up, forgather, form, gather, get, goose*, goose up*, heighten, hike, hike up*, honor, inflate, intensify, jack up, jump, jump up, levy, look up, magnify, mass, mobilize, mushroom*, muster, obtain, perk up, pick up, promote, put up, pyramid, rally, recruit, reinforce, rendezvous, run up*, send through the roof*, shoot up, snowball*, strengthen, up; SEE CONCEPTS 236,244,245

raise [v3] *start up, motivate; introduce*
abet, activate, advance, arouse, awaken, bring up, broach, cause, evoke, excite, foment, foster, incite,

instigate, kindle, moot, motivate, provoke, put forward, resurrect, set, set on, stir up, suggest, whip up; SEE CONCEPTS 75,221

raise [v4] *nurture, care for*
breed, bring up, cultivate, develop, drag up, fetch up, foster, group, grow, nourish, nurse, plant, produce, propagate, provide, rear, sow, suckle, support, train, wean; SEE CONCEPTS 253,257,295

rake [n] *man who frequently seeks casual sex*
Casanova*, chaser, debauchee, dissolute man, Don Juan*, gigolo, lecher*, libertine, Lothario*, philanderer, playboy*, player*, profligate, rascal, roué, seducer, sensualist, sport*, swinger, tomcat*, voluptuary*, wolf*, womanizer; SEE CONCEPTS 412,419

rake [v] *scrape up, hoe*
break up, clean up, clear, clear up, collect, comb, enfilade, examine, finecomb, fine-tooth-comb*, gather, grade, graze, grub, harrow, hunt, ransack, rasp, remove, rummage, scan, scour, scrape, scratch, scrutinize, search, smooth, sweep, weed; SEE CONCEPTS 109,165,178,216

rakish [adj] *charming and immoral*
abandoned, chic, dashing, debauched, depraved, devil-may-care*, dissipated, dissolute, fashionable, fast*, flashy, gay, jaunty, lecherous, licentious, loose*, natty, prodigal, profligate, raffish, saucy, sinful, smart, sporty, wanton, wild; SEE CONCEPTS 401,545

rally [n1] *celebratory meeting*
assemblage, assembly, celebration, clambake*, convention, convocation, get-together, mass meeting, meet, pep rally, pow-wow*, session; SEE CONCEPTS 377,386

rally [n2] *turn for the better*
comeback, improvement, recovery, recuperation, renewal, resurgence, revival, turning point; SEE CONCEPT 700

rally [v1] *reorganize, unite*
arouse, assemble, awaken, bestir, bond together, bring together, bring to order, call to arms*, challenge, charge, collect, come about, come together, come to order, convene, counterattack, encourage, fire, gather, get together, inspirit, kindle, marshal, mobilize, muster, organize, reassemble, redouble, reform, refresh, regroup, rejuvenate, renew, restore, resurrect, resuscitate, revive, round up, rouse, summon, surge, urge, wake, waken, whet, wreak havoc*; SEE CONCEPTS 7,22,117,320

rally [v2] *revive; take a turn for the better*
bounce back, brace up, come along, come around, come from behind, enliven, get act together*, get back in shape*, get better, get second wind*, grow stronger, improve, invigorate, make a comeback, perk up, pick up, pull through, recover, recuperate, refresh, regain strength, shape up, snap out of it, surge, turn around, turn things around*; SEE CONCEPT 700

ram [*v*] *bang into; pack forcibly*
beat, butt, collide with, cram, crash, crowd, dash, dig, drive, drum, force, hammer, hit, hook, impact, jack, jam-pack, pack, plunge, poke, pound, run, run into, sink, slam, smash, stab, stick, strike, strike head-on, stuff, tamp, thrust, wedge; SEE CONCEPTS *189,208,209*

ramble [*n*] *aimless walk*
constitutional, excursion, hike, perambulation, peregrination, roaming, roving, saunter, stroll, tour, traipse, trip, turn; SEE CONCEPTS *151,224*

ramble [*v1*] *wander about; travel aimlessly*
amble, bat around*, be all over the map*, branch off, clamber, climb, cruise, depart, digress, divagate, diverge, drift, excurse, extend, fork, gad, gallivant, get sidetracked*, knock about*, knock around*, meander, perambulate, percolate, peregrinate, promenade, range, roam, rove, saunter, scramble, snake, sprangle, sprawl, spread, spread-eagle, straddle, straggle, stray, stroll, trail, traipse, turn, twist, walk, wind, zigzag; SEE CONCEPTS *151,154,581,692*

ramble [*v2*] *talk aimlessly, endlessly*
amplify, babble, beat around bush*, be diffuse, blather, chatter, depart, descant, digress, divagate, diverge, drift, drivel, dwell on, enlarge, excurse, expatiate, get off the subject*, go astray, go off on tangent*, go on and on*, gossip, harp on, lose the thread*, maunder, meander, prose, protract, rant and rave*, rattle on*, stray, talk nonsense, talk off top of head*, talk randomly, wander; SEE CONCEPT *51*

rambling [*adj1*] *disconnected, wordy*
circuitous, confused, desultory, diffuse, digressive, discursive, disjointed, incoherent, incongruous, irregular, long-winded, periphrastic, prolix; SEE CONCEPT *267*

rambling [*adj2*] *sprawling, spread out*
at length, covering, gangling, here and there, irregular, random, scattered, spreading, straggling, strewn, trailing, unplanned; SEE CONCEPTS *485,772*

rambunctious [*adj*] *loud, energetic*
boisterous, noisy, raucous, rough, rowdy, rude, termagant, tumultous/tumultuous, turbulent, unruly; SEE CONCEPT *542*

ramification [*n*] *consequence, development*
bifurcation, branch, branching, breaking, complication, consequence, divarication, division, excrescence, extension, forking, offshoot, outgrowth, partition, radiation, result, sequel, subdividing, subdivision, upshot; SEE CONCEPTS *98,230,824*

ramp [*n*] *incline*
access, adit, grade, gradient, hill, inclination, inclined plane, rise, slope; SEE CONCEPTS *443,757*

rampage [*n*] *storm, violence*
binge, blowup, boiling point*, destruction, disturbance, ferment, fling, frenzy, fury, mad*, more heat than light*, orgy, rage, ruckus, splurge, spree, tear, tempest, tumult, turmoil, uproar, wingding; SEE CONCEPT *86*

rampage [*v*] *go crazy; storm*
go berserk, rage, run amuck, run riot, run wild, tear; SEE CONCEPTS *86,384*

rampant [*adj*] *uncontrolled, out of hand*
aggressive, blustering, boisterous, clamorous, dominant, epidemic, exceeding bounds, excessive, extravagant, exuberant, fanatical, flagrant, furious, growing, impetuous, impulsive, luxuriant, on the rampage, out of control, outrageous, pandemic, predominant, prevalent, profuse, raging, rampaging, rank, rife, riotous, spreading, tumultous/tumultuous, turbulent, unbridled, unchecked, uncontrollable, ungovernable, unrestrained, unruly, vehement, violent, wanton, widespread, wild; SEE CONCEPTS *544,554,772*

rampart [*n*] *fortification, stronghold*
barricade, barrier, bastion, breastwork, bulwark, defense, earthwork, elevation, embankment, fence, fort, guard, hill, mound, parapet, protection, ridge, security, support, vallation, wall; SEE CONCEPTS *321,439,509*

ramshackle [*adj*] *falling apart; in poor condition*
broken-down, crumbling, decrepit, derelict, dilapidated, flimsy, jerry-built*, rickety, shabby, shaky, tottering, tumble-down, unfirm, unsafe, unsteady; SEE CONCEPTS *485,488*

rancid [*adj*] *rotten, strong-smelling*
bad, carious, contaminated, curdled, decomposing, disagreeable, disgusting, evil-smelling, feculent, fetid, foul, frowzy, fusty, gamy, high, impure, loathsome, malodorous, moldy, musty, nasty, nidorous, noisome, noxious, off, offensive, olid, polluted, putrefactive, putrefied, putrescent, putrid, rank, reeky, repulsive, sharp, smelly, sour, soured, stale, stinking, strong, tainted, turned, unhealthy, whiffy; SEE CONCEPTS *462,570,598,613*

rancor [*n*] *bitterness, hatefulness*
acerbity, acrimony, animosity, animus, antagonism, antipathy, aversion, bad blood*, bile*, dudgeon, enmity, grudge, hardness of heart*, harshness, hate, hatred, hostility, ill feeling, ill will, malevolence, malice, malignity, mordacity, pique, resentfulness, resentment, retaliation, revengefulness, ruthlessness, spite, spitefulness, spleen, umbrage, uncharitableness, unfriendliness, variance, vengeance, vengefulness, venom, vindictiveness, virulence; SEE CONCEPTS *29,410,633*

random [*adj*] *haphazard, chance*
accidental, adventitious, aimless, arbitrary, casual, contingent, designless, desultory, driftless, fluky, fortuitous, hit-or-miss*, incidental, indiscriminate, irregular, objectless, odd, promiscuous, purposeless, slapdash*, spot, stray, unaimed, unconsidered, unplanned, unpremeditated; SEE CONCEPTS *535,548,557*

range [*n1*] *sphere, distance, extent*
ambit, amplitude, area, bounds, circle, compass, confines, diapason, dimension, dimensions, domain, earshot*, elbowroom*, expanse, extension, exten-

sity, field, gamut, hearing, ken, latitude, leeway, length, limits, magnitude, matter, neighborhood, orbit, order, panorama, parameters, play, province, purview, radius, reach, realm, run, run of, scope, space, span, spectrum, sphere, spread, stretch, sweep, swing, territory, tune, vicinity, width; SEE CONCEPTS *651,743,745,756,761,787*

range [*n2*] *order, series*
assortment, chain, class, collection, file, gamut, kind, line, lot, rank, row, selection, sequence, sort, string, tier, variety; SEE CONCEPTS *727,769*

range [*v1*] *order, categorize*
align, allineate, arrange, array, assort, bias, bracket, catalogue, categorize, class, classify, dispose, draw up, file, grade, group, incline, line, line up, pigeonhole*, predispose, rank; SEE CONCEPTS *84,158*

range [*v2*] *wander, roam*
circumambulate, cover, cross, cruise, drift, encompass, explore, float, follow one's nose*, gallivant, globe-trot*, hit the road*, hit the trail*, make circuit, meander, pass over, ply, prowl, ramble, reach, reconnoiter, rove, scour, search, spread, straggle, stray, stroll, sweep, traipse, tramp, travel, traverse, trek; SEE CONCEPTS *151,224*

range [*v3*] *extend; change within limits*
differ, diverge from, fluctuate, go, reach, run, stretch, vary, vary between; SEE CONCEPT *697*

rangy [*adj*] *long and lean*
gangling, gangly, lanky, leggy, long-legged, long-limbed, reedy, skinny, spindling, spindly, thin, weedy; SEE CONCEPTS *491,779*

rank [*n1*] *standing in a system, often a social one*
ancestry, authority, birth, blood, cachet, capacity, caste, circumstance, class, classification, condition, consequence, degree, dignity, distinction, division, echelon, estate, esteem, family, footing, grade, hierarchy, level, nobility, note, order, paramountcy, parentage, pecking order, pedigree, place, position, primacy, privilege, quality, reputation, seniority, situation, slot, sort, sovereignty, sphere, state, station, stature, status, stock, stratum, supremacy, type; SEE CONCEPTS *296,378,388,744*

rank [*n2*] *column, tier of individuals*
echelon, file, formation, group, hierarchy, line, queue, range, row, series, string; SEE CONCEPT *727*

rank [*adj1*] *stinking, foul*
bad, dank, disagreeable, disgusting, evil-smelling, feculent, fetid, funky, fusty*, gamy*, graveolent, gross*, high, humid, loathsome, mephitic, moldy, musty, nasty, nauseating, noisome, noxious, obnoxious, off, offensive, olid, pungent, putrescent, putrid, rancid, reeking, repulsive, revolting, smelly, sour, stale, strong, strong-smelling, tainted, turned; SEE CONCEPT *598*

rank [*adj2*] *abundant, luxurious*
coarse, dense, excessive, extreme, exuberant, fertile, flourishing, fructiferous, grown, high-growing, junglelike, lavish, lush, luxuriant, overabundant, overgrown, productive, profuse, prolific, rampant, rich,

semitropical, tropical, vigorous, wild; SEE CONCEPT *485*

rank [*adj3*] *utter, absolute*
arrant, blatant, capital, complete, conspicuous, consummate, downright, egregious, excessive, extravagant, flagrant, glaring, gross, noticeable, outright, outstanding, perfect, positive, rampant, sheer, thorough, total, undisguised, unmitigated; SEE CONCEPTS *531,535*

rank [*adj4*] *obscene, vulgar*
abusive, atrocious, coarse, crass, dirty*, filthy, foul, gross*, indecent, nasty, outrageous, raunchy, scurrilous, shocking, smutty*, wicked; SEE CONCEPT *545*

rank [*v1*] *line up; classify in system*
align, arrange, array, assign, assort, button down*, class, dispose, establish, estimate, evaluate, fix*, give precedence, grade, include, judge, list, locate, marshal, order, peg, pigeonhole*, place, place in formation, position, put, put away, put down as, put down for, put in line, range, rate, regard, settle, size up, sort, tab, typecast, valuate, value; SEE CONCEPTS *37,84,158*

rank [*v2*] *be worthwhile; have supremacy*
antecede, be classed, belong, be worth, come first, count among, forerun, go ahead of, go before, have the advantage, outrank, precede, stand, take the lead; SEE CONCEPTS *388,671*

rankle [*v*] *annoy, irritate*
aggravate, anger, bother, chafe, embitter, exasperate, fester, fret, gall, get one's goat*, harass, hurt, inflame, irk, irritate, mortify, nettle, obsess, pain, pester, plague, rile, torment, vex; SEE CONCEPTS *7,14,19*

ransack [*v*] *turn inside out in search; ravage*
appropriate, comb, despoil, explore, ferret, filch, fine-tooth-comb*, go through, gut*, hunt, investigate, lay waste, leave no stone unturned*, lift, look all over for*, look high and low*, look into, loot, make off with*, maraud, overhaul, peer, pilfer, pillage, pinch, plunder, poach, probe, pry, purloin, raid, rake, rape, ravish, rifle, rob, rummage, rustle, sack, scan, scour, scrutinize, search, seek, seize, shake down*, sound, spoil, spy, steal, strip, take away, thieve; SEE CONCEPTS *103,139,142,216*

ransom [*n*] *blackmail money paid for return of possession or person*
bribe, compensation, deliverance, expiation, liberation, money, payment, payoff, price, redemption, release, rescue; SEE CONCEPT *344*

ransom [*v*] *pay blackmail money for return of possession or person*
buy freedom of, buy out, deliver, emancipate, extricate, free, liberate, manumit, obtain release of, pay for release of, recover, redeem, regain, release, reprise, repurchase, rescue, save, set free, unchain, unfetter; SEE CONCEPTS *127,131,341*

rant [*n*] *yelling, raving*
bluster, bombast, diatribe, fustian, harangue, oration, philippic, rhapsody, rhetoric, rodomontade, tirade, vociferation; SEE CONCEPTS *44,49,52*

rant [v] *yell, rave*
bellow, bloviate, blow one's top*, bluster, carry on, clamor, cry, declaim, fume, harangue, mouth, objurgate, orate, perorate, rage, rail, roar, scold, shout, sizzle*, soapbox*, sound off*, spiel*, spout*, storm*, stump*, take on*, vociferate; SEE CONCEPTS *44,49,52*

rap [n1/v1] *hit quickly and lightly*
beat, blow, conk, crack, knock, lick, pat, strike, swat, swipe, tap, whack; SEE CONCEPT *189*

rap [n2] *conversation*
causerie, chat, chin, colloquy, confabulation, conference, deliberation, dialogue, discourse, discussion, prose, talk, ventilation, yarn; SEE CONCEPTS *56,266*

rap [n3] *blame; criticism*
admonishment, admonition, censure, chiding, flak, knock, pan*, punishment, rebuke, reprimand, reproach, reproof, responsibility, sentence, swipe; SEE CONCEPTS *52,123,317*

rap [v2] *talk casually; speak abruptly*
babble, bark, chat, chatter, chitchat, confabulate, converse, discourse, jabber, palaver, run off at the mouth*, spit, talk; SEE CONCEPTS *56,266*

rap [v3] *criticize*
blame, castigate, censure, condemn, denounce, denunciate, knock*, pan*, reprehend, reprimand, reprobate, scold, skin, tick off*; SEE CONCEPT *52*

rape [n] *defilement, sexual assault*
abduction, abuse, criminal attack, criminal ravishment, defloration, deflowering, depredation, desecration, despoilment, despoliation, devirgination, forcible violation, maltreatment, molestation, outrage, perversion, pillage, plunder, plundering, rapine, ravishment, sack, seduction, sexual assault, spoliation, statutory offense, violation; SEE CONCEPTS *192,375*

rape [v] *sexually assault; defile*
abuse, attack, betray, compromise, corrupt, debauch, deceive, deflorate, deflower, despoil, devirginate, dishonor, entice, force, loot, lure, maltreat, mislead, molest, outrage, pillage, plunder, ransack, ravish, ruin, sack, seduce, seize, shame, spoliate, tempt, violate, wrong; SEE CONCEPTS *192,375*

rapid [adj] *very quick*
accelerated, active, agile, breakneck*, brisk, double time, expeditious, expeditive, express, fast, fleet, fleet of foot*, flying, hasty, hurried, in nothing flat*, light-footed*, like house on fire*, lively, mercurial, nimble, on the double*, precipitate, prompt, quick as a wink*, quickened, ready, really rolling*, screaming*, speedy, spry, swift, winged; SEE CONCEPTS *541,588,799*

rapidity [n] *quickness*
acceleration, alacrity, bat, briskness, celerity, dispatch, expedition, fleetness, gait, haste, hurry, pace, precipitateness, promptitude, promptness, rapidness, rush, speed, speediness, swiftness, velocity; SEE CONCEPTS *755,805*

rapidly [adv] *very quickly*
at speed, briskly, expeditiously, fast, flat-out*, full tilt*, hastily, hurriedly, immediately, in a hurry, in a rush, in haste, lickety-split*, like a shot*, posthaste*, precipitately, promptly, speedily, swiftly, with dispatch; SEE CONCEPTS *544,588,799*

rapport [n] *understanding between people*
affinity, agreement, bond, compatibility, concord, cotton, empathy, good vibes*, good vibrations, groove, harmony, hitting it off*, interrelationship, link, relationship, same wavelength*, simpatico*, soul, sympathy, the groove*, togetherness, unity; SEE CONCEPT *388*

rapprochement [n] *restoration of harmony*
agreement, cordiality, detente, friendliness, friendship, harmonizing, harmony, reconcilement, reconciliation, reunion, softening; SEE CONCEPTS *384,388*

rapt [adj] *absorbed, fascinated*
absent, absent-minded, abstracted, beguiled, bewitched, blissful, busy, captivated, carried away*, caught up in*, charmed, daydreaming, deep*, delighted, dreaming, ecstatic, employed, enamored, engaged, engrossed, enraptured, enthralled, entranced, gripped*, happy, held*, hung up*, hypnotized, immersed, inattentive, intent, involved, lost, oblivious, occupied, overwhelmed, preoccupied, rapturous, ravished, spellbound, taken*, transported, unconscious, wrapped*, wrapped up*; SEE CONCEPT *403*

rapture [n] *extreme happiness and delight in something*
altitudes, at-oneness*, beatitude, bliss, buoyancy, cheer, cloud nine*, communion, contentment, cool*, delectation, delight, ecstasy, elation, elysium, enchantment, enjoyment, enthusiasm, euphoria, exaltation, exhilaration, felicity, gaiety, gladness, glory, good spirits, gratification, heaven, inspiration, joy, jubilation, nirvana, paradise, passion, pleasure, ravishment, rhapsody, satisfaction, seventh heaven*, spell, transport, well-being; SEE CONCEPTS *32,410*

rare [adj1] *exceptional, infrequent*
attenuate, attenuated, deficient, extraordinary, few, few and far between*, flimsy, inconceivable, isolated, light, limited, occasional, out of the ordinary, rarefied, recherché, scanty, scarce, scattered, seldom, semioccasional, short, singular, sparse, sporadic, strange, subtile, subtle, tenuous, thin, uncommon, unfrequent, unheard of, unimaginable, unique, unlikely, unthinkable, unwonted; SEE CONCEPTS *530,576*

rare [adj2] *precious, excellent*
admirable, choice, dainty, delicate, elegant, exquisite, extreme, fine, great, incomparable, invaluable, matchless, peerless, priceless, recherché, rich, select, superb, superlative, unique; SEE CONCEPT *574*

rare [adj3] *not fully cooked*
bloody, half-cooked, half-raw, moderately done, nearly raw, not done, rarely done, red, undercooked, underdone; SEE CONCEPT *462*

rarely [adv] not often; exceptionally
almost never, barely, extra, extraordinarily, extremely, finely, hardly, hardly ever, infrequently, little, notably, now and then, once in a while, once in blue moon, on rare occasions, remarkably, scarcely ever, seldom, singularly, uncommon, uncommonly, unfrequently, unoften, unusually; SEE CONCEPTS 530,541

rascal [n] person who is unprincipled, does not work hard
bastard, beggar, blackguard, black sheep*, bully, bum, cad, cardsharp*, charlatan, cheat, delinquent, devil, disgrace, felon, fraud, good-for-nothing*, grafter, hooligan*, hypocrite, idler, imp, knave, liar, loafer, miscreant, mountebank, ne'er-do-well*, opportunist, pretender, prodigal, profligate, rake, rapscallion, recreant, reprobate, robber, rogue, rowdy, ruffian, scallawag, scamp, scoundrel, shyster, sinner, skunk*, sneak, swindler, tough*, tramp, trickster, varmint*, villain, wastrel, wretch; SEE CONCEPT 412

rash [n] outbreak of disease or condition
breakout, epidemic, eruption, flood, hives, plague, series, spate, succession, wave; SEE CONCEPTS 230,306

rash [adj] careless, impulsive
adventurous, audacious, bold, brash, daring, determined, devil-may-care*, fiery, foolhardy, frenzied, furious, harebrained, hasty, headlong, headstrong, heedless, hotheaded, ill-advised, ill-considered, immature, impetuous, imprudent, incautious, indiscreet, injudicious, insuppressible, irrational, jumping to conclusions*, madcap, overhasty, passionate, precipitant, precipitate, premature, reckless, thoughtless, unguarded, unthinking, unwary, venturesome, venturous, wild; SEE CONCEPT 401

rasp [v] grind, rub
abrade, bray, excoriate, file, grate, irk, irritate, jar, pound, raze, rub, sand, scour, scrape, scratch, vex, wear; SEE CONCEPTS 7,19,186,215

rate [n1] ratio, proportion
amount, comparison, degree, estimate, percentage, progression, quota, relation, relationship, relative, scale, standard, weight; SEE CONCEPT 768

rate [n2] fee charged for service, privilege, goods
allowance, charge, cost, dues, duty, estimate, figure, hire, price, price tag, quotation, tab, tariff, tax, toll, valuation; SEE CONCEPTS 329,766

rate [n3] speed, pace
clip, dash, flow, gait, gallop, hop, measure, motion, movement, pace, spurt, tempo, time, tread, velocity; SEE CONCEPT 755

rate [v1] judge, classify
adjudge, admire, appraise, apprise, assay, assess, button down*, calculate, class, consider, count, deem, determine, esteem, estimate, evaluate, fix, grade, guess at, measure, peg, pigeonhole*, price, put away, put down as*, put down for*, rank,

reckon, redline, regard, relate to standard, respect, score, set at, size up*, stand in with, survey, tab*, tag, take one's measure, think highly of, typecast, valuate, value, weigh; SEE CONCEPTS 12,37

rate [v2] be entitled to
be accepted, be favorite, be welcome, be worthy, deserve, earn, merit, prosper, succeed, triumph; SEE CONCEPTS 129,376,388

rather [adv1] moderately
a bit, a little, averagely, comparatively, enough, fairly, in a certain degree, kind of, more or less, passably, pretty, quite, ratherish, reasonably, relatively, slightly, some, something, somewhat, sort of, so-so*, tolerably, to some degree, to some extent; SEE CONCEPTS 544,548

rather [adv2] significantly
a good bit, considerably, noticeably, quite, somewhat, very, well; SEE CONCEPTS 544,772

rather [adv3] preferably; instead
alternately, alternatively, as a matter of choice, by choice, by preference, first, in lieu of, in preference, just as soon, more readily, more willingly, much sooner, sooner, willingly; SEE CONCEPT 529

ratify [v] affirm, authorize
accredit, approve, authenticate, bear out, bind, bless, certify, commission, confirm, consent, corroborate, endorse, establish, give stamp of approval*, go for*, license, okay*, rubber stamp*, sanction, sign, substantiate, uphold, validate; SEE CONCEPTS 50,88

ratio [n] percentage, relation of part to whole
arrangement, correlation, correspondence, equation, fraction, proportion, proportionality, quota, quotient, rate, relationship, scale; SEE CONCEPT 768

ration [n] allotment of limited supply
allowance, apportionment, assignment, bit, consignment, cut, distribution, division, divvy*, dole, drag, food, helping, measure, meed, part, piece of action*, portion, provender, provision, quantum, quota, share, store, supply; SEE CONCEPTS 457,835

ration [v] divide something into portions
allocate, allot, apportion, assign, budget, conserve, control, deal, distribute, divvy*, dole, give out, issue, limit, measure out, mete, mete out, parcel, parcel out, proportion, prorate, quota, restrict, save, share; SEE CONCEPTS 98,140

rational [adj] realistic; of sound mind
all there*, analytical, balanced, calm, cerebral, circumspect, cognitive, collected, cool*, deductive, deliberate, discerning, discriminating, enlightened, farsighted, impartial, intellectual, intelligent, judicious, knowing, levelheaded, logical, lucid, normal, objective, perspicacious, philosophic, prudent, ratiocinative, reasonable, reasoning, reflective, sagacious, sane, sensible, sober, sound, stable, synthetic, thinking, thoughtful, together, well-advised, wise; SEE CONCEPT 402

rationale [n] logic for belief, action
account, excuse, explanation, exposition, grounds, hypothesis, justification, motivation, motive, philos-

ophy, principle, raison d'être, rationalization, reason, reasons, song and dance*, sour grapes*, story*, the big idea*, theory, the whole idea*, whatfor*, why and wherefore*, whyfor*; SEE CONCEPT *661*

rationalize [*v*] *make excuse; justify*
account for, apply logic, cop a plea*, cop out*, deliberate, elucidate, excise, excuse, explain away, extenuate, give alibi*, intellectualize, justify, make allowance, reason, reason out, reconcile, resolve, think, think through, vindicate; SEE CONCEPT *57*

rattle [*v1*] *bang, jiggle*
bicker, bounce, clack, clatter, drum, jangle, jar, jolt, jounce, knock, shake, shatter, sound, vibrate; SEE CONCEPTS *65,152*

rattle [*v2*] *talk aimlessly, endlessly*
babble, cackle, chat, chatter, clack, gab, gabble, gush, jabber, jaw, list, prate, prattle, reel off, run on, run through, yak; SEE CONCEPT *51*

rattle [*v3*] *disconcert, upset someone*
abash, addle, bewilder, bother, confound, confuse, discombobulate*, discomfit, discompose, discountenance, distract, disturb, embarrass, faze, flummox*, frighten, get to*, muddle, nonplus, perplex, perturb, psych out*, put off, put out, put out of countenance, rattle one's cage*, scare, shake, throw, unnerve; SEE CONCEPT *16*

raucous [*adj1*] *noisy, rough*
absonant, acute, atonal, blaring, blatant, braying, brusque, cacophonous, discordant, dissonant, dry, ear-piercing, grating, grinding, gruff, harsh, hoarse, husky, inharmonious, jarring, loud, piercing, rasping, sharp, squawking, stertorous, strident, thick, unharmonious, unmusical; SEE CONCEPTS *592,594*

raucous [*adj2*] *rowdy*
boisterous, disorderly, intemperate, rambunctious, termagant, tumultous/tumultuous, turbulent, unruly; SEE CONCEPT *401*

ravage [*v*] *destroy, ransack*
annihilate, break up, capture, consume, cream, crush, damage, demolish, desecrate, desolate, despoil, devastate, dismantle, disorganize, disrupt, exterminate, extinguish, forage, foray, gut, harry, impair, lay waste, leave in ruins, loot, overrun, overthrow, overwhelm, pillage, pirate, plunder, prey, prostrate, pull down, raid, rape, raze, rob, ruin, sack, seize, shatter, sink, smash, spoil, spoliate, stamp out, strip, sweep away, total, trample, trash, waste, wreak havoc, wreck, wrest; SEE CONCEPTS *86,252*

rave [*v1*] *talk endlessly*
babble, be delirious, bloviate, blow one's top*, carry on*, come unglued*, declaim, flip one's lid*, freak out*, fume, gabble, go ape*, go bananas*, go crazy, go mad, harangue, jabber, make a to-do*, mouth, orate, perorate, prate, prattle, rage, rail, rant, rattle on, roar, run amuck*, splutter, storm, talk wildly, thunder, wander; SEE CONCEPTS *51,54*

rave [*v2*] *be very enthusiastic*
be delighted, be excited, be mad about, be wild about, bubble*, carry on about*, cry up*, effervesce,

enthuse, fall all over*, go on about*, gush, make a to-do*, praise, rhapsodize, rhapsody; SEE CONCEPTS *49,410*

ravel [*v*] *come apart; unwind*
disentangle, free, loosen, make plain, smooth out, unbraid, unravel, unsnarl, untangle, untwine, untwist, unweave, unwind, weave out; SEE CONCEPTS *250,469*

ravenous [*adj*] *very hungry; desirous*
avaricious, could eat a horse*, covetous, devouring, edacious, empty, famished, ferocious, gluttonous, grasping, greedy, insatiable, insatiate, omnivorous, predatory, rapacious, ravening, starved, starved to death*, starving, voracious, wolfish*; SEE CONCEPT *406*

ravine [*n*] *gap in earth's surface*
abyss, arroyo, break, canyon, chasm, clove, coulee, crevasse, crevice, cut, defile, ditch, fissure, flume, gorge, gulch, gulf, gully, notch, pass, valley, wash; SEE CONCEPTS *509,513*

ravish [*v1*] *enchant*
allure, attract, bewitch, captivate, charm, delight, draw, enrapture, enthrall, entrance, fascinate, hold, hypnotize, magnetize, mesmerize, overjoy, please, spellbind, trance, transport; SEE CONCEPT *11*

ravish [*v2*] *sexually assault*
abduct, abuse, carry off, defile, deflorate, deflower, force, outrage, rape, seduce, shanghai, spoil, violate; SEE CONCEPTS *192,375*

raw [*adj1*] *not cooked, prepared*
basic, bloody, callow, coarse, crude, fibrous, fresh, green, hard, immature, impure, native, natural, organic, rough, roughhewn, rude, unbaked, uncooked, undercooked, underdone, undressed, unfashioned, unformed, unfried, ungraded, unpasteurized, unprepared, unprocessed, unrefined, unripe, unsorted, unstained, untreated, virgin; SEE CONCEPTS *462,485*

raw [*adj2*] *exposed, tender, referring to skin*
abraded, au naturel, blistered, bruised, chafed, cut, dressed, galled, grazed, naked, nude, open, pared, peeled, scraped, scratched, sensitive, skinned, sore, unclad, unclothed, uncovered, wounded; SEE CONCEPTS *406,485*

raw [*adj3*] *inexperienced*
callow, fresh, green*, ignorant, immature, inexperienced, new, unconversant, undisciplined, unpracticed, unseasoned, unskilled, untaught, untrained, untried, unversed, young; SEE CONCEPT *527*

raw [*adj4*] *vulgar, nasty*
coarse, crass, crude, dirty*, filthy, foul, gross*, indecent, inelegant, low*, mean, obscene, pornographic, rank, rough, rude, smutty*, uncouth, unrefined, unscrupulous; SEE CONCEPTS *372,545*

raw [*adj5*] *harsh, unpleasant, referring to weather*
biting, bitter, bleak, breezy, chill, chilly, cold, damp, freezing, piercing, wet, wind-swept, windy; SEE CONCEPT *525*

ray [n] *beam; indication*
bar, blaze, blink, emanation, flash, flicker, gleam, glimmer, glint, glitter, hint, incandescence, irradiation, light, moonbeam, patch, pencil, radiance, radiation, scintilla, shaft, shine, spark, sparkle, streak, stream, sunbeam, trace, wave; SEE CONCEPTS *624,628*

raze [v] *flatten, knock down; wipe out*
batter, blow down, bomb, break down, bulldoze, capsize, cast down, crash, decimate, delete, demolish, destroy, dynamite, efface, erase, expunge, extinguish, extirpate, fell, level, mow down, obliterate, overthrow, overturn, pull down, reduce, remove, rub out, ruin, scatter, scratch out, smash, spill, strike out, subvert, tear down, tear up, throw down, topple, total, unbuild, undo, unmake, upset, wipe out, wrack, wreck, zap*; SEE CONCEPT *252*

reach [n] *extent, range; stretch*
ability, ambit, capacity, command, compass, distance, extension, gamut, grasp, horizon, influence, jurisdiction, ken, latitude, magnitude, mastery, orbit, play, power, purview, radius, scope, spread, sweep, swing; SEE CONCEPTS *651,756*

reach [v1] *arrive at*
arrive, attain, catch up to, check in, clock in*, come, come to, enter, gain on*, get as far as, get in, get to, hit, hit town*, land, make, make it, make the scene*, overtake, ring in*, roll in, show, show up, sign in, turn up*, wind up at; SEE CONCEPT *159*

reach [v2] *stretch to; touch*
approach, attain, buck, carry to, come at, come up to, contact, continue to, encompass, end, equal, extend to, feel for, get a hold of, get hold of, get to, go, go as far as, go on, go to, grasp, hand, hold out, join, lead, lunge, make, make contact with, overtake, pass, pass along, put out, roll on, seize, shake hands, shoot, span, spread, stand, strain, strike; SEE CONCEPTS *108,612,756*

reach [v3] *attain; rise*
accomplish, achieve, amount to, arrive at, climb to, come to, drop, fall, gain, move, rack up, realize, score, sink, win; SEE CONCEPTS *706,763,780*

reach [v4] *communicate with*
affect, approach, contact, get, get in touch, get through, get to, influence, keep in contact, keep in touch, maintain, move, sway, touch; SEE CONCEPTS *7,19,22,266*

react [v] *respond; conduct oneself*
acknowledge, act, answer, answer back, backfire, back talk*, be affected, behave, boomerang*, bounce back*, counter, echo, feel, function, get back at, give a snappy comeback*, give back, have a funny feeling*, have vibes*, operate, perform, proceed, rebound, reciprocate, recoil, recur, reply, return, revert, take, talk back, turn back, work; SEE CONCEPTS *45,633*

reaction [n1] *response*
acknowledgment, answer, attitude, backfire, backlash, back talk*, boomerang*, comeback, compensation, counteraction, counterbalance, counterpoise, double-take*, echo, feedback, feeling, hit, kick, kickback, knee-jerk*, lip*, opinion, reagency, rebound, reception, receptivity, reciprocation, recoil, reflection, reflex, rejoinder, repercussion, reply, retort, return, reverberation, revulsion, sass*, snappy comeback*, take*, vibes*, wisecrack; SEE CONCEPTS *45,633*

reaction [n2] *political conservativism*
backlash, backsliding, counter-revolution, obscurantism, regression, relapse, retreat, retrenchment, retrogression, right, right wing, status quo, Toryism, withdrawal; SEE CONCEPTS *300,689*

reactionary [n] *person who is politically conservative*
bitter-ender*, counter-revolutionary, diehard*, hard hat*, intransigent, obscurantist, reactionist, rightist*, right-winger, royalist, standpatter*, Tory*, traditionalist, ultraconservative; SEE CONCEPT *359*

reactionary [adj] *conservative*
counter-revolutionary, die-hard*, obscurantist, old-line*, orthodox, regressive, retrogressive, right, rightist*, rigid, standpat*, Tory*, traditionalist, traditionalistic; SEE CONCEPTS *529,542*

read [v1] *look at and understand written word*
apprehend, bury oneself in*, comprehend, construe, decipher, dip into*, discover, flip through*, gather, glance, go over, go through, interpret, know, leaf through*, learn, make out*, perceive, peruse, pore over*, refer to, scan, scratch the surface*, see, skim, study, translate, unravel, view; SEE CONCEPT *72*

read [v2] *express, state*
affirm, announce, assert, declaim, deliver, display, explain, expound, hold, indicate, mark, paraphrase, pronounce, recite, record, register, render, restate, say, show, speak, utter; SEE CONCEPT *266*

readable [adj1] *understandable, legible*
clear, coherent, comprehensible, decipherable, distinct, explicit, flowing, fluent, graphic, intelligible, lucid, orderly, plain, precise, regular, simple, smooth, straightforward, tidy, unequivocal, unmistakable; SEE CONCEPTS *272,529*

readable [adj2] *pleasurable to peruse*
absorbing, amusing, appealing, brilliant, clever, easy, eloquent, engaging, engrossing, enjoyable, entertaining, enthralling, exciting, fascinating, gratifying, gripping, ingenious, interesting, inviting, pleasant, pleasing, relaxing, rewarding, satisfying, smooth, stimulating, well-written, worthwhile; SEE CONCEPT *272*

readily [adv] *quickly; effortlessly*
at drop of hat*, at once, cheerfully, eagerly, easily, facilely, freely, gladly, hands down*, immediately, in a jiffy*, in no time*, lightly, no sweat*, nothing to it*, piece of cake*, promptly, quick as a wink*, right away, slick as whistle*, smoothly, speedily, straight away, swimmingly, unhesitatingly, well, willingly, without delay, without demur, without difficulty, without hesitation; SEE CONCEPTS *544,820*

readiness [*n*] *skill; eagerness*
address, adroitness, alacrity, aptness, deftness, dexterity, dispatch, ease, eloquence, expedience, expedition, facility, fitness, fluency, good will, handiness, inclination, keenness, maturity, preparation, preparedness, promptitude, promptness, prowess, quickness, rapidity, ripeness, sleight, volubility, willingness; SEE CONCEPTS *630,633,678*

reading [*n*] *interpretation of written word*
account, book-learning, commentary, conception, construction, edification, education, erudition, examination, grasp, impression, inspection, knowledge, learning, lesson, paraphrase, perusal, rendering, rendition, review, scholarship, scrutiny, study, translation, treatment, understanding, version; SEE CONCEPTS *72,271,274*

ready [*adj1*] *prepared; available*
accessible, adjusted, all set, all systems go*, anticipating, apt, arranged, at beck and call*, at fingertips*, at hand, at the ready, bagged, champing at bit*, close to hand, completed, convenient, covered, equal to, equipped, expectant, fit, fixed for, handy, in line, in order, in place, in position, in readiness, in the saddle*, near, on call, on hand, on tap*, on the brink*, open to, organized, primed, qualified, ripe, set, waiting, wired*; SEE CONCEPTS *560,576,799*

ready [*adj2*] *willing, inclined*
agreeable, apt, ardent, disposed, eager, enthusiastic, fain, game, game for, glad, happy, keen, minded, predisposed, prompt, prone, psyched up*, wired*, zealous; SEE CONCEPTS *401,542*

ready [*adj3*] *skillful, intelligent*
active, acute, adept, adroit, alert, apt, astute, bright, brilliant, clever, deft, dexterous, dynamic, expert, handy, keen, live, masterly, perceptive, proficient, prompt, quick, quick-witted, rapid, resourceful, sharp, skilled, smart; SEE CONCEPTS *402,527*

ready [*v*] *prepare*
arrange, brace, brief, clear the decks*, equip, fill in, fit, fit out, fix, fortify, gear up*, get, get ready, get set, gird, keep posted*, let in on*, make, make ready, make up, order, organize, pave the way*, post, prep, provide, psych up*, put on to*, set, strengthen, warm up, wise up*; SEE CONCEPTS *35,60,202*

real [*adj*] *genuine in existence*
absolute, actual, authentic, bodily, bona fide, certain, concrete, corporal, corporeal, de facto, embodied, essential, evident, existent, existing, factual, firm, heartfelt, honest, incarnate, indubitable, in the flesh, intrinsic, irrefutable, legitimate, live, material, original, palpable, perceptible, physical, positive, present, right, rightful, sensible, sincere, solid, sound, stable, substantial, substantive, tangible, true, unaffected, undeniable, undoubted, unfeigned, valid, veritable; SEE CONCEPT *582*

realistic [*adj1*] *sensible, matter-of-fact*
astute, businesslike, commonsense, down-to-earth, earthy, hard, hard-boiled, levelheaded, practical, pragmatic, pragmatical, prudent, rational, real, reasonable, sane, sensible, shrewd, sober, sound, unfantastic, unidealistic, unromantic, unsentimental, utilitarian; SEE CONCEPTS *403,542,548*

realistic [*adj2*] *genuine*
authentic, faithful, graphic, lifelike, natural, original, representational, representative, true, true to life, truthful; SEE CONCEPT *582*

reality [*n*] *facts of existence*
absoluteness, actuality, authenticity, being, bottom line*, brass tacks*, certainty, concreteness, corporeality, deed, entity, existence, genuineness, how things are*, like it is*, materiality, matter, name of the game*, nuts and bolts*, object, palpability, perceptibility, phenomenon, presence, realism, realness, real world*, sensibility, solidity, substance, substantiality, substantive, tangibility, truth, validity, verisimilitude, verity, way of it*, what's what*; SEE CONCEPTS *689,725*

realize [*v1*] *appreciate, become aware of*
apprehend, be cognizant of, become conscious of, catch, catch on*, comprehend, conceive, discern, envisage, envision, fancy*, feature*, get, get it*, get the idea*, get the picture*, get through one's head*, grasp, image, imagine, know, pick up*, recognize, see daylight*, take in*, think, understand, vision, visualize; SEE CONCEPT *15*

realize [*v2*] *accomplish*
actualize, bring about, bring off, bring to fruition, carry out, carry through, complete, consummate, corporealize, do, effect, effectuate, fulfill, make concrete*, make good*, make happen, materialize, perfect, perform, reify; SEE CONCEPT *91*

realize [*v3*] *gain, earn*
accomplish, achieve, acquire, attain, bring in, clear, get, go for, make, make a profit, net, obtain, produce, rack up*, reach, receive, score*, sell for, take in, win; SEE CONCEPTS *120,124,330*

really [*adj*] *without a doubt*
absolutely, actually, admittedly, amen*, as a matter of fact, assuredly, authentically, be assured, believe me, beyond doubt, categorically, certainly, de facto, easily, for real*, genuinely, honestly, in actuality, indeed, indubitably, in effect, in fact, in point of fact, in reality, legitimately, literally, no ifs ands or buts*, nothing else but, of course, positively, precisely, surely, truly, undoubtedly, unmistakably, unquestionably, verily, well, why sure*, you bet*; SEE CONCEPTS *535,582*

realm [*n*] *area of responsibility or rule*
branch, compass, country, department, dimension, domain, dominion, empire, expanse, extent, field, ground, kingdom, land, monarchy, neck of the woods*, neighborhood, orbit, place, principality, province, purview, radius, range, reach, region, scope, sphere, state, stomping grounds*, sweep, territory, turf, world, zone; SEE CONCEPTS *349, 362,512,651*

reap [v] *collect, harvest*
acquire, bring in, come to have, crop, cull, cut, derive, draw, gain, garner, gather, get, get as a result, glean, ingather, mow, obtain, pick, pick up, pluck, procure, produce, profit, realize, receive, recover, retrieve, secure, strip, take in, win; SEE CONCEPTS *109,120,124,257*

rear [n] *back or end part*
afterpart, back, back door*, back end, back seat*, backside, behind, bottom, butt, buttocks, end, heel, hind, hind part, hindquarters, posterior, postern, rear end, rear guard, rearward, reverse, rump, seat, stern, tail, tail end, tailpiece, tush*; SEE CONCEPTS *825,827*

rear [adj] *back, end*
aft, after, astern, backward, behind, dorsal, following, hind, hinder, hindermost, hindmost, last, mizzen, posterior, postern, rearmost, rearward, retral, reverse, stern, tail; SEE CONCEPT *583*

rear [v1] *raise young*
breed, bring up, care for, cultivate, educate, foster, grow, nurse, nurture, propagate, train; SEE CONCEPT *295*

rear [v2] *lift, rise*
bring up, elevate, hoist, hold up, jump, leap, loom, pick up, raise, set upright, soar, spring up, support, take up, tower, turn up, uphold, uplift, upraise; SEE CONCEPTS *194,196,741*

rear [v3] *build*
construct, erect, fabricate, put up, raise, set up, uprear; SEE CONCEPT *168*

reason [n1] *mental analysis*
acumen, apprehension, argumentation, bounds, brain*, brains*, comprehension, deduction, dialectics, discernment, generalization, induction, inference, intellect, intellection, judgment, limits, logic, lucidity, marbles, mentality, mind*, moderation, propriety, ratiocination, rationalism, rationality, rationalization, reasonableness, reasoning, saneness, sanity, sense*, senses*, sensibleness, sound mind, soundness, speculation, understanding, wisdom, wit; SEE CONCEPTS *37,409*

reason [n2] *intention, aim*
antecedent, argument, basis, cause, consideration, design, determinant, end, goal, grounds, idea, impetus, incentive, inducement, motivation, motive, object, occasion, proof, purpose, rationale, root, spring, target, ulterior motive, warrant, wherefore, why, why and wherefore, whyfor; SEE CONCEPT *659*

reason [n3] *explanation for an action*
account, apologia, apology, argument, case, cover, defense, excuse, exposition, ground, idea, justification, notion, proof, rationale, rationalization, song and dance*, sour grapes*, stall, the whole idea*, vindication, whatfor*, wherefore*, why*, why and wherefore*, whyfor*; SEE CONCEPT *661*

reason [v1] *mentally analyze*
adduce, cerebrate, cogitate, conclude, contemplate, decide, deduce, deduct, deliberate, draw conclusion, draw from, examine, figure out, gather, generalize, infer, make out, philosophize, ratiocinate, rationalize, reflect, resolve, solve, speculate, study, suppose, syllogize, think, think through, thresh out, work out; SEE CONCEPT *37*

reason [v2] *argue, persuade*
bring around, contend, debate, demonstrate, discourse, discuss, dispute, dissuade, establish, expostulate, justify, move, point out, prevail upon, prove, remonstrate, show error of ways*, talk into, talk out of, trace, urge, win over; SEE CONCEPTS *46,56,68*

reasonable [adj1] *moderate, tolerable*
acceptable, analytical, average, cheap, circumspect, conservative, controlled, discreet, equitable, fair, feasible, fit, honest, humane, impartial, inexpensive, judicious, just, justifiable, knowing, legit, legitimate, low-cost, low-priced, making sense, modest, objective, okay, plausible, politic, proper, prudent, rational, reflective, restrained, right, sane, sapient, sensible, sound, standing to reason, temperate, understandable, unexcessive, unextreme, valid, within reason; SEE CONCEPTS *547,558*

reasonable [adj2] *intelligent, practical*
advisable, all there*, arguable, believeable, cerebral, clear-cut, cognitive, commonsensical, conscious, consequent, consistent, cool*, credible, in one's right mind*, judicious, justifiable, levelheaded, logical, perceiving, percipient, plausible, ratiocinative, rational, reasoned, reasoning, reflective, sane, sensible, sober, sound, tenable, thoughtful, thought-out, together, tolerant, unbiased, unprejudiced, well-advised, wise; SEE CONCEPT *402*

reasoning [n] *logic, interpretation*
acumen, analysis, apriority, argument, case, cogitation, concluding, corollary, deduction, dialectics, exposition, generalization, hypothesis, illation, induction, inference, interpretation, logistics, premise, proof, proposition, ratiocination, rationale, rationalizing, reason, syllogism, syllogization, thinking, thought, train of thought; SEE CONCEPTS *37,529*

reassure [v] *restore confidence to*
assure, bolster, brace, buoy, cheer, comfort, console, convince, encourage, give a lift*, give confidence, guarantee, hearten, inspire, inspirit, perk up, pick up*, put one's mind to rest*, relieve, snap out of it*; SEE CONCEPTS *7,22*

rebate [n] *refund given to purchaser*
abatement, allowance, bonus, deduction, discount, kickback, payback, reduction, reimbursement, remission, repayment, subtraction; SEE CONCEPT *344*

rebel [n] *person who does not obey*
agitator, anarchist, antagonist, apostate, demagogue, deserter, disectarian, dissenter, experientialist, experimenter, frondeur, guerrilla, heretic, iconoclast, independent, individualist, innovator, insurgent, insurrectionary, malcontent, mutineer, nihilist, nonconformist, opponent, overthrower, recreant, renegade, resistance, revolter, revolutionary, revolutionist, rioter, schismatic, secessionist, seditionist,

separatist, subverter, traitor, turncoat; SEE CONCEPTS *359,412,423*

rebel [*adj*] *not obeying*
insubordinate, insurgent, insurrectionary, mutinous, rebellious, revolutionary; SEE CONCEPT *401*

rebel [*v*] *refuse to obey*
be insubordinate, boycott, break with*, censure, combat, come out against, criticize, defy, denounce, disobey, dissent, drop out*, fight, get out of line*, insurrect, make waves*, mutiny, oppose, opt out*, overthrow, overturn, remonstrate, renounce, resist, revolt, riot, rise up*, rock the boat*, run amok*, secede, strike, take up arms, turn against, upset; SEE CONCEPTS *106,633*

rebellion [*n*] *disobedience; revolt*
apostasy, defiance, disobedience, dissent, heresy, insubordination, insurgence, insurgency, insurrection, nonconformity, revolution, rising, schism, uprising; SEE CONCEPTS *106,300,320,633*

rebellious [*adj*] *disobedient, unmanageable*
alienated, anarchistic, attacking, bellicose, contumacious, defiant, difficult, disaffected, disloyal, disobedient, disorderly, dissident, factious, fractious, iconoclastic, incorrigible, individualistic, insurgent, insurrectionary, intractable, mutinous, obstinate, pugnacious, quarrelsome, radical, rebel, recalcitrant, refractory, resistant, restless, revolutionary, rioting, riotous, sabotaging, seditious, threatening, treasonable, turbulent, ungovernable, unruly, warring; SEE CONCEPTS *401,529,542*

rebuff [*n*] *turning away; ignoring*
brushoff, check, cold shoulder*, cut, defeat, denial, discouragement, go-by*, hard time*, insult, kick in the teeth*, nix*, nothing doing*, opposition, rebuke, refusal, rejection, reprimand, repulse, slight, snub, thumbs down*, turndown; SEE CONCEPTS *30,278*

rebuff [*v*] *turn away; give the cold shoulder*
beat off, brush off, check, chide, cold-shoulder*, cross, cut, decline, deny, disallow, discourage, dismiss, disregard, fend off, hold off, ignore, keep at a distance*, keep at arm's length*, keep at bay, lash out at, neglect, not hear of, oppose, pass up, push back, put in one's place*, put off, rebuke, refuse, reject, repel, reprove, repudiate, repulse, resist, send away, slight, snub, spurn, stave off, tell off, turn down, ward off; SEE CONCEPTS *30,54*

rebuke [*n*] *reprimand; harsh criticism*
admonishment, admonition, affliction, bawling-out*, berating, blame, castigation, censure, chewing-out*, chiding, comeuppance, condemnation, correction, disapproval, dressing-down*, earful*, expostulation, going-over*, hard time*, kick in the teeth*, lecture, lesson, objurgation, ostracism, punishment, putdown, rap*, rating, rebuff, refusal, remonstrance, reprehension, reproach, reproof, reproval, repulse, row, scolding, slap in the face*, snub, talking-to*, telling-off*, tongue-lashing*, upbraiding; SEE CONCEPTS *44,52,278*

rebuke [*v*] *reprimand; criticize harshly*
admonish, bawl out*, berate, blame, call on the carpet*, carp on, castigate, censure, chew out*, chide, climb all over*, dress down*, fry*, go after*, jawbone*, jump down one's throat*, jump on*, lay into*, lean on*, lecture, lesson, monish, oppose, pay, rake, read*, reprehend, reprimand, reproach, reprove, rip*, scold, sit on*, sound off*, take to task*, tear apart*, tell off, tick off, upbraid, zap*; SEE CONCEPTS *44,52*

rebut [*v*] *argue against; prove wrong*
break, come back at, confound, confute, controvert, cross, defeat, deny, disconfirm, disprove, evert, fend off, get back at, hold off, invalidate, keep off, negate, negative, overturn, prove false, quash, refute, repel, repulse, stave off, take on, top, ward off; SEE CONCEPTS *46,54*

recalcitrant [*adj*] *disobedient, uncontrollable*
contrary, contumacious, defiant, fractious, indomitable, insubmissive, insubordinate, intractable, obstinate, opposing, radical, rebellious, refractory, resistant, resisting, stubborn, undisciplinable, undisciplined, ungovernable, unmanageable, unruly, untoward, unwilling, wayward, wild, willful, withstanding; SEE CONCEPT *401*

recall [*n1*] *remembrance*
anamnesis, memory, recollection, reminiscence; SEE CONCEPT *529*

recall [*n2*] *request for return*
annulment, cancellation, nullification, recision, repeal, rescindment, rescission, retraction, revocation, withdrawal; SEE CONCEPTS *662,685*

recall [*v1*] *remember*
arouse, awaken, bethink, bring to mind, call to mind, call up, cite, come to one, educe, elicit, evoke, extract, flash, flash on*, look back, mind, nail it down*, recollect, reestablish, reinstate, reintroduce, remind, reminisce, renew, retain, retrospect, revive, ring a bell, rouse, stir, strike a note*, summon, think back*, think of, waken; SEE CONCEPT *40*

recall [*v2*] *ask for return of offending thing*
abjure, annul, call back, call in, cancel, countermand, discharge, dismantle, dismiss, disqualify, forswear, lift, nullify, palinode, recant, repeal, rescind, retract, reverse, revoke, suspend, take back, unsay, withdraw; SEE CONCEPTS *50,88,131,143*

recant [*v*] *take back something said*
abjure, abnegate, abrogate, annul, apostatize, back down, back off, back out, backtrack*, call back, cancel, contradict, countermand, deny, dial back*, disavow, disclaim, disown, eat one's words*, forswear, go back on one's word*, nullify, palinode, recall, renege, renounce, repeal, repudiate, rescind, retract, revoke, take back, unsay, void, weasel out*, welsh*, withdraw, worm out of*; SEE CONCEPTS *25,266*

recapitulate [*v*] *go over something again*
epitomize, go over same ground*, go the same round*, outline, paraphrase, recap*, recount, rehash,

reiterate, repeat, rephrase, replay, restate, review, reword, run over*, run through again*, summarize, sum up; SEE CONCEPT *266*

recede [v] *withdraw; diminish*
abate, back, close, decline, decrease, depart, die off, diminish, drain away, draw back, drop, dwindle, ebb, fade, fall back, flow back, go away, go back, lessen, reduce, regress, retire, retract, retreat, retrocede, retrograde, retrogress, return, shrink, sink, subside, taper, wane; SEE CONCEPTS *195,698,776*

receipt [n1] *acknowledgment of delivery*
cancellation, certificate, chit, counterfoil, declaration, discharge, letter, notice, proof of purchase, quittance, release, sales slip, slip, stub, voucher; SEE CONCEPTS *271,332*

receipt [n2] *delivery of goods*
acceptance, accession, acquiring, acquisition, admission, admitting, arrival, getting, intaking, receiving, reception, recipience, taking; SEE CONCEPT *124*

receipts [n] *money earned in business venture*
bottom line*, cash flow, comings in*, earnings, gain, gate, get*, gross, handle*, income, net, proceeds, profit, return, revenue, revenue stream, royalty, take*, take-in*, taking*; SEE CONCEPT *344*

receive [v1] *accept delivery of something*
accept, acquire, admit, apprehend, appropriate, arrogate, assume, be given, be informed, be in receipt of, be told, catch, collect, come by, come into, cop*, corral*, derive, draw, earn, gain, gather, get, get from, get hands on*, get hold of*, grab, hear, hold, inherit, latch on to*, make, obtain, perceive, pick up, pocket*, procure, pull, pull down*, reap, redeem, secure, seize, snag*, take, take in, take possession, win; SEE CONCEPT *124*

receive [v2] *endure, sustain*
bear, be subjected to, encounter, experience, go through, meet with, suffer, undergo; SEE CONCEPT *23*

receive [v3] *take in guest or member*
accept, accommodate, admit, allow entrance, bring in, entertain, greet, host, induct, initiate, install, introduce, invite, let in, let through, make comfortable, make welcome, meet, permit, roll out red carpet*, shake hands*, show in, take in, usher in, welcome; SEE CONCEPTS *50,83,88,140*

recent [adj] *current*
contempo, contemporary, fresh, hot off the fire*, hot off the press*, just out, late, latter, latter-day, modern, modernistic, neoteric, new, newborn, newfangled, novel, present-day, the latest*, today, up-to-date, young; SEE CONCEPTS *578,797,820*

recently [adv] *currently*
afresh, anew, freshly, in recent past, in recent times, just a while ago, just now, lately, latterly, new, newly, not long ago, of late, short while ago, the other day; SEE CONCEPT *820*

receptacle [n] *container for disposal, storage*
bowl, box, holder, hopper, repository, vessel, wastebasket; SEE CONCEPT *494*

reception [n1] *acceptance; acknowledgment*
accession, acquisition, admission, disposition, encounter, gathering, greeting, induction, introduction, meeting, reaction, receipt, receiving, recipience, recognition, response, salutation, treatment, welcome; SEE CONCEPTS *83,124,384*

reception [n2] *celebratory party*
buffet, dinner, do*, entertainment, function, gathering, levee, matinee, soiree, supper, tea; SEE CONCEPT *383*

receptive [adj] *open to new ideas*
acceptant, acceptive, accessible, alert, amenable, approachable, bright, favorable, friendly, hospitable, influenceable, interested, observant, open, open-minded, open to suggestions, perceptive, persuadable, pushover, quick on the uptake, ready, recipient, responsive, sensitive, suggestible, susceptible, swayable, sympathetic, welcoming, well-disposed; SEE CONCEPT *404*

recess [n1] *niche, corner*
alcove, ambush, angle, apse, bay, break, carrel, cavity, cell, closet, cove, cranny, crutch, crypt, cubicle, dent, depression, depths, embrasure, fork, heart, hiding place, hole, hollow, indentation, mouth, nook, opening, oriel, penetralia, reaches, retreat, secret place, slot, socket; SEE CONCEPTS *440,513*

recess [n2] *break, interval in action*
break-off, breather*, breathing spell*, cessation, closure, coffee break, cutoff, downtime*, halt, happy hour*, hiatus, holiday, interlude, intermission, interregnum, layoff, letup, lull, pause, respite, rest, stop, suspension, ten*, time-out, vacation; SEE CONCEPT *807*

recess [v] *stop action*
adjourn, break off*, break up*, call time*, dissolve, drop, drop it, pigeonhole*, prorogate, prorogue, put on hold, rise, shake, sideline, take a break, take a breather*, take five*, take ten*, terminate; SEE CONCEPTS *119,121*

recession [n] *reversal of action; reduction of business activity*
bad times*, bankruptcy, big trouble*, bottom-out*, bust, collapse, decline, deflation, depression, downturn, hard times*, inflation, rainy days*, return, shakeout*, slide, slump, stagnation, unemployment; SEE CONCEPT *335*

recipe [n] *directions, formula*
compound, ingredients, instructions, method, modus operandi, prescription, procedure, process, program, receipt, technique; SEE CONCEPT *274*

reciprocal [adj] *exchanged, alternate*
changeable, companion, complementary, convertible, coordinate, correlative, corresponding, dependent, double, duplicate, equivalent, exchangeable, fellow, give-and-take*, interchangeable, interdependent, matching, mutual, reciprocative, reciprocatory, twin; SEE CONCEPTS *566,577*

reciprocate [*v*] *exchange, alternate; equal*
barter, be equivalent, correspond, equal, feel in return, interchange, make up for*, match, pay one's dues*, recompense, render, repay, reply, requite, respond, retaliate, retort, return, return the compliment, scratch one's back*, serve out, share, square, swap, swing, tit for tat*, trade, vacillate, wave; SEE CONCEPTS *45,104,384*

recital [*n*] *narrative, rendering*
account, concert, description, detailing, enumeration, fable, musical, musicale, narration, narrative, performance, portrayal, presentation, reading, recapitulation, recitation, recountal, recounting, rehearsal, relation, repetition, report, statement, story, tale, telling; SEE CONCEPTS *263,264*

recitation [*n*] *reading to audience*
address, appeal, declaiming, delivery, discourse, discoursing, discussion, exercise, holding forth, lecture, monologue, narrating, narration, oration, passage, performance, piece, playing, proclamation, recital, recounting, rehearsal, rendering, report, selection, soliloquizing, speaking, talk, telling; SEE CONCEPTS *72,263,266*

recite [*v*] *read out loud; narrate*
account for, address, answer, chant, communicate, convey, declaim, delineate, deliver, describe, detail, discourse, dramatize, enact, enlarge, enumerate, expatiate, explain, give an account, give a report, give verbal account, hold forth, impart, interpret, itemize, mention, narrate, parrot*, perform, picture, portray, quote, recapitulate, recount, reel off*, rehearse, relate, render, repeat, reply, report, retell, soliloquize, speak, state, tell, utter; SEE CONCEPTS *55,57,72,266*

reckless [*adj*] *irresponsible in thought, deed*
adventuresome, adventurous, any which way, audacious, brash, breakneck*, carefree, careless, daredevil*, daring, desperate, devil-may-care*, fast and loose*, feckless, foolhardy, harebrained, hasty, headlong, heedless, helter-skelter, hopeless, hotheaded*, ill-advised, imprudent, inattentive, incautious, inconsiderate, indiscreet, kooky*, madcap*, mindless, negligent, overventuresome, playing with fire*, precipitate, rash, regardless, temerarious, thoughtless, uncareful, venturesome, venturous, wild; SEE CONCEPTS *401,542*

reckon [*v1*] *add up; evaluate*
account, appraise, approximate, calculate, call, cast, cipher, compute, conjecture, consider, count, count heads*, count noses*, deem, enumerate, esteem, estimate, figure, figure out, foot, gauge, guess, hold, judge, keep tabs*, look upon, number, place, put, rate, regard, run down, square, sum, surmise, take account of, tally, think of, tick off*, tot, total, tote*, tote up*, tot up, view; SEE CONCEPTS *37,764*

reckon [*v2*] *suppose, imagine*
assume, bank on, bargain for, believe, be of the opinion, build on, conjecture, count on, depend on, expect, fancy, gather, guess, plan on, rely on, surmise,

suspect, take, think, trust in, understand; SEE CONCEPTS *12,26*

reckoning [*n*] *computation, account*
adding, addition, arithmetic, bad news*, bill, calculation, charge, check, ciphering, cost, count, counting, debt, due, estimate, estimation, fee, figuring, grunt*, invoice, IOU*, score, settlement, statement, summation, tab, working; SEE CONCEPT *331*

recline [*v*] *lie down*
be recumbent, cant, heel, lay down, lean, lie, list, loll, lounge, repose, rest, slant, slope, sprawl, stretch, stretch out, tilt, tip; SEE CONCEPTS *154,201*

recluse [*n*] *person who does not want social contact*
anchoress, anchorite, ascetic, cenobite, eremite, hermit, monk, solitaire, solitary, troglodyte; SEE CONCEPT *423*

recluse/reclusive [*adj*] *hermitlike, unsociable*
antisocial, ascetic, cloistered, eremetic, hermetic, isolated, misanthropic, monastic, reserved, retiring, secluded, secluse, seclusive, sequestered, solitary, standoffish, withdrawn; SEE CONCEPTS *404,555*

recognition [*n1*] *identification, acknowledgment*
acceptance, acknowledging, admission, allowance, apperception, appreciation, apprehending, assimilation, avowal, awareness, cognizance, concession, confession, consciousness, detection, discovery, double take, high sign, identifying, memory, notice, noticing, perceiving, perception, realization, recall, recalling, recognizance, recollection, recurrence, remembering, remembrance, respect, salute, sensibility, tumble, understanding, verifying; SEE CONCEPT *38*

recognition [*n2*] *appreciation given*
acceptance, acknowledgment, approval, attention, credit, esteem, gratitude, greeting, honor, notice, pat on back*, pat on head*, plum*, puff*, puffing up*, pumping up*, rave, regard, renown, salute, strokes*; SEE CONCEPTS *10,337,689*

recognize [*v1*] *identify*
admit, be familiar, button down*, descry, determinate, diagnose, diagnosticate, distinguish, espy, finger*, flash on*, know, know again, make*, make out, nail*, note, notice, observe, peg*, perceive, pinpoint, place, recall, recollect, remark, remember, ring a bell*, see, sight, spot, tab, tag, verify; SEE CONCEPT *38*

recognize [*v2*] *acknowledge, understand; approve*
accept, admit, agree, allow, appreciate, assent, avow, be aware of, comprehend, concede, confess, grant, greet, honor, make, own, perceive, realize, respect, salute, sanction, see; SEE CONCEPT *15*

recoil [*v*] *shrink away*
backfire, balk, blanch, blench, blink, carom, cringe, demur, dodge, draw back, duck, falter, flinch, hesitate, jerk, kick, pull back, quail, quake, react, rebound, reel, resile, shake, shirk, shrink, shudder, shy away, spring, start, step back, stick, stickle, swerve, tremble, turn away, waver, wince, withdraw; SEE CONCEPTS *150,194,195*

recollect [v] *remember*
arouse, awaken, bethink, bring to mind, call to mind, cite, come to one, flash, flash on*, look back on, mind, place, recall, recognize, remind, reminisce, retain, retrospect, revive, rouse, stir, summon, waken; SEE CONCEPT *40*

recommend [v] *advise, approve*
acclaim, advance, advocate, applaud, back, be all for*, be satisfied with, celebrate, commend, compliment, confirm, counsel, endorse, enjoin, esteem, eulogize, exalt, exhort, extol, favor, front for, glorify, go on record for*, hold up, justify, laud, magnify, plug*, praise, prescribe, prize, propose, put forward, put in a good word*, put on to*, sanction, second, speak highly of, speak well of, stand by, steer, suggest, think highly of, uphold, urge, value, vouch for; SEE CONCEPTS *10,75*

recommendation [n] *advice, approval*
advocacy, approbation, blessing, certificate, character reference, charge, commendation, counsel, direction, endorsement, esteem, eulogy, favorable mention, good word*, guidance, injunction, instruction, judgment, letter of support, order, pass, plug*, praise, proposal, proposition, reference, sanction, steer*, suggestion, support, testimonial, tip, tribute, two cents' worth*, urging; SEE CONCEPTS *274,278*

recompense [n] *something returned, paid back*
amends, atonement, bus fare*, compensation, cue, damages, emolument, expiation, gravy*, indemnification, indemnity, little something*, overcompensation, pay, payment, propitiation, quittance, recoupment, recovery, redemption, redress, remuneration, reparation, repayment, requital, restitution, retrieval, retrievement, return, reward, salvo, satisfaction, solatium, sweetener*, tip, wages; SEE CONCEPTS *340,344*

recompense [v] *pay back, make restitution*
ante up, atone, atone for, balance, comp*, compensate, cough up*, counterbalance, counterpoise, countervail, do business*, equalize, expiate, fix, give satisfaction, grease, indemnify, make amends, make good*, make up for, offset, overcompensate, pay, pay for, propitiate, put out*, reciprocate, recoup, recover, redress, reimburse, remunerate, repay, requite, retaliate, retrieve, return, reward, satisfy, spring for, square*, sweeten the pot*, swing for*, take care of; SEE CONCEPTS *126,341*

reconcile [v1] *make peace; adjust*
accommodate, accord, accustom, appease, arbitrate, arrange, assuage, attune, bring together, bring to terms, bury the hatchet*, come together, compose, conciliate, conform, cool*, coordinate, fit, fix up, get together on, harmonize, integrate, intercede, kiss and make up*, make matters up, make up, mediate, mitigate, pacify, patch things up*, patch up*, placate, propitiate, proportion, reconciliate, rectify, reestablish, regulate, resolve, restore harmony, reunite, settle, suit, tune, win over; SEE CONCEPTS *384,697*

reconcile [v2] *resign oneself to something*
accept, accommodate, get used to*, make the best of*, put up with*, resign, submit, yield; SEE CONCEPT *23*

recondite [adj] *mysterious, obscure*
abstruse, academic, acroamatic, arcane, cabalistic, concealed, cryptic, dark, deep, difficult, erudite, esoteric, hard, heavy, hermetic, hidden, involved, learned, little-known, mystic, mystical, occult, orphic, pedantic, profound, scholarly, secret; SEE CONCEPTS *529,576*

reconsider [v] *think about again*
amend, change one's mind, consider again, correct, emend, go over, have second thoughts*, polish, rearrange, reassess, recheck, reevaluate, reexamine, rehash, replan, rethink, retrace, review, revise, reweigh, rework, run through, see in a new light*, sleep on, take another look, think better of*, think over, think twice*, work over; SEE CONCEPT *17*

reconstruct [v] *reorganize, build up*
copy, deduce, doctor*, do up*, fix, fix up, make over, modernize, overhaul, patch, piece together, reassemble, rebuild, recast, recondition, reconstitute, recreate, reestablish, refashion, reform, regenerate, rehabilitate, rejuvenate, remake, remodel, remold, renovate, reorient, repair, replace, reproduce, reshuffle, restore, retool, revamp, rework; SEE CONCEPTS *84,168,171*

record [n1] *account of event or proceedings*
almanac, annals, archive, archives, chronicle, comic book*, diary, directory, document, documentation, entry, evidence, file, history, inscription, jacket, journal, legend, log, manuscript, memo, memoir, memorandum, memorial, minutes, monument, note, paper trail*, register, registry, remembrance, report, script, scroll, story, swindle sheet*, testimony, trace, track record*, transcript, transcription, witness, writing, written material; SEE CONCEPTS *271,281*

record [n2] *background, experience*
accomplishment, administration, career, case history, conduct, curriculum vitae, history, past behavior, performance, reign, studies, track record*, way of life*, work; SEE CONCEPT *678*

record [n3] *achievement*
ceiling, maximum; SEE CONCEPT *706*

record [v1] *write down; store information*
book, can*, catalog, chalk up*, chronicle, copy, cut, cut a track, document, dub, enroll, enter, enumerate, file, inscribe, insert, jot down, keep account, lay down, list, log, make a recording, mark, mark down, matriculate, note, post, preserve, put down, put in writing, put on file*, put on paper*, put on tape*, register, report, set down, tabulate, take down, tape, tape-record, transcribe, video, videotape, wax, write in; SEE CONCEPT *125*

record [v2] *give evidence of*
contain, designate, explain, indicate, mark, point out, point to, read, register, say, show; SEE CONCEPT *261*

recount [v] *tell a story*
break a story*, convey, delineate, depict, describe, detail, echo, enumerate, give an account of, itemize, narrate, picture, play back, portray, recap*, recite, rehash, rehearse, relate, repeat, report, run by again*, run down*, run through*, say again, state, tell, track, unload, verbalize; SEE CONCEPTS *55,266*

recoup [v] *recover, make up for*
compensate, get back, get out from under*, get well, make good, make redress for, make well, redeem, refund, regain, reimburse, remunerate, repay, repossess, requite, retrieve, satisfy, win back; SEE CONCEPTS *124,126,342,700*

recourse [n] *alternative*
aid, appeal, choice, expediency, expedient, help, makeshift, option, refuge, remedy, resort, resource, shift, stand-by, stopgap*, substitute, support, way out*; SEE CONCEPTS *693,712*

recover [v1] *find again*
balance, bring back, catch up, compensate, get back, make good, obtain again, offset, reacquire, recapture, reclaim, recoup, recruit, redeem, rediscover, regain, reoccupy, repair, replevin, replevy, repossess, rescue, restore, resume, retake, retrieve, salvage, take back, win back; SEE CONCEPTS *120,183*

recover [v2] *improve in health*
be out of woods*, better, bounce back*, come around, convalesce, feel oneself again*, forge ahead, gain, get back on feet*, get better, get in shape, get out from under*, get over, get well, grow, heal, increase, make a comeback*, mend, overcome, perk up*, pick up, pull through, rally, reach, realize, rebound, recuperate, refresh, regain one's health, regain one's strength, rejuvenate, renew, restore, return to form, revive, snap back*, sober up*, start anew, take turn for better; SEE CONCEPTS *303,700*

recreation [n] *sports, games, special interests*
amusement, avocation, ball*, disport, dissipation, distraction, diversion, divertissement, ease, enjoyment, entertainment, exercise, festivity, field day*, frolic, fun, fun and games*, game, hilarity, hobby, holiday, jollity, laughs*, leisure activity, mirth, pastime, picnic, play, playtime, pleasure, R and R*, rec, refreshment, relaxation, relief, repose, rollick, sport, vacation; SEE CONCEPTS *363,364*

recruit [n] *person beginning service*
apprentice, beginner, convert, draftee, enlisted man/woman, fledgling, freshman, GI*, greenhorn*, helper, initiate, learner, neophyte, newcomer, new man/woman, novice, novitiate, plebe*, proselyte, rookie, sailor, selectee, serviceman/woman, soldier, tenderfoot*, trainee, volunteer; SEE CONCEPTS *348,358*

recruit [v] *gather resources*
augment, better, build up, call to arms, call up, deliver, draft, engage, enlist, enroll, fill up, find manpower, gain, impress, improve, induct, levy, mobilize, muster, obtain, procure, proselytize, raise, reanimate, recoup, recover, recuperate, refresh, re-

gain, reinforce, renew, repair, replenish, repossess, restore, retrieve, revive, round up, select, sign on, sign up, store up, strengthen, supply, take in, take on, win over; SEE CONCEPTS *41,109,120,320*

rectify [v] *correct a situation; make something right*
adjust, amend, clean up, clean up act*, debug, dial back*, doctor, emend, fix, fix up, go over, improve, launder, make good*, make up for*, mend, pay one's dues*, pick up, put right, recalibrate, redress, reform, remedy, repair, revise, right, scrub, shape up, square, straighten out, straighten up, turn things around*; SEE CONCEPT *126*

recuperate [v] *improve in health*
ameliorate, be on the mend*, be out of woods*, bounce back*, convalesce, gain, get back on feet*, get better, get well, heal, look up, make a comeback*, mend, perk up*, pick up, pull out of it*, pull through, rally, recover, regain health, snap out of it*, turn the corner*; SEE CONCEPTS *303,700*

recur [v] *happen again; repeat in one's mind*
be remembered, be repeated, come again, come and go, come back, crop up again*, haunt thoughts*, iterate, persist, reappear, recrudesce, reiterate, repeat, return, return to mind, revert, run through one's mind*, turn back; SEE CONCEPTS *3,242*

recurrent [adj] *repeating*
alternate, chain, continued, cyclical, frequent, habitual, intermittent, isochronal, isochronous, periodic, periodical, recurring, regular, reoccurring, repeated, repetitive, rolling; SEE CONCEPTS *541,544*

red [n/adj] *color of blood; shade resembling such a color*
bittersweet, bloodshot, blooming, blush, brick, burgundy, cardinal, carmine, cerise, cherry, chestnut, claret, copper, coral, crimson, dahlia, flaming, florid, flushed, fuchsia, garnet, geranium, glowing, healthy, inflamed, infrared, magenta, maroon, pink, puce, rose, roseate, rosy, rubicund, ruby, ruddy, russet, rust, salmon, sanguine, scarlet, titian, vermilion, wine; SEE CONCEPTS *618,622*

redden [v] *blush, make rosy*
bloody, color, crimson, dye, encarmine, encarnadine, flush, glow, go red, mantle, paint, pink, pinken, rose, rouge, rubify, rubric, rubricate, ruby, rud, ruddle, ruddy, rust, suffuse, tint, turn red, vermilion; SEE CONCEPTS *250,469*

redeem [v1] *recover possession*
buy back, buy off, call in, cash, cash in, change, cover, defray, discharge, exchange, get back, make good, pay off, purchase, ransom, recapture, reclaim, recoup, regain, reinstate, repay, replevin, replevy, repossess, repurchase, restore, retrieve, settle, take in, trade in, win back; SEE CONCEPTS *104,131,327*

redeem [v2] *free; buy the freedom of*
deliver, disenthrall, disimprison, emancipate, extricate, liberate, loose, manumit, pay ransom, ransom, release, rescue, save, set free, unbind, unchain, unfetter; SEE CONCEPTS *127,327*

redeem [v3] *atone for; compensate*
abide by, absolve, acquit, adhere to, balance, carry out, compensate, counterbalance, counterpoise, countervail, defray, discharge, fulfill, hold to, keep, keep the faith*, make amends, make good*, make up for, meet, offset, outweigh, perform, redress, rehabilitate, reinstate, restore, satisfy, save, set off; SEE CONCEPTS *91,126*

redress [n] *help, compensation*
aid, amendment, amends, assistance, atonement, balancing, change, conciliation, correction, cure, ease, indemnity, justice, offsetting, payment, quittance, recompense, rectification, reestablishment, reformation, rehabilitation, relief, remedy, remission, remodeling, renewal, repair, reparation, reprisal, requital, restitution, retribution, return, revision, reward, reworking, satisfaction, vengeance; SEE CONCEPTS *344,712*

redress [v] *change, rectify*
adjust, amend, annul, balance, cancel, compensate, correct, counteract, countercheck, dial back*, ease, even out, frustrate, make amends, make reparation, make restitution, make up for, mend, negate, negative, neutralize, pay for, pay one's dues*, put right*, recalibrate, recompense, reform, regulate, relieve, remedy, repair, restore, revise, square, turn around, turn over new leaf*, turn things around*, vindicate; SEE CONCEPTS *126,697*

reduce [v1] *make less; decrease*
abate, abridge, bankrupt, bant, break, cheapen, chop, clip, contract, curtail, cut, cut back, cut down, debase, deflate, depreciate, depress, diet, dilute, diminish, discount, drain, dwindle, go on a diet, impair, impoverish, lessen, lose weight, lower, mark down, moderate, nutshell, pare, pauperize, rebate, recede, roll back, ruin, scale down, shave, shorten, slash, slim, slow down, step down, take off weight, taper, taper off, tone down, trim, truncate, turn down, weaken, wind down; SEE CONCEPTS *137,236,240,247,698*

reduce [v2] *defeat*
bear down, beat down, break, bring, conquer, cripple, crush, disable, drive, enfeeble, force, master, overcome, overpower, ruin, subdue, subjugate, undermine, vanquish, weaken; SEE CONCEPT *95*

reduce [v3] *humble, humiliate*
abase, break, bring low, bump, bust, declass, degrade, demerit, demote, disgrade, disrate, downgrade, lower, take down a peg; SEE CONCEPTS *7,19,384*

redundant [adj] *excessive; repetitious*
bombastic, de trop*, diffuse, extra, extravagant, inessential, inordinate, iterating, long-winded*, loquacious, oratorical, padded*, palaverous, periphrastic, pleonastic, prolix, reiterating, spare, supererogatory, superfluous, supernumerary, surplus, tautological, unnecessary, unwanted, verbose, wordy; SEE CONCEPTS *553,781*

reef [n] *underwater or partially submerged ledge*
atoll, bank, bar, beach, cay, coral reef, ridge, rock, rock barrier, sand bar, shoal; SEE CONCEPT *509*

reek [n] *strong odor*
effluvium, fetor, mephitis, smell, stench, stink; SEE CONCEPT *600*

reek [v] *smell of; be characterized by*
be permeated by, be redolent of, emit, fume, funk, give off odor, have an odor, smell, smoke, steam, stench, stink; SEE CONCEPT *600*

reel [v] *wobble; spin around*
bob, careen, falter, feel giddy, go around, lurch, pitch, revolve, rock, roll, shake, stagger, stumble, sway, swim, swing, swirl, teeter, titubate, totter, turn, twirl, waver, weave, wheel, whirl; SEE CONCEPTS *151,153*

refer [v1] *mention*
accredit, adduce, advert, allude, ascribe, assign, associate, attribute, bring up, charge, cite, credit, designate, direct attention, excerpt, exemplify, extract, give as example, glance, hint, impute, indicate, insert, instance, interpolate, introduce, invoke, lay, make allusion, make mention of, make reference, name, notice, point, point out, put down to, quote, speak about, speak of, specify, touch on; SEE CONCEPT *73*

refer [v2] *direct, guide*
commit, consign, deliver, hand in, hand over, introduce, pass on, point, put in touch, recommend, relegate, send, submit, transfer, turn over; SEE CONCEPTS *143,187*

refer [v3] *concern, apply*
answer, appertain, be about, be a matter of, bear upon, be directed to, belong, be relevant, connect, correspond with, cover, deal with, encompass, have a bearing on, have reference, have relation, have to do with, hold, include, incorporate, involve, pertain, point, regard, relate, take in, touch; SEE CONCEPT *532*

refer [v4] *seek information*
advise, apply, commune, confer, consult, go, have recourse, look up, recur, repair, resort, run, turn, turn to; SEE CONCEPTS *72,216*

referee [n] *person who mediates, judges*
adjudicator, arbiter, arbitrator, conciliator, judge, ref*, umpire; SEE CONCEPTS *348,366*

referee [v] *judge, mediate*
adjudge, adjudicate, arbitrate, umpire; SEE CONCEPT *18*

reference [n1] *remark, citation*
advertence, allusion, associating, attributing, bringing up, connecting, hint, implication, indicating, innuendo, insinuation, mention, mentioning, note, plug*, pointing out, quotation, relating, resource, source, stating; SEE CONCEPT *278*

reference [n2] *testimonial of good character*
certificate, certification, character, credentials, endorsement, good word, recommendation, tribute; SEE CONCEPTS *69,274*

reference [*n3*] *printed matter with information*
archives, cyclopedia, dictionary, encyclopedia, evidence, source, thesaurus, writing; SEE CONCEPTS *271,280*

refine [*v1*] *purify*
clarify, cleanse, distill, filter, process, rarefy, strain; SEE CONCEPT *165*

refine [*v2*] *perfect, polish*
better, civilize, clarify, cultivate, elevate, explain, hone, improve, make clear, round, sleek, slick, smooth, temper; SEE CONCEPT *244*

refined [*adj1*] *cultured, civilized*
aesthetic, civil, classy*, courteous, courtly, cultivated, delicate, discerning, discriminating, elegant, enlightened, exact, fastidious, fine, finespun, genteel, gentlemanly, gracious, high-brow*, high-minded, ladylike, nice, plush, polished, polite, posh, precise, punctilious, restrained, ritzy*, sensitive, snazzy*, sophisticated, spiffy, suave, sublime, subtle, swanky*, tasteful, urbane, well-bred, well-mannered; SEE CONCEPTS *401,555,589*

refined [*adj2*] *cleaned of impurities*
aerated, boiled down, clarified, clean, cleansed, distilled, drained, expurgated, filtered, processed, pure, purified, rarefied, strained, washed; SEE CONCEPT *621*

refinement [*n1*] *cleansing*
clarification, cleaning, depuration, detersion, distillation, draining, filtering, processing, purification, rarefaction, rectification; SEE CONCEPT *165*

refinement [*n2*] *cultivation, civilization*
affability, civility, courtesy, courtliness, delicacy, dignity, discrimination, elegance, enlightenment, erudition, fastidiousness, fineness, fine point*, finesse, fine tuning*, finish, gentility, gentleness, good breeding, good manners, grace, graciousness, knowledge, lore, nicety, nuance, polish, politeness, politesse, precision, sophistication, style, suavity, subtlety, tact, taste, urbanity; SEE CONCEPTS *388,633,655*

reflect [*v1*] *give back*
be resonant, cast, catch, copy, echo, emulate, flash, follow, give forth, imitate, match, mirror, rebound, repeat, repercuss, reply, reproduce, resonate, resound, return, reverberate, reverse, revert, shine, take after, throw back; SEE CONCEPTS *65,171,624*

reflect [*v2*] *think about*
cerebrate, chew*, cogitate, consider, contemplate, deliberate, meditate, mull over, muse, ponder, reason, ruminate, speculate, stew*, study, think, weigh, wonder; SEE CONCEPTS *17,24*

reflect [*v3*] *demonstrate, indicate*
bear out, bespeak, communicate, display, evince, exhibit, express, indicate, manifest, reveal, show; SEE CONCEPT *261*

reflection [*n1*] *thought, thinking*
absorption, brainwork, cerebration, cogitation, consideration, contemplation, deliberation, idea, imagination, impression, meditation, musing, observation, opinion, pensiveness, pondering, rumination, speculation, study, view; SEE CONCEPTS *17,24*

reflection [*n2*] *mirror image*
appearance, counterpart, duplicate, echo, idea, image, impression, light, likeness, picture, representation, reproduction, shadow; SEE CONCEPT *628*

reflection [*n3*] *criticism*
animadversion, aspersion, blame, censure, derogation, discredit, disesteem, imputation, obloquy, reproach, slam, slur, stricture; SEE CONCEPT *52*

reflective [*adj*] *thoughtful*
cogitating, contemplative, deliberate, meditative, pensive, pondering, reasoning, ruminative, speculative, studious; SEE CONCEPT *403*

reform [*v*] *correct, rectify*
ameliorate, amend, better, bring up to code*, change one's ways*, clean up, clean up one's act*, convert, correct, cure, emend, go straight*, improve, make amends, make over, mend, rearrange, rebuild, reclaim, reconstitute, reconstruct, redeem, refashion, regenerate, rehabilitate, remake, remedy, remodel, renew, renovate, reorganize, repair, resolve, restore, revise, revolutionize, rework, shape up, standardize, swear off, transform, turn over a new leaf*, uplift; SEE CONCEPTS *35,110,126,202*

refrain [*n*] *chorus of musical piece*
burden, melody, music, song, strain, theme, tune, undersong; SEE CONCEPTS *264,595*

refrain [*v*] *do without; keep from doing*
abstain, arrest, avoid, be temperate, cease, check, curb, desist, eschew, forbear, forgo, give up, go on the wagon*, halt, inhibit, interrupt, keep, leave off, not do, pass, pass up, quit, renounce, resist, restrain, sit out*, stop, take the cure*, take the pledge*, withhold; SEE CONCEPTS *121,681*

refresh [*v*] *make like new; give new life*
brace, breathe new life into, bring around, brush up, cheer, cool, enliven, exhilarate, freshen, inspirit, jog, modernize, prod, prompt, quicken, reanimate, recreate, regain, reinvigorate, rejuvenate, renovate, repair, replenish, restore, resuscitate, revitalize, revive, revivify, stimulate, update, vivify; SEE CONCEPTS *35,202,697*

refreshment [*n*] *small amount of food or drink*
bite, pick-me-up*, snack, spread, tidbit; SEE CONCEPT *457*

refrigerate [*v*] *chill, usually in storage*
air-condition, air-cool, cool, freeze, ice, keep cold, make cold; SEE CONCEPTS *202,255*

refuge [*n*] *place to hide, have privacy*
ambush, anchorage, asylum, cover, covert, den, escape, exit, expedient, fortress, harbor, harborage, haven, hideaway, hideout, hiding place, hole, home, immunity, ivory tower*, makeshift, opening, outlet, port, preserve, protection, recourse, resort, resource, retreat, safe place, sanctuary, security, shelter,

shield, stopgap*, stronghold, way out*; SEE CONCEPTS *198,515*

refugee [*n*] *person running from something, often oppression*

alien, boat person, castaway, defector, derelict, deserter, displaced person, DP*, emigrant, émigré, escapee, evacuee, exile, expatriate, expellee, foreigner, foundling, fugitive, homeless person, leper, maroon, outcast, outlaw, pariah, prodigal, renegade, runaway, stateless person; SEE CONCEPTS *359,413*

refund [*n*] *returned money*

acquittance, allowance, compensation, consolation, discharge, discount, give-back*, give-up*, kickback, money back, payment, rebate, reimbursement, remuneration, repayment, restitution, retribution, return, satisfaction, settlement; SEE CONCEPTS *340,344*

refund [*v*] *return money; rebate*

adjust, balance, compensate, give back, honor a claim, indemnify, kickback*, make amends, make good*, make repayment, make up for, pay back, recompense, recoup, redeem, redress, reimburse, relinquish, remit, remunerate, repay, restore, reward, settle; SEE CONCEPT *341*

refurbish [*v*] *spruce up*

clean up, do up*, fix up, gussy up*, mend, modernize, overhaul, recondition, redo, reequip, refit, refresh, rehab, rehabilitate, rejuvenate, remodel, renew, renovate, repair, restore, retread, revamp, set to rights, spruce, update; SEE CONCEPTS *177,202*

refusal [*n*] *denial of responsibility; unwillingness*

abnegation, ban, choice, cold shoulder*, declension, declination, defiance, disallowance, disapproval, disavowal, disclaimer, discountenancing, disfavor, dissent, enjoinment, exclusion, forbidding, interdiction, knockback*, negation, nix*, no, nonacceptance, noncompliance, nonconsent, option, pass, prohibition, proscription, rebuff, refutation, regrets, rejection, renouncement, renunciation, repudiation, repulse, repulsion, reversal, thumbs down*, turndown, veto, withholding, writ; SEE CONCEPTS *278,633*

refuse [*n*] *garbage*

debris, dregs, dross, dump, dust, hogwash*, junk, leavings, litter, muck, offal, rejectamenta*, remains, residue, rubbish, scraps, scum*, sediment, slop*, sweepings, swill, trash, waste, waste matter; SEE CONCEPT *260*

refuse [*v*] *deny; say no*

beg off, brush off*, decline, demur, desist, disaccord, disallow, disapprove, dispense with, dissent, dodge, evade, hold back, hold off, hold out, ignore, make excuses, nix*, not budge, not budget, not buy*, not care to*, pass up, protest, rebuff, refuse to receive, regret, reject, repel, reprobate, repudiate, send off*, send regrets*, set aside*, shun, spurn, thumbs down*, turn away, turn deaf ear to*, turn down, turn from, turn one's back on*, withdraw, withhold; SEE CONCEPTS *30,49,266*

refute [*v*] *prove false; discredit*

abnegate, argue against, blow sky high*, break, burn, burn down, cancel, cancel out, confute, contend, contradict, contravene, convict, counter, crush, debate, demolish, disclaim, disconfirm, dispose of, disprove, dispute, evert, explode, expose, gainsay, give the lie to*, invalidate, negate, oppose, overthrow, parry, quash, rebut, reply to, repudiate, shoot down, shoot full of holes*, show up, silence, squelch, take a stand against, tear down*, thumbs down*, top*; SEE CONCEPT *54*

regain [*v*] *get back, get back to*

achieve, attain, compass, gain, get out from under, get well, make well, reach, reach again, reacquire, reattain, recapture, reclaim, recoup, recover, recruit, redeem, repossess, retake, retrieve, return to, save, take back, win back; SEE CONCEPTS *120,124,131*

regal [*adj*] *fit for royalty*

august, glorious, imposing, kinglike, kingly, magnificent, majestic, monarchial, monarchical, noble, princely, proud, queenly, resplendent, royal, sovereign, splendid, stately, sublime; SEE CONCEPT *589*

regale [*v*] *throw a party; have fun*

amuse, delight, divert, entertain, feast, fracture, give a party, grab, gratify, have a get-together, laugh it up, nurture, party, please, ply, refresh, satisfy, serve, toss a party; SEE CONCEPTS *292,384*

regard [*n1*] *attention, look*

care, carefulness, cognizance, concern, consciousness, curiosity, gaze, glance, heed, interest, interestedness, mark, mind, note, notice, observance, observation, once-over*, remark, scrutiny, stare, view; SEE CONCEPTS *596,623,626,690*

regard [*n2*] *affection, good opinion*

account, appreciation, approbation, approval, attachment, care, cherishing, concern, consideration, curiosity, deference, devotion, esteem, estimation, favor, fondness, homage, honor, interest, interestedness, liking, love, note, opinion, prizing, reputation, repute, respect, reverence, satisfaction, store, sympathy, thought, value, valuing, veneration, worship; SEE CONCEPTS *10,532,689*

regard [*n3*] *feature, detail*

aspect, bearing, concern, connection, item, matter, particular, point, reference, relation, relevance, respect; SEE CONCEPTS *532,644*

regard [*v1*] *look at; listen to*

advertise, attend, beam, behold, contemplate, eagle eye*, eye, eyeball*, flash, gaze, get a load of*, give attention, heed, look on, mark, mind, note, notice, observe, overlook, pay attention, pipe*, pore over*, read, remark, respect, scan, scrutinize, see, spy, stare at, take into consideration, take notice of, view, watch, witness; SEE CONCEPTS *596,623,626*

regard [*v2*] *believe, judge*

account, adjudge, admire, assay, assess, consider, deem, esteem, estimate, look upon, rate, reckon, respect, revere, see, suppose, surmise, think, treat, value, view; SEE CONCEPTS *10,12*

regard [*v3*] *have something to do with*
apply to, bear upon, be relevant to, concern, have a bearing on, have to do with*, interest, pertain to, refer to, relate to; SEE CONCEPT *532*

regardful [*adj*] *attentive, observant*
advertent, arrect, aware, careful, considerate, deferential, duteous, dutiful, heedful, intentive, mindful, observative, observing, respectful, thoughtful, watchful; SEE CONCEPT *401*

regardless [*adj*] *indifferent, unconcerned*
behindhand, blind, careless, coarse, crude, deaf, delinquent, derelict, disregarding, heedless, inadvertent, inattentive, inconsiderate, insensitive, lax, listless, mindless, neglectful, negligent, nonobservant, rash, reckless, remiss, rude, slack, unfeeling, unheeding, uninterested, unmindful; SEE CONCEPT *401*

regardless [*adv*] *despite everything*
against, although, anyway, aside from, at any cost, but, come what may, despite, distinct from, for all that, in any case, in spite of everything, leaving aside, nevertheless, no matter what, nonetheless, notwithstanding, without considering, without regard to; SEE CONCEPTS *544,548*

regards [*n*] *best wishes*
commendations, compliments, deference, devoirs, good wishes, greeting, love, love and kisses*, remembrances, respects, salutation, salutations; SEE CONCEPT *278*

regenerate [*v*] *breathe new life into*
change, exhilarate, inspirit, invigorate, produce, raise from the dead*, reanimate, reawaken, reconstruct, recreate, reestablish, refresh, reinvigorate, rejuvenate, renew, renovate, reproduce, restore, revive, revivify, uplift; SEE CONCEPTS *7,22, 173,202,251*

regime [*n*] *leadership of organization*
administration, dynasty, establishment, government, incumbency, management, pecking order*, reign, rule, system, tenure; SEE CONCEPTS *299,325*

region [*n*] *area, domain; scope*
arena, bailiwick, belt, block, clearing, country, demesne, district, division, domain, dominion, environs, expanse, field, ghetto, ground, inner city, jungle, land, locale, locality, neck of woods*, neighborhood, part, place, precinct, province, quarter, range, realm, scene, section, sector, shire, sphere, stomping ground*, suburb, terrain, territory, tract, turf, vicinity, walk, ward, world, zone; SEE CONCEPTS *198,508,512*

register [*n*] *list, record*
annals, archives, book, catalog, catalogue, chronicle, diary, entry, file, ledger, log, memorandum, registry, roll, roll call, roster, schedule, scroll; SEE CONCEPT *281*

register [*v1*] *enter in list, record*
catalogue, check in, chronicle, enlist, enroll, file, inscribe, join, list, note, record, schedule, set down,

sign on, sign up, sign up for, subscribe, take down, weigh in; SEE CONCEPTS *79,114,125*

register [*v2*] *indicate, reveal*
be shown, bespeak, betray, disclose, display, exhibit, express, manifest, mark, point out, point to, read, record, reflect, say, show; SEE CONCEPT *261*

register [*v3*] *make an impression*
come home, dawn on, get through, have an effect, impress, sink in, tell; SEE CONCEPTS *7,19,22*

regress [*v*] *return to earlier way of doing things*
backslide, degenerate, deteriorate, ebb, fall away, fall back, fall off, go back, lapse, lose ground, recede, relapse, retreat, retrogress, revert, rollback, sink, throw back, turn back; SEE CONCEPTS *633,698*

regret [*n*] *upset over past action*
affliction, anguish, annoyance, apologies, apology, bitterness, care, compunction, concern, conscience, contrition, demur, disappointment, discomfort, dissatisfaction, dole, grief, heartache, heartbreak, lamentation, misgiving, nostalgia, pang, penitence, qualm, regretfulness, remorse, repentance, ruefulness, scruple, self-accusation, self-condemnation, self-disgust, self-reproach, sorrow, uneasiness, woe, worry; SEE CONCEPTS *21,410*

regret [*v*] *be upset about*
apologize, be disturbed, bemoan, be sorry for, bewail, cry over*, cry over spilled milk*, deplore, deprecate, disapprove, feel remorse, feel sorry, feel uneasy, grieve, have compunctions*, have qualms*, kick oneself*, lament, look back, miss, moan, mourn, repent, repine, rue, weep*, weep over*; SEE CONCEPTS *21,410*

regretful [*adj*] *sad, sorry*
apologetic, ashamed, attritional, compunctious, contrite, disappointed, mournful, penitent, remorseful, repentant, rueful, sorrowful; SEE CONCEPT *403*

regrettable [*adj*] *unfortunate, wrong*
afflictive, calamitous, deplorable, dire, disappointing, distressing, dreadful, grievous, heartbreaking, ill-advised, lamentable, pitiable, pitiful, sad, shameful, unfavorable, unhappy, woeful; SEE CONCEPTS *548,571*

regular [*adj1*] *normal, common*
approved, bona fide, classic, commonplace, correct, customary, daily, established, everyday, formal, general, habitual, lawful, legitimate, natural, normal, official, ordinary, orthodox, prevailing, prevalent, proper, routine, run-of-the-mill*, sanctioned, standard, time-honored, traditional, typic, typical, unexceptional, unvarying, usual; SEE CONCEPTS *530, 533,547*

regular [*adj2*] *orderly, consistent, balanced*
accordant, alternating, arranged, automatic, classified, congruous, consonant, constant, cyclic, dependable, efficient, established, even, exact, expected, fixed, flat, formal, harmonious, in order, invariable, level, measured, mechanical, methodical, momentary, ordered, organized, patterned, periodic, precise, probable, punctual, rational, recurrent, regulated,

rhythmic, routine, serial, set, smooth, standardized, stated, steady, straight, successive, symmetrical, systematic, uniform; SEE CONCEPTS *326,544,566,585*

regulate [v] *manage, organize*
adapt, adjust, administer, allocate, arrange, balance, classify, conduct, control, coordinate, correct, determine, direct, dispose, fit, fix, govern, guide, handle, improve, legislate, measure, methodize, moderate, modulate, monitor, order, oversee, pull things together*, put in order, readjust, reconcile, rectify, rule, run, set, settle, shape up, square, standardize, straighten up, superintend, supervise, systematize, temper, time, true, tune, tune up; SEE CONCEPTS *94,117*

regulation [n1] *managing, organizing*
adjustment, administration, arrangement, classification, codification, control, coordination, direction, governance, governing, government, guidance, handling, management, moderation, modulation, reconciliation, regimentation, reorganization, settlement, standardization, superintendence, supervision, systematization, tuning; SEE CONCEPTS *94,117*

regulation [n2] *rule, requirement*
bible, book, canon, chapter and verse*, code, commandment, decree, decretum, dictate, direction, edict, law, no-nos*, numbers, order, ordinance, precept, prescript, principle, procedure, reg*, standing order, statute; SEE CONCEPTS *318,687*

rehabilitate [v] *renovate, adjust*
change, clear, convert, fix up, furbish, improve, make good*, mend, rebuild, reclaim, recondition, reconstitute, reconstruct, recover, redeem, reestablish, reform, refurbish, rehab*, reinstate, reintegrate, reinvigorate, rejuvenate, renew, restitute, restore, save; SEE CONCEPTS *35,126,134,202*

rehash [v] *talk over again*
change, discuss, reiterate, repeat, rephrase, restate, reuse, rework, rewrite, say again, state differently; SEE CONCEPT *56*

rehearsal [n] *preparation for performance*
call, description, drill, dry run*, experiment, going-over, practice, practice session, prep*, reading, readying, recital, recitation, recounting, rehearsing, relation, retelling, run-through, shakedown, test flight, trial balloon*, trial performance, tryout, workout; SEE CONCEPTS *264,292,363*

rehearse [v] *prepare for performance*
act, depict, describe, do over, drill, dry run*, experiment, go over, go through, hold a reading*, hone, iterate, learn one's part, narrate, practice, ready, recapitulate, recite, recount, reenact, reiterate, relate, repeat, review, run lines, run through, state, study, take from the top*, tell, test, train, try out, tune up, walk through*, warm up, work out; SEE CONCEPTS *266,292,363*

reign [n] *rule, dominion*
administration, ascendancy, command, control, dynasty, empire, hegemony, incumbency, influence, monarchy, power, regime, sovereignty, supremacy, sway, tenure; SEE CONCEPTS *198,376*

reign [v] *have power over; prevail*
administer, be in power, be in the driver's seat*, be supreme, boss, command, dominate, domineer, govern, head up, helm, hold power, hold sway*, influence, manage, obtain, occupy, overrule, predominate, preponderate, rule, rule the roost*, run the show*, run things*, sit, superabound, wear the crown*; SEE CONCEPTS *117,298*

reimburse [v] *pay back something owed*
balance, compensate, indemnify, make reparations, make up for, offset, pay, recompense, recover, refund, remunerate, repay, requite, restore, return, square, square up; SEE CONCEPT *341*

rein [n] *restraint, control*
bit, brake, bridle, check, curb, deterrent, governor, halter, harness, hold, line, restriction, strap; SEE CONCEPT *499*

rein [v] *restrain, control*
bridle, check, collect, compose, cool, curb, halt, hold, hold back, limit, repress, restrict, simmer down, slow down, smother, suppress; SEE CONCEPT *130*

reinforce [v] *strengthen, augment*
add fuel to fire*, add to, back up, beef up*, bolster, boost, build up, buttress, carry, emphasize, energize, enlarge, fortify, harden, heat up, hype, increase, lend a hand, multiply, pick up, pillar, prop, prop up, punch up, shore up, soup up*, stand up for, stiffen, stress, stroke, supplement, support, sustain, toughen, underline; SEE CONCEPTS *5,236,245,250*

reinstate [v] *give back responsibility*
bring back, put back, put in power again, recall, redeem, reelect, reestablish, rehabilitate, rehire, reintroduce, reinvest, renew, replace, restore, return, revive; SEE CONCEPTS *351,384*

reiterate [v] *say or do again*
come again, ditto*, double-check, echo, go over again, ingeminate, iterate, one more time, play back, recap*, recapitulate, recheck, rehash, renew, repeat, reprise, resay, restate, retell, rewarn, say again; SEE CONCEPTS *100,171,266*

reject [v] *say no to*
burn, cashier*, cast, cast aside, cast off, chuck, decline, deny, despise, disallow, disbelieve, discard, discount, discredit, disdain, dismiss, eliminate, exclude, jettison, jilt, kill*, nix*, not buy*, pass by, pass on, pass up, put down, rebuff, refuse, renounce, repel, reprobate, repudiate, repulse, scoff, scorn, scout, scrap, second, shed, shoot down*, shun, slough, spurn, throw away, throw out, thumbs down*, turn down, veto; SEE CONCEPTS *21,30,180*

rejection [n] *denial, refusal*
bounce, brushoff*, cold shoulder*, disallowance, dismissal, elimination, exclusion, hard time*, kick in teeth*, nix*, no dice*, no go*, nothing doing*, no way*, pass, rebuff, renunciation, repudiation, slap in the face*, thumbs down*, turndown, veto; SEE CONCEPTS *21,30,180*

rejoice [v] *be very happy about something*
be glad, be overjoyed, celebrate, delight, enchant, enjoy, exult, feel happy, glory, joy, jump for joy, make merry, revel, triumph; SEE CONCEPT *410*

rejuvenate [v] *make new again*
breathe new life into*, do, do up*, exhilarate, face lift*, give new life to, make young again, modernize, reanimate, reclaim, recondition, reconstruct, recover, refresh, refurbish, regenerate, rehab, reinvigorate, renew, renovate, restitute, restore, retread, revitalize, revivify, spruce, spruce up, update; SEE CONCEPTS *35,202*

relapse [n] *deterioration, weakening*
backsliding, fall, fall from grace*, lapse, loss, recidivism, recurrence, regression, repetition, retrogression, return, reversion, setback, turn for the worse*, worsening; SEE CONCEPT *698*

relapse [v] *deteriorate, weaken*
backslide, be overcome, be overtaken, degenerate, fade, fail, fall, fall back, lapse, recidivate, regress, retrogress, revert, sicken, sink, slide back, slip back, suffer, turn back, worsen; SEE CONCEPT *698*

relate [v1] *give an account of*
break a story*, chronicle, clue one in*, depict, describe, detail, disclose, divulge, express, get off one's chest*, give the word*, impart, itemize, lay it on the line*, let one's hair down*, narrate, particularize, picture, present, recite, recount, rehearse, report, retell, reveal, run down, run through, set forth, shoot the breeze*, sling*, spill, spill the beans*, spin a yarn*, state, tell, track, verbalize; SEE CONCEPT *55*

relate [v2] *correlate, pertain*
affect, ally, appertain, apply, ascribe, assign, associate, bear upon, be joined with, be relevant to, bracket, combine, compare, concern, conjoin, connect, consociate, coordinate, correspond to, couple, credit, have reference to, have to do with, identify with, impute, interconnect, interdepend, interrelate, join, link, orient, orientate, pertain, refer, tie in with, touch, unite, yoke; SEE CONCEPT *532*

related [adj] *connected, accompanying*
affiliated, agnate, akin, alike, allied, analogous, associated, cognate, complementary, concomitant, connate, connatural, consanguine, convertible, correlated, correspondent, dependent, enmeshed, fraternal, germane, incident, interchangeable, interconnected, interdependent, interrelated, intertwined, interwoven, in the same category, in touch with, joint, knit together*, like, linked, mutual, of that ilk, parallel, pertinent, reciprocal, relevant, similar, tied up; SEE CONCEPTS *487,573,577*

relation [n] *connection, family connection*
affiliation, affinity, alliance, association, consanguinity, kin, kindred, kinship, kinsman/woman, liaison, propinquity, relationship, relative, sibling, similarity; SEE CONCEPTS *296,414,421,714*

relationship [n] *connection; friendship*
accord, affair, affiliation, affinity, alliance, analogy, appositeness, association, bond, communication, conjunction, consanguinity, consociation, contact, contingency, correlation, dependence, dependency, exchange, homogeneity, hookup, interconnection, interrelation, interrelationship, kinship, liaison, likeness, link, marriage, nearness, network, parallel, pertinence, pertinency, proportion, rapport, ratio, relation, relativity, relevance, similarity, tie, tie-in, tie-up; SEE CONCEPTS *388,714*

relative [n] *member of a family*
agnate, aunt, blood, brother-in-law, clansman/woman, cognate, connection, cousin, father, father-in-law, folk, folks, grandparents, great-grandparents, in-laws, kinsman/woman, mother, mother-in-law, nephew, niece, relation, sib*, sibling, sister-in-law, stepbrother/sister, stepparent, uncle; SEE CONCEPT *414*

relative [adj1] *comparative, respective*
about, allied, analogous, approximate, associated, concerning, conditional, connected, contingent, corresponding, dependent, in regard to, near, parallel, proportionate, reciprocal, referring, related, relating to, reliant, with respect to; SEE CONCEPT *563*

relative [adj2] *pertinent, applicable*
apposite, appropriate, appurtenant, apropos, contingent, dependent, germane, pertaining, referring, related, relevant; SEE CONCEPT *558*

relatively [adv] *in or by comparison*
almost, approximately, comparably, comparatively, nearly, proportionately, rather, somewhat, to some extent; SEE CONCEPTS *544,772*

relax [v1] *be or feel at ease*
breathe easy*, calm, calm down*, collect oneself, compose oneself, cool off*, ease off, feel at home, hang loose*, knock off*, laze, let oneself go*, lie down, loosen up, make oneself at home*, put one's feet up*, recline, repose, rest, settle back, simmer down*, sit around, sit back, soften, stop work, take a break*, take a breather*, take it easy*, take one's time*, take ten*, take time out*, tranquilize, unbend, unlax, unwind; SEE CONCEPT *210*

relax [v2] *diminish, lessen*
abate, ease, ease off, ebb, lax, let up, loose, loosen, lose speed, lower, mitigate, moderate, modify, modulate, reduce, relieve, remit, slack, slacken, slow, slow down, untighten, weaken; SEE CONCEPTS *240,698*

relaxation [n] *entertainment; resting or recovering*
alleviation, amusement, assuagement, diversion, enjoyment, fun, leisure, loosening, mitigation, pleasure, reclining, recreation, refreshment, relief, repose, requiescence, rest; SEE CONCEPTS *210, 292,363*

relay [v] *pass on, transmit*
broadcast, carry, communicate, deliver, hand down, hand on, hand over, send, send forth, spread, transfer, turn over; SEE CONCEPT *143*

release [n1] *delivery; dispensation*
absolution, acquittal, acquittance, charge, clemency, commute, deliverance, discharge, dispensation,

emancipation, exemption, exoneration, floater, freedom, freeing, let-off*, liberation, liberty, lifeboat, lifesaver, manumission, relief, spring, turnout, walkout; SEE CONCEPTS *127,685*

release [*n2*] *publication*
announcement, flash*, handout, issue, leak, news, notice, offering, proclamation, propaganda, publicity, story; SEE CONCEPTS *271,280*

release [*v*] *let go, let out*
absolve, acquit, bail out, cast loose, clear, commute, deliver, discharge, disengage, dispense, drop, emancipate, exculpate, excuse, exempt, exonerate, extricate, free, give off, give out, go easy on, issue, leak, let off, let off steam*, let up on*, liberate, lifeboat, loose, loosen, manumit, open up, set at large, set free, set loose, spring, surrender, take out, turn loose, turn out, unbind, unchain, undo, unfasten, unfetter, unleash, unloose, unshackle, untie, vent, wipe slate clean*, yield; SEE CONCEPTS *50,60,88,127,143*

relegate [*v1*] *assign, transfer*
accredit, charge, commend, commit, confide, consign, credit, delegate, entrust, hand over, pass on, refer, turn over; SEE CONCEPTS *41,143*

relegate [*v2*] *banish, downgrade*
demote, deport, dismiss, displace, eject, exile, expatriate, expel, expulse, lag, ostracize, remove, throw out, transport; SEE CONCEPTS *30,121,211*

relent [*v*] *die down; let up*
acquiesce, be merciful, capitulate, cave in*, change one's mind, come around, comply, cool it*, die away, drop, ease, ease off, ease up on*, ebb, fall, fold, forbear, give in, give quarter*, give some slack*, give up, give way, go along with, go easy on*, have mercy, have pity, lay back, let go, let it happen*, lighten up*, mellow out*, melt, moderate, quit, relax, say uncle*, show mercy, slacken, slow, soften, subside, wane, weaken, yield; SEE CONCEPTS *35,698,776*

relentless [*adj1*] *cruel, merciless*
adamant, bound, bound and determined, dead set on*, determined, dogged, ferocious, fierce, go for broke*, grim, hang in*, hang-tough*, hard, harsh, implacable, inexorable, inflexible, inhuman, mean business, mortal, obdurate, pitiless, remorseless, rigid, rigorous, ruthless, single-minded, stiff, stop at nothing, strict, stringent, unappeasable, unbending, uncompromising, undeviating, unflinching, unforgiving, unrelenting, unstoppable, unyielding, vindictive; SEE CONCEPT *401*

relentless [*adj2*] *continuous, neverending*
incessant, nonstop, persistent, pertinacious, punishing, sustained, tenacious, unabated, unbroken, unfaltering, unflagging, unrelenting, unrelieved, unremitting, unstoppable; SEE CONCEPTS *326,534,798*

relevant [*adj*] *appropriate; to the purpose*
accordant, admissible, ad rem, allowable, applicable, applicatory, apposite, appurtenant, apt, becoming, cognate, compatible, concerning, conformant,

conforming, congruent, congruous, consistent, consonant, correlated, correspondent, fit, fitting, germane, harmonious, have direct bearing, having to do with, important, material, on the button*, on the nose*, pat*, pertaining to, pertinent, pointful, proper, referring, related, relative, significant, suitable, suited, to the point, weighty; SEE CONCEPT *558*

reliable [*adj*] *trustworthy*
candid, careful, certain, conscientious, constant, decent, decisive, definite, dependable, determined, devoted, faithful, firm, good, high-principled, honest, honorable, impeccable, incorrupt, loyal, okay, positive, predictable, proved, reputable, respectable, responsible, righteous, safe, sincere, solid, sound, stable, staunch, steadfast, steady, sterling, strong, sure, there, tried, tried-and-true*, true, true-blue*, true-hearted, trusty, unequivocal, unfailing, unimpeachable, upright, veracious; SEE CONCEPTS *535,542,544*

reliance [*n*] *confidence*
assurance, belief, credence, credit, dependence, faith, hope, interdependence, interdependency, stock, trust; SEE CONCEPT *689*

relic [*n*] *something saved from the past*
antique, antiquity, archaism, artifact, curio, curiosity, evidence, fragment, heirloom, keepsake, memento, memorial, monument, remains, remembrance, remembrancer, reminder, remnant, residue, ruins, scrap, souvenir, survival, testimonial, token, trace, trophy, vestige; SEE CONCEPT *446*

relief [*n*] *remedy, aid; relaxation*
abatement, allayment, alleviation, amelioration, appeasement, assistance, assuagement, balm, break, breather, cheer, comfort, comforting, consolation, contentment, cure, deliverance, diversion, ease, easement, extrication, fix, hand, happiness, help, letup, lift, lightening, load off one's mind*, maintenance, mitigation, mollification, palliance, quick fix*, refreshment, release, remedy, remission, reprieve, respite, rest, restfulness, satisfaction, softening, solace, succor, support, sustenance; SEE CONCEPTS *681,712*

relieve [*v1*] *make less painful; let up on*
abate, allay, alleviate, appease, assuage, break, brighten, calm, comfort, console, cure, decrease, diminish, divert, dull, ease, free, interrupt, lighten, mitigate, moderate, mollify, palliate, qualify, quiet, relax, salve, slacken, soften, solace, soothe, subdue, take load off one's chest*, take load off one's mind*, temper, vary; SEE CONCEPTS *244,700*

relieve [*v2*] *help; give assistance*
aid, assist, bring aid, give a break*, give a hand*, give a rest, spell, stand in for, substitute for, succor, support, sustain, take over from, take the place of; SEE CONCEPT *110*

relieve [*v3*] *remove blame, responsibility*
absolve, deliver, discharge, disembarrass, disencumber, dismiss, dispense, excuse, exempt, force to re-

sign, free, let off, privilege, pull, release, spare, throw out, unburden, yank; SEE CONCEPTS *50,88,351*

religion [n] *belief in God*
adoration, ceremonial, church, communion, consecration, creed, cult, denomination, devotion, devoutness, doctrine, faithfulness, fidelity, godliness, higher power, morality, myth, mythology, observance, orthodoxy, persuasion, pietism, piety, prayer, preference, religiosity, rites, ritual, sacrifice, sanctification, sect, spirituality, spiritual-mindedness, standards, superstition, theology, veneration; SEE CONCEPTS *368,689*

religious [*adj1*] *concerning belief in God*
believing, born-again, canonical, churchgoing, churchly, clerical, deistic, devotional, devout, divine, doctrinal, ecclesiastical, ethical, faithful, god-fearing, godly, holy, honest, honorable, just, ministerial, moral, noble, orthodox, pietistic, pious, pontifical, prayerful, priestly, pure, reverent, righteous, sacerdotal, sacred, sacrosanct, saintlike, saintly, scriptural, sectarian, spiritual, staunch, steadfast, supernatural, theistic, theological, upright; SEE CONCEPTS *536,545*

religious [*adj2*] *conscientious, scrupulous*
exact, faithful, fastidious, meticulous, punctilious, rigid, rigorous, unerring, unswerving; SEE CONCEPT *538*

relinquish [v] *give up, let go*
abandon, abdicate, abnegate, back down, cast, cast off, cede, cut loose*, desert, discard, ditch*, drop, drop like hot potato*, drop out, dump*, forbear, forgo, forsake, forswear, hand over, kick, kiss goodbye*, lay aside, leave, opt out, quit, quit cold turkey*, release, renounce, repudiate, resign, retire from, sacrifice, shed, stand down, surrender, swear off, take the oath, take the pledge, vacate, waive, withdraw, yield; SEE CONCEPTS *119,127,234*

relish [n] *great appreciation of something*
appetite, bias, delectation, diversion, enjoying, enjoyment, fancy, flair, flavor, fondness, gusto, heart, leaning, liking, love, loving, palate, partiality, penchant, pleasure, predilection, prejudice, propensity, sapidity, sapor, savor, smack, stomach, tang, taste, zest; SEE CONCEPTS *20,32*

relish [v] *look forward to; appreciate*
admire, be fond of, cherish, delight in, dig, enjoy, fancy, go, go for, like, luxuriate in, mind, prefer, revel in, savor, taste; SEE CONCEPT *32*

reluctant [*adj*] *unenthusiastic, unwilling*
afraid, averse, backward, calculating, cautious, chary, circumspect, demurring, diffident, discouraged, disheartened, disinclined, grudging, hanging back, hesitant, hesitating, indisposed, involuntary, laggard, loath, opposed, queasy, recalcitrant, remiss, shy, slack, slow, squeamish, tardy, uncertain, uneager, wary; SEE CONCEPT *401*

rely [v] *have confidence in*
await, bank, be confident of, believe in, be sure of, bet, bet bottom dollar on*, build, calculate, commit,

confide, count, depend, entrust, expect, gamble on, have faith in, hope, lay money on*, lean, look, reckon, ride on coattails*, swear by*, trust; SEE CONCEPTS *12,26*

remain [v] *stay, wait*
abide, be left, bide, bivouac, bunk*, cling, continue, deep-freeze*, delay, dwell, endure, freeze, go on, halt, hang, hang out, hold over, hold the fort*, hover, inhabit, keep on, last, linger, live, lodge, make camp, nest, outlast, outlive, pause, perch, persist, prevail, put on hold, remain standing, reside, rest, roost, sit out, sit through, sit tight, sojourn, squat, stand, stay behind, stay in, stay over, stay put, stick around, stop, survive, tarry, visit, wait; SEE CONCEPTS *23,239,681,804*

remainder [n] *balance, residue*
bottom of barrel*, butt, carry-over, detritus, dregs, excess, fragment, garbage, hangover*, heel, junk, leavings, leftover, obverse, oddment, odds and ends*, overplus, refuse, relic, remains, remnant, residuum, rest, ruins, salvage, scrap, stump, surplus, trace, vestige, waste, wreck, wreckage; SEE CONCEPTS *260,835*

remark [n] *comment, observation*
acknowledgment, annotation, assertion, attention, back talk, bon mot*, cognizance, comeback, commentary, conclusion, consideration, crack*, declaration, elucidation, exegesis, explanation, explication, exposition, expression, gloss*, heed, illustration, interpretation, mention, mind, note, notice, obiter dictum*, observance, observation, opinion, point, recognition, reflection, regard, saying, statement, talk, thought, two cents' worth*, utterance, wisecrack, witticism, word; SEE CONCEPTS *51,278*

remark [v] *notice and comment*
animadvert, behold, catch, commentate, crack*, declare, descry, espy, heed, make out, mark, mention, mouth off*, note, observe, pass comment, perceive, pick up on, reflect, regard, say, see, speak, spot, state, take note, take notice, utter, wisecrack; SEE CONCEPTS *38,51,626*

remarkable [*adj*] *extraordinary, unusual*
arresting, arrestive, conspicuous, curious, distinguished, exceptional, famous, gilt-edged*, greatest, important, impressive, marked, miraculous, momentous, notable, noteworthy, noticeable, odd, outstanding, peculiar, phenomenal, preeminent, primo*, prominent, rare, salient, signal, significant, singular, smashing, solid, splash*, strange, striking, super, surprising, uncommon, uncustomary, unique, unordinary, unwonted, weighty, wicked, wonderful, world class, zero cool*; SEE CONCEPT *574*

remedial [*adj*] *healing, restorative*
alleviative, antidotal, antiseptic, corrective, curative, curing, healthful, health-giving, invigorating, medicating, medicinal, purifying, recuperative, reformative, remedying, repairing, restitutive, restorative, sanative, sanatory, solving, soothing, therapeutic,

tonic, treating, vulnerary, wholesome; SEE CONCEPT
537

remedy [*n*] *cure, solution*
antidote, assistance, biologic, corrective, counteractant, counteraction, counteractive, counteragent,
countermeasure, counterstep, cure-all*, drug, elixir,
fix, improvement, medicament, medicant, medicine,
panacea, pharmaceutical, pharmacon, physic, pill,
quick fix*, redress, relief, restorative, support, therapy, treatment; SEE CONCEPTS *307,311,693,712*

remedy [*v*] *fix, cure*
aid, alleviate, ameliorate, amend, assuage, attend,
change, clean up, clean up one's act*, control, correct, debug*, doctor, ease, fiddle with, fix up, go
over, heal, help, launder, make up for, mitigate, palliate, pick up, put right, recalibrate, rectify, redress,
reform, relieve, renew, repair, restore, revise, right,
scrub, set right, set to rights*, shape up, solve,
soothe, square*, square up*, straighten out, treat,
upgrade; SEE CONCEPTS *126,212,310*

remember [*v*] *keep in mind; summon into mind*
bear in mind, bethink, brood over, call to mind, call
up, cite, commemorate, conjure up, dig into the
past*, dwell upon, educe, elicit, enshrine, extract,
fix in the mind, flash, flash on*, get, go back, have
memories, hold dear, keep forever, know by heart,
learn, look back, master, memorialize, memorize,
mind, nail down, recall, recognize, recollect, refresh
memory, relive, remind, reminisce, retain, retrospect, revive, revoke, ring a bell*, strike a note*,
summon up, think back, treasure; SEE CONCEPT *40*

remembrance [*n1*] *memory, recollection*
afterthought, anamnesis, flash*, flashback, hindsight*, mental image, mind, recall, recognition, reconstruction, regard, reminiscence, retrospect,
thought; SEE CONCEPTS *40,529*

remembrance [*n2*] *gift, testimonial*
commemoration, favor, keepsake, memento, memorial, monument, present, relic, remembrancer, reminder, reward, souvenir, token, trophy; SEE
CONCEPT *337*

remind [*v*] *awaken memories of something*
admonish, advise, bethink, bring back to, bring to
mind, call attention, call to mind, call up, caution,
cite, emphasize, give a cue*, hint, imply, intimate,
jog one's memory*, make one think, make remember, mention, note, point out, prod, prompt, put in
mind, recall, recollect, refresh memory, remember,
reminisce, retain, retrospect, revive, stir up, stress,
suggest, warn; SEE CONCEPTS *7,19,22,40,78*

reminder [*n*] *warning, notice; keepsake*
admonition, expression, gesture, hint, indication, intimation, memento, memo, memorandum, memorial,
note, notice, relic, remembrance, remembrancer,
sign, souvenir, suggestion, token, trinket, trophy; SEE
CONCEPTS *271,278,529*

reminisce [*v*] *go over in one's memory*
bethink, call up, cite, hark back, live in the past, look
back, mind, muse over, recall, recollect, remember,

remind, retain, retrospect, review, revive, think
back; SEE CONCEPTS *17,40*

reminiscent [*adj*] *suggestive of something in the past*
bringing to mind, evocative, implicative, mnemonic,
nostalgic, recollective, redolent, remindful, similar;
SEE CONCEPT *529*

remiss [*v*] *careless, thoughtless*
any old way*, any which way*, asleep at switch*,
asleep on job*, behindhand, culpable, daydreaming,
defaultant, delinquent, derelict, dilatory, disregardful, faineant, forgetful, heedless, inattentive, indifferent, indolent, lackadaisical, lax, lazy, neglectful,
negligent, regardless, slack, slapdash, slipshod,
sloppy, slothful, slow, tardy, uninterested, unmindful, woolgathering*; SEE CONCEPT *401*

remission [*n1*] *acquittal, pardon*
absolution, amnesty, discharge, excuse, exemption,
exoneration, forgiveness, indulgence, mercy, pardon, release, reprieve; SEE CONCEPT *685*

remission [*n2*] *pause; lessening*
abatement, abeyance, alleviation, amelioration,
break, decrease, delay, diminution, ebb, interruption, let-up, lull, moderation, reduction, relaxation,
release, respite, suspension; SEE CONCEPTS
303,698,807

remit [*v1*] *send, transfer*
address, consign, dispatch, forward, mail, make payment, pay, post, route, settle, ship, square, transmit;
SEE CONCEPTS *217,341*

remit [*v2*] *stop, postpone*
abate, absolve, alleviate, amnesty, cancel, condone,
decrease, defer, delay, desist, diminish, dwindle,
ease up, excuse, exonerate, fall away, forbear, forgive, halt, hold off, hold up, intermit, mitigate, moderate, modify, modulate, pardon, prorogue, put off,
reduce, relax, release, repeal, reprieve, rescind, respite, shelve, sink, slack, slacken, soften, stay, suspend, wane, weaken; SEE CONCEPTS *234,698*

remnant [*n*] *leftover part*
balance, bit, dregs, dross, end, end piece, excess,
fragment, hangover*, heel, leavings, lees, leftovers,
odds and ends*, orts, part, particle, piece, portion,
remainder, remains, residual, residue, residuum,
rest, rump, scrap, shred, strip, surplus, survival, vestige; SEE CONCEPTS *260,835*

remonstrate [*v*] *argue against*
animadvert, blame, censure, challenge, combat,
complain, criticize, decry, demur, deprecate, disapprove, disparage, dispute, dissent, except, expostulate, fight, find fault, frown upon, inveigh, kick*,
nag, object, oppose, pick at, protest, rain, recriminate, resist, scold, sound off*, take exception, take
issue, withstand; SEE CONCEPTS *46,52,54*

remorse [*n*] *guilty or bad conscience*
anguish, attrition, compassion, compunction, contriteness, contrition, grief, guilt, pangs of conscience, penance, penitence, penitency, pity, regret,

remorsefulness, repentance, rue, ruefulness, self-reproach, shame, sorrow; SEE CONCEPTS *410,728*

remorseful [*adj*] *guilty, ashamed*
apologetic, attritional, chastened, compunctious, conscience-stricken, contrite, guilt-ridden, mournful, penitent, penitential, regretful, repentant, rueful, sad, self-reproachful, sorrowful, sorry; SEE CONCEPT *401*

remorseless [*adj*] *without guilt in spite of wrongdoing*
avaricious, barbarous, bloody, callous, cruel, fierce, forbidding, greedy, grim, hard, hard-bitten, hardened, hard-hearted, harsh, impenitent, implacable, inexorable, inhuman, inhumane, insensitive, intolerant, merciless, murderous, obdurate, pitiless, relentless, rigorous, ruthless, sanguinary, savage, shameless, sour, tough, tyrannical, unchristian, uncompassionate, uncontrite, unforgiving, unmerciful, unregenerate, unrelenting, unremitting, unrepenting, unyielding, vindictive; SEE CONCEPT *401*

remote [*adj1*] *out-of-the-way; in the distance*
alien, back, backwoods, beyond, boondocks*, devious, distant, far, faraway, far-flung, far-off, foreign, frontier, godforsaken*, god-knows-where*, in a backwater*, inaccessible, isolated, lonely, lonesome, middle of nowhere*, obscure, off-lying, off the beaten path*, outlandish, outlying, private, removed, retired, secluded, secret, undiscovered, unknown, unsettled, wild; SEE CONCEPT *583*

remote [*adj2*] *irrelevant, unrelated*
abstracted, alien, alone, apart, detached, exclusive, extraneous, extrinsic, farfetched, foreign, immaterial, inappropriate, indirect, nongermane, obscure, outside, pointless, removed, strange, unconnected; SEE CONCEPTS *564,575*

remote [*adj3*] *unlikely, improbable*
doubtful, dubious, faint, fat chance*, implausible, inconsiderable, meager, negligible, off, outside, poor, slender, slight, slim, small; SEE CONCEPT *552*

remote [*adj4*] *cold, detached; unapproachable*
abstracted, aloof, casual, cool*, disinterested, distant, faraway, icy, incurious, indifferent, introspective, introverted, laid-back*, offish, putting on airs, removed, reserved, standoffish, stuck up, uncommunicative, unconcerned, uninterested, uninvolved, uppity, withdrawn; SEE CONCEPTS *401,404*

remove [*v1*] *lift or move object; take off, away*
abolish, abstract, amputate, carry away, carry off, cart off, clear away, cut out, delete, depose, detach, dethrone, dig out, discard, discharge, dislodge, dismiss, displace, disturb, do away with, doff, efface, eject, eliminate, erase, evacuate, expel, expunge, extract, get rid of, junk*, oust, pull out, purge, raise, relegate, rip out, separate, shed, ship, skim, strike out, take down, take out, tear out, throw out, transfer, transport, unload, unseat, uproot, wipe out*, withdraw; SEE CONCEPT *211*

remove [*v2*] *do away with; kill*
assassinate, blot out*, clear away, dispose of, do away with, do in, drag, drag down, efface, eliminate,

eradicate, erase, exclude, execute, expunge, exterminate, extirpate, get rid of, liquidate, murder, obliterate, purge, scratch, sterilize, take down, take out, waste*, wipe out*; SEE CONCEPTS *121,252*

remunerate [*v*] *compensate, reward*
accord, ante up*, award, dish out*, do business*, grant, guerdon, indemnify, pay, pay off, pay up, post, recompense, redress, reimburse, repay, requite, shell out*, spring for*, vouchsafe; SEE CONCEPT *341*

render [*v1*] *contribute*
cede, deliver, distribute, exchange, furnish, give, give back, give up, hand over, impart, make available, make restitution, minister, part with, pay, pay back, present, provide, relinquish, repay, restore, return, show, submit, supply, surrender, swap, tender, trade, turn over, yield; SEE CONCEPTS *108,140*

render [*v2*] *show; execute*
act, administer, administrate, carry out, delineate, depict, display, do, evince, exhibit, give, govern, image, interpret, limn, manifest, perform, picture, play, portray, present, represent; SEE CONCEPTS *91,261*

render [*v3*] *translate, explain*
construe, deliver, interpret, paraphrase, pass, put, reproduce, restate, reword, state, transcribe, transliterate, transpose, turn; SEE CONCEPTS *57,266*

rendezvous [*n1*] *get-together*
affair, appointment, assignation, blind date, date, double date, engagement, heavy date, matinee, meet, meeting, one night stand*, tête-à-tête, tryst; SEE CONCEPT *384*

rendezvous [*n2*] *place for get-together*
gathering point, hangout*, haunt, love nest*, meeting place, purlieu, resort, spot, stomping ground*, venue, watering hole*; SEE CONCEPT *198*

rendezvous [*v*] *meet, often secretly*
assemble, be closeted, be reunited, collect, come together, congregate, congress, converge, forgather, gather, get together, join up, meet behind closed doors, meet privately, muster, raise, rally; SEE CONCEPT *384*

rendition [*n*] *explanation; interpretation*
arrangement, construction, delivery, depiction, execution, interpretation, performance, portrayal, presentation, reading, rendering, transcription, translation, version; SEE CONCEPTS *263,278*

renegade [*n*] *person who is rebellious*
abandoner, apostate, backslider, betrayer, defector, deserter, dissident, double-crosser*, escapee, exile, forsaker, fugitive, heretic, iconoclast, insurgent, mutineer, outlaw, rebel, recreant, refugee, runaway, schismatic, snake*, snake in the grass*, tergiversator, traitor, turnabout, turncoat; SEE CONCEPTS *359,412*

renegade [*adj*] *rebellious*
apostate, backsliding, disloyal, dissident, heterodox, mutinous, outlaw, radical, reactionary, rebel, recre-

ant, revolutionary, runaway, schismatic, traitorous, unfaithful, untraditional; SEE CONCEPTS *401,542*

renew [*v*] *start over*
begin again, brace, breathe new life into*, bring up to date*, continue, exhilarate, extend, fix up, freshen, gentrify, go over, mend, modernize, overhaul, prolong, reaffirm, reawaken, recommence, recondition, recreate, reestablish, refit, refresh, refurbish, regenerate, rehabilitate, reinvigorate, rejuvenate, remodel, renovate, reopen, repair, repeat, replace, replenish, restate, restock, restore, resume, resuscitate, retread, revitalize, revive, spruce, stimulate, transform; SEE CONCEPTS *35,202,221*

renounce [*v*] *abandon, reject*
abdicate, abjure, abnegate, abstain from, apostacize, arrogate, cast off, decline, defect, demit, deny, desert, disavow, discard, disclaim, disown, divorce oneself from*, drop out, dump*, eschew, forgo, forsake, forswear, get on the bandwagon*, give up, leave flat*, leave off, opt out, quit, rat*, recant, reject, relinquish, repudiate, resign, sell out*, spurn, swear off, take the pledge*, tergiversate, tergiverse, throw off, throw over, toss over, turn, waive, walk out on, wash hands of*; SEE CONCEPTS *30,54,195*

renovate [*v*] *fix up, modernize*
clean, cleanse, do*, do up*, face-lift*, gussy up, make over, overhaul, reactivate, recondition, reconstitute, recreate, refit, reform, refresh, refurbish, rehabilitate, rekindle, remake, remodel, renew, repair, restore, resurrect, resuscitate, retread, retrieve, revamp, revitalize, revive, revivify, spruce, spruce up*, update; SEE CONCEPTS *168,177,202*

renown [*adj*] *fame*
acclaim, celebrity, distinction, éclat, eminence, glory, honor, illustriousness, kudos*, luster, mark, note, notoriety, preeminence, prestige, prominence, prominency, rep*, reputation, repute, stardom; SEE CONCEPT *668*

renowned [*adj*] *famous*
acclaimed, celebrated, celebrious, distinguished, eminent, esteemed, extolled, famed, great, illustrious, in the limelight*, lauded, monster, name, notable, noted, of note, outstanding, praised, prominent, redoubted, signal, somebody, splashy, star, superstar, well-known; SEE CONCEPTS *568,574*

rent [*n1*] *fee paid for use, service, or privilege*
hire, lease, payment, rental, tariff; SEE CONCEPT *329*

rent [*n2*] *opening, split*
breach, break, chink, cleavage, crack, discord, dissension, division, faction, fissure, flaw, fracture, gash, hole, perforation, rift, rip, rupture, schism, slash, slit, tatter, tear; SEE CONCEPTS *513,665*

rent [*v*] *pay or charge fee for use, service, or privilege*
allow the use of, borrow, charter, contract, engage, hire, lease, lend, let, loan, make available, put on loan, sublet, take it; SEE CONCEPTS *89,115*

renunciation [*n*] *abandonment, rejection*
abdication, abjuration, abnegation, abstention, cancellation, denial, disavowal, disclaimer, eschewal,

eschewing, forbearing, forswearing, giving up, rebuff, refusal, relinquishment, remission, renouncement, repeal, repudiation, resignation, sacrifice, self-abnegation, self-denial, self-sacrifice, spurning, surrender, veto, waiver, yielding; SEE CONCEPTS *30,54,195*

repair [*n*] *restoration, fixing*
adjustment, darn, improvement, mend, new part, overhaul, patch, reconstruction, reformation, rehabilitation, replacement, substitution; SEE CONCEPTS *513,700,824*

repair [*v1*] *fix, restore*
compensate for, correct, darn, debug, doctor*, do up*, emend, face-lift*, fiddle with, heal, improve, make good, make up for, mend, overhaul, patch, patch up, put back together, put in order, put right, rebuild, recondition, recover, rectify, redline, redress, reform, refresh, refurbish, rejuvenate, remedy, renew, renovate, restore, retread, retrieve, revamp, revive, right, settle, sew, square*, touch up; SEE CONCEPT *212*

repair [*v2*] *leave; retire*
apply, betake oneself, fare, go, head for, hie, journey, move, pass, proceed, process, push on, recur, refer, remove, resort, run, set off for, travel, turn, wend, withdraw; SEE CONCEPT *195*

reparation [*n*] *compensation, amends*
adjustment, apology, atonement, damages, dues, emolument, expiation, indemnification, indemnity, making good, payment, penance, propitiation, quittance, recompense, redemption, redress, remuneration, renewal, repair, repayment, reprisal, requital, restitution, retribution, reward, satisfaction, settlement, squaring things*; SEE CONCEPTS *337,344,712*

repartee [*n*] *pleasant conversation*
answer, badinage, banter, bon mot*, comeback, humor, irony, persiflage, pleasantry, quip, raillery, rejoinder, reply, response, retort, riposte, sally, sarcasm, satire, wit, witticism, wittiness, wordplay; SEE CONCEPTS *45,56,266*

repay [*v1*] *give back money or possession*
accord, award, balance, compensate, indemnify, make amends, make restitution, make up for, offset, pay back, pay dues, rebate, recompense, refund, reimburse, remunerate, requite, restore, return, reward, settle up, square*; SEE CONCEPTS *131,341*

repay [*v2*] *get even; obtain restitution for past injustice*
avenge, even the score, get back at, get revenge, make reprisal, pay back, reciprocate, requite, retaliate, return, return the compliment*, revenge, settle the score*, square accounts*; SEE CONCEPTS *7,19,246,384*

repeal [*n*] *cancellation*
abolition, abrogation, annulment, invalidation, nullification, rescinding, rescindment, rescission, revocation, withdrawal; SEE CONCEPTS *121,318,685*

repeal [v] *declare null and void*
abolish, abrogate, annul, back out, backpedal, blow, call off*, cancel, countermand, dismantle, forget it, invalidate, kill*, KO*, lift, nix*, nullify, opt out, recall, renig, rescind, reverse, revoke, scrub, set aside, shoot down, stand down, throw over, vacate, void, wash out, weasel out*, wipe out, withdraw, worm out*, X-out*, zap*; SEE CONCEPTS *50,88,121,317*

repeat [n] *something done over; duplicate*
echo, recapitulation, reiteration, repetition, replay, reproduction, rerun, reshowing; SEE CONCEPT *695*

repeat [v] *duplicate, do again*
chime, come again, din, ditto*, drum into*, duplicate, echo, go over again, hold over, imitate, ingeminate, iterate, make like, occur again, play back, play over, quote, read back, reappear, recapitulate, recast, reciprocate, recite, reconstruct, recrudesce, recur, redo, refashion, reform, rehash*, rehearse, reissue, reiterate, relate, remake, renew, reoccur, replay, reprise, reproduce, rerun, resay, reshow, restate, retell, return, revert, revolve, rework*, run over, sing same old song*; SEE CONCEPTS *91,111,171*

repeatedly [adv] *over and over again*
again, again and again, frequently, many a time, many times, much, oft, often, oftentimes, oftimes, regularly, time after time, time and again; SEE CONCEPT *553*

repel [v1] *push away; repulse*
beat back, beat off, brush off, buck, cast aside, chase away, check, cold shoulder*, confront, cool*, cut, decline, dismiss, disown, dispute, drive away, drive back, drive off, duel, fend off, fight, force back, force off, hold back, hold off, keep at arm's length*, keep at bay*, keep off, kick, knock down, oppose, parry, push back, put down, put to flight, rebuff, rebut, refuse, reject, resist, stand up against, stave off, traverse, turn down, ward off, withstand; SEE CONCEPTS *30,208*

repel [v2] *induce aversion*
disgust, give a pain in neck*, make sick*, offend, put off*, reluct, repulse, revolt, sicken, turn off*, turn one's stomach*; SEE CONCEPTS *7,19,303*

repent [v] *ask forgiveness*
apologize, atone, be ashamed, be contrite, be sorry, bewail, deplore, feel remorse, have qualms, lament, reform, regret, relent, reproach oneself, rue, see error of ways*, show penitence, sorrow; SEE CONCEPTS *48,410*

repentance [n] *feeling bad for past action*
attrition, compunction, conscience, contriteness, contrition, grief, guilt, penitence, penitency, regret, remorse, rue, ruth, self-reproach, sorriness, sorrow; SEE CONCEPTS *410,728*

repercussion [n] *consequence*
backlash, chain reaction, echo, effect, fallout, feedback, flak, follow-through*, follow-up, impact, imprint, influence, kickback*, mark, reaction, rebound,

recoil, re-echo, result, reverberation, side effect, spinoff, waves*; SEE CONCEPT *230*

repertory [n] *collection*
bit, cache, depot, list, range, rep, repertoire, repository, routine, schtick*, stock, stockroom, store, storehouse, stunt*, supply; SEE CONCEPTS *263, 432,712*

repetition [n] *duplication; doing again*
alliteration, broken record*, chant, chorus, copy, echo, encore, ingemination, iteracy, iterance, iteration, litany, paraphrase, periodicity, perseveration, practice, reappearance, recapitulation, recital, recurrence, redundancy, rehearsal, reiteration, relation, renewal, reoccurrence, repeat, repetitiousness, replication, report, reproduction, restatement, return, rhythm, rote, tautology; SEE CONCEPT *695*

repetitious [adj] *wordy, tedious*
alliterative, boring, dull, echoic, iterant, iterative, long-winded, plangent, pleonastic, prolix, recapitulatory, redundant, reiterative, repeating, repetitive, resonant, tautological, verbose, windy; SEE CONCEPT *553*

replace [v] *take the place of; put in place of*
alter, back up, change, compensate, displace, fill in, follow, front for, give back, mend, oust, outplace, patch, pinch hit for*, put back, reconstitute, recoup, recover, redeem, redress, reestablish, refund, regain, reimburse, reinstate, repay, restitute, restore, retrieve, ring, ring in, shift, sit in, stand in, stand in lieu of, step into shoes of*, sub, substitute, succeed, supersede, supplant, supply, swap places, take out, take over, take over from; SEE CONCEPTS *104,211,697*

replenish [v] *fill, stock*
furnish, make up, provide, provision, refill, refresh, reload, renew, replace, restock, restore, stock, top; SEE CONCEPTS *140,209*

replete [adj] *full, well-stocked*
abounding, abundant, alive, awash, brimful, brimming, charged, chock-full*, complete, crammed, crowded, filled, full up*, glutted, gorged, jammed, jam-packed, lavish, loaded, luxurious, overfed, overflowing, packed, plenteous, rife, sated, satiated, stuffed, swarming, teeming, thronged, well-provided; SEE CONCEPTS *483,740*

replica [n] *duplicate*
carbon, carbon copy, chip off old block*, clone, copy, ditto*, dupe*, facsimile, flimsy*, imitation, likeness, lookalike, mimeo, mimic, miniature, model, photocopy, reduplication, repeat, replication, repro, reproduction, stat, workalike, Xerox*; SEE CONCEPTS *260,670,688*

reply [n] *answer*
acknowledgment, antiphon, back talk*, comeback, counter, echo, feedback, knee-jerk reaction*, lip, reaction, reciprocation, rejoinder, respond, response, retaliation, retort, return, riposte, sass*, snappy comeback*, vibes*, wisecrack; SEE CONCEPT *278*

reply [*v*] *answer*
acknowledge, be in touch*, come back*, counter, echo, feedback, field the question*, get back to, react, reciprocate, rejoin, respond, retaliate, retort, return, riposte, shoot back*, squelch*, top*, write back; SEE CONCEPT *45*

report [*n1*] *account, story*
address, announcement, article, blow by blow*, brief, broadcast, cable, chronicle, communication, communique, declaration, description, detail, digest, dispatch, handout, history, hot wire*, information, message, narration, narrative, news, note, opinion, outline, paper, picture, piece, precis, proclamation, pronouncement, recital, record, relation, release, résumé, rundown, scoop*, statement, summary, tale, telegram, tidings, version, wire, word*, write-up; SEE CONCEPTS *274,282,283*

report [*n2*] *gossip, talk*
advice, blow by blow*, buzz*, canard, chat, chatter, chitchat, comment, conversation, cry*, dirt*, earful, grapevine*, hash*, hearsay, intelligence, murmur, news, prating, rumble, rumor, scandal, scuttlebutt*, small talk*, speech, tattle, the latest*, tidings, whispering, word*; SEE CONCEPTS *51,278*

report [*n3*] *loud noise*
bang, blast, boom, crack, crash, detonation, discharge, explosion, reverberation, sound; SEE CONCEPT *595*

report [*n4*] *reputation*
character, esteem, fame, name, regard, rep*, repute; SEE CONCEPT *388*

report [*v1*] *communicate information, knowledge*
account for, advise, air, announce, bring word, broadcast, cable, circulate, cover, debrief, declare, describe, detail, disclose, document, enunciate, give an account of, give the facts, impart, inform, inscribe, itemize, list, make known, make public, mention, narrate, note, notify, pass on, present, proclaim, promulgate, provide details, publish, radio, recite, record, recount, rehearse, relate, relay, retail, reveal, set forth, spread, state, summarize, telephone, tell, trumpet, wire, write up; SEE CONCEPT *60*

report [*v2*] *present oneself*
appear, arrive, be at hand, be present, clock in*, come, get to, reach, show, show up, turn up*; SEE CONCEPT *159*

reporter [*n*] *person who informs*
anchorman/woman, anchorperson, announcer, columnist, correspondent, cub*, editor, ink slinger*, interviewer, journalist, legman/woman*, newscaster, newshound*, newspaperman/woman, newswriter, pressman/woman, scribe, scrivener, star, stringer, writer; SEE CONCEPTS *348,356*

repose [*n*] *restfulness; calm*
ease, inaction, inactivity, leisure, peace, quiet, quietness, quietude, refreshment, relaxation, relaxing, renewal, requiescence, respite, rest, restoration, sleep, slumber, stillness, tranquillity; SEE CONCEPTS *410,681,720*

repose [*v*] *relax; recline*
deposit, lay down, lie, lie down, loaf, loll, lounge, place, rest, settle, settle down, slant, sleep, slumber, stretch, stretch out, take it easy, tilt; SEE CONCEPTS *154,210*

reprehensible [*adj*] *very bad; shameful*
amiss, blamable, blameworthy, censurable, condemnable, culpable, delinquent, demeritorious, discreditable, disgraceful, errant, erring, guilty, ignoble, objectionable, opprobrious, remiss, sinful, unholy, unworthy, wicked; SEE CONCEPT *571*

represent [*v1*] *present image of; symbolize*
act as, act as broker, act for, act in place of, appear as, assume the role of, be, be agent for, be attorney for, be proxy for, betoken, body, buy for, copy, correspond to, do business for, emblematize, embody, enact, epitomize, equal, equate, exemplify, exhibit, express, factor, hold office, imitate, impersonate, mean, perform, personify, play the part, produce, put on, reproduce, sell for, serve, serve as, show, speak for, stage, stand for, steward, substitute, symbolize, typify; SEE CONCEPTS *87, 317,682,716*

represent [*v2*] *depict, show*
body forth, delineate, denote, describe, design, designate, display, draft, enact, evoke, exhibit, express, hint, illustrate, interpret, limn, mirror, narrate, outline, picture, portray, realize, relate, render, reproduce, run down, run through, sketch, suggest, track; SEE CONCEPTS *138,261*

representative [*n1*] *person who acts in the stead of another*
agent, assemblyman/woman, assemblyperson, attorney, commissioner, congressman/woman, congressperson, councilman/woman, councilor, councilperson, counselor, delegate, deputy, lawyer, legislator, member, messenger, proxy, rep*, salesman/woman, senator, spokesman/woman; SEE CONCEPTS *348,354*

representative [*n2*] *typical example*
archetype, case, case history, embodiment, epitome, exemplar, illustration, instance, personification, sample, sampling, specimen, type; SEE CONCEPT *688*

representative [*adj*] *characteristic, typical*
adumbrative, archetypal, classic, classical, delineative, depictive, emblematic, evocative, exemplary, ideal, illustrative, model, nature of beast*, presentational, prototypal, prototypical, quintessential, rep*, symbolic, symbolical, what you see is what you get*; SEE CONCEPTS *487,573*

repress [*v*] *keep back, hold in*
black out*, bottle, chasten, check, collect, compose, control, cool*, cork*, crush, curb, gridlock*, hinder, hold back, inhibit, jam up, keep in, keep in check, keep under wraps*, kill*, lock, master, muffle, overcome, overpower, quash, quelch, quell, rein, restrain, shush, silence, simmer down*, smother,

squelch, stifle, subdue, subjugate, suppress, swallow, throw cold water on*, tie up*; SEE CONCEPTS *121,130*

reprieve [*n*] *relief of blame, responsibility*
abatement, abeyance, absolution, acquittal, alleviation, amnesty, anchor*, clearance, clemency, commute, deferment, freeing, let-up*, lifeboat*, lifesaver*, mitigation, palliation, pardon, postponement, release, remission, respite, spring*, stay, suspension, truce; SEE CONCEPTS *318,685*

reprieve [*v*] *relieve of blame, responsibility*
abate, absolve, allay, alleviate, amnesty, excuse, forgive, grant a stay, let go, let off, let off the hook*, let off this time*, let up on*, lifeboat*, mitigate, palliate, pardon, postpone, remit, respite; SEE CONCEPTS *50,88,317*

reprimand [*n*] *oral punishment*
admonishment, admonition, bawling out*, blame, calling down*, castigation, censure, chiding, comeuppance, dressing-down*, going over*, grooming, hard time*, lecture, piece of one's mind*, ragging*, rap*, rebuke, reprehension, reproof, scolding, slap on wrist*, talking-to, telling-off, tongue-lashing*, what for*; SEE CONCEPTS *123,278*

reprimand [*v*] *blame, scold*
admonish, call on the carpet*, castigate, censure, check, chew out*, chide, come down on*, criticize, denounce, dress down*, give piece of one's mind*, give the dickens*, lecture, lesson, light into*, lower the boom*, monish, rap, rebuke, reprehend, reproach, reprove, take to task*, tell off, tick off*, upbraid; SEE CONCEPTS *44,52*

reprisal [*n*] *revenge*
avengement, avenging, counterblow, counterstroke, eye for an eye*, paying back, requital, retaliation, retribution, vengeance; SEE CONCEPT *384*

reproach [*n*] *strong criticism; dishonor*
abuse, admonishment, admonition, blame, blemish, censure, chiding, condemnation, contempt, disapproval, discredit, disgrace, disrepute, ignominy, indignity, obloquy, odium, opprobrium, rap*, rebuke, reprehension, reprimand, reproof, scorn, shame, slight, slur, stain, stigma; SEE CONCEPTS *44,52,123,388*

reproach [*v*] *find fault with*
abuse, admonish, blame, call down, call to task*, cavil, censure, chide, condemn, criticize, defame, discredit, disparage, give comeuppance*, give the devil*, jawbone*, lay on, lesson, rake, ream, rebuke, reprehend, reprimand, reprove, scold, sit on*, take to task*, trim, upbraid; SEE CONCEPTS *44,52*

reproduce [*v1*] *make more copies of*
carbon*, clone, copy, do again, dupe*, duplicate, echo, emulate, engross, follow, imitate, knock off, manifold, match, mimeo*, mimeograph*, mirror, parallel, photocopy, photograph, Photostat, pirate, portray, print, reawaken, recount, recreate, redo, reduplicate, reenact, reflect, relive, remake, repeat,

replicate, represent, reprint, restamp, revive, stereotype, transcribe, type, Xerox*; SEE CONCEPTS *111,171*

reproduce [*v2*] *make something new; give birth*
bear, beget, breed, engender, father, fecundate, generate, hatch, impregnate, mother, multiply, procreate, produce young, progenerate, proliferate, propagate, repopulate, sire, spawn; SEE CONCEPTS *173,251,374*

reproduction [*n*] *something duplicated; duplication*
breeding, carbon*, carbon copy, chip off old block*, clone, copy, ditto*, dupe*, facsimile, fake, flimsy, generation, imitation, increase, look-alike, mimeo*, mimeograph, mirror image*, multiplication, offprint, photocopy, photograph, Photostat, pic*, picture, portrayal, print, procreation, proliferation, propagation, recreation, reduplication, reenactment, renewal, replica, replication, reprinting, repro*, revival, stat, transcription, twin, Xerox*, X ray*; SEE CONCEPTS *173,625,670,716*

repudiate [*v*] *reject; turn one's back on*
abandon, abjure, apostatize, banish, be against, break with, cast, cast off, cut off, decline, default, defect, demur, deny, desert, disacknowledge, disapprove, disavow, discard, disclaim, dishonor, disinherit, dismiss, disown, dump, flush, fly in the face of*, forsake, nix*, oust, rat*, recant, refuse, renounce, repeal, reprobate, rescind, retract, reverse, revoke, spurn, tergiversate, tergiverse, turn, turn down, wash one's hands of*; SEE CONCEPTS *13,21,30*

repugnant [*adj*] *bad, obnoxious; hostile*
abhorrent, abominable, adverse, against, alien, antagonistic, antipathetic, averse, conflicting, contradictory, counter, creepy, different, disagreeable, disgusting, distasteful, extraneous, extrinsic, foreign, foul, hateful, horrid, incompatible, inconsistent, inconsonant, inimical, in opposition, invidious, loathsome, nasty, nauseating, noisome, objectionable, odious, offensive, opposed, opposite, repellent, revolting, revulsive, sickening, unconformable, unfitted, unfriendly, vile; SEE CONCEPTS *401,564,571*

repulse [*n*] *snub; rejection*
brush-off*, check, cold shoulder*, defeat, disappointment, failure, nix*, nothing doing*, rebuff, refusal, reverse, slap in the face*, spurning, thumbs down*, turndown; SEE CONCEPTS *388,674*

repulse [*v1*] *push away*
beat off, brush off*, check, defeat, drive back, fend off, fight off, heave-ho*, hold off, keep off, kick in the teeth*, nix*, overthrow, push back, put down, rebuff, rebut, reject, repel, resist, set back, stave off, throw back, ward off; SEE CONCEPTS *96,208*

repulse [*v2*] *make sick*
disdain, disgust, disregard, give a pain*, rebuff, refuse, reject, reluct, repel, revolt, sicken, snub, spurn, turn down, turn off; SEE CONCEPTS *21,410*

repulsion [*n*] *hatred, disgust*
abhorrence, abomination, antipathy, aversion, denial, detestation, disrelish, distaste, hate, horror,

loathing, malice, rebuff, refusal, repugnance, repugnancy, resentment, revolt, revulsion, snub; SEE CONCEPT *29*

repulsive [*adj*] *very disgusting, offensive*
abhorrent, abominable, animal*, creepy*, disagreeable, distasteful, forbidding, foul, gross*, hateful, hideous, horrid, loathsome, nasty, nauseating, noisome, objectionable, obnoxious, odious, off-putting, pugnacious, repellent, revolting, sickening, sleazy*, ugly, undesirable, unpleasant, unsightly, vile; SEE CONCEPTS *529,571,579*

reputable [*adj*] *worthy of respect*
acclaimed, celebrated, conscientious, constant, creditable, dependable, distinguished, eminent, esteemed, estimable, excellent, fair, faithful, famed, famous, favored, good, high-principled, high-ranking, honest, honorable, honored, illustrious, in high favor, just, legitimate, notable, of good repute, popular, prominent, redoubted, reliable, renowned, respectable, righteous, salt of earth*, sincere, straightforward, trustworthy, truthful, upright, well-known, well-thought-of; SEE CONCEPTS *545,567,574*

reputation [*n*] *commonly held opinion of person's character*
acceptability, account, approval, authority, character, credit, dependability, distinction, éclat, eminence, esteem, estimation, fame, favor, honor, influence, mark*, name*, notoriety, opinion, position, prestige, privilege, prominence, rank, regard, reliability, renown, rep*, report, repute, respectability, standing, stature, trustworthiness, weight; SEE CONCEPTS *388,411,689*

reputed [*adj*] *believed*
accounted, alleged, assumed, conjectural, considered, deemed, estimated, gossiped, held, hypothetical, ostensible, putative, reckoned, regarded, reported, rumored, said, seeming, supposed, suppositional, supposititious, suppositive, suppository, thought; SEE CONCEPT *529*

request [*n*] *question or petition*
appeal, application, asking, begging, call, commercial, demand, desire, entreaty, inquiry, invitation, offer, prayer, recourse, requisition, solicitation, suit, supplication; SEE CONCEPT *662*

request [*v*] *ask for*
appeal, apply, beg, beseech, bespeak, call for, demand, desire, entreat, hit, hit up for*, hold out for*, hustle*, inquire, petition, pray, promote, put in for*, requisition, seek, solicit, sponge*, sue, supplicate, touch; SEE CONCEPT *53*

require [*v1*] *need, want*
crave, depend upon, desire, feel necessity for, have need, hurting for, lack, miss, stand in need, wish; SEE CONCEPTS *20,646*

require [*v2*] *ask, demand; necessitate*
assert oneself, beg, beseech, bid, call for, call upon, cause, challenge, claim, command, compel, constrain, crave, demand, direct, enjoin, entail, exact,

expect, insist upon, instruct, involve, look for, obligate, oblige, order, postulate, push for, request, requisition, solicit, take; SEE CONCEPTS *53,646*

required/requisite [*adj*] *necessary*
appropriate, called for, compulsatory, compulsory, condign, demanded, deserved, due, enforced, essential, imperative, imperious, indispensable, just, mandatory, needed, needful, obligatory, prerequisite, prescribed, recommended, right, rightful, set, suitable, unavoidable, vital; SEE CONCEPT *546*

requirement/requisite [*n*] *necessity, want*
claim, compulsion, concern, condition, demand, desideratum, element, engrossment, essential, exaction, exigency, extremity, fulfillment, fundamental, imperative, lack, must, need, obligation, obsession, pinch, precondition, preliminary, preoccupation, prepossession, prerequisite, prescription, provision, proviso, qualification, sine qua non, specification, stipulation, stress, terms, urgency, vital part; SEE CONCEPTS *646,709*

requisition [*n*] *demand; application for need*
appropriation, call, commandeering, demand, occupation, request, seizure, summons, takeover; SEE CONCEPT *662*

requisition [*v*] *ask for; apply for something needed*
buy, call for, challenge, claim, demand, dibs on*, exact, order, postulate, put in for, request, require, solicit; SEE CONCEPTS *48,53*

requite [*v*] *compensate, give in return*
indemnify, make, make amends, make good, pay, pay off, quit, reciprocate, recompense, redeem, redress, reimburse, remunerate, repay, respond, restitution, retaliate, return, revenge, reward, satisfy, settle; SEE CONCEPTS *126,131,341,384*

rescind [*v*] *declare null and void*
abolish, abrogate, annul, back out of, backpedal*, backwater*, call off, cancel, countermand, crawl out of*, dismantle, forget, invalidate, lift, nix*, overturn, pull the plug*, quash, recall, remove, renege, repeal, retract, reverse, revoke, scrub*, set aside, void, wangle out*, weasel out*, X-out*; SEE CONCEPTS *121,234,317*

rescue [*n*] *saving from danger*
deliverance, delivery, disembarrassment, disentanglement, emancipation, exploit, extrication, feat, heroics, heroism, liberation, performance, ransom, reclaiming, reclamation, recovering, recovery, redemption, release, relief, salvage, salvation, saving; SEE CONCEPT *134*

rescue [*v*] *save from danger*
bail one out*, conserve, deliver, disembarrass, disentangle, emancipate, extricate, free, get off the hook*, get out, get out of hock*, give a break, hold over, keep, liberate, manumit, preserve, protect, pull out of the fire*, ransom, recapture, recover, redeem, regain, release, retain, retrieve, safeguard, salvage, save life of, set free, spring*, unleash, unloose; SEE CONCEPT *134*

research [n] *examination, study*
analysis, delving, experimentation, exploration, fact-finding, fishing expedition*, groundwork, inquest, inquiry, inquisition, investigation, legwork*, probe, probing, quest, R and D*, scrutiny; SEE CONCEPTS *349,362*

research [v] *examine, study*
analyze, consult, do tests, experiment, explore, inquire, investigate, look into, look up, play around with, probe, read up on, scrutinize; SEE CONCEPTS *31,103*

resemblance [n] *correspondence, similarity*
affinity, alikeness, analogy, birds of a feather*, carbon*, carbon copy, clone, closeness, coincidence, comparability, comparison, conformity, counterpart, double, facsimile, image, kinship, likeness, like of, look-alike, parallel, parity, peas in pod*, ringer*, sameness, semblance, simile, similitude, spitting image*, two of a kind*, Xerox*; SEE CONCEPTS *664,670,716*

resemble [v] *look or be like*
appear like, approximate, bear resemblance to, be similar to, be the very picture of*, bring to mind, coincide, come close to, come near, correspond to, double, duplicate, echo, favor, feature, follow, have earmarks of*, have signs of, match, mirror, parallel, pass for, relate, remind one of, seem like, simulate, smack of*, sound like, take after; SEE CONCEPTS *664,670,716*

resent [v] *be angry about*
bear a grudge, begrudge, be in a huff*, be insulted, be offended by, be put off by*, be rubbed wrong way*, be vexed, dislike, feel bitter, feel sore*, frown at, get nose out of joint*, grudge, harbor a grudge*, have hard feelings*, object to, take amiss, take as an insult, take exception, take offense, take umbrage; SEE CONCEPTS *29,410*

resentment [n] *hate, anger*
acerbity, acrimony, animosity, animus, annoyance, antagonism, bad feeling, bitterness, choler, cynicism, displeasure, dudgeon, exacerbation, exasperation, fog, fury, grudge, huff, hurt, ill feeling, ill will, indignation, ire, irritation, malice, malignity, miff, offense, outrage, passion, perturbation, pique, rage, rancor, rise, spite, umbrage, vehemence, vexation, wrath; SEE CONCEPTS *29,410*

reservation [n1] *condition, stipulation*
catch, circumscription, demur, doubt, fine print*, grain of salt*, hesitancy, kicker*, provision, proviso, qualification, restriction, scruple, skepticism, string*, strings*, terms; SEE CONCEPTS *646,711*

reservation [n2] *holding or thing held for future use*
bespeaking, booking, exclusive possession, isolation, limitation, place, reserving, restriction, retaining, retainment, setting aside, spot, withholding; SEE CONCEPT *710*

reservation [n3] *habitat for large group*
enclave, homeland, preserve, reserve, sanctuary, territory, tract; SEE CONCEPTS *512,516*

reserve [n1] *supply*
ace in hole*, assets, backlog, cache, capital, drop, emergency fund*, fund, hoard, insurance, inventory, nest egg*, plant, provisions, rainy day fund*, reservoir, resources, savings, stash, stock, stockpile, store, wealth; SEE CONCEPTS *340,710,712*

reserve [n2] *coolness of manner*
aloofness, backwardness, calmness, caution, coldness, constraint, coyness, demureness, diffidence, formality, inhibition, modesty, quietness, reluctance, repression, reservation, restraint, reticence, secretiveness, self-restraint, shyness, silence, suppression, taciturnity, uncommunicativeness, unresponsiveness; SEE CONCEPT *633*

reserve [v1] *keep, hold back*
conserve, defer, delay, duck*, have, hoard, hold, husband, keep back, keep out, lay up, maintain, plant, possess, postpone, preserve, put away, put by, put off, retain, save, set aside, squirrel*, squirrel away*, stash, stockpile, store, store up, stow away, withhold; SEE CONCEPT *129*

reserve [v2] *hold for future use*
bespeak, book, contract, engage, prearrange, preengage, retain, schedule, secure; SEE CONCEPT *53*

reserved [adj1] *silent, unsociable; constrained*
aloof, backward, bashful, cautious, ceremonious, close, close-mouthed, cold*, collected, composed, conventional, cool, demure, diffident, distant, eremitic, formal, frigid, gentle, icy*, mild, misanthropic, modest, noncommittal, offish, peaceful, placid, prim, quiet, reclusive, restrained, reticent, retiring, secretive, sedate, self-contained, serene, shy, soft-spoken, solitary, standoffish, taciturn, unapproachable, uncommunicative, uncompanionable, undemonstrative, unresponsive, withdrawn; SEE CONCEPTS *401,404*

reserved [adj2] *held for future use*
appropriated, arrogated, booked, claimed, engaged, kept, laid away, limited, preempted, private, qualified, restricted, retained, roped off, set apart, set aside, spoken for, taken; SEE CONCEPTS *576,710*

reservoir [n] *accumulation, repository*
backlog, basin, cistern, container, fund, holder, lake, nest egg*, pond, pool, receptacle, reserve, source, spring, stock, stockpile, storage, store, supply, tank, tarn; SEE CONCEPTS *514,712*

reside [v] *live or exist in*
abide, be intrinsic to, be vested, bide, consist, continue, crash, dig, dwell, endure, hang one's hat*, inhabit, inhere, lie, locate, lodge, nest, occupy, park, people, perch, populate, remain, rest with, roost, settle, sojourn, squat, stay, take up residence, tenant; SEE CONCEPTS *226,407*

residence [n] *place for living*
abode, address, apartment, condo, co-op, domicile, dwelling, habitation, hall, headquarters, hole, home, homeplate*, house, household, inhabitancy, inhabitation, living quarters, lodging, manor, mansion, oc-

cupancy, occupation, palace, rack*, roof*, roost*, seat, settlement, villa; SEE CONCEPT *516*

resident [*n*] *person living in a particular place*
citizen, cliff dweller, denizen, dweller, habitant, householder, indweller, inhabitant, inmate, liver, local, lodger, native, occupant, resider, squatter, suburbanite, tenant, urbanite; SEE CONCEPT *413*

residual [*adj*] *leftover*
balance, continuing, enduring, extra, lingering, net, remaining, surplus, unconsumed, unused, vestigal; SEE CONCEPTS *560,771*

residue [*n*] *leftover part*
balance, debris, dregs, dross, excess, extra, garbage, heel, junk, leavings, leftovers, orts, parings, remainder, remains, remnant, residual, residuum, rest, scourings, scraps, scum, sewage, shavings, silt, slag, surplus, trash; SEE CONCEPTS *260,432*

resign [*v*] *give up responsibility*
abandon, abdicate, bail out, bow out, capitulate, cease work, cede, demit, divorce oneself from, drop, drop out, end service, fold, forgo, forsake, give notice, give up the ship*, hand in resignation, hand over, hang it up*, leave, quit, relinquish, renounce, retire, secede, separate oneself from, sign off, stand aside, stand down, step down, surrender, terminate, throw in the towel*, turn over, vacate, waive, walk out, wash hands of*, yield; SEE CONCEPTS *119,195,351*

resignation [*n1*] *relinquishment of responsibility*
abandonment, abdication, departure, giving up, leaving, notice, quitting, renunciation, retirement, surrender, tendering, termination, vacating, withdrawal; SEE CONCEPTS *119,195,351*

resignation [*n2*] *endurance, passivity*
acceptance, acquiescence, compliance, conformity, deference, docility, forbearing, fortitude, humbleness, humility, longanimity, lowliness, meekness, modesty, nonresistance, patience, patientness, resignedness, submission, submissiveness, sufferance; SEE CONCEPTS *410,657*

resigned [*adj*] *enduring, passive*
accommodated, acquiescent, adapted, adjusted, agreeable, amenable, biddable, calm, compliant, cordial, deferential, docile, genial, gentle, long-suffering, manageable, nonresisting, obedient, patient, peaceable, philosophical, pliant, quiescent, quiet, ready, reconciled, relinquishing, renouncing, satisfied, stoical, subdued, submissive, subservient, tame, tolerant, tractable, unassertive, unprotesting, unresisting, well-disposed, willing, yielding; SEE CONCEPTS *401,542*

resilient [*adj*] *bouncy, flexible*
airy, buoyant, effervescent, elastic, expansive, hardy, irrepressible, plastic, pliable, quick to recover, rebounding, rolling with punches*, rubbery, snapping back, springy, stretchy, strong, supple, tough, volatile; SEE CONCEPTS *488,489*

resist [*v*] *withstand, oppose*
abide, abstain from, antagonize, assail, assault, battle, bear, brook, buck, check, combat, confront, contend, continue, counteract, countervail, curb, defy, die hard, dispute, duel, endure, fight back, forbear, forgo, hinder, hold, hold off, hold out against, keep from, leave alone, maintain, persevere, persist, prevent, put up a fight, refrain, refuse, remain, remain firm, repel, stand up to, stay, stonewall, struggle against, suffer, thwart, traverse, turn down, weather, withstand; SEE CONCEPTS *23,35,96,106*

resistance [*n*] *fighting, opposition*
battle, blocking, check, combat, contention, counteraction, cover, defiance, detention, fight, friction, halting, hindrance, holding, impedance, impediment, impeding, intransigence, obstruction, parrying, protecting, protection, rebuff, refusal, retardation, safeguard, screen, shield, stand, striking back, struggle, support, warding off, watch, withstanding; SEE CONCEPTS *23,96,106,410*

resolute [*adj*] *determined, strong-willed*
adamant, bold, constant, courageous, dead set on*, decided, dogged, faithful, firm, fixed, immutable, inflexible, intent upon, intrepid, loyal, meaning business*, obstinate, persevering, persistent, persisting, purposeful, relentless, resolved, serious, set, settled, staunch, steadfast, steady, strong, stubborn, tenacious, true, unbending, unchanging, uncompromising, undaunted, unfaltering, unflagging, unflinching, unshakable, unshaken, unwavering, unyielding, valiant; SEE CONCEPTS *403,542*

resolution [*n1*] *determination, strong will*
aim, boldness, constancy, courage, dauntlessness, decidedness, decision, declaration, dedication, determination, doggedness, earnestness, energy, firmness, fixed purpose, fortitude, guts*, heart*, immovability, intent, intention, judgment, mettle, moxie*, obstinacy, perseverance, pluck, purpose, purposefulness, purposiveness, relentlessness, resoluteness, resolve, settlement, sincerity, spirit, spunk, staunchness, staying power, steadfastness, stubbornness, tenacity, verdict, willpower; SEE CONCEPTS *410,657*

resolution [*n2*] *answer, judgment*
analysis, assertion, breakdown, call, conclusion, decision, declaration, determination, dissection, elucidation, end, exposition, finding, interpretation, motion, nod, outcome, pay dirt*, presentation, proposal, proposition, quick fix*, recitation, recommendation, resolve, settlement, solution, solving, sorting out, ticket*, unravelling, upshot, verdict, working out; SEE CONCEPTS *18,230,274*

resolve [*n*] *decision, determination*
boldness, conclusion, courage, decidedness, design, earnestness, firmness, fixed purpose, intention, objective, project, purpose, purposefulness, purposiveness, resoluteness, resolution, steadfastness, undertaking, will, willpower; SEE CONCEPTS *410,659,689*

resolve [v] *make up one's mind; find solution*
agree, analyze, anatomize, answer, break, break down, choose, clear up, clinch*, conclude, deal with, decide, decipher, decree, design, determine, dissect, dissolve, elect, elucidate, fathom, figure, fix, intend, iron out*, lick*, make a point of, pan out*, pass upon, propose, purpose, puzzle out, remain firm, rule, settle, solve, take a stand, undertake, unfold, unravel, untangle, unzip*, will, work, work out, work through; SEE CONCEPTS *15,18,24*

resonant [adj] *vibrant in sound*
beating, booming, clangorous, consonant, deep, deep-toned, earsplitting, echoing, electrifying, enhanced, full, heightened, intensified, loud, mellow, noisy, orotund, plangent, powerful, profound, pulsating, pulsing, resounding, reverberant, reverberating, rich, ringing, roaring, round, sonorant, sonorous, stentorian, strident, thrilling, throbbing, thundering, thunderous; SEE CONCEPT *594*

resort [n1] *vacation place*
camp, fat farm*, hangout, harbor, haunt, haven, hideaway, hideout, holiday spot*, hotel, hot spring*, inn, lodge, mineral spring, motel, nest, park, purlieu, refuge, rendezvous, retreat, spot, spring, stomping ground*, tourist center, tourist trap*; SEE CONCEPTS *198,516*

resort [n2] *alternative, recourse*
chance, course, device, expediency, expedient, hope, makeshift, opportunity, possibility, reference, refuge, relief, resource, shift, stopgap, substitute, surrogate; SEE CONCEPTS *693,712*

resort [v] *have recourse to; make use of*
address, affect, apply, avail oneself of, benefit by, bring into play, devote, direct, employ, exercise, fall back on, frequent, go, go to, haunt, head for, look to, make use of, put to use, recur, recur to, refer to, repair, run, take up, try, turn, turn to, use, utilize, visit; SEE CONCEPT *225*

resource [n] *supply drawn upon, either material or nonmaterial*
ability, appliance, artifice, assets, capability, capital, cleverness, contraption, contrivance, course, creation, device, expedient, fortune, hoard, ingenuity, initiative, inventiveness, makeshift, means, measure, method, mode, nest egg*, property, quickwittedness, recourse, refuge, relief, reserve, resourcefulness, riches, shift, source, step, stock, stockpile, store, stratagem, substance, substitute, support, surrogate, system, talent, way, wealth, worth; SEE CONCEPTS *340,523,658,710,712*

resourceful [adj] *imaginative*
able, active, adventurous, aggressive, bright, capable, clever, creative, enterprising, ingenious, intelligent, inventive, original, quick-witted, sharp, talented, venturesome; SEE CONCEPT *402*

resources [n] *money, possessions, natural resources*
ace in hole*, assets, backing, bankroll, basics, belongings, budget, capital, collateral, effects, funds, holdings, income, kitty*, material goods, means, nest egg*, nut*, property, reserves, revenue, riches, saved for a rainy day*, savings, sock*, stuff, supplies, the goods*, ways and means*, wealth, wherewithal*; SEE CONCEPTS *340,446,523,710,712*

respect [n1] *admiration given by others*
account, adoration, appreciation, approbation, awe, consideration, courtesy, deference, dignity, esteem, estimation, favor, fear, homage, honor, obeisance, ovation, recognition, regard, repute, reverence, testimonial, tribute, veneration, worship; SEE CONCEPT *689*

respect [n2] *way, sense*
aspect, bearing, character, connection, detail, facet, feature, matter, particular, point, reference, regard, relation; SEE CONCEPT *682*

respect [v] *admire; obey*
abide by, adhere to, adore, appreciate, attend, awe, be kind to, comply with, defer to, esteem, follow, have good opinion of, have high opinion, heed, honor, look up to, note, notice, observe of, pay attention, recognize, regard, revere, reverence, set store by, show consideration, show courtesy, spare, take into account, think highly of, uphold, value, venerate; SEE CONCEPTS *10,32*

respectable [adj1] *good, honest*
admirable, appropriate, august, becoming, befitting, comely, conforming, correct, creditable, decent, decorous, dignified, done, estimable, fair, honorable, mediocre, moderate, modest, nice, ordinary, passable, presentable, proper, redoubtable, redoubted, reputable, reputed, respected, satisfactory, seemly, sublime, suitable, tolerable, upright, venerable, virtuous, well-thought-of, worthy; SEE CONCEPT *572*

respectable [adj2] *substantial, ample*
appreciable, considerable, decent, fair, fairly good, good, goodly, presentable, reasonable, sensible, sizable, tidy, tolerable; SEE CONCEPT *771*

respectful [adj] *courteous, mannerly*
admiring, appreciative, civil, considerate, courtly, deferential, duteous, dutiful, gracious, humble, obedient, obeisant, polite, recognizing, regardful, regarding, reverent, reverential, self-effacing, solicitous, submissive, upholding, venerating, well-mannered; SEE CONCEPT *401*

respective [adj] *particular, specific*
corresponding, each, individual, own, personal, relevant, separate, several, singular, various; SEE CONCEPT *556*

respects [n] *good wishes*
best wishes, compliments, courtesies, deference, devoirs, greetings, kind wishes, regards, salaam, salutations; SEE CONCEPT *278*

respite [n] *pause, suspension in activity*
acquittal, adjournment, break, breath*, breather, breathing space*, cessation, coffee break*, deadlock, deferment, delay, deliverance, discharge, downtime*, ease, exculpation, five*, forgiveness, halt, hi-

atus, immunity, intermission, interregnum, interruption, interval, layoff, leisure, let-up*, lull, moratorium, pardon, postponement, protraction, recess, relaxation, release, relief, reprieve, rest, stay, stop, ten*, time, time out*, truce; SEE CONCEPTS *121,681,807*

resplendent [*adj*] *bright, radiant*
beaming, blazing, brilliant, dazzling, effulgent, flaming, gleaming, glittering, glorious, glossy, glowing, gorgeous, irradiant, luminous, lustrous, magnificent, proud, refulgent, shining, shiny, splendid, splendiferous, splendorous, sublime, superb; SEE CONCEPTS *579,589,617*

respond [*v*] *act in answer to something*
acknowledge, act in response, answer, answer back, behave, be in touch with, come back, come back at, come in, counter, feedback, feel for, field the question*, get back to, get in touch, react, reciprocate, rejoin, reply, retort, return, talk back; SEE CONCEPTS *45,384*

response [*n*] *answer, reaction*
acknowledgment, antiphon, back talk*, comeback, counter, double-take*, echo, feedback, hit, kickback*, knee-jerk reaction*, lip*, rejoinder, reply, respond, retort, return, reverberation, riposte, sass*, snappy comeback*, vibes*, wisecrack; SEE CONCEPT *278*

responsibility [*n1*] *accountability, blame*
albatross*, amenability, answerability, authority, boundness, burden, care, charge, contract, contraint, culpability, duty, encumbrance, engagement, fault, guilt, holding the bag*, importance, incubus, incumbency, liability, obligation, obligatoriness, onus, pledge, power, rap, restraint, subjection, trust; SEE CONCEPT *645*

responsibility [*n2*] *maturity, trustworthiness*
ability, capableness, capacity, competency, conscientiousness, dependability, dependableness, efficiency, faithfulness, firmness, honesty, levelheadedness, loyalty, rationality, reliability, sensibleness, soberness, stability, steadfastness, trustiness, uprightness; SEE CONCEPTS *411,633*

responsible [*adj1*] *accountable, in charge*
answerable, at fault, at the helm, authoritative, bonded, bound, bound to, carrying the load, censurable, chargeable, compelled, constrained, contracted, culpable, decision-making, devolving on, duty-bound, engaged, executive, exposed, fettered, guilty, hampered, held, high, important, in authority, in control, incumbent, liable, minding the store*, obligated, obliged, on the hook*, open, pledged, subject, susceptive, sworn to, tied, to blame, under contract, under obligation; SEE CONCEPT *545*

responsible [*adj2*] *trustworthy, mature*
able, adult, capable, competent, conscientious, dependable, dutiful, effective, efficient, faithful, firm, levelheaded, loyal, qualified, rational, reliable, self-reliant, sensible, sober, sound, stable, steadfast,

steady, tried, trusty, upright; SEE CONCEPTS *401,404*

responsive [*adj*] *quick to react*
acknowledging, active, alive, answering, awake, aware, compassionate, conscious, forthcoming, impressionable, influenceable, kindhearted, open, passionate, perceptive, persuadable, reactive, receptive, replying, respondent, sensible, sensile, sensitive, sentient, sharp, softhearted, susceptible, susceptive, sympathetic, tender, warm, warmhearted; SEE CONCEPTS *401,542*

rest [*n1*] *inactivity*
break, breather, breathing space*, calm, calmness, cessation, coffee break*, comfort, composure, cut-off, downtime*, doze, dreaminess, ease, forty winks*, halt, holiday, hush, idleness, interlude, intermission, interval, leisure, let-up*, lull, motionlessness, nap, pause, peace, quiescence, quiet, quietude, recess, recreation, refreshment, relaxation, relief, repose, respite, siesta, silence, sleep, slumber, somnolence, standstill, stay, stillness, stop, time off, tranquillity, vacation; SEE CONCEPTS *315,681,807*

rest [*n2*] *remainder of something*
balance, bottom of barrel*, dregs, dross, excess, heel, leavings, leftovers, odds and ends*, orts, others, overplus, remains, remnant, residual, residue, residum, rump, superfluity, surplus; SEE CONCEPTS *260,835*

rest [*n3*] *base, foundation*
basis, bed, bottom, footing, ground, groundwork, holder, pedestal, pediment, pillar, prop, seat, seating, shelf, stand, stay, support, trestle; SEE CONCEPTS *442,825*

rest [*v1*] *be calm; sleep*
be at ease, be comfortable, breathe, compose oneself, doze, dream, drowse, ease off, ease up, idle, laze, lean, let down, let up, lie by, lie down, lie still, loaf, loll, lounge, nap, nod, put feet up*, recline, refresh oneself, relax, repose, sit down, slack, slacken, slack off, sleep, slumber, snooze, spell, stretch out, take a break, take a nap, take five*, take it easy*, take life easy*, take ten*, take time out, unbend, unlax, unwind, wind down; SEE CONCEPTS *210,315,681*

rest [*v2*] *lie, recline*
be quiet, be supported, lay, lean, lie still, loll, lounge, pause, prop, repose, roost, settle, sit, stand, stand still, stretch out; SEE CONCEPTS *154,681*

rest [*v3*] *depend, hinge*
base, be based, be contingent, be dependent, be founded, be seated on, be supported, be upheld, bottom, count, establish, found, ground, hang, lie, predicate, rely, reside, stay, turn; SEE CONCEPT *711*

restaurant [*n*] *business establishment serving food and drink*
bar, café, cafeteria, canteen, chophouse*, coffee shop, diner, dining room, dive*, doughnut shop, drive-in, eatery, eating house, eating place, fast-food place, greasy spoon*, grill, hamburger stand, hash-

ery*, hideaway*, hotdog stand, inn, joint*, luncheonette, lunchroom, night club, outlet*, pizzeria, saloon, soda fountain, watering hole*; SEE CONCEPTS *439,448,449*

restitution [*n*] *compensation, repayment*
amends, dues, indemnification, indemnity, payment, quittance, rebate, recompense, redress, refund, reimbursement, remuneration, reparation, reprisal, requital, restoration, return, satisfaction, squaring things*; SEE CONCEPT *344*

restive [*adj*] *impatient, nervous*
agitated, balky, contrary, edgy, fidgety, fractious, fretful, froward, ill at ease, jittery, jumpy, nervy, obstinate, on edge, ornery, perverse, recalcitrant, refractory, restless, stubborn, tense, uneasy, unruly, unyielding, uptight; SEE CONCEPTS *401,542*

restless [*adj*] *not content; moving about*
active, agitated, antsy*, anxious, bundle of nerves*, bustling, changeable, disturbed, edgy, fidgeting, fidgety, fitful, footloose*, fretful, hurried, ill at ease*, inconstant, intermittent, irresolute, itchy*, jumpy, nervous, nomadic, on edge, perturbed, restive, roving, sleepless, spasmodic, strung out*, tossing and turning*, transient, troubled, turbulent, uneasy, unpeaceful, unquiet, unrestful, unruly, unsettled, unstable, unsteady, wandering, worried; SEE CONCEPTS *403,542,584*

restlessness [*n*] *constant motion; discontent*
activity, agitation, ailment, ants*, antsy*, anxiety, bustle, disquiet, disquietude, disturbance, edginess, excitability, ferment, fitfulness, fretfulness, hurry, inconstancy, inquietude, insomnia, instability, jitters, jumpiness, movement, nervousness, restiveness, transience, turbulence, turmoil, uneasiness, unrest, unsettledness, worriedness; SEE CONCEPTS *410,657,748*

restore [*v1*] *fix, make new*
bring back, build up, cure, heal, improve, make healthy, make restitution, mend, modernize, reanimate, rebuild, recall, recondition, reconstitute, reconstruct, recover, redeem, reenforce, reerect, reestablish, refresh, refurbish, rehabilitate, reimpose, reinstate, reintroduce, rejuvenate, renew, renovate, repair, replace, rescue, retouch, revitalize, revive, revivify, set to rights, strengthen, touch up, update, win back; SEE CONCEPTS *126,212,244*

restore [*v2*] *give back*
hand back, put back, replace, return, send back; SEE CONCEPTS *131,232*

restrain [*v*] *keep under control; hold back*
arrest, bind, bottle up*, box up*, bridle, chain, check, choke back, circumscribe, confine, constrain, contain, control, cool*, cork*, crack down*, curb, curtail, debar, delimit, detain, deter, direct, fetter, gag, govern, guide, hamper, handicap, harness, hem in, hinder, hogtie*, hold, impound, imprison, inhibit, jail, keep, keep down, keep in line*, kill*, limit, lock up, manacle, muzzle, pinion, prescribe,

prevent, pull back, repress, restrict, sit on, stay, subdue, suppress, tie down, tie up; SEE CONCEPTS *121,130,191*

restrained [*adj*] *calm, quiet*
bottled up*, calm and collected, chilled, conservative, controlled, cool, corked up*, discreet, in charge, in check*, inobtrusive, laid-back, mild, moderate, muted, on leash*, plain, reasonable, reticent, retiring, self-controlled, shrinking, soft, steady, subdued, tasteful, temperate, unaffable, undemonstrative, under control, under wraps*, unexcessive, unexpansive, unextreme, unobtrusive, uptight, withdrawn; SEE CONCEPTS *401,542*

restraint [*n1*] *self-control*
abstemiousness, abstinence, caution, coercion, command, compulsion, confines, constraint, control, coolness, curtailment, economy, forbearance, grip, hindrance, hold, inhibition, limitation, moderation, prevention, repression, reserve, restriction, secretiveness, self-denial, self-discipline, self-government, self-possession, self-restraint, silence, suppression, unnaturalness, withholding; SEE CONCEPT *633*

restraint [*n2*] *limitation; something that holds*
abridgment, arrest, ban, bar, barrier, bondage, bridle, captivity, chains, check, command, confinement, constraint, cramp, curb, decrease, deprivation, detention, determent, deterrence, embargo, fetters, hindrance, impediment, imprisonment, instruction, interdict, limit, manacles, obstacle, obstruction, order, pinions, prohibition, reduction, rein, repression, restriction, rope, stop, stoppage, straitjacket, string*, taboo, violence, weight; SEE CONCEPTS *5,666,674*

restrict [*v*] *confine, limit situation or ability to participate*
bind, bottle up*, bound, chain, check, circumscribe, come down on, constrict, contain, contract, cool down, cramp, curb, decrease, define, delimit, delimitate, demarcate, demark, diminish, encircle, hamper, handicap, hang up, hem in, hold back, hold down, impede, inclose, inhibit, keep within bounds, keep within limits, moderate, modify, narrow, pin down, prelimit, put away, put on ice*, qualify, reduce, regulate, restrain, send up, shorten, shrink, shut in, surround, temper, tether, tie; SEE CONCEPT *130*

restriction [*n*] *limit*
ball and chain*, bounds, brake, catch, check, circumscription, condition, confinement, constraint, containment, contraction, control, cramp, curb, custody, demarcation, excess baggage*, fine print*, glitch*, grain of salt*, handicap, hang-up*, inhibition, limitation, limits, lock*, no-no*, qualification, regulation, reservation, restraint, rule, small difficulty, stint, stipulation, stricture, string*, stumbling block*; SEE CONCEPTS *666,674*

result [*n*] *effect brought about by something*
aftereffect, aftermath, arrangement, backwash*, byproduct, close, completion, conclusion, conse-

quence, consummation, corollary, creature, crop, decision, denouement, determination, development, emanation, end, ensual, event, eventuality, execution, finish, fruit*, fruition, harvest, issue, offshoot*, outcome, outcropping, outgrowth, payoff, proceeds, product, production, reaction, repercussion, returns, sequel, sequence, settlement, termination, upshot; SEE CONCEPT *230*

result [v] *happen, develop*
accrue, appear, arise, attend, become of, be due to, come about, come forth, come from, come of, come out, conclude, culminate, derive, effect, emanate, emerge, end, ensue, eventualize, eventuate, finish, flow, follow, fruit, germinate, grow, happen, issue, occur, originate, pan out, proceed, produce, rise, spring, stem, terminate, turn out, wind up, work out; SEE CONCEPTS *4,119,242*

résumé [n] *outline of experience*
abstract, bio*, biography, curriculum vitae, CV*, digest, epitome, precis, recapitulation, review, rundown, sum, summary, summation, summing-up, synopsis, vita, work history; SEE CONCEPTS *271,283*

resume [v] *begin again*
assume again, carry on, come back, continue, go on, go on with, keep on, keep up, occupy again, pick up, proceed, reassume, recapitulate, recommence, recoup, regain, reinstitute, reoccupy, reopen, repossess, restart, retake, return to, take back, take up; SEE CONCEPTS *221,239*

retain [v1] *hold on to physically or mentally*
absorb, bear in mind, cling to, clutch, contain, detain, enjoy, grasp, hand onto, have, hold, hold fast, husband, keep, keep in mind, keep possession, maintain, memorize, mind, own, possess, preserve, put away, recall, recognize, recollect, remember, reminisce, reserve, restrain, retrospect, save, withhold; SEE CONCEPTS *40,190,710*

retain [v2] *hire*
commission, contract, employ, engage, maintain, pay, reserve; SEE CONCEPT *351*

retaliate [v] *get even with someone*
even the score*, exact retribution, get, get back at, give and take*, make reprisal, pay, pay back, reciprocate, recompense, repay, requite, retrospect, return, return the compliment, revenge, revive, settle, square accounts*, strike back, take eye for an eye*, take revenge, turn the tables on*, turn upon, wreak vengeance; SEE CONCEPTS *126,384*

retard [v] *hinder, obstruct*
arrest, back off, baffle, balk, bog, bog down, brake, bring to screeching halt*, check, choke, choke off, clog, close off, crimp, dawdle, decelerate, decrease, defer, delay, detain, down, encumber, falter, fetter, flag, hamper, handicap, hang up, hesitate, hold back, hold up, impede, lessen, let up, loaf, loiter, mire, poke, postpone, reduce, retardate, set back, shut down, shut off, slacken, slow down, slow up, stall, take down; SEE CONCEPTS *121,130,190,240*

retarded [adj] *intellectually limited*
backward, defective, dim, dim-witted, dull, exceptional, feeble-minded, half-witted, held back, imbecile, mentally defective, moronic, not all there*, opaque, simple, simple-minded, slow, slow-witted, stupid, subnormal, touched, underachieving, weak; SEE CONCEPT *402*

reticent [adj] *secretive, quiet*
bashful, clammed up*, close, close-mouthed, dried up*, dummied up*, hesitant, mum, reserved, restrained, shy, silent, taciturn, tight-lipped, uncommunicative, unforthcoming, unspeaking, uptight*; SEE CONCEPTS *267,401*

retire [v] *leave a place or responsibility*
absent oneself, decamp, deny oneself, depart, draw back, ebb, exit, fall back, get away, get off, give ground, give up work, give way, go, go away, go to bed, go to one's room*, go to sleep, hand over, hit the sack*, leave service, make vacant, part, pull back, pull out, recede, regress, relinquish, remove, repeal, rescind, resign, retreat, revoke, run along, rusticate, secede, seclude oneself, separate, sever connections, stop working, surrender, take off, turn in, withdraw, yield; SEE CONCEPTS *195,234,351*

retiring [adj] *shy, undemonstrative*
backward, bashful, coy, demure, diffident, humble, meek, modest, nongregarious, not forward, quiet, rabbity, recessive, reclusive, reserved, restrained, reticent, self-effacing, shrinking, timid, timorous, unaffable, unassertive, unassuming, unexpansive, unsociable, withdrawing, withdrawn; SEE CONCEPT *401*

retort [n] *snappy answer*
antiphon, back answer, back talk, comeback, cooler, counter, crack*, gag*, jape*, jest, joke, lip*, parting shot*, quip, rejoinder, repartee, reply, reprisal, respond, response, retaliation, return, revenge, riposte, sally*, snappy comeback*, topper*, wisecrack, witticism; SEE CONCEPT *278*

retort [v] *answer*
answer back, back talk*, come back at*, counter, crack*, rebut, rejoin, repay, reply, requite, respond, retaliate, return, riposte, sass*, shoot back*, snap back*, squelch*, talk back, top*; SEE CONCEPT *45*

retract [v] *take back; renege on*
abjure, back, back down, back off, back out of, call off, cancel, change one's mind, countermand, deny, disavow, disclaim, disown, draw in, eat one's words*, eliminate, exclude, fall back, forget in, forswear, go back on, have change of heart*, nig*, palinode, pull back, pull in, recall, recant, recede, reel in*, renege, renounce, repeal, repudiate, rescind, retreat, retrocede, retrograde, reverse, revoke, rule out, sheathe, suspend, take back, take in, unsay, welsh*, withdraw; SEE CONCEPTS *25,49,119,697*

retreat [n1] *departure*
ebb, evacuation, flight, retirement, withdrawal; SEE CONCEPTS *30,195*

retreat [*n2*] *place one goes for peace*
adytum, ark, asylum, cell, cloister, convent, cover, covert, defense, den, habitat, harbor, haunt, haven, hermitage, hideaway, hiding place, ivory tower*, port, privacy, refuge, resort, retirement, safe house, safe place, sanctuary, seclusion, security, shelter, solitude; SEE CONCEPT *516*

retreat [*v*] *pull back, go away*
abandon, avoid, back, back away, back down, back off, back out, backtrack, beat it, cave in, decamp, depart, disengage, draw back, ebb, elude, escape, evacuate, evade, fall back, fold, give ground, go, go along with, go back, hand over, hide, keep aloof, keep apart, lay down, leave, move back, opt out, pull out, quail, quit, recede, recoil, reel, regress, relinquish, resign, retire, retrocede, retrograde, reverse, run, seclude oneself, sequester, shrink, start back, turn tail*, vacate, withdraw; SEE CONCEPTS *30,195*

retribution [*n*] *payback for another's action*
avengement, avenging, comeuppance, compensation, counterblow, eye for an eye*, just deserts*, justice, punishment, reckoning, recompense, redress, repayment, reprisal, requital, retaliation, revanche, revenge, reward, satisfaction, vengeance, what for*; SEE CONCEPTS *123,126,384*

retrieve [*v*] *get back*
bring back, fetch, get back, reacquire, recall, recapture, reclaim, recoup, recover, recruit, redeem, regain, repair, repossess, rescue, restore, salvage, save, win back; SEE CONCEPTS *120,124,131*

retrospect [*n*] *afterthought*
hindsight, recollection, reconsideration, reexamination, remembering, remembrance, reminiscence, retrospection, review, revision, survey; SEE CONCEPTS *17,40,410*

return [*n1*] *coming again*
acknowledgment, answer, appearance, arrival, coming, entrance, entry, homecoming, occurrence, reaction, reappearance, rebound, recoil, recoiling, recompense, recompensing, recovery, recrudescence, recurrence, reestablishment, reinstatement, rejoinder, reoccurrence, replacement, repossession, restitution, restoration, restoring, retreat, reversion, revisitation; SEE CONCEPTS *4,695*

return [*n2*] *earnings, benefit*
accrual, accruement, advantage, avail, compensation, gain, gate, income, interest, lucre, proceeds, profit, reciprocation, recompense, reimbursement, reparation, repayment, requital, results, retaliation, revenue, reward, take, takings, yield; SEE CONCEPTS *340,710*

return [*n3*] *answer*
antiphon, comeback, rejoinder, reply, respond, response, retort, riposte; SEE CONCEPT *278*

return [*n4*] *summary*
account, form, list, record, report, statement, tabulation; SEE CONCEPTS *283,331*

return [*v1*] *go back, turn back*
back up, bounce back, circle back, come again, come back, double back, go again, hark back to, move back, react, reappear, rebound, recoil, reconsider, recrudesce, recur, reel back, reenter, reexamine, reoccur, repair, repeat, retire, retrace steps, retreat, revert, revisit, revolve, rotate, turn, turn back; SEE CONCEPTS *159,242*

return [*v2*] *give back, send back*
bestow, carry back, convey, give, hand back, make restitution, pay back, put back, react, rebate, reciprocate, recompense, reestablish, refund, reimburse, reinsert, reinstate, remit, render, repay, replace, requite, reseat, restitute, restore, retaliate, roll back, send, take back, thrust back, toss back, transmit; SEE CONCEPTS *108,131,217*

return [*v3*] *earn*
bring in, cash in on*, clean up*, clear*, make, make a killing*, net, pay, pay dividend, pay off, repay, score, show profit, yield; SEE CONCEPT *330*

return [*v4*] *answer*
announce, arrive at, bring in, come back, come in, come to, communicate, declare, deliver, pass, rejoin, render, reply, report, respond, retort, state, submit; SEE CONCEPT *45*

reveal [*v1*] *disclose, tell*
acknowledge, admit, affirm, announce, avow, betray, break the news*, bring out into open*, bring to light*, broadcast, come out with, communicate, concede, confess, declare, divulge, explain, expose, get out of system*, give away, give out, give the lowdown*, impart, inform, leak, let cat out of the bag*, let fall, let on, let out, let slip*, make known, make plain, make public, notify, proclaim, publish, put cards on table*, report, talk, tell, unfold, utter; SEE CONCEPT *60*

reveal [*v2*] *show, uncover*
bare, disclose, display, exhibit, expose, flash, lay bare, manifest, open, unclothe, unearth, unmask, unveil; SEE CONCEPT *138*

revel [*n*] *celebration, merrymaking*
bacchanal, carousal, carouse, debauch, festivity, frolic, gaiety, gala, high jinks*, jollification, jollity, merriment, party, reveling, revelment, saturnalia, skylarking*, spree, wassail, whoopee*; SEE CONCEPTS *292,377*

revel [*v*] *take pleasure; celebrate*
bask, blow off steam*, carouse, carry on, crow, cut loose*, delight, enjoy, fool around*, frolic, gloat, go on a spree*, indulge, kick up heels*, kid around*, lap up*, lark, let go*, let loose*, live it up*, luxuriate, make merry, paint the town*, rejoice, relish, riot, roister, roll, rollick, run around, savor, step out, thrive, wallow, whoop it up*; SEE CONCEPTS *292,377,384*

revelation [*n*] *disclosure, telling*
adumbration, announcement, apocalypse, betrayal, blow by blow*, break, broadcasting, clue, commu-

nication, cue, discovery, display, divination, divulgement, earful, exhibition, expose, exposition, exposure, eye-opener*, flash, foreshadowing, inspiration, leak, lightning bolt*, manifestation, news, oracle, proclamation, prophecy, publication, scoop*, showing, sign, the latest*, tip, uncovering, unearthing, unveiling, vision; SEE CONCEPTS *60,274*

revelry [*n*] *merrymaking*
carousal, carouse, celebration, debauch, debauchery, entertainment, festival, festivity, fun, gaiety, high jinks*, jollification, jollity, party, reveling, revelment, saturnalia, spree, whoop-de-do*, whoopla*; SEE CONCEPTS *377,384*

revenge [*n*] *retaliation for wrong, grievance*
animus, attack, avenging, avengment, counterblow, counterinsurgency, counterplay, eye for an eye*, fight, getting even*, ill will, implacability, malevolence, measure for measure, rancor, repayment, reprisal, requital, retribution, return, ruthlessness, satisfaction, sortie, spitefulness, tit for tat*, vengeance, vengefulness, vindictiveness; SEE CONCEPTS *86,122,384*

revenge [*v*] *retaliate for wrong, grievance*
avenge, be out for blood*, defend, even the score*, fight back, fix, fix one's wagon*, get, get back at, get even, give comeuppance, give just deserts*, hit back, justify, kick back, make reprisal, match, pay back, pay back in spades*, pay off, punish, reciprocate, redress, repay, requite, retort, return, return the compliment*, score, settle up, settle with, square, stick it to, take eye for an eye*, turn the tables on*, venge, vindicate; SEE CONCEPTS *86,122,384*

revenue [*n*] *income, profit*
acquirement, annuity, bottom line*, cash flow, credit, dividend, earnings, emolument, fruits*, fund, gain, gate*, get*, gravy*, handle*, interest, means, net, pay, payoff, perquisite, proceeds, receipt, resources, return, reward, salary, split*, stock, strength, take*, take in*, taking*, wages, wealth, yield; SEE CONCEPTS *329,332,344*

reverberate [*v*] *vibrate in sound*
echo, react, rebound, recoil, redound, re-echo, resound, ring; SEE CONCEPT *65*

revere/reverence [*v*] *have a high opinion of*
admire, adore, apotheosize, appreciate, be in awe of, cherish, defer to, deify, enjoy, esteem, exalt, hold in awe*, honor, look up to*, love, magnify, pay homage, prize, put on pedestal*, regard, respect, think highly of, treasure, value, venerate, worship; SEE CONCEPTS *10,32*

reverence [*n*] *high opinion of something*
admiration, adoration, apotheosis, approbation, approval, awe, bow, deference, deification, devotion, devoutness, esteem, fealty, fear, genuflection, high esteem, homage, honor, love, loyalty, obeisance, obsequiousness, piety, praise, prostration, religiousness, respect, veneration, worship; SEE CONCEPTS *10,32*

reverie [*n*] *daydream*
absent-mindedness, absorption, abstraction, castle-building*, castles in the air*, contemplation, daydreaming, detachment, dreaminess, dreaming, fantasy, fool's paradise*, head trip*, inattention, meditation, mind trip*, muse, musing, pensiveness, phantasy, pipe dream*, preoccupation, study, thought, trance, trip*, woolgathering*; SEE CONCEPTS *529,532*

reverse [*n1*] *opposite*
about-face*, antipode, antipole, antithesis, back, bottom, change of mind, contra, contradiction, contradictory, contrary, converse, counter, counterpole, flip-flop*, flip side*, inverse, other side, overturning, rear, regression, retrogression, retroversion, reversal, reversement, reversion, switch, turn, turnabout, turn around, turning, underside, verso, volte-face, wrong side; SEE CONCEPTS *665,697,738*

reverse [*n2*] *bad luck; failure*
adversity, affliction, bath, blow, catastrophe, check, conquering, defeat, disappointment, hardship, misadventure, misfortune, mishap, repulse, reversal, setback, trial, turnabout, vanquishment, vicissitude; SEE CONCEPTS *674,679*

reverse [*v1*] *turn upside down or backwards*
about-face*, back, backpedal, backtrack, back up, capsize, double back*, evaginate, evert, exchange, flip-flop*, go back, go backwards, interchange, inverse, invert, move backwards, overturn, rearrange, retreat, revert, shift, switch, transfer, transplace, transpose, turn around, turn back, turn over, upend, upset; SEE CONCEPTS *158,213,697*

reverse [*v2*] *cancel, change*
alter, annul, backpedal, backtrack, convert, countermand, declare null and void*, dismantle, double back*, flip-flop*, invalidate, lift, modify, negate, nullify, overrule, overset, overthrow, overturn, quash, recall, renege, repeal, rescind, retract, revoke, set aside, turn around, turn the tables*, undo, upset; SEE CONCEPTS *13,234,697*

revert [*v*] *return to an earlier, less-developed condition*
about-face*, backslide, change, come back, decline, degenerate, deteriorate, fall off the wagon*, flip-flop*, go back, hark back, inverse, invert, lapse, react, recrudesce, recur, regress, relapse, resume, retrograde, retrogress, return, take up where left off*, throw back, transpose, turn, turn back; SEE CONCEPTS *13,385,698*

review [*n1*] *examination, study*
analysis, another look*, audit, check, checkup, drill, file, fresh look*, inspection, march past*, once-over*, parade, procession, reassessment, recapitulation, reconsideration, reflection, report, rethink, retrospect, revision, scan, scrutiny, second look, second thought, survey, view; SEE CONCEPTS *24,103*

review [*n2*] *critique; summary*
abstract, analysis, appraisal, article, assessment, blurb, book review, canvass, column, comment,

commentary, criticism, discourse, discussion, dissertation, essay, evaluation, exposition, inspection, investigation, journal, judgment, magazine, mention, monograph, notice, organ, outline, pan*, periodical, recapitulation, redraft, reviewal, revision, study, synopsis, theme, thesis, treatise, write-up; SEE CONCEPTS *280,283*

review [*v1*] *go over again*
analyze, brush up*, call to mind, check out, check thoroughly, debrief, go over, hash over*, look at again, look back on, polish up, reassess, recall, recap*, recapitulate, recollect, reconsider, reevaluate, reexamine, reflect on, rehash*, remember, rethink, revise, revisit, run over, run through, run up flagpole*, summon up, take another look, think over; SEE CONCEPT *103*

review [*v2*] *criticize, scrutinize*
assess, bad-mouth*, correct, discuss, evaluate, examine, give one's opinion, inspect, judge, knock*, pan*, put down*, rave, read through, reedit, revise, rip, skin alive*, slam*, study, swipe at*, take down*, trash*, weigh, write a critique, zap*; SEE CONCEPTS *49,52*

revise [*v*] *correct, edit*
alter, amend, blue pencil*, change, clean up, compare, cut, debug, develop, emend, go over, improve, launder, look over, modify, overhaul, perfect, polish, recalibrate, recast, reconsider, redo, redraft, redraw, reexamine, rehash, reorganize, restyle, revamp, review, rework, rewrite, run through, scan, scrub, scrutinize, study, tighten, update, upgrade; SEE CONCEPTS *79,126,244*

revision [*n*] *change; rewriting*
afterlight, alteration, amendment, correction, editing, emendation, homework, improvement, modification, overhauling, polish, recension, reconsideration, rectification, rectifying, redaction, redraft, reediting, reexamination, rescript, restyling, retrospect, retrospection, review, revisal, revise, updating; SEE CONCEPTS *79,126,244,700*

revival [*n*] *rebirth, reawakening*
awakening, cheering, consolation, enkindling, freshening, invigoration, quickening, reanimation, recovery, recrudescence, regeneration, rejuvenation, renaissance, renascence, renewal, restoration, resurgence, resurrection, resuscitation, revitalization, revivification, risorgimento; SEE CONCEPTS *119,221*

revive [*v*] *start again; bring back to life*
animate, arouse, awaken, bounce back*, breathe new life into*, brighten, bring around*, bring to*, cheer, come around*, come to life, comfort, console, encourage, energize, enkindle, enliven, exhilarate, gladden, inspirit, invigorate, make whole*, overcome, please, quicken, rally, reanimate, recondition, recover, refresh, rejuvenate, rekindle, relieve, renew, renovate, repair, restore, resurrect, resuscitate, revitalize, rouse, snap out of it*, solace, spring up*,

strengthen, touch up*, wake up; SEE CONCEPTS *13,221,469,697*

revoke [*v*] *take back; cancel*
abjure, abolish, abrogate, annul, back out of, backpedal, call back, call off, countermand, counterorder, declare null and void*, deny, disclaim, dismantle, dismiss, disown, erase, expunge, forswear, Indian give, invalidate, lift, negate, nix*, nullify, obliterate, quash*, recall, recant, remove, renounce, repeal, repudiate, rescind, retract, reverse, rub out*, scrub*, set aside, vacate, void, wipe out*, withdraw; SEE CONCEPTS *50,88,121,234*

revolt [*n*] *uprising*
defection, displeasure, insurgency, insurrection, mutiny, rebellion, revolution, rising, sedition; SEE CONCEPTS *106,300,320*

revolt [*v1*] *rebel, rise up against*
arise, boycott, break, defect, defy, drop out, get out of line*, insurrect, make waves*, mutiny, oppose, opt out, overthrow, overturn, rebel, renounce, resist, riot, rock the boat*, strike, take up arms, turn against; SEE CONCEPTS *106,300,320*

revolt [*v2*] *disgust, nauseate*
crawl*, gross out*, make flesh crawl*, make sick, offend, pain, reluct, repel, repulse, shock, sicken, turn off*, turn stomach*; SEE CONCEPTS *7,19*

revolting [*adj*] *disgusting, nauseating*
abhorrent, abominable, appalling, awful, distasteful, foul, gross*, horrible, horrid, loathsome, nasty*, nauseous, noisome, obnoxious, obscene, offensive, repellent, repugnant, repulsive, rotten*, shocking, sickening, sleazy*, vile; SEE CONCEPT *529*

revolution [*n1*] *drastic action or change, often in politics*
anarchy, bloodshed, cabal, coup, coup d'état, crime, debacle, destruction, disorder, foment, golpe, guerrilla activity, innovation, insubordination, insurgency, metamorphosis, mutiny, outbreak, overthrow, overturn, plot, radical change, rebellion, reformation, reversal, revolt, rising, row, shake-up, shift, strife, strike, subversion, transformation, tumult, turbulence, turmoil, turnover, underground activity, unrest, upheaval, uprising, uproar, upset, violence; SEE CONCEPTS *106,300,320,697*

revolution [*n2*] *circuit around something*
circle, circumvolution, cycle, gyration, gyre, lap, orbit, pirouette, reel, revolve, revolving, roll, rotation, round, spin, swirl, turn, turning, twirl, wheel, whirl; SEE CONCEPTS *436,484,738,792*

revolve [*v1*] *turn, circle*
circumduct, go around, gyrate, gyre, orbit, roll, rotate, spin, turn around, twist, wheel, whirl; SEE CONCEPTS *147,738*

revolve [*v2*] *think about*
consider, deliberate, meditate, mull over, muse, ponder, reflect, roll, ruminate, study, think over, turn over in mind; SEE CONCEPT *17*

revulsion [n] *disgust, hatred*
abhorrence, abomination, aversion, detestation, dislike, distaste, hate, horror, loathing, recoil, repugnance, repulsion; SEE CONCEPT 29

reward [n] *payment, prize*
accolade, award, benefit, bonus, bounty, carrot*, comeuppance, compensation, crown*, cue, dividend, feather in cap*, fringe benefit, gain, garland, goodies*, gravy*, grease*, guerdon, honor, just deserts*, meed, merit, perks*, plum*, premium, profit, punishment, recompense, remuneration, repayment, requital, retribution, return, salve, strokes*, sweetener*, tip, wages; SEE CONCEPTS *337,344*

reward [v] *pay; give prize*
compensate, honor, recompense, remunerate, repay, requite, stroke, sugarcoat*, take care of*, tip; SEE CONCEPTS *108,132,341*

rewarding [adj] *beneficial, pleasing*
advantageous, edifying, fruitful, fulfilling, gainful, gratifying, productive, profitable, remunerative, satisfying, valuable, worthwhile; SEE CONCEPTS *548,572*

rhetoric [n] *wordiness; long speech*
address, balderdash*, big talk*, bombast, composition, discourse, elocution, eloquence, flowery language, fustian, grandiloquence, hot air*, hyperbole, magniloquence, oration, oratory, pomposity, rant, verbosity; SEE CONCEPTS *51,277,278*

rhetorical [adj] *wordy; flowery in speech*
articulate, aureate, bombastic, declamatory, eloquent, embellished, euphuistic, exaggerated, flamboyant, flashy*, florid, fluent, glib*, grand, grandiloquent, grandiose, high-flown*, hyperbolic, imposing, inflated, magniloquent, mouthy, oratorical, ornate, ostentatious, overblown, overdone, overwrought, pompous, pretentious, showy, silver-tongued*, sonorous, stilted, swollen, tumescent, tumid, turgid, verbose, vocal, voluble, windy*; SEE CONCEPT *267*

rhyme [n] *prose in which lines end with like sounds*
alliteration, beast, cadence, couplet, doggerel, half-rhyme, harmony, iambic pentameter, measure, meter, nursery rhyme, ode, poem, poesy, poetry, rhythm, rune, slant rhyme, song, tune, verse, vowel-chime; SEE CONCEPTS *278,595*

rhythm [n] *beat, accent of sound, music*
bounce, cadence, cadency, downbeat, flow, lilt, measure, meter, metre, movement, pattern, periodicity, pulse, regularity, rhyme, rise and fall, swing, tempo, time, uniformity; SEE CONCEPT *595*

ribald [adj] *vulgar, obscene*
base, bawdy, blue*, coarse, devilish, earthy, fast*, filthy*, foul-mouthed, gross*, indecent, indecorous, juicy, lascivious, lewd, licentious, low-down and dirty*, naughty*, off-color*, out of line*, purple*, racy, rascally, raunchy, raw*, risqué, rogue, rough, rude, salacious, salty*, scabrous, scurrilous, sly,

smutty*, spicy*, unbecoming, ungentlemanly, unladylike; SEE CONCEPTS *267,401*

rich [n] *wealthy people or institutions*
bountiful, haves*, landed, monied, nouveau riche, old money, upper class, upper crust*, well-to-do*; SEE CONCEPT *423*

rich [adj1] *having a lot of money*
affluent, bloated, comfortable, easy, fat, filthy rich*, flush, gilded, in clover*, independent, in the money*, loaded*, made of money*, moneyed, opulent, plush, propertied, prosperous, rolling in it*, swimming, upscale, uptown, wealthy, well-heeled*, well-off*, well provided for*, well-to-do*, worth a million*; SEE CONCEPT *334*

rich [adj2] *abundant, well-supplied*
abounding, ample, chic, classy, copious, costly, deluxe, elaborate, elegant, embellished, expensive, exquisite, extravagant, exuberant, fancy, fecund, fertile, fine, fruitful, full, gorgeous, grand, high-class, lavish, lush, luxurious, magnificent, ornate, palatial, plenteous, plentiful, plush, posh, precious, priceless, productive, prolific, resplendent, ritzy*, smart, snazzy*, spiffy, splendid, stylish, sumptuous, superb, swank*, swanky*, swell, valuable, well-endowed; SEE CONCEPTS *334,589,771*

rich [adj3] *flavorful*
creamy, delicious, fatty, full-bodied, heavy, highly flavored, juicy, luscious, nourishing, nutritious, oily, satisfying, savory, spicy, succulent, sustaining, sweet, tasty; SEE CONCEPT *613*

rich [adj4] *full in color or sound*
bright, canorous, deep, dulcet, eloquent, expressive, intense, mellifluous, mellow, resonant, rotund, significant, silvery, sonorous, strong, vibrant, vivid, warm; SEE CONCEPTS *406,594,618*

rich [adj5] *very funny*
absurd, amusing, comical, diverting, droll, entertaining, farcical, foolish, hilarious, humorous, incongruous, laughable, ludicrous, odd, preposterous, queer, ridiculous, risible, side-splitting*, slaying*, splitting*, strange; SEE CONCEPTS *267,529*

riches [n] *money and possessions*
abundance, affluence, assets, clover, fortune, gold, lap of luxury*, means, opulence, plenty, property, resources, richness, substance, treasure, wealth, worth; SEE CONCEPTS *335,340,446,710*

rickety [adj] *unsound, broken-down*
broken, decrepit, derelict, dilapidated, feeble, flimsy, fragile, frail, imperfect, infirm, insecure, jerry-built*, precarious, ramshackle, rattletrap*, rocky, shaky, tottering, tottery*, tumble-down*, unsteady, wavering, weak, wobbly; SEE CONCEPT *488*

rid [v] *do away with; free*
abolish, clear, deliver, disabuse, disburden, disembarrass, disencumber, dump*, eject, eliminate, eradicate, expel, exterminate, extinguish, extirpate, fire, give the brush*, heave-ho*, junk*, kiss goodbye*, liberate, make free, purge, release, relieve, remove,

roust, scrap, send packing*, shake off, shed, throw away, throw out, toss out, unburden, unload, uproot; SEE CONCEPTS *180,211*

riddle [*n*] *brain-teaser*
bewilderment, brain-twister*, charade, Chinese puzzle*, closed book*, complexity, complication, confusion, conundrum, cryptogram, dilemma, distraction, doubt, embarrassment, enigma, entanglement, intricacy, knotty question*, labyrinth, maze, mind-boggler*, mystery, mystification, perplexity, plight, poser, predicament, problem, puzzle, puzzlement, quandary, question, rebus, sixty-four dollar question*, stickler*, strait, stumper*, teaser, tough nut to crack*, tough proposition, twister*; SEE CONCEPT *532*

riddle [*v*] *perforate, permeate*
bore, corrupt, damage, honeycomb*, impair, infest, mar, pepper, pervade, pierce, pit, puncture, spoil; SEE CONCEPTS *156,220*

ride [*n*] *journey, trip in vehicle*
airing, commute, drive, excursion, expedition, hitch, jaunt, joyride*, lift, outing, pick up*, run, spin, Sunday drive, tour, transportation, turn, whirl; SEE CONCEPT *224*

ride [*v1*] *carry or be carried*
be supported, control, cruise, curb, direct, drift, drive, float, go, go with, guide, handle, hitch a ride*, hitchhike, journey, manage, motor, move, post, progress, restrain, roll, sit, sit on, thumb a ride*, tool around*, tour, travel; SEE CONCEPTS *94,148,224*

ride [*v2*] *dominate, oppress*
afflict, annoy, badger, bait, be arbitrary, be autocratic, berate, disparage, domineer, enslave, grip, harass, harry, haunt, hector, hound, override, persecute, rate, reproach, revile, scold, torment, torture, tyrannize, upbraid; SEE CONCEPTS *7,14,19*

ridge [*n*] *raised part of solid*
backbone, chine, corrugation, crease, crinkle, elevation, esker, fold, furrow, hill, hogback, moraine, parapet, plica, pole, range, rib, rim, rimple, rivel, ruck, seam, spine, upland, wrinkle; SEE CONCEPTS *471,509,513*

ridicule [*n*] *contemptuous laughter at someone or something*
badinage, banter, buffoonery, burlesque, caricature, chaff, comeback, contempt, derision, dig*, disdain, disparagement, farce, foolery, gibe, irony, jab*, jeer, laughter, leer, mockery, mordancy, needling, parody, parting shot*, persiflage, putdown*, put-on*, raillery, rally, razz*, rib*, roast*, sarcasm, sardonicism, satire, scorn, slam*, sneer*, swipe*, taunt*, taunting, travesty; SEE CONCEPTS *54,59*

ridicule [*v*] *make contemptuous fun of something or someone*
banter, caricature, cartoon, chaff, deflate, deride, expose, fleer, gibe, haze, humiliate, jape, jeer, jive, jolly, josh, kid, lampoon, laugh at, make a fool of*, make a game of*, make fun of, make laughing

stock*, mimic, mock, needle, pan*, parody, poke fun at*, pooh-pooh*, pull one's leg*, put down*, quiz, rag, rail at, rally, raz*, rib*, ride*, roast*, run down*, satirize, scoff, scorn, send up*, show up, sneer, takeoff, taunt, travesty, twit, unmask; SEE CONCEPTS *54,59*

ridiculous [*adj*] *stupid, funny*
absurd, antic, bizarre, comic, comical, contemptible, daffy*, derisory, droll, fantastic, farcical, foolheaded*, foolish, gelastic, goofy*, grotesque, harebrained*, hilarious, impossible, incredible, jerky*, laughable, ludicrous, nonsensical, nutty*, outrageous, preposterous, risible, sappy*, silly, slaphappy*, unbelievable, wacky*; SEE CONCEPTS *529, 548,552*

rife [*adj*] *overflowing*
abounding, abundant, alive, common, current, epidemic, extensive, frequent, general, many, multitudinous, numerous, pandemic, plentiful, popular, prevailing, prevalent, profuse, raging, rampant, regnant, replete, ruling, swarming, teeming, thronged, ubiquitous, universal, widespread; SEE CONCEPTS *771,772*

rifle [*v*] *ransack*
burglarize, burgle, despoil, go through, grab, gut, loot, pillage, plunder, rip, rip off*, rob, rummage, sack, smash and grab*, strip, take, tip over*, trash*, waste*; SEE CONCEPT *139*

rift [*n1*] *break, crack*
breach, chink, cleavage, cleft, cranny, crevice, fault, fissure, flaw, fracture, gap, hiatus, interruption, interval, opening, parting, rent, rima, rime, space, split; SEE CONCEPT *513*

rift [*n2*] *difference of opinion*
alienation, breach, break, clash, disagreement, division, estrangement, falling out*, misunderstanding, quarrel, rupture, schism, separation, split; SEE CONCEPTS *46,106,388*

rig [*n*] *equipment*
accouterments, apparatus, equipage, fittings, fixtures, gear, machinery, outfit, paraphernalia, tackle; SEE CONCEPT *496*

rig [*v1*] *outfit, supply*
accouter, appoint, arm, array, attire, clothe, costume, dress, equip, fit out, furnish, gear, kit, provision, set up, turn out; SEE CONCEPTS *140,167,182*

rig [*v2*] *arrange for certain outcome*
doctor, engineer, fake, falsify, fiddle with*, fix, gerrymander*, juggle, manipulate, tamper with, trump up*; SEE CONCEPTS *202,697*

right [*n1*] *privilege*
advantage, appanage, authority, benefit, birthright, business, claim, comeuppance, desert, deserving, due, exemption, favor, franchise, freedom, immunity, interest, liberty, license, merit, permission, perquisite, power, preference, prerogative, priority, title; SEE CONCEPT *376*

right [n2] *justice, morality*
correctness, emancipation, enfranchisement, equity, freedom, good, goodness, honor, independence, integrity, lawfulness, legality, liberty, morality, properness, propriety, reason, rectitude, righteousness, rightness, straight, truth, uprightness, virtue; SEE CONCEPT *645*

right [adj1] *fair, just*
appropriate, condign, conscientious, deserved, due, equitable, ethical, fitting, good, hold together*, hold water*, honest, honorable, justifiable, lawful, legal, legitimate, merited, moral, proper, requisite, righteous, rightful, scrupulous, stand-up*, suitable, true, upright, virtuous; SEE CONCEPT *545*

right [adj2] *accurate, precise*
absolute, admissible, amen, authentic, bona fide, complete, correct, exact, factual, faithful, free of error, genuine, immaculate, indubitable, inerrant, infallible, just, nice, on the money*, on the nose*, out-and-out*, perfect, proper, punctilious, real, right as rain*, righteous, right on*, rigorous, satisfactory, solemn, sound, strict, sure, thoroughgoing, true, undistorted, undoubted, unerring, unmistaken, utter, valid, veracious, veridical, veritable, watertight*; SEE CONCEPTS *535,557,582*

right [adj3] *appropriate, fitting*
acceptable, adequate, advantageous, all right, becoming, befitting, comely, comme il faut*, common, condign, convenient, correct, decent, decorous, deserved, desirable, done*, due, favorable, felicitous, fit, good, happy, ideal, merited, nice, opportune, proper, propitious, requisite, rightful, satisfactory, seemly, sufficient, suitable, tolerable; SEE CONCEPTS *558,572*

right [adj4] *sane, healthy*
all there, balanced, circumspect, compos mentis, discerning, discreet, enlightened, far-sighted, fine, fit, hale, in good health*, in the pink*, judicious, lucid, normal, penetrating, rational, reasonable, sound, unimpaired, up to par*, well, wise; SEE CONCEPTS *314,403*

right [adj5] *conservative politically*
die-hard*, old-line*, orthodox, reactionary, right wing, traditionalistic; SEE CONCEPTS *529,689*

right [adj6] *opposite of left*
clockwise, dexter, dextral, right-handed; SEE CONCEPT *581*

right [v] *fix, correct*
adjust, amend, balance, clean up, compensate for, debug, dial back, doctor*, do justice, emend, fiddle with*, fix up, go straight, launder, make up for, mend, overhaul, patch, pick up, put in place, put right, recalibrate, recompense, recondition, reconstruct, rectify, redress, repair, restore, reward, scrub, set straight, settle, set upright, shape up, sort out, square, straighten, straighten out, turn around, vindicate; SEE CONCEPTS *126,212*

right [adv1] *accurately, precisely*
absolutely, all the way, altogether, bang*, clear, completely, correctly, entirely, exactly, factually, fully, genuinely, just, perfectly, precisely, quite, sharp, slap, smack-dab*, square, squarely, thoroughly, totally, truly, utterly, well, wholly; SEE CONCEPTS *531,557,582*

right [adv2] *appropriately, suitably*
acceptably, adequately, amply, aptly, becomingly, befittingly, fittingly, properly, satisfactorily, well; SEE CONCEPTS *558,572*

right [adv3] *fairly, justly*
conscientiously, decently, dispassionately, equitably, ethically, evenly, honestly, honorably, impartially, lawfully, legitimately, morally, objectively, properly, reliably, righteously, sincerely, squarely, virtuously, without bias, without prejudice; SEE CONCEPT *545*

right [adv4] *beneficially*
advantageous, exceedingly, extremely, favorably, for the better, fortunately, highly, notably, perfectly, remarkably, to advantage, very, well; SEE CONCEPTS *537,572*

right [adv5] *directly, without delay*
at once, away, direct, due, first off, forthwith, immediately, instanter, instantly, now, promptly, quickly, right away, straight, straightaway, straightly, undeviatingly; SEE CONCEPT *799*

righteous [adj] *good, honest*
angelic, blameless, charitable, commendable, conscientious, creditable, deserving, devoted, devout, dutiful, equitable, ethical, exemplary, fair, faithful, godlike, guiltless, holy, honorable, impartial, innocent, irreproachable, just, laudable, law-abiding, matchless, meritorious, moral, noble, peerless, philanthropic, philanthropical, praiseworthy, punctilious, pure, reverent, right-minded, saintly, scrupulous, sinless, spiritual, sterling, trustworthy, upright, virtuous, worthy; SEE CONCEPT *545*

rightful [adj] *legitimate*
applicable, appropriate, apt, authorized, befitting, bona fide, canonical, card-carrying*, condign, deserved, due, ethical, fair, fit, fitting, holding water, honest, just, kosher*, lawful, legal, legit*, merited, moral, moralistic, noble, official, on the level*, on the up and up*, orthodox, permitted, principled, proper, real, requisite, right, right-minded, suitable, true, twenty-four carat*, valid, virtuous; SEE CONCEPTS *545,558*

rigid [adj] *stiff, strict, severe*
adamant, adamantine, austere, bullheaded*, changeless, chiseled*, dead set*, definite, determined, exact, firm, fixed, hard, hard-line*, harsh, incompliant, inelastic, inexorable, inflexible, intransigent, invariable, locked in*, obdurate, rigorous, set, set in stone*, single-minded, solid, static, stern, straitlaced*, stringent, tough nut to crack*, unalterable, unbending, unbreakable, unchanging, uncompromis-

ing, undeviating, unmoving, unpermissive, unrelenting, unyielding; SEE CONCEPTS *403,534,535*

rigor [*n*] *strictness, exactness*
accuracy, affliction, asperity, austerity, conscientiousness, conventionalism, difficulty, exactitude, firmness, hardness, hardship, harshness, inclemency, inflexibility, intolerance, meticulousness, obduracy, ordeal, preciseness, precision, privation, punctiliousness, rigidity, roughness, severity, sternness, stiffness, stringency, suffering, tenacity, thoroughness, traditionalism, trial, tribulation, vicissitude, visitation; SEE CONCEPTS *638,654,666*

rigorous [*adj*] *severe; exact*
accurate, ascetic, austere, bitter, brutal, burdensome, correct, definite, dogmatic, exact, exacting, hard, harsh, inclement, inflexible, intemperate, ironhanded, meticulous, nice, onerous, oppressive, precise, proper, punctilious, right, rigid, rugged, scrupulous, stern, stiff, strict, stringent, uncompromising, unpermissive; SEE CONCEPTS *535,557,565*

rile [*v*] *anger, upset*
acerbate, aggravate, annoy, bother, bug*, disturb, exasperate, gall, get one's goat*, get under skin*, grate, inflame, irk, irritate, nettle, peeve, pique, provoke, put out*, roil, rub wrong way*, try one's patience*, vex; SEE CONCEPTS *7,19*

rim [*n*] *border; top edge*
band, brim, brink, brow, circumference, confine, curb, end, fringe, hem, ledge, limit, line, lip, margin, outline, perimeter, periphery, ring, skirt, strip, terminus, top, verge; SEE CONCEPTS *484,836*

ring [*n1*] *circle; circular object*
arena, band, brim, circlet, circuit, circus, enclosure, eye, girdle, halo, hoop, loop, ringlet, rink, round; SEE CONCEPTS *436,446*

ring [*n2*] *group participating together*
association, band, bloc, bunch, cabal, camp, cartel, cell, circle, clan, clique, coalition, combination, combine, corner, coterie, crew, crowd, faction, gang, in-group, junta, junto, knot, Mafia, mob, monopoly, organization, outfit, party, pool, push, racket, syndicate, troop, troupe, trust; SEE CONCEPTS *325,381*

ring [*n3*] *chime, bell-like noise*
buzz, call, clangor, clank, jangle, jingle, knell, peal, reverberation, tinkle, toll, vibration; SEE CONCEPT *595*

ring [*v1*] *encircle*
begird, belt, circle, circumscribe, compass, confine, enclose, encompass, gird, girdle, hem in, inclose, loop, move around, rim, round, seal off, surround; SEE CONCEPT *758*

ring [*v2*] *chime; make bell-like noise*
bang, beat, bong, buzz, clang, clap, jangle, jingle, knell, peal, play, pull, punch, resonate, resound, reverberate, sound, strike, tinkle, tintinnabulate, toll, vibrate; SEE CONCEPT *65*

rinse [*v*] *wash off, out*
bathe, clean, cleanse, dip, flush, soak, splash, wash, water, wet; SEE CONCEPTS *165,256*

riot [*n1*] *uprising, disorder*
anarchism, anarchy, branigan, brawl, burst, commotion, confusion, distemper, disturbance, flap, fray, free-for-all*, fuss, hassle, lawlessness, misrule, mix-up, mob violence, protest, quarrel, racket, raising Cain*, row, ruckus, ruction, rumble, rumpus, run-in, scene, shivaree, shower, snarl, stir, storm, street fighting, strife, to-do*, trouble, tumult, turbulence, turmoil, uproar, wingding*; SEE CONCEPTS *106,300*

riot [*n2*] *very funny happening*
boisterousness, carousal, confusion, excess, extravaganza, festivity, flourish, frolic, high jinks*, howl, jollification, lark, merrymaking, panic*, revelry, romp, scream*, sensation, show, sidesplitter*, skylark*, smash*, splash*, tumult, uproar, wow*; SEE CONCEPTS *384,386*

riot [*v*] *protest; cause an uproar*
arise, debauch, dissipate, fight, go on rampage, racket, rampage, rebel, revolt, rise, run riot*, stir up trouble*, take to the streets*; SEE CONCEPTS *106,300*

rip [*n*] *tear, cut*
cleavage, gash, hole, laceration, rent, slash, slit, split; SEE CONCEPTS *309,513*

rip [*v*] *tear, cut*
be rent, burst, claw, cleave, fray, frazzle, gash, hack, lacerate, rend, rive, score, shred, slash, slit, split; SEE CONCEPT *214*

ripe [*adj1*] *fully developed; experienced*
accomplished, adult, aged, completed, concummate, conditioned, enlightened, enriched, filled out, finished, fit, full, full-blown, full-fledged, fully grown, grown, grown-up, increased, informed, in readiness, judicious, learned, mature, matured, mellow, overdue, perfected, plump, prepared, prime, ready, ripened, sagacious, seasoned, skilled, skillful, sound, timely, usable, versed, well-timed, wise; SEE CONCEPTS *462,560,578,797*

ripe [*adj2*] *favorable, ideal*
auspicious, opportune, right, suitable, timely; SEE CONCEPT *558*

rip-off [*n*] *trick; robbery*
cheat, con*, exploitation, fraud, gyp*, larceny, lift*, pinch*, purloining, racket*, steal, stealing, swindle, theft, thievery, thieving; SEE CONCEPTS *139,192*

rip off [*v*] *rob; trick*
abuse, appropriate, bleed*, cheat, con*, cop*, defraud, dupe, exploit, filch*, fleece*, gyp*, heist, impose on*, lift*, nab*, pilfer, pinch*, plunder, ransack, relieve, rifle, skin*, soak*, stick*, swindle, swipe, thieve, use; SEE CONCEPTS *139,192*

rise [*n1*] *increase, improvement*
acceleration, accession, accretion, addition, advance, advancement, aggrandizement, ascent, augmentation, boost, breakthrough, climb, distention, doubling, enlargement, growth, heightening, hike,

increment, inflation, intensification, intensifying, multiplication, piling up, progress, promotion, raise, stacking up, step-up, surge, swell, upgrade, upsurge, upswing, upturn, waxing; SEE CONCEPTS *700,780*

rise [*n2*] *movement upward; upward slope*
acclivity, ascension, ascent, climb, elevation, eminence, highland, hillock, incline, lift, mount, rising, rising ground, soaring, surge, towering, upland, upsurge; SEE CONCEPTS *166,738,752*

rise [*v1*] *get up; ascend*
arise, arouse, aspire, awake, be erect, be located, be situated, blast off*, bob up*, climb, come up, get out of bed, get steeper, get to one's feet*, go uphill, grow, have foundation, levitate, lift, mount, move up, pile out*, push up, reach up, rise and shine*, rise up, rocket, roll out*, rouse, scale, sit up, slope upwards, soar, sprout, stand up, straighten up, surface, surge, surmount, sweep upward, tower, turn out, up*, upspring; SEE CONCEPTS *154,166,738*

rise [*v2*] *increase, grow*
accelerate, add to, advance, aggravate, arise, ascend, augment, billow, build, bulge, climb, deepen, distend, double, enhance, enlarge, expand, go through the roof*, go up, heighten, improve, inflate, intensate, intensify, levitate, lift, magnify, mount, move up, multiply, perk up, pick up, pile up, raise, redouble, rouse, soar, speed up, spread, stack up, swell, take off, upsurge, wax; SEE CONCEPTS *700,780*

rise [*v3*] *progress in business*
advance, be elevated, be promoted, better oneself, climb the ladder*, flourish, get on, get somewhere*, go places*, progress, prosper, succeed, thrive, work one's way up*; SEE CONCEPTS *351,704*

rise [*v4*] *become apparent*
appear, arise, befall, begin, betide, chance, come, crop up, dawn, derive, develop, emanate, emerge, eventuate, fall out*, flare up, flow, go, happen, head, issue, loom, occur, originate, proceed, spring, stem, surface, transpire, turn up*; SEE CONCEPTS *4,716*

rise [*v5*] *rebel*
insurrect, mount, mutiny, resist, revolt, riot, take up arms; SEE CONCEPT *106*

risk [*n*] *chance taken*
accident, brinksmanship, contingency, danger, exposedness, exposure, flyer*, fortuity, fortune, gamble, hazard, header, jeopardy, liability, liableness, luck, openness, opportunity, peril, plunge, possibility, prospect, shot in the dark*, speculation, stab*, uncertainty, venture, wager; SEE CONCEPTS *675,693*

risk [*v*] *take a chance*
adventure, beard, be caught short*, brave, chance, compromise, confront, dare, defy, defy danger, encounter, endanger, expose to danger, face, gamble, go out of one's depth*, hang by a thread*, hazard, imperil, jeopardize, jeopardy, leap before looking*, leave to luck*, meet, menace, peril, play with fire*, plunge, put in jeopardy, run the chance, run the risk, skate on thin ice*, speculate, tackle, take a flyer*,

take a header*, take a plunge*, take on*, take the liberty*, venture, wager; SEE CONCEPTS *87,100*

risky [*adj*] *dangerous*
chancy, delicate, dicey*, endangered, fraught with danger*, going for broke*, hairy*, hanging by a thread*, hazardous, iffy*, insecure, jeopardous, long shot*, not a prayer*, off the deep end*, on slippery ground*, on the spot*, on thin ice*, out on a limb*, perilous, playing with fire*, precarious, rocky*, sensitive, speculative, ticklish, touch-and-go*, touchy, treacherous, tricky, uncertain, unhealthy, unsafe, unsound, venturesome, wicked, wide-open; SEE CONCEPT *548*

risqué [*adj*] *improper, referring to sex*
amoral, bawdy*, blue*, breezy, crude, daring, dirty*, earthy, erotic, filthy*, foul, gross*, hot*, immodest, immoral, indecent, indecorous, indelicate, indiscreet, inelegant, lewd, lurid, naughty, obscene, off-base*, off-color*, offensive, out-of-line, provocative, purple*, racy, raw, ribald, salacious, salty*, shady, sizzling, smart, smutty*, spicy*, suggestive, unrefined, vulgar, wanton, warm, wicked, X-rated*; SEE CONCEPTS *267,545,548*

rite [*n*] *ceremony, tradition*
act, celebration, ceremonial, communion, custom, form, formality, liturgy, observance, occasion, ordinance, practice, procedure, ritual, sacrament, service, solemnity; SEE CONCEPTS *377,386*

ritual [*n*] *ceremony, tradition*
act, ceremonial, communion, convention, custom, form, formality, habit, liturgy, observance, ordinance, practice, prescription, procedure, protocol, red tape*, rite, routine, sacrament, service, solemnity, stereotype, usage; SEE CONCEPTS *386,634,687*

rival [*n*] *person who opposes in competition*
adversary, antagonist, bad guy*, bandit, buddy, challenger, competition, competitor, contender, contestant, emulator, entrant, equal, equivalent, fellow, match, opponent, opposite number, peer; SEE CONCEPTS *348,366,423*

rival [*adj*] *opposing*
battling, combatant, combating, competing, competitive, conflicting, contending, contesting, cutthroat, disputing, emulating, emulous, equal, opposed, striving, vying; SEE CONCEPTS *542,564*

rival [*v*] *oppose; be a match for*
amount, approach, approximate, bear comparison with*, come near to*, come up to*, compare with, compete, contend, contest, correspond, emulate, equal, go after, go for, jockey for position*, match, measure up to, meet, near, partake, resemble, rivalize, scramble for, seek to displace, tie, touch, vie with; SEE CONCEPTS *92,667*

road [*n*] *path upon which travel occurs*
alley, artery, asphalt, avenue, back street, boulevard, byway, cobblestone, concrete, course, crossroad, direction, drag*, dragway, drive, expressway, highway, lane, line, main drag*, parking lot*, parkway,

passage, pathway, pavement, pike, roadway, route, street, subway, terrace, thoroughfare, throughway, thruway, track, trail, turnpike, viaduct, way; SEE CONCEPT 501

roam [v] *wander about*
bum*, bum around*, drift, gad, gallivant, hike, hit the road*, knock around*, meander, peregrinate, prowl, ramble, range, rove, saunter, straggle, stray, stroll, struggle along, traipse, tramp, travel, traverse, trek, vagabond, walk; SEE CONCEPTS 151,224

roar [n1] *growl, howl*
barrage, bawl, bay, bellow, blast, bluster, boom, clamor, clash, crash, cry, detonation, din, drum, explosion, holler, outcry, reverberation, rumble, shout, thunder, uproar, yell; SEE CONCEPTS 77,595

roar [n2/v2] *laugh loudly*
belly laugh, guffaw, hoot, howl, scream; SEE CONCEPT 77

roar [v1] *growl, howl*
bark, bawl, bay, bellow, blast, bluster, boom, brawl, bray, clamor, crash, cry, detonate, din, drum, explode, holler, rebound, reecho, repercuss, resound, reverberate, roll, rout, rumble, shout, sound, thunder, trumpet, vociferate, yell; SEE CONCEPTS 64,77

rob [v] *steal, deprive*
abscond, appropriate, bereave, break into, burglarize, burgle, cheat, con, cop*, defalcate, defraud, despoil, disinherit, dispossess, divest, do out of*, embezzle, filch*, gyp*, heist, hijack, hold up*, hustle, liberate, lift*, loot, lose, mug, oust, peculate, pilfer, pillage, pinch*, plunder, promote, purloin, raid, ransack, relieve, requisition, rifle*, rip off*, roll*, sack*, scrounge, snitch*, stick up*, strip, strong-arm*, swindle, swipe, take, thieve, withhold; SEE CONCEPTS 139,142,192

robber [n] *person who steals*
bandit, brigand, buccaneer, burglar, cardsharper*, cat burglar, cattle thief*, cheat*, chiseler*, con man/woman, corsair, crook, desperado, despoiler, fence, forager, fraud, grafter, highwayman, hijacker, holdup man/woman, housebreaker, looter, marauder, mugger, operator, pickpocket, pilferer, pillager, pirate, plunderer, prowler, punk*, raider, rustler, safecracker, sandbagger*, second-story operator*, shoplifter, stealer, stickup, swindler, thief, thug; SEE CONCEPT 412

robe [n] *gown, often for wearing at home*
bathrobe, cape, costume, covering, dress, dressing gown, frock, garment, habit, housecoat, kimono, mantle, muumuu, negligee, outfit, peignoir, vestment, wrapper; SEE CONCEPT 451

robust [adj] *healthy, strong*
able-bodied, athletic, boisterous, booming, brawny, built, concentrated, fit, fit as fiddle*, flourishing, full-bodied, hale, hardy, hearty, hefty, hulk, hunk, husky, in fine fettle*, in good health, in good shape, in the pink*, live, lusty, muscular, peppy, potent, powerful, powerhouse, prospering, prosperous, roar-

ing, rough, rugged, sinewy, snappy, sound, stout, strapping, sturdy, thriving, tiger*, tough, vigorous, well, wicked*, zappy*, zippy*; SEE CONCEPTS 314,489,613

rock [n1] *stone*
bedrock, boulder, cobblestone, crag, crust, earth, gravel, lava, lodge, mass, metal, mineral, ore, pebble, promontory, quarry, reef, rubble, shelf, slab, slag; SEE CONCEPTS 470,474,477,478,509,523

rock [n2] *foundation*
anchor, bulwark, cornerstone, defense, mainstay, protection, Rock of Gibraltar*, strength, support; SEE CONCEPTS 442,712

rock [v] *move back and forth*
agitate, billow, careen, concuss, convulse, falter, heave, jiggle, jog, jolt, jounce, lurch, move, oscillate, pitch, push and pull, quake, quaver, quiver, reel, roll, roll about, shake, shock, stagger, sway, swing, toss, totter, tremble, undulate, vibrate, wobble; SEE CONCEPTS 147,149

rocky [adj1] *rugged, stony*
bouldered, craggy, flinty, hard, inflexible, jagged, lapidarian, lithic, pebbly, petrified, petrous, rockbound, rock-ribbed, rough, solid, stonelike; SEE CONCEPTS 485,604

rocky [adj2] *unyielding, inflexible*
adamant, bloodless, firm, flinty, hard, impassible, insensate, insensible, insensitive, obdurate, pitiless, rocklike, rough, rugged, solid, steady, tough; SEE CONCEPT 401

rocky [adj3] *doubtful, undependable*
dizzy, ill, rickety, shaky, sick, sickly, staggering, ticklish, tottering, tricky, uncertain, unreliable, unstable, unsteady, unwell, weak, wobbly; SEE CONCEPTS 314,488,489

rod [n] *bar, pole*
baton, billet, birch, cane, cylinder, dowel, ingot, mace, pin, rodule, scepter, sceptre, shaft, slab, spike, staff, stave, stick, strip, switch, wand; SEE CONCEPTS 436,470,479

rogue [n] *person who deceives, swindles*
bad egg*, bad news*, blackguard*, black sheep*, charlatan, cheat, cheater, con man/woman, crook, defrauder, devil, enfant terrible*, fraud, gyp*, heel*, hooligan*, knave, lowlife*, mischief, miscreant, monstrosity, mountebank, ne'er-do-well*, outlaw, problem*, rapscallion, rascal, reprobate, scalawag, scamp, scoundrel, swindler, trickster, villain; SEE CONCEPT 412

role [n1] *impersonation of a character*
act, acting, appearance, aspect, bit, character, clothing, execution, extra, guise, hero, heroine, ingenue, lead, look, part, performance, personification, piece, player, portrayal, presentation, representation, seeming, semblance, show, star, stint, super, title, walk-on; SEE CONCEPTS 263,716

role [n2] *duty, function*
act, bit, business, capacity, execution, game*, guise, job, office, part, piece, pose, position, post, posture,

province, stint, task, what one is into*; SEE CONCEPTS *362,694*

roll [*n1*] *revolving, turning*
cycle, gyration, reel, revolution, rotation, run, spin, trundling, turn, twirl, undulation, whirl; SEE CONCEPTS *147,201*

roll [*n2*] *cylindrical object*
ball, barrel, bobbin, cartouche, coil, cone, convolution, cornucopia, cylinder, fold, reel, rundle, scroll, shell, spiral, spool, trundle, volute, wheel, whorl; SEE CONCEPT *436*

roll [*n3*] *list, roster*
annals, catalog, census, chronicle, directory, head count*, index, muster, nose count*, register, roll call, schedule, scroll, table; SEE CONCEPT *281*

roll [*n4*] *growl, reverberation*
barrage, boom, booming, clangor, drone, drumbeat, drumming, echoing, grumble, quaver, racket, rat-a-tat*, resonance, roar, rumble, rumbling, thunder; SEE CONCEPT *595*

roll [*v1*] *revolve, turn; proceed smoothly*
alternate, be in sequence, bowl, circle, circumduct, coil, curve, drape, drive, eddy, elapse, enfold, entwine, envelop, flow, fold, follow, furl, go around, go past, gyrate, gyre, impel, pass, pirouette, pivot, propel, reel, rock, rotate, run, spin, spiral, succeed, swaddle, swathe, swing around, swirl, swivel, trundle, twirl, twist, undulate, wheel, whirl, wind, wrap; SEE CONCEPTS *147,201*

roll [*v2*] *spread out*
even, flatten, grind, level, press, pulverize, smooth; SEE CONCEPTS *137,208,250*

roll [*v3*] *thunder, reverberate*
bombinate, boom, cannonade, drum, echo, growl, grumble, hum, pattern, quaver, rattle, re-echo, resound, roar, ruffle, rumble, rustle, sound, trill, whirr; SEE CONCEPT *65*

roll [*v4*] *rock, sway*
billow, drift, flow, glide, heave, incline, jibe, lean, lumber, lurch, pitch, ramble, range, reel, roam, rove, run, stagger, stray, surge, swagger, swing, toss, tumble, undulate, waddle, wallow, wave, welter, yaw; SEE CONCEPTS *147,149*

rollicking [*adj*] *fun-loving, lively*
antic, boisterous, carefree, cavorting, cheerful, devil-may-care*, exuberant, frisky, frolicsome, glad, happy, hearty, jaunty, jovial, joyful, joyous, light hearted, merry, playful, rip-roaring*, romping, spirited, sportive, sprightly; SEE CONCEPTS *401,548*

romance [*n1*] *love affair*
affair, affair of the heart*, amour, attachment, courtship, enchantment, fairy tale*, fascination, fling, flirtation, intrigue, liaison, love, love story, passion, relationship; SEE CONCEPTS *375,384*

romance [*n2*] *written work about love affair*
ballad, fairy tale, fantasy, fiction, idealization, idyll, legend, love story, lyric, melodrama, novel, story, tale, tear-jerker*; SEE CONCEPT *280*

romance [*n3*] *adventure, flight of fancy*
charm, color, excitement, exoticness, fairy tale, fancy, fantasy, fascination, glamour, hazard, idealization, idyll, mystery, nostalgia, risk, sentiment, venture; SEE CONCEPT *673*

romantic [*adj*] *sentimental, idealistic*
adventurous, amorous, bathetic, charming, chimerical, chivalrous, colorful, corny*, daring, dreamy, enchanting, erotic, exciting, exotic, extravagant, fairy-tale, fanciful, fantastic, fascinating, fond, glamorous, idyllic, impractical, lovey-dovey*, loving, maudlin, mushy*, mysterious, nostalgic, passionate, picturesque, poetic, quixotic, sloppy*, soppy*, starry-eyed, syrupy, tear-jerking*, tender, unrealistic, utopean, visionary, whimsical, wild; SEE CONCEPTS *403,542,548*

romp [*n*] *fun; caper*
antic, cakewalk*, cavort, dance, escapade, frisk, frolic, gambol, hop, lark, leap, play, rollick, rout, skip, sport; SEE CONCEPTS *292,384*

romp [*v*] *have fun, enjoy oneself*
caper, cavort, celebrate, cut capers*, cut up*, fool around*, frisk, frolic, gambol, go on the town*, kid around*, lark, let loose*, make merry, play, prance, revel, roister, rollic, skip, skylark, sport, whoop it up*; SEE CONCEPTS *292,384*

room [*n1*] *space, range*
allowance, area, capacity, chance, clearance, compass, elbowroom, expanse, extent, latitude, leeway, license, margin, occasion, opening, opportunity, place, play, range, reach, rein, rope, scope, sway, sweep, territory, vastness, volume; SEE CONCEPTS *651,756*

room [*n2*] *enclosed section of building designed for specific purpose*
accommodation, alcove, apartment, cabin, cave*, chamber, cubbyhole*, cubicle, den, flat, flop*, joint*, lodging, niche, office, setup*, suite, turf, vault; SEE CONCEPT *448*

roomy [*adj*] *having ample space*
ample, broad, capacious, commodious, extensive, generous, large, sizable, spacious, wide; SEE CONCEPT *583*

root [*n*] *base, core*
basis, bedrock*, beginnings, bottom, cause, center, crux, derivation, essence, essentiality, footing, foundation, fountain, fountainhead*, fundamental, germ, ground, groundwork, heart, inception, infrastructure, mainspring, marrow, motive, nub, nucleus, occasion, origin, pith, provenance, provenience, quick, quintessence, radicle, radix, reason, rhizome, rock bottom*, seat, seed, soul, source, starting point, stem, stuff, substance, substratum, tuber, underpinning, well; SEE CONCEPTS *442,648,661,826,829*

root [*v*] *dig and search*
burrow, delve, embed, ferret, forage, grub, grub up, hunt, ingrain, lodge, nose, place, poke, pry, rummage; SEE CONCEPT *178*

rope [n] *cord, line*
braiding, cable, cordage, hawser, lace, lanyard, lariat, lasso, strand, string, tape, thread, twine; SEE CONCEPT *475*

roster [n] *list of items, names*
agenda, catalog, head count*, index, inventory, listing, muster, nose count*, program, record, register, roll, roll call, rote, schedule, scroll, table; SEE CONCEPTS *281,283*

rosy [adj1] *pink, reddish in color*
aflush, blooming, blushing, colored, coral, deep pink, fresh, glowing, healthy-looking, high-colored, incarnadine, pale red, peach, red, red-complexioned, red-faced, roseate, rose-colored, rubicund, ruddy; SEE CONCEPT *618*

rosy [adj2] *cheerful, hopeful*
alluring, auspicious, bright, encouraging, favorable, glowing, likely, optimistic, pleasing, promising, reassuring, roseate*, rose-colored*, sunny*; SEE CONCEPTS *529,548*

rot [n1] *corrosion, disintegration*
blight, canker, corrosion, decay, decomposition, deterioration, mold, putrefaction, putrescence; SEE CONCEPTS *469,698*

rot [n2] *garbage, nonsense*
balderdash*, bilge, bunk, claptrap, drivel, foolishness, guff, hogwash, hooey*, moonshine*, poppycock*, rubbish, silliness, stuff and nonsense*, tommyrot*; SEE CONCEPTS *278,529*

rot [v] *corrode, deteriorate*
break down, corrupt, crumble, debase, debauch, decay, decline, decompose, degenerate, demoralize, deprave, descend, disimprove, disintegrate, fester, go bad*, go downhill*, go to pot*, languish, molder, perish, pervert, putrefy, retrograde, sink, spoil, stain, taint, turn, warp, waste away, wither, worsen; SEE CONCEPTS *240,469,698*

rotary [adj] *turning*
encircling, gyral, gyratory, revolving, rotating, rotational, rotatory, spinning, vertiginous, vorticular, whirligig, whirling; SEE CONCEPTS *581,584*

rotate [v1] *go around in circle*
circle, circumduct, circumvolve, gyrate, gyre, move, pirouette, pivot, reel, revolve, roll, spin, swivel, troll, trundle, turn, twirl, twist, waltz, wheel, whirl, whirligig, whirr; SEE CONCEPTS *147,738*

rotate [v2] *alternate*
bandy, ensue, exchange, follow, follow in sequence, interchange, relieve, spell, succeed, switch, take turns; SEE CONCEPTS *104,697*

rotten [adj1] *decayed, decaying*
bad, bad-smelling, corroded, corrupt, crumbled, crumbling, decomposed, decomposing, disgusting, disintegrated, disintegrating, fecal, feculent, festering, fetid, foul, gross*, infected, loathsome, loud, mephitic, moldering, moldy, noisome, noxious, offensive, overripe, perished, polluted, purulent, pustular, putrescent, putrid, putrified, rancid, rank, rotting, smelling, sour, spoiled, stale, stinking, strong, tainted, touched, unsound; SEE CONCEPTS *462,485*

rotten [adj2] *dishonest, immoral*
bent, bribable, contaminated, corrupt, crooked, debauched, deceitful, defiled, degenerate, depraved, dirtied, dishonorable, disloyal, faithless, filthy, flagitious, impure, mercenary, nefarious, perfidious, perverse, polluted, soiled, sullied, tainted, treacherous, unclean, untrustworthy, venal, vicious, villainous, vitiated; SEE CONCEPTS *404,545*

rotten [adj3] *despicable, inferior, bad*
amiss, base, below par, bruised, bum, contemptible, crummy*, defective, deplorable, dirty, disagreeable, disappointing, diseased, displeasing, dissatisfactory, filthy, impaired, inadequate, injured, lousy*, lowgrade, mean, nasty, poor, punk*, regrettable, rough, scurrilous, shaky, sorry, sour, substandard, unacceptable, unfortunate, unhappy, unlucky, unpleasant, unsatisfactory, unsound, vile, wasted, wicked, withering, wrong; SEE CONCEPTS *570,571,574*

rough [adj1] *uneven, irregular*
asperous, bearded, brambly, bristly, broken, bumpy, bushy, chapped, choppy, coarse, cragged, craggy, cross-grained, disheveled, fuzzy, hairy, harsh, jagged, knobby, knotty, nappy, nodular, not smooth, ridged, rocky, ruffled, rugged, scabrous, scraggy, shaggy, sharp, stony, tangled, tousled, tufted, unequal, uneven, unfinished, unlevel, unshaven, unshorn, woolly, wrinkled, wrinkly; SEE CONCEPTS *485,606*

rough [adj2] *stormy; not quiet*
agitated, blustering, blustery, boisterous, buffeting, cacophonous, choppy, coarse, discordant, dry, furious, grating, gruff, harsh, hoarse, husky, inclement, inharmonious, jarring, raging, rasping, raucous, rugged, squally, stridulent, tempestuous, tumultous/tumultuous, turbulent, unmusical, wild; SEE CONCEPTS *525,592,594*

rough [adj3] *rude, impolite*
bearish, bluff, blunt, boisterous, boorish, brief, brusque, churlish, coarse, crass, crude, cruel, crusty, curt, discourteous, drastic, extreme, gross*, hairy*, hard, harsh, ill-mannered, improper, inconsiderate, indecorous, indelicate, inelegant, loud, loutish, mean, nasty, raw, rowdy, severe, sharp, short, tough, unceremonious, uncivil, uncouth, uncultivated, uncultured, unfeeling, ungracious, unjust, unmannerly, unpleasant, unpolished, unrefined, untutored, violent, vulgar; SEE CONCEPTS *267,401*

rough [adj4] *basic, incomplete*
austere, crude, cursory, formless, hard, imperfect, raw, rough-and-ready*, roughhewn*, rudimentary, shapeless, sketchy, spartan, uncompleted, uncut, undressed, unfashioned, unfinished, unformed, unhewn, unpolished, unprocessed, unrefined, unwrought; SEE CONCEPT *531*

rough [*adj5*] *approximate*
amorphous, estimated, foggy, general, hazy, imprecise, inexact, proximate, rude, sketchy, uncertain, unprecise, vague; SEE CONCEPT *557*

rough out [*v*] *do preliminary design*
adumbrate, block out, chalk, characterize, delineate, draft, outline, plan, skeleton, sketch, suggest; SEE CONCEPTS *36,79,174*

rough up [*v*] *beat up*
bash, batter, hit, knock about, knock around, maltreat, manhandle, mistreat, roughhouse, slap around, thrash; SEE CONCEPTS *189,246*

round [*n1*] *globe, ball; semicircular area*
arc, arch, band, bend, bow, circle, circlet, curvation, curvature, curve, disc, disk, equator, eye, gyre, hoop, loop, orb, orbit, ring, ringlet, sphere, wheel; SEE CONCEPT *436*

round [*n2*] *cycle, stage*
ambit, beat, bout, circuit, circulation, circumvolution, compass, course, division, gyration, lap, level, performance, period, revolution, rotation, round trip, routine, schedule, sequence, series, session, succession, tour, turn, wheel, whirl; SEE CONCEPTS *364, 727,807*

round [*n3*] *unit of ammunition*
bullet, cartridge, charge, discharge, load, shell, shot; SEE CONCEPTS *498,500*

round [*adj1*] *ball-shaped; semicircular area*
annular, arced, arched, arciform, bent, bowed, bulbous, circular, coiled, curled, curved, curvilinear, cylindrical, discoid, disk-shaped, domical, egg-shaped, elliptical, globose, globular, looped, orbed, orbicular, orbiculate, oval, ringed, rotund, rounded, spherical, spheroid, spiral; SEE CONCEPT *486*

round [*adj2*] *complete*
accomplished, done, entire, finished, full, rounded, solid, unbroken, undivided, whole; SEE CONCEPT *531*

round [*adj3*] *full-bodied, ample in size*
chubby*, expansive, fleshy, generous, large, plump, plumpish, pudgy*, roly-poly*, rotund, rounded, tubby*; SEE CONCEPTS *491,773*

round [*adj4*] *resonant, rich in sound*
consonant, full, mellifluous, orotund, plangent, resounding, ringing, rotund, sonorous, vibrant; SEE CONCEPT *594*

round [*adj5*] *honest, direct*
blunt, candid, frank, free, outspoken, plain, straightforward, unmodified, vocal; SEE CONCEPT *267*

round [*v1*] *turn; encircle*
begird, bypass, circle, circulate, circumnavigate, compass, encompass, flank, gird, girdle, go around, gyrate, hem, pivot, revolve, ring, roll, rotate, skirt, spin, surround, wheel, whirl; SEE CONCEPTS *147,149,187*

round [*v2*] *make curved; remove angles*
arch, bend, bow, coil, convolute, crook, curl, curve, form, loop, mold, perfect, polish, recurve, refine,

shape, sleek, slick, smooth, whorl; SEE CONCEPTS *184,202*

round [*adv1*] *approximate*
about, all but, almost, around, as good as, close to, in the neighborhood of, just about, most, near, nearly, practically, roughly; SEE CONCEPT *762*

roundabout [*adj*] *indirect*
ambiguous, circuitous, circular, circumlocutory, collateral, deviating, devious, discursive, evasive, meandering, oblique, obliquitous, periphrastic, taking the long way*, tortuous; SEE CONCEPTS *559,581,584*

round off [*v*] *finish*
bring to a close, cap, climax, close, complete, conclude, crown, culminate, finish off, settle, top off; SEE CONCEPT *234*

roundup [*n*] *collection, collation*
assembly, branding, gathering, herding, marshalling, muster, rally, summary, survey; SEE CONCEPTS *257,397*

round up [*v*] *collect, gather*
assemble, bring in, bring together, cluster, drive, group, herd, marshal, muster, rally; SEE CONCEPTS *109,257*

rouse [*v1*] *wake*
arouse, awake, awaken, call, get up, raise, rise, stir, wake up; SEE CONCEPT *250*

rouse [*v2*] *stimulate, excite*
aggravate, agitate, anger, animate, arouse, ask for it*, awaken, bestir, bug*, challenge, craze, deepen, disturb, enhance, enliven, exhilarate, fire up*, foment, galvanize, get going, heighten, incite, inflame, innervate, innerve, instigate, intensate, intensify, key up*, kindle, magnify, make waves*, mount, move, needle, pep up*, pique, provoke, quicken, rally, redouble, rile, rise, startle, steam up*, stir, trigger, urge, vivify, wake, waken, wake up, whet, whip up*, work up; SEE CONCEPTS *7,22,244*

rout [*n*] *overwhelming defeat*
beating, cakewalk*, clobbering*, comedown, confusion, debacle, disaster, drubbing*, embarrassment, flight, hiding, overthrow, retreat, romp, ruin, shambles, shutout, thrashing, trashing*, upset, vanquishment, walkover*, washout*, waxing, whipping; SEE CONCEPTS *95,119,363*

rout [*v*] *defeat overwhelmingly*
bash, beat, blow out of water*, bulldoze*, bury*, chase, clean up on*, clobber, conquer, cream*, crush, cut to pieces*, destroy, discomfit, dispel, drive off, expel, finish*, hunt, kill*, lambaste, larrup, murder*, outmaneuver, overpower, overthrow, put to flight*, repulse, scatter, scuttle, shut out*, skunk*, subdue, subjugate, swamp*, torpedo*, total*, trounce, vanquish, wallop, wax*, whip, wipe off map*, wipe out*, worst, zap*; SEE CONCEPT *95*

route [*n*] *path over which someone or something travels*
avenue, beat, beeline, byway, circuit, course, detour, digression, direction, divergence, itinerary,

journey, line, meandering, passage, pavement, pike, plot, program, rambling, range, road, round, rounds, run, short cut, tack, track, trail, wandering, way; SEE CONCEPTS *501,660*

route [*v*] *send along a path*
address, conduct, consign, convey, direct, dispatch, escort, forward, guide, lead, pilot, remit, see, shepherd, ship, show, steer, transmit; SEE CONCEPTS *187,217*

routine [*n*] *habitual activity*
act, beaten path*, bit, channels, custom, cycle, daily grind*, drill, formula, grind*, groove*, habit, line, method, order, pace, pattern, piece, practice, procedure, program, rat race*, rote, round, rut, schtick*, spiel*, system, tack, technique, treadmill, usage, way, wont; SEE CONCEPTS *6,362,770*

routine [*adj*] *habitual*
accepted, accustomed, chronic, conventional, customary, everyday, familiar, general, methodical, normal, ordinary, periodic, plain, quotidian, regular, seasonal, standard, typical, unremarkable, usual, wonted, workaday; SEE CONCEPTS *530,547,548*

row [*n1*] *sequence, series*
bank, chain, column, consecution, echelon, file, line, order, progression, queue, range, rank, string, succession, tier, train; SEE CONCEPTS *432,727,744*

row [*n2*] *fight, ruckus*
affray, altercation, bickering, brawl, castigation, commotion, controversy, dispute, disturbance, falling-out*, fracas, fray, fuss, knock-down-drag-out*, lecture, melee, noise, quarrel, racket, reprimand, reproof, riot, rumpus, run-in*, scrap*, set-to*, shouting match*, squabble, talking-to*, telling-off*, tiff, tongue-lashing*, trouble, tumult, uproar, words*, wrangle; SEE CONCEPTS *46,52,106*

row [*v1*] *move boat with paddle*
drag, oar, paddle, pull, punt, sail, scud, scull, sky an oar, swim*; SEE CONCEPT *187*

row [*v2*] *argue, fight*
bawl out, berate, bicker, brawl, call on the carpet*, dispute, jaw, quarrel, ream, scold, scrap, spat, squabble, tiff, tongue-lash*, wrangle; SEE CONCEPTS *46,106*

rowdy [*n*] *person who is boisterous, noisy*
brawler, bully, hellion*, hooligan*, lout, punk, roughneck*, ruffian, terror*, troublemaker; SEE CONCEPT *412*

rowdy [*adj*] *boisterous, noisy*
disorderly, lawless, loud, loudmouthed, loutish, mischievous, obstreperous, rambunctious, raucous, rebellious, rough, roughhouse, rude, turbulent, unruly, uproarious, wild; SEE CONCEPT *401*

royal [*adj*] *kingly, grand*
aristocratic, august, authoritative, baronial, commanding, dignified, elevated, eminent, grandiose, high, high-born, honorable, illustrious, imperial, imposing, impressive, kinglike, lofty, magnificent, majestic, monarchical, noble, princelike, princely,

queenly, regal, regnant, reigning, renowned, resplendent, ruling, sovereign, splendid, stately, superb, superior, supreme, worthy; SEE CONCEPTS *549,574*

rub [*n1*] *stroke, massage*
abrasion, attrition, brushing, caress, friction, grinding, kneading, pat, polish, rasping, scouring, scraping, shine, smear, smoothing, stroking, swab, swipe, wear, wipe; SEE CONCEPT *215*

rub [*n2*] *difficulty, problem*
bar, catch, crimp, dilemma, drawback, hamper, hindrance, hitch, hurdle, impediment, obstacle, predicament, snag, stumbling block*, traverse, trouble; SEE CONCEPTS *666,674*

rub [*v*] *stroke, massage*
abrade, anoint, apply, bark, brush, buff, burnish, caress, chafe, clean, coat, cover, curry, daub, erase, erode, excoriate, file, fray, fret, furbish, glance, glaze, gloss, grate, graze, grind, knead, mop, paint, pat, plaster, polish, put, rasp, scour, scrape, scrub, shine, slather, smear, smooth, spread, swab, triturate, wear, wear down, wipe; SEE CONCEPT *215*

rubbish [*n1*] *garbage*
debris, dregs, dross, junk, litter, lumber, offal, refuse, rubble, rummage, scrap, sweepings, trash, waste; SEE CONCEPT *260*

rubbish [*n2*] *nonsense*
balderdash*, bilge*, bunkum, drivel, gibberish, hogwash, hooey*, poppycock*, rot*, stuff and nonsense*, tommyrot*; SEE CONCEPTS *230,278*

ruddy [*adj*] *pinkish, blushing*
blooming, blowsy, bronzed, crimson, florid, flush, flushed, fresh, full-blooded, glowing, healthy, pink, red, red-complexioned, reddish, roseate, rosy, rubicund, ruby, sanguine, scarlet; SEE CONCEPT *618*

rude [*adj1*] *disrespectful, rough*
abrupt, abusive, bad-mannered, barbarian, barbaric, barbarous, blunt, boorish, brusque, brutish, cheeky, churlish, coarse, crabbed, crude, curt, discourteous, graceless, gross, gruff, ignorant, illiterate, impertinent, impolite, impudent, inconsiderate, insolent, insulting, intrusive, loutish, low, obscene, offhand, peremptory, raw, savage, scurrilous, short, surly, uncivil, uncivilized, uncouth, uncultured, uneducated, ungracious, unmannerly, unpolished, unrefined, vulgar, wild; SEE CONCEPTS *267,401*

rude [*adj2*] *crude, primitive*
angular, artless, barbarous, callow, coarse, formless, fresh, green*, ignorant, inartistic, inelegant, inexperienced, inexpert, makeshift, primal, raw, rough, roughhewn, roughly made, rudimental, rudimentary, shapeless, simple, uncivilized, unconversant, uncultivated, unfashioned, unfinished, unformed, unhewn, unpolished, unprocessed, unrefined, wild; SEE CONCEPTS *490,531*

rude [*adj3*] *sudden; approximate*
abrupt, guessed, harsh, imperfect, imprecise, inexact, in the ballpark*, proximate, rough, sharp, star-

tling, stormy, surmised, turbulent, unpleasant, unprecise, violent; SEE CONCEPTS *557,799*

rudimentary [*adj*] *basic, fundamental*
ABCs*, abecedarian, basal, beginning, early, elemental, elementary, embryonic, immature, initial, introductory, larval, nuts and bolts*, primary, primitive, simple, simplest, three Rs*, uncompleted, undeveloped, vestigial; SEE CONCEPTS *546,549*

ruffle [*v1*] *mess up*
cockle, confuse, crease, crinkle, crumple, crush, derange, disarrange, discompose, dishevel, disorder, pucker, purse, rifle, rumple, tangle, tousle, wrinkle; SEE CONCEPT *158*

ruffle [*v2*] *upset, irritate*
abrade, agitate, anger, annoy, bluster, bother, browbeat, bully, chafe, confuse, cow*, disconcert, disquiet, disturb, excite, floor*, flummox, flurry, fluster, fret, fuddle, gall, get to*, harass, intimidate, irk, nettle, peeve, perturb, provoke, put off*, put out*, rattle, rattle one's cage*, shake up*, stir, stump, throw into tizzy*, torment, trouble, unsettle, vex, wear, worry; SEE CONCEPTS *7,14,19*

rugged [*adj1*] *bumpy, weathered*
asperous, broken, coarse, craggy, difficult, furrowed, harsh, hilly, irregular, jagged, leathery, lumpy, mountainous, ragged, rocky, rough, rough-hewn, scabrous, scraggy, stark, uneven, unlevel, unpolished, unrefined, unsmooth, weather-beaten, worn, wrinkled; SEE CONCEPTS *490,606*

rugged [*adj2*] *severe, violent*
bitter, brutal, difficult, hard, harsh, inclement, intemperate, rigorous, rough, stormy, tempestuous, turbulent; SEE CONCEPTS *525,537*

rugged [*adj3*] *uncouth, crude*
barbarous, blunt, boorish, churlish, graceless, ill-bred, loutish, rude, uncultured, unpolished, unrefined; SEE CONCEPT *401*

rugged [*adj4*] *difficult, rigorous*
arduous, demanding, exacting, formidable, hairy*, hard, harsh, heavy*, heavy sledding*, knotty*, laborious, large order*, mean, murder*, no picnic*, operose, rough, stern, strenuous, taxing*, tough, trying, uncompromising, uphill*; SEE CONCEPTS *538,565*

rugged [*adj5*] *big, strong*
brawny, burly, energetic, hale, hardy, healthy, husky, indefatigable, lusty, muscular, robust, sturdy, tough, unflagging, vigorous, well-built; SEE CONCEPTS *314,489*

ruin [*n*] *situation of devastation*
atrophy, bane, bankruptcy, bath, belly-up*, breakdown, collapse, confusion, crackup, crash, crumbling, damage, decay, defeat, degeneracy, degeneration, demolition, destitution, destruction, deterioration, dilapidation, disintegration, disrepair, dissolution, downfall, downgrade, extinction, failure, fall, havoc, insolvency, loss, nemesis, overthrow, ruination, skids, subversion, the end*,

undoing, waste, Waterloo*, wreck, wreckage; SEE CONCEPT *674*

ruin [*v*] *devastate, destroy*
bankrupt, beggar, botch, break, bring down, bring to ruin, bust, clean out, crush, decimate, deface, defeat, defile, demolish, deplete, deplore, depredate, desecrate, despoil, devour, dilapidate, disfigure, do in*, drain, exhaust, fleece, impoverish, injure, lay waste, maim, make a mess of, mangle, mar, mutilate, overthrow, overturn, overwhelm, pauperize, pillage, rape, ravish, raze, reduce, sack, shatter, smash, spoil, spoilate, total, use up, wipe out*, wrack, wreak havoc*, wreck; SEE CONCEPTS *234,246,252*

ruinous [*adj*] *disastrous, devastating*
annihilative, baleful, baneful, calamitous, cataclysmic, catastrophic, crippling, damaging, deadly, deleterious, depleting, dire, disastrous, draining, exhausting, extravagant, fatal, fateful, harmful, hurtful, immoderate, impoverishing, injurious, murderous, noxious, pernicious, shattering, suicidal, unfortunate, wasteful, withering, wrackful; SEE CONCEPTS *537,548,570*

ruins [*n*] *buildings that are dilapidated*
ashes, debris, destruction, detritus, foundation, relics, remains, remnants, residue, rubble, traces, vestiges, wreck, wreckage; SEE CONCEPTS *439,733*

rule [*n1*] *standard, principle of behavior*
aphorism, apothegm, assize, axiom, basis, brocard, canon, chapter and verse*, command, commandment, criterion, decorum, decree, decretion, dictum, direction, edict, etiquette, formula, fundamental, gnome, guide, guideline, keynote, keystone, law, maxim, model, moral, no-no's*, order, ordinance, precedent, precept, prescription, propriety, regimen, regulation, ruling, statute, tenet, test, the book*, the numbers*, truism; SEE CONCEPT *687*

rule [*n2*] *leadership of organization*
administration, ascendancy, authority, command, control, direction, domination, dominion, empire, government, influence, jurisdiction, mastery, power, regime, regnancy, reign, sovereignty, supremacy, sway; SEE CONCEPTS *299,376*

rule [*n3*] *method, way*
course, custom, formula, habit, normalcy, normality, order of things, policy, practice, procedure, routine; SEE CONCEPTS *6,647*

rule [*v1*] *govern, manage*
administer, be in authority, be in driver's seat*, be in power, bridle, command, conduct, control, crack the whip*, curb, decree, dictate, direct, dominate, domineer, guide, hold sway*, hold the reins*, keep under one's thumb*, lay down the law*, lead, order, overrule, predominate, preponderate, preside, prevail, regulate, reign, restrain, rule the roost*, run, run the show*, sit on top of*, sway, take over; SEE CONCEPTS *117,298*

rule [v2] *judge, decide*
adjudge, adjudicate, conclude, decree, deduce, determine, establish, figure, find, fix, gather, hold, infer, lay down, pass upon, postulate, prescribe, pronounce, resolve, settle, theorize; SEE CONCEPTS *18,81*

rule out [v] *exclude, reject*
abolish, avert, ban, bate, cancel, count out, debar, deter, dismiss, eliminate, except, forbid, forestall, forfend, leave out, not consider, obviate, preclude, prevent, prohibit, proscribe, recant, revoke, stave off, suspend, ward off; SEE CONCEPTS *25,121*

ruler [n1] *person in charge of organization*
adjudicator, boss, captain, chief, chieftain, commander, controller, crowned head, director, emperor, empress, governor, head, head of state, king, leader, lord, manager, master, mastermind, matriarch, mistress, monarch, patriarch, potentate, prince, princess, queen, regent, senior, sovereign; SEE CONCEPTS *347,354*

ruler [n2] *tool for measuring or calculating length*
folding rule, measure, measuring stick, rule, slide rule, straightedge, T-square, yardstick; SEE CONCEPT *499*

ruling [n] *judgment, decree*
adjudication, decision, directive, edict, finding, judgment, law, order, precept, pronouncement, resolution, rule, ukase, verdict; SEE CONCEPT *318*

ruling [adj1] *dominant, governing*
cardinal, central, commanding, controlling, leading, overriding, overruling, pivotal, regnant, reigning, sovereign, supreme, upper; SEE CONCEPT *574*

ruling [adj2] *prevailing, main*
chief, current, dominant, pivotal, popular, predominant, preeminent, preponderant, prevalent, principal, rampant, rife, widespread; SEE CONCEPT *568*

rumble [v] *growl, thunder*
boom, grumble, resound, roar, roll; SEE CONCEPT *65*

ruminate [v] *think about seriously*
brainstorm*, brood, chew over, cogitate, consider, contemplate, deliberate, excogitate, figure, meditate, mull over, muse, ponder, rack one's brains*, reflect, revolve, stew about*, think, turn over, use one's head*, weigh; SEE CONCEPT *24*

rummage [v] *ransack, search*
beat the bushes*, comb, delve, dig out, disarrange, disarray, disorder, disorganize, disrupt, disturb, examine, explore, ferret out, fish, forage, grub, hunt, jumble, leave no stone unturned*, look high and low*, mess up, mix up, poke, rake, root, scour, search high heaven*, seek, shake, shake down, spy, toss, turn inside out*, turn upside down*; SEE CONCEPTS *158,216*

rumor [n] *talk about supposed truth*
back-fence talk*, breeze*, bruit, canard, clothesline*, comment, cry, dispatch, earful*, fabrication, falsehood, fame, fiction, gossip, grapevine*, hearsay, hoax, innuendo, intelligence, invention, lie, news, notoriety, on-dit*, report, repute, rumble,

scandal, scuttlebutt*, story, suggestion, supposition, tale, tattle, tidings, whisper, wire*, word; SEE CONCEPTS *274,277,278*

rumor [v] *tell a supposed truth*
bruit, buzz*, circulate, gossip, noise about*, pass around, publish, report, say, talk, tattle, whisper; SEE CONCEPTS *49,54*

rump [n] *bottom, posterior of animal or human*
back, backside, beam, behind, breech, bum*, butt, butt end, buttocks, can*, croup, derrière, duff*, fanny*, haunches, hind end, hindquarters, keister*, moon*, prat, rear, rear end, sacrum, seat, tail*, tail end, tush*; SEE CONCEPTS *392,825*

rumple [v] *crush, wrinkle*
bedraggle, cockle, crease, crimp, crinkle, crumple, derange, dishevel, disorder, fold, mess up, muss up, pucker, ruck up, ruffle, screw up, scrunch, seam, tousle, wreathe; SEE CONCEPTS *137,219,250*

run [n1] *fast moving on foot*
amble, bound, break, canter, dart, dash, drop, escape, fall, flight, gallop, jog, lope, pace, race, rush, scamper, scuttle, spring, sprint, spurt, tear, trot, whisk; SEE CONCEPTS *150,195*

run [n2] *journey*
drive, excursion, jaunt, joy ride*, lift, outing, ride, round, spin, tour, travel, trip; SEE CONCEPT *224*

run [n3] *sequence, course*
bearing, chain, continuance, continuation, continuity, current, cycle, drift, duration, endurance, field, flow, line, motion, movement, passage, path, period, persistence, progress, prolongation, round, route, season, series, spell, streak, stream, stretch, string, succession, swing, tendency, tenor, tide, trend, way; SEE CONCEPTS *721,727,738*

run [v1] *move fast on foot*
abscond, amble, barrel, beat it*, bolt, bound, bustle, canter, career, clear out, course, cut and run*, dart, dash, decamp, depart, dog it*, escape, flee, flit, fly, gallop, go like lightning*, hasten, hie, hotfoot*, hurry, hustle, jog, leg it*, light out*, lope, make a break*, make off*, make tracks*, pace, race, rush, scamper, scoot, scorch, scramble, scud, scurry, shag, shoot, skedaddle*, skip, skitter, smoke*, speed, spring, sprint, spurt, take flight, take off, tear, tear out, travel, trot, whisk; SEE CONCEPTS *150,195*

run [v2] *move rapidly, flowingly*
bleed, cascade, course, deliquesce, diffuse, discharge, dissolve, drop, fall, flow, flux, fuse, glide, go, go soft, gush, issue, leak, leap, liquefy, melt, pass, pour, proceed, roll, sail, scud, skim, slide, spill, spin, spout, spread, stream, thaw, tumble, turn to liquid, whirl, whiz; SEE CONCEPT *146*

run [v3] *operate, drive*
act, bear, carry, command, control, convey, go, govern, handle, manage, maneuver, move, perform, ply, propel, tick, transport, use, work; SEE CONCEPTS *225,680*

run [v4] *manage, supervise*
administer, be in charge, be in driver's seat*, be in saddle*, boss, carry on, conduct, control, coordinate, direct, head, head up, helm, keep, lead, look after, mastermind, operate, ordain, oversee, own, pull the strings*, regulate, ride herd on*, superintend, take care of*; SEE CONCEPT *117*

run [v5] *continue, range*
be current, circulate, cover, encompass, extend, go, go around, go on, last, lie, move past, persevere, proceed, reach, spread, stretch, trail, vary; SEE CONCEPTS *651,721*

run [v6] *attempt to be elected to public office*
be a candidate, challenge, compete, contend, contest, hit the campaign trail*, kiss babies*, oppose, politick, race, ring doorbells*, shake hands*, stand, stump, whistlestop*; SEE CONCEPT *300*

run-around [n] *avoidance*
come-off, delay, detour, difficulty, diversion, elusion, escape, escaping, eschewal, evasion, inertia, postponement, roundabout, shunning; SEE CONCEPTS *30,121*

runaway [n] *person who is trying to escape*
absconder, delinquent, deserter, escapee, escaper, fugitive, lawbreaker, maroon, offender, truant, wanted person; SEE CONCEPT *412*

runaway [adj] *out of control*
delinquent, disorderly, escaped, fleeing, fugitive, loose, out of hand*, running, uncontrolled, wild; SEE CONCEPT *401*

rundown [n] *summary*
briefing, outline, precis, recap, report, résumé, review, run-through, sketch, synopsis; SEE CONCEPT *283*

run-down [adj] *shabby, in bad shape*
abandoned, beat-up, below par, broken-down, crumbling, debilitated, decrepit, derelict, deserted, desolate, dilapidated, dingy, dog-eared*, down-at-the-heel*, drained, enervated, exhausted, fatigued, forsaken, frowzy*, in a bad way*, neglected, old, out of condition, peaked, ramshackle, ratty*, rickety, seedy, shabby*, tacky, tattered, tired, tumble-down, uncared-for, under the weather*, unhealthy, untended, used up, weak, weary, worn-out; SEE CONCEPTS *314,485,570*

run down [v] *ridicule*
belittle, criticize, decry, defame, denigrate, depreciate, derogate, detract, diminish, disparage, dispraise, downcry, knock*, make fun of*, opprobriate, revile, speak ill of, vilify; SEE CONCEPTS *52,54*

rung [n] *notch, step*
bar, board, crossbar, crosspiece, degree, grade, level, rod, round, rundle, stage, tread; SEE CONCEPTS *471,744*

run-in [n] *argument*
altercation, bickering, brush, confrontation, contretemps, dispute, encounter, falling-out*, fight, hassle, quarrel, row, set-to*, skirmish, tussle; SEE CONCEPTS *46,106*

run in [v] *arrest*
apprehend, bust, collar, cop*, detain, handcuff, jail, nab, pick up, pinch*, pull in, put the cuffs on*, take into custody, throw in jail*; SEE CONCEPTS *298,317*

running [n] *management of organization*
administration, care, charge, conduct, control, coordination, direction, functioning, handling, intendance, leadership, maintenance, operation, organization, oversight, performance, regulation, superintendency, supervision, working; SEE CONCEPT *117*

running [adj] *continuous, flowing, operating*
active, alive, constant, cursive, dynamic, easy, effortless, executing, fluent, functioning, going, in action, incessant, in operation, in succession, live, moving, operative, perpetual, proceeding, producing, smooth, together, unbroken, unceasing, uninterrupted, working; SEE CONCEPTS *538,560,584*

running [adv] *continually*
consecutively, continuously, night and day*, successively, together, unintermittedly, uninterruptedly; SEE CONCEPTS *482,798*

run out [v] *fail, be exhausted*
be cleaned out*, be out of, cease, close, come to a close, depart, dissipate, dry up, end, exhaust, expire, finish, give out, go, have no more, have none left, lose, peter out*, stop, terminate, tire, waste, waste away, weaken, wear out; SEE CONCEPTS *105,699*

runt [n] *very small person*
dwarf, half-pint*, homunculus, Lilliputian, manikin, midget, peewee*, punk*, pygmy, shrimp*; SEE CONCEPT *424*

run through [v] *use up; waste*
blow, consume, dissipate, exhaust, expend, finish, fritter away, lose, spend, squander, throw away, wash up; SEE CONCEPT *156*

rupture [n1] *break, split*
breach, burst, cleavage, cleft, crack, division, fissure, fracture, hernia, herniation, parting, rent, schism, tear; SEE CONCEPTS *309,513*

rupture [n2] *disagreement, dissolution*
altercation, breach, break, break-up, bust-up*, clash, contention, detachment, disruption, disunion, division, divorce, divorcement, estrangement, falling-out, feud, hostility, misunderstanding, parting, partition, quarrel, rift, schism, separation, split, split-up*; SEE CONCEPTS *46,388*

rupture [v1] *break open*
breach, burst, cleave, crack, disrupt, divide, erupt, fracture, hold, open, part, puncture, rend, rive, separate, sever, shatter, split, sunder, tear; SEE CONCEPTS *98,246,308*

rupture [v2] *disagree; dissolve union*
break off, break up, come between, disjoin, disrupt, dissect, dissever, disunite, divide, divorce, part,

separate, split, split up, sunder; SEE CONCEPTS *297,384*

rural [*adj*] *country, not urban*
agrarian, agricultural, agronomic, Arcadian, backwoods, bucolic, countrified, farm, georgic, idyllic, natural, outland, pastoral, provincial, ranch, rustic, rustical, simple, sylvan, unsophisticated; SEE CONCEPT *583*

ruse [*n*] *trick, deception*
angle, artifice, blind, booby trap*, curveball*, deceit, device, dodge*, feint, gambit, game, game plan*, gimmick, hoax, imposture, jig*, maneuver, ploy, scenario, sham*, shenanigans*, shift*, stratagem, stunt, subterfuge, switch*, twist*, wile; SEE CONCEPTS *59,674*

rush [*n1*] *hurry, speed*
blitz, charge, dash, dispatch, expedition, flood, flow, flux, haste, hastiness, hurriedness, precipitance, precipitancy, precipitation, race, scramble, stream, surge, swiftness, urgency; SEE CONCEPTS *145,748,818*

rush [*n2*] *attack*
assault, blitz, charge, onslaught, push, storm, surge, violence; SEE CONCEPT *86*

rush [*v1*] *hurry, speed*
accelerate, barrel, bolt, break, career, charge, chase, course, dart, dash, dispatch, expedite, fire up*, fleet, fling, flit, fly, get cracking*, get the lead out*, go like lightning*, haste, hasten, hotfoot*, hurry up, hustle, lose no time*, make haste, make short work of*, press, push, quicken, race, roll, run, scramble, scud, scurry, shake a leg*, shoot, speed up, sprint, step on gas*, streak, surge, tear, whiz*, zip*, zoom*; SEE CONCEPTS *91,150,152*

rush [*v2*] *charge, attack*
capture, overcome, storm, surge, take by storm*; SEE CONCEPT *86*

rust [*n*] *corrosion*
blight, corruption, decay, decomposition, dilapidation, mold, oxidation, rot, wear; SEE CONCEPTS *309,720*

rust [*v*] *corrode*
decay, decline, degenerate, deteriorate, oxidize, stale, tarnish, wither; SEE CONCEPT *469*

rustic [*n*] *person from the country, with little experience*
backwoodsman/woman, boor, cornfed*, country boy/girl, country cousin*, countryman/woman, farmer, hayseed*, hick*, hillbilly, mountaineer, peasant, provincial, redneck*, rural, yokel*; SEE CONCEPT *413*

rustic [*adj1*] *country, rural*
agrarian, agricultural, Arcadian, artless, austere, bucolic, countrified, homely, homespun, homey, honest, natural, outland, pastoral, picturesque, plain, primitive, provincial, simple, sylvan, unaffected, unpolished, unrefined, unsophisticated, verdant; SEE CONCEPTS *583,589*

rustic [*adj2*] *crude, uncouth*
awkward, boorish, churlish, clodhopping, clownish, coarse, countrified, dull, foolish, graceless, ignorant, inelegant, loutish, maladroit, rough, rude, stupid, uncultured, uneducated, ungainly, unmannerly, unpolished, unsophisticated; SEE CONCEPT *401*

rustle [*n*] *whisper, swish*
crackle, crepitation, crinkling, friction, noise, patter, ripple, rustling, sound, stir; SEE CONCEPT *595*

rustle [*v*] *swish, whisper*
crackle, crepitate, crinkle, hum, murmur, patter, sigh, stir, tap, whir, whish, whoosh; SEE CONCEPT *65*

rusty [*adj1*] *corroded*
decayed, oxidized, rust-covered, rusted; SEE CONCEPT *485*

rusty [*adj2*] *out of practice; inexperienced*
deficient, impaired, neglected, not what it was*, sluggish, soft, stale, unpracticed, unqualified, weak; SEE CONCEPT *527*

rut [*n1*] *groove, indentation*
furrow, gouge, hollow, pothole, rabbet, score, track, trench, trough; SEE CONCEPT *513*

rut [*n2*] *routine of daily life*
circle, circuit, course, custom, daily grind*, dead end*, grind*, groove, habit, humdrum*, pace, pattern, performance, practice, procedure, rote, round, system, treadmill, usage, wont; SEE CONCEPTS *6,647*

ruthless [*adj*] *mean, heartless*
adamant, barbarous, brutal, callous, cold, cold-blooded*, cruel, cutthroat, dog-eat-dog*, feral, ferocious, fierce, grim, hard, hard-hearted*, harsh, implacable, inexorable, inhuman, ironfisted, killer, malevolent, merciless, mortal, obdurate, pitiless, rancorous, relentless, remorseless, revengeful, sadistic, savage, severe, stern, stony, surly, unappeasable, unfeeling, unforgiving, unmerciful, unrelenting, unsympathetic, unyielding, vicious, vindictive, without pity; SEE CONCEPTS *401,404*

S

sable [*adj*] *very dark in color*
black, dark, dusky, dusty, ebon, ebony, gloomy, inky, jet, jetty, murky, pitch-black, pitch-dark, raven, somber; SEE CONCEPT *618*

sabotage [*n*] *damage*
demolition, destruction, disruption, impairment, injury, mischief, overthrow, subversion, subversiveness, treachery, treason, undermining, vandalism, wreckage, wrecking; SEE CONCEPTS *86,246,252*

sabotage [*v*] *incapacitate, damage*
attack, block, bollix, break up, cripple, deep six*, destroy, disable, disrupt, do*, do in*, foul up*, frustrate, hamper, hinder, louse up*, mess up*, obstruct, put out of action, put out of commission*, screw up*, subvert, take out*, throw monkey wrench into*, torpedo*, undermine, vandalize, wreck; SEE CONCEPTS *86,246,252*

sack [*v1*] *remove from position of responsibility*
ax*, bounce*, can*, cashier*, discharge, dismiss, drop, expel, fire, give a pink slip*, give marching orders*, give the boot*, kick out, send packing*, ship, terminate; SEE CONCEPT *351*

sack [*v2*] *raid, plunder*
demolish, depredate, desecrate, desolate, despoil, destroy, devastate, devour, fleece, gut, lay waste, loot, maraud, pillage, ravage, rifle, rob, ruin, spoil, spoliate, strip, waste; SEE CONCEPTS *139,252*

sacred [*adj1*] *holy, blessed*
angelic, cherished, consecrated, divine, enshrined, godly, hallowed, numinous, pious, pure, religious, revered, sacramental, saintly, sanctified, solemn, spiritual, unprofane, venerable; SEE CONCEPT *574*

sacred [*adj2*] *protected*
dedicated, defended, guarded, immune, inviolable, inviolate, invulnerable, sacrosanct, secure, shielded, untouchable; SEE CONCEPT *587*

sacrifice [*v*] *give up, let go*
cede, drop, endure, eschew, forfeit, forgo, immolate, kiss goodbye*, lose, offer, offer up, part with, renounce, resign oneself to*, spare, suffer, surrender, waive, yield; SEE CONCEPTS *108,116*

sacrilege [*n*] *irreverence*
blasphemy, crime, curse, desecration, heresy, impiety, mockery, offense, profanation, profaneness, profanity, sin, violation; SEE CONCEPT *645*

sad [*adj1*] *unhappy, depressed*
bereaved, bitter, blue*, cheerless, dejected, despairing, despondent, disconsolate, dismal, distressed, doleful, down, downcast, down in dumps*, down in mouth*, forlorn, gloomy, glum, grief-stricken, grieved, heartbroken, heartsick, heavyhearted, hurting, in doldrums*, in grief, in the dumps*, languishing, low, low-spirited, lugubrious, melancholy, morbid, morose, mournful, out of sorts*, pensive, pessimistic, sick at heart*, somber, sorrowful, sorry, troubled, weeping, wistful, woebegone; SEE CONCEPT *403*

sad [*adj2*] *unfortunate, distressing*
bad, calamitous, dark, dejecting, deplorable, depressing, disastrous, discomposing, discouraging, disheartening, dismal, dispiriting, dreary, funereal, grave, grievous, hapless, heart-rending*, joyless, lachrymose, lamentable, lugubrious, melancholic, miserable, moving, oppressive, pathetic, pitiable, pitiful, poignant, regrettable, saddening, serious, shabby, sorry, tearful, tear-jerking*, tragic, unhappy, unsatisfactory, upsetting, wretched; SEE CONCEPTS *529,548*

sadden [*v*] *upset, depress*
break one's heart*, bring one down*, bum out*, cast down, dampen spirits, damper, dash, deject, deplore, desolate, discourage, dishearten, dispirit, distress, down, drag down*, grieve, make blue, oppress, press, put a damper on*, put into a funk*, throw cold water on*, turn one off*, weigh down*; SEE CONCEPTS *7,19*

sadistic [*adj*] *cruel, perverted*
barbarous, brutal, fiendish, perverse, ruthless, vicious; SEE CONCEPTS *542,545*

sadness [*n*] *unhappiness, depression*
anguish, blahs*, bleakness, blue devils*, blue funk*, broken heart*, bummer, cheerlessness, dejection, despondency, disconsolateness, dismals, dispiritedness, distress, dolefulness, dolor, downcastness, downer*, dysphoria, forlornness, funk, gloominess, grief, grieving, heartache, heartbreak, heavy heart*, hopelessness, letdown, listlessness, melancholy, misery, moodiness, mopes*, mournfulness, mourning, poignancy, sorrow, sorrowfulness, the blues*, the dumps*, tribulation, woe; SEE CONCEPT *410*

safe [*adj1*] *free from harm*
buttoned up*, cherished, coast is clear*, free from danger, guarded, home-free*, impervious, impregnable, in safety, intact, inviolable, invulnerable, maintained, okay*, out of danger, out of harm's way*, preserved, protected, safe and sound, safeguarded, secure, sheltered, shielded, sitting pretty*, snug, tended, unassailable, undamaged, under lock and key*, under one's wing*, unharmed, unhurt, uninjured, unmolested, unscathed, unthreatened, vindicated, watched; SEE CONCEPT *587*

safe [*adj2*] *not dangerous*
certain, checked, clear, competent, decontaminated, dependable, harmless, healthy, innocent, innocuous, innoxious, inoffensive, neutralized, nonpoisonous, nontoxic, pure, reliable, risk-free, riskless, secure, sound, tame, trustworthy, uninjurious, unpolluted, wholesome; SEE CONCEPTS *314,537,548*

safe [*adj3*] *cautious, conservative*
calculating, careful, chary, circumspect, competent, considerate, dependable, discreet, gingerly, guarded, on safe side*, prudent, realistic, reliable, sure, tried and true*, trustworthy, unadventurous, wary; SEE CONCEPTS *401,542*

safeguard [*n*] *protection*
aegis, armament, armor, buffer, bulwark, convoy, defense, escort, guard, screen, security, shield, surety, ward; SEE CONCEPT *712*

safeguard [*v*] *protect*
assure, bulwark, conserve, cover, defend, ensure, fend, guard, insure, look after, preserve, save, screen, secure, shield, shotgun*, watch over; SEE CONCEPT *96*

safety [*n*] *protection from harm*
assurance, asylum, cover, defense, freedom, immunity, impregnability, inviolability, invulnerability, refuge, safeness, sanctuary, security, shelter; SEE CONCEPT *729*

sag [*n*] *drop, decline*
basin, cant, concavity, depression, dip, distortion, downslide*, downswing*, downtrend, downturn, droop, fall, falloff, hollow, list, settling, sink, sink-

age, sinkhole*, sinking, slant, slip, slump, tilt; SEE CONCEPTS *181,698,776*

sag [v] *droop*
bag, bend, bow, bulge, cave in, curve, dangle, decline, dip, drop, drop off, fail, fall, fall away, fall off, flag, flap, flop, give way, hang, hang down, languish, lean, settle, sink, slide, slip, slump, swag, wilt; SEE CONCEPTS *181,698,776*

saga [n] *story, often long*
adventure, chronicle, epic, legend, narrative, soap opera, tale, yarn; SEE CONCEPT *282*

sagacious [adj] *smart, judicious*
acute, apt, astucious, astute, cagey*, canny, clear-sighted, clever, cool*, discerning, discriminating, far-sighted, foxy*, gnostic, heady, hip, insightful, intelligent, keen, knowing, knowledgeable, perceptive, perspicacious, prudent, rational, sage, sapient, savvy, sensible, sharp, shrewd, smooth, sophic, wise, witty; SEE CONCEPT *402*

sail [v] *travel through water, air; glide*
boat, captain, cast anchor, cast off, cross, cruise, dart, drift, embark, flit, float, fly, get under way*, leave, make headway, motor, move, navigate, pilot, put to sea*, reach, run, scud, set sail, shoot, skim, skipper, skirr, soar, steer, sweep, tack, voyage, weigh anchor, wing; SEE CONCEPT *224*

sailor [n] *person who travels by sea*
able-bodied seaman/woman, bluejacket*, boater, boatman/woman, cadet, circumnavigator, deck hand, frogman/woman, hearty*, jack*, lascar*, marine, mariner, mate, middy, midshipman/woman, navigator, old salt*, pilot, pirate, sailorman/woman, salt*, sea dog*, seafarer, seaman/woman, shellback*, shipmate, swab, swabber*, swabbie*, tar*, tarpaulin*, water dog*, windjammer*, yachtsman/woman; SEE CONCEPTS *348,358,366*

saintly [adj] *good, righteous*
angelic, beatific, blameless, blessed, devout, divine, god-fearing, godly, holy, pious, pure, religious, sainted, saintlike, seraph, sinless, upright, upstanding, virtuous, worthy; SEE CONCEPT *404*

sake [n1] *benefit, gain*
account, advantage, behalf, consideration, good, interest, profit, regard, respect, welfare, well-being; SEE CONCEPT *693*

sake [n2] *reason, objective*
aim, cause, consequence, end, final cause, motive, principle, purpose, score; SEE CONCEPTS *659,661*

salary [n] *money paid for work done*
bacon*, bread*, earnings, emolument, fee, hire, income, pay, payroll, recompense, remuneration, scale, stipend, take, take-home*, wage, wages; SEE CONCEPT *344*

sale [n] *exchange of object for money*
auction, barter, business, buying, clearance, closeout, commerce, consuming, deal, demand, disposal, dumping, enterprise, marketing, negotiation, purchase, purchasing, reduction, selling, trade, transac-

tion, unloading, vending, vendition; SEE CONCEPTS *324,345*

salient [adj] *noticeable, important*
arresting, arrestive, conspicuous, famous, impressive, intrusive, jutting, marked, moving, notable, obtrusive, obvious, outstanding, pertinent, projecting, prominent, pronounced, protruding, remarkable, signal, significant, striking, weighty; SEE CONCEPT *567*

sallow [adj] *pale, unhealthy*
anemic, ashen, ashy, bilious, colorless, dull, greenish-yellow, jaundiced, muddy, olive, pallid, pasty, sickly, wan, waxy, yellowish; SEE CONCEPT *618*

saloon [n] *business establishment that primarily serves liquor*
alehouse, bar, barroom, beer joint*, cocktail lounge, dive*, drinkery, gin mill*, hangout*, joint*, night club, place, pub, public house, speakeasy*, taproom, tavern, watering hole*; SEE CONCEPTS *439,448,449*

salt away [v] *save, store up*
accumulate, amass, bank, cache, hide, hoard, invest, lay aside, lay away, put away, put by, put in the bank, save, save for rainy day*, set aside, spare, stash, stockpile; SEE CONCEPT *330*

salty [adj1] *flavored with sodium chloride*
acrid, alkaline, brackish, briny, highly flavored, oversalted, pungent, saliferous, saline, salt, salted, saltish, sour; SEE CONCEPTS *462,613*

salty [adj2] *spicy, colorful*
humorous, lively, piquant, pungent, racy, sharp, snappy, tangy, tart, witty, zestful; SEE CONCEPTS *401,589*

salubrious [adj] *health-giving*
beneficial, good, healthful, healthy, hygienic, invigorating, salutary, sanitary, wholesome; SEE CONCEPTS *560,572*

salute/salutation [n] *greeting, recognition*
address, bow, howdy*, kiss, obeisance, salaam*, tribute, welcome; SEE CONCEPT *38*

salute [v] *greet; honor*
accost, acknowledge, address, bow, call to, congratulate, hail, pay homage, pay respects, pay tribute, present arms, receive, recognize, salaam*, snap to attention*, speak, take hat off to*, welcome; SEE CONCEPTS *38,69,320*

salvage [v] *save, rescue*
deliver, get back, glean, ransom, reclaim, recover, redeem, regain, restore, retrieve, salve; SEE CONCEPT *134*

salvation [n] *rescue, saving*
conservancy, conservation, deliverance, emancipation, escape, exemption, extrication, husbanding, keeping, liberation, lifeline, pardon, preserval, preservation, redemption, release, reprieve, restoration, safekeeping, sustentation; SEE CONCEPT *134*

salve [n] *ointment for relief of pain or illness*
aid, balm, cerate, counterirritant, cream, cure, dressing, emollient, help, liniment, lotion, lubricant, med-

ication, medicine, remedy, unction, unguent; SEE CONCEPTS *311,466*

same [*adj1*] *alike, identical*
aforementioned, aforesaid, carbon*, carbon copy*, clone, coequal, comparable, compatible, corresponding, ditto*, double, dupe*, duplicate, equal, equivalent, indistinguishable, interchangeable, in the same manner, like, likewise, look-alike, related, same difference, selfsame, similar, similarly, synonymous, tantamount, twin, very, Xerox*; SEE CONCEPTS *487,566,573*

same [*adj2*] *unchanging*
changeless, consistent, constant, invariable, perpetual, unaltered, unchanged, unfailing, uniform, unvarying; SEE CONCEPT *534*

sameness [*n*] *likeness, similarity*
adequation, alikeness, analogy, equality, equivalency, identicalness, identity, indistinguishability, monotony, no difference, oneness, par, parity, predictability, repetition, resemblance, selfsameness, standardization, tedium, uniformity, unison, unity, unvariedness; SEE CONCEPTS *667,670*

sample [*n*] *example, model*
bit, bite, case, case history, constituent, cross section, element, exemplification, fragment, illustration, indication, individual, instance, morsel, part, pattern, piece, portion, representative, sampling, segment, sign, specimen, typification, unit; SEE CONCEPTS *688,835*

sample [*v*] *taste, try*
examine, experience, experiment, inspect, partake, savor, sip, test; SEE CONCEPTS *103,616*

sanctify [*v*] *hold in highest esteem*
absolve, anoint, bless, cleanse, consecrate, dedicate, deify, enshrine, glorify, hallow, purify, set apart, worship; SEE CONCEPTS *10,12*

sanctimonious [*adj*] *self-righteous*
bigoted, canting, deceiving, false, goody-goody*, holier-than-thou*, hypocritical, insincere, pharisaical, pietistic, pious, preachy, self-satisfied, smug, stuffy, unctuous; SEE CONCEPTS *401,404*

sanction [*n1*] *authorization*
acquiescence, allowance, approbation, approval, assent, authority, backing, confirmation, consent, countenance, encouragement, endorsement, fiat, go-ahead, green light*, leave, nod, okay*, permission, permit, ratification, recommendation, seal of approval*, stamp of approval*, sufferance, support, word; SEE CONCEPT *685*

sanction [*n2*] *embargo, punishment*
ban, boycott, coercive measure, command, decree, injunction, penalty, punitive measure, sentence, writ; SEE CONCEPT *123*

sanction [*v*] *authorize, confirm*
accredit, allow, approve, back, bless, certify, commission, countenance, empower, endorse, get behind*, give the go-ahead*, give the green light*, give the nod*, go for*, license, okay*, permit, rat-

ify, support, vouch for, warrant; SEE CONCEPTS *50,88*

sanctuary [*n1*] *church; holiest room or area in religious building*
altar, chancel, holy place, sanctorium, sanctum, shrine, temple; SEE CONCEPTS *368,439,448*

sanctuary [*n2*] *place to hide, be safe*
asylum, church, convent, cover, covert, defense, den, harbor, harborage, haven, hideaway, hideout, hole, hole-up*, ivory tower*, oasis, port, protection, refuge, resort, retreat, safe house, screen, shelter, shield; SEE CONCEPTS *515,516*

sanctuary [*n3*] *safe place for wildlife*
asylum, conservation area, game refuge, harborage, national park, nature preserve, park, preserve, refuge, reserve, retreat, shelter; SEE CONCEPT *517*

sane [*adj*] *mentally sound; reasonable*
all there*, balanced, both oars in water*, commonsensical, compos mentis, discerning, fair-minded, fit, having all marbles*, healthy, in one's right mind*, intelligent, judicious, levelheaded, logical, lucid, moderate, normal, of sound mind*, oriented, playing with full deck*, prudent, rational, right, right-minded, sagacious, sage, sapient, self-possessed, sensible, sober, sound, steady, together, well, wise; SEE CONCEPTS *314,402,403*

sanguine [*adj1*] *happy; optimistic*
animated, assured, buoyant, cheerful, confident, enthusiastic, expectant, hopeful, lively, positive, secure, self-assured, self-confident, spirited, undoubtful, upbeat; SEE CONCEPTS *403,542*

sanguine [*adj2*] *reddish; flushed*
bloody, florid, flush, glowing, red, rubicund, ruddy, scarlet; SEE CONCEPT *618*

sanitary [*adj*] *clean, germ-free*
healthful, healthy, hygienic, purified, salubrious, sanative, sterile, uncontaminated, uninfected, unpolluted, unsullied, wholesome; SEE CONCEPT *621*

sanity [*n*] *mental health; soundness of judgment*
acumen, balance, clear mind, common sense, comprehension, good judgment, healthy mind, intelligence, judiciousness, levelheadedness*, lucidity, lucidness, marbles*, normality, prudence, rationality, reason, reasonableness, right mind*, sagacity, saneness, sense, sound mind*, soundness, stability, understanding, wit; SEE CONCEPTS *409,410*

sap [*n*] *stupid person*
chump, dolt, dupe, fall guy*, fool, idiot, jerk, nitwit, pigeon*, simpleton, sucker*, weakling; SEE CONCEPT *412*

sap [*v*] *squeeze out; weaken*
attenuate, bleed, blunt, cripple, debilitate, deplete, destroy, devitalize, disable, drain, enervate, enfeeble, erode, exhaust, impair, prostrate, rob, ruin, subvert, undermine, vitiate, wear down, wreck; SEE CONCEPTS *142,156,240,246*

sappy [*adj*] *foolish, sentimental*
absurd, balmy, bathetic, crazy*, drippy*, idiotic, illogical, insane, loony*, maudlin, mushy*, prepos-

terous, silly, slushy*, soppy*, sticky*, stupid; SEE CONCEPTS *403,542*

sarcasm [n] *mocking remark*
acrimony, aspersion, banter, bitterness, burlesque, causticness, censure, comeback, contempt, corrosiveness, criticism, cut*, cynicism, derision, dig*, disparagement, flouting, invective, irony, lampooning, mockery, mordancy, put-down*, raillery, rancor, ridicule, satire, scoffing, scorn, sharpness, sneering, superciliousness, wisecrack; SEE CONCEPTS *52,54,277,278*

sarcastic [adj] *nasty, mocking in speech*
acerb, acerbic, acid, acrimonious, arrogant, austere, backhanded, biting, bitter, brusque, captious, carping, caustic, chaffing, contemptuous, contumelious, corrosive, cussed, cutting, cynical, derisive, disillusioned, disparaging, disrespectful, evil, hostile, irascible, ironical, mean, mordant, needling, offensive, ornery, salty*, sardonic, satirical, saucy*, scorching, scornful, scurrilous, severe, sharp, smart-alecky*, snarling, sneering, taunting, trenchant, twitting, weisenheiming*; SEE CONCEPT *267*

satiate [v] *stuff, satisfy completely or excessively*
cloy, content, feed to gills*, fill, glut, gorge, gratify, indulge, jade, nauseate, overdose, overfill, pall, sate, saturate, slake, surfeit; SEE CONCEPTS *169,740*

satire [n] *ridicule intended to expose truth*
banter, burlesque, caricature, causticity, chaffing, irony, lampoon, lampoonery, mockery, parody, pasquinade, persiflage, play-on, put-on*, raillery, sarcasm, send-up*, skit, spoof, squib*, takeoff*, travesty, wit, witticism; SEE CONCEPTS *263,271,280*

satirical/satiric [adj] *mocking*
abusive, bantering, biting, bitter, burlesque, caustic, censorious, chaffing, cutting, cynical, farcical, incisive, ironical, lampooning, mordant, paradoxical, parodying, pungent, ridiculing, sarcastic, sardonic, spoofing, taunting; SEE CONCEPT *267*

satisfaction [n] *giving or enjoying a state of comfort, content*
achievement, amends, amusement, atonement, bliss, cheerfulness, comfort, compensation, complacency, conciliation, contentedness, contentment, delight, ease, enjoyment, fulfillment, gladness, good fortune, gratification, happiness, indemnification, indulgence, joy, justice, peace of mind, pleasure, pride, propitiation, recompense, redress, refreshment, reimbursement, relief, reparation, repletion, resolution, reward, satiety, serenity, settlement, vindication, well-being; SEE CONCEPTS *344,410,720*

satisfactory [adj] *acceptable, sufficient*
adequate, all right, ample, A-OK*, appeasing, assuaging, assuasive, average, cogent, comfortable, competent, cool*, decent, delighting, enough, fair, fulfilling, good, good enough, gratifying, groovy*, passable, peachy*, pleasing, satisfying, solid, sound, sufficing, suitable, tolerable, unexceptional, up to snuff*, valid; SEE CONCEPTS *529,558,560*

satisfy [v1] *please, content*
amuse, animate, appease, assuage, befriend, brighten up, captivate, capture, cheer, cloy, comfort, conciliate, content, delight, do the trick*, elate, enliven, entertain, enthrall, exhilarate, fascinate, fill, fill the bill*, flatter, get by, gladden, glut, gorge, gratify, hit the spot*, humor, indulge, make merry, make the grade*, mollify, pacify, placate, propitiate, quench, rejoice, sate, satiate, score, sell, sell on, slake, suit, surfeit; SEE CONCEPTS *7,22*

satisfy [v2] *answer, persuade*
accomplish, appease, assuage, assure, avail, be adequate, be enough, be sufficient, come up to, complete, comply with, conform to, convince, dispel doubt, do, equip, fill, fulfill, furnish, get by, induce, inveigle, keep promise, make good, make the grade*, meet, observe, pass muster*, perform, provide, put mind at ease*, qualify, quiet, reassure, score, sell, serve the purpose*, suffice, tide over*, win over; SEE CONCEPTS *108,140,656*

satisfy [v3] *pay, compensate*
answer, atone, clear up, disburse, discharge, indemnify, liquidate, make good*, make reparation, meet, pay off, quit, recompense, remunerate, repay, requite, reward, settle, square*; SEE CONCEPTS *126,341*

saturate [v] *drench, wet through*
bathe, douche, douse, imbue, immerse, impregnate, infuse, overfill, penetrate, percolate, permeate, pervade, sate, satiate, soak, sop, souse, steep, suffuse, surfeit, transfuse, wash, waterlog; SEE CONCEPT *256*

saucy [adj] *disrespectful*
arch, audacious, bold, brash, brazen, cheeky*, combative, contumelious, flip*, flippant, forward, fresh, impertinent, impudent, insolent, intrusive, meddlesome, minx*, nervy, obtrusive, pert, presumptuous, rude, sassy, smart, smart-alecky*, smug, snippy*, volatile, weisenheiming*, wise; SEE CONCEPTS *267,401*

saunter [n] *stroll*
airing, amble, constitutional, promenade, ramble, turn, walk; SEE CONCEPT *151*

saunter [v] *stroll along*
amble, ankle, dally, drift, linger, loiter, meander, mope*, mosey*, ooze*, percolate, promenade, ramble, roam, rove, sashay, stump, take a stroll, tarry, toddle, traipse, trill, wander; SEE CONCEPT *151*

savage [adj1] *wild, untamed*
aboriginal, ancient, archaic, barbarian, barbaric, bestial, brutal, brute, crude, earliest, feral, ferocious, fierce, first, fundamental, harsh, in a state of nature, lupine, native, natural, nonliterate, original, primary, primeval, primitive, primordial, pristine, rough, rude, rugged, rustic, simple, turbulent, unbroken, uncivilized, uncultivated, uncultured, undomesticated, unmodified, unrestrained, unspoiled, vicious; SEE CONCEPTS *401,485*

savage [adj2] *cruel, vicious*
atrocious, barbarous, beastly, bestial, bloodthirsty, bloody, brutal, brutish, cold-blooded, crazed, demo-

niac, destructive, devilish, diabolical, fell, feral, ferine, ferocious, fierce, frantic, furious, grim, harsh, heartless, hellish, infernal, inhuman, inhumane, malevolent, malicious, merciless, murderous, pitiless, rabid, raging, rapacious, ravening, relentless, remorseless, ruthless, sadistic, truculent, unrelenting, violent, wolfish; SEE CONCEPTS *401,540,542*

save [*v1*] *rescue*
bail out, come to rescue, defend, deliver, emancipate, extricate, free, get off the hook*, get out of hock*, give a break, liberate, pull out of fire*, ransom, recover, redeem, salvage, save one's neck*, set free, spring, unchain, unshackle; SEE CONCEPTS *127,134*

save [*v2*] *economize; set money aside for later use*
amass, be frugal, be thrifty, cache, collect, conserve, cut corners*, deposit, economize, feather nest*, gather, hide away, hoard, hold, husband, keep, lay aside, lay away, maintain, make ends meet*, manage, penny-pinch*, pile up, put by, reserve, retrench, roll back, salt away*, save for rainy day*, scrimp, skimp, sock away*, spare, squirrel*, stash, stockpile, store, stow away, tighten belt*, treasure; SEE CONCEPTS *120,129,330*

save [*v3*] *guard, protect*
conserve, defend, keep safe, keep up, look after, maintain, preserve, safeguard, screen, shield, sustain, take care of; SEE CONCEPTS *96,117*

savings [*n*] *provision for future*
accumulation, ace in hole*, cache, fund, funds, gleanings, harvest, hoard, investment, kitty*, mattress full*, means, money in the bank, nest egg*, property, provision, provisions, rainy day fund*, reserve, reserves, resources, riches, sock, stake, stockpile, store; SEE CONCEPTS *335,340,446,710*

savior [*n*] *person who redeems, aids in time of difficulty*
conservator, defender, deliverer, friend in need*, Good Samaritan*, guardian, guardian angel, hero, knight, liberator, messiah, preserver, protector, rescuer, salvager, salvation; SEE CONCEPTS *370,416*

savor [*n1*] *taste, flavor*
odor, piquancy, relish, salt, sapidity, sapor, scent, smack, smell, spice, tang, tinge, zest; SEE CONCEPT *614*

savor [*n2*] *distinctive quality*
affection, attribute, character, characteristic, excitement, feature, flavor, interest, mark, property, salt, spice, trait, virtue, zest; SEE CONCEPTS *411,543*

savor [*v*] *delight in, enjoy*
appreciate, experience, feel, gloat, know, like, luxuriate in, partake, relish, revel in, sample, sip, smack, smell, taste; SEE CONCEPTS *32,616*

savory [*adj*] *pleasing, delicious in flavor*
agreeable, ambrosial, aperitive, appetizing, aromatic, dainty, decent, delectable, exquisite, fragrant, full-flavored, good, luscious, mellow, mouthwatering, palatable, perfumed, piquant, pungent, redolent,

relishing, respectable, rich, sapid, savorous, scrumptious, spicy, sweet, tangy, tasty, tempting, toothsome, wholesome; SEE CONCEPT *613*

say [*v*] *make declaration*
add, affirm, allege, announce, answer, assert, break silence*, claim, come out with, communicate, conjecture, convey, declare, deliver, disclose, divulge, do, estimate, express, flap*, gab*, give voice*, guess, imagine, imply, jaw, judge, lip*, maintain, make known, mention, opine, orate, perform, pronounce, put forth, put into words, rap*, read, recite, rehearse, relate, remark, render, repeat, reply, report, respond, reveal, rumor, speak, spiel*, state, suggest, tell, utter, verbalize, voice, yak*; SEE CONCEPTS *51,266*

saying [*n*] *maxim, proverb*
adage, aphorism, apophthegm, axiom, byword, daffodil*, dictum, epigram, motto, precept, saw, statement, truism; SEE CONCEPT *278*

scale [*n1*] *graduated system*
calibration, computation, degrees, extent, gamut, gradation, hierarchy, ladder, order, pecking order*, progression, proportion, range, ranking, rate, ratio, reach, register, rule, scope, sequence, series, spectrum, spread, steps, system, way; SEE CONCEPTS *651,744,770,787*

scale [*n2*] *thin covering, skin*
film, flake, incrustation, lamina, layer, plate, scurf; SEE CONCEPTS *399,484*

scale [*v1*] *ascend, climb*
clamber, escalade, escalate, go up, mount, surmount; SEE CONCEPT *166*

scale [*v2*] *measure*
adjust, balance, calibrate, compare, compute, estimate, gauge, graduate, proportion, prorate, regulate, size; SEE CONCEPT *764*

scamper [*v*] *run, dash*
bolt, dart, flee, fly, hasten, hie, hurry, light out, make off, race, romp, rush off, scoot, scurry, scuttle, shoot, skedaddle*, skip, speed, speed away, sprint, tear, trot, whip, zip*; SEE CONCEPT *150*

scan [*v*] *look over, scrutinize lightly*
browse, check, consider, contemplate, dip into*, examine, flash*, flip through, give the once-over*, glance at, glance over, inquire, investigate, leaf through*, look, look-see*, look through, look up and down*, overlook, regard, riff, riffle, rumble, run over, run through, scour, search, size up, skim, study, survey, sweep, take a gander*, take stock of*, thumb through*; SEE CONCEPTS *103,623*

scandal [*n*] *public embarrassment*
aspersion, backbiting, backstabbing, belittlement, calumny, crime, defamation, depreciation, detraction, dirty linen*, discredit, disgrace, dishonor, disparagement, disrepute, dynamite, eavesdropping, gossip, hearsay, idle rumor, ignominy, infamy, mud, obloquy, opprobrium, reproach, rumor, scorcher,

shame, sin, skeleton, slander, tale, talk, turpitude, wrongdoing; SEE CONCEPTS *278,645,674*

scandalous [*adj*] *disreputable*
atrocious, backbiting, calumnious, crying, defamatory, desperate, detracting, detractive, disgraceful, gossiping, heinous, ignominious, infamous, libelous, maligning, monstrous, odious, opprobrious, outrageous, red hot*, scurrilous, shameful, shocking, slanderous, traducing, unseemly, untrue, vilifying; SEE CONCEPT *545*

scant/scanty [*adj*] *inadequate*
bare, barely sufficient, close, deficient, exiguous, failing, insufficient, limited, little, meager, minimal, narrow, poor, rare, restricted, scrimpy, short, shy, skimpy, slender, spare, sparing, sparse, stingy, thin, tight, wanting; SEE CONCEPTS *766,767,789*

scapegoat [*n*] *person who takes blame for another's action*
dupe, fall guy*, goat*, mark*, patsy*, sacrifice, substitute, sucker, target, victim, whipping boy*; SEE CONCEPT *412*

scar [*n*] *blemish from previous injury or illness*
blister, cacatrice, cicatrix, crater, defect, discoloration, disfigurement, flaw, hurt, mark, pockmark, scab, track, wound; SEE CONCEPT *580*

scar [*v*] *mark, hurt*
beat, blemish, brand, cut, damage, deface, disfigure, flaw, injure, maim, mar, pinch, score, scratch, slash, stab, traumatize; SEE CONCEPTS *7,19,137,176,246*

scarce [*adj*] *insufficient, infrequent*
at a premium, deficient, failing, few, few and far between*, in short supply, limited, occasional, rare, scant, scanty, seldom, seldom met with, semioccasional, short, shortened, shy, sparse, sporadic, truncated, uncommon, unusual, wanting; SEE CONCEPTS *541,789*

scarcely [*adv*] *barely*
hardly, imperceptibly, infrequently, just, just barely, only just, rarely, scantily, seldom, slightly; SEE CONCEPTS *541,789*

scare [*n*] *frightened state*
alarm, alert, fright, panic, shock, start, terror; SEE CONCEPTS *230,410*

scare [*v*] *frighten someone*
affright, alarm, awe, chill, daunt, dismay, freeze, give a fright*, give a turn, intimidate, panic, paralyze, petrify, scare silly*, scare stiff*, scare the pants off*, shake up*, shock, spook, startle, strike terror in*, terrify, terrorize; SEE CONCEPTS *7,19,42*

scared [*adj*] *frightened*
afraid, aghast, anxious, fearful, have cold feet*, panicked, panicky, panic-stricken, petrified, shaken, startled, terrified, terror-stricken; SEE CONCEPT *403*

scary [*adj*] *frightening, terrifying*
alarming, bloodcurdling, chilling, creepy, eerie, hair-raising*, hairy*, horrendous, horrifying, intimidating, shocking, spine-chilling*, spooky, unnerving; SEE CONCEPTS *529,548*

scathing [*adj*] *nasty, critical in remarks*
belittling, biting, brutal, burning, caustic, cruel, cutting, harsh, mordacious, mordant, salty*, sarcastic, scorching, scornful, searing, severe, sulphurous, trenchant, withering; SEE CONCEPT *267*

scatter [*v*] *strew, disperse*
besprinkle, broadcast, cast, derange, diffuse, disband, discard, disject, dispel, disseminate, dissipate, distribute, disunite, diverge, divide, expend, fling, intersperse, litter, migrate, part, pour, put to flight*, run away, scramble, separate, set, set asunder, sever, shatter, shed, shower, sow, spend, split up, spray, spread, sprinkle, sunder, take off in directions*, throw around, throw out; SEE CONCEPTS *179,217,222*

scatterbrained [*adj*] *not thinking clearly*
birdbrained*, careless, dizzy, empty-headed*, featherbrained*, flighty, forgetful, frivolous, giddy, harebrained*, illogical, inattentive, irrational, irresponsible, madcap, silly, slaphappy*, stupid, thoughtless; SEE CONCEPT *402*

scenario [*n*] *master plan; sequence of events*
book, outline, pages, plot, résumé, rundown, scheme, sides, sketch, story line, summary, synopsis; SEE CONCEPTS *282,283,660*

scene [*n1*] *setting of a performance or event*
arena, backdrop, background, blackout, display, exhibition, flat, flats, landscape, locale, locality, location, mise en scène, outlook, pageant, picture, place, representation, scenery, seascape, set, setting, show, sight, site, spectacle, spot, stage, tableau, theater, view; SEE CONCEPTS *263,625,628*

scene [*n2*] *part of a dramatic performance*
act, bit, episode, incident, part, piece, routine, shtick, spot; SEE CONCEPT *264*

scene [*n3*] *display of emotion*
carrying-on*, commotion, confrontation, exhibition, fit, fuss, performance, row, tantrum, temper tantrum, to-do*, upset; SEE CONCEPT *633*

scene [*n4*] *field of interest*
arena, business, compass, culture, environment, field, milieu, setting, sphere, world; SEE CONCEPT *349*

scenery [*n*] *surroundings*
backdrop, decor, flat, flats, furnishings, furniture, landscape, mise en scène, neighborhood, properties, props, prospect, set, setting, spectacle, sphere, stage set, stage setting, terrain, view, vista; SEE CONCEPTS *263,628*

scenic [*adj*] *beautiful, picturesque*
breathtaking, dramatic, grand, impressive, panoramic, spectacular, striking; SEE CONCEPTS *485,579*

scent [*n*] *smell, aroma*
aura, balm, bouquet, essence, fragrance, incense, odor, perfume, redolence, spice, tang, track, trail, whiff; SEE CONCEPT *599*

scent [*v*] *detect, smell*
be on the track of*, be on the trail of*, discern, get wind of*, nose, nose out*, recognize, sense, sniff; SEE CONCEPTS *601,602*

schedule [*n*] *plan for one's time*
agenda, appointments, calendar, catalog, chart, diagram, docket, inventory, itinerary, lineup, list, order of business, program, record, registry, roll, roster, sked, table, timetable; SEE CONCEPTS *271,283,660*

schedule [*v*] *plan one's time*
appoint, arrange, be due, book, card, catalog, engage, get on line*, line up*, list, note, organize, pencil in, program, record, register, reserve, set, set up, sew up*, slate, time, write in one's book*; SEE CONCEPTS *36,125*

scheme [*n1*] *course of action*
arrangement, blueprint, chart, codification, contrivance, design, device, diagram, disposition, draft, expedient, game plan, layout, order, ordering, outline, pattern, plan, presentation, program, project, proposal, proposition, purpose, schedule, schema, strategy, suggestion, system, tactics, theory; SEE CONCEPTS *271,625,660*

scheme [*n2*] *plot, maneuver to get result*
action, angle*, brainchild*, cabal, conspiracy, covin, dodge*, frame-up*, game, game plan*, gimmick, hookup*, hustle, hype*, intrigue, layout, machination, picture*, pitch, ploy, practice, proposition, put-up job*, ruse, scenario, scene, setup*, shift*, story, stratagem, subterfuge, tactics, trick*, twist*; SEE CONCEPTS *59,645,660*

scheming [*adj*] *deceitful, sly*
artful, calculating, conniving, crafty, cunning, designing, duplicitous, foxy, slippery, tricky, underhand, wily; SEE CONCEPT *542*

scholar [*n*] *person who is very involved in education and learning*
academic, augur, bookman/woman, bookworm, brain*, critic, disciple, doctor, egghead*, gnome, grind*, intellectual, learned person, learner, litterateur, man/woman of letters, philosopher, professor, pupil, sage, savant, schoolboy/girl, scientist, student, teacher, tool, wise man/woman; SEE CONCEPT *350*

scholarly [*adj*] *academic*
bookish, cultured, educated, erudite, intellectual, learned, lettered, literate, longhair*, scholastic, schooled, studious, taught, trained, well-read; SEE CONCEPT *402*

school [*n1*] *place, system for educating*
academy, alma mater, blackboard*, college, department, discipline, establishment, faculty, hall, halls of ivy*, institute, institution, jail*, schoolhouse, seminary, university; SEE CONCEPTS *287,289*

school [*n2*] *persons receiving education*
academy, adherents, circle, class, clique, denomination, devotees, disciples, faction, followers, following, group, party, pupils, sect, set; SEE CONCEPTS *288,350*

school [*n3*] *body of philosophy on subject*
belief, creed, faith, outlook, persuasion, school of thought, stamp*, way, way of life*; SEE CONCEPTS *349,689*

school [*v*] *teach*
advance, coach, control, cultivate, direct, discipline, drill, educate, guide, indoctrinate, inform, instruct, lead, manage, prepare, prime, show, train, tutor, verse; SEE CONCEPT *285*

science [*n*] *methodical study of part of material world*
art, body of knowledge, branch, discipline, education, erudition, information, learning, lore, scholarship, skill, system, technique, wisdom; SEE CONCEPTS *274,349,360*

scientific [*adj*] *systematic; discovered through experimentation*
accurate, clear, controlled, deductive, exact, experimental, logical, mathematical, methodical, objective, precise, sound; SEE CONCEPT *535*

scintillating [*adj*] *bright, stimulating*
animated, brilliant, clever, dazzling, ebullient, exciting, flashing, gleaming, glimmering, glinting, glittering, lively, shining, smart, sparkling, sprightly, twinkling, witty; SEE CONCEPTS *401,529,617*

scion [*n*] *offshoot, descendant*
begat, branch, brood, child, chip off old block*, graft, heir, issue, junior, offspring, progeny, seed, shoot, slip, sprout, successor, twig; SEE CONCEPTS *414,428*

scoff [*v*] *make fun of; despise*
belittle, boo*, contemn, deride, dig at*, disbelieve, discount, discredit, disdain, flout, gibe, jeer, knock*, laugh at, make light of*, mock, pan*, poke fun at, pooh-pooh*, rag*, rally, reject, revile, ride, ridicule, scorn, show contempt, sneer, tease; SEE CONCEPT *54*

scold [*v*] *find fault with*
abuse, admonish, asperse, berate, blame, castigate, cavil, censure, chasten, chide, criticize, denounce, disparage, dress down*, expostulate, give a talking-to*, jump on*, keep aft, lay down the law*, lecture, light into*, nag, objurate, preach, put down, rail, rake over the coals*, rate, ream, rebuke, recriminate, reprimand, reproach, reprobate, reprove, revail, take to task*, taunt, tell off*, upbraid, vilify, vituperate; SEE CONCEPTS *44,52,54*

scoop [*n1*] *utensil, tool for shovelling*
bail, dipper, ladle, shovel, spade, spoon, trowel; SEE CONCEPTS *493,499*

scoop [*n2*] *previously secret information that is suddenly public*
beat, exclusive, exposé, inside story*, news, revelation, sensation; SEE CONCEPT *274*

scoop [*v*] *dig up; shovel*
bail, clear away, dig, dig out, dip, empty, excavate, gather, gouge, grub, hollow, lade, ladle, lift, pick up, remove, scrape, spade, sweep away, sweep up, take up; SEE CONCEPT *178*

scope [*n*] *extent or range of something*
ambit, amplitude, area, breadth, capacity, compass, comprehensiveness, confines, elbowroom, extension, field, field of reference, freedom, fullness, latitude, leeway, liberty, margin, opportunity, orbit, outlook, play, purview, radius, reach, room, run,

space, span, sphere, wideness; SEE CONCEPTS *651,739,787*

scorch [*v*] *burn*
bake, blacken, blister, broil, char, cook, melt, parch, roast, scald, sear, seethe, shrivel, simmer, singe, stale, stew, swelter, wither; SEE CONCEPTS *249,255*

score [*n1*] *total, points*
account, addition, aggregate, amount, average, count, final count, grade, mark, number, outcome, rate, reckoning, record, result, stock, sum, summary, summation, tab, tally; SEE CONCEPTS *364,784*

score/scores [*n2*] *large group; a great number*
army, cloud, crowd, drove, flock, host, hundred, legion, lot, mass, million, multitude, myriad, rout, swarm, throng, very many; SEE CONCEPT *432*

score [*n3*] *musical arrangement*
charts, composition, music, orchestration, transcript; SEE CONCEPT *262*

score [*n4*] *obligation; account payable*
account, amount due, bill, charge, debt, grievance, grudge, injury, injustice, invoice, reckoning, statement, tab, tally, total; SEE CONCEPTS *332,645*

score [*v1*] *achieve, succeed*
accomplish, amass, arrive, attain, chalk up*, connect, flourish, gain, gain advantage, get*, hit pay dirt*, impress, luck out*, make a killing*, make an impression*, make the grade*, notch, procure, prosper, pull off*, put over*, rack up*, reach, realize, secure, take the cake*, thrive, triumph, win; SEE CONCEPTS *704,706*

score [*v2*] *keep count*
add, calculate, chalk up, count, enumerate, keep tally, rack up, reckon, record, register, tally, total; SEE CONCEPTS *125,764*

score [*v3*] *cut, nick*
cleave, crosshatch, deface, furrow, gash, gouge, graze, groove, indent, line, mark, mill, notch, scrape, scratch, serrate, slash, slit; SEE CONCEPTS *137,176*

score [*v4*] *write a musical arrangement*
adapt, arrange, compose, orchestrate, set; SEE CONCEPTS *79,292*

scorn [*n*] *contempt toward something*
contemptuousness, contumely, derision, despisal, despisement, despite, disdain, disparagement, disregard, jeering, mockery, ridicule, sarcasm, scoffing, scornfulness, slight, sneer, sport, taunting, teasing; SEE CONCEPTS *29,54*

scorn [*v*] *hold in contempt; look down on*
abhor, avoid, be above, confute, consider beneath one*, contemn, defy, deride, despise, disdain, disregard, flout, gibe, hate, ignore, make fun of, mock, put down, refuse, refute, reject, renounce, repudiate, ridicule, run down*, scoff at, shun, slight, sneer, spurn, taunt, trash*, turn back on*, turn nose up at*; SEE CONCEPTS *21,30,52,54*

scoundrel [*n*] *person who is deceptive and uncaring of others*
bad egg*, bad news*, blackguard*, black sheep*, caitiff, cheat, creep, crook, dastard, good-for-nothing*, heel, imp, incorrigible, knave, lowlife*, maggot*, mischiefmaker, miscreant, ne'er-do-well*, rascal, reprobate, rogue, scalawag, scamp, thief, vagabond, villain, wretch; SEE CONCEPT *412*

scour [*v1*] *clean, polish thoroughly*
abrade, brush, buff, burnish, cleanse, flush, furbish, mop, pumice, purge, rub, sand, scrub, wash, whiten; SEE CONCEPT *165*

scour [*v2*] *search thoroughly*
beat, comb, ferret out, find, fine-tooth-comb*, forage, grub, hunt, inquire, leave no stone unturned*, look for, look high and low*, look up and down*, rake, ransack, rout, rummage, seek, track down, turn inside out*, turn upside-down*; SEE CONCEPT *216*

scourge [*n*] *plague, torment*
affliction, bane, correction, curse, infliction, misfortune, penalty, pest, pestilence, punishment, terror, visitation; SEE CONCEPTS *674,675*

scourge [*v*] *beat, punish, often physically*
afflict, belt, cane*, castigate, chastise, curse, discipline, excoriate, flail, flog, harass, hit, horsewhip*, lambaste, lash, penalize, plague, scathe, scorch*, tan*, terrorize, thrash, torment, trounce, wallop*, whale*, whip; SEE CONCEPTS *14,52,122,189*

scout [*n*] *person who is searching, investigating*
advance, adventurer, detective, escort, explorer, guard, lookout, outpost, outrider, patrol, picket, pioneer, precursor, reconnoiterer, recruiter, runner, sleuth, spotter, spy, vanguard; SEE CONCEPTS *348,358*

scout [*v*] *investigate, check out*
case, examine, explore, ferret, have a look-see*, hunt, inspect, look for, observe, probe, reconnoiter, run reconnaissance, rustle up*, search, seek, set eyes on*, spot, spy, stake out, survey, take in, track down, watch; SEE CONCEPTS *103,216,623*

scowl [*n*] *frown*
black look*, dirty look*, evil eye*, glower, grimace; SEE CONCEPTS *185,716*

scowl [*v*] *frown*
disapprove, glare, gloom, glower, grimace, look daggers at*, lour, lower, make a face*; SEE CONCEPT *185*

scram [*v*] *leave quickly*
beat it*, clear out*, decamp, depart, disappear, get lost*, go away, hightail*, make oneself scarce*, make tracks*, scoot*, skedaddle*, take off, vamoose*; SEE CONCEPT *195*

scramble [*n*] *mix-up, confusion*
clutter, commotion, competition, conglomeration, free-for-all*, hash*, hassle, hustle, jumble, jungle, litter, melee, mishmash, muddle, race, rat race*, rush, shuffle, struggle, tumble, tussle; SEE CONCEPTS *230,388,432*

scramble [*v*] *race; get into position clumsily*
clamber, climb, contend, crawl, hasten, jockey for position*, jostle, look alive*, make haste, move, push, run, rush, scrabble, scurry, scuttle, strive, struggle, swarm, trek, vie; SEE CONCEPTS *87,150*

scrap [*n1*] *tiny bit of something*
atom, bite, bits and pieces*, butt, castoff, chip, chunk, crumb, cutting, discard, end, fragment, glob, gob, grain, hunk, iota, jot, junk, leaving, leftover, lump, mite, modicum, morsel, mouthful, odds and ends*, orts, part, particle, piece, portion, remains, shred, slice, sliver, smithereen*, snatch, snippet, speck, stump, trace, waste; SEE CONCEPTS *831,835*

scrap [*n2*] *argument, fight*
affray, battle, brawl, broil*, disagreement, dispute, fracas, fray, quarrel, row, scuffle, set-to*, squabble, tiff*, wrangle; SEE CONCEPTS *46,106*

scrap [*v1*] *abandon; throw away*
abandon, break up, cast, chuck, consign to heap*, demolish, discard, dismiss, dispense with, ditch, do away with*, drop, forsake, get rid of*, jettison, junk, put to pasture*, reject, retire, shed, slough, throw out, toss out, write off; SEE CONCEPTS *121,180*

scrap [*v2*] *fight, argue*
battle, bicker, caterwaul, come to blows*, fall out, have shouting match*, have words*, quarrel, row, spat, squabble, tiff, wrangle; SEE CONCEPTS *46,106*

scrape [*n*] *bad or embarrassing situation*
awkward situation, corner*, difficulty, dilemma, discomfiture, distress, embarrassment, fix*, hole*, jam*, mess*, pickle*, plight, predicament, tight spot*, trouble; SEE CONCEPT *674*

scrape [*v1*] *scratch, remove outer layer*
abrade, bark, bray, chafe, clean, erase, file, grate, graze, grind, irritate, pare, peel, rasp, rub, scour, scuff, shave, skin, squeak, thin, triturate; SEE CONCEPTS *165,186,215*

scrape [*v2*] *be very frugal*
cut it close, get along, get by, have a close shave*, pinch, save, scrimp, shave, skimp, stint, struggle; SEE CONCEPT *330*

scratch [*n*] *small cut or mark*
blemish, claw mark, gash, graze, hurt, laceration, score, scrape; SEE CONCEPTS *309,513*

scratch [*v1*] *cut; make a mark on*
claw, damage, etch, grate, graze, incise, lacerate, mark, prick, rasp, rub, scarify, score, scrape, scrawl, scribble; SEE CONCEPTS *79,176*

scratch [*v2*] *cancel*
annul, delete, eliminate, erase, pull, pull out, strike, withdraw; SEE CONCEPT *121*

scrawl [*v*] *write erratically*
doodle, inscribe, scrabble, scratch, scribble, squiggle; SEE CONCEPT *79*

scrawny [*adj*] *unhealthily thin*
angular, bony, gaunt, lank, lanky, lean, rawboned, scraggy, skeletal, skin-and-bones*, skinny, spare, undernourished, underweight; SEE CONCEPTS *490, 491,773*

scream [*n1*] *outcry*
cry, high-pitched sound, holler, howl, screech, shriek, wail, yell, yelp; SEE CONCEPT *595*

scream [*n2*] *person or thing that is very funny*
card*, character*, comedian, comic, entertainer, guffaw*, hoot*, howl*, joker, laugh, panic, riot, sensation, sidesplitter*, wit*; SEE CONCEPTS *423,529*

scream [*v*] *cry out*
bawl, bellow, blare, caterwaul, holler, howl, jar, roar, screak, screech, shout, shriek, shrill, sing out, squeal, voice, wail, yell, yip, yowl; SEE CONCEPT *77*

screen [*n*] *protection used in or as furniture, motion picture display*
awning, canopy, cloak, concealment, cover, covering, curtain, divider, envelope, guard, hedge, mantle, mask, net, partition, security, shade, shelter, shield, shroud, veil; SEE CONCEPTS *277,440,443, 445,473*

screen [*v1*] *hide, protect*
blind, block out, bulwark, bury, cache, camouflage, cloak, close, conceal, cover, cover up, defend, disguise, ensconce, fend, guard, inumbrate, mask, obscure, obstruct, safeguard, seclude, secrete, secure, separate, shade, shadow, shelter, shield, shroud, shut off, shut out, shutter, stash, umbrage, veil, wall off; SEE CONCEPTS *96,188*

screen [*v2*] *examine and choose*
cull, eliminate, evaluate, extract, filter, gauge, grade, pick out, process, riddle, scan, select, separate, sieve, sift, sort, winnow; SEE CONCEPT *41*

screw [*v1*] *twist in*
spiral, tighten, turn, twine, wind, work; SEE CONCEPTS *85,160*

screw [*v2*] *twist, contort*
contract, crimp, crinkle, crumple, distort, pucker, rimple, ruck up, rumple, scrunch, wrinkle; SEE CONCEPT *219*

screw [*v3*] *pressure*
bilk, bleed, cheat, chisel, coerce, constrain, defraud, do*, exact, extort, extract, force, gyp*, hold a knife to*, oppress, pinch*, pressurize, put screws to*, ream*, shake down*, squeeze, wrench, wrest, wring; SEE CONCEPTS *14,192*

screw up [*v*] *make a mess of*
blow, bobble, bollix*, botch, bungle, confuse, flub*, foul up*, goof*, goof up*, louse, make hash of*, mess, mess up, mishandle, mismanage, muck up*, muddle, muff, queer, snafu*, spoil; SEE CONCEPT *101*

script [*n1*] *handwriting*
calligraphy, characters, chirography, fist, hand, letters, longhand, penmanship, writing; SEE CONCEPTS *79,284*

script [*n2*] *story for a performance*
article, book, copy, dialogue, libretto, lines, manuscript, playbook, scenario, text, typescript, words; SEE CONCEPTS *263,271*

scrounge [*v*] *beg, forage for*
bum, freeload, hunt, sponge, wheedle; SEE CONCEPTS *48,216*

scrub [*v1*] *clean with force*
abrade, brush, buff, cleanse, mop, polish, rub, scour, wash; SEE CONCEPT *165*

scrub [v2] *cancel*
abandon, abolish, abort, call off, delete, discontinue, do away with, drop, forget about, give up; SEE CONCEPTS *121,234*

scruffy [adj] *rough, bedraggled*
badly groomed, frowzy*, mangy*, messy, ragged, run-down, seedy, shabby, slovenly, tacky*, tattered, threadbare, ungroomed, unkempt, untidy; SEE CONCEPTS *485,589*

scrumptious [adj] *delicious*
ambrosial, appetizing, delectable, delightful, exquisite, heavenly, inviting, luscious, lush, magnificent, mouthwatering, rich, succulent, tasty, yummy; SEE CONCEPTS *529,613*

scruple [n] *misgiving, doubt*
anxiety, caution, censor, compunction, conscience, demur, difficulty, faltering, hesitancy, hesitation, pause, perplexity, qualm, reconsideration, reluctance, reluctancy, second thought*, squeamishness, superego, twinge, uneasiness; SEE CONCEPTS *532,690*

scruple [v] *balk, have misgivings*
be loath, be reluctant, be unwilling, boggle, demur, doubt, falter, fret, gag, have qualms, hesitate, question, shy, stick, stickle, stumble, think twice about*, vacillate, waver, worry; SEE CONCEPT *21*

scrupulous [adj] *extremely careful*
conscientious, conscionable, critical, exact, fastidious, fussy, heedful, honest, honorable, just, meticulous, minute, moral, nice, painstaking, particular, precise, principled, punctilious, punctual, right, rigorous, strict, thinking twice*, true, upright; SEE CONCEPTS *401,538,542*

scrutinize [v] *examine closely*
analyze, burn up, candle, canvass, case, check, check out, check over, comb*, consider, contemplate, dig, dissect, explore, eyeball*, fine-toothcomb*, get a load of*, inquire into, inspect, investigate, look over, overlook, peg*, penetrate, perlustrate, peruse, pierce, pore over, probe, put under microscope*, scan, scope, scrutinate, search, sift, smoke*, stare, study, survey, take the measure of, view, watch, weigh; SEE CONCEPTS *24,103, 623*

scrutiny [n] *close examination*
analysis, audit, close-up, eagle eye*, exploration, inquiry, inspection, investigation, long hard look*, perlustration, perusal, review, scan, search, sifting, study, surveillance, survey, tab*, the eye*, view; SEE CONCEPTS *24,103,623*

scuffle [n] *fight*
affray, brawl, broil, commotion, disturbance, fracas, fray, fuss*, go*, jump, mix-up, row*, ruckus, ruction, rumpus, scrap, set-to*, shuffle, strife, tussle, wrangle; SEE CONCEPT *106*

scuffle [v] *fight*
clash, come to blows, contend, cuff, grapple, jostle, skirmish, struggle, tussle, wrestle; SEE CONCEPT *106*

sculpture [v] *form a three-dimensional art object*
carve, cast, chisel, cut, engrave, fashion, hew, model, mold, sculp, sculpt, shape; SEE CONCEPTS *137,174,184*

scum [n1] *superficial impurities, dirt*
algae, crust, dross, film, froth, residue, scruff, spume, waste; SEE CONCEPT *260*

scum [n2] *people who are bad, despicable*
curs*, dregs*, lowest*, mass, mob, proletariat, rabble, riffraff, rubbish*, scum of the earth*, trash*, unwashed, vermin; SEE CONCEPT *412*

scurrilous [adj] *foul-mouthed, vulgar*
abusive, coarse, contumelious, defamatory, dirty*, filthy*, foul, gross*, indecent, infamous, insulting, invective, lewd, low*, nasty, obscene, offending, offensive, opprobrious, outrageous, raunchy, ribald, salacious, scabrous, scandalous, shameless, slanderous, smutty*, truculent, vituperative, vituperatory, vituperous; SEE CONCEPTS *267,542,545*

scurry [v] *move along swiftly*
barrel, bustle, dart, dash, dust, fly, hasten, hop along, hurry, race, rip, run, rush, scamper, scoot, scud, scutter, scuttle, shoot, skim, sprint, step along, tear, whirl, whisk, zip*; SEE CONCEPT *150*

sea [n] *large body of water; large mass*
abundance, blue*, bounding main*, brine, briny*, briny deep*, Davy Jones' locker*, deep, drink*, expanse, lake, main, multitude, number, ocean, plethora, pond, profusion, sheet, splash*, surf, swell, waves*; SEE CONCEPT *514*

seal [n] *authentication; stamp*
allowance, assurance, attestation, authorization, cachet, confirmation, imprimatur, insignia, notification, permission, permit, ratification, signet, sticker, tape, tie; SEE CONCEPTS *284,685*

seal [v1] *make airtight*
close, cork, enclose, fasten, gum, isolate, paste, plaster, plug, quarantine, secure, segregate, shut, stop, stopper, stop up, waterproof; SEE CONCEPTS *85,160*

seal [v2] *ensure, finalize*
assure, attest, authenticate, clinch, conclude, confirm, consummate, establish, ratify, settle, shake hands on*, stamp, validate; SEE CONCEPTS *234,324*

seam [n] *line where two objects are connected*
bond, closure, connection, coupling, gore, gusset, hem, joint, junction, juncture, pleat, stitching, suture, tuck, union; SEE CONCEPTS *452,471*

seamy [adj] *corrupt, unwholesome*
bad, dark, degraded, disagreeable, disappointing, disreputable, disturbing, low, nasty, rough, sordid, squalid, unpleasant; SEE CONCEPT *545*

sear [v] *dry, burn*
blight, brand, brown, burn up, cauterize, cook, dehydrate, desiccate, dry out, dry up, exsiccate, harden, parch, scorch, seal, shrivel, sizzle, tan, toast, wilt, wither; SEE CONCEPTS *170,249*

search [*n*] *seeking to find something*
chase, examination, exploration, fishing expedition*, frisking*, going-over*, hunt, inquest, inquiry, inspection, investigation, legwork*, perquisition, pursual, pursuance, pursuing, pursuit, quest, research, rummage, scrutiny, shakedown*, wild-goose chase*, witch hunt*; SEE CONCEPT *216*

search [*v*] *seek to find something*
beat, beat about, cast about, chase after, check, comb, examine, explore, ferret, fine-tooth-comb*, forage, frisk, go in quest of, go through, grope, grub, gun for, hunt, hunt for, inquire, inspect, investigate, leave no stone unturned*, look, look for, look high and low*, look over, poke into, probe, prospect, pry, quest, rake, ransack, rifle through, root, rummage, run down, scan, scour, scout, scrutinize, seek, shake down, sift, smell around, study, track down, turn inside out*, turn upside down*; SEE CONCEPT *216*

season [*n*] *time of year governed by annual equinoxes*
division, fall, interval, juncture, occasion, opportunity, period, spell, spring, summer, term, time, while, winter; SEE CONCEPT *814*

season [*v1*] *flavor food*
color, enliven, lace, leaven, pep, pepper, salt, spice, zest; SEE CONCEPT *170*

season [*v2*] *acclimatize, prepare*
acclimate, accustom, anneal, climatize, discipline, fit, habituate, harden, inure, mature, qualify, school, steel, temper, toughen, train; SEE CONCEPTS *35,202*

seasonable [*adj*] *timely, appropriate*
apropos, apt, auspicious, convenient, favorable, fit, opportune, pertinent, propitious, prosperous, providential, relevant, seasonal, suitable, timeous, towardly, welcome, well-timed; SEE CONCEPT *558*

seasoning [*n*] *flavoring for food*
condiment, dressing, gravy, herb, pepper, pungency, relish, salt, sauce, spice, zest; SEE CONCEPTS *457,461*

seat [*n1*] *furniture for sitting, reclining*
bench, chair, chaise lounge, chesterfield, couch, davenport, lounge, loveseat, pew, recliner, settee, settle, stall, stool, wing chair; SEE CONCEPT *443*

seat [*n2*] *central location of organization*
abode, axis, capital, center, cradle, focal point, fulcrum, headquarters, heart, house, hub, location, mansion, nerve center, place, polestar, post, residence, site, situation, source, spot, station; SEE CONCEPT *198*

seat [*n3*] *base, foundation*
basement, basis, bed, bottom, cause, fitting, footing, ground, groundwork, rest, seating, support; SEE CONCEPT *442*

seat [*n4*] *buttocks*
backside, behind, bottom, breech, derrière, duff*, fanny*, fundament*, keister*, posterior, rear, rear end, rump, tush*; SEE CONCEPTS *392,825,827*

seat [*v*] *place in furniture, position*
accommodate, deposit, establish, fix, hold, install, locate, lounge, nestle, perch, plant, put, roost, set, settle, sit, squat, take; SEE CONCEPTS *154,201,384*

secede [*v*] *pull away; split from*
abdicate, apostatize, break with, disaffiliate, leave, quit, resign, retire, retract, retreat, separate, withdraw; SEE CONCEPTS *119,298,384*

seclude [*v*] *isolate, hide*
blockade, boycott, cloister, closet, conceal, confine, cover, embargo, enclose, evict, immure, ostracize, quarantine, retire, screen, segregate, separate, sequester, shut off, withdraw; SEE CONCEPTS *121,135,188*

secluded [*adj*] *isolated, sheltered*
abandoned, alone, aloof, beleaguered, blockaded, cloistered, close, closet, confidential, covert, cut off*, deserted, hermetic, hidden, incommunicado*, insular, isolate, lonely, lonesome, off the beaten track*, out-of-the-way*, personal, private, quarantined, quiet, reclusive, remote, removed, reserved, retired, screened, secluse, seclusive, secret, segregated, sequestered, shut off*, shy, singular, solitary, tucked away*, unapproachable, unfrequented, uninhabited, unsociable, withdrawn; SEE CONCEPTS *401,576,583*

seclusion [*n*] *isolation*
aloneness, aloofness, beleaguerment, blockade, concealment, desolation, detachment, hiding, monkhood, privacy, privateness, quarantine, reclusion, reclusiveness, remoteness, retirement, retreat, seclusiveness, separateness, separation, sequestration, shelter, solitude, withdrawal; SEE CONCEPTS *135,188,388,631*

second [*n1*] *shortest interval of time*
bat of an eye*, flash, instant, jiffy*, moment, nothing flat*, sec*, shake*, split second, twinkling*, wink; SEE CONCEPTS *803,821*

second [*n2*] *support; duplicate*
assistant, backer, double, exponent, helper, placer, proponent, reproduction, runner-up, supporter, twin; SEE CONCEPTS *423,670*

second [*adj*] *next; subordinate*
additional, alternative, another, double, duplicate, extra, following, further, inferior, lesser, lower, next, next in order, other, place, repeated, reproduction, runner-up, secondary, subsequent, succeeding, supporting, twin, unimportant; SEE CONCEPTS *575,585*

second [*v*] *support, advance a suggestion*
aid, approve, assist, back, back up, encourage, endorse, forward, further, give moral support, go along with, promote, stand by, uphold; SEE CONCEPTS *298,324,384*

secondary [*adj1*] *subordinate; less important*
accessory, alternate, auxiliary, backup, bush-league*, collateral, consequential, contingent, dependent, dinky*, extra, inconsiderable, inferior, insignificant, lesser, lower, minor, minor-league*, petty, relief, reserve, second, second-rate*, small, small-fry*, small-time*, subject, subservient, sub-

sidiary, substract, supporting, tributary, trivial, under, unimportant; SEE CONCEPTS *574,575*

secondary [*adj2*] *derivative*

auxiliary, borrowed, consequent, dependent, derivate, derivational, derived, developed, eventual, indirect, proximate, resultant, resulting, second-hand, subordinate, subsequent, subsidiary, vicarious; SEE CONCEPT *549*

second-rate/second-class [*adj*] *inferior, cheap*

cheap and dirty*, common, commonplace, déclassé, hack*, low-grade, low-quality, mean, mediocre, poor, shoddy*, substandard, tacky*, tawdry; SEE CONCEPTS *334,567,574*

secrecy [*n*] *concealment*

clandestineness, confidence, confidentiality, covertness, dark, darkness, furtiveness, hiding, hush, isolation, mystery, privacy, reticence, retirement, seclusion, secretiveness, secretness, silence, solitude, stealth, suppression, surreptitiousness; SEE CONCEPT *631*

secret [*n*] *something kept hidden, unrevealed*

classified information, code, confidence, confidential information, enigma, formula, key, magic number*, mystery, occult, oracle, password, privileged information, puzzle, skeleton in cupboard*, unknown; SEE CONCEPTS *274,631*

secret [*adj1*] *hidden, unrevealed*

abstruse, ambiguous, arcane, backdoor, camouflaged, classified, cloak-and-dagger*, close, closet, clouded, conspiratorial, covered, covert, cryptic, dark, deep, disguised, enigmatical, esoteric, furtive, hush-hush*, mysterious, mystic, mystical, obscure, occult, on the QT*, out-of-the-way*, private, recondite, reticent, retired, secluded, shrouded, strange, undercover, underground, under wraps*, undisclosed, unenlightened, unfrequented, unintelligible, unknown, unpublished, unseen, veiled; SEE CONCEPTS *529,576*

secret [*adj2*] *underhand, clandestine*

backdoor, backstairs, camouflaged, classified, close, confidential, covert, cryptic, discreet, disguised, dissembled, dissimulated, furtive, hush-hush*, in ambush, incognito, inside, restricted, secretive, sly, sneak, sneaky, stealthy, subrosa, surreptitious, top secret, unacknowledged, under false pretense*, underhanded, under-the-table*; SEE CONCEPTS *545,576*

secrete [*v1*] *hide*

bury, cache, conceal, cover, cover up, deposit, disguise, ditch, ensconce, finesse, harbor, hide out, keep quiet, keep secret, keep to oneself, keep under wraps*, palm*, paper, plant, screen, seclude, secure, shroud, squirrel*, stash, stash away, stonewall*, stow, sweep under rug*, veil, whitewash*, withhold; SEE CONCEPTS *188,266*

secrete [*v2*] *give off, emit*

discharge, emanate, excrete, extravasate, extrude, exude, perspire, produce, sweat; SEE CONCEPTS *146,179*

secretive [*adj*] *uncommunicative*

backstairs*, buttoned up*, cagey, clammed up*, close, close-mouthed*, covert, cryptic, enigmatic, feline, furtive, hushed, in chambers*, in privacy*, in private, in the background*, in the dark*, on the QT*, reserved, reticent, silent, taciturn, tight-lipped*, undercover, unforthcoming, withdrawn, zipped*; SEE CONCEPTS *267,548*

secretly [*adv*] *in hidden manner*

behind closed doors*, behind someone's back*, by stealth, clandestinely, confidentially, covertly, furtively, hush-hush*, in camera*, in confidence*, in holes and corners*, in secret, insidiously, in strict confidence, intimately, obscurely, on the QT*, on the quiet*, on the sly*, personally, privately, privily, quietly, slyly, stealthily, sub rosa, surreptitiously, underhandedly, under the table*, unobserved; SEE CONCEPTS *267,548*

sect [*n*] *school of thought*

camp, church, communion, connection, creed, crew, cult, denomination, division, faction, faith, following, group, order, party, persuasion, religion, school, splinter group, team, wing; SEE CONCEPTS *381,382*

sectarian [*n*] *person who is narrow-minded*

adherent, bigot, cohort, disciple, dissenter, dissident, dogmatist, extremist, fanatic, henchman/woman, heretic, maverick, misbeliever, nonconformist, partisan, radical, rebel, revolutionary, satellite, schismatic, separatist, supporter, true believer, zealot; SEE CONCEPTS *359,423*

sectarian [*adj*] *narrow-minded, exclusive*

bigoted, clannish, cliquish, dissident, doctrinaire, dogmatic, factional, fanatic, fanatical, hidebound, insular, limited, local, nonconforming, nonconformist, parochial, partisan, provincial, rigid, schismatic, skeptical, small-town*, splinter; SEE CONCEPT *403*

section [*n*] *division, portion*

area, belt, bite, branch, category, chunk, classification, component, cross section, cut, department, district, drag, end, field, fraction, fragment, hunk, installment, locality, lump, member, moiety, parcel, part, passage, piece, precinct, quarter, region, sample, sector, segment, share, slice, slot, sphere, split, subdivision, territory, tier, tract, vicinity, zone; SEE CONCEPT *835*

sectional [*adj*] *localized, divided*

exclusive, factional, local, narrow, partial, regional, selfish, separate, separatist; SEE CONCEPTS *557,785*

sector [*n*] *area, subdivision*

category, district, division, part, precinct, quarter, region, stratum, zone; SEE CONCEPTS *508,835*

secular [*adj*] *not spiritual or religious*

civil, earthly, laic, laical, lay, material, materialistic, nonclerical, nonreligious, of this world, profane, temporal, unsacred, worldly; SEE CONCEPTS *529,549*

secure [*adj1*] *safe*

defended, guarded, immune, impregnable, out of harm's way, protected, riskless, safe, sheltered,

shielded, unassailable, undamaged, unharmed; SEE
CONCEPT *587*

secure [*adj2*] *fastened, stable*
adjusted, anchored, bound, buttoned down*, fast,
firm, fixed, fortified, immovable, iron, locked,
nailed, safe and sound*, set, solid, solid as a rock*,
sound, staunch, steady, strong, sure, tenacious, tight;
SEE CONCEPT *488*

secure [*adj3*] *certain, definite*
able, absolute, assured, at ease, balanced, carefree,
cinch, conclusive, confident, determined, easy, established, firm, hopeful, in the bag*, locked on*,
nailed down*, on ice*, reassured, reliable, resolute,
sanguine, self-assured, self-confident, settled, shoo-
in*, solid, sound, stable, steadfast, steady, strong,
sure, sure thing*, tried and true*, unanxious, undoubtful, well-founded; SEE CONCEPTS *403,535*

secure [*v1*] *obtain*
access, achieve, acquire, annex, assure, bag*, buy,
capture, catch, chalk up*, cinch, come by, ensure,
gain, get, get hold of, grasp, guarantee, have, hook,
insure, land, lock, lock up, make sure, pick up, procure, rack up*, take, win; SEE CONCEPT *120*

secure [*v2*] *attach, tie up*
adjust, anchor, batten down, bind, bolt, button, button down, catch, cement, chain, clamp, clinch,
close, fasten, fix, hitch, hook on, lash, lock, lock up,
make fast, moor, nail, padlock, pinion, rivet, settle,
slough, tack, tie, tie down, tighten; SEE CONCEPTS
85,160

secure [*v3*] *protect, make safe*
assure, bulwark, cover, defend, ensure, fend, guarantee, guard, insure, safeguard, screen, shield; SEE
CONCEPT *96*

security [*n1*] *safety, protection*
aegis, agreement, armament, armor, asylum, bail,
bond, care, collateral, compact, contract, covenant,
cover, custody, defense, earnest, freedom, guarantee, guard, immunity, insurance, pact, pawn, pledge,
precaution, preservation, promise, protection, redemption, refuge, retreat, safeguard, safekeeping,
safeness, safety measure, salvation, sanctuary, shelter, shield, surety, surveillance, token, ward, warrant; SEE CONCEPTS *712,729*

security [*n2*] *peace of mind*
assurance, calm, certainty, confidence, conviction,
ease, freedom, positiveness, reliance, soundness,
sureness, surety; SEE CONCEPT *410*

sedate [*adj*] *calm, collected*
cold sober*, composed, cool, cool as cucumber*,
decorous, deliberate, demure, dignified, dispassionate, earnest, grave, imperturbable, laid-back*, no-
nonsense, placid, proper, quiet, seemly, serene,
serious, sober, solemn, somber, staid, steady, tranquil, unflappable, unruffled; SEE CONCEPTS *404,542*

sedative [*n*] *soothing agent, medicine*
analgesic, anodyne, barbiturate, calmant, calmative,
depressant, dope*, downer, drug, hypnotic, knock-

out pill, medication, narcotic, nerve medicine, opiate, pacifier, pain-killer, pain pill*, quietive, sleeping
pill, tranquilizer; SEE CONCEPT *307*

sedative [*adj*] *soothing*
allaying, anodyne, calmative, calming, lenitive, relaxing, sleep-inducing, soporific, tranquillizing; SEE
CONCEPT *537*

sedentary [*adj*] *motionless, lazy*
desk, desk-bound, idle, inactive, seated, settled, sitting, sluggish, stationary, torpid; SEE CONCEPTS
542,584

sediment [*n*] *solid residue from liquid solution*
debris, deposit, dregs, dross, gook, grounds, gunk,
lees, matter, powder, precipitate, precipitation, residuum, settling, silt, slag, solids, trash, waste; SEE
CONCEPT *260*

seduce [*v*] *tempt, ensnare*
abduct, allure, attract, bait, beguile, betray, bribe,
captivate, coax, corrupt, debauch, deceive, decoy,
defile, deflower, delude, demoralize, deprave, draw,
entice, entrance, entrap, hook, induce, inveigle, invite, lead astray*, lead on*, lure, mislead, mousetrap*, overpower, overwhelm, pervert, pull, ravish,
rope in, ruin, score, steer, stimulate, string along*,
sucker*, tease, vamp, violate, wheedle; SEE CON-
CEPTS *11,375*

seductive [*adj*] *alluring, sexy*
attracting, attractive, beguiling, bewitching, captivating, charming, come-hither*, desirable, drawing,
enchanting, enticing, fascinating, flirtatious, inviting, irresistible, magnetic, provocative, ravishing, siren, specious, tempting; SEE CONCEPTS *372,579*

see [*v1*] *perceive with eyes*
beam, be apprised of, behold, catch a glimpse of,
catch sight of, clock*, contemplate, descry, detect,
discern, distinguish, espy, examine, eye, flash, gape,
gawk, gaze, get a load of*, glare, glimpse, heed,
identify, inspect, lay eyes on*, look, look at, make
out, mark, mind, note, notice, observe, pay attention
to, peek, peep, peer, peg*, penetrate, pierce, recognize, regard, remark, scan, scope, scrutinize, sight,
spot, spy, stare, survey, take notice, view, watch,
witness; SEE CONCEPTS *590,626*

see [*v2*] *appreciate, comprehend*
appraise, ascertain, behold, catch, catch on, conceive, descry, determine, discern, discover, distinguish, envisage, envision, espy, experience, fancy,
fathom, feature, feel, find out, follow, get, get the
drift*, get the hang of*, grasp, have, hear, imagine,
investigate, know, learn, make out, mark, mind,
note, notice, observe, perceive, ponder, realize, recognize, remark, study, suffer, sustain, take in, think,
tumble, undergo, understand, unearth, view, visualize, weigh; SEE CONCEPTS *15,31,43*

see [*v3*] *accompany, guide*
associate with, attend, bear company, call, come by,
come over, conduct, consort with, date, direct, drop
by, drop in, encounter, escort, go out with, go with,

keep company with, lead, look up, meet, pilot, pop in, receive, route, run into, shepherd, show, speak to, steer, stop by, stop in, take out, usher, visit, walk; SEE CONCEPTS *187,227,384*

see [*v4*] *visualize*
anticipate, conceive, divine, envisage, envision, fancy, feature, foresee, foretell, imagine, picture, realize, think, vision; SEE CONCEPT *12*

seed [*n1*] *beginning, source*
berry, bud, cell, conceit, concept, conception, core, corn, ear, egg, embryo, germ, grain, image, impression, inkling, kernel, notion, nucleus, nut, ovule, ovum, particle, rudiment, semen, spark, sperm, spore, start, suspicion; SEE CONCEPTS *393,428,648*

seed [*n2*] *children*
begats, brood, descendants, heirs, issue, offspring, posterity, progenitor, progeny, race, scions, spawn, successors; SEE CONCEPT *414*

seedy [*adj*] *run-down, dilapidated*
ailing, beat up, bedraggled, crummy*, decaying, decrepit, dingy, dog-eared*, down-at-the-heel*, drooping, droopy, faded, flagging, frowzy, gone to seed*, grubby, in a bad way*, mangy, messy, neglected, old, overgrown, poor, poorly, ragged, ratty, sagging, scruffy, shabby, sickly, sleazy*, slovenly, squalid, tacky, tattered, threadbare, tired, torn, unkempt, untidy, unwell, used up, wilted, wilting, worn; SEE CONCEPTS *485,570*

seek [*v1*] *look for*
be after, beat the bushes*, bird-dog*, bob for, cast about, chase, comb, delve, delve for, dig for, dragnet, explore, fan, ferret out, fish, fish for*, follow, go after, gun for*, hunt, inquire, investigate, leave no stone unturned*, look about, look around, look high and low*, mouse*, nose*, prowl, pursue, quest, ransack, root, run after, scout, scratch, search for, search out, sniff out*, track down; SEE CONCEPT *216*

seek [*v2*] *try, attempt*
aim, aspire to, assay, endeavor, essay, have a go*, offer, pursue, strive, struggle, undertake; SEE CONCEPT *87*

seek [*v3*] *ask, inquire*
beg, entreat, find out, invite, petition, query, request, solicit; SEE CONCEPT *48*

seem [*v*] *appear; give the impression*
assume, be suggestive of, convey the impression, create the impression, give the feeling of*, give the idea*, have the appearance of, have the aspects of, have the earmarks of*, have the features of, have the qualities of, hint, imply, insinuate, intimate, look, look as if, look like, look to be, make a show of, pretend, resemble, show, show every sign of, sound, sound like, strike one as being, suggest; SEE CONCEPT *543*

seeming [*adj*] *apparent*
appearing, illusive, illusory, ostensible, outward, professed, quasi-, semblant, specious, surface; SEE CONCEPTS *487,573*

seemly [*adj*] *appropriate, suitable*
becoming, befitting, comme il faut*, compatible, conforming, congenial, congruous, consistent, consonant, correct, decent, decorous, fit, fitting, in good taste, meet, nice, pleasing, proper, suited, timely; SEE CONCEPT *558*

seep [*v*] *leak*
bleed, drain, drip, exude, flow, ooze, percolate, permeate, soak, sweat, transude, trickle, weep, well; SEE CONCEPTS *146,179*

seethe [*v*] *be very angry*
be furious, be incensed, be livid, be mad, be on the warpath*, blow one's stack*, blow up*, boil, breathe fire*, bristle, burn, ferment, flare, flip, foam, foam at mouth*, froth, fume, hit the ceiling*, rage, see red*, simmer, smolder, spark, stew*, storm*; SEE CONCEPTS *29,34*

segment [*n*] *part of something*
articulation, bit, compartment, cut, division, member, moiety, parcel, piece, portion, section, sector, slice, subdivision, wedge; SEE CONCEPT *835*

segregate [*v*] *discriminate and separate*
choose, close off, cut off, disconnect, dissociate, divide, insulate, island, isolate, quarantine, select, sequester, set apart, sever, single out, split up; SEE CONCEPTS *21,135,645*

seize [*v1*] *grab, take*
appropriate, catch, catch hold of, clasp, clench, clinch, clutch, compass, embrace, enclose, enfold, envelope, fasten, grapple, grasp, grip, hang onto, hold fast, lay hands on*, lay hold of*, pinch, pluck, snag, snatch, squeeze, take hold of; SEE CONCEPTS *142,164,190*

seize [*v2*] *abduct; take by force*
ambush, annex, apprehend, appropriate, arrest, arrogate, bag, bust, capture, carry off, catch, claw, clutch, commandeer, confiscate, conquer, exact, force, gain, get, grab, grasp, hijack, hook, impound, incorporate, kidnap, lift, nab, nail*, occupy, overcome, overpower, overrun, overwhelm, pick up, pounce, secure, shanghai, snag, snare, spirit away*, subdue, take, take by storm*, take captive, take over, take possession of, throttle, trap, usurp, wrench; SEE CONCEPT *90*

seizure [*n1*] *convulsive attack*
access, breakdown, convulsion, fit, illness, paroxysm, spasm, spell, stroke, throe, turn; SEE CONCEPT *308*

seizure [*n2*] *capture, taking*
abduction, annexation, apprehension, arrest, bust*, collar*, commandeering, confiscation, drop, grab, grabbing, hook*, pinch*, seizing, snatch; SEE CONCEPT *90*

seldom [*adv*] *infrequently*
a few times, every now and then, from time to time, hardly, hardly ever, in a few cases, inhabitually, irregularly, little, not often, not very often, occasionally, on and off, once in a blue moon*, once in a

while, rarely, scarcely, scarcely ever, semioccasionally, sometimes, sporadically, uncommonly, unoften, unusually, whimsically; SEE CONCEPT *541*

select [*adj*] *excellent, elite, preferable*
best, blue-chip*, boss*, choice, chosen, cool*, cream*, culled, delicate, discriminating, eclectic, elect, elegant, exclusive, exquisite, favored, first-class*, first-rate*, handpicked, limited, number one*, pick, picked, posh, preferred, prime, privileged, rare, recherché, screened, selected, selective, special, superior, top, topnotch, tops, weeded*, winner, winnowed, world-class*; SEE CONCEPTS *574,653*

select [*v*] *pick out, prefer from among choices*
choose, cull, decide, elect, make, make a choice, make a selection, mark, name, opt, optate, opt for, peg*, pick, pin down, say so*, single out, slot*, sort out, tab*, tag*, take, tap*, winnow; SEE CONCEPT *41*

selection [*n*] *preference from among choices*
alternative, choice, choosing, collection, culling, draft, druthers*, election, excerpt, option, pick, picking; SEE CONCEPT *529*

selective [*adj*] *discriminating*
careful, choicy, choosy, discerning, discriminatory, eclectic, fussy, judicious, particular, persnickety*, picky, scrupulous, select; SEE CONCEPTS *404,542*

self-centered [*adj*] *absorbed with oneself*
egocentric, egomaniacal, egotistic, egotistical, grandstanding, independent, inward-looking, know-it-all*, narcissistic, on an ego trip*, self-absorbed, self-indulgent, self-interested, self-involved, selfish, self-seeking, self-serving, self-sufficient, stuck on oneself*, swelled head*, wrapped up with oneself*; SEE CONCEPT *404*

self-confident [*adj*] *secure with oneself*
assured, fearless, hotdog*, hotshot*, know-it-all*, poised, sanguine, self-assured, self-reliant, sure of oneself, undoubtful; SEE CONCEPT *404*

self-conscious [*adj*] *insecure with oneself*
affected, anxious, artificial, awkward, bashful, diffident, discomfited, embarrassed, ill-at-ease, mannered, nervous, out of countenance, shamefaced, sheepish, shy, stiff, stilted, uncertain, uncomfortable, uneasy, unsure; SEE CONCEPTS *401,404*

self-control [*n*] *willpower over one's actions*
abstemiousness, aplomb, balance, constraint, dignity, discipline, discretion, poise, repression, reserve, restraint, reticence, self-constraint, self-discipline, self-government, self-mastery, sobriety, stability, stoicism, strength of character; SEE CONCEPT *633*

self-evident/self-explanatory [*adj*] *obvious*
apparent, axiomatic, clear, comprehensible, incontrovertible, inescapable, manifest, patently true, plain, prima facie*, undeniable, understandable, unmistakable, unquestionable, visible; SEE CONCEPTS *529,548*

selfish [*adj*] *thinking only of oneself*
egocentric, egoistic, egoistical, egomaniacal, egotistic, egotistical, greedy*, hog*, mean, mercenary, mi-

serly, narcissistic, narrow, narrow-minded, out for number one*, parsimonious, prejudiced, self-centered, self-indulgent, self-interested, self-seeking, stingy, ungenerous, wrapped up in oneself*; SEE CONCEPTS *404,542*

self-respect/self-esteem [*n*] *pride in oneself*
amour-propre, conceit, confidence, dignity, egotism, faith in oneself, morale, narcissism, self-assurance, self-content, self-regard, self-satisfaction, vanity, worth; SEE CONCEPTS *411,689*

self-righteous [*adj*] *smug*
affected, canting, complacent, egotistical, goody-goody*, holier-than-thou*, hypocritical, noble, pharisaic, pietistic, pious, preachy, sanctimonious, self-satisfied, superior; SEE CONCEPTS *401,542*

self-satisfaction [*n*] *pride, contentment*
complacency, conceit, glow, peace of mind, self-approbation, self-approval, self-pleasure, smugness; SEE CONCEPTS *410,689*

self-satisfied [*adj*] *proud, content*
complacent, conceited, egotistic, flushed, pleased, puffed up*, self-congratulatory, smug, vain; SEE CONCEPTS *404,542*

self-sufficient [*adj*] *able to take care of oneself*
arrogant, closed, competent, conceited, confident, do one's own thing*, efficient, egotistic, haughty, independent, individual, one-man/woman, on one's own, out for number one*, self-confident, self-dependent, self-sufficing, self-supported, self-supporting, self-sustained, self-sustaining, smug, unit; SEE CONCEPTS *334,404*

sell [*v1*] *exchange an object for money*
advertise, auction, bargain, barter, be in business*, boost, clinch the deal, close, close the deal, contract, deal in, dispose, drum, dump, exchange, handle, hawk, hustle, market, merchandise, move, peddle, persuade, pitch, plug, puff*, push, put across, put up for sale, retail, retain, snow, soft sell*, soft soap*, spiel*, stock, sweet talk*, trade, traffic, unload, vend, wholesale; SEE CONCEPT *345*

sell/sell out [*v2*] *betray*
beguile, break faith, bunk, cross, deceive, deliver up, delude, disappoint, double-cross*, fail, four-flush*, give away, give up, mislead, play false, rat on*, sell down the river*, stab in the back*, surrender, take in, violate; SEE CONCEPTS *14,63*

seller [*n*] *person who gives object in exchange for money*
agent, auctioneer, businessman/woman, businessperson, dealer, marketer, merchant, peddler, representative, retailer, sales help, salesman/woman, salesperson, shopkeeper, storekeeper, trader, tradesman/woman, vendor; SEE CONCEPTS *347,348*

semblance [*n*] *aura, appearance*
affinity, air, alikeness, analogy, aspect, bearing, comparison, facade, face, false front*, feel, feeling, figure, form, front, guise, image, likeness, mask, mien, mood, pose, pretense, resemblance, seeming,

show, showing, similarity, simile, similitude, simulacrum, veil, veneer; SEE CONCEPTS *673,716*

send [*v1*] *transmit, transfer through a system*
accelerate, address, advance, assign, broadcast, cast, circulate, commission, commit, communicate, consign, convey, delegate, deliver, detail, direct, dispatch, drop, emit, expedite, express, fire, fling, forward, freight, get under way, give off, grant, hasten, hurl, hurry off, impart, issue, let fly, mail, post, propel, put out, radiate, relay, remit, route, rush off, ship, shoot, televise, troll, wire; SEE CONCEPTS *217,223*

send [*v2*] *please*
charm, delight, electrify, enrapture, enthrall, enthuse, excite, intoxicate, move, please, ravish, stir, thrill, titillate, turn on; SEE CONCEPTS *7,11,22*

senile [*adj*] *failing in physical and mental capabilities due to old age*
aged, ancient, anile, decrepit, doddering, doting, enfeebled, feeble, imbecile, infirm, in second childhood*, old, senescent, shattered, sick, weak; SEE CONCEPTS *314,402,403*

senior [*n*] *older person*
ancient, dean, doyen, doyenne, elder, elderly person, first-born, golden-ager*, grandfather, grandmother, head, master, matriarch, old folk*, oldster*, oldtimer*, patriarch, pensioner, pops*, relic*, retired person, senior citizen, superior; SEE CONCEPTS *414,424*

senior [*adj*] *older or of higher rank*
chief, elder, higher, leading, major, more advanced, next higher, superior; SEE CONCEPTS *574,578, 585,797*

seniority [*n*] *rank in organization due to length of service*
advantage, antiquity, eldership, precedence, preference, priority, rank, ranking, standing, station, superiority; SEE CONCEPTS *671,727*

sensation [*n1*] *feeling, perception*
awareness, consciousness, emotion, gut reaction*, impression, passion, response, sense, sensibility, sensitiveness, sensitivity, sentiment, susceptibility, thought, tingle, vibes*; SEE CONCEPTS *34,410,529*

sensation [*n2*] *something wonderful or awe-inspiring*
agitation, bomb*, bombshell*, commotion, excitement, flash, furor, hit, marvel, miracle, phenomenon, portent, prodigy, scandal, stir, stunner, surprise, thrill, wonder, wow*; SEE CONCEPTS *293,529*

sensational [*adj1*] *startling, exaggerated*
amazing, arresting, astounding, breathtaking, coarse, colored, conspicuous, dramatic, electrifying, emotional, excessive, exciting, extravagant, hairraising*, horrifying, juicy*, livid, lurid, marked, melodramatic, noticeable, outstanding, piquant, pointed, prominent, pungent, remarkable, revealing, rough, salient, scandalous, sensationalistic, shocking, signal, spectacular, staggering, stimulating, sul-

try, tabloid*, thrilling, vulgar, X-rated*; SEE CONCEPTS *267,537,545*

sensational [*adj2*] *excellent, superb*
agitating, astonishing, breathtaking, cool*, dandy, divine, dramatic, eloquent, exceptional, exciting, fabulous, first-class, glorious, impressive, incredible, keen, marvelous, mind-blowing, most*, moving, out of this world*, smashing, spectacular, stirring, surprising, thrilling, zero cool*; SEE CONCEPT *574*

sense [*n1*] *feeling of animate being*
faculty, feel, function, hearing, impression, kinesthesia, sensation, sensibility, sensitivity, sight, smell, taste, touch; SEE CONCEPT *405*

sense [*n2*] *awareness, perception*
ability, appreciation, atmosphere, aura, brains, capacity, clear-headedness, cleverness, cognizance, common sense, consciousness, discernment, discrimination, feel, feeling, gumption, imagination, impression, insight, intellect, intelligence, intuition, judgment, knowledge, mentality, mind, premonition, presentiment, prudence, quickness, reason, reasoning, recognition, sagacity, sanity, sentiment, sharpness, smarts, soul, spirit, tact, thought, understanding, wisdom, wit; SEE CONCEPTS *33,409*

sense [*n3*] *point, meaning*
acceptation, advantage, bottom line*, burden, core, definition, denotatiton, drift, gist, good, heart, implication, import, intendment, interpretation, logic, matter, meat*, meat and potatoes*, message, name of the game*, nature of the beast*, nitty-gritty*, nuance, nub, nuts and bolts*, punch line*, purport, purpose, reason, short, significance, significancy, signification, stuff, substance, thrust, understanding, upshot, use, value, worth; SEE CONCEPTS *668,682*

sense [*v*] *become aware of*
anticipate, apperceive, appreciate, apprehend, believe, be with it, catch, catch on, catch the drift*, consider, credit, deem, dig, discern, divine, feel, feel in bones*, feel in gut*, get the drift*, get the idea*, get the impression*, get the picture*, get vibes*, grasp, have a feeling*, have a hunch*, hold, just know, know, notice, observe, perceive, pick up, read, realize, savvy, suspect, take in, think, understand; SEE CONCEPT *34*

senseless [*adj*] *silly, meaningless*
absurd, asinine, batty, crazy, daft, doublespeak*, double talk*, fatuous, flaky, foolish, idiotic, illogical, imbecilic, inane, incongruous, inconsistent, insignificant, irrational, ludicrous, mad, mindless, moronic, nonsensical, nutty, pointless, purportless, purposeless, ridiculous, simple, stupid, trivial, unimportant, unintelligent, unmeaning, unreasonable, unsound, unwise, wacky*, without rhyme or reason*; SEE CONCEPTS *548,558*

sensibility [*n*] *responsiveness; ability to feel*
affection, appreciation, awareness, discernment, emotion, feeling, gut reaction*, heart*, insight, in-

tuition, judgment, keenness, perceptiveness, rationale, sensation, sense, sensitiveness, sensitivity, sentiment, susceptibility, taste, vibes*; SEE CONCEPTS *409,410*

sensible [*adj*] *realistic, reasonable*
all there*, astute, attentive, au courant, aware, canny, cognizant, commonsensical, conscious, consequent, conversant, cool*, discerning, discreet, discriminating, down-to-earth, far-sighted, having all one's marbles*, informed, in right mind, intelligent, judicious, knowing, logical, matter-of-fact, practical, prudent, rational, sagacious, sage, sane, sentient, shrewd, sober, sound, together, well-reasoned, well-thought-out, wise, witting; SEE CONCEPTS *402,542*

sensitive [*adj1*] *impressionable*
acute, cognizant, conscious, delicate, easily affected, emotionable, emotional, feeling, fine, high-strung*, hung up*, hypersensitive, impressible, irritable, keen, knowing, nervous, oversensitive, perceiving, perceptive, precarious, precise, psychic, reactive, receptive, responsive, seeing, sensatory, sensile, sensorial, sensory, sentient, supersensitive, susceptible, tense, ticklish, touchy, touchy feely*, tricky, tuned in*, turned on to*, umbrageous, understanding, unstable, wired; SEE CONCEPT *403*

sensitive [*adj2*] *easily hurt*
delicate, easily harmed, painful, sore, tender; SEE CONCEPT *406*

sensitivity [*n*] *responsiveness to stimuli*
acuteness, affectibility, awareness, consciousness, delicacy, feeling, impressionability, nervousness, reactiveness, reactivity, receptiveness, sensation, sense, sensitiveness, subtlety, susceptibility, sympathy; SEE CONCEPTS *405,410*

sensory [*adj*] *affecting animate nerve organs*
acoustic, afferent, audible, audiovisual, auditory, aural, auricular, clear, discernible, distinct, gustative, gustatory, hearable, lingual, neural, neurological, ocular, olfactive, olfactory, ophthalmic, optic, perceptible, phonic, plain, receptive, sensational, sensatory, sensible, sensual, sonic, tactile, visual; SEE CONCEPT *406*

sensual [*adj*] *physical, erotic*
animal, animalistic, arousing, bodily, carnal, debauched, delightful, epicurean, exciting, fleshly, heavy, hedonic, hot, irreligious, lascivious, lecherous, lewd, libidinous, licentious, lustful, moving, pleasing, rough, sensuous, sexual, sexy, sharpened, steamy, stimulating, stirring, tactile, unchaste, unspiritual, voluptuous, X-rated*; SEE CONCEPTS *372,401*

sensuous [*adj*] *gratifying to senses*
carnal, epicurean, exciting, fleshly, fleshy, hedonistic, luscious, lush, luxurious, passionate, physical, pleasurable, pleasure-loving, pleasure-seeking, primrose, rich, self-indulgent, sensory, sensual, sensualistic, sumptuous, sybaritic, voluptuous; SEE CONCEPTS *372,537*

sentence [*n*] *punishing decree*
book, censure, clock, condemnation, considered opinion, decision, determination, dictum, doom, edict, fall, getup*, hitch, jolt, judgment, knock, order, penalty, pronouncement, punishment, rap*, ruling, sending up the river*, sleep, stretch, term, time, trick, vacation, verdict; SEE CONCEPT *318*

sentence [*v*] *decide punishment*
adjudge, adjudicate, blame, condemn, confine, convict, damn, denounce, devote, doom, impound, imprison, incarcerate, jail, judge, mete out, ordain, pass judgment, penalize, proscribe, punish, put away*, put on ice*, railroad*, rule, send to prison, send up the river*, settle, take the fall*, throw the book at*; SEE CONCEPTS *122,317*

sentiment [*n*] *emotion, belief*
affect, affectivity, attitude, bias, conception, conviction, disposition, emotionalism, eye, feeling, hearts and flowers*, idea, inclination, inclining, judgment, leaning, mind, opinion, overemotionalism, partiality, passion, penchant, persuasion, position, posture, predilection, propensity, romanticism, sensibility, sentimentality, slant, softheartedness, tendency, tender feeling, tenderness, thought, view, way of thinking; SEE CONCEPTS *32,410,689*

sentimental [*adj*] *emotional, romantic*
affected, affectionate, corny*, demonstrative, dewy-eyed, dreamy, effusive, gushing, gushy, idealistic, impressionable, inane, insipid, jejune, languishing, lovey-dovey*, loving, maudlin, moonstruck*, mushy*, nostalgic, overacted, overemotional, passionate, pathetic, rosewater*, saccharine*, sappy*, schmaltzy*, schoolgirlish, silly, simpering, sloppy*, slushy*, soapy*, soft, softhearted*, sugary*, sweet, syrupy*, tearful, tear-jerking*, tender, touching, vapid, visionary, weepy; SEE CONCEPTS *267,401,542*

separate [*adj1*] *disconnected*
abstracted, apart, apportioned, asunder, cut apart, cut in two, detached, disassociated, discrete, disembodied, disjointed, distant, distributed, disunited, divergent, divided, divorced, far between, free, independent, in halves, isolated, loose, marked, parted, partitioned, put asunder, removed, scattered, set apart, set asunder, severed, sovereign, sundered, unattached, unconnected; SEE CONCEPT *577*

separate [*adj2*] *alone, individual*
apart, autonomous, detached, different, discrete, distinct, distinctive, diverse, free, independent, lone, one, only, particular, peculiar, several, single, sole, solitary, unique, various; SEE CONCEPTS *557,564*

separate [*v1*] *remove something from group; keep or set apart*
break, break off, cleave, come apart, come away, come between, detach, dichotomize, disconnect, disentangle, disjoin, disjoint, dissect, dissever, distribute, divide, divorce, intersect, part, rupture, sever,

split, split up, sunder, uncombine, uncouple, undo; SEE CONCEPT *135*

separate [*v2*] *isolate, segregate*
assign, break up, classify, close off, comb, compartment, compartmentalize, cut off, discriminate, distribute, draw apart, group, insulate, interval, intervene, island, order, put on one side, rope off, seclude, sequester, sift, single out, sort, space, split up, stand between, winnow; SEE CONCEPTS *158,201*

separate [*v3*] *part company in a romantic relationship or marriage*
alienate, bifurcate, break it off*, break off, break up, dedomicile, depart, discontinue, disunify, disunite, diverge, divorce, drop, estrange, go away, go different ways*, go separate ways*, leave, part, pull out, split up, take leave, uncouple, unlink, untie the knot*; SEE CONCEPTS *297,384*

separately [*adv*] *alone, individually*
apart, clearly, definitely, disjointly, distinctly, independently, one at a time, one by one, personally, severally, singly, solely; SEE CONCEPTS *544,577*

separation [*n*] *being apart; break-up*
break, break-up, dedomiciling, departure, detachment, disconnection, disengagement, disjunction, disrelation, dissociation, dissolution, disunion, division, divorce, divorcement, embarkation, estrangement, farewell, gap, leave-taking*, on out and out*, on the rocks*, parting, parting of the ways*, partition, pffft, rift, rupture, segregation, severance, split, split-up*; SEE CONCEPTS *135,195,297,388*

sequel [*n*] *follow-up*
aftereffect, aftermath, alternation, causatum, chain, close, closing, conclusion, consecution, consequence, continuation, development, effect, end, ending, epilogue, eventuality, finish, finishing, issue, order, outcome, part two*, payoff, progression, result, row, sequence, sequent, series, spin-off*, termination, train, upshot; SEE CONCEPTS *271, 293,824,832*

sequence [*n*] *series, order*
arrangement, array, catenation, chain, classification, concatenation, consecution, consecutiveness, continuance, continuity, continuousness, course, cycle, disposition, distribution, flow, graduation, grouping, ordering, pecking order*, perpetuity, placement, procession, progression, row, run, sequel, skein, streak, string, subsequence, succession, successiveness, track, train; SEE CONCEPTS *721,727*

sequential [*adj*] *occurring in an order*
consecutive, constant, continuous, following, incessant, later, next, persistent, regular, sequent, serial, steady, subsequent, subsequential, succedent, succeeding, successive; SEE CONCEPTS *482,548,585*

sequester [*v*] *isolate, seclude*
cloister, close off, cut off, draw back, enisle, hide, insulate, island, secrete, segregate, separate, set apart, set off, withdraw; SEE CONCEPTS *90,188*

serene [*adj*] *calm, undisturbed*
at peace, clear, collected, comfortable, composed, content, cool*, cool as cucumber*, dispassionate, easy, easygoing, fair, halcyon, imperturbable, laid-back*, limpid, patient, peaceful, pellucid, phlegmatic, placid, poised, quiescent, quiet, reconciled, resting, satisfied, sedate, self-possessed, smooth, still, stoical, tranquil, undisturbed, unflappable, unruffled, untroubled; SEE CONCEPTS *401,485*

serenity [*n*] *calm, peacefulness*
calmness, composure, cool, patience, peace, peace of mind, placidity, quietness, quietude, stillness, tranquillity; SEE CONCEPTS *633,673*

serial [*adj*] *in continuing order*
consecutive, continual, continued, continuing, ensuing, following, going on, sequent, sequential, succedent, succeeding, successional, successive; SEE CONCEPTS *482,585*

series [*n*] *order, succession*
alternation, arrangement, array, category, chain, classification, column, consecution, continuity, course, file, gradation, group, line, list, procession, progression, range, row, run, scale, sequel, sequence, set, skein, streak, string, suit, suite, tier, train; SEE CONCEPTS *721,727,769*

serious [*adj1*] *somber, humorless*
austere, bound, bound and determined*, businesslike, cold sober*, contemplative, deadpan*, deliberate, determined, downbeat, earnest, funereal, genuine, go for broke*, grave, grim, honest, intent, long-faced*, meditative, no-nonsense, pensive, pokerfaced*, reflective, resolute, resolved, sedate, set, severe, sincere, sober, solemn, staid, steady, stern, thoughtful, unhumorous, unsmiling, weighty; SEE CONCEPTS *403,542*

serious [*adj2*] *crucial, weighty*
arduous, dangerous, deep, difficult, far-reaching, fateful, fell, formidable, grave, grievous, grim, hard, heavy, important, laborious, major, mean business*, meaningful, menacing, momentous, no joke*, no laughing matter*, of consequence, operose, out for blood*, playing hard ball*, pressing, severe, significant, smoking*, sobering, strenuous, strictly business*, threatening, tough, ugly, unamusing, unhumorous, urgent, worrying; SEE CONCEPTS *538,565,568*

seriously [*adv1*] *not humorously*
actively, all joking aside*, cool it*, cut the comedy*, determinedly, down, earnestly, fervently, for real*, gravely, in all conscience, in all seriousness, in earnest, intently, passionately, purposefully, quit horsing around*, resolutely, save it*, sedately, simmer down*, sincerely, soberly, solemnly, sternly, straighten out, thoughtfully, vigorously, with a straight face*, with forethought, with sobriety, zealously; SEE CONCEPTS *535,542,544*

seriously [*adv2*] *dangerously, critically*
acutely, badly, decidedly, deplorably, distressingly, gravely, grievously, harmfully, intensely, menac-

ingly, perilously, precariously, quite, regrettably, severely, sorely, threateningly, very; SEE CONCEPTS *544,565,568*

seriousness [*n1*] *humorlessness*
calmness, coolness, earnest, earnestness, gravity, intentness, sedateness, serious-mindedness, sincerity, sober-mindedness, sobriety, solemnity, staidness, sternness, thoughtfulness; SEE CONCEPTS *410,657*

seriousness [*n2*] *danger; criticalness*
enormity, gravity, importance, moment, significance, urgency, weight; SEE CONCEPTS *668,675*

sermon [*n*] *instructive speech with a moral*
address, advice, discourse, doctrine, exhortation, harangue, homily, lecture, lesson, moralism, pastoral, preach, preaching, preachment, tiracle; SEE CONCEPTS *278,368*

serrated [*adj*] *jagged*
denticulate, indented, notched, ragged, sawlike, sawtooth, saw-toothed, scored, serrate, serried, serriform, serrulate, toothed; SEE CONCEPT *486*

servant [*n*] *person who waits on another*
assistant, attendant, cleaning man/woman, dependent, domestic, drudge, help, helper, hireling, houseboy, live-in, maid, man, menial, minion, retainer, serf, server, slave, woman; SEE CONCEPT *348*

serve [*v1*] *aid, help; supply*
arrange, assist, attend to, be of assistance, be of use, care for, deal, deliver, dish up*, distribute, do for, give, handle, hit, minister to, mother, nurse, oblige, play, present, provide, provision, set out, succor, wait on, work for; SEE CONCEPTS *110,140*

serve [*v2*] *act, do*
accept, agree, attend, be employed by, carry on, complete, discharge, follow, fulfill, function, go through, hearken, labor, obey, observe, officiate, pass, perform, subserve, toil, work; SEE CONCEPT *91*

serve [*v3*] *suffice; do the work of*
advantage, answer, answer the purpose, apply, avail, be acceptable, be adequate, be good enough, benefit, be of use, be useful, content, do, do duty as, fill the bill*, fit, function, make, profit, satisfy, service, suit, work, work for; SEE CONCEPTS *656,658*

service [*n1*] *aid, help*
account, advantage, applicability, appropriateness, assistance, avail, benefit, business, check, courtesy, dispensation, duty, employ, employment, favor, fitness, indulgence, kindness, labor, maintenance, ministration, office, overhaul, relevance, serviceability, servicing, supply, use, usefulness, utility, value, work; SEE CONCEPTS *110,324,658*

service [*n2*] *rite of a church*
ceremonial, ceremony, formality, function, liturgy, observance, ritual, sermon, worship; SEE CONCEPT *368*

service [*n3*] *time in military operation*
action, active duty, combat, duty, fighting, sting; SEE CONCEPTS *320,321*

serviceable [*adj*] *useful, functional*
advantageous, aiding, assistive, beneficial, convenient, dependable, durable, efficient, handy, hard-wearing, helpful, invaluable, operative, practical, profitable, usable, utile, utilitarian, valuable; SEE CONCEPT *560*

servile [*adj*] *grovelling, subservient*
abject, base, beggarly, bootlicking*, craven, cringing, despicable, eating crow*, eating humble pie*, fawning, humble, ignoble, low, mean, obedient, obeisant, obsequious, passive, slavish, submissive, sycophantic, toadying, unctuous, unresisting; SEE CONCEPTS *401,404*

servitude [*n*] *slavery*
bondage, bonds, chains, confinement, enslavement, obedience, peonage, serfdom, serfhood, subjection, subjugation, thrall, thralldom, vassalage, yoke; SEE CONCEPTS *388,410*

session [*n*] *meeting, gathering*
affair, assembly, concourse, conference, discussion, get-together, hearing, huddle, jam session*, meet, period, showdown, sitting, term; SEE CONCEPTS *114,324*

set [*n1*] *physical bearing*
address, air, attitude, carriage, comportment, demeanor, deportment, fit, hang, inclination, mien, port, position, posture, presence, turn; SEE CONCEPT *757*

set [*n2*] *stage setting*
flats, mise en scene, scène, scenery, setting, stage set; SEE CONCEPT *263*

set [*n3*] *group, assortment*
array, assemblage, band, batch, body, bunch, bundle, camp, circle, clan, class, clique, clump, cluster, clutch, collection, company, compendium, coterie, crew, crowd, faction, gaggle, gang, kit, lot, mob, organization, outfit, pack, push, rat pack, sect, series; SEE CONCEPTS *417,432,769*

set [*adj1*] *decided*
agreed, appointed, arranged, bent, brick wall*, certain, concluded, confirmed, customary, dead set on*, decisive, definite, determined, entrenched, established, firm, fixed, hanging tough*, immovable, intent, inveterate, ironclad, locked in, obstinate, pat, pigheaded*, prearranged, predetermined, prescribed, regular, resolute, resolved, rigid, rooted, scheduled, set in stone*, settled, solid as a rock*, specified, stated, steadfast, stiff-necked*, stipulated, stubborn, unflappable, usual, well-set; SEE CONCEPTS *535,542*

set [*adj2*] *firm, hardened; inflexible*
entrenched, fixed, hard and fast, hidebound, immovable, jelled, located, placed, positioned, rigid, settled, sited, situate, situated, solid, stable, stiff, strict, stubborn, unyielding; SEE CONCEPT *488*

set [*v1*] *position, place*
affix, aim, anchor, apply, arrange, bestow, cast, deposit, direct, embed, ensconce, establish, fasten, fix, head, insert, install, introduce, lay, level, locate,

lock, lodge, make fast, make ready, mount, park, plank, plant, plop, plunk, point, post, prepare, put, rest, seat, settle, situate, spread, station, stick, train, turn, wedge, zero in*; SEE CONCEPTS *201,202*

set [*v2*] *decide upon*
agree upon, allocate, allot, appoint, arrange, assign, conclude, decree, designate, determine, dictate, direct, establish, estimate, fix, fix price, impose, instruct, lay down, make, name, ordain, prescribe, price, rate, regulate, resolve, schedule, settle, specify, stipulate, value; SEE CONCEPT *18*

set [*v3*] *harden*
become firm, cake, clot, coagulate, condense, congeal, crystallize, fix, gel, gelate, gelatinize, jell, jellify, jelly, solidify, stiffen, thicken; SEE CONCEPT *250*

set [*v4*] *decline*
descend, dip, disappear, drop, go down, sink, subside, vanish; SEE CONCEPT *181*

set [*v5*] *start, incite*
abet, begin, commence, foment, initiate, instigate, provoke, put in motion, raise, set on*, stir up*, whip up*; SEE CONCEPT *221*

setback [*n*] *disappointment*
about-face*, backset, bath*, blow, bottom, check, comedown, defeat, delay, difficulty, drawing board*, flip-flop*, hindrance, hitch*, hold-up, impediment, misfortune, obstacle, rebuff, regress, regression, retardation, reversal, reversal of fortune, reverse, slowdown, square one*, stumbling block*, trouble, upset, whole new ballgame*; SEE CONCEPTS *388,674,679*

set back [*v*] *delay, hinder*
bog down*, decelerate, defeat, detain, embog, hang up*, hold up, impede, mire, retard, reverse, slow, slow down, slow up; SEE CONCEPT *130*

setting [*n*] *scene, background*
ambience, backdrop, context, distance, environment, frame, framework, horizon, jungle, locale, location, mise en scène*, mounting, perspective, set, shade, shadow, site, stage set, stage setting, surroundings; SEE CONCEPTS *198,263*

settle [*v1*] *straighten out, resolve*
achieve, adjudicate, adjust, appoint, arrange, call the shots*, choose, cinch, clean up, clear, clear up, clinch, come to a conclusion, come to a decision, come to an agreement, complete, concert, conclude, confirm, decide, determine, discharge, dispose, end, establish, figure, fix, form judgment, judge, make a decision, make certain, mediate, nail down*, negotiate, order, pay, put an end to, put into order, reconcile, regulate, rule, satisfy, seal, set to rights*, square, verify, work out; SEE CONCEPTS *18,126,341*

settle [*v2*] *calm, relieve*
allay, assure, becalm, compose, lull, pacify, quell, quiet, quieten, reassure, relax, sedate, soothe, still, tranquilize; SEE CONCEPTS *7,22,469*

settle [*v3*] *come to rest; fall*
alight, bed down, decline, descend, flop, immerse, land, lay, light, lodge, perch, place, plop, plunge, put, repose, roost, seat, set down, settle down, sink, sit, submerge, submerse, subside, touch down; SEE CONCEPT *181*

settle [*v4*] *make one's home*
abide, colonize, dwell, establish, hang up hat*, inhabit, keep house, live, locate, lodge, move to, park, put down roots, reside, set up home, squat, take root*, take up residence; SEE CONCEPT *226*

settlement [*n1*] *decision, conclusion*
adjustment, agreement, arrangement, clearance, compact, compensation, completion, conclusion, confirmation, contract, covenant, deal, defrayal, determination, discharge, disposition, establishment, happy medium*, liquidation, pay, payment, payoff, quietus, reimbursement, remuneration, resolution, satisfaction, showdown, termination, trade-off, working out; SEE CONCEPTS *230,684*

settlement [*n2*] *community*
colonization, colony, encampment, establishment, foundation, habitation, hamlet, inhabitancy, occupancy, occupation, outpost, plantation, principality, residence; SEE CONCEPTS *512,515*

set up [*v*] *start*
arrange, assemble, back, begin, build, build up, compose, constitute, construct, create, elevate, erect, establish, excite, exhilarate, found, inaugurate, initiate, inspire, install, institute, introduce, launch, make provision for, open, organize, originate, prearrange, prepare, put together, put up, raise, rear, stimulate, strengthen, subsidize, usher in; SEE CONCEPT *221*

sever [*v1*] *cut apart*
bisect, carve, cleave, cut, cut in two, detach, disconnect, disjoin, dissect, dissever, dissociate, disunite, divide, part, rend, rive, separate, slice, split, sunder; SEE CONCEPTS *98,176*

sever [*v2*] *dissociate*
abandon, break off, disjoint, dissolve, divide, divorce, put an end to, separate, terminate; SEE CONCEPTS *297,384*

several [*adj*] *assorted, various*
a few, a lot, any, certain, considerable, definite, different, disparate, distinct, divers, diverse, handful, hardly any, indefinite, individual, infrequent, manifold, many, not many, numerous, only a few, particular, personal, plural, proportionate, quite a few, rare, respective, scant, scanty, scarce, scarcely any, separate, single, small number, some, sparse, special, specific, sundry; SEE CONCEPTS *564,762*

severe [*adj1*] *uncompromising, stern*
astringent, austere, biting, caustic, close, cold, cruel, cutting, disapproving, dour, earnest, firm, flinty, forbidding, grave, grim, hard, hard-nosed*, harsh, inconsiderate, inexorable, inflexible, iron-handed*, obdurate, oppressive, peremptory, pitiless, relent-

less, resolute, resolved, rigid, satirical, scathing, serious, sober, stern, stiff*, strait-laced*, strict, tight-lipped*, unalterable, unbending, unchanging, unfeeling, unrelenting, unsmiling, unsparing; SEE CONCEPTS *401,534,542*

severe [*adj2*] *difficult, harsh*
acute, arduous, ascetic, austere, bitter, bleak, consequential, critical, dangerous, dear, demanding, despotic, distressing, domineering, drastic, effortful, exacting, extreme, fierce, forbidding, grave, grim, grinding, hard, heavy, hefty, implacable, inclement, intemperate, intense, mordant, oppressive, overbearing, pitiless, punishing, rigorous, rugged, serious, sharp, sore, strenuous, stringent, taxing, toilsome, tough, tyrannical, unpleasant, unrelenting, violent, weighty, wicked; SEE CONCEPTS *565,569*

severely [*adv*] *harshly*
acutely, badly, critically, dangerously, extremely, firmly, gravely, hard, hardly, intensely, markedly, painfully, rigorously, roughly, seriously, sharply, sorely, sternly, strictly, with an iron hand; SEE CONCEPT *569*

sew [*v*] *prepare fabric for clothing, covering*
baste, bind, embroider, fasten, piece, seam, stitch, tack, tailor, work; SEE CONCEPT *218*

sex [*n1*] *male or female gender*
femininity, manhood, manliness, masculinity, sexuality, womanhood, womanliness; SEE CONCEPT *648*

sex [*n2*] *intercourse between animate beings*
birds and the bees*, coition, coitus, copulation, facts of life*, fornication, generation, intimacy, lovemaking, magnetism, procreation, relations, reproduction, sensuality, sexuality; SEE CONCEPT *375*

sexual [*adj*] *concerning reproduction, intercourse*
animal, animalistic, bestial, carnal, erotic, fleshly, generative, genital, genitive, intimate, loving, passionate, procreative, reproductive, sensual, sharing, venereal, voluptuous, wanton; SEE CONCEPT *372*

sexy [*adj*] *being attractive to another*
arousing, come-hither*, cuddly, erotic, flirtatious, hot*, inviting, kissable, libidinous, mature, provocative, provoking, racy, risqué, seductive, sensual, sensuous, slinky*, spicy*, steamy*, suggestive, titillating, voluptuous; SEE CONCEPT *372*

shabby [*adj1*] *broken-down; in poor shape*
bare, bedraggled, crummy, decayed, decaying, decrepit, degenerated, desolate, deteriorated, deteriorating, dilapidated, dingy, disfigured, disreputable, dog-eared*, faded, frayed, gone to seed*, mangy, meager, mean, miserable, moth-eaten, neglected, pitiful, poor, poverty-stricken, ragged, ramshackle, ratty, rickety, ruined, ruinous, run-down, scrubby, scruffy, seedy, shoddy, sleazy, slipshod, squalid, tacky, tattered, threadbare, tired, worn, worn-out, worse for wear*, wretched; SEE CONCEPT *485*

shabby [*adj2*] *despicable*
beggarly, cheap, contemptible, despisable, dirty, disgraceful, dishonorable, disreputable, ignoble, igno-

minious, inconsiderate, inglorious, low, low-down, mean, mercenary, miserly, rotten, scummy, selfish, shady, shameful, shoddy, sordid, sorry, stingy, thoughtless, ungentlemanly, unkind, unworthy; SEE CONCEPTS *401,404*

shade [*n1*] *dimness*
adumbration, blackness, coolness, cover, darkness, dusk, gloominess, obscuration, obscurity, penumbra, screen, semidarkness, shadiness, shadow, shadows, umbra, umbrage; SEE CONCEPT *620*

shade [*n2*] *blind, shield*
awning, canopy, cover, covering, curtain, screen, veil; SEE CONCEPT *445*

shade [*n3*] *color, hue*
brilliance, cast, saturation, stain, tinge, tint, tone; SEE CONCEPTS *620,622*

shade [*n4*] *slight difference*
amount, cast, dash, degree, distinction, gradation, hint, nuance, proposal, semblance, soupçon, spice, streak, suggestion, suspicion, tincture, tinge, trace, variation, variety; SEE CONCEPT *665*

shade [*n5*] *ghost*
apparition, bogey*, haunt, manes, phantasm, phantom, revenant, shadow, specter, spirit, umbra, wraith; SEE CONCEPT *370*

shade [*v*] *shut out the light*
adumbrate, be overcast, blacken, cast a shadow, cloud, cloud over, cloud up, conceal, cover, darken, deepen, dim, eclipse, gray, hide, inumbrate, mute, obscure, overshadow, protect, screen, shadow, shelter, shield, shutter, tone down, umbrage, veil; SEE CONCEPTS *250,526*

shadow [*n1*] *darkness*
adumbration, cover, dark, dimness, dusk, gloom, obscuration, obscurity, penumbra, protection, shade, shelter, umbra, umbrage; SEE CONCEPTS *620,622*

shadow [*n2*] *hint, suggestion*
breath, intimation, memento, relic, smack, suspicion, tincture, tinge, touch, trace, vestige; SEE CONCEPT *278*

shadow [*v1*] *make dark*
adumbrate, becloud, bedim, cast a shadow, cloud, darken, dim, gray, haze, inumbrate, obscure, overcast, overcloud, overhang, overshadow, screen, shade, shelter, shield, umbrage, veil; SEE CONCEPT *250*

shadow [*v2*] *follow secretly*
dog, keep in sight, pursue, spy on, stalk, tag, tail, trail, watch; SEE CONCEPT *207*

shady [*adj1*] *dark, covered*
adumbral, bosky, cloudy, cool, dim, dusky, indistinct, leafy, out of the sun*, screened, shaded, shadowed, shadowy, sheltered, umbrageous, umbrous, under a cloud, vague; SEE CONCEPTS *485,617*

shady [*adj2*] *disreputable, suspicious*
crooked, disgraceful, dishonest, dishonorable, dubious, fishy, ignominious, infamous, inglorious, notorious, questionable, scandalous, shabby, shameful,

shifty, shoddy, slippery, suspect, suspicious, under-handed, unethical, unrespectable, unscrupulous, untrustworthy; SEE CONCEPT *545*

shaggy [*adj*] *hairy, unkempt*
furry, hirsute, long-haired, ragged, rough, ruffled, rugged, uncombed, unshorn; SEE CONCEPT *485*

shake [*v1*] *quiver, tremble*
agitate, brandish, bump, chatter, churn, commove, concuss, convulse, discompose, disquiet, disturb, dither, dodder, flap, flicker, flit, flitter, flourish, fluctuate, flutter, jar, jerk, jog, joggle, jolt, jounce, move, oscillate, palpitate, perturb, quail, quake, quaver, rattle, reel, rock, roil, ruffle, set in motion, shimmer, shimmy, shiver, shudder, stagger, stir up, succuss, sway, swing, totter, tremble, tremor, twitter, upset, vibrate, waggle, water, wave, whip, wobble; SEE CONCEPTS *150,152*

shake [*v2*] *upset deeply*
appall, bother, consternate, daunt, discompose, dismay, distress, disturb, frighten, horrify, impair, intimidate, jar, knock props out*, make waves*, move, rattle, throw, throw a curve*, undermine, unnerve, unsettle, unstring, upset, weaken, worry; SEE CONCEPTS *7,19*

shake off [*v*] *lose by getting away*
clear, dislodge, drop, elude, get away from, get rid of, give the slip*, leave behind, remove, rid oneself of, throw off, unburden; SEE CONCEPTS *102,195*

shake up [*v*] *upset, unsettle*
agitate, break with past*, cause revolution*, churn up*, clean out, clean up, clear out, disturb, liquidate, make a clean sweep*, mix, overturn, purge, remove, reorganize, rid, shock, stir up, turn upside down*; SEE CONCEPTS *14,324*

shaky [*adj1*] *trembling*
all-a-quiver*, aquake, aquiver, ashake, faltering, fluctuant, infirm, insecure, jellylike, jerry-built*, jittery, nervous, not set, precarious, quaking, quivery, rattletrap*, rickety, rocky, rootless, shaking, tottering, tottery, trembling, tremorous, tremulous, tumble-down, unfirm, unsettled, unsound, unstable, unsteady, unsure, vacillating, wavering, weak, wobbly, yielding; SEE CONCEPT *488*

shaky [*adj2*] *doubtful*
dubious, indecisive, not dependable, not reliable, precarious, problematic, questionable, suspect, uncertain, unclear, undependable, unreliable, unsettled, unsound, unsteady, unsupported, unsure; SEE CONCEPT *535*

shallow [*adj1*] *not deep*
cursory, depthless, empty, flat, hollow, inconsiderable, sand bar, shelf, shoal, slight, superficial, surface, trifling, trivial, unsound; SEE CONCEPTS *737,777*

shallow [*adj2*] *unintelligent, ignorant*
cursory, empty, empty-headed, farcical, feather-brained, flighty, flimsy, foolish, frivolous, frothy, half-baked*, hollow, idle, inane, lightweight, mean-

ingless, paltry, petty, piddling, puerile, simple, sketchy, skin-deep*, slight, superficial, surface, trifling, trivial, uncritical, unthinking, vain, wishy-washy*; SEE CONCEPT *402*

sham [*n*] *hoax, trick*
burlesque, cant, caricature, cheat, counterfeit, cover-up, deceit, deception, facade, fake, fakery, false front*, farce, feint, flimflam*, forgery, fraud, hypocrisy, hypocriticalness, imitation, impostor, imposture, jive*, mock, mockery, pharisaism, phony, pretend, pretense, pretext, pseudo*, put-on, sell, smoke*, snow job*, spoof, travesty, whitewash; SEE CONCEPTS *59,192*

sham [*adj*] *artificial, counterfeit*
adulterated, affected, assumed, bogus*, dummy, ersatz*, fake, false, feigned, fictitious, forged, fraudulent, imitation, lying, make-believe, misleading, mock, phony, plaster*, pretend, pretended, pseudo*, simulated, so-called, spurious, substitute, synthetic, untrue; SEE CONCEPT *582*

sham [*v*] *trick; pull a hoax*
act, affect, ape, assume, bluff, copy, counterfeit, create, do a number*, fake, fake it, feign, imitate, invent, lie, make like, mislead, mock, play possum*, pretend, put on, put up a front*, shuck and jive*, simulate, sucker*; SEE CONCEPTS *59,111,171*

shambles [*n*] *a mess*
anarchy, babel*, bedlam, botch, chaos, confusion, disarray, disorder, disorganization, hash, havoc, hodge-podge, madhouse, maelstrom, mess-up, mix-up, muddle; SEE CONCEPTS *230,674*

shame [*n*] *disgrace, embarrassment*
abashment, bad conscience*, blot, chagrin, compunction, confusion, contempt, contrition, degradation, derision, discomposure, discredit, disesteem, dishonor, disrepute, guilt, humiliation, ignominy, ill repute, infamy, irritation, loss of face*, mortification, obloquy, odium, opprobrium, pang, pudency, remorse, reproach, scandal, self-disgust, self-reproach, self-reproof, shamefacedness, skeleton in cupboard*, smear, stigma, stupefaction, treachery; SEE CONCEPTS *388,410*

shame [*v*] *disgrace, embarrass*
abash, blot, confound, cut down to size*, debase, defile, degrade, disconcert, discredit, dishonor, give a black eye*, humble, humiliate, mortify, reproach, ridicule, shoot down*, smear, stain, take down*, take down a peg*; SEE CONCEPTS *7,14,19*

shameful [*adj*] *atrocious; disreputable*
base, carnal, contemptible, corrupt, dastardly, debauched, degrading, diabolical, disgraceful, dishonorable, drunken, embarrassing, flagrant, heinous, humiliating, ignominious, immodest, immoral, impure, indecent, infamous, intemperate, knavish, lewd, low, mean, mortifying, notorious, obscene, opprobrious, outrageous, profligate, reprehensible, reprobate, ribald, scandalous, shaming, shocking,

sinful, unbecoming, unclean, unworthy, vile, villainous, vulgar, wicked; SEE CONCEPTS *401,545,571*

shameless [*adj*] *corrupt, indecent*
abandoned, arrant, audacious, barefaced, bold, brash, brassy, brazen, cheeky*, depraved, dissolute, flagrant, forward, hardened, high-handed*, immodest, immoral, improper, impudent, incorrigible, insolent, lewd, outrageous, overbold, presumptuous, profligate, reprobate, rude, unabashed, unashamed, unblushing, unchaste, unprincipled, wanton; SEE CONCEPTS *401,545*

shape [*n1*] *form, structure*
appearance, architecture, aspect, body, build, cast, chassis, circumscription, configuration, conformation, constitution, construction, contour, cut, embodiment, figure, format, frame, guise, likeness, lineation, lines, look, make, metamorphosis, model, mold, outline, pattern, profile, semblance, shadow, silhouette, simulacrum, stamp, symmetry; SEE CONCEPTS *436,754,757*

shape [*n2*] *condition, health*
case, estate, fettle*, fitness, kilter*, order, repair, state, trim, whack; SEE CONCEPTS *316,720*

shape [*v1*] *form, create*
assemble, block out, bring together, build, carve, cast, chisel, construct, crystallize, cut, embody, fabricate, fashion, forge, frame, hew, knead, make, mint, model, mold, pat, pattern, produce, roughhew, sculpture, sketch, stamp, streamline, throw together*, trim, whittle; SEE CONCEPTS *137,184*

shape [*v2*] *devise, plan*
accommodate, adapt, become, define, develop, form, frame, grow, guide, modify, prepare, regulate, remodel, tailor, take form, work up; SEE CONCEPT *36*

shapeless [*adj*] *formless*
abnormal, amorphic, amorphous, anomalous, assymetrical, baggy, deformed, disfigured, embryonic, ill-formed, inchoate, indefinite, indeterminate, indistinct, invisible, irregular, malformed, misshapen, mutilated, nebulous, undeveloped, unformed, ungraceful, unmade, unshapely, unstructured, unsymmetrical, vague, without character, without form; SEE CONCEPTS *486,589*

shapely [*adj*] *well-proportioned*
balanced, beautiful, built, comely, curvaceous, elegant, full-figured, graceful, neat, pleasing, proportioned, regular, rounded, sightly, statuesque, sylphlike, symmetrical, trim, well-formed, well-turned; SEE CONCEPTS *406,490*

share [*n*] *portion, allotment*
allowance, apportionment, bite, chunk, claim, commission, contribution, cut, cut in, cut up, divide, dividend, division, divvy*, dose, drag, due, end, fifty-fifty*, fraction, fragment, halver, helping, heritage, interest, lagniappe*, lot, measure, meed, parcel, part, partage, percentage, piece, pittance, plum, points, proportion, quantum, quota, quotient, quo-

tum, rake-off*, ration, segment, serving, slice, split, stake, taste, whack*; SEE CONCEPTS *710,835*

share [*v*] *use in common with others*
accord, administer, allot, apportion, assign, be a party to, bestow, cut the pie*, deal, dispense, distribute, divide, divide with, divvy*, divvy up*, dole out, experience, give and take, give out, go Dutch*, go fifty-fifty*, go halves*, go in with, have a hand in, have a portion of, mete out, parcel out, part, partake, participate, partition, pay half, piece up, prorate, quota, ration, receive, shift, slice, slice up, split, split up, take a part of, yield; SEE CONCEPTS *98,100,384*

sharp [*adj1*] *knifelike, cutting*
aciculate, acuate, acuminate, acuminous, acute, apical, barbed, briery, cuspate, cuspidate, edged, fine, ground fine, honed, horned, jagged, keen, keen-edged, knife-edged, needlelike, needle-pointed, peaked, pointed, pointy, prickly, pronged, razor-sharp, salient, serrated, sharp-edged, sharpened, spiked, spiky, spiny, splintery, stinging, tapered, tapering, thorny, tined, tipped, unblunted, whetted; SEE CONCEPT *486*

sharp [*adj2*] *sudden*
abrupt, distinct, extreme, intense, marked; SEE CONCEPTS *581,799*

sharp [*adj3*] *perceptive, quick-witted*
acute, adroit, alert, apt, astute, brainy, bright, brilliant, canny, clever, critical, cute, discerning, discriminating, fast, foxy*, have smarts*, ingenious, intelligent, keen, knowing, nimble, nobody's fool*, not born yesterday*, observant, on the ball*, original, penetrating, penetrative, quick, quick on the trigger*, quick on uptake*, ready, resourceful, savvy, sensitive, slick, smart, smart as a tack*, subtle, wise; SEE CONCEPT *402*

sharp [*adj4*] *dishonest, deceitful*
artful, bent, crafty, cunning, designing, ornery, salty, shady, shrewd, slick, slippery, sly, smart, snake, two-faced*, underhand, unethical, unscrupulous, wily; SEE CONCEPT *545*

sharp [*adj5*] *severe, intense*
acute, agonizing, biting, cutting, distinct, distressing, drilling, excruciating, fierce, keen, knifelike, painful, paralyzing, penetrating, piercing, shooting, smart, sore, stabbing, stinging, violent; SEE CONCEPTS *537,569*

sharp [*adj6*] *distinct, well-defined*
audible, clear, clear-cut, crisp, definite, explicit, obvious, visible; SEE CONCEPT *535*

sharp [*adj7*] *stylish*
chic, classy, dashing, distinctive, dressy, excellent, fashionable, fine, first-class*, fly*, in style, smart, snappy*, swank*, tony*, trendy; SEE CONCEPT *589*

sharp [*adj8*] *hurtful, bitter in speech*
acrimonious, angry, barbed, biting, caustic, cutting, double-edged, harsh, incisive, inconsiderate, penetrating, peppery, piercing, pointed, pungent, sarcas-

tic, sardonic, scathing, severe, short, stabbing, stinging, tart, thoughtless, trenchant, unceremonious, ungracious, virulent, vitriolic; SEE CONCEPT *267*

sharp [*adj9*] *having strong affect on animate senses*
acerbic, acid, acrid, active, astringent, austere, bitter, brisk, burning, harsh, hot, lively, odorous, piquant, pungent, sour, strong-smelling, suffocating, tart, vigorous, vinegary; SEE CONCEPTS *537,598,613*

sharp [*adv*] *on time*
abruptly, accurately, bang, exactly, just, on the button*, on the dot*, precisely, promptly, punctually, right, smack-dab*, square, squarely, suddenly, without warning; SEE CONCEPT *799*

sharpen [*v*] *make knifelike*
acuminate, dress, edge, file, grind, hone, make acute, make sharp, put an edge on, put a point on, sharp, stroke, strop, taper, whet; SEE CONCEPTS *137,250*

shatter [*v1*] *break into small pieces*
blast, blight, burst, crack, crash, crunch, crush, dash, demolish, destroy, disable, exhaust, explode, fracture, fragment, fragmentalize, fragmentize, impair, implode, overturn, pulverize, rend, rive, ruin, scrunch, shiver, smash, smash to smithereens*, smatter, snap, splinter, splinterize, split, torpedo*, total*, wrack up, wreck; SEE CONCEPTS *246,252*

shatter [*v2*] *hurt someone badly*
break a heart*, crush, destroy, devastate, dumbfound, rattle, ruin, upset; SEE CONCEPTS *7,19*

shave [*v*] *cut outer covering off*
barber, brush, clip, crop, cut, cut back, cut down, decorticate, graze, kiss, make bare, pare, peel, plane, prune, shear, shingle, shred, skim, skin, slash, slice thin, sliver, strip, touch, trim; SEE CONCEPTS *137,162,176,202*

shed [*v*] *cast off*
afford, beam, cashier, cast, diffuse, disburden, discard, doff, drop, emit, exude, exuviate, give, give forth, jettison, junk, let fall, molt, pour forth, radiate, reject, scatter, scrap, send forth, shower, slip, slough, spill, sprinkle, take off, throw, throw away, throw out, yield; SEE CONCEPTS *179,180,181,211*

sheen [*n*] *brightness, shine*
burnish, finish, glaze, gleam, glint, gloss, luster, patina, polish, shimmer, shininess, wax; SEE CONCEPT *620*

sheepish [*adj*] *shy, embarrassed*
abashed, ashamed, chagrined, diffident, docile, foolish, guilty, mortified, retiring, self-conscious, shamefaced, silly, tame, timid, timorous, uncomfortable; SEE CONCEPT *401*

sheer [*adj1*] *abrupt, steep*
arduous, erect, headlong, perpendicular, precipitate, precipitous, sideling, upright, very steep; SEE CONCEPTS *490,581*

sheer [*adj2*] *utter, absolute*
altogether, arrant, blasted, blessed, complete, confounded, downright, gross, infernal, out-and-out*,

outright, perfect, pure, quite, rank, simple, single, thoroughgoing, total, unadulterated, unalloyed, undiluted, unmitigated, unmixed, unqualified; SEE CONCEPTS *531,535,544*

sheer [*adj3*] *see-through, thin*
airy, chiffon, clear, cobwebby*, delicate, diaphanous, filmy, fine, flimsy, fragile, gauzy, gossamer, lacy, limpid, lucid, pellucid, pure, slight, smooth, soft, tiffany, translucent, transparent; SEE CONCEPT *606*

sheet [*n*] *coating, covering; page*
area, blanket, coat, expanse, film, foil, folio, lamina, layer, leaf, membrane, overlay, pane, panel, piece, plate, ply, slab, stratum, stretch, surface, sweep, veneer; SEE CONCEPTS *172,270,475,484*

shelf [*n*] *jutting, flat area or piece*
bank, bracket, console, counter, cupboard, ledge, mantelpiece, mantle, rack, reef, ridge, rock, shallow, shoal; SEE CONCEPTS *445,509,513*

shell [*n*] *structure; covering*
carapace, case, chassis, crust, frame, framework, hull, husk, integument, nut, pericarp, plastron, pod, scale, shard, shuck, skeleton, skin; SEE CONCEPTS *399,428,484*

shell out [*v*] *give*
ante up, disburse, expend, fork over*, hand over, lay out, outlay, pay, pay for, pay out, spend; SEE CONCEPT *341*

shelter [*n*] *protection, habitat*
apartment, asylum, cave, condo, co-op, cover, covert, crib, defense, den, digs*, dwelling, guard, guardian, harbor, harborage, haven, hermitage, hide, hideaway, hideout, hole in the wall*, home, homeplate, house, housing, hut, joint*, lodging, pad*, pen, port, preserve, protector, quarterage, rack, refuge, retirement, retreat, roof, roof over head*, roost*, safety, sanctuary, screen, security, shack, shade, shadow, shed, shield, tent, tower, turf, umbrella; SEE CONCEPTS *515,712*

shelter [*v*] *provide safety, cover*
chamber, conceal, cover, cover up, defend, enclose, guard, harbor, haven, hide, house, lodge, preserve, protect, roof, safeguard, screen, secure, shield, surround, take care of, take in, ward, watch over; SEE CONCEPTS *134,188*

shelve [*v*] *defer, postpone*
delay, dismiss, drop, freeze*, give up, hang up, hold, hold off, hold over, hold up, lay aside, mothball*, pigeonhole*, prolong, prorogue, put aside, put off, put on back burner*, put on hold, put on ice*, scrub, sideline, slow up, stay, suspend, table, tie up, waive; SEE CONCEPT *121*

shield [*n*] *protection*
absorber, aegis, armament, armor, buckler, buffer, bulwark, bumper, cover, defense, escutcheon, guard, mail, rampart, safeguard, screen, security, shelter, ward; SEE CONCEPTS *712,729*

shield [v] *protect*
bulwark, chamber, conceal, cover, cover all bases*, cover up, defend, fend, give cover, give shelter, go to bat for*, guard, harbor, haven, house, ride shotgun*, roof, safeguard, screen, secure, shelter, shotgun*, stonewall*, take under one's wing*, ward off; SEE CONCEPTS *96,134*

shift [n1] *switch, fluctuation*
about-face*, alteration, bend, change, changeover, conversion, deflection, deviation, displacement, double, fault, modification, move, passage, permutation, rearrangement, removal, shifting, substitution, switch, tack, transfer, transference, transformation, transit, translocation, turn, variation, veering, yaw; SEE CONCEPTS *213,697*

shift [n2] *trick, stratagem*
artifice, contrivance, craft, device, dodge, equivocation, evasion, expediency, expedient, gambit, hoax, makeshift, maneuver, move, ploy, recourse, refuge, resort, resource, ruse, stopgap*, strategy, substitute, subterfuge, wile; SEE CONCEPTS *59,660*

shift [n3] *time served doing work*
bout, go, period, spell, stint, time, tour, trick, turn, working time; SEE CONCEPT *802*

shift [v] *switch, fluctuate*
about-face*, alter, blow hot and cold*, bottom out*, budge, change, change gears, cook*, deviate, dial back, dislocate, displace, disturb, do up, drift, exchange, fault, flip-flop*, hem and haw*, move, move around, move over, rearrange, recalibrate, relocate, remove, replace, reposition, ship, shuffle, slip, stir, substitute, swap places, swerve, switch over, tack, transfer, transmogrify, transpose, turn, turn around, turn the corner*, turn the tables*, vacillate, vary, veer, waffle, yo-yo*; SEE CONCEPTS *213,232,697*

shifty [adj] *deceitful, untrustworthy*
cagey, collusive, conniving, contriving, crafty, crooked, cunning, devious, dishonest, dodging, duplicitous, elusive, equivocating, evasive, fly-by-night*, foxy, fraudulent, furtive, insidious, knavish, lying, mendacious, prevaricative, prevaricatory, roguish, scheming, shady, shrewd, shuffling, slick, slimy*, slippery, sly, sneaky, treacherous, tricky, underhand, unhonest, unprincipled, untruthful, wily; SEE CONCEPTS *401,404*

shimmer [n] *gleam*
blinking, coruscation, diffused light, flash, glimmer, glint, glisten, glitter, gloss, glow, incandescence, iridescence, luster, phosphorescence, scintillation, sheen, spangle, spark, sparkle, twinkle; SEE CONCEPTS *620,624*

shimmer [v] *glisten*
blaze, coruscate, dance, flare, flash, gleam, glint, glow, jiggle, phosphoresce, scintillate, shimmy, shine, sparkle, twinkle, wiggle; SEE CONCEPT *624*

shine [n] *brightness; polish*
flash, glare, glaze, gleam, glint, glitz, gloss, lambency, light, luminosity, luster, patina, polish, radiance, rub, sheen, shimmer, show, sparkle; SEE CONCEPT *620*

shine [v1] *give off or reflect light*
beam, bedazzle, blaze, blink, burn, dazzle, deflect, emit light, flare, flash, flicker, give light, glare, gleam, glimmer, glisten, glitter, glow, illuminate, illumine, incandesce, irradiate, luminesce, mirror, radiate, scintillate, shimmer, sparkle, twinkle; SEE CONCEPT *624*

shine [v2] *polish, burnish*
brush, buff, buff up, finish, furbish, give a sheen, glance, glaze, gloss, make brilliant, put a finish on, put a gloss on, rub, scour, sleek, wax; SEE CONCEPT *202*

shiny [adj] *bright, glistening*
agleam, burnished, clear, gleaming, glossy, lustrous, polished, satiny, sheeny, slick, sparkling, sunny; SEE CONCEPT *617*

ship [v] *send, transport*
address, consign, direct, dispatch, drop, embark, export, forward, freight, go aboard, haul, move, put on board, remit, route, shift, ship out, smuggle, transfer, transmit; SEE CONCEPTS *148,217*

shirk [v] *avoid, get out of responsibility*
bypass, cheat, creep, dodge, dog*, duck, elude, eschew, evade, fence, get around, goldbrick*, lie down on job*, lurk, malinger, parry, pussyfoot*, quit, shuffle off, shun, sidestep, skulk, slack, slink, slip, sluff off, snake, sneak, steal; SEE CONCEPTS *30,59,681*

shiver [v1] *shake, tremble*
be cold, dither, flutter, freeze, have the quivers, have the shakes, palpitate, quake, quaver, quiver, shudder, tremor, twitter, vibrate, wave; SEE CONCEPTS *152,185*

shiver [v2] *shatter; break into small pieces*
burst, crack, fragment, fragmentalize, pash, rive, smash, smash to smithereens*, smatter, splinter, splinterize; SEE CONCEPTS *246,252*

shock [n] *complete surprise; blow*
awe, bombshell*, breakdown, bump, clash, collapse, collision, concussion, confusion, consternation, crash, distress, disturbance, double whammy*, earthquake, encounter, excitement, eye-opener*, hysteria, impact, injury, jarring, jolt, percussion, prostration, ram, scare, start, stroke, stupefaction, stupor, trauma, traumatism, turn, upset, whammy*, wreck; SEE CONCEPTS *33,309,529*

shock [v] *completely surprise*
abash, agitate, anger, antagonize, appall, astound, awe, bowl over*, daze, disgust, dismay, displease, disquiet, disturb, electrify, flabbergast, flood, floor*, give a turn*, hit like ton of bricks*, horrify, insult, jar, jolt, knock out*, nauseate, numb, offend, outrage, overcome, overwhelm, paralyze, revolt, rock, scandalize, shake, shake up, sicken, stagger, startle, stun, stupefy, throw a curve*, traumatize, unsettle; SEE CONCEPT *42*

shocking [*adj*] *outrageous; very surprising*
abominable, appalling, atrocious, awful, burning, crying, desperate, detestable, direful, disgraceful, disgusting, disquieting, distressing, dreadful, fearful, formidable, foul, frightful, ghastly, glaring, hateful, heinous, hideous, horrible, horrific, horrifying, loathsome, monstrous, nauseating, odious, offensive, repulsive, revolting, scandalous, shameful, sickening, stupefying, terrible, ugly, unspeakable; SEE CONCEPTS *548,571*

shoddy [*adj*] *in bad shape*
base, borax, broken-down, cheap, cheesy*, common, dilapidated, dingy*, discreditable, disgraceful, dishonorable, disreputable, gaudy, ignominious, inferior, inglorious, junky*, makeshift, mean, not up to snuff*, paltry, plastic, poor, pretentious, rundown, scruffy*, second-rate*, seedy, shabby, shady, shameful, sleazy*, slipshod, tacky*, tawdry, trashy*, unrespectable; SEE CONCEPTS *485,571*

shoot [*v1*] *discharge a projectile, often to injure or kill*
bag*, barrage, blast, bombard, bring down, catapult, dispatch, drop the hammer*, emit, execute, expel, explode, fire, fling, gun, hit, hurl, ignite, kill, launch, let fly, let go with, loose, murder, open fire*, open up*, pick off*, plug, pop*, project, propel, pull the trigger, pump*, set off, throw lead*, torpedo, trigger, zap*; SEE CONCEPTS *179,246,252*

shoot [*v2*] *dash*
boil, bolt, charge, chase, dart, flash, fling, fly, gallop, hotfoot*, hurry, hurtle, lash, pass, race, reach, run, rush, scoot, skirr, speed, spring, spurt, streak, tear, whisk, whiz; SEE CONCEPTS *150,152*

shop [*n*] *place of retail business*
boutique, chain, deli, department store, emporium, five-and-dime, market, mill, outlet, showroom, stand, store, supermarket; SEE CONCEPTS *439, 441,448,449*

shop [*v*] *look for merchandise to buy*
buy, go shopping, hunt for, look for, market, purchase, try to buy; SEE CONCEPTS *327,330*

shore [*n*] *waterside*
bank, beach, border, brim, brink, coast, coastland, embankment, lakeshore, lakeside, littoral, margin, river bank, riverside, sand, sands, seaboard, seacoast, seashore, shingle, strand, waterfront; SEE CONCEPT *509*

shore [*v*] *reinforce*
bear up, bolster, brace, bulwark, buttress, carry, hold, prop, strengthen, support, sustain, underpin, upbear, uphold; SEE CONCEPTS *110,190*

short [*adj1*] *abridged*
abbreviate, abbreviated, aphoristic, bare, boiled down, breviloquent, brief, compendiary, compendious, compressed, concise, condensed, curtailed, curtate, cut short, cut to the bone*, decreased, decurtate, diminished, epigrammatic, fleeting, in a nutshell*, laconic, lessened, little, long story made short*, momentary, not protracted, pithy, pointed, precise, sen-

tentious, short and sweet*, shortened, short-lived, short-term, succinct, summarized, summary, terse, undersized, unprolonged, unsustained; SEE CONCEPTS *267,272,798*

short [*adj2*] *not tall*
abbreviated, chunky, close to the ground, compact, diminutive, dwarf, dwarfed, dwarfish, little, low, not long, petite, pint-sized*, pocket, pocket-sized*, runty, sawed-off*, skimpy, slight, small, squat, squatty, stocky, stubby, stunted, thick, thickset, tiny, undersized, wee*; SEE CONCEPTS *773,779,782*

short [*adj3*] *insufficient*
deficient, exiguous, failing, inadequate, lacking, limited, low on, meager, needing, niggardly*, poor, scant, scanty, scarce, short-handed*, shy, skimpy, slender, slim, sparse, tight, wanting; SEE CONCEPTS *527,560,762*

short [*adj4*] *abrupt, discourteous*
bad-tempered, blunt, breviloquent, brief, brusque, curt, direct, gruff, impolite, inconsiderate, irascible, offhand, rude, sharp, short-spoken, short-tempered, snappy*, snippety*, snippy*, straight, terse, testy, thoughtless, unceremonious, uncivil, ungracious; SEE CONCEPTS *267,401*

short [*adj5*] *crumbly*
brittle, crisp, crunchy, delicate, fragile, friable; SEE CONCEPT *462*

short [*adv*] *abruptly*
aback, by surprise, forthwith, sudden, suddenly, unanticipatedly, unaware, unawares, unexpectedly, without delay, without hesitation, without warning; SEE CONCEPT *799*

shortage [*n*] *deficiency*
curtailment, dearth, defalcation, deficit, failure, inadequacy, insufficiency, lack, lapse, leanness, paucity, pinch, poverty, scantiness, scarcity, shortfall, tightness, underage, want, weakness; SEE CONCEPTS *646,709,767*

shortcoming [*n*] *weak point*
bug*, catch*, defect, deficiency, demerit, drawback, failing, fault, flaw, frailty, imperfection, infirmity, lack, lapse, sin, weakness; SEE CONCEPTS *411,666,674,679*

shorten [*v*] *diminish, decrease*
abbreviate, abridge, blue pencil*, bob, boil down*, chop, clip, compress, condense, contract, curtail, cut, cut back, cut down, cut to the bone*, dock, edit, elide, excerpt, lessen, lop, minimize, put in a nutshell*, reduce, retrench, shrink, slash, snip, trim; SEE CONCEPTS *137,236,240,247*

short-lived [*adj*] *temporary*
brief, ephemeral, evanescent, fleeting, fugacious, fugitive, impermanent, momentary, passing, short, short-haul, short-run, short-term, transient, transitory; SEE CONCEPT *798*

shortly [*adv*] *right away*
anon, any minute now, before long, by and by, in a little while, presently, proximately, quickly, soon; SEE CONCEPT *820*

short-sighted [adj] *unmindful of future consequences*
astigmatic, blind, careless, foolish, headlong, ill-advised, ill-considered, imperceptive, impolitic, impractical, improvident, imprudent, injudicious, myopic, near-sighted, rash, stupid, unsagacious, unwary; SEE CONCEPTS *401,542*

shot [n1] *try, chance*
attempt, break, conjecture, effort, endeavor, fling*, go*, guess, occasion, opening, opportunity, pop*, show, slap*, stab*, surmise, time, turn, whack*, whirl*; SEE CONCEPT *693*

shot [n2] *discharge; ammunition*
ball, buckshot, bullet, dart, lead, lob, missile, pellet, projectile, slug, throw; SEE CONCEPT *498*

shoulder [v1] *be responsible for*
accept, assume, bear, carry, take on, take upon oneself; SEE CONCEPT *23*

shoulder [v2] *push, jostle*
bulldoze*, elbow, hustle, nudge, press, push aside, shove, thrust; SEE CONCEPT *208*

shout [n] *loud outcry*
bark, bawl, bellow, call, cheer, clamor, cry, howl, hue, roar, salvo, scream, screech, shriek, squall, squawk, tumult, vociferation, whoop*, yammer*, yap*, yawp*, yell; SEE CONCEPTS *77,595*

shout [v] *cry out loudly*
bawl, bay, bellow, call out, cheer, clamor, exclaim, holler, raise voice, roar, scream, screech, shriek, squall, squawk, vociferate, whoop*, yammer*, yap*, yawp*, yell; SEE CONCEPT *77*

shove [v] *push without gentleness*
boost, buck, bulldoze*, cram, crowd, dig, drive, elbow, hustle, impel, jab, jam, jostle, nudge, poke, press, prod, propel, shoulder, thrust; SEE CONCEPT *208*

shove off [v] *leave quickly*
blow, clear out, depart, exit, get off, go, go away, pull out, push off, quit, run along, start out, take off, vamoose*; SEE CONCEPT *195*

show [n1] *demonstration, exhibition*
appearance, array, display, expo*, exposition, fair, fanfare, fireworks, grandstand, manifestation, occurrence, pageant, pageantry, panoply, parade, pomp, presentation, program, representation, shine*, showboat*, showing, sight, spectacle, splash*, view; SEE CONCEPT *261*

show [n2] *entertainment event*
act, appearance, burlesque, carnival, cinema, comedy, drama, entertainment, film, flick, motion picture, movie, pageant, picture, play, presentation, production, showing, spectacle; SEE CONCEPTS *263,293*

show [n3] *false front; appearance given*
affectation, air, display, effect, face*, front, grandstand play*, guise, illusion, impression, likeness, make-believe*, ostentation, parade, pose, pretense, pretext, profession, seeming, semblance, sham*,

shine*, showboat*, showing, simulacrum, splash*; SEE CONCEPTS *633,716*

show [v1] *actively exhibit something*
afford, air, arrive, attend, bare, blazon, brandish, deal in, demonstrate, display, disport, exhibit, expose, flash, flaunt, flourish, lay bare, lay out, mount, offer, parade, present, produce, proffer, put on, reveal, sell, set out, showcase, show off, sport, spread, stage, streak, submit, supply, trot out, unfold, unfurl, unveil, vaunt, wave; SEE CONCEPT *138*

show [v2] *passively exhibit something*
appear, arrive, assert, be visible, blow in, clarify, come, demonstrate, determine, disclose, discover, display, divulge, elucidate, emerge, establish, evidence, evince, explain, get, get in, illustrate, indicate, instruct, lay out, loom, make known, make out, make the scene*, manifest, mark, materialize, note, ostend, point, present, proclaim, project, prove, put in appearance, reach, register, reveal, show face*, show up, teach, testify to, turn up, unveil; SEE CONCEPT *261*

show [v3] *grant*
accord, act with, bestow, confer, dispense, give; SEE CONCEPT *108*

show [v4] *accompany*
attend, conduct, direct, escort, guide, lead, pilot, route, see, shepherd, steer; SEE CONCEPTS *187,384*

showdown [n] *confrontation*
breaking point, clash, climax, crisis, culmination, exposé, moment of truth, unfolding; SEE CONCEPTS *388,674*

showoff [n] *person who brags about him- or herself*
boaster, braggadocio, braggart, egotist, exhibitionist, swaggerer, vulgarian; SEE CONCEPT *412*

show off [v] *flaunt; brag*
advertise, boast, brandish, demonstrate, display, disport, exhibit, expose, flash*, hand a line*, make a spectacle of, parade, spread out, swagger, trot out*; SEE CONCEPTS *49,261*

show up [v1] *arrive, attend*
appear, be conspicuous, be visible, blow in*, come, get, get in, make an appearance, put in appearance, reach, show, stand out, turn up; SEE CONCEPT *159*

show up [v2] *expose, embarrass*
belittle, convict, debunk, defeat, discover, discredit, highlight, invalidate, lay bare*, let down, mortify, pinpoint, put spotlight on*, put to shame*, reveal, shame, show in bad light*, uncloak, undress, unmask, unshroud, worst; SEE CONCEPTS *54,60*

showy [adj] *flamboyant, flashy*
classy, dashing, flash, garish, gaudy, glaring, histrionic, jazzy*, loud, luxurious, meretricious, opulent, ornate, ostentatious, overdone, overwrought, peacocky, pizzazz*, pompous, pretentious, resplendent, screaming, sensational, snazzy*, splashy, splendiferous, sumptuous, swank*, tawdry, tinsel*, tony*; SEE CONCEPT *589*

shred [n] *tiny piece*
atom, bit, cantlet, crumb, fragment, grain, iota, jot, modicum, ounce, part, particle, rag, ray, ribbon, scintilla, scrap, shadow, sliver, smidgen, snippet, speck, stitch, tatter, trace, whit; SEE CONCEPT *831*

shred [v] *cut into ribbons*
cut, fray, frazzle, make ragged, reduce, shave, sliver, strip, tatter, tear; SEE CONCEPT *176*

shrew [n] *female who is very vicious*
amazon*, calumniator, carper, detractor, harpy*, harridan, nag, ogress, reviler, termagant, tigress*, virago, vituperator; SEE CONCEPTS *412,415*

shrewd [adj] *clever, intelligent*
acute, argute, artful, astucious, astute, brainy*, cagey*, calculating, canny, crafty, cunning, cutting*, deep*, discerning, discriminating, far-sighted, foxy*, heady*, ingenious, inside, in the know*, judicious, keen, knowing, on the inside*, on top of*, penetrating, perceptive, perspicacious, piercing, probing, profound, prudent, quick-witted, sagacious, savvy, sensible, shark, sharp, slick*, slippery*, sly, smart, smooth, streetwise, tricky, underhand, up on*, wily, wise, wised up*; SEE CONCEPTS *401,402*

shriek [n/v] *high-pitched scream*
blare, cry, howl, screech, shout, shrill, squawk, squeal, wail, whoop, yell; SEE CONCEPTS *77,595*

shrill [adj] *high-pitched, harsh in sound*
acute, argute, blaring, blatant, cacophonous, clanging, clangorous, deafening, discordant, ear-piercing, ear-splitting, high, metallic, noisy, penetrating, piercing, piping, raucous, screeching, sharp, strident, thin, treble; SEE CONCEPTS *592,594*

shrine [n] *tribute to a god, idol, or spirit*
altar, chapel, church, enshrinement, grave, hallowed place, holy place, mausoleum, reliquary, sacred place, sanctorium, sanctuary, sanctum, sepulcher, temple; SEE CONCEPTS *368,439,448*

shrink [v1] *become smaller*
compress, concentrate, condense, constrict, contract, decrease, deflate, diminish, drop off, dwindle, fail, fall off, fall short, grow smaller, lessen, narrow, reduce, shorten, shrivel, wane, waste, waste away, weaken, wither, wrinkle; SEE CONCEPTS *137,698,776*

shrink [v2] *recoil, shy away*
blench, boggle, contract, cower, cringe, crouch, demur, draw back, flinch, hang back, huddle, quail, recede, refuse, retire, retreat, scruple, shudder, slink, wince, withdraw; SEE CONCEPTS *188,195*

shrivel [v] *dehydrate, dry up*
burn, contract, desiccate, dwindle, fossilize, mummify, mummy, parch, scorch, sear, shrink, stale, welter, wilt, wither, wizen, wrinkle; SEE CONCEPTS *137,250,255*

shudder [v] *shake, quiver*
convulse, dither, gyrate, jitter, quake, shimmy, shiver, tremble, tremor, twitter, wave; SEE CONCEPTS *34,150,152*

shuffle [v1] *move along lazily*
drag, limp, muddle, pad, scrape, scuff, scuffle, shamble, straggle, stumble, trail; SEE CONCEPT *151*

shuffle [v2] *rearrange, mix up*
break the deck, change, change the order, confuse, disarrange, disarray, discompose, dislocate, disorder, disorganize, disrupt, disturb, intermix, jumble, mess up, shift; SEE CONCEPTS *158,363*

shun [v] *avoid, ignore*
bilk, cold-shoulder*, cut, decline, despise, disdain, ditch*, dodge, double, duck, elude, escape, eschew, evade, get around, give a wide berth*, give the runaround*, have no part of*, have nothing to do with*, hide out, keep away from, keep clear of, neglect, palm off*, pass up, refuse, reject, scorn, shake, shake off, shy, snub, stall, stand aloof from, stay shy of, steer clear of*, turn back on*; SEE CONCEPTS *30,384*

shut [v] *close*
bar, batten down*, cage, close down, close up, confine, draw, drop the curtain*, enclose, exclude, fasten, fold, fold up, imprison, lock, push, put to, seal, secure, shut down, slam, wall off; SEE CONCEPTS *85,121,160,206,208,324*

shut off/shut out [v] *exclude; screen*
bar, beleaguer, blockade, block out, close, conceal, cover, debar, discontinue, evict, fence off, hide, keep out, lock out, mask, obstruct, ostracize, refuse, seclude, shroud, veil; SEE CONCEPTS *25,121,188*

shut up [v] *be or make quiet*
bottle up*, choke, dry up*, dummy up*, fall silent, gag, hold tongue*, hush, keep trap shut*, muzzle, pipe down*, quiet, quieten, quit chattering, shush*, silence, soft-pedal*, still, stop talking; SEE CONCEPT *77*

shy [adj1] *quiet and self-conscious*
afraid, apprehensive, averse, backward, bashful, cautious, chary, circumspect, conscious, coy, demure, diffident, disinclined, distrustful, fearful, hesitant, humble, indisposed, introvert, introverted, loath, loner, modest, nervous, recessive, reluctant, reserved, reticent, retiring, self-effacing, shamefaced, sheepish, shrinking, skittish, suspicious, timid, unassertive, unassured, uneager, uneffusive, unresponsive, unsocial, unwilling, wallflower*, wary; SEE CONCEPTS *401,404*

shy [adj2] *lacking, failing*
deficient, inadequate, insufficient, scant, scanty, scarce, short, unsufficient, wanting; SEE CONCEPTS *546,762,789*

sick [adj1] *not healthy, not feeling well*
ailing, bedridden, broken down, confined, debilitated, declining, defective, delicate, diseased, disordered, down, feeble, feverish, frail, funny*, green*, hospitalized, ill, impaired, imperfect, in a bad way, incurable, indisposed, infected, infirm, in poor health, invalid, laid-up, lousy, mean, nauseated, not so hot*, peaked, poorly, qualmish, queasy, rickety,

rocky, rotten, run down, sick as a dog*, suffering, tottering, under medication, under the weather*, unhealthy, unwell, weak, wobbly; SEE CONCEPT *314*

sick [*adj2*] *morbid, gross*
black, ghoulish, macabre, morose, sadistic, sickly; SEE CONCEPTS *537,571*

sick [*adj3*] *fed up, displeased*
blasé, bored, disgusted, jaded, revolted, satiated, tired, up to here with*, weary; SEE CONCEPT *403*

sicken [*v*] *revolt, make ill*
affect, afflict, derange, disgust, disorder, gross out*, nauseate, offend, reluct, repel, repulse, turn, turn one's stomach*, unhinge, unsettle, upset; SEE CONCEPTS *14,246*

sickening [*adj*] *disgusting, awful*
diseased, distasteful, foul, gross*, icky*, loathsome, nasty, nauseating, nauseous, noisome, offensive, putrid, repugnant, repulsive, revolting, rotten, stinking*, stomach-turning*, tainted, turn-off*; SEE CONCEPTS *529,571*

sickly [*adj1*] *not healthy*
ailing, below par, bilious, cranky, delicate, diseased, down, dragging, faint, feeble, indisposed, infirm, in poor health, lackluster, laid-low, languid, low, mean, off-color*, out of action*, out of shape*, pallid, peaked, peaky, pining, poorly, rocky, run-down, seedy, sickish, unhealthy, wan, weak; SEE CONCEPT *314*

sickly [*adj2*] *revolting*
bilious, cloying, insalubrious, mawkish, morbid, morose, nauseating, noisome, noxious, sick, unwholesome; SEE CONCEPTS *537,571*

sickness [*n*] *ill or abnormal condition*
affection, affliction, ailment, bug*, complaint, condition, disease, diseasedness, disorder, flu, ill, ill health, illness, indisposition, infirmity, malady, nausea, queasiness, syndrome, unhealth, unhealthfulness, unwellness; SEE CONCEPT *306*

side [*n1*] *edge, exteriority of object*
aspect, attitude, border, bottom, boundary, direction, disposition, division, elevation, face, facet, flank, front, hand, haunch, jamb, lee, limit, loin, margin, part, perimeter, periphery, posture, quarter, rear, rim, sector, stance, stand, surface, top, verge, view, wing; SEE CONCEPTS *513,835*

side [*n2*] *point of view*
angle, appearance, aspect, belief, direction, facet, hand, light, opinion, outlook, phase, position, slant, stand, standpoint, viewpoint; SEE CONCEPT *689*

side [*n3*] *opposing person or view*
behalf, belligerent, camp, cause, combatant, competition, contestant, crew, enemy, faction, foe, interest, part, party, rival, sect, team; SEE CONCEPTS *301,365*

side [*adj*] *minor; flanking*
ancillary, incidental, indirect, lateral, lesser, marginal, not the main, oblique, off-center, postern, roundabout, secondary, sidelong, sideward, side-

ways, sidewise, skirting, subordinate, subsidiary, superficial; SEE CONCEPT *575*

sideways [*adv*] *to the edge, exteriority*
alongside, aside, aslant, aslope, athwart, broadside, crabwise, edgeways, indirectly, laterally, obliquely, side by side, sidelong, sidewards, slanting, slantingly, slantwise, sloping, to the side; SEE CONCEPTS *581,583*

sift [*v*] *take out residue; remove impurities*
analyze, clean, colander, comb, delve into, dig into, drain, evaluate, examine, explore, fathom, filter, go into, go through, grade, inquire, investigate, look into, pan, part, pore over, probe, prospect, purify, riddle, screen, scrutinize, search, separate, sieve, size, sort, strain, winnow; SEE CONCEPTS *103,165*

sigh [*v1*] *breathe out heavily*
blow, complain, cry, exhale, gasp, grieve, groan, howl, lament, moan, murmur, pant, respire, roar, sob, sorrow, sough, suspire, wheeze, whine, whisper, whistle; SEE CONCEPT *163*

sigh [*v2*] *long for*
ache, crave, dream, hanker, hunger, languish, lust, mourn, pine, suspire, thirst, yearn; SEE CONCEPT *20*

sight [*n1*] *ability to perceive with eyes*
afterimage, appearance, apperception, apprehension, eye, eyes, eyeshot, eyesight, field of vision, ken, perception, range of vision, seeing, view, viewing, visibility, vision; SEE CONCEPT *629*

sight [*n2*] *spectacle*
display, exhibit, exhibition, outlook, pageant, parade, point of interest, scene, show, view, vista; SEE CONCEPTS *261,293*

sight [*n3*] *horrifying person or thing*
blot, eyesore, fright, mess, monstrosity, ogre, ogress, scarecrow, slob, spectacle, tramp; SEE CONCEPTS *412,513*

sight [*v*] *see*
behold, discern, distinguish, eyeball*, make out*, observe, perceive, spot, view, witness; SEE CONCEPT *626*

sign [*n1*] *indication, evidence*
assurance, augury, auspice, badge, beacon, bell, caution, clue, divination, flag, flash, foreboding, foreknowledge, foreshadowing, foretoken, forewarning, gesture, giveaway, handwriting on wall*, harbinger, herald, high sign*, hint, light, manifestation, mark, nod, note, omen, portent, precursor, prediction, premonition, presage, presentiment, prognostic, proof, signal, suggestion, symbol, symptom, token, trace, vestige, warning, wave, whistle, wink; SEE CONCEPTS *274,529,673,689*

sign [*n2*] *document with information; symbol*
badge, board, character, cipher, crest, device, emblem, ensign, guidepost, insignia, logo, mark, notice, placard, proof, representation, signboard, signpost, symbolization, token, type, warning; SEE CONCEPTS *271,284*

sign [*v1*] *write name*
acknowledge, authorize, autograph, confirm, endorse, initial, ink, inscribe, put John Hancock on*, put John Henry on*, rubber-stamp*, set one's hand to*, signature, subscribe, witness; SEE CONCEPT *79*

sign [*v2*] *motion to another*
beckon, express, flag, gesticulate, gesture, indicate, motion, signal, signalize, signify, use sign language, wave; SEE CONCEPT *74*

signal [*n*] *indication; authorization*
alarm, alert, beacon, bleep, blinker, cue, flag, flare, gesture, go-ahead*, green light*, high sign*, indicator, mark, Mayday*, movement, nod, okay*, omen, sign, SOS*, token, tocsin, wink; SEE CONCEPTS *74,284,529,685*

signal [*adj*] *extraordinary, outstanding*
arresting, arrestive, characteristic, conspicuous, distinctive, distinguished, eminent, exceptional, eye-catching, famous, illustrious, individual, marked, memorable, momentous, notable, noteworthy, noticeable, peculiar, prominent, pronounced, remarkable, renowned, salient, significant, striking; SEE CONCEPTS *568,574*

signal [*v*] *indicate; give a sign to*
beckon, communicate, flag, flash, gesticulate, gesture, motion, nod, semaphore, sign, signalize, warn, wave, wink; SEE CONCEPT *74*

significance [*n1*] *meaning*
acceptation, bottom line*, connotation, drift, force, heart, implication, import, intendment, kicker*, meat*, message, name of the game*, nature of the beast*, nitty-gritty*, nub, nuts and bolts*, point, punch line*, purport, score, sense, significancy, signification, stuff, understanding; SEE CONCEPT *682*

significance [*n2*] *importance*
authority, consequence, consideration, credit, excellence, gravity, import, impressiveness, influence, magnitude, matter, merit, moment, momentousness, perfection, pith, prestige, relevance, signification, virtue, weight, weightiness; SEE CONCEPT *668*

significant [*adj1*] *telling, meaningful*
cogent, compelling, convincing, denoting, eloquent, expressing, expressive, facund, forceful, heavy, important, indicative, knowing, meaning, momentous, powerful, pregnant, representative, rich, sententious, serious, sound, suggestive, symbolic, valid, weighty; SEE CONCEPTS *267,567*

significant [*adj2*] *important, critical*
big, carrying a lot of weight*, consequential, considerable, heavy, material, meaningful, momentous, notable, noteworthy, serious, substantial, vital, weighty; SEE CONCEPT *568*

signify [*v1*] *mean, indicate*
add up to, announce, bear, be a sign of, bespeak, betoken, carry, communicate, connote, convey, denote, disclose, evidence, evince, exhibit, express, flash, imply, import, insinuate, intend, intimate, manifest, matter, portend, proclaim, purport, repre-sent, show, sign, spell, stand for, suggest, symbolize, talk, tell, wink; SEE CONCEPTS *55,266,682*

signify [*v2*] *be of importance*
be of consequence, be of significance, carry weight, count, import, matter, mean, weigh; SEE CONCEPT *668*

silence [*n*] *absence of sound, speech*
blackout, calm, censorship, dead air, death, dumbness, hush, hush-hush*, inarticulateness, iron curtain, laconism, lull, muteness, noiselessness, peace, quiescence, quiet, quietness, quietude, quietus, reserve, reticence, saturninity, secrecy, sleep, speechlessness, still, stillness, sulk, sullenness, taciturnity, uncommunicativeness; SEE CONCEPT *65*

silence [*v*] *make or be quiet*
choke off*, clam, clam up*, close up, cool it*, cut off, cut short, dampen, deaden, decrease the volume, dry up*, dull, dumb, dummy up*, extinguish, gag, hold one's tongue*, hush, hush-hush*, hush one's mouth*, keep it down*, lull, muffle, mute, muzzle, overawe, pipe down*, quash, quell, quiet, quiet down, quieten, say nothing, shush*, shut up, sit on*, soft-pedal*, squelch, stifle, still, strike dumb*, subdue, suppress, tongue-tie*; SEE CONCEPT *266*

silent [*adj1*] *quiet; speechless*
bashful, buttoned up*, checked, clammed up*, close, closed up, closemouthed, curbed, dumb, dummied up*, faint, Garbo*, hush, hushed, iced*, inarticulate, incoherent, inconversable, indistinct, inhibited, laconic, mousy, mum, mute, muted, noiseless, nonvocal, not talkative, reserved, restrained, reticent, shy, silentious, soundless, still, struck dumb, taciturn, tongue-tied, unclear, uncommunicative, unheard, unsociable, unspeaking, voiceless, wordless, zipped*; SEE CONCEPT *594*

silent [*adj2*] *understood, implied*
aphonic, implicit, indescribable, inexpressible, nameless, tacit, unexpressed, unpronounced, unspoken, unuttered, unvoiced, wordless; SEE CONCEPT *267*

silhouette [*n*] *outline*
contour, delineation, etching, figuration, form, likeness, line, lineament, lineation, portrait, profile, shade, shadow, shape; SEE CONCEPTS *259,625*

silky [*adj*] *very smooth; like satin*
cottony, delicate, glossy, like silk, luxurious, plush, satiny, silk, silken, sleek, soft, tender, velvety; SEE CONCEPT *606*

silly [*adj*] *absurd, giddy, foolish*
asinine, balmy, brainless, childish, crazy, dippy*, dizzy*, empty, empty-headed*, fatuous, feather-brained*, flighty, foolhardy, frivolous, harebrained*, idiotic, ignorant, illogical, immature, imprudent, inane, inappropriate, inconsistent, irrational, irresponsible, ludicrous, meaningless, muddle-headed*, nitwitted, nonsensical, pointless, preposterous, puerile, ridiculous, senseless, sheepheaded*, simple, simple-minded, stupid, unintelligent, unreasonable,

unwise, vacuous, witless; SEE CONCEPTS *401, 403,542*

silver [*adj*] *shiny gray in color*
argent, argentate, bright, lustrous, pale, pearly, plated, resplendent, silvered, silvery, sterling, white; SEE CONCEPT *618*

similar [*adj*] *very much alike*
agnate, akin, allied, analogous, coincident, coincidental, coinciding, collateral, companion, comparable, complementary, congruent, congruous, consonant, consubstantial, correlative, corresponding, homogeneous, identical, in agreement, kin, kindred, like, matching, much the same, parallel, reciprocal, related, resembling, same, twin, uniform; SEE CONCEPTS *487,573*

similarity [*n*] *likeness, correspondence*
affinity, agreement, alikeness, analogy, approximation, association, closeness, coincidence, collation, community, comparability, comparison, concordance, concurrence, conformity, congruence, congruity, connection, correlation, dead ringer*, harmony, homogeneity, identity, interrelation, kinship, likes of, look-alike, parallel, parallelism, parity, peas in a pod*, proportion, reciprocity, relation, relationship, resemblance, sameness, semblance, simile, similitude, synonymity, two of a kind; SEE CONCEPT *670*

simmer [*v*] *boil, smolder*
be agitated, be angry, be tense, be uptight, bubble, burn, churn, cook, effervesce, ferment, fizz, fret, fricassee, fume, parboil, rage, seethe, smart, sparkle, stew, stir, warm; SEE CONCEPTS *35,170,410*

simple [*adj1*] *clear, understandable; easy*
child's play*, cinch*, clean, easy as pie*, effortless, elementary, facile, incomplex, intelligible, light, lucid, manageable, mild, no problem*, no sweat*, not difficult, picnic*, piece of cake*, plain, quiet, royal, self-explanatory, simple as ABC*, smooth, snap*, straightforward, transparent, uncomplicated, uninvolved, unmistakable, untroublesome, walkover*; SEE CONCEPTS *529,538*

simple [*adj2*] *uncluttered, natural*
absolute, austere, classic, clean, discreet, elementary, folksy, homely, homey, humble, inelaborate, lowly, mere, modest, not complex, open and shut*, plain, pure, pure and simple*, rustic, sheer, single, Spartan, unadorned, unadulterated, unaffected, unalloyed, unblended, uncombined, uncomplicated, uncompounded, undecorated, unelaborate, unembellished, unfussy, unmitigated, unmixed, unornamented, unostentatious, unpretentious, unqualified, vanilla*; SEE CONCEPTS *562,589*

simple [*adj3*] *childlike, innocent*
amateur, artless, bald, basic, childish, direct, frank, green*, guileless, honest, ingenuous, naive, naked, natural, plain, sincere, square, stark, trusting, unaffected, unartificial, undeniable, unexperienced, un-

pretentious, unschooled, unsophisticated, unstudied, unvarnished; SEE CONCEPTS *267,401,542*

simple [*adj4*] *feeble-minded; not intelligent*
amateur, asinine, backward, brainless, credulous, dense, dimwitted, dull, dumb, fat, feeble, foolish, green*, gullible, half-witted, idiotic, ignorant, illiterate, imbecile, inane, inexperienced, inexpert, insensate, mindless, moronic, nitwitted, obtuse, retarded, senseless, shallow, silly, simple-minded, slow, soft, soft-headed*, stupid, thick, uneducated, unintelligent, witless; SEE CONCEPT *402*

simplicity [*n*] *absence of complication, sophistication*
artlessness, candor, chastity, clarity, classicality, clean lines, clearness, directness, ease, easiness, elementariness, guilelessness, homogeneity, ingenuousness, innocence, integrity, lack of adornment, modesty, monotony, naïveté, naivety, naturalness, obviousness, openness, plainness, primitiveness, purity, restraint, severity, singleness, straightforwardness, uniformity, unity; SEE CONCEPTS *633,655,663*

simplify [*v*] *make easy, intelligible*
abridge, analyze, boil down, break down, break it down, chasten, clarify, clean it up, clean up, clear up, cut down, cut the frills*, decipher, disentangle, disinvolve, draw a picture*, elucidate, explain, facilitate, get down to basics*, get to the meat*, hit the high spots*, interpret, lay out, let daylight in*, let sunlight in*, make clear, make perfectly clear, make plain, nutshell*, order, put one straight*, reduce, shorten, spell out, streamline, unscramble; SEE CONCEPTS *57,110,261*

simply [*adv1*] *plainly, clearly*
artlessly, candidly, commonly, directly, easily, frankly, guilelessly, honestly, ingenuously, intelligibly, matter-of-factly, modestly, naturally, openly, ordinarily, quietly, sincerely, straightforwardly, unaffectedly, unpretentiously, without any elaboration; SEE CONCEPTS *544,562*

simply [*adv2*] *merely*
barely, but, just, only, purely, solely, utterly; SEE CONCEPTS *544,557*

simply [*adv3*] *absolutely, completely*
altogether, in fact, really, totally, unreservedly, utterly, wholly; SEE CONCEPTS *531,535*

simulate [*v*] *pretend, imitate*
act, act like, affect, ape*, assume, bluff, borrow, cheat, concoct, copy, counterfeit, crib*, deceive, disguise, dissemble, do, do a take-off*, do like, equivocate, exaggerate, fabricate, fake, favor, feature, feign, fence, gloss over, invent, knock off*, lie, lift, make believe, mimic, mirror, misrepresent, phony, pirate, play, playact, pose, prevaricate, put on*, put on an act*, replicate, reproduce, resemble, steal; SEE CONCEPTS *59,63,111,171*

simultaneous [*adj*] *happening at about the same time*
accompanying, agreeing, at the same time, coetaneous, coeval, coexistent, coexisting, coincident, coinciding, concurrent, concurring, contemporaneous,

contemporary, dead heat*, in sync*, synchronal, synchronic, synchronous, with the beat*; SEE CONCEPTS *548,799*

sin [n] *illegal or immoral action*
anger, covetousness, crime, damnation, debt, deficiency, demerit, disobedience, envy, error, evil, evildoing, fault, gluttony, guilt, immorality, imperfection, iniquity, lust, misdeed, offense, peccability, peccadillo, peccancy, pride, shortcoming, sinfulness, sloth, tort, transgression, trespass, ungodliness, unrighteousness, veniality, vice, violation, wickedness, wrong, wrongdoing, wrongness; SEE CONCEPTS *101,645*

sin [v] *commit illegal or immoral action*
backslide*, break commandment, break law, cheat, commit crime, deviate, do wrong, err, fall, fall from grace*, go astray*, lapse, live in sin, misbehave, misconduct, offend, sow wild oats*, stray, take primrose path*, transgress, trespass, wallow in the mire*, wander; SEE CONCEPTS *101,375,645*

sincere [adj] *straightforward, honest*
aboveboard, actual, artless, bona fide, candid, deadlevel*, dear, devout, earnest, faithful, forthright, frank, genuine, guileless, heartfelt, honest to God*, like it is, meant, natural, no fooling*, no-nonsense*, on the level*, on the line*, on up and up*, open, outspoken, plain, pretensionless, real, regular, righteous, saintly, serious, square*, sure enough, true, true-blue*, trustworthy, twenty-four carat*, unaffected, undesigning, undissembled, unfeigned, unpretentious, up-front*, wholehearted; SEE CONCEPTS *267,401,542*

sincerely [adv] *seriously, honestly*
aboveboard, candidly, deeply, earnestly, frankly, from bottom of heart, genuinely, in all conscience, in all sincerity, ingenuously, in good faith, naturally, profoundly, really, truly, truthfully, wholeheartedly, without equivocation; SEE CONCEPTS *267,582*

sincerity [n] *straightforwardness, honesty*
artlessness, bona fide, candor, earnestness, frankness, genuineness, good faith, goodwill, guilelessness, heart, honor, impartiality, innocence, justice, openness, probity, reliability, seriousness, sincereness, singleness, trustworthiness, truth, truthfulness, veracity, wholeheartedness; SEE CONCEPTS *633,657*

sinful [adj] *immoral, criminal*
amiss, bad, base, blamable, blameful, blameworthy, censurable, corrupt, culpable, damnable, demeritorious, depraved, disgraceful, erring, evil, guilty, iniquitous, irreligious, low, morally wrong, reprehensible, reprobate, shameful, ungodly, unholy, unregenerate, unrighteous, vicious, vile, wicked, wrong; SEE CONCEPTS *545,548*

sing [v1] *carry a tune with one's voice*
belt out*, burst into song*, buzz*, canary*, cantillate, carol, chant, chirp, choir, croon, descant, duet, groan*, harmonize, hum, hymn, intone, lift up a voice*, line out*, lullaby, make melody*, mouth,

pipe, purr*, resound, roar, serenade, shout, singsong, solo, trill, troll, tune, vocalize, wait, warble, whine, whistle, yodel; SEE CONCEPTS *47,77,292*

sing [v2] *tattle on someone*
betray, blow the whistle*, fink, inform, peach*, rat*, snitch, spill the beans*, talk, turn in; SEE CONCEPTS *60,317*

singer [n] *person who can carry a tune*
accompanist, artist, artiste, chanter, chanteuse, choralist, chorister, crooner, diva, intoner, melodist, minstrel, musician, nightingale, serenader, soloist, songbird, songster, troubadour, vocalist, voice, warbler, yodeler; SEE CONCEPT *352*

single [adj1] *alone, distinct*
distinct, distinguished, especial, exceptional, exclusive, individual, indivisible, isolated, lone, loner, not general, not public, odd, one, only, original, particular, peerless, personal, private, rare, restricted, secluded, separate, separated, simple, singled-out, singular, sole, solitary, special, specific, strange, unalloyed, unblended, uncommon, uncompounded, undivided, unique, unitary, unmixed, unrivaled, unshared, unusual, without equal; SEE CONCEPTS *564,577,762*

single [adj2] *not married*
bachelor, celibate, companionless, divorced, eligible, free, living alone, loner, separated, sole, solo, spouseless, unattached, unfettered, unmarried, unwed, virgin; SEE CONCEPT *555*

singly [adv] *individually*
apart, independently, one at a time, one by one, particularly, respectively, separately, severally; SEE CONCEPT *577*

singular [adj1] *unique, odd*
atypical, avant-garde, bizarre, breaking new ground*, conspicuous, cool*, curious, eccentric, eminent, exceptional, extraordinary, loner, noteworthy, original, outlandish, out-of-the-way, outstanding, peculiar, prodigious, puzzling, queer, rare, remarkable, special, strange, uncommon, unimaginable, unordinary, unparalleled, unprecedented, unthinkable, unusual, unwonted, weird; SEE CONCEPT *564*

singular [adj2] *alone, separate*
certain, definite, discrete, exclusive, individual, one, only, particular, respective, single, sole, solitary, solo, unique, unrepeatable; SEE CONCEPT *577*

sinister [adj] *nasty, menacing*
adverse, apocalyptic, bad, baleful, baneful, blackhearted, corrupt, deleterious, dire, disastrous, dishonest, disquieting, doomful, evil, foreboding, harmful, hurtful, ill-boding, inauspicious, injurious, lowering, malefic, malevolent, malign, malignant, menacing, mischievous, obnoxious, ominous, pernicious, perverse, poisonous, portentous, threatening, unfavorable, unfortunate, unlucky, unpropitious, woeful; SEE CONCEPTS *401,548,571*

sink [v1] *fall in, go under*
bore, bring down, capsize, cast down, cave in, couch, decline, demit, depress, descend, dig, dip,

disappear, drill, drive, droop, drop, drown, ebb, engulf, excavate, fall, flounder, force down, founder, go down, go to the bottom, immerse, lay, let down, lower, overturn, overwhelm, plummet, plunge, put down, ram, regress, run, sag, scuttle, set, settle, shipwreck, slope, slump, stab, stick, stoop, submerge, subside, swamp, thrust, tip over, touch bottom, wreck; SEE CONCEPTS *181,213*

sink [*v2*] *fall, decrease*
abate, collapse, diminish, drop, lapse, lessen, relapse, retrogress, slip, slump, subside, wane; SEE CONCEPTS *698,776*

sink [*v3*] *deteriorate*
decay, decline, decrease, degenerate, depreciate, descend, deteriorate, die, diminish, disimprove, disintegrate, dwindle, fade, fail, flag, go downhill*, lessen, retrograde, rot, spoil, waste, weaken, worsen; SEE CONCEPTS *469,698*

sink [*v4*] *be humble or humbled*
abase, bemean, be reduced to, cast down, debase, degrade, demean, humiliate, lower, stoop, succumb; SEE CONCEPTS *7,19,35*

sinuous [*adj*] *winding, twisting*
anfractuous, circuitous, coiling, convoluted, crooked, curved, curvy, deviative, devious, flexuous, indirect, meandering, meandrous, serpentine, snaky*, supple, tortuous, twisting and turning*, undulating, vagrant; SEE CONCEPT *581*

sip [*v*] *drink slowly*
drink in, extract, imbibe, partake, quaff, sample, savor, sup, swallow, taste, toss; SEE CONCEPT *169*

sit [*v1*] *rest on one's behind*
bear on, be seated, cover, ensconce, give feet a rest*, grab a chair*, have a place, have a seat, hunker*, install, lie, park*, perch*, plop down*, pose, posture, put it there*, relax, remain, rest, seat, seat oneself, settle, squat, take a load off*, take a place, take a seat; SEE CONCEPTS *154,201*

sit [*v2*] *hold a meeting*
assemble, be in session, come together, convene, deliberate, hold an assembly, meet, officiate, open, preside; SEE CONCEPTS *324,384*

site [*n*] *place of activity*
fix, ground, habitat, hangout, haunt, home, lay, layout, locale, locality, location, locus, mise-en-scène, plot, point, position, post, range, scene, section, situation, slot, spot, station, wherever, X marks the spot*; SEE CONCEPT *198*

situation [*n1*] *place of activity*
bearings, direction, footing, latitude, locale, locality, location, locus, longitude, position, post, seat, setting, site, spot, stage, station, where, whereabouts; SEE CONCEPT *198*

situation [*n2*] *circumstances, status*
ballgame*, bargain, capacity, case, character, condition, footing*, how things stack up*, like it is*, mode, picture, place, plight, position, posture, rank, scene, size of it*, sphere, stage, standing, standpoint,

state, state of affairs, station, status quo*; SEE CONCEPTS *388,696*

situation [*n3*] *employment status*
appointment, berth, billet, capacity, connection, employment, engagement, hire, job, office, place, placement, position, post, profession, spot, trade; SEE CONCEPTS *351,360,668*

sizable [*adj*] *considerable, large*
ample, big, burly, capacious, comprehensive, decent, decent-sized, extensive, good, goodly, great, gross, hefty, husky, jumbo*, king-size, largish, major, massive, ponderous, respectable, sensible, spacious, strapping, substantial, tidy, voluminous, whopping*; SEE CONCEPT *781*

size [*n*] *extent or bulk of some dimension*
admeasurement, amount, amplitude, area, bigness, body, breadth, caliber, capaciousness, capacity, content, diameter, dimensions, enormity, extension, extent, greatness, height, highness, hugeness, immensity, intensity, largeness, length, magnitude, mass, measurement, proportion, proportions, range, scope, spread, stature, stretch, substance, substantiality, tonnage, vastness, volume, voluminosity, width; SEE CONCEPTS *730,792*

sizzle [*v*] *hiss, fry*
broil, brown, buzz, cook, crackle, fizz, fizzle, frizzle, grill, roast, sear, sibilate, spit, sputter, swish, wheeze, whisper, whiz; SEE CONCEPTS *65,170*

skeleton [*n*] *structure of bones in animate being or supports in an object*
bones, bony structure, cage, design, draft, frame, framework, Mr./Ms. Bones, osteology, outline, scaffolding, sketch, support; SEE CONCEPTS *393,733*

skeptic [*n*] *person who is leery, unbelieving*
agnostic, apostate, atheist, cynic, disbeliever, dissenter, doubter, doubting Thomas*, freethinker, heathen, heretic, infidel, materialist, misanthrope, misbeliever, nihilist, pagan, pessimist, profaner, questioner, rationalist, scoffer, unbeliever; SEE CONCEPTS *361,423*

skeptical [*adj*] *disbelieving, leery*
agnostic, aporetic, cynical, dissenting, doubtful, doubting, dubious, freethinking, hesitating, incredulous, mistrustful, questioning, quizzical, scoffing, show-me*, suspicious, unbelieving, unconvinced; SEE CONCEPT *403*

sketch [*n*] *drawing, outline*
account, adumbration, aperçu, blueprint, cartoon, chart, compendium, configuration, copy, delineation, depiction, description, design, diagram, digest, doodle, draft, figuration, figure, form, illustration, likeness, monograph, painting, picture, piece, plan, portrayal, precis, report, representation, rough, shape, skeleton, summary, survey, syllabus, version, vignette; SEE CONCEPTS *268,283,625*

sketch [*v*] *draw, outline*
adumbrate, block out*, blueprint*, chalk, characterize, chart, delineate, depict, describe, design, detail,

develop, diagram, doodle, draft, lay out*, line, map out*, paint, plan, plot, portray, represent, rough out*, skeleton, skeletonize, trace; SEE CONCEPTS *36,174*

sketchy [adj] *rough, incomplete*
coarse, crude, cursory, defective, depthless, faulty, imperfect, inadequate, insufficient, introductory, outline, perfunctory, preliminary, rough, scrappy, shallow, skimpy, slight, superficial, uncritical, unfinished, vague; SEE CONCEPT *531*

skid [v] *slide against will*
drift, glide, go into skid, move, sheer, skew, slip, slue, swerve, veer; SEE CONCEPT *152*

skill [n] *ability, talent to do something*
accomplishment, address, adroitness, aptitude, art, artistry, cleverness, clout, command, competence, craft, cunning, deftness, dexterity, dodge*, ease, experience, expertise, expertism, expertness, facility, finesse, goods*, handiness, ingenuity, intelligence, job, knack*, know-how*, line, makings, mastership, mastery, moxie*, one's thing*, profession, proficiency, prowess, quickness, readiness, right stuff*, savvy, skillfulness, sleight, smarts*, stuff*, technique, trade, what it takes*; SEE CONCEPTS *409,630*

skillful [adj] *able, talented*
accomplished, adept, adroit, a hand at*, apt, brainy, clever, competent, cool*, crack*, crackerjack*, dexterous, experienced, expert, good, handy, into*, learned, masterful, masterly, old*, on the ball*, practical, practiced, prepared, pretty, primed, pro, professional, proficient, quick, ready, really into, savvy, seasoned, sharp, skilled, smart, smooth, there*, trained, tuned in*, versant, versed, vet*, veteran, well-versed, whiz, wicked*, wised up*, workmanlike; SEE CONCEPTS *402,527*

skim [v1] *remove the top part*
brush, cream, dip, get the cream, glance, graze, kiss, ladle, ream, scoop, separate, shave, top; SEE CONCEPT *211*

skim [v2] *glide over quickly, lightly*
brush, carom, coast, dart, float, fly, graze, ricochet, sail, scud, shoot, skate, skip, skirr, skitter, smooth along, soar, trip; SEE CONCEPTS *150,152*

skim [v3] *look through cursorily*
browse, brush over, dip, examine, flip through, get the cream*, give the once-over*, glance, glance over, hit the high spots*, leaf through*, once over lightly*, read, read swiftly, riff, riffle, run eye over*, scan, skip, thumb through*, turn the pages*; SEE CONCEPTS *72,103,623*

skimp [v] *be cheap or frugal about*
be mean with, be niggardly, be sparing, cut corners*, make ends meet*, penny-pinch*, pinch, roll back, save, scamp, scant, scrape, screw, scrimp, slight, spare, stint, tighten one's belt*, withhold; SEE CONCEPT *330*

skimpy [adj] *sparse, inadequate*
deficient, exiguous, failing, insufficient, meager, miserly, niggardly, poor, scant, scanty, scrimp,

scrimpy, short, shy, spare, stingy, thin, tight, unsufficient, wanting; SEE CONCEPTS *334,762,789*

skin [n] *outer covering, especially of animate being*
bark, carapace, case, casing, coating, crust, cutis, derma, dermis, epidermis, fell, film, fur, hide, hull, husk, integument, jacket, membrane, outside, parchment, peel, pelt, rind, sheath, sheathing, shell, shuck, slough, surface, tegument, vellum; SEE CONCEPTS *392,428,484*

skin [v] *remove outer covering*
abrade, bare, bark, cast, cut off, decorticate, excoriate, exuviate, flay, gall, graze, hull, husk, lay bare, pare, peel, pull off, remove, rind, scale, scalp, scrape, shave, shed, shuck, slough, strip, trim; SEE CONCEPTS *176,211*

skinny [adj] *very thin*
angular, bony, emaciated, gaunt, lank, lanky, lean, like a rail*, malnourished, rawboned, scraggy, scrawny, skeletal, skin-and-bone*, slender, spare, twiggy*, undernourished, underweight; SEE CONCEPTS *490,491*

skip [v1] *bounce or jump over*
bob, bolt, bound, buck, canter, caper, carom, cavort, dance, flee, flit, fly, frisk, gambol, glance, graze, hippety-hop*, hop, leap, lope, make off, prance, ricochet, run, scamper, scoot, skedaddle*, skim, skirr, skitter, spring, step, tiptoe, trip; SEE CONCEPTS *150,194*

skip [v2] *avoid, miss*
cut, desert, disregard, escape, eschew, flee, leave out, miss out, neglect, omit, pass over, pass up, play hooky*, run away, skim over, split; SEE CONCEPTS *30,681*

skirt [n1] *border, edge*
brim, brink, fringe, hem, margin, outskirts, perimeter, periphery, purlieus, rim, skirting, verge; SEE CONCEPTS *484,825*

skirt [n2] *ladies' garment that hangs from waist*
culottes, dirndl, dress, hoop, kilt, midi, mini, muumuu, pannier, petticoat, sarong, tutu; SEE CONCEPT *451*

skirt [v1] *border; be on the edge*
bound, define, edge, flank, fringe, hem, lie along, lie alongside, margin, rim, surround, verge; SEE CONCEPT *751*

skirt [v2] *avoid; get around*
burke, bypass, circumnavigate, circumvent, detour, dodge, duck, elude, equivocate, escape, evade, hedge, ignore, sidestep, skip, steer clear of; SEE CONCEPTS *30,102,147*

skittish [adj] *very nervous*
agitable, alarmable, capricious, changeable, combustible, dizzy*, edgy, excitable, excited, fearful, fickle, fidgety, flighty, frivolous, giddy, harebrained,* high-strung*, irresponsible, jumpy, lightheaded, lively, peppy, playful, restive, scatterbrained*, sensitive, spirited, undependable, unreliable, volative, whimsical, zippy*; SEE CONCEPT *401*

sky [*n*] *earth's atmosphere*
azure, celestial sphere, empyrean, firmament, heavens, lid*, the blue*, upper atmosphere, vault, vault of heaven*, welkin, wild blue yonder*; SEE CONCEPT *437*

slab [*n*] *chunk of solid object*
bar, billet, bit, board, boulder, chip, cut, cutting, hunk, ingot, lump, muck, piece, plate, portion, rod, slice, stave, stick, stone, strip, wedge; SEE CONCEPTS *471,835*

slack [*n*] *looseness, excess*
give, leeway, play, room, slackening, slowdown, slow-up; SEE CONCEPTS *513,807*

slack [*adj1*] *loose, baggy; inactive*
dull, easy, feeble, flabby, flaccid, flexible, flimsy, inert, infirm, laggard, lax, leisurely, limp, not taut, passive, quaggy, quiet, relaxed, sloppy, slow, slow-moving, sluggish, soft, supine, unsteady, weak; SEE CONCEPTS *485,584,589*

slack [*adj2*] *lazy, negligent*
asleep on the job*, behindhand, careless, delinquent, derelict, dilatory, disregardful, dormant, dull, easygoing, faineant, idle, inactive, inattentive, indolent, inert, lackadaisical, lax, lethargic, neglectful, not busy, permissive, quiescent, quiet, regardless, remiss, slothful, slow, slow-moving, sluggish, stagnant, tardy; SEE CONCEPT *538*

slack/slacken [*v*] *do little or nothing; loosen*
abate, decrease, diminish, dodge, drop off, dwindle, ease, ease off, featherbed*, flag, goldbrick*, goof off*, idle, lax, lay back, lessen, let up, lie down on job*, loose, moderate, neglect, reduce, relax, release, shirk, slack off, slow down, taper, tire, untighten, wane; SEE CONCEPTS *210,681,698*

slam [*n1*] *loud noise from impact*
bang, bash, blast, blow, boom, burst, clap, crack, crash, ding, pound, smack, smash, whack, wham; SEE CONCEPTS *189,595*

slam [*n2*] *harsh criticism*
animadversion, aspersion, jab, obloquy, potshot*, slap*, slur*, stricture, swipe*; SEE CONCEPTS *52,278*

slam [*v1*] *throw or push very hard*
bang, bat, batter, beat, belt, blast, clobber, close, crash, cudgel, dash, fling, hammer, hit, hurl, knock, pound, shut, slap, slug, smash, strike, swat, thump, thwack, wallop; SEE CONCEPTS *189,208,222*

slam [*v2*] *criticize very harshly*
attack, castigate, damn, excoriate, flay, lambaste, lash into, pan, scathe, scourge, shoot down, slap, slash, vilify; SEE CONCEPTS *52,54*

slander [*n*] *scandalous remark*
aspersion, backbiting*, backstabbing*, belittlement, black eye*, calumny, defamation, depreciation, detraction, dirt*, dirty linen*, disparagement, hit*, libel, lie, misrepresentation, muckraking, mud*, mudslinging*, obloquy, rap*, scandal, slam*, slime*, smear*, tale; SEE CONCEPTS *54,192,278*

slander [*v*] *make a scandalous remark*
asperse, assail, attack, backbite*, bad-mouth*, belie, belittle, besmirch, blacken name*, blaspheme, blister, blot, calumniate, cast a slur on, curse, damage, decry, defame, defile, denigrate, depreciate, derogate, detract, dishonor, disparage, give a bad name*, hit*, hurt, injure, libel, malign, muckrake, mudslinging*, pan*, plaster, revile, roast*, run smear campaign*, scandalize, scorch, slam*, slur, smear, smirch, sneer, strumpet, sully, tarnish, tear down, traduce, vilify; SEE CONCEPTS *54,192*

slang [*n*] *casual dialect*
argot, cant, colloquialism, informal speech, jargon, lingo, neologism, patois, patter, pidgin, shoptalk, slanguage* street talk, vernacular, vulgarism, vulgarity; SEE CONCEPT *276*

slant [*n1*] *angle, slope*
camber, cant, declination, diagonal, grade, gradient, inclination, incline, lean, leaning, pitch, rake, ramp, tilt; SEE CONCEPT *738*

slant [*n2*] *particular opinion*
angle, attitude, bias, direction, emphasis, judgment, leaning, one-sidedness, outlook, point of view, predilection, predisposition, prejudice, prepossession, sentiment, side, standpoint, view, viewpoint; SEE CONCEPT *689*

slant [*v1*] *angle off, slope*
aim, bank, beam, bend, bevel, cant, decline, descend, deviate, direct, diverge, grade, heel, incline, lean, level, lie obliquely, list, point, skew, splay, swerve, tilt, tip, train, veer; SEE CONCEPTS *201,738*

slant [*v2*] *change to suit; distort*
aim, angle, bias, color, concentrate, direct, focus, influence, orient, point, prejudice, train, twist, warp, weight; SEE CONCEPTS *63,266*

slap [*n/v*] *hard hit, often with hand*
bang, bash, blip, blow, box, buffet, bust, chop, clap, clout, crack, cuff, pat, percuss, poke, potch, punch, slam, smack, sock, spank, strike, swat, wallop, whack, wham; SEE CONCEPT *189*

slash [*v1*] *cut*
carve, chop, gash, hack, incise, injure, lacerate, open up, pierce, rend, rip, score, sever, slice, slit, wound; SEE CONCEPTS *137,176*

slash [*v2*] *reduce greatly*
abbreviate, abridge, clip, curtail, cut, cut back, cut down, drop, hack, lower, mark down, pare, retrench, shave, shorten; SEE CONCEPTS *236,240,247*

slaughter [*n*] *killing*
annihilation, bloodbath, bloodshed, butchery, carnage, destruction, extermination, liquidation, massacre, murder, slaying; SEE CONCEPT *252*

slaughter [*v*] *kill*
butcher, crush, decimate, defeat, destroy, do in* exterminate, finish, liquidate, maim, mangle, massacre, murder, mutilate, overwhelm, rout, slay, stick, thrash, torture, total* trounce, vanquish, waste, wipe out*; SEE CONCEPT *252*

slave [n] *person who serves, often under duress*
bondservant, bondsman/woman, captive, chattel, drudge, help, laborer, menial, peon, retainer, serf, servant, skivvy, subservient, thrall, toiler, vassal, victim, worker, workhorse; SEE CONCEPT *348*

slave [v] *work very hard*
be servile, drudge, grind, grovel, grub, muck, plod skivvy, slog, toil, work fingers to bone*; SEE CONCEPT *87*

slavery [n] *state of working under duress or without freedom*
bondage, bullwork, captivity, chains* constraint, drudge, drudgery, enslavement, enthrallment, feudalism, grind, helotry, indenture, labor, menial labor, moil, peonage, restraint, serfdom, serfhood, servitude, subjection, subjugation, thrall, thralldom, toil, vassalage, work; SEE CONCEPTS *324,388*

slay [v] *kill*
annihilate, assassinate, butcher, cut off, destroy, dispatch, do*, do away with, do in*, down*, eliminate, erase, execute, exterminate, finish, hit, knock off*, liquidate, massacre, murder, neutralize, put away*, rub out*, slaughter, snuff*, waste*; SEE CONCEPT *252*

sleazy [adj] *disreputable*
base, broken-down, cheap, common, dilapidated, flimsy, limp, low, mean, paltry, poor, run-down, seedy, shabby, shoddy, sordid, squalid, tacky*, trashy*, unsubstantial; SEE CONCEPTS *334,485,589*

sleek [adj] *smooth, glossy*
glassy, glistening, lustrous, polished, satin, shiny, silken, silky; SEE CONCEPT *606*

sleep [n] *suspension of consciousness*
bedtime*, catnap, coma, dormancy, doze, dream, dullness, few z's*, forty winks*, hibernation, lethargy, nap, nod, repose, rest, sack time*, sandman*, shuteye*, siesta, slumber, slumberland*, snooze, torpidity, torpor, trance; SEE CONCEPT *315*

sleep [v] *suspend consciousness*
bed down*, bunk*, catch a wink*, catch forty winks*, catnap, cop some z's*, crash*, doze, dream, drop off*, drowse, fall asleep, fall out*, flop*, hibernate, hit the hay*, hit the sack*, languish, nap, nod, nod off, oversleep, relax, repose, rest, retire, sack out*, saw wood*, slumber, snooze, snore, take a nap, turn in*, yawn, zonk out*, zzz*; SEE CONCEPT *315*

sleepy [adj] *tired, dull*
asleep, blah*, comatose, dopey*, dozy, draggy, drowsy, heavy, hypnotic, inactive, lethargic, listless, out*, out of it*, quiet, sleeping, sleepyhead*, slow, sluggish, slumberous, slumbersome, snoozy*, somnolent, soporific, torpid, yawning; SEE CONCEPTS *315,539*

slender/slim [adj1] *thin, not heavy*
attenuate, beanpole*, beanstalk*, fine, insubstantial, lean, lithe, narrow, reedy*, skeleton, skinny, slight, spare, stalky*, stick, svelte, sylphlike, tenuous,
threadlike, trim, twiggy*, willowy; SEE CONCEPTS *490,491*

slender/slim [adj2] *inadequate, flimsy*
bare, deficient, faint, feeble, fragile, inconsiderable, insufficient, little, meager, poor, remote, scant, scanty, scarce, short, shy, slight, small, spare, tenuous, thin, wanting, weak; SEE CONCEPTS *552,771*

slice [n] *piece; share*
allotment, allowance, bite, chop, cut, cut of pie*, helping, lot, part, portion, quota, segment, sliver, thin piece, triangle, wedge; SEE CONCEPT *835*

slice [v] *cut into portions, shares*
carve, chiv, cleave, dissect, dissever, divide, gash, hack, incise, pierce, segment, sever, shave, shred, slash, slit, split, strip, subdivide, sunder; SEE CONCEPTS *98,137,176*

slick [adj1] *smooth, polished*
glossy, greasy, icy, lubricious, oily, oleaginous, shiny, sleek, sleeky, slippery, slithery, soapy; SEE CONCEPT *606*

slick [adj2] *smart, clever*
adroit, cagey*, canny, deft, dextrous, foxy, glib, knowing, meretricious, plausible, professional, quick, sharp, shrewd, skillful, sly, smooth, smooth-spoken, sophisticated, specious, streetwise*, unctuous, urbane, wise; SEE CONCEPTS *401,402*

slide [v] *move smoothly; move down*
accelerate, coast, drift, drive, drop, fall, fall off, flow, glide, glissade, launch, move, move along, move over, propel, sag, scooch*, shift, shove, skate, skid, skim, slip, slither, slump, smooth along, spill, stream, thrust, toboggan, tumble, veer; SEE CONCEPTS *150,152*

slight [n] *insult, disrespect*
affront, brush-off, call-down, cold shoulder*, contempt, cut*, discourtesy, disdain, disregard, inattention, indifference, kick, neglect, put-down*, rebuff, rejection, slap in the face*, snub; SEE CONCEPTS *30,384,529*

slight [adj1] *insignificant, small*
fat, feeble, inconsiderable, insubstantial, meager, minor, modest, negligible, off, outside, paltry, petty, piddling, remote, scanty, slender, slim, sparse, superficial, trifling, trivial, unessential, unimportant, weak; SEE CONCEPTS *575,762,789*

slight [adj2] *thin, small in build*
attenuate, broomstick*, dainty, delicate, feeble, flimsy, fragile, frail, light, reedy, shadow, skeleton, skinny, slender, slim, spare, stick, twiggy*; SEE CONCEPTS *490,491*

slight [v] *offend, insult*
affront, blink at, brush off, chill, cold-shoulder*, contemn, cool*, cut*, despise, discount, disdain, disparage, disregard, fail, flout, forget, give the brush*, ignore, make light of, neglect, not give time of day*, omit, overlook, pooh-pooh*, reject, scoff, scorn, show disrespect, shrug off, skip, slur, sneeze at*,

snub, treat with contempt, turn deaf ear to*, upstage; SEE CONCEPTS *7,19,30,384*

slightly [*adv*] *a little*
hardly, hardly at all, hardly noticeable, imperceptibly, inappreciably, inconsiderably, insignificantly, kind of, lightly, marginally, more or less, on a small scale, pretty, scarcely any, somewhat, to some degree, to some extent; SEE CONCEPTS *544,772*

slim [*v*] *lose weight*
diet, reduce, slenderize; SEE CONCEPT *202*

slime [*n*] *muck, gelled waste*
fungus, glop*, goo*, gunk*, mire, mucus, mud, ooze, scum, sludge; SEE CONCEPT *260*

slimy [*adj*] *oozy, gooey*
clammy, glutinous, miry, mucky, mucous, muculent, muddy, scummy, viscous, yukky*; SEE CONCEPTS *485,621*

sling [*v*] *throw or hang over*
bung, cast, catapult, chuck, dangle, fire, fling, heave, hoist, hurl, launch, lob, peg, pitch, raise, send, shoot, suspend, swing, toss, weight; SEE CONCEPTS *181,222*

slink/slither [*v*] *creep by*
coast, cower, glide, glissade, go stealthily, gumshoe*, lurk, meander, pass quietly, prowl, pussyfoot*, shirk, sidle, skitter, skulk, slick, slide, slip, snake, sneak, steal, undulate; SEE CONCEPT *151*

slip [*n1*] *error, goof*
blooper*, blunder, bungle, failure, fault, flub*, fluff*, foul-up*, gaff, howler*, imprudence, indiscretion, lapse, misdeed, misstep, mistake, muff*, omission, oversight, screw-up*, slip of the tongue*, slip-up*, trip; SEE CONCEPT *101*

slip [*n2*] *piece of paper*
label, leaf, page, sheet, sliver, strip, tag, ticket; SEE CONCEPTS *270,475*

slip [*v1*] *fall; glide*
drop, glissade, lose balance, lose footing, lurch, move, shift, skate, skid, slick, slide, slither, smooth along, totter, trip; SEE CONCEPTS *150,152*

slip [*v2*] *err*
blunder, drop the ball*, flub*, fluff*, goof*, go wrong, make a mistake, miscalculate, misjudge, mistake, muff*, put foot in mouth*, slip up, stumble, trip; SEE CONCEPT *101*

slippery [*adj1*] *smooth, slick*
glace, glassy, glazed, glistening, greasy, icy, like a skating rink*, lubricious, lustrous, perilous, polished, satiny, silky, sleek, slimy, soapy, unctuous, unsafe, unstable, unsteady, waxy, wet; SEE CONCEPT *606*

slippery [*adj2*] *uncertain, unreliable*
cagey*, changeable, crafty, cunning, devious, dishonest, duplicitous, elusive, evasive, false, fly-by-night*, foxy, inconstant, insecure, mutable, shifty, slick, slithery, smooth, sneaky, treacherous, tricky, two-faced*, unpredictable, unsafe, unstable, unsteady, untrustworthy, variable; SEE CONCEPTS *401,534,535*

slipshod [*adj*] *careless; not well done*
bedraggled, botched*, disheveled, faulty, fly-by-night*, fouled-up*, haphazard, imperfect, inaccurate, inexact, junky*, loose, messed-up, messy, neglected, negligent, raunchy, screwed-up*, scrubby*, scruffy*, shabby*, shoddy*, slapdash*, sloppy, slovenly, tacky*, tattered, threadbare, unkempt, unmeticulous, unsystematic, unthorough, untidy; SEE CONCEPTS *485,570,589*

slit [*n*] *small opening, cut*
aperture, breach, cleavage, cleft, crack, crevice, fissure, gash, hole, incision, rent, split, tear; SEE CONCEPT *513*

slit [*v*] *cut open*
gash, incise, knife, lance, pierce, rip, sever, slash, slice, slot, split open, tear; SEE CONCEPT *176*

sliver [*n*] *tiny piece, usually of wood or metal*
bit, flake, fragment, paring, shaving, shred, slice, slip, snip, snippet, splinter, thorn; SEE CONCEPTS *471,831*

slobber [*v*] *drool*
dribble, drip, drivel, froth, salivate, slabber, slaver, water at the mouth; SEE CONCEPT *185*

slogan [*n*] *motto*
byword, catchphrase, catchword, expression, idiom, jingle, phrase, proverb, rallying cry*, saying, shibboleth*, trademark*, war cry*, watchword; SEE CONCEPT *278*

slop [*v*] *splash; make a mess*
dash, drip, flounder, let run out, let run over, overflow, slosh, smear, smudge, spatter, spill, splatter, spray, wallow; SEE CONCEPT *250*

slope [*n*] *slant, tilt*
abruptness, bank, bend, bevel, bias, cant, declination, declivity, deflection, descent, deviation, diagonal, downgrade, gradient, hill, inclination, incline, lean, leaning, obliqueness, obliquity, pitch, ramp, rise, rising ground, shelf, skew, steepness, swag, sway, tip; SEE CONCEPTS *738,757*

slope [*v*] *slant, tilt*
angle, ascend, bank, bevel, cant, descend, dip, drop, drop away, fall, heel, incline, lean, list, pitch, rake, recline, rise, shelve, skew, splay, tip; SEE CONCEPTS *201,738*

sloppy [*adj*] *messy*
awkward, bedraggled, botched, careless, clumsy, dingy*, dirty, disheveled, inattentive, mediocre, muddy, not clean, poor, slapdash, slipshod, slovenly, sludgy*, slushy*, splashy*, tacky*, unkempt, unthorough, untidy, watery, wet; SEE CONCEPTS *531,603,621*

slot [*n*] *opening, place*
aperture, channel, cut, groove, hole, niche, position, recess, slit, socket, space, time, vacancy; SEE CONCEPT *513*

slouch [v] *slump over*
be lazy, bend, bow, crouch, droop, lean, loaf, loll, lounge, sag, stoop, wilt; SEE CONCEPTS *154,201*

slovenly [adj] *dirty, disordered*
bedraggled, botched, careless, dingy*, disheveled, disorderly, dowdy, down-at-the-heel*, frowzy*, frumpy*, grody*, grubby*, grungy*, heedless, icky*, loose, messed up*, messy, mussy, negligent, pigpen*, raunchy, seedy, slack, slapdash, sleazy*, slipshod, sloppy, tacky, topsy-turvy, unfastidious, unkempt, unthorough, untidy; SEE CONCEPTS *485,621*

slow [adj1] *unhurried, lazy*
apathetic, crawling, creeping, dawdling, delaying, deliberate, dilatory, disinclined, dreamy, drowsy, easy, gradual, heavy, idle, imperceptible, inactive, indolent, inert, lackadaisical, laggard, lagging, leaden, leisurely, lethargic, listless, loitering, measured, moderate, negligent, passive, phlegmatic, plodding, ponderous, postponing, procrastinating, quiet, reluctant, remiss, slack, sleepy, slothful, slow-moving, sluggish, snaillike, stagnant, supine, tardy, torpid, tortoiselike; SEE CONCEPTS *538,584,588*

slow [adj2] *behind, late*
backward, behindhand, belated, conservative, dead, delayed, detained, dilatory, down, draggy*, dull, gradual, hindered, impeded, inactive, lingering, long-delayed, long-drawn-out*, low, moderate, off, overdue, prolonged, protracted, reduced, slack, sleepy, sluggish, stagnant, stiff, tame, tardy, tedious, time-consuming, uneventful, unproductive, unprogressive, unpunctual; SEE CONCEPTS *529,537,548*

slow [adj3] *unintelligent*
backward, dense, dim, dimwitted, dull, dumb, dunce, imbecile, limited, moronic, obtuse, retarded, simple, slow on uptake*, stupid, thick*, unresponsive; SEE CONCEPT *402*

slow [v] *delay, restrict*
abate, anchor it, back-water*, bog down, brake, check, choke, curb, curtail, cut back, cut down, decelerate, decrease, detain, diminish, ease off, ease up, embog, handicap, hinder, hit the brakes*, hold back, hold up, impede, keep waiting, lag, lessen, let down flaps*, loiter, lose speed, lose steam*, mire, moderate, postpone, procrastinate, qualify, quiet, reduce, reduce speed, reef, regulate, rein in, relax, retard, retardate, set back, slacken, stall, stunt, temper, wind down; SEE CONCEPTS *130,234,250*

slowdown [n] *slacking off; gradual decrease*
arrest, deceleration, decline, delay, downtrend, downturn, drop, drop-off, falloff, freeze, inactivity, retardation, retardedness, slack, slackening, slow-up, stagnation, stoppage, strike; SEE CONCEPTS *121,130*

sluggish [adj] *dull, slow-moving*
apathetic, blah*, comatose, dopey*, down, dragging, draggy*, drippy*, heavy, hebetudinous, inactive, indolent, inert, laid-back*, languid, languorous, leaden, lethargic, lifeless, listless, lumpish, mooney*, off, phlegmatic, pokey*, slack, sleepyhead*,

slothful, slow, sluggard, slumberous, stagnant, stiff, sullen, torpid, unresponsive; SEE CONCEPTS *401,584*

slumber [n] *sleep*
coma, dormancy, doze, drowse, forty winks*, inactivity, languor, lethargy, nap, repose, rest, sack time*, shut-eye*, snooze, stupor, torpor; SEE CONCEPT *315*

slump [n] *decline, failure*
bad period, bad times, blight, blue devils*, blue funk*, bottom, bust, collapse, crash, depreciation, depression, descent, dip, downer*, downslide*, downswing*, downtrend, downturn, drop, dumps*, fall, falling-off*, funk, hard times*, letdown*, low, rainy days*, recession, reverse, rut, sag, slide, slip, stagnation, the skids*, trough; SEE CONCEPTS *335,410,674*

slump [v] *decline, sink*
bend, blight, cave in, collapse, crash, decay, deteriorate, droop, drop, fall, fall off*, go down, go downhill*, go to ruin*, hunch, keel over, loll, pitch, plummet, plunge, reach new low*, sag, slide, slip, slouch, topple, tumble; SEE CONCEPTS *181,698, 699,763*

slur [n] *insult*
accusation, affront, animadversion, aspersion, bar sinister*, black eye*, blemish, blot, blur, brand, brickbat*, calumny, dirty dig*, discredit, disgrace, dump, expose, hit, innuendo, insinuation, knock, obloquy, odium, onus, put-down*, rap, reflection, reproach, slam, smear, stain, stigma, stricture, zinger*; SEE CONCEPTS *44,54,278*

slur [v1] *insult*
blacken, blemish, blister, blot, blow off*, brand, calumniate, cap, chop*, cut to the quick*, cut up*, defame, denigrate, detract, discredit, disgrace, dump on*, give a black eye*, hit where one lives*, insinuate, kick in the teeth*, libel, malign, miff, offend, push, put down*, reproach, roast*, scorch*, skin alive*, slander, slap in the face*, slight, smear*, snub, spatter, stain, tear down, traduce, vilify, zing*; SEE CONCEPTS *7,19,44,54*

slur [v2] *mumble words*
garble, mispronounce, miss, skip, stutter; SEE CONCEPT *47*

sly [adj] *clever, devious*
arch, artful, astute, bluffing, cagey, calculating, canny, captious, conniving, covert, crafty, crooked, cunning, deceitful, deceptive, delusive, designing, dishonest, dishonorable, dissembling, double-dealing, elusive, foxy, furtive, guileful, illusory, impish, ingenious, insidious, intriguing, mean, mischievous, plotting, roguish, scheming, secret, sharp, shifty, shrewd, slick, smart, smooth, sneaking, stealthy, subtle, traitorous, treacherous, tricky, underhand, unscrupulous, wily; SEE CONCEPTS *401,542*

smack [n/v] *strike, often with hand*
bang, blip, blow, box, buffet, chop, clap, clout, crack, cuff, hit, pat, punch, slap, snap, sock, spank, tap; SEE CONCEPT *189*

smack [*adv*] *directly, exactly*
accurately, bang*, clearly, just, plumb, point-blank*, precisely, right, sharp, square, squarely, straight; SEE CONCEPT *557*

small [*adj1*] *tiny in size, quantity*
baby, bantam, bitty*, cramped, diminutive, dwarf, humble, immature, inadequate, inconsequential, inconsiderable, insufficient, limited, little, meager, microscopic, mini*, miniature, minuscule, minute, modest, narrow, paltry, petite, petty, picayune, piddling*, pint-sized*, pitiful, pocket-sized*, poor, puny*, pygmy, runty*, scanty, scrubby, short, shrimp*, slight, small-scale, stunted, teensy*, teeny, toy, trifling, trivial, undersized, unpretentious, wee*, young; SEE CONCEPTS *773,789*

small [*adj2*] *unimportant*
bush-league*, inadequate, inconsiderable, ineffectual, inferior, insignificant, lesser, light, limited, lower, mean, minor, minor-league*, minute, narrow, negligible, paltry, petty, secondary, set, small-fry*, small-time*, trifling, trivial, unessential; SEE CONCEPT *575*

small [*adj3*] *narrow-minded, nasty*
base, grudging, ignoble, illiberal, limited, little, mean, narrow, petty, selfish, set, vulgar; SEE CONCEPT *401*

smart [*adj1*] *intelligent*
acute, adept, agile, alert, apt, astute, bold, brainy*, bright, brilliant, brisk, canny, clever, crafty, effective, egghead*, fresh, genius, good, impertinent, ingenious, keen, knowing, long-haired*, nervy, nimble, on the ball*, pert, pointed, quick, quick-witted, ready, resourceful, sassy, sharp, shrewd, skull, slick*, whiz*, wise; SEE CONCEPT *402*

smart [*adj2*] *stylish, fashionable*
chic, dapper, dashing, dressed to kill*, elegant, exclusive, fine, fly*, in fashion, last word*, latest thing*, modish, natty, neat, snappy, spruce, swank, trendy, trim, well turned-out, with-it*; SEE CONCEPT *589*

smart [*adj3*] *brisk, lively*
active, bold, brazen, cracking, energetic, forward, good, jaunty, nervy, pert, quick, saucy, scintillating, spanking, spirited, sprightly, vigorous; SEE CONCEPTS *401,542*

smart [*v*] *hurt, pain*
ache, be painful, bite, burn, prick, prickle, sting, suffer, throb, tingle; SEE CONCEPTS *246,728*

smash [*n1*] *collision; defeat*
accident, bang, bash, blast, blow, boom, breakdown, breaking, breakup, burst, clap, collapse, crack, crack-up, crash, debacle, destruction, disaster, downfall, failure, pile-up, ruin, shattering, slam, smash-up, sock, wallop, welt, whack, wham, wreck; SEE CONCEPTS *674,675*

smash [*n2*] *great success*
hit, knockout, sensation, wow; SEE CONCEPT *706*

smash [*v1*] *break into pieces*
bang, belt, blast, break to smithereens*, burst, clobber, collide, crack, crash, crush, demolish, disinte-grate, fracture, fragment, hit, make mincemeat of*, pound, powder, pulverize, rive, scrunch, shatter, shiver, slam, slug, splinter, squash, squish, trash, wallop; SEE CONCEPTS *246,252*

smash [*v2*] *defeat, destroy*
annihilate, break up, decimate, demolish, destruct, disrupt, lay in ruins*, lay waste*, overthrow, overturn, put out of action*, put out of commission*, raze, ruin, shatter, tear down, topple, trash, tumble, wreck; SEE CONCEPTS *95,252*

smear [*v1*] *rub on, spread over*
apply, bedaub, besmirch, blur, coat, cover, dab, daub, defile, dirty, discolor, overlay, overspread, patch, plaster, slop, smudge, soil, spatter, spray, sprinkle, stain, sully, taint, tar, tarnish; SEE CONCEPTS *172,202,215*

smear [*v2*] *tarnish a reputation*
asperse, bad-mouth*, befoul, besmirch, blacken, blackguard*, blister, calumniate, defame, defile, denigrate, discolor, drag through mud*, give a black eye*, hit, libel, malign, mud-sling*, pan*, poor-mouth*, rap*, rip up*, scorch*, slam*, slander, slur, sully, taint, traduce, vilify; SEE CONCEPTS *54,63*

smell [*n*] *odor*
aroma, bouquet, emanation, essence, flavor, fragrance, incense, perfume, redolence, savor, scent, spice, stench, stink, tang, trace, trail, whiff; SEE CONCEPT *590,599*

smell [*v1*] *perceive with the nose*
breathe, detect, discover, find, get a whiff*, identify, inhale, nose, scent, sniff, snuff; SEE CONCEPTS *590,601,602*

smell [*v2*] *have an odor*
be malodorous, funk*, reek, smell to high heaven*, stench, stink, whiff; SEE CONCEPT *600*

smelly [*adj*] *having a bad odor*
evil-smelling, fetid, foul, foul-smelling, funky*, high, malodorous, mephitic, noisome, olid, putrid, rancid, rank, reeking, stinking, strong, strong-smelling, whiffy*; SEE CONCEPT *598*

smile [*v*] *put on a happy expression*
beam, be gracious, express friendliness, express tenderness, grin, laugh, look amused, look delighted, look happy, look pleased, simper, smirk; SEE CONCEPT *185*

smirk [*n*] *sly smile*
beam, grin, leer, simper, smug look, sneer; SEE CONCEPT *185*

smoky [*adj*] *hazy, sooty*
begrimed, black, burning, caliginous, dingy, fumy, gray, grimy, messy, murky, reeking, silvery, smoke-colored, smoldering, thick, vaporous; SEE CONCEPTS *485,618*

smolder [*v*] *burn, simmer*
boil, bubble, churn, consume, erupt, explode, ferment, fester, fulminate, fume, seethe, smoke, steam, stir; SEE CONCEPTS *35,249*

smooth [*adj1*] *level, unwrinkled; flowing*
bland, continuous, creamy, easy, effortless, equable, even, flat, fluent, fluid, flush, frictionless, gentle,

glassy, glossy, hairless, horizontal, invariable, lustrous, mild, mirrorlike, monotonous, peaceful, plain, planate, plane, polished, quiet, regular, rhythmic, rippleless, serene, shaven, shiny, silky, sleek, soft, soothing, stable, steady, still, tranquil, unbroken, undeviating, undisturbed, uneventful, uniform, uninterrupted, unruffled, untroubled, unvarying, velvety; SEE CONCEPTS *406,480,606*

smooth [*adj2*] *suave in behavior*
agreeable, bland, civilized, courteous, courtly, facile, genial, glib, ingratiating, mellow, mild, persuasive, pleasant, polite, slick, smarmy*, unctuous, urbane; SEE CONCEPT *401*

smooth [*v1*] *make level*
burnish, clear, even, flatten, flush, glaze, gloss, grade, iron, lay, level, make uniform, perfect, plane, polish, press, refine, round, sand, sleek, slick, varnish; SEE CONCEPTS *137,250*

smooth [*v2*] *make peace*
allay, alleviate, appease, assuage, calm, comfort, cool*, ease, extenuate, facilitate, iron out, mellow, mitigate, mollify, palliate, pat, pave the way*, soften, stroke, take the edge off*, take the sting out*; SEE CONCEPTS *7,22*

smother [*v*] *extinguish; cover, hide*
asphyxiate, choke, collect, compose, conceal, control, cool, cork, douse, envelop, heap, hush up*, inundate, keep back, kill, muffle, overwhelm, quash, quell, quench, rein, repress, restrain, shower, shroud, simmer down, snuff, squelch, stamp out, stifle, strangle, suffocate, suppress, surround, throttle; SEE CONCEPTS *130,172,188,234*

smudge [*n*] *dirt smear*
blemish, blot, blur, macule, smut, smutch, soiled spot, spot; SEE CONCEPT *723*

smudge [*v*] *smear, dirty*
begrime, blacken, blotch, blur, daub, defile, foul, grime, mark, plaster, slop, smirch, soil, spatter, sully, taint, tarnish; SEE CONCEPT *254*

smug [*adj*] *pleased with oneself*
complacent, conceited, egoistic, egotistical, holier-than-thou*, hotshot*, pompous, priggish, puffed-up*, self-contented, self-righteous, self-satisfied, snobbish, stuck on oneself*, stuck-up*, stuffy, superior, vainglorious; SEE CONCEPTS *404,542*

smuggle [*v*] *transfer illegal goods*
bootleg, deal, export, hide, moonshine*, pirate, push, run, run contraband*, run rum*, snake in*; SEE CONCEPT *192*

smutty [*adj*] *obscene, vulgar*
bawdy, blue*, coarse, crude, dirty, filthy, foul, immoral, improper, indecent, indelicate, lewd, nasty, off-color*, pornographic, prurient, racy, raunchy, raw, risqué, rough, salacious, salty, scatological, suggestive, X-rated*; SEE CONCEPTS *267,372,545*

snack [*n*] *tiny meal*
bite, bite to eat*, break, eats*, goodies*, grub*, light meal, lunch, luncheon, midnight snack, morsel, munch*, nibble, nosh*, pickings, piece, refreshment, tea, tidbit; SEE CONCEPTS *457,459*

snag [*n*] *complication in situation*
bar, barrier, blockade, brake, bug*, catch, Catch-22, clog, crimp, cropper, crunch, curb, difficulty, disadvantage, drag*, drawback, fix*, glitch, hamper, hitch, hold-up*, hole*, hurdle, impediment, inconvenience, knot, obstacle, obstruction, pickle*, problem, puzzler, scrape, spot, stumbling block*, the rub*, tight spot*; SEE CONCEPTS *666,674*

snag [*v*] *catch on something*
hole, nail, rip, run into, tear; SEE CONCEPT *214*

snaky [*adj1*] *winding*
anfractuous, convoluted, entwined, flexuous, indirect, meandering, meandrous, serpentine, sinuous, tortuous, twisted, twisting, writhing, zigzag; SEE CONCEPT *581*

snaky [*adj2*] *devious, sly*
crafty, insidious, lurking, perfidious, slinking, sneaky, subtle, treacherous, venomous, vipery, virulent; SEE CONCEPT *401*

snap [*n*] *easy thing to accomplish*
breeze*, child's play*, cinch, duck soup*, ease, easy as pie*, easy job, kid stuff*, no problem, picnic*, pie*, smooth sailing*, soft touch*, walkover*; SEE CONCEPT *693*

snap [*v1*] *separate, break*
click, come apart, crack, crackle, fracture, give way, pop; SEE CONCEPTS *98,246*

snap [*v2*] *bite, seize*
bite at, catch, clutch, grab, grasp, grip, jerk, lurch, nip, snatch, twitch, yank; SEE CONCEPTS *90,191*

snap [*v3*] *speak sharply*
bark, flare, flash, fly off the handle*, get angry, growl, grumble, grunt, jump down throat*, lash out, retort, roar, snarl, snort, take it out on*, vent, yell; SEE CONCEPTS *54,77*

snappy [*adj1*] *nasty, irritable*
cross, disagreeable, edgy, fractious, hasty, huffy, petulant, quick-tempered, snappish, tart, testy, touchy, waspish; SEE CONCEPTS *267,401*

snappy [*adj2*] *fashionable*
chic, classy, dapper, dashing, fly*, in good taste, modish, natty, sharp, smart, stylish, swank*, tony*, trendy, up-to-the-minute, with style; SEE CONCEPT *589*

snappy [*adj3*] *fast*
abrupt, breakneck*, expeditious, fleet, harefooted, hasty, immediate, instant, on-the-spot, quick, rapid, speedy, sudden, swift, unpremeditated; SEE CONCEPTS *588,799*

snare [*n*] *trap*
allurement, bait, booby trap*, catch, come-on*, deception, decoy, enticement, entrapment, inveiglement, lure, net*, noose*, pitfall, quicksand*, seducement, temptation, trick, wire*; SEE CONCEPTS *529,674*

snare [v] *catch, trap*
arrest, bag*, corral*, decoy, enmesh, entangle, entrap, get fingers on*, involve, land, lure, net, pull in, round up, seduce, seize, tempt, wire*; SEE CONCEPTS *11,90*

snarl [n] *complication, mess*
chaos, clutter, complexity, confusion, disarray, disorder, entanglement, intricacy, intricateness, jam, jungle, knot, labyrinth, maze, mishmash, morass, muddle, muss, skein, swarm, tangle, web; SEE CONCEPTS *663,666,674*

snarl [v1] *grumble*
abuse, bark, bluster, bully, champ the bit*, complain, fulminate, gnarl, gnash teeth, growl, mumble, murmur, mutter, quarrel, show teeth, snap, threaten, thunder, yelp; SEE CONCEPT *77*

snarl [v2] *complicate, mess up*
confuse, embroil, enmesh, ensnarl, entangle, entwine, involve, muck, muddle, perplex, ravel, tangle; SEE CONCEPTS *16,158*

snatch [n] *small part*
bit, fragment, piece, smattering, snippet, spell; SEE CONCEPTS *264,832*

snatch [v] *grab away*
abduct, catch, clap hands on, clutch, collar*, gain, get fingers on*, grapple, grasp, grip, jerk, jump, kidnap, make off with, nab, nail, pluck, pull, rescue, seize, snag, spirit away, steal, take, win, wrench, wrest, yank; SEE CONCEPTS *90,191*

sneak [n] *person who is very dishonest*
cheater, con man/woman, coward, cur, dastard, heel*, informer, knave, louse, rascal, reptile, scoundrel, skunk*, slink*, snake*, snake in grass*, toad*, weasel*, wretch; SEE CONCEPT *412*

sneak [v] *move stealthily*
ambush, case, cheat, cower, crawl, creep, deceive, delude, evade, glide, gumshoe*, hide, lurk, mooch, move secretly, ooze, pad, pass, prowl, pussyfoot*, secrete, shirk, sidle, skulk, slide, slink, slip, slither, sly, smuggle, snake, snook, spirit, steal, worm; SEE CONCEPTS *151,188*

sneaky [adj] *underhanded, dishonest*
base, contemptible, cowardly, deceitful, devious, disingenuous, double-dealing*, duplicitous, furtive, guileful, indirect, low, malicious, mean, nasty, recreant, secretive, shifty, slippery, sly, sneaking, snide, stealthy, surreptitious, tricky, underhand, unreliable, unscrupulous, untrustworthy, yellow*; SEE CONCEPTS *267,401,542*

sneer [v] *mock, condemn*
affront, belittle, burlesque, caricature, crack, curl lip*, decry, deride, detract, disdain, disparage, dump, fleer, flout, gibe, gird, give Bronx cheer, grin, hold in contempt*, hold up to ridicule*, insult, jeer, jest, lampoon, laugh at, leer, look down on, put down, quip at, rally, rank out, ridicule, satirize, scoff, scorn, slam, slight, smile, sneeze at*, sniff at*, snigger, swipe, taunt, travesty, turn up

one's nose*, twit, underrate; SEE CONCEPTS *30,52,54*

snicker/snigger/sniggle [v] *laugh at mockingly*
chortle, chuckle, giggle, guffaw, hee-haw, smirk, sneer, teehee, titter; SEE CONCEPT *77*

snide [adj] *hateful, nasty*
base, cynical, disparaging, hurtful, insinuating, malicious, mean, sarcastic, scornful, sneering, spiteful, unkind; SEE CONCEPT *401*

sniff [v] *breathe in*
detect, inhale, inspire, nose, scent, smell, snift, snuff, snuffle; SEE CONCEPTS *601,602*

snob [n] *person who looks down on others*
braggart, highbrow, name-dropper, parvenu, pretender, smarty pants*, stiff neck*, upstart; SEE CONCEPT *423*

snobbish [adj] *stuck-up, conceited*
aloof, arrogant, condescending, egotistic, haughty, high-and-mighty*, high-flown*, high-hat*, ostentatious, overbearing, patronizing, persnickety*, pompous, pretentious, putting on airs*, remote, sniffy*, snippy*, snooty*, snotty*, supercilious, superior, swanky, tony*, uppish, uppity*; SEE CONCEPT *401*

snoop [n] *person who noses around*
busybody, butt-in*, detective, eavesdropper, ferret, gumshoe*, meddler, peeping Tom*, pragmatist, pry, pryer, quidnunc, rubberneck*, scout, sleuth, snooper; SEE CONCEPTS *348,423*

snoop [v] *nose around*
busybody*, interfere, intrude, meddle, mess with, mouse*, nose, peek, peep, peer, poke, poke nose in*, pry, snook, spy, stare; SEE CONCEPTS *216,384,623*

snooze [n] *light sleep*
catnap, doze, forty winks*, nap, siesta, slumber; SEE CONCEPT *315*

snooze [v] *sleep lightly*
catnap, doze, drop off, drowse, nap, nod off*, siesta, slumber, take forty winks*; SEE CONCEPTS *210,315*

snore [v] *make sounds when sleeping*
breathe heavily, saw logs*, saw wood*, sleep, snort, snuffle, wheeze; SEE CONCEPTS *77,315*

snub [v] *give someone the cold shoulder*
act cool*, boycott, brush off*, burr, censure, chill, cold-shoulder*, cool, cut, cut dead*, disdain, disregard, duck, give the brush*, humble, humiliate, ice*, ice out*, ignore, look coldly upon, look right through*, mortify, neglect, not give time of day*, offend, ostracize, pass up, put down, put the chill on*, rebuff, scold, scorn, scratch, shame, shun, slight, slur, snob, swank, upstage; SEE CONCEPTS *30,54,384*

snug [adj] *cozy, warm*
close, comfortable, comfy, compact, convenient, cushy, easeful, easy, homelike, homely, intimate, neat, restful, sheltered, snug as bug in rug*, soft, substantial, tight, trim, well-off; SEE CONCEPT *485*

snuggle [v] *cuddle*
bundle, burrow, curl up, grasp, huddle, hug, nestle, nuzzle, snug, spoon; SEE CONCEPTS *190,201*

soak [v] *drench, wet*
absorb, assimilate, bathe, damp, dip, drink, drown, dunk, flood, imbrue, immerge, immerse, impregnate, infiltrate, infuse, macerate, marinate, merge, moisten, penetrate, percolate, permeate, pour into, pour on, saturate, seethe, soften, sop, souse, steep, submerge, take in, wash, water, waterlog; SEE CONCEPT *256*

soar [v] *climb, fly*
arise, ascend, aspire, escalate, glide, lift, mount, rise, rocket, sail, shoot, shoot up, skyrocket, top, tower, up, uprear, wing; SEE CONCEPTS *148,150*

sob [v] *cry hard*
bawl, blub, blubber, boohoo*, break down, cry a river*, cry convulsively, cry eyes out*, howl, lament, shed tears, snivel, turn on waterworks*, wail, weep, whimper; SEE CONCEPTS *185,410*

sober [adj1] *not partaking of alcohol*
abstaining, abstemious, abstinent, ascetic, calm, clear-headed, cold sober*, continent, controlled, dry, moderate, nonindulgent, not drunk, on the wagon*, restrained, sedate, self-possessed, serious, steady, temperate, took the pledge*; SEE CONCEPT *401*

sober [adj2] *calm, peaceful; dull*
abnegating, abstaining, calm, clear-headed, cold, collected, composed, constrained, cool, dark, disciplined, dispassionate, down-to-earth*, drab, earnest, eschewing, forgoing, grave, hard-boiled*, imperturbable, inhibited, levelheaded, low-key, lucid, no-nonsense, pacific, peaceful, plain, practical, quiet, rational, realistic, reasonable, reserved, restrained, sedate, serene, serious, severe, soft, solemn, somber, sound, staid, steady, subdued, toned down, unexcited, unimpassioned, unruffled; SEE CONCEPTS *401,542*

so-called [adj] *supposed*
alleged, allegedly, commonly named, formal, nominal, ostensible, pretended, professed, purported, self-named, self-styled, supposed, titular, wrongly named; SEE CONCEPT *552*

sociable [adj] *friendly, outgoing*
accessible, affable, approachable, close, clubby*, companionable, conversable, convivial, cordial, familiar, genial, good-natured, gregarious, intimate, neighborly, regular, social, warm; SEE CONCEPT *555*

social [adj] *public, friendly*
amusing, civil, collective, common, communal, communicative, community, companionable, convivial, cordial, diverting, entertaining, familiar, general, gracious, gregarious, group, hospitable, informative, mannerly, neighborly, nice, organized, pleasant, pleasurable, polished, polite, popular, public, sociable, societal; SEE CONCEPTS *536,555*

socialize [v] *be friendly at gatherings*
associate, chum with*, club*, consort, entertain, fraternize, get about, get around, get together, go out, hang around with*, hobnob, join, keep company, make advances, make the rounds*, mingle, mix, pal around*, run with*, tie up with*; SEE CONCEPT *384*

society [n1] *humankind, people*
association, camaraderie, civilization, commonality, commonwealth, community, companionship, company, comradeship, culture, fellowship, friendship, general public, humanity, jungle*, nation, population, public, rat race*, social order, world, zoo*; SEE CONCEPTS *379,417*

society [n2] *organization, institution*
alliance, association, brotherhood, circle, clan, clique, club, companionship, comradeship, corporation, coterie, fellowship, fraternity, gang, group, guild, hookup, institute, league, mob, order, outfit, ring, sisterhood, sodality, syndicate, tie-in, tie-up, union; SEE CONCEPTS *381,387*

society [n3] *upper class of people*
aristocracy, beau monde*, beautiful people*, country set*, elite, flower*, gentry, glitterati*, haut monde, high society*, jet set*, main line, patriciate, polite society*, quality, smart set*, top drawer*, upper crust*, who's who*; SEE CONCEPTS *387,388,417*

sock [n/v] *hit hard*
beat, belt, bop, buffet, chop, clout, cuff, ding, nail, paste, punch, slap, smack, smash, soak, whack; SEE CONCEPT *189*

soft [adj1] *cushioned, squishy*
bendable, comfortable, comfy, cottony, cozy, creamy, cushiony, cushy, delicate, doughy, downy, ductile, easeful, easy, elastic, feathery, fine, flabby, fleecy, fleshy, flexible, flimsy, flocculent, flowing, fluffy, fluid, formless, furry, gelatinous, impressible, limp, malleable, moldable, mushy, pappy, pithy, plastic, pliable, pulpy, quaggy, rounded, satiny, silken, silky, smooth, snug, spongy, squashy, supple, thin, velvety, yielding; SEE CONCEPTS *488,606*

soft [adj2] *faint, temperate*
ashen, balmy, bland, caressing, comfortable, cool, cushy, delicate, diffuse, dim, dimmed, dulcet, dull, dusky, faint, gentle, hazy, lenient, light, low, low-key, mellifluous, mellow, melodious, mild, misty, murmured, muted, pale, pallid, pastel, pleasing, quiet, restful, shaded, smooth, sober, soothing, subdued, sweet, tinted, toned down, twilight, understated, wan, whispered; SEE CONCEPTS *525,537,592,618*

soft [adj3] *compassionate*
affectionate, amiable, benign, courteous, easy, easygoing, effortless, gentle, gracious, indulgent, kind, kindly, lax, lenient, liberal, manageable, overindulgent, permissive, pitying, sensitive, sentimental, simple, spineless, sympathetic, tender, tenderhearted, undemanding, weak; SEE CONCEPT *401*

soft [adj4] *out of condition*
doughy, fat, flabby, flaccid, fleshy, formless, gone to seed*, limp, out of shape*, overindulged, pampered, untrained, weak; SEE CONCEPTS *314,485*

soft [adj5] *stupid*
daft, fatuous, feeble-minded, foolish, silly, simple, witless; SEE CONCEPT *402*

soften [v] *calm, soothe*
abate, allay, alleviate, appease, assuage, become tender, bend, cushion, diminish, disintegrate, dissolve, ease, enfeeble, give, knead, lessen, lighten, lower, mash, mellow, melt, mitigate, moderate, modify, moisten, mollify, palliate, qualify, quell, relax, relent, still, subdue, temper, tenderize, thaw, tone down, turn down, weaken, yield; SEE CONCEPT *250*

soggy [adj] *damp or soaking*
clammy, dank, dripping, heavy, humid, moist, mucky, muggy, mushy, pasty, pulpy, saturated, soaked, sodden, soft, sopping, spongy, sticky, sultry, waterlogged; SEE CONCEPT *603*

soil [n1] *earth, dirt*
clay, dry land, dust, grime, ground, land, loam, soot, terra firma; SEE CONCEPT *509*

soil [n2] *land where one lives*
country, fatherland, home, homeland, mother country, motherland, region, terra firma; SEE CONCEPTS *198,510,511*

soil [v] *make dirty*
bedraggle, befoul, begrime, besmirch, contaminate, crumb, debase, defile, degrade, dirty, discolor, disgrace, foul, grime, maculate, mess, mess up, muck*, muck up*, muddy, muss*, muss up*, pollute, shame, smear, smudge, spatter, spoil, spot, stain, sully, taint, tar, tarnish; SEE CONCEPT *254*

sojourn [n] *brief travel; visit*
layover, residence, rest, stay, stop, stopover, tarriance, vacation; SEE CONCEPTS *224,226,227*

sojourn [v] *travel briefly; visit*
abide, dwell, inhabit, linger, lodge, nest, perch, reside, rest, roost, squat, stay, stay over, stop, tarry, vacation; SEE CONCEPTS *224,226,227*

solace [n] *comfort, peace*
alleviation, assuagement, condolement, condolence, consolation, pity, relief; SEE CONCEPTS *7,22,410*

solace [v] *give comfort, peace*
allay, alleviate, buck up, cheer, comfort, condole with, console, mitigate, soften, soothe, upraise; SEE CONCEPTS *7,22*

soldier [n] *person serving in military*
airman/woman, cadet, cavalryman, commando, conscript, draftee, enlisted man/woman, fighter, fighting man/woman, GI*, Green Beret, guardsman/woman, guerrilla, gunner, infantry, infantryman/woman, man-at-arms, marine, mercenary, military man/woman, musketeer, officer, paratrooper, pilot, private, rank, recruit, scout, selectee, serviceman/woman, serviceperson, trooper, veteran, volunteer, warmonger, warrior; SEE CONCEPT *358*

sole [adj] *alone, singular*
ace, exclusive, individual, lone, one, one and only, onliest, only, only one, particular, remaining, separate, single, solitary, solo, spouseless, unique, unmarried, unshared, unwed; SEE CONCEPTS *555,564,577*

solely [adv] *only, alone*
barely, but, completely, entirely, exclusively, individually, merely, onliest, purely, simply, singlehandedly, singly, singularly, totally, undividedly, wholly; SEE CONCEPTS *544,577*

solemn [adj1] *quiet, serious*
austere, brooding, cold sober*, deliberate, dignified, downbeat, earnest, funereal, glum, grave, heavy, intense, matter of life and death*, moody, no fooling*, no-nonsense*, pensive, portentous, reflective, sedate, sober, somber, staid, stern, thoughtful, weighty; SEE CONCEPTS *403,542*

solemn [adj2] *impressive, sacred*
august, awe-inspiring, ceremonial, ceremonious, conventional, devotional, dignified, divine, formal, full, grand, grave, hallowed, holy, imposing, impressive, magnificent, majestic, momentous, ostentatious, overwhelming, plenary, religious, reverential, ritual, sanctified, stately, venerable; SEE CONCEPT *574*

solicit [v] *plead for; try to sell*
accost, apply, approach, ask, beg, beseech, bespeak, bum, cadge, call, canvass, challenge, claim, come on to*, crave, demand, desire, drum*, drum up*, entreat, exact, go, hawk, hit on*, hit up*, hustle, implore, importune, inquire, mooch, panhandle, pass the hat*, peddle, petition, postulate, pray, promote, proposition, query, question, refer, request, require, requisition, resort, seduce, seek, sponge, steer, sue for, supplicate, touch, tout, turn, whistle for*; SEE CONCEPTS *53,345*

solicitous [adj] *worried*
anxious, appetent, apprehensive, ardent, athirst, attentive, avid, beside oneself, careful, caring, concerned, devoted, eager, earnest, heedful, impatient, keen, loving, mindful, raring, regardful, tender, thirsty, troubled, uneasy, worried sick*, worried stiff*, zealous; SEE CONCEPT *403*

solicitude [n] *worry, anxiety*
attention, attentiveness, care, compunction, concern, concernment, considerateness, consideration, disquiet, disquietude, heed, presentiment, qualm, regard, scruple, tender loving care*, TLC*, unease, uneasiness, watchfulness; SEE CONCEPT *410*

solid [adj1] *hard, dimensional*
brick wall*, close, compact, compacted, concentrated, concrete, consolidated, dense, firm, fixed, heavy, hefty, hulk, hunk, husky, massed, material, physical, rock, rocklike, rooted, secure, set, sound, stable, strong, sturdy, substantial, thick, tight, unshakable; SEE CONCEPTS *483,604*

solid [adj2] *continuous, complete*
agreed, brick wall, consecutive, consentient, continued, firm, like a rock, regular, set in stone*, stable, steady, unalloyed, unanimous, unbroken, undivided,

uninterrupted, united, unmixed; SEE CONCEPTS *482,488,531*

solid [*adj3*] *dependable, reliable*
cogent, constant, decent, estimable, genuine, good, law-abiding, levelheaded, pure, real, satisfactory, satisfying, sensible, serious, sober, sound, stalwart, steadfast, trustworthy, trusty, upright, upstanding, valid, worthy; SEE CONCEPTS *401,534*

solitary [*adj*] *alone, single; unsociable*
aloof, antisocial, cloistered, companionless, deserted, desolate, distant, eremetic, forsaken, friendless, hermitical, hidden, individual, introverted, isolated, lone, lonely, lonesome, lorn, misanthropic, offish, only, out-of-the-way*, particular, reclusive, remote, reserved, retired, secluded, separate, sequestered, singular, sole, solo, stag, standoffish, unaccompanied, unapproachable, unattended, uncompanionable, unfrequented, unique, unsocial, withdrawn; SEE CONCEPTS *555,577,583*

solitude [*n*] *aloneness*
confinement, desert, detachment, emptiness, isolation, loneliness, loneness, lonesomeness, peace and quiet*, privacy, quarantine, reclusiveness, retirement, seclusion, separateness, shelf, silence, solitariness, waste, wasteland, wilderness, withdrawal; SEE CONCEPTS *388,673,714*

solution [*n1*] *answer, resolution*
band-aid*, clarification, elucidation, explanation, explication, key, pay dirt*, quick fix*, result, solving, the ticket*, unfolding, unravelling, unravelment; SEE CONCEPTS *230,661,712*

solution [*n2*] *mixture of liquid and another substance*
blend, compound, dissolvent, elixir, emulsion, extract, fluid, juice, mix, sap, solvent, suspension; SEE CONCEPTS *260,467*

solve [*v*] *answer, resolve*
break*, clarify, clear up, construe, crack*, deal with, decide, decipher, decode, determine, disentangle, divine, do, elucidate, enlighten, explain, expound, fathom, figure out, find out, fix, get, get right, get to the bottom*, have, hit, hit upon*, illuminate, interpret, iron out*, lick*, make a dent*, make out*, pan out*, put two and two together*, puzzle, reason, settle, think out, unfold, unlock, unravel, unriddle, untangle, work, work out; SEE CONCEPTS *15,18,37*

somber [*adj*] *sad, depressing*
black, bleak, blue, caliginous, cloudy, dark, depressive, dim, dingy, dire, dismal, dispiriting, doleful, down, drab, dragged, dreary, dull, dusky, earnest, funereal, gloomy, grave, grim, hurting, joyless, lugubrious, melancholy, mournful, murky, nononsense, obscure, sad, sedate, sepulchral, serious, shadowy, shady, sober, solemn, sourpuss, staid, tenebrous, weighty; SEE CONCEPTS *403,485,529*

somebody [*n*] *person of fame, importance*
celebrity, dignitary, heavyweight*, household name*, luminary, name*, notable, one, personage, person of note, public figure, so-and-so*, someone*,

some person*, star, superstar, VIP*, whoever*; SEE CONCEPT *423*

someday [*adv*] *eventually*
after a while, anytime, at a future time, finally, in a time to come, on a day, one day, one fine day, one of these days, one time, one time or another, sometime, sooner or later, subsequently, ultimately, yet; SEE CONCEPTS *548,820*

somehow [*adv*] *by some means*
after a fashion, anyhow, anyway, anywise, by hook or crook*, come what may*, every man for himself*, in one way or another, in some such way, in some way, one way or another, somehow or another, somehow or other; SEE CONCEPT *544*

something [*n*] *entity*
article, being, commodity, existence, existent, individual, object, substance, thing; SEE CONCEPT *433*

sometimes [*adv*] *every now and then*
at intervals, at times, consistently, constantly, ever and again, every so often, frequently, from time to time, here and there, intermittently, now and again, now and then, occasionally, off and on, once in a blue moon*, once in a while, on occasion, periodically, recurrently; SEE CONCEPT *805*

somewhat [*adv*] *to some extent*
adequately, a little, bearably, considerably, fairly, far, incompletely, in part, insignificantly, kind of, moderately, more or less, not much, partially, pretty, quite, rather, ratherish, significantly, slightly, some, something, sort of, to a degree, tolerably, well; SEE CONCEPTS *548,569,772*

somewhere [*adv*] *in, at some place*
about, any old place, around, around somewhere, elsewhere, here and there, in one place or another, kicking around*, parts unknown*, scattered, someplace, someplace or another, someplace or other, somewheres; SEE CONCEPT *583*

song [*n*] *melody sung or played with musical instrument*
air, anthem, aria, ballad, canticle, carol, chant, chorale, chorus, ditty, expression, golden oldie*, hymn, lay, lullaby, lyric, melody, number, oldie*, opera, piece, poem, psalm, refrain, rock, rock and roll, round, shanty, strain, tune, verse, vocal; SEE CONCEPTS *262,293,595*

soon [*adv*] *in the near future*
anon, any minute now, before long, betimes, by and by, coming down the pike*, directly, early, ere long, expeditiously, fast, fleetly, forthwith, hastily, in a little while, in a minute, in a second, in a short time, in due time, in short order, instantly, in time, licketysplit*, on time, posthaste, presently, promptly, pronto, quick, quickly, rapidly, short, shortly, speedily; SEE CONCEPTS *548,798,820*

soothe [*v*] *calm, ease*
allay, alleviate, appease, assuage, balm, becalm, butter up, calm down, cheer, compose, console, cool, cool off*, dulcify, help, hush, lighten, lull, make

nice, make up, mitigate, mollify, pacify, patch things up*, play up to*, pour oil on*, quiet, quieten, relieve, settle, smooth down, soften, square, still, stroke, subdue, take the edge off*, take the sting out*, tranquilize, unburden, untrouble; SEE CONCEPTS *7,22,110,384*

sophisticated [*adj1*] *cosmopolitan, cultured*
adult, artificial, been around, blasé, bored, citified, cool*, couth, cultivated, cynical, disenchanted, disillusioned, experienced, in, in the know*, into*, jaded, jet-set*, knowing, laid-back*, mature, mondaine, on to, practical, practiced, refined, schooled, seasoned, sharp, skeptical, smooth, stagy*, streetwise, studied, suave, svelte, switched on*, uptown*, urbane, well-bred, wised up*, wise to*, with it*, worldly, worldly wise*, world-weary; SEE CONCEPTS *401,404,589*

sophisticated [*adj2*] *complex, advanced*
complicated, delicate, elaborate, highly developed, intricate, involved, knotty, labyrinthine, modern, multifaceted, refined, subtle; SEE CONCEPT *562*

sophistication [*n*] *culture, style*
composure, elegance, finesse, poise, refinement, savoir faire, savoir vivre, social grace, tact, urbanity, worldliness, worldly wisdom; SEE CONCEPTS *388,633,655*

sophomoric [*adj*] *inexperienced*
brash, foolish, naive, reckless, young; SEE CONCEPT *401*

soporific [*adj*] *sleepy; sleep-inducing*
anesthetic, balmy, calming, deadening, dozy*, drowsy, dull, hypnotic, mesmerizing, narcotic, nodding, numbing, opiate, quietening, sedative, slumberous, snoozy*, somniferous, somnolent, soothing, tranquilizing; SEE CONCEPTS *537,539*

sorcery [*n*] *black magic, witchcraft*
abracadabra*, alchemy, bewitchment, black art, charm, conjuring, devilry, divination, enchantment, evil eye, hocus-pocus*, hoodoo*, incantation, jinx, magic, mumbo-jumbo*, necromancy, spell, thaumaturgy, voodoo, witchery, witching, wizardry; SEE CONCEPTS *370,689*

sordid [*adj*] *dirty, bad, low*
abject, avaricious, base, black, calculated, corrupt, covetous, debauched, degenerate, degraded, despicable, disreputable, dowdy, filthy, foul, frowzy, grasping, grubby, ignoble, impure, low-down, mean, mercenary, miserable, miserly, nasty, niggardly, poor, scurvy, seedy, selfish, self-seeking, servile, shabby, shameful, slatternly, sleazy, slovenly, slum, slummy, small, small-minded, squalid, unclean, uncleanly, ungenerous, venal, vicious, vile, wretched; SEE CONCEPTS *334,545,571*

sore [*adj1*] *hurt physically*
abscessed, aching, acute, afflicted, annoying, bruised, burned, burning, chafed, critical, distressing, extreme, hurtful, hurting, inflamed, irritated, pained, painful, raw, reddened, sensitive, severe,

sharp, smarting, tender, ulcerated, uncomfortable, unpleasant, vexatious; SEE CONCEPT *314*

sore [*adj2*] *angry; hurt mentally*
afflicted, aggrieved, annoyed, annoying, critical, distressing, grieved, grieving, indignant, irked, irritated, pained, peeved, pressing, resentful, sensitive, smarting, stung, troubled, upset, urgent, vexed, weighty; SEE CONCEPT *403*

sorrow [*n*] *extreme upset, grief*
affliction, agony, anguish, bad news*, big trouble*, blow, blues*, care, catastrophe, dejection, depression, distress, dolor, grieving, hardship, heartache, heartbreak, lamenting, melancholy, misery, misfortune, mourning, pain, rain*, regret, remorse, repentence, rue, sadness, suffering, trial, tribulation, trouble, unhappiness, weeping, woe, worry, wretchedness; SEE CONCEPT *410*

sorrow [*v*] *be very upset, grieved*
agonize, bemoan, be sad, bewail, carry on, cry a river*, deplore, eat heart out*, grieve, groan, hang crepe*, lament, moan, mourn, regret, sing the blues*, sob, take on, weep; SEE CONCEPTS *34,410*

sorrowful [*adj*] *very upset; grieving*
affecting, afflicted, dejected, depressed, disconsolate, distressing, doleful, dolent, full of sorrow, grievous, heartbroken, heart-rending*, heavyhearted, hurting, in mourning, in pain, in sorrow, lamentable, lugubrious, melancholy, miserable, mournful, painful, piteous, plaintive, rueful, ruthful, sad, sick at heart*, singing the blues*, sob story*, sorry, tearful, tear-jerking*, unhappy, woebegone, woeful, wretched; SEE CONCEPT *403*

sorry [*adj1*] *remorseful, regretful*
apologetic, attritional, compunctious, conscience-stricken, contrite, guilt-ridden, melted, penitent, penitential, repentant, self-accusing, self-condemnatory, self-reproachful, shamefaced, softened, touched; SEE CONCEPTS *403,545*

sorry [*adj2*] *sad, heartbroken*
bad, disconsolate, distressed, grieved, heavyhearted, melancholy, mournful, pitiful, rueful, saddened, sorrowful, unhappy; SEE CONCEPT *403*

sorry [*adj3*] *despicable, pathetic*
abject, base, beggarly, cheap, contemptible, deplorable, despisable, disgraceful, dismal, distressing, inadequate, insignificant, mean, miserable, paltry, piteous, pitiable, pitiful, poor, sad, scruffy*, scummy*, scurvy, shabby, shoddy, small, trifling, trivial, unimportant, vile, worthless, wretched; SEE CONCEPTS *485,529*

sort [*n*] *type, variety*
array, batch, battery, body, brand, breed, category, character, class, clutch, denomination, description, family, genus, group, ilk, kind, likes, likes of*, lot, make, nature, number, order, parcel, quality, race, set, species, stamp, stripe, style, suite; SEE CONCEPT *378*

sort [v] *place in order*
arrange, assort, button down*, catalogue, categorize, choose, class, classify, comb, cull, distribute, divide, file, grade, group, order, peg, pick, pigeonhole*, put down as, put down for, put in order, put in shape, put to rights*, rank, riddle, screen, select, separate, sift, size up, systematize, tab, typecast, winnow; SEE CONCEPTS *84,158*

so-so [adj] *adequate, passable*
average, enough, fair, fairish, fair to middling*, indifferent, mediocre, medium, middling*, moderate, not bad*, okay*, ordinary, respectable, run-of-the-mill*, tolerable, undistinguished; SEE CONCEPTS *533,575*

soul [n1] *psyche, inspiration, energy*
anima, animating principle, animation, animus, ardor, bosom, bottom, breast, breath of life, cause, conscience, courage, disposition, ego, elan vital, essence, feeling, fervor, force, genius, heart, individuality, intellect, intelligence, life, marrow, mind, nobility, noumenon, personality, pith, pneuma, principle, quintessence, reason, recesses of heart*, secret self*, spirit, spiritual being, stuff, substance, thought, vital force, vitality, vivacity; SEE CONCEPTS *409,410,411*

soul [n2] *being*
body, character, creature, ghost, human being, individual, living soul, man, mortal, person, personage, phantom, shadow, spirit, umbra, woman; SEE CONCEPT *389*

sound [n] *something heard or audible*
accent, din, harmony, intonation, loudness, melody, modulation, music, noise, note, pitch, racket, report, resonance, reverberation, ringing, softness, sonance, sonancy, sonority, sonorousness, static, tenor, tonality, tone, vibration, voice; SEE CONCEPT *595*

sound [adj1] *complete, healthy*
alive and kicking*, effectual, entire, firm, fit, flawless, hale, hearty, intact, in the pink*, perfect, right, right as rain*, robust, safe, sane, solid, stable, sturdy, substantial, thorough, total, unblemished, undamaged, undecayed, unhurt, unimpaired, uninjured, up to snuff*, vibrant, vigorous, virile, vital, well, well-constructed, whole, wholesome, wrapped tight; SEE CONCEPTS *314,488*

sound [adj2] *logical, reasonable*
accurate, advisable, all there*, cogent, commonsensical, consequent, convincing, cool*, correct, deep, exact, fair, faultless, flawless, got it together*, impeccable, intellectual, judicious, just, levelheaded, orthodox, precise, profound, proper, prudent, rational, reliable, responsible, right, right-minded, right-thinking, satisfactory, satisfying, sensible, sober, solid, telling, thoughtful, together, true, trustworthy, valid, well-advised, well-founded, well-grounded, wise; SEE CONCEPTS *403,529,558*

sound [adj3] *accepted, established*
all there*, authoritative, canonical, dependable, fair, faithful, fly*, go*, hang together*, hold together*, hold up*, hold up in wash*, hold water*, kosher*, legal, legit*, loyal, orthodox, proper, proven, received, recognized, reliable, reputable, safe, sanctioned, secure, significant, solid, solvent, stable, stand up*, tried-and-true*, true, valid, wash; SEE CONCEPTS *535,552,582*

sound [v1] *produce noise*
babble, bang, bark, blare, blow, boom, burst, buzz, cackle, chatter, clack, clang, clank, clap, clatter, clink, crash, creak, detonate, echo, emit, explode, hum, jabber, jangle, jar, moan, murmur, patter, play, rattle, reflect, resonate, resound, reverberate, ring, roar, rumble, shout, shriek, shrill, sing, slam, smash, snort, squawk, thud, thump, thunder, toot, trumpet, vibrate, whine, whisper; SEE CONCEPT *65*

sound [v2] *give the impression*
appear, appear to be, look, seem, strike as being; SEE CONCEPTS *543,716*

sour [adj1] *bad-tasting; gone bad*
acerb, acetic, acetose, acetous, acid, acidic, acidulated, acrid, astringent, bad, biting, bitter, briny, caustic, curdled, cutting, dry, fermented, green, keen, musty, peppery, piquant, pungent, rancid, salty, sharp, soured, sourish, stinging, tart, turned, unpleasant, unripe, unsavory, unwholesome, vinegary, with a kick*; SEE CONCEPTS *462,613*

sour [adj2] *in a bad mood*
acid, acrid, acrimonious, bitter, churlish, crabby*, cynical, disagreeable, discontented, displeasing, embittered, grouchy, grudging, ill-natured, ill-tempered, irritable, jaundiced, on edge*, peevish, rotten, tart, ungenerous, unhappy, unpleasant, waspish; SEE CONCEPTS *403,542*

sour [v] *alienate*
acidify, curdle, disenchant, embitter, envenom, exacerbate, exasperate, make sour, spoil, turn, turn off; SEE CONCEPTS *14,250*

source [n] *beginning; point of supply*
antecedent, author, authority, authorship, begetter, birthplace, cause, commencement, connection, dawn, dawning, derivation, determinant, expert, father, fount, fountain, fountainhead, horse's mouth*, inception, informant, mother, onset, opening, origin, origination, originator, parent, paternity, provenance, provenience, rise, rising, root, specialist, spring, start, starting point, wellspring; SEE CONCEPT *648*

souse [v] *make very wet*
brine, deluge, dip, douse, drench, drown, duck, dunk, immerse, impregnate, marinate, pickle, preserve, seethe, soak, sop, steep, submerge, submerse, waterlog, wet; SEE CONCEPT *256*

souvenir [n] *keepsake from event*
gift, memento, memorial, relic, remembrance, remembrancer, reminder, token, trophy; SEE CONCEPTS *337,446*

sovereign [n] *person in total control*
autocrat, chief, czar, emperor, empress, king, majesty, monarch, potentate, prince, queen, ruler, shah, supreme ruler, tsar; SEE CONCEPT *354*

sovereign [*adj*] *dominant, effective*
absolute, ascendant, autonomous, chief, commanding, directing, effectual, efficacious, excellent, guiding, highest, imperial, independent, kinglike, kingly, lofty, majestic, master, monarchal, monarchial, overbearing, paramount, predominant, predominate, preponderant, prevalent, principal, queenly, regal, regnant, reigning, royal, ruling, self-governed, supreme, unlimited; SEE CONCEPTS *536,568*

sovereignty [*n*] *domination*
ascendancy, ascendant, dominance, dominion, jurisdiction, masterdom, preeminence, prepotence, prepotency, primacy, supremacy, supreme power, sway; SEE CONCEPT *299*

sow [*v*] *plant*
broadcast, disject, disseminate, drill, fling, grow, implant, inseminate, lodge, pitch, propagate, put in, raise, scatter, seed, strew, toss; SEE CONCEPTS *253,257*

space [*n1*] *room, scope*
amplitude, area, arena, blank, breadth, capacity, compass, distance, elbowroom, expanse, expansion, extension, extent, field, gap, headroom, headway, infinity, interval, lacuna, leeway, location, margin, omission, play, range, reach, slot, spaciousness, sphere, spot, spread, stretch, territory, tract, turf, volume, zone; SEE CONCEPTS *739,746,756*

space [*n2*] *time interval*
bit, duration, period, season, span, spell, stretch, term, time, while; SEE CONCEPT *807*

spacious [*adj*] *extensive, expansive*
ample, big, boundless, broad, capacious, cavernous, comfortable, commodious, endless, enormous, extended, generous, great, huge, immense, infinite, large, limitless, roomy, sizable, spacy, uncrowded, vast, voluminous, wide, widespread; SEE CONCEPTS *481,482,774*

span [*n*] *distance, duration*
amount, compass, extent, interval, length, measure, period, reach, space, spell, spread, stretch, term, time; SEE CONCEPTS *756,807,822*

span [*v*] *stretch over*
arch, bridge, connect, cover, cross, extend, ford, go across, link, pass over, range, reach, traverse, vault; SEE CONCEPT *756*

spank [*v*] *slap, usually on bottom*
belt, blip, box, buffet, cane, chastise, clobber, clout, cuff, flax, flog, hide, larrup, lash, lather, leather*, lick, paddle, punch, punish, put over one's knee*, smack, sock, tan*, tan one's hide*, thrash, trim, wallop, welt, whip, whup*; SEE CONCEPT *189*

spare [*adj1*] *extra, reserve*
additional, backup, de trop, emergency, free, in excess, in reserve, in store, lagniappe, leftover, more than enough*, odd, option, over, supererogatory, superfluous, supernumerary, surplus, unoccupied, unused, unwanted; SEE CONCEPTS *771,824*

spare [*adj2*] *thin; sparse*
angular, bony, economical, exiguous, frugal, gaunt, lank, lanky, lean, meager, modest, poor, rangy, raw-boned, scant, scanty, scraggy, scrawny, shadow, skimpy, skinny, slender, slight, slim, sparing, sparse, stick, stilt, stingy, wiry; SEE CONCEPTS *490,491,771*

spare [*v1*] *do or manage without*
accommodate with, afford, allow, bestow, dispense with, give, grant, indulge in, lay aside, lay away, lay by, lay in, lay up, let have, part with, pinch, put by, relinquish, salt away*, save, scrape, scrimp, short, skimp, stint; SEE CONCEPT *129*

spare [*v2*] *forgive; have mercy upon*
absolve, bail out, be lenient, be merciful, discharge, dispense, excuse, exempt, forbear, get off the hook*, get out of hock*, give a break*, give quarter to*, go easy on*, leave, let go, let off*, pardon, pity, privilege from, pull out of the fire*, refrain from, release, relent, relieve from, save bacon*, save from, save neck*, spring; SEE CONCEPTS *50,88,134*

sparing [*adj*] *careful, economical*
avaricious, canny, chary, close, cost-conscious, frugal, humane, mean, money-conscious, parsimonious, provident, prudent, saving, stewardly, stingy, thrifty, tight, tight-fisted, tolerant, ungiving, unwasteful, wary; SEE CONCEPTS *334,401*

spark [*n*] *flash, trace*
atom, beam, fire, flare, flicker, gleam, glint, glitter, glow, hint, jot, nucleus, ray, scintilla, scintillation, scrap, sparkle, spit, vestige; SEE CONCEPTS *519,624,828,831*

spark [*v*] *start, inspire*
animate, excite, kindle, precipitate, provoke, set in motion, set off, stimulate, stir, touch off, trigger; SEE CONCEPT *221*

sparkle [*n*] *glitter, shine*
animation, brilliance, coruscation, dash, dazzle, élan, flash, flicker, gaiety, gleam, glimmer, glint, glitz, glow, life, panache, radiance, scintillation, shimmer, show, spark, spirit, twinkle, vim, vitality, vivacity, zap, zip; SEE CONCEPTS *411,624,628*

sparkle [*v*] *glitter, shine*
beam, bubble, coruscate, dance, effervesce, fizz, fizzle, flash, flicker, gleam, glimmer, glint, glisten, glow, scintillate, shimmer, spark, twinkle, wink; SEE CONCEPT *624*

sparse [*adj*] *very few and scattered*
dispersed, exiguous, few and far between, inadequate, infrequent, meager, occasional, poor, rare, scant, scanty, scarce, scrimpy, skimpy, spare, sporadic, thin, uncommon; SEE CONCEPTS *762,789*

spasm [*n*] *twitch, fit*
access, attack, burst, contraction, convulsion, eruption, frenzy, jerk, outburst, pain, paroxysm, seizure, throe, yank; SEE CONCEPTS *185,728*

spasmodic [*adj*] *twitching, erratic*
bits and pieces*, changeable, choppy, convulsive, desultory, fitful, fits and starts*, intermittent, irregular, jerky, on-again-off-again*, periodic, shaky, spastic, sporadic, spotty, spurtive, uncertain; SEE CONCEPTS *482,530,541*

spatter [v] *splash, sprinkle*
bespatter, bestrew, broadcast, dash, daub, dirty, discharge, disperse, dot, douse, dribble, mottle, polka-dot, scatter, shower, slop, smudge, soil, spangle, speck, speckle, splutter, spot, spray, sputter, stipple, strew, swash, wet; SEE CONCEPTS *172,179,256*

spawn [v] *produce*
bring forth, create, father, generate, give rise to, hatch, issue, make, originate, parent, procreate, reproduce, sire; SEE CONCEPTS *173,251,374*

speak [v1] *talk*
allege, articulate, assert, aver, blab*, break silence, chat, chew*, communicate, converse, convey, declare, deliver, descant, discourse, drawl, enunciate, expatiate, express, gab*, gas*, go*, jaw*, lip*, make known, make public, modulate, mouth, mumble, murmur, mutter, open one's mouth, perorate, pop off*, pronounce, put into words, rap*, say, shout, sound, speak one's piece*, spiel*, spill, state, tell, utter, verbalize, vocalize, voice, whisper, yackety-yak*, yak*, yammer; SEE CONCEPTS *47,266*

speak [v2] *address; give a lecture*
argue, declaim, descant, discourse, get across, harangue, hold forth, orate, pitch, plead, prelect, recite, sermonize, spiel*, spout*, stump, talk; SEE CONCEPTS *60,285*

speak out/speak up [v] *make one's position known*
assert, come out with, declare, have one's say*, insist, let voice be heard*, make oneself heard, make plain, say loud and clear, sound off, speak loudly, speak one's mind*, stand up for; SEE CONCEPTS *49,57*

special [adj] *distinguished, distinctive; important in own way*
appropriate, best, certain, characteristic, chief, choice, defined, definite, designated, determinate, different, earmarked, especial, exceptional, exclusive, express, extraordinary, festive, first, gala, individual, limited, main, major, marked, memorable, momentous, out of the ordinary, particular, peculiar, personal, primary, proper, rare, red-letter*, reserved, restricted, select, set, significant, smashing, sole, specialized, specific, uncommon, unique, unreal*, unusual; SEE CONCEPTS *557,564,567*

specialist [n] *person who is an expert in a field*
ace, adept, authority, connoisseur, consultant, devotee, doctor, guru*, high priest*, master, maven, old hand*, old pro*, pro, professional, pundit, sage, savant, scholar, technician, veteran, virtuoso; SEE CONCEPTS *347,357*

specialize [v] *concentrate on specific area*
be into, develop oneself in, do one's thing*, go in for, have a weakness for, limit oneself to, practice, practice exclusively, pursue, study intensively, train, work in; SEE CONCEPTS *91,324*

specially [adv] *particularly*
distinctively, especially, expressly, in specie, specifically, uniquely; SEE CONCEPT *557*

specialty [n] *distinctive feature; concentration*
career, claim to fame, cup of tea*, distinguishing feature, field of concentration, forte, game*, hobby, job, long suit*, magnum opus, major, masterpiece, minor, number, object of attention, object of study, occupation, pièce de résistance*, practice, profession, pursuit, racket*, special, speciality, special project, thing*, vocation, weakness, work; SEE CONCEPT *349*

species [n] *class, variety*
breed, category, collection, description, division, group, kind, likes*, lot, nature, number, order, sort, stripe*, type; SEE CONCEPT *378*

specific [adj] *particular, distinguishing*
bull's eye*, categorical, characteristic, clean-cut, clear-cut, cut fine*, dead on*, definite, definitive, different, distinct, downright, drawn fine, especial, exact, explicit, express, flat out*, hit nail on head*, individual, limited, on target, outright, peculiar, precise, reserved, restricted, right on, set, sole, special, specialized, straight-out, unambiguous, unequivocal, unique; SEE CONCEPTS *535,557,564*

specifically [adv] *expressly, particularly*
accurately, categorically, characteristically, clearly, concretely, correctly, definitely, distinctively, especially, exactly, explicitly, in detail, indicatively, individually, in specie, minutely, peculiarly, pointedly, precisely, respectively, specially; SEE CONCEPTS *557,564*

specification [n] *requirement, qualification*
blueprint, condition, designation, detail, item, particular, particularization, spec, stipulation, term; SEE CONCEPTS *270,646*

specify [v] *designate; decide definitely*
be specific, blueprint*, button down*, cite, come to the point, condition, define, detail, determine, draw a picture*, enumerate, establish, finger*, fix, get down to brass tacks*, get to the point*, go into detail, indicate, individualize, instance, inventory, itemize, lay out, limit, list, make, mention, name, particularize, peg, pin down, point out, precise, put down, put finger on, set, settle, show clearly, slot, specialize, specificate, specificize, spell out, stipulate, tab, tag, tick off; SEE CONCEPTS *18,57*

specimen [n] *example, sample*
case, case history, copy, cross section, embodiment, exemplar, exemplification, exhibit, illustration, individual, instance, model, part, pattern, proof, representation, representative, sampling, sort, species, type, unit, variety; SEE CONCEPTS *688,831*

specious [adj] *misleading*
apparent, apparently right, beguiling, captious, casuistic, colorable, credible, deceptive, delusive, empty, erroneous, fallacious, false, flattering, hollow, idle, illogical, inaccurate, incorrect, likely, nugatory, ostensible, ostentatious, plausible, presumable, presumptive, pretentious, probable, seeming, sophistic,

sophistical, sophisticated, spurious, unsound, untrue, vain, wrong; SEE CONCEPTS *552,582*

speck [*n*] *tiny bit*
atom, blemish, blot, crumb, defect, dot, fault, flaw, fleck, flyspeck, grain, iota, jot, mark, mite, modicum, molecule, mote, particle, point, shred, smidgen, speckle, splotch, spot, stain, trace, whit; SEE CONCEPT *831*

speckled [*adj*] *dotted*
brindled, dappled, flaked, flecked, freckled, mosaic, motley, mottled, particolored, patchy, peppered, punctate, spotted, spotty, sprinkled, stippled, studded, variegated; SEE CONCEPTS *485,618*

spectacle [*n*] *something showy; exhibition*
comedy, curiosity, demonstration, display, drama, event, exposition, extravaganza, marvel, movie, pageant, parade, performance, phenomenon, play, production, representation, scene, show, sight, spectacular, tableau, view, wonder; SEE CONCEPTS *261,529*

spectacular [*adj*] *wonderful, impressive*
amazing, astonishing, astounding, breathtaking, daring, dazzling, dramatic, eye-catching, fabulous, fantastic, grand, histrionic, magnificent, marked, marvelous, miraculous, prodigious, razzle-dazzle*, remarkable, sensational, splendid, staggering, striking, stunning, stupendous, theatrical, thrilling, wondrous; SEE CONCEPTS *529,537,574*

spectator [*n*] *person who watches event*
beholder, bystander, clapper, eyewitness, fan, gaper, gazer, kibitzer, looker, looker-on, moviegoer, observer, onlooker, perceiver, playgoer, seer, showgoer, sports fan, standee, stander-by, theatergoer, viewer, watcher, witness; SEE CONCEPTS *366,423*

speculate [*v1*] *think about deeply and theorize*
beat one's brains*, brainstorm, build castles in air*, call it, call the turn, cerebrate, chew over*, cogitate, conjecture, consider, contemplate, deliberate, dope*, dope out*, excogitate, figure, figure out*, guess, guesstimate, have a hunch*, hazard a guess, head trip*, hypothesize, kick around*, meditate, muse, pipe-dream*, psych out*, read, read between lines*, reason, reflect, review, ruminate, run it up flagpole*, scheme, size up, study, suppose, surmise, suspect, weigh, wonder; SEE CONCEPTS *17,24,28,37*

speculate [*v2*] *gamble, risk*
dare, hazard, make book*, margin up*, play, play the market*, plunge, pour money into*, spec*, stick neck out*, take a chance, take a flier*, take a fling*, venture, wildcat; SEE CONCEPTS *28,330,363*

speculation [*n1*] *theory, guess*
belief, brainwork*, cerebration, cogitation, conjecture, consideration, contemplation, deliberation, excogitation, guesstimate*, guesswork, hunch, hypothesis, meditation, opinion, reflection, review, shot, shot in the dark*, sneaking suspicion*, stab, stab in the dark*, studying, supposition, surmise,

thinking, thought, weighing; SEE CONCEPTS *24,28,529,689*

speculation [*n2*] *risk, gamble*
backing, flier*, flutter, gambling, hazard, hunch, piece, plunge, right money, risky business*, risky venture, shot, shot in the dark*, smart money*, spec*, speculative enterprise, stab*, venture, wager; SEE CONCEPTS *192,330,363*

speech [*n1*] *talk*
accent, articulation, communication, conversation, dialect, dialogue, diction, discussion, doublespeak*, double talk*, elocution, enunciation, expressing, expression, idiom, intercourse, jargon, language, lingo, locution, mother tongue, native tongue, oral communication, palaver, parlance, prattle, pronunciation, prose, speaking, spiel, tone, tongue, utterance, verbalization, vernacular, vocal expression, vocalization, vocalizing, voice, voicing; SEE CONCEPTS *47,266,276*

speech [*n2*] *formal talk to audience*
address, allocution, appeal, bombast, chalk talk*, commentary, debate, declamation, diatribe, discourse, disquisition, dissertation, eulogy, exhortation, harangue, homily, invocation, keynote, lecture, opus, oration, oratory, panegyric, paper, parlance, parley, pep talk*, pitch, prelection, recitation, rhetoric, salutation, sermon, spiel*, stump*, tirade, valedictory; SEE CONCEPTS *60,285*

speechless [*adj*] *without ability to talk*
aghast, amazed, aphonic, astounded, buttoned up*, clammed up*, close-mouthed, cool*, cool as cucumber*, dazed, dumb, dumbfounded, dumbstruck, inarticulate, mum, mute, not saying boo*, reserved, shocked, silent, taciturn, thunderstruck*, tight-lipped*, tongue-tied*, uncommunicative, unflappable, voiceless, wordless; SEE CONCEPT *267*

speed [*n*] *rate of motion, often a high rate*
acceleration, activity, agility, alacrity, breeze, briskness, celerity, clip, dispatch, eagerness, expedition, fleetness, gait, haste, headway, hurry, hustle, legerity, lick, liveliness, momentum, pace, precipitancy, precipitation, promptitude, promptness, quickness, rapidity, rapidness, readiness, rush, rustle, snap, steam, swiftness, urgency, velocity; SEE CONCEPT *755*

speed [*v*] *move along quickly*
advance, aid, assist, barrel, belt, bomb, boost, bowl over, career, cover ground*, cut along, dispatch, expedite, facilitate, flash, fly, further, gallop, gather momentum, gear up*, get a move on*, get moving, get under way, go all out, go fast, go like the wind*, hasten, help, hightail, hurry, impel, lose no time*, make haste, open up throttle*, press on, promote, quicken, race, ride, run, rush, sail, spring, step on it*, tear, urge, whiz, zoom; SEE CONCEPTS *110,150,152*

speedy [*adj*] *fast, quick*
accelerated, agile, alacritous, breakneck*, brisk, expeditious, express, fleet, harefooted, hasty, head-

long, hurried, immediate, lissome, lively, nimble, precipitate, prompt, quick-fire, rapid, rapid-fire, ready, snappy, summary, supersonic, swift, ultrasonic, winged*; SEE CONCEPTS *548,584,588*

spell [*n1*] *interval, period*
bit, bout, course, go, hitch, interlude, intermission, patch, relay, season, shift, space, stint, streak, stretch, term, time, tour, tour of duty, trick, turn, while; SEE CONCEPTS *807,817,822*

spell [*n2*] *magical aura over an entity*
abracadabra*, allure, amulet, bewitching, bewitchment, charm, conjuration, enchanting, enchantment, exorcism, fascination, glamour, hex, hexing, hocus-pocus*, incantation, jinx, magic, mumbo-jumbo*, rune, sorcery, talisman, trance, voodoo*, whack*, whammy*, witchery; SEE CONCEPTS *370,673,689*

spell [*n3*] *seizure*
access, attack, fit, illness, jag, paroxysm, spasm, stroke, throe, turn; SEE CONCEPTS *306,308*

spell [*v1*] *mean, imply*
add up to, amount to, augur, connote, denote, express, herald, import, indicate, intend, point to, portend, presage, promise, signify, suggest; SEE CONCEPTS *55,74,75*

spell [*v2*] *give rest, relief*
allow, breathe, free, lay off, lie by, release, relieve, stand in for, take over, take the place of; SEE CONCEPTS *83,110*

spellbound [*adj*] *enchanted, fascinated*
agape, amazed, bemused, bewildered, bewitched, breathless, captivated, caught up, charmed, enthralled, gripped, held, hooked, mesmerized, open-mouthed, petrified, possessed, rapt, transfixed, transported, under a spell; SEE CONCEPT *403*

spend [*v1*] *give, pay out*
absorb, allocate, ante up*, apply, bestow, blow*, cast away, come across, come through, concentrate, confer, consume, contribute, cough up*, defray, deplete, disburse, dispense, dissipate, donate, drain, drop, employ, empty, evote, exhaust, expend, foot the bill*, fritter, give, hand out, invest, lavish, lay out, liquidate, misspend, outlay, pay down, pay up, prodigalize, put in, run through, settle, shell out*, spring for*, squander, throw away, use, use up, waste; SEE CONCEPTS *156,169,225,341*

spend [*v2*] *use time; occupy*
consume, devote, drift, employ, fill, fool around*, fritter, go, idle, kill, laze, let pass, misuse, pass, put in, squander, waste, while away*; SEE CONCEPT *100*

spendthrift [*n*] *person careless with money*
big spender*, dissipater, high-roller, improvident, imprudent, prodigal, profligate, spender, sport, squanderer, waster, wastrel; SEE CONCEPTS *348,353,423*

spent [*adj*] *used up, gone; tired out*
all in*, bleary, blown, burnt-out*, bushed, consumed, dead*, debilitated, depleted, disbursed, dissipated, dog-tired*, done-in*, down the drain*, drained, effete, enervated, exhausted, expended,

fagged, far-gone*, finished, had it*, limp, lost, played-out*, prostrate, ready to drop*, shattered, shot, thrown away, used, washed-up*, wasted, weakened, wearied, weary, worn out; SEE CONCEPTS *314,560,771*

spew [*v*] *spit out*
belch, bring up, cascade, disgorge, eject, eruct, erupt, expel, flood, gush, heave, irrupt, puke*, regurgitate, scatter, spit, spit up, spread, spritz, throw up*, urp, vomit; SEE CONCEPTS *179,308*

sphere [*n1*] *globular object*
apple*, ball, big blue marble*, circle, earth, globe, globule, orb, pellet, pill, planet, rondure, round, spaceship Earth*; SEE CONCEPTS *436,511*

sphere [*n2*] *domain of influence*
bailiwick, capacity, champaign, circle, class, compass, demesne, department, dominion, employment, field, function, ground, jungle, jurisdiction, level, neck of the woods*, orbit, pale, position, precinct, province, range, rank, realm, scope, station, stomping ground*, stratum, terrain, territory, turf, walk of life, zone; SEE CONCEPTS *349,388,686*

spice [*n*] *flavor, zest*
aroma, color, excitement, fragrance, gusto, guts*, kick, pep, piquancy, pungency, relish, salt, savor, scent, seasoning, tang, zap*, zip*; SEE CONCEPTS *614,673*

spicy [*adj1*] *pungent, flavorful*
ambrosial, appetizing, aromal, aromatic, distinctive, fiery, flavorsome, fragrant, fresh, herbaceous, highly seasoned, hot, keen, odoriferous, peppery, perfumed, piquant, poignant, racy, redolent, savory, scented, seasoned, snappy, spirited, sweet, tangy, tasty, zesty, zippy; SEE CONCEPT *613*

spicy [*adj2*] *off-color, vulgar*
breezy, broad, erotic, hot*, indelicate, racy, red hot*, ribald, risqué, salty*, scandalous, sensational, sophisticated, suggestive, titillating, unseemly, wicked, X-rated*; SEE CONCEPTS *267,372,545*

spike [*v*] *pierce*
fasten, impale, lance, make fast, nail, pin, prick, skewer, spear, spit, stick, transfix; SEE CONCEPT *220*

spill [*v1*] *slop, drop*
discharge, disgorge, dribble, drip, empty, flow, lose, overfill, overflow, overrun, overturn, pour, run, run out, run over, scatter, shed, spill over, splash, splatter, spray, sprinkle, spurt, squirt, stream, throw off, upset, well over; SEE CONCEPTS *179,181*

spill [*v2*] *reveal*
betray, blab, blow, disclose, divulge, give away, inform, let cat out of bag*, mouth, squeal, tattle, tell; SEE CONCEPT *60*

spin [*n*] *circular motion*
circuit, gyration, revolution, roll, rotation, spiral, turn, twist, whirl; SEE CONCEPT *748*

spin [*v*] *go around, make go around*
gyrate, gyre, oscillate, pendulate, pirouette, purl, reel, revolve, rotate, spiral, swim, turn, twirl, twist, wheel, whirl; SEE CONCEPTS *150,152,218*

spine [n] *backbone*
back, bone, chine, rachis, ridge, spinal column, vertebrae, vertebral column; SEE CONCEPTS *393,420*

spineless [adj] *cowardly*
amoeba*, emasculate, faint-hearted, fearful, feeble, forceless, frightened, gutless*, impotent, inadequate, ineffective, ineffectual, invertebrate, irresolute, lily-livered*, nerveless, pithless, soft, spiritless, squeamish, submissive, timid, vacillating, weak, weak-kneed, weak-willed, yellow*, yellow-bellied*; SEE CONCEPTS *401,542*

spiral [n] *curled shape*
coil, corkscrew, curlicue, flourish, gyration, gyre, helix, quirk, screw, volute, whorl; SEE CONCEPT *436*

spiral [adj] *curling, winding*
circling, circular, circumvoluted, cochlear, coiled, corkscrew, curled, helical, helicoid, radial, rolled, screw-shaped, scrolled, tendrillar, tortile, voluted, whorled, wound; SEE CONCEPT *486*

spirit [n1] *soul, attitude*
air, animation, ardor, backbone*, boldness, breath, character, complexion, courage, dauntlessness, disposition, earnestness, energy, enterprise, enthusiasm, essence, fire, force, frame of mind, gameness, grit*, guts*, heart, humor, jazz*, life, life force, liveliness, mettle, mood, morale, motivation, nerve, oomph*, outlook, psyche, quality, resolution, resolve, sparkle, spunk*, stoutheartedness, substance, temper, temperament, tenor, vigor, vitality, vital spark, warmth, will, willpower, zest; SEE CONCEPTS *407,411*

spirit [n2] *atmosphere, essence*
feeling, genius, gist, humor, intent, intention, meaning, purport, purpose, quality, sense, substance, temper, tenor, timbre, tone; SEE CONCEPTS *673,682*

spirit [n3] *ghost*
apparition, eidolon, phantasm, phantom, poltergeist, shade, shadow, soul, specter, spook, sprite, supernatural being, umbra, vision, wraith; SEE CONCEPT *370*

spirited [adj] *lively, vivacious*
active, alert, animate, animated, ardent, audacious, avid, bold, bouncy, brave, bright, burning, chirpy, courageous, dauntless, eager, effervescent, energetic, enthusiastic, fearless, fiery, full of life, game, gingery*, gritty, gutsy*, high-spirited, hot, hyper, intrepid, jumping, keen, mettlesome, nervy, passionate, peppery, peppy, plucky, resolute, rocking, sharp, snappy, sparkling, sprightly, spunky, valiant, vigorous, zappy*, zealous, zesty, zingy*, zippy*; SEE CONCEPTS *404,542*

spiritless [adj] *depressed*
apathetic, blah*, blue*, broken, cast down, could care less*, dejected, despondent, disconsolate, dispirited, dopey*, down, downcast, downhearted, down in the dumps*, down in the mouth*, draggy, drippy, droopy, dull, enervated, flat*, flat tire*, inanimate, indifferent, lackadaisical, lackluster, languid, languishing, languorous, lifeless, limp, listless,

low, melancholic, melancholy, mopy, slothful, subdued, submissive, tame, torpid, unconcerned, unenthusiastic, unmoved, zero*; SEE CONCEPTS *403,542*

spiritual [adj] *religious, otherworldly*
airy, asomatous, devotional, discarnate, disembodied, divine, ethereal, extramundane, ghostly, holy, immaterial, incorporeal, intangible, metaphysical, nonmaterial, nonphysical, platonic, pure, rarefied, refined, sacred, supernal, unfleshly, unphysical; SEE CONCEPTS *536,582*

spit [n] *saliva*
discharge, dribble, drool, slaver, spittle, sputum, water; SEE CONCEPT *467*

spit [v] *eject saliva or substance*
discharge, drool, expectorate, hawk, hiss, sibilate, sizz, slobber, spatter, spew, splutter, spritz, sputter, throw out; SEE CONCEPTS *179,185*

spite [n] *hateful feeling*
animosity, antipathy, bad blood*, contempt, despite, enmity, gall, grudge, harsh feeling, hate, hatred, ill will, malevolence, malice, maliciousness, malignity, peeve, pet peeve*, pique, rancor, resentment, revenge, spitefulness, spleen, umbrage, vengeance, vengefulness, venom, vindictiveness; SEE CONCEPT *29*

spite [v] *offend, hurt*
annoy, begrudge, beset, crab*, cramp style*, discomfit, gall, get even*, grudge, hang up*, harass, harm, injure, louse up*, needle, nettle, persecute, pique, provoke, put out*, upset apple cart*, vex; SEE CONCEPTS *7,19,121*

spiteful [adj] *hurtful, nasty*
accidentally on purpose*, angry, barbed, catty*, cruel, cussed, despiteful, dirty, evil, hateful, ill-disposed, ill-natured, malevolent, malicious, malign, malignant, mean, ornery, rancorous, snide, spleenful, splenetic, venomous, vicious, vindictive, waspish, wicked; SEE CONCEPTS *401,542*

splash [n] *spattering, impact*
burst, dash, display, effect, patch, sensation, splurge, stir, touch; SEE CONCEPT *676*

splash [v] *throw liquid*
bathe, bespatter, broadcast, dabble, dash, douse, drench, drown, get wet, moisten, paddle, plash, plunge, shower, slop, slosh, soak, sop, spatter, splatter, spray, spread, sprinkle, squirt, strew, throw, wade, wallow, wet; SEE CONCEPTS *222,256*

splendid [adj1] *luxurious, expensive*
baroque, beaming, beautiful, bright, brilliant, costly, dazzling, elegant, fab*, fat*, flamboyant, glittering, glowing, gorgeous, grand, grandiose, imposing, impressive, lavish, lustrous, mad*, magnificent, magnifico, marvelous, ornate, plush, posh, radiant, refulgent, resplendent, rich, solid gold*, splashy, splendiferous, splendrous, sumptuous, superb, swanky; SEE CONCEPTS *334,485,589*

splendid [adj2] *excellent, illustrious*
admirable, brilliant, celebrated, distinguished, divine, eminent, exceptional, exquisite, fantastic, fine,

first-class, glorious, gorgeous, grand, great, heroic, impressive, magnificent, marvelous, matchless, outstanding, peerless, premium, proud, rare, remarkable, renowned, resplendent, royal, splendiferous, splendorous, sterling, sublime, superb, superlative, supreme, transcendent, unparalleled, unsurpassed, very good, wonderful; SEE CONCEPTS *568,574*

splendor [*n*] *radiance, glory*
brightness, brilliance, ceremony, dazzle, display, effulgence, gorgeousness, grandeur, luster, magnificence, majesty, pageant, pomp, refulgence, renown, resplendence, richness, show, solemnity, spectacle, stateliness, sumptuousness; SEE CONCEPTS *620, 655,673*

splice [*v*] *join, interweave*
braid, entwine, graft, hitch, interlace, intertwine, intertwist, knit, marry, mate, mesh, plait, tie, unite, weave, wed, yoke; SEE CONCEPT *193*

splinter [*n*] *thin piece of solid*
bit, chip, flake, fragment, needle, paring, shaving, sliver, wood; SEE CONCEPTS *471,479,831*

splinter [*v*] *break into thin, small pieces*
break to smithereens*, burst, disintegrate, fracture, fragment, pash, rive, shatter, shiver, smash, split; SEE CONCEPT *246*

split [*n1*] *opening*
breach, chasm, chink, cleavage, cleft, crack, damage, division, fissure, gap, rent, rift, rima, rimation, rime, rip, rupture, separation, slash, slit, tear; SEE CONCEPT *513*

split [*n2*] *difference, disunion*
alienation, breach, break, break-up, discord, disruption, dissension, divergence, division, estrangement, fissure, fracture, partition, rent, rift, rupture, schism; SEE CONCEPTS *297,388*

split [*v1*] *break up, pull apart*
bifurcate, branch, break, burst, cleave, come apart, come undone, crack, dichotomize, disband, disjoin, dissever, disunite, diverge, divide, divorce, fork, gape, give way, go separate ways, hack, isolate, open, part, part company, put asunder, rend, rip, rive, separate, sever, slash, slit, snap, splinter, sunder, tear, whack; SEE CONCEPTS *135,176,297*

split [*v2*] *divide into parts*
allocate, allot, apportion, carve up, distribute, divide, divvy*, divvy up*, dole, go even-steven*, go fifty-fifty*, halve, mete out, parcel out, partition, share, slice, slice the pie*, slice up; SEE CONCEPT *98*

splurge [*v*] *spend lavishly*
be extravagant, binge, celebrate, fling, give a party, rampage, spred; SEE CONCEPTS *327,377*

spoil [*v1*] *ruin, hurt*
blemish, damage, debase, deface, defile, demolish, depredate, desecrate, desolate, despoil, destroy, devastate, disfigure, disgrace, harm, impair, injure, make useless, mar, mess up*, muck up*, pillage, plunder, prejudice, queer, ravage, sack, smash, spo-

liate, squash, take apart, tarnish, trash, undo, upset, vitiate, waste, wreck; SEE CONCEPTS *246,252*

spoil [*v2*] *baby, indulge*
accommodate, cater to, coddle, cosset, favor, humor, kill with kindness*, mollycoddle*, oblige, overindulge, pamper, spoon-feed*; SEE CONCEPTS *14,136*

spoil [*v3*] *decay, turn bad*
addle, become tainted, become useless, break down, crumble, curdle, decompose, deteriorate, disintegrate, go bad, go off, mildew, molder, putrefy, rot, taint, turn; SEE CONCEPTS *456,469*

spoils [*n*] *possessions stolen or gained*
booty*, cut*, gain, goods, graft, hot goods*, loot, make*, pickings, pillage, plunder, prey, prize, squeeze, swag, take*; SEE CONCEPTS *337,710*

spoken [*adj*] *by word of mouth*
announced, articulate, communicated, expressed, lingual, mentioned, oral, phonetic, phonic, put into words, said, sonant, told, traditional, unwritten, uttered, verbal, viva voce, voiced; SEE CONCEPT *267*

spokesman/woman/person [*n*] *person who communicates for another*
agent, champion, delegate, deputy, mediator, mouth, mouthpiece*, prolocutor, prophet, protagonist, representative, speaker, stand-in, substitute, talker; SEE CONCEPTS *348,354,359*

spongy [*adj*] *cushioned, absorbent*
absorptive, cushiony, elastic, light, mushy, pappy, porous, pulpous, pulpy, resilient, rubbery, soft, springy, squishy, yielding; SEE CONCEPT *606*

sponsor [*n*] *person who helps, promotes another*
adherent, advocate, angel*, backer, benefactor, godparent, grubstaker, guarantor, mainstay, patron, promoter, supporter, surety, sustainer, underwriter; SEE CONCEPTS *348,423*

sponsor [*v*] *help, promote*
answer for, back, bankroll, be responsible for, finance, fund, grubstake, guarantee, patronize, put up money, stake, subsidize, vouch for; SEE CONCEPTS *110,341*

spontaneous [*adj*] *impulsive, willing*
ad-lib*, automatic, break loose, casual, down, extemporaneous, extempore, free, free spirited, from the hip*, impetuous, impromptu, improvised, inevitable, instinctive, involuntary, irresistible, natural, offhand, off the cuff*, off top of head*, simple, unartful, unavoidable, unbidden, uncompelled, unconscious, unconstrained, uncontrived, uncontrolled, unforced, unintentional, unplanned, unpremeditated, unprompted, unsophisticated, unstudied, up front, voluntary; SEE CONCEPTS *401,542,548*

spoof [*n*] *trick, mockery*
bluff, bon mot, burlesque, caricature, cheat, deceit, deception, fake, flim-flam*, game, hoax, imposture, jest, joke, lampoon, parody, phony, prank, put-on, quip, satire, sell, send-up*, sham, take-off, travesty, trickery, wisecrack; SEE CONCEPTS *59,273*

spooky [adj] frightening
chilling, creepy, eerie, ghostly, mysterious, ominous, scary, spine-chilling, supernatural, uncanny, unearthly, weird; SEE CONCEPTS 529,537

sporadic [adj] on and off
bits and pieces*, desultory, few, fitful, fits and starts*, hit-or-miss*, infrequent, intermittent, irregular, isolated, occasional, on-again-off-again*, random, rare, scarce, scattered, seldom, semioccasional, spasmodic, spotty, uncommon, unfrequent; SEE CONCEPT 541

sport [n1] recreational activity; entertainment
action, amusement, athletics, ball, disport, diversion, exercise, frolic, fun, fun and games*, gaiety, game, games, pastime, physical activity, picnic, play, pleasure, recreation; SEE CONCEPT 363

sport [n2] fun, joking
antics, badinage, banter, derision, drollery, escapade, frolic, horseplay, jest, jesting, joke, jollification, jollity, kidding, laughter, merriment, mirth, mockery, mummery, nonsense, pleasantry, practical joke, raillery, scorn, teasing, tomfoolery, trifling; SEE CONCEPTS 59,273

sport [n3] person who takes kidding
buffoon, butt, jestee, joke, laughingstock, mock, mockery, object of derision, object of ridicule, plaything, target; SEE CONCEPT 423

sport [v] display, wear
be dressed in, don, exhibit, have on, model, show off; SEE CONCEPTS 167,261

sporting/sportive [adj] playful and fair
antic, coltish, considerate, devil-may-care*, frisky, frolicsome, full of fun*, game, gamesome, gay, generous, gentlemanly, impish, jaunty, joyous, larkish, lively, merry, mischievous, reasonable, roguish, rollicking, sportsmanlike, sportsmanly, sprightly, square, wild; SEE CONCEPT 401

spot [n1] mark, stain
atom, blemish, blot, blotch, daub, discoloration, dollop, dram, drop, flaw, iota, jot, little bit, mite, molecule, mote, nip, particle, pimple, pinch, shot, smidgen, smudge, snort, speck, taint, whit; SEE CONCEPTS 284,831

spot [n2] location
hangout*, hole*, joint*, layout, locality, locus, office, pad, place, plant, point, position, post, roof, scene, seat, section, sector, site, situation, slot, station, wherever*, X*, X marks the spot*; SEE CONCEPT 198

spot [n3] bad situation
box*, corner*, difficulty, dilemma, fix, hole*, jam, mess, pickle*, plight, predicament, quandary, scrape, trouble; SEE CONCEPTS 666,674

spot [n4] position in organization
appointment, berth, billet, connection, job, office, place, post, responsibility, situation, station, work; SEE CONCEPTS 351,362

spot [v1] mark, stain
besmirch, bespatter, blot, blotch, dapple, dirty, dot, fleck, maculate, marble, mottle, pepper, pimple, soil, spatter, speck, speckle, splash, splotch, stipple, streak, stripe, stud, sully, taint, tarnish; SEE CONCEPTS 79,179

spot [v2] see, recognize
catch, catch sight of, descry, detect, determinate, diagnose, discern, discover, distinguish, encounter, espy, ferret out, find, identify, locate, make out, meet with, observe, pick out, pinpoint, place, point out, sight, trace, track, turn up; SEE CONCEPTS 38,183,626

spotless [adj] very clean; innocent
above reproach, blameless, chaste, clean, decent, faultless, flawless, gleaming, hygienic, immaculate, irreproachable, modest, pure, sanitary, shining, snowy, stainless, unblemished, undefiled, unimpeachable, unsoiled, unstained, unsullied, untarnished, virgin, virginal, white; SEE CONCEPTS 404,621

spotlight [n] attention; bright beam of light
center stage, fame, flashlight, floodlight, interest, light, limelight, notoriety, public attention, public eye, publicity; SEE CONCEPTS 388,624,668

spotlight [v] focus attention on
accentuate, draw attention, feature, floodlight*, give prominence, highlight, illuminate, limelight*, point up, publicize, put on center stage*; SEE CONCEPTS 261,292

spotty [adj] blotchy, irregular
desultory, erratic, flickering, fluctuating, not uniform, on-again-off-again*, patchy, pimply, spasmodic, sporadic, unequal, uneven; SEE CONCEPT 534

spouse [n] one of a married couple
better half, breadwinner*, bride, companion, groom, helpmate, husband, man, mate, partner, roommate, wife, woman; SEE CONCEPT 414

spout [v1] spurt, emit
cascade, discharge, eject, erupt, expel, exude, gush, jet, pour, roll, shoot, spill, spray, squirt, stream, surge; SEE CONCEPT 179

spout [v2] talk forcefully
boast, brag, chatter, declaim, expatiate, go on, gush, harangue, hold forth, orate, pontificate, ramble, rant, sermonize, shoot off mouth*, speechify, spellbind, spiel, vapor, yell; SEE CONCEPTS 49,51

sprawl [v] sit or lie spread out
drape, extend, flop, lie, loll, lounge, ramble, recline, sit, slouch, slump, spread, spread-eagle*, straddle, straggle, stretch, trail; SEE CONCEPT 201

spray [n] fine mist
aerosol, atomizer, drizzle, droplets, duster, fog, froth, moisture, spindrift, splash, sprayer, sprinkler, vaporizer; SEE CONCEPTS 514,680

spray [v] sprinkle, diffuse
atomize, drizzle, dust, scatter, shoot, shower, smear, spatter, splash, spritz, squirt, throw around; SEE CONCEPTS 179,256

spread [n1] *expansion, development; extent*
advance, advancement, compass, diffusion, dispersion, dissemination, enlargement, escalation, expanse, extension, increase, period, profusion, proliferation, radiation, ramification, range, reach, scope, span, spreading, stretch, suffusion, sweep, term, transfusion, transmission; SEE CONCEPTS *651,704,721,787*

spread [n2] *outlay of food, meal*
array, banquet, blowout, dinner, feast, lunch, regale, repast; SEE CONCEPT *459*

spread [v1] *open or fan out*
arrange, array, be displayed, be distributed, bloat, branch off, broaden, cast, circulate, coat, cover, daub, develop, diffuse, dilate, disperse, diverge, enlarge, escalate, even out, expand, extend, flatten, flow, gloss, increase, lay, lengthen, level, lie, multiply, mushroom, open, outstretch, overlay, paint, pervade, prepare, proliferate, radiate, reach, roll out, set, settle, smear, sprawl, spray, stretch, strew, suffuse, swell, uncoil, unfold, unfurl, unroll, untwist, unwind, widen; SEE CONCEPTS *158,172,201*

spread [v2] *publicize*
advertise, blazon, broadcast, cast, circulate, declare, diffuse, disseminate, distribute, make known, make public, proclaim, promulgate, propagate, publish, radiate, scatter, shed, sow, strew, transmit; SEE CONCEPT *60*

spree [n] *wild activity*
bacchanalia, ball, bash, binge, caper, carousal, carouse, carousing, celebration, field day*, fling, frolic, high jinks*, high time*, jag, jamboree, junket, lark, merry-go-round*, orgy, party, rampage, revel, rip*, spending expedition, spending spree, splurge, tear*; SEE CONCEPTS *327,377,384*

sprightly [adj] *fun, vivacious*
active, agile, airy, alert, animate, animated, blithe, bouncy, breezy, bright, brisk, cheerful, cheery, chipper, chirpy, clever, dapper, dashing, energetic, fairylike, frolicsome, gay, good, grooving, hyper, jaunty, jolly, joyous, jumping, keen, keen-witted, light, lively, nimble, peppy, perky, playful, quick, quick-witted, saucy, scintillating, smart, snappy, spirited, sportive, spry, swinging, zappy*, zingy*, zippy*; SEE CONCEPTS *401,404,542*

spring [n1] *jump, skip*
bounce, bounciness, bound, buck, buoyancy, elasticity, flexibility, give, hop, leap, recoil, resilience, saltation, springiness, vault; SEE CONCEPTS *194,731*

spring [n2] *season following winter*
blackberry winter*, budding, budtime, flowering, prime, seedtime, springtide, springtime, vernal equinox, vernal season; SEE CONCEPT *814*

spring [n3] *origin*
beginning, cause, consideration, fount, fountain, fountainhead, impetus, motive, root, source, stimulus, well, wellspring, whence; SEE CONCEPTS *648,661*

spring [n4] *body of rushing waters*
artesian well, baths, fountain, geyser, hot spring, hydrolysate, spa, thermal spring, watering place, wells; SEE CONCEPT *514*

spring [v1] *jump, skip*
bolt, bounce, bound, hippety hop*, hop, hurdle, leap, lop, lope, rebound, recoil, skitter, start, startle, trip, vault; SEE CONCEPT *194*

spring [v2] *originate, emerge*
appear, arise, arrive, be derived, be descended, begin, birth, burgeon, come, come into being, come into existence, come out, commence, derive, descend, develop, emanate, flow, grow, hatch, head, issue, loom, mushroom, proceed, rise, shoot up, start, stem, upspring; SEE CONCEPTS *105,302,373*

sprinkle [v] *scatter, disseminate*
baptize, christen, dampen, dot, dredge, dust, freckle, mist, moisten, pepper, powder, rain, shake, shower, smear, speck, speckle, spit, spot, spray, spritz, squirt, strew, stud; SEE CONCEPTS *179,222,256*

sprinkling [n] *hint, dash*
admixture, dust, dusting, few, handful, lick, mixture, powdering, scattering, several, smattering, sprinkle, strain, taste, tinge, touch, trace; SEE CONCEPT *831*

sprint [v] *run very fast*
dart, dash, go at top speed, hotfoot*, race, rush, scamper, scoot, scurry, shoot, tear*, whiz*; SEE CONCEPT *150*

sprout [v] *develop*
bud, burgeon, germinate, grow, push, shoot, shoot up, spring, take root, vegetate; SEE CONCEPT *257*

spruce [adj] *stylish, neat*
classy, clean, dainty, dapper, elegant, prim, smart, tidy, trim, well-groomed; SEE CONCEPT *589*

spruce up [v] *make neat, well-groomed*
brush, deck out*, dress up, fix up, groom, prim, primp, sleek, slick, smarten, tidy, titivate, wash; SEE CONCEPTS *162,167,202*

spry [adj] *active, vivacious*
agile, alert, brisk, energetic, fleet, full of pep, healthy, in full swing*, lithe, nimble, on the go*, prompt, quick, quick on the draw*, ready, robust, rocking, sound, spirited, sprightly, supple, vigorous; SEE CONCEPT *401*

spunk [n] *courage, nerve*
backbone, determination, doggedness, fortitude, gameness, grit*, gumption*, guts*, intestinal fortitude*, mettle, moxie*, pluck, resolution, spirit, toughness, true grit*; SEE CONCEPTS *411,633*

spur [n] *incitement, stimulus*
activation, actuation, catalyst, excitant, goad, goose*, impetus, impulse, incentive, incitation, inducement, motivation, motive, needle*, prick, stimulant, trigger, turn-on*, urge; SEE CONCEPT *661*

spur [v] *incite, prompt*
animate, arouse, awaken, countenance, drive, egg on*, exhort, favor, fire up*, goad, goose*, impel,

instigate, key up, press, prick, prod, propel, push, put up to, rally, rouse, sic*, spark, stimulate, stir, trigger, turn on, urge, work up; SEE CONCEPTS *14,68*

spurious [*adj*] *counterfeit, fake*
affected, apocryphal, artificial, assumed, bastard*, bent, bogus, bum, contrived, deceitful, deceptive, dummy*, ersatz*, faked, false, feigned, forged, framed, illegitimate, imitation, make-believe, mock, phony, pirate, pretend, pretended, pseudo*, put-on*, sham*, simulated, specious, substitute, unauthentic, ungenuine, unreal; SEE CONCEPT *582*

spurn [*v*] *turn away; ignore*
air, cold-shoulder*, contemn, cut, decline, despise, disapprove, disdain, dismiss, disregard, drop, dump, flout, flush, hold in contempt, look down on*, nix*, not hear of*, pass by, rebuff, refuse, reject, reprobate, repudiate, repulse, scoff, scorn, slight, sneer, sneeze at*, snub, steer clear*, turn down, turn nose up at*; SEE CONCEPTS *21,30,384*

spurt [*n*] *burst of activity*
access, commotion, discharge, eruption, explosion, fit, jet, outburst, rush, spate, spritz, squirt, stream, surge; SEE CONCEPTS *1,119,179*

spurt [*v*] *erupt*
burst, emerge, flow, flow out, gush, issue, jet, ooze, pour out, shoot, spew, spout, spritz, squirt, stream, surge, well; SEE CONCEPT *179*

spy [*n*] *person who secretly finds out about another's business*
agent, detective, double agent, emissary, espionage agent, foreign agent, informer, inside man/woman, intelligencer, investigator, lookout, mole*, observer, operative, patrol, picket, plant*, scout, secret agent, secret service, sleeper, sleuth, snoop, spook, spotter, undercover agent, watcher; SEE CONCEPTS *348,412*

spy [*v*] *secretly follow, watch another's actions*
case, catch sight of, discover, examine, eyeball*, fish out*, get a load of*, glimpse, keep under surveillance, look for, meddle, notice, observe, peep, pry, recon, reconnoiter, scout, scrutinize, search, set eyes on, shadow, sleuth, snoop, spot, stag, stake out, tail, take in, take note, trail, view, watch; SEE CONCEPTS *103,623*

squabble [*n*] *argument*
altercation, bickering, controversy, difference, difference of opinion, disagreement, dispute, feud, fight, flap*, fuss*, hassle, quarrel, row*, scene*, scrap*, set-to*, spat*, tiff*, words*, wrangle; SEE CONCEPT *46*

squabble [*v*] *argue*
argufy, bicker, brawl, clash, disagree, dispute, encounter, fall out*, fight, hassle, have words*, quarrel, quibble, row, scrap, spat, tiff*, wrangle; SEE CONCEPT *46*

squad [*n*] *team, crew*
band, battalion, company, division, force, gang, group, regiment, squadron, troop; SEE CONCEPTS *322,365,417*

squalid [*adj*] *poor, run-down*
abominable, base, broken-down, decayed, despicable, dingy, dirty, disgusting, disheveled, fetid, filthy, foul, grimy, gruesome, horrible, horrid, ignoble, impure, low, mean, miry, moldy, muddy, musty, nasty, odorous, offensive, poverty-stricken, ramshackle, reeking, repellent, repulsive, scurvy, seedy, shabby, shoddy, sloppy, slovenly, soiled, sordid, ugly, unclean, unkempt, vile, wretched; SEE CONCEPTS *334,485,570*

squander [*v*] *fritter away, use up*
be prodigal with, be wasteful, blow*, cash out*, consume, dissipate, expend, frivol, frivol away, go through, lavish, misspend, misuse, prodigalize, put out*, run through, scatter, spend, spend like water*, spring for*, throw away, throw money around*, trifle, waste; SEE CONCEPTS *156,225,327*

square [*n1*] *person who is old-fashioned, conventional*
antediluvian, conservative, diehard*, fuddy-duddy*, reactionary, stick-in-the-mud*, traditionalist; SEE CONCEPT *423*

square [*n2*] *municipal park*
area, center, circle, common, green, plaza, space, village green; SEE CONCEPT *509*

square [*adj1*] *honest, genuine*
aboveboard, decent, equal, equitable, ethical, even, fair, fair-and-square, impartial, impersonal, just, nonpartisan, objective, on-the-level, sporting, sportsmanlike, sportsmanly, straight, straightforward, unbiased, unprejudiced, upright; SEE CONCEPTS *267,542*

square [*adj2*] *four-sided*
boxlike, boxy, equal-sided, equilateral, foursquare, orthogonal, quadrate, quadratic, quadratical, rectangular, rectilinear, right-angled, squared, squarish; SEE CONCEPT *486*

square [*adj3*] *old-fashioned, conventional*
behind the times, bourgeois, button-down*, conservative, dated, orthodox, out-of-date, straight*, straitlaced*, stuffy*; SEE CONCEPTS *401,404*

square [*v1*] *correspond, agree*
accord, balance, check out, coincide, conform, dovetail*, fit, fit in, gee, harmonize, jibe, match, reconcile, tally; SEE CONCEPT *664*

square [*v2*] *pay off, satisfy*
balance, bribe, buy, buy off, clear, clear off, clear up, corrupt, discharge, fix, have, liquidate, make even, pay, pay up, quit, rig, settle, tamper with; SEE CONCEPT *341*

square [*v3*] *adapt, regulate*
accommodate, adjust, align, conform, even up, fit, level, quadrate, reconcile, suit, tailor, tailor-make, true; SEE CONCEPTS *126,202*

squash [*v*] *compress*
annihilate, bear, bruise, crowd, crush, distort, extinguish, flatten, jam, kill, macerate, mash, pound, press, pulp, push, put down, quash, quell, scrunch, shut down, sit on, smash, squeeze, squish, stamp on,

suppress, trample, triturate; SEE CONCEPTS *121,208, 219*

squat [*adj*] *short and stocky*
broad, chunky, dumpy*, fat, heavy, heavyset, splay, thick, thick-bodied, thickset, tick; SEE CONCEPTS *491,773,779*

squat [*v*] *lower body by bending knees*
bow, cower, crouch, hunch, hunker down, perch, roost, settle, sit, stoop; SEE CONCEPT *201*

squawk [*v1*] *make high-pitched, animal-like sound*
cackle, caw, crow, cry, hoot, screech, yap, yawp, yelp; SEE CONCEPTS *64,77*

squawk [*v2*] *gripe*
bellyache*, complain, kick up a fuss*, protest, raise Cain*, squeal, yammer; SEE CONCEPTS *52,54*

squeak [*v*] *make sharp, high-pitched sound*
cheep, creak, cry, grate, peep, pipe, scream, screech, scritch, shrill, sing, sound, squeal, talk, whine, yelp; SEE CONCEPTS *64,65*

squeal [*n/v1*] *yell in a loud and high-pitched manner*
bleat, cheep, creak, grate, howl, peep, rasp, scream, scream bloody murder*, screech, shout, shriek, shrill, squawk, wail, yelp, yip, yowl; SEE CONCEPTS *64,77*

squeal [*v2*] *inform on*
betray, blab*, complain, protest, rat on*, sell down the river*, sing*, snitch*, squawk*, talk, tattle, tattletale, tell; SEE CONCEPTS *54,60*

squeamish [*adj*] *nauseated; finicky*
annoyed, captious, delicate, disgusted, dizzy, exacting, fastidious, fussy, hypercritical, mincing, particular, prim, prudish, puritanical, qualmish, queasy, queer, scrupulous, shaky, sick, sickly, sick to one's stomach*, strait-laced, unsettled, upset, vertiginous; SEE CONCEPTS *314,401,404*

squeeze [*n*] *pressure, crushing*
clasp, clutch, congestion, crowd, crunch, crush, embrace, force, handclasp, hold, hug, influence, jam, press, restraint, squash; SEE CONCEPTS *219, 674,686*

squeeze [*v1*] *exert pressure on sides, parts of something*
bear, choke, clasp, clip, clutch, compress, contract, cram, crowd, crush, cuddle, embrace, enfold, force, grip, hold tight, hug, jam, jostle, nip, pack, pinch, press, quash, ram, scrunch, squash, squish, strangle, stuff, throttle, thrust, wedge, wring; SEE CONCEPT *219*

squeeze [*v2*] *try to get money out of*
bleed*, bring pressure to bear, eke out, extort, extract, lean on*, milk*, oppress, pinch*, pressure, pressurize, put screws to*, shake down*, wrench, wring; SEE CONCEPTS *53,192,342*

squelch [*v*] *suppress, restrain*
black out, censure, crush, extinguish, kill, muffle, oppress, quelch, quench, repress, settle, shush, sit on, smother, squash, stifle, strangle, thwart; SEE CONCEPT *130*

squint [*v*] *scrunch up eyes when viewing*
cock the eye, look, look askance, look cross-eyed, peek, peep, screw up eyes, squinch; SEE CONCEPTS *185,623*

squire [*v*] *accompany*
assist, attend, chaperon, companion, date, escort, serve; SEE CONCEPTS *384,714*

squirm [*v*] *wiggle, fidget*
agonize, flounder, shift, skew, squiggle, toss, twist, wind, worm, wriggle, writhe; SEE CONCEPT *213*

squirt [*v*] *squeeze out liquid*
eject, emit, flow, jet, pour, spatter, spit, splash, splur, spray, sprinkle, spritz, spurt, stream, surge; SEE CONCEPTS *179,256*

stab [*n1*] *piercing cut*
ache, blow, gash, hurt, incision, jab, jag, pang, piercing, prick, puncture, rent, stick, thrust, transfixion, twinge, wound; SEE CONCEPT *309*

stab [*n2*] *attempt*
attempt, crack*, endeavor, essay, fling*, go*, one's best*, shot*, try, venture, whack*, whirl*; SEE CONCEPT *87*

stab [*v*] *puncture, pierce with sharp, pointed object*
bayonet, brand, carve, chop, cleave, clip, cut, drive, gore, hit, hurt, injure, jab, jag, knife, open up, penetrate, pierce, plow, plunge, prick, prong, punch, ram, run through, saber, shank, sink, slice, spear, stick, thrust, transfix, wound; SEE CONCEPT *220*

stability [*n*] *resistance of some degree*
adherence, aplomb, assurance, backbone, balance, cohesion, constancy, dependability, determination, durability, endurance, establishment, firmness, immobility, immovability, maturity, permanence, perseverance, resoluteness, security, solidity, solidness, soundness, stableness, steadfastness, steadiness, strength, substantiality, support, toughness; SEE CONCEPTS *411,731*

stabilize [*v*] *make or keep in steady state; make resistant to change*
balance, ballast, bolt, brace, counterbalance, counterpoise, equalize, fasten, firm, firm up*, fix, freeze*, maintain, ossify, poise, preserve, prop, secure, set, settle, stabilitate, steady, stiffen, support, sustain, uphold; SEE CONCEPTS *110,250*

stable [*adj*] *constant, fixed; resistant*
abiding, anchored, balanced, brick-wall*, calm, deep-rooted, durable, enduring, equable, established, even, fast, firm, immutable, invariable, lasting, nailed, perdurable, permanent, poised, reliable, resolute, safe, secure, set, set in stone*, solid, solid as a rock*, sound, stabile, stalwart, stationary, staunch, stay put, steadfast, steady, stout, strong, sturdy, substantial, sure, together, tough, unalterable, unchangeable, unfluctuating, uniform, unvarying, unwavering, well-built, well-founded; SEE CONCEPTS *404,488*

stack [*n*] *pile*
assemblage, bank, bundle, cock, drift, heap, hill, hoard, load, mass, mound, mountain, pack, pyramid, sheaf; SEE CONCEPTS *432,440,509*

stack [v] *pile up*
accumulate, amass, bank up, cock, drift, heap, hill, load, mound, pile, rick, stockpile; SEE CONCEPTS *109,158*

stadium [n] *arena for recreation or spectating*
amphitheater, athletic field, bowl, coliseum, diamond, field, garden, gridiron, gymnasium, pit, ring, stade, strand; SEE CONCEPT *438*

staff [n1] *employees of organization*
agents, assistants, cadre, cast, crew, deputies, faculty, force, help, officers, operatives, organization, personnel, savages, servants, shop, slaves, teachers, team, workers, work force; SEE CONCEPT *325*

staff [n2] *stick, usually for walking*
cane, club, pikestaff, pole, prop, rod, stave, walking stick, wand; SEE CONCEPTS *311,479*

stage [n1] *level, period within structure or system*
date, degree, division, footing, grade, juncture, lap, leg, length, moment, node, notch, phase, plane, point, point in time, rung, standing, status, step; SEE CONCEPTS *727,744,816*

stage [n2] *theater platform; theater life*
arena, boards*, Broadway, dais, drama, footlights, frame, legit*, limelight*, mise-en-scène, off-Broadway, play, scaffold, scaffolding, scene, scenery, set, setting, show biz*, show business, spotlight, stage set, staging, theater; SEE CONCEPTS *263,349,438,439,448*

stage [v] *arrange, produce*
bring out, do, engineer, execute, give, mount, open, orchestrate, organize, perform, play, present, put on, show; SEE CONCEPTS *94,292*

stagger [v1] *walk falteringly*
alternate, careen, dither, falter, halt, hesitate, lurch, overlap, pitch, reel, shake, stammer, step, sway, swing, teeter, titubate, topple, totter, vacillate, waver, wheel, whiffle, wobble, zigzag; SEE CONCEPT *151*

stagger [v2] *astound, shock*
amaze, astonish, boggle, bowl over*, confound, consternate, devastate, dumbfound, flabbergast, floor*, give a shock, nonplus, overpower, overwhelm, paralyze, perplex, puzzle, shake, shatter, startle, strike dumb*, stump, stun, stupefy, surprise, take aback, take breath away*, throw off balance*; SEE CONCEPTS *7,19,42*

stagnant [adj] *motionless, dirty*
brackish, dead, dormant, filthy, foul, idle, immobile, inactive, inert, lifeless, listless, passive, putrid, quiet, sluggish, stale, standing, static, stationary, still, unmoving; SEE CONCEPTS *584,621*

stagnate [v] *deteriorate by lack of action*
constipate, decay, decline, fester, go to seed*, hibernate, idle, languish, lie fallow, not move, putrefy, rot, rust, stall, stand, stand still, stifle, stultify, trammel, vegetate; SEE CONCEPTS *698,748*

staid [adj] *restrained, set*
calm, cold sober*, collected, composed, cool, decorous, demure, dignified, earnest, formal, grave, nonsense*, quiet, sedate, self-restrained, serious, settled, sober, solemn, somber, starchy, steady, stuffy, weighty; SEE CONCEPTS *401,404*

stain [n] *spot of dirt, blot*
bar sinister*, black eye*, blemish, blot, blotch, blur, brand, color, discoloration, disgrace, dishonor, drip, dye, infamy, ink spot, mottle, odium, onus, reproach, shame, slur, smirch, smudge, spatter, speck, splotch, spot, stigma, tint; SEE CONCEPTS *230,622*

stain [v] *dirty, taint*
animalize, bastardize, besmirch, bestialize, blacken, blemish, blot, brutalize, color, contaminate, corrupt, daub, debase, debauch, defile, demoralize, deprave, discolor, disgrace, drag through the mud*, dye, mark, pervert, smear, smudge, soil, spot, sully, tar, tarnish, tinge, tint; SEE CONCEPTS *54,250,254*

stake [n1] *pole*
pale, paling, picket, post, rod, spike, stave, stick; SEE CONCEPTS *471,479*

stake [n2] *bet, wager*
ante, chance, hazard, peril, pledge, pot, risk, venture; SEE CONCEPTS *329,363*

stake [n3] *share, investment*
award, claim, concern, interest, involvement, prize, purse; SEE CONCEPTS *344,710,835*

stake [v] *bet, wager*
back, bankroll, capitalize, chance, finance, gamble, game, grubstake, hazard, imperil, jeopardize, lay, play, pledge, put, put on, risk, set, stake down, venture; SEE CONCEPTS *330,363*

stale [adj1] *old, decayed*
dried, dry, faded, fetid, flat, fusty, hard, insipid, malodorous, musty, noisome, parched, rank, reeking, smelly, sour, spoiled, stagnant, stenchy, stinking, tasteless, watery, weak, zestless; SEE CONCEPTS *462,485,598*

stale [adj2] *overused, out-of-date*
antiquated, banal, bent, cliché, clichéd, cliché-ridden, common, commonplace, corny*, dead, dinosaur*, drab, dull, dusty, effete, flat, fusty, hackneyed, insipid, mawkish, moth-eaten*, out*, passé, past, platitudinous, repetitious, shopworn, stereotyped, threadbare, timeworn, tired, trite, unoriginal, well-worn, worn-out, yesterday*, zestless; SEE CONCEPTS *267,578,589,797*

stalemate [n] *deadlock*
arrest, Catch-22*, check, delay, draw, gridlock, impasse, pause, standoff, standstill, tie; SEE CONCEPTS *230,807,832*

stalk [n] *stem of plant*
axis, bent, helm, pedicel, pedicle, reed, shaft, spike, spire, support, trunk, twig, upright; SEE CONCEPT *428*

stalk [v] *follow, creep up on*
ambush, approach, chase, drive, flush out, haunt, hunt, pace, pursue, shadow, striddle, stride, tail, track, trail, walk up to; SEE CONCEPTS *149,159,749*

stall [v] *delay for own purposes*
arrest, avoid the issue*, beat around the bush*, brake, check, die, drag one's feet*, equivocate,

fence, filibuster, halt, hamper, hedge, hinder, hold off, interrupt, not move, play for time*, postpone, prevaricate, put off, quibble, shut down, slow, slow down, stand, stand off, stand still, stay, still, stonewall*, stop, suspend, take one's time*, tarry, temporize; SEE CONCEPT 121,234

stalwart [*adj*] *strong, valiant*
athletic, bold, bound, bound and determined*, brave, brawny, brick-wall*, courageous, daring, dauntless, dead set on*, dependable, fearless, forceful, gutsy*, hanging tough*, hefty, husky, indomitable, intrepid, lusty, manly, muscular, nervy*, powerhouse*, redoubtable, robust, rugged, sinewy, solid, spunky*, staunch, steamroller*, stout, stouthearted, strapping, sturdy, substantial, tenacious, tough, unafraid, undaunted, valorous, vigorous; SEE CONCEPTS 404,489

stamina [*n*] *strength, vigor*
backbone*, endurance, energy, force, fortitude, grit*, guts*, gutsiness, heart, indefatigability, intestinal fortitude*, legs*, lustiness, moxie*, power, power of endurance, resilience, resistance, starch*, staying power, tolerance, toleration, vim, vitality, zip*; SEE CONCEPTS 411,732

stammer [*v*] *stutter in speech*
falter, halt, hammer, hem and haw*, hesitate, jabber, lurch, pause, repeat, splutter, sputter, stop, stumble, wobble; SEE CONCEPTS 47,266

stamp [*n1*] *impression, symbol, seal*
brand, cast, earmark, emblem, hallmark, impress, imprint, indentation, mark, mold, print, signature, sticker; SEE CONCEPTS 259,284

stamp [*n2*] *character*
breed, cast, cut, description, fashion, form, ilk, kind, lot, mold, sort, stripe, type; SEE CONCEPT 411

stamp [*v1*] *step on hard*
beat, clomp, clump, crush, stomp, stump, tramp, trample, tromp; SEE CONCEPT 149

stamp [*v2*] *imprint; press mark on*
brand, cast, drive, engrave, etch, fix, grave, hammer, impress, infix, inscribe, letter, mark, mold, offset, pound, print; SEE CONCEPTS 79,174

stampede [*n*] *rush of animals*
charge, chase, crash, dash, flight, fling, hurry, panic, rout, run, scattering, shoot, smash, tear; SEE CONCEPT 152

stance [*n*] *position, posture*
attitude, bearing, carriage, color, deportment, posture, say-so*, slant, stand, standpoint, viewpoint; SEE CONCEPTS 689,757

stand [*n1*] *position, opinion*
angle, attitude, belief, carriage, determination, notion, poise, pose, sentiment, slant, sound, stance, standpoint, twist, two cents' worth*, view; SEE CONCEPT 689

stand [*n2*] *base, stage*
board, booth, bracket, counter, dais, frame, gantry, grandstand, place, platform, rack, rank, staging, stall, station, support, table; SEE CONCEPTS 442,443

stand [*v1*] *be or get upright*
be erect, be on feet, be vertical, cock, dispose, erect, jump up, locate, mount, place, poise, position, put, rank, rise, set, settle; SEE CONCEPT 201

stand/stand for [*v2*] *endure, bear*
abide, allow, bear with, brook, cope, countenance, experience, handle, hang on, hold, last, live with, put up with, resign oneself to, stay the course*, stomach*, submit, suffer, support, sustain, swallow*, take, tolerate, undergo, wear, weather, withstand; SEE CONCEPT 23

stand [*v3*] *be in force, exist*
be located, belong, be situated, be valid, continue, endure, fill, halt, hold, last, obtain, occupy, pause, prevail, remain, rest, stay, stop, take up; SEE CONCEPT 407

standard [*n1*] *guideline, principle*
archetype, average, axiom, barometer, beau ideal*, belief, benchmark*, canon, code, criterion, ethics, example, exemplar, fundamental, gauge, grade, guide, guideline, ideal, ideals, law, mean, measure, median, mirror, model, morals, norm, par, paradigm, pattern, principle, requirement, rule, rule of thumb*, sample, specification, test, touchstone*, type, yardstick; SEE CONCEPT 687

standard [*n2*] *flag*
banderole, banner, bannerol, color, colors, emblem, ensign, figure, insignia, jack, pennant, streamer, symbol; SEE CONCEPT 475

standard [*adj*] *regular, approved*
accepted, authoritative, average, basic, boilerplate*, canonical, classic, common, customary, definitive, established, everyday, garden variety*, general, normal, official, orthodox, popular, prevailing, recognized, regulation, run-of-the-mill*, set, staple, stock, typical, usual, vanilla*; SEE CONCEPT 533

standardize [*v*] *make regular, similar*
assimilate, bring into line, homogenize, institute, institutionalize, mass produce, normalize, order, regiment, stereotype, systematize; SEE CONCEPT 126

stand for [*v*] *signify, mean*
answer for, appear for, betoken, denote, exemplify, imply, indicate, represent, signify, suggest, symbol, symbolize; SEE CONCEPT 682

standing [*n*] *position, rank*
cachet, capacity, character, condition, consequence, credit, dignity, eminence, estimation, footing, place, prestige, reputation, repute, scene, situation, slot, state, station, stature, status, term; SEE CONCEPTS 388,727

standing [*adj*] *permanent*
continuing, existing, fixed, perpetual, regular, repeated; SEE CONCEPT 551

standoffish [*adj*] *cold, distant*
aloof, antisocial, cool, distant, eremitic, haughty, indifferent, misanthropic, reclusive, remote, reserved, solitary, unapproachable, unapproachable, uncom-

panionable, unsociable, withdrawn; SEE CONCEPTS *401,404*

stand out [*v*] *be conspicuous, prominent*
attract attention, be distinct, beetle, be highlighted, be striking, bulge, bulk, catch the eye, emerge, jut, loom, overhang, poke, pouch, project, protrude, stick out; SEE CONCEPT *716*

standstill [*n*] *stop*
arrest, cessation, check, checkmate, corner*, dead end*, deadlock, dead stop*, delay, gridlock, halt, hole, impasse, inaction, pause, stalemate, standoff, wait; SEE CONCEPTS *119,832*

staple [*adj*] *necessary, basic*
chief, essential, fundamental, important, in demand, key, main, popular, predominant, primary, principal, standard; SEE CONCEPT *546*

star [*n*] *person who is famous*
celebrity, draw*, favorite, headliner, hero, idol, lead, leading lady, leading man, luminary, name, starlet, superstar, topliner*; SEE CONCEPTS *352,366*

star [*adj*] *famous, illustrious*
brilliant, capital, celebrated, chief, dominant, leading, main, major, outstanding, paramount, predominant, preeminent, principal, prominent, talented, well-known; SEE CONCEPT *568*

stare [*v*] *gape, watch*
beam*, bore*, eagle eye*, eye, eyeball*, fix, focus, gawk, gaze, glare, glim, goggle*, lay eyes on*, look, look fixedly, ogle, peer, rivet, rubberneck*, take in; SEE CONCEPT *623*

stark [*adj1*] *utter, absolute*
abrupt, arrant, bald, bare, blasted, blessed, blunt, complete, confounded, consummate, downright, entire, firm, flagrant, gross*, infernal, out-and-out*, palpable, patent, pure, rank, severe, sheer, simple, stiff, unalloyed, unmitigated; SEE CONCEPTS *531,569*

stark [*adj2*] *bare, unadorned*
au naturel*, austere, bald, barren, bleak, chaste, clear, cold, depressing, desolate, dreary, empty, forsaken, grim, harsh, naked, nude, plain, raw, severe, solitary, stripped, unclad, unclothed, uncovered, undraped, vacant, vacuous, void; SEE CONCEPT *485*

start [*n1*] *beginning*
alpha*, birth, bow, commencement, countdown, dawn, dawning, day one*, derivation, embarkation, exit, first step, flying start*, foundation, inauguration, inception, initiation, jump-off, kickoff, leaving, onset, opening, origin, outset, running start, setting out, source, spring, square one*, start-off, takeoff; SEE CONCEPTS *648,832*

start [*n2*] *advantage*
allowance, backing, break, bulge, chance, draw, edge, handicap, head start, helping hand, introduction, lead, odds, opening, opportunity, sponsorship, vantage; SEE CONCEPT *693*

start [*n3*] *flinch*
convulsion, jar, jump, scare, shock, spasm, turn, twitch; SEE CONCEPTS *150,194*

start [*v1*] *begin; come into existence*
activate, appear, arise, arouse, come into being, commence, create, depart, embark, engender, enter upon, establish, father, found, get going, get under way*, go ahead, hit the road*, inaugurate, incite, initiate, instigate, institute, introduce, issue, launch, lay foundation, leave, light, make a beginning, open, originate, pioneer, rise, rouse, sally forth, see light, set in motion, set out, set up, spring, take first step*, take the plunge*, turn on; SEE CONCEPTS *221,241*

start [*v2*] *flinch*
blanch, blench, bolt, bounce, bound, buck, dart, draw back, jerk, jump, jump the gun*, leap, quail, recoil, shrink, shy, spring, squinch, startle, twitch, wince; SEE CONCEPTS *150,194*

startle [*v*] *frighten, surprise*
affright, agitate, alarm, amaze, astonish, astound, awe, bolt, consternate, floor, fright, give a turn*, jump, make jump, rock, scare, scare to death*, shake up, shock, spook, spring, spring something on*, stagger, start, stun, take aback, terrify, terrorize; SEE CONCEPTS *7,19,42*

starving/starved [*adj*] *deprived of food*
could eat a horse*, craving, dehydrated, drawn, dying, emaciated, empty, faint, famished, haggard, hungering, hungry, malnourished, peaked, peckish, perishing, pinched, ravenous, skinny, thin, underfed, undernourished, weakened; SEE CONCEPTS *406,546*

state [*n1*] *condition or mode of being*
accompaniment, attitude, capacity, case, category, chances, character, circumstance, circumstances, contingency, element, environment, essential, estate, event, eventuality, fix, footing, form, frame of mind, humor, imperative, juncture, limitation, mood, nature, occasion, occurrence, outlook, pass, phase, plight, position, posture, predicament, prerequisite, proviso, reputation, requirement, shape, situation, spirits, stand, standing, state of affairs, station, status, stipulation, time, welfare; SEE CONCEPTS *410,639,696,701,720*

state [*n2*] *dignity, grandeur*
cachet, ceremony, consequence, display, glory, majesty, pomp, position, prestige, rank, splendor, standing, stature, status, style; SEE CONCEPT *388*

state [*n3*] *government, country*
body politic*, commonwealth, community, federation, kingdom, land, nation, republic, sovereignty, territory, union; SEE CONCEPTS *508,510*

state [*v*] *declare, assert*
affirm, air, articulate, asseverate, aver, bring out, chime in*, come out with, deliver, describe, elucidate, enounce, enumerate, enunciate, explain, expound, express, give, give blow-by-blow*, give rundown*, interpret, narrate, pitch, present, pronounce, propound, put, recite, recount, rehearse, relate, report, say, set forth, speak, specify, spiel*,

tell, throw out*, utter, vent, ventilate, voice; SEE CONCEPTS *49,51,55*

stately [*adj*] *dignified, impressive*
august, ceremonial, ceremonious, conventional, courtly, deliberate, elegant, elevated, formal, gallant, gracious, grand, grandiose, haughty, high, highfaluting*, high-minded*, imperial, imperious, imposing, kingly, large, lofty, lordly, luxurious, magnificent, majestic, massive, masterful, measured, monumental, noble, opulent, palatial, pompous, portly, princely, proud, regal, royal, solemn, stiff, sumptuous, superb, towering; SEE CONCEPTS *401,574,589*

statement [*n1*] *declaration, assertion*
ABCs*, account, acknowledgment, affidavit, affirmation, allegation, announcement, articulation, aside, asseveration, assurance, averment, avowal, blow-by-blow*, charge, comment, communication, communiqué, description, dictum, ejaculation, explanation, make, manifesto, mention, narrative, observation, picture, presentation, presentment, proclamation, profession, protestation, recital, recitation, relation, remark, report, rundown, testimony, utterance, ventilation, verbalization, vocalization, voice, word; SEE CONCEPTS *271,274,278*

statement [*n2*] *account of finances*
affidavit, audit, bill, budget, charge, invoice, reckoning, record, report, score, tab; SEE CONCEPT *331*

static [*adj*] *motionless, changeless*
at a standstill, constant, deadlocked, fixed, format, gridlocked, immobile, immovable, inactive, inert, latent, passive, rigid, stabile, stable, stagnant, stalled, standing still, stationary, sticky, still, stopped, stuck, unchanging, unfluctuating, unmoving, unvarying; SEE CONCEPTS *534,584*

station [*n1*] *headquarters, base*
base of operations, depot, home office, house, location, locus, main office, place, position, post, seat, site, situation, spot, stop, terminal, where, whereabouts; SEE CONCEPT *198*

station [*n2*] *social or occupational status*
appointment, business, calling, capacity, caste, character, class, duty, employment, estate, footing, grade, level, occupation, order, place, position, post, rank, service, situation, sphere, standing, state, stratum; SEE CONCEPTS *349,376,388*

station [*v*] *place at a location*
allot, appoint, assign, base, commission, establish, fix, garrison, install, lodge, park, plant, post, put, set; SEE CONCEPTS *50,88,201,320,351*

stationary [*adj*] *not moving; fixed*
anchored, at a standstill, immobile, inert, moored, motionless, nailed*, nailed down*, parked*, pat*, permanent, stable, stagnant, standing, static, stockstill, unmoving; SEE CONCEPTS *488,551*

statue [*n*] *trophy or memorial*
bronze, bust, cast, effigy, figure, icon, image, ivory, likeness, marble, piece, representation, sculpture,

simulacrum, statuary, statuette, torso; SEE CONCEPT *259*

statuesque [*adj*] *tall and dignifed*
beautiful, graceful, grand, imposing, majestic, regal, shapely, stately, trim, well-proportioned; SEE CONCEPTS *579,589,779*

stature [*n*] *importance*
ability, cachet, caliber, capacity, competence, consequence, development, dignity, elevation, eminence, growth, merit, position, prestige, prominence, qualification, quality, rank, size, standing, state, station, status, tallness, value, virtue, worth; SEE CONCEPTS *668,741*

status [*n*] *rank*
cachet, caliber, capacity, character, condition, consequence, degree, dignity, distinction, eminence, footing, grade, merit, mode, place, position, prestige, prominence, quality, rating, renown, situation, stage, standing, state, station, stature, worth; SEE CONCEPTS *388,668*

statute [*n*] *rule, law*
act, assize, bill, canon, decree, decretum, edict, enactment, measure, ordinance, precept, regulation; SEE CONCEPT *318*

staunch [*adj*] *resolute, dependable*
allegiant, ardent, constant, faithful, fast, firm, inflexible, liege, loyal, reliable, secure, sound, stable, stalwart, steadfast, stiff, stout, strong, sure, tough, tried-and-true, true, true-blue, trustworthy, trusty; SEE CONCEPTS *401,534,542*

stay [*n1*] *visit*
break, halt, holiday, sojourn, stop, stopover, vacation; SEE CONCEPT *227*

stay [*n2*] *hold, delay*
deferment, halt, pause, postponement, remission, reprieve, standstill, stop, stopping, suspension; SEE CONCEPTS *121,832*

stay [*n3*] *support, underpinning*
brace, buttress, column, hold, prop, reinforcement, shore, shoring, stanchion, truss, underpropping; SEE CONCEPTS *440,445*

stay [*v1*] *wait*
abide, bide, bunk, continue, dally, delay, endure, establish oneself, halt, hang, hang about, hang around, hang in, hang out, hold the fort*, hover, lag, last, linger, loiter, nest, outstay, pause, perch, procrastinate, put down roots*, remain, reprieve, reside, respite, roost*, settle, sit tight*, sojourn, squat, stand, stay out, stay put, stick around*, stop, sweat*, sweat it out*, tarry; SEE CONCEPTS *210,681*

stay [*v2*] *visit*
be accommodated, bide, dwell, live, lodge, put up, sojourn, stop, stop over, tarry; SEE CONCEPTS *226,227*

stay [*v3*] *hold in abeyance*
adjourn, arrest, check, curb, defer, delay, detain, discontinue, halt, hinder, hold, hold over, impede, intermit, interrupt, obstruct, postpone, prevent, pro-

rogue, put off, shelve, stall, stop, suspend, ward off; SEE CONCEPT *121*

steadfast [*adj*] *loyal, steady*

abiding, adamant, allegiant, ardent, bound, changeless, constant, dedicated, dependable, enduring, established, faithful, fast, firm, fixed, immobile, immovable, inexorable, inflexible, intense, intent, liege, never-failing, obdurate, persevering, relentless, reliable, resolute, rigid, single-minded, stable, staunch, stubborn, sure, tried-and-true*, true, trueblue, unbending, unfaltering, unflinching, unmovable, unqualified, unquestioning, unswerving, unwavering, unyielding, wholehearted; SEE CONCEPTS *401,534,542*

steady [*adj1*] *stable, fixed*

abiding, brick-wall*, certain, changeless, constant, durable, enduring, equable, even, firm, immovable, never-failing, patterned, regular, reliable, safe, set, set in stone*, solid, solid as a rock*, stabile, steadfast, steady-going, substantial, sure, unchangeable, unchanging, unfaltering, unfluctuating, uniform, unqualified, unquestioning, unshaken, unvarying, unwavering; SEE CONCEPTS *488,534*

steady [*adj2*] *continuing*

ceaseless, confirmed, consistent, constant, continuous, equable, eternal, even, faithful, habitual, incessant, never-ending, nonstop, persistent, regular, rhythmic, stabile, stable, steady-going, unbroken, unfaltering, unfluctuating, uniform, uninterrupted, unremitting, unvarying, unwavering; SEE CONCEPT *798*

steady [*adj3*] *balanced, faithful in mind*

allegiant, ardent, calm, constant, cool, dependable, equable, fast, imperturbable, intense, levelheaded, liege, loyal, poised, reliable, reserved, resolute, sedate, self-possessed, sensible, serene, seriousminded, settled, single-minded, sober, staid, staunch, steadfast, unswerving, unwavering, wholehearted; SEE CONCEPTS *403,542*

steal [*v1*] *take something without permission*

abduct, appropriate, blackmail, burglarize, carry off, cheat, cozen, defraud, despoil, divert, embezzle, heist, hold for ransom, hold up, housebreak*, keep, kidnap, lift*, loot, make off with*, misappropriate, peculate, pilfer, pillage, pinch*, pirate, plagiarize, plunder, poach, purloin, ransack, remove, rifle, rip off*, run off with*, sack*, shanghai*, shoplift, snitch*, spirit away*, stick up*, strip, swindle, swipe, take, take possession of, thieve, walk off with*, withdraw; SEE CONCEPT *139*

steal [*v2*] *sneak around*

creep, flit, glide, go stealthily, insinuate, lurk, pass quietly, skulk, slide, slink, slip, snake, tiptoe; SEE CONCEPTS *151,207*

stealthy [*adj*] *quiet and secretive*

catlike, catty*, clandestine, covert, crafty, cunning, enigmatic, feline, furtive, hush-hush*, noiseless, private, secret, shifty, silent, skulking, slinking, sly,

sneak, sneaking, sneaky, sub-rosa*, surreptitious, undercover, underhand, under wraps*, wily; SEE CONCEPTS *401,576*

steam [*n*] *energy*

beef, force, might, muscle, potency, power, puissance, sinew, strength, vigor, vim; SEE CONCEPT *633*

steel [*v*] *prepare oneself*

animate, brace, buck up*, cheer, embolden, encourage, fortify, gird, grit teeth*, harden, hearten, inspirit, make up one's mind*, prepare, rally, ready, reinforce, strengthen; SEE CONCEPT *35*

steep [*adj1*] *extreme in direction, course*

abrupt, arduous, breakneck, declivitous, elevated, erect, headlong, high, hilly, lifted, lofty, perpendicular, precipitate, precipitous, prerupt, raised, sharp, sheer, straight-up; SEE CONCEPT *581*

steep [*adj2*] *very expensive*

dizzying, excessive, exorbitant, extortionate, extreme, high, immoderate, inordinate, overpriced, stiff, towering, uncalled-for, undue, unmeasurable, unreasonable; SEE CONCEPTS *334,762*

steep [*v*] *let soak*

bathe, damp, drench, fill, imbue, immerse, impregnate, infuse, ingrain, invest, macerate, marinate, moisten, permeate, pervade, saturate, soak, sodden, sop, souse, submerge, suffuse, waterlog; SEE CONCEPT *256*

steer [*v*] *guide, direct on a course*

beacon, be in the driver's seat*, captain, conduct, control, drive, escort, govern, head for, helm, herd, lead, pilot, point, route, run, run things, see, shepherd, show, skipper, take over, take the helm, take the reins; SEE CONCEPTS *94,187*

stem [*n*] *stalk of plant*

axis, branch, pedicel, pedicle, peduncle, petiole, shoot, stock, trunk; SEE CONCEPT *428*

stem [*v1*] *come from*

arise, be bred, be brought about, be caused, be generated, derive, develop, emanate, flow, head, issue, originate, proceed, rise, spring; SEE CONCEPT *648*

stem [*v2*] *prevent, stop*

arrest, bring to a standstill, check, contain, control, curb, dam, hinder, hold back, oppose, resist, restrain, stay, withstand; SEE CONCEPT *121*

stench [*n*] *foul odor*

fetor, funk*, malodor, mephitis, noisomeness, redolence, smell, stink*; SEE CONCEPTS *599,600*

step [*n1*] *pace of feet in walking*

footfall, footprint, footstep, gait, impression, mark, print, spoor, stepping, stride, trace, track, trail, tread, vestige, walk; SEE CONCEPT *149*

step [*n2*] *action, move*

act, advance, advancement, deed, degree, expedient, gradation, grade, level, maneuver, means, measure, motion, notch, phase, point, procedure, proceeding, process, progression, rank, remove, rung, stage, start; SEE CONCEPTS *1,832*

step [n3] *one level of stairs*
doorstep, gradation, notch, rest, round, run, rung, stair, tread; SEE CONCEPTS *440,445*

step [v] *move foot to walk*
advance, ambulate, ascend, dance, descend, go backward, go down, go forward, go up, hoof, mince, move backward, move forward, pace, prance, skip, stride, tiptoe, traipse, tread, trip, troop, walk; SEE CONCEPT *149*

step in [v] *become involved*
arrive, be invited, chip in*, come, enter, intercede, interfere, intermediate, interpose, intervene, lend a hand*, mediate, negotiate, take action; SEE CONCEPTS *100,324,384*

step up [v] *accelerate*
augment, boost, escalate, hasten, hurry, improve, increase, intensify, lift, quicken, raise, shake up, speed, speed up, up; SEE CONCEPTS *236,244,245*

stereotype [n] *idea held as standard, example*
average, boilerplate*, convention, custom, fashion, formula, institution, mold, pattern, received idea; SEE CONCEPT *688*

stereotype [v] *categorize as being example, standard*
catalogue, conventionalize, define, dub, institutionalize, methodize, normalize, pigeonhole*, regulate, standardize, systematize, take to be, typecast; SEE CONCEPTS *38,49*

stereotyped [adj] *standard, conventional*
banal, clichéd, cliché-ridden, commonplace, corny*, dull, hackneyed, mass-produced, ordinary, overused, platitudinous, played out*, stale, standardized, stock, threadbare*, tired*, trite, unoriginal, wellworn, worn-out, worn thin; SEE CONCEPT *530*

sterile [adj] *unproductive, clean*
antiseptic, arid, aseptic, bare, barren, bleak, dead, decontaminated, desert, desolate, disinfected, dry, effete, empty, fallow, fruitless, futile, gaunt, germfree, hygienic, impotent, infecund, infertile, pasteurized, sanitary, septic, sterilized, unfruitful, uninfected, unprofitable, unprolific, vain, waste, without issue; SEE CONCEPTS *485,621*

sterilize [v] *make clean*
alter, antisepticize, asceptize, aseptify, autoclave, castrate, change, clean, decontaminate, desexualize, disinfect, emasculate, fix, fumigate, incapacitate, make sterile, neuter, pasteurize, purify, sanitize, spay; SEE CONCEPTS *231,250*

stern [adj] *serious, authoritarian*
ascetic, astringent, austere, bitter, bullheaded*, by the book*, cruel, disciplinary, dyed-in-the-wool*, flinty, forbidding, frowning, grim, hang-tough*, hard, hard-boiled*, hard-core*, hardheaded*, hardline*, hard-nosed*, hard-shell*, harsh, implacable, inexorable, inflexible, mortified, mule, mulish, relentless, rigid, rigorous, rough, severe, steely, stiff-necked*, strict, stubborn, tough, unrelenting, unsparing, unyielding; SEE CONCEPTS *401,542*

stew [n1] *mixture, miscellany*
brew, goulash*, hash, jumble, medley, mélange, mishmash, mulligan*, olio*, pasticcio*, pie*, potpourri, salmagundi*, soup; SEE CONCEPTS *432,457, 460,461*

stew [n2] *commotion; mental upset*
agitation, confusion, dither, flap, fretting, fuming, fuss, lather, pother, snit, sweat, tizzy, tumult, turbulence, turmoil, worry; SEE CONCEPT *410*

stew [v] *worry; steam*
boil, chafe, cook, fret, fume, fuss, pother, seethe, simmer; SEE CONCEPT *35*

stick [n] *pole, often wooden*
bar, bat, baton, billet, birch, bludgeon, board, branch, cane, club, cudgel, drumstick, ferrule, ingot, mast, rod, rule, ruler, shoot, slab, slat, staff, stake, stalk, stave, stem, strip, switch, timber, twig, wand, wedge; SEE CONCEPTS *470,479*

stick [v1] *adhere, affix*
attach, be bogged down, become embedded, become immobilized, bind, bond, braze, catch, cement, clasp, cleave, cling, cling like ivy*, clog, cohere, fasten, fix, freeze to, fuse, glue, hold, hold fast, hold on, hug, jam, join, linger, lodge, paste, persist, remain, snag, solder, stay, stay put, stick like barnacle*, stick together, unite, weld; SEE CONCEPTS *85,160*

stick [v2] *poke with pointed object*
dig, drive, gore, impale, insert, jab, penetrate, pierce, pin, plunge, prod, puncture, ram, run, sink, spear, stab, thrust, transfix; SEE CONCEPT *220*

stick [v3] *position, lay*
deposit, drop, establish, fix, install, place, plant, plonk, plunk, put, set, settle, store, stuff; SEE CONCEPT *201*

stick [v4] *endure*
abide, bear, bear up under, brook, get on with, go, grin and bear it*, last, persist, put up with, see through, stand, stay, stomach*, suffer, support, take, take it, tolerate, weather; SEE CONCEPT *23*

stick-in-the-mud [n] *person set in their ways*
antediluvian, conservative, diehard*, fossil*, mossback*, old fogy*, reactionary; SEE CONCEPT *423*

stick out [v] *bulge*
beetle, come through, extend, extrude, jut, obtrude, outthrust, overhang, poke, pouch, pout, project, protend, protrude, push, show, stand out; SEE CONCEPT *751*

sticky [adj1] *gummy, adhesive*
agglutinative, clinging, gluey, glutinous, ropy, syrupy, tacky, tenacious, viscid, viscous; SEE CONCEPT *606*

sticky [adj2] *humid and hot*
clammy, close, dank, mucky, muggy, oppressive, soggy, sultry, sweltering; SEE CONCEPT *525*

sticky [adj3] *difficult, embarrassing*
awkward, delicate, discomforting, formidable, hairy*, hard, heavy*, knotty*, laborious, nasty, op-

erose, painful, rough, rugged, strenuous, thorny, tricky, unpleasant; SEE CONCEPT *565*

stiff [*adj1*] *hard, inflexible*
annealed, arthritic, benumbed, brittle, buckram, cemented, chilled, congealed, contracted, creaky, firm, fixed, frozen, graceless, hardened, immalleable, impliable, incompliant, indurate, inelastic, jelled, mechanical, numbed, ossified, petrified, refractory, resistant, rheumatic, rigid, set, solid, solidified, starched, starchy, stark, steely, stiff as a board*, stony, taut, tense, thick, thickened, tight, unbending, unbending, unflexible, ungraceful, unsupple, unyielding, wooden; SEE CONCEPT *604*

stiff [*adj2*] *formal, standoffish*
angular, artificial, austere, ceremonious, cold, constrained, forced, hardheaded, headstrong, inflexible, intractable, labored, mannered, obstinate, pertinacious, pompous, priggish, prim, punctilious, relentless, starchy, stilted, strong, stubborn, uneasy, ungainly, ungraceful, unnatural, unrelaxed, unrelenting, wooden; SEE CONCEPT *401*

stiff [*adj3*] *difficult*
arduous, exacting, fatiguing, formidable, hard, laborious, tough, trying, uphill; SEE CONCEPT *565*

stiff [*adj4*] *extreme, severe*
austere, brisk, cruel, drastic, exact, excessive, exorbitant, extravagant, great, hard, harsh, heavy, immoderate, inexorable, inordinate, oppressive, pitiless, potent, powerful, rigorous, sharp, steep, strict, stringent, strong, towering, unconscionable, undue, vigorous; SEE CONCEPTS *540,569*

stiffen [*v*] *make or become harder*
anneal, benumb, brace, cake, candy, cement, chill, clot, coagulate, condense, congeal, crystallize, curdle, firm, fix, freeze, gel, harden, inflate, inspissate, jell, jelly, ossify, petrify, precipitate, prop, reinforce, set, solidify, stabilize, starch, steady, strengthen, tauten, tense, thicken; SEE CONCEPTS *137,250,469*

stifle [*v*] *prevent, restrain*
asphyxiate, black out, bring to screeching halt*, burke, check, choke, choke back, clamp down*, clam up*, constipate, cork, cover up, crack down*, curb, dry up*, extinguish, gag, hold it down, hush, hush up, kill*, muffle, muzzle, prevent, put the lid on*, queer*, repress, restrain, shut up, silence, sit on*, smother, spike, squash, squelch, stagnate, stop, strangle, stultify, suffocate, suppress, torpedo*, trammel; SEE CONCEPTS *121,130,191*

stigma [*n*] *shame*
bar sinister*, besmirchment, black mark*, blame, blemish*, blot*, brand, disfigurement, disgrace, dishonor, imputation, lost face*, mark*, odium, onus, reproach, scar*, slur, spot*, stain*, taint; SEE CONCEPTS *230,388,689*

still [*n*] *quiet*
hush, noiselessness, peace, quietness, quietude, silence, soundlessness, still, stillness, tranquillity; SEE CONCEPTS *65,748*

still [*adj*] *calm, motionless, quiet*
at rest, buttoned up*, clammed up*, closed, close-mouthed, deathlike, deathly, deathly quiet, deathly still, fixed, halcyon, hushed, hushful, inert, lifeless, noiseless, pacific, peaceful, placid, restful, sealed, serene, silent, smooth, soundless, stable, stagnant, static, stationary, stock-still, tranquil, undisturbed, unruffled, unstirring, untroubled, whist; SEE CONCEPTS *584,594*

still [*v*] *make quiet, motionless, calm*
allay, alleviate, appease, arrest, balm, becalm, calm, choke, compose, decrease volume, fix, gag, hush, lull, muffle, muzzle, pacify, quiet, quieten, settle, shush*, shut down, shut up, silence, slack, smooth, smooth over, soothe, squash, squelch, stall, stop, subdue, tranquilize; SEE CONCEPTS *7,22,65,121*

still [*conj*] *however*
after all, besides, but, even, for all that, furthermore, howbeit, nevertheless, nonetheless, notwithstanding, still and all, though, withal, yet; SEE CONCEPT *544*

stilted [*adj*] *artificial, pretentious*
affected, angular, aureate, bombastic, constrained, decorous, egotistic, euphuistic, flowery, forced, formal, genteel, grandiloquent, high-flown, high-sounding, inflated, labored, magniloquent, mincing, overblown, pedantic, pompous, prim, rhetorical, sonorous, stiff, unnatural, wooden*; SEE CONCEPTS *267,401*

stimulant [*n*] *substance that invigorates*
analeptic, bracer, catalyst, drug, energizer, excitant, goad, impetus, impulse, incentive, incitation, incitement, motivation, motive, pick-me-up*, restorative, reviver, shot in the arm*, spark plug*, spur, stimulus, tonic, upper; SEE CONCEPTS *240,307,661*

stimulate [*v*] *excite, provoke*
activate, animate, arouse, build a fire under*, commove, dynamize, elate, encourage, energize, enliven, exhilarate, fan, fire, fire up*, foment, foster, galvanize, get one going*, get one started*, goad, grab, hook, impel, incite, inflame, innervate, innerve, inspire, instigate, jazz*, juice*, key up*, motivate, move, perk, pique, prod, prompt, quicken, rouse, send, set up, spark, spirit, spur, steam up*, stir up*, support, trigger, turn on*, urge, vitalize, vivify, wake up*, whet, work up*; SEE CONCEPTS *14,242*

stimulus [*n*] *provocation*
bang*, boost, catalyst, cause, charge, encouragement, eye-opener*, fillip, fireworks*, flash*, goad, impetus, impulse, incentive, incitation, incitement, inducement, instigation, invitation, kick*, motivation, motive, piquing, propellant, provocation, push, shot in the arm*, spur, stimulant, stimulation, sting*, turn-on*, urging; SEE CONCEPTS *240,307,661*

sting [*v*] *prick, pain*
bite, burn, electrify, hurt, injure, inspire, needle, pique, poke, prickle, smart, tingle, wound; SEE CONCEPTS *220,246,313,728*

stingy [*adj*] *penny-pinching, averse to spending money*
acquisitive, avaricious, chary, cheap, chintzy*, churlish, close, close-fisted, costive, covetous, curmudgeonly, economical, extortionate, frugal, grasping, greedy, grudging, ignoble, illiberal, ironfisted, mean, miserly, narrow, near, niggard, niggardly*, parsimonious, pennywise*, penurious, petty, pinchpenny*, rapacious, saving, scrimping, scurvy, selfish, skimping, sordid, sparing, thrifty, tightfisted, uncharitable, ungenerous, ungiving; SEE CONCEPTS *326,334,401*

stink [*n*] *bad smell*
fetor, foulness, foul odor, malodor, noisomeness, offensive smell, stench; SEE CONCEPTS *599,600*

stink [*v1*] *smell badly*
be offensive, be rotten, funk*, have an odor, offend, reek*, smell up, stench, stink to high heaven*; SEE CONCEPT *600*

stink [*v2*] *be lousy, bad*
be abhorrent, be detestable, be held in disrepute, be no good, be offensive, be rotten, have a bad name*, smell; SEE CONCEPTS *230,388*

stint [*n*] *period of responsibility*
assignment, bit, chore, consignment, duty, job, participation, quota, share, shift, spell, stretch, task, term, time, tour, turn, work; SEE CONCEPTS *362, 807,822*

stint [*v*] *economize; hold back*
be frugal, begrudge, be parsimonious, be sparing, be stingy, confine, cut corners*, define, go easy on, grudge, limit, make ends meet*, penny-pinch*, pinch, restrain, roll back*, save, save for rainy day*, scrape, scrimp, skimp on*, sock away*, spare, squirrel*, stash, tighten belt*, withhold; SEE CONCEPT *330*

stipend [*n*] *payment for services*
allowance, award, consideration, emolument, fee, gratuity, hire, pay, pension, salary, take*, wage; SEE CONCEPT *344*

stipulate [*v*] *decide on conditions*
agree, arrange, bargain, condition, contract, covenant, designate, detail, engage, guarantee, impose, insist upon, lay down, lay finger on, make, make a point, name, particularize, pin down, pledge, postulate, promise, provide, put down for, require, settle, slot, specificate, specificize, specify, spell out, state; SEE CONCEPTS *8,18,60*

stipulation [*n*] *condition of agreement*
agreement, arrangement, circumscription, clause, contract, designation, engagement, fine print*, limit, obligation, precondition, prerequisite, provision, proviso, qualification, requirement, reservation, restriction, settlement, sine qua non, small print*, specification, string attached*, term, terms; SEE CONCEPTS *270,318,684*

stir [*n*] *commotion, excitement*
activity, ado, agitation, backwash*, bustle, din, disorder, disquiet, disturbance, ferment, flap*, flurry, furor, fuss, movement, pandemonium, pother, racket, row, scene, to-do*, tumult, turmoil, uproar, whirl, whirlwind; SEE CONCEPTS *230,388*

stir [*v1*] *mix up, agitate*
beat, blend, disturb, flutter, mix, move, move about, quiver, rustle, shake, toss, tremble, whip, whisk; SEE CONCEPTS *158,170*

stir [*v2*] *incite, stimulate*
abet, actuate, add fuel to fire*, adjy, affect, agitate, animate, arouse, awaken, bestir, challenge, craze, drive, electrify, energize, excite, feed the fire*, foment, galvanize, impel, inflame, inspire, kindle, make waves*, motivate, move, prompt, provoke, psych*, quicken, raise, rally, rile, rouse, roust, rout, set, spark, spook*, spur, stimulate, stir embers*, stir up, switch on, thrill, touch, trigger, urge, vitalize, wake, waken, whet, whip up*, work up*; SEE CONCEPTS *14,221*

stir [*v3*] *get up and going*
awake, awaken, bestir, be up and about, budge, exert, get a move on*, get moving, hasten, look alive, make an effort, mill about, move, rouse, shake a leg*, wake, waken; SEE CONCEPT *149*

stock [*n1*] *merchandise*
accumulation, array, articles, assets, assortment, backlog, cache, choice, commodities, fund, goods, hoard, inventory, nest egg*, produce, range, reserve, reservoir, selection, stockpile, store, supply, variety, wares; SEE CONCEPT *338*

stock [*n2*] *animals raised on a farm*
animals, beasts, cattle, cows, domestic, farm animals, flock, fowl, herd, hogs, horses, livestock, pigs, sheep, swine; SEE CONCEPTS *394,397*

stock [*n3*] *ancestry*
background, breed, clan, descent, extraction, family, folk, forebears, house, kin, kindred, line, lineage, line of descent, parentage, pedigree, race, species, strain, tribe, type, variety; SEE CONCEPTS *296,378*

stock [*n4*] *investment in company*
assets, blue chips, bonds, capital, convertible, funds, over-the-counter*, paper, property, share; SEE CONCEPT *332*

stock [*n5*] *estimation, faith*
appraisal, appraisement, assessment, confidence, count, dependence, estimate, evaluation, figure, hope, inventory, judgment, reliance, review, trust; SEE CONCEPTS *37,689,764*

stock [*adj*] *commonplace*
banal, basic, common, conventional, customary, dull, established, formal, hackneyed, normal, ordinary, overused, regular, routine, run-of-the-mill*, set, standard, staple, stereotyped, traditional, trite, typical, usual, worn-out; SEE CONCEPTS *530,547*

stock [*v*] *supply with merchandise*
accumulate, amass, carry, deal in, equip, fill, furnish, gather, handle, have, hoard, keep, keep on hand, lay in, provide, provision, put away, reserve, save, sell, stockpile, store, stow away, trade in; SEE CONCEPTS *140,182,324*

stocky [*adj*] *short and overweight; short and muscular*
chunky*, corpulent, fat, heavyset, plump, solid, squat, stout, stubby*, sturdy, thick, thickset; SEE CONCEPTS *491,773*

stodgy [*adj*] *dull, stuffy*
banausic, boring, dim, dreary, formal, heavy, labored, monotonous, pedantic, pedestrian, plodding, ponderous, staid, tedious, turgid, unexciting, unimaginative, uninspired, uninteresting, weighty; SEE CONCEPTS *401,404*

stoic/stoical [*adj*] *philosophic, calm*
aloof, apathetic, cool, cool as cucumber*, detached, dispassionate, dry, enduring, impassive, imperturbable, indifferent, indomitable, long-suffering, matter-of-fact, patient, phlegmatic, resigned, roll with punches*, self-controlled, sober, stolid, unconcerned, unemotional, unflappable, unmoved; SEE CONCEPTS *401,404*

stolid [*adj*] *apathetic, stupid*
blunt, bovine, dense, doltish, dry, dull, dumb, heavy, impassive, inactive, indifferent, inert, lumpish, matter-of-fact, obtuse, passive, phlegmatic, slow, stoic, supine, unemotional, unexcitable, wooden; SEE CONCEPTS *401,402*

stomach [*n1*] *digestive organ of animate being; exterior abdominal region*
abdomen, belly, below the belt*, breadbasket*, gut, inside, insides, maw*, paunch, pot*, potbelly*, solar plexus, spare tire*, tummy; SEE CONCEPTS *393,420*

stomach [*n2*] *appetite*
appetence, desire, inclination, mind, relish, taste, tooth; SEE CONCEPT *20*

stomach [*v*] *endure, tolerate*
abide, bear, bear with, bite the bullet*, brook, digest, grin and bear it*, live with*, put up with, reconcile oneself, resign oneself, stand, submit to, suffer, swallow, sweat, take, take it, tolerate; SEE CONCEPT *23*

stone [*n*] *hard piece of earth's surface*
boulder, crag, crystal, gem, grain, gravel, jewel, metal, mineral, ore, pebble, rock; SEE CONCEPTS *474,477*

stony [*adj*] *hard, icy in appearance, response*
adamant, blank, callous, chilly*, cold, cold-blooded*, coldhearted*, cruel, expressionless, firm, frigid, hard-boiled*, hardened, heartless, hostile, indifferent, inexorable, inflexible, merciless, obdurate, pitiless, rough, tough, uncompassionate, unfeeling, unforgiving, unrelenting, unresponsive, unsympathetic; SEE CONCEPTS *401,485*

stoop [*n*] *slouched posture*
bad posture, droop, round shoulders, sag, slouch, slump; SEE CONCEPT *757*

stoop [*v1*] *bow down*
be bowed, bend, be servile, bow, cringe, crouch, descend, dip, duck, hunch, incline, kneel, lean, relax, sink, slant, squat; SEE CONCEPTS *181,201*

stoop [*v2*] *condescend; lower oneself to another*
accommodate, act beneath oneself, concede, debase oneself, deign, demean oneself, descend, favor, oblige, patronize, relax, resort, sink, thaw, unbend, vouchsafe; SEE CONCEPTS *35,384*

stop [*n1*] *end, halt; impediment*
bar, barricade, blank wall*, block, blockade, break, break off, brick wall*, cease, cessation, check, close, closing, conclusion, control, cutoff, desistance, discontinuation, ending, fence, finish, freeze*, grinding halt*, hindrance, layoff, letup, lull, pause, plug, roadblock*, screeching halt*, standstill, stay, stoppage, termination, wall; SEE CONCEPTS *240,832*

stop [*n2*] *visit; place of rest*
break, depot, destination, halt, rest, sojourn, stage, station, stay, stopover, termination, terminus; SEE CONCEPTS *198,227*

stop [*v1*] *bring or come to a halt or end*
be over, blow off*, break, break off, call it a day*, cease, close, cold turkey*, come to a standstill*, conclude, cool it*, cut out*, cut short, desist, discontinue, draw up, drop, end, finish, halt, hang it up*, hold, kill, pause, pull up, put an end to, quit, quit cold*, refrain, run its course*, scrub*, shut down, sign off*, stall, stand, stay, tarry, terminate, wind up*, wrap up*; SEE CONCEPTS *119,234,237*

stop [*v2*] *prevent, hold back*
arrest, avoid, bar, block, bottle, break, check, choke, choke off, clog, close, congest, cut off, disrupt, fill, fix, forestall, frustrate, gag, hinder, hush, impede, intercept, interrupt, muzzle, obstruct, occlude, plug, put a stop to, rein in, repress, restrain, seal, shut down, shut off, shut out, silence, stall, staunch, stay, stem, still, stopper, suspend, throw over, turn off, ward off; SEE CONCEPT *121*

stopgap [*n*] *temporary help*
band-aid*, expediency, expedient, improvisation, makeshift, pis aller*, recourse, refuge, resort, resource, shift, substitute, temporary expedient; SEE CONCEPT *712*

stopgap [*adj*] *temporarily helping*
band-Aid, emergency, expedient, impromptu, improvised, makeshift, practical, provisional, rough-and-ready*, rough-and-tumble*, substitute, temp, temporary, throwaway*; SEE CONCEPTS *551,560*

stoppage [*n*] *halt, curtailment*
abeyance, arrest, blockage, check, close, closure, cutoff, deduction, discontinuance, down, downtime*, hindrance, interruption, layoff, lockout, obstruction, occlusion, shutdown, sit-down, standstill, stopping, walkout; SEE CONCEPT *832*

store [*n1*] *collection, supply*
abundance, accumulation, backlog, cache, fount, fountain, fund, hoard, inventory, lode, lot, mine, nest egg*, plenty, plethora, provision, quantity, reserve, reservoir, savings, spring, stock, stockpile, treasure, wares, wealth, well; SEE CONCEPTS *432,710*

store [n2] *place for keeping supply*
arsenal, bank, barn, box, cache, conservatory, depository, depot, magazine, pantry, repository, reservoir, stable, storehouse, storeroom, tank, treasury, vault, warehouse; SEE CONCEPTS *439,441,448,494*

store [n3] *business establishment that sells goods*
boutique, chain store, convenience store, deli, department store, discount house, discount store, drugstore, emporium, five-and-dime*, five-and-ten*, grocery store, market, mart, outlet, repository, shop, shopping center, showroom, specialty shop, stand, storehouse, super*, superette, supermarket; SEE CONCEPTS *325,439,448,449*

store [v] *collect and put aside*
accumulate, amass, bank, bin, bottle, bury, cache, can, cumulate, deposit, freeze, garner, hide, hive, hoard, husband, hutch, keep, keep in reserve, lay away, lay up*, lock away, lock up, mothball*, pack, pack away, park, plant, put, put away, put by, put in storage, reserve, roll up, salt away*, save, save for rainy day*, sock away*, squirrel*, stash, stock, stockpile, treasure, victual, warehouse; SEE CONCEPTS *109,129*

storm [n1] *strong weather*
blast, blizzard, blow, cloudburst, cyclone, disturbance, downpour, gale, gust, hurricane, monsoon, precip*, raining cats and dogs*, snowstorm, squall, tempest, tornado, twister, whirlwind, windstorm; SEE CONCEPT *526*

storm [n2] *commotion, turmoil*
agitation, anger, annoyance, assault, attack, barrage, blitz, blitzkrieg, bluster, bomb, bombardment, broadside, burst, bustle, cannonade, clamor, clatter, convulsion, disturbance, drumfire, furor, fury, fusillade, hail, hassle, hysteria, offensive, onset, onslaught, outbreak, outburst, outcry, passion, perturbation, pother, rabidity, racket, rage, rampancy, roar, row, ruction, rumpus, rush, salvo, squall, stir, strife, temper, tumult, upheaval, violence, volley; SEE CONCEPTS *86,230,674*

storm [v] *attack, rush*
aggress, assail, assault, beset, blow violently, bluster, breathe fire*, burn up, carry on*, charge, come at*, complain, drizzle, drop, fly, fume, go on, howl, pour, rage, rain, rant, rave, rip, roar, scold, set in, sizzle, sound off, spit, squall, stalk, steam up*, stomp, strike, take by storm*, take on*, tear, thunder*; SEE CONCEPTS *52,86,150,526*

stormy [adj] *rough (referring to weather)*
bitter, blowy, blustering, blustery, boisterous, cold, coming down*, damp, dirty, foul, frigid, furious, gusty, howling, menacing, murky, pouring, raging, raining cats and dogs*, rainy, riproaring, roaring, savage, squally, stormful, storming, tempestuous, threatening, torrid, turbulent, violent, wet, wild, windy; SEE CONCEPT *525*

story [n1] *account, news*
adventure, allegory, anecdote, apologue, article, autobiography, beat, biography, book, chronicle, cliff-hanger*, comedy, conte, description, drama, epic, fable, fairy tale, fantasy, feature, fiction, folktale, gag, history, information, legend, long and short of it*, memoir, myth, narration, narrative, news item, nonfiction, novel, old saw*, old wives' tale*, parable, potboiler*, recital, record, relation, report, romance, saga, scoop*, sequel, serial, spiel*, tale, tragedy, version, yarn*; SEE CONCEPTS *270,274,282*

story [n2] *lie*
canard, fabrication, falsehood, falsity, fib, fiction, misrepresentation, prevarication, tale, untruism, untruth, white lie; SEE CONCEPTS *278,282*

stout [adj1] *overweight*
big, bulky, burly, corpulent, fat, fleshy, heavy, obese, on the heavy side*, plenitudinous, plump, porcine, portly, rotund, substantial, thick-bodied, tubby*, upholstered, weighty, zaftig*; SEE CONCEPTS *491,773*

stout [adj2] *strong, brawny*
able-bodied, athletic, hard, hardy, hulking, husky, indomitable, invincible, lusty, muscular, robust, stable, stalwart, staunch, strapping, sturdy, substantial, tenacious, tough, vigorous; SEE CONCEPTS *489,490*

stout [adj3] *courageous*
bold, brave, dauntless, fearless, gallant, heroic, intrepid, lionhearted, manly, plucky, resolute, stalwart, undaunted, valiant, valorous; SEE CONCEPTS *403,542*

stow [v] *reserve, store*
bundle, deposit, load, pack, pack like sardines*, put away, secrete, stash, stuff, top off, tuck, warehouse*; SEE CONCEPT *209*

straggle [v] *wander, stray*
be late, dawdle, drift, lag, loiter, maunder, meander, poke, poke around, ramble, range, roam, rove, scramble, spread, straddle, string out, tail, trail; SEE CONCEPT *151*

straight [adj1] *aligned; not curved*
beeline*, collinear, consecutive, continuous, direct, erect, even, horizontal, in a line, in a row, inflexible, in line, invariable, level, like an arrow*, lineal, linear, near, nonstop, perpendicular, plumb, precipitous, rectilineal, rectilinear, right, running, sheer, short, smooth, solid, square, straightforward, successive, through, true, unbent, unbroken, uncurled, undeviating, undistorted, uninterrupted, unrelieved, unswerving, upright, vertical; SEE CONCEPTS *482,486,581*

straight [adj2] *honest, fair*
aboveboard, accurate, authentic, bald, blunt, candid, categorical, decent, equitable, fair and square*, forthright, frank, good, honorable, just, law-abiding, moral, outright, plain, point-blank*, reliable, respectable, straightforward, summary, trustworthy, unqualified, upright; SEE CONCEPTS *267,542*

straight [adj3] *orderly*
arranged, correct, exact, in order, neat, organized, put to rights, right, shipshape*, sorted, tidy; SEE CONCEPTS *535,585*

straight [*adj4*] *unmixed*
concentrated, neat, out-and-out*, plain, pure, strong, thoroughgoing, unadulterated, undiluted, unmodified, unqualified; SEE CONCEPTS *462,621*

straight [*adj5*] *conventional, square*
bourgeois, buttoned-down*, conservative, orthodox, traditional; SEE CONCEPT *404*

straight [*adv1*] *immediately, directly*
as the crow flies*, at once, away, dead*, direct, due, exactly, first off, forthwith, in direct line, instanter, instantly, lineally, now, point-blank*, right, right away, straightaway, straightforwardly, straightly, undeviatingly; SEE CONCEPTS *581,820*

straight [*adv2*] *honestly*
candidly, frankly, in plain English*, no holds barred*, no punches*, point-blank*; SEE CONCEPTS *267,544*

straighten [*v*] *put in neat or aligned order*
align, arrange, compose, correct, even, level, make plumb, make straight, neaten, order, put in order, put perpendicular, put straight, put to rights, put upright, put vertical, rectify, set to rights, smarten up*, spruce up*, tidy, unbend, uncoil, uncurl, unfold, unravel, unsnarl, untwist; SEE CONCEPTS *158,202,231*

straightforward [*adj1*] *honest*
aboveboard, barefaced*, candid, direct, forthright, frank, genuine, guileless, honorable, just, laid on the line*, level, like it is*, mellow, open, outspoken, plain, plain-dealing*, pretenseless, right-on*, sincere, square-shooting*, straight, straight-arrow*, talking turkey*, truthful, unconcealed, undisguised, undissembled, undissembling, unequivocal, unvarnished, up front*, upright, upstanding, veracious; SEE CONCEPT *267*

straightforward [*adj2*] *simple, easy*
apparent, clear, clear-cut, direct, distinct, elementary, evident, manifest, palpable, patent, plain, routine, straight, through, unambiguous, uncomplicated, undemanding, unequivocal, uninterrupted; SEE CONCEPTS *535,538*

strain [*n1*] *pain, due to exertion*
ache, anxiety, bruise, brunt, burden, constriction, effort, endeavor, exertion, force, injury, jerk, pressure, pull, sprain, stress, stretch, struggle, tautness, tension, tensity, twist, wrench; SEE CONCEPT *728*

strain [*n2*] *ancestry*
blood, breed, descent, extraction, family, lineage, pedigree, race, species, stock; SEE CONCEPTS *296,380*

strain [*n3*] *suggestion, hint*
humor, manner, mind, shade, soupçon, spirit, streak, style, suspicion, temper, tendency, tinge, tone, touch, trace, trait, vein, way; SEE CONCEPTS *410,529,682*

strain [*n4*] *melody*
air, descant, diapason, lay, measure, song, tune, warble; SEE CONCEPTS *262,595*

strain [*v1*] *stretch, often to limit*
constrict, distend, distort, draw tight, drive, exert, extend, fatigue, injure, overexert, overtax, over-work, pull, push, push to the limit, rack, sprain, task, tauten, tax, tear, tighten, tire, twist, weaken, wrench; SEE CONCEPTS *156,206,208,313*

strain [*v2*] *work very hard*
bear down, endeavor, exert, go all out*, go for broke*, grind, hammer hustle, labor, moil, peg away*, plug, push, strive, struggle, sweat, toll, try; SEE CONCEPT *87*

strain [*v3*] *filter*
exude, percolate, purify, refine, riddle, screen, seep, separate, sieve, sift; SEE CONCEPTS *135,202*

strain [*v4*] *cause mental stress*
distress, harass, hassle, irk, pain, pick at, push, stress, trouble, try; SEE CONCEPTS *7,19*

strained [*adj*] *forced, pretended*
artificial, at end of rope*, awkward, choked, constrained, difficult, embarrassed, false, farfetched, hard put*, in a state*, labored, nervous wreck*, put, self-conscious, stiff, strung out*, taut, tense, tight, uncomfortable, uneasy, unglued, unnatural, unrelaxed, uptight, wired*, wreck*; SEE CONCEPTS *267,401*

strait [*n1*] *crisis, difficulty*
bewilderment, bind, bottleneck*, choke point*, contingency, crossroad, dilemma, distress, embarrassment, emergency, exigency, extremity, hardship, hole*, mess*, mystification, pass, perplexity, pinch*, plight, predicament, rigor, squeeze*, turning point*, vicissitude, zero hour*; SEE CONCEPT *674*

strait [*n2*] *water channel*
inlet, narrows, sound; SEE CONCEPT *514*

strand [*n*] *fine thread*
fiber, filament, length, lock, rope, string, tress; SEE CONCEPTS *392,452,475*

stranded [*adj*] *marooned, abandoned*
aground, ashore, beached, cast away, godforsaken*, grounded, helpless, high and dry*, homeless, left at the altar*, left in the lurch*, on the rocks*, out in left field*, passed up, penniless, run aground*, shipwrecked, sidelined, sidetracked*, wrecked*; SEE CONCEPT *577*

strange [*adj1*] *deviating, unfamiliar*
aberrant, abnormal, astonishing, astounding, atypical, bizarre, curious, different, eccentric, erratic, exceptional, extraordinary, fantastic, far-out*, funny, idiosyncratic, ignorant, inexperienced, irregular, marvelous, mystifying, new, newfangled*, odd, oddball*, off, offbeat*, outlandish, out-of-the-way*, peculiar, perplexing, quaint, queer, rare, remarkable, singular, unaccountable, unaccustomed, uncanny, uncommon, unheard of, unseasoned, unusual, weird, wonderful; SEE CONCEPT *564*

strange [*adj2*] *exotic, foreign*
alien, apart, awkward, detached, external, faraway, irrelevant, isolated, lost, new, novel, out of place, outside, remote, romanesque, romantic, unexplored, unfamiliar, unknown, unrelated, untried; SEE CONCEPTS *549,576*

stranger [n] *person who is unfamiliar*
alien, drifter, foreign body, foreigner, guest, immigrant, incomer, interloper, intruder, itinerant person, migrant, migratory worker, new arrival, new boy/girl, newcomer, outcomer, outlander, out-of-stater*, outsider, party crasher*, perfect stranger*, squatter*, transient, uninvited person, unknown, unknown person, visitor, wanderer; SEE CONCEPTS *413,423*

strangle [v] *choke, stifle*
asphyxiate, gag, garrote/garrotte, inhibit, kill, muffle, quelch, repress, restrain, shush, smother, squelch, strangulate, subdue, suffocate, suppress, throttle; SEE CONCEPTS *130,191,252*

strap [n] *long piece of material*
band, belt, harness, leash, strop, switch, thong, tie, whip; SEE CONCEPTS *471,475*

strapped [adj] *destitute*
beggared, broke*, dirt poor*, flat*, fortuneless, impoverished, out of money, penniless, penurious, poor, stone-broke*; SEE CONCEPT *334*

strapping [adj] *big and strong*
brawny, bruiser, burly, hefty, hulk, hulking, hunk, husky, ox, powerful, powerhouse, robust, stalwart, stout, sturdy, tall, vigorous, well-built; SEE CONCEPTS *489,773*

strategem [n] *trick*
action, angle, artifice, bit*, booby trap*, brainchild*, con, deception, device, dodge, feint, gambit, game, game plan*, gamesmanship, gimmick, grift, intrigue, layout, maneuver, method, one-upmanship*, pitch, plan, play, plot, ploy, pretext, proposition, racket, ruse, scenario, scene, scheme, setup, shift, slant, stall, story, subterfuge, switch, twist, wile; SEE CONCEPTS *59,660*

strategic [adj1] *crucial*
cardinal, critical, decisive, imperative, important, key, necessary, vital; SEE CONCEPTS *546,567*

strategic [adj2] *clever, calculated*
cunning, deliberate, diplomatic, dishonest, planned, politic, tricky; SEE CONCEPT *544*

strategy [n] *plan of action*
action, angle, approach, artifice, blueprint*, brainchild*, craft, cunning, design, game, game plan*, gimmick, grand design, layout, maneuvering, method, plan, planning, policy, procedure, program, project, proposition, racket*, scenario, scene, scheme, setup, slant, story, subtlety, system, tactics; SEE CONCEPT *660*

stray [adj] *abandoned, wandering*
devious, erratic, homeless, lost, roaming, roving, vagrant; SEE CONCEPT *583*

stray [v1] *deviate, err*
circumlocute, depart, digress, divagate, diverge, do wrong, excurse, get off the subject*, get off the track*, get sidetracked*, go off on a tangent*, ramble, sin, wander; SEE CONCEPTS *101,266*

stray [v2] *wander; get lost*
be abandoned, be lost, deviate, drift, err, gad*, gallivant, go all over the map*, go amiss, go astray, lose one's way, meander, ramble, range, roam, rove, straggle, swerve, traipse, turn, wander away, wander off; SEE CONCEPT *149*

streak [n] *vein, line; small part*
band, bar, beam, dash, element, hint, intimation, layer, ray, ridge, rule, shade, slash, smear, strain, stream, strip, stripe, stroke, suggestion, suspicion, touch, trace; SEE CONCEPTS *436,628,657,727*

streak [v] *make a line on*
band, dapple, daub, fleck, marble, slash, smear, spot, strake, striate, stripe, variegate, vein; SEE CONCEPT *250*

stream [n] *small river*
beck, branch, brook, burn, course, creek, current, drift, flood, flow, freshet, race, rill, rindle, rivulet, run, runnel, rush, spate, spritz, surge, tide, torrent, tributary, watercourse; SEE CONCEPT *514*

stream [v] *flow from*
cascade, continue, course, emerge, emit, flood, glide, gush, issue, move past, pour, roll, run, shed, sluice, spill, spout, spritz, spurt, surge; SEE CONCEPTS *146,179*

street [n] *path upon which travel occurs*
artery, avenue, back alley*, boulevard, byway, court, dead end, drag*, drive, highway, lane, parkway, passage, pavement, place, road, roadway, route, row, stroll, terrace, thoroughfare, track, trail, turf*, way; SEE CONCEPT *501*

strength [n1] *stamina, mental or physical*
backbone, body, brawn, brawniness, brute force*, clout, courage, durability, energy, firmness, force, fortitude, hardiness, health, healthiness, lustiness, might, muscle, nerve, physique, pith, potency, pow*, power, powerhouse*, robustness, security, sinew, sock*, soundness, stability, stableness, stalwartness, steadiness, steamroller, stoutness, strong arm*, sturdiness, substance, tenacity, toughness, verdure, vigor, vim*, virility, vitality, zip*; SEE CONCEPTS *410,732*

strength [n2] *intensity*
clout, cogency, concentration, depth, effectiveness, efficacy, energy, extremity, fervor, force, juice*, kick*, potency, power, resolution, spirit, vehemence, vigor, virtue; SEE CONCEPT *669*

strength [n3] *advantage, substance*
anchor, asset, body, burden, connection, core, gist, guts, in, intestinal fortitude, license, mainstay, meat, pith, purport, security, sense, strong point, succor, upper hand, weight, wire; SEE CONCEPTS *682,693*

strengthen [v1] *make more forceful, powerful*
add, add fuel to fire*, anneal, ascend, bolster, brace, build up, buttress, confirm, corroborate, empower, enhance, enlarge, establish, extend, fortify, harden, heighten, increase, intensify, invigorate, justify, make firm, mount, multiply, regenerate, reinforce, rejuvenate, reman, renew, restore, rise, set up, sinew*, steel*, step up, substantiate, support, sustain,

temper, tone, tone up, toughen, wax*; SEE CONCEPTS *244,250*

strengthen [v2] *encourage, hearten*
animate, back, back up, bear out, bloom, brace, brace up, burgeon, carry weight, cheer, consolidate, embolden, enhearten, enliven, flourish, flower, fortify, gather resources, gird, give weight, harden, inspirit, invigorate, nerve, nourish, prepare, prosper, rally, ready, refresh, rejuvenate, restore, steel, substantiate, temper, thrive, toughen, uphold; SEE CONCEPTS *7,22,35*

strenuous [adj1] *difficult; requiring hard work*
arduous, demanding, effortful, energy-consuming, exhausting, hard, Herculean*, laborious, mean, operose, taxing, toilful, toilsome, tough, tough going*, uphill*, uphill battle*, wicked; SEE CONCEPT *538*

strenuous [adj2] *energetic, zealous*
active, aggressive, ardent, bold, determined, dynamic, eager, earnest, lusty, persistent, red-blooded, resolute, spirited, strong, tireless, vigorous, vital; SEE CONCEPTS *401,542*

stress [n1] *emphasis*
accent, accentuation, beat, force, import, importance, significance, urgency, weight; SEE CONCEPTS *65,668*

stress [n2] *physical or mental pressure*
affliction, agony, alarm, albatross, anxiety, apprehensiveness, burden, clutch, crunch, disquiet, disquietude, distention, draw, dread, expectancy, extension, fear, fearfulness, ferment, flutter, force, hardship, hassle, heat, impatience, intensity, misgiving, mistrust, nervousness, nervous tension, oppression, overextension, passion, protraction, pull, restlessness, spring, strain, stretch, tautness, tenseness, tension, tensity, tightness, traction, trauma, trepidation, trial, urgency, worry; SEE CONCEPTS *410,720,728*

stress [v1] *accentuate, emphasize*
accent, belabor, dwell on, feature, harp on*, headline*, italicize*, lay emphasis on, make emphatic, play up, point up, repeat, rub in*, spot, spotlight*, underline*, underscore*; SEE CONCEPTS *49,68*

stress [v2] *put under physical or mental pressure*
afflict, burden, crunch, distend, force, fret, hassle, overdo, overextend, pull, put in traction*, put on trial*, spring, strain, stretch, tense, tense up*, traumatize, worry; SEE CONCEPTS *7,19,246,313*

stretch [n1] *expanse*
amplitude, area, branch, breadth, bridge, compass, dimension, distance, expansion, extension, extent, gamut, length, orbit, proliferation, purview, radius, range, reach, region, scope, space, span, spread, sweep, tract, wing; SEE CONCEPTS *651,721,746*

stretch [n2] *period of time*
bit, continuance, duration, extent, length, run, space, span, spell, stint, term, time, while; SEE CONCEPTS *807,822*

stretch [v] *extend, elongate*
amplify, branch out, bridge, burst forth, cover, crane, develop, distend, drag out, draw, draw out, expand, fill, go, grow, inflate, lengthen, lie out, magnify, make, make taut, make tense, open, overlap, pad, prolong, prolongate, protract, pull, pull out, pyramid, rack, range, reach, recline, repose, run, shoot up, span, spin out, spread, spread out, spring up, strain, string out, swell, tauten, tighten, unfold, unroll, widen; SEE CONCEPTS *137,250*

strict [adj1] *authoritarian*
austere, dead set*, disciplinary, dour, draconian*, exacting, firm, forbidding, grim, hard, hard-boiled*, harsh, iron-fisted*, no-nonsense*, oppressive, picky, prudish, punctilious, puritanical, rigid, rigorous, scrupulous, set, severe, square, stern, stickling, straight, strait-laced*, stringent, stuffy*, tough, unpermissive, unsparing, uptight*; SEE CONCEPTS *401,542*

strict [adj2] *accurate, absolute*
close, complete, exact, faithful, just, meticulous, particular, perfect, precise, religious, right, scrupulous, total, true, undistorted, utter, veracious, veridical; SEE CONCEPTS *535,557*

stride [v] *walk purposefully*
clump, drill, march, pace, parade, pound, stalk, stamp, stomp, striddle, stump, traipse, tramp, tromp; SEE CONCEPT *149*

strident [adj] *harsh, shrill*
blatant, boisterous, clamorous, clashing, discordant, grating, hoarse, jangling, jarring, loud, noisy, obstreperous, rasping, raucous, screeching, squawky, squeaky, stentorian, stertorous, stridulant, stridulous, unmusical, vociferant, vociferous; SEE CONCEPTS *592,594*

strife [n] *struggle, battle*
affray, altercation, animosity, argument, bickering, blowup, brawl, clash, combat, competition, conflict, contention, contest, controversy, difference, disagreement, discord, dispute, dissension, dissent, dissidence, disunity, emulation, faction, factionalism, fighting, friction, fuss, hassle, quarrel, rivalry, spat, squabble, squabbling, static, striving, tug of war*, variance, warfare, words, wrangle, wrangling; SEE CONCEPTS *46,106,674*

strike [v1] *hit hard*
bang, bash, beat, boff, bonk, box, buffet, bump into, chastise, clash, clobber, clout, collide, conk*, crash, cuff*, drive, force, hammer, impel, knock, percuss, plant*, pop*, pound, pummel, punch, punish, run into, slap, slug, smack, smash into, sock, swat, thrust, thump, touch, wallop, whop*; SEE CONCEPT *189*

strike [v2] *make an impact*
affect, be plausible, carry, come to mind*, dawn on*, get*, have semblance, hit*, impress, influence, inspire, look, move, occur to, reach, register*, seem, sway, touch; SEE CONCEPTS *7,19,22,716*

strike [v3] *find, discover*
achieve, arrive at, attain, catch, chance upon*, come across, come upon, dig up*, effect, encounter, hap-

pen upon*, hit upon*, lay bare*, light upon, open up, reach, seize, stumble across*, take, turn up*, uncover, unearth; SEE CONCEPTS *120,183*

strike [*v4*] *devastate, affect*
afflict, aggress, assail, assault, attack, beset, deal a blow, excruciate, fall upon, harrow, hit, invade, martyr, rack, set upon, smite, storm, torment, torture, try, wring; SEE CONCEPTS *7,19*

strike [*v5*] *walk out of job in protest*
arbitrate, be on strike, boycott, go on strike, hit the bricks*, hold out, mediate, mutiny, negotiate, picket, quit, refuse to work, resist, revolt, sit down*, sit in*, slow down, stick out, stop, tie up; SEE CONCEPT *351*

strike out [*v*] *leave to begin new venture*
bear, begin, get under way*, head, initiate, light out*, make, set out, start, start out, take off*; SEE CONCEPT *195*

striking [*adj*] *extraordinary; beautiful*
arresting, arrestive, astonishing, attractive, bizarre, charming, cogent, commanding, compelling, confounding, conspicuous, dazzling, distinguished, dynamite, electrifying, eye-catching*, fascinating, forceful, forcible, handsome, impressive, jazzy*, lofty, marked, memorable, noteworthy, noticeable, out of the ordinary*, outstanding, powerful, prominent, remarkable, salient, showy, signal, singular, staggering, startling, stunning, surprising, telling, unusual, wonderful, wondrous; SEE CONCEPTS *574,579*

string [*n1*] *long fiber*
cord, rope, strand, twine, twist; SEE CONCEPT *475*

string [*n2*] *succession, series*
chain, consecution, echelon, file, line, order, procession, queue, rank, row, sequel, sequence, strand, tier, train; SEE CONCEPTS *727,769*

string along [*v*] *play with; keep dangling*
bluff, coquet, dally, deceive, dupe, flirt, fool, hoax, lead on*, put one over on*, take for a ride*, toy, trifle, wanton; SEE CONCEPT *59*

stringent [*adj*] *rigid, tight*
acrimonious, binding, brick-wall*, by the book*, by the numbers*, compelling, confining, convincing, dead set on*, demanding, draconian*, drawing, dyed-in-the-wool*, exacting, forceful, hard, hard-nosed*, harsh, inflexible, ironclad, iron-fisted, picky, poignant, powerful, rigorous, rough, set, severe, stiff, strict, tough, unpermissive, valid; SEE CONCEPTS *401,535,569*

stringy [*adj*] *long, thin*
fibrous, gangling, gristly, lank, lanky, muscular, reedy, ropy, sinewy, spindling, spindly, threadlike, tough, wiry; SEE CONCEPT *490*

strip [*n*] *thin piece of material*
band, banding, bar, belt, billet, bit, fillet, ingot, layer, ribbon, rod, section, segment, shred, slab, slip, stick, stripe, swathe, tape, tongue; SEE CONCEPTS *471,834*

strip [*v*] *bare, uncover*
decorticate, denude, deprive, despoil, dismantle, displace, disrobe, divest, empty, excorticate, expose, gut, hull, husk, lay bare, lift, peel, pillage, plunder, ransack, ravage, remove, rob, scale, shave, shed, shuck, skin, slip out of, spoil, take off, tear, unclothe, undress, withdraw; SEE CONCEPT *211*

stripe [*n*] *line, strip*
band, banding, bar, border, decoration, division, fillet, layer, ribbon, rule, streak, striation, stroke; SEE CONCEPTS *284,622*

strive [*v*] *try for, exert oneself*
aim, assay, attempt, bear down, bend over backward*, break one's neck*, compete, contend, do one's best*, do one's utmost*, drive, endeavor, essay, fight, go after, go all out*, go for broke*, go for the jugular*, go the limit*, hassle, jockey*, knock oneself out*, labor, leave no stone unturned*, make every effort, moil, offer, push, scramble, seek, shoot for*, strain, struggle, sweat, tackle, take on, toil, try hard, tug*, work; SEE CONCEPT *87*

stroke [*n1*] *accomplishment*
achievement, blow*, feat, flourish, hit*, move, movement; SEE CONCEPT *706*

stroke [*n2*] *seizure*
apoplexy, attack, collapse, convulsion, fit, shock; SEE CONCEPTS *33,308*

stroke [*v*] *pat lengthwise*
brush, caress, chuck, comfort, fondle, pet, rub, smooth, soothe, tickle; SEE CONCEPT *612*

stroll [*n*] *lazy walk*
airing, breath of fresh air*, constitutional, cruise, excursion, promenade, ramble, saunter, turn; SEE CONCEPT *151*

stroll [*v*] *walk along lazily*
amble, cruise, drift, gallivant, linger, make one's way*, mope*, mosey*, promenade, ramble, roam, rove, sashay*, saunter, toddle, traipse, tramp, wander; SEE CONCEPT *151*

strong [*adj1*] *healthy, powerful*
able, able-bodied, active, athletic, big, capable, durable, enduring, energetic, firm, fixed, forceful, forcible, hale, hard as nails*, hardy, hearty, heavy, heavy-duty*, in fine feather*, mighty, muscular, reinforced, robust, rugged, secure, sinewy, solid, sound, stable, stalwart, stark, staunch, steady, stout, strapping, sturdy, substantial, tenacious, tough, unyielding, vigorous, well-built, well-founded, well-made; SEE CONCEPTS *314,489,540*

strong [*adj2*] *determined, resolute*
aggressive, brave, clear, cogent, courageous, dedicated, deep, eager, fervent, fervid, fierce, firm, forceful, gutsy*, handful*, hardball*, hard-nosed*, independent, intelligent, intense, iron-willed, keen, mean, perceptive, plucky, potent, pushy, resilient, resourceful, sagacious, self-assertive, severe, staunch, steadfast, take charge*, tenacious, tough, unbending, uncompromising, unyielding, vehement,

violent, wicked*, zealous; SEE CONCEPTS *403,542*

strong [*adj3*] *distinct, unmistakable*

clear, clear-cut, cogent, compelling, convincing, effective, fast, firm, forceful, formidable, great, hard, influential, marked, mighty, overpowering, persuasive, potent, powerful, redoubtable, secure, sharp, sound, stiff, stimulating, telling, trenchant, urgent, weighty, well-established, well-founded; SEE CONCEPTS *535,537*

strong [*adj4*] *extreme*

acute, draconian*, drastic, forceful, intense, keen, severe, sharp, strict; SEE CONCEPT *569*

strong [*adj5*] *forceful on the senses*

biting, bold, bright, brilliant, concentrated, dazzling, effective, fetid, full-bodied, glaring, hard, heady, high, highly flavored, highly seasoned, hot, inebriating, intoxicating, loud, malodorous, noisome, piquant, potent, powerful, pungent, pure, rancid, rank, rich, robust, sharp, spicy, stark, stimulating, stinking, straight, strong-flavored, undiluted, unmixed; SEE CONCEPTS *462,598,618*

stronghold [*n*] *refuge*

bastion, bulwark, castle, citadel, fastness, fort, fortification, fortress, garrison, keep, presidio, redoubt; SEE CONCEPTS *439,712*

structure [*n1*] *makeup, form*

anatomy, architecture, arrangement, build, complex, configuration, conformation, construction, design, fabric, fabrication, format, formation, frame, framework, interrelation, make, morphology, network, order, organization, skeleton, system, texture; SEE CONCEPT *733*

structure [*n2*] *building*

cage, construction, edifice, erection, fabric, house, pile, pile of bricks*, rockpile, skyscraper; SEE CONCEPT *439*

struggle [*n*] *hard try; fight to win*

attempt, battle, brush, clash, combat, conflict, contest, effort, encounter, endeavor, essay, exertion, free-for-all*, grind, hassle, jam, jump, labor, long haul*, pains*, roughhouse*, row*, scramble, set-to*, skirmish, strife, striving, toil, trial, tussle, undertaking, work, wrangle; SEE CONCEPTS *87,106,674*

struggle [*v1*] *labor, work*

assay, attempt, bend over backwards*, break one's back*, break one's neck*, cope, dig, endeavor, exert oneself, give it best shot*, give old college try*, go all out*, grind, hassle, have nose to grindstone*, hustle, make every effort*, offer, plug, plug away*, scratch, seek, slave, strain, strive, sweat, tackle, take a crack*, take a stab*, take on, toil, try, try one's hardest*, undertake, valiant attempt*, work like a dog*; SEE CONCEPT *87*

struggle [*v2*] *fight, wrestle*

battle, brawl, buck, bump heads*, compete, contend, contest, cross swords*, go up against*, grapple, hassle, lock horns*, put up a fight*, romp, rough-

house*, row, scrap, scuffle, shuffle, slug, smack, tangle; SEE CONCEPT *106*

strut [*v*] *walk pompously*

flaunt, flounce, grandstand*, mince, parade, peacock*, play to audience, prance, put on airs*, sashay*, show off, stalk, stride, swagger, swank, sweep; SEE CONCEPTS *149,261*

stub [*n*] *stumpy end*

butt, counterfoil, dock, remainder, remnant, root, short end*, snag, stump, tag, tail, tail end*; SEE CONCEPTS *825,827*

stubborn [*adj*] *obstinate, unyielding*

adamant, balky, bullheaded*, cantankerous, contumacious, cussed*, determined, dogged, firm, fixed, hardheaded, headstrong, inexorable, inflexible, insubordinate, intractable, mulish, obdurate, opinionated, ornery, persevering, persistent, pertinacious, perverse, pigheaded*, rebellious, recalcitrant, refractory, relentless, rigid, self-willed, set in one's ways*, single-minded, steadfast, stiff-necked*, tenacious, tough, unbending, unmanageable, unreasonable, unshakable, untoward, willful; SEE CONCEPTS *401,404*

stubby [*adj*] *short and thick*

fat, heavyset, squat, stocky, stout, stumpy*, thick-bodied, thickset; SEE CONCEPTS *491,773,779*

student [*n*] *person actively learning*

apprentice, coed, disciple, docent, freshman, grad, graduate, junior, learner, novice, observer, pupil, registrant, scholar, schoolboy/girl, skill, sophomore, undergrad*, undergraduate; SEE CONCEPT *350*

studied [*adj*] *intentional*

advised, affected, aforethought, calculated, conscious, considered, deliberate, designed, examined, gone into, investigated, planned, plotted, premeditated, prepared, prepense, purposeful, reviewed, studious, thought-about, thoughtful, thought-out, thought-through, voluntary, well-considered, willful, willing; SEE CONCEPTS *538,548*

studious [*adj*] *scholarly, attentive*

academic, assiduous, bookish*, bookworm*, busy, careful, contemplative, diligent, eager, earnest, grubbing, hard-working, industrious, intellectual, learned, lettered, meditative, reflective, sedulous, serious, thoughtful, well-informed, well-read; SEE CONCEPTS *402,538*

study [*n*] *learning, analysis*

abstraction, academic work, analyzing, application, attention, class, cogitation, comparison, concentration, consideration, contemplation, course, cramming, debate, deliberation, examination, exercise, inquiry, inspection, investigation, lesson, meditation, memorizing, muse, musing, pondering, questioning, reading, reasoning, reflection, research, reverie, review, rumination, schoolwork, scrutiny, subject, survey, thought, trance, weighing; SEE CONCEPTS *31,103*

study [*v1*] *contemplate, learn*

apply oneself, bone up*, brood over, burn midnight oil*, bury oneself in*, coach, cogitate, consider, crack the books*, cram, dig*, dive into*, examine, excogitate, go into, go over, grind, hit the books*, inquire, learn, learn the ropes*, lucubrate, meditate, mind, mull over, perpend, peruse, plug*, plunge, polish up*, ponder, pore over*, read, read up, refresh, think, think out, think over, tutor, weigh; SEE CONCEPT *31*

study [*v2*] *examine, analyze*
brainstorm, canvass, case, check out, check over, check up, compare, deliberate, do research, eagle eye*, figure, inspect, investigate, keep tabs*, look into, peruse, read, research, scope, scrutinize, sort out, survey, view; SEE CONCEPT *103*

stuff [*n1*] *personal belongings*
being, effects, equipment, gear, goods*, impedimenta, individual, junk*, kit, luggage, objects, paraphernalia, possessions, substance, tackle, things*, trappings; SEE CONCEPTS *432,446*

stuff [*n2*] *essence, substance*
bottom, bottom line*, essentiality, heart*, marrow*, matter, meat*, nitty-gritty*, nuts and bolts*, pith*, principle, quintessence, soul, staple, virtuality; SEE CONCEPTS *668,682*

stuff [*n3*] *fabric*
cloth, material, raw material, textile, woven material; SEE CONCEPT *167*

stuff [*v*] *load with*
choke up, clog up, compress, congest, cram, crowd, fill, fill to overflowing, fill to the brim, force, glut, gobble, gorge, gormandize, guzzle, jam, jam-pack, overfill, overindulge, overstuff, pack, pad, push, ram, sate, satiate, shove, squeeze, stow, wad, wedge; SEE CONCEPTS *169,209*

stuffy [*adj1*] *close, oppressive*
airless, breathless, confined, fetid, heavy, humid, muggy, stagnant, stale, stifling, suffocating, sultry, thick, unventilated; SEE CONCEPT *525*

stuffy [*adj2*] *old-fashioned, prim*
arrogant, bloated, conventional, dreary, dull, fusty, genteel, humorless, important, magisterial, musty, narrow-minded, pompous, priggish, prim and proper*, prissy, prudish, puffy, puritanical, self-important, staid, stilted, stodgy, straitlaced*, uninteresting, Victorian*; SEE CONCEPTS *401,404*

stumble [*v1*] *slip, stagger*
blunder, bumble, careen, err, fall, fall down, falter, flounder, hesitate, limp, lose balance, lumber, lurch, muddle, pitch, reel, shuffle, stammer, swing, tilt, topple, totter, trip, wallow, waver, wobble; SEE CONCEPTS *101,181*

stumble [*v2*] *happen upon*
blunder upon*, bump, chance, chance upon*, come across, come up against, discover, encounter, fall upon, find, happen upon*, hit, light, light upon*, luck*, meet, run across, stub toe on*, tumble, turn up; SEE CONCEPTS *183,693*

stump [*n*] *end piece*
butt, end, projection, stub, tail end*, tip; SEE CONCEPTS *825,827*

stump [*v1*] *confuse, bewilder*
baffle, bring up short, confound, dumbfound, foil, mystify, nonplus, outwit, perplex, puzzle, stagger, stick, stop, stymie; SEE CONCEPT *16*

stump [*v2*] *walk with deliberation*
barge, clomp, clump, galumph, lumber, plod, stamp, stomp, stumble, trudge; SEE CONCEPT *149*

stun/stupefy [*v*] *amaze, shock*
astonish, astound, bemuse, bewilder, blow away*, bowl over*, confound, confuse, daze, dumbfound, flabbergast, floor*, fog*, give a turn*, hit like ton of bricks*, knock out*, knock over*, knock unconscious, muddle, overcome, overpower, overwhelm, paralyze, petrify, rock*, shake up*, stagger, strike dumb*, surprise, take breath away*, throw a curve*; SEE CONCEPT *42*

stunning [*adj*] *beautiful, marvelous*
beauteous, bonny, brilliant, comely, dazzling, devastating, excellent, fair, famous, fine, first-class*, first-rate*, gorgeous, great, handsome, heavenly, impressive, lovely, number one*, out of this world*, pretty, ravishing, remarkable, royal, sensational, smashing, spectacular, striking, superior, top, wonderful; SEE CONCEPTS *574,579*

stunt [*n*] *deed, trick*
achievement, act, antic, caper, exploit, feat, feature, performance, sketch, skit, tour de force; SEE CONCEPTS *264,384*

stunted [*adj*] *kept from growing*
bantam, diminutive, dwarf, dwarfed, dwarfish, half-pint*, little, measly, mite, peanut*, peewee*, pint-sized*, runted, runtish, runty, scrub, short, shot, shrimp*, small, small fry*, tiny, undergrown, undersized, wee*, yea big*, yea high*; SEE CONCEPTS *773,779*

stupendous [*adj*] *wonderful, amazing*
astonishing, astounding, breathtaking, colossal, dynamite, enormous, fab*, fabulous, fantastic, fat*, gigantic, great, huge, marvelous, mind-blowing*, mind-boggling*, miraculous, monster, monumental, overwhelming, phenomenal, prodigious, radical*, smashing, spectacular, staggering, stunning, super, superb, surprising, terrific, titantic, too much, tremendous, unreal*, utmost*, vast, wonderful, wondrous; SEE CONCEPTS *574,781*

stupid [*adj*] *not intelligent; irresponsible*
brainless, dazed, deficient, dense, dim, doltish, dopey*, dull, dumb, dummy*, foolish, futile, gullible, half-baked*, half-witted*, idiotic, ill-advised, imbecilic, inane, indiscreet, insensate, irrelevant, irresponsible, laughable, loser*, ludicrous, meaningless, mindless, moronic, naive, nonsensical, obtuse, out to lunch*, pointless, puerile, rash, senseless, shortsighted, simple, simpleminded, slow, sluggish, stolid, stupefied, thick, thick-headed*, trivial, unintelligent, unthinking, witless; SEE CONCEPTS *402,548*

stupor [*n*] *daze, unconsciousness*
amazement, anaesthesia, apathy, asphyxia, bewilderment, coma, dullness, fainting, hebetude, hypnosis,

inertia, inertness, insensibility, languor, lassitude, lethargy, narcosis, numbness, petrifaction, sleep, slumber, somnolence, sopor, stupefaction, suspended animation, swoon, swooning, torpor, trance; SEE CONCEPTS *315,316*

sturdy [*adj*] *solid, durable*
athletic, built to last*, bulky, determined, durable, firm, flourishing, hardy, hearty, hefty, hulking, husky, lusty, muscular, powerful, powerhouse*, resolute, robust, rugged, secure, solid, sound, stalwart, staunch, steadfast, stiff, stout, stouthearted, strapping, strong, strong-arm*, substantial, tenacious, tough, unyielding, vigorous, well-built, well-made; SEE CONCEPTS *314,488,489*

stutter [*v*] *speak haltingly*
dribble, falter, hesitate, splutter, sputter, stammer, stumble; SEE CONCEPT *77*

style [*n1*] *fashion, manner*
appearance, approach, bearing, behavior, carriage, characteristic, cup of tea*, custom, cut*, description, design, druthers*, flash*, form, genre, groove*, habit, hand, idiosyncrasy, kind, method, mode, number, pattern, peculiarity, rage*, sort, spirit, strain, technique, tenor, thing*, tone, trait, trend, type, variety, vein, vogue, way; SEE CONCEPTS *411,655*

style [*n2*] *fashionableness*
chichi*, comfort, cosmopolitanism, craze, dash, delicacy, dernier cri*, dressiness, ease, élan, elegance, fad, flair, grace, grandeur, luxury, mode, panache, polish, rage, refinement, savoir-faire, smartness, sophistication, stylishness, taste, thing*, urbanity, vogue; SEE CONCEPTS *655,668*

style [*n3*] *way of speaking, writing, expressing oneself*
diction, expression, mode of expression, phraseology, phrasing, treatment, turn of phrase*, vein, wording; SEE CONCEPT *276*

style [*v*] *name, title*
address, baptize, call, christen, denominate, designate, dub, entitle, label, name, term; SEE CONCEPT *62*

stylish [*adj*] *fashionable*
à la mode*, beautiful, chic, chichi*, classy, clotheshorse*, dap, dapper, dashing, dressed to kill*, dressed to the teeth*, dressy, fly*, groovy*, high-class*, in, in fashion, in the mainstream*, in vogue, jazzy*, latest, mod*, modernistic, new, nifty, now*, ostentatious, polished, pretentious, rakish, ritzy, sassy*, sharp, showy, sleek, slick*, smart, snappy*, snazzy*, swank*, swell, tony*, trendy, upscale, up-to-date, uptown, urbane, voguish; SEE CONCEPTS *579,589*

stymie [*v*] *frustrate, hinder*
balk, block, choke off, confound, corner, crab*, cramp, cramp one's style*, crimp, cut off, dead-end*, defeat, foil, give the run around*, hang fire*, hang up*, hold off, hold up, impede, mystify, nonplus, obstruct, pigeonhole*, prevent, put on back burner*, put on hold, puzzle, queer*, shelve, snook-er*, stall, stonewall*, stump, throw monkey wrench*, thwart; SEE CONCEPTS *121,130*

suave [*adj*] *charming, smooth*
affable, agreeable, bland, civilized, cordial, courteous, courtly, cultivated, cultured, diplomatic, distingué, fulsome, genial, glib, gracious, ingratiating, obliging, oily*, pleasant, pleasing, polished, polite, politic, refined, smooth-tongued*, sociable, soft*, soft-spoken, sophisticated, svelte, unctuous, urbane, well-bred, worldly; SEE CONCEPTS *401,404*

subconscious [*n*] *inner thoughts*
essence, mind, psyche, soul, subconsciousness, subliminal, subliminal self, submerged mind, underconsciousness, undersense; SEE CONCEPT *410*

subconscious [*adj*] *innermost in thought*
hidden, inmost, inner, intuitive, latent, mental, repressed, subliminal, suppressed, unconscious; SEE CONCEPT *529*

subdivision [*n*] *smaller entity of whole*
class, community, development, group, lower group, minor group, subclass, subsidiary, tract; SEE CONCEPTS *513,835*

subdue [*v*] *keep under control; moderate*
bear down, beat down, break, break in, check, conquer, control, crush, defeat, discipline, drop, extinguish, gentle, get the better of*, get the upper hand*, get under control, humble, master, mellow, overcome, overpower, overrun, put own, quash, queer, quell, quench, quiet, quieten, reduce, repress, restrain, shut down, soften, squelch, subjugate, suppress, tame, temper, tone down, trample, triumph over, vanquish; SEE CONCEPTS *121,130,252*

subdued [*adj*] *quiet, controlled*
chastened, crestfallen, dejected, dim, domestic, domesticated, downcast, down in the mouth*, grave, hushed, inobtrusive, low-key, mellow, moderated, muted, neutral, out of spirits*, repentant, repressed, restrained, sad, serious, shaded, sober, soft, softened, solemn, submissive, subtle, tasteful, tempered, toned down, unobtrusive; SEE CONCEPTS *401,403,594*

subject [*n1*] *issue, matter*
affair, argument, business, case, chapter, class, core, course, discussion, field of reference, gist, head, idea, item, material, matter at hand, meat*, motif, motion, motive, object, point, principal object, problem, proposal, question, resolution, study, subject matter, substance, text, theme, theorem, thesis, thought, topic; SEE CONCEPTS *529,532,689*

subject [*n2*] *one under authority or control of another*
case, client, customer, dependent, guinea pig*, liege, liegeman/woman, national, patient, serf, subordinate, vassal; SEE CONCEPTS *413,423*

subject [*adj*] *at the mercy of; answerable*
accountable, apt, at one's feet*, bound by, captive, collateral, conditional, contingent, controlled, dependent, directed, disposed, enslaved, exposed, governed, in danger of, inferior, liable, likely, obedient, open, prone, provisional, ruled, satellite, secondary,

sensitive, servile, slavish, sub, subaltern, subjugated, submissive, subordinate, subservient, substract, susceptible, tentative, tributary, under, vulnerable; SEE CONCEPTS *552,575*

subjective [*adj*] *emotional; based on inner experience rather than fact*
abstract, biased, fanciful, idiosyncratic, illusory, individual, instinctive, introspective, introverted, intuitive, nonobjective, nonrepresentative, personal, prejudiced, unobjective; SEE CONCEPTS *529,542*

subjugate [*v*] *overpower, defeat*
bear down, beat down, bring to heel*, bring to knees*, coerce, compel, conquer, crush, enslave, enthrall, force, hold sway, keep under thumb*, kick around*, master, overcome, overthrow, put down, quell, reduce, reel back in*, rule, rule over, subdue, suppress, tame, triumph, vanquish; SEE CONCEPTS *95,117,133*

sublime [*adj*] *great, magnificent*
abstract, august, divine, dynamite, elevated, eminent, evil, exalted, glorious, gorgeous, grand, heavenly, high, holy, ideal, imposing, lofty, majestic, noble, outrageous, proud, resplendent, sacred, spiritual, splendiferous, splendorous, stately, super, superb, the most*, too much*, transcendent, transcendental; SEE CONCEPT *574*

submerge [*v*] *dunk in liquid*
deluge, descend, dip, douse, drench, drown, duck, engulf, flood, go down, go under, immerse, impregnate, inundate, overflow, overwhelm, plunge, sink, sound, souse, submerse, subside, swamp, whelm; SEE CONCEPTS *181,256*

submission [*n*] *compliance*
acquiescence, appeasement, assent, backing down, bowing, capitulation, cringing, defeatism, deference, docility, giving in, humbleness, humility, malleability, meekness, nonresistance, obedience, passivism, passivity, pliabilty, prostration, recreancy, resignation, servility, subjection, submissiveness, submitting, surrender, tractability, unassertiveness, yielding; SEE CONCEPT *633*

submissive [*adj*] *compliant*
abject, accommodating, acquiescent, amenable, bowing down, comfortable, complying, deferential, docile, domesticated, dutiful, giving-in*, humble, ingratiating, lowly, malleable, meek, menial, nonresistant, nonresisting, obedient, obeisant, obeying, obsequious, passive, patient, pliable, pliant, resigned, servile, slavish, subdued, tame, tractable, uncomplaining, unresisting, yes*, yielding; SEE CONCEPT *401*

submit [*v1*] *comply, endure*
abide, accede, acknowledge, acquiesce, agree, appease, bend, be submissive, bow, buckle, capitulate, cave, cede, concede, defer, eat crow*, fold, give away, give ground, give in, give way, go with the flow*, grin and bear it*, humor, indulge, knuckle, knuckle under*, kowtow*, lay down arms, obey, put

up with, quit, relent, relinquish, resign oneself, say uncle*, stoop, succumb, surrender, throw in the towel*, toe the line*, tolerate, truckle, withstand, yield; SEE CONCEPT *23*

submit [*v2*] *present, offer; argue for*
advance, advise, affirm, argue, assert, claim, commit, contend, hand in, make a pitch*, move, proffer, propose, proposition, propound, put, put forward, refer, state, suggest, table, tender, theorize, urge, volunteer; SEE CONCEPT *66*

subordinate [*n*] *person or thing that serves another*
aide, assistant, attendant, dependent, deputy, flunky*, gofer*, helper, inferior, junior, low man, peon, poor relation*, scrub*, second, second fiddle*, second string*, serf, servant, slave, subaltern, third string*, underling; SEE CONCEPTS *348,423*

subordinate [*adj*] *lesser, supplementary*
accessory, adjuvant, ancillary, auxiliary, baser, below par, collateral, contributory, dependent, inferior, insignificant, junior, low, lower, minor, paltry, satellite, secondary, second-fiddle*, second-string*, smaller, sub, subaltern, subalternate, subject, submissive, subnormal, subservient, subsidiary, substract, tributary, under, underaverage, unequal; SEE CONCEPT *575*

subscribe [*v1*] *pay for use; contribute*
advocate, ante up*, buy, chip in*, come through*, consent, donate, do one's part*, endorse, enroll, give, grant, ink*, make a deal*, offer, pitch in*, pledge, promise, put up*, register, second, set, sign, signature, sign up*, support; SEE CONCEPTS *129,341*

subscribe [*v2*] *agree*
accede, acquiesce, advocate, approve, assent, autograph*, back, bless, boost, consent, cosign, countenance, ditto*, endorse, favor, get behind*, give stamp of approval* give the go-ahead*, go along with*, hold with*, ink*, obey, okay*, put John Hancock on*, rubber-stamp*, sanction, sign, signature, support, take, undersign, underwrite, yes*; SEE CONCEPTS *10,50,88*

subsequent [*adj*] *after*
consecutive, consequent, consequential, ensuing, following, later, next, posterior, postliminary, proximate, resultant, resulting, sequent, sequential, serial, subsequential, succeeding, successional, successive; SEE CONCEPTS *585,820*

subsequently [*adv*] *afterward*
after, afterwards, afterwhile, at a later date, behind, by and by, consequently, finally, infra, in the aftermath, in the end, later, latterly, next; SEE CONCEPTS *585,820*

subservient [*adj1*] *extremely compliant*
abject, acquiescent, a slave to*, at one's beck and call*, at one's mercy*, bootlicking*, cowering, cringing, dancing, deferential, docile, fawning, ignoble, inferior, in one's clutches*, in one's pocket*, in one's power*, mean, menial, obeisant, obsequious, resigned, servile, slavish, subject, submissive,

sycophantic, under one's thumb*; SEE CONCEPTS *401,404*

subservient [*adj2*] *secondary, useful*
accessory, adjuvant, ancillary, appurtenant, auxiliary, bush-league*, collateral, conducive, contributory, flunky, helpful, inferior, instrumental, minor, serviceable, subordinate, subsidiary, supplemental, supplementary; SEE CONCEPTS *560,575*

subside [*v*] *die down; decrease*
abate, cave in, collapse, decline, de-escalate, descend, die away, diminish, drop, dwindle, ease, ease off, ebb, fall, let up, level off, lower, lull, melt, moderate, peter out*, quieten, recede, settle, sink, slacken, taper, wane; SEE CONCEPTS *181,698,776*

subsidiary [*adj*] *secondary, helpful*
accessory, adjuvant, aiding, ancillary, appurtenant, assistant, assisting, auxiliary, backup, branch, collateral, contributory, cooperative, lesser, minor, serviceable, subject, subordinate, subservient, supplemental, supplementary, tributory, useful; SEE CONCEPTS *560,575*

subsidize [*v*] *give money to get started*
angel*, back, bankroll, contribute, endow, finance, fund, grubstake*, help, juice*, pick up the check*, pick up the tab*, prime the pump*, promote, put up the money for, sponsor, stake, support, underwrite; SEE CONCEPTS *110,341*

subsidy [*n*] *money given to help another*
aid, alimony, allowance, appropriation, assistance, bequest, bonus, bounty, contribution, endowment, fellowship, financial aid, gift, grant, gratuity, help, honorarium, indemnity, payment, pension, premium, reward, scholarship, subsidization, subvention, support, tribute; SEE CONCEPTS *337,344*

subsist [*v*] *keep going, living*
barely exist*, be, breathe, continue, eke out a living*, eke out an existence*, endure, exist, get along*, get by*, hang in*, hang on*, hang tough*, just make it*, last, live, make ends meet*, make it*, manage, move, remain, remain alive, ride out*, scrape by*, stay alive, stick it out*, stick with it*, survive, sustain; SEE CONCEPTS *23,330,407*

subsistence [*n*] *provisions for survival*
affluence, aliment, alimentation, bread*, bread and butter*, capital, circumstances, competence, earnings, existence, food, fortune, gratuity, income, independence, keep, legacy, livelihood, living, maintenance, means, money, necessities, nurture, pension, property, provision, ration, resources, riches, salary, salt*, substance, support, sustenance, upkeep, victuals, wages, wealth, wherewithal*; SEE CONCEPTS *446,457,646,710*

substance [*n1*] *entity, element*
actuality, animal, being, body, bulk, concreteness, core, corpus, fabric, force, hunk, individual, item, mass, material, matter, object, person, phenomenon, reality, something, staple, stuff, texture, thing; SEE CONCEPTS *433,478,523*

substance [*n2*] *essence, meaning*
ABCs*, amount, basis, body, bottom, bottom line*, brass tacks*, burden, center, core, corpus, crux, drift, effect, essentiality, focus, general meaning, gist, gravamen, guts*, heart, import, innards, kernel, marrow, mass, matter, meat*, name of the game*, nitty-gritty*, nub, nuts and bolts*, pith, point, purport, quintessence, sense, significance, soul, staple, strength, stuff, subject, sum total*, tenor, theme, thrust, upshot, virtuality, way of it*; SEE CONCEPTS *682,689*

substance [*n3*] *wealth*
affluence, assets, estate, fortune, means, property, resources, riches, worth; SEE CONCEPT *335*

substantial [*adj1*] *important, ample*
abundant, big, big-deal*, bulky, consequential, considerable, durable, extraordinary, firm, generous, goodly, heavy, heavyweight, hefty, key, large, major-league*, massive, material, meaningful, momentous, plentiful, principal, serious, significant, sizable, solid, sound, stable, steady, stout, strong, sturdy, superabundant, tidy, valuable, vast, weighty, well-built, worthwhile; SEE CONCEPTS *568,773,781*

substantial [*adj2*] *material, real*
actual, card-carrying*, concrete, corporeal, existent, for real*, honest-to-god*, legit*, objective, phenomenal, physical, positive, righteous, sensible, solid, sure enough*, tangible, true, twenty-four-carat*, valid, visible, weighty; SEE CONCEPT *582*

substantial [*adj3*] *rich*
affluent, comfortable, easy, opulent, prosperous, snug, solid, solvent, wealthy, well, well-heeled, well-off, well-to-do; SEE CONCEPT *334*

substantially [*adv*] *to a large extent*
considerably, essentially, extensively, heavily, in essence, in fact, in reality, in substance, in the main, largely, mainly, materially, much, really; SEE CONCEPTS *569,772*

substantiate [*v*] *back up a statement, idea*
actualize, affirm, approve, attest to, authenticate, bear out, check out, check up, complete, confirm, corroborate, debunk, demonstrate, establish, incarnate, justify, manifest, materialize, objectify, personify, prove, ratify, realize, reify, support, test, try, try on, try out, validate, verify; SEE CONCEPTS *49,138,317*

substitute [*n*] *someone or something that takes the place of another*
agent, alternate, assistant, auxiliary, backup, changeling, delegate, deputy, dernier ressort, double, dummy, equivalent, expediency, expedient, fill-in, ghost, ghost writer, locum, locum tenens, makeshift, pinch-hitter*, procurator, proxy, recourse, refuge, relay, relief, replacement, representative, reserve, resort, resource, stand-by, stand-in, stopgap*, sub, succedaneum, successor, supplanter, supply, surrogate, symbol, temp, temporary, temporary expedient, understudy, vicar; SEE CONCEPTS *423,712*

substitute [adj] alternative
acting, additional, alternate, another, artificial, backup, counterfeit, dummy, ersatz*, experimental, false, imitation, makeshift, mock, near, other, provisional, proxy, pseudo*, replacement, representative, reserve, second, sham*, simulated, spurious, stopgap*, substitutive, supplemental, supplementary, supposititious, surrogate, symbolic, temporary, tentative, vicarial, vicarious; SEE CONCEPTS 560,575

substitute [v] interchange, exchange
act for, alternate, answer for, back up, be in place of, change, commute, cover for, deputize, displace, do the work of, double for, fill in for, fill one's position, go as, proxy, relieve, replace, serve in one's stead, spell, stand for, stand in for, sub, supercede, supplant, swap, swap places with*, switch, take another's place, take over; SEE CONCEPTS 87,104

subtle [adj1] nice, quiet, delicate
attenuate, attenuated, deep, discriminating, ethereal, exquisite, faint, fine, finespun, hairline, hairsplitting, illusive, implied, inconspicuous, indirect, indistinct, inferred, ingenious, insinuated, mental, penetrating, profound, refined, slight, sophisticated, suggestive, tenuous, thin, understated; SEE CONCEPTS 537,544

subtle [adj2] clever, cunning
analytic, analytical, artful, astute, complex, crafty, deep, designing, detailed, devious, dexterous, exacting, foxy, guileful, insidious, intriguing, keen, penetrating, perceptive, precise, ratiocinative, scheming, shrewd, skillful, sly, wily; SEE CONCEPT 402

subtract [v] take away
decrease, deduct, detract, diminish, discount, draw back, knock off, remove, take, take from, take off, take out, withdraw, withhold; SEE CONCEPTS 211,764

suburb [n] neighborhood outside of but reliant on nearby large city
bedroom community*, burb*, country, countryside, environs, fringe, hamlet, hinterland, outlying area, outpost, outskirts, precinct, purlieu, residential area, slub, suburbia, village; SEE CONCEPTS 508,512

subversive [adj] rebellious, destructive
incendiary, inflammatory, insurgent, insurrectionary, overthrowing, perversive, riotous, ruinous, seditious, treasonous, underground, undermining; SEE CONCEPT 401

subvert [v] rebel, destroy
capsize, contaminate, corrupt, debase, defeat, demolish, deprave, depress, extinguish, invalidate, invert, level, overthrow, overturn, pervert, poison, pull down, raze, reverse, ruin, sabotage, supersede, supplant, suppress, topple, tumble, undermine, upset, vitiate, wreck; SEE CONCEPTS 86,95,252

succeed [v1] attain good outcome
accomplish, achieve, acquire, arrive, avail, benefit, be successful, carry off*, come off*, conquer, distance, do all right*, do the trick*, earn, flourish, fulfill, gain, get, get to the top*, grow famous, hit*, make a fortune*, make good*, make it*, make out*,

master, obtain, outdistance, outwit, overcome, possess, prevail, profit, prosper, pull off*, realize, reap, receive, recover, retrieve, score, secure, surmount, thrive, triumph, turn out*, vanquish, win, work, worst; SEE CONCEPTS 141,706

succeed [v2] come after; take the place of
accede, assume, become heir to, be subsequent, come into, come into possession, come next, displace, ensue, enter upon, follow, follow after, follow in order, go next, inherit, postdate, replace, result, supersede, supervene, supplant, take over; SEE CONCEPTS 727,749,813

succeeding/successive [adj] following
alternating, consecutive, ensuing, following after, in a row, in line, next, next in line for, next in order, next off, next up, rotating, sequent, sequential, serial, seriate, subsequent, subsequential, succedent, successional; SEE CONCEPTS 585,811,812,818,820

success [n] favorable outcome
accomplishment, achievement, advance, arrival, ascendancy, attainment, bed of roses*, benefit, big hit*, boom*, clover*, consummation, do well, Easy Street*, éclat, eminence, fame, flying colors*, fortune, fruition, gain, good luck*, good times*, grand slam*, gravy train*, happiness, happy days*, hit, killing, lap of luxury*, laugher*, mastery, maturation, profit, progress, prosperity, realization, reward, savvy, sensation, snap, strike, successfulness, triumph, victory, walkaway*, walkover*, win; SEE CONCEPTS 693,706

successful [adj] favorable, profitable
acknowledged, advantageous, ahead of the game*, at the top*, at top of ladder*, auspicious, bestselling, blooming, blossoming, booming, champion, crowned, efficacious, extraordinary, flourishing, fortuitous, fortunate, fruitful, happy, lucky, lucrative, moneymaking, notable, noteworthy, on track*, out in front*, outstanding, paying, prosperous, rewarding, rolling, strong, thriving, top, triumphant, unbeaten, undefeated, victorious, wealthy; SEE CONCEPT 528

succinct [adj] brief, to the point
blunt, boiled down*, breviloquent, brusque, compact, compendiary, compendious, concise, condensed, curt, cut to the bone*, in a nutshell*, in few words*, laconic, pithy, short, summary, terse; SEE CONCEPT 267

succulent [adj] juicy, delicious
divine, heavenly, luscious, lush, mellow, moist, mouthwatering, pulpy, rich, sappy, tasty, yummy; SEE CONCEPTS 462,613

succumb [v] die or surrender
accede, bow, break down, buckle, capitulate, cave, cave in*, cease, collapse, croak, decease, defer, demise, depart, drop, eat crow*, expire, fall, fall victim to, flake out, fold, give in, give into, give out, give up the ghost*, give way, go, go down, go under, knuckle, knuckle under*, meet Waterloo*, pack it in*, pass, pass away, perish, quit, say uncle*,

show white flag*, submit, take the count*, toss in the towel*, wilt, yield; SEE CONCEPTS 35,105,385

such [conj/adj] aforementioned, specific
aforesaid, akin, alike, analogous, comparable, corresponding, equivalent, like, parallel, said, similar, such a one, such a person, such a thing, suchlike, that, the like, this; SEE CONCEPT 557

sudden [adj] unexpected; happening quickly
abrupt, accelerated, acute, expeditious, fast, flash, fleet, hasty, headlong, hurried, immediate, impetuous, impromptu, impulsive, out of the blue*, precipitant, precipitate, precipitous, quick, quickened, rapid, rash, rushing, spasmodic, speeded, subito, swift, unforeseen, unusual; SEE CONCEPT 799

suddenly [adv] unexpectedly
aback, abruptly, all at once, all of a sudden, asudden, forthwith, on spur of moment*, quickly, short, sudden, swiftly, unanticipatedly, unaware, unawares, without warning; SEE CONCEPT 799

sue [v] bring legal charges against
accuse, appeal, beg, beseech, bring an action, charge, claim, claim damages, contest, demand, drag into court, enter a plea, entreat, file, file a claim, file suit, follow up, haul into court, have the law on, have up, indict, institute legal proceedings, litigate, petition, plead, prefer charges against, prosecute, pull up, put away, see in court, solicit, summon, supplicate, take out after, take to court; SEE CONCEPT 317

suffer [v1] be in pain
ache, agonize, ail, be affected, be at disadvantage, be convulsed, be handicapped, be impaired, be racked, be wounded, brave, complain of, deteriorate, droop, endure, experience, fall off, feel wretched, flag, get, go through, grieve, have a bad time*, hurt, languish, pain, sicken, smart, undergo, writhe; SEE CONCEPTS 308,313

suffer [v2] endure, permit
abide, accept, acquiesce, admit, allow, bear, bear with, bleed, bow, brave, brook, carry the torch*, concede, countenance, encounter, experience, feel, go through, have, hurt, indulge, know, let, license, live with, put up with, receive, sanction, see, sit and take it, stand, stomach*, submit, support, sustain, swallow*, sweat*, take*, take it*, tolerate, undergo, wait out, yield; SEE CONCEPTS 23,83

suffering [n] pain, agony
adversity, affliction, anguish, difficulty, discomfort, distress, dolor, hardship, martyrdom, misery, misfortune, ordeal, passion, torment, torture; SEE CONCEPT 728

suffice [v] be adequate, enough
answer, avail, be good enough, be sufficient, be the ticket*, content, do, do the trick*, fill the bill*, get by, go over big*, hack it*, hit the spot*, make a hit*, make the grade*, meet, meet requirement, satisfy, serve, suit; SEE CONCEPT 713

sufficient [adj] enough, adequate
acceptable, agreeable, all right*, ample, aplenty, appreciate, comfortable, commensurable, commensu-

rate, common, competent, copious, decent, due, galore, pleasing, plenteous, plentiful, plenty, proportionate, satisfactory, sufficing, tolerable, unexceptionable, unexceptional, unobjectionable; SEE CONCEPTS 558,560,771

suffocate [v] choke
asphyxiate, drown, smother, stifle, strangle; SEE CONCEPTS 163,246

suggest [v1] convey advice, plan, desire
advance, advise, advocate, broach, commend, conjecture, exhort, give a tip*, move, offer, offer suggestion, plug*, pose, prefer, propone, propose, proposition, propound, put, put forward, put in two cents*, put on to something*, recommend, steer, submit, theorize, tip, tip off*, tout; SEE CONCEPT 75

suggest [v2] imply; bring to mind
adumbrate, advert, allude, be a sign of, connote, cross the mind, denote, evoke, hint, indicate, infer, insinuate, intimate, lead to believe, occur, point, point in direction of, promise, put in mind, refer, represent, shadow, signify, symbolize, typify; SEE CONCEPTS 74,682

suggestion [n1] advice, plan
advancement, angle, approach, bid, big idea*, bit*, brainchild*, charge, commendation, exhortation, game plan*, gimmick, hot lead*, idea, injunction, instruction, invitation, lead, motion, opinion, outline, pitch, presentation, proffer, proposal, proposition, recommendation, reminder, resolution, scheme, setup, sneaking suspicion*, steer*, submission, telltale, tender, testimonial, thesis, tip, tip-off*; SEE CONCEPTS 278,689

suggestion [n2] hint, implication
allusion, association, autosuggestion, breath, clue, connotation, cue, indication, inkling, innuendo, insinuation, intimation, notion, overtone, reminder, self-suggestion, shade, signification, smack, soupçon, strain, suspicion, symbol, symbolism, symbolization, symbology, telltale, thought, tinge, trace, undertone, vein, whisper, wind; SEE CONCEPT 529

suggestive [adj1] signifying
evocative, evocatory, expressive, giving an inkling*, indicative, intriguing, pregnant, redolent, remindful, reminiscent, significative, symbolic, symptomatic; SEE CONCEPTS 267,529

suggestive [adj2] dirty, vulgar
bawdy, blue*, broad, erotic, immodest, improper, indecent, indelicate, obscene, off-color*, provocative, prurient, racy, ribald, risqué, rude, seductive, sexy, shady, tempting, titillating, unseemly, wicked; SEE CONCEPTS 372,545

suit [n1] matching top and bottom clothing
clothing, costume, dress, ensemble, getup*, gray flannel*, habit, livery, outfit, threads*, tuxedo, uniform, wardrobe; SEE CONCEPT 451

suit [n2] legal action
case, cause, lawsuit, litigation, proceeding, prosecution, trial; SEE CONCEPT 318

suit [n3] *appeal, request*
address, application, asking, attention, court, court-ship, entreaty, imploration, imprecation, invocation, petition, plea, prayer, requesting, solicitation, solic-iting, supplication, wooing; SEE CONCEPT *662*

suit [v1] *be acceptable, appropriate*
accord, agree, answer, answer a need, become, befit, benefit, be proper for, beseem, be seemly, check, check out, conform, correspond, cut the mustard, do, enhance, fill the bill*, fit, fit in, flatter, fulfill, get by, go, go together, go with, gratify, harmonize, make the grade*, match, pass muster*, please, satisfy, serve, square, suffice, tally; SEE CONCEPT *656*

suit [v2] *adapt, tailor*
accommodate, adjust, amuse, change, conform, en-tertain, fashion, fill, fit, fit in, gratify, modify, please, proportion, quadrate, readjust, reconcile, re-vise, satisfy, tailor-make, toe the mark*; SEE CON-CEPTS *126,697*

suitable [adj] *appropriate, acceptable*
advisable, applicable, apposite, apt, becoming, be-fitting, commodious, condign, convenient, copace-tic, correct, cut out for*, deserved, due, expedient, felicitous, fit, fitting, good, good enough*, handy, happy, in character, in keeping*, just, kosher*, le-git*, meet, merited, nice, okay*, opportune, peachy, pertinent, politic, presentable, proper, reasonable, relevant, requisite, right, righteous, rightful, satis-factory, seemly, sufficient, suited, swell, up to snuff*, useful, user friendly; SEE CONCEPT *558*

suite [n1] *set of rooms or furniture*
apartment, array, batch, body, chambers, collection, flat, group, lodging, lot, parcel, rental, series, set, tenement; SEE CONCEPTS *441,516*

suite [n2] *entourage of people*
array, attendants, batch, body, clutch, cortege, court, escort, faculty, followers, group, lot, retainers, reti-nue, servants, set, staff, train; SEE CONCEPT *417*

suite [n3] *series*
chain, concatenation, consecution, line, order, pro-gression, row, scale, sequel, sequence, string, suc-cession, train; SEE CONCEPT *727*

suitor [n] *person who admires another*
admirer, beau, boyfriend, cavalier*, courter, date, follower, girlfriend, lover, man, paramour, suppli-cant, swain, woman, wooer; SEE CONCEPT *423*

sulk [v] *pout*
be down in the mouth*, be in a huff*, be morose, be out of sorts*, be silent, brood, frown, gloom, glower, gripe, grouse, grump*, look sullen, lower, moon*, mope*, scowl, take on; SEE CONCEPTS *35,52*

sullen [adj] *brooding, upset*
bad-tempered, cheerless, churlish, crabbed*, crab-by*, cross, cynical, dismal, dour, dull, fretful, frowning, gloomy, glowering, glum, gruff, grumpy*, heavy, hostile, ill-humored, inert, irrita-ble, malevolent, malicious, malign, mean, moody, morose, obstinate, ornery, out of sorts*, peevish,

perverse, pessimistic, petulant, pouting, pouty, quer-ulous, saturnine, silent, somber, sour, sourpussed, stubborn, sulking, sulky, surly, tenebrific, tenebrous, ugly, unsociable, uptight*; SEE CONCEPT *403*

sultry [adj1] *hot and humid*
baking, broiling, burning, close, hot, mucky, muggy, oppressive, red-hot*, scorching, sizzling, smothering, soggy, sticky, stifling, stuffy, suffocat-ing, sweltering, sweltry, torrid, wet; SEE CONCEPTS *525,605*

sultry [adj2] *sensuous*
desirable, erotic, heavy*, hot*, lurid, passionate, provocative, seductive, sexy, steamy*, voluptuous, X-rated*; SEE CONCEPT *372*

sum [n] *total*
aggregate, all, amount, body, bulk, entirety, entity, epitome, gross, integral, mass, quantity, reckoning, résumé, score, structure, summary, summation, sum total*, synopsis, system, tally, totality, value, whole, works*, worth; SEE CONCEPTS *432,784,787*

summarily [adv] *without delay*
arbitrarily, at short notice, expeditiously, forthwith, immediately, on the spot, peremptorily, promptly, readily, speedily, swiftly, without waste; SEE CON-CEPTS *544,799*

summarize [v] *give a rundown*
abridge, abstract, boil down*, cipher, compile, con-dense, cut, cut back, cut down, digest, encapsulate, epitomize, get to meat*, give main points, inventory, nutshell*, outline, pare, precis, prune*, recap*, re-capitulate, rehash*, résumé, retrograde, review, run down*, run through*, shorten, skim, snip, sum, sum-mate, sum up, synopsize, trim; SEE CONCEPTS *55,236,247*

summary [n] *short statement of main points*
abbreviation, abridgment, abstract, analysis, apercu, brief, capitulation, case, compendium, condensation, conspectus, core, digest, epitome, essence, extract, inventory, long and short of it*, nutshell*, outline, pandect, precis, prospectus, recap*, recapitulation, reduction, rehash*, report, résumé, review, roundup, rundown, run-through, sense, skeleton*, sketch, sum and substance*, summing-up*, survey, syllabus, synopsis, version, wrap-up*; SEE CONCEPT *283*

summary [adj] *concise, to the point*
arbitrary, boiled down*, breviloquent, brief, com-pact, compacted, compendiary, compendious, con-densed, cursory, curt, hasty, in a nutshell*, laconic, perfunctory, pithy*, recapped, rehashed, run-down, run-through, short, short and sweet*, succinct, terse; SEE CONCEPTS *267,272*

summer [n] *hot season of year*
daylight savings time, dog days*, heat, midsummer, picnic days*, riot time*, summer solstice, sum-mertide, summertime, sunny season, vacation; SEE CONCEPT *814*

summit [n] *top, crowning point*
acme, apex, apogee, capstone, climax, crest, crown, culmination, head, height, max, meridian, most,

peak, pinnacle, roof, vertex, zenith; SEE CONCEPT *836*

summon [*v*] *call to a place*
arouse, ask, assemble, beckon, beep, bid, call, call back, call for, call forth, call in, call into action, call together, call upon, charge, cite, command, conjure, convene, convoke, direct, draft, draw on, enjoin, gather, hail, invite, invoke, mobilize, motion, muster, order, petition, rally, recall, request, ring, rouse, send for, sign, signal, subpoena, toll; SEE CONCEPT *53*

sumptuous [*adj*] *luxurious, splendid*
awe-inspiring, beautiful, costly, dear, deluxe, elegant, expensive, extravagant, gorgeous, grand, grandiose, imposing, impressive, lavish, luscious, luxuriant, magnificent, opulent, out of this world, palatial, plush, pompous, posh, prodigal, profuse, rich, ritzy, splendiferous, superb, swank, ultra, upholstered; SEE CONCEPTS *334,485,574*

sum up [*v*] *form an opinion of; summarize*
close, conclude, condense, digest, epitomize, estimate, examine, get the measure of, inventory, nutshell*, put in a nutshell*, recapitulate, review, size up, sum, synopsize, total; SEE CONCEPT *55*

sundry [*adj*] *miscellaneous*
assorted, different, divers, manifold, many, quite a few, several, some, varied, various; SEE CONCEPTS *564,772*

sunny [*adj1*] *bright, clear (referring to weather)*
brilliant, clarion, cloudless, fine, light, luminous, pleasant, radiant, rainless, shining, shiny, summery, sunlit, sunshiny, unclouded, undarkened; SEE CONCEPTS *525,617*

sunny [*adj2*] *happy*
beaming, blithe, buoyant, cheerful, cheery, chirpy, genial, joyful, lighthearted, lightsome, optimistic, pleasant, smiling, sunbeamy; SEE CONCEPTS *401,542*

sunrise [*n*] *rise of sun above horizon*
aurora, break of day*, bright, cockcrow*, dawn, dawning, daybreak, daylight, early bright*, light, morn*, morning, sunup; SEE CONCEPT *810*

sunset [*n*] *fall of sun below horizon*
close of day, crepuscular light, dusk, eve, evening, eventide, gloaming, nightfall, sundown, twilight; SEE CONCEPT *810*

super [*adj*] *excellent*
cool*, divine, glorious, great, groovy*, hot*, incomparable, keen, magnificent, marvelous, matchless, neat, outstanding, peerless, sensational, smashing, superb, terrific, topnotch, wonderful; SEE CONCEPT *574*

superb [*adj*] *excellent, first-rate*
admirable, august, best, breathtaking, choice, elegant, elevated, exalted, exquisite, fine, glorious, gorgeous, grand, great, lofty, magnificent, majestic, marvelous, matchless, noble, optimal, optimum, outstanding, peerless, prime, proud, resplendent, solid, splendid, splendiferous, splendorous, standout, state-

of-the-art, stunning, sublime, super, superior, superlative, unrivaled, very best; SEE CONCEPT *574*

supercilious [*adj*] *arrogant, stuck-up*
bossy, cavalier, cocky*, condescending, contemptuous, disdainful, egotistic, haughty, high-and-mighty*, imperious, insolent, lofty, lordly, nervy*, overbearing, patronizing, proud, putting on airs*, scornful, snobby, superior, uppity*, vainglorious; SEE CONCEPT *401*

superficial [*adj*] *without depth, detail*
apparent, casual, cosmetic, cursory, depthless, desultory, empty, evident, exterior, external, flash, flimsy, frivolous, general, glib, half-baked*, hasty, hurried, ignorant, inattentive, lightweight, nodding, one-dimensional, on the surface, ostensible, outward, partial, passing, perfunctory, peripheral, quick-fix*, seeming, shallow, shoal, silly, sketchy, skin-deep*, slapdash*, slight, smattery, summary, surface, tip of the iceberg*, trivial, uncritical, warped; SEE CONCEPTS *557,777*

superficially [*adv*] *lightly; without care*
apparently, at first glance, carelessly, casually, externally, extraneously, flimsily, frivolously, hastily, ignorantly, not profoundly, not thoroughly, once over lightly*, on the surface, ostensibly, outwardly, partially, skim, to the casual eye*; SEE CONCEPTS *531,544*

superfluous [*adj*] *extra, unnecessary*
abounding, de trop*, dispensable, excess, excessive, exorbitant, expendable, extravagant, extreme, gratuitous, inessential, in excess, inordinate, lavish, leftover, needless, nonessential, overflowing, overmuch, pleonastic, profuse, redundant, remaining, residuary, spare, superabundant, supererogatory, superfluent, supernumerary, surplus, unasked, uncalled-for, unneeded, unrequired, unwanted, useless; SEE CONCEPTS *546,560,824*

superintendent [*n*] *person who oversees organization*
administrator, boss, caretaker, chief, conductor, controller, curator, custodian, director, foreman/woman, governor, head, head man/woman, inspector, manager, overseer, sitter, slave driver*, straw boss*, super*, supervisor, zookeeper*; SEE CONCEPT *347*

superior [*n*] *person higher or highest in rank*
boss, brass*, CEO*, chief, chieftain, czar, director, elder, exec*, executive, guru*, head, head honcho*, heavyweight*, higher-up*, key player*, leader, manager, principal, ruler, senior, supervisor, VIP*; SEE CONCEPT *347*

superior [*adj1*] *better, greater, higher; excellent*
above, a cut above*, admirable, capital, choice, dandy, deluxe, distinguished, exceeding, excellent, exceptional, exclusive, expert, famous, fine, finer, first-class, first-rate, first-string, five-star*, good, good quality, grander, high-caliber, high-class, major, more advanced, more skillful, noteworthy, of higher rank, over, overlying, paramount, predominant, preferable, preferred, premium, prevailing, pri-

mary, remarkable, senior, superhuman, super-incumbent, surpassing, unrivalled; SEE CONCEPT *574*

superior [*adj2*] *arrogant, haughty*
airy, bossy, cavalier, cocky*, condescending, cool, disdainful, high-and-mighty*, high-hat*, insolent, lofty, lordly, overbearing, patronizing, pretentious, proud, snobbish, stuck-up*, supercilious, uppity*, upstage*, wiseguy*; SEE CONCEPT *401*

superiority [*n*] *advantage, predominance*
ahead, ascendancy, authority, better, bulge, dominance, edge, eminence, excellence, influence, lead, meliority, nobility, perfection, position, power, predomination, preeminence, preponderance, prestige, prevalence, pull, rank, spark, supremacy, top, transcendence, upper hand*, vantage, victory, whip hand*; SEE CONCEPT *671*

superlative [*adj*] *excellent, first-class*
A-1*, accomplished, all-time*, best, capital, consummate, crack, effusive, exaggerated, excessive, extreme, finished, gilt-edge*, greatest, highest, hundred-proof*, inflated, magnificent, matchless, of highest order*, optimum, outstanding, peerless, standout*, superb, supreme, surpassing, tops*, transcendent, unexcelled, unparalleled, unrivaled, unsurpassed, winner, world-class; SEE CONCEPT *574*

supernatural [*adj*] *mysterious, not of this world*
abnormal, celestial, concealed, dark, fabulous, fairy, ghostly, heavenly, hidden, impenetrable, invisible, legendary, metaphysical, miraculous, mystic, mythical, mythological, numinous, obscure, occult, paranormal, phantom, phenomenal, preternatural, psychic, rare, secret, spectral, superhuman, superior, supermundane, superordinary, supranatural, transcendental, uncanny, uncomprehensible, unearthly, unfathomable, unintelligible, unknowable, unknown, unnatural, unrevealed, unusual; SEE CONCEPT *582*

supersede [*v*] *take the place of; override*
abandon, annul, desert, discard, displace, forsake, oust, outmode, outplace, overrule, reject, remove, replace, repudiate, set aside, succeed, supplant, supplement, suspend, take over, usurp; SEE CONCEPTS *128,141*

superstition [*n*] *belief in sign of things to come*
false belief, fear, irrationality, notion, old wives' tale*, shibboleth*, unfounded fear; SEE CONCEPT *689*

supervise [*v*] *manage people, project*
administer, be in charge*, be in driver's seat*, be in the saddle, be on duty, be responsible for, boss, call the play*, call the shots*, chaperon, conduct, control, crack the whip*, deal with, direct, handle, inspect, keep an eye on*, look after, overlook, oversee, preside over, quarterback*, ride herd on*, run, run the show*, run things*, sit on top of*, superintend, survey, take care of; SEE CONCEPT *117*

supervision [*n*] *management of people, project*
administration, auspices, care, charge, conduct, control, direction, guidance, handling, instruction, in-tendance, oversight, running, stewardship, superintendence, superintendency, surveillance; SEE CONCEPT *117*

supervisor [*n*] *person who manages people, project*
administrator, boss, brass hat*, caretaker, chief, curator, custodian, director, executive, foreman/woman, head, inspector, king of the hill*, manager, overseer, slave driver*, steward, straw boss*, super*, superintendent, zookeeper*; SEE CONCEPT *347*

supplant [*v*] *displace, replace*
back up, bounce, cast out, crowd, cut out, eject, expel, fill in, force, force out, front for, oust, outplace, overthrow, remove, ring, ring in, sit in, stand in, substitute, succeed, supersede, swap places with, take out, take over, take the place of, transfer, undermine, unseat, usurp; SEE CONCEPT *128*

supple [*adj*] *bendable*
adaptable, agile, bending, ductile, elastic, flexible, graceful, limber, lissome, lithe, lithesome, malleable, moldable, plastic, pliable, pliant, resilient, rubber, springy, stretch, stretchy, svelte, willowy, wiry, yielding; SEE CONCEPTS *488,604*

supplement [*n*] *something added*
added feature*, addendum, addition, additive, appendix, bell, bells and whistles*, codicil, complement, continuation, extra, insert, option, postscript, pullout, rider, sequel, spin-off, subsidiary; SEE CONCEPTS *270,824*

supplement [*v*] *add to*
add fuel to fire*, augment, beef up*, build up, buttress, complement, complete, enhance, enrich, extend, fill out, fill up, fortify, heat up*, improve, increase, jazz up*, pad*, punch up*, reinforce, step up, strengthen, subsidize, supply, top; SEE CONCEPTS *236,244,245*

supplies [*n*] *equipment, provisions*
food, foodstuffs, items, material, materials, necessities, provender, rations, raw materials, replenishments, stock, store, stores; SEE CONCEPTS *446,451,457*

supply [*n*] *reserve of goods*
accumulation, amount, backlog, cache, fund, hoard, inventory, number, quantity, reservoir, source, stock, stockpile, store, surplus; SEE CONCEPT *712*

supply [*v*] *furnish, provide, give a resource*
afford, cater, cater to, come across with*, come through*, come up with, contribute, deliver, dispense, drop, endow, equip, feed, fill, find, fix up, fulfill, give with, grant, hand, hand over, heel*, kick in*, minister, outfit, pony up*, produce, provide, provision, purvey, put out, put up, replenish, satisfy, stake, stock, store, transfer, turn over, victual, yield; SEE CONCEPTS *107,140*

support [*n1*] *something that holds up structure*
abutment, agency, back, backing, base, bed, bedding, block, brace, buttress, collar, column, cornerstone, device, flotation, foothold, footing, foundation, fulcrum, groundwork, guide, hold, lin-

ing, means, medium, pillar, platform, pole, post, prop, rampart, reinforcement, rest, rib, rod, shore, stake, stanchion, stave, stay, stiffener, stilt, substratum, substructure, sustentation, timber, underpinning; SEE CONCEPTS *440,442,445,471*

support [n2] *help, approval*
aid, assist, assistance, backing, blessing, championship, comfort, encouragement, friendship, furtherance, hand, lift, loyalty, moral support, patronage, protection, relief, succor, sustenance; SEE CONCEPTS *10,110,388,712*

support [n3] *food, money, possessions for staying alive*
alimentation, alimony, allowance, care, keep, livelihood, living, maintenance, necessities, nutriment, payment, provision, relief, responsibility, stock, stores, subsidy, subsistence, sustenance, upkeep, victuals; SEE CONCEPTS *340,446,457,712*

support/supporter [n4/n] *person who helps another*
adherent, advocate, ally, angel*, apologist, backbone, backer, benefactor, champion, cohort, comforter, confederate, coworker, defender, disciple, endorser, espouser, exponent, expounder, fan, follower, friend, helper, mainstay, maintainer, partisan, patron, patroness, pillar, preserver, prop, proponent, satellite*, second, sponsor, stalwart, stay, subscriber, supporter, sustainer, tower of strength*, upholder, well-wisher*; SEE CONCEPT *423*

support [v1] *hold up*
base, be a foundation for, bear, bed, bolster, bottom, brace, buttress, carry, cradle, crutch, embed, found, ground, hold, keep from falling, keep up, mainstay, poise, prop, reinforce, shore, shore up, shoulder, stand, stay, strut, sustain, undergird, upbear, uphold; SEE CONCEPT *190*

support [v2] *take care of, provide for*
angel*, attend to, back, bankroll, be a source of strength*, bring up, buoy up, care for, chaperon, cherish, earn one's keep, encourage, feed, finance, fortify, foster, fund, give a leg up*, guard, keep, keep an eye on*, look after, maintain, make a living, nourish, nurse, pay expenses of, pay for, pick up the check*, prop, put up money for*, raise, set up, sponsor, stake, stiffen, strengthen, stroke, subsidize, succor, sustain, underwrite, uphold; SEE CONCEPTS *7,19,22,140,295,341*

support [v3] *defend, advocate belief*
abet, advance, agree with, aid, approve, assist, back, bear out, bolster, boost, boost morale, carry, champion, cheer, comfort, countenance, endorse, establish, forward, foster, get behind*, go along with, go to bat for*, help, hold, justify, keep up, lot with, maintain, plead for, promote, pull for, put forward, rally round, second, side with, stand behind, stand up for, stay, stick by*, stick up for*, substantiate, sustain, take one's side*, take the part of*, throw in with*, uphold, verify; SEE CONCEPTS *10,49,110*

support [v4] *endure*
abide, bear, bear with, brook, carry on, continue, countenance, go, go through, handle, keep up, live with*, maintain, put up with*, stand, stand for*, stay the course*, stick it out*, stomach*, submit, suffer, swallow*, sweat out*, take, tolerate, undergo, wait out; SEE CONCEPT *23*

suppose [v1] *assume, guess*
accept, admit, brainstorm, calculate, conjecture, cook up*, dare-say*, deem, divine, dream, expect, figure, go out on a limb*, grant, guess, guesstimate*, hazard a guess*, hypothesize, imagine, infer, judge, opine, posit, predicate, presume, presuppose, pretend, spark, speculate, surmise, suspect, take, take for granted, theorize, think, understand; SEE CONCEPT *28*

suppose [v2] *believe*
assume, be afraid, conceive, conclude, conjecture, consider, deem, dream, expect, fancy, feel, gather, have a hunch*, have sneaking suspicion*, hypothesize, imagine, judge, postulate, pretend, reckon, regard, suspect, swear by, take, take as gospel truth*, take stock in*, think, understand, view; SEE CONCEPT *12*

supposition [n] *guess, belief*
apriorism, assumption, condition, conjecture, doubt, guessing, guesstimate*, guesswork, hunch, hypothesis, idea, likelihood, notion, opinion, perhaps, posit, postulate, postulation, premise, presumption, presupposition, rough guess*, shot in the dark*, sneaking suspicion*, speculation, stab in the dark*, suppose, surmise, suspicion, theory, thesis, view; SEE CONCEPT *689*

suppress [v] *restrain, hold in check*
abolish, annihilate, beat down, bottle, bring to naught, burke, censor, check, clamp, conceal, conquer, contain, cover up, crack down on, crush, curb, cut off, extinguish, hold back, hold down, hold in, interrupt, keep in, keep secret, muffle, muzzle, overcome, overpower, overthrow, put an end to, put down, put kibosh on*, put lid on*, quash, quell, quench, repress, shush*, silence, sit on*, smother, snuff out*, spike, squash*, stamp out*, stifle, stop, subdue, trample, withhold; SEE CONCEPTS *121,130,252*

supremacy [n] *total domination*
absolute rule, ascendancy, authority, command, control, dominance, dominion, driver's seat*, lordship, mastery, paramountcy, power, predominance, preeminence, preponderance, prepotence, primacy, principality, sovereignty, superiority, supreme authority, sway, transcendence; SEE CONCEPTS *133,376*

supreme [adj] *greatest, principal*
absolute, best, cardinal, chief, closing, crowning, culminating, excellent, extreme, final, first, foremost, head, highest, incomparable, last, leading, marvelous, master, matchless, maximum, paramount, peerless, perfect, predominant, preeminent,

prevailing, prime, sovereign, superb, superlative, surpassing, terminal, top, top-drawer*, towering, transcendent, ultimate, unequaled, unmatched, unparalleled, unsurpassable, unsurpassed, utmost; SEE CONCEPTS *568,574*

sure [*adj1*] *certain, definite*
abiding, assured, changeless, clear, confident, constant, convinced, convincing, decided, doubtless, enduring, firm, fixed, for a fact, free from doubt, genuine, incontestable, incontrovertible, indisputable, indubitable, never-failing, persuaded, positive, real, satisfied, set, steadfast, steady, telling, unchangeable, unchanging, uncompromising, undeniable, unequivocal, unfailing, unfaltering, unqualified, unquestionable, unquestioning, unshakable, unshaken, unvarying, unwavering, valid; SEE CONCEPT *535*

sure [*adj2*] *physically stable*
fast, firm, fixed, safe, secure, solid, staunch, steady, strong; SEE CONCEPT *488*

sure [*adj3*] *inevitable*
assured, bound, certain, guaranteed, indisputable, ineluctable, inerrant, inescapable, infallible, irrevocable, surefire, unavoidable, unerring, unfailing; SEE CONCEPT *548*

sure [*adj4*] *self-confident*
arrogant, assured, certain, composed, confident, decided, decisive, positive, self-assured, self-possessed; SEE CONCEPT *401*

surely [*adv*] *without doubt*
absolutely, admittedly, assuredly, beyond doubt, beyond shadow of doubt*, certainly, clearly, come what may*, conclusively, decidedly, definitely, distinctly, doubtlessly, evidently, explicitly, fixedly, for certain, for real, indeed, indubitably, inevitably, inexorably, infallibly, irrefutably, manifestly, nothing else but, plainly, positively, rain or shine*, to be sure, undoubtedly, unequivocally, unerringly, unfailingly, unmistakably, unquestionably, unshakably, with certainty, without fail; SEE CONCEPT *535*

surface [*n*] *external part of something*
area, cover, covering, expanse, exterior, exteriority, externality, facade, face, facet, level, obverse, outside, peel, periphery, plane, rind, side, skin, stretch, superficiality, superficies, top, veneer; SEE CONCEPT *484*

surface [*adj*] *external*
apparent, covering, depthless, exterior, facial, outer, outside, outward, shallow, shoal, superficial, top; SEE CONCEPTS *485,583*

surface [*v*] *come to the top of*
appear, arise, come to light, come up, crop up, emerge, flare up, materialize, rise, transpire; SEE CONCEPTS *166,716*

surfeit [*n*] *excess*
bellyful*, excess, glut*, overabundance, overflow, overfullness, overindulgence, overkill, overmuch, overplus, plenitude, plethora, profusion, remainder, repletion, satiety, satisfaction, saturation, superabundance, superfluity, surplus, up to here*; SEE CONCEPT *740*

surfeit [*v*] *overfill*
cloy, cram, eat, fill, glut, gorge, jade, overfeed, overindulge, pall, sate, satiate, satisfy, stuff; SEE CONCEPTS *209,740*

surge [*n*] *rush, usually of liquid*
billow, breaker, deluge, efflux, flood, flow, growth, gush, intensification, outpouring, rise, roll, surf, swell, upsurge, wave; SEE CONCEPTS *432,467,787*

surge [*v*] *rush, usually in liquid form*
arise, billow, climb, deluge, eddy, flow, grow, gush, heave, mount, pour, ripple, rise, roll, sluice, stream, swell, swirl, tower, undulate, well forth; SEE CONCEPTS *146,179*

surly [*adj*] *gruff, bearish*
boorish, brusque, churlish, cross, crusty*, curmudgeonly, discourteous, dour, fractious, glum, grouchy*, ill-mannered, ill-natured, irritable, morose, perverse, rude, saturnine, sulky, sullen, testy, ugly, uncivil, ungracious; SEE CONCEPT *401*

surmise [*n*] *guess, conclusion*
assumption, attempt, conjecture, deduction, guesstimate*, guesswork, hunch, hypothesis, idea, inference, notion, opinion, possibility, presumption, sneaking suspicion*, speculation, supposition, suspicion, theory, thought; SEE CONCEPTS *529,689*

surmise [*v*] *come to a conclusion*
assume, conclude, conjecture, consider, deduce, fancy, guess, guesstimate*, hazard a guess*, hypothesize, imagine, infer, opine, presume, pretend, regard, risk assuming, speculate, suppose, suspect, take a shot*, take a stab*, theorize, think, venture a guess; SEE CONCEPTS *18,28*

surmount [*v*] *overcome, triumph over*
best, better, cap, clear, conquer, crest, crown, defeat, down, exceed, hurdle, leap, lick*, master, negotiate, outdo, outstrip, over, overpower, overtop, pass, prevail over, rise above, subdue, surpass, throw*, top*, vanquish, vault; SEE CONCEPTS *95,141*

surpass [*v*] *outdo something or someone*
beat, best, better, cap, eclipse, exceed, excel, go beyond, go one better*, improve upon, outdistance, outgo, outmatch, outpace, outperform, outrank, outrival, outrun, outshine, outstep, outstrip, outweigh, override, overshadow, overstep, pass, put to shame*, rank*, surmount, top, tower, tower above*, transcend, trump*; SEE CONCEPT *141*

surplus [*n*] *extra material*
balance, excess, overage, overflow, overkill, overmuch, overrun, overstock, oversupply, plethora, plus, remainder, residue, something extra, superabundance, superfluity, surfeit, surplusage, the limit, too much; SEE CONCEPTS *260,658,824*

surplus [*adj*] *extra*
de trop*, excess, in excess, leftover, odd*, over, remaining, spare, superfluent, superfluous, supernu-

merary, too much*, unused; SEE CONCEPTS *560, 781,824*

surprise [*n*] *something amazing; state of amazement*
abruptness, amazement, astonishment, astoundment, attack, awe, bewilderment, bombshell*, consternation, curiosity, curveball, disappointment, disillusion, eye-opener*, fortune, godsend*, incredulity, jolt*, kick*, marvel, miracle, miscalculation, phenomenon, portent, precipitance, precipitation, precipitousness, prodigy, rarity, revelation, shock, start, stupefaction, suddenness, thunderbolt*, unexpected, unforeseen, whammy*, wonder, wonderment; SEE CONCEPTS *410,529*

surprise [*v1*] *astonish; cause amazement*
amaze, astound, awe, bewilder, blow away*, bowl over*, cause wonder, confound, confuse, consternate, daze, dazzle, discomfit, disconcert, dismay, dumbfound, electrify, flabbergast, floor, jar, jolt, leave aghast, leave open-mouthed, nonplus, overwhelm, perplex, petrify, rattle, rock, shake up, shock, spring something on, stagger, startle, strike dumb*, strike with awe, stun, stupefy, take aback, take one's breath away*, throw a curve*, unsettle; SEE CONCEPT *42*

surprise [*v2*] *sneak up on; catch*
ambush, bushwhack*, burst in on, capture, catch in the act*, catch off-balance*, catch off-guard*, catch red-handed*, catch unawares*, come down on, discover, drop in on, grab, grasp, lay for, lie in wait*, nab, seize, spring on, startle, take, take by surprise, waylay; SEE CONCEPTS *42,86*

surrender [*n*] *giving up; resignation*
abandonment, abdication, acquiescence, appeasement, capitulation, cessation, dedition, delivery, giving way, relenting, relinquishment, renunciation, submission, succumbing, white flag*, yielding; SEE CONCEPTS *67,108,119,320*

surrender [*v*] *give up; resign*
abandon, buckle under*, capitulate, cave in*, cede, commit, concede, consign, cry uncle*, deliver up, eat crow*, eat humble pie*, entrust, fall, fold, forego, give in, go along with, go down, go under, hand over, knuckle, knuckle under*, leave, let go, pack it in*, part with, play dead*, put up white flag*, quit, relinquish, renounce, roll over*, submit, succumb, throw in the towel*, toss it in*, waive, yield; SEE CONCEPTS *67,108,119,320*

surreptitious [*adj*] *sneaky, secret*
clandestine, covert, fraudulent, furtive, hidden, hush-hush*, in holes and corners*, on the QT*, on the sly*, private, skulking, slinking, sly, sneaking, stealthy, sub-rosa, unauthorized, undercover, underhand, under-the-table*, under wraps*, veiled; SEE CONCEPT *548*

surrogate [*n*] *person or thing that acts as substitute*
agent, alternate, backup, delegate, deputy, expediency, expedient, fill-in, makeshift, pinch hitter*, proxy, recourse, refuge, replacement, representative,

resort, resource, stand-in, stopgap*, sub*; SEE CONCEPTS *348,414,423*

surround [*v*] *enclose, encircle something*
beleaguer, beset, besiege, blockade, border, bound, box in, circle, circumscribe, circumvent, close around, close in, close in on, compass, confine, edge, enclave, encompass, envelop, environ, fence in, fringe, gird, girdle, go around, hem in, inundate, invest, lay siege to, limit, loop, margin, outline, rim, ring, round, shut in, skirt, verge; SEE CONCEPT *758*

surroundings [*n*] *environment*
ambience, atmosphere, background, climate, community, environs, home, location, medium, milieu, neighborhood, setting, vicinity; SEE CONCEPTS *198,673*

surveillance [*n*] *close observation, following*
body mike*, bug, bugging*, care, control, direction, eagle eye*, examination, eye, inspection, lookout, peeled eye*, scrutiny, spying, stakeout, superintendence, supervision, surveyance, tab*, tail*, tap*, track*, vigil, vigilance, watch, wiretap; SEE CONCEPTS *103,298,749*

survey [*n*] *scrutiny, examination*
analysis, aperçu, audit, check, compendium, critique, digest, inquiry, inspection, outline, overview, pandect, perlustration, perusal, precis, review, sample, scan, sketch, study, syllabus, view; SEE CONCEPTS *37,103,197,271,291*

survey [*v*] *scrutinize, take stock of*
appraise, assay, assess, canvass, case, check, check out, check over, check up, contemplate, estimate, evaluate, examine, give the once over*, inspect, look over, look upon, measure, observe, overlook, oversee, plan, plot, prospect, rate, read, reconnoiter, research, review, scan, scope, scrutinize, set at, size, size up, stake out, study, summarize, superintend, supervise, take stock of*, test the waters*, valuate, value, view; SEE CONCEPTS *37,48,103,197,291*

survive [*v*] *continue to live*
bear, be extant, be left, carry on, carry through, come through, cut it, endure, exist, get on, get through, go all the way*, go the limit*, handle, hold out, keep, keep afloat, last, live, live down, live on, live out, live through, make a comeback*, make the cut*, outlast, outlive, outwear, persevere, persist, pull out of it*, pull through, recover, remain, remain alive, revive, ride out*, see through, stand up, subsist, suffer, sustain, tough it out*, weather, withstand; SEE CONCEPTS *23,239,407*

susceptible [*adj*] *exposed, naive*
affected, aroused, be taken in, disposed, easily moved, easy, fall for, given, gullible, impressed, impressible, impressionable, inclined, influenced, liable, mark, movable, nonresistant, obnoxious, open, out on a limb*, persuadable, predisposed, prone, pushover, ready, receptive, responsive, roused, sensible, sensile, sensitive, sentient, sitting duck*, soft, stirred, subject, sucker*, suggestible, susceptive,

swallow, swayed, tender, touched, tumble for*, vulnerable, wide open; SEE CONCEPTS *403,542*

suspect [*adj*] *doubtful*

doubtable, dubious, fishy*, incredible, open, problematic, pseudo*, questionable, ridiculous, shaky*, suspected, suspicious, thick*, thin*, unbelievable, uncertain, unclear, unlikely, unsure; SEE CONCEPTS *529,582*

suspect [*v*] *distrust; guess*

assume, be afraid, believe, conceive, conclude, conjecture, consider, disbelieve, doubt, expect, feel, gather, harbor suspicion*, have a hunch*, have doubt, have sneaking suspicion*, hazard a guess*, hold, imagine, mistrust, presume, reckon, smell a rat*, speculate, suppose, surmise, think, think probable, understand, wonder; SEE CONCEPTS *21,28*

suspend [*v1*] *hang from above*

append, attach, be pendent, dangle, depend, hang down, hang up, hook up, sling, swing, wave; SEE CONCEPTS *181,190*

suspend [*v2*] *delay, hold off*

adjourn, arrest, bar, break up, can, cease, check, count out, cut short, debar, defer, discontinue, eject, eliminate, exclude, file, halt, hang, hang fire*, hang up, hold up, inactivate, intermit, interrupt, lay aside, lay off, lay on the table*, lay over, omit, pigeonhole*, pink-slip*, postpone, procrastinate, prorogue, protract, put an end to, put a stop to, put off, put on back burner*, put on hold, put on ice*, put on the shelf*, reject, retard, rule out, shelve, stave off, stay, waive, withhold; SEE CONCEPTS *119,121,130,351*

suspense [*n*] *anticipation*

anxiety, apprehension, chiller*, cliff-hanger*, cloak and dagger*, confusion, dilemma, doubt, eagerness, expectancy, expectation, grabber*, hesitancy, hesitation, impatience, indecision, indecisiveness, insecurity, irresolution, page-turner*, perplexity, potboiler*, tension, thriller*, uncertainty, wavering; SEE CONCEPTS *410,679*

suspension [*n*] *delay*

abeyance, abeyancy, adjournment, break, breather*, breathing spell*, cessation, coffee break*, concluding, conclusion, cutoff, deferment, disbarment, discontinuation, discontinuing, doldrums, dormancy, downtime*, end, ending, finish, five*, freeze, halt, heave-ho*, intermission, interruption, latency, layoff, letup, moratorium, pause, period, postponement, quiescence, quiescency, remission, respite, stay, stoppage, suspense, ten*, termination, time-out; SEE CONCEPTS *119,807,832*

suspicion [*n1*] *doubt*

bad vibes*, chariness, conjecture, cynicism, distrust, dubiety, dubiosity, funny feeling*, guess, guesswork, gut feeling*, hunch, idea, impression, incertitude, incredulity, jealousy, lack of confidence, misgiving, mistrust, nonbelief, notion, qualm, skepticism, sneaking suspicion*, supposition, surmise,

uncertainty, wariness, wonder; SEE CONCEPTS *532,689,690*

suspicion [*n2*] *hint, trace*

cast, glimmer, intimation, shade, shadow, smell, soupçon, strain, streak, suggestion, tinge, touch, whiff; SEE CONCEPTS *529,831*

suspicious [*adj1*] *distrustful*

apprehensive, cagey*, careful, cautious, doubtful, green-eyed*, incredulous, in doubt, jealous, leery, mistrustful, not born yesterday* on the lookout*, questioning, quizzical, skeptical, suspect, suspecting, unbelieving, uptight*, wary, watchful, without belief, without faith, wondering; SEE CONCEPTS *403,542*

suspicious [*adj2*] *doubtful, fishy*

borderline, debatable, different, disputable, doubtable, dubious, equivocal, farfetched, funny*, irregular, not kosher*, open, open to doubt, open to question, out of line*, overt, peculiar, phony, problematic, queer, questionable, reaching, rings untrue*, shady, shaky*, suspect, too much*, uncertain, uncommon, unsure, unusual, won't wash*; SEE CONCEPTS *529,564*

sustain [*v1*] *keep up, maintain*

aid, approve, assist, back, bankroll, bear, befriend, bolster, brace, buoy, buttress, carry, comfort, confirm, continue, convey, defend, endorse, favor, feed, foster, go for, help, keep alive, keep from falling, keep going, lend a hand*, lug, nourish, nurse, nurture, pack, preserve, prolong, prop, protract, provide for, ratify, relieve, save, shore up, stand by, stick up for, supply, support, tote, transfer, transport, uphold, validate, verify; SEE CONCEPTS *110,140,190*

sustain [*v2*] *endure, experience*

abide, bear, bear up under, bear with, brook, digest, encounter, feel, go, hang in, have, know, live with*, put up with*, see, stand*, stand up to, stomach*, suffer, take it, tolerate, undergo, withstand; SEE CONCEPTS *23,678*

sustenance [*n*] *necessities for existence*

aid, aliment, bacon*, bread*, bread and butter*, comestible, daily bread*, eatables, edibles, food, keep, livelihood, maintenance, nourishment, nutrition, pap*, provender, provision, ration, refreshment, salt*, subsistence, support, victual, wherewithal*; SEE CONCEPTS *340,446,457,709*

svelte [*adj*] *thin and well-built*

graceful, lean, lissom, lithe, slender, slinky, smooth, sylphlike, willowy; SEE CONCEPTS *490,491*

swagger [*v*] *show off; walk pompously*

bluster, boast, brag, brandish, bully, cock, flourish, gasconade, gloat, grandstand*, hector, look big*, lord, parade, parade one's wares*, peacock*, play to the crowd*, pontificate, prance, put on, put on airs*, sashay*, saunter, strut, swank*, swashbuckle*, sway, sweep, swell; SEE CONCEPTS *49,149,716*

swallow [*v1*] *consume*

absorb, belt*, bolt*, chugalug*, devour, dispatch, dispose, down, drink, drop, eat, gobble, gulp, imbibe, ingest, ingurgitate, inhale, put away, quaff, sip, slurp, swig, swill, take, toss*, wash down*, wolf*; SEE CONCEPT *169*

swallow [*v2*] *believe without much thought*
accept, be naive, buy, fall for; SEE CONCEPT *12*

swamp [*n*] *wet land covered with vegetation*
bog, bottoms, everglade, fen, glade, holm, marsh, marshland, mire, moor, morass, mud, muskeg, peat bog, polder, quag, quagmire, slough, swale, swampland; SEE CONCEPT *509*

swamp [*v*] *overwhelm, flood*
beset, besiege, crowd, drench, drown, engulf, inundate, overcrowd, overflow, overload, satiate, saturate, sink, snow*, submerge, submerse, surfeit, swallow up, upset, wash, waterlog*, whelm; SEE CONCEPTS *146,179,641*

swank/swanky [*adj*] *plush, stylish*
chichi*, classy, deluxe, exclusive, expensive, fancy, fashionable, flamboyant, flashy, glamorous, grand, lavish, luxurious, ostentatious, peacocky, plushy, posh, pretentious, rich, ritzy*, sharp, showy, smart, snappy, splashy, sumptuous, tony*, trendy, with-it*; SEE CONCEPT *589*

swap/swop [*v*] *exchange*
bandy, bargain, barter, change, interchange, substitute, switch, trade, traffic, truck; SEE CONCEPT *104*

swarm [*n*] *large, moving group*
army, bevy, blowout, concourse, covey, crowd, crush, drove, flock, herd, horde, host, jam, mass, mob, multitude, myriad, pack, press, push, school, shoal, throng, troop, turnout; SEE CONCEPTS *397,417,432*

swarm [*v*] *move forward as a group*
abound, be alive, be numerous, be overrun, cluster, congregate, crawl, crowd, flock, flow, gather, gather like bees*, jam, mass, mob, move in a crowd, pullulate, rush together, stream, teem, throng; SEE CONCEPTS *113,114,159*

swarthy [*adj*] *dark-complexioned*
black, brown, brunet, dark, dark-hued, darkish, dark-skinned, dusky, exotic, swart, tan, tawny; SEE CONCEPT *618*

swat [*v*] *hit*
beat, belt, biff, box, buffet, clobber, clout, cuff, ding, knock, slap, slug, smack, smash, sock, strike, wallop, whack; SEE CONCEPT *189*

sway [*n*] *strong influence*
amplitude, authority, clout, command, control, dominion, empire, expanse, government, jurisdiction, mastery, might, power, predominance, range, reach, regime, reign, rule, run, scope, sovereignty, spread, stretch, sweep; SEE CONCEPTS *376,686*

sway [*v1*] *move back and forth*
bend, blow hot and cold*, careen, fluctuate, hem and haw*, incline, lean, lurch, oscillate, pendulate, pulsate, rock, roll, stagger, swagger, swing, undulate, vibrate, wave, waver, weave, wobble, yo-yo*; SEE CONCEPTS *13,145,151*

sway [*v2*] *influence, affect*
bias, brainwash, carry, conduct, control, crack*, direct, dispose, dominate, get*, govern, guide, hold sway over, hook, impact on, impress, incline, induce, inspire, lead by the nose*, manage, move, overrule, persuade, predispose, prevail on, put across, reign, rule, rule over, sell*, soften up*, strike, suck in*, touch, turn one's head*, twist one's arm*, whitewash*, win over, work on; SEE CONCEPTS *14,68,117*

swear [*v1*] *declare under oath*
affirm, assert, attest, avow, covenant, cross one's heart*, depend on, depose, give one's word*, give witness, have confidence in, maintain, make an affidavit, pledge oneself, plight, promise, rely on, say so*, state, state under oath, swear by, swear to God*, swear up and down*, take an oath, testify, trust, vouch, vow, warrant; SEE CONCEPT *49*

swear [*v2*] *speak profanely; be vulgar*
bedamn, be foul-mouthed, blaspheme, curse, cuss, execrate, flame*, imprecate, take name in vain*, talk dirty*, use language*, utter profanity; SEE CONCEPTS *52,54*

swearing [*n*] *foul language*
bad language*, blasphemy, cursing, cuss, cussing, dirty language*, dirty name*, dirty talk*, dirty word*, execration, expletives, four-letter word*, imprecation, malediction, no-no*, pardon my French*, profanity, swearword; SEE CONCEPTS *54,276,278*

sweat [*n1*] *body's perspiring*
diaphoresis, excretion, exudation, perspiration, steam, transudation; SEE CONCEPTS *185,467*

sweat [*n2*] *hard work*
backbreaker*, chore, drudgery, effort, grind, labor, moil, slavery, task, toil, travail, work; SEE CONCEPTS *362,677*

sweat [*v1*] *perspire*
break out in a sweat, drip, eject, exude, glow, ooze, secrete, seep, spout, swelter, transude, wilt; SEE CONCEPT *185*

sweat [*v2*] *worry about; bear*
abide, agonize, be on pins and needles*, be on tenterhooks*, brook, chafe, endure, exert, fret, go, labor, lose sleep over*, stand, stay the course*, stick it out*, stomach*, suffer, take, toil, tolerate, torture, work hard; SEE CONCEPTS *23,35*

sweaty [*adj*] *damp with perspiration*
bathed, clammy, covered with sweat, drenched, dripping, drippy, glowing, hot, moist, perspiring, perspiry, soaked, sticky, stinky, sweating, wet; SEE CONCEPT *406*

sweep [*n1*] *range, extent*
ambit, breadth, compass, extension, latitude, length, orbit, purview, radius, reach, region, scope, span, stretch, vista; SEE CONCEPTS *651,756,787*

sweep [*n2*] *movement*
arc, bend, course, curve, gesture, move, play, progress, stroke, swing; SEE CONCEPTS *145,748*

sweep [v1] *brush off, away*
broom, brush, brush up, clean, clear, clear up, mop, ready, remove, scrub, tidy, vacuum; SEE CONCEPT *165*

sweep [v2] *fly, glide*
career, fleet, flit, flounce, glance, hurtle, pass, sail, scud, skim, tear, wing, zoom; SEE CONCEPTS *150,152*

sweeping [adj] *wide-ranging*
across-the-board, all-around, all-embracing, all-encompassing, all-inclusive, all-out, bird's-eye*, blanket, broad, complete, comprehensive, exaggerated, exhaustive, extensive, full, general, global, inclusive, indiscriminate, out-and-out*, overall, overdrawn, overstated, radical, thorough, thoroughgoing, unqualified, vast, wall-to-wall*, whole-hog*, wholesale*, wide; SEE CONCEPTS *531,772*

sweet [n] *sugary food*
bonbon, candy, chocolate, confection, confectionery, confiture, delight, dessert, enjoyment, final course, gratification, joy, pleasure, pudding, snack, sugarplum, sweetmeat; SEE CONCEPTS *457,461*

sweet [adj1] *sugary*
candied, candy-coated, cloying, delicious, honeyed, like candy, like honey, like sugar, luscious, nectarous, saccharine, sugar-coated, sugared, sweetened, syrupy, toothsome; SEE CONCEPTS *462,613*

sweet [adj2] *friendly, kind*
affectionate, agreeable, amiable, angelic, appealing, attractive, beautiful, beloved, charming, cherished, companionable, considerate, darling, dear, dearest, delectable, delicious, delightful, dulcet, engaging, fair, generous, gentle, good-humored, good-natured, heavenly, lovable, loving, luscious, mild, mushy, patient, pet, pleasant, pleasing, precious, reasonable, saccharine, sweet-tempered, sympathetic, taking, tender, thoughtful, treasured, unselfish, winning, winsome; SEE CONCEPTS *401,404,542*

sweet [adj3] *nice-smelling*
ambrosial, aromal, aromatic, balmy, clean, fragrant, fresh, new, perfumed, perfumy, pure, redolent, savory, scented, spicy, sweet-smelling, wholesome; SEE CONCEPT *598*

sweet [adj4] *nice-sounding*
dulcet, euphonic, euphonious, harmonious, mellifluous, mellow, melodic, melodious, musical, orotund, rich, rotund, silver-tongued, silvery, smooth, soft, sonorous, soothing, sweet-sounding, tuneful; SEE CONCEPT *594*

sweeten [v1] *add sugar*
add sweetening, candy, candy-coat, honey, make sweet, make toothsome, mull, sugar, sugar-coat; SEE CONCEPT *170*

sweeten [v2] *make happy; appease*
alleviate, assuage, conciliate, mollify, pacify, placate, propitiate, soften up, soothe; SEE CONCEPTS *7,22*

sweetheart [n] *person whom another loves*
admirer, beau, beloved, boyfriend, companion, darling, dear, dear one, flame, girlfriend, heartthrob, honey, inamorata, inamorato, love, lovebird, lover, one and only*, paramour, pet, significant other, steady, suitor, swain, sweet, treasure*, truelove, valentine; SEE CONCEPTS *414,423*

swell [n] *large increase, flow*
billow, crescendo, growth, ripple, rise, seat, surf, surge, undulation, uprise, wave; SEE CONCEPT *780*

swell [adj] *wonderful*
awesome, cool*, dandy, deluxe, desirable, excellent, exclusive, fashionable, fine, fly*, grand, groovy*, keen, marvelous, neat, nifty, plush, posh, ritzy*, smart, stylish, super, terrific; SEE CONCEPTS *548,574*

swell [v] *become larger*
accumulate, add to, aggravate, amplify, augment, balloon, become bloated, become distended, become swollen, be inflated, belly, billow, blister, bloat, bulge, dilate, distend, enhance, enlarge, expand, extend, fatten, fill out, grow, grow larger, heighten, increase, intensity, mount, plump, pouch, pout, protrude, puff, puff up, rise, round out, surge, tumefy, uprise, well up; SEE CONCEPTS *236,245,780*

swelling [n] *physical growth; lump*
abscess, blister, boil, bruise, bulge, bump, bunion, carbuncle, contusion, corn, dilation, distention, enlargement, hump, increase, inflammation, injury, knob, knurl, node, nodule, pimple, pock, protuberance, puff, puffiness, pustule, ridge, sore, tumescence, tumor, wale, wart, weal, welt; SEE CONCEPTS *306,309*

sweltering [adj] *very hot*
airless, baking, broiling, burning, close, fiery, humid, oppressive, perspiring, scorching, sizzling, stewing, sticky, stifling, stuffy, sultry, sweaty, sweltry, torrid; SEE CONCEPT *605*

swerve [v] *turn aside, often to avoid collision*
bend, deflect, depart, depart from, deviate, dip, diverge, err, get off course, go off course, incline, lurch, move, sheer, sheer off, shift, sideslip, sidestep, skew, skid, slue, stray, swing, tack, train off, turn, veer, wander, waver, wind; SEE CONCEPTS *150,195,201*

swift [adj] *very fast*
abrupt, alacritous, barrelling, breakneck, cracking*, double-quick*, expeditious, express, fleet, fleet-footed*, flying, hasty, headlong, hurried, in nothing flat*, like crazy*, like mad*, nimble, on the double*, precipitate, prompt, pronto, quick, rapid, ready, screaming, shake a leg*, short, short-lived, snappy*, spanking*, speedball*, speedy, sudden, supersonic, unexpected, winged; SEE CONCEPTS *588,799*

swiftly/swift [adv] *very fast*
apace, double-quick*, expeditiously, flat-out*, fleetly, full tilt*, hastily, hurriedly, in no time*, posthaste, promptly, quick, quickly, rapidly, speedily, without losing time*, without warning*; SEE CONCEPTS *588,799*

swim [v] *make way through water using arms, legs*
bathe, breast-stroke, crawl, dive, dog paddle, float, freestyle, glide, go for a swim, go swimming, go-

wading, high-dive, move, paddle, practice, race, skinny-dip, slip, stroke, submerge, take a dip, wade; SEE CONCEPT *363*

swimmingly [*adv*] *very well*
as planned, cosily, easily, effectively, effortlessly, favorably, fortunately, happily, like a dream*, like clockwork*, prosperously, quickly, satisfyingly, smoothly, successfully, well, with flying colors*, with no trouble, without a hitch*; SEE CONCEPTS *528,544*

swindle [*n*] *cheating, stealing*
blackmail, cheat, con, crooked deal*, deceit, deception, dirty pool*, double-cross*, double-dealing*, extortion, fake, fast one*, fast shuffle*, frame-up, fraud, gyp, hoax, hustle, imposition, imposture, knavery, racket*, rip-off*, roguery, scam, sell, shady deal*, shakedown, sham, sharp practice*, shell game*, sting, trick, trickery; SEE CONCEPTS *59,139,192*

swindle [*v*] *cheat, steal*
bamboozle, beat*, bilk, clip*, con*, cozen, deceive, defraud, diddle*, do*, dupe, extort, fleece*, flim-flam*, fool, frame*, fudge*, gouge*, gull*, gyp*, hoodwink, overcharge, pluck, pull a fast one*, put one over on*, rip off*, rogue*, rook, run a game on*, sandbag, scam, sell a bill of goods*, set up, shaft, stiff*, sting*, sucker, take for a ride*, take to the cleaners*, trick, trim*, victimize; SEE CONCEPTS *59,139,192*

swindler [*n*] *person who cheats another*
absconder, charlatan, cheat, cheater, chiseler, clip, confidence man/woman, con man/woman, counterfeiter, crook, deceiver, defrauder, dodger, double-dealer, falsifier, forger, four-flusher*, fraud, gouger, grifter, gyp, impostor, knave, mechanic, mountebank, operator, rascal, rogue, rook, scammer, scoundrel, shark, sharp, sharper, slicker, thief, trickster; SEE CONCEPT *412*

swing [*n*] *moving back and forth*
beat, cadence, cadency, fluctuation, lilt, measure, meter, motion, oscillation, rhythm, stroke, sway, swaying, tempo, undulation, vibration; SEE CONCEPTS *65,748*

swing [*v*] *move back and forth; be suspended*
avert, away, be pendent, curve, dangle, deflect, divert, flap, fluctuate, hang, lurch, oscillate, palpitate, pendulate, pitch, pivot, reel, revolve, rock, roll, rotate, sheer, shunt, suspend, sway, swerve, swivel, turn, turn about, turn on an axis, twirl, undulate, vary, veer, vibrate, volte-face, wag, waggle, wave, wheel, whirl, wiggle, wobble; SEE CONCEPT *145*

swipe [*n/v1*] *hit*
bash, blow, clip, clout, clump, cuff, knock, lash out, lick, rap, slap, smack, sock, strike, swat, wallop, wipe; SEE CONCEPT *189*

swipe [*v2*] *steal*
appropriate, cop, filch, heist, hook, lift, make off with, nab, nick, pilfer, pinch, purloin, sneak, snitch; SEE CONCEPT *139*

swirl [*v*] *spin around*
agitate, boil, churn, coil, crimp, crisp, curl, eddy, purl, roil, roll, snake, surge, swoosh, twirl, whirl, whirlpool, whorl, wriggle; SEE CONCEPTS *145,738*

swish [*adj*] *fashionable, elegant*
classy, deluxe, exclusive, grand, in, plush, posh*, ritzy*, smart, stylish, sumptuous, swank, swell, tony*, trendy, with-it*; SEE CONCEPT *589*

switch [*n*] *change, exchange*
about-face, alteration, change of direction, reversal, shift, substitution, swap, transformation; SEE CONCEPT *697*

switch [*v*] *change, exchange*
change course, convert, deflect, deviate, divert, interchange, rearrange, replace, shift, shunt, sidetrack, substitute, swap, trade, turn, turnabout, turn aside, veer; SEE CONCEPTS *104,232,697*

swivel [*v*] *spin around axis*
hinge, pirouette, pivot, revolve, rotate, swing around, turn, whirl; SEE CONCEPT *145*

swollen [*adj*] *enlarged*
bloated, bulgy, distended, distent, inflamed, inflated, puffed, puffy, tumescent, tumid; SEE CONCEPT *485*

swoop [*v*] *descend quickly*
dive, fall, plummet, plunge, pounce, rush, slide, stoop, sweep; SEE CONCEPTS *150,181*

sycophant [*n*] *person who caters to another*
adulator, backscratcher*, backslapper*, bootlicker*, brownnoser*, doormat*, fan, fawner, flatterer, flunky*, groupie*, groveler, handshaker*, hanger-on*, lackey, minion, parasite, politician, puppet, slave, yes-man; SEE CONCEPT *423*

symbol [*n*] *letter, character, sign of written communication*
attribute, badge, denotation, design, device, emblem, figure, image, indication, logo, mark, motif, note, numeral, pattern, regalia, representation, stamp, token, type; SEE CONCEPT *284*

symbolic [*adj*] *representative*
allegorical, characteristic, denotative, emblematic, figurative, indicative, indicatory, significant, suggestive, symptomatic, token, typical; SEE CONCEPT *267*

symbolize [*v*] *represent; stand for*
betoken, body forth, connote, denote, emblematize, embody, epitomize, exemplify, express, illustrate, indicate, mean, mirror, personify, show, signify, suggest, symbol, typify; SEE CONCEPTS *74,138,682*

symmetrical [*adj*] *well-proportioned*
balanced, commensurable, commensurate, equal, in proportion, proportional, regular, shapely, well-formed; SEE CONCEPTS *480,485,579*

symmetry [*n*] *proportion*
agreement, arrangement, balance, centrality, conformity, correspondence, equality, equilibrium, equipoise, equivalence, evenness, finish, form, harmony, order, proportionality, regularity, rhythm, shapeliness, similarity; SEE CONCEPTS *716,717*

sympathetic [*adj1*] *concerned, feeling*
affectionate, all heart*, appreciating, benign, benignant, caring, commiserating, compassionate, comprehending, condoling, considerate, heart in right place*, interested, kind, kindhearted, kindly, loving, pitying, responsive, sensitive, soft, softhearted*, supportive, sympathizing, tender, thoughtful, understanding, vicarious, warm, warmhearted*; SEE CONCEPT *542*

sympathetic [*adj2*] *agreeable, friendly*
amenable, appreciative, approving, companionable, compatible, congenial, congruous, consistent, consonant, cool, down, encouraging, favorably disposed, having a heart*, in sympathy with, likeminded, on same wavelength*, open, open-minded, pro, receptive, responsive, simpatico, tuned in*, vicarious, well-disposed, well-intentioned; SEE CONCEPTS *401,542,563*

sympathize [*v*] *feel for, be compassionate*
ache, agree, appreciate, be in accord, be in sympathy, be kind to, be there for*, be understanding, bleed for*, comfort, commiserate, compassionate, comprehend, condole, emphathize, feel heart go out to*, go along with, grieve with, have compassion, identify with, love, offer consolation, pick up on, pity, share another's sorrow, show kindliness, show mercy, show tenderness, side with*, tune in*, understand; SEE CONCEPTS *34,110*

sympathy [*n1*] *shared feeling*
accord, affinity, agreement, alliance, attraction, benignancy, close relation, commiseration, compassion, concord, congeniality, connection, correspondence, empathy, feelings, fellow feeling, grandstand play*, harmony, heart, kindliness, kindness, mutual attraction, mutual fondness, rapport, responsiveness, sensitivity, tenderness, understanding, union, unity, warmheartedness, warmth; SEE CONCEPTS *388,410,664*

sympathy [*n2*] *pity*
aid, cheer, comfort, commiseration, compassion, condolence, consolation, empathy, encouragement, reassurance, rue, ruth, solace, tenderness, thoughtfulness, understanding; SEE CONCEPTS *410,633*

symptom [*n*] *sign of illness or problem*
evidence, expression, index, indication, indicia, manifestation, mark, note, significant, syndrome, token, warning; SEE CONCEPTS *306,316*

syndicate [*n*] *group of business entities*
association, board, bunch, cabinet, cartel, chain, chamber, combine, committee, company, conglomerate, council, crew, gang, group, megacorp*, mob, multinational*, organization, outfit, partnership, pool, ring, trust, union; SEE CONCEPTS *323,325*

syndrome [*n*] *disease, condition*
affection, ailment, complaint, complex, diagnostics, disorder, infirmity, malady, problem, prognostics, sickness, sign, symptoms; SEE CONCEPTS *306,316,674*

synonymous [*adj*] *equivalent*
alike, apposite, coincident, compatible, convertible, correspondent, corresponding, equal, identical, identified, interchangeable, like, one and the same, same, similar, synonymic, tantamount; SEE CONCEPTS *487,573*

synopsis [*n*] *digest, summary*
abridgment, abstract, aperçu, breviary, brief, capsule, compendium, condensation, conspectus, epitome, outline, précis, recap*, résumé, review, rundown, run-through, short and sweet*, sketch; SEE CONCEPT *283*

synthesis [*n*] *combining; combination*
amalgam, amalgamation, blend, building a whole, coalescence, composite, compound, constructing, construction, entirety, forming, fusion, integrating, integration, making one, organism, organization, structure, unification, union, unit, welding, whole; SEE CONCEPTS *113,837*

synthesize [*v*] *combine; make whole*
amalgamate, arrange, blend, harmonize, incorporate, integrate, manufacture, orchestrate, symphonize, unify; SEE CONCEPTS *113,205*

synthetic [*adj*] *artificial*
constructed, counterfeit, ersatz*, fabricated, factitious, fake, false, hokey*, made, makeshift, manmade, manufactured, mock, phony, plastic, unnatural; SEE CONCEPTS *485,582*

system [*n1*] *order, whole*
arrangement, classification, combination, complex, conformity, coordination, entity, fixed order, frame of reference, ideology, integral, integrate, logical order, orderliness, organization, philosophy, red tape*, regularity, rule, scheme, setup, structure, sum, theory, totality; SEE CONCEPTS *770,837*

system [*n2*] *method, plan*
arrangement, artifice, course of action, custom, definite plan, fashion, logical process, manner, methodicalness, methodology, mode, modus, modus operandi, operation, orderliness, orderly process, pattern, policy, practice, procedure, proceeding, process, regularity, routine, scheme, strategy, structure, systematic process, systematization, tactics, technique, theory, usage, way, wise; SEE CONCEPT *6*

systematic [*adj*] *orderly*
analytical, arranged, businesslike, complete, efficient, logical, methodic, methodical, ordered, organized, out-and-out*, precise, regular, standardized, systematized, thoroughgoing, well-ordered; SEE CONCEPTS *557,585*

systematize [*v*] *put in order*
arrange, array, contrive, design, devise, dispose, establish, frame, get act together, institute, make uniform, marshal, methodize, order, organize, plan, project, pull together, rationalize, regulate, schematize, shape up, standardize, straighten up, systemize, tighten up; SEE CONCEPTS *84,94*

T

tab [n1] *ticket, label*
bookmark, clip, flag, flap, holder, logo, loop, marker, slip, sticker, stop, strip, tag; SEE CONCEPTS *270,475*

tab [n2] *bill for service*
account, charge, check, cost, invoice, price, price tag, rate, reckoning, score, statement, tariff; SEE CONCEPT *329*

table [n1] *furniture upon which to work, eat*
bar, bench, board, buffet, bureau, console, counter, desk, dining table, dinner table, dresser, lectern, pulpit, sideboard, sink, slab, stand, wagon; SEE CONCEPT *443*

table [n2] *meal*
bill of fare, board, cuisine, diet, fare, food, meat and drink, menu, spread, victuals; SEE CONCEPT *459*

table [n3] *flatland*
flat, mesa, plain, plateau, tableland, upland; SEE CONCEPT *509*

table [n4] *diagram with columns of information*
agenda, appendix, canon, catalogue, chart, compendium, digest, graph, illustration, index, inventory, list, plan, record, register, roll, schedule, statistics, summary, synopsis, table of contents, tabulation; SEE CONCEPTS *283,625*

table [v] *postpone a proposition*
cool*, defer, delay, enter, hang*, hold off, hold up, move, pigeonhole*, propose, put aside, put forward, put off, put on back burner*, put on hold, put on ice*, put on the shelf*, shelve, submit, suggest; SEE CONCEPTS *121,324*

tableau [n] *scene, often painted*
illustration, picture, representation, spectacle, view; SEE CONCEPTS *625,716*

tablet [n1] *sheaf of papers that are connected*
book, folder, memo pad, notebook, pad, quire, ream, scratch, scratch pad, sheets; SEE CONCEPT *475*

tablet [n2] *encapsulated medicine*
cake, capsule, dose, lozenge, medicine, pellet, pill, square, troche; SEE CONCEPT *307*

taboo [n] *something not allowed, permitted*
anathema, ban, disapproval, don't*, forbiddance, inhibition, interdict, law, limitation, no-no*, prohibition, proscription, regulation, religious convention, reservation, restraint, restriction, sanction, social convention, stricture, superstition, thou-shalt-not*; SEE CONCEPTS *532,687*

taboo [adj] *not allowed, permitted*
anathema, banned, beyond the pale*, disapproved, forbidden, frowned on*, illegal, off limits*, outlawed, out of bounds*, prohibited, proscribed, reserved, restricted, ruled out, unacceptable, unmentionable, unthinkable; SEE CONCEPT *548*

tabulate [v] *figure, classify*
alphabetize, arrange, catalogue, categorize, chart, codify, digest, enumerate, formulate, grade, index, list, methodize, order, range, register, systematize, tabularize; SEE CONCEPTS *84,764*

tacit [adj] *taken for granted; not said aloud*
alluded to, allusive, assumed, hinted at, implicit, implied, inarticulate, indirect, inferred, intimated, silent, suggested, undeclared, understood, unexpressed, unsaid, unspoken, unstated, unvoiced, wordless; SEE CONCEPTS *529,548*

taciturn [adj] *uncommunicative*
aloof, antisocial, brooding, clammed up*, close, close-mouthed*, cold, curt, distant, dour, dried-up*, dumb, laconic, mum, mute, quiet, reserved, reticent, sententious, silent, sparing, speechless, tight-lipped*, unexpressive, unforthcoming, withdrawn; SEE CONCEPTS *267,401*

tack [n1] *course of movement*
aim, alteration, approach, bearing, bend, deflection, deviation, digression, direction, double, echelon, heading, line, method, oblique course, path, plan, point of sail, procedure, set, shift, siding, sidling, sweep, swerve, switch, tactic, tangent, turn, variation, way, yaw, zigzag; SEE CONCEPTS *692,738*

tack [n2] *short pin for attaching*
brad, nail, point, pushpin, staple, thumbtack; SEE CONCEPT *475*

tack [v] *attach*
add, affix, annex, append, baste, fasten, fix, hem, mount, nail, paste, pin, sew, staple, stitch, tag, tie; SEE CONCEPTS *85,160,218*

tackle [n] *equipment for activity*
accouterment, apparatus, appliance, gear, goods, habiliments, hook, impedimenta, implements, line, machinery, materiel, outfit, paraphernalia, rig, rigging, tools, trappings; SEE CONCEPT *496*

tackle [v1] *make an effort*
accept, apply oneself, attack, attempt, bang away at*, begin, come to grips with*, deal with, devote oneself to, embark upon, engage in, essay, give a try*, give a whirl*, go for it*, launch, make a run at*, pitch into, set about, square off*, start the ball rolling*, take a shot at*, take in hand*, take on, take up, try, try on for size*, turn one's hand to*, turn to, undertake, work on; SEE CONCEPTS *87,100*

tackle [v2] *jump on and grab*
attack, block, bring down, bring to the ground*, catch, challenge, clutch, confront, down, grapple, grasp, halt, intercept, nail, put the freeze on*, sack, seize, smear, stop, take, take hold of, throw, throw down, upset; SEE CONCEPTS *90,164,191*

tacky [adj] *cheap, tasteless*
broken-down, crude, dilapidated, dingy*, dowdy, down-at-heel*, faded, frumpy*, gaudy, inelegant, mangy*, messy, nasty*, outmoded, out-of-date, poky*, ratty, run-down, seedy*, shabby*, shoddy*, sleazy*, sloppy*, slovenly, stodgy, threadbare, unbecoming, unkempt, unstylish, unsuitable, untidy, vulgar; SEE CONCEPTS *485,589*

tact [n] *finesse, thoughtfulness*
acumen, acuteness, address, adroitness, amenity, aptness, care, common sense, consideration, control, courtesy, delicacy, delicatesse, diplomacy, discernment, discretion, discrimination, gallantry, good taste, head, horse sense*, intelligence, judgment, penetration, perception, perspicacity, poise, policy, politicness, presence, prudence, refinement, repose, savoir-faire, sensitivity, skill, smoothness, suavity, subtlety, tactfulness, understanding, urbanity; SEE CONCEPT *633*

tactful [adj] *thoughtful, careful*
adroit, aware, cautious, civil, considerate, courteous, deft, delicate, diplomatic, discreet, gentle, judicious, observant, perceptive, poised, polished, polite, politic, prudent, sensitive, skilled, skillful, statesmanlike, suave, subtle, sympathetic, tactical, understanding, urbane, wise; SEE CONCEPT *401*

tactics [n] *strategy*
approach, campaign, channels, course, defense, device, disposition, generalship, line, maneuver, maneuvering, means, method, move, plan, plan of attack, ploy, policy, procedure, red tape*, scheme, stratagem, system, tack, technique, trick, way; SEE CONCEPT *660*

tactless [adj] *unthinking, careless*
awkward, blundering, boorish, brash, bungling, clumsy, crude, discourteous, gauche, gruff, harsh, hasty, impolite, impolitic, imprudent, inconsiderate, indelicate, indiscreet, inept, injudicious, insensitive, maladroit, misunderstanding, rash, rough, rude, sharp, stupid, thoughtless, uncivil, unconsiderate, undiplomatic, unfeeling, unkind, unperceptive, unpolished, unsubtle, unsympathetic, untactful, vulgar; SEE CONCEPT *401*

tag [n] *label, ticket*
badge, button, card, check, chip, docket, emblem, flap, ID*, identification, inscription, insignia, logo, mark, marker, motto, note, pin, slip, stamp, sticker, stub, tab, tally, trademark, voucher; SEE CONCEPTS *270,284,475*

tag [v1] *label; attach label*
add, adjoin, affix, annex, append, call, check, christen, designate, docket, dub, earmark, fasten, hold, identify, mark, name, nickname, style, tack, tally, tap, term, ticket, title, touch; SEE CONCEPTS *62,85,160*

tag [v2] *follow*
accompany, attend, bedog, chase, dog, heel, hunt, pursue, shadow, tail, trace, track, track down, trail; SEE CONCEPT *207*

tail [n] *end piece, part*
appendage, behind, butt*, buttocks, caudal appendage, conclusion, empennage, end, extremity, fag end*, hind end, hindmost part, hind part, last part, posterior, rear, rear end, reverse, rudder, rump*, stub, tag, tag end, tailpiece, train, tush*, wagger*; SEE CONCEPTS *392,825,827*

tail [v] *follow*
bedog, dog*, eye*, hound*, keep an eye on, pursue, shadow, stalk, tag, track, trail; SEE CONCEPT *207*

tailor/tailoress [n] *person who sews clothing*
clothier, costumier, couturier, dressmaker, garment maker, needle worker*, outfitter, seamstress, suit maker; SEE CONCEPT *348*

tailor [v] *make to fit; adjust*
accommodate, adapt, alter, conform, convert, custom-make, cut, cut to fit, dovetail*, fashion, fit, make to order, modify, mold, quadrate, reconcile, shape, shape up, square, style, suit, tailor-make; SEE CONCEPTS *126,202,218*

taint [n] *contamination, corruption*
black mark, blemish, blot, contagion, defect, disgrace, dishonor, fault, flaw, infection, pollution, shame, smear, spot, stain, stigma; SEE CONCEPTS *230,388*

taint [v] *dirty, contaminate; ruin*
adulterate, besmirch, blacken, blemish, blight, blot, blur, brand, break down, cast a slur, cloud, cook, corrupt, crud up, crumble, cut, damage, debase, decay, decompose, defile, deprave, discolor, discredit, disgrace, dishonor, disintegrate, doctor, foul, give a bad name*, harm, hurt, infect, muddy, poison, pollute, putrefy, rot, shame, smear, soil, spike, spoil, stain, stigmatize, sully, tar, tarnish, trash, turn, water, water down; SEE CONCEPTS *246,254,384*

take [n] *profit*
booty*, catch, catching, cut, gate, haul*, holding, part, proceeds, receipts, return, returns, revenue, share, takings, yield; SEE CONCEPT *344*

take [v1] *get; help oneself to*
abduct, accept, acquire, arrest, attain, capture, carry off, carve out, catch, clasp, clutch, collar*, collect, earn, ensnare, entrap, gain possession, gather up, get hold of, grab, grasp, grip, handle, haul in, have, hold, lay hold of, obtain, overtake, pick up, prehend, pull in, reach, reap, receive, secure, seize, snag, snatch, strike, take hold of, take in, win; SEE CONCEPTS *120,142*

take [v2] *steal*
abduct, abstract, accroach, annex, appropriate, arrogate, borrow, carry off, commandeer, confiscate, expropriate, filch*, haul in, liberate, lift*, misappropriate, nab*, nail*, nip*, pick up, pinch*, pluck, pocket*, preempt, pull in, purloin, rip off*, run off with*, salvage, seize, sequester, snag, snare, snatch*, snitch*, swipe*, take in; SEE CONCEPT *139*

take [v3] *buy; reserve*
book, borrow, charter, choose, cull, decide on, derive, draw, elect, engage, gain, get, hire, lease, mark, obtain, optate, opt for, pay for, pick, prefer, procure, purchase, rent, select, single out; SEE CONCEPTS *41,327*

take [v4] *endure*
abide, accept, accommodate, bear, bear with, brave, brook, contain, give access, go, go through, grin and

bear it*, hack*, hang in*, hang on*, hang tough*, hold, let in, live with, put up with, receive, ride out*, stand, stand for, stick it out*, stomach, submit to, suffer, swallow, take it, take lying down*, take on the chin*, tolerate, undergo, weather, welcome, withstand; SEE CONCEPT 23

take [v5] *consume*
devour, down, drink, eat, feed, feed on, imbibe, ingest, inhale, meal, partake of, swallow; SEE CONCEPT 169

take [v6] *accept, adopt; use*
accommodate, admit, appropriate, assume, be aware of, behave, bring, deal with, delight in, do, effect, enjoy, enter upon, execute, exercise, exert, experience, function, give access, have, include, let in, like, luxuriate in, make, observe, operate, perform, play, practice, put in practice, react, receive, relish, sense, serve, take in, treat, undertake, utilize, welcome, work; SEE CONCEPTS 100,124,225

take [v7] *understand*
accept, apprehend, assume, be aware of, believe, catch, compass, comprehend, consider, deem, expect, experience, feel, follow, gather, grasp, hold, imagine, interpret as, know, look upon, observe, perceive, presume, receive, reckon, regard, see, see as, sense, suppose, suspect, take in, think, think of as; SEE CONCEPT 15

take [v8] *win; be successful*
beat, be efficacious, do the trick, have effect, operate, prevail, succeed, triumph, work; SEE CONCEPT 706

take [v9] *carry, transport; accompany*
attend, back, bear, bring, buck, cart, conduct, convey, convoy, drive, escort, ferry, fetch, go with, guide, gun, haul, heel, jag, journey, lead, lug, move, pack, piggyback*, pilot, ride, schlepp*, shoulder, steer, tote, tour, trek, truck, usher; SEE CONCEPTS 114,187,217

take [v10] *captivate, enchant*
allure, attract, become popular, bewitch, charm, delight, draw, entertain, fascinate, magnetize, overwhelm, please, wile, win favor; SEE CONCEPT 11

take [v11] *require*
ask, call for, crave, demand, necessitate, need; SEE CONCEPT 646

take [v12] *subtract*
deduct, discount, draw back, eliminate, knock off, remove, subtract, take away, take off, take out; SEE CONCEPTS 211,236,247

take [v13] *cheat, deceive*
bamboozle*, beat*, bilk, con, cozen, defraud, do*, dupe, fiddle, flimflam*, gull, gyp*, hoodwink, pull a fast one*, swindle, take for a ride*, trick; SEE CONCEPTS 59,192

take [v14] *contract, catch*
be seized, come down with*, derive, draw, get, sicken with, take sick with; SEE CONCEPT 308

take down [v1] *write down*
inscribe, jot down, make a note of, minute, note, note down, put on record, record, set down, transcribe; SEE CONCEPT 125

take down [v2] *humble*
deflate, humiliate, let down, lower, mortify, pull down, put down, take apart; SEE CONCEPTS 7,19,52

take in [v1] *deceive, fool*
beguile, betray, bilk, bluff, cheat, con*, defraud, delude, do*, double-cross*, dupe, flimflam*, fourflush*, gull, hoodwink, lie, mislead, pull wool over eyes*, swindle, trick; SEE CONCEPT 59

take in [v2] *understand*
absorb, assimilate, comprehend, digest, get, grasp, perceive, receive, savvy, see, soak up, take; SEE CONCEPT 15

takeoff [n1] *leaving*
ascent, climb, departure, hop, jump, launch, liftoff, rise, upward flight; SEE CONCEPTS 148,195,224

takeoff [n2] *mockery, satire*
burlesque, caricature, cartoon, comedy, imitation, lampoon, mocking, parody, ridicule, send-up, spoof, travesty; SEE CONCEPTS 111,263,292

take off [v1] *leave; leave the ground*
ascend, bear, beat it, become airborne, begone, blast off, blow*, clear out*, decamp, depart, disappear, exit, get off, get out, go, go away, head, hightail*, hit the road*, hit the trail*, lift off, light out*, make*, pull out, quit, scram*, set out*, shove off*, soar, split, take to the air*, vamoose*, withdraw; SEE CONCEPTS 148,195,224

take off [v2] *mock, satirize*
ape, burlesque, caricature, imitate, lampoon, mimic, parody, ridicule, send up, spoof, travesty; SEE CONCEPTS 111,273,292

take on [v1] *assume, accept*
acquire, add, address oneself to, adopt, agree to do, annex, append, attempt, become, begin, come to have, commence, develop, embrace, employ, endeavor, engage, enlist, enroll, espouse, handle, have a go at*, hire, launch, put on, retain, set about, tackle, take in hand*, take up, take upon oneself*, try, turn, undertake, venture; SEE CONCEPTS 87,221

take on [v2] *compete*
attack, battle, contend, contest, encounter, engage, face, fight, match, meet, oppose, pit, vie; SEE CONCEPT 92

take up [v] *begin or start again*
adopt, assume, become involved in, carry on, commence, continue, embrace, engage in, enter, espouse, follow through, get off, go on, initiate, kick off, open, pick up, proceed, recommence, renew, reopen, restart, resume, set to, start, tackle, take on, tee off, undertake; SEE CONCEPTS 221,239

tale [n1] *story*
account, anecdote, fable, fairy tale, fiction, folk tale, legend, myth, narration, narrative, novel, relation,

report, romance, saga, short story, yarn*; SEE CONCEPT 282

tale [n2] *made-up story*
canard, chestnut*, clothesline*, defamation, detraction, exaggeration, fabrication, falsehood, falsity, fib, fiction, lie, misrepresentation, prevarication, rigmarole*, rumor, scandal, slander, spiel*, tall story*, untruism, untruth, yarn*; SEE CONCEPTS 278,282

talent [n] *ability*
aptitude, aptness, art, a way with*, bent*, capability, capacity, craft, endowment, expertise, facility, faculty, flair, forte, genius, gift, green thumb*, head*, inventiveness, knack*, know-how*, nose*, power, savvy*, set, skill, smarts*, the formula*, the goods*, the right stuff*, thing*, turn*, what it takes*; SEE CONCEPT 630

talk [n1] *speech, address to group*
allocution, chalk talk*, declamation, descant, discourse, disquisition, dissertation, epilogue, exhortation, expatiation, harangue, homily, lecture, monologue, oration, peroration, prelection, recitation, screed, sermon, spiel*; SEE CONCEPTS 60,285

talk [n2] *gossip*
allusion, badinage, banter, blather*, bombast, bunk*, buzz*, cant, chat, chatter, chitchat, conversation, cry, gab, grapevine*, hearsay, hint, hot air*, idle talk, innuendo, insinuation, jaw*, jive*, lip*, noise, nonsense*, on-dit*, palaver, persiflage, prose, racket*, raillery, report, rot*, rubbish*, rumble*, rumor, scuttlebutt*, small talk, tête-à-tête*, trash*, yarn*; SEE CONCEPTS 51,278

talk [n3] *discussion*
argument, colloquy, conclave, confabulation, conference, consultation, conversation, deliberation, dialogue, earful, encounter, eyeball-to-eyeball*, huddle*, interlocution, interview, meeting, negotiation, palaver, parlance, parley, powwow*, seminar, spiel*, straight talk, symposium, ventilation, visit; SEE CONCEPT 56

talk [n4] *communication with language*
argot, chatter, dialect, discourse, jargon, lingo, locution, nasalization, parlance, patois, slang, speaking, speech, utterance, verbalization, words; SEE CONCEPTS 47,65

talk [v1] *produce words; inform*
articulate, babble, broach, chant, chat, chatter, comment on, communicate, confess, converse, describe, divulge, drawl, drone, express, flap one's tongue*, gab, gabble*, give voice to, gossip, influence, intone, notify, palaver, parley, patter, persuade, prate, prattle*, pronounce, reveal, rhapsodize, run on*, say, sing*, soliloquize, speak, spill the beans*, spout, squeak*, squeal*, talk one's leg off*, tell, tell all*, use, utter, ventriloquize, verbalize, voice, yak*; SEE CONCEPTS 60,266

talk [v2] *discuss with another*
argue, be in contact, canvass, carry on conversation, chew*, collogue, commune, confabulate, confer,

confide, consult, contact, deliberate, dialogue, engage in conversation, exchange, go into a huddle*, groupthink*, have a meet*, hold discussion, huddle*, interact, interface, interview, join in conversation, keep in touch, negotiate, network, palaver, parley, reach out, reason, relate, thrash out*, touch*, touch base*, vent, visit; SEE CONCEPT 56

talk [v3] *address group*
accost, deliver a speech, discourse, give a talk, give speech, harangue, hold forth, induce, influence, lecture, orate, persuade, pitch, prelect, sermonize, speak, spiel*, spout*, stump*, sway*; SEE CONCEPTS 60,285

talkative [adj] *excessively communicative*
articulate, big-mouthed*, chattering, chatty*, effusive, eloquent, fluent, full of hot air*, gabby*, garrulous, glib, gossipy, long-winded*, loose-lipped*, loquacious, loudmouthed*, mouthy*, multiloquent, prolix, rattling, slick*, smooth*, talky, verbal, verbose, vocal, voluble, windy*, wordy; SEE CONCEPT 267

tall [adj1] *high in stature, length*
alpine, altitudinous, beanstalk*, big, elevated, giant, great, high-reaching, lank, lanky, lofty, rangy, sky-high, skyscraping, soaring, stick*, towering; SEE CONCEPTS 779,782

tall [adj2] *exaggerated, unreasonable*
absurd, demanding, difficult, embellished, exorbitant, farfetched, hard, implausible, impossible, outlandish, overblown, preposterous, steep, unbelievable; SEE CONCEPTS 529,565

tally [n] *count, record*
account, mark, poll, reckoning, running total, score, summation, tab, total; SEE CONCEPTS 283,786

tally [v] *add up; count, record*
catalog, compute, enumerate, inventory, itemize, keep score, mark, mark down, number, numerate, reckon, register, sum, tale, tell, total, write down; SEE CONCEPTS 125,764

tame [adj1] *domesticated, compliant*
acclimatized, amenable, biddable, bridled, broken, busted, civilized, cultivated, disciplined, docile, domestic, fearless, gentle, gentle as a lamb*, habituated, harmless, harnessed, housebroken, kindly, manageable, mastered, meek, mild, muzzled, obedient, overcome, pliable, pliant, subdued, submissive, tractable, trained, unafraid, unresisting, yoked*; SEE CONCEPT 401

tame [adj2] *dull, uninteresting*
bland, bloodless, boiled down*, boring, conventional, diluted, feeble, flat*, halfhearted, humdrum*, insipid, lifeless, limp, mild, monotonous, prosaic, routine, spiritless, tedious, unexciting, uninspiring, vapid, weak, wearisome, white-bread*, without punch*; SEE CONCEPTS 529,542,548

tame [v] *domesticate, make compliant*
break, break in, break the spirit*, bridle, bring to heel*, bust, check, conquer, curb, discipline, domes-

ticize, domiciliate, enslave, gentle, housebreak, house-train, humble, master, mitigate, mute, pacify, repress, restrain, soften, subdue, subjugate, suppress, temper, tone down, train, vanquish, water down*; SEE CONCEPTS *14,250*

tamper [v1] *interfere, alter*
busybody, butt in*, change, cook, cut, damage, destroy, diversify, doctor, fiddle with*, fool, horn in*, interfere, interlope, interpose, intrude, irrigate, manipulate, meddle, mess around with*, monkey around*, muck about*, phony up*, plant*, poke nose into*, spike*, tinker, vary, water*; SEE CONCEPT *232*

tamper [v2] *bribe*
buy, buy off, corrupt, fix, get to, have, influence, lubricate, manipulate, reach, rig, square; SEE CONCEPT *192*

tan [n/adj] *light brown*
beige, biscuit, bronze, brown, brownish, buff, cream, drab, ecru, gold, khaki, leather-colored, natural, olive, olive-brown, saddle, sand, suntan, tawny, umber, yellowish; SEE CONCEPTS *618,622*

tang [n] *biting taste or odor*
aroma, bite, flavor, guts*, kick*, nip, piquancy, pungency, reek, relish, sapidity, sapor, savor, scent, smack*, smell, spiciness, tanginess, thrill, twang, zap*, zest; SEE CONCEPTS *599,600,614*

tangible [adj] *real, concrete*
actual, appreciable, corporeal, definite, detectable, discernible, distinct, embodied, evident, factual, gross, incarnated, manifest, material, objective, observable, obvious, palpable, patent, perceivable, perceptible, phenomenal, physical, plain, positive, sensible, solid, stable, substantial, tactile, touchable, verifiable, visible, well-grounded; SEE CONCEPTS *529,582*

tangle [n] *knot, confusion*
coil, complication, entanglement, jam, jungle, labyrinth, mass, mat, maze, mesh, mess, mix-up, morass, muddle, rummage, skein, snag, snarl, twist, web; SEE CONCEPTS *230,674,720*

tangle [v] *knot, complicate*
catch, coil, confuse, derange, discompose, disorganize, drag into, embroil, enmesh, ensnare, entangle, entrap, foul up*, hamper, implicate, interlace, interlock, intertwist, interweave, involve, jam, kink, make a party to*, mat, mesh, mess up*, mix up*, muck*, obstruct, perplex, ravel, snarl, tie up, trap, twist, unbalance, upset; SEE CONCEPTS *112,190*

tantalize [v] *provoke, tease*
annoy, badger, baffle, bait, bedevil, beleaguer, charm, entice, fascinate, frustrate, gnaw, harass, harry, keep hanging*, lead on, make mouth water*, pester, plague, taunt, thwart, titillate, torment, torture, worry; SEE CONCEPTS *7,11,19,22*

tantamount [adj] *same*
alike, as good as, commensurate, duplicate, equal, equivalent, identical, indistinguishable, like, paral-

lel, same as, selfsame, synonymous, uniform, very; SEE CONCEPTS *487,573*

tantrum [n] *fit*
anger, animosity, conniption, dander*, flare-up, hemorrhage*, huff*, hysterics, outburst, storm*, temper, temper tantrum, wax; SEE CONCEPTS *306,384*

tap [n] *faucet*
bibcock, cock, egress, hydrant, nozzle, petcock, spigot, spout, stopcock, valve; SEE CONCEPTS *445,464*

tap [v1] *hit lightly*
beat, bob, dab, drum, knock, palpate, pat, percuss, rap, strike, tag, thud, thump, tip, touch; SEE CONCEPT *189*

tap [v2] *pierce to drain*
bleed, bore, broach, draft, drain, draw, draw forth, draw off, draw out, drill, empty, lance, milk, mine, open, penetrate, perforate, pump, riddle, siphon, spear, spike, stab, unplug, unstopper, use, utilize; SEE CONCEPTS *142,220*

tape [n] *ribbon of material*
band, braid, edging, line, rope, strip; SEE CONCEPT *475*

tape [v1] *stick together with material*
bandage, bind, bond, fasten, hold together, rope, seal, secure, support, swathe, tie, tie up, truss, wire, wrap; SEE CONCEPTS *85,160*

tape [v2] *record sounds, sights*
audiotape, make a tape, register, tape-record, video, videotape; SEE CONCEPTS *125,292*

taper/taper off [v] *decrease to a point*
abate, bate, close, come to a point, die away, die out, diminish, drain, dwindle, fade, lessen, narrow, recede, reduce, rescind, subside, thin, thin out, wane, weaken, wind down; SEE CONCEPTS *137,698,776*

tardy [adj] *late*
backward, behindhand, belated, dawdling, delayed, delinquent, detained, dilatory, held up, hung up*, in a bind, jammed, laggard, loitering, not arrived, not done, overdue, procrastinating, retarded, slack, slow, sluggish, strapped for time*, too late, unpunctual; SEE CONCEPTS *542,548,799*

target [n1] *aim, goal*
ambition, bull's-eye*, destination, duty, end, function, ground zero*, intention, mark, object, objective, point, purpose, spot, use; SEE CONCEPT *659*

target [n2] *person as object of ridicule*
butt*, byword, fall guy*, game, mark*, pigeon*, prey, quarry, scapegoat*, scorn, sitting duck*, sport, victim, whipping boy*; SEE CONCEPT *423*

tariff [n] *tax or fee*
assessment, charge, cost, duty, excise, impost, levy, price, price tag, rate, tab, tax, toll; SEE CONCEPT *329*

tarnish [v] *dirty, corrupt*
befoul, begrime, blacken, blemish, blot, contaminate, damage, darken, defame, defile, dim, discolor, disgrace, dull, embarrass, grime, harm, hurt, impair, injure, lose luster, lose shine, mar, muddy, pale,

pollute, rust, slander, smear, smudge, soil, spoil, spot, stain, sully, taint, tar, vitiate; SEE CONCEPTS *246,254,469*

tarry [*v*] *dawdle, delay*
abide, bide, dally, drag, drag one's feet*, dwell, filibuster, get no place fast*, goof around*, hang around*, hold the phone*, lag, linger, lodge, loiter, lose time, pause, poke, procrastinate, put off, remain, rest, sojourn, stall, stay, stick around, stop, stop over, tail, take one's time*, temporize, tool, trail, visit, wait, warm a chair*; SEE CONCEPTS *35,151,210*

tart [*n*] *pastry*
bun, Danish, eclair, fruit tart, pie, popover, roll, turnover; SEE CONCEPT *457*

tart [*adj*] *bitter, sour in taste or effect*
acerb, acerbic, acetose, acid, acidulous, acrimonious, astringent, barbed, biting, caustic, cutting, dry, harsh, nasty, piquant, pungent, scathing, sharp, short, snappish, snappy, snippy, tangy, testy, trenchant, vinegary, wounding; SEE CONCEPTS *267,613*

task [*n*] *job or chore, often assigned*
assignment, bother, burden, business, calling, charge, daily grind*, deadweight*, duty, effort, employment, enterprise, errand, exercise, fun and games*, function, gig*, grind*, grindstone*, headache*, job, labor, load, long row to hoe*, millstone*, mission, nuisance, occupation, office, onus, pain, project, province, responsibility, stint, strain, tax, toil, trouble, undertaking, vocation, work; SEE CONCEPTS *362,666*

task [*v*] *assign, burden*
charge, encumber, entrust, exhaust, lade, load, oppress, overload, push, saddle, strain, tax, test, weary, weigh, weight; SEE CONCEPTS *14,112,666*

taste [*n1*] *flavor of some quality*
aftertaste, aroma, bang*, bitter, drive, ginger, jolt, kick*, oomph*, palatableness, piquancy, punch*, relish, salt, sapidity, sapor, savor, savoriness, smack, sour, sting*, suggestion, sweet, tang*, wallop, zest, zing*, zip*; SEE CONCEPT *614*

taste [*n2*] *tiny sample*
appetizer, bit, bite, canapé, chaw, chomp, dash, delicacy, drop, fragment, hint, hors d'oeuvre, morsel, mouthful, nip, sampling, sip, soupçon, spoonful, sprinkling, suggestion, swallow, tidbit, tincture, tinge, titbit, touch, trifle, whiff*, wink*; SEE CONCEPTS *458,835*

taste [*n3*] *inclination, preference*
affection, appetence, appetite, attachment, bent*, comprehension, cup of tea*, desire, disposition, druthers, fancy, fondness, gusto, heart, leaning, liking, palate, partiality, penchant, predilection, predisposition, prepossession, relish, soft spot*, stomach*, tendency, thing*, type, understanding, weakness, zest; SEE CONCEPTS *20,32,529,659*

taste [*n4*] *capacity to sense flavor*
appetence, appetite, gout, gustation, palate, stomach, taste buds, tongue; SEE CONCEPTS *590,615*

taste [*n5*] *judgment, propriety*
acumen, acuteness, aestheticism, appreciation, correctness, cultivation, culture, decorum, delicacy, discernment, discretion, discrimination, distinction, elegance, feeling, finesse, good taste, grace, nicety, penetration, perception, polish, politeness, refinement, restraint, style, susceptibility, tact, tactfulness, tastefulness; SEE CONCEPTS *388,411,655,689*

taste [*v1*] *judge, try*
assay, bite, chew, criticize, differentiate, discern, distinguish, eat, enjoy, lick, nibble, partake, perceive, relish, sample, savor, sense, sip, test, touch, try, try the flavor of; SEE CONCEPTS *169,616*

taste [*v2*] *experience*
appreciate, be exposed to, come up against, encounter, feel, have knowledge of, know, meet with, partake of, perceive, run up against, savor, undergo; SEE CONCEPT *678*

tasteful [*adj*] *nice, refined*
aesthetically pleasing, artistic, beautiful, charming, chaste, classical, classy, cultivated, cultured, delectable, delicate, discriminating, elegant, esthetic, exquisite, fastidious, fine, graceful, gratifying, handsome, harmonious, in good taste, pleasing, plush, polished, posh, precise, pure, quiet, restrained, rich, savory, smart, snazzy*, spiffy*, splendiferous, stylish, subdued, swank, tasty, unaffected, unobtrusive, uptown; SEE CONCEPTS *529,574,589*

tasteless [*adj1*] *without flavor*
big zero*, blah*, bland, boring, distasteful, dull, flat, flavorless, insipid, mild, nowhere*, pabulum*, plain, plain vanilla*, savorless, stale, tame, thin, unappetizing, uninspired, uninteresting, unpalatable, unpleasurable, unsavory, unseasoned, vanilla*, vapid, watered-down*, watery, weak, without spice, zero*; SEE CONCEPT *613*

tasteless [*adj2*] *cheap, vulgar*
artificial, barbaric, barbarous, coarse, crass, crude, flashy, foolish, garish, gaudy, graceless, hideous, impolite, improper, indecorous, indelicate, indiscreet, inelegant, loud, low, low-down, low-down-and-dirty*, makeshift*, off-color*, ornate, ostentatious, outlandish, pretentious, raunchy*, rough, rude, showy, stupid, tacky, tactless, tawdry, trivial, uncouth, unlovely, unpolished, unrefined, unseemly, unsightly, useless, wild; SEE CONCEPTS *401,570, 589*

tasty [*adj*] *delicious*
appetizing, delectable, delish*, divine, fit for a king*, flavorful, flavorsome, flavory, full-flavored, good-tasting, heavenly, luscious, mellow, palatable, piquant, pungent, sapid, savory, scrumptious, spicy, sugar-coated, sweetened, tasteful, toothsome, toothy, yummy, zestful; SEE CONCEPT *613*

tattle [*v*] *gossip; tell rumor*
babble, blab*, chat, chatter, give away, give the show away*, gossip, have a big mouth*, jabber,

leak, noise, prate, prattle*, rumor, snitch, spill, spill the beans*, spread rumor*, squeal, talk, talk idly, tell on, tell tale*, yak*; SEE CONCEPTS *54,60*

tattletale/tattler [*n*] *person who gossips, tells rumor*
bigmouth*, blabberer, blabbermouth*, busybody, canary*, fat mouth*, fink*, gossip, informer, rat*, rumormonger, scandalmonger, snitch*, squealer*, stool pigeon*, talebearer, taleteller, telltale*, tipster, troublemaker, whistleblower, windbag*; SEE CONCEPTS *412,423*

taunt [*n*] *provocation; teasing*
backhanded compliment*, barb, brickbat*, censure, comeback, crack, cut, derision, dig, dirty dig*, dump, gibe, insult, jab, jeer, mockery, outrage, parting shot*, put-down*, reproach, ridicule, sarcasm, slam*, slap*, snappy comeback*, swipe*; SEE CONCEPTS *7,19,266*

taunt [*v*] *provoke, reproach; tease*
affront, bother, deride, dig*, disdain, dump on*, flout, insult, jab*, jeer, lout, mock, offend, outrage, put down, quiz, rally, revile, ridicule, scoff at, scorn, scout, slam*, slap*, sneer, swipe at, tantalize, torment, twitter, upbraid; SEE CONCEPTS *7,19,54*

taut [*adj*] *rigid, tight*
close, firm, flexed, snug, stiff, strained, stressed, stretched, tense, tightly drawn, trim, unyielding; SEE CONCEPTS *488,604*

tavern [*n*] *business establishment for serving drink, food*
alehouse, bar, barroom, beer joint*, dive*, drinkery, gin mill*, grog shop*, honky tonk*, hostelry, hotel, inn, joint*, lodge, lounge, night spot, nineteenth hole*, pub, public house, roadhouse, saloon, speakeasy*, suds*, taphouse*, taproom, watering hole*; SEE CONCEPTS *439,448,449*

tawdry [*adj*] *cheap, tasteless*
blatant, brazen, chintzy*, common, crude, dirty, flaring, flashy, flaunting, garish, gaudy, gimcrack*, glaring, glittering, glitzy, jazzy, junky*, loud, meretricious, obtrusive, offensive, plastic, poor, raffish, screaming, showy, sleazy*, sporty, tacky*, tinsel, vulgar; SEE CONCEPTS *334,589*

tax [*n1*] *charge levied by government on property, income*
assessment, bite*, brokerage, capitation, contribution, cost, custom, dues, duty, excise, expense, fine, giveaway*, imposition, impost, levy, obligation, pork barrel*, price, rate, salvage, tariff, tithe, toll, towage, tribute; SEE CONCEPT *329*

tax [*n2*] *burden*
albatross*, charge, deadweight*, demand, difficulty, drain, duty, imposition, load, millstone*, onus, pressure, strain, task, weight; SEE CONCEPTS *362,666*

tax [*v1*] *levy charge on property, income*
assess, charge, charge duty, demand, demand toll, enact, exact, exact tribute, extract, impose, lay an impost, rate, require contribution, tithe; SEE CONCEPT *298*

tax [*v2*] *burden*
charge, cumber, drain, encumber, enervate, exhaust, lade, load, make demands on, oppress, overburden, overtax, overuse, overwork, press hard on, pressure, prey on, push, put pressure on, saddle, sap, strain, stress, stretch, task, tire, try, weaken, wear out, weary, weigh, weigh down, weigh heavily on, weight; SEE CONCEPTS *14,208,240*

tax [*v3*] *accuse*
arraign, blame, censure, charge, criminate, impeach, impugn, impute, incriminate, inculpate, indict, reproach, reprove; SEE CONCEPT *44*

taxing [*adj*] *burdensome*
demanding, difficult, disturbing, enervating, exacting, exigent, grievous, heavy, onerous, oppressive, punishing, sapping, stressful, tedious, tiring, tough, troublesome, trying, wearing, wearisome, weighty; SEE CONCEPT *565*

teach [*v*] *educate; instill knowledge*
advise, brainwash*, break in*, brief, catechize, coach, communicate, cram, demonstrate, develop, direct, discipline, drill, edify, enlighten, exercise, explain, expound, fit, form, give instruction, give lessons, give the facts, ground, guide, illustrate, imbue, impart, implant, improve mind, inculcate, indoctrinate, inform, initiate, instruct, interpret, lecture, nurture, open eyes*, polish up*, pound into*, prepare, profess, rear, school, sharpen, show, show the ropes*, train, tutor; SEE CONCEPT *285*

teacher [*n*] *person who educates*
abecedary, adviser, assistant, baby-sitter, coach, disciplinarian, docent, don, educator, faculty member, governess, guide, guru*, instructor, lecturer, maestro, master, mentor, mistress, pedagogue, preceptor, professor, pundit, scholar, schoolmaster, schoolmistress, schoolteacher, supervisor, teach*, trainer, tutor; SEE CONCEPT *350*

team [*n*] *group, crew*
aggregation, band, body, bunch, club, company, contingent, duo, faction, foursome, gang, lineup, organization, outfit, pair, partners, party, rig, sect, set, side, span, squad, stable, string, tandem, trio, troop, troupe, unit, workers, yoke; SEE CONCEPTS *365,397,417*

tear [*n1*] *rip, cut*
breach, break, crack, damage, fissure, gash, hole, imperfection, laceration, mutilation, rent, run, rupture, scratch, split, tatter; SEE CONCEPT *513*

tear/tears [*n2*] *droplets from eyes, often caused by emotion*
blubbering*, crying, discharge, distress, drops, grieving, lachryma, lamentation, lamenting, moisture, mourning, pain, regret, sadness, sob, sob act*, sobbing, sorrow, teardrop, wailing, water, waterworks*, weep, weeping, weeps, whimpering, woe; SEE CONCEPTS *185,467*

tear [*n3*] *wild action*
bender, binge, bust, carousal, carouse, drunk, spree, wassail; SEE CONCEPTS *383,384*

tear [*v1*] *cut, rip an object*
break, claw, cleave, crack, damage, divide, evulse, extract, fray, frazzle, gash, grab, impair, incise, injure, lacerate, mangle, mutilate, pluck, pull, pull apart, rend, ribbon, rift, rive, run, rupture, scratch, seize, separate, sever, shred, slash, slit, snatch, split, sunder, wrench, wrest, yank; SEE CONCEPTS *206,214*

tear [*v2*] *move very fast*
boil, bolt, career, charge, chase, course, dart, dash, fling, fly, gallop, hurry, lash, race, run, rush, shoot, speed, spring, zoom; SEE CONCEPTS *150,152*

tearful [*adj*] *crying, very upset*
bawling*, blubbering*, blubbery*, distressed, dolorous, in tears, lachrymose, lamentable, lamenting, moist, mournful, pathetic, pitiable, pitiful, poignant, sad, Sarah Benhardt*, sniveling*, sobbing, sorrowful, teary, watery, weeping, weepy, wet, whimpering, woeful; SEE CONCEPTS *401,403*

tease [*v*] *aggravate, provoke*
annoy, badger, bait, banter, be at, bedevil, beleaguer, bother, chaff, devil, disturb, dog*, gibe, give a hard time*, gnaw, goad, harass, harry, hector, importune, jive*, josh, lead on*, mock, needle*, nudge, pester, pick on*, plague, put down*, rag*, rally, razz*, rib*, ride, ridicule, roast*, send up*, slam, snap, sound, spoof, swipe at, tantalize, taunt, torment, vex, worry; SEE CONCEPTS *7,11,19,22*

technical [*adj*] *concerning details, mechanics*
abstruse, high-tech*, industrial, mechanical, methodological, occupational, professional, restricted, scholarly, scientific, special, specialized, technological, vocational; SEE CONCEPT *536*

technique [*n*] *method*
address, approach, art, artistry, capability, capacity, course, craft, delivery, execution, facility, fashion, knack*, know-how*, manner, means, mode, modus, modus operandi, performance, procedure, proficiency, routine, skill, style, system, tactics, technic, touch, usage, way, wise; SEE CONCEPTS *6,630*

tedious [*adj*] *dull, monotonous*
annoying, arid, banal, boring, bromidic, drab, dragging, draggy*, dreary, drudging, dry, dull as dishwater*, dusty*, endless, enervating, exhausting, fatiguing, ho-hum*, humdrum*, insipid, irksome, laborious, lifeless, long-drawn-out*, mortal, pabulum*, poky*, prosaic, prosy, slow, snooze, soporific, tiresome, tiring, unexciting, uninteresting, vapid, wearful, wearisome; SEE CONCEPTS *529,548*

tedium [*n*] *dullness, monotony*
banality, boredom, deadness*, doldrums, drabness, dreariness, ennui, irksomeness, lack of interest, lifelessness, routine, sameness, tediousness, tiresomeness, wearisomeness, yawn*; SEE CONCEPTS *388,410,668*

teem [*v*] *be abundant, full*
abound, bear, be crawling with, be full of, be numerous, be plentiful, be prolific, brim, bristle, burst, burst at seams*, bustle, crawl, crowd, flow, grow, jam, overflow, overrun, pack, pour, pour out, produce, prosper, pullulate, rain, roll in, shower, superabound, swarm, swell, swim in, wallow in; SEE CONCEPTS *146,179,740*

teeming [*adj*] *abundant, full*
alive, brimful, brimming, bristling, bursting, chockfull, crammed, crawling, filled, fruitful, multitudinous, numerous, overflowing, packed, plentiful, populous, pregnant, replete, rife, swarming, thick, thronged; SEE CONCEPTS *481,483,774*

teeny/teensy [*adj*] *very small*
diminutive, Lilliputian*, microscopic, miniature, minuscule, minute, teensy-weensy*, teeny-weeny*, tiny, wee*, weeny*; SEE CONCEPTS *773,789*

teeter [*v*] *wobble back and forth*
balance, dangle, falter, flutter, lurch, pivot, quiver, reel, rock, seesaw, stagger, stammer, stumble, sway, teeter-totter*, topple, totter, tremble, tremble precariously, waver, weave, wiggle; SEE CONCEPT *145*

telegram [*n*] *message sent by coded radio signals*
buzzer, cable, cablegram, call, coded message, flash, radiogram, report, signal, summons, telegraph, telegraphic message, teletype, telex, wire; SEE CONCEPTS *269,271*

telepathy [*n*] *ability to know another's thoughts*
clairvoyance, ESP*, extrasensory perception, insight, mind-reading, parapsychology, premonition, presentiment, second sight*, sixth sense*, spiritualism, telepathic transmission, telesthesia, thought transference; SEE CONCEPTS *410,630*

telephone [*v*] *communicate through telephone system*
buzz*, call, call up, contact, dial, get back to*, get on the horn*, get on the line*, give a call, give a jingle*, give a ring*, make a call, phone, pick up*, put a call through*, ring, ring up*, touch base with*; SEE CONCEPTS *225,266,269*

television [*n*] *visual and audio entertainment transmitted via radio waves*
audio, baby-sitter*, boob tube*, box*, eye*, idiot box*, receiver, small screen, station, telly*, tube, TV, TV set, vid*, video; SEE CONCEPTS *277,279,293,463*

tell [*v1*] *communicate*
acquaint, advise, announce, apprise, authorize, bid, break the news*, call upon, clue in, command, confess, declare, direct, disclose, divulge, enjoin, explain, express, fill in*, give facts, give out, impart, inform, instruct, keep posted*, lay open*, leave word, let in on*, let know, let slip*, level, make known, mention, notify, open up, order, proclaim, put before, recite, reel off*, report, represent, require, reveal, say, speak, spit it out*, state, summon, utter; SEE CONCEPT *266*

tell [*v2*] *narrate, describe*
chronicle, depict, express, give an account of, portray, recount, rehearse, relate, report, set forth, speak, state; SEE CONCEPT *55*

tell [*v3*] *understand, discern*
ascertain, be sure, clinch, comprehend, deduce, determine, differentiate, discover, discriminate, distin-

guish, divine, find out, identify, know, know for certain, learn, make out, perceive, recognize, see; SEE CONCEPT *15*

tell [*v4*] *carry weight*
count, have effect, have force, make presence felt, make presence known, militate, register, take effect, take its toll*, weigh; SEE CONCEPT *676*

tell [*v5*] *calculate*
compute, count, count one by one, enumerate, number, numerate, reckon, tale, tally; SEE CONCEPT *764*

telling [*adj*] *effective, significant*
cogent, considerable, conspicuous, convincing, crucial, decisive, devastating, effectual, forceful, forcible, important, impressive, influential, marked, operative, potent, powerful, satisfactory, satisfying, solid, sound, striking, trenchant, valid, weighty; SEE CONCEPTS *537,567*

tell off [*v*] *reprimand; criticize harshly*
berate, censure, chide, give piece of one's mind*, lecture, rail, rake over the coals*, rebuke, reproach, reprove, revile, scold, take to task*, tick off*, tongue-lash*, upbraid, vituperate; SEE CONCEPTS *44,52*

temerity [*n*] *nerve, audacity*
assurance, boldness, brass*, carelessness, daring, effrontery, foolhardiness, forwardness, gall*, hardihood, hastiness, heedlessness, impertinence, impetuosity, imprudence, impudence, impulsiveness, indiscretion, intrepidity, intrusiveness, nerve, overconfidence, pluck*, precipitancy, precipitateness, precipitation, presumption, rashness, recklessness, rudeness, thoughtlessness, venturesomeness; SEE CONCEPTS *411,633*

temper [*n1*] *state of mind*
atmosphere, attitude, attribute, aura, character, climate, complexion, condition, constitution, disposition, drift, frame of mind, humor, individualism, individuality, leaning, makeup, mind, mood, nature, orientation, outlook, peculiarity, personality, posture, property, quality, scene, soul, spirit, state, strain, style, temperament, tendency, tenor, thing*, timbre, tone, trend, type, vein, way; SEE CONCEPTS *410,411*

temper [*n2*] *angriness; bad mood*
acerbity, anger, annoyance, bad-humor, cantankerousness, crossness, dander*, excitability, fit, fretfulness, furor, fury, grouchiness, heat*, hotheadedness, huffiness, ill-humor, impatience, irascibility, ire, irritability, irritation, miff, outburst, passion, peevishness, petulance, pugnacity, rage, resentment, sensitivity, short fuse*, slow burn*, snit*, sourness, stew*, sullenness, surliness, tantrum, tartness, tear*, tiff, tizzy*, touchiness, wax*; SEE CONCEPTS *29,410*

temper [*n3*] *calmness*
calm, composure, cool, coolness, equanimity, good humor, moderation, poise, self-control, tranquility; SEE CONCEPTS *32,410*

temper [*v1*] *calm, moderate*
abate, adjust, admix, allay, alleviate, assuage, chill out*, cool, cool out*, curb, dilute, ease, fine tune,

lessen, make reasonable, mitigate, modulate, mollify, monkey around with*, pacify, palliate, relieve, restrain, revamp, soften, soft-pedal*, soothe, switch, take the bite out*, take the edge off*, take the sting out*, tone down, transmogrify, weaken; SEE CONCEPTS *7,22,110,126*

temper [*v2*] *harden*
anneal, bake, braze, cement, chill, congeal, dry, indurate, mold, petrify, set, solidify, starch, steel, stiffen, strengthen, toughen, toughen up; SEE CONCEPTS *250,726*

temperament [*n*] *disposition, personality*
attitude, bent, capacity, cast, character, complexion, constitution, distinctiveness, ego, emotions, frame of mind, humor, idiosyncrasy, inclination, individualism, individuality, inner nature, intellect, kind, makeup, mentality, mettle, mood, nature, outlook, peculiarity, quality, soul, spirit, stamp, structure, susceptibility, temperament, tendency, turn, type, way; SEE CONCEPTS *410,411*

temperamental [*adj*] *angry most of the time; moody*
capricious, changeable, cussed*, easily upset, emotional, erratic, excitable, explosive, fickle, fiery, froward, headstrong, highly strung*, hotheaded*, hyper*, hypersensitive, impatient, in bad mood, inconsistent, irritable, mean, mercurial, neurotic, ornery, passionate, petulant, sensitive, thin-skinned*, ticklish, touchy, uncertain, undependable, unpredictable, unreliable, unstable, variable, volatile, willful; SEE CONCEPT *403*

temperance [*n*] *self-restraint; abstinence*
abnegation, abstemiousness, asceticism, astringency, austerity, conservatism, constraint, continence, control, discretion, eschewal, forbearance, forgoing, frugality, golden mean*, happy medium*, measure, moderateness, moderation, moderatism, mortification, prohibition, prudence, reasonableness, refrainment, restraint, sacrifice, self-control, self-denial, self-deprivation, self-discipline, soberness, sobriety, stoicism, teetotalism, uninebriation, unintoxication; SEE CONCEPTS *410,633*

temperate [*adj1*] *calm, moderate*
agreeable, balmy, checked, clement, collected, composed, conservative, constant, cool, curbed, discreet, dispassionate, equable, even, even-tempered, fair, gentle, levelheaded, medium, mild, modest, pleasant, reasonable, regulated, restrained, self-controlled, self-restrained, sensible, sober, soft, stable, steady, unexcessive, unextreme, unimpassioned, warm; SEE CONCEPTS *525,542,547*

temperate [*adj2*] *controlled, sober*
abstemious, abstentious, abstinent, continent, moderate, restrained, self-restraining; SEE CONCEPT *401*

temperature [*n*] *hotness, coldness of some degree*
body heat, calefaction, climate, cold, condition, degrees, febricity, feverishness, heat, incalescence, pyrexia, thermal reading, warmth; SEE CONCEPT *610*

tempest [*n*] *wild storm; commotion*
blizzard, bluster, chaos, convulsion, cyclone, disturbance, ferment, furor, gale, hurricane, squall, tor-

nado, tumult, typhoon, upheaval, uproar, wildness, windstorm; SEE CONCEPTS *230,526*

tempestuous [*adj*] *wild, stormy*
agitated, blustering, blustery, boisterous, breezy, coarse, emotional, excited, feverish, furious, gusty, heated, hysterical, impassioned, intense, passionate, raging, rough, rugged, squally, storming, tumultous/ tumultuous, turbulent, unbridled, uncontrolled, unrestrained, violent, windy; SEE CONCEPTS *401,525,542*

temple [*n*] *house of worship*
cathedral, chapel, church, holy place, house, house of God*, house of prayer*, mosque, pagoda, pantheon, place of worship, sanctuary, shrine, synagogue, tabernacle; SEE CONCEPTS *368,439*

tempo [*n*] *beat, rhythm*
bounce, cadence, downbeat, measure, meter, momentum, pace, pulse, rate, speed, time, velocity; SEE CONCEPT *65*

temporal [*adj1*] *material, worldly*
banausic, carnal, civil, earthly, earthy, fleshly, lay, materialistic, mortal, mundane, nonsacred, nonspiritual, physical, profane, secular, sensual, subcelestial, sublunary, terrestrial, unhallowed, unsacred, unsanctified, unspiritual; SEE CONCEPT *582*

temporal [*adj2*] *momentary*
chronological, ephemeral, evanescent, fleeting, fugacious, fugitive, impermanent, momentary, of time, passing, short-lived, temporary, transient, transitory; SEE CONCEPT *799*

temporary [*adj*] *lasting only a short while*
acting, ad hoc, ad interim, alternate, band-aid*, brief, changeable, ephemeral, evanescent, fleeting, for the time being*, fugacious, fugitive, impermanent, interim, limited, make-do*, makeshift*, momentary, mortal, overnight, passing, perishable, pro tem, protempore, provisional, provisory, shifting, short, short-lived, slapdash*, stopgap*, substitute, summary, supply, temp, transient, transitory, unfixed, unstable, volatile; SEE CONCEPTS *551,798*

tempt [*v*] *lure, entice*
allure, appeal to, attract, bait, butter up*, captivate, charm, coax, court, dare, decoy, draw, draw out, entrap, fascinate, honey*, hook*, incite, induce, influence, instigate, intrigue, inveigle, invite, lead on, make mouth water*, motivate, mousetrap*, move, oil, persuade, play up to, promote, provoke, risk, rouse, seduce, solicit, stimulate, tantalize, test, train, try, turn one's head*, wheedle, whet, woo*; SEE CONCEPTS *11,68*

temptation [*n*] *lure, attraction*
allurement, appeal, attractiveness, bait, blandishment, coaxing, come-on*, decoy*, draw, enticement, fancy, fascination, hankering, inducement, inveiglement, invitation, provocation, pull, seducement, seduction, snare, tantalization, trap*, yen; SEE CONCEPTS *20,529,532,690,709*

tempting [*adj*] *alluring, inviting*
appetizing, attractive, charming, divine, enticing, fascinating, fetching, heavenly, intriguing, luring, magnetic, mouth-watering*, provoking, rousing, scrumptious, seductive, tantalizing, yummy*; SEE CONCEPTS *462,529*

tenable [*adj*] *reasonable*
arguable, believable, condonable, credible, defendable, defensible, excusable, impregnable, justifiable, maintainable, plausible, rational, reliable, secure, sound, strong, trustworthy, viable, vindicable, warrantable; SEE CONCEPTS *552,558*

tenacious [*adj1*] *strong, unyielding*
adamant, bound, clinging, coherent, cohesive, determined, dogged, fast, firm, forceful, inflexible, intransient, iron, meaning business*, mulish, obdurate, obstinate, persevering, persistent, persisting, pertinacious, possessive, purposeful, relentless, resolute, retentive, set, solid, spunky, stalwart, staunch, steadfast, stout, strong-willed, stubborn, sturdy, sure, tight, tough, true, unforgetful, unshakable, unswerving; SEE CONCEPTS *326,401,489,542*

tenacious [*adj2*] *sticky*
adhesive, clinging, clingy, fast, firm, fixed, glutinous, gummy, inseparable, mucilaginous, resisting, retentive, secure, set, tacky, tight, viscid, viscose, viscous, waxy; SEE CONCEPTS *488,606*

tenacity [*n*] *diligence, stubbornness*
application, backbone, chutzpah*, clock*, courage, determination, doggedness, firmness, grit, guts*, gutsiness, guttiness, heart*, inflexibility, intestinal fortitude*, intransigence, moxie*, nerve, obduracy, obstinacy, perseverance, persistence, pertinacity, resoluteness, resolution, resolve, spunk, starch*, staunchness, steadfastness, stick-to-itiveness*, stomach*, strength of purpose, true grit*, what it takes*, willfulness; SEE CONCEPTS *411,657*

tenant [*n*] *person who leases a place*
addressee, boarder, dweller, holder, householder, indweller, inhabitant, leaseholder, lessee, lodger, occupant, occupier, possessor, renter, rent payer, resident, roomer; SEE CONCEPTS *348,423*

tend [*v1*] *be apt, likely*
aim, bear, be biased, be conducive, be disposed, be inclined, be in the habit of, be liable, bend, be predisposed, be prejudiced, conduce, contribute, dispose, drift, favor, go, gravitate, have an inclination, have a tendency, head, impel, incline, influence, lead, lean, look, make for, move, move toward, point, redound, result in, serve to, trend, turn, verge on; SEE CONCEPTS *411,650*

tend [*v2*] *care for*
accomplish, administer, attend, baby-sit, cater to, cherish, control, corral, cultivate, defend, direct, do, do for, feed, foster, guard, handle, keep, keep an eye on*, keep tabs on*, look after, maintain, manage, mind, minister to, nurse, nurture, oversee, perform, protect, ride herd on*, safeguard, see after, see to,

serve, shepherd, shield, sit, superintend, supervise, take care of, take under wing*, wait on, watch, watch out for, watch over; SEE CONCEPTS *136,257,295*

tendency [*n1*] *inclination to think or do in a certain way*
addiction, affection, bent*, bias, current, custom, disposition, drift, habit, impulse, inclining, leaning, liability, mind, mindset*, partiality, penchant, predilection, predisposition, proclivity, proneness, propensity, readiness, run, set, shift, slant, susceptibility, temperament, thing*, trend, turn, type, usage, way*, weakness; SEE CONCEPT *657*

tendency [*n2*] *direction of movement*
aim, bearing, bent, bias, course, current, curve, drift, drive, heading, inclination, leaning, movement, purport, run, shift, tenor, trend, turn, turning, way; SEE CONCEPTS *692,738*

tender [*adj1*] *fragile, soft*
breakable, dainty, delicate, effete, feeble, frail, supple, weak; SEE CONCEPTS *604,606*

tender [*adj2*] *young, inexperienced*
callow, childish, childlike, green*, immature, impressionable, new, raw*, rookie, sensitive, unripe, vernal, vulnerable, wet behind the ears*, youthful; SEE CONCEPTS *578,797*

tender [*adj3*] *affectionate, loving*
all heart*, amorous, benevolent, bleeding-heart*, caring, charitable, commiserative, compassionate, considerate, demonstrative, emotional, evocative, fond, forgiving, gentle, humane, kind, lenient, lovey-dovey, merciful, mild, moving, mushy, poignant, responsive, romantic, sensitive, sentimental, soft, softhearted, solicitous, sympathetic, tenderhearted, thoughtful, ticklish, tolerant, touching, touchy, warm, warmhearted, yielding; SEE CONCEPTS *401,542*

tender [*adj4*] *painful, sore*
aching, acute, bruised, delicate, hypersensitive, inflamed, irritated, oversensitive, raw, sensitive, smarting, thin-skinned, ticklish, touchy; SEE CONCEPTS *314,403,548*

tenebrous [*adj*] *dark, ominous*
ambiguous, amphibological, caliginous, dim, dingy, dusk, dusky, equivocal, gloomy, lightless, murky, obscure, shadowy, shady, somber, sunless, uncertain, unclear, unexplicit, unilluminated, unintelligible, unlit, vague; SEE CONCEPTS *535,617*

tenet [*n*] *belief, principle*
article of faith, assumption, canon, conception, conviction, credo, creed, doctrine, dogma, faith, impression, maxim, opinion, persuasion, position, precept, presumption, profession, rule, selfconviction, system, teaching, thesis, trust, view; SEE CONCEPTS *687,689*

tenor [*n1*] *meaning, intent*
aim, body, burden, core, course, course of thought, current, direction, drift, evolution, gist, inclination, meat, mood, path, pith, purport, purpose, run, sense, stuff, substance, tendency, theme, tone, trend, way; SEE CONCEPTS *529,682*

tenor [*n2*] *high male voice*
alto, countertenor, falsetto; SEE CONCEPT *65*

tense [*adj1*] *tight, stretched*
close, firm, rigid, stiff, strained, taut; SEE CONCEPTS *485,604*

tense [*adj2*] *under stress, pressure*
agitated, anxious, apprehensive, beside oneself*, bundle of nerves*, choked, clutched, concerned, edgy, excited, fidgety, fluttery, high-strung*, hung up*, hyper*, in a tizzy*, jittery, jumpy, keyed up*, moved, moving, nerve-racking, nervous, nervous wreck*, on edge, overanxious, overwrought, queasy, restive, restless, shaky, shot, shot to pieces*, strained, stressful, strung out*, uneasy, unnerved, unquiet, up the wall*, uptight*, white knuckled*, wired*, worried, worrying, wound up*, wreck*; SEE CONCEPTS *401,403,548*

tension [*n1*] *tightness*
astriction, balance, constriction, force, pressure, rigidity, stiffness, strain, straining, stress, stretching, tautness, tenseness, tensity; SEE CONCEPTS *723,726*

tension [*n2*] *mental stress*
agitation, ants*, ants in pants*, anxiety, apprehension, bad feeling*, brunt, concern, discomfort, disquiet, edginess, hostility, jitters, jumps*, nail-biter*, nerves, nervousness, pins and needles*, pressure, restlessness, shakes, strain, suspense, unease, uneasiness, worriment, worry; SEE CONCEPT *410*

tentative [*adj1*] *conditional, experimental*
acting, ad interim, conjectural, contingent, dependent, iffy*, indefinite, makeshift, not final, not settled, on trial, open for consideration, probationary, provisional, provisionary, provisory, speculative, subject to change, temporary, test, trial, unconfirmed, undecided, unsettled; SEE CONCEPTS *551,552*

tentative [*adj2*] *indefinite, uncertain*
backward, cautious, diffident, disinclined, doubtful, faltering, halting, hesitant, irresolute, reluctant, timid, undecided, unsure, vacillating, vacillatory, wobbly; SEE CONCEPTS *534,535,542*

tenuous [*adj*] *weak, thin*
aerial, airy, attenuate, attenuated, delicate, doubtful, dubious, ethereal, fine, flimsy, gossamer, insignificant, insubstantial, light, narrow, nebulous, questionable, rare, rarefied, reedy, shaky, sketchy, slender, slight, slim, subtle, twiggy; SEE CONCEPTS *489,491,575*

tenure [*n*] *time in position of responsibility*
administration, clamp, clasp, clench, clinch, clutch, dynasty, grasp, grip, hold, holding, incumbency, occupancy, occupation, ownership, possession, proprietorship, regime, reign, residence, security, tenancy, term; SEE CONCEPTS *287,816*

tepid [*adj*] *lukewarm*
apathetic, cool, disinterested, dull, halfhearted, indifferent, languid, lifeless, mild, milk-warm, mod-

erate, slightly warm, spiritless, temperate, unenthusiastic, unlively, warm, warmish; SEE CONCEPTS 542,605

term [n1] *description of a concept*
appellation, article, caption, denomination, designation, expression, head, indication, language, locution, moniker, name, nomenclature, phrase, style, terminology, title, vocable, word; SEE CONCEPTS 275,683

term [n2] *time period*
course, cycle, duration, go*, hitch*, interval, phase, quarter, season, semester, session, space, span, spell, standing, stretch, time, tour, turn, while; SEE CONCEPTS 807,822

term [n3] *limit*
bound, boundary, close, conclusion, confine, confines, culmination, end, finish, fruition, limitation, terminus; SEE CONCEPTS 745,832

term [v] *name something*
baptize, call, christen, denominate, describe, designate, dub, entitle, label, style, subtitle, tag, title; SEE CONCEPT 62

terminal [n1] *end of road; limit*
boundary, depot, end, end of the line, extremity, station, termination, terminus; SEE CONCEPTS 198,745

terminal [n2] *computer screen, computer input/output device*
cathode ray tube, CRT*, display, input device, monitor, screen, VDT*, video display; SEE CONCEPT 463

terminal [adj] *final, deadly*
bitter end*, bounding, check out*, closing, concluding, eventual, extreme, fatal, hindmost, incurable, killing, lag, last, last hurrah*, latest, latter, lethal, limiting, mortal, number is up*, on way out*, period, ultimate, utmost; SEE CONCEPTS 314,548

terminate [v] *stop, finish*
abolish, abort, achieve, adjourn, annul, bounce, bound, bring to an end, cancel, cease, close, come to an end, complete, conclude, confine, cut off, define, desist, determine, discharge, discontinue, dismiss, dissolve, drop, eliminate, end, expire, extinguish, fire, halt, issue, lapse, limit, perfect, prorogate, prorogue, put an end to, recess, restrict, result, run out, sack, scratch, scrub, tether, ultimate, wind down, wind up*, wrap*, wrap up*; SEE CONCEPTS 119,121,234

termination [n] *end*
abortion, ballgame*, cease, cessation, close, completion, conclusion, consequence, curtains*, cutoff*, desistance, discontinuation, effect, ending, end of the line, expiry, fag end*, finale, finis, finish, issue, kiss-off*, outcome, payoff*, period, result, stop, terminus, windup*, wrap-up*; SEE CONCEPTS 119,832

terms [n1] *conditions, agreement*
charge, circumstances, conclusion, condition, details, fee, fine print*, items, nitty-gritty*, particulars,

payment, points, premise, premises, price, provision, provisions, proviso, provisos, qualifications, rate, reservation, size of it*, small print*, specifications, stipulation, stipulations, strings*, treaty, understanding, what it is*; SEE CONCEPTS 270,318,684

terms [n2] *status of relationship*
balance, equality, equivalence, footing, par, parity, position, relations, relationship, standing; SEE CONCEPT 388

terrain [n] *landscape*
area, bailiwick, contour, country, domain, dominion, field, form, ground, land, profile, province, region, shape, soil, sphere, territory, topography, turf; SEE CONCEPTS 508,509

terrestrial [adj] *earthly*
earthbound, earthlike, earthy, global, mundane, physical, profane, prosaic, secular, sublunary, subsolar, telluric, temporal, terrene, uncelestial, unspiritual, worldly; SEE CONCEPT 536

terrible [adj] *bad, horrible*
abhorrent, appalling, atrocious, awe-inspiring, awesome, awful, beastly, dangerous, desperate, dire, disastrous, disturbing, dread, dreaded, dreadful, extreme, fearful, frightful, ghastly, gruesome, harrowing, hateful, hideous, horrendous, horrible, horrid, horrifying, inconvenient, loathsome, monstrous, obnoxious, odious, offensive, petrifying, poor, repulsive, revolting, rotten, serious, severe, shocking, unfortunate, unnerving, unpleasant, unwelcome, vile; SEE CONCEPT 571

terribly [adv] *very*
awfully, badly, decidedly, desperately, discouragingly, disturbingly, drastically, dreadfully, exceedingly, extremely, fearfully, frightfully, gravely, greatly, highly, horribly, intensely, markedly, mightily, much, notoriously, remarkably, seriously, staggeringly, thoroughly, unbelievably, unfortunately, unhappily; SEE CONCEPTS 569,570

terrific [adj1] *intense*
agitating, appalling, awesome, awful, deafening, disquieting, dreadful, enormous, excessive, extreme, fearful, fierce, formidable, frightful, gigantic, great, harsh, horrible, horrific, huge, immense, large, monstrous, severe, shocking, terrible, terrorizing, thunderous, tremendous, upsetting; SEE CONCEPT 569

terrific [adj2] *wonderful*
ace*, amazing, breathtaking, divine, excellent, fabulous, fantastic, fine, glorious, great, groovy*, hot*, keen, magnificent, marvelous, outstanding, sensational, smashing, stupendous, super, superb, swell, very good; SEE CONCEPT 572

terrify [v] *scare*
alarm, appall, awe, chill, dismay, freeze, fright, frighten, horrify, intimidate, paralyze, petrify, put fear of God into*, scare pants off of*, scare stiff*, scare to death*, shock, spook, startle, strike fear, stun, stupefy, terrorize; SEE CONCEPTS 7,19,42

territory [n] *domain, region*
area, belt, block, boundary, colony, commonwealth, country, district, dominion, empire, enclave, exclave, expanse, extent, field, land, mandate, nation, neck of the woods*, neighborhood, province, quarter, section, sector, sphere, state, stomping grounds*, street, terrain, terrene, township, tract, turf, walk, zone; SEE CONCEPTS *198,349,508*

terror [n] *intense fear*
alarm, anxiety, awe, consternation, dismay, dread, fearfulness, fright, horror, intimidation, panic, shock, trepidation, trepidity; SEE CONCEPTS *27,690*

terrorize [v] *upset, threaten*
alarm, appall, awe, bludgeon, browbeat, bulldoze*, bully, coerce, cow, dismay, dragoon, fright, frighten, hector, horrify, intimidate, menace, oppress, petrify, scare, scare to death*, shock, spook, startle, strike terror*, strong-arm*, terrify; SEE CONCEPTS *7,14,19*

terse [adj] *brief, short*
abrupt, aphoristic, boiled down*, breviloquent, brusque, clear-cut, clipped, close, compact, compendiary, compendious, concise, condensed, crisp, cryptic, curt, cut to the bone*, elliptical, epigrammatic, exact, gnomic, in a nutshell*, incisive, laconic, lean, long story short*, neat, pithy, pointed, precise, sententious, short and sweet*, snappy, succinct, summary, taut, to the point, trenchant; SEE CONCEPTS *267,272*

test [n] *examination, quiz*
analysis, approval, assessment, attempt, blue book*, catechism, check, comp, confirmation, corroboration, countdown, criterion, dry run*, elimination, essay, evaluation, exam, experiment, final, fling*, go*, inquest, inquiry, inspection, investigation, lick*, oral*, ordeal, pop quiz, preliminary, probation, probing, proof, questionnaire, scrutiny, search, shibboleth, standard, substantiation, touchstone*, trial, trial and error*, trial run, try, tryout, verification, yardstick*; SEE CONCEPTS *5,290*

test [v] *examine, quiz*
analyze, assay, assess, check, confirm, demonstrate, experiment, experimentalize, give a tryout, inquire, investigate, look into, make a trial run, match up, prove, prove out, put to the test*, question, run idea by someone*, run up flagpole*, see how it flies*, see how wind blows*, send up a balloon*, shake down*, stack up, substantiate, try, try on, try on for size*, try out, validate, verify; SEE CONCEPTS *5,103,291*

testament [n] *tribute; last wishes*
attestation, colloquy, confirmation, covenant, demonstration, earnest, evidence, exemplification, instrument, proof, testimonial, testimony, will, witness; SEE CONCEPT *318*

testify [v] *vouch for; give testimony*
affirm, announce, argue, assert, attest, bear witness, bespeak, betoken, certify, corroborate, cross one's heart*, declare, demonstrate, depone, depose,

evince, give evidence, give facts, give one's word*, indicate, make evident, mount, point to, prove, say so*, show, sing*, stand up for, state, swear, swear to, swear up and down*, token, warrant, witness; SEE CONCEPTS *49,317*

testimonial [n] *tribute*
affidavit, appreciation, attestation, certificate, character, commemoration, commendation, confirmation, credential, degree, endorsement, evidence, homage, honor, indication, manifestation, memorial, memorialization, monument, ovation, plug*, proof, recommendation, reference, remembrance, salute, salvo, say-so*, show, sign, symbol, testament, testimony, token, voucher, witness; SEE CONCEPTS *49,278,318*

testimony [n] *declaration about truth; proof*
affidavit, affirmation, attestation, avowal, confirmation, corroboration, data, demonstration, deposition, documentation, evidence, facts, grounds, illustration, indication, information, manifestation, profession, statement, submission, substantiation, support, testament, verification, witness; SEE CONCEPTS *49,278,318*

testy [adj] *irritable, touchy*
annoyed, bad-tempered, cantankerous, captious, choleric, crabbed*, cranky*, cross, crotchety*, edgy, exasperated, fretful, grouchy*, grumpy*, impatient, irascible, mean, ornery, out of sorts, peevish, peppery, petulant, quarrelsome, quick-tempered, short-tempered, snappy*, splenetic, sullen, thin-skinned*, uptight*, waspish; SEE CONCEPTS *401,403,542*

tether [n] *fastening*
binding, bond, chain, cord, fetter, halter, harness, lead, leash, picket, restraint, rope, shackle; SEE CONCEPT *475*

tether [v] *fasten*
batten, bind, chain, fetter, leash, manacle, moor, picket, restrain, rope, secure, shackle, tie; SEE CONCEPTS *85,160*

text [n1] *subject matter of document*
argument, body, consideration, content, contents, context, document, extract, fundamentals, head, idea, issue, line, lines, main body, matter, motify, motive, paragraph, passage, point, quotation, sentence, stanza, subject, theme, thesis, topic, verse, vocabulary, wording, words; SEE CONCEPTS *270,682*

text [n2] *book used in education*
assignment, class book, course book, handbook, manual, reader, reference, reference book, required reading, schoolbook, source, syllabus, textbook, workbook; SEE CONCEPTS *280,287*

texture [n] *characteristics of a surface*
arrangement, balance, being, character, coarseness, composition, consistency, constitution, disposition, essence, essentiality, fabric, feel, feeling, fiber, fineness, flexibility, form, framework, grain, intermixture, make, makeup, nap, nature, organization, pattern, quality, roughness, scheme, sense, smooth-

ness, stiffness, strategy, structure, surface, taste, tissue, touch, warp, weave, web, woof; SEE CONCEPTS *611,673,682*

thank [v] *express gratitude*
acknowledge, be grateful, be indebted, be obligated, be obliged, bless, bow down*, give thanks, kiss*, praise, say thank you, show appreciation, show courtesy, show gratitude, smile on*; SEE CONCEPTS *60,69,76*

thankful [adj] *appreciative*
beholden, content, contented, grateful, gratified, indebted, much obliged, obliged, overwhelmed, pleased, relieved, satisfied; SEE CONCEPTS *401,403*

thankless [adj1] *unappreciated*
barren, disagreeable, distasteful, fruitless, futile, miserable, not worth it*, ungrateful, unpleasant, unprofitable, unrecognized, unrequited, unreturned, unrewarding, useless, vain, wretched; SEE CONCEPTS *538,548*

thankless [adj2] *unappreciative, inconsiderate (in behavior)*
careless, cruel, heedless, inappreciative, rude, self-centered, thoughtless, ungracious, ungrateful, unmindful, unthankful; SEE CONCEPT *401*

thanks [n] *spoken or written appreciation*
acknowledgment, benediction, blessing, credit, grace, gramercy, gratefulness, gratitude, praise, recognition, thankfulness, thanksgiving, thank you note; SEE CONCEPTS *60,69,278*

thaw [v] *unfreeze, warm*
become liquid, become soft, defrost, deliquesce, dissolve, flow, flux, fuse, liquefy, loosen, melt, mollify, open up, relax, relent, run, soften, unbend, warm up; SEE CONCEPTS *13,255,469*

theater/theatre [n] *stage, building for performance*
amphitheater, arena, assembly hall, auditorium, barn, boards*, cinema, coliseum, concert hall, deck, drama, drive-in, footlights, hall, hall, hippodrome, house, locale, movie, movie house, oak*, odeum, opera house, playhouse, room, scene, show hall, site; SEE CONCEPTS *263,293,439,448*

theatrical [adj] *dramatic*
affected, amateur, artificial, campy*, ceremonious, comic, dramaturgic, exaggerated, ham*, hammy*, histrionic, legitimate, mannered, melodramatic, meretricious, operatic, ostentatious, pompous, schmaltzy*, show, showy, staged, stilted, superficial, theatric, thespian, tragic, unnatural, unreal, vaudeville; SEE CONCEPTS *401,536*

theft [n] *stealing*
annexation, appropriation, break-in, burglary, caper, cheating, crime, defrauding, deprivation, embezzlement, extortion, filch, fleece*, fraud, grab*, heist, holdup, hustle*, job*, larceny, lift*, looting, mugging, peculation, pilferage, pilfering, pillage, pinch*, piracy, plunder, purloining, racket*, rapacity, rip-off*, robbery, robbing, score*, shoplifting, snatch*, snitch*, steal, stickup, swindle, swindling,

swiping*, thievery, thieving, touch*, vandalism; SEE CONCEPTS *139,192*

theme [n1] *idea, subject matter*
affair, argument, burden, business, case, head, keynote, leitmotif, line, matter, matter in hand, motif, motive, point, point at issue, problem, proposition, question, stuff, subject, text, thesis, thought, topic; SEE CONCEPTS *278,682,689*

theme [n2] *written composition*
article, description, dissertation, essay, exercise, exposition, manuscript, paper, report, statement, thesis; SEE CONCEPT *271*

then [adv1] *before; at another time*
again, all at once, anon, at that instant, at that moment, at that point, at that time, before long, formerly, later, next, on that occasion, soon after, suddenly, thereupon, when, years ago; SEE CONCEPT *799*

then [adv2] *therefore*
accordingly, consequently, ergo, from that time, from then on, from there on, hence, so, thence, thenceforth, thereupon, thus, whence; SEE CONCEPT *548*

theological [adj] *religious, concerning a god-centered philosophy*
apostolic, canonical, churchly, deistic, divine, doctrinal, ecclesiastical, metaphysical, scriptural, theistic; SEE CONCEPT *536*

theorem [n] *explanation based on hypothesis and experiments*
assumption, axiom, belief, deduction, dictum, doctrine, formula, fundamental, law, postulate, principium, principle, proposition, rule, statement, theory, thesis; SEE CONCEPTS *529,687,689*

theoretical [adj] *hypothetical*
abstract, academic, analytical, as a premise, assumed, codified, conjectural, contingent, formalistic, formularized, general, ideal, idealized, ideational, ideological, imaginative, impractical, instanced, intellectual, in the abstract, in theory, logical, metaphysical, notional, on paper*, pedantic, philosophical, postulated, presumed, problematical, pure, quixotic, speculative, suppositional, tentative, transcendent, transcendental, unearthly, unproved, unsubstantiated, vague; SEE CONCEPT *529*

theorize [v] *hypothesize*
conjecture, formulate, guess, project, propound, speculate, submit, suggest, suppose, think; SEE CONCEPT *43*

theory [n] *hypothesis, belief*
approach, argument, assumption, base, basis, belief, code, codification, concept, conditions, conjecture, doctrine, dogma, feeling, formularization, foundation, grounds, guess, guesswork, hunch, idea, ideology, impression, method, outlook, philosophy, plan, position, postulate, premise, presentiment, presumption, proposal, provision, rationale, scheme, shot*, speculation, stab*, supposal, suppose, suppo-

sition, surmise, suspicion, system, systemization, theorem, thesis, understanding; SEE CONCEPTS *529,689*

therapeutic [*adj*] *healing*
ameliorative, analeptic, beneficial, corrective, curative, good, remedial, restorative, salubrious, salutary, sanative; SEE CONCEPT *537*

therapy [*n*] *healing treatment*
analysis, cure, healing, medicine, remedial treatment, remedy, therapeutics; SEE CONCEPT *310*

thereafter [*adv*] *from that time forward*
after that, consequently, following, forever after, from that day forward, from that day on, from there on, hereafter, thenceforth, thenceforward; SEE CONCEPT *799*

therefore [*adv*] *as a result; for that reason*
accordingly, and so, consequently, ergo, for, forasmuch as, for this reason, hence, inasmuch as, in consequence, in that event, on account of, on the grounds, since, so, then, thence, therefrom, thereupon, thus, to that end, whence, wherefore; SEE CONCEPTS *230,676*

thesis [*n1*] *belief, assumption to be tested*
apriorism, contention, contestation, hypothesis, idea, line, opinion, point, posit, position, postulate, postulation, premise, presumption, presupposition, principle, proposal, proposition, sentiment, statement, supposition, surmise, theory, view; SEE CONCEPTS *529,689*

thesis [*n2*] *written dissertation*
argument, argumentation, composition, discourse, disquisition, essay, exposition, memoir, monograph, monography, paper, research, theme, tractate, treatise; SEE CONCEPTS *271,287*

thick [*adj1*] *deep, bulky*
blubbery*, broad, bulky, burly, chunky, compact, concrete, consolidated, fat, firm, hard, heavy, high, husky, massive, obese, pudgy, solid, squat, stocky, stubby*, stumpy*, substantial, thickset, wide; SEE CONCEPTS *491,773*

thick [*adj2*] *concentrated, dense*
caked, clabbered, close, clotted, coagulated, compact, compressed, concrete, condensed, congealed, consolidated, crowded, curdled, deep, firm, fixed, gelatinous, gloppy*, gooey, gummous, gummy, gunky*, heavy, impenetrable, impervious, jelled, jellied, opaque, ossified, ropy, set, sloppy, solid, solidified, stiff, syrupy, thickened, turbid, viscid, viscous, vitrified; SEE CONCEPTS *483,606*

thick [*adj3*] *crowded, packed*
abundant, brimming, bristling, bursting, chock-full*, close, compact, compressed, concentrated, condensed, considerable, covered, crammed, crawling*, dense, frequent, full, great, heaped, impenetrable, impervious, inspissated, like sardines*, localized, multitudinous, numerous, populated, populous, profuse, rank, replete, several, solid, swarming, teeming, tight; SEE CONCEPT *771*

thick [*adj4*] *stupid*
blockheaded*, boneheaded*, brainless, dense, dimwitted, doltish, dopey*, dull, dumb, ignorant, insensitive, moronic, numbskulled, obtuse, slow, slow-witted*, thickheaded*; SEE CONCEPT *402*

thick [*adj5*] *dense (referring to weather)*
cloudy, dull, foggy, heavy, impenetrable, indistinct, muddy, obscure, soupy*, turbid; SEE CONCEPT *525*

thick [*adj6*] *friendly*
chummy*, close, confidential, cordial, devoted, familiar, fraternal, hand in glove*, inseparable, intimate, on good terms; SEE CONCEPT *555*

thick [*adj7*] *unreasonable*
excessive, flimsy*, implausible, improbable, inconceivable, incredible, thin*, too much*, unbelievable, unconvincing, unfair, unjust, unsubstantial; SEE CONCEPTS *529,548*

thicken [*v*] *set; make more dense*
add, buttress, cake, clabber, clot, coagulate, condense, congeal, curdle, deepen, enlarge, expand, freeze, gel, grow thick, harden, inspissate, jell, jelly, ossify, petrify, reinforce, solidify, stiffen, swell, widen; SEE CONCEPTS *137,250,469*

thief [*n*] *person who steals*
bandit, burglar, cat burglar, cheat, clip*, criminal, crook, defalcator, embezzler, heister*, highwayman, hijacker, holdup man/woman, housebreaker, kleptomaniac, larcener, larcenist, lifter*, moonlighter*, mugger, owl*, pickpocket, pilferer, pirate, plunderer, porch climber*, prowler, punk*, purloiner, robber, scrounger, shoplifter, sniper, spider*, stealer, stickup man/woman*, swindler; SEE CONCEPT *412*

thieving/thievish [*adj*] *criminal*
crooked, cunning, dishonest, fraudulent, furtive, kleptomaniacal*, larcenous, light-fingered*, pilfering, piratic*, plunderous, predatory, rapacious, secretive, sly, spoliative, stealthy, sticky-fingered*; SEE CONCEPT *401*

thin [*adj1*] *fine, light, slender*
anorexic, attenuate, attenuated, beanpole*, beanstalk*, bony*, cadaverous, delicate, emaciated, ethereal, featherweight, fragile, gangling, gangly, gaunt, haggard, lank, lanky, lean, lightweight, meager, narrow, peaked, pinched, pole*, puny*, rangy, rarefied, rawboned, reedy, rickety, scraggy*, scrawny*, shadow, shriveled, skeletal, skinny*, slight, slim, slinky, small, spare, spindly, stalky*, starved, stick*, stilt*, subtle, threadlike, twiggy*, twiglike*, undernourished, underweight, wan, wasted, wizened; SEE CONCEPTS *491,773*

thin [*adj2*] *transparent, fine*
attenuate, attenuated, delicate, diaphanous, filmy, flimsy, gossamer, paper-thin, permeable, rare, rarefied, refined, see-through, sheer, slight, slim, subtile, subtle, tenuous, translucent, unsubstantial, wafer-thin, wispy; SEE CONCEPT *606*

thin [*adj3*] *deficient, weak*
diluted, feeble*, flat*, flimsy*, implausible, improbable, inadequate, inconceivable, incredible, insubstantial, insufficient, lame, meager, poor, questionable, scant, scanty, scarce, scattered, shallow, sketchy, skimpy*, slight, sparse, stretched, superficial, thick*, transparent, unbelievable, unconvincing, unpersuasive, unsubstantial, untenable, vapid, weak-kneed*; SEE CONCEPT *771*

thin [*adj4*] *diluted*
diffuse, dilute, dispersed, fine, light, rarefied, refined, runny, subtle, watery, weak, wishy-washy*; SEE CONCEPT *485*

thin [*v*] *make diluted or less dense*
attenuate, cook, cut, cut back, decrease, delete, diminish, disperse, doctor, edit, emaciate, expand, extenuate, irrigate, lace*, needle*, prune, rarefy, reduce, refine, shave, spike, trim, water, water down*, weaken, weed out; SEE CONCEPTS *137,250*

thing [*n1*] *something felt, seen, perceived*
affair, anything, apparatus, article, being, body, business, circumstance, commodity, concept, concern, configuration, contrivance, corporeality, creature, device, element, entity, everything, existence, existent, fact, figure, form, gadget, goods, implement, individual, information, instrument, item, machine, material, materiality, matter, means, mechanism, object, part, person, phenomenon, piece, point, portion, shape, situation, stuff, subject, substance, tool, word; SEE CONCEPT *433*

thing [*n2*] *act*
accomplishment, action, circumstance, deed, doing, duty, episode, event, eventuality, exploit, feat, happening, incident, job, movement, obligation, occasion, occurrence, phenomenon, proceeding, stunt, task, work; SEE CONCEPT *3*

thing [*n3*] *aspect, characteristic*
article, attribute, detail, element, facet, factor, feature, item, particular, point, property, quality, statement, thought, trait; SEE CONCEPTS *411,657,834*

thing/things [*n4*] *personal possession(s)*
apparel, attire, baggage, belongings, chattels, clothes, clothing, duds*, effects, equipment, gear, goods, habiliments, impedimenta, luggage, odds and ends*, paraphernalia, personal effects, personals*, property, raiment, stuff, trappings, tricks; SEE CONCEPTS *446,451*

thing [*n5*] *idea, obsession*
attitude, bee in bonnet*, craze, fad, fetish, fixation, hang-up*, idée fixe, impression, mania, notion, opinion, phobia, preoccupation, quirk, style, thought; SEE CONCEPT *529*

think [*v1*] *believe; anticipate*
assume, be convinced, comprehend, conceive, conclude, consider, credit, deem, determine, envisage, envision, esteem, estimate, expect, fancy, feature, feel, foresee, gather, guess, hold, image, imagine, judge, plan for, presume, project, realize, reckon,

regard, see, sense, suppose, surmise, suspect, take, understand, vision, visualize; SEE CONCEPTS *12,26*

think [*v2*] *contemplate*
analyze, appraise, appreciate, brood, cerebrate, cogitate, comprehend, conceive, consider, deduce, deliberate, estimate, evaluate, examine, figure out, have in mind, ideate, imagine, infer, intellectualize, judge, logicalize, meditate, mull, mull over, muse, ponder, rack one's brains*, rationalize, reason, reflect, resolve, revolve, ruminate, sort out, speculate, stew*, stop to consider, study, take under consideration, turn over, use one's head*, weigh; SEE CONCEPTS *17,33,43*

think [*v3*] *remember*
call to mind, recall, recollect, reminisce; SEE CONCEPT *40*

thinkable [*adj*] *believable, feasible*
cogitable, comprehendible, comprehensible, conceivable, convincing, imaginable, likely, possible, practicable, practical, presumable, reasonable, supposable, within realm of possibility*, within the limits; SEE CONCEPT *529*

thirst [*n*] *craving (especially for liquid)*
appetite, aridity, desire, drought, dryness, eagerness, hankering, hunger, keenness, longing, lust, passion, thirstiness, yearning, yen; SEE CONCEPTS *20,709*

thirsty [*adj*] *dry, desirous (especially for liquid)*
agog*, anxious, appetent, ardent, arid, athirst, avid, bone-dry*, breathless, burning, cottonmouthed*, craving, crazy for*, dehydrated, droughty, dry as dust*, dying*, eager, greedy, hankering, hungry, impatient, inclined, itching for*, juiceless, keen, longing, lusting, parched, partial to, sapless, thirsting, waterless, wild for*, yearning; SEE CONCEPTS *403,603*

thorny [*adj1*] *sharp, pointed*
barbed, briery, bristling, bristly, prickly, spiked, spiky, spinous, spiny, stinging, thistly; SEE CONCEPT *485*

thorny [*adj2*] *difficult, problematic*
awkward, baffling, bothersome, formidable, harassing, hard, irksome, nettlesome, perplexing, prickly, severe, sticky, ticklish, tough, tricky, troublesome, trying, unpleasant, upsetting, vexatious, worrying; SEE CONCEPT *565*

thorough/thoroughgoing [*adj1*] *exhaustive*
absolute, all-embracing, all-inclusive, all-out*, all the way*, assiduous, blow-by-blow*, careful, circumstantial, clocklike, complete, comprehensive, conscientious, detailed, efficient, exact, from A to Z*, full, full-dress, in-depth, intensive, itemized, meticulous, minute, painstaking, particular, particularized, plenty, royal, scrupulous, slam bang*, soup to nuts*, sweeping, tough, whole-hog*; SEE CONCEPTS *531,538*

thorough/thoroughgoing [*adj2*] *absolute, utter*
arrant, complete, consummate, downright, entire, out-and-out*, outright, perfect, pure, rank, sheer,

straight-out*, total, unmitigated, unqualified; SEE CONCEPTS *531,535,557*

thoroughbred [*adj*] *pure, unmixed*
blood, full-blooded, graded, papered, pedigree, pedigreed, pure-blooded, purebred; SEE CONCEPT *549*

thoroughly [*adv1*] *exhaustively*
all, assiduously, carefully, completely, comprehensively, conscientiously, earnestly, efficiently, exceedingly, exceptionally, extremely, flat out*, from A to Z*, from top to bottom*, fully, hard, highly, hugely, in and out*, in detail, inside out*, intensely, intensively, meticulously, notably, painstakingly, remarkably, scrupulously, strikingly, sweepingly, through and through*, throughout, unremittingly, up and down*, very, whole hog*, wholly; SEE CONCEPTS *531,538*

thoroughly [*adv2*] *utterly*
absolutely, altogether, completely, downright, entirely, fully, perfectly, plumb, quite, totally, to the full, well, wholly, without reservation; SEE CONCEPTS *531,535,557*

though [*adv*] *however*
after all, all the same, for all that, howbeit, nevertheless, nonetheless, notwithstanding, still, still and all, withal, yet; SEE CONCEPT *544*

though [*conj*] *while*
albeit, allowing, although, but, despite, despite the fact, even if, even supposing, even though, granted, howbeit, if, much as, notwithstanding, when, whereas; SEE CONCEPT *544*

thought [*n1*] *formation of mental objects*
anticipation, apprehending, attention, brainwork, cerebration, cogitation, cognition, concluding, consideration, considering, contemplation, deducing, deduction, deliberation, deriving, discerning, heed, hope, ideation, inducing, inferring, introspection, intuition, judging, knowing, logic, meditation, musing, perceiving, rationalization, rationalizing, realizing, reasoning, reflection, regard, rumination, scrutiny, seeing, speculation, study, theorization, thinking, understanding; SEE CONCEPTS *17,43,409,410*

thought [*n2*] *idea, concept*
aim, anxiety, appreciation, aspiration, assessment, assumption, attentiveness, belief, brainchild*, brainstorm*, caring, compassion, conception, concern, conclusion, conjecture, conviction, design, dream, drift, estimation, expectation, fancy, feeling, guess, hope, hypothesis, image, inference, intention, intuition, judgment, kindness, knowledge, notion, object, opinion, plan, premise, prospect, purpose, regard, reverie, solicitude, supposition, sympathy, theory, thinking, understanding, view, worry; SEE CONCEPT *529*

thoughtful [*adj1*] *caring, mindful*
anxious, astute, attentive, aware, benign, canny, careful, cautious, charitable, chivalrous, circumspect, civil, concerned, considerate, cooperative, courteous, deliberate, diplomatic, discreet, friendly, gallant, gracious, heedful, helpful, indulgent, kind, kindly, mindful, neighborly, obliging, observant, observative, observing, polite, prudent, regardful, responsive, sensitive, social, solicitous, tactful, unselfish, wary, well-bred, well thought-out; SEE CONCEPTS *401,555*

thoughtful [*adj2*] *contemplative, introspective*
absorbed, analytical, attentive, brainy*, calculating, cerebral, cogitative, deep, deliberative, discerning, earnest, engrossed, farsighted, grave, intellectual, intent, keen, levelheaded, logical, lost in thought*, meditative, melancholy, museful, musing, pensive, philosophic, pondering, preoccupied, rapt, rational, reasonable, reasoning, reflecting, reflective, retrospective, ruminative, serious, sober, studious, subjective, thinking, wise, wistful; SEE CONCEPTS *402,403,542*

thoughtless [*adj1*] *inconsiderate*
antisocial, apathetic, asocial, blind, boorish, brash, deaf, discourteous, egocentric, hasty, heedless, hotheaded*, impolite, inattentive, incautious, indelicate, indifferent, indiscreet, insensitive, listless, madcap*, neglectful, negligent, primitive, rash, reckless, rude, self-centered, selfish, sharp, short, tactless, uncaring, unceremonious, unconcerned, undiplomatic, ungracious, unheeding, unkind, unmindful, unrefined; SEE CONCEPTS *401,555*

thoughtless [*adj2*] *absent-minded, unobservant*
bovine, careless, confused, doltish, dull, empty-headed*, flighty*, foolish, heedless, ill-advised, ill-considered, imprudent, inadvertent, inane, inattentive, incomprehensible, inept, injudicious, irrational, irreflective, lamebrained*, loony*, mindless, neglectful, negligent, obtuse, puerile, rash, reckless, regardless, remiss, senseless, silly, stupid, undiscerning, unheeding, unmindful, unreasonable, unreasoning, unreflective, unthinking, vacuous, witless; SEE CONCEPTS *402,403,542*

thrash [*v*] *flail about; beat*
batter, beat up, belabor, belt, birch, buffet, bury, cane, chasten, chastise, clobber, crush, defeat, flagellate, flog, jerk, kill, lambaste, lick, maul, murder, overwhelm, paste, pelt, pitch, pound, pummel, punish, rout, rush, scourge, seesaw, slaughter, spank, stir, strike, surge, tan, tan one's hide*, thresh, toss, toss and turn*, trash, trim, trounce, wallop, wax*, whip, work over*, writhe; SEE CONCEPTS *95,189*

threadbare [*adj1*] *worn, frayed*
beat up*, damaged, dilapidated, dingy*, dog-eared*, down-at-the-heel*, faded, frowzy*, impaired, injured, old, ragged, ratty*, run-down*, scruffy*, seedy*, shabby, shopworn, tacky, tattered, time-worn, used, used-up, worn-out*, worse for wear*; SEE CONCEPTS *485,606*

threadbare [*adj2*] *trite, corny*
banal, bathetic, cliché, clichéd, cliché-ridden, common, commonplace, conventional, dull, everyday,

familiar, hackneyed, imitative, moth-eaten*, musty, overused, poor, set, stale, stereotyped, stock, tedious, tired, uncreative, well-worn, worn-out; SEE CONCEPT *267*

threat [*n*] *warning; danger*
blackmail, bluff, commination, fix, foreboding, foreshadowing, fulmination, hazard, impendence, intimidation, menace, omen, or else*, peril, portent, presage, risk, thunder, writing on the wall*; SEE CONCEPTS *278,675*

threaten [*v1*] *warn, pressure*
abuse, admonish, augur, blackmail, bluster, browbeat, bully, caution, comminate, cow, enforce, flex muscles*, forebode, forewarn, fulminate, growl, intimidate, look daggers*, make threat, menace, portend, presage, pressurize, push around*, scare, scowl, shake fist at*, snarl, spook, terrorize, torment, walk heavy*; SEE CONCEPTS *7,19,78*

threaten [*v2*] *endanger*
advance, approach, be dangerous, be gathering, be imminent, be in the air*, be in the offing*, be on the horizon*, brewing, come on, forebode, foreshadow, frighten, hang over*, impend, imperil, jeopardize, loom, overhang, portend, presage, put at risk, put in jeopardy, warn; SEE CONCEPTS *231,407*

threatening [*adj*] *menacing, ominous*
aggressive, alarming, apocalyptic, at hand, baleful, baneful, black, bullying, cautionary, close, comminatory, dangerous, dire, fateful, forthcoming, grim, ill-boding, imminent, impendent, impending, inauspicious, intimidatory, looming, loury, lowering, lowery, minacious, minatory, near, overhanging, portending, portentous, scowling, sinister, terrorizing, ugly, unlucky, unpropitious, unsafe, upcoming, warning; SEE CONCEPTS *525,548,570*

threshold [*n*] *opening; beginning*
brink, dawn, door, doorstep, doorway, edge, entrance, gate, inception, origin, outset, point, point of departure, sill, start, starting point, verge, vestibule; SEE CONCEPTS *440,513,648,832*

thrift [*n*] *economy*
austerity, carefulness, economizing, frugality, husbandry, parsimony, providence, prudence, saving, stinginess, thriftiness; SEE CONCEPT *335*

thrifty [*adj*] *economical*
canny, careful, chary, cheap, chintzy*, close*, close-fisted, conserving, frugal, mean, parsimonious, penny-pinching, preserving, provident, prudent, saving, scrimpy*, sparing, steal, stingy*, tight*, unwasteful; SEE CONCEPTS *334,401*

thrill [*n*] *sudden excitement*
adventure, bang*, blast, charge*, circus, fireworks, flash*, flush*, fun, good feeling, inspiration, kicks*, lift*, pleasure, refreshment, response, sensation, stimulation, tingle*, titillation, turn-on*, twitter*, upper*, wallop*; SEE CONCEPTS *32,529*

thrill [*v*] *excite, stimulate*
animate, arouse, blow away*, delight, electrify, enchant, enthuse, fire up*, flush, flutter, galvanize,

glow, go over big*, grab, inspire, juice*, key up*, knock socks off*, move, palpitate, quicken, quiver, race one's motor*, rally, rouse, score, send, stir, stir up, tickle*, tingle*, titillate, tremble, turn on*, wow*; SEE CONCEPTS *7,22*

thrilling [*adj*] *exciting*
blood-tingling*, boss*, breathtaking, electrifying, enchanting, exquisite, fab*, fabulous, frantic, gripping, hair-raising*, large, mad, magnificent, mind-bending*, mind-blowing*, miraculous, overwhelming, rip-roaring*, riveting, rousing, sensational, shivering, stimulating, stirring, swinging, trembling, wild, wondrous, zero cool*; SEE CONCEPTS *548,572*

thrive [*v*] *do well*
advance, arrive, batten, bear fruit, bloom, blossom, boom, burgeon, develop, flourish, get ahead*, get fat*, get on*, get places*, get there*, grow, grow rich, increase, make a go*, mushroom*, progress, prosper, radiate, rise, score*, shine, shoot up, succeed, turn out well, wax*; SEE CONCEPTS *704,706*

thriving [*adj*] *successful*
advancing, arrived, blooming, booming, burgeoning, cooking*, developing, doing well, flourishing, going strong*, growing, have it made*, have the wherewithal*, healthy, home free*, on top of heap*, progressing, prolific, prospering, prosperous, rich, roaring, robust, rolling*, sitting pretty*, wealthy, well; SEE CONCEPTS *334,528*

throb [*v*] *pulsate, beat*
flutter, palpitate, pitpat, pound, pulse, resonate, thrill, thump, tingle, tremble, twitter, vibrate; SEE CONCEPTS *152,185*

throng [*n*] *large crowd*
assemblage, assembly, bunch, collection, concourse, congregation, crush, drove, everybody, flock, gathering, horde, host, jam, mass, mob, multitude, pack, press, push, sellout, swarm, wall-to-wall*; SEE CONCEPTS *417,432*

throttle [*v*] *choke*
burke, control, gag, inhibit, silence, smother, stifle, strangle, strangulate, suppress; SEE CONCEPT *191*

through [*adj1*] *done*
buttoned up*, complete, completed, concluded, ended, finis*, finished, in the bag*, over, terminated, wound up*, wrapped up*; SEE CONCEPTS *531,548*

through [*adj2*] *direct*
constant, free, nonstop, one-way, opened, rapid, regular, straight, straightforward, unbroken, unhindered, uninterrupted; SEE CONCEPTS *482,581*

through [*prep1*] *by way of*
as a consequence, as a result, at the hand of, because of, by means of, by, by dint of, by reason, by the agency of, by virtue of, for, in consequence of, in virtue of, per, through the medium of, using, via, with, with the help of; SEE CONCEPT *544*

through [*prep2*] *between, during*
about, by, clear, for the period, from beginning to end, in, in and out, in the middle, into, past, round,

straight, throughout, within; SEE CONCEPTS *583,798*

throughout [*adj*] *during the whole of*
all over, all the time, all through, around, at full length, completely, during, every bit, everyplace, everywhere, far and near, far and wide, for the duration, from beginning to end, from end to end, from one end to the other, from start to finish, from the start, from the word go*, head and shoulders*, high and low, in all respects, in every place, in everything, inside and out, on all accounts*, over, overall, right through, round, the whole time, through the whole of, to the end, up and down; SEE CONCEPTS *482,531,798*

throw [*v1*] *propel something through the air*
bandy, barrage, bombard, buck, bunt, butt, cant, cast, catapult, chuck, dash, deliver, discharge, dislodge, drive, fell, fire, flick, fling, fling off, flip, floor, force, heave, hurl, impel, lapidate, launch, let fly*, let go, lift, lob, overturn, overwhelm, peg, pellet, pelt, pepper, pitch, precipitate, project, push, put, scatter, send, shove, shower, shy, sling, splatter, spray, sprinkle, start, stone, strew, thrust, toss, tumble, unhorse, unseat, upset, volley, waft; SEE CONCEPT *222*

throw [*v2*] *confuse*
addle, astonish, baffle, befuddle, bewilder, confound, disconcert, distract, disturb, dizzy*, dumbfound, fluster, mix up*, throw off*, unsettle, upset; SEE CONCEPT *16*

throw away [*v1*] *dispose of*
abandon, cast, cast off, chase, clear, discard, dismiss, dispense with, ditch*, drop*, dump*, eject, eliminate, evict, extrude, free oneself of, get rid of, jettison, junk*, lose, refuse, reject, rid oneself of, scrap*, shake off*, shed, slip, throw off, throw out, turn down, unburden; SEE CONCEPT *180*

throw away [*v2*] *waste*
be wasteful, blow, consume, dissipate, fail to exploit, fritter, lose, refuse, reject, squander, trifle, turn down; SEE CONCEPT *156*

throw off [*v*] *elude, escape*
abuse, deceive, evade, get away from, give the slip*, leave behind, lose, outdistance, outrun, shake off, trick; SEE CONCEPT *102*

throw out [*v*] *comment*
bring forward, bring to light*, bring up, chime in*, come out with, declare, deliver, produce, reveal, say, state, suggest, tell, utter; SEE CONCEPT *51*

throw over [*v*] *abandon, leave*
break up with, break with, desert, discard, drop, eighty-six*, finish with, forsake, jilt*, quit, renounce, split up with, walk out on*; SEE CONCEPTS *195,384*

throw up [*v1*] *vomit, be nauseous*
be sick, bring up, disgorge, heave, puke*, regurgitate, retch, spew, spit up, upchuck*; SEE CONCEPTS *179,308*

throw up [*v2*] *build quickly*
build overnight*, jerrybuild*, knock together*, patch, put together, roughcast, roughhew, run up*, slap together*, throw together; SEE CONCEPT *168*

thrust [*n1*] *point of communication*
burden, core, effect, gist, meaning, meat*, pith*, purport, sense, short, substance, upshot; SEE CONCEPT *682*

thrust [*n2*] *forward movement*
advance, blitz, boost, drive, impetus, impulsion, jump, lunge, momentum, onset, onslaught, poke, pressure, prod, propulsion, punch, push, shove, stab, whack, wham; SEE CONCEPTS *208,222*

thrust [*v*] *push hard*
advance, assail, assault, attack, bear down, boost, buck, butt, chuck, chunk, clip, clout, crowd, cut, dig, drive, elbow*, embed, fire, force, heave, hump, impale, impel, interject, jab, jam, jostle, lob, lunge, nick, nudge, peg, pierce, pitch, plunge, poke, pour it on, press, prod, propel, punch, push forward, put, railroad*, ram, run, shove, sink, sling, smack, stab*, stick, toss, transfix, urge, wham*; SEE CONCEPTS *208,222*

thud/thump [*n/v*] *dull crash; dull sound*
bang, beat, blow, clonk, clout, clump, clunk, fall, flutter, hammer, hit, knock, plop, poke, pound, pounding, pulse, rap, slap, smack, strike, throb, thunk*, thwack*, wallop*, whack*; SEE CONCEPTS *65,181,189*

thunder [*n*] *crashing sound*
barrage, blast, boom, booming, cannonade, clap, cracking, crash, crashing, detonation, discharge, drumfire, explosion, fulmination, outburst, peal, pealing, roar, rumble, rumbling, thunderbolt, thundercrack, uproar; SEE CONCEPTS *524,595*

thunder [*v1*] *boom, crash*
blast, clamor, clap, crack, deafen, detonate, drum, explode, peal, resound, reverberate, roar, rumble, storm; SEE CONCEPTS *65,521,526*

thunder [*v2*] *yell at*
bark, bellow, curse, declaim, denounce, fulminate, gnarl, growl, rail, roar, shout, snarl, threaten, utter threat; SEE CONCEPTS *52,54*

thus [*adv1*] *in this manner*
along these lines, as follows, hence, in kind, in such a way, in this fashion, in this way, just like that, like so, like this, so, thus and so, thus and thus, thusly, to such a degree; SEE CONCEPT *544*

thus [*adv2*] *accordingly*
consequently, ergo, for this reason, hence, on that account, so, then, therefore, thereupon; SEE CONCEPT *544*

thwart [*v*] *stop, hinder*
baffle, balk, beat, bilk, check, circumvent, confuse, counter, crab*, cramp, crimp, cross, curb, dash, defeat, disappoint, ditch, dodge, double-cross*, duck, foil, foul up*, frustrate, give the slip*, hold up, impede, louse up*, match, obstruct, oppose, outwit,

pit, play off, prevent, queer, restrain, ruin, scotch*, skin, snafu*, stymie, take down, take wind out of*, trammel, upset, upset apple cart*; SEE CONCEPTS *121,130*

tic [*n*] *spasm*
contraction, fit, jerk, twitch; SEE CONCEPT *308*

tick [*n1*] *clicking sound; one beat*
beat, blow, clack, click, clicking, flash, instant, metallic sound, minute, moment, pulsation, pulse, rap, second, shake, tap, tapping, throb, ticktock, twinkling, wink; SEE CONCEPTS *595,808,810*

tick [*n2*] *checkmark*
check, cross, dash, flick, indication, line, mark, stroke, X*; SEE CONCEPT *284*

tick [*v*] *click*
beat, clack, pulsate, tap, thump, ticktock; SEE CONCEPTS *65,189*

ticket [*n*] *authorization on paper*
admission, badge, board, card, certificate, check, chit, coupon, credential, docket, document, invite, key, label, license, marker, note, notice, open sesame, paper, pass, passage, passport, password, permit, raincheck, receipt, record, slip, sticker, stub, tab, tag, token, voucher; SEE CONCEPTS *271,685*

tickle [*v*] *make laugh*
amuse, brush, caress, convulse, creep, delight, divert, enchant, entertain, excite, gratify, itch, pat, pet, please, stimulate, stroke, thrill, tingle, titillate, touch, vellicate; SEE CONCEPTS *7,22,612*

ticklish [*adj*] *difficult, tricky*
awkward, capricious, chancy, changeable, critical, dangerous, delicate, fickle, inconstant, mercurial, nice, precarious, risky, rocky, sensitive, temperamental, thorny, touchy, trying, uncertain, unstable, unsteady, variable, volatile; SEE CONCEPTS *548,565*

tidbit [*n*] *tiny portion*
bit, bite, delicacy, goody*, morsel, mouthful, snack, soupçon, titbit, treat; SEE CONCEPTS *458,835*

tide [*n*] *flow, current*
course, direction, drag, drift, ebb, eddy, flood, flow, flux, movement, race, run, rush, sluice, spate, stream, tendency, torrent, trend, undercurrent, undertow, vortex, wave, whirlpool; SEE CONCEPT *514*

tide over [*v*] *help along*
aid, assist, bridge the gap*, keep head above water*, keep one going, see through; SEE CONCEPT *110*

tidings [*n*] *greetings, news*
advice, bulletin, communication, dirt, information, intelligence, message, report, word; SEE CONCEPT *274*

tidy [*adj1*] *clean, neat*
apple-pie order*, businesslike, chipper*, cleanly, in good shape, methodical, neat as a pin*, ordered, orderly, shipshape*, sleek, snug, spick-and-span*, spruce, systematic, to rights*, trim, uncluttered, well-groomed, well-kept, well-ordered; SEE CONCEPTS *485,585,621*

tidy [*adj2*] *considerable*
ample, fair, generous, good, goodly, handsome, healthy, large, largish, respectable, sizable, substantial, vast; SEE CONCEPTS *762,781*

tidy [*v*] *make neat and orderly*
clean, clear the decks*, fix up, frame*, get act together*, groom, neaten, order, police, pull together, put in good shape, put in order, put in shape, put to rights*, shape up, spruce, spruce up*, straighten, straighten up, tauten, whip into shape*; SEE CONCEPT *250*

tie [*n1*] *fastening*
attachment, band, bandage, bond, brace, connection, cord, fastener, fetter, gag, hookup, joint, knot, ligament, ligature, link, network, nexus, outfit, rope, strap, string, tackle, tie-in, tie-up, yoke, zipper; SEE CONCEPT *680*

tie [*n2*] *deadlock*
dead heat*, draw, drawn battle*, equivalence, even game, level, photo finish*, push, stalemate, standoff; SEE CONCEPTS *364,667*

tie [*n3*] *relationship*
affiliation, allegiance, association, bond, commitment, connection, duty, hookup, kinship, liaison, network, obligation, outfit, tie-in; SEE CONCEPT *388*

tie [*v1*] *connect, interlace*
anchor, attach, band, bind, cinch, clinch, do up, fasten, gird, join, knot, lash, link, make a bow, make a hitch, make a knot, make fast, marry, moor, rivet, rope, secure, splice, tether, tie up, tighten, truss, unite, wed; SEE CONCEPTS *85,160,193*

tie/tie up [*v2*] *hamper, hinder*
bind, clog, confine, curb, delay, entrammel, fetter, hog-tie*, hold, leash, limit, lock up, obstruct, restrain, restrict, shackle, stop, tie one's hands*, trammel; SEE CONCEPT *130*

tie [*v3*] *equal*
balance, be even, be neck and neck*, be on a par, break even*, deadlock*, draw, even off, keep up with, match, measure up, meet, parallel, rival, touch; SEE CONCEPTS *92,667*

tier [*n*] *level*
bank, category, class, course, echelon, file, grade, group, grouping, layer, league, line, order, pigeonhole*, queue, range, rank, row, series, story, stratum, string; SEE CONCEPTS *378,727,744*

tiff [*n*] *argument*
altercation, bad mood, bickering, difference, disagreement, dispute, falling-out*, fit, huff*, miff*, pet, quarrel, row*, run-in*, scrap, spat, squabble, sulk, tantrum, temper, words*, wrangle; SEE CONCEPTS *46,674*

tight [*adj1*] *close, snug*
bound, clasped, close-fitting, compact, constricted, contracted, cramped, crowded, dense, drawn, enduring, established, fast, firm, fixed, hidebound, inflexible, invulnerable, narrow, quick, rigid, secure, set, skintight, solid, stable, steady, stiff, strained,

stretched, strong, sturdy, taut, tenacious, tense, thick, tightened, unbending, unyielding; SEE CONCEPTS *483,485*

tight [*adj2*] *sealed*
airtight, blind, blocked, bolted, choking, clumped, cramping, crushing, cutting, fast, fastened, firm, fixed, hermetic, hermetically sealed, impenetrable, impermeable, impervious, locked, nailed, obstructed, padlocked, pinching, plugged, proof, sealed, secure, short, shrunken, shut, skintight, slammed, smothering, snapped, sound, stopped up, tied, tied up, uncomfortable, watertight; SEE CONCEPTS *489,576*

tight [*adj3*] *stingy*
cheap, close, grasping, mean, miserly, niggardly, parsimonious, penny-pinching*, penurious, sparing, tightfisted; SEE CONCEPTS *334,401*

tight [*adj4*] *difficult, troublesome*
arduous, close, critical, dangerous, distressing, disturbing, exacting, hazardous, near, perilous, precarious, punishing, rough, sticky, tense, ticklish, tough, tricky, trying, upsetting, worrisome; SEE CONCEPTS *548,565*

tight [*adj5*] *intoxicated*
boozy*, buzzed*, drunk, drunken, high*, inebriated, loaded*, pickled*, plastered*, smashed*, stewed*, stoned*, tipsy, under the influence; SEE CONCEPTS *401,406*

tighten [*v*] *constrict*
bind, clench, close, compress, condense, congeal, contract, cramp, crush, fasten, fix, grip, harden, narrow, pinch, pressure, rigidify, screw, secure, squeeze, stiffen, strain, strangle, stretch, tauten, tense, toughen; SEE CONCEPTS *250,469,697*

till [*n*] *cash box*
box, cash drawer, cash register, kitty*, money box, safe, tray, treasury, vault; SEE CONCEPT *339*

till [*v*] *cultivate land*
dig, dress, farm, grow, harrow, hoe, labor, mulch, plant, plough, plow, prepare, raise crops, sow, tend, turn, turn over, work; SEE CONCEPTS *253,257*

tilt [*n1*] *lean, slope*
angle, cant, dip, drop, fall, grade, gradient, inclination, incline, leaning, list, pitch, rake, slant, slide; SEE CONCEPT *738*

tilt [*n2*] *fight*
attack, bout, clash, collision, combat, conflict, contest, duel, encounter, fracas, joust, meet, scrimmage, scuffle, set-to, skirmish, struggle, tournament, tourney, tussle; SEE CONCEPT *106*

tilt [*v1*] *lean, slant*
bend, cant, careen, dip, heel, incline, list, lurch, pitch, rake, recline, seesaw, set at an angle, shift, slope, slouch, swag, sway, tip, turn, yaw; SEE CONCEPTS *147,149*

tilt [*v2*] *attack, fight*
break, charge, clash, combat, contend, cross swords*, duel, encounter, joust, overthrow, spar, thrust; SEE CONCEPT *106*

timber [*n*] *trees, wood*
balk, beam, board, boom, club, forest, frame, girder, grove, hardwood, log, mast, plank, pole, rafter, rib, stake, timberland, weald, woodland, wood lot, woods; SEE CONCEPTS *430,479*

time [*n1*] *temporal length of event or entity's existence, period*
age, allotment, bit, bout, chronology, clock, continuance, date, day, duration, epoch, era, eternity, extent, future, generation, go*, hour, infinity, instance, instant, interval, juncture, lastingness, life, life span*, lifetime, many a moon*, moment, month, occasion, pace, past, point, present, season, second, shift, space, span, spell, stage, stint, stretch, tempo, term, tide, tour, turn, week, while, year; SEE CONCEPTS *801,806,809,819,823*

time [*n2*] *opportunity*
break, chance, heyday, look-in*, occasion, opening, peak, shot, show, squeak*; SEE CONCEPT *693*

timely [*adj*] *at the right time*
appropriate, auspicious, convenient, favorable, fit, fitting, in good time*, in nick of time*, judicious, likely, meet, modern, now, opportune, pat, promising, prompt, proper, propitious, prosperous, punctual, seasonable, suitable, timeous, towardly, up-to-date, up-to-the-minute, well-timed, with it*; SEE CONCEPTS *558,799*

timid [*adj*] *shy*
afraid, ambivalent, apprehensive, badgered, bashful, browbeaten, bullied, capricious, coldfooted*, cowardly, cowed, cowering, coy, daunted, demure, diffident, fainthearted*, fearful, feeble, frightened, gentle, humble, intimidated, irresolute, milquetoast, modest, mousy, nervous, pusillanimous, retiring, shaky, shrinking, shy, soft, spineless*, spiritless, submissive, timid, timorous, trembling, unassertive, unassured, unnerved, vacillating, wavering, weak, yellow*; SEE CONCEPT *401*

tinge [*n1*] *color*
cast, colorant, coloration, coloring, dye, dyestuff, hue, nib, pigment, shade, stain, tincture, tint, tone, wash; SEE CONCEPT *622*

tinge [*n2*] *hint*
bit, dash, drop, intimation, nib, pinch, shade, smack, smattering, soupçon, sprinkling, strain, streak, suggestion, tincture, touch, trace; SEE CONCEPTS *529,831*

tinge [*v*] *color*
complexion, dye, imbue, impregnate, infiltrate, saturate, shade, stain, streak, suffuse, tincture, tinge, tint; SEE CONCEPT *250*

tingle [*v*] *feel tickled, itchy*
creep, get excited, have goose bumps*, itch, prickle, shiver, sting, thrill, throb, tickle, twitter; SEE CONCEPT *612*

tinker [*v*] *fiddle with*
dabble, doodle*, fix, mess*, mess with*, monkey*, muck about*, niggle*, play, play with, puddle,

putter, repair, take apart, toy, trifle with; SEE CON-CEPTS *87,212*

tinkle [v] *jingle, ring*
chime, chink, chinkle, clink, ding, jangle, make bell sound, plink, sound, ting, tingle, tintinnabulate; SEE CONCEPT *65*

tint [n] *shade of color*
cast, chroma, color, coloration, complexion, dash, dye, flush, glow, hint, hue, luminosity, pigmentation, rinse, stain, suggestion, taint, tinct, tincture, tinge, tone, touch, trace, wash; SEE CONCEPT *622*

tint [v] *color with a certain shade*
affect, complexion, dye, influence, rinse, shade, stain, taint, tincture, tinge, touch, wash; SEE CONCEPT *250*

tiny [adj] *very small*
bitsy*, bitty, diminutive, dwarf, dwarfish, infinitesimal, insignificant, itsy-bitsy*, itty-bitty*, Lilliputian, little, microscopic, midget, mini*, miniature, minikin, minimum, minuscular, minuscule, minute, negligible, pee-wee*, petite, pint-sized*, pocket, pocket-size*, puny, pygmy, slight, teensy*, teensyweensy*, teeny*, trifling, wee*, yea big*; SEE CONCEPTS *762,773,789*

tip/tipoff [n1/n] *inside information*
bang, bug*, buzz*, clue, cue, dope*, forecast, hint, in*, information, inkling, inside wire, kibitz, knowledge, news, point, pointer, prediction, prompt, secret information, steer*, suggestion, two cents' worth*, warning, whisper, word, word of advice, word to the wise*; SEE CONCEPT *274*

tip [n2] *very top*
apex, cap, crown, cusp, edge, end, extremity, head, nip, peak, point, stub, summit, tiptop, vertex; SEE CONCEPT *836*

tip [n3] *gratuity paid*
compensation, cue, fee, gift, handout, lagniappe, money, one-way*, perk, perquisite, pourboire*, reward, small change, something*, sweetener*; SEE CONCEPT *344*

tip [v1] *knock over; cause to lean*
bend, cant, capsize, careen, dump, empty, heel, incline, lean, list, overset, overturn, pour, recline, shift, slant, slope, spill, tilt, topple, topple over, turn over, unload, upend, upset, upturn; SEE CONCEPTS *189,201,208*

tip [v2] *give inside information*
advise, caution, clue, cue, forewarn, give a clue, give a hint, give the low-down*, hint, prompt, steer, suggest, tip off, warn; SEE CONCEPT *60*

tipsy [adj] *inebriated*
addled, dazed, drunk, drunken, fuddle, happy, high*, intoxicated, irrigated*, lit*, loaded*, mellow, merry, stewed*, tight, unsteady, woozy; SEE CONCEPTS *401,406*

tirade [n] *abuse, outburst*
anger, berating, censure, condemnation, denunciation, diatribe, dispute, fulmination, harangue, invec-tive, jeremiad*, lecture, malediction, philippic*, ranting, revilement, screed, sermon, tongue-lashing*, vituperation; SEE CONCEPTS *44,54,278*

tire [v] *exhaust, weary*
annoy, bore, burn out*, bush*, collapse, crawl, debilitate, deject, depress, disgust, dishearten, dispirit, displease, distress, drain, droop, drop, enervate, ennui, exasperate, fag, fail, faint, fatigue, flag, fold, give out, go stale, grow weary, harass, irk, irritate, jade, nauseate, overburden, overstrain, overtax, overwork, pain, pall, peter out*, poop out*, prostrate, put to sleep, sap, sicken, sink, strain, tax, vex, weaken, wear, wear down, wear out, weary, wilt, worry, yawn*; SEE CONCEPTS *13,14,469*

tired [adj] *exhausted, weary*
all in*, annoyed, asleep, beat*, bored, broken-down, burned out*, collapsing, consumed, dead on one's feet*, distressed, dog-tired*, done for*, done in*, drained, drooping, droopy, drowsy, empty, enervated, exasperated, fagged, faint, fatigued, fed up*, finished, flagging, haggard, irked, irritated, jaded, narcoleptic, overtaxed, overworked, petered out*, played out*, pooped*, prostrated, run-down, sick of, sleepy, spent, stale, tuckered out, wasted, weary, worn, worn out; SEE CONCEPTS *314,403,406*

tireless [adj] *determined*
active, ball of fire*, eager, energetic, enthusiastic, grind, hard-working*, hyper*, incessant, indefatigable, industrious, jumping, on the go*, perky, persevering, resolute, steadfast, strenuous, unflagging, untiring, unwearied, unwearying, vigorous; SEE CONCEPTS *538,542*

tiresome [adj] *irritating, exasperating*
a bit much*, annoying, arduous, boresome, boring, burdensome, demanding, difficult, drag, dragging, drudging, dull, enervative, exacting, exhausting, fatiguing, flat, hard, heavy, hefty, ho-hum*, humdrum*, irksome, jading, laborious, monotonous, nowhere, onerous, oppressive, pain in the neck*, strenuous, tedious, tired, tiring, too much*, tough, trying, uncool*, uninteresting, unrelieved, vexatious, wearing, wearisome, wearying, yawn*; SEE CONCEPTS *529,537,538*

titillate [v] *excite, stimulate*
amuse, arouse, entertain, grab, grapple, hook, interest, palpate, provoke, switch on, tantalize, tease, thrill, tickle, tickle pink*, turn on; SEE CONCEPTS *7,11,22*

title [n1] *heading, label*
appellation, banner, caption, close, description, head, headline, inscription, legend, name, rubric, salutation, sign, streamer, style, subtitle; SEE CONCEPT *283*

title [n2] *name*
appellation, appellative, brand, cognomen, denomination, designation, epithet, handle*, honorific, label, moniker, nom de plume*, nomen, pseudonym, sobriquet, style, tab*, tag*, term; SEE CONCEPT *683*

title [*n3*] *possession, laurel*
authority, championship, claim, commission, crest, crown, decoration, deed, degree, desert, dibs*, due, entitlement, holding, justification, license, medal, merit, ownership, power, prerogative, pretense, pretension, privilege, proof, ribbon, right; SEE CONCEPTS *376,710*

title [*v*] *name*
baptize, call, christen, denominate, designate, dub, entitle, label, style, term; SEE CONCEPT *62*

toast [*n*] *salutation when drinking alcohol*
acknowledgment, celebration, ceremony, commemoration, compliment, down, drink, health, honor, pledge, proposal, salute, sentiment, shingle, thanksgiving, tribute; SEE CONCEPT *278*

toast [*v*] *brown with heat*
cook, crisp, dry, grill, heat, parch, roast, warm; SEE CONCEPT *170*

to-do [*n*] *commotion, excitement*
agitation, bother, brouhaha*, bustle, clamor, disorder, disturbance, flap*, furor, fuss, hassle, hoo-ha*, hoopla*, hubbub*, hurly-burly*, hurrah, performance, pother, quarrel, racket, ruction, rumpus, stir, tumult, turmoil, unrest, uproar, whirl; SEE CONCEPTS *230,674*

together [*adj*] *composed*
calm, cool*, in sync*, stable, well-adjusted, well-balanced, well-organized; SEE CONCEPT *542*

together [*adv1*] *as a group; all at once*
all together, as one, at one fell swoop*, closely, coincidentally, collectively, combined, commonly, concertedly, concomitantly, concurrently, conjointly, contemporaneously, en masse, hand in glove*, hand in hand*, in a body, in concert, in cooperation, in one breath*, in sync*, in unison, jointly, mutually, on the beat*, side by side, simultaneously, synchronically, unanimously, unitedly, with one accord, with one voice, with the beat; SEE CONCEPTS *538,544,548*

together [*adv2*] *in a row*
consecutively, continually, continuously, in succession, night and day, one after the other, on end, running, successively, unintermittedly, without a break, without interruption; SEE CONCEPTS *482,585*

toil [*n*] *hard work*
application, drudgery, effort, exertion, industry, labor, moil, nine-to-five*, occupation, pains*, sweat, travail; SEE CONCEPTS *100,362,677*

toil [*v*] *work hard*
drive, drudge, grind, knock oneself out*, labor, moil, peg away*, plod, plug, push oneself, slave, strain, strive, struggle, sweat, tug, work, work like a dog*; SEE CONCEPTS *100,677*

token [*n*] *indication, remembrance*
badge, clue, demonstration, earnest, evidence, expression, favor, gift, index, indicia, keepsake, manifestation, mark, memento, memorial, note, omen, pawn, pledge, presage, proof, relic, reminder, representation, sample, security, sign, significant, souvenir, symbol, symptom, trophy, warning, warrant; SEE CONCEPTS *284,337,529*

tolerable [*adj*] *acceptable, good enough*
adequate, allowable, all right, average, bearable, better than nothing*, common, decent, endurable, fair, fairly good, fair to middling*, goodish*, indifferent, livable, mediocre, middling*, not bad*, okay*, ordinary, passable, presentable, respectable, run-of-the-mill*, satisfactory, so-so*, sufferable, sufficient, supportable, sustainable, tidy, unexceptionable, unexceptional, unimpeachable; SEE CONCEPTS *529,548*

tolerance [*n1*] *open-mindedness*
altruism, benevolence, broad-mindedness, charity, clemency, compassion, concession, endurance, forbearance, freedom, good will, grace, humanity, indulgence, kindness, lenience, leniency, lenity, liberalism, liberality, liberalness, license, magnanimity, mercifulness, mercy, patience, permission, permissiveness, sensitivity, sufferance, sympathy, toleration, understanding; SEE CONCEPTS *410,657*

tolerance [*n2*] *fortitude, grit*
endurance, guts*, hardiness, hardness, opposition, patience, resilience, resistance, stamina, staying power*, steadfastness, steadiness, strength, sufferance, toughness, vigor; SEE CONCEPT *732*

tolerant [*adj*] *open-minded, easygoing*
advanced, benevolent, big, broad, broad-minded*, catholic, charitable, clement, complaisant, condoning, easy on, easy with, excusing, fair, forbearing, forgiving, free and easy*, humane, indulgent, kindhearted*, lax, lenient, liberal, long-suffering*, magnanimous, merciful, patient, permissive, progressive, radical, receptive, soft, sophisticated, sympathetic, understanding, unprejudiced, wide; SEE CONCEPTS *403,542*

tolerate [*v*] *allow, indulge*
abide, accept, admit, authorize, bear, bear with, blink at*, brook, condone, consent to, countenance, endure, go, go along with, have, hear, humor, live with, permit, pocket, put up with, receive, sanction, sit and take it*, sit still for, stand, stand for, stay the course*, stomach*, string along, submit to, suffer, sustain, swallow*, take, tough out*, undergo, wink at*; SEE CONCEPTS *23,83*

toll [*n1*] *fee*
assessment, charge, cost, customs, demand, duty, exaction, expense, impost, levy, payment, price, rate, tariff, tax, tribute; SEE CONCEPT *329*

toll [*n2*] *damage, deaths*
casualties, cost, expense, inroad, loss, losses, penalty, price; SEE CONCEPT *230*

toll [*v*] *ring out*
announce, bell, bong, call, chime, clang, knell, peal, signal, sound, strike, summon, warn; SEE CONCEPT *65*

tomb [*n*] *burial place*
box, burial, burial chamber, catacomb, coffin, crypt, grave, mausoleum, monument, pit, sepulcher, trough, vault; SEE CONCEPT *305*

tone [*n1*] *pitch, volume*
accent, emphasis, force, inflection, intonation, modulation, resonance, strength, stress, timbre, tonality; SEE CONCEPT *65*

tone [*n2*] *attitude, spirit*
air, approach, aspect, character, condition, current, drift, effect, expression, fashion, feel, frame, grain, habit, humor, manner, mind, mode, mood, movement, nature, note, quality, state of things, strain, style, temper, tenor, trend, vein; SEE CONCEPTS *655,673,682*

tone [*n3*] *color*
blend, cast, coloration, hue, shade, tinge, tint, value; SEE CONCEPT *622*

tone [*n4*] *condition of the body*
elasticity, health, healthiness, resiliency, strength, tonicity, tonus, vigor; SEE CONCEPT *316*

tone down [*v*] *moderate*
chill out*, cloud, dampen, darken, deepen, dim, mitigate, modulate, play down, reduce, restrain, shade, sober, soften, soft-pedal*, subdue, temper; SEE CONCEPT *240*

tongue [*n*] *language*
argot, articulation, dialect, discourse, expression, idiom, language, lingo, parlance, patois, speech, talk, utterance, vernacular, voice; SEE CONCEPT *276*

tonic [*n*] *restorative drink, medicine*
analeptic, boost, bracer, conditioner, cordial, drug, fillip, invigorator, livener, pick-me-up*, pickup, refresher, restorative, roborant, shot in the arm*, stimulant, strengthener; SEE CONCEPT *307*

too [*adv1*] *also*
additionally, along, as well, besides, further, furthermore, in addition, into the bargain, likewise, more, moreover, to boot, withal; SEE CONCEPTS *544,771*

too [*adv2*] *excessively*
awfully, beyond, ever, exceptionally, exorbitantly, extremely, greatly, highly, immensely, immoderately, in excess, inordinately, notably, over, over and above, overly, overmuch, remarkably, strikingly, unconscionably, unduly, unreasonably, very; SEE CONCEPTS *569,772*

tool [*n1*] *instrument used to shape, form, finish*
apparatus, appliance, contraption, contrivance, device, engine, gadget, gizmo*, implement, job, machine, means, mechanism, utensil, weapon, whatchamacallit*; SEE CONCEPT *499*

tool [*n2*] *person who allows himself to be used*
accessory, accomplice, agent, auxiliary, chump*, creature, dupe, easy mark*, figurehead, flunky*, go-between, greenhorn*, hireling, idiot, intermediary, jackal, lackey, mark, medium, messenger, minion, patsy*, pawn, peon, puppet, stooge, stool pigeon*, sucker*; SEE CONCEPTS *348,412,423*

top [*n1*] *highest point*
acme, apex, apogee, cap, capital, ceiling, climax, cork, cover, crest, crown, culmination, cusp, face, fastigium, finial, head, height, high point, lid, limit, maximum, meridian, peak, pinnacle, point, roof, spire, stopper, summit, superficies, surface, tip, utmost, vertex, zenith; SEE CONCEPT *836*

top [*n2*] *highest rank*
best, captain, chief, choice, cream, elite, first place, flower, head, lead, leader, master, pick, pride, prime, prize, utmost; SEE CONCEPT *668*

top [*adj*] *best, most important; highest*
apical, capital, chief, crack, crowning, culminating, dominant, elite, excellent, fine, finest, first, first-class, first-rate, five-star*, foremost, greatest, head, lead, leading, loftiest, maximal, maximum, outside, paramount, preeminent, primary, prime, principal, ruling, sovereign, superior, supreme, tiptop*, top-drawer*, topmost, top-notch, upper, uppermost; SEE CONCEPTS *567,574,583*

top [*v1*] *place on or reach highest part*
ascend, cap, climb, cloak, clothe, cover, crest, crown, face, finish, garnish, piggyback*, protect, reinforce, roof, scale, spread over, superimpose, surmount, tip; SEE CONCEPTS *172,201,750*

top [*v2*] *surpass*
bash, beat, be first, best, better, blow away*, clobber*, eclipse, exceed, excel, fake out*, finagle*, fox*, go beyond, goose*, outdo, outfox, outshine, outstrip, overrun, run circles around*, shut out*, total*, transcend; SEE CONCEPTS *95,141*

top [*v3*] *remove the upper part*
amputate, cream, crop, curtail, cut off, decapitate, detruncate, dock, file off, lop off, pare, pollard, prune, ream, scrape off, shave off, shear, shorten, skim, trim, truncate; SEE CONCEPT *211*

topic [*n*] *subject matter*
affair, argument, business, case, division, field, head, issue, material, matter, matter in hand, moot point, motif, motion, motive, point, point in question, problem, proposition, question, resolution, subject, text, theme, theorem, thesis; SEE CONCEPT *532*

topical [*adj1*] *current*
contemporary, modern, newsworthy, nominal, popular, subjective, thematic, up-to-date; SEE CONCEPT *820*

topical [*adj2*] *restricted, local*
confined, insular, limited, parochial, particular, regional, sectional; SEE CONCEPTS *557,583*

topple [*v*] *fall or knock over; overthrow*
belly up*, bring down, capsize, collapse, do a pratfall*, fall, falter, founder, go down, hit the dirt*, keel over, knock down, land, lose it*, lurch, nosedive, oust, overbalance, overturn, pitch, plunge, slump, stagger, stumble, take a header*, teeter, tip over, totter, tumble, turn over, unhorse, unseat, upset; SEE CONCEPTS *95,147,181,208*

topsy-turvy [*adj*] *mixed-up*
chaotic, cluttered, cockeyed, confused, disarranged, disheveled, disjointed, dislocated, disordered, disorderly, disorganized, downside-up*, inside-out, inverted, jumbled, littered, messy, muddled, over-

turned, pell-mell*, riotous, tangled, tumultous/ tumultuous, unhinged, untidy, upended, upside-down, upturned; SEE CONCEPTS *485,548,585*

torment [n] *severe mental distress*

affliction, agony, anguish, annoyance, bane, bother, excruciation, harassment, hell*, irritation, misery, nag, nagging, nuisance, pain, pain in the neck*, persecution, pest, plague, provocation, rack, scourge, suffering, torture, trouble, vexation, worry; SEE CONCEPTS *410,728*

torment [v] *be or make very upset*

abuse, afflict, agonize, annoy, bait, bedevil, bone, bother, break, crucify, devil, distress, drive bananas, drive up the wall*, excruciate, give a hard time*, harass, harrow, harry, heckle, hound, hurt, irritate, mistreat, molest, nag, pain, persecute, pester, plague, play cat and mouse*, provoke, punish, put through wringer*, rack, rub salt in wound*, smite, tease, torture, trouble, try, vex, worry, wring; SEE CONCEPTS *7,19,313*

torn [adj1] *cut open*

broken, burst, cleaved, cracked, damaged, divided, fractured, gashed, impaired, lacerated, mangled, ragged, rent, ripped, ruptured, severed, shabby, slashed, sliced, slit, snapped, split, wrenched; SEE CONCEPT *485*

torn [adj2] *undecided*

divided, irresolute, of two minds*, split, uncertain, unsure, vacillating, wavering; SEE CONCEPTS *403,542*

torpid [adj] *lazy, slow*

apathetic, benumbed, comatose, dopey*, dormant, drowsy, dull, faineant, heavy, hebetudinous, idle, inactive, indifferent, indolent, inert, lackadaisical, languid, languorous, latent, leaden, lethargic, listless, lymphatic, motionless, numb, paralyzed, passive, slothful, slow-moving, sluggish, slumberous, sodden, somnolent, stagnant, static, stupid, stuporous; SEE CONCEPTS *401,538*

torrent [n] *heavy flow*

cascade, cataclysm, cataract, cloudburst, deluge, downpour, effusion, flood, flooding, flux, gush, inundation, niagara, outburst, overflow, pour, rush, shower, spate, stream, tide, waterfall; SEE CONCEPTS *146,179,526*

torrid [adj1] *very hot*

arid, austral, blazing, blistering, boiling, broiling, burning, dried, dry, fiery, heated, parched, parching, red-hot*, scalding, scorched, scorching, sizzling, stifling, sultry, sweltering, tropic, tropical; SEE CONCEPT *605*

torrid [adj2] *sensuous*

ardent, blazing, burning, erotic, fervent, flaming, hot*, hot-blooded*, impassioned, intense, passionate, red-hot*, sexy, steamy*, sultry, white-hot*; SEE CONCEPT *372*

tortuous [adj1] *very twisted*

anfractuous, bent, circuitous, convoluted, crooked, curved, flexuous, indirect, involute, labyrinthine,

mazy, meandering, meandrous, roundabout, serpentine, sinuous, snaky, twisting, vermiculate, winding, zigzag; SEE CONCEPT *581*

tortuous [adj2] *complicated*

ambiguous, convoluted, cunning, deceptive, devious, indirect, involute, involved, misleading, perverse, roundabout, tricky; SEE CONCEPT *562*

torture [n] *severe mental or physical pain*

ache, affliction, agony, anguish, cruciation, crucifixion, distress, dolor, excruciation, hell*, hell on earth*, impalement, laceration, martyrdom, misery, pang, persecution, rack, suffering, third degree*, torment, tribulation, twinge; SEE CONCEPTS *410,728*

torture [v] *upset or hurt severely*

abuse, afflict, agonize, annoy, beat, bother, crucify, distress, disturb, excruciate, grill, harrow, impale, injure, irritate, lacerate, maim, mangle, martyr, martyrize, mistreat, mutilate, oppress, pain, persecute, rack, smite, torment, try, whip, wound, wring, wrong; SEE CONCEPTS *7,19,246,313*

toss [n/v1] *throw*

bung, cast, chuck, chunk, fire, fling, flip, heave, hurl, launch, lob, peg, pitch, project, propel, sling, twirl, wing; SEE CONCEPT *222*

toss [v2] *move back and forth*

agitate, agonize, bob, buffet, disturb, flounder, heave, jiggle, joggle, jolt, labor, lurch, move restlessly, oscillate, pitch, rise and fall, rock, roll, seesaw, shake, squirm, stir, sway, swing, thrash, tumble, undulate, wallow, wave, wobble, wriggle, writhe; SEE CONCEPT *147*

total [n] *whole*

aggregate, all, amount, body, budget, bulk, entirety, flat out*, full amount, gross, jackpot*, mass, quantity, quantum, result, sum, sum total*, tale, the works*, totality; SEE CONCEPTS *786,837*

total [adj] *complete, thorough*

absolute, all-out, comprehensive, consummate, downright, entire, every, full, full-blown, full-scale, gross, inclusive, integral, out-and-out, outright, overall, perfect, plenary, positive, sheer, sweeping, thoroughgoing, totalitarian, unconditional, undisputed, undivided, unlimited, unmitigated, unqualified, unreserved, unrestricted, utter, whole; SEE CONCEPTS *531,762*

total [v] *add up*

add, aggregate, amount to, calculate, cast, come, come to, comprise, consist of, equal, figure, figure, foot, mount up to, number, pile up, reach, reckon, result in, ring up*, run into, run to, stack up, summate, sum up, totalize, tote, yield; SEE CONCEPT *764*

totalitarian [adj] *dictatorial*

absolute, authoritarian, autocratic, communist*, despotic, fascistic, monolithic, Nazi*, one-party, oppressive, total, totalistic, tyrannical, undemocratic; SEE CONCEPT *536*

totally [adv] *completely*

absolutely, all, all in all, altogether, comprehensively, consummately, entirely, exactly, exclusively, flat out*, full blast*, fully, in toto*, just, perfectly, quite, thoroughly, top to bottom*, unconditionally, unmitigatedly, utterly, wholeheartedly, wholly; SEE CONCEPT *531*

totter [*v*] *move falteringly*
blunder, careen, dodder, falter, flounder, hesitate, lurch, quake, quiver, reel, rock, roll, seesaw, shake, shimmy, slide, slip, stagger, stammer, stumble, sway, teeter, topple, tremble, trip, walk unsteadily, waver, weave, wheel, wobble, zigzag; SEE CONCEPT *151*

touch [*n1*] *physical contact*
blow, brush, caress, collision, communication, contact, contingence, crash, cuddling, embrace, feel, feeling, fondling, graze, grope, handling, hit, hug, impact, junction, kiss, licking, manipulation, nudge, palpation, pat, peck, perception, percussion, petting, push, rub, rubbing, scratch, shock, stroke, stroking, tactility, taction, tap, taste, touching; SEE CONCEPTS *590,608,612*

touch [*n2*] *tiny amount*
bit, dash, detail, drop, hint, inkling, intimation, jot, pinch, scent, shade, smack, small amount, smattering, soupçon, speck, spot, streak, suggestion, suspicion, taste, tincture, tinge, trace, whiff; SEE CONCEPTS *529,831,832*

touch [*n3*] *manner, method*
ability, acquaintance, adeptness, adroitness, approach, art, artistry, awareness, characteristic, command, communication, contact, deftness, direction, effect, facility, faculty, familiarity, finish, flair, hand, handiwork, influence, knack, mastery, skill, style, talent, technique, trademark, understanding, virtuosity, way; SEE CONCEPTS *6,630,655*

touch [*v1*] *make physical contact*
abut, adjoin, be in contact, border, brush, butt on, caress, come together, communicate, contact, converge, dab, examine, feel, feel up, finger, fondle, frisk, glance, graze, grope, handle, hit, impinge upon, inspect, join, kiss, lay a finger on, lick, line, manipulate, march, massage, meet, neighbor, osculate, palm, palpate, partake, pat, paw, percuss, pet, probe, push, reach, rub, scrutinize, sip, smooth, strike, stroke, suck, sweep, tag, tap, taste, thumb, tickle, tip, toy, verge; SEE CONCEPT *612*

touch [*v2*] *have an effect on*
affect, arouse, carry, disturb, excite, feel out, get through to*, get to, grab, impress, influence, inspire, make an impression*, mark, melt, move, quicken, soften, stimulate, stir, strike, strike a chord*, stroke, sway, tug at the heart*, upset; SEE CONCEPTS *7,19,22*

touch [*v3*] *have to do with; regard*
affect, be a party to, bear on, bear upon, be associated with, belong to, center upon, concern, concern oneself with, consume, deal with, drink, eat, get involved in, handle, have to do with, interest, involve, partake of, pertain to, refer to, use, utilize; SEE CONCEPT *532*

touch [*v4*] *make mention*
allude to, bring in, cover, deal with, discuss, go over, mention, note, refer to, speak of, treat; SEE CONCEPT *51*

touch [*v5*] *compare with; correspond to*
amount, approach, be a match for*, be in the same league*, be on a par*, come near, come to, come up to, equal, hold a candle to*, match, measure up, meet, parallel, partake, rival, tie, verge on; SEE CONCEPT *561*

touched [*adj*] *deeply moved emotionally*
affected, disturbed, feel for*, feel in gut*, got to*, grabbed*, impressed, melted*, softened, stirred, swayed, turned on by*, turned on to*, upset; SEE CONCEPTS *403,542*

touched [*adj2*] *crazy*
batty*, bizarre, bonkers*, cuckoo*, daft, eccentric, fanatic, flighty, insane, neurotic, not all there*, not right*, nuts*, nutty*, obsessed, out of one's mind*, peculiar, pixilated, queer, unhinged; SEE CONCEPTS *402,403*

touching [*adj1*] *affecting, moving emotionally*
compassionate, emotive, grabbed by, heartbreaking, heart-rending, impressive, melting, mind-blowing, pathetic, piteous, pitiable, pitiful, poignant, responsive, sad, stirring, stunning, sympathetic, tear-jerking, tender, wistful; SEE CONCEPTS *529,537*

touch up [*v*] *fix up; improve*
amend, brush up, do up, enhance, finish off, give a face-lift*, gloss, make improvements, modify, patch up, perfect, polish, put finishing touches on*, remodel, renew, renovate, repair, retouch, revamp, rework, round off, tease*; SEE CONCEPTS *212,244*

touchy [*adj*] *easily offended*
bad-tempered, bundle of nerves*, cantankerous, captious, choleric, crabbed, cranky, cross, delicate, dicey*, grouchy*, grumpy*, hazardous, hypersensitive, irascible, irritable, jumpy*, mean, ornery, oversensitive, peevish, perturbable, pettish, petulant, precarious, querulous, quick-tempered, risky, sensitive, splenetic, surly, temperamental, testy*, thin-skinned*, ticklish*, tricky, unpredictable, unsafe, uptight, volatile, wired up*, wound up*; SEE CONCEPTS *401,542,548*

tough [*n*] *person who is rowdy, mean*
bruiser, brute, bully, criminal, gangster, goon*, hood*, hoodlum, hooligan, punk*, rough*, roughneck, rowdy, ruffian, thug, villain; SEE CONCEPT *412*

tough [*adj1*] *sturdy, strong*
brawny, cohesive, conditioned, dense, durable, fibrous, firm, fit, flinty, hard, hard as nails*, hard-bitten*, hardened, hardy, healthy, indigestible, inflexible, leathery, lusty, mighty, molded, resilient, resistant, rigid, robust, rugged, seasoned, sinewy, solid, stalwart, steeled, stiff, stout, strapping, tenacious, tight, tough as nails*, unbreakable, uncooked, unyielding, vigorous, withstanding; SEE CONCEPTS *314,489*

tough [*adj2*] *obstinate, rough*
adamant, arbitrary, callous, confirmed, cruel, desperate, drastic, exacting, ferocious, fierce, firm, fixed, hard, hard-bitten*, hard-boiled*, hard-line*, hard-nosed*, hard-shelled*, harsh, headstrong, immutable, inflexible, intractable, merciless, narrow, obdurate, pugnacious, refractory, resolute, ruffianly, ruthless, savage, severe, stern, stiff, strict, stubborn, taut, terrible, unalterable, unbending, uncompromising, uncontrollable, unforgiving, unmanageable, unyielding, vicious, violent; SEE CONCEPTS *403,542*

tough [*adj3*] *difficult, laborious*
arduous, backbreaking*, baffling, burdensome, demanding, effortful, exacting, exhausting, exigent, grievous, hairy*, handful*, hard, heavy*, intractable, intricate, irksome, knotty*, labored, mean, no piece of cake*, onerous, oppressive, perplexing, puzzling, resisting, severe, stiff, strenuous, taxing, thorny*, toilsome, troublesome, trying, unyielding, uphill*, weighty*, wicked; SEE CONCEPTS *538,565*

toughen [*v*] *harden*
acclimate, acclimatize, anneal, brutalize, climatize, develop, inure, make difficult, season, strengthen, temper; SEE CONCEPTS *202,250*

tour [*n*] *journey; stint*
bout*, circle tour, circuit, course, cruise, excursion, expedition, getaway*, go*, hitch*, hop*, jaunt*, junket, outing, overnight, peregrination, progress, road, round*, roundabout*, round trip, run, shift, spell, stretch, stump*, swing*, time, travel, trek, trick*, trip, turn, voyage, weekend, whistle-stop*; SEE CONCEPTS *81,224,807*

tour [*v*] *visit, journey*
barnstorm*, cruise, explore, globe-trot*, go on the road*, holiday*, hop*, jaunt, jet, junket, peregrinate, sightsee, stump*, swing*, take a trip, travel, vacation, voyage; SEE CONCEPTS *224,227*

tourist [*n*] *person who visits a place*
day-tripper, excursionist, globetrotter, jet-setter, journeyer, rubberneck*, sightseer, stranger, traveler, tripper*, vacationist, visitor, voyager, wayfarer; SEE CONCEPT *423*

tournament [*n*] *sporting competition*
clash, contest, duel, event, fight, games, joust, match, meet, meeting, series, sport, test, tilt, tourney; SEE CONCEPT *363*

tousled [*adj*] *disarrayed*
beat-up*, dirty, disarranged, disheveled, disordered, grubby*, messed-up*, messy, mussed-up*, ruffled, rumpled, sloppy, tangled, uncombed, unkempt; SEE CONCEPTS *485,589*

tout [*v*] *brag about, show off*
acclaim, ballyhoo*, boost, give a boost*, herald, laud, plug*, praise, proclaim, promote, publicize, push, steer, tip, tip off*, trumpet; SEE CONCEPTS *69,138*

tow [*v*] *pull along*
drag, draw, ferry, haul, lug, propel, push, trail, trawl, tug, yank; SEE CONCEPT *206*

toward/towards [*prep1*] *on the way to; near*
against, almost, approaching, close to, coming up, contra, en route, facing, for, fronting, headed for, in relation to, in the direction of, in the vicinity, just before, moving, nearing, nearly, not quite, on the road to, over against, pointing to, proceeding, shortly before, to, via, vis-à-vis; SEE CONCEPT *586*

toward/towards [*prep2*] *concerning*
about, against, anent, apropos, as for, as to, for, in re, re, regarding, with regard to, with respect to; SEE CONCEPT *532*

tower [*n*] *very high building or building part*
belfry, castle, citadel, cloud buster, column, fort, fortification, fortress, high rise, keep, lookout, mast, minaret, monolith, obelisk, pillar, refuge, skyscraper, spire, steeple, stronghold, turret; SEE CONCEPTS *439,440*

tower [*v*] *rise above*
ascend, be above, dominate, exceed, extend above, look down, look over, loom, mount, overlook, overtop, rear, soar, surmount, surpass, top, transcend; SEE CONCEPTS *141,752*

towering [*adj*] *huge, excessive*
aerial, airy, colossal, elevated, extraordinary, extravagant, extreme, fantastic, gigantic, great, high, immoderate, imperial, imposing, impressive, inordinate, intense, lofty, magnificent, massive, mighty, monumental, outstanding, paramount, preeminent, prodigious, skyscraping, soaring, spiring, stately, stupendous, sublime, superior, supreme, surpassing, tall, towery, transcendent, tremendous, ultimate, undue, unmatchable, unmeasurable; SEE CONCEPTS *567,779*

town [*n*] *incorporated community*
apple*, boondocks, borough, burg*, city, hamlet, metropolis, municipality, seat, sticks*, township, whistle-stop*; SEE CONCEPTS *507,508*

toxic [*adj*] *poisonous*
baneful, deadly, harmful, lethal, mephitic, noxious, pernicious, pestilential, poison, septic, toxicant, venomous, virulent; SEE CONCEPT *537*

toy [*n*] *entertainment article*
bauble, curio, doll, game, knickknack, novelty, plaything, trifle, trinket; SEE CONCEPT *446*

toy [*v*] *play with*
amuse oneself, coquet, cosset, dally, dandle, fiddle, flirt, fool, fool around*, jest, lead on, mess around*, pet, play, play around, play games, sport, string along*, tease, trifle, wanton; SEE CONCEPT *384*

trace [*n*] *evidence; small bit*
breath, crumb, dab, dash, drop, element, footmark, footprint, fragment, hint, indication, intimation, iota, jot, mark, memento, minimum, nib, nuance, particle, pinch, proof, record, relic, remains, remnant, scintilla, shade, shadow, shred, sign, slot, smell, smidgen, snippet, soupçon, speck, spoor, spot, sprinkling, strain, streak, suggestion, survival, suspicion, taste, tincture, tinge, tittle, token, touch, track, trail,

tread, trifle, vestige, whiff, whisper; SEE CONCEPTS *529,831*

trace [*v1*] *seek, follow*
ascertain, detect, determine, discern, discover, ferret out, find, hunt, perceive, pursue, run down, search for, shadow, smell out, spoor, spot, stalk, track, trail, unearth; SEE CONCEPTS *207,216*

trace [*v2*] *draw around*
chart, copy, delineate, depict, duplicate, map, mark out, outline, record, reproduce, show, sketch; SEE CONCEPTS *79,174*

track [*n1*] *mark, print made by something*
clue, footmark, footprint, footstep, groove, impress, impression, imprint, indication, memorial, monument, path, print, record, remains, remnant, rut, scent, sign, slot, spoor, step, symbol, token, trace, tract, trail, tread, vestige, wake; SEE CONCEPTS *513,628*

track [*n2*] *path, way*
alley, artery, avenue, beaten path*, boulevard, clearing, course, cut*, drag*, footpath, highway, lane, line, orbit, passage, pathway, rail, rails, road, roadway, route, street, thoroughfare, track, trackway, trail, trajectory, walk; SEE CONCEPT *501*

track/track down [*v*] *follow, pursue*
apprehend, beat the bushes*, be hot on trail*, birddog*, bring to light*, capture, catch, chase, cover, dig up, discover, do, dog*, dog footsteps of*, draw an inference, expose, ferret out, find, go after, hunt, piece together, put together, run down, scout, shadow, smell out*, sniff out*, stalk, stick to, tail, trace, trail, travel, traverse, unearth; SEE CONCEPTS *183,207,216*

tract [*n*] *area, lot*
amplitude, belt, district, estate, expanse, extent, field, parcel, part, piece, plat, plot, portion, quarter, region, section, sector, spread, stretch, zone; SEE CONCEPTS *508,513*

tractable [*adj*] *manageable*
acquiescent, amenable, biddable, complaisant, compliant, controllable, docile, ductile, facile, flexible, game, go along with*, governable, hang loose*, malleable, meek, obedient, persuadable, plastic, pliable, pliant, putty in hands*, roll with punches*, subdued, submissive, tame, tractile, willing, workable, yielding; SEE CONCEPTS *401,488,542*

traction [*n*] *physical resistance, friction*
absorption, adherence, adhesion, constriction, contraction, drag, draught, drawing, grip, haulage, pull, pulling, purchase, resorption, strain, stress, stretch, suck, suction, towage; SEE CONCEPTS *731,748*

trade [*n1*] *buying and selling*
barter, business, clientele, commerce, contract, custom, customers, deal, dealing, enterprise, exchange, industry, interchange, market, merchantry, patronage, public, sales, swap, traffic, transaction, truck; SEE CONCEPTS *324,327,330,345*

trade [*n2*] *profession, work*
art, avocation, business, calling, craft, employment, game, handicraft, job, line, line of work, métier, nine-to-five*, occupation, position, pursuit, skill, thing*, vocation; SEE CONCEPTS *349,360*

trademark [*n*] *logo, symbol*
brand, brand name, identification, initials, label, logo, logotype, mark, stamp, tag; SEE CONCEPTS *259,284*

tradition [*n*] *established practice*
attitude, belief, birthright, conclusion, convention, culture, custom, customs, ethic, ethics, fable, folklore, form, habit, heritage, idea, inheritance, institution, law, legend, lore, mores, myth, mythology, mythos, opinion, practice, praxis, ritual, unwritten law, usage, wisdom; SEE CONCEPT *687*

traditional [*adj*] *usual, established*
acceptable, accustomed, acknowledged, ancestral, classic, classical, common, conventional, customary, doctrinal, fixed, folk, habitual, historic, immemorial, long-established, old, oral, popular, prescribed, regular, rooted, sanctioned, taken for granted, time-honored, transmitted, universal, unwritten, widely used, widespread; SEE CONCEPTS *530,533*

traffic [*n1*] *coming and going*
cartage, flux, freight, gridlock, influx, jam, movement, parking lot*, passage, passengers, rush hour, service, shipment, transfer, transit, transport, transportation, travel, truckage, vehicles; SEE CONCEPTS *224,505,770*

traffic [*n2*] *buying and selling*
barter, business, closeness, commerce, communication, communion, connection, custom, dealing, dealings*, doings*, exchange, familiarity, industry, interchange, intercourse, intimacy, merchantry, patronage, peddling, relations, relations, relationship, soliciting, trade, transactions, truck*; SEE CONCEPTS *330,335*

traffic [*v*] *buy and sell; do business*
bargain, barter, black-market*, bootleg*, connect with, contact, deal, deal in*, dicker, exchange, fence, handle, have dealings, have transaction, horse trade*, interact, interface, make a deal, market, moonshine*, negotiate, network, peddle, push, reach out, relate, shove, swap, touch, touch base*, trade, truck*, work out; SEE CONCEPTS *324,327,330,345*

tragedy [*n*] *disaster*
adversity, affliction, bad fortune, bad luck, blight, blow*, calamity, cataclysm, catastrophe, contretemps, curse, curtains*, dole, dolor, doom, downer*, failure, hard knocks*, hardship, humiliation, lot, misadventure, mischance, misfortune, mishap, reverse, shock, struggle, the worst*, unluckiness, Waterloo*, woe, wreck; SEE CONCEPTS *674,675*

tragic [*adj*] *catastrophic, very bad*
adverse, anguished, appalling, awful, calamitous, cataclysmic, crushing, deadly, deathly, deplorable,

desolate, destructive, dire, disastrous, doleful, dreadful, fatal, fateful, forlorn, grievous, grim, hapless, harrowing, heartbreaking, heart-rending, ill-fated, ill-starred, lamentable, miserable, mournful, painful, pathetic, pitiable, pitiful, ruinous, sad, shocking, sorrowful, terrible, unfortunate, unhappy, woeful, wretched; SEE CONCEPTS **548,571**

trail [n] *path, track*
aisle, beaten track*, byway, footpath, footprints, footsteps, groove*, mark, marks, pathway, road, route, rut, scent, spoor, stream, stroll, tail, trace, train, wake, way; SEE CONCEPT **501**

trail [v] *lag behind, follow*
bedog, bring up the rear*, chase, dally, dangle, dawdle, delay, dog*, drag, draggle, draw, droop, drop back, extend, fall back, fall behind, falter, flag, follow a scent*, halt, hang, hang back, hang down, haul, hunt, lag, linger, loiter, nose out*, plod, poke, poke along*, procrastinate, pull, pursue, shadow, shag, spook*, spoor, stalk, straggle, stream, string along*, tag along*, tail, take out after, tarry, tow, trace, track, traipse, trudge; SEE CONCEPTS **207,727,753**

train [n] *series*
alternation, appendage, caravan, chain, column, concatenation, consecution, convoy, cortege, course, court, entourage, file, following, gradation, line, order, procession, progression, retinue, row, run, scale, sequel, sequence, set, string, succession, suite, tail, thread, tier, track, trail, wake; SEE CONCEPTS **432,727**

train [v1] *prepare*
accustom, brainwash*, break in, care for, coach, cultivate, develop, discipline, drill, drum into, dry run*, educate, enlighten, equip, exercise, get a workout, get in shape, ground, grow strong, guide, habituate, harden, hone, improve, instruct, inure, make ready, mold, prime, qualify, rear, rehearse, run through, school, season, shape, sharpen, show the ropes*, study, tame, teach, tutor, update, warm up, whip into shape*, wise up*, work out; SEE CONCEPTS **35,202,285**

train [v2] *aim at*
beam, bring to bear, cast, cock, direct, draw a bead*, focus, get in one's sights*, head, incline, lay, level, line up, point, slant, turn, zero in*; SEE CONCEPT **201**

training [n] *preparation*
background, basics, buildup, chalk talk*, coaching, cultivation, discipline, domestication, drill, education, exercise, foundation, grounding, groundwork, guidance, indoctrination, instruction, practice, preliminaries, preparation, principles, readying, schooling, seasoning, sharpening, teaching, tuition, tune-up*, tutelage, upbringing, warm-up, workout; SEE CONCEPTS **202,285,678**

trait [n] *characteristic*
affection, attribute, birthmark, cast, character, custom, denominator, feature, habit, idiosyncrasy, lineament, manner, mannerism, mark, nature of the beast*, oddity, peculiarity, point, property, quality, quirk, savor, thing*, trick, virtue; SEE CONCEPTS **411,644,834**

traitor [n] *person who is disloyal*
apostate, backslider*, back-stabber*, Benedict Arnold*, betrayer, conspirator, deceiver, defector, deserter, double-crosser*, fink*, hypocrite, impostor, informer, intriguer, Judas*, miscreant, quisling, rebel, renegade, snake*, sneak*, snitch*, snitcher*, spy, squealer*, stool pigeon*, tattletale, traducer, treasonist, turncoat*, two-timer*, whistle-blower*, wolf*; SEE CONCEPT **412**

tramp [n1] *person who is poor, desperate*
beggar, bum, derelict, down-and-out*, drifter, floater, gypsy, hitchhiker, hobo, loafer, outcast, panhandler, prostitute, vagabond, vagrant, wanderer; SEE CONCEPT **412**

tramp [n2] *heavy walk*
cruise, excursion, expedition, footfall, footstep, hike, jaunt, march, ramble, saunter, slog, stomp, stroll, tour, traipse, tread, trek, turn, walking trip; SEE CONCEPTS **151,224**

tramp [v] *walk heavily*
crush, footslog, gallop, hike, hop, march, navigate, plod, pound, ramble, range, roam, rove, slog, stamp, stodge, stomp, stroll, stump, thud, toil, tour, traipse, trample, tread, trek, trip, tromp, trudge, walk over; SEE CONCEPTS **151,224**

trample [v] *walk forcibly over*
bruise, crush, encroach, flatten, grind, hurt, infringe, injure, override, overwhelm, pound, ride roughshod over*, run over, squash, stamp, step on, stomp, tramp, tread, tromp, violate; SEE CONCEPTS **137,208,246**

trance [n] *hypnotic state*
abstraction, coma, daze, dream, ecstasy, glaze, insensibility, muse, petrifaction, rapture, reverie, spell, study, stupor, transfixion, transfixture, unconsciousness; SEE CONCEPT **410**

tranquil [adj] *quiet, peaceful*
agreeable, amicable, at ease, at peace, balmy, calm, collected, comforting, composed, cool, easy, easygoing, even, even-tempered, gentle, halcyon, hushed, lenient, low, measured, mild, moderate, murmuring, pacific, paradisiacal, pastoral, patient, placid, pleasing, poised, possessed, quiet, reasonable, restful, sedate, sedative, serene, smooth, sober, soft, soothing, stable, still, tame, temperate, undisturbed, unexcitable, unexcited, unperturbed, unruffled, untroubled, whispering; SEE CONCEPTS **525,542,594**

tranquility [n] *peace, quiet*
ataraxia, calm, calmness, composure, coolness, equanimity, hush, imperturbability, imperturbation, law and order, order, peacefulness, placidity, quietness, quietude, repose, rest, restfulness, sedateness, serenity, stillness; SEE CONCEPTS **65,673**

tranquilize [v] *make calm, quiet*
balm, calm, calm down, compose, hush, lull, pacify, put at rest, quell, quiet, quieten, relax, sedate, settle one's nerves*, soothe, still, subdue, unruffle; SEE CONCEPTS *7,22,310*

transact [v] *do business, carry out*
accomplish, button down*, button up*, buy, carry on, clinch, close, conclude, conduct, discharge, do*, effectuate, enact, execute, finish, handle, jell, manage, move, negotiate, operate, perform, prosecute, pull off, run with the ball*, see to, sell, settle, sew up*, take care of, TCB*, work out a deal*, wrap up*; SEE CONCEPTS *91,223,324,330,706*

transaction [n] *business dealing; undertaking*
act, action, activity, affair, agreement, bargain, bond, business, buying, compact, contract, convention, coup, covenant, deal, deed, disposal, doings*, enterprise, event, execution, goings-on*, happening, intercourse, matter, negotiation, occurrence, pact, performance, play, proceeding, purchase, purchasing, sale, selling, step; SEE CONCEPTS *223,324, 330,684*

transcend [v] *go beyond; surpass*
beat, best, be superior, better, eclipse, exceed, excel, go above, leave behind, leave in the dust*, outdo, outrival, outshine, outstrip, outvie, overstep, overtop, rise above, top, transform; SEE CONCEPT *141*

transcendent/transcendental [adj] *extraordinary, superior*
absolute, abstract, accomplished, beyond grasp, boundless, consummate, entire, eternal, exceeding, fantastic, finished, hypothetical, ideal, incomparable, infinite, innate, intact, intellectual, intuitive, matchless, obscure, original, otherworldly, peerless, perfect, preeminent, primordial, second to none*, sublime, supernatural, supreme, surpassing, theoretical, towering, transcending, transmundane, ultimate, unequalable, unequalled, unique, unparalleled, unrivalled, whole; SEE CONCEPT *574*

transcribe [v] *transfer to another medium*
copy out, decipher, duplicate, engross, interpret, note, record, render, reprint, reproduce, rewrite, set out, take down, tape, tape-record, transfer, translate, transliterate, write out; SEE CONCEPTS *79,125,171*

transfer [n] *change of possession*
alteration, assignment, conduction, convection, deportation, displacement, move, relegation, relocation, removal, shift, substitution, transference, translation, transmission, transmittal, transposition, variation; SEE CONCEPTS *108,143,217,223*

transfer [v] *pass possession to*
assign, bear, bring, carry, cart, cede, change, consign, convert, convey, deed, delegate, deliver, dislocate, dispatch, dispense, displace, disturb, express, feed, ferry, find, forward, give, hand, hand over, haul, lug, mail, make over, metamorphose, move, pass on, pass the buck*, post, provide, relegate, relocate, remove, sell, send, shift, ship, shoulder, sign

over, supply, taxi, tote, transfigure, translate, transmit, transmogrify, transmute, transplant, transport, transpose, turn over; SEE CONCEPTS *108,143, 217,223,243*

transfix [v1] *hold one's attention*
bewitch, captivate, enchant, engross, fascinate, hold, hypnotize, mesmerize, palsy, paralyze, petrify, rivet, root, spellbind, stop dead*, stop in one's tracks*, stun; SEE CONCEPTS *11,14*

transfix [v2] *pierce*
fix, impale, lance, nail down, penetrate, pin down, puncture, run through, skewer, skiver, spear, spike, spit, stick, transpierce; SEE CONCEPT *220*

transform [v] *change completely*
alter, commute, convert, cook, denature, doctor, make over, metamorphose, mold, mutate, reconstruct, remodel, renew, revamp, revolutionize, shift gears*, sing different tune*, switch, switch over, transfer, transfigure, translate, transmogrify, transmute, transpose, turn around, turn over new leaf*, turn the corner*, turn the tables*; SEE CONCEPTS *232,697*

transformation [n] *complete change*
about-face*, alteration, changeover, conversion, flip-flop*, metamorphosis, radical change, renewal, revolution, shift, switch, transfiguration, transmogrification, transmutation; SEE CONCEPT *697*

transgression [n] *violation, misbehavior*
breach, breaking of the law, contravention, crime, defiance, disobedience, encroachment, erring, error, fault, infraction, infringement, iniquity, lapse, misdeed, misdemeanor, offense, overstepping, sin, slip, trespass, vice, wrong, wrongdoing; SEE CONCEPTS *101,192,645*

transient/transitory [adj] *temporary, brief*
changeable, deciduous, emigrating, ephemeral, evanescent, flash, fleeting, flitting, fly-by-night*, flying, fugacious, fugitive, going by, impermanent, insubstantial, migrating, momentary, moving, passing, provisional, short, short-lived, short-term, temporal, transmigratory, unstable, vacating, volatile; SEE CONCEPT *798*

transit [n] *transportation*
alteration, carriage, carrying, conveyance, crossing, infiltration, motion, movement, osmosis, passage, penetration, permeation, portage, shift, shipment, transfer, transference, transport, transporting, travel, traverse; SEE CONCEPTS *155,224*

transition [n] *change, often major*
alteration, changeover, conversion, development, evolution, flux, growth, metamorphosis, metastasis, passage, passing, progress, progression, realignment, shift, transformation, transit, transmutation, turn, turning point, upheaval; SEE CONCEPT *697*

translate [v1] *interpret, explain*
construe, convert, decipher, decode, do into, elucidate, explicate, gloss, make clear, metaphrase, paraphrase, put, render, reword, simplify, spell out,

transcribe, transliterate, transpose, turn; SEE CON-
CEPTS *55,57*

translate [*v2*] *change*
alter, commute, convert, metamorphose, transfigure,
transform, transmogrify, transmute, transpose, turn;
SEE CONCEPT *232*

translation [*n*] *rewording; interpretation*
adaptation, construction, crib*, decoding, elucidation, explanation, gloss, key, metaphrase, paraphrase, reading, rendering, rendition, rephrasing,
restatement, simplification, transcription, translitera-
tion, version; SEE CONCEPTS *268,277,278*

translucent [*adj*] *clear*
clear-cut, crystal, crystalline, diaphanous, glassy,
limpid, lucent, lucid, luminous, pellucid, see-
through, semiopaque, semitransparent, translucid,
unblurred; SEE CONCEPT *618*

transmit [*v*] *communicate, send*
address, bear, bequeath, break, broadcast, carry,
channel, conduct, consign, convey, diffuse, dispatch, disseminate, drop a line*, drop a note*, forward, funnel, give a call*, give a ring*, hand down,
hand on, impart, instill, issue, mail, pass on, pipe,
put on the air, radio, relay, remit, route, send, send
out, ship, siphon, spread, take, traject, transfer,
transfuse, translate, transport; SEE CONCEPTS
217,266,292

transparent [*adj1*] *see-through*
cellophane, clear, crystal-clear, crystalline, diaphanous, filmy, gauzy, glassy, gossamer, hyaline, limpid, lucent, lucid, pellucid, permeable, plain, sheer,
thin, tiffany, translucent, transpicuous, vitreous; SEE
CONCEPTS *606,618*

transparent [*adj2*] *obvious, understandable*
apparent, articulate, artless, candid, clear-cut, direct,
distinct, distinguishable, easily seen, easy, evident,
explicit, forthright, frank, guileless, honest, ingenuous, manifest, open, patent, perspicuous, plain,
plain-spoken, recognizable, self-explanatory, sincere, straight, straightforward, unambiguous, undisguised, unequivocal, unmistakable, unsophisticated,
visible; SEE CONCEPT *267*

transpire [*v1*] *occur, happen*
arise, befall, betide, chance, come about, come to
pass, develop, ensue, eventuate, fall out*, gel, go,
occur, result, shake, take place, turn up, what goes*;
SEE CONCEPT *3*

transpire [*v2*] *become known*
be disclosed, be discovered, be made public, break,
come out, come to light, emerge, get out, leak; SEE
CONCEPTS *261,266*

transplant [*v*] *relocate*
displace, emigrate, graft, immigrate, move, readapt,
recondition, remove, reorient, reset, resettle, revamp, shift, transfer, transpose, uproot; SEE CON-
CEPTS *213,310*

transport [*n1*] *move, transfer*
carriage, carrier, carrying, carting, conveyance, conveying, conveyor, freightage, hauling, lift, move-

ment, mover, moving, passage, removal, shipment,
shipping, transference, transferring, transit, transportation, transporting, transshipment, truckage, vehicle; SEE CONCEPTS *155,503*

transport [*n2*] *delight*
ardor, bliss, cloud nine*, ecstasy, enchantment, enthusiasm, euphoria, fervor, happiness, heaven, passion, rapture, ravishment, rhapsody, seventh
heaven*; SEE CONCEPTS *32,410*

transport [*v1*] *move, transfer*
back, bear, bring, carry, conduct, convey, ferry,
fetch, haul, heel*, jag, lug, pack, piggyback*, remove, ride, run, schlepp*, ship, shoulder*, take,
tote, truck; SEE CONCEPTS *147,187,217*

transport [*v2*] *exile*
banish, cast out, deport, displace, expel, expulse,
oust, relegate, sentence; SEE CONCEPTS *211,317*

transport [*v3*] *captivate, delight*
agitate, carry away, electrify, elevate, enchant, enrapture, entrance, excite, inflame, move, provoke,
quicken, ravish, send, slay, spellbind, stimulate, stir,
thrill, trance, uplight, wow; SEE CONCEPTS *7,22*

transpose [*v*] *swap, switch*
alter, backtrack*, change, commute, convert, double
back, exchange, flip-flop*, interchange, inverse, invert, metamorphose, move, put, rearrange, relocate,
render, reorder, reverse, revert, shift, substitute,
transfer, transfigure, transform, translate, transmogrify, transmute, turn, turn the tables*; SEE CONCEPTS
104,232,697

trap [*n*] *snare, trick*
allurement, ambuscade, ambush, artifice, bait, booby
trap*, come-on*, conspiracy, deception, decoy, device, dragnet, enticement, feint, gambit, hook*, intrigue, inveiglement, lasso*, lure, machination,
maneuver, net*, noose*, pitfall*, plot, ploy, prank,
quagmire*, quicksand*, ruse, seducement, snag*,
stratagem, subterfuge, temptation, wile; SEE CON-
CEPT *674*

trap [*v*] *catch, snare; trick*
ambuscade, ambush, beguile, box in*, circumvent,
collar*, corner*, corral*, deceive, decoy, dupe, enmesh, ensnare, entangle, entrap, fool, grab, hook,
inveigle, land*, mousetrap*, nab, nail*, net, overtake, rope in*, seduce, snag, suck in*, surprise, take,
tangle, trammel, trip up*; SEE CONCEPTS *59,90*

trappings [*n*] *paraphernalia, equipment*
accouterment, adornment, apparel, appointment,
decoration, dress, embellishment, finery, fitting, fixture, furnishing, gear, livery, ornament, panoply,
personal effects, raiment, rigging, things, trimming;
SEE CONCEPTS *446,451,496*

trash [*n1*] *garbage*
debris, dregs, droppings, dross*, excess, filth*, fragments, junk, leavings, litter, oddments, odds and
ends*, offal, pieces, refuse, residue, rubbish, rubble,
rummage, scourings, scrap, scraps, scum*, sedi-

ment, shavings, sweepings, waste; SEE CONCEPTS *260,834*

trash [*n2*] *worthless person*
beggar, dregs*, good-for-nothing*, hobo, outlaw, rabble, raff*, rascal, riffraff*, scum*, thief, tramp, unwashed, varmint, vermin; SEE CONCEPTS *412,417*

trash [*n3*] *ridiculous communication*
balderdash*, bilge*, drivel, foolish talk, hogwash, inanity, malarkey*, nonsense, rot*, rubbish*, tripe*, twaddle*; SEE CONCEPT *278*

trauma [*n*] *severe mental or physical pain*
agony, anguish, blow, collapse, confusion, damage, derangement, disturbance, hurt, injury, jolt, ordeal, outburst, shock, strain, stress, suffering, torture, traumatization, upheaval, upset, wound; SEE CONCEPT *728*

travel [*n*] *journey*
biking, commutation, cruising, drive, driving, excursion, expedition, flying, globe-trotting*, hop*, junket, movement, navigation, overnight, passage, peregrination, ramble, ride, riding, sailing, seafaring, sightseeing, swing, tour, touring, transit, trek, trekking, trip, voyage, voyaging, walk, wandering, wanderlust, wayfaring, weekend; SEE CONCEPT *224*

travel [*v*] *journey on a trip or tour*
adventure, carry, cover, cover ground, cross, cruise, drive, explore, fly, get through, go, go abroad, go camping, go into orbit*, go riding, hop*, jaunt, jet*, junket*, knock around, make a journey, make one's way*, migrate, motor, move, overnight*, proceed, progress, ramble, roam, rove, sail, scour, set forth, set out, sightsee, take a boat, take a plane, take a train, take a trip, tour, transmit, traverse, trek*, vacation, visit, voyage, walk, wander, weekend*, wend; SEE CONCEPT *224*

traveler [*n*] *person who journeys*
adventurer, barnstormer*, bum*, commuter, displaced person, drifter, excursionist, expeditionist, explorer, floater, gadabout*, globetrotter, gypsy, hiker, hobo, itinerant, jet-setter, journeyer, junketer, migrant, navigator, nomad, passenger, peddler, pilgrim, rambler, roamer, rover, sailor, salesman/woman, salesperson, seafarer, sightseer, tourist, tramp, transmigrant, trekker, tripper, trouper, truant, vagabond, vagrant, voyager, wanderer, wayfarer; SEE CONCEPTS *348,423*

traverse [*v1*] *cross over; travel*
bisect, bridge, cover, crisscross, cross, cut across, decussate, do, go across, go over, intersect, move over, negotiate, pace, pass over, pass through, perambulate, peregrinate, ply, quarter, range, roam, span, track, transverse, travel over, tread, walk, wander; SEE CONCEPTS *147,201,692,750*

traverse [*v2*] *resist, contradict*
balk, buck, check, combat, contest, contravene, counter, counteract, cross, deny, disaffirm, dispute, duel, fight, frustrate, gainsay, go against, hinder, impede, impugn, negate, negative, obstruct, oppose, repel, thwart, withstand; SEE CONCEPTS *54,121*

travesty [*n*] *spoof, ridicule*
burlesque, caricature, distortion, exaggeration, farce, lampoon, lampoonery, mimicry, mock, mockery, parody, perversion, play, put-on*, roast*, satire, send-up*, sham*, takeoff*; SEE CONCEPTS *273,292*

travesty [*v*] *ridicule, spoof*
ape, burlesque, caricature, deride, distort, imitate, lampoon, make a mockery of, make fun of, mimic, mock, parody, pervert, play on*, put on*, satire, send up*, sham*, take off*; SEE CONCEPTS *273,292*

treacherous [*adj1*] *dishonest, disloyal*
betraying, catchy, deceitful, deceptive, double-crossing*, double-dealing*, duplicitous, faithless, false, false-hearted, fly-by-night*, insidious, misleading, perfidious, recreant, shifty*, slick*, slippery*, snake in the grass*, traitorous, treasonable, tricky, two-faced*, two-timing*, undependable, unfaithful, unloyal, unreliable, untrue, untrustworthy; SEE CONCEPTS *401,404*

treacherous [*adj2*] *dangerous*
alarming, chancy, deceptive, difficult, dissembled, faulty, hairy*, hazardous, icy*, insecure, jeopardous, menacing, misleading, ominous, perilous, precarious, risky, shaky, slippery, ticklish, tricky, undependable, unhealthy, unreliable, unsafe, unsound, unstable, wicked; SEE CONCEPTS *565,587*

treachery [*n*] *disloyalty, dishonesty*
betrayal, bunco, corruption, dirty dealing*, dirty pool*, dirty trick*, dirty work*, disaffection, dodge, double-cross*, double-dealing*, duplicity, faithlessness, fake, falseness, fast shuffle*, flimflam*, grift, gyp*, infidelity, perfidiousness, perfidy, put-on*, racket*, recreancy, scam*, sellout, shell game*, skin game*, spoof, stab in the back*, sweet talk*, treacherousness, treason, two-timing*, whitewash*; SEE CONCEPTS *633,645*

tread [*n*] *walk*
footstep, footsteps, gait, march, pace, step, stride, trace, track, tramp; SEE CONCEPTS *149,284*

tread [*v*] *walk; bear down*
ambulate, crush, foot, hike, hoof, march, oppress, pace, plod, quell, repress, squash, stamp, stamp on, step, step on, stride, subdue, subjugate, suppress, traipse, tramp, trample, troop, trudge; SEE CONCEPT *149*

treason [*n*] *disloyalty*
breach of faith, crime, deceit, deceitfulness, deception, disaffection, dishonesty, duplicity, faithlessness, lèse majesté, mutiny, perfidy, revolt, revolutionary, sedition, seditious act, seditiousness, subversion, traitorousness, treachery; SEE CONCEPTS *192,645*

treasure [*n*] *prized possession or entity*
abundance, apple of one's eye*, cache, capital, cash, catch*, darling, find, fortune, funds, gem, gold, hoard, jewel, money, nest egg*, nonpareil, paragon,

pearl*, pile*, plum*, pride and joy*, prize, reserve, riches, richness, store, treasure trove, valuable, wealth; SEE CONCEPTS *332,337,446,710*

treasure [v] *hold dear*
adore, appreciate, apprize, cherish, conserve, dote on, esteem, guard, idolize, love, preserve, prize, revere, reverence, save, value, venerate, worship; SEE CONCEPT *32*

treasury [n] *place where money, valuables are kept*
archive, bank, bursar, bursary, cache, chest, coffer, damper, depository, exchange, exchequer, Fort Knox*, gallery, hoard, museum, register, repository, safe, storage, store, storehouse, strongbox, treasure house, vault; SEE CONCEPTS *339,439,449*

treat [n] *pleasing entity or occurrence*
amusement, banquet, celebration, dainty, delicacy, delight, enjoyment, entertainment, feast, fun, gift, goody*, gratification, joy, party, pleasure, refreshment, satisfaction, surprise, sweet, thrill, tidbit; SEE CONCEPTS *457,529,693*

treat [v1] *act, behave towards*
account, act with regard to, appraise, conduct, conduct oneself toward, consider, deal with*, employ, estimate, evaluate, handle, have business with*, have recourse to*, have to do with*, hold, look upon, manage, negotiate, play, rate, react toward, regard, respect, serve, take, use, value, wield; SEE CONCEPT *633*

treat [v2] *doctor, medicate*
administer, apply treatment, attend, care for, cure, dose, dress, heal, medicament, minister to, nurse, operate, prescribe; SEE CONCEPT *310*

treat [v3] *pay the bill for someone else*
amuse, blow, buy for, divert, entertain, escort, feast, foot the bill*, give, indulge, on one*, on the house*, pay for, pick up the check*, pick up the tab*, play host*, provide, regale, satisfy, set up, spring for*, stake, stand*, take out, wine and dine*; SEE CONCEPTS *327,384*

treat [v4] *be concerned with; discuss*
advise, approach, arrange, comment, confabulate, confer, consider, consult, contain, criticize, deal with, deliberate, discourse on, discuss, enlarge upon, explain, go into, interpret, manipulate, reason, review, speak about, study, tackle, talk about, think, touch upon, weigh, write about; SEE CONCEPTS *17,56*

treatise [n] *written study of a subject*
argument, book, commentary, composition, discourse, discussion, disquisition, dissertation, essay, exposition, memoir, monograph, pamphlet, paper, review, script, thesis, tract, tractate, work, writing; SEE CONCEPTS *271,280*

treatment [n1] *medical care*
analysis, cure, diet, doctoring, healing, hospitalization, medication, medicine, operation, prescription, regimen, remedy, surgery, therapeutics, therapy; SEE CONCEPT *310*

treatment [n2] *handling of entity, situation*
action towards, angle, approach, behavior towards, conduct, custom, dealing, employment, execution, habit, line, management, manipulation, manner, method, mode, modus operandi*, practice, procedure, proceeding, processing, reception, strategy, usage, way; SEE CONCEPTS *117,633*

treaty [n] *agreement, contract*
accord, alliance, arrangement, bargain, bond, cartel, charter, compact, concord, concordat, convention, covenant, deal, entente, league, negotiation, pact, reconciliation, sanction, settlement, understanding; SEE CONCEPTS *684,685*

tree [n] *large plant enclosed in bark and shedding leaves*
forest, hardwood, pulp, sapling, seedling, shrub, softwood, stock, timber, wood, woods; SEE CONCEPT *430*

trek [n] *long journey*
expedition, footslog, hike, long haul, march, odyssey, peregrination, slog, tramp, travel, trip; SEE CONCEPT *224*

trek [v] *journey*
be on the move*, be on the trail*, foot, hike, hit the road*, march, migrate, plod, range, roam, rove, slog, traipse, tramp, travel, trudge, walk; SEE CONCEPT *224*

tremble [v] *shake, vibrate*
flutter, have the shakes*, jar, jitter, oscillate, palpitate, quake, quaver, quiver, rock, shiver, shudder, teeter, throb, totter, tremor, wobble; SEE CONCEPT *152*

tremendous [adj] *huge, overwhelming*
amazing, appalling, astounding, awesome, awful, blimp, colossal, cracking, deafening, dreadful, enormous, excellent, exceptional, extraordinary, fabulous, fantastic, fearful, formidable, frightful, gargantuan, gigantic, great, great big*, huge, humongous, immense, incredible, jumbo*, large, mammoth, marvelous, massive, mondo*, monstrous*, monumental, prodigious, stupendous, super, terrible, terrific, titanic*, towering, vast, whale*, whopper, whopping, wonderful; SEE CONCEPTS *574,773,781*

tremor [n] *shaking, shock*
agitation, earthquake, flutter, quake, quaking, quaver, quiver, quivering, ripple, shake, shiver, shivering, tremble, trembling, trepidation, upheaval, vibration, wobble; SEE CONCEPTS *145,526*

trench [n] *ditch, channel dug in earth*
arroyo, canal, cut, depression, dike, drain, drill, dugout, earthwork, entrenchment, excavation, fosse, foxhole, furrow, gorge, gulch, gully, gutter, hollow, main, moat, pit, rut, sink, trough, tube, waterway; SEE CONCEPTS *509,513*

trenchant [adj] *sarcastic, scathing*
acerbic, acid, acidulous, acute, astringent, biting, caustic, clear, clear-cut, crisp, critical, crushing, cutting, distinct, driving, dynamic, effective, effectual,

emphatic, energetic, explicit, forceful, forcible, graphic, hurtful, impressive, incisive, intense, keen, mordant, penetrating, piquant, pointed, potent, powerful, pungent, razor-sharp*, salient, salty*, sententious, severe, sharp, significant, strong, tart, to the point, unequivocal, unsparing, vigorous, weighty, well-defined; SEE CONCEPTS *267,537*

trend [*n1*] *flow, current*
aim, bearing, bent, bias, course, direction, drift, inclination, leaning, movement, orientation, progression, run, swing, tendency, tenor, wind; SEE CONCEPTS *230,657,738*

trend [*n2*] *style, fashion that is in favor*
craze, cry, fad, furor, in-thing*, latest thing*, look, mode, newest wrinkle*, rage, thing*, vogue; SEE CONCEPT *655*

trendy [*adj*] *in fashion, style*
à la mode*, contemporary, fashionable, fly*, in, in vogue, latest, modish*, now*, popular, stylish, swank*, tony*, up-to-the-minute, voguish, with-it*; SEE CONCEPT *589*

trepidation [*n*] *anxiety, worry*
agitation, alarm, apprehension, blue funk*, butterflies*, cold feet*, cold sweat*, consternation, creeps*, dismay, disquiet, disturbance, dread, emotion, excitement, fear, fright, goose bumps*, horror, jitters, nervousness, palpitation, panic, perturbation, shock, terror, trepidity, uneasiness, worriment; SEE CONCEPT *27*

trespass [*n*] *invasion, offense*
breach, contravention, crime, delinquency, encroachment, entrenchment, error, evildoing, fault, infraction, infringement, iniquity, injury, intrusion, misbehavior, misconduct, misdeed, misdemeanor, obtrusion, poaching, sin, transgression, unlawful entry, violation, wrongdoing, wrongful entry; SEE CONCEPTS *101,192,645,691*

trespass [*v*] *infringe, offend*
butt in*, chisel in*, crash, crash the gates*, deviate, displease, do wrong by, encroach, entrench, err, horn in*, interlope, intrude, invade, kibitz*, lapse, meddle, misbehave, mix in, muscle in*, nose in*, obtrude, overstep, penetrate, poach, poke, sin, stick nose in*, transgress, violate, wrong; SEE CONCEPTS *101,159,192,384*

trial [*n1*] *test*
analysis, assay, attempt, audition, check, crack*, dry run*, effort, endeavor, essay, examination, experience, experiment, experimentation, fling*, go*, hassle, investigation, lick*, probation, proof, R and D*, research and development, shakedown*, shot*, showcase, stab*, striving, struggle, testing, test run, trial and error*, trial run, try, try on*, tryout, undertaking, venture, whack*, workout; SEE CONCEPTS *87,290,291*

trial [*n2*] *legal proceeding*
action, arraignment, case, citation, claim, contest, counterclaim, court action, court martial, cross-

examination, habeas corpus, hearing, impeachment, indictment, lawsuit, litigation, prosecution, rap*, seizure, suit, tribunal; SEE CONCEPTS *317,691*

trial [*n3*] *trouble, big problem*
adversity, affliction, albatross*, anguish, annoyance, bane, blow, bother, burden, calvary, care, complication, cross to bear*, crucible*, difficulty, distress, drag*, grief, hardship, hard time*, hassle, heartbreak, inconvenience, irritation, load, misery, misfortune, nightmare, nuisance, ordeal, pain, pain in the neck*, pest, plague, rigor, severe test, sorrow, suffering, thorn, tribulation, trying time, unhappiness, vexation, vicissitude, visitation, woe, wretchedness; SEE CONCEPTS *674,728*

trial [*adj*] *experimental*
balloon, exploratory, pilot, preliminary, probationary, provisional, tentative, test, testing; SEE CONCEPTS *548,560*

tribe [*n*] *ethnic group; family*
association, blood, caste, clan, class, division, dynasty, horde, house, ilk, kin, kind, kindred, lineage, people, race, seed, society, sort, stock, type; SEE CONCEPTS *296,380,421*

tribulation [*n*] *pain, unhappiness*
adversity, affliction, albatross*, bad luck*, blow*, bummer*, burden, care, cross to bear*, crucible*, curse, difficulty, distress, double whammy*, downer*, drag*, grief, hard knock*, hard time*, headache*, heartache*, misery, misfortune, oppression, ordeal, persecution, rainy day*, reverse, sorrow, suffering, trial, trouble, vexation, visitation, woe, worry, wretchedness, wronging; SEE CONCEPTS *666,728*

tributary [*adj*] *secondary; branch*
accessory, dependent, feeding, minor, satellite, shoot, side, sub, subject, subordinate, under; SEE CONCEPT *560*

tribute [*n*] *testimonial, praise*
accolade, acknowledgment, applause, appreciation, citation, commendation, compliment, encomium, esteem, eulogy, gift, gratitude, honor, laudation, memorial, offering, panegyric, recognition, recommendation, respect, salutation, salvo; SEE CONCEPTS *69,278*

trick [*n1*] *deceit*
ambush, artifice, blind, bluff, casuistry, cheat, chicanery, circumvention, con, concealment, conspiracy, conundrum, cover, deception, decoy, delusion, device, disguise, distortion, dodge*, double-dealing, duplicity, equivocation, evasion, fabrication, fake, falsehood, feint, forgery, fraud, game, gimmick*, gyp*, hoax, illusion, imposition, imposture, intrigue, invention, machination, maneuver, perjury, plot, ploy, pretense, ruse, snare, stratagem, subterfuge, swindle, trap, treachery, wile; SEE CONCEPTS *59,645*

trick [*n2*] *prank, joke*
accomplishment, antic, caper, catch, device, escapade, feat, frolic, funny business, gag*, gambol, jape*, jest, lark, monkeyshine*, practical joke, put-

on*, shenanigan*, sleight of hand, sport, stunt, tomfoolery; SEE CONCEPTS *59,273,384*

trick [*n3*] *expertise, know-how*
ability, art, command, craft, device, facility, gift, hang, knack, method, secret, skill, swing, technique; SEE CONCEPT *630*

trick [*n4*] *characteristic, habit*
crotchet, custom, foible, habitude, idiosyncrasy, manner, mannerism, peculiarity, practice, praxis, quirk, trait, usage, use, way, wont; SEE CONCEPTS *411,657*

trick [*n5*] *time working at something*
bout, go*, hitch, shift, spell, stint, tour, turn; SEE CONCEPT *807*

trick [*v*] *fool; play joke on*
bamboozle, catch*, cheat, con, deceive, defraud, delude, disinform, double deal*, dupe, fake, flimflam*, fool, gull, hoax, hocus-pocus*, hoodwink, impose upon, jive*, mislead, outwit, play for a fool*, pull wool over*, put one over on*, rook*, screw*, set up*, swindle, take for a ride*, take in*, throw, trap, victimize; SEE CONCEPT *59*

trickery [*n*] *deception, joke*
bait and switch*, cheat, cheating, chicane, chicanery, con, deceit, dishonesty, dodge, double-cross*, double-dealing*, dupery, fast shuffle*, flimflam*, fourberie, fraud, funny business*, guile, hoax, imposture, knavery, pretense, quackery, razzle-dazzle*, scam, sharp practice, shell game*, shenanigans*, snow job*, sting*, stunt, swindling, underhandedness; SEE CONCEPTS *59,645*

trickle [*v*] *run out*
crawl, creep, distill, dribble, drip, drop, exude, flow, issue, leak, ooze, percolate, seep, stream, trill, weep; SEE CONCEPTS *146,179*

tricky [*adj1*] *complicated, difficult*
catchy, complex, critical, delicate, intricate, involved, knotty*, perplexing, precarious, problematic, quirky, risky, rocky, sensitive, sticky, thorny*, ticklish, touch-and-go*, touchy, undependable, unstable; SEE CONCEPT *562*

tricky [*adj2*] *deceptive, sly*
artful, astute, cagey, catchy, clever, crafty, cunning, deceitful, deep, delusive, delusory, devious, dishonest, foxy*, greasy*, guileful, insidious, intelligent, keen, misleading, scheming, shady, sharp, shifty, shrewd, slick*, slippery*, smooth, streetwise*, subtle, treacherous, wily, witted, wry; SEE CONCEPT *401*

tried [*adj*] *reliable*
approved, certified, constant, demonstrated, dependable, faithful, proved, secure, staunch, steadfast, tested, tried-and-true*, true-blue*, trustworthy, trusty, used; SEE CONCEPT *535*

trifle [*n1*] *novelty item*
bagatelle, bauble, bibelot, curio, gewgaw*, knickknack, nothing*, novelty, objet d'art, plaything, toy, trinket, triviality, whatnot*; SEE CONCEPT *446*

trifle [*n2*] *very small amout*
bit, dash, diddly*, drop, eyelash*, fly speck*, fraction, hint, jot, little, no big deal*, particle, picayune*, piece, pinch, shade, smack, soupçon, speck, spice, spot, squat, suggestion, suspicion, touch, trace; SEE CONCEPTS *668,831*

trifle [*v*] *toy with; mess around*
amuse oneself, be insincere, coquet, dabble, dally, dawdle, dilly-dally*, doodle, fidget, flirt, fool, fool around*, fool with*, fribble*, fritter, futz around*, horse around*, idle, indulge in, lead on, loiter, lollygag*, lounge, mess with*, misuse, monkey, monkey with*, palter, philander, play, play games with*, play with, potter, putter, squander, string along*, toy, twiddle, use up, wanton, waste, waste time, wink at*; SEE CONCEPTS *210,292,363*

trifling [*adj*] *insignificant, worthless*
banal, dinky*, empty, forget it*, frivolous, hollow, idle, idling, inane, inconsequential, inconsiderable, insipid, jejune, loitering, measly, minuscule, negligible, niggling*, no big deal*, no big thing*, nugatory, paltry, petty, picayune, piddling, puny, shallow, silly, slight, small, tiny, trivial, unimportant, vain, valueless, vapid; SEE CONCEPTS *575,789*

trigger [*v*] *cause to happen*
activate, bring about, cause, elicit, generate, give rise to, produce, prompt, provoke, set in motion, set off, spark, start; SEE CONCEPT *242*

trim [*n1*] *decoration*
adornment, border, edging, embellishment, frill, fringe, garnish, gingerbread*, ornamentation, piping, trimming; SEE CONCEPTS *475,824*

trim [*n2*] *condition, health*
commission, fettle*, fitness, form, kilter*, order, repair, shape, situation, state, whack*; SEE CONCEPT *316*

trim [*adj1*] *neat, orderly*
apple-pie order*, clean, clean-cut, compact, dapper, fit, in good shape, neat as a pin*, nice, shipshape*, slick, smart, snug, spick-and-span*, spruce, streamlined, symmetrical, tidy, to rights*, uncluttered, well-groomed; SEE CONCEPTS *485,621*

trim [*adj2*] *shapely*
beautiful, clean, comely, fit, graceful, in fine fettle*, in good shape, sleek, slender, slick, slim, statuesque, streamlined, svelte, well-balanced, well-proportioned, willowy; SEE CONCEPTS *314,490,491*

trim [*v1*] *cut shorter*
abbreviate, barber, blue pencil*, bob, boil down*, clip, crop, curtail, cut, cut back, cut down, dock, edit, even up, lop, mow, pare, pare down, plane, prune, put in a nutshell*, shave, shear, shorten, slice off, snip, tidy, truncate, whittle down; SEE CONCEPTS *176,236,247*

trim [*v2*] *decorate*
adorn, array, beautify, bedeck, beribbon, deck*, dress, dress up, embellish, emblazon, embroider,

garnish, ornament, prank, pretty up*, prink*, spangle, spruce up*; SEE CONCEPTS *162,177*

trim [*v3*] *beat, defeat*
clobber, drub, lambaste, lick, smother, thrash, trounce, wax*, whip; SEE CONCEPT *95*

trinket [*n*] *knickknack*
bagatelle, bauble, bead, bibelot, curio, doodad*, gadget, gewgaw*, gimcrack*, glass*, hardware, jewel, jewelry, junk, nothing*, novelty, objet d'art, ornament, plaything, rock*, sparkler*, stone, toy, trifle, whatnot*; SEE CONCEPT *446*

trio/triple [*n*] *three of something*
leash, set of three, ternion, threesome, trey, triad, triangle, trilogy, trine, trinity, triplet, triplicate, triptych, triumvirate, triune, troika; SEE CONCEPTS *784,786*

trip [*n1*] *journey, excursion*
cruise, errand, expedition, foray, hop*, jaunt, junket, outing, overnight, peregrination, ramble*, run, swing*, tour, travel, trek, voyage, weekend; SEE CONCEPT *224*

trip [*n2*] *error, blunder*
bungle, fall, false move, false step, faux pas*, indiscretion, lapse, misstep, mistake, slip, stumble; SEE CONCEPTS *101,230*

trip [*v*] *fall, err*
buck, canter, confuse, disconcert, fall, fall over, founder, frolic, go headlong*, go wrong, hop, lapse, lope, lose balance, lose footing, lurch, make a faux pas*, miscalculate, misstep, pitch, play, plunge, skip, slide, slip, slip on, slip up, sprawl, spring, stumble, throw off, topple, tumble, unsettle; SEE CONCEPTS *101,149*

trite [*adj*] *silly, commonplace*
banal, bathetic, bromidic, chain, cliché, clichéd, common, cornball*, corny*, drained, dull, exhausted, familiar tune*, flat, hackneyed, hokey*, jejune, mildewed*, moth-eaten*, musty*, old hat*, ordinary, pedestrian, platitudinous, prosaic, readymade, routine, run-of-the-mill*, set, shopworn, stale, stereotyped, stock, threadbare, timeworn, tired, uninspired, unoriginal, used-up, vapid, warmed-over*, well-worn, worn, worn-out; SEE CONCEPTS *267,530*

triumph [*n1*] *extreme happiness*
celebration, elation, exultance, exultation, festivity, joy, jubilance, jubilation, jubilee, merriment, pride, rejoicing, reveling; SEE CONCEPT *410*

triumph [*n2*] *victory, achievement*
accomplishment, ascendancy, attainment, big hit*, big win*, cinch, clean sweep*, conquest, coup, feat, feather in cap*, gain, grand slam*, hit, hole in one*, homer*, mastery, pushover, riot, score, sell, sensation, shoo-in*, smash-hit*, splash, success, sure bet*, sure thing*, surmounting, takeover, the gold*, tour de force*, vanquishing, vanquishment, walkover*, win; SEE CONCEPT *706*

triumph [*v1*] *be very happy*
celebrate, crow, delight, exult, gloat, glory, jubilate, rejoice, revel, swagger; SEE CONCEPT *32*

triumph [*v2*] *achieve, succeed*
beat the game*, beat the system*, best, blow away*, carry the day*, come out on top*, conquer, dominate, flourish, get last laugh*, master, overcome, overwhelm, prevail, prosper, sink, strike it big*, subdue, sweep, take it all*, take the cake*, thrive, trounce, vanquish, win, win hands down*, win out*; SEE CONCEPTS *95,141,706*

triumphant [*adj*] *successful*
boastful, celebratory, champion, conquering, dominant, elated, exultant, glorious, happy, in the lead, jubilant, looking good, lucky, on top, out front, prizewinning, proud, rejoicing, swaggering, triumphal, unbeaten, undefeated, victorious, winning; SEE CONCEPT *528*

trivia [*n*] *details*
fine points, memorabilia, minutiae, trifles, trivialities; SEE CONCEPTS *274,543*

trivial [*adj*] *not important*
atomic, beside the point*, commonplace, diminutive, evanescent, everyday, flimsy, frivolous, immaterial, inappreciable, incidental, inconsequential, inconsiderable, insignificant, irrelevant, little, meager, mean, meaningless, microscopic, minor, minute, momentary, negligible, nonessential, nugatory, of no account*, paltry, petty, piddling*, puny, scanty, skindeep*, slight, small, superficial, trifling, trite, unimportant, valueless, vanishing, worthless; SEE CONCEPT *575*

troop/troops [*n*] *group, often military*
armed forces, army, assemblage, assembly, band, body, bunch, collection, combatants, company, contingent, corps, crew, crowd, delegation, drove, fighting forces, flock, forces, gang, gathering, herd, horde, host, legion, military, multitude, number, outfit, pack, party, personnel, servicemen/women, service personnel, soldiers, soldiery, squad, swarm, team, throng, troopers, troupe, unit; SEE CONCEPTS *322,417*

trophy [*n*] *physical award*
blue ribbon*, booty, citation, crown, cup, decoration, gold*, gold star*, guerdon, keepsake, laurels, medal, memento, memorial, palm, prize, reminder, ribbon, souvenir, spoils*, token; SEE CONCEPT *337*

tropical [*adj*] *warm and humid*
close, equatorial, hot, lush, steamy, sticky, stifling, sultry, sweaty, sweltering, torrid, tropic; SEE CONCEPTS *525,605*

trot [*v*] *move along briskly*
amble, canter, go, hurry, jog, lope, pad, rack, ride, run, scamper, step lively; SEE CONCEPT *150*

trot out [*v*] *bring forward*
brandish, bring up, come out with, display, disport, drag up, exhibit, expose, flash, flaunt, parade, recite, rehearse, reiterate, relate, repeat, represent, show, show off; SEE CONCEPT *138*

trouble [*n1*] *annoyance, worry*
agitation, anxiety, bad news*, bind, bother, commotion, concern, danger, difficulty, dilemma, dire

straits, discontent, discord, disorder, disquiet, dissatisfaction, distress, disturbance, grief, hang-up*, heartache, hindrance, hot water*, inconvenience, irritation, mess, misfortune, nuisance, pain, pest, pickle*, predicament, problem, puzzle, row, scrape*, sorrow, spot, strain, stress, strife, struggle, suffering, task, torment, tribulation, tumult, unrest, vexation, woe; SEE CONCEPTS *532,674,675,690,728*

trouble [*n2*] *something requiring great effort*
ado, attention, bother, bustle, care, concern, difficulty, effort, exertion, flurry, fuss, hardship, inconvenience, labor, pains, pother, rigor, strain, stress, struggle, thought, trial, while, work, worry; SEE CONCEPTS *666,677*

trouble [*n3*] *bad health*
affliction, ailment, complaint, curse, defect, disability, disease, disorder, failure, illness, malady, malfunction, upset; SEE CONCEPT *316*

trouble [*v1*] *bother, worry*
afflict, agitate, ail, annoy, bug*, burden, burn up*, concern, discommode, discompose, disconcert, disoblige, disquiet, distress, disturb, drive up the wall*, flip out*, fret, get to, give a bad time*, give a hard time*, grieve, harass, harry, impose on, inconvenience, irk, irritate, make a fuss*, make a scene*, make waves*, pain, perplex, perturb, pester, plague, psych*, put out*, sadden, spook*, stir up, strain, stress, torment, try, upset, vex; SEE CONCEPTS *7,19*

trouble [*v2*] *make an effort*
be concerned with, exert, go to the effort of, take pains*, take the time*; SEE CONCEPT *100*

troublemaker [*n*] *person who causes a problem*
agent provocateur, agitator, bad actor*, firebrand*, gremlin*, heel*, hellion, incendiary, inciter, inflamer, instigator, knave, loose cannon*, meddler, mischief-maker, nuisance, phony*, punk*, rabble-rouser*, rascal, recreant, rogue, smart aleck*, snake*, stormy petrel*, weasel*, wise guy*; SEE CONCEPT *412*

troublesome [*adj*] *bothersome, worrisome*
alarming, annoying, arduous, burdensome, damaging, dangerous, demanding, difficult, disquieting, harassing, hard, heavy, importunate, inconvenient, infestive, intractable, irksome, irritating, laborious, mean, messy, murder, oppressive, painful, pesky, pestiferous, pestilential, problematic, refractory, repressive, rough, taxing, tiresome, tough, tricky, troublous, trying, ugly, ungovernable, unruly, uphill, upsetting, vexatious, vexing, wearisome, wicked, worrying; SEE CONCEPTS *529,565*

trough [*n*] *gutter, depression*
canal, channel, crib, cup, dike, dip, ditch, duct, flume, furrow, gully, hollow, manger, moat, trench, watercourse; SEE CONCEPTS *509,513*

trounce [*v*] *defeat overwhelmingly*
bash, beat, blank, bury, bust*, cap, clobber, conquer, cook one's goose*, crush, drub, dust*, fix one's wagon*, flog*, hammer*, lambaste*, lather*,

lick*, make mincemeat of*, murder, overcome, overwhelm, paste*, pommel*, put away*, rout, swamp, thrash*, total*, trash*, walk over*, wallop*, waste*, wax*, whip, win, wipe off the mat*; SEE CONCEPT *95*

truce [*n*] *peaceful solution*
accord, agreement, amnesty, armistice, break, breather, cease-fire, cessation, de-escalation, halt, intermission, interval, letup, lull, moratorium, olive branch*, pause, peace, reconciliation, reprieve, respite, rest, stay, suspension, temporary peace, terms, treaty, white flag*, wind-down*; SEE CONCEPTS *230,298,684*

truck [*n1*] *commerce, merchandise*
barter, business, buying and selling, commercial goods, commodities, communication, communion, connection, contact, dealings, exchange, goods*, intercourse, relations, stock, stuff*, trade, traffic, wares*; SEE CONCEPTS *324,330,338*

truck [*n2*] *wheeled vehicle for hauling*
buggy*, car, carryall, crate*, dump, eighteen-wheeler*, four by eight*, four by four*, four-wheel drive*, freighter, jeep, lorry, pickup, rig*, semi*, van, wagon, wheels*; SEE CONCEPT *505*

truck [*v*] *buy and sell*
bargain, barter, deal, deal in*, do business, exchange, handle, have dealings, negotiate, peddle, retail, swap, trade, traffic, transact, wholesale*; SEE CONCEPTS *324,327,345*

truculent [*adj*] *belligerent, hateful*
abusive, aggressive, antagonistic, bad-tempered, barbarous, bellicose, browbeating, brutal, bullying, caustic, combative, contentious, contumelious, cowing, cross, defiant, ferocious, fierce, frightening, harsh, hostile, inhuman, inhumane, intimidating, invective, mean, militant, mordacious, mordant, obstreperous, opprobrious, ornery, pugnacious, quarrelsome, rude, savage, scathing, scrappy, scurrilous, sharp, sullen, terrifying, terrorizing, trenchant, violent, vituperative, vituperous; SEE CONCEPTS *267,401*

trudge [*v*] *walk heavily*
clump, drag oneself*, footslog, hike, lumber, march, plod, plug along*, schlepp*, slog, step, stumble, stump, traipse, tramp, tread, trek, wade; SEE CONCEPT *151*

true [*adj1*] *real, valid; concordant with facts*
accurate, actual, appropriate, authentic, authoritative, bona fide, correct, dependable, direct, exact, factual, fitting, genuine, honest, indubitable, kosher*, lawful, legal, legitimate, natural, normal, on target*, perfect, precise, proper, pure, regular, right, rightful, sincere, straight, sure-enough, trustworthy, truthful, typical, undeniable, undesigning, undoubted, unerring, unfaked, unfeigned, unquestionable, veracious, veridical, veritable, very, wash*; SEE CONCEPTS *267,535,582*

true [*adj2*] *loyal*
allegiant, ardent, confirmed, conscientious, constant, creditable, dedicated, dependable, devoted, dutiful,

estimable, faithful, fast, firm, high-principled, honest, honorable, just, liege, no lie*, on the up and up*, pure, reliable, resolute, right, right-minded, scrupulous, sincere, square, staunch, steadfast, steady, straight, strict, sure, true-blue*, truehearted, trustworthy, trusty, unaffected, undistorted, unfeigned, unswerving, up front*, upright, veracious, veridical, wholehearted, worthy; SEE CONCEPTS *267,401,542*

true [*adv*] *honestly, accurately*
correctly, on target, perfectly, precisely, properly, rightly, truthfully, unerringly, veraciously, veritably; SEE CONCEPTS *267,535,544*

truly [*adv*] *really, doubtlessly*
absolutely, accurately, actually, authentically, beyond doubt, beyond question, confirmedly, constantly, correctly, de facto, definitely, devotedly, exactly, factually, faithfully, firmly, genuinely, honestly, honorably, in actuality, in fact, in reality, in truth, legitimately, loyally, positively, precisely, reliably, righteously, rightly, sincerely, staunchly, steadily, surely, truthfully, unequivocally, veraciously, veritably, very, with all one's heart*, with devotion, without a doubt; SEE CONCEPTS *267,535,582*

truncate [*v*] *shorten*
abbreviate, abridge, clip, crop, curtail, cut, cut off, cut short, lop, pare, prune, shear, top, trim; SEE CONCEPTS *137,236,247*

trunk [*n1*] *body, core*
block, bole, butt, column, log, soma, stalk, stem, stock, thorax, torso; SEE CONCEPTS *392,428,826*

trunk [*n2*] *long nose of animal*
beak, proboscis, prow, snoot, snout; SEE CONCEPT *399*

trunk [*n3*] *container, box*
bag, baggage, bin, case, chest, coffer, coffin, crate, foot locker, locker, luggage, portmanteau, suitcase, wardrobe; SEE CONCEPTS *494,502*

trust [*n1*] *belief in something as true, trustworthy*
assurance, certainty, certitude, confidence, conviction, credence, credit, dependence, entrustment, expectation, faith, gospel truth*, hope, positiveness, reliance, stock, store, sureness; SEE CONCEPT *689*

trust [*n2*] *responsibility, custody*
account, care, charge, duty, guard, guardianship, keeping, liability, moment, obligation, protection, safekeeping, trusteeship, ward; SEE CONCEPTS *376,645*

trust [*n3*] *large company*
bunch, business, cartel, chain, combine, conglomerate, corporation, crew, crowd, gang, group, institution, megacorp*, mob, monopoly, multinational, organization, outfit, pool, ring, syndicate; SEE CONCEPTS *323,325*

trust [*v1*] *believe, place confidence in*
accredit, assume, bank on, be convinced, bet bottom dollar on*, bet on, build on, calculate on, confide in,

count on, depend on, expect, gamble on, have faith in, hope, imagine, lay money on*, lean on, look to, place confidence in, place trust in, presume, reckon on, rely upon, suppose, surmise, swear by, take, take at face value*, think likely; SEE CONCEPT *12*

trust [*v2*] *give to for safekeeping*
advance, aid, assign, command, commission, commit, confer, confide, consign, delegate, entrust, give over, grant, lend, let, let out, loan, make trustee, patronize, put into hands of, sign over, store, transfer, turn over; SEE CONCEPT *115*

trustworthy/trusty [*adj*] *reliable, believable*
accurate, always there*, authentic, authoritative, convincing, credible, dependable, ethical, exact, honest, honorable, kosher*, levelheaded, mature, on the level*, on up and up*, open, plausible, principled, realistic, responsible, righteous, rock*, saintly, secure, sensible, square, steadfast, straight, there*, to be trusted, tried, tried-and-true*, true, true-blue*, trustable, truthful, unfailing, up-front*, upright, valid, veracious; SEE CONCEPTS *267,404,535*

truth [*n1*] *reality, validity*
accuracy, actuality, authenticity, axiom, case, certainty, certainty, correctness, dope*, exactitude, exactness, fact, facts, factualism, factuality, factualness, genuineness, gospel*, gospel truth*, honest truth, infallibility, inside track*, legitimacy, maxim, naked truth*, nitty-gritty*, perfection, picture, plain talk, precision, principle, rectitude, rightness, scoop, score, trueness, truism, truthfulness, unvarnished truth, veracity, verisimilitude, verity, whole story*; SEE CONCEPTS *278,638,725*

truth [*n2*] *honesty, loyalty*
authenticity, candor, constancy, dedication, devotion, dutifulness, faith, faithfulness, fidelity, frankness, integrity, openness, realism, revelation, sincerity, uprightness, veridicality, verity; SEE CONCEPT *657*

truthful [*adj*] *accurate, honest*
believable, candid, correct, exact, factual, faithful, forthright, frank, guileless, ingenuous, just, kosher*, legit*, like it is*, literal, on the level*, on the up and up*, open, outspoken, plainspoken, precise, real, realistic, reliable, righteous, scrupulous, sincere, square, straight, straightforward, true, true-blue*, trustworthy, truth-telling, unfeigned, unreserved, veracious, veritable; SEE CONCEPTS *267,542*

try [*n*] *attempt*
all one's got*, best shot*, bid, crack*, dab, effort, endeavor, essay, fling*, go*, jab*, pop*, shot*, slap*, stab*, striving, struggle, trial, undertaking, whack*, whirl*; SEE CONCEPTS *87,677*

try [*v1*] *attempt*
aim, aspire, attack, bear down, chip away at*, compete, contend, contest, do one's best*, drive for, endeavor, essay, exert oneself, go after, go all out*, go for, have a crack*, have a go*, have a shot*, have a stab*, have a whack*, knock oneself out*, labor, lift

a finger*, make a bid, make an attempt, make an effort, make a pass at*, propose, put oneself out*, risk, seek, shoot for*, speculate, strive, struggle, tackle, undertake, venture, vie for, work, wrangle; SEE CONCEPT *87*

try [*v2*] *experiment, test*
appraise, assay, check, check out, evaluate, examine, inspect, investigate, judge, prove, put to the proof*, put to the test*, sample, scrutinize, taste, try out, weigh; SEE CONCEPTS *103,291*

try [*v3*] *bother, afflict*
agonize, annoy, crucify, distress, excruciate, harass, inconvenience, irk, irritate, martyr, pain, plague, rack, strain, stress, tax, tire, torment, torture, trouble, upset, vex, weary, wring; SEE CONCEPTS *7,19*

try [*v4*] *bring before a judge*
adjudge, adjudicate, arbitrate, decide, examine, give a hearing, hear, judge, referee, sit in judgment; SEE CONCEPT *317*

trying [*adj*] *difficult, bothersome*
aggravating, annoying, arduous, demanding, exacting, exasperating, exigent, fatiguing, hard, irksome, irritating, onerous, oppressive, pestilent, provocative, rough, severe, sticky, strenuous, stressful, taxing, tight, tiresome, tough, tricky, troublesome, upsetting, vexing, wearisome, weighty; SEE CONCEPTS *548,565*

try on/try out [*v*] *evaluate, test*
appraise, audition, check out, demonstrate, dry run*, experiment, fit, give a try, have a fitting*, inspect, practice, probe, prove, put into practice, put to the test, sample, scrutinize, taste, try for size, wear; SEE CONCEPTS *103,167,291,453*

tryst [*n*] *meeting during a love affair*
appointment, assignation, date, engagement, meet, meeting, rendezvous, union; SEE CONCEPTS *375, 384*

tuck [*v*] *fold together*
constrict, contract, draw together, enfold, gather, hem, insert, make snug, pinch, plait, pleat, push, put in, seam, squeeze in, swaddle, wrap; SEE CONCEPTS *193,218*

tuft [*n*] *clump of strands of something*
bunch, cluster, collection, cowlick, feathers, group, knot, plumage, ruff, shock, topknot, tussock; SEE CONCEPTS *392,432,471*

tug [*n/v*] *quick pull*
drag, draw, haul, heave, jerk, lug, strain, toil, tow, traction, wrench, yank; SEE CONCEPT *206*

tuition [*n*] *education; education costs*
charge, expenditure, fee, instruction, lessons, price, schooling, teaching, training, tutelage, tutoring; SEE CONCEPT *287*

tumble [*v*] *fall or make fall awkwardly*
belly up*, bowl down, bring down, descend, dip, disarrange, disarray, disorder, disturb, do a pratfall, down, drop, fall headlong*, flatten, floor, flop, go down, hit the dirt*, jumble, keel, keel over, knock down, knock over, level, lose footing, lose it*, mess up, nose-dive, pitch, plummet, plunge, roll, sag, skid, slip, slump, spill, stumble, take a header*, tip over, topple, toss, trip, unsettle, upset; SEE CONCEPTS *147,149,181*

tumor [*n*] *abnormal growth in animate being*
bump, cancer, carcinoma, cyst, lump, neoplasm, sarcoma, swelling, tumefaction; SEE CONCEPT *316*

tumult [*n*] *uproar, confusion*
ado, affray, agitation, altercation, babel, bedlam, brawl, clamor, commotion, convulsion, din, disorder, disturbance, dither, excitement, ferment, fight, fracas, fuss, hassle, jangle, lather, maelstrom, noise, outbreak, outcry, pandemonium, paroxysm, pother, quarrel, racket, riot, row, ruction, seething, stir, strife, turbulence, turmoil, unrest, unsettlement, upheaval, upturn, wildness; SEE CONCEPTS *230,674*

tumultous/tumultuous [*adj*] *confused; in an uproar*
agitated, boisterous, clamorous, disorderly, disturbed, excited, fierce, hectic, irregular, lawless, noisy, obstreperous, passionate, raging, rambunctious, raucous, restless, riotous, rowdy, rowdy-dowdy, rumbunctious, stormy, termagant, turbulent, unrestrained, unruly, uproarious, violent, vociferous, wild; SEE CONCEPT *548*

tune [*n1*] *melody, harmony*
air, aria, carol, chorus, composition, concert, consonance, descant, diapason, ditty*, harmony, jingle, lay, measure, melodia, motif, number, piece, song, strain, theme, warble; SEE CONCEPTS *264,595*

tune [*n2*] *agreement*
accord, chime, chorus, concert, concord, concordance, consonance, euphony, harmony, pitch, sympathy, unison; SEE CONCEPTS *670,714*

tune, tune up [*v*] *bring into harmony*
accommodate, adapt, adjust, attune, conform, coordinate, dial, fix, harmonize, integrate, modulate, pitch, proportion, reconcile, regulate, set, string, tighten; SEE CONCEPTS *65,126*

tunnel [*n*] *covered passageway*
adit, burrow, channel, crawl space, crawlway, crosscut, drift, hole, hole in the wall*, mine, passage, pit, shaft, subway, tube, underpass; SEE CONCEPTS *509,513*

tunnel [*v*] *dig a passage through*
burrow, excavate, mine, penetrate, sap, scoop out, undermine; SEE CONCEPT *178*

turbulent [*adj1*] *unsettled, raging (referring to weather)*
agitated, bitter, blustering, blustery, boiling, bumpy, choppy, coarse, confused, destructive, disordered, disturbed, fierce, foaming, furious, howling, inclement, moiling, noisy, restless, riotous, roaring, rough, ruffled, rugged, stirred up, stormful, storming, stormy, swirling, tempestuous, thunderous, tremulous, tumultous/tumultuous, unstable, violent, wild; SEE CONCEPT *525*

turbulent [*adj2*] *rebellious, unmanageable*
agitated, anarchic, angry, bitter, boisterous, chaotic, demonstrative, destructive, disorderly, excited, fierce, fiery, foaming, insubordinate, lawless, mutinous, obstreperous, passionate, perturbed, quarrelsome, rabid, rambunctious, rampant, raucous, refractory, riotous, rough, roughhouse*, rowdy, rude, seditious, shaking, stern, storming, termagant, tumultous/tumultuous, unbridled, uncontrolled, undisciplined, ungovernable, unruly, untamed, uproarious, vehement, violent, vociferous, wild; SEE CONCEPT *401*

turmoil [*n*] *chaos*
agitation, ailment, anxiety, anxiousness, bedlam, bustle, commotion, confusion, disorder, disquiet, disquietude, distress, disturbance, dither, ferment, flap*, flurry, free-for-all*, fuss, hassle, hectic, hubbub*, lather, mix-up, noise, pandemonium, pother, restiveness, restlessness, riot, row, ruckus, stir, strife, to-do*, topsy-turvy, trouble, tumult, turbulence, unrest, uproar, violence, whirl; SEE CONCEPTS *230,674*

turn [*n1*] *revolution, curving*
about-face, angle, bend, bias, bow, branch, change, changeabout, circle, circuit, circulation, circumvolution, corner, curve, cycle, departure, detour, deviation, direction, drift, flection, flexure, fork, gyration, gyre, heading, hook, pirouette, pivot, quirk, retroversion, reversal, reverse, reversion, right-about, roll, rotation, round, shift, spin, spiral, swing, tack, tendency, trend, turnabout, turning, twist, twisting, wheel, whirl, wind, winding, yaw; SEE CONCEPTS *198,738,754*

turn [*n2*] *sudden change*
alteration, bend, branch, crotch, deflection, departure, detour, deviation, digression, distortion, divarication, double, fork, modification, mutation, shift, tack, twist, variation, warp, yaw; SEE CONCEPT *697*

turn [*n3*] *chance, opportunity*
accomplishment, act, action, bit, bout, crack*, deed, favor, fling*, gesture, go*, go around*, move, period, round, routine, say*, service, shift, shot*, spell, stint, succession, time, tour, trick, try; SEE CONCEPT *693*

turn [*n4*] *walk, outing*
airing, circuit, constitutional, drive, excursion, jaunt, promenade, ramble, ride, saunter, spin, stroll; SEE CONCEPTS *147,224,363*

turn [*n5*] *aptitude, knack*
affinity, aptness, bent, bias, bump, disposition, faculty, flair, genius, gift, head, inclination, leaning, predisposition, propensity, talent; SEE CONCEPTS *411,630*

turn [*n6*] *scare*
attack, blow, fit, fright, jolt, seizure, shock, spell, start, surprise; SEE CONCEPTS *230,410*

turn [*v1*] *revolve, curve*
arc, bend, circle, circulate, circumduct, come around, corner, cut, eddy, go around, go round, ground, gyrate, gyre, hang a left*, hang a right*, incline, loop, make a left, make a right, move in a circle, negotiate, orbit, oscillate, pass, pass around, pirouette, pivot, revolve, roll, rotate, round, spin, sway, swing, swivel, take a bend*, twirl, twist, vibrate, weave, wheel, whirl, wind, yaw; SEE CONCEPTS *147,201,738,748*

turn [*v2*] *reverse; change course*
about-face, aim, alter, alternate, backslide, call off, capsize, change, change position, convert, curve, depart, detour, detract, deviate, digress, direct, diverge, double back, face about, go back, incline, inverse, invert, loop, move, pivot, rechannel, recoil, redirect, regress, relapse, retrace, return, revert, sheer, shift, shunt, shy away, sidetrack, subvert, sway, swerve, swing, swirl, switch, tack, transform, twist, upset, vary, veer, volte-face, wheel, whip, whirl, zigzag; SEE CONCEPTS *195,198,213*

turn [*v3*] *adapt, fit*
alter, become, change, change into, come, convert, divert, fashion, form, get, go, grow into, metamorphose, modify, mold, mutate, pass into, put, refashion, remake, remodel, render, run, shape, transfigure, transform, translate, transmute, transpose, vary, wax; SEE CONCEPTS *232,697*

turn [*v4*] *become sour or tainted*
acidify, become rancid, break down, crumble, curdle, decay, decompose, disintegrate, dull, ferment, go bad, molder, putrefy, rot, sour, spoil, taint; SEE CONCEPTS *456,469*

turn [*v5*] *use; resort to*
adapt, address, appeal, apply, approach, bend, be predisposed to, devote, direct, employ, favor, give, go, have recourse, incline, lend, look, prefer, recur, repair, run, tend, throw, turn energies to*, turn hand to*, undertake, utilize; SEE CONCEPTS *100,225*

turn [*v6*] *sicken*
derange, discompose, disgust, disorder, make one sick*, nauseate, revolt, unbalance, undo, unhinge*, unsettle, upset; SEE CONCEPTS *7,19,250*

turn [*v7*] *change one's mind; defect*
apostatize, bring round, change sides, desert, go over, influence, persuade, prejudice, prevail upon, rat*, renege, renounce, repudiate, retract, talk into, tergiversate, tergiverse; SEE CONCEPTS *21,41,54*

turn [*v8*] *twist a body part*
bruise, crick, dislocate, hurt, sprain, strain, wrench; SEE CONCEPT *246*

turn down [*v*] *reject*
decline, disapprove, dismiss, rebuff, refuse, reprobate, repudiate, say no, scorn, spurn, throw out; SEE CONCEPTS *18,54*

turn in [*v*] *go to bed*
bed, catch some z's*, flop*, go to sleep, hit the hay*, hit the sack*, lie down, nap, pile in, rest, retire, roll in; SEE CONCEPT *210*

turning point [*n*] *crucial occurrence*
axis, change, climacteric, climax, contingency, crisis, critical moment, critical period, crossing, cross

roads, crux, culmination, decisive moment, development, emergency, exigency, hinge, juncture, moment of truth*, pass, peak, pinch, pivot, shift, strait, transition, twist, zero hour*; SEE CONCEPTS *679,832*

turn off [*v1*] *disgust*
alienate, bore, disenchant, disinterest, displease, irritate, lose one's interest, make one sick*, nauseate, offend, put off, repel, sicken; SEE CONCEPTS *7,19*

turn off [*v2*] *stop from operating*
close, cut, cut out, douse, extinguish, halt, hit the switch, kill*, log off, put out, shut, shut down, shut off, switch off, turn out, unplug; SEE CONCEPTS *121,234*

turn on [*v1*] *excite, please*
arouse, attract, captivate, enchant, get started, initiate, introduce, show, stimulate, stir up, thrill, titillate, work up; SEE CONCEPT *11*

turn on [*v2*] *start the operation of*
activate, begin, energize, get started, ignite, initiate, introduce, log on, put in gear, put on, set in motion, start up, switch on; SEE CONCEPT *221*

turnout [*n1*] *group assembling for event*
assemblage, assembly, attendance, audience, congregation, crowd, gate, gathering, number, throng; SEE CONCEPT *417*

turnout [*n2*] *amount produced*
aggregate, output, outturn, product, production, productivity, quota, turnover, volume, yield; SEE CONCEPTS *338,786*

turn out [*v1*] *equip; produce*
accouter, appoint, arm, bear, bring out, build, clothe, dress, fabricate, finish, fit, fit out*, furnish, make, manufacture, outfit, process, put out, rig*, rig out*, yield; SEE CONCEPTS *167,205*

turn out [*v2*] *get out of bed*
appear, arise, come, emerge, get up, pile out, rise, rise and shine, roll out, show up, uprise, wake, wake up; SEE CONCEPT *159*

turn over [*v1*] *give, transfer*
assign, come across with, commend, commit, confer, confide, consign, convey, delegate, deliver, entrust, feed, find, furnish, give over, give up, hand, hand over, pass on, provide, relegate, relinquish, render, supply, surrender, yield; SEE CONCEPTS *108,143*

turn over [*v2*] *think about seriously*
consider, contemplate, deliberate, give thought to, meditate, mull over, muse, ponder, reflect on, revolve, roll, ruminate, think over, wonder about; SEE CONCEPTS *17,24*

turn up [*v1*] *come, arrive*
appear, attend, blow in*, come, come in, enter, get, get in, make an appearance*, materialize, pop in*, punch in*, put in an appearance*, reach, roll in*, show, show up*, weigh in*; SEE CONCEPT *159*

turn up [*v2*] *discover or be discovered*
become known, be found, bring to light*, catch, come across, come to light*, come to pass, crop up, descry, detect, dig up*, disclose, encounter, espy,

expose, find, hit upon*, learn, meet, meet with*, pop up*, reveal, see, spot, track, track down*, transpire, uncover, unearth; SEE CONCEPTS *31,183*

tutor [*n*] *person who teaches another privately*
baby-sitter, coach, educator, governess, governor, grind, guardian, guide, guru*, instructor, lecturer, master, mentor, preceptor, private teacher, prof*, schoolmaster/mistress, teach*, teacher; SEE CONCEPT *350*

tutor [*v*] *teach someone privately*
clue, coach, direct, discipline, drill, drum into*, edify, educate, guide, instruct, lay it out for*, lecture, let in on*, ready, school, train, update; SEE CONCEPT *285*

twilight [*n*] *onset of darkness at end of day*
afterglow, afterlight, crepuscular light, decline, dimness, dusk, early evening, ebb, end, evening, eventide, gloaming, half-light, last phase, late afternoon, night, nightfall, sundown, sunset; SEE CONCEPTS *810,832*

twin [*n*] *something exactly like another*
clone, companion, coordinate, corollary, counterpart, doppelgänger*, double, duplicate, fellow, fraternal twin, identical twin, likeness, lookalike, match, mate, reciprocal, ringer*, Siamese twin; SEE CONCEPTS *414,664,670*

twin [*adj*] *duplicate, similar*
accompanying, bifold, binary, copied, corresponding, coupled, double, dual, duplicating, geminate, identical, joint, like, matched, matching, paired, parallel, same, second, selfsame, twofold, very same; SEE CONCEPTS *487,563,573*

twine [*n*] *rope, cord*
braid, coil, convolution, cordage, knot, snarl, string, tangle, thread, twist, whorl, yarn; SEE CONCEPT *475*

twine [*v*] *coil, twist together*
bend, braid, corkscrew, curl, encircle, enmesh, entangle, entwine, interlace, interweave, knit, loop, meander, plait, spiral, splice, surround, tangle, twist, undulate, weave, wind, wrap, wreathe; SEE CONCEPTS *147,201,742*

twinge [*n*] *sharp pain*
ache, bite, gripe, lancination, misery, pang, pinch, prick, shiver, smart, spasm, stab, stitch, throb, throe, tic, tweak, twist, twitch; SEE CONCEPT *728*

twinkle [*v*] *glimmer, shine*
blink, coruscate, flash, flicker, gleam, glint, glisten, glitter, glow, illuminate, light, light up, scintillate, shimmer, sparkle, wink; SEE CONCEPT *624*

twirl [*v*] *turn around circularly*
gyrate, gyre, pirouette, pivot, purl, revolve, rotate, spin, turn, twist, wheel, whirl, whirligig, wind; SEE CONCEPTS *150,152*

twist [*n1*] *curl, spin*
arc, bend, braid, coil, convolution, curlicue, curve, flourish, hank, helix, jerk, meander, plug, ply, pull, roll, spiral, swivel, torsion, turn, twine, undulation,

warp, wind, wrench, yank, zigzag; SEE CONCEPTS *738,754*

twist [*n2*] *sudden development; oddity*
aberration, bent, change, characteristic, confusion, crotchet, eccentricity, entanglement, foible, idiosyncrasy, kink, knot, mess, mix-up, peculiarity, proclivity, quirk, revelation, slant, snarl, surprise, tangle, trait, turn, variation; SEE CONCEPTS *411,832*

twist [*v1*] *curl, spin*
coil, contort, corkscrew, encircle, entwine, intertwine, rick, screw, spiral, sprain, squirm, swivel, turn, turn around, twine, twirl, warp, weave, wiggle, wind, wrap, wrap around, wreathe, wrench, wriggle, wring, writhe, zigzag; SEE CONCEPTS *80,147, 184,201,206,738*

twist [*v2*] *misrepresent*
alter, belie, change, color, contort, distort, falsify, garble, misquote, misstate, pervert, screw up*, warp; SEE CONCEPT *63*

twitch [*v*] *have a spasm*
beat, blink, clasp, clutch, flutter, grab, grasp, grip, jerk, jiggle, jump, kick, lug, lurch, nip, pain, palpitate, pluck, pull, seize, shiver, shudder, snap, snatch, squirm, tic, tremble, tug, twinge, vellicate, yank; SEE CONCEPTS *185,206*

tycoon [*n*] *person who has a lot of money, power*
administrator, baron, big shot*, boss, businessman/woman, business person, capitalist, captain of industry*, czar*, director, entrepreneur, executive, fat cat*, financier, industrialist, investor, magnate, mogul, wealthy person; SEE CONCEPT *347*

type [*n1*] *class, kind*
blazon, brand, breed, cast, category, character, classification, cut, description, feather, form, genre, group, ilk, likes, lot, mold, nature, number, order, persuasion, rubric, sample, sort, species, specimen, stamp, standard, strain, subdivision, variety, way; SEE CONCEPTS *378,411*

type [*n2*] *example, model*
archetype, epitome, essence, exemplar, original, paradigm, pattern, personification, prototype, quintessence, representative, sample, specimen, standard; SEE CONCEPT *688*

type [*n3*] *printed characters*
case, emblem, face, figure, font, point size, print, printing, sign, symbol; SEE CONCEPTS *79,284*

type [*v1*] *classify*
arrange, button down*, categorize, class, peg, pigeonhole*, put away, put down as, sort, standardize, stereotype, tab*, typecast; SEE CONCEPTS *18,84*

type [*v2*] *hit keys on machine to print document*
copy, dash off*, hunt-and-peck*, teletype, touch, touch-type, transcribe, typewrite, write; SEE CONCEPTS *79,199,203*

typical [*adj*] *usual, conventional*
archetypal, archetypical, average, characteristic, classic, classical, common, commonplace, emblematic, essential, everyday, exemplary, expected, general, habitual, ideal, illustrative, in character, indicative, in keeping, matter-of-course*, model, natural, normal, old hat*, ordinary, orthodox, paradigmatic, patterned, prevalent, prototypal, prototypical, quintessential, regular, representative, standard, standardized, stock, suggestive, symbolic, typic, unexceptional; SEE CONCEPTS *530,533,547*

typify [*v*] *represent, characterize*
body forth, characterize, describe, emblematize, embody, epitomize, exemplify, feature, illustrate, incarnate, mean, mirror, model, personify, stand for, sum up, symbolize; SEE CONCEPTS *55,261,682*

tyranny [*n*] *dictatorship*
absolutism, authoritarianism, autocracy, coercion, cruelty, despotism, domination, fascism, highhandedness, imperiousness, monocracy, oppression, peremptoriness, reign of terror, severity, terrorism, totalitarianism, totality, unreasonableness; SEE CONCEPTS *299,301*

tyrant [*n*] *person who dictates, oppresses*
absolute ruler, absolutist, authoritarian, autocrat, bully, czar, despot, dictator, Hitler*, inquisitor, martinet, oppressor, slave driver*, Stalin*; SEE CONCEPTS *354,412*

U

ubiquitous [*adj*] *ever-present*
all-over, everywhere, omnipresent, pervasive, ubiquitary, universal, wall-to-wall; SEE CONCEPT *530*

ugly [*adj1*] *unattractive*
animal, appalling, awful, bad-looking, beastly, deformed, disfigured, foul, frightful, grisly, gross*, grotesque, hard-featured, hideous, homely, horrid, ill-favored, loathsome, misshapen, monstrous, not much to look at*, plain, repelling, repugnant, repulsive, revolting, unbeautiful, uncomely, uninviting, unlovely, unprepossessing, unseemly, unsightly; SEE CONCEPT *579*

ugly [*adj2*] *unpleasant, disagreeable*
base, despicable, dirty, disgusting, distasteful, filthy, foul, frightful, hideous, horrid, ignoble, low, lowdown, mean, messy, monstrous, nasty, nauseous, noisome, objectionable, odious, offensive, pesky, repellent, repugnant, repulsive, revolting, scandalous, servile, shocking, sickening, sordid, sorry, terrible, troublesome, troublous, vexatious, vile, wicked, wretched; SEE CONCEPTS *403,571*

ugly [*adj3*] *dangerous, threatening*
angry, bellicose, black, cantankerous, crabbed, crabby, dark, disagreeable, dour, evil, fell, forbidding, formidable, gloomy, glum, grave, grievous, major, malevolent, menacing, morose, nasty, obnoxious, ominous, pugnacious, quarrelsome, rough, saturnine, scowling, serious, sinister, spiteful, sullen, surly, treacherous, truculent, vicious, vinegary, violent, wicked; SEE CONCEPTS *401,548*

ulterior [*adj*] *secret; pertaining to a hidden goal*
ambiguous, buried, concealed, covert, cryptic, dark, enigmatic, equivocal, guarded, hidden, implied, obscure, obscured, personal, privy, remote, secondary, selfish, shrouded, under cover, under wraps*, undisclosed, undivulged, unexpressed, unsaid; SEE CONCEPTS *544,576*

ultimate [*adj1*] *last, final*
bitter end*, bottom line*, capping, chips down*, closing, concluding, conclusive, decisive, end, eventual, extreme, far out*, farthermost, farthest, final curtain*, furthermost, furthest, hindmost, last hurrah*, latest, latter, lattermost, most distant, payoff*, swan song*, terminal; SEE CONCEPTS *799,820*

ultimate [*adj2*] *best, greatest*
extreme, highest, incomparable, living end*, max*, maxi*, maximum, most, paramount, preeminent, significant, superlative, supreme, surpassing, the most, topmost, towering, transcendent, unequalable, unmatchable, unsurpassable, utmost; SEE CONCEPTS *568,574*

ultimate [*adj3*] *fundamental*
absolute, basic, categorical, elemental, empyreal, empyrean, primary, radical, sublime, transcendental; SEE CONCEPTS *535,546*

ultimately [*adv*] *eventually*
after all, after a while, as a conclusion, at last, at long last, at the close, basically, by and by, climactically, conclusively, finally, fundamentally, hereafter, in conclusion, in consummation, in due time, in future, in the end, in the sequel, presently, sequentially, someday, sometime, somewhere, sooner or later, yet; SEE CONCEPT *820*

ultra [*adj*] *extreme*
all out*, drastic, excessive, extremist, fanatical, far-out*, gone*, immoderate, outlandish, out of bounds*, outré, rabid, radical, revolutionary, too much*; SEE CONCEPTS *562,569*

umbrage [*n*] *personal displeasure*
anger, annoyance, chagrin, exasperation, fury, grudge, high dudgeon*, huff, indignation, injury, ire, irking, irritation, miff*, nettling*, offense, pique, provoking, rage, resentment, sense of injury, vexation, wrath; SEE CONCEPTS *29,410*

umpire [*n*] *person who settles dispute*
adjudicator, arbiter, arbitrator, assessor, compromiser, inspector, judge, justice, mediator, moderator, negotiator, peacemaker, proprietor, ref*, referee, settler, ump*; SEE CONCEPTS *348,366,423*

unable [*adj*] *not having talent, skill*
can't cut it*, can't hack it*, can't make the grade*, clumsy, helpless, hog-tied*, impotent, impuissant, inadequate, incapable, incapacitated, incompetent, ineffectual, inefficacious, inefficient, inept, inoperative, no can do*, no good*, not able, not cut out for*, not equal to*, not up to*, out of commission*, powerless, sidelined, unfit, unfitted, unqualified, unskilled, weak; SEE CONCEPT *527*

unabridged [*n*] *not shortened*
complete, entire, full-length, intact, total, unabbreviated, uncondensed, uncut, unexpurgated, unshortened, whole; SEE CONCEPTS *267,531*

unacceptable [*adj*] *not suitable or satisfactory*
below par, damaged, disagreeable, displeasing, distasteful, exceptionable, half-baked*, ill-favored, improper, inadmissible, insupportable, lemon*, lousy*, not up to snuff*, objectionable, obnoxious, offensive, reject, repugnant, seconds, unappealing, undesirable, uninviting, unpleasant, unsatisfactory, unwanted, unwelcome, won't do*; SEE CONCEPTS *529,558*

unaccompanied [*adj*] *alone*
abandoned, a cappella*, apart, by oneself, deserted, detached, hermit, individual, isolate, isolated, lone, loner, odd, on one's own, removed, single, solitary, solo, stag, traveling light*, unattended, unescorted; SEE CONCEPTS *555,577*

unaccountable [*adj*] *not explainable; mysterious*
arcane, astonishing, baffling, extraordinary, impenetrable, incomprehensible, inexplicable, inscrutable, mystic, odd, peculiar, puzzling, strange, uncommon, unexplainable, unfathomable, unheard-of, unintelligible, unknowable, unusual, unwonted; SEE CONCEPTS *529,564*

unaccustomed [*adj1*] *not prepared, ready; new to*
green*, ignorant, incompetent, inexperienced, newcomer, not given to*, not used to, novice, unacquainted, unfamiliar with, uninformed, uninstructed, unpracticed, unseasoned, unskilled, untaught, untrained, unused to, unversed in; SEE CONCEPTS *527,678*

unaccustomed [*adj2*] *new, strange*
alien, altered, bizarre, different, eccentric, exceptional, exotic, foreign, imported, novel, outlandish, out of the ordinary, quaint, remarkable, singular, special, surprising, uncommon, unconventional, uncustomary, unexpected, unfamiliar, unknown, unorthodox, unprecedented, unusual, unwonted, variant; SEE CONCEPTS *547,564*

unadvised [*adj*] *not smart; careless*
brash, hasty, heedless, hot-headed, ignorant, ill-advised, imprudent, inadvisable, incautious, inconsiderate, indiscreet, injudicious, in the dark*, rash, reckless, thoughtless, unaware, unconsidered, uninformed, unknowing, unsuspecting, unwarned, unwary, unwise; SEE CONCEPTS *403,548*

unaffected [*adj1*] *honest, unsophisticated*
artless, candid, direct, folksy*, forthright, frank, genuine, guileless, homey*, ingenuous, modest, naive, natural, plain, simple, sincere, single, spontaneous, straightforward, true, unartificial, unassuming, unpretentious, unschooled, unspoilt, unstudied, up front*; SEE CONCEPTS *401,404*

unaffected [*adj2*] *unchanged, unmoved*
aloof, callous, calm, casual, cold fish*, cool, easygoing, hard-boiled*, hard-hearted*, impassive, im-

pervious, laid-back*, not influenced, not to worry*, proof, steady, thick-skinned*, unaltered, unconcerned, unexcited, unimpressed, uninfluenced, unresponsive, unruffled, unstirred, untouched; SEE CONCEPTS *542,548*

unanimous [*adj*] *in agreement; uncontested*
accepted, accordant, agreed, agreeing, as one, assenting, collective, combined, common, communal, concerted, concordant, concurrent, consensus, consentient, consistent, consonant, harmonious, homogeneous, in complete accord, like-minded, of one mind, popular, public, shared, single, solid, undisputed, undivided, unified, united, universal, unquestioned, with one voice*; SEE CONCEPTS *8,267,563*

unappetizing [*adj*] *distasteful*
flat, flavorless, grody*, gross*, icky*, insipid, savorless, stinky, tasteless, unappealing, unattractive, uninteresting, uninviting, unpalatable, unpleasant, unsavory, vapid, yucky*; SEE CONCEPTS *462,529*

unapproachable [*adj1*] *unfriendly*
aloof, chilly*, cold, cool, distant, frigid, hesitant, inaccessible, remote, reserved, standoffish, uncommunicative, unsociable, withdrawn; SEE CONCEPTS *404,555*

unapproachable [*adj2*] *difficult to get to*
inaccessible, out of reach, out-of-the-way, remote, unattainable, unobtainable, unreachable; SEE CONCEPT *576*

unasked [*adj*] *voluntary*
arrogant, gratuitous, impudent, not asked, of one's own accord, overbearing, presumptuous, spontaneaous, supererogatory, unbidden, uncalled-for, undemanded, undesired, uninvited, unprompted, unrequested, unsought, unwanted, unwelcome, voluntarily, wanton, willing, without prompting; SEE CONCEPTS *401,558*

unassuming [*adj*] *shy*
backward, bashful, diffident, humble, lowly, meek, modest, mousy*, plain, prim, quiet, reserved, retiring, self-effacing, simple, unambitious, unassertive, unobtrusive, unostentatious, unpretending, unpretentious; SEE CONCEPTS *401,404*

unauthorized [*adj*] *not sanctioned, permitted*
crooked*, dirty*, illegal, illegitimate, no-no*, off base*, out of bounds*, out of line*, over the line*, pirated, shady*, unapproved, unconstitutional, under the table*, unjustified, unlawful, unofficial, unsanctioned, unwarranted, wildcat*, wrongful; SEE CONCEPTS *319,548*

unavoidable [*adj*] *bound to happen*
certain, compulsory, fated, impending, ineluctable, ineludible, inescapable, inevasible, inevitable, inexorable, locked up*, necessary, obligatory, open and shut*, set, sure, unescapable; SEE CONCEPT *535*

unaware [*adj*] *ignorant*
blind, careless, caught napping*, daydreaming, deaf, deaf to*, doped*, forgetful, heedless, ignorant, in a daze*, inattentive, incognizant, inconversant, insen-

sible, mooning, negligent, nescient, not all there*, not cognizant, oblivious, out cold*, out of it*, out to lunch*, spacey*, unacquainted, unconcerned, unconscious, unenlightened, unfamiliar, uninformed, uninstructed, unknowing, unmindful, unsuspecting, unwitting; SEE CONCEPT *402*

unawares [*adv*] *without warning; suddenly*
aback, abruptly, accidentally, by accident, by mistake, by surprise, carelessly, ignorantly, inadvertently, mistakenly, off guard, short, sudden, surprisingly, unconsciously, unexpectedly, unintentionally, unknowingly, unprepared, unready, unwittingly, without warning; SEE CONCEPTS *544,548,799*

unbalanced [*adj1*] *not even, stable*
asymmetric, asymmetrical, disproportionate, irregular, lopsided, not balanced, off-balance, shaky, top-heavy, treacherous, unequal, uneven, unstable, unsteady, unsymmetrical, wobbly; SEE CONCEPT *480*

unbalanced [*adj2*] *crazy; mentally disturbed*
batty*, daft, demented, deranged, eccentric, erratic, flaky*, freaky*, insane, irrational, kinky*, kooky*, lunatic, mad, nobody home*, non compos mentis*, not all there*, nutty*, out to lunch*, psychotic, touched, troubled, unglued*, unhinged*, unscrewed*, unsound, unstable; SEE CONCEPT *403*

unbearable [*adj*] *very bad; too much*
a bit much*, enough, heavy-handed*, inadmissible, insufferable, insupportable, intolerable, last straw*, oppressive, unacceptable, unendurable, unsurpassable; SEE CONCEPTS *537,571*

unbecoming [*adj*] *improper, unsuitable*
awkward, clumsy, discreditable, gauche, ill-suited, inappropriate, inapt, incongruous, indecent, indecorous, indelicate, inept, maladroit, malapropos, offensive, rough, salacious, tacky*, tasteless, unattractive, unbefitting, uncomely, undue, unfair, unfit, unfitting, unflattering, ungodly, unhandsome, unlovely, unseasonable, unseemly, unsightly, unsuited, untimely, untoward, unworthy; SEE CONCEPTS *558,579,589*

unbelievable [*adj*] *beyond the imagination*
astonishing, beyond belief, cockamamie*, cockeyed*, doubtful, dubious, far-fetched, fishy*, flaky*, flimsy*, for the birds*, full of holes*, harebrained*, implausible, impossible, improbable, incogitable, inconceivable, incredible, kooky*, lamebrained, open to doubt, outlandish, past belief, phony, preposterous, questionable, reaching, scatterbrained*, screwy*, staggering, suspect, thick*, thin*, too much*, unconvincing, unimaginable, unsubstantial, unthinkable, weak, won't hold water*, won't wash*; SEE CONCEPTS *529,548*

unbending [*adj*] *rigid, tough*
aloof, crisp, distant, do or die*, dug in*, firm, formal, hard as nails*, hard-line*, hold one's ground*, hold the fort*, hold the line*, incompliant, inelastic, inexorable, inflexible, intractable, locked in*, obdurate, obstinate, relentless, reserved, resolute, set in

stone*, severe, single-minded, stand one's ground*, stand pat*, stick to one's guns*, stiff, strict, stubborn, uncompromising, unflexible, unrelenting, unswayable, unyielding, uptight; SEE CONCEPTS *401,534,604*

unbiased [*adj*] *not prejudiced*
aloof, cold, color blind*, disinterested, dispassionate, equal, equitable, even-handed, fair, honest, impartial, just, neutral, nondiscriminatory, nonpartisan, objective, on the fence*, open-minded, straight, unbigoted, uncolored, uninterested, unprejudiced; SEE CONCEPT *542*

unblemished [*adj*] *not flawed*
chaste, clean, decent, faultless, flawless, immaculate, intact, modest, perfect, pure, sound, spotless, stainless, undamaged, undefiled, unflawed, unhurt, unimpaired, uninjured, unmarked, unmarred, unspotted, unstained, unsullied, untarnished, whole; SEE CONCEPTS *485,621*

unbreakable [*adj*] *strong, tough*
adamantine, armored, brass-bound, durable, everlasting, firm, incorruptible, indestructible, infrangible, invulnerable, lasting, nonbreakable, perdurable, resistant, rugged, shatterproof, solid, tight, toughened, unshakable, unyielding; SEE CONCEPTS *488,489,798*

unbroken [*v*] *continuous, whole*
ceaseless, constant, deep, endless, entire, even, fast, incessant, intact, perfect, perpetual, profound, progressive, regular, solid, sound, successive, total, undisturbed, unimpaired, uninterrupted, unremitting, unruffled, untroubled; SEE CONCEPTS *482,485,798*

unburden [*adj*] *get rid of*
clear, confess, confide, disburden, discharge, disclose, disencumber, dispose of, divulge, dump, ease, empty, get off one's chest*, lay bare*, let hair down*, lighten, lose, out with it*, own, relieve, relinquish, reveal, shake, shake off*, tell all, throw off, unbosom, unload; SEE CONCEPTS *60,211,244*

uncanny [*adj*] *very strange, unusual*
astonishing, astounding, creepy, devilish, eerie, exceptional, extraordinary, fantastic, ghostly, ghoulish, incredible, inexplicable, inspired, magical, miraculous, mysterious, mystifying, preternatural, prodigious, queer, remarkable, scary, secret, singular, spooky, superhuman, supernatural, supernormal, supranormal, unearthly, unheard-of, unnatural, weird; SEE CONCEPTS *537,564*

uncertain [*adj*] *doubtful, changeable*
ambiguous, ambivalent, chancy, conjectural, dubious, erratic, fitful, hanging by thread*, hazy, hesitant, iffy, incalculable, inconstant, indefinite, indeterminate, indistinct, insecure, irregular, irresolute, on thin ice*, precarious, questionable, risky, speculative, touch and go*, unclear, unconfirmed, undecided, undetermined, unfixed, unforeseeable, unpredictable, unreliable, unresolved, unsettled, un-

sure, up for grabs*, up in the air*, vacillating, vague, variable, wavering; SEE CONCEPTS *529,534,535*

uncertainty [*n*] *doubt, changeableness*
ambiguity, ambivalence, anxiety, bewilderment, concern, confusion, conjecture, contingency, dilemma, disquiet, distrust, doubtfulness, dubiety, guesswork, hesitancy, hesitation, incertitude, inconclusiveness, indecision, irresolution, lack of confidence, misgiving, mistrust, mystification, oscillation, perplexity, puzzle, puzzlement, qualm, quandary, query, questionableness, reserve, salt*, scruple, skepticism, suspicion, trouble, uneasiness, unpredictability, vagueness, wonder, worry; SEE CONCEPTS *388,410,696*

unchangeable [*adj*] *constant, steadfast*
changeless, continuing, firm, fixed, immovable, immutable, inalterable, inevitable, inflexible, invariable, irreversible, permanent, resolute, stable, strong, unalterable, unmodifiable, unmovable; SEE CONCEPT *534*

unchanging [*adj*] *constant, permanent*
abiding, changeless, consistent, continuing, enduring, equable, eternal, even, fixed, immutable, imperishable, invariable, lasting, perpetual, rigid, same, stabile, static, unchanged, unfading, unfailing, unfluctuating, uniform, unvarying; SEE CONCEPTS *534,551,649*

uncivilized [*adj*] *wild, uncultured*
barbarian, barbaric, barbarous, boorish, brutish, churlish, coarse, crass, crude, discourteous, disrespectful, gross*, ill-bred, illiterate, impertinent, impolite, loutish, mannerless, outrageous, philistine, primitive, rude, rugged, savage, unconscionable, uncontrolled, uncouth, uncultivated, uneducated, ungodly, unholy, unmannered, unpolished, unrefined, unsophisticated, vulgar, wicked; SEE CONCEPT *401*

unclean [*adj*] *dirty*
bedraggled, befouled, besmirched, black, blurred, common, contaminated, corrupt, decayed, defiled, desecrated, dusty, evil, feculent, fetid, filthy, foul, grimy, impure, messy, muddy, nasty, polluted, profaned, putrescent, putrid, rancid, rank, rotten, sloppy, slovenly, smeared, smudged, soiled, sooty, sordid, spotted, squalid, stable, stained, stall, stinking, sullied, tainted, tarnished, unhealthful, vile; SEE CONCEPT *621*

uncomfortable [*adj1*] *painful, rough*
afflictive, agonizing, annoying, awkward, bitter, cramped, difficult, disagreeable, distressing, dolorous, excruciating, galling, grievous, hard, harsh, ill-fitting, incommodious, irritating, thorny, torturing, troublesome, vexatious, wearisome; SEE CONCEPTS *529,537,583*

uncomfortable [*adj2*] *distressed, upset*
aching, angry, anguished, annoyed, awkward, chafed, cheerless, comfortless, confused, discomfited, discomposed, disquieted, disturbed, embarrassed, exhausted, fatigued, galled, harsh, hurt, ill at

ease, in pain, miserable, nervous, pained, restless, self-conscious, smarting, sore, stiff, strained, suffering, tired, troubled, uneasy, vexed, weary, worn, wracked, wretched; SEE CONCEPTS *403,485*

uncommitted [*adj*] *free; not involved*
cut loose*, don't care*, fence-sitting*, floating, free-spirited, laid-back*, middle ground*, middle of the road*, neutral, nonaligned, nonpartisan, on the fence*, restrained, unaffiliated, unattached, uninvolved, unpledged; SEE CONCEPTS *403,542*

uncommon [*adj1*] *very different*
aberrant, abnormal, anomalous, arcane, bizarre, curious, eccentric, egregious, exceptional, exotic, extraordinary, extreme, fantastic, few, freakish, infrequent, irregular, nondescript, noteworthy, novel, odd, original, out of the ordinary, out of the way*, outré, peculiar, prodigious, queer, rare, remarkable, scarce, seldom, singular, sporadic, startling, strange, surprising, unaccustomed, unconventional, uncustomary, unfamiliar, unheard of, unique, unorthodox, unusual, weird; SEE CONCEPT *564*

uncommon [*adj2*] *wonderful, exceptional*
distinctive, extraordinary, incomparable, inimitable, notable, noteworthy, outstanding, rare, remarkable, singular, special, superior, unimaginable, unique, unparalleled, unprecedented, unthinkable, unwonted; SEE CONCEPT *574*

uncommonly [*adv*] *infrequently*
exceptionally, extra, extremely, hardly ever, in few instances, irregularly, not often, now and then, occasionally, oddly, on occasion, particularly, peculiarly, rarely, remarkably, scarcely ever, seldom, sporadically, strangely, unusually, very; SEE CONCEPT *541*

uncommunicative [*adj*] *shy, silent*
aloof, buttoned up*, clammed up*, close, close-mouthed*, curt, distant, dried up*, evasive, Garbo*, guarded, hush-hush*, offish*, on the QT*, quiet, reserved, reticent, retiring, secretive, short, standoffish, taciturn, tight-lipped*, unapproachable, unresponsive, unsociable; SEE CONCEPT *267*

uncompromising [*adj*] *stubborn*
brick-wall*, decided, determined, firm, hard-core*, hard-line*, inexorable, inflexible, intransigent, locked, obdurate, obstinate, pigheaded*, relentless, resolute, rigid, set in stone*, single-minded, steadfast, stiff-necked*, strict, strong, tough, unbending; SEE CONCEPTS *401,542*

unconcerned [*adj*] *carefree; apathetic*
aloof, blind, blithe, callous, careless, cold, cool, deaf, detached, dispassionate, distant, easy, feckless, forgetful, hardened, hard-hearted, heedless, impassive, inattentive, incurious, indifferent, insensible, insensitive, insouciant, lackadaisical, lukewarm, negligent, neutral, nonchalant, oblivious, phlegmatic, relaxed, reserved, self-centered, serene, stony, supine, unbothered, uninterested, uninvolved,

unmoved, unperturbed, unruffled, unsympathetic, untroubled, unworried; SEE CONCEPTS *403,542*

unconditional [*adj*] *absolute, total*
actual, all out, assured, categorical, certain, clear, complete, decisive, definite, determinate, downright, entire, explicit, final, flat out, full, genuine, indubitable, no catch*, no fine print*, no holds barred*, no ifs ands or buts*, no kicker*, no strings*, open, out-and-out*, outright, plenary, positive, straight out, thorough, thoroughgoing, unconstrained, unequivocal, unlimited, unmistakable, unmitigated, unqualified, unquestionable, unreserved, unrestricted, utter, whole, wide; SEE CONCEPTS *531,535,544*

unconscionable [*adj*] *immoral, immoderate*
amoral, barbarous, conscienceless, criminal, dishonest, excessive, exorbitant, extravagant, extreme, inordinate, knavish, outrageous, preposterous, sneaky, too much*, uncivilized, undue, unethical, unfair, ungodly, unholy, unjust, unprincipled, unreasonable, unscrupulous, wanton, wicked; SEE CONCEPTS *545,569*

unconscious [*adj1*] *not awake; out cold*
benumbed, blacked out*, bombed*, cold*, comatose, dead to the world*, drowsy, entranced, feeling no pain*, flattened*, inanimate, in a trance, inert, insensate, insensible, knocked*, lethargic, numb, on the canvas*, out, out like a light*, palsied, paralyzed, passed out*, put away*, raving, senseless, stunned, stupefied, swooning, torpid, tranced, zonked*; SEE CONCEPTS *314,539*

unconscious [*adj2*] *ignorant; automatic*
accidental, gut*, ignorant, inadvertent, inattentive, inherent, innate, instinctive, involuntary, latent, lost, reflex, repressed, subconscious, subliminal, suppressed, unaware, uncalculated, undeliberate, unheeding, unintended, unintentional, unmindful, unpremeditated, unrealized, unwitting; SEE CONCEPTS *542,544*

uncontrollable [*adj*] *wild; carried away*
beside oneself, disorderly, excited, fractious, frantic, freaked, furious, headstrong*, indocile, indomitable, insuppressible, insurgent, intractable, irrepressible, irresistible, lawless, loose cannon*, mad, obdurate, obstinate, recalcitrant, strong, stubborn, uncontainable, undisciplinable, undisciplined, ungovernable, unmanageable, unrestrainable, unruly, violent; SEE CONCEPT *401*

unconventional [*adj*] *very different; odd*
anarchistic, atypical, avant-garde, beat, bizarre, crazy, eccentric, far-out*, freakish, freaky, free and easy*, idiosyncratic, individual, individualistic, informal, irregular, kinky*, kooky*, nonconformist, oddball*, offbeat, off-beaten track*, off the wall*, original, out in left field, out of the ordinary, unceremonious, uncommon, uncustomary, unique, unorthodox, unusual, way-out*, weirdo*; SEE CONCEPT *564*

uncouth [adj] *clumsy, uncultivated*
awkward, barbaric, boorish, cheap, clownish, clumsy, coarse, crass, crude, discourteous, disgracious, gawky, graceless, gross*, heavy-handed, ill-bred, ill-mannered, impertinent, impolite, inelegant, loud, loud-mouthed, loutish, oafish, raunchy, raw, rough, rude, strange, tacky*, uncalled-for*, uncivil, uncivilized, uncultivated, ungainly, ungenteel, ungentlemanly, unpolished, unrefined, unseemly, vulgar; SEE CONCEPT *401*

uncover [v] *reveal, disclose*
bare, betray, break, bring to light*, crack, denude, dig up*, disclose, discover, display, divulge, expose, give away, hit upon, lay bare, lay open, leak, make known, open, open up, reveal, show, strike, strip, stumble on, subject, tap, tell, tip one's hand*, unclothe, unearth, unmask, unveil, unwrap; SEE CONCEPTS *60,183,261*

uncritical [adj] *casual, unfussy*
careless, cursory, easily pleased, imperceptive, imprecise, imprudent, inaccurate, indiscriminate, offhand, perfunctory, shallow, slipshod, superficial, undiscerning, undiscriminating, unexacting, uninformed, unperceptive, unselective, unthinking; SEE CONCEPT *542*

undaunted [adj] *brave, bold*
audacious, coming on strong*, courageous, dauntless, fearless, fire-eating*, gallant, icy*, indomitable, intrepid, not discouraged, not put off*, resolute, spunky, steadfast, unafraid, unalarmed, unapprehensive, undeterred, undiscouraged, undismayed, unfaltering, unflinching, unshrinking, valiant, valorous; SEE CONCEPT *401*

undecided [adj] *not sure, not definite*
ambivalent, betwixt and between*, blowing hot and cold*, borderline, debatable, dithering*, doubtful, dubious, equivocal, hemming and hawing*, hesitant, iffy*, indecisive, indefinite, in the middle*, irresolute, moot, of two minds*, on the fence*, open, pendent, pending, running hot and cold*, tentative, torn, uncertain, unclear, uncommitted, undetermined, unfinished, unsettled, unsure, up in the air*, vague, waffling, wavering, wishy-washy*; SEE CONCEPTS *403,529*

undeniable [adj] *definite, proven*
actual, beyond doubt, beyond question, binding, certain, clear, compulsory, evident, for sure, inarguable, incontestable, incontrovertible, indisputable, indubitable, irrefutable, manifest, necessary, no ifs and or buts*, obligatory, obvious, open and shut*, patent, positive, real, sound, sure, sure thing*, true, unanswerable, unassailable, undoubted, unquestionable; SEE CONCEPT *535*

undependable [adj] *irresponsible*
bum, capricious, careless, changeable, dubious, erratic, fickle, fly-by-night*, inconsistent, inconstant, indefinite, indeterminate, loose*, no bargain*, no-good*, treacherous, trick, tricky, trustless, unas-sured, uncertain, unpredictable, unreliable, unsafe, unsound, unstable, unsure, untrustworthy, variable; SEE CONCEPTS *401,535*

under [adv1/prep1] *below*
beneath, bottom, concealed by, covered by, down, downward, held down, inferior, lower, nether, on the bottom, on the nether side, on the underside, pinned, pressed down, supporting, to the bottom, underneath; SEE CONCEPTS *586,735,793*

under [adv2/prep2] *secondary*
amenable, belonging, collateral, consequent, corollary, dependent, directed, following, governed, included, inferior, in the power of, junior, lesser, low, lower, obedient, obeying, reporting, sub, subject, subjugated, subordinate, subsequent, subservient, subsidiary, substract, subsumed; SEE CONCEPTS *560,575,577*

undercover [adj] *secret, spy*
clandestine, concealed, confidential, covert, creep, furtive, hidden, hole-and-corner*, hush-hush*, incognito*, intelligence, on the QT*, private, stealth, stealthy, sub-rosa*, surreptitious, underground, underhand, underneath, under wraps*; SEE CONCEPTS *544,576*

undercurrent [n] *drift, pull*
atmosphere, aura, crosscurrent, direction, eddy, feeling, flavor, hint, inclination, indication, insinuation, intimation, murmur, overtone, propensity, riptide, sense, suggestion, tendency, tenor, tinge, trace, trend, underflow, undertone, undertow, vibes*, vibrations; SEE CONCEPTS *673,738*

underdog [n] *person who is not expected to succeed*
casualty, failure, fall guy*, little guy*, loser, low man/woman*, prey, underling, victim; SEE CONCEPTS *366,423*

underestimate [v] *minimize; rate too low*
belittle, deprecate, depreciate, disesteem, disparage, make light of*, miscalculate, miscarry, not do justice*, put down*, sell short*, slight, think too little of*, underrate, undervalue; SEE CONCEPTS *12,54,764*

undergo [v] *be subjected to*
abide, bear, bear up, bow, defer, encounter, endure, experience, feel, go through, have, know, meet with, put up with, see, share, stand, submit to, suffer, support, sustain, tolerate, weather, withstand, yield; SEE CONCEPT *23*

underground [adj1] *below the surface*
below ground, buried, covered, in the recesses, subterranean, subterrestrial, sunken, underfoot; SEE CONCEPT *583*

underground [adj2] *secret, subversive*
alternative, avant-garde, clandestine, concealed, covert, experimental, hidden, hush-hush*, on the QT*, on the sly*, private, radical, resistant, resistive, revolutionary, surreptitious, unbowed, unconventional, undercover, under wraps*, unusual; SEE CONCEPTS *564,576*

underhand [*adj*] *deceitful*
clandestine, concealed, crafty, crooked, cunning, deceptive, devious, dirty-dealing*, dishonest, dishonorable, double-crossing*, duplicitous, fraudulent, furtive, guileful, hush-hush*, indirect, insidious, oblique, on the QT*, on the quiet*, secret, secretive, shady, shifty, slippery*, sly*, sneaking, sneaky, stealthy, subrosa*, surreptitious, treacherous, tricky, two-faced*, two-timing*, undercover, underhanded, under wraps*, unethical, unfair, unjust, unscrupulous, wily; SEE CONCEPTS *401,544*

underline [*v*] *emphasize; mark*
accentuate, bracket, call attention to, caption, check off, draw attention to, feature, give emphasis, highlight, indicate, interlineate, italicize, play up, point to, point up, rule, stress, underscore; SEE CONCEPTS *49,79*

underlying [*adj*] *fundamental, latent*
basal, basic, bottom, bottom-line*, cardinal, concealed, critical, crucial, elemental, elementary, essential, hidden, indispensable, intrinsic, lurking, necessary, needful, nitty-gritty*, nub, primary, prime, primitive, radical, root, substratal, veiled, vital; SEE CONCEPTS *546,549*

undermine [*v*] *weaken*
attenuate, blunt, clip one's wings*, corrode, cripple, debilitate, dig, dig out*, disable, eat away*, enfeeble, erode, excavate, foil, frustrate, hollow out, hurt, impair, knock bottom out*, mine, poke full of holes*, ruin, sabotage, sandbag*, sap, soften, subvert, threaten, thwart, torpedo*, tunnel, undercut, wear, whittle away, wreck; SEE CONCEPTS *14,240*

underneath [*adv/prep*] *below*
beneath, bottom, covered, lower, neath, nether, under; SEE CONCEPTS *586,735*

underprivileged [*adj*] *poor*
badly off*, depressed, deprived, destitute, disadvantaged, down and out*, handicapped, hapless, hard up*, have-not*, ill-fated, ill-starred, impoverished, indigent, in dire straits, in need, in want, needy, unfortunate, unlucky; SEE CONCEPT *334*

understand [*v1*] *appreciate, comprehend*
accept, apprehend, be aware, be conscious of, be with it*, catch, catch on, conceive, deduce, discern, distinguish, explain, fathom, figure out, find out, follow, get*, get the hang of*, get the idea*, get the picture*, get the point*, grasp, have knowledge of, identify with, infer, interpret, ken*, know, learn, make out*, make sense of, master, note, penetrate, perceive, possess, read, realize, recognize, register, savvy, see, seize, sense, sympathize, take in*, take meaning, tolerate; SEE CONCEPT *15*

understand [*v2*] *think, believe*
accept, assume, be informed, concede, conceive, conclude, conjecture, consider, count on, deduce, expect, fancy, feel for, gather, guess, hear, imagine, infer, learn, presume, reckon, suppose, surmise, suspect, take for granted, take it, think; SEE CONCEPT *12*

understanding [*n1*] *comprehension, appreciation*
acumen, apperception, apprehension, assimilation, awareness, decipherment, discernment, discrimination, grasp, grip, insight, intellect, intelligence, intuition, judgment, ken, knowing, knowledge, mastery, penetration, perception, perceptiveness, perceptivity, percipience, perspicacity, prehension, realization, reason, recognition, savvy, sense, sharpness, wit; SEE CONCEPT *409*

understanding [*n2*] *belief*
acceptation, conception, conclusion, estimation, idea, import, impression, inkling, intendment, interpretation, judgment, knowledge, meaning, message, notion, opinion, perception, purport, sense, significance, significancy, signification, sympathy, view, viewpoint; SEE CONCEPTS *682,689*

understanding [*n3*] *informal agreement*
accord, common view, concord, deal, handshake*, harmony, meeting of minds*, pact; SEE CONCEPT *684*

understanding [*adj*] *accepting, tolerant*
compassionate, considerate, discerning, empathetic, forbearing, forgiving, generous, kind, kindly, patient, perceptive, responsive, sensitive, sympathetic; SEE CONCEPTS *401,542*

understood [*adj*] *assumed, implicit*
accepted, appreciated, axiomatic, down pat*, got it*, implied, inferential, inferred, known, on to*, pat, presumed, roger*, tacit, taken for granted, undeclared, unexpressed, unsaid, unspoken, unstated, wise to, wordless; SEE CONCEPT *529*

undertake [*v*] *attempt, engage in*
address oneself, agree, answer for, bargain, begin, commence, commit, commit oneself, contract, covenant, devote, embark, endeavor, enter upon, fall into, go about, go for, go in for, go into, guarantee, have a hand in*, have a try, hazard, initiate, launch, make a run at*, move, offer, pitch in, pledge, promise, set about, set in motion, set out, shoulder, stake, stipulate, tackle, take on, take the plunge*, take upon oneself, try, try out, venture, volunteer; SEE CONCEPTS *87,100*

undertaking [*n*] *endeavor, attempt*
adventure, affair, business, deal, effort, engagement, enterprise, essay, experiment, game, happening, hassle, hazard, job, move, operation, outfit, play, project, proposition, pursuit, shop, striving, struggle, task, thing*, trial, try, venture, what one is into*, work; SEE CONCEPTS *87,324,349,362*

undertone [*n*] *suggestion, whisper*
association, atmosphere, buzz, connotation, feeling, flavor, hint, hum, implication, low tone, mumble, murmur, mutter, overtone, rumor, tinge, touch, trace, undercurrent; SEE CONCEPTS *65,682*

underwear [*n*] *clothing worn under outerwear*
bikini, boxers, boxer shorts, bra, briefs, BVDs*, corset, drawers*, intimate things, jockeys, jockey shorts, lingerie, long johns, panties, shorts, skivvy*, smallclothes, underclothes, underclothing, undergar-

ment, underpants, undershirt, underthings, undies; SEE CONCEPT *451*

underweight [*adj*] *thin*
angular, anorexic, bony, gangly, malnourished, puny, scrawny, shadow, skeleton*, skin and bones*, skinny, starved, stringbean*, undernourished, undersized; SEE CONCEPT *491*

underworld [*n*] *criminal activity, element*
abyss, Cosa Nostra, criminals, felonry, gangland, gangsters, Mafia, mob*, organized crime, racket*, riffraff*, syndicate; SEE CONCEPTS *412,645*

underwrite [*v*] *endorse, insure*
accede, agree to, angel*, approve, back, bankroll, collateral, consent, countersign, endow, finance, float, fund, guarantee, help, initial, okay*, pay, provide, provide financing, sanction, seal, secure, sign, sponsor, stake, subscribe, subsidize, support; SEE CONCEPTS *50,88,110,341*

undesirable [*adj*] *offensive, unacceptable*
abominable, annoying, bothersome, defective, disagreeable, disliked, displeasing, distasteful, dreaded, icky, inadmissible, incommodious, inconvenient, inexpedient, insufferable, loathed, loathsome, objectionable, obnoxious, offensive, outcast, out of place, rejected, repellent, repugnant, scorned, shunned, to be avoided, troublesome, unacceptable, unattractive, unlikable, unpleasing, unpopular, unsatisfactory, unsavory, unsought, unsuitable, unwanted, unwelcome, unwished for, useless; SEE CONCEPTS *529,570*

undeveloped [*adj*] *immature*
abortive, backward, behindhand, embryonic, halfbaked, ignored, inchoate, incipient, inexperienced, latent, potential, primitive, primordial, unactualized, underdeveloped, unevolved, unprogressive, untaught, untrained; SEE CONCEPTS *485,578,797*

undisputed/undisputable [*adj*] *positive, accepted*
acknowledged, admitted, arbitrary, assured, authoritative, beyond question, certain, conclusive, decided, dogmatic, final, incontestable, incontrovertible, indisputable, indubitable, irrefutable, not disputed, positive, recognized, sure, tyrannous, unchallenged, uncontested, undeniable, undoubted, unequivocal, unerring, unquestioned; SEE CONCEPT *535*

undivided [*adj*] *whole*
absorbed, circumspect, collective, combined, complete, concentrated, concerted, continued, deliberate, detailed, diligent, engrossed, entire, exclusive, fast, fixed, full, intense, intent, jackpot*, joined, lock stock and barrel*, minute, rigid, scrupulous, single, solid, steady, thorough, unanimous, unbroken, uncut, undistracted, unflagging, united, unswerving, vigilant, whole enchilada*, wholehearted, whole nine yards*, whole shebang*, works*; SEE CONCEPTS *482,531*

undo [*v1*] *open*
disengage, disentangle, free, loose, loosen, release, unbind, unblock, unbutton, unclose, unfasten, unfix, unlock, unloose, unloosen, unravel, unshut, unstop, untie, unwrap; SEE CONCEPT *135*

undo [*v2*] *nullify, invalidate*
abate, abolish, abrogate, annihilate, annul, break, bring down, bring to naught*, cancel, cramp*, craze, crimp*, decimate, defeat, demolish, destroy, have*, impoverish, injure, make waves*, mar, negate, neutralize, offset, outfox, outmaneuver, outsmart, overreach, overthrow, overturn, quash, queer, raze, reverse, ruin, screw up*, shatter, skin*, smash, spoil, stymie*, subvert, unbuild, undermine, unsettle, upset, vitiate, wipe out*, wrack, wreck; SEE CONCEPTS *7,19,121,252*

undoing [*n*] *destruction, misfortune*
accident, adversity, affliction, bad luck, bad omen, bane, blight, blow, blunder, calamity, casualty, catastrophe, collapse, curse, defeat, destroyer, difficulty, disgrace, doom, downfall, error, failure, fault, faux pas*, flaw, fumble, grief, humiliation, last straw*, misadventure, miscalculation, mischance, mishap, misstep, omission, overthrow, overturn, reversal, reverse, ruin, ruination, shame, slip, smash, stumble, subversion, trial, trip, trouble, visitation, weakness, wreck; SEE CONCEPTS *230,674,679*

undoubtedly [*adv*] *certainly*
assuredly, beyond question, beyond shadow of a doubt*, definitely, doubtless, easily, indeed, of course, really, surely, truly, undeniably, unmistakably, unquestionably, well, without doubt; SEE CONCEPT *535*

undress [*v*] *take off clothes*
denude, disarray, dismantle, disrobe, divest oneself, doff, get off, get out of, husk, peel, shed, shock, slip off, slip out of, strip, unattire, uncloak, unclothe, unmask; SEE CONCEPTS *211,453*

undue [*adj*] *excessive, unnecessary*
disproportionate, exceeding, exorbitant, extravagant, extreme, forbidden, illegal, ill-timed, immoderate, improper, inappropriate, inapt, indecorous, inept, inordinate, intemperate, needless, overmuch, sinister, too great, too much, unapt, uncalled-for, unconscionable, underhanded, undeserved, unfair, unfitting, unjust, unjustifiable, unjustified, unmeasurable, unreasonable, unseasonable, unseemly, unsuitable, untimely, unwarrantable, unwarranted; SEE CONCEPTS *546,558,569*

unduly [*adv*] *excessively*
disproportionately, ever, extravagantly, extremely, illegally, immensely, immoderately, improperly, indecorously, inordinately, out of proportion, over, overfull, overly, overmuch, too, underhandedly, unfairly, unjustifiably, unjustly, unnecessarily, unreasonably; SEE CONCEPTS *544,546,569*

undying [*adj*] *never-ending*
constant, continuing, deathless, eternal, everlasting, immortal, imperishable, indestructible, inextinguishable, infinite, interminable, perennial, permanent,

perpetual, persistent, unceasing, undiminished, unended, unending, unfading; SEE CONCEPT *798*

unearth [v] *dig up*
ascertain, bring to light*, catch on*, delve, determine, discover, disinter, dredge up, excavate, exhibit, exhume, expose, ferret, find, find out, hear, hit upon, learn, reveal, root, see, see the light, show, spark, spotlight*, strike, stumble on, turn up, unbury, uncover, uproot; SEE CONCEPTS *178,183*

unearthly [adj] *supernatural; very strange*
abnormal, absurd, appalling, demoniac, devilish, eerie, ethereal, extraordinary, fiendish, frightening, funereal, ghastly, ghostly, ghoulish, hair-raising, haunted, heavenly, hyperphysical, miraculous, nightmarish, not of this world, phantom, preternatural, ridiculous, scary, sepulchral, spectral, spooky, sublime, superhuman, uncanny, ungodly, unholy, unreasonable, weird; SEE CONCEPTS *536,564,582*

uneasy [adj] *awkward, uncomfortable*
afraid, agitated, alarmed, all nerves*, anguished, anxious, apprehensive, bothered, constrained, discomposed, dismayed, disquieted, disturbed, edgy, fearful, fidgety, fretful, harassed, ill at ease, impatient, insecure, in turmoil, irascible, irritable, jittery, jumpy, nervous, on edge, on the qui vive*, palpitant, peevish, perplexed, perturbed, precarious, restive, restless, shaken, shaky, strained, suspicious, tense, tormented, troubled, unquiet, unsettled, unstable, upset, vexed, worried, wrung; SEE CONCEPTS *403,548,690*

uneducated [adj] *lacking knowledge*
benighted, empty-headed, ignoramus, ignorant, illiterate, inerudite, know-nothing*, lowbrow*, uncultivated, uncultured, uninstructed, unlearned, unlettered, unread, unrefined, unschooled, untaught, untutored; SEE CONCEPT *402*

unemotional [adj] *not responsive*
along for the ride*, apathetic, blah*, callous, chill*, cold, cold fish*, coldhearted*, cool, deadpan, dispassionate, emotionless, flat, frigid, glacial, go with the flow*, hard-boiled*, hard-hearted*, heartless, impassive, indifferent, insensitive, laid-back*, listless, marble*, obdurate, passionless, phlegmatic, quiet, reserved, reticent, roll with the punches*, thick-skinned*, uncompassionate, undemonstrative, unexcitable, unfeeling, unimpressionable, unresponsive, unsympathetic; SEE CONCEPTS *401,403*

unemployed [adj] *without a job*
at liberty*, between jobs*, closed down*, disengaged, down, fired, free, idle, inactive, jobless, laid off, leisured, loafing*, on layoff, on the bench*, on the dole*, on the shelf*, out of action*, out of a job, out of work, resting, unapplied, underemployed, unengaged, unexercised, unoccupied, unused, without gainful employment, workless; SEE CONCEPT *538*

unending [adj] *continuing*
amaranthine, ceaseless, constant, continual, continuous, endless, eternal, everlasting, immortal, incessant, infinite, interminable, never-ending, perpetual, steady, unceasing, uninterrupted, unremitting; SEE CONCEPTS *482,798*

unequal [adj1] *different*
differing, disparate, dissimilar, distant, divergent, diverse, incommensurate, like night and day*, mismatched, not uniform, odd, poles apart*, unalike, unequivalent, uneven, unlike, unmatched, unsimilar, variable, various, varying, weird*; SEE CONCEPT *564*

unequal [adj2] *not balanced; lopsided*
asymmetrical, disproportionate, ill-matched, inequitable, irregular, nonsymmetrical, off-balance, one-sided, overbalanced, unbalanced, uneven, unproportionate, unsymmetrical; SEE CONCEPT *480*

unequaled [adj] *supreme, pre-eminent*
alone, beyond compare, incomparable, inimitable, matchless, nonpareil, only, paramount, peerless, second to none*, surpassing, towering, transcendent, ultimate, unique, unmatched, unparagoned, unparalleled, unrivaled, unsurpassed, without equal; SEE CONCEPT *574*

unequivocal [adj] *definite, positive*
absolute, apparent, categorical, certain, clear, clearcut, decided, decisive, direct, distinct, downright, evident, explicit, flat out*, incontestable, incontrovertible, indisputable, indubitable, manifest, no catch*, no fine print*, no holds barred*, no ifs ands or buts*, no strings attached*, obvious, open and shut*, palpable, patent, plain, straight, straightforward, straight out, unambiguous, uncontestable, undeniable, undisputable, univocal, unmistakable, unquestionable; SEE CONCEPT *535*

unerring [adj] *accurate*
certain, errorless, exact, faultless, impeccable, inerrable, inerrant, infallible, invariable, just, perfect, reliable, sure, true, trustworthy, unfailing; SEE CONCEPTS *535,574*

unethical [adj] *dishonest, immoral*
cheating, corrupt, crooked, dirty*, dirty-dealing*, dishonorable, disreputable, double-crossing*, fake, fishy*, flimflam*, fly-by-night*, gyp*, illegal, improper, mercenary, scam*, shady*, sharp*, slick*, slippery*, sneaky*, two-faced*, two-timing*, underhand, unfair, unprincipled, unprofessional, unscrupulous, wrong; SEE CONCEPT *545*

uneven [adj] *not smooth or balanced*
asperous, asymmetrical, broken, bumpy, changeable, craggy, differing, discrepant, disparate, disproportionate, fitful, fluctuating, harsh, ill-matched, intermittent, irregular, jagged, jerky, leftover, lopsided, nonsymmetrical, notched, not flat, not level, not parallel, odd, off-balance, one-sided, overbalanced, patchy, remaining, rough, rugged, scabrous, scraggy, serrate, spasmodic, spotty, unbalanced, unequal, unfair, unlevel, unsmooth, unsteady, unsymmetrical, variable; SEE CONCEPTS *480,566,606*

uneventful [adj] *monotonous, dull*
boring, common, commonplace, humdrum*, inconclusive, indecisive, ordinary, prosaic, quiet, routine,

tedious, unexceptional, unexciting, unfateful, uninteresting, unmemorable, unnoteworthy, unremarkable, unvaried; SEE CONCEPT 548

unexpected [adj] surprising
abrupt, accidental, amazing, astonishing, chance, electrifying, eye-opening*, fortuitous, from left field*, impetuous, impulsive, instantaneous, not bargained for*, not in the cards*, out of the blue*, payback, prodigious, staggering, startling, stunning, sudden, swift, unanticipated, unforeseen, unheralded, unlooked-for, unpredictable, unpredicted, wonderful; SEE CONCEPTS 544,548

unfailing [adj] certain, unchanging
absolute, assiduous, bottomless, boundless, ceaseless, come-through, consistent, constant, continual, continuing, continuous, count on, delivering, dependable, diligent, dyed-in-the-wool*, endless, eternal, faithful, inexhaustible, infallible, invariable, loyal, never-failing, persistent, reliable, rock*, same, staunch, steadfast, straight, sure, surefire, there*, tried-and-true*, true, trustworthy, unflagging, unlimited, unrelenting; SEE CONCEPTS 534,535,538

unfair [adj] prejudiced, wrongful
arbitrary, bad, base, biased, bigoted, blameworthy, cheating, criminal, crooked*, cruel, culpable, discreditable, discriminatory, dishonest, dishonorable, foul, grievous, illegal, immoral, improper, inequitable, inexcusable, iniquitous, injurious, low, mean, one-sided, partial, partisan, petty, shameful, shameless, uncalled-for, undue, unethical, unjust, unjustifiable, unlawful, unprincipled, unreasonable, unrightful, unscrupulous, unsporting, unwarranted, vicious, vile, wicked, wrong; SEE CONCEPTS 544,545,548

unfaithful [adj] disloyal, adulterous
adulterine, cheating, deceitful, double-crossing*, faithless, false, false-hearted, fickle, foresworn, inconstant, incontinent, moonlighting*, not true to, of bad faith, perfidious, philandering, recreant, shifty*, snaky*, sneaking, traitorous, treacherous, treasonable, two-faced*, two-timing*, unchaste, unreliable, untrue, untrustworthy, wicked, worm*; SEE CONCEPT 545

unfaltering [adj] steadfast
abiding, bent on*, bound, bound and determined*, dead set on*, enduring, firm, going all the way*, indefatigable, meaning business*, mulish*, never-failing, persevering, pigheaded*, resolute, set, steady, stiff-necked*, stubborn, sure, tireless, unfailing, unflagging, unflappable, unflinching, unqualified, unquestioning, unswerving, untiring, unwavering, wholehearted; SEE CONCEPTS 403,535,538

unfamiliar [adj1] different, strange
alien, anomalous, bizarre, curious, exotic, extraordinary, fantastic, foreign, little known, new, novel, obscure, original, outlandish, out-of-the-way*, peculiar, recondite, remarkable, remote, unaccustomed, uncommon, unexpected, unexplored, uninvestigated, unknown, unusual; SEE CONCEPT 564

unfamiliar [adj2] inexperienced; not knowing about
ignorant, incognizant, inconversant, not associated, not versed in, oblivious, out of contact, unaccustomed, unacquainted, unaware, unconversant, uninformed, uninitiated, uninstructed, unknowing, unknown, unpracticed, unskilled, unversed, unwitting; SEE CONCEPTS 402,678

unfathomable [adj1] bottomless
abysmal, boundless, deep, eternal, immeasurable, infinite, soundless, unending, unmeasured, unplumbed; SEE CONCEPTS 482,777

unfathomable [adj2] hard to believe; difficult to understand
abstruse, baffling, beats me*, clear as mud*, deep*, enigmatic, esoteric, heavy, impenetrable, incognizable, incomprehensible, indecipherable, inexplicable, obscure, profound, too deep*, uncomprehensible, ungraspable, unintelligible, unknowable; SEE CONCEPT 529

unfavorable [adj] very bad
adverse, antagonistic, calamitous, contrary, damaging, destructive, disadvantageous, discommodious, hostile, ill, ill-advised, improper, inadvisable, inauspicious, inconvenient, inexpedient, infelicitous, inimical, inopportune, late, low, malapropos*, negative, objectionable, ominous, opposed, poor, regrettable, tardy, threatening, troublesome, unfit, unfortunate, unfriendly, unlucky, unpromising, unpropitious, unseasonable, unseemly, unsuited, untimely, untoward, wrong; SEE CONCEPTS 529,571

unfeeling [adj] hard-hearted, numb
anesthetized, apathetic, asleep, benumbed, brutal, callous, cantankerous, churlish, cold, cold-blooded*, cold fish*, coldhearted*, crotchety, cruel, deadened, exacting, feelingless, hard, hardened, heartless, icy*, inanimate, inhuman, insensate, insensible, insensitive, iron-hearted, merciless, obdurate, pitiless, ruthless, sensationless, senseless, severe, stony, surly, thick-skinned*, tough, unamiable, uncaring, uncompassionate, uncordial, unemotional, unkind, unsympathetic; SEE CONCEPTS 314,403,542

unfinished [adj] not completed
amateurish, bare, crude, cut short, dabbling, defective, deficient, dilettante, faulty, formless, found wanting, fragmentary, half-baked*, half-done*, immature, imperfect, incomplete, in the making, in the rough*, lacking, natural, not done, plain, raw, rough, roughhewn, shapeless, sketchy, tentative, unaccomplished, unadorned, unassembled, uncompleted, unconcluded, under construction, undeveloped, undone, unexecuted, unfashioned, unfulfilled, unperfected, unpolished, unrefined, wanting; SEE CONCEPTS 485,531

unfit [adj1] not appropriate or suited
below par*, can't make the grade*, debilitated, decrepit, discordant, down, dragging, feeble, flimsy,

ill-adapted, ill-equipped, ill-suited, improper, inadequate, inapplicable, inappropriate, incompatible, incongruous, incorrect, ineffective, inexpedient, infelicitous, inharmonious, laid low*, mistaken, not fit, out of element*, out of place, out of shape, poorly, rocky*, unbecoming, uncongenial, uncool, unhealthy, unlikely, unmeet, unpromising, unsuitable, unsuited, useless, valueless; SEE CONCEPT *558*

unfit [*adj2*] *not ready*
amateur, awkward, blundering, bungling, bush league*, butter-fingered*, clumsy, debilitated, disqualified, feeble, heavy-handed, ill-equipped, impotent, inadequate, incapable, incapacitated, incompetent, ineffective, inefficient, ineligible, inept, inexperienced, inexpert, maladjusted, maladroit, no good*, not cut out for*, not equal to, not up to*, unable, unapt, unfitted, unhandy, unpracticed, unprepared, unproficient, unqualified, unskilled, unskillful, untrained, useless, weak; SEE CONCEPT *527*

unflagging [*adj*] *persistent*
active, assiduous, constant, diligent, dynamic, energetic, fixed, indefatigable, inexhaustible, persevering, staunch, steady, tireless, unceasing, undeviating, unfailing, unfaltering, unrelenting, unremitting, unretiring, untiring, unwearied; SEE CONCEPTS *538,798*

unflappable [*adj*] *cool and calm*
collected, composed, deliberate, disimpassioned, easy, impassive, imperturbable, level-headed, nonchalant, relaxed, self-possessed, unruffled; SEE CONCEPTS *401,542*

unfold [*v1*] *spread out*
disentangle, display, expand, extend, fan, fan out, flatten, loosen, open, outspread, outstretch, reel out, release, shake out, spread, straighten, stretch out, unbend, uncoil, uncrease, uncurl, undo, unfurl, unravel, unroll, untwist, unwind, unwrap; SEE CONCEPT *201*

unfold [*v2*] *make known*
announce, clarify, clear up, decipher, describe, disclose, discover, display, divulge, dope out, elucidate, explain, explicate, expose, figure out, illustrate, present, publish, resolve, reveal, show, solve, uncover, unravel; SEE CONCEPTS *55,261*

unfold [*v3*] *develop*
bear fruit, demonstrate, elaborate, evidence, evince, evolve, expand, grow, manifest, mature; SEE CONCEPT *704*

unforeseen [*adj*] *surprising*
abrupt, accidental, from left field*, not bargained for*, out of the blue*, startling, sudden, surprise, unanticipated, uncalculated, unexpected, unlooked-for; SEE CONCEPTS *544,548*

unfortunate [*adj*] *unlucky, bad*
adverse, afflicted, broken, burdened, calamitous, cursed, damaging, deplorable, desperate, destitute, disastrous, doomed, forsaken, hapless, hopeless, ill-fated, ill-starred, in a bad way*, inappropriate, infelicitous, inopportune, jinxed, lamentable, luckless, out of luck*, pained, poor, regrettable, ruined, ruinous, shattered, star-crossed*, stricken, troubled, unbecoming, unfavorable, unhappy, unpropitious, unprosperous, unsuccessful, unsuitable, untoward, wretched; SEE CONCEPTS *334,548,570*

unfounded [*adj*] *not based on fact*
baseless, bottomless, deceptive, fabricated, fallacious, false, foundationless, gratuitous, groundless, hot air*, idle, illogical, just talk*, mendacious, misleading, off-base, spurious, trumped up*, uncalled-for, unjustified, unproven, unreal, unsubstantiated, untrue, untruthful, unwarranted, vain, without basis, without foundation; SEE CONCEPTS *267,582*

unfriendly [*adj*] *nasty, hostile*
acrimonious, against, alien, aloof, antagonistic, antisocial, censorious, chilly, chip on shoulder*, cold*, combative, competitive, conflicting, contrary, disaffected, disagreeable, distant, estranged, grouchy, grudging, gruff, hateful, ill-disposed, inauspicious, inhospitable, inimical, malicious, malignant, misanthropic, not on speaking terms*, opposed, opposite, quarrelsome, sour, spiteful, surly, uncharitable, uncongenial, unfavorable, unneighborly, unpropitious, unsociable, vengeful, warlike; SEE CONCEPTS *401,548*

ungodly [*adj1*] *immoral*
blasphemous, corrupt, depraved, godless, impious, improper, indecent, indecorous, indelicate, irreligious, malevolent, profane, rough, sinful, undecorous, unhallowed, unholy, unseemly, untoward, vile, wicked; SEE CONCEPTS *542,545*

ungodly [*adj2*] *outrageous*
atrocious, barbarous, dreadful, horrendous, horrid, intolerable, nasty, unbelievable, uncivilized, unconscionable, unearthly, unholy, unreasonable, unseemly; SEE CONCEPTS *529,548,570*

ungrateful [*adj*] *not appreciative*
careless, demanding, dissatisfied, faultfinding, forgetful, grasping, grumbling, heedless, ingrate, insensible, oblivious, self-centered, selfish, thankless, unappreciative, unmindful, unnatural, unthankful; SEE CONCEPT *401*

unguarded [*adj*] *thoughtless; unwary*
accessible, artless, candid, careless, casual, direct, foolhardy, frank, headlong, heedless, honest, ill-considered, impolitic, imprudent, impulsive, incautious, indiscreet, ingenuous, naive, offhand, rash, spontaneous, straightforward, unalert, uncircumspect, unconscious, undiplomatic, unpremeditated, unreflective, unthinking, unvigilant, unwatchful, unwise, vulnerable, weak; SEE CONCEPT *401*

unhappy [*adj1*] *sad*
bleak, bleeding*, blue*, blue funk*, bummed out*, cheerless, crestfallen, dejected, depressed, despondent, destroyed, disconsolate, dismal, dispirited, down*, down and out*, downbeat, downcast, down in the mouth*, dragged, dreary, gloomy, grim, heavy-hearted, hurting, in pain, in the dumps*, let-

down*, long-faced, low, melancholy, mirthless, miserable, mournful, oppressive, put away*, ripped*, sad, saddened, sorrowful, sorry, teary, troubled; SEE CONCEPT *403*

unhappy [*adj2*] *unfortunate, unlucky*
afflicted, cursed, hapless, ill-fated, ill-starred, luckless, misfortunate, troubled, untoward, wretched; SEE CONCEPT *548*

unhealthy [*adj1*] *sick*
ailing, below par, debilitated, delicate, diseased, down, dragging, feeble, frail, ill, in a decline, infirm, in ill health, in poor health, invalid, laid low*, out of action*, out of shape, peaked, poorly, rundown, shaky, sickly, unsound, unwell, weak; SEE CONCEPT *314*

unhealthy [*adj2*] *very bad in effect on well-being*
baneful, chancy, corrupt, corrupting, dangerous, degenerate, degrading, deleterious, demoralizing, depraved, detrimental, harmful, hazardous, insalubrious, jeopardous, morbid, nefarious, negative, noisome, noxious, perilous, perverse, risky, rotten, treacherous, undesirable, unhealthful, unsanitary, unsound, unwholesome, villainous, virulent, wicked; SEE CONCEPTS *537,571*

unheard-of [*adj*] *unique, obscure*
exceptional, inconceivable, little-known, nameless, new, novel, outlandish, preposterous, rare, shocking, singular, unbelievable, undiscovered, unfamiliar, unknown, unlikely, unprecedented, unrenowned, unsung, unusual; SEE CONCEPTS *564,576*

unholy [*adj1*] *sacreligious*
base, blameful, corrupt, culpable, depraved, dishonest, evil, godless, guilty, heinous, immoral, impious, iniquitous, irreligious, irreverent, irreverential, profane, sinful, ungodly, unhallowed, unsanctified, vile, wicked; SEE CONCEPTS *542,548*

unholy [*adj2*] *outrageous*
appalling, awful, barbarous, dreadful, horrendous, shocking, uncivilized, unearthly, ungodly, unnatural, unreasonable; SEE CONCEPT *537*

unidentified [*adj*] *secret*
anonymous, mysterious, nameless, not known, pseudonymous, unclassified, unfamiliar, unknown, unmarked, unnamed, unrecognized, unrevealed; SEE CONCEPT *576*

unification [*n*] *joining together*
affinity, alliance, amalgamation, coalescence, coalition, combination, concurrence, confederation, connection, consolidation, coupling, federation, fusion, hookup, interlocking, linkage, melding, merger, merging, union, uniting; SEE CONCEPTS *230,388*

uniform [*n*] *coordinated outfit*
attire, costume, dress, garb, gown, habit, khaki, livery, monkey suit*, OD*, olive drab*, regalia, regimentals, robe, stripes*, suit; SEE CONCEPT *451*

uniform [*adj1*] *consistent*
compatible, consonant, constant, equable, even, fated, fateful, fixed, habitual, homogeneous, immu-

table, incorrigible, inflexible, invariable, irreversible, level, methodical, monolithic, normal, of a piece*, ordered, orderly, ossified, plumb, regular, reliable, rigid, smooth, stable, static, steady, straight, symmetrical, systematic, true, unalterable, unbroken, unchanging, undeviating, undiversified, unfluctuating, unmodifiable, unvarying, well-balanced, well-proportioned; SEE CONCEPT *534*

uniform [*adj2*] *alike*
agnate, akin, analogous, carbon*, carbon copy, comparable, consistent, consonant, correspondent, ditto*, double, equal, identical, like, mated, monotonous, parallel, same, same difference*, selfsame, similar, treadmill*, undifferentiated, unvaried, Xerox*; SEE CONCEPTS *487,573*

unimaginable [*adj*] *mind-boggling*
beyond wildest dreams*, doubtful, exceptional, extraordinary, fantastic, impossible, improbable, inapprehensible, incogitable, incomprehensible, inconceivable, incredible, indescribable, ineffable, not understandable, rare, singular, unbelievable, uncommon, unheard-of, unique, unknowable, unordinary, unthinkable; SEE CONCEPTS *529,548*

unimaginative [*adj*] *dull, predictable*
banal, barren, bromidic, common, commonplace, derivative, dime a dozen*, dry, dull as dishwater*, flat, hackneyed, ho hum*, lifeless, matter-of-fact, ordinary, pabulum*, pedestrian, prosaic, routine, square*, tame, tedious, trite, uncreative, uninspired, unoriginal, unromantic, usual, vanilla*, well-worn, zero*; SEE CONCEPTS *542,547,548*

unimportant [*adj*] *of no real worth, value*
beside the point*, casual, frivolous, frothy, immaterial, inconsequential, inconsiderable, indifferent, insignificant, irrelevant, little, low-ranking, meaningless, minor, minute, negligible, nonessential, nothing*, nugatory, null, of no account*, of no consequence*, paltry, petty, picayune, second-rate*, shoestring*, slight, trifling, trivial, unnecessary, useless, worthless, zero*, zilch*, zip*; SEE CONCEPT *575*

uninhibited [*adj*] *free and easy; without restraint*
audacious, candid, cut loose*, expansive, fancy-free*, footloose*, frank, free, hanging out*, informal, instinctive, liberated, natural, no holds barred*, off the cuff*, open, relaxed, spontaneous, unbridled, unchecked, unconstrained, uncontrolled, uncurbed, ungoverned, unhampered, unrepressed, unreserved, unrestrained, unrestricted, unself-conscious, unsuppressed; SEE CONCEPTS *267,401*

uninspired [*adj*] *dull, unoriginal*
bromidic, commonplace, corny*, everyday, flat, heavy-handed, humdrum*, indifferent, old hat*, ordinary, phoned in*, ponderous, prosaic, stale, sterile, stock, uncreative, unexciting, unimaginative, unimpressed, uninspiring, uninteresting, uninventive, unmoved, yawn*; SEE CONCEPTS *542,547,548*

unintelligible [*adj*] *not understandable*
ambiguous, equivocal, fathomless, Greek, illegible, impenetrable, inarticulate, incognizable, incoherent,

incomprehensible, indecipherable, indistinct, inexplicit, jumbled, meaningless, muddled, obscure, opaque, tenebrous, uncertain, unclear, unexplicit, unfathomable, ungraspable, unknowable, unreadable, vague; SEE CONCEPT *267*

unintentional/unintended [*adj*] *not planned*
accidental, aimless, casual, chance, erratic, extemporaneous, fortuitous, haphazard, inadvertent, involuntary, purposeless, random, unconscious, undesigned, undevised, unexpected, unforeseen, unintended, unplanned, unpremeditated, unthinking, unthought, unwitting; SEE CONCEPTS *401,548*

uninterested [*adj*] *oblivious to*
aloof, apathetic, blasé, bored, bored stiff*, casual, could not care less*, detached, disinterested, distant, going through motions*, hard-hearted*, impassive, incurious, indifferent, listless, remote, thick-skinned*, turned off*, unconcerned, uncurious, uninvolved, unresponsive, weary, withdrawn; SEE CONCEPTS *401,403*

uninteresting [*adj*] *boring, uneventful*
arid, banal, big yawn*, bromidic, common, commonplace, depressing, dismal, drab, dreary, dry, dull, dusty*, fatiguing, flat, ho hum*, humdrum*, insipid, irksome, jejune, monotonous, nothing*, nowhere*, pedestrian, prosaic, prosy, soporific, stale, stupid, tedious, tired, tiresome, trite, unenjoyable, unentertaining, unexciting, uninspiring, wearisome; SEE CONCEPTS *529,548*

uninterrupted [*adj*] *continuing; unbroken*
ceaseless, consecutive, constant, continual, continuous, direct, endless, interminable, nonstop, peaceful, perpetual, steady, straight, straightforward, sustained, through, unceasing, undisturbed, unending, unremitting; SEE CONCEPTS *482,798*

union [*n1*] *merger, joining*
abutment, accord, agglutination, agreement, amalgam, amalgamation, blend, centralization, coadunation, combination, coming together, commixture, compound, concatenation, conciliation, concord, concurrence, confluence, congregation, conjunction, consolidation, correlation, coupling, fusion, harmony, hookup, incorporation, intercourse, joint, junction, juncture, meeting, melding, merging, mixture, seam, symbiosis, synthesis, tie-in, tie-up, unanimity, unification, unison, uniting, unity; SEE CONCEPTS *113,664,714*

union [*n2*] *group with shared interest, cause*
alliance, association, brotherhood, club, coalition, confederacy, confederation, congress, employees, federation, guild, labor union, league, local, order, society, sodality, syndicate, trade union; SEE CONCEPTS *325,381*

unique [*adj1*] *alone, singular*
different, exclusive, individual, lone, one, one and only*, onliest*, only, particular, rare, separate, single, solitary, solo, sui generis*, uncommon, unexampled; SEE CONCEPTS *564,577*

unique [*adj2*] *one-of-a-kind; without equal*
anomalous, best, exceptional, extraordinary, far-out*, incomparable, inimitable, matchless, most, nonpareil, novel, only, peerless, primo*, rare, singular, something else*, special, standout, strange, uncommon, unequaled, unexampled, unimaginable, unmatched, unparagoned, unparalleled, unprecedented, unreal, unrivaled, utmost, weird*; SEE CONCEPTS *564,574*

unison [*n*] *harmony*
accord, accordance, agreement, alliance, community, concert, concord, concordance, conjunction, consent, consonance, cooperation, federation, fellowship, league, reciprocity, sympathy, unanimity, union, unity; SEE CONCEPT *664*

unit [*n1*] *whole*
assemblage, assembly, bunch, complement, crew, crowd, detachment, entirety, entity, gang, group, mob, one, outfit, ring, section, system, total, totality; SEE CONCEPTS *432,837*

unit [*n2*] *part*
arm, block, component, constituent, detachment, detail, digit, element, factor, feature, fraction, ingredient, integer, item, joint, layer, length, link, member, module, piece, portion, section, segment, square, wing; SEE CONCEPT *834*

unite [*v*] *combine; join together*
affiliate, ally, amalgamate, associate, band, band together, become one, blend, close ranks*, coadjute, coalesce, commingle, concur, confederate, conjoin, connect, consolidate, cooperate, couple, embody, fuse, gather together, hang together*, harden, hook up with, incorporate, intertwine, join, join forces, keep together, league, link, marry, meet, merge, mix, pool, pull together, relate, solidify, stay together, stick together, strengthen, throw in with*, unify, wed; SEE CONCEPTS *113,193*

united [*adj*] *combined; in agreement*
affiliated, agreed, allied, amalgamated, assembled, associated, banded, coadunate, cognate, collective, concerted, concordant, confederated, congruent, conjoint, conjugate, conjunctive, consolidated, cooperative, corporate, federal, homogeneous, hooked up, in accord, in cahoots*, incorporated, integrated, joined up, leagued, like-minded*, lined up*, linked, of one mind, of the same opinion, one, plugged in*, pooled, tied in, unanimous, undivided, unified, unitary; SEE CONCEPTS *563,577*

unity [*n*] *wholeness*
accord, agreement, alliance, coadunation, combination, concord, concurrence, confederation, consensus, consent, consonance, entity, federation, harmony, homogeneity, homogeneousness, identity, individuality, indivisibility, integral, integrality, integrity, interconnection, oneness, peace, rapport, sameness, singleness, singularity, soleness, solidarity, synthesis, totality, unanimity, undividedness,

unification, uniformity, union, unison; SEE CONCEPTS *664,714,837*

universal [*adj*] *worldwide, entire*
accepted, all, all-embracing, all-inclusive, all-over, astronomical, broad, catholic, celestial, common, comprehensive, cosmic, cosmopolitan, customary, diffuse, earthly, ecumenical, empyrean, extensive, general, generic, global, multinational, mundane, omnipresent, planetary, prevalent, regular, stellar, sweeping, terrestrial, total, ubiquitous, undisputed, unlimited, unrestricted, usual, whole, widespread, worldly; SEE CONCEPTS *536,772*

universe [*n*] *everything in creation*
cosmos, everything, macrocosm, natural world, nature, world; SEE CONCEPTS *370,511*

unjust [*adj*] *not fair*
below the belt*, biased, cheap shot*, dirty pool*, fixed*, inequitable, influenced, low-down*, one-sided, partial, partisan, prejudiced, raw deal*, shabby*, underhand, undeserved, unfair, unforgivable, unjustified, unmerited, unrighteous, wrong, wrongful; SEE CONCEPT *545*

unkempt [*adj*] *shabby, sloppy*
bedraggled, coarse, crude, dilapidated, dirty, disarranged, disarrayed, disheveled, disordered, grubby*, grungy*, messed up, messy, mussed up*, neglected, rough, rumpled, scruffy, shaggy, slipshod, slovenly, tousled, unclean, uncombed, unfastidious, ungroomed, unimproved, unneat, unpolished, untidy, vulgar; SEE CONCEPTS *485,621*

unkind [*adj*] *not nice*
barbarous, brutal, cold-blooded*, coldhearted*, cruel, hard-hearted, harsh, hateful, heartless, inconsiderate, inhuman, inhumane, insensitive, malevolent, malicious, malignant, mean, nasty, sadistic, savage, spiteful, thoughtless, uncaring, uncharitable, unfeeling, unfriendly, unsympathetic; SEE CONCEPT *401*

unknown [*adj*] *obscure, mysterious*
alien, anonymous, concealed, dark, desolate, distant, exotic, far, faraway, far-off, foreign, hidden, humble, incog*, incognito, Jane/John Doe*, little known, nameless, new, remote, secret, so-and-so*, strange, such-and-such*, unapprehended, unascertained, uncelebrated, uncharted, undiscovered, undistinguished, unexplained, unexplored, unfamiliar, unheard-of, unidentified, unnamed, unnoted, unperceived, unrecognized, unrenowned, unrevealed, unsung, untold, whatchamacallit*, X*; SEE CONCEPT *576*

unlawful [*adj*] *against the law*
actionable, banned, bootleg*, criminal, flagitious, forbidden, illegal, illegitimate, illicit, improper, iniquitous, lawless, nefarious, outlawed, prohibited, taboo, unauthorized, under-the-counter*, unlicensed, wrongful; SEE CONCEPT *319*

unlike [*adj*] *different*
apples and oranges*, clashing, conflicting, contradictory, contrary, contrasted, discordant, disharmonious, disparate, dissimilar, dissonant, distant, distinct, divergent, diverse, far cry*, heterogeneous, hostile, incompatible, incongruous, inconsistent, mismatched, night and day*, not alike, offbeat, opposed, opposite, poles apart*, separate, unalike, unequal, unrelated, variant, various, weird; SEE CONCEPT *564*

unlikely [*adj*] *not probable*
absurd, contrary, doubtful, dubious, faint, implausible, improbable, inconceivable, incredible, not likely, out of the ordinary, outside chance, questionable, rare, remote, slight, strange, unbelievable, unconvincing, unheard-of, unimaginable, untoward; SEE CONCEPT *552*

unlimited [*adj*] *extensive, complete*
absolute, all-encompassing, all-out*, boundless, countless, endless, full, full-blown*, full-out*, full-scale, great, illimitable, immeasurable, immense, incalculable, incomprehensible, indefinite, infinite, interminable, limitless, measureless, no end of*, no end to*, no strings*, numberless, total, totalitarian, unbounded, unconditional, unconfined, unconstrained, unfathomed, unfettered, universal, unqualified, unrestrained, unrestricted, untold, vast, wide open; SEE CONCEPT *772*

unload [*v*] *take off; empty*
break bulk, cast, clear out, disburden, discharge, discommode, disencumber, disgorge, dump, get rid of, jettison, lighten, off-load, relieve, remove, rid, slough, take a load off, unburden, unlade, unpack, void; SEE CONCEPTS *180,211*

unlucky [*adj*] *unfortunate, doomed*
afflicted, bad break*, behind eight ball*, black*, calamitous, cataclysmic, catastrophic, cursed, dire, disastrous, down on luck*, hapless, hard luck, ill-fated, ill-starred, inauspicious, luckless, miserable, ominous, out of luck, rotten luck*, star-crossed*, tough luck, tragic, unfavorable, unhappy, unsuccessful, untimely, untoward; SEE CONCEPTS *529,548*

unmarried [*adj*] *not presently wed*
bachelor, celibate, chaste, eligible, husbandless, maiden, single, sole, spouseless, unattached, uncoupled, unwed, unwedded, virgin, virginal, widowed, wifeless; SEE CONCEPT *555*

unmerciful [*adj*] *cruel*
bestial, bloodthirsty, brutal, coldhearted*, hard, heartless, hurtful, implacable, inhumane, merciless, monstrous, pitiless, relentless, remorseless, ruthless, tyrannous, uncaring, unfeeling, unpitying, unrelenting, unsparing, vengeful, vindictive; SEE CONCEPT *401*

unmistakable [*adj*] *certain, definite*
apparent, clear, conspicuous, decided, distinct, evident, explicit, for certain, glaring, indisputable, manifest, no ifs ands or buts*, obvious, open and shut*, palpable, patent, plain, positive, pronounced, self-explanatory, straightforward, sure, transparent, unambiguous, unequivocal, univocal; SEE CONCEPT *535*

unmitigated [adj] *absolute, pure*
arrant, austere, clear-cut, complete, consummate, damned, downright, gross, intense, oppressive, out-and-out*, outright, perfect, persistent, rank, relentless, rigid, severe, sheer, simple, straight-out*, thorough, thoroughgoing, unabated, unabridged, unadulterated, unalleviated, unbending, unbroken, undiluted, unmixed, unqualified, unrelieved, utter; SEE CONCEPTS 531,535,569

unnatural [adj] *not regular; artificial*
aberrant, abnormal, affected, anomalous, assumed, bizarre, concocted, contrary, contrived, ersatz*, extraordinary, fabricated, factitious, false, feigned, forced, freakish, freaky, imitation, incredible, insincere, irregular, labored, made-up*, make-believe*, odd, outlandish, outrageous, perverse, perverted, phony, preposterous, pseudo*, put-on*, queer*, staged, stiff, stilted*, strained, strange, studied, supernatural, synthetic, theatrical, unaccountable, uncanny, unconforming, unorthodox, unusual; SEE CONCEPTS 564,582

unnecessary [adj] *not required*
accidental, additional, avoidable, beside the point*, casual, causeless, chance, dispensable, excess, exorbitant, expendable, extraneous, extrinsic, fortuitous, futile, gratuitous, haphazard, inessential, irrelevant, lavish, needless, noncompulsory, nonessential, optional, prodigal, profuse, random, redundant, supererogatory, superfluous, surplus, uncalled-for, uncritical, undesirable, unessential, unneeded, unrequired, useless, wanton, worthless; SEE CONCEPT 546

unnerve [v] *upset, intimidate*
agitate, bewilder, bowl over*, buffalo*, castrate*, chill*, confound, daunt, demoralize, disarm, discombobulate, disconcert, discourage, dishearten, dismay, dispirit, distract, emasculate, enervate, enfeeble, floor*, fluster, frighten, get to*, give a turn*, intimidate, needle*, perturb, psych out*, rattle, ride, sap*, shake, spook, throw, throw off*, uncalm, undermine, unhinge, unman, unsettle, weaken; SEE CONCEPTS 7,14,19

unnoticed [adj] *ignored*
disregarded, glossed over, hidden, inconspicuous, neglected, overlooked, passed by, pushed aside, secret, unconsidered, undiscovered, unheeded, unobserved, unobtrusive, unperceived, unrecognized, unremarked, unremembered, unrespected, unseen, winked at; SEE CONCEPT 529

unobtrusive [adj] *keeping a low profile*
humble, inconspicuous, low-key, low-profile, meek, modest, quiet, reserved, restrained, retiring, self-effacing, soft-pedaled*, subdued, tasteful, unassuming, unnoticeable, unostentatious, unpretentious; SEE CONCEPTS 401,548

unorthodox [adj] *abnormal; other than accepted*
beatnik*, crazy*, different, dissident, eccentric, far-out, flaky*, heretical, heterodox, irregular, kinky*, nonconformist, off the beaten path*, schismatic, sec-

tarian, unconventional, uncustomary, unusual, unwonted, way-out*, weird*; SEE CONCEPT 564

unpaid [adj1] *free, voluntary*
contributed, donated, due, freewilled, gratuitous, honorary, unindemnified, unrewarded, unsalaried, volunteer; SEE CONCEPT 538

unpaid [adj2] *not settled; taken without remuneration*
delinquent, due, in arrears, , mature, not discharged, outstanding, overdue, owing, past due, payable, undefrayed, unliquidated, unsettled; SEE CONCEPT 334

unparalleled [adj] *superlative*
all-time*, alone, beyond compare, champ*, champion, consummate, exceptional, greatest, incomparable, matchless, most, only, peerless, rare, single, singular, solid gold*, ten*, tops*, unequaled, unique, unmatched, unprecedented, unrivaled, unsurpassed, winner, without equal, world-class*; SEE CONCEPT 574

unpleasant [adj] *bad*
abhorrent, bad news*, bad scene*, disagreeable, displeasing, distasteful, fierce, grody*, gross*, hard-time*, icky*, irksome, lousy, nasty, objectionable, obnoxious, poisonous, repulsive, rotten, sour, troublesome, unacceptable, unattractive, uncool*, undesirable, unhappy, unlikable, unlovely, unpalatable, yucky*; SEE CONCEPTS 529,570

unpopular [adj] *not liked or sought after*
abhorred, avoided, creepy, despised, detested, disesteemed, disfavored, disliked, drip*, dumpy*, execrated, gross*, loathed, loser*, lousy, nerd*, obnoxious, ostracized, out, out of favor, pain*, rejected, scorned, shunned, unaccepted, unattractive, uncared for, undesirable, unloved, unvalued, unwanted, unwelcome, weird, wimpy*; SEE CONCEPTS 529,555

unprecedented [adj] *exceptional, original*
aberrant, abnormal, anomalous, bizarre, eccentric, exotic, extraordinary, fantastic, freakish, idiosyncratic, marvelous, miraculous, modern, new, new-fangled, novel, odd, outlandish, out-of-the-way*, outré*, preternatural, prodigious, remarkable, signal, singular, sui generis*, uncommon, unexampled, unheard-of, unique, unparalleled, unrivaled, unusual; SEE CONCEPTS 549,564,574

unpredictable [adj] *changeable*
capricious, chance, chancy, dicey*, doubtful, erratic, fickle, fluctuating, fluky*, from left field*, hanging by a thread*, iffy*, incalculable, inconstant, random, touch and go*, touchy, uncertain, unforeseeable, unreliable, unstable, up for grabs*, variable, whimsical; SEE CONCEPT 534

unprejudiced [adj] *fair*
balanced, dispassionate, equal, equitable, even-handed, fair-minded, impartial, just, liberal, nondiscriminatory, nonpartisan, objective, open-minded, straight, unbiased, unbigoted, uncolored, uninfluenced; SEE CONCEPTS 319,401,542

unpretentious [adj] simple, honest
discreet, down, down home*, easy-going, folksy*, free-spirited, homey*, humble, inelaborate, laid-back*, lowly, modest, plain, prosaic, straightforward, unaffected, unambitious, unassuming, unbeautified, uncomplex, unembellished, unimposing, unobtrusive, unostentatious, unpresumptuous, unspoiled, up front; SEE CONCEPTS *401,404*

unprincipled [adj] corrupt
abandoned, amoral, bent*, cheating, conscienceless, crooked, deceitful, devious, dirty-dealing*, dishonest, dissolute, double-crossing*, double-dealing*, immoral, licentious, mercenary, praetorian, profligate, reprobate, shady, sly, stop-at-nothing*, tricky, two-faced*, two-timing*, unconscionable, underhand, unethical, unprofessional, unscrupulous, venal, wanton; SEE CONCEPT *545*

unprofessional [adj] not done well or skillfully
amateur, amateurish, ignorant, improper, inadequate, incompetent, inefficient, inexperienced, inexpert, lax, negligent, nonexpert, unethical, unfitting, unsuitable, untrained, unworthy; SEE CONCEPTS *527,538*

unqualified [adj1] not prepared, competent
amateur, bush, bush-league*, disqualified, ill-equipped, inadequate, incapable, incompetent, ineligible, inexperienced, not equal to, not up to*, unequipped, unfit, unfitted, unprepared, unskilled; SEE CONCEPT *527*

unqualified [adj2] outright, absolute
abiding, blasted, blessed, categorical, certain, clear, complete, confounded, consummate, downright, enduring, entire, explicit, express, firm, flat out*, infernal, never-failing, no catch*, no ifs ands or buts*, out-and-out*, perfect, positive, rank, sheer, simple, steadfast, steady, sure, thorough, thoroughgoing, total, unadulterated, unalloyed, unconditional, unfaltering, unlimited, unmitigated, unreserved, unrestrained, unrestricted, utter, wholehearted, without reservation; SEE CONCEPTS *531,535*

unquestionable [adj] definite; beyond doubt
absolute, accurate, authentic, bona fide*, certain, clear, cold, conclusive, dependable, down pat*, downright, established, faultless, flat*, flawless, for certain, genuine, incontestable, incontrovertible, indisputable, indubitable, irrefutable, manifest, no ifs ands or buts*, obvious, pat, patent, perfect, positive, real, reliable, self-evident, superior, sure, sure-enough, true, undeniable, undisputable, undoubted, unequivocal, unimpeachable, unmistakable, veritable, well-founded, well-grounded; SEE CONCEPTS *529,535*

unreal [adj] fake, make-believe; hypothetical
aerial, artificial, chimerical, delusive, dreamlike, fabled, fabulous, false, fanciful, fictitious, fictive, figmental, hallucinatory, ideal, illusory, imaginary, imagined, immaterial, impalpable, insincere, insubstantial, intangible, invented, legendary, misleading, mock, mythical, nebulous, nonexistent, notional, ostensible, phantasmagoric*, pretended, reachy, romantic, seeming, sham*, storybook*, suppositious, supposititious, theoretical, unbelievable, unsubstantial, visionary; SEE CONCEPT *582*

unrealistic [adj] not believable or practical
blue sky*, castles in the air*, floating, gone, half-baked*, impossible, impracticable, impractical, improbable, ivory-tower*, nonrealistic, nonsensical, not applicable, not sensible, on cloud nine*, pie in the sky*, pipe dream*, quixotic, reachy, romantic, silly, starry-eyed, theoretical, unreal, unworkable; SEE CONCEPTS *552,560*

unreasonable [adj1] not logical or sensible
absurd, all wet*, arbitrary, biased, capricious, contradictory, erratic, fallacious, far-fetched, foolish, full of hot air*, headstrong, illogical, incoherent, incongruous, inconsequential, inconsistent, invalid, irrational, loose, mad, nonsensical, off the wall*, opinionated, preposterous, quirky, reasonless, senseless, silly, stupid, thoughtless, unreasoned, vacant, wrong; SEE CONCEPTS *401,548*

unreasonable [adj2] extravagant; beyond normal limits
absonant, arbitrary, arm and a leg*, dear*, excessive, exorbitant, extortionate, extreme, far-out*, illegitimate, immoderate, improper, inordinate, intemperate, out of bounds*, overkill, overmuch, peremptory, posh, pricey*, senseless, steep*, stiff*, too great, too much, too-too*, uncalled-for*, unconscionable, undue, unfair, unjust, unjustifiable, unlawful, unrightful, unwarrantable, unwarranted, up to here*, way out*, wrongful; SEE CONCEPTS *334,762,771*

unrelated [adj] independent; different
beside the point*, dissimilar, extraneous, inapplicable, inappropriate, irrelative, irrelevant, mismatched, nongermane, not germane, not kin, not kindred, not related, separate, unassociated, unattached, unconnected, unlike; SEE CONCEPTS *563,564*

unrelenting [adj] merciless
bound, bound and determined, brick-wall*, ceaseless, constant, continual, continuous, cruel, dead set on*, endless, grim, hanging tough*, hard-headed*, implacable, incessant, inexorable, intransigent, iron-fisted, mortal, perpetual, persistent, pitiless, relentless, remorseless, rigid, ruthless, set, steady, stern, stiff, stiff-necked*, tenacious, tough, unabated, unbending, unbroken, unflinching, unremitting, unsparing, unwavering, unyielding; SEE CONCEPTS *401,548,798*

unreliable [adj] not trustworthy, not true
capricious, deceitful, deceptive, delusive, disreputable, dubious, erroneous, fake, fallible, false, fickle, fly-by-night*, furtive, hallucinatory, hollow, implausible, inaccurate, inconstant, irresponsible, makeshift, meretricious, mistaken, pretended, pseudo*, questionable, sham*, shifty, specious, treacherous,

tricky, uncertain, unconvincing, undependable, underhand, underhanded, unfaithful, unsound, unstable, unsure, untrue, untrustworthy, vacillating, wavering, weak; SEE CONCEPTS *542,552,587*

unresolved [*adj*] *uncertain; not settled*
betwixt and between*, changing, doubtful, faltering, hesitant, hesitating, hot and cold*, incomplete, indecisive, irresolute, jury's out*, moot, open to question*, pending, problematical, pussyfooting*, unanswered, unconcluded, undecided, undetermined, unfinished, unsettled, unsolved, up in the air*, vacillating, vague, waffling; SEE CONCEPTS *529,534*

unrest [*n*] *state of agitation; disturbance*
altercation, anarchy, annoyance, anxiety, bickering, bother, chagrin, change, confusion, contention, controversy, crisis, debate, disaffection, discontent, discord, disease, disquiet, dissatisfaction, dissension, distress, dither*, ennui, grief, insurrection, irritation, malaise, moodiness, mortification, perplexity, perturbation, protest, quarrel, rebellion, restlessness, sedition, sorrow, strife, tension, tizzy*, trouble, tumult, turmoil, unease, uneasiness, uproar, upset, vexation, worry; SEE CONCEPTS *410,674*

unruly [*adj*] *disobedient*
assertive, bawdy, disorderly, drunken, forward, fractious, headstrong, heedless, impervious, impetuous, imprudent, impulsive, incorrigible, inexorable, insubordinate, intemperate, intractable, lawless, mean, mutinous, obstreperous, opinionated, ornery, out of control, out of line*, perverse, quarrelsome, rash, rebellious, recalcitrant, reckless, refractory, restive, riotous, rowdy, turbulent, uncontrollable, ungovernable, unmanageable, unyielding, violent, wayward, wild, wilful; SEE CONCEPT *401*

unsafe [*adj*] *dangerous*
alarming, chancy, erratic, explosive, fearsome, hanging by a thread*, hazardous, insecure, on a limb*, on thin ice*, perilous, precarious, risky, shaky*, slippery, threatening, ticklish*, touch and go*, touchy*, treacherous, uncertain, undependable, unreliable, unsound, unstable, untrustworthy; SEE CONCEPT *587*

unsaid [*adj*] *not expressed or partially expressed*
implicit, implied, inferred, left to the imagination*, silenced, tacit, undeclared, understood, unexpressed, unspoken, unstated, unuttered, unvoiced, wordless; SEE CONCEPT *267*

unsatisfactory [*adj*] *insufficient, inadequate*
amiss, bad, damaged, deficient, disappointing, disconcerting, displeasing, disquieting, distressing, disturbing, for the birds*, junky*, lame, mediocre, no good, not good enough, not up to par*, offensive, poor, regrettable, rotten, schlocky*, second, thin, unacceptable, undesirable, unsuitable, unwelcome, unworthy, upsetting, vexing, weak, wrong; SEE CONCEPTS *529,558,570*

unsavory [*adj*] *revolting, sickening*
acid, bitter, bland, disagreeable, distasteful, dull, flavorless, gross*, icky*, insipid, lousy, nasty, nauseating, no good*, objectionable, obnoxious, offensive, rancid, rank, raunchy*, repellent, repugnant, repulsive, rough, sad, shady, sharp, shifty, sour, stinking, tart, tasteless, tough, unappetizing, unpalatable, unpleasant, wrong; SEE CONCEPTS *462,571,613*

unscathed [*adj*] *not hurt*
in one piece*, safe, sound, unharmed, unhurt, uninjured, unmarked, unscarred, unscratched, untouched, whole; SEE CONCEPT *314*

unscrupulous [*adj*] *immoral*
arrant, base, casuistic, conscienceless, corrupt, crafty, crooked, deceitful, degraded, degrading, disgraceful, dishonest, dishonorable, exploitative, illegal, improper, knavish, low-down*, mercenary, perfidious, petty, questionable, recreant, roguish, ruthless, scandalous, scheming, selfish, self-seeking, shady, shameless, shifty, sinister, slippery, sly, two-faced*, unconscientious, unconscionable, underhand, underhanded, unethical, unfair, unprincipled, unworthy, venal, wicked, wrongful; SEE CONCEPTS *401,545*

unseemly [*adj*] *improper; in bad taste*
cheap, coarse, crude, discreditable, disreputable, inappropriate, inapt, incorrect, indecent, indecorous, indelicate, inelegant, inept, in poor taste, malapropos, malodorous, out of keeping, out of place, poor, raffish, rough, rowdy, rude, ruffian, tawdry, unapt, unbecoming, unbefitting, undignified, ungodly, unrefined, unsuitable, untoward, vulgar, wrong; SEE CONCEPTS *401,558*

unseen [*adj*] *hidden*
concealed, curtained, dark, imaginary, imagined, impalpable, impenetrable, imperceptible, inconspicuous, invisible, lurking, not in sight, obscure, occult, out of sight, shrouded, undetected, undiscovered, unnoticed, unobserved, unobtrusive, unperceived, unsuspected, veiled; SEE CONCEPT *576*

unselfish [*adj*] *kind, giving*
altruistic, benevolent, charitable, chivalrous, denying, devoted, disinterested, extroverted, generous, helpful, humanitarian, incorruptible, indulgent, liberal, loving, magnanimous, noble, open-handed, self-effacing, self-forgetting, selfless, self-sacrificing; SEE CONCEPTS *401,404*

unsettle [*v*] *bother, upset*
agitate, confuse, dement, derange, disarrange, disarray, discommode, discompose, disconcert, disorder, disorganize, displace, disquiet, disrupt, disturb, down, flurry, fluster, fuddle, get to*, jumble, needle, perturb, psych out*, put off, rattle, ruffle, rummage, sicken, spook, throw, throw off*, trouble, turn, unbalance, unhinge*, unnerve; SEE CONCEPTS *7,19,242*

unsettled [*adj1*] *bothered, upset*
active, agitated, antsy*, anxious, busy, changeable, changeful, changing, complex, complicated, con-

fused, disorderly, disturbed, explosive, fidgety, fluid, flustered, inconstant, insecure, kinetic, mobile, mutable, on edge*, perilous, perturbed, precarious, rattled, restive, restless, shaken, shaky, shifting, shook up*, tense, thrown, ticklish, troubled, unbalanced, uncertain, uneasy, unnerved, unpeaceful, unpredictable, unquiet, unrestful, unstable, unsteady, variable, wavering, wobbling; SEE CONCEPTS *401,403*

unsettled [*adj2*] *not decided, taken care of*
betwixt and between*, clouded*, debatable, doubtful, dubious, dubitable, due, immature, in arrears, moot, open, outstanding, overdue, owing, payable, pendent, pending, problematic, uncertain, unclear, undecided, undetermined, unfixed, unpaid, unresolved, up for grabs*, waffling; SEE CONCEPTS *334,535*

unsightly [*adj*] *not pretty*
deformed, disagreeable, drab, dull, hideous, homely, horrid, lackluster, repulsive, revolting, ugly, unattractive, unpleasant, unprepossessing, unshapely; SEE CONCEPT *579*

unsociable [*adj*] *unfriendly*
aloof, antagonistic, brooding, cold, cool, distant, easy-going, hostile, inaccessible, inhospitable, introverted, laid-back*, loner, nongregarious, recessive, reclusive, reserved, retiring, secretive, sensitive, shy, standoffish*, stuck-up*, timid, unapproachable, unbending, uncommunicative, uncongenial, unforthcoming, unneighborly, unsocial, uppity*, withdrawn; SEE CONCEPTS *401,555*

unsolicited [*adj*] *unasked for*
free, freewilled, gratis*, gratuitous, offered, spontaneous, uncalled-for*, undesirable, undesired, unforced, uninvited, unrequested, unsought, unwelcome, voluntary, volunteered; SEE CONCEPT *538*

unsophisticated [*adj*] *natural, simple*
artless, authentic, bona fide*, bush-league*, callow, childlike, clean, cornball*, corny*, crude, folksy, genuine, green*, guileless, homey*, inexperienced, ingenuous, innocent, kid, naive, plain, pure, raw, rookie, straightforward, unadulterated, unaffected, unartificial, uncomplicated, uninvolved, unrefined, unschooled, unstudied, untutored, unworldly, wide-eyed*; SEE CONCEPTS *401,548,562*

unsound [*adj*] *not well; flimsy*
ailing, crazed, dangerous, decrepit, defective, delicate, demented, deranged, diseased, erroneous, fallacious, false, faulty, flawed, fragile, frail, ill, illogical, inaccurate, incongruous, incorrect, infirm, in poor health, insane, insecure, insubstantial, invalid, lunatic, mad, not solid, rickety, shaky, specious, tottering, unbacked, unbalanced, unhealthy, unhinged, unreliable, unsafe, unstable, unsteady, unsubstantial, unwell, weak, wobbly; SEE CONCEPTS *314,403,587*

unspeakable [*adj*] *very bad; beyond description*
abominable, alarming, appalling, atrocious, awful, beastly, beyond words, calamitous, detestable, dire,

disgusting, dreadful, evil, execrable, fearful, frightening, frightful, heinous, horrible, horrid, incommunicable, inconceivable, indefinable, indescribable, ineffable, inexpressible, inhuman, loathsome, monstrous, nameless, obnoxious, odious, offensive, outrageous, overwhelming, preternatural, repellent, repugnant, repulsive, revolting, shocking, unbelievable, unimaginable, unutterable; SEE CONCEPTS *548,571*

unstable/unsteady [*adj*] *doubtful, weak*
ambiguous, borderline, capricious, changeable, dizzy, dubious, erratic, fickle, fitful, fluctuating, giddy, inconsistent, inconstant, insecure, irrational, lubricious, mercurial, mobile, movable, moving, mutable, not fixed, precarious, rickety, risky, rocky, sensitive, shaky, shifty, slippery, suspect, teetering, temperamental, ticklish, tricky, uncertain, unpredictable, unsettled, unsteady, untrustworthy, vacillating, variable, volatile, wavering, weaving, wiggly, wobbly; SEE CONCEPTS *488,534,542*

unsuitable [*adj*] *not proper, appropriate*
clashing, disagreeable, discordant, discrepant, disparate, disproportionate, dissident, dissonant, ill-suited, improper, inadequate, inadmissible, inapposite, inappropriate, inapt, incompatible, incongruous, inconsistent, ineligible, infelicitous, inharmonious, interfering, irrelevant, jarring, malapropos, out of character, out of keeping, out of place, senseless, unacceptable, unbecoming, unbefitting, uncalled-for, undue, unfit, unfitting, unmatched, unseasonable, unseemly, unsuited; SEE CONCEPT *558*

unsure [*adj*] *doubtful, insecure*
betwixt and between*, borderline, distrustful, dubious, fluctuant, fly-by-night*, hesitant, iffy*, in a quandary, indecisive, indeterminate, irresolute, lacking, mistrustful, open, problematic, rootless, shaky, skeptical, suspicious, touch and go*, unassured, uncertain, unclear, unconfident, unconvinced, undecided, undependable, unreliable, unstable, untrustworthy, untrusty, up for grabs*, vacillating, wavering, weak, wimpy*, wobbly; SEE CONCEPT *535*

unsuspecting [*adj*] *gullible*
confiding, credulous, easy, inexperienced, ingenuous, innocent, naive, off guard*, simple, swallowing, taken in*, trustful, trusting, unconscious, undoubting, unsuspicious, unwarned, unwary; SEE CONCEPTS *401,404*

unsympathetic [*adj*] *heartless*
aloof, antipathetic, apathetic, aversive, callous, cold*, cold-blooded*, cool*, cruel, disinterested, frigid*, halfhearted, hard, harsh, icy*, indifferent, insensitive, lukewarm*, mean, nasty, obdurate, repellent, repugnant, stony, tough, uncompassionate, unconcerned, uncongenial, unemotional, unfeeling, unkind, unmoved, unpitying, unpleasant, unresponsive; SEE CONCEPTS *401,542*

untangle [*v*] *straighten out*
clear up, disembroil, disencumber, disentangle, explain, extricate, put in order, solve, unravel, unscramble, unsnarl, untwist, unweave; SEE CONCEPT *126*

unthinkable [*adj*] *incredible, unusual*
absurd, beyond belief, beyond possibility, exceptional, extraordinary, illogical, implausible, impossible, improbable, incogitable, inconceivable, insupportable, outlandish, out of the question*, preposterous, rare, singular, unbelievable, uncommon, unimaginable, unique, unlikely, unordinary, unreasonable; SEE CONCEPTS *564,582*

unthinking [*adj*] *careless*
blundering, brutish, feckless, foolish, heedless, impulsive, inadvertent, inconsiderate, indelicate, insensitive, instinctive, mechanical, napping, negligent, oblivious, outrageous, rash, rude, selfish, senseless, tactless, thoughtless, uncaring, unconscious, undiplomatic, unheeding, unintended, unmeant, unmindful, unpremeditated, unreasoning, untactful, unwise, vacant, witless; SEE CONCEPT *401*

untidy [*adj*] *dirty, disorderly*
bedraggled, careless, chaotic, cluttered, disarranged, disarrayed, disheveled, dowdy*, frowzy*, in disorder, jumbled, littered, mess, messy, mixed up*, muddled, rumpled, slapdash*, slipshod*, sloppy, slovenly, snarled, tacky*, tangled, topsy-turvy, tousled, uncombed, unfastidious, unkempt, unneat, unorderly, unsettled, upset; SEE CONCEPTS *589,621*

until [*prep*] *just before*
as far as, before, before the coming, continuously, down to, in advance of, in expectation, prior to, till, to, up till, up to; SEE CONCEPT *820*

untimely [*adj*] *inappropriate*
a bit previous, abortive, anachronistic, awkward, badly timed, bright and early*, disagreeable, early, early bird, early on, ill-timed, improper, inappropriate, inauspicious, inconvenient, inexpedient, inopportune, intrusive, malapropos, mistimed, out-of-date, overearly, oversoon, premature, previous, soon, too early, too late, undue, unfavorable, unfit, unfortunate, unlucky, unpropitious, unseasonable, unseemly, unsuitable, unsuited, wrong; SEE CONCEPTS *548,799*

untiring [*adj*] *determined, persevering*
ball of fire*, constant, continued, continuing, dedicated, devoted, dogged, eager beaver*, fireball*, firm, go-go*, grind*, hyper*, incessant, indefatigable, indomitable, inexhaustible, jumping, patient, perky, persistent, pertinacious, plodding, plugging, resolute, staunch, steady, strong, tenacious, tireless, unceasing, undeterred, unfailing, unfaltering, unflagging, unflinching, unremitting, unstinted, unswerving, unwavering, unwearied; SEE CONCEPT *538*

untold [*adj*] *very many; enormous*
beyond measure, countless, gigantic, hidden, huge, immense, incalculable, indescribable, inexpressible, innumerable, innumerous, mammoth, manifold, many, measureless, mighty, monstrous, multiple, multitudinous, myriad, numberless, private, prodigious, staggering, suppressed, titanic, uncountable, uncounted, undreamed of, unexpressed, unimaginable, unknown, unnumberable, unnumbered, unspeakable, unthinkable, vast; SEE CONCEPTS *529,762,781*

untouched [*adj*] *whole; not spoiled*
clear, entire, flawless, fresh, good, immaculate, incorrupt, indifferent, in good condition, intact, out of danger, perfect, pure, safe and sound, sanitary, secure, shipshape, sound, spotless, unaffected, unblemished, unbroken, unconcerned, undamaged, unharmed, unhurt, unimpressed, uninjured, unmarred, unmoved, unscathed, unstained, unstirred, untried, virgin, virginal, without a scratch; SEE CONCEPTS *403,485,621*

untoward [*adj1*] *troublesome*
adverse, annoying, awkward, contrary, disastrous, disturbing, fractious, hapless, ill-starred, inauspicious, inconvenient, indocile, inimical, inopportune, intractable, irritating, luckless, misfortunate, perverse, recalcitrant, refractory, star-crossed, undisciplined, unfavorable, unfortunate, ungovernable, unhappy, unlucky, unmanageable, unpliable, unpropitious, unruly, untimely, unyielding, vexatious, wild; SEE CONCEPTS *542,548,570*

untoward [*adj2*] *improper; not suitable*
improprietous, inappropriate, indecent, indecorous, indelicate, malodorous, out of place*, rough*, unbecoming, uncouth, unfitting, ungodly*, unseemly; SEE CONCEPTS *401,558*

untroubled [*adj*] *calm, peaceful*
composed, cool, halcyon, hushed, placid, quiet, serene, steady, still, tranquil, unagitated, unconcerned, undisturbed, unflappable, unflustered, unperturbed, unruffled, unstirred, unworried; SEE CONCEPTS *403,548,594*

untrue [*adj*] *dishonest*
apocryphal, cheating, counterfactual, crock*, deceitful, deceptive, delusive, deviant, disloyal, dissembling, distorted, erroneous, faithless, fallacious, false, fictitious, forsworn, hollow, imprecise, inaccurate, inconstant, incorrect, inexact, lying, meretricious, misleading, mistaken, off*, out of line*, perfidious, perjured, prevaricating, recreant, sham*, specious, spurious, traitorous, treacherous, two-faced*, unfaithful, unloyal, unsound, untrustworthy, untruthful, wide, wrong; SEE CONCEPTS *267,545,582*

untrustworthy [*adj*] *not dependable, faithful*
capricious, conniving, crooked, deceitful, devious, dishonest, disloyal, dubious, fair-weather*, faithless, false, fickle, fink*, fly-by-night*, guileful, irresponsible, questionable, shady, sharp, shifty*, slippery, sneaky, treacherous, tricky, trustless, two-faced*, two-timing*, unassured, undependable, unfaithful, unreliable, unsafe, unsure, untrue, untrusty; SEE CONCEPTS *401,542,545*

unusual [adj] different
abnormal, amazing, astonishing, atypical, awe-inspiring, awesome, bizarre, conspicuous, curious, different, distinguished, eminent, exceptional, extraordinary, far-out*, inconceivable, incredible, memorable, noteworthy, odd, out of the ordinary*, outstanding, phenomenal, prodigious, prominent, queer, rare, refreshing, remarkable, significant, singular, something else*, special, strange, surprising, uncommon, unconventional, unexpected, unfamiliar, unique, unparalleled, unwonted, weird*; SEE CONCEPT 564

unusually [adv] extremely
almighty, awful, awfully, curiously, especially, extra, extraordinarily, mighty, oddly, peculiarly, plenty, powerful, rarely, real, really, remarkably, right, so, so much, strangely, surprisingly, terribly, terrifically, too much, uncommon, uncommonly, very; SEE CONCEPTS 544,569

unvarnished [adj] plain, honest
bare, candid, clean, folksy*, for real*, frank, genuine, homey*, naked, open, open and shut*, pure, pure and simple*, simple, sincere, stark, straight, straightforward, unadorned, unconcealed, undisguised, undissembled, unembellished, vanilla*; SEE CONCEPTS 267,582

unveil [v] reveal
bare, betray, bring to light*, come out, disclose, discover, display, divulge, expose, give away, lay bare*, lay open*, let it all hang out*, make known, make public, open, open up, show, spring, tell, tip one's hand*, unbosom, uncover; SEE CONCEPTS 60,138

unwarranted [adj] not reasonable or right
baseless, bottomless, foundationless, gratuitous, groundless, indefensible, inexcusable, uncalled-for*, unconscionable, undue, unfair, unfounded, ungrounded, unjust, unjustifiable, unjustified, unprovoked, unreasonable, unwarrantable, wrong; SEE CONCEPTS 545,548,558

unwary [adj] thoughtless, heedless
brash, careless, credulous, hasty, ignorant, ill-advised, impetuous, imprudent, incautious, inconsiderate, indiscreet, negligent, rash, reckless, unadvised, unalert, uncircumspect, unguarded, unprepared, unsuspecting, unsuspicious, unvigilant, unwatchful; SEE CONCEPTS 401,403

unwavering [adj] consistent, unchanging
abiding, brick-wall*, dead set on*, dedicated, determined, enduring, firm, fixed, intense, never-failing, pat, regular, resolute, set, set in stone*, single-minded, solid, staunch, steadfast, steady, sure, undeviating, unfaltering, unflagging, unflappable, unqualified, unshakable, unshaken, unswerving, untiring; SEE CONCEPTS 488,535,542

unwelcome [adj] not wanted, desired
blackballed*, disagreeable, displeasing, distasteful, exceptionable, excess baggage*, excluded, ill-favored, inadmissible, left out in cold*, lousy, not in the picture*, objectionable, obnoxious, rejected, repellent, shut out, thankless, unacceptable, unasked, undesirable, uninvited, unpleasant, unpopular, unsought, unwanted, unwished for; SEE CONCEPTS 529,555,570

unwieldy [adj] awkward, bulky
burdensome, clumsy, cumbersome, cumbrous, encumbering, gross, hefty, inconvenient, lumbering, massive, onerous, ponderous, uncontrollable, ungainly, unhandy, unmanageable, weighty; SEE CONCEPTS 562,781

unwilling [adj] not in the mood
afraid, against, against the grain*, averse, backward, begrudging, compelled, contrary, demurring, disinclined, disobliging, evasive, forced, grudging, hesitating, indisposed, indocile, involuntary, laggard, loath, malcontent, opposed, recalcitrant, refractory, reluctant, remiss, resistant, shrinking, shy, slack, slow, unaccommodating, uncheerful, uncooperative, uneager, unenthusiastic, uninclined, unobliging, unready, unwishful, wayward; SEE CONCEPTS 401,542

unwind [v1] undo, untangle
disentangle, free, loose, loosen, ravel, separate, slacken, unbend, uncoil, unfurl, unravel, unreel, unroll, untwine, untwist, unwrap; SEE CONCEPT 158

unwind [v2] relax
calm down*, ease off*, loosen up*, quiet down*, quieten, recline, rest, sit back*, slow down*, take a break*, take it easy*, wind down*; SEE CONCEPT 210

unwise [adj] stupid, irresponsible
childish, fat, foolhardy, foolish, ill-advised, ill-considered, immature, impolitic, improvident, imprudent, inadvisable, inane, inappropriate, indiscreet, inept, injudicious, misguided, naive, rash, reckless, senseless, short-sighted, silly, thoughtless, undesirable, unfortunate, unintelligent, unsound, witless; SEE CONCEPTS 401,402,548

unwitting [adj] without fully realizing
accidental, aimless, chance, comatose, forgetful, haphazard, ignorant, inadvertent, incognizant, inconversant, innocent, involuntary, numb, oblivious, senseless, unacquainted, unaware, unconscious, undesigned, unfamiliar, uninformed, uninstructed, unintended, unintentional, unknowing, unmeant, unmindful, unplanned, unsuspecting, unthinking; SEE CONCEPTS 401,544,548

unworldly [adj1] spiritual
abstract, astral, celestial, daydreaming, daydreamy, dreamy, ethereal, extraterrestrial, fantastic, incorporeal, metaphysical, nonmaterialistic, otherworldly, religious, supersensory, transcendental, unearthly, unreal, visionary; SEE CONCEPTS 536,582

unworldly [adj2] not sophisticated; inexperienced
artless, babe in woods*, clean, corn-fed*, country, folksy*, green*, idealistic, ingenuous, innocent, naive, natural, raw*, simple, trusting, unaffected, unartificial, uncool, unschooled, unsophisticated,

unstudied, wide-eyed*; SEE CONCEPTS *401,555,589*

unworthy [adj] *not of value*

base, beneath, blamable, contemptible, degrading, disgraceful, dishonorable, disreputable, good-for-nothing, ignoble, improper, inappropriate, ineligible, inexcusable, no-account*, no-good*, not deserving, not fit, not good enough, nothing, not worth, offensive, out of place*, recreant, reprehensible, shameful, unbecoming, unbefitting, undeserving, unfit, unmerited, unseemly, unsuitable, valueless, vile, wretched, wrong; SEE CONCEPTS *404,558,571*

unwritten [adj] *understood*

accepted, conventional, customary, oral, spoken, tacit, traditional, unformulated, unrecorded, unsaid, verbal, vocal, word-of-mouth; SEE CONCEPTS *267,533*

unyielding [adj] *steadfast, resolute*

adamant, dead set on*, determined, firm, fixed, hard, hard-core*, hardheaded*, hard-line*, hard-nosed*, headstrong*, immalleable, immovable, implacable, impliable, inexorable, inflexible, intractable, locked in, merciless, mulish, obdurate, obstinate, pertinacious, pigheaded*, refractory, relentless, resolute, rigid, ruthless, single-minded, solid, staunch, stiff, stiff-necked*, stubborn, tough, unbending, uncompliant, uncompromising, unmovable, unrelenting, unswayable, unwavering; SEE CONCEPTS *401,542*

upbeat [adj] *cheerful*

buoyant, cheery, encouraging, favorable, fond, happy, heartening, hopeful, optimistic, positive, promising, rosy, sanguine; SEE CONCEPTS *403,572*

update [v] *bring up to date*

amend, modernize, refresh, refurbish, rejuvenate, renew, renovate, restore, revise; SEE CONCEPT *244*

upheaval [n] *major change*

about-face, alteration, cataclysm, catastrophe, clamor, commotion, convulsion, disaster, disorder, disruption, disturbance, eruption, explosion, ferment, flip-flop*, new ball-game*, new deal*, outbreak, outburst, outcry, overthrow, revolution, shakeout, stirring, switch, temblor, tremor, tumult, turmoil, turnaround, upturn; SEE CONCEPT *230*

uphill [adj1] *going up*

acclivous, ascending, climbing, mounting, rising, skyward, sloping upward, toward summit, up, uprising; SEE CONCEPT *581*

uphill [adj2] *difficult, laborious*

arduous, effortful, exhausting, grueling, hard, labored, operose, punishing, rugged, strenuous, taxing, toilsome, tough, wearisome; SEE CONCEPTS *538,565*

uphold [v] *maintain, support*

advocate, aid, assist, back, back up, bolster, boost, brace, buoy up, buttress, carry, champion, confirm, countenance, defend, elevate, encourage, endorse, help, hoist, hold to, hold up one's end*, justify, pick up, promote, prop, raise, rear, second, shore up, side with, stand by, stick by, stick up for*, sustain, take

up, upbear, uplift, upraise, uprear, vindicate; SEE CONCEPT *110*

upkeep [n] *maintenance*

budget, conservation, costs, expenditure, expenses, keep, outlay, overhead, preservation, price, repair, running, subsistence, support, sustenance, sustentation; SEE CONCEPTS *117,344*

upper [adj1] *above*

high, higher, loftier, more elevated, overhead, top, topmost, uppermost, upward; SEE CONCEPT *583*

upper [adj2] *superior*

beautiful, elevated, elite, eminent, greater, important, more important; SEE CONCEPTS *555,567*

uppermost [adj1] *top*

apical, culminating, highest, loftiest, most elevated, topmost, upmost; SEE CONCEPT *583*

uppermost [adj2] *most important; chief*

best, big, boss, dominant, executive, foremost, greatest, high-up*, leading, main, paramount, predominant, preeminent, primary, principal, supreme, the most*, tops*, winner, world-class*; SEE CONCEPTS *568,632*

upright [adj1] *straight-up*

cocked, end on, end up, erect, on end, perpendicular, plumb, raised, sheer, standing, stand-up, steep, straight, upended, upstanding, upward, vertical; SEE CONCEPTS *581,583*

upright [adj2] *honorable, honest*

aboveboard, blameless, circumspect, conscientious, correct, equitable, ethical, exemplary, fair, faithful, good, high-minded, impartial, incorruptible, just, kosher*, legit*, moral, noble, principled, punctilious, pure, right, righteous, square, straight, straightforward, true, true-blue*, trustworthy, unimpeachable, up front*, virtuous; SEE CONCEPTS *404,545*

uprising [n] *disturbance*

insurgence, insurrection, mutiny, outbreak, rebellion, revolt, revolution, riot, upheaval; SEE CONCEPTS *106,674*

uproar [n] *commotion, pandemonium*

ado, babble, babel*, bedlam, bickering, big scene*, brawl, broil*, bustle, chaos, clamor, clangor, clatter, confusion, din, disorder, flap*, fracas*, free-for-all*, furor, fuss, hassle, jangle, mayhem, melee, noise, outcry, racket*, riot, roughhouse*, row, ruction, shivaree*, stink*, stir, strife, to-do*, turbulence, turmoil, violence; SEE CONCEPTS *46,65,106,674*

uproot [v] *destroy; rip out of a place*

abate, abolish, annihilate, blot out*, demolish, deracinate, dig up, displace, do away with*, eliminate, eradicate, excavate, exile, exterminate, extirpate, extract, move, overthrow, overturn, pull up, remove, root out, tear up, weed, weed out, wipe out; SEE CONCEPTS *147,178,211,252*

upset [n] *problem*

agitation, bother, complaint, defeat, destruction, disorder, disquiet, distress, disturbance, free-for-all*, goulash*, hassle, illness, malady, overthrow, quea siness, reverse, reversion, screw-up*, shake-up*, shock, sickness, stew*, subversion, surprise, tizzy*, trouble, turmoil, worry; SEE CONCEPT *674*

upset [adj] *disturbed, bothered*
agitated, all torn up*, amazed, antsy*, apprehensive, blue*, broken up*, capsized, chaotic, come apart, confused, disconcerted, dismayed, disordered, disquieted, distressed, disturbed, dragged*, frantic, grieved, hurt, ill, in disarray, jittery, jumpy, low, muddled, overturned, overwrought, psyched out*, rattled, ruffled*, shocked, shook up*, sick, spilled, thrown, tipped over, toppled, troubled, tumbled, unglued*, unsettled, unzipped*, upside-down, worried; SEE CONCEPTS *403,485,570*

upset [v1] *disorder; knock over*
capsize, change, derange, disarray, disorganize, disturb, invert, jumble, keel over, mess up*, mix up, muddle, overset, overturn, pitch, put out of order, reverse, rummage, spill, spoil, subvert, tilt, tip over, topple, tumble, turn, turn inside-out*, turn topsy-turvy*, turn upside-down, unsettle, upend, upturn; SEE CONCEPTS *147,208,213*

upset [v2] *bother, trouble*
adjy, afflict, agitate, ail, bewilder, bug*, confound, cramp, craze, debilitate, derange, discombobulate*, discompose, disconcert, dismay, disquiet, distract, distress, disturb, egg on*, fire up*, flip*, flip out*, floor*, flurry, fluster, get to*, give a hard time*, grieve, incapacitate, indispose, key up*, lay up, make a scene*, make waves*, perturb, pick on*, pother, psych*, rattle, rock the boat*, ruffle, sicken, spook, stir up, throw off balance*, turn, turn on, unhinge*, unnerve, unsettle; SEE CONCEPTS *7,19*

upset [v3] *defeat*
beat, be victorious, conquer, get the better of*, outplay, overcome, overpower, overthrow, overturn, topple, triumph over, win; SEE CONCEPT *95*

upshot [n] *end result*
aftereffect, aftermath, burden, climax, completion, conclusion, consequence, core, culmination, denouement, development, effect, end, ending, event, eventuality, finale, finish, gist, issue, meaning, meat*, outcome, payoff, pith*, purport, result, sense, sequel, substance, termination, thrust; SEE CONCEPTS *230,682*

upside-down [adj] *overturned, inverted*
backward, bottom-side up, bottom up, confused, disordered, downside-up*, haywire*, helter-skelter*, in chaos, in disarray, jumbled, mixed-up, on head, reversed, tangled, topsy-turvy*, upendedong way, wrong-side-up; SEE CONCEPT *583*

upstanding [adj] *honorable*
ethical, good, honest, incorruptible, moral, principled, straightforward, true, trustworthy, upright; SEE CONCEPT *545*

uptight [adj] *nervous*
anxious, apprehensive, cautious, concerned, conventional, edgy, nervy, old-fashioned, on edge*, on the

defensive*, restive, strict, tense, troubled, uneasy, withdrawn, worried; SEE CONCEPT *401*

up-to-date [adj] *current, modern*
abreast, advanced, à la mode*, all the rage*, au courant, avant-garde, brand-new, contemporary, cutting edge*, dashing, expedient, faddish*, fashionable, fitting, hot*, in, in fashion, in-thing*, in vogue, modernistic, modish, neoteric, new, newest, newfangled, now*, opportune, popular, red-hot*, state-of-the-art, stylish, suitable, timely, today*, trendy, up*, up-to-the-minute, with it*; SEE CONCEPTS *578,589,797,799*

urban [adj] *city*
burghal, central, citified, civic, civil, downtown, inner-city, metropolitan, municipal, nonrural, oppidan, popular, public, town, village; SEE CONCEPT *536*

urbane [adj] *civilized*
affable, balanced, bland, civil, cosmopolitan, courteous, cultivated, cultured, debonair, elegant, genteel, gracious, mannerly, metropolitan, obliging, poised, polished, polite, refined, smooth, sophisticated, suave, well-bred, well-mannered; SEE CONCEPT *401*

urchin [n] *young deprived person*
brat*, cub, dickens*, gamin, guttersnipe, imp, juvenile delinquent, mudlark, punk*, pup*, ragamuffin, waif; SEE CONCEPT *423*

urge [n] *very strong desire*
appetite, appetition, compulsion, craving, drive, druthers, fancy, fire in belly*, goad, impetus, impulse, incentive, itch*, longing, lust, motive, passion, pressure, stimulant, stimulus, sweet tooth*, weakness, wish, yearning, yen; SEE CONCEPTS *20,532*

urge [v] *beg, push for, encourage*
adjure, advance, advise, advocate, appeal to, ask, attract, beseech, champion, charge, commend, compel, conjure, counsel, countenance, drive, egg on*, endorse, entreat, exhort, favor, fire up*, force, further, goad, hasten, impel, implore, incite, induce, influence, insist on, inspire, instigate, maneuver, move, plead, press, promote, prompt, propel, propose, push, put up to*, rationalize, recommend, request, sanction, solicit, speak for, spur, stimulate, support, tempt, wheedle; SEE CONCEPTS *68,75*

urgent [adj] *needing immediate attention*
burning*, called-for, capital, chief, clamant, clamorous, compelling, critical, crucial, crying*, demanded, demanding, driving, essential, exigent, foremost, heavy*, hurry-up, immediate, impelling, imperative, important, importunate, indispensable, insistent, instant, leading, life and death*, momentous, necessary, paramount, persuasive, pressing, primary, principal, required, salient, serious, top-priority, touch and go*, touchy, vital, wanted, weighty*; SEE CONCEPTS *548,568*

usable [adj] *available, working*
accessible, adaptable, advantageous, applicable, at disposal, at hand, beneficial, consumable, convenient, current, employable, exhaustible, expendable,

exploitable, fit, functional, good, helpful, in order, instrumental, open, operative, practicable, practical, profitable, ready, running, serviceable, subservient, unused, useful, utile, utilizable, valid, valuable, wieldy; SEE CONCEPTS *560,576*

usage [n] *habit, custom*
acceptance, control, convention, currency, form, formula, habitude, handling, management, matter of course, method, mode, operation, practice, praxis, procedure, regime, regulation, rote, routine, rule, running, tradition, treatment, trick, use, way, wont; SEE CONCEPTS *6,658*

use [n] *application; employment*
account, adoption, advantage, appliance, applicability, appropriateness, avail, benefit, call, capitalization, cause, convenience, custom, end, exercise, exercising, exertion, fitness, good, habit, handling, help, helpfulness, mileage, mobilization, necessity, need, object, occasion, operation, point, practice, profit, purpose, reason, relevance, service, serviceability, treatment, usability, usage, usefulness, utility, value, way, wear and tear*, wont, worth; SEE CONCEPTS *225,658,709*

use [v] *work with; consume*
accept, adopt, apply, avail oneself of, bestow, bring into play*, bring to bear*, capitalize, control, do with, draw on, employ, exercise, exert, exhaust, expend, exploit, find a use, govern, handle, make do*, make the most of*, make use, manage, manipulate, operate, play on, ply, practice, press into service*, put forth*, put into action, put to use, put to work, regulate, relate, run, run through, set in motion, spend, take advantage of*, turn to account, utilize, waste, wield, work; SEE CONCEPTS *169,225*

useful [adj] *beneficial, valuable*
advantageous, all-purpose, applied, appropriate, brave, commodious, convenient, effective, favorable, fit, fruitful, functional, good, handy, helpful, instrumental, meet, of assistance, of service, of use, practicable, practical, pragmatic, profitable, proper, propitious, purposive, salutary, serviceable, subsidiary, suitable, suited, toward, utile, utilitarian, workaday, worthwhile; SEE CONCEPT *560*

useless [adj] *not working; not valuable*
abortive, bootless*, counterproductive, disadvantageous, dysfunctional, expendable, feckless, fruitless, futile, good-for-nothing*, hopeless, idle, impracticable, impractical, incompetent, ineffective, ineffectual, inept, inoperative, inutile, meaningless, no good, nonfunctional, of no use, pointless, profitless, purposeless, scrap, stupid*, unavailable, unavailing, unfunctional, unproductive, unprofitable, unpurposed, unusuable, unworkable, vain, valueless, waste, weak, worthless; SEE CONCEPT *560*

usher [n] *person who guides others to place*
attendant, conductor, doorkeeper, doorman/woman, doorperson, escort, guide, herald, lead, leader, page, pilot, precursor, usherette; SEE CONCEPT *352*

usher [v] *guide*
bring in, conduct, direct, escort, herald, inaugurate, initiate, institute, introduce, launch, lead, marshal, open the door, originate, pave the way*, pilot, precede, preface, receive, set up, show around, show in, show out, steer; SEE CONCEPTS *187,221*

usual [adj] *common, typical*
accepted, accustomed, average, chronic, commonplace, constant, conventional, current, customary, cut and dried*, everyday, expected, familiar, fixed, frequent, garden variety*, general, grind, habitual, mainstream, matter-of-course, natural, normal, ordinary, plain, plastic, prevailing, prevalent, quotidian, regular, rife, routine, run-of-the-mill*, so-so*, standard, stock, typic, unremarkable, vanilla*, whitebread*, wonted, workaday; SEE CONCEPTS *530,547*

usually [adv] *for the most part*
as a rule, as is the custom, as is usual, as usual, by and large, commonly, consistently, customarily, frequently, generally, habitually, in the main, mainly, more often than not, mostly, most often, normally, now and again, now and then, occasionally, once and again, on the whole, ordinarily, regularly, routinely, sometimes; SEE CONCEPTS *530,541*

usurp [v] *take over*
accroach, annex, appropriate, arrogate, assume, barge in*, butt in*, clap hands on*, commandeer, cut out, displace, elbow in*, get hands on*, grab, grab hold of, highjack*, infringe upon, lay hold of, muscle in*, preempt, seize, squeeze in, supplant, swipe, take, work in, worm in*, wrest; SEE CONCEPTS *142,384*

utensil [n] *tool, usually for eating*
apparatus, appliance, contrivance, convenience, device, equipment, fork, gadget, implement, instrument, knife, silverware, spoon, tableware, ware; SEE CONCEPTS *493,499*

utilitarian [adj] *practical*
commonsensical, down-to-earth, effective, efficient, functional, hard, hardheaded, matter-of-fact, nuts and bolts*, pragmatic, pragmatical, realistic, sensible, serviceable, unidealistic, unromantic, useful; SEE CONCEPT *560*

utility [n] *serviceableness*
account, adequacy, advantage, advantageousness, applicability, appropriateness, avail, benefit, convenience, efficacy, efficiency, expediency, favor, fitness, function, point, practicality, productiveness, profit, relevance, service, serviceability, use, usefulness; SEE CONCEPT *658*

utilize [v] *make use of*
advance, apply, appropriate, avail oneself of, bestow, employ, exercise, exploit, forward, further, handle, have recourse to, profit by, promote, put to use, resort to, take advantage of, turn to account, use; SEE CONCEPT *225*

utmost [adj] *extreme, maximum*
absolute, all-out*, chief, complete, entire, exhaustive, farthest, final, full, furthermost, greatest, highest, last, last straw*, maximal, most, most distant,

outermost, out of bounds*, outside, paramount, plenary, preeminent, remotest, sheer, supreme, thorough, thoroughgoing, too much*, too-too*, top, topmost, total, ultimate, ultra*, unconditional, undiminished, unlimited, unmitigated, unqualified, unreserved, uttermost, whole, worst case*; SEE CONCEPTS *531,574,772*

utopia [n] *ideal place and life*
Arcadia, bliss, dreamland, dreamworld, Eden*, Elysian Fields*, Erehwon*, fairyland, Garden of Eden*, heaven, land of milk and honey*, never-never land*, paradise, perfection, pie in the sky*, promised land*, seventh heaven*, Shangri-La*, wonderland; SEE CONCEPTS *370,689*

utopian [adj] *imaginary, ideal*
abstract, airy, ambitious, arcadian, chimerical, dream, fanciful, fantasy, grandiose, hopeful, idealist, idealistic, ideological, illusory, impossible, impractical, lofty, otherworldly, perfect, pie in the sky*, pretentious, quixotic, romantic, transcendental, unfeasible, visionary; SEE CONCEPTS *572,574, 582*

utter [adj] *outright, absolute*
all-fired*, arrant, blasted*, blessed*, blooming*, complete, confounded, consummate, downright, entire, flat-out*, infernal, out-and-out*, perfect, pure, sheer, stark, straight-out*, thorough, thoroughgoing, total, unmitigated, unqualified; SEE CONCEPTS *531, 535*

utter [v] *say, reveal*
affirm, air, announce, articulate, assert, asseverate, blurt, bring out, chime, chin*, come out with*, declaim, declare, deliver, disclose, divulge, ejaculate, enunciate, exclaim, express, give words to*, go, jaw, lip, make known, modulate, mouth*, mutter, proclaim, promulgate, pronounce, publish, put into words, recite, say, shout, speak, spiel*, state, talk, throw out, verbalize, vocalize, voice, whisper; SEE CONCEPTS *47,55*

utterance [n] *revelation*
announcement, articulation, assertion, asseveration, declaration, delivery, discourse, ejaculation, expression, opinion, oration, peroration, pronouncement, rant, recitation, remark, reply, response, saying, sentence, speaking, speech, spiel, statement, talk, vent, verbalization, vocalization, vociferation, voice, word, words; SEE CONCEPTS *47,278*

utterly [adv] *completely*
absolutely, all, all in all, altogether, entirely, exactly, extremely, fully, in toto*, just, perfectly, plumb*, purely, quite, thoroughly, to nth degree*, totally, to the core*, well, wholly; SEE CONCEPT *531*

uttermost [adj] *extreme*
farthest, final, furthermost, furthest, last, outermost, outmost, remotest, utmost; SEE CONCEPTS *585,778*

V

vacancy [n] *opening*
abstraction, blankness, desertedness, emptiness, gap, job, lack, opportunity, position, post, room, situa-

tion, space, vacuity, vacuousness, vacuum, void, voidness; SEE CONCEPTS *513,516,693*

vacant [adj1] *empty; unoccupied*
abandoned, available, bare, clear, deserted, devoid, disengaged, free, idle, not in use, stark, tenantless, to let, unemployed, unengaged, unfilled, uninhabited, unlived in, untaken, untenanted, unused, void, without contents; SEE CONCEPTS *481,560,740,774*

vacant [adj2] *absent-minded; expressionless*
abstracted, blank, daydreaming, deadpan, dreaming, dreamy, empty-headed, foolish, idle, inane, incurious, inexpressive, silly, stupid, thoughtless, unexpressive, unintelligent, unthinking, vacuous, vapid, witless; SEE CONCEPT *402*

vacate [v] *leave empty*
abandon, abrogate, annul, clear, depart, discharge, dissolve, empty, evacuate, give up, go away, leave, move out, move out of, part with, quash, quit, relinquish, renounce, rescind, retract, reverse, revoke, void, withdraw; SEE CONCEPTS *195,234*

vacation [n] *planned time spent not working*
break, breathing space*, day of rest, few days off*, fiesta, furlough, gone fishing*, holiday, intermission, layoff, leave, leave of absence, liberty, long weekend*, recess, recreation, respite, rest, sabbatical, spell, time off, two weeks with pay*; SEE CONCEPTS *363,807*

vaccinate [v] *give a shot to treat or prevent disease*
immunize, inject, inoculate, mitigate, prevent, protect, treat, variolate; SEE CONCEPT *310*

vacillate [v] *go back and forth*
alternate, be indecisive, be irresolute, change, change mind, dither, fence-straddle*, fluctuate, hedge, hem and haw*, hesitate, hover, oscillate, pause, pussyfoot around*, reel, rock, run hot and cold*, seesaw*, shilly-shally*, stagger, straddle, sway, swing, waffle, waver, whiffle*, yo-yo*; SEE CONCEPT *13*

vacuous [adj] *empty; unintelligent*
airheaded*, birdbrain*, blank, drained, dull, dumb, emptied, foolish, half-baked*, inane, lamebrain*, minus*, shallow, silly*, stupid, superficial, uncomprehending, unreasoning, vacant, void; SEE CONCEPT *402*

vacuum [n] *emptiness*
exhaustion, free space, gap, nothingness, rarefaction, space, vacuity, void; SEE CONCEPTS *513,740*

vagabond/vagrant [n] *person who wanders from place to place*
beggar, bum, deadbeat, derelict, down-and-outer*, drifter, floater, gypsy, hobo, idler, itinerant, loafer*, migrant, nomad, outcast, rascal, rogue, rolling stone*, rover, stray, street person*, tramp*, transient, traveler, wanderer, wayfarer; SEE CONCEPTS *412,423*

vagabond [adj] *poor and homeless*
aimless, begging, bumming, destitute, down-and-out*, drifting, errant, fancy-free*, fly-by-night*, footloose*, idle, itinerant, itinerate, journeying,

mendicant, migratory, mooching*, moving, no-madic, panhandling*, perambulant, perambulatory, peripatetic, prodigal, profligate, rambling, roaming, rootless*, roving, sauntering, shifting, shiftless, straggling, stray, strolling, transient, travelling, un-settled, vagrant, wandering, wayfaring, wayward; SEE CONCEPT 539

vague [adj] not definite or clear
ambiguous, amorphous, amphibological, bewilder-ing, bleary, blurred, cloudy, dark, dim, doubtful, dreamlike, dubious, enigmatic, equivocal, faint, fuzzy, generalized, hazy, ill-defined, impalpable, im-precise, indefinite, indeterminate, indistinct, inexpli-cable, lax, loose, misunderstood, muddy, nebulous, obscure, perplexing, problematic, puzzling, ques-tionable, shadowy, superficial, tenebrous, uncertain, unclear, undetermined, unexplicit, unintelligible, un-known, unsettled, unspecified, unsure; SEE CONCEPTS 267,485,529

vain [adj1] egotistical
arrogant, big-headed, boastful, cocky*, conceited, egocentric, egoistic, haughty, high-and-mighty*, in-flated, narcissistic, ostentatious, overweening, pleased with oneself*, proud, puffed up*, self-important, stuck-up*, swaggering*, swollen-headed*, vainglorious; SEE CONCEPTS 401,404

vain [adj2] futile, useless
abortive, barren, bootless, delusive, delusory, empty, frivolous, fruitless, going nowhere*, hollow, idle, inefficacious, insignificant, in vicious circle*, misleading, needle in haystack*, not a prayer*, no-win*, nugatory, on a treadmill*, otiose, paltry, petty, pointless, profitless, puny, senseless, shuck, slight, sterile, time-wasting, trifling, trivial, unavailing, un-important, unnotable, unproductive, unprofitable, valueless, void, wild-goose chase*, worthless; SEE CONCEPTS 552,575

valedictory [adj] farewell
departing, final, goodbye, last, parting, terminal; SEE CONCEPT 267

valiant [adj] brave
adventurous, assertive, audacious, bold, brave, chiv-alrous, courageous, dauntless, fearless, fire-eating*, gallant, game, grand, great, gritty*, gutsy*, gutty*, heroic, high-spirited, indomitable, intrepid, lion-hearted, magnanimous, nervy*, noble, plucky*, powerful, puissant, redoubtable, self-reliant, spunky*, stalwart, steadfast, stout, stouthearted, strong-willed, unafraid, undaunted, undismayed, valorous, venturesome, venturous, vigorous, worthy; SEE CONCEPTS 401,404,538

valid [adj] right, genuine
accurate, attested, authentic, authoritative, binding, bona fide, cogent, compelling, conclusive, con-firmed, convincing, credible, determinative, effica-cious, efficient, good, in force, irrefutable, just, kosher*, lawful, legal, legit*, legitimate, logical, of-ficial, original, persuasive, potent, powerful, proven, pure, solid, sound, stringent, strong, substantial, tell-ing, tested, true, trustworthy, ultimate, unadulter-ated, unanswerable, uncorrupted, weighty, well-founded, well-grounded; SEE CONCEPTS 319,545,582

validate [v] ascertain the truth, authenticity of some-thing
approve, authenticate, authorize, bear out, certify, confirm, constitute, corroborate, endorse, give stamp of approval*, give the go-ahead*, give the green light*, give the nod*, John Hancock*, justify, legal-ize, legitimize, make binding*, make legal*, make stick*, okay*, ratify, rubber-stamp*, sanction, set seal on*, sign off on*, substantiate, verify; SEE CON-CEPTS 50,88,317

validity [n] genuineness, lawfulness
authority, cogency, effectiveness, efficacy, force, foundation, gravity, grounds, legality, legitimacy, persuasiveness, point, potency, power, punch, right, soundness, strength, substance, validness, weight; SEE CONCEPTS 645,691,725

valley [n] hollow in the land
basin, bottom, canyon, channel, coulee, dale, dell, depression, dingle, glen, gorge, lowland, notch, plain, swale, trough, vale; SEE CONCEPTS 509,513

valor [n] bravery
backbone*, boldness, chivalry, courage, dash*, de-fiance, derring-do*, determination, fearlessness, fight, firmness, fortitude, gallantry, grit*, guts*, har-dihood, heart, heroism, indomitableness, intestinal fortitude*, intrepidity, invincibility, manliness, met-tle, moxie*, nerve, pluck, prowess, resolution, sand, spirit, spunk, starch*, stomach*, tenacity, valiance, valiancy; SEE CONCEPTS 411,633

valuable [n] prized possession
advantage, antique, asset, benefit, collectible, com-modity, heirloom, nugget*, plum*, treasure; SEE CONCEPT 446

valuable [adj] very important; priceless
admired, appreciated, beneficial, cherished, collect-ible, costly, dear, esteemed, estimable, expensive, heirloom, held dear, helpful, high-priced, hot*, hot property*, important, in demand, inestimable, in-valuable, of value, precious, prized, profitable, rel-evant, respected, scarce, serviceable, treasured, useful, valued, worthwhile, worthy; SEE CONCEPTS 334,560,568

value [n1] financial worth
amount, appraisal, assessment, charge, cost, equiv-alent, expense, market price, monetary worth, price, profit, rate; SEE CONCEPTS 335,336

value [n2] advantage, worth
account, bearing, benefit, caliber, condition, conno-tation, consequence, content, denotation, desirabil-ity, distinction, drift, eminence, esteem, estimation, excellence, finish, force, goodness, grade, help, im-plication, import, importance, interpretation, mark, marketability, meaning, merit, power, preference, profit, purpose, quality, regard, repute, sense, ser-viceableness, significance, state, stature, substance,

superiority, use, usefulness, utility, valuation; SEE
CONCEPTS *346,658,668,682*

valve [*n*] *on-and-off device*
cock, faucet, flap, gate, hydrant, lid, pipe, plug,
shutoff, spigot, stopper, tap; SEE CONCEPTS
445,464,499

vandal [*n*] *person who defiles property*
defacer, despoiler, destroyer, hoodlum, looter,
mischief-maker, pillager, pirate, plunderer, ravager,
thief; SEE CONCEPT *412*

vanish [*v*] *disappear*
become invisible, be lost, clear, dematerialize, die,
die out, dissolve, evanesce, evaporate, exit, fade,
fade away, go away, melt; SEE CONCEPT *105*

vanity [*n*] *conceit, egotism*
affected way, affection, airs, arrogance, big-
headedness*, conceitedness, display, egotism, ego
trip*, narcissism, ostentation, pretension, pride, self-
admiration, self-love, self-worship, show*, showing
off*, smugness, vainglory; SEE CONCEPT *410*

vanquish [*v*] *defeat soundly*
bear down, beat, conquer, crush, humble, master,
overcome, overpower, overturn, overwhelm, put
down, quell, reduce, repress, rout, subdue, subjugate, subvert, surmount, trample, triumph over; SEE
CONCEPT *95*

vapid [*adj*] *flat, dull*
bland, boring, colorless, dead*, driveling, flat, flat
tire*, flavorless, inane, innocuous, insipid, jejune,
least, lifeless, limp, milk-and-water*, milk-toast*,
nothing, nowhere, stale, tame, tasteless, tedious,
tiresome, unimaginative, uninspiring, uninteresting,
unpalatable, vacant, vacuous, watery, weak, wishy-
washy*, zero*; SEE CONCEPTS *529,537,575*

vapor [*n*] *fumes, mist*
breath, condensation, dampness, dew, effluvium, exhalation, fog, gas, haze, miasma, moisture, reek,
smog, smoke, steam; SEE CONCEPTS *437,524*

variable [*adj*] *changing, changeable*
capricious, changeful, fickle, fitful, flexible, fluctuating, fluid, iffy*, inconstant, irregular, mercurial,
mobile, mutable, protean, shifting, shifty, slippery*,
spasmodic, temperamental, ticklish, uncertain, uneq-
uable, unsettled, unstable, unsteady, vacillating, volatile, waffling, wavering, yo-yo*; SEE CONCEPT *534*

variance [*n*] *difference*
about-face*, argument, change, conflict, contention,
deviation, difference of opinion, different strokes,
disaccord, disagreement, discord, discrepancy, dissension, dissent, dissidence, disunity, divergence, diversity, division, flip-flop*, fluctuation, incongruity,
inconsistency, mid-course correction*, mutation,
separation, severing, strife, sundering, switch, transmogrification, unharmoniousness, variation, variety;
SEE CONCEPTS *388,665,697*

variant [*n*] *derived form*
alternative, branch, development, exception, irregularity, modification, result, spinoff, variation, version; SEE CONCEPT *665*

variant [*adj*] *different*
alternative, derived, differing, divergent, exceptional, modified, various, varying; SEE CONCEPT *564*

variation [*n*] *difference; alternative*
aberration, abnormality, adaptation, alteration, bend,
break, change, contradistinction, contrast, curve, deflection, departure, departure from the norm*, deviation, digression, discrepancy, disparity, displacement, dissimilarity, dissimilitude, distinction, divergence, diversification, diversity, exception, fluctuation, inequality, innovation, modification, mutation,
novelty, shift, swerve, turn, unconformity, variety;
SEE CONCEPTS *665,697*

varied [*adj*] *different*
assorted, conglomerate, discrete, diverse, heterogeneous, indiscriminate, miscellaneous, mixed, motley, multifarious, separate, sundry, various; SEE
CONCEPT *564*

variety [*n1*] *difference*
array, assortment, change, collection, combo, conglomeration, cross section, departure, discrepancy,
disparateness, divergency, diversification, diversity,
fluctuation, heterogeneity, incongruity, intermixture,
many-sidedness, medley, mélange, miscellany,
mishmash, mixed bag, mixture, modification, multifariousness, multiplicity, potpourri, range, shift,
soup, stew, variance, variation; SEE CONCEPTS
432,665

variety [*n2*] *type, sort*
assortment, brand, breed, category, character, class,
classification, description, division, family, genus,
grade, ilk, kidney, kind, make, nature, order, quality, race, rank, species, strain, stripe, tribe; SEE CON-
CEPT *378*

various [*adj*] *miscellaneous, differing*
all manner of*, assorted, changeable, changing, different, discrete, disparate, distinct, distinctive, diverse, diversified, heterogeneous, individual, legion,
manifold, many, many-sided, multifarious, multitudinal, multitudinous, numerous, omnifarious, peculiar, populous, separate, several, sundry, unalike,
unequal, unlike, variant, varied, variegated; SEE CON-
CEPTS *564,771*

varnish [*v*] *add a layer to; embellish*
adorn, coat, cover, decorate, enamel, finish, gild,
glaze, gloss, japan, lacquer, luster, paint, polish,
shellac, surface, veneer, wash, wax; SEE CONCEPTS
172,177

vary [*v*] *change*
alter, alternate, assort, be unlike, blow hot and cold*,
convert, depart, deviate, differ, digress, disagree,
displace, dissent, divaricate, diverge, diversify, divide, fluctuate, hem and haw*, inflect, interchange,
modify, mutate, part, permutate, range, separate,
shilly-shally*, swerve, take turns, transform, turn,
variegate, yo-yo*; SEE CONCEPT *697*

vast [*adj*] *very large; wide in range*
all-inclusive, ample, astronomical, big, boundless,
broad, capacious, colossal, comprehensive, detailed,

endless, enormous, eternal, expanded, extensive, far-flung*, far-reaching, forever, giant, gigantic, great, huge, illimitable, immeasurable, immense, infinite, limitless, mammoth, massive, measureless, monstrous, monumental, never-ending*, prodigious, prolonged, spacious, spread-out, stretched-out, sweeping, titanic, tremendous, unbounded, unlimited, voluminous, widespread; SEE CONCEPTS 772,773,781

vault [n] *depository*
basement, box, can, catacomb, cavern, cellar, crib, crypt, dungeon, grave, mausoleum, pit, repository, safe, safe-deposit box, sepulcher, strongroom, tomb; SEE CONCEPT 494

vault [v] *jump over; span*
arch, ascend, bend, bounce, bound, bow, clear, curve, hop, hurdle, leap, mount, negotiate, over, overleap, rise, soar, spring, surmount; SEE CONCEPTS 194,752

veer [v] *change direction*
angle off, avert, bear, be deflected, bend, change, change course, curve, cut, deflect, depart, deviate, digress, dip, diverge, divert, drift, get around, make a left*, make a right*, pivot, sheer, shift, skew, skid, swerve, swing, swivel, tack, train off, turn, twist, volte-face, wheel, whip, whirl; SEE CONCEPTS 148,150,213

vegetable [n] *edible part of plant*
edible, green, greens, herb, herbaceous plant, legume, produce, root, salad, truck, yellow; SEE CONCEPT 431

vegetate [v1] *be very passive*
be inert, decay, deteriorate, exist, go to pot*, go to seed*, hibernate, idle, languish, loaf*, pass time, stagnate, weaken; SEE CONCEPTS 210,698

vegetate [v2] *grow, sprout*
bloom, blossom, bud, burgeon, germinate, shoot, spring, swell; SEE CONCEPTS 253,257

vehement [adj] *passionate, opinionated*
angry, ardent, ball of fire*, come on strong*, concentrated, delirious, desperate, eager, earnest, emphatic, enthusiastic, exquisite, fervent, fervid, fierce, fiery, forceful, forcible, frantic, furious, hearty, heated, hopped up*, hot*, hyper*, impassioned, impetuous, inflamed, intense, lively, on the make*, potent, powerful, pronounced, rabid, strong, terrible, vicious, violent, wild, zealous; SEE CONCEPTS 401,542

vehicle [n1] *machine used for transportation*
agent, automobile, bicycle, boat, buggy, bus, cab, car, carrier, chariot, conveyance, crate, jalopy, jeep, mechanism, motorcycle, taxi, transport, truck, van, vector, wagon, wheels; SEE CONCEPT 503

vehicle [n2] *means of attaining end*
agency, agent, apparatus, channel, expedient, implement, instrument, instrumentality, intermediary, means of expression*, mechanism, medium, ministry, organ, tool, vector, way, ways and means*; SEE CONCEPTS 6,277,278,694,712

veil [n] *disguise*
blind, cloak, coloring, cover, curtain, facade, false front, film, front, guise, mantilla, mask, screen, shade, shroud, veiling; SEE CONCEPTS 451,673

veil [v] *hide*
beard*, blanket, camouflage, cloak, conceal, cover, cover up, curtain*, dim, disguise, drape, enclose, enfold, enshroud, envelop, finesse, invest, launder, mantle, mask, obscure, put up a front*, screen, secrete, shield, shroud, stonewall*, whitewash*, wrap; SEE CONCEPT 172

vein [n1] *mood, tone*
attitude, bent, character, characteristic, complexion, dash, disposition, faculty, fashion, fettle, hint, humor, line, manner, mind, mode, nature, note, spice, spirit, strain, streak, style, suggestion, suspicion, tang, temper, temperament, tenor, tinge, touch, trace, turn, wave, way; SEE CONCEPTS 411,673,682

vein [n2] *blood vessel*
capillary, course, current, duct, follicle, hair, lode, nerve, seam, stratum, streak, stripe, thread, venation; SEE CONCEPTS 393,420

velocity [n] *speed*
acceleration, celerity, dispatch, expedition, fleetness, gait, haste, headway, hurry, impetus, momentum, pace, quickness, rapidity, rapidness, rate, swiftness, tempo; SEE CONCEPTS 755,792

vendor [n] *person who sells wares*
businessman/woman, businessperson, dealer, hawker, huckster*, merchant, outcrier, peddler, pitchman/woman, roadman/woman, traveler, traveling salesperson; SEE CONCEPT 348

veneer [n] *pretence, front*
appearance, coating, cover, covering, disguise, exterior, facade, face, finish, gloss, guise, layer, leaf, mask, overlay, semblance, show, surface, window dressing*; SEE CONCEPTS 633,673,716

veneer [v] *cover, overlay*
blanch, coat, extenuate, face, finish, gloss, palliate, plate, shellac, sugarcoat, surface, varnish, whiten, whitewash; SEE CONCEPT 172

venerable [adj] *respected*
admirable, aged, august, dignified, esteemed, estimable, experienced, grand, grave, honorable, honored, imposing, matriarchal, noble, patriarchal, philosophical, revered, reverenced, reverend, sacred, sage, sedate, serious, stately, venerated, wise, worshipful, worshipped; SEE CONCEPT 574

vengeance [n] *retaliation for another's act*
avengement, avenging, counterblow, evening of score*, eye for an eye*, getting even*, repayment, reprisal, requital, retribution, return, revenge, settling of score*, tit for tat*, vengefulness, wrath; SEE CONCEPTS 29,384

vengeful [adj] *retaliating; hating*
antagonistic, avenging, hostile, implacable, inimical, punitive, rancorous, relentless, retaliatory, revenge-

ful, spiteful, unforgiving, vindictive; SEE CONCEPTS *401,542*

venom [*n*] *poison; hating*
acidity, acrimony, anger, bane, bitterness, contagion, gall, grudge, hate, hatred, ill will, infection, malevolence, malice, maliciousness, malignity, rancor, spite, spitefulness, spleen, taint, toxin, virulence, virus; SEE CONCEPTS *29,399*

venomous [*adj*] *poisonous; hateful*
accidentally on purpose*, antagonistic, baleful, baneful, catty*, cussed, deadly, destructive, dirty, evil, hostile, lethal, malefic, malevolent, malicious, malign, malignant, mean, mephitic, noxious, ornery, poisonous, rancorous, savage, spiteful, toxic, toxicant, vicious, vindictive, viperish, viperous, virulent, waspish; SEE CONCEPTS *537,542,544*

vent [*n*] *outlet*
aperture, avenue, chimney, drain, duct, exit, flue, hole, opening, orifice, pipe, split, spout, ventilator; SEE CONCEPTS *440,464*

vent [*v*] *let out; express*
air, assert, come out with, declare, discharge, drive out, emit, empty, express, give, give off, give out, issue, loose, pour out, provide escape, put, release, state, take out on, throw off*, unleash, utter, ventilate, verbalize, voice; SEE CONCEPTS *49,51,179*

ventilate [*v*] *air out; make known*
advertise, air, bring into the open, bring up, broach, broadcast, circulate, debate, deliberate, discourse, discuss, examine, express, free, give, go into, introduce, moot, publish, put, scrutinize, sift, state, take up, talk about, talk of, talk over, thresh out, vent, verbalize; SEE CONCEPTS *51,60*

venture [*n*] *gamble, attempt*
adventure, baby*, chance, deal, endeavor, enterprise, essay, experiment, exploit, feat*, hazard, header, investment, jeopardy, peril, pet project*, project, proposition, pursuit, risk, setup*, shot*, spec*, speculation, stab*, stake, test, thing*, trial, undertaking, wager; SEE CONCEPTS *87,675*

venture [*v*] *take a chance*
advance, assay, attempt, bet, brave, challenge, chance, dare, dare say*, defy, endanger, essay, experiment, expose, feel, front*, gamble, get down*, go out on a limb*, grope, have a fling at*, hazard, imperil, jeopardize, lay open, make a stab at*, make bold, operate, play for, play the market*, presume, put in jeopardy*, put up*, risk, speculate, stake, stick one's neck out*, take a crack at*, take a flyer*, take a plunge*, try, try out, volunteer, wager; SEE CONCEPTS *87,330,363*

venturesome [*adj*] *courageous*
adventurous, aggressive, audacious, bold, brave, daredevil, daring, enterprising, fearless, foolhardy, gutsy, intrepid, moxie*, overbold, plucky, pushy, rash, reckless, resourceful, risky, spirited, spunky, stalwart, stout, sturdy, temerarious, venturous; SEE CONCEPTS *401,548*

veracious [*adj*] *true*
accurate, credible, dependable, direct, ethical, factual, faithful, frank, genuine, high-principled, honest, just, kosher*, legit*, like it is*, on the level*, on the line*, on the up and up*, open, reliable, right, righteous, straight arrow, straightforward, strict, true-blue*, trustworthy, truthful, undeceptive, up front*, valid, veridical; SEE CONCEPTS *267,545,582*

veracity [*n*] *truth*
accuracy, actuality, authenticity, candor, correctness, credibility, exactitude, exactness, fact, fairness, fidelity, frankness, genuineness, gospel*, honest-to-god truth*, honesty, honor, impartiality, integrity, like it is*, openness, precision, probity, reality, real McCoy*, rectitude, rightness, sincerity, straight stuff*, trueness, truism, trustworthiness, truthfulness, uprightness, verisimilitude, verity, word*; SEE CONCEPTS *278,645*

verbal [*adj*] *spoken*
exact, expressed, lingual, literal, oral, rhetorical, said, stated, told, unwritten, verbatim, word-for-word*, word-of-mouth*; SEE CONCEPT *267*

verbatim [*adj*] *exactly*
accurately, direct, directly, literally, literatim, precisely, sic*, to the letter*, word-for-word*; SEE CONCEPTS *267,535*

verbiage [*n*] *repetition, wordiness*
circumlocution, expansiveness, floridity, long-windedness, loquacity, periphrase, periphrasis, pleonasm, prolixity, redundancy, tautology, verbosity; SEE CONCEPTS *278,695*

verbose [*adj*] *wordy, long-winded*
bombastic, circumlocutory, diffuse, flowery, full of air*, fustian, gabby*, garrulous, grandiloquent, involved, loquacious, magniloquent, palaverous, periphrastic, pleonastic, prolix, redundant, repeating, repetitious, repetitive, rhetorical, talkative, talky*, tautological, tautologous, tedious, tortuous, windy*, yacking*; SEE CONCEPT *267*

verdant [*adj*] *green, blooming*
flourishing, fresh, grassy, leafy, lush, verdurous; SEE CONCEPTS *485,618*

verdict [*n*] *law judgment*
adjudication, answer, arbitrament, award, conclusion, decision, decree, deduction, determination, finding, opinion, ruling, sentence; SEE CONCEPT *318*

verge [*n*] *extremity, limit*
border, borderline, boundary, brim, brink, edge, extreme, fringe, hem, lip, margin, point, rim, selvage, skirt, terminus, threshold; SEE CONCEPT *484*

verge [*v*] *come near*
abut, adjoin, approach, be on the edge*, border, bound, brink on, butt on*, communicate, edge, end, fringe, gravitate toward, hem, incline, join, lean, line, march, margin, neighbor, outline, rim, skirt, surround, tend, touch, trench, trend; SEE CONCEPTS *657,749*

verify [v] *confirm, validate*
add up*, attest, authenticate, bear out, certify, check, check out, check up, check up on*, confirm, corroborate, debunk, demonstrate, document, double-check, establish, eye*, eyeball*, find out, hold up, justify, make certain, make sure, pan out*, peg*, prove, settle, size*, size up*, stand up*, substantiate, support, test, try; SEE CONCEPTS *291,317*

verisimilitude [n] *authenticity*
color, credibility, genuineness, likeliness, likeness, plausibility, realism, resemblance, semblance, show, similarity; SEE CONCEPT *725*

veritable [adj] *authentic*
actual, bona fide, factual, for real, genuine, indubitable, kosher*, legit*, real, true, undoubted, unquestionable, very; SEE CONCEPT *582*

vernacular [n] *native language*
argot, cant, dialect, idiom, jargon, jive talk*, language, lingo, mother tongue*, parlance, patois, patter, phraseology, slang, speech, street talk*, tongue; SEE CONCEPT *276*

vernacular [adj] *native, colloquial*
common, dialectal, domesticated, idiomatic, indigenous, informal, ingrained, inherent, local, mother, natural, ordinary, plebian, popular, vulgar; SEE CONCEPTS *267,549*

versatile [adj] *adjustable, flexible*
able, accomplished, adaptable, adroit, all-around, all-purpose, ambidextrous, conversant, dexterous, elastic, facile, functional, gifted, handy, ingenuous, many-sided, mobile, multifaceted, plastic, pliable, protean, putty*, ready, resourceful, skilled, skillful, talented, variable, varied; SEE CONCEPTS *527,542*

verse [n] *written composition*
ballad, epic, jingle, lay, lyric, ode, poem, poesy, poetry, rhyme, rune, song, sonnet, stanza; SEE CONCEPT *282*

versed [adj] *experienced, informed*
abreast, accomplished, acquainted, au courant*, au fait*, competent, conversant, familiar, in the know*, knowledgeable, learned, practical, practiced, proficient, qualified, savvy, seasoned, skilled, trained, tuned in*, up*, up on*, versant, veteran, well-informed; SEE CONCEPTS *402,403,527*

version [n] *account of a happening*
adaptation, chronicle, clarification, condensation, construction, exercise, form, history, interpretation, narrative, paraphrase, portrayal, reading, redaction, rendering, rendition, report, restatement, rewording, side, simplification, sketch, statement, story, tale, transcription, translation, variant; SEE CONCEPT *282*

vertex [n] *top*
acme, apex, apogee, cap, cope, crest, crown, culmination, extremity, fastigium, height, peak, pinnacle, roof, summit, tip, upper extremity, zenith; SEE CONCEPT *836*

vertical [adj] *upright*
bolt upright, cocked, erect, on end, perpendicular, plumb, sheer, steep, straight-up, up-and-down, upward; SEE CONCEPTS *581,583*

very [adj] *real, exact*
actual, appropriate, authentic, bare, bona fide, correct, especial, express, genuine, ideal, identical, indubitable, mere, model, perfect, plain, precise, pure, right, same, selfsame, sheer, simple, special, sure-enough, true, undoubted, unqualified, unquestionable, veritable, very same; SEE CONCEPTS *535,557*

very [adv] *much, really; to a high degree*
absolutely, acutely, amply, astonishingly, awfully, certainly, considerably, dearly, decidedly, deeply, eminently, emphatically, exaggeratedly, exceedingly, excessively, extensively, extraordinarily, extremely, greatly, highly, incredibly, indispensably, largely, notably, noticeably, particularly, positively, powerfully, pressingly, pretty, prodigiously, profoundly, remarkably, substantially, superlatively, surpassingly, surprisingly, terribly, truly, uncommonly, unusually, vastly, wonderfully; SEE CONCEPTS *544,569,772*

vessel [n1] *ship*
barge, bark, bateau, boat, bottom, bucket*, can*, craft, liner, ocean liner, steamer, tanker, tub*, wagon; SEE CONCEPT *506*

vessel [n2] *container, bowl*
basin, kettle, pitcher, pot, receptacle, urn, utensil; SEE CONCEPT *494*

vest [v] *authorize, entrust*
belong, bestow, confer, consign, empower, endow, furnish, invest, lodge, pertain, place, put in the hands of*, settle; SEE CONCEPTS *50,88*

vestibule [n] *small room for arrivals*
antechamber, anteroom, doorway, entrance, entrance hall, entry, entryway, foyer, gateway, hall, hallway, lobby, narthex, porch, portal, portico; SEE CONCEPT *448*

vestige [n] *sign, indication*
evidence, glimmer, hint, memento, print, relic, remainder, remains, remnant, residue, scrap, shadow, suspicion, token, trace, track; SEE CONCEPTS *260,284,673*

veteran [n] *person with much experience; particularly in war*
expert, GI*, master, old guard*, old hand*, old pro*, old salt*, old soldier*, old-timer*, past master, past mistress, pro, shellback*, sourdough*, trouper, vet*, warhorse*; SEE CONCEPTS *358,423*

veteran [adj] *experienced, seasoned*
adept, battle-scarred*, been around*, disciplined, exercised, expert, from way back*, hardened, inured, knows one's stuff*, long-serving, long-time, not born yesterday*, of the old school*, old, old-time, practical, practiced, pro, proficient, skilled, sophisticated, steady, trained, up to speed*, versed, vet*, weathered, wise, wise to ways*, worldly; SEE CONCEPTS *402,527,678*

veto [n] *refusal of permission*
ban, blackball*, declination, denial, embargo, interdict, interdiction, negative, nonconsent, prohibition; SEE CONCEPTS *81,121,298,685*

veto [*v*] *refuse permission*
ban, blackball*, burn, cut, decline, defeat, deny, disallow, disapprove, discountenance, forbid, give thumbs down*, interdict, kill, negate, negative, nix*, not go for*, pass, pass by, pass on, prohibit, put down, refuse, reject, rule out*, shoot down*, throw away*, throw out*, thumbs down*, turn down; SEE CONCEPTS *50,81,88,121,298*

vex [*v*] *distress, bother*
abrade, afflict, aggravate, agitate, anger, annoy, be at, chafe, depress, displease, disquiet, disturb, eat*, embarrass, exasperate, fret, gall*, get in one's hair*, get under one's skin*, give a bad time*, give a hard time*, grate on*, harass, harry, hassle, infuriate, irk, irritate, molest, needle, nettle, offend, peeve, perplex, pester, pique, plague, provoke, put out*, rasp, ride, rile, tease, tick off*, torment, trouble, turn off*, upset, worry; SEE CONCEPTS *7,19*

vexatious [*adj*] *distressing, bothersome*
afflicting, aggravating, annoying, burdensome, disagreeable, disappointing, disturbing, exasperating, irksome, irritating, mean, nagging, pesky, provoking, teasing, tormenting, troublesome, troublous, trying, ugly, unpleasant, upsetting, wicked, worrisome, worrying; SEE CONCEPTS *529,537*

via [*prep*] *by way of*
along, as a means, by, by dint of*, by means of, by this route, by virtue of, on the way, over, per, through, through the medium of*, through this medium*, with; SEE CONCEPT *544*

viable [*adj*] *reasonable, practicable*
applicable, doable, feasible, operable, possible, usable, within possibility, workable; SEE CONCEPTS *552,560*

vibrant [*adj1*] *alive, colorful*
active, animated, dynamic, electrifying, energetic, lively, peppy, responsive, sensitive, sound, sparkling, spirited, vigorous, virile, vital, vivacious, vivid, zesty*, zippy*; SEE CONCEPTS *401,618*

vibrant [*adj2*] *throbbing*
aquiver, consonant, oscillating, palpitating, pulsating, pulsing, quaking, quivering, resonant, resounding, reverberant, ringing, sonoránt, sonorous, trembling; SEE CONCEPT *584*

vibrate [*v*] *shake, quiver*
beat, echo, fluctuate, flutter, jar, oscillate, palpitate, pulsate, pulse, quake, resonate, resound, reverberate, ripple, shiver, sway, swing, throb, tremble, tremor, undulate, wave, waver; SEE CONCEPTS *152,748*

vibration [*n*] *shaking, quivering*
beating, fluctuation, judder, oscillation, pulsation, pulse, quake, quiver, resonance, reverberation, shake, shimmy, throb, throbbing, trembling, tremor, vacillation, wave, wavering; SEE CONCEPTS *152,748*

vicarious [*adj*] *acting in another's place*
commissioned, delegated, deputed, empathetic, eventual, indirect, pretended, secondary, substituted, substitutional, surrogate, sympathetic; SEE CONCEPTS *401,538*

vice [*n1*] *bad habit; sin*
carnality, corruption, debasement, debauchery, decay, degeneracy, depravity, evil, evildoing, ill, immorality, indecency, iniquity, lechery, lewdness, libidinousness, licentiousness, looseness, lubricity, lust, maleficence, malignance, offense, perversion, profligacy, rot, sensuality, squalor, transgression, trespass, venality, wickedness, wrong; SEE CONCEPTS *372,645*

vice [*n2*] *weakness*
blemish, defect, demerit, failing, fault, flaw, foible, frailty, imperfection, mar, shortcoming, weak point; SEE CONCEPTS *411,657,666*

vice versa [*adv*] *contrary, oppositely*
about-face*, again, contra, contrariwise, conversely, far from it*, in reverse, on the contrary, the other way around*, turn about*; SEE CONCEPTS *544,564*

vicinity [*n*] *local area*
around*, ballpark*, district, environment, environs, hood, locality, nearness, neck of the woods*, neighborhood, precinct, pretty near*, propinquity, proximity, purlieus, range, region, surroundings, territory, turf, vicinage; SEE CONCEPTS *198,747*

vicious [*adj1*] *corrupt, wrong*
abandoned, abhorrent, atrocious, bad, barbarous, base, contaminated, cruel, dangerous, debased, degenerate, degraded, demoralized, depraved, diabolical, faulty, ferocious, fiendish, flagitious, foul, heinous, immoral, impious, impure, indecent, infamous, iniquitous, insubordinate, lewd, libidinous, licentious, miscreant, monstrous, nefarious, perverse, profligate, putrid, reprehensible, reprobate, rotten, savage, sinful, unprincipled, untamed, vile, villainous, violent, wicked, wild, worthless; SEE CONCEPTS *401,545,571*

vicious [*adj2*] *nasty, hateful*
backbiting*, beastly, bloodthirsty, brutal, cruel, cussed*, defamatory, despiteful, dirty*, evil, fierce, frightful, furious, horrid, intense, lousy*, malevolent, malicious, malign, mean, murderous, ornery, poisonous, rancorous, rough, savage, slanderous, spiteful, tough, vehement, venomous, vindictive, violent, wicked; SEE CONCEPTS *267,401,542*

vicissitude [*n*] *change*
about-face*, alteration, alternation, diversity, flip-flop*, fluctuation, innovation, mid-course correction*, mutability, mutation, novelty, permutation, progression, reversal, revolution, shift, sport, switch, switchover, transposition, turnaround, uncertainty, ups and downs*, variation, variety; SEE CONCEPT *697*

victim [*n*] *someone or something sacrificed, preyed upon*
babe in woods*, butt*, casualty, clown, dupe, easy make*, easy mark*, fall guy*, fatality, fool, gambit, gopher*, gudgeon*, gull*, hireling, hunted, immolation, injured party, innocent, mark, martyr, patsy, pawn*, pigeon*, prey, pushover*, quarry, sacrifice*,

scapegoat*, sitting duck*, sitting target*, soft touch*, stooge*, sucker*, sufferer, underdog, wretch*; SEE CONCEPTS *423,659*

victimize [v] *cheat, fool*
bamboozle*, burn*, chisel*, clip*, con, cozen, deceive, defraud, discriminate against, dupe, exploit, fleece*, flimflam*, gull*, have it in for*, hoax, hoodwink, immolate, persecute, pick on, pigeon*, prey on, rope in*, screw*, set up*, snow*, stack the deck*, stiff*, sting*, sucker*, swindle, take advantage of, trick, use; SEE CONCEPTS *14,59,192*

victor [n] *person who wins*
champ, champion, conquering hero/heroine*, conqueror, defeater, first*, gold medallist, greatest, hero/heroine, king, master, medalist, prizewinner, queen, subjugator, title holder, top*, top dog*, vanquisher, winner; SEE CONCEPTS *366,416*

victorious [adj] *successful, winning*
arrived, champion, conquering, mastering, on top, prizewinning, triumphant, vanquishing; SEE CONCEPT *528*

victory [n] *win, success*
achievement, advantage, ascendancy, bull's-eye*, clean sweep*, conquest, control, defeat, defeating, destruction, dominion, feather in cap*, gain, grand slam*, hit, hole in one*, killing*, laurels, mastery, mission accomplished*, overthrow, prize, subjugation, superiority, supremacy, sweep, the gold*, triumph, upper hand*, upset, winning; SEE CONCEPTS *95,671,706,832*

vie [v] *compete*
be rivals, buck, challenge, contend, contest, counter, go for*, go for broke*, go for the gold*, go for the jugular*, jockey for position*, match, oppose, pit, play, play off, push, rival, scramble for, strive, struggle, sweat; SEE CONCEPTS *92,363*

view [n1] *something that is seen*
appearance, aspect, composition, contour, design, field of vision, glimpse, illustration, landscape, look, opening, outline, outlook, panorama, perspective, picture, prospect, range of vision, representation, scene, seascape, show, sight, spectacle, stretch, tableau, vision, vista, way; SEE CONCEPT *628*

view [n2] *examination*
analysis, audit, check, contemplation, display, eyeball*, flash*, gander*, inspection, lamp*, look, looksee, perlustration, review, scan, scrutiny, sight, slant, squint*, survey, viewing; SEE CONCEPTS *24,103*

view [n3] *belief*
attitude, belief, close-up, concept, conception, consideration, conviction, deduction, eye*, feeling, impression, inference, judgment, judgment call*, mind, notion, opinion, persuasion, point of view, say-so*, sentiment, slant*, thought, twist, two cents' worth*, value judgment, way of thinking; SEE CONCEPT *689*

view [v1] *look at*
beam, behold, canvass, check out, check over, consider, contemplate, descry, dig, discern, distinguish,

eagle eye*, espy, examine, explore, eye*, feast eyes on*, flash*, gaze, get a load of*, inspect, lay eyes on, mark, notice, observe, perceive, pipe*, read, regard, rubberneck*, scan, scope, scrutinize, see, set eyes on, spot, spy, stare, survey, take in*, watch, witness; SEE CONCEPTS *623,626*

view [v2] *believe*
account, consider, deem, judge, look on, reckon, regard, think about; SEE CONCEPT *12*

viewpoint [n] *way of thinking*
angle, aspect, attitude, direction, estimation, eye*, frame of reference, ground, light, long view, outlook, perspective, point of observation, point of view, position, posture, respect, side, slant, stance, stand, standpoint, twist, two cents' worth*, vantage point, view; SEE CONCEPT *689*

vigilance [n] *carefulness*
acuity, alertness, attention, attentiveness, caution, circumspection, diligence, lookout, observance, surveillance, vigil, watch, watchfulness; SEE CONCEPTS *644,657*

vigilant [adj] *careful, watchful*
acute, agog, alert, anxious, attentive, aware, cautious, circumspect, got it covered*, guarded, keen, looking for, looking to, observant, on alert, on guard, on the ball*, on the job*, on the lookout, on the qui vive*, on toes*, open-eyed*, sharp, sleepless, unsleeping, waiting on, wakeful, wary, wide-awake, with eyes peeled*, with weather eye open*; SEE CONCEPTS *401,542,576*

vigor [n] *power, energy*
ability, action, activity, agility, alertness, bang*, birr, bounce, capability, capacity, dash, drive, dynamism, endurance, enterprise, exercise, fire, force, get-up-and-go*, go*, hardiness, healthiness, intensity, juice*, kick*, liveliness, lustiness, manliness, might, motion, moxie*, muscle*, nimbleness, pep*, pith, potency, puissance, punch*, push, quickness, snap*, sock, soundness, starch*, steam*, strength, tuck*, urgency, vehemence, vim, vitality, well-being, zing*, zip*; SEE CONCEPTS *316,411,732*

vigorous [adj] *energetic, powerful*
active, athletic, ball of fire*, bouncing, brisk, dashing, driving, dynamic, effective, efficient, enterprising, exuberant, fertile, flourishing, forceful, forcible, hale, hard-driving, hardy, healthy, hearty, intense, lively, lusty, masterful, mettlesome, peppy, persuasive, potent, red-blooded*, robust, rugged, snappy, sound, spanking, spirited, steamroller*, strapping, strenuous, strong, strong as an ox*, sturdy, take-charge*, take-over*, tough, virile, vital, zealous, zippy*; SEE CONCEPTS *314,404,489*

vile [adj] *offensive, horrible*
abandoned, abject, appalling, bad, base, coarse, contemptible, corrupt, debased, degenerate, depraved, despicable, dirty, disgraceful, disgusting, evil, filthy, foul, horrid, humiliating, ignoble, immoral, impure, iniquitous, loathsome, low, mean, miserable, nasty,

nauseating, nefarious, noxious, perverted, repellent, repugnant, repulsive, revolting, shocking, sickening, sinful, sleazy*, stinking*, ugly, vicious, vulgar, wicked, worthless, wretched; SEE CONCEPTS **529,545,571**

vilify [v] *criticize very harshly*
abuse, asperse, assail, attack, bad-mouth*, berate, blister, call down*, caluminate, censure, cuss, damn, debase, decry, defame, denigrate, denounce, dig*, disparage, dress down*, dump on*, give a black eye*, jinx, knock, libel, malign, mistreat, mudsling*, pan*, put a whammy on*, put down*, rag on*, rap*, revile, rip up*, roast*, run down, scorch, skin alive*, slam*, slander, slur, smear*, speak ill of, tear down*, tear into*, traduce, vituperate, voodoo*; SEE CONCEPTS **44,52**

village [n] *small town*
center, crossroads, hamlet, suburb; SEE CONCEPT **507**

villain [n] *evil person*
antihero, bad guy*, blackguard*, brute, caitiff, creep*, criminal, devil, enfant terrible*, evildoer, heel, knave, libertine, lowlife*, malefactor, mischief-maker*, miscreant, offender, profligate, rapscallion, rascal, reprobate, rogue, scoundrel, sinner, wretch; SEE CONCEPT **412**

vindicate [v] *prove one's innocence*
absolve, acquit, advocate, argue, assert, bear out, claim, clear, confute, contend, corroborate, defend, disculpate, disprove, do justice to, establish, exculpate, excuse, exonerate, extenuate, free, free from blame, guard, justify, maintain, plead for, protect, prove, rationalize, refute, rehabilitate, second, shield, substantiate, support, uphold, warrant, whitewash*; SEE CONCEPTS **49,57,317**

vindictive [adj] *hateful, revengeful*
avenging, cruel, grim, grudging, implacable, malicious, malignant, merciless, rancorous, relentless, resentful, retaliatory, ruthless, spiteful, unforgiving, unrelenting, vengeful, venomous, wreakful; SEE CONCEPTS **401,542**

vintage [n] *crop, especially of wine*
collection, epoch, era, generation, grapes, harvest, origin, wine, year; SEE CONCEPT **429**

vintage [adj] *superior*
best, choice, classic, classical, excellent, mature, old, prime, rare, ripe, select, selected, venerable; SEE CONCEPTS **574,578,797**

violate [v1] *break a law, agreement*
breach, contaminate, contravene, defy, disobey, disregard, disrupt, encroach, err, infract, infringe, meddle, offend, oppose, outrage, profane, resist, sacrilege, sin, tamper with, trample on, transgress, trespass, withstand; SEE CONCEPTS **101,192**

violate [v2] *rape, defile*
abuse, assault, befoul, debauch, defile, deflorate, deflower, desecrate, dishonor, force, invade, outrage, pollute, profane, ravish, spoil; SEE CONCEPTS **246,375**

violation [n1] *breach; breaking of the law*
abuse, break, breaking, contravention, encroachment, illegality, infraction, infringement, misbehavior, misdemeanor, negligence, nonobservance, offense, rupture, transgressing, transgression, trespass, trespassing, violating, wrong; SEE CONCEPTS **101,192**

violation [n2] *rape, defilement*
assault, blasphemy, debasement, defacement, defacing, degradation, desecration, destruction, devastation, dishonor, invasion, mistreatment, outrage, pollution, profanation, rapine, ravishment, ruin, sacrilege, spoliation; SEE CONCEPTS **246,252,375**

violence [n] *extreme force, intensity*
abandon, acuteness, assault, attack, bestiality, bloodshed, blowup, brutality, brute force, clash, coercion, compulsion, confusion, constraint, cruelty, destructiveness, disorder, disturbance, duress, ferocity, fervor, fierceness, fighting, flap, foul play, frenzy, fury, fuss, harshness, murderousness, onslaught, passion, power, raging, rampage, roughness, ruckus, rumble, savagery, severity, sharpness, storm, storminess, struggle, terrorism, tumult, turbulence, uproar, vehemence, wildness; SEE CONCEPTS **29,641,669,675**

violent [adj1] *destructive*
agitated, aroused, berserk, bloodthirsty, brutal, coercive, crazy, cruel, demoniac, desperate, distraught, disturbed, enraged, fierce, fiery, forceful, forcible, frantic, fuming, furious, great, headstrong, homicidal, hotheaded*, hysterical, impassioned, impetuous, inflamed, intemperate, mad, maddened, maniacal, mighty, murderous, passionate, potent, powerful, raging, riotous, rough, savage, strong, uncontrollable, ungovernable, unrestrained, urgent, vehement, vicious, wild; SEE CONCEPTS **401,540,544**

violent [adj2] *severe, extreme*
acute, agonizing, biting, blustery, coercive, concentrated, devastating, excruciating, exquisite, forceful, forcible, gale force*, great, harsh, immoderate, inordinate, intense, mighty, outrageous, painful, potent, powerful, raging, rough, ruinous, sharp, strong, tempestuous, terrible, tumultous/tumultuous, turbulent, wild; SEE CONCEPTS **525,569**

virgin/virginal [adj] *brand-new, unused*
abstinent, celibate, chaste, first, fresh, idle, immaculate, initial, innocent, intact, modest, natural, new, original, primeval, pristine, pure, single, snowy*, spotless, uncorrupted, undefiled, undisturbed, unmarred, unmarried, unspoiled, unsullied, untapped, untested, untouched, untried, unwed, vestal, white*; SEE CONCEPTS **372,560,578,797**

virile [adj] *potent, powerful*
brave, driving, energetic, forceful, generative, lusty, macho*, male, manlike, mannism, masculine, procreative, red-blooded*, reproductive, robust, sound, strong, vibrant, vigorous, vital; SEE CONCEPTS **372,401,404**

virtual [adj] in essence
basic, constructive, essential, fundamental, implicit, implied, in all but name*, in conduct, indirect, in effect, in practice, potential, practical, pragmatic, tacit, unacknowledged; SEE CONCEPTS 487,537,544, 573

virtually [adv] for all practical purposes
around, as good as, basically, effectually, essentially, for all intents and purposes*, fundamentally, give or take a little*, guesstimate*, implicitly, in all but name*, in effect, in essence, in substance, in the ballpark*, in the neighborhood*, morally, nearly, not absolutely, not actually, practically, something like, upwards of; SEE CONCEPTS 487,544,573

virtue [n] honor, integrity
advantage, asset, character, charity, chastity, consideration, credit, ethic, ethicality, ethicalness, excellence, faith, faithfulness, fineness, fortitude, generosity, goodness, good point*, high-mindedness, hope, ideal, incorruptibility, innocence, justice, kindness, love, merit, morality, plus, probity, prudence, purity, quality, rectitude, respectability, righteousness, temper, temperance, trustworthiness, uprightness, value, virginity, worth, worthiness; SEE CONCEPTS 411,645

virtuoso [n] person who is an expert
ace, adept, artist, artiste, authority, big league*, brain*, celebrity, champ*, champion, crackerjack*, dillettante, egghead, genius, hotshot*, hot stuff*, intelligent, maestro, magician, master, maven, musician, natural*, no slouch*, old hand*, old pro*, past master, performer, pro, prodigy, professional, pundit, sharp*, star, superstar, whiz*, wizard; SEE CONCEPTS 348,352,416

virtuous [adj] good, ethical; innocent
blameless, celibate, chaste, clean-living, effective, effectual, efficient, excellent, exemplary, faithful, guiltless, high-principled, honest, honorable, incorruptible, inculpable, in the clear*, irreprehensible, kosher*, legit*, moral, moralistic, noble, on the level*, on the up and up*, praiseworthy, principled, pure, regular, righteous, right-minded, spotless, straight, true-blue*, unsullied, untainted, untarnished, up front*, upright, virginal, wholesome, without reproach, worthy; SEE CONCEPTS 401,545

virulent [adj1] poisonous, lethal
baneful, deadly, destructive, fatal, harmful, infective, injurious, malign, malignant, mephitic, pernicious, poison, septic, toxic, toxicant, unhealthy, unwholesome, venomous; SEE CONCEPTS 537,571

virulent [adj2] hostile
acrimonious, antagonistic, bitter, cutting, hateful, malevolent, malicious, rancorous, resentful, scathing, sharp, spiteful, splenetic, stabbing, unfriendly, venomous, vicious, vindictive, vitriolic; SEE CONCEPTS 267,542

viscous [adj] sticky, gummy
adhesive, clammy, gelatinous, gluey*, glutinous, gooey*, mucilaginous, ropy, slimy*, stiff, syrupy, tenacious, thick, tough, viscid; SEE CONCEPT 606

visible [adj] apparent, seeable
arresting, big as life*, bold, clear, conspicuous, detectable, discernible, discoverable, distinguishable, evident, inescapable, in sight, in view, macroscopic, manifest, marked, not hidden, noticeable, observable, obtrusive, obvious, ocular, open, out in the open, outstanding, palpable, patent, perceivable, perceptible, plain, pointed, pronounced, revealed, salient, seen, signal, striking, to be seen, unconcealed, under one's nose*, unhidden, unmistakable, viewable, visual; SEE CONCEPTS 529,576,619

vision [n1] ability to perceive with eyes
eyes*, eyesight, faculty, optics, perceiving, perception, range of view, seeing, sight, view; SEE CONCEPT 629

vision [n2] mental image, concept
angle, aspect, astuteness, breadth of view, castles in the air*, conception, daydream, discernment, divination, dream, facet, fancy, fantasy, far-sightedness, foreknowledge, foresight, head trip*, idea, ideal, ideality, imagination, insight, intuition, keenness, mental picture, muse, nightmare, outlook, penetration, perspective, phantasm, pie in the sky*, pipe dream*, point of view, prescience, retrospect, slant, standpoint, trip, understanding, view; SEE CONCEPTS 529,532,689

vision [n3] apparition
apocalypse, chimera, delusion, ecstasy, fantasy, ghost, hallucination, haunt, illusion, mirage, nightmare, oracle, phantasm, phantom, phenomenon, presence, prophecy, revelation, specter, spirit, spook, trance, warlock, wraith; SEE CONCEPTS 370,529

vision [n4] very beautiful thing or person
angel*, dazzler, dream, eyeful*, feast for the eyes*, perfect picture*, picture, sight, sight for sore eyes*, spectacle, stunner; SEE CONCEPTS 424,529

visionary [n] person who dreams, is idealistic
castle-builder*, daydreamer, Don Quixote*, dreamer, enthusiast, idealist, mystic, prophet, romancer, romantic, seer, stargazer, theorist, utopian, zealot; SEE CONCEPTS 361,416

visionary [adj] idealized, romantic
abstracted, ambitious, astral, chimerical, daydreaming, delusory, dreaming, dreamy, exalted, fanciful, fantastic, grandiose, ideal, idealist, idealistic, illusory, imaginary, impractical, in the clouds*, introspective, lofty, musing, noble, otherworldly, pretentious, prophetic, quixotic, radical, speculative, starry-eyed, unreal, unrealistic, unworkable, unworldly, utopian; SEE CONCEPTS 529,560,582

visit [n] social call upon another
appointment, call, evening, holiday, interview, sojourn, stay, stop, stopover, talk, tarriance, vacation, visitation, weekend; SEE CONCEPTS 226,227

visit [v1] be a guest of
call, call on, chat, come around, come by, converse, crash, drop by, drop in, drop over, dwell, frequent,

go over to, go to see, hit, inspect, look around, look in on, look up, pay a call*, pay a visit to, play, pop in*, reside, see, sojourn, stay at, stay with, step in, stop by, stop off, swing by*, take in, talk, tarry, tour; SEE CONCEPTS 226,227

visit [v2] *bother, haunt*
afflict, assail, attack, avenge, befall, bring down on, descend upon, force upon, impose, inflict, pain, punish, smite, trouble, wreak, wreck; SEE CONCEPTS *7,14,19*

visitor [n] *person temporarily in a foreign location*
caller, company, guest, habitué, inspector, invitee, out-of-towner, transient, visitant; SEE CONCEPT *423*

visual [adj] *able to be seen with eyes*
beheld, discernible, imaged, observable, observed, ocular, optic, optical, perceptible, seeable, seen, viewable, viewed, visible, visional; SEE CONCEPTS *485,576,619*

visualize [v] *make a picture of in the mind*
anticipate, apprehend, bring to mind, call to mind, call up, conceive of, conjure up, create, divine, dream up, envisage, envision, fancy, feature, foresee, get the picture*, image, imagine, object, picture, reflect, see, see in the mind's eye*, think, view, vision; SEE CONCEPTS *17,34*

vital [adj1] *essential*
basic, bottom-line*, cardinal, coal-and-ice*, constitutive, critical, crucial, decisive, fundamental, heavy*, imperative, important, indispensable, integral, key, life-or-death*, meaningful, meat-and-potatoes*, name, name-of-the-game*, necessary, needed, nitty-gritty*, prerequisite, required, requisite, significant, underlined, urgent; SEE CONCEPTS *546,567*

vital [adj2] *lively*
animated, dynamic, energetic, forceful, lusty, red-blooded, spirited, strenuous, vibrant, vigorous, virile, vivacious, zestful; SEE CONCEPT *401*

vital [adj3] *alive*
animate, animated, breathing, generative, invigorative, life-giving, live, living, quickening; SEE CONCEPT *539*

vitality [n] *energy, spirit*
animation, ardor, audacity, bang, being, bloom, bounce, clout, continuity, drive, endurance, existence, exuberance, fervor, force, get-up-and-go*, go, guts*, intensity, life, liveliness, lustiness, pep, pizzazz*, power, pulse, punch, robustness, snap, sparkle, spunk*, stamina, starch*, steam, strength, stuff*, venturesomeness, verve, vigor, vim, virility, vivaciousness, vivacity, zest*, zing*, zip*; SEE CONCEPTS *407,411,633*

vitiate [v1] *cancel*
abate, abolish, abrogate, annihilate, annul, delete, deny, invalidate, negate, nullify, quash, recant, revoke, undermine, undo; SEE CONCEPTS *121,317*

vitiate [v2] *hurt, corrupt*
blemish, blight, brutalize, contaminate, damage, debase, debauch, defile, deprave, deteriorate, devalue, harm, impair, injure, mar, pervert, pollute, prejudice, spoil, sully, taint, tarnish, violate, warp, water down, weaken; SEE CONCEPTS *246,250*

vituperate [v] *criticize harshly*
abuse, accuse, asperse, bark at*, bawl out*, berate, blame, calumniate, castigate, censure, chew out*, condemn, curse, denounce, find fault, growl, insult, lambaste, lash, malign, rail, rate, reproach, revile, rip into*, run down*, scold, smear, tear into*, tongue-lash*, traduce, upbraid, vilify, yell at; SEE CONCEPTS *44,52,54*

vivacious [adj] *lively, spirited*
active, alert, animate, animated, bouncy, brash, breezy, bubbling, cheerful, ebullient, effervescent, exuberant, frolicsome, full of life, gay, happy, high-spirited, jolly, jumping, keen, lighthearted, merry, playful, rocking, scintillating, sparkling, sportive, sprightly, swinging, upbeat, vibrant, vital, zesty; SEE CONCEPTS *401,404*

vivid [adj] *intense, powerful*
active, animated, bright, brilliant, clear, colorful, definite, distinct, dramatic, dynamic, eloquent, energetic, expressive, flamboyant, gay, glowing, graphic, highly colored, lifelike, lively, lucid, meaningful, memorable, picturesque, realistic, resplendent, rich, sharp, shining, spirited, stirring, striking, strong, telling, theatrical, true-to-life, vigorous; SEE CONCEPTS *537,569,618*

vocabulary [n] *language of a person or people*
cant, dictionary, glossary, jargon, lexicon, palaver, phraseology, terminology, thesaurus, wordbook, word-hoard*, words, word-stock; SEE CONCEPTS *276,280*

vocal [adj1] *spoken*
articulate, articulated, choral, expressed, intonated, lyric, modulated, operatic, oral, phonetic, phonic, pronounced, put into words*, said, singing, sonant, sung, uttered, verbal, viva voce, vocalic, vocalized, voiced, vowel; SEE CONCEPTS *267,594*

vocal [adj2] *extroverted about opinion*
articulate, blunt, clamorous, eloquent, expressive, facile, fluent, forthright, frank, free, free-spoken, glib, noisy, outspoken, plain-spoken, round, smooth-spoken, stentorian, strident, venting, vociferous; SEE CONCEPTS *267,404*

vocalize [v] *put into words or song*
belt out*, canary*, chant, chirp, communicate, convey, croon, emit, enunciate, express, give out*, groan, impart, let out*, moan, pronounce, say, shout, sing, sound, speak, talk, utter, vent, verbalize, voice, warble, yodel; SEE CONCEPT *77*

vocation [n] *life's work*
art, business*, calling, career, craft, do*, dodge*, duty, employment, field, game, handicraft, job, life-work, line*, line of business, métier, mission, nine-to-five*, occupation, office, post, profession, pursuit, racket*, role, thing*, trade, undertaking; SEE CONCEPTS *349,360*

vociferous [*adj*] *loud, insistent*
boisterous, clamant, clamorous, distracting, loud-mouthed, noisy, obstreperous, ranting, shouting, shrill, strident, uproarious, vehement, vociferant; SEE CONCEPTS *267,592,594*

vogue [*n*] *fashion; current practice*
chic, craze*, currency, custom, dernier cri*, fad*, fashionableness, favor, in thing*, last word*, latest, mode, popularity, practice, prevalence, rage*, style, stylishness, thing*, trend, usage, use, way; SEE CONCEPT *655*

vogue [*adj*] *fashionable*
faddy*, in*, latest, mod*, modish, now, popular, prevalent, rage*, state-of-the-art, trendy, up-to-the-minute*, with it*; SEE CONCEPT *589*

voice [*n1*] *expression, language*
articulation, call, cry, delivery, exclamation, inflection, intonation, modulation, murmur, mutter, roar, shout, song, sound, speech, statement, tone, tongue, utterance, vent, vocalization, vociferation, words, yell; SEE CONCEPTS *77,276*

voice [*n2*] *opinion*
approval, choice, decision, expression, option, part, participation, preference, representation, right of free speech, say, say-so*, suffrage, vent, view, vote, vox populi*, will, wish; SEE CONCEPTS *278,376*

voice [*v*] *express opinion; put into words*
air, announce, articulate, assert, come out with*, cry, declare, deliver, divulge, emphasize, enunciate, give expression, give utterance, inflect, intonate, modulate, present, proclaim, pronounce, put, recount, say, sound, speak, talk, tell, utter, vent, verbalize, vocalize; SEE CONCEPTS *49,51*

void [*n*] *emptiness, want*
blank, blankness, cavity, gap, hole, hollow, lack, nihility, nothingness, nullity, opening, space, vacuity, vacuum; SEE CONCEPTS *513,646,709*

void [*adj1*] *empty*
abandoned, bare, barren, bereft, clear, deprived, destitute, devoid, drained, emptied, free, lacking, scant, short, shy, tenantless, unfilled, unoccupied, vacant, vacuous, without; SEE CONCEPTS *481,583,740,774*

void [*adj2*] *nullified, meaningless*
avoided, bad, dead, forceless, fruitless, ineffective, ineffectual, inoperative, invalid, negated, not viable, nugatory, null, null and void, set aside, sterile, unconfirmed, unenforceable, unfruitful, unratified, unsanctioned, unsuccessful, useless, vain, voided, worthless; SEE CONCEPT *560*

void [*v1*] *get rid of; empty*
clear, deplete, discharge, dispose, drain, dump, eject, eliminate, emit, evacuate, flow, give off, go, pour, relieve, remove, throw out, vacate; SEE CONCEPTS *179,180*

void [*v2*] *nullify, cancel*
abnegate, abrogate, annul, black out*, bleep*, blue pencil*, clean up, cut, declare null and void*, discharge, dissolve, drop*, gut*, invalidate, launder,

rescind, sanitize, sterilize, take out, trim, vacate; SEE CONCEPTS *50,88,121,211*

volatile [*adj*] *explosive, changeable*
airy, buoyant, capricious, effervescent, elastic, elusive, ephemeral, erratic, expansive, fickle, fleeting, flighty, flippant, frivolous, fugacious, fugitive, gaseous, gay, giddy, impermanent, imponderable, inconsistent, inconstant, light, lively, lubricious, mercurial, momentary, playful, resilient, short-lived, sprightly, subtle, temperamental, ticklish, transient, transitory, unsettled, unstable, unsteady, up and down, vaporous, variable, whimsical; SEE CONCEPTS *401,534*

volition [*n*] *free will*
accord, choice, choosing, conation, desire, determination, discretion, election, option, preference, purpose, resolution, selection, will, willingness, wish; SEE CONCEPTS *20,41*

volume [*n1*] *capacity, measure of capacity*
aggregate, amount, body, bulk, compass, content, contents, cubic measure, dimensions, extent, figure, mass, number, object, quantity, size, total; SEE CONCEPTS *719,740,794*

volume [*n2*] *loudness of a sound*
amplification, degree, intensity, power, sonority, strength; SEE CONCEPTS *65,792*

volume [*n3*] *book*
album, edition, publication, tome, treatise, version; SEE CONCEPT *280*

voluminous [*adj*] *big, vast*
abundant, ample, billowing, bulky, capacious, cavernous, comprehensive, convoluted, copious, covering, expansive, extensive, full, great, large, legion, many, massive, multifarious, multitudinous, numerous, prolific, roomy, several, simple, spacious, sundry, swelling, various; SEE CONCEPTS *773,781*

voluntarily [*adv*] *of one's own free will*
at one's discretion, by choice, by preference, deliberately, freely, intentionally, of one's own accord*, on one's own, on one's own initiative*, optionally, spontaneously, willingly, with all one's heart*, without being asked, without prompting; SEE CONCEPTS *538,544*

voluntary [*adj*] *willing*
autonomous, chosen, deliberate, designful, discretional, elected, free, freely, free-willed, gratuitous, honorary, independent, intended, intentional, opted, optional, spontaneous, unasked, unbidden, uncompelled, unconstrained, unforced, unpaid, unprescribed, volitional, volunteer, willed, willful, wished, witting; SEE CONCEPTS *538,544*

volunteer [*v*] *offer to do something*
advance, bring forward, chip in*, come forward, do on one's own volition*, enlist, go in*, let oneself in for*, offer services, present, proffer, propose, put at one's disposal*, put forward, sign up, speak up, stand up, step forward, submit oneself, suggest, take

bull by the horns*, take initiative*, take the plunge*, take upon oneself*, tender; SEE CONCEPTS *66,67*

voluptuous [*adj*] *well-developed, erotic*
ample, buxom, curvaceous, curvy, enticing, fleshly, full-bosomed, luscious, lush, luxurious, provocative, seductive, sensual, sensuous, shapely, wanton; SEE CONCEPTS *372,485*

vomit [*v*] *disgorge*
be seasick*, be sick, bring up*, dry heave*, eject, emit, expel, gag*, heave*, hurl*, puke*, regurgitate, retch, ruminate, spew, spit up, throw up, upchuck*; SEE CONCEPTS *179,185,308*

voracious [*adj*] *very hungry, greedy*
avid, covetous, devouring, dog-hungry, edacious, empty, gluttonous, gorging, grasping, gross, insatiable, omnivorous, piggy, prodigious, rapacious, ravening, ravenous, sating, starved, starved to death*, starving, uncontrolled, unquenchable; SEE CONCEPTS *20,401*

vote [*n*] *decision or right to decide representation*
aye*, ballot, choice, franchise, majority, nay*, plebiscite, poll, referendum, secret ballot, show of hands*, suffrage, tally, ticket, will, wish, yea*, yes or no*; SEE CONCEPTS *300,376*

vote [*v*] *decide on representation*
ballot, cast ballot, cast vote, choose, confer, declare, determine, effect, elect, enact, enfranchise, establish, go to the polls*, grant, judge, opt, pronounce, propose, put in office*, recommend, return, second, suggest; SEE CONCEPTS *41,300*

vouch [*v*] *give assurance*
act as a witness, affirm, answer for, assert, asseverate, assure, attest to, avert, avow, back, bear testimony, be responsible for, certify, confirm, contend, corroborate, cosign, declare, get behind*, give an affidavit, guarantee, maintain, okay*, predicate, profess, prove, put forth, rubber-stamp*, say so*, sign for, sponsor, stand up for*, substantiate, support, swear to, swear up and down*, testify, uphold, verify, vow, warrant, witness; SEE CONCEPTS *49,71,317*

vow [*n*] *promise*
affiance, assertion, asseveration, oath, pledge, profession, troth, word of honor; SEE CONCEPTS *278,689*

vow [*v*] *make a solemn promise*
affirm, assure, consecrate, covenant, cross one's heart*, declare, dedicate, devote, give word of honor*, pledge, plight, promise, swear, swear up and down*, testify, undertake solemnly*, vouch, warrant; SEE CONCEPTS *71,297*

voyage [*n*] *journey, often by water*
boating, crossing, cruise, excursion, hop, jaunt, junket, overnight, passage, sail, swing, tour, travel, travels, trek, trip, weekend; SEE CONCEPTS *155,224*

vulgar [*adj1*] *rude, offensive*
base, blue*, boorish, cheap, coarse, common, contemptible, crude, dirty, disgusting, dishonorable, filthy, fractious, gross*, hard-core*, ignoble, impolite, improper, indecent, indecorous, indelicate, in-

ferior, low, malicious, nasty, naughty, obscene, odious, off-color*, profane, raw, repulsive, ribald, risqué, rough, rude, scatological, slippery, smutty*, sneaking, soft-core*, sordid, suggestive, tasteless, tawdry, uncouth, unmannerly, unrefined, unworthy, villainous, X-rated*; SEE CONCEPTS *267,372,545*

vulgar [*adj2*] *common, general*
colloquial, conversational, dime a dozen*, everyday, familiar, garden variety*, low, native, ordinary, plastic, plebeian, popular, public, run-of-the-mill*, unrefined, vernacular; SEE CONCEPT *530*

vulnerable [*adj*] *open to attack*
accessible, assailable, defenseless, exposed, liable, naked, on the line*, on the spot*, out on a limb*, ready, sensitive, sitting duck*, sucker*, susceptible, tender, thin-skinned*, unguarded, unprotected, unsafe, weak, wide open*; SEE CONCEPTS *403,587*

W

wacky [*adj*] *acting crazy*
absurd, balmy, crazed, crazy, daft, demented, deranged, eccentric, erratic, foolish, hare-brained, insane, irrational, loony*, lunatic, mad, nuts*, nutty*, odd, preposterous, screwy*, silly, unpredictable, wild, zany*; SEE CONCEPTS *401,403*

wad [*n*] *ball of something*
back, block, boodle, bunch, bundle, chunk, clump, cushion, fortune, gathering, heap, hunk, lining, lump, mass, mint, nugget, packet, pad, pile, plug, pot, ream, roll, slew, stuff, tuft, wadding; SEE CONCEPTS *432,436*

waddle [*v*] *walk like a duck*
rock, shuffle, sway, toddle, totter, wiggle, wobble; SEE CONCEPT *151*

wade [*v*] *plod, often through water*
attack, attempt, bathe, drudge, fall to, ford, get feet wet*, get stuck in*, go for, initiate, jump in, labor, launch, light into, paddle, pitch in, set about, set to, splash, start, stumble, tackle, tear into*, toil, trek, walk, work through; SEE CONCEPTS *87,151*

waft [*v*] *carry*
bear, be carried, blow, carry, convey, drift, float, ride, transmit, transport; SEE CONCEPTS *147,217*

wag [*n*] *person who is very funny*
a million laughs*, card*, clown, comedian, comic, cutup*, droll*, farceur*, funnyman/woman, funster, humorist, jester*, joker, jokester, kibitzer*, kidder, life of the party*, madcap*, prankster, punster, quipster, show-off*, trickster, wisecracker, wit, zany; SEE CONCEPTS *416,423*

wag [*v*] *wiggle back and forth*
beat, bob, fish-tail*, flutter, lash, move side to side, nod, oscillate, quiver, rock, shake, shimmy, stir, sway, swing, switch, twitch, vibrate, waggle, wave; SEE CONCEPTS *150,152*

wage/wages [*n*] *earnings for work*
allowance, bacon*, bacon and eggs*, bread*, compensation, cut, emolument, fee, hire, pay, payment,

price, receipts, recompense, remuneration, return, returns, reward, salary, share, stipend, sugar*, take*, take-home*; SEE CONCEPT *344*

wage [v] *carry on*
carry out, conduct, do, engage in, fulfill, make, practice, proceed with, prosecute, pursue, undertake; SEE CONCEPTS *91,100*

wager [n] *money or something gambled*
action, ante*, bet, challenge, chunk, fifty-fifty*, fighting chance*, flyer*, gamble, handle, hazard, hedge, hunch, long shot*, odds on*, outside chance*, parlay, play, pledge, plunge, pot*, risk, stake, toss-up, venture; SEE CONCEPTS *329,363,364*

wager [v] *bet money or something else in a gamble*
adventure, chance, gamble, game, hazard, hedge, hustle, lay, lay a wager, parlay, play, play the market*, pledge, plunge, put on*, put on the line*, put up, risk, set*, shoot*, shoot the works*, spec*, speculate, stake, take action, venture; SEE CONCEPTS *28,363*

waif [n] *young person who is poor*
drop, fetch, foundling, guttersnipe, homeless child, mudlark, orphan, ragamuffin, stray; SEE CONCEPTS *414,423*

wail [v] *cry loudly*
bawl*, bay, bemoan, bewail, carry on*, complain, cry the blues*, deplore, fuss, grieve, howl, jowl, keen, kick, lament, moan, mourn, repine, sob, squall, ululate, weep, whimper, whine; SEE CONCEPTS *77,185*

wait [n] *pause, delay*
down, downtime*, halt, hold*, hold-up, interim, interval, on hold*, rest, stay, time wasted*; SEE CONCEPT *807*

wait [v] *pause, rest*
abide, anticipate, await, bide, bide one's time*, cool it*, dally, delay, expect, fill time, foresee, hang, hang around, hang onto your hat*, hang out, hold back, hold everything*, hold on, hold the phone*, hole up*, keep shirt on*, lie in wait*, lie low*, linger, look for, look forward to, mark time*, put on hold*, remain, save it*, sit tight*, sit up for*, stall, stand by, stay, stay up for, stick around*, sweat it*, tarry, watch; SEE CONCEPTS *210,681*

wait on [v] *serve*
arrange, attend, care for, deal, deliver, help, minister, mother, nurse, portion, ready, set, tend; SEE CONCEPTS *136,324*

waive [v] *give up; let go*
abandon, allow, cede, defer, delay, disclaim, disown, dispense with, forgo, grant, hand over, hold off, hold up, leave, neglect, postpone, prorogue, put off, refrain from, reject, relinquish, remit, remove, renege, renounce, reserve, resign, set aside, shelve, stay, surrender, suspend, table, turn over, yield; SEE CONCEPTS *121,234,317*

waiver [n] *giving up; letting go*
abandonment, abdication, disclaimer, forgoing, postponement, refusal, rejection, relinquishment, remis-

sion, renunciation, reservation, resignation, setting aside, surrender, tabling; SEE CONCEPTS *121,318,685*

wake [n1] *formal observance of a body before funeral*
deathwatch, funeral service, last rites, obsequies, rites, vigil, watch; SEE CONCEPTS *367,377*

wake [n2] *trail behind something*
aftermath, backwash, furrow, path, track, train, wash, wave; SEE CONCEPTS *753,824*

wake/waken [v1] *stop sleeping*
arise, awake, awaken, be roused, bestir, bring to life*, call, come to, get out of bed*, get up, nudge, open one's eyes*, prod, rise, rise and shine*, roll out, rouse, shake, stir, stretch, tumble out*, turn out, wake up; SEE CONCEPT *105*

wake/waken [v2] *excite, stimulate*
activate, animate, arouse, awaken, challenge, enliven, fire, fire up*, freshen, galvanize, grasp, jazz up*, key up*, kindle, notice, pep up*, provoke, quicken, rally, renew, rouse, see, steam up*, stir up, switch on*, understand, whet, zip up*; SEE CONCEPTS *7,14,22*

wakeful [adj] *alert, restless*
alive, astir, attentive, careful, heedful, insomniac, insomnious, observant, on guard, on the alert*, on the lookout*, on the qui vive*, sleepless, unsleeping, vigilant, waking, wary, watchful, wide-awake; SEE CONCEPTS *539,542*

walk [n1] *brief travel on foot*
airing, carriage, circuit, constitutional, gait, hike, jaunt, march, pace, parade, perambulation, peregrination, promenade, ramble, saunter, schlepp*, step, stretch, stride, stroll, tour, traipse, tramp, tread, turn; SEE CONCEPTS *149,224*

walk [n2] *pathway*
aisle, alley, avenue, boardwalk, boulevard, bricks, bypath, byway, catwalk, cloister, course, court, crossing, esplanade, footpath, gangway, lane, mall, passage, path, pavement, pier, platform, promenade, road, sidewalk, street, track, trail; SEE CONCEPT *501*

walk [n3] *discipline*
area, arena, bailiwick, calling, career, course, domain, dominion, field, line, metier, profession, province, sphere, terrain, territory, trade, vocation; SEE CONCEPTS *349,360*

walk [v] *move along on foot*
advance, amble, ambulate, canter, escort, exercise, file, foot, go, go on foot*, hike, hit the road*, hoof it, knock about*, lead, leg*, locomote, lumber, march, meander, pace, pad, parade, patrol, perambulate, plod, prance, promenade, race, roam, rove, run, saunter, scuff, shamble, shuffle, slog, stalk, step, stride, stroll, strut, stump, take a walk, toddle, tour, traipse, tramp, travel on foot*, traverse, tread, trek, troop, trudge, wander, wend one's way*; SEE CONCEPT *149*

wall [n] *obstruction, divider*
bank, bar, barricade, barrier, block, blockade, bulwark, curb, dam, embankment, enclosure, facade,

fence, fortification, hindrance, hurdle, impediment, levee, limitation, palisade, panel, paneling, parapet, partition, rampart, restriction, retainer, roadblock, screen, side, stockade, stop, surface; SEE CONCEPTS *440,666*

wallop [*n*] *strong hit*
bash, belt, blow, bop, bump, clash, collision, crash, haymaker, impact, jar, jolt, kick, percussion, punch, shock, slam, slug, smack, smash, thump, thwack, whack; SEE CONCEPT *189*

wallop [*v1*] *beat, hit*
bam, bash, batter, belt, blast, boff, bop, buffet, bushwhack, clobber*, drub*, hide, lambaste*, paste, pelt, plant one*, pound, pummel, punch, slam, slog, slug, smack, smash, sock, strike, swat, take out, tan*, thrash, thump, whack, wham, whomp, zap*; SEE CONCEPT *189*

wallop [*v2*] *defeat soundly*
beat, best, clobber*, crush*, drub*, lambaste*, lick*, rout, shellac*, thrash*, trim*, trounce, vanquish, whip*; SEE CONCEPT *95*

wallow [*v1*] *slosh around in*
bathe in, be immersed, blunder, flounder, get stuck, immerse, lie, loll, lurch, move around in, reel, roll, roll about, roll around in, splash around, sprawl, stagger, stumble, sway, toss, totter, tumble, wade, welter; SEE CONCEPTS *149,201*

wallow [*v2*] *become very involved in*
bask, delight, enjoy, glory, grovel, humor, indulge oneself, luxuriate, pamper, relish, revel, roll, rollick, spoil, take pleasure; SEE CONCEPT *384*

wan [*adj*] *colorless, weak*
anemic, ashen, ashy, bilious, blanched, bleached, bloodless, cadaverous, dim, discolored, faint, feeble, forceless, ghastly, haggard, impotent, ineffective, ineffectual, livid, pale, pallid, pasty, peaked, sickly, washed-out, waxen, white, worn; SEE CONCEPTS *314,618*

wand [*n*] *rod*
baton, caduceus, scepter, sprig, staff, stick, twig; SEE CONCEPTS *470,499*

wander [*v1*] *move about aimlessly*
aberrate, amble, circumlocute, circumnutate, cruise, deviate, divagate, diverge, drift, float, follow one's nose*, gad*, gallivant*, globe-trot, hike, hopscotch*, jaunt, maunder, meander, peregrinate, ramble, range, roam, roll, rove, saunter, straggle, stray, stroll, take to the road*, trail, traipse*, tramp, trek, vagabond, walk the tracks*; SEE CONCEPTS *151,224*

wander [*v2*] *digress; get lost*
babble, depart, deviate, divagate, diverge, err, get off the track*, get sidetracked*, go astray*, go off on a tangent*, lose one's way, lose train of thought*, ramble, rave, shift, stray, swerve, talk nonsense*, veer; SEE CONCEPTS *101,266,665*

wanderer [*n*] *person who travels aimlessly*
adventurer, beachcomber, bum, drifter, explorer, floater, gad*, gadabout, gallivanter, globe-trotter,

gypsy, itinerant, meanderer, nomad, pilgrim, rambler, ranger, roamer, rolling stone*, rover, straggler, stray, stroller, traveler, vagabond, vagrant, voyager; SEE CONCEPT *423*

wane [*v*] *diminish, lessen*
abate, atrophy, decline, decrease, die away, die down, die out, dim, draw to a close*, drop, dwindle, ease off, ebb, fade, fade away, fail, fall, fall short, let up, moderate, peter out*, relent, shrink, sink, slacken, slack off, subside, taper off, waste away, weaken, wind down, wither; SEE CONCEPTS *698,776*

want [*n1*] *desire*
appetite, craving, demand, fancy, hankering, hunger, longing, necessity, need, requirement, thirst, wish, yearning, yen; SEE CONCEPT *20*

want [*n2*] *lack, need*
absence, dearth, default, defect, deficiency, destitution, exigency, exiguousness, famine, impecuniousness, impoverishment, inadequacy, indigence, insufficiency, meagerness, neediness, paucity, pauperism, penury, poorness, poverty, privation, scantiness, scarcity, shortage, skimpiness; SEE CONCEPTS *646,709*

want [*v1*] *desire*
ache, aspire, be greedy, choose, could do with, covet, crave, desiderate, fancy, feel a need, hanker, have ambition, have an urge for, have a passion for*, have eyes for*, hunger, incline toward, itch for, long, lust, need, pine, prefer, require, spoil for, thirst, wish, yearn, yen for; SEE CONCEPT *20*

want [*v2*] *lack, need*
be deficient, be deprived of, be found wanting, be insufficient, be poor, be short of, be without, call for, demand, fall short in, have need of, miss, require, stand in need of, starve; SEE CONCEPT *646*

wanting [*adj*] *lacking, inadequate*
absent, away, bankrupt, bereft, burned out*, cooked*, cut off, defective, deficient, deprived, destitute, devoid, disappointing, empty, failing, faulty, gone, half-baked*, imperfect, incomplete, in default, inferior, less, minus, missing, needed, not good enough, not up to par*, omitted, out of gas*, patchy, poor, scant, scanty, scarce, short, shy, sketchy, substandard, too little too late*, unfulfilled, unsound; SEE CONCEPTS *531,546,560*

wanton [*n*] *profligate person*
debauchee, libertine, pampered person, prostitute, rake, spoiled person; SEE CONCEPTS *412,415,419*

wanton [*adj1*] *extravagant, lustful*
abandoned, dissipated, dissolute, fast*, fickle, inconsiderate, lax, lewd, libertine, libidinous, licentious, of easy virtue*, of loose morals*, outrageous, profligate, promiscuous, rakish, shameless, speedy, unchaste, unconscionable, unprincipled, unscrupulous, wayward, X-rated*; SEE CONCEPTS *372,401,545*

wanton [*adj2*] *cruel, malicious*
accidentally on purpose*, arbitrary, contrary, double-crossing*, evil, gratuitous, groundless, malevolent,

malicious, mean, merciless, motiveless, needless, ornery, perverse, senseless, spiteful, unasked,
uncalled-for*, unfair, unjust, unjustifiable, unjustified, unprovoked, vicious, wayward, wicked, willful; SEE CONCEPT *401*

wanton [*adj3*] *careless*
capricious, changeable, devil-may-care*, extravagant, fanciful, fickle, fitful, fluctuating, free, frivolous, heedless, hot and cold*, immoderate,
inconstant, intemperate, lavish, outrageous, prodigal, profuse, rash, reckless, spendthrift, spoiled,
thriftless, unfettered, unreserved, unrestrained, up
and down*, variable, volatile, wasteful, whimsical,
wild; SEE CONCEPTS *534,542*

war [*n*] *armed conflict*
battle, bloodshed, cold war, combat, conflict, contention, contest, enmity, fighting, hostilities, hostility, police action, strife, strike, struggle, warfare;
SEE CONCEPT *320*

war [*v*] *fight, battle*
attack, attempt, bombard, campaign against, challenge, clash, combat, contend, contest, differ, disagree, endeavor, engage in combat, go to war, kill,
make war, march against, meet, murder, oppugn,
shell, shoot, strive, struggle, take on, take the field
against*, take up arms, tug, wage war; SEE CONCEPTS
106,320

ward [*n1*] *district*
area, canton, department, diocese, division, parish,
precinct, quarter, territory, zone; SEE CONCEPTS
508,513

ward [*n2*] *custody; person in one's custody*
adopted child, care, charge, child, client, dependent,
foster child, godchild, guardianship, keeping, minor,
orphan, pensioner, protection, protégé, protégée, pupil, safekeeping, trust; SEE CONCEPTS *414,691*

ward/ward off [*v*] *defend, guard*
avert, avoid, beat off, block, check, deflect, deter,
divert, fend, foil, forestall, frustrate, halt, hold off,
interrupt, keep at arm's length*, keep at bay*, keep
off, obviate, parry, preclude, prevent, rebuff, rebut,
repel, repulse, rule out, stave off, stop, stymie*,
thwart, turn, turn aside, turn away; SEE CONCEPTS
96,134

warden [*n*] *person who guards and manages*
administrator, bodyguard, caretaker, curator, custodian, deacon, dogcatcher, gamekeeper, governor,
guard, guardian, jailer/jailor, janitor, keeper, officer,
overseer, prison head, ranger, skipper, steward, superintendent, watchdog, watchman/woman; SEE
CONCEPT *347*

wardrobe [*n*] *clothes or furniture for storing clothes*
apparel, attire, buffet, bureau, chest, chiffonier,
closet, clothing, commode, costumes, cupboard,
drapes*, dresser, dry goods, duds*, ensembles, garments, locker, outfits, rags*, suits, threads*, toggery, togs, trousseau, trunk, vestments, weeds*; SEE
CONCEPTS *443,451*

warehouse [*n*] *storage place*
barn, bin, depository, depot, distribution center, establishment, repository, shed, stash house, stockpile,
stockroom, store, storehouse; SEE CONCEPTS *439,449*

wares [*n*] *merchandise for sale*
articles, commodities, goods, line, lines, manufac-
tures, material, produce, product, products, range,
seconds, stock, stuff, vendibles; SEE CONCEPT *338*

warfare [*n*] *armed conflict*
armed struggle, arms, battle, blows, campaigning,
clash, combat, competition, contest, counterinsurgency, discord, emulation, fighting, hostilities, military operation, passage of arms, rivalry, strategy,
strife, striving, struggle, tug-of-war*, war; SEE CON-
CEPT *320*

warlike [*adj*] *hostile, battling*
aggressive, attacking, bellicose, belligerent, bloodthirsty, combative, contending, contentious, contrary, fighting, gladiatorial, hawkish, inimical,
martial, militant, militaristic, military, offensive,
pugnacious, quarrelsome, ructious, soldierly, truculent, unfriendly, warmongering, warring; SEE CON-
CEPTS *401,548*

warm [*adj1*] *moderately hot*
balmy, broiling, clement, close, flushed, glowing,
heated, hot, lukewarm, melting, mild, perspiring,
pleasant, roasting, scorching, sizzling, snug, summery, sunny, sweating, sweaty, sweltering, temperate, tepid, thermal, toasty, warmish; SEE CONCEPT
605

warm [*adj2*] *friendly, kind*
affable, affectionate, amiable, amorous, ardent,
cheerful, compassionate, cordial, empathetic, fervent, genial, gracious, happy, heartfelt, hearty, hospitable, kindhearted, kindly, loving, pleasant,
responsive, sincere, softhearted, sympathetic, tender, warmhearted, wholehearted; SEE CONCEPTS
267,401,404

warm [*adj3*] *enthusiastic*
amorous, angry, animated, ardent, earnest, effusive,
emotional, excitable, excited, fervent, fervid, glowing, gung-ho*, heated, hot*, intense, irascible, keen,
lively, nutty*, passionate, spirited, stormy, vehement, vigorous, violent, zealous; SEE CONCEPTS
401,542

warm [*v*] *heat up*
bake, chafe, cook, fix, heat, melt, microwave, prepare, put on the fire, thaw, toast, warm over, warm
up; SEE CONCEPTS *170,255*

warn [*v*] *give notice of possible occurrence*
acquaint, address, admonish, advise, advocate, alert,
apprise, caution, clue, clue in*, counsel, cry wolf*,
deprecate, direct, dissuade, enjoin, exhort, fill in,
forbid, forearm, forewarn, give fair warning, give
the high sign*, give warning*, guide, hint, inform,
instruct, lay it out*, make aware, notify, order, post,
predict, prepare, prescribe, prompt, put on guard*,
recommend, remind, remonstrate, reprove, signal,

suggest, summon, tell, threaten, tip, tip off*, urge, wise up*; SEE CONCEPT *78*

warning [n] *notice of possible occurrence*
admonition, advice, alarm, alert, augury, caution, caveat, distress signal, example, exhortation, fore, foretoken, forewarning, guidance, handwriting on wall*, heads up*, hint, indication, information, injunction, intimation, lesson, look out*, Mayday*, notification, omen, portent, prediction, premonition, presage, recommendation, sign, signal, SOS*, suggestion, threat, tip, tip-off*, token, watch-it*, wink, word, word to the wise*; SEE CONCEPTS *78,274*

warning [adj] *cautionary*
admonishing, admonitory, cautioning, exemplary, exhortatory, monitorial, monitory, ominous, premonitory, threatening; SEE CONCEPT *267*

warp [v] *bend, distort*
bastardize*, brutalize, color, contort, corrupt, crook, curve, debase, debauch, deform, deprave, deviate, misrepresent, misshape, pervert, swerve, torture, turn, twist, vitiate, wind; SEE CONCEPTS *63,137,213,250*

warrant [n] *authorization*
accreditation, assurance, authentication, authority, basis, carte blanche, certificate, commission, credential, credentials, ducat, earnest, foundation, go-ahead*, green light*, guarantee, license, official document, okay*, pass, passport, pawn, permission, permit, pledge, right, sanction, security, shingle, sticker, subpoena, summons, tag, testimonial, ticket, token, verification, warranty, word; SEE CONCEPTS *376,685*

warrant [v] *guarantee, justify, authorize*
affirm, answer for, approve, argue, assert, assure, attest, avouch, back, bear out, call for, certify, claim, commission, contend, declare, defend, delegate, demand, empower, endorse, ensure, entitle, excuse, explain, give grounds for, guarantee, guaranty, insure, license, maintain, necessitate, permit, pledge, privilege, promise, require, sanction, secure, sponsor, stand behind, state, stipulate, swear, take an oath, undertake, underwrite, uphold, vindicate, vouch for, vow; SEE CONCEPTS *50,57,71,88*

warranty [n] *promise*
assurance, bail, bond, certificate, contract, covenant, guarantee, guaranty, pledge, security, surety, written promise; SEE CONCEPTS *684,685*

warrior [n] *person who fights in combat*
battler, champion, combatant, conscript, enlisted man/woman, enlisted person, fighter, fighting man/woman, fighting person, GI*, GI Joe*, hero, man-at-arms, serviceman/woman, serviceperson, soldier, trooper; SEE CONCEPT *358*

wary [adj] *careful, cautious*
alert, attentive, cagey*, calculating, canny, chary, circumspect, considerate, discreet, distrustful, doubting, frugal, gingerly, guarded, handling with kid gloves*, heedful, keeping on one's toes*, leery, on guard, on the lookout*, on the qui vive*, provident, prudent, safe, saving, sly, sparing, suspicious, thinking twice*, thrifty, unwasteful, vigilant, walking on eggs*, watchful, watching one's step*, watching out, wide-awake; SEE CONCEPTS *401,403*

wash [n1] *laundry, bath*
ablution, bathe, cleaning, cleansing, dirty clothes, laundering, rinse, scrub, shampoo, shower, washing; SEE CONCEPTS *451,514*

wash [n2] *wave; water movement*
ebb and flow, eddy, flow, gush, heave, lapping, murmur, roll, rush, spurt, surge, surging, sweep, swell, swirl, swishing, undulation; SEE CONCEPT *748*

wash [n3] *coloring*
coat, coating, film, layer, overlay, rinse, stain, suffusion, swab; SEE CONCEPT *475*

wash [v1] *bathe, clean*
bath, brush up, bubble, cleanse, clean up, dip, do the dishes*, do the laundry*, douse, drench, float, freshen up*, fresh up, hose, imbue, immerse, lap, launder, lave, moisten, rinse, scour, scrub, shampoo, shine, shower, slosh, soak, soap, sponge, starch, swab, take a bath*, take a shower*, tub, wash up*, wet, wipe; SEE CONCEPT *165*

wash [v2] *be convincing*
be acceptable, bear scrutiny, be plausible, be reasonable, carry weight, convince, endure, hold up, hold water*, stand up*, stick*; SEE CONCEPT *676*

waste [n1] *spending, use without thought*
decay, desolation, destruction, devastation, dilapidation, dissipation, disuse, exhaustion, expenditure, extravagance, fritter, havoc, improvidence, lavishness, loss, lost opportunity*, misapplication, misuse, overdoing, prodigality, ravage, ruin, squander, squandering, unthriftiness, wastage, wastefulness; SEE CONCEPTS *156,252*

waste [n2] *land that is uncultivated*
badlands, barren, bog, brush, brushland, bush, desert, dust bowl, fen, jungle, marsh, marshland, moor, quagmire, solitude, swamp, tundra, void, wasteland, wild, wilderness, wilds; SEE CONCEPT *509*

waste [n3] *garbage, refuse*
debris, dreck, dregs, dross, excess, hogwash, junk, leavings, leftovers, litter, offal, offscourings, rubbish, rubble, ruins, rummage, scrap, slop, sweepings, swill, trash; SEE CONCEPT *260*

waste [v1] *spend or use without thought; dwindle*
atrophy, be of no avail*, blow, burn up, consume, corrode, crumble, debilitate, decay, decline, decrease, deplete, disable, disappear, dissipate, divert, drain, droop, eat away, ebb, emaciate, empty, enfeeble, exhaust, fade, fritter away*, frivol away*, gamble away, gnaw, go to waste, lavish, lose, misapply, misemploy, misuse, perish, pour down the drain*, prodigalize, run dry, run through*, sap, sink, splurge, squander, thin, throw away, trifle away, undermine, wane, wear, wear out, wilt, wither; SEE CONCEPT *156*

waste [v2] *ruin, destroy*
depredate, desecrate, desolate, despoil, devastate, devour, lay waste, pillage, rape, ravage, raze, reduce, sack, spoil, spoliate, wreak havoc; SEE CONCEPT *252*

wasteful [*adj*] *not economical*
careless, cavalier, destructive, dissipative, extravagant, immoderate, improvident, incontinent, lavish, liberal, overdone, overgenerous, pound-foolish*, prodigal, profligate, profuse, reckless, ruinous, spendthrift, squandering, thriftless, uneconomical, unthrifty, wanton, wild; SEE CONCEPT *401*

watch [*n1*] *clock worn on body*
analog watch, chronometer, digital watch, pocket watch, stopwatch, ticker*, timepiece, timer, wristwatch; SEE CONCEPT *463*

watch [*n2*] *lookout*
alertness, attention, awareness, duty, eagle eye*, eye*, gander, guard, hawk, heed, inspection, notice, observance, observation, patrol, picket, scrutiny, sentinel, sentry, supervision, surveillance, tab, tout, vigil, vigilance, watchfulness, weather eye*; SEE CONCEPTS *134,623*

watch [*v1*] *look at*
attend, case, check out, concentrate, contemplate, eagle-eye*, examine, eye*, eyeball*, focus, follow, gaze, get a load of*, give the once over*, have a look-see*, inspect, keep an eye on*, keep tabs on*, listen, look, mark, mind, note, observe, pay attention, peer, pipe, regard, rubberneck*, scan, scope, scrutinize, see, spy, stare, take in, take notice, view, wait; SEE CONCEPT *623*

watch [*v2*] *guard, protect*
attend, be on alert*, be on the lookout*, be vigilant*, be wary, be watchful, care for, keep, keep eyes open*, keep eyes peeled*, keep watch over, look after, look out, mind, oversee, patrol, pick up on, police, ride shotgun for*, superintend, take care of, take heed*, tend, wait; SEE CONCEPTS *134,623*

watchful [*adj*] *on the lookout*
alert, all ears*, attentive, careful, cautious, chary, circumspect, glued*, guarded, heedful, hooked*, keen, not missing a trick*, observant, on guard, on one's toes*, on the ball*, on the job*, on the qui vive*, on the watch, open-eyed, prepared, ready, see after, see to, suspicious, unsleeping, vigilant, wakeful, wary, wide-awake, with eyes peeled*; SEE CONCEPT *401*

watchman/woman [*n*] *person who guards, is on lookout*
caretaker, curator, custodian, detective, flagman/woman, guard, keeper, lookout, observer, patrol, patrolman/woman, picket, policeman/woman, ranger, scout, security guard, security man/woman, sentinel, sentry, signalman/woman, spotter, spy, ward, warden, watch, watcher; SEE CONCEPT *348*

water [*n*] *pure liquid hydrogen and oxygen*
Adam's ale*, aqua, aqua pura*, drink, H_2O, rain, rainwater, saliva, tears; SEE CONCEPT *467*

water [*v*] *dampen; put water in*
baptize, bathe, damp, dilute, doctor, douse, drench, drool, flood, hose, imbue, inundate, irrigate, moisten, saturate, soak, sodden, souse, spatter, spray, sprinkle, steep, thin, wash, weaken, wet; SEE CONCEPT *256*

watery [*adj*] *liquid, diluted*
adulterated, anemic, aqueous, bloodless, colorless, damp, dilute, doused, flavorless, fluid, humid, insipid, marshy, moist, pale, runny, serous, sodden, soggy, tasteless, thin, washed, watered-down, waterlike, water-logged, weak, wet; SEE CONCEPTS *485,603,618*

wave [*n*] *sea surf, current*
bending, billow, breaker, coil, comber, convolution, corkscrew, crest, crush, curl, curlicue, drift, flood, foam, ground swell, gush, heave, influx, loop, movement, outbreak, rash, ridge, ripple, rippling, rocking, roll, roller, rush, scroll, sign, signal, stream, surge, sweep, swell, tendency, tide, tube, twirl, twist, undulation, unevenness, uprising, upsurge, whitecap, winding; SEE CONCEPTS *147,436,514*

wave [*v*] *move back and forth; gesture*
beckon, billow, brandish, coil, curl, direct, falter, flap, flourish, flow, fluctuate, flutter, fly, gesticulate, indicate, motion, move to and fro, oscillate, palpitate, pulsate, pulse, quaver, quiver, reel, ripple, seesaw, shake, sign, signal, stir, stream, surge, sway, swell, swing, swirl, swish, switch, tremble, twirl, twist, undulate, vacillate, vibrate, wag, waggle, waver, whirl, wield, wigwag, wobble; SEE CONCEPTS *74,147,149*

waver [*v*] *shift back and forth; be indecisive*
be irresolute, be unable to decide*, blow hot and cold*, change, deliberate, dilly-dally*, dither, falter, flicker, fluctuate, halt, hedge, hem and haw*, hesitate, oscillate, palter, pause, pussyfoot around*, quiver, reel, run hot and cold*, seesaw*, shake, stagger, sway, teeter, totter, tremble, trim, undulate, vacillate, vary, waffle, wave, weave, whiffle, wobble, yo-yo*; SEE CONCEPTS *18,147,410*

wax [*v*] *become large, fuller*
augment, become, build, come, develop, dilate, enlarge, expand, fill out, get bigger, get to, grow, grow full, heighten, increase, magnify, mount, multiply, rise, run, swell, turn, upsurge; SEE CONCEPTS *704,780*

way [*n1*] *method, technique*
action, approach, contrivance, course, course of action, custom, design, expedient, fashion, form, groove*, habit, habitude, hang-up*, hook*, idea, instrument, kick, manner, means, measure, mode, modus, move, outline, plan, plot, policy, practice, procedure, process, scheme, shot, step, stroke, style, system, tack, thing*, usage, use, vehicle, wise, wont; SEE CONCEPT *6*

way [*n2*] *direction, route*
access, admission, admittance, advance, alternative, approach, artery, avenue, bearing, boulevard, by-

way, channel, course, distance, door, drag*, elbow-room, entrance, entrée, entry, extent, forward motion, gate, gateway, headway, highway, ingress, journey, lane, length, line, march, movement, opening, orbit, passage, path, pathway, progress, progression, ride, road, room, row, space, stone's throw*, street, stretch, tendency, thataway*, thoroughfare, track, trail, trend, walk; SEE CONCEPTS *501,738,739*

way [*n3*] *characteristic, habit*
aspect, behavior, circumstance, condition, conduct, consuetude, custom, detail, fashion, feature, fettle, form, gait, groove, guise, habit, hook, idiosyncrasy, kick*, manner, nature, particular, personality, point, practice, praxis, respect, sense, shape, shot, situation, state, status, style, thing*, tone, trait, trick, usage, use, wont; SEE CONCEPT *411*

wayfaring [*adj*] *traveling*
drifting, gadabout, globe-trotting, itinerant, itinerate, jet-setting*, journeying, nomadic, perambulant, perambulatory, peripatetic, rambling, roving, rubbernecking*, vagabond, vagrant, voyaging, walking, wandering; SEE CONCEPT *401*

waylay [*v*] *intercept, ambush*
accost, ambuscade, assail, attack, box*, bushwhack*, catch, hold up, intercept, jump, lay for*, lie in wait, lurk, pounce on, prowl, set upon, skulk, slink, surprise, swoop down*; SEE CONCEPTS *86,121*

wayward [*adj*] *contrary, unmanageable*
aberrant, arbitrary, balky, capricious, changeable, contumacious, cross-grained, delinquent, disobedient, disorderly, errant, erratic, fickle, flighty, fractious, froward, headstrong, immoral, inconstant, incorrigible, insubordinate, intractable, mulish, obdurate, obstinate, ornery, perverse, rebellious, recalcitrant, refractory, restive, self-indulgent, self-willed, stubborn, uncompliant, undependable, ungovernable, unpredictable, unruly, unstable, variable, whimsical, willful; SEE CONCEPT *401*

weak [*adj1*] *not strong*
anemic, debilitated, decrepit, delicate, effete, enervated, exhausted, faint, feeble, flaccid; flimsy, forceless, fragile, frail, hesitant, impotent, impuissant, infirm, insubstantial, irresolute, lackadaisical*, languid, languorous, limp, makeshift, out of gas*, powerless, prostrate, puny, rickety*, rocky*, rotten, senile, shaky, sickly, sluggish, spent, spindly, supine, tender, torpid, uncertain, undependable, unsound, unsteady, unsubstantial, wasted, wavering, weakened, weakly, wobbly; SEE CONCEPTS *314,488,489*

weak [*adj2*] *cowardly*
faint-hearted, fluctuant, frightened, hesitant, impotent, indecisive, ineffectual, infirm, insecure, irresolute, laid-back*, nerveless, nervous, palsied, powerless, shaky, soft, spineless, tender, timorous, uncertain, undependable, unmanly, unreliable, unstable, unsure, vacillating, wavering, weak-kneed*,

wimpy*, wishy-washy*, wobbly, zero*; SEE CONCEPTS *402,403,542*

weak [*adj3*] *faint, soft*
bated, dim, distant, dull, feeble, gentle, imperceptible, inaudible, indistinct, low, muffled, pale, poor, quiet, reedy, slight, small, stifled, thin, unaccented, unstressed, whispered; SEE CONCEPT *594*

weak [*adj4*] *deficient, feeble*
faulty, flabby, flimsy, forceless, green*, handicapped, hollow, immature, implausible, impotent, improbable, inadequate, incompetent, incomplete, inconceivable, inconclusive, incredible, ineffective, ineffectual, inept, invalid, lacking, lame, limited, pathetic, poor, raw, shaky, shallow, slight, slim, small, spineless, substandard, thick, thin, unbelievable, unconvincing, unprepared, unqualified, unsatisfactory, unsubstantial, unsure, untrained, wanting; SEE CONCEPTS *537,558,570*

weak [*adj5*] *exposed, vulnerable*
accessible, assailable, defenseless, helpless, indefensible, unguarded, unprotected, unsafe, untenable, wide open, woundable; SEE CONCEPTS *576,587*

weak [*adj6*] *watered-down*
dilute, diluted, insipid, milk-and-water*, runny, tasteless, thin, washy, waterish, watery, wishy-washy*; SEE CONCEPTS *462,485*

weaken [*v*] *reduce the strength of*
abate, adulterate, break up, castrate, cripple, crumble, cut, debase, debilitate, decline, decrease, depress, devitalize, dilute, diminish, droop, dwindle, ease up, emasculate, enervate, exhaust, fade, fail, faint, flag, give way, halt, impair, impoverish, invalidate, languish, lessen, limp, lose, lose spirit, lower, minimize, mitigate, moderate, reduce, relapse, relax, sap, slow down, soften, temper, thin, thin out, tire, totter, tremble, undermine, unman, vitiate, wane, water down, wilt; SEE CONCEPTS *240,698*

weakling [*n*] *person who has no strength*
baby, chicken*, chicken heart*, coward, cream puff*, crybaby, dotard, invertebrate, jellyfish*, misfit, pushover, wimp*, yellow belly*; SEE CONCEPTS *412,423*

weakness [*n*] *defect, proneness*
Achilles heel*, appetite*, blemish, chink in armor*, debility, decrepitude, deficiency, delicacy, enervation, failing, faintness, fault, feebleness, flaw, fondness, fragility, frailty, gap, impairment, imperfection, impotence, inclination, inconstancy, indecision, infirmity, instability, invalidity, irresolution, lack, languor, lapse, liking, passion, penchant, powerlessness, predilection, proclivity, prostration, senility, shortcoming, soft spot*, sore point*, taste*, vice, vitiation, vulnerability; SEE CONCEPTS *411,674,732*

wealth [*n*] *money, resources*
abundance, affluence, assets, belongings, bounty, cache, capital, cash, clover*, commodities, copiousness, cornucopia, dough*, estate, fortune, funds,

gold, goods, hoard, holdings, lap of luxury*, long green*, lucre, luxuriance, luxury, means, opulence, pelf, plenitude, plenty, possessions, profusion, property, prosperity, prosperousness, revenue, riches, richness, security, stocks and bonds, store, substance, substantiality, treasure, velvet*, worth; SEE CONCEPTS 340,710

wealthy [adj] rich; having a lot of money
affluent, booming, comfortable, have it made*, independent, in the money*, loaded, made of money*, moneyed, of independent means, opulent, pecunious, prosperous, rolling in it*, substantial, upscale, well-heeled*, well-off*, well-to-do*; SEE CONCEPT 334

wear [n] use, corrosion
abrasion, attrition, damage, depreciation, deterioration, dilapidation, diminution, disappearance, employment, erosion, friction, impairment, inroads, loss, mileage, service, usefulness, utility, waste, wear and tear; SEE CONCEPTS 658,698

wear [v1] be clothed in
array, attire, bear, be dressed in, carry, clothe oneself, cover, display, don, draw on, dress in, effect, exhibit, fit out, get into, get on, harness, have on, put on, show, slip on, sport, suit up*, turn out*, wrap; SEE CONCEPTS 167,453

wear [v2] corrode, use
abrade, become threadbare, become worn, be worthless, chafe, consume, crumble, cut down, decay, decline, decrease, deteriorate, diminish, drain, dwindle, erode, exhaust, fade, fatigue, fray, gall, go to seed*, graze, grind, impair, jade, overuse, overwork, rub, scrape, scrape off, scuff, shrink, tax, tire, use up, wash away, waste, wear out, wear thin, weary, weather; SEE CONCEPTS 156,225,240,698

wear [v3] bother, undermine
annoy, drain, enervate, exasperate, exhaust, fatigue, get the better of, harass, irk, pester, reduce, tax, vex, weaken, wear down, weary; SEE CONCEPTS 7,19

wear [v4] endure
bear up, be durable, hold up, last, remain, stand, stand up; SEE CONCEPT 23

weary [adj] tired
all in*, beat*, bone-tired*, bored, burned out*, bushed, dead*, dead tired*, discontented, disgusted, dog-tired*, done in*, drained, drooping, drowsy, enervated, exhausted, fagged, fatigued, fed up, flagging, had it*, impatient, indifferent, jaded, knocked out, out of gas*, overworked, pooped*, punchy*, ready to drop*, sick, sick and tired*, sleepy, spent*, taxed, wearied, wearing, wiped out*, worn out*, zonked*; SEE CONCEPTS 314,403,485

weary [v] make tired
annoy, bore, burden, cause ennui, cloy, debilitate, depress, disgust, dishearten, distress, drain, droop, drowse, enervate, enfeeble, exasperate, exhaust, fade, fag, fail, fall off, fatigue, flag, glut, grow tired, harass, have had enough*, irk, jade, leave one cold*, lose interest, make discontented, nauseate, oppress,

overwork, pain, plague, sap, sicken, sink, strain, take it out of*, tax, tire, tire out, try the patience of*, tucker out*, vex, weaken, wear down, wear out, weigh; SEE CONCEPTS 13,250,303

weather [n] atmospheric conditions
climate, clime, elements; SEE CONCEPTS 522,524

weather [v] endure
acclimate, bear the brunt of*, bear up against*, become toughened, brave, come through, expose, get through, grow hardened, grow strong, harden, make it, overcome, pull through, resist, ride out*, rise above*, season, stand, stick it out*, suffer, surmount, survive, toughen, withstand; SEE CONCEPTS 23,35,202

weave [v] blend, unite; contrive
braid, build, careen, complect, complicate, compose, construct, create, criss-cross, crochet, cue, entwine, fabricate, fold, fuse, incorporate, interfold, interlace, interlink, intermingle, intertwine, introduce, knit, knot, loop, lurch, make, make up, manufacture, mat, merge, mesh, move in and out, net, piece together, plait, ply, put together, reticulate, sew, snake, spin, splice, twine, twist, twist and turn, whip through, wind, wreathe, writhe, zigzag; SEE CONCEPTS 147,158

web [n] netting
cobweb, complexity, entanglement, fabric, fiber, filigree, gossamer, interconnection, interlacing, involvement, labyrinth, lacework, lattice, mat, matting, maze, mesh, meshwork, morass, net, network, plait, reticulation, screen, skein, snarl, tangle, texture, tissue, toil, trellis, warp, weave, webbing, weft, wicker, woof; SEE CONCEPTS 260,473

wed [v1] marry
become man and wife, be married, couple, espouse, get hitched*, get married, join, lead to the altar, make one*, receive in marriage, say I do*, take in marriage, tie*, tie the knot*, unite; SEE CONCEPT 297

wed [v2] join, unite
ally, associate, blend, coalesce, cojoin, combine, commingle, connect, couple, dedicate, fuse, interweave, link, marry, merge, relate, unify, yoke; SEE CONCEPTS 113,193

wedding [n] marriage rite
bells, bridal, espousal, hook, marriage, marriage ceremony, matrimony, nuptial rite, nuptials, spousal, union, wedlock; SEE CONCEPT 297

wedge [n] solid piece, often triangular
block, chock, chunk, cleat, cotter, cusp, keystone, lump, prong, quoin, shim, spire, taper; SEE CONCEPTS 471,499

weep [v] cry
bawl, bemoan, bewail, blubber*, boohoo*, break down*, burst into tears*, complain, deplore, drip, grieve, howl, keen, lament, let go*, let it out*, mewl, moan, mourn, shed tears, snivel, sob, squall, ululate, wail, whimper, yowl; SEE CONCEPTS 49,185

weigh [v1] *measure heaviness*
counterbalance, have a weight of, heft, measure, put in the balance, put on the scale, scale, tip the scales at; SEE CONCEPT *103*

weigh [v2] *consider, contemplate*
analyze, appraise, balance, brainstorm*, deliberate, estimate, evaluate, examine, excogitate, give thought to, hash over*, meditate, mind, mull over, perpend, ponder, rate, reflect upon, rehash, sort out, study, sweat, think about, think out, think over, track; SEE CONCEPT *24*

weigh [v3] *have influence*
be heavy, be important, be influential, be something, burden, carry weight, charge, count, cumber, cut, cut some ice, encumber, import, impress, lade, load, matter, mean, militate, press, pull, register, saddle, show, signify, stack up against*, tax, tell, weight; SEE CONCEPTS *7,19,22,237,682*

weigh down [v] *depress*
bear down, burden, cumber, get down, hold down, oppress, overburden, overload, press, press down, prey on, pull down, sadden, task, trouble, weight, weigh upon, worry; SEE CONCEPTS *7,19*

weight [n1] *heaviness*
adiposity, avoirdupois, ballast, burden, density, G-factor*, gravity, gross, heft, heftiness, load, mass, measurement, net, ponderosity, ponderousness, poundage, pressure, substance, tonnage; SEE CONCEPT *795*

weight [n2] *something used to measure heaviness*
anchor, ballast, bob, counterbalance, counterpoise, counterweight, mass, pendulum, plumb, plumb bob, poundage, pressure, rock, sandbag, sinker, stone; SEE CONCEPTS *290,470*

weight [n3] *importance*
access, authority, clout, connection, consequence, consideration, credit, effectiveness, efficacy, emphasis, forcefulness, forcibleness, impact, import, influence, magnitude, moment, momentousness, persuasiveness, pith, potency, power, powerfulness, prestige, pull, significance, signification, substance, sway, value, weightiness; SEE CONCEPTS *668,682*

weight [n4] *burden*
albatross*, ball and chain*, charge, cumber, cumbrance, deadweight*, duty, encumbrance, excess baggage*, incubus, load, millstone*, onus, oppression, pressure, responsibility, strain, task, tax; SEE CONCEPTS *532,674,679,690*

weighty [adj1] *heavy*
burdensome, cumbersome, cumbrous, dense, fat*, fleshy, hefty, massive, obese, overweight, ponderous, porcine, portly, stout; SEE CONCEPT *491*

weighty [adj2] *serious, important*
big, big deal*, consequential, considerable, critical, crucial, earnest, forcible, grave, heavy, heavyweight, life and death*, material, meaningful, momentous, no-nonsense*, portentous, sedate, severe, significant, sober, solemn, somber, staid, substantial, underlined; SEE CONCEPTS *548,568*

weighty [adj3] *troublesome, difficult*
backbreaking, burdensome, crushing, demanding, exacting, exigent, grievous, onerous, oppressive, superincumbent, taxing, tough, worrisome, worrying; SEE CONCEPTS *538,565*

weird [adj] *odd, bizarre*
awe-inspiring, awful, creepy*, curious, dreadful, eccentric, eerie*, far-out*, fearful, flaky*, freaky*, funky*, ghastly, ghostly, grotesque, haunting, horrific, inscrutable, kinky*, kooky*, magical, mysterious, occult, oddball*, ominous, outlandish, peculiar, preternatural, queer, secret, singular, spooky, strange, supernal, supernatural, uncanny, uncouth, unearthly, unnatural; SEE CONCEPTS *564,570*

welcome [n] *greeting*
acceptance, entertainment, entrée, friendliness, handshake, hello, hospitality, howdy*, key to the city*, ovation, reception, red carpet*, rumble, salutation, salute, tumble; SEE CONCEPT *278*

welcome [adj] *gladly received*
acceptable, accepted, agreeable, appreciated, cherished, congenial, contenting, cordial, delightful, desirable, desired, esteemed, favorable, genial, good, grateful, gratifying, honored, invited, nice, pleasant, pleasing, pleasurable, refreshing, satisfying, sympathetic, wanted; SEE CONCEPTS *555,572*

welcome [v] *receive gladly*
accept, accept gladly, accost, admit, bid welcome, embrace, entertain, flag*, greet, hail, hug, meet, offer hospitality, receive, roll out red carpet*, salute, show in, take in, tumble*, usher in; SEE CONCEPTS *266,384*

weld [v] *bind, connect*
bond, braze, cement, combine, fix, fuse, join, link, solder, unite; SEE CONCEPT *193*

welfare/well-being [n] *health and prosperity*
abundance, advantage, benefit, contentment, ease, easy street*, euphoria, felicity, good, good fortune, happiness, interest, luck, profit, progress, satisfaction, success, thriving; SEE CONCEPTS *316,693,706*

well [n] *water hole*
abyss, bore, chasm, depression, derivation, fount, fountain, fountainhead, geyser, hole, inception, mine, mouth, origin, pit, pool, repository, reservoir, root, shaft, source, spa, spout, spring, springs, watering place, wellspring; SEE CONCEPTS *509,513,514*

well [adj1] *healthy*
able-bodied, alive and kicking*, blooming, bright-eyed*, bushy-tailed*, chipper*, fine, fit, flourishing, fresh, great, hale, hardy, hearty, husky, in good health, in the pink*, right, right as rain*, robust, sane, solid as a rock*, sound, strong, strong as an ox*, together, trim, up to par*, vigorous, whole, wholesome, wrapped tight*; SEE CONCEPT *314*

well [adj2] *lucky, fortunate*
advisable, agreeable, bright, comfortable, fine, fitting, flourishing, good, happy, pleasing, profitable,

proper, prosperous, providential, prudent, right, satisfactory, thriving, useful; SEE CONCEPTS *548,572*

well [*adv1*] *happily, pleasantly; capably*
ably, accurately, adeptly, adequately, admirably, agreeably, attentively, capitally, carefully, closely, commendably, competently, completely, conscientiously, correctly, effectively, efficiently, excellently, expertly, famously, favorably, fully, in a satisfactory manner, irreproachably, nicely, proficiently, profoundly, properly, rightly, satisfactorily, skillfully, smoothly, soundly, splendidly, strongly, successfully, suitably, thoroughly, with skill; SEE CONCEPTS *527,528,544*

well [*adv2*] *sufficiently*
abundantly, adequately, amply, appropriately, becomingly, by a wide margin, completely, considerably, easily, effortlessly, entirely, extremely, far, fittingly, freely, fully, greatly, heartily, highly, luxuriantly, plentifully, properly, quite, rather, readily, right, satisfactorily, smoothly, somewhat, substantially, suitably, thoroughly, very much, wholly; SEE CONCEPTS *558,772*

well-bred [*adj*] *mannerly*
aristocratic, blue-blooded*, civil, considerate, courteous, courtly, cultivated, cultured, gallant, genteel, gentle, gentlemanly, ladylike, noble, patrician, polished, polite, refined, taught, trained, upper-crust*, urbane, well-behaved, well-mannered; SEE CONCEPTS *334,401*

well-known [*adj*] *familiar, famous*
acclaimed, big, big name*, celeb*, celebrated, common, conspicuous, eminent, face, illustrious, important, infamous, in the limelight*, in the public eye*, known, large, leading, name, notable, noted, notorious, outstanding, popular, prominent, public, recognized, renowned, reputable, somebody, splash, star, superstar, VIP*, widely known, WK*; SEE CONCEPT *568*

well-off [*adj*] *successful, wealthy*
affluent, comfortable, easy, flourishing, flush, fortunate, loaded, lucky, moneyed, prosperous, rich, snug, substantial, thriving, well, well-to-do; SEE CONCEPT *334*

welt [*n*] *red mark*
bruise, contusion, injury, mouse, ridge, scar, streak, stripe, wale, weal, wheal, wound; SEE CONCEPT *309*

wet [*n*] *dampness, moisture*
clamminess, condensation, damp, drizzle, humidity, liquid, rain, rains, water, wetness; SEE CONCEPT *607*

wet [*adj*] *damp, moist*
aqueous, clammy, dank, dewy, drenched, dripping, drizzling, foggy, humid, misty, moistened, muggy, pouring, raining, rainy, saturate, saturated, showery, slimy, slippery, slushy, snowy, soaked, soaking, sodden, soggy, sopping, soppy, soused, stormy, teary, teeming, water-logged, watery, wringing-wet; SEE CONCEPT *603*

wet [*v*] *cause to become damp, moist*
bathe, damp, dampen, deluge, dip, douse, drench, drown, hose, humidify, imbue, irrigate, moisten, rinse, saturate, soak, sop, souse, splash, spray, sprinkle, steep, wash, water; SEE CONCEPTS *161,256*

whack [*n1/v*] *hit*
bang, bash, bat, beat, belt, biff, box, buffet, clobber, clout, crack, cuff, ding, lambaste, nail, rap, slap, slug, smack, smash, sock, strike, thrash, thump, thwack, wallop, wham; SEE CONCEPT *189*

whack [*n2*] *try, attempt*
bash, crack, fling, go, pop, shot, slap, stab, turn, whirl; SEE CONCEPT *87*

wharf [*n*] *boat storage*
berth, breakwater, dock, jetty, landing, landing stage, levee, pier, quay, slip; SEE CONCEPT *439*

wheedle [*v*] *talk into*
banter, blandish, butter up, cajole, charm, coax, con, court, draw, entice, finagle, flatter, inveigle, kowtow*, lay it on*, oil*, persuade, seduce, snow*, soap*, soften up*, soft-soap*, spread it on*, sweeten up*, sweet-talk*, work on*, worm*; SEE CONCEPT *68*

wheel [*n*] *circle, revolution*
caster, circuit, circulation, circumvolution, cycle, disk, drum, gyration, gyre, hoop, pivot, pully, ratchet, ring, roll, roller, rotation, round, spin, trolley, turn, twirl, whirl; SEE CONCEPTS *436,464,502*

wheel [*v*] *turn, rotate*
circle, gyrate, orbit, pirouette, pivot, reel, revolve, roll, spin, swing, swivel, trundle, twirl, whirl; SEE CONCEPT *147*

wheeze [*v*] *breathe roughly, heavily*
buzz, catch one's breath, cough, gasp, hiss, murmur, pant, puff, rasp, sibilate, snore, whisper, whistle; SEE CONCEPTS *163,308*

when [*conj*] *though*
albeit, although, at, at the same time, during, howbeit, immediately upon, just after, just as, meanwhile, much as, whereas, while; SEE CONCEPT *799*

where [*n*] *place*
location, locus, point, position, site, situation, spot, station; SEE CONCEPT *198*

where/wherever [*adv*] *at which point*
anywhere, everywhere, in whatever place, in which, to what end, to which, whereabouts, whither; SEE CONCEPT *583*

whet [*v1*] *make sharp*
edge, file, finish, grind, hone, sharpen, strop; SEE CONCEPTS *137,250*

whet [*v2*] *arouse, excite*
animate, awaken, challenge, enhance, incite, increase, kindle, pique, provoke, quicken, rally, rouse, stimulate, stir, wake, waken; SEE CONCEPTS *7,11,22*

whiff [*n*] *smell of an odor*
aroma, blast, breath, dash, draught, flatus, fume, gust, hint, inhalation, odor, puff, scent, shade, smack, sniff, snuff, soupçon, trace, trifle, waft; SEE CONCEPTS *599,601,602*

while [*n*] *time interval*
bit, instant, interim, meantime, moment, occasion, period, space, spell, stretch, time; SEE CONCEPTS *807,822*

while [*conj1*] *as long as*
although, at the same time, during, during the time, in the time, throughout the time, whilst; SEE CONCEPT *799*

while [*conj2*] *even though*
albeit, although, howbeit, much as, though, when, whereas; SEE CONCEPT *544*

whim [*n*] *sudden idea*
caprice, conceit, craze, desire, disposition, dream, fad, fancy, fantasy, freak, humor, impulse, inclination, notion, passing thought, quirk, sport, spur of the moment*, thought, urge, vagary, vision, whimsy; SEE CONCEPTS *529,661*

whimper [*v*] *cry softly*
bleat, blubber, complain, fuss, mewl, moan, object, pule, snivel, sob, weep, whine; SEE CONCEPTS *77,185*

whimsical [*adj*] *playful, fanciful*
amusing, arbitrary, capricious, chancy, chimerical, comical, curious, dicey, droll, eccentric, erratic, fantastic, flaky*, freakish, funny, kinky*, mischievous, odd, peculiar, quaint, queer*, quizzical, singular, uncertain, unpredictable, unusual, wagish, wayward, weird*; SEE CONCEPTS *401,548*

whine [*n*] *complaint, cry*
gripe, grouse, grumble, moan, plaintive cry, sob, wail, whimper; SEE CONCEPTS *54,77*

whine [*v*] *complain, cry*
bellyache, carp, drone, fuss, gripe, grouse, grumble, howl, kick, mewl, moan, murmur, pule, repine, snivel, sob, wail, whimper, yowl; SEE CONCEPTS *54,77*

whip [*n*] *length of material for hitting*
bat, belt, birch, bullwhip, cane, cat-o'-nine-tails, crop, goad, horsewhip, knout, lash, prod, push, rawhide, rod, ruler, scourge, strap, switch, thong; SEE CONCEPT *499*

whip [*v1*] *hit repeatedly*
bash, beat, birch, bludgeon, cane, castigate, chastise, cudgel, drub, ferule, flagellate, flog, hide, larrup, lash, lather, punish, scourge, spank, strap, strike, switch, tan, thrash, trash, wallop, whale, whomp; SEE CONCEPT *189*

whip [*v2*] *defeat soundly*
beat, best, blast, clobber, conquer, drub, hammer*, kill*, lambaste, lick*, mop up*, outdo, overcome, overpower, overrun, overwhelm, put away*, rout, run circles around*, settle, steamroller*, subdue, take apart*, thrash, top, trim*, trounce, vanquish, wallop, wax*, whomp*, worst*; SEE CONCEPT *95*

whip [*v3*] *dash, dart*
avert, deflect, dive, divert, flash, flit, fly, jerk, pivot, pull, rush, seize, sheer, shoot, snatch, surge, tear, turn, veer, wheel, whirl, whisk; SEE CONCEPTS *150,152*

whip [*v4*] *agitate, stir up*
beat, blend, mix, whisk, work up; SEE CONCEPTS *152,170*

whip up [*v*] *incite, excite*
abet, agitate, arouse, compel, disturb, drive, foment, goad, hound, inflame, instigate, kindle, prick, prod, provoke, push, raise, set, set on, spur, start, stir, stir up, urge, work up; SEE CONCEPTS *14,221*

whirl [*n1*] *spin, revolution*
circle, circuit, circulation, circumvolution, flurry, gyration, gyre, pirouette, reel, roll, rotation, round, spin, surge, swirl, turn, twirl, twist, wheel, whir, whirlpool; SEE CONCEPTS *152,738*

whirl [*n2*] *commotion, confusion*
ado*, agitation, bustle, clatter, daze, dither, ferment, flurry, fluster, flutter, furor, fuss, hubbub*, hurly-burly*, hurry, merry-go-round, moil, pother, round, ruction, rush, series, spin, stir, storm, succession, tempest, tumult, turbulence, uproar, whirlwind; SEE CONCEPTS *230,388*

whirl [*n3*] *attempt*
bash, crack, fling, go, pop, shot, slap, stab, try, whack; SEE CONCEPT *87*

whirl [*v*] *spin around*
circle, eddy, gyrate, gyre, pirouette, pivot, purl, reel, revolve, roll, rotate, swirl, swoosh, turn, turn around, twirl, twist, wheel, whir; SEE CONCEPT *152*

whirlpool [*n*] *spinning water*
eddy, maelstrom, stir, undercurrent, undertow, vortex, whirl; SEE CONCEPT *514*

whirlwind [*adj*] *very fast*
cyclonic, hasty, headlong, hurricane, impetuous, impulsive, lightning, quick, rapid, rash, short, speedy, swift, tornado; SEE CONCEPTS *588,798*

whisk [*v*] *brush quickly; hasten*
barrel, bullet, dart, dash, flick, flit, flutter, fly, hurry, race, rush, shoot, speed, sweep, tear, whip, whiz, wipe, zip; SEE CONCEPT *152*

whisper [*n1*] *rumor; information expressed in soft voice*
buzz, confidence, disclosure, divulgence, gossip, hint, hum, hushed tone, innuendo, insinuation, low voice, mumble, murmur, mutter, report, secret, secret message, sigh, sighing, susurration, undertone, word; SEE CONCEPTS *274,278*

whisper [*n2*] *trace, suggestion*
breath, dash, fraction, hint, shade, shadow, soupçon, suspicion, tinge, touch, whiff; SEE CONCEPTS *529,673,831*

whisper [*v*] *speak softly*
breathe, buzz*, confide, gossip, hint, hiss, insinuate, intimate, mumble, murmur, mutter, say softly, say under one's breath*, sibilate, sigh, speak confidentially, spread rumor, susurrate, talk into someone's ear*, talk low, tell, tell a secret; SEE CONCEPTS *60,266*

whistle [v] *make sharp, shrill sound*
blare, blast, fife, flute, hiss, pipe, shriek, signal, skirl, sound, toot, tootle, trill, warble, wheeze, whine, whiz; SEE CONCEPTS *65,77*

whit [n] *very tiny bit*
atom, crumb, dash, drop, fragment, grain, hoot, iota, jot, little, mite, modicum, particle, piece, pinch, scrap, shred, speck, trace; SEE CONCEPTS *831,835*

white [adj] *extremely pale; clean*
achromatic, achromic, alabaster, ashen, blanched, bleached, bloodless, Caucasian, chalky, clear, fair, frosted, ghastly, gray, hoary, immaculate, ivory, light, milky, neutral, pallid, pasty, pearly, pure, silver, silvery, snowy, spotless, stainless, transparent, unblemished, unsullied, wan, waxen; SEE CONCEPT *618*

whiten [v] *make or become extremely pale*
blanch, bleach, blench, chalk, decolor, decolorize, dull, etiolate, fade, frost, grizzle, lighten, pale, silver, turn pale, white, whitewash; SEE CONCEPT *250*

whitewash [v] *cover up the truth*
blanch, camouflage, conceal, exonerate, extenuate, gloss over, launder, liberate, make light of*, paint, palliate, sugarcoat*, suppress, varnish, veneer, vindicate, white, whiten; SEE CONCEPTS *49,63*

whittle [v] *cut away at; reduce*
carve, chip, consume, decrease, diminish, eat away, erode, fashion, form, hew, lessen, model, mold, pare, sculpt, shape, shave, trim, undermine, wear away; SEE CONCEPTS *176,184,236,247*

whiz [n] *very intelligent person*
adept, expert, genius, gifted person, marvel, master, past master, pro, prodigy, professional, star, virtuoso, wizard, wonder; SEE CONCEPT *416*

whiz [v] *move quickly by*
bullet, buzz, dart, flit, fly, hiss, hum, hurry, hurtle, race, speed, swish, whir, whirl, whisk, whoosh, zip; SEE CONCEPT *150*

whole [n] *total made up of parts*
aggregate, aggregation, all, amount, assemblage, assembly, being, big picture, body, bulk, coherence, collectivity, combination, complex, ensemble, entirety, entity, everything, fullness, gross, hook line and sinker*, integral, jackpot, linkage, lock stock and barrel*, lot, lump, oneness, organism, organization, piece, quantity, quantum, result, sum, summation, sum total*, supply, system, the works*, totality, unit, unity, whole ball of wax*, whole enchilada*, whole nine yards*, whole shebang*; SEE CONCEPTS *432,635,837*

whole [adj1] *entire, complete*
accomplished, aggregate, all, choate, completed, concentrated, conclusive, consummate, every, exclusive, exhaustive, fixed, fulfilled, full, full-length, gross, inclusive, in one piece, integral, outright, perfect, plenary, rounded, total, unabbreviated, unabridged, uncut, undivided, unexpurgated, unqualified, utter; SEE CONCEPT *531*

whole [adj2] *unbroken, perfect*
complete, completed, developed, faultless, flawless, good, in good order*, in one piece*, intact, inviolate, mature, mint, plenary, preserved, replete, safe, ship-shape, solid, sound, thorough, together, undamaged, unharmed, unhurt, unimpaired, uninjured, unmarred, unmutilated, unscathed, untouched, without a scratch; SEE CONCEPTS *485,574*

whole [adj3] *healthy*
able-bodied, better, cured, fit, hale, healed, hearty, in fine fettle, in good health, recovered, right, robust, sane, sound, strong, well, wholesome; SEE CONCEPT *314*

wholehearted/whole-hearted [adj] *enthusiastic, sincere*
abiding, ardent, authentic, bona fide, candid, committed, complete, dedicated, determined, devoted, earnest, emphatic, enduring, fervent, frank, genuine, heartfelt, hearty, impassioned, never-failing, passionate, real, serious, steadfast, steady, sure, true, unfaltering, unfeigned, unqualified, unquestioning, unreserved, unstinting, unwavering, warm, zealous; SEE CONCEPTS *542,548,582*

wholesale [adj] *all-inclusive*
broad, bulk, complete, comprehensive, extensive, far-reaching, general, in bulk, indiscriminate, in quantity, in the mass, large-scale, mass, overall, quantitative, sweeping, total, wide-ranging, widespread; SEE CONCEPTS *771,772*

wholesome [adj] *healthy, decent*
all there, beneficial, clean, edifying, ethical, exemplary, fit, good, hale, healthful, health-giving, helpful, honorable, hygienic, in fine feather*, innocent, in the pink*, invigorating, moral, nice, normal, nourishing, nutritious, nutritive, pure, respectable, restorative, right, righteous, safe, salubrious, salutary, sane, sanitary, sound, strengthening, together, virtuous, well, worthy; SEE CONCEPTS *314,462,537,545*

wholly [adv1] *completely, entirely*
all, all in all*, all the way*, altogether, comprehensively, from A to Z*, fully, heart and soul*, in every respect*, in toto*, one hundred percent*, outright, perfectly, quite, roundly, thoroughly, top to bottom*, totally, utterly, well; SEE CONCEPTS *531,772*

wholly [adv2] *exclusively*
individually, just, only, purely, solely, specifically, without exception; SEE CONCEPT *557*

whoop [n/v] *hurrah*
bellow, boo, cheer, cry, cry out, holler, hoot, howl, jeer, scream, shout, shriek, squawk, yell; SEE CONCEPT *77*

whopping [adj] *enormous*
big, colossal, extraordinary, gargantuan, giant, gigantic, great, huge, immense, large, mammoth, massive, mighty, monstrous, mountainous, prodigious, tremendous; SEE CONCEPTS *773,781*

whorl [n] *spiral*
coil, corkscrew, curl, eddy, helix, swirl, twirl, twist, vortex, whirlpool; SEE CONCEPT *436*

wicked [*adj1*] *corrupt, bad*
abandoned, abominable, amoral, arch, atrocious, bad news*, base, contemptible, debased, degenerate, depraved, devilish, dissolute, egregious, evil, fiendish, flagitious, foul, gross*, guilty, heartless, heinous, immoral, impious, impish, incorrigible, indecent, iniquitous, irreligious, low-down, mean, mischievous, nasty, naughty, nefarious, profane, reprobate, rotten, scandalous, shameful, shameless, sinful, unethical, unprincipled, unrighteous, vicious, vile, villainous, wayward, worthless; SEE CONCEPTS *401,545*

wicked [*adj2*] *destructive, troublesome*
acute, agonizing, awful, barbarous, bothersome, chancy, crashing, dangerous, difficult, distressing, dreadful, fearful, fierce, galling, harmful, hazardous, injurious, intense, mean, mighty, offensive, outrageous, painful, perilous, pesky, risky, severe, terrible, treacherous, troublous, trying, ugly, uncivilized, unconscionable, ungodly, unhealthy, unholy, unpleasant, unsound, vexatious; SEE CONCEPTS *537,565,571*

wicked [*adj3*] *expert*
able, adept, adroit, au fait, capable, clever, competent, deft, good, masterly, mighty, outstanding, powerful, pretty, qualified, skillful, strong; SEE CONCEPT *527*

wide [*adj1*] *expansive, roomy*
advanced, all-inclusive, ample, baggy, broad, capacious, catholic, commodious, comprehensive, deep, dilated, distended, encyclopedic, expanded, extensive, far-ranging, far-reaching, full, general, immense, inclusive, large, large-scale, liberal, loose, open, outspread, outstretched, progressive, radical, scopic, spacious, splay, squat, sweeping, tolerant, universal, vast, voluminous; SEE CONCEPTS *772,773,796*

wide [*adj2*] *off-course*
astray, away, distant, far, far-off, inaccurate, off, off-target, off the mark, remote; SEE CONCEPTS *581,583*

widen [*v*] *open up*
add to, augment, broaden, dilate, distend, enlarge, expand, extend, grow, grow larger, increase, multiply, open, open out, open wide, ream, spread, spread out, stretch, swell, unfold; SEE CONCEPTS *236,245,780*

widespread [*adj*] *extensive*
across the board*, all over the place*, boundless, broad, common, comprehensive, current, diffuse, epidemic, far-flung*, far-reaching, general, on a large scale, outspread, overall, pandemic, pervasive, popular, prevailing, prevalent, public, rampant, regnant, rife, ruling, sweeping, universal, unlimited, unrestricted, wall-to-wall*, wholesale; SEE CONCEPTS *530,536,772*

width [*n*] *breadth, wideness of some amount*
amplitude, area, broadness, compass, cross measure, diameter, distance across, expanse, extent, girth, measure, range, reach, scope, span, squatness, stretch, thickness; SEE CONCEPTS *760,787,792*

wield [*v*] *control, use*
apply, brandish, command, conduct, employ, exercise, exert, flourish, handle, have, have at one's disposal, hold, maintain, make use of, manage, maneuver, manipulate, operate, ply, possess, put to use, shake, swing, throw, utilize, wave, work; SEE CONCEPTS *94,147,225*

wife [*n*] *married woman*
bride, companion, consort, helpmate, mate, monogamist, other half, partner, roommate, spouse; SEE CONCEPTS *414,415*

wiggle [*n/v*] *shake back and forth*
jerk, jiggle, shimmy, squirm, twist, twitch, wag, waggle, wave, worm, wriggle, writhe, zigzag; SEE CONCEPTS *80,150,152*

wild [*adj1*] *untamed*
agrarian, barbarian, barbaric, barbarous, dense, desert, deserted, desolate, escaped, feral, ferocious, fierce, free, indigenous, lush, luxuriant, native, natural, neglected, overgrown, overrun, primitive, rampant, rude, savage, unbroken, uncivilized, uncultivated, undomesticated, uninhabited, untouched, vicious, virgin, waste; SEE CONCEPTS *406,583*

wild [*adj2*] *disorderly, rowdy*
avid, berserk, boisterous, chaotic, crazed, crazy, eager, enthusiastic, extravagant, flighty, foolhardy, foolish, giddy, hysterical, impetuous, impracticable, imprudent, incautious, irrational, lawless, licentious, mad, madcap, noisy, nuts, outrageous, preposterous, profligate, rabid, rash, raving, reckless, riotous, rough, self-willed, turbulent, unbridled, uncontrolled, undisciplined, unfettered, ungovernable, unmanageable, unrestrained, unruly, uproarious, violent, wayward; SEE CONCEPT *401*

wild [*adj3*] *intense, stormy*
blustering, blustery, choppy, disturbed, furious, howling, inclement, raging, rough, storming, tempestuous, turbulent, violent; SEE CONCEPTS *525, 569*

wilderness/wilds [*n*] *uninhabited area*
back country, back of beyond*, badland, barrens, boondocks, bush, desert, forest, hinterland, jungle, middle of nowhere*, no-man's land*, outback, primeval forest, sticks*, waste, wasteland, wild; SEE CONCEPT *517*

wile [*n*] *cunning*
angle, artfulness, artifice, cheating, chicane, chicanery, con*, contrivance, craft, craftiness, deceit, deception, device, dishonesty, dissimulation, dodge, feint, flimflam*, fraud, gambit, game, gimmick, guile, hoax, horseplay, imposition, little game, lure, maneuver, monkey business*, monkeyshines*, plot, ploy, racket*, ruse, scam*, scheming, setup*, shenanigans*, skullduggery*, slant, slyness, stratagem,

stunt, subterfuge, switch, trick, trickery, twist; SEE CONCEPTS *59,63*

will [*n1*] *personal choice*
aim, appetite, attitude, character, conviction, craving, decision, decisiveness, decree, design, desire, determination, discipline, discretion, disposition, fancy, feeling, hankering, heart's desire*, inclination, intention, liking, longing, mind, option, passion, pining, pleasure, power, preference, prerogative, purpose, resolution, resolve, self-control, self-discipline, self-restraint, temperament, urge, velleity, volition, willfulness, willpower, wish, wishes, yearning; SEE CONCEPTS *20,411,659*

will [*n2*] *last wishes; command*
bequest, bestowal, declaration, decree, device, directions, dispensation, disposition, estate, heritage, inheritance, insistence, instructions, legacy, order, property, testament; SEE CONCEPT *318*

will [*v1*] *cause*
authorize, bid, bring about, command, decide on, decree, demand, determine, direct, effect, enjoin, exert, insist, intend, ordain, order, request, resolve; SEE CONCEPT *242*

will [*v2*] *choose*
be inclined, crave, desire, elect, have a mind to*, incline, like, opt, please, prefer, see fit*, want, wish; SEE CONCEPT *20*

will [*v3*] *give, bequeath to another*
bequest, confer, cut off, devise, disherit, disinherit, leave, legate, pass on, probate, transfer; SEE CONCEPTS *108,317*

willful [*adj1*] *stubborn, obstinate*
adamant, bullheaded, contumacious, determined, dogged, factious, froward, headstrong, inflexible, intractable, intransigent, mulish, obdurate, persistent, pertinacious, perverse, pigheaded*, refractory, resolved, self-willed, stiffnecked*, uncompromising, unyielding; SEE CONCEPTS *401,542*

willful [*adj2*] *voluntary*
conscious, contemplated, deliberate, designed, intended, intentional, planned, premeditated, purposeful, studied, unforced, volitional, willed, willing, witting; SEE CONCEPTS *401,535*

willing [*adj*] *agreeable, ready*
accommodating, active, amenable, cheerful, compliant, consenting, content, deliberate, desirous, disposed, eager, energetic, enthusiastic, fair, favorable, feeling, forward, game, go along with, happy, in accord with, inclined, in favor, intentional, in the mood, like, minded, obedient, one, pleased, predisposed, prepared, prompt, prone, reliable, responsible, tractable, unasked, unbidden, unforced, voluntary, well-disposed, willful, witting, zealous; SEE CONCEPTS *401,403,576*

willpower [*n*] *personal determination*
discipline, drive, firmness, fixity, force, grit, resolution, resolve, self-control, self-discipline, self-government, self-restraint, single-mindedness, strength, will; SEE CONCEPT *411*

wilt [*v*] *sag, fail*
become limp, break down, cave in, collapse, diminish, droop, drop, dry up, dwindle, ebb, fade, faint, flaccid, flag, give out, languish, melt, mummify, shrivel, sink, succumb, wane, waste, waste away, weaken, wither, wizen; SEE CONCEPTS *181,427,469,699*

wily [*adj*] *crafty, clever*
arch, artful, astute, cagey*, crazy like a fox*, crooked, cunning, deceitful, deceptive, deep, designing, foxy, greasy*, guileful, insidious, intriguing, knowing, sagacious, scheming, sharp, shifty, shrewd, slick*, slippery*, sly, smooth, sneaky, streetwise, tricky, underhanded; SEE CONCEPTS *401,545*

win [*n*] *victory*
accomplishment, achievement, conquest, gain, gold*, gold star*, kill*, killing*, pay dirt*, score, slam, success, sweep, triumph; SEE CONCEPTS *95,141,832*

win [*v1*] *finish first; succeed*
achieve, beat, be first, be victorious, carry the day*, come in first, conquer, edge, finish in front, finish off, gain, gain victory, overcome, overwhelm, prevail, run circles around*, shut out*, sink*, take the prize, triumph, upset, walk away with*, walk off with*; SEE CONCEPTS *95,141,363*

win [*v2*] *achieve, obtain*
accomplish, acquire, annex, approach, attain, bag*, bring in, catch, collect, come away with*, derive, earn, effect, gain, get, harvest, have, make, net, pick up, procure, rack up*, reach, realize, receive, score, secure; SEE CONCEPTS *120,706*

win/win over [*v3*] *influence, persuade*
allure, argue into, attract, bring around, carry, charm, convert, convince, disarm, draw, get, induce, overcome, prevail upon, prompt, slay, sway, talk into, wow; SEE CONCEPTS *11,68*

wince [*v*] *draw back*
back off, blanch, blench, cower, cringe, dodge, duck, flinch, grimace, jib, make a face*, quail, recoil, shrink, shy, start, swerve, turn; SEE CONCEPTS *154,185*

wind [*n1*] *air currents*
air, blast, blow, breath, breeze, chinook, cyclone, draft, draught, flurry, flutter, gale, gust, mistral, puff, tempest, typhoon, wafting, whiff, whirlwind, whisk, zephyr; SEE CONCEPT *524*

wind [*n2*] *warning, report*
babble, clue, cue, gossip, hint, hot air*, idle talk, inkling, intimation, notice, rumor, suggestion, talk, tidings, whisper; SEE CONCEPT *278*

wind [*v*] *bend, turn*
coil, convolute, corkscrew, cover, crook, curl, curve, deviate, distort, encircle, enclose, entwine, envelop, fold, furl, loop, meander, ramble, reel, roll,

screw, slither, snake, spiral, swerve, twine, twist, weave, wrap, wreathe, wriggle, zigzag; SEE CONCEPTS *201,738*

winding [*adj*] *bending, turning*
ambiguous, anfractuous, circuitous, convoluted, crooked, curving, devious, flexuous, gyrating, indirect, intricate, involved, labyrinthine, mazy, meandering, roundabout, serpentine, sinuous, snaky, spiraling, tortuous, twisting, wriggly, zigzag; SEE CONCEPTS *581,584*

wind up [*v*] *finish*
be through with, bring to a close, clean up*, close, close down, come to the end, complete, conclude, determine, do, end, end up*, finalize, finish up, halt, liquidate, settle, terminate, tie up loose ends*, wrap up*; SEE CONCEPT *234*

windy [*adj1*] *breezy*
airy, blowing, blowy, blustering, blustery, boisterous, brisk, drafty, fresh, gusty, raw, squally, stormy, tempestuous, wild, windswept; SEE CONCEPT *525*

windy [*adj2*] *talkative; boastful*
bombastic, diffuse, empty, garrulous, inflated, lengthy, long-winded, loquacious, meandering, palaverous, pompous, prolix, rambling, redundant, turgid, verbose, wordy; SEE CONCEPT *267*

wing [*n1*] *organ, device of flight*
aileron, airfoil, appendage, feather, pennon, pinion; SEE CONCEPTS *399,502*

wing [*n2*] *section; extension*
addition, adjunct, annex, arm, block, branch, bulge, circle, clique, coterie, detachment, division, ell, expansion, faction, group, part, projection, prolongation, protrusion, protuberance, section, segment, set, side, unit; SEE CONCEPTS *440,441,824,835*

wink [*n1/v*] *flutter, flick*
bat, blink, flash, gleam, glimmer, glitter, nictate, nictitate, sparkle, squinch, squint, twinkle; SEE CONCEPTS *185,624*

wink [*n2*] *moment*
flash*, instant, jiffy*, minute, second,.shake*, split second*, twinkle*, twinkling*; SEE CONCEPTS *808,821*

winner [*n*] *someone or something that succeeds*
champ, champion, conquering hero, conqueror, first, hero, king, master, medalist, medalwinner, number one*, prizewinner, title-holder, top dog*, vanquisher, victor; SEE CONCEPTS *366,416*

winning/winsome [*adj1*] *attractive, charming*
acceptable, adorable, agreeable, alluring, amiable, bewitching, captivating, cute, delectable, delightful, disarming, dulcet, enchanting, endearing, engaging, fascinating, fetching, gratifying, lovable, lovely, pleasing, prepossessing, sweet, taking; SEE CONCEPTS *401,404*

winning [*adj2*] *triumphant*
champion, conquering, leading, successful, victorious; SEE CONCEPTS *528,632*

winter [*n*] *cold season of the year*
chill, cold, frost, Jack Frost*, wintertide, wintertime; SEE CONCEPT *814*

wintry [*adj*] *cold, snowy*
biting, bleak, brumal, chilly, cutting, desolate, dismal, freezing, frigid, frosty, frozen, harsh, hibernal, hiemal, icebox*, icy, raw, snappy, three-dog night*; SEE CONCEPTS *525,605*

wipe [*v*] *brush, swab*
clean, clean off, clear, dry, dust, erase, mop, obliterate, remove, rub, sponge, take away, towel, wash; SEE CONCEPT *165*

wipe out [*v*] *destroy; get rid of*
abate, abolish, annihilate, black out, blot out, cancel, decimate, delete, efface, eliminate, eradicate, erase, expunge, exterminate, extinguish, extirpate, kill, massacre, obliterate, remove, root out, slaughter, slay, uproot, X-out*; SEE CONCEPT *252*

wiry [*adj*] *thin and strong*
agile, athletic, bristly, fibrous, lean, light, limber, muscular, ropy, sinewy, stiff, strapping, stringy, supple, tough; SEE CONCEPTS *490,491*

wisdom [*n*] *insight, common sense*
acumen, astuteness, balance, brains*, caution, circumspection, clear thinking, comprehension, discernment, discrimination, enlightenment, erudition, experience, foresight, good judgment, gumption, horse sense*, information, intelligence, judgment, judiciousness, knowledge, learning, pansophy, penetration, perspicacity, poise, practicality, prudence, reason, sagacity, sageness, sanity, sapience, savoir faire, savvy, shrewdness, solidity, sophistication, stability, understanding; SEE CONCEPT *409*

wise [*adj*] *intelligent, reasonable*
astute, aware, calculating, careful, clever, cogitative, contemplative, crafty, cunning, discerning, discreet, educated, enlightened, erudite, experienced, foresighted, grasping, informed, insightful, intuitive, judicious, keen, knowing, knowledgeable, perceptive, perspicacious, politic, prudent, rational, reflective, sagacious, sage, sane, sapient, scholarly, sensible, sensing, sharp, shrewd, smart, sophic, sound, tactful, taught, thoughtful, understanding, wary, well-informed, witty; SEE CONCEPT *402*

wish [*n*] *desire*
ambition, aspiration, choice, disposition, hankering, hope, hunger, inclination, intention, invocation, itch, liking, longing, pleasure, prayer, preference, request, thirst, urge, want, whim, will, yearning, yen; SEE CONCEPTS *20,709*

wish [*v*] *desire*
aspire, beg, choose, command, covet, crave, desiderate, elect, entreat, envy, expect, fancy, hanker, hope, hunger, invoke, itch, like, long, look forward to*, need, order, please, pray for, prefer, request, set one's heart on*, sigh for, solicit, spoil for, thirst, want, will, yearn, yen; SEE CONCEPT *20*

wishy-washy [adj] bland, dull
banal, characterless, cowardly, enervated, feeble, flat, flavorless, indecisive, ineffective, ineffectual, insipid, irresolute, jejune, languid, listless, mediocre, namby-pamby*, sapless, spiritless, tasteless, thin, vacillating, vapid, watered-down, watery, wavering, weak, weak-kneed*; SEE CONCEPT **404**

wisp [n] strand
bit, lock, piece, shock, shred, snippet, string, thread, tuft, twist; SEE CONCEPTS **392,831**

wistful [adj] daydreaming, longing
contemplative, desirous, disconsolate, dreaming, dreamy, forlorn, hopeless, meditative, melancholy, mournful, musing, nostalgic, pensive, plaintive, reflective, sad, thoughtful, wishful, yearning; SEE CONCEPT **403**

wit [n1] humor
aphorism, badinage, banter, bon mot, burlesque, drollery, facetiousness, fun, gag, jest, jocularity, joke, lark, levity, pleasantry, practical joke, prank, pun, quip, raillery, repartee, sally, satire, trick, whimsicality, wisecrack, wittiness, wordplay; SEE CONCEPTS **59,273,411**

wit [n2] person who is very funny
a million laughs*, banterer, card, comedian, comic, cutup*, epigrammatist, farceur, funnyman/woman, funster, gagman/woman, humorist, jester, joker, jokesmith, jokester, kibitzer*, life of the party*, madcap, punster, quipster, trickster, wag, wisecracker, wise guy; SEE CONCEPTS **352,416**

wit/wits [n3] judgment, intelligence
acumen, acuteness, astucity, astuteness, awareness, balance, brainpower, brains*, cleverness, common sense, comprehension, depth of perception, discernment, discrimination, esprit, grasp, ingenuity, insight, keenness, lucidity, marbles, mentality, mind, perception, perspicacity, practicality, prudence, rationality, reason, sagaciousness, sagacity, sageness, saneness, sanity, sapience, sense, shrewdness, soundness, understanding, wisdom; SEE CONCEPT **409**

witch [n] woman who casts spells over others
beldam, charmer, crone, enchantress, hag, hellcat, magician, minx, necromancer, occultist, she-devil, siren, sorceress; SEE CONCEPTS **361,412,415**

witchcraft [n] spell-casting, magic
abracadabra*, bewitchment, black art, black magic, charisma, conjuring, demonology, devil worship, divination, enchantment, hocus-pocus*, hoodoo*, incantation, jinx, magnetism, mumbo-jumbo*, necromancy, occult, occultism, sorcery, spell, thaumaturgy, voodoo, voodooism, whammy*, witchery, witching, wizardry; SEE CONCEPTS **367,370,689**

withdraw [v1] remove something or someone from situation
abjure, absent oneself, back out, bail out, blow, book, bow out, check out, depart, detach, disengage, draw away, draw back, drop out, ease out, eliminate, exfiltrate, exit, extract, fall back, get away, get lost, get off, give ground, give way, go, keep aloof, keep apart, leave, make oneself scarce, phase out, pull back, pull out, quail, quit, recede, recoil, retire, retreat, run along, secede, seclude oneself, shrink, switch, take a hike, take away, take leave, take off, take out, vacate; SEE CONCEPTS **195,211**

withdraw [v2] retract; declare void
abjure, abolish, abrogate, annul, ban, bar, call off, disavow, disclaim, dissolve, forswear, invalidate, nullify, palinode, quash, recall, recant, renege, renig, repress, repudiate, rescind, retire, reverse, revoke, stamp out, suppress, take back, unsay; SEE CONCEPTS **50,88,121,697**

withdrawal [n] removal; retraction
abandonment, abdication, abjuration, alienation, departure, disavowal, disclaimer, disengagement, egress, egression, exit, exiting, exodus, extraction, marooning, recall, recantation, relinquishment, repudiation, rescission, resignation, retirement, retreat, revocation, revulsion, secession; SEE CONCEPTS **195,211,685**

withdrawn [adj1] unsociable
aloof, aseptic, casual, cool, detached, disinterested, distant, incurious, indifferent, introverted, nongregarious, offish, quiet, recluse, reclusive, remote, reserved, restrained, retired, retiring, retreated, shrinking, shy, silent, solitary, standoffish, taciturn, timorous, uncommunicative, uncompanionable, unconcerned, uncurious, undemonstrative, unforthcoming, uninterested; SEE CONCEPT **401**

withdrawn [adj2] hidden, remote
cloistered, departed, isolated, out-of-the-way, private, recluse, removed, retreated, secluded, solitary, taken out; SEE CONCEPT **583**

wither [v] droop, decline
atrophy, become stale, blast, blight, collapse, constrict, contract, decay, deflate, desiccate, deteriorate, die, disintegrate, dry, dry up, fade, fold, languish, perish, shrink, shrivel, wane, waste, waste away, wilt, wizen; SEE CONCEPTS **427,698**

withhold [v] keep back
abstain, bridle, check, clam up, conceal, constrain, curb, deduct, deny, detain, disallow, dummy up*, hide, hold, hold back, hold down, hold out, hold out on, inhibit, keep, keep secret, keep to oneself*, keep under one's hat*, keep under wraps*, kill, refrain, refuse, repress, reserve, resist, restrain, retain, sit on, spike, stop oneself, suppress; SEE CONCEPTS **35,121,188**

within [adv] inside
in, in a period, indoors, inner, in reach, interior, inward, not beyond, not outside, not over; SEE CONCEPTS **586,772**

without [adv] outside
after, beyond, externally, left out, on the outside, out, outdoors, out-of-doors, outwardly, past; SEE CONCEPTS **586,772**

withstand [v] *endure, bear*
brace, brave, buck, combat, confront, contest, cope, cross, defy, dispute, duel, face, fight, fly in the face of*, grapple with, hang on*, hang tough*, hold off*, hold one's ground*, hold out*, oppose, prevail against, put up struggle, put up with, remain firm, repel, resist, ride out*, sit and take it*, stand, stand fast*, stand firm*, stand one's ground*, stand up against*, stand up to*, stick*, stick fast*, suffer, take, take it, take on, thwart, tolerate, traverse, violate, weather, win out*; SEE CONCEPTS *23,96*

witness [n] *person who observes an event*
attestant, attestor, beholder, bystander, corroborator, deponent, eyewitness, gawker, looker-on, observer, onlooker, proof, rubbernecker*, signatory, signer, spectator, testifier, testimony, viewer, watcher; SEE CONCEPTS *355,423*

witness [v1] *observe*
attend, be a witness, behold, be on hand*, be on the scene*, be present, eyeball*, flash on*, get a load of*, look on, mark, note, notice, perceive, pick up on, pipe*, read, see, sight, spot, spy, take in, view, watch; SEE CONCEPT *626*

witness [v2] *testify; authenticate*
affirm, announce, argue, attest, bear out, bear witness, be a witness, bespeak, betoken, certify, confirm, corroborate, countersign, depone, depose, endorse, give evidence, give testimony, indicate, say under oath, sign, stand for, subscribe, vouch for; SEE CONCEPTS *49,50,88,317*

witty [adj] *funny and clever*
amusing, bright, brilliant, campy, crazy, diverting, droll, entertaining, epigrammatic, facetious, fanciful, gay, humorous, ingenious, intelligent, jocose, jocular, joshing, keen, lively, original, penetrating, piercing, piquant, quick-witted, ridiculous, scintillating, screaming, slapstick, sparkling, waggish, whimsical; SEE CONCEPTS *267,542*

wizard [n1] *person who can perform magic*
astrologer, augurer, clairvoyant, conjurer, diviner, enchanter, fortuneteller, hypnotist, magician, magus, medium, necromancer, occultist, palmist, seer, shaman, soothsayer, sorcerer, thaumaturge, warlock, witch; SEE CONCEPT *361*

wizard [n2] *person who is highly skilled*
ace*, adept, artist, authority, crackerjack*, expert, genius, hot shot*, maestro, marvel, master, past master, pro*, prodigy, professional, proficient, shark*, star, virtuoso, whiz*, whiz kid*, wiz*; SEE CONCEPTS *348,423*

wizened [adj] *dried, shriveled up*
diminished, gnarled, lean, macerated, mummified, old, reduced, shrunk, shrunken, wilted, withered, worn, wrinkled; SEE CONCEPTS *485,603*

wobble [v] *stagger, quake*
be unsteady, careen, falter, flounder, lurch, oscillate, quiver, reel, rock, roll, seesaw, shake, shimmy, stumble, sway, swing, teeter, totter, tremble, vacillate, vibrate, waver, weave, wiggle; SEE CONCEPTS *150,152*

wobbly [adj] *shaky*
fluctuant, insecure, precarious, rattletrap, rickety, rocky, teetering, tottering, unbalanced, uneven, unsafe, unstable, unsteady, unsure, vacillating, wavering, wavy, weak, wiggling; SEE CONCEPT *488*

woe [n] *suffering*
adversity, affliction, agony, anguish, bemoaning, blues*, burden, calamity, care, cataclysm, catastrophe, curse, dejection, deploring, depression, disaster, distress, dole, drag, gloom, grief, grieving, hardship, headache*, heartache*, heartbreak, lamentation, melancholy, misadventure, misery, misfortune, pain, rain*, regret, rue, sadness, sorrow, tragedy, trial, tribulation, trouble, unhappiness, wretchedness; SEE CONCEPTS *410,532,690,728*

woebegone [adj] *depressed, troubled*
black, bleak, blue*, bummed out*, chapfallen, cheerless, crestfallen, dejected, despondent, disconsolate, dismal, dispirited, doleful, down, downcast, downhearted, down-in-the-mouth*, dreary, forlorn, gloomy, grief-stricken, grim, hangdog*, hurting, in pain*, long-faced*, low, lugubrious, melancholy, miserable, mournful, sad, shot down*, sorrowful, unhappy, woeful, wretched; SEE CONCEPT *403*

woeful [adj] *terrible, sad*
afflicted, agonized, anguished, appalling, awful, bad, calamitous, catastrophic, cruel, deplorable, disappointing, disastrous, disconsolate, disgraceful, distressing, doleful, dreadful, feeble, gloomy, grieving, grievous, grim, heartbreaking, heartrending, heartsick, hopeless, inadequate, lamentable, lousy, mean, miserable, mournful, paltry, pathetic, piteous, pitiable, pitiful, plaintive, poor, racked, rotten, shocking, sorrowful, sorry, tortured, tragic, unfortunate, unhappy, wretched; SEE CONCEPTS *548,571*

wolf [v] *consume sloppily and fast*
bolt, cram, devour, gobble, gorge, gulp, guzzle, ingurgitate, pack, slop, slosh, stuff, swallow; SEE CONCEPT *169*

woman [n] *female human*
aunt, daughter, gal, gentlewoman, girl, girlfriend, grandmother, lady, ma'am, maid, maiden, matron, mistress, mother, Ms/Miss/Mrs, niece, she, spouse, wife; SEE CONCEPTS *414,415*

wonder [n1] *amazement*
admiration, astonishment, awe, bewilderment, concern, confusion, consternation, curiosity, doubt, fascination, fear, incredulity, jar, jolt, marveling, perplexity, perturbation, puzzlement, reverence, shock, skepticism, start, stupefaction, stupor, surprise, suspicion, uncertainty, wondering, wonderment; SEE CONCEPTS *410,532,690*

wonder [n2] *something that is amazing*
act of God*, curiosity, cynosure, freak, marvel, miracle, nonpareil, oddity, phenomenon, portent, prod-

igy, rara avis*, rarity, sensation, sight, spectacle, stunner, wonderment; SEE CONCEPTS *529,686*

wonder [*v1*] *doubt; ponder*
ask oneself, be curious, be inquisitive, conjecture, disbelieve, inquire, meditate, puzzle, query, question, speculate, think; SEE CONCEPTS *17,21*

wonder [*v2*] *be amazed*
admire, be astonished, be awestruck, be confounded, be dumbstruck, be fascinated, be flabbergasted, be startled, be taken aback, boggle, gape, gawk, look aghast, marvel, stare; SEE CONCEPT *34*

wonderful [*adj*] *great, extraordinary*
admirable, amazing, astonishing, astounding, awe-inspiring, awesome, brilliant, cool, divine, dynamite, enjoyable, excellent, fabulous, fantastic, fine, groovy*, incredible, magnificent, marvelous, miraculous, outstanding, peachy*, phenomenal, pleasant, pleasing, prime, remarkable, sensational, something else*, staggering, startling, strange, stupendous, super, superb, surprising, swell, terrific, too much*, tremendous, unheard-of, wondrous; SEE CONCEPTS *529,574*

woo [*v*] *seek as romantic partner*
address, aim for, beg, bill and coo*, butter up*, caress, charm, chase, court, cultivate, curry favor*, date, entreat, gallant, go steady, importune, keep company, make advances, make love, press one's suit with*, propose, pursue, run after, rush, seek in marriage*, seek the hand of*, set one's cap for, solicit, spark*, spoon*, sue; SEE CONCEPTS *297,375,384*

wood/woods [*n*] *forest*
copse, grove, lumber, thicket, timber, timberland, trees, weald, woodland; SEE CONCEPTS *430,509,517*

wooden [*adj1*] *made of timber*
board, clapboard, frame, ligneous, log, peg, plant, slab, timber, timbered, woody; SEE CONCEPT *485*

wooden [*adj2*] *stiff, inflexible*
awkward, bumbling, clumsy, gauche, gawky, graceless, heavy, heavy-handed, inelegant, inept, maladroit, obstinate, ponderous, rigid, stilted, unbending, ungainly, ungraceful, unhandy, unyielding, weighty; SEE CONCEPTS *488,542*

word [*n1*] *discussion*
chat, chitchat*, colloquy, confab*, confabulation, consultation, conversation, discussion, talk, tête-à-tête; SEE CONCEPT *56*

word [*n2*] *statement*
account, adage, advice, announcement, bulletin, by-word, comment, communication, communiqué, declaration, directive, discourse, dispatch, expression, gossip, hearsay, information, intelligence, intimation, introduction, message, news, notice, pronouncement, proverb, remark, report, rumble, rumor, saw, saying, scuttlebutt, speech, talk, tidings, utterance; SEE CONCEPTS *274,278*

word [*n3*] *unit of language*
concept, designation, expression, idiom, lexeme, locution, morpheme, name, phrase, sound, term, usage, utterance, vocable; SEE CONCEPT *275*

word [*n4*] *command*
behest, bidding, charge, commandment, decree, dictate, edict, go-ahead*, green light*, injunction, mandate, order, signal, ukase, will; SEE CONCEPT *685*

word [*n5*] *promise*
affirmation, assertion, assurance, commitment, declaration, engagement, guarantee, oath, parole, pledge, plight, solemn oath, solemn word, vow, warrant, word of honor; SEE CONCEPTS *71,278,689*

word [*n6*] *password*
countersign, slogan, watchword; SEE CONCEPTS *684,685*

wording [*n*] *way of expressing a thought*
choice of words, diction, language, locution, manner, mode, parlance, phraseology, phrasing, style, terminology, turn of phrase, wordage, words; SEE CONCEPTS *278,682*

wordy [*adj*] *talkative*
bombastic, chatty*, diffuse, discursive, flatulent, gabby*, garrulous, inflated, lengthy, long-winded, loquacious, palaverous, pleonastic, prolix, rambling, redundant, rhetorical, tedious, turgid, verbose, voluble, windy*; SEE CONCEPT *267*

work [*n1*] *labor, chore*
assignment, attempt, commission, daily grind*, drudge, drudgery, effort, elbow grease*, endeavor, exertion, functioning, grind, grindstone*, industry, job, moil, muscle, obligation, pains*, performance, production, push, salt mines*, servitude, slavery, slogging, stint, stress, striving, struggle, sweat*, task, toil, travail, trial, trouble, undertaking; SEE CONCEPTS *87,362,677*

work [*n2*] *business, occupation*
activity, art, calling, commitment, contract, craft, do*, duty, employment, endeavor, gig*, grind*, industry, job, line, line of business, livelihood, manufacture, métier, moonlight*, nine-to-five*, obligation, office, practice, profession, pursuit, racket*, responsibility, skill, slot*, specialization, stint, swindle, task, thing*, trade, vocation, walk; SEE CONCEPTS *349,351,360*

work [*n3*] *achievement*
act, application, article, composition, creation, deed, end product, function, handicraft, handiwork, oeuvre, opus, output, performance, piece, product, production, workmanship; SEE CONCEPTS *260,706*

work [*v1*] *be employed; exert oneself*
apply oneself, be gainfully employed, buckle down*, carry on, dig, do a job, do business, drive, drudge, earn a living*, freelance, have a job, hold a job, hustle, knuckle down*, labor, manage, moil, moonlight*, nine-to-five it*, peg away*, plug away*, ply, punch a clock*, pursue, report, scratch, slave, slog*, specialize, strain, strive, sweat*, take on, toil, try; SEE CONCEPTS *100,351*

work [*v2*] *manipulate, operate*
accomplish, achieve, act, behave, bring about, carry out, cause, contrive, control, create, direct, drive, effect, execute, force, function, go, handle, imple-

ment, manage, maneuver, move, perform, ply, progress, react, run, serve, take, tick, use, wield; SEE CONCEPTS *94,117,199,204*

work [*v3*] *cultivate, form*
care for, dig, dress, farm, fashion, handle, knead, labor, make, manipulate, mold, process, shape, tend, till; SEE CONCEPTS *173,184,257*

workable [*adj*] *feasible*
applicable, breeze*, cinch*, doable, duck soup*, easy, easy as pie*, exploitable, functional, no sweat*, piece of cake*, possible, practicable, practical, simple as ABC*, snap, usable, useful, viable, working; SEE CONCEPTS *538,552,560*

worker [*n*] *person who is employed*
artisan, blue collar*, breadwinner, company man/woman, craftsman/woman, craftsperson, employee, hand, help, laborer, mechanic, nine-to-fiver*, operative, peasant, pink collar*, proletarian, serf, slave, stiff, toiler, trader, tradesman/woman, wage earner, white collar*, working man/woman, working stiff*; SEE CONCEPT *348*

working [*adj*] *active, occupied*
alive, busy, dynamic, effective, employed, engaged, functioning, going, hot*, in a job, in force, in full swing, in gear, in process, laboring, live, moving, on fire*, on the job, on track*, operative, practical, running, useful, viable; SEE CONCEPTS *538,560*

workmanship [*n*] *expertise in production*
ability, achievement, art, artistry, competence, craft, craftsmanship, execution, handicraft, handiwork, manufacture, proficiency, quality, skill, technique, work; SEE CONCEPTS *630,706*

workout [*n*] *exercise, practice*
conditioning, constitutional, drill, rehearsal, routine, session, test, training, tryout, warm-up, work; SEE CONCEPTS *290,363*

work out [*v*] *solve; satisfy*
accomplish, achieve, arrange, attain, be effective, bring off, clear, come out, come to terms*, complete, compromise, construct, contrive, develop, devise, elaborate, evolve, figure out, find out, finish, fix, form, formulate, get something done, go, go well, handle, happen, manipulate, pan out*, plan, prosper, pull off*, put together, reach agreement, resolve, result, succeed, swing*, turn out, up, win; SEE CONCEPTS *706,713*

work up [*v*] *stimulate*
agitate, animate, arouse, breed, cause, develop, engender, excite, generate, get up, hatch, improve, incite, induce, inflame, instigate, move, muster up*, occasion, produce, rouse, spur, stir up; SEE CONCEPTS *14,242*

world [*n1*] *planet, globe*
cosmos, creation, earth, heavenly body, macrocosm, microcosm, nature, sphere, star, terrene, universe; SEE CONCEPTS *511,770*

world [*n2*] *class of existing beings*
class, division, everybody, everyone, group, humanity, humankind, human race, man, mankind, men

women and children, race, realm; SEE CONCEPTS *378,391*

world [*n3*] *person's environment, experience*
ambience, area, atmosphere, business, domain, field, kingdom, life, matters, memory, province, pursuits, realm, sphere, system; SEE CONCEPT *678*

worldly [*adj1*] *material, nonreligious*
carnal, earthly, earthy, fleshly, human, lay, materialistic, mundane, natural, physical, practical, profane, secular, sublunary, telluric, temporal, terrene, terrestrial, ungodly; SEE CONCEPTS *536,582*

worldly [*adj2*] *sophisticated, materialistic*
avaricious, been around, blasé, callous, cool*, cosmopolitan, covetous, disenchanted, grasping, greedy, hardened, knowing, opportunistic, power-loving, practical, self-centered, selfish, unprincipled, uptown*, urbane, worldly-wise; SEE CONCEPT *401*

worldwide [*adj*] *general*
catholic, common, comprehensive, cosmic, ecumenical, extensive, global, international, multinational, omnipresent, pandemic, planetary, ubiquitous, universal; SEE CONCEPT *536*

worn/worn-out [*adj*] *used, tired*
beat, burned out*, bushed*, busted*, clichéd, consumed, depleted, destroyed, deteriorated, drained, drawn, effete, exhausted, fatigued, frayed, gone, hackneyed, had it*, haggard, jaded, kaput*, knocked out*, old, out of gas*, overused, overworked, pinched, played out*, pooped*, ragged, ruined, shabby, shot, spent, stale, tattered, the worse for wear*, threadbare, timeworn, tired out, totaled*, used up, useless, wearied, weary, well-worn, wiped out, worn down, wrung out*; SEE CONCEPTS *485,560*

worried [*adj*] *anxious, troubled*
afraid, apprehensive, beside oneself, bothered, clutched, concerned, distracted, distraught, distressed, disturbed, fearful, fretful, frightened, hung up*, ill-at-ease, nervous, on edge*, on pins and needles*, overwrought, perturbed, solicitous, tense, tormented, uneasy, upset, uptight, worried stiff*; SEE CONCEPT *403*

worry [*n*] *anxiety, trouble*
anguish, annoyance, apprehension, bad news*, care, concern, disquiet, distress, disturbance, doubt, fear, headache*, heartache*, irritation, misery, misgiving, nag*, pain*, perplexity, pest, plague, presentiment, problem, torment, torture, trial, uncertainty, uneasiness, vexation, woe, worriment; SEE CONCEPTS *532,690*

worry [*v*] *be or make anxious, troubled*
afflict, aggrieve, agonize, ail, annoy, attack, bedevil, beleaguer, beset, bite one's nails*, bother, brood, bug*, chafe, concern oneself, depress, despair, disquiet, distress, disturb, dun, feel uneasy, fret, gnaw at, goad, go for*, harass, harry, hassle, have qualms, hector, importune, irritate, needle*, oppress, persecute, perturb, pester, plague, stew*, sweat out*, take on, tantalize, tear, tease, test, torment, torture, trou-

ble, try, unsettle, upset, vex, wince, writhe, wrong; SEE CONCEPTS *7,14,19,410*

worsen [*v*] *diminish, decay*
aggravate, corrode, damage, decline, degenerate, depress, descend, deteriorate, disintegrate, exacerbate, fall off, get worse, go downhill*, impair, lower, retrograde, retrogress, rot, sink; SEE CONCEPTS *240,698*

worship [*n*] *honoring, glorification*
adoration, adulation, awe, beatification, benediction, chapel, church service, deification, devotion, exaltation, genuflection, glory, homage, honor, idolatry, idolization, invocation, laudation, love, offering, praise, prayer, prostration, regard, respect, reverence, rite, ritual, service, supplication, veneration, vespers; SEE CONCEPTS *69,367*

worship [*v*] *honor, glorify*
admire, adore, adulate, bow down, canonize, celebrate, chant, deify, dote on, esteem, exalt, extol, idolize, laud, love, magnify, offer prayers to, pay homage to, praise, pray to, put on a pedestal*, respect, revere, reverence, sanctify, sing, sing praises to*, venerate; SEE CONCEPTS *69,367*

worth [*n*] *value, estimation associated with something*
account, aid, assistance, avail, benefit, caliber, class, consequence, cost, credit, desirability, dignity, equivalence, excellence, goodness, help, importance, mark, meaningfulness, merit, moment, note, perfection, price, quality, rate, significance, stature, use, usefulness, utility, valuation, virtue, weight, worthiness; SEE CONCEPTS *335,346*

worthless [*adj*] *of no use; without value*
abandoned, abject, barren, base, bogus, cheap, contemptible, counterproductive, despicable, empty, futile, good-for-nothing, ignoble, inconsequential, ineffective, ineffectual, inferior, insignificant, inutile, meaningless, mediocre, miserable, no-account*, no-good*, nothing, nugatory, paltry, pointless, poor, profitless, sterile, trashy, trifling, trivial, unavailing, unessential, unimportant, unproductive, unprofitable, unusable, useless, valueless, waste, wretched; SEE CONCEPTS *560,570,575*

worthwhile [*adj*] *helpful*
advantageous, beneficial, constructive, estimable, excellent, gainful, good, important, invaluable, justifiable, lucrative, meritorious, money-making, paying, priceless, productive, profitable, remunerative, rewarding, serviceable, useful, valuable, worthy; SEE CONCEPTS *560,567,572*

worthy [*adj*] *honorable, respectable*
A-1*, aces*, admirable, best, blameless, choice, commendable, creditable, decent, dependable, deserving, desirable, divine, estimable, ethical, excellent, exemplary, first-class*, first-rate*, good, honest, incorrupt, invaluable, laudable, meritorious, model, moral, noble, pleasing, praiseworthy, precious, priceless, pure, reliable, reputable, righteous, right-minded, salt of the earth*, satisfying, sterling, top-drawer*, top-notch*, true, trustworthy, upright,

valuable, virtuous, winner, worthwhile; SEE CONCEPTS *545,567,572*

wound [*n*] *injury*
anguish, bruise, cut, damage, distress, gash, grief, harm, heartbreak, hurt, insult, laceration, lesion, pain, pang, shock, slash, torment, torture, trauma; SEE CONCEPT *309*

wound [*v1*] *cause bodily damage*
bruise, carve, clip*, contuse, cut, damage, ding*, gash, harm, hit, hurt, injure, irritate, lacerate, nick, open up, ouch*, pierce, rough up*, scrape, scratch, slash, slice, stick, total; SEE CONCEPTS *137,246,313*

wound [*v2*] *cause mental hurt*
bother, cut to the quick*, distress, disturb, do in*, dump on*, get*, grieve, hurt, hurt one's feelings, mortify, offend, outrage, pain, put down*, shake up*, sting, traumatize, trouble, upset; SEE CONCEPTS *7,14,19*

wrangle [*n*] *fight, argument*
altercation, battle royal*, bickering, blow-off*, blowup*, branigan, brawl, brouhaha*, clash, contest, controversy, disagreement, dispute, exchange, falling-out*, flap*, fracas, hassle, knock-down drag-out*, quarrel, row, ruckus*, ruction, rumble, rumpus, scene, set-to*, squabble, tiff; SEE CONCEPTS *46,106*

wrangle [*v*] *fight, argue*
altercate, bicker, brawl, bump heads*, contend, cross swords*, disagree, dispute, fall out*, hassle, have at it*, have words*, lock horns*, pick a bone*, put up a fight, quarrel, quibble, row, scrap, spat, squabble, take on, tangle, tiff; SEE CONCEPTS *46,106*

wrap [*n*] *clothing that is worn over for warmth*
blanket, cape, cloak, coat, cover, fur, jacket, mantle, shawl, stole; SEE CONCEPT *451*

wrap [*v*] *surround with a covering*
absorb, bandage, bind, bundle, bundle up, camouflage, cloak, clothe, cover, drape, encase, encircle, enclose, enfold, envelop, fold, gift-wrap*, hide, immerse, invest, mask, muffle, pack, package, protect, roll up, sheathe, shelter, shroud, swaddle, swathe, twine, veil, wind; SEE CONCEPT *172*

wrap up [*v*] *finish*
bring to a close, close, complete, conclude, determine, end, halt, polish off, terminate, wind up; SEE CONCEPT *234*

wrath [*n*] *extreme anger*
acrimony, asperity, boiling point*, conniption*, dander, displeasure, exasperation, flare-up, fury, hate, hatefulness, huff, indignation, ire, irritation, mad, madness, offense, passion, rage, resentment, rise, stew*, storm, temper, vengeance; SEE CONCEPTS *29,410*

wrathful [*adj*] *very angry*
beside oneself, displeased, enraged, furious, heated, incensed, indignant, infuriated, irate, ireful, mad, on the warpath*, raging, storming; SEE CONCEPT *403*

wreak [v] *force, cause*
bring about, carry out, create, effect, execute, exercise, force upon, inflict, unleash, vent, visit, work, wreck; SEE CONCEPT *242*

wreath [n] *circular decoration*
band, bay, bouquet, chaplet, circlet, coronal, coronet, crown, festoon, garland, laurel, lei, loop, ring, ringlet; SEE CONCEPTS *259,260,429*

wreck [n] *severe damage or severely damaged goods*
collapse, crash, crate, debacle, debris, derelict, destruction, devastation, disruption, fender bender*, heap*, hulk*, jalopy*, junk*, junker*, litter, mess, pile-up*, rear-ender*, relic, ruin, ruins, shipwreck, smashup*, total*, waste, wreckage; SEE CONCEPTS *260,674*

wreck [v] *ruin, destroy*
bash, batter, beach, break, capsize, crack up*, crash, cripple, dash, decimate, demolish, devastate, dilapidate, disable, do in*, efface, founder, impair, injure, mangle, mar, mess up*, pile up*, put out of commission*, ravage, raze, run aground, sabotage, scuttle, shatter, shipwreck, sink, smash, smash up, spoil, strand, subvert, take apart, take out, tear up, torpedo*, total, trash, undermine, vandalize, wrack*, wrack up*; SEE CONCEPT *252*

wrench [v] *jerk, force violently*
bend, coerce, compel, contort, dislocate, dislodge, distort, drag, exact, extract, pervert, pinch, pull, rend, rip, screw, sprain, squeeze, strain, tear, tug, tweak, twist, wrest, wring, yank; SEE CONCEPTS *80,206*

wrestle [v] *struggle physically or mentally with something*
battle, combat, contend, endeavor, essay, exert, fight, grapple, grunt, scuffle, strain, strive, tangle, tussle, work; SEE CONCEPTS *17,191,208*

wretched [adj] *terrible, very bad*
abject, afflicted, base, bummed, calamitous, cheap, contemptible, dejected, deplorable, depressed, despicable, disconsolate, distressed, dolorous, down, down and out*, downcast, faulty, flimsy, forlorn, gloomy, hapless, hopeless, hurting, inferior, in the pits*, low, low-down*, mean, melancholy, miserable, paltry, pathetic, pitiable, pitiful, poor, shabby, shameful, sordid, sorrowful, sorry, spiritless, tragic, unfortunate, unhappy, vile, weak, woebegone, woeful, worthless; SEE CONCEPTS *403,571*

wriggle [v] *maneuver out of; wiggle*
convulse, crawl, dodge, extricate oneself, glide, jerk, jiggle, ooze, skew, slink, slip, snake, sneak, squirm, turn, twist, twitch, wag, waggle, worm, writhe, zigzag; SEE CONCEPTS *30,149*

wring [v] *twist, contort*
choke, coerce, compress, draw out, exact, extort, extract, force, gouge, hurt, pain, pinch, pry, push, screw, shake down, squeeze, strain, strangle, throttle, turn, wrench, wrest; SEE CONCEPTS *142,206,208*

wrinkle [n] *crinkle, fold*
contraction, corrugation, crease, crow's-foot*, crumple, depression, furrow, gather, line, pleat, plicate, pucker, ridge, rimple, rumple, tuck; SEE CONCEPTS *418,513*

wrinkle [v] *crinkle, fold*
compress, corrugate, crease, crimp, crisp, crumple, furrow, gather, line, prune up, pucker, purse, rimple, ruck, rumple, screw up, scrunch, seam, shrivel, twist; SEE CONCEPTS *185,201*

writ [n] *court order*
command, decree, document, habeas corpus, mandate, paper, prescript, process, replevin, subpoena, summons, warrant; SEE CONCEPT *318*

write [v] *put language down on paper*
address, author, autograph, bang out*, chalk*, commit, communicate, comp*, compose, copy, correspond, create, dash off*, draft, draw up, drop a line, drop a note*, engross, formulate, ghost, indite, ink, inscribe, jot down, knock off, knock out, letter, note, note down, pen, pencil, print, push a pencil*, put in writing, record, reproduce, rewrite, scrawl, scribble, scribe, scriven, set down, set forth, sign, take down, tell, transcribe, turn out, typewrite, write down, write up; SEE CONCEPTS *79,203*

write off [v] *devalue; forget about*
cancel, cross out, decry, depreciate, disregard, downgrade, give up, lower, mark down, shelve, take a loss on, underrate, undervalue; SEE CONCEPT *54*

writer [n] *person who composes with language*
author, biographer, columnist, contributor, correspondent, critic, dramatist, editor, essayist, freelancer, ghostwriter, journalist, man/woman of letters, newspaperman/woman, newspaper person, novelist, poet, reporter, screenwriter, scribbler, scribe, scripter, stenographer, stringer, wordsmith; SEE CONCEPTS *348,356*

writhe [v] *contort; toss back and forth*
agonize, bend, distort, jerk, recoil, squirm, struggle, suffer, thrash, thresh, twist, wiggle, wince, worm, wriggle; SEE CONCEPTS *80,150*

writing [n1] *printing on paper*
autograph, calligraphy, chirography, hand, handwriting, hieroglyphics, longhand, manuscript, penmanship, print, scrawl, scribble, script, shorthand; SEE CONCEPTS *79,284*

writing [n2] *printed composition*
article, belles-lettres, book, discourse, dissertation, document, editorial, essay, letter, literature, manuscript, novel, ode, opus, pamphlet, paper, piece, play, poem, prose, publication, record, review, signature, theme, thesis, tract, treatise, work; SEE CONCEPT *271*

wrong [n] *offense, sin*
abuse, bad deed, bias, blunder, crime, cruelty, damage, delinquency, discourtesy, error, evil, faux pas*, favor, foul play, grievance, harm, hurt, immorality,

imposition, indecency, inequity, inhumanity, iniquity, injury, injustice, insult, libel, malevolence, miscarriage, misdeed, misdemeanor, misdoing, mistake, oppression, persecution, prejudice, sinfulness, slander, slight, spite, tort, transgression, trespass, turpitude, unfairness, vice, villainy, violation, wickedness, wrongdoing; SEE CONCEPT *645*

wrong [*adj1*] *incorrect*
amiss, askew, astray, at fault, awry, bad, counterfactual, defective, erratic, erring, erroneous, fallacious, false, faulty, fluffed, goofed*, inaccurate, in error, inexact, miscalculated, misconstrued, misfigured, misguided, mishandled, mistaken, not precise, not right, not working, off-target, on the wrong track*, out, out of commission*, out of line*, out of order*, perverse, rotten, sophistical, specious, spurious, ungrounded, unsatisfactory, unsound, unsubstantial, untrue, wide; SEE CONCEPTS *571,582*

wrong [*adj2*] *immoral, dishonest*
amoral, bad, base, blamable, blameworthy, blasphemous, censurable, corrupt, criminal, crooked, debauched, depraved, dishonorable, dissipated, dissolute, evil, felonious, illegal, illicit, indecent, iniquitous, naughty, profane, profligate, reprehensible, reprobate, risqué, sacrilegious, salacious, shady, sinful, smutty, unethical, unfair, ungodly, unholy, unjust, unlawful, unrighteous, vicious, wanton, wicked, wrongful; SEE CONCEPT *545*

wrong [*adj3*] *inappropriate, not suitable*
amiss, awkward, bad, disproportionate, funny, gauche, ill-advised, improper, inapt, incongruous, incorrect, indecorous, infelicitous, malapropos, misplaced, not done, off-balance, rotten, unacceptable, unbecoming, unconventional, undesirable, unfit, unfitted, unfitting, unhappy, unsatisfactory, unseemly, unsuitable; SEE CONCEPT *558*

wrong [*adj4*] *reverse, opposite*
back, inside, inverse, obverse; SEE CONCEPT *586*

wrong [*v*] *hurt, mistreat another*
abuse, aggrieve, cheat, damage, defame, discredit, dishonor, harm, hurt, ill-treat, impose upon, injure, malign, maltreat, misrepresent, mistreat, offend, oppress, outrage, persecute, take advantage of; SEE CONCEPTS *7,19,246,313*

wrong [*adv*] *astray*
afield, amiss, askew, badly, erroneously, inaccurately, incorrectly, mistakenly, unfavorably, wrongly; SEE CONCEPTS *544,548*

wrongful [*adj*] *evil, illegal*
blameworthy, criminal, dishonest, dishonorable, felonious, illegitimate, illicit, immoral, improper, lawless, reprehensible, unethical, unfair, unjust, unlawful, wicked; SEE CONCEPTS *319,545*

wry [*adj*] *sarcastic, distorted*
askew, aslant, awry, contorted, crooked, cynical, deformed, droll, dry, ironic, mocking, sardonic, twisted, uneven, warped; SEE CONCEPTS *267,581*

X

x-ray [*n*] *picture of inside a body*
actinism, cathode rays, encephalogram, fluoroscope, radioactivity, radiograph, refractometry, Roentgen rays, ultraviolet rays; SEE CONCEPT *311*

Y

yacht [*n*] *pleasure boat*
cabin cruiser, cruiser, racer, sailboat, sailing boat, sloop; SEE CONCEPT *506*

yak/yap [*n/v*] *talk a lot*
babble, blather, chat, chatter, clack, confabulate, gab, gossip, jabber, jaw, prate, prattle, run on, tattle, yammer; SEE CONCEPTS *51,266*

yank [*v*] *pull hard and fast*
draw, evulse, extract, hitch, jerk, lug, snap, snatch, tear, tug, twitch, vellicate, wrench; SEE CONCEPT *206*

yard [*n*] *grassy area around a structure*
backyard, barnyard, clearing, close, corral, court, courtyard, enclosure, fold, garden, grass, lawn, lot, patch, patio, playground, quadrangle, terrace; SEE CONCEPT *509*

yarn [*n1*] *fiber for knitting*
cotton fiber, flaxen thread, fleece, spun wool, thread, twist, wool; SEE CONCEPT *473*

yarn [*n2*] *story, often long and made-up*
adventure, alibi, anecdote, fable, fabrication, fairy tale, lie, line, narrative, potboiler*, prose, sea story*, song*, song and dance*, string*, tale, tall story*, tall tale; SEE CONCEPT *282*

yawn [*v*] *open mouth wide, usually sign of fatigue in animate being*
catch flies*, divide, doze, drowse, expand, gap, gape, give, nap, part, sleep, snooze, spread, yaw, yawp; SEE CONCEPTS *163,185*

yearly [*adj*] *every twelve months*
annual, annually, once a year, per annum, perennial, regularly, year by year, yearlong; SEE CONCEPTS *541,823*

yearn [*v*] *desire strongly*
ache, be desirous of, be eager for, be passionate, chafe, covet, crave, dream, hanker, have a crush on*, hunger, itch, languish, long, lust, pine, set one's heart on*, thirst, want, wish for, yen; SEE CONCEPT *20*

years [*n*] *old age*
age, agedness, caducity, dotage, elderliness, oldness, second childhood*, senescence, senility; SEE CONCEPT *715*

yell [*n/v*] *loud communication*
bawl, bellow, call, cheer, complain, cry, holler, hoot, howl, lament, roar, scream, screech, shout, shriek, shrill, squawk, squeal, ululate, vociferate, wail, weep, whoop, yap, yelp, yip; SEE CONCEPTS *47,595*

yellow [*n/adj1*] *sunny color*
amber, bisque, blond, buff, chrome, cream, gold, ivory, lemon, saffron, sand, tawny; SEE CONCEPTS *618,622*

yellow [*adj2*] *cowardly*
chicken*, craven, deceitful, gutless, lily-livered*, low, offensive, pusillanimous, sneaking, treacherous, tricky, unethical, unprincipled; SEE CONCEPTS *267,401*

yelp [*n/v*] *short, high cry*
bark, hoot, howl, screech, yap, yip, yowl; SEE CONCEPT *64*

yen [*n*] *strong want*
craving, desire, hankering, hunger, itch, longing, lust, passion, thirst, urge, yearning; SEE CONCEPTS *20,709*

yes [*adv*] *agreed*
affirmative, all right*, amen, aye*, beyond a doubt, by all means, certainly, definitely, even so, exactly, fine, gladly, good, good enough, granted, indubitably, just so, most assuredly, naturally, of course, okay*, positively, precisely, surely, sure thing*, true, undoubtedly, unquestionably, very well, willingly, without fail, yea*, yep*; SEE CONCEPTS *535,572*

yesterday [*n*] *the day before today*
bygone, foretime, lang syne*, last day, not long ago, past, recently, the other day; SEE CONCEPT *815*

yet [*adv1*] *up until now*
as yet, earlier, hitherto, prior to, so far, still, thus far, till, until now, up to now; SEE CONCEPT *820*

yet [*adv2*] *in spite of*
after all, although, at any rate, but, despite, even though, howbeit, however, nevertheless, nonetheless, notwithstanding, on the other hand, still, still and all, though, withal; SEE CONCEPT *544*

yet [*adv3*] *in addition*
additionally, along, also, as well, besides, further, furthermore, likewise, more, moreover, over and above, still, still further, to boot*, too; SEE CONCEPT *548*

yet [*adv4*] *in the future*
after a while, at some future time, beyond this, even, eventually, finally, in due course, in the course of time, someday, sometime, sooner or later, still, ultimately; SEE CONCEPT *799*

yield [*n*] *production of labor*
crop, earnings, harvest, income, output, outturn, produce, profit, return, revenue, takings, turnout; SEE CONCEPTS *260,338*

yield [*v1*] *produce*
accrue, admit, afford, allow, beam, bear, blossom, bring forth, bring in, discharge, earn, furnish, generate, give, give off, hold out, net, offer, pay, proffer, provide, return, sell for, supply, tender, turn out; SEE CONCEPT *205*

yield [*v2*] *give in, surrender*
abandon, abdicate, admit defeat, back down, bend, bow, break, buy, call it quits*, capitulate, cave in, cede, collapse, come to terms*, crumple, defer, fold, fold up, give oneself over, give up, give way*, go, hand over, knuckle, knuckle under*, lay down arms*, leave, let go*, part with, relax, relent, relinquish, resign, sag, say uncle*, submit, succumb, suffer defeat, surrender, throw in the towel*; SEE CONCEPTS *14,18,35*

yield [*v3*] *grant, allow*
accede, accept, acknowledge, acquiesce, admit, agree, assent, bow, break, comply, concede, concur, consent, defer, fail, fit in, go along with*, go with the flow*, permit, play the game*, surrender, toe the line*, toe the mark*, waive; SEE CONCEPT *8*

yielding [*adj1*] *accommodating*
acquiescent, biddable, compliant, docile, easy, flexible, humble, nonresistant, obedient, passive, pliable, pliant, putty in one's hands, resigned, submissive, tractable; SEE CONCEPTS *401,404*

yielding [*adj2*] *soft, flexible*
elastic, malleable, mushy, pappy, plastic, pliable, pulpy, quaggy, resilient, spongy, springy, squishy, squshy, supple, tractable, tractile, unresisting; SEE CONCEPTS *488,606*

yoke [*n*] *bondage, bond*
burden, chain, coupling, enslavement, helotry, knot, ligament, ligature, link, nexus, oppression, peonage, serfdom, service, servility, servitude, slavery, tie; SEE CONCEPTS *513,677*

yoke [*v*] *bond together; join*
associate, attach, bracket, buckle, combine, conjoin, conjugate, connect, couple, fasten, fix, harness, hitch, link, secure, splice, strap, tack, tie, unite, wed; SEE CONCEPTS *85,160,193*

yokel [*n*] *person who is mired in local custom*
backwoodsman/woman, boor*, country boy/girl, country cousin*, countryman/woman, hayseed*, peasant, rustic; SEE CONCEPT *413*

yonder [*adv*] *faraway*
away, beyond, distant, farther, further, remote, yon; SEE CONCEPTS *586,778*

young [*n*] *animate beings that are not mature*
babies, baby, brood, family, issue, litter, little ones*, offspring, progeny; SEE CONCEPTS *394,414,424*

young [*adj*] *immature*
adolescent, blooming, blossoming, boyish, boylike, budding, burgeoning, callow, childish, childlike, crude, developing, early, fledgling, fresh, girlish, girllike, green*, growing, half-grown, ignorant, inexperienced, infant, inferior, junior, juvenile, little, modern, new, newborn, newish, not aged, pubescent, puerile, punk, raw, recent, tender, tenderfoot*, undeveloped, undisciplined, unfinished, unfledged, unlearned, unpracticed, unripe, unseasoned, untried, unversed, vernal, youthful; SEE CONCEPTS *578,678,715,797*

youngster/youth [*n/n1*] *person before the age of maturity*
boy, chick*, cub*, fledgling, girl, junior, juvenile, juvenile delinquent*, kid*, lad, lass, pup, pupil,

puppy, student, teenager, young adult, young person; SEE CONCEPTS *414,424*

youth [*n2*] *early period in life of animate being*
adolescence, awkward age, bloom, boyhood, childhood, girlhood, greenness, ignorance, immaturity, inexperience, innocence, juvenescence, minority, prime, puberty, salad days*, springtide, springtime of life, teens, tender age*, virginity, youthfulness; SEE CONCEPT *817*

youthful [*adj*] *new, immature*
active, adolescent, boyish, budding, buoyant, callow, childish, childlike, enthusiastic, fresh, full of life, girlish, green*, inexperienced, infant, juvenile, keen, pubescent, puerile, tender, underage, vernal, vigorous, virginal, young; SEE CONCEPTS *542,578,797*

yowl [*n/v*] *long, loud animate sound*
bawl, bay, caterwaul, cry, holler, howl, mewl, scream, screech, squall, squeal, ululate, wail, whine, yell, yelp, yip; SEE CONCEPT *77*

Z

zany [*n*] *person who is wildly funny*
buffoon, card*, clown, comedian, comic, cutup*, farceur, funnyman/woman, gagman/woman, humorist, idiot, jester, joker, madcap*, moron, nut*, practical joker, prankster, screwball*, show-off, simpleton*, wag*, wisecracker*; SEE CONCEPTS *352,423*

zany [*adj*] *crazy, funny*
camp*, campy*, clownish, comical, dumb, eccentric, fool, foolish, goofy, hare-brained*, humorous, joshing, kooky*, loony*, madcap*, nutty*, sappy*, wacky*, witty; SEE CONCEPTS *267,401*

zeal [*n*] *enthusiasm*
alacrity, ardor, bustle, determination, devotion, diligence, dispatch, drive, eagerness, earnestness, enterprise, fanaticism, fervor, fierceness, fire, gusto, hustle, inclination, initiative, intensity, intentness, keenness, mania, passion, perseverance, push, readiness, sincerity, spirit, stick-to-itiveness*, urgency, vehemence, verve, warmth, what-it-takes*, yen, zest; SEE CONCEPTS *32,410,411*

zealous [*adj*] *enthusiastic*
afire, antsy, ardent, avid, burning, coming on strong*, dedicated, devoted, eager, earnest, fanatic, fanatical, fervent, fervid, fireball*, fired, frenetic, gung-ho*, hot*, impassioned, itchy*, keen, obsessed, passionate, possessed, pushy*, rabid, ripe, self-starting, spirited, wild-eyed*; SEE CONCEPTS *326,401,404*

zenith [*n*] *top*
acme, altitude, apex, apogee, bitter end*, cap, capper, capstone, climax, crest, crown, culmination, elevation, eminence, height, high noon*, high point, meridian, payoff, peak, pinnacle, roof, summit, tiptop, topper, vertex; SEE CONCEPTS *706,832,836*

zero [*n*] *nothing*
·aught, blank, bottom, cipher, insignificancy, love*, lowest point, nada*, nadir, naught, nil*, nix*, nobody*, nonentity, nought, nullity, oblivion, ought, rock bottom*, scratch, shutout, void, zilch*, zip*, zot*; SEE CONCEPTS *407,784*

zero hour [*n*] *vital moment*
appointed hour*, climax, contingency, countdown, crisis, crossroad, D-day*, emergency, exigency, jumping-off point*, juncture, moment of truth*, pinch, strait, target, the time*, turning point*; SEE CONCEPTS *668,815,832*

zest [*n1*] *taste, flavor*
bite, body, charm, flavoring, ginger, guts*, interest, kick*, nip, piquancy, punch*, pungency, relish, salt, savor, seasoning, smack*, snap*, spice, tang, zap*, zip*; SEE CONCEPT *614*

zest [*n2*] *energy, gusto*
appetite, ardor, bliss, bounce, cheer, delectation, delight, eagerness, ecstasy, elation, enjoyment, enthusiasm, fervor, guts*, happiness, keenness, moxie*, passion, pep*, pleasure, relish*, satisfaction, zeal, zing*; SEE CONCEPTS *410,411*

zigzag [*adj*] *moving side to side*
askew, awry, bent, crinkled, crooked, devious, diagonal, erratic, fluctuating, inclined, indirect, irregular, jagged, meandering, oblique, oscillating, rambling, serrated, sinuous, sloping, snaking, tortuous, transverse, twisted, twisting, undulating, waggling, winding; SEE CONCEPT *581*

zip [*n*] *enthusiasm, energy*
brio*, drive, get-up-and-go*, go*, gusto*, life, liveliness, oomph*, pep*, pizzazz*, punch, sparkle, spirit, verve, vigor, vim, vitality, zest, zing*; SEE CONCEPTS *411,633*

zip [*v*] *move about quickly*
bustle, dash, flash, fly, hasten, hurry, run, rush, shoot, speed, tear, waltz, whisk, whiz, zoom; SEE CONCEPT *150*

zone [*n*] *district*
area, band, belt, circuit, ground, realm, region, section, sector, segment, sphere, territory, tract; SEE CONCEPTS *508,513*

zoom [*v*] *move very quickly*
buzz, dart, dash, dive, flash, fly, hum, hurtle, outstrip, rip, rocket, rush, shoot, shoot up, skyrocket, speed, streak, surge, tear, whirl, whiz, zip*; SEE CONCEPT *150*

ROGET'S 21ST CENTURY CONCEPT INDEX

Simply put, a thesaurus is a collection of words grouped according to idea. 17,000 words appear in the A to Z listings of *Roget's 21st Century Thesaurus* with over 450,000 synonyms to choose from. This selection alone would seem generous enough to satisfy the lexicographer's expectation of what a thesaurus should contain. But a wealth of new alternatives is created when we begin to think about the higher connections that can be made between words and ideas in the language. This is the purpose of *Roget's 21st Century's* Concept Index.

The Concept Index not only helps writers and thinkers to *organize* their ideas but leads them from those very ideas to the words that can best express them. It is a semantic hierarchy of the most common concepts we use in American English, as it is spoken and written today. 837 concepts are classified according to their subject and usage, and are grouped under ten general categories of interest: Actions, Causes, Fields of Human Activity, Life Forms, Objects, the Planet, Qualities, Senses, States, and Weights and Measures.

Each of *Roget's 21st Century Thesaurus's* 17,000 main entries is cross-referenced to any concept(s) to which it can be related. For example, when you look up the entry for "knowledgeable" in the A to Z listing, it is referenced to concept #402. Turning in the index to concept #402, "attribute of intelligence," you will see over 100 other main entries that are also related to this concept:

MAIN ENTRY
with synonym list as it appears in the A to Z listing

knowledgeable [*adj*] *aware, educated*
abreast, acquainted, alert, appreciative, apprised, au courant, au fait, brainy, bright, brilliant, clever, cognizant, conscious, conversant, discerning, erudite, experienced, familiar, informed, insightful, intelligent, in the know, knowing, learned, lettered, omniscient, perceptive, plugged in*, posted, prescient, privy, quick-witted, sagacious, sage, savvy, scholarly, sensible, sharp, smart, sophic, sophisticated, tuned-in*, understanding, versed, well-informed, well-rounded, wise, with-it; SEE CONCEPT *402*

CONCEPT
with collection of main entry words referenced to it in the index

402 attribute of intelligence: able, abreast, abstruse, academic, acute, adept, alert, amenable, analytic/analytical, appreciative, apt, astute, awake, aware, backward, bewildered, blank, blind, bright, brilliant, calculable, canny, childish, clairvoyant, clear, clever, clumsy, cognizant, coherent, common-sense, complex, comprehensible, conscious, considered, contemplative, conversant, creative, cunning, dark, deducible, deep, delirious, dense, designedly, dexterous, dim, discerning, dizzy, dopey, down-to-earth, dull, dumb, educated, efficient, elevated, empty, empty-headed, enlightened, erudite, experienced, expert, familiar, farsighted, fatuous, forgotten, frivolous, gifted, gullible, harebrained, hazy, idiotic, ignorant, illiterate, imbecile, impressionable, incisive, incomprehensible, inefficient, ineligible, inept, inexperienced, informed, ingenious, inquiring, inquisitive, insipid, intellectual, intelligent, intuitive, inventive, irrational, judicious, keen, knowing, knowledgeable, learned, logical, lucid, mental, mindful, mistaken, nimble, oblivious, observant, obtuse, omniscient, penetrating, perceptive, perspicacious, philosophical/philosophic, precocious, privy, professional, proficient, profound, psychic, quick, quick-witted, rational, ready, reasonable, resourceful, retarded, sagacious, sane, scatterbrained, scholarly, senile, sensible, shallow, sharp, shrewd, simple, skillful, slick, slow, smart, soft, stolid, studious, stupid, subtle, thick, thoughtful, thoughtless, touched, unaware, uneducated, unfamiliar, unwise, vacant, vacuous, versed, veteran, weak, wise

Any of these main entry words appearing together as attributes of intelligence in the Concept Index—from "astute" to "ingenious" to "perspicacious" to "veteran"—may be the one perfect word you are looking for. Or, intrigued by the associations the word "veteran" brings to mind, you could return to the A to Z listing to explore its synonyms:

veteran [adj] *experienced, seasoned*
adept, battle-scarred*, been around*, disciplined, exercised, expert, from way back*, hardened, inured, knows one's stuff*, long-serving, long-time, not born yesterday*, of the old school*, old, old-time, practical, practiced, pro, proficient, skilled, sophisticated, steady, trained, up to speed*, versed, vet*, weathered, wise, wise to ways*, worldly; SEE CONCEPTS *402,527,678*

Even further possibilities exist, when you realize that "veteran" is referenced to two additional concepts: #527, the quality of "ability" and #678, the state of "experience." Main entries are often referenced to as many as three or four different concepts.

Simple to use, the Concept Index becomes invaluable in the effort to turn an idea into a specific word. By linking together the main entries that share similar concepts, but may not be direct synonyms, the index makes possible creative semantic connections between words in our language, stimulating thought and broadening vocabulary.

Whether you begin by browsing through the Concept Index for ideas, or in the A to Z listing with a particular word in mind, you will find that *Roget's 21st Century Thesaurus* goes beyond traditional thesauri and synonym-finders to offer thousands of word choices through access to its unique Concept Index.

QUICK REFERENCE GUIDE TO CONCEPTS

ACTIONS

Class of
SEE CONCEPTS **1–6**
Cognitive
SEE CONCEPTS **7–43**
Communicative
SEE CONCEPTS **44–79**
General
SEE CONCEPTS **80–143**
Motion
SEE CONCEPTS **144–155**
Physical
SEE CONCEPTS **156–227**

CAUSES

Abstract
SEE CONCEPTS **228–247**
Physical
SEE CONCEPTS **248–256**

FIELDS OF HUMAN ACTIVITY

Agriculture
SEE CONCEPTS **257–258**

The Arts
SEE CONCEPTS **259–265**
Communications
SEE CONCEPTS **266–284**
Education
SEE CONCEPTS **285–291**
Entertainment
SEE CONCEPTS **292–294**
Family
SEE CONCEPTS **295–297**
Government and Politics
SEE CONCEPTS **298–301**
Health
SEE CONCEPTS **302–316**
Legal
SEE CONCEPTS **317–319**
Military
SEE CONCEPTS **320–322**
Monetary and Financial Affairs
SEE CONCEPTS **323–346**
Professions
SEE CONCEPTS **347–362**
Recreation
SEE CONCEPTS **363–366**

Actions

1 **action:** act, action, activity, behave, feat, spurt, step
2 **event:** affair, anything, be, event, eventuate, experience, fact, incident, milestone, move, movement, occasion, outbreak, pass, proceeding
3 **occurrence:** development, episode, proceeding, recur, thing, transpire
4 **occurrence with one participant:** act, befall, behave, break, chance, coincidence, come, come off, deed, episode, fall out, fluke, go, happen, happening, intervene, occur, occurrence, result, return, rise
5 **occurrence with two participants:** boundary, limit, measure, obstruct, reinforce, restraint, test
6 **series of related actions:** channel, commit, disposition, elapse, form, instrument, maneuver, manner, means, mechanism, method, mode, path, pattern, policy, procedure, process, routine, rule, rut, system, technique, touch, usage, vehicle, way

7 **affect:** abandon, abase, affect, afflict, affront, aggravate, agitate, agonize, alarm, alienate, allay, alleviate, allure, anger, annoy, antagonize, appall/appal, appeal, appease, appeasement, arouse, arrest, assuage, attract, awaken, baffle, bait, beckon, bedazzle, befuddle, beguile, beleaguer, bemuse, beset, besiege, bewitch, bias, bombard, bore, bother, brighten, bring down, bug, buoy (up), burden, captivate, chafe, chagrin, charm, cheer, chill, clear, cloud, comfort, complicate, compose, concern, console, content, cow, craze, cross, crucify, crush, dampen, dash, daunt, debase, deceive, deception, defame, deflate, degrade, delight, demean, demoralize, deprecate, depreciate, depress, disaffect, disappoint, disarm, discomfit, discomfort, discommode, discompose, disconcert, discountenance, disgust, dishearten, dismay, disoblige, disparage, displease, disquiet, distress, disturb, divert, double-cross, downgrade, draw, dwarf, electrify, elevate, embarrass, embitter, embroil, enamor, enchant, encourage, encouragement, encroach, endear, energize, enliven, enrage, enrapture, enthrall, entice, enticement, entrance, estrange, exacerbate, exasperate, excite, exercise, exhilarate, fail, fascinate, faze, ferment, flurry, fluster, fortify, freak, fret, frustrate, fulfill, gall, galling, galvanize, get, govern, grate, gratify, grieve, grip, gripe, harass, harm, harry, hearten, horrify, hound, hurt, impress, inflame, ingratiate, inspire, instigate, interest, intimidate, intrigue, invigorate, irk, irritate, jar, kindle, let

down, lighten, lower, lull, madden, matter, menace, miff, mock, molest, mollify, mortify, move, nag, needle, nerve, nettle, occupy, offend, oppress, outrage, pacify, pain, pall, peeve, pep up, perk up, persecute, perturb, pester, petrify, pick at/pick on, pique, placate, plague, please, prejudice, pressure, prime, prod, provoke, puncture, put out, quell, quicken, rack, rally, rankle, rasp, reach, reassure, reduce, regenerate, register, remind, repay, repel, revolt, ride, rile, rouse, ruffle, sadden, satisfy, scar, scare, send, settle, shake, shame, shatter, sink, slight, slur, smooth, solace, soothe, spite, stagger, startle, still, strain, strengthen, stress, strike, support, sweeten, take down, tantalize, taunt, tease, temper, terrify, terrorize, threaten, thrill, tickle, titillate, torment, torture, touch, tranquilize, transport, trouble, try, turn, turn off, undo, unnerve, unsettle, upset, vex, visit, wake/waken, wear, weigh, weigh down, whet, worry, wound, wrong
8 **agree:** accede, accept, acceptance, accession, accord, acknowledge, acknowledgment, acquiesce, acquiescence, agree, align, assent, back, bear, cleave, cohere, comply, compromise, concur, consent, conspire, contract, covenant, draft, encourage, enlist, follow, give in/give up, go, go along/go along with, go by, grant, league, negotiate, stipulate, unanimous, yield
9 **amuse:** bait, divert, entertain, humor
10 **approve:** acquiesce, acquiescence, advocate, agree, applaud, appreciate, approbation, approval, approve, authorize, blessing, champion, concur, condone, countenance, defend, deference, endorse, envy, espouse, exalt, exculpate, excuse, exonerate, favor, go for, honor, idolize, league, nod, okay, overlook, pardon, pity, pride, prize, recognition, recommend, regard, respect, revere/reverence, reverence, sanctify, subscribe, support
11 **attract:** attract, fascinate, grip, interest, intrigue, inveigle, lure, mesmerize, pull, ravish, seduce, send, snare, take, tantalize, tease, tempt, titillate, transfix, turn on, whet, win, win over
12 **believe:** accept, acceptance, acknowledge, appreciate, appreciation, assume, authenticate, bank on, bear, believe, bleed, consider, convert, count on/count upon, credit, deem, disagree, embrace, esteem, expect, feel, forgive, glorify, glory, hold, imagine, infer, lean, make believe, misjudge, object, overrate, postulate, predispose, presume, rate, reckon, regard, rely, sanctify, see, suppose, swallow, think, trust, underestimate, understand, view
13 **change conception:** ache, alternate, awakening, caprice, catharsis, concession, conform, conformity, crack, crack up, fit, flare, fluctuate, give, go back/go back on, oscillate, perish, repudiate, re-

verse, revert, revive, sway, thaw, tire, vacillate, weary

14 compel: abet, alarm, attraction, badger, bait, bewilder, bind, brainwash, browbeat, brutality, bulldoze, bully, burden, coerce, coercion, come between, compel, confusion, conjure, constrain, constraint, convert, corrupt, dare, debauch, defeat, demoralize, deprave, discourage, disgrace, dispel, distract, domineer, duress, embitter, engross, enrage, enslave, entrance, excite, fan, fire, foment, force, freeze, frighten, galvanize, get back at, goad, grate, grind, harass, harassment, hassle, haunt, horrify, humble, humiliate, hurt, impel, impinge, imposition, incense, incite, inconvenience, inculcate, indoctrinate, induce, infest, inflame, infuriate, instill, interject, intimidate, intrude, inveigle, invigorate, jinx, jog, kindle, load, lumber, make, manipulate, meddle, mesmerize, mistreat, molest, motivate, nauseate, nerve, nettle, nonplus, oblige, offend, oppress, oppression, panic, paralyze, pervert, petrify, pique, plague, poison, pound, predispose, prejudice, press, pressure, prey on, provocation, push, put, put out, rankle, ride, ruffle, scourge, screw, sell/sell out, shake up, shame, sicken, sour, spoil, spur, stimulate, stir, sway, tame, task, tax, terrorize, tire, transfix, undermine, unnerve, victimize, visit, wake/waken, whip up, work up, worry, wound, yield

15 comprehend: appreciate, appreciation, apprehend, assimilate, catch, comprehend, conceive, decipher, deduce, deduction, derive, determine, differentiate, dig, digest, discern, discriminate, distinguish, do, draw, embrace, familiarize, fathom, feel, figure, follow, gather, get, grasp, hear, identify with, infer, know, make, make out, misapprehend, misconstrue, mistake, misunderstand, outwit/outsmart, penetrate, perceive, realize, recognize, resolve, see, solve, take, take in, tell, understand

16 confuse: confound, confuse, daze, dazzle, decoy, derange, disconcert, disrupt, distract, dumbfound, floor, fluster, foul up, get, hassle, humble, jumble, mix up, muddle, mystify, nonplus, obscure, overwhelm, perplex, perturb, puzzle, rattle, snarl, stump, throw

17 consider: absorb, ache, balance, begrudge, bleed, brood, buckle down, cogitate, commune, concentrate, consult, contemplate, cook up, cram, daydream, deliberate, deliberation, devote, dream, dream up, dwell on/dwell upon, engross, entertain, envisage/envision, excogitate, eye, fancy, fantasize, focus, gnaw, grieve, harbor, heed, hide, immerse, marvel, meditate, mull, muse, occupy, picture, ponder, puzzle, reconsider, reflect, reflection, reminisce, retrospect, revolve, speculate, think, thought, treat, turn over, visualize, wonder, wrestle

18 decide: abnegation, adjudicate, adopt, adoption, appraisal, appraise, cancel, circumscribe, classification, classify, conclude, convict, count, credit, date, decide, dedicate, define, derive, destine, determine, disapprove, disavow, dispose of, distinguish, evaluate, falter, figure, fix, go along/go along with, go by, ground, group, hedge, impose, influence, intend, judge, make out, misjudge, moderate, ordain, plant, premise, provide, purpose, referee, resolution, resolve, rule, set, settle, solve, specify, stipulate, surmise, turn down, type, waver, yield

19 depress: abandon, abase, affect, afflict, affront, aggravate, agitate, agonize, alarm, alienate, anger, annoy, antagonize, appall/appal, appeal, arouse, arrest, awaken, awe, baffle, bait, befuddle, beguile, beleaguer, bemuse, beset, besiege, bias, bombard, bore, bother, bring down, bug, burden, chafe, chagrin, chill, cloud, complicate, concern, cow, craze, cross, crucify, crush, dampen, dash, daunt, debase, deceive, deception, defame, deflate, degrade, demean, demoralize, deprecate, depreciate, depress, disaffect, disappoint, disarm, discomfit, discomfort, discommode, discompose, disconcert, discountenance, disgust, dishearten, dismay, disoblige, disparage, displease, disquiet, distress, disturb, divert, double-cross, downgrade, draw, dwarf, embarrass, embitter, embroil, encroach, enrage, enthrall, entice, enticement, estrange, exacerbate, exasperate, excite, exercise, fail, faze, ferment, flurry, fluster, freak, fret, frustrate, gall, galling, get, govern, grate, grieve, gripe, harass, harm, harry, horrify, hound, hurt, impress, inflame, instigate, intimidate, irk, irritate, jar, let down, lower, madden, matter, menace, miff, mock, molest, mortify, move, nag, needle, nettle, occupy, offend, oppress, outrage, pain, pall, peeve, persecute, perturb, pester, petrify, pick at/pick on, pique, plague, prejudice, pressure, prime, prod, provoke, puncture, put out, quicken, rack, rankle, rasp, reach, reduce, register, remind, repay, repel, revolt, ride, rile, ruffle, sadden, scar, scare, shake, shame, shatter, sink, slight, slur, spite, stagger, startle, strain, stress, strike, support, take down, tantalize, taunt, tease, terrify, terrorize, threaten, torment, torture, touch, trouble, try, turn, turn off, undo, unnerve, unsettle, upset, vex, visit, wear, weigh, weigh down, worry, wound, wrong

20 desire: addiction, advance(s), affinity, aim, ambition, angle for, appetite, aspiration, aspire, avid, behest, burn, care, covet, crave, craving, crush, cupidity, curiosity, dependence/dependency, desire, drool, eagerness, envy, expect, famished, fancy, fantasy, fascination, fish for, free will, goad, greed, hanker after/hanker for, hankering, hope, hunger, hungry, impulse, inclination, indulge, insatiable, interest, itch, lack, languish, lean, leaning, like, liking, long, longing, lust, mania, mind, miss, moon, mope, motivation, motive, need, nostalgia, notion, obsession, pant, penchant, pine, please, pleasure, predilection, predisposition, prefer, preference, proclivity, propensity, purport, purpose, pursue, relish, require, sigh, stomach, taste, temptation, thirst, urge, volition, voracious, want, will, wish, yearn, yen

21 **doubt:** begrudge, controvert, deplore, despair, disallow, disapprove, disbelief, disbelieve, discount, discountenance, discredit, dissent, distrust, doubt, frown, fume, grudge, hesitate, hesitation, mind, misgiving, mistrust, object, objection, oppose, query, question, regret, reject, rejection, repudiate, repulse, scorn, scruple, segregate, spurn, suspect, turn, wonder

22 **elate:** affect, allay, alleviate, allure, appeal, appease, appeasement, arouse, arrest, assuage, attract, awaken, awe, beckon, bedazzle, beguile, bemuse, bewitch, brighten, buoy (up), captivate, charm, cheer, clear, comfort, compose, concern, console, content, delight, disarm, divert, draw, electrify, elevate, enamor, enchant, encourage, encouragement, endear, energize, enliven, enrapture, enthrall, entice, enticement, entrance, excite, exhilarate, fascinate, ferment, fortify, fulfill, galvanize, get, govern, gratify, grip, hearten, impress, inflame, ingratiate, inspire, instigate, interest, intrigue, invigorate, kindle, lighten, lull, matter, mollify, move, nerve, occupy, pacify, pep up, perk up, pique, placate, please, pressure, prime, prod, provoke, quell, quicken, rally, reach, reassure, regenerate, register, remind, rouse, satisfy, send, settle, smooth, solace, soothe, still, strengthen, strike, support, sweeten, tantalize, tease, temper, thrill, tickle, titillate, touch, tranquilize, transport, wake/waken, weigh, whet

23 **endure:** abide, accept, accommodate, acquiesce, bear, bear with, bow, brave, brook, come in for, come through, condone, cope, descend, digest, do without, endure, face, go, go through, hang on, have, keep at, keep up, linger, lump, make out, manage, mind, mourn, pay, persist, receive, reconcile, remain, resist, resistance, shoulder, stand/stand for, stick, stomach, submit, subsist, suffer, support, survive, sustain, sweat, take, tolerate, undergo, wear, weather, withstand

24 **examine:** analysis, analyze, assay, assess, assessment, bury, canvass, check, chew, cogitate, compare, comparison, consider, consideration, debate, decompose, deduce, deduction, deliberate, deliberation, dissect, dissection, evaluate, evaluation, examine, excogitate, experiment, go into, go over, inquire, inquiry, introspection, observe, ponder, pore, reflect, reflection, resolve, review, ruminate, scrutinize, scrutiny, speculate, speculation, turn over, view, weigh

25 **exclude:** abnegation, abstain, blacklist, boycott, count out, disallow, disavow, disinherit, except, exception, exclude, exclusion, jump, omission, omit, ostracize, oust, parry, pass, pass by, pass over, proscribe, recant, retract, rule out, shut off/shut out

26 **expect:** anticipate, anticipation, assume, await, bargain for, calculate, count, count on/count upon, demand, depend, expect, foresee, imagine, lean, look, mean, plan, postulate, predispose, presume, propose, reckon, rely, think

27 **fear:** apprehension, blanch, dismay, dread, fear, funk, horror, mistrust, panic, phobia, terror, trepidation

28 **guess:** believe, bet, calculation, call, conjecture, deem, divine, estimate, estimation, forecast, gamble, guess, hazard, implication, presume, project, projection, speculate, speculation, suppose, surmise, suspect, wager

29 **hate:** abhor, abominable, abomination, aggression, anarchy, anger, animosity, antagonism, antipathy, atrocity, aversion, blow up, boil, burn, contempt, deplore, despise, detest, discrimination, disdain, disfavor, disinclination, dislike, disrespect, dissatisfaction, dissent, distaste, enmity, exasperation, execrate, execration, frown, fume, fury, grudge, hate, hatred, horror, ill will, indignation, lament/lamentation, loath, loathe, look down on, malice, mind, odium, opposition, outrage, phobia, pique, rage, rancor, repulsion, resent, resentment, revulsion, scorn, seethe, spite, temper, umbrage, vengeance, venom, violence, wrath

30 **ignore:** blink, brush aside/brush off, bypass, disallow, discount, disdain, disobey, dispense with, disregard, drop, eliminate, elude, eschew, evade, except, exception, exclude, exclusion, fence, forget, forsake, hedge, ignore, leave, lose, neglect, overlook, parry, pass, pass by, pass over, rebuff, refuse, reject, rejection, relegate, renounce, renunciation, repel, repudiate, retreat, run-around, scorn, shirk, shun, skip, skirt, slight, sneer, snub, spurn, wriggle

31 **learn:** absorb, acquaint, ascertain, catch, decipher, determine, dig, discover, discovery, edification, find out, get, glean, hear, learn, master, orientation, pick up, probe, research, see, study, turn up

32 **love:** acceptance, activity, admiration, admire, adoration, adore, adulation, affair, affection, affinity, amour, appetite, appreciate, appreciation, approval, attachment, attention, bag, bask, bewitched, bliss, canonize, care, charity, cherish, consideration, consolation, constancy, court, delight in, devotion, dig, discriminate, discrimination, dote on/dote upon, empathy, enamored, endear, enjoy, enjoyment, esteem, exaltation, exult, exultation, fall for, fancy, fascinated, fascination, favor, fidelity, flame, flirtation, fond, fondness, go for, gratitude, homage, idolize, infatuated, leaning, liaison, like, liking, love, lure, mad, mania, mercy, partiality, passion, penchant, predilection, predisposition, prize, proclivity, rapture, relish, respect, revere/reverence, reverence, savor, sentiment, taste, temper, thrill, transport, treasure, triumph, zeal

33 **mental event:** learn, sense, shock, stroke, think

34 **mental perception:** ascertain, attend, behold, be-

ware, burn, come at, feel, gnaw, gravitate, grope, hallucinate, learn, mind, note, notice, observe, occur, pity, presage, seethe, sensation, sense, shudder, sorrow, sympathize, visualize, wonder

35 **mental preparation:** abide, adjust, bottle up, capitulate, center, centralize, comply, concede, conceive, condition, convert, cope, crawl, dare, deign, descend, design, determine, dismiss, dispel, face, forbear, get over, habituate, harden, look out, manufacture, melt, orient, plan, preparation, prepare, prime, quail, ready, reform, refresh, rehabilitate, rejuvenate, relent, renew, resist, season, simmer, sink, smolder, steel, stew, stoop, strengthen, succumb, sulk, sweat, tarry, train, weather, withhold, yield

36 **plan:** arrange, assure, base, block out, book, brew, budget, calculate, chart, coin, concoct, connive, conspire, contemplate, contrive, cook up, coordinate, daydream, design, devise, draft, dream up, engineer, fabricate, finesse, fix, formulate, frame, hatch, intend, intrigue, invent, lay, lay out, machinate, maneuver, manufacture, mastermind, mean, organize, outline, plan, plot, program, project, propose, purpose, pursue, rough out, schedule, shape, sketch

37 **reason:** analyze, cipher, clear up, conclude, construe, crack, criticize, date, decipher, dialectic, do, educe, equate, estimate, figure, forecast, gauge, generalize, induction, infer, judgment, logic, make, premise, project, rank, rate, reason, reasoning, reckon, solve, speculate, stock, survey

38 **recognize:** acknowledge, ascertain, come across, conjure up, crack, cut, detect, detection, diagnose, differentiate, discern, discriminate, distinguish, elude, encounter, familiarize, fathom, feel, identify, know, mark, perceive, pinpoint, place, recognition, recognize, remark, salute/salutation, salute, spot, stereotype

39 **relate:** ascribe, associate, association, categorize, class, classification, classify, codify, compare, comparison, contrast, correlate, equate, identify with, implication

40 **remember:** block out, forget, mind, recall, recollect, remember, remembrance, remind, reminisce, retain, retrospect, think

41 **select:** aim, allocate, allot, allow, appoint, appointment, assign, assignment, cast, choice, choose, cull, designate, designation, elect, election, excerpt, favoritism, finger, like, name, nominate, nomination, opt, pick, prefer, recruit, relegate, screen, select, take, turn, volition, vote

42 **surprise:** alarm, amaze, appall/appal, astonish, astound, awe, backfire, baffle, bedazzle, befuddle, bewilder, confound, daze, dazzle, deluge, dumbfound, electrify, flabbergast, frighten, jolt, overwhelm, petrify, scare, shock, stagger, startle, stun/stupefy, surprise, terrify

43 **think:** count, design, devise, envisage/envision, fancy, imagine, mint, occur, originate, picture, proceed, see, theorize, think, thought

COMMUNICATIVE

44 **accuse:** accuse, affront, arraign, bastardize, betray, betrayal, blame, blow up, charge, condemn, condemnation, decry, denounce, discredit, forswear, gripe, groan, grumble, heckle, humble, humiliate, impeach, implicate, impute, indict, indictment, invective, inveigh, malign, persecute, profane, rant, rebuke, reprimand, reproach, scold, slur, tax, tell off, tirade, vilify, vituperate

45 **answer:** acknowledge, agree, answer, counter, decline, denial, fill in, give in/give up, react, reaction, reciprocate, repartee, reply, respond, retort, return

46 **argue:** agitate, altercation, argue, argument, back talk, battle, beard, bicker, brawl, clash, conflict, confront, confrontation, confute, contend, contention, contest, contradict, contradiction, contravene, controversy, controvert, demur, deny, dicker, differ, difference, difficulty, disagree, disagreement, dispute, dissension, dissent, diverge, divide, encounter, expostulate, fall out, feud, fight, fracas, friction, fuss, haggle, hassle, imbroglio, maintain, misunderstanding, negate, object, objection, protest, quarrel, quibble, reason, rebut, remonstrate, rift, row, run-in, rupture, scrap, squabble, strife, tiff, uproar, wrangle

47 **articulate:** articulate, call, cry, delivery, diction, elocution, enunciate, exclaim, expression, hail, heckle, mumble, parrot, pipe, pronounce, put, sing, slur, speak, speech, stammer, talk, utter, utterance, yell

48 **ask:** accost, apologize, apology, appeal, application, apply, approach, ask, beg, beseech, canvass, catechize, charter, conjure, consult, consultation, crave, crawl, cross-examine, desire, entreat, examine, grill, hearing, implore, inquest, inquire, inquiry, interrogate, interview, investigate, investigation, invitation, invite, invocation, invoke, pester, petition, plead, poll, pray, prayer, propose, proposition, pump, query, quest, question, quiz, repent, requisition, scrounge, seek, survey

49 **assert:** accredit, acknowledge, advance, advocate, affirm, affirmation, allegation, allege, announce, announcement, ascribe, assert, assertion, attest, avow, bemoan, blow up, bluster, boast, brag, bravado, color, come clean, corroborate, crow, debunk, declaim, declaration, declare, defend, deny, dramatize, drum into, embellish, emphasize, establish, exclaim, exclamation, exult, generalize, gloat, glory, gloss, gush, impress, impute, insinuate, insist, intimate, justify, lay, level, magnify, maintain, mock, mockery, overrate, pass, play down, play up, plead, plug, point out, pound, proclaim, profess, promote, promotion, pronounce, puff, punctuate, purport, push, rant, rave, refuse, retract, review, rumor, show off, speak out/speak up, spout, state, stereotype, stress, substantiate, support, swagger, swear, testify, testimonial, tes-

timony, underline, vent, vindicate, voice, vouch, weep, whitewash, witness

50 authorize: accede, accord, accredit, acknowledge, acknowledgment, acquit, affirm, aggrandize, appoint, appointment, approve, arm, assign, authorize, back, ban, bar, bear out, bless, blessing, certify, charter, commission, concession, consent, constitute, contract, countenance, countermand, crown, decree, dedicate, delegate, delegation, detail, disown, empower, enable, enact, endorse, enforce, enjoin, entitle, entrust, establish, exempt, fire, forgive, grant, induct, inflict, invest, invoke, lay, let, let off, license, make, name, negate, nod, nominate, nomination, nullify, okay, ordain, order, override/overrule, pardon, permission, permit, place, prescribe, prohibit, ratify, recall, receive, release, relieve, repeal, reprieve, revoke, sanction, spare, station, subscribe, underwrite, validate, vest, veto, void, warrant, withdraw, witness

51 comment: accost, acknowledge, add, air, annotate, aside, babble, badger, bemoan, brag, bravado, bring up, broach, circumlocution, comment, commentary, congratulate, conjecture, couch, critique, declaim, decline, deliver, discourse, enunciate, express, extemporize, greet, greeting, harangue, hearsay, interject, interrupt, jabber, jaw, observation, observe, preach, ramble, rattle, rave, remark, report, rhetoric, say, spout, state, talk, throw out, touch, vent, ventilate, voice, yak/yap

52 criticize: abuse, admonish, air, aspersion, assail, assault, attack, barb, baste, beef, belittle, berate, blast, browbeat, carp, castigate, censure, chasten, chastise, chew out, chide, come down on, complain, complaint, condemn, condemnation, confront, correct, cow, criticism, criticize, critique, crucify, cut, cut up, damn, debase, decry, denigrate, denounce, denunciation, deny, deprecate, depreciate, deride, derision, detract, detraction, diatribe, disapprove, disparage, disparagement, dress down, excoriate, flak, fulminate, fulmination, gainsay, gibe, gird, grievance, gripe, groan, grouch, grumble, hiss, humble, humiliate, impeach, impugn, insult, invective, inveigh, jaw, kick, knock, lambaste, lament, lash, lay into, lecture, malign, moan, mortify, mutter, nag, offense, pan, pick at/pick on, profane, protest, quibble, rail, rant, rap, rebuke, reflection, remonstrate, reprimand, reproach, review, row, run down, sarcasm, scold, scorn, scourge, slam, sneer, squawk, storm, sulk, swear, take down, tell off, thunder, vilify, vituperate

53 demand: ask, beckon, beg, behest, bid, bidding, bribe, call, challenge, charge, claim, command, countermand, crave, cross-examine, dare, decree, demand, dictate, direct, enjoin, entreat, exact, extort, extortion, grill, importune, impose, inflict, insist, instruct, interrogate, necessitate, obligate, order, petition, pump, query, question, request,

require, requisition, reserve, solicit, squeeze, summon

54 deny: abuse, accusation, affront, aspersion, attack, backbiting, barb, belie, belittle, blacken, blame, blemish, casuistry, confront, contradict, curse, damn, debase, defamation, defame, defile, demean, demur, denial, denigrate, deride, detract, detraction, dig, diminish, disclaim, discountenance, discredit, disgrace, dishonor, disown, disparage, disparagement, downgrade, embarrass, explode, flout, forswear, fulminate, fulmination, gainsay, gibe, gird, insult, invective, inveigh, jeer, lambaste, lament, laugh at, lecture, lip, malign, mimic, minimize, mortify, mouth, needle, oath, oppose, protest, puncture, put-down, put down, rave, rebuff, rebut, refute, remonstrate, renounce, renunciation, ridicule, rumor, run down, sarcasm, scoff, scold, scorn, show up, slam, slander, slur, smear, snap, sneer, snub, squawk, squeal, stain, swear, swearing, tattle, taunt, thunder, tirade, traverse, turn, turn down, underestimate, vituperate, whine, write off

55 describe: articulate, articulation, blab, define, denote, describe, detail, mean, narrate, narration, outline, paraphrase, phrase, portray, recite, recount, relate, signify, spell, state, summarize, sum up, tell, translate, typify, unfold, utter

56 discuss: argue, bargain, canvass, communicate, confer, conference, consult, debate, deliberate, deliberation, dialogue/dialog, discourse, discuss, discussion, gossip, huddle, intercede, interchange, jabber, jaw, negotiate, negotiation, powwow, rap, reason, rehash, repartee, talk, treat, word

57 explain: account for, admission, admit, annotate, cite, clarification, clarify, clear up, come clean, comment, concede, confide, confirm, construe, corroborate, declare, defense, define, demonstrate, detail, dilate, elaborate, elucidate, emphasize, enlighten, enumerate, evidence, excuse, expand, explain, explicate, expound, gloss, illuminate, illustrate, interpret, itemize, justify, let on, own, palliate, paraphrase, plea, preface, prove, rationalize, recite, render, simplify, speak out/speak up, specify, translate, vindicate, warrant

58 fabricate: aspersion, backbiting, belie, bluff, disprove, embroider, impugn, profane

59 fool: affect, artifice, assume, bamboozle, banter, beguile, bilk, blow up, bluff, burn, cajole, charade, cheat, chicanery, circumvent, color, con, copy, corner, counterfeit, cross, deceit, deceive, deception, decoy, default, defraud, delude, disguise, dishonesty, dissemble, dissimulate, do, dodge, do out of, double-cross, double-dealing, dramatize, dupe, duplicity, elude, enmesh, ensnare, entangle, entrap, evasion, excuse, extort, fake, feign, fence, finesse, flatter, flattery, fleece, fool, fooling, forge, forgery, fraud, frolic, fudge, gag, game, garble, gimmick, gyp, hanky-panky, have, hoax, hocus-pocus, impersonate, imposition, imposture, inveigle, invent, juggle, kid, make believe, maneuver, masquerade, mimic, mince, mislead, mock, outwit/outsmart, overplay, palliate, pander, parody, play down, ploy, pose, posture, prank, pretend, pretense, pretext, put on, ridicule, ruse, scheme, sham, shift, shirk, simulate, spoof, sport, strategem, string along, swindle, take, take in, trap, trick, trickery, victimize, wile, wit

60 **inform:** acknowledge, acquaint, address, advance, advertise, advise, allow, allude, allusion, announce, avow, bare, betray, betrayal, bill, blab, break, breathe, brief, briefing, broadcast, buzz, chronicle, circulate, clue, come out, come out with, confess, confession, convene, convey, cover, debunk, declare, define, deliver, detail, develop, dictate, disclose, divulge, enlighten, expose, exposure, feature, furnish, get across, give, give away, gossip, herald, hint, impart, inform, instruct, intimate, introduce, issue, leak, lecture, let on, notify, pass, plug, post, prescribe, proclaim, program, promulgate, propagate, publication, publicize, ready, release, report, reveal, revelation, show up, sing, speak, speech, spill, spread, squeal, stipulate, talk, tattle, thank, thanks, tip, unburden, uncover, unveil, ventilate, whisper

61 **instruct:** bar, direct, educate, instruct, prescribe
62 **label:** attach, call, christen, define, designate, dub, entitle, identify, label, name, style, tag, term, title
63 **lie:** backbiting, belie, bunk, cant, casuistry, color, default, detraction, distort, distortion, duplicity, embroider, equivocate, equivocation, evasion, exaggerate, exaggeration, fabricate, fabrication, falsehood, falsify, feign, fib, fiction, fudge, garble, gloss, hoax, hypocrisy, invent, invention, juggle, libel, lie, malign, misinform, mislead, misrepresent/misquote, mock, obscure, pad, perjure, pervert, play down, pose, pretend, pretense, prevaricate, profane, profess, sell/sell out, simulate, slant, smear, twist, warp, whitewash, wile

64 **noise, animal:** bark, bay, call, cheep, chirp, howl, peep, roar, squawk, squeak, squeal, yelp
65 **noise-making:** bang, blare, blast, blow, boom, buzz, cadence, chant, chime, clank, clash, clatter, click, clink, clump, cough, crash, creak, crinkle, drone, drum, grumble, gurgle, harmony, hum, hush, inflection, jangle, jar, jingle, measure, meter, muffle, murmur, mute, patter, peal, pipe, pitch, play, quiet, racket, rattle, reflect, reverberate, ring, roll, rumble, rustle, silence, sizzle, sound, squeak, still, stress, swing, talk, tempo, tenor, thud/thump, thunder, tick, tinkle, toll, tone, tranquility, tune/tune up, undertone, uproar, volume, whistle

66 **offer:** allude, extend, lay, offer, pose, present, proffer, propose, put, submit, volunteer
67 **offer to give:** amends, apologize, apology, bid, bidding, come forward, concession, expiate, ex-

tend, furnish, offer, pose, present, proffer, put, surrender, volunteer

68 **persuade:** advance, argue, argument, assure, bend, bring around, budge, cajole, carry, coax, coerce, coercion, convince, disarm, discourage, dissuade, draw, drive, drum up, egg on, elicit, eloquence, entice, enticement, forward, get, goad, hammer away/hammer into, impel, induce, inducement, influence, ingratiate, invite, lead, lobby, maintain, motivate, negotiate, negotiation, occasion, persuade, persuasion, pitch, predispose, prevail upon/prevail on, procure, prompt, push, reason, spur, stress, sway, tempt, urge, wheedle, win, win over

69 **praise:** accent, acclaim, acclamation, accolade, accredit, adulation, aggrandize, applaud, applause, approbation, benediction, blarney, bless, champion, cheer, citation, commemorate, commend, commendation, compliment, congratulate, congratulations, consecrate, credit, crown, dedicate, dedication, deify, distinguish, elevate, elevation, endorse, enshrine, eulogize, eulogy, exalt, exaltation, extol, felicitate, flatter, flattery, further, glorify, hail, homage, kudos, laud, laurels, magnify, ovation, praise, puff, reference, salute, thank, thanks, tout, tribute, worship

70 **predict:** announce, anticipate, astrology, augur, augury, call, forebode, forecast, foreordain, foresee, foreshadow, foretell, oracle, precursor, predict, prediction, presage, prognosticate, project, prophecy, prophesy

71 **promise:** assurance, assure, avow, commitment, covenant, ensure, go back/go back on, guarantee, oath, pledge, portend, promise, vouch, vow, warrant, word

72 **read:** leaf, look up, narrate, narration, peruse, pore, read, reading, recitation, recite, refer, skim

73 **refer:** attach, attribute, drive at, instance, intend, mean, mention, oppose, point out, refer

74 **signal:** beckon, call, flag, gesture, gesture/gesticulate, hail, harbinger, hint, indicate, indication, nod, omen, page, sign, signal, spell, suggest, symbolize, wave

75 **suggest:** advice, advise, advocate, approach, ask, cajole, come up with, commend, connote, counsel, drum into, enlighten, exhort, exhortation, fish for, foreshadow, get at, guidance, guide, hint, imply, innuendo, insinuate, intimate, motion, move, nominate, nomination, pointer, pose, preach, proffer, propose, raise, recommend, spell, suggest, urge

76 **thank:** appreciate, gratitude, thank
77 **vocalize:** accent, air, bark, bawl, bellow, blare, cackle, caterwaul, chant, cheer, chortle, chuckle, clamor, croak, cry, drawl, drone, exclamation, giggle, groan, growl, grumble, hail, harmonize, hiss, howl, hum, laugh/laughter, laugh, moan, mumble, murmur, mutter, outcry, parrot, pipe, roar, scream, shout, shriek, shut up, sing, snap, snarl, snicker/snigger/sniggle, snore, squawk,

squeal, stutter, vocalize, voice, wail, whimper, whine, whistle, whoop, yowl

78 warn: admonish, alert, bluster, caution, caveat, charge, defy, dissuade, enjoin, exhort, exhortation, forebode, foreboding, forecast, foretell, forewarn, page, portend, remind, threaten, warn, warning

79 write: abstract, address, annotate, autograph, chronicle, compile, compose, correspond, correspondence, cover, depict, dot, draft, draw, draw up, edit, endorse, engrave, engraving, enroll, extract, fill in, fleck, hand, inscribe, label, line, list, mark, notify, page, pen, picture, plot, point, punctuate, put down, quote, register, revise, revision, rough out, score, scratch, scrawl, script, sign, spot, stamp, trace, transcribe, type, underline, write, writing

GENERAL

80 act abstractly: freak, jerk, lurch, twist, wiggle, wrench, writhe

81 act over an area: decree, rule, tour, veto

82 admit: accede, accept, acquiesce, admit, allow, concede, concur, grant

83 allow: absolve, accord, acquit, admission, admit, allow, approve, authorize, capitulate, capitulation, contribute, defer, enable, entitle, excuse, exempt, grant, have, leave, let, let off, liberate, license, overlook, patronage, permission, permit, pity, receive, reception, spell, suffer, tolerate

84 arrange: adjust, alphabetize, antedate, arrange, arrangement, array, center, centralize, codify, collate, collocate, compile, concentrate, coordinate, derange, dispose, disrupt, distribute, disturb, divide, file, graduate, group, index, jumble, line, marshal, muddle, order, organization, organize, perplex, pile, place, program, range, rank, reconstruct, sort, systematize, tabulate, type

85 attach: adhere, adjoin, affix, anchor, annex, append, attach, batten, bind, bond, cement, chain, clamp, clasp, cling, cohere, connect, engage, fasten, fix, hitch, knot, latch, lock, moor, nail, paste, peg, pin, screw, seal, secure, shut, stick, tack, tag, tape, tether, tie, yoke

86 attack: aggression, ambush, assail, assault, attack, besiege, blast, blitz, bomb, bombard, brutality, burst, charge, combat, come at, coup d'état, descent, embroil, encounter, encroach, engage, fire, fix, foray, fray, go for, incursion, infest, inroad, insurrection, invade, invasion, lambaste, lay into, maraud, occupation, occupy, offensive, onset, onslaught, outbreak, overrun, overwhelm, pillage, plunder, pounce, prey on, raid, rampage, ravage, revenge, rush, sabotage, storm, subvert, surprise, waylay

87 attempt: adhere, angle for, answer, apply, assume, attempt, bid, bother, buckle down, campaign, chance, commit, counteract, counterbalance, crack, dabble, dare, defy, delve, dip

into, direct, drill, drive, drudge, effort, emulate, endeavor, engage, enterprise, essay, exercise, exert, exertion, experiment, fiddle, function, further, go, hammer away/hammer into, hazard, hush, imitate, keep at, keep up, labor, mess around, monkey, offer, overdo, overplay, persevere, persist, plod, practice, presume, purpose, pursue, putter, represent, risk, scramble, seek, slave, stab, strain, strive, struggle, substitute, tackle, take on, tinker, trial, try, undertake, undertaking, venture, wade, whack, whirl, work

88 authorize: accede, accord, accredit, acknowledge, acknowledgment, acquit, affirm, aggrandize, appoint, appointment, approve, arm, assign, authorize, back, ban, bar, bear out, bless, blessing, certify, charter, commission, concession, consent, constitute, contract, countenance, countermand, crown, decree, dedicate, delegate, delegation, detail, disown, empower, enable, enact, endorse, enforce, enjoin, entitle, entrust, establish, exempt, fire, forgive, grant, induct, inflict, invest, invoke, lay, let, let off, license, make, name, negate, nod, nominate, nomination, nullify, okay, ordain, order, override/overrule, pardon, permission, permit, place, prescribe, prohibit, ratify, recall, receive, release, relieve, repeal, reprieve, revoke, sanction, spare, station, subscribe, underwrite, validate, vest, veto, void, warrant, withdraw, witness

89 borrow: borrow, charter, lease, let, rent

90 capture: apprehend, apprehension, arrest, bag, besiege, capture, catch, collar, commandeer, confinement, conquer, corner, coup d'état, custody, enslave, ensnare, entangle, entrap, expropriate, fetch, foray, get, grab, grasp, imprison, incarcerate, kidnap, nab, nail, net, occupation, occupy, pinch, pull in, seize, seizure, sequester, snap, snare, snatch, tackle, trap

91 carry out: accomplish, action, application, assure, avail, complement, complete, comply, conclude, contrive, discharge, do, duplicate, echo, effect, enact, execute, execution, fill, finalize, finish, follow, follow through, fulfill, hammer out, handle, hustle, implement, make, make out, manage, meet, mind, obey, observe, operate, perfect, perform, perpetrate, persist, practice, proceed, prosecute, pull off, realize, redeem, render, repeat, rush, serve, specialize, transact, wage

92 compete: bout, boxing, compete, competition, contend, contention, contest, opposition, pit, play, rival, take on, tie, vie

93 contract: catch, come down with, contract, get, incur

94 control: auspices, contain, contrive, deal/deal with, determine, direct, discipline, dominate, domineer, harness, manage, moderate, monopolize, operate, overlook, predominate, preside, prevail, regulate, regulation, ride, stage, steer, systematize, wield, work

95 defeat: beat, best, confute, conquer, conquest,

coup de grâce, crush, defeat, discomfit, edge, extinguish, finish, floor, lick, master, outdo, overcome, overpower, overrun, overtake, overthrow, overwhelm, prevail, prostrate, put down, quash, quell, reduce, rout, smash, subjugate, subvert, surmount, thrash, top, topple, trim, triumph, trounce, upset, vanquish, victory, wallop, whip, win

96 defend: beard, bulwark, convoy, counteract, counterbalance, cover, defend, ensure, fend, fend off, fight back/fight off, guard, protect, repulse, resist, resistance, safeguard, save, screen, secure, shield, ward/ward off, withstand

97 demonstrate: advertising, bear out, demonstrate, establish, evidence, exemplify, give, illustrate, imply

98 divide: allocate, apportion, bestow, bisect, cleave, disconnect, dismember, disrupt, dissect, distribute, distribution, divide, division, fork, fragment, halve, mete, part, partition, place, portion, punctuate, quarter, ramification, ration, rupture, sever, share, slice, snap, split

99 enable: allow, enable, implement, qualify

100 engage in: address, anticipate, apply, collaborate, dig in, drudge, embark on, exist, fall to, fare, fend for, fight, give, go about, go into, go on, grub, immerse, labor, make, participate, pitch in, plunge, ply, practice, pursue, reiterate, risk, share, spend, step in, tackle, take, toil, trouble, turn, undertake, wage, work

101 err: blunder, botch, bungle, butcher, compromise, err, error, fault, faux pas, flounder, frailty, fumble, gaffe, guilt, impropriety, inaccuracy, indiscretion, lapse, malpractice, miscalculate, mishandle/mismanage, misjudge, miss, misstep, mistake, neglect, overlook, oversight, screw up, sin, slip, stray, stumble, transgression, trespass, trip, violate, violation, wander

102 escape: abscond, avoid, avoidance, bail out, break, break out, bypass, circumvent, disappear, disappearance, dodge, duck, elude, equivocate, escape, eschew, evade, evasion, extricate, flee, flight, flinch, fly, getaway, get out, lose, make off, shake off, skirt, throw off

103 examine: analysis, analyze, assay, audit, authenticate, autopsy, case, check, compare, confirm, criticize, decompose, delve, dig, evaluate, evaluation, examination, examine, experiment, explore, follow up, go into, go over, go through, grade, graduate, hearing, inspect, inspection, investigate, investigation, judgment, look into, measure, nose, observe, peer, peruse, pore, postmortem, probe, quest, ransack, research, review, sample, scan, scout, scrutinize, scrutiny, sift, skim, spy, study, surveillance, survey, test, try, try on/try out, view, weigh

104 exchange: alternate, amends, barter, commute, exchange, interchange, reciprocate, redeem, replace, rotate, substitute, swap/swop, switch, transpose

105 existential change: age, arise, awaken, awakening, begin, come from, date, demise, disappear, disappearance, dissipate, dissolution, dissolve, emerge, fade, form, go, go out, languish, materialize, originate, pass, perish, peter out, run out, spring, succumb, vanish, wake/waken

106 fight: altercation, battle, bout, box, brawl, brush, clamor, clash, combat, conflict, confrontation, contend, contention, contest, contravene, dispute, encounter, engage, engagement, faction, ferment, feud, fight, fight back/fight off, fighting, fracas, fray, free-for-all, friction, fuss, grapple, hassle, imbroglio, mayhem, melee, misunderstanding, oppose, opposition, quarrel, racket, rebel, rebellion, resist, resistance, revolt, revolution, rift, riot, rise, row, run-in, scrap, scuffle, strife, struggle, tilt, uprising, uproar, war, wrangle

107 fuel: charge, feed, fill, fuel, supply

108 give: administer, afford, allocate, allot, allow, apportion, atone, bear, bequeath, bestow, cast, cede, commend, commit, compensate, confide, consign, consignment, contribute, deal, deliver, delivery, descend, devote, disburse, disseminate, dole out, donate, drop off, emit, endow, entrust, finance, furnish, give, give away, hand out, hand over, impart, leave, mete, pass, pass off, present, provide, reach, render, return, reward, sacrifice, satisfy, show, surrender, transfer, turn over, will

109 group: aggregate, alloy, amass, bank, blend, bunch, cluster, collect, collection, commingle, compilation, compile, compound, concentrate, confluence, congregate, consolidate, consolidation, cull, distribution, flock, garner, gather, get together, group, heap, herd, muster, pick, pile, rake, reap, recruit, round up, stack, store

110 help: abet, aid, alleviate, assist, assistance, attend, baby, backing, bail out, befriend, benefit, bolster, boost, break, care, chip in, coddle, commiserate, contribute, convoy, cooperate, cooperation, cover, cultivate, cultivation, cure, defend, dispense, doctor, do for, ease, encourage, encouragement, facilitate, favor, fawn, forward, foster, free, further, furtherance, guarantee, guide, hand, help, hold, indulge, intercede, intervene, invigorate, keep, kindness, lavish, liberate, lift, lighten, mind, minister, nurse, nurture, oblige, patronage, patronize, pitch in, profit, promote, promotion, provide, quell, reform, relieve, serve, service, shore, simplify, soothe, speed, spell, sponsor, stabilize, subsidize, support, sustain, sympathize, temper, tide over, underwrite, uphold

111 imitate: ape, mimic, mirror, mock, mockery, parallel, parody, pattern, pretend, repeat, reproduce, sham, simulate, takeoff, take off

112 involve: attack, coalesce, confuse, contain, cooperate, cooperation, count, devote, embody, embrace, enclose, encompass, enmesh, entangle, entrap, figure in, implicate, include, incorporate, interpolate, introduce, involve, mire, overdo, tangle, task

113 join: accompany, add, adhere, adjoin, affiliate,

affix, alloy, amalgamate, annex, annexation, append, articulate, articulation, assemble, assembly, attach, band, bridge, butt, cleave, close, coalesce, cohere, combine, compound, connect, converge, couple, dovetail, embody, engage, fasten, fix, fuse, fusion, get together, graft, hitch, incorporate, integrate, intermingle, intersect, intertwine/interweave, introduce, join, knit, knot, lace, link, meeting, meld, merge, mesh, mix, pair, piece, pool, swarm, synthesis, synthesize, union, unite, wed

114 **join socially:** affiliate, align, assemble, associate, attach, attend, band, belong, bump into, call, cavort, chaperon, collect, collusion, confluence, congregate, consort, consultation, convene, convention, converge, convocation, couple, dalliance, dally/dally with, date, enroll, enter, escort, gather, group, hang about/hang around/hang out, huddle, integrate, intermingle, intertwine/interweave, join, league, link, matriculate, meet, mix, register, session, swarm, take

115 **lend:** finance, fund, invest, lease, lend, let, loan, pawn, rent, trust

116 **lose:** deliver, fall, forfeit, forget, leak, lose, misplace, omission, sacrifice

117 **manage:** adjust, administer, administration, boss, carry on, charge, compose, conduct, control, custody, deal/deal with, direct, dispense, dispose, dominate, drill, economy, face, fare, farm, farming, fend for, get along, get by, get on, guide, handle, handling, head, lead, manage, management, marshal, master, monitor, officiate, operate, orchestrate, organization, overlook, oversee, oversight, predominate, preside, rally, regulate, regulation, reign, rule, run, running, save, subjugate, supervise, supervision, sway, treatment, upkeep, work

118 **manifest:** agree, comprehend, connote, embodiment, embody, emerge, exemplify, exude, give, indicate, loom, manifest, mirror, point, presage, promise, prove, radiate

119 **modify an event:** abide, advent, balk, birth, cancellation, cessation, close, closure, come on, come out, come up, coming, commence, complement, completion, conception, conclude, conclusion, culminate, dawn, desist, develop, discontinuance, disposal, embargo, end, ending, end up, ensue, entrance, expiration, expire, fall, finish, genesis, give in/give up, halt, knock off, lapse, lay off, matriculate, pass, pause, pull out, pull up, quit, recess, relinquish, resign, resignation, result, retract, revival, rout, secede, spurt, standstill, stop, surrender, suspend, suspension, terminate, termination

120 **obtain:** acquire, acquisition, amass, attain, capitalize, earn, gain, get, get at, get back, land, lay up/lay by, make, obtain, pick up, possess, procure, pull in, realize, reap, recover, recruit, regain, retrieve, save, secure, strike, take, win

121 **prevent:** abolish, abolition, abort, abrogate, abstain, adjourn, adjournment, anticipate, arrest, asphyxiate, avert, avoid, avoidance, baffle, balk, ban, banish, bar, birth control, block, bog down, brake, break, bridle, censor, cheat, check, choke, circumvent, clog, close, confine, constrain, constraint, contravene, cop out, counter, cripple, cross, curb, cut short, dash, defeat, defer, deferment/deferral, delay, deprivation, deprive, deter, discharge, discontinue, discourage, disqualify, dissolve, drop, drop out, encumber, exclude, exclusion, foil, forbear, forbid, forgo, freeze, frustrate, gag, halt, hesitate, hesitation, hinder, hold back/hold off, hold up, impede, incapacitate, inhibit, intercept, interfere, interference, interrupt, invalidate, jam, keep, kill, mire, muffle, muzzle, negate, negation, neutralize, nip, nullify, obstruct, obviate, occlude, omit, outlaw, override/overrule, paralyze, parry, pause, preclude, preempt, prevent, procrastinate, prohibit, prohibition, proscribe, pull out, pull up, put off, quash, quell, recess, refrain, relegate, remove, repeal, repress, rescind, respite, restrain, retard, revoke, rule out, run-around, scrap, scratch, scrub, seclude, shelve, shut, shut off/shut out, slowdown, spite, squash, stall, stay, stem, stifle, still, stop, stymie, subdue, suppress, suspend, table, terminate, thwart, traverse, turn off/turn out, undo, veto, vitiate, void, waive, waiver, waylay, withdraw, withhold

122 **punish:** avenge, chasten, chastise, correct, correction, discipline, evict, exile, expel, fine, pay, penalize, punish, revenge, scourge, sentence

123 **punishment:** blackmail, damage(s), discipline, eviction, fine, forfeit, lesson, punishment, rap, reprimand, reproach, retribution, sanction

124 **receive:** accept, acceptance, acquire, acquisition, bring in, come by, come in for, fetch, find, gain, have, inherit, make, object, profit, realize, reap, receipt, receive, reception, recoup, regain, retrieve, take

125 **record:** enroll, enter, enumerate, itemize, list, record, register, schedule, score, take down, tally, tape, transcribe

126 **rectify:** accommodate, amend, appease, appeasement, arbitrate, arbitration, atone, atonement, avenge, compensate, conclude, correct, correction, counteract, counterbalance, cover, cure, do up, edit, emend, equalize, expiate, fix, iron out, make up, mediate, mediation, mend, offset, overhaul, penance, placate, quiet, recompense, recoup, rectify, redeem, redress, reform, rehabilitate, remedy, requite, restore, retaliate, retribution, revise, revision, right, satisfy, settle, square, standardize, suit, tailor, temper, tune/tune up, untangle

127 **release:** acquittal, cede, clear, deliver, delivery, discharge, disentangle, dismiss, dismissal, emancipate, exculpate, exempt, exonerate, extricate, free, loose/loosen, ransom, redeem, release, relinquish, save

128 **replace:** change, fill in, follow, supersede, supplant

129 reserve: allocate, assign, assignment, assumption, claim, clear, come by, deserts, deserve, designate, earmark, earn, engage, enroll, entitle, gain, intend, merit, put away/put aside/put by, rate, reserve, save, spare, store, subscribe

130 restrict: bar, barricade, bind, block, bound, boycott, brake, check, circumscribe, clog, cocoon, confine, constrain, constraint, constrict, constriction, control, cramp, curb, curtail, dam, deaden, defer, deferment/deferral, delay, disable, embargo, encumber, enjoin, enslave, expatriate, expel, expulsion, fetter, fetters, foil, forbear, forgo, gag, govern, grind, ground, hamper, handicap, harness, hem/hem in, hinder, hobble, hold back/hold off, hold up, impair, impede, imposition, inhibit, limit, matter, moderate, narrow, obligate, obstruct, postpone, prohibit, prohibition, rein, repress, restrain, restrict, retard, set back, slow, slowdown, smother, squelch, stifle, strangle, stymie, subdue, suppress, suspend, thwart, tie/tie up

131 return: deliver, fetch, hand over, ransom, recall, redeem, regain, repay, requite, restore, retrieve, return

132 reward: award, commend, confer, decorate, reward

133 rule: abdicate, accession, command, depose, deposition, dictatorship, displace, enforce, enforcement, govern, impose, oppress, subjugate, supremacy

134 save: cocoon, conservation, conserve, deposit, guard, harbor, lay up/lay by, maintain, maintenance, pad, patrol, preservation, preserve, protect, put away/put aside/put by, rehabilitate, rescue, salvage, salvation, save, shelter, shield, spare, ward/ward off, watch

135 separate: abstract, analyze, appropriate, appropriation, assign, class, classification, classify, dedicate, detach, disaffect, disconnect, disengage, disentangle, dislocate, dismantle, dismember, disperse, disrupt, dissociate, divide, division, filter, fragment, gape, garner, glean, hoard, open, part, partition, seclude, seclusion, segregate, separate, separation, split, strain, undo

136 serve: accommodate, administer, board, bondage, cater, obey, oblige, pamper, pander, provide, quench, spoil, tend, wait on

137 shape change: beat, bisect, bruise, carve, chip, chisel, cleave, clip, compact, crimp, crinkle, cut, desiccate, disfigure, disguise, distort, disturb, divide, do in, edge, elongate, enlarge, fatigue, file, flatten, fragment, gash, hack, lacerate, nick, notch, pierce, prune, puncture, reduce, roll, rumple, scar, score, sculpture, shape, sharpen, shave, shorten, shrink, shrivel, slash, slice, smooth, stiffen, stretch, taper/taper off, thicken, thin, trample, truncate, warp, whet, wound

138 show: advertising, bare, circulate, model, point, prove, represent, reveal, show, substantiate, symbolize, tout, trot out, unveil

139 steal: abduct, appropriate, appropriation, assume,

bilk, break in, burglary, cheat, confiscate, copy, divest, do out of, embezzle, embezzlement, extort, extortion, filch, fleece, hold up, kidnap, knock off, larceny, lift, loot, maraud, milk, misappropriate, pilfer, pillage, pinch, plagiarism, plunder, poach, pocket, ransack, rifle, rip-off, rip off, rob, sack, steal, swindle, swipe, take, theft

140 supply: appoint, contribute, deal, deluge, dish out, dispensation, dispense, disseminate, distribute, distribution, divide, dole out, equip, feed, foster, fuel, furnish, glut, hand out, infuse, issue, keep, lend, maintain, make out, nourish, nurse, nurture, portion, provide, provision, quarter, ration, receive, render, replenish, rig, satisfy, serve, stock, supply, support, sustain

141 surpass: abound, beat, better, break, cap, conquer, eclipse, exceed, excel, flourish, get ahead, go by, lead, lick, outdo, outweigh, overtake, pass, predominate, prevail, succeed, supersede, surmount, surpass, top, tower, transcend, triumph, win

142 take: acquire, acquisition, arrogate, assume, assumption, broach, burn, commandeer, compass, confiscate, cull, deplete, deprivation, deprive, disarm, disarmament, divest, drain, draw, educe, elicit, exact, excerpt, expropriate, extract, filch, harvest, have, milk, nip, peel, pilfer, pocket, preempt, pump, ransack, rob, sap, seize, take, tap, usurp, wring

143 transfer abstractly: afford, bear, bring, commit, consign, consignment, conveyance, delegate, delegation, infect, recall, refer, relay, release, relegate, transfer, turn over

MOTION

144 be moved: earthquake, elapse, flop, hang, lap

145 change of place: flicker, motion, movement, passage, pop, rush, sway, sweep, swing, swirl, swivel, teeter, tremor

146 flow: flow, pour, run, secrete, seep, stream, surge, swamp, teem, torrent, trickle

147 move: bob, budge, careen, churn, circulate, circulation, contort, cruise, curl, curve, dandle, deflect, descend, descent, dislocate, dislodge, displace, dive, drift, drive, entwine, falter, fidget, flex, flourish, gyrate, haul, lean, loop, move, oscillate, overturn, paddle, pitch, pivot, pulsate/pulse, pulse, revolve, rock, roll, rotate, round, skirt, tilt, topple, toss, transport, traverse, tumble, turn, twine, twist, uproot, upset, waft, wave, waver, weave, wheel, wield

148 move mechanically: aviation, bank, carriage, carry, cart, drive, fly, haul, mobilize, navigate, operate, pack, park, ride, ship, soar, takeoff, take off, veer

149 move oneself: ascend, ascension, bend, constitutional, flap, flex, flounce, gad, gait, gallivant, gambol, go ahead, go for, gyrate, hike, jerk, motion, mount, move, negotiate, pace, pad, pass, patter, progress, quail, rock, roll, round, stalk, stamp, step, stir, stray, stride, strut, stump, swagger, tilt, tread, trip, tumble, walk, wallow, wave, wriggle

150 move oneself quickly: barge in/barge into, beat, bolt, bounce, bustle, capsize, coast, course, dart, dash, flash, flee, flinch, flit, flutter, fly, gallop, glide, hasten, hurry, hurtle, hustle, jerk, jiggle, lurch, make off, march, plunge, pound, prance, race, recoil, run, rush, scamper, scramble, scurry, shake, shoot, shudder, skim, skip, slide, slip, soar, speed, spin, sprint, start, storm, sweep, swerve, swoop, tear, trot, twirl, veer, wag, whip, whiz, wiggle, wobble, writhe, zip, zoom

151 move oneself slowly: amble, crawl, creep, cruise, dalliance, dally, decline, drag, hobble, jog, knock about/knock around, lag, limp, linger, loiter, lumber, lurk, meander, plod, poke, prowl, pussyfoot, ramble, range, reel, roam, saunter, shuffle, slink/slither, sneak, stagger, steal, straggle, stroll, sway, tarry, totter, tramp, trudge, waddle, wade, wander

152 move quickly: advance, advancement, agitate, capsize, convulsion, course, discharge, dispatch, fall, flicker, flourish, flutter, hasten, jerk, jiggle, jostle, keel over, lurch, palpitate, plunge, precipitate, quake, quiver, rattle, rush, shake, shiver, shoot, shudder, skid, skim, slide, slip, speed, spin, stampede, sweep, tear, throb, tremble, twirl, vibrate, vibration, wag, whip, whirl, whisk, wiggle, wobble

153 move slowly: dangle, float, lag, reel

154 position oneself: arise, bow, cant, duck, get down, get off, get up, hover, huddle, hunch, kneel, lie, list, loll, lounge, mount, nestle, obeisance, perch, poise, pose, ramble, recline, repose, rest, rise, seat, sit, slouch, wince

155 travelling: lift, navigation, procession, transit, transport, voyage

PHYSICAL

156 abuse: abuse, charge, consumption, cop out, corrode, defile, dissipate, dope, enervate, exploit, force, frazzle, fritter, impinge, lose, malpractice, milk, misappropriate, mishandle/mismanage, mistreat, misuse, overdo, pervert, prostitute, riddle, run through, sap, spend, squander, strain, throw away, waste, wear

157 anatomical change: distend, flake, neuter

158 arrange: align, arrange, bundle, collate, coordinate, crease, deploy, dispose, file, group, indent, lay, lay out, mess up, mix up, muss, order, organize, position, range, rank, reverse, ruffle, rummage, separate, shuffle, snarl, sort, spread, stack, stir, straighten, unwind, weave

159 arrive: admission, advent, appear, appearance, approach, arrival, arrive, billow, board, come, come in, coming, cross, cruise, disembark, dock, embark, encroach, enter, entrance, foray, get, get back, get in, get on, go, go ahead, gravitate, immigrate, infiltrate, influx, insinuate, intrude, in-

vade, invasion, jaunt, land, light, loom, lunge, make, penetrate, permeate, pierce, pounce, progress, pull up, reach, report, return, show up, stalk, swarm, trespass, turn out, turn up

160 attach: adhere, adjoin, affix, anchor, annex, append, attach, batten, bind, bond, cement, chain, clamp, clasp, cling, cohere, connect, engage, fasten, fix, hitch, knot, latch, lock, moor, nail, paste, peg, pin, screw, seal, secure, shut, stick, tack, tag, tape, tether, tie, yoke

161 bathe: bath, bathe, clean, wet

162 beautify: adorn, adornment, bask, beautify, comb, decorate, decoration, doll up, embellish, enhance, fix up, flatter, furbish, groom, ornament, primp, shave, spruce up, trim

163 breathe: breath, breathe, draw, exhale, expire, gasp, heave, huff, inhale, pant, puff, sigh, suffocate, wheeze, yawn

164 catch: catch, field, intercept, seize, tackle

165 clean: bath, bathe, brush, catharsis, clarify, clean, cleanse, clear, disinfect, distill, do up, expurgate, filter, flush, furbish, gut, housework, lather, mop, purge, purification, purify, rake, refine, refinement, rinse, scour, scrape, scrub, sift, sweep, wash, wipe

166 climb: arise, ascend, ascension, ascent, climb, get on, mount, rise, scale, surface

167 clothe: array, attire, clothe, deck, disrobe, doll up, dress, dress up, garb, get on, ornament, outfit, primp, rig, sport, spruce up, stuff, try on/try out, turn out, wear

168 construct: build, compose, construct, construction, dismantle, erect, establish, fashion, forge, form, found, frame, make, modernize, pave, pitch, put up, raise, rear, reconstruct, renovate, throw up

169 consume: absorption, bolt, chew, consume, consumption, contract, corrode, crunch, demolish, deplete, devour, diet, digest, dig in, dine, dispatch, dissipate, draft, drink, eat, engulf, exhaust, fast, feast, feed on, finish, gargle, glut, gnaw, gobble, gorge, go through, graze, gulp, guzzle, imbibe, munch, nibble, nip, partake, peck, polish off, prey on, put away, quaff, satiate, sip, spend, stuff, swallow, take, taste, use, wolf

170 cook: bake, barbecue, baste, beat, boil, brew, broil, butcher, can, churn, coddle, cook, cure, distill, fix, flavor, foam, fry, grill, housework, knead, mash, pickle, preservation, preserve, sear, season, simmer, sizzle, stir, sweeten, toast, warm, whip

171 copy: ape, copy, counterfeit, duplicate, echo, emulate, follow, forge, forgery, imitate, imitation, mimic, mirror, multiply, parallel, parrot, pattern, pretend, quote, reconstruct, reflect, reiterate, repeat, reproduce, sham, simulate, transcribe

172 cover: blanket, bury, camouflage, coat, cover, daub, disguise, dissimulate, drape, dress, dust, engulf, envelop, face, finish, funeral, gild, glaze, insulate, inter, inundate, laminate, lap, line, mask, masquerade, muzzle, obscure, oil, overrun, paint, palliate, paper, pave, pervade, plate, sheet, smear, smother, spatter, spread, top, varnish, veil, veneer, wrap

173 create: bear, beget, breed, coin, come up with, compose, conceive, concoct, constitute, construct, contrive, create, creation, design, draft, engineer, establish, establishment, fabricate, fashion, father, film, forge, form, formation, formulate, frame, generate, generation, hatch, improvise, institute, invent, make, make up, mastermind, materialize, mint, mold, originate, piece, pioneer, procreate, regenerate, reproduce, reproduction, spawn, work

174 create art: chart, compose, depict, dot, draw, engrave, engraving, etch, illustrate, impress, imprint, lay out, mount, outline, paint, photograph, picture, plot, portray, pose, pottery, print, rough out, sculpture, sketch, stamp, trace

175 create with effort: beat, forge, mold

176 cut: amputate, ax/axe, behead, bisect, carve, chisel, chop, cleave, clip, crop, cut, cut up, dent, dismember, dissect, dissection, engrave, engraving, etch, fell, gash, hack, knife, lacerate, mangle, mince, mutilate, nick, notch, pare, peel, pierce, pink, prune, scar, score, scratch, sever, shave, shred, skin, slash, slice, slit, split, trim, whittle

177 decorate: adorn, adornment, decorate, decoration, embellish, embellishment, embroider, enhance, enrich, furnish, gild, modernize, ornament, paper, refurbish, renovate, trim, varnish

178 dig: bore, burrow, claw, dig, embed, excavate, excavation, exhume, grub, hollow, inter, mine, plant, plow, rake, root, scoop, tunnel, unearth, uproot

179 discharge: blast, blowout, blow up, bubble, burst, cascade, come from, deliver, detonate, discharge, drain, dribble, drop, effusion, eject, emanate, emanation, emission, emit, erupt, eruption, evacuate, excrete, expel, explode, explosion, express, exude, fire, flare, flood, flow, flush, gag, give off/give out, go off, gush, heave, impregnate, infest, infiltrate, influx, infuse, inject, inundate, issue, jet, launch, leak, mushroom, ooze, outbreak, overflow, overrun, pass, penetrate, percolate, permeate, pervade, pour, proceed, project, scatter, secrete, seep, shed, shoot, spatter, spew, spill, spit, spot, spout, spray, sprinkle, spurt, squirt, stream, surge, swamp, teem, throw up, torrent, trickle, vent, void, vomit

180 dispose: boot, buck, chuck, discard, disposal, dispose of, ditch, do away with, dump, jettison, kick out, reject, rejection, rid, scrap, shed, throw away, unload, void

181 drop: clatter, crash, crumble, decline, descend, descent, dip, dive, drip, droop, drop, duck, dump, fall, fell, flop, founder, fumble, go down, go under, ground, keel over, land, light, lower, percolate, pitch, plumb, plummet, plunge, sag, set, settle, shed, sink, sling, slump, spill, stoop, stumble, submerge, subside, suspend, swoop, thud/thump, topple, tumble, wilt

182 equip: arm, do up, equip, fit, furnish, gear, outfit, rig, stock

183 find: come across, detect, detection, discover, discovery, ferret out, find, find out, learn, locate, meet, pick up, pinpoint, recover, spot, strike, stumble, track/track down, turn up, uncover, unearth

184 form: arch, bend, bloat, braid, carve, chisel, constitute, contort, crumple, curl, curve, fold, materialize, model, mold, pat, round, sculpture, shape, twist, whittle, work

185 gesture: bawl, beam, beat, belch, bite, bleed, blink, blow, chew, clap, drag, dribble, drivel, drool, excrete, expire, frown, gnaw, grimace, grin, gulp, itch, kink, kiss, laugh/laughter, laugh, lick, munch, nod, perspire, pucker, puff, pulsate/pulse, pulse, purse, scowl, shiver, slobber, smile, smirk, sob, spasm, spit, squint, sweat, tear/tears, throb, twitch, vomit, wail, weep, whimper, wince, wink, wrinkle, yawn

186 grind: abrasion, corrode, creak, crunch, file, frazzle, granulate, grate, grind, mash, mill, pound, powder, pulverize, rasp, scrape

187 guide: aviation, channel, conduct, convey, direct, divert, drive, ease, ferry, funnel, guide, infuse, inject, lay, lead, level, maneuver, marshal, mobilize, navigate, navigation, point, refer, round, route, row, see, show, steer, take, transport, usher

188 hide: ambush, balk, bury, cache, camouflage, cloak, conceal, concealment, cover, cower, cringe, cut, disguise, dissemble, dissimulate, eavesdrop, embed, ensconce, envelop, harbor, hide, isolate, lurk, mask, masquerade, obscure, palliate, screen, seclude, seclusion, secrete, sequester, shelter, shrink, shut off/shut out, smother, sneak, withhold

189 hit: applaud, applause, bang, baste, bat, batter, battery, beat, belt, blow, boot, box, buffet, bump, bunt, butt, chip, clap, clash, clatter, clip, clobber, club, collide, collision, concussion, crack, crash, crown, cuff, dash, deflect, dent, drive, drum, flog, glance, hail, hammer, hand, hit, impact, jab, jar, jostle, kick, knock, lash, lick, manhandle, maul, nail, pat, peck, pelt, poke, pound, punch, ram, rap, rough up, scourge, slam, slap, smack, sock, spank, strike, swat, swipe, tap, thrash, thud/thump, tick, tip, wallop, whack, whip

190 hold: anchor, cling, clog, clutch, cradle, cuddle, dandle, dangle, embrace, fondle, grab, hold, hook, hug, nip, nuzzle, pin, prop, retain, retard, seize, shore, snuggle, support, suspend, sustain, tangle

191 hold forcefully: apprehend, brace, cage, captivity, clasp, clench, clinch, clutch, confinement, constrict, constriction, contain, cramp, dam, detain, detention, embrace, enfold, enslave, fetter, fetters, grapple, grasp, grip, gripe, harness, hold, imprison, incarcerate, leash, overpower, pen, press, restrain, snap, snatch, stifle, strangle, tackle, throttle, wrestle

192 illegal behavior: blackmail, bleed, breach, break, break in, bribe, bug, buy, cheat, conspire, contraband, contravene, crime, delinquency, depredation, disobey, entrench, extortion, fault, fix, fraud, graft, have, holdup, hold up, imposture, infraction, infringe, injustice, intrigue, jinx, kickback, knock off, larceny, libel, loot, mischief, misconduct, misdeed/misdemeanor, murder, offense, outrage, pick, pilfer, plagiarism, poach, racket, rape, ravish, rip-off, rip off, rob, screw, sham, slander, smuggle, speculation, squeeze, swindle, take, tamper, theft, transgression, treason, trespass, victimize, violate, violation

193 join physically: link, meld, merge, mesh, mingle, mix, piece, pool, splice, tie, tuck, unite, wed, weld, yoke

194 jump: bounce, bound, clear, deflect, dive, flip, gallop, gambol, hop, hurdle, jump, leap, lunge, lurch, plunge, pounce, rear, recoil, skip, spring, start, vault

195 leave: abandon, abscond, back, blow, board, bolt, break, break out, clear out, cringe, dart, defection, depart, departure, desert, desertion, deviate, digress, disappear, disappearance, dismount, distance, diverge, draw back, drop, ebb, egress, embark, evacuate, exit, exodus, fall back, farewell, flee, flight, fly, forsake, get along, get off, get out, go, goodbye, go off, go out, jaunt, jilt, leave, light out, make off, maroon, part, parting, pull out, push off/push on, quail, quit, recede, recoil, renounce, renunciation, repair, resign, resignation, retire, retreat, run, scram, separation, shake off, shove off, shrink, strike out, swerve, takeoff, take off, throw over, turn, vacate, withdraw, withdrawal

196 lift: boost, dip, elevate, heave, hoist, lift, pick up, pry, raise, rear

197 measure: balance, figure, measure, survey

198 move living quarters: anyplace, anywhere, approach, arena, battlefield, camp, colonization, cover, defect, defection, deport, deportation, destination, dominion, element, emigrate, empire, evict, eviction, exile, expatriate, expel, jurisdiction, landmark, locale/locality, location, lookout, migrate, move, neighborhood, outdoors, outside, point, position, post, premises, province, refuge, region, reign, rendezvous, resort, seat, setting, site, situation, soil, spot, station, stop, surroundings, terminal, territory, turn, vicinity, where

199 perform: fan, hit, perform, type, work

200 physical action: application, apply, drop, hit, hold, lift, push

201 position: aim, barricade, bow, cant, close, cock, coil, deposit, dial, dip, direct, disseminate, ensconce, entwine, fix, hang, indent, insert, install, installation, interpolate, intersperse, isolate, jut, lap, lay, lean, lie, list, lodge, loop, misplace, occlude, park, pile, pitch, place, plant, point, position, post, prop, put, recline, roll, seat, separate, set, sit, slant, slope, slouch, snuggle, sprawl,

spread, squat, stand, station, stick, stoop, swerve, tip, top, train, traverse, turn, twine, twist, unfold, wallow, wind, wrinkle

202 prepare physically: acclimate, adjust, braid, brush, brush up, buff, bundle, burnish, coat, condition, disguise, doll up, domesticate, do up, dress, embalm, face, finish, fix up, formulate, fortify, gear, get, gild, glaze, gloss, grace, groom, habituate, housework, knit, lubricate, make up, modernize, modulate, orient, overhaul, pack, pad, pare, plaster, plate, polish, preparation, prepare, preservation, preserve, prime, primp, ready, reform, refresh, refrigerate, refurbish, regenerate, rehabilitate, rejuvenate, renew, renovate, rig, round, season, set, shave, shine, slim, smear, spruce up, square, straighten, strain, tailor, toughen, train, training, weather

203 print: edit, print, type, write

204 process: grind, process, work

205 produce: agriculture, fabricate, fabrication, father, film, forge, form, generate, generation, lay, make, manufacture, mint, output, print, produce, production, synthesize, turn out, yield

206 pull: drag, draw, extract, lug, pick, pluck, pry, pull, pump, shut, strain, tear, tow, tug, twist, twitch, wrench, wring, yank

207 pursue: chase, dog, follow, hound, hunt, pursue, pursuit, shadow, steal, tag, tail, trace, track/track down, trail

208 push: advance, advancement, back, balloon, barge in/barge into, billow, bloat, blow up, boost, bulge, bulldoze, burst, compact, compress, cram, crowd, crumple, crush, dent, depress, dig, drive, elbow, extrude, fan, force, hit, indent, inject, insinuate, intrude, jam, jog, jolt, jostle, knead, level, manhandle, mash, massage, mob, nick, notch, nudge, poke, press, prod, propel, protrude, pulp, pump, purse, push, ram, repel, repulse, roll, shoulder, shove, shut, slam, squash, strain, tax, thrust, tip, topple, trample, upset, wrestle, wring

209 put in container: box, enclose, fill, flood, fold, glut, imbue, inject, insert, interpolate, introduce, load, pack, plug, pour, ram, replenish, stow, stuff, surfeit

210 relax: asleep, bask, dalliance, dally, dawdle, drop off, loaf, loiter, loll, lounge, lull, nap, nod, putter, relax, relaxation, repose, rest, slack/slacken, snooze, stay, tarry, trifle, turn in, unwind, vegetate, wait

211 remove: abstract, amputate, blot, bounce, break off, cancel, cashier, clear, clear out, cut out, delete, deport, deportation, disarm, disarmament, discharge, distill, divest, drain, eliminate, empty, eradicate, erase, evict, eviction, except, exception, excerpt, excise, excoriate, expatriate, expulsion, expunge, extirpate, extract, extraction, free, gut, hollow, omit, oust, peel, pry, purge, relegate, remove, replace, rid, shed, skim, skin, strip, subtract, take, top, transport, unburden, undress, unload, uproot, void, withdraw, withdrawal

212 **repair:** adjust, compensate, fix, overhaul, patch, remedy, repair, restore, right, tinker, touch up

213 **reposition:** bank, bow, bump, crimp, crinkle, crook, crouch, curl, curve, deploy, descend, descent, dislocate, dislodge, displace, divert, drag, draw back, invert, jump, reverse, shift, sink, squirm, transplant, turn, upset, veer, warp

214 **rip:** claw, fray, lacerate, rip, snag, tear

215 **rub:** bite, buff, burnish, chafe, creak, erase, excoriate, file, fret, friction, gall, glaze, gloss, grate, grind, polish, rasp, rub, scrape, smear

216 **search:** comb, delve, dig, exploration, explore, ferret out, forage, frisk, grope, grub, hunt, investigate, investigation, look up, nose, pan, plumb, probe, prospect, pry, quest, rake, ransack, refer, rummage, scour, scout, scrounge, search, seek, snoop, trace, track/track down

217 **send:** banish, carriage, carry, cart, channel, commit, consign, consignment, convey, deliver, delivery, deport, deportation, direct, dismiss, dismissal, dispatch, disperse, distribute, distribution, export, extradite, ferry, forward, funnel, mail, pack, pass, passage, pipe, radiate, remit, return, route, scatter, send, ship, take, transfer, transmit, transport, waft

218 **sew:** baste, embroider, embroidery, knit, line, patch, sew, spin, tack, tailor, tuck

219 **squeeze:** choke, clasp, clinch, constrict, constriction, crease, crush, distill, enfold, gripe, pinch, pucker, pulp, pulverize, rumple, screw, squash, squeeze

220 **stab:** claw, drill, impale, knife, lacerate, penetrate, perforate, pierce, prick, punch, puncture, riddle, spike, stab, stick, sting, tap, transfix

221 **start:** actuate, emanate, emanation, embark on, engage, engender, erect, establish, establishment, fall to, father, foment, found, impel, implement, inaugurate, incite, initiate, initiation, inspire, install, installation, instigate, instill, institute, introduce, kindle, launch, lead, make, mobilize, onset, open, originate, pioneer, plant, preface, propel, provoke, raise, renew, resume, revival, revive, set, set up, spark, start, stir, take on, take up, turn on, usher, whip up

222 **throw:** buck, cast, chuck, dart, dash, deliver, disseminate, dust, eject, erupt, extrude, fire, fling, flip, heave, hurl, intersperse, jettison, launch, pelt, pitch, powder, project, propagate, propel, scatter, slam, sling, splash, sprinkle, throw, thrust, toss

223 **transfer of an object:** give, send, transact, transaction, transfer

224 **travel:** accompany, commute, cover, cross, cruise, do, double back, drive, embark, excursion, expedition, exploration, explore, flight, fly, gad, gallivant, hike, jaunt, journey, knock about/knock around, make, migrate, navigate, navigation, negotiate, outing, passage, pick up, pilgrimage, ramble, range, ride, roam, run, sail, sojourn, takeoff, take off, tour, traffic, tramp, transit, travel, trek, trip, turn, voyage, walk, wander

225 **use:** apply, avail, bolt, borrow, broach, consume, consumption, deplete, devour, dip, drain, draw on, eat, employ, employment, enervate, exercise, exert, exhaust, expend, exploit, fatigue, finish, maneuver, manipulate, milk, occupy, partake, ply, polish off, resort, run, spend, squander, take, telephone, turn, use, utilize, wear, wield

226 **use living quarters:** abide, accommodate, cohabit, dwell, exist, hang about/hang around/hang out, inhabit, live, locate, lodge, occupy, reside, settle, sojourn, stay, visit

227 **visit:** call, come by, drop in, frequent, see, sojourn, stay, stop, tour, visit

Causes

ABSTRACT

228 **affect:** affect, cause, change, evoke

229 **event that causes another:** cause, origin, precipitous/precipitate

230 **state of causation:** adaptation, aftermath, amazement, anticlimax, armistice, astonishment, awe, backlash, backwash, bang, bedlam, bereavement, bind, blessing, bliss, blot, blunder, boom, bottom line, break, buildup, catharsis, certainty, change, chaos, check, coincidence, collapse, collision, comfort, complication, compromise, congestion, consequence, consternation, contamination, corollary, culmination, decay, deception, decomposition, decoy, degeneracy, degradation, descent, destruction, deterioration, disadvantage, disappointment, disarray, disorder, disposal, disrepair, dissipation, dissolution, effect, end, ending, error, event, eventuality, fall, flap, flurry, frailty, frenzy, fruit, fulfillment, furor, gaffe, headway, hubbub, huddle, impact, imperfection, impression, improvement, inaccuracy, infection, irony, issue, jinx, jitters, lapse, lather, mess, miscarriage, mistake, mix-up, morass, muddle, muss, nonsense, occurrence, outcome, outgrowth, payoff, phenomenon, portent, press, price, proceed, product, racket, ramification, rash, repercussion, resolution, result, rubbish, scare, scramble, settlement, shambles, solution, stain, stalemate, stigma, stink, stir, storm, taint, tangle, tempest, therefore, to-do, toll, trend, trip, truce, tumult, turmoil, turn, undoing, unification, upheaval, upshot, whirl

231 **to be:** alienate, animate, antagonize, awake, awaken, awakening, calm, cause, compound, en-

ergize, even, materialize, sterilize, straighten, threaten

232 to change: adapt, adjust, alter, alternate, assimilate, attune, cancel, change, commute, conversion, convert, differentiate, distort, diversify, double back, equalize, expurgate, fashion, fit, fix, invert, modify, neutralize, offset, overturn, restore, shift, switch, tamper, transform, translate, transpose, turn

233 to change abstractly: demote, intensify, mitigate

234 to change an event: abbreviate, accelerate, acceleration, activate, actuate, adjourn, approach, arrest, bed, begin, break off, break up, build, cancel, cease, close, commence, complement, conclude, consummate, continue, crown, cut in, cut off, cut short, desist, determine, discontinue, dispatch, dispose of, disrupt, dissolve, end, enter, finish, foul up, graduate, halt, hurry, intervene, invalidate, kick, knock off, lay off, leave, leave off, lift, manipulate, nip, nullify, pause, pick up, preclude, preempt, put off, quash, quell, quench, quit, relinquish, remit, rescind, retire, reverse, revoke, round off, ruin, scrub, seal, slow, smother, stall, stop, terminate, turn off/turn out, vacate, waive, wind up, wrap up

235 to change cognitively: agree, change, concede, harden, lay

236 to change number or quantity: abbreviate, abridge, abstract, accumulate, add, addition, advance, aggrandize, alleviate, amplification, amplify, augment, blow up, boost, build, build up, commute, compress, condense, contract, curtail, cut, cut back, deduct, deepen, deflate, detract, digest, dilate, discount, double, draw out, enlarge, escalate, evolve, expand, extend, extension, fatten, hike, imbue, increase, inflate, jump, lengthen, lift, lower, magnify, modify, narrow, pare, prune, raise, reduce, reinforce, shorten, slash, step up, summarize, supplement, swell, take, trim, truncate, whittle, widen

237 to change or affect an event: delay, procrastinate, protract, stop, weigh

238 to change state of being: dispatch, do for

239 to continue: abide, bear, broaden, carry on, come, come back, continue, create, drag on/drag out, draw, drawl, draw out, dwell on/dwell upon, eke out, elongate, endure, extend, go, go on, hammer away/hammer into, hang on, hold, kill, lengthen, linger, perpetuate, persevere, persist, prolong, protract, pursue, remain, resume, survive, take up

240 to diminish: abate, account, adulterate, aggravate, aggravation, alloy, attenuate, beginning, blot, blunt, break, canker, cheapen, compound, compromise, cool, corrupt, cut, deaden, debase, debauch, debilitate, decay, decline, decrease, degrade, depress, disorder, doctor, downgrade, emasculate, enfeeble, fatigue, impair, imperil, let up, lower, minimize, mitigate, moderate, modify, muffle, mute, pale, provocation, qualify, reduce, relax, retard, rot, sap, shorten, slash, stimulant,

stimulus, stop, tax, tone down, undermine, weaken, wear, worsen

241 to function: animate, begin, cause, start

242 to happen: accelerate, boomerang, breathe, bring, copy, engender, ensue, entail, eventuate, evoke, expedite, expedition, facilitate, follow, impel, incite, inconvenience, induce, inflict, influence, inspire, instigate, institute, intervene, make, motivate, move, muddle, necessitate, oblige, occasion, occur, orchestrate, pass, precipitate, prod, produce, prompt, provoke, put, recur, result, return, stimulate, trigger, unsettle, will, work up, wreak

243 to have: accent, give, push, transfer

244 to improve: advance, allay, ameliorate, amend, assuage, augment, augmentation, become, benefit, better, betterment, boost, brighten, bring about, brush up, civilize, confirm, contribute, cultivate, cure, dignify, enhance, enrich, freshen, garnish, help, improve, lift, lighten, magnify, mend, mollify, pad, perfect, perk up, polish, quench, quiet, raise, refine, relieve, restore, revise, revision, rouse, step up, strengthen, supplement, touch up, unburden, update

245 to increase quantity: accumulate, add, addition, advance, aggrandize, amplification, amplify, augment, augmentation, blow up, boost, build, build up, deepen, dilate, double, draw out, enlarge, escalate, evolve, expand, extend, extension, fatten, hike, imbue, increase, inflate, jump, lengthen, lift, magnify, raise, reinforce, step up, supplement, swell, widen

246 to injure: abuse, afflict, asphyxiate, batter, battery, beat, blemish, bruise, chip, cost, cripple, crush, damage, debilitate, decay, deface, defile, deform, dent, desecrate, desecration, devastate, disable, disagree, discomfort, disfigure, endanger, expose, fragment, get back at, gripe, handicap, harm, hurt, impair, incapacitate, infect, injure, irritate, knife, lacerate, lay up, maim, mangle, manhandle, mar, maul, mistreat, molest, mutilate, outrage, pain, paralyze, persecute, poison, pollute, rack, repay, rough up, ruin, rupture, sabotage, sap, scar, shatter, shiver, shoot, sicken, smart, smash, snap, splinter, spoil, sting, stress, suffocate, taint, tarnish, torture, trample, turn, violate, violation, vitiate, wound, wrong

247 to reduce quantity: abbreviate, abridge, abstract, alleviate, commute, compress, condense, contract, curtail, cut, cut back, deduct, deflate, detract, digest, discount, lessen, lower, minimize, modify, narrow, pare, prune, reduce, shorten, slash, summarize, take, trim, truncate, whittle

PHYSICAL

248 to break: collide, crack, crash, crumble, dash

249 to burn: arson, blaze, burn, char, conflagration, fire, flame, flare, glow, ignite, inflame, kindle, lick, light, parch, scorch, sear, smolder

250 to change physically: awake, bite, blacken, black out, bleach, blush, brighten, bruise, buttress, chip, color, compact, confirm, congeal, consolidate, corrode, crimp, crinkle, cross, darken, daub, debase, deepen, deform, dehydrate, desiccate, dilute, dim, discolor, disfigure, disorder, disorganize, distort, disturb, do in, douse, dry, dye, eclipse, edge, elongate, emasculate, enervate, exhaust, fade, fatigue, fatten, ferment, file, flatten, flush, fog, foul, gird, harden, hypnotize, intensify, jell, lay, level, light, lighten, loose/loosen, mark, melt, muzzle, neuter, numb, open, pacify, pale, petrify, prolong, prostrate, protract, quicken, ravel, redden, reinforce, roll, rouse, rumple, set, shade, shadow, sharpen, shrivel, slop, slow, smooth, soften, sour, stabilize, stain, sterilize, stiffen, streak, strengthen, stretch, tame, temper, thicken, thin, tidy, tighten, tinge, tint, toughen, turn, vitiate, warp, weary, whet, whiten

251 to create: bear, beget, breed, conceive, concoct, constitute, construct, create, engineer, establish, fabricate, father, forge, form, generate, hatch, materialize, mint, mold, originate, piece, procreate, regenerate, reproduce, spawn

252 to destroy: abolish, abolition, annihilate, annul, assassinate, batter, blight, bomb, break, bring down, bulldoze, burst, bust, butcher, carnage, clobber, collapse, consume, consumption, contaminate, coup de grâce, crucify, crumple, crush, cut down, damage, deface, demolish, demolition, depredation, desecrate, desecration, desolate, despoil, destroy, destruction, devastate, disintegrate, dismantle, disorganize, dispatch, dissolve, do away with, do for, do in, drown, end, endanger, enfeeble, eradicate, erode, erosion, execute, execution, expunge, exterminate, extinguish, extirpate, finish, hang, homicide, hunt, kill, knock off, level, liquidate, mangle, manslaughter, massacre, mess up, murder, obliterate, overthrow, paralyze, pervert, pillage, plunder, poison, prostrate, pull down, pulverize, purge, put away, put down, put out, quash, quench, ravage, raze, remove, ruin, sabotage, sack, shatter, shiver, shoot, slaughter, slay, smash, spoil, strangle, subdue, subvert, suppress, undo, uproot, violation, waste, wipe out, wreck

253 to grow: cultivate, develop, farm, farming, flower, plant, raise, sow, till, vegetate

254 to make dirty: adulterate, blur, clutter, contaminate, dirty, litter, mess up, pollute, smudge, soil, stain, taint, tarnish

255 to make hot or cold: air, boil, chill, cool, freeze, heat, melt, numb, parch, refrigerate, scorch, shrivel, thaw, warm

256 to make wet: absorb, absorption, dampen, deluge, dip, douse, drench, drivel, drool, drown, dunk, engulf, extinguish, immerse, moisten, oil, overflow, permeate, rinse, saturate, soak, souse, spatter, splash, spray, sprinkle, squirt, steep, submerge, water, wet

Fields of human activity

AGRICULTURE

257 action: agriculture, bed, bury, conservation, cross, cultivate, cultivation, culture, erosion, fertilize, gather, graft, harvest, husbandry, preservation, raise, reap, roundup, round up, sow, sprout, tend, till, vegetate, work

258 organization: farm, grange

THE ARTS

259 art object: antique, antiquity, canvas, classic, coat, collage, composition, creation, decoration, depiction, design, dye, emblem, embroidery, enamel, etching, exhibit, figure, flourish, glaze, handicraft, illustration, image, insignia, knickknack, landscape, lattice, masterpiece, medium, model, monument, ornament, pattern, picture, piece, pigment, portrait, pottery, print, profile, silhouette, stamp, statue, trademark, wreath

260 created object: alloy, amulet, apparatus, ash(es), badge, brew, camouflage, capsule, card, change, cinder, composite, composition, compound, concoction, contrivance, creation, curiosity, debris, decoration, derivative, dip, discovery, embers, enamel, essence, fabrication, fake, fence, fertilizer, filth, foam, folder, formation, froth, fusion, fuzz, garbage, garland, gimmick, glass, grime, grit, grounds, half-breed, hash, hodgepodge, hook, huddle, hybrid, imitation, innovation, invention, junk, knickknack, lather, leftover, litter, mess, mix/mixture, novelty, oddity, odds and ends, offshoot, original, outgrowth, output, pack, pad, paper, patchwork, pennant, potpourri, preparation, refuse, remainder, remnant, replica, residue, rest, rubbish, scum, sediment, slime, solution, surplus, trash, vestige, waste, web, work, wreath, wreck, yield

261 exhibition: appear, appearance, boast, brandish, demonstrate, demonstration, develop, display, exhibit, exhibition, expose, exposure, flash, flaunt, foreshadow, impress, look, loom, manifest, mark, mount, parade, peep/peer, personify, point out, portend, posture, pout, present, presentation, produce, record, reflect, register, render, represent, show, show off, sight, simplify, spectacle, sport, spotlight, strut, transpire, typify, uncover, unfold

262 musical instrument: accompaniment, arrangement, baton, bugle, compact disk, harmony, hymn, measure, medley, melody, meter, note, piece, score, song, strain

263 **performance:** anthem, aria, ballet, broadcasting, burlesque, carol, chant, character, comedy, composition, concert, drama, enactment, event, extravaganza, farce, impression, lampoon, medium, movie, music, opus, part, performance, piece, play, premiere, presentation, preview, program, recital, recitation, rendition, repertory, role, satire, scene, scenery, script, set, setting, show, stage, takeoff, theater/theatre

264 **performance part:** act, chorus, encore, epilogue, ovation, plot, prelude, recital, refrain, rehearsal, scene, snatch, stunt, tune

265 **photograph:** observe, photograph, portray, print, proof

COMMUNICATIONS

266 **communication:** address, ad-lib, answer, arrogate, audience, babble, back down, bewail, bid, build up, call, carry, censor, chat, chatter, circumlocution, colloquy, commune, communicate, communication, contact, conversation, converse, correspond, digress, discourse, divide, drivel, effusion, emit, exult, falter, gab, get, give, hush up, improvise, indicate, interact, intercourse, interplay, intervene, intrude, lecture, magnify, mince, monologue, oration, patter, punctuate, quash, quiet, rap, reach, read, recant, recapitulate, recitation, recite, recount, refuse, rehearse, reiterate, render, repartee, say, secrete, signify, silence, slant, speak, speech, stammer, stray, talk, taunt, telephone, tell, transmit, transpire, wander, welcome, whisper, yak/yap

267 **communicative quality:** abusive, acerbity, acid, acidulous, acrid, acrimonious, ad-lib, ambiguous, amusing, apologetic, articulate, artless, biting, bitter, bluff, blunt, boastful, bombastic, brazen, brief, broken, brusque, candid, captious, caustic, censorious, chatty, close, closemouthed, colloquial, communicative, complimentary, confidential, confidentially, convincing, courteous, crisp, critical, crude, cryptic, curt, cutting, cynical, debatable, defamatory, demonstrative, derisive, derogatory, descriptive, destructive, diffuse, direct, directly, disconnected, dishonest, disjointed, disrespectful, doctrinaire, dogmatic, droll, dry, effusive, eloquent, emphatic, encyclopedic, erroneous, et cetera, evasive, even, exaggerated, expansive, explanatory, explicit, expository, expressive, extemporaneous/extempory, facetious, fallacious, false, falsely, farcical, feeble, fictitious, figurative, filthy, firm, firsthand, flaming, flatulent, flimsy, florid, flowery, fluent, forceful, forcible, foreign, forensic, forthright, foul, fractious, frank, frankly, fresh, fulsome, funny, gabby, garrulous, genuine, glib, glowing, grandiloquent, graphic, gross, grouchy, groundless,

gruff, guileless, hackneyed, harsh, hateful, heartfelt, heated, hollow, honest, humorous, hypocritical, idle, illogical, illustrative, imperative, imperious, implicit, implied, importunate, impromptu, improvised, imprudent, inarticulate, incisive, incoherent, indescribable, indicative, ineffable, inelegant, inexplicable, inflated, informative, ingenuous, inoffensive, insincere, insistent, insolent, ironic/ironical, jocular/jocose/jocund, jolly, keen, laconic, laudatory, laughable, left-handed, legendary, legible, lengthy, libelous, literal, literally, literary, loose, loquacious, lurid, lying, malicious, malign, matter-of-fact, mean, meaningful, meaty, mendacious, misleading, mushy, musty, mythical/mythological, naked, nameless, narrative, natural, negative, noncommittal, oblique, obnoxious, obscene, offensive, offhand, oily, open, openly, opinionated, opprobrious, oracular, oral, outspoken, overblown, parting, pejorative, penetrating, peppery, persuasive, pithy, plain, poetic, poignant, pointed, pompous, ponderous, pornographic, pregnant, priceless, private, privileged, privy, profane, prophetic, prosaic, public, pulp, pungent, quick-witted, quizzical, racy, rambling, reticent, rhetorical, ribald, rich, risqué, rough, round, rude, sarcastic, satirical/satiric, saucy, scathing, scurrilous, secretive, secretly, sensational, sentimental, sharp, short, significant, silent, simple, sincere, sincerely, smutty, snappy, sneaky, speechless, spicy, spoken, square, stale, stilted, straight, straightforward, strained, succinct, suggestive, summary, symbolic, taciturn, talkative, tart, terse, threadbare, transparent, trenchant, trite, truculent, true, truly, trustworthy/trusty, truthful, unabridged, unanimous, uncommunicative, unfounded, uninhibited, unintelligible, unsaid, untrue, unvarnished, unwritten, vague, valedictory, veracious, verbal, verbatim, verbose, vernacular, vicious, virulent, vocal, vociferous, vulgar, warm, warning, windy, witty, wordy, wry, yellow, zany

268 **description:** denotation, depiction, description, design, exposition, expression, formula, gloss, history, hyperbole, identification, illustration, kudos, label, legend, name, news, nickname, notation, obituary, outline, paraphrase, plan, poem, poetry, portrait, profile, prose, pseudonym, sketch, translation

269 **devices used for:** alarm, computer, copy, photocopy, telegram, telephone

270 **document, part:** addendum, advertisement, amendment, appendix, article, banner, body, chapter, clause, codicil, condition, entry, epilogue, excerpt, extract, feature, foreword, introduction, item, label, leaf, legend, margin, obituary, passage, preface, provision/proviso, sheet, slip, specification, stipulation, story, supplement, tab, tag, terms, text

271 **document, physical object:** act, affidavit, agreement, album, analysis, annal(s), annual, archive,

article, balance sheet, bill, book, bulletin, card, caricature, catalog/catalogue, certificate, chronicle, circular, commitment, compact, composition, concord, constitution, contract, convention, corpus, credentials, criticism, critique, declaration, deed, deposition, digest, diploma, direction(s), directive, dispatch, dissertation, docket, document, draft, drama, enclosure, epistle, essay, explanation, exposition, facsimile, fiction, file, form, guarantee, history, identification, injunction, journal, letter, life, line, log, mail, material, memoir, memorandum/memo, message, missive, monument, narrative, note/notes, notice, opus, pact, pamphlet, paper/papers, paper, pass, passport, patent, permit, petition, piece, plan, policy, poster, proceedings, proclamation, promotion, pronouncement, proposal, prose, reading, receipt, record, reference, release, reminder, résumé, satire, schedule, scheme, script, sequel, sign, statement, survey, telegram, theme, thesis, ticket, treatise, writing

272 document quality: readable, short, summary, terse

273 humorous tale: banter, chaff, crack, jest, joke, kid, lampoon, levity, parody, pleasantry, pun, quip, spoof, sport, take off, travesty, trick, wit

274 information: advice, allusion, analysis, annotation, announcement, answer, broadcast, bulletin, buzz, calendar, caution, caveat, charge, clarification, clue, command, commitment, communication, confession, conjecture, construction, counsel, data, declaration, definition, dictate, direction(s), directive, disclosure, dope, evidence, excerpt, exhortation, explanation, exposé, fact, facts, gossip, grounds, groundwork, guidance, guide, herald, hint, illumination, information, instruction, intelligence, intimation, key, knowledge, lead, learning, lesson, light, lore, material, message, news, notice, particular, plug, point, pointer, prescription, prognosis, program, prompt, pronouncement, proof, publication, publicity, quotation/quote, reading, recipe, recommendation, reference, report, resolution, revelation, rumor, science, scoop, secret, sign, statement, story, tidings, tip/tipoff, trivia, warning, whisper, word

275 integral language parts: adjective, adverb, antonym, aphorism, banality, barbarism, byword, cant, catchword, clause, cliché, euphemism, expletive, figure of speech, grammar, idiom, jargon, metaphor, neologism, nomenclature, phrase, proverb, term, word

276 language: adage, adieu, alphabet, code, dialect, diction, expression, grammar, jargon, language, lexicon, lingo, nomenclature, patter, slang, speech, style, swearing, tongue, vernacular, vocabulary, voice

277 media: advertisement, banner, correspondence, criticism, dispatch, memorandum/memo, pen, rhetoric, rumor, sarcasm, screen, television, translation, vehicle

278 object used in: address, advertisement, alert, analogy, anathema, answer, aphorism, approach, assertion, assurance, axiom, babble, back talk, banner, banter, breath, bunk, call, cant, catchword, chat, chatter, claim, cliché, comeback, comment, commentary, commonplace, compliment, congratulations, contact, contention, contradiction, controversy, correspondence, criticism, cry, cue, curse, decision, declaration, defense, definition, derision, dialogue/dialog, dictum, digression, disapproval, dispatch, disputation, dispute, dissension, dissidence, dissonance, double entendre, double-talk, drivel, edict, eloquence, embellishment, epigram, epilogue, epitaph, equivocation, eulogy, euphemism, exaggeration, exaltation, fabrication, falsehood, falsity, farewell, fib, figure of speech, flak, fulmination, gab, gibberish, gibe, goodbye, gossip, grace, gratitude, grievance, gripe, groan, guidance, harangue, hearsay, hiss, hocus-pocus, hogwash, honor, implication, impropriety, indication, indignity, innuendo, instruction, insult, invective, invention, invocation, irony, issue, knock, lament/lamentation, laurels, lecture, letter, lie, line, lip, litany, malediction, maxim, meaning, memorandum/memo, mention, missive, mockery, monologue, moral, motion, motto, mouth, negation, negative, notice, oath, obscenity, observation, offense, offer, omen, oracle, oration, order, outcry, overtone, overture, password, patter, phrase, pitch, platform, platitude, plea, pleasantry, pledge, portent, praise, precursor, prediction, pretension, proclamation, profanity, profession, projection, promise, pronouncement, propaganda, prophecy, proverb, puff, pun, put-down, quip, quotation/quote, rebuff, rebuke, recommendation, reference, refusal, regards, remark, reminder, rendition, reply, report, reprimand, respects, response, retort, return, rhetoric, rhyme, rot, rubbish, rumor, sarcasm, saying, scandal, sermon, shadow, slam, slander, slogan, slur, statement, story, suggestion, swearing, tale, talk, testimonial, testimony, thanks, theme, threat, tirade, toast, translation, trash, tribute, truth, utterance, vehicle, veracity, verbiage, voice, vow, welcome, whisper, wind, word, wording

279 organization: media, newspaper, radio, television

280 publication: advertisement, almanac, anthology, article, authority, autobiography, bible, bill, biography, book, brochure, cartoon, catalog/catalogue, dictionary, directory, edition, fiction, handbook, issue, journal, lexicon, literature, magazine, manual, memoir, newspaper, novel, organ, pamphlet, paper, periodical, press, print, publication, publicity, reference, release, review, romance, satire, text, treatise, vocabulary, volume

281 record: annal(s), archive, calendar, itinerary, list, program, record, register, roll, roster

282 story: account, allegory, anecdote, biography, chronicle, epic, fable, fib, fiction, folklore, legend, lore, memoir, mystery, myth, mythology, narration, narrative, plot, poem, poetry, report, saga, scenario, story, tale, verse, version, yarn

283 **summary:** abbreviation, abridgement, abstract, agenda, annotation, bill, breakdown, brief, caption, citation, compendium, condensation, diagnosis, diary, directory, epitome, inventory, menu, moral, precis, profile, program, prospectus, report, résumé, return, review, roster, rundown, scenario, schedule, sketch, summary, synopsis, table, tally, title

284 **symbol:** arms, augury, autograph, badge, brand, capital, character, charm, check, code, crest, cue, device, dot, emblem, exponent, flag, fleck, flourish, hallmark, handwriting, harbinger, herald, impression, imprint, index, indication, insignia, label, landmark, lead, letter, line, mark, notation, note, numeral, script, seal, sign, signal, spot, stamp, stripe, symbol, tag, tick, token, trademark, tread, type, vestige, writing

EDUCATION

285 **educate:** address, break in, breed, care, catechize, coach, domesticate, drill, educate, education, form, groom, ground, illuminate, inculcate, indoctrinate, initiate, instill, instruct, instruction, lesson, preach, preparation, school, speak, speech, talk, teach, train, training, tutor

286 **education level:** class, freshman/woman, grade, level

287 **objects used in:** class, college, course, dissertation, edification, education, erudition, lesson, lore, school, tenure, text, thesis, tuition

288 **organization:** academy, alma mater, class, college, enrollment, faculty, institute/institution, school

289 **place of:** academy, alma mater, class, college, school

290 **test:** assay, audition, criterion, dissection, drill, examination, exercise, experiment, index, inquest, inquiry, inspection, investigation, probe, quiz, test, trial, weight, workout

291 **testing:** fiddle, grade, pace, plumb, survey, test, trial, try, try on/try out, verify

ENTERTAINMENT

292 **action:** act, acting, amuse, amusement, antic, appear, arrange, bet, bill, broadcast, cruise, dance, diversion, dramatize, enact, enactment, entertain, featuring, feign, game, host, hype, impersonate, interpret, issue, overplay, pageant, parody, perform, play, prance, pretend, preview, produce, publication, publicize, put on, regale, rehearsal, rehearse, relaxation, revel, romp, score, sing, spotlight, stage, takeoff, take off, tape, transmit, travesty, trifle

293 **object:** auditorium, balloon, bet, broadcast, broadcasting, cinema, circus, comedy, distraction,

drama, extravaganza, farce, film, fireworks, humor, lounge, medium, movie, news, nightclub, picture, publicity, sensation, sequel, show, sight, song, television, theater/theatre

294 **organization:** band, cast, chorus, corps, ensemble, following, gallery

FAMILY

295 **child raising:** baby, baby-sit, breed, bring up, care, coddle, cradle, cultivate, form, foster, mind, mother, nourish, nurse, nurture, pamper, raise, rear, support, tend

296 **family:** aristocracy, birth, blood, bride, bridegroom, brood, clan, class, consanguinity, court, darling, descendant, descent, extraction, family, folk, genealogy, gentility, heritage, house, household, issue, kin, kindred, line, lineage, mate, mistress, offspring, origin, pedigree, people, posterity, progeny, rank, relation, stock, strain, tribe

297 **marriage:** annul, annulment, betroth, betrothal, couple, desert, desertion, divorce, elope, engage, engagement, espouse, estrange, estrangement, jilt, marriage, marry, match, mate, matrimony, nuptials, part, parting, propose, rupture, separate, separation, sever, split, vow, wed, wedding, woo

GOVERNMENT AND POLITICS

298 **government action:** abdicate, abolish, abolition, accession, administer, administration, amnesty, bust, colonization, command, depose, deposition, dethrone, displace, dominate, enact, enforce, enforcement, exile, expulsion, filibuster, legalize, override/overrule, pass, reign, rule, run in, secede, second, surveillance, tax, truce, veto

299 **government organization:** administration, ally, cabinet, capitalism, capitol, chamber, confederacy, congress, council, court, delegation, democracy, dictatorship, direction, empire, fascism, government, house, jury, legislature, police/police officer, post, regime, rule, sovereignty, tyranny

300 **political action:** amnesty, arbitrate, arbitration, ballot, campaign, canvass, crusade, demonstrate, demonstration, displace, drive, drum up, elect, election, endorse, lobby, mutiny, nominate, nomination, patronage, picket, politics, poll, protest, reaction, rebellion, revolt, revolution, riot, run, vote

301 **political organization:** alliance, ballot, caucus, commonwealth, communism, confederacy, delegation, faction, fascism, machine, party, politics, side, tyranny

HEALTH

302 **birth:** bear, birth, breed, childbirth, conception, confinement, delivery, spring

303 change in: ache, black out, come down with, faint, fit, look up, mend, pull through, recover, recuperate, remission, repel, weary

304 death: abort, abortion, death, decease, demise, die, dissolution, end, expiration, expire, fatality, pass away, passing, perish

305 deathplace: cemetery, crypt, grave, graveyard, monument, tomb

306 disease: affliction, ailment, bacteria, blight, bug, cancer, canker, complaint, condition, contagion, contamination, cyst, disease, disorder, epidemic, germ, growth, illness, indigestion, infection, infirmity, microbe, pest, pimple, plague, rash, sickness, spell, swelling, symptom, syndrome, tantrum

307 drug: analgesic, anesthetic/anaesthetic, antidote, antiseptic, antitoxin, balm, capsule, contraceptive, cure, dope, dose, drug, medicine/medication, narcotic, nostrum, panacea, pill, poison, pot, potion, prescription, remedy, sedative, stimulant, stimulus, tablet, tonic

308 event: abort, abortion, ache, attack, catch, contract, convulsion, cough, cramp, crick, faint, gag, gargle, heal, massage, nauseate, palpitate, paroxysm, pass out, perk up, rupture, seizure, spell, spew, stroke, suffer, take, throw up, tic, vomit, wheeze

309 injury: abrasion, affliction, bite, blister, boil, bruise, concussion, contusion, cut, damage, defect, detriment, disability, disadvantage, disservice, fracture, gash, harm, injury, prick, puncture, rip, rupture, rust, scratch, shock, stab, swelling, welt, wound

310 medical action: alter, analyze, autopsy, bandage, castrate, cure, diagnose, dissection, doctor, dope, dress, drug, ease, examination, heal, inject, malpractice, massage, operate, operation, postmortem, practice, remedy, therapy, tranquilize, transplant, treat, treatment, vaccinate

311 medical instruments: bandage, cure, injection, lotion, matter, nostrum, ointment, panacea, prescription, remedy, salve, staff, x-ray

312 medical organization: asylum, clinic, hospital, madhouse, office

313 pain: ache, afflict, anesthesia/anaesthesia, discomfort, distress, gripe, harassment, harm, hurt, itch, pinch, sting, strain, stress, suffer, torment, torture, wound, wrong

314 quality of: able-bodied, ailing, anemic, bad, benign, better, burning, catching, clean, communicable, congenital, contagious, convalescent, crippled, curable, curative, delicate, disabled, diseased, dizzy, doddering, done in, drugged, drunk, epidemic, excruciating, faint, febrile, fit, game, genetic, giddy, gory, groggy, haggard, hale, hardy, healthy, hearty, high, hurt, ill, immune, indisposed, inebriated, infectious, infirm, insane, invalid, irreparable, lame, light headed, low, lusty, malignant, mental, morbid, nauseous, neurotic, normal, palsied, paralytic, peaked, pestilent/

pestilential, poor, poorly, queasy, queer, right, robust, rocky, rugged, run-down, safe, sane, senile, sick, sickly, soft, sore, sound, spent, squeamish, strong, sturdy, tender, terminal, tired, tough, trim, unconscious, unfeeling, unhealthy, unscathed, unsound, vigorous, wan, weak, weary, well, whole, wholesome

315 sleep: anesthesia/anaesthesia, asleep, awake, coma, doze, drop off, hibernate, insomnia, lethargy, nap, nightmare, nod, quiet, rest, sleep, sleepy, slumber, snooze, snore, stupor

316 state of: ache, addiction, ailment, apoplexy, beat, collapse, complaint, condition, confinement, cough, debility, disability, dislocation, epidemic, faint, fatigue, fitness, form, gestation, hangover, health, hurt, hygiene, ill, immunity, insanity, lapse, malaise, maternity, nausea, neurosis, pain, paroxysm, pink, shape, stupor, symptom, syndrome, tone, trim, trouble, tumor, vigor, welfare/well-being

LEGAL

317 legal action: absolve, acquit, acquittal, action, adjudicate, adopt, adoption, annul, annulment, apprehend, apprehension, arraign, arrest, bequeath, book, bring, bust, charge, cite, collar, commute, condemn, condemnation, convict, conviction, counsel, covenant, cross-examine, cut off, decree, detain, detention, disinherit, enact, enforce, enforcement, evidence, excommunicate, exculpate, exonerate, extradite, hearing, impeach, imprison, incarcerate, indict, indictment, inherit, insure, jail, judge, leave, legalize, let off, lift, litigate, moderate, nab, nail, ordain, outlaw, override/overrule, pardon, pass, perjure, pick up, pinch, plead, practice, prohibit, proscribe, prosecute, pull in, put away, raid, rap, repeal, represent, reprieve, rescind, run in, sentence, sing, substantiate, sue, testify, transport, trial, try, validate, verify, vindicate, vitiate, vouch, waive, will, witness

318 objects used in legal practice: acquittal, act, affidavit, article, bail, bar, bench, bequest, bill, bond, brief, canon, case, claim, code, constitution, court, decree, deed, deposition, dictate, enactment, entreaty, evidence, indictment, injunction, inquest, institute, insurance, jury, law, lawsuit, legislation, libel, litigation, mandate, measure, ordinance, paper/papers, pardon, passage, patent, plea, pledge, precept, prescription, principle, regulation, repeal, reprieve, ruling, sentence, statute, stipulation, suit, terms, testament, testimonial, testimony, verdict, waiver, will, writ

319 quality of law: administrative, authoritarian, authoritative, autocratic, canonical, clear, constitutional, contraband, democratic, effectual, exempt, forensic, free, illegal, illegitimate, illicit, inadmissible, judicial, just, lawful, lawless, legal, legislative, legitimate, misbegotten, permissible, punitive, unauthorized, unlawful, unprejudiced, valid, wrongful

320 **military action:** action, aggression, barrage, blitz, blow up, campaign, conflict, contest, coup d'état, defeat, deploy, depose, deposition, descent, dethrone, disarm, disarmament, draft, engage, engagement, enlist, explode, explosion, fire, incursion, induct, induction, insurrection, invade, invasion, maneuver, mobilize, occupation, occupy, offensive, oppression, overthrow, rally, rebellion, recruit, revolt, revolution, salute, service, station, surrender, war, warfare

321 **object used by military:** armory, barracks, battery, battlefield, citadel, defense, draft, fort/fortress, magazine, post, rampart, service

322 **organization:** ally, army, artillery, battalion, brigade, cavalry, corps, defense, detachment, detail, enemy, fleet, force, legion, military, platoon, squad, troop/troops

323 **association:** board, cartel, conglomerate, establishment, federation, firm, industry, market/mart, merger, patronage, syndicate, trust

324 **business action:** advertise, advertising, annexation, appear, appointment, auction, aviation, cashier, commercialize, commission, conclave, conference, consultation, convene, convention, cry, deal, dealings, depression, dictate, discharge, dismiss, drudge, enterprise, exchange, export, farm, farming, fold, gathering, hold, hype, incorporate, intercourse, malpractice, management, manufacture/manufacturing, market, mediate, mediation, meet, meeting, merge, merger, monopolize, operation, patronage, patronize, pioneer, popularize, position, powwow, practice, produce, project, promote, promotion, proposal, publicize, puff, push, put up, sale, seal, second, service, session, shake up, shut, sit, slavery, specialize, step in, stock, table, trade, traffic, transact, transaction, truck, undertaking, wait on

325 **business organization:** agency, airport, association, bakery, bar, branch, bureau, bureaucracy, business, cartel, clientele, commerce, company, concern, conglomerate, corporation, council, direction, dispensation, enterprise, establishment, exchange, field, firm, house, industry, labor, management, operation, outfit, partnership, personnel, practice, regime, ring, staff, store, syndicate, trust, union

326 **business quality:** accomplished, ambitious, businesslike, busy, careful, concentrated, diligent, discipline, eager, earnest, enterprising, grasping, greedy, methodical/methodic, miserly, orderly, painstaking, persistent, practical, professional,

proper, purposeful, regular, relentless, stingy, tenacious, zealous

327 **buying:** buy, charge, lavish, lay out, order, patronize, pay, procure, purchase, redeem, shop, splurge, spree, squander, take, trade, traffic, treat, truck

328 **cost:** appraisal, cost, expense

329 **fee:** amount, bet, bill, bribe, charge, commission, damage(s), debt, duty, excise, expense, fare, fee, levy, obligation, overhead, pay, price, rate, rent, revenue, stake, tab, tariff, tax, toll, wager

330 **financial action:** assess, audit, bank, bargain, bet, bid, bidding, bill, bring, bring in, budget, bust, cash, charge, deduct, default, deposit, depress, depression, devalue, dicker, discount, earn, economize, economy, endorse, fail, frugality, gross, insure, invest, investment, levy, liquidate, net, pawn, pay, pinch, price, profit, realize, return, salt away, save, scrape, shop, skimp, speculate, speculation, stake, stint, subsist, trade, traffic, transact, transaction, truck, venture

331 **financial document:** account, agreement, book, coupon, reckoning, return, statement

332 **financial object:** account, adjustment, arrears, assessment, asset(s), backing, bail, balance, balance sheet, bargain, bill, budget, capital, cheap, draft, equity, fund, insurance, interest, investment, liability, loan, means, order, overhead, patronage, pawn, pay, pension, pledge, principal, profit, quotation/quote, receipt, revenue, score, stock, treasure

333 **financial organization:** bank, board, market/mart

334 **financial quality:** affluent, balanced, bankrupt, behind, broke, charitable, cheap, close, comfortable, commercial, complimentary, costly, dear, depressed, destitute, disadvantaged, disadvantageous, down-and-out, due, economic, economical, exorbitant, expensive, extravagant, fat, financial, finished, fiscal, flush, free, frugal, gainful, generous, good, grasping, gratis, gratuitous, high, humble, impecunious, impoverished, improvident, indebted, indigent, inexpensive, insolvent, invaluable, lavish, liberal, liquid, low, lucrative, marketable, mean, miserly, modest, monetary, moneyed, moneymaking, munificent, narrow, needy, net, nominal, opulent, outstanding, overdue, owing, palatial, paltry, parsimonious, patrician, payable, penniless, plush, poor, posh, poverty-stricken, precious, priceless, privileged, prodigal, profitable, profligate, prohibitive, prosperous, provident, rich, second-rate/second-class, self-sufficient, skimpy, sleazy, sordid, sparing, splendid, squalid, steep, stingy, strapped, substantial, sumptuous, tawdry, thrifty, thriving, tight, underprivileged, unfortunate, unpaid, unreasonable, unsettled, valuable, wealthy, well-bred, well-off

335 **financial state:** afford, arrears, avarice, bankruptcy, boom, bring, circumstances, credit, cutback, default, deficit, depression, devalue,

discount, economy, extravagance, fail, fortune, frugality, inadequacy, inflation, living, misery, need, obligation, owe, panic, paucity, pile, pomp, poverty, prosperity, recession, riches, savings, slump, substance, thrift, traffic, value, worth

336 financial value state: cost, decline, expense, value

337 gift: acquisition, allowance, arrival, atonement, award, balm, benefit, bequest, bonus, boon, bounty, charity, citation, comfort, commendation, compensation, contribution, courtesy, decoration, diploma, dispensation, dividend, dole, donation, due, endowment, extravagance, find, fruit, gain, gem, gift, godsend, good, grant, gratuity, haul, heirloom, honor, indulgence, inheritance, laurels, legacy, loot, luxury, medal, memento, memorial, offering, plum, premium, present, presentation, prize, purse, recognition, remembrance, reparation, reward, souvenir, spoils, subsidy, token, treasure, trophy

338 merchandise: bargain, cargo, commodity, consignment, contraband, fabrication, freight, goods, hardware, harvest, haul, inventory, line, load, merchandise, order, product, stock, truck, turnout, wares, yield

339 monetary container: bag, bank, purse, till, treasury

340 money: advance, allowance, appropriation, asset(s), bill, bread, cash, change, chips, coin, contribution, currency, deposit, dollar, donation, endowment, estate, finances, financing, fund, funds, income, investment, loot, maintenance, means, mint, money, offering, pay, pile, pool, recompense, refund, reserve, resource, resources, return, riches, savings, support, sustenance, wealth

341 money giving: advance, blow, buy, compensate, disburse, discharge, endow, expend, finance, fritter, fund, invest, lavish, lay out, misappropriate, patronage, patronize, pay, play, ransom, recompense, refund, reimburse, remit, remunerate, repay, requite, reward, satisfy, settle, shell out, spend, sponsor, square, subscribe, subsidize, support, underwrite

342 money taking: bill, blackmail, bleed, clear, collect, extort, extortion, fine, fleece, recoup, squeeze

343 ownership part: hold, owner, possession, proprietor

344 payment: advance, alimony, bounty, collateral, commission, compensation, consideration, cut, deal, debt, deposit, disbursement, discharge, dividend, dole, draft, dues, earnings, equity, expenditure, expense, fee, financing, gain, graft, grant, gratuity, gross, income, installment, interest, kickback, outlay, pay, payment, penalty, pension, perk, pittance, premium, prize, proceeds, profit, purse, raise, ransom, rebate, receipts, recompense, redress, refund, reparation, restitution, revenue, reward, salary, satisfaction, stake, stipend, subsidy, take, tip, upkeep, wage/wages

345 selling: auction, bazaar, charge, handle, market, merchandise, peddle, sale, sell, solicit, trade, traffic, truck

346 value state: appreciation, benefit, decline, import, importance, mark, quality, value, worth

PROFESSIONS

347 business manager: administrator, banker, boss, businessman/businesswoman, capitalist, captain, chief, commander, dealer, director, employer, entrepreneur, establishment, executive, farmer, father/mother, financier, foreman/woman, founder, head, landlord, leader, magnate, manager, master, merchant, mistress, mogul, notable, officer, official, owner, principal, professional, proprietor, ruler, seller, specialist, superintendent, superior, supervisor, tycoon, warden

348 businessperson: accountant, adjutant, adviser/advisor, agent, aid/aide, analyst, announcer, applicant, apprentice, arbitrator, archaeologist, architect, assistant, associate, astronaut, attendant, auditor, author, authority, aviator, baker, banker, barber, bearer, broker, builder, businessman/businesswoman, butcher, butler, buyer, caretaker, carpenter, cartoonist, cashier, chair, chairperson, clerk, client, collaborator, colleague, commuter, connection, consumer, cook, correspondent, courier, court, craftsperson, creator, critic, custodian, customer, dabbler, deputy, detective, domestic, drudge, emissary, employee, engineer, envoy, expert, farmer, fellow, financier, flyer, fortune-teller/fortuneteller, friend, go-between, gourmet, groom, guard, guide, hack, hand, help, inferior, informant/informer, intermediary, investigator, janitor, journalist, labor, liaison, machine, maid, mariner, mastermind, matron, maverick, mediator, messenger, middleman/woman, miser, model, monitor, negotiator, novice, opposition, page, partner, patriarch, patron, picket, pilot, pioneer, playwright, poet, porter, prodigal, professional, prostitute, recruit, referee, reporter, representative, rival, sailor, scout, seller, servant, slave, snoop, spendthrift, spokesman/woman/person, sponsor, spy, subordinate, surrogate, tailor/tailoress, tenant, tool, traveler, umpire, vendor, virtuoso, watchman/woman, wizard, worker, writer

349 discipline: affair, anatomy, anthropology, appointment, archaeology, architecture, arithmetic, art, astronomy, botany, career, cinema, communications, department, discipline, domain, employment, field, geography, lifework, line, livelihood, logic, matter, occupation, orbit, passion, philosophy, poetry, position, press, project, province, psychology, pursuit, realm, research, scene, school, science, specialty, sphere, stage, station, territory, trade, undertaking, vocation, walk, work

350 educator: academic, adviser/advisor, alumnus/

alumna, brain, coach, dean, disciplinarian, expert, faculty, freshman/woman, genius, graduate, guru, instructor, intellectual, learner, master, mastermind, mentor, mistress, monitor, novice, principal, professor, pupil, scholar, school, student, teacher, tutor

351 **employment:** ax/axe, bounce, can, collaborate, commission, demote, discharge, dismiss, dismissal, earn, elevate, elevation, employ, employment, engage, fire, gross, hire, interview, job, kick out, labor, layoff, lay off, live, livelihood, living, make, occupation, office, oust, pay, picket, post, promote, promotion, raise, reinstate, relieve, resign, resignation, retain, retire, rise, sack, situation, spot, station, strike, suspend, work

352 **entertainer:** acrobat, actor, artist, ballet dancer, buff, character, comedian, comic, connoisseur, creator, director, fan, fanatic, fledgling, follower, freak, hero/heroine, host/hostess, idol, joker, luminary, magician, mimic, musician, name, notable, participant, personage/personality, player, protagonist, singer, star, usher, virtuoso, wit, zany

353 **financier:** accountant, banker, bearer, broker, financier, spendthrift

354 **government officer:** administrator, ally, ambassador, arbiter, authoritarian, authority, autocracy, conqueror, consul, delegate, deputy, despot, dictator, diplomat, disciplinarian, envoy, establishment, executive, exile, expatriate, figure, figurehead, governor, informant/informer, inhabitant, intermediary, justice, king, leader, legislator, liaison, lord, master, minister, mogul, monarch, negotiator, officer, official, page, patrol, peacemaker, personage/personality, police/police officer, representative, ruler, sovereign, spokesman/woman/person, tyrant

355 **legal practitioner:** attorney, bench, beneficiary, consul, counsel, counselor, heir, investigator, judge, lawyer, officer, party, proponent, witness

356 **media person:** commentator, journalist, press, reporter, writer

357 **medical practitioner:** analyst, doctor, nurse, patient, physician, psychiatrist, specialist

358 **military person:** commander, conqueror, deserter, fighter, lookout, mercenary, militant, officer, patrol, private, recruit, sailor, scout, soldier, veteran, warrior

359 **politician:** advocate, ally, anarchist, apostate, apostle, applicant, arbitrator, backer, bigot, candidate, conservative, demagogue, diehard, diplomat, dissident, donor, extremist, fanatic, hostage, idealist, insurgent, militant, nonconformist, partisan, patron, picket, politician, proponent, protagonist, radical, reactionary, rebel, refugee, renegade, sectarian, spokesman/woman/person

360 **profession:** business, calling, career, craft, employment, finance, job, labor, lifework, line, livelihood, mission, occupation, place, position, profession, psychology, science, situation, trade, vocation, walk, work

361 **religious person:** acolyte, agnostic, angel, apostle, believer, chaplain, clergyman/woman, convert, creator, cynic, disciple, doubter, father, hermit, layman/woman, magician, minister, missionary, monk, nun, pagan, pastor, preacher, priest, prophet, skeptic, visionary, witch, wizard

362 **task:** affair, assignment, bee, berth, chore, commission, concern, drudgery, duty, effort, enterprise, errand, exercise, exertion, function, grind, groove, job, labor, mission, office, part, picnic, post, project, province, realm, research, role, routine, spot, stint, sweat, task, tax, toil, undertaking, work

RECREATION

363 **action:** angle, athletics, boating, bowl, boxing, bunt, chance, coach, competition, contest, cruise, dance, deal, defeat, dissipation, diversion, engage, event, exercise, fish, gamble, gambol, game, gymnastics, hike, hobby, hunt, keep up, lay, leisure, match, meet, meeting, mess around, oppose, pastime, pit, play, race, raffle, recreation, rehearsal, rehearse, relaxation, rout, shuffle, speculate, speculation, sport, stake, swim, tournament, trifle, turn, vacation, venture, vie, wager, win, workout

364 **objects used in:** amusement, avocation, bicycle, club, equipment, field, game, gymnasium, hobby, holiday, lap, point, pool, raffle, recreation, round, score, tie, wager

365 **organization:** conference, field, league, side, squad, team

366 **participants:** amateur, athlete, aviator, champion, coach, competitor, contestant, dabbler, entrant, entry, fan, fanatic, fighter, fledgling, follower, freak, mariner, master, name, opponent, opposition, participant, pedestrian, player, referee, rival, sailor, spectator, star, umpire, underdog, victor, winner

RELIGIOUS

367 **action:** anoint, baptism, baptize, bless, blessing, burial, bury, canonize, christen, communion, consecrate, dedicate, dedication, defect, defection, deify, enshrine, excommunicate, inter, penance, pray, prayer, preach, purification, purify, wake, witchcraft, worship

368 **objects used in:** abbey, beads, bible, casket, cathedral, cemetery, church, cloister, coffin, convent, deity, denomination, divinity, faith, grace, holiness, invocation, litany, liturgy, monastery, pulpit, religion, sanctuary, sermon, service, shrine, temple

369 **organization:** church, clergy, congregation, cult, parish

370 **supernatural:** angel, apparition, black magic, deity, demon, devil, divinity, elf, eternity, fairy, ghost, God, heaven, hell, hereafter, incantation, magic, monster, paradise, phantom, presence, sav-

ior, shade, sorcery, spell, spirit, universe, utopia, vision, witchcraft

SEX AND REPRODUCTION

371 attribute of gender: buxom, femininity/feminine, male, masculinity/masculine

372 attribute of sex: adulterous, amatory, amorous, aphrodisiac, bisexual, carnal, celibate, chaste, close, desirable, erotic, femininity/feminine, fertile, fertility, fleshly, gay, homosexual, hot, kinky, lascivious, lecherous, lewd, libidinous, licentious, loose, loving, nasty, naughty, obscene, passion, passionate, pornographic, potent, promiscuous, provocative, pure, raw, seductive, sensual, sensuous, sexual, sexy, smutty, spicy, suggestive, sultry, torrid, vice, virgin/virginal, virile, voluptuous, vulgar, wanton

373 birth: bear, birth, breed, childbirth, conception, confinement, delivery, spring

374 child bearing: beget, deliver, delivery, father, fertilize, generate, generation, get, have, labor, multiply, procreate, produce, propagate, reproduce, spawn

375 sex act: affair, alter, assignation, birth control, caress, climax, cohabit, conception, copulate, coquet, couple, cuddle, dalliance, dally/dally with, debauch, deflower, enamor, fertilize, flirt, flirtation, fondle, hug, impregnate, intercourse, kiss, love, love affair, mate, molest, pass, paw, pet, play around, proposition, rape, ravish, romance, seduce, sex, sin, tryst, violate, violation, woo

SOCIAL INTERACTIONS

376 authority: agency, agent, ascendancy/ascendency, auspices, authority, carte blanche, censorship, chair, chairperson, chief, choice, claim, clearance, cogency, command, connoisseur, control, curb, custody, dominance, domination, dominion, duty, ease, empire, franchise, immunity, impunity, independence, jurisdiction, justice, leadership, leave, mastery, office, option, permission, permit, power, prerogative, privilege, rate, reign, right, rule, station, supremacy, sway, title, trust, voice, vote, warrant

377 celebration: acclamation, affair, banquet, baptism, carnival, celebrate, celebration, commemorate, commemoration, commencement, entertain, fair, fanfare, feast, festival, festivity, fete, fiesta, gaiety, gala, keep, observance, observe, orgy, pageant, parade, pomp, rally, revel, revelry, rite, splurge, spree, wake

378 class: branch, brand, breed, caste, category, class, classification, cut, denomination, description, division, echelon, estate, family, form, genre/genus, gradation, grade, kind, manner, mob, model, mold, nature, nobility, order, position, quality, rank, sort, species, stock, tier, type, variety, world

379 community: colony, commune, community, constituency, country, folk, neighborhood, people, population, public, society

380 ethnic group: nationality, people, race, strain, tribe

381 organization: affiliate, affiliation, agency, apparatus, assembly, bar, brigade, brotherhood, coalition, combination, commission, committee, council, crew, crowd, department, federation, foundation, guild, institute/institution, league, membership, movement, network, organization, partnership, party, ring, sect, society, union

382 part of a group: chapter, division, plurality, sect

383 party: affair, blowout, dance, entertainment, festivity, gala, masquerade, orgy, party, reception, tear

384 social action: abuse, accept, advance(s), adventure, amends, amuse, appeal, appointment, associate, befriend, betray, bite, blooper, bounce, caper, carouse, cavort, cohabit, collaborate, commemorate, compel, conclave, conduct, consort, cool, coquet, court, cower, cultivate, cut up, disaffect, discriminate, disgrace, disobey, disorganize, dissociate, encounter, endanger, engagement, enjoy, entertain, entertainment, escapade, escort, estrange, excursion, faux pas, fawn, fete, fight, flirt, flirtation, flock, forsake, fraternize, frequent, frisk, frolic, go together/go with, grovel, hanky-panky, haunt, hold, host, hubbub, induct, induction, infringe, insinuate, interfere, interference, interrupt, introduce, invitation, invite, jilt, kick out, know, kowtow, lose, love, make up, maroon, mask, meddle, mediate, mediation, meet, meeting, mingle, mishandle/mismanage, mutiny, obeisance, oblige, observance, observe, ostracize, overture, pander, part, parting, pass, patch up, patronize, penance, pick up, play, play around, poke, popularize, powwow, prance, prank, pretend, program, proposition, prostrate, pry, pursue, put up, rampage, rapprochement, reception, reciprocate, reconcile, reduce, regale, reinstate, rendezvous, repay, reprisal, requite, respond, retaliate, retribution, revel, revelry, revenge, riot, romance, romp, rupture, seat, secede, second, see, separate, sever, share, show, shun, sit, slight, snoop, snub, socialize, soothe, spree, spurn, squire, step in, stoop, stunt, taint, tantrum, tear, throw over, toy, treat, trespass, trick, tryst, usurp, vengeance, wallow, welcome, woo

385 social change: breakup, civilize, give in/give up, revert, succumb

386 social event: adventure, assignation, ball, bee, benefit, binge, blast, bustle, caper, caricature, carnival, ceremony, clamor, clown, come between, conference, date, debut, display, dissipation, diversion, entertainment, escapade, exhibition, exposition, fair, feature, fiesta, fling, frolic, fun, function, funeral, gathering, inauguration, initiation, memorial, merriment/merrymaking, occasion, outing, parade, picnic, rally, riot, rite, ritual

387 social organization: association, band, brotherhood, circle, clan, class, clique, club, congregation, congress, crowd, cult, elite, entourage, faction, fellowship, following, fraternity, gang, guild, league, legion, order, society

388 social state: amity, association, attendance, awkwardness, behind, belong, belonging, bigotry, bond, brand, breach, break, breeding, brotherhood, calm, camaraderie, care, caste, celebrity, celibacy, censorship, ceremony, circumstances, civilization, class, clutches, coherence, commotion, companionship, compatibility, complicity, concert, concord, conflict, conjunction, connection, consanguinity, consequence, contact, contempt, cooperation, correlation, courtesy, courtship, credit, crunch, culture, dalliance, degree, detachment, difference, dignity, diplomacy, disaffection, disagreement, discord, disfavor, disgrace, disharmony, dishonor, disorder, dissociation, dissolution, distinction, disturbance, division, duty, ease, echelon, elite, eminence, enrollment, entertainment, entree, entry, equality, estate, estrangement, excitement, face, fame, familiarity, favoritism, fellowship, feud, fidelity, footing, friendliness, friendship, frivolity, fun, furor, fuss, gaiety, genre/genus, gentility, get along, get on, glory, harmony, height, hospitality, housing, hubbub, humiliation, immunity, importance, infidelity, intimacy, intrigue, juncture, kick, laissez-faire, lapse, lather, league, level, liaison, liberty, love affair, luxury, marriage, match, mirth, mourning, mutiny, name, network, nobility, nonsense, notch, notoriety, obligation, odium, onus, pandemonium, partnership, peace, pink, place, platitude, pleasure, polish, popularity, position, predicament, prestige, privacy, rage, rank, rapport, rapprochement, rate, refinement, relationship, report, reproach, repulse, reputation, rift, rupture, scramble, seclusion, separation, servitude, setback, shame, showdown, situation, slavery, society, solitude, sophistication, sphere, split, spotlight, standing, state, station, status, stigma, stink, stir, support, sympathy, taint, taste, tedium, terms, tie, uncertainty, unification, variance, whirl

Life forms

BEINGS

389 beings: being, body, cell, creation, creature, cur, egg, form, individual, life, organism, soul
390 former beings: body, cadaver, carcass/carcase, corpse
391 group of beings: band, flock, group, world
392 limb or appendage of: ankle, arm, back, backside, beak, behind, branch, bust, butt/buttocks, calf, chest, claw, digit, egg, extremity, eye, fiber, finger, flank, flesh, foot, freckle, germ, hair, hand, head, jaw, leg, limb, lip, member, mop, mouth, nose, posterior, rump, seat, skin, strand, tail, trunk, tuft, wisp
393 organ: abdomen, abdominal, bacteria, belly, blood, bone, bowels, brain, gut, heart, joint, mind, molecule, muscle, nucleus, seed, skeleton, spine, stomach, vein

BEINGS, ANIMAL

394 animal: adult, animal, beast, brute, buck, calf, cat, cattle, chicken, clam, cock, colt, cur, fawn, frog, game, goat, half-breed, hound, hybrid, litter, mongrel, monkey, monster, mother, parasite, pet, pig, prey, stock, young
395 bird: bird, chicken
396 fish: aquarium, aquatic
397 group of animals: drove, family, herd, horde, litter, pack, roundup, stock, swarm, team
398 insect: bee, bug, grub, pest
399 limb or appendage of: bill, chin, coat, crest, feather, fertilizer, fur, meat, mop, paunch, pelt, pulp, scale, shell, trunk, venom, wing
400 mammal: cat, dog, donkey, fawn, goat, hound, mother, pig

GENERAL CHARACTERISTICS

401 attribute of behavior: abstemious, acerbity, acid, acrid, acrimonious, active, adamant, adolescent, affable, affected, affectionate, agreeable, agreeably, aimless, alive, aloof, amiable, amuck, animate, animated, anxious, apathetic, arbitrary, arch, ardent, argumentative, arrogant, artificial, assured, attentive, audacious, austere, authoritarian, avid, babyish, backward, bad, balky, barbarian, barbaric, barbarous, barefaced, beaming, beastly, belligerent, benevolent, big, bland, blindly, boisterous, bold, brash, brassy, brave, brazen, brittle, brusque, brutal, calculating, calm, cantankerous, capricious, carnivorous, casual, cautious, cavalier, chary, childish, chill, chivalrous, chummy, civil, clumsy, coarse, cocky/cocksure, collected, combative, comic/comical, common, compassionate, complacent, complaisant, composed, compulsive, concerned, conciliatory, condescending, considerate, constructive, contemptuous, contrary, contumacious, convivial, cool, cordial, correct, corrupt, country, courageous, courteous, courtly, covetous, cowardly, coy, crabby/crabbed, crafty, cranky, crass, craven, cross, crotchety, crude, cruel, crusty, cunning, daring, dark, dauntless, deaf, debonair, deceitful, decent, deceptive, decided, decorous, defensive, deferential, defiant, deliberate, deliberately, delicate, delightful, delinquent, delirious, demonstrative, demure, desperate, detached, devious, diffident, diplomatic, disagreeable, disarming, discourteous, discreet, disdainful, disgruntled, disingenuous, disinterested, disloyal, disobedient, disobliging, disorderly, dispassionate, disputatious, disrespectful, disruptive, dissipated, dissolute, distant, distraught, docile, doctrinaire, dogged, dolorous, domineering, doting, double-dealing, dour, eager, earnest, easy, ebullient, edgy, effeminate, effervescent, emotionless, enthusiastic, envious, epicurean, equable, equal, evasive, even, exacting, excitable, excited, exuberant, faithful, faithless, fake, false, falsely, fanatical, fatherly, favorable, favorably, fawning, fearful, fearless, feigned, ferocious, fervent/fervid, feverish, fickle, fidgety, fiery, fighting, finicky, flagrant, flamboyant, flexible, flighty, flippant, flirtatious, flushed, foolhardy, foolish, foolishly, forceful, formal, forward, foxy, fractious, fraternal, free, freely, fresh, fretful, frisky, frivolous, fulsome, fussy, genial, genteel, gentlemanly, giddy, glacial, glowing, good, graceless, gracious, grandiose, grave, gritty, grouchy, gruff, grumpy, halfhearted, hard, hardhearted, haughty, headstrong, heartless, hearty, heedless, helpless, heroic, high-strung, hostile, hot, huffy, humane, humble, hypocritical, icy, idle, ill at ease, ill-mannered, ill-natured, impatient, impersonal, impertinent, impish, impolite, impolitic, importunate, impossible, impudent, impulsive, inactive, inclement, inconsiderate, inexorable, ingratiating, inhospitable, inhuman/inhumane, inimical, innocuous, insensitive, insidious, insolent, insubordinate, insurgent, intractable/intransigent, intrepid, invidious, irascible, irreconcilable, irrepressible, irreverent, irritable, jaded, jaundiced, jaunty, jovial, jubilant, jumpy, juvenile, keen, kind, kittenish, ladylike, lax, lazy, lecherous, lenient, lethargic, level, liberal, licentious, lifeless, light, light headed, listless, lively, lofty, loose, loquacious, lordly, loud, loving, lunatic, maladroit, malevolent, malicious, manly, mannered, mannerly, martial, masterful, maternal, mawkish, mean, meek, menacing, mercenary, merciful, merciless, mercurial, mild, militant, mincing, mischievous, miscreant, miserly, modest, motherly, mousy, munificent, naive, narcissistic, nasty, natural, naughty, nefarious, neglectful, negligent, neighborly, nerveless, nervy, noble, nomadic, nonchalant, noncompliant, nonconformist, nonviolent, nosy, obdurate, obedient, obliging, obnoxious, obsequious, obstinate, obtrusive, odious, offhand, oily, orderly, ostentatious, outlandish, overbearing, overconfident, overwrought, parsimonious, partisan, passionate, paternal, pedantic, peevish, pent-up, peppery, peppy, peripatetic, perky, permissive, persistent, pert, perverse, petulant,

philosophical/philosophic, pious, pitiless, placid, plaintive, playful, polite, politic, pompous, possessed, pragmatic, precious, precipitous/precipitate, precise, predatory, premature, presumptuous, pretentious, prickly, prim, prissy, prodigal, profane, profligate, prompt, proper, propitious, proud, provident, prudent, prudish, puerile, pugnacious, punctilious, pushy, quarrelsome, querulous, quick-tempered, quiet, racy, radiant, raffish, rakish, rash, raucous, ready, rebel, rebellious, recalcitrant, reckless, refined, regardful, regardless, relentless, reluctant, remiss, remorseful, remorseless, remote, renegade, repugnant, reserved, resigned, respectful, responsible, responsive, restive, restrained, reticent, retiring, ribald, rocky, rollicking, rough, rowdy, rude, rugged, runaway, rustic, ruthless, safe, salty, sanctimonious, saucy, savage, scintillating, scrupulous, secluded, self-conscious, self-righteous, sensual, sentimental, serene, servile, severe, shabby, shameful, shameless, sheepish, shifty, short, short-sighted, shrewd, shy, silly, simple, sincere, sinister, skittish, slick, slippery, sluggish, sly, small, smart, smooth, snaky, snappy, sneaky, snide, snobbish, sober, soft, solid, sophisticated, sophomoric, sparing, spineless, spiteful, spontaneous, sporting/sportive, sprightly, spry, square, squeamish, staid, standoffish, stately, staunch, steadfast, stealthy, stern, stiff, stilted, stingy, stodgy, stoic/stoical, stolid, stony, strained, strenuous, strict, stringent, stubborn, stuffy, suave, subdued, submissive, subservient, subversive, sunny, supercilious, superior, sure, surly, sweet, sympathetic, taciturn, tactful, tactless, tame, tasteless, tearful, temperate, tempestuous, tenacious, tender, tense, testy, thankful, thankless, theatrical, thieving/thievish, thoughtful, thoughtless, thrifty, tight, timid, tipsy, torpid, touchy, tractable, treacherous, tricky, truculent, true, turbulent, ugly, unaffected, unasked, unassuming, unbending, uncivilized, uncompromising, uncontrollable, uncouth, undaunted, undependable, underhand, understanding, unemotional, unflappable, unfriendly, ungrateful, unguarded, uninhibited, unintentional/unintended, uninterested, unkind, unmerciful, unobtrusive, unprejudiced, unpretentious, unreasonable, unrelenting, unruly, unscrupulous, unseemly, unselfish, unsettled, unsociable, unsophisticated, unsuspecting, unsympathetic, unthinking, untoward, untrustworthy, unwary, unwilling, unwise, unwitting, unworldly, unyielding, uptight, urbane, vain, valiant, vehement, vengeful, venturesome, vibrant, vicarious, vicious, vigilant, vindictive, violent, virile, virtuous, vital, vivacious, volatile, voracious, wacky, wanton, warlike, warm, wary, wasteful, watchful, wayfaring, wayward, well-bred, whimsical, wicked, wild, willful, willing, wily, winning/winsome, withdrawn, worldly, yellow, yielding, zany, zealous

402 attribute of intelligence: able, abreast, abstruse, academic, acute, adept, alert, amenable, analytic/analytical, appreciative, apt, astute, awake, aware, backward, bewildered, blank, blind, bright, brilliant, calculable, canny, childish, clairvoyant, clear, clever, clumsy, cognizant, coherent, common-sense, complex, comprehensible, conscious, considered, contemplative, conversant, creative, cunning, dark, deducible, deep, delirious, dense, designedly, dexterous, dim, discerning, dizzy, dopey, down-to-earth, dull, dumb, educated, efficient, elevated, empty, empty-headed, enlightened, erudite, experienced, expert, familiar, farsighted, fatuous, forgotten, frivolous, gifted, gullible, harebrained, hazy, idiotic, ignorant, illiterate, imbecile, impressionable, incisive, incomprehensible, inefficient, ineligible, inept, inexperienced, informed, ingenious, inquiring, inquisitive, insipid, intellectual, intelligent, intuitive, inventive, irrational, judicious, keen, knowing, knowledgeable, learned, logical, lucid, mental, mindful, mistaken, nimble, oblivious, observant, obtuse, omniscient, penetrating, perceptive, perspicacious, philosophical/philosophic, precocious, privy, professional, proficient, profound, psychic, quick, quick-witted, rational, ready, reasonable, resourceful, retarded, sagacious, sane, scatterbrained, scholarly, senile, sensible, shallow, sharp, shrewd, simple, skillful, slick, slow, smart, soft, stolid, studious, stupid, subtle, thick, thoughtful, thoughtless, touched, unaware, uneducated, unfamiliar, unwise, vacant, vacuous, versed, veteran, weak, wise

403 attribute of mentality: abashed, absentee, absent-minded, absorbed, absorbing, accustomed, addled, affected, affectionate, afraid, aggrieved, aghast, agonizing, alert, amatory, amorous, angry, anxious, apathetic, appreciative, apprehensive, aspiring, assumed, attentive, automatic, averse, avid, bad, balmy, beaten, beholden, believable, bent, bewildered, bewitched, bigoted, black, bleak, blissful, blue, boiling, breathless, broad, broad-minded, broken, brokenhearted, buoyant, burning, calculating, captive, carnal, cautious, certain, cheerful, cheerless, chipper, circumspect, clairvoyant, clear, compassionate, complacent, concerned, confident, confused, conscious, contemplative, content, contented, contrite, crabby/crabbed, cranky, crazy, crestfallen, cross, crotchety, curious, cynical, daft, dearly, decided, dejected, delighted, delirious, demented, depressed, deranged, desolate, despairing, desperately, despondent, disaffected, disappointed, disbelieving, disconcerted, disconsolate, discontented/discontent, discouraged, discouraging, disenchanted, disgruntled, disgusted, disillusioned, disinclined, disinterested, disoriented, dispirited, dissatisfied, dissident, distraught, distressed, distrustful, doleful, dolorous, doubtful, down, downcast, downhearted, dumb-

founded, ecstatic, elated, emotional, emotionless, enamored, engrossed, envious, excited, expectant, exultant, fascinated, fed up, festive, firm, flaming, flushed, foggy, forgetful, forgotten, forlorn, frantic, frenetic, fretful, frightened, frustrated, fulfilled, funereal, furious, gay, glad, gladly, gleeful, gloomy, grateful, greedy, grumpy, gut, half-baked/half-witted, happily, happy, hard, headstrong, healthy, heavy, high, hopeful, hot, huffy, hurt, hysterical, ill at ease, impartial, impassioned, impressionable, inattentive, incensed, inconsolable, incredulous, indifferent, indignant, indiscriminate, infatuated, insane, insatiable, insecure, insular, intent, intently, interested, intolerant, intoxicated, invidious, irate, irrational, irresolute, irritable, jaundiced, jealous, jovial, joyful/joyous, joyless, jubilant, judicious, keen, lackadaisical, languid, lascivious, lethargic, levelheaded, livid, lonely, lonesome, longing, lost, low, lucid, lukewarm, lunatic, mad, malleable, manic/maniacal, melancholy, mental, merry, mindful, mindless, miserable, moody, morbid, morose, narrow, narrow-minded, negative, nerveless, nervous, neurotic, neutral, noncommittal, normal, nostalgic, numb, nuts/nutty, objective, oblivious, observant, obsessed, opposed/opposing, overcome, overjoyed, overwrought, partial, penitent, pensive, pent-up, pessimistic, petty, platonic, predisposed, preoccupied, prepared, prepossessed, profound, proud, provincial, psychic, psychological, psychotic, purposeful, puzzled, queasy, rabid, radical, raging, rapt, realistic, reflective, regretful, resolute, restless, right, rigid, romantic, sad, sane, sanguine, sappy, scared, sectarian, secure, senile, sensitive, serious, sick, silly, skeptical, solemn, solicitous, somber, sore, sorrowful, sorry, sound, sour, spellbound, spiritless, steady, stout, strong, subdued, sullen, susceptible, suspicious, tearful, temperamental, tender, tense, testy, thankful, thirsty, thoughtful, thoughtless, tired, tolerant, torn, touched, tough, ugly, unadvised, unbalanced, uncomfortable, uncommitted, unconcerned, undecided, uneasy, unemotional, unfaltering, unfeeling, unhappy, uninterested, unsettled, unsound, untouched, untroubled, unwary, upbeat, upset, versed, vulnerable, wacky, wary, weak, weary, willing, wistful, woebegone, worried, wrathful, wretched

404 attribute of personality: aboveboard, abrasive, adventurous, aggressive, airy, altruistic, amenable, amorphous, approachable, ardent, arrogant, artful, assertive, assuming, assured, audacious, august, bashful, belligerent, big, bitter, blasé, blessed, blithe, bloodless, boastful, bold, boorish, brash, bright, buoyant, busy, callous, calm, captious, carefree, catty, charitable, charming, chaste, cheerful, childlike, chill, chilly, choosy, churlish, clean, clear, clement, clinical, close, cocky/cocksure, cold, colorful, colorless, combative, conceited, confident, convivial, cool, courageous, coy, credulous, culpable, cursed, cute, dainty, dashing, decent, dedicated, deep, delicate, delightful, demonic/demoniac/demoniacal, demure, dependent, deserving, despicable, detached, determined, devious, die-hard, difficult, dignified, discriminating, dispassionate, disreputable, distant, docile, dynamic, easy, easygoing, effeminate, egocentric, egotistic/egoistic, elastic, enchanting, energetic, engaging, enterprising, exacting, exalted, excitable, exemplary, feckless, finicky, finished, flatulent, flirtatious, forbearing, fortunate, forward, foxy, free, fresh, frigid, fussy, gallant, game, garrulous, gauche, generous, genial, genteel, gentle, glacial, glib, good, good-humored, good-natured, green, gregarious, gritty, gutless, gutsy, happy-go-lucky, hardened, hard-hearted, hard-nosed/hardheaded, hateful, heroic, high-strung, humble, icy, ill-natured, immaculate, immovable, impassive, imperturbable, impetuous, individual, indomitable, indulgent, inexperienced, infamous, inflexible, inherent, inhibited, innocent, insipid, insouciant, intolerant, intrinsic, inveterate, inviting, irresponsible, jaunty, kind, kind-hearted, kindly, latent, lazy, liberal, lighthearted, likable, little, lovable, low, lowly, loyal, magnanimous, magnetic, mercurial, meritorious, mild, mincing, misanthropic, miserly, modest, narcissistic, native, natural, nice, noble, nonchalant, notorious, obedient, obliging, obsequious, obsessed, odd/oddball, odious, officious, opinionated, opprobrious, optimistic, outgoing, outspoken, overbearing, particular, patient, peculiar, peppy, perky, persistent, persnickety, personable, pert, philanthropic, picky, pigheaded, pliable, predictable, prepossessing, prim, prissy, proper, pushy, queer, quick-tempered, receptive, recluse/reclusive, remote, reserved, responsible, rotten, ruthless, saintly, sanctimonious, sedate, selective, self-centered, self-confident, self-conscious, selfish, self-satisfied, self-sufficient, servile, shabby, shifty, shy, smug, sophisticated, spirited, spotless, sprightly, square, squeamish, stable, staid, stalwart, standoffish, stodgy, stoic/stoical, straight, stubborn, stuffy, suave, subservient, sweet, treacherous, trustworthy/trusty, unaffected, unapproachable, unassuming, unpretentious, unselfish, unsuspecting, unworthy, upright, vain, valiant, vigorous, virile, vivacious, vocal, warm, winning/winsome, wishy-washy, yielding, zealous

405 essential property of life forms: awkwardness, body, complexion, dotage, fatigue, hygiene, physique, sense, sensitivity

406 essential quality of life forms: adult, alimentary, animal, athletic, awake, awkward, barefoot, bearded, blank, bodily, breathless, brunette/brunet, bushy, buxom, cadaverous, corpulent, curly, curvaceous, dark, decrepit, drowsy, empty, exhausted, expectant, expressionless, fair, famished, fleshy, florid, full, gaunt, glassy, haggard, hairless, hairy, high, human, hungry, impercepti-

ble, inborn/inbred, infertile, innate, insensitive, intestinal/intestine, intoxicated, intrinsic, jaded, light, limber, lumbering, piercing, predatory, pregnant, primitive, private, promising, prostrate, ravenous, raw, rich, sensitive, sensory, shapely, smooth, starving/starved, sweaty, tight, tipsy, tired, wild

407 existential state: be, being, casualty, coexistence, endure, exist, existence, flesh, gone, live, loss, manage, matter, mortality, nature, none, nothing/nothingness, oblivion, outlast, presence, reside, spirit, stand, subsist, survive, threaten, vitality, zero

408 gender: female, femininity/feminine, male, masculinity/masculine

409 intelligence: acquaintance, acumen, anticipation, appreciation, apprehension, aptitude, attention, awareness, bent, brain, capacity, clairvoyance, clarity, cleverness, cognizance/cognition, common sense, comprehension, conception, consciousness, craft, dark, darkness, delusion, depth, dexterity, education, efficiency, empathy, enlightenment, erudition, experience, expertise/expertness, familiarity, fancy, feeling, finesse, foresight, forte, genius, gift, grasp, grip, head, idiocy, ignorance, illumination, imagination, innocence, insight, intellect, intelligence, intuition, invention, judgment, knack, know-how, knowledge, learning, light, literacy, memory, mentality, mind, misconception, misunderstanding, observance, observation, originality, perception, proficiency, reason, sanity, sense, sensibility, skill, soul, thought, understanding, wisdom, wit/wits

410 mentality: absorption, abstraction, accession, ache, aggravation, agility, agonize, agony, alarm, alienation, alter ego, amazement, anger, anguish, anticipation, anxiety, apathy, application, assurance, astonishment, attention, attitude, attrition, avarice, awe, behalf, belief, belonging, bigotry, bitterness, blues, boast, boredom, bosom, breakdown, breast, bristle, buoyancy/buoyance, capitulation, caprice, care, caution, censure, chagrin, cheer, clairvoyance, clemency, cogitation, collapse, comfort, compassion, complex, composure, compulsion, compunction, conception, concern, confusion, conquest, consideration, consolation, constancy, contemplation, content, contentment, contrition, conviction, corollary, credit, cult, curiosity, dark, darkness, daze, decision, defeat, deference, degradation, delight, delight in, delirium, delusion, dependence/dependency, depression, design, desolation, despair, desperation, difficulty, disability, disaffection, disappointment, discipline, discomfiture, discomfort, discontent, discouragement, discrimination, disgust, disinclination, dismay, disorder, displeasure, disquiet, dissatisfaction, distraction, distress, disturbance, doldrums, dolor, doubt, ease, ecstasy, elation, embarrassment, emotion, encouragement, enjoyment, ennui, envy, equanimity, euphoria, exaltation, exasperation, excitement, exhaustion, exhilaration, expectancy, expectation, exultation, fallacy, feeling, fever, firmness, fluster, fog, folly, forbearance, force, foresight, forethought, forgetfulness, fortitude, frazzle, free will, frenzy, fret, fright, frustration, fume, funk, furor, fury, gladness, glee, gloom, gratification, gratitude, grief, grieve, happiness, health, heart, heartbreak, heat, heaven, hesitation, hope, huff, humiliation, humor, hysteria, idiocy, imagination, impulse, indifference, indignity, insanity, insight, instability, introspection, ire, jitters, joy, kick, lament/lamentation, letdown, lethargy, levity, lunacy, malaise, mania, martyrdom, melancholy, merriment/merrymaking, mirth, mistake, monotony, mood, mope, morale, mourn, mourning, muddle, nausea, neglect, nerves, nervousness, neurosis, nostalgia, objection, oblivion, observance, observation, obsession, offense, optimism, originality, outlook, pain, panic, paradise, paroxysm, passion, pathos, peace, penance, penitence, perception, perspective, pessimism, pique, pity, pleasure, posture, pout, precaution, predisposition, premonition, presage, presence, presentiment, psyche, psychology, push, pussyfoot, qualm, quarter, rage, rancor, rapture, rave, regret, rejoice, remorse, repent, repentance, repose, repulse, resent, resentment, resignation, resistance, resolution, resolve, restlessness, retrospect, sadness, sanity, satisfaction, scare, security, self-satisfaction, sensation, sensibility, sensitivity, sentiment, seriousness, servitude, shame, simmer, slump, sob, solace, solicitude, sorrow, soul, state, stew, strain, strength, stress, subconscious, surprise, suspense, sympathy, tedium, telepathy, temper, temperament, temperance, tension, thought, tolerance, torment, torture, trance, transport, triumph, turn, umbrage, uncertainty, unrest, vanity, waver, woe, wonder, worry, wrath, zeal, zest

411 personality: aggression, ardor, arrogance, art, artifice, assumption, atrocity, attribute, audacity, backbone, bearing, being, best, bounce, bravery, buoyancy/buoyance, caliber, calm, candor, character, characteristic, charisma, charity, charm, complexion, compliance, conceit, confidence, constraint, courage, cultivation, dash, decision, dedication, demeanor, determination, dignity, disposition, disrepute, distinction, drive, effrontery, ego, egoism/egotism, élan, empathy, endowment, endurance, energy, enterprise, entity, essence, eye, failing, fiber, fight, fire, foible, fortitude, frailty, gall, gallantry, generosity, geniality, gentility, go, goodness, good will/goodwill, greatness, grit, gumption, gusto, guts, heart, heroism, honor, humor, identity, idiosyncrasy, inclination, individuality, infamy, inhibition, initiative, innocence, integrity, kind, kink, laziness, life, loyalty, magnetism, makeup, manner, mark, martyrdom, mentality, mettle, mien, might, mold, mood, morale, morals, motivation, mystique, nature, nerve,

notoriety, obedience, oddity, panache, patience, peculiarity, penchant, pep, perseverance, personality, pluck, point, possibilities, potency, presence, pride, probity, proclivity, propensity, property, prowess, psyche, push, qualify, quirk, reputation, responsibility, savor, self-respect/self-esteem, shortcoming, soul, sparkle, spirit, spunk, stability, stamina, stamp, style, taste, temerity, temper, temperament, tenacity, tend, thing, trait, trick, turn, twist, type, valor, vein, vice, vigor, virtue, vitality, way, weakness, will, willpower, wit, zeal, zest, zip

HUMANS

412 bad person: accessory, accomplice, addict, adversary, agitator, anarchist, antagonist, apostate, ass, assailant, assassin, authoritarian, bandit, barbarian, beggar, braggart, bum, bungler, burglar, cad, cannibal, captive, character, cheat, clod, clown, confederate, convict, criminal, critic, crook, culprit, cur, delinquent, demagogue, demon, derelict, deserter, desperado, despot, devil, dolt, dope, drone, dumbbell, dummy, dunce, enemy, exile, expatriate, fake, felon, fiend, fighter, foe, fool, fraud, fugitive, gangster, glutton, good-for-nothing, gossip, grouch, hypocrite, idiot, imbecile, imp, impostor, incendiary, insurgent, interloper, intruder, joke, knave, kook, liar, loafer, loser, lunatic, madman/madwoman, maniac, menace, mercenary, misanthrope, miscreant, miser, monster, murderer, nuisance, nut, oaf, ogre, outlaw, parasite, pawn, pervert, pessimist, pest, pill, playboy/playgirl, prisoner, prodigal, profligate, prostitute, psychopath, quack, ragamuffin, rake, rascal, rebel, renegade, robber, rogue, rowdy, runaway, sap, scapegoat, scoundrel, scum, showoff, shrew, sight, sneak, spy, swindler, tattletale/tattler, thief, tool, tough, traitor, tramp, trash, troublemaker, tyrant, underworld, vagabond/vagrant, vandal, villain, wanton, weakling, witch

413 ethnic group member: black, citizen, denizen, emigrant, foreigner, immigrant, inhabitant, local, migrant, native, newcomer, nomad, outsider, patriot, pioneer, plebeian, refugee, resident, rustic, stranger, subject, yokel

414 family member: ancestor, ancestry, antecedent(s), babe, baby, bastard, brother, child, descendant, father, fiancé/fiancée, forefather, forerunner, guardian, half-breed, heir, husband, hybrid, infant, issue, kid, kin, kindred, man, matriarch, mother, nurse, occupant, offspring, orphan, owner, parent, partner, patriarch, predecessor, progeny, relation, relative, scion, seed, senior, spouse, surrogate, sweetheart, twin, waif, ward, wife, woman, young, youngster/youth

415 female: beauty, bride, female, girl, hag, lady, maid, matriarch, matron, miss, mistress, mother, nymph, playboy/playgirl, prostitute, shrew, wanton, wife, witch, woman

416 good person: ace, angel, benefactor, expert, genius, hero/heroine, humanitarian, idealist, intellect, intellectual, intimate, missionary, peacemaker, pet, prodigy, pundit, savior, victor, virtuoso, visionary, wag, whiz, winner, wit

417 group of people: anybody, anyone, army, assemblage, attendance, audience, band, board, body, cadre, caucus, circle, civilization, class, clientele, clique, cloud, company, congregation, contingent, convention, corps, corpse, crew, crowd, crush, elite, enrollment, entourage, everybody/everyone, expedition, federation, field, flesh, following, force, gallery, gathering, horde, host, huddle, human, legion, man, mankind, masses, member, membership, mob, mortal, mortality, multitude, muster, outfit, pack, party, people, person, personnel, platoon, practice, public, set, society, squad, suite, swarm, team, throng, trash, troop/troops, turnout

418 limb or appendage: ankle, beard, bosom, bottom, braid, breast, bristle, brow, can, cheek, coiffure, curl, elbow, features, pore, wrinkle

419 male: bachelor, bastard, boy, boyfriend, bridegroom, brother, buck, dude, escort, father, fellow, gentleman, groom, guy, husband, lad, male, man, patriarch, philanderer, playboy/playgirl, prostitute, rake, wanton

420 organ: backbone, blood, bone, brain, heart, muscle, spine, stomach, vein

421 racial group member: kin, kindred, relation, tribe

422 royalty: crown, king, lord, monarch, noble/nobleman/noblewoman

423 social group member: acquaintance, addict, admirer, adventurer, advocate, alien, alliance, alter ego, another, apprentice, aristocracy, aristocrat, arrival, assistant, associate, augur, auxiliary, bachelor, beatnik, beau, beggar, beginner, believer, beloved, benefactor, beneficiary, bigot, boor, bore, boyfriend, braggart, brother, brute, buddy, buff, buffoon, bully, bum, bungler, busybody, butt, bystander, captive, casualty, celebrity, chaperon, character, chicken, chum, churl, civilian, clairvoyant, clod, clown, cohort, collaborator, colleague, comedian, comic, companion, company, competitor, comrade, confidant, connection, conquest, consort, convoy, correspondent, coward, craven, crony, cynic, darling, date, dear, derelict, deserter, devotee, diehard, dilettante, disciple, disciplinarian, dissident, dolt, donor, dope, doubter, driver, drunk/drunkard, dude, dumbbell, dummy, dunce, dupe, eccentric, emigrant, emissary, enthusiast, entrant, epicurean, equal, escort, exception, exile, expatriate, exponent, extremist,

extrovert, eyewitness, failure, fan, father/mother, favorite, fellow, fiancé/fiancée, fiend, figure, figurehead, flame, flirt, follower, fool, fop, forerunner, fortune-teller/fortuneteller, founder, freak, freshman/woman, friend, gentleman, goat, go-between, gourmet, greenhorn, grouch, guardian, guest, guide, hag, hanger-on, hedonist, herald, hermit, hostage, humanitarian, idealist, idol, inferior, informant/informer, interloper, intimate, introvert, intruder, jerk, jester, joke, joker, kook, layman/woman, liaison, local, loser, love, lover, luminary, machine, madman/madwoman, master, mate, maverick, mediator, miser, mistress, moron, mother, negotiator, neighbor, newcomer, noble/nobleman/noblewoman, nobody/nonentity, nonconformist, notable, novice, nut, oddity/oddball, old hand, onlooker, original, outcast, outsider, pagan, pal, participant, partisan, partner, passenger, patrician, patron, pauper, peer, personage/personality, pessimist, philanderer, pill, pillar, playboy/playgirl, plebeian, poet, prey, prophet, proponent, protagonist, pundit, puppet, pushover, ragamuffin, rebel, recluse, rich, rival, scream, second, sectarian, skeptic, snob, snoop, somebody, spectator, spendthrift, sponsor, sport, square, stick-in-the-mud, stranger, subject, subordinate, substitute, suitor, support/supporter, surrogate, sweetheart, sycophant, target, tattletale/tattler, tenant, tool, tourist, traveler, umpire, underdog, urchin, vagabond/vagrant, veteran, victim, visitor, wag, waif, wanderer, weakling, witness, wizard, zany

424 traits: adolescent, adult, babe, baby, beauty, beginner, boy, brat, child, dwarf, elder, eyeful, fledgling, freak, giant, girl, gnome, grown-up, infant, invalid, juvenile, kid, lad, midget, minor, nymph, runt, senior, vision, young, youngster/youth

PLANTS

425 flower: bloom, blossom, bouquet, flower

426 fruit: berry, fruit, produce

427 growth or death of: bloom, blossom, bud, develop, germinate, grow, growth, wilt, wither

428 part: bark, bough, branch, bud, fiber, flavoring, flower, foliage, fruit, grain, husk, juice, leaf, limb, log, nut, peel, pod, pulp, scion, seed, shell, skin, stalk, stem, trunk

429 plant: algae, bouquet, bramble, brush, bush, creation, crop, fertilizer, fossil, garland, grove, harvest, hedge, hybrid, nature, organism, plant, produce, vintage, wreath

430 tree: timber, tree, wood/woods

431 vegetable: produce, vegetable

Objects

432 group of: accumulation, aggregate, amalgam, anthology, archive, armada, array, arsenal, assembly, assortment, backlog, bale, batch, battery, bevy, blend, body, bolt, bunch, bundle, cadre, caravan, cavalcade, chain, clot, cloud, clump, cluster, clutter, collection, column, combination, compilation, complex, composite, compound, concentration, concoction, concourse, congestion, conglomeration, couple, crush, deluge, deposit, drift, drove, ensemble, everything, fleet, flock, fusion, group, hash, heap, herd, hodgepodge, host, huddle, jumble, junk, knot, litter, load, lot, lump, many, mass, medley, mélange, miscellany, mix/mixture, mob, mound, mountain, multitude, muster, number, odds and ends, pack, package, pair, parcel, party, patchwork, pile, pool, potpourri, press, queue, repertory, residue, row, score, scores, scramble, set, stack, stew, store, stuff, sum, surge, swarm, throng, train, tuft, unit, variety, wad, whole

433 object: anything, article, entity, fact, individual, loser, matter, object, something, substance, thing

434 part of: aspect, barb, carcass/carcase, compartment

435 place: asylum, barrier, base, center, depository, depot, dynasty, haunt, haven, heaven, hell, place

436 shape: angle, arc, arch, ball, bead, bend, bulb, bulge, check, circle, coil, cone, contortion, contour, convolution, corner, crescent, curl, curve, disk, dummy, effigy, elbow, globe, kink, knot, labyrinth, lap, line, loaf, loop, maze, mold, orb, orbit, outline, revolution, ring, rod, roll, round, shape, sphere, spiral, streak, wad, wave, wheel, whorl

437 air: air, atmosphere, billow, blast, breath, breeze, bubble, cloud, draft, dust, effervescence, firmament, fumes, lather, puff, sky, vapor

438 arena: aquarium, arena, bazaar, center, coliseum, dump, field, gymnasium, hall, stadium, stage

439 building: abbey, airport, architecture, archives, armory, arsenal, asylum, auditorium, bakery, bank, bar, barn, booth, building, cathedral, clinic, club, conservatory, construction, consulate, court, dock, domicile, edifice, embassy, enclosure, factory, fort/fortress, fortification, framework, fraternity, garage, gymnasium, hall, hang-out, harbor, hospital, hotel, house, inn, installation, institute/institution, jail, joint, mansion, mill, monastery, motel, museum, nightclub, office, outlet, pavilion, pen, penitentiary, pier, plant, post, prison, pub, rampart, restaurant, ruins, saloon, sanctuary, shop, shrine, stage, store, stronghold, structure, tavern, temple, theater/theatre, tower, treasury, warehouse, wharf

440 building part: aisle, alcove, annex, archway, attic, awning, balcony, basement, bay, belfry, bleachers, booth, buttress, canopy, ceiling, cellar, chimney, chute, closet, column, concourse, corner, corridor, cranny, den, department, dome, door, egress, entrance, entry, exit, fireplace, floor, foyer, gallery, gate, gutter, hall, niche, nook, partition, passage/passageway, pillar, platform, pole, post, prop, recess, screen, stack, stay, step, support, threshold, tower, vent, wall, wing

441 business place: agency, annex, building, bureau, factory, foyer, hall, lobby, office, shop, store, suite, wing

442 foundation: backbone, base, basis, bed, bottom, core, foot, footing, foundation, frame, groundwork, rest, rock, root, seat, stand, support

443 furniture: altar, antique, banister, bed, bench, bleachers, booth, buffet, bunk, bureau, cabinet, can, chair, cot, couch, cradle, crib, cupboard, fireplace, furniture, mirror, partition, pen, perch, pier, platform, podium, pulpit, rack, rail/railing, ramp, screen, seat, stand, table, wardrobe

444 furniture accessory: bedding, bedspread, candlestick, canopy, chandelier, curtain, cushion

445 furniture part: gate, handle, knickknack, knob, latch, ledge, novelty, picket, pivot, post, quilt, screen, shade, shelf, stay, step, support, tap, valve

446 personal item: adornment, album, amulet, backpack, beads, belongings, bracelet, briefcase, brooch, cache, cargo, chain, charm, contraceptive, curio, disguise, doll, equipment, favorite, fetish, gem, glasses, goods, handbag, jewel, jewelry, keepsake, lotion, luggage, makeup, memento, novelty, odds and ends, pack, paraphernalia, plaything, pledge, pocketbook, possession, pouch, pride, property, puppet, purchase, purse, relic, resources, riches, ring, savings, souvenir, stuff, subsistence, supplies, support, sustenance, thing/things, toy, trappings, treasure, trifle, trinket, valuable

447 recreation area: cabaret, casino, hang-out, landmark

448 room: alcove, apartment, attic, auditorium, bath, bathroom, bedroom, chamber, cell, cellar, den, enclosure, foyer, gallery, hall, kitchen, lobby, loft, office, outlet, parlor, pub, restaurant, room, saloon, sanctuary, shop, shrine, stage, store, tavern, theater/theatre, vestibule

449 **workplace:** bakery, base, bazaar, brothel, bureau, business, cabaret, cafe, canteen, capitol, church, clinic, conservatory, consulate, dairy, depot, diner, dive, dump, embassy, emporium, establishment, exchange, factory, farm, field, gallery, garage, hang-out, hospital, hotel, inn, jail, joint, lounge, madhouse, market/mart, mill, mine, motel, museum, nightclub, office, outlet, penitentiary, plant, port, prison, pub, restaurant, saloon, shop, store, tavern, treasury, warehouse

CLOTHING

450 **accessory:** bag, bandanna, belt, boot, buckle, cap, collar, mask, pocketbook, pouch, purse
451 **clothing:** apparel, armor, array, attire, bathing suit, blouse, cape, cloak, clothes/clothing, coat, costume, disguise, dress, ensemble, finery, frock, garb, garment, gear, glove, gown, habit, hat, jacket, masquerade, nightgown, outfit, pajamas, pants, quilt, robe, skirt, suit, supplies, thing/things, trappings, underwear, uniform, veil, wardrobe, wash, wrap
452 **part:** collar, crease, crown, patch, pocket, seam, strand
453 **state of dress:** bareness, try on/try out, undress, wear

FOOD AND DRINK

454 **beverage:** alcohol, ale, beverage, brew, coffee, draft, drink
455 **beverage, alcoholic:** beer, liquor
456 **change in:** curdle, spoil, turn
457 **food:** appetizer, batter, bite, bread, brew, broth, bun, candy, casserole, confection, cracker, delicacy, diet, dish, doughnut, fare, food, frankfurter, game, grub, hamburger, helping, leftover, loaf, maintenance, meat, morsel, nourishment, nurture, nutrition, pancake, pastry, preserves, produce, ration, refreshment, seasoning, snack, stew, subsistence, supplies, support, sustenance, sweet, tart, treat
458 **food part:** morsel, nibble, nip, pat, taste, tidbit
459 **meal:** banquet, barbecue, bite, board, buffet, diet, dinner, fare, feast, meal, picnic, plate, snack, spread, table
460 **produced from animal:** dish, food, frankfurter, game, grub, hamburger, loaf, meat, stew
461 **produced from plant:** dish, doughnut, food, loaf, pancake, pastry, preserves, produce, seasoning, stew, sweet
462 **quality of:** acerbity, alcoholic, baked, crusty, done, eatable, edible, effervescent, mellow, natural, nourishing, nutritious, perishable, rancid, rare, raw, ripe, rotten, salty, short, sour, stale, straight, strong, succulent, sweet, tempting, unappetizing, unsavory, weak, wholesome

MACHINES

463 **machine:** alarm, apparatus, appliance, brake, catapult, clock, computer, contrivance, device, engine, fan, furnace, gadget, installation, instrument, jet, machine, machinery, mechanism, model, plant, television, terminal, watch
464 **machine part:** anchor, antenna, axle, bank, cog, cushion, engine, gear, pivot, pointer, tap, valve, vent, wheel

MATTER, CONDITIONS OF

465 **gas:** gas, jet
466 **gel:** balm, batter, clot, cream, dip, gum, lotion, ointment, ooze, paste, plaster, salve
467 **liquid:** alcohol, broth, cream, drop, enamel, eruption, essence, flow, fluid, froth, fuel, gush, jet, juice, liquid, matter, milk, moisture, ooze, paint, potion, precipitation, solution, spit, surge, sweat, tear/tears, water
468 **liquid part:** cream, drop, froth
469 **physical change:** attrition, bubble, clot, cloud, coagulate, coagulation, collapse, color, congeal, consolidation, contraction, crack, crumble, cry, darken, decay, decompose, degeneracy, degenerate, dehydrate, die, discolor, disintegrate, dissipate, dissolution, dissolve, distend, dry, eat, erode, evaporate, evaporation, exhaust, fade, fester, fizz, flake, flare, flatten, fluctuate, flush, foam, foul, fragment, give, glow, go out, grow, growth, harden, heat, jell, languish, metamorphose, metamorphosis, open, ossify, perspire, putrefy, ravel, redden, revive, rot, rust, settle, sink, spoil, stiffen, tarnish, thaw, thicken, tighten, tire, turn, wilt
470 **solid:** band, bar, barricade, barrier, baton, block, blockade, bolt, brace, bulge, cake, cast, clot, club, clump, cord, dam, deposit, fossil, glass, hedge, hunk, hurdle, ice, jump, lump, matter, mirror, monument, obstacle, obstruction, partition, pill, pole, post, prop, rock, rod, stick, wand, weight
471 **solid part:** arm, attachment, back, bar, beam, block, bolt, branch, chunk, chute, closure, corner, deposit, flap, hinge, hump, hunk, knob, knot, leg, ligature, link, lump, node/nodule, nub, nugget, outgrowth, patch, plug, powder, projection, protuberance, ridge, rung, seam, slab, sliver, splinter, stake, strap, strip, support, tuft, wedge

MATTER, DIVISIONS OF

472 **chemical:** alkali, alkaline, ammonia, antiseptic
473 **fabric:** apparel, awning, bedding, blanket, canvas, carpet, cloth, fabric, flag, lace, nap, net, pad/padding, pennant, quilt, screen, web, yarn
474 **gem:** gem, jewel, rock, stone
475 **material:** appointment, binding, blanket, brace, cast, cement, cloak, coat, coating, glaze, glue, lace, leash, line, material, pad/padding, pad, page,

paint, paper, patchwork, pipe, plaster, plate, poison, pole, rope, sheet, slip, standard, strand, strap, string, tab, tablet, tack, tag, tape, tether, trim, twine, wash

476 metallic: alloy, armor, badge, can, chain, fence, iron, medal, metal, ornament

477 mineral: rock, stone

478 natural element: blaze, carbohydrate, cell, conflagration, embers, ferment, film, fire, flame, jewel, rock, substance

479 wood: beam, board, cane, coffin, fence, framework, log, paddle, perch, picket, pier, pole, post, rack, rail/railing, rod, splinter, staff, stake, stick, timber

MATTER, QUALITIES OF

480 balance: awkward, dizzy, even, lopsided, odd, proportionate/proportional, smooth, symmetrical, unbalanced, unequal, uneven

481 capacity: brimming/brimful, capacious, capacity, close, compact, congested, crowded, empty, full, packed, spacious, teeming, vacant, void

482 continuity: broken, connected, continuous, direct, disconnected, discontinuous, disjointed, dragging, durable, endless, entire, episodic, eternal, fitful, flowing, indelible, intermittent, lengthy, long, never-ending, nonstop, numberless, old, ongoing, patchy, perfect, running, sequential, serial, solid, spacious, spasmodic, straight, through, throughout, together, unbroken, undivided, unending, unfathomable, uninterrupted

483 density: airtight, anemic, close, compact, concentrated, congested, cramped, crowded, dense, devoid, fraught, full, hollow, impenetrable, packed, replete, solid, teeming, thick, tight

484 exteriority: adjunct, adornment, annex, border, bound/bounds, boundary, brink, buffer, circuit, circumference, compass, confines, corner, cover, crust, cushion, edge, exterior, extreme, extremity, face, fringe, hem, horizon, hull, husk, jacket, lip, margin, membrane, outer, outside, peel, perimeter, periphery, pod, revolution, rim, scale, sheet, shell, skin, skirt, surface, verge

485 physical: ablaze, acid, acute, adulterated, aesthetic/esthetic, agile, alimentary, antiseptic, atomic, austere, bad, bald, bare, barren, bearded, beautiful, bland, blank, bloody, blunt, brawny, broken, burning, caustic, clean, combustible, comfortable, corrugated, corrupt, cozy, crippled, crumbly, cuddly, curable, damaged, decayed, decrepit, deformed, deserted, desolate, devoid, dilapidated, diluted/dilute, dingy, dirty, disgusting, disheveled, disordered, disorderly, disorganized, disrepair, done in, drained, drawn, droopy, dusty, effervescent, enervated, erect, exhausted, expectant, exposed, failing, faint, fallow, fat, fatigued, fatty, fertile, filthy, fireproof, fit, flaccid, flaming, flammable, flexible, foamy, forked, formless,

foul, fragile, frail, free, fresh, frothy, game, gaping, ghastly, ghostly, gnarled, good, green, grimy, grubby, gruesome, hardy, immature, impaired, impalpable, impervious, impotent, inchoate, inconspicuous, incorruptible, incurable, indistinct, infirm, inflammable, insubstantial, intact, invisible, irreparable, laden, leafy, lean, lifeless, liquid, livable, loathsome, loose, lusty, magnificent, malleable, mangy, marked, material, mature, mean, messy, mild, miserable, mixed, muddy, muscular, naked, nasty, natural, neat, neutral, noxious, nude, oblique, obtuse, obvious, open, orderly, outstanding, palatial, palpable, palsied, paltry, paralytic, pathetic, peaceful, pendulous/pendent, perfect, perishable, perverted, physical, piteous, pitiful, placid, plain, pregnant, premature, prepared, prickly, primitive, prolific, prominent, prostrate, puffy, pure, putrid, quizzical, ragged, rambling, ramshackle, rank, raw, rocky, rotten, rough, run-down, rusty, savage, scenic, scruffy, seedy, serene, shabby, shady, shaggy, shoddy, slack, sleazy, slimy, slipshod, slovenly, smoky, snug, soft, somber, sorry, speckled, splendid, squalid, stale, stark, sterile, stony, sumptuous, surface, swollen, symmetrical, synthetic, tacky, tense, thin, thorny, threadbare, tidy, tight, topsy-turvy, torn, tousled, trim, unblemished, unbroken, uncomfortable, undeveloped, unfinished, unkempt, untouched, upset, vague, verdant, visual, voluptuous, watery, weak, weary, whole, wizened, wooden, worn/worn-out

486 shape: angular, baggy, beaten, bent, billowy, blunt, checkered, circular, concave, conical/conic, convex, crescent, crooked, curly, curved, deformed, dull, elliptical, flabby, flat, flush, gnarled, grotesque, kinky, malformed, oblong, obtuse, oval, round, serrated, shapeless, sharp, spiral, square, straight

487 similarity: akin, alike, analogous, approximate, closely, cognate, comparable, comparative, conformable, different, equal, equivalent, faithful, homogenous, identical, interchangeable, like, parallel, related, representative, same, seeming, similar, synonymous, tantamount, twin, uniform, virtual, virtually

488 stability: adhesive, adrift, brittle, choppy, doddering, ductile, durable, fast, firm, firmly, fixed, flexible, hard, immobile, immovable, insecure, limber, lithe, motionless, movable, moving, pliable, ramshackle, resilient, rickety, rocky, secure, set, shaky, soft, solid, sound, stable, stationary, steady, sturdy, supple, sure, taut, tenacious, tractable, unbreakable, unstable/unsteady, unwavering, weak, wobbly, wooden, yielding

489 strength: able-bodied, athletic, brawny, breakable, brute, durable, failing, feeble, firmly, flimsy, fragile, frail, full-bodied, hale, hardy, indestructible, indomitable, infirm, invincible, lame, leathery, lusty, mighty, muscular, potent, powerful, powerless, puny, resilient, robust, rocky, rugged, stalwart, stout, strapping, strong, sturdy, tenacious, tenuous, tight, tough, unbreakable, vigorous, weak

490 **structure:** airtight, airy, amorphous, baggy, bare, beaten, bleak, blind, budding, cavernous, cleancut, clear, cleft, composite, conglomerate, craggy, crooked, curvaceous, curved, dainty, delicate, depressed, detached, diaphanous, ductile, elastic, emaciated, even, flabby, flat, flush, gaping, gaunt, hollow, incarnate, irregular, jagged, level, limp, oblique, plane, pointed, precipitous, rude, rugged, scrawny, shapely, sheer, skinny, slender/slim, slight, spare, stout, stringy, svelte, trim, wiry

491 **weight:** bantam, beaten, buoyant, cadaverous, chubby, chunky, corpulent, dainty, emaciated, ethereal, fat, fine, fleshy, gargantuan, gaunt, giant, gigantic, haggard, heavy, hefty, lanky, lean, light, lightweight, lithe, meager, obese, overweight, plump, ponderous, portable, portly, pudgy, rangy, round, scrawny, skinny, slender/slim, slight, spare, squat, stocky, stout, stubby, svelte, tenuous, thick, thin, trim, underweight, weighty, wiry

TOOLS

492 **cleaner:** antiseptic, cleanser, deodorant, polish
493 **cooking:** barbecue, bowl, china, pan, plate, scoop, utensil
494 **container:** bag, baggage, barrel, basin, basket, bottle, bowl, box, briefcase, bucket, cabinet, cage, can, chamber, canteen, carton, case, cask, casket, cell, chest, coffer, coffin, container, crate, cup, dish, envelope, flask, glass, hamper, jar, jug, keg, kit, luggage, main, package, packet, pan, parcel, portfolio, pot, pottery, pouch, purse, receptacle, store, trunk, vault, vessel

495 **cutting:** blade, chisel, knife
496 **equipment:** equipment, gear, harness, installation, kit, outfit, pack, paraphernalia, plant, rig, tackle, trappings
497 **grasping:** bond, bridle, catch, clasp, curb
498 **part:** ammunition, hinge, hook, pivot, pointer, round, shot
499 **tool:** apparatus, ax/axe, blade, brace, broom, brush, cart, chain, chisel, clamp, club, conduit, connection, contrivance, device, drill, gadget, hardware, implement, instrument, key, knife, latch, lock, mop, organ, paddle, pen, pipe, rein, ruler, scoop, tool, utensil, valve, wand, wedge, whip
500 **weapon:** ammunition, armament(s), arms, artillery, atom bomb, baton, battery, bomb, bullet, catapult, cudgel, defense, explosive, fetters, gun, magazine, missile, nuclear weapon, round

TRANSPORTATION

501 **object used for:** access, alley, approach, artery, avenue, boulevard, bridge, career, channel, circuit, concourse, conduit, conveyance, course, crossing, detour, diversion, drain, duct, expressway, highway, intersection, line, passage/passageway, path, road, route, street, track, trail, walk, way
502 **part, vehicle:** anchor, bow, fender, handle, portal, trunk, wheel, wing
503 **vehicle:** caravan, conveyance, jet, transport, vehicle
504 **vehicle, air:** airplane, armada, balloon, craft, plane
505 **vehicle, land:** ambulance, automobile, bicycle, cab, car, cart, coach, hack, model, traffic, truck
506 **vehicle, water:** armada, barge, boat, canoe, craft, ferry, fleet, vessel, yacht

The Planet

GEOGRAPHY

507 **city:** capital, center, city, town, village
508 **geographic division:** area, country, county, department, desert, district, dynasty, grounds, kingdom, land, outskirts, province, quarter, region, sector, state, suburb, terrain, territory, town, tract, ward, zone
509 **land:** abyss, avalanche, backwoods, bank, basin, bay, beach, bed, bluff, bog, canyon, cape, cave, cavern, clay, cliff, coast, compost, court, cove, crevice/crevasse, culvert, dirt, ditch, downgrade, drop, earth, elevation, eminence, excavation, expanse, farm, field, forest, fossil, frontier, garden, geography, glacier, glen, gorge, green, ground, gulf, gully, harbor, hill, horizon, inlet, island,

land, landscape, lawn, lot, marsh, meadow, mine, mire, morass, mound, mountain, nature, outlook, parcel, park, pass, peak, pit, plain, plateau, plaza, plot, port, precipice, projection, property, prospect, quagmire, rampart, ravine, reef, ridge, rock, shelf, shore, soil, square, stack, swamp, table, terrain, trench, trough, tunnel, valley, waste, well, wood/woods, yard
510 **nation:** country, home, kingdom, land, nation, nationality, soil, state
511 **planet:** cosmos, earth, globe, moon, nature, planet, soil, sphere, universe, world
512 **region:** capital, colony, commonwealth, community, quarter, realm, region, reservation, settlement, suburb
513 **section:** aisle, alcove, backyard, barrier, beat,

bed, belt, berth, blank, border, breach, brink, canyon, cavity, cell, chasm, clearance, clearing, cleavage, cleft, corner, country, county, court, crack, cranny, crevice/crevasse, crossing, den, depression, dip, ditch, edge, enclosure, excavation, expanse, fracture, frontier, furrow, gap, green, groove, gulf, gully, gutter, hem, hole, hump, interstice, lawn, leak, ledge, limit, lip, margin, marginal, mouth, niche, nook, notch, opening, outlet, outskirts, parcel, park, pass, patch, pit, plaza, plot, pocket, precipice, projection, prominence, puncture, ravine, recess, rent, repair, ridge, rift, rip, rupture, rut, scratch, shelf, side, sight, slack, slit, slot, split, subdivision, tear, threshold, track, tract, trench, trough, tunnel, vacancy, vacuum, valley, void, ward, well, wrinkle, yoke, zone

514 water: abyss, aquarium, aqueduct, arm, basin, bay, beach, billow, brine, brook, canal, cape, cascade, channel, coast, condensation, course, creek, current, deep, fountain, gulf, harbor, ice, inlet, lake, ocean, pond, pool, race, reservoir, sea, spray, spring, strait, stream, tide, wash, wave, well, whirlpool

HABITATS

515 habitat: abode, asylum, environment, habitat/habitation, harbor, haven, home, lair, land, oasis, paradise, place, premises, property, refuge, sanctuary, settlement, shelter

516 habitat, human: accommodations, address, apartment, asylum, barracks, berth, cabin, camp, castle, cloister, convent, cottage, domicile, dwelling, element, embassy, environs, estate, flat, grange, grounds, haunt, home, hotel, house, household, housing, hovel, hut, inn, jail, lodge, lodging, madhouse, mansion, monastery, motel, neighborhood, palace, penitentiary, prison, quarters, reservation, residence, resort, retreat, sanctuary, suite, vacancy

517 habitat, rural: barn, belt, burrow, cobweb, conservatory, dairy, desert, desolation, farm, field, forest, garden, grange, grove, jungle, lawn, sanctuary, wilderness/wilds, wood/woods

518 state of: domain, entrench, occupancy, occupation, presence

NATURAL RESOURCES

519 electricity: beam, current, spark
520 energy: electricity, energy, fuel, power
521 expression of energy: blast, blaze, boom, chill, combustion, concussion, crash, discharge, explosion, fire, flame, flash, freeze, noise, thunder
522 natural event: eclipse, effervescence, weather
523 resources: fuel, material, resource, resources, rock, substance

WEATHER

524 object connected with: avalanche, blast, breeze, chill, climate, cloud, cold, deluge, drift, film, flood, flurry, fog, frost, gale, gust, hail, haze, humidity, hurricane, mist, moisture, precipitation, puff, thunder, vapor, weather, wind
525 quality of: breezy, bright, clear, clement, close, cloudy, crisp, dirty, dismal, dreary, fair, fierce, fiercely, filmy, fine, foggy, furious, gentle, gloomy, gusty, hazy, heavy, humid, inclement, mild, misty, muggy, oppressive, overcast, raw, rough, rugged, soft, sticky, stormy, stuffy, sultry, sunny, temperate, tempestuous, thick, threatening, tranquil, tropical, turbulent, violent, wild, windy, wintry
526 type of: blizzard, blow, cloud, downpour, drizzle, earthquake, fog, gale, hail, hurricane, mist, precipitation, puff, quake, rain, shade, storm, tempest, thunder, torrent, tremor

Qualities

ABSTRACT

527 ability: able, accountable, adept, adroit, agile, artistic, awkward, barren, capable, commendable, competent, deft, dexterous, dilettante, disabled, effete, efficient, eligible, executive, experienced, expert, facile, feeble, gifted, good, great, handy, inapt, incapable, incompetent, inefficient, inept, inexperienced, master, masterful, mistress, neat, nimble, powerful, powerless, practical, professional, proficient, qualified, raw, ready, rusty, short, skillful, unable, unaccustomed, unfit, unprofessional, unqualified, versatile, versed, veteran, well, wicked

528 achievement: able, abortive, accomplished, ace, artful, attainable, complete, consummate, crack, defensible, done, effectual, efficacious, feasible, fine, finished, flourishing, forward, fruitful, fruitless, futile, gifted, great, obtainable, possible, potential, practical, professional, proficient, prosperous, successful, swimmingly, thriving, triumphant, victorious, well, winning

529 cognitive: academic, afraid, afterthought, alternative, amicable, anathema, appalling, attractive, axiomatic, bad, bag, balm, bane, bearable, belief, black, boring, bothersome, breast, breathtaking, burdensome, cheering, chimera, comforting, comic/comical, comparison, complex, comprehensible, conceivable, considered, considering, corollary, crazy, daydream, deducible, deep, demonstrable, deplorable, depressing, derivable, desirous, detestable, dialectic, difficult, discouraging, disputable, disquieting, distasteful, doleful, doubtful, dream, dry, dull, elusive, enchanting, engrossing, enigmatic/enigmatical, enjoyable, entertaining, equivocal, esoteric, evident, exalted, exciting, exhilarating, explicit, fabulous, fanciful, fantasy, farfetched, fascinating, favored, favorite, fearful, fetish, figment, flat, fleshly, forerunner, forgotten, foul, frightful/frightening, frightful, funny, ghastly, glad, golden, good, grating, half-baked/half-witted, hallucination, harbinger, hard, harebrained, harrowing, hazy, heady, heartbreaking, heinous, heretical, hilarious, hopeless, horizon, horrible/horrendous/horrid, humorous, hypnotic, hypothetical, idea, ideal, idyllic, illogical, illusory/illusive, image, imaginable, imaginary, imaginative, impalpable, impenetrable, impression, inadvisable, incomprehensible, inconceivable, incredible, incredulous, indelible, inexplicable, inner, innovation, innovative, inscrutable, inside, insoluble, inspiration, instinct, insufferable, intelligible, interesting, intimate, intolerable, inviting, inward, irrational, irrefutable, irresistible, itch, jocular/jocose/jocund, joy, knotty, knowledge, known, lamentable, leery, left, liberal, liking, limit, loathsome, logical, loose, lucid, luminous, lure, mad, make-believe, mania, manifest, marvel, marvelous, matter, maudlin, maze, measurable, memorable, memory, metaphysical, miraculous, mirage, mistaken, mode, monotonous, moving, mysterious, mystic/mystical, naked, nauseous, nondescript, nostalgic, note, noticeable, notion, obscure, observable, obsession, obvious, offensive, opaque, open, painful, palatable, palpable, panorama, pathetic, pedagogic, pedantic, perceptible, perspicuous, pesky, phantom, phenomenon, phobia, pick, piquant, piteous, pitiful, plain, plaintive, poignant, pointless, ponderous, portent, precious, preference, premise, premonition, preposterous, presage, problem, problematic, profound, provocative, psychedelic, pure, purposely, putative, puzzling, questionable, radical, rather, reactionary, readable, reasoning, rebellious, recall, recondite, remembrance, reminder, reminiscent, repulsive, reputed, reverie, revolting, rich, ridiculous, right, rosy, rot, sad, satisfactory, scary, scintillating, scream, scrumptious, secret, secular, selection, self-evident/self-explanatory, sensation, shock, sickening, sign, signal, simple, slight, slow, snare, somber, sorry, sound, spectacle, spectacular, speculation, spooky, strain, subconscious, subject, subjective, suggestion, suggestive, surmise, surprise, suspect, suspicion, suspicious, tacit, tall, tame, tangible, taste, tasteful, tedious, temptation, tempting, tenor, theorem, theoretical, theory, thesis, thick, thing, thinkable, thought, thrill, tinge, tiresome, token, tolerable, touch, touching, trace, treat, troublesome, unacceptable, unaccountable, unappetizing, unbelievable, uncertain, uncomfortable, undecided, understood, undesirable, unfathomable, unfavorable, ungodly, unimaginable, uninteresting, unlucky, unnoticed, unpleasant, unpopular, unquestionable, unresolved, unsatisfactory, untold, unwelcome, vague, vapid, vexatious, vile, visible, vision, visionary, whim, whisper, wonder, wonderful

530 commonality: accidental, antiquated, antique, automatic, banal, bourgeois, common, commonly, commonplace, conventional, current, customarily, customary, diffuse, dogmatic, dull, everyday, fair, familiar, frequent, frequently, general, generally, generic, habitual, hackneyed, infrequent, less, little, mainly, much, musty, natural, occasional, occasionally, old, ordinarily, ordinary, pedestrian, popular, prevailing, prevalent, proverbial, public, rare, rarely, regular, routine, spasmodic, stereotyped, stock, traditional, trite, typical, ubiquitous, usual, usually, vulgar, widespread

531 completeness: absolutely, all-out, almost, altogether, blank, bodily, capsule, clean, complete, completely, comprehensive, conscientious, crowning, dead, deeply, deficient, definitive, demonstrative, done, downright, entire, entirely, every, exhaustive, fatal, final, finished, fulfilled, full, full-scale, fully, halfway, incomplete, inseparable, intact, integral, intensive, outright, over, partial, partially, partly, past, perfectly, piecemeal, plenary, practically, pretty, primarily, principally, profound, pure, purely, quite, rank, right, rough, round, rude, sheer, simply, sketchy, sloppy, solid, stark, superficially, sweeping, thorough/thoroughgoing, thoroughly, through, throughout, total, totally, unabridged, unconditional, undivided, unfinished, unmitigated, unqualified, utmost, utter, utterly, wanting, whole, wholly

532 concerned with: about, anxiety, appertain, apply, apropos, barrier, bear on/bear upon, beat, behalf, behind, belong, bother, bug, burden, business, care, challenge, charge, compulsion, concept, concern, consideration, conundrum, craze, debate, difficulty, discovery, disputation, disquiet, distraction, distress, ear, enigma, fancy, fascination, feeling, fixation, focus, guilt, hallucination, hangup, heed, horror, include, interest, issue, keynote/keystone, matter, mystery, notice, notion, object, obstacle, obstruction, pain, paradox, part, particular, passion, peeve, pertain, pivot, place, presentiment, priority, problem, province, provocation, qualm, quandary, question, refer, regard, relate, reverie, riddle, scruple, subject, suspicion, taboo, temptation, topic, touch, toward/towards, trouble, urge, vision, weight, woe, wonder, worry

533 conformity: acceptable, adequate, admissible, befitting, classic, decent, formal, ideal, mediocre, medium, moderate, ordinary, orthodox, practical, proper, regular, so-so, standard, traditional, typical, unwritten

534 constancy: ambivalent, arbitrary, borderline, changeable, chronic, consistent, constant, continual, fickle, firmly, fitful, fluid, forever, formative, frozen, grim, halting, hesitant, immovable, immutable, impervious, incessant, inconsistent, indecisive, indestructible, indomitable, inexorable, insistent, intermittent, intractable/intransigent, invariable, inveterate, iron, irregular, irrevocable, monotonous, relentless, rigid, same, severe, slippery, solid, spotty, static, staunch, steadfast, steady, tentative, unbending, uncertain, unchangeable, unchanging, unfailing, uniform, unpredictable, unresolved, unstable/unsteady, variable, volatile, wanton

535 definiteness: absolute, absolutely, accurate, aimless, airtight, ambiguous, apparent, apparently, assured, automatic, canonical, categorical, certain, certainly, clean, clean-cut, clear-cut, clearly, close, complete, conclusive, concrete, conscious, controversial, debatable, decided, decidedly, decisive, definite, definitely, definitive, demonstrable, designedly, dicey, discernible, disordered, disorderly, disputable, distinct, doubtful, doubtless, dubious, easily, elective, emphatic, entirely, equivocal, erratic, especial, especially, evident, evidently, exact, exactly, experimental, explicit, express, expressly, factual, final, finally, finite, fixed, flat, formless, graphic, gross, guaranteed, haphazard, hard, hard-core, hesitant, illegible, impeccable, implicit, implied, inalienable, incalculable, incontrovertible, indecisive, indeed, indefinite, indeterminate, indisputable, indistinct, inevitable, infallible, ingrained, intangible, irrefutable, irresolute, just, legible, limpid, main, marked, markedly, mere, moot, nebulous, necessarily, necessary, official, only, open, outright, overt, palpable, pat, peremptory, perfect, plain, positive, positively, precarious, precise, precisely, pronounced, pure, questionable, random, rank, really, reliable, right, rigid, rigorous, scientific, secure, seriously, set, shaky, sharp, sheer, simply, slippery, sound, specific, straight, straightforward, strict, stringent, strong, sure, surely, tenebrous, tentative, thorough/thoroughgoing, thoroughly, tried, true, trustworthy/trusty, ultimate, unavoidable, uncertain, unconditional, undeniable, undependable, undisputed/undisputable, undoubtedly, unequivocal, unerring, unfailing, unfaltering, unmistakable, unmitigated, unqualified, unquestionable, unsettled, unsure, unwavering, utter, verbatim, very, willful, yes

536 domain: absolute, academic, administrative, agrarian, agricultural, aquatic, athletic, authoritative, autocratic, blessed, bridal, captive, celestial, chemical, city, civic, civil, classical, clerical, commanding, commercial, communal, confederate, constituent, country, democratic, dismal, domestic, drab, earthly, economic, fleshly, foreign, free, global, home, household, industrial, infernal, internal, international, itinerant, literary, local, marine/maritime, metropolitan, military, municipal, national, native, nautical/naval, nomadic, pedagogic, personal, prevalent, psychological, public, religious, social, sovereign, spiritual, technical, terrestrial, theatrical, theological, totalitarian, unearthly, universal, unworldly, urban, widespread, worldly, worldwide

537 effects: advisory, aphrodisiac, awesome, awry, bad, baleful, baneful, beastly, benign, bitter, bleak, bracing, bright, burning, calamitous, cogent, combustible, coming, consequent, convincing, corrective, corrosive, costly, cultural, curative, damaging, deadly, deathly, deep, defamatory, deleterious, demonstrative, desperate, destined, destructive, detrimental, dire, direful, disadvantageous, disagreeable, disastrous, disruptive, done for, doomed, dramatic, drastic, dread, dreadful, eclectic, ecumenical, eerie, effective, effectual, efficacious, embarrassing, emergent, entertaining, epidemic, exigent, expressive, extenuating, faint, fatal, fateful, favorable, favorably, fearful, fecund, fetching, fierce, fiercely, flat, fooled, forbidding, forcible, foreign, formative, formidable, fortunately, foul, fresh, frightful/frightening, fruitful, fruitless, fun, funereal, funny, furious, general, gentle, ghastly, ghostly, gloomy, good, gory, grateful, grave, greatly, grievous, grisly, gross, grotesque, harmful, harmless, harsh, healthful/healthy, heartbreaking, heavenly, helpful, hideous, highly, horrible/horrendous/horrid, hurtful, hypnotic, ill, ill-fated/ill-starred, imperceptible, imposing, incendiary, inconclusive, inconvenient, ineffective/ineffectual, inflammatory, influential, inimical, injurious, insipid, insufferable, intoxicating, invigorating, inviting, jazzy, juicy, lamentable, lethal, lovely, lucky, lurid, macabre, madly, magic/magical, magnetic, malign, memorial, menacing, mighty, mild, monstrous, morbid, mortal, moving, narcotic, nasty, neutral, noisome, nondescript, noticeable, nourishing, noxious, offensive, oppressive, outstanding, painful, pale, penetrating, peremptory, pernicious, persuasive, pesky, pestilent/pestilential, piercing, pleasing/pleasurable, poison/poisonous, prejudicial, prepossessing, productive, profitable, prosaic, provocative, psychedelic, remedial, right, rugged, ruinous, safe, sedative, sensational, sensuous, sharp, sick, sickly, slow, soft, soporific, spectacular, spooky, strong, subtle, telling, therapeutic, tiresome, touching, toxic, trenchant, unbearable, uncanny, uncomfortable, unhealthy, unholy, vapid, venomous, vexatious, virtual, virulent, vivid, weak, wholesome, wicked

538 efforts: ambitious, applied, assiduous, automated, automatic, concerted, conscientious, cooperative, difficult, diligent, employed, gladly, go-ahead, hard, heavy, idle, indolent, industrious, labored, laborious, laden, light, lightly, mindless, murderous, onerous, painstaking, persistent, religious, rugged, running, scrupulous, serious, simple, slack, slow, straightforward, strenuous, studied, studious, thankless, thorough/thoroughgoing, thoroughly, tireless, tiresome, together, torpid, tough, unemployed, unfailing, unfaltering, unflagging, unpaid, unprofessional, unsolicited, untiring, uphill, valiant, vicarious, voluntarily, voluntary, weighty, workable, working

539 existential: alive, almighty, animate, comatose, conscious, consist, dead, deadly, deceased, defunct, dormant, drowsy, dying, extant, extinct, fallen, fatal, immaterial, immortal, inanimate, incarnate, late, lifeless, live, living, lost, luxuriate, missing, nil, nonexistent, obsolete, out, perennial, present, sleepy, soporific, unconscious, vagabond, vital, wakeful

540 forcefulness: almighty, bang, blatant, bloody, brute, cumulative, desperate, driving, dynamic, effective, electric/electrical, fierce, fiercely, hard, insistent, invincible, madly, mightily, mighty, potent, powerful, powerfully, savage, stiff, strong, violent

541 frequency: annual, annually, casual, commonly, daily, hardly, nightly, occasional, occasionally, often, periodic, rapid, rarely, recurrent, scarce, scarcely, seldom, spasmodic, sporadic, uncommonly, usually, yearly

542 inclination: abrupt, accommodating, acquisitive, active, addicted, adrift, adventurous, affirmative, aggressive, agreeable, alive, aloof, ambitious, amicable, anxious, apt, arbitrary, arid, assiduous, base, beastly, benign, besides, blindly, brisk, busy, careful, carefully, careless, casual, characteristic, charitable, cheap, cold-blooded, competitive, conducive, confirmed, conflicting, conservative, conspicuous, constant, contradictory, corporal, corporeal, correct, crack, creditable, curious, decent, dedicated, deep, deliberate, deliberately, delicate, delicately, demanding, dependable, derelict, designing, determined, detestable, devoted, devout, dictatorial, die-hard, difficult, dilatory, diligent, dim, diplomatic, dirty, discriminating, disinclined, disingenuous, disposed, disputatious, distrustful, dogged, dogmatic, domestic, doubtful, dour, downtrodden, dull, dutiful, dynamic, eager, earnest, earthy, easy, economical, effervescent, effusive, elusive, emotional, emotionless, energetic, engaged, engrossed, enterprising, enthusiastic, equable, equal, equitable, errant, erratic, evasive, even, exact, exaggerated, exciting, execrable, exigent, exotic, expeditious, explosive, factious, fair, fairly, fallible, farcical, fast, fastidious, feckless, ferocious, fervent/fervid, fiery, firm, firmly, flexible, fluid, fly-by-night, fond, foolish, foolishly, forbearing, forced, fortunate, frantic, free, frenzied, fresh,

frisky, frolicsome, funereal, gaily, gallant, gay, generous, gentle, genuine, gingerly, given to, gladly, go-ahead, godless, godly, good, gracious, grandiose, grasping, gratuitous, greedy, gross, guarded, guileless, gullible, gutless, gutsy, half-hearted, happily, happy-go-lucky, hard, hardcore, hardened, hard-nosed/hardheaded, harsh, hasty, headlong, heartless, hearty, helpless, hesitant, hospitable, hostile, humane, humanitarian, hurtful, hypocritical, hysterical, idle, ignoble, ignorant, imaginative, immersed, impartial, impassive, impatient, impersonal, impetuous, implacable, improper, improvident, imprudent, impulsive, inadvertent, inane, inattentive, incautious, indefatigable, indifferent, indignant, indiscriminate, indisposed, indolent, indulgent, inelegant, inert, infant/infantile, inflammatory, ingenuous, inhibited, innocent, inoffensive, inquiring, insecure, insidious, insincere, insouciant, intent, intolerant, intractable/intransigent, inventive, involved, irate, jaundiced, jealous, jolly, joyful/joyous, joyless, judicious, kind, kindhearted, kindly, kinky, lackadaisical, lackluster, languid, lax, lenient, levelheaded, lewd, liable, liberal, lifeless, light, lighthearted, live, lively, livid, loath, loud, loving, low, low-key, lukewarm, magnanimous, malevolent, malicious, malign, masterful, materialistic, maudlin, mawkish, mean, melodramatic, merciful, merciless, meretricious, methodical/methodic, meticulous, mindful, mushy, naive, narrow, narrow-minded, neat, neglectful, negligent, nerveless, nervous, neutral, nice, nonchalant, noncommittal, noncompliant, nonconformist, nonpartisan, obdurate, objective, objectively, oblivious, obnoxious, obstinate, obtrusive, occupied, odd/oddball, offhand, open, opposed/opposing, opprobrious, optimistic, overconfident, overwrought, pagan, parochial, partial, particular, partisan, passionate, passive, paternal, patient, peaceful, peevish, penitent, peppery, perceptive, peremptory, perfunctory, persuasive, perverse, petulant, philanthropic, pigheaded, plastic, playful, pleasant, pompous, ponderous, poor, practical, pragmatic, precipitous/precipitate, precise, predictable, premature, premeditated, prepossessed, presumptuous, pretentious, productive, progressive, prolific, prone, prostrate, protective, proud, prudent, pugnacious, punctilious, purposeful, quarrelsome, querulous, radical, raging, rambunctious, reactionary, ready, realistic, rebellious, reckless, reliable, renegade, resigned, resolute, responsive, restive, restless, restrained, rival, romantic, sadistic, safe, sanguine, sappy, savage, scheming, scrupulous, scurrilous, sedate, sedentary, selective, selfish, self-righteous, self-satisfied, sensible, sentimental, serious, seriously, set, severe, short-sighted, silly, simple, sincere, sly, smart, smug, sneaky, sober, solemn, sour, spineless, spirited, spiritless, spiteful, spontaneous, sprightly, square, staunch, steadfast, steady, stern, stout, straight, strenuous, strict, strong, subjective, sunny, susceptible, suspicious, sweet, sympathetic, tame, tardy, temperate, tempestuous, tenacious, tender, tentative, tepid, testy, thoughtful, thoughtless, tireless, together, tolerant, torn, touched, touchy, tough, tractable, tranquil, true, truthful, unaffected, unbiased, uncommitted, uncompromising, unconcerned, unconscious, uncritical, understanding, unfeeling, unflappable, ungodly, unholy, unimaginative, uninspired, unprejudiced, unreliable, unstable/unsteady, unsympathetic, untoward, untrustworthy, unwavering, unwilling, unyielding, vehement, vengeful, venomous, versatile, vicious, vigilant, vindictive, virulent, wakeful, wanton, warm, weak, wholehearted/whole-hearted, willful, witty, wooden, youthful

543 is an attribute of: appear, appearance, belong, quality, savor, seem, sound, trivia

544 manner: abominable, absurd, advisedly, aimless, although, anyhow, anyway, as, beautifully, blah, blind, breezy, broken, brutal, brutally, busily, businesslike, busy, by, calm, camp, casual, catchy, circuitous, circumspect, counter, covert, covertly, cumbersome, delicately, despite, dreary, easy, equable, ergo, even, foolish, foolishly, for, forcibly, forthwith, fortunately, freely, frenzied, frequently, gradual, gradually, grievous, grim, grisly, hastily, helter-skelter, how, however, ill-advised, immediately, immoderate, impersonal, impolitic, inadvertent, incautious, incidentally, indelicate, indirect, individually, instant, instantly, instinctive, intentional, intently, involuntary, irregularly, irresponsible, just, justly, kindly, lackadaisical, largely, leisurely, less, lightly, little, long, low-key, luckily, luxuriate, luxurious, madly, mainly, manual, markedly, mechanical, methodical/methodic, meticulous, mightily, misguided, misspent, moderately, monotonous, more, moreover, most, mostly, much, mutually, narrowly, naturally, necessarily, nevertheless, notwithstanding, objectively, of course, openly, otherwise, outwardly, over, overly, parenthetical, partially, pell-mell, perfectly, perfunctory, per se, personally, piecemeal, poorly, positively, possibly, posthaste, powerfully, presumably, primarily, principally, progressive, promptly, providing/provided, punctual, purely, purposeless, purposely, quick, rampant, rapidly, rather, readily, recurrent, regardless, regular, relatively, reliable, separately, seriously, sheer, simply, slightly, solely, somehow, still, straight, strategic, subtle, summarily, superficially, swimmingly, though, through, thus, together, too, true, ulterior, unawares, unconditional, unconscious, undercover, underhand, unduly, unexpected, unfair, unforeseen, unusually, unwitting, venomous, very, via,

vice versa, violent, virtual, virtually, voluntarily, voluntary, well, while, wrong, yet

545 morality: abandoned, answerable, astray, atrocious, bad, badly, bawdy, black, blasphemous, blue, broad, coarse, common, conscientious, contraband, corrupt, criminal, crooked, culpable, cunning, damnable, damned, dark, debauched, decadent, degenerate, demonic/demoniac/demoniacal, depraved, devilish, diabolic, dirty, disorderly, dissipated, dissolute, drunk, egregious, elevated, equitable, erotic, errant, ethical, evil, faithful, faithless, fast, faultless, fickle, filthy, flagrant, fleshly, fraudulent, frightful, good, gross, guileless, guiltless, guilty, heathen, heretical, holy, honest, ignoble, ill, illegal, illicit, immaculate, immoral, impious, improper, impure, incorruptible, indecent, indefensible, indelicate, inexcusable, infamous, infernal, inhuman/inhumane, innocent, insidious, insincere, involved, irreproachable, just, justifiable, justly, lawful, lawless, lewd, liable, libidinous, licentious, loose, loyal, mischievous, miscreant, moral, nasty, naughty, nefarious, obscene, off-color, perverted, pornographic, prejudicial, pretended, profane, profligate, promiscuous, racy, rakish, rank, raw, religious, reputable, responsible, right, righteous, rightful, risqué, rotten, sadistic, scandalous, scurrilous, seamy, secret, sensational, shady, shameful, shameless, sharp, sinful, smutty, sordid, sorry, spicy, suggestive, unconscionable, unethical, unfair, unfaithful, ungodly, unjust, unprincipled, unscrupulous, untrue, untrustworthy, unwarranted, upright, upstanding, valid, veracious, vicious, vile, virtuous, vulgar, wanton, wholesome, wicked, wily, worthy, wrong, wrongful

546 necessity: absent, applied, auxiliary, bereft, binding, capital, chosen, collateral, component, compulsory, controversial, deciding, dependent, dire, discretionary, dispensable, elementary, enough, essential, expendable, extra, extraneous, famished, fresh, fundamental, gratuitous, imperative, inadequate, inapplicable, indebted, indispensable, insatiable, insufficient, integral, intrinsic, introductory, lacking, main, mandatory, marketable, meager, necessary, needless, nonessential, obligatory, preparatory, prerequisite, providing/provided, provisional, radical, required/requisite, rudimentary, shy, staple, starving/starved, strategic, superfluous, ultimate, underlying, undue, unduly, unnecessary, vital, wanting

547 normality: aberrant, abnormal, accepted, accustomed, all right, anomalous, astonishing, atypical, average, bizarre, characteristic, classic, common, conventional, curious, customarily, customary, disguised, eccentric, everyday, exorbitant, extreme, familiar, formal, general, generally, habitual, incidental, incongruous, irregular, lowly, macabre, mean, mediocre, medium, middle, middling, moderate, modest, mundane, natural, nondescript, normal, normally, ordinary, pedestrian, plain, prevalent, prosaic, reasonable, regular, routine, stock, temperate, typical, unaccustomed, unimaginative, uninspired, usual

548 occurrence: amusing, atrocious, ceremonial, ceremonious, chaotic, chronological, closed, coincident, coincidental, consequent, covert, covertly, crowning, cumulative, cursed, dangerous, dangerously, dark, desperate, didactic, dire, disagreeable, disastrous, disgusting, dismal, dramatic, droll, dull, egregious, embarrassing, empirical/empiric, endurable, enjoyable, ensuing, eventful, exciting, excruciating, exhilarating, exigent, exposed, express, festive, forbidden, forced, forcibly, forthcoming, fortuitous, foul, furious, furtive, futile, gala, gloomy, grateful, grave, grievous, gruesome, hairy, half-baked/half-witted, hapless, happily, harrowing, hazardous, heavy, hectic, heinous, historic, historical, hopeful, hopeless, humdrum, hurried, ill-advised, ill-fated/ill-starred, ill-timed, imminent, impending, inane, inauspicious, incidental, inconclusive, inconvenient, incurable, indefensible, informal, insane, ironic/ironical, irregularly, jolly, joyful/joyous, joyless, juicy, lackluster, late, limit, lively, low-key, ludicrous, madcap, magic/magical, maiden, memorable, menacing, meritorious, merry, meteoric, miraculous, misguided, misleading, mostly, much, murderous, nasty, nearing, necessary, nefarious, nice, objectionable, offensive, ominous, oncoming, opportune, oppressive, outlandish, over, overall, overblown, overdue, partisan, peaceable, penal, pending, perilous, permissible, pernicious, pessimistic, pleasant, poignant, pointless, poor, predetermined, predictable, premeditated, preposterous, pressing, primarily, privileged, promising, propitious, prospective, prosperous, queer, random, rather, realistic, regardless, regrettable, rewarding, ridiculous, risky, risqué, rollicking, romantic, rosy, routine, ruinous, sad, safe, scary, secretive, secretly, self-evident/self-explanatory, senseless, sequential, shocking, simultaneous, sinful, sinister, slow, someday, somewhat, soon, speedy, spontaneous, studied, stupid, sure, surreptitious, swell, taboo, tacit, tame, tardy, tedious, tender, tense, terminal, thankless, then, thick, threatening, thrilling, through, ticklish, tight, together, tolerable, topsy-turvy, touchy, tragic, trial, trying, tumultous/tumultuous, ugly, unadvised, unaffected, unauthorized, unawares, unbelievable, uneasy, uneventful, unexpected, unfair, unforeseen, unfortunate, unfriendly, ungodly, unhappy, unholy, unimaginable, unimaginative, uninspired, unintentional/unintended, uninteresting, unlucky, unobtrusive, unreasonable, unrelenting, unsophisticated, unspeakable, untimely, untoward, untroubled, unwarranted, unwise, unwitting, urgent,

venturesome, warlike, weighty, well, whimsical, wholehearted/whole-hearted, woeful, wrong, yet

549 original: aboriginal, ancestral, automated, automatic, bastard, born, built-in, classical, colonial, congenital, constitutional, counterfeit, derivative, domestic, essential, ethereal, ethnic, exotic, extraneous, extrinsic, foreign, from, genetic, hereditary, human, humble, ignoble, illegitimate, implicit, imported, inborn/inbred, indigenous, ingrained, inherent, innate, intimate, low, lowly, man-made, medieval, misbegotten, mortal, mystic/mystical, native, noble, organic, original, patrician, pedigree, plebeian, preliminary, premature, primary/prime, proper, provincial, racial, radical, royal, rudimentary, secondary, secular, strange, thoroughbred, underlying, unprecedented, vernacular

550 peculiarity: ablaze, adaptable, aggressive, airy, ashamed, austere, authoritative, babyish, born, characteristic, clement, closed, contemptible, continent, conventional, corny, craven, cultured, dead, defensive, dreadful, fastidious, forbidding, forceful, forgetful, gawky, gingerly, halting, laborious, laughable, leisurely, protective, punctual

551 permanency: abiding, always, chronic, endless, fixed, fleeting, fly-by-night, forever, fugitive, invincible, irrevocable, lasting, makeshift, passing, permanent, perpetual, standing, stationary, stopgap, temporary, tentative, unchanging

552 probability: absurd, accidental, alleged, apparent, apparently, attainable, chance, chancy, clearly, conceivable, contingent, convincing, credible, definitely, dicey, disposed, doubtless, dubious, earthly, easily, eventual, eventually, farfetched, feasible, fishy, fluky, fortuitous, funny, groundless, hardly, hypothetical, ideal, iffy, illusory/illusive, imaginable, immune, implausible, impossible, impractical/impracticable, improbable, inconceivable, incredible, inevitable, insurmountable, intended, invalid, legendary, liable, likely, logical, marvelous, maybe, negligible, odd, off, optional, ostensible, out, outside, perhaps, plausible, possible, possibly, potential, preposterous, presumably, probable, probably, prone, prospective, remote, ridiculous, slender/slim, so-called, sound, specious, subject, tenable, tentative, unlikely, unrealistic, unreliable, vain, viable, workable

553 repetition: again, alternate, away, redundant, repeatedly, repetitious

554 restrictiveness: absolute, all, autonomous, beyond, binding, bound, bounded, boundless, captive, cloistered, concentrated, conditional, confined, exclusive, exclusively, exclusive of, exempt, finite, fixed, independent, independently, limited, narrow, numbered, permissible, prohibited, prohibitive, provisional, qualified, rampant

555 social: accommodating, allied, amorous, antisocial, aristocratic, awkward, bigoted, blameless, brotherly, burlesque, busy, chummy, civilian, clandestine, clannish, close, commemorative, companionable, compatible, congenial, conjugal, connubial, cooperative, cultural, dear, defenseless, depressed, difficult, dignified, disadvantaged, disadvantageous, disaffected, disgraceful, dishonorable, elite, eminent, engaged, fallen, familiar, forsaken, friendless, friendly, frisky, gentle, homeless, hospitable, hot, important, inelegant, intimate, lonely, lonesome, marital, matrimonial, meddlesome, near, noble, nuptial, platonic, popular, preferred, prestigious, recluse/reclusive, refined, single, sociable, social, sole, solitary, thick, thoughtful, thoughtless, unaccompanied, unapproachable, unmarried, unpopular, unsociable, unwelcome, unworldly, upper, welcome

556 **specialization:** alone, circumstantial, express, expressly, finicky, respective

557 **specificity:** accurate, all right, approximate, careless, catholic, certain, closely, correct, definite, descriptive, detailed, exact, exactly, extra, fine, general, just, lax, limited, literal, literally, meticulous, minute, namely, nice, particular, particularly, pat, peculiar, perfect, photographic, precise, precisely, proper, punctilious, random, right, rigorous, rough, rude, sectional, separate, simply, smack, special, specially, specific, specifically, strict, such, superficial, systematic, thorough/thoroughgoing, thoroughly, topical, very, wholly

558 **suitability:** absurd, acceptable, accepted, accordingly, adequate, adequately, agreeable, all right, ample, amply, applicable, appropriate, apropos, apt, awkward, becoming, befitting, best, conformable, congruous, correct, correctly, cut out for, decent, decorous, de rigeur, discordant, done, down-to-earth, due, duly, eligible, enough, excusable, exorbitant, expedient, extreme, favorable, favorably, feasible, felicitous, fit, fitted, fitting, full-grown/full-fledged, fully, germane, good, granted, happy, improper, inadmissible, inadvisable, inapplicable, inappropriate, inapt, incongruous, incorrect, ineligible, inept, inopportune, just, justifiable, lame, legitimate, livable, meet, nice, objectionable, okay, old, orthodox, passable, pat, perfect, pertinent, presentable, previous, proper, reasonable, relative, relevant, right, rightful, ripe, satisfactory, seasonable, seemly, senseless, sound, sufficient, suitable, tenable, timely, unacceptable, unasked, unbecoming, undue, unfit, unsatisfactory, unseemly, unsuitable, untoward, unwarranted, unworthy, weak, well, wrong

559 **transmission:** infectious, passable, roundabout

560 **usefulness:** acting, adequately, barren, broken, convenient, damaged, dead, defective, defunct, dependable, derelict, desert, desirable, desolate, dilapidated, dissipated, drained, effective, effete, efficient, employed, enervated, excessive, exhausted, expedient, extravagant, faded, fallow, faulty, finished, fitted, fixed, fruitful, fruitless,

functional, futile, good, handy, helpful, hollow, idle, impaired, impoverished, inactive, ineffective/ineffectual, inefficient, infallible, infertile, instead, instrumental, interim, invalid, irrelevant, leftover, live, living, lost, makeshift, misspent, null, obsolete, occupied, old, open, operative, outmoded, practicable, practical, prepared, prodigal, productive, propitious, purposeless, ready, residual, ripe, running, salubrious, satisfactory, serviceable, short, spent, stopgap, subservient, subsidiary, substitute, sufficient, superfluous, surplus, trial, tributary, under, unrealistic, usable, useful, useless, utilitarian, vacant, valuable, viable, virgin/virginal, visionary, void, wanting, workable, working, worn/worn-out, worthless, worthwhile

COMPARATIVE

561 **compared with:** contrast, mark, touch

562 **complexity:** abstruse, artless, backward, bare, baroque, bilateral, blank, clarion, clear, complex, complicated, crude, cursory, elaborate, elementary, exaggerated, fancy, graphic, intricate, involved, modest, pell-mell, simple, simply, sophisticated, tortuous, tricky, ultra, unsophisticated, unwieldy

563 **correspondence:** akin, allied, applicable, close, commensurate, concurrent, conformable, congruent, congruous, consistent, consonant, duplicate, harmonious, kindred, likewise, moderate, mutual, proportionate/proportional, relative, sympathetic, twin, unanimous, united, unrelated

564 **difference:** alien, altered, alternative, ambivalent, another, assorted, atypical, avant-garde, averse, bizarre, converse, curious, deviant, diametric/diametrical, different, differently, discordant, discrepant, discrete, disparate, disproportionate, dissimilar, dissonant, distinct, distinctive, divergent, diverse, eccentric, especial, especially, exceptional, extraordinary, fantastic, freakish, funny, heterogeneous, incompatible, inconsistent, individual, inverse, irreconcilable, manifold, miscellaneous, mixed, monstrous, motley, multiple/multifarious, new, novel, odd/oddball, offbeat, opposed/opposing, opposite, other, particular, peculiar, phenomenal, polar, preternatural, quaint, queer, remote, repugnant, rival, separate, several, single, singular, sole, special, specific, specifically, strange, sundry, suspicious, unaccountable, unaccustomed, uncanny, uncommon, unconventional, underground, unearthly, unequal, unfamiliar, unheard-of, unique, unlike, unnatural, unorthodox, unprecedented, unrelated, unthinkable, unusual, variant, varied, various, vice versa, weird

565 **difficulty:** agonizing, arduous, awkward, complicated, defective, deficient, delicate, demanding, easily, easy, effortless, facile, formidable, gruel-

ing, hard, heavy, inaccurate, insurmountable, knotty, laborious, murderous, onerous, ponderous, prickly, rigorous, rugged, serious, seriously, severe, sticky, stiff, tall, taxing, thorny, ticklish, tight, tough, treacherous, troublesome, trying, uphill, weighty, wicked

566 equivalence: alike, alternate, approximately, balanced, commensurate, comparable, comparative, coordinate, corresponding, disproportionate, duplicate, equal, equivalent, even, identical, indistinguishable, level, matching, mock, model, nearly, reciprocal, regular, same, uneven

567 importance: above, august, below, beneath, beneficial, central, chiefly, chosen, climactic/climacteric, collateral, component, conspicuous, costly, dear, dogmatic, elevated, essential, estimable, exclusive, front, fundamental, grave, high, holy, immediate, important, inferior, known, main, majestic, material, meaningful, noteworthy, noticeable, operative, precious, pregnant, primary/prime, prodigious, reputable, salient, second-rate/second-class, significant, special, strategic, telling, top, towering, upper, vital, worthwhile, worthy

568 importance, extreme: acute, basic, basically, beloved, best, better, big, blessed, bright, brilliant, burning, capital, cardinal, celebrated, chief, consequential, considerable, critical, crucial, deciding, dire, divine, dominant, earnest, eminent, exigent, fabled, famous, fatal, fateful, favored, favorite, first, foremost, glorious, grand, great, hallowed, head, historic, illustrious, immortal, influential, invaluable, key, legendary, major, master, momentous, monumental, necessary, notable, noted, noteworthy, outstanding, overriding, paramount, pet, pivotal, praiseworthy, predominant, preeminent, premier, pressing, prestigious, priceless, principal, prominent, renowned, ruling, serious, seriously, signal, significant, sovereign, splendid, star, substantial, supreme, ultimate, uppermost, urgent, valuable, weighty, well-known

569 intensity: acute, almighty, awfully, bad, badly, biting, blatant, bloody, concentrated, considerably, desperate, desperately, drastic, exceedingly, exquisite, extra, extreme, extremely, greatly, harsh, heavy, high, highly, immoderate, insanely, intense, mightily, most, notably, outrageous, powerfully, pretty, profound, quite, severe, severely, sharp, somewhat, stark, stiff, stringent, strong, substantially, terribly, terrific, too, ultra, unconscionable, undue, unduly, unmitigated, unusually, very, violent, vivid, wild

570 negative: adverse, affected, amiss, apocryphal, awful, awfully, bad, baleful, baneful, base, black, conflicting, creepy, cruel, damnable, damned, defiled, degenerate, deleterious, delinquent, deplorable, derogatory, despicable, detrimental, dire, direful, done for, egregious, empty, erroneous, evil, fallacious, false, faulty, fearful, filthy, grim,

grisly, heinous, icky, ill, imperfect, inadequate, inauspicious, incendiary, incorrect, incorrigible, inexcusable, infamous, injurious, inordinate, insecure, lame, loathsome, miserable, misguided, misspent, negative, null, objectionable, off, poor, prejudicial, rancid, rotten, ruinous, run-down, seedy, slipshod, squalid, tasteless, terribly, threatening, undesirable, unfortunate, ungodly, unpleasant, unsatisfactory, untoward, unwelcome, upset, weak, weird, worthless

571 negative, extreme: abject, abominable, atrocious, awful, awfully, bad, badly, cursed, lousy, nasty, noisome, outrageous, pernicious, perverse, poorly, regrettable, reprehensible, repugnant, repulsive, rotten, shameful, shocking, shoddy, sick, sickening, sickly, sinister, sordid, terrible, tragic, ugly, unbearable, unfavorable, unhealthy, unsavory, unspeakable, unworthy, vicious, vile, virulent, wicked, woeful, wretched, wrong

572 positive: admirable, affirmative, agreeable, agreeably, all right, angelic, astonishing, auspicious, awesome, beloved, beneficial, benign, best, better, boss, comfort, comfortable, commendable, consummate, cool, decent, delicious, desirable, estimable, exceptional, exemplary, extraordinary, fabulous, fanciful, fantastic, faultless, favorable, favorably, fortunate, fortunately, fun, good, grateful, heavenly, idyllic, incredible, innocuous, interesting, luckily, lucky, magnificent, majestic, meritorious, merry, miraculous, nice, nifty, noble, opportune, pleasant, pleasing/pleasurable, positive, prodigious, profitable, propitious, prosperous, proud, respectable, rewarding, right, salubrious, terrific, thrilling, upbeat, utopian, welcome, well, worthwhile, worthy, yes

573 similarity: akin, alike, analogous, approximate, closely, cognate, comparable, comparative, conformable, different, equal, equivalent, faithful, homogenous, identical, interchangeable, like, parallel, related, representative, same, seeming, similar, synonymous, tantamount, twin, uniform, virtual, virtually

574 superiority: absolute, admirable, advanced, advantage, advisable, all right, all-time, arch, capital, cardinal, champion, chief, choice, chosen, classic/classical, coarse, commanding, correct, crack, dandy, definitive, delectable, delicate, deluxe, dependent, deplorable, dignified, distinctive, distinguished, divine, dominant, elegant, elite, eminently, enviable, especial, especially, excellent, exceptional, exemplary, exquisite, fantastic, fine, first-class/first-rate, flawless, glorious, golden, grand, great, head, holy, ideal, impeccable, imperative, imperfect, imperious, important, imposing, impressive, incomparable, ineffable, infallible, inferior, inimitable, irreproachable, irresistible, junior, laudable, lay, leading, less, lofty, lordly, low, luscious, lush, luxuriant, luxurious, majestic, major, marvelous, matchless, maximum, menial, mint, model, omnipotent, optimum, outstanding, paramount, peerless, perfect, perfectly, pet, phenomenal, poor, poorly, powerful, praiseworthy, predominant, preeminent, preferred, premium, prevalent, primary/prime, principal, privileged, prize, prodigious, proud, rare, remarkable, renowned, reputable, rotten, royal, ruling, sacred, secondary, second-rate/second-class, select, senior, sensational, signal, solemn, spectacular, splendid, stately, striking, stunning, stupendous, sublime, sumptuous, super, superb, superior, superlative, supreme, swell, tasteful, top, transcendent/transcendental, tremendous, ultimate, uncommon, unequaled, unerring, unique, unparalleled, unprecedented, utmost, utopian, venerable, vintage, whole, wonderful

575 unimportance: empty, expendable, frivolous, immaterial, inconsequential/inconsiderable, insignificant, irrelevant, lesser, lightweight, little, meaningless, menial, minor, minute, moderate, needless, negligible, nominal, nonessential, ordinary, peripheral, petty, piddling, puny, remote, second, secondary, side, slight, small, so-so, subject, subordinate, subservient, subsidiary, substitute, tenuous, trifling, trivial, under, unimportant, vain, vapid, worthless

PHYSICAL

576 accessibility: accessible, adaptable, approachable, arcane, available, bereft, blind, broad, clandestine, close, closed, concealed, confidential, confidentially, cryptic, dark, defenseless, depleted, discernible, dissipated, distant, dubious, engaged, enigmatic/enigmatical, esoteric, exposed, furtive, glaring, graphic, hidden, hush-hush, illegible, impenetrable, inaccessible, incognito, inconspicuous, inner, inscrutable, inside, insoluble, known, latent, legible, lost, manifest, missing, mobile, mysterious, nameless, obscure, observable, obtainable, occult, open, optional, out, outward, outwardly, passable, patent, perceptible, permeable, plain, possible, private, privy, prohibited, pronounced, public, rare, ready, recondite, reserved, secluded, secret, stealthy, strange, tight, ulterior, unapproachable, undercover, underground, unheard-of, unidentified, unknown, unseen, usable, vigilant, visible, visual, weak, willing

577 accompaniment: abandoned, again, alone, along, also, and, attendant, complementary, concomitant, connected, deserted, each, en masse, en route, ensemble, et cetera, except, furthermore, incidental, including, isolated, joint, jointly, left, lone, mutually, odd, one, only, parenthetical, per se, personally, reciprocal, related, separate, separately, single, singly, singular, sole, solely, solitary, stranded, unaccompanied, under, unique, united

578 age: adolescent, advanced, afresh, aged, ancient, antediluvian, antiquarian, antiquated, antique, archaic, big, boyish, callow, contemporary, crotchety, crude, doddering, elder, elderly, fresh, full-grown/full-fledged, green, immature, immemorial, inchoate, infant/infantile, innovative, junior, juvenile, late, mature, medieval, mellow, mint, modern, modish, musty, new, newfangled, novel, old, older, old-fashioned, original, originally, outdated/out-of-date, outmoded, passé, puerile, quaint, recent, ripe, senior, stale, tender, undeveloped, up-to-date, vintage, virgin/virginal, young, youthful

579 beauty: adorable, aesthetic/esthetic, artistic, attractive, beautiful, becoming, brunette/brunet, comely, cosmetic, crisp, cute, dapper, deathly, decorative, delectable, desirable, disheveled, dressy, elegant, exquisite, fair, fancy, fashionable, fetching, fine, flawless, glamorous, glorious, good-looking, gorgeous, graceful, grotesque, handsome, hideous, homely, imperfect, irresistible, lovely, ornamental, ornate, picturesque, plain, presentable, pretty, repulsive, resplendent, scenic, seductive, statuesque, striking, stunning, stylish, symmetrical, ugly, unbecoming, unsightly

580 deformity: blemish, blot, blotch, chip, contortion, defect, deformity, dent, distortion, fault, flaw, frailty, freak, scar

581 direction: about, across, adrift, along, around, astern, astray, at, away, awry, backward, below, centrifugal, circuitous, counter, crooked, crosswise/crossways, devious, diagonal, diagonally, direct, directly, due, erect, errant, erratic, forked, forth, forward, haphazard, horizontal, indirect, inward, lateral, left, north, outgoing, outward, parallel, perpendicular, plane, plumb, ramble, right, rotary, roundabout, sharp, sheer, sideways, sinuous, snaky, steep, straight, through, tortuous, uphill, upright, vertical, wide, winding, wry, zigzag

582 genuineness: abstract, actual, actually, airy, alias, allegorical, apocryphal, apparent, apparently, artificial, arty, assumed, authentic, authoritative, baseless, believable, bogus, certain, circumstantial, colored, concrete, conjectural, counterfeit, credible, dark, deceptive, de facto, delusive, dogmatic, dreamy, effective, empirical/empiric, enigmatic/enigmatical, erroneous, ersatz, esoteric, ethereal, extant, factual, fake, fallacious, false, fantastic, farfetched, feigned, fictitious, figurative, frank, fraudulent, genuine, good, groundless, hard, heartfelt, historical, hypothetical, illusory/illusive, imaginary, imitative, inaccurate, indisputable, intangible, invisible, irrefutable, just, legitimate, made-up, magic/magical, make-believe, man-made, matter-of-fact, metaphysical, mock, monstrous, mystic/mystical, mythical/mythological, nominal, nonexistent, occult, ostensible, ostensibly, palpable, phony, physical, plastic, positive, positively, pretended, pseudo, quack, quasi, quite, real, realistic, really, right, sham, sincerely, sound, specious, spiritual, spurious, substantial, supernatural, suspect, synthetic, tangible, temporal, true, truly, unearthly, unfounded, unnatural, unreal, unthinkable, untrue, unvarnished, unworldly, utopian, valid, veracious, veritable, visionary, wholehearted/whole-hearted, worldly, wrong

583 location: aboard, about, abroad, absent, absentee, advance, aerial, agricultural, aground, airy, alone, ashore, astride, at, beached, center, central, civic, civil, cloistered, coastal, diffuse, down, everywhere, exterior, external, fixed, forward, from, front, here, horizontal, inside, insular, interior, isolated, lateral, leafy, left, lonely, low, middle, north, off, out, outdoor, outer, outlying, outside, outward, over, overseas, pastoral, penal, peripheral, perpendicular, polar, populous, posterior, precipitous, present, private, prominent, prone, prostrate, quiet, rear, remote, roomy, rural, rustic, secluded, sideways, solitary, somewhere, stray, surface, through, top, topical, uncomfortable, underground, upper, uppermost, upright, upside-down, vertical, void, where/wherever, wide, wild, withdrawn

584 movement: ambulatory, billowy, brisk, centrifugal, clumsy, destined, fleet, flowing, fluent, flying, frozen, fugitive, gawky, graceful, graceless, heavy, immobile, inactive, indolent, inert, itinerant, languid, left-handed, leisurely, lethargic, lifeless, lightly, liquid, listless, lithe, lumbering, maladroit, migrant/migratory, mobile, motionless, movable, moving, nimble, nomadic, nonstop, outgoing, passive, pendulous/pendent, peripatetic, portable, quiet, restless, rotary, roundabout, running, sedentary, slack, slow, sluggish, speedy, stagnant, static, still, vibrant, winding

585 order: advance, advanced, alphabetical, avant-garde, bottom, center, chronological, collective, confused, consecutive, direct, disjointed, disorganized, first, following, fore, foregoing, foremost, former, formerly, forward, front, immediate, incipient, indiscriminate, initial, intermediate, internal, introductory, last, lastly/last, latter, leading, least, maiden, mean, median, methodical/methodic, next, older, on, onward, onwards, orderly, original, originally, past, pell-mell, pioneer, posterior, preceding, preliminary, premier, preparatory, previous, primary/prime, regular, second,

senior, sequential, serial, straight, subsequent, subsequently, succeeding/successive, systematic, tidy, together, topsy-turvy, uttermost

586 relative placement: about, abreast, adjacent, adjoining, after, ahead, ajar, almost, along, alongside, amid/amidst, among, apart, approximate, around, aside, askew, behind, below, beneath, beside, between, bottom, by, close, cockeyed, contiguous, convenient, direct, down, elsewhere, en route, far, faraway, farther, farthest, furthest, gone, halfway, handy, hard, immediate, lower, near, nearby, next, on, overhead, parallel, preceding, toward/towards, under, underneath, within, without, wrong, yonder

587 safety: chancy, chary, perilous, precarious, sacred, safe, secure, treacherous, unreliable, unsafe, unsound, vulnerable, weak

588 speed: agile, cursory, expeditious, express, fast, fleet, gradual, gradually, hastily, hasty, headlong, hurried, instant, instantly, posthaste, precipitous/precipitate, quick, rapid, rapidly, slow, snappy, speedy, swift, swiftly/swift, whirlwind

589 style: adorable, bald, baroque, beautiful, becoming, bedraggled, black, bland, bold, bourgeois, brassy, casual, cheap, chic, class, classical, classy, conglomerate, contemporary, cosmopolitan, country, crude, cultural, cursory, dashing, distasteful, dowdy, dressy, elegant, exquisite, fashionable, fitted, flamboyant, flashy, floral, florid, flowery, formless, gaily, garish, gaudy, gay, generous, glamorous, glaring, gorgeous, graceful, grand, grandiose, graphic, homely, hot, humble, improvised, incognito, informal, ingenuous, innovative, jazzy, kinky, lavish, loud, lovely, lush, luxuriate, luxurious, marked, mean, mere, meretricious, modern, modish, naked, neat, new, newfangled, obsolete, old-fashioned, opulent, orderly, original, ornamental, ornate, ostentatious, outdated/out-of-date, outmoded, palatial, passé, picturesque, plain, plush, popular, posh, pretentious, prevalent, provincial, quaint, quiet, refined, regal, resplendent, rich, rustic, salty, scruffy, shapeless, sharp, showy, simple, slack, sleazy, slipshod, smart, snappy, sophisticated, splendid, spruce, stale, stately, statuesque, stylish, swank/swanky, swish, tacky, tasteful, tasteless, tawdry, tousled, trendy, unbecoming, untidy, unworldly, up-to-date, vogue

Senses

590 physical: burn, caress, hear, see, smell, taste, touch

591 attribute of hearing: audible, deaf, distinct
592 attribute of noise: blatant, brassy, cacophonous,

clarion, discordant, dissonant, grating, loud, noisy, piercing, quiet, raucous, rough, shrill, soft, strident, vociferous

593 attribute of noise-making: dumb, mute

594 attribute of sound: aloud, audible, blatant, brassy, cacophonous, clarion, deep, discordant, dissonant, dull, faint, full, gentle, grating, gruff, guttural, high, hoarse, hollow, husky, loud, low, mellow, melodious/melodic, muffled, musical, noiseless, noisy, off-key, piercing, quiet, raucous, resonant, rich, rough, round, shrill, silent, still, strident, subdued, sweet, tranquil, untroubled, vocal, vociferous, weak

595 audible object: acknowledgment, air, alert, anthem, aria, arrangement, ballad, bang, bell, blast, boom, buzz, carillon, carol, chant, clamor, clank, clap, clatter, click, clink, clump, crack, crash, delivery, din, dirge, discord, dissonance, drone, echo, gasp, groan, growl, gurgle, harmony, hiss, howl, hymn, inflection, jangle, melody, murmur, music, noise, peal, pop, psalm, refrain, report, rhyme, rhythm, ring, roar, roll, rustle, scream, shout, shriek, slam, song, sound, strain, thunder, tick, tune, yell

596 hearing: attend, bug, commiserate, eavesdrop, hear, listen, mind, monitor, regard

597 sound perception: hearing

598 attribute of odor: aromatic, astringent, fetid, fragrant, high, malodorous, musty, noisome, odorless, odorous, putrid, rancid, rank, sharp, smelly, stale, strong, sweet

599 object that can be smelled: aroma, bouquet, breath, incense, odor, perfume, scent, smell, stench, stink, tang, whiff

600 odor: fragrance, fumes, incense, perfume, reek, smell, stench, stink, tang

601 olfactory perception: breathe, inhale, nose, scent, smell, sniff, whiff

602 smelling: scent, smell, sniff, whiff

603 attribute of dryness: absorbent, arid, balmy, clammy, damp, dank, dry, filmy, fluid, humid, juicy, liquid, misty, moist, muggy, musty, oily, parched, sloppy, soggy, thirsty, watery, wet, wizened

604 attribute of hardness: adamant, concrete, downy, erect, firm, firmly, flaccid, hard, impenetrable, impervious, inflexible, iron, limp, mushy, permeable, plastic, rocky, solid, stiff, supple, taut, tender, tense, unbending

605 attribute of temperature: ablaze, arctic, balmy, benign, biting, bland, boiling, bracing, brisk, broiling, burning, chill, chilly, close, cold, cool, cozy, crisp, febrile, feverish, fiery, freezing,

frigid, frosty, frozen, glacial, heated, hot, icy, lukewarm, polar, sultry, sweltering, tepid, torrid, tropical, warm, wintry

606 attribute of texture: abrasive, adhesive, beaten, bias, breakable, brittle, bushy, coarse, corrugated, cozy, craggy, creamy, crisp, crumbly, crusty, dainty, delicate, diaphanous, diluted/dilute, downy, elastic, ethereal, fibrous, filmy, fine, firm, fleecy, flimsy, fluffy, fuzzy, gauzy, gelatinous, glassy, glossy, gooey, gossamer, greasy, gritty, icy, irregular, jagged, lacy, leathery, lucid, matted, mottled, muddy, mushy, oily, opaque, paper, pasty, permeable, pointed, porous, powdery, rough, rugged, sheer, silky, sleek, slick, slippery, smooth, soft, spongy, sticky, tenacious, tender, thick, thin, threadbare, transparent, uneven, viscous, yielding

607 dryness: drought, evaporation, humidity, wet

608 tactile perception: feeling, itch, touch

609 tactile quality: excruciating, numb

610 temperature: cold, fever, frost, glow, heat, temperature

611 texture: consistency, delicacy, feel, fiber, finish, gloss, grain, mesh, nap, polish, texture

612 touching: brush, caress, dab, feel, finger, graze, grope, handle, itch, lick, manipulate, meet, monkey, nestle, nudge, nuzzle, pat, paw, pet, reach, stroke, tickle, tingle, touch

613 attribute of taste: acerbity, acid, acidulous, acrid, appetizing, astringent, bad, bitter, bland, corrupt, delectable, delicious, distasteful, done, eatable, edible, full-bodied, hot, insipid, luscious, palatable, peppery, piquant, poignant, pungent, racy, rancid, rich, robust, salty, savory, scrumptious, sharp, sour, spicy, succulent, sweet, tart, tasteless, tasty, unsavory

614 taste: bite, bitterness, flavor, savor, spice, tang, taste, zest

615 taste perception: taste

616 tasting: bite, gargle, sample, savor, taste

617 attribute of brightness: ablaze, beaming, bold, bright, brilliant, clear, colorful, crystal, dark, dim, dingy, drab, dull, dusky, effulgent, faded, faint, glaring, gloomy, glossy, glowing, incandescent, lackluster, light, lucid, luminescent, luminous, lustrous, misty, murky, nebulous, obscure, opaque, radiant, resplendent, scintillating, shady, shiny, sunny, tenebrous

618 attribute of color: amber, anemic, beige, black, blond/blonde, bloodless, blue, bold, bright, bronze, brown, brunette/brunet, buff, cadaverous, cherry, clear, colored, colorful, colorless, crystal, dappled, dark, deathly, deep, drab, dusky, faded, fair, florid, flushed, gaudy, gay, gloomy, glowing, gold/golden, gray/grey, green, iridescent, jet, light, livid, mauve, milky, motley, mottled, mousy, muddy, multicolored, murky, neutral, opaque, orange, pale, pastel, pasty, peaked, pearly, purple, red, rich, rosy, ruddy, sable, sallow, sanguine, silver, smoky, soft, speckled, strong, swarthy, tan, translucent, transparent, verdant, vibrant, vivid, wan, watery, white, yellow

619 attribute of vision: appreciable, blind, clear, concealed, conspicuous, discernible, disguised, distinct, fuzzy, glaring, glassy, graphic, impalpable, invisible, lucid, myopic, prominent, pronounced, visible, visual

620 brightness: dark, darkness, gleam, glitter, gloom, gloss, glow, illumination, light, luster, night, overshadow, pall, polish, radiance, radiate, shade, shadow, sheen, shimmer, shine, splendor

621 clean: grimy, grubby, hygienic, immaculate, impeccable, impure, mangy, messy, neat, pure, refined, sanitary, slimy, sloppy, slovenly, spotless, stagnant, sterile, straight, tidy, trim, unblemished, unclean, unkempt, untidy, untouched

622 color: auburn, beige, blush, cast, color, complexion, decor, fade, flush, gloom, glow, hue, orange, pigment, pink, purple, red, shade, shadow, stain, stripe, tan, tinge, tint, tone, yellow

623 looking: attend, avert, browse, contemplate, contemplation, dip into, eye, face, fix, focus, gape, gawk, gaze, glance, glare, glimpse, glower, heed, inspect, leaf, leer, look, lookout, look out, mind, monitor, patrol, peek/peep, peer, point, pry, regard, scan, scout, scrutinize, scrutiny, skim, snoop, spy, squint, stare, view, watch

624 occurrence of light: beam, blink, bolt, cast, eclipse, flash, flicker, glance, glare, gleam, glimmer, glisten, glitter, glow, halo, illuminate, illumination, light, lighten, ray, reflect, shimmer, shine, spark, sparkle, spotlight, twinkle, wink

625 picture: arms, caricature, cartoon, chart, design, diagram, drawing, emblem, engraving, facsimile, figure, handwriting, impression, imprint, layout, map, model, outline, pattern, picture, plan, portrait, profile, reproduction, scene, scheme, silhouette, sketch, table, tableau

626 seeing: behold, distinguish, eye, gaze, make out, mark, meet, note, notice, observe, perceive, regard, remark, see, sight, spot, view, witness

627 visibility change: blur, clear, dim, fog

628 visible object: acknowledgment, alert, aspect, beacon, beam, blaze, buoy, cue, glance, glare, hallmark, halo, handwriting, light, mirage, model, outlook, panorama, prospect, ray, reflection, scene, scenery, sparkle, streak, track, view

629 visual perception: blindness, perspective, sight, vision

States

ABSTRACT

630 ability: ability, agility, artifice, artistry, awkwardness, bent, can, capability, capacity, competence, dexterity, disqualification, ease, efficiency, eloquence, endowment, expertise/expertness, facility, faculty, feebleness, flair, gift, hand, handicraft, head, inability, inclination, knack, know-how, league, literacy, master, mastery, mind, niche, performance, power, productivity, proficiency, promise, propensity, prowess, qualification, qualify, readiness, skill, talent, technique, telepathy, touch, trick, turn, workmanship

631 accessibility: access, circulation, concealment, privacy, seclusion, secrecy, secret

632 be ahead: ahead, first, front, uppermost, winning

633 behavior: abandon, abstinence, acquit, acrimony, act, adultery, affectation, airs, alacrity, amenity, antithesis, apathy, arrogance, asperity, audacity, austerity, balance, barbarism, barbarity, bearing, behave, behavior, benevolence, betrayal, bitterness, bluster, brass, bravery, carriage, carry on, chastity, cheek, chivalry, coarseness, compassion, complaisance, condescend, condescension, condolence, conduct, cordiality, correctness, corruption, countenance, courage, courtesy, cruelty, culture, custom, cut, debauchery, deceit, decency, decorum, deference, defiance, demeanor, deportment, desperation, detachment, diffidence, diplomacy, dishonesty, disloyalty, disobedience, disregard, disrespect, dissidence, dissipation, distance, do, eagerness, earnestness, ebullience, effervescence, effrontery, endurance, enthusiasm, equanimity, equilibrium, etiquette, excess, excitement, exuberance, face, faithfulness, faithlessness, fanaticism, feint, fervor, firmness, flightiness, flippancy, folly, foolishness, forbearance, formality, freedom, frivolity, fuss, gall, geniality, grace, grit, grovel, haughtiness, heroism, honesty, honor, hostility, humility, hypocrisy, impatience, impertinence, indecency, indiscretion, insolence, irreverence, kindness, laziness, lethargy, license, lunacy, manhood/womanhood, manner, manners, mercy, misbehave, misbehavior, mischief, misconduct, misdeed/misdemeanor, moderation, modesty, mutiny, naiveté, nonconformity, nonsense, obedience, oblivion, observance, order, ostentation, outburst, pep, perseverance, piety, poise, polish, pose, precaution, presumption, pretense, pretension, pride, propriety, prowess, purpose, quarter, radiance, rancor, react, reaction, readiness, rebel, rebellion, refinement, refusal, regress, reserve, responsibility, restraint, scene, self-control, serenity, show, simplicity, sincerity, sophistication, spunk, steam, submission, sympathy, tact, temerity, temperance, treachery, treat, treatment, valor, veneer, vitality, zip

634 **commonality:** diffusion, frequency, ritual

635 **completeness:** bulk, complement, culmination, deficiency, entirety, finality, fullness, integrity, whole

636 **conformity:** adequacy, adhere, archetype, cohere, fidelity, par

637 **constancy:** consistency, constancy, continuance, instability, monotony

638 **definiteness:** accuracy, ambiguity, certainty, clarity, correctness, exactness, finality, precision, rigor, truth

639 **exist in a condition:** blame, condition, existence, state

640 **extension:** addition, continuation

641 **forcefulness:** clasp, clutches, dictatorship, efficacy, force, gravity, impact, impetus, impulse, intensity, kick, might, momentum, muscle, power, pressure, push, swamp, violence

642 **made of:** compose, have, inclusion, manifestation

643 **make up:** accompany, comprise, consist of, cover, form, include, make up

644 **mannerism:** air, attention(s), austerity, characterize, clemency, courtesy, custom, earmark, entity, fashion, foible, forgetfulness, habit, idiosyncrasy, manner, mannerism, mark, mien, mode, propriety, purpose, quirk, regard, trait, vigilance

645 **morality:** abandon, atrocity, blasphemy, coarseness, conscience, corruption, craft, debauchery, decadence, degeneracy, delinquency, depravity, dirt, disservice, enormity, equality, equity, ethics/ethic, evil, excess, fairness, faithfulness, faithlessness, falsity, favoritism, fraud, good, goodness, good will/goodwill, greatness, guile, guilt, guise, holiness, honesty, honor, ideals, imposition, imposture, indecency, infamy, infidelity, infraction, iniquity, injustice, innocence, justice, liability, license, loyalty, misbehave, misbehavior, mischief, misconduct, misdeed/misdemeanor, morality, morals, obligation, obscenity, outrage, principle/principles, probity, profanity, prostitute, responsibility, right, sacrilege, scandal, scheme, score, segregate, sin, transgression, treachery, treason, trespass, trick, trickery, trust, underworld, validity, veracity, vice, virtue, wrong

646 **necessity:** absence, behoove, call for, dearth, defect, deficit, demand, do, do without, drought, enough, entail, essential, exigency/exigence, frill, go without, have, lack, mainstay, must, necessitate, necessity, need, obligate, oblige, paucity, prerequisite, provide, qualification, require, requirement/requisite, reservation, shortage, specification, subsistence, take, void, want

647 **normality:** aberration, abnormality, anomaly, average, eccentricity, gauge, norm, rule, rut

648 **origin:** ancestry, birth, bottom, counterfeit, cradle, derivation, derive from, emanate, emanation, extraction, femininity/feminine, fountain, germ, hail, head, heredity, heritage, home, inception, issue, masculinity/masculine, matrix, mortality, origin, parent, precursor, root, seed, sex, source, spring, start, stem, threshold

649 **permanency:** constant, fixed, forever, permanent, perpetual, unchanging

650 **probability:** absurdity, chance, contingency, credibility, eventuality, liability, likelihood, must, odds, possibilities, possibility, potential, probability, promise, tend

651 **range:** area, breadth, circulation, compass, continuation, degree, diffusion, dissemination, dissipation, distance, diversity, expanse, extent, gamut, go, jurisdiction, latitude, length, matter, overrun, panorama, play, radius, range, reach, realm, room, run, scale, scope, spread, stretch, sweep

652 **restrictiveness:** abbreviation, abridgement, autonomy, bar, block, blockade, bondage, captivity, constraint, curb, exemption, flexibility, prohibition, qualification

653 **specialization:** alone, circumstantial, express, precise, select

654 **specificity:** accuracy, correctness, exactness, model, point, precision, property, rigor

655 **style:** appeal, approach, artistry, behavior, clash, classic, classicism, cultivation, cut, dash, discrimination, elegance, fad, fashion, finish, frill, frippery, genre/genus, glamour, glitter, grace, look, mode, ostentation, polish, pomp, popularity, rage, refinement, simplicity, sophistication, splendor, style, taste, tone, touch, trend, vogue

656 **suitability:** absurdity, adequacy, agree, awkwardness, blend, consistency, correctness, do, expediency/expedience, fitness, propriety, satisfy, serve, suit

657 **tendency:** acrimony, alacrity, animation, aptitude, atrocity, care, charity, cultivation, dedication, defiance, determination, devotion, diligence, direction, discretion, dishonesty, disinclination, eagerness, earnestness, effervescence, enterprise, enthusiasm, equity, face, fairness, fashion, fervor, finesse, gallantry, generosity, grace, guile, gusto, guts, heat, hospitality, hostility, humility, hurry, hypocrisy, idleness, impatience, incline, indifference, indignation, indulgence, inertia, inhibition, initiative, kindness, liability, mind, moderation, naiveté, neglect, nervousness, nonconformity, patience, pity, posture, presence, pretension, rage, resignation, resolution, restlessness, seriousness, sincerity, streak, tenacity, tendency, thing, tolerance, trend, trick, truth, verge, vice, vigilance

658 **usefulness:** agency, agent, convenience, efficiency, employment, expediency/expedience,

good, help, makeshift, malfunction, medium, operation, practice, purpose, resource, serve, service, surplus, usage, use, utility, value, wear

COGNITIVE

659 goal: aim, ambition, aspiration, destination, dream, end, function, goal, intent/intention, mark, meaning, mission, object, objective, pleasure, point, prize, purport, purpose, quarry, reason, resolve, sake, target, taste, victim, will

660 plan: angle, approach, architecture, calculation, channel, chart, chicanery, collusion, complicity, concoction, conspiracy, contrivance, craft, deceit, design, device, diagram, diet, dispensation, disposition, dodge, draft, expediency/expedience, expedient, feint, form, gambit, game, gimmick, groundwork, idea, innovation, intrigue, invention, itinerary, layout, machination, maneuver, manner, method, move, plan, plot, policy, program, purport, purpose, route, scenario, schedule, scheme, shift, strategem, strategy, tactics

661 reason: alibi, angle, asset, basis, benefit, blame, boon, cause, confirmation, essence, essential, excuse, explanation, footing, fuel, goad, grounds, groundwork, hypothesis, idea, impetus, incentive, inducement, inspiration, justification, keynote/keystone, lesson, meaning, message, motive, nub, occasion, origin, pretext, rationale, reason, root, sake, solution, spring, spur, stimulant, stimulus, whim

662 request: command, demand, desire, directive, edict, entreaty, petition, plea, prayer, proposal, proposition, query, recall, request, requisition, suit

COMPARATIVE

663 complexity: complexity, exaggeration, labyrinth, simplicity, snarl

664 correspondence: accord, answer, approximate, balance, clash, community, conform, conformity, connection, consonance, consort, correspond, correspondence, double, dovetail, duplicate, fit, flatter, go, go together/go with, harmonize, harmony, identity, jibe, likeness, make, match, mate, proportion, resemblance, resemble, square, sympathy, twin, union, unison, unity

665 difference: aberration, antithesis, assortment, contradict, contradiction, contrast, controversy, converse, depart, departure, deviate, deviation, differ, difference, digression, disagree, disagreement, discrepancy, disharmony, disparity, disproportion, dissension, dissent, dissimilarity, dissonance, distinction, diverge, divergence, diversity, eccentricity, exception, foil, gap, gradation, grade, inequality, innovation, miscellany, mutation, novelty, nuance, oddity, opposite, opposition, peculiarity, rent, reverse, shade, variance, variant, variation, variety, wander

666 difficulty: abomination, awkwardness, conundrum, deficiency, delay, disadvantage(s), drawback, enormity, entanglement, facility, handicap, hindrance, hitch, impediment, labyrinth, limitation, matter, misery, muddle, obstacle, obstruction, plight, pressure, problem, quagmire, question, restraint, restriction, rigor, rub, shortcoming, snag, snarl, spot, task, tax, tribulation, trouble, vice, wall

667 equivalence: alternate, amount, balance, border on, cancel, cohere, coincide, coincidence, come up to, copy, correlation, counterpart, disproportion, duplicate, equal, equality, equate, equivalence, equivalent, image, make, match, model, par, parallel, parity, rival, sameness, tie

668 importance: accent, aspect, bearing, beauty, berth, best, celebrity, character, cipher, consequence, core, count, cream, crux, dignity, dominance, element, elevation, eminence, emphasis, essence, flower, forefront/foreground, fundamental, glory, grandeur, gravity, greatness, height, honor, import, importance, kernel, key, lead, magnitude, mark, matter, moment, name, nobility, nothingness, overshadow, peak, prestige, pride, priority, prominence, quality, renown, sense, seriousness, significance, signify, situation, spotlight, stature, status, stress, stuff, style, tedium, top, trifle, value, weight, zero hour

669 intensity: intensity, strength, violence

670 similarity: affinity, agree, analogy, community, consistency, equivalence, equivalent, identity, likeness, parallel, parity, replica, reproduction, resemblance, resemble, sameness, second, similarity, tune, twin

671 superiority: ascendancy/ascendency, distinction, elegance, eminence, excel, excellence, ideal, imperfection, importance, jewel, marvel, miracle, paragon, perfection, pick, power, precedence, preponderance, prodigy, rank, seniority, superiority, victory

OF BEING

672 abstraction: manifestation, oblivion

673 aura: air, allure, ambience, appeal, appearance, aspect, atmosphere, attribute, aura, background, being, blaze, celestial, charm, chorus, climate, cultivation, dash, dump, ease, environment, feel, feeling, flavor, glory, glow, kind, look, medium, milieu, monotony, mood, orbit, presence, quiet, romance, semblance, serenity, sign, solitude, spell, spice, spirit, splendor, surroundings, texture, tone, tranquility, undercurrent, veil, vein, veneer, vestige, whisper

674 bad situation: abortion, accident, adversity, affliction, anarchy, anticlimax, atrophy, backwash, bane, beaten, bedlam, bereavement, bind, blight, blooper, blow, brunt, calamity, casualty, cataclysm, catastrophe, catch, chagrin, chaos, clamor, clog, clutter, cobweb, collapse, collision, comedown, commotion, complication, conflict, contamination, contempt, corner, crisis, crunch, curse, damage, deadlock, dearth, debacle, decay, decline, decomposition, deficiency, descent, detriment, devastation, difficulty, dilemma, disadvantage(s), disappointment, disaster, discomfiture, discouragement, disorganization, disrepair, disservice, distress, disturbance, downfall, drag, drama, drawback, dud, duress, embarrassment, emergency, entanglement, error, exigency/exigence, eyesore, failing, fall, famine, ferment, fiasco, filth, fix, flap, flaw, flop, frenzy, friction, frustration, handicap, hang-up, hardship, harm, hassle, havoc, hell, hindrance, hitch, holdup, hole, hurdle, ill, impasse, imposture, impropriety, inadequacy, inconvenience, indiscretion, infirmity, injustice, jam, jump, kink, lapse, liability, limitation, load, lose, loss, madhouse, malfunction, matter, maze, mess, mire, misadventure, misery, misfortune/mishap, misstep, mix-up, muss, neglect, nightmare, nuisance, obstacle, obstruction, onus, oppression, ordeal, outrage, pall, pandemonium, pass, pell-mell, pest, pickle, pinch, pitfall, pity, plague, plight, poison, predicament, press, pressure, problem, puncture, quagmire, quandary, question, repulse, restraint, restriction, reverse, rub, ruin, ruse, scandal, scourge, scrape, setback, shambles, shortcoming, showdown, slump, smash, snag, snare, snarl, spot, squeeze, storm, strait, strife, struggle, syndrome, tangle, tiff, to-do, tragedy, trap, trial, trouble, tumult, turmoil, undoing, unrest, uprising, uproar, upset, weakness, weight, wreck

675 danger: calamity, cataclysm, corner, crunch, curse, danger, dilemma, disaster, emergency, fatality, hardship, hazard, ill, jeopardy, mayhem, menace, peril, poison, risk, scourge, seriousness, smash, threat, tragedy, trouble, venture, violence

676 effect: amount, attraction, because, cogency, combustion, cost, culmination, effectiveness, efficacy, feebleness, magnetism, potency, proceed, punch, splash, tell, therefore, wash

677 effort: concentration, cooperation, difficulty, diligence, direct, effort, exertion, force, go, groove, idleness, industry, plod, sweat, toil, trouble, try, work, yoke

678 experience: background, callow, career, culture, heritage, history, ignorance, lead (a life), life, live, maturity, mellow, memory, naive, naiveté, phenomenon, practical, readiness, record, sustain, taste, training, unaccustomed, unfamiliar, veteran, world, young

679 fate: accident, blessing, break, catch, chaff, chance, contingency, cost, demise, destiny, disadvantage, doom, downfall, dues, duty, fate, fluke, fortune, freak, future, godsend, good, jinx, judgment, limbo, lot, luck, misfortune/mishap, oblivion, outlook, payoff, penalty, pitfall, plague,

portion, reverse, setback, shortcoming, suspense, turning point, undoing, weight

680 function: application, avail, bar, begin, bolt, cloak, closure, cord, cushion, decoy, deterrent, disguise, dump, gauge, operate, operation, run, spray, tie

681 inaction: abeyance, abide, asleep, bide, dalliance, dally, dawdle, doze, drag, fool around, forbear, forgo, hang, hesitate, hesitation, idleness, inertia, leisure, linger, loaf, loiter, lounge, neglect, nod, procrastinate, refrain, relief, remain, repose, respite, rest, shirk, skip, slack/slacken, stay, wait

682 meaning: ambiguity, connotation, content, context, cryptic, denotation, denote, double entendre, drift, drive at, emphasis, express, fiber, gist, imply, import, importance, light, matter, mean, meaning, meat, message, nature, nub, point, punch, purport, quintessence, represent, respect, sense, significance, signify, spirit, stand for, strain, strength, stuff, substance, suggest, symbolize, tenor, text, texture, theme, thrust, tone, typify, understanding, undertone, upshot, value, vein, weigh, weight, wording

683 name: alias, anonymous, denomination, designation, epithet, handle, name, nickname, nomenclature, pseudonym, term, title

684 of agreement: accord, agreement, alliance, armistice, arrangement, assent, bargain, bond, charter, chorus, coherence, coincidence, communion, compact, compliance, compromise, concert, concord, consensus, consent, contract, convention, covenant, deal, faction, meeting, negotiation, okay, order, pact, protocol, provision/proviso, settlement, stipulation, terms, transaction, treaty, truce, understanding, warranty, word

685 of authorization: approval, authority, certificate, charter, confirmation, consent, credentials, decree, delegation, determination, dispensation, enactment, endorsement, enforcement, entree, entry, exemption, fiat, finding, forgiveness, go-ahead, grace, guarantee, induction, leave, license, mandate, negation, nod, order, pardon, pass, passage, passport, patent, permission, permit, recall, release, remission, repeal, reprieve, sanction, seal, signal, ticket, treaty, veto, waiver, warrant, warranty, withdrawal, word

686 of being an influence: bolt, contact, effect, effectiveness, fetish, gush, influence, instrument, leadership, leverage, muscle, orbit, persuasion, preponderance, pressure, sphere, squeeze, sway, wonder

687 of being a rule: authority, axiom, ban, basis, benchmark, canon, code, condition, convention, creed, criterion, custom, democracy, dictate, doctrine, dogma, edict, essence, ethics/ethic, fact, form, formality, formula, fundamental, gauge, generality, ideology, institute, keynote/keystone, law, line, measure, model, morals, norm, observance, parameter, philosophy, policy, practice, precept, principle, protocol, regulation, ritual, rule, standard, taboo, tenet, theorem, tradition

688 of being an example: archetype, case, classic, embodiment, epitome, example, exemplar, exponent, guide, ideal, illustration, instance, lesson, light, measure, model, norm, original, paradigm, paragon, pattern, picture, precedent, prototype, replica, representative, sample, specimen, stereotype, type

689 of belief: advocacy, allegiance, anticipation, aphorism, apparition, assumed, assumption, atheism, attitude, attrition, axiom, basis, belief, bias, black magic, capitalism, cause, chauvinism, church, commonplace, complaint, concept, conception, conclusion, confidence, conformity, conjecture, connotation, conscience, consensus, contention, conviction, credence, creed, cult, culture, decision, deduction, definition, delusion, democracy, denomination, dependence/dependency, derision, determination, diagnosis, dictum, disapproval, disbelief, discrimination, dissent, dissidence, dissonance, distrust, divinity, doctrine, dogma, doubt, estimate, estimation, ethics/ethic, evaluation, expectancy, expectation, eye, faith, faithfulness, fallacy, fanaticism, fantasy, fascism, fatalism, favor, feeling, fetish, foreboding, forgiveness, generality, gospel, grievance, guess, heresy, honor, hunch, hypothesis, idea, ideals, ideology, illusion, image, impression, incantation, induction, inkling, instinct, intimation, intuition, judgment, leaning, line, logic, magic, make-believe, maxim, mind, miracle, misconception, misgiving, motivation, motive, nihilism, nonconformity, notion, objection, obsession, omen, opinion, optimism, oracle, outlook, perception, perspective, persuasion, pessimism, philosophy, piety, platform, position, preconception, prediction, prejudice, premise, premonition, presage, presentiment, presumption, pride, principle/principles, prognosis, prophecy, prospect, purport, purpose, racism, reaction, reality, recognition, regard, reliance, religion, reputation, resolve, respect, right, school, self-respect/self-esteem, self-satisfaction, sentiment, side, sign, slant, sorcery, speculation, spell, stance, stand, stigma, stock, subject, substance, suggestion, superstition, supposition, surmise, suspicion, taste, tenet, theme, theorem, theory, thesis, trust, understanding, utopia, view, viewpoint, vision, vow, witchcraft, word

690 of concern: afraid, aghast, alarm, anxiety, anxious, apprehension, burden, concern, conundrum, craze, difficulty, dismay, disquiet, distraction, distraught, distress, doubt, fascination, feeling, fixation, foreboding, frightened, guilt, hallucination, hang-up, horror, interest, jitters, jumpy, misgiving, mistrust, obsession, panic, passion, peeve, premonition, puzzled, quandary, question, regard,

scruple, suspicion, temptation, terror, trouble, uneasy, weight, woe, wonder, worry

691 of law: abomination, annulment, autocracy, custody, exemption, freedom, independence, justice, laissez-faire, liberty, offense, order, peace, prohibition, trespass, trial, validity, ward

692 on a course: career, pitch, ramble, tack, tendency, traverse

693 opportunity: contingency, facility, fluke, freedom, handicap, hazard, hearing, interest, juncture, lead, leverage, luck, merit, miracle, occasion, odds, opening, opportunity, outlet, picnic, plus, possibility, preference, prize, profit, prospect, pushover, recourse, remedy, resort, risk, sake, shot, snap, start, strength, stumble, success, time, treat, turn, vacancy, welfare/well-being

694 purpose: application, employment, help, purpose, role, vehicle

695 repetition: boomerang, echo, repeat, repetition, return, verbiage

696 situation: case, circumstance, condition, context, environment, experience, instance, landmark, matter, medium, mystery, occurrence, point, position, situation, state, uncertainty

OF CHANGE

697 abstract: about-face, accommodation, adapt, adaptation, adjust, adjustment, back down, balance, deepen, depart, departure, deviate, deviation, digress, digression, dip, diversify, fluctuate, flux, get, interchange, metamorphose, metamorphosis, movement, mutation, novelty, oscillate, range, reconcile, redress, refresh, replace, retract, reverse, revive, revolution, rig, rotate, shift, suit, switch, tighten, transform, transformation, transition, transpose, turn, variance, variation, vary, vicissitude, withdraw

698 diminish: abate, atrophy, come down, cut, decline, decrease, degenerate, depreciate, deteriorate, deterioration, die, diminish, diminution, drain, drop, drop off, dwarf, dwindle, ebb, erosion, evaporate, evaporation, fade, fester, flag, go, go down, lapse, lessen, let up, lull, mollify, peter out, plummet, qualify, recede, reduce, regress, relapse, relax, relent, remission, remit, revert, rot, sag, shrink, sink, slack/slacken, slump, stagnate, subside, taper/taper off, vegetate, wane, weaken, wear, wither, worsen

699 fail: blow, bomb, comedown, decline, default, disappoint, disqualify, downfall, droop, error, fail, failure, fall, fault, fizzle, flag, flop, flounder, fold, founder, go, go down, go under, miscarriage, miss, misstep, neglect, omission, overlook, run out, slump, wilt

700 improve: accession, advance, advancement, amendment, boom, boost, clear up, come along, correction, develop, development, dignify, edification, elevate, embellish, embellishment, energize, expansion, furbish, grace, improve, improvement, lift, look up, mend, pay, pick up, progress, pull through, rally, recoup, recover, recuperate, relieve, repair, revision, rise

701 **of state:** acclimate, aging, alteration, alternate, approach, assimilate, backfire, become, break out, change, come, come about, conversion, convert, metamorphose, metamorphosis, state

702 **of structure:** buckle, collapse, degenerate, dissolve, flatten

703 **organizational:** adjournment, dissolution, growth, merger

704 **progress:** advance, advancement, batten, boom, breakthrough, breeze, bring off, buildup, click, climax, coast, come on, consummate, course, develop, development, evolution, evolve, expansion, fare, flourish, flower, form, fruition, furtherance, gestation, get along, get on, go, go ahead, go far, grow, growth, headway, inroad, jump, mature, mellow, mount, mushroom, passage, precipitate, progress, push off/push on, rise, score, spread, thrive, unfold, wax

705 **unchanged:** abeyance, calm, limbo, peace, quiet

OF NEED OR ACHIEVEMENT

706 **achievement:** ability, accomplish, accomplishment, achieve, achievement, acme, action, apex, arrive, art, attain, attainment, background, bloom, blossom, bring about, bring off, carry, carry out, climax, clinch, come at, comeback, come through, compass, completion, conquer, conquest, consummate, consummation, coup, craft, crown, deed, degree, discharge, distinction, doing, draw, drive, effect, efficacy, excel, execute, execution, exercise, exploit, extreme, extremity, failure, feat, find, finish, flair, flourish, fruition, fulfill, fulfillment, gain, get, get ahead, gift, go far, go over, hammer out, hit, land, manage, maximum, milestone, operate, pan out, pass, perfect, perfection, performance, pinnacle, potential, prodigy, proficiency, progress, prosper, prosperity, pull off, pull through, reach, record, score, smash, stroke, succeed, success, take, thrive, transact, triumph, victory, welfare/well-being, win, work, workmanship, work out, zenith

707 **lack:** lack, loss, nothing/nothingness

708 **mutual possession:** communal, joint, mutual

709 **need:** addiction, affinity, bait, call, charge, claim, craving, cupidity, dearth, default, dependence/dependency, deprivation, desire, exigency/exigence, famine, hankering, hope, hunger, inadequacy, lack, longing, lust, must, necessity, need, partiality, penchant, poverty, predilection, predisposition, preference, prerequisite, prize, propensity, requirement/requisite, shortage, sustenance, temptation, thirst, use, void, want, wish, yen

710 **possession:** abundance, acquisition, asset(s), belongings, boast, buy, cache, capital, cash, clutches, commodity, custody, deserts, desolation, division, domain, dominion, due, dynasty, enjoy, enjoyment, entrench, estate, exuberance, finances, fortune, fund, funds, gain, get, grasp, have, hoard, hold, keep, legacy, lot, monopolize, monopoly, occupancy, occupation, own, ownership, plunder, possess, possession, presence, prize, property, purchase, reservation, reserve, reserved, resource, resources, retain, return, riches, savings, share, spoils, stake, store, subsistence, title, treasure, wealth

711 **requirement:** depend, hinge, provision/proviso, provisional, reservation, rest

712 **resource:** amenity, arrival, ballast, bastion, catalyst, comfort, convenience, edge, expediency/expedience, expedient, facility, find, guard, hoard, indulgence, luxury, mainstay, maintenance, makeshift, medium, mine, momentum, nurture, option, organ, pillar, plum, protection, provision, recourse, redress, relief, remedy, reparation, repertory, reserve, reservoir, resort, resource, resources, rock, safeguard, security, shelter, shield, solution, stopgap, stronghold, substitute, supply, support, vehicle

713 **satisfaction:** afford, suffice, work out

PHYSICAL

714 **accompaniment:** attend, both, chaperon, coincide, coincidence, conjunction, escort, friendship, go, privacy, relation, relationship, solitude, squire, tune, union, unity

715 **age:** antiquity, dotage, freshness, majority, manhood/womanhood, maturity, novelty, old age, years, young

716 **appearance:** appear, appearance, beard, blind, braid, cast, color, copy, countenance, decay, dissemble, double, dummy, duplicate, echo, expression, eyesore, facade, face, facsimile, favor, forgery, front, glare, grimace, grin, guise, illusion, image, imitation, likeness, look, mark, mask, match, personify, pose, pout, presence, pretense, pretext, radiate, represent, reproduction, resemblance, resemble, rise, role, scowl, semblance, show, sound, stand out, strike, surface, swagger, symmetry, tableau, veneer

717 **balance:** awkwardness, poise, proportion, symmetry

718 **beauty:** beauty, coiffure, countenance, elegance, embellishment, fright, glamour, glory, grace, hairstyle, imperfection

719 **capacity:** content, fill, hold, volume

720 **condition:** allure, apoplexy, beat, calm, carriage, comfort, connection, disability, disgust, dislocation, dissipation, distress, disturbance, emptiness, exhaustion, form, frazzle, health, maturity, peace, pollution, repose, rust, satisfaction, shape, state, stress, tangle

721 **continuity:** bridge, concatenation, continuity, durability, halt, length, run, sequence, series, spread, stretch

722 **density:** consistency, density, firmness

723 **essential:** austerity, brawn, corruption, decor, fat, fertility, fitness, poke, posture, smudge, tension

724 **force:** combustion, effort, force, push

725 **genuineness:** actuality, appear, certainty, counterfeit, credibility, fact, fallacy, falsity, feint, make-believe, reality, truth, validity, verisimilitude

726 **hardness:** firmness, temper, tension

727 **order:** arrangement, chain, column, concatenation, confusion, cosmos, course, disarray, dislocation, disorganization, distribution, file, form, gradation, grade, head, introduction, line, mean, median, method, order, organization, pattern, precede, precedence, precursor, priority, procession, queue, range, rank, round, row, run, seniority, sequence, series, stage, standing, streak, string, succeed, suite, tier, trail, train

728 **pain:** ache, affliction, agony, anesthesia/anaesthesia, cramp, crick, discomfort, distress, grief, harm, heartbreak, hurt, injury, itch, kink, letdown, misery, ordeal, pain, pang, pinch, remorse, repentance, smart, spasm, sting, strain, stress, suffering, torment, torture, trauma, trial, tribulation, trouble, twinge, woe

729 **safety:** buffer, bulwark, fortification, precaution, protection, safety, security, shield

730 **size:** brevity, bulk, caliber, condensation, dimensions/dimension, enormity, extent, fullness, greatness, infinity, magnitude, measurement, miniature, proportion, size

731 **stability:** anchor, durability, equilibrium, firmness, flexibility, instability, spring, stability, traction

732 **strength:** brawn, durability, feebleness, firmness, infirmity, kick, might, potency, power, stamina, strength, tolerance, vigor, weakness

733 **structure:** anatomy, architecture, composition, delicacy, emptiness, fabric, figure, frame, framework, mesh, ruins, skeleton, structure

734 **weight:** buoyancy/buoyance, fat, fatness, pressure

SPATIAL

735 **below:** below, bottom, down, under, underneath

736 **containment:** capacity, contain, fill

737 **depth:** deep, depth, shallow

738 **direction:** ascent, circulation, crook, cross, current, curve, decline, descent, deviation, dip, direction, diverge, divergence, diversion, downgrade, fork, grade, gradient, inclination, incline, intersect, lean, level, line, list, meander, orbit, pitch, reverse, revolution, revolve, rise, rotate, run, slant, slope, swirl, tack, tendency, tilt, trend, turn, twist, undercurrent, way, whirl, wind

739 **distance:** altitude, bearing/bearings, distance, latitude, leeway, scope, space, way

740 **fill:** brim, charge, cloy, content, cram, crowd, flood, glut, hollow, overflow, packed, replete, satiate, surfeit, teem, vacant, vacuum, void, volume

741 **height:** dominate, dwarf, elevation, eminence, height, rear, stature

742 **inside:** contain, have, hold, interior, twine

743 **length:** extent, height, length, range

744 **level:** gradation, grade, layer, level, line, notch, plane, plateau, rank, row, rung, scale, stage, tier

745 **limits, physical:** boundary, confines, curb, demarcation, end, extent, extreme, extremity, frontier, limit, perimeter, periphery, play, range, term, terminal

746 **location:** absence, absenteeism, bearing/bearings, dissemination, front, hang, junction/juncture, lie, look, median, middle, protrude, space, stretch

747 **location, relative:** adjoin, border, butt, contact, cross, detachment, face, join, precede, precedence, presence, project, proximity, vicinity

748 **motion:** activity, agility, convulsion, discharge, hurry, lethargy, restlessness, rush, spin, stagnate, still, sweep, swing, traction, turn, vibrate, vibration, wash

749 **nearness:** abut, border on, intersect, stalk, succeed, surveillance, verge

750 **on:** cover, on, pile, top, traverse

751 **outside:** band, edge, skirt, stick out

752 **over:** above, altitude, dominate, overhang, overlook, rise, tower, vault

753 **sequential:** line, trail, wake

754 **shape:** bag, conformation, curvature, cut, entwine, figure, fold, form, hollow, loop, pucker, shape, turn, twist

755 **speed:** celerity, dispatch, expedition, haste, hurry, pace, rapidity, rate, speed, velocity

756 **spread:** balloon, branch off/branch out, breadth, bridge, go, latitude, range, reach, room, space, span, sweep

757 **structure:** aperture, ascent, attitude, bag, beef, break, build, composition, condition, conformation, constitution, construction, crease, curvature, even, fabric, figure, fluid, form, frame, grade, gradient, makeup, physique, plane, ramp, set, shape, slope, stance, stoop

758 **surrounding:** circle, coil, compass, define, edge, encircle, enclose, encompass, fence, frame, gird, hedge, hem/hem in, mob, pen, ring, surround

759 **touching:** meet, neighbor, overlap

760 **width:** breadth, diameter, width

761 **within a group:** middle, range

Weights and measures

MATHEMATICS

762 **attribute of a number:** any, apiece, average, calculable, countless, dual, immeasurable, infinite, innumerable, just about, legion, less, light, limitless, manifold, many, mathematical, maximum, minimal, minimum, more, multiple/multifarious, multitudinous, myriad, nil, numberless, numeric/numerical, numerous, one, plentiful/plenty, plus, profuse, round, several, short, shy, single, skimpy, slight, sparse, steep, tidy, tiny, total, unreasonable, untold

763 **change in number:** accrue, appreciate, appreciation, deduction, discount, increase, increment, inflation, jump, peak, plummet, raise, reach, slump

764 **mathematic reasoning:** add, addition, appraise, arithmetic, average, balance, calculate, calculation, cast, computation, compute, count, enumerate, estimate, figure, gauge, measure, number, pace, page, reckon, scale, score, stock, subtract, tabulate, tally, tell, total, underestimate

765 **numeric symbol:** digit, fraction, number

766 **numeric value:** appraisal, count, couple, majority, maximum, peak, percentage, rate, scant/scanty

767 **quantity:** abundance, copiousness, enough, exuberance, greatness, overabundance, paucity, peak, plenty, plethora, preponderance, scant/scanty, shortage

768 **ratio:** quota, rate, ratio

769 **series:** array, chain, range, series, set, string

770 **system:** apparatus, automation, bureaucracy, business, capitalism, channel, circuit, commerce, communications, complex, cosmos, dispensation, file, finance, grammar, machinery, mail, method, net, network, pattern, post, routine, scale, system, traffic, world

QUANTIFIERS

771 **attribute of quantity:** about, additional, affluent, all, altogether, amply, below, best, better, big, bountiful, brimming/brimful, copious, depleted, disproportionate, double, dual, enough, excessive, extremely, few, flush, fraught, further, good, hardly, huge, inadequate, insufficient, just about, lacking, leftover, liberal, limited, limitless, lush, luxuriant, many, more, most, much, new, nil, other, outrageous, over, plus, residual, respectable, rich, rife, slender/slim, spare, spent, sufficient, thick, thin, too, unreasonable, various, wholesale

772 **attribute of range:** abysmal, all, all-out, barely, besides, beyond, blanket, bodily, bounded, bound-less, broad, capacious, catholic, chiefly, comprehensive, cosmic, dead, dearly, deeply, different, diffuse, diverse, eclectic, ecumenical, encyclopedic, exhaustive, expansive, extended, extensive, far, far-reaching, full-scale, fully, general, generally, global, greatly, inclusive, increasingly, indiscriminate, international, largely, lower, mainly, mixed, moderately, more, moreover, most, mostly, motley, much, multiple/multifarious, only, overall, pervasive, practically, primarily, principally, quite, rambling, rampant, rather, relatively, rife, slightly, somewhat, substantially, sundry, sweeping, too, universal, unlimited, utmost, vast, very, well, wholesale, wholly, wide, widespread, within, without

773 **attribute of size:** angular, atomic, baby, bantam, better, big, brief, broad, burly, capacious, capsule, cavernous, chubby, chunky, commodious, compact, compendious, concise, corpulent, cramped, cumbersome, dwarf, enormous, extensive, fleshy, full, gargantuan, giant, gigantic, grand, great, gross, hearty, hefty, huge, husky, immeasurable, immense, imposing, impressive, incalculable, infinitesimal, inflated, laconic, large, little, major, mammoth, massive, microscopic, midget, mighty, miniature, minimal, minor, minute, monstrous, monumental, narrow, petite, pocket, portable, prodigious, pudgy, puny, round, scrawny, short, small, squat, stocky, stout, strapping, stubby, stunted, substantial, teeny/teensy, thick, thin, tiny, tremendous, vast, voluminous, whopping, wide

774 **capacity:** brimming/brimful, capacious, capacity, close, compact, congested, crowded, empty, full, packed, spacious, teeming, vacant, void

775 **change of quantity:** accession, allowance, develop, development, grow, growth

776 **decreasing:** attrition, contraction, cut, cutback, deduction, deflate, depreciate, diminish, diminution, drop, drop off, dwindle, fall, lessen, recede, relent, sag, shrink, sink, subside, taper/taper off, wane

777 **depth:** abysmal, deep, profound, shallow, superficial, unfathomable

778 **distance:** about, afar, away, beyond, contiguous, directly, distant, extreme, far, faraway, farther, farthest, furthest, immediate, last, near, nearby, off, onward, onwards, uttermost, yonder

779 **height:** alpine, elevated, giant, gigantic, high, lanky, lofty, long, low, midget, petite, precipitous, rangy, short, squat, statuesque, stubby, stunted, tall, towering

780 **increasing:** accretion, accrue, accumulation, amplification, boost, bulge, distend, enlarge, enlargement, expansion, gather, increase, increment,

inflate, inflation, leap, mount, peak, proliferate, reach, rise, swell, wax, widen

781 **large:** abundant, aggregate, ample, appreciable, bulky, colossal, commodious, considerable, countless, excessive, extreme, extremely, exuberant, fantastic, far, generous, giant, gigantic, good, great, gross, handsome, handsomely, immeasurable, incalculable, infinite, inordinate, jumbo, large, lavish, legion, manifold, massive, maximum, mighty, monstrous, much, multitudinous, myriad, numberless, numerous, opulent, plentiful/ plenty, prodigal, prodigious, profuse, redundant, sizable, stupendous, substantial, surplus, tidy, tremendous, untold, unwieldy, vast, voluminous, whopping

782 **length:** extended, high, lengthy, low, short, tall

783 **measurement:** degree, extent, mark, proportion

784 **number:** amount, digit, estimate, figure, number, numeral, pair, percentage, point, quotation/quote, score, sum, trio/triple, zero

785 **portion:** among, apart, asunder, fractional, fragmentary, gross, half, sectional

786 **quantity:** all, amount, array, avalanche, average, backlog, barrage, batch, buildup, bundle, calculation, cascade, cipher, deal, deluge, duo, excess, extravagance, few, figure, flood, flow, glut, gust, heap, influx, lot, many, mass, measure, minimum, mint, myriad, number, overabundance, pile, pittance, plenty, plethora, quantity, sum, surge, tally, total, trio/triple, turnout

787 **range:** bound/bounds, breadth, compass, confines, expanse, extent, gamut, latitude, length, range, scale, scope, spread, sweep, width

788 **relative:** cumulative, empty, fairly, full

789 **small:** compendious, diminutive, dinky, exiguous, few, handful, infinitesimal, least, less, light, little, low, marginal, meager, measly, microscopic, miniature, minimal, minimum, minor, minute, negligible, nominal, one, outside, petite, piddling, scant/scanty, scarce, scarcely, shy, skimpy, slight, small, sparse, teeny/teensy, tiny, trifling

790 **unit of distance measure:** depth, distance, foot, inch, mile

791 **unit of height measure:** altitude, foot, height, inch, mile

792 **unit of measure:** acre, area, degree, dimensions/ dimension, gauge, mass, measure, measurement, perimeter, revolution, size, velocity, volume, width

793 **unit of scalar measure:** above, abysmal, lesser, low, over, under

794 **unit of volume measure:** capacity, fill, volume

795 **unit of weight measure:** ounce, pound, weight

796 **width:** broad, cavernous, wide

TIME

797 **attribute of age:** adolescent, advanced, afresh, aged, ancient, antediluvian, antiquarian, anti-

quated, antique, archaic, big, boyish, callow, contemporary, crotchety, crude, doddering, elder, elderly, fresh, full-grown/full-fledged, green, immature, immemorial, inchoate, infant/infantile, innovative, junior, juvenile, late, mature, medieval, mellow, mint, modern, modish, musty, new, newfangled, novel, old, older, old-fashioned, original, originally, outdated/out-of-date, outmoded, passé, puerile, quaint, recent, ripe, senior, stale, tender, undeveloped, up-to-date, vintage, virgin/virginal, young, youthful

798 **attribute of duration:** ad infinitum, all-time, always, annual, awhile, brief, ceaseless, chronic, compact, concise, confirmed, constant, continual, continuous, dragging, endless, ephemeral, eternal, eternally, ever, everlasting, extended, fleeting, forever, fugitive, immortal, incessant, indefinitely, infinite, interminable, inveterate, laconic, lasting, lifelong, limitless, long, meteoric, momentary, never-ending, nonstop, old, ongoing, passing, perennial, permanent, perpetual, relentless, running, short, short-lived, soon, steady, temporary, through, throughout, transient/ transitory, unbreakable, unbroken, undying, unending, unflagging, uninterrupted, unrelenting, whirlwind

799 **attribute of time:** actual, advance, afterward/ afterwards, again, almost, already, antediluvian, anterior, at, behind, bottom, colonial, coming, concurrent, consecutive, dilatory, dire, due, duly, early, effective, ever, extemporaneous/ extemporary, fast, felicitous, finally, foremost, forever, forthcoming, forward, frequently, gradual, gradually, hasty, hence, hereafter, hurried, immemorial, initial, instant, instantly, intermittent, irregular, irregularly, just about, last, lastly/ last, late, later, latter, leisurely, meantime, meanwhile, meteoric, narrowly, never, next, nightly, nocturnal, old, old-fashioned, once, oncoming, originally, overdue, pell-mell, periodic, perpetual, posterior, posthaste, postmortem, preceding, precipitous/precipitate, preliminary, previous, primarily, primary/prime, primeval, primitive, primordial, prompt, promptly, punctual, rapid, rapidly, ready, right, rude, sharp, short, simultaneous, snappy, sudden, suddenly, summarily, swift, swiftly/swift, tardy, temporal, then, thereafter, timely, ultimate, unawares, untimely, up-to-date, when, while, yet

800 **date:** anniversary, date

801 **day:** afternoon, almanac, anniversary, daily, date, day, ephemeral, evening, journal, morning, night, nightly, nocturnal, noon, time

802 **definite period:** date, day, holiday, instant, leave, morning, noon, present, shift

803 **division of:** day, minute, second

804 **duration:** brevity, continuance, continuation, course, duration, endurance, endure, eternity, extent, go, halt, length, remain

805 frequency: rapidity, sometimes
806 hour: afternoon, evening, morning, night, noon, time
807 indefinite period: age, antiquity, anytime, bit, bout, break, breath, continuance, convenience, era, future, generation, hiatus, history, infinity, interim, interlude, intermission, interruption, interval, lapse, leave, leisure, let-up, lull, meantime, minute, moment, past, pause, period, present, recess, remission, respite, rest, round, slack, space, span, spell, stalemate, stint, stretch, suspension, term, tour, trick, vacation, wait, while
808 minute: flash, instant, jiffy, moment, tick, wink
809 month: almanac, calendar, gestation, lunatic, moon, time
810 part of a day: afternoon, dark, dawn, day, daybreak, daylight, dusk, evening, gloom, light, morning, night, nightfall, sunrise, sunset, tick, twilight
811 past or future: following, future, past, preceding, previous, prior, succeeding/successive
812 proximity: immediate, near, now, prior, succeeding/successive
813 relative order: follow, precede, succeed
814 season: autumn, season, spring, summer, winter
815 specific: anniversary, beginning, date, dawn, daybreak, instance, juncture, point, present, yesterday, zero hour
816 stage of existence: administration, age, boyhood, childhood, cycle, day, era, generation, life, past, phase, prime, stage, tenure
817 stage of life form: adolescence, age, babyhood, cradle, cycle, landmark, life, lifetime, majority, maternity, old age, prime, puberty, spell, youth
818 temporal association: anachronism, clockwork, dispatch, elapse, eternity, fly, following, future, haste, pace, past, precede, precedence, preceding, previous, prior, rush, succeeding/successive
819 temporal object: anytime, clock, time
820 time relative to present: abrupt, after, ago, ahead, amid/amidst, anew, antecedent, back, before, beforehand, behind, belated, between, bygone, circa, coincident, contemporary, current, deferred, destined, directly, during, early, ensuing, erstwhile, eventual, eventually, final, first, following, fore, foregoing, former, formerly, forthwith, future, historical, immediate, immediately, imminent, impending, infant/infantile, instantaneous, just, lately, momentarily, near, nearing, new, newly, now, once, past, present, presently, previous, previously, prior, readily, recent, recently, shortly, someday, soon, straight, subsequent, subsequently, succeeding/successive, topical, ultimate, ultimately, until, yet
821 unit of time measure: day, flash, minute, second, wink
822 within a time period: interim, interval, period, span, spell, stint, stretch, term, while

823 year: almanac, anniversary, annual, annually, time, yearly

824 added part: arm, attachment, auxiliary, complement, complementary, excess, extension, extra, fitting, flap, fresh, frill, frippery, furthermore, garnish, new, offshoot, outgrowth, protuberance, ramification, repair, sequel, spare, superfluous, supplement, surplus, trim, wake, wing
825 bottom part: fringe, rear, rest, rump, seat, skirt, stub, stump, tail
826 core part: base, bosom, bottom, constituent, core, crux, element, essential, filling/filler, focus, foundation, fundamental, germ, heart, hub, inner, interior, internal, kernel, marrow, meat, nub, nucleus, quintessence, root, trunk
827 end part: addendum, back, border, butt, end, point, posterior, rear, seat, stub, stump, tail
828 first part: appetizer, early, initial, introduction, lead, nucleus, overture, precursor, predecessor, preliminary, spark
829 main part: body, bulk, capital, chief, element, feature, flower, focus, fundamental, hulk, hull, main, majority, parcel, plurality, root
830 middle part: aisle, axis, axle, bowels, center, central, filling/filler, inner, inside, interior, intermediate, internal, joint, junction/juncture, mean, median, middle, midst, pivot
831 minor part: atom, bit, breath, chip, collateral, component, crumb, dash, detail, dot, drop, factor, feature, fiber, flake, fleck, flicker, glimmer, grain, grit, handle, iota, item, joint, lick, ligature, minimum, modicum, molecule, morsel, nibble, nip, node/nodule, particle, patch, peripheral, pinch, point, powder, scrap, shred, sliver, spark, specimen, speck, splinter, spot, sprinkling, suspicion, tinge, touch, trace, trifle, whisper, whit, wisp
832 of an event: chapter, close, conclusion, dawn, end, ending, finale, finality, finish, genesis, germ, head, height, highlight, inception, installation, interruption, last, leg, limit, meridian, onset, opening, orientation, origin, outbreak, overture, particular, peak, period, preliminary, prelude, premiere, preview, prime, sequel, snatch, stalemate, standstill, start, stay, step, stop, stoppage, suspension, term, termination, threshold, touch, turning point, twilight, twist, victory, win, zenith, zero hour
833 of an order: back, beginning, end, front, middle
834 part: accessory, accompaniment, attribute, component, constituent, counterpart, feature, member, part, phase, piece, strip, thing, trait, trash, unit
835 portion: accompaniment, addition, adjunct, allotment, ancillary, appendage, arm, bit, bite, branch, constituent, contents, dab, deal, division, dose, drop, end, excerpt, excess, extract, facet, factor, feature, fraction, fragment, front, half, ingredient,

installment, interest, item, layer, link, little, lot, majority, mass, measure, member, morsel, parcel, pat, percentage, piece, portion, quarter, quota, ration, remainder, remnant, rest, sample, scrap, section, sector, segment, share, side, slab, slice, stake, subdivision, taste, tidbit, whit, wing

836 top part: acme, alpine, apex, barb, brim, ceiling, citadel, climax, crest, crown, extreme, extremity, face, front, head, height, lid, maximum, meridian, peak, pinnacle, plug, point, prominence, rim, summit, tip, top, vertex, zenith

837 whole: all, amount, entirety, everything, gross, synthesis, system, total, unit, unity, whole